The Cambridge Guide to Children's Books in English

THE CAMBRIDGE GUIDE TO

CHILDREN'S BOOKS IN ENGLISH

Victor Watson

ADVISORY EDITORS

Elizabeth L. Keyser
Hollins College, Roanoke

Juliet Partridge
University of Tasmania

Morag Styles
Homerton College, Cambridge

CAMBRIDGE
UNIVERSITY PRESS

PUBLISHED BY THE PRESS SYNDICATE OF THE UNIVERSITY OF CAMBRIDGE
The Pitt Building, Trumpington Street, Cambridge, United Kingdom

CAMBRIDGE UNIVERSITY PRESS
The Edinburgh Building, Cambridge CB2 2RU, UK
40 West 20th Street, New York, NY 10011–4211, USA
10 Stamford Road, Oakleigh, VIC 3166, Australia
Ruiz de Alarcón 13, 28014 Madrid, Spain
Dock House, The Waterfront, Cape Town 8001, South Africa

http: //www.cambridge.org

First published 2001

Printed in United Kingdom at the University Press, Cambridge

Typeface Lexicon A (*The Enschede Type Foundry*) 8.25/10.5pt *System* QuarkXPress™ [SE]

A catalogue record for this book is available from the British Library

Library of Congress Cataloguing in Publication data
The Cambridge Guide to Children's Books in English / [edited by] Victor Watson;
advisory editors, Elizabeth L. Keyser, Juliet Partridge, Morag Styles.
p. cm.
Includes bibliographical references and index.
ISBN 0 521 55064 5
1. Children's literature, English – Encyclopedias. 2. Children's literature,
American – Encyclopedias. 3. Children's literature, Commonwealth
(English) – Encyclopedias. 4. Children – Books and reading – Encyclopedias. I. Watson,
Victor.
PR990.C36 2001
820.9′9282′03 – dc21 00-065163

ISBN 0 521 55064 5 hardback

Contents

Editor's introduction

The Cambridge Guide to Children's Books in English is a reference work providing a critical and appreciative overview of children's books written in English across the world. It gives due weight to the history of children's books from pre-Norman times as well as acknowledging recent and current developments in publishing practices and in children's own reading.

This book is not a 'Guide to Children's Literature'. A strictly literary work would inevitably have been a rather narrow account of the canonical texts which have come – quite rightly in most cases – to be seen as constituting the great and long-established traditions of children's literature on both sides of the Atlantic. Such a work would have found it difficult to avoid retreading paths that have been mapped before and are now rather well-trodden. *The Cambridge Guide to Children's Books in English* has set itself a wider task: to include authors, or illustrators, or works published in English, believed by the editors to have made a significant impact on young readers anywhere in the world, or to have in some way influenced the production of children's books.

It must be apparent to everyone that an account of children's reading is significantly different from an account of children's literature. In recognition of the fact that a great deal of what children read has little to do with classrooms or with what many adults think of as 'literary', I have included entries on drama, television, comics, children's annuals, adventure game-books, and the growing range of media texts. I have also tried to ensure that entries are neither blandly descriptive nor loftily patronising towards young readers – whose reading interests should wherever possible, I believe, be acknowledged alongside the more available and articulate views of literary critics.

Children's books reflect and are bound up in cultural changes; they are particularly susceptible to developing assumptions about the nature of childhood, adolescence and education. They also have a lot in common with popular literature and share a good deal of ground with wider popular cultures. Their survival is directly dependent on the enthusiasm of their readers – though that enthusiasm may derive from the affectionate remembered allegiance of adult readers as well as from the loyalty of new young readers. I have attempted in the *Guide* to reflect and account for this enthusiasm while at the same time evaluating and explaining how individual writers, artists and works have expressed and contributed to the changing culture of the young.

Children's books exist in a world of social, political and economic change. The entries in the *Guide* take account of the fact that children's writers – and children themselves – are directly affected by both publishing practices and school literacy policies, as well as by poverty, bias and the terrible strains of war, exile and victimisation. We must also remember that children's books exist in a world of adult judgement, often passionate, sometimes bigoted. A Guide which did not pay due regard to the contexts in which children's books are produced and judged, and to those other – more private – contexts in which they are read, would be seriously incomplete. Accordingly, there are entries on publishing, reviewing, critical approaches to children's books, war stories, multicultural books, gay and lesbian books, abridgement, and other contextual topics.

The Cambridge Guide to Children's Books in English breaks new ground in a number of ways. In addition to the two great and long-established traditions of children's writing from Britain and the United States, I have tried, with the help of my advisory Editors, to do justice to the increasing and impressive range of successful children's books produced in Canada, Australia, New Zealand, West and East Africa and India; and to the exciting and extraordinary renaissances in children's books that are currently taking place – for different reasons – in Ireland and South Africa. There are distinguished reference works available in most of these countries, but in this *Guide* these separate traditions of writing for children have been brought together for the first time – each with its own national and regional cultures but all linked by history and language, publishing and marketing practices, and shared assumptions about children and childhood – to indicate the existence of a world-wide amplitude of provision for children.

As editor, I have become increasingly aware that book illustration has traditionally been undervalued, especially in the United Kingdom. Although picturebook artists have in the last two decades received considerable recognition, illustrators from the past are generally neglected, often not even named in the great library catalogues, and – until recently – publishers of children's books were often culpably casual about the ownership of illustration copyright. Much careful scholarship is still needed in this area; and while the *Guide* cannot claim to have set this injustice to rights, I have taken a few steps in the right direction by ensuring that there are entries on more individual illustrators than in comparable reference works, and others on related topics such as wood engraving, lithography and cover art.

Another innovative feature of the *Guide* is its recognition of the significance of series fiction. Since the publication of *Swallows and Amazons,* there have been more than 500 series titles published for children, along with sequels, trilogies and quartets. Reading all the books in a series implies a special commitment on the part of the young reader which is, I believe, quite different from the cautious curiosity many readers feel about an unfamiliar book. Series fiction has been treated rather shabbily by many previous critical works, with the first title receiving some consideration and the rest either not mentioned at all or being summarily listed. By concentrating on an entire series (*The Chronicles of Prydain*, for example), *The Guide* will bring its accounts of children's books closer to the experience of children's own reading.

A selection of notable awards and previous winners is to be found in the appendix; additionally there is an entry in the text on awards and medals.

While *The Cambridge Guide to Children's Books in English* is not primarily a bibliographical resource, every effort has been made to ensure accuracy. However, as experienced editors will not be surprised to learn, I have found that the achievement of total factual accuracy is an impossibility: dates of publication and even titles of books are, I have found, surprisingly flexible. Readers should also note that some authors regard their date of birth as confidential and this information has therefore not always been included.

Children's books are produced in such prolific abundance that an editor of a work such as this occasionally despairs of achieving completeness. This reference work is a critical snapshot, a little blurred in places because its subject is fast-moving and multifaceted. When I began this project, Harry Potter and Hogwarts had not been heard of; and subsequently many new and exciting writers (Katherine Roberts) and illustrators (Helen Cooper) have appeared; well-established writers have unexpectedly produced startlingly new fiction (Louis Sachar); new writers with uncertain reputations have in a few dazzling years established their stature as major authors (Henrietta Branford, Nick Warburton); novels with sequels have turned into major completed trilogies (the *Earthfasts* trilogy); new perspectives on works by earlier writers have become available (Anne Frank); and the great classics are repeatedly remade for contemporary readers with new illustrations (*Alice's Adventures in Wonderland*, *The Wind in the Willows*).

I owe a great debt of gratitude to the many contributors whose names are listed and who have responded to my editorial suggestions with such good grace. However, there are a number of individuals to whom I owe an additional debt for their helpful assistance far beyond the requirement of contracts. They are, of course, my three hardworking advisory editors, Morag Styles, Juliet Partridge and Elizabeth Keyser; a number of individual colleagues whose constantly available advice was as valuable as their written contributions – Kate Agnew, Susan Ang, Valerie Coghlan, Judith Graham, Elwyn Jenkins, Pat Schaefer, Nick Tucker and Mary Nathan; the Chris Beetles Gallery; and my press editor, Caroline Bundy, for her patience, helpfulness and sense of humour; and, finally, my wife Judith, whose support – psychological at first, directly practical in the later stages – has been invaluable.

Victor Watson

A note to the reader

There are four kinds of entry: *author entries*, *title entries*, some longer *topic entries* (see below) and a few, mostly short, entries covering *technical terms* (e.g. childness, recontextualisation, crosshatching) from both book production and literary criticism. There are also entries on literary awards, periodicals and, in a few cases, notable critics, editors and librarians.

Author and title entries are arranged alphabetically, authors by surname. Mc is alphabetised as Mac, Dr as Doctor and St as Saint. Historical, legendary and fictional figures (such as Robin Hood, Wild Bill Hickok and Mickey Mouse) are listed according to their first used name. Definite and indefinite articles in titles are ignored in the alphabetisation as are apostrophes. Author names are sorted before titles: **Little, Jean** appears before **Little Bear series**.

The headwords – names of authors, titles, series, movements, topics, characters – are in **bold** type. A name or part of a name which is unused is placed in round brackets: e.g. **Ahlberg, (George) Allan**. Where a writer is known by more than one name, or started life with a different one, the alternative name appears in square brackets after the more familiar one: e.g. **Turner** [**Burwell**], **Ethel** (**Mary**).

Titles or names in SMALL CAPITALS in the course of a text indicate that they have a separate entry in the *Guide*. Cross-references may be shortened: for example, NATIVE AMERICANS IN CHILDREN'S LITERATURE may appear as NATIVE AMERICANS.

A note on less obvious entries

In addition to the expected *topic entries* on subjects such as fairy tales, nursery rhymes, adventure stories, fantasy, picturebooks and so on, there are a number of less obvious topics. These include:

- abridgement
- adult fiction
- African American literature
- *Alice* imitations
- ballads
- ballet stories
- bias
- books for blind readers
- the [Australian] bush
- camping and tramping fiction

child authors
drugs in children's books
fairy fantasy
gay and lesbian literature
Guiding and Scouting fiction
Latin lessons and Latin masters
Latin versions
lithography
movable books
music and story
Native Americans in children's books
neglected authors
nudity in children's books
pantomime
playground rhymes
pony stories
reviewers and reviewing
riddles and jokes
sex in children's books
soap operas
superheroes
'The Big Five'
time-slip fantasy
US Latino children's literature
wood engraving

Finally, there are entries on the many *folktales and myths* which have found their way into children's stories:

Aboriginal culture in children's books
African mythology and folktales
classical mythology
English folktales
folktales and legends
Indian myths, legends and folktales
Irish mythology and folklore
Maori writing for children
Scottish folktales
Welsh mythology and folklore

Abbreviations

ABC	Australian Broadcasting Commission
ALA	American Library Association
AWGIE	Australian Writers' Guild annual award
BAFTA	British Academy of Film and Television Awards
BBC	British Broadcasting Corporation
CBC	Canadian Broadcasting Corporation
CBCA	Children's Book Council of Australia
CBS	Columbia Broadcasting System
CLA	Canadian Library Association
IBBY	International Board on Books for Young People
ITV	Independent Television
MGM	Metro Goldwyn Meyer
MLA	Modern Language Association
NYT	National Youth Theatre
OBE	Order of the British Empire
PBS	Public Broadcasting Service
RAF	Royal Air Force
RSPCA	Royal Society for the Prevention of Cruelty to Animals
TIE	Theatre in Education
UNESCO	United Nations Educational, Scientific and Cultural Organisation
YABBA	Young Australians' Best Book Award

A

A Apple Pie (1886) ALPHABET BOOK designed by KATE GREENAWAY and based on an ancient rhyme. Her bold banner-style capitals were innovatory and the pages are peopled by her characteristic drawings of children engaged in fun and games, their quaint dress harmonising with the quaint language of the text. PC

Aardema, Verna 1911–2000 American reteller of African and Mexican FOLKTALES for children. Born in New Era, Michigan, Aardema was so interested in books as a child that she frequently failed to complete her chores. She began her career as a teacher and later became city staff correspondent for the *Muskegon Chronicle*, frequently having to juggle her roles as a writer, mother and teacher. She became interested in children's stories through telling them, often African folktales, to her own children, and she published her first collection of stories, *Tales from the Story Hat*, in 1960. Aardema is not of African or Mexican descent, but she carefully researches the cultural background of each story. She received the CALDECOTT MEDAL for *Why Mosquitoes Buzz in People's Ears* (1975), which was adapted and animated by Weston Woods, the Lewis Carroll Shelf Award for *Who's in Rabbit's House?* (1977), and several Parents' Choice Awards including one for *Oh, Kojo! How Could You!* (1984). *BRINGING THE RAIN TO KAPITI PLAIN* (1981) was featured on *READING RAINBOW*. Aardema has worked with some of the most respected illustrators of children's books, including LEO and DIANE DILLON, Marc Brown, and JERRY PINKNEY. JGJ

see also AFRICAN MYTHOLOGY AND FOLKTALES

Abbott, Jacob see *ROLLO* SERIES; see also AMERICAN TRACT SOCIETY; INFORMATION BOOKS PUBLISHING AND PUBLISHERS; SCHOOL STORIES

ABCs see ALPHABET BOOKS; see also CHAPBOOKS

Aboriginal culture in children's books The representation of Aboriginal culture in children's books in Australia has reflected the changing attitudes of the newly dominant culture towards Aborigines. In the early days of white settlement, for example, Aborigines were seen by many as a race apart, a lower form of life akin to animals, to be feared and treated with hostility.

Illustration from *Lielle's Spirit Bird* by Lisa Kennedy (1995), with imagery deriving from her Aboriginal ancestry.

In *A MOTHER'S OFFERING TO HER CHILDREN* (1841) by Charlotte Barton, for example – believed to be the first children's book to be published in Australia – a mother describes the 'atrocities' of Aboriginal culture to her children. In *Tasmanian Friends and Foes, Feathered, Furred and Finned* (Meredith, 1880) Aborigines are described as 'the very lowest type of humanity; the ugliest, least intelligent, and least teachable of savages'. In boys' ADVENTURE STORIES it was common for Aborigines to be seen as sporting targets to be shot at.

There were those, however, who were sympathetic towards Aborigines, although in a very paternalistic way. This became more prevalent towards the end of the 19th century when Social Darwinist theories led people to believe that Aborigines would soon become extinct, thus justifying the policies of dispossession and 'protection'. *The Little Black Princess* (1905), by MRS AENEAS GUNN, tells the story of Bett Bett (the 'little black princess') who is treated very affectionately by her 'owner', but who, effectively, has the status of a lovable pet. Even the gardener 'Goggle Eye', described by the author as a 'king' of his people, is treated as a silly child. The Aborigines were portrayed in a similar way in the popular stories of the *BILLABONG* books (1910–42) by MARY GRANT BRUCE, although there was some lessening of the stereotyping towards the end of the series. Tarlton Rayment in *The Prince of the Totem: a Simple Black Tale for Clever White Children* (1933), despite the unfortunate title of the book, nevertheless gave some sense of the complexity of Aboriginal societies and their religious beliefs. In *THE WAY OF THE WHIRLWIND* (1941), written and illustrated by Mary and Elizabeth Durack, the traditions of a European FOLKTALE were combined with Aboriginal myth to reflect changing feelings about Australian identity.

As the 20th century continued, many fictional and non-fiction texts reinforced the widely accepted notion that the only way forward for Aborigines was to forget their Aboriginal heritage and go the 'white man's way', to become fully 'civilised'. At the same time, Aboriginal characters in books were sometimes romanticised and given miraculous gifts and insights, especially in a crisis, including characters who had not previously been aware of their Aboriginality. *Aranda Boy* (1952) by Rex Ingamells, *Picaninny Walkabout* (1957) by Axel Poignant, and *Tangara* (1960) by NAN CHAUNCY were some of the first books to give relatively enlightened portrayals of Aboriginal characters. The sensitively written *The Rocks of Honey* (1960) by PATRICIA WRIGHTSON deals with one person's difficulties related to his black and white inheritance. The award-winning Wrightson has continued to write many other novels which deal with Aboriginal issues, including issues of spirituality.

An important factor affecting the portrayal of Aborigines and Aboriginal culture in children's books is that until comparatively recently the books have been produced by non-Aboriginal writers, illustrators and publishers. While the situation is now changing, it has meant that most writers have been ethnocentric in their approach, often leading to inaccuracies, distortions and misappropriation of sensitive material, particularly in relation to Dreaming stories. While many collections of Aboriginal 'myths and legends' have been published over the past 100 years, including the well-known *Australian Legendary Tales* (1896) by Langloh Parker, most have been criticised, because the source of the stories has not been acknowledged, permission to publish has often not been given (or fully understood), and because the stories have often been trivialised and reworked to meet European expectations of what constitutes a story, particularly with stories published for young children. Catherine Berndt, however, did follow the correct protocols in collecting, retelling and publishing stories from the Gunwinggu women to produce *Land of the Rainbow Snake* (1979). Notable collections of Dreaming stories by Aboriginal authors include *Stradbroke Dreamtime* (1972) by OODGEROO NOONUCCAL (Kath Walker), Tulo Gordon's *Milbi: Aboriginal Tales for Queensland's Endeavour River* (1979), PICTUREBOOKS by Dick Roughsey and PERCY TREZISE, and the *Bawoo* stories by May O'Brien. The bilingual *Tjarany/Roughtail: The Dreaming of the Roughtail Lizard and other stories told by the Kukatja* (1992), published by the Aboriginal publisher Magabala Books, has won several awards, setting a high standard in terms of presentation, illustration and contextualisation of the stories. Magabala Books has published many books by Aboriginal writers, including *Do Not Go Around the Edges* (1990), DAISY UTEMORRAH's life story in verse and prose, illustrated by Pat Torres.

Aboriginal voices are increasingly being heard and seen in various types of stories. Ian Abdulla's picturebooks, such as *As I Grew Older* (1993), tell stories of his childhood on the Murray River through text and illustration. The *Badudu Stories* (by O'Brien and Leaney) deal with problems that Aboriginal children may face in terms of language and prejudice. BRONWYN BANCROFT's vibrant illustrations interpret historical and Dreaming stories in books like *The Whalers* (1996), a new edition of *Stradbroke Dreamtime* (1993), and novels with contemporary urban settings like *The Fat and Juicy Place* (1992) by DIANA KIDD. The distinguished indigenous artist and academic Donna Leslie, with her imaginative illustrations for the bilingual *Alitji in Dreamland* (1992), has given new life to CARROLL's *ALICE'S ADVENTURES IN WONDERLAND*.

Non-Aboriginal writers who include Aboriginal characters in their work are now, on the whole, much more aware of Aboriginal points of view and sensitivities. Books like *The Burnt Stick* (1994) by ANTHONY HILL, which deals with issues related to the 'stolen generation', *Songman* (1994) by ALLAN BAILLIE, set on the Arnhem Land coast in 1720, and JAMES MOLONEY's *Dougy* (1993) and *Gracey* (1994), which deal with racial tensions in a country town, have been well received. Aboriginal involvement in all aspects of the writing, illustrating, editing and publishing of books for children is steadily increasing, resulting in many exciting and innovative books which reflect the many voices of Aboriginal Australia. AH

abridgement The concept of abridging adult works for children as a form of editing, whether for length, content or style, dates back almost as far as the notion of children as a literary audience. With the Protestant Reformation and its emphasis on personal interpretation, Bibles for children appeared in a variety of forms – pictorial, versified, alphabetised and miniature. Thomas Cranmer's translation and adaptation for children of Luther's *Catechismus* was published in 1548 and Calvin's *Catechisme*, also for children, in 1556. Later abridgements of religious works included numerous 18th-century hieroglyphic editions of the Bible and also an illustrated *Juvenile Martyrology* (c. 1820), an abridgement of Foxe's *Book of Martyrs* (1563). By the early 20th century juvenile retellings of miracle plays were available in Netta Syrett's *Old Miracle Plays of England* (1911).

While AESOP's fables and classical texts had been available to schoolchildren since the early days of printing, the popularity of JOHN LOCKE's theories on pleasant learning and the reform and broadening of the curriculum in the 18th century reduced the emphasis on classical studies, and more and more material was revised for children. Greek and Roman myths (see CLASSICAL MYTHOLOGY), legends and histories began to appear in English-language editions for juvenile leisure reading including, by the 19th century, translations from the French of François de Fénelon's *Les Aventures de Télémaque* (1699), an adaptation of Homer, CHARLES LAMB's *Adventures of Ulysses* (1808) and an abridged edition of Flavius Josephus' history of *The Wars of the Jews* (1823).

The new children's book publishers of the second half of the 18th century soon produced juvenile abridgements of the popular adult novels of the day. In 1768–9 Francis Newbery published, simplified and abridged *Pamela, Clarissa, Tom Jones, Joseph Andrews, Sir Charles Grandison*, ROBINSON CRUSOE and, in the 1770s, *GULLIVER'S TRAVELS* and *Don Quixote*. But it was not until the end of the century that the editing of adult works for children became driven primarily by moral concerns rather than by a perception of the child's interests or reading level. Thomas Bowdler's *Family Shakespeare* reflected this change in attitude so clearly that his name has become synonymous with this form of editing. But CHARLES and MARY LAMB's *TALES FROM SHAKESPEAR* (1807) was intended chiefly for young ladies, 'because boys are generally permitted the use of their fathers' libraries at a much earlier age than girls are'.

Medieval romances such as *ROBIN HOOD, Valentine and Orson* or *The Seven Champions of Christendom* were retold in CHAPBOOK form in the 18th century, and in the early 1790s *The Oriental Moralist*, the first English edition of the *ARABIAN NIGHTS* for children, was published, the stories having begun to appear in English for an adult audience in 1706. When FAIRY TALES finally began to be published regularly in collections more substantial than chapbooks, they were often revised to emphasise a moral, overtly, as in PERRAULT'S *HISTOIRES OU CONTES DU TEMPS PASSÉ* (1697), or more often subtly within the text of the tale itself.

The revival of interest in, and anthropological collecting of, traditional material – BALLADS, FOLKTALES and romances – was a largely 19th-century phenomenon, but Thomas Percy's *Reliques of Ancient English Poetry* (1765) was influential in popularising antiquarian and, eventually, popular interest in published versions of *ROBIN HOOD, THE CHILDREN [or BABES] IN THE WOOD* and similar ballads and stories. In 1807 *Ancient Ballads 'Selected from Percy's collection; with explanatory notes, taken from different authors'* was published 'for the use and entertainment of young persons'. The early 19th-century fashion for medievalism, best seen in the popularity of the historical novels of SIR WALTER SCOTT, resulted in works like Clara Reeves's *Edwin, King of Northumberland* (1802), a retelling of part of THE VENERABLE BEDE'S *Historia Ecclesiastica* (early 8th century). In 1841 *True Tales of the Olden Time Selected from Froissart* made this historical work available to children also. After the publication of two important series – the *Home Treasury* (1843–7), edited by Sir Henry Cole under the pseudonym of FELIX SUMMERLY, and *The Old Story Books of England* (1845), edited by William John Thoms – collectors and antiquarians offered increasing numbers of ballads, romances, legends and folktales in attractive, well-produced editions with illustrations by notable artists. Fairy tales were retold in verse, in dramatic form or to teach specific lessons. In the 1840s the artist GEORGE CRUIKSHANK rewrote several fairy tales as temperance tracts (for which he was reviled by DICKENS).

By the mid-19th century, traditional material began to appear in alternative formats such as playing-cards or puzzles. The idea of using an abridged form of a tale to illustrate a novelty item was not new. In the 18th century the engraved borders of calligraphic samplers (writing sheets) had displayed scenes from Aesop's fables, the Bible, fairy tales and children's fiction. In 1777 *A New Years Gift for Little Masters and Misses* was published. This collection of woodcuts by THOMAS BEWICK, a number of which illustrate the stories of *CINDERELLA, PUSS IN BOOTS* and *LITTLE RED RIDING HOOD*, was printed without any accompanying text. Much later, the publisher William Spooner included versions of both *Fortunio and His Seven Gifted Servants* (1846) and *The Hare and the Tortoise* (1849) in his stock of table games, and illustrations of NURSERY RHYMES often appeared on puzzles.

Legends, other than English or Greek and Roman, were late arrivals as children's stories and some are still uncommon, although over the last 30 years a number of prominent children's authors and artists have created PICTUREBOOK versions for young children of myths, legends and folktales from many cultures. *Beowulf*, which was first published in a modern English translation in 1837, was first retold for children in Alfred Church's *Heroes of Chivalry and Romance* (1898). Even the KING ARTHUR stories, although popular in adult editions, were not retold as a group for children until the second half of the 19th century. SIDNEY LANIER's series of retellings of legends and histories, *The Boy's King Arthur* (1880), *The Boy's Mabinogion* (1881), *The Boy's Percy* (1882) and *The Boy's Froissart* (1879) remained popular in both Britain and America until well into this century.

By the beginning of this century sets and series were common at all price levels. Alongside collections such as Andrew Lang's 'COLOURED' *FAIRY BOOKS* was, the *Told to the Children* series by T.C. and E.C. Jack: 38 volumes of legends, medieval romances and ballads edited by Louey Chisholm and published between 1905 and 1909. The review in the *Pall Mall Gazette* declared: 'The shortening and simplification of the originals has been admirably done.' W.T. Stead's *Books for the Bairns*, printed on cheap paper and illustrated with line drawings, was geared to a more working-class market. Stead was concerned to bring both adult and juvenile classics to the children of the poor in an affordable form, and 288 titles were created and published between 1896 and 1920. By 1897 sales had reached 150,000 per month.

Individual authors have, at various times, retold particular adult works that they felt would be suitable for or attractive to children. Frequently including didactic interpolation, some of these are isolated efforts; others became part of the juvenile canon. Two stories from Spenser's *Faerie Queene* (1590s), 'The Knight of the Red Cross' and 'Sir Guyon', were retold in 1829 by Elisa W. Bradburn. Mrs H.R. Haweis, who was devoted to making CHAUCER accessible to children, produced five works abridged or retold from Chaucer between 1877 and 1887. Edwardian children had access to abridgements and retellings of, among others, Chaucer, Boccaccio, Cervantes, Coleridge, Scott, Dickens and Tennyson.

It is not only adult works that are abridged for children. As expectations of children's reading levels change, children's books are sometimes abridged or edited. BEATRIX POTTER is one author who is periodically cited as offering too sophisticated a vocabulary for today's pre-school reader; in the 1980s, LADYBIRD BOOKS, in association with Frederick Warne, published controversial adaptations of her stories with simplified language and puppet photographs replacing Potter's original illustrations.

As printing became increasingly mechanised and books correspondingly cheaper to purchase, a new form of ephemeral publication appeared. These were advertising pamphlets, their text often taken from fairy tales or nursery rhymes, abridged or rewritten to advertise the product. Colman's Mustard brought out one such series in the 1890s, and in the 1930s the Kellogg Company printed a series of brief retellings of fairy tales which doubled as games and in which the heroes or heroines benefited from the consumption of Kellogg's Corn Flakes.

In 1942 Simon & Schuster published a new series, *Little Golden Books*, which sold in enormous numbers through the 1940s and 1950s. At 25 cents a copy, they were designed for pre-school children and were marketed through bookshops, department stores and supermarkets. The text was very simple, sometimes an original story, more often a simplified retelling of a traditional story or popular novel for older children. The emphasis was on the quality of the illustrations rather than of the text, and artists working on the series included LEONARD WEISGARD, FEODOR ROJANKOVSKY and MARTIN and ALICE PROVENSEN. Abridged or reillustrated versions, sometimes new, sometimes from the WALT DISNEY cartoon, of *PETER RABBIT*, *MARY POPPINS*, *Peter and the Wolf* (see MUSIC AND STORY), *The Tin Woodman of Oz*, *ALICE'S ADVENTURES IN WONDERLAND*, and many other classics were included in the titles. By 1953 nearly 300 million books had been sold in over ten countries.

Abridged versions of both juvenile and adult fiction classics have also appeared in COMIC form. In 1941 the first *Classics Illustrated*, 'featuring stories by the world's greatest authors', 'endorsed by educators' and 'on sale at newsstands everywhere', were published monthly by Famous Authors Ltd. and sold for 10¢. The series included works as diverse as *Alice in Wonderland*, *TOM BROWN'S SCHOOLDAYS*, the *Iliad*, *A Midsummer Night's Dream*, *Lord Jim* and *Crime and Punishment*, and there was a separate series of *Classics Illustrated* fairy tales. JSh

absey books see ALPHABET BOOKS

Ace: The Very Important Pig see *THE SHEEP-PIG*

Achebe, Chinua 1930– Nigerian novelist who, in partnership with the poet Christopher Okigbo, founded the Citadel Press in Enugu, one aim being to publish children's stories with an African perspective. Okigbo's death during the Biafran War (1967–70) blocked the enterprise, though Achebe had already completed *CHIKE AND THE RIVER* (1966) and later wrote, with John Iroaganachi, the animal fable *How the Leopard Got His Claws*. PR

see also AFRICAN MYTHOLOGY AND FOLKTALES

Across the Barricades see *KEVIN AND SADIE* SERIES

acteme Theoretical term of uncertain provenance which denotes units of narrative, usually but not exclusively fictional in origin, which have broken free of their verbal and literary moorings and come to acquire an almost universal familiarity and resonance within a culture, as if innately known. CHARLES DICKENS provides many notable examples, among them Oliver Twist asking for more, and Tiny Tim's 'God bless us, every one.' Many instances are rooted in children's literature, not only in FAIRY TALE but also in modern works such as *PETER PAN* (the ticking crocodile), *THE WIND IN THE WILLOWS* (Mole's little home, the Wild Wood), or the *NARNIA* series (Lucy's passage through the wardrobe to the Narnian snow). PH

Adams, Adrienne 1906– Illustrator of children's books, greeting cards and other materials. She was born in Fort Smith, Arkansas, and trained as an artist. As a schoolteacher in the 1920s, she rose early every morning to paint for a few hours before school began. Moving to New York City, she attended the American School of Design and designed greeting cards, textiles, murals and furniture. Her first children's book was *Bag of Smoke* (1942), written by her husband, John Lonzo Anderson. Since then she has illustrated more than 30 children's books, usually working in colourful paints, pastels or crayons. Among her most popular books are two Caldecott runners-up, *Houses from the Sea* (1959) and *The Day We Saw the Sun Come Up* (1961); and two stories by the Brothers GRIMM, *The Shoemaker and the Elves* (1960) and *Jorinda and Joringel* (1968). All four books were selected as ALA Notable Books. Adams has often used her talent to bring new life to old stories, including tales by the Brothers GRIMM, Andrew Lang (see *'COLOURED' FAIRY BOOKS*), KENNETH GRAHAME and HANS CHRISTIAN ANDERSEN, FOLKTALES from around the world, and traditional carols. For *The Easter Egg Artists* (1976), *A Halloween Happening* (1981) and three other books, she created the text as well as the illustrations. CAB

Adams, Gillian see CRITICAL APPROACHES TO CHILDREN'S LITERATURE

Adams, Harriet Stratemeyer see *NANCY DREW* SERIES

Adams, Jeanie (Elsie Jean) 1945– Australian writer and illustrator, with a background in anthropology and indigenous arts, who has lived with the Wik Mungkan people of North Queensland. Her first award-winning PICTUREBOOK, *Pigs and Honey* (1989), is set in a contemporary Far North Queensland Aboriginal community. Together with *Going for Oysters* (1991) and *Tucker's Mob* (1992) with author CHRISTOBEL MATTINGLEY, this picturebook broke new ground in portraying daily community life from an Aboriginal perspective, and is illustrated in a distinctive batik style. FK

Adams, Richard see *WATERSHIP DOWN*; NICOLA BAYLEY; BIAS IN CHILDREN'S BOOKS; ANIMALS IN FICTION

Adams, William Taylor see *OLIVER OPTIC*

Adamson, George see *THE IRON MAN*

Adamson, Jean and Gareth see *TOPSY AND TIM* SERIES

adaptations see ABRIDGEMENT

Addams Family, The Created by cartoonist Charles Addams for *The New Yorker Magazine*, *The Addams Family* became a TELEVISION series from 1964 to 1966. The films, *The Addams Family* (1991) and *Addams Family Values* (1993), provide a dark and morbidly satirical spoof of American family life, capitalising on interest in the supernatural, the morose and the paranormal. *The Addams Family* offers a humorous look at the outsiders as they persistently attempt, despite their abnormalities, to fit into the seemingly 'normal' world in which they live, thus demonstrating that the concept of 'normalcy' is merely a perception, not a reality. CLR

***Addy Walker* series** see *AMERICAN GIRLS COLLECTION* SERIES

Ademola, Lady Kofo 1913– Nigerian educationist and voluntary social worker, born in Lagos. Her ten titles of *Lady K Tales* (1991, 1992), illustrated with amusing line drawings, present a tortoise up to his usual tricks, unlikely suitors winning princesses, and other folkloric themes. VD

Adkins, Jan 1944– American author and illustrator for readers of all ages. Born in Ohio, Adkins has worked as a designer for an architecture firm, a mathematics and science teacher, and an assistant art director for *National Geographic*. His books are charming and informative, and explore such diverse subjects as sandcastles, wine, sailing and baking. His first book, enjoyed equally by children and adults, was *The Art and Industry of Sandcastles* (1970), for which he wrote and hand-lettered the text and created ILLUSTRATIONS of real medieval castles and their copies built of sand. The book, nominated for the National Book Award, is not only visually appealing but also provides useful information for the building of sandcastles. Among his other children's books are *Toolchest: A Primer of Woodcraft* (1973), *Moving Heavy Things* (1980), *How a House Happens* (1983) and *String: Tying It Up, Tying It Down* (1992). These books and others combine technical information and whimsical illustrations. Adkins is adamant that he will not oversimplify texts to make them more accessible; if children understand everything the first time they look at a book, he reasons, they will not return to it. Adkins has also written fiction for young adults and for adults, and he is a regular contributor to magazines including CRICKET and *Smithsonian*. CAB

Adoff, Arnold 1935– American writer of poetry and prose, anthologist, editor and teacher. Adoff was born in the East Bronx, New York City. While working as a teacher in Harlem in the 1960s, he collected the works of AFRICAN AMERICAN poets to use in his classroom; this eventually resulted in the anthology *I Am the Darker Brother* (1968; rev. 1997). He has since compiled eight anthologies with the aim of introducing reading audiences to the wealth of literature by black writers. Adoff has also published over 25 books of his own poetry, which is known both for its musicality and for its 'shaped speech' style which highlights the way the arrangement of the words on the page contributes to the meaning. He has received numerous honours and distinctions for his works and in 1988 was the recipient of the National Council of Teachers of English Award for Excellence in Poetry for Children. Adoff has also written a BIOGRAPHY of Malcolm X and several PICTUREBOOKS. His works, both poetry and prose, tend to focus on a sense of family, the celebration of diversity, and children's imagination. Adoff married the author VIRGINIA HAMILTON in 1960. EB

adolescent fiction see YOUNG ADULT FICTION

adult fiction A number of adult writers have held a special appeal for young readers and have played an important transitional role in leading them towards adult fiction. In the case of *GULLIVER'S TRAVELS* and *ROBINSON CRUSOE*, this appeal has lasted almost 300 years and has been worldwide. In 19th-century Britain, the *Waverley* novels of SIR WALTER SCOTT – in their numerous attractively bound and illustrated editions – were read by thousands of young people. Some of the works of Jane Austen, CHARLES DICKENS, the BRONTËS, CHARLES KINGSLEY and other Victorian novelists achieved a similar popularity. This was partly because a good deal of fiction was serialised in the great periodicals of the time and was a central part of family reading, and partly because – as R. L. STEVENSON fully appreciated – the ADVENTURE STORY in particular could be made to appeal equally to young and adult readers.

In the early part of the 20th century the five Richard Hannay thrillers by JOHN BUCHAN were widely read by the young, as were the *Bulldog Drummond* books by 'Sapper' (Herman Cyril McNeile) and later the works of DOROTHY L. SAYERS, Agatha Christie, Edgar Wallace, Nicholas Monsarrat, ERIC LINKLATER, ALEXANDRE DUMAS, JULES VERNE, HISTORICAL FICTION by Jean Plaidy and Georgette Heyer, and war fiction (especially 'great escape' stories). Anthony Hope's *The Prisoner of Zenda* (1894) – described by one of Agatha Christie's characters as 'the first romance one was allowed to read' – and Daphne Du Maurier's *Rebecca* (1938), remained popular for many years. Later, Mary Renault's *The Mask of Apollo* (1966) came to be almost as popular as *Rebecca*, though probably for different reasons. Enid Bagnold's *National Velvet* (1935) became almost a cult book for riding enthusiasts, and in the 1960s the James Bond novels by Ian Fleming, popularised by the film versions, were read by thousands of young readers. In the 80s and 90s thousands of young FANTASY enthusiasts were easily drawn towards the enormous range of adult fantasy.

However, three series stood head-and-shoulders above all others in their special appeal to young readers in the 20th century: the *Sherlock Holmes* stories by Sir Arthur Conan Doyle (from 1887), the *SCARLET PIMPERNEL* stories by Baroness Orczy (from 1905), and C.S. Forrester's *Hornblower* stories (from 1937). For *Hornblower* enthusiasts, it was easy to graduate to the *Ramage* novels by Dudley Pope, secretly enjoyed by the fictional Nicola Marlow in the *MARLOW* series by ANTONIA FOREST. VW

see also LITERATURE IN CHILDREN'S BOOKS; WAR STORIES; YOUNG ADULT FICTION

***Adventure* (comic)** see 'THE BIG FIVE'

adventure game books Interactive texts which enable readers to pick characters which are then moved into conflict situations by making certain choices, usually decided by rolling dice. The complex FANTASY and SCIENCE FICTION settings are described at great length, and games may take days to complete. The popularity of the game books reached cult-like proportions in the 1970s and 80s, before computers replaced them with alternatives. HA

see also ADVENTURE STORIES; *DUNGEONS AND DRAGONS*

adventure stories Narratives about action or events involving danger and conflict and developing with speed and urgency. The protagonist at the centre of the action is a child, or youthfully-minded adult, who struggles to meet a challenge and achieve the required happy ending. The protagonists characteristically display more than ordinary abilities in single-mindedly pursuing a moral cause, and in the best stories they are changed and enriched by their adventures. The form has been adapted as the mores and concerns of society have changed; the hegemony of 19th-century boy/youth heroes, intimately connected with the ideology of empire, was gradually eroded during the latter part of the 20th century. There is still an emphasis on action, but the nature of both the protagonists and their challenges has mutated and diversified.

The modern adventure story has two principal origins, one of which is *ROBINSON CRUSOE* (1719). In ROBINSONNADES the challenge is survival and taking possession of a remote, often exotic place. Confident empire-building was integral to early adventure stories: the shipwrecked family in *SWISS FAMILY ROBINSON* (1812–13) adapt to tropical island life. CAPTAIN MARRYAT, irritated by Johann David Wyss's inaccuracies in natural history, geography and seamanship, wrote *Masterman Ready* (1841). In BALLANTYNE's *Coral Island* (1858) three exuberant British boys survive pirates, cannibals, a hurricane and a volcanic explosion. William Golding used *Coral Island* as an ironic contrast in *LORD OF THE FLIES* (1954). Alongside the theme of survival is the theme of the quest, for example in R.L. STEVENSON's *TREASURE ISLAND* (1883), which inspired H. RIDER HAGGARD's *KING SOLOMON'S MINES* (1885) and J. Meade Falkner's *MOONFLEET* (1898).

The robinsonnade was adapted by Richard Jefferies in his influential and innovatory *Bevis* (1882), sequel to *WOOD MAGIC* (1881). Two boys, free from adult direction, make boats and rafts in an idyllic English rural landscape, infusing their activity with imaginary adventures and heroic roles. *Bevis* was a strong influence on ARTHUR RANSOME's stories about the sailing adventures of both girls and boys in *SWALLOWS AND AMAZONS* (1930) and its sequels. Independent children are similarly integral to the children-versus-criminals genre started by Erich Kästner in *EMIL AND THE DETECTIVES* (1929) and its many sequels, but here the adventures take place in a dangerously real urban world. Cecil Day Lewis anglicised the form in *THE OTTERBURY INCIDENT* (1948), and the formula proved adaptable. Rural, holiday versions were written by ENID BLYTON in *THE FAMOUS FIVE* (1945–63) and *THE SECRET SEVEN* (1949–63), and by MALCOLM SAVILLE in *THE LONE PINE* series (1943–78). American versions include Franklin W. Dixon's *HARDY BOYS* series (from 1970s), Carolyn Keene's *NANCY DREW* series (from 1970s), and the *Adventure* series by WILLARD PRICE (1951–80). The form has also been used more creatively to explore serious social issues. Adventure stories about children escaping from, or struggling with, the injustices of poverty or abuse include BERNARD ASHLEY's *A WILD KIND OF JUSTICE* (1977), NINA BAWDEN's *Squib* (1971) and *Kept in the Dark* (1982), JOHN ROWE TOWNSEND's *GUMBLE'S YARD* (1961), RUTH THOMAS's *The Runaways* (1987) and ROBERT SWINDELLS's *STONE COLD* (1993). The strong sense of moral challenge, of battle between good and evil, links these books with FANTASY adventure stories; between 1960 and 1979 such adventure stories set in imaginary, mythical worlds were written by SUSAN COOPER, ALAN GARNER and URSULA LE GUIN. PHILIP PULLMAN has redefined and reworked these elements of adventure stories in *Northern Lights* (1995) (see *HIS DARK MATERIALS*).

The second strand derives from the Romanticism of SIR WALTER SCOTT's historical works, and is evident in G.A. HENTY's numerous historical adventure stories written for boys – but also read by girls – between 1871 and 1906. Henty deliberately set out to inspire a sense of historic destiny in his readers, his choice of settings, character and action expressing the ideals of contemporary British imperialism. In *BIGGLES* (1930s–1970s), W.E. Johns created a hero with stereotypical Henty qualities of dash, honour and innocence. In spite of its anachronistic attitudes to race, gender, class and patriotism the series is still widely read by children. As society's attitudes to conflict and morality shifted, the historical adventure story of the 19th century changed. The change began with GEOFFREY TREASE's *Bows Against the Barons* (1934), a radical version of the *ROBIN HOOD* stories. Trease followed it with adventure stories in which young people are caught up in the effects of historical events: *Cue for Treason* (1940), *Hills of Varna* (1948) and *Popinjay Stairs* (1973). The liberalisation of the historical adventure story continued in HENRY TREECE's *VIKING* saga (1955–64), ROSEMARY SUTCLIFF's *Roman* trilogy (1954–9) and *WARRIOR SCARLET* (1958), and LEON GARFIELD's Dickensian *Smith* (1967) and *BLACK JACK* (1968). More recent historical adventure stories that cross the class and gender divide are *Tulku* (1979) by PETER DICKINSON, *The Elephant Chase* (1992) by GILLIAN CROSS and *Kezzie* (1993) by THERESA BRESLIN.

Alongside the *Biggles* stories, other adventure stories about the Second World War became explorations of the way children's lives are affected by war, and of the attitudes and morality of both enemy and hero. In IAN SERRAILLIER's *THE SILVER SWORD* (1956) and Ann Holm's *I AM DAVID* (1963), displaced and persecuted children, caught up in the war, escape to safety across Europe. JILL PATON WALSH in *The Dolphin Crossing* (1967) and ROBERT WESTALL in *THE MACHINE GUNNERS* (1975) and its sequel *Fathom Five* (1979), describe the adventures of children entangled in the confusing adult world of war. The contemporary realities and dilemmas of terrorism and political aggression are faced by young people in Peter Dickinson's

The Seventh Raven (1981) and *A.K.* (1990), ROBERT CORMIER's *After the First Death* (1982) and John Rowe Townsend's *The Invaders* (1992).

American adventure stories can be categorised to some extent by their dramatic situations: there are, for example, robinsonnades, survival stories, sea stories and frontier tales. Typically the protagonist is separated from the familiarity of home and family. Robinsonnades and survival stories pit the protagonist against the indifference of nature and against the self; sea adventures provide a somewhat foreign but self-contained society in miniature; finally, frontier stories take place in locations where the popular imagination sees a conflict between civilisation and savagery. While 19th- and early 20th-century British stories were set in India, South Africa and Arctic Canada, American stories typically took place either in the 'wild west' or the competitive world of commerce in the city.

Many 19th- and early 20th-century American adventure stories had entertainment as their primary aim. They are frequently called DIME NOVELS, after the series begun by Irwin Beadle in 1860. The vast majority of these stories take place in the 'Wild West', but they also borrow themes from the *LEATHER-STOCKING TALES* as well as a fractured comic sense from the humorists of the old Southwest. Ann Sophia Stephens's novel, *Malaeska: The Indian Wife of the White Hunter* (1860), the first in the original dime series, sold 300,000 copies. The series numbered 300 volumes, and they were patterned after the thrillers that Gleason and Ballou published in their Boston-based magazine, *Gleason's Pictorial Drawing-Room Companion* of the 1850s. Ed Ellis's *Seth Jones*, the eighth novel in the series, sold 400,000 copies. Edward Wheeler created the popular *DEADWOOD DICK*, an English-born frontiersman, noted Indian-fighter and express guard for Black Hills gold shipments.

Not all early American popular adventure stories were set in the West. HORATIO ALGER wrote nearly 130 books for boys; the *Ragged Dick* stories (from 1867) were his most popular series. MARK TWAIN's *THE ADVENTURES OF TOM SAWYER* is a work that exploits and parodies the literary tradition of adventure begun by Sir Walter Scott. *The Adventures of Huckleberry Finn* is the most celebrated adventure story in American literature. *The Prince and the Pauper*, a work that Twain intended as the companion piece to *Huck*, is an adventure of traded places and a move towards self-knowledge. Perhaps the most popular adventure tale at the turn of the century was Edgar Rice Burroughs's bestseller *TARZAN OF THE APES* (1914), a tale that has achieved the status of popular myth in American culture.

The dime novel was superseded by 'pulp fiction' around 1895. These works celebrated the adventures of such characters as Frank Merriwell, the Rover Boys and Tom Swift. The most successful purveyor of this type of fiction was EDWARD STRATEMEYER, who created the *Rover Boys* series, which ran from 1899 to 1926. Howard Garis wrote *Uncle Wiggily's Adventures* in 1912, followed by many popular sequels. He also wrote the *Tom Swift* books. Leslie McFarlane, under the pseudonym 'Frank Dixon', began the *HARDY BOYS* series in 1927. Edward Stratemeyer plotted the first three *NANCY DREW* stories; his daughter Harriet Adams took over the pseudonym 'Carolyn Keene' and has written almost a volume a year since 1930. The popularity of the adventure genre was extended in the thirties and forties to other media – comic books (*SUPERMAN* first appeared in 1938; *BATMAN*, 1939), Saturday matinée thrillers and radio drama (*The Green Hornet*, *The Shadow* and *Jack Armstrong, The All-American Boy*).

Many notable American adventure stories of the 20th century appeared before the end of World War II, including JACK LONDON's *The Sea Wolf* (1904), William Bowen's *The Old Tobacco Shop* (1921) and Charles Hawes's *The Dark Frigate* (1923). Historical adventure is represented in Anne Kyle's *The Apprentice of Florence* (1933). The idea of the frontier as an indifferent or even hostile environment is depicted in Jack London's *The Call of the Wild* (1903) and *White Fang* (1906), Grace Moon's *Runaway Papoose* (1928), Marian McNeely's *The Jumping-Off Place* (1929), CORNELIA MEIGS's *Swift Rivers* (1932), Walter Edmonds's *The Matchlock Gun* and LOIS LENSKI's *Indian Captive: The Story of Mary Jemison* (1941).

Post-war writers have continued the traditions of adventure fiction. HAROLD KEITH's *Rifles for Watie* (1957) continues the historical adventure genre. AVI's *The True Confessions of Charlotte Doyle* (1990) combines sea adventure, historical fiction and an exploration of gender roles. Robinsonnades and tales of survival abound. SCOTT O'DELL's *ISLAND OF THE BLUE DOLPHINS* (1960) and *The Black Pearl* (1996), JEAN CRAIGHEAD GEORGE's *My Side of the Mountain* (1959) and *JULIE OF THE WOLVES* (1972), GARY PAULSON's *Dogsong* (1985) and *Hatchet* (1987), and Ivy Ruckman's *Night of the Twisters* (1986) are representative examples.

The extension of the adventure genre into FANTASY and SCIENCE FICTION has produced valuable works in Britain and the USA. These include MADELEINE L'ENGLE's *A WRINKLE IN TIME* (1962), URSULA LEGUIN's *EARTHSEA* quartet, SUSAN COOPER's *THE DARK IS RISING* series, LLOYD ALEXANDER's *THE CHRONICLES OF PRYDAIN*, and ORSON SCOTT CARD's *Ender's Game* (1992).

Australia, with its pioneer and outback heritage, provides some particularly exciting settings for a range of adventure stories. However, Australian writers have not limited themselves to this; city and townscapes, TIME-SLIP settings, science fiction and fantasy worlds, past times and other places, have all provided scope for adventure stories. Set in THE BUSH, the *BILLABONG* series (1910–42) by MARY GRANT BRUCE recounts family adventures which span many years. *THE SILVER BRUMBY* series (1958–96), by ELYNE MITCHELL, is set in the Australian alps; the stories feature wild horses and typically involve traps, rescues and injuries. COLIN THIELE, in *Fire in the Stone* (1973), focuses not only on environmental issues and the problems of mining opals but also on parental rejection, revealing how individuals can overcome both personal and external challenges. The sea has been the inspiration for many Australian writers – MAX FATCHEN'S *The Spirit Wind* (1973) is an adventure set on land and sea in which an old and dignified Aboriginal and a young European form an alliance against a bully; and in ALLAN BAILLIE'S *Adrift* (1984) two young children, while playing an imaginative pirate game, are carried out to sea in an old crate. Colin Thiele, while offering a commentary upon the problems associated with tuna fishing in *Blue Fin* (1969), also provides a story of disaster, survival and the sea.

IVAN SOUTHALL'S trilogy *Hill's End* (1962), *Ash Road* (1965) and *To the Wild Sky* (1967), dealing with courageous responses from young people following an inundation, bush fire or air crash, set the style for many subsequent Australian adventure stories which reveal characters personally transformed while involved in disasters. LILITH NORMAN'S *Climb a Lonely Hill* (1970) focuses upon immediate social reality and describes children's successful response to a physical ordeal while overcoming adult weaknesses and developing their own personal strengths.

The adventure genre has been dramatically extended in the *SPACE DEMONS* trilogy (1986–96) by GILLIAN RUBINSTEIN, when a computer game imbued with hate adjudicates among different adult and young personalities. PATRICIA WRIGHTSON'S *Down to Earth* (1965) combines adventure and science fiction to depict both extra-terrestrial life and interplanetary voyages. VICTOR KELLEHER'S *Master of the Grove* (1982) presents a world where magic is possible, and has many of the features of the DETECTIVE STORY, with a final climax of confrontation between good and evil, domination and liberation. JOHN MARSDEN'S series, curiously called a trilogy but including seven titles beginning with *TOMORROW, WHEN THE WAR BEGAN* (1993–9), tells the story of a group of young people faced with a national disaster, who conduct a guerrilla war against an overwhelming invading force which has taken over Australia. These books concern the personal and moral problems, challenges and development of young people facing immediate and direct threats, and show how they are transformed by meeting the challenges they encounter. VCH, HMcC, MRA

see also COMICS; SUPERHEROES

Adventures of a Doll, The see DOLL STORIES

Adventures of Huckleberry Finn, The see *THE ADVENTURES OF TOM SAWYER*; see also MARK TWAIN; BIAS IN CHILDREN'S BOOKS

Adventures of Tom Bombadil, The see J.R.R. TOLKIEN

Adventures of Tom Sawyer, The (1876) MARK TWAIN'S classic novel for children and adults. While it was followed by the highly successful yet controversial 'twin' work, *The Adventures of Huckleberry Finn* (1884), the other sequels, *Tom Sawyer Abroad* (1894) and *Tom Sawyer, Detective* (1896), were not as well written or as well received. Reacting against the genre of children's literature which depicted only the good child or the unacceptable bad boy, Twain created Tom Sawyer from his own memories of growing up in Hannibal, the basis for the St Petersburg of the novel. Tom is a 'real' boy who is acceptable to the small Missouri town despite his 'bad boy' pranks, trickery and adventures. Into the episodic adventures in each chapter, Twain has woven four storylines. The first, which Twain loosely follows throughout the novel, involves Tom's relationship with his Aunt Polly, his half-brother Sid and his cousin Mary, and includes the famous scene in which Tom convinces his friends of the joys of whitewashing the fence. The second storyline traces Tom's infatuation with Becky Thatcher and their frightening adventure in the cave, while the third follows Tom, Joe Harper and Huck Finn's week-long adventures on Jackson Island culminating in their supposed deaths and their resurrections at their own funeral. Finally, in the most complex storyline Tom and Huck witness Injun Joe's murder of Doc Robinson, discover Joe's hide-out, and, after his death, become heroes by finding his cache of gold.

While not his most controversial book, *Tom Sawyer* has certainly produced a myriad of reactions to its realistic depiction of an American boyhood which, as he states in the introduction, Twain hopes will also appeal to the adult audience and 'pleasantly remind them of what they once were themselves'. Throughout *Tom Sawyer* and his career, Twain was concerned with the authentic portrayal of childhood and of the American frontier. He elucidates these concerns through Tom, who directs the boys' play as pirates and other 'high-toned robbers' according to the books he has read. Tom is realistically portrayed as the show-off, the superstitious voyeur and the impetuous, love-struck pre-teen.

Initial negative reactions came from those who considered Tom's actions and language too improper for their children to read, whereas recent criticism tends to focus on Tom's questionable maturation and his capitulation to St Petersburg society as he ultimately becomes the 'good bad' boy. He is the proclaimed hero while his companion, Huck Finn, remains the town's 'pariah' and escapes St Petersburg society in his own book, the sequel to *Tom Sawyer*. In this century *Tom Sawyer* has been the subject of numerous cinematic and TELEVISION adaptations as well as paintings by artist Norman Rockwell. Mark Twain's bestselling *The Adventures of Tom Sawyer* has become synonymous with American boyhood.

The Adventures of Huckleberry Finn (1884), Twain's sequel to *The Adventures of Tom Sawyer* (1876), has been labelled by critics *the* great American novel, from which 'all modern American literature comes' (Hemingway). Whereas the title character of *Tom Sawyer* is the 'good bad' boy who eventually fully acquiesces to societal dictates despite his mischievous ways, Huckleberry Finn is the 'bad bad' boy who is never accepted by the Missouri society from which he escapes on his convoluted journey to freedom on the Mississippi River. On this archetypal coming-of-age quest during the American antebellum period, Huck aligns himself with the runaway slave Jim and defies those who would say that a slave is not a man. During the trip down the river, Huck and Jim go ashore and encounter all segments of southern society, including the comic burlesque of the King and the Duke, the tragic feud of the Grangerfords and Sheperdsons, and the irony of Tom Sawyer's fantastically engineered plan to free the already liberated Jim. At his epiphanic moment, Huck decides not to turn Jim in and to 'go to hell' for him. Huck does not capitulate to society, nor to Tom Sawyer, and he forsakes 'sivilization' to 'light out for the territory ahead of the rest'.

Historically, *Huckleberry Finn* has been both praised and denigrated for its realistic depiction of life during the pre-Civil War period. Twain uses authentic vernacular language remembered from his childhood and includes at least three different dialects – the educated 'white' dialect, the dialect of the uneducated title character, who is also the narrator, and the slave dialect of Jim. Among the contextualised terms used in the book, the word 'nigger' appears over 200 times and has incited almost continual controversy. Such objections notwithstanding, *Huckleberry Finn* addresses many societal and personal issues, of both its author's times and our own. Twain illuminated, through the metaphorical journey down the Mississippi River, the social stratification of American society as the outsider Huck runs away from his drunken and abusive Pap to affiliate with the other – and even lower – outsider Jim, who ultimately becomes his spiritual father. With characteristic wit and sarcasm, Twain looks satirically at the southern slave society of his youth, pointing out its foibles and inconsistencies as Huck and Jim face both the tragedy and comedy of life.

While Mark Twain sarcastically disclaims in his own introduction to Huckleberry Finn any 'motive . . . moral . . . or plot' to his classic tale of American adolescence, and thereby ironically associates himself in name only with those literary scholars who would seek to exclude Huck from the ranks of children's literature, the book is a children's tale of the highest order. Perhaps its greatness as children's literature and its contribution to the genre lie precisely in its ability to transcend the arbitrary boundaries between texts; it is intended for all audiences, for all times, and for all generations. CLR

Adventures of Two Dutch Dolls and a 'Golliwogg', The see ILLUSTRATION IN CHILDREN'S BOOKS

Ælfric 955?–1020? Abbot of Eynsham. He compiled the first Latin grammar in the vernacular, for 'little boys of tender years', with brief examples in dialogue form and a Latin/Anglo-Saxon vocabulary of words, from colours to farming gear, arranged by category. He is best known for his *Colloquium*, a lively manual of Latin conversation with an Anglo-Saxon interlinear gloss that is cast as a dialogue between some pupils and their master who, after a playful preliminary conversation about being good and avoiding flogging, questions the boys about their various professions (real or imagined), such as monk, farmer, hunter, merchant and shoemaker. GA

Ælfric Bata (Early 11th century) Student of ÆLFRIC of Eynsham, with whom he is sometimes confused. His *Colloquia* comprise an expansion of Ælfric's *Colloquium* plus two further *colloquia*, one easier, one more difficult. They contain a series of dialogues on different subjects ostensibly for the teaching of Latin vocabulary, including one between lively, often abusive students who misbehave and are subsequently whipped, and another between a young monk (a 'sweet boy') training to be a professional scribe and a customer who wants to commission a copy of a missal. The *Colloquia* provide a vivid picture of Anglo-Saxon student life and teaching. GA

Aesop (sixth century BC) Notional author of the most important body of FABLES in Western literature. It is not certain that Aesop actually existed as a historical figure; the first extant written collection of fables attributed to him is by the Latin poet Phaedrus in the first century AD. However there are a number of references to him in earlier classical literature – particularly Herodotus, Plutarch and Plato – which appear to establish key features of his identity: that he was a slave originally living in Asia Minor who achieved fame as a result of his extraordinary talent for telling apt and memorable stories. Herodotus suggests that he moved to Greece and eventually met his death at the hands of the people of Delphi. To this bare outline was later added a whole series of almost certainly apocryphal incidents detailing his life and career, including the ascription of physical deformity. The qualities ascribed to him in these stories include a unique capacity for survival and gaining an edge in politically dangerous situations. Having been sold as a slave to the philosopher Xanthus, for instance, Aesop is depicted as outdoing his master in correctly interpreting a particularly obscure omen for the Samians. But Aesop strikes a bargain before doing so; he will interpret the omen only on the condition that a successful result will secure his release from slavery. Several incidents also play on the notion of Aesop as an ironic commentator on human pretensions to escape the earthbound – indeed scatological – regime of the body. When the famous philospher Xanthus urinates on a journey without pausing at the wayside, for instance, Aesop comments wryly on his lack of concern for the inessential. Aesop's association with animals – he is pictured surrounded by them in the famous Steinhowel woodcut which CAXTON imitated in the first English printed edition of the fables – is another essential ingredient in his character which goes some way towards accounting for the enduring popularity of this author with children.

The absorption of Aesop's fables into the canon of literature deemed suitable for children occurred at a relatively early stage. The fable was a form recommended as exemplar in the study of grammar and rhetoric by Quintillian in the first century AD, and Aesop appears regularly as a curriculum author for 'minores' at least from the 11th century. Whether or not any of the details of his 'life' have a real historical basis, they give a particular focus to qualities in the stories he is said to have written, and they gave him a distinct identity within the pantheon of classical writers at the heart of the educational curriculum in the medieval and Renaissance world. Aesop's unique position among this galaxy of esteemed writers as a – probably illiterate – member of an underclass of slaves seems apt, at least, if one considers how sharp-eyed the fables are about relationships between the powerful and apparently powerless in the natural world, and the lessons for human conduct that can be drawn. DWh

African American literature Fiction, non-fiction, poetry, folklore and illustrative art focusing on African Americans: their present-day lives, cultural experiences, and history in America and Africa. In the beginning were the slave narratives, told, retold, remembered, eventually written down, published, read, reread, and ultimately recreated, transformed, and available today in collections by such writers as JULIUS LESTER, VIRGINIA HAMILTON and PATRICIA MCKISSACK. Then came the Harlem Renaissance of the 1920s and an interest by black writers to refute stereotypes and to promote a theme of struggle shared by many African American writers through the production of black art. African American literature and visual art forms were to come from black, rather than white, models. The magazine founded by W. E. B. DU BOIS, *THE BROWNIES' BOOK* (1920–1), reflected this same goal.

In the 1930s, two prominent members of the Harlem literary establishment, LANGSTON HUGHES and ARNA BONTEMPS, discovered a way to wed adult aims for African American art and children's literature in *Popo and Fifina, Children of Haita* (1932). Hughes's poetic language complemented Bontemps' understanding of both childhood playfulness and parental concerns. 'Langston had the story and . . . I had the children', said Bontemps, a father of six. During the 1930s Bontemps went on to produce more books without Hughes, at the same time searching for a more realistic way to depict black children's speech. After using standard English in *Popo and Fifina*, he used regional Alabama dialect in *You Can't Pet a Possum* (1934). Eventually he produced in *Sad Faced Boy* (1937) an early version of Black English, as he moved from reproducing phonemic levels of speech to replicating syntactic levels. Bontemps' books are even more important for their degree of authenticity. For the first time, black children could read books written by a black adult who had observed both the segregated worlds of rural Alabama and those of urban Harlem.

Several white writers of the 1930s were trying to portray black children accurately and sympathetically. Ellis Credle's *Across the Cotton Patch* (1935), set in her native region of Eastern North Carolina, reveals both black and white children eating watermelon, riding hogs and saying 'Sho nuff'. But the white children in these books do not continuously speak an unreadable, comic dialect, as do the black characters. Finding dialect difficult for her own kindergarten students in Atlanta, Eva Knox Evans eliminated it in the stories she wrote about black children – *Araminta* (1935) and *Jerome Anthony* (1936). Credle eventually did the same; she also discovered that the way she had been portraying black children in ILLUSTRATIONS was not well accepted. For a later book, she eliminated the use of dialect and substituted photographs for drawings in order to avoid any question of caricature. *The Flop Eared Hound* (1938) stands today as an important early 20th-century regional document.

More PICTUREBOOKS illustrated by photographs followed Credle's books. Stella Sharpe produced *Tobe* (1939), another realistic story of rural Southern life, and Ellen Tarry and MARIE ETS co-authored *My Dog Rinty* (1946), in which Northern black families in Harlem could be seen advancing economically, in great contrast to the simple, fixed existence portrayed in Sharpe's and Credle's earlier books. Each of these writers presented pictures of segregated worlds, whether of North Carolina or Harlem, foreshadowing issues that were to trouble books about the black child for the next two decades.

Ellen Tarry's *Hezekiah Horton* (1942) and MARGUERITE DE ANGELI'S *Bright April* (1946) represent changes occurring in the 40s. Black author Tarry emphasised the new economic possibilities for black children: Hezekiah dreams of owning an automobile and finally learns that some day he can become the white man's chauffeur. The white author De Angeli educated the white child in values of brotherhood at the same time that she informed the black child about white expectations and the politics of accommodation: the black child April aspires to own a hat shop but is told that 'many people cannot do the things they want to do' and that 'homely work is important too'.

De Angeli's text and illustrations, although showing no caricatures of race, reveal no distinguishing ethnic traits; the more like the white child the black child could be, the better, white writers of the 40s suggest. A notable exception was FLORENCE CRANNELL MEANS, a white writer whose earlier work, *Shuttered Windows* (1938), had told the story of a black girl from Minnesota who goes to live with her great-grandmother in the Sea Islands of South Carolina and has her first encounter with racial discrimination. In 1946, Means produced *Great Day in the Morning*, the story of a young black girl in Alabama experiencing racial prejudice at Tuskegee. In both books, she sets class differences among American blacks against the backdrop of the white, mainstream bigotry of her day. Wisdom, kindness and dignity are the universal traits that black characters display in Means's books, set in a socio-historical context.

Many books of the 50s and 60s spoke of the problem of integrating schools and neighbourhoods, and because most of the authors were writing from a white perspective, the mood was similar to that of the 40s: injustice was usually given quick and simple cures and optimism prevailed: 'Colored is just another color', says the lone bigot at the end of Jerrold Beim's *Swimming Hole* (1950). The attitude of black writers was very different. Ed Williams of LORENZ GRAHAM'S *South Town* (1958) is a quiet, even-handed person, but even he is reduced to hatred by the bigotry of his white employer. 'He's got too much dirt in him for me to go near him', Williams says at the end of the book. 'And I got too much hate in me.'

By the 1960s, when EZRA KEATS produced *A SNOWY DAY* and won the Caldecott Award for his striking pictures of a black child in a bright red snowsuit discovering the joy of the year's first snowfall, the children's publishing world seemed open to a new idea: the black child as world 'player'. Less ethnic than universal in behaviour, action and supposed feelings, Peter was any child – Everychild – playing in the snow. The problem, however, was cultural completeness. The notion that the black child might have separate feelings because of separate experiences was a new one to white writers, who for so long had followed the credo of the 40s – that all people have similar basic emotions. At the same time, as outsiders to the black experience themselves, they were simply unable to produce richly detailed, authentic portraits of African American culture. Thus white writers in this era continued to see the 'universal' condition as more significant than differences of heritage and culture. In the wake of a burgeoning civil rights movement and conflicts over school and housing integration, the vision of a black child as universal child appealed to those who foresaw a 'white' world in which black children might become peacefully assimilated.

Black children needed black writers like JOHN STEPTOE, black critics began to say. Steptoe's *Stevie*, published in 1969 when Steptoe was only 19, is a story of sibling jealousy, but here, unlike Keats's book, a universal theme is dramatised in terms of ethnic differences. As with Bontemps some 37 years earlier, the language replicated the dialogue Steptoe had heard black children speak. Ethnic characteristics in language, artwork and setting filled the pages of Steptoe's next two books, *Uptown* (1970) and *Train Ride* (1971). The children in these books often appear as miniature adults – serious, belligerent, even sad – and the colours add a bright solemn intensity. The black family is also clearly delineated – the frightened parents of missing children in *Train Ride*, and Robert's sturdy mother in *Stevie*, comforting the fearful child she has taken in.

Others thought that more needed to be done. Significant research, conducted by NANCY LARRICK in 1965, indicated that only 6.7 per cent, or 349 out of 5,206 children's trade books for a three-year period, contained any reference in text or illustrations to the black child. When the references did appear, they were often misleading. In *Black Pilgrimage* (1971), black artist TOM FEELINGS tells of turning down many jobs illustrating children's books in the 1960s because he felt that white writers of these books were presenting a distorted view of African American life. Returning from a visit to Ghana, Feelings co-authored with his wife Muriel *Zamani Goes to Market* (1970), a story of

African family life. Soon afterward, they produced an African ALPHABET and an African COUNTING BOOK. All three books were created to provide positive representations of the black heritage, and they revealed a new method of illustration that Feelings conceived in Africa: he combined black ink, white tempera with tissue paper overlay and final ink wash, in order to convey the feeling of the hot sun upon the black skin.

The white mainstream children's publishing industry began to see that writers of African American literature also needed to explore the complexities of cultural differences, as VIRGINIA HAMILTON had done in 1967, when she produced her first children's book. *Zeely* is the story of a young black girl, Geeder, who in visiting her uncle's farm one summer fantasises that her neighbour, six-feet-tall Zeely Tabor, is a Watusi Queen. By the time Geeder realises the extent of her illusion, she has discovered, through Zeely, the beauty and mystery of her own African heritage and a great deal about pride, courage and self-esteem.

Once the idea of cultural differences gained the attention of publishers, the doors opened wider for many distinguished black writers and artists. A golden age of African American children's literature, long in the making, was well underway. In 1974, Virginia Hamilton was the first African American writer to win the Newbery Award, and in 1978 Mildred Taylor became the second. Writing from the black perspective about the cultural fabric of black life in America, many notable writers and artists have recorded their own African American experiences and have remembered or imagined fascinating stories of their ancestors.

What makes African American children's literature unique is the strong sense of family, especially the extended family, and the importance for cultural survival of keeping and transmitting the knowledge of family and cultural history. What gives African American children's literature its particular artistic strength is the medley of richly varied ethnic voices. African American traditions, values, beliefs, idioms, people and stories flow through these works, and the ways writers and artists of so many culturally diverse black communities in America find to inscribe readers into their own cultural worlds give this particular branch of American children's literature its own unique identity. NM

see also ASHLEY BRYAN; LUCILLE CLIFTON; DONALD CREWS; LEO DILLON; NIKKI GIOVANNI; ELOISE GREENFIELD; JOYCE HANSEN; SHARON BELL MATHIS; BRIAN PINKNEY; JERRY PINKNEY; JAMES RANSOME; FAITH RINGGOLD; JOYCE CAROL THOMAS; JACQUELINE WOODSON

African mythology and folktales The oral traditions of the peoples of Africa have provided material for many children's books, some in the original languages, but most in translation. English-language books draw primarily on tales from countries that fell under British colonial rule. Hundreds of books contain stories from the peoples of Ghana and Nigeria, Central and East Africa, and all the countries from Malawi and Zambia southward.

The majority of these books have been published by South Africans – in fact, they have constituted one of the largest genres of children's books in South Africa in the 20th century, which suggests that writers have seen such stories as contributing to inter-cultural understanding in that country. Geraldine Elliot and Phyllis Savory are among many of the South African writers worthy of notice. Writers who have published elsewhere include Harold Courlander, Kathleen Arnott, VERNA AARDEMA and Elizabeth Helfman.

The stories come from many sources. Since the 19th century thousands have been collected and published by white anthropologists, and writers have drawn on these, as well as on their own collections, for children's books. Tales are frequently recycled, both from classic collections and from more recent books. Excellent stories have been written in the style of FOLKTALES by MARGUERITE POLAND and CICELY VAN STRATEN, among others.

Books of folktales raise the question as to what constitutes a children's book: while some, in format, illustration and style, are obviously intended for children, there are many that are vaguely addressed to 'children of all ages'. All too often the stories are written in a cumbersome and pedestrian style, with ILLUSTRATIONS that are unlikely to appeal to children. On the other hand, some authors have taken particular care to make their versions of the stories lively enough to be read to, or by, children. Some books have been beautifully illustrated and more recently single tales have appeared as PICTUREBOOKS.

It is unfortunate that westerners have tended to see African folktales as primarily suitable for children, as this smacks of cultural condescension. Nevertheless, there is no reason why those told to children in traditional African society should not be passed on through children's books, and the results have made a considerable contribution to the children's literature of the world. African oral tradition can be said to include myths of creation and cosmology, legends of historical events and people, praise songs, stories of humans and supernatural beings, FABLES, RIDDLES and tales explaining proverbs. It must be recognised, however, that this sort of classification, and the way the material is selected and adapted by (white) writers, inevitably distorts the original material.

Some children's writers (such as JENNY SEED and DIANA PITCHER) have assembled creation stories which tell of the creator and what the San of Southern

Africa call the 'people of the early race'. However, books in English seem to favour talking-animal stories, and some include songs, riddles and proverbs. A popular kind is the aetiological, or 'pourquois', story, such as 'How the leopard got his spots'. Often animal stories are satirical. Well-known characters include the frog, the lightning-bird and the milk-bird.

Stories about a TRICKSTER figure are common. He can be a hare, tortoise, spider, jackal, mantis (in San tales) or diminutive boy. As a hare, he was carried to North America, where he appears as Brer Rabbit in the *Uncle Remus* stories (see JOEL CHANDLER HARRIS). Animal stories often contain a contest, usually set up by the trickster, and other stratagems by which animals outwit each other. Widespread plots include the tug o' war between huge beasts such as the elephant, hippopotamus, rhinoceros or crocodile, and the race between the tortoise and the hare.

Usually African tales, while reflecting African customs and values, do not point a simple moral. Tales are told about chiefs and their sons, beautiful maidens, magic bowls and spoons, animals and birds that talk to people, enchanters, diviners, witches, ogres, cannibals, dangerous spirits and monsters. Quests, tests and journeys feature, as they do in folktales around the world.

Many folktales are common to peoples widely spread across the African continent. Beginning at least with AESOP, African tales have also been carried to other parts of the world. Similarly, some tales found in Africa today show elements drawn from the folklore of other continents, such as the BROTHERS GRIMM, the Hindu *Pancha-tantra* and the Buddhist *Jataka* tales, or they include modern elements reflecting European colonisation. In South Africa, the tales of the Cape Malays (descendants of slaves), recorded by I.D. du Plessis, are largely based on stories from the *ARABIAN NIGHTS*.

The publication of folktales in African languages has been mostly for school readers, such as C.L.S. Nyembezi's use of Zulu tales for his *Igoda* series. Only a few African writers have published stories in English, for example Bob Leshoai and GCINA MHLOPHE in South Africa, and CHINUA ACHEBE and Amos Tutuola in West Africa. In South Africa, the publishing market is strengthened by a great deal of cross-translation between the indigenous languages, English and Afrikaans. ERJ

Agard, John 1949– British/Guyanese poet who moved to England in 1977. Agard worked for the Commonwealth Institute for many years promoting Caribbean culture. He describes himself as a 'Poetsonian', emphasising the links between poetry and other arts and the satirical spirit of the Caribbean calypsonian. Popular with youthful and adult audiences, Agard is also a gifted performer of poetry. After a highly successful stint at London's South Bank Arts Centre, he became the first Poet in Residence at the BBC in 1998.

Agard's poetry has wide appeal, from very young children to teenagers and adults. Key poetry collections include *I Din Do Nuttin* (1983), *SAY IT AGAIN, GRANNY* (1986), *Laughter is an Egg* (1988), *We Animals Would Like a Word With You* (1996) and *Get Back, Pimple* (1997). *No Hickory No Dickory No Dock* (1991) and *A CARIBBEAN DOZEN* (1996) are collaborations with his partner, GRACE NICHOLS; the latter is an excellent introduction to 13 Caribbean poets. Agard's work focuses on direct, everyday experience in Britain as well as his roots in the Caribbean, mixing universal themes with ordinary domestic life and tackling issues like racism, using irony and humour rather than invective to make his point in poetry that dances and sings. He has also published plays and PICTUREBOOKS and received the Casa de Las Americas Prize for an adult collection in 1982. HT

Agarwal, Deepa 1947– Indian fiction writer, translator, scriptwriter, author of PICTUREBOOKS for the young, and of mystery, adventure and ghost stories for the 9–12 age group. Agarwal believes that reading is an essential part of growing up. Her work therefore deals with a variety of complex themes, such as class and gender divisions, or the growth and transformation of children through struggle and perseverance. Stories like the *Everyday Tales* (1995) deal with problems such as parental pressure to perform well in school; the true meaning of friendship; or the tensions in a divided family. Her clumsy, well-meaning character Lippo, in *Lippo Goes to the Park* (1994), was appreciated enough to lead to a series of *Lippo* books. Her picturebook *Ashok's New Friends* (1990), on the theme of equality between girls and boys, received the National Award for Children's Literature. The desire to demolish gender stereotypes leads her to construct stories where girls play significant roles, as in the daring search for a rare Himalayan herb in *Hunt for the Miracle Herb* (1995), a book packed with interesting descriptive passages which highlight her concern for the preservation of the environment. MBh

Agwu, Ada K. 1936– Nigerian writer and teacher, born in Ohafia, Imo State. Her juvenile novel, *Tunji the Motor Mechanic* (1973), gives a blue-collar twist to the popular theme of a disadvantaged child succeeding through education. Works for younger readers include *Spider's Land* (1977), a paean to hard work and perseverance, and adaptations of two Bible stories, *The Dreamer Boy* (1973) and *The Boy in the Ark* (1977). VD

Ahlberg, (George) Allan 1938– and **Ahlberg, Janet (Elizabeth Mary) [née Hall]** 1944–94 British husband-and-wife team who wrote and illustrated PICTUREBOOKS. Allan and Janet met whilst training to be teachers, although Janet turned quickly to ILLUSTRATION after studying Art and Design. Allan, however, taught for ten years before they collaborated on their first project, a series of books entitled *The Brick Street Boys*, first published in 1975. The series grew out of Janet's request that Allan should write her a story to illustrate, and from the beginning they worked as a team, collaborating closely on each book.

Within a very few years they had achieved success and popularity with books such as *Jeremiah in the Dark Woods* (1977) and *EACH PEACH PEAR PLUM* (1978), both of which reveal the Ahlbergs' intuitive understanding of the child's world of story. Throughout the 1980s and into the 1990s the Ahlbergs created a series of ingenious and original picturebooks including: the *Happy Families* series (from 1980), *Funnybones* (from 1980), *Peepo* (1981), *The Baby's Catalogue* (1982), *THE JOLLY POSTMAN* (1986), *STARTING SCHOOL* (1988) and *It Was a Dark and Stormy Night* (1993). Much of their work has been innovative and has extended the range of the picturebook, but it has always stayed very close to the world of child readers and their desires. In 1986 they won the KURT MASCHLER AWARD for *The Jolly Postman*. Allan Ahlberg's output has been prolific and he has worked with a number of other illustrators including ANDRÉ AMSTUTZ, COLIN MCNAUGHTON, CHARLOTTE VOAKE and FRITZ WEGNER. Recent publications include *The Hen House* (1999) and *Slow Dog Falling* (1999), and *The Snail House* (2000), beautifully illustrated by Gillian Tyler. DL

see also *PLEASE MRS BUTLER*

From *Burglar Bill* by Allan and Janet Ahlberg.

Aiken, Joan 1924– British novelist, daughter of the American writer Conrad Aiken, born in Sussex, England. Joan Aiken has published more than 50 books for children and adults. Her most popular books for children are the *JAMES III* SERIES. Like the first in the series, *The Wolves of Willoughby Chase*, the sequels are full of fast-paced, fantastic adventures set in an imaginary historical period. Aiken has written short stories, plays and poetry, and is also known for her horror stories and mystery novels. In 1982 she published a guide to writing skills, *The Way to Write for Children*. Some of her collections of stories comprise versions of traditional FOLKTALES; others contain her own composed stories. Among Aiken's books for younger children are the hilarious adventures of the eccentric pet raven, Mortimer, who always ends up causing trouble for Arabella and her parents (*Mortimer's Cross*, 1983, *Mortimer Says Nothing*, 1985, *Arabella and Mortimer*, 1989).

Dido Twite, Mr Slighcarp and Margrave of Nordmarck are some of the unforgettable characters Aiken has created, aided by her sense of humour and her inventive skill for names reminiscent of Dickens. Characters border on the caricature and the action is satisfyingly predictable: wicked villains' plots are foiled again and again by innocent heroes and heroines – particularly in the historical FANTASIES. In these and other stories, the readers enter a world of magic which guarantees happy endings with punishments and rewards. In her horror stories, on the other hand, the readers get a chilling glimpse of the more sinister edges of the unreal. EA

Aikin, John see ANNA LAETITIA BARBAULD; see also LUCY AIKIN

Aikin, Lucy 1781–1864 English writer, born into a liberal, intellectual Unitarian family based in Stoke Newington, London. Lucy was the daughter of John Aikin (the biographer, essayist and critic) and niece of ANNA LAETITIA BARBAULD. She edited one of the earliest anthologies for the young, *Poetry for Children* (1801), which includes an enlightened and intelligent preface and several of her own poems of modest ambition. An anti-slavery activist with feminist leanings, Aikin produced prolific works of fiction and history for children and turned her hand to a range of writing for adults. MCCS

Ajayi, Christie Ade 1930– Nigerian writer and early childhood educator, born in Ile-Oluri, Ondo State. Seeing the need for children's books with local flavour, she wrote the escapades of *Ade, Our Naughty Little Brother* (1975), Yoruba FOLKTALES in *The Old Storyteller* (1975), and *Akin Goes to School* (1978), co-authored with

Illustration by Jessie McDermott for *Lulu's Library* by Louisa May Alcott.

Michael Crowder. Ajayi has also written PICTUREBOOKS portraying familiar everyday experiences, in *Alli's Bicycle, Tinu's Doll, Emeka's Dog* and *My Book of Animal Riddles,* all published in 1982. VD

Akan folktales see OSAFOA DANKYI; MESHACK ASARE

Aladdin see *ARABIAN NIGHTS' ENTERTAINMENTS*; see also DAVID WOOD; MOVABLE BOOKS

Alcock, Vivien 1924– British author born in Worthing, Sussex. Alcock worked as a commercial artist and married LEON GARFIELD in 1948. Characteristically her novels feature female protagonists poised between childhood and adolescence, who feel alienated from their parents. Strong elements of FANTASY and the supernatural direct lively plots in which contemporary relationships and issues are explored within powerfully evoked settings. Her first novel, *The Haunting of Cassie Palmer* (1980), praised for its originality and social relevance, contained themes which recur in later books. Probably her most distinctive work is *The Monster Garden* (1988). Several, including *The Sylvia Game* (1984) and *The Cuckoo Sister* (1985), were serialised for TELEVISION. CMN

Alcott, Louisa May 1832–88 American novelist who has suffered in recent decades by losing her intended audience of young adolescent girls and attracting the attentions of adult critics who have their own political agenda to promote. Best known for the four books, beginning with *LITTLE WOMEN* (1868), which comprise the March family saga, and for numerous novels and short stories for children, she also wrote sensational stories for newspaper publication under the pseudonym A.M. Barnard.

Much is made of the autobiographical content of the March family novels but this is really true only of *Little Women,* and even that gives scant indication of the Alcotts' circumstances during Louisa's childhood and adulthood up to the point of its publication, when it launched her career as a successful, sought-after writer. Daughter of Abigail May and Bronson Alcott, the Transcendentalist philosopher, she and her sisters were raised in poverty and desperate insecurity. Bronson, whose advanced and – to 19th-century parents – alarming views on education resulted in the closure of a number of schools he founded, and who abhorred the notion of working for hire, was not a provider. This obligation fell first of all upon his wife who, although sharing his high ideals, needed to feed her daughters, and later upon Louisa, whose dream, realised by the success of *Little Women,* was to provide for her family and relieve them from the burden of debt.

Thereafter Alcott's output was regular but uneven in quality. Although she never returned to the didactic whimsy of her first published fiction, *Flower Fables* (1855), and only once to the rousing excesses of A.M. Barnard, her work rarely achieved the confident fluency of the March novels or the grittiness of *Hospital Sketches* (1864), based closely upon her own experiences as an army nurse at the outbreak of the Civil War (although she omitted the disastrous and permanent damage inflicted on her own health).

The fate of her first novel, *Moods* (1864), is revealed in *Good Wives* (1869). Chopped about as a result of conflicting advice, it is a flawed but interesting début and remarkably outspoken upon the subject of divorce. She always used her fiction as a vehicle for the propagation of educational, social and feminist theory, and her relatively early death robbed her of the audience she was preparing for herself. In *An Old Fashioned Girl* (1870) – the title of which belies the content – she contrasted the idle rich family, supported by an overworked father, with the healthy independence of the women who went out to work for their living, though she never underestimated the toll this took in a world still unadjusted to the idea of female emancipation. She pursued this further in *Work* (1873), which, being written for adults, allowed her greater frankness about the experiences of women surviving alone. *Eight Cousins* (1875) and its sequel, *Rose in Bloom* (1876), are more overtly polemical. The main character, Rose, is orphaned and consigned to the care of her father's brother Alec, a doctor. In the teeth of opposition from her six aunts, Alec educates Rose to take care of herself, the message of the books being that if women were to assume their place alongside men as equals, their first duty was to free themselves from the self-inflicted ailments that enfeebled them. That a badly nourished woman in a suffocating corset and clothes that virtually crippled her was ill-equipped to call herself anyone's equal, seems self-evident now. In 1875 these were contentious ideas and, coupled with Alcott's dedicated suffragism, would have drawn severe disapproval had she not already established herself as a popular favourite. The book is no sermon, though, but an entertaining read, as is the sequel which follows Rose into adulthood with her boy cousins. Rose herself is not a particularly interesting figure, but she is surrounded by lively characters, not least of whom is Uncle Alec, one of those vigorous and outgoing men that Alcott was so skilled at creating in spite of having been surrounded in her formative years by the solipsistic Transcendentalists who haunted the woods around Concord.

Alcott's reaction to her success was always ambivalent. She loved the money and, for a short while, the fame, but lending her experiences to the middle-aged Jo of *Jo's Boys* (1886), she allows herself some sarcastic jabs at her public, at herself as a 'literary nursemaid who provides moral pap for the young', and at her publisher, Thomas Niles of Roberts Brothers, who in a riverine pun is translated into Mr Tiber, who 'sits at his desk like a sort of king . . . for the greatest authors are humble to him, and wait his Yes and No with anxiety'. One chapter of *An Old Fashioned Girl* features a visit to a group of women artists among whom is a farouche young writer, sulking at her unexpected celebrity. The ambivalence was compounded by her persona of benign literary auntie, purveyor of moral pap, who was a front woman for the caustic, depressive realist whose sardonic tongue cut through the bromides. The laconic Yankee diction of her young protagonists was a voice she suppressed in herself, preferring to make her authorial interventions in the admonitory tones of Aunt Jo, rather than the scathing social and political critic she might have allowed herself to be.

In *Little Women* Jo dreams of becoming a great author. So, one must assume, did Alcott. Like Jo, she settled for less, understanding that her reach exceeded her grasp, but her best work was popular for a century and influenced many who followed her. *Little Women* has been filmed three times and Jo March became a role model for generations of girls. Alcott has been criticised for withholding glittering prizes from Jo, who so clearly deserved them, but there were no glittering prizes for Alcott either. Nevertheless, she changed the face of children's fiction forever. JMM

Alcuin 735?–804 Director of the Cathedral School at York and, after 762, of the Emperor Charlemagne's Palace School. Alcuin was a major figure in the reform of European education, both secular and religious. He also tutored the royal sons and daughters and other members of the nobility. Among his many works, including educational texts, are his *Disputatio Pippini cum Albino Scholastico*, a dialogue with Pippin, Charlemagne's young son, which represents an imaginative method of learning vocabulary, and his poem 'Versus de Gallo' ('A Poem about a Cock') which is the first extant version of the tale of the fox and the cock. GA

Alden, Isabella MacDonald see *PANSY*

Alderson, Brian see REVIEWING AND REVIEWERS; see also EDWARD ARDIZZONE; CRITICAL APPROACHES TO CHILDREN'S LITERATURE; HAROLD JONES; ANTONY MAITLAND; CHRIS RIDDELL

Alderson, Valerie see REVIEWING AND REVIEWERS

Aldhelm 639?–709 Abbot of Malmsbury and Bishop of Sherborne. His *De Septenario* or *Epistola ad Acircum* (685?) – a Latin letter to King Aldfrith of Northumbria, his godson – contains a discussion of the number seven, and two technical treatises on metre in the form of question and answer between pupil and teacher, the first English example of this ancient genre. The letter includes 101 poetic 'enigmata' or riddles with a title providing the solution. Intended to illustrate Latin verse composition, the riddles subsequently had their own manuscript tradition, becoming a popular and influential school text in Britain and on the Continent. GA

see also JOKES AND RIDDLES

Aldin, Cecil see CHRISTMAS ISSUES; EVELYN EVERETT GREEN; see also ILLUSTRATION IN CHILDREN'S BOOKS; LAWSON WOOD

Aldrich, Thomas Bailey see *THE STORY OF A BAD BOY*; see also *OUR YOUNG FOLKS*; GEORGE WILBUR PECK

Aldridge, (Harold Edward) James 1918– Australian writer who spent his childhood in Swan Hill on the River Murray, in Victoria. After some years working as a journalist and novelist in the United Kingdom, Aldridge wrote a series of books, the *St Helen* novels, set in a town on the River Murray in the 1920s and 1930s. His reputation as a writer for children is based on this body of work. *The True Story of Lilli Stubeck* (1984), winner of the CHILDREN'S BOOK COUNCIL OF

AUSTRALIA BOOK OF THE YEAR AWARD (1985) and remarkable for its singularly independent heroine, exemplifies features of all of Aldridge's work and has lent support to the argument that Aldridge writes of childhood, rather than for children. The narrator is Kit Quayle who, as a boy, took part in the events he describes, but whose account is given from the perspective of an adult with an understanding enhanced by time and experience. Aldridge reconstructs, in telling detail, rural Australia of the early 20th century, focusing on traits celebrated in BUSH tradition. *The True Story of Lola MacKellar* (1992), *The True Story of Spit MacPhee* (1986) – winner of the GUARDIAN AWARD – and *A Sporting Proposition* (1973) are the *St Helen* titles most commonly regarded as children's books. MN

Alembi, Ezekiel Writer of books for the Kenya Literature Bureau, and author of *High Adventure* (1994), which exposes its hero Philip to a world of FANTASY when he tries to make an aeroplane. He has also written *Don't be Long John* and *Setting the Score* (1995), the latter an exciting ADVENTURE STORY. ABO

Alex Quartet, The Series of novels by New Zealander TESSA DUDER, which features feisty, multi-talented Alex, a dominant cult character in New Zealand Young Adult fiction. The quartet comprises *Alex* (1987) (published in the USA as *In Lane Three, Alex Archer*); *Alex in Winter* (1989); *Alex in Rome* (1992); and *Songs for Alex* (1992). Alex struggles to be selected for the 1960 New Zealand Olympic swimming team, to succeed at Rome, and to discover what she wants to achieve in life. She faces strong competition (especially from Maggie, who becomes a friend), dilemmas concerning female identity, destructive skulduggery from some adults (though her own family fully supports her), multiple demands at school, and, above all, grief following her boyfriend's accidental death in *Alex*. Driven to achieve as much for Andy as for herself, Alex has to grow, through grief, before forming a new relationship with future opera singer, Tom. A powerful subplot concerns issues of female identity. Duder's quartet received almost universal acclaim, winning six New Zealand awards, and other commendations in the USA. A film version of *Alex* increased its popularity. DAH

Alexander, Cecil Frances 1818–95 Irish writer of children's verse, born in County Wicklow. Married to the Archbishop of Armagh, Alexander was more interested in the devotional than the poetic. Nevertheless, she produced some of the most popular hymns for children ever written, such as 'All things bright and beautiful'. *Hymns for Little Children* (1848) is typical of her ability to communicate simply and directly with a young audience. MCCS

Alexander, Lloyd (Chudley) 1924– American author of a number of works for adults and children, and translator of Sartre's *Nausea* and *The Wall and Other Stories*, and works by other French writers. Alexander is best known for his work for children, and in particular his *PRYDAIN CHRONICLES*. He has also written two other, less well-known series: *Vesper Holly* and *Westmark*, and many shorter works for the young. The *Westmark* series consists of *Westmark* (1981), *The Kestrel* (1982) and *The Beggar Queen* (1984). Unlike the *Prydain Chronicles*, the *Westmark* books are not set in a universe operated by magic, but in an environment reminiscent of the French Revolution. However, the two series share the theme of 'remaking' the world. Both see the end of an old order, whether defined by political doctrine or by magic, and the establishment of a new system in its place. Vesper Holly is a rich young girl, who, accompanied by her guardian, Professor Brinton Garrett, is caught up in a series of adventures in Illyria, El Dorado, Drackenberg, Jedera and Philadephia. The swashbuckling flavour of the *Vesper Holly* series is evocative of Ruritania, James Bond and Indiana Jones; its heroine is a very modern one, though the series is ostensibly set in the 1880s, and she appears to be equal to all challenges. Of note among Alexander's single novels is *The Remarkable Adventures of Prince Jen* (1991), an allegorical tale with an Oriental setting about a prince on a journey of self-discovery. His most recent work is *Gypsy Ryska* (1999). SA

***Alfie* series** (from 1981) Stories written and illustrated by SHIRLEY HUGHES, whose images of childhood, with their use of sepia and black line and free brushwork, continue to delight young readers, who readily identify with Alfie, his toddler sister Annie Rose and their predicaments. The restricted vocabulary makes the series ideal for reading to very young children or by emergent readers. The rosy, cherub-faced children are depicted in familiar, well-observed groupings, and facial expressions and many finer details tell their own story, slightly different from the text. The series began with *Alfie Gets In First* and has continued through to *Alfie Weather* (2001). JSW

See also ALPHABET BOOKS

Alfred 840–901 King of the West Saxons, noted for his revival of learning after the ravages of the Danes. Among his translations into West Saxon were Orosius' *Historia adversus Paganos*, used as a history and geography textbook, and Boethius' *Consolations of Philosophy*, long a basic text in the schools. Exemplary stories about Alfred, originating in Asser's *Life of Alfred* (c. 893), such as his quickly memorising a book of Saxon poems in order to win it from his mother, and his allowing the griddle cakes to burn when he was in hiding, have long been a part of children's culture. GA

Alger, Horatio, Jr. 1832–99 American novelist, educated for the ministry at Harvard. He was a Unitarian minister in Brewster, Massachusetts, until quitting in 1866. The reason for his departure from the pulpit was shrouded in secrecy for many years, until it was revealed, fairly recently, that he was forced to resign his position as a result of having sexual relations with a number of the boys and young men in his parish. He published his first boys' book, *Frank's Campaign*, in 1864.

His name has become synonymous with a particular kind of American FAIRY TALE, the 'rags-to-riches' story of a boy who moves from poverty to financial and social success, thanks to the beneficial role of capitalism in an industrialised late 19th-century America. His novels are typically described as male *CINDERELLA* stories and this analogy succeeds if one keeps in mind that in most versions of *Cinderella* the heroine succeeds with the assistance of a magical helper; Alger's heroes, despite their inherent pluck, are usually dependent on 'luck' to succeed (indeed a series of his novels was known by the title 'Luck and Pluck'). The dozens of novels he wrote between the late 1860s and his death in 1899 have similar if not identical plots: a young boy, 'adrift in the city' (to use another of his titles), manages, through industry, a positive outlook and good fortune, to rise above his squalid origin and become a successful capitalist. His boys are not simply cardboard figures: while one cannot say that they possess psychological depth, they are a step beyond the one-dimensional figures of previous CAUTIONARY TALES in that they are often slightly mischievous, while at core honest and ethical.

Dick Hunter, the title character of his best-known and most commercially successful novel, *Ragged Dick*, is a good example of this: he is not above stealing and lying when these are necessary for survival, but he would never turn on one of his fellow boot-blacks, and most of his lying seems more in the realm of exaggeration and teasing than that of true deception. He is brave, kind and loving, and is rewarded for these qualities with a position in a bank. Paradoxically, Alger's heroes often lose their distinctiveness and charm when they rise above the squalor in which Alger has initially 'found' them. Alger also depicts self-made households of homo-social, arguably homo-erotic boys and young men, perhaps reflecting his own dreams and fantasies of a utopia peopled by male youths.

His novels have never been critical successes, most critics taking them to task for the improbability of their plots, the sameness of characterisations, and the flat and unimaginative use of language. Their influence on young readers of their time and on ensuing generations of writers of boys' books should not, however, be underestimated. BH

Algonquin stories see FOLKTALES AND LEGENDS; see also NATIVE AMERICANS IN CHILDREN'S LITERATURE; EGERTON R. YOUNG

Ali Baba and the Forty Thieves see *ARABIAN NIGHTS' ENTERTAINMENTS*; TONY SARG

Alias Madame Doubtfire see *MRS DOUBTFIRE*

***Alice* imitations** A large corpus of novels, poems and stories which emulate, appropriate, continue or critique LEWIS CARROLL'S *ALICE'S ADVENTURES IN WONDERLAND* (1865) and/or *Through the Looking-Glass* (1871). Approximately 200 such works have been identified, most produced between 1869 and 1920.

Although the term 'imitation' is often used to signify redundant works which are derivative of and inferior to an 'authentic' original, the *Alice* books were themselves influenced by a tradition of Victorian FANTASY already established by such authors as Catherine Sinclair, F.E. Paget, Frances Browne and CHARLES KINGSLEY. Rather than being mere imitations of Carroll's originals, literary responses to the *Alice* books trace the larger process by which new works for children engage in dialogical relationships with powerful and popular cultural icons, enacting in literary form broader cultural debates about childhood, children's literature, the FANTASY genre and the icons themselves. These *Alice*-inspired works thus dramatise the various kinds of cultural work the books performed as authors both reinscribed and resisted popular perceptions of the *Alice* books and their effects on child readers.

The majority of works based on the *Alice* books are emulations – dream fantasies following an episodic journey plot within an imaginary 'wonderland', and featuring an adventurous heroine or hero similar to Alice, nonsense poetry and language, characters familiar from popular works for children (including the *Alice* books), and a sentimental return to the domestic 'real' world of home and family. Such works include TOM HOOD'S *From Nowhere to the North Pole: a Noah's Ark-Æological Narrative* (1875), CHARLES CARRYL'S *Davy and the Goblins, or What Followed Reading 'Alice's Adventures in Wonderland'* (1885), G.E. Farrow's *The Wallypug of Why* and its sequels (1895–1906), and John Rae's *New Adventures of 'Alice'* (1917).

Women writers published some of the more subversive appropriations of the Alice mythos. These works – including Jean Ingelow's *MOPSA THE FAIRY* (1869), CHRISTINA ROSSETTI'S *Speaking Likenesses* (1874), JULIANA EWING'S *Amelia and the Dwarfs* (1870), FRANCES HODGSON BURNETT'S *Behind the White Brick* (1879), Maggie Browne's *Wanted – A King; or, How Merle Set the Nursery Rhymes to Right* (1890), Anna Matlack Richards' *A New Alice in the Old Wonderland*

(1895), and several works by E. NESBIT – present Alices who embody women's power and influence in late Victorian middle-class culture.

Imitations of his work both frustrated and fascinated Carroll, whose diary mentions what became a substantial collection 'of books of the *Alice* type'. He considered a lawsuit against Anna Richards over her unauthorised sequel; yet, unable to recreate the *Alice* books' appeal in his own works, for example in *The Nursery Alice* (1889) and *Sylvie and Bruno* (1889), Carroll may have looked to these imitations for a key to understanding his own success. CS

Alice's Adventures Under Ground see ALICE'S ADVENTURES IN WONDERLAND

Alice's Adventures in Wonderland and *Through the Looking Glass* (1865, 1871) The story of how Charles Lutwidge Dodgson, a mathematics don at Christ Church, Oxford, came to write *Alice's Adventures in Wonderland* has long since grown into literary myth. While rowing up the river to Godstow on a hot summer afternoon in 1862 with Robinson Duckworth (the Duck) and three Liddell sisters: Lorina (the Lory), Alice and Edith (the Eaglet), Dodgson (the Dodo in *Alice* – the nickname arose from his stammer in pronouncing his name) was prevailed upon to tell them a story, which he did, extemporising as he went along. He later wrote up the story which he called *Alice's Adventures Under Ground* and illustrated it himself, presenting it to Alice Liddell in 1864 as a Christmas present. Dodgson was encouraged by his friends Henry Kingsley (brother of CHARLES KINGSLEY) and GEORGE MACDONALD to put it into print; it was revised and published a year later by Macmillan. *Alice's Adventures in Wonderland*, as its title became, emerged as the work of 'LEWIS CARROLL', with new ILLUSTRATIONS provided by the *Punch* cartoonist JOHN TENNIEL. It was a much expanded version of the earlier text, introducing 'The Caucus Race', 'Pig and Pepper', 'A Mad Tea-Party' and the Cheshire Cat, all of which had been absent in the original telling. *Alice's Adventures in Wonderland* was later adapted by Dodgson for younger readers in *The Nursery 'Alice'* (1890), in which 20 of the original illustrations by Tenniel were printed in colour.

From his correspondence with Macmillan, it would appear that Dodgson was thinking about *Through the Looking Glass* as early as the latter half of 1866; it was, however, 1871 before he finished writing it and Tenniel completed the illustrations; the book came out in December of that year. Both the *Alice* books have been continuously in print since their first publication, and what might be called an 'Alice industry' has grown up around them which began during Dodgson's own lifetime, he himself inventing and commercially producing such items as the Wonderland Postage-Stamp Case. The first professional stage adaptation of *Alice* was produced by Henry Savile Clark in 1886; the work has also been adapted for the ballet and inspired a good many composers. David Del Tredici (1937–), an American composer, deserves mention here as having apparently been more than ordinarily struck by the *Alice* books. His love-affair with them has produced *Vintage Alice* (1972), *Adventures Underground* (1973), *In Wonderland* (parts 1 and 2) (1969–75), *An Alice Symphony* (1976), *Final Alice* (1976), *Annotated Alice* (1976) and the four-part *Child Alice* (1977–81): *In Memory of a Summer Day*, *Happy Voices*, *All in the Golden Afternoon*, and *Quaint Events*, most of which are works for voice with accompaniment (see also MUSIC AND STORY). *Alice's Adventures in Wonderland* were also rendered as a WALT DISNEY cartoon entitled *Alice in Wonderland* (1951), which failed to observe the integrity of the text, and there have been many film versions, including one using puppets and a soft-porn version in 1976. *Dreamchild* (1985) is a more serious film exploring the relationship between 'Carroll' and Alice Liddell/Hargreaves.

ALICE IMITATIONS are legion, for example G.E. Farrow's *The Wallypug of Why*, Gilbert Adair's *Through the Needle's Eye* and the more recent *Castle of Inside Out* (1997) by David Henry Wilson, which begins with an encounter between a child named Lorina and a Black Rabbit. Plays on the title itself are even more prolific, one of the better-known perhaps being *Malice in Wonderland*, used as a title by C. Day Lewis writing as Nicholas Blake.

Alice's Adventures in Wonderland and its sequel are landmarks in children's literature. In *Through the Looking Glass*, Humpty Dumpty says to Alice, 'The piece I'm going to repeat . . . was written entirely for your amusement.' The statement is also true of the *Alice* books, which were among the earliest works for children to be written for the entertainment and delight of the child rather than for instruction or improvement. The *Alice* books were among the first 'bestselling' children's works: Morton Cohen's *Lewis Carroll: A Biography* (1995) states that by 1898, the year of Dodgson's death, more than 150,000 copies of *Alice's Adventures in Wonderland* and 100,000 copies of *Through the Looking Glass* had been printed.

The *Alice* books confront questions related to the issue of identity: what forms it, whether it is a thing externally constructed by society, its categories, rules and behavioural patterns, or something that is internally made. Rosemary Jackson, in *Fantasy: the Literature of Subversion* (1981), has suggested that the fantastic, as an alternative and oppositional mode to realism, constitutes a form of subversion, its departure from the assumptions and workings of the real everyday world serving to question and undercut those assumptions.

The playfulness of Carroll's fantasies may indeed function to critique and deconstruct Victorian society and 'Anglo-Saxon attitudes', and also the philosophy or ethos governing its literature, by examining how identity is affected when the usual rules governing the individual are removed.

Questioning is a prominent feature of *Alice's Adventures in Wonderland*; a good many of Alice's utterances begin with 'I wonder', and Wonderland is less a world of wondrous things (though it is this as well) than it is a place of investigation and speculative thinking. Play may work to disrupt or unsettle the engraved patterns of things in its refusal to treat them seriously, and one of the dominant metaphors of the two books is that of games: we have the caucus race and croquet, where rules are cast to the wind, and playing cards and chess. As Alice tumbles down the rabbit-hole in *Alice's Adventures in Wonderland,* the rules and assumptions which operate in the everyday world are found no longer to apply. Institutions and practices are gently mocked; Victorian education and mannerisms, for example, are simultaneously targeted in the Mock Turtle's description of his education in 'Reeling and Writhing . . . Mystery, ancient and modern . . . Drawling, Stretching and Fainting in Coils'. The forms and rituals of social etiquette are dissolved in the chaos of the Mad Hatter's Tea Party, where dormice are stuffed into teapots, people move round the table in search of clean crockery, and the meaninglessness of polite conversation emerges under the scrutiny of the Hare and Hatter as they break down and examine the way words are put together. Matters religious may be read as being treated with equal irreverence if we accept Humphrey Carpenter's interpretation, in *Secret Gardens: the Golden Age of Children's Literature* (1985), of the invitation to 'eat me' and 'drink me' as being parodic of the eucharist. The notion of law-as-system is also shown to collapse in the trial sequence. Rules are made up or changed on the spur of the moment and the topsy-turvy nature of the proceedings becomes fully evident as the King asks the jury to consider the verdict before the evidence has even been heard, the Queen calling for sentence first and verdict after. Time itself has ceased to signify as structure: the March Hare's watch, greased with the best butter, is no longer accurate and it is always six o' clock and thus always tea-time. In *Through the Looking Glass*, the converse is true: 'The rule is, jam to-morrow and jam yesterday – but never jam today.' The eternity of Wonderland exists in the interstices of Looking-Glass time.

Alice asks, while falling, 'I wonder what Latitude or Longitude I've got to?' But latitude and longitude no longer serve as reference points by which to orient oneself. The sense of Wonderland's innocence of formal directionality is reinforced when Alice asks the Cheshire Cat, 'Would you tell me, please, which way I ought to go from here?' and is told that that 'depends a good deal on where you want to get to'. The world is denuded of its structures and signposts, and this releases the individual from all social strictures. However, the implication of the Cheshire Cat's speech is that direction is dependent upon desire and thus determined from within rather than externally; individuals are in the end responsible for themselves and their own destination.

In a world characterised by changeability (babies turn into pigs, pebbles into cakes etc.) and impermanence (cats fade away), the self's sense of its own concreteness and identity becomes all-important. Certainly the structure of both the *Alice* books, especially *Through the Looking Glass* where she progresses from pawn to queen, is somewhat suggestive of a *rite de passage*, a quest to achieve selfhood and the heart's desire, though this reading is not without its own problems.

Alice's alterations in size occur at a dizzying rate, and are at first not voluntary but occur accidentally. On drinking from the bottle marked 'drink me', she shrinks till she begins to worry that 'it might end . . . in (her) going out altogether, like a candle'. When she eats the cake marked 'eat me', she grows so large that she loses the sense of herself, unable to see her far-off feet which she then speaks of as things separate from her. (It is interesting to note that in her fantasies of sending presents to her feet by post, her right foot is 'Esq.', i.e. male and not even of the same gender as herself.) Identity may easily be lost as we see in the passage when Alice, fanning herself, becomes unsure of who she is:

> Dear, dear! How queer everything is to-day! And yesterday things went on just as usual. I wonder if I've been changed in the night . . . But if I'm not the same, the next question is Who in the world am I? Ah, *That's* the great puzzle! . . . I'm sure I can't be Mabel, for I know all sorts of things, and she, oh! she knows such a very little! Besides, *she's* she, and *I'm* I, and – oh dear, how puzzling it all is!

Alice's Adventures in Wonderland and *Through the Looking Glass* show that neither the sense of concrete identity nor desire are things easily achieved. In *Through the Looking Glass* one can only reach a place by walking away from it. In *Alice's Adventures in Wonderland* the space towards which the work is tensed is the garden of bright flower-beds and cool fountains, and Alice spends a good deal of time trying to get there. When she does, she finds that the garden, the symbolic place of desire, is no Eden re-discovered but a sham: the roses are not natural but painted over, and in this Arcadia, death, in the person of the Queen of Hearts, is all-too present. The work in fact conveys the extreme tenuousness of existence – accentuated by the Queen of Hearts' constant calls for beheadings – and the sense of self. Nor is reaching the garden symbolic of finally achieving selfhood, which appears to be always delayed, just as, in *Through the Looking Glass*, jam is always out of reach.

The *Alice* books remain almost as often-read today as they were a century ago, though this popularity may be a self-sustaining one, as much due to their status as classics as anything else. The wit of their parodies is bound to be less appreciated today, since the verse being parodied is no longer in currency, and the liberating value of Alice's adventures to her own contemporaries – a children's book intended purely to amuse rather than to educate – is perforce less in this time when the basic assumptions regarding children and their needs have altered greatly and there is so much good writing for children available. However, despite the challenge of comparison with Tenniel and ARTHUR RACKHAM, contemporary illustrators are continually attracted to the *Alice* books, two distinguished recent examples being by ANTHONY BROWNE (1988) and HELEN OXENBURY (1999). For whatever reasons, Carroll's works continue to maintain their cultural presence, with even strangers to the complete texts being familiar with quotations and characters from it. SA

Aliki (Liacouras Brandenburg) 1929– Author-illustrator of PICTUREBOOKS. Born unexpectedly on the New Jersey seashore, where her Greek immigrant parents were spending Labor Day, Aliki later recaptured the atmosphere of beach vacations in *Those Summers* (1996), and the warmth of her extended family in such stories as *The Two of Them* (1970). Her first children's book, inspired by her first European trip, was *The Story of William Tell* (1960). Although she has illustrated many books by others, Aliki's own books have increasingly reflected her varied interests – palaeontology in *Digging Up Dinosaurs* (1981), publishing in *How a Book Is Made* (1986), and Louis XIV in *The King's Day* (1989). With her particular gift for INFORMATION BOOKS, she achieves both essential clarity and richly fascinating detail; to present information at different levels of complexity, for example, she may surround a simple text in large type with sequences of detailed ILLUSTRATIONS captioned in fine print. In *Mummies Made in Egypt* (1979) this technique combines with a style and palette suggestive of Egyptian tomb-painting, while in *A Medieval Feast* (1983) jewel-toned illustrations and decorative borders evoke medieval illuminations. Similarly, in *The King's Day* a single process – burial, feasting, Louis' daily routine – sums up an entire culture. SR

Alkali, Zaynab Nigerian author from the North, best known for her portrayal of a young woman's plight in *The Stillborn*. Alkali's YOUNG ADULT novel, *The Virtuous Woman* (1986), presents a more hopeful view – the young heroine, though disabled and unsure of herself, finds a soul mate and new maturity on a fateful train journey. VD

All Creatures Great and Small see JAMES HERRIOT

All-Nite Cafe, The (1993) This winner of the *SIGNAL* Award for Poetry is one of PHILIP GROSS's well-written collections for young adults. Whether mingling multi-storey car parks with ghosts, or balloons and the edge of sleep, Gross's poems explore the silent imaginings, the forgotten places and the significance of fleeting moments, bringing the internal and external world together through inventive use of language and image. HT

Allan Quatermain see SIR RIDER HAGGARD

Allan, Mabel Esther see BALLET STORIES; *DRINA* SERIES

Allan, Nicholas 1956– British illustrator. Early training at the Slade School of Art and work in many different fields led to Allan's first PICTUREBOOK in 1989. His spare line-and-wash drawings are used to good effect in books such as *Jesus' Christmas Party* (1991) and *Heaven* (1996), which deal with serious topics with wit and warmth. *Hilltop Hospital* (1992) is a well-shaped medical soap-opera in picturebook form, complete with calamities, unrequited love, missing children and distinct hospital (animal) characters. JAG

Allcroft, Brit see *CAPTAIN PUGWASH* SERIES

Alldridge, Elizabeth see *WORZEL GUMMIDGE* SERIES

Allen Lane see PUBLISHERS AND PUBLISHING

Allen, Judy 1941– British writer of fiction and non-fiction born in Old Sarum. Prolific and highly diverse, a concerned environmentalist, her great strengths of sympathy and humour are seen in such prize-winning novels as *Awaiting Developments* (1988) and *Between the Moon and the Rock* (1992), which entertainingly handle sensitive and contentious issues that a less even-handed approach might reduce to propaganda. She also writes adult drama and guide books, and for younger children texts that are simple without being simplistic, such as *The Dim Thin Ducks* (1990) and *What is a Wall after All?* (1993) JMM

Allen, Pamela (Kay) 1934– Australian author and illustrator, born in New Zealand, who began by illus-

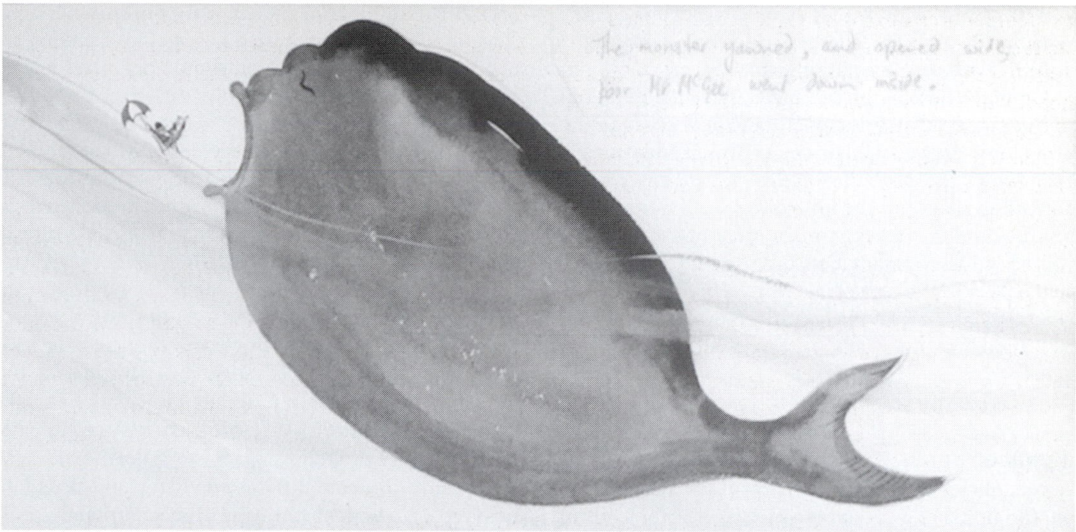

Illustration by Pamela Allen for *Mr McGee Goes to Sea.*

trating the work of others but whose most successful books have been those she has both written and illustrated herself. Her work is particularly appealing to very young children and is notable for careful layout, the use of white backgrounds, the movement denoted in the ILLUSTRATIONS and her exuberant use of language. Her wryly humorous stories are laced with strong rhythms, frequent repetition and much play on words. She has covered a great range of themes and topics in her books; science in *Mr Archimedes' Bath* (1980), *Who Sank the Boat?* (1982) and *The Pear in the Pear Tree* (1999); sibling rivalry in *I Wish I Had a Pirate Suit* (1989); a series of FANTASIES about the comical Mr McGee written in verse; caring for animals in *My Cat Maisie* (1990) and *Clippity-Clop* (1994). Other titles include *Bertie and the Bear* (1984), *A Lion in the Night* (1986), *Belinda* (1992) and *Alexander's Outing* (1993). An illustration from *Who Sank the Boat?* was included in a series of children's literature stamps produced by Australia Post in 1996. She has won numerous awards for her books, including CHILDREN'S BOOK COUNCIL OF AUSTRALIA PICTUREBOOK OF THE YEAR in 1983 and 1984. MLH

Allen, Stephen T. see *MERRY'S MUSEUM*

Allingham, William 1824–89 Anglo-Irish poet who spent much of his working life as a customs inspector. Friendly with members of the Pre-Raphaelite circle, he edited *Fraser's Magazine* from 1874 to 1879. His poetry for children was popular in his day. *The Fairies* (1850) appeared as a separate book in 1883; *In Fairyland* (1870) was wonderfully illustrated by RICHARD DOYLE. *Rhymes for the Young Folk* (1887) is the best-known collection. MCCS

Ally Sloper see COMICS

Almond, David British writer whose first children's novel, *Skellig* (1998), had the rare distinction of being awarded both the CARNEGIE MEDAL and the WHITBREAD CHILDREN'S BOOK OF THE YEAR AWARD. It was followed in 1999 by *Kit's Wilderness*. Both novels are set in the Northeast of England, successfully employing a bold combination of realism and magic. In *Skellig* this mixture is exemplified by the character of Skellig himself, who is simultaneously a ruined down-and-out and an angel of hope and joy. Michael's discovery of Skellig – behind piles of filthy rubbish at the back of a dilapidated garage – coincides with the family's fear that their new baby is dying. The story of the baby and the story of Skellig converge in an almost rapturous and entirely convincing closure. *Kit's Wilderness* addresses different causes of unhappiness – old age, death, social rejection, and the cruelty endured by past generations.

Friendship is at the heart of both novels. They celebrate – entirely without sentimentality – the power of imagination and storytelling to transcend suffering and fear; so that it was perhaps not surprising that in 1999 David Almond should make a strong attack on the British Government's education policy, which he said was so obsessed with raising standards that it was destroying the creativity of childhood and ignoring 'the mysterious zone of imagination, intuition, insight'. What was unprecedented about this incident was that HM Chief Inspector for Schools, Chris Woodhead, took the charge sufficiently seriously to publish a rebuttal in a national newspaper.

Almond's next children's novel, *Heaven Eyes* (2000), was less successful. It is a poetic and at times thought-provoking exploration of the confused identities of abandoned and orphaned children, held together by an authorial faith in the unitedness of all human existence. Almond makes similar imaginative use of a ruined industrial landscape, but the pace and urgency characteristic of his previous work is here almost overwhelmed by an uneven narrative structure and stylised dialogue. VW

Alor, Ogbonne see *THE MAGIC APPLE TREE*

alphabet books Sometimes known as ABC Books, Abcee, Abcie, or Absey books. From the 15th century on, the alphabet was seen as a prerequisite for learning to read and was frequently published as part of a HORNBOOK. This would include an upper- and lower-case alphabet, along with a syllabary and prayers such as the Grace and The Lord's Prayer. Hornbooks were sometimes referred to as Criss-Cross Rows in recognition of the common practice of stringing the first nine letters of the alphabet on wire into a cross form and crossing oneself before beginning lessons, while reciting 'God spede me, ABC'.

The element of instruction was reinforced with the development of PRIMERS. Although originally meaning the prayerbook itself, the word came to refer to those that possessed an opening page displaying the alphabet. Sometimes a separate page or booklet containing an ABC, a syllabary and certain prayers was produced so that it could be slipped into a prayerbook or catechism. The best known of such early primers was published, under licence, by Thomas Petyt in 1538; he provided 'The BAC [sic] bothe in latyn and in Englysshe'. A desire to aid rote learning led to the introduction of woodcut ILLUSTRATIONS to the alphabet, as early as 1570, by John Hart in *A method or comfortable beginning for all unlearned*, 'whereby they may be taught to read English in a very short time with pleasure'. This led to the development of battledores containing an illustrated alphabet, and these continued to be produced into the 19th century, sometimes still in the hornbook shape so that they could be used for hitting shuttlecocks.

The picturing and naming of common objects in alphabetical order was to continue as the pattern, and it became common to add rhyming couplets or short verses beneath the pictures, thereby creating the separate alphabet book. With word and image to play with, it was possible to take the ABC book beyond instruction and add elements of pleasure and play. This was also in accordance with the advice of JOHN LOCKE, the influential 17th-century philosopher and educationalist, who suggested in 1693 that learning to read and learning the alphabet should begin as soon as children could talk. Some decades earlier, the popular translation of Commenius' *ORBIS SENSUALIUM PICTUS* (1658, trans. 1659) – considered by some to be the first children's PICTUREBOOK – contained an illustrated alphabet. Locke's ideas influenced the work of 'T.W.' and, later, JOHN NEWBERY. Thomas White, a Puritan writer, published *A Little Book for Little Children* in 1660. It contains little to comfort and much to frighten the young reader, even in the ABC section. The second edition (probably around 1712), was still under the authorship of 'T.W.' but influenced by someone evidently of a different mind since it balances instruction with the pleasure principle. The opening page was a representation of a hornbook with an alphabet illustrated with woodcuts, and possibly the first printing of the traditional alphabet text beginning 'A was an Archer and shot at a frog.' This version, along with the even older *A, Apple Pie or The Tragical Death of A, Apple Pie* belongs to the tradition of rhymed alphabets. John Newbery, the 18th-century bookseller, discovered the economic viability of publishing books specifically for children. His *A LITTLE PRETTY POCKET-BOOK* uses the alphabet to organise an exploration of children's games. Both the upper- and lower-case letters are used with woodcuts linked to four-line verses about each specific activity, with either a Moral or Rule of Life tacked on to each one. *A Little Pretty Pocket Book* was an immediate success and was later published (1787) in America by ISAIAH THOMAS. It is interesting to note that one 18th-century London bookshop, associated with publishers noted for their illustrated books, was called 'GREAT A, little a AND BIG BOUNCING B'.

The basic aims and formats of ABC books were now set and their continuing development was a reflection of the main changes in the history of children's book illustration. John Newbery made the link between picture, theme and letter, and sought to improve the quality of the blocks themselves. Angus, a printer in Newcastle, received a commission to publish *The Only Method to Make Reading Easy*, written by a local schoolmaster. It was the good fortune of both that the illustrations were entrusted to an apprentice, THOMAS BEWICK, later to be revered for his graphic brilliance and for his refinement of the craft of WOOD ENGRAVING. He designed 24 miniature cuts of birds and animals. The pictures missing were for the letters U and X; in fact, X has often caused problems for the picture-maker, no matter what the theme. Xerxes has done valiant service in many an ABC book. In *An Alphabet of Animals for Little Naturalists* (1821), the reader not only has some unusual images of animals but is introduced to U for urchin and X for xiphia, the swordfish.

During the 19th century increasing attention was paid to the quality of the illustrations. *The Alphabet of Goody Two Shoes* (1808) is a good example. It was published by Newbery's successor, using a character that Newbery had first made popular. It is beautifully though anonymously illustrated with hand-coloured engravings of scenes full of contemporary details. It begins traditionally with 'A, was an apple'. The picture shows a child, who is the narrator, watching the cook while the verse hints at a favourite recipe. In some cases the details set out in the verses of two letters are combined to make one composite picture as with Y and Z: the Youth in the park playing his flute while a young Zealander girl passes by, concerned by the barking dogs protesting at the music.

The end of the century saw Alphabet books printed by the pioneering EDMUND EVANS, who did so much to improve the quality of children's books, especially in colour printing. WALTER CRANE created a number of ABC books for Evans, including *The Railway Alphabet, The Farmyard Alphabet, The Baby's Own Alphabet, Noah's Ark Alphabet, An Alphabet of Old Friends* and *The Absurd Alphabet*. IONA AND PETER OPIE list 25 editions of *A, Apple Pie* before 1900, which indicates its popularity both with readers and with illustrators keen to demonstrate their ingenuity in their interpretations of it; one of these was KATE GREENAWAY, who reworked it in 1866 for Evans, filling it with her unmistakable children in their Regency dress.

This listing of Crane's alphabet books underlines another feature – the proliferation of themes to match the growing interest of children in the world around them. These themes included names, animals, birds, the farmyard, flowers, railways and ships. There were comic alphabets and nonsense ABC books. One earlier nonsense alphabet is noteworthy for its challenge to its readers' phonic skills, or their familiarity with Greek: *Aldiborontiphosskyphorniostikos* (1820) was inspired by the *ARABIAN NIGHTS* stories. Some publishers latched onto the idea of using family characters – 'Aunts', 'Uncles' and 'Cousins' – to sell their books. *Cousin Honeycomb's Railway Alphabet* (c. 1850) is one such, depicting the contemporary trials of train travel: 'G is the GUARD that sits perched above,/And sees that no parcel or passengers move.'

The 20th century has seen the popularity of the ABC book continue, a challenge to the ingenuity and imagination of many current illustrators, for example HELEN OXENBURY, SHIRLEY HUGHES, MITSUMASO ANNO and QUENTIN BLAKE. BRIAN WILDSMITH was awarded the Kate Greenaway Medal in 1962 for his version. In 1986 GRAEME BASE created an international bestseller with an alphabet book, *ANIMALIA*, that challenged adult readers. Interactive possibilities were explored by Robert Crowther in his very successful *The Most Amazing Hide and Seek Alphabet Book* (1977) and more recently in *Robert Crowther's Incredible Animal Alphabet* (1994). The development of new paper technology has also led to pop-up ABC books. AR

see also JANE JOHNSON; EDWARD LEAR; MOVABLE BOOKS

Althea [Braithwaite] 1940– American writer, illustrator and editor, and managing editor of Dinosaur Publications. Althea filled a gap in the children's book market in the 1970s, providing a range of modestly priced story and INFORMATION BOOKS for younger children. Books in *The Althea Series* were typically straightforward and uncompromising, intended to help children with new experiences or understanding – the first day at school, a visit to the dentist, fear of the dark, a new baby, death; others dealt with a range of topics and issues, such as *Making a Road, What is a Union?* EAG

Altsheler, Joseph 1862–1919 American author of HISTORICAL FICTION and boys' adventure series. Born in Kentucky, Altsheler grew up hearing pioneer tales of wilderness survival. He graduated from Vanderbilt University and embarked on a lifelong career as a journalist, first writing for the Louisville *Courier-Journal*. In 1892 Altsheler became an editor for the *New York World*. He began writing novels in 1897 and published 44 titles in the next 21 years. His most popular series, which includes *Scouts of the Valley* and *The Young Trailers: A Story of Early Kentucky* (1907), features a young hero, Henry Ware. This series romanticises the beauty of the American wilderness while celebrating survival skills and comradeship. Altsheler also wrote fictional accounts of the American Revolutionary War, the French and Indian War, the American Civil War, the battle for Texas independence, and the exploration of the Great Plains and Rocky Mountains. At the time of his death, his books were considered among the most popular books for boys in America. KKW

see also ADVENTURE STORIES

Amalgamated Press see 'THE BIG FIVE'; see also COMICS; *PIP AND SQUEAK; PLAYBOX ANNUAL; RADIO FUN; THE SCHOOL FRIEND*

Amber Spyglass, The see *HIS DARK MATERIALS*

Ambrus, Victor 1935– Illustrator and artist. Born in Budapest, Ambrus came to England in 1956 as a refugee when Russia invaded Hungary. Already in his third year of art training, Ambrus spent two terms at Farnham Art College, then went on to the Royal College of Art where he studied engraving and LITHOGRAPHY, and gravitated towards print-making.

He began his career as a book-illustrator with the publisher Blackie; Mabel George of Oxford University Press was quick to spot his ability, and he was soon to become one of her recruited 'stable' of artists, which included CHARLES KEEPING and BRIAN WILDSMITH. Ambrus is a brilliant colourist and has an expressive line capable of delicacy of touch or weight of attack. He is particularly skilled in the drawing of horses, and for historical texts – his special enthusiasm – his research is meticulous. Ambrus has won the Kate Greenaway Medal twice, in 1965 for *Three Poor Tailors*, and in 1975 for *Mishka* and *Horses in Battle*. Ambrus has illustrated over 300 titles ranging from classics, stories and historical novels for older children, to collections of tales and anthologies, educational resource books, his own PICTUREBOOKS for younger children, and the *Dracula* and *Blackbeard* cartoon stories. JD

see also KING ARTHUR

Amelia Bedelia see PEGGY PARISH

Ameliaranne Series of single-story books, all illustrated by Susan B. Pearse. *Ameliaranne and the Green Umbrella* (1920), the first of over ten books, is by Constance Heward; later writers include ELEANOR FARJEON and Margaret Gilmour. The eponymous heroine is the spirited and resourceful daughter of a poor village washerwoman with six younger children to support. The intrusive 'r' in Ameliaranne's name is indicative of a genial condescension in presentation. Individual titles were reissued as late as the 1970s, but attempts to update the new stories while keeping the original social situation, have led to anachronism. PP

American Boy, The see *THE YOUTH'S COMPANION*

American Girls Collection Historical fictions developed by Pleasant Rowland intended to teach American history from the point of view of a nine-year-old girl. Each of the six series is composed of six CHAPTER BOOKS featuring an assertive female protagonist living at a significant point in American history. The first series, published in the 1940s, features Felicity Merriman and explores colonial Williamsburg in 1774 prior to the American Revolutionary War. The *Kirsten* series traces the journey of Kirsten Larson and her family as they immigrate from Sweden to Minnesota in 1854. Samantha Parkington is an orphan who lives with her wealthy grandmother in New York in 1904. Molly McIntire experiences World War II on the home front during 1944. The most recent series attempts to be more multicultural: the *Addy Walker* series examines the escape from slavery of the African-American protagonist, while the *Josefina Montoya* series features a Hispanic heroine growing up on a ranch near Santa Fe, New Mexico, in 1824. While the books are the heart of the American Girls Collection, the Pleasant Company also markets dolls of each of the characters and accessories which are prominently featured in the ILLUSTRATIONS. The carefully researched series promotes positive role models for middle-school girls, but it is difficult to separate the books from the well-made but expensive dolls and accessories. JCS

see also HISTORICAL FICTION

American Spelling Book, The A primer, the first published work of Noah Webster (1758–1843), originally issued in 1783 as Part I of *A Grammatical Institute of the English Language, Comprising An Easy, Concise, and Systematic Method of Education, Designed for the Use of English Schools in America*. A new edition revised by Webster was published in 1787 and re-titled *The American Spelling Book*. Webster revised it again in 1804 and once more in 1829 and re-named it *The Elementary Spelling Book*. The noted American publisher ISAIAH THOMAS favoured Webster's book as a school text and printed a great number. The spelling book represented only one of Webster's efforts to promote standardised American English and punctuation and thereby establish a separate American culture. In text, the speller differed little from other primers of the era except that it included an 'Analysis of Sounds in the English Language'. The so-called 'Porcupine' Edition of *The American Spelling Book* included a portrait of Webster so badly cut that the renowned lexicographer resembled a prickly porcupine, causing many children to shrink from their primers with alarm. KSB

American Sunday School Union An interdenominational organisation, founded in 1817, whose goal was to establish Sunday Schools 'without distinction of sect, or creed, or custom'. It published such periodicals as *The Youth's Friend*, *Scholar's Magazine* and *The Infant's Magazine*, as well as books of doctrinal teachings, memoirs of pious children, BIOGRAPHIES, history, poetry, hymns, travels and moral fiction. By 1830 it claimed to have sold over six million publications, and began creating American literature for children. These publications were similar to HANNAH MORE'S *CHEAP REPOSITORY TRACTS* published in England, but were written by American authors and featured native subjects and settings. Reflecting the Union's interdenominational emphasis, the anonymously written books did not receive the ASSU imprint until approved by a committee including at least three members from different denominations. The Union took care to present attractive books of a high moral and religious character, employing skilled writers and illustrators to create entertaining and memorable stories. Sunday School libraries, stocked with the books of the ASSU and similar organisations, were the earliest children's libraries and inspired other free, circulating libraries. Union books and Sunday School libraries provided much of the reading material available to children in antebellum America. JJB

American Tract Society An interdenominational organisation founded in 1825 to 'promote the interests of vital godliness and sound morality, by the circulation of Religious Tracts'. Established in the wake of the Second Great Awakening, its tracts promoted Evangelical Christian teachings about salvation and damnation, Sabbath observance, and church attendance. It began publishing tracts for children in 1827, initially reprinting such RELIGIOUS TRACT SOCIETY tracts as *The Dairyman's Daughter* (1809); it later published American works, such as the bestseller *The Young Christian* (1832) by Jacob Abbott. The Society initially opposed publishing fiction, preferring children to take up 'solid, practical, doctrinal reading'. Writers gradually used fictional elements, however, to engage children's interest. JJB

Amstutz, André British illustrator. After training at Brighton School of Art and pursuing a career in advertising, Amstutz entered the children's book world through a collaboration with ALLAN AHLBERG on *Ten in a Bed*, *Happy Families*, the *Funnybones* series, *Slow Dog Falling*, *Chicken, Chips and Peas* and *The Hen House*. Blocks of bold, flat colour and inventive page design, including white text on black page, characterise these books. His illustrations for Browning's *PIED PIPER OF HAMELIN* (1993) show him at his best, with warm, subtle colour, apt characterisation, well-researched and witty detail bringing the medieval period alive, and layouts which amplify his representation of scenes, both interior and exterior. JAG

Anancy, Anansi or **Anance the spider man** Hero of TRICKSTER stories originating in West Africa (Ananse is Ashanti for spider) which are now more commonly associated with Caribbean, particularly Jamaican, folklore and culture. Also known as Kwaku Anance, Ceiling Thomas, Br'er Ananci or Nancy, this chameleon-like figure, whose powers of transformation rendered him a creature of many worlds, was thought to possess extraordinary qualities and the wisdom of a god. Ananse is both human and spider and was believed to be the creator of man.

Embedded in the original, orally transmitted narratives were meanings which related to Ashanti life. The formulaic opening to a traditional Anancy story – 'We do not mean, we do not really mean what we say' – suggested an element of parable within the diversion of the storytelling experience. More recently, the generic term Anansesem is used to describe gatherings for singing and storytelling.

Outrageously mischievous, subversive and clever, Anancy is customarily depicted engaged in deeds of audacious benevolence or self-gratification. Moving with ease between the human and animal world, he overcomes seemingly insuperable challenges and flaunts societal conventions. His clever antics and frequently foolish endeavours are synonymous with those of BRER RABBIT.

Notable collections and retellings are by Peggy Appiah (1966), GERALD MCDERMOTT (1972), Eric Kimmel (1988), and JAMES BERRY (1988). Outstanding versions for younger children are GAIL HALEY'S *A Story, A Story* (Caldecott Medal 1971) – in which Anancy, outwitting Nyame the sky-god, releases all the stories of the world – and the contemporary PICTUREBOOK by FIONA FRENCH, *Anancy and Mr Dry Bone* (1991). CMN

Anand, Paro 1957– Indian fiction writer and editor at the National Centre for Children's Literature. Anand is the recipient of the 1998 Award for Significant Contribution to Children's Literature from the Russian Centre for Science and Culture. A practised storyteller, her fiction focuses on issues like peer pressure, facing challenges, falling in love, and the domestic violence that confronts and troubles children and teenagers. *Pepper the Capuchin Monkey and Other Stories* (1992) is a collection of stories depicting contemporary life. Although rooted in the Indian context the stories have a wider appeal with which children all over the world can empathise. *The Little Bird* (1993) is a modern FABLE of courage and sacrifice emphasising the fact that the smallest is not necessarily the weakest. The book is informed by a consciousness of the environment and a desire to bring the child closer to it. Continuing these concerns, *Born to Lead* (1994) is the saga of a tiger cub in a jungle destroyed by man. *Impossible? Tales of the Unknown* (1996) and *School Soup* (1996) are two books for teenagers narrated with warmth and wit to alleviate the loneliness of the adolescent reader. She has also written *Superzero* (1996), a collection of witty, thought-provoking stories for younger children. MBh

***Anastasia Krupnik* series** A series of nine humorous children's novels by LOIS LOWRY. In 1979, Lois Lowry created her most popular literary figure, the title character of *Anastasia Krupnik*. In her first book, Anastasia, the daughter of a poet and English professor and an artist, aspires to become a writer herself and struggles with the difficulty of developing memories worth writing about. Unlike BEVERLY CLEARY'S Ramona Quimby, to whom she has been compared, Anastasia is upper-middle-class, living in Boston,

'It was the old soldier.' Illustration (probably by Helen Stratton) for Hans Christian Andersen's *Fairy Tales.*

Massachusetts. Despite her background, Anastasia faces typical childhood problems such as making friends and coming to terms with the death of a grandparent and a younger sibling. Anastasia proved such a rich character that Lowry continued her adventures in eight more novels, advancing her from age ten to thirteen. As Eric Kimmel has suggested, the *Anastasia* books often tread the fine line between humour and tragedy. In subsequent novels, Anastasia has endured moving to the suburbs, weathered various unsuccessful infatuations, and solved school problems such as learning to climb a rope in gym class, completing a science project on gerbils, and passing a seemingly meaningless class on ethics. Anastasia has also appeared as a minor character in three popular books focusing on her younger brother, Sam. JDC

Ancient Mariner, The see THE RIME OF THE ANCIENT MARINER

Andersen, Hans Christian 1805–75 Danish writer. The story of Hans Christian Andersen's life is, as he so often described it, A FAIRY TALE: the son of a cobbler and an illiterate washer woman becomes a bestselling and internationally renowned author, a friend of princes, kings and queens. However, it is a fairy tale in the style of one of Andersen's own stories, no simple journey from 'once upon a time' to 'happily ever after' but a complex tale open to many interpretations, where a possibly mysterious beginning leads to a bitter-sweet end. Indeed, the stories are the Life, containing as they do so much more of what he actually felt and longed for than his autobiographies ever reveal.

Andersen was brought up in straitened circumstances in Odense. At about the time of his birth an illegitimate son was born to Prince Christian Frederik, the Crown Prince of Denmark, and the daughter of an army General. The birth of this child was hushed up and he vanished. Was he given to a servant and her new shoemaker husband to bring up?

From the start Andersen was an outsider. Too tall, too awkward, an ugly child whom neighbours condemned as behaving more like a girl than a boy, he was above all an exhibitionist who would sing, dance or recite poetry for anyone who wanted to listen and many who did not. He adored his father, Hans, who introduced Hans Christian to reading. He also built a puppet theatre which was Hans Christian's solace for years to come.

It was this fascination with the theatre that took him to Copenhagen at the age of 14. His father had died and because of his inability to mix with others Andersen had had very little schooling, despite education having been made compulsory in Denmark. He bombarded the Royal Theatre board with requests for acting auditions and then later with plays. This eventually led to his being sent to grammar school, very much against his will. He was unhappy there partly due to what is now thought to have been dyslexia. His education was overseen by Jonas Collin, the director of the Royal Theatre, who later managed his finances. Andersen's relationships with the different members of the Collin family were the most important in his life. The feelings of love, duty and resentment that they engendered were to be the catalyst for many of his best-known stories.

His first real success came in 1835 with *The Improvisatore*. Set in Italy, this novel centres on the friendship between two young men. This was the first but not the last time that Andersen explored his relationship with Edvard Collin, one of Jonas' sons, in print. Andersen loved Edvard with a passion that lasted his whole life. It is now thought that the unrequited love that Andersen claimed to have for various engaged and unattainable women, including the singer Jenny Lind, were merely blinds to hide his homosexuality.

Reviewers were extremely surprised and disappointed that Andersen followed *The Improvisatore* with a small book of four stories for children, *The Tinderbox*, *Little Claus and Big Claus*, *The Princess and the Pea* and

Little Ida's Flowers (1835). The stories were criticised for lacking any obvious moral and also for being written in a colloquial style. For his part, Andersen felt that this was their point. As Alison Prince puts it in her excellent biography (*The Fan Dancer*, 1998) he was writing for children not at them. Andersen describes how his intention was to set the stories down just as one would tell them aloud to children, using ordinary everyday language. In doing so, he injected a vitality and freshness into the stories that made them appeal not only to the readers of his own time but also to those of today. Andersen had finally found his own voice.

The first three stories were based on folktales but the last was entirely his own. He took the positive reception of this as a cue to write his own fairy tales. Collections followed every year and – as Andersen said himself – no Christmas tree was complete without that year's new volume. The GRIMM BROTHERS had started a trend and at last the middle classes felt that fairy tales printed in proper books were safe to give to their children. Andersen's timing was perfect.

The stories proved to be more than a financial success. They enabled Andersen to explore the turbulent feelings that he could not express in any other way. *The Little Mermaid* (1837) concerns the pain of a lover who can never be accepted by her beloved for who and what she is; it was first conceived at the time of Edvard's marriage. *The Emperor's New Clothes*, published at the same time, can be read as a fable about the flimsiness of trying to use conventional notions to hide one's true self. *The Ugly Duckling* (1843) describes his feelings towards so many who ridiculed him and who would never accept that he was a great writer, particularly within the Collin family. *The Gardener and the Family* is Andersen's attack on Denmark itself for not truly appreciating the contribution that he made to literature even though he was widely acclaimed abroad. As well as the fairy tales, he wrote novels, poetry, verse plays and travel books and was fêted throughout Europe.

Yet he was an outsider twice over, and the very factors that alienated him were those that contributed to his success and enduring popularity. Whatever he achieved, he would always be the poor boy from Odense, never quite accepted as a social equal by the bourgeois families of Copenhagen. However, he never sought to overthrow the social system. Instead he wanted a meritocracy where talented individuals like himself could rise to any level. His tales espouse very middle-class values of belief in God, hard work and achieving a sustainable income (something that worried him even at his death, even though by then he was lending others money). Even princesses, if they did not follow the bourgeois code, could lose their place in society (*The Swineherd*). This reinforcement of their beliefs was part of his stories' appeal to the middle classes and why they became so popular. Andersen's background also gave him the strong, fresh authorial voice that we can still hear today.

Illustration by Anne Anderson for *Blackie's Children's Annual.*

The other separating factor was his sexuality. He longed for love, and once he had achieved his writing ambitions he became all the more aware of the hole in his life. Whether Andersen would ever have become the writer that he did if he had been cherished as he yearned to be is very much to be doubted. His best-loved and most famous tales have endured because of the psychological truths they contain and the writer's desperate need that drives them. AMN

Anderson, Anne 1874–1930 Writer and illustrator of children's books, and artist. Scottish-born Anderson spent her childhood in Argentina before settling in England. Influenced by Jessie M. King and MABEL LUCIE ATTWELL, she illustrated over 100 books, including several with the artist Alan Wright (her husband from 1912). Though she rarely tackled strictly fairy subjects, she always imbued her watercolour ILLUSTRATIONS with an atmosphere of delicate FANTASY, making her particularly popular in the nursery of the 1920s. Maleen Matthews has enthused that 'from the point of view of creating the child mind

she is perhaps more important than either [RACKHAM or CHARLES ROBINSON]'. DW
see also FAIRY FANTASY

Anderson, C(larence) W(illiam) 1891–1971 American author and illustrator of HORSE STORIES. Born in Nebraska, Anderson studied at the Art Institute of Chicago before settling in the East. His classic early reader *Billy and Blaze* (1936), the story of a young boy's adventures with his first horse, was followed by nearly a dozen more books about them. He was equally at home writing and illustrating for older readers, producing such popular longer fiction as *Afraid to Ride* (1957). Perhaps even more significant for older readers were his multitude of non-fiction works, including straightforward guides to horsemanship, collective equine BIOGRAPHIES, and more general explorations of the world of horses, especially thoroughbreds. Probably the American author with the greatest impact on early equestrian dreams, Anderson was unerring in his depiction of horses (he was a qualified show judge) and perceptive and sympathetic about his young readers' yearnings. His art, which has also been displayed in museums and galleries, ranged from the less formal early drawings to more meticulous portraits but always demonstrated his technical mastery; his horses exude character, and his books evince a passion for the subject matter that endeared them to generations of like-minded readers. DS

Anderson, Rachel see DISABILITY IN CHILDREN'S BOOKS; see also BIAS IN CHILDREN'S BOOKS

Anderson, Wayne 1946– British illustrator. Anderson made a dramatic début with his haunting illustrations for *Ratsmagic* (Christopher Logue, 1976) and he has given dramatic, disturbing illustrations to *Thumbelina* (James Riordan, 1991). Misty and mystical illustrations accompany his own mythic story, *Dragon* (1992). JAG

Andrews, Jane 1833–87 American author of instructive fiction. Forced by illness to abandon college teaching, Andrews started her own school; her integrative approach to education inspired several experimental children's books. *The Seven Little Sisters Who Live on the Round Ball That Floats in the Air* (1861) not only found a (much-imitated) way to teach geography through visits to imaginary children, but was one of the earliest attempts to further inter-cultural understanding through children's literature. *Ten Boys Who Lived on the Road From Long Ago to Now* (1885) focused attention not on historical facts, but on conceptualising cultural change. SR

Androcles and the Lion Play by Bernard Shaw, first produced in 1913. Shaw intended his play as an 'antidote to *PETER PAN*', which would 'show what a play for children should be like . . . It should never be childish; nothing offends children more than to play down to them.' In practice Shaw's comedy of Christian martyrdoms in the Roman amphitheatre has never seriously challenged *Peter Pan* in popularity. Some comic incongruities work well, notably the reluctant bravery of timid Androcles, and the triumph of violence over Christian pacifism in the Samson-like Ferovius, but Shaw cannot resist a vein of intellectual satire which children are liable to find tedious and perplexing. PH

Andy Pandy see *ROBIN*; see also TELEVISION; *WATCH WITH MOTHER*

Anecdotes and Adventures of Fifteen Gentlemen (c.1821) Probably by Richard Scrafton Sharpe, a London grocer who tried to keep his authorship a secret. It was published shortly after *The History of Sixteen Wonderful Old Women* (1820). One of the earliest examples of the LIMERICK form, it pre-dates EDWARD LEAR, whose first limericks, in *A BOOK OF NONSENSE*, were not published until 1846, and who admired Sharpe's book. This typical example shows Sharpe's sense of fun:

> There was once an old miser at Reading,
> Had a house and a yard with a shed in;
> 'Twas meant for a cow,
> But so small that I vow
> The poor creature could scarce get her head in.

MCCS

Angel for May, An see MELVYN BURGESS; see also WAR STORIES

Angelou, Maya see TOM FEELINGS

Anglicus, Bartholomaeus English Franciscan whose *De Proprietatibus Rerum* (c. 1241–51) is a Latin encyclopaedia designed to fulfill the needs of his pupils and to serve as a basis for the interpretation of scripture. Extant in many manuscripts, its popularity increased with translations into the vernaculars, one of which was John Trevisa's in 1398, printed by Wynkyn de Worde in 1495 as *All the Proprytees of Things*. The 1582 edition, *Batman uppon Bartholome*, is referred to as 'Shakespeare's Encyclopaedia'. Book Six is often cited by historians for its evidence of the clear distinction between infancy, boyhood/girlhood (until puberty), adolescence (until 21) and adulthood. GA

Anglund, Joan Walsh 1926– American author and illustrator. Born in Hinsdale, Illinois, Anglund spent much of her childhood drawing and writing stories in the margins of books, and later became a professional illustrator. *A Friend is Someone Who Likes You* (1958) was written to counteract loneliness after a move to New York City, and was followed by more than 75 books for children and adults, in which briefly expressed comforting thoughts are accompanied by nostalgic pictures of children with large faces and widely spaced eyes. Tiny details like toys, snails or butterflies give added appeal. FEA

Angry Arthur (1982) Picturebook by HIAWYN ORAM, illustrated by SATOSHI KITAMURA, which tells of Arthur's frustration when denied the chance to watch a Western on TELEVISION. Each member of his family – who constitute his real world – tries to intervene to end the tantrum. But this only fuels it, and the threat to his personal world is translated into an escalating natural violence (storm, hurricane, typhoon and universequake) which wrecks his home, town, city and eventually the world and the universe.

Satoshi Kitamura has created a rich, detailed and inventive visual text, touching both the humour and the psychological depth of Arthur's predicament. He uses mainly paired double spreads (without framing to draw in the reader), washed with strong colour, typically blues and violets with some golds. One of the pair depicts the rampage of the anger-storm, all chaos and distorting movement; the other, the lull and silence following the outburst. There are many touches of brilliance – the shadow-figure of the mother, large and threatening, the fracturing of the whole picture as the tantrum takes off, the reverberating figure of boy and cat in the universequake, and the spinning multiple image of the pair tumbling through space. AR

***Angus* series** see MARJORIE FLACK

Anholt, Catherine 1958– and **Anholt, Laurence** 1959– Prolific and versatile British husband-and-wife partnership who have produced separately and collaboratively more than 60 books for children. Together, they have published a wide range of board books for babies and PICTUREBOOKS for slightly older preschool children, mostly based on family life and important childhood events. They support a range of literacy activities for very young children and in 1998 were commissioned by the UK government to produce a booklet for the BOOKSTART project, *Babies Love Books*. Several of their books have been reproduced in CD-ROM and Braille versions (see also BOOKS FOR BLIND READERS).

In the acclaimed *Amazing Artists* series Laurence Anholt incorporates reproductions within his own illustrations to introduce young readers to great artists – Van Gogh, Picasso, Degas. He has also collaborated with Arthur Robins on the *Seriously Silly Stories*, a series which includes *Cinderboy* (1996), *Daft Jack and the Beanstack* (1968) – 'Daft Jack and his mother were so poor, they lived under a cow in a field. His mother slept at the front end and Jack slept at the udder end' – *Rumply Crumply Stinky Pin* (1996) and *The Fried Piper of Hamstring* (1998). The *One and Only* series is the result of a collaboration with TONY ROSS and includes stories about Harry the Hairiest Man, Ruby the Rudest Girl and other zany protagonists.

The *Big Book of Families* (1998) exemplifies the Anholts' work at its best: told mostly in verse employing the familiar rhythms and rhyme-patterns of NURSERY RHYMES and PLAYGROUND RHYMES, this engaging book is an invitation to very young children to peer into the daily lives of a wide range of loving families. VW

Aniakor, Chika see *THE MAGIC APPLE TREE*

***Animal Ark* series** (from 1994) Extraordinarily popular British series of 'vet' stories for younger readers, based on a brief by Ben Baglio and written under the name of Lucy Daniels. Several authors have worked on the series, including Jenny Oldfield. By 1998 there were 44 titles, including 'internal' trilogies such as *Animal Ark in Africa*, *Animal Ark in Australia* and *Animal Ark in America*. The stories feature Mandy Hope, adopted daughter of two practising vets, and her friend James. Realistic veterinary detail and information on animal care (checked by a veterinary practitioner) help the books to avoid sentimentality, though there is always a happy outcome.

Each book, with its alliterative title, deals with a different animal – pet, farm or wild – and the rescue of that animal from some unfortunate circumstance. Unsentimental attitudes to animals are voiced but not allowed to predominate. Any unsympathetic characters are seen in the context of the causes of their behaviour and usually change into happier, more understanding or fulfilled individuals. Where the stories deal with conservation issues, alternative points of view are given.

The series has appeared on TELEVISION and there is a prequel series, *Animal Ark Pets*. JSW

See also ANIMALS IN FICTION

Animal Farm see ANIMALS IN FICTION; ANIMATED CARTOONS; see also RALPH STEADMAN

Animal Magic see TELEVISION

Animalia (1986) Australian PICTUREBOOK which took writer and illustrator GRAEME BASE three years to create. It is a bold, elaborate ALPHABET, which, with its sophisticated vocabulary, humorous use of strong alliteration, juxtaposition of ideas and allusions, and lavishly detailed ILLUSTRATIONS of

Illustration by Graeme Base for *Animalia.*

anthropomorphic animals, is enjoyed by both children and adults as they seek to find the hundreds of objects for each letter, and the boy, Graeme, who is hidden on every page. HE

animals in fiction The association between children and stories about animals is very ancient. Not only do animals figure strongly in many Myths, Folktales and Legends but they also constitute the core of the Fable tradition which, from Roman times, has featured centrally in the early stages of children's literacy development. The reasons for this association probably include the fact that animals can be made more distinctive and memorable than different kinds of people for young readers and listeners. The sense that animals share some human qualities but are also fundamentally different can also be exploited in a variety of ways. The gap between humans and animals can be used to make moral points clearer by analogy, to say strong things with a degree of protection, and to provoke laughter and ridicule. Above all, the gap between animals and humans keeps alive a sense that the world is strange and full of wonder, a sense which has been at the heart of much good children's fiction.

Animals in traditional stories drew on three main functions – exemplary, symbolic and environmental – which more recent writing has picked up and developed in diverse and creative new ways. The fable tradition can be characterised as predominantly exemplary, though it has always included both satire and stories whose primary focus is survival rather than ethics. Modern children's versions have drawn extensively not only on the western traditions of Aesop and *Reynard the Fox,* but also on fables from other cultures. Particularly notable have been Trickster Tales, the *Anancy* stories from West Africa, the Coyote stories from the American Southwest, and the adventures of *Brer Rabbit* (also originally from Africa). These last were collected from plantations in the southern United States by Joel Chandler Harris and published in vivid, colloquial literary form in *Uncle Remus* (1880) and other volumes. The full-blown tradition of animal satire is rarer than might be supposed, though it includes such famous examples as George Orwell's *Animal Farm* (1945), the final section of Swift's *Gulliver's Travels* (1726), and Don Marquis' *archy and mehitabel* (1931).

Fairy Tales and folktales often use animals to shape their symbolic structures. The story of the frog who turns into a prince, for example, or the lycanthrope stories of men who periodically become wolves, engage with multiple strands of symbolic meaning in the transformations they portray. Although the symbolic function is drawn on lightly in more recent children's fiction involving animals, it remains important in Fantasy literature. C. S. Lewis develops a symbolic association between the lion Aslan and Christ in the *Narnia* series, for instance. Even in more secular writing such uses are common: the hero of Ursula Le Guin's *Earthsea Quartet,* for example, takes the name 'Sparrowhawk', a title whose totemic resonances are developed at different points in the story.

The environmental or realistic use of animals in traditional forms provided some access to knowledge of what we would now call 'natural history'. In early forms – such as the bestiaries – natural history deriving from the observation of animals was mixed with traditions representing fantastical beasts and dragons, folklore and allegorically derived links to spiritual truths and morality. But the fascination which many children have with the natural world has always been mediated through animal stories, and in the 17th century the rise of scientifically based knowledge and observation provided opportunities for writers to contextualise animal stories within increasingly realistic environments incorporating detailed observation of the natural world. There are some signs of such observation of country life in the extended literary fables of medieval writers such as GEOFFREY CHAUCER and Robert Henryson, but the conventions of extended realism developed within the 19th-century novel made available a much more sustained use of environmental detail in children's fiction, particularly from the late 19th century onwards. Richard Jefferies' novels of country life for older readers, *WOOD MAGIC* (1880) and *Bevis; the Story of a Boy* (1882), influenced a range of later authors (Henry Williamson, KENNETH GRAHAME and ARTHUR RANSOME were all indebted to him), even though Jefferies is not much read today. Both Henry Williamson (in *TARKA THE OTTER*, 1927, and *Salar the Salmon*, 1929) and JACK LONDON in his dog stories (*The Call of the Wild*, 1903, *White Fang*, 1905) dispensed with the conventions which allow animals to think and talk like humans in stories in order to get greater verisimilitude and a kind of tough, fully realised 'otherness' into their depictions of the natural world. This tendency was taken in different directions by authors such as ERNEST THOMPSON SETON, J.W. Fortescue and Denys Watkins Pitchford (see B.B.), sometimes described as 'naturalist' writers of animal fiction. But even authors who retain conventions of verbal communication and human psychology in their animal characters have often done so against a backdrop of a detailed sense of environment and authentic animal behaviour. This has set up quite other resonances than traditions within which animals become direct ciphers for human experience. RUDYARD KIPLING'S *THE JUNGLE BOOKS* (1893–4), for instance, have been described as the first attempt to enter an animal world, while later novels such as FELIX SALTEN'S *BAMBI* (1928) (much more heavily anthropomorphised in DISNEY's film version) rely as much on realistic insights into animals' life histories as on verbalising essentially human responses to the dangers and exigencies of forest life.

From the middle of the 18th century animal stories figured strongly within the newly constituted corpus of books produced specifically for child readers. After fables, the most important animal narratives were moral tales. These might serve either as parables for human behaviour or as exhortations to children to treat all animals with kindness and respect, in a move reflecting changing attitudes towards the natural world inspired partly by ROUSSEAU and the cult of sentimentalism. SARAH TRIMMER'S *HISTORY OF THE ROBINS* (1786), for instance, combined both these ethical perspectives. A number of devices which have a central place in the development of animal fiction have their origins in the moral tales of late 18th and early 19th centuries. DOROTHY KILNER'S *The Life and Perambulations of a Mouse* (1783), for instance, is a moral story about filial obedience. But it also instigated the device of a tale told in autobiographical fashion from the perspective of the animal itself. The device was used repeatedly in moral tales about a whole gamut of animal species – hare, cat, baboon, even goldfinch – in the early 19th century. It was exploited to full effect in at least one of the classics of children's literature, Anna Sewell's *BLACK BEAUTY* (1877), and in an inferior imitation, the dog story *Beautiful Joe* (1894) by the Canadian author MARSHALL SAUNDERS. A variant on this device, the human being with fully employed consciousness trapped for a period in an animal body, has been employed with imaginative flair in a number of other fine children's texts of the 20th century, including T. H. WHITE'S *The Sword in the Stone* (1938) (see *THE ONCE AND FUTURE KING*) and JOHN MASEFIELD'S *The Box of Delights* (1935). The moral perspective on the human treatment of animals – including, latterly, animal rights and conservation issues – has also continued as a vital imaginative strand in children's fiction. It is a major component in novels as diverse as ANNE FINE'S *The Chicken Gave it to Me* (1992), the *ANIMALS OF FARTHING WOOD* series (1979–82) and HUGH LOFTING'S *DOCTOR DOLITTLE* series (1920–52).

The heavy moralising strand in early animal stories for children began to be cut across, from the early 19th century, by stories in which the dominant tone was lighter, charming, even self-consciously absurd. The work normally credited with initiating this sea change was WILLIAM ROSCOE'S *THE BUTTERFLY'S BALL* (1806/7). Harvey Darton described Roscoe's work and its equally popular imitations – *The Lion's Parliament* (1807) and *THE PEACOCK 'AT HOME'* (1807) – as 'cheerful good fun of a simple kind'. The lighter tone predominating in these verse narratives paved the way for experiments in NONSENSE VERSE with animal subjects by authors such as EDWARD LEAR, LESLIE L. BROOKE and OGDEN NASH. More profound, but equally absurd, was the use of animal types within the topsy-turvy dream worlds of LEWIS CARROLL'S unique masterpieces, the *ALICE* stories (1865, 1871).

A lull in the production of animal stories can be discerned from around 1860 to 1880 – the principal exceptions being *Black Beauty* and CHARLES KINGSLEY'S fantasy, *THE WATER-BABIES* (1863). When animal stories again became popular, a marked shift from the exemplary to the realistic-environmental had occurred. Victorian fascination with the natural world had led both to the acceptance of nature study in the school curriculum and to a new interest in wild creatures. In America especially, the realisation that many native species of birds and animals were in imminent danger of extinction encouraged the development of environmental awareness in both adults and children. The Canadian contribution was particularly influential, taking the form of fictionalised wild animal biographies based on years of close observation. In the 1880s, for example, Ernest Thompson Seton was already publishing the remarkable stories later collected in *Wild Animals I Have Known* (1898); two other Canadian authors, CHARLES G.D. ROBERTS and RODERICK HAIG-BROWN, were to develop the form in their turn. Unlike the bloodthirsty ADVENTURE STORIES of the mid-19th century, which pitted trigger-happy protagonists against wild animals and native people alike, the animal stories of the *fin de siècle* often showed human protagonists living in harmony with the untamed natural world: Mowgli in *The Jungle Books*, for example; Jefferies' Bevis; Yan and Sam in Seton's *Two Little Savages* (1903); Elnora in GENE STRATTON-PORTER's *A Girl of the Limberlost* (1909). As animal protagonists, wild animals – even predators – were now preferred to small, harmless, semi-domesticated creatures. Instead of Sarah Trimmer's robins and Dorothy Kilner's mice, children could share the dangers of the wild with Sir John Fortescue's heroic stag in *The Story of a Red Deer* (1897), with Charles G.D. Roberts' *Red Fox* (1905), with KENNETH GRAHAME's mole and water-rat, with Selma Lagerlöf's wild geese in *THE WONDERFUL ADVENTURES OF NILS* (originally *Nils Holgersson*, 1901), or with Kipling's mongoose, black panther and fur seal. In Jack London's *The Call of the Wild* (1903), the heroic dog Buck finally chooses life with a wolf pack in the wilderness in preference to humankind and domesticity – a choice inconceivable 20 years earlier. Even BEATRIX POTTER's stories revealed the many hungry enemies that frogs, geese and rabbits had to fear.

In the 19th century, the uniqueness of Australian fauna, coupled with the opportunity for adventure, produced such novels as Anne Bowman's *Kangaroo Hunters* (1858) and Arthur Ferres' *His First Kangaroo* (1896). However, there was a transition towards fantasy, most notably with the publication of Ethel Pedley's *Dot and the Kangaroo* (1899), followed by MAY GIBBS's *SNUGGLEPOT AND CUDDLEPIE* and Norman Lindsay's classic, *THE MAGIC PUDDING* (both 1918). The comparative realism of the Australian native animals in the first two books was overwhelmed by anthropomorphism in the third. Lindsay satirised Australians and their institutions with his depictions of the gentlemanly koala, Bunyip Bluegum, and the aggressive penguin, Sam Sawnoff, who try to protect their puddin' from thieves, a wombat and a possum. *BLINKY BILL* (1933) by DOROTHY WALL continued this tradition, with Blinky (another koala) getting into frequent scrapes. Wall, like Pedley, promoted the conservation of native animals.

In the 20th century, the animal story progressed steadily. The popularity of toy stories in the 1920s clearly influenced Margery Williams Bianco's *Poor Cecco* (1925) and A.A. MILNE's *WINNIE-THE-POOH* (1926), both of which combined animal characters with live toys. Although animal biographies were still being produced – notably Felix Salten's *Bambi, A Life in the Woods* (1923, trans. 1928), Will James's *SMOKY, THE COWHORSE* (1926), DHAN GOPAL MUKERJI's *Gay-Neck, the Story of a Pigeon* (1927), and the first PONY STORY, *MOORLAND MOUSIE* (1929) by 'Golden Gorse', – the dominance of humorous, light-hearted fantasy tended to discourage the realistic approach. More typical were *The Story of Doctor Dolittle* (1922) and its successors, by Hugh Lofting; *To and Again* (1927), the first of Walter R. Brooks' *FREDDY THE PIG* series; and, on a different level, THORNTON W. BURGESS's whimsical stories of 'Old Mother West Wind' and her animal friends.

The charm of representing animals in more normalised human settings has been regularly exploited in Britain. As in *The Butterfly's Ball*, to name just one example, the illustrations are generally a key facet of the appeal and quality of such stories. In the 19th and early 20th centuries such stories were often connected in nostalgic ways to the life and mores of small rural communities. BEATRIX POTTER's tales and, somewhat later, the *LITTLE GREY RABBIT* books written by ALISON UTTLEY are perhaps prime examples of this kind of story. Superficially these writers appear to have much in common: both idealise rural settings in the North of England and use small animals, often dressed like humans, whose lives mix animal characteristics with domestic concerns. Yet they are actually two very different kinds of narrative. Beatrix Potter is a subtle ironist, whose evocation of rural domesticity is tempered by the harsher imperatives of rivalry and survival reminiscent of the more exposed world of the fables. Alison Uttley's stories are more comfortable and cosy; her Little Grey Rabbit is unequivocally good, and the appeal derives more from a blend of homely folklore and rural custom with the aura of a lost ideal of cherished wholesomeness embodied by small animals.

As the Great Depression, the rise of fascism and the threat of war cast their shadow over the 1930s, the realistic mode began once more to dominate the animal story – but with a difference: wild creatures were, in the main, replaced by domestic horses, ponies, dogs and the occasional cat. At a time when human civilisation seemed intent on self-destruction, the simple bond of devotion between human and animal may have comforted young and old readers alike. As in the 1890s, realistic animal stories originally written for adults were often read by children; well-known examples published between 1930 and 1950 include Enid Bagnold's *National Velvet* (1930), MARJORIE KINNAN RAWLINGS's *The Yearling* (1938), Eric Knight's *LASSIE COME-HOME* (194), MARY O'HARA's *Flicka* trilogy which began with *My Friend Flicka* in 1941, and PAUL GALLICO's *Jennie* (in America, *The Abandoned*; 1950). In America, HORSE STORIES were especially popular; unlike British pony stories, they were free from class distinctions and more varied in setting, being strongly influenced by the regionalism of the 1930s and the rising popularity of HISTORICAL FICTION. STEPHEN MEADER's *Red Horse Hill* (1930) is a memoir of rural New Hampshire as well as an early example of the 'boy and his horse' theme. MARGUERITE HENRY not only raised the genre to its highest literary level, but introduced her readers to numerous cultures and historical periods – early 19th-century New England in *Justin Morgan Had a Horse* (1945), Virginia's off-shore islands in *Misty of Chincoteague* (1947), 18th-century Morocco in *King of the Wind* (1948), Theodore Roosevelt's Arizona in *Brighty of the Grand Canyon* (1953), Siena and Vienna in *Gaudenzia, Pride of the Palio* (1960) and *White Stallion of Lipisza* (1964). Even the first of Walter Parley's still popular *BLACK STALLION* series (from 1941) begins its adventures on the Red Sea and ends in New York City. American writers of dog stories, such as Colonel S.P. Meek and James Kjelgaard, also employed a variety of settings, both regional and international. Horse and dog stories tended to follow the same basic pattern: the boy (or girl) wants a horse (or dog), gets one but then loses it, and finally recovers it.

In 1931, Frank Dalby Davison's *Man-Shy*, Australia's first 'symbolic' animal novel, appeared. Man-Shy, a wild heifer, barely surviving the fencing of the waterholes, represented the 'battler' of the Depression. Realism was emphasised, also, in LESLIE REES's series of illustrated books for younger readers, which included *The Story of Karrawingi the Emu* (1946), the first winner of the Australian Children's Book of the Year Award. The tradition of realistic animal stories in Australia continued in the 1950s and 60s, with the most successful of these novels being ELYNE MITCHELL's *THE SILVER BRUMBY* (1958) and COLIN THIELE's *STORM BOY* (1963), both of which were filmed. The latter, with the pelican Mr Percival in a major role, has become a classic.

In the 1950s, as fantasy assumed a more dominant role in children's literature, animal fantasy rebounded to the forefront. Humanised animals had persisted mainly in books for younger children by such authors as KATHLEEN HALE, MUNRO LEAF and MARGARET WISE BROWN; now new authors, with a somewhat older audience, were experimenting with a range of anthropomorphic possibilities. E.B. WHITE, who had already startled reviewers with a mouse-child born to human parents in *Stuart Little* (1945), described, unforgettably, a devoted friendship between a pig and a spider in *CHARLOTTE'S WEB* (1952). URSULA MORAY WILLIAMS shipwrecked, a tomcat on a desert island in *The Nine Lives of Island Mackenzie* (in America, *Island Mackenzie*; 1959). Freddy the Pig encountered Men from Mars and taught them to play baseball. Complex animal societies sometimes existed secretly below the threshold of human awareness – the mice of Margery Sharp's *The Rescuers* (1959) (see *MISS BIANCA* SERIES), the animal network of DODIE SMITH'S *THE ONE HUNDRED AND ONE DALMATIONS* (1956) and Esther Averill's *CAT CLUB*. This type of fantasy was to achieve its ultimate expression in Richard Adams's rabbit epic, *WATERSHIP DOWN* (1972).

One variety of anthropomorphism was to become highly influential in the following decades: the story whose animal characters are in fact human beings in fur, identified as 'animal' only through their illustrations. Some critics refuse to consider them animal stories at all. The protagonists of ELSE MINARIK's *Little Bear* – which may have initiated the trend in 1957 – has, typically, nothing bear-like in his personality or way of life; he is a human child, dressed by MAURICE SENDAK in a cute bear suit. RUSSELL HOBAN's *Bedtime for Frances* (1960) goes a step further: Frances (who is not called 'Little Badger') and her parents resemble not so much badgers as blobby, furry human beings. Here, as in ARNOLD LOBEL's *FROG AND TOAD* series (from 1970), animal disguises make the exposé of immaturity palatable to beginning readers. By the 1990s, the animal connection had become even more tenuous: MARC BROWN's Arthur, in his multi-animal classroom, really looks nothing like an anteater, while ROSEMARY WELLS's Max and Ruby are recognisable as 'rabbits' only by their ears. Increasing sensitivity towards racism and sexism in children's books doubtless accounts in part for the popularity of this device; animal characters are not only free of ethnicity, but can be free of gender too. Not coincidentally, the 1960s, when this type of animal story became prominent, was also the period when African-American child characters were often identified as such only in the illustrations.

The social and cultural changes associated with the 1960s and early 70s left their mark on the animal story in more direct ways, the most important being the widespread rise in environmental consciousness. As the pendulum swung back once more towards the mode of realism, writers of animal stories were influenced by their personal awareness of the environmental crisis as well as the revolutionary studies of animal communication and social behaviour by such scientists as Konrad Lorenz, Jane Goodall and Dian Fossey. *Watership Down* (1972), for example, was directly influenced by Richard Adams's concern for the natural environment and by recent research into rabbit behaviour.

Stories such as WALT MOREY'S *Gentle Ben* (1965) – a boy and his grizzly – attempted to dispel the negative images associated with wild predators. Of these ecologically oriented writers, none proved of greater importance than JEAN CRAIGHEAD GEORGE. Although her earliest wild animal biographies date back to the late 1940s, *My Side of the Mountain* (1959), in which a boy spends a winter 'living wild' in the Catskills, was her pivotal work – looking back to such predecessors as *Bevis* and *Two Little Savages* and forward to such overtly environmentalist novels as *Who Really Killed Cock Robin?* (1971), *JULIE OF THE WOLVES* (1972) and *The Missing Gator of Gumbo Limbo* (1992)

In America in the 1970s, the bleak 'new realism' can be discerned in the horse and dog stories of Lynn Hall, where the bond between child and animal often proves illusory or even dangerous. The boy protagonist of *Ride a Wild Dream* (1975) never succeeds in taming the wild stallion; and the girl protagonist of *Flowers of Anger* (1976) becomes obsessed with her desire for revenge when her beloved horse is killed. The 1980s and 90s, however, saw some evidence of a return to the optimistic, flamboyant type of animal fantasy in such authors as DICK KING-SMITH, whose *THE SHEEP-PIG* (in America, *Babe the Gallant Pig*; 1983) was translated with great success into a feature-length film. Brian Jacques' *REDWALL* series (from 1985), with its feasts and quests and bloody battles, has also proved highly popular with children.

At about the same time, in New Zealand Neil McNaughton's *Tat: the Story of a Sheepdog* (1970) became probably the first successful animal story from that country. Tat's life is dominated by his relationship with his master but, as is common, there is considerable emphasis on human unkindness towards animals. It seems, however, that the majority of the more important New Zealand animal stories – unsurprising given the geography of the country – are about sea creatures. ANNE DE ROO'S *Boy and the Sea Beast* (1971) and JOY COWLEY'S *The Silent One* (1981) are cases in point: in the former, Thunder the dolphin is the catalyst for Boy's education, entertainment and even his dreams.

In the 1980s and 90s, the utilisation of animals as symbols became a real literary force, especially in GILLIAN RUBINSTEIN'S award-winning *FOXSPELL* (1994), with the man-fox representing both feral fauna in Australia and human freedom. Numerous titles by VICTOR KELLEHER, especially the SCIENCE FICTION novels *TARONGA* (1986) and *Parkland* (1994), draw on animals as symbols – the zoo tiger in the former and the hybrids in the latter are equated to humans, as are the baboons which are used for experimental purposes in the realistic *Papio* (1984). New Zealander Kate de Goldi's *SANCTUARY* (1996) also has a symbolic animal, a caged panther which matches the central character's caged spirit.

While in New Zealand the fictional replacement of native animals with domesticated, feral and even foreign species seems almost complete, in Britain there has been a drift towards portraying animals largely stripped of their domestic human accoutrements in stories which retain versions of Beatrix Potter's tougher-edged ironies. ROALD DAHL'S *The Fantastic Mr Fox* and, for younger children, PAT HUTCHINS' *ROSIE'S WALK* (1970) are two examples among many which could be cited. Meanwhile, perhaps in response to children's changing social experience of the world outside the home, the cosier type of domestic narrative exemplified by Alison Uttley has moved increasingly from a rural to a suburban setting, often ending up in the garden or playroom. In the move into the town or home, animals have tended to become pets or cuddly toys. In *WINNIE-THE-POOH* (1926), A.A. MILNE was able to give his playroom animals the imaginative expanse of the hundred acre wood to roam in, and in the apparently inimitable *RUPERT BEAR* stories the locus of the old-fashioned rural community, Nutwood, becomes a launching-pad for the most far-flung adventures. But in MICHAEL BOND'S *PADDINGTON BEAR* (1958–74) the journey from the wilds of Peru to London marks the steady incursion of animal figures into suburbia, and a wide range of modern fiction for children – from the bear stories of MICK INKPEN to the work of JANE HISSEY – is set largely within the domestic confines of the house.

A number of contemporary writer/illustrators have drawn with imaginative skill on different potentialities within animal writing, but the work of the British illustrator, ANTHONY BROWNE, is perhaps particularly distinguished in its range, complexity and force. His use of animals blends satire and surrealism with psychological depth, often producing subtle, probing kinds of moral questioning. His work is one index of the enduring popularity, as well as the potential quality, of animal stories in children's fiction.

DWh, JF, SR

Animals of Farthing Wood, The Popular series of novels for children by Colin Dann, first published between 1979 and 1982. The original story concerned the hazardous journey of a group of disparate animals from their home in Farthing Wood, threatened by developers, to sanctuary in White Deer Park. In the books which continued the series, not quite as successfully, the epic journey was replaced by a kind of family saga between rival foxes established in the new White Deer Park environment. The book and series are perhaps the most popular example of a new genre for children – the 'eco-narrative' – in which contemporary concerns for ecological and conservation issues are dramatised through an adaptation of older literary genres. The form of the original story is essentially that of epic – a journey involving varied battles, threats and dangers whose endpoint is the consolidation of a new, more settled way of life. The popularity of the series was considerably enhanced by being reproduced by the BBC in a serialised cartoon version broadcast from 1993. Although conservation issues received less extended consideration in the cartoon version, the animals' characters were made more colourful, the slightly earnest dialogue of the novels being replaced by interactions with a sharper, more humorous edge. Characterisation in the series (especially of badger and mole) owes something to children's classics such as THE WIND IN THE WILLOWS. However, this is combined with realistic snippets of natural history and, as in Richard Adams's WATERSHIP DOWN, considerable emphasis is given to struggles for power and social cohesion between the animals. DWh

see also ECOLOGY

animated cartoons Animation of drawings for the cinema grew out of the pre-cinema flicker books which were published in the last century and which showed simple visual gags such as figures walking along and falling over. The principle was applied to magic lantern slides, especially by Émile Reynaud in Paris who created the Praxinoscope (1888). This showed complete stories running for up to 15 minutes on a screen for audiences, a decade before Lumière's cinematographe projected one-minute photographed films.

The first British animated cartoon designed for children was a series based on the *Daily Mirror*'s popular strip, PIP, SQUEAK AND WILFRED (1921). Twenty-six one-reel films were produced under the supervision of Lancelot Speed, a newspaper cartoonist who had first won animation acclaim with his wartime series of topical films, *Bully Boy* (1914). Speed was closely followed by a former church architect, Anson Dyer, who made cartoon films of *Bobby the Scout* (1921) and a *Kiddigraph* series (1922) for Hepworth Productions. When Pathe Pictures dropped the American *Felix the Cat* from their magazine films, they replaced him with *Pongo the Pup*, animated by Dudley Buxton, who had begun making cartoons during World War I and Joe Noble. The same year, 1924, the first truly successful cartoon series was based on G.E. STUDDY's popular pup, *Bonzo*, a series which had taken England by storm through his coloured magazine cartoons and comic strips. There were 26 *Bonzo* films in all, directed by William Ward, who eventually became a cartoonist for *Mickey Mouse Weekly* (see MICKEY MOUSE ANNUAL), drawing strips starring Donald Duck. Another animator on the *Bonzo* films was Brian White, who later worked in strips, creating the long-running *Nipper* for the *Daily Mail* and the *Nipper Annual* throughout the 1930s.

Felix the Cat, produced in America by Pat Sullivan and created and animated by Otto Messmer, became the first world 'star' of cartoon films, running from 1918 to 1930. A brilliant creation, who used his detachable tail for almost any gag, Felix had a theme song, 'Felix Keeps on Walking', and a newspaper strip. This was published in England with great success and collated into *The Felix Annual* which ran from 1923 until 1930. The continual revival of *Felix* as a TELEVISION cartoon prompted a rebirth of his annual in 1956, when the cartoonist was John Mortimer, who later gave up drawing to become a television comedy writer.

Animation thrived in the USA during the 1920s but it was not until the advent of sound films via Warner Brothers' Vitaphone system (1927) that cartoon films finally caught on with the public. WALT DISNEY, who had been working in cartoons for years (*Alice in Cartoonland, Oswald the Lucky Rabbit*), finally met with immediate success with *Steamboat Willie* (1928). This musical cartoon starred Mickey Mouse, and within a year or so books for children depicting the rodent's adventures were bestsellers. In England, Dean & Son bought the rights and produced the first *Mickey Mouse Annual* (1930), a thick Christmas ANNUAL which was to run until 1965. The original cartoonist was Wilfred Haughton, the first man in England to become an official Mickey Mouse artist. Later he drew and painted the coloured covers of *Mickey Mouse Weekly* (1936) before being dismissed by the film-makers as too old-fashioned to depict the newly-modelled Mickey Mouse. Mickey's chum, the quarrelsome, short-tempered Donald Duck, soon received his own *Donald Duck's Annual* (1939), which ceased publication in 1942 because of wartime paper shortages.

The thirties brought a revival of British animation, first with Anson Dyer and his *Old Sam* series, based on Stanley Holloway's recordings of the famous comic monologues, then with Roland Davies, who formed his own small cartoon studio and made films starring his cart-horse character, *Come on Steve*, which ran in the *Sunday Express*. Two children's books were based on Steve, and there was a short-lived post-war *Come on Steve Annual* (1948–9).

Although the first full-length animated feature, *Adventures of Prince Achmed*, was produced by the German director Lotte Reiniger in 1926, the escalating expense of producing even short cartoon sequences meant that, from the 1930s, the world market in children's animated cartoons was dominated by a few American companies. This was particularly so when speech and, from the early 1930s, colour began to be extensively used, adding very significantly to production costs. Foremost amongst the large studio producers was, of course, the Disney corporation, which pioneered and, for a considerable period, effectively monopolised production of feature-length cartoons. Prior to World War II, Max Fleisher had produced a full-length colour feature film of GULLIVER'S TRAVELS (1939), designed to compete with the phenomenal success of Disney's *Snow White and the Seven Dwarfs* (1937). But despite reasonable box office returns Fleischer attempted only one more feature-length cartoon, and it was not for another 20 years that Disney had any serious competition in this field.

However, within the format of the short cartoon more diversity remained possible. Disney's great innovation had been the creation of fully developed animated characters within cartoons, rather than reliance largely on the action to hold the audience's attention. This innovation gave rise, from the 30s onwards, to a plethora of animated cartoon 'stars'. Disney's Donald Duck and MICKEY MOUSE were joined by an astonishing variety of other characters, from Fleisher's Betty Boop to POPEYE, Daffy Duck and later BUGS BUNNY, each very distinctively characterised in terms of personality and movement. Where Disney tended to combine character with smoothness in movement and with sentiment in the script, in the 1940s and 1950s other studios began to deck out their character stars with increasingly anarchic and boisterous styles of presentation. Animators such as Hanna and Barbera at MGM and Tex Avery, Walter Lanz and Chuck Jones at Warner Brothers were responsible for a new range of characters and approaches. Perhaps the most popular figure to emerge in this mid-period was BUGS BUNNY, created by Avery for Warner Brothers' long-running *Looney Tunes* series, whose fast-talking, sardonically cool demeanour led to him being compared to Groucho Marx.

The advent of TELEVISION, combined with a legal decision in 1949 which meant that American film companies could no longer force distributors to take a package of feature film and cartoon shorts together, led to a sharp decline in the US production of short cartoons. While some studios closed or scaled down their cartoon departments, Hanna and Barbera became hugely influential in developing a format, first devised by Jay Ward in 1949, which cut the production costs of making cartoons dramatically so they could compete in the new television market. The process, which was called 'limited animation', enabled producers to use a variety of angles, cuts and camera moves to give pace to the story, while using far fewer cels or drawings. A number of the shows developed during the 50s and early 60s using these techniques were crossovers from successful television comedy series. Hanna and Barbera's cartoon *The Flintstones*, for instance, derived from the classic situation comedy *The Honeymooners*, while the long-running *Top Cat* was based on the artful chicanery of Sergeant Bilko in *The Phil Silvers Show.*

While American-produced short cartoons dominated the world market for children's television, many other countries have sustained independent and diverse traditions within the field of animation. Within Britain, post-war production was initially very small scale. David Hand, the director of *Snow White* and *BAMBI* for Disney, set up a company called GB Animation in 1944; the company's ambition was to rival Disney and the team was trained to strive for similar qualities of production. However their major series *Animaland* was not a great success, despite high technical achievements, and the group was dissolved in 1949. John Halas, a disciple of the Bauhaus philosophy of social art, had more lasting influence; working with Joy Batchelor he produced a version of *Animal Farm*, the first British animated feature film, in 1949. Together they founded a production company, Halas and Batchelor, which became one of the most highly regarded in the world.

From the 1960s, production of animated cartoons within Britain increased steadily. Notable achievements among feature films have been *WATERSHIP DOWN* (1978), produced by the American Martin Rosen with directors John Hubley and Tony Guy, and George Dunning's innovative cult movie *Yellow Submarine* (1967). Dunning founded the company TVC in 1957 with John Coates, which under Coates's direction produced a stream of successful animation films (including THE SNOWMAN and *When the Wind Blows*) even after Dunning's death. *The Snowman* (1982) was directed by Diane Jackson, who began her career working as an animator on *Yellow Submarine.* Output from British animation studios has been very varied with no single central tradition in evidence. An increasing number of productions have been funded on the model of co-sponsorship developed by Channel 4 television, often with international collaboration. The series *THE ANIMALS OF FARTHING WOOD*, for instance, was co-produced in Britain and France, with funding from 19 public broadcast networks, while *Count Duckula*, whose unlikely subject is a vegetarian vampire duck, was made as a co-production with the American cable company Nickelodeon. Such ventures look set to continue in an era of increasing globalisation. DG, DWh

Anne of Green Gables Distinguished and popular series by the Canadian author L.M. MONTGOMERY. In *Anne of Green Gables* (1908), Anne Shirley, a red-headed orphan, is sent by mistake to the elderly Matthew and Marilla Cuthbert, who had 'ordered a boy' but end by adopting her. The book and its seven sequels trace the bringing up, education, escapades, marriage etc. of Anne, following a pattern established in 19th-century American books for girls, such as COOLIDGE'S *KATY* books, though the *Anne* books are themselves Canadian, being set on Prince Edward

Island. The prototypes for these books were LOUISA M. ALCOTT'S *LITTLE WOMEN* books, and one may even trace an inheritance of incident between the works: when in *Anne of Green Gables* Anne breaks her slate over Gilbert Blythe's head and is stood in front of the class to the 'excruciating' hurt of her feelings, this recalls Amy March's mortification in *Little Women* when similarly punished for eating limes in class. The *Anne* books were themselves to inspire imitation: POLLYANNA, the orphan who softens the heart of her aunt and changes the lives of those around her, is a literary descendant of Anne.

Anne, like Jo March, is uneasily situated between two worlds: the traditional 19th-century female domain of house and family, and the more modern sphere shaped by the claims of individualism, where personal fulfilment in other terms is envisaged and encouraged. The dichotomy may be perceived in the values espoused by the series. On the one hand, *Anne of Green Gables*, *Anne of Avonlea* (1909), *Anne of the Island* (1915) and *Anne of Windy Poplars* (1936) all show Anne pursuing an education and career with great zest and ability. (*Anne of Windy Poplars* was also published as *Anne of Windy Willows* and – though published after *Rilla of Ingleside* (1921) which is chronologically the last of the series – it refers to the period of Anne's teaching before she marries Gilbert.) Unlike Edith in CHARLOTTE YONGE'S *DAISY CHAIN*, who is dissuaded from pursuing her academic interests because she is a girl, Anne is very well educated indeed for her time, both being formally trained as a teacher and having a tertiary education. Here, the individual appears to be encouraged to develop her potential, abilities and interests to the fullest.

Furthermore, one of the qualities most strongly asserted throughout the series is that of imagination – the cornerstone of the Romantic ethos, which invests the drab world with colour and meaning. When Anne first arrives at Green Gables, the whitewashed walls of her room appear to her 'so painfully bare and staring that she thought they must ache over their own bareness'. This may perhaps be symbolic of Green Gables' inhabitants, the Cuthberts, who until Anne's arrival have lived a sparse, neat, but unexpanded life. Anne, whose waking hours are spent in imagining things, brings a new dimension to the house and its occupants, Marilla's underdeveloped sense of humour and capacity for affection being brought out more and more. Anne is thus a child in the Wordsworthian tradition, both as ambassador of the imagination and in her conformation to the Romantic idea of the innocent and feeling child as teacher to adults who have lost their way. This should, however, not be taken to mean that the series takes its own Romantic allegiances too seriously. When Anne, 'devoured by secret regret that she had not been born in Camelot' and feeling that those days were 'so much more romantic than the present', decides to dramatise Tennyson's poem on the Lily Maid of Astolat, the flat in which she is sitting begins to leak and sink – this, with mild humour, working to deflate all romantic pretensions.

However, all this is strangely at variance with a different system of values in the series, one that is more old-fashioned and traditional. Early on in *Anne of Green Gables*, upon Matthew's declaring himself a Conservative, Anne says decidedly, 'Then I'm Conservative too', and this youthful assertion of political loyalties is prophetic of the values which will ultimately be embraced: in the end, the series sees Anne's education and career become subsidiary to the claims of the home and family. If one considers the structure of the series in terms of the date of publication, leaving aside the *Chronicles* and *Further Chronicles of Avonlea* which are collections of short stories not about Anne, we have: *Anne of Green Gables*, *Anne of Avonlea*, *Anne of the Island*, *Anne's House of Dreams* (c.1915), *Rainbow Valley* (1919), *Rilla of Ingleside* (1921), *Anne of Windy Poplars* and *Anne of Ingleside* (1937). The order of publication suggests that the series is tensed towards Anne's marriage as its point of climax, *Rainbow Valley* and *Rilla of Ingleside* in a sense focusing more on her children than on her, and the last two obviously being afterthoughts, novels which go back to fill in the spaces. While Anne continues to be dreamy and imaginative until the last, she nonetheless appears to have been reclaimed by a system in which the valid life is that which is devoted to social duties rather than the pursuit of individualistic desires. This might perhaps be said to constitute a retreat of sorts from the modern way of life.

In any case, part of the charm of the *Anne* books resides in the apparently unchanging and idyllic nature of life within them. The characters are comfortably predictable even to each other: the Pyes, for example, are difficult and unpleasant, and everywhere Anne settles has its local version of them. *Rilla of Ingleside*, which depicts the Blythe family during the First World War, is the most sombre of the series, but even here the shadow of the war falls only distantly. Rilla, who has grown up during the war, relapses, when Kenneth returns to propose to her, into her old lisp, and with it, into a symbolic childlikeness. Apart from the one irreversible tragedy of Walter Blythe's death, the close of the novel sees the old dispensation re-established, the old way of life restored. SA

Annie John (1983) An autobiographical novel by Jamaica Kincaid, based on her childhood and adolescence on Antigua. The novel depicts the protagonist's great childhood attachment to her mother and the dissolution of that bond as Annie moves into adolescence. The novel blends island customs and English culture; Annie's mother adheres to native beliefs while her father has become Anglicised. When Annie succumbs to a mysterious illness, the white doctor's medicines are of no use; only her grandmother, Ma Chess, an Obeah woman, is able to save her. Annie herself is punished at school for refusing to regard Christopher Columbus as a hero. Nonetheless, Annie continues to attend an English school on the island and at the end of the novel she leaves for England to continue her education at nursing school. Roni Natov has written a psychoanalytic analysis of *Annie John*, 'Mothers and Daughters: Jamaica Kincaid's Pre-Oedipal Narrative' (*Children's Literature* 18, 1990), which applies Nancy Chodorow's feminist psychoanalytic theories on female children and separation anxiety to Annie's relationship with her mother. Moira Ferguson's chapter on *Annie John* in *Jamaica Kincaid: Where the Land Meets the Body* (1994) offers a post-colonial interpretation. AKP

Anno (Mitsumaso) 1926– Japanese illustrator, born in the old town of Tsuwano, in western Japan. He was a primary school teacher for several years before becoming one of Japan's leading book illustrators. His work was first seen outside Japan in the early 1970s when his books began to be published in other countries, and by the middle of that decade he was widely recognised as an artist of extraordinary imagination and creativity. Anno has produced an individual and accomplished body of work which may be enjoyed by anyone of any age who is intrigued by representational art that plays with maths, science and paradox. Anno has a meticulous graphic style using pen, fine outlines and precisely applied water colour for his detailed compositions. He delights in optical illusion, for which he is sometimes compared with M.C. Escher. Whilst in each of his PICTUREBOOKS there is a total unity of graphic style as well as the invitation to the reader to respond creatively, there is a great variety in the body of work itself which includes pedagogic, 'wordless' and literary picturebooks.

Anno's Alphabet: An Adventure in Imagination appeared in 1974, showing paradoxical paintings in *trompe l'oeil* in which each letter of the alphabet purports to be carefully made in wood, but the super-real details are used to indicate an implausible construction. Art with a scientific approach continues in *Anno's Magical ABC: An Anamorphic Alphabet* (1981), produced in collaboration with his son Masaichiro Anno. In Anno's opinion, to be numerate is not to be able to count up to ten, but to have an understanding of such basic concepts as matching, comparisons, ordering, sorting and identifying. *Anno's Counting Book* (1977), *Anno's Counting House* (1982) and *Anno's Mysterious Multiplying Jar* (1982), another collaboration with Masaichiro Anno, help children to enjoy grasping the meaning of number. *Anno's Three Little Pigs* (1986) with Tuyosi Mori, which may be relished as a story about Socrates the wolf, his ever-hungry wife, and his friend Pythagoras the frog, is also an accessible demonstration of combinational analysis, mathematical permutations and combinations.

The best-known of Anno's 'wordless' picturebooks, which have their origins in the artist's travels, are four which record a lone traveller, journeying through recognisable landscapes with inhabitants who include characters historical or created – from popular and high culture. In *Anno's Journey* (1977) Beethoven sits at his window, Shylock is on the Rialto in *Anno's Italy* (1979) and Constable and WINNIE-THE-POOH appear in *Anno's Great Britain* (1982). In *Anno's USA* (1983) at the end of the book, the lone traveller completes his journey from West to East Coast, just as The Mayflower arrives three hundred years before he set off. Anno's most remarkable literary picturebook is *Anno's Aesop* (1990) in which he illustrates the FABLES, playing mischievously with at least 25 literary or graphic conventions, thus foxing a pre-literate Mr Fox who is 'reading' to his young son by interpreting the pictures. In 1984 Anno received the Hans Christian Andersen Illustrator Award. JD

annuals The earliest annuals were published in the 1820s, but the most notable favourite of the Victorian era first appeared in 1840. *PETER PARLEY'S ANNUAL* ran for 52 years, drawing originally on the varied works of the American writer SAMUEL GOODRICH (1793–1860). In the 1872 edition, 'Peter Parley' hoped his gift was 'not simply harmless, but beneficial; not simply entertaining, but useful'. Its longevity was exceeded only by that of *CHATTERBOX*, which ran for 90 volumes from 1867.

In the late 1800s and the early 20th century, almost all the major children's publishers packed their annuals with stories, features, rhymes, black-and-white ILLUSTRATIONS and colour plates. Frequently, the year's issues of a weekly or monthly publication were bound together within handsome covers; thus devotees of *Boy's Own Paper*, *Chums* or *The Captain* could re-read a favourite serial story (by writers such as TALBOT BAINES REED or P.G. WODEHOUSE) as complete adventures.

In the first half of the 20th century, the major player in the field in Britain was the Amalgamated Press (AP), founded in the 1890s by Alfred Harmsworth (later Lord Northcliffe, whose newspaper empire included *The Daily Mail*, *The Daily Mirror* and *The Times*). AP exploited a niche in the market for the youngest readers, and *Tiny Tots* (1899) was followed in 1909 by *Playbox Annual*, featuring the ubiquitous Tiger Tim who, with his pals the Bruin Boys, appeared in comics and annuals for well over half a century. For older readers, AP capitalised on the success of their weeklies, *Magnet* and *Gem*, with THE GREYFRIARS HOLIDAY ANNUAL (1920). Their other popular weekly, *The Champion*, appeared in annual format in 1924, with new adventures of such heroes as The Modern Methods Detective, Panther Grayle, and later the boxing flying ace, Rockfist Rogan. For girls, there were *The Schoolgirls' Own Annual* (1923) with stories of Morcove School, *The School Friend Annual* (1927) and *Girls' Crystal Annual* (1940). Films, radio and television have always been mirrored in comics, and AP's *Film Fun* and RADIO FUN duly appeared as annuals in 1938 and 1940. Comic strips about stars such as Laurel and Hardy and Tommy Handley ran alongside lengthier prose stories. *The Knockout Fun Book* (1941) employed a similar combination, with such contrasting heroes as Sexton Blake and Billy Bunter.

From the early 1920s, AP's greatest rivals as publishers of weekly story papers were D.C. Thomson & Co. of Dundee, Scotland. Their five weekly story papers (see 'THE BIG FIVE') spawned annuals, but their success was surpassed by that of annuals for younger readers derived from Thomson's BEANO (1940) and DANDY (1939), celebrating such timeless characters as Desperate Dan, Korky the Cat and Lord Snooty and his Pals. (Early editions of these two annuals, in good condition, have subsequently commanded prices approaching £1000.) In the post-war period, the most innovative comic was undoubtedly Hulton Press's EAGLE (1952), with its companions GIRL, SWIFT, and ROBIN, all of which appeared in annual format. Adventure stories with fine artwork (including the outstanding DAN DARE strip drawn by Frank Hampson) were balanced by attractively presented information items.

Titles have proliferated in the last 30 years. Many have been short-lived, reflecting the popularity of a band or a television series. By contrast, *Roy of the Rovers* still scored for Melchester Rovers after 40 seasons in his own annual; and the work of such artists as Leo Baxendale and Reg Parlett has kept *Buster* (1962) and *Whizzer and Chips* (1971) very much alive. *2000 AD* (1978) and *Judge Dredd* (1981), modelled on American SUPERHERO comics, have faithful older readerships. Several successful annuals featured characters serialised in newspapers, such as 'TEDDY TAIL of the *Daily Mail*' (1915), the *Daily Herald*'s BOBBY BEAR (1922) and the *Daily Mirror*'s PIP, SQUEAK AND WILFRED (1923). RUPERT BEAR has outlived them all, first appearing in the *Daily Express Annual* of 1930. Early *Rupert* annuals and some of the wartime editions are much prized by collectors. *Rupert, Dandy* and *Beano* prompt fond memories among parents and grandparents, and these three are still very likely to be among a child's Christmas presents at the beginning of the 21st century. GPF

'There, sitting up in a row, were my three children.' Illustration by Honor Appleton for *Blackie's Children's Annual* (1917).

see also ANIMATED CARTOONS; *BLACKIE'S CHILDREN'S ANNUAL*; COMICS; *JOY STREET*; PERIODICALS AND MAGAZINES

Anstey, E. see DRAMA FOR CHILDREN; E. NESBIT

anthropomorphism see ANIMALS IN FICTION; FANTASY

Appiah, Peggy see ANANCY

Applebee, A.N. see FAIRY TALES

Appleton, Honor Charlotte 1879–1951 British illustrator of over 150 children's books in the first half of the 20th century. Honor Appleton was born in Brighton in 1879. She lived there all her life apart from periods studying at the Royal Academy Schools and Frank Calderon's School of Animal Painting. Early commissions included a poster for the Sussex Women's Art Club in 1905, showing the influence of the Art Nouveau movement, and in 1911 she illustrated William Blake's *SONGS OF INNOCENCE*. Her most enduring work is the series of eleven *Josephine* books written by Mrs H.C. Cradock and published by Blackie from 1916 to 1940. In these Appleton develops a distinctive water-colour style which takes the reader into

Illustration by PAULINE BAYNES for *The Arabian Nights.*

the child's perception. The perspective of the painted scene is taken from just above floor level, allowing the skirting board to occupy a significant space in the composition. The delicate water-colours bring to life the toys in Josephine's adventures, to which Appleton was able to add movement and interaction – for example, in *The Fancy House* a girl steps into the picture she has drawn on the wall of her bedroom. An exhibition of her work travelled to galleries around the country from Hove Public Library in 1952. SM

Appleton, Jonathan see REVIEWING AND REVIEWERS

Apprentices, The (1976–8) First published as twelve separate volumes superbly illustrated either by FAITH JAQUES or ANTONY MAITLAND, these novellas by LEON GARFIELD later reappeared as one unillustrated volume in 1982. The dozen apprentices, be they lamp-lighter, undertaker or buckle-maker, live in 18th-century London and occasionally intrude upon each other's stories. All have to choose between moral right or wrong, but despite having to cope with an overriding sense of menace and squalor, they all come through as better, wiser people. The author's genius for atmosphere, language and vivid detail is evident on every page. NT

Arabian Nights' Entertainments, The Title by which the collection of tales in Arabic called *The Thousand and One Nights* is best known to the English-speaking world. The collection is initiated by a frame story in which the vizier's daughter, Sheherazade, escapes execution by King Shahriyar by telling stories that arouse his curiosity.

The stories recounted by Sheherazade are extremely diverse in kind and quality. They include lengthy heroic epics, devotional tales, chronicles of low life, FABLES, pornography, scatological jokes and cosmological FANTASY. Those which have gained most favour with young readers, however, have been ADVENTURE STORIES, often involving quests for fabulous treasure with strong magical dimensions. The most widely circulated of these are the stories of *Sinbad*, *Aladdin* and *Ali Baba*. The best tales are distinguished by the extraordinary inventiveness of the plots and by their ability to combine magical elements with a fine-grained realism. No doubt it was these qualities which made the stories so powerfully attractive to Romantic writers. Coleridge was both thrilled and terrorised by the *Nights* as a child; Horace Walpole even went so far in his enthusiasm as to proffer the advice: 'read *Sinbad* and you will be sick of *Aeneas*'.

The early history of the tales is obscure. The nucleus of the story collection appears to derive from a translation into Arabic of sections from a now lost Persian book of FAIRY TALES called the *Hazar Afsahah* (A Thousand Legends). The influence of the stories on the West began with a translation by the Frenchman Antoine Galland, whose *Mille et Une Nuits*, published in 12 volumes between 1704 and 1717, was enormously popular and served as the basis for further translations into several other European languages. In England 'Grub Street' versions were circulated by CHAPBOOK publishers from around 1708.

The first English collection specifically designed for children (heavily expurgated and moralised) was *The Oriental Moralist or Beauties of the Arabian Nights Entertainments* published by Elizabeth Newbery (c.1791). A series of more scholarly translations of the full text (most famously Sir Richard Burton's, 1885–8) were produced in the 19th century, but the *Nights* gradually ceased to be part of the common literary culture for adults. A few stories became popular in PANTOMIME, however, and excellent new editions for children continued to be published (including ANDREW LANG'S, 1898, and *Dalziels' Illustrated Arabian Nights' Entertainment*, 1863–5, with pictures by TENNIEL, Millais and others). Although the *Nights* formed the imaginative background to some important new series of tales for children (E. NESBIT'S *PSAMMEAD* stories, for instance, and R. L. STEVENSON'S reworking of the material in *New Arabian Nights*, 1882), there was an increasing tendency for a few tales to be extracted from the corpus and retold separately.

This tendency has continued in the 20th century with *Aladdin*, particularly, having some claim to being one of the most popular – and adaptable – children's stories of all time. Alongside its adoption within pantomime it has recently become a key text in Disney's film repertoire, and in 2000 the BBC transmitted a new television version employing special effects by the *JIM HENSON Creature Shop*. DWh

Arbuthnot, May Hill 1884–1969 American lecturer, teacher and author. Born in Iowa, Arbuthnot spent most of her life in Ohio. After her retirement as an associate professor at Western Reserve University, she became a full-time writer and lecturer. In her long and distinguished career, she brought children and books together, believing that a good children's book was one enjoyed by children, not just critics. Co-author of *Children and Books*, an influential textbook, and collections of poetry, short stories and biographies, Arbuthnot also wrote and reviewed books. She received many AWARDS, including Scott Foresman's named lectureship in her honour presented at the ALA's annual meeting. SPI

Ardizzone, Edward 1900–79 British artist and illustrator, and author of the *LITTLE TIM* series. Born in Haiphong in China, Ardizzone came to England when he was five. He was educated at Clayesmore school, and then worked for seven years as a clerk in London, for some of this period attending evening classes at the Westminster School of Art, where he was taught by Bernard Meminsky. He held his first exhibition in 1930, followed by a series of exhibitions at the Leger Gallery, and his work became more widely known through his illustrations for the *Radio Times*. He painted for the most part in water colour, and explored aspects of urban life, especially the Maida Vale district of London where he lived, with subjects such as the saloon-bars of various public houses, the canal, the street-life, and Paddington recreation ground.

One early commission was a set of line drawings for J. Sheridan Le Fanu's *In a Glass Darkly*, published in 1929, the year of Ardizzone's marriage to Catherine Anderson. In 1936, when his own children were five and six, he published his first children's book, *Little Tim and the Brave Sea Captain*, followed the next year by *Lucy Brown and Mr Grimes*. (This story caused consternation among American librarians, since it featured an old man talking to an unknown girl in a public park, and it was later rewritten and reillustrated, with Mr

Illustration from *Tim All Alone* by Edward Ardizzone (1956).

Grimes as a family friend.) Tim and Lucy were then brought together in *Tim and Lucy go to Sea* (1938). These three, though forming part of the longer series that was to come, are linked together through their special format, which imitated the sketchbooks in which they were created, with the author's handwriting lettered by Grace Hogarth.

In 1940, Ardizzone was appointed as a war artist on the recommendation of Sir Kenneth Clark. He served in France, North Africa, Sicily, Italy, Normandy and Germany, as well as recording life in England between 1940 and 1942. His extensive and moving collection of drawings and watercolours is in the Imperial War Museum in London, and he published vivid illustrated accounts of two phases of his experience, *Baggage to the Enemy* (1941) and *Diary of a War Artist* (1974).

After the war, Ardizzone's reputation steadily increased. In addition to regular exhibitions, his work was seen in *Punch*, the *Strand Magazine* and the *London Magazine*. He published a number of illustrated diaries, most notably his *Indian Diary* (1953). In addition to his own books, he became one of the best known and most prolific illustrators of his time, both of children's books and other literature, especially classics. Outstanding examples include *THE PILGRIM'S PROGRESS* (1947), *Barchester Towers* (1953) and *Travels with a Donkey*. Characteristically, Ardizzone visited the Cevennes to search out the atmosphere and locations which inspired STEVENSON.

In the field of children's books, Ardizzone proved as sympathetic and perceptive in collaboration with other authors as he was with his own writing. He demonstrated his skill and sensitivity as an illustrator of

Original artwork by Kerry Argent for *Wombat Divine* by MEM FOX.

poetry in a new edition of WALTER DE LA MARE'S *PEACOCK PIE* (1946). He then found a creative partnership with JAMES REEVES, and in 1952 they published *The Blackbird in the Lilac*, the first of ten books produced together. A second happy relationship was with ELEANOR FARJEON. The first of their six books was *THE LITTLE BOOKROOM* (1955), which won the 1955 Carnegie Medal, and the 1956 Hans Christian Andersen Medal. A third successful combination was with his cousin Christianna Brand (Mary Lewis) and the *NURSE MATILDA* books. Other highlights include PHILIPPA PEARCE'S *The Minnow on the Say* (1955), CLIVE KING'S *STIG OF THE DUMP* (1963), Freda P. Nichols's *The Milldale Riot* (1965) – a story about the lives of children in British factories during the Industrial Revolution – *The Second-best Children in the World* (1972) by the Irish writer Mary Lavin, and a reissue of GRAHAM GREENE'S *The Little Fire Engine* (1973); this last was one of four books by Greene, originally published in the 1940s with illustrations by Dorothy Craigie, which Ardizzone reillustrated.

After the war, Ardizzone resumed his success as an author/illustrator with a steady stream of books. *Tim to the Rescue* (1949) relaunched the *Little Tim* series. In between, he also produced other books, for example *Nicholas and the Fast Moving Diesel* (1947), *Titus in Trouble* (1959) – commended for the Kate Greenaway Award – *Johnny the Clockmaker* (1960), *Diana and her Rhinoceros* (1964) and *Johnny's Bad Day* (1969).

Brian Alderson, whose comprehensive 'preliminary hand list' of Ardizzone's illustrated books appeared in *The Private Library* (second series, 5.1, spring 1972), located his mastery of the art of illustration in his 'felicitous ability to capture the spirit and mood of a moment or a place in a vignette of deceptive simplicity'. Ardizzone manages to reflect, and often to extend and deepen, the mood of a poem or a scene without dominating or distracting from the original. He wrote himself that 'the illustrator draws to some extent like a child. He does not copy from life, but makes it up. He has a "think" and puts a line around his "think".' He defined the illustrator's job as being 'to stimulate the reader's imagination rather than to do all his imagining for him'. He also suggested that the best PICTUREBOOKS were created by artists who had written their own texts. Not being visually minded, a writer who is not an artist 'cannot leave out enough; he must elaborate; he cannot visualise how the picture will tell the story'. In Ardizzone's best work, the pictures blend effortlessly with words which convey the rhythms and tones of the speaking voice.

Ardizzone's style is both subtle and robust. Much of his painting contains a satiric edge, sometimes in the manner of Honoré Daumier, or, within the English tradition, of Thomas Rowlandson. His illustrations for children's books convey the richness and pleasure of everyday life, but with an acute eye for the small human dramas and quirks of behaviour which decorate it. At the same time, as his titles often indicate, he does not ignore the less harmonious elements which may threaten a child. As in the best comedies, his stories move towards reconciliation and reunion, and his pictures, taken as a whole, convey a sense of enjoyment and generous celebration. PR

Argent, Kerry 1960– Australian illustrator who uses soft rich pencil and water-colour to portray the movement, warmth and humour of animals and people. *One Woolly Wombat* (1982), a COUNTING BOOK in rhyming text, began Argent's illustrating career, and introduced the appealing wombat character which also features in MARGARET WILD'S *Thank You Santa*

(1991) and MEM FOX's *Wombat Divine* (1995), both of which have become perennial Australian Christmas titles. Thelma Catterwell's *Sebastian Lives in a Hat* (1985), about rearing a motherless wombat, and *A Bush Birthday* (1985), written by ELEANOR NILSSON, are just two of the many picture stories in which Argent depicts Australian bush animals. FK

Aris, Ernest see *LITTLE FOLKS*

Armitage, Ronda 1943– and **Armitage, David** 1943– A New Zealander and an Australian living in England, the Armitages have produced varied PICTUREBOOKS since the 1970s, the most popular being the *Lighthouse Keeper* series. Ronda's stories are of small problems revealing adult weaknesses. The continually inept, lovable and irascible Mr Grinling, first appearing in *The Light House Keeper's Lunch* (1977), is escorted through rescues and life by his tough, imaginative wife. Mrs Grinling, a subtly drawn complex character, is the chief source of the humanity emanating from the series. David's delicate, layered ILLUSTRATIONS, strongly structured with action freely depicted, flow outward and hint at life beyond. They complement rather than document the text. *Flora and the Strawberry Red Birthday Party* (1997) maintains the Armitages' trademark humour. *Queen of the Night* was published in 1999. The themes in the Armitages' books are often topical – such as Dad doing the washing – but they are always presented with sharp humour and complexity. MJH

Armstrong, Jennifer 1961– American editor and writer of children's and YOUNG ADULT FICTION. After graduating from Smith College in 1983, Armstrong began writing serials for the *Sweet Dreams* and *Private Eye* series under the pseudonym of Julia Winfield. While working on her most impressive novel, *Steal Away* (1992), she also published four books for middle-grade readers, the *Pets, Inc.* series. She defends her right to publish many kinds of books, recognising that series books are popular with young readers, and critics generally acknowledge that her series books are usually a cut above the norm. When she published *Steal Away* it was well received, earning her a Best Book Award, an ALA and Golden Kite Honor Award, a Society of Children's Book Writers and Illustrators Award, and a Notable Book Citation. *Steal Away* is a historical novel in which a young orphan befriends a slave girl and finds she must contend with the prejudice of her uncle as well as the anger of the slaves. Armstrong has also published a number of children's PICTUREBOOKS, including *Hugh Can Do* (1992), which won a Notable Book Citation, and *Chin Yu Min and the Ginger Cat* (1993). JGJ

Armstrong, William H(oward) 1914– American educator and author of books for children. Armstrong, winner of the 1970 Newbery Medal for SOUNDER (1969), was born in Virginia and taught high school history for over 30 years. His love of history helped shape his writing. *Sounder*, set in rural southern America at the turn of the century, met with some criticism: it was published during a time of civil unrest in the United States and its nameless characters were black. In fact, it was not until the publication of *Sour Land* (1971) that readers learned the name of the main character in *Sounder*. According to *Children's Books and Their Creators* (ed. Anita Silvey, 1995), Armstrong did not realise *Sounder* was a book for children until it was published. RSH

see also BIAS IN CHILDREN'S BOOKS

Arowolo, Femi see *WITHOUT A SILVER SPOON*

art paper An ultra-smooth paper required for colour printing. The smooth finish is achieved by a coating of china clay and heavy rolling, making the paper brittle and unsuitable for conventional binding. ILLUSTRATIONS on such paper therefore have to be TIPPED IN to a book. Together with the introduction of three- and four-colour processes, the use of art paper enabled coloured illustrations to be used more frequently in children's books, most spectacularly in the years before and after World War I in GIFT BOOKS such as DULAC'S *ARABIAN NIGHTS*, but also in less expensive story books and ANNUALS. GCB

Arthurian legend see KING ARTHUR

Artzybasheff, Boris (Mikhailovitch) 1899–1965 Russian-born author and illustrator. Artzybasheff became a seaman in 1919 after the Russian Revolution, worked briefly in an engraver's shop in New York, and within three months published some of his caricatures in *New York World*. Discouraged that this initial success failed to earn him a raise, he went back to sea for five months on an oil tanker, returning to New York speaking English. He established himself as an independent artist with an assortment of assignments, among them designing sets for Michel Fontine's ballets. In 1926, he became a US citizen and later won acclaim for a number of endeavours, notably 219 covers of *Time* (1941–65). During World War II he served as graphic consultant to the Department of State and supervised the production of an atlas used by the Army Training Command. He illustrated a number of children's books by other authors and wrote and illustrated *Poor Shaydullah* (1931) and *Seven Simeons: A Russian Tale* (1937), which won a *New York Herald Tribune* Spring Book Festival Award (1937) and was runner-up for the Caldecott Medal (1938). *Gay Neck*

Illustration from *THE BRASSMAN'S SECRET* by Meshack Asare.

written by DHAN GOPAL MUKERJI and illustrated by Artzybasheff won the Newberry Medal in 1928. KSB

see also PADRAIC COLUM

Arundel, Honor (Morfydd) 1919–73 Once popular British writer of novels for girls, though her work is now seldom seen on library bookshelves. Whilst her underlying themes are the eventual acceptance of adult responsibilities and values, the world of the child with all its subtle perceptions is still sensitively represented in her work. This individualist approach owes much more to the transatlantic tradition of writers for teenage girls in which the reader's interest is generated by the heroine's personal problems and perceptions, rather than the popular British formula of hockey-sticks and ponies.

The concerns with which Arundel's teenage heroines have to deal cover a wide range. There is, for instance, the realisation in *Emma in Love* (1970) that first love may not be life-long; in *The Longest Weekend* (1969) that a liaison with the father of one's illegitimate child, whilst no bed of roses, is in fact more satisfying than the stifling tyranny of an over-indulgent mother and grandmother; in *A Family Failing* (1972) that the break-up of one's parents' marriage is a tragedy to be endured; and ultimately, in *The Blanket Word* (1973), that the death of a parent with cancer is a trauma that must be confronted. Most of her books are written from an autobiographical standpoint and are instantly arresting. *The Girl in the Opposite Bed* (1970), a minor classic in which two girls from different backgrounds learn to live – and face death – in a hospital ward, has been sadly undervalued. CWB

Asare, Meshack 1945– Ghanaian writer and artist, and author/illustrator of award-winning books for children. His PICTUREBOOK *Tawia Goes to Sea* (1970), cited by UNESCO as the first successful picturebook from Africa, is about a boy's fascination with the boats in his small coastal fishing village. Never getting the chance to go with the men in their real boats because he is too small, he makes himself a FANTASY boat, complete with big, strong fishermen. In *THE BRASSMAN'S SECRET* (1981), an Ashanti boy is enticed with a pot of gold by a magical goldweight. The gold will be his to take if he can give the meaning of all the goldweight symbols along his way. He explains all but one – the symbol which says, 'Learn from the past'– so the pot of gold eludes him.

Asare's book *Chipo and the Bird on the Hill* (1984) reconstructs one day in the lives of two children in the acropolis Great Zimbabwe on the basis of archaeological data and the oral history of the people of Zimbabwe. Likewise, *Children of the Omumborombonga Tree* (1990) is a creation story about the common ancestry of the people of Namibia. *Cat in Search of a Friend* (1984), based on an Akan folktale, won both the BIB Golden Plaque and the Austrian National Book Prize in 1985.

Asare also writes about more contemporary issues – for example in *Halima* (1990), which is about the experiences of a teenage girl who is sent to learn a trade in the city. She runs away from the city to avoid being exploited, but finds herself in a Dogon town where, although her hostesses are very kind to her, this is only because she is being prepared to become the wife of a very important person, the priest.

Ascham, Roger 1515–68 English humanist, and tutor to Queen Elizabeth I. Ascham's most famous publication in English, *The Scholemaster* (1570), was a conduct book for young gentlemen and their teachers. He thought children should be taught 'cheerfully and plainly', warning against the excessive use of discipline and physical punishment. DWh

Ashabranner, Brent 1921– American writer of over 20 non-fiction titles for children that frequently highlight cross-cultural issues. Ashabranner began writing in high school and published stories while in college. After service in the Navy during World War II, he completed his education and taught English. In 1955 he began a 25-year career in foreign development, working for the US Government, the Peace Corps and the Ford Foundation in Africa and Southeast Asia. Though Ashabranner collaborated on several books for children, he did not write full-time until he returned to the United States in 1980. Since then he has written 17 books, two with his daughter Melissa (1950–). Ashabranner credits his extensive work abroad as well as his youth in a mixed culture of Anglos, Native Americans and Arab-Americans for his interest in cross-cultural experiences. *To Live in Two Worlds: American Indian Youth Today* (1984) and *The New Americans: Changing Patterns in US Immigration* (1983) highlight the difficulties individuals face as they move between cultures. His sensitivity to human experience is also evident in his treatment of other topics such as migrant workers (*Dark Harvest: Migrant Farmworkers in America*, 1985), the Vietnam War Memorial (*Always to Remember: The Story of the Vietnam Veterans Memorial*, 1988), and the US Census (*Counting America: The Story of the United States Census*, 1989). EBD

see also: INFORMATION BOOKS.

Ashencoatie see ENGLISH FOLKTALES

Ashford, Daisy [Margaret Mary Julia] 1881–1972 Britain's best-known juvenile novelist, Ashford spent an affluent childhood in Lewes, Sussex. At the age of four she dictated her first story, and thereafter she wrote fiction for her own pleasure. In 1919 she rediscovered a story written when she was nine bearing the misspelled title *The Young Visiters*. Published the same year with an introduction by J.M. BARRIE, its unconscious humour, double meanings and artless innocence turned it into a bestseller that was never subsequently out of print. Other manuscripts written when she was a child were later published as *Love and Marriage* (1965) and *The Hangman's Daughter* (1982). NT

see also CHILD AUTHORS

Ashley, Bernard 1935– Writer of contemporary stories with a working-class setting. Ashley was born and educated in London. As the head teacher of a South London Primary School, his first-hand experience of the difficulties facing some of his pupils encouraged him to write a series of hard-hitting novels. These described typical urban problems such as juvenile delinquency in *Terry on the Fence* (1977), bullying in *All My Men* (1978), disintegrating family life in *A KIND OF WILD JUSTICE* (1978) and the disruption caused by war in *Johnnie's Blitz* (1996). Always well plotted, many of Ashley's books were successfully adapted for children's TELEVISION. *The Little Soldier* (1999) was shortlisted for the CARNEGIE MEDAL NT

see also WAR STORIES

Ashling see *THE OBERNEWTYN CHRONICLES*

Asian American children's literature The term 'Asian American' refers to American authors and illustrators from a plethora of cultural backgrounds, including, among many others, Hawaiian, Japanese, Chinese, Korean, Hmong, Vietnamese, Indonesian, Thai and Indian. Within this field there is also a diversity of genres, including, for example, Cynthia Chin-Lee and Yumi Heo's ALPHABET BOOK *A is for Asia* (1997), Kara Dalkey's FANTASY novel *Little Sister* (1996), Ed Young's FOLK TALE *Lon Po Po* (1989), the PICTUREBOOKS of ALLEN SAY, the HISTORICAL FICTION of LAURENCE YEP, LENSEY NAMIOKA and YUSHIKO UCHIDA, and contemporary novels by the latter authors as well as Mitali Perkins' *The Sunita Experiment* (1993). There are also anthologies of fiction, drama and poetry – such as *American Dragons* (1993) – and compelling non-fiction books such as Huynh Quang Nhoung's memoir *The Land I Lost* (1982), illustrated by Vo-Dinh Mai and Ken Mochizuki, and Dom Lee's *Passage to Freedom: The Sugihara Story* (1997).

Illustrators such as SHEILA HAMANAKA (*A Visit to Amy-Claire*, 1992), along with Mai, Young, Say, Lee and Heo, among others, strive to provide accurate visual portrayals of the Asian American experience, and many Asian American novelists have addressed neglected or misrepresented historical situations. For example, Yep relates the almost unheard-of story of a Chinese-American aviator who replicated the work of the Wright brothers in *Dragon Wings* (1975). In *The Journey Home*, Uchida presents a Japanese family who were interned in the US containment camps where Japanese Americans were held during World War II. In the humorous tale *The Year of the Boar and Jackie Robinson*

(1984), BETTE BAO LORD dramatises her experience of immigrating to the US in 1947 and learning what it means to be both Chinese and American.

Many books tell stories about Asian homelands. Several Korean American authors have thoughtfully examined the effects of war on the country of their birth, as do SOOK NYUL CHOI in *The Year of Impossible Goodbyes* (1991) and Helen Lee in *The Long Season of Rain* (1996). In *Shisuko's Daughter* (1993), Kyoko Mori tells the traumatic story of her own teenage years in Japan. Although these books present a portion of history that many children are unfamiliar with, they also tell human stories with universal themes. And an equal number of authors and books explore the contemporary experiences of Asian Americans, such as Lensey Namioka's novel about the Yang family, *Yang the Third and Her Impossible Family* (1995), Marie G. Lee's *Finding My Voice* (1992) and Allen Say's picturebook *Stranger in the Mirror* (1995).

Bi-culturalism, cultural discrimination and family traditions are common issues that are dealt with in Asian American literature, but in general the field is concerned with all aspects of childhood – from the trials and tribulations of inter-cultural dating in Kevin Kyung's story 'Autumn Rose' (in *A Gathering of Flowers*, 1990) to the exploration of relationships with grandparents in Visalya Hirunpidok's 'Yai' (*American Dragons*, 1993). ARTL

Asimov, Isaac [George E. Dale, Dr. A, Paul French] 1920–92 American biochemist turned author, Asimov was born in Petrovichi, USSR. He was brought to the US in 1923 and became a citizen in 1928. As a writer Asimov had an exceptional ability to explain complex scientific ideas in terms understood by children and in a manner entertaining to both children and adults. A prolific author of both fiction and INFORMATION BOOKS, his works number over 350 with about half still in print, an achievement in itself. He is best known for his adult SCIENCE FICTION, especially the award-winning *Foundation* series. In addition to science fact and science fiction he has written mysteries, short stories, history, poems, limericks, and guides to the Bible, SHAKESPEARE and CLASSICAL MYTHOLOGY.

Asimov began writing as a child, with his first published piece appearing in a high school literary publication. By the time he was 18 he had had his first science fiction story accepted by the pulp magazines popular in the 30s and 40s. He attended Columbia University, enrolled in the pre-med programme and continued to appease his need to write through short stories. In his second year of medical school he decided to pursue a degree in chemistry and went on to receive his PhD from Columbia in 1948. He took a teaching position at Boston University School of Medicine, continuing to write science fiction for children and adults.

He is credited with helping to establish and define the genre of science fiction. Through his stories the three laws of robots evolved and have since been followed by other science fiction writers. These laws are also held in high regard within the scientific community as necessary in theory. His first science fiction novel for adults, *Pebble in the Sky,* was published in 1950. A science fiction series for children, the *Lucky Star* series (1953–8), appeared under the pseudonym Paul French. Though many of the science elements in the series were later proven inaccurate, the series was reissued in the 70s, under Asimov's own name, with a foreword explaining the scientific inconsistencies.

During the early 1950s Asimov collaborated on a textbook for medical students with two colleagues at Boston University. He was delighted to be writing non-fiction, regarding it as another form of teaching, and went on to write books for the general public on various science topics. He eventually branched into writing articles for professional and general audience science magazines, columns for science fiction magazines, and information books on science subjects for children.

In 1958, Asimov was forced to decide between writing and teaching. At the level of associate professor, he left to pursue writing, but in 1979, owing to his prominence, he was promoted to the status of full professor, though this was an honour in title only. Boston University's archives house Asimov's writings, notes and manuscripts. LAW

***Asmir* series** Three books by Australian author CHRISTOBEL MATTINGLEY based on the plight of a Bosnian boy and his family caught up in civil war. The first, *No Gun for Asmir* (1993), tells of the escape from Bosnia to Vienna of seven-year-old Asmir, his mother and younger brother; *Asmir in Vienna* (1995) describes their life in that city, and *Escape from Sarajevo* (1996) is the story of Asmir's father, who had been left behind in Sarajevo, and his reunion with his family in Austria. Asmir's family is known personally to Mattingley, and she has written their story compassionately and movingly, but without sensationalising it. This emphasis on a single family is in part responsible for the success of the books in developing awareness of the fate and powerlessness of children who are victims of war. Young readers empathise with Asmir – his fear, his courage, his distress at being parted from his father, and his difficulties in a new country. The ease with which readers, even from entirely different backgrounds, can identify with Asmir is enhanced by the photographs of the family and the maps of their journey which are included in each volume. MLH

Asterix (from 1959) French satirical COMIC book adventure series, joint creation of writer René

Goscinny (1926–77) and artist Albert Uderzo (1927–). Set in 50 BC, it pits anarchic and warm-hearted Ancient Gauls against the flat-footed might of occupying Rome. *Asterix* fever gripped France in the 1960s, conferring respectability to 'bandes dessinées' and fuelling an industry (films, theme park). Wittily translated into English by Anthea Bell and Derek Hockridge, there are 31 titles to date, translated into 70 languages.

Diminutive Asterix and his friends enjoy a simple life in their village, the last to hold out against Julius Caesar's legions. Their irreverent confidence is a major irritant to the Empire. A magic potion concocted by the druid, 'Getafix', ensures superhuman strength. Like the other delightfully dim-witted and petty-minded characters (scheming centurions, nervous conscripts), the invincible Gauls are themselves naive and flawed ('Unhygenix' the irritable fishmonger, the self-absorbed bard 'Cacofonix'). Only Asterix and the elderly druid remain alert, good-natured observers of absurdities all around.

Asterix works at many levels. Immediately accessible is the knockabout comedy. Illustrations teem with incidental detail, long-running gags (like the progressive wisening up of a nerdy new legionary), old jokes (Chief 'Vitalstatistix's' chronic failure to control his shield-bearers). Effortlessly bashing Roman soldiers is a way of life, the mayhem intricately captured in 'before' and 'after' panels. Accurate and informative about the ancient world, the books are packed with visual and verbal jokes: 'ancient' names ('Nefarius Purpus', 'Crismus Bonus'), puns and anachronisms. There are sophisticated cultural allusions in text and pictures (Alexandrians speak in 12-syllable alexandrines). The praised English translators seek equivalents rather than literal renderings, and capture the spirit of the original, some wordplay actually enhancing the original (British Chieftain 'Zebigbos' becomes 'Mykingdomforanhos').

Packing contemporary references into the ancient setting, *Asterix* celebrates wit, freedom and a relaxed hedonism, debunking regimentation and mindlessness. The medieval satirical animal epic *Le Roman de Renart*, and Laurel and Hardy, were inspirations for this figure of the little man who triumphs against the odds. Translated for struggling regions like the Baltic, *Asterix* also had positive resonances for French people wanting to resist American cultural domination alongside President De Gaulle. However the satire is double-edged, vigorously mocking the self-important French and their own earnestly revered institutions. The heroes' ubiquitous refrain, 'these foreigners are crazy!', reveals their own blinkers. The entertaining anachronisms (chauvinistic tourists, advertising breaks during the circus) have bite: Ancient Rome shows up our own absurd modern 'civilisation', with its conformities, inefficiencies and sterility, equally cracking at the seams.

The humour is gentle and affectionate; it 'hurts, degrades, humiliates no-one' (Kessler). Nervous Romans are victims of their own system, most want a quiet life. Stereotypes (goose-stepping Goths, unflappable Brits) are a send-up of stereotyping itself. The 'violence' is equally benign: knocked-out legionaries wear blissful liberated smiles, the thumping giant 'Obelix' is an incurable softy. The central characters are bachelors, however, and women remain background caricatures: powerful but stroppy housewives or shapely girls. CMP

At Ardilla (1991) Coming-of-age novel by Australian writer GILLIAN RUBINSTEIN – an eerie portrait of a girl's struggle, conscious and subconscious, between childhood and adulthood, FANTASY and reality. 'Tense and difficult' 12-year-old Jen is deeply troubled when a new family disturbs her annual summer holiday at the seaside house 'Ardilla'. When her sister and friends abandon their usual 'club' and its protective rituals in favour of the newcomers, Jen's fears for the safety of Ardilla unbalance her mind and judgement. Tragedy is narrowly avoided and Jen is 'cleansed of imagining and superstition', whilst gaining satisfying insight into the adult she may become. NLR

At the Back of the North Wind see GEORGE MACDONALD; see also FANTASY; ARTHUR HUGHES; ILLUSTRATION IN CHILDREN'S BOOKS; LAUREN MILLS; PUBLISHING AND PUBLISHERS

Atkinson, M(ary) E(velyn) see CAMPING AND TRAMPING FICTION; see also NEGLECTED WORKS

atlases see INFORMATION BOOKS

Atterton, Julian 1956– British author of six historical novels for children set between the sixth and fourteenth centuries. These do not settle on what might be called the 'establishment' narratives of British history, but attempt to reconstruct the shape of things and events in ancient Northumbria and Rheged. Three of these novels follow the fortunes of the de Falaise family over two centuries, the family chronicle being the vehicle through which the larger events are traced and set in perspective. He has also reworked two of the *ROBIN HOOD* legends for younger readers. SA

Attwell, Mabel Lucie 1879–1964 British illustrator. With a career starting in her twenties and lasting, in the case of her popular ANNUALS, until her death, Mabel Lucie Attwell's distinctive, rubbery babies and wispy fairies dominated books, greetings cards, children's clothes, toys and artefacts for several decades.

Indeed, her cute children appear to have influenced many adults' views of children and childhood. Her early covers and colour plates, for such classics as *Mother Goose Rhymes* (1909), *ALICE'S ADVENTURES IN WONDERLAND* (1910) and HANS CHRISTIAN ANDERSEN'S *Fairy Tales* (1913), were respected for their sensitive line and pleasing composition, but her output grew to lack variety and care in content and approach even though it assured her instant recognition and a steady income. JAG

Atwater, Florence 1896–1979 and **Atwater, Richard** 1892–1948 American authors noted primarily for the creation of *Mr. Popper's Penguins* (1938). Richard Atwater began his writing career as a journalist and newspaper reporter, producing columns for two Chicago newspapers and a collection of verse, *Rickety Times of Riq* (1925). The publication of his first children's book, *Doris and the Trolls* (1931), encouraged Richard to write *Mr. Popper's Penguins*, inspired in part by Admiral Byrd's expedition to the Antarctic. In 1934, after completing the book, Richard suffered a debilitating stroke, leaving the job of marketing the manuscript to his wife, Florence, who had worked as a high school teacher and had also published articles in national magazines. After two rejections, Florence rewrote the book, making it less whimsical and somewhat more realistic by adding a new beginning and ending. *Mr. Popper's Penguins* has been praised for its matter-of-fact style and charming absurdity, earning the Atwaters a variety of awards including a Newbery Honour, Lewis Carroll Shelf Award, and a Young Reader's Choice Award from the Pacific Northwest Library Association. The book continues to be popular with contemporary young readers who enjoy ROBERT LAWSON'S humorous illustrations and the chaos created when twelve penguins come into the life of a house painter. JDC

Atwood, Margaret see *UP IN THE TREE*; see also JOYCE BARKHOUSE; CHILD AUTHORS

audio-tapes see STORYTAPES

Aulnoy, Marie-Catherine le Jumel de Barnville de la Motte, Comtesse d' c. 1650–1705 French writer of over 20 stories in the fashionable court style and the first to introduce FAIRY STORIES to the female salons. Her tales were aimed at an adult audience but subsequently several have become popular with children, although more so in France than in England. Her stories include 'The Blue Bird', 'The White Cat' and 'The Yellow Dwarf'. Her work first appeared in English in 1699 and Francis Newbery published a selection entitled *Mother Bunch's Fairy Tales* in 1773. JHD

Aunt Effie see JANE EUPHEMIA BROWNE

Aunt Judy's Magazine Popular British sixpenny monthly children's magazine, founded by Margaret Gatty in 1866 to counter sensationalist literature, and catering to the broad age range of the Victorian family. Its major contributor was Mrs Gatty's daughter, JULIANA HORATIA EWING, most of whose published work made its first appearance in the magazine. Promising parents that they need fear no 'overflowing of mere amusement', it nevertheless maintained a balance between instruction and entertainment. Although it attracted writers and illustrators of note, including HANS CHRISTIAN ANDERSEN, LEWIS CARROLL and RANDOLPH CALDECOTT, cost and content restricted its commercial success, and the magazine closed in 1885, soon after Mrs Ewing's death. BW

see also COMICS, PERIODICALS AND MAGAZINES

Austen, Jane see LITERATURE IN CHILDREN'S LITERATURE; see also *MARLOW* SERIES; ADULT FICTION

***Austin Family* series** Domestic fiction by MADELEINE L'ENGLE, including *Meet the Austins* (1960), *The Moon by Night* (1963), *The Young Unicorns* (1968), *The Anti-Muffins* (1980), *A Ring of Endless Light* (1980), *The Twenty-Four Days Before Christmas* (1984), and *Troubling a Star* (1994). The Austins are to some extent autobiographical: events in the early novels, such as the family's temporary adoption of the daughter of a family friend, are loosely based on the L'Engle family's real-life experiences. Although all of the family members are well-developed characters, the eldest daughter, Vicky, is the primary protagonist, and the books focus on her anxieties about adolescence. In *A Ring of Endless Light*, a Newbery Honour Book, Vicky's beloved grandfather is dying; as she struggles with feelings of loss and doubts about her faith, she encounters three very different young men whose values help her clarify her beliefs. The books reflect more global concerns as well: *The Moon by Night* depicts anxiety about nuclear war, *The Young Unicorns* comments on youth gangs and urban crime, and *Troubling a Star* focuses on third-world espionage and environmentalism. Donald R. Hettinga includes a chapter on the Austin books in *Presenting Madeleine L'Engle* (1993). AKP

Australian Book Review see REVIEWING AND REVIEWERS

Australian Christmas Story Book, The (1871) Short stories by Cyrus Mason, the grandson of Robert and Elizabeth Browning, and one of the first Australian children's books to include coloured ILLUS-

TRATIONS. It was an attempt to establish the practice of reading aloud in Australia and to provide suitable material. MSax

autobiography see BIOGRAPHY AND AUTOBIOGRAPHY

Avenger, The see SUPERHEROES

Averill, Esther see *CAT CLUB* SERIES; see also ANIMALS IN FICTION

Avery, Gillian 1926– British novelist, editor and historian of children's books. Avery lives and works in Oxford and Victorian Oxford provides a setting for many of her most popular children's novels, including *THE WARDEN'S NIECE* (1957). *James Without Thomas* (1959) and *The Elephant War* (1960) make use of the same setting and reintroduce characters familiar to readers of the earlier novel. Though neither has been as successful as *The Warden's Niece*, each retains the familiar sense of humour and adventure. Avery builds a complex world around her characters, both within each individual book and in the links between novels. The Victorian setting is recreated by attention to detail; uncomfortable clothing, cold and dreary rooms and monotonous routines oppress the heroes and heroines, but their concerns are familiar to contemporary readers. Avery is particularly good at describing characters who know their own limitations, whether social or educational, and strive to overcome them. In *The Greatest Gresham* (1962) the two older Gresham children are acutely conscious of a need to win their father's approval. They hope to do so by achieving greatness, but are at a loss as to how to do this successfully. The youngest child, like many of Avery's younger-sibling characters, is irritatingly and irrepressibly self-confident, while the next-door family, with their desirable – if unsuitable – scruffiness and independence, provides a vehicle for humour as well as social commentary.

Social snobbery is mocked in *A Likely Lad* (1971), winner of the Guardian Award in 1972. The relations who are obsessed with class and money are shown to be dishonest and unpleasant, while education rather than breeding is seen as the key to success. The hero, Willy, is typically diffident and unsure of himself, but determined to fight for what he believes to be right. Willy's father, like many of the fathers in Avery's novels, appears strict and frightening, and is preoccupied with his place in the community. The book gained additional popularity when it was televised by the BBC.

The comic side of life features strongly in Avery's novels. She has an eye for the quirky and the satirical and creates child characters who are skilful at seeing through adult pretences. Mr Copplestone, the maverick tutor from *The Warden's Niece*, reappears in *To Tame A Sister* (1961), gawky and quixotic as ever, but determined to master his penny-farthing bicycle. Although providing humour himself, he also draws attention to the ridiculous pretensions of the other adults ('Your excellent cousin expects me to help organise her abominable croquet meeting . . . She confidently expects the weather to be fine – the Fulkes have never known disappointment she says').

Avery was chair of the Children's Books History Society and has written extensively about the history of children's books and other aspects of childhood. *Behold The Child* (1994) provides a detailed history of American children's books, while other work has included a history of independent girls' schools and a study of the Victorians in life and literature. She has also edited, with Julia Briggs, *Children And Their Books* (1989) a collection of essays celebrating the life and work of the OPIES. KA

Avi [Wortis] 1937– American librarian, storyteller, teacher and writer of children's books, YOUNG ADULT FICTION and plays. Born in New York City, Avi – his given name (pronounced ah-vee) – overcame dysgraphia, failure and the harsh criticism of many teachers in order to pursue his ambition of becoming a writer. His family environment of writers, artists and political activists stimulated his own interest in words and helped him to overcome his handicap and the criticism which hounded him throughout his early school career. Although Avi is best known for his young adult fiction, he began as a playwright, achieving an award and magazine publication for one of the plays he wrote in college. While working as a librarian and writing a novel, Avi began telling stories to his children. He published his first children's book, *Things That Sometimes Happen*, in 1970 and began to write books with his sons in mind, slowly advancing as their reading level did. With his first young adult novel, *No More Magic* (1975), which won a Mystery Writers of America Special Award, Avi found his creative niche. Since then he has become one of the most widely read and respected authors of novels for young adults.

Avi is perhaps most noted for a changing and developing style which keeps his writing fresh and exciting. While much of his early work was primarily HISTORICAL FICTION – *Captain Grey* (1977), *Night Journeys* (1979), *Encounter at Easton* (1980) and *The Fighting Ground* (1984), which won the Scott O'Dell Award for Historical Fiction – he has also written mysteries, adventures, supernatural tales, coming-of-age books, fantasies and humorous novels. His background as a playwright has helped him develop an ability to tell an intense and dramatic story. However, he is not content to write in familiar patterns allowing his writing to become formulaic or stale, and he constantly examines new and different ways of storytelling. *The True Confessions of Charlotte Doyle* (1990), winner of several awards including a Newbery Honor Medal and Golden Kite Award, is told from the viewpoint of a young girl through her journal, while *Nothing But The Truth* (1991) – also a Newbery Honour Book – does not have a single point of view but is told through diaries, letters and newspaper clippings. *City of Light, City of Dark* (1993) is one of his most recent contributions to young adult literature. In this futuristic FANTASY, Avi is able to recreate contemporary concerns and traditional fantasy elements in what is truly a 'novel' (new) form, the comic-book novel (see GRAPHIC NOVEL). While the book contains customary quest motifs and conflicts between light and dark, its mutlicultural characterisation, multilingual dialogue, and comic-book art work (by Brian Floca) make it a collage of words and images, something which has become commonplace in contemporary culture. In examining Avi's work, particularly the two Newbery books and his comic-book novel, it is clear that the postmodernist's concern with the ability of language to 'mean' informs Avi's current work and makes readers responsible for discovering meaning for themselves. JGJ

awards and medals The oldest award for children's literature in the English-speaking world is the Newbery Medal, first awarded in 1922 to the author of the most distinguished book published for children in the United States by an American citizen or resident. The award was established by Frederic G. Melcher, American bookseller and publisher, and has since been given annually by the Association for Library Services to Children, a divison of the American Library Association. Named after the publisher of *A LITTLE PRETTY POCKET* Book, the first award was presented to HENRIK VAN LOON for *The Story of Mankind*. The Newbery Medal was introduced because of the lack of quality in children's literature of its time, as was the first British children's book award, also administered by librarians: the CARNEGIE MEDAL has a long and distinguished history and its recipients include ELEANOR FARJEON, C.S. LEWIS, PHILIPPA PEARCE, PETER DICKINSON and ANNE FINE. Its first recipient, in 1937, was ARTHUR RANSOME for *Pigeon Post* (the author grumbled that 'it would have been better to send the blessed thing by post'). Both of these awards, and the Australian equivalent, the Children's Book Council of Australia Book of the Year Award, remain premier awards in the children's book world. In New Zealand the Esther Glen Award is the most distinguished, a frequent winner having been MARGARET MAHY. The major international prize is the Hans Christian Andersen Award, first presented in 1956 by the International Board on Books for Young People (IBBY). The main award for children's poetry in the UK is the *Signal* Poetry award, established in 1979.

However, such is the nature of international publishing that few have access to the work of many award-winners, though there is some compensation in the form of awards for books published in translation, such as the Mildred L. Batchelder award in America – presented annually since 1966 by the American Library Association to encourage American publishers to seek out superior children's books abroad – and the more recent Marsh award in Britain. In South Africa, most literary awards were for many years awarded for books in Afrikaans, such as the Scheepers prize and the Tienie Holloway medal. The Percy FitzPatrick Award (named after the author of *Jack of the Bushveld*) is a gold medal awarded every second year by the South African Institute for Librarianship and Information Science, for the best children's book written in English by a South African author.

Because of their long standing, many of these awards have often been regarded as recognising staid and respectable works rather than experimental and exciting material. Other awards were introduced to counteract this, such as the *Guardian Award*, first established in 1966, although just over ten years later, its instigator, JOHN ROWE TOWNSEND, at that time the *Guardian*'s literary editor, admitted that 'there has been rather more overlap between the *Guardian* and the Carnegie than I expected'. There has also been a proliferation of awards designed to highlight areas of publishing which have been neglected in the past. Examples include the Coretta Scott King Award, inaugurated in 1969 to honour the life of Dr Martin Luther King and his wife Coretta Scott King; the award, first presented in 1970, is given annually to an author for promoting an understanding and appreciation of different cultures. The Orbis Pictus Award – named in commemoration of *ORBIS SENSUALIUM PICTUS*, published by Johannes Comenius in 1657 and considered to be the first children's information book – was established in the United States in 1990 by the National Council of Teachers of English to promote and recognise excellence in non-fiction writing. The Aesop Prize was established in 1994 by the children's folklore section of the American Folklore Society to acknowledge outstanding children's books incorporating folklore. In Australia the Multicultural Children's Literature Award had only five suitable titles in its first year, 1990, but only three years later this had grown to 49. The Te Kura Pounamu Award was established in 1995 and is New Zealand's first book award for literature in Maori. The remit of the United Kingdom's Other Award, first introduced in 1975 and discontinued just over ten years later, was wider: it was designed to highlight those books which portray positive images of minorities – although its main criterion was that winning books (in true egalitarian style, there was no single outright winner) should be 'accessible, in form and content, to children and young people' and 'give pleasure and enjoyment'. Similar awards include Australia's Children's Peace Literature Award and America's A Book Can Develop Empathy Award.

In Ireland, the CBI/BISTO Book Awards are made annually by CHILDREN'S BOOKS IRELAND for books by an author or illustrator born or resident in Ireland. One award is made for the 'Bisto Book of the Year' and one in the 'First Children's Book' category – the Eilis Dillon Memorial Award. Merit Awards are made to three other titles. Both fiction and non-fiction works are eligible, and they are judged by a panel of independent judges. The Reading Association of Ireland Children's Book Award and Special Merit Award are both biennial awards made for works of fiction or non-fiction for books published in Ireland. The independent judging panel is composed of teachers and librarians. The Special Merit Award is presented for a book which the judges consider has made a significant contribution to a particular aspect of publishing for children in Ireland.

The Tom Fitzgibbon Award is administered by the NEW ZEALAND CHILDREN'S BOOK FOUNDATION and sponsored by Scholastic New Zealand Ltd. It is awarded annually to a best first manuscript by a previously unpublished writer of a work of fiction for children aged from 7 to 13. The Award recognises the outstanding contribution made by the late Tom Fitzgibbon to children's literature in New Zealand. Past winners include *Summer of Shadows* (1997) by Iona McNaughton, *Dark Horses* (1997) by Heather Cato, *2MUCH4U* (1999) by Vince Ford, and *The Stolen* (2000) by Shirley Corlett. The Gaelyn Gordon Award for a Much-Loved Book – also given by the New Zealand Children's Book Foundation – commemorates the life and work of writer GAELYN GORDON and honours a book by a New Zealand author that has proved itself a long-standing favourite with New Zealand children. ELSIE LOCKE'S *The Runaway Settlers* (1965) won the inaugural award in 1998, while the 1999 winnner was *Grandpa's Slippers* (1989), written by Joy Watson and illustrated by Wendy Hodder.

Although awards presented for fiction have often provoked controversy, there appears to be less dispute when awards are given for ILLUSTRATION. Even when there is media attention such as that given to GREGORY ROGERS'S Kate Greenaway Medal winner, *WAY HOME* (1994), it is more often the subject matter of the book which causes concern. However, judges of awards for both creative writing and illustration believe that the illustration award is more difficult because it depends more on immediate personal preference. In America the Randolph Caldecott Medal was first awarded in 1938 and the British Kate Greenaway Medal followed in 1955, both named after Victorian children's book illustrators and both selected by librarians. The Caldecott was presented to MAURICE SENDAK'S *WHERE THE WILD THINGS ARE* and to illustrators as diverse as CHRIS VAN ALLSBURG, ARNOLD LOBEL and EZRA JACK KEATS. The award was established by Frederic Melcher, and has since been given annually by the Association for Library Services to Children. It was designed to encourage excellence in pictorial presentation.The Kate Greenaway Medal was first given to EDWARD ARDIZZONE, and other winners have included SHIRLEY HUGHES, QUENTIN BLAKE, ANTHONY BROWNE, JANET AHLBERG and MICHAEL FOREMAN. Invariably the awards are presented for PICTUREBOOKS rather than any other form of illustration, and as the judges are librarians there is often some feeling that the award shortlist is composed of picturebooks that work in storytelling sessions rather than of works with the highest-quality illustration. However, there are some awards in which artists themselves become involved as judges, such as the Mother Goose Award presented to new illustrators. Other awards involve children's book critics, such as the Kurt Maschler Award–established by Kurt Maschler in memory of Erich Kästner and Walter Trier, author and illustrator respectively of *EMIL AND THE DETECTIVES* and given for the combination of text and illustration. This award has been presented for, among others, JOHN BURNINGHAM'S *GRANPA*, the AHLBERGS' *JOLLY POSTMAN* and two Anthony Browne titles, *GORILLA* and his illustrations for *ALICE'S ADVENTURES IN WONDERLAND*.

An increasing trend has been to introduce awards in which the majority of judges (if not the total number) has been children. The paradox of adults producing and selecting what children are supposed to want to read is one which has long been discussed; the concern is that they tend to present prizes to worthy books which their target audience finds unreadable. 'Children's choice awards' are an attempt to go some way to resolving that problem, at least as far as awards are concerned. There are many awards of this kind in America, where JUDY BLUME is often a winner (whereas she has only received one award chosen by adults), and in Australia, where the Western Australia Young Readers' Book Award has been presented since 1980, most frequently to ROALD DAHL (who has rarely had an award from adult judges). In Britain the most established children's choice award is that presented by the Federation of Children's Book Groups, an organisation composed mainly of parents who are interested in children's books; and in New Zealand a children's choice award was initiated in 1997.

The fact that the selectors of the longest established awards in America and Britain are practitioners, i.e. librarians, has led some critics to doubt their ability to select quality material. However, these awards are invariably the most democratic of children's book prizes as they are recommended by those working daily with children and titles have to go through a rigorous process before reaching a shortlist. Other awards are judged principally by other authors and rely on publishers to submit selected titles.

One of the major problems for children's literature is to attract attention in the media. This has been compensated in recent years by more awards being sponsored, with more money to put into publicity. The Whitbread Award is an early example of this, while Britain's financially most generous children's book award, the Smarties Prize, is sponsored by the sweets manufacturer – much to the disgust of JANET and ALLAN AHLBERG who made it known they did not want to win the award for that reason. The Smarties, incidentally, seems to have achieved the best of both worlds as far as selection goes – the shortlist is compiled by adults and children choose the winners from this list.

If writers and illustrators do not win awards for their books in a particular year, they can still hope for an award which goes to their work in general, such as America's Laura Ingalls Wilder Award – established in 1954 by the Association for Library Services to Children, a division of the American Library Association, and given every three (originally five) years to an author or illustrator whose body of work has made a substantial and lasting contribution to children's literature; or Australia's Dromkeen Medal – named after the Dromkeen homestead, where Joyce and Courtney Oldmeadow established the Dromkeen Collection of Australian Children's Literature in 1974, – awarded annually to an Australian citizen who has made a significant contribution to the appreciation and development of children's literature. They could also be considered for Britain's Eleanor Farjeon Award, which is presented to personalities in the children's book world. And if they miss out on these awards, they might still be eligible for America's Phoenix Award which is presented to a book published 20 years earlier and which was not recognised at the time. KB, VC, JKB

see also the appendix

Awdry, Christopher see *THOMAS THE TANK ENGINE* SERIES

Awdry, Revd W(ilbert) (Vere) see *THOMAS THE TANK ENGINE* SERIES

Ayckbourn, Alan 1939– British dramatist whose plays for adults have enjoyed international critical and popular success. Unlike most 'commercial' dramatists, Ayckbourn has shown repeated interest in writing and producing original works for children. They usually receive their premiere at the Stephen Joseph Theatre in the Round at Scarborough, England, where Ayckbourn is Artistic Director. He described his Christmas show for children, *Xmas v Mastermind* (1962) as 'the most disastrous play I've ever done', and has suppressed it, but nevertheless went on to write *Mr A's Amazing Maze Plays* (1989), an ingenious comedy thriller in which the youthful audience directs much of the action, and most recently, *The Champion of Paribanou* (1996), a typically challenging piece which uses classic plot devices from the *ARABIAN NIGHTS* but embellishes them with allusions to *STAR WARS* and the *Faust* legend. *Invisible Friends* (1991) is designed for older children, but characteristically blends comedy with undertones of menace and an unemphatic but uncompromising moral base. This CAUTIONARY TALE points children to the perils of wish fulfilment, and parents to the risks of inattentiveness, but it does so through constant dramatic surprise and technical wizardry. Ayckbourn says of children's theatre that 'you've got to keep the action going', and he uses elaborate technical resources and spectacular effects to introduce young audiences to the sheer fun of live theatre. PH

B

'Baa Baa Black Sheep' see MUSIC AND STORY; see also RUDYARD KIPLING

***Baba Yaga* stories** see FOLKTALES AND LEGENDS; see also BLAIR LENT; MARIANNA MAYER

***Babar* series** (1932–93) Picturebooks about the eponymous elephant character, the first seven of which were written and illustrated by Jean de Brunhoff between 1931 and his death in 1937 and made a major contribution to the development of the picturebook as a serious genre. The giant format, bold colours, detailed double-page spreads, the handwritten text, the humour and seriousness in both the text and the pictures of de Brunhoff books were original and innovative. In each book a serious moral tone is balanced by humour and echoed in the illustrations which are distinguished by their confident draughtsmanship and attention to detail. His son Laurent has continued the series but with less acclaim. *The Story of Babar* (1934) was the first of a series of adventures in which the eponymous hero becomes king of the elephants and, dressed in his vivid green suit and jaunty gold crown, rules wisely and firmly; he is urbane, dignified, and French. The first English version, *The Story of Babar the Little Elephant* was published in 1934, the most recent, *The Rescue of Babar*, in 1993. Long since reduced from the scale of the original texts, the series is available in standard paperback format. The early classic illustrations are often better known as greetings cards. Six of the early stories were retold by ENID BLYTON in a cheap hardback edition published in 1941, with illustrations redrawn in black-and-white by Olive F. Openshaw. This popular version ran into several editions. EAG

Babbitt, Natalie (Zane Moore) 1932– American author-illustrator noted as a gifted storyteller whose FANTASY novels appeal to all ages. She has received several AWARDS, including the 1976 Christopher Award, a Newbery Honour for *Kneeknock Rise* (1970) and numerous honour citations and ALA Notable Book citations. Her best-known novel is *Tuck Everlasting* (1975), which was later made into a family film. In 1977 it earned the US Honour Book citation and the Congress of the International Board on Books for Young People citation. Babbitt's stories include entertaining narratives with strong characters struggling to gain love and acceptance, and to learn to make independent decisions and overcome fears.

Babbitt was born in 1932 in Dayton, Ohio. After high school Babbitt enrolled in a fashion ILLUSTRATION course before attending Smith College to pursue an art degree. While there, she met and married her husband, Samuel Fisher Babbitt, an aspiring writer who later became vice-president of Brown University. Raising a family kept Babbitt busy until 1966 when, after illustrating *The Forty-Ninth Magician*, written by her husband, she was encouraged to continue illustrating books and to try writing stories of her own. She wrote two PICTUREBOOKS, *Dick Foote and the Shark* (1967) and *Phoebe's Revolt* (1968), both told in rhyming verse.

Her remaining books are for older readers. Though criticised for using humour and references to SHAKESPEARE beyond the grasp of young readers, Babbitt says in *Contemporary Authors* that she believes children are 'far more perceptive and wise than American books give them credit for being'. Her novels combine an entertaining story on the surface with something deeper. In *The Devil's Storybook* (1974), for example, a TRICKSTER continues to be fooled by those he tries to fool. After giving a goat a voice, the Devil is annoyed by the animal's continuous complaining. Despite its humorous and light-hearted parody, the book imparts a subtle lesson about meddling.

Tuck Everlasting is a masterpiece. It tells the story of the Tuck family who happen upon a spring of immortality and the miseries this 'blessing' entails for them. When their secret is discovered by ten-year-old Winnie, they must convince her of the importance of death in the cycle of living things. In the end, however, it is Winnie who must choose between mortality and immortality. A weighty subject, and Babbitt handles it skilfully, not overwhelming the reader, nor compromising the tale. Underlying threads include acceptance of death, breaking from familial controls, and expanding one's horizons. LAW

Babe: The Gallant Pig see THE SHEEP-PIG

Babes in the Wood see CHILDREN THE WOOD

Baby Books Three PICTUREBOOKS for very young children by WALTER CRANE. Building on his considerable artistic experience and reputation, Crane created two innovative song books, supported by the craft of EDMUND EVANS, an outstanding printer who had pioneered high-quality colour printing. Together they produced *The Baby's Opera* (1877) and *The Baby's Bouquet* (1879). Both are books of old rhymes with musical settings, some occupying one half of the double spread with Crane's ILLUSTRATIONS on the other, and others framed within pictorial decorations and marginal designs. Each opening is carefully composed: one of the 'Three Blind Mice' on a lefthand page, for example, is to be seen running up the grandfather clock of 'Dickory Dock' on the right. The tunes were arranged by Crane's sister Lucy.

The commercial success of these picturebooks was to a large extent due to the process devised by Evans for reproducing colour illustrations with extraordinary brilliancy and faithfulness to the original artwork. The two *Baby Books* were so popular that a third was created, *The Baby's Own Aesop* (1887). The rhyming text was written by W. J. Linton, the engraver to whom Crane had been apprenticed. Crane paid particular attention to the front covers, with colour prints mounted on board and the details of the design reflecting the content; the cover of *The Baby's Opera*, for example, shows an opera stage on which 'Hey Diddle Diddle' is being performed in front of a Chinese willowpattern backcloth, with a cat playing the fiddle on one side of the footlights and a little dog laughing and clapping on the other. The three *Baby Books* exemplify Crane's conviction that the design of a book for children was a matter of supreme importance and that every detail should contribute to the book's aesthetic integrity. In 1889 the three were combined for reprinting as triplets. AR

Baby literacy projects see BOOKSTART

***Baby* series** Eight books for parents and very young children, written and illustrated by JAN ORMEROD: *Dad's Back, Messy Baby, Reading, Sleeping* (1985), *Bend and Stretch, Making Friends, Mum's Home* and *This Little Nose* (1987). The books are based on close and accurate observation of unremarkable events in the domestic lives of a baby and its mother or father. They are designed for parents to read with their own children, so the actions of each are equally interesting and recognisable. The events are unobtrusively and carefully structured to lead the readers through to an emotionally satisfying conclusion. In *Reading*, for example, the father sits imperturbably undisturbed in the same position in each frame while his baby clambers around him and finishes, in the last frame, sitting in his lap, also reading the book. The ILLUSTRATIONS are in simple watercolour and line; there are few props, no intrusive settings. Each spread is conceived as a whole and as two separate squares. The individual volumes are out of print but they were collected in one volume, *Mum and Dad and Me* (1996), which loses the exquisite sense of space and structure of the originals. RC

***Baby-Sitters Club* series** A popular series written by Ann M. Martin featuring the realistic adventures of eight girls who run a cooperative babysitting service in Stoneybrook, Connecticut. With more than 100 books in the series, it began with *Kristy's Great Idea* (1986) where Kristy Thomas, Claudia Kishi, Mary Anne Spier and Stacey McGill form a babysitting service as an aid to their community and as a way to make money. The group meets regularly to receive assignments and record notes of their jobs in the Club Notebook, which functions as a group diary and is a major feature of the books. The original group is enlarged when Dawn Schaefer arrives from California and later when Abby Stevenson joins the group. The club also adds two junior members: Jessi Ramsey and Mallory Pike. Martin provides a range of personalities in her characters: Kristy is a talkative, sometimes bossy leader, Claudia, who is Asian-American, is artistic, Stacey comes from a divorced family and is discovered to have diabetes, Mary Anne is quiet and shy and wears glasses. The Baby-Sitters Club has been made into a TELEVISION series and a film, *The Baby-Sitters Club* (1995). JCS

Back In The Jug Agane see RONALD SEARLE; GEOFFREY WILLANS; see also SCHOOL STORIES

Bacon, Ron(ald) Leonard 1924– New Zealand storyteller and writer for children, who began his writing career with an adult novel in 1964. Much of Bacon's writing has been the retelling of traditional stories, especially the myths and legends of the MAORI people. He has a strong belief in the power of myths and legends to develop mutual respect in multicultural societies. His meticulously researched books interpret traditional Maori life for a modern urban population. *Again, the Bugle Blows* (1972), an historical novel, tells a gripping story of the courage of the Maori in a little-known battle. When published, it marked a key point in the development of children's literature, validating New Zealand history, traditional stories and the life of New Zealand children as central themes. However Bacon is best known for his PICTUREBOOKS, which feature well-researched and sensitively retold stories of traditional Maori life. *The House of the People* (1977) and *The Fish of our Fathers* (1984), both illustrated by Robert Jahnke, are two picturebooks which have received awards. He has worked with a range of illustrators including CHRIS GASKIN and Para Machitt. Among his best known and loved titles are *The Legend of Kiwi* (1987), *The Clay Boy* (1990), *The Banjo Man* (1990), *The Kite* (1991), and his books featuring Hemi, an appealing and lively Maori boy. Bacon has also written many titles for educational series. LL

Bad Child's Book of Beasts, The (1896) First collection of parodic verse by HILAIRE BELLOC, illustrated by B.T.B. (Basil Blackwood), which sold so well he immediately produced a sequel, *More Beasts (for Worse Children)*, in 1897. The short, ingeniously rhymed poems mock the 'improving' moral verse that was predominant earlier in the century, promising, 'if rightly understood', to make the child reader 'unnaturally good'. 'The Elephant' ('such a *little* tail behind/ so *LARGE* a trunk before') and 'The Frog' are frequently anthologised examples. The animal poems are more accessible to young readers than the later, more sophisticated *Cautionary Tales* (1907). ML

Baden-Powell, Agnes see GUIDING AND SCOUTING FICTION

Baden-Powell, Robert Stephenson Smyth see CAMPING AND TRAMPING FICTION; GUIDING AND SCOUTING FICTION; KING ARTHUR

Badger on the Barge (1984) A set of five long short stories by JANNI HOWKER. Though the author was only 27 when this collection appeared, she was already an accomplished craftswoman; the stories are subtle, sensitive and carefully framed, and show a writerly gift for the sounding and memorable phrase. Each of them is about the relationship between a young and an old person, and in each there is a second relationship, or web of relationships, interwoven with the main one: thus, in *The Egg-man*, a crazy old man's loving delusion that he is giving a new dress to his long-dead wife is echoed and transfigured in the loving and fragile birthday present that Jane helps her dad make for her mum. In *The Topiary Garden*, Liz meets the old woman Sally Beck who could only make a life for herself by pretending to be a boy. Liz, in the macho context of the motor-bike trials which are the only way in which her father and older brother will let the summer holiday be spent, is in a comparable situation, and has to assert her identity as a girl. 'We're a long-living breed, us women', says Sally Beck. 'Gives us a chance to see the world change, lass.' Most touching and atmospheric of these stories is *Jakey*, about the old boatman whose death is closing in on him and is seen by young Steven as 'a great grey shape, like a shark, swimming behind, slowly, secretly'. JRT

Badger's Parting Gifts (1984) Picturebook by the British illustrator SUSAN VARLEY. This gentle book tells the twin stories of Badger's dying and how his friends come to terms with his absence from them. Death is presented as a positive for the very old: a laying aside of pain and a restoration of youth. Meanwhile, Badger's friends pass through the succeeding seasons of grief as the year turns from Badger's dying in the autumn. By summer they have realised that, since they still have the skills that Badger taught them, they can still feel his presence in their lives. The rather bare narrative is fleshed out by the ILLUSTRATIONS which bring warmth, wit and life to the story. AMN

Badudu stories see ABORIGINAL CULTURE IN CHILDREN'S BOOKS

Bagnold, Enid see ADULT FICTION; ANIMALS IN FICTION; PONY STORIES

Bagthorpe Saga Ongoing series of stories by HELEN CRESSWELL which chronicle the domestic disasters of the eccentric Bagthorpe family whose manifest intelligence is not complemented by practical talents. The prosaic child Jack of the introductory book *Ordinary Jack* (1977) fails to emulate the scholarly brilliance of his three siblings or the self-promotion of his extraordinary parents. *Absolute Zero* (1978), which followed to similar critical acclaim, exemplifies how the combination of slapstick incidents, whimsical humour and a witty narrative, rich in literary allusion, appeals to both child and adult readers. *Bagthorpes Besieged* (1996) forms the ninth part of the saga. CMN

Bagpuss see OLIVER POSTGATE AND PETER FIRMIN

Bailey, Carolyn Sherwin 1875–1961 American editor and author of fiction, plays, poetry and non-fiction for children. Titles such as *Tops and Whistles: True Stories of Early American Toys and Children* (1937) and *Lincoln Time Stories* (1924) are representative of the love of early American history, folk customs and crafts that runs through Bailey's enormous output. Only a few of her books are still in print, most notably *Miss Hickory*, which won the Newbery award in 1946. Miss Hickory is a doll made from an applewood twig and a hickory nut who finds herself abandoned by a child owner and left to survive the countryside winter out of doors. Both literally and figuratively hard-headed, Miss Hickory exhibits considerable ingenuity and courage as she finds clothes, shelter and worthwhile pastimes to sustain herself. A comical mood pervades the story until the disconcerting conclusion in which a squirrel bites off her head. The headless twig then grafts itself onto an apple tree, causing it to burst into blossom and thus creating an inanimate but sensuous afterlife for itself. The story's ending has been variously interpreted as an

Illustration by Di Wu for *Old Magic* by Allan Baillie.

anti-feminist symbolic rape and as a miraculous rebirth. RUTH STILES GANNETT's black-and-white ILLUSTRATIONS are graceful and vigorous. As a book, *Miss Hickory* continues to flourish among young readers by virtue of its appealing toy heroine and lively plot. CV

Baillie, Allan (Stuart) 1943– Much-travelled Australian journalist of Scottish birth, author of novels, stories and PICTUREBOOKS exploring history, culture and identity. *Adrift* (1983), his first published novel, is an ADVENTURE STORY in which a boy, his sister and her cat are accidentally cast adrift on a packing crate. *Little Brother* (1985) moves offshore and, through the flight of ten-year-old Vithy from the Khmer Rouge, brings home to Australian readers the horrors of war and the plight of refugees on their doorstep. Baillie's research is clearly evident in *Riverman* (1986), a novel of the mining and logging communities of Tasmania's rugged West Coast, in which 12-year-old Tim journeys up the Gordon River to the giant Huon pines, on a trip of self-discovery, after his father's death in a mine disaster. While *Eagle Island* (1987) and *Hero* (1990) are ADVENTURE STORIES, *Megan's Star* (1988) and *Magician* (1992) are SCIENCE FICTION or FANTASY tales. The excitement of the Tiananmen Square democracy movement is the backdrop for *THE CHINA COIN* (1991). Baillie moves the setting to Arnhem Land in northern Australia, before the European invasion, for the mature and historically rich *Songman* (1994). *Secrets of Walden Rising* (1996) presents a cavalcade of Australian history in a haunting story of the almost surreal, drought-induced emergence of an old mining town from an artificial lake. English boy Brendan, transplanted to rural Australia like the young Allan Baillie himself, is the outsider, the seeker after understanding, knowledge and acceptance. Baillie's picturebooks include *Bawshou Rescues the Sun* (1991), a Han folktale; *The Boss* (1992), which explores a contemporary Chinese childhood, and *Rebel!* (1993) set in Burma, and illustrated by Di Wu, which exposes arrogant authoritarianism. *Drac and the Gremlin* (1988), in collaboration with illustrator JANE TANNER, places a science fiction print text in counterpoint with a lush visual text, depicting two children playing in their backyard. It won the 1989 Children's Book Council of Australia Picture Book of the Year Award. Baillie's well-researched works are highly popular, presenting readers with strong storylines and complex realistic characters in a web of rich historical and cultural ideas. SNJ

Baker, Augusta 1911–98 American Children's librarian, editor, author, and storyteller. Born in Baltimore and educated at the State University of New York at

Albany, Baker began her library career in the New York Public Library in 1937, where she served for 37 years. She initiated a special collection of black children's books and edited a bibliography, *The Black Experience in Children's Books* (1971). Well known as a storyteller and lecturer, she is co-author of *Storytelling, Art and Technique* (1977). Her many honours include the American Library Association's Grolier Award in 1968 for outstanding achievement in guiding and stimulating children's reading. AL

Baker, Eric see REVIEWING AND REVIEWERS

Baker, Jeannie 1950– Artist, PICTUREBOOK maker, animated-film director, tutor and lecturer, born in England and later living in Australia. Since 1972 she has worked on her collage constructions, many of which are designed to illustrate picturebooks but stand individually as works of art. They have been exhibited in galleries in London, New York and throughout Australia and are part of many private and public art collections. Since 1977 she has made many highly acclaimed picturebooks, using her own texts and collages. The collage constructions, tactile, intriguing and impressive, are made of mostly natural and authentic materials, selected to support the subject matter, treated, painted, made in sections, then assembled to give the illusion of solidity and depth. Questions about human responsibility for our actions are implicit in Baker's work, as can be seen for example in *Home in the Sky* (1984), a story set in New York about a boy unselfishly relinquishing a pigeon which he has rescued and taking consolation in the bird's flight. Baker expands the theme of responsible action to include the way we personally affect the environment in *WHERE THE FOREST MEETS THE SEA* (1988) and in *Windows* (1991), both of which are concerned with the extinction of plant and animal life as human beings encroach on the wilderness; and in *THE STORY OF ROSY DOCK* (1995), which addresses subtly in microcosm the bigger issues of the devastation of native habitats by the introduction of a non-native species. JD

Baldwin, James 1924–87 African-American novelist and essayist born in Harlem. Baldwin used his considerable verbal skills to preach the gospel during his adolescent years. However, his attention quickly switched from religious to racial issues, and he became an impassioned critic of black inequality. In works like *Go Tell It On the Mountain* (1953), *Notes of a Native Son* (1955), *Nobody Knows My Name* (1961) and *The Fire Next Time* (1963), Baldwin uncompromisingly and often poetically examined questions of identity and race. He moved to Europe in 1948 and spent most of the remainder of his life in Paris. Widely read in Europe, his works have become part of the American literary canon, read by adolescents as well as adults. MJKP

Illustration by Jeannie Baker from *The Story of Rosy Dock.*

ballads Forms of poetry, originally oral, recited, or more often sung, on social occasions within communities where literate culture was marginal. In these settings they represented a kind of popular or folk art, the themes of early ballads often reflecting the harsh living conditions of the people for whom they were composed. Traditions of ballad composition and performance of this kind still exist in northern Greece, parts of the central Balkans and Sicily. In Britain many of the finest ballads came from the border regions between Scotland and England and between the Scottish Highlands and Lowlands.

Since they derive from oral culture, ballads tend to have a form which is easily memorable; many have musical versions, so ballads are often sung. The most common ballad stanza is a quatrain, rhyming abcb, in which the lines ending a and c contain three strongly stressed syllables and the rhymed lines have four stresses. Other forms, including rhyming couplets, are also possible. Many ballads contain refrains, which slow down and intensify the action being narrated, use of repetition making the poems more hauntingly memorable.

Ballads invariably tell a story, often romantic and dramatic, generally focusing on a single episode and often narrated in a spare, impersonal style, but sometimes full of emotion, such as when the mother begs her son to tell her what ails him in *Lord Randal*. Although the subject matter of traditional ballads tends to be tragic, some are composed in a lighter, comic vein, such as the warring old couple who lose all their possessions out of obstinacy in *Get Up and Bar the Door*, or the farmer who finally has to admit that his wife can do more work in one day than he can do in seven! There has also been a strong tradition linking ballads to protest against different forms of injustice.

Given these qualities – memorable poetry, links to oral culture, musicality and strong dramatic focus – it is not surprising that ballads should have long appealed to children. Indeed, a number of the most popular children's stories – including those associated with ROBIN HOOD – appeared from an early date in ballad form. Some of the border ballads share that spirit of adventure and daring (and plenty of blood) which are also popular with the young. When in the 18th century traditional ballads began to be collected and written down, they served as a model for more literary forms of imitation.

This mixture of the literary and the oral has been the basis for the continued vitality of the ballad form within children's culture over the past 200 years. Examples of earlier 'literary' ballads which have been regularly anthologised for children include Coleridge's *THE RIME OF THE ANCIENT MARINER*, KEATS's *La Belle Dame sans Merci*, TENNYSON's *THE LADY OF SHALOTT*, Alfred Noyes's *THE HIGHWAYMAN* and Oscar Wilde's *The Ballad of Reading Gaol*. The greatest balladeer for children (and adults) of the 20th century was CHARLES CAUSLEY, whose collections for the young contain more ballads – often about the sea or Cornish folklore – than any other form. DW, MCCS

Ballantyne, R(obert) M(ichael) 1825–94 Born in Scotland, Ballantyne made his reputation writing and lecturing about his experiences in Canada, where he lived for a time when employed by the Hudson's Bay Company. He made his first venture into juvenile publishing, an abridged version of a book about North America, while working for the family printing firm in Edinburgh. On the basis of its success he wrote his first novel, set in Canada and containing considerable detail about hunting and the lives and practices of the native populations. Originally titled *Snowflakes and Sunbeams; or, The Young Fur Traders* (1856) it survives as *The Young Fur-Traders*. Although there is a love interest in the text, it primarily chronicles its protagonists' adventures in the wilds of North America. Young men in isolated settings became Ballantyne's stock-in-trade for the novels which followed, the best of which is *The Coral Island* (1858). This text shows clearly Ballantyne's preoccupations with action and the religious justification of empire.

The Coral Island tells two stories: it begins with three youths, Jack, Peterkin and Ralph (the narrator), being shipwrecked off the coast of an idyllic South Sea island. The first half of the book is concerned with their efforts to make themselves safe and comfortable on the island. Survival is not the issue; the island is benign, and the only serious threats the boys encounter come from outside – sharks and pirates. Their friendship and respect for the territory they settle make rescue superfluous; the second half of the book, therefore, consists of a barrage of problems including cannibals and pirates. Ralph is abducted by the pirates, and in their company witnesses both the hideous lack of concern for human life which Ballantyne offers as characteristic of natives, and the transformations brought about by missionaries – who also facilitate trade. Whatever the problems and dangers encountered by the three protagonists, they remain true Englishmen, never faltering in their determination to do right. Except for gaining some practical knowledge, they are unchanged by their adventures, and the reader is left in no doubt as to their reception and future happiness when they arrive in 'dear old England'.

Despite its loose and episodic construction – little effort is made to unite the two halves of the book – it is vividly told. Frequently criticised today for its depiction of the South Sea islanders as barbarians held in check only by the strenuous efforts of British missionaries, *The Coral Island* spawned many island ADVENTURE STORIES, notably *TREASURE ISLAND* and *THE LORD OF THE FLIES*. It typifies the Victorian boys' adventure novel in its unwavering belief in the superiority of the British boy, and its determination to teach history, duty, manliness and benevolent responsibility.

After *The Coral Island* Ballantyne's reputation as a writer for boys was established. He contributed to periodicals and wrote a number of books, few of which are now remembered; his illustrated books, including a version of *Pilgrim's Progress* told through the characters of three little kittens, are similarly forgotten. KR

see also ROBINSONNADES

Ballet Shoes (1937) BALLET STORY by NOEL STREATFEILD which traces the fortunes of three sisters, Pauline, Petrova and Posy. 'Found' and adopted by Great Uncle Matthew, they choose their own surname: Fossil, vowing to make it great and 'put it into the history books', this suggesting the theme of self-making that runs through the book. Because of money problems, the children are sent to Madame Fidolia's academy to acquire a training in ballet and drama in order to earn a living; this aspect of the book has led to its being thought of as a 'career novel'. The novel's emphasis, however, is less on the idea of training for an occupation than on self-discovery. This is linked to the understanding and accommodation of what might be called 'otherness', or other realities. Much of this is learned through the literature and drama which inform the book richly: by reading, the heroines live out alternative lives, knowing what it means to be hungry, frightened, homesick, etc. However, just as *Ballet Shoes* values 'otherness' it also values uniqueness of self, for each of the Fossil sisters is encouraged to preserve and develop that which marks them as individuals, namely their separate loves of drama, dance and mechanics. SA

ballet stories Stories of or about ballet, falling into three categories: fictional, often featuring a ballet school, a performance, classes and tutors; stories about real ballet stars such as Margot Fonteyn, which have been adapted for a young readership; and compilations of tales of the ballet retold for children, such as *Swan Lake* (e.g. by CATHERINE STORR, 1987, and by ADÈLE GERAS, illustrated by EMMA CHICHESTER CLARK, 2000), *The Nutcracker* (e.g. by Geras and Clark, 1999) and *Coppelia*.

Of the fictional stories, the best-known and best-loved is *BALLET SHOES* (1936) by NOEL STREATFEILD, featuring the adopted Fossil family and full of backstage rivalry, auditions and 'The Show', all of which have become essential ingredients for a good ballet story. Extended series of stories involving the ballet have been written by Lorna Hill in the *SADLER'S WELLS* and *Dancing Peel* sequences in the 1950s; there were also the *DRINA* and *Ballet Family* series by Mabel Esther Allan (Jean Estoril). Some writers – Lorna Hill, for example – took the opportunity provided by an extended series to develop characters from young ballet students in their teens to adulthood and feature their children following in their footsteps. More recently, boys have been appearing in ballet stories, as in Jean Ure's *A Proper Little Nooreyeff* (1982). The actress Susan Hampshire has tried her hand at the ballet story with *Lucy Jane at the Ballet* (1985). Often seen as the lesser sister of the pony story, the ballet story is coming to terms with the 1990s, for example in the excellent compilation *Ballet Stories* (1997).

Serialised in many girls' comics, ballet stories have always been regarded as standard girls' fiction, often with a thriller aspect involved. For example, the sixth *GIRL* annual includes the comic-strip tale 'Belle of the Ballet tells the story of the famous Rag-Bag Ballet'. The *SCHOOL FRIEND* annual for 1962 features a picture story, 'The Masked Ballerina', with Madame Élisse as the ballet mistress, and Jean Lester as the ballet pupil. Madame has a French accent, which always adds to the sense of romance and the exotic found in this genre.The story contains Russian spies, a country house and the kidnap of a world-famous ballerina. All these ingredients emphasise the excitement and danger girls have come to expect in this type of story. Gladys Malvern's *The Dancing Star* is a fictionalised account of the life of Anna Pavlova, making it more accessible for the younger readership than a biography. Ruth Tilden's *Sophie's Ballet Class* (1996), a 'Pull-the-Tab' Book, is aimed at the younger child, who can pull tabs to illustrate the ballet movements such as pirouette and plié. Mal Lewis Jones's ballet school series, with such titles as *On Tour with the Ballet School* (1995), are the latest ones written, proving that the genre shows no signs of disappearing from the streetwise child's reading. SET

see also ANNUALS; RUMER GODDEN; MUSIC AND STORY

Bambi Novel by Felix Salten (1923; trans. 1928) and animated feature film by WALT DISNEY (1942). *Bambi* tells the story of a young fawn, Bambi, as he lives through his childhood and enters adulthood in an unspecified woodland setting. The novel follows a calendrical structure. Along the way, Bambi experiences many of the pleasures and dangers of nature, learning to be alert for the greatest of all dangers, man (or 'He', as he is referred to in the novel). Salten also wrote a sequel, *Bambi's Children: The Story of a Forest Family*.

The Disney film has probably replaced the novel for most children. It was the first film in which Disney told a story entirely populated by animals. The plot is consolidated for dramatic reasons, focusing more tightly on Bambi's growth from childhood to adulthood, with less attention to other animals, though he does have two friends, Thumper, a rabbit, and Flower, a skunk, as well as his sweetheart, Feline, carried over from the novel. The scenes of infancy and childhood are charming. The death of Bambi's mother is handled with subtlety and taste, and the scene has remained etched in the minds of generations of children, as a traumatic dramatisation of parent-child separation. The last part of the film, when Bambi and his friends go through puberty and experience first love, are a little too coy, and the anthropmorphising of the animals becomes less plausible. BH

Bancroft, Bronwyn 1958– Acclaimed Aboriginal Australian artist of the Bandjalung people, who has illustrated not only PICTUREBOOKS and novels, but also murals, posters, logo designs and garments. Bancroft's artworks are represented in Australian and international collections. Books include *The Fat and Juicy Place* (1991), written by DIANA KIDD; the new edition of OODGEROO NOONUCCAL's *Stradbroke Dreamtime* (1993); and three collections by Roland Robinson and other contributors: *Dirrangun* (1994), *Minah* (1995) and *The Whalers* (1996). Her work is informed by her passionate commitment to extending the reader's knowledge of Aboriginal beliefs and history. She has collaborated with the Aboriginal writer SALLY MORGAN to produce *Dan's Grandpa* (1996), *In Your Dreams* (1997) and *Just a Little Brown Dog* (1997), and illustrated *Big Rain Coming* (1999) by Katrina Germein. Bancroft's artwork conveys a powerful sense of spirituality. Her ILLUSTRATIONS glow with the strong use of colour, black outlines, and her distinctive interpretation of traditional Aboriginal designs and patterns. RS

see also ABORIGINAL CULTURE IN CHILDREN'S BOOKS

Bang, Molly (Garrett) 1943– American author and illustrator, sometimes writing as Garrett Bang. She has lived and worked in Japan and Bangladesh. From 1973 she has published many translations of FOLK TALES from around the world, some by her mother, Betsy Bang, and a number of original stories, and she has received several Caldecott and American Library Association AWARDS. Her own stories capture the charm and simplicity of the folk tales which provided her early inspiration, and her work is distinctive for its MULTICULTURAL content, arising naturally from the internationalism of her sources. She is endlessly inventive and her illustration has never become predictable. She deploys a variety of painterly techniques, COLLAGE, paper cut-outs and reliefs, but her illustrations all reflect the influence of oriental art in their abandonment of traditional western perspective. *Wiley and the Hairy Man* (1976) was adapted from an old American tale. *Ten, Nine, Eight* (1983) used a simple bedtime rhyme invented by a black father settling his baby daughter to sleep; the sumptuously dense flat fields of colour offer a child's eye view of her nursery with lovingly observed details. *The Paper Crane* (1985) conveys a simple moral message within a magical narrative; an oriental stranger welcomed by an impecunious café-proprietor fashions an origami bird which comes to life and restores the fortunes of the host. *Red Dragonfly on My Shoulder* (1992) is a collection of Japanese HAIKU; *From Sea to Shining Sea* (1993) presents a selection of American folklore and folk-song; and *Chattanooga Sludge* (1996) deals with environmental issues. PC

Banks, Lynne Reid 1929– English writer of books for children, young adults, and adults, best known for her series *The Indian in the Cupboard* (1981–93), an important contribution to the literature of miniatures and toys come to life. Young Omri has the power to enliven his plastic toys, and through his adventures with Little Bear learns responsibility. The books were the basis of a 1995 film directed by Frank Oz. Banks has also written a series of books for teens, including two Jewish novels (*Secrets and Affairs*; *One More River*) which make use of her extensive knowledge of Israel and Israeli society, obtained during several years of teaching in kibbutzim. MDK

see also YOUNG ADULT FICTION

Bannerman [née Watson], Helen (Brodie Cowan) see *LITTLE BLACK SAMBO*; see also BIAS IN CHILDREN'S BOOKS; ILLUSTRATION IN CHILDREN'S BOOKS; JULIUS LESTER

***Bannermere* series** see GEOFFREY TREASE; see also SCHOOL STORIES

Barbauld, Anna Laetitia 1743–1825 Prolific English poet and writer, noted for her pioneering series of first readers, *Lessons for Children* (1777–9) and her popular *HYMNS IN PROSE FOR CHILDREN* (1781). The daughter of dissenters and educated at home, her first published *Poems* (1774) established her early literary and intellectual reputation. Setting up a boys' school after her marriage in 1774, she began writing for children, believing in quality production, with content drawn from everyday life. She moved to London and continued to write, contributing to her brother, John Aikin's, series for young readers, *Evenings at Home* (1792–6). Her children's writing – informed by her mistrust of imaginative flights of fancy and her belief that children should see the hand of God in all things – was criticised by CHARLES LAMB for being dull and didactic: 'Damn them! – I mean the cursed Barbauld Crew, those blights and blasts of all that is Human in man and child.' BW

Barber, Antonia see NICOLA BAYLEY; ERROL LE CAIN; P.J. LYNCH; MUSIC AND STORY

Barbour, Ralph Henry 1870–1944 American writer of sports stories for young readers. His works were outwardly didactic, expressing his belief in the nobility of sportsmanship and its ability to transform boys' lives for the better. Typically set in private preparatory schools, they focus on a poor outsider ridiculed by his fellow schoolmates but redeemed at last through his school spirit and his willingness to be a team player. His best-known works are *For the Honor of the School* (1900), *The Spirit of the School* (1907), and the *Ferry Hill* series, including *The Crimson Sweater* (1906) and its sequels, which are notable for their refreshingly unconventional portrayal of women. DLR

Barker, Cicely Mary see *FLOWER FAIRY* SERIES; see also BLACKIE'S CHILDREN'S ANNUAL; FAIRY FANTASY; ALICE B. WOODWARD

Barkhouse, Joyce 1913– Canadian writer of short stories, verse, plays, MYTHS, LEGENDS, HISTORICAL FICTION and BIOGRAPHIES, born in the Annapolis Valley. Barkhouse's subjects and themes involve historical figures and the difficulties experienced in the past and present lives of humans and animals. Her biography *George Dawson, The Little Giant* (1989) is based upon the life of one of Canada's earliest and greatest geologists and explorers, after whom Dawson Creek and Dawson City were named. Barkhouse's work also includes *Abraham Gesner* (1980), *The Witch of Port Lajoye* (1983), *A Name for Himself: A Biography of Thomas Head Raddall* (1990) and *Yesterday's Children* (1992), a collection of 12 stories set in Atlantic Canada. *Anna's Pet* (1980), co-authored with Margaret Atwood and illustrated by Ann Blades, describes a child's relationship with various pets. *Pit Pony* (1989), winner of the Ann Connor Brimer Award in 1991 and filmed as a CBC family movie, concerns a ten-year-old boy and a pit pony – one of the wild horses of Sable Island – who are both forced to work in the mines. *Smallest Rabbit* (1996), a PICTUREBOOK, concerns difficulties in finding food during winter months. MRS

Barklem, Jill see *BRAMBLY HEDGE* SERIES

Barne, Kitty [Marion Catherine] 1883–1957 Now largely forgotten British writer of outstanding FAMILY STORIES (curiously described by Humphrey Carpenter and Mari Prichard as 'a few unremarkable novels'). Unusually for the time, the contemporary World War II background – though not stressed – is unequivocally present in much of her fiction: Axel, the musical child prodigy in *Family Footlights* (1939) who is deprived of his violin, has probably just escaped from Nazi Germany or Austria, and *Visitors From London* (winner of the 1940 Carnegie Medal) describes with sympathy and humour how a group of East Londoners coped with evacuation to the country. *We'll Meet in England* (1942) tells how two children escape from Nazi-occupied Norway and sail to Britain. These, with *She Shall Have Music* (1938), show a perceptive eye for both adult and child behaviour, an engaging style and a sympathetic understanding of the need for the arts in the lives of children. After the war, Kitty Barne went on to write PONY STORIES.

Barne also published a BIOGRAPHY, *Elizabeth Fry* (1950), an excellent model of how biographies for children might be written. She dedicated it to 'Elizabeth Fry's great-great-grand-daughter NOEL STREATFEILD', a writer whose novels about music and theatre – though much better known – are arguably much less accomplished than her own. VW

Barney and Friends 1992– An American educational children's TELEVISION programme. Sheryl Leach and Kathy Parker, mothers and educators, created *Barney & the Backyard Gang* as a children's home video. In 1992, PBS began producing a version called *Barney and Friends*. Barney, a large purple dinosaur, is joined in a variety of learning experiences by a multiethnic group of children. Although the show is obviously didactic in nature, it uses song as its primary learning tool and small children are enthralled. The music is comfortable and familiar and the children on the show face a variety of common social and educational problems. JGJ

Barney Boko see COMICS

Baron Münchausen Eponymous baron whose name has become a byword for TALL TALES. Karl Friedrich Hieronymous von Münchhausen (1720–97) actually existed. Indeed he outlived the creator of his literary exploits, librarian and professor Rudolf Erich Raspe (1737–94). Raspe escaped arrest for stealing jewellery in his native Germany by fleeing to England, where he concocted and published in English *The Travels and Surprising Adventures of Baron Münchausen* (1785), a series of anecdotes attributed to Münchausen. The Baron's outrageous adventures appealed to the popular imagination and ensured the book's enduring success across Europe. The tales have taken many forms: CHAPBOOK editions were once sold at fairs; retellings for children began to appear at the end of the 19th century, and film versions have revived the popularity of the Baron's stories in recent times by allowing free reign to special effects. GL

Barongo, Evangeline Ugandan librarian and writer of *The Lazy Crocodile* and *Wise Monkey*, intended for primary schools. Her stories, which are highly entertaining and make interesting reading, are meant to stimulate children's reading and impart Ugandan and African values. Mrs Barongo and Mrs. R.M. Mwayi (also a librarian) have co-authored another children's book, *The African Children's Stories*, published in Kenya in 1996. ABO

Barrett, Angela 1955– British PICTUREBOOK author. One of the many successful graduates of the Royal College of Art, London, Angela Barrett has worked almost entirely in the field of children's book ILLUSTRATION since 1983, contributing her characteristically highly finished illustrations to the work of many well-known PICTUREBOOK authors and collectors of tales. Whilst there is a distinctive Barrett style which consists of stylised, elongated figures, unusual perspectives, precise detail and high drama in the composition, she is nevertheless always sensitive to the particular qualities of the work she is illustrating, so that we find illuminated letters and symbolism in the medieval *Proud Knight, Fair Lady*, retold by NAOMI LEWIS (1989), great settings and contrasts in *Snow White*, retold by Josephine Poole (1991), which for many readers is a perfect interpretation, and proper use of half pages in the mysterious and beautifully designed *Beware, Beware* by SUSAN HILL (1993). JAG

Barrett, Peter 1935– Popular and prolific natural history illustrator. His eye for the detail of flora and fauna and the sunlit charm of his water-colour technique made him an ideal choice for successful reworkings of E.H. SHEPARD's *THE WIND IN THE WILLOWS* (1986) and Gerald Durrell's *My Family and Other Animals* (1987). CB

Barrie, Sir J(ames) M(atthew) 1860–1937 Scottish playwright and novelist, Barrie was born in Kirriemuir, a small town North of Dundee. The ninth child of a weaver, he grew up in comparative poverty. As a child he played numerous imaginary games in the wash-house opposite the family home, later recalled in a series of stories. In 1866 Barrie's older brother David died in a skating accident. Barrie's formidable mother was inconsolable until finally transferring her considerable emotional needs onto her younger son. This was a relationship he never subsequently grew away from, writing to his mother every day as an adult. At Edinburgh University Barrie started writing professionally as a journalist and later as an author. His first play was staged in London in 1892; later successes included *Quality Street* and *The Admirable Crichton*, both produced in 1902. Neither equalled the fame of PETER PAN in 1904, although *Dear Brutus* (1917) and *Mary Rose* (1920) both had large followings. Barrie's fiction, especially *Sentimental Tommy* (1896) and *Tommy and Grizel* (1920), has also been overshadowed by what he later described as his 'terrible masterpiece', the immortal play about the boy who never grew up – for some, an apt description of Barrie himself. NT

Barrytown Trilogy see RODDY DOYLE

Barton, Griselda see *THE COOL WEB*

basal readers see READING SCHEMES

Base, Graeme (Rowland) 1958– Australian illustrator and author with a passion for representing real and imaginary animals in different media, best known for his intricate ALPHABET BOOK, *ANIMALIA* (1986). Sophisticated, alliterative language and complex links between his involved and involving illustrations ensure that his multi-level works appeal as family books across a broad age range. As a creator he has continued to refine his work, integrating shape, colour, sound and movement in imaginative ways. His years of research, and the influences of travel to Africa and Asia, are apparent in the innovative ideas and detailed ILLUSTRATIONS of *The Discovery of Dragons* (1996) and *The Sign of the Seahorse* (1992), and the mysterious verses of *The Eleventh Hour* (1988), where readers are enticed with cryptic clues. Earlier, Base illustrated the work of others, such as *Jabberwocky* (1987) by LEWIS CARROLL, but since the publication of his *My Grandma Lived in Gooligulch* (1983), Base has created his own stories, many of which are now being considered for animation with music. *The Worst Band in the Universe: A Totally Cosmic Adventure* (1999) combines Base's love of poetry, art and music in a wild space FANTASY quest in which the hero, Sprocc, seeks to release his world from musical mediocrity. Base's significance lies not only in the scope and variety of his ideas, but also in the range of media for which they may be adapted. HE

Basile, Giambattista see 'BLUEBEARD'; FAIRY TALES; WARWICK GOBLE; 'PUSS IN BOOTS'; 'SLEEPING BEAUTY'

***Bastable* series** A group of stories by E. NESBIT. The series was begun in 1899 with *The Story of the Treasure Seekers* and continued with *The Wouldbegoods* (1901) and *New Treasure Seekers* (1904). *Oswald Bastable and Others* (1905) is a collection of short stories, some of which relate to the doings of the Bastable family. Though each of the books is ostensibly governed by an overarching idea, for example the need 'to restore the fallen fortunes of the House of Bastable' or trying to be good, the structure of the works is in fact loosely episodic, and the final outcome is seldom reliant on any kind of narrative build-up in the rest of the text.

An emphasis on play rather than on character-building, soul-making and work differentiates Nesbit's books from the general run of children's books of the same period. They also differ in making the children and their value systems the point of reference: adults are judged and evaluated by the children rather than the other way around. The willingness to accommodate and fall in with the spirit of play characterises those adults who win the approval of the Bastable children. Albert-next-door is considered a poor specimen who cries and does not know how to make-believe; his uncle, on the other hand, faced with the 'capture' of his nephew by the 'desperate band of brigands', responds with, 'Albert, you are more highly privileged than I ever was. No one ever made me a nice dungeon when I was your age.' The 'Indian uncle' who finally restores the fallen fortunes of their house also proves his worth on being invited to dinner by the

Illustration by Suddasattwa Basu for *The Homecoming*.

children, when he elects to have 'play dinner' rather than 'grown-up dinner', 'hunting' the main course and slaying the pudding in 'the good-old fashioned way'.

Literature is another important component of the 'Bastable' books. The children's reading fertilises their imaginations and provides the basic 'plots' of their schemes, which are then reworked to comic effect. The series is energised by the tension between the 'real' world and the world of fiction. By borrowing the romance of the fictional world the mundane world is recreated and reshaped as enchanted space: the dinginess of the house in Lewisham Road, for example, is forgotten as the children play at being diviners, bandits, treasure seekers. In turn, the clichés of romantic fiction are given a new life and validity constituting as they do a species of truth to the children, and inspiring them to action. On another level, literature is also important as an index to authenticity, for without necessarily being able to articulate it, the children are aware that some of the books they read, the sentimental and 'improving' kind, contain a certain insincerity of ethos: Dickie does not wish to join the Wouldbegoods if it means 'reading books about children who die'. There is scant patience with humbug and dying among the Bastables, who were the forerunners of a new and energetic generation of literary children. SA

Basu, Suddhasattwa 1956– Well-known Indian illustrator, painter, and maker of animated films, Basu is a product of the Art College, Calcutta, and is regarded as one of the foremost illustrators for children in India today. It was his experience with the children's magazine *Target* which transformed this shy, self-effacing man from a painter to an illustrator. His soft, lyrical drawings are marked by a rare fluidity and are devoid of intellectualised abstraction, as amply demonstrated by his ILLUSTRATIONS for RUSKIN BOND's *To Live in Magic* (1985). Technically sound, his work displays a tremendous sense of drawing composition, colour and space. He is acutely sensitive to the nuances and demands of the text and demonstrates a delicacy and subtlety that few have been able to match. The rare visual treat of the lavish, detailed illustrations of V. Suleiman's *The Homecoming* (1997) virtually carries the text on its shoulders. The illustrations reveal his basic belief that the contemporary world can be interpreted meaningfully only through tradition. He works in various fastidiously selected media to capture the mood of the text, to which he remains faithful without ever falling into the trap of being literal. He is opposed to the formulation of a typical, identifying style that would interfere with the appreciation of the text. MBh

Bates Di(anne Nancy) 1948– Australian writer of fiction, best known for her *Grandma Cadbury* series

(1988–93) about a truck-driving grandmother, who also rides a Harley Davidson. Outrageous humour and zany characters typify Bates's writing. Her satirical *Bushrangers* (1996) includes opera singer Dame Nellie Nickabocka, and other eccentrics. By contrast, *The Last Refuge* (1996), with its delicate emotional balancing, narrated by Mitch, a young girl witnessing violence, shows Bates's ability to touch upon more serious issues. A Special Prize in the 1993 Australian Multicultural Children's Literature Awards, and reader nominations for the West Australian Young Readers' Book Award 1988, indicate Bates's popularity. HE

Batman Comic-book figure, created by Bob Kane and Bill Finger, who first appeared in 1939 in no. 27 of the American series *Detective Comics*. Batman is the secret persona of millionaire Bruce Wayne who (sometimes with his sidekick Robin) fights crime in Gotham City, a gothicised version of New York. Its 'caped crusader' is an ambiguous figure who, while an ostensible champion of good, has obvious affiliations with the night and all that this conventionally connotes, as another of his soubriquets, 'The Dark Knight', suggests. The figure has undergone many alterations in conceptualisation since its creation almost 60 years ago. SA

Batman: The Dark Knight Returns see GRAPHIC NOVELS; SUPERHEROES

Battle of St. George Without, The (1966) Novel by JANET MCNEILL, set in a run-down city square. A group of young inhabitants of Dove Square take on an older gang intent on stealing lead from the roof of a disused church in the centre of the square. The plot is simple but given firm substance by McNeill's creation of a strong sense of place and unforced dialogue between the protagonists, who are portrayed sympathetically but realistically. Both young and old play a part in an outcome which is satisfying, while avoiding the trap of making everything right in the end. It was followed by a sequel, *Goodbye Dove Square*, in which the square's inhabitants are moved to new flats in a process of urban renewal. VC

battledores see HORNBOOKS AND BATTLEDORES

Baum, L(yman) Frank [Floyd Akers, Laura Bancroft, Captain Hugh Fitzgerald, Suzanne Metcalf, Schuyler Staunton, Edith Van Dyne] 1856–1919 American writer, best known for his *Oz* books. L. Frank Baum had a wide and varied career; educated mainly at home because of poor health as a child, Baum read extensively and showed an early interest in writing through the publication of an amateur newspaper. His other great love was the theatre, and he eventually managed some of his father's opera houses as well as producing his own play, *The Maid of Arran*, which toured from New York to Chicago with Baum himself as the lead. Although he would remain primarily interested in writing and the theatre, Baum worked at several other odd jobs as an adult, including breeding chickens, selling crockery door-to-door, inventing a new brand of axel grease and running a general store. Despite many failures in these occupations, Baum maintained an optimistic, ready-for-anything spirit which would infect his *Oz* series, one of the factors in their continued popularity.

His first success as a fiction writer came from some prose retellings of NURSERY RHYMES. The 1897 edition of *Mother Goose in Prose*, with ILLUSTRATIONS by the then unknown MAXFIELD PARRISH, sold well enough to interest another publisher in producing Baum's follow-up effort, *Father Goose: His Book* in 1899. The droll pictures by the artist W.W. DENSLOW helped to make *Father Goose* popular with the public, and Baum capitalised on the sudden burst of fame in 1900 with *The Wonderful Wizard of Oz*. This book, his most famous, again teamed Baum's writing with Denslow's artwork, creating characters and images which would become a part of the American psyche, such as the Yellow Brick Road, the Tin Woodman and the humbug Wizard of Oz. Baum's protagonist Dorothy, a self-confident and unperturbable girl from Kansas, embodied the spirit of a frontier America, where people hoped for the best despite all obvious reasons to doubt. *The Wonderful Wizard of Oz* cemented Baum's fame as an author of modern, American FAIRY TALES for children, and he never wrote any other type of story under his own name.

While the success of *The Wonderful Wizard of Oz* expanded, both from continued sales of the book and from its various spin-offs – which included a comic strip illustrated by Denslow and a musical play partly produced by Baum – the book's author tried to branch out, creating stories of other fairy lands and characters, including Santa Claus. However, the public demanded more about Oz, and so Baum eventually satisfied the children by producing an *Oz* book a year. In the meantime, he amused himself with other projects, including both boys' series books (*The Boy Fortune Hunters* and *Sam Steele* adventures) and girls' series books (particularly the popular *Aunt Jane's Nieces* series) under pseudonyms, and producing silent films based on the *Oz* books, which, though unsuccessful commercially, used interesting early film techniques. The more commercially successful film based on Baum's book, *The Wizard of Oz* directed by Victor Fleming, was made in 1939. Unusually for a children's author, Baum's death in 1919 received notice across the country, including an obituary in the New York Times. KS

Bawden, Edward 1903–89 British illustrator, and highly versatile artist and designer. Though Bawden produced few children's books, his work has had an immense influence on other illustrators, particularly through its appealing use of false naivety and its communication of humour. DW

Bawden, Nina 1925– One of the most accomplished British children's writers of her time, Bawden was born in London and went to Oxford University. She began writing for adults in 1953. Ten years later she decided to write a children's book in response to what she saw as the general lack of social and emotional realism in the stories she was then reading to her own growing family. Although *The Secret Passage* (1963) was still written in an orthodox, holiday ADVENTURE mode, its child characters went to state schools, talked back to their parents and were generally as lively, inquisitive and occasionally headstrong as the real thing. More novels followed, notably *The Witch's Daughter* (1966) where the adolescent heroine was blind, and *A Handful of Thieves* (1967), a small masterpiece about a botched episode of child detective work. In *Squib* (1971) Bawden wrote a more disturbing story about child neglect, drawing on her experience as a magistrate. But however occasionally grim their circumstances, her young characters always come through by the end, even if they sometimes have to settle for a little less than they wanted. This is particularly true of *CARRIE'S WAR* (1973), her most successful novel, set during the war-time evacuation and memorably adapted for TELEVISION. Although the story ends on a note of tragedy and loss, the children themselves have survived and grown in understanding. *THE PEPPERMINT PIG* (1975) continued the theme of children transplanted into unaccustomed circumstances. *Rebel on a Rock* (1978) took the same characters from *Carrie's War*, but now adult and with their own children. All become dangerously involved in a Mediterranean political coup. More sinister in a different way, *Kept in the Dark* (1982) describes the arrival of a disturbing stranger into a formerly tranquil household made up of grandparents and grandchildren. Neither old nor young have the power to see him off, and tension increases before an electrifying climax. Another frightening story, *Devil by the Sea* (1976), was originally published for adults in 1957 and re-appeared in slightly abridged form for children. In this novel a child witnesses a murder, but is unable to persuade anyone else of the truth. The murderer meanwhile is closing in; strong meat even for a writer who has never believed in pulling her punches with a child audience when it comes to describing life as it sometimes is.

Later novels increasingly touch on the way the present can become a victim of the past. *Outside Child* (1989) describes a family racked by secrets, while *The Real Plato Jones* (1994) writes about the way a tragic conflict of loyalties in wartime Greece continues to have repercussions for those originally involved some fifty years later. *In My Own Time; Almost an Autobiography* (1994) provides useful background to the author's books both for adults and children, which with *Granny the Pag* (1996) now amount to 40 titles in all. This is an outstanding achievement from an author who has always been popular with children as well as critics. NT

see also WAR STORIES

Bayley, Nicola 1949– Nicola Bayley's illustrating career took off while she was a student at the Royal College of Art in England when her meticulous, highly finished and brilliantly coloured work attracted the attention of Tom Maschler of Jonathan Cape. Bayley's first half-dozen books included *The Tyger Voyage* (Richard Adams, 1976) and *The Patchwork Cat* (WILLIAM MAYNE, 1981), in which can be discerned, as well as her attention to detail – which she achieves by using tiny brushes – her love affair with cats. The immensely successful *The Mousehole Cat* (Antonia Barber, 1990) includes both a real cat and a symbolic storm cat who is magically realised, and in *Fun with Mrs. Thumb* (JAN MARK, 1993), there are dramatic and witty contrasts of the huge cat inside a dolls' house and a quiet reference to KATHLEEN HALES's *ORLANDO*. JAG

Baynes, Pauline (Diana) 1922– Distinguished British illustrator, much of whose work descends directly from the attention to detail, and the joy in colour, of the monks in the medieval scriptorium. Her margin decoration for Grant Uden's *A Dictionary of Chivalry* won her the Kate Greenaway Medal in 1968, whilst her black-and-white illustrations for J. Westwood's *Mediaeval Tales* have the vigour of 15th-century woodcuts. Baynes was the illustrator for both C.S. LEWIS's *NARNIA* series and J.R.R. TOLKIEN's *LORD OF THE RINGS*, for which she designed the box and the maps – as well as his two books of verse: *The Adventures of Tom Bombadil and Other Verses from the Red Book* and *Bilbo's Last Song*, and Amabel Williams-Ellis's retelling of *The Arabian Nights*. Her jewel-like book-jackets have conferred an accolade on many a novel. EM

Baynton, Martin 1953– New Zealand illustrator, who emigrated from England in 1987. Baynton's ILLUSTRATIONS were first published in *Jim Frog* (1983), with text by RUSSELL HOBAN. Three more collaborative works with Hoban followed. Since then Baynton has developed his considerable skills as an illustrator, writer, playwright, actor and speaker. The *Fifty* series established his international reputation as a writer/illustrator, along with several highly

Illustration by Nicola Bayley for *The Mousehole Cat* by Antonia Barber.

successful PICTUREBOOKS such as *Jane and the Dragon* (1988) and *Why Do You Love Me?* (1989). *Daniel's Dinosaurs* (1990), with text by Mary Carmine, achieved a New Zealand record with an American print run of over 100,000. Baynton's gentle, detailed and colourful illustrations, using the single medium of coloured pencils, have ensured his popularity with young readers. Recent ventures into script-writing, acting, directing and novel-writing indicate that Baynton still has much to contribute to the New Zealand literary scene. LO

BB [Denys (James) Watkins-Pitchford] 1905–90 British writer, illustrator and artist. Watkins-Pitchford illustrated under his own name, but wrote as 'BB', letters which define a size of shot. This characterised him as a countryman, and his work communicated his love of nature to adults and children. While teaching art at Rugby School, he produced his first children's books, the ANIMAL STORIES *Wild Lone* (1938) and *Sky Gipsy* (1939). *THE LITTLE GREY MEN* (Carnegie Medal winner for 1942) and *Down the Bright Stream* (1948) are tales of gnomes which display a developing vein of FANTASY. It is thus no wonder that as an illustrator he admired and was sometimes influenced by ARTHUR RACKHAM. DW

BBC (British Broadcasting Corporation) see TELEVISION; see also *THE BORROWERS*; *CHILDREN'S HOUR ANNUAL*; *PROFESSOR BRANESTAWM*; *TOYTOWN*

Beach York, Carol see DOLL STORIES

Beake, Lesley 1949– Much-honoured South African author, twice winner of the Percy FitzPatrick Award, for *The Strollers* (1987) and *A Cageful of Butterflies* (1989). Beake writes for a full range of young readers from beginners to young adults, on difficult and challenging topics and often with shifts in chronology and voice. Her YOUNG ADULT FICTION tackles serious and unusual subjects, some of them historical, such as a deaf-and-dumb African boy, a blind 19th-century globe-trotter, and street children. *Song of Be* (1991), one of several of her books set in Namibia, has as its protagonist a young San woman experiencing the transition of her people to a modern way of life at the time of Namibian independence. This remarkable novel was named a 'Best Book for Young Adults' by the American Library Association in 1995. ERJ

Beale, Fleur 1945– New Zealand writer of sports-oriented novels. Since 1990, Beale has written ten action novels, whose clipped dialogue in current slang ensures their popularity. Protagonists succeed in sports, solve immediate crises and care for chronically ill parents. Whether surfing, off-road driving or aerobic dancing, through toughness and peer support these teenagers come to understand themselves. In *Slide the Corner* (1993) a car enthusiast from a rigid academic family builds his world through work and rally driving. Parents may be inept or cruel, but Beale creates a pragmatic world where effective help comes from peers and from responsible adults. MJH

Beaman, S.G. Hulme see TOYTOWN SERIES

Beames, Margaret 1935– New Zealand historical novelist since 1977. Initially writing informative, slightly didactic historical novels, in the late 1980s, Beames widened her oeuvre to include PICTUREBOOKS and straightforward ADVENTURE STORIES. *The Parkhurst Boys* (1986) tells of the life of convict apprentices sent to New Zealand in 1842. The hero's treatment by his cruel boss, his near starvation and escape to live with local Maoris build up to his not unexpected rescue by his long-lost family. In *Archway Arrow* (1996), a junior novel driven chiefly by dialogue, Beames confidently eschews 'issues', using a quintessential rural New Zealand children's summer obsession, making rafts, to show that honesty and honour bring rewards. MJH

Beano The second weekly COMIC for children to be published by D.C. Thomson of Dundee. The first issue was dated 30 July 1938. Modelled closely on the company's first comic, *DANDY,* it soon exceeded that comic's circulation and ever since has been Thomson's best-selling title. Its popularity also extends to *The Beano Book*, the Christmas ANNUAL which was first published in the autumn of 1939 (undated). Consisting mostly of reprints of favourite characters, like its companion annual it also contained strips that were never published in the weekly. These were trial strips drawn by hopeful contributors. From 1942 the title changed to *The Magic Beano Book* for eight editions, incorporating Thomson's discontinued *Magic Fun Book* (1940–1). DG

beast epic see ANIMALS IN FICTION; REYNARD THE FOX

Beastly Tales from Here and There (1991) The puckish and sparkling humour of Indian author Vikram Seth's animal FABLES in verse has made *Beastly Tales* attractive fare for both the young and the old. Well-known characters – such as the deceitful crocodile who is caught out by the quick-thinking monkey – are clothed in novel and enchanted garb, and made to rub shoulders with freshly created characters and creatures who are kinky, droll and hilarious. Of the ten tales told here, two come from India, two from the Ukraine, and two, as the author claims, 'came directly to [him] from the land of Gup'. Scintillating ILLUSTRATIONS by RAVI SHANKAR back the remarkably versatile poetic talent of the writer. MBh

see also ANIMALS IN FICTION

Beatty, Patricia 1922–91 American author. Writing both with her first husband (John Beatty, 1922–75) and alone, Beatty has written more than 45 historical novels, including *The Royal Dirk* (1966), *Charley Skedaddle* (1987) and *Jayhawker* (1991). Her young characters are participants in exciting events, maturing as they make choices in difficult and often dangerous situations. The books range widely in both time period and physical location, and Beatty attempts, through dialect, to give a sense of how people actually talked in their respective time and place. She often includes extensive notes which provide additional related information and historical context. WH

see also HISTORICAL FICTION

Beaumont, Mme Marie Le Prince de 1711–80 French writer of over 70 books, mainly didactic and for children. She fled an unhappy marriage to live in England, where she stayed for nearly 20 years. There she supported herself as a governess and by writing. Her fame rests on one work, *Le Magasin des Enfants* (1756), translated by the author as *The Young Misses Magazine, Containing Dialogues between a Governess and Several Young Ladies of Quality, Her Scholars* (1761). This contains, among other stories, her FAIRY TALE *BEAUTY AND THE BEAST*, which has been accepted as a classic ever since. PP

'Beauty and the Beast' FAIRY TALE by MME DE BEAUMONT, in which Beauty – to save her father's life – consents to live in an enchanted palace with a Beast who begs her, in vain, to marry him. The Beast is dying before Beauty realises she has grown to love him. Her avowal releases the Beast from a wicked spell: he becomes a handsome prince, and they marry. De Beaumont belonged to a tradition of French salon culture in which sophisticated ladies played creatively with such fairy tales. Mme de Villeneuve (1695–1755) wrote an intolerably long and involved version, in which, for instance, Beauty is entertained in her palace by parrots who 'declaimed verses composed by the best authors'. The COMTESSE D'AULNOY (c. 1650–1705) wrote another version, in which the Beast is horrifically violent. The motif of monster bridegroom (occasionally, bride) is older than French culture and widespread. The story of 'Cupid and Psyche' involves an invisible husband, suspected of being a monster. Meanwhile, in Norwegian FOLKTALE the Beast is a bear; in Russia, a goat; in India, a tamarind tree; in

Illustration by Ian Beck for *Ian Beck's Picture Book*.

Germany, an iron stove. The story has inspired adult works of distinction, such as Cocteau's film, *La Belle et la Bête* (1946), and ANGELA CARTER's short story, *The Courtship of Mr Lyon* (1979). The tale, in its recreations, has emphasised different elements according to period: filial piety; courtly love; a woman's right to choose. The theme of redemption through love appeals timelessly to children and adults alike. PP

Beaver Scout Annual, The see GUIDING AND SCOUTING FICTION

Bechtel, Louise Seaman 1894–1985 American children's book editor, critic, and author of several books for and about children. Born in Brooklyn and educated at Vassar, Bechtel looked to a career in journalism, which materialised after several years of teaching. She began work at Macmillan in the advertising department and moved to head the juvenile department, the first children's book department in the United States, which she directed from 1919 to 1934. She later became editor of the children's book section of the *New York Herald Tribune Book Review* (1949–56). Bechtel was the author of several books, including *The Brave Bantam* (1946), *Mr. Peck's Pets* (1947), and *Books in Search of Children* (1969). She was associate editor and honorary director of *THE HORN BOOK*, beginning in 1935. As editor at Macmillan, Bechtel worked with many outstanding children's book figures, including RACHEL FIELD, HELEN SEWELL, Margery Bianco, ELIZABETH COATSWORTH and PADRIAC COLUM. While at Macmillan, she wrote her own catalogues (of which she was proud), lectured, contributed reviews, and hosted a weekly radio programme on children's books. Considered a creative shaper and maker in the burgeoning period of American children's book production, Bechtel experimented and, in her words, 'stepped away from its traditions'. AL

Beck, Ian 1947– British illustrator. After Brighton College of Art, where he was taught by RAYMOND BRIGGS, Beck became a freelance illustrator, working in many different fields, including book covers and greetings cards. His first book, *Round and Round the Garden* (Sarah Williams, 1983) was followed by his own *The Teddy Robber* (1989), and both typify his precise line drawing, hatching and sure use of watercolour. Both these titles were shortlisted for the Best Books for Babies Award. *Emily & the Golden Acorn* (1992) and *Tom and the Island of Dinosaurs* (1993) have eventful and satisfying story lines and are enhanced by generously detailed and affecting ILLUSTRATIONS. Similar characteristics distinguish his three teddy-bear books, *Home Before Dark* (1997), *Lost in the Snow* (1998) and *Alone in the Woods* (2000). In 1999 Beck illustrated an anthology, *Poems for Christmas*, a compilation of traditional and contemporary poems by Jill Bennett. JAG

Beck, Jennifer 1939– New Zealand short story and PICTUREBOOK writer. Born in Auckland and trained as a clinical psychologist, Beck began writing in the early 1980s, specialising in short texts. More than 30 of her stories have been included in 'school reader' programmes, published world-wide. In a notable collaboration with Dunedin illustrator ROBYN BELTON, she is the author of three acclaimed picturebooks: *The Choosing Day* (1988), *David's Dad* (1991) and especially *The Bantam and the Soldier* (1996), which is a poignant story, based on a family wartime anecdote, of friendship, loyalty and loss set in the World War I trenches in France. TD

Beckett, Mary 1926– Belfast-born author of adult and children's books, the latter characterised by a gentle style, suiting their domestic settings and emphasis on family life. In *Hannah or Pink Balloons* (1995), her strongest work to date, she explores 12-year-old Hannah's developing maturity through her relationship with her grandmother. VC

Beckett, Sandra see CRITICAL APPROACHES TO CHILDREN'S LITERATURE

Bedard, Michael 1949– Canadian children's writer. Born in Toronto and educated at the University of

Toronto, Bedard has written FAIRY TALES, PICTUREBOOKS and novels that are decidedly intellectual yet accessible. His novels explore symbolically a theme based on William Blake's works, the continual conflict between light and darkness. Emphasising the need to understand connections between past and present, they focus on relationships between the young and the elderly, who must co-operate to prevent evil or to realise good. In *A Darker Magic* (1987) and its sequel, *Painted Devil* (1994), older women, symbols of wisdom because they know past evils, work with young girls, symbols of imaginative hope, to prevent a magic show and a puppet theatre, respectively, from enslaving and killing children. In *Redwork* (1990), winner of the Governor General's Award and the Canadian Library Association Book of the Year Award, references to Blake, alchemy and classic movies underscore a conflict between a juvenile delinquent, who represents the darkness of ignorance and hatred, and two sensitive teenagers, who represent sympathetic acceptance. The teens help an old alchemist seek the Philosopher's Stone, symbol of imaginative fulfillment, thereby ending the old man's lonely isolation while gaining purpose in their own lives. REJ

see also *SONGS OF INNOCENCE*

Beddows, Eric [Ken Nutt] 1951– Canadian gallery artist and illustrator of children's books. Born Ken Nutt in Woodstock, Ontario, Beddows was initially best known for his gently humorous black-and-white pencil drawings. Award-winning collaborations with TIM WYNNE-JONES on the *Zoom at Sea* trilogy (1983–92) and SID FLEISCHMAN on *I Am Phoenix* (1985) and *Joyful Noise* (1988) exemplify his love of FANTASY and the natural world. *Shadow Play* (1990), also by Fleischman, reveals Beddows's characteristic sophisticated use of light and shadow. His colour ILLUSTRATIONS are equally impressive: the toddler's-eye view of a city street in *Night Cars* (1988), by Teddy Jam, won Beddows two major awards; and the 1940s-style paintings for Pam Conrad's *The Rooster's Gift* (1996) earned him the Governor General's Literary Award for Children's Book Illustration. Since 1985 he has used two names for his dual career: Eric Beddows – a combination of his middle name and his mother's maiden name – for his children's illustration, and Ken Nutt for his gallery art. AG

Bede, the Venerable 673?–735 Anglo-Saxon monk. While at Jarrow, Bede wrote brief instructional manuals for children on spelling, figures of speech, writing Latin verse, time and methods of reckoning it. His *De Natura Rerum* contains stories about fanciful creatures such as mermaids and served as a text for children until the Norman Conquest. Stories from the *Ecclesiastical History of the English People* – such as the Pope calling English boys 'angeli' (angels), not 'angli' (Angles), life compared to the flight of a sparrow through a room, and the hymn of Caedman – formed part of children's culture until well into the 20th century. GA

Bedford, F(rancis) D(onkin) 1864–1954 British illustrator best known for his illustration of verses by E.V. LUCAS (1868–1938). The first of their many titles, *The Book of Shops* (1899), is typical with its large, landscape-format, full-colour illustrations. Bedford's early architectural training is detectable in the content and design of his page, and RANDOLPH CALDECOTT is an obvious influence on his line, use of colour and introduction of witty extra stories in the illustrations. Illustrations for CHARLES DICKENS, J.M. BARRIE and GEORGE MACDONALD, and an acclaimed centenary edition of ANN AND JANE TAYLOR'S *ORIGINAL POEMS* (1903), were highlights in Bedford's long, productive career. JAG

Bedknob and Broomstick (1957) Acclaimed and popular novel by British author MARY NORTON, originally published as two short novels, *The Magic Bedknob* and *Bonfires and Broomsticks*. The story, in the tradition of E. NESBIT and EDWARD EAGER, concerns the danger, comedy and moral uncertainty that arise when children experiment with magic and time travel. Written with the author's characteristic sharpness and irony, it has less of the melancholy of *THE BORROWERS* series, and shows a sympathetic interest in the character of the village spinster whose secret study of magic – and whose oblique and equivocal relationship with Paul, the youngest of the children – leads to the children's adventures. VW

Beginner Books see *THE CAT IN THE HAT* SERIES; *DR SEUSS*; see also STAN AND JAN BERENSTAIN

Behn, Harry 1898–1973 American author and poet, who was born in territorial Arizona. Behn played as a child with the Yavapai Indian children near his home in Prescott, and learned from them 'a ceremonial response to the earth, to the dancing sun and singing winds; how to live in a world as magical as a dream; to speak with a soft voice as white-wing doves do on evenings in summer'. Behn graduated from Harvard in 1922, wrote screenplays for 20th Century Fox and MGM in Hollywood, taught creative writing at the University of Arizona, and founded the *Arizona Quarterly* and the University of Arizona Press. He was 50 years old when he began writing poetry for children, inspired by his three-year-old daughter who pointed to the stars and said 'moon-babies'. Although he wrote children's stories, translated Japanese HAIKU and wrote books for adults, it is for his seven books of children's poetry, all but one illustrated by him, that he is best-known. His best poems are about the mysteries of time and nature as experienced from the perspective of a solitary child. Behn has said that his *Chrysalis: Concerning Children and Poetry* (1968) contains 'almost everything that matters to me'. LH

Bell, Anthea see WAR STORIES; ASTERIX; CHRISTIAN MORGENSTERN

Bell, Krista see REVIEWING AND REVIEWERS

Belloc, (Joseph) Hilaire (Pierre René) 1870–1953 English author, who wrote comic verse for children. He published *THE BAD CHILD'S BOOK OF BEASTS* (1896) and followed this with further illustrated parodies of 19th-century moralising verse in *Cautionary Tales for Children* (1907), cleverly rhymed, tongue-in-cheek warnings to errant children. ML

Belton, Robyn 1947– One of New Zealand's most accomplished illustrators, Belton was born in Wanganui and studied with RUSSELL CLARK at the Canterbury University School of Fine Arts. Since 1978 she has worked as a freelance illustrator and tertiary lecturer, and her work has appeared in more than twenty 'school readers' and in many issues of the *SCHOOL JOURNAL*. Her hardback PICTUREBOOKS include the anti-war *THE DUCK IN THE GUN* (1984) with JOY COWLEY; *Donkey* (1986) with George Ciantar; and *The Choosing Day* (1988) and *David's Dad* (1990), both with JENNIFER BECK. In 1996, with Beck, she published to critical acclaim a second anti-war book, *The Bantam and the Soldier*, which also features a farmyard bird as a main character and a catalyst to the story. Belton is widely admired for her meticulous research, mastery of watercolour, and her belief that a successful illustrator builds around the author's text as both an accompanist and interpreter. TD

Bemelmans, Ludwig see *MADELEINE* SERIES; see also ILLUSTRATION IN CHILDREN'S BOOKS; MUNRO LEAF; PICTUREBOOKS

Benét, Rosemary (Carr) 1897?–1962 and **Benét, Stephen Vincent** 1898–1943 Stephen Vincent – twice recipient of the Pulitzer Prize for Poetry, as well as numerous awards for stories – collaborated with his wife Rosemary on one children's text, *A Book of Americans* (1933). A collection of verse describing famous historical figures, mostly presidents, it avoids banal jingoism with an adroit sense of humour. Many of the poems are sensitive to the fact that American history contains much that is shameful as well as heroic. For instance, 'Indian' considers the European conquerors' mixed accomplishment:

They'll kill his deer and net his fish
And clear away his wood,
And frequently remark to him
They do it for his good.

Benjamin Franklin's poem pokes fun at his taste for 'pretty girls', while praising him because

all our humming dynamos and our electric light
Go back to what Ben Franklin found, the day he flew
his kite.

Though males dominate this collection, Rosemary's contribution offsets this: she is known for her poem in which the ghost of Nancy Hanks wonders, 'What happened to Abe?' For children over 12, these poems provide an enjoyable introduction to many personages who ought to be familiar. RAM

Bennett, John 1865–1956 American author and illustrator. Bennett's historical novels were noteworthy in that they so effectively captured the period and events they portrayed. His *Master Skylark: A Story of Shakespeare's Time* first appeared as a serial in *ST NICHOLAS* (1896–7) and then in a volume illustrated by REGINALD BIRCH. Master Skylark is a Stratford singing boy kidnapped and taken off to London, where he meets SHAKESPEARE and is taken to sing for the queen. The Bard's London is captured in vivid splashes of colourful details and crammed with fascinating characters and events, evoking the glories of the Elizabethan age. His second book, *Barnaby Lee* (1902), employs the same artistry in its portrayal of Peter Styvesant's forced surrender of New Amsterdam to the British, and handles a complex plot with ease and clarity. Here again, Bennett's ability to make the past come alive creates an excitement as he skillfully blends well-rounded characters, historical information and appreciation of moral values. A certain exuberance infuses both books so that the reader is drawn into the period in full participation. KSB

See also HISTORICAL FICTION

Benson, Gerard 1931– British poet. He won the *SIGNAL* Award in 1991 for *This Poem Doesn't Rhyme*, which was intended 'to help readers to see other possibilities' (than rhyme) in poetry. Other collections, such as *The Magnificent Callisto* (1992), have been commended for poetic craftmanship, range of forms and the poems about his own childhood. A member of the Barrow poets group, translator and columnist for the *Times Education Supplement*, Benson started 'Poems on the Underground' in London tube trains in 1986. He writes for children and adults and works in schools. EAG

Benson, Patrick 1956– British illustrator. Trained in Florence and in London, Benson made an auspicious start with his meticulous cross-hatched and colour-washed work for WILLIAM MAYNE's *Hob Stories* (1984) which won the Mother Goose Award for new illustrators. He has partnered several notable authors with ILLUSTRATIONS that are both elegant and energetic. He pays great attention to characterisation, viewpoint and detail. His own text, *Little Penguin* (1990), successfully makes use of line drawing, frames and a limited palette to tell its touching tale. *Owl Babies* (MARTIN WADDELL, 1992) sees Benson dramatically meeting the challenge of an affecting but relatively static text. *The Little Boat* (Kathy Henderson, 1995) won the Kurt Maschler Award and *The Sea-Thing Child* (RUSSELL HOBAN) was shortlisted for the Kate Greenaway Award. He has also illustrated books by CHARLES DICKENS, KENNETH GRAHAME and ROALD DAHL. JAG

Benson, Sally 1900–72 American writer, born in St Louis, Missouri. In New York, Benson became best known for her short stories for adults and her stories which were more *about* than *for* young people. Benson wrote newspaper interviews, and reviews of movies and mystery stories. She also wrote more than 20 screenplays, 108 short stories for *The New Yorker*, and won the O. Henry prize twice. Although her story collection *Emily* (1938) was not written for children, Benson does describe the character development and poignant concerns that accompany the experience of growing up. *Junior Miss* (1941) is a collection of bittersweet, at times humorous stories of female maturation with its accompanying feelings of anguish, inadequacy and the necessity for manipulation. *Meet Me in St. Louis* (1942), a collection of 12 stories based upon her sister's diary, describes family life at the turn of the century when the World's Fair was held in St. Louis. The film version starred Judy Garland. *Stories of the Gods and Heroes* (1940) confirmed Benson's remarkable gift for STORYTELLING. MRS

Beowulf see *DRAGON SLAYER*; see also ABRIDGEMENT; KEVIN CROSSLEY-HOLLAND; FOLKTALES AND LEGENDS

Berenstain, Jan(ice Grant) 1923– and **Stan(ley)** 1923– Writers and illustrators of the *Berenstain Bears* series of PICTUREBOOKS. Having met in art school, the Berenstains married in 1946 and worked and collaborated originally on cartoons. They published a book with cartoon bear characters, *The Big Honey Hunt* (1962), for DR SEUSS and his *Beginner Books* for young children learning to read. This led to a series of more than 80 picturebooks about the family of a boy, a girl, a mother and a father bear. These use simple situations which small children would encounter growing up, and also include important issues, in such books as *The Berenstain Bears Go to the Doctor* (1981), *The Berenstain Bears and Too Much Junk Food* (1985), and *The Berenstain Bears Learn About Strangers* (1985). With a restricted vocabulary, brightly coloured pictures and simplified plots, the books offer easy solutions to contemporary problems and present an energetic, optimistic view of life for younger readers. TELEVISION specials and other products support the series. Along with Dr Seuss and RICHARD SCARRY, this has been one of the most popular and prolific of contemporary picturebook series. GRB

Beresford, Elisabeth British author, born in Paris. Although she is best known as the creator of the *Wombles*, Beresford has written many other books for both children and adults. Many of her children's stories are about magical things happening to ordinary children, such as *Dangerous Magic* (1972), or plausible adventures often set in London. An example is *Lizzy's War* (1993), in which a little girl is evacuated to the countryside where she shares some hair-raising escapades with the eccentric Mrs Damps. The *Wombles* stories (from 1968) are about a group of benign furry creatures living on Wimbledon Common in London who collect litter and transform it into useful objects. The craze which followed the televising of the stories and the heavy merchandising of Wombles paraphernalia makes it hard to view the stories objectively, but despite some criticisms of the series, Beresford was undoubtedly satisfying a popular demand. She has also written romantic thrillers for adults. HCE

Berg, Leila 1917– Born in Salford, England, Berg has written a great many stories for children. Berg conceived the *Nippers* READING SCHEME and wrote many of its titles, aiming to reflect the vitality of contemporary children's literature. The *Nippers* scheme was criticised for stereotyping working-class life, but Berg felt strongly that children should see representations of children like themselves in their reading. The informal and authentic dialogue was ground-breaking in its time. Berg received the Eleanor Farjeon Award in 1974 for services to children's literature. HCE

Berna, Paul see *A HUNDRED MILLION FRANCS*

Berridge, Celia see *POSTMAN PAT* SERIES

Berry, James 1924– Major poet who was born in Jamaica, moved to Britain in 1948, and was awarded the OBE in 1990. He was the first black writer to win the National Poetry Competition in Britain and one of the first to use his native Caribbean 'Nation Language' as well as standard English in his poetry. There was no poetry in his childhood, just the Bible and ANANCY stories. Berry worked as a telegraphist to support his family before becoming a full-time writer. A cultural activist in schools and writers' workshops, he championed black writing by editing two ground-breaking anthologies of West Indian British poetry, *Bluefoot Traveller* (1981) and *News for Babylon* (1984). His collections for children, *When I Dance* (1988) (Signal Poetry Award 1989) and *Playing a Dazzler* (1996), reflect his concern to write about children's experience in Britain and the Caribbean. Berry's poems combine a rich Jamaican lyricism with an unfailing faith in the child's imagination. He captures moments with passionate intensity, celebrating humanity and diversity, but always putting the child centre-stage. *A Thief in the Village* (1987), a collection of short stories set in the Caribbean which won the Smarties Prize, demonstrates Berry's belief in literature and education as a means of bridging different cultures. Other fictional works include *Anancy Spiderman* (1988) and *The Future Telling Lady* (1991). *Celebration Song* (1994), which puts the story of Jesus' birth in a Caribbean setting, is the first of several PICTUREBOOKS. HT

Berry, Liz [Shirley Elizabeth Pountney] Contemporary British painter, and novelist for teenage readers. Berry has been both an art teacher and a careers guidance officer in East London, and has run her own art gallery. In all her four novels she combines a strong understanding of young people with a gift for particularly vivid description. When her first book, *Easy Connections* (1983), was published, it was immediately successful among its intended readers. *Junior Bookshelf* praised Berry as 'a novelist of rare promise' and the book was shortlisted for the *Observer* Young Adult Fiction prize. Its sequel, *Easy Freedom* (1985), was particularly popular with girls. However, both novels were controversial; because of their subject matter – rape, for example – and perhaps because the love story is set in the world of powerful, wealthy and glamorous rock musicians, some critics, educators and parents were outraged. Berry's next novel, *Mel* (1988), sold even more copies than *Easy Connections* and is more clearly successful in representing its heroine's maturation towards independence. Her latest work, *The China Garden* (1994), is a mystery/FANTASY exploring the theme of rebirth and renewal, and at the same time a powerful modern love story with pace, poetically visualised imagery and a sure grasp of the theme of female autonomy. MT

Bessie Bunter see *School Friend*; see also CHARLES HAMILTON; SCHOOL STORIES

Bestall, Alfred see *Blackie's Children's Annual*; RUPERT BEAR; *Rupert and the Frog Song*

bestiaries see ANIMALS IN FICTION; see also ILLUSTRATION IN CHILDREN'S BOOKS

Bethancourt, T. Ernesto [Tom Paisley] 1932– Hispanic-American author of over 20 novels for young adults. Bethancourt often examines minority groups and the prejudice displayed toward any individual whose appearance, background, race or ethnicity varies from what is perceived as the norm. He also analyses relationships between generations, and estranged family members learn to understand and accept one another. Bethancourt's books are informational and mirror his own interests: *Tune In Yesterday* (1978) is partially set in the New York City jazz clubs of 1942, while escape artist Harry Houdini makes an appearance in *The Tomorrow Connection* (1984). Teen protagonists usually narrate in a breezy style which incorporates wordplay and contemporary slang. His most popular books are the *Doris Fein* mystery series. Critics have commented that Fein, an intelligent, overweight, Jewish girl, is a more realistic NANCY DREW displaying a feisty spirit and a sense of humour. Bethancourt's humour rarely masks the seriousness of the point he is making. In *The Great Computer Dating Caper* (1984), two boys set up a dating service for unpopular girls. The situations they find themselves in are amusing, but the boys also learn about sadness, vulnerability and the price of using others to benefit themselves. WH

Bethnal Green Museum of Childhood see COLLECTIONS OF CHILDREN'S BOOKS

***Betsy Biggalow* series** see MALORIE BLACKMAN

***Betsy-Tacy* series** Books by Maud Hart Lovelace (1893–1980) based on her childhood in Mankato, Minnesota. The title characters meet at Betsy's fifth birthday party; they remain best friends throughout the series, which includes short volumes about their childhood adventures as well as longer volumes about their adolescence and adulthood. Betsy travels to Europe in 1914 and observes events that lead to World War I. The final volume, *Betsy's Wedding*, provides a thoughtful look at the challenges and triumphs of married life. In addition to the ten Betsy-Tacy adventures, the series includes three volumes in which Betsy and her friends appear peripherally: *Carney's House Party* (1949), *Emily of Deep Valley* (1950) and *Winona's Pony Cart* (1953). The books are domestic stories; they are also detailed representations of life in a small midwestern town in the late 19th and early 20th century. For a demonstration of the historical accuracy of the series, see Sharla Scannell Whalen's *Betsy-Tacy Companion* (1995). The *Betsy-Tacy* books are also discussed by Suzanne Rahn in *Rediscoveries in Children's Literature* (1995). In 1990, The Betsy-Tacy Society was formed in Mankato; it now includes over a thousand members. AKP

Bettelheim, Bruno see FAIRY TALES; GRIMM BROTHERS; CHARLES PERRAULT

Betty Boop see ANIMATED CARTOONS; POPEYE

Bevis: The Story of a Boy see *WOOD MAGIC*; see also CAMPING AND TRAMPING FICTION

Bewick, Thomas 1753–1828 Wood engraver, praised by John Ruskin for his 'magnificent artistic power, the flawless virtue, veracity, tenderness, the infinite humour of the man'. The eldest of eight children, Bewick was raised at Eltringham, a village 11 miles west of Newcastle. His father was a farmer and managed a colliery. Bewick's *Memoir* (1862) records a vigorous boyhood spent roaming the countryside with his friends, and a passion for drawing what he had seen. Apart from one unhappy year working in London, Bewick rarely left the landscape which sustained him as man and artist. His famous two-volume *History of British Birds* (1797/1804) is decorated by wonderfully observed vignettes of a rural life which is idyllic, harsh and comical in turn. CHARLOTTE BRONTË's young Jane Eyre was entranced by the stories implicit in these cameos. Much of Bewick's apprentice work was published in CHAPBOOKS for children; in later life, he illustrated Croxall's *AESOP*. Bewick's delicate images, with their sense of three-dimensional depth, resulted from his innovative technique of 'white line' engraving on hardwoods such as box, concentrating as much on what was cut away as on what remained. He was a committed teacher, and his influence and that of his pupils is still acknowledged by present-day wood engravers. GPF

see also WOOD ENGRAVING

BFG, The (1982) One of ROALD DAHL's sunnier and more inventive novels, with the audacious use of the United Kingdom's reigning monarch as a character. The many felicitous ideas – dream-catching, the giants' ultra-sensitive hearing, the linguistic convolutions of the Big Friendly Giant – are matched by a cheerful vulgarity – notably the BFG's predilection for 'whizzpopping'. The central character, Sophie, is typical of Dahl's resourceful heroines. Journalists applied the Big Friendly Giant image to Dahl himself. PLH

Bhatty, Margaret 1930– Indian fiction writer. A sense of commitment is the reason for Bhatty's persistence in writing for children in spite of the low remuneration and the unsympathetic attitude of some Indian publishers. As a humanist she prefers to stand outside all traditional belief systems, believing that the conscience is a faculty that can be cultivated, that it is the rational outcome of an educative process. Reasonableness is therefore, to her, the best approach to life's problems. These concerns pervade her work. She has written extensively for children since 1976, starting with *The Adventures of Bhim the Bold* (1976), a traditional FANTASY with a male as the hero. She tries to reverse stereotypes by making girls take the initiative, as in *The Mystery of the Zamorin's Treasure* (1982) and *The Secret of Sickle-Moon Mountain* (1994). *Zamorin's Treasure* also has valuable background information about the wildlife of the Laccadive Islands, the history of the Portuguese explorers, and the early European trade with India. Her books display a rare secular spirit that transcends religious boundaries and emphasises the human capacity for compassionate relationships, as in *Travelling Companions* (1982). She has also written a successful SCIENCE FICTION thriller, *The Evil Empire* (1992). MBh

bias Human beings are inevitably inclined towards certain attitudes, and authors often reveal theirs by uncritical acceptance of opinions held by the majority of their contemporaries. Children's books are as likely to be biased as any other literature, and attempts to produce totally impartial writing are doomed to failure. Nevertheless, some forms of bias are probably more dangerous or offensive than others, and since the 1970s many attempts have been made to alert authors, publishers and readers to the desirability of avoiding overt expressions of prejudice. Although some of these endeavours have been regarded as over-reactions, recent children's authors are on the whole likely to portray society more fairly. However, bias may arise when certain sectors of the community – notably females, disabled or handicapped people, the elderly, those of a particular class, ethnicity, nation, culture, sexual orientation, political persuasion or religion – are depicted in, or excluded from, either text or illustration.

Gender bias has frequently led to plots in which most of the interesting adventures are performed by boys, while the girls are shown to conform to the stereotype of females as reliant on male assistance. In E. NESBIT's work, however, there is sometimes a clash between what is explicitly said about the female characters ('girls are so much softer and weaker than we are', says the doctor in *THE RAILWAY CHILDREN*, 1906) and the active and resourceful way in which Bobbie and the females in Nesbit's other books behave. There has also been concern about female characters in FAIRY TALES, and many recent writers and illustrators (such as ALISON LURIE, ROBERT MUNSCH, CATHERINE STORR, MARTIN WADDELL and ANGELA CARTER) have provided alternative views, particularly of princesses. BABETTE COLE, Ann Jungman and Gail Carson Levine have also depicted strong females and sensitive males in their fairy tale rewrites, thus addressing the gender bias of authors who consistently portray females as weepy and passive, and males as exhibiting an unemotional stoicism. SUSAN COOPER in *Dawn of Fear* (1972) and her many FANTASY works has emphasised sensitivity in both males and females. She has been criticised for producing unassertive females who are excluded from the interesting adventures of the story. But Cooper's work also provokes the question: what is an 'interesting' adventure – or what is an 'adventure'? Is it the same for males as for females? Is it the same for all males, or all females?

A remaining bastion of gender bias is to be found today in some ANIMAL FICTION, for such books often have a preponderance of male characters. Richard Adams, whose *WATERSHIP DOWN* (1972) was criticised for presenting the female rabbits as more passive than the males, has in *Tales from Watership Down* (1996) portrayed some dominant does, but the message still seems to be that females need males more than males need females.

Evidence of eurocentric bias in writings of the past is abundant. The imperialism of such British writers as BALLANTYNE, HENTY, KIPLING and HAGGARD is apparent to readers with some knowledge of history, while the often blatant racial prejudice in children's popular fiction by ENID BLYTON, W.E. Johns (see *BIGGLES* SERIES), ROALD DAHL and Hugh Lofting (see *DOCTOR DOLITTLE* SERIES) has also been frequently analysed. More recent editions of these authors have revealed successful attempts to change offending words or pictures, but older copies remain in existence.

Helen Bannerman's *LITTLE BLACK SAMBO* (1905) is an especially telling case of eurocentrism. Here a family supposedly from India reveals a curious mixture of physical and cultural traits: straight hair, large accentuated lips, an African bandana for the mother, and a trio of rhyming family names – Mambo, Jambo and Sambo – that spanned Spanish, African and French origins. The child's name was unfortunately adopted by white supremacists in America as a denigrating term for black males generally. Bannerman, having lived in West Africa as a child, the daughter of a Scottish clergyman, and in India as an adult, the wife of a physician, mixed African and Indian cultural traits when she created her pictures. She also placed tigers of northern India in her setting of southern India. Despite all its incongruities, the book underwent numerous reprintings – for what child could resist tigers turning into melted butter? The book had delicious colours and word patterns (who could resist purple shoes with crimson soles and crimson linings?). In 1931 RCA Victor produced a musical rendition, which may explain why some adult readers reminisce fondly about the book. For those who are less nostalgic, there are two recently revised editions: JULIUS LESTER's inventive *Sam and the Tigers* (1990) and Fred Marcellino's elegant *The Story of Little Babaji* (1996).

Bias in INFORMATION BOOKS can be particularly dangerous as prejudice may be masquerading under the guise of fact, and young readers are more likely to be alert to the creative role of the author in fiction than to the selective role of compilers of textbooks, atlases and encyclopedias. The bias in many children's reference books published in the first half of the 20th century is easy to detect today: ARTHUR MEE'S *CHILDREN'S ENCYCLOPEDIA* (1925) includes a colour plate headed 'Brothers and Sisters are we all', portraying about 50 children in national dress, with a transparent overlay indicating their racial identities; in the foreground are large depictions of European children, while a few tiny 'negroes' and 'hottentots' represent a huge section of the human race. *Jolly Families* (1946) by David Seth-Smith, 'the Zoo man of the BBC', after some descriptions and grotesque pictures of 'Eskimos', 'Negroes' and 'Red Indians', goes straight on to portray monkeys and other animals as if there were no significant distinction between the 'subordinate' humans and the lower species.

Since many children's authors, even today, tend to come from a middle-class background, it has often been difficult for them to avoid bias in favour of behaviour and standards they take for granted. Despite her obvious good intentions, EVE GARNETT'S *THE FAMILY FROM ONE END STREET* (1937) is nearly as patronising and comic in its treatment of the Ruggles family as ARTHUR RANSOME's admittedly comic portrayal of the subservience of a policeman confronted by the imperious middle-class Nancy Blackett. A similar situation prevails in RUTH SAWYER'S *Roller Skates* (1936), in which the heroine's upper-class status and liberated condition enable her to mingle freely with a variety of New York City residents during the early years of the 20th century and to offer her liberal sympathies to them. Lucinda helps such deserving cases as the Irish policeman, the Polish violinist, the Jewish theatre family, and a Chinese princess. Readers lamenting their plight might overlook the fact that the black servant is given no last name and no problem of her own for Lucinda to solve.

With the social changes after World War II, some authors – such as PENELOPE LIVELY in *Going Back* (1975) and ANTHONY BROWNE in *A WALK IN THE PARK* (1977) – have seriously tried to supply a critique of class prejudice, but such attempts may often fail to be detected by their child audience. How many readers of VIRGINIA HAMILTON's novels see that she is examining class differences among African Americans in *M.C. Higgins the Great* (1974) and *The House of Dies Drear* (1968), or that she is playing on class, cultural, regional and language differences within one African-American extended family in *Second Cousins* (1998)?

Bias in the representation of disabled people (see DISABILITY) is also evident in children's literature from the past, ranging from the saintly 'cripples' of CHARLES DICKENS and SUSAN COOLIDGE to R.L. STEVENSON's villainous Blind Pew and Long John Silver. Seldom until the latter half of the 20th century, notably in the work of ROSEMARY SUTCLIFF, have authors portrayed disabled people as individuals. More recently, JEAN URE and IAN STRACHAN have featured several kinds of physical disability, while Rachel Anderson has tackled the often more delicate subject of children with severe learning difficulties. ELAINE KONIGSBURG has revealed a particular interest in mental and physical illness in her many books, and Virginia Hamilton has described families dealing with aging relatives and critical illness.

If bias has always been present in books for young people, is there any great need for concern about it? Debate has focused on what happens when girls and children from minority groups are continually reading literature in which characters resembling themselves are either subordinate to white Anglo-Saxon males or totally absent. Although readers often identify with characters different from themselves in appearance and behaviour, critics have argued that never seeing someone like themselves in a leading role may affect readers' expectations about life. The effect on young readers, in particular, may be considerable. Additionally, some biased literature may give offence to readers whose ethnic or religious group is tactlessly portrayed. The effect on readers from a group consistently portrayed as powerless also needs acknowledgement. American children's authors have often portrayed Native Americans as cruel, sadistic, physically ugly and subhuman, and Asian Americans as generic non-persons with comical speech patterns, hairstyles or behaviours. African American children have often had to read books in which white supremacy was an unquestioned 'given', and Hispanic and Latino children in America have had, until recently, very few books to call their own.

The late 1970s saw a big increase in the awareness of race and gender bias in children's literature. In Britain in 1975, the Children's Rights' Workshop founded the 'Other Award', in an attempt to encourage writers to produce books without race, gender or class bias. The American Library Association initiated the Coretta Scott King Award in 1969 for distinguished work by African American authors and illustrators, and the Pura Belpre Award in 1996 for Latino writers and illustrators (see AWARDS AND MEDALS).

Accompanying both British and American equality legislation of this period, many books and sets of guidelines were published with the intention of alerting those involved with children's books to the effect of problematic illustrations, plot, characterisation and language. Inevitably, allegations were made that this smacked of censorship. Among the books which became controversial at this stage were William Armstrong's *SOUNDER* (1969), Theodore Taylor's *THE CAY* (1970), PAULA FOX's *The Slave Dancer* (1973) and BERNARD ASHLEY's *THE TROUBLE WITH DONOVAN CROFT* (1974), all written by white authors and initially highly acclaimed for their powerful condemnation of racism but later censured because the black characters were seen as too passive. This divergence of opinion highlights a characteristic problem faced by writers trying to overcome bias – that the very process in which they are active is sometimes later directed against their own work, as not having gone far enough.

Another problem faced by these and other authors is whether or not to include racist or sexist language or attitudes. MARK TWAIN's *Huckleberry Finn* (1884) continues to evoke controversy in American schools for use of the word 'nigger' and for Huck's unconscious acceptance of institutionalised racism. The remarks of Mary Lennox in FRANCES HODGSON BURNETT's *THE SECRET GARDEN* (1910) have, more recently, come under scrutiny by the East-Indian American child character in Mitali Perkins's *The Sunita Experiment* (1993), her insights having been drawn from Perkins's own response to *A Secret Garden* in childhood.

Although provocative language may be necessary for authenticity, the very appearance of such terms in a book may seem to legitimise their use; and so it is important that child readers see clearly the way that bigoted characters' experiences are broadened or their awareness heightened by exposure to a different perspective, as in the case of MILDRED TAYLOR's white child character Jeremy Simms in her *Logan* family saga. Difficulties arise at times in the production of HISTORICAL FICTION, especially since well-intentioned readers may not always be aware of their own preconditioned attitudes. Taylor's depiction of white supremacist behaviour in the American South of the 1930s has at times evoked defensive responses from white readers who have never confronted their own deep-seated cultural attitudes or who are facing for the first time lamentable facts of their own national history. Devices such as figurative language and the use of an unreliable narrator may also be misunderstood by young readers, who will therefore be resistant to the way in which the author may be intending to guide their sympathies.

Until recently there have been fewer attempts to remove from children's books any bias against elderly or disabled people, although during the 1980s there were attempts in Britain to portray gay individuals in a more positive light, which received strong criticism. The focus of the controversy was Susanne Bosche's *Jenny Lives with Eric and Martin* (1983); interestingly, a more explicit depiction of a gay relationship in AIDAN CHAMBERS's *Dance on My Grave* (1982), for older readers, attracted much less attention. In earlier decades in America, authors disposed of gay characters by the end of the story, just as they killed off fallen women in adult literature. In the 1990s, however, JACQUELINE WOODSON's work, which sometimes focuses on lesbian relationships, has been well received.

It would be idle to claim that writing today is free of bias. There have been, in the work of many distinguished white authors and illustrators, disturbing examples of stereotypes, caricatured artwork, cultural inaccuracies in pictorial details, unconvincing narrative voice, and condescending or superficial treatment of the ethnicity portrayed, when outsiders have coopted the insiders' stories. Some would suggest that there is now a bias against outsiders of particular races and ethnicities writing or illustrating books for insider cultural groups. In fact outsiders have been successful in such efforts in a few recent cases. The notable picturebooks of PAUL GOBLE depicting Native American culture, those of EZRA JACK KEATS, Ann Grifalconi and RACHAEL ISADORA portraying inner-city children of African American heritage, and the poetry of ARNOLD ADOFF often featuring children of bi-cultural heritage, all come to mind. The work of English writers GERALDINE KAYE and BEVERLEY NAIDOO, focusing on African children, has been similarly well received.

Sometimes an author's attempt to eliminate one form of bias succeeds but the book fails in authenticity, as in the case of *Amazing Grace* (1991) and *Boundless Grace* (1995), both by MARY HOFFMAN and CAROLINE BINCH. In the first book, the authors deal ably with a female child's quest to fulfil the role she chooses for herself – to dance the part of Peter Pan in the school play. But neither author nor illustrator is of African American or African Caribbean heritage and there is no exploration of ethnic differences in these books. No ethnic world view and no cultural references are built into the texture of the book itself – its focus, emphasis or subject matter. In the sequel, Grace (supposedly an American black child in the American edition and an English black child in the English edition) travels to Gambia to meet her father's family, but the author focuses only on observable details of surface features, rather than on values, beliefs, traditions and world view of Gambian and African American or African Caribbean life. Hoffman's Grace is a generic child whose identity changes whenever the book crosses a national border, and the books about her treat child readers of African ancestry in a similar generic manner. The bias here resides not only in the high-handed way that white publishers of children's books treat ethnic groups, but also in the way they treat child readers generally; for literary quality – in plot, conflict, theme, and especially depth of characterisation – suffers when people are treated in generic ways.

Children's literature can certainly not expect to change society by portraying people, idealistically, in roles that they are unlikely to hold. On the other hand, it does have the responsibility to respect cultural differences and to explore cultural identities with the breadth and depth they deserve. Over-enthusiastic measures against bias may be self-defeating, and in many cases they have certainly led to resentment and counter-reaction. Children cannot be insulated from prejudice, stereotypes, misunderstandings and superficial thinking, so probably the most important single aspect is the need to educate young readers to recognise bias – in themselves, in literature, in society, and so take it into account in their reading. Books that display bias may even be a useful tool in this process.

PAP, NM

Bible stories Prose retellings of the Holy Scriptures edited for different readerships. Bible stories – or children's Bibles as they have often been called – have formed an integral part of Catholic, Protestant and Jewish religious education for centuries. Editing inevitably incorporates contemporaneous social and religious expectations and results in broad variability in the telling of individual stories. For example, in Bible stories for children 23 different sequences of events have been cited to account for the parting of the Red Sea in the Exodus story of Moses leading the Israelites out of Egypt. Although at any given date Protestants, Catholics and Jews have told the Moses story differently, variant tellings of this story, like other Old and New Testament narratives, have smoothly crossed denominational borders from one generation to another.

With roots deep in the Middle Ages in the *Historia Scholastica* of Peter Comestor (c.1170), Bible stories reemerged with Martin Luther's 'Passionalbüchlein' (1529) and began to flourish with Nicolas Fontaine's (French-language) *History of the Old and New Testament* (1670), Johann Hübner's (German-language) *Twice Fifty-Two Bible Histories* (1714), and in England with JOHN NEWBERY's *Holy Bible Abridged* (1755 (New Testament); 1757 (Old and New Testament)).

The first book of Bible stories to be printed in the United States was *The Children's Bible* by 'N.H.' in Philadelphia in 1763. Its extended title accurately defined and described the genre's purpose: *An History of the holy Scriptures. In which, the several Passages of the Old and New Testament are laid down in a Method never before attempted; being reduced to the tender capacities of the little*

Readers, by a lively and striking Abstract, so as, under God, to make those excellent Books take such a firm Hold of their young Minds and Memories and leave such Impressions there, both of Moral and Religious Virtue, as no Accidents of their future Lives will ever be able to blot out . . . The book claimed a novelty it did not possess, for the Genesis stories of Fontaine's Bible had already been translated into English, and besides Newbery's *Holy Bible Abridged*, two other native English productions already existed: *A Compendious History* (1726) and *The Bible in Miniature* (1727).

American Protestant readers had little taste for Bible stories for children until the 1780s, when Newbery's *Holy Bible Abridged* was pirated by one Massachusetts publisher after another. It enjoyed great success in America in both full and abbreviated versions, with or without illustrations. In small 16° (sextodecimo) format or as a tiny 64°, it was produced easily on local presses from Brattleboro, Vermont to Wilmington, Delaware and penetrated every corner of the American Northeast. Its text was often contracted, and its title varied: *The History of the Holy Bible*, *The Bible in Miniature*, *A Concise History of the Holy Bible*, *The History of the Bible* or sometimes the original title. In short, wherever a handpress existed, a version of *The Holy Bible Abridged* was sure to follow.

Initially undifferentiatedly Protestant, Bible stories in America were soon joined by a Catholic collection in 1784, Joseph Reeve's *The History of the Old and New Testament*. A new translation of Fontaine's Bible stories, it served the growing population of English-speaking Catholics who had emigrated to the United States, and remained in use until the early 20th century.

Non-English-speaking Protestant immigrants also required Bible stories for their English-speaking children. The first was a translation of the Hübner Bible histories that was printed wherever large numbers of German immigrants settled: Harrisburg (1826), Philadelphia (until the 1830s), and St. Louis (until 1878). Hübner's Bible stories were followed by further German Bible stories, as well as by Greek, Norwegian and Swedish versions such as *Etthundra fyra bibliska historien* (1881), *Volrath Vogts Bibelhistorie: me nogle foran-dringer* (1882), and *Solstralen: textblad for de minsta barnen*. Until the late 19th century, American and Canadian English-language books of Bible stories were reprints of English originals. Thus MRS SARAH TRIMMER's *Abridgment of Scripture History* was available in 1804, and *Mamma's Bible Stories* appeared on both sides of the Atlantic in 1855 and was still in print 30 years later.

Bible stories for Jewish children written in English made their first appearance in the 1880s, when Sakolki's Hebrew Book Store in New York City offered the 84-page *Scripture history: simply arranged for the use of Jewish schools*. It began a tradition of Bible stories for Jewish children in the vernacular that has remained vigorous to the present day, with authors such as Hyman Goldin, Scholem Asch, Lenore Cohen, Ruth Samuels, Sidney Brichto and Shirley Newman.

Denominationally specific Protestant children's Bibles co-existed during most of the 20th century with supra-confessional bestsellers like *The Golden Bible*, whose advisers included Catholic, Protestant and Jewish clergy. A further homogenisation of story traditions has occurred in conjunction with the internationalisation of publishing houses (see also PUBLISHING AND PUBLISHERS). As a consequence, many 'American' Bible stories are in fact translations of Dutch, Italian, German or French originals.

Throughout its history the Bible story genre has been irresistible to established writers: HANNAH MORE produced a sacred drama about Joseph and his brothers (1811); SAMUEL GOODRICH (as 'Peter Parley') produced a *Book of Bible Stories* in 1834, as did the populariser Henrik Willem van Loon in 1923, the poet WALTER DE LA MARE in 1929, the novelist Pearl Buck in 1971, the public preacher Norman Vincent Peale in 1973, the pop singer Pat Boone in 1984, and the children's TELEVISION personality SHARI LEWIS in 1986. Equally eager to guide the young were many anonymous authors, who identified themselves modestly with pen names such 'A Lady of Cincinnati' (1834) or simply, 'A Mother' (1846).

A consequential American innovation in the field of Bible stories was M.C. Gaines's 1942 COMIC-STRIP in the New York *Sunday Herald*. Serialised in seven installments, Gaines's comic-strip Bible stories sold millions of copies and provided a prototype that was further developed in the 1980s, in France by Larousse and in Germany by the Deutsche Bibelgesellschaft. RBB

bibliotherapy The practice of recommending appropriate works of fiction for children experiencing social or personal problems (such as drug addiction, abuse or bereavement) in the expectation that accounts of fictional children coping with similar difficulties – followed by discussion of the issues – will help young readers. The practice was especially prevalent in the USA during the 1980s. VW

Bierhorst, John 1936– American author, editor, translator and musicologist. Bierhorst was born in Boston, Massachusetts, and raised in Ohio. He attended Cornell University. As an adult, Bierhorst became fascinated with Indian culture after a trip to Peru. His first book, *The Fire Plume* (1969), has been followed by collections of myths, songs, stories and riddles of the native people of North and South America, and he has received eight ALA Notable Book awards, as well as a National Endowment of the Arts Fellowship and various research grants from the

National Endowment for the Humanities. In *A Cry from the Earth* (1979), the regional differences among Native Americans are studied through their dance, instrumentation and vocalisation. Bierhorst explores their music both as a unique art form and as a cultural artefact. *The Naked Bear, Folktales of the Iroquois* (1987), illustrated by Dirk Zimmer, retells the stories of the tribes of New York and southern Canada. These stories are particularly attractive to children with their happy endings of virtue overcoming the powers of evil. In *Dancing Fox, Arctic Tales* (1997), stories about TRICKSTERS and SUPERHEROES are illustrated by Inuit artist Mary K. Okeena. JRG

see also MUSIC AND STORY

big books Books reissued in large-format editions to enable teachers in primary schools to share them with groups or whole classes of children. In the United Kingdom from the late 1990s, big books came to be associated with the 'literacy hour'. The Walker Big Books series includes PICTUREBOOKS by MARTIN WADDELL, MICHAEL ROSEN and JILL MURPHY, and, for more confident readers, chapter books by JAN MARK and ANNE FINE. VW

see also PUBLISHING AND PUBLISHERS

'Big Five, The' Collective title given to a highly successful group of weekly story papers published by D.C. Thomson & Co. of Dundee. *Adventure* (first published 1921), *Rover* (1922), *Wizard* (1922), *Skipper* (1930) and *Hotspur* (1933) challenged the domination of the schoolboy market by Amalgamated Press's *Magnet* and *Gem*. Only *Skipper* did not survive the paper shortages of World War II.

Where the Amalgamated Press papers chronicled an unchanging public school world throughout their 30 years of publication, Thomson's readers escaped to the ranges of the Wild West, the Sahara with the Foreign Legion or Lost Cities in the Jungle. Their heroes regularly tangled with monsters or robots. Closer to home, stories featured county cricket or league soccer, while the pupils of boarding schools such as *Hotspur's* Red Circle were more like their devoted readers than the chaps of Amalgamated's St Jim's or St Frank's.

In 1939, George Orwell attacked all the weeklies for their élitism and their ridicule of the habits of foreigners. The childlike eccentricities of the 'Nigs' on Spadger's Isle continued on the cover of *Wizard* until 1950, but, as if to contradict Orwell, anti-establishment figures flourished in the Thomson papers during and after the war. Alf Tupper, 'The Tough of the Track', worked as an apprentice welder, trained on fish and chips, and delighted in getting the better of the toffs from the local athletic academy. Tom Smith attended Lipstone College, but as a scholarship boy from the backstreets of Ironborough. Matt Braddock VC, *Rover's* daring flying ace, was a non-conforming Sergeant with no time for toffee-nosed officers. Wilson, the Wonder Athlete, rejected society entirely; well over 100 years old, he lived as a recluse on the Yorkshire Moors, emerging only to don his old black running costume to defeat all-comers.

Romance was of no concern to readers of the Big Five. Apart from a brief flirtation with a 'damsels in distress' series in the early *Rover*, girls played almost no part in the papers. The advertisements suggest stronger interests in model trains, stamps, bikes and Mars Bars.

The Thomson papers have rarely been credited with the part they played in encouraging boys to read substantial tracts of prose. A single issue usually contained around 40,000 words, and many boys devoured two or three papers a week. The stories were well-shaped if formulaic, economically written and accurate in detail; a reader could learn the technical mysteries of spin bowling, for example, from 'It's Wickets That Count'.

By the mid-1970s, readers were accustomed to more visual media, and comic strips increasingly crowded out the prose stories; finally, the titles were absorbed into other comics where some of the old stories reappeared in graphic format. Big Five heroes such as the detective Dixon Hawke (who bore a close resemblance to Sexton Blake) did not hesitate to punch a crook on the jaw, but they never countenanced violence for its own sake, and detested any form of cheating. In an issue of *Buddy* in 1982, Tom Smith cut off part of the course to win a cross-country race at Lipstone; his 1940s incarnation would rather have cut off a limb. GPF

Big Golden Books see *GOLDEN BOOKS*

Biggles and **Worrals** Hero and heroine of 102 novels, the creations of Captain W.E. Johns. In 1930 this former British pilot founded the magazine *Popular Flying*, in whose pages first appeared the adventures of Biggles, or to give him his full name, Major James Bigglesworth, D.S.O., M.C. An intrepid flyer, brilliant detective and fearless adventurer, he was the leader of an intimate group of friends composed of Captain Algernon Lacy ('Algy'), Flying Officer 'Ginger' Hebblethwaite, and Lord 'Bertie' Lissie. Slightly in awe of Biggles, whose authoritarian style included regularly lecturing his attentive group on matters as diverse as the habits of elephants or the history of piracy, everyone always offered unfailing support to each other in their frequent moments of shared danger. While never given to excessive violence, Biggles himself was a tough proposition, though also, at times, a sensitive, rather lonely individual. Happy to do his duty, he always preferred working in the background to any vulgar show of ostentatious bravery.

The outbreak of World War II saw him and his friends in action against the German foe. For Biggles, this was the renewal of a vendetta carried over from 1914–18 arising from his many dog-fights pitting his Sopwith Camel against the Prussian ace pilot Erich von Stalhein. Battle of Britain pilots, often little more than late adolescents themselves, also occasionally read these stirring, action-packed stories. In 1941 Johns created a young heroine in response to an Air Ministry drive to encourage recruitment into the Women's Auxiliary Air Force. This was Worrals of the WAAF, in fact Flight Officer Joan Worralson. With her chum, Section Officer Betty 'Frecks' Lovell, both were qualified pilots who ferried planes from the manufacturers out to squadrons sometimes fighting abroad. Very much a new woman ahead of her time, Worrals was highly skilled in her own right and always properly impatient with any sign of masculine condescension. Her last adventure, *Worrals Investigates*, appeared in 1950.

A bestseller topped only by ENID BLYTON, Johns came in for criticism in the 1960s for some of his attitudes. He had, for example, a particular dislike for racial mixing, with Biggles reserving biting comments for those he habitually described as 'half-breeds'. On a more harmless level, the Edwardian slang Biggles was apt to use ('By Jingo!') began to sound ridiculous, as did his penchant for drinking lemonade – suggested to Johns early on by his publisher as preferable to his consuming whisky. The last story, *Biggles Sees Too Much*, appeared in 1970 and showed signs of age. But in his prime Biggles, and to a lesser extent Worrals, gave enormous pleasure to young readers in search of lively adventure and uncomplicated heroics, set against a variety of exciting backgrounds and always at some stage involving aerial dog-fights of breath-taking audacity. Those many children who at some stage enjoyed nothing so much as running along with arms outstretched making loud aeroplane noises found in Biggles the very hero they were always looking for. NT

see also WAR STORIES

Bilgewater (1976) Novel by JANE GARDAM about a solitary and intelligent girl growing up in a boys' boarding school. Marigold is known to the school only by her relationship with her father, who is a housemaster. As a teenager Marigold becomes more involved with the life of the school, and by the end of the novel she has become not only satisfyingly central to the well-being of both her father and the school, but has also retained her own academic individuality, eventually becoming the head of a Cambridge college. First published as a children's novel, *Bilgewater* now appears on its publisher's adult lists. KA

Bilibin, Ivan 1876–1942 Russian illustrator. Bilibin's work was published in the UK in the 1970s in translations of fairy and folk tales by Alexander Afanasiev and stories by A.N. Pushkin. The strongest influences discernible in his ILLUSTRATIONS are Art Nouveau, especially WALTER CRANE, and Russian peasant art, as can be seen in the rich colouring, patterning and decorated borders. *The Tale of Tsar Sultan* (Pushkin, 1905), a narrative in rhyming couplets, has an intensity of colouring in its ornate illustrations that derives from early lithography. JAG

Bill and Ben, the Flowerpot Men see ROBIN; see also TELEVISION; *WATCH WITH MOTHER*

Bill's New Frock (1989) Smarties prize-winning novel by ANNE FINE which takes a humorous look at gender stereotyping in primary schools. Bill wakes up one morning to find that he is a girl. His mother sends him to school in a pretty pink frock and Bill has a horrible day. Being a girl is limitation enough, but it is the dress itself and not his gender which presents the real problem – 'If this was the sort of thing that kept happening to you if you came to school in a frilly pink frock, no wonder all the girls wore jeans.' KA

***Billabong* series** Fifteen novels by Australian MARY GRANT BRUCE, published in book form between 1910 and 1942. With the notable exception of *From Billabong to London* (1915), *Jim and Wally* (1916) and *Captain Jim* (1919), which use World War I as a focus, the books are set on 'Billabong', a sheep station in rural Victoria, country which Bruce knew well. *A Little Bush Maid* (1910), which introduces the characters, was originally serialised between 1905 and 1907 in the *Leader*. Other well-known titles include *Mates at Billabong* (1911) and *Billabong's Daughter* (1924). The books involve the Linton family, father David who provides a role model for them all, and son and daughter Jim and Norah. The close relationship between brother and sister is a feature of Bruce's work. Also becoming a part of the family very early on is Jim's friend Wally Meadows, who subsequently marries Norah. Other important characters who appear throughout the Billabong books are the housekeeper Brownie, Irish stockman Murty O'Toole, Chinese vegetable gardener Lee Wing, Hogg, the Scottish flower-gardener and Black Billy, the Aboriginal rouseabout.

This series did much to establish notions of heroism and comradeship amongst its readers. Jim and Wally are tall, laconic, courageous, patriotic, hard working, protective of women and gentlemanly – values they also admire in others. Rural life is seen as the best way of inculcating these values. Norah loves the outdoor life but also learns more traditional female pursuits from Brownie. The Linton family is always happiest at

Billabong, which remains largely unchanged throughout the series. The books retained their readership for many years, although from a contemporary perspective they now seem conservative, with unacceptable attitudes about class, the role of women, and people other than white Anglo-Saxons. MH

Billings, Hammatt Nineteenth-century American illustrator. His work appears in the first edition of Harriet Beecher Stowe's *UNCLE TOM'S CABIN* and in NATHANIEL HAWTHORNE's *A Wonderbook for Boys and Girls* (1852) and *Tanglewood Tales* (1853), in both of which classic tales are retold, according to Hawthorne, in the stead of 'classical coldness which is as repellant as the touch of marble'. Billings's ILLUSTRATIONS, while effective in context, somehow fail to rescue the two volumes from Hawthorne's dreary framework, in which a young student tells the stories to children with names like Primrose and Sweet Fern. Billings also illustrated some of the six *Little Purdy* books (from 1863) by SOPHIE MAY. Intended for younger children, Billings's artwork here decorates the antics of a little girl who climbs ladders to get to Heaven and plays doctor with her little sister Dorothy. By responding to these three radically different textual requirements, Billings demonstrated the artistic versatility for which he was renowned. KSB

Billy Bunter see ANNUALS; *GREYFRIARS*; CHARLES HAMILTON; see also LATIN LESSONS AND LATIN MASTERS; SCHOOL STORIES; TELEVISION

Billy the Kid 1855?–81 Nickname of Henry McCarty who also used the name William H. Bonney as an alias. He was one of several cowboy outlaws involved in the Lincoln County (New Mexico) War among cattle ranchers who were vying for political power and control of government beef contracts. He was killed by Deputy Sheriff Pat Garrett after escaping jail. Although not the brutal murderer portrayed by his enemies, neither was he the innocent and misunderstood youth portrayed in popular fiction, such as Edmund Fable's *Billy the Kid, The New Mexico Outlaw: Or, The Bold Bandit of the West* (1881) or the more recent *Anything for Billy* (1988) by Larry McMurtry, or in the film *Billy the Kid* (MGM, 1930, 1941). EBD

Binch, Caroline 1947– Binch is notable for her realistic settings, confident use of colour and layout, and convincing portraits. The latter are frequently of black characters, as in ROSA GUY's *Paris, Pee Wee and Big Dog* (1984), in GRACE NICHOLS'S *COME ON INTO MY TROPICAL GARDEN* (1988) and in her first PICTUREBOOK, *Billy the Great* (Rosa Guy, 1991). *Amazing Grace* and its sequel, *Grace & Family* (MARY HOFFMAN, 1991, 1995) are internationally successful, and *Hue Boy* (R.P. Mitchell, 1992) was winner in the 0–5 category of the SMARTIES AWARD for 1993. *Gregory Cool* (1994) and *Since Dad Left* (1998) are her own picturebooks. JAG

biography and autobiography Biography for children in English may be said to begin with John Foxe's *Book of Martyrs* (1563), James Janeway's *A TOKEN FOR CHILDREN* (1632), and JOHN NEWBERY's edition of *Plutarch's Lives* for children (1762–3). These earlier books were followed by Victorian contributions such as CHARLOTTE YONGE's *Book of Golden Deeds of all Times* (1864), a collection of 'soul-stirring deeds that give life and glory to the record of events', MARY LOUISA MOLESWORTH's *Stories of the Saints for Children* (1892), and WILLIAM CANTON's *A Child's Book of Saints* (1898), published in the United States as *W.V.'s Golden Legend*. In the same period, Andrew Lang wrote biographies of Charles Edward Stuart, John Knox and Joan of Arc.

Many notable writers have produced biographies for children, including LAURA E. RICHARDS (on Florence Nightingale and Abigail Adams), ALBERT BIGELOW PAINE (on MARK TWAIN), GEOFFREY TREASE (on D.H. Lawrence, Elizabeth I and LORD BYRON) and JILL PATON WALSH (on Grace Darling). JEAN FRITZ, MILTON MELTZER, Rhoda Blumberg, JUDITH ST. GEORGE and RUSSELL FREEDMAN are among the most highly regarded contemporary American writers of biography for children.

The genre received increased attention when Freedman's *Lincoln: A Photobiography* (1987), a book as strongly written and emotionally compelling as any novel, became the fifth biography to win the Newbery Medal for the most distinguished contribution to American literature for children. The previous winning biographies were CORNELIA MEIGS's *Invincible Louisa* (1934), JAMES DAUGHERTY's *Daniel Boone* (1940), ELIZABETH YATES's *Amos Fortune, Free Man* (1951), and JEAN LATHAM's *Carry On Mr. Bowditch* (1956).

Since the 1970s standards of accuracy and authenticity have risen, and the range of subjects considered suitable for children and the frankness with which they are handled have increased. Yet, as Judith Lechner points out in a study of biographies of Pocahontas and John James Audubon, 'Accuracy in Biographies for Children' (*New Advocate* 10), problems remain, including carelessness and oversimplification, inadequate data, unreliable sources and taboos. She concludes that 'one of the most valuable lessons children can learn from reading biographies is that "getting the facts straight" is a continuous and exciting process'.

Fully 75 per cent of all biographies written for children today are published in series, a few of which are excellent, but many of which are not. As Leo Zanderer has commented: 'One feels the diligent work of scissors

Illustration by Reginald Birch for *St Nicholas Magazine* (1892).

and paste, but not a reflective mind at work' ('Evaluating Contemporary Children's Biography', LION AND UNICORN 5). Many of these, however, appeal to the interests of children, especially the well-illustrated small biographies of sports heroes and entertainers. Many children who have difficulty reading are willing to tackle these simply written books about someone who interests them.

One old-fashioned series that continues to be reprinted, and read and loved by at least some children (or their parents), despite, or perhaps because of, a degree of fictionalisation no longer acceptable to most critics, is the *Childhood of Famous Americans* series. Books with titles such as *Merriweather Lewis, Boy Explorer* (1962, 1997), *Abe Lincoln, Frontier Boy* (1932), and *Jane Addams, Little Lame Girl* (1944) emphasise their subjects' childhoods and the seeds of greatness revealed therein.

Jo Carr in *Matters of Fact* (1972) recommends autobiography as an alternative to badly written biographies, although the veracity of autobiography is also unreliable. Many children's writers and illustrators, including ERIC BLEGVAD, ERIC CARLE, BEVERLY CLEARY, ROALD DAHL, TRINA SCHART HYMAN, LEO LIONNI, GARY PAULSEN, CYNTHIA RYLANT and MARGOT ZEMACH, have produced engaging autobiographies.

Recent biographies and autobiographies have taken increasingly interesting and innovative approaches and formats. There are PICTUREBOOKS such as CATHERINE BRIGHTON's *Nijinsky: Scenes from the Childhood of a Great Dancer* (1989), Diane Stanley's *Peter the Great* (1986), William Joyce's *William Joyce Scrapbook* (1997), and PETER SIS's *The Starry Messenger* (1996). There have also been numerous illustrated biographies focused on particular incidents in the lives of ordinary people, such as *Orphan Train Rider: One Boy's True Story* by Andrea Warren (1996), *Hiding from the Nazis* (1997) by David A. Adler, illustrated by Karen Ritz, and *Passage to Freedom: The Sugihara Story* (1997) by Ken Mochizuki, illustrated by Dom Lee. Judith St George traces the friendship between Alexander Graham Bell and Helen Keller in *Dear Dr. Bell . . . Your Friend, Helen Keller* (1992), well-illustrated with photographs, and PAUL FLEISCHMAN's *Townsend's Warbler* (1992) chronicles the converging journeys of Townsend and the bird that bears his name. From non-English-speaking countries have come books that combine biography with information on the work and the historical and physical contexts of their subjects' lives. Christina Bjork and Lena Anderson's *Linnea in Monet's Garden* (1987), originally published in Sweden, and Claudio Pescio's and Sergio's *Master of Art* series such as *Rembrandt and Seventeenth-Century Holland* (1995), originally published in Italy, have been extremely successful. LH

Birch, Reginald B(athurst) 1856–1943 Illustrator born in London. Birch studied painting in Munich where he learned German pen-draughtsmanship. He settled in the United States in 1871 and illustrated for *ST NICHOLAS* as well as for many newspapers and other magazines. His drawings for FRANCES HODGSON BURNETT's *LITTLE LORD FAUNTLEROY* (1886) and *SARA CREWE* (1888) brought him fame and commissions to illustrate hundreds of other books, including JOHN BENNETT's *Master Skylark* (1897). His drawing style declined in popularity during the 1920s but later came back into vogue with his ILLUSTRATIONS for books like LOUIS UNTERMEYER's edition of stories from Gilbert and Sullivan's operas, *The Last Pirate* (1934), OGDEN NASH's *Bad Parent's Book of Verse*

'Bidibidi squeezed into Maxine's kennel.' Illustration from *Bidibidi* by Gavin Bishop.

(1936) and Francis Hodgson Burnett's *A Little Princess* (1938). Birch's artistic technique has been compared to the line drawing of late 19th-century British illustrators. His child characters have distinctly British and aristocratic attributes, especially those in Burnett's books. His portrayal of Little Lord Fauntleroy's long curls, velvet suit and lace collar began a children's fashion rage in America that dismayed Birch. Praised for its strong picture sense, storytelling power and integrity of line and design, Birch's graceful, humorous style helped to establish a refreshing new trend in American children's book illustration in the late 19th century. DAC

Birmingham, Christian 1970– British illustrator. A graduate from Exeter College of Art and Design, Birmingham came to public attention in 1995 when Michael Morpurgo's *The Wreck of the Zanzibar*, which Birmingham had illustrated, won the Whitbread Children's Book Award. In the same year, Birmingham's first picturebook, *The Magical Bicycle* (text by Berlie Doherty), was nominated for the Kurt Maschler Award. Both Birmingham's drawing and his picturebook work reveal a distinctive, soft-focus, impressionist style; work in colour reveals an adventurous use of the page, perspective and composition. In Dickens's *Oliver Twist* (1996), Birmingham employs both small cameos and rich, atmospheric colour plates. *Wombat Goes Walkabout* (by Michael Morpurgo) was shortlisted for the 1999 Kate Greenaway Award. JAG

Biro, Val (Balint Stephen) see *Gumdrop* series

Birthday Books see Kate Greenaway

Bishop, Claire Huchet 1899?–1993 French-American author, storyteller and librarian. In 1924 Bishop helped to create L'Heure Joyeuse, the first children's library in France. Storytelling here led to her first book, a retelling of the Chinese folktale *The Five Chinese Brothers* (1938). After World War II, Bishop became increasingly prominent in France as an opponent of anti-Semitism, eventually serving as president of the Jewish-Christian Fellowship of France (1968–81) and of the International Council of Christians and Jews (1975–7); among other accomplishments, she was instrumental in the expunging of anti-Semitic language from the Catholic catechism.

Author of several biographies for children – including *Martin de Porres: Hero* (1954), about Latin America's patron saint of inter-racial harmony – she is best known for three stories with French settings. *Pancakes-Paris* (1947) describes with unusual frankness the deprivations French children endured during and after the war. *All Alone* (1953) depicts the solitary lives of young shepherds in the Pyrenées; both of these were Newbery Honour Books. More closely related to Bishop's political activism, *Twenty and Ten* (1952) is a moving and suspenseful war story of French Catholic children who hide a group of Jewish children from the Nazis. SR

Bishop, Gavin 1946– Foremost New Zealand picturebook illustrator and writer since 1978, and the winner of many national prizes. In 1984 he won the Grand Prix in the Noma Concours in Japan with *Mr Fox* (1982), while *Bidibidi* (1983) had been the runner-up the previous year. Bishop's accomplished visual contradictions of bold sweeping brushwork against intimate interior details make the books intriguing. Strong waves of dark colour in *The Horror of Hickory Bay* (1984) are unequivocal, the illustrations' surreal complexity recognised immediately by children. His texts are equally complex. Bidibidi, a sheep of lasting good sense, is a distillation of people who decide to control their own lives. In his retelling of the MAORI legend *Maui and the Sun* (1996), Bishop's skilled watercolours are perfectly integrated with the measured text: layered earth and grand, disturbed waves of colour echo the archetypal emotions of triumph and despair when Maui discovers the sun's name. Bishop is a prolific writer and illustrator who has deservedly dominated the New Zealand picturebook scene for more than a decade. MJH

Biswas, Pulak 1941– Pioneering Indian illustrator and painter. Biswas is credited with raising book ILLUSTRATION to the level of serious art in a context where illustrating is considered a poor cousin of painting. He believes that 'a good illustration should not only help understand the text; it should go beyond that on its own as a work of art'. He has incorporated elements of India's folk art forms in his illustrations. Always trying to overcome the barriers imposed by the pre-determination of a text, the first success of his iconoclastic efforts was seen in the illustrations to Mulk Raj Anand's *A Day in the Life of Maya of Mohenjodaro* (1968). Here he succeeded in demolishing the stereotypical fair heroine by portraying Maya as a dark little snub-nosed girl. Biswas's first full-time illustrating job was with the Children's Book Trust, where he worked on a broad range of titles with a great degree of freedom. He has been associated with all leading publishing houses for children in India, and has also worked for publishers in the United States, Austria and Germany. He was awarded the Grand Honorary Diploma in the Biennale of Illustrations, Bratislava, in 1967. His exquisite stylised illustrations of the great Indian classics, the *Ramayana* (1989) and the *Pancatantra* (1969), stand out as the best examples of his work. MBh

Illustration from *Tiger on a Tree* by Pulak Biswas.

Black Beauty sequels see CHRISTINE, JOSEPHINE AND DIANA PULLEIN-THOMPSON; see also ANIMALS IN FICTION

Black Beauty: the Autobiography of a Horse (1877) Novel by Anna Sewell (1820–78) cast in the form of fictional animal autobiography which first gained popularity in the eighteenth century. *Black Beauty* is one of the best-selling novels of all time. Originally written as a didactic story for adults, especially working men and boys responsible for horses and their welfare, it became popular with children almost immediately and has remained so ever since. The story recounts Black Beauty's life as a working horse, from idyllic beginnings as a foal on a country estate, through gradual physical deterioration and worsening treatment under successive ownerships, to a consolatory happy ending. The story is episodic, told in simple prose and short chapters, each chapter embodying a moral and educational point. Written for adults with modest literacy and little leisure for reading, the book is linguistically undemanding but narratively powerful, its episodes unified by its sympathetic central figure, his moving life-story, and his naive but telling perspective on human behaviour. Anna Sewell was a Quaker, and the book articulates Quaker values not only concerning the human treatment of animals but in its loathing of warfare and its exposure of social ills such as drunkenness. It defends – and in itself impressively represents – the Quaker virtues of plain speaking and moral courage. PH

see also ANIMAL STORIES

Black Book of Carmarthen, The see KING ARTHUR

Black Bull of Norroway, The see 'BEAUTY AND THE BEAST'; see also SCOTTISH FOLKTALES

Black Hearts in Battersea see *JAMES III* SERIES

Black Holes and Uncle Albert see UNCLE ALBERT SERIES

Endpaper design by Honor Blackman for *Blackie's Children's Annual* (1923/4).

Black Jack (1968) Tale by British author LEON GARFIELD which starts with the outsize eighteenth-century villain of the title apparently rising from the dead. In fact, he cheated the hangman by first swallowing a silver pipe through which he could breathe – a detail also found in JOHN MASEFIELD's adventure story *Dead Ned* (1938). Thereafter Black Jack forces Tolly, an innocent London apprentice, into a life of crime. But when Tolly falls for delicate Belle, he finds the strength to save his and her situation. Black Jack finally recognises Tolly's moral authority and helps him to escape back to normality. NT

***Black Stallion* series** American HORSE BOOKS by Walter Farley. Starting in 1941 with the publication of *The Black Stallion*, the series followed the adventures of Alec Ramsay and his magnificent stallion, the Black, from their first dramatic encounter at sea through the Black's impressive racing career (with Alec as his jockey) and the achievements of the Black's offspring. The combination of solid equestrian detail and romantic wish-fulfillment was a resoundingly successful one, and Farley rang the changes on the mystical bond between horse and young man through 16 titles (two more connect only peripherally with Alec and the Black), twice allowing the worlds of *The Black Stallion* and *The Island Stallion*, his other equine series, to overlap. Alec's exploits include a multitude of racing victories, journeys to the Black's home country of Saudi Arabia, an exploration of the world of harness racing, a brush with the supernatural, falling in love with a talented free spirit, and coping with her death. Since Farley's death, his son Steven Farley has taken up the series, but his contribution lacks the compelling drama of his father's books. The series has prompted one near-classic film *The Black Stallion*, directed by Carroll Ballard (1980), and a less memborable sequel. DS

***Blackberry Farm* series** A popular series of simple anthropomorphic stories written for very young readers in the 1950s and 1960s by Jane Pilgrim, illustrated by F. Stocks May, and subsequently re-issued many times. VW

Blacker, Terence 1948– British author and journalist, best known for the *Ms Wiz* series, illustrated first by Kate Simpson and then by TONY ROSS. The first in the series, *Ms Wiz Spells Trouble* (1988), was shortlisted for the CHILDREN'S BOOK AWARD and selected for the Children's Book of the year, 1989. Excellent for the emergent reader, the pacy narrative relates the exploits of the 'Paranormal Operative', Ms Wiz, who uses spells 'wherever things need livening up'. The offbeat, wish-fulfilling humour is guaranteed to appeal to young readers. Other titles by Blacker include the *Hot Shot* series of four football stories, beginning with *Pride and Penalties* (1994), aimed at secondary-school children. Featuring a girls' football team, the stories appeal through a blend of popular contemporary subject matter, footballing detail, and the treatment – often humorous – of adolescent insecurities. *The Transfer* (1998) is a FANTASY football story for 9–12-year-olds about a boy who is obsessed by football and who uses his computer and 'cybertelekinesis' to materialise a magnificent striker. JSW

Blackie's Children's Annual British ANNUAL published from 1904 until 1940, and one of the best annuals ever produced for young children in the United Kingdom. Because it did not consist of the bound copies of a weekly or monthly paper, it was possible to design each annual as a single complete volume. The result was a lively and colourful publication, in striking contrast to the double-columned black-and-white drabness of *CHATTERBOX* and other annuals of the period. The emphasis was on stories, poetry and pictures, with contributions from the best writers and illustrators of the time, including E. NESBIT, Hugh Walpole and ANGELA BRAZIL; later Constance Heward (writer of the *AMELIARANNE* stories) and BARBARA EUPHAN TODD (*WORZEL GUMMIDGE*) contributed. In the late 1920s Norman Hunter contributed comic stories (with characters like His Oriental Utterness the Emperor of Schutem-sydewaiz), and an early *PROFESSOR BRANESTAWM* story appeared in the 1937 issue. Illustrators included CHARLES ROBINSON, JOHN HASSALL, H.M. BROCK, Florence Harrison, H.R. and C.M. Millar, ALICE B. WOODWARD, Helen Stratton and ANNE ANDERSON, and later there was work by Alfred Bestall (see *RUPERT BEAR*) and MABEL LUCIE ATTWELL. From 1925, S.G. Hulme Beaman's early illustrations in the *TOYTOWN* manner began to appear, and CICELY M. BARKER designed an *Alphabet of Flowers* for the 1934 issue.

What made *Blackie's Children's Annual* distinctive was the careful and imaginative editorial attention to detail, the high-quality printing in colour and tint, and artwork mostly in the manner of Art Nouveau and poster prints. Numerous vignettes, end-pieces and marginal decorations were thoughtfully designed to appeal to young readers. The early issues had coloured pictorial endpapers, and at one period there were two related endpapers; the 1913 front endpaper, for example, showed MOTHER GOOSE piloting an airship with six children and several piles of books; the back endpaper depicted the children distributing the books – which are, of course, *Blackie's Children's Annuals* – to the star-fairies. After 1917 there was a change of editorial style and the artistic character of the *Annual* became strongly influenced by HONOR C. APPLETON (best known for her *Josephine* stories). The best of the *Annuals* were produced in this period, and for a few years there was a parallel publication for younger readers, *Blackie's Little Ones' Annual*. Throughout the 1920s the high standard was sustained in competition with Blackwell's *JOY STREET*, which first appeared in 1923. In the late 1930s, however, there was a slackening of editorial control and a lowering of standards. The final volume had no date and no number (possibly because it was not issued on time, or in the assumption that sales would be slow), and the features which had formerly distinguished the *Annual* from its cheaper rivals vanished. There were no tinted illustrations, the pages were printed on thick paper and designed in cramped double columns, with close print and a small type-face. Nevertheless, *Blackie's Children's Annual* was distinguished by its unusually careful child-centredness, and for 30 years it was colourful, varied, often funny, never dull, and always carefully designed with the amusement and interests of young readers in mind. VW

Blackman, Malorie 1962– London-born writer of lively and humorous novels and short stories for young people of all age groups. All her books provide positive gender and race models, portraying active and confident females in everyday adventures with which her readers can easily identify. Blackman's series for young children includes Caribbean stories featuring Betsey Biggalow, and two stories for Tamarind (a black publishing house): *Dizzy's Walk* (1999) and *Marty Monster* (1999). In *Hacker* (1992), for older children, the author uses her experience as a systems programmer to create an exciting and suspense-filled story which readers who are not computer-literate can follow, provided they are prepared to disregard some technical details. PAP

Illustration from *Clown* by Quentin Blake.

Blackwood, Basil see *THE BAD CHILD'S BOOK OF BEASTS*; see also CAUTIONARY VERSE

Blackwood, William see *MCGUFFEY ECLECTIC READERS*

Blake, Quentin (Saxby) 1932– Prolific British illustrator and recipient of countless AWARDS. Blake conveys a joyous anarchy suited to the characters he most commonly portrays: RUSSELL HOBAN'S *Captain*

Najork, John Yeoman's *Wild Washerwoman*, ROALD DAHL's *Twits*, *WITCHES* and *BFG*, and the cast of MICHAEL ROSEN's poems, are the most notorious. Nils-Olof Franzen's *Agaton Sax* and J.P. Martin's *UNCLE* were also portrayed in Blake's dynamic pen-strokes, and he was the original illustrator of JOAN AIKEN's *Arabel and Mortimer* (1974 onwards), produced for TELEVISION in animated and puppet versions. He has interpreted traditional NURSERY RHYMES and HILAIRE BELLOC's *Cautionary Tales*, whilst his affectionate depiction of *Monster* in the Longman series by Ellen Blance and Ann Cook (1977 onwards) has lightened the load of many a beginning reader. *Patrick* (1968) was the first of his own creations, and *Angelo* (1970) followed soon after. *Mr Magnolia* (1980) (Kate Greenaway Medal 1981) derives its comic absurdity from the pursuit of a single rhyme, in the manner of DR SEUSS. Blake's witty pathos is best seen in *The Story of the Dancing Frog* (1985). Unruly and eccentric characters appear and reappear throughout his own work (for example, in *Mrs Armitage on Wheels*, 1987, and *Mrs Armitage and The Big Wave*, 1997), depicted in sprightly sketches and colourful washes creating artistic unity with the delightfully mad text. The mischief of children, and the horror and bewilderment of their adult victims, emerge vividly in Blake's spiky figures with bulging eyes. In 1999 Quentin Blake was appointed the first CHILDREN'S LAUREATE. PC

Blake, William see *SONGS OF INNOCENCE AND EXPERIENCE*

bleed In PICTUREBOOKS an illustration bleeds if it extends to the trimmed edge of the paper. An illustration may bleed on one, two, three or all four edges. The effect suggests a life going on beyond the confines of the page, and diminishes the separation between the pictured world and that of the viewer. JD

Blegvad, Erik 1923– Artist and illustrator, translator of HANS CHRISTIAN ANDERSEN and author of his own picturebook AUTOBIOGRAPHY, *Self-Portrait* (1979), a small masterpiece. Blegvad has illustrated almost 100 children's books. Born in Copenhagen, Denmark, into a family that valued art, Blegvad grew up to attend the Copenhagen School of Arts, where he met N.M. BODECKER, who was to become a lifelong friend. In 1947 Blegvad moved to Paris, where he created ILLUSTRATIONS for magazines and newspapers, and met his wife, Lenore Hochman, an American who later became a writer of children's books. After several years in the United States the Blegvads moved to London in 1966, and divided their time between Vermont, London and the south of France. Blegvad is best known for his detailed pen-and-ink line-drawings,though some of his illustrations are watercolours with very little line. His style has consequently been compared to that of E.H. SHEPARD. Of Andersen's *Twelve Tales* (1993), Blegvad writes in the introduction: 'If the English in these translations sounds old-fashioned, well, so does the original Danish.' The language does have an old-fashioned feel, but the stories have a delightfully conversational tone, and are perfectly complemented by Blegvad's ink and watercolour illustrations. LH

Blinky Bill Mischievous koala character, created by Australian writer DOROTHY WALL, who featured in *Blinky Bill* (1933), *Blinky Bill Grows Up* (1934), *Blinky Bill and Nutsy* (1937) and *Blinky Bill Joins the Army* (1941). The books are episodic, recounting Blinky's escapades. Although he occasionally does good deeds, he is frequently rude and disobedient, sometimes cruel, and unfailingly condescending to girl koalas. The books are a plea for the conservation of koalas, which were hunted nearly to extinction at the time. Blinky Bill has appeared in an animated TELEVISION series, and was the symbol of the Australian Republican Movement. JF

Blishen, Edward 1920–96 British author, editor and reviewer. Blishen first worked as a secondary school teacher in an under-privileged area of London. This experience turned him into a lifelong champion of books for all children previously deprived of attractive and appropriate literature. From 1961 he compiled the *Junior Pears Encyclopedia*, and in 1964 edited the *Oxford Book of Poetry*. A perceptive critic, Blishen was in constant demand at the many book conferences springing up in the 1960s, witness to the new interest in children's literature following the arrival of significant fresh talents on the children's scene. In 1975 he included a number of these figures in his edited volume *The Thorny Paradise; Writers on Writing for Children*. One of the writers featured in this collection was LEON GARFIELD, with whom Blishen had earlier collaborated in *THE GOD BENEATH THE SEA*, a brilliant retelling of Ancient Greek legend designed, as Blishen put it later, 'to chase the moths out of myths'. This volume won the Carnegie Medal in 1970. Its sequel, *The Golden Shadow*, appeared in 1973. Blishen later collaborated with his wife Nancy on a series of *Story Book Treasuries* designed for children aged between five and eight. Much of the rest of his time was spent on a series of autobiographical studies, often recalling his own enthusiasm for a whole range of literature. Incapable of writing a dull sentence, passionate about reading and always encouraging in his criticism of new writers, Blishen was an important and unfailingly positive influence upon children's literature during all his professional life. NT

see also CLASSICAL MYTHOLOGY

Block, Francesca Lia 1962– American writer of postmodern FAIRY TALES known collectively as the *DANGEROUS ANGELS* series which begins with *Weetzie Bat* (1989). Block, like her characters, lives in Los Angeles. In addition to *Dangerous Angels*, Block has written the adolescent novel *The Hanged Man* (1994), a dark tale of father–daughter incest, and *Girl Goddess #9: Nine Stories* (1996), short stories featuring assertive young women trying to make sense of adolescence in the 1990s. JCS

blocking Impressed lettering and ornamental or pictorial designs on the covers of a book, made by the use of a heated brass stamp. The blocked surface may be covered with gold leaf, metal foil or coloured with ink, or it may be left plain. The latter method is known as blind blocking. GCB

Bloom, Valerie 1956– Jamaican-born poet. Her first children's collection, *Duppy Jamboree* (1992), celebrates the language and oral traditions of the Caribbean. Bloom writes about the adventures of a Jamaican childhood with gently ironic humour and with a strong sense of narrative. The poems use modified Jamaican patois and are characterised by vigorous rhyming and rhythmical structures. This rich sound-patterning, though perfectly crafted for the page, also lends itself to reading aloud. *Fruits* (1992), illustrated by David Axtell, is a delicious counting poem for younger readers taken from the first collection. She has also published *Ackee, Bread Fruit, Callaloo* (1994). ML

Blos, Joan W(insor) 1928– American award-winning author of HISTORICAL FICTION who has also written many popular PICTUREBOOKS. She has received the most recognition for *A Gathering of Days: A New England Girl's Journal, 1830–32* (1979), which won both the Newbery Medal and the American Book Award in 1980. Born in New York City, Blos was the only child of parents who emphasised the importance of reading and education. She attended an experimental elementary school where a variety of academic, creative and practical experiences was stressed. With this foundation it is no surprise that she eventually put her love for literature and her interest in child development and language together. Her picturebooks, such as *Martin's Hats* (1984), celebrate the power of children's imaginations. Her books for older readers are historical fiction in which factual truth is evident in the well-researched details and authentic language. They also address social truth and personal growth. In *A Gathering*, Catherine's journal reveals her deepest thoughts in coping with a friend's death and in deciding to offer assistance to a runaway slave. Lame Shem learns self-worth, trust and forgiveness through perseverence in *Brothers of the Heart* (1985). LAW

Blue Bird, The (1909) Allegorical children's play by the Belgian symbolist poet and dramatist Maurice Maeterlinck (1862–1949), first published in England in 1909. Dedicated to J. M. BARRIE, the author of *PETER PAN*, it clearly shows the influence of Barrie's play (not least in its idealisation of motherhood) but has a more coherent moral and allegorical structure. It tells of Tyltyl and Mytyl, a woodcutter's children, who are sent by a fairy on a dream quest for the Blue Bird of happiness which will cure a sick child. Unsuccessful in their mission, they at last find the Blue Bird in their own home. Though immensely difficult to stage, *The Blue Bird* is historically important in the evolution of children's theatre. PH

***Blue Door Theatre* series** see *THE SWISH OF THE CURTAIN*; see also PAMELA BROWN

Blue Lagoon, The see H. DE VERE STACPOOLE

Blue Peter Book, The (1964–) Annual and sometimes intermittent publication in association with *Blue Peter*, the BBC's flagship children's TELEVISION programme, which was first transmitted on 16 October 1958, and is believed to be the longest-running children's programme in the world. *The Blue Peter Book* appeared in 1964 and was issued regularly until 1992, edited mostly by Biddy Baxter and Edward Barnes. However, there was no publication in 1986 and 1990, and it was discontinued altogether after the 1992 issue. Young readers in Britain rejoiced when, in 1998, annual publication was resumed to coincide with the programme's 40th anniversary.

The Blue Peter Book is characterised by high-quality ILLUSTRATIONS – mainly photographic – and lively factual articles, especially about animal life and the environment. The books make a great feature of the programme's own pets. The *Blue Peter* Christmas Appeal has traditionally involved millions of British children and this too is featured in the books, along with the annual Special Assignment which takes the presenters overseas. In the early issues there were usually two or three stories, including a *PADDINGTON BEAR* story, by MICHAEL BOND.

With the 26th issue came a change of editorship and a greater emphasis on contemporary youth culture; the already minimal element of fiction disappeared altogether, and the personalities of the presenters – their interests, favourite sports, and so on – became a key element. This self-referential approach backfired somewhat in 1998 when one of the presenters was involved in a highly publicised drug scandal. However, the editor and presenters showed great skill and sensitivity in the way they publicly handled this issue. Both the programme and *The Blue Peter Book* have remained consistently dedicated to the involvement of

'The heads of six Ladies / All lovely as life; / With this writing on each, / "An Inquisitive Wife."' Chapbook illustration from *Bluebeard.*

young viewers and are affectionately regarded as a national institution by both adults and children.

In November 2000, in a special programme devoted entirely to children's books, the inaugural *Blue Peter* Awards for children's books were made in several categories: the first *Blue Peter* Book of the Year Award was presented to GERALDINE MCCAUGHREAN for her retelling of JOHN BUNYAN's *Pilgrim's Progress* illustrated by Jason Cockroft. VW

see also TELEVISION FOR CHILDREN

Blue Poetry Book, The (1891) Anthology edited by Andrew Lang, with well-chosen poems for the young drawn from adult rather than children's verse, strongly favouring the Romantics. In his Introduction, Lang takes anthologists to task for failing to represent adequately Scottish poetry; he himself omits women poets almost entirely. MCCS

'Bluebeard' FAIRY TALE included in *Histoires ou contes du temps passé* (1697) (see CONTES DE MA MÈRE L'OYE) by CHARLES PERRAULT, originally entitled 'La Barbe Bleue'. It is the story of a blue-bearded man who gives his new wife all the keys to his house but forbids her to use one of them. Driven by curiosity she opens the prohibited door to discover the bodies of her husband's former wives. Bluebeard, seeing blood on the key, realizes that his wife has disobeyed him and determines to murder her. She is saved, however, and Bluebeard is killed. The story was first translated into English in 1729 by Robert Samber and later became the subject of CHAPBOOKS. A variant published by the GRIMM BROTHERS under the title 'Marienkind', in which the punitive figure is the Virgin Mary, was described by Marina Warner as one of their 'nastier morality tales'.

The story, founded on traditional materials, has its origins before Perrault. In *Pentamerone* (1634/6) by Giambattista Basile, the ogress tells Princess Marchetta that she may enter any room except that to which she is given the key. Also predating Perrault's version is *Mr Fox*, in which a lady discovers her neighbour's house to be full of blood and bones. Mr Fox's denial of the killing is quoted in SHAKESPEARE's *Much Ado About Nothing*. Suppositions have been made that this story has a historical basis and suitable candidates for Bluebeard have been put forward. One of these is Gilles de Rais (1404–40) who was tried for the murder of around 140 victims; however, a more probable Bluebeard is Comorre the Cursed (c. AD 500) who was the reputed killer of four wives and whose fifth wife found out his crimes and was nearly killed herself. JHD

Blume, Judy 1938– For some years America's most popular writer of teenage fiction. Blume was born in New Jersey in the type of white, middle-class area later to feature as the background to many of her novels. Her first successful story, *Are You There, God? It's Me, Margaret* (1970), set the pattern for other 'problem' stories still to come. Its main character is an 11-year-old girl just about to enter adolescence. Her most urgent inner thoughts touch on hopes and fears seen as typical of this age-group. Will she soon be able to wear a bra? Will she one day have a boyfriend? The success of this story was instantaneous. Written in an informal, chatty style, it openly discussed topics such as menstruation, which up to then had been taboo in children's fiction. Teenagers reading Blume could recognise their own occasional worries and obsessions. Younger readers were allowed a vivid glimpse of the type of emotional and physical changes they were soon to experience yet which were comparatively undiscussed with them by parents or teachers. Other titles treating different problems followed. *Then Again, Maybe I Won't* (1971) is about a boy who is receiving psychiatric help, and *Deenie* (1973) features a heroine with severe curvature of the spine. *Blubber* (1974), perhaps Blume's best novel, describes how one slightly overweight girl is subjected to cruel classroom humour. When a brave pupil decides to take her side, she too becomes a victim of the chief bully. As a study of gleeful childhood malevolence for its own sake, *Blubber* packs a powerful punch. It is also well written, with a good ear for adolescent dialogue.

Forever (1975) made Blume into the well-known controversial figure she has remained ever since. This was the first children's story which not only featured teenage SEX but did so calmly, at length and in some technical detail. Still banned in a number of American States, it was some time before a paperback edition finally appeared in Britain. Children then flocked to it; rarely can a children's book have been passed from reader to reader quite so eagerly. Blume had by now become something of a guru for teenagers; her visits to bookshops produced record crowds, and thousands of young readers wrote to her describing similar problems in their own lives. Some of these letters were later collected and published in *Letters to Judy; What Your Kids Wish They Could Tell You* (1986). More novels followed, still mostly focusing on adolescent problems, including tensions with parents.

Critics have questioned the narrow social background to her books and the way that awkward emotional problems sometimes seem to resolve themselves with deceptive ease. But Blume's ability to reach young readers cannot be questioned, and her sense of humour and sharp eye for detail ensure that her stories never drift into self-conscious BIBLIOTHERAPY. An author who also writes successfully for adults, she is never less than a skilled practitioner with a determination to describe important stages of growing up still too often ignored elsewhere. NT

Blythe, Gary 1959– British illustrator, born and trained in Liverpool. Blythe's oil paintings for *THE WHALES' SONG* (Dyan Sheldon, 1990), which won the KATE GREENAWAY MEDAL had an immediate impact with their dramatically lit scenes and touching close-ups. *The Garden* (Dyan Sheldon, 1993), also in oil, showed similar strengths and great range as he moved from the close-up of a trowel to wide landscapes, from suburban garden to wigwam and camp fire. *This is the Star* (Joyce Dunbar, 1996) tells the Christmas story with photographic realism, fused with something altogether more dramatic and mystical. JAG

Blyton, Enid (Mary) 1897–1968 British novelist and educational writer, best known for her *NODDY* and *FAMOUS FIVE* series, and arguably the best-selling children's writer of all time. She was the eldest child of lower middle-class parents who split up when Blyton was 13, when her beloved father left home. Many think that this event arrested Blyton's emotional development, thus explaining her facility in writing for children. But this explanation is offered of too many children's writers. In fact, Blyton had a large amount of material rejected before her eventual success with her first book, *Child Whispers* (1922), a collection of verse in the manner of ROSE FYLEMAN. However, she had trained to be a teacher, and was also starting to publish educational material, eventually writing the equivalent of National Curricula single-handedly. The launch of *SUNNY STORIES* (1926) allowed Blyton to expand her fictional output, leading to some of her best work. Her first full-length work of fiction appeared here, the episodic *Adventures of the Wishing Chair* (1937). Later came *The Enchanted Wood* (1939), the first of one of her most enduring series, *THE MAGIC FARAWAY TREE* books. These stories whimsically combine the everyday world with a cosy FANTASY realm, with no problematisation of the interrelation between the two. Also in *Sunny Stories* appeared what was thought to be the first of her more realistic adventures, *The Secret Island* (1938). However, *The Wonderful Adventures* (1927) has now come to light, a far earlier and very uneven attempt at what would later become a winning formula.

Imogen Smallwood, Blyton's younger daughter, has suggested that her mother's best writing came out of periods when she was most under stress. This certainly applies to her books of the late 30s mentioned above, and to the *FAMOUS FIVE*, *Mystery*, *Adventure* and school series (*St. Clare's* and *MALORY TOWERS*), all of which started life around the time of the breakdown of her first marriage – to the Newnes editor, Hugh Pollock, by whom she had two daughters – and the hushed-up, fairly turbulent early years of her second marriage, to surgeon Kenneth Darrell Waters (from 1943). Blyton seems to have been adept at fictionalising her own life, too, for her autobiography, *The Story of My Life* (1952), presents a seemingly ideal family unit, erasing all trace of her daughters' real father.

With an increasing number of children clamouring for Blyton's books in post-war Britain, a critical backlash began, focusing especially on her 1949 creation, *NODDY*. Blyton's simple, sometimes slapdash style did not endear her to adults, and neither did her incredible facility in composition. She could write 10,000 words a day, describing the process as like watching action unfold on a 'private cinema screen', her only intervention being to type it up. This productivity peaked in 1951, when she averaged over 50 publications a year, notching up a record 69 in 1955. Overall, it is estimated that she wrote over 700 books, and some 4,500 short stories. Consequently, she hardly ever revised, forever producing new titles which covered the entire span of childhood, from toddler to young teenager. It was feared that children might grow up on an exclusive diet of Blyton, ending up developmentally stunted. Although this moral panic now seems histrionic, at the time LIBRARIES in many countries sought to ration their Blyton stocks, and a few even banished them altogether.

By the 1960s, stylistic criticism of her work had become secondary to accusations of sexism and racism (see BIAS). Despite several powerful female characters, the general stereotyping of gender roles – epitomised by the domesticated Anne in the *FAMOUS FIVE* – was felt to be unacceptable. Likewise, her use of golliwogs, once a staple of toy-cupboards, was seen as insensitive in an increasingly multicultural society. More generally, the middle-class norm of her work was thought dated and unpalatable. Most of this criticism was beyond Blyton's comprehension; it also went unheeded by children, who wrote in their thousands to 'Green Hedges', probably the most famous address in the world during its owner's lifetime. Blyton's policy of encouraging this communication ensured that she kept close links with her audience, which provided her with invaluable market research. After 1963 she wrote very little, due to an illness that may have been Alzheimer's disease. By her death her work had been translated into 128 languages, making her the third most translated author in the world. Thirty years on, Blyton is still rated amongst the most popular children's writers in Britain, refuting all those who called her work ephemeral. To adapt W. H. AUDEN's famous saying, Blyton raises the notion that some writers might be good only for children.

An adult lack of understanding certainly adds to Blyton's appeal; for if she is guilty of anything it is 'ageism', in that she empowers her child characters at the expense of adults, showing the latter to be inadequate and deceitful. Children are shown solving their own problems, with companionship always central. To read her work is therefore to join that world-wide club of children entering it with a good deal of insider knowledge. Blyton is best seen in these terms, as a storyteller in the oral tradition, relating safe but exciting tales in which children feature as heroes. Her plain style with its straightforward vocabulary – easily digestible by the newly literate – provides a skeletal framework capable of accommodating almost any child's fantasies. It is hardly surprising, therefore, that not only are her books read but they also provide a focus for imaginative play, games, clubs and storywriting. The accusations of stereotyping are also more productively seen in terms of the oral tradition, where stock figures are drawn from an age-old repository of NURSERY RHYME, FAIRY TALE, MYTH and LEGEND. From this perspective, Blyton's enduring, worldwide popularity (with the notable exception of America) becomes more comprehensible. With the sale of her copyright to entertainments giant the Trocadero (later Chorion) in 1996, her name and works have seen even greater exposure, often through spin-offs in other media. DR

Bobbsey Twins, The (1904–92) A phenomenally successful American children's series created by EDWARD STRATEMEYER under the pseudonym Laura Lee Hope. The series was originally written by Stratemeyer himself, and then by various ghost writers. The first Bobbsey Twin book, *The Bobbsey Twins or Merry Days Indoors and Out*, appeared in 1904, and new titles and modified reprints continued to be issued until 1992. *The Bobbsey Twins* is, in fact, the longest-running juvenile series in the history of children's literature, with over 160 titles, of which over 50 million copies have been sold and translated into multiple languages.

The series features the adventures of two sets of twins, Nan and Bert and Flossie and Freddie Bobbsey, and follows the twins from one frolic or mystery to another. The books are a good example of the innocent and warm FAMILY STORY. The series has gone through extensive revisions over the years: the original ages of the twins have been changed, dated references, ethnic slurs and extraneous material have been removed, and the overall length of the books has been reduced by approximately one fifth. Many of the original stories have been reissued in modernised and adapted versions, some under new titles. JKB

Bobby Bear (1919) Character in the children's pages of the new left-wing British newspaper the *Daily Herald*, strikingly similar to the later, more famous and longer-running teddy-bear hero of the *Daily Express* children's feature, *RUPERT BEAR*. Beginning as a single-panel drawing with supporting serialised story, the series later became a COMIC strip which also ran in *MICKEY MOUSE WEEKLY*. The first artist signed herself 'Meg', and the stories were by Dora McLaren. The feminine influence continued when 'Aunt' Kitsie Bridges took over the writing, but the best-remembered artist was Wilfred Haughton, who drew the *MICKEY MOUSE ANNUAL*. The *Bobby Bear Annual* began as a paperback in 1920 and ran through until 1969, changing to standard hardback in 1931. DG

Bobby Brewster (1949–82) Series of stories popular in the 1960s, 70s and 80s, written by H(erbert) E(atton) Todd (1908–88), an accomplished public STORYTELLER who was persuaded after the first series had been broadcast on radio in 1946 to put more than 20 of the tales into print. The stories centre upon Bobby Brewster – three-and-a-half years old in the first stories but nine in the later books – and on simple objects and situations in his life. The stories, often a series of episodic adventures, are told with humour and simplicity and look at life in a magical, comical, even whimsical way. The storyteller's voice is strong and the reader is invited into Bobby's world by the use of asides.

The first book, *Bobby Brewster and the Winkers' Club*, starts with Bobby's inability to wink. His success in overcoming this enables him to become a member of an animals' left-eye Winkers' Club and to see life from an individual animal's point of view, as he shrinks to join a cuckoo in a cuckoo-clock or accompanies a horse on a milk round. Amongst the best stories are *Bobby Brewster and the Ghost* (1966) and *Bobby Brewster's Typewriter* (1971). JSW

Bodecker, N(iels) M(ogens) 1922–88 Danish-born illustrator and author who lived in the United States after 1952. Although Bodecker worked as an illustrator of magazines and books (including Edward Eager's *HALF MAGIC* and its sequels), he is best remembered for his NONSENSE VERSES and other poems for children. He attributed his lifelong love of poetry to the influence of his mother, who read, sang and made rhymes with him, and taught him the names of plants as they walked in the fields: 'cornflower, poppy, pimpernel, plantain and cinquefoil', and 'wildrose, broom, and Lady Mary's shift sleeve – a poetry all its own'. His first book in English, *It's Raining Said John Twaining: Danish Nursery Rhymes* (1973), was a translation of Danish NURSERY RHYMES for his sons. Highly successful, it was followed by several well-received collections of his own verses, including *Let's Marry Said the Cherry* (1974), *Hurry, Hurry, Mary Dear!* (1976), and a book of LIMERICKS, *A Person from Britain Whose Head Was the Shape of a Mitten* (1980), all illustrated with his own whimsical drawings, many of them integral to the verses. A posthumous collection, *Water Pennies and Other Poems*, a gentle book of verses about pond creatures, was illustrated by Bodecker's lifelong friend ERIK BLEGVAD. LH

Bodleian Library see COLLECTIONS OF CHILDREN'S BOOKS; see also IONA AND PETER OPIE; *THE WARDEN'S NIECE*

Bodsworth, Nan(ette) (Elizabeth) 1936– Australian PICTUREBOOK writer and illustrator of her own stories, including *Mike's Birthday Bulldozer* (1981) and *Hello Kangaroo!* (1986). Her most successful work for younger readers, *A Nice Walk In The Jungle* (1989), is a humorous story of a teacher taking a class on a nature walk in the jungle. The teacher, eager to make the children aware of their environment, fails to notice, however, that one by one her students are being eaten by a huge snake. Young readers particularly enjoy a shared reading of Bodsworth's humorous stories.

CH, HMcC

Bogdanov, Michael British theatre director with a distinguished record of work at the National Theatre and the Royal Shakespeare Company. Bogdanov's contribution to children's theatre lies in his adaptations of Longfellow's *THE SONG OF HIAWATHA* (1978) and Coleridge's *THE RIME OF THE ANCIENT MARINER* (1979), both performed as Christmas shows initially at the Young Vic and subsequently at the National Theatre. Using the original texts, Bogdanov creates spectacular theatrical effects, making liberal use of music, dance, acrobatics, sound effects and lighting. The adaptations place great demands on actors and technicians, but they are deeply sensitive to the atmosphere and meanings of the poems, while mediating them as dynamic children's entertainment. PH

Bolt, Robert 1924–95 Dramatist whose main successes were *Flowering Cherry* (1958) and *A Man For All Seasons* (1960), the latter having been widely studied and performed by older students in schools. Bolt also wrote several major screenplays, including *Lawrence of Arabia* (1962) and *Dr Zhivago* (1966). His only important work for children is the play *The Thwarting of Baron Bolligrew* (1966). This has been a popular piece in the repertoire of professional theatre for children, and has often been successfully acted by children in school productions. Skilfully accommodating variants on key figures and situations in PANTOMIME, the play is a mock-heroic comedy taking a satirical view of traditional 'St George and the Dragon' chivalry. Its engaging comic hero is Sir Oblong Fitz Oblong, a soft-hearted knight with a loathing of blood sports, whose scrupulous anxiety to avoid all bloodshed conflicts entertainingly with his earnest desire to defend the poor and confront the wicked. The play's strength lies in its neat intermingling of comedy and suspense, and its satiric reversals of habitual expectations, for example in Sir Oblong's declaration that 'duelling is utterly against my principles', and in the dragon's eventual slaughter not by the hero's sword but the villain's gunfire. Bolt achieves an unusual and effective blend of dramatic forms. PH

Bonanza see COMICS

Bond, Michael 1926– British writer. Born in Newbury, Berkshire, and educated at Presentation College, Reading, Bond joined the RAF for a year before becoming a BBC cameraman from 1947 to 1966. His acclaim as a children's writer began in 1958 with the creation of *A Bear Called Paddington*. The appeal and adventures of this marmalade-loving and hilariously unlucky child bear have continued well into the 1990s with the republication of numerous sequels and an animated TELEVISION series. Bond invented other characters: the eponymous orphan mouse and guinea pig whose adventures first appear in *Here Comes Thursday* (1966) and *The Adventures of Olga da Polga* (1971). Where Paddington is included as a member of the Brown family as if he was another child, Olga and Thursday inhabit an animal world very different to the magic realism of Paddington. Despite taking on distinctly human characteristics, Olga, Thursday and their companions are restricted to the natural world of the garden and the organ-loft cupboard. In these stories the child reader takes the position of a wise spectator, the omniscient representative of the human world of which, unlike Paddington, these animals will never be a part. Bond has collaborated on numerous productions for both television and radio, including the 1960s children's programme *The Herbs*. He has also written articles and short stories for newspapers and magazines. KR

Bond, Nancy 1945– American author for young adults. Bond has written seven novels, all longer than most books for children. She creates richly detailed settings that extend far beyond her native New England. *A String in the Harp* (1976), a Newbery Honour Book, is a legendary TIME-SLIP FANTASY set in Wales. *Another Shore* (1988), a historical TIME-SLIP fantasy, moves from Boston to Nova Scotia. In *Truth to Tell* (1994), a realistic coming-of-age book, the English protagonist emigrates to New Zealand. In each story, Bond dramatises an international conflict and various patterns of adjustment; young adults are often uprooted and their cultural displacement produces personal and social conflicts. When her protagonists are not crossing cultures, they are confronting either the separations that occur within families – as in *The Best of Enemies* (1978) – or other life changes that occur in families, communities and the world at large, as in *Country of Broken Stone* (1980), *The Voyage Begun* (1981) and *A Place to Come Back To* (1984). Whether she is producing classic realism – her usual genre – or time-slip fantasy, specificity of place and depth of character are Bond's major strengths, human complexity her subject. Bond's leisurely pace makes her an old-fashioned storyteller of timeless young adult concerns. NM

Bond, Ruskin 1934– Anglo-Indian writer whose fiction includes over 30 stories for children. These sensitively reflect a life spent almost entirely in India. Bond received the Llewellyn Rhys Memorial Prize for his novel, *A Room on the Roof* (1956), the story of a teenage boy torn between his English and his Indian cultural heritage. Not all Bond's fiction is available outside India. In Britain his stories have included *Angry River* (1972), *The Blue Umbrella* (1972) (or *Binya's Blue Umbrella*, 1996, in the USA); and *Getting Granny's Glasses* (1985). PP

Bonfires and Broomsticks see ***Bedknob and Broomstick***

Bonham, Frank 1914– American author. His works include such realistic contemporary novels as *Durango Street* (1965) and *Gimme an H, Gimme an E, Gimme an L, Gimme a P* (1980), in which his protagonists attempt to escape their mental, emotional, physical or ethnic-based societal problems. Although his plots have been described as contrived, Bonham has won praise for his evocative settings, well-motivated, believable characters and for his descriptions of traditional beliefs of the time. He has also written *Mystery in Little Tokyo* (1966), *Mystery of the Fat Cat* (1968), *The Nitty Gritty* (1968) and *Viva Chicano* (1970). MRS

Bonnie Pit Laddie, The (1960) Historical novel by Frederick Grice, winner of the Other Award, realistically describing the lives of working people in a Northumberland mining community. In unsentimental style, it charts Dick Ullathorne's growing awareness of social inequalities and his realisation that through education he can break the cycle of son following father into the pit. However, it is not until the whole community suffers the hardship of a strike due to unfair treatment at the hands of the mine-owner, and Dick is injured in a pit accident, that he manages to break loose to seek his future elsewhere. MSS

Bontemps, Arna (Wendell) 1902–73 African American writer and anthologist. Born in Louisiana and raised in California, Bontemps was an important Harlem Renaissance poet, wrote three adult novels, and anthologised poetry and folklore. He was a pioneer of literature about and for AFRICAN AMERICAN children. His first book for children, *Popo and Fifina: Children of Haiti* (1932), co-authored with LANGSTON HUGHES, presented a sympathetic portrait of Haitian peasant life. In four subsequent fictions, three histories and three BIOGRAPHIES, Bontemps presented rich African American characters and detailed, accurate accounts of the black American experience. His *Story of the Negro* (1948) was a runner-up for the Newbery Award, and the revised 1956 edition won the Jane Addams Children's Book Award.

His best children's fiction, in *Sad-Faced Boy* (1937), *Lonesome Boy* (1955) and *Mr. Kelso's Lion* (1970), portrays young boys awakening to the richness of African American culture and the dangers of racism in America. The latter two, in their use of the metaphoric, have something in common with FABLES, and Bontemps' collaborations with Jack Conroy on three TALL TALES confirms his interest in American FOLK TALES. Bontemps wrote his books to provide characters and histories with which black children could identify, thereby filling a void he found in his own youthful reading experiences. DWR

Boock, Paula 1964– New Zealand writer of prize-winning teen novels. Beginning with *Out Walked Mel* (1991), Boock has written four books investigating intelligent, decisive girls sorting out their lives and relationships. In *Home Run* (1995), Bryony, successful academic and athlete, has to choose between her tough, shoplifter friends and moving to a middle-class school. She moves. Social class and inter-ethnic relationships are issues Boock also investigates in plays and short stories. *Night Creatures* (1995), a short story, is a subtle, funny episode of lesbian teen love. In *Dare, Truth or Promise* (1997) Boock has written the first New Zealand young lesbian novel. The familial, school and social implications of being lesbian are secondary to the story of the girls themselves, told with warmth and humour. Her writing is notable for the stark rendition of first love, whatever the sexual orientation of the lovers. MJH

see also SEX IN CHILDREN'S BOOKS

book clubs see PUBLISHERS AND PUBLISHING

book covers see COVER ART

Book for Boys and Girls, A see JOHN BUNYAN; *COUNTRY RHIMES FOR CHILDREN*

Book of Knowledge, The Authorised American version of *The Children's Encyclopaedia* edited in Britain by ARTHUR MEE and published from 1908. Unconventional in its arrangement, entries were divided into 14 sections with such headings as 'The Child's Book of Golden Deeds', 'Poetry', 'Stories', 'Familiar Things' and 'Things to Make and Do'. Story material included AESOP'S *Fables*, legends of KING ARTHUR and longer, serialised works such as *Don Quixote*, all lavishly illustrated. Produced by the Grolier Society, *The Book of Knowledge* was even more successful than the British version, and by 1946 more than 50 million volumes had been sold. KSB

Book of Nonsense, A (1846) First collection of limericks and drawings by EDWARD LEAR, dedicated to the children of his patron, for whom he wrote them. A 'much enlarged' second edition followed in 1861. Lear's collection first established the LIMERICK as popular NONSENSE VERSE, though the form had been invented earlier, probably by Richard Scrafton Sharpe. ML

Book of Verses for Children, A (1897) Anthology edited by the British critic and essayist, E.V. LUCAS, followed by *Another Book of Verses for Children* (1907). Unlike most editors, Lucas's excellent selection features verse with genuine appeal to the young by poets who concentrated on writing for children. Like most of his contemporaries, he regarded poetry for children as 'a stepping stone . . . to the better thing' rather than as a genre of quality in its own right. MCCS

Book of Wirrun, The see WIRRUN TRILOGY; see also THE BUSH

Book Tower, The Yorkshire Television magazine programme dedicated to children's books, which was networked on Children's ITV from 1979 to 1989. Devised by Joy Whitby, the creator of the BBC's *Playschool*, it was originally set in an actual tower but later in different locations. Its format mixed features on writers, interviews and dramatised book extracts, and latterly employed guest presenters for themed programmes, such as Bruce Grobelaar on football or MICHAEL ROSEN on war. The participation of publishers and booksellers was encouraged with the weekly issue of a *Book Tower Watcher's Guide*. SG

Book Trust see COLLECTIONS OF CHILDREN'S BOOKS; see also REVIEWING AND REVIEWERS

***Bookano* books** see PICTUREBOOKS; MOVABLE BOOKS

Bookbird (1957–) International (irregular) quarterly journal of children's literature, sponsored by the IBBY. Issued in English, the journal was established by Jella Lepman and Dr Richard Bamberger, who co-edited the publication during its early years. Covering the international children's book scene, *Bookbird* reviews recent materials about children's literature, lists recommended books for translation, and publishes in-depth articles relevant to the field. MS

Bookchat (1976–) South African periodical. Started by Jay Heale for a Children's Book Group, this newsletter has grown into a magazine which celebrated its 21st birthday with a special issue to mark the 'State of the Nation' with regard to South African children's books. As the only children's literature periodical in South Africa, *Bookchat* has played an appreciated role in promoting the importance of youth literature (for which its editor, Jay Heale, was given the Carl Lohann

Award in 1992) and its coverage eased South Africa's acceptance into the IBBY in 1992. JHe

books for blind readers Many organisations worldwide provide services for blind and visually impaired children and young adults. The Royal New Zealand Foundation for the Blind, for example, provides a number of training services, including assistance for parents with blind and visually impaired children. In Australia, The Royal Blind Society of New South Wales offers advice on equipment, toys and books, as does the Royal Victorian Institute for the Blind and the Royal Society for the Blind of South Australia.

In the United States, many regional organisations offer similar services and some organisations offer booklists specifically for children. The Library of Congress National Library Service for the Blind and Physically Disabled issues the *Braille Book Review* six times a year, and lists fiction and non-fiction Braille and cassette books for young adults, including works by JOSEPH BRUCHAC, PAUL ZINDEL, ROBERT LIPSYTE, MARK TWAIN, ROBERT CORMIER and ROBERT C. O'BRIEN. The Canadian National Institute for the Blind provides an extensive range of fiction and non-fiction Braille and audio-books. In the United Kingdom the Royal National Institute for the Blind produces books in Braille, mostly for young adults, by major writers, including JUDITH KERR, JENNY NIMMO, NINA BAWDEN, DOROTHY EDWARDS, PENELOPE LIVELY, CYNTHIA VOIGT and JANE GARDAM, as well as a number of titles from the *POINT* series published by Scholastic. The National Library for the Blind at Stockport, England, aims to provide visually impaired readers, including children, with the same access to library services as other readers enjoy. It provides books in both Braille and Moon (see below), as well as a number of 'Two-Ways' books, in which a Braille text is bound with the original print and pictures. It offers a Fiction Café website for young readers, and *Read On*, a quarterly magazine. Its lending library includes work by JOAN AIKEN, MALORIE BLACKMAN, LYNNE REID BANKS, NICK WARBURTON, BETSY BYARS and ROALD DAHL.

In the past, provision has concentrated mainly on the supply of fiction for confident and independent readers. However, in recent years a number of charities in Britain have recognised the importance of providing PICTUREBOOKS for much younger children. The Living Paintings Trust – an organisation dedicated to bringing art to people with impaired sight – has instituted the 'Feel Happy' project for children. It reproduces well-known picturebooks with the main characters presented in raised images which are also brightly coloured for readers with partial sight; these are bound into the book along with clear plastic sheets of Braille text. This combination with the original text allows the book to be shared with a sighted adult, or by a visually impaired adult with a sighted child. An audio-cassette explains how to understand the raised images and describes the other pictures. Titles available from the 'Feel Happy' postal library include works by JOHN BURNINGHAM, PAT HUTCHINS, MARTIN WADDELL, COLIN MCNAUGHTON, NICK BUTTERWORTH and SATOSHI KITAMURA. Another charity in Britain – which also interleaves texts in Braille on clear plastic sheets with the original print text – is the ClearVision Project, a nationwide postal lending library based in London; this organisation co-operates with the 'Feel Happy' project and has over 1,500 books available for very young readers, as well as board books and 'lift-the-flap' books.

There are also a number of support groups concentrating mainly on helping adults to make tactile books for visually impaired children. The London-based charity Bag Books provides books for children with visual impairment and/or severe learning difficulties; their books are made of pages of A3-sized card to which is fixed an object appropriate to the story and which a child may feel, hear or smell, along with the story on laminated card sheets for the teller to use when sharing the book with the child.

Braille is a universally accepted system of writing for visually impaired readers, consisting of a code of 63 characters of between one and six raised dots. The system was invented in 1824 by Louis Braille. The Moon system was developed in 1845 by William Moon of Brighton, England. It differs from Braille in that the raised letters resemble the shapes of letters in the normal alphabet; this familiarity is helpful to people who become blind in later life. Both systems are currently used in the provision of books for children. VW

Books for Keeps (1980–) Bi-monthly British periodical concerned with current children's literature. It was founded in 1980 by Richard Hill, who is still managing director, with Pat Triggs as editor. In 1989 CHRIS POWLING took over the editorship, succeeded in 1997 by Rosemary Stones. The periodical contains articles surveying the whole of children's literature, from the revaluation of classics to accounts of current publishing practice. Regular features such as 'authorgraphs' give insights into authors' backgrounds and methods. Authoritative reviewers contribute short but discriminating reviews of books, usually when they reach paperback stage. More recently, a star-rating system was added, which caused some controversy. The readership has four main constituencies: librarians, book-buying parents and children, authors, and teachers. All have been encouraged to contribute, both with articles and to the lively letters page. Teachers especially have had much influence, so that the periodical has become perhaps the most important forum for debate in the field. Its voice has always been controversial, sometimes even subversive, but it has undoubtedly set standards and defined agendas for action by publishers as well as teachers and readers. Its accompanying booklists have broken new ground, particularly with regard to minorities, both ethnic and social. DCH

see also REVIEWING AND REVIEWERS

Books for Keeps Guide to Poetry, The (1996) An invaluable collection of articles and REVIEWS of poetry for children aged 0–13, edited by CHRIS POWLING and Morag Styles, and published jointly with the Reading and Language Information Centre, University of Reading, UK. The reviews are genuinely critical engagements with the texts, by writers who know about and love poetry. The *Guide* updates the highly successful *Poetry 0–16* (1988). ML

Bookstart Project initiated in 1993 by Barrie Wade and Maggie Moore from the University of Birmingham in the United Kingdom, designed to investigate and encourage book-sharing among families with infants aged approximately nine months. A group of inner-city families received a free pack which contained a book, a poem card and information about book purchase and joining the library. These packs were highly valued and resulted in more book-sharing for babies and increased book ownership. Evaluations have found that parents in the pilot study acted in ways which encouraged young children's interest in and enthusiasm for books.

Following the success of Bookstart, many similar baby literacy projects have been set up throughout the United Kingdom. The aim of all the projects is to encourage parents and carers to involve their children in interaction with books from a very early age. These are usually multi-agency projects, involving health visitors and librarians as well as the education service. Families receive a free pack containing books, rhyme cards and other materials related to literacy, and are also offered advice and support from a project officer who works with the families, promoting library membership and encouraging the sharing of books. Some projects have included contact with mothers before the birth of the baby, with information relating to the benefits of reading with young children being distributed at pre-natal classes.

A powerful rationale for such projects can be found in the work of DOROTHY BUTLER. In *Babies Need Books* she outlines the ways in which books can be used with the youngest children, and offers a convincing argument for their place in everyone's daily routine. Her emphasis is on the pleasure that books can bring both parents and children, and each chapter, covering ages from birth to five, is accompanied by a lengthy list of suggested titles. In *Cushla and her Books* she describes the progress of a handicapped child from babyhood to confident child and explains how books played an important part in this development, providing further powerful justification for the use of books with the very youngest children. HB

Boreman, Thomas 17??–1743 Early publisher of children's books whose work predates that of JOHN NEWBERY. Boreman's *Description of Three Hundred Animals* (1730) was in fact adapted by Newbery within his own publications. Boreman's principal work for children was *Gigantick Histories*, published in ten volumes between 1740 and 1743. These were historical and descriptive accounts of famous London buildings, written for children and incorporating specially designed new woodcuts. The books were printed in a very small format, their tininess being a topic for jokes by Boreman designed to create an air of easy familiarity with his young readers. DWh

Borrowers, The (1952–82) Series of five novels written by MARY NORTON, about a family of tiny people who are driven from their home under the floorboards of a large country house, where everything they need is 'borrowed' from the 'human beans' who live upstairs. The novels are set in the period between 1907 and 1911. The main characters are Pod, Homily and their daughter Arrietty, who is tempted repeatedly to break the sacred law forbidding Borrowers from allowing themselves to be 'seen' by human beings. This invariably leads to trouble, and the wilful and passionate Arrietty is the cause of the family's homelessness. The five novels are an account of their wanderings – their dramatic escapes from danger, their subsequent imprisonment, and their discovery after many adventures of a safe new home in a half-empty rectory.

The appeal to young readers lies largely in the resourcefulness and courage of the Borrowers, whose every possession has to be taken from 'upstairs' at great personal risk and adapted for use in their miniature world. From the first story, *The Borrowers* (1952), Norton makes great use of the narrative possibilities of perspective and the ingenuity needed to make big objects serve the needs of tiny people. She also tantalises her readers by constantly reminding them of the evocative unreliability of STORYTELLING. The origin of *The Borrowers* is wrapped up in mystery: the narrator is Kate, who heard the tale from Mrs May, who heard it from her fanciful young brother, who might have made it up. In *The Borrowers Afield* (1955), the first four chapters are devoted to establishing a dubious authenticity for the tale, and in *The Borrowers Afloat* (1959), the mystery of the telling is intensified as the source is described as 'the biggest liar in five counties'.

There is a good deal of social comedy and family realism in the series, especially in the character of Homily. A working-class mother who pronounces parquet 'parkett', she is prickly, proud, ignorant and brave. DIANA STANLEY'S ILLUSTRATIONS indicate a bony, graceless figure with spikey hair. Arrietty is represented as a recognisably rebellious and disruptive teenager chafing at restrictions.

The character of Arrietty gives unity to the series. Although her thinking is shaped largely by her parents, she is a reader and knows of wider possible horizons than her literally small-minded parents can understand. The theme of escape, and Arrietty's yearning for an expansion of her limited world, provides a powerful emotional impetus beneath the narrative surface and is reflected in the titles, which indicate a progressive movement outwards – abroad, afloat, aloft. It also leads to moments of lyricism, as here, where radiance and colour burst upon Arrietty's eyes for the first time after a lifetime in the darkness under the floorboards:

> She saw the gleaming golden stone floor of the hall stretching away into distance; she saw the edges of rugs, like richly coloured islands in a molten sea, and she saw, in a glory of sunlight – like a dreamed-of gateway to fairyland – the open front door. Beyond she saw grass and, against the clear, bright sky, a waving frond of green.

Throughout the series, Norton uses Arrietty's developing perceptions to combine a celebration of light and colour with the painstaking description of minute detail:

> Standing up, she picked a primrose. The pink stalk felt tender and living in her hands and was covered with silvery hairs, and when she held the flower, like a parasol, between her eyes and the sky, she saw the sun's pale light through the veined petals.

But expansion leads to danger. In *The Borrowers Afield*, Norton again provides a surface ADVENTURE STORY of danger, risk, and temporary periods of rest and sanctuary, while at a deeper level the allegory of adolescence continues to explore the widening of Arrietty's cultural landscape. The tiny Borrowers are like pioneers discovering a huge new landscape – with frogs, snakes, wild strawberries, torrential rain. Respite comes with the discovery of an old boot where they take up temporary residence. There are long lyrical accounts of Arrietty's almost Wordsworthian joy in the beauty of a transfigured landscape, the realisation of everything she had imagined. But there is one discovery she had not imagined – Spiller, an unknown Borrower, male, young, independent, slightly mysterious, resourceful and unruffled. In the end Spiller saves their lives.

Arrietty precipitates the final catastrophe because of her fatal desire to make friends with 'human beans'. Every time it happens, she is involved in confessions, shame, disapproval – yet she cannot help herself. The ending cleverly combines an invitation to a sequel with another expression of this weakness of the heroine's.

The Borrowers Afloat is probably unique in that almost a whole flashback chapter is a reprint of the ending of the previous book. Like its predecessor, it begins with an escape, this time down a water drain with the help of Spiller. Then, through many dangers, they sail down the river in a kettle, and later in Spiller's boat, a converted knife-box covered with an old gaiter. Their destination is the miniature village of Little Fordham. *The Borrowers Aloft* (1961) is, like the others, a short story of escape expanded into a longer one by concentration on minute details, but it also includes several chapters devoted to the human characters of village life. A date is given: it is 1911, and the writing of these adult chapters has a quiet pastoral quality reminiscent of 'Miss Read'. The narrative does not turn to the Borrowers until Chapter 6, testing the patience of young readers somewhat. The Borrowers are imprisoned in an attic by a greedy pair of 'human beans' who intend to show them for money. The account of their escape by balloon is told with careful and convincing attentiveness to mechanical minutiae. Diana Stanley's illustrations occasionally fail to match the accuracy of the account: a careful young reader might spot an error where Pod is depicted trying to unscrew the wrong part of the musical box which is to be used for a winding-gear.

In 1966 Mary Norton published a short story called *Poor Stainless*, in which Homily tells Arrietty a story about happier times when the house was full of Borrowers. But the series was not properly resumed until *The Borrowers Avenged* (1982). Arrietty's need to expand her horizons had earlier been explicitly associated with her fascination with Spiller. She had decided to marry him because 'he likes the out-of-doors, you see, and I like it too'. But these hints are not developed in this last novel of the series; Spiller simply walks out with a fierce glance which seems to Arrietty 'almost one of loathing'. He remains a mystery throughout the series – amoral, resourceful, coming and going according to unknown dictates.

The central authorial interest now seems to be the life of the village church. The daily activities associated with it – and the half-empty old rectory to which the Borrowers escape – are described with a gentle nostalgic affection suggesting the memories of an Edwardian lady – and at more length than some young readers might like. The long-lost Lupy and Hendreary now live in a disused harmonium in the vestry, and several pages are devoted to Arrietty's discovery of the church interior. The final climax of the story is set within the floral decoration of the church for Easter. It is difficult not to suspect that Norton had become less interested in the Borrowers than she was in the village, its social hierarchy, the eccentricities of its people, and the modest loveliness of its church. It is possible to read the series as an account of economic and cultural dependence. One might equally well argue that it is an allegory that leads the reader ultimately to the certainties of the Anglican Church – and there is certainly some delicate comedy arising from Aunt Lupy's religious conversion, her pointed pleasure in the words of the hymn 'All things bright and beautiful, all creatures great and *small*', and from Arrietty's misunderstanding of the difference between a high vicar and a low one.

The Borrowers' last home is under a window-seat, with a grating that opens out to the sunshine – an important symbol for Arrietty. Nevertheless, the final chapter leaves her in some ways worse off than she was at the start: she has had to make a 'grave and sacred' promise never again to speak to a human being. 'Would anyone, ever, begin to understand . . .?' says the tearful Arrietty. Her new friend – a Borrower-poet called Peregrine (pronounced Peagreen) – is impatient with her interest in human beings. Imagination and hope have given way to narrow and pragmatic notions of safety. Arrietty's sustaining dreams of a radiant fairyland future are defeated by the author's nostalgic elegy for a vanished past and the dim coloured lights of a village church. Norton does not tie up the loose ends and there is no closure, just a distancing shift of perspective and a final elegiac sentence referring a little sadly to 'the ladies who come on Wednesdays and Fridays to do the flowers in the church'.

In the 1990s the BBC broadcast TELEVISION serialisations of *The Borrowers*. The adaptations took drastic liberties with the original narratives, inventing a pair of sneering young bully-Borrowers whose adolescent pranks almost lead to the deaths of Pod, Homily and Arrietty. This transformed the series into a crude thriller about teenage violence, a villainy undreamed of by Norton. Nevertheless, the adaptation was something of a triumph for the BBC, partly because of the sophisticated special effects for contrasting the big world with the miniature one. Even more important was the casting of two major actors, Penelope Wilton as Homily and Ian Holm as Pod. Rebecca Callard as the young Arrietty was loving, animated and passionate – with just the right hint of wilfulness and wistfulness.

VW

Boston, L(ucy) M(aria) 1892–1990 British author best known for the *GREEN KNOWE* SERIES of novels. As with several of her short works for younger children, including *The Castle of Yew* (1965) and *The Guardians of the House* (1975), and also her first book, *Yew Hall* (1954), a novel for adults which was later reissued for teenage readers, the *Green Knowe* books centre upon Lucy Boston's own house, the 12th-century manor at Hemingford Grey near Cambridge. This house forms the key to virtually all her best work; the only major exception is *The Sea Egg* (1967), a lyrical FANTASY set in Cornwall, in which two small boys swim secretly at night with seals and Triton.

Boston did not start writing until she was 60, inspired by the ancient house which she had bought just before World War II and lovingly restored. Its Norman hall, she said, 'imposes that intense stillness that suggests an awakened revelation'. The revelation to her – and the young reader's – alerted imagination, is the depth and continuity of past time, the magical interplay of history and MYTH, and the power of buildings to absorb and transmit the lives they contain. Hers is one of the earliest and most intensely realised of modern time fantasies for children. PH

Boston, Peter see *GREEN KNOWE* SERIES

Bottersnikes and Gumbles (1967) The first of the Australian series created by S.A. Wakefield, with witty line drawings by Desmond Digby. It was followed by *Gumbles on Guard* (1975), *Gumbles in Summer* (1979) and *Gumbles in Trouble* (1989). The Bottersnikes are lazy, uncouth, ugly creatures that inhabit unsavoury areas of the Australian bush and press the giggly, easy-going, utterly pliable Gumbles into their service. A review in the *Times Literary Supplement* claimed that Wakefield and Digby had 'invented a complete mythology of the rubbish dump and produced one of the most brilliantly funny books to appear for a long time'. Certainly children have taken the series to their hearts, responding to the ludicrous nature of the creatures themselves, the ongoing battle between the 'Snikes and the Gumbles – which takes on almost epic proportions – and also to the disgusting decadence of the 'Snikes. In each book the feud between the two extremes of temperament is intensified. The plump, pliable Gumbles grow more endearing, the 'Snikes, who glower and glow, but who shrink when wet, more revolting. Without ever becoming didactic, Wakefield implies that as long as litter persists 'Snikes will pollute the landscape. Happily, there will be a Gumble not too far away. MSax

Bottigheimer, Ruth see CRITICAL APPROACHES TO CHILDREN'S LITERATURE

Bourgeois, Paulette 1951– Manitoba-born occupational therapist, newsprint and TELEVISION reporter, and writer of fiction and non-fiction. Her first published book, *Franklin in the Dark* (1986), illustrated by Brenda Clark, launched the world-renowned series of *Franklin the Turtle* PICTUREBOOKS. In this series

'The Huguenot'. Illustration from *The Boy's Own Paper.*

Bourgeois treats the hidden fears and concerns of younger children with gentle humour and understanding. Franklin – an anthropomorphised turtle who faces problems similar to those faced by preschoolers and older children – either adapts to his situation or solves his problems through the application of courage and ingenuity. In her non-fiction, Bourgeois also provides concrete, practical, down-to-earth answers that tend to dispel emotional distress or confusion both in her *In My Neighbourhood* series and also in her reassuring books about physical and emotional change in adolescents. MRS

bowdlerisation see ABRIDGEMENT

Box of Delights, The see *THE MIDNIGHT FOLK*; see also FANTASY

'Boy stood on the burning deck, The' see FELICIA HEMANS

Boy's Own Paper, The (1879–1967) British juvenile periodical founded by the Religious Tract Society (RTS) with the intention of combating the spread of PENNY DREADFULS and other forms of popular publishing generally regarded as pernicious by educationists and others with responsibility for young people. According to the writer and critic Edward Salmon, it succeeded in its aims and became, 'the only first-class journal of its kind to find its way into the slums as well as into the best homes'. Salmon was writing in 1888 – nine years after the first edition of the *BOP* appeared. The first editor of the paper was George Andrew Hutchinson, and it was he who conceived the magazine's successful mixture of fiction, practical articles and lighter features, all written by experts in their fields.

Hutchinson's ideas for the *BOP* were at odds with the RTS's original plans for a wholesome boy's paper. The RTS Committee had envisaged a vigorously Christian publication which would be part of the Society's missionary work. After a series of prototypes and sustained arguments, Hutchinson convinced the Committee that it could best counteract the popular press with a more secular kind of publication. His efforts were so successful that far from being the loss-making enterprise the Society (and every commercial publisher they had approached) expected, the *BOP* turned out to be highly profitable. Perhaps for this reason a companion paper for girls (*THE GIRL'S OWN PAPER*) was launched the following year.

The success of the *BOP* was immediate. Within three months it had achieved a circulation of 200,000, which probably represented a readership of 600,000. Priced at only one penny (the price was fixed until 1916), it could be afforded by the same audience as purchased the penny dreadfuls, but with its high quality design, lavish illustrations and incorporation of features such as full-colour pull-out sections printed on good-quality paper, it represented much better value for money. Perhaps such attributes alone would not have attracted habitual readers of thrilling adventures, but Hutchinson made a point of including exciting serialised fiction by the best writers of the day – including JULES VERNE, Gordon Stables, W.H.G. KINGSTON and R.M. BALLANTYNE. He was equally adamant about the need to employ first-class illustrators.

The magazine ceased weekly publication in 1914 and became a 'monthly'. Hutchinson's editorship came to an end with his death in 1913. He was succeeded by a succession of editors, culminating in the appointment of Jack Cox, the paper's last editor and one of its historians. Cox oversaw the paper's last issue in February 1967. By the time of its demise the *BOP* was no longer the eclectic paper of Hutchinson's day but had become solidly middle-class. Its readership declined steadily throughout the 20th century and the magazine became increasingly slim until it was a shade of its former self. The last *Boy's Own Annual* was issued in 1940. KR

Boylston, Helen Dore 1895–1984 American author of career novels for girls. Trained as a nurse, Boylston served with the British Expeditionary Force in France during World War I and with the Red Cross afterwards. She held several nursing positions in New England before pursuing writing full-time. Her nursing experience is the basis of many of her books, including *Sister: The War Diary of a Nurse* (1927), *Clara Barton, Founder of the American Red Cross* (1955), and the *Sue Barton* series (1936–52) for which she is best known. Seven novels trace Sue Barton's career from her training days to her work as a visiting nurse, a superintendent of nurses and a staff nurse. The series also addresses the development of strong female friendships and Sue's romance with Dr William Barry, whom she marries in the fifth book. Boylston's *Carol* series (1941–6) is about the life of an actress from her apprenticeship and first summer stock position to modest success on Broadway and with a touring Shakespearean production. Though criticised for lack of depth, Boylston is praised for her honest portrayal of vocations often unrealistically romanticised in fiction, for her promotion of working women and for her humour. Boylston's series were the first career novels published in America. JLB

bracelet shading In PICTUREBOOK illustration, a line used within a contour line, to give the impression of volume to a shape. Forearms, legs, cloth covering body shapes, tree trunks and any cylindrical shape can be modelled by bracelet shading. JD

Bradbury, Ray Douglas 1920– Writer of SCIENCE FICTION and FANTASY novels and short stories for adults and young adults. Born in Waukegan, Illinois, Bradbury moved to Los Angeles as a teenager. He began his writing career in the late 1930s as a contributor to the pulp magazines that were then popular. In Los Angeles he continued to be an active writer, creative consultant, and speaker. He has received many AWARDS, among them the O. Henry Memorial Award (1948), the World Fantasy Award for Lifetime Achievement (1977), the Jules Verne Award (1984), the Grand Master Nebula Award (1988), the Bram Stoker Award (1989), and the Los Angeles Citizen of the Year Award (1995).

His successful writing career has covered a wide variety of genres, including novels, short stories, plays and poems, but he is best known as a writer of science fiction. *The Martian Chronicles* (1950) established Bradbury as a writer who was keenly concerned about the social problems of his own world, such as the nuclear arms race and censorship. In one of his most famous works, *Fahrenheit 451* (1953), he continued to explore issues of social justice, focusing on a futuristic totalitarian world in which books are strictly controlled and sometimes burned by the government.

Bradbury's fame as a writer of science fiction, however, should not overshadow his literary successes in different genres, including horror and fantasy. *Something Wicked This Way Comes* (1962) is one of his novels that best demonstrates his unique blend of horror and fantasy. He has also written numerous short story collections that focus on the horrid and macabre, including *The Illustrated Man* (1951) and *Long After Midnight* (1976). Bradbury uses horror to provoke readers to recognise that even the small sins with which most individuals must struggle every day – greed, sloth and envy, for instance – can lead to disastrous results, as they do in Bradbury's dark and sinister world. SAI

Bradford, Clare see PAPERS: EXPLORATIONS INTO CHILDREN'S LITERATURE

Bradford, Karleen 1936– Ontario-born writer of fiction and non-fiction. Her first books, *Wrong Again, Robbie* (1983) – originally published as *A Year for Growing Up* (1983) – *I Wish There Were Unicorns* (1983) and *Thirteenth Child* (1994) are contemporary problem novels concerned with the troubles and difficulties of young adult experience. Bradford's TIME-SLIP novels, which often portray protagonists who go back in time to change history, include *The Other Elizabeth* (1982), the historical FANTASY, *Haunting at Cliff House* (1985) and *Nine Days Queen* (1986), about Lady Jane Grey. Her non-fiction includes *Animal Heroes* (1995) and *Write Now!* (1996). *There Will Be Wolves* (1992) – the first in her historical series about the Crusades – won the 1993 Canadian Library Association's Young Adult Book Award. *Shadows on a Sword* (1996) is the second book in her *Crusades* quartet; the last to appear so far is *Lionheart's Scribe* (1999), which is about Richard the Lionheart. MRS

Bradman, Tony, 1954– British author and promoter of children's books. As a journalist with an interest in popular culture, he worked on a magazine for parents, introducing REVIEWS of children's books and a 'babies' book' AWARD. From 1984 he published a wide variety of books for toddlers and young readers. Inspired by his own experience of parenthood, his humorous recreation of chaotic family life and his sympathetic portrayal of naughtiness appeal to children. Best known as the creator of *DILLY THE DINOSAUR*, his other writing includes PICTUREBOOKS, novels, poetry, and anthologies of poetry and prose. *Look Out, He's Behind You!* (1988) and *A Bad Week for the Three Bears* (1992) provide witty twists on traditional nursery tales. *Sam The Girl Detective* (1989) and its sequels are snappy whodunits quite accessible to readers too young to recognise the clever parody of

Chandler. Bradman's poetry anthologies, such as *The Mad Family* (1987), frequently deal with aspects of family life and relationships, whilst *Amazing Adventure Stories* (1994) and similar compilations bring together stories by established authors on themes that will attract young, fluent readers. In 1998 he wrote *The Tale of Joseph and His Brothers*. British public lending library statistics for 1996 ranked Bradman within the top ten children's authors. PC

Bragg, Mabel see *The Little Engine That Could*

***Bramley Hedge* series** (from 1980) British series written and illustrated by Jill Barklem, the first four of which were named after the seasons. The well-written and decriptive texts serve mainly as vehicles for the pictures, which are deservedly popular and widely marketed in spin-off products. The tales tell of a family of anthropomorphic mice, living in the roots and trunks of hedgerow trees, who enjoy a cosy life, celebrating different festivals and seasonal changes. The pictures – which vary in format from double page-openings to vignettes – invite imaginative and attentive readers to enter a fascinating miniature world, the story often leading them into a new location illustrated with a feast of fine detail. Colours are used subtly to enhance mood and show changes in light and weather conditions. The ENDPAPERS are sepia-toned pictorial maps, and the printing and packaging are reminiscent of ALISON UTTLEY'S *LITTLE GREY RABBIT* series. JSW

Brancato, Robin 1936– American author of YOUNG ADULT FICTION. A graduate of the University of Pennyslvania, Brancato taught high school and junior high school English and also worked as a copy-editor. Her popular contemporary novels for young adults include *Winning* (1977), winner of the ALA Best Book for Young Adults, *Blinded by the Light* (1978), a Literary Guild Selection made into a CBS Movie of the Week, and *Come Alive at 505* (1980), another ALA Best Book for Young Adults. *Don't Sit Under the Apple Tree* (1975) and *Sweet Bells Jangled Out of Tune* (1982) are other novels in which Brancato explores the personal experiences, defeats and triumphs, fears and reassurances of young people. In *Facing Up* (1984) the theme is the gains and losses of affection, while in the FANTASY, *Uneasy Money* (1986), the rueful theme deals with the losses and gains that accompany a lottery win. MRS

Brand, Christianna see *Nurse Matilda series*

Brandt, Katrin 1942– German illustrator. Brandt studied painting and graphic design in Hannover and published her first children's book, *The Elves and the Shoemaker*, in 1967. In the following year, this book was awarded the German Children's Book Prize and Brandt's work was then published in the United Kingdom and the United States. Detail, vigour and subtle watercolour characterise Brandt's work. JAG

Branford, Henrietta 1946–99 Prolific and versatile children's author, born in India and brought up in Jordan and England. Branford's novels for older readers are characterised by taut narrative and a sharp, precise style appropriate to uncompromising representations of cruelty and suffering. *Fire, Bed and Bone* (1998), winner of the *Guardian* Children's Fiction Prize and the Bronze Smarties Prize, is an animal AUTOBIOGRAPHY set during the peasant rebellion of 1381; *White Wolf* (1998) – another animal biography – is set in the American West. *The Fated Sky* (1997), however, has a Norse setting, while *Chance of Safety* (1998) is a pacy and chilling thriller set in a futuristic dystopian Britain.

Branford's other works could hardly be more different, providing for very young children and newly independent readers. The *Spacebaby* stories (from 1996) are fast-moving, hi-tech comic thrillers about a benevolent space traveller who arrives in the form of a baby, while the *Royal Blunder* stories (from 1994) are gentle, rather dreamy stories about a magical cat companion. The *Dimanche Diller* stories (from 1994) are outstanding thrillers for very young readers – about a little girl orphaned in the opening paragraph and subsequently fought over for her wealth. In all her stories for younger readers – including the more quirky *Ruby Red* (1998) and *Dipper's Island* (1999) – Branford's heroes and heroines possess a determined resourcefulness reminiscent of *PIPPI LONGSTOCKING* and suggest a world of danger which can always be defeated in the end by love, friendship and cleverness – a characteristic which made her an especially appropriate choice to write *Hansel and Gretel* (1998) in Scholastic's series of FAIRY TALE retellings. VW

see also *Song Quest*

Bransby, Lawrence 1951– South African writer of novels for teenagers who made a striking début with *Down Street* (1989) and *Homeward Bound* (1990), which are searing attacks on the racism, sexism and brutal masculine values that were to be found in typical South African schools for white pupils prior to the end of apartheid. Two subsequent novels continued to combine adolescent angst with the turmoil that accompanied the transition to democracy. *Outside the Walls* (1995) is written in a bitter, facetious style with the crude language that Bransby often unashamedly adopts. *The Boy who Counted to a Million* (1995) represents the gentler, religious side of his writing. In a skilful combination of two plots, a white boy is weaned off his craze for war as real violence increases around him. Bransby's stories with girl protagonists also reflect these two sides to his writing. *The Geek in Shining Armour* (1992) is a typical, and unexceptional, teenage problem novel about a girl getting mixed up in the wrong crowd. *A Mountaintop Experience* (1992), on the other hand, is unusual in that it concerns a girl's search for a religious answer to her sordid family life.

ERJ

Brassman's Secret, The African PICTUREBOOK by MESHACK ASARE, published in Ghana in 1981 under conditions in which the design and printing of a children's picturebook amounted in itself to a major achievement. Through the story of a boy and his longing for gold, Asare celebrates the life and history of an Asante village. The boy passes many tests, returning from a FANTASY adventure wiser but no richer, to be welcomed by 'real boys and real girls, the hardworking, noisy, happy children of the Asante town'. The sharp irony of the storytelling is reinforced by dramatic illustrations in black ink. VW

Brathwaite, Edward Kamau see *POETRY JUMP UP*; *I LIKE THAT STUFF*

Bratton, J.S. see CRITICAL APPROACHES TO CHILDREN'S BOOKS

Brazil, Angela 1869–1947 British SCHOOL STORY writer, best known for her representations of a new breed of jolly schoolgirls, full of japes and racy slang. Brazil was born in Preston, Lancashire, where her father was a cotton mill manager, and the family moved frequently during her childhood, which is vividly recalled in her autobiography, *My Own Schooldays* (1925). Brazil went to the preparatory department of Manchester High School and then to Ellerslie, before joining her older sister, Amy, at art school in London. After the death of her father and the publication of her first work, *The Mischievous Brownie*, in 1899, she travelled with her mother and sister. In 1911 she moved to Coventry to keep house for her brother, Walter, who was in medical practice, and after the death of their mother in 1915 they were joined by their sister. None of the three ever married, sharing the same house in Coventry until Angela's death in 1947.

Throughout her writing life Brazil contributed to a variety of magazines, children's ANNUALS and story collections. Her indisputable influence on the shape and style of the girls' school story began with *The Fortunes of Philippa* (1906), based loosely on her mother's girlhood experience. Written in the first person, the book had stylistic imperfections but its intentions were clear: Brazil had rescued the girls' school story from the moralistic strictures of writers like L.T. MEADE and Mrs. de Horne Vaizey, and the modern fictional schoolgirl was about to come into her own. *The Third Class at Miss Kaye's* (1908), *The Nicest Girl in the School* (1909), *Bosom Friends* (1909) and *A Fourth Form Friendship* (1911), all written in the third person, rapidly established Brazil's reputation.

The outbreak of war in 1914 enabled Brazil to incorporate new features from its crises into the girls' school story and marked her most productive and vigorous writing period. Despite their immediate popularity, *The School by the Sea* (1914), *The Madcap of the School* (1917), *A Patriotic Schoolgirl* (1918) and *For the School Colours* (1918) are flawed by a ruthless authorial determination to bend character to plot, and by a sometimes painfully ingenuous schoolgirl response to events.

Unconstrained by narrative judgement, her schoolgirl creations work their way through acts of enormous condescension (starting a society for the 'Poor Brave Things' – crippled children – for whom they plan a 'romp' in *For the School Colours*) and unselfconscious snobbery. To the modern reader, however, the schoolgirl pride in 'Britishness' and strong anti-German sentiments are reminders that Brazil's work has few of the qualities of timelessness.

In her later novels, such as *The School on the Cliff* (1938) and *Five Jolly Schoolgirls* (1941), the artless intensity of passionate schoolgirl friendships has diminished, but the zest of the earlier books is lacking. Brazil's prolific output was maintained to the last but became increasingly formulaic, with repetitions of old plots and adventures, and her final volume, *The School on the Loch* (1946), is no exception.

In spite of their dated quality, the stories have retained a popularity, in part because the schoolgirl ethic, however risible it seems in pastiche, is a compelling feature for modern readers whose experience of school may be very different. BW

Breaktime (1978) The first in a series of linked experimental novels about adolescence by AIDAN CHAMBERS; an early British example of serious books for teenagers, dealing with the complexities of their lives in the late 20th century. Chambers overturns two sets of conventions: sex taboos and the accepted forms of romantic fiction. Paradoxically, in demonstrating the inadequacy of language to represent teenage thought and feeling, he shows how the constructed power of a text both disturbs and extends young readers' perspectives on literature. The narrator is the hero, Ditto (i.e. just like all the rest). Challenged by his rationalist schoolfriend, Morgan, to prove that literature is more than fictive wordplay, Ditto keeps a diary of his first break from home constraints, when he goes camping, looking for 'action, event, drama' and sexual initiation with the more experienced Helen. In witty self-deprecation he relates the facts of his adventures.

Memories and feelings intrude to break up the linear account, interweaving it with graphics, quotations, play-script, shifts of viewpoint and other narrative and semiotic devices associated with the metafictive in Joyce, Kundera, Calvino, CORMIER and GARNER. Critics select the textual daring of the representation of the sex act as Chambers's most strenuous challenge to his readers. The page is divided to calibrate Ditto's commentaries on the event and a quotation from Benjamin Spock's sex manual. This experience of textual jouissance extends the readers' understanding of partnership with the author and prepares them for adult texts in contemporary literature. MM

see also SEX IN CHILDREN'S BOOKS

Bregin, Elana 1954– South African author. Her *The Kayaboeties*, which won the Young Africa Award in 1989, is a novel set in Durban where Bregin grew up and spent much of her adult life. It is a humorous yet tense tale of the transition to a post-apartheid society, and shows white children discovering friendship with a black boy. Since then, Bregin has won that award twice more with strong, politically aware youth novels, *The Boy From the Other Side* (1992) and *The Red-Haired Khumalo* (1994). Her concern about the ill-treatment of animals led to such environmentally minded books as *Warrior of Wilderness* (1989) and *Bert the Crusher* (1995). JHe

Brent-Dyer, Elinor M. see *CHALET SCHOOL* SERIES; see also SCHOOL STORIES; WAR STORIES

Brer Rabbit see JOEL CHANDLER HARRIS; see also BUGS BUNNY

Breslin, Theresa Contemporary Scottish author of novels for young people and a children's librarian in Glasgow. A realistic, dramatic storyteller who draws on Scottish speech, history and environment, Breslin's stories concern the vulnerabilities and tensions of growing up in challenging, often extreme circumstances and illustrate the redemptive power of relationships. She won the Carnegie Medal in 1995 with *Whispers in the Graveyard* (1994). Impoverished, dyslexic Solomon is empowered by a younger child and a teacher to overcome macabre supernatural forces. In the process he gains the fortitude to start facing up to and engaging with the painful realities of his life. It is a gripping story in which Breslin makes some pertinent, ironic observations about schools. In *Kezzie* (1993) a fatherless family endures the 1930s Depression in Glasgow until Kezzie's sister is taken to Canada as part of the Child Emigration scheme. Kezzie's perseverance and loving family loyalty are tested and strengthened on her heroic journey to rescue Lucy. In the sequel, *A Homecoming For Kezzie* (1995), the reunited family experience the Clydebank Blitz. *Alien Force* (1995) is a SCIENCE FICTION thriller and *Death or Glory Boys* (1996) is a terrorist thriller. Recent work, for younger readers, includes *Name Games* (1997) and *Blair, the Winner* (1997). VCH

Brett, Jan (Churchill) 1949– American author, painter and illustrator of children's books from 1970s to the present. A native of New England, Brett always hoped to illustrate books, and she became an avid art lover and student. After developing a notably detailed and ornate style as she illustrated books by other authors, Brett then began adapting old folktales and creating stories of her own. Her texts are usually surrounded by eye-catching borders and side panels, which often foreshadow or tell a parallel story that observant readers will pick out and follow. For example, in her retelling of the Ukrainian folktale *The Mitten* (1989), eight animals squeeze one by one into a lost mitten lying in the snow. The animals, which become progressively larger as the story unfolds, are subtly revealed by Brett within her intricate borders. Like *The Mitten*, many of her stories are set in natural surroundings, and her characters are often animals, although she uses Scandinavian trolls, as, for example, in *The Trouble With Trolls* (1992). Brett's books have been published in several foreign languages, including Norwegian, German and French. CHW

'Briar Rose' see 'SLEEPING BEAUTY'; see also JANE YOLEN

Bridwell, Norman (Ray) 1928– American author and illustrator of the series beginning with *Clifford, the Big Red Dog* (1962). Clifford, huge but lovable, continues to be extremely popular with young children. A new series of board books, about 'Clifford, the small red puppy' has subsequently been produced, including *Clifford's Peekaboo* (1991) and *Clifford's Bedtime* (1991). PDS

Brierley, Louise 1958– British illustrator particularly known for her *The Twelve Days of Christmas* (1986), illustrated with elongated, elfin figures in mysterious, medieval, wintry pastel-coloured settings. Similar figures haunt her *Songs for Shakespeare* (1992) where tiny cameos perfectly echo and reflect the moods of the different songs. But Brierley refuses to be pigeon-holed. Maud, the central character of *The Fisherwoman* (Anne Carter, 1990) is as robust as any Henry Moore sculpture, and *Celebration Song* (JAMES BERRY, 1994) gives us a black Mary and infant Jesus amidst elemental and rust-coloured symbolic landscapes. *Creation Stories* (Margaret Mayo, 1995) and *Beauty and the Beast* (ADÈLE GERAS, 1996) confirm Brierley as a powerful and original interpreter of MYTH and FAIRY STORY. JAG

Briggs, K(atharine) M(ary) 1898–1980 British academic and folklorist who wrote two novels for adults, *Hobberdy Dick* (1955) and *Kate Crackernuts* (1963) both of which have been appropriated by children since Kestrel reissued them in 1978 and 1979 respectively. The social upheaval caused by the 17th-century Civil War is at the root of each: in *Hobberdy Dick* the loyalty of a helpful and caring hob 'in charge' of a Royalist manor house is challenged when his beloved family is supplanted by Puritans. Setting *Kate Crackernuts* (a long novel based on the brief FOLKTALE) in Scotland enabled Briggs to explore the horrors of witchcraft rife there at this period. Her four-volume *Dictionary of English Folktales* was published in 1970–71. EM

Briggs, Raymond (Redvers) 1934– British author and illustrator of PICTUREBOOKS, best known for his work in comic-strip form. Briggs was born in South London and attended Wimbledon Art School between 1949 and 1953. There followed two years National Service and then two years at the Slade School of Art, where he realised that his talents were as an illustrator rather than a painter. In the early 60s Briggs wrote some stories of his own and illustrated three small collections of NURSERY RHYMES, but recognition came only with the publication in 1966 of *The Mother Goose Treasury* for which he had produced nearly 900 illustrations and for which he won the Kate Greenaway Medal.

Briggs continued to illustrate the work of others, and in 1969, with ELFRIDA VIPONT, he created *THE ELEPHANT AND THE BAD BABY*, a book that has remained popular with parents, teachers and young children ever since. In 1970 Briggs published his own *Jim and the Beanstalk*, an ironic reinterpretation of the traditional tale, in which the giant is treated with some light-hearted realism and turned into one of the illustrator's characteristically grumpy old men. In the next few years Briggs gradually ceased to illustrate the work of others and began to concentrate upon producing his own picturebooks. *FATHER CHRISTMAS*, published in 1973, was many months in the making and won its creator the Kate Greenaway Medal for the second time. The sequels, *Father Christmas Goes on Holiday* and *Father Christmas Having a Wonderful Time* appeared in 1975 and 1993 respectively. The depiction in *Fungus the Bogeyman* (1977) of an imaginary world that was deliberately repulsive perplexed many of its original readers. The *Fungus the Bogeyman Plop-up Book*, the result of a collaboration with paper engineer Ron van der Meer, appeared in 1982 (see also MOVABLE BOOKS).

Briggs is perhaps best known for the wordless picturebook *THE SNOWMAN* (1978), a book which has a directness and narrative drive that stem from Briggs's long apprenticeship as a storyteller in pictures. It was, and still is, deservedly popular. Briggs's sympathy for the underdog and his contempt for officialdom and authority emerged in *Gentleman Jim* (1980), and two years later he placed the same bemused but well-meaning everyman figure at the heart of *When the Wind Blows* (1982), his moving tale of nuclear war and its aftermath. In 1984 Briggs's talent for satire and his distaste for authoritarianism came together in *The Tin-Pot Foreign General and the Old Iron Woman* where he bitingly caricatured the political leaders involved in the Falklands war. He returned to the theme of the misfit and the underdog with *Unlucky Wally* (1987) and *Unlucky Wally Twenty Years On* (1989), and then in 1992 published *The Man*, a book which revealed Briggs to be experimenting once again with the possibilities of the picturebook form, this time combining pictures with direct speech to create a vividly realised FANTASY in the vein of *The Snowman*. A similar tale, *The Bear*, followed in 1994. In 1999 Briggs published *ETHEL & ERNEST: A TRUE STORY*, a touching account of his parents' marriage. DL

'The Raven and the Pea Pod Man'. Illustration from *Creation Stories* by Louise Brierley.

Brighton, Catherine 1943– British illustrator and creator of BIOGRAPHIES for children. Her reputation rests on her re-creation in words and pictures of the childhoods of the famous, such as *Nijinsky* (1989), *Mozart* (1990) and *The Brontës* (1994), and of the lives of children living through famous eras – *Dearest Grandmama* (1991), *Rosalee and the Great Fire of London* (1994) and *My Napoleon* (1997). The dramas and imagined feelings of her child

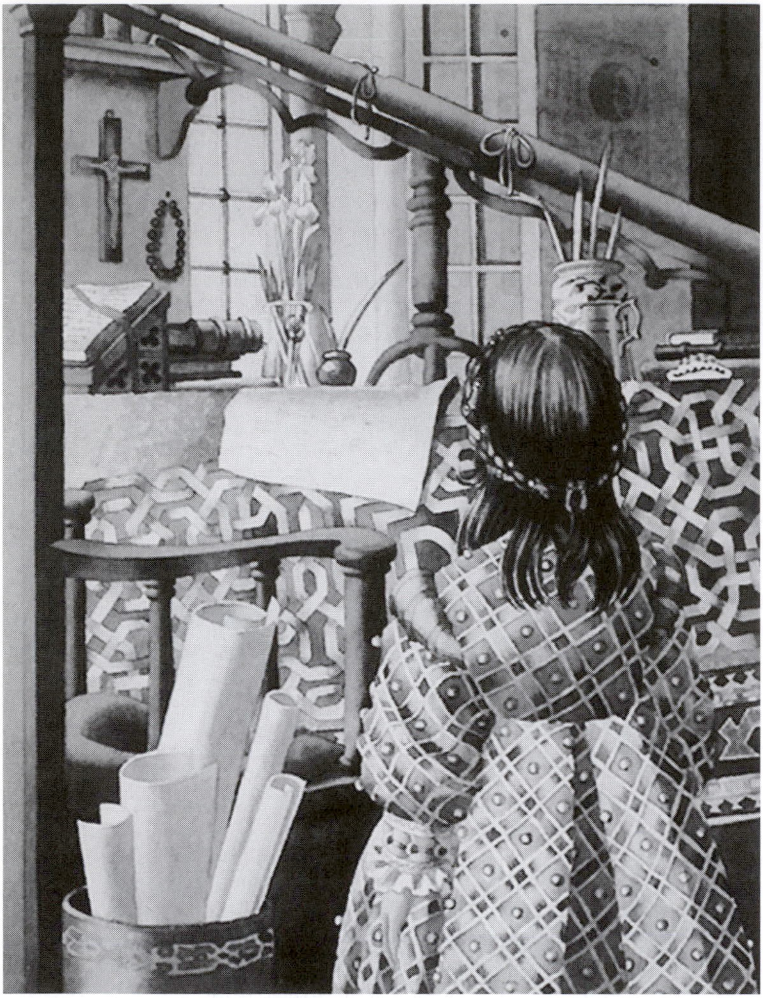

Illustration from *Five Secrets in a Box* by Catherine Brighton, the story of Galileo's daughter.

characters are placed in carefully researched, historically accurate contexts, but they also have an emotional truth which reaches the reader of today. Her stylised, watercolour illustrations make dramatic use of frames, of light and shade, of pattern and of colour, and she includes much detail for her readers to discover. JAG

Bringing the Rain to Kapiti Plain (1981) African FOLKTALE first recorded in the early years of the 20th century. It is retold by VERNA AARDEMA in strong rhythmic verse, using the cumulative patterning of *The House that Jack Built*. Beatriz Vidal illustrates it with stylised images capturing the Kenyan countryside and its inhabitants. AR

Brink, Carol Ryrie 1895–1981 American author of over 30 novels for children and adults. Born in Moscow, Idaho, Brink described her childhood as happy, but also marked 'by death, disaster and loneliness'. Indeed, before she was nine her father had died of consumption, her grandfather had been murdered and her mother had committed suicide. Brink was subsequently raised by her grandmother and aunt. These tragedies, she felt, intensified the joys in her life and contributed to her development as a writer. After college, she married her childhood sweetheart, with whom she had two children.

Brink is known for her historical and realistic fiction. She is praised for her sympathetic and humorous depiction of family life and childhood, with an emphasis on self-reliance and steadfastness. She based many of her stories on her own family's adventures and travels, often in Europe. Her best-known novel, *Caddie Woodlawn* (1935), won the 1936 Newbery Medal, and is a recounting of her grandmother's childhood. It is the warm and enduring story of a lively tomboy and her family's struggle to make a home for themselves in the wilderness of Wisconsin during the 1860s; it was followed by a sequel, *Magical Melons* (1944). JKB

see also FAMILY STORIES; HISTORICAL FICTION

Brinsmead, H(esba) F(ay) 1922– Australian writer of over 20 novels, whose first book for teenagers, *Pastures of the Blue Crane* (1964), winner of the Children's Book Council of Australia Book of the Year Award (1965), is considered a watershed in the depiction of racial prejudice; Amaryllis (Rhyl) Merewether meets Perry, a part South Sea Islander, who turns out to be her brother. Often referred to as a writer of realistic novels for and about teenagers, Brinsmead's version of reality is coloured by her strong value-system – principally, the belief that constructive action through hard work will lead to self-fulfilment and overcome inner weaknesses, or even external misfortunes. Brinsmead relies on several devices to enable her romantic heroines to achieve success – a fortuitous absence of parents, timely coincidences and convenient acquisition of wealth.

Like MAVIS THORPE CLARK, Brinsmead draws upon her wide first-hand experiences of Australia to provide accurate detail and settings for her books – fossicking in the outback for *A Sapphire for September* (1967); weed-spraying in south-west Tasmania for *Season of the Briar* (1965); and ocean fishing for *Listen to the Wind* (1970). *Bianca and Roja* (1992), set in Yugoslavia, moves away from realism to a FAIRY TALE genre, but it lacks the vigour of her earlier work. *Longtime Dreaming* (1982) and *Christmas at Longtime* (1983) are semi-factual and based on her 1920s childhood, set in the Blue Mountains of New South Wales, but her writing is at its best in the first of these reminiscences, *Longtime Passing* (1971). Told with a humour tinged with nostalgia and warmth, this book gives insight into Brinsmead's roots and explains her concern to give young people, through her writing, the same kind of character-building experiences. JAP

Brisley, Joyce Lankester see *MILLY-MOLLY-MANDY* SERIES

Brock, C(harles) E(dmund) 1870–1938 and **H(enry) M(atthew)** 1875–1960 British illustrators. The fine line ILLUSTRATIONS in the first edition of E. NESBIT'S *THE RAILWAY CHILDREN* (1906) are typical of the work of C.E. Brock, the elder of the two brothers. Often called 'costume' illustrations, they successfully illuminate period, plot and character. Much of C.E. Brock's considerable output is found in the line illustrations for classics such as *GULLIVER'S TRAVELS* (1894) and FRANCIS HODGSON BURNETT'S *LITTLE LORD FAUNTLEROY* (1925). H.M. Brock was an equally prolific illustrator, contributing to many children's magazines, ANNUALS and SCHOOL and ADVENTURE STORIES. He is best remembered for his colour and line work for Warne's series of FAIRY TALES. Both brothers also illustrated adult fiction. JAG

'The sisters visited her every night.' Illustration by H.M. Brock for HANS CHRISTIAN ANDERSEN'S *Fairy Tales.*

broken outline A characteristic of an artist's style which allows the ground space to enter the figure. The effect imparts a liveliness to the figure because the pen itself seems to have skipped over the paper as it made the marks. PICTUREBOOKS illustrated by QUENTIN BLAKE, TONY ROSS and JOHN BURNINGHAM furnish examples. JD

Brontë, Charlotte 1816–55, **Emily** 1818–48 and **Anne** 1820–49 British authors. In any study of children and literature the Brontë sisters must be considered important figures. There are substantial reasons for this, one being that like Jane Austen, they and their brother Branwell were precocious and prolific child-authors. The four Brontë children grew up at Haworth Parsonage in Yorkshire with their father, the Reverend Patrick Brontë, with whom they enjoyed an unconventional upbringing, reading freely and eclectically.

Their juvenilia, written around the imaginary places and inhabitants of Verdopolis (Glasstown), Gondal and Angria, shows influences as diverse as the *ARABIAN NIGHTS' ENTERTAINMENTS*, the Bible, SIR WALTER SCOTT, and *Blackwood's Magazine*, whose tales of terror and travelogues were devoured with equal avidity. Although bearing the unmistakeable imprint of Gothic romances, the writings of the young Brontës experiment with a range of voices and perspectives, and there is a developing sense of the complexities of character and motivation which lend interest to these works. A fascination with humanity's darker potential is also evident in these early pieces.

In their adult novels a different kind of contribution was made, one which may have helped to reshape the notion of the child and thus the literature produced for children. All three sisters show an impatience with literary stereotypes of the child, and the representation of children in them is firmly unsentimental; in describing Adèle, Jane Eyre writes:

> She had no great talents, no marked traits of character, no peculiar development of feeling or taste which raised her one inch above the ordinary level of childhood; but neither had she any deficiency or vice which sunk her below it . . . This, *par parenthèse*, will be thought cool language by persons who entertain solemn doctrines about the *angelic nature of children*, and the duty of those charged with their education to conceive for them an idolatrous devotion. But I am not writing to flatter parental egotism, to echo cant, or prop up humbug; I am merely telling the truth.

Jane Eyre (1847) – which is one of the first works of serious adult fiction to be encountered by many young readers – may fairly claim to be the first English novel to have closely scrutinised children rather than merely utilising them as symbols. Furthermore, it traces the development of the adult from his or her childhood beginnings, and ironically displays the discrepancy between the doting view of the Reed and Brocklehurst children as angels and the hypocritical, even vicious, reality. A similar point is made by Anne Brontë in *Agnes Grey* (1847), and in Emily Brontë's *Wuthering Heights* (1847), Cathy and Heathcliff peer through a window of Thrushcross Grange to find the Linton children screaming and fighting, the private view a far cry from the public image.

But children in the Brontë novels are also shown to possess a deep imaginative and emotional life, and this insight may have been a factor in the development of children's literature as children's authors began to cater for aspects of children other than their moral development. In Jane's response to *Bewick's Book of British Birds*, where the child contemplates pictures and weaves her own narratives around them, her imagination stimulated by the images, we may perhaps also see a foreshadowing of the idea of the PICTUREBOOK for the child; less than 30 years later, in ALICE'S ADVENTURES IN WONDERLAND, another famous fictional child would ask what good a book without pictures or conversations was, the remark demonstrating a radical shift in assumptions governing children's books.

Finally, the Brontës have contributed to children's literature through the way in which their lives, writings and doings have continued to inspire later children's books. ANTONIA FOREST'S *Peter's Room* (1961), PAULINE CLARKE'S *The Twelve and the Genii* (1963), JANE GARDAM'S *THE SUMMER AFTER THE FUNERAL* (1973) and GARY KILWORTH'S *The Brontë Girls* (1995) are some examples of this. SA

Bronzeville Boys and Girls (1956) First and best-known children's book by the distinguished AFRICAN AMERICAN author Gwendolyn Brooks. Her initial volumes of poetry for adults, *A Street in Bronzeville* (1945) and the Pulitzer-Prize-winning *Annie Allen* (1949), established childhood as central to Brooks's exploration of the complex lives of Chicago's black urban poor. *Bronzeville Boys and Girls* presents the early years of those lives when the rich interior life of dreams does not negate but still outweighs material circumstance. Thirty-four poems, each featuring its title's character(s), show children at play and in moments of reflection about self, family, pets, glimpses of nature, the necessity of moving house again or of hiding disappointments from anxious parents. Brooks varies form and metre, and employs a variety of poetic devices coupled with striking images: for example, 'no door-screen dust' smudges a child's clean face. Contemporary reviewers praised the poems' 'universal' appeal and sensitivity to the child's inner world, and Ronni Solbert's ILLUSTRATIONS reinforced that view by downplaying racial identifiers. Later critics have appreciated the book's subtle signifiers of urban African American experience, and it continues to inspire favourable comparison with more recent works such as ELOISE GREENFIELD'S *Night on Neighborhood Street*. JMA

Brook, Judy 1926– British illustrator. Brook has produced several, sprightly, line and colour wash PICTUREBOOKS from 1966 onwards in the *Tim Mouse* series. The resourceful Tim heroically acts, rescues and leads against a background of idyllic English countryside. JAG

Brooke, L(eonard) Leslie 1862–1940 British author and illustrator, at his most ingenious working with the wit and eccentricities of NONSENSE VERSE. His *Nursery Rhyme Book* (1897), edited by Andrew Lang, foreshadowed his exuberant versions of EDWARD LEAR'S longer poems. His pictures complement and extend his own whimsical rhymes most delightfully in *Johnny Crow's Garden* (1903) and its two sequels: *Johnny Crow's Party* (1907) and, almost 30 years later, *Johnny Crow's New Garden* (1935). Hidden within the detail of his finest ILLUSTRATIONS, including those for four FAIRY TALES in *The Golden Goose Book* (1905), there are amusing stories-within-stories for children to discover. GPF

Brooks, Ron(ald George) 1948– Australian-born illustrator who did much to establish the modern PICTUREBOOK in that country. With text by JENNY WAGNER, *The Bunyip of Berkeley's Creek* (1973) won the Children's Book Council of Australia Picture Book of the Year AWARD, as did *JOHN BROWN, ROSE AND THE MIDNIGHT CAT* (1977), also with text by Wagner. Brooks's ILLUSTRATIONS for *Aranea: A Story about a Spider* (1975) and *Motor Bill and the Lovely Caroline* (1994), both with Wagner, and for *Old Pig* (1995), with text by MARGARET WILD, demonstrate his sensitive interpretation of the text. His own books, *Annie's Rainbow* (1975) and *Timothy and Gramps* (1978) explore the inner imaginative life of children. Whether using fine line and intricate CROSS-HATCHING (both in colour and black and white) in his early books, or luminous free-flowing colour with line in his later work, Brooks suggests rather than states, inviting his audience to explore the meaning constructed by his paintings. While he is never aggressively Australian he did introduce local icons into his early work, such as a platypus, a kookaburra perched in a tree, and of course the bunyip; his fences, too, are peculiarly Australian. Yet Brooks's art is universal, drawing on archetypal folk images in *Annie's Rainbow* and using animals as symbols of timeless human emotions and characteristics. MSax

see also ANIMALS IN FICTION

Browin, Frances Williams 1898– American editor, essayist, and author of children's and adult books. Born in Media, Pennsylvania, Browin attended Swarthmore College and moved to Philadelphia. She is particularly interested in reconstructing the past, taking special pleasure and interest in letters, diaries, old newspaper articles, and other materials relating to America's history. Her writings tend to be historical and informational and usually demonstrate careful research and attention to detail. In 1953 Browin received an award from the Freedoms Foundation for several of her essays. Among her children's books are *Ginger's Cave* (1954), *The Whozits* (1955), *Bridge to Brooklyn* (1956), *Looking for Orlando* (1961) and *Coins Have Tales to Tell* (1966). She has also co-authored books with Seale Harris and Florence Aiken Banks. JGJ

see also HISTORICAL FICTION; INFORMATION BOOKS

Brown, Jeff see *FLAT STANLEY* SERIES; TOMI UNGERER

Brown, Marc (Tolon) 1946– American author and illustrator whose best-known series of books involve an anteater called Arthur. From the first title, *Arthur's Nose* (1976), these books describe situations with which children readily identify, such as losing a tooth, having to wear glasses, or dealing with an obnoxious friend. *Arthur Writes a Book* (1998) is a recent adventure. *Arthur's Baby* (1987) introduced a new baby sister, D.W., who eventually joined forces alongside Arthur with several titles of her own including *D.W.! Go to Your Room!* (1999). Brown, whose preferred media are pencil and watercolour, has also illustrated FOLKTALES and numerous other books. One of his own non-fiction series depicts dinosaurs dealing with issues of safety, travel, the environment, divorce and death. He is also the editor and illustrator for a series on finger, hand, play and party rhymes. PDS

Brown, Marcia (Joan) 1918– American translator, reteller, author, and illustrator of PICTUREBOOKS. Born in Rochester, New York, and educated at the Woodstock School of Painting and New York College for Teachers, Brown worked as a storyteller at the New York Public Library. Her skilful use of different media to illustrate and enhance her retellings of stories from different cultures and periods has often been praised. She was the first artist to receive the prestigious CALDECOTT MEDAL from the ALA three times: in 1955 for her pen-and-inks with pastel colour overwashes for *CINDERELLA*, in 1962 for woodblocks in *Once a Mouse*, and in 1983 for her COLLAGE illustrations for Blaise Cendrars's *Shadow*. In addition, Brown has received six Caldecott Honour Book Awards: *Stone Soup: An Old Tale* (1947); *Henry-Fisherman: A Story of the Virgin Islands* (1949); *DICK WHITTINGTON AND HIS CAT* (1950); *Skipper John's Cook* (1951); *PUSS IN BOOTS* (1952); and *The Steadfast Tin Soldier* (1953). *All Butterflies: An ABC* (1974) was named a Boston Globe-Horn Honour Book in 1974. Brown was nominated for the Hans Christian Andersen Award in 1966 and 1975, received the University of Southern Mississippi Medallion for Distinguished Service for Children's Literature in 1972, and the Regina Medal in 1977. DJH

see also ALPHABET BOOKS; *STONE SOUP*

Brown, Margaret Wise 1910–52 Author of nearly 90 PICTUREBOOKS for young children and one of the genre's outstanding writers, known in the United States as the 'laureate of the nursery'. Graduating from Hollins College, Brown briefly attended Columbia University where – inspired by Gertrude Stein and Virginia Woolf – she intended to be a writer of experimental fiction. After dropping out of

Columbia, Brown attended the Writers Laboratory at the Bank Street School of Education. She became an assistant at the Publication Office at Bank Street, working with LUCY SPRAGUE MITCHELL, its founder. Bank Street pioneered the systematic study of child development in the United States.

Using Mitchell's educational concept of children as little empiricists living in the here and now, Brown developed her concept that in order to be a successful writer for young children, one 'must not love children, but what children love'. The publisher William R. Scott had a child attending the school and Mitchell convinced him of the need for quality books for young children and recommended Brown as his first children's book editor. As an editor at William R. Scott Inc., Brown published innovative books for children, including Gertrude Stein's *THE WORLD IS ROUND* (1939), which was a response to her contacting established authors to write for children. Working with illustrators from the Writers Laboratory, Brown published picturebooks, beginning with *When The Wind Blew* (1938), as well as editing the influential Bank Street reader, *Another Here and Now Storybook* (1937). A prolific writer, Brown worked with a number of publishers since none was able to release as the many titles as she was capable of producing in a single year. She used humorous pen names such as Timothy Hay, Juniper Sage and Golden MacDonald, the latter being the name that appeared on *The Little Island* (1947), illustrated by LEONARD WEISGARD, which was awarded the Caldecott medal as the outstanding picturebook of the year.

Brown was particularly attuned to sound: she said a good picturebook shows its musical origins. This musical quality of her books is especially clear in *The Noisy Book* (1939) and its seven sequels, in which the dog Muffin listens to the world around him. Brown was also sensitive to the intimate details of a child's world, as is seen in her *Goodnight Moon* (1947), illustrated by CLEMENT HURD, in which her rhythmical prose captures a child ritualistically saying goodnight to various objects before going to sleep. JCS

Brown, Palmer 1919– American writer and illustrator of FANTASY for young readers. A small but exquisite oeuvre of delicate, whimsical stories has established Brown as a fantasist of unique sensibility. His work reflects a profound and poignant awareness of the fragility of childhood, the irrevocableness of passing time, the comfort of home and the beauty of the natural world. His first two books, *Beyond the Pawpaw Trees* (1956) and *The Silver Nutmeg* (1957), recount the adventures of young Anna Lavinia, who, like Alice in Wonderland, travels to other worlds full of humorously odd imaginary creatures and nonsensical situations. *Cheerful* (1957), *Something for Christmas* (1958) and *Hickory* (1978) feature mouse protagonists who introduce the reader to the intimate yet passionately felt world of small animals. *Hickory* exemplifies the height of Brown's artistry, as he introduces a note of deep melancholy in this story of a tender-hearted young mouse who befriends a doomed grasshopper. Brown embellishes his work by having his characters sing and recite NONSENSE VERSE, some of which has been anthologised. His books are all illustrated with his own charming, intricate drawings and watercolours, dense with intriguing details. CV

Brown, Pamela 1924– British writer of theatre stories best known for her first novel, *THE SWISH OF THE CURTAIN* (1941), which introduces the Blue Door Theatre Company. Brown's career as an actor and television producer has provided her with much detail about early TELEVISION and life in repertory. JG

Brown, Ruth 1941– British writer and illustrator, born in Devon. Associate of The Royal College of Art, she has provided ILLUSTRATIONS for BBC children's programmes and for several stories by JAMES HERRIOT. Her first book was *Crazy Charlie* (1978) and since then she has published around 20 books including *A Dark, Dark Tale* (1981), which received international acclaim, *The Big Sneeze* (1985), nominated for the Kate Greenaway Medal, *The World that Jack Built* (1991) and *One Stormy Night* (1992). Simple texts, sometimes patterning the form of familiar tales, complement expansive, richly detailed illustrations in which small animals roam wide landscapes, inhabit spooky haunts, or reside in domestic contentment. In 1997 she illustrated HIAWYN ORAM's *The Wise Doll*, a traditional Russian tale. CMN

Browne, Anthony (Edward Tudor) 1946– British author and illustrator of PICTUREBOOKS, best known for his use of surreal imagery. Browne was born in Yorkshire and attended Leeds College of Art from 1963 to 1967. He then spent a number of years working first as a medical artist – a job he enjoyed and which influenced his approach to illustration – and then in advertising and as a designer of greetings cards. His first book, *Through the Magic Mirror* (1976), seems weak in comparison to his later work but with hindsight it can be seen as something of a manifesto, marking out his terrain as an illustrator. *A Walk in the Park* appeared in 1977 and *Bear Hunt* in 1979. In the latter work Browne humorously undermines readers' expectations by handing over to his hero the power to author his own story with a magic pencil.

GORILLA (1983), the book in which Browne first gave free rein to his fascination with the great apes, received both the Kate Greenaway and Kurt Maschler awards and has proved to be an enduring success. In

Illustration from *The Tale of the Monstrous Toad* by Ruth Brown.

1984 Willy the chimpanzee appeared for the first time in *Willy the Wimp*. Here and in the sequels, *Willy the Champ* (1985), *Willy and Hugh* (1991), *Willy the Wizard* (1995) and *Willy the Dreamer* (1997), Browne let his beloved primates take centre stage with stories all of their own. In *Zoo* (1992), which won the Kate Greenaway Medal for a second time, Browne contrasts the dignity of wild animals in captivity with the vulgarity and ugliness of the human visitors. His *King Kong* (1994) takes up a similar theme. The style of *Gorilla*, where colour, point of view and pictorial ambiguity are employed to give the story density, was first trialled in Browne's multilayered reworking of *Hansel and Gretel* (1981). He returned to FAIRY TALE themes in 1989 with *THE TUNNEL* and then in 1990 published *CHANGES*, where he tied his fondness for surreal, mutating imagery to a story of childlike misunderstanding. PIGGYBOOK (1986) and *The Big Baby: a Little Joke* (1993) both satirise male weaknesses.

From 1984 onwards Browne began to work occasionally with other writers. That year saw his first collaboration with Annalena McAfee, *THE VISITORS WHO CAME TO STAY*. *Kirsty Knows Best* followed in 1987. In both these books Browne remained alert to the ways in which his own pungent pictorial manner could enhance someone else's text rather than overwhelm it. Other collaborations include *Knock, Knock! Who's There?* (1985) with Sally Grindley, *Trail of Stones* (1990) and *The Night Shimmy* (1991) with Gwen Strauss, and illustrations for books by Janni Howker and Ian McEwan. In 1988 Browne reinterpreted *Alice's Adventures in Wonderland* – a book beloved of the Surrealists – and largely side-stepped comparison with TENNIEL. The book won Browne a second EMIL. It also proved to be a showcase for the full range of his talents, including his liking for pictorial quotation, a form of intertextuality that he has always exploited freely. Browne won a third Kurt Maschler award for *Voices in the Park* in 1998 and in 2000 he was awarded the Hans Christian Andersen medal in recognition of his entire body of work. DL

Browne, Eileen British illustrator. Browne has illustrated stories by several modern children's writers but her own text, *Handa's Surprise*, which appeared in 1994, brought her into prominence. It is the story of a small African girl's walk to her friend in a neighbouring village. She carries a basket of tropical fruit on her head as a present. On her journey her fruit is stolen by various animals, but all ends surprisingly well. The delight of the story lies in the clever dual narrative, shared between brilliantly coloured pictures and rhythmic text. JAG

Browne, Frances see *GRANNY'S WONDERFUL CHAIR*

Browne, Jane Euphemia 1811–98 English poet for children whose pseudonym was 'Aunt Effie'. Daughter of a rich landowner in Cumberland, she wrote verse which proved very popular with the young in volumes such as *Aunt Effie's Rhymes for Little Children* (1852) and *Aunt Effie's Gift for the Nursery* (1854). Her hallmarks were simplicity, sweetness and, unfortunately, sentimentality. MCCS

***Brownie* magazine** see GUIDING AND SCOUTING FICTION

Brownies Book, The (1920–1) Magazine for African American families published during the Harlem Renaissance. W.E.B. Du Bois, editor of the official magazine of the NAACP (National Association for the Advancement of Colored People), *The Crisis*, published a popular, special issue for children annually – filled with games, stories, pictures and accounts of black achievement – which grew into a separate magazine for 'Children of the Sun' – the young black readers of his era who were constantly being ridiculed. (The famous children's magazine, *St Nicholas*, often used the word 'niggers' and filled its pages with demeaning cartoons, as did the mainstream press.) 'To make coloured children realize that being "colored" is a normal, beautiful thing', as his first goal, he selected many photographs of striking black children; and so that children would 'become familiar with the history and achievements of the Negro race', he included copious biographical accounts of heroic black people. Alongside the poetry and stories written by child readers like Langston Hughes, regular columns included letters to the editor from children and parents, stories and pictures of children and their accomplishments, and 'As the Crow Flies', written by Du Bois to instruct children about contemporary events in America and around the world. NM

see also African American literature

Browning, Elizabeth Barrett see child authors

Browning, Robert see *The Pied Piper of Hamelin*

Brownjohn, Alan 1931– English author and critic who worked in schools and teacher training before devoting himself entirely to writing. Chair of the Poetry Society from 1982 until 1988, Brownjohn is a poet who has always been interested in including children in his audience. *Brownjohn's Beasts* (1970) is his best-known collection for children, but his poetry also features in *Six of the Best: A Puffin Sextet* (1989). His poem most regularly anthologised for the young is the prescient 'We Are Going to See the Rabbit', written long before 'green' poetry was fashionable, in Brownjohn's first collection, *The Railings* (1961). MCCS

Brownjohn, Sandy 1946– English educationalist and poet. Author of books on language and teaching Shakespeare, she is best known for three popular books about teaching poetry, collected and expanded in *To Rhyme or Not to Rhyme* (1994). Based on her own classroom experience, Brownjohn's techniques emphasising form and poetic language have been adopted enthusiastically by many teachers. Her first collection of poetry, *Both Sides of the Catflap* (1969), reveals a characteristic technical assurance. FRBS

Bruce, Dorita Fairlie see *Dimsie series*; see also *Chalet School series*; school stories; war stories

Bruce, Mary (Minnie) Grant 1878–1958 Australian novelist, born in Sale, Victoria, who began her career as a journalist, most notably running the children's page of the *Leader* in Melbourne. After her marriage to her second cousin, Major George Bruce, she and her husband divided their time between Australia and Ireland. Although best remembered for the *Billabong series*, she wrote many others. Bruce, like Ethel Turner, was usually published by Ward Lock, who, as Brenda Niall points out, did their best to establish rivalry between the two women in order to encourage them to increase their output. Despite her lengthy sojourns overseas, the Australian bush was always Bruce's preferred setting, and she used it to test and develop character, as in *Dick Lester of Kurrajong* (1920) and *Robin* (1938), or to bring happiness to those whose life had been corrupted in some way by the city, as in *Golden Fiddles* (1928). Bruce's books, with their depiction of Australia as a largely rural culture, had a long-lasting influence on Australian children's literature, with the pastoral adventure remaining an important genre long after she had ceased to write. MLH

Bruchac, Joseph 1942– American writer of children's books, storyteller, editor and publisher. Bruchac was raised by his grandparents in the Adirondack foothills of upper New York State. He is a member of the Abenaki nation and since 1975 has worked to preserve Abenaki culture and language through his poetry, prose and folklore. With his wife, Carol, he also created The Greenfield Review Press, which promotes the works of multi-ethnic writers. Bruchac has written over 60 works for children, most of which explore Native American experiences and environmental themes. The *Keepers of the Earth* series (co-authored with Michael Caduto) encourages exploration of the delicate balance between environmental and social worlds. Bruchac is also one of the best-known contemporary Native American storytellers. Although he writes in numerous styles and genres, his works tend to reflect Native American oral traditions and he draws extensively on Native American folklore. Among other honours, Bruchac has received the Boston Globe-Horn Book Award for non-fiction for *The Boy Who Lived with the Bears* (1996), an ALA Notable Book award for *A Boy Called Slow* (1995), and a Young Reader's Book Award for *The Story of the Milky Way* (1995), co-authored with Gayle Ross. EB

see also ecology; Native Americans in children's books

Bruin Boys, The see annuals

Bruna, Dick 1927– Dutch author and graphic artist who in the 1950s introduced a new style in books for very young children. The simplicity and directness of Bruna's pictures with their use of opaque primary colours and black outlines gained international popularity in the 1960s and 70s. Bruna's is a considered and crafted simplicity; his images and texts are pared down to essentials. The characters in Bruna's books – Miffy the rabbit is his most memorable creation – engage attention by looking directly at the reader. GL

Bryan, Ashley (F.) 1923– American writer, reteller and illustrator of children's books, FOLKTALES and spirituals, and professor emeritus of art and visual studies at Dartmouth College. Born in New York City and educated at Cooper Union Art School and Columbia University, Bryan has worked as a storyteller, lecturer and artist. Editor Jean Karl encouraged him to write and illustrate his own books. The result was *The Ox of the Wonderful Horns and Other African Folktales* (1971), a collection of five stories he illustrated with stylised paintings which reflect his knowledge of African masks, art and sculpture. Bryan has received numerous awards, including the 1981 Coretta Scott King Award for *Beat the Story-Drum, Pum-Pum* (1980), and honourable mentions from the Coretta Scott King committee for his ILLUSTRATIONS for *I'm Going to Sing: Black American Spirituals, Volume Two* (1982) and for the text of *The Lion and the Ostrich Chicks and Other African Folk Tales* (1986); and in 1988 for his illustrations for John Langstaff's *What a Morning! the Christmas Story in Black Spirituals* (1987). Although his paintings have often been mistaken for silk screens or wood blocks, only *Walk Together Children* (1974) and *I'm Going to Sing* (1982), his volumes on Black American spirituals, are block prints. DJH

Buchan, John 1875–1940 British author and public servant. As well as serving as a Member of Parliament and as Governor-General of Canada, John Buchan wrote over 60 books, including biographies, history and novels. But, although he produced several books for children, including *Prester John* (1910), an African adventure, and the FANTASY *The Magic Walking Stick* (1932), his adult suspense stories about Richard Hannay seems most likely still to engage some young readers. *The Thirty-Nine Steps* (1915) in particular, in which Hannay uncovers a foreign plot against Britain, has proved enduringly popular, and has been filmed at least twice, notably by Alfred Hitchcock in 1935. DB

Buck, Pearl S. 1892–1973 American writer of children's and adult fiction that frequently focused on experiences in Asia. The daughter of missionaries, Buck spent much of her youth in China, an experience that deeply influenced her writing. She developed into a prolific writer, writing dozens of books and a number of plays and movie adaptations of her works. Her well-known novel *The Good Earth* (1932) received the Pulitzer Prize, and in 1938 she won the Nobel Prize for Literature. As in her adult works, Buck often used Asian settings in her children's stories. *Yu Lan: Flying Boy of China* (1945) describes a Chinese boy with a passion for airplanes. One of Buck's best-known children's books, *The Big Wave* (1947), describes what happens to two Japanese friends when a tidal wave swamps the village where one of them lives. These books and others established Buck as an early champion of the belief that all children are created equal. As well as being a writer, she was actively involved for most of her life with promoting children's rights in Asia and the United States, an interest that is evident in many of her books. SAI

Buckeridge, Anthony see *JENNINGS* SERIES; see also SCHOOL STORIES

Buddha stories see MARIE SHEDLOCK

Buffalo Bill [William F. Cody] 1846–1917 Frontier scout and hunting guide nicknamed for the number of buffalo he shot. Ned Buntline and Prentiss Ingraham wrote popular DIME NOVELS that romanticised his character, some of which were made into plays in which Cody starred as himself. In 1883 he began his Wild West Show, which provided audiences in the Eastern United States and Europe with entertainment based on frontier experiences: stagecoach attacks, cattle drives, cavalry and Indian battles, and shooting and riding exhibitions. Buffalo Bill's Wild West show remained popular and relatively profitable until its last tour in 1914. EBD

Buffie, Margaret 1945– Canadian teacher, advertising artist, freelance illustrator and painter, and writer of YOUNG ADULT FICTION, born in Manitoba. Buffie's 'lifelong interest in the supernatural' is reflected in her themes. Her first novel, *Who is Frances Rain?* (1987), based on her own experiences as well as her imagination, won the 1987 CLA Young Adult Book Award and the Young Adult Canadian Book Award. This novel was followed by *The Guardian Circle* (1989). *My Mother's Ghost* (1992) was televised and the American version, renamed *Someone Else's Ghost*, was selected by the American Junior Library Guild as an outstanding book for 1995 and featured in the Junior Library Guild Magazine. Buffie's fourth young adult novel, *The Dark Garden* (1995), chosen for the 'Books for Everyone' selection, won the McNally Robinson Book for Young People Award, and was shortlisted for the Ruth Schwartz Award. Buffie won the Vicky Metcalfe Award for a Body of Work Inspirational to Children in 1996. In *The Warnings* and *The Dark Garden*, Buffie's spirit and FANTASY worlds intrude upon the real world as she features ghosts, haunted settings and time travel. MRS

Bugs Bunny Cartoon character featured in theatrical and televised short subjects and features, beginning in 1940 and continuing to the present day. Created and developed by Tex Avery and Chuck Jones, Bugs Bunny is the most famous ANIMATED CARTOON character to come out of the Warner Brothers studio, and the rise of his popularity symbolised a challenge to WALT DISNEY's virtual monopoly on animation in the 1930s. A wisecracking TRICKSTER, with a New York City dialect, Bugs always defeated his antagonists, most notably the human Elmer Fudd, through wit and cunning: he is a more aggressive descendant of Brer Rabbit and other rabbit and hare trickster figures from world folklore. BH

Bulla, Clyde Robert 1914– American writer of children's fiction and non-fiction, and composer. Born in the small farming community of King City, Missouri, Bulla won a writing prize when he was ten which convinced him he should become a writer. He taught himself piano during his teenage years and spent his spare time writing stories and studying opera. In 1946 his first children's book, *The Donkey Cart*, was published and he began a prolific and award-winning career. The diversity of his material belies his farming background, but his early work contains authentic portrayals of farm life. He has written HISTORICAL FICTION, often focusing on the difficulties of being a child during the early days of America's development. He has also viewed America's growth through the eyes of her native peoples in books such as *Pocahontas and the Strangers* (1971), a Christopher Medal winner. *Shoeshine Girl* (1975) is one of his most honoured books, winning the Charlie May Simon Award, and both the Sequoyah and South Carolina's Children's Book Awards. He has written non-fiction books about opera, holidays and science projects. He has also composed music for a number of song books, collaborating with lyricist LOIS LENSKI. JGJ

see also INFORMATION BOOKS; MUSIC AND STORY

Bumppo, Natty see *LEATHER-STOCKING TALES*

Bunting, (Anne) Eve(lyn) 1928– Prolific Irish American author. Bunting is extremely perceptive about societal trends; she estimates that perhaps 90 per cent of her ideas come by way of newspapers and magazines. Thus, she writes on an astonishing range of subjects: *Our Sixth-Grade Sugar Babies* (1990) charts the problems of sixth-graders who must spend a week playing parent to a five-pound sack of sugar; *Sharing Susan* (1991) examines the feelings of a 12-year-old girl who was inadvertently switched at birth and now must return to her biological parents; *The Wall* (1990), a book for young readers, presents inter-generational relationships along with an understanding of grief and loss; *One More Flight* (1976) comments on birds of prey that have been injured by man and must now be protected, as well as the plight of damaged children who need special care. Bunting received the 1995 NEWBERY MEDAL for *Smoky Night* (1994), a sensitive look at the Los Angeles riots through the uncomprehending eyes of a child. Bunting's books are not always serious; her *Night of the Gargoyles* (1994) is a poetic romp which reveals what gargoyles do when night falls and they are no longer observed. WH

Bunyan, John 1628–88 English author and preacher. Bunyan is one of very few writers to come from an impoverished background, achieve fame in his own day, and whose works continue to be well known and highly regarded many generations later. His most famous work, *THE PILGRIM'S PROGRESS* (1678–84), which is a classic of the Puritan tradition, was enormously influential for at least two centuries after its publication and has been translated into dozens of languages. Lovers of *LITTLE WOMEN* will remember that it is peppered with references to Bunyan.

Bunyan began life as a tinsmith in Elstow, Bedfordshire, learning to read and write at the village school. He was famously a 'Jack the lad', and anything but pious as a young man, turning to religion after fighting in the Civil War and around the time of his first marriage in 1648. Study of religious works led to Bunyan's spiritual conversion to Nonconformist beliefs, and he became unswervingly devoted to converting others. He was persecuted for his faith and in 1660 he was arrested for preaching, spending most of the following 12 years in prison, where he wrote several books, including his spiritual autobiography, *Grace Abounding to the Chief of Sinners* (1666). On release from prison in 1672 (he served another short stint in 1676 for once again refusing to give up preaching), Bunyan became pastor of the Bedford separatist church.

The Pilgrim's Progress was not written with the young in mind, though Bunyan was pleased that his extraordinary, dramatic, allegorical narrative was enjoyed by children as well as adults. It included the hymn 'To Be a Pilgrim', still popular today. The critically underrated *A Book for Boys and Girls* (1686), also known as *COUNTRY RHIMES FOR CHILDREN*, is arguably the first poetry book for young readers. Although it contains some stern lessons, it also demonstrates Bunyan's realisation that children needed to be wooed with a bit of fun if his religious exhortations were to work. The everyday subject matter and simple homeliness of the 'rhimes' added to their appeal; the 'comparisons' to help children understand his allegories are much less powerful, however, than in *The Pilgrim's Progress*. GERALDINE MCCAUGHREAN's retelling of *The Pilgrim's Progress* won the inaugural *BLUE PETER* Award. MCCS

Burch, Robert 1925– American author of PICTUREBOOKS and realistic novels. After serving in the military, then working and travelling world-wide, Burch returned to his native Fayette County, Georgia. His best writing, novels for middle-grade readers, chronicles life in the rural South during the Depression. *Queenie Peavey* (1966), winner of the Jane Addams Book Award, the Phoenix Award, and others, exemplifies Burch's unsentimental but sympathetic character portrayals. Queenie's trouble-making masks her defensiveness over her father's imprisonment. Two later novels – *Ida Early Comes Over the Mountain* (1980) and *Christmas with Ida Early* (1983) – feature a housekeeper reminiscent of Mary Poppins. In these books, Burch effectively uses humour to make points about human nature. KKP

Burgess, (Frank) Gelett 1866–1951 American author, editor, illustrator and humorist. Born in Boston, Burgess graduated from Massachusetts Institute of Technology and began work as a draftsman with the Southern Pacific Railroad in 1887, becoming an instructor of topographical drawing at the University of California in 1890. Four years later he changed careers when he became designer and associate editor for *Wave Magazine*. In 1895 he became editor of *The Lark* and famous for his 'Purple Cow' quatrain, which appeared in the first issue:

I never saw a Purple Cow,
I never hope to see one;
But I can tell you, anyhow,
I'd rather see than be one.

Another creation by Burgess to appear first in *The Lark* was a series of balloon-headed children who satirised different intellectual postures. So successful were the Goops, that Burgess reshaped them into a long series of children's books characterising different kinds of misbehaviour, beginning with *Goops and How To Be Them* (1900). In *Goop Tales Alphabetically Told* (1904), each letter features a different Goop: Abednego for the one who wouldn't go to bed, Bawlfred, 'because he bawls when he is hurt', and Cawlomar, because he 'always calls his Ma' and tattles on his siblings. KSB

Ah, Yes! I Wrote the "Purple Cow"—
I'm Sorry, now, I Wrote it!
But I can Tell you Anyhow,
I'll Kill you if you Quote it!

Illustration by Gelett Burgess from *The Burgess Nonsense Book* (1914).

Burgess, Melvin 1954– British writer born in London, who published his first novel, *The Cry of the Wolf*, in 1990. This and two other novels, *An Angel for May* (1992) and *The Baby and Fly Pie* (1993), were shortlisted for the Library Association's Carnegie Medal. Burgess, who writes challenging novels for young adults and imaginative fiction for younger readers, is regarded as one of the rising stars of contemporary children's literature. Issues of current and enduring concern such as the hunting of animals, DISABILITY, homelessness, witchcraft, child abuse and drugs are boldly confronted. The human and animal characters that feature in his books often exist on the margins of society, and in depicting their situations and experiences Burgess reveals tough, uncompromising aspects of modern life. *Junk* (1996) won both the 1997 *Guardian* Award for Children's Fiction and the Carnegie Medal. Based on first-hand research, the book is set in inner-city Bristol in the early 1980s. Successive monologues sustain the narrative drive which documents the viewpoints of teenage characters caught up in the seductive lure and downward spiral of drug addiction. Accessible to a wide range of young people the book generated strong debate as to its suitability for teenage readers. Because of its uncompromising representation of violence, under-age sex and psychological ambiguities, similar controversy greeted *Bloodtide* (1999), in which aspects of the *Volsund* saga are transported to an urban gangland setting. *The Earth Giant* (1997) is for younger readers, a powerful FANTASY about secrecy, jealousy and fear.

CMN

see also AWARDS AND MEDALS; DRUGS IN CHILDREN'S BOOKS

Burgess, Thornton 1874–1965 American writer, born in Sandwich, Massachusetts. Burgess worked as a reporter and associate editor of *Good Housekeeping Magazine*; he wrote monthly nature calendars, a daily newspaper column for 45 years, articles on nature studies and more than 70 children's books. Burgess's first book, *Old Mother West Wind* (1910), became the first in his series of eight *Mother West Wind* books. In addition to these, his most popular titles include *The Adventure of Danny Meadow Mouse* (1915), *Happy Jack* (1918) and *Lightfoot the Deer* (1921). Burgess, who said he wrote his fiction for children in the hope of stimulating their imagination, has been criticised for humanising nature and animals and for his sentimental style. Nevertheless, he was a pioneer in his field who made facts about animals' lives and habitats available to a wide reading public, which included adults and children. His non-fiction books include *The Burgess Bird Book for Children* (1919) and *The Burgess Sea Shore Book for Children* (1929). His work has been translated into many languages. In 1938, Burgess was granted an honorary degree by Northeastern University. MRS

Burkert, Nancy Ekholm 1933– American illustrator of highly acclaimed and exquisitely executed PICTUREBOOKS, including Caldecott Honour Book *Snow White and the Seven Dwarfs* (1972), translated by RANDALL JARRELL. Other picturebooks include HANS CHRISTIAN ANDERSEN's *The Nightingale* (1965), translated by EVA LEGALLIENNE; EDWARD LEAR's *The Scroobious Pip* (1968), completed by OGDEN NASH; Andersen's *The Fir Tree* (1970); and *Valentine & Orson* (1989), Burkert's own re-creation in verse and art of a medieval romance. She also illustrated ROALD DAHL's *James and the Giant Peach* (1961) and books by NATALIE SAVAGE CARLSON, MEINDERT DEJONG and John Updike.

Burkert is known for her painstaking research and attention to detail. She enlisted her daughter as the model for Snow White, and studied dwarfism in order to draw the dwarfs accurately. She also researched and incorporated the symbolic and iconic traditions of medieval and renaissance art, surrounding Snow White with a basket of cherries, a white dog and lilies, all symbols of purity and virginity. The meadow rue embroidered on her apron symbolises protection against witches, while the wicked queen is accompanied by bats, moths, skulls, snuffed candles and deadly nightshade, all symbols of witchcraft or death. For John Gardner, 'her pictures are what book ILLUSTRATIONS are supposed to be – interpretations . . . visual ways of elaborating, justly and harmoniously, what the words say'. LH

Burnett, Frances Hodgson 1849–1924 British author remembered for her three children's classics, *LITTLE LORD FAUNTLEROY* (1886), *A LITTLE PRINCESS* (1905) and *THE SECRET GARDEN* (1911). She was born in Manchester and removed to America at the age of sixteen, beginning her writing career two years later. In 1873 she married Swan Burnett, and they had two sons. She later divorced her husband; her second marriage to Stephen Townsend in 1900 was equally ill-fated. Though she wrote many novels and plays for adults, the interest these works inspire today is minimal and then only a by-product of her fame as the creator of Sara Crewe and Mary Lennox. Of her other work for children, *The Lost Prince* (1915), the story about the lost heir to Samavia, is the best known. It is a romantic tale with a Ruritanian flavour, and like the other three more famous works, moves towards a scene where the child is recognised and comes into its rightful heritage. In *Little Lord Fauntleroy*, this occurs with the confirmation of Fauntleroy's right to the title and the false heir being exposed. In *The Secret Garden*, Colin runs out of the garden into the arms of his father who has avoided him for years. Mr Carrisford's 'It is the child!' is paralleled by the announcement in *The Lost Prince*: 'It is the Lost Prince. It is Ivor!' These scenes suggest that Burnett's books are all concerned at some level with a *rite de passage* and are about recognition and coming into one's own.

The stories begin with the children as outsiders just arrived from India, America or Russia and trace their movement towards integration. This is perhaps most obvious in *A Little Princess*, a work which strongly recalls CHARLOTTE BRONTË's unfinished *Emma*, about a purportedly wealthy girl abandoned at a school. Sara Crewe loses her father and is forced to become a drudge at Miss Minchin's seminary for Young Ladies. She is later found by Mr Carrisford, a friend of her father's, who adopts her. Mary Lennox (another orphan) comes to Misselthwaite Manor from India, and *The Secret Garden*, which is generally considered Burnett's most satisfying work, follows the growth of her relationships with her cousin Colin and the others around her. All Burnett's books are in their own ways representations of the search for a family and a home, and her own restless life might be thought to mirror this desire (she crossed the Atlantic 33 times).

The strengths of Burnett's books are many. The plots are absorbing and the descriptions detailed; the children in her books are (at least eventually) likeable and interesting people, even though Fauntleroy has frequently been criticised as sentimentally rendered, a Wordsworthian innocent reclaiming and redeeming the corrupt adult. The values espoused by her works are admirable, old-fashioned ones; a high value is placed on the imagination and also on kindness, goodness and courage. SA

Illustration from *Aldo* by John Burningham.

Burnford, Sheila C. see *The Incredible Journey*

Burningham, John (Mackintosh) 1936– Innovative British writer and illustrator of PICTUREBOOKS born in Farnham, Surrey. He attended Summerhill, the school founded and run by A.S. Neill, and went on to the Central School of Art and Design in 1956 after having been drafted into work in hospitals, forestry and farming having refused National Service. On completing his course in 1959, his first job in ILLUSTRATION was designing posters for London Transport. Work in educational publishing followed, but in the early 1960s Burningham's frustration with his inability to secure the kind of work he wanted drove him to write and illustrate *Borka, the Adventures of a Goose with No Feathers* (1963). The book was published by Jonathan Cape and gained for Burningham his first Kate Greenaway Medal. The popularity of *Borka* created a demand for more of the same, and over the next four years Burningham wrote and illustrated four tales that are all very much in the *Borka* mould – classic realist texts accompanied by striking, painterly illustrations.

Many of his books of the 1970s and 1980s, however, were distinctly innovative. *Mr Gumpy's Outing* (1970) won for Burningham a second Kate Greenaway Medal and is a key book in Burningham's oeuvre, for in it he not only dropped his painterly style in favour of a lighter, more linear mode but also radically revised his approach to the design and organisation of picturebooks. From *Mr Gumpy's Outing* onwards his pictures no longer simply illustrate words but are integrated with them in fully composite texts. In COME AWAY FROM THE WATER, SHIRLEY (1977), *Time to get Out of the Bath, Shirley* (1978), *Where's Julius?* (1986) and *John Patrick Norman McHennessy – the Boy Who was Always Late* (1987), Burningham developed the technique of using the book's central GUTTER and the turn of the page to separate distinct narrative or textual elements. In this way he was able to suggest narrative complexity with great economy of means, often mingling FANTASY and realism in provocative and humorous ways. Burningham also followed other avenues during this period. *Would You Rather . . .* (1978) directly invites its readers to choose from ghastly, comic or pleasurable alternatives. *The Shopping Basket* (1980) and *Avocado Baby* (1982) are more conventional as picturebooks, but in GRANPA (1984) – a book composed of fragments and gaps, and winner of the Kurt Maschler Award – Burningham created what is possibly his most challenging and moving work.

It has been characteristic of Burningham that he has always maintained a varied output. In the 1960s he produced a series of wall friezes and in the 1970s and 1980s he published several series of books for the very young, such as *First Words* (1984) and *Rhyme Time* (1988/89). In 1983 he illustrated THE WIND IN THE WILLOWS. During the 1990s Burningham has never quite equalled the achievements of the previous two decades but has nonetheless produced substantial work, sometimes strikingly illustrated in mixed media, in *Oi! Get Off Our Train* (1989), *Aldo* (1991), *Courtney* (1994), *Cloudland* (1996) and *Whadayamean* (1999). DL

Burns, Robert 1759–96 Scottish poet, and precursor of Romantic poetry. Burns came from an impoverished background in rural Ayrshire and was largely self-taught. He enjoyed some celebrity for his poetry in his lifetime, though he died in poverty. His songs and verse, often in Scots dialect, are lyrical, witty and often simple, making them accessible to a wide audience. His poetry has regularly been anthologised for children since the beginning of the 19th century. MCCS

Burroughs, Edgar Rice, see *TARZAN OF THE APES*; see also ADVENTURE STORIES; SCIENCE FICTION

Burton, Hester (Wood-Hill) 1913–2000 British historical novelist who won the Carnegie Medal for *Time of Trial* (1963). Burton's work is set against a background of national historical events which include the Great Fire of London, the Battle of Trafalgar and the evacuation of Dunkirk. It is not the events themselves which seem important, however, but the effect they have on the lives of the characters who are bound up in them. Burton depicts strong heroines who are often at odds with the frighteningly brutal world in which they live and who courageously fight for justice despite their apparent ordinariness. KA

Burton, Virginia Lee 1909–68 American illustrator and writer of PICTUREBOOKS. Born in Massachusetts and raised in California, Burton recognised early on that she wished to pursue a career in art. She entered the world of children's picturebooks because she wanted complete artistic control over the books in which her ILLUSTRATIONS would appear, but she was always more interested in the pictures than their accompanying texts. Since she considered herself more a designer than a writer, she also maintained an active design career as one of the founding members of the Folly Cove Designers, a group of artisans who lived in Gloucester, Massachusetts, and were famous for their textile designs.

Despite her fame as a designer, Burton is best remembered as the illustrator and writer of seven picturebooks and the illustrator of several more. Her most famous books are *Mike Mulligan and His Steam Shovel* (1939) and *The Little House* (1942), the winner of the 1943 CALDECOTT MEDAL. In both works, Burton shows her ability to create engaging, simple stories that appealed to the youngest of readers. As Mike Mulligan and his outdated steam shovel, Mary Anne, race to dig the town-hall cellar and demonstrate to the town of Popperville that they can do the work of 100 men in a single week, they are surely two of the most memorable characters in children's literature, mesmerising new generations of readers for over 50 years. As in many of her books, in both the story and pictures Burton records urban development and portrays the contrast between the bucolic countryside and the sprawling city.

Burton also wrote a number of other well-received picturebooks: *Choo Choo: The Story of a Little Engine Who Ran Away* (1937), *Calico the Wonder Horse; or, The Saga of Stewy Stinker* (1941), *Katy and the Big Snow* (1943) and *Maybelle the Cable Car* (1952). Many of her works, like *Mike Mulligan*, demonstrate Burton's ability to give human characteristics to inanimate objects, such as a steam shovel, train engine or cable car, and to write lively narratives for young readers. Burton also illustrated a number of other works, including HANS CHRISTIAN ANDERSEN's *The Emperor's New Clothes*. Her most comprehensive illustration project was Anne Malcomson's *The Song of Robin Hood* (1947), a Caldecott Honour Book in 1948 that provides one of the finest examples of Burton's artistic talent. SAI

bush, the This concept is a dominating presence in Australia's fiction. It includes the immensity of the Outback, desert and farm alike, wide plains and mountain ranges, isolated homesteads and small towns. It can also be the patch of greenery beginning just outside the suburban fence, but the more distant from the city one is, the more its influence can be felt. The term not only denotes the countryside; it defines itself in opposition to urban life and values. It evokes a spirit of simple decency, of independence, resilience and comradeship in rural communities, and can be a setting for pastoral idyll and didactic FABLE. The bush has changing moods, too: it can express the innocence of sunlit open landscape on a picnic excursion, or the malevolence of enclosing forest as night draws in. It is the sternest judge of human endeavour, and sometimes executioner of those who fail its test of character.

The bush has played a central part in Australian children's literature from its beginnings. In *Alfred Dudley or The Australian Settlers* (1830) – by the English author, Sarah Porter, but published anonymously – and the works that followed it over the next 60 years, it typifies Australia as a welcoming land that rewards labour, honesty, courage and generosity with wealth. In these ADVENTURE STORIES, largely for British audiences, the bush is a place of opportunity, danger and conflict with the elemental forces of flood, fire and drought. Australia became quite literally 'a golden land' from mid-century, although many children's authors were ambivalent about easily won riches, and saw true reward as the virtues gained from perseverance and hard work. In the more overtly instructive works, such as the first children's book published in Australia, *A MOTHER'S OFFERING TO HER CHILDREN* (1841), the bush primarily provides a setting for descriptions of exotic wildlife and alien native peoples.

During the period of Australia's movement towards an independent national identity, marked in the writings of Henry Lawson and Joseph Furphy (writing as Tom Collins), and the art of Tom Roberts and Arthur Streeton, the emerging country's children's books – now embracing a significant local readership – depicted the character of bush life more realistically. SEVEN LITTLE AUSTRALIANS (1894), a story of domestic life where 'not one of the seven is really good, for the excellent reason that Australian children never are', begins at 'Misrule' a little way from Sydney. When the children move to their grandparents' remote property at Yarrahappini, the excitement and tragedy associated so firmly in fiction with bush life is set in motion. This creative compromise in Australian children's books, between domestic naturalism and adventurous romance, is the field which served MARY GRANT BRUCE so well in the *BILLABONG* SERIES. In the first of these, *A Little Bush Maid* (1910), Norah is described as having 'grown just as the wild bush flowers grow – hardy, unchecked, almost untended'. The next, *Mates at Billabong* (1911), has as its villain Norah's cousin Cecil from Sydney; he belongs to the tradition of effete 'new-chums' from the old country who peopled the previous century's yarns, but no sympathy is accorded him and he remains unredeemed by his bush sojourn. The familiar Australian theme, which contrasts the city where the majority of people live and the bush as the genuine home for the national spirit, had found its full expression.

FANTASY writing inspired by the bush emerged at the same time as a national strain of the realist novel. It was largely made up of FAIRY TALES awkwardly adapted from European models, and animal stories, the most notable of which was Ethel Pedley's *Dot and the Kangaroo* (1899). Lost in the bush, a little girl learns, and by example teaches young readers, to be kind to the innocent and gentle bush creatures (see also ANIMALS IN FICTION). The most remarkable story to link animals to the bush, however, is neither strictly a fantasy nor about native animals; it is Frank Dalby Davison's *Man-Shy* (1931). It follows the career of a heifer who escapes into the unfenced hills above a station to join a wild herd of scrub cattle; there is little in Australian children's books to match its evocation of the joy of freedom or the poignancy of her lonely end: 'gaunt and solitary, she stood, waiting to join the shadowy company of her kind – the wild herd that had passed from the ranges for ever'. The passing away of the bush and the cultures it sustained, indigenous and settler alike, is a story that will maintain its hold despite, or perhaps because of, Australia's increasingly sophisticated and urbanised society.

The need to find a strain of fantasy to fit an Australian setting has led to the creation of a succession of bush spirits: from the Gumnut Babies and fearsome Banksia Men of MAY GIBBS'S *SNUGGLEPOT AND CUDDLEPIE* (1918) and the displaced fairies and pixies of Annie Rentoul and IDA RENTOUL OUTHWAITE in *The Little Green Road to Fairyland* (1922), through to the careful adaptations by PATRICIA WRIGHTSON from Aboriginal folklore of creatures such as Nyols and Potkooroks who are associated with the rocks and trees of a wholly indigenous setting; as Wrightson puts it, 'the magic must be real in place'. Wrightson's *SONG OF WIRRUN* trilogy (1977–81) is the most thoroughgoing attempt so far in Australian children's literature to establish a mythology that truly represents the land and the right relation of its inhabitants to it.

Illustrators have played an important part in relocating the spirit of place. The artwork of Gibbs and Outhwaite had as much to do with the success of their work as their stories, and RON BROOKS'S drawings in *The Bunyip of Berkeley's Creek* (1973) equally evocatively capture both the creature and the swampy surroundings from which it emerges. Surprisingly, it was not until nearly a century after the Australian Impressionists found a style to catch the forms and colours of the bush that Desmond Digby deployed it effectively in *WALTZING MATILDA* (1970). As the means of production of PICTUREBOOKS have become more sophisticated, there has been an increasing tendency to use a visual idiom drawn from the nation's art, and apply it to the reinterpretation of landscape. DICK ROUGHSEY and ARONE MEEKS have adapted traditional Aboriginal styles and motifs to this purpose, while ROBERT INGPEN and JOHN ANTHONY KING have portrayed the colonial past in contrasting moods of affection and bitterness. One can see in JEANNIE BAKER'S COLLAGES of a magical and vulnerable Daintree in *WHERE THE FOREST MEETS THE SEA* (1987) a revaluation of the brutal, impenetrable North Queensland swamps and rainforests that broke the will of its first explorers, and in *THE STORY OF ROSIE DOCK* (1995) how a seemingly harsh environment has succumbed to colonisation by stealth. Her *Window* (1991) has the strongest of these messages, showing how the cities' advance means destruction of the bush.

The bush remains a force in contemporary children's books in Australia, both in fiction and non-fiction. It has become a site for the contestation of new values; conservation, not exploitation, is the theme. Historical novels like those of HESBA BRINSMEAD (*Longtime Passing*, 1971) and JAMES ALDRIDGE (*The True Story of Lilli Stubeck*, 1984) are tinged with nostalgia for what has been lost and a desire to cherish what remains of life based in the bush. The earlier menace and drabness that met the European eye have been transformed in the visions of a culture that now feels at home there. Yet the world beyond suburban streets still excites the imagination of authors and young readers in a literature given to examining the problem of human nature. David Malouf has perceptively remarked that: 'the landscape in Australia raises existential issues rather than moral ones'. A tradition of adventure tales is not easily given up, especially where the environment is a metaphor for challenge. IVAN SOUTHALL has repeatedly used the bush as a testing place for self-discovery, as have COLIN THIELE, LILITH NORMAN and others. In JOHN MARSDEN'S series beginning with *TOMORROW, WHEN THE WAR BEGAN* (1993) the bush refuge may be called Hell, but it is the source of resistance and renewal of a society subdued by invasion. In a nation where the city and the beach are claiming precedence, the legend of the bush is still alive in children's fiction. MMcC

bush stories see THE BUSH; TALL TALES

bushman mythology see AFRICAN MYTHOLOGY AND FOLKTALES; see also MARY PHILLIPS; JENNY SEED

Bustani, Juma Kenyan author of ADVENTURE STORIES for children. *Adventure in Nakuru* (1988), *Adventure in Mombasa* (1988), and *Adventure in Nairobi* (1990) are intended to encourage reading for pleasure and the improvement of written and spoken English among children. The books have black-and-white ILLUSTRATIONS with attractive covers in full colour. ABO

Buster see ANNUALS

Butler, Dorothy, O.B.E. 1925– Author best known for *Cushla and her Books: Three Years of Enrichment in the Life of a Handicapped Child* (1979), a study of the part played by PICTUREBOOKS in the early life of her granddaughter. Further titles develop this theme: *Babies Need Books* (1980), *Five to Eight* (1985) and *Children, Books and Families* (1995). Between 1965 and 1990, she ran a highly acclaimed children's bookshop in Auckland while writing many books for younger readers. AWARDS for her contribution to children's literature include the Eleanor Farjeon Award (1979), the Children's Literature Association of New Zealand Honour for Distinguished Services to New Zealand Children's Literature (1991) and the Margaret Mahy Lecture Award (1992). EAG

Butler, Francelia 1913–98 American writer, scholar and teacher of children's literature. Butler almost single-handedly initiated the scholarly study of children's literature in the United States. She chaired the first seminar in children's literature at the Modern Language Association meeting in 1971; founded and edited the first scholarly journal in the field, *Children's Literature* (1972); founded and presided over the first professional organisation for children's literature, The Children's Literature Association (1972); and finally founded the International Peace Games Festival (1990). She spent most of her career as a professor of English at the University of Connecticut and has produced editorials, scholarly articles and books, anthologies for classroom use, and works of fiction. JZo

Butterfly's Ball, The, and the Grasshopper's Feast (1806–7) Narrative poem by Liverpool member of parliament, William Roscoe. This delightful extended verse story about the imaginary doings of various insects – with such minute details as 'With Step so majestic the Snail did advance, / And promised the gazers a Minuet to dance' – set off a craze with about a dozen alternative versions by other authors appearing within a year, the best of which is *The Peacock at Home* by CATHERINE ANN DORSET. A version by Alan Aldridge and William Plomer won the Whitbread Award in 1973. MCCS

Butterworth, Hezekiah 1839–1905 American writer and editor, who is chiefly remembered for his 17 travelogue books, beginning with *Zig Zag Journeys in Europe: Vacation Rambles in Historic Lands* (1880). In the first eight volumes, the travellers are imaginary members of the Zig Zag Club of the Academy of Yule, located in Massachusetts. Butterworth was interested in folk literature, BALLADS and LEGENDS, emphasising cultural differences rather than travel routes. The author took his idea from the French teacher Rodolphe Toepffer, who took his boys on a zig-zag tour through Switzerland, described in *Voyages en ZigZag*. Butterworth was connected with *THE YOUTH'S COMPANION* from 1870 to 1894. KSB

Butterworth, Nick see *PERCY SERIES*

Butterworth, Oliver 1915– American author of humorous SCIENCE FICTION fantasies for children. Although Butterworth's output was small – three books altogether – the first two were historically remarkable for their satirical treatment of socio-political issues in a period when children's books avoided any hint of controversy. In his popular story *The Enormous Egg* (1956), a fast-growing triceratops, hatched from a hen's egg in Freedom, New Hampshire, is donated by the boy who raised him to the National Zoo in Washington DC. An outraged Senator proposes to outlaw dinosaurs as outmoded, un-American and a waste of tax-payers' money, but the boy saves his pet by appearing on TELEVISION; an outpouring of support, with public demonstrations, promptly puts the Dinosaur Bill to rest. Butterworth's concern for civil liberties is equally apparent in *The Trouble With Jenny's Ear* (1960), in which two boys interested in science experiment with electronic surveillance and their six-year-old sister develops the ability to hear people's thoughts. This commentary on the right to privacy and distance education, and the clash between community values and property rights, still seems topical. SR

Byars, Betsy 1928– American writer who was born in Charlotte, North Carolina. Byers has lived in West Virginia and South Carolina, settings that supply her realistic fiction with Southern folkways of a variety of social classes and educational backgrounds. Her protagonists – emergent adolescent children coping with problems often caused by self-absorbed and quirky adults – produce an unusual blend of humour and pathos in her plots.

Early in her career, Byars, the author of over 48 books, produced a modern classic in *The Midnight Fox* (1968). Here she discovered her theme: a young person discovering self-worth in the midst of family tensions and adult misdemeanors, and her own special way of dramatising it through strong evocation of place, depth of characterisation, and empathetic humour. In subsequent books, she often emphasised the one-parent family. The adult would be immature, irresponsible, neglectful of the parent role in some respect, or simply absent, and the child would either be mothering a younger sibling who falls prey to life-threatening danger or left to resolve problems alone. Such is the case in *Summer of the Swans* (1970), Byars's Newbery winner; *The Cartoonist* (1978), one of her best books in terms of characterisation; *The Night Swimmers* (1980), an American Book Award winner; and *The Not-Just-Anybody Family* (1986), part of a series about the Blossom family.

Sometimes both parents are present and the child is less a mothering figure than an outsider trying to come to terms with a dysfunctional family, as in *The Glory Girl* (1983). Sometimes more than one adult is problematic. In *The Pinballs* (1977) – her best-known work in Britain – children from three troubled families end up together as foster children in the same home. Sometimes the child is coming to terms with a failure to mother an irresponsible adult – an uncle in *Goodbye Chicken Little* (1979); a baby-sitter in *Cracker Jackson* (1985); or a teacher in *The Burning Questions of Bingo Brown* (1988).

Byars's major strength is emotional resonance, a quality she achieves by allowing readers to enter children's minds and observe the way they perceive life and work through problems. A common problem for children in these books is having adult responsibilities foisted upon them before they are ready, losing their childhood in the process. But her books avoid being tragedies, since nearly always an adult steps in just in time to save the child's failed heroic act, to set things right or give the child the courage or insight to push on. Her problem novels, published primarily between 1968 and 1986, mark an era when social upheaval (working mothers, increased divorce, spousal abuse, and baby-boomer lifestyles) was being reflected in children's books. Byars reveals the inner thoughts of children and their preoccupations and fears with humour, compassion and insight, a multi-faceted talent that has won her critical acclaim and popularity at home and abroad. NM

Byron, Lord (George Gordon Noel) 1788–1824 English Romantic poet. His *The Destruction of Sennacherib* (1815) ('The Assyrian came down like a wolf on the fold . . .') tends to be anthologised for children, although Byronic energy, idealism and cynicism are better represented by the *Weltschmerz* of *Childe Harold* (1812) and the scandalously satirical autobiographical realism of *Don Juan* (1819–24). His fame and reputation were equivalent to those of a modern pop star, an appeal he to some extent retains. His journals describe, with vivid wit and self-knowledge, a recklessly adventurous life. His letters include replies, gently discouraging and invitingly seductive, to young female fans. RC

C

Cabinet des Fées, Le see FAIRY TALES

Cady, (Walter) Harrison 1877?–1970 American author and illustrator of books for children, born in Gardner, Massachusetts. He began his career as an artist by illustrating a *MOTHER GOOSE* book for McLoughlin Brothers. He wrote and illustrated several of his own books including *Caleb Cottontail: His Adventures in Search of the Cotton Plant* (1921), *Animal Alphabet* (1927) and several books about Johnny Funny-Bunny. He was the primary illustrator for more than 40 *Green Meadow* story books by THORNTON W. BURGESS, and he also illustrated books by FRANCES HODGSON BURNETT. JGJ

Cairo Jim's Adventures A series of seven (to date) novels by Australian GEOFFREY MCSKIMMING. Archaeologist-poet Cairo Jim, his 'good friend' flight attendant Jocelyn Osgood, Doris the Shakespeare-quoting macaw, and Brenda the Wonder Camel seek ancient sites and artefacts worldwide – and in dashing style defend these from the evil Neptune Bone, the raven Desdemona, and other wrong-doers. Laden with improbabilities, puns and references, the books (like the *ASTERIX* books) provide idiosyncratic information on history, geography and culture. There are no child protagonists, and McSkimming never writes down to his audience. Despite – or because of – this, the books are extremely popular. NLR

Calamity Jane A famous character of the American West, primarily in the DIME NOVELS of Edward L. Wheeler. As the companion and sometime love interest of DEADWOOD DICK, Calamity Jane wears men's clothing, drinks, swears, shoots and rides expertly. The character is loosely based on the adventures and personality of Martha Jane Cannary (1852?–1906), who received her nickname because she was always at the scene of a calamity. In the 20th century Calamity Jane appears in several novels including Pete Dexter's *Deadwood* (1986) and Larry McMurtry's *Buffalo Girls* (1990), and in films such as *The Plainsman* (1936), *Calamity Jane* (1953) and *The Pale Face* (1948). EBD

Caldecott, Randolph 1846–86 British illustrator born in Chester, son of an accountant. Although he was always drawing, Caldecott initially became a bank clerk, a job that was to take him eventually to Manchester in 1866. Here he attended evening art school, where the emphasis was mainly on line, a reflection of the design needs of local industry. Caldecott contributed illustrations to local newspapers and magazines and, encouraged by his success, moved to London in 1871, deciding to become a full-time artist in 1872. He made friends among the art establishment and knew both WALTER CRANE and KATE GREENAWAY, the other two great Victorian illustrators. A close friend introduced Caldecott to the art history of the 18th century and to artists such as Hogarth, Rowlandson and Gillray, whose work profoundly influenced him. His first published book illustrations, as opposed to the magazine work he continued to do, was in a travel book which led in 1874 to a commission to provide illustrations to Washington Irving's Sketchbook, published as *Old Christmas* in 1876. Caldecott's sketches recreated an 18th-century image of England and developed the visual repertoire he would return to later in his toy books.

Old Christmas brought Caldecott to the attention of EDMUND EVANS, the printer. Both men were constantly experimenting to improve the production of ILLUSTRATION, and Caldecott accepted a commission to produce two PICTUREBOOKS a year. Sixteen books were published, each based on the words of a NURSERY RHYME or well-known nonsense verse: *The House that Jack Built, John Gilpin, Elegy on the Death of a Mad Dog, The Babes in the Wood, Sing a Song of Sixpence, Three Jovial Huntsmen, The Farmer's Boy, The Queen of Hearts, The Milkmaid* with *Hey Diddle Diddle, Bye, Baby Bunting, A Frog he Would A-Wooing Go, The Fox Jumps over the Parson's Gate, Come Lasses and Lads, Ride a Cock Horse to Banbury Cross* with *A Farmer went Trotting upon his Grey Mare, An Elegy on the Glory of her Sex, Mrs. Mary Blaise* and *The Great Panjandrum Himself.* Evans recognised Caldecott's ability to capture characters and movement in his free pen-and-ink sketches and encouraged him to alternate double spreads of full colour with plain sketch sequences in brown ink. He allowed Caldecott to develop original and often witty and ironic alternative narratives to the familiar words. Caldecott regularly depicted the world of the 18th-century country squire.

Caldecott earned himself an international reputation, was admired by Van Gogh and Gauguin and sought after in America. He travelled to America in 1885, seeking to alleviate the poor heath he had suffered from all his life, but died there early in 1886. The American connection continues with the CALDECOTT MEDAL, awarded annually since 1938 to the outstanding American illustrator of the year. AR

Caldecott Medal see APPENDIX

Calhoun, Frances Boyd 1867–1909 American author of short verses and one novel. Calhoun, born in Virginia and an avid member of the Daughters of the American Confederacy, considered herself 'a Southerner of Southerners'. She wrote only one book, *Miss Minerva and William Green Hill* (1909) and died shortly after it was published. The book met with great success at the time and is still in print. Because of its popularity, a series of five more titles about Miss Minerva followed, written by another author. Calhoun's depiction of Miss Minerva is a reflection of the perception of womanhood at the turn of the century in America. The story is about a Southern spinster and her humorous relationship with her six-year-old orphaned nephew who comes to live with her. The novel is full of Southern dialect typical of the time and setting of the story. ESC

Call of the Wild, The see JACK LONDON; see also ANIMALS IN FICTION

***Callendar* series** see SIR JOHN VERNEY

Came Back to Show You I Could Fly (1989) Australian novel by ROBIN KLEIN. Beautiful, erratic, troubled 20-year-old Angie and old-fashioned, over-protected, 11-year-old Seymour are an unlikely duo. Both outsiders, their relationship reveals the power of friendship to comfort and heal. Seymour naively sees Angie as an exotic free spirit, but as the narrative progresses the scales fall away from his eyes and he takes a pivotal role in her rehabilitation. The writing is rich in illustrative, evocative description, carefully crafted with symbolic details (e.g. Angie's Pegasus tattoo, Seymour's ironic name). Angie's interspersed letters, verse and notes subtly reveal the people behind the facades. Although never judgmental of Angie, through Seymour's eyes Klein allows readers to observe and evaluate Angie's tragic life. The novel won the 1990 Children's Book Council of Australia Book of the Year: Older Readers Award, and a Human Rights Award for Literature. SNJ

Cameron, Ann see *JULIAN* STORIES

Cameron, Eleanor (Frances) 1912–96 American writer and critic. Cameron established her reputation as a writer for children with *The Wonderful Flight to the Mushroom Planet* (1954) and the succeeding series, tales of space travel that hover between FANTASY and SCIENCE FICTION. These stories reflect contemporary fascination with space exploration and also a profound sense of wonder at the marvellous nature of the universe. Written at the request of her son, the *Mushroom Planet* books tell of two boys who, with the help of an extra-terrestrial scientist, Mr Bass, explore the planet Basidium and, in a thinly-disguised commentary on the collision between colonialism and indigenous cultures, seek to protect the Mushroom People from the encroachments of external forces. Heroism and personal character, however, rather than political commentary, remain the focal themes of these novels.

Cameron's work as a critic reflects her intense convictions about the craft of writing. In her collections of essays, *The Green and Burning Tree* (1969) and *The Seed and the Vision* (1993), she celebrated her indebtedness to writers such as Virginia Woolf and RANDALL JARRELL. Through close, appreciative readings of a wide range of literary works, she sought to describe her aesthetics of literary experience. She believed passionately that 'children's literature is not something separate in its requirements of excellence, but a branch of the tree of all literature, sharing the same elements and depending upon the same surge of life and artistry.' She was not afraid to criticise popular figures such as WALT DISNEY and ROALD DAHL, or to respond publicly to critics of her own writing, and was embroiled in controversy at times as a result.

Her most distinguished fiction begins with a semi-autobiographical novel, *A Room Made of Windows* (1971), in which she poetically evokes the Berkeley hills of her childhood in the 1920s and a talented child figure, Julia Redfern, who is intensely devoted to words and comes to discover – sometimes painfully – her talent as a writer. Cameron continued the *Julia Redfern* series with four other novels, in which Julia is either older or younger than in the first.

In several beautifully written novels, Cameron explored the idea of time travel, not as science fiction but as a reflection of the fundamentally mysterious co-existence of all times. The award-winning book *The Court of the Stone Children* (1973) memorably connects the experience of art with the encounter with people of another time. *To the Green Mountains* (1975) is the story of a young woman's maturation against a backdrop of rural life and acute memories and perceptions. *Beyond Silence* (1980), set in Scotland, concerns the quest of a young man to return to an earlier, happier period of his life, which he succeeds in doing through what Cameron has called 'extra-sensory experiences'.

Camping and tramping: illustration by J. Kiddell-Monroe from *A Cabin for Crusoe* by David Severn.

Cameron's pervasive theme is the mystery and awe of human existence in time. Her writing is characterised by elegance and precision of word choice, poetic insight, depth of understanding of personality, and a strong sense of place. JDS

camp-fire sing-songs see COMMUNITY SONGS

Campbell, Rod 1946– British book designer. Campbell is principally known for his bright, simple and successful children's novelty book, *Dear Zoo* (1982). The unsuitable gifts that the zoo sends to the narrator arrive in various packing crates; cracks and bars offer glimpses but the animals are fully revealed only when the reader lifts the flaps. All Campbell's subsequent flap-books successfully relate the paper engineering to the narrative action of the text. JAG

see also MOVABLE BOOKS

camping and tramping fiction A term used here to refer to a popular kind of British novel in which the narrative was mostly devoted to the excitements of hiking, exploring, boating, map-reading and the practicalities of camping. The term covers some popular individual novels and some major series, published for children between 1930 and 1960, as well as numerous stories published in children's ANNUALS. Their fictional children had ready access to camping equipment or a handy horse-drawn caravan, free entry to friendly farm-houses, and the guaranteed loyalty of passing gypsies and circus-folk.

Camping and tramping fiction sets itself apart from the fiction associated with GUIDING AND SCOUTING; in fact, in *Fell Farm Campers* (1960) a group of incompetent working-class Boy Scouts are given some friendly but patronising assistance by the *real* campers – and taught how to behave. This was one of the *Fell Farm* series by Marjorie Lloyd, in which a family of children spend their school holidays on a farm in the Lake District. The series exhibits both the worst and the best features of this type of fiction – not much action, characters who are of little interest, a stereotypical farmer's wife fussily providing huge meals, and a generally cheerful and trusting world. On the other hand, the camping and exploring adventures of the children are represented with a detailed and affectionate authenticity which appealed to thousands of young readers. Another popular series, beginning with *Out With Romany* (1937), by 'Romany of the BBC' (G. Bramwell Evens) and running through several titles and many reprints until 1949, was committed to the observation and understanding of British wildlife. In David Severn's *Crusoe* series the narrative voice reinforces its passion for its subject with some beautiful wood-engravings by J. Kiddell-Monroe. The fictional world represented was fundamentally conservative, the narrative posture reclusive, and the tone elegiac, but the combination of rapturous lyrical description with sharply defined illustrations was often genuinely affecting.

Like much camping and tramping fiction, Severn's narratives are essentially love stories in which the loved one is the English countryside, and the authorial desire is to initiate young readers into a similar devotion. The influence of RUDYARD KIPLING – especially *PUCK OF POOK'S HILL* – was a powerful factor, especially in works like *South Country Secrets* by 'Euphan' (BARBARA EUPHAN TODD) and her husband 'Klaxon', in which a group of children returning from South Africa explore not only the geography but also the history of southern England. Another revered text was BEVIS (see WOOD MAGIC). Such fiction assumed an ideology of patriotism: a specifically English continuity was implicitly celebrated, stretching from Bronze Age settlers to the defeat of Germany.

Despite its popularity, most camping and tramping fiction lacked the imaginative and meditative quality of works like ALISON UTTLEY'S *THE COUNTRY CHILD*, and it had none of the dramatic pace of ENID BLYTON'S famous series. A distinguished exception, however, is the work of ELINOR LYON, whose series of novels set in Scotland subtly represents an intensely realised but understated friendship between its three protagonists, and their relationship with the romantic landscape of remote lochs and mountains on the west coast. Elsewhere, however, as if they sensed their own narrowness, camping and tramping narratives were constantly having to turn into other kinds of story – PONY STORIES (such as *Five Proud Riders* by Ann Stafford), natural history books, and especially ADVENTURE STORIES.

David Severn's *The Cruise of the Maiden Castle* is typical of the genre: its first eight chapters describe movingly and accurately the practicalities of taking a longboat on England's canals in the 1940s. The leisurely plot is given some urgency when the four longboat children have a fight with some local working-class boys, and the novel turns into an adventure story as the children discover a disused factory full of stolen goods. (This tendency to turn into adventure stories is shared by BALLET STORIES too.) However, there are no self-indulgent heroics: Severn's child-protagonists are described as frankly terrified. When they report their find to a local policeman, he suspects the 'young whippersnappers' are pulling his leg. The case is reported in the national press and the children become reluctant heroes. It is easy to ridicule this, but the formula was extraordinarily popular with young readers for three decades. A girl-centred series was produced by M.E. Atkinson between 1936 and 1961: her novels were about the Lockett family and were set mostly in the south of England. The series extended to 21 titles, all published in hardback and each running to several editions. Like ARTHUR RANSOME and MALCOLM SAVILLE, Atkinson rose above the limitations of the subject matter.

Nothing more powerfully demonstrates cultural change than the popularity of these books, with their assumption that the entire British countryside was a safe playground for middle-class youngsters. They were eclipsed by the 'new wave' of young writers in the 1960s, by rapid changes in reading habits, and by the overwhelming popularity of Enid Blyton's series, many of which derived from the camping and tramping fiction they helped to displace. VW

see also PUBLISHING AND PUBLISHERS; NEGLECTED AUTHORS

Canadian Children's Literature/Littérature canadienne pour la jeunesse see PUBLISHING AND PUBLISHERS; CRITICAL APPROACHES TO CHILDREN'S LITERATURE; see also REVIEWING AND REVIEWERS

Canadian Library Association Book of the Year for Children see APPENDIX

Cannan, Joanna see PONY STORIES; CHRISTINE, JOSEPHINE AND DIANA PULLEIN-THOMPSON

Canterbury Tales see GEOFFREY CHAUCER; see also REG CARTWRIGHT; SELINA HASTINGS

Cap o' Rushes see FOLKTALES AND LEGENDS

Capp, Al see *LI'L ABNER*

Captain America see SUPERHEROES

Captain Marvel see COMICS, PERIODICALS AND MAGAZINES; SUPERHEROES

Captain Planet see SUPERHEROES

Captain Pugwash British cartoon series by John Ryan (1921–). It was originally created for the early *EAGLE*, appeared in book form from 1957, as an ANIMATED CARTOON for BBC TELEVISION and a *Radio Times* comic strip in the 1960s, and was animated again for Brit Allcroft's company in the 1990s. The cowardly pirate captain of 'The Black Pig' features in uncomplicated stories of treasure hunts and rivalry with the villanous Cut-Throat Jake, made unique by Ryan's inventive dialogue, eye for comic incident and richly detailed drawing, whilst the good sense of Tom the cabin boy provides an ironical perspective on a world of large but foolish adults. SG

Captain Stormalong see TALL TALES

Captain Toby (1987) PICTUREBOOK by SATOSHI KITAMURA. Responding to a storm raging outside, Toby dreams that his house is carried far out to sea to be attacked by a giant octopus and saved by his grandparents in their house-submarine. Kitamura orchestrates his line to create not only character and setting but a powerful sense of movement, whether depicting trees thrashing in the wind or the house far out in billowing waters. There are touches of *ANGRY ARTHUR* in the humorous details and the battle with the octopus. It also recalls TED HUGHES's poem 'Wind': 'This house has been far out to sea all night.' AR

Captain, The see ANNUALS; see also JOHN HASSALL; P.G. WODEHOUSE

***Carbonel* series** Stories by Barbara Sleigh (1906–82), including *Carbonel* (1957), *The Kingdom of Carbonel* (1960) and *Carbonel and Calidor* (1977). In the first book, Rosemary buys Carbonel from a witch who wants to retire, only to discover that he is the King of the Cats under a spell that keeps him bound to his owner, the 'minion of the twiggy broom'; Rosemary's task is to break the spell. In *The Kingdom of Carbonel*, Rosemary and her friend John have to rescue Carbonel's kittens, who have been kit-napped by the witch, his ex-owner. The theme of freedom or self-ownership runs through the books, this extending even to the witch, who, as we see at the end of *The Kingdom of Carbonel*, also desires to be set free from her wickedness. She has to be 'unwitched' just as Carbonel has been unspelled, through the children's sacrifice of their most treasured possession. Although *Carbonel and Calidor*, which was written many years later, is as witty and humorous as its predecessors, it remains a work apart from the first two books which form a coherent imaginative unit. Carbonel possesses few real cat characteristics, having a lot more in common with E. NESBIT's *PSAMMEAD* and Mouldiwarp, superior magical (animal) creatures who speak with the voice of tart and faintly impatient adulthood. SA

card mounts Pages of thin card or thick paper, often in a contrasting colour to the text pages, onto which coloured illustrations printed on ART PAPER were TIPPED IN in GIFT BOOKS. GCB

Card, Orson Scott 1951– American writer in genres as various as SCIENCE FICTION, FANTASY, HISTORICAL FICTION, contemporary realism, horror, technical writing and creative non-fiction. Card was born in Richland, Washington, and grew up in California, Arizona and Utah; he also lived in Brazil for two years as a missionary for the Mormon Church.

Card's most successful works are his series which initially feature young protagonists. Series still in progress include: the *Ender* series (*Ender's Game*, 1985; *Children of the Mind*, 1996), the *Homecoming Saga* (*The Memory of Earth*, 1992; *Earthborn*, 1995), and the *Tales of Alvin Maker* (*Seventh Son*, 1987; *Alvin Journeyman*, 1995). These series share many characteristics of children's literature in general: the issues of the coming-of-age of young protagonists, the importance of the home both as a theme and as a means for organising the plot, and the use of fantasy as a tool to create alternative worlds in which to examine the place of children in religious, scientific, social and ethical contexts. MC

Carey, Peter 1943– Australian novelist, author of the Booker Prize winner *Oscar and Lucinda*. Carey's only children's book is *The Big Bazoohley* (1995), a short comical novel about a boy kidnapped and forced to enter the 'Perfecto Kiddo Competition', unwittingly solving his parents' financial crisis. Its STORYTELLING style and irreverence have led to comparisons with ROALD DAHL's fiction. NLR

Caribbean Dozen, A (1994) Collection of poems by Caribbean poets, edited by JOHN AGARD and GRACE NICHOLS. The 'dozen' refers to 13 poets, a reference to the Caribbean market tradition whereby vendors 'throw in' extra food to supplement orders. Thus readers are given an extra poet, constituting their 'mek-up'. The voices of the poets are informed by the circumstances of a Caribbean childhood, and the language used is heavy with rhythm and texture. Reference is made to the oral culture which the contributors feel significantly influenced their collective interest in words. Cathie Felstead provides bold and colourful illustrations which serve to complement both the richness of the language and the vibrancy of Caribbean life. GD

Carle, Eric 1929– Distinguished American illustrator who for nearly three decades has produced PICTUREBOOKS which are aesthetically satisfying and consistently original in approach. He was born of German parents in New York. The family returned to Germany in 1935, where he was educated. In 1952 Carle went back to America, where he worked as a graphic designer, art editor and illustrator before writing his own texts to illustrate in the mid-60s. Carle is particularly concerned with smoothing the transition from home to school for the young child; consequently his picturebooks are half-book, half-toy – teaching a number of useful things, containing jokes and humorous surprises, and always expressive. Carle has a self-confessed abiding love for the small insignificant animals which appear as his characters, mostly involved in their natural activities, and often exhibiting human emotions and foibles. Carle's exuberant expressionist style is manifested in COLLAGES of tissue papers, woodcut and linocut, embellished with oil, tempera, pastel, crayons and photography; he is an inspired colourist. He tears the paper animal shapes, and articulates the limbs by overlapping to suggest muscle, or he allows the tiniest gaps between the tissue at the joints, which gives the impression of the lightest of movements.

Carle's second picturebook, *The Very Hungry Caterpillar* (1968), has become a modern classic. It shows the life cycle of the insect in split page format and featuring cut-out holes in the pages. The width of the split page increases to match the caterpillar's appetite as the days go by. First it 'eats' a hole just the right size for a small finger in the image of an apple. When the strip is turned we see the caterpillar/finger coming through the fruit. The next strip shows two pears and two holes, and so on. The child learns about metamorphosis and the sequence of the days of the week, listens to the story, pantomimes the action, and empathises with the caterpillar. In *The Bad-Tempered Ladybird* (1977) – called *The Grouchy Ladybug* in the United States

– Carle uses the split-page format again, and equally wittily, this time with a developed narrative and painterly backgrounds. A bad-tempered ladybird who flies through the hours of the day looking for a fight and challenging everything it meets is finally silenced by a slap from the (pop-up) tail of a whale. The picturebook can teach telling the time, left and right, size concepts, and, by implication, how literary irony works.

The Very Busy Spider (1985) has a multi-sensory approach through thermography, using non-toxic slip-proof ink which leaves a perceptible trace on the surface of the paper, for images of the spider, web and a pesky fly. On the succession of page openings the spider diligently shows – and the beholder, whether sighted or visually impaired, can feel – how a web is gradually woven. Sound effects accompany *The Very Quiet Cricket* (1990), which comes complete with built-in battery. The eponymous hero and the reader are given a natural history lesson which concludes with a mating call. JD

Carlson, Natalie Savage 1906– American author of more than 40 novels, PICTUREBOOKS and collections of stories. She was born in Virginia to a French Canadian mother and an American father. Much of her childhood was spent at Shady Grove Farm in rural Maryland, the setting for *The Half-Sisters* (1972). Later the family moved to California, where Carlson went to work as a reporter for *The Long Beach Morning Sun* after graduating from high school. After her marriage to a career naval officer and the birth of her two daughters – to whom she loved to read – Carlson began to write for children. *The Talking Cat and Other Stories of French Canada* (1952), illustrated by ROGER DUVOISIN, was based on stories told to her mother by her Uncle Michel Meloche. It received the *New York Herald Tribune* Children's Spring Book Festival Award and widespread critical acclaim. While living in Paris for three years following World War II, Carlson gathered the material for some of her best-loved books: *The Happy Orpheline* (1957) and its sequels, and Newbery Honour Book *The Family Under the Bridge* (1958), illustrated by GARTH WILLIAMS. Carlson has been praised for her light and graceful style, fine dialogue and vividly depicted characters and settings. LH

Carmody, Isobelle (Jane) 1958– Australian writer who wrote her first novel, *Obernewtyn* (1987), the first of the *OBERNEWTYN CHRONICLES*, while still at high school. Since then she has proved to be a prolific writer. Her works can be classed as science FANTASY but go beyond the escapism which is common to this genre. Although Carmody's main audience is young adults, her talent as a storyteller and her accessible style of writing make her work appealing to all ages. Carmody uses a number of devices to plunge the reader straight into the worlds she creates. In *Scatterlings* (1991), for example, Merlin awakes to a foreign yet not completely unrecognisable world. Many of Carmody's characters have an inner vulnerability which affects their relationships with other characters and colours the events of the story – Jack in *Greylands* (1997) is trying to come to terms with the death of his mother and the emotional distance of his father. The 'greylands' of the story reflect Jack's grief and sense of dislocation. Carmody often uses the transition between the imaginary and the real to highlight discordances in social and personal life. In her collection of short stories, *Green Monkey Dreams* (1996), characters must grapple with inner demons, as in 'The Beast', or with feelings of isolation, as in 'Corfu'. A setting often used by Carmody is that of the post-apocalyptic world. Frequent references to the 'time before' seem to point to flaws in contemporary western society. *Darkfall*, book I of *The Legendsong*, was published in 1997. Carmody's creative talents have been recognised on a formal level in her numerous shortlistings for book AWARDS and her 1994 CHILDREN'S BOOK COUNCIL OF AUSTRALIA BOOK OF THE YEAR AWARD for *The Gathering* (1993), which also won the 1994 Children's Literature Peace Prize. SKS

Carnan, Thomas 1737–88 Bookseller, who became the partner, stepson and later heir of the most important early publisher of children's books, JOHN NEWBERY. Thomas Carnan's father, William, was editor of the *Reading Mercury* and ran a business largely concerned with newspaper printing. After William died in 1737, John Newbery married his widow and became a partner in the firm from around 1740. Thomas Carnan was an active partner with his stepfather from the 1750s, and with John Newbery's son Francis until the latter transferred his interests to selling patent medicines around 1780. DWh

Carnegie Medal see APPENDIX

Carousel: The Guide to Children's Books (1995–) British magazine established when the groundbreaking *Books for Your Children* ceased publication after 30 years. The vacuum was filled by *Carousel*, currently published in Birmingham, England, three times a year. Its aim was to continue its predecessor's mission to inform, entertain and guide those readers – especially parents – seeking to encourage the enjoyment of books and the reading habit in their children. The magazine contains in-depth articles, and interviews with authors, illustrators and those working in the world of children's books. Its strength lies in the numerous pages of signed REVIEWS ranging widely over the entire spectrum of children's books, from books for babies to YOUNG ADULT FICTION. Fiction, non-fiction, poetry and audio-tapes (see STORYTAPES) are assessed, and the magazine's editors seek to give impartial advice and comment. *Carousel* is closely linked to the Federation of Children's Book Groups, a voluntary organisation devoted to encouraging the reading habit in children. VB

see also REVIEWS AND REVIEWING; AWARDS AND MEDALS; CHILDREN'S BOOK AWARD

Carpenter, Humphrey see CRITICAL APPROACHES TO CHILDREN'S BOOKS; see also *ALICE'S ADVENTURES IN WONDERLAND*

Carrie's War (1975) Acclaimed novel by the British author NINA BAWDEN. The moral complexity and themes of *Carrie's War* perhaps render it more suitable for slightly older readers. It is about two children, Carrie and her brother Nick, who are evacuated to Wales during World War II. The 'war' of the title, however, while referring on one level to the actual combat going on in the background, is more usefully thought of as operative on the metaphorical plane. For there are many kinds of conflict depicted in the book. There is the conflict between their host, Councillor Evans, and his two sisters, Auntie Lou and Mrs Gotobed. Carrie and Nick are caught up in this war, which in Carrie's case becomes internalised as she acquires an understanding of, and sympathy for, both parties. The 'war' is also a war against the inauthenticity which avoids the unpleasantness of confrontation and prevents one from finding the courage to speak the truth. Ultimately, the book is about the attempt to conquer the fear of the past and its mistakes. When Carrie comes back 30 years later to the house for whose destruction she has thought herself responsible, this war is finally won. SA

Carroll, Lewis [Charles Lutwidge Dodgson] 1832–98 British mathematician and author. Dodgson's father was the curate of the parish of Daresbury in Cheshire, and Dodgson was born at the parsonage there on 27 January 1832, the eldest of 11 children. He showed early signs of an unusual precociousness; his headmaster James Tate at Richmond School where he was first educated said that he had 'a very uncommon share of genius'. He was educated at Rugby, a few years after Dr Thomas Arnold's death in 1846, and in 1851 went to Christ Church, Oxford, where he was to remain for the rest of his life. Taking first-class honours in the Final Mathematical School in 1854, Dodgson went on to tutor and then to become Mathematical Lecturer at Christ Church in 1855, in the same year that Henry George Liddell, Alice Liddell's father, became the dean of the college.

Dodgson was for a time fascinated with photography and lionised as one of the best amateur photographers of his day. Recent scholarship has commented a good deal on his photography of young girls in the nude, speculating on Dodgson's psychological make-up and motives. He seems to have been an extraordinarily shy man, perhaps only really comfortable with children, upon whom he lavished the wealth of his creative genius, devising puzzles and tales for them. However, odd and unconventional as his dealings with children might have been, all the evidence suggests that Dodgson was careful to ensure that his young subjects were, in that Victorian phrase, 'uncompromised', their mothers or other guardians being present throughout. It was through his photography that he encountered the Liddell children, and he spent much of his time at the deanery until the 'break' with the Liddells (the exact cause of which is still unknown) in 1862.

The occasion which gave birth to *ALICE'S ADVENTURES IN WONDERLAND* is well-documented: *Alice* was invented while Dodgson, Robinson Duckworth and the three Liddell sisters, Lorina, Alice and Edith, were on a rowing party to Godstow, in order to keep the children entertained. It was illustrated by JOHN TENNIEL, the political cartoonist from *Punch*, and published by Macmillan in 1865 under the name 'Lewis Carroll'. From Dodgson's letters, it appears that a sequel was thought of as early as 1866, but it was not till 1871 that *Through the Looking Glass* actually made its appearance.

His next work for juveniles was the long nonsense poem, *THE HUNTING OF THE SNARK* (1876) which met with mixed reviews. *The Nursery 'Alice'*, an adaptation of his first book made for younger children, came out in 1890. His last works for children were *Sylvie and Bruno* (1889) and *Sylvie and Bruno Concluded* (1893), which were illustrated by Harry Furniss. These too failed to please most critics, though their author himself said that he took 'a far deeper interest in [them], as having tried to put more real *thought* into [them].' Despite this assertion of partiality, they are indeed less successful works, suffering from a sentimentality in the depiction of children absent in the earlier works (Bruno lisps sweetly) and a certain self-consciousness.

Along with EDWARD LEAR, Carroll initiated a tradition of NONSENSE VERSE in British poetry for children which has continued strongly to the present day. It is a reversal of expectations which Carroll might have relished that his best nonsense poems are in his *Alice* novels and his worst in his small book of poems *Phantasmagoria* (1883). *Alice's Adventures in Wonderland* contains a variety of poems and parodies which have becomes classics of nonsense: one of the first shape poems for children in 'The Mouse's Tale'; 'The Lobster Quadrille', with its lively dance-rhythms; parodies of ISAAC WATTS such as 'How doth the little crocodile' and 'You are old, Father William'. All these demonstrate Carroll's technical mastery of different forms alongside his inventive play with words and meanings: the regularity of the verse perfectly counterpointing the illogicality of the sense. In *Through the Looking Glass*, Carroll included, amongst other nonsense verse, the mock-heroic ballad of 'Jabberwocky', with its 'portmanteau words' like 'slithy' and 'mimsy' packing together multiple meanings, and Tweedledum and Tweedledee's poems such as 'The Walrus and the Carpenter'. The nonsense poems form an integral part of the novels, which in turn supply a narrative context (for example, when Alice tries to recite known poems but they come out 'very queer indeed') which is lost when the poems are collected separately. *The Hunting of the Snark* (1876), a long narrative ballad which Carroll subtitled 'An Agony in Eight Fits', was his last substantial piece of nonsense verse. The poem shares some of the vocabulary of 'Jabberwocky', but has none of the triumphant joy of the earlier ballad, since the hunt ends this time in failure and the mood is more anxious throughout.

Though today remembered mainly for his achievements in the field of children's literature, Dodgson was also well-reputed as a mathematician in his own day and was published widely in this area. He was an inveterate creator of word and mathematical puzzles, which again were mainly intended for the amusement of his many young friends; many of these still exist and have been collected and published. Charles Dodgson never married. He died in 1898 of a bronchial infection, shortly before his 66th birthday. SA, ML

Carryl, Charles 1862–1924 American stockbroker turned writer of nonsense, considered during his lifetime to be 'America's LEWIS CARROLL'. Carryl's popular *Davy and The Goblin, Or What Followed Reading 'Alice's Adventures in Wonderland'* (1885), written for his son Guy, attempts to bring Carroll's sense of FANTASY to an American setting as Davy climbs aboard a Dutch clock which carries him to Carryl's wonderland. In the less successful *The Admiral's Caravan* (1892), Dorothy rides a Ferry to Nowhere as the Ferryman entertains her with a Ferry Tale and meets a series of fantastic creatures. Both novels are illustrated by REGINALD BIRCH and first appeared in serial form in *ST NICHOLAS*. JCS

see also ALICE IMITATIONS

Carson, Kit (Christopher) 1809–68 Hero of adventure stories. Born in Kentucky, Carson was an American trapper and guide with Charles Fremont during his famous expeditions to the West. He was prominent in the acquisition of California during the Mexican War. Because of his brave exploits as a fighter against the Indians and as an officer in the Civil War, he was idolised and made the hero of many boys' action-packed stories, some based on actual exploits and some based on legends which had grown up around him. He is also the hero of the frontier poet JOAQUIN MILLER's poem 'Kit Carson's Ride' (1871), in which he is described as courageously rescuing his Native American bride from a prairie fire while riding his faithful horse 'Pache'. MS

Carter, Angela 1940–92. British writer renowned in the realm of children's fiction as an authoritative editor of FAIRY TALES. She found acclaim for her translation of CHARLES PERRAULT's nursery tales from their original French – *The Fairy Tales of Charles Perrault* (1977). Further editorships produced *Sleeping Beauty and Other Favourite Fairy Tales* (1982), illustrated by MICHAEL FOREMAN – winner of the KURT MASCHLER AWARD – and two collections for Virago Press: *The Virago Book of Fairy Tales* (1990) and *The Second Virago Book of Fairy Tales* (1992). Carter also completed four works of children's fiction, although these are no longer in print. In *Miss Z, The Dark Young Lady* (1970), illustrated by Eros Keith, Miss Z, clad in magic dress, embarks upon a fantastic quest in order to counter the rash behaviour of her father and return some parrots to their native habitat. The young adventurer encounters all manner of wonderful creatures, such as Unicorns and Green Lions, and ultimately restores good fortune to the Parrot Jungle. Carter also supplied the text for *Moonshadow* (1982), a book conceived and illustrated by JUSTIN TODD. The adventure sees Tom, the central character, pursuing the Moonshadow Cat across land and sea. Classically, the tale is borne out of Tom's dreams, but it teaches him to respect his own shadow. In *Martin Leman's Comic and Curious Cats* (1979) Carter's writing complements Leman's bold and colourful paintings to produce an ALPHABET BOOK of cats. She collaborated, too, on *The Donkey Prince* (1970), illustrated by Eros Keith. Sadly her fiction, which echoes the kind of 'pleasure principle' seen at work in fairy tales, remains largely undiscovered. GD

Carter, Peter 1929–99 British novelist who has twice been awarded the *Observer* prize for teenage fiction. He uses irony and stark realism to describe the lives of ordinary characters caught up in political events of the present and the past. In *Under Goliath* (1977), Alan realises that he has involuntarily taken sides when he joins a Belfast Orange band. In *Bury the Dead* (1986), in a bleak East Berlin dominated by the Wall, Erika has to confront the consequences for her own future of the horrors of Nazism. Eschewing easy solutions, Carter's novels force readers to reconsider the present in view of the weight of the past. EA

cartoons see ANIMATED CARTOONS; COMICS, PERIODICALS AND MAGAZINES; SUPERHEROES

Cartwright, Pauline 1944– Prolific New Zealand writer of titles for educational publishers. *What Is It Like to Be Old?* (1988), a PICTUREBOOK, is an outstanding exploration of this topic. Cartwright's first novel, *Meg's Last Springtime* (1990), is a sensitive coming-of-age story, highlighting the author's ability to create strong contemporary characters in believable situations and settings. Other titles include *Saved by Ryan Kane* (1994) and *What! No TV?* (1993); in the latter, a boy meets his grandfather for the first and only time, and learns that 'life and death were a circle and every person was a part of it'. BN

Cartwright, Reg 1938– Self-taught British illustrator. Cartwright's early career was in advertising but then he won the MOTHER GOOSE AWARD for his oil illustrations in *Mr. Potter's Pigeon* (Patrick Kinmouth, 1980). He has worked with the author SELINA HASTINGS (*Peter and the Wolf*, 1987; *The Canterbury Tales*, 1988; *The Man who Wanted to Live Forever*, 1988), and he has produced several books with Ann Cartwright, frequently about animals, such as *The Winter Hedgehog* (1989). His *Birds, Beasts and Fishes* collection (ed. Anne Carter, 1991) reveals his particular style: naive, formal, robust, well-defined blocks of bright colour, with lush Rousseau-like settings. JAG

Casabianca see FELICIA HEMANS

Cassedy, Sylvia 1930–89 American writer and poet well known for her use of a FANTASY world to relieve the anxieties and problems of young people. The strong, imaginative characters in *Behind the Attic Wall* (1983), *M.E. and Morton* (1987) and *Lucie Babbidge's House* (1989) are unforgettable personalities. Cassedy's poetry includes *Roomrimes: Poems* (1987) and *Zoomrimes: Poems About Things That Go* (1993), both in alphabetical format. She also translated poetry from India and Japan. PDS

see also ALPHABET BOOKS

Castlemon, Harry [Charles Austin Fosdick] 1842–1915 American author of ADVENTURE STORIES for boys. His 58 books indicate the popularity of series books for boys at the time and also reflect Castlemon's own adventurous life. As a youth, he ran away from his home in Buffalo, New York, and joined the navy. He experienced perilous duty aboard Federal gunboats during the Civil War and used that background as the basis for his most popular stories, the *Gunboat* series, in which young Frank Nelson is introduced in the first two books, *Frank the Young Naturalist* and *Frank on a Gunboat*, both published in 1864. According to Castlemon, 'Boys don't like fine writing. What they want is adventure, and the more of it you can get into 250 pages of manuscript, the better fellow you are.' Other series – *Go Ahead, Roughing It* and *Rocky Mountain* – take their events from the making of America in the expansion of the frontier, again from the author's own youthful experience. Dangerous mountain climbs, encounters with large brown bears, hurtling rides through frothing rapids – these and similar adventures kept his readers turning pages even if other aspects of his books remained undeveloped. KSB

Caswell, Brian (Paul) 1954– Welsh-born Australian writer and former teacher who has published 13 titles, from MERRYLL OF THE STONES (1989) to *Only The Heart* (1997). Caswell uses cinematic techniques to structure intricate narratives, frequently exploring themes of 'otherness', the outsider and the migrant's experience in a new land. In *A Cage of Butterflies* (1992) Caswell writes for a post-Spielberg generation accustomed to the sophisticated demands of electronic and digital mass media. The plot concerns the use for medical research of Miriam and the other think-tank children, and the super-intelligent, almost autistic 'Babies', with whose minds they are able to communicate. This chilling SCIENCE FICTION novel uses five narrators to create a continuously shifting mixture of voices, insights and opinions from which the reader constructs the narrative, much like in the viewing of a film. This multi-persona style of narration, with shifting perspectives and multiple settings, is a trademark of Caswell's work, whether in *Mike* (1993), *Lisdalia* (1994), *Maddie* (1995) – a trilogy of linked characters' stories dealing with perspectives on the migrant experience in suburban Australia – or in *Only The Heart* (1997), which is co-authored with Vietnamese Australian David Phu An Chiem. *Deucalion* (1995), another science fiction multi-narrative novel, works as an allegory of colonialism, and addresses the subjugation of indigenous peoples. *Deucalion* won the 1995 Children's Peace Literature Award, and the Aurealis Award for Young Adult Science Fiction/Fantasy; a sequel, *The View from Ararat*, was published in 1999. *Asturias* (1996) draws upon the author's experiences in the music industry, which are cross-cut with an historian's fascination with the Spanish Civil War. SNJ

Cat Among the Pigeons (1987) A collection of poems by KIT WRIGHT, exuberantly illustrated by POSY SIMMONDS. The poems demonstrate Wright's skill in word-craft, with a rich variety of stanza patterns. They vary from short nature lyrics to longer narrative verse, often looking at animals and humans in unexpected ways. HA

***Cat Club* series** American series of 13 cat stories for young children, written and illustrated by Esther Averill (1902–92). Averill's first books were written in Paris for her own experimental Domino Press, with

ILLUSTRATIONS by a young Russian emigré, FEODOR ROJANKOVSKY; their *Daniel Boone* (1931) broke new ground in PICTUREBOOK design. Later she worked as a children's librarian in New York City. In *The Cat Club* (1944) she introduced Jenny Linsky, a shy little black cat with a red scarf – based, according to Averill, on a cat of her own who seemed too shy and plain ever to be a heroine. The members of the Cat Club who became Jenny's friends were also city cats whom Averill owned or knew well; in *The Hotel Cat* (1969) and *The Fire Cat* (1960) two of them were given stories of their own. Jenny's adventures and her feelings – meeting strangers, losing her scarf, apprehensively attending her first party – are essentially any child's. In *Jenny's Adopted Brothers* (1952), she welcomes two strays into her home, but becomes jealous when they seem to usurp her place. Deceptively ingenuous illustrations add to the charm of these simply told, warm-hearted, but never sentimental stories. SR

Cat in the Hat, The (1957) DR SEUSS's best-known PICTUREBOOK epitomises the concept of instruction through delight. *The Cat in the Hat* was composed as a controlled vocabulary book with only 223 different words. Seuss created the book as a response to a 1954 article in *Life* magazine by John Hersey which speculated that the decline in children's reading abilities in the United States was due to the dull basal readers used in school (see READING SCHEMES) and suggested that children's writers, such as Seuss, might try to write a school primer. Seuss found the limited vocabulary a challenge and, after a period of frustration, simply chose the first two words that rhymed – 'cat' and 'hat' – from the list of approved words and created his most memorable character.

Few readers who have enjoyed the book's much-imitated anapaestic tetrameter stanzas, or viewed the bright, cartoon ILLUSTRATIONS, would suspect it was intended to be educational rather than entertaining. Two children are left at home alone on a rainy day with nothing to do. The Cat arrives and promises to show them 'Good fun that is funny'. This forbidden fun involves a series of messy activities, including the Cat's failed attempt to juggle, and flying kites in the house with the Cat's companions, Thing One and Thing Two. These wild things are the alter egos of the children, just as the disapproving fish, who insists that they make the Cat go away, is their conscience. At the last moment, the Cat cleans up the chaos with a zany Seuss machine before Mother returns. The book concludes with a question to the reader, 'What would YOU do, IF your mother asked YOU' what had happened during the day?

The popularity of *The Cat in the Hat* led to the founding of the Beginner Book division of Random House in 1957 with Dr Seuss as president. The image of the Cat in the Hat became the logo for this controlled vocabulary series, which included the sequel *The Cat in the Hat Comes Back* (1958) as well as *Green Eggs and Ham* (1960). The Cat reappears in *The Cat in the Hat Songbook* (1967), *The Cat's Quizzer* (1976) and *I Can Read with My Eyes Shut* (1978), in which he teaches a younger cat to read. A TELEVISION special based on the book with a script by Seuss was broadcast in 1971, followed by *The Grinch Grinches the Cat in the Hat* (1982).

Seuss franchised the Cat to Coleco Toy Company, but was unhappy with the toy Cat's expression. *The Cat in the Hat* has been widely translated, and a selection from it appears in the 16th edition of *Bartlett's Familiar Quotations*. Since Seuss's death in 1991, the Seuss Estate has authorised an increasing number of *Cat* products ranging from a CD-Rom version and a board game to clothing featuring the character. A six-foot statue of The Cat in the Hat is planned for the Dr Seuss National Memorial in Geisel's birthplace of Springfield, Massachusetts. JCS

Cat Who Went to Heaven, The see LYNN WARD; see also ELIZABETH COATSWORTH

Catalogue of the Universe, The (1985) Novel for teenagers by CARNEGIE MEDAL winner, MARGARET MAHY, distinguished by a complexity of effect masked by an apparent narrative simplicity. The story concerns the young Tycho Potter, a shy and reflective boy with a wry deprecatory humour and an interest in philosophy and astronomy. It tells with frankness and humour how his lifelong friendship with the beautiful and sexy Angela May – whose own problems arise from her eccentric mother and her need to meet her unknown father – transforms itself into sexual love, thus linking philosophy with romance, sincerity with humour, and intelligence with passion. VW

Catcher in the Rye, The (1951) Novel by J.D. Salinger (1919–), *about* adolescence rather than *for* adolescents, and widely seen as a precursor of (or to blame for) probably the most common form of writing for young adults. Since the 1960s, thousands of novels, especially in the United States, have used a first-person demotic narrative and are concerned with teenage *angst*. Salinger's novel has been criticised for its complete absorption in its solipsistic teenage 'hero', which does not allow for any ironic (or other) distancing – which is precisely the criticism levelled at other books in the genre. It is, of course, difficult to say how directly *The Catcher in the Rye* has influenced YOUNG ADULT FICTION, although Holden Caulfield's sad weekend journey from school to nervous breakdown was highly influential for teenagers on its first publication. Certainly, the shock tactic of its famous opening sentence: 'If you really want to hear about it, the first thing you'll probably want to know is where I was born . . . and all that David Copperfield kind of crap . . .' has been widely echoed, if not imitated. JUDY BLUME's *Forever* (USA, 1975; UK, 1976), for example, begins: 'Sybil Davison has a genius IQ and has been laid by at least six different guys.' Ironically, *The Catcher in the Rye* is uncharacteristic of Salinger's small but intense oeuvre, only hinting at the mysticism which is characteristic of his later novellas, such as *Franny and Zooey* (USA, 1961; UK, 1962). PLH

***Cathedral* series** see CHOIR SCHOOL SERIES

Catnach, James (Jemmy) 1792–1841 London printer of street literature, broadsides, songs and CHAPBOOKS. Born in Alnwick, Catnach was apprenticed to his father, eventually moving to Monmouth Court, Seven Dials, London, in 1813. When news was short he contrived scandalous headlines for his news sheets, 'catchpennies' and 'cocks', which were the forerunners of the 'gutter' press. He was sentenced to six months in prison for suggesting that a local butcher made his sausages out of dead bodies. Popular titles in his list of halfpenny and farthing books for children were *Cries of London*, 'COCK ROBIN' and *Jack and Gill*. SD

Catran, Ken 1944– New Zealand writer, who began his writing career as a TELEVISION scriptwriter, but is now best known for his SCIENCE FICTION for young adults. Catran's two series, *Deepwater Trilogy* and *The Solar Colonies*, have been adapted for television. They take the reader into the future, to a world that transcends time and yet is believable. Familiar issues for young readers, such as relationships with peers and striving for independence, are examined from a new perspective in imaginative settings. *Golden Prince* (1999), set in Troy, exemplifies Catran's ability to make an historical story relevant to modern youth. By contrast, *Black Sister* (1999) is a fast-paced horror story. Two books, *Dream Bite* (1995) and *The Onager* (1996), have been shortlisted for children's book awards in New Zealand. LL

Cattle Raid of Cuailgne, The see IRISH MYTHOLOGY AND FOLKLORE

Caudill, Rebecca 1899–1985 American author of more than 20 books for children and adults. Caudill was born in the mountains of Kentucky and attended college in Georgia where she was the first woman to work her way through school. She received a master's degree from Vanderbilt University in 1922. After graduate school, Caudill taught in Tennessee and Brazil, and travelled throughout Canada and Europe. She edited a girls' magazine, *Torchbearer*, from 1924 to 1930. In 1931 she married James Ayars, an editor, and the couple had two children. Caudill's work is inspired and flavoured by her Appalachian upbringing, and she is known for her realistic fiction and simple but eloquent prose. One of her early works was a trilogy based on her own childhood: *Happy Little Family* (1947); *Schoolhouse in the Woods* (1949); *Up and Down the River* (1951). She won a Newbery Honour Medal for *Tree of Freedom* (1949), a historical novel set in Kentucky and Carolina in the 1780s. The novel follows a pioneer family facing the threat of the Revolutionary War. Other works include *The Best-Loved Doll* (1962); *A Pocketful of Cricket* (1964); *A Certain Small Shepherd* (1965); *Did you Carry the Flag Today, Charley?* (1966). JKB

see also FAMILY STORIES; HISTORICAL FICTION

Causley, Charles 1917– British poet, writer, onetime teacher, and one of the most distinctive voices in children's poetry today. Many of his poems are classics of the school anthology, among them 'I Saw a Jolly Hunter', 'Timothy Winters' – with his 'ears like bombs and teeth like splinters' – and 'My Mother saw a Dancing Bear'. All three are included in both *Collected Poems* (1992) and *Collected Poems for Children* (1996), indicating that, like Auden, Causley believes 'there are no good poems which are only for children'.

Causley's roots are in Cornwall, and after serving in the Navy during the War years he returned to teach in his old primary school. He knows children well, their capabilities, imagination, discernment; he never undermines them with weak craftsmanship or subject matter. He respects the fact that they need not fully understand a poem to gain a glimmer, a shiver, of enjoyment. The sea made an early impression; he was both fearful of it and fascinated by it, as many poems reflect.

An early adult collection, *Underneath the Water* (1968), includes one of his best-loved poems, which has been adopted by children's editors – 'By St Thomas Water', with its haunting childhood fear of the churchyard dead, remembered by the grown-up poet: 'Waiting in the cold grass / Under a crinkled bough.' 'Crinkled' is a choice word, characteristic of the writer of phrases like 'the claw of the pawing sea'; 'a nothingness of air'; 'stubborn as a stone'; 'a blitz of a boy'.

In the Navy it was the sailors' jargon he found irresistible, and he found his first poetic subjects then – separation, death, loss, odd-ball characters. He has held his own place for 30 years in the children's literature world, unconcerned with 'political correctness' or current trends. WALTER DE LA MARE, if not his mentor, is one influence. Like the earlier poet, Causley had musical training, is inspired by rhyme, structure, rhythm, and handles nonsense, lyrics, oddities and enchantments with expertise. He relishes, too, an underlying menace and unease – shadows, a chill wind, the darker side of light. De la Mare would recognise Causley's 'Tom Bone' who 'lived all alone / In a deep house on Winter Street'; 'The Jolly Hunter', shot with his own jolly gun; 'Sarah Jane', enticed by mermaids. All these appear in *FIGGIE HOBBIN* (1970, reissued with some extra poems in 1990, illustrated by GERALD ROSE) – a delicious Cornish plum-pudding. The passing of time, death, lost innocence, war, creep in amongst much bubbling humour and word-play.

Causley is the ballad-writer of today, bringing fresh originality to a well-explored genre. His BALLADS are rich in story, vivid, colourful, passionate and moving. Some young readers also respond to the starker themes of crime, poverty, or broken romance of his adult poetry. The hard-hitting, streetwise 'My Friend Maloney' – an ageing Timothy Winters – is one favourite. Notes accompany many poems based on history, myth and tradition, giving a sense of place, time, reality: An Italian ship wrecked near Tintagel in 1893; a tale of Nelson's corpse at Trafalgar; the 1941 Cretan Campaign. The haunting 'Mary, Mary Magdalene' – transporting many readers seeking out the saint's granite figure on Launceston church wall to recite (perhaps from memory?) 'I throw a pebble on your back/Will it lie or fall?' – King Ezra the drover; St Brigid; the Obby Loss; Lady Jane Grey; Aesop; Solomon Fingergreen; the Young Snowman of Churton-le-Grice – these are some of the characters who bound through two sparkling collections, *Jack the Treacle Eater* (1987) and *The Young Man of Cury* (1991). *Early One Morning* (1986), for younger readers, has been set to music by Anthony Castro. *The Ballad of Aucassin & Nicolette* (1982), with music by Stephen McNeff, has had radio and stage productions. *The Gift of a Lamb* (1978), drawn from the *Second Shepherd's Play*, is slick, funny and serious, immensely actable; the villain, Thieving Jack, a razor-sharp wide-boy, modern and medieval. Causley is a religious, entirely un-pious writer; themes involving the nativity, crucifixion and resurrection spring out with startling imagery, always immediate.

As an anthologist, Causley has impeccable judgement and breadth of vision. In a revealing introduction to *A PUFFIN BOOK OF MAGIC VERSE* (1974), he tells us: 'Properly examined a good poem, however simple-seeming on the surface, never stops giving us fresh and exciting secrets . . . One thing seems certain: that the language of magic has always been, always must be, the language of poetry.' AHa

Cautionary Tales for Children see CAUTIONARY VERSE; HILAIRE BELLOC

cautionary verse A tradition of verse principally dating from the Victorian period, generally delivered in rhyming couplets, that relates the seemingly minor misdemeanors of children, acquiring its ruthless humour from the punishment or misfortune that befalls them. This is usually excessive and wildly out of proportion to the original transgression. HILAIRE BELLOC's *THE BAD CHILD'S BOOK OF BEASTS* (1896) and *Cautionary Tales* (1907) are the most celebrated, including Jim, who ran away from his nurse and was eaten by a Lion ('And always keep a-hold of nurse / For fear of finding something worse'), and Matilda, who told lies and was burned to death.

These verses openly parodied Victorian values and stereotypes; respectable gentlemen and ladies were made to sound – and to look, in B.T.B.'s (Basil Blackwood's) ILLUSTRATIONS – eccentric or just plain silly. Belloc's amusing verse was also a reaction to the didactic, moral tales prevalent in children's literature before and during the first half of the 19th century. These were either Puritan, fiercely evangelical or part of a materialistic, utilitarian world-view giving secular warnings against failings typical of childhood – greed, selfishness, curiosity, disobedience – usually carrying a note of admonition.

In 1845 HEINRICH HOFFMANN's *STRUWWELPETER*, with its collection of both terrifying and comical cautionary verse, accompanied by his own exaggeratedly expressive drawings, was an early and clear reaction to the moral tale in verse. Hoffmann, Belloc and HARRY GRAHAM (*Ruthless Rhymes for Heartless Homes*, 1899) countered Victorian sentiment about children. These 'over-the-top', amusingly cruel Awful Warnings were developed in the second half of the 20th century by OGDEN NASH, whose Jabez Dawes, the Boy Who Laughed at Santa Claus (*Custard and Company*, 1979) was turned into a Jack-in-the-Box.

Best known today in this genre is ROALD DAHL for *REVOLTING RHYMES* (1982), though his famous story, *Charlie and the Chocolate Factory*, is in many ways a cautionary tale, considering the fate that befalls greedy or spoilt children in Wonka's factory and the lessons that are sung after each punishment by the Oompa Loompas. In *Revolting Rhymes* Dahl retells FAIRY TALES and, in time-honoured cautionary tale tradition, he ends with a tongue-in-cheek moral lesson. In contrast to his Victorian forbears, Dahl invokes the benefits of being street-wise, quick-witted and more ruthless than one's adversaries. Knowingness is rewarded as opposed to innocence. A favourite with children is the heroine of his *LITTLE RED RIDING HOOD*, a resourceful gun-slinger, who doesn't need a father figure to chase the wolf away – she 'slips a pistol from her knickers' instead and ends the tale dressed in a wolf-skin coat. JL

Cavanna, Betty 1909– American writer of YOUNG ADULT FICTION. Cavanna graduated from Douglass College and worked as a journalist, advertising manager and art director until 1943, when she became a writer of books in various genres – non-fiction, HISTORICAL FICTION, suspense and mystery – mainly for young adults. As an author of popular fiction, Cavanna's light romances feature well-drawn settings, as well as believable characters. Her heroines, often innocent small-town girls, are suddenly faced with the necessity of escaping from their familiar environments. Cast out into the unknown, they must make their own way, often in an alien world. Her themes include alienation, displacement and the vulnerability of innocence. In Cavanna's historical novel *Runaway Voyage* (1978), for example, a maidservant, Elisa, escapes from her employer's attempts to exploit her and courageously embarks upon a journey from New York City to Seattle, where she succeeds in finding a new life for herself in frontier country. Cavanna's mystery novels include *Stamp Twice for Murder* (1981). She also writes under the pseudonyms of Elizabeth Headley and Betsy Allen. MRS

(Cavoukian), Raffi 1948– Internationally popular singer/songwriter for young children, known professionally by his first name only. After spending his first ten years in Egypt, Raffi moved with his Armenian family to Toronto, Canada, where he learned a new language and culture. A self-taught guitarist by the age of 16, Raffi early aspired to a career as a musician. In 1976 Raffi released his first album, *Singable Songs for the Very Young*, which he produced and distributed with his own money. Over the next decade his popularity grew rapidly, primarily by word of mouth. By the late 1980s, Raffi had received two Grammy Award nominations in addition to the Order of Canada – the country's highest distinction – for his contributions to the lives of Canadian children. With his gentle voice, immense respect for children, and light-hearted, folksy tunes, Raffi continues to gain a young following. When asked about his craft in 1986, Raffi told *Publisher's Weekly*: 'Well-made children's records are right up there with well-made children's books, in terms of what they can offer the young child . . . They both evoke feelings, images and moods.' CHW

see also MUSIC AND STORY

Caxton, William c. 1422–91 The first English printer. Although none of the texts Caxton printed were intended specifically for a child readership, his choices included many of the most popular stories in the early children's literature canon. The most important book he printed, from a child's perspective, was his own translation of AESOP'S FABLES (1484). This incorporated woodcuts copied from Steinhowell, establishing an important precedent for the tradition of illustrated children's stories. Caxton also printed Arthurian romances (sufficiently important within chivalric education to be attacked by humanists in the 16th century), as well as *REYNARD THE FOX*, COURTESY BOOKS and works by CHAUCER. DWh

see also KING ARTHUR

Cay, The (1969) American ROBINSONNADE by THEODORE TAYLOR. A World War II bombing and shipwreck leave Phillip, an American boy, first on a raft and then on a tiny uncharted island with Timothy, an old black Caribbean man. Because Phillip goes blind and they have so few tools or natural resources, this is a more brutal portrayal of castaways at the mercy of nature than many other survival stories for children. Forced to make a home in a cramped hut, and dependent on Timothy, Phillip abandons his mother's biases about racial separatism. Timothy teaches Phillip survival skills that make him self-sufficient after a hurricane kills Timothy. As in other novels by Taylor, the child protagonist develops an enduring attachment to the place where he learns self-reliance and to the friend who helps him form independent values. Dramatised on television in 1974, *The Cay* remains popular with children and teachers. Defending it against charges of racism, Taylor emphasises that the story was based on his Caribbean experience and people he knew. *Timothy of the Cay* (1993) is both a prequel about Timothy's life and a sequel about Phillip's quest to regain his sight and revisit the island. TLH

CBI/Bisto Book Award see APPENDIX

CD-ROMs Disks (the meaning 'compact disk–read only memory') storing information which can be viewed on personal computers. CD-ROMs use many media, including words, still and moving images, sound and hypertext links which, in turn, provide a setting for interactivity. They are created by a team of developers, rather than a traditional book's single author. While CD-ROMs are used for many purposes – including archives, databases, encyclopedias and games – the format became popular in the 1990s for interactive literature and 'edutainment', particularly for children. Because the cost of owning a computer and purchasing CD-ROMs is considerable, the audience for children's CD-ROMs is middle and upper-class; parents and children with home computers use them more than schools hampered by tight budgets and limited technology. Consequently, these CD-ROMs emphasise their entertainment value and limit – or pleasantly conceal – their didactic elements.

Some of the first CD-ROMs were enhancements of programs created on the floppy-disk format for personal computers. *Amanda Stories* (1988) by Amanda Goodenough were first developed as lively, black-and-white interactive texts created in HyperCard for Macintosh computers. In CD-ROM format, these were enhanced with colour and more sound. *The Oregon Trail* (1990) was also created on floppy disks for several computer platforms but became more complicated and sophisticated in CD-ROM. The popular, entertaining story follows pioneers trekking across the western United States on the Oregon Trail.

Many books have been adapted for the CD-ROM format. BEATRIX POTTER's 1902 *THE TALE OF PETER RABBIT* was delightfully adapted by Discis Books in 1993 and included annotations, definitions of vocabulary, and voices reading the text in several languages. Mark Schlichting adapted AESOP's *The Tortoise and The Hare* (1993) with illustrations by Michael Dashow and Barbara Lawrence Webster for Broderbund Books, which has published some of the most innovative children's CD-ROMs. This version's updated FABLE includes cartoon-like characters, jazzy music, hidden minor characters and a narrator who reads the story aloud. While the storyline is true to Aesop, the added multimedia dimensions enable the reader to have more control of the text and to play with it. *AlphaBonk Farm* (1994) takes a humorous, interactive approach to traditional ALPHABET BOOKS while sneaking in farm facts; young viewers can play any of the letter games repeatedly.

While the CD-ROMs so far noted are mainly for children under 12, the most groundbreaking texts in this format are *Myst* (1993) and its sequel *Riven* (1997), both created by brothers Rand and Robyn Miller. With three-dimensional artistic images, an original soundtrack and an imaginative story, the bestselling *Myst* created a multimedia text appealing both to junior high children and adults. Readers collect clues, click on images, solve puzzles, watch videos, and record notes in a book to unravel the story. CD-ROMs are an important leap forward in multimedia texts, but other formats, with more advanced technology such as DVD, may eclipse them. CD-ROMs can be used in tandem with the world wide web, but the latter also has different interactive aspects which CD-ROMs cannot duplicate. JAS

censorship Strictly speaking, censorship refers to official or governmental control of published, broadcast or performed material. However, the term is frequently applied loosely to any attempt by an individual or organisation to restrict the availability or content of books, films and videos. Children's literature has always been a flashpoint for censorship concerns. Since children have traditionally been thought of as easily influenced, adults have been prescriptive about what is appropriate for children to read (or hear, or view). The history of children's literature demonstrates that there has often been a conflict between pleasure and instruction.

One of the first and still prevalent issues in censorship focuses on the truth/fiction dichotomy so stressed in Western culture. JEAN-JACQUES ROUSSEAU, one of the first to recognise the developmental stages of children's mental growth, discouraged all novels and FAIRY TALES for his fictional young pupil except for *ROBINSON CRUSOE*, partly because it was based on an actual account. When FANTASY stories began being published widely for children in the late 1700s and 1800s, they were attacked using this same logic. Allied with this concern was the ethical issue that story characters should model moral behaviour. Although the Victorian period witnessed a flowering of fairy stories, SAMUEL GOODRICH, known as Peter Parley, denounced all such stories, while Anthony Comstock in the United States led a campaign against children's DIME NOVELS of adventure and mystery. In the 20th century, popular versions of fairy tales have been variously challenged for promoting alcoholism, sexism, ageism, materialism, class discrimination, violence, and, again, for being unreal.

In contrast to earlier centuries, the late 20th century has bred concerns not just about fantasy, but about realism, though the concern still centres upon protecting children from corruption. As children's writers have begun exposing young readers to more realistic situations, they have challenged the traditional restrictions on swearing, explicit sexual accounts, graphic violence, and disturbing accounts of social issues such as racism, homelessness or child abuse.

Western culture still adheres to the Romantic image of the child whose innocence should be protected, while realising that children must be exposed to the real world if they are to survive. It is a difficult balance. However, a more moderate application of censorship sees the issue in terms of appropriateness to age: a book which is mentally, emotionally or psychologically appropriate for a 14-year-old may not be appropriate for an eight-year-old.

Although attempts at censorship are often seen as expressions of power, strongly held beliefs and ethical views on matters of education are also at stake. Censorship is on the rise perhaps because many parents feel they have little control over their children in a technologically advanced society. However, in the United States the one way they can maintain influence is through the schools, where their complaints are taken seriously, so that public schools and LIBRARIES have become common targets. In such situations, whatever a teacher reads or makes available to students – or whatever is on the shelves of school or public libraries – is a possible target.

In South Africa, rigorous censorship by government authorities during the apartheid era (1948–94) affected children's reading in that many books and films were banned or had cuts imposed and certain people could not be quoted, thus narrowing the range from which education departments and libraries could select. In addition, institutions were cautious not to facilitate reading that might be considered politically subversive. A small number of YOUNG ADULT novels were published that questioned racial discrimination and its consequences, but these usually escaped attention from the Publications Control Board. Some anti-racist adult works, such as Alan Paton's *Cry, the Beloved Country* and the Canadian novel *I Heard the Owl Call My Name* by MARGARET CRAVEN, were never banned and were read in some schools during this period.

In the United States, most censorship attacks derive from the far right. Primarily Christian fundamentalists, these politically influential if not always cohesive groups have made their presence known nationally and at the local level by being elected to school boards, where textbook selections are made. A famous couple in Texas, the Geblers, came to influence the publishing industry itself, since Texas selects all its textbooks state-wide. As a result, for many years evolution was not included in any textbooks selected for Texas schoolchildren. On the far left, California used a similar process, but the textbooks selected for their schoolchildren had to pass the 'politically correct' test. *Huckleberry Finn* (see TOM SAWYER), which is one of the most censored books ever, can be challenged by the far right for Huck's questioning of the law, and by the far left for his use of the word 'nigger'. Conservative organisations known for promoting censorship include the Eagle Forum, Citizens for Excellence in Education, and Focus on the Family. Challenges from these groups have begun to include attacks on magic, environmentalism, globalism, and independent thinking on many other issues. There are, however, several organisations devoted to fighting censorship, most notably the American Library Association, the National Organisation of Women, and the American Civil Liberties Union. The People for the American Way exists exclusively to monitor censorship attacks and report to the media. In general, these organisations believe censorship is abhorrent in any form.

In Britain, attempts to censor children's books have been less organised; the campaign by public libraries against the work of ENID BLYTON in the 1960s was a rare exception. Though a school or library may at any time be challenged by a local individual or group (for example, a clergyman objecting to the use in schools of books about witches), teachers and librarians enjoy a considerable degree of freedom. Whether this is likely to endure as the central government gains a tighter control of the school curriculum remains to be seen. At present, censorship becomes important only when a tabloid newspaper takes issue with a particular book or author (for example, Susanne Bosche's *Jenny Lives with Eric and Martin*, denounced because it concerned gay parents). Since the popular press in Britain is predominantly right-wing, its main targets are what it sees as absurd examples of 'political correctness'. However, a more insidious form of hidden censorship – a fear on the part of publishers to take risks with challenging or controversial material – is believed by many to be a serious inhibiting factor on the actual publication of children's books. Similarly, where there is a threat of public controversy, teachers and booksellers are less likely to promote innovative and challenging books.

Authors of children's books – from LEWIS CARROLL and MARK TWAIN to E. NESBIT and beyond – have often been subtly subversive; today, however, they are under so much public scrutiny that implied or explicit challenges to current assumptions are less probable. It is likely, therefore, that overt censorship is less of a danger than assumed and unacknowledged expectations which have the effect of imposing a bland and safe ideological orthodoxy on the provision of children's books. CAT, VW, EJ

Centre for the Children's Book An institution developed in the 1990s in Newcastle-upon-Tyne to raise the status of children's books in the United Kingdom. A primary aim was to establish a national archive of children's books and organise events and exhibitions centred upon post-war and contemporary children's writers, illustrators and PICTUREBOOK authors. The concept grew partly out of a conviction that the opportunity for children to exchange ideas with practising authors and illustrators can profoundly influence their creative lives. The inspiration for this enterprise lay mostly in the enthusiasm of two people, Mary Briggs and Elizabeth Hammill (see also CHILD AUTHORS), who over several years acquired a substantial archive, raised funding, and negotiated with publishers and national and regional bodies in search of accommodation. The Centre's first exhibition, held at the Discovery Museum in Newcastle in 1998, was called *Daft as a Bucket* and featured the work of COLIN MCNAUGHTON; it was genuinely child-centred and interactive, involving art and drama produced by local students. Along with a number of smaller-scale projects, a second major exhibition – devoted to the *TINTIN* stories by the Belgian artist Hergé – was held in 1999, launched by QUENTIN BLAKE, Britain's first CHILDREN'S LAUREATE. VW

Chalet School, The Girls' school story series which begins with the arrival of 24-year-old Madge Bettany and her younger sister, Joey, in the Austrian Tyrol, and the foundation there of a new trilingual, non-denominational school (*The School in the Chalet*, 1925). By 1970, when the last book (*The Prefects at the Chalet School*) was published posthumously, the author, Elinor Brent-Dyer, had written 58 volumes about the same school.

The series takes the school, impelled by political tensions and war, from Austria to Guernsey, to the British mainland, and finally, in peacetime, to Switzerland. Joey, 'a Chalet girl to the end', follows the school wherever it goes.

Joey is the series' key figure and, like her heroine, LOUISA MAY ALCOTT's Jo March, she is headstrong and impish as a girl and resistant to the prospect of womanhood. Elements of her fictional life echo those of her creator; neither had the full complement of parents, both spent their lives involved in education and wrote stories for girls, and both were received into the Roman Catholic church.

Born Gladys Eleanor May Dyer in South Shields in 1894 shortly before her father deserted the family, Brent-Dyer entered the City of Leeds Training College in 1915 and then taught in the boys' department of a local elementary school. Like other major writers of girls' school fiction, she never married. The fictional Joey, on the other hand, sustains her connection with a privileged world of 'rollicking girlhood' and boarding school in adult life, while becoming a wife and then the mother of 11 children.

The books retain a devoted readership, at one time boasting a fan club of over 4,000. Their strength lies in the teacher's insights of their author: readers are as familiar with the staff common room as they are with the pupils' classrooms. Mistresses, such as Kathie Ferrars, straight from Oxford, with her 'crisp way of dealing' with her pupils (*The New Mistress at the Chalet School*, 1957), are generally likeable and efficient, and among the girls 'sentimental grand passions' are severely discouraged (*A Problem for the Chalet School*, 1956). Dialogue has a robustness lacking in the contrived slang of the school stories of ANGELA BRAZIL. Although the momentous events of a world war touch the life of the school, there is none of the patriotic jingoism evident in the work of Dorita Fairlie Bruce.

While it may be true, as Rosemary Auchmuty claims, that the books present a compelling picture of single-sex school life which has largely vanished from the modern educational scene, they have attracted some criticism, notably from Mary Cadogan and Patricia Craig for their 'religious sentimentality', 'assembly line' plots and for the 'artifical prolongation' of Joey's association. Nevertheless, Brent-Dyer attempted to chart the changes in the social values affecting the lives of girls and women, and her final book leaves Joey's daughters contemplating, not a life at home as their mother had done, but the prospect of university and careers. BW

Chalmers, Mary (Eileen) 1927– American author and illustrator of books for children. A New Jersey native, Chalmers studied at the Philadelphia Museum College of Art and at the Barnes Foundation. Because publishers found it difficult to find books suitable to her style, she was encouraged to write her own. The birth of her niece provided the incentive she needed to launch her career, and in 1955 she published her first book *Come For a Walk With Me*. In addition to writing and illustrating several of her own books, she has also illustrated books by CHARLOTTE ZOLOTOW, URSULA NORDSTROM, RUTH KRAUSS and Nancy Jewell. JGJ

Chambers, Aidan 1934– British novelist, dramatist, critic, editor and publisher. In the United Kingdom he is known as a distinguished lecturer and teacher who was once a monk. His considerable reputation in Europe and North America comes from his boundary-breaking postmodern novels about adolescence. For his teenage pupils in the 60s, 'an oppressed people', he wrote plays: *Johnny Salter* (1966), *The Car* (1967), *The Chicken Run* (1968) and, later, *The Dream Cage* (1982), to reflect their lives and language. The same concerns prompted a series of anthologies, mostly ghost stories, and *Topliners* (1966), a list of paperback novels for inexperienced readers whose needs are also highlighted in *The Reluctant Reader* (1969). This pedagogic strand continues in *Booktalk* (1985), *The Reading Environment* (1991) and the much-admired *Tell Me: Children, Reading and Talk* (1993).

As a critic, Chambers championed the work of ALAN GARNER. His true authorial voice emerges in *BREAKTIME* (1978), followed by *Dance on My Grave* (1982), *Now I Know* (1987), *The Toll Bridge* (1992) and *Postcards from No Man's Land* (1999), metafictive novels that divide critical opinion, the last of which won the 1999 CARNEGIE MEDAL. The narrators, young males, explore their new awareness of sexuality, spiritual experience and friendship in terms of relationships, language and cultural symbols. Readers are expected to engage in meaning-making with texts that reflect their understanding of other contemporary forms of communication. The novels have an affinity with the writing of CORMIER in the United States and Pohl in Sweden. Chambers is co-proprietor, with his wife Nancy, of The Thimble Press, which publishes *SIGNAL*. As Turton & Chambers he published translations of European fictions for young people. MM

Chambers, Nancy see *SIGNAL*; see also CRITICAL APPROACHES TO CHILDREN'S LITERATURE

Chambers, Robert see SCOTTISH FOLKTALES; see also NURSERY RHYMES

Champion the Wonder Horse see TELEVISION

Champion, The see ANNUALS

Chanail, An see *THE SLEEPING GIANT*

She went to the fruiterer's
To buy him some fruit;
When she came back,
He was playing the flute.

She went to the shoe-mart
To buy him some shoes;
And when she came back,
He sat reading the news.

From J.G. Rusher's chapbook version of *Old Mother Hubbard.*

Chance Child, A (1978) Novel by Jill Paton Walsh recounting two stories that interweave and unfold along different historical periods. Creep is a neglected child who runs away and somehow fades from the world of his siblings into the time of the Industrial Revolution, with its hellish working conditions for children. He is invisible to all but those he befriends until he becomes real, and as an adult in 1833 he writes an autobiography which is read by his brother 150 years later. The ill-treated, half-starved children who work and live in the imaginary landscape haunt the readers as they follow Creep in his journey. EA

Changeover, The (1984) New Zealand novel, winner of a second Carnegie Medal for Margaret Mahy, who continues her exploration of the extraordinary in ordinary life, deploying the supernatural as a metaphor for the reality of adolescent preoccupations. Fourteen-year-old Laura Chant suspects Carmody Braque, a lemure, of taking the spirit of her sick brother, Jacko. A classmate, his mother and his grandmother, all witches, enchant Laura, working a changeover which enables her to rescue Jacko. Wordplay, symbolism and other subtle forms of familiar Mahy magic combine here to produce a finely wrought romance and a truly scary description of a changeover, along with delicately insightful explorations of the tangle of human relationships. RS

Changes (1990) Picturebook by Anthony Browne in which everyday objects are shown mutating under the gaze of a little boy, Joseph, who waits alone in the house for his father and mother to return. Alerted by his father to expect changes, he sees them everywhere, but the reader only discovers what kind of changes are really in store at the end when the parents return with a new baby. Browne foreshadows this event, and hints at Joseph's disquiet, with embedded pictures such as a framed Madonna and Child on the wall and a cuckoo in a nest on the television screen. DL

Changes, The Trilogy by the British author Peter Dickinson recounting independent yet related episodes during the Changes – a futuristic Britain where the vast majority of the population has degenerated to a medieval state, hating and fearing anything technological. The trilogy was published in reverse order: *The Weathermonger* (1968) tells how the Changes are brought to an end by two children, while *Heartsease* (1969) relates the adventure of one group of children as they assist in the escape of an outsider accused of witchcraft. *The Devil's Children* (1970) is set at the beginning of the Changes. *The Weathermonger* has been criticised for the implausibility of its ending, in which a drug-dependent Merlin is found to be causing the Changes, but while this criticism is harsh for a novel of fantasy, there is a marked difference between this book and the later two, which more convincingly portray the dark atmosphere of an ignorant, feudal world, filled with xenophobia and violence. In these books the simple fact of the Changes hangs largely unexplained over the country and adds menace to the well-paced adventure present in all three books. In *The Devil's Children* a young girl called Nicola, having been abandoned by her parents and herself prone to machine-hatred, makes a new home with a community of Sikhs who are immune to the Changes. Dickinson's portrayal of the Sikhs is never tokenistic; they are central protagonists in a book which is noteworthy for one of the earliest depictions of an ethnic minority in British children's literature. MSed

chapbooks Cheap pamphlets sold by pedlars or 'chapmen' who travelled around the British Isles from the 16th to the 19th century. Usually formed from one sheet of printed paper folded to make a small booklet of a few pages, they seldom had wrappers. The title appeared on the upper page, and they often contained one or more crude woodcuts. They were first described as histories, romances, and Godly books, and the name 'chapbook' evolved in the 19th century from the men who sold them. Chapbooks were the popular literature of ordinary people, containing religious and ADVENTURE STORIES, historical and political events, histories of heroes and notorious criminals, and advice on everyday subjects. They were not considered suitable for children, though they were often read by them.

During the Industrial Revolution a more sophisticated public became disenchanted by their old-fashioned style, and publishers, realising the increasing demand for children's literature, began to adapt chapbooks for the juvenile market. From 1780 onwards many booksellers advertised children's chapbooks. Smaller than before, they contained *ABCs*, catechisms, RIDDLES, stories and rhymes. Costing one penny or less, they were better printed than earlier adult chapbooks, included a wide selection of woodcuts, and many had attractive coloured paper or card wrappers. SD

see also J.G. RUSHER; JAMES CATNACH; JOHN MARSHALL; JAMES KENDREW

Chapman, Jean (Erica Sherlock) Australian writer of PICTUREBOOKS, short stories and information texts, as well as a prodigious compiler of anthologies comprising stories, verse and activities. A scriptwriter with ABC Educational Programmes for over 25 years, Chapman has focused on extending Australian children's knowledge not only of their own land, but of other countries, through her numerous picturebooks and stories based on personal travel experiences, or by adapting traditional stories from other countries. Early picturebooks, such as *The Wish Cat* (1966) and *Wombat* (1969), are gentle, well-told stories, with an exquisite control of language. Precise and imaginative use of vocabulary and meticulous research are clearly evident in the Italian-inspired story of a stray cat, *Moon-Eyes* (1978), illustrated by ASTRA LACIS. The English Easter tradition of producing the Paschal candle is celebrated in bouncing verse in *The Great Candle Scandal* (1982), with witty illustrations by ROLAND HARVEY. *Tell Me a Tale* (1975), the first of Chapman's anthologies, illustrated by DEBORAH and KILMENY NILAND, was followed by collections for Christmas, Easter and Halloween. *The Bush Jumper* (1998) is a picturebook for younger children. A bicentenary anthology, *Cockatoo Soup* (1987), illustrated by RODNEY MCRAE, is a celebration of Australia's multicultural society, to which Chapman has made such a significant contribution. JAP

chapter books Term used to describe REAL BOOKS for children who have mastered basic reading skills but still require simple, illustrated texts with a story that is more complicated than that found in a READING SCHEME book. Well-known examples include *FLAT STANLEY* (1964) and *THE WORST WITCH* (1974). KA

Charles, His Royal Highness, Prince see DAVID WOOD

Charlie and the Chocolate Factory see ROALD DAHL; see also CAUTIONARY VERSE

Charlie and the Great Glass Elevator see ROALD DAHL; see also COVER ART

Charlot, Jean 1898–1979 Painter, writer, muralist, lithographer and illustrator of books for both children and adults. Born in Paris, Charlot lived in Mexico in the 1920s where he studied and was active in the mural movement as well as working as a staff artist in archaeological excavations of the Yucatan. From this experience came a number of books about the Mayan culture and Mexican art movements. In 1929 he moved to the United States where he illustrated many books, both his own and by others, and taught art at several universities, including 17 years at the University of Hawaii. His ILLUSTRATIONS for PICTUREBOOKS, including MARGARET WISE BROWN's *A Child's Good Night Book* (1942), *A Child's Good Morning Book* (1952) and *Sneakers: Seven Stories about a Cat* (1955), show the influence of his mural painting: figures are round and sturdy, with a monumentality as though carved from stone, drawn with a simple line and shaded in pencil. Charlot was an established artist when he began illustrating books for children, and he brought a sense of design, layout and aesthetic sensibility to the American picturebook. GRB

Charlotte's Web (1952) Novel by E.B. WHITE, found on most lists of favourite children's books some 50 years after publication. It touches the hearts of readers because it tells honestly the story of animals who live in a barn and behave as they are programmed to behave. Charlotte is a spider who must continue to spin webs and trap insects because that is her job. When she befriends the lonely pig, Wilbur, and ingeniously saves his life by spinning words into her web, she cannot prolong her own life. She must die after she lays her egg sac and Wilbur will have to be content with the friendship of several of her more than 500 offspring who remain living in the barn.

Each of the creatures is true to its nature. Templeton, the rat, is a selfish scavenger. The stuttering goose bosses the other creatures and hisses her comments about everything that happens on the farm. Wilbur eats his slops and rests in the cool mud just as all pigs do. Even Fern and Avery behave like siblings in their interactions. Fern saves Wilbur from the

Illustration by ANNETTE MACARTHUR-ONSLOW from *The Roaring 40* by Nan Chauncy.

axe in the beginning of the story, but as she begins to grow up and become interested in school, and boys and Ferris wheels, she no longer sits in the barn and listens to the animals every day as she used to.

White studied spiders in books and in their natural settings, making sure he understood how they lived and died. He insisted the illustrator, GARTH WILLIAMS, should not try to make Charlotte look like a human being. He definitely wanted her to be a spider.

White loved living on a saltwater farm in Maine where he became very knowledgeable about the animals in his barn. He raised many of them for food but found it disturbing when one of his pigs became sick. Although he nursed it, he could not save it from death. It was a puzzle: he had been raising that pig so that he could kill it for food. The event troubled him so much that he wrote an essay about it and then decided to explore the ironies in his next book for children.

White struggled to find a strong beginning for the book. He wrote at least eight different versions attempting to use the barn as a setting before he created Fern's strong opening lines, 'Where's Papa going with that ax?', which actively pulls us into the story. His ending words were in his mind from the beginning: 'It is not often that someone comes along who is a true friend and a good writer. Charlotte was both.'

Critics loved the story. One was prophetic: 'If there's only one book of the current season still in circulation 50 years hence, it will be *Charlotte's Web*.' Another deemed it 'one of those rare stories for young people which bid fair to last longer than their author – a minor classic beyond question.' BG

Chatterbox (1866–1955) A weekly halfpenny magazine, founded by Rev. J. Erskine Clarke and intended for a wide age range of young readers and aiming to substitute improving reading for popular juvenile 'blood-and-thunder' fiction. Also published as an ANNUAL and a threepenny monthly from January 1867, the paper, with its 'ideals of piety and virtue', was a heavy mixture of serial stories, illustrations and informative articles. By January 1901, editorship had passed to J.F. Harvey Darton who held it until 1931, transforming its sombre purpose and tone by introducing a livelier content, including adventure stories, puzzles and competitions. JOHN MASEFIELD was a contributor, J.M. BARRIE and ANGELA BRAZIL two of its many child readers. By 1948 *Chatterbox* had lost its appeal and zest, surviving only as an annual, entirely secular in outlook and indistinguishable from the many others published for the Christmas market by its new owners, Dean and Son. Containing lacklustre school and adventure stories, puzzles and articles, the volumes attracted few writers of note. In terms of quality of content and production, *Chatterbox* failed to compete in a changing market for children's magazines and it finally ceased publication in 1955. BW

Chaucer, Geoffrey 1340?–1400 Writer and minor court official, affectionately regarded as the father of English poetry. Chaucer did not write specifically for children (apart from an instruction manual on the astrolabe for his son). But his classic status has created a niche in the market of older children's literature for modernised versions of selections from the *Canterbury Tales*. The most popular selections are largely from the comic fabliaux, whose high-spirited, scatological naturalism often appeals strongly to children in abridged, mildly bowdlerised versions, and from the tales of romance and chivalry. A number of these versions have been illustrated. Re-tellings of the *Canterbury Tales* by GERALDINE MCCAUGHREAN (1984) and SELINA HASTINGS (1993) are currently available. DWh

Chauncy, Nan 1900–70 Australian writer who had the most significant influence on children's literature of her generation. Chauncy focused on realistic fiction, yet used the TIME-SLIP narrative as a means of allowing the past and the present to intermingle. Settled in Tasmania, and an early advocate of wilderness life, Chauncy showed a deep compassion for the past of the Tasmanian Aborigines. *Tangara* (1960), the tale of a lonely child slipping into the past to make friends with a mysterious Aboriginal girl, is particularly memorable. *Mathinna's People* (1967), a less compelling narrative, tells of the tragic colonisation of

Tasmania. Without overt didacticism, it makes the past poignantly and morally relevant to the present. Her portrayal of character has been praised, though she is more successful with goodness than with badness. Her interest in landscape, landforms and the natural BUSH is pervasive. She received the AUSTRALIAN CHILDREN'S BOOK OF THE YEAR AWARD in 1958, 1959 and 1961 for *Tiger in the Bush* (1957), *Devil's Hill* (1958) and *Tangara*. Together with *They Found a Cave* (1948), which was made into a children's film in 1962, these titles are her best known.

CH, HMcC

Cheap Repository Tracts A series of tracts published between 1795 and 1798 by S. Hazard (Bath), J. MARSHALL (London) and, later, Evans and Hatchard (London), which imitated CHAPBOOKS and ballad sheets in both form and content. The evangelical writer HANNAH MORE conceived the idea of the Tracts, fearing the effects on the recently literate poor of both traditional chapbook literature and seditious political pamphlets. The first was published in March 1795 and by May a regular series of three titles per month – a ballad, a tract, and a Sunday reading – had been established, the tract tales sometimes appearing in parts over several months. Sold to chapmen and booksellers, they were also bought in large numbers by moral philanthropists for distribution to Sunday Schools, prisons, and the army and navy. By March 1796, 2,000,000 copies had been sold and the initial subscription funding became superfluous. More wrote over 50 of the 114 Tracts, under the pseudonym 'Z'. Other authors included her sister Sarah and several members of the Clapham Sect, a group of prominent Anglican evangelicals and anti-slavery activists with whom More was associated. Both the interdenominational RELIGIOUS TRACT SOCIETY and individual evangelicially minded publishers used the *Cheap Repository Tract* as a model throughout the 19th century.

JSh

Chear, Abraham d. 1668 English Baptist from Plymouth who wrote poems while in prison for his dissenting beliefs. *A Looking-Glass for Children* was published posthumously in 1672 and often reprinted. Although he addresses children kindly enough, his 'lessons and instructions to youth' are delivered in severe verse which focuses more on the avoidance of sin than on the love of God or the pleasures of childhood.

MCCS

Chesterton, G.K. see *JOY STREET*; see also GEORGE CRUIKSHANK

Chichester Clark, Emma 1955– British illustrator. Since graduating from the Chelsea School of Art and the Royal College of Art, Clark has been a freelance illustrator, specialising in book covers and recently in work for children. She won the MOTHER GOOSE AWARD in 1988 for *Listen to This* (stories selected by Laura Cecil) and has continued to make an impact with such books as *I Never saw a Purple Cow* (a selection of NONSENSE rhymes, 1990), *The Minstrel and the Dragon Pup* (ROSEMARY SUTCLIFFE, 1993), *Something Rich and Strange* (selections from SHAKESPEARE, 1997) and *The Adventures of Robin Hood and Marian* (ADRIAN MITCHELL, 1997). Her adventurously coloured ink and crayon ILLUSTRATIONS decorate, clarify and dramatise all at the same time.

JAG

Chicken Licken see *STORY OF CHICKEN LICKEN, THE*

Chike and the River (1966) Novel by the Nigerian writer CHINUA ACHEBE. Chike is an 11-year-old boy who leaves the security of his home village and goes to live with his uncle in the city of Onitsha, on the east bank of the Niger. The story traces the different stages of Chike's encounters with the world, and his plans to acquire a shilling, the fare that will allow him to cross the river by ferry. Each episode tests Chike, and the apparently random series of small adventures forms a pattern, culminating in his discovery of a robbery and the reward of a scholarship. The novella shares the narrative strength, humour and immediacy of Achebe's adult fiction, and has a refreshing range and richness of language. It has sold over half a million copies.

PR

See also AFRICAN MYTHOLOGY AND FOLKTALES

Child, Lydia Maria 1802–80 American author, abolitionist and reformer. Lydia, youngest child of the Francis family of Medford, Massachusetts, was allowed little formal education and discouraged from reading, but with the support of her brother Convers Francis she wrote her first novel, *Hobomok* (1824), at the age of 22. This account of a successful interracial marriage horrified some readers and pleased others; Child remained a controversial figure throughout her life.

Determined to write for and about her own American society, Child completed *Evenings in New England: Intended for Juvenile Amusement and Instruction* (1824) and went on to become editor of the first American children's magazine, *THE JUVENILE MISCELLANY*, in 1826. *Emily Parker* (1827) and *The First Settlers of New England* (1829) were intended for young people, and *The Little Girl's Own Book* (1831) – full of suggestions for games and a wide variety of other activities – was revised and reprinted many times, later as *The Girl's Own Book*.

Always alert to the needs of the less powerful members of society, Child also wrote books of advice for mothers and for housewives on small budgets; but in 1833 she focused her attention on the problem of slavery, and *An Appeal in Favor of that Class of Americans Called Africans* infuriated many readers. Supporters of slavery withdrew their support of Child as a writer for children, and although she continued to produce collections of stories such as *Flowers for Children* (three volumes, 1844–7), *Fact and Fiction* (1846) and *A New Flower for Children* (1856), she devoted more of her time and energy to other concerns, particularly to the abolition of slavery and to the rights of women.

Within children's literature Child has perhaps been known best for her poem 'Boy's Thanksgiving', with its opening line, 'Over the river and through the wood,/To grandfather's house we go.' Some of her children's stories have recently been reprinted, however, and make interesting reading, since Child's egalitarian stance encourages readers to identify with the feelings and opinions of all kinds of characters, and to be willing to abandon prejudices as those characters do. In 'Louisa Preston' (*Juvenile Miscellany*, 1828), the problem of Louisa's poverty is seen through the eyes of her mother, her schoolteacher, Louisa herself, and several schoolfriends. 'Jumbo and Zairee' (*Juvenile Miscellany*, 1831) places its black and white characters first in Africa and then in the American South, so that they all experience the loneliness of being a stranger as well as the power of being on home ground – which is seen as the power to do good. In these stories kindness is a natural quality, and kind acts bring a generous response. FEA

child authors The slogan of the young writers Katharine Hull and Pamela Whitlock in the 1930s was: 'By children, about children, for children . . . Do without the grown-up author altogether.' However, dispensing with 'grown-up authors' has proved problematical as the attitude of established writers to young newcomers is crucial. Nevertheless, far more young people have successfully got their work into print than is generally appreciated. Aside from children's oral culture, the writings of child authors are arguably the only true 'children's literature'. But that writing is not always directed at a child audience, and children often try to imitate adult models or, willingly or not, have their writing overseen by an adult. Diaries and journals are probably the least corrupted by adult influence (e.g. those of ANNE FRANK, Anaïs Nin).

In America, some of this writing by young authors appears in publications directed primarily at other children, either yearbooks and school newspapers and the like, or magazines such as *OUR YOUNG FOLKS*, *ST NICHOLAS*, *CRICKET*, *STONE SOUP*, *Merlyn's Pen*, or *Seventeen*; occasionally it finds an adult audience in journals for teachers such as the *English Journal*. Nevertheless children's writing rarely attracts much attention beyond the immediate audience for it, with three exceptions.

The first occurs when a child is greeted by adults as a child prodigy; the writing satisfies adult expectations for innocent childhood creations and as a result is commercially published: for example, the American child authors Horace Wade, David Putnam, Hilda Conkling, Opal Whitely, Nathalia Crane and Barbara Newhall Follett. These child authors are often controversial, and there are adults who doubt the authenticity of their writing (see David Sadler, 'Innocent Hearts', *Children's Literature Association Quarterly* 17.4, 1992–3). Such authors may publish for a while as adults, but they are not critically well received and do not continue to find commercial success.

Second, an adult author's fame directs attention to the juvenilia, which may then be published, even filmed, as with LOUISA MAY ALCOTT and Edith Wharton, or become the subject of exhibitions, as with E. E. CUMMINGS. Scholars may find themes already present in the juvenilia that reappear in the adult writing, as is the case with NATHANIEL HAWTHORNE, F. Scott Fitzgerald and Ernest Hemingway. But from a recent collection of the juvenilia of 42 contemporary United States and Canadian authors, from ISAAC ASIMOV to Tobias Wolff, only four have gone on to write for children: Margaret Atwood, Stephen King, URSULA K. LE GUIN and MADELEINE L'ENGLE (*First Words: Earliest Writing from Favorite Contemporary Authors*, edited by Paul Mandelbaum, 1993).

Finally a child author may satisfy in adolescence the standards for commercial publication as an adult, as, for example, EDGAR ALLAN POE in the United States, who may have written 'To Helen' at 14. In the days when adolescents were welcomed as apprentices at newspapers, such authors as Benjamin Franklin, MARK TWAIN, and W.E. DU BOIS were publishing articles at the age of 16. More recent examples of successful teenage writers for young adults are MAUREEN DALY, *Seventeenth Summer*, written at 17; S.E. HINTON, *The Outsiders*, at 16; and the Canadian GORDON KORMAN, *This Can't Be Happening at MacDonald High*, at 13. Such young writers are now actively sought by at least one publishing company, Landmark Editions, which has published over 24 titles since 1986 and sold more than 345,000 copies; a major requirement is no adult interference.

Although poetry by children is a rich field for literary research, aside from studies by educators and by critics of individual authors whose juvenilia survive, little attention has been paid to it. Beside a few journal articles, there seem to exist only five anthologies and a study by MYRA COHN LIVINGSTON, *The Child as Poet: Myth or Reality* (1984). Apart from the juvenilia of established poets like Elizabeth Barrett Browning, the 19th century produced child poets like Marjorie Fleming, whose writings survive as curiosities rather than glimpses into childhood. It was not until the late 1950s, when Herbert Read said that children's poetry could aspire to the highest literary standards, that it came to be seen as a distinct art form. CHARLES CAUSLEY – in his foreword to Timothy Rogers' *Those First Affections: An Anthology of Poems Composed Between the Ages of Two and Eight* (1979) – speaks of a child as a 'creature emerging from a world of semi-darkness, in a dazzling, new-found map of speech'. The key is often spontaneous metaphor, as a child as young as three – Patrick Buxton, quoted in *Those First Affections* – can show: 'The owl is the mother of the dark/And the moon comes up/ From under the mud.' Properly nurtured, this basic facility survives into adolescence. The celebration of prodigies like eight-year-old Nika Turbina, whose poetry filled Russian stadia in the 1980s, has suggested a latent poetic sensibility within all children. In his foreword to her collection, *First Draft* (Moscow, 1984; translated by Marion Boyars in 1988), Yevgeny Yevtushenko says, 'children . . . perceive the world in a much more adult way than we think'.

This belief in children's innate seriousness has impelled British poets like TED HUGHES, ADRIAN MITCHELL and GILLIAN CLARKE to work alongside teachers. The groundbreaking work of Marjorie Hourd, David Holbrook and others has encouraged many teachers to help children discover the conscious, structured language of poetry for themselves. Belief in children as writers was also the inspiration behind projects such as W.H. Smith's 'Poets in Schools' and Arvon Foundation initiatives in the second half of the 20th century, which funded poets to work in classrooms. In 1959 the *Daily Mirror* launched what became known as the W.H. Smith 'Young Writers' competition. Anthologies of children's prose and poetry published over three decades demonstrate the wisdom of the judges' advice: 'Write about your own experiences . . . and find a way of expressing them which is your own and nobody else's.' Later Cadburys sponsored regular art and writing competitions. While some young winners such as Glyn Maxwell survived to become adult poets, most do not. 'What happens to all this talent?' asked Ted Hughes as Chair of a judging panel. The distinguishing mark of the ROALD DAHL Competition's *Wondercrump* books (1994–6) was a brave eclecticism which spurned exclusivity and yet retained a high level of interest. Bloodaxe published *Bossy Parrot* (1984), the best poems from a children's poetry competition based in the Newcastle area; *Apple Fire* (1993), edited by JILL PIRRIE, draws on poetry from Halesworth Middle School in Suffolk. Like the 100 poems chosen by Gillian Clarke in *I Can Move the Sea*, they testify to the power of myth and nature as the impetus for so much good poetry by children. Publication not only encourages young writers; it enlightens the adult world about the fact that with encouragement and good teaching many children are capable of writing fine poetry.

A considerable number of children in Britain have written novels and had them published. DAISY ASHFORD's *The Young Visiters* (1919) – written when the writer was nine, and an immediate bestseller, reprinted 16 times in its first six months – constituted a children's literature in reverse, a child writing for adults. It has a preface by J. M. BARRIE and retains the original child's spelling and grammar – clearly part of the appeal to adult readers of the time. The same cannot be said of Katharine Hull and Pamela Whitlock, who at the ages of 15 and 16 sent their manuscript of *THE FAR-DISTANT OXUS* to ARTHUR RANSOME suggesting with an ironic disingenuousness that, if he was too busy to bother with it, he might like to 'ask Titty or Roger'. The work was published in 1937 and two successful sequels followed it. How genuinely they were writing for other children cannot be known, but they were certainly aiming to produce a *SWALLOWS AND AMAZONS* lookalike, with – shrewdly – the additional interest of ponies. Works by children are often imitative in form and genre: *THE SWISH OF THE CURTAIN* (1941), which was begun by Pamela Brown when she was 14 and later developed into a successful series, was almost certainly influenced by the recent success of NOEL STREATFEILD's career novel, *Ballet Shoes* (1936). When genuine originality did appear, it was not always greeted with generosity: *Black Marigolds* by Gillian Bell was published in 1953 with illustrations by JOHN VERNEY – and a patronising introduction by Streatfeild, who commented that the young 16-year-old would one day 'grow up to be a real writer'.

PONY STORIES were produced by an unusually large number of young British writers in the early years of the genre – the 1930s, 40s and 50s. Many of the adolescent girls who read pony books felt a compulsion to write as well as ride during the pony-mad phase, and the formula of pony stories was easily imitated. The relationship between girl and horse, which could be perceived as a rehearsal for future sexual and maternal emotions, was less complex than the human variety, offering no threats to an adolescent author. All that was needed was the expertise, and since girls who could afford to ride ponies were likely to be middle-class and literate, they were also more likely to write a book. The novelty value of a teenage writer and the great demand for pony stories also made it easier for the young writers to be published in the 1930s, 40s and 50s than it would be now.

The youngest of these writers was Moyra Charlton who started *Tally Ho, the story of an Irish Hunter* just after her 11th birthday and finished it 13 months later. It was published in 1930 (and reprinted five times in the next 14 months), the first of her several books. Primrose

Cumming was also a teenager when her first book, *Doney*, later admired by RUDYARD KIPLING, was accepted in 1934 by *Country Life*, publishers of her inspiration, *MOORLAND MOUSIE*. In 1936, 15-year-old Shirley Faulkner-Horne wrote a book of instruction, *Riding for Children*. The most prolific and consistent exponents of the genre, the three PULLEIN-THOMPSON sisters, Josephine and the twins Diana and Christine, also started as teenagers. Their first book, written jointly, *It Began with Picotee*, was published in 1946, and was quickly followed by others written individually. K.M. Peyton started writing at the age of 9 and her first story was published when she was 15. She was 19 when *Sabre, The Horse from the Sea* – a passionate girl-and-horse love-story – appeared under her maiden name Kathleen Herald in 1948, and was followed by two others. She never lost her all-consuming interest and continued to write pony books. Other early starters were Mary Colville, who published *Plain Jane* (1938) when she was 13 – a *BLACK BEAUTY* story about a Shetland pony; Daphne Winstone, who wrote *Flame* (1945) when she was 12 and had it illustrated by Lionel Edwards, the 'great draughtsman of the hunting field'; and Garland Bullivant, who wrote *Fortune's Foal* (1939) as a teenager. April Jaffe was 14 when she wrote *Satin and Silk* (1948); Catherine Harris in her teens when she wrote *We Started a Riding Club* (1954); Gillian Baxter 18 when she wrote *Jump to the Stars* (1957), the first of many. Lindsay Campbell wrote *Horse of Air* (1957) at 15; and Bernagh Brims wrote *Runaway Riders* (1963) at the same age.

Many children – as schoolteachers know – can make perceptive REVIEWERS and critics. In 1990 this ability was harnessed and given a marketing format when Elizabeth Hammill, with a group of teenagers from schools in the Newcastle area, founded *In Brief*, with the slogan 'for teenagers, by teenagers', a thrice-yearly in-house review magazine distributed free at all Waterstone's bookshops in Britain and Ireland. After six years of working without assistance, this constantly changing team of young reviewers eventually received professional help with design and production, though the writing remained entirely their own. Their reviews of YOUNG ADULT FICTION, and accounts of interviews with major children's authors, established new standards both for intelligent and uncompromising directness, and for clarity and accessibility, in reviews for teenage readers. *BOOKS FOR KEEPS* features some excellent reviews of 'good reads' by younger readers. Ireland for a period was especially rich in young authors. The popular writer of teenage fiction Martina Murphy, author of *Fast Car* (1998), *Free Fall* (1999) and *Dirt Tracks* (2000), wrote an unpublished series of gang-stories when she was 11 and her first published novel, *LiveWire* (1997), when she was 16; Aislinn O'Loughlin had her first work – *Cinderella's Fella* – published when she was 14 and wrote four more while still at school; and Claire Hennessy's popular work, *Dear Diary* (2000), was published when she was 13.

Australia and New Zealand seem to have been particularly careful to encourage young writers. In New Zealand LISA VASIL published her first book at 13: *Just an Ordinary Kid* (1988) is a poignant account of Carol, who has cerebral palsy, striving to be treated like everyone else. Notable Australian authors whose first books were published by the time they were 18 include novelist SONYA HARTNETT and poet DOUG MACLEOD. Kathie Armstong (pseudonym Katie Lee), now well-known for her plays and TELEVISION scripts, had two teenage novels in print at the age of 16. Nicki Greenberg's series of 12 little books for young children were published when she was 16. Recently-published child authors include Kate Mahon (with a junior novel, *Just One Tear*, in 1992) and Jessica Carroll (only 12 when she wrote the text for the PICTUREBOOK *Billy the Punk*, illustrated by CRAIG SMITH and shortlisted for the 1996 CHILDREN'S BOOK COUNCIL OF AUSTRALIA'S BOOK OF THE YEAR AWARDS). SIMON FRENCH's first novel, *Hey Phantom Singlet* (1975), written at the age of 15 to amuse classmates, was published two years later.

The *Starfish Generation*, a journal composed of children's writing and information for children on how to write and be published, is part of a programme which includes video tutorials, feedback from established authors and some book production. The first Starfish Books publication, *Creation* (text by Sarah Crawford, aged 12), was listed as a Notable Book in the Children's Book of the Year Awards, 1995.

The aim articulated by the young writers of *The Far-Distant Oxus* – 'By children, about children, for children' – may at last have been achieved, for many young writers both of fiction and poetry have recently discovered that the future for child authors probably lies in the INTERNET and have started to make vigorous and independent use of websites set aside for child authors. ARH, LJL, JP, VW, GA

see also ANNE, CHARLOTTE AND EMILY BRONTË; MAUREEN DALY; INTERNET; *STONE SOUP; MSINGA*

Child Education see REVIEWING AND REVIEWERS

child poets see CHILD AUTHORS

Child's Christmas in Wales, A (1952) The first record made by Caedmon, on which Dylan Thomas reads his poetry and the story *Christmas in Wales*, which had been previously published by *Harper's Bazaar*. Thus Thomas immortalised his memories of childhood, where 'All the Christmases roll down the hill toward the two-tongued sea.' In 1978 an edition illustrated by EDWARD ARDIZZONE was published. HA

Child's Garden of Verses, A (1885) Celebrated collection of poems by ROBERT LOUIS STEVENSON. E.V. LUCAS said: 'It stands alone. There is nothing like it, so intimate, so simply truthful, in our language, in any language . . . he has recaptured in maturity the thoughts, ambitions, purposes, hopes, fears, philosophy of the child.' Lucas was not alone in suggesting that Stevenson was the first poet to write 'with the voice of a child'.

And does it not seem hard to you,
When all the sky is clear and blue,
And I should like so much to play,
To have to go to bed by day?

The apparent authenticity of such a statement – it takes art to make it seem childlike – is what was missing from children's poetry before Stevenson. A landmark in publishing, it has never been out of print.

Most of the 66 poems in the collection are outstanding. One of the most powerful impressions is of a child's deep absorption in the world of play and the imagination, accompanied by the paraphernalia of domestic, daily life:

We built a ship upon the stairs
All made of the back-bedroom chairs,
And filled it full of sofa pillows
To go a-sailing on the billows.

This is a near-perfect account of how children recognise the boundaries of the FANTASY world they create, yet how imagination allows them the escape-route of adventure. Some poems deal with loneliness and illness, Stevenson's own experience of childhood. 'The Land of Counterpane' was written by someone who knew what it was like to spend weeks in bed; the experience in 'The Lamplighter' was that of the isolated observer. Stevenson also writes of the everyday – of summer fun with his cousins outside Edinburgh, of grown-ups seen from the child's point of view, of night fears and the pleasures of books.

Stevenson had modest expectations for his little volume of children's poetry, confiding in Sidney Colvin, 'I would as soon call 'em "Rimes for Children" as anything else. I am not proud or particular . . . These are rhymes, jingles; I don't go in for eternity.' He was proved wrong, however. Stevenson has been well-served by a number of illustrators. The most outstanding interpreters of the poems are CHARLES ROBINSON (1895), whose *art nouveau* ink drawings are richly textured, ornamental and atmospheric; Henriette Willebeek Le Mair (1926), whose young, beautiful, romantic innocents are painted in art deco style; EVE GARNETT (1948), whose faint line drawings evoke an enchanting world; BRIAN WILDSMITH (1966), whose vibrant primary colours blaze off the page; and MICHAEL FOREMAN (1985), who puts the poems in a contemporary setting, while hanging on to links wih the past through an 'Everychild' motif which runs through the book. MCCS

Child's Instructor, or a New and Easy Primer see PRIMERS

childist criticism A term used by Peter Hunt in two essays in *SIGNAL* in 1984 to refer to a radical new approach to the criticism of children's books which would involve a complete re-reading of texts from 'a childist point of view', making possible the 're-seeing of a whole culture' in ways similar to those achieved by feminist criticism. Hunt expressed dissatisfaction with the practices of traditional criticism and reviewing of children's books based on adult preferences, bland predictions about the supposed responses of children, and patronising assumptions about what young readers might be capable of. He argued that such criticism should be challenged by alternative approaches seeking to understand children's books in the economic, psychological, educational and personal contexts in which they are read by children.

Although the term 'childist criticism' has not passed into the common currency of critical practice, the critical approaches Hunt recommended have subsequently been adopted by many practitioners, notably such distinguished writers as Peter Hollindale, Perry Nodelman, Shirley Brice Heath and Charles Sarland. A particularly seminal work in the United Kingdom has been *How Texts Teach What Readers Learn* (1988) by MARGARET MEEK, which provided an exemplary model: it did not ask how 'good' or 'appealing' a child's book might be, but what it made possible for young readers. Probably the most important 'childist' approaches to children's books in the United Kingdom are to be found in the unacknowledged work of thousands of teachers and teacher-educators influenced in particular by Meek's innovative work.
VW

childness A term proposed by Peter Hollindale in his development of a critical theory for children's literature. The word itself, used by Shakespeare and a few other writers, denotes the 'quality of being a child', but Hollindale extends it to include an adult's capacity to invest childhood with memories, values and hopes. Accordingly 'childness' for children is composed of their developing and varying sense of self in the world, while for adults it involves a remembered childhood, expectations of child-behaviour, and a sense of continuity between the child self and the adult self. 'Childness . . . is shared ground, though differently experienced and understood, between child and adult.' It follows that an imaginative concern for childness is 'the distinguishing property of a text in

Illustration from J.G. RUSHER's chapbook version of *Children in the Wood.*

children's literature' – brought to life when the text is read by a child.

Hollindale further argues that an aesthetic of linear narrative is necessarily involved in texts of 'childness' because it provides the adult writer with a basis for remembered continuity while also appealing to child readers' evolving and provisional sense of their developing selves. Hollindale's theory is explained in *Signs of Childness in Children's Books* (1997), published by the Thimble Press (see *SIGNAL*). VW

Children of Green Knowe, The see GREEN KNOWE SERIES

Children of the New Forest see CAPTAIN FREDERICK MARRYAT; see also HISTORICAL FICTION

Children in the Wood Popular ballad of orphan siblings entrusted to the guardianship of an uncle who covets their inheritance and arranges for their murder. It ends with the death of the children, abandoned in a wood, and retribution for the uncle and the hired murderer. According to the Stationers' Register, it was in print in 1593. Available throughout the 17th and 18th centuries in CHAPBOOK or broadside form, it was included in Percy's *Reliques of Ancient English Poetry* (1765). Numerous editions for children were published in the late 18th and early 19th centuries, both in the traditional verse form and in prose and verse retellings. One chapbook version, published by J.G. RUSHER of Banbury, was followed by a sequel, *The Children in the Wood Restored, or Perfidy Detected*, in which the children were brought back to life. RANDOLPH CALDECOTT illustrated the ballad for his PICTUREBOOK series in 1879, and JOSEPH JACOBS included it in *More English Fairy Tales* (1894). Also popular were toy theatre and PANTOMIME versions of the tale. EDWARD ARDIZZONE illustrated a picturebook version of the tale in 1972, but the story has generally fallen out of popularity in recent years. JS

Children Who Lived in a Barn, The (1938) Novel by ELEANOR GRAHAM about five children left homeless and without their parents. Despite a rather contrived opening, the novel is distinguished from others written in the 1930s by the authenticity of its representation of children's behaviour. There is no idealising of childhood companionship: there are quarrels, sulks and disloyalty. The oldest sister, Sue, is an endearing character – patient (mostly), resourceful, often despairing, and good-humoured. The most interesting aspects of the narrative are the accounts of the children's battle with the DV (District Visitor) to avoid their being separated and sent off to different institutions. VW

Children's Book Award see APPENDIX

Children's Book Council of Australia, The Volunteer organisation dating from 1945 when several Australian states formed committees to celebrate Children's Book Week and, in the following year, presented the first Book of the Year AWARD. It was not until 1958, however, that a truly national body was instituted. The aim of the CBCA is to foster children's reading, and to this end it publishes a journal, *READING TIME*, and booklists; sponsors activities which promote books and reading; and holds a biennial conference. Of pre-eminent importance, though, is the presentation of its Book of the Year awards for different categories of Australian children's and adolescent fiction and for non-fiction. JF

see also APPENDIX

Children's Book Foundation of New Zealand, The National clearing-house for individuals and organisations concerned with children's literature and literacy, established in 1990. It has established the Margaret Mahy Lecture Award which is awarded annually to a person who has made an especially distinguished and significant contribution to children's literature, publishing or literacy, and the Tom Fitzgibbon Award for a work of fiction for children by a previously unpublished writer. The Children's Book Foundation also co-ordinates the Storylines New Zealand Children's Writers and Illustrators Festival and sponsors an annual Spring Lecture series which it co-ordinates with children's literature groups throughout the country. FP

Children's Book Review see REVIEWING AND REVIEWERS

Children's Books Ireland An organisation launched in 1997 as a result of a merger between the CHILDREN'S LITERATURE ASSOCIATION OF IRELAND and the IRISH CHILDREN'S BOOK TRUST. It maintains the membership base of the former and continues the activities of both organisations. VC

Children's Encyclopaedia, The First produced in magazine form at the beginning of the 1930s, ARTHUR MEE's immensely popular and impressive *Encyclopaedia* was then published in 10 volumes, as a *Big Book for Little People*. There were 19 main divisions – 17 of 'knowledge' and two of 'practical teaching' – for example, 'Stories', 'Familiar Things', 'Ideas', 'Things to Make and Do' and 'School Lessons'. The attraction of the format lay in the way the themes were interspersed throughout the volumes, in the variety of ILLUSTRATIONS, including colour and photographs, and in the user-friendly language, which, although highly moralistic, did not talk down to young readers. HA

Children's Garland, The (1862) Influential anthology full of poetry for adults, edited by Coventry Patmore, who famously declared: 'I have excluded all verse written expressly for children and most of the poetry written about children for grown people', thus setting a precedent for the extraordinary omission of children's verse in anthologies for the young. MCCS

Children's Hour see *CHILDREN'S HOUR ANNUAL*; see also TELEVISION; *PROFESSOR BRANESTAWM*; *JENNINGS* SERIES

Children's Hour Annual Published in association with the famous BBC children's programme (1922–64), the *Children's Hour Annual* appeared as early as 1924 but failed. The annuals were relaunched in 1935 with Derek McCullock (Uncle Mac) as the first editor. McCulloch selected items – mostly stories, with some poetry and a few information articles – to reflect both the wide variety of broadcast programmes and the contributions made by all the regions. The annuals were presented as very much an extension of the programme itself. Contributors included S.G. HULME BEAMAN, H.E. TODD, NOEL STREATFEILD, ALISON UTTLEY and RUTH MANNING-SANDERS. Other publications went on to make use of the Children's Hour connection, e.g. *Uncle Mac's Own Story Book*, and *Good Afternoon, Children*. AR

Children's Laureate British laureateship established in 1999 and first awarded to honour the work of the illustrator QUENTIN BLAKE. The author MICHAEL MORPURGO conceived the idea, which was backed by the booksellers Waterstone's, the government, and the poet TED HUGHES. The laureateship is not a royal appointment and does not involve the holder in compositions to celebrate public occasions. The post is awarded every two years by an awarding panel which includes young readers in its membership. Early plans to require the laureate to campaign on behalf of children's literature were abandoned as unrealistic: it was appreciated that such activities would interfere with the holder's creative work. VW

Children's Literature Annual of the Modern Language Association Division on Children's Literature and the CHILDREN'S LITERATURE ASSOCIATION, published by Yale University Press. Founded by FRANCELIA BUTLER in 1972 as a forum for sustained critical discussion of children's literature, on her retirement from the University of Connecticut in 1992 the journal moved to Hollins University, where it was for some time edited by Elizabeth Lennox Keyser and R.H.W. Dillard. The most prestigious of the children's literature journals, it is refereed by children's literature experts and by Yale; articles are expected to be well-researched and significant contributions to the field. It includes reviews of current scholarly books. GA

Children's Literature Abstracts see REVIEWING AND REVIEWERS

Children's Literature Association Organisation founded in 1973 by Anne Devereaux Jordan and FRANCELIA BUTLER to encourage serious scholarship and research in children's literature. A non-profit-making international group for professors, teachers, librarians, critics, students and institutions, CLA provides fellowships and scholarships for worthy research projects and sponsors an annual conference including papers, panels, workshops and discussion. The group presents awards at its conference for the most significant critical article, book or undergraduate paper, as well as the Phoenix Award for a book published 20 years earlier still considered worthy of recognition. CLA publishes an annual, a quarterly and a semi-annual newsletter, and selected books about children's literature. SPI

Children's Literature Association of Ireland Founded in 1988, this organisation aimed to promote quality reading by young people in Ireland by means of a magazine, seminars and conferences, mainly through an adult membership base. In 1996 it merged with the IRISH CHILDREN'S BOOK TRUST to form CHILDREN'S BOOKS IRELAND. VC

Children's Literature Association of Nigeria see MABEL SEGUN

Children's Literature Association Quarterly Begun in 1974 as the newsletter of the CHILDREN'S LITERATURE ASSOCIATION, and until winter 1980 called the *Quarterly Newsletter*. Since 1983 the journal has been refereed and the editorship has changed every five years or so. Some issues are themed, with a guest editor. The *Quarterly* has to date been particularly interested in recent critical trends and in working with younger scholars just beginning to publish. It includes critical theory, parallel cultures, and lively arts columns and book reviews. GA

Children's Literature Center see COLLECTIONS OF CHILDREN'S BOOKS

Children's Literature in Education International critical quarterly established in 1970 after a series of conferences at St Luke's College, England (now Exeter University School of Education). As the journal's circulation expanded, a North American editor was appointed alongside the British board. Typically, an issue includes five or six lengthy articles contributed by academics, children's writers, librarians or teachers. The policy is 'to promote lively discussion of poetry and prose . . . and to heighten professional understanding'. Two collections of articles have appeared: *Writers, Critics and Children* (1976) and *Celebrating Children's Literature in Education* (1995). The present publisher is Kluwer Academic / Human Sciences Press, New York. GPF

Children's Newspaper see SIR ARTHUR MEE

Children's Television Workshop see *SESAME STREET*

children's theatre see DRAMA FOR CHILDREN

Childress, Alice 1920–94 American novelist, playwright and actress, best-known for her bold explorations of the social problems faced by African Americans in contemporary society. Her principal work for young readers is *A Hero Ain't Nothin' but a Sandwich* (1973), a powerful novel about the drug addiction of a young African American boy in the inner city. The story is told from multiple points of view, including the boy's own and that of his teachers, mother, step-father, grandmother, friends and acquaintances. Childress captures a wide variety of voices, including those of street-wise drug-pushers, complacent middle-class white educators, militant middle-class African Americans, struggling working-class African Americans, and teenagers caught in the middle. Many of the book's chapters read like dramatic monologues, a technique undoubtedly deriving from her extensive theatrical experience and requiring the reader to judge first-hand the characters and their actions. The book's stark realism, its frank language and its ambiguous ending have made it the subject of considerable controversy, not to mention frequent banning. Her treatment of issues of incest, sexual preference and race is equally sharp in *Those Other People* (1989). Childress also wrote the screenplay for *A Hero Ain't Nothin' but a Sandwich*. Her play *Wedding Band*, about interracial marriage, met with similar censure, but Childress was unshaken in her commitment to social justice. DLR

China Coin, The (1991) Novel by Australian writer ALLAN BAILLIE which focuses on themes of finding oneself, and reconciliation with one's identity and heritage. After her father's death, Australian-born Leah reluctantly goes with her mother, Joan, to China on a quest to locate Joan's ancestral village and relatives, and for Leah to discover the origin of a broken Chinese coin given to her by her father. Leah's journey of self-discovery takes place against the backdrop of unrest over democracy leading to the massacres in Tiananmen Square in July 1989. The narrative captures the heady excitement and urgency of the democracy movement, which Baillie witnessed first-hand in China while researching settings and history for Leah and Joan's quest. SNJ

Chips see COMICS, PERIODICALS AND MAGAZINES

Chitty Chitty Bang Bang Fantastical adventure by Ian Fleming (author of the *James Bond* novels), first published as three separate tales (1964/65), illustrated by JOHN BURNINGHAM. It is best known through the omnibus edition (1971) and the film (1968), with a screenplay co-written by ROALD DAHL. Restored from dilapidation by Commander Caractacus Potts, the eponymous car becomes embroiled with smugglers, along with the Commander, his wife and their twins, Jeremy and Jemima. Chitty saves the day through her use of various tricks, such as her ability to fly and float. The simple, powerful atmosphere of intrigue in the stories is traded for a more involved plot in the film version, which also features different characters. MSed

Choi, Sook N. 1937– Korean writer who immigrated to the United States as a student in the 1950s. Choi has published three autobiographical novels for children and young adults, as well as a PICTUREBOOK. The first novel, *Year of Impossible Goodbyes* (1992), with a ten-year-old female protagonist who reveals great courage during the most trying times, is the most important for the portrayal of Korean life during World War II and the transmission of cultural knowledge and values. Its sequels, *Echoes of the White Giraffe* (1993) and *Gathering of Pearls* (1994), are important both as coming-of-age female novels and as portraits of contemporary Korean life. In the second book, Sookan is five years older; in the final book, set in 1954, she is 18 and feeling caught between two very different ways of life after leaving her home in Seoul to become a college student in America.

The picturebook, *Halmoni and the Picnic* (1993), features eight-year-old Hunmi's shy grandmother who has just immigrated to America. Choi's fiction is sensitive, fine-tuned and insightful, similar to the strong, quiet females that she creates. NM

***Choir School* series** (1955–63) A sequence of four novels by WILLIAM MAYNE, set in the choir school of an English cathedral which is almost certainly based on Canterbury, where Mayne had been a pupil. Each novel is concerned with a different schoolboy and his friends, and is set in the continuity of school life affectionately but firmly sustained by the school and cathedral staff. The first in the sequence, *A Swarm in May* (1955), established Mayne's reputation as an exciting and innovative writer for children. It was followed by *Choristers' Cake* (1956), *Cathedral Wednesday* (1960) and *Words and Music* (1963).

This sequence is distinguished from other SCHOOL STORIES by Mayne's extraordinary ability to capture the physicality of place intimately perceived from within a child's sensual understanding, as in this description of a choirboy waking up in winter:

> Andrew found his breath on the windows when he got up. There was sunshine on the cathedral, splashed on the South side, so that there were columns of shadow up the tower. Andrew looked out of the window at it, then closed the window against the air, and put more breath on the pane, close and hot, to clear a peep-hole on to the city.

Mayne also demonstrates a unique ability to concentrate in a few apparently easy sentences the complex connections between a boy's thought and his physical movements, exemplified in these opening sentences from *Cathedral Wednesday*:

> Andrew Young overtook a bus and raced down the London Road. The thing he had in mind was to get to the level-crossing before the gates were closed for the four-fifteen train from the North; but he was too late, and the gates began to swing as he came near. He put his left foot down to the ground and let the bicycle droop whilst he felt in his pocket for the book with the engine-numbers in. The engine was almost certain to be one of the Ashford tankers; but – sometimes – Stanhope had said so – a Midland engine did the whole journey.

Like his contemporary, ALAN GARNER, Mayne provides few narrative explanations. The choir school novels refer to a culture of grammar schools and boarding schools familiar to many young readers in the 1950s and 1960s; but they would make considerable demands on young readers today. They make full use of the shared idiom of a closed community, with numerous jokes requiring a knowledge of music, the Bible, or LATIN ('knottus grannius fecit'). However, the effect for the determined – probably adult – reader is a dynamic sense of private and communal experience, often muddled, fleetingly grasped, and only partly understood by the young characters. To this is added a sense of the enduring seriousness of the choir school's purpose; towards the end of the last novel, the headmaster explains: 'We are dedicated to a certain job: we have our choir work; that's all we are here for, in fact; and you know a choir isn't a collection of soloists each obeying his own rule. We have to sing together, or not at all.' VW

Chorpenning, Charlotte 1875–1955 American playwright, teacher, director and producer, one of the earliest and most prolific of playwrights for children. She is most closely associated with the Goodman Theatre and its School of Drama, where she developed and ran its Children's Theatre department for many years. She is the first writer to treat children's theatre seriously as an art with principles that could be codified and used critically. Chorpenning had a number of rules she believed necessary for successful children's theatre, all of which revolve around the importance of understanding the nature of the child as an audience. These rules include allowing the child to identify with the protagonist of the story; permitting no interruption of the flow of the action; creating character and message strictly in terms of the story (i.e. without artificial moralising); and providing 'exercise spots' for the child audience, in order to keep them involved and to encourage them to participate actively in the theatrical experience. The Children's Theatre Association of America presents the Charlotte B. Chorpenning Cup to 'a writer of outstanding plays for children'. BH

see also DRAMA FOR CHILDREN

***Chrestomanci* series** (1977–88) Novels and stories by DIANA WYNNE JONES, linked by the figure of Christopher Chant, who occupies the post of the Chrestomanci – a government-employed nine-lifed enchanter. The four novels *Charmed Life* (1977), *The Magicians of Caprona* (1980), *Witch Week* (1982) and *The Lives of Christopher Chant* (1988) and the short stories do not otherwise form a series in the sense of needing to be read sequentially in a given order. While magic with its possibilities is obviously something that the author takes pleasure in for its own sake, it also functions as a multivalent metaphor for creativity, self-expression, and that which renders an individual different from everyone else. For instance, the many witches in *Witch Week* each have their own individual style of magic. The fantasies are set in a universe where worlds exist in series, each series created by the splitting off of a world when, as Gwendolyn Chant in *Charmed Life* explains, 'there is a big event in History, like a battle or earthquake when the result can be two or more quite diferent [sic] things.' (Gwendolen can cast spells, but she cannot spell.) Three of the four novels take place in some alternative England during this century, and *The Magicians of Caprona* in an alternative Italy.

All four of the novels take as their subject the rites of passage of their protagonist(s): the coming into magical power, knowledge of one's magical abilities and the control of that power, control and knowledge being an index to self-awareness. Within each novel there is an agent that acts to negate or inhibit the powers of the individual. In *The Lives of Christopher Chant*, this agent is silver, which is also Christopher's mother's maiden-name (Argent); it is his mother's brother, Uncle Ralph, who is responsible for sending him into the series of worlds to undertake (this all unknowingly) illegal activities, and many of his nine lives are lost in the process. Cat Chant, his nephew, who is the protagonist of *Charmed Life*, also loses most of his lives to that which inhibits him and steals his power; in his case, this is his sister Gwendolyn. In the other two novels, it is the system that causes the repression. The world of *Witch Week* is one that burns witches, and hence symbolically attempts to stifle creativity and difference. *The Magicians of Caprona* sees the decline of magical ability in two rival houses, and this is later discovered to be caused by the Duchess of Caprona, who is Caprona's ancient enemy, the White Rat, in disguise; as its ruler, she may perhaps also be read as representing the system. If they are to defeat the White Rat, the houses need to band together and be integrated; the individual alone has no power against society.

Diana Wynne Jones' work may thus be read at many levels, as FANTASY and also as psychological, sociological and perhaps even political comment. Magic may be a means of exploring an individual's development in terms of familial dynamics such as sibling rivalry, or as it takes place within the constraints, the norms and expectations of the society he or she lives in.

The *Chrestomanci* novels and short stories were reissued in 2000 under the series title *Worlds of Chrestomanci*. *Mixed Magics*, a new title, is a collection of short stories featuring Chrestomanci, some of which have been previously anthologised elsewhere. SA

Chrisman, Arthur Bowie 1889–1953 American collector and writer of FOLKTALES for children. Born in Virginia, Chrisman never physically travelled abroad, but he is best known for his collection of Chinese folktales *Shen of the Sea* (1925), illustrated by Else Hassalriis in a series of silhouettes, which won the Newbery Medal. The book conveys a clear sense of the Chinese spirit while using readily recognisable western symbols and motifs. *Shen* consists of 16 original tales, told to Chrisman by a Chinese storekeeper whom he consulted while researching Chinese foods and with whom he became close friends. Other collections include *The Wind That Wouldn't Blow: Stories of the Merry Middle Kingdom for Children and Myself* (1927), and *Treasures Long Hidden; Old Tales and New Tales from the East* (1941), illustrated by Weda Yap. Chrisman's tales maintain the folkloric spirit while allowing something of the writer's personal sense of humour and excitement to shine through. They are filled with details evoking the culture from which they are drawn and display a keen sense of audience. SCWA

Christmas Carol, A see CHARLES DICKENS; see also MICHAEL FOREMAN; ARTHUR RACKHAM; *MUPPETS*

Christmas issues The development and widespread availability of photographic means of reproducing ILLUSTRATIONS led to a proliferation of illustrated popular magazines in the 1890s. In the years before and immediately after World War I these magazines would vie with one another to see who could produce the most sumptuous and lavishly illustrated Christmas issues. These usually had double the number of pages of the regular issues and made much greater use of colour, and they frequently included specially commissioned stories and pictures for younger readers. Well to the fore in this contest was the weekly *Illustrated London News*; the special issue for Christmas 1912 reads like a catalogue of the best illustrators of the day, with work by EDMUND DULAC, KAY NIELSEN, E.J. DETMOLD, WARWICK GOBLE, CHARLES ROBINSON and WILLIAM HEATH ROBINSON. The *Illustrated London News* and their competitors, *The Graphic*, *The Sketch* and *The Tatler*, maintained this quality of illustration throughout the 1920s with notable examples of work by these artists, and others such as ARTHUR RACKHAM, George Barbier and Cecil Aldin. The smaller-format monthly magazines such as *The Strand*, *Pall Mall*, *Pearson's*, *The Windsor* and *The London* also competed fiercely. Leading children's authors were also kept busy by the Christmas specials: in 1905 E. NESBIT had serialisations of THE RAILWAY CHILDREN in *The London*, of *The Story of the Amulet* in *The Strand*, and her short story 'Septimus Septimuson' in the Christmas issue of *Pall Mall*. F. Anstey, MRS MOLESWORTH, Mrs Speilmann and L.T. MEADE all remained popular contributors in the early years of the century. GCB

Christopher, John [C.S. Youd] 1922– Writer of SCIENCE FICTION novels for young people. Christopher wrote many books for adults before turning to the children's list with *The White Mountains* (1967). This thoughtful, stylish novel set a new standard in Britain, appealing both to young readers and to commentators on children's literature who had hitherto looked down on science fiction. It expanded into the *TRIPODS* TRILOGY, and was followed by *THE PRINCE IN WAITING* and *Fireball* trilogies and several other novels, notably *The Lotus Caves* and *The Guardians*. Christopher's later work is less innovative, tending to re-explore earlier themes. JRT

Chronicles of Avonlea see *ANNE OF GREEN GABLES*

Chronicles of Narnia, The (1950–6) Seven novels by C. S. LEWIS relating to the history of Narnia. Narnia was first discovered at the back of a wardrobe by Lucy Pevensie, and this discovery is chronicled in *The Lion, the Witch and the Wardrobe* (1950). The creation of Narnia is described in *The Magician's Nephew* (1955) and its ending in *The Last Battle* (1956). The chronicles, which Marion Lochhead has called the *Narniad*, belong to the FANTASY genre. Except in *The Horse and His Boy* (1954), which takes place wholly in Narnia, the characters in the other works move between this world and Narnia. The chronicles are regarded by many as modern classics of children's literature, and have been made into TELEVISION series and turned into opera by John McCabe in 1969, the libretto written by Gerald Larner (see MUSIC AND STORY).

The *Chronicles of Narnia* have frequently been compared with E. NESBIT's work. Naomi Lewis, for example, comments in *20th Century Children's Writers* that *The Magician's Nephew* is the 'most Nesbit-like of the novels' – indeed the novel itself explains that it is set in a time when 'Sherlock Holmes was still living in Baker Street and the Bastables were still looking for treasure in the Lewisham Road', and might thus appear to be invoking a relation with Nesbit's books. But any resemblance is at best superficial: Lewis's work has a dark edge which is missing in Nesbit's fantasies, and the illustrations by PAULINE BAYNES tend on the whole to accentuate this. David Holbrook has criticised the inherent sadism, the infliction of pain, that is permitted within the series, and also the fear which the works are capable of evoking. The visit of the Babylonian Queen to London in Nesbit's *The Story of the Amulet* (1906) is treated comically, and the magic that (temporarily) transforms London is benign. The episode is 'reworked' in *The Magician's Nephew*, when the Witch-Empress Jadis follows Digory and Polly to London, but the scenes which follow are anything but humorous; they are in fact violent and frightening. The witch throws Aunt Letty across the room; later, she wrenches off the top of a lamp-post which she then uses as a weapon. This is rough magic compared to that which operates in Nesbit's fiction. The fear which Lewis's writing calls forth gives point to his meanings. That is to say, Lewis's novels work (as Nesbit's do not) within a universe structured by moral conflict – a war between good and evil – and the more menacing and sombre colouring of his work serves to emphasise the seriousness of the business: evil has genuine power and should not be taken lightly.

This war is the main burden of the novels; the evil that is being fought, however, is not always figured as 'supernatural' (for example, the witches in *The Lion, the Witch and the Wardrobe* and *The Silver Chair*, or the Calormene god Tash). It may be represented in human terms, as for example in *Prince Caspian* (1951), where Caspian's uncle, Miraz the usurper, is the enemy to be fought, or in *The Voyage of the Dawn Treader* (1953), in the person of the Governer of the Lone Islands who countenances and encourages slavery. The common denominator in the manifestations of evil found in the various novels is repression, the desire to subjugate and control response. Miraz tries to repress Old Narnia and knowledge of it and of Aslan, paralleling the White Witch's refusal to allow the name of Aslan to be spoken. It is always winter and never Christmas in Narnia under the witch, symbolising stasis and eternal non-fulfillment, a theme repeated in stone as the witch turns dissenters into statues. In all this, the Chronicles maintain the right of the individual to free will, even if that will is towards evil; to repress that free will is itself the ultimate sin. The Dwarfs in *The Last Battle* are shown the truth but reject it. In the pain of moral choice meaning is made. As Aslan says to Digory in *The Magician's Nephew* after he has been tempted by Jadis to eat the apple of immortality which he has been commanded to bring back, 'For this fruit you have hungered and thirsted and wept. No hand but yours shall sow the seed of the Tree that is to be the protection of Narnia.'

In spite of this sobriety, the novels are also governed by a poetics of desire as indicated by the quest structure within many of the individual works. This desire, however, often fails to properly identify its object, either manifesting itself as a general sense of lack and yearning, or else projecting itself onto something else. All of this is perhaps most evident in *The Voyage of the Dawn Treader*. The apparent quest is Caspian's search for the seven lords of Narnia who were his father's friends. But the end point of the quest, his discovery of the last three lords, also coincides with his meeting with Ramandu's daughter, the structure suggesting that in some way she is Caspian's true goal. Furthermore, Caspian's quest is also intertwined with Reepicheep's, which is to seek out the 'utter East' and to find Aslan's country. Thus, each quest is a shadow of another, Reepicheep's quest the clearest representation of how all quests within the series are tensed towards Aslan and whatever he stands for. As Aslan says to Emeth the Calormene in *The Last Battle*: 'Beloved . . . unless thy desire had been for me thou wouldst not have sought so long and so truly. For all find what they truly seek.' The Chronicles of Narnia, then, are about not just achieving quests, but discovering the true nature of a long desire, naming and identifying it, and in so doing, finding oneself. SA

Chronicles of Prydain, The (1964–79) Series by the American author LLOYD ALEXANDER, comprising the five books: *The Book of Three* (1964), *The Black Cauldron* (1967), *The Castle of Llyr* (1968), *Taran Wanderer* (1979) and *The High King* (1979). There is also a collection of short stories, *The Foundling and Other Tales of Prydain* (1973) which, though not generally conceived of as part of the Chronicles, nonetheless amplifies them; Dallben's beginnings and the tale of Coll's rescue of Hen Wen are given here. The books take as their effective protagonist the character of Taran, whose progress from Assistant Pig Keeper to High King of Prydain structures the series. The *Mabinogion* (see WELSH MYTHOLOGY AND FOLKLORE) stands behind the *Chronicles of Prydain*, providing many of the series' characters and tropes. However, though the action takes place within an apparently mythic framework, the myths of the *Mabinogion* do not inform the narrative in the same way that the story of Bloddeuwedd functions to shape ALAN GARNER's *THE OWL SERVICE*. They lend a cultural coherence to the world of Prydain, but do not determine its narrative paths.

The series might be said to describe the transition between phases or modes: the mythic, the heroic and the human. Though this is only made clear in *The High King*, Taran and his companions have been living in the last days of an age of myths and heroes. Prydain was once upon a time ruled by Queen Achren, and her age of myth and enchantment has been superseded by an age of heroes, represented by Prydain under the Sons of Don. The Sons of Don are themselves bound by the ruling that when the Lord of Annuvin, Arawn, has been overcome, they, and all those with magic, must depart for the Summer Country, leaving 'one who comes of no station in life', Taran, as High King. The mythic only remains as memory; the age of man has begun.

At the beginning of *The Book of Three* Taran is shown wishing for the life of a hero instead of that of an Assistant Pig Keeper; he wants to make swords, not horseshoes. Then, he is flung with a horrifying suddenness into a narrative crowded with the resonant figures of myth: Gwydion himself, the evil queen Achren and Spiral Castle, the Horned King, the fabled sword Dyrnwyn. However, he appears uncomfortably out of place in the heroic mode: his actions lack the purposefulness of a hero on quest; he achieves the things of importance almost by accident – as he says, 'what I mostly did was to make mistakes'. As the series continues, it becomes ever clearer that while Taran does grow closer to the traditional configuration of the war-hero, his real gain in stature is achieved in terms that have to do with the knowledge of himself and his limitations (*Taran Wanderer*), and the ability to give up his place within the company of heroes to do the quiet work that will earn him no place in songs. The *Chronicles* thus ultimately locate themselves not within the aesthetics of high FANTASY, but within an aesthetic of the quotidian, which has its own heroisms. SA

see also TALIESIN

Chums see ANNUALS

***Church Mice* series** (1972–99) Picturebooks by Graham Oakley. The current titles are *The Church Mouse* (1972), *The Church Cat Abroad* (1973), *The Church Mice on the Moon* (1974), *The Church Mice Spread Their Wings* (1975), *The Church Mice Adrift* (1976), *The Church Mice at Bay* (1978), *The Church Mice at Christmas* (1980), *The Church Mice in Action* (1982), *The Diary of a Church Mouse* (1986), *The Church Mice and the Ring* (1992) and *The Church Mice Take a Break* (1999). *The Church Mouse* not only introduced the adventurous and inventive mouse Arthur but also Sampson the cat with whom he shares a home in a gloomy Gothic church. Arthur invites a tidal wave of endangered mice to join them, among them Humphrey the school mouse. These are memorable characters, beautifully realised, in a world of stereotypical human beings. Oakley makes full use of his control over word, picture and page design to create extended storylines, highly detailed pictures demanding careful reading, and a very varied and intriguing layout. His pictures exist in an organic relationship with the words, as in good film comedy. His work is capable of appealing to a wide age range but, because of the erroneous notion that PICTUREBOOKS are for the very young, it does not always reach a wider audience with the competencies to appreciate his subtleties. AR

Ciardi, John (Anthony) 1916–86 An influential figure in the post-war American poetry establishment. Ciardi's poems for children exploit the NONSENSE tradition of CARROLL and LEAR, though hints of a grim humour occasionally find their way into this playfulness. His ironic side is visualised by artist EDWARD GOREY, whose quirky ILLUSTRATIONS accompany *You Read to Me, I'll Read to You* (1962), with its comical poems set in type of alternating colour to encourage parents and children to take turns reading. He also illustrated *The King Who Saved Himself from Being Saved* (1965), a verse tale expressing a scepticism about heroism that works as an effective counter to commercial values. In 1982 Ciardi received the National Council of Teachers of English Award for Excellence in Poetry for Children.

In Ciardi's only work of fiction for children, *The Wish Tree* (1962), a boy who must learn that keeping a pet entails responsibility takes a dream journey into the wish tree. This is a beautifully conceived image, enhanced by Louis S. Glanzman's black-and-white illustrations. Whatever a child may long for, the idea of a tree that one enters, ascending infinite steps into the higher regions of the self, serves as a powerful symbol. RAM

Cider with Rosie (1959) An idyllic account by Laurie Lee of his formative years in a remote Cotswold village in the early 20th century. He describes, often with wry humour, the eccentricities of his large, extended family and key events in their lives – schooldays, village outings, games, first love. Written in a poetic prose style, Lee's nostalgic view of a pastoral, pre-motorised England, is a popular text in schools. Subsequently, Lee wrote *As I Walked Out One Midsummer Morn* (1969), recounting his experiences as a young man initially in London, then in Spain. The book ends as he joins the International Brigade in the Spanish Civil War. MSS

'Cinderella' A popular FAIRY TALE that has been told the world over for centuries. Some 700 accounts have been recorded. In most versions the essential details of the story remain the same: a cruel stepmother, a beautiful but ill-treated stepdaughter who is left behind when her sisters go to a royal festival or ball, and something magical that comes to her aid. Her wishes granted, the heroine arrives at the ball and captivates her prince. Escaping home by midnight to preserve her identity, she leaves behind a slipper or ring. The prince, overcome by her beauty, searches for the girl, eventually finding and marrying her. The earliest written version, about 850–60 AD, comes from China and is very similar to the present-day story, though Yeh-hsien, the heroine, has her wishes granted by a fish. The earliest variant found in Europe was published in Italy in 1634, called *La Gatta Cenerentola*. In the Scottish account, the girl *Rashin Coatie* wears a coat of rushes, and owns a magical red calf which grants her wishes. A French story, *Finetta the Cinder-girl*, written by MADAME D'AULNOY, was translated into English in 1721, but the English version we know today comes from a French story written by CHARLES PERRAULT, or possibly his son, in *Histoires ou Contes du temps passé*, Paris, 1697. This was translated into English as *Histories or Tales of Past Times* in 1729. This story has been enjoyed as a nursery story in CHAPBOOKS, verse, PANTOMIME, film and opera. SD

See also JOHN STEPTOE; JOYCE CAROL THOMAS

Cisneros, Sandra 1954– Latina writer frequently read by young adults. Raised in a Chicago *barrio*, Sandra Cisneros managed to attend the prestigious University of Iowa writing programme, where her sense of difference from the more privileged participants prompted the writing of *The House on Mango Street* (1983), a prize-winning collection of stories. Dedicated to 'las Mujeres' (the women), *The House on Mango Street* is a series of vignettes, many of them poetic, narrated by the pre-adolescent Esperanza Cordero. For Esperanza and other women, the house serves as both sanctuary and prison; to escape the inequities of the male-dominated culture, she moves inward and upward to the house of literature. A blind aunt admonishes her to keep writing, for writing offers her a way to free herself from the *barrio*. But by the end of this coming-of-age story, Esperanza knows, like Cisneros herself, that she goes away only 'to come back. For the ones I left behind. For the ones who cannot get out.' Although *The House on Mango Street* portrays poverty, violence (including sexual violence) and despair, it also captures the exhilaration and energy of childhood. Subsequent works include *Woman Hollering Creek and Other Stories* (1991) and two volumes of poetry. NV

Clapp, Patricia 1912– American author and playwright best known for her works of HISTORICAL FICTION. She was awarded the Lewis Carroll Shelf Award and National Book Award runner-up for *Constance: A Story of Early Plymouth* (1969). As a child Clapp dreamt of becoming a professional dancer. After marrying she became involved in community theatre, and this led to her being asked to produce a play for her daughters' Girl Scout troop. Her writing career bloomed, for she could find no suitable play and so wrote one tailored to the number of girls in the troop. She continued to write plays for children and adults, publishing them in the late 1950s. Her first novel for children, *Constance*, was the result of typing up genealogy notes for a family friend. She could not put from her mind the young girl who came to America with her family on the *Mayflower*. This book and several others, including *I'm Deborah Simpson* (1977) and a BIOGRAPHY of Elizabeth Blackwell, use the diary format. In each, Clapp's extensive research is apparent. From the privacy of a journal, the narration focuses on the internal life of the character while drawing the reader into the action. LAW

Clare, Helen see CLARKE, PAULINE

Clare, John 1793–1864 British poet famous for *The Shepherd's Calendar* (1827), which portrays rural life throughout the year with references to childhood and includes versified FAIRY TALES such as *CINDERELLA* and *JACK AND THE BEANSTALK*. 'Little Trotty Wagtail', 'Hares at Play', 'Badger' and 'Clock a Clay' are among Clare's poems found in children's anthologies. PDS

Clark, Ann Nolan, 1896–1995 American author of numerous books for children and young adults, many of them featuring Native Americans and other peoples of the southwestern United States among whom she lived and worked. Born in Las Vegas, New Mexico Territory in 1896, the young Ann Nolan grew up in a multicultural environment that prepared her well for her later work as a writer and as a teacher of Native American children. Her first book, *In My Mother's House* (1941), grew out of her need for a book that related to the lives of her third-grade students at Tesuque Pueblo. Clark's *Secret of the Andes* (1952) is, unfortunately, better known for winning the Newbery Medal over E.B. WHITE's *CHARLOTTE'S WEB*, than for its own intrinsic merits. Clark's moving story of the young boy Cusi and his quest for a family and his destiny, is written in highly poetic language that communicates the rhythmic language patterns and the mysterious cadences of the lives of Inca Indians living in the high mountain valleys of Peru. Clark wrote in *Journey to the People* (1969) that she expected her books to have five qualities: honesty, accuracy, reality, imagination, and also appreciation of 'all that life holds and all that life means'. LH

see also NATIVE AMERICANS IN CHILDREN'S BOOKS

Clark, Catherine Anthony 1892–1977 Canadian writer who was born in England and emigrated to Canada in 1914 where she lived for the rest of her life. She wrote the first truly Canadian FANTASIES for children: *The Golden Pinecone* (1950); *The One-Winged Dragon* (1955); *The Silver Man* (Toronto, 1958; London, 1959); *The Diamond Feather; or, The Door in the Mountain: A Magic Tale for Children* (1962); and *The Hunter and the Medicine Man* (1966). These stories blend realistic depictions of the Kootenay mountains region of British Columbia with supernatural events and characters drawn from local Native traditions and tales. In each story, a boy and a girl travel into the mountains or wilderness and help solve a problem within the natural and/or supernatural world, maturing as they do so. Clark's style, methods and concerns are similar to those of Australian writer PATRICIA WRIGHTSON. A seventh novel, *The Man with the Yellow Eyes* (Toronto, 1962; New York, 1963; London, 1964), is a boy's ADVENTURE STORY, written for the *Buckskin Book* series. TR

Clark, Leonard 1905–81 British poet and editor, and from 1936 until 1970 one of Her Majesty's Inspectors of Schools. He was awarded the OBE for 'Services to Poetry in Education'. Although his work is not well known today, many poems continue to be anthologised. In 'Early Portrait' he describes himself: 'an odd mixture, loved music and poetry,/all strange and rural things, the changing seasons / . . . an eager bespectacled reader'. He is best represented in *Collected Poems and Verses* (1975) and *Six of the Best* (1989). He was general editor of the series *Chatto Poets for the Young* (1970s), and fine anthologies include *Common Ground* (1964) and *All Things New* (1965). AHa

Clark, Margaret (Dianne) 1943– Australian writer of comic popular fiction, born in Geelong, Victoria. A former teacher, Clark has written much character-based humour for younger children, including the *Mango Street Primary School* series, in which pupils grapple with personal weaknesses such as clumsiness, bossiness and anxiety. Her current role as a drug counsellor informs her insightful, issue-filled young adult novels, especially *Back on Track: Diary of a Street Kid* (1995). Clark's underlying message is that individuality is acceptable and desirable. She has published over 30 books since 1987, including the *Hair-Raiser* junior horror novels, written under the pseudonym Lee Striker. NLR

Clark, Mavis Thorpe 1912–99 Australian writer of BIOGRAPHY, educational books, and over 20 works of children's fiction. She had her first book, a boy's adventure, *Hatherly's First Fifteen* (1930), published at the age of 18. Considered a pioneer, she was one of the first contemporary writers to give children historically accurate yet entertaining novels with varied Australian settings. *The Brown Land was Green* (1956), reissued as *Kammoora* (1990), is a fast-moving ADVENTURE STORY, set in pastoral Victoria in the 1840s, and shows Clark was ahead of her time with her strong-willed, resourceful heroine, Henrietta, and her genuine empathy for the plight of Aboriginal people. *The Min-Min* (1966), considered her best novel, was an early attempt at a realistic teenage problem novel. It won the CHILDREN'S BOOK COUNCIL OF AUSTRALIA BOOK OF THE YEAR AWARD in 1967. In the young adult novel *Solomon's Child* (1981), Clark manages to evoke some sympathy for her protagonist, Jude, a shop-lifting delinquent, but other works tend to be overlaid with didacticism arising from Clark's concern to present factually accurate detail, which sometimes overwhelms the telling of a good story. JAP

Clark, Russell 1905–66 New Zealand artist after whom the New Zealand Library and Information Association's annual award for the most distinguished ILLUSTRATIONS in a children's book is named. Clark was a versatile artist best known for his illustrations during the 1940s and 1950s in the *Listener* and the SCHOOL JOURNAL. His *Journal* work is regarded as particularly significant; he drew clear detailed pictures of ordinary activities in a style that conveyed drama or humour, but was never patronising. The Russell Clark Award has been running since 1975, and is a fitting tribute to one of New Zealand's best illustrators for children. LO

see also RUSSELL CLARK AWARD (Appendix)

Clarke, Gillian 1937– Welsh poet, best known for her distinguished adult poetry. Recently chair of the T.S. Eliot Poetry Prize panel of judges, Gillian Clarke has always been committed to children's poetry. She works regularly in schools, often encouraging teachers to publish children's work locally. Clarke produced her first anthology for children, *The Whispering Room*, in 1996 and a collection of poetry for children, *The Animal Wall and Other Poems*, in 1999. MCCS

Clarke, Judith 1943– Australian novelist and short story writer with a penchant for horror, the bizarre and humour. Clarke has won acclaim for most of her works. The three Al Capsella books reveal Clarke's wry humour, acute ear and her insights into the fears and foibles of teenage boys (or young men) and their anxious and often bemused parents. *The Heroic Life of Al Capsella* (1988), *Al Capsella and the Watchdogs* (1990) and *Al Capsella on Holidays* (1992) all contain experiences universal enough for the books to find an American readership. In similar vein, the novella *Big Night Out* (1995) depicts a night of mayhem as a group of teenage boys stumble around in pursuit of fun and freedom. Two collections of stories, *The Boy on the Lake – Stories of the Supernatural* (1989) and *Panic Stations* (1995), enhance Clarke's reputation for creating spooky, funny and wildly imaginative fiction, grounded in everyday reality. *Luna Park at Night* (1991) is described as an 'irreverent novel for young teenagers'. *The Ruin of Kevin O'Reilly* (1996) is for younger children. Three major novels for older teenagers reveal a writer of maturity, depth and sophistication writing at the height of her powers: *Friend Of My Heart* (1994) melds a number of love stories with a subtle exploration of old age and dementia; *The Lost Day* (1997) is the intricate and chilling city story of a boy who 'disappears' for a day, with a focus on how his friends, family and society respond. *Angels Passing By* was published in 1998, as was the emotionally charged *Nighttrain*, in which Luke, pressured by parents and anxious and threatened at school, is plagued by doubts, and by the night train that only he can hear. AN

Clarke, Pauline 1921– British writer who also writes books for younger children as Helen Clare. Clarke was born in Nottinghamshire and educated at Somerville College, Oxford, where she read English. She is best known for *The Twelve and the Genii*, which won the CARNEGIE MEDAL as well as the Lewis Carroll Shelf Award in 1963. This is a work about the 'Twelves' or 'Young Men' – the wooden soldiers of Branwell BRONTË – which a young boy discovers in a house near Haworth, and which are found to have the ability to come to life. In order to avoid being sold to an American academic, they escape with the help of the 'Genii', the children, to the Haworth Museum. It is, however, stressed that the Twelves are not dolls but individuals with distinct personalities, and this non-patronising attitude is also discernible in the *Five Doll* books Clarke wrote as Helen Clare. The genre of 'doll fiction' (see DOLL STORIES) becomes in her hands, as in RUMER GODDEN's, a mode that combines creativity and play with learning about the dynamics of human relationships and making friends. SA

Clarke, Rebecca Sophia see SOPHIE MAY

classical mythology A body of myths and legends comprising probably the best-known secular stories in western culture. Arising from oral stories, they were not composed and later written down with children in mind. A very brief introduction to Greek, Roman and Norse myth would strongly suggest that they are remarkably unsuitable for the young; yet they have remained popular with children and with the adults who make choices on behalf of children about what texts they should read. Many of the Greek stories are drawn from Homer's *Iliad* and *Odyssey*, and from the poetry of Hesiod, while Virgil celebrated the glories of Rome through the heroic adventures depicted in the *Aeneiad*. Life as reflected in these stories is perilous and so is taken on with verve, energy and an element of cunning.

In Greek myth, the world was created out of Chaos which gave birth to Gaea, the Earth, who in turn gave birth to Uranus. Together they produced the Titans, the Cyclopes and the Hecatoncheires. Uranus tried to destroy his children and only Cronus was brave enough to attack his father. He castrated him and married Rhea, fathering many children. However, since these were destined to destroy him he swallowed each one as it was born until Rhea saved one, Zeus, by trickery. In time, Zeus gave Cronus a potion which made him vomit up the other gods and goddesses, and then began a long battle against the Titans. Eventually, Zeus and the other deities prevailed and established a stronghold on Mount Olympus. There are different versions of the creation of humans, including the Pandora story, but perhaps the most influential one describes 'five ages of man', the first of which was a golden age of innocence.

Although there are many Roman myths they are largely imported from the Greek stories. From the third century BC, when the Romans adopted the Greek gods, they gave them new names and domesticated them to conform to Roman culture and religion. Many of the Roman stories derive from the writings of Virgil and Livy, celebrating heroic adventures, notably of Aeneas and Ulysses, but there are also mythological stories of love drawn from Ovid, Apuleius and Musaeus.

Much of Norse mythology is drawn from the Icelandic sagas, *The Elder Edda* and *The Younger Edda*, compiled in the Middle Ages. According to these myths, the world was created from a great void when Odin and his brothers killed the Frost Giant Ymir and it will end when the Giants kill Odin and his comrades in battle. Fighting is a central element in the stories and is the way in which a warrior can die nobly and reach the warriors' paradise, Valhalla. Nevertheless, as with Greek and Roman myths, although life might be, in Hobbes' terms, 'nasty, brutish and short', there is a good deal of drinking, eating, lovemaking, trickery, friendship, treachery and revenge to be got through before attaining paradise. The Aesir are the primary race of gods, including Odin, Thor and Balder, and the Vanir, including Frey and Freya, are the secondary race of gods, at first in conflict with the Aesir but later assimilated with them into Asgard. The Giants wield magic powers and the Dwarves live underground. The female warrior Valkyries are attendants on Odin, 'choosers of the slain' who are visible only to brave mortal fighters about to die and whom they select to live in Valhalla in Asgard. The world is supported on an enormous ash tree, Yggdrassil, whose roots descend to the netherworld, to the land of the Giants, to Midgard, where people live, and to Asgard, the dwelling place of the gods. The serpent Nidhogg gnaws away at the roots of Yggdrasil, which will collapse at the end of time. The Norns, or Fates, water the tree to keep it from dying.

This is not the stuff of children's literature as many people would understand it. However, it is because of the elemental issues which myth presents that the stories recommend themselves to readers who are, like the mythic figures they read about, shaping and facing up to their growing experience of everyday reality. In myth, imagination is mingled with fact. Divine experiences very often represent human strivings, fears and interests and, where men's and women's lives become entangled with those of gods and goddesses, there is often an aspect of authentic history mingled with tales of heroic feats. From the very first these mythic stories were taken and used to represent the characteristics of the age in which they were being told, and once the stories became established fare for young minds, the editors of the tales presented them deliberately for young readers. Some notable collections and retellings particularly aimed to give lessons in life and morality. In 1808 CHARLES LAMB published *The Adventures of Ulysses*, based on Chapman's version of Homer's epic, which recounted tales of human effort in the face of adversity. Later, in America, two noteworthy collections were made: NATHANIEL HAWTHORNE produced a version of the tales which would be suitable for children in *A Wonder Book* (1851) and *Tanglewood Tales* (1853); and another American, Thomas Bulfinch, aimed to popularise mythology in *The Age of Fable* (1855), one of the most significant collections of classical myths, including the Norse. This was not specifically aimed at young readers but it omitted 'everything offensive to pure taste and good morals'.

At about the same time, CHARLES KINGSLEY in Britain published *The Heroes* (1856). This remained one of the most popular retellings for many years, but again reflects Kingsley's own interests as he interpolates comment and addresses the reader, drawing morals from the tales. ANDREW LANG, famous for his COLOURED FAIRY BOOKS, also produced *Tales of Troy and Greece* in 1907; and ROBERT GRAVES published *The Siege and Fall of Troy* and *Myths of Ancient Greece* between 1958 and 1960, reviving the heroic and uncompromising nature of many of the stories. In all retellings, myths are invested with particular significance; they are never innocent of the influence of their tellers. The Norse myths have enjoyed fame through Wagner's adaptation of them in *The Ring Cycle* and this in its turn was absorbed into Nazi ideology. Modern versions of myths offer different perspectives, though many remain true to the sinewy strength of the first tales. KEVIN CROSSLEY-HOLLAND's *Axe Age, Wolf Age* (1985) is a vibrant and dramatic introduction to Norse mythology. TONY ROBINSON presents Theseus and Odysseus as flawed heroes in his humorous and compassionate *Theseus: the King Who Killed the Minotaur* (1988) and *The Odyssey* (1992), which older readers find compelling. MARCIA WILLIAMS's delightful cartoon-style *Greek Myths* (1991) and the clear and well-illustrated *Orchard Book of Greek Myths* (1992), retold by GERALDINE MCCAUGHREAN and illustrated by EMMA CHICHESTER CLARK, are particularly geared to younger readers, although they pull no punches. In the 1980s the BBC TELEVISION *Storyteller* series evocatively portrayed the origins of the tales as oral stories where the teller could comment on the actions of heroes. In a more traditional but highly approachable version, Katherine Lines's fine *Faber Book of Greek Legends* (1973) maintains the vigour and challenge of the original content; but perhaps the most impressive retellings are two books by LEON GARFIELD and EDWARD BLISHEN: *THE GOD BENEATH THE SEA* (1992) takes the Greek myths from chaos through to the end of the golden age of humans and the fall of Haephaestus, linking the stories in a continuous narrative; *The Golden Shadow* (1991) tells the story of Heracles. Both are hauntingly illustrated by CHARLES KEEPING. These robust retellings capture the authors' sense that the Greek myths embodied 'the nature of human destiny and the quality and force of human passion'.

The appeal of myth for young readers is remarkable given that the content of the stories is very much related to the adult world, but this paradox is just one of a number of tensions and conflicts surrounding myth as a form of literature. One of the most appealing aspects of myth is that it refuses to be pinned down. Many writers and thinkers over the ages have tried to define myth and its relationship with people, societies and cultures. Dante saw myth as truth hidden behind a beautiful fiction; Voltaire asserted that the study of myth was the occupation of blockheads; Frazer saw the tales as mistaken explanations of real phenomena. The psychologist Jung thought that all human beings have an inherent myth-making potential, and the anthropologist Malinowski saw myth as representing cultural truths. However scholarship tries to define or interpret myths, they seem to defy explanation, and in chasing interpretations there may be a risk of missing the potency of the stories themselves.

But even if capturing the essence of traditional myth proves elusive, it is possible to identify some common features which seem to carry the power of the stories. Myths are often stories of creation or explanation. They are sacred stories, telling how gods created people and describing the relationships between humans and the natural and supernatural worlds they inhabit. Modern scholarship divides myth into the categories of pure myth, heroic saga and FOLKTALE. Pure myth is seen as both primitive science and primitive religion consisting of stories that explain natural phenomena or stories of how people should behave towards the supernatural beings who have power over their destinies. These myths recount how the world began, who the various gods and goddesses are, what powers they control and the effects of this power; they also tell how humankind can propitiate supernatural rulers. Myths often deal with the tributes due to gods and goddesses, perhaps the most important one being piety and subordination. Quixotic and incomprehensible, the dwellers on Olympus or Asgard were ever ready to raise storms, sink ships, ravage crops – and people – and generally create trouble. The world depicted in classical myth is harsh and risky, from the punishment meted out to Prometheus for daring to steal fire to the Norse mythic knowledge that certain doom awaits both gods and people and the only resolution is to reach Valhalla by dying courageously in combat.

The starkness of 'pure' myth is balanced by the potential offered in the tales of heroes – and heroines. In the stories which survive, heroic feats are mostly carried out by men, but they are also often aided by women, whose acts of courage are perhaps less showy and aggressive but nevertheless contribute to outwitting or evading the power of gods and goddesses. Some commentators have seen classical myth as excluding the interests of women and girls, being tales written by men largely about the exploits of men and gods. A more careful analysis, however, reveals that far from depicting women and goddesses as submissive to the whims of men and gods, there is good evidence of women's strength, bravery and intellect. The goddesses themselves wield formidable power, and while they could not prevail against the might of Zeus, Jupiter or Odin, neither could the lesser gods. Indeed, goddesses often managed to prevail where gods failed, since they did not pit physical or magical power against the supreme deity but used their intellectual and intuitive powers. Stories about Atalanta, the Amazon fighters, Medea, Ariadne, Penelope and Freya bear witness to women's strength, quick-wittedness and fortitude. While physically active gods and men are foregrounded in the tales, the female characters are by no means depicted as weak and winsome.

As stories which have been transmitted through generations they have also been transformed by those retellings. It is possibly because of their origins in oral tellings that myths offer such rich and multifaceted possibilities for readers and tellers. They deal with the large matters of life and death, the soul and the afterlife, power and powerlessness, courage and fear, and the force of the passions – love, lust, anger, retribution, revenge. Symbol, metaphor, imagery and oblique meanings abound as the myths give shape to the big matters of existence. They tackle important questions of morality, although that morality may sometimes seem ambiguous or questionable to different cultures. They also offer what Jerome Bruner calls 'possible worlds' or, as Garfield and Blishen put it, the potential 'if not to explain life, then to provide a pattern that would act as a vast imaginative alternative to an explanation'. Myths offer possibilities of sharing experiences which can sometimes be terrifying; in forming these experiences into crafted stories, potentially devastating forces are contained and controlled. By making art from the raw material of knowledge of a violent and threatening universe, myths create a fine thread between acknowledging fearful realities and transforming them into fantasy to make them more manageable.

Mythical stories are threaded with paradoxes and dualities – the golden age of innocence balanced against the responsibilities of knowledge; the power of deities against the vulnerability of humankind. In standing up to the gods and goddesses of classical mythological tales, men and women showed inventiveness, cleverness, bravery, craft and cunning. The actions of the central characters are often selfish, foolhardy, ignoble according to western views of morality, and downright stupid, yet they are heroes. They undertake difficult journeys and overcame hazards. In some cases they are aided by divine powers and magic; in others they are punished for seeming to challenge that power in acts of hubris. They tell of individuals who have thoughts and feelings just like you or me who, through metaphorical transformation, experience more than the here-and-now; they place those individuals in settings with all the tensions, contradictions and passions engendered within families and social groups, but offer the possibility of magically transporting the courageous individual from that setting. If the immediate content – rape, incest, murder and mayhem – is not what would conventionally be encouraged for young readers, the struggles against adversity, the journeys and tests of strength do have resonance for children growing in understanding of themselves and the world. The particular power of myth lies in its ability to offer something both specific and general, in stories which are permeated with the dualities and paradoxes of human experience. ECB

see also ABORIGINAL CULTURE; AFRICAN MYTHOLOGY; FAIRY TALES; FOLKTALES AND LEGENDS; IRISH MYTHOLOGY; KING ARTHUR; MAORI WRITING; NATIVE AMERICANS; ROBIN HOOD; SCOTTISH FOLKTALES; SUPERHEROES; WELSH MYTHOLOGY AND FOLKLORE

claymation cartoons (1908–present) Animated films created by photographing three-dimensional plasticine or clay figures. While this process has been employed in American films from as early as 1908, its use in children's cartoons was popularised through Art Clokey's series of 127 TELEVISION shorts featuring a blue-green clay adolescent named Gumby and his orange horse, Pokey (1955–71). The term 'Claymation', was adopted as a trademark by Will Vinton, who produced the first full-length film using this technique, *The Adventures of Mark Twain* (1985), and created the popular California Raisins, who starred in advertisements and television specials from 1986. JDC

Cleary, Beverly 1916– American author of classic children's fiction – FANTASY, SCHOOL STORIES and the perennially popular *RAMONA* series. Cleary attended elementary and high school in Portland and the University of California, Berkeley. She later studied library science at the University of Washington in order to become a children's librarian. While working in Yakima, she noticed a lack of funny, family books for primary school children, and when her twin children were born she decided to try her hand at writing. Her first published work, *Henry Huggins* (1950), is set in Portland and recounts the misadventures of a boy who wants a dog. Henry and his dog were to appear in five other books. Other popular books by Cleary include *The Mouse and the Motorcycle* (1965), *Ralph S. Mouse* (1982) and *Runaway Ralph* (1989), about the adventures of a young mouse and his human friends. But it is her books about Ramona Quimby and her family, beginning with *Ramona the Pest* (1968), that have endeared her to generations of schoolchildren who readily identify with the comedic ups and downs of life in and out of the playground. In Britain and Ireland, a book which made a major impact was *Fifteen* (US, 1956; UK, 1962), which explores, with sympathy and understanding, the anxieties, self-doubt and confusions of a teenage girl falling in love for the first time.

Cleary has always understood the language and lore of childhood and is able to communicate the realities of everyday life in an amusing and engaging way that appeals to young readers. Her popularity is evidenced by the fact that she has received the Young Reader's Choice Award from the Pacific Northwest Library Association five times – for *Henry and Ribsy* (1957), *Henry and the Paper Route* (1960), *The Mouse and the Motorcycle*, *Ramona the Pest* and *Ramona and her Father* (1980). PBS made the *Ramona* books into a TELEVISION series, and *The Mouse and the Motorcycle* and *Runaway Ralph* were made into films. In 1984, *Dear Mr Henshaw*, about a boy who writes to his favourite author detailing his problems, received the NEWBERY MEDAL. Cleary has written two autobiographical works: *A Girl from Yamhill* (1988) and *My Own Two Feet: A Memoir* (1995). DJH

Cleaver, Elizabeth 1935–1980 Canadian illustrator of children's books. Born in Montreal, Canada, Cleaver studied art in Hungary and in Canada. After a brief job in advertising she devoted her full time to ILLUSTRATION. Although her career was cut short by premature death from cancer, she illustrated 13 books that won her international recognition and many awards. Her first book was *The World Has Wings* (1969) and subsequent work was marked by her fascination with various genres of storytelling and an interest in experimentation with unusual artistic techniques. Cleaver pioneered the illustration of Canadian native tales in *How Summer Came to Canada* (1969), *The Mountain Goats of Temlaham* (1969), *The Loon's Necklace* (1977) and *The Fire Stealer* (1979). For these books, she researched native culture in depth and experimented with innovations in the use of colour symbolism, COLLAGE, line patterning, and the incorporation of natural materials. She applied the visual designs of the performing arts in illustrating *Petrouchka* (1980), a retelling of

Stravinsky's ballet, and in *The Enchanted Caribou* (1985), an Arctic transformation tale for which she used Inuit shadow puppetry. Cleaver's artistic originality and her creative use of multicultural backgrounds helped establish a distinctively Canadian school of children's book illustration. DAC

Cleaver, Vera 1919–92 and **Cleaver, Bill** 1920–81 American authors. The Cleavers, writing together, produced a number of prize-winning books, often featuring a heroine in her early teens who faces an enormous personal challenge. These young women are often exceptionally insightful and articulate for their age; they are also bossy, self-confident and prickly. Readers enjoy their success in coping with problems such as divorce (*Ellen Grae*, 1967), an emotionally destructive parent (*Hazel Rye*, 1983), a parent's suicide (*Grover*, 1970) and an 'exceptional' sibling (*Me Too*, 1973). The Cleavers' writing is always spare and understated; Bill once remarked that the basis of fiction is what is left unsaid as it forces the reader to become involved. Critics have commented that survival is an ever-present theme; this is especially true in *Where the Lilies Bloom* (1969), a 1970 Newbery Honour Book. The Luther children, directed by the capable Mary Call, are determined to stay together as a family after the death of their father. Their fight for emotional unity is mirrored by their physical struggle in the face of food shortages inside the house and raging blizzards outside. The Cleavers continually provide a non-predictable story line, lively dialogue and well-developed characters. WH

Clemens, Samuel see MARK TWAIN

Clement, Rod 1961– Australian illustrator, cartoonist and writer, whose PICTUREBOOKS reflect an eye for visual humour, irony, double-entendre and the absurd. His first major success was *EDWARD THE EMU* by Sheena Knowles (1988), followed in 1990 by his first self-authored title, the bitter and hilarious *Counting on Frank*, which shows a child using maths to escape family mediocrity. This has been developed into a CD-ROM game. He wrote and illustrated *Eyes in Disguise* (1992) and the well-received *Just Another Ordinary Day* (1995), which blends a gentle description of a child's normal day with stylised, fantastical images that belie the verbal text. NLR

Clever Bill see SIR WILLIAM NICHOLSON; see also ILLUSTRATION IN CHILDREN'S BOOKS; PICTUREBOOKS

***Clever Polly* series** (1955–90) Four CHAPTER BOOKS written by CATHERINE STORR. Polly first appeared in a collection of stories, *Clever Polly and Other Stories* published in 1952, and this story is retold in the first full book of the series. The stories are based on well-known FAIRY TALES whose ending Polly always knows better than the wolf, so that where he expects to end the story having caught his dinner, she knows that wolves never succeed in eating little girls. The earlier books in the series are written from Polly's point of view, with little sympathy for the stupid wolf, who never presents Polly with any real threat. Each chapter begins with an account of Polly's activities, stressing her cleverness so that the reader is confident in her ability to outwit the wolf.

Between the first and last book of the series there is a considerable change in both the structure and ethos of the books. By *Last Stories of Polly and the Wolf*, the wolf has abandoned traditional fairy tales and adopted a more complex approach to catching Polly. The perspective has changed too and we are encouraged to feel more sympathy for the traditional villain. Polly herself remains equally down-to-earth, though her instructions to the wolf are now couched in more colloquial language. In a final demonstration that he is not as stupid as the stories suggest, he manages to outwit Polly and the adults and escape their trap. KA

Illustration from *Counting on Frank* by Rod Clement.

Clifton, (Thelma) Lucille (Sayles) 1936– AFRICAN AMERICAN poet and author of fiction, non-fiction and 19 children's books. Clifton grew up in Buffalo, New York, and attended Howard University and Fredonia State College. Her writing, like that of Gwendolyn Brooks (see *BRONZEVILLE BOYS AND GIRLS*) and ELOISE GREENFIELD, affirms the importance of family and childhood. Clifton's adult volumes of poetry during her years of active parenting – she had six children in rapid succession – reflect the anxieties of mothering black children in a racist society; her children's books are Clifton's way of nurturing the strength and self-esteem those children need in order to survive. Central to this project is her *Everett Anderson* series (1970–83), seven PICTUREBOOKS in verse about an engaging young boy proud of his black identity and secure in his mother's love. The series' last book, *Everett Anderson's Goodbye* (1983), sensitively depicts Everett's mourning and recovering from the death of his father. Other notable titles include *The Times They Used to Be* (1974) and *My Friend Jacob* (1980). Early in her career, Clifton was criticised for using Black English in some of her children's books; her vigorous defence of this usage is seconded by the high esteem now accorded to the body of her work for children. JMA

Coatsworth, Elizabeth (Jane) 1893–1986 American author of HISTORICAL FICTION, contemporary stories, and ADVENTURE STORIES set in foreign countries. Born into a family accustomed to travelling, Coatsworth toured Europe and Egypt at five, and Mexico at twelve. After earning a Master's degree from Columbia in 1916, she spent a year exploring Java, China, Korea and the Philippines. This wide acquaintance with other cultures helps explain her lifelong fascination with otherness; her Newbery Award winner, *The Cat Who Went to Heaven* (1930), for example, remains a rare attempt to interpret Buddhist beliefs and values for western children. Although the majority of her historical novels are set in colonial and post-Revolutionary America – including *The Golden Horseshoe* (1935), *Old Whirlwind* (1953) and *Away Goes Sally* (1934), first of five *Sally* books – she has also opened doors to Guatemala (*The Boy with the Parrot*, 1930), Viking Greenland (*Jon the Unlucky*, 1963), medieval Ireland (*The Wanderers*, 1972), 18th-century Ethiopia (*The Princess and the Lion*, 1963) and Tristan da Cunha (*Jock's Island*, 1963). Her clear, graceful style – adaptable to an exceptional range of age groups – attests to her training as a poet; some of the poems accompanying her stories have become favourites on their own merits; her most quoted poem is the mysterious 'On a Night of Snow'. SR

Cobblestone An American history magazine designed for children aged between nine and twelve. In publication since 1980 and originally issued monthly, *Cobblestone* is now published nine times a year to coincide with the traditional American school year. Each issue is devoted to a particular aspect of American history. In 1999 *Cobblestone* dealt with topics ranging from the First Amendment: Freedom of the Press, to Andrew Carnegie and the Spanish American War. Given its obvious ties to the school curriculum, the primary venues for the magazine are the library and the classroom. Lively in style and layout, the magazine also appeals to young history enthusiasts who include it as a regular part of their pleasure reading. The magazine is the premier product of the Cobblestone Publishing Company, which also produces *Faces*, a magazine of world cultures and geography; *Calliope*, a world history publication; and *Footsteps*, a magazine devoted to AFRICAN AMERICAN heritage. VAG

Cock-House at Fellsgarth, The see TALBOT BAINES REED

***Cock-Olly* series** (1941–4) South African talking-animal stories by Mary Henderson, popular in the 1940s, illustrated by Patricia Shepherd in a comic style typical of the period. The narrative is interspersed with verse and includes much lively and rather twee dialogue. Though written in the whimsical European style that had been popular since the 1920s, the stories mark a significant step towards giving South African children's books an essentially local content. It is likely that they were written and published in Durban because of the scarcity of British publications during the War. They are set in the Kruger National Park and feature creatures such as the Cock-Olly Bird, mice, termites, Wise Owl and Mangy the Jackal. The four books in the series are *The Cock-Olly Book: Tales of Veld, Fun and Frolic* (1941), *Looma, Teller of Tales: More Stories of Kruger Park* (1943), *Tortoo the Tortoise: Ruler of Kruger Park* (1943) and *Mrs Mouse of Kruger Park* (1944). ERJ

'Cock Robin' The song of 'Who killed Cock Robin?', with its powerfully affecting ending, 'All the birds in the air fell a-sighing and a-sobbing, When they heard the bell toll for poor Cock Robin', has equivalents all over Europe in which different birds are mourners. Thus it is likely to be a very old song, much older than its first printed appearance in the second volume of *TOMMY THUMB'S PRETTY SONG BOOK* in 1744 (first four verses only) would seem to indicate. 'Cock Robin' formed a substantial part of the late 18th-century CHAPBOOK trade, the earliest known being R. Marshall's 'pretty gilded toy' of c. 1770; in these all 14 verses are given. When children's books began to be coloured, 'Cock Robin' was a favourite subject. Major publishers such as W. Darton (1806), J. HARRIS (1822), E. Marshall (1823), Dean & Munday and AK. Newman (c.1830) had to have at least one 'Cock Robin' in their list, sometimes with the addition of *The Courtship, Marriage, and Pic Nic Dinner of Cock Robin and Jenny Wren*. J.G. RUSHER, the Banbury printer of children's chapbooks, included a 'Cock Robin' in his list, as did THOMAS KENDREW of York. The story is in the same vein as John Skelton's poem 'Phyllyp Sparrow', written about 1508, which was possibly suggested by Catullus' *Luctus in morte Passeris*. (It is almost certain that 'bull' was a shortened form of 'bullfinch' and did not refer to the bovine creature often depicted in illustrations.) It has been suggested that 'Cock Robin' originated as a satire against Robert Walpole, at the time his ministry fell in 1742, but this is unlikely. Parodies abound, notably that by Byron, mourning the death of Keats: 'Who kill'd John Keats? I says the Quarterly, So savage and Tartarly; 'Twas one of my feats.' IO

Cocking, Percy see COMICS, PERIODICALS AND MAGAZINES

Cody, William F. see BUFFALO BILL

Cole, Babette (Steele) 1949– British illustrator and PICTUREBOOK maker, born in Jersey, British Channel Islands. Cole graduated from Canterbury College of Art in 1973 and has worked in TELEVISION animation and as a designer of greetings cards. She is best known for her zestful, *faux naïf* style and for themes which frequently nudge at the boundaries of taste. In *The Trouble with Mum* (1983) and its sequels she created a bizarre family including a grandmother who is an alien. *The Hairy Book* (1984), *The Slimy Book* (1985) and *The Smelly Book* (1987) celebrated the indecorous, and in *Princess Smartypants* (1986) and *Prince Cinders* (1987) Cole turned the traditional tale on its head. As with all satirists Cole's work has a didactic streak. The silliness in *Supermoo* (1993) is stiffened with a spine of ecological awareness, and *Three Cheers for Errol* (1988) champions the underdog who is a failure at school. *Mummy Laid an Egg* (1993) and *Dr Dog* (1994) are both overtly pedagogical. In the former, two level-headed young siblings instruct their foolish parents in the facts of life and in the latter a dog teaches its owners how to take care of their bodies and avoid common illnesses. Cole won the KURT MASCHLER AWARD in 1996 for *Drop Dead*. *Bad Habits!* (1998) is about an uncivilised heroine whose vulgar habits have to be corrected. DL

Cole, Sir Henry see FELIX SUMMERLY

Cole, Joanna 1944– American editor and writer of fiction and non-fiction for children. She has also written under the pseudonym of Ann Cooke. Cole is best known for her *Magic School Bus* series in which science is presented humorously in PICTUREBOOK format. She credits Craig Walker, editor at Scholastic, for the basic idea of a science teacher who leads her students on magical science adventures. Since 1986, the teacher Ms Frizzle has driven the Magic School Bus to such diverse places as the city waterworks and inside the human body. In writing the series, Cole makes 'science the skeleton of the book'. Bruce Degen is the illustrator. Katherine Bouton of the *New York Times Book Review* has lauded the series as making 'science so much fun that the information is almost incidental'. An animated PBS TELEVISION series based on the *Magic School Bus* books was first transmitted in 1994. Cole has garnered numerous awards including the *Washington Post* / Children's Book Guild Nonfiction Award, 1991. Her many fiction titles include the recent easy-to-read series in collaboration with Stephanie Calmenson, *Gator Girls* (1995). GIK

'Cock Robin': engraving by the DALZIEL BROTHERS for *National Nursery Rhymes and Nursery Songs.*

Cole, William 1919– Editor and writer of children's poetry. He has compiled numerous volumes of children's poetry under distinctive themes – such as animals, magic, seasons and ships – including the award-winning *Beastly Boys and Ghastly Girls* (1964). His *Humorous Poetry for Children* (1955), and collections of 'knock-knock' jokes, cartoons and RIDDLES, show his preference for humour. He has also written original verse books, including *Aunt Bella's Umbrella* (1970) and *Have I Got Dogs!* (1993). SCWA

Cole's Funny Picturebook: the Funniest Picturebook in the World (1879) A quirky compilation of humorous stories, verse, RIDDLES, pictures, puzzles, drawings and other oddities, conceived and published by the Australian entrepreneurial owner of Cole's Book Arcade in Melbourne, E.W. Cole. Cole cut and pasted material gleaned from English and

American periodicals and augmented with his own inimical satirical comments to produce an affordable PICTUREBOOK, 'to delight the children and make home happier'. Reprints of *Book No 2* (1872) exceeded one million copies by 1973, while from 1951 new books and editions were published by Cole Turnley, E.W. Cole's grandson. Although outdated, and with little Australian content, the books, with the distinctive rainbow arch on their covers, have continued to entertain many generations of Australian children, perhaps because they truly promoted family reading. JAP

Coleman, Charlotte see *MARMALADE ATKINS*

Coleridge, Samuel Taylor see *THE RIME OF THE ANCIENT MARINER*; see also *LYRICAL BALLADS*; LULLABIES

Coleridge, Sara see *PRETTY LESSONS IN VERSE FOR ALL GOOD CHILDREN*

collage The technique of pasting cloth, paper, photographs, prints or other materials onto the picture surface. Collage is capable of generating visual tension since the materials are perceived both as their material selves and as whatever they represent in the composition. A picture made entirely of collage has a static quality. This may be exploited to serve the seriousness of the themes as in the PICTUREBOOKS of JEANNIE BAKER. EZRA JACK KEATS balances the flat two-dimensional pasted elements with areas of rich painting, whilst ERIC CARLE often breaks the edge of his collage shapes with drawn lines, crayon and paint, which brings to the whole a sense of vitality. JD

Collected Animal Poems (1995) Four small volumes of collected poems by Ted Hughes, attractively produced by Faber publishers. The set includes a reissue of the outstanding *WHAT IS THE TRUTH* (1984), arguably HUGHES's finest collection for children and winner of the *Signal* Award, with delightful new illustrations by Lisa Flather; and *The Iron Wolf* (1995), with its superb black-and-white line drawings by CHRIS RIDDELL. Both are aimed at younger readers, especially the latter, which includes previously unpublished, short, amusing and accessible poems that retain Hughes's observant honesty about the animal kingdom; and some from earlier collections, *Under the North Star* (1981) and *The Cat and the Cuckoo* (1987). The two remaining volumes, *A March Calf* and *The Thought-Fox* are without illustrations and geared towards pupils in secondary schools and adult readers. *A March Calf* draws on distinguished early work by Hughes, such as *Season Songs* (1976) and *The Hawk in the Rain* (1957), while *The Thought-Fox* contains some of his most popular poems, including 'Hawk Roosting' and the title poem, taken from collections as various as *Wolfwatching* (1989), *Lupercal* (1960) and *River* (1983). MCCS

collections of children's books Many special collections of children's books and related materials originated in the interests of antiquarians and librarians. These specialist and idiosyncratic collections can be set alongside those of the national libraries which, while they may have had the advantage of legal deposit to ensure breadth of coverage over time, do not necessarily compare so favourably in depth, for example in collections of ephemera. For scholars, a compact and accessible library such as the Osborne Collection in Toronto, which has brought together games and harlequinades as well as one of the most comprehensive of all collections of early children's books, has particular value in enabling access to the range of materials available in any one period. The Victoria and Albert Museum's Renier Collection has similar strengths. The size of library is therefore not necessarily a guide to its utility for scholars.

Despite the above caveat, the British Library is still the best single collection in the United Kingdom, notwithstanding its unsystematic acquisition of children's books before 1950. (The Newspaper Library at Colindale houses newspapers and serials.) At present, around half of its collections are out-housed, but the move from Bloomsbury to the new St Pancras building is intended to bring many more together. Pre-1800 books are separately shelved and include many rare works, including the only known copies of *TOMMY THUMB'S PRETTY SONG BOOK VOL. 2* (1744) and the first edition of *THE HISTORY OF LITTLE GOODY TWO-SHOES* (1765). Special collections include CHAPBOOKS and a collection of books by Isaac Taylor. The Department of Manuscripts holds the work of many important writers: LEWIS CARROLL, RUDYARD KIPLING and ROBERT LOUIS STEVENSON, among others. The 18th Century Short-Title Catalogue has revolutionised access to many of the Library's most important holdings.

The Bodleian Library, Oxford University, has become especially significant as a resource since its acquisition of the 20,000-volume Opie Collection in 1988, which was famously assembled by PETER AND IONA OPIE and formed the basis for their *Oxford Dictionary of Nursery Rhymes* (1951). Because their work was broadly based in social and cultural history and in anthropology, the Collection reflects wide-ranging interests – from 17th- and 18th-century rarities to Victorian TOY BOOKS. The Opie Collection, Harding Chapbooks, and the John Johnson Collection of children's books and ephemera are catalogued separately from the main Bodleian library. The Bodleian also possesses the earliest known manuscript of a story for children, written by JANE JOHNSON in 1744. Cambridge University Library, like the British Library and the Bodleian a copyright library, contains over four million books, but has become comprehensive in coverage only since the mid-19th century. Chapbooks are a particularly strong feature: around 2,500 in the general collection, with further titles in the Glaisher and Munby Collections. Other academic libraries with notable, if smaller, collections include: Leicester University, the School of Education Collection, which spans the 16th to early 20th centuries, to 1914 (c. 3,500 volumes); the University of London Institute of Education Library, covering all aspects of education, with a historical collection of pre-1919 monographs and pre-1860 periodicals, the National Reference Library of Schoolbooks and Classroom Materials and the National Library for the Handicapped Child; Manchester Metropolitan University Collection, from 1840 to 1939 (c. 4,000 volumes); Manchester University John Rylands Library which contains fine 19th-century illustrated books and the ALISON UTTLEY Collection; Nottingham University, the Briggs Collection of early educational literature and the William and Mary Howitt Special Collection (c. 1,700 volumes); Reading University Children's Collection (c. 5,000 volumes). All have catalogues, of varying quality.

The Victoria and Albert Museum National Art Library has approximately one million volumes, including sale and exhibition catalogues. Its illustrated books, especially those of THOMAS BEWICK, are especially fine. The Guy Little Collection and the Linder Bequest of BEATRIX POTTER items are also included. The V&A Bethnal Green Museum of Childhood houses the Renier Collection of Historic and Contemporary Children's Books, the largest special collection of children's books in the United Kingdom with around 80,000 items, and arguably the finest: many of its ephemera are unique. A computerised catalogue is currently being compiled, but access to the collection is limited and its future home is uncertain. The Book Trust's Collection of current children's books published in the United Kingdom over the previous two years is passed on to the Bethnal Green Museum after display. The Book Trust for Scotland retains a similar collection of current books for consultation.

The National Library of Scotland, Edinburgh, a copyright library since 1710 with around five million items, has a substantial collection of children's books, especially the Eudo Mason Collection (c. 3,600 volumes) and the Lauriston Castle collection (c. 11,000 volumes) with many chapbooks and school prize books. The National Library of Wales, Aberystwyth, also a copyright library, contains books in Welsh for children in the D.J. Williams Collection, while the nearby Welsh National Centre for Children's Literature collects current and retrospective children's books in Welsh and English-Welsh. Trinity College, Dublin, a copyright library since 1801, has few children's books before the mid-19th-century, but the Pollard Collection of school books includes many 19th-century text books.

A further considerable and largely untapped resource is the number of significant collections amassed by public libraries, local museums and colleges of education. Some have been integrated with university collections, but many still languish in store-rooms and stacks, inadequately catalogued and with poor access for scholars. Bletchley Library, Milton Keynes, has a collection of about 1,100 volumes of early children's books from 1711 to 1940; Hertfordshire has a fine special collection of children's books originally collected by Mary Thwaite, mainly post-1945; the London Borough of Camden has a KATE GREENAWAY Collection in Hampstead Library with over 1,000 items, including a complete collection of her works from 1878, plus original drawings and rare greetings cards; Preston (Harris) Public Library has the Spencer Collection of c. 5,000 volumes; Wiltshire has a collection of c. 3,000 volumes of Victorian and Edwardian children's books, including the Tatham Collection of girls' and girls' school stories. Birmingham Central Library's Parker Collection of Early Children's Books is a particularly well-catalogued and well-housed example, with c. 10,000 items and 105 games. The PICTUREBOOKS and MOVABLE BOOKS are very fine.

In Scotland, the Jordanhill College Library collection, which contains c. 15,000 contemporary children's books, and the Museum of Childhood in Edinburgh, with c. 11,000 books from the early 19th century, are further significant resources.

In the United States the Library of Congress became a copyright library only in 1870, but with the establishment of the Children's Book Section, later to become the Children's Literature Center, the largest collection of children's books in the United States became accessible to scholars. Cataloguing is of high quality. Other collections in the Library of Congress include the Jean Hersholt Collection of HANS CHRISTIAN ANDERSEN materials, including manuscripts.

The large academic library collections in the United States have specialised not only in historical materials but also in collections of contemporary authors' works, manuscripts and archive materials. Scholars of contemporary children's literature therefore need to look to America for much primary source material. The University of Minnesota Kerlan Collection contains manuscripts by many of the NEWBERY MEDAL winners, together with illustrations by WANDA GÁG; the University of Southern Mississippi has the growing deGrummond Collection, which includes material on EZRA JACK KEATS and on Kate Greenaway; Stanford University houses the Mary L. Schofield Collection of Children's Literature, with c. 10,000 volumes; the Temple University, Philadelphia, houses the WALTER DE LA MARE Collection; the Wheaton College, Illinois, has the Wade Collection with books, manuscripts and related materials of C.S. LEWIS, GEORGE MACDONALD and J. R. R. TOLKIEN.

Rich historical collections are housed in the American Antiquarian Society in Worcester, Massachusetts, with c. 3,000 volumes from around 1700 – mainly the d'Alte Welch collection of books printed in the USA before 1821; the University of California, Los Angeles, which has c. 200 books published by JOHN NEWBERY and his successors and a collection of 19th-century children's books; the University of Florida in Gainseville, which has the Ruth Baldwin Collection of c. 70,000 volumes, most of which are pre-1900, and the Peabody and Essex Museum in Salem, Massachusetts, with c. 5,000 titles.

As in Britain, there are rich collections in American Public libraries, but these are generally much better housed and catalogued. The Philadelphia Free Public Library, Pennsylvania, contains early Sunday School texts, together with modern authors and illustrators including EVALINE NESS.

Private institutional libraries which contain some of the most rare items from the historical to the modern periods include the Pierpont Morgan Library in New York, the Henry E. Huntington Library in San Marino, California, and the Rosenbach Museum and Library in Philadelphia; the latter has an extensive collection of MAURICE SENDAK material. Exhibition catalogues have become invaluable bibliographical tools.

The Osborne Collection of children's books, in Toronto, Canada, remains one of the best known and most widely accessible collections due to the excellence of its catalogue – still an invaluable bibliographical tool (J. St John, *The Osborne Collection of Early Children's Books: A Catalogue*, 2 vols., Toronto Public Library, 1958–75). This details some 5,600 items, with scholarly annotations which provide key insights into the span of children's publishing over the period 1566–1910, the scope of the collection. Toronto Public Library has also developed the Lillian H. Smith Collection, comprising the 'best' children's books published in English since 1910.

In Australia and New Zealand the most significant special collection, Dromkeen, is in Riddell's Creek, Victoria, with particular emphasis on Australian authors from the early 20th century, including manuscripts of works by IVAN SOUTHALL and PATRICIA WRIGHTSON. Other significant collections of children's literature can be found in all states of Australia. The Research Collection of Children's Literature in Western Australia was begun in 1979 and now contains over 6000 volumes of Australian works, arranged chronologically. It provides a clear view of the attitudes and range of writing available to children in particular periods. The Mitchell Library, part of the State Library of New South Wales, has a vast collection of published Australian children's literature, dating from 1841 to the present. The Lu Rees Archives Collection, housed at the University of Canberra, comprises more than 6,500 titles, including over 500 foreign-language editions of Australian children's books. There are also original manuscripts, pieces of artwork and a full set of New South Wales *SCHOOL MAGAZINES*. The collection also publishes a regular update, entitled *The Lu Rees Archives: Notes, Books and Authors*. In Tasmania, the Australian Children's Literature Collection of over 4,000 titles, housed in the State Library, includes books from 1920 onwards.

The National Library of New Zealand has two 'closed access' heritage collections of children's literature. The first is the Dorothy Neal White Collection which contains 19th-century and early 20th-century children's books, up until 1940. It also owns the Susan Price Collection, which in 1995 totalled more than 10,000 books written and published both in New Zealand and overseas, from the 1930s to the present day. This is a growing collection, curated and held in her lifetime by Susan D. Price. New Zealand writers, notably MARGARET MAHY, have gained greater world-wide prominence in recent years and scholarly studies have been encouraged by the New Zealand Children's Literature Association.

Much of the recent upsurge of interest in the study of children's literature which has fuelled the demand for primary sources has come from a reawakening of interest in cultural diversity. Scholars from a range of disciplines – sociology, philosophy, social and economic history, politics, communication and media studies, art history – as well as from literature, are using collections such as those above, and it has therefore become more pressing to develop adequate bibliographical aids facilitating searches from a range of perspectives: subject, illustrator, publisher, printer, as well as author. Access through the internet is also becoming a reality for many scholars as national and academic libraries mount their catalogues on the World-Wide Web. The Library of Congress collections were some of the first to become available worldwide, and the British Library has followed suit. The availabilty of children's book collections to scholars is likely to be transformed through these new media, with the 'national' collections – already a less appropriate term given the global export of children's literature – becoming less confined by their geographic boundaries. ME, JAP

see also THE CENTRE FOR THE CHILDREN'S BOOK

Collier, James Lincoln 1928– and **Collier, Christopher** 1930– American brothers who work together as authors of historical novels for children. Born in New York City, James Lincoln Collier was educated at Hamilton College, has worked as a magazine editor and has written books for adults on music and jazz, fiction for children, non-fiction books on music for children and seven works of HISTORICAL FICTION for young adults with his brother. The academic half of the writing team, Christopher, was born in New York City and educated at Clark University and Columbia University, where he received his PhD. Christopher has taught history at university and served as the Connecticut State Historian. He is the author of numerous articles and academic books and – together with his brother – of *Decision in Philadelphia: The Constitutional Convention of 1787* (1986), a book for adults.

The brothers' historical fiction for children and young adults is mainly set in the Revolutionary War period and skilfully blends historical facts, accurate settings and historical personages with fictional protagonists to create historical novels which deal with contemporary themes. These complex and well-researched novels have received numerous awards, including a Newbery Honour Award, a Jane Addams Honour Book, and finalist citation for the National Book Award for *My Brother Sam is Dead* (1974). DJH

Collington, Peter 1948– British illustrator who has carved a unique niche for himself as an illustrator whose favoured medium is the wordless story. In his first book *Little Pickle* (1986), he found not only the form (the use of scores of framed 'shots') but also the content that characterises all his stories: the journey from reality to FANTASY and back. Often his characters fall asleep at the start of the story; this enables toys to come to life (*The Angel and the Soldier Boy*, 1987) or fairies to work their magic (*On Christmas Eve*, 1990; *The Tooth Fairy*, 1995). *The Coming of the Surfman* (1993) – which does employ words – and *A Small Miracle* (1997) move into social parable. Recent titles also show Collington moving away from the use of coloured crayons into gouache, which allows a greater depth of colour whilst preserving the spontaneity necessary for stories told only through pictures. JAG

Collins, Heather 1946– Canadian illustrator of INFORMATION BOOKS and PICTUREBOOKS for children. Born in Montreal, Collins was always aware of her ability and desire to draw. After graduating from the Ontario College of Art, Collins designed and illustrated textbooks. She was sought after in the educational market and soon asked to illustrate picturebooks, most notably KATHY STINSON's *The Bare Naked Book* (1986). Collins has illustrated over 30 books, using a variety of techniques and materials. Pencil drawings, her best-known style, are found in the author BARBARA GREENWOOD's *A Pioneer Story: The Daily Life of a Canadian Family in 1840* (1994), which won The Mr. Christie's Book Award and the Ruth Schwartz Children's Book Award. Here, Collins combined fanciful, imaginative touches with the realist requirements of an informational text. She has done the same in Pamela Hickman's *A New Duck* (1999), Jane Drake's and Ann Love's *The Kids Cottage Games Book* (1998) and Barbara Greenwood's *The Last Safe House: The Story of the Underground Railroad* (1998). A NURSERY RHYME series, including *One, Two Buckle My Shoe* (1997), represents a new direction, as Collins reinterprets the rhymes as stories. SJ

Collins Magazine for Boys and Girls see *THE YOUNG ELIZABETHAN*

Collodi [Lorenzini], Carlo see *PINOCCHIO*; see also ROBERTO INNOCENTI

colour reproduction see ILLUSTRATION IN CHILDREN'S BOOKS; see also WOOD ENGRAVING

'coloured' *Fairy Books* In 1889, Andrew Lang edited and published what was to be the first of 12 'coloured' *Fairy Books*, *The Blue Fairy Book*, collections of traditional FOLK and FAIRY TALES, the bulk of which are European. Lang's own interest in fairy tales was mainly scholarly and anthropological, but the work proved so popular that it was quickly followed by the other collections, though Lang eventually passed on the work of editing them to his wife. H.J. Ford's 'pre-Raphaelite' ILLUSTRATIONS, which still accompany most editions of the *Fairy Books*, add immeasurably to the sense of the enchanted world that one enters in the tales themselves. Related collections published in the same format included *The True Story Book* (1894), *THE ARABIAN NIGHTS ENTERTAINMENTS* (1898), *The Book of Romance* (1902) and *The Red Book of Heroes* (1909). Early copies in good condition are highly valued by collectors. SA

Colum, Padraic 1881–1972 Irish-born novelist, folklorist, poet and dramatist. Colum was already well respected as an adult author when he wrote his first major work for children, *A Boy in Eireann* (1913), a semi-autobiographical novel. It intersperses a retelling of the legends of Finn McCool with the contemporary story of Finn O'Donnell and his family living in an

Ireland of political unrest. Emigrating to the United States in 1914, Colum developed a career in writing for children with retellings and adaptations of MYTHS AND LEGENDS from many countries. These are told simply and with a direct appeal to the reader. A collection of stories, *The King of Ireland's Son* (1916), is among the best-known of these. Distinguished illustrators such as JACK B. YEATS, BORIS ARTZYBASHEFF and WILLY POGANY worked with Colum, and a number of his books are notable for their art deco illustration and presentation. VC

see also IRISH MYTHOLOGY AND FOLKLORE

Colvin, Sidney see *A CHILD'S GARDEN OF VERSES*

Colwell, Eileen (Hilda) 1904– British children's librarian, storyteller and writer. A pioneer in her profession, Colwell reacted against the meagreness and gloom of the few children's LIBRARIES already existing, their books on high shelving and uniformly rebound in drab colours. From 1926 to 1967 she worked at the Hendon Public Library in London, creating its first children's library, which was well-stocked and welcoming, with regular Story Hours. Her library served as a prototype. Colwell was internationally known as a storyteller; and *How I Became a Librarian* (1956) is still in print in Japan, where it has been influential in the development of children's libraries. PP

see also STORYTELLING

Come Away From the Water, Shirley (1977) PICTUREBOOK by JOHN BURNINGHAM. A deceptively simple work of great interest both formally and stylistically and typical of the pared-down approach to picturebook-making adopted by Burningham in the 1970s and 80s. The story is superficially slight and tells of a trip to the beach by Shirley and her dull parents. However, by using the central GUTTER of each double page spread to separate story worlds rather than pictures in sequence, Burningham is able to show the reader two distinct perspectives on events. Thus the VERSO has the parents sitting in deck-chairs doing little other than make largely cautionary remarks to their daughter. The latter is visible only on the RECTO where, in a sequence of vividly coloured, wordless images, she appears to become caught up in an adventure aboard a pirate ship. By eschewing explanation and removing cues to interpretation, Burningham creates gaps in the text larger than is customary in picturebooks and thus gives the reader more work to do. Older children and adults tend to see Shirley as wrapped up in imaginative play or fantasy. Younger, less experienced – and less easily satisfied – readers are frequently intrigued by the lack of a clear relationship between the two sets of images and will often openly try to puzzle out how they are connected. *Come Away from the Water, Shirley* thus exemplifies the picturebook rule of 'less is more'. A sequel, *Time to Get Out of the Bath, Shirley*, was published in 1978. DL

Come Hither: A Collection of Rhymes and Poems for the Young of All Ages (1923) The most important and distinguished Bristish anthology of the century, compiled by WALTER DE LA MARE. In an allegorical introduction a boy, Simon, finds a house in a hollow called Threa (earth), where he encounters Miss Taroone (nature) and Nahum Taroone (human nature), and a book of poems – 500 poems by 260 poets spanning six centuries, under headings like 'Evening and Dream', 'War' and 'Dance, Music & Bells'. In 'Around and Roundabout' detailed notes, anecdotes and more verse reveal de la Mare's vast love and knowledge of literature and his desire to pass it on. In his introduction to *Tom Tiddler's Ground* (1932), a slighter, but equally vital anthology, he says: 'We can . . . particularly when we are young, delight in the sounds of words of a poem, immensely enjoy . . . the music and rhythm and lilt, feel its enchantment, without realising its full meaning . . . It is best to find your way to a poem yourself.' AHa

Come on into my Tropical Garden (1988) First collection of poems for children by GRACE NICHOLS, illustrated with photographic realism by CAROLINE BINCH. The poems invite the reader to meet family and friends, and sample the tastes and sounds of a Guyanese childhood. The collection effectively brings together the exotic and the familiar, child and adult perspectives, as well as Creole and standard English. ML

Comenius, John Amos see *ORBIS SENSUALIUM PICTUS*; EMBLEM BOOKS; see also ILLUSTRATION IN CHILDREN'S BOOKS

Comfort Herself (1984) Prize-winning novel by GERALDINE KAYE about a girl trying to find her own identity after the tragic death of her mother. Comfort struggles to reconcile the two different sides to her personality inherited from her Ghanaian father and her English mother as she spends time in each country. Life with her English grandparents is shown to be dull and repetitive, but it is comforting and allows her to prolong her childhood. The Ghanaian way of life also clearly has its drawbacks – her father is distant, her Ghanaian grandmother as easily offended as her English one, and each country has different moral codes and restrictions on the behaviour of young women. Colour imagery is used throughout the books to symbolise the differences between the two ways of life: her English village is green and grey, with a garden filled with traditional flowers, while life in Ghana is multi-coloured and vibrant and Comfort herself wears clothes in colours that symbolise the power of life. Comfort adopts a different personality for each country, but in the sequel, *Great Comfort* (1988), she is compared to a chameleon changing its colour as she finally learns to reconcile the two different aspects of her life and personality. KA

Comic Adventures of Old Mother Hubbard and Her Dog, The (1805) Sarah Catherine Martin (1768–1826) wrote and illustrated the first published version of this rhyme which became one of the earliest best-sellers of the nursery – John Harris noted that 10,000 copies were sold in a few months – though Mother Hubbard and other old dames with dogs had already featured in the oral tradition. MCCS

Comic Cuts see COMICS, PERIODICALS AND MAGAZINES

comic books see COMICS, PERIODICALS AND MAGAZINES

comics, periodicals and magazines It is hard to conceive of a period when comics and children were not meant for each other. But comics in Britain began as an adult entertainment, born in the early 19th century when caricature sheets and prints developed. The first regular publication was *The Glasgow Looking Glass*, published fortnightly in Scotland only, beginning in June, 1825. Publisher John Watson changed his title to *The Northern Looking Glass* after no. 5, hoping for wider sales. This four-pager, all cartoons, had no appeal for children and none was expected. The format was copied by London's famous print publisher, Thomas McLean, who launched his evident imitation, *The Looking Glass*, in January 1830. The cartoonist was William Heath, and it was sold plain or hand-coloured, also as a bound volume containing twelve editions – the first ever comic ANNUAL.

Ally Sloper, the first recurring comic-strip hero, was created as a weekly strip in the magazine *Judy*, by the prolific writer/editor/cartoonist Charles Ross in 1867. This laughable layabout, later drawn by Ross's French wife Marie Duval, became such a public favourite that he soon appeared in the annual *Ally Sloper's Comic Kalendar* (1875–87), then in his *Summer Number* (1880–7), and finally his own weekly comic, *Ally Sloper's Half Holiday*, which ran from 1884 to 1916. A number of paperback reprints of the comic strip were issued from 1873 to 1883, and there was at least one colour book designed for children, *The True Story of Ally Sloper and the Paint Pot*, undated but indicating the way comics would develop.

The boom in weekly comics began when Alfred Harmsworth issued no. 1 of *Comic Cuts* (17 May 1880), destined to last the longest of any British comic, through 3,003 issues, closing on 12 September 1953. 'The Harmsworth Touch', as it became known throughout publishing, was to halve the price of contemporary publications, and in this case *Comic Cuts*' success was due to its price of one halfpenny instead of the penny of its rivals. Comics were still published for adults, and, apart from one failed attempt in 1885 called *Jack and Jill*, it was not until 1904, when Harmsworth's coloured comic *Puck* was issued, that the children's comic was born. Even this was a process of evolution, as it seemed for a while that adults would not buy a coloured comic. After several experiments in design and content, it became a children's comic before Christmas 1904. It remained a comic that adults bought for children, finally expiring in the wartime paper shortage of 1940.

The first weekly comic designed exclusively for children was *The Rainbow* (from 14 February 1914), which starred the already popular magazine characters 'Tiger Tim and the Hippo Boys'. An immediate success, the comic was even delivered to Buckingham Palace tucked inside *The Times*. A rare headline marked this moment: 'The Popular Paper for Home and Palace.'

Soon all other comics on the market lowered their sights to the juvenile market, either creating new characters or converting old ones. The longest run was 'Weary Willie and Tired Tim', created for *Illustrated Chips* by the great postcard artist Tom Browne. These characters ran from 1896 to the last issue on 12 September 1953, always on the front page but not always, of course, by Tom Browne. He gave them up around 1900, well before they were subtly changed to appeal to children, still tramps but not the rather villainous pair they had been at their beginning.

Tom Browne may be said to have defined British comic style, with his clean, crisp artwork and slapstick action, uncluttered by the usual CROSSHATCHING so prevalent in this period. He had been inspired by the revolutionary artwork of cartoonist Phil May, and in turn inspired such successive comic artists as Percy Cocking (who took over Willie and Tim in 1908), Roy Wilson, Hugh McNeil, Robert Nixon and many others. Comics were divided into two classes, 'penny plain and twopence coloured': the penny comic was printed in black on coloured paper, and the twopenny comic was printed on white paper with full colour front pages. This held until World War II when paper shortage caused all comics to convert to the smaller half-tabloid size and raise their prices to twopence and threepence respectively.

Mickey Mouse Weekly (8 February 1936) burst on the British scene as a great surprise to the reading and publishing world. It was a large tabloid printed in photogravure – for the first time in comics – with four pages in full colour, the rest in halftones. It was a huge success, carrying strips starring WALT DISNEY's animation creations in American reprints and British-drawn originals. Top artists were Basil Reynolds (Skit and Skat), William Ward, a former animator (Donald Duck) and Wilfred Haughton, a cartoonist from the earlier *MICKEY MOUSE ANNUAL*, who painted the front pages. The comic also fathered the first Christmas specials (1936–9), sold at sixpence with 64 pages. This idea was revived after the War when almost every comic produced its own Christmas – and, later, summer – specials, a policy which continues to this day.

The late 1930s saw the birth of a new style of comic weekly. From D.C. Thomson of Dundee in Scotland came no. 1 of *THE DANDY* (4th December 1937), now on its way to breaking *Comic Cuts*' record as the longest-running comic. This half-tabloid 28-page comic introduced a 'new look' in characters and styling. Concentrating on working-class schoolchildren and rough, even violent, action, it introduced such varied heroes as Korky the Cat, who behaved like a human being, Desperate Dan, a super-tough cowboy who would eventually be tamed by his Aunt Aggie and her cow-pies, Invisible Dick, a schoolboy who sniffed a magic bottle to disappear and kick policemen where it hurts, and oddball freaks like Barney Boko, a tramp whose nose was six feet long. The comic was such a success that Thomson followed it with the similar BEANO (1938), *Magic* (1939) and many more. Harmsworth's old firm, the Amalgamated Press, sought to follow the Scottish format with the similarly styled *RADIO FUN* (1938) and *Knockout* (1939), and later reduced their tabloid *Playbox*, *Puck* and *Crackers* to the *Dandy* format.

The war years and the associated paper shortages reduced the traditional comics in size and circulation, but they were a boon to minor publishers. The leading producer was Gerald G. Swan, a market trader who, unable to import American comic-books, created his own. *New Funnies* (1940) was the first British original in the smaller comic-book format, selling at 64 pages for sixpence. Many other titles followed from Swan and his rivals, starting a whole new comic scene. After the war the influence of the American SUPERHERO was felt and many of the independent comic-books developed their own. None was more successful than *Marvelman* who, modelled on the American series *Captain Marvel*, ran from 1954 to 1963, 346 issues plus annuals – and the same run was scored by his clone, *Young Marvelman*.

The mid-century was marked by the creation of EAGLE, an outsize comic in photogravure colour designed by cleric REV. MARCUS MORRIS. Led by its sci-fi hero, *DAN DARE, PILOT OF THE FUTURE*, the comic was selling a million copies a week before another publisher took over the paper and decline set in.

The TELEVISION age brought a rash of related comics. *T.V. Fun* (1953–9) was for slightly older readers and featured stars from adult television: Arthur Askey, Jack Warner, Jimmy Edwards, Max Bygraves and 'Sally Barnes the tv charlady'. No great success, the comic converted to *T.V. Fan*, a romantic weekly, but that too soon collapsed. Other television comics were *T.V. Heroes* (1958–60), a monthly featuring non-copyright characters from such series as *ROBIN HOOD*, *Wyatt Earp* and *Daniel Boone*; *T.V. Land* (1960–2), a weekly starring *Larry the Lamb* (originally a great radio favourite), *IVOR THE ENGINE* and *Twizzle*; *T.V. Express* (1960–2), including W.E. Johns's pilot BIGGLES and some American features like *Gun Law*; *T.V. Features* (1960–1) with *William Tell*; and *T.V. Century 21* (1965–9). This latter was constructed around the popular Gerry Anderson SCIENCE FICTION series filmed with puppets, including *Stingray*, *Supercar*, *Thunderbirds* and *Captain Scarlet*, as well as *The Munsters* and other series from the United States. *T.V. Toyland* (1966–8) starred *Pinky and Perky* and *THE MAGIC ROUNDABOUT*; *T.V. Tornado* (1967–8) featured *The Saint* and some American series such as *Bonanza*; and *T.V. Action* (1972–3) reintroduced *DOCTOR WHO*, *Stingray* and added *Dad's Army*. Most of these comics had annuals, as well as summer and Christmas specials. In recent years British comics have concentrated on picturisations of contemporary television animation characters, running just so long as the parent series are popular.

In Australia, after a few earlier and spectacularly unsuccessful attempts, the industry sprang into life in 1940 when the importation of newsprint – and, with it, the popular American comics – was banned. The local creators and publishers moved in any (or all) of four directions as a response to the resultant yawning hole in the market: they produced clones of American comics (*Yarmak*, 1949, for example, was an imitation of TARZAN); parodies of those same comics (*Tripalong Hoppity*, 1944, and *Speed Umplestoop*, 1943, were parodies of *Hopalong Cassidy* and *Flash Gordon* respectively); carefully 'international' stories with no evidence of their Australian origin (e.g. *The Phantom Pirate*, 1946); or aggressively Australian strips with obviously local idiom, characterisation and setting (e.g. *Ben Barbary Bushranger*, 1947). This golden age of the Australian comic lasted until the introduction of television in 1956 and the lifting of the ban on the importation of newsprint in 1959, both of which had a devastating effect. These two blows killed the local comic industry which, despite a flirtation with the so-called 'underground comix' of the 1960s and a brief renaissance, especially of superhero comics, in 1987 and 1988, is now moribund. The great artists of past decades, amongst them Stanley Pitt, Emile Mercier and Monty Wedd, are now forgotten, and their work is found only in private collections and the closed stacks of large libraries. The days when a locally produced comic like *The Scorpion* (1954) could have a monthly circulation of some 100,000 copies in a population of seven million are a distant, nostalgic memory.

In America, periodicals for children emerged in the late 1700s, but it was not until a combination of market forces and improvements in technology and distribution combined to make it possible to publish a juvenile magazine at a profit in the 1820s that significant journals such as *The Juvenile Miscellany* (1826–36) and the long-lived and popular *Youth's Companion* (1827–1929) appeared.

Many of the early periodicals were religious in their orientation, either under denominational control or supported by non-sectarian groups like the American Sunday School Union or the American Temperance Union. But Samuel Griswold Goodrich's *Parley's Magazine: for Children and Youth* (1833–44) and his *Merry's Museum* (1841–70) presented educational features and amusing, realistic fiction. Two influential magazines with high standards appeared in the 1860s: *Our Young Folks: An Illustrated Monthly for Boys and Girls* (1865–73), edited by John Townsend Trowbridge, Lucy Larcom and 'Gail Hamilton' (Mary Abigail Dodge), and *The Riverside Magazine for Young People* (1867–70), edited by Horace Elisha Scudder. *The Riverside* had a large and elegant format and was brilliantly edited. One of its early contributors was Mary Mapes Dodge, whose correspondence with Scudder shows she shared many of his editorial views, though her superior ability to project a warm and engaging editorial persona was one of the factors which made for the greater success of her own *St Nicholas* (1873–1943). Scribner and Company, later the Century Company, publishers of *St Nicholas*, paid contributors generously and offered access to many distinguished artists and authors on their adult list as well the services of printer Theodore DeVinne and art director Alexander Drake. Authors whose work appeared in *St Nicholas* include Mark Twain, Frances Hodgson Burnett, Louisa May Alcott, John Townsend Trowbridge, Frank Stockton, Sarah Orne Jewett, Rebecca Harding Davis, and L. Frank Baum. Generally conceded to have been the best children's periodical ever produced in the United States, *St Nicholas* absorbed a number of its rivals and continued publication (though it never regained its primary place in American children's publishing after Dodge's death in 1905) until the 1940s.

The late 19th century also saw the rise of sensational magazines for young people such as *Frank Leslie's Boys' and Girls' Weekly* (1866–84), as well as a quality rival to *St Nicholas* in *Harper's Young People: An Illustrated Weekly* (1879–99). But literary magazines for children did not thrive after the turn of the century, giving way to journals directed toward readers of certain age groups, like *Seventeen*, or those interested in special subjects such as wildlife (*Ranger Rick's Nature Magazine*), or scouting (*The American Boy*), or designed to support school curricula. However, since 1973 Open Court Publishing Company has been producing *Cricket: The Magazine for Children* and a related family of magazines that maintain high literary and artistic standards in the *St Nicholas* tradition. Good sources for further information on American magazines for children are *Children's Periodicals of the United States* (1984), edited by R. Gordon Kelly, and Frank Luther Mott's *History of American Magazines* (1938–68). SRG, DG, JF

see also annuals; animated cartoons; 'The Big Five'

Commonwealth Annual see Empire Youth Annual

community songs Songs sung in youth hostels and clubs, on long coach journeys, and on many other communal occasions, including 'D'ye ken John Peel', 'Ten green bottles', 'Clementine', 'Old Macdonald had a farm', 'There was an old woman who swallowed a fly', and many others. They are part of most children's verbal experience and are, in particular, associated with the camp-fire sing-songs of Girl Guides and Boy Scouts (see Guiding and Scouting fiction). Covering a wide range of British and American folk and comic songs, action songs, national and student songs, their chief criterion is familiarity. The standard collection is still Sid G. Hedges' *Youth Sing Book* (1945). IO

Compleet Molesworth, The see Ronald Searle; Geoffrey Willans; see also school stories

Complete Nonsense of Edward Lear, The (1947) An edition, edited by Holbrook Jackson, which includes all of Lear's limericks, the longer verses, prose stories, alphabets and comic botany. It is a seminal work which utilises puns, spoonerisms and mis-pronunciations, invents words, and ultimately challenges the boundaries of accepted language use to establish new freedoms for future writers. JL

Conlon-McKenna, Marita 1956– Dublin-born author whose work has been translated into many languages and who has received awards in Ireland and abroad. Conlon-McKenna sees herself very much as a storyteller, and the outstanding feature of her work is its strong narrative thrust. She has written three novels in the FAMINE series. Apart from this trilogy, her other works are set in different places and at different times. *The Blue Horse* (1993) is concerned with a modern-day travelling family, and *Safe Harbour* (1994) is set in London and Wicklow during World War II. In *No Goodbye* (1994) the reactions of a family unexpectedly deserted by their mother are given from the separate viewpoints of each of the four children. Conlon-McKenna has written the text for two PICTUREBOOKS, illustrated by Christopher Coady, *Little Star* (1993) and *The Very Last Unicorn* (1994). VC

Conly, Jane Leslie 1947– American writer whose first two books, *Racso and the Rats of NIMH* (1986) and *R-T, Margaret, and the Rats of NIMH* (1990), follow the adventures of a race of super-intelligent rats. The rats first appeared in a book by her father, ROBERT C. O'BRIEN, *MRS. FRISBY AND THE RATS OF NIMH* (1972). Conly's books continue her father's emphasis on the theme of social responsibility while weaving in new characters with more complex personal problems. Racso, who appears in both books, is Conly's most distinctive FANTASY character, an impulsive, boastful, vain, yet charming and warm-hearted young rat. Conly's subsequent novels have turned to realism, with a focus on character development. *Crazy Lady!* (1993) features a mentally ill woman and other members of an impoverished urban neighbourhood. In *Trout Summer* (1995), Conly evokes rural and suburban settings as she portrays a family that is redefining itself after a divorce. Conly has earned critical acclaim for her engaging, thought-provoking stories. In both her FANTASY and realistic novels, she creates nuanced psychological landscapes that involve the reader intimately with the characters' thoughts and feelings as they evolve throughout the story. Conly's books have garnered many awards and citations, most notably the Newbery Honour award for *Crazy Lady!*. CV

Connor, Ralph [Charles William Gordon] 1860–1937 Canadian novelist. Born in Ontario, Canada, of Scottish immigrants, Connor was educated for the Presbyterian ministry at the University of Toronto. In 1890 he undertook mission work for three years in the frontier camps of western Canada. On the basis of these experiences he created many action-packed melodramas that depicted robust clergymen saving the souls of rough frontiersmen through a struggle between good and evil. His first three novels, *Black Rock* (1898), *Sky Pilot* (1899) and *The Man from Glengarry* (1901), were international bestsellers that combined simple morality and violence in a formula of 'muscular Christianity' that projected the Canadian West as the locale of the nation's destiny. Of the 19 novels Connor wrote, *Glengarry Schooldays* (1902) was most popular with its scenes of his early childhood life, the idealised depiction of pioneer activities, and the nostalgic portrayal of virtuous characters modelled on his parents. Connor's escapist romances matched the mood of the times and filled the country's need for a powerful Canadian myth. DAC

conservation see ECOLOGY IN CHILDREN'S BOOKS; see also ANIMALS IN FICTION

Constant Tin Soldier, The see HANS CHRISTIAN ANDERSEN; P.J. LYNCH; MUSIC AND STORY

Contes de ma mère l'Oye (1697) Collection of tales ascribed to CHARLES PERRAULT (1628–1703), originally published as *Histoires ou contes du temps passé: avec des Moralitez*. The collection contains the first known written versions of *BLUEBEARD*, *CINDERELLA*, *Diamonds and Toads*, *HOP O MY THUMB*, *LITTLE RED RIDING HOOD*, *PUSS IN BOOTS*, *Riquet of the Tuft* and *SLEEPING BEAUTY*. The tales were told in prose but concluded with a brief 'Moralité' in verse.

The origins of the tales are ambiguous. Some scholars believe Perrault drew upon Italian and French writings, but no such sources have been traced for three of the tales. Others suggest that he gleaned the stories from peasant women working as servants in Paris, or that he might have remembered hearing them in childhood. It is possible that he was told the stories by the nurse of his own son, Pierre, whose name appears as the author of the *Contes* after a dedication to 'Mademoiselle', the 19-year-old Elizabeth Charlotte d'Orléans, niece to Louis XIV. Pierre was 17 in 1697, and it is just feasible that he compiled the collection; however, contemporary evidence suggests that in Parisian literary circles, Charles Perrault was widely assumed to be the author.

The tales probably had two, or even three, intended audiences: the court and the elegant salons of Paris, where the affectation of rustic simplicity was much in vogue; the children of wealthy families; and the Academy, where Perrault offered the tales to his fellow Academicians as evidence of the superiority of modern stories over those of classical authors – ammunition in the furious 'Quarrel of the Ancients and the Moderns' in which Perrault was embroiled for many years.

The first English translation by Robert Samber, entitled *Histories or Tales of Past Times. Told by Mother Goose* (1729) was well received by a British public already familiar with tales invented (rather than retold) by the Countess d'Aulnoy, translated into English some 20 years earlier. The name of MOTHER GOOSE, associated in France with traditional tales and rhymes, had appeared in the frontispiece illustration decorating Perrault's edition. In England and the United States, 'Mother Goose' frequently became linked with NURSERY RHYMES rather than prose tales – JOHN NEWBERY adopted her name for a collection of rhymes published in 1765, for example – and Perrault's stories are usually published as 'FAIRY TALES'.

Some editions of the tales include three verse narratives, first published by Perrault in 1695, including a version of 'Patient Griselda' which, like Chaucer, Perrault probably encountered in Boccaccio. Perrault's retellings have often fused with oral versions and been re-cast by storytellers (notably the GRIMM BROTHERS) to suit the needs and tastes of other cultures and other generations. Perhaps the stories found their most dramatic illustrator in Gustave Doré's *Fairy Tales Told Again* (1872).

Often the tales appear separately rather than within the complete collection. They are so widely known that writers can assume children will know the essential storylines, and so the tales have been reworked in countless versions from pop-ups to pantomime and parody. However, it may be that such retellings as the immensely popular *Revolting Rhymes* of ROALD DAHL (1982) delight their readers with their undercutting wit at the expense of the embedded power which fuelled the original tales. GPF

Contes des feés see FAIRY TALES

continuous narrative Term used in PICTUREBOOK illustration to show one character portrayed in more than one place, and possibly in more than one setting, across a single picture plane. JD

Cool Web, The: The Pattern of Children's Reading (1977) Edited by MARGARET MEEK, Aidan Warlow and Griselda Barton, this distinguished work has made a major contribution to the study of children's literature in Britain and has become a classic text. The editors offer a critical synthesis of a number of different ideas and approaches from critics and children's authors. They have drawn together observations and insights which have convincingly affected the status of children's literature as an academic discipline and helped to lay the foundations for the increasing development of critical theory and children's literature courses in higher education. EAG

Coolidge, Olivia E(nsor) British writer of juvenile historical BIOGRAPHIES. Born in London, Coolidge was the daughter of historian and journalist Sir Robert Charles Kirkwood. After studying at Oxford she taught English and Classics. Coolidge is best known for her biographies, including the award-winning *The King of Men* (1966) and her Newbery Honor Award winner, *Men of Athens* (1963). Trying to build her works on facts, but not to the extent that they might overwhelm an interesting story, Coolidge believed that good biographies should concern themselves with the value of a hero's achievements in the effect his or her deeds might have on others. Her works – which include *Cromwell's Head* (1955), *Edith Wharton* (1964), *Tom Paine, Revolutionary* (1969), and *Gandhi* (1971) – try to simplify and clarify without reducing the subject's life through sentimentality or by making it appear too one-dimensional. Also interested in myth, she produced a number of collections, including *Greek Myths* (1949) and *Legends of the North* (1951), a collection of Norse mythology, illustrated by Edouard Sandoz. SCWA

see also: CLASSICAL MYTHOLOGY

Frontispiece by Addie Ledyard for *Nine Little Goslings* by Susan Coolidge.

Coolidge, Susan [Sarah Chauncey Woolsey] 1835–1905 American novelist, writer and translator, best known for the *KATY* SERIES. Born in Cleveland, Ohio, she was the oldest daughter in a cultured, intellectual family closely connected with Yale University where her uncle Theodore Dwight Woolsey was President. Like her contemporary LOUISA MAY ALCOTT, she was a nurse in the American Civil War. Unlike Alcott, Coolidge was comfortably settled, moving permanently to Newport, Rhode Island, after her father's death in 1870. All her books for girls and most of her flood of poems, essays, belles lettres and magazine articles appeared between 1871 and 1894. The first two *Katy* books, *What Katy Did* (1872) and *What Katy Did At School* (1873), are strongly autobiographical, reflecting a robust energetic girl leading her younger siblings in their ploys in the large garden of their New Haven home. *What Katy Did At School* derives from Coolidge's own schooldays at Mrs Hubbard's Boarding School in Hanover, New Hampshire. Coolidge allowed Katy a freedom Jo March would have envied. *What Katy Did Next* (1886) and its sequel *In The High Valley* (1891) become less successful as Katy grows up. Coolidge wrote 12 other books for girls: *The New Year's Bargain* (1871), *Mischief's Thanksgiving* (1874), *Nine Little Goslings* (1875), *For Summer Afternoons* (1876), *Eyebright* (1879), *A Guernsey Lily* (1880), *Cross Patch* (1881), *A Round Dozen* (1883), *A Little Country Girl* (1885), *Just Sixteen* (1889), *The Barberry Bush* (1893) and *Not Quite Eighteen* (1894). None of her 16 books is in print in America and only the *Katy* books are available in Britain. Readers may have outgrown Katy the reformed tomboy as they have not outgrown the eternally rebellious Jo March. KP

Coombs, Patricia 1926– American illustrator and author of PICTUREBOOKS. Born in Los Angeles, Coombs moved frequently during childhood. Although she earned undergraduate and graduate degrees in English, family demands left little time for writing until her children entered school. Her first book, *Dorrie's Magic* (1962), received accolades in the *New York Times Book Review*. That encouragement and a supportive editor prompted Coombs to continue the series about the young witch Dorrie and her cat Gink, who live with Big Witch and Cook. Dorrie's curiosity may get her into trouble, but several times her ingenuity and courage save the day for Witchville residents. Coombs's other picturebooks often include FAIRY TALE or FOLKTALE elements. For example, in *Mouse Café* (1972), a *New York Times* Best Illustrated Book, a beautiful young mouse is driven from home by her mean sisters and tormented by her fellow waitresses before marrying rich Mr Hodges. In *Molly Mullet* (1975), the heroine plays a non-traditional role by saving her village from an ogre despite her father's and the king's lack of confidence in a 'sneezley, wheezley girl'. Coombs has also illustrated picturebooks by other authors, but her most enduring work undoubtedly will be her popular series about the plucky young witch. KKP

Cooney, Barbara 1917–2000 Much-loved American writer and illustrator. Born in Maine, this versatile illustrator perfected the scratch-board technique in *The American Speller: An Adaptation of Noah Webster's Blue-Backed Speller* (1961) but prefers illustrating in full colour. She illustrated over 100 books, often dealing with the themes of self-reliance, the search for beauty and the naturalness of ageing. She received the ALA's CALDECOTT MEDAL for *Chanticleer and the Fox* (1958), an adaptation of CHAUCER's *The Nun's Priest's Tale*. In 1980 she received the CALDECOTT AWARD for DONALD HALL's *Ox-Cart Man* (1979), for which she painted on wood using a technique reminiscent of American primitives to depict a 19th-century New Hampshire farmer making his annual trek to market.

Cooney received many other awards, including the 1983 American Book Award for *Miss Rumphius* (1982), in which she combined New England scenes with the interior of her grandmother's house to illustrate the life of 'the lupine lady'. Miss Rumphius was given this affectionate title because of her habit of sowing lupine (lupin) seeds throughout the community to make the world more beautiful. Its sequel was *Island Boy* (1988), which Cooney believed was her best work; the trilogy was completed with *Hattie and the Wild Waves* (1990), another picturebook biography.

Cooney received the Silver Medallion from the University of Southern Mississippi (1975); the Smith College Medal (1976); and in 1989 the Maine Library Association created the Lupine Award in her memory. Cooney's work reflects her skills both as an artist and as a book designer. It must have come as a shock to her to find that a respected reference work on children's writers recorded her as having died in 1994. In fact, she went on to illustrate Michael Beyard's *Emily* (1993) – based on an incident in the life of EMILY DICKINSON – *Only Opal: The Diary of a Young Girl* (1994) by Opal Whitely, and her own *Eleanor* (1996), a story about Eleanor Roosevelt's early life. Her last work was *Basket Moon* (1999). DJH

Cooney, Caroline B. see *POINT* SERIES

Cooper, Helen 1963– British illustrator. Though she has been writing and illustrating children's PICTUREBOOKS since 1986, it was in 1993 with the publication of two remarkable picturebooks, *The Bear under the Stairs* and *The House Cat*, that Helen Cooper came to public attention. In the first she explores fears and fantasies with great sensitivity and visual flair, and in the second she documents, with understated side-swipes at class difference, the astonishing journeys of a cat, both to and from its new home. *The Baby who Wouldn't Go to Bed* (1996), winner of the KATE GREENAWAY MEDAL is possibly even more inventive with its story of bedtime resistance amid a surreal nursery wonderland. *Pumpkin Soup* (1998) – a deceptively simple story of friendship, patience and loyalty, set in a richly coloured magical landscape – won its author a second Kate Greenaway Award. JAG

Cooper, James Fenimore see *LEATHER-STOCKING TALES*; F.O.C. DARLEY; ROBINSONNADES

Cooper, Mary see *TOMMY THUMB'S SONG BOOK*; *TOMMY THUMB'S PRETTY SONG BOOK*; see also ILLUSTRATION IN CHILDREN'S BOOKS; NURSERY RHYMES

Cooper, Susan (Mary) 1935– British author living in America best known for *THE DARK IS RISING* sequence; other novels include *Dawn of Fear* (1970), set during World War II, and *Seaward* (1983), a complex FANTASY and the most difficult of all her novels. More recently she has written *The Boggart* (1993), an entertaining story about a family who inherit a castle in Scotland with a boggart which makes its way back to Canada with them. The mayhem it causes there produces a humorous novel which successfully combines Cooper's skill in writing fantasy with a convincing portrayal of family life. Her *King of Shadows* (1999) was shortlisted for the CARNEGIE AWARD. KA

Cope, Wendy 1945– English poet whose first adult title, *Making Cocoa for Kingsley Amis* (1986), shot into the bestselling list as the literary hit of the year. Cope spent many years as a primary teacher in London with a specialist interest in music before becoming a full-time writer. She has written and edited collections for young readers, and she has reviewed children's books on a regular basis. *Twiddling Your Thumbs* (1988), illustrated by Sally Kindberg, contains delightful finger rhymes for under-sixes. Excellent edited volumes include *The Orchard Book of Funny Poems* (1993). Cope is highly regarded as a humorist, but her much anthologised poems often carry a serious message; she is especially noted for her witty use of irony and parody. MCCS

copyright see PUBLISHING AND PUBLISHERS

Coral Island: A Tale of the Pacific Island see R.M. BALLANTYNE; see also ADVENTURE STORIES; *THE LORD OF THE FLIES*; ROBINSONNADES

Corbett, W.J. see *PENTECOST* TRILOGY

Coretta Scott King Award see APPENDIX

Corlett, William 1938– British novelist best known for his *Magician's House* eco-fantasy quartet and *Now and Then* (1995), winner of the Dillons First Fiction Award, an adult exploration of the unspoken gay subtext of his *Gate of Eden* trilogy (1974–5), which was written for young adults. Born in Darlington, County Durham, England, Corlett trained at the Royal Academy of Dramatic Art, first working as an actor and playwright. Award-winning TELEVISION scripts and adaptations of children's novels such as *THE MACHINE-GUNNERS* followed, work which is reflected in the complex experimental mixed-narrative technique of Corlett's adolescent fiction and in his acute ear for dialogue. His use of letters, journals, scripts, essays and cutting and mixing introduces alternative viewpoints and challenges for readers experiencing the intense emotional crises or choices facing his central characters. In *The Secret Line* (1988), these devices encapsulate troubled Joanna's inner inventions and outer realities as she learns to accept her 'mixed skin' and family, choosing truth and community, not FANTASY and racial self-isolation. A concern with betrayal and its effects, with ensuring the survival of civilising values, with finding one's identity, and with parallel or psychological time underpins Corlett's fiction, providing his adolescent work with a far bleaker edge than his quartet for younger readers, *Magician's House*.

This sequence (1990–92) is a confident, inventive interweaving of contemporary family tensions, alliances and concerns with holiday ADVENTURE STORY, TIME-SLIP FANTASY and ancient magic. Its origins lie in the classic conflict between the forces of light and dark, unusually played out through Stephen Tyler, a 16th-century alchemist, and his assistant Morden. This conflict erupts into the present when the three Constant children visit their uncle and his partner at the magician's house in Golden Valley. Stephen, who is dying in his own time, chooses the children to be his apprentices in the 'Great task' – countering greed (the destruction of Golden Valley for financial gain) with environmental awareness and true moral alchemy. Despite the quartet's contemporary and ecological concerns it also contains timeless fantasy ingredients with its remote setting on the Welsh borders, the Tudor house and its secret room, the alchemists' ability to slip through time in animal form, the children's quest and the palpable sense of unease and danger conveyed through the natural world by snow, darkness and beast fighting beast. Corlett's concern for moral alchemy occasionally verges on the polemical in Stephen's homilies. This aside, the quartet is consummately composed and tautly paced as the children discover that their greatest hope for success lies in themselves and richly repay the magician's trust. EMH

Cormier, Robert 1925–2000 American novelist and journalist, Cormier is one of the most pessimistic of 20th-century children's writers. While it has never been an unassailable convention that all children's stories should end happily, the common understanding up to the 1970s was that there should always be at least some element of hope and moral justice at the conclusion of a children's story. Leaving young readers with a sense of bleak injustice and general despair has not been considered generally desirable in the post-war western world. But Cormier challenged such attitudes with his powerful and disturbing teenage novel *The Chocolate War* (1974). In this story, the playground bully, working closely with a corrupt school administration, ends up triumphant while the one pupil brave enough to stand up to him is savagely beaten, with no indication that his particular stand will ever be vindicated. While many critics disliked this book and its message, many young readers seemed to find it much to their taste, often writing to the author to tell him so. With so many other writers to turn to when they wanted a more upbeat message, children seemed to want at least one author who echoed any pessimistic feelings they might sometimes have about life.

Keeping pace with this feeling, succeeding novels grew if anything more gloomy. *I am the Cheese* (1977) is a story about a boy, somewhat incongruously suffering political interrogation, who discovers that he has been betrayed by his own manipulative father. Deprived of all hope, the boy's mind finally gives way. *After the First Death* (1979) tells the story of a hijacked busload of children. The teenage terrorist at the heart of the action begins to establish a relationship with the young woman in charge of the children. Yet by the end of the story she is shot dead and the terrorist, slightly wounded, is already planning his next outrage. *The Bumblebee Flies Anyway* (1983) has the even bleaker setting of a harshly run hospital ward for children with terminal illnesses. Total nihilism is avoided, however, when some of these young patients plan to speed up their deaths by making a final, boldly defiant gesture. Out of utter hopelessness, some sort of hope is finally restored. Following next, *Beyond the Chocolate War* (1985) also marks a retreat from pessimism, with Cormier urging the case for non-violence and the importance of dissent. But *Fade* (1988), a harrowing story of child abuse, shows a return to the despair of former novels.

Cormier is not a great writer, but certainly an effective one. He has a gift for pacey narrative and deft characterisation. His insistence on the vulnerability of innocence faced by the power of evil is not an attractive message but was a necessary one at a time when children's literature still took a rose-tinted attitude to most of life's harsher realities. Since Cormier started writing, other British and American authors have also written bleak, occasionally despairing stories. This greater diversity of mood and message does not please everyone, but older child readers often seem to relish such stories along with other types of reading. NT

Corrin, Ruth 1939– New Zealand author of FAMILY NOVELS and PICTUREBOOKS. Corrin moved into writing through *Grampa's Place* (1985), her widely acclaimed radio series for pre-schoolers. In early books, all driven by issues, passive protagonists suffer lives in fractured families. In the thematically complex novel *Secrets* (1990), which confronts incest, an absent father, wealthy neglect, and honesty, the author uses more thoughtful characters who do investigate choices. In *Get Real* (1996), the hero braves floods, helps release his father from jail and establishes solid friendships at school. Corrin here deftly blends thinking, action and social issues. In 1990 and 1992 Corrin was awarded major writing grants. MJH

Cotton, John see *MILK FOR BABES*; see also *THE NEW-ENGLAND PRIMER*; PUBLISHING AND PUBLISHERS

Cotton, Nathaniel 1705–88 Minor English writer, doctor and manager of a mental asylum. Cotton cared kindly for the poet WILLIAM COWPER, who suffered from mental health problems. He wrote *Visions in Verse* (1751) which, though 'reprinted more than a dozen times during the next half century' (OPIE, 1973), now seems worthy but dull, offering little light relief to young readers. MCCS

Count Duckula see ANIMATED CARTOONS

counting books Learning to count is one of the earliest lessons, alongside the alphabet and NURSERY RHYMES. Along with ALPHABET BOOKS, counting books offer the opportunity to teach important cultural knowledge through book-sharing. Indeed, counting rhymes such as 'One, two, buckle my shoe' often form a large part of a very young child's first encounters with strongly 'tuned' language. Counting books can be found in a wide variety of forms; they may be collections of number rhymes, labelling books – where the aim is merely to promote the notion of one-to-one correspondence – or they may be far greater in complexity, using narrative devices as well as mathematical concepts.

The recitation of numbers has an inherent rhythmic quality, and it is possibly because of this that so many counting books use rhyme. One of the earliest known examples is *Marmaduke Multiply's Merry Method of Making Minor Mathematicians* (1817). Through the use of somewhat contrived rhyming couplets this book aimed to support children in the learning of their multiplication tables, for example 'Seven times 10 *are* 70, We're sailing very pleasantly.' The appeal of the book was increased by its attractive hand-coloured

ILLUSTRATIONS. In the middle of the 19th century a number of counting books were published as TOY BOOKS. These included *Amusing Addition* and *Amusing Subtraction* (both c. 1850). Both of these used rhyme as a device not only for making the text memorable, but also for involving the readers in RIDDLES or encouraging them to count from the illustrations. This verse, from *Amusing Addition*, shows how humour and problem solving were seen as a natural part of learning:

> Now see if you can pussy spell,
> With letters only three;
> Ah, that is right, you've done it well,
> For 'tis just C A T.

Jacko's Merry Method of Learning the Pence Table (c. 1850) used a device which is still commonplace today – embedding the counting within a narrative. The counting was also linked to the illustrations, five shillings being represented by sixty buttons on a gentleman's jacket, each one being worth a penny. The author thus makes an abstract concept more accessible by linking new knowledge to familiar images and understandings.

Modern counting books tend to concentrate not on the multiplication tables, addition or subtraction, but rather on cardinal numbers and the development of one-to-one correspondence. Exactly how authors and illustrators try to achieve these goals varies considerably. Some methods are apparently simple and straightforward, such as the photographic work of Fiona Pragoff. In *How Many?* her work is of exceptional clarity, and her subjects so carefully chosen that there is much to discuss with the young reader. Her book includes 20 toes, one very old-fashioned key and 15 buttons. Another excellent example of a photographic counting book is Jane Miller's *Farm Counting Book* (1990), with similarly uncluttered backgrounds, numerals, and a simple explanatory text. Counting books using the farm as a theme have always been popular, possibly because the ability to name familiar domestic animals has traditionally been considered important for young children. *The Farm*, published by LADYBIRD BOOKS in 1958, had knowledgeable illustrations and rhythmic text, written by a member of the UK National Farmer's Union, and no doubt supported many children of that generation in learning to count because of its affordability and easy availability.

More recently, many PICTUREBOOK authors have contributed to the development of counting books both as a sophisticated genre in its own right and also as a bridge to other texts. MAURICE SENDAK wrote and illustrated *One was Johnny* (1962) and *Seven Little Monsters* (1975). Both these books used rhyme and rhythm to support both the counting and the reading of the text. Readers familiar with Sendak's other work may recognise some of the monsters. *1, 2, 3, to the Zoo* (1968) by ERIC CARLE is an excellent introduction not only to counting, but also to Carle's particular style of illustration, with a small engine chugging through the book, towing trucks containing the number of animals already counted in previous pages.

COLIN MCNAUGHTON'S *1, 2, 3, of Things* (1976) is not for young children alone, but would also appeal to older readers who share its sense of humour. Entries include 'One on the run from a vast cream bun' and (the last entry) 'Fifty thousand and eighty four could not believe just what they saw'. Visual humour is also employed in *One Bear at Bedtime* (1987) by MICK INKPEN, in which a young boy has difficulties with various animals, all of whom seem to want to prevent him going to bed; hidden in each of the pictures are tiny caterpillars which the author explicitly asks the reader to search for, thus involving them in more counting. Such counting books view the child as a problem-solving learner, using curiosity to their advantage. This curiosity combined with a desire to be a 'knower of things' is used to good effect by Bert Kitchen in *Animal Numbers* (1987); the reader is invited into the counting game by use of a riddle: 'Answer me this if you're in the mood, How many babies in each mother's brood?' The following pages combine illustrations and numerals in a stunning fashion – the woodpecker drills into the upright of the number four, whilst its babies nest within it. The thirst for further knowledge is rewarded at the end of the book, with names and simple facts about each animal illustrated.

There are many counting books which attempt to involve the reader not only through the counting, which is an inevitable part of the reading, but also through the use of pictorial or written narrative devices. In *Anno's Counting Book* (1977), MITSUMASA ANNO portrays a landscape which changes depending on the time of day, seasons or year. Unusually, this book begins with zero, showing only a cold winter landscape – no village. The ending is magical – the twelfth month with a Christmas scene showing twelve reindeer in the sky. The reader is involved in discovering just how many sets of each number are present on each page so that a desire to count is built into the construction of the book. *1 Hunter* (1982) by PAT HUTCHINS tells the story of a walk through the jungle; the words tell only half the story – the two trees past which the hunter stalks turn out to be the legs of elephants. The ENDPAPERS of this book add to the invitation to count, as many eyes peek from a wide variety of hiding-places. In SATOSHI KITAMURA'S *When Sheep Cannot Sleep* (1987), the reader has to learn how to do the counting without the help of the narrative text, which tells the story of Woolly, an insomniac sheep. The subtitle 'a counting book' appears enigmatic when the book is first opened, as none of the reader's expectations of ordinary counting books are met.

Counting books do not have to be completely original in order to be effective. Many picturebook versions of traditional songs and rhymes support the reader not only through the familiarity of the rhyme but also by offering a variety of interpretations. *Ten in a Bed* is one such example. In the version illustrated by Mary Rees (1987), the rhyme is excellently interpreted by illustrations which tell a story of far greater complexity than the words. The endpapers provide the beginning and end to a narrative which will appeal to all children, with the naughty 'little one' being dealt with most effectively. In *Ten in the Bed* (1990) and *Ten out of Bed* (1996) by Penny Dale the story is retold from the point of view of a child who has far too many soft toys in the bed. In both versions a simple counting song is turned into a complex narrative by the addition of pictures.

Another song to have been interpreted in a variety of ways is 'Over in the Meadow'. It is a counting rhyme that has many qualities, not least the atmosphere of contentment that pervades it. It has been interpreted by various authors including EZRA JACK KEATS. The most recent version illustrated by Louise Voce is charming, and the rhyme benefits from the humorous nature of her drawings. *Over on the Farm* (1995) by Christopher Gunson respects the qualities of the traditional version but uses new animals and settings, for example 'Over in the forest on an oak leaf floor . . .'. The adaptation of the song 'The ants came marching . . .' has resulted in two particularly memorable counting books. In *Amazing Anthony Ant* (1993) this simple song has been imaginatively transformed into a picturebook of incredible complexity. Ants march across the page, as the verses dictate, but there are also puzzles to solve and puns to enjoy, including 'The Beetles in Concert in Cavern Club Close'. This is a counting book which can be savoured for many years. In *One by One, Garth Pig's Rain Song* (1994), MARY RAYNER uses the same song to tell the story of Garth Pig and his fellow piglets' journey home, and how they avoid the impending thunderstorm. The narrative told in the song is augmented by the illustrations, showing the adventures of the various piglets.

The universality of number is reflected in many counting books. In *One Smiling Grandma* (1992), the setting is the Caribbean. This is apparent not only in the illustrations, but also in the creatures and objects to be counted: 'Three hummingbirds sipping nectar sweet, four steel drums tapping out the beat.' In *Emeka's Gift* (1995) by Ifeoma Onyefulu the objects to be counted are shown through photographs of a Nigerian village which illustrate the story of Emeka, a little boy from the Igala tribe. This book offers much information about life in an African village, as well as the opportunity to develop number skills. A more familiar domestic situation is used in MOLLY BANG's *Ten, Nine, Eight* (1983) when, starting with ten toes, a father begins a countdown until his daughter is in bed. In *Feast for Ten* (1993), by Cathryn Falwell, an African American family are depicted shopping for and preparing a sumptuous feast. This book is unusual in that it encourages the reader to count to ten twice. The counting is well supported by the use of clear COLLAGE illustrations and effective rhyming couplets – 'two pumpkins for pie, three chickens to fry'.

Counting books are more than concept books – they are valuable not just as a way to learn numbers, but also for teaching many valuable lessons about reading and authorship. HB

Country Child, The (1931) This evocative book by the British author ALISON UTTLEY describes the yearly cycle of life on a farm at the end of the 19th century. It is also a portrait (perhaps a self-portrait) of an imaginative child who is solitary but not lonely, finding friends and enemies everywhere from the moon who lights her walk home in the winter to the stuffed fox who menaces her climb to bed each night. This book differs from others Uttley wrote about the countryside of her childhood: we see, hear, taste and touch through the senses of a child encountering her present environment, rather than seeing through the mind's eye of an adult recalling her past. AMN

see also *LITTLE BROWN MOUSE* SERIES; *LITTLE GREY RABBIT* SERIES; *A TRAVELLER IN TIME*

Country Rhimes for Children (1686) Collection of poems by JOHN BUNYAN. Bunyan's 'Book for Boys and Girls' is probably the first book of poetry for children in England. The preface defines Bunyan's intended audience and his didactic aim and method: to save the souls of children of all ages by 'playing the fool' or writing about things that interest children in a childlike way. The form used is that of the EMBLEM BOOK: the poems are descriptions of everyday things with accompanying morals, called 'comparisons'. The rhyme and metre, as well as the comparisons, are sometimes rather forced. ML

courtesy books Advice manuals, often written in the form of dialogues, offering models of the attitudes, behaviour and skills needed for social advancement. The form became popular in the later Middle Ages, when it was associated particularly with training for positions in noble households and at court, as in the most famous of all courtesy books, Castiglione's *Il Cortegiano* [The Courtier]. However, the genre outlived its feudal origins, flourishing in the 18th century when courtesy books addressed a whole range of topics associated with manners, decorum and the nurture of children. Many were produced by well-known publishers of children's books. DWh

Cousins, Lucy 1964– British illustrator whose creation, Maisy, is set to become a best-loved character in children's books. She appeared first in *Maisy Goes Swimming* (1990), a novelty book where the paper engineering is intrinsic to the narrative. Maisy has to be divested of each item of her clothes before she can go swimming. The simple black-outlined mouse and the flat bold colour won Maisy instant recognition, and there are now a score of *Maisy* books and a range of merchandising. Cousins has received various prizes, special mentions and commendations for her work. JAG

see also MOVABLE BOOKS

cover art The cover of a book is much more than a protective jacket. It should provide an ideogram for the theme of the book. In a simple visual statement it must aesthetically interpret the feelings, themes, atmosphere, genre and characters. It is the symbol which represents for the reader all that the book says in terms of its ideas, emotion, atmosphere and values or 'moral view'. Moreover, it is a vital element in the selling, marketing and promotion of the book to its readers. The cover, in competition with the many advertising images which assault the reader's senses every day, has to present an arresting image to entice the attention of younger readers. The relationship between the text and this image must be intimate and subtle. The cover has become virtually a poster advertising a book's contents. While describing the process involved in the creation of symbolic reference for the cover of GARY CREW's *No Such Country*, GREGORY ROGERS, asked why he did not provide an 'artist's note' on the inside book jacket to explain the illustrative symbols he had used on the cover, replied that there already was one – the text.

The cover has changed dramatically since its inception as a purely protective dustjacket in the 19th century. Embossed spines and lurid covers advertised popular favourites, such as ETHEL TURNER's famous stories of family life published by Ward Lock from the 1890s, but World War I and the Depression arrested the development of children's book marketing. The poor quality of reproduction during the 1940s began to improve dramatically after World War II, with the growth of paperbacks, improved printing techniques, and the availability of more subtle and sophisticated reproductive media, changing covers from the matt-finish wrap-around jackets illustrated by earlier artists such as SHIRLEY HUGHES, BRIAN WILDSMITH, CHARLES KEEPING, NOELA YOUNG, Walter Stackpool, MARGARET HORDER and WALTER CUNNINGHAM to the eye-catching artwork we know today.

In the 1960s Hughes, Wildsmith and Keeping were major contributors to cover art in Britain; Shirley Hughes's cover for *THE SECRET GARDEN* (1970) reflects the garden and characters in a free-flowing style, while Keeping's cover for ALAN GARNER's *THE OWL SERVICE* (1967) reflects the geometric designs popular in the 1960s. The later practice of using less well-known illustrators to design book covers – who have subsequently often become famous in their own right – can be seen through the covers of ROALD DAHL's books. Today QUENTIN BLAKE is especially associated with Dahl's work, his quick humorous line-and-colour drawings appropriately reflecting the plots and characters; but other illustrators, notably BABETTE COLE, FAITH JACQUES and TONY ROSS, have also illustrated Dahl covers. MICHAEL FOREMAN's cover for *Charlie and the Great Glass Elevator* (1986) exemplifies the illustrator's gentle style and use of blue tones, while EMMA CHICHESTER CLARK's design for *James and the Giant Peach* (1990) suggests the spiky characters of the narrative.

Publishers sometimes use a common design format for the covers of an author. The books of PHILIPPA PEARCE, reissued by Puffin in the 1990s, all have the same design – a royal blue border with the author's name written as a cartouche within a box, along with the title. Her covers have been illustrated by two different artists, LOUISE BRIERLEY and Stephen Lambert; Brierley's cover for *Tom's Midnight Garden* (1993) has a dreamlike quality richly suggestive of Pearce's theme, while Lambert's cover for *The Battle of Bubble and Squeak* (1994) is similar in style but uses a bolder palette of colour. CAROLINE BINCH has also illustrated some of Pearce's work, as well as the cover of *The Friends* (1988) by ROSA GUY, this last showing how artists are now capable of representing black characters in realistic and positive ways. Kaye Hodges has illustrated ANNE FINE's books; Bruce Hogarth and Alun Hood were responsible for MARGARET MAHY's dramatic YOUNG ADULT covers. In the United States, significant artists include the experienced jacket artist, Wendell Minor, who describes the demand for visually arresting covers as 'attention deficit design'. Other American artists are Mike Wimmer, DAVID SHANNON, THOMAS LOCKER and Troy Howell. The latter created the covers for Brian Jacques's *REDWALL* SERIES.

Some writers have worked closely with particular illustrators who contribute both to the cover and within the text. The relationship between MICHAEL MORPURGO and CHRISTIAN BIRMINGHAM has been very successful; Birmingham's work for *The Butterfly Lion* (1996) and *The Wreck of the Zanzibar* (1995) is a delight, as the covers reflect scenes from the stories in a gentle and appealing way to engage the reader's imagination. JILL PATON WALSH's partnership with ALAN MARKS has been an equal success: Marks's line-and-colour illustrations for *Matthew and the Sea Singer* (1992) and *Thomas and the Tinners* (1995) show energy and movement, and give a sense that the characters are alive. Some artists have become entirely identified with a particular writer; in Australia, PAUL JENNINGS's works were until recently always jacketed with Keith McEwan's ILLUSTRATIONS and had a recognisable style, as have MORRIS GLEITZMAN's covers done by KIM GAMBLE. Some authors, however, prefer to have a different artist chosen according to the demands of each title. Other prominent Australian cover artists in recent years have included Lorraine Hannay, JANE TANNER, David Wong, KERRY ARGENT and Anne Spudvilas. GREGORY ROGERS, winner of the 1995 Kate Greenaway Medal, is one of Australia's most prolific cover artists, having designed hundreds of covers, but he only came to prominence as an illustrator when he published his own PICTUREBOOKS.

Artists focus variously on incident, theme, character, symbol or a combination of all these elements. For example, the cover of ROBIN KLEIN's *CAME BACK TO SHOW YOU I COULD FLY* (1989) by VIVIENNE GOODMAN was a masterful character portrait of the teenage drug addict who is the subject of the young male character's adulation. The butterfly tattooed on her shoulder is laden with symbolic resonance – flight, beauty and tragic lack of permanence. Vivienne Goodman's exquisite work has transformed expectations of what is necessary to the sophisticated marketing of a title. Her fine detailing has created photo-realistic portraiture which resonates with feeling and intellectual appreciation of the writer's intentions. Gregory Rogers' cover for STEVEN HERRICK's *Water Bombs* (1992) is a portrait of the poet being bombarded by a water bomb, but it is also a thematic statement: the poet is shown as an adult victim of the childish pranks he perpetrated as a boy.

The commissioning of covers is an interesting case study in publishing processes. The manuscript is usually presented with a brief to a cover artist. The rough is created and discussed, usually with the publishing 'covers' committee and the writer, and then ultimately completed to a deadline well in advance of publication, to promote the book. The various factors which influence the final selection include not only artistic and thematic integrity, but also marketing and promotional potential. However, despite the careful consideration which publishers give to the choice of cover, often the process fails when too many people offer input and make bad compromises in the final selection. The integrity of many books has been betrayed by short-sighted marketing, and many publishers seem out of touch with their markets and produce unappealing covers. There is also a tendency for publishers to intervene too much in the illustration process, forgetting that the commissioned artist is likely to have more knowledge of the power of imagery, and of the cognitive meaning of spatial dimensions and format, than does the publicist.

Successive eras have different social and cultural agenda, which may make an earlier cover look outmoded or even offensive, and in recent years there has been a move to edit texts to make them more politically sensitive; it is easier to simply repackage a book in a new cover than it is to change or censor its contents. Covers also vary according to the multiple markets in which they may be released (educational/trade; hardback/paperback; adult/young adult/junior), or the series of which they form part. Publishers are also influenced by the media, and the television or film 'tie-in' cover is a relatively new development.

The body of cover art also provides a focus on differing art techniques employed by varying artists, on a range of commissions. Photo-realism and more recently the usage of computer-manipulated photographs are the techniques currently most favoured in the young adult fiction area. For younger readers, the Quentin Blake style of pen-and-ink caricatures is more popular, as with the work of illustrators such as David Mackintosh and Kim Gamble. Some contemporary covers feature holograms, embossing, foil, diecuts, day-glo inks and matt lamination in order to attract their readers.

Visual texts are as readable as the written word, and the artist who designs and illustrates a cover is as challenged by the task as the picturebook artist, but is often not acknowledged for his or her talents. RS, FMC

see also LEO AND DIANE DILLON

Cowcher, Helen 1951– British illustrator. Cowcher is known for her wild, wondrous but disquieting PICTUREBOOKS which are concerned with endangered environments and animals: *Jaguar* (1987), *Rainforest* (1988), *Antarctica* (1990), *Tigress* (1991) and *Whistling Thorn* (1993). The threat posed by humans provides the narrative drama, and her full-page water-colours and close-ups reinforce the tension and atmosphere. JAG

Cowley, Joy 1936– New Zealand writer with an international reputation for her work, and noted for her active support of the community of children's writers and illustrators. Cowley is an exemplary storyteller, able to convey serious messages with sensitivity, imagination and humour, while showing a deep respect for people. Many of her books have become modern classics, such as *The Silent One* (1981), which is set on a Fijian island and tells the story of Jonasi, who is unable to hear or to speak, and his mystical relationship with a turtle. *Bow Down Shadrach* (1991), which relates the fate of a beloved draught horse, is a lively narrative with natural, humorous dialogue and warm characters. Humour is also used to advantage to convey a strong anti-war message in *THE DUCK IN THE GUN* (1969), (republished in 1984 with new illustrations by ROBYN BELTON). Cowley is a prolific and successful writer for children and adults, with over 350 texts published in educational series, including *Greedy Cat*, a story familiar to most New Zealand children. Cowley has received numerous awards, which include the *NEW ZEALAND POST* CHILDREN'S BOOK AWARD, the ESTHER GLEN AWARD, the RUSSELL CLARK MEDAL and the 1990 Commemoration Medal for services to New Zealand. LL

Cowper, William 1731–1800 English poet and one-time Clerk at the House of Lords. Cowper was born in Hertfordshire and lived mostly in London, Norfolk and Olney. His move to Olney, where he lived from 1767 until 1786 and where his best poems were written, was partly on account of its preacher, John Newton, whose oratory made him famous throughout the country and who, with Cowper at his side, established the parish of Olney as a humane, evangelical community. Newton became a close friend and in 1771 they began work on what are now known as the Olney Hymns. Sadly, Cowper suffered from bouts of mental illness throughout his life. A precursor of Romantic poetry, Cowper is well known as a nature poet and was often included in anthologies for children until the end of the Victorian period. A lively sense of humour is also evident in poems like 'John Gilpin', which found its way into many nurseries and – about 100 years after it was composed – was illustrated by RANDOLPH CALDECOTT and issued as one of EDMUND EVANS's TOY BOOKS. MCCS

Cox, David (Dundas) 1933– Australian writer and illustrator, born in Goondiwindi, who spent his early life on the land before studying at the St Martin's School of Art in London. Head artist for the *Courier Mail* for 27 years, he left in 1991 to concentrate on his ILLUSTRATION career. His many books include *Bossyboots* (1985), *Tin Lizzie and Little Nell* (1982), *The Slumber Party* (1992), *Miss Bunkle's Umbrella* (1981), *Ayu and the Perfect Moon* (1984) and *Shock Monday* (1999). Illustrations for other authors include *The Sugar-Gum Tree* (1983) by PATRICIA WRIGHTSON; *Our Excusion* (1994) by KATE WALKER; and *Leaves for Mr Walter* (1998) by Janeen Brian. He works in pen and ink, and liquid acrylic, and has a distinctively whimsical style which is much in evidence in *The Biography of Gilbert Alexander Pig* (1999), written by Gael Cresp. His awards include the Walkley Award (1978) and numerous Children's Book Council of Australia nominations and Honour Book awards. RS

Cox, Palmer 1840–1924 American author and illustrator. Cox was born in Granby, Quebec, but spent much of his adult life in San Francisco and New York. In 1880 he illustrated an ALPHABET BOOK by Arthur Gilman with pictures of Brownies, small comic characters with round heads and bodies and spindly legs, based on stories from SCOTTISH FOLKTALES heard as a child. The first *Brownie* story by Cox himself was published in 1883 in *ST NICHOLAS*; written in rhyming couplets, it was followed by many more stories in that magazine and in the *Ladies' Home Journal*, and by 13 volumes of *Brownie* stories. Cox returned to Granby and built 'Brownie Castle' where he lived until his death. Cox's Brownies are sociable creatures, all male, differentiated by their hats and clothing and sometimes individually identifiable as a Scotsman or an Arab, a policeman or a sailor. They are technologically adept, able for instance to put together bicycle parts to make a machine on which scores of Brownies can ride together. Having no power to make again what they have made before, they constantly exercise their ingenuity as they travel the world. FEA

see also TRICKSTER (illustration)

Crabtree, Anthony 1930–95 Prolific writer of children's novels and Professor of Children's Literature at Cavendish College, Cambridge, England, from 1974 until his death. He is best known for his *Crispin* series (1952–96). Crabtree's work has been praised for the skill with which it maps the ambiguous parameters of childhood and negotiates the dramas of cultural reproduction. In *Crispin's Little Friend* (1959) Crabtree resists popular perceptions of play and reinscribes the mythos of the doll's house, while *Up and Around With Crispin* (1977) interrogates the ideology of the MOVABLE BOOK. As a series, the *Crispin* books resist the valorisation of the diminutive and engage in dialogical relationships with powerful cultural icons, enacting in narrative form broader cultural debates about childhood, historicism and the closure of adolescence. Crabtree's writing career began with *Crispin's Christmas* (1952) and this was followed by 189 sequels. *Crusoe Crispin* was awarded the 1984 We Wallow in Water award for its contribution to the world's appreciation of the importance of learning to swim. Plans for a televised serial version of the *Crispin* stories came to nothing because the author insisted on a complete run of the entire series, which would have lasted 26 years. Crabtree's reputation for obscurity was second to none. VW

Crabtree, Judith (Helen) 1931– Australian author and illustrator. Meticulous detail characterises Crabtree's allegorical PICTUREBOOK illustrations.

'The Brownies in Canada.' Illustration by Palmer Cox from *The Brownies Around the World.*

European-style folk FANTASY is created in *Night of the Wild Geese* (1990), *A Strange and Powerful Magic* (1996) and *Skew-Whiff* (1996). In *The Sparrow's Story at the King's Command* (1983) a sparrow saves a story in his head, after the pages of a book are spoiled. Crabtree believes that ILLUSTRATIONS should 'offer small gaps – an incident not fully explained, through which the readers can enter their own dreaming'. Her realistic junior novels include *The High Rise Gang* (1975) with contemporary characters, but Crabtree prefers archetypal figures and mythological motifs. HE

Crackers see COMICS, PERIODICALS AND MAGAZINES

Cradock, Mrs H.C. see APPLETON, HONOR C.

Craft, K(inuko) Y(amabe) 1940– Commercial artist and illustrator, born and raised in Japan. Known since her move to the United States for her elaborate ILLUSTRATIONS of MYTHS and FAIRY TALES, Craft has often collaborated with MARIANNA MAYER (*The Twelve Dancing Princesses*, 1989, and *Baba Yaga and Vasilisa the Brave*, 1994), and has also worked with her daughter, M. Charlotte Craft (*Cupid and Psyche*, 1996, and *King Midas and the Golden Touch*, 1999). Craft illuminates the first letter of each page, and illustrates each text spread with two paintings, one full-page and one with the text. These techniques allow her to depict several aspects of the narrative. She frames each painting, often breaking the border, giving each illustration a luminous and life-like appeal. Her more recent publications include *Pegasus* (1998) and *Cinderella* (2000). CEJ

Craig, Helen 1934– British illustrator. From a talented family of writers, designers, actors and illustrators, Helen Craig received no formal training but started illustrating when she had a child of her own. With Katherine Holabird she has produced, from 1982 onwards, 11 popular titles about the spirited mouse Angelina, and with Sarah Hayes she has created several *This is the Bear* books from 1986 onwards. She illustrated Blake Morrison's *The Yellow House* (1987)

'But when she drew back her hand, the finger had gone.' Illustration by Judith Crabtree from *A Strange and Powerful Magic.*

using etchings and aquatints, but she usually works in delicate watercolour and the lightest line, as in her own *The Town Mouse and the Country Mouse* (1992) and *Charlie and Tyler at the Seaside* (1995). JAG

Cranch, Christopher Pearse 1813–1892 American author of FANTASY for children. A follower of American transcendentalism, Cranch was also a minister, a poet and a painter. Though he published numerous poems for children in periodicals such as *ST NICHOLAS* and *RIVERSIDE MAGAZINE FOR YOUNG PEOPLE*, Cranch is best known for his full-length fantasies for children, *The Last of the Huggermuggers: A Giant Story* (1855) and *Kobboltozo: A Sequel to The Last of the Huggermuggers* (1856), in which he gently satirises American ingenuity and opportunism and incorporates numerous puns (Kobboltozo is a cobbler; other characters include a tailor, Stitchkin, and a historian, Mark Scrawler). Cranch's fantasies draw on the traditions of the ROBINSONNADE and the tales of *JACK THE GIANT-KILLER* as well as the FAIRY TALES of the GRIMM BROTHERS and HANS CHRISTIAN ANDERSEN. Reprinted many times throughout the 19th century, they were republished in a single volume in 1993, along with Cranch's final full-length fantasy for children, *The Legend of Doctor Theophilus; or, The Enchanted Clothes*, which Cranch had completed in the late 1850s but never published. Edited by Greta D. Little and Joel Myerson, *Three Children's Novels by Christopher Pearse Cranch* includes a useful biographical entry and Cranch's own woodcut ILLUSTRATIONS for the stories. AKP

Crane, Walter 1845–1915 Victorian illustrator who, along with KATE GREENAWAY and RANDOLPH CALDECOTT, set new standards for the TOY BOOK in the closing years of the 19th century. Crane was born in Liverpool, son of Thomas Crane, a miniaturist portrait painter. He showed early promise and developed his own style while young. He was apprenticed to a well-known wood engraver, W.J. Linton, which accounts for his strong use of line. One can detect a number of influences on his work: he was interested in William Blake's careful integration of words and images; he knew the work of John Ruskin and the Pre-Raphaelites; and later in life he met and worked with William Morris, whose ideas can be seen in the way Crane decorated his images and in the whole idealised, archaic world he created. Crane himself acknowledged the influence that Japanese prints had on his work, with their strong outlines, use of flat colour, resistance to perspective, solid blacks and asymmetry of design. Influenced by William Blake's *SONGS OF INNCOCENCE* and by his association with William Morris and the Arts and Crafts Movement, Crane believed that the overall design of a book for children – and every element of it – was a matter of profound aesthetic importance.

He began with hackwork but in 1863 he was introduced to EDMUND EVANS, an artist in his own right but also an innovative craftsman-printer with a serious commitment to high-quality books for children. Evans believed it was possible to produce artistically satisfying coloured printed books for the mass market and that people would be willing to pay sixpence for them. He quickly recognised Crane's ability and recruited him for the experiment, which was also backed by Frederick Warne, a newly established publisher. Their first books included *Song of Sixpence, 1, 2, Buckle my Shoe, The House That Jack Built* and *The Farmyard ABC*. These were a great success and established Crane's reputation. Between 1869 and 1876 Crane created some 35 more PICTUREBOOKS with Evans for the publisher George Routledge (Warne's brother-in-law). These titles include *I Saw Three Ships*, *The Frog Prince*, *Cinderella* and *Jack and the Bean Stalk*. Crane's success earned him his own named series, the *Walter Crane's Toy Books*. In 1874 he used a larger-format book, known as the 'shilling series'; this gave him more scope for decoration and for experimenting with graphic layout. Between 1875 and 1890 Crane illustrated many of MRS MOLESWORTH's novels and worked on OSCAR WILDE's *The Happy Prince and Other Tales* (1888), and during a year spent in America (1891–2) he was invited to illustrate NATHANIEL HAWTHORNE's *Wonderbook for Boys and Girls*. He illustrated several of Margaret Deland's floral fantasies between 1893 and 1905. He also collaborated on the production of reading primers: *The Golden Primer* (with M.D. Meikeljohn) and *Steps to Reading* (with Nellie Dale). They were first published in 1898/9 and stayed in print for some 40 years. In 1898 Crane was appointed Principle of the Royal College of Art and Design. AR

Craven, Margaret 1901–80 American author. Although Craven wrote short stories for over 30 years (published in *Ladies' Home Journal*, *Collier's* and *Saturday Evening Post*), her first novel, *I Heard the Owl Call My Name* (1973), is her masterpiece. The manuscript was initially refused by a number of American publishers; it was published in Canada and soon became an international success. The novel tells the story of a young priest's experience in Kingcome, a small Indian village in British Columbia; it is quietly told, yet is full of tensions between modern expansion and ancient tradition, between young and old, between men and women, and between things spiritual and things secular. In her autobiography, Craven writes of receiving letters from all over the world which attempted to communicate what her book had meant to its readers. The success of *I Heard the Owl Call My Name* was not repeated in Craven's other novel, *Walk Gently This Good Earth* (1977), a family epic which stretches over three generations. Craven's autobiography, *Again Calls the Owl* (published the year of her death), provides a brief update on Kingcome after the conclusion of *I Heard the Owl Call My Name*. WH

creation myths see AFRICAN MYTHOLOGY AND FOLKTALES; CLASSICAL MYTHOLOGY

creative dramatics see DRAMA FOR CHILDREN

Creature Shop see JIM HENSON

Creech, Sharon 1945– American author of books for children. Born in Cleveland, Ohio, Creech moved to England to teach in 1979 and stayed, raising her family and teaching literature in Surrey. *Walk Two Moons* (1994), her first book published in the United States (though not the first in Britain), received the ultimate accolade of the NEWBERY MEDAL. Relying on an uncondescendingly colloquial storytelling voice, the novel features the life and times of Salamanca Tree Hiddle, who journeys across America with her grandparents to the place of her mother's fatal accident, and who passes the time by relating the unusual story of her friend Phoebe's own search for family knowledge. Creech deftly allows plot layers to become tangled and then sort themselves out, relying on a combination of distinctive detail, serendipitous occurrence, and warm empathy to create an ultimately strong and optimistic vision in the face of grief. The theme of death and its complicated impact on families recurs in her other novels, but only *Chasing Redbird* (1997) approaches the unforced humour and successful tonal balance found in *Walk Two Moons*. DS

see also YOUNG ADULT FICTION

Cresswell, Helen 1934– British writer born in Nottinghamshire, prolific author of over 60 books for children. Commended for her purity of style, for the poetic language of her FANTASY stories, and for the easy way she manipulates the fusion between comedy and fantasy, she has been widely acclaimed as a diverse and original writer. Several of her books have been nominated for major British awards but narrowly missed ultimate distinction. *The Piemakers* (1967), *The Nightwatchman* (1969), *Up the Pier* (1971) and *The Bongleweed* (1973) were all runners-up for the CARNEGIE MEDAL and some were contenders for the *GUARDIAN* and WHITBREAD AWARDS. Many of her stories have been serialised on the BBC's *JACKANORY* programme and several were written in tandem with screenplays of popular TELEVISION serials, in particular the *Lizzie Dripping* series (1972–4), *The Secret World of Polly Flint* (1982), *Moondial* (1987) and the BAGTHORPE SAGA series. Cresswell suggests that this dual purpose for writing helps to shape a work by controlling the plot. She has ensured that television adaptations of her fantasies have been filmed in their originally conceived settings, local to her home. Other successful television adaptations include books by E. NESBIT, ENID BLYTON and GILLIAN CROSS. *The Return of the Psammead* (1992) – Cresswell's 'act of imaginative homage to Nesbit' – has also enjoyed serialisation.

The diversity of Cresswell's writing is evident in its wide range of appeal. For very young children the stories in *At the Stroke of Midnight* (1971) are retellings of classic FAIRY TALES and for readers in the seven-plus range titles such as *A Game of Catch* (1969) and the *Two Hoots* (1978) series have received acclaim. Generally her stories for older children can be categorised as examples of poetic fantasy or eccentric comedy. A fine blend of these two elements is exemplified in her first significant success, *The Piemakers*, which was praised for its 'richness of humour and inner truthfulness'. Set within a timeless, pastoral landscape, the absurdly fanciful tale concerns the making of a monumental royal pie. Cresswell's admiration for dedicated craftsmanship shines through the prose as, with due ritual and ceremony, Arthy the master piemaker fashions his culinary masterpiece. Her distinctive authorial flair is evident in the authentically observed family relationships and the joyful celebration of rural community. *The Night-Watchmen* traces the friendship between Henry, a boy recovering from illness, and two romantic scholar-vagabonds who pose as night-watchmen. Roaming the indistinct borders between fantasy and reality and infused with philosophical and poetic language, the book has generated much critical discussion. A similar symbolic dimension steers a powerful route through the comic fantasy of *The Bongleweed*. Cresswell suggests that young Becky, who has been responsible for the creation of a gloriously abundant and wilful plant can, whilst mourning its demise, exult in the fact that life retains the capacity for 'infinite possibility'. *Moondial* is a time-travel fantasy set in the National Trust property of Belton House in Lincolnshire, England. Place and atmosphere, good and evil, are strongly evoked as a contemporary child becomes involved with two unhappy ghost children.

CMN

Crew, Gary (David) 1947– One of Australia's most accomplished and challenging writers for young people. Born in Brisbane, Crew has been a draftsman, teacher, editor and university lecturer, and holds an MA in Commonwealth Literature. His studies are evident in his novels, which explore postcolonial concerns of place and identity, frequently employing multiple (and unreliable) voices, less-than-pleasant characters, a blend of genre and literary fiction, and an edge of the uncanny. His first novel, *The Inner Circle* (1986), reverses stereotype in that an Aboriginal teenager assists an emotionally deprived white boy, whilst symbolically promising spiritual and racial unity. In *The House of Tomorrow* (1988), cultural identity is again at the fore: troubled schoolboy Danny hears 'voices' which stem from his part-Asian background. As in many of Crew's texts there is betrayal, death and disintegration, but also rebirth. *Strange Objects* (1990), by contrast, is an uneasy, semi-historical FANTASY which stretched the Australian notion of young adult fiction. A fragmented collection of documents, it tells two stories: the (imagined) fate of two murderous sailors set adrift off West Australia in 1629 (a historical fact), and that of a (fictional) disturbed boy who finds their leavings 350 years later. Slippage between the stories interrogates 'truth' and colonialism, and leads to psychotic or supernatural events. *No Such Country* (1991) again explores colonisation, in an extraordinary allegory of guilt and atonement. The book is dense with biblical references, whilst sustaining accessible mystery and romance narratives. *Angel's Gate* (1993) is a return to realism, albeit with biblical and gothic resonances. Set in a repressive small town (a favourite Crew setting), it tells of the hunt for two 'wild children', witnesses to their father's murder, and considers wildness of both character and landscape. *Inventing Anthony West* (1994) is a supernatural spoof on the teenage romance.

Crew has also shifted PICTUREBOOK boundaries, both in content and format. His first picturebook, *Tracks* (1992), illustrated by GREGORY ROGERS, is a simple backyard adventure for young children; but with his second, *Lucy's Bay* (1992), also illustrated by Gregory Rogers, Crew began to write picturebooks for older readers, then a largely new concept in Australia. *Lucy's Bay* is the highly-crafted story of a boy returning to the seaside site of his sister Lucy's death – a death caused by his own inattentiveness – then moving into the future. Despite a mixed critical response, Crew's next book, *First Light* (1993), illustrated by PETER GOULDTHORPE, showed similar emotional subtlety as it tells of a sensitive boy and his intolerant father. *Gulliver in the South Seas* (1994), illustrated by John Burge, reflects Crew's rejection of Eurocentric representation by situating Lilliput in the Indonesian archipelago. *THE WATERTOWER* (1994) is a horror story, while *THE LOST DIAMONDS OF KILLIECRANKIE* (1995), a picturebook for teenagers, blends mystery and history. *Caleb* (1996), illustrated by STEVEN WOOLMAN, a gothic tale of entomology, is similarly suitable for older readers, as is *Memorial* (1999), a thought-provoking picturebook sensitively illustrated by SHAUN TAN. Crew embraces complex structure, imagery and ideas. An outspoken advocate for writers and youth fiction, he speaks knowledgeably and articulately of writing and history. NLR

Crews, Donald 1938– Highly regarded AFRICAN AMERICAN author-illustrator of concept books and PICTUREBOOKS. Born in Newark, New Jersey, Crews is married to the picturebook author Ann Jonas; their daughter Nina Crews is also an author-illustrator. After Crews graduated from Cooper Union, he created his first picturebook, *We Read: A to Z* (1967), as an exercise for his graphics portfolio. Like many author-illustrators, he continued his 'apprenticeship' by following the ALPHABET BOOK with one on numbers, *Ten Black Dots* (1968). Crews illustrated other authors for ten years before producing two benchmarks of the concept genre: *Freight Train* (1978) and *Truck* (1980). His bold designs, influenced by the graphic artists Paul

Rand and Bruno Munari as well as by cubism, constructivism, futurism and pop art, skilfully employ colour and the play of dark and light to capture sensations. Motion, sound and touch become visible in books such as *Carousel* (1982), *Parade* (1983), *Flying* (1986) and *Sail Away* (1995); story lines are secondary to presenting the concepts. In contrast, *Bigmama's* (1991) and *Shortcut* (1992) tell stories from Crews's childhood, when he visited grandparents in Cottondale, Florida. The allure of the trains that took Crews there combines with love of family in these evocative and welcomed additions to the Crews canon. JMA

Cricket in Times Square, The see GEORGE SELDEN

Cricket Magazine Award-winning American children's magazine published by Carus Publishing Company since 1973, renowned for its literary and artistic quality. The magazine, designed for readers aged 9–14, was intentionally created to be in the tradition of ST NICHOLAS, the distinguished children's periodical (1873–1943). Many of the most distinguished authors and illustrators of the 20th century have been contributors, including LLOYD ALEXANDER, URSULA LE GUIN, ISAAC BASHEVIS SINGER, VIRGINIA HAMILTON, TRINA SCHART HYMAN, TOMIE DE PAOLA, QUENTIN BLAKE and ERIC CARLE. Almost all of the art is original, and the covers are particularly noteworthy. The magazine's founder, Marianne Carus, is editor-in-chief and an active member of the international children's book community. The firm publishes three other children's magazines for younger ages: *Spider* (6–9), *Ladybug* (2–6), and *Babybug* (6 months–2 years).

Cricket's mission is to create a love of reading and an appreciation of good writing and ILLUSTRATION; to stimulate children's imaginations; and to introduce multicultural values. The content includes literature, nature, science, history, astronomy, art, music, social science, sports, crafts, cartoons, puzzles and children's letters. The magazine has received awards from Parents' Choice, the Educational Press Association and the International Reading Association. For a short period from October 1974, a companion magazine, *Cricket and Co.*, was published in Britain. AL

***Cricklepit Combined School* series** Tales by GENE KEMP, who won both the CARNEGIE MEDAL and the Other Award for the first – *The Turbulent Term of Tyke Tiler* (1977). Each story – except *Juniper* (1986) – is told as a first-person narrative and has the lively and authentic feel of the junior school playground in both language and action. When *The Turbulent Term of Tyke Tiler* was first published it was greeted as 'a truly innovatory book which has given new horizons to the day-school story' (*BOOKS FOR KEEPS*), and ROBERT LEESON in *Reading and Righting* (1985) saw it as a 'turning-point' because of its working-class characters and setting. It was hailed by feminists for raising gender issues, though Kemp has since admitted that her clever delay in revealing that the active and engaging narrator is female until the final pages was more of a narrative twist than an ideological statement.

Kemp's later *Cricklepit* stories – *Gowie Corby Plays Chicken* (1979) and *Charlie Lewis Plays for Time* (1984) – whilst remaining realistically grounded in an urban school setting, reveal a darker society of underprivileged and isolated children whose lives are often painful and distressing. There is, however, always an optimistic ending and the occasionally naive theme of redemption is seasoned by witty descriptions and the kind of excruciating puns that children love ('What did the cross-eyed teacher say? – I can't control my pupils!'). *Juniper*, whilst also set in the Cricklepit world, deals in a more sober manner with themes of violence, fear and DISABILITY, in the mode of the mystery story instead of the SCHOOL STORY. Kemp has subsequently written more *Cricklepit* stories, for example *Just Ferret* (1990) and *Zowey Corby's Story* (1995). PJR

critical approaches to children's literature These are revised in each generation by adults who read, select, annotate and discuss texts created by writers, artists, publishers and other adults whose implied readers are young people. Most commentators, including historians of this literature, derive their perspectives from their own reading (including their early experiences), their ideologies of childhood and their textual preferences. In her periodical *The Guardian of Education* (1802–6), SARAH TRIMMER reviewed systematically the publications of the previous 50 years so as to distinguish texts designed to promote sound learning and good behaviour from those 'replete with hidden mischief'. She rejected *CINDERELLA*, a family favourite: 'it paints some of the worst passions that can enter the human breast'. This strain, variously interpreted by later historians, permeates 19th-century writing about and for the young. F.J. HARVEY DARTON, whose *Children's Books in England* (1932) chronicles this period in detail, is aware of the continuing conflict 'between hesitant morality and spontaneous happiness'. He is also clear-eyed about the fact that children's books are material objects produced for profit. His wide knowledge and close reading of texts helped to establish children's literature of the 19th century as a matrix for later studies. Brian Alderson, the editor of the third edition of Darton's history (1982), is his obvious successor. GILLIAN AVERY's *19th Century Children* (1965) and Lance Salway's *A Peculiar Gift* (1976) confirm the cultural embeddedness of books for children, while encouraging the study of them as a significant enterprise. It is worth comparing and contrasting J.S. Bratton's *The Impact of Victorian Children's Fiction* (1981), a detailed socio-literary analysis of Sunday school 'reward' fictions, Humphrey Carpenter's *Secret Gardens* (1985) – a collection of nostalgic biographical studies of writers of the so-called 'golden age', 1860–1930 – and John Goldthwaite's deeply researched, idiosyncratic views of FANTASY writings in *The Natural History of Make Believe* (1996).

Twentieth-century critical perspectives reveal a growing self-consciousness on the part of writers, illustrators and critics. Asked why they choose to write for children, authors are quick to reject the implication that their work is either childish, easy or simply ephemeral. WILLIAM MAYNE says he 'doesn't care what adults think'. In his apologia *Tales out of School* (1949), GEOFFREY TREASE is more robust: his sense of young readers' enjoyment of a good yarn helped him to conceptualise his view of HISTORICAL FICTION and to continually adapt his art over more than half a century. JILL PATON WALSH sees herself as 'making a serious adult statement and making it utterly simple and transparent'. During the 60s and 70s and beyond, conscientious REVIEWING kept up with the growing output of fiction, poetry and, less regularly, INFORMATION BOOKS. ELAINE MOSS's autobiographical collection of reviews and other writing, *Part of the Pattern* (1986), is close to contemporary publishing and critical practices at a time of growing readership, experimental productions, and the gradual filtering of trade books into school reading.

GROWING POINT, MARGERY FISHER's reviewing journal (1962–92), remains unmatched in its contribution to serious writing about books for the young. In the context of prizes and rewards (see AWARDS AND MEDALS), discussions about 'the best' came to a head with the complaint, continually repeated in ideological arguments, that books selected by adults are rarely chosen, or even enjoyed, by children. The creation of the Other Award (1975) for books with social sensitiveness to the multicultural nature of children's literature within British culture, and ROBERT LEESON's *Reading and Righting* (1985), loosened the by now traditional, middle-class humanist hold on children's reading. These complexities, other refinements and a rich array of comment and serious reviewing are visible in the journal SIGNAL, APPROACHES TO CHILDREN'S BOOKS (from 1970), edited by Nancy Chambers at the Thimble Press, which is accompanied by a series of monographs and other critical writings, including *The Signal Companion*, a classified guide to the contents of the journal from 1970 to 1994. The *SIGNAL* Poetry Prize established the importance of and continues to promote critical writing about poetry for children.

As the culture of childhood has changed, defining children's literature continued to be a 20th-century obsession. The critical domain has been extended by philosophical, psychological and cultural studies and an increasing range of literary theories derived from academic approaches to texts. The editors of *THE COOL WEB* (1977) suggested the universality of narrative as a starting point for considering the complex nature of the topic. Discussions founder on the perceived differences between experienced (adult) readers and the nature of children's reading, notably their 'responses' to different kinds of text. Brian Alderson's essay 'The Irrelevance of Children to the Children's Book Reviewer' (1969) is still a point of departure for discussions of textual criticism. It shares with JOHN ROWE TOWNSEND's 'Standards of Criticism for Children's Literature' (1971) the Leavisite insistence on a critic's responsibility to recognise that a text has 'value in itself'. Psychological approaches are benchmarked by Nicholas Tucker's *The Child and the Book* (1981). In her interpretation of *PETER PAN*, Jacqueline Rose includes the judgement that children's fiction is 'impossible' because it 'hangs on . . . the impossible relation between adult and child' (1984). This notion is developed in Karin Lesnik-Oberstein's *Children's Literature: Criticism and the Fictional Child* (1994). Challenges to approaches regarded as conventional have come from new (as distinct from renewed) forms of text-making, notably in PICTUREBOOKS where the versatility of artists in response to new printing techniques now demands descriptions of visualisation more akin to the subtleties of Jane Doonan. Likewise, changes in narrative modes in novels for adolescents are now described in terms of narratology, derived from adult literary criticism. In this the work of AIDAN CHAMBERS is important. As an experimental novelist he makes plain to his implied readers the constructedness of texts. Together with teacher-critics Geoff Fox, Victor Watson, Morag Styles, MARGARET MEEK and others, he has theorised his insights and practices. His work is acknowledged by Maria Nikolajeva in *Children's Literature Comes of Age; Towards a New Aesthetic* (1996), which claims that postmodern children's books are best served by postmodern adult critical practices (in her case, psychoanalytic ones) which declare the grown-upness of selected contemporary books.

The emergence of this kind of critical writing is one aspect of the argument that theoretical studies of children's literature should be acknowledged in institutions of higher education. In terms of research, Peter Hunt has been the foremost champion. From a small collection of conference papers (Benton, 1979) to the *International Companion Encyclopedia of Children's Literature* (1996), he has been instrumental in creating a world network of those whose research concerns are located in this domain. He argues for a distinctive CHILDIST CRITICISM, parallel to 'feminist' criticism, which accepts an obligation to children's reading as a necessary aspect of criticism more generally.

Well supported by critical works like NEIL PHILIP's study of ALAN GARNER (*A Fine Anger*, 1981) and Barbara Wall's *The Narrator's Voice* (1991), significant studies of individual children (Hugh Crago, 1983; Carol Fox, 1993) and ever-growing bibliographies, children's literature may be said to have found its academic feet in the second half of the 20th century. It is served well by collaborative efforts, such as the searching and productive conferences held at Homerton College in Cambridge since 1991, following which the evidence of textual criticism and of children's readings are brought together in books edited by Morag Styles, Eve Bearne and Victor Watson.

However, as at the beginning, not all critical approaches to children's literature win recognition in the mainstream of academic literary studies. What counts as research evidence is still a matter for debate. In addition, academic criticism has not found it easy to accept the fact that 20th-century children's books were transformed not only by a widening of their audience, but also by the growing, and now dominant, influence of other media: cheaper productions of books in series, COMICS, PERIODICALS AND MAGAZINES, compendia, and multimedia presentations, where photography, film and graphics are most influential. Books of information, a particular kind of investment publishing for the young, do not attract critical attention to any significant extent. Questions of definition remain. In *Signs of Childness in Children's Books* (1997) Peter Hollindale, whose critical approaches have always confronted the complexity of this topic (see CHILDNESS), has proposed 'multiple' definitions which involve the author, the text and the young reader.

In the United States, Canada and Australia critical approaches to children's literature are as diverse as those to adult literature, as is evidenced by two useful works by the Canadian scholars Perry Nodelman and Roderick McGillis. Nodelman's *The Pleasures of Children's Literature* (1992, rev. 1996), although focused on teaching, covers reader response and the implied reader, narratology, metafiction, ideology and Marxist criticism, gender, women's writing, multiculturalism, intertextuality, structuralism (Lévi-Strauss, Vladimir Propp, Barthesian codes), psychoanalytic theory (Bettelheim and Lacan), Jungian archetypes and those of Northrop Frye. Most importantly, it includes an area distinct to children's literature, the relationship of text to ILLUSTRATION, a subject on which Nodelman himself has written a seminal book, *Words about Pictures: The Narrative Art of Children's Picturebooks* (1989). McGillis's *The Nimble Reader: Literary Theory and Children's Literature* (1996) covers somewhat the same ground but focuses rather on how these theoretical schools evolved, beginning with formalism and New Criticism and ending with a discussion of poststructuralist criticism (feminism and deconstruction). Anyone embarking on an investigation of children's literature, particularly in regard to critical approaches, would benefit greatly from these two books and their extensive references.

There have been critical works by single authors on subjects such as feminism (Roberta Seelinger Trites, *Waking Sleeping Beauty: Feminist Voices in Children's Literature*, 1997), linguistics and ideology (the Australian John Stephens's *Language and Ideology in Children's Fiction*, 1992), fantasy (Brian Attebery, *Strategies of Fantasy*, 1992) and metanarratives (John Stephens and Robyn McCallum, *Retelling Stories, Framing Culture*, 1998). Much of the most significant theoretical work, however, has appeared in festschrifts, special issues of adult's literature journals such as *Studies in the Literary Imagination* (fall 1985) and *Poetics Today* (spring 1992), and above all, in the journals devoted to academic approaches to children's literature: *Canadian Children's Literature, Children's Literature* (Yale University Press), the *CHILDREN'S LITERATURE ASSOCIATION QUARTERLY*, *CHILDREN'S LITERATURE IN EDUCATION*, *THE LION AND THE UNICORN* and *PAPERS* (Australia). These journals often have special issues that are devoted to one topic; the *Children's Literature Association Quarterly* has a critical theory column. So much work of theoretical significance on children's literature is now appearing that there is a tendency for those who ignore the periodical record and only consult books to reinvent the wheel.

Comprehensive as the books by McGillis and Nodelman are, they do not cover author studies; examples of recent well-researched BIOGRAPHIES informed by a feminist critical approach are Elizabeth Keyser's award-winning *Whispers in the Dark* (1993) on LOUISA MAY ALCOTT, and Nancy Huse's *Noel Streatfeild* (1994). Nor do they cover the important recent work in children's literature that has to do largely with context. The Marxist critic Jack Zipes set higher American standards for research and scholarship with the first of his numerous books on FAIRY TALES, *Breaking the Magic Spell* (1979), a subject he and other scholars such as Ruth Bottigheimer and Maria Tartar have further pursued. The historical and cultural researches of such scholars as Gillian Adams have addressed children's literature prior to the invention of printing, for example in the special issue of the *Children's Literature Association Quarterly* on medieval children's literature (spring 1998); and the books and essays of children's literature historians such as

GILLIAN AVERY and Anne MacLeod have also contributed much to our understanding of American children's literature. Also in terms of context, the research of new historicists, initiated by Mitzi Myers and including Claudia Nelson (*Boys Will Be Girls*, 1991) and Lynne Vallone (*Disciplines of Virtue*, 1995), has radically revised our judgements about the value and role of didacticism, the changing constructions of childhood, and our perception of 18th- and 19th-century children's literature; see, for example, the special issue of the *Children's Literature Association Quarterly* on new historicism (fall 1996).

Because Australia, Canada and the United States have become increasingly aware both of the territorial and cultural rights of their first inhabitants and of an immigrant multiethnicity that is no longer limited primarily to white Europeans, multicultural and postcolonial theoretical approaches have flourished, as in, for example, the special issue of *ARIEL* 28.1 (1997), edited by Roderick McGillis. The portrayal of the other is an important part of children's films as well, and recent approaches to their history have led to a new level of critical sophistication; see, for example, the special issues of *The Lion and the Unicorn* 21.3 (1997) and *Children's Literature Association Quarterly* 22.1 (1997). Another segment of children's culture involves the material; it has been provided with a model by Lois Kuznets's award-winning *When Toys Come Alive* (1994); there are also studies on such subjects as Barbie dolls and advertising. Cultural and historical context is also the basis for much of the work involving sexuality and queer theory; see the special issues of the *Lion and the Unicorn* (fall 1999) and the *Children's Literature Association Quarterly* (fall 1998).

It would seem that the critical approaches most appropriate to children's literature would be those that address the special nature of its audience, but reader response and reception theory have proved highly problematic. Since critics who write about children's literature are no longer children, they have three choices: to address what they or others (sometimes their older students) remember their responses were as children (Michael Steig's *Stories of Reading*, 1989); to study intensively one or more children in their family (Maureen and Hugh Crago's *Prelude to Literacy*, 1983; and Shelby Wolf and Shirley Brice Heath's *The Braid of Literature*, 1992); or to study the responses of groups of children, usually in a classroom situation. Although there have been numerous studies in American education journals such as *The New Advocate*, *English Journal*, *Language Arts* and *The Reading Teacher* of individual child audiences in a given locality and of a specified economic and racial make-up, academic reader response theorists apparently have yet to come to terms with these in any comprehensive way. There is also the question of adult manipulation (or 'colonising', in Nodelman's terms) of responses – children, in the subject position as they are, have always been expert at producing what they think a teacher or other interlocutor wants. Add to these difficulties the fact that elsewhere in the world, as evidenced by the international journal BOOKBIRD, children are very differently constructed, any kind of global pronouncement about 'childist' criticism becomes suspect. It is all a question of which children one is talking about.

A final problem that has to do with the audience for children's literature involves the line between children and adults. It is difficult to define children's literature at all: should it be defined by its *intended* audience – whether the intention is the author's or the publisher's – or by its *actual* audience, that is when there is evidence that a text has been read by a substantial number of children regardless of adult intentions? An examination of the ambiguous nature of the border between the child and adult audience and the propensity of certain authors to write for both of them at the same time (cross-writing) has led to an interest in border theory: see the special issue of *CHILDREN'S LITERATURE* in 1997. And the increasing recognition of the amorphous nature of children's literature has led to a fluid kind of criticism, one that is more fully appropriate to the postmodern condition; see *Reflections of Change: Children's Literature Since 1945*, edited by Sandra Beckett (1997). MM, GA

Crockett, Davy see DAVY CROCKETT

Crompton, Richmal see *JUST WILLIAM* SERIES

Cross, Gillian 1945– British novelist who has been writing for readers of different ages since 1979. Cross won the CARNEGIE MEDAL for *WOLF* in 1990 and the SMARTIES PRIZE and WHITBREAD CHILDREN'S NOVEL AWARD for *The Great Elephant Chase* in 1992. She is a versatile writer, with works ranging from HISTORICAL FICTION (*The Iron Way*, 1979) to SCHOOL STORIES (*The Mintyglo Kid*, 1983, and *Swimathon*, 1986). Two books – *THE DEMON HEADMASTER* (1982) and *The Demon Headmaster Strikes Again* (1996) – have been serialised for BBC TELEVISION. In 1998 she wrote a version of *The Goose Girl* for Scholastic's series of paperback FAIRY TALES. Her novels for young adults deal with contemporary issues; the protagonists in *ON THE EDGE* (1985), *A MAP OF NOWHERE* (1989) and *Wolf* contend with situations where the certainties and security of childhood have gone awry and they are alone in an adult world. In *Wolf*, teenage Cassie confronts terrorism, environmental issues and family breakdown, in a tightly wrought, intertextual, postmodern text. The heroine of *Tightrope* (1999) seeks relief from caring for her bedridden mother in the form of nocturnal graffiti raids, becoming embroiled in local gang warfare and protectionism. Tad and Cissie in *The Great Elephant Chase*, set in 19th-century America, are tested to their limits attempting to rescue a performing elephant. In biographical notes, Cross describes herself as a storyteller – 'But I am aware of certain themes running through my writing . . . personal responsibility, the importance of moral decisions and the power of people to change their own lives.' *Tightrope* (1999) was shortlisted for the CARNEGIE AWARD. EAG

Cross, Peter 1951– British illustrator and writer. His first books, *Trouble for Trumpets* (1982) and *Trumpet in Grumpetland* (1984), had a cult following for their richly detailed FANTASY land. Four simple and enchanting books for young children followed, featuring a family of dinosaurs (1985), and then a series of five popular books about Dudley, a characterful dormouse. Anniversary celebrations *1588 and All This* (1988) – an Armada spoof – and *The Boys' Own Battle of Britain* (1989) appealed to older children and adults with their relentless humour and invention. Since 1991 Cross has been a bestselling and innovative greetings card artist for Gordon Fraser. CB

crosshatching Technique in drawing where parallel strokes in one direction (hatching) are crossed with rows of parallel strokes at a different angle. Crosshatching is a means to achieve tone (or different 'colours' of grey) with line, and has its origins in etching and engraving where it is used for shading and modelling. The technique has the effect of settling the image on the paper. The traditional association with the past gives an old-fashioned quality to contemporary PICTUREBOOK illustrations that are hatched and crosshatched. MAURICE SENDAK's pictures for *WHERE THE WILD THINGS ARE* and his drawings for *The Juniper Tree* show the technique in conjunction with colour, or in monochrome, respectively. JD

Crossley-Holland, Kevin 1941– British writer who has made his name as poet, teller and reteller of tales, editor, translator, librettist and broadcaster. Although many of his publications are for adults, the tales of *Havelok the Dane* (1964) and *The Green Children* (1966) began his distinguished and distinctive contribution to literature for children. MYTH, LEGEND, the mystical and the magical, are the fields Crossley-Holland has made his own. For very young children, he has been successful with simple retellings of GRIMM tales, for example *The Fox and the Cat*, illustrated by SUSAN VARLEY (1985). For slightly older readers there is a flawless ghost story, *Storm*, which won the CARNEGIE MEDAL (illustrated by ALAN MARKS, 1985). Alan Marks was also the illustrator for a new, tender retelling of *The Green Children* (1994) in which, through the first-person narrator of the girl, the author recreates the human world in all its sensuous strangeness.

A much-praised, dramatic prose version of *Beowulf* illustrated by CHARLES KEEPING (1982) led readers to Crossley-Holland's collections, such as his *The Norse Myths* (1980) or *British Folk Tales* (1987) or *Tales from Europe* (1991), all of which demonstrate his ability to speak in a contemporary voice whilst retaining the imagery, rhythms and mystery of the past. With Gwyn Thomas, he has translated and written a definitive, scholarly, spirited retelling of *The Mabinogion* (1984) and also *The Quest of Olwen* (1988) and *The Tale of Taliesin* (1992). *THE SEEING STONE* (2000) is the first part of a proposed trilogy about KING ARTHUR. Two of his stories, *The Green Children* and *The Wildman*, have been performed as operas with music by Nicola LeFanu. Above all, Crossley-Holland is associated with the Fens and East Anglia in England. In the collections *The Old Stories* (1997), with illustrations by JOHN LAWRENCE, the strange, shadowy, watery world of the fens is poetically and powerfully evoked. JAG

Crouch, Marcus see *PETER PAN*; NATIVE AMERICANS IN CHILDREN'S LITERATURE

Crouch, Nathaniel 1632–1725 English hack writer who worked under the pseudonym of Richard Burton [R.B.] and was successful at 'digesting . . . other peoples' books and passing them off as his own' (OPIES, 1973). The resulting stories for the young, sometimes in verse, include *Youth's Divine Pastime* (1691) which made at least 18 editions. MCCS

Cruickshank, Margrit 1942– Scottish writer and bookseller, born in Aberdeen and now living in Dublin. She has produced five *S.K.U.N.K.* novels, rollicking ADVENTURE STORIES, all with an underlying environmental theme, and several other works for younger readers. Her writing displays more complexity, however, in her novels for older readers. *Circling the Triangle* (1991) realistically addresses the inner conflict and uncertainties of the central protagonist, Stephen, which are heightened by the three alternative endings to the novel. *The Door* (1996) also has a young male narrator, Hugh. Here the emphasis is partly on social issues, and in particular it focuses on sexual harassment in a Dublin comprehensive school. VC

Cruikshank, George 1792–1878 British political caricaturist and book illustrator. His long life was driven by an extraordinary and sometimes unpredictable energy. In its obituary for him, *Punch* noted his 'childlike nature' and 'high opinion of himself', but praised 'a rare and original genius, a pioneer in the arts of illustration'. Children knew Cruikshank best through the first English version (by Edgar Taylor) of *Grimms' Fairy Tales* (1823), where the caricaturist's hand is evident in the volatile, minutely detailed etchings. Ruskin judged them 'the finest thing next to Rembrandt done since etching was invented'; though Percy Muir thought the prancing hobgoblins and wizened grotesques charged with a repellent 'leeriness'. Young readers must have relished his illustrations for *John Gilpin* (1828), ROBINSON CRUSOE (1831) and UNCLE TOM'S CABIN (1852). *Oliver Twist* (1838) included his haunting image of Fagin in the condemned cell. 'It does not look merely like a picture of Fagin', wrote G.K. Chesterton, 'it looks like a picture by Fagin'. In his fifties, Cruikshank became a relentless campaigner against the demon drink, and (to Dickens's published disgust), the texts for his *Fairy Library* (1853–4) are permeated by temperence dogma, though the etchings, especially for JACK AND THE BEANSTALK, retain the aery mystery and excitement of his finest work. GPF

Crystal, The see GIRL'S CRYSTAL ANNUAL

Cuckoo Clock, The (1877) The best-known story by the British author MRS MOLESWORTH, concerning a lonely young girl forced to live with two kind but over-anxious aunts. Griselda has much in common with LEWIS CARROLL's Alice: she is lively, challenging and anxious to be good. Although the story was written in the same period as GEORGE MACDONALD's great fantasies, it is closer in spirit to E. NESBIT: the story is not overloaded with morbidity, the dialogue is lively, and the irritable Cuckoo who guides Griselda in her imaginary adventures is kindly, magical, and a convincing psychological function of the young heroine's loneliness. VW

Cue for Treason see GEOFFREY TREASE; ADVENTURE STORIES

Cullen, Countee 1903–46 African American poet and major figure of the Harlem Renaissance. His children's books are *The Lost Zoo (A Rhyme for the Young, But Not Too Young)* (1940), about the animals who missed (and almost missed) Noah's ark, and *My Lives and How I Lost Them* (1942), an account by Cullen's cat Christopher of his adventures. *The Lost Zoo*, in verse, is more significant. On the surface an amusing tale, it was meant to be understood by its black audience as a warning against the stereotypes whites imposed upon them. Both books were reprinted in 1992. GA

cummings, e(dward) e(stlin) 1894–1962 American poet who abandoned traditional conventions of punctuation and capitalisation. A Harvard graduate, he wrote his name in lower-case letters and experimented with parentheses, spelling and stanza forms. Son of a Unitarian minister, cummings could be flippant, profound, satirical, romantic and funny. *Tulips and Chimneys* (1923), his first collection, established love and nature as strong themes in his poetry. He was influenced by transcendentalism and Ralph Waldo Emerson. His best-known poems include 'Chanson Innocent', 'Since Feeling Is First' and '1 (a'. NV

Cunliffe, John see POSTMAN PAT SERIES

Cunning Little Vixen, The see MUSIC AND STORY

Cunningham, Julia W(oolfolk) 1916– American author of books for children, often allegorical and combining the realistic and the fantastic in original ways. Cunningham is always interested in complex themes, often involving psychological isolation and spiritual freedom, topics unusual in children's books. Her best-known and most controversial book is *Dorp Dead* (1965), an intense and allegorical work in which the orphan Gilly Ground – a poor speller – is apprenticed to the carpenter Kobalt. Kobalt at first seems a caring parent, but in fact he wishes to cage and enslave Gilly. Gilly is saved by himself, by his connection to nature and his love for the dog Mash, and by the mysterious figure of the Hunter. The novel is rich in allegorical suggestion, disturbing in its portrayal of destructive psychological tendencies, and hopeful about human nature in its resolution.

The orphan Gilly is one of many in Cunningham's novels, which at times seem preoccupied with the theme of orphanhood. Her protagonists are either actual orphans, like Gilly, or virtual orphans, like the girl in *Macaroon* (1961), whose parents are perpetually absent and have psychologically orphaned her. In the very powerful *Tupenny* (1978) an orphan girl comes to a mysterious town where parents have banished or killed their children and where the preacher has an unhealthy psychological sway over the town. The orphan Tupenny manages to restore the town, but in the process banishes herself to loneliness and isolation yet again. It is a fable of the necessity and cost of love and compassion.

A number of Cunningham's allegorical novels almost resemble animal FABLES. *Dear Rat* (1961) stars Andrew the Rat, a detective from Wyoming who successfully deals with three thieves intent on stealing jewels from Chartres Cathedral. *Oaf* (1986) is the tale of a young boy whose motto is 'fifty-fifty', and who always shares half of what he has with the talking animals he meets on his travels, ultimately saving a number of them from a cruel master. *Viollet* (1966) is the somewhat gothic tale of a lovely thrush who can sing only while alone in a ruined castle and garden.

The gothic and romantic tendency of much of Cunningham's writing can be seen in her series of books about Auguste, a French deaf-mute mime. These novels, beginning with *Burnish Me Bright* (1970), appear to take place in the modern world but contain elements of both the gothic and the romantic. There are mysterious strangers and houses, abandoned street children who perform for pennies, and other elements that some critics have found too centred in 19th-century sentimentality and melodrama. Nonetheless, this series is at heart an allegory about people who, through lack of understanding, destroy things of psychological, emotional and even spiritual value. The destruction often involves physical violence, and the books include scenes of arson and mob behaviour.

Cunningham's novels, despite some criticism and despite the sometimes confusing overlap between FANTASY, allegory and realism in them, remain important. The best of Cunningham's work presents challenging themes in unique and memorable ways. MDK

see also ANIMALS IN FICTION

Cunningham, Walter 1910–88 Prolific and versatile Australian illustrator, best known for his carefully executed drawings and watercolours for LESLIE REES's animal life-cycle books, as well as his *Digit Dick* series (1942–57). While the perky diminutive character of Digit Dick shows the influence of WALT DISNEY, whose animated cartoons were popular in the early 1940s, Cunningham had a versatility of styles and demonstrated a deep affinity for all things Australian, especially the natural world and its plants and animals. A frequent illustrator for the New South Wales *SCHOOL MAGAZINE*, Cunningham is also remembered as producing the first Australian PICTUREBOOKS with coloured ILLUSTRATIONS spreading across two pages to form one united design. JAP

Cunto de li Cunti, Lo see 'Bluebeard'; FAIRY TALES; 'Puss in Boots'; 'Sleeping Beauty'

***Curious George* series** A series of seven books published from 1941 to 1966 that chronicle the adventures of the monkey Curious George (known as 'Zozo' in England) and his friends. His adventures began with the publication of *Curious George* (1941), a brightly illustrated PICTUREBOOK which authors H.A. (Hans Augusto) Rey and Margret Elizabeth Rey had to smuggle out of Germany on a bicycle after the Nazis' rise to power. The Reys ended up in the United States, where the original *Curious George* volume was followed by six others. In books such as *Curious George Rides a Bike* (1952), *Curious George Flies a Kite* (1958), *Curious George Learns The Alphabet* (1963) and *Curious George Goes to the Hospital* (1966), the always mischievous monkey encounters numerous comic mishaps because of his boundless curiosity. Fortunately, the man with the yellow hat, George's constant companion, is always around to rescue his friend. Curious George's adventures have gained world-wide popularity, perhaps because the small monkey runs into many of the everyday problems of any curious child, yet never comes to any lasting harm. Over half a century after his first appearance, Curious George has continued to attract countless enthusiastic new readers. SAI

Cushman, Karen 1941– American writer of HISTORICAL FICTION. Born in Chicago, Cushman grew up writing but did not publish until she was 52. Her first book, *Catherine, Called Birdy* (1994), became a Newbery Honour Book, and her second, *The Midwife's Apprentice* (1995), won the NEWBERY AWARD. The theme of her fiction is also the theme of her life as she describes it in her Newbery speech: 'the painful search for a place to belong' and the need to find out about 'identity and responsibility, compassion and kindness and belonging, and being human in the world'. Thus she can choose heroines from the medieval period in England, as in her first two books, or the Gold Rush days in California, as with her third, *The Ballad of Lucy Whipple* (1996), and succeed in overcoming the wide gap of cultural differences. Cushman is an important new writer with a strong and gifted imagination, and the voices of her child characters are similarly important. She represents strong, courageous, risk-taking and outspoken feminists, who learn never to give up. NM

Custer, George Armstrong 1839–76 A controversial and flamboyant army officer who became the model of the brave and patriotic soldier. Custer began his military service early in the Civil War after his graduation from West Point. His courage and daring drew the attention of high-ranking officers, and before the end of the Civil War he was promoted to major general at the age of 23, thereby gaining the nickname 'the Boy General'. After the Civil War Custer served in the western campaigns designed to force Native Americans onto tribal reservations or to exterminate them. Custer, at the Little Big Horn River, misjudged the strength of a Sioux encampment and in characteristically rash fashion attacked before a feasible battle plan had been developed. He and his troops were killed. The battle, known as Custer's Last Stand, became a potent symbol in American culture for courage in the face of overwhelming odds.

Custer gained heroic stature almost immediately. Writers for the popular press frequently romanticised Custer, portraying him with flowing hair and dressed in white buckskin. BUFFALO BILL reorganised his Wild West Show to climax with a re-enactment of Custer's Last Stand. DIME NOVELS frequently included Custer as a model for boys. However, in the latter half of the 20th century opinion about Custer shifted, primarily because of the Indian Rights Movement, which refocused public attention on these events through the perspective of Native Americans.

EBD

Cycles of the Kings, The see IRISH MYTHOLOGY AND FOLKLORE

D

D'Aulaire, Edgar 1898–1986 and **D'Aulaire, Ingri Parin** 1904–80 American husband-and-wife team who created PICTUREBOOKS for children. The D'Aulaires, who produced more than 20 picturebooks during their lifelong collaboration, were diligent and methodical about researching the locality and backgrounds for each book. Most have Norwegian or Norwegian American themes, including FOLKTALES and MYTHS, although the D'Aulaires also produced BIOGRAPHIES of Americans such as Benjamin Franklin and Abraham Lincoln, and other picturebooks with themes related to the culture and history of the United States, to which they emigrated in 1929. They used painstaking lithographic processes to illustrate their books. The combination of method and lush pastel colouring lends a slightly folkloric effect to their work. The biographies are uncontroversial and straightforward, with text artfully selected to appeal to a child's sensibilities. Other works are less constrained and more fanciful, with glints of quiet, childlike humour. Today, both illustrations and texts seem dated, but the richness of the colours and detail of the pictures are still appealing. The D'Aulaires won a CALDECOTT MEDAL for *Abraham Lincoln* (1939). MJKP

see also ILLUSTRATION IN CHILDREN'S BOOKS; LITHOGRAPHY

Dadd, Richard see FAIRY FANTASY

Daddy Long-Legs see JEAN WEBSTER; see also SCHOOL STORIES

Daffy Duck see ANIMATED CARTOONS

Dahl, Roald 1916–1990 British short-story writer, one of the most successful writers for children ever, and one of the most contentious. His stories owe much to PANTOMIME and farce, and are full of violence, vulgarity, revenge and strongly held opinions. They often feature downtrodden but resilient children pitted against adult grotesques. Although he claimed to be on the child's side he has been widely seen as manipulative, and has been accused variously of racism, anti-Semitism, misogyny and cruelty. On the other hand, his supporters (who far outnumber his detractors) argue that he speaks to childhood values (such as love of simple justice), and to children's delight in excess, cartoon-like extravagance, and verbal ingenuity.

His (unauthorised) biographer, Jeremy Treglown, suggested in 1994 that his books are 'like FOLKTALES . . . [they] draw on deep, widespread longings and fears. They bind characters, readers and writer into a private fantasy. They make you laugh and cry. They do this with well-tried technical expertise, and in a way that is often a cryptogram of the life which produced them.' The biographical school of critics has much to work on in Dahl's life. He was born of Norwegian parents in Llandaff, Wales, and from the age of six he spent his childhood and youth as an unhappy and rebellious schoolboy. This period is vividly (and bitterly) described in the first of his autobiographical books, *Boy* (1984). The second, *Going Solo* (1986), describes his brief period working for Shell Oil in Africa, how he joined the RAF, crashed and was seriously injured in Libya, and how he fought as a fighter pilot in Greece in 1941. He then moved to the British Embassy in Washington as an intelligence officer, where C.S. Forester encouraged him to take up writing.

After the war he returned to England and over the next 20 years established an international reputation as a short-story writer, with stories which generally explore the darker side of human nature – his major collections are *Someone Like You* (USA, 1974; UK, 1975), *Kiss Kiss* (1960) and *Switch Bitch* (1974). He was involved (often acrimoniously) in film scripts for *You Only Live Twice* (1967), *CHITTY CHITTY BANG BANG* (1968), *Willy Wonka and the Chocolate Factory* (1971) and *The Night Digger* (1971), a vehicle for his actress wife, Patricia Neal, which flopped.

The 1960s were a period both of personal tragedy and literary success. In 1960, his four-month-old son Theo suffered brain damage when his pram was hit by a taxi in New York. In 1962 his daughter Olivia died at the age of seven; and in 1965 Patricia Neal had a massive stroke. In the cases of Theo and Patricia, Dahl used all his resources and contacts to restore both of them as far as possible to normal life: the death of his daughter affected him deeply. But in 1961 he had published (in the United States) a FANTASY based on stories told to his daughters, *James and the Giant Peach* (filmed in 1996). This quirky picaresque can be read both as cheerful fantasy and as psychological allegory.

Charlie and the Chocolate Factory, among the most popular children's books of all time, appeared in the United States in 1964. Ironically, several major British publishers had turned it down before Allen & Unwin published it in 1967. It is in many ways an old-fashioned, STRUWWELPETER-like moral tale, with ruthless punishments being meted out to revolting children, and the poor and honest child being inordinately rewarded. The book was famously attacked by the critic ELEANOR CAMERON (and others) for its black pygmy workers, the 'Oompa-Loompas' (their colour was later changed by Dahl to a politically correct pink), and for its alleged sadism and general tastelessness. In some ways this and other attacks forced Dahl to formulate an attitude to children's writing, fundamentally that 'children are much more vulgar than grown ups. They have a coarser sense of humour. They are basically more cruel. So often, though, adults judge a children's book by their own standards rather than by the child's standards.'

Fantastic Mr Fox (1970) confirmed Dahl as a major writer for children, and even his relative failures, such as *The Magic Finger* (USA, 1966; UK, 1970) or *Charlie and the Great Glass Elevator* (USA, 1972; UK, 1973) – he regretted being persuaded to write a sequel to *Charlie and the Chocolate Factory* – sold well. His output was variable, ranging from cruder pieces like *The Twits* (UK, 1980; USA, 1981) to finely tuned books like *The BFG* (1982), and from verses such as *Dirty Beasts* (1983), which had a varied reception, to happy PICTUREBOOKS such as *The Giraffe, the Pelly and Me* (1985). The illustrating of his books by QUENTIN BLAKE, which began with *The Enormous Crocodile* (1978) and which eventually extended retrospectively to *Charlie and the Chocolate Factory* and *Fantastic Mr Fox*, often subtly toned down the savagery of Dahl's work.

There is no question that his books demonstrate a remarkable intelligence, and at their best – in *Going Solo* or *The BFG* – more than competent craftsmanship. It may be that Dahl rode his hobby horses a little hard at times, and that the fact that he remained, as AIDAN CHAMBERS observed, a ten-year-old boy in many ways, did not necessarily produce balanced work. Dahl suffered fools – and, latterly, it has been suggested, almost anyone who disagreed with him – not at all. As he said in his last interview (and he appears to have been fond of playing with interviewers): 'If I don't like what people say or write about me, I simply say they're wrong. Sod 'em.' And yet he was proud to think that 'if he were to knock on any door in the world at a house with children, he would be offered a cup of tea'. Rather too much of the criticism of Dahl has been partisan, leaning heavily on biography and personality, and on a very simplistic cause–effect concept of reading, but it cannot be denied that he was both skilled craftsman and shrewd businessman.

Part of Dahl's posthumous income is distributed by The Roald Dahl Foundation. Set up by his second wife, Felicity, this has made substantial grants to medical and educational causes, and a major Roald Dahl Children's Arts Centre in Cardiff's dockland, centred on the Norwegian Church where he was baptised, has been proposed. PLH

Daily Mail Annual for Boys and Girls British ANNUAL edited first by ENID BLYTON (1945) and later by Susan French. The first issue is a highly valued collectors' item, featuring as it does strip cartoons of pre-war features such as *Come on Steve* by Roland Davies and *The Nipper* by Brian White, as well as the *Mail*'s juvenile hero *TEDDY TAIL*, revived by Arthur Potts, who signed himself 'Spot'. Story illustrators included the famous and individualistic Eric Parker, remembered for his stylish pictures of SEXTON BLAKE the detective. The annual divided into two from 1956, one for boys and the other for girls, and together they ran well into the 1960s. DG

Dale, Penny 1954– British illustrator. A graduate from Exeter College of Art and Design, Dale's early career was in community art and theatre projects and in graphic design. Her children's PICTUREBOOKS are characterised by delicate drawing and close and warm observation of domestic incident. She has won awards and commendations for such books as *Wake up, Mr. B!* (1988), *Once There Were Giants* (MARTIN WADDELL, 1989) and *Rosie's Babies* (Martin Waddell, 1990). She has produced a series of three COUNTING BOOKS, *Ten in the Bed* (1990), *Ten out of Bed* (1996) and *Ten Play Hide-and-Seek* (1998), and in 2000 she illustrated Waddell's picturebook *Night Night, Cuddly Bear*. An early title, *Bet You Can't!* (1987) portrays black children with humour and faithful realism, and makes imaginative use of frames and speech bubbles. JAG

***Dalemark* series** Novels by DIANA WYNNE JONES, comprising *Cart and Cwidder* (1975), *Drowned Ammet* (1977), *The Spellcoats* (1979) and *The Crown of Dalemark* (1993). They are set in a world where magic operates and which is split by political tension. The first three novels are independent of each other, though the fourth volume, written 14 years later, brings the threads and some of the protagonists of the earlier novels together in a quest for the lost crown of Dalemark. The series, while managing to avoid its clichés, conforms more closely to the configurations of traditional FANTASY than most of Wynne Jones's other work. SA

Dalgliesh, Alice 1893–1979 Author and editor of children's books. Born and raised in Trinidad, educated in England and the United States, Dalgliesh worked as a kindergarten and elementary school teacher and taught courses in children's literature at Columbia

University before becoming children's book editor for Scribner's in 1934, where she published the work of such writers as MARCIA BROWN, KATHERINE MILHOUSE and LEO POLITI. Meanwhile she continued to work at her own writing. Among her best-known books are several Newbery Honour Books – *The Silver Pencil* (1945), *The Bears on Hemlock Mountain* (1953) and *The Courage of Sarah Noble* (1955). *The Thanksgiving Story*, illustrated by HELEN SEWELL, was a Caldecott Honour Book. Two fictionalised autobiographies (see BIOGRAPHY AND AUTOBIOGRAPHY) provide fascinating insights into her life and personality. The deeply moving *The Silver Pencil* tells of her childhood and early adulthood, and her quest to become a writer and find a place she could call home. *Along Janet's Road* (1946) depicts her beginnings as an editor, and contains fascinating sketches of several famous authors for children and adults whose identity is fun to guess. All of Dalgliesh's children's books reflect her love and understanding of real children, and the best are excellent for reading aloud. LH

Dallas [Mumford], Ruth 1919– New Zealand historical writer and poet, whose strength comes from her exact observation of the South Island landscape, her understanding of people and her firm grasp of reality. For Dallas there is no escapism, no FANTASY. Four of her books, *The Children in the Bush* (1969), *The Wild Boy in the Bush* (1971), *The Big Flood in the Bush* (1972) and *Holiday Time in the Bush* (1983), are based on her mother's childhood in the 1890s. In these stories, the children's widowed mother, a nurse, struggles to support her youngsters in a remote New Zealand sawmilling community. Dallas took her pen-name from her admired grandmother, Mrs Dallas, the nurse. Her books reflect sympathy for the old and the poor. *Shining Rivers* (1979), set during Otago's gold rush, explores Johnnie's growing friendship with an elderly prospector, and in *The House on the Cliffs* (1975) a child learns to understand an old woman's need to be independent. *A Dog called Wig* (1970) is about a boy in the 1930s who longed for a dog. All the stories grapple with the real problems of life, and make an earlier New Zealand come alive for young readers. SDP

Dalton, Annie 1948– British writer of FANTASY for young adults and children, whose work has been slowly gaining a reputation for itself. Though she only began her writing career at the age of 40 with *Out of the Ordinary* in 1988, she has produced 12 books in nine years, of which *The Afterdark Princess* (1990) won the Nottingham Library Oak Award, *Night Maze* (1989) was shortlisted for the CARNEGIE MEDAL, and *The Real Tilly Beany* (1991) received a Carnegie Medal commendation.

These marks of recognition are well deserved; her FANTASY is fresh and original, written in natural, modern idiom and uncluttered by tired, purple prose. Her studies of the emotionally or socially underprivileged manage to avoid coyness, sentimentality and aggressiveness. It is noticeable, for instance, that with the exception of the *Tilly Beany* books, the children in her works, even in those for young readers, tend to come from broken or troubled homes. However, the child 'victims' of these situations are not only un-self-pitying but capable of great love, and it is through them that the healing within the various work eventually comes. Though much of Dalton's work examines familial unhappiness, her work is nonetheless essentially protective and tender towards the child. Parents, even when unable to get along with each other, are seen to do their best by their children and are positively presented, unlike in many 'problem novels' which show parents as helpless, inadequate and the source of their children's problems.

Dalton's fantasies operate simultaneously on two planes: as fantasy and as studies of children or adolescents with emotional or family problems. And though the different aspects of her work are in general well integrated, the narrative moving fluidly from one mode to another, on the whole one gains the impression that the novels are weighted in favour of one aspect, the fantasy plots being somewhat subordinated to the working out of the 'problem novel' plots. In *Naming the Dark* (1993), for example, the fantasy plot which involves the fall of Atlantis only tantalisingly sketches in the Atlantean background of the children, and the Atlantean element fades off at the end, its outcome uncompleted.

The fantasy elements in Annie Dalton's books may be seen to be closely related to the emotional and psychological states of her characters, and the working out of the fantastic plots to correspond to changes in their inner lives. In *Night Maze*, the 'curse' lying upon the Noone family which dooms each member to a life of non-fulfillment is tagged to emotional isolation and the failure to value human relationships – these things lying at the symbolic heart of the maze. In order to undo the curse, Gerald and Harriet have first to break through the barriers which surround the individuals within the household. In *The Afterdark Princess*, a work for younger children, Joe Quail, transported from our world to the realm of Afterdark and sent on a hero's quest, loses both his cowardice and friendlessness. Dalton's latest work is *The Dream Snatcher* (1998), a sequel to *The Afterdark Princess*. SA

Daly, Maureen 1921– American writer of a classic girls' coming-of-age novel. Although Daly has written many books for children and young adults, her most famous novel was her first, written when she was a teenager. *Seventeenth Summer* (1942) has become a classic of YOUNG ADULT LITERATURE. Though reti-

Engraving by the Dalziel Brothers of an illustration by A.W. Bayes for HANS CHRISTIAN ANDERSEN's 'The Wild Swans'.

cent by today's standards, Daly's story of a young girl's first romance was considered frank in the 1940s: the heroine, Angie Morrow, experiences her first dance, beer, kiss and unmistakable erotic stirrings. The novel ends on a practical note, however, when Angie parts from her working-class boyfriend to go to college. The novel was a great success and Daly even received fan mail from soldiers stationed overseas. She graduated from Rosy College and married the writer William P. McGivern, winner of the Edgar Award and author of *Soldiers of '44* (1979). In the 1960s Daly wrote several books for younger readers, including *The Ginger Horse* (1964) and *The Small War of Sergeant Donkey* (1966), both illustrated by WESLEY DENNIS. Other titles dealt with a young boy's visits to a farm, a library, a zoo, and Europe, where the Dalys raised their own children. Later, Daly was prompted by the death of her daughter Megan to return to girls' fiction; in *Acts of Love* (1986) and *First a Dream* (1990) the heroine, Henrietta is modelled on Megan. NV

Daly, Niki 1946– Internationally acclaimed South African illustrator and writer, as well as a recorded song-writer. Daly has been an inspiration and trend-setter for South African book ILLUSTRATION. Born in Cape Town, he has lectured in graphic design, worked as a series editor and now freelances. His award-winning *Not So Fast, Songololo* (1985) was the first ever South African PICTUREBOOK featuring a black urban child and has been animated on video by Weston Woods in the United States with the voice of GCINA MHLOPHE. Daly's illustrations for *Charlie's House* by Reviva Schermbrucker (1989) showed that a child living in a tin shack in a township was not robbed of imagination. *The Dancer* (with co-author Nola Turkington, 1997) captures the dream quality of San (Bushman) life and vision. JHe

see also AFRICAN MYTHOLOGY AND FOLKTALES

Dalziel, George 1815–1902 and **Dalziel, Edward** 1817–1903 Leading British WOOD ENGRAVERS in the second half of the 19th century. They were raised in Newcastle-upon-Tyne and trained as engravers in the tradition of THOMAS BEWICK. Their vast output included work as varied as RICHARD DOYLE's illustrations for JOHN RUSKIN's *THE KING OF THE GOLDEN RIVER*, plates re-engraved for EDWARD LEAR's *BOOK OF NONSENSE*, and SIR JOHN TENNIEL's designs for *ALICE'S ADVENTURES IN WONDERLAND* and *Through the Looking Glass*. Though Dante Gabriel Rossetti in his 'Address to Dalziel Brothers' pleaded:

> O woodman spare that block,
> O gash not anyhow!

other more appreciative artists greatly admired the brothers' skill in reproducing and sometimes enhancing their original drawings. JMB

Dan Dare, Pilot of the Future Hero of the cover story of the most important British COMIC of the 1950s, *EAGLE*. The first issue (14 April 1950) introduced readers to a level of quality and presentation never seen before: the full-colour photogravure printing allowed Frank Hampson's meticulous and imaginative artwork to make an unforgettable impact. Colonel Dare himself, with his faithful batman Digby, became an immediate favourite with hundreds of thousands (possibly millions) of readers. His long-jawed face with the inverted tick at the end of the eyebrows was as much an icon of the atomic age as the Skylon at the Festival of Britain. His most formidable enemy was the Mekon, the leader of the Venusian Treens. The tiny spindly figure of the Mekon under his vast domed head, hovering on a little saucer above his green-faced troops, contributed a great deal to the success of the strip. Dan Dare's heyday lasted 20 years or so. For all the modernistic glamour of the settings, he was too old-fashioned a figure to function competently in the uneasy morality of the 1970s and 80s, despite attempts to revive him. PNP

Dandy The first weekly comic paper for children to be published by the Scottish firm D.C. Thomson of Dundee. It first appeared on 4 December 1937, and is still published, having celebrated its golden jubilee in 1997 with a double-sized special. The *Dandy* ANNUAL commenced the following year in September 1938 (undated) and for its first 14 years was called *The Dandy Monster Comic*, switching to *The Dandy Book* from the 1952 edition. The first edition cost 2s.6d and is now worth some £4,000. Originally only the covers and preliminary pages were newly drawn, but more recent issues contain especially drawn adventures of favourite characters. DG

***Dangerous Angels* series** The collection of FRANCESCA LIA BLOCK's five postmodern FAIRY TALES that trace the 'almost-family' saga of a group of colourful but unconventional characters living in contemporary Los Angeles; the first was *Weetzie Bat* (1989). Block's vivid glimpse into contemporary youth culture is conveyed in a highly poetic style that is part magical realism and part MTV (Music Television); it combines popular culture and sub-cultures with fairy tales and myth. Some adults find Block's reporting of alternative lifestyles troubling.

Weetzie Bat is the story of an idealist adolescent girl, Weetzie, and her best friend Dirk, a young gay punk rocker. Weetzie and Dirk live together in a fairy-tale cottage left to them by Dirk's grandmother. Block's richly textured descriptions of LA and ear for language make these slender novels fascinating. For Weetzie and her company, Los Angeles is a fabulous wonderland. They refer to it as 'Shangri-L.A.' where it 'was hot and cool, glam and slam, rich and trashy, devils and angels, Los Angeles'. Dirk and Weetzie are given a magical lamp which provides them with three wishes. Both seek true love, but quickly learn in the age of AIDS that 'Love is a dangerous angel'. Dirk finds happiness with a young surfer named Duck, while Weetzie eventually falls in love with an older film-maker, My Secret Agent Lover Man. When Weetzie wants a baby, Secret Agent Lover Man refuses, but Dirk and Duck help Weetzie conceive, which results in the birth of Cherokee Bat. Shocked by Weetzie's actions, her lover temporarily leaves but commits his own infidelity, resulting in the arrival of the mysterious infant, Witch Baby. Adjusting to the changes in this unconventional family, the couple reunite, realising that life, unlike fairy tales, rarely comes with 'a happily ever after' conclusion.

In *Witch Baby* (1991) the protagonist, now an adolescent, who has always felt 'not one of them', has to discover her birth mother, before she can take her place in her extended family. *Cherokee Bat and the Goat Guys* (1992) deals with the sexual awakening of Weetzie's two daughters, Cherokee and Witch Baby. They are members of the band The Goat Guys, with their boyfriends, Raphael and Angel Juan, and learn the power and destruction of making music, making love and using drugs. Witch Baby searches for her boyfriend in New York City with the help of her grandfather's ghost in *Missing Angel Juan* (1993), and *Baby Be-Bop* (1995) tells the story of Dirk's coming out as a gay teen before he met Weetzie. Block is one of the most original and controversial voices of adolescent literature to emerge in the 1990s. JCS

see also GAY AND LESBIAN LITERATURE; SEX IN CHILDREN'S LITERATURE

Daniel Boone 1734–1820 American frontiersman, woodsman and pioneer. James Fennimore Cooper, in his *LEATHER-STOCKING TALES*, used as sources events in Boone's life. Timothy Flint's *Biographical Memoir of Daniel Boone, the First Settler of Kentucky* (1833) was the most widely read BIOGRAPHY in antebellum America. DAVY CROCKETT self-consciously adopted mannerisms popularly associated with Boone to heighten his legendary status. Stories of the two later became confounded when the same actor, Fess Parker, played both of them on TELEVISION. EDB

Dankyi, Osafoa Ghanaian writer and broadcaster. One of the older generation of writers, Osafoa Dankyi brings the oral and literary traditions together in her work. Well-versed in her native Akan customs and traditions, she takes most of the material for her children's books from folklore. Her children's book *Ananse Searches for a Fool and Other Stories* (1994) – an excellent example of her work – is a collection of popular Akan folktales written to capture the excitement of traditional STORYTELLING and the pleasure of reading. MAs

see also ANANCY

Dann, Colin see *THE ANIMALS OF FARTHING WOOD* SERIES

Dann, Max 1955– Australian writer whose witty titles (backed up by racy writing) such as *Adventures with My Worst Best Friend* (1982), *Going Bananas* (1983), *Bernice Knows Best* (1983) and *Dusting in Love* (1990) have won Dann an enthusiastic following among Australian junior readers. More than most, Dann can dramatise the fears, embarrassments, confusion, obsessions, the ineptness and frustrations of childhood, yet show with affection and sympathy the vulnerability and absurdities that make life for the young both painful and challenging. In *Clark* (1987), for instance, a seemingly sadistic teacher, aptly named Mr Grimwraither, is actually driven by loneliness, as the fearful, even wimpish young Clark comes to realise. MSax

Danny Fox (1966) Animal story by David Thomson. The title character possesses many of the qualities of the FOLKTALE fox: greed, cunning and egotism. Like many anthropomorphic animals, he combines adult responsibilities with childlike behaviour and language. The main plot shows him devoting his talents to furthering the marriage between a poor fisherman (whom he previously robbed) and a princess, against the wishes of her cruel step-mother. Despite an abundance of animal and female stereotypes and some didacticism, the effect is humorous and sometimes original. In *Danny Fox Meets a Stranger* (1968) Thomson also includes some REYNARD THE FOX legends. PAP

see also ANIMALS IN FICTION

Danziger, Paula 1944– American writer of children's books and YOUNG ADULT FICTION. One of the best-selling authors for children in the United States, Danziger repeatedly comes under critical fire for her formulaic problem novels. Most of her protagonists are young teenage girls oppressed by parents and coping with divorce, low self-esteem and the opposite sex. Her earliest work, characterised by extreme anger moderated by dry humour, features repressive, emotionally unaware parents whose children must learn to define themselves as individuals. Danziger's first novel, *The Cat Ate My Gymsuit* (1974), featured the puns, sarcasm and zany humour which Danziger has maintained as her hallmark. She has written sequels to most of her books for older readers and has made two forays into series books. In the four *Matthew Martin* books, Danziger experimented for the first time with a male protagonist. *Amber Brown is Not a Crayon* (1994), intended for beginning readers, introduced third-grader Amber Brown, who must cope with her parents' divorce and the move of a friend. Unlike many series, the *Amber Brown* books are not static; Amber moves from grade to grade, making progress and facing occasional set-backs. Danziger is as popular in Britain as she is in the United States, appearing regularly on BBC TELEVISION. She has collaborated with Ann M. Martin (author of *THE BABY-SITTERS CLUB* series) on *P.S. Longer Letter Later* (1998) and its sequel, *Snail Mail No More* (2000). CEJ

Dark is Rising, The FANTASY series by British author SUSAN COOPER, taking its title from its second volume (1973), the other books being, *Over Sea, Under Stone* (1965), *Greenwitch* (1974), *The Grey King* (Newbery Medal, 1975) and *Silver on the Tree* (1977). The series is structured as a quest whose ultimate aim is the final defeat of the Dark forces. Will Stanton, the last of the Old Ones (the forces of Light), Jane, Barney and Simon Drew, and Bran the son of Arthur Pendragon, have to fulfill certain prophecies and recover various things of power which are necessary to their fight against the Dark: the Grail, the six signs, the sword Eirias and the harp of gold. The action of the quest shifts between the real world and a plane of magical and mythic other-reality, which lies outside time, the plane on which the Lost Land still exists and on which Herne the Hunter rides.

The quest structure and the search for magical items is a familiar one to readers of fantasy, but Cooper's treatment of these things, and of the Arthurian legends, rehabilitates and gives them new life. Merlin surfaces as Merriman Lyon, one of the most powerful Old Ones, and the adultery of Guinevere results in her coming momentarily into the 20th century where she leaves Arthur's son, fearing that Arthur might refuse to acknowledge him. The mythic is not merely employed for its archetypal value, its ability to universalise the struggle between good and evil; myth is also explored on the human level at which it is significant only to the individuals involved.

Cooper's treatment of the tropes of the series and its dichotomised terms of reference – Light and Dark – is far from naive. While the Light is weighted as the positive term in this binary structure, its absolutism is spoken of in terms that ironically institute a comparison with the Dark: 'At the heart of the Light there is a cold white flame, just as at the centre of the Dark there is a great black pit bottomless as the Universe' (*The Grey King*). The absolute good is necessary from the cosmic perspective, but this is sharply perspectivised against the sacrifices the individual may often be called upon to make in order that the Light might triumph. John Rowlands, Bran's friend, says, 'I would take the one human being over all the principle, all the time' (*The Grey King*). The tragedy and sense of loss he feels prevents there being any easy valorisation of absolute good, though paradoxically his sacrifice, and those of others on behalf of the Light, act as a powerful testimony to the reality of the war they are engaged in and the importance of the victory going to the Light.

SA

Darke, Marjorie 1929– British novelist, many of whose novels have a historical theme. *The First of Midnight* (1977) is set in 18th-century Bristol, after the legal abolition of slavery but before it had disappeared in practice. Neither Midnight the slave nor the servant Jess have much to hope for from life, but both are determined not to be worn down by circumstances. This strength of character – particularly in the face of historical adversity – is a feature of many of Darke's novels. Her heroes and heroines are often working-class, with little money. In *A Long Way To Go* (1982) the young black British hero is determined not to fight in the First World War despite the reactions of those around him. The same tenacity and determination are shown by Emily Palmer, the heroine of *A Question of Courage* (1975) and *A Rose From Blighty* (1990). In the first of the two novels she fights for women to get the vote and in the second she goes to work as a Voluntary Aid Department nurse in France. Both novels show how many of the difficulties affect both Emily and her richer friend, regardless of class.

KA

Darley, F(elix) O(ctavius) C(arr) 1822–88 Popular American illustrator of the 19th century, so well-known that publishers would often print his name on a book's cover as a selling point. Born in Philadelphia, the first publication Darley illustrated, *Scenes in Indian Life* (1843), displayed his love for western subjects. Darley was promoted early on in his career by EDGAR ALLAN POE, who in 1845 published his designs in *Saturday Museum*. Working in a variety of media and styles, Darley went on to illustrate more than 200 books, including many of James Fenimore Cooper's *LEATHER-STOCKING TALES* and works by NATHANIEL HAWTHORNE and CHARLES DICKENS. He is perhaps best known for the ILLUSTRATIONS he produced for his friend WASHINGTON IRVING in *Rip Van Winkle* (1848) and *The Legend of Sleepy Hollow* (1849). Darley's work is marked by his frequent use of numerous figures moulded into fluid and dramatic scenes. They are often types rather than individuals, and very staged, but they display a keen sense of gesture and movement.

SCWA

Darton, J. Harvey see DARTON FAMILY; see also *CHATTERBOX*; CRITICAL APPROACHES TO CHILDREN'S LITERATURE; *HOLIDAY HOUSE*; *ORIGINAL STORIES FROM REAL LIFE*; *PETER PAN*; ANN AND JANE TAYLOR

Darton family Children's publishers. William Darton set up as a bookseller in London in 1787, himself writing and illustrating some of his first children's publications. He was joined in 1791 by Joseph Harvey, beginning a partnership between the two Quaker families at Gracechurch Street which continued until the 1840s. Priscilla Wakefield's prose works and ANN and JANE TAYLOR's verse established their reputation. In 1804 Darton's eldest son, also William, started his own independent house at Holborn Hill. Though his output was rather similar to his father's, it differed in that it included traditional NURSERY RHYMES. William Junior's son John, who succeeded him (and at about the same time left the Society of Friends), had as partner Samuel Clark and later Frederick Hodge. The Holborn Hill firm, which published *PETER PARLEY'S ANNUAL* and many of MRS SHERWOOD's later works, came to an end in 1866. Of Wells Gardner, Darton & Co., the third Darton family firm, John's son Joseph, formerly a partner, became sole proprietor in 1880. Its publications included E. NESBIT's *THE RAILWAY CHILDREN* and JOHN MASEFIELD's *Martin Hyde* and *Jim Davis*. Masefield's two works were first serialised in *CHATTERBOX* under the editorship of F.J. Harvey Darton. In 1928 the Darton family ceased to be connected with the firm, thus ending 141 years' involvement in PUBLISHING children's books.

LD

Dasent, Sir George see *THREE BILLY GOATS GRUFF*

Daugherty, James 1889–1974 American author and illustrator who specialised in BIOGRAPHY and history. Initially an artist, his first notable work was the illustration of S.E. White's *Daniel Boone* (1926). He illustrated a number of historical works, including *Abe Lincoln* (1943), *Knickerbocker's History of New York* (1928) and UNCLE TOM'S CABIN (1852), and then turned to writing himself, his first book being *Andy and the Lion* (1938), based on the Androcles legend. The book has been praised as a model of PICTUREBOOK design, with its skilful integration of text and pictures. His earthy, fluid drawings earned him a Caldecott Honor citation. Daugherty eventually turned to writing longer works, which he also illustrated, but he abandoned the picturebook format altogether. The first full-length book which he both wrote and illustrated, *Daniel Boone* (1939), won the NEWBERY MEDAL and was followed by two other notable biographies, *Poor Richard* (1941), a life of Benjamin Franklin, and *Abraham Lincoln* (1943), both of which he illustrated. These works, for older children, are robust celebrations of the American spirit. He wrote several books about the American western frontier, which had always fascinated him, and continued to illustrate the works of others, including several books by his wife. DLR

Daughter of the Wind (1989) Novel by Suzanne Fisher Staples about the lives of the nomadic people in the Cholistan desert and the heroine's struggle to accept the idea of an arranged marriage. Shabanu is an independent heroine determined not to submit to the pressures of society, but even she has to sacrifice herself for the sake of her family. Written after the author spent time in the Cholistan desert, the book depicts life for the nomads as harsh and brutal, though the view of the marriage customs is clearly that of an outsider. A sequel, *Haveli*, was published in 1994. KA

Davidson, Andrew 1958– British wood engraver, taught by JOHN LAWRENCE whilst at the Royal College of Art. Davidson is best known for his dark, intense ILLUSTRATIONS for the second edition of *THE IRON MAN* (TED HUGHES), which won the KURT MASCHLER AWARD in 1985. He also illustrated Hughes's *Tales from the Early World* (1988) and *The Iron Woman* (1993) with equally highly charged and deftly designed WOOD ENGRAVINGS. JAG

Davies, Andrew (Wyndham) 1936– British playwright and novelist, born in Cardiff, who worked as an English teacher and university lecturer before his success as a writer and adaptor of TELEVISION drama. *The Fantastic Feats of Doctor Boox* (1972) and the *Marmalade Atkins* series (from 1979) are episodically surreal, but in *Alfonso Bonzo* (1986) a schoolboy's swapped television set leaks 3D images into his life in ways that are frightening as well as funny. Davies has written sympathetically about the teaching profession in the play *Prin* (1989), which urges teachers to be 'extraordinary people' and teach children to be 'extraordinary people', and in the PICTUREBOOKS *Raj in Charge* (1994) and *Poonam's Pets* (1992) children are empowered by fantastical encounters in realistic classroom settings. The dangerous yet liberating power of FANTASY is more penetratingly explored in the award-winning *Conrad's War* (1978). Through his obsession with war games, a boy is drawn into TIME-SLIP experiences as a World War II bomber pilot, prisoner and enemy soldier, and comes finally to understand the 'sad and serious' aspects of war. Davies is a sharp and often provocative observer of contemporary British culture, creating especially convincing male characters and relishing the eruption of comic and often transformational anarchy into ordinary family life. SG

Davies, W.H. 1871–1940 Welsh writer, known as the 'tramp poet'. Davies had a wild boyhood in which he lost his foot in an accident. He enjoyed some critical acclaim and popularity for his often simple lyrical verse. He has a small place in *THE OXFORD BOOK OF CHILDREN'S VERSE* but is now best known for poems like 'The Cat' and 'Leisure', a mainstay of the school anthology, which includes the memorable couplet: 'What is this life if, full of care, / We have no time to stand and stare.' MCCS

Davison, Frank Dalby see ANIMALS IN FICTION; see also THE BUSH; PUBLISHING AND PUBLISHERS

Davy Crockett 1786–1836 An expert bear hunter from Tennessee who became an American folk hero because of his exaggerated TALL TALES about himself and because of his death at the Battle of the Alamo. When he ran for Congress, Crockett described himself as half-horse, half-alligator, with a touch of snapping turtle, and such descriptions plus his outrageous hunting boasts made him a popular character in plays and DIME NOVELS of the 19th century. As with many figures in the American West, the reality of Crockett's life was much more sedate than the stories that developed around him. DISNEY revived interest in the Crockett character in 1955 with a movie and TELEVISION show. EBD

Day, Thomas 1748–1789 British writer often referred to as the English ROUSSEAU. Day tried to apply the Frenchman's philosophy to the upbringing of his wards and his friend's child, Dick Edgeworth, but their response to his training was unenthusiastic. Neverthless, in *THE HISTORY OF LITTLE JACK* (1787) and *SANDFORD AND MERTON* (1789), Day's fictional heroes embodied his egalitarian conviction that birth and breeding are meaningless encumbrances compared with an intelligent resourcefulness. Day's

A Day of Rhymes: illustration from *A Night of Lullabies* by Sarah Pooley.

humanitarian approach, encompassing a hatred of slavery and of cruelty to animals, was absorbed by many 19th-century schoolboys who had few realistic fictional role models with whom to identify. CWB

Day Lewis, C. see *OTTERBURY INCIDENT, THE*; see also ADVENTURE STORIES; *ALICE'S ADVENTURES IN WONDERLAND*

Day of Rhymes, A (1987) Popular British collection of NURSERY RHYMES for children, selected and illustrated by Sarah Pooley, and winner of the *Parents' Magazine* Best Book for Babies award. Traditional action rhymes (like 'Ring a ring a roses' and 'Two fat gentlemen met in a lane') are accompanied by pictures demonstrating the movements. The multicultural ILLUSTRATIONS are bright, vigorous and cartoon-like, with a strong emphasis on smiling faces. The originality of the collection lay in the inclusion of some less well-known rhymes, and in the ingenuity of some of the pictures – 'Hey diddle, diddle', for example, shows a child miming a cow while jumping over another with a moon on his pyjamas, as a third child runs off with a dish and a spoon. Sarah Pooley has also illustrated INFORMATION BOOKS and other collections of poetry for younger children, including a companion anthology, *A Night of Lullabies* (1991). VW

Day of the Triffids, The (1951) SCIENCE FICTION novel by the British author John Wyndham. A man wakes to find everyone else blinded overnight in a global catastrophe. His gripping personal chronicle documents the secretly longed-for civilisation breakdown that ensues, and the moral choices facing the survivors. CMP

Day They Came to Arrest the Book, The (1982) Provocative novel by the American Nat Hentoff, which examines the issue of CENSORSHIP in public schools. A small town is divided when a group of parents attempt to have *Huckleberry Finn* (see *ADVENTURES OF TOM SAWYER*) eradicated from a high-school curriculum and library. Hentoff does an admirable job of defending the book while giving a fair amount of coverage to some of the common arguments in support of censorship. While the novel lacks depth and thematic intensity, the variety and attitude of the characters help to make it an informative and a useful book for instigating a discussion about censorship. JGJ

de Angeli, Marguerite (Lofft) 1889–1987 American writer and illustrator best known for her children's books focusing on minority groups. She won the 1950 NEWBERY MEDAL for *The Door in the Wall* (1949), depicting a handicapped child's courage and determination to live a meaningful life in medieval England. This was followed in 1956 by *Black Fox of Lorne*, another historical novel, set in 10th-century Scotland at the time of the Norse invasions. LAW

see also HISTORICAL FICTION

de Brunhoff, Jean and Laurent see *BABAR* SERIES; see also MUSIC AND STORY

***De Danann* trilogy** see MICHAEL SCOTT

de Genlis, Mme see DRAMA FOR CHILDREN

de Graft-Hanson, J.O. Ghanaian Professor of Classics and writer, who has written much-loved story books for children and young adults. He explores the oral and narrative traditions in both folklore and history, blurring the line between the two as is the tradition of most pre-literate societies. The finest example of the deftness in his use of folk legend and oral history is his book *Amanfi's Gold* (1996). In this story, a small group of students are fired by their imagination and the hint from a palmwine drunkard. They go in search of the caves in which the last major battle was fought between two warring tribes. One of the tribes was led by Amanfi, the legendary giant who carried his sister round in a hut so that he could have an endless supply of popcorn. The youngsters find the caves and stumble upon heaps of gold, but an explosion shakes the ground and the cave collapses and disappears. MAs

de Hamel, Joan 1924– New Zealand writer whose first book, *X Marks the Spot* (1973), set in the New Zealand BUSH, gives detailed and child-centred descriptions of flora and fauna. Just as important are de Hamel's child characters who provide unexpected depths, considering the holiday ADVENTURE genre. De Hamel's English origins are highlighted in this novel by expressions such as 'jolly decent', but she showed her commitment to high-quality indigenous literature by producing *Take the Long Path* (1978), winner of the ESTHER GLEN AWARD which explores with great sensitivity a boy discovering his Maori identity. *The Third Eye* (1987) is a complex, multilayered text about Maori/Pakeha relationships, conservation and establishing a sense of place within the landscape. BN

de Horne Vaisey, Mrs see *GIRL'S OWN PAPER*; ANGELA BRAZIL; SCHOOL STORIES

de La Fontaine, Jean 1621–95 French writer associated with the court of Louis XIV and most famous for his *Fables* (1668–93). La Fontaine rewrote AESOP'S FABLES in lively and sophisticated verse forms, bringing qualities of freshness, gaiety and mordant wit to the ancient genre which have never been surpassed. When British publishers began to produce collections of fables specifically designed for children in the 18th century, texts were initially based mainly on the prose versions of Sir Roger L'Estrange or Samuel Croxall. Translations and adaptations from La Fontaine began to supplant these English models from the 19th century onwards. DWh

de la Mare, Walter [John] 1873–1956 British poet and writer. Any survey of 20th-century children's literature will cite Walter de la Mare as a much-loved major influence. One particular poem, 'The Listeners', still appears in any 'favourite poems' listing, but de la Mare is now less well known to young readers than he was. A pupil at St Paul's Choir School, at 16 he became a clerk for the Anglo-American Oil Company in London, remaining there for 20 years. A lover of books from childhood, he spent his evenings writing adult stories, poems and tales for children. His first published story, *Kismet* (1895), a macabre piece in the 90s fashion, appeared under his pseudonym, Walter Ramal, and showed a taste for the supernatural that would remain.

His first poems, *Songs of Childhood* (1902), displayed the influences of SHAKESPEARE, Blake (see *SONGS OF INNOCENCE*), Herrick and CHRISTINA ROSSETTI, although his unmistakable, individual voice was clear. Among poems of imagination, not specifically for any age group, were some that would be much quoted and still anthologised 40 years later: 'How large unto the tiny fly / must little things appear'; 'If I were Lord of Tartary / Myself and me alone'; 'I spied John Mouldy in his cellar.' *The Three Mulla-Mulgars* (1910), a full-length ADVENTURE STORY, relates the quest of three Royal Monkey brothers for their father. Children were either captivated or bewildered by the allegorical romance and, though once highly praised, it has not survived. *PEACOCK PIE* (1913) is the collection which established him. Frequently reissued in different illustrated editions, the contents seem as fresh and sparkling today as ever.

Down-Adown-Derry (1922) gathered de la Mare's fairy poems, and *Stuff and Nonsense* (1927), a quirky collection, included his variations on the LIMERICK, revealing a tongue-in-cheek dark humour: Dr Jones's cure for aching bones is 'to take them out'.

The poems for *This Year, Next Year* (1931) were written to complement Harold Jones's ILLUSTRATIONS – a task in no way inhibiting, resulting in an attractive, now collectable book. *Bells and Grass* (1941) featured poems rediscovered in a 35-year-old commonplace book, although 'the time intervening seemed to have vanished away like smoke'. New rhymes added were 'written with precisely the same hope as the old had been'. Here is Dainty Miss Apathy; Old Mr Jones who 'every hour is growing younger'; Master Proud-Face, 'pale as a pudding'; and Old Ben Baily who has 'Been and done / For a small brown bunny / With his long gun.'

Critics who label de la Mare fey and whimsical, his mysterious other-wordliness a cheat, forget his robust humour, meticulous craftsmanship, and above all his clear intention and respect for the reader. If, finally, too many poems poured from his fertile imagination and eager pen, enough of true brilliance affirm his belief that 'only the rarest kind of best in anything can be good enough for the young'.

Collected Stories for Children, the work of over 40 years, won the 1947 CARNEGIE MEDAL. These stories are dense and detailed, and the ideas very widely ranged, from what are almost FAIRY STORIES to stories narrated by one character to another, often an elderly person to a child. Old ladies and old houses were favourite subjects. In *The Riddle*, the shortest, most enigmatic story, seven children are warned by their grandmother 'not to meddle in the old oak-chest' – one by one each disappears into its depth. A lover of unanswered questions – who were the 'phantom listeners' of that poem? – de la Mare supplied no solution, unless, perhaps, the end of childhood was implied.

His occasional essays and introductions would form a rare collection, and he was also a discerning editor. *COME HITHER* (1923) remains the best anthology of the 20th century. In 'Around and Roundabout' detailed notes, anecdotes and more verse reveal de la Mare's inquisitive research, tireless enthusiasm, vast love and knowledge of literature and his desire to pass it on. He was made a Companion of Honour in 1948 and awarded the Order of Merit in 1953. LEONARD CLARK, in a Bodley Head Monograph (1960), writes: 'To meet this man was an unforgettable experience' – to discover his work is another. AHa

see also *JOY STREET*

de Regniers, Beatrice Schenk 1914–2000 American writer. De Regniers grew up in Indiana, and originally wanted to pursue a theatrical life. Dissuaded by her father, she became a social worker, but danced professionally in her free time. After marriage she moved to New York and became an editor and writer, founding the *Scholastic* Lucky Book Club in 1961. De Regniers was a prolific writer, with more than 30 books to her credit since 1953, including nearly a dozen books written during the 1960s under the pen name 'Tamara Kitt'. Most of de Regniers' books are based on retellings or adaptations of traditional tales, and her works in general are characterised by simple, precise and lyrical language which seems almost choreographed. Books like *Little Sister and the Month Brothers* (1976) and *A Little House of Your Own* (1954) are gentle and reassuring in tone, and easy to read aloud. Occasionally, de Regniers' attempts to overtly explore children's emotions or experience can seem obscure, as in *The Boy, The Rat, and The Butterfly* (1971). De Regniers published several volumes of original poetry for children, and a number of books which feature cats, including the still-favoured *So Many Cats!* (1984). Artist BENI MONTRESOR won a CALDECOTT MEDAL for his ILLUSTRATION of de Regniers' *May I Bring a Friend?* (1964). MJKP

de Roo, Anne (Louise) 1931– New Zealand writer of historical novels, winner of the New Zealand Children's Book of the Year in 1984. Since 1969 de Roo has written over 15 children's books, mostly HISTORICAL FICTION covering the period from the 1850s to the 1950s. This is a unique body of work, unmatched in capturing early and rural New Zealand life. Nineteenth-century settlers' journeys, burning off and breaking in the land, the coming of age of young men and women in a physically tough land, and the flattening of class barriers are the themes of these precisely constructed books. De Roo advocates animal care, hard farm-work, mountain walking and country space for the emotional rebuilding of her characters. She has a sure touch when working with the English settler or colonial family, but displays a slight awkwardness as she explicates, rather than reveals, issues of race relations. Prize-winning, historically accurate *Jacky Nobody* (1983) is set in the early Northland wars between British soldiers and sympathetically drawn Maori warriors. Reflecting de Roo's liberal 1970s view, the hero, mixed-race orphan Jacky, must acknowledge both sides of his parentage to become a strong adult – as must New Zealand, in De Roo's eyes. MJH

de Villeneuve, Mme see *BEAUTY AND THE BEAST*

Deadwood Dick A literary character created by Edward L. Wheeler in 33 stories for Beadle and Adams' DIME NOVELS (1877–85). Deadwood Dick turns to noble outlawry in Deadwood, Dakota Territory, in order to escape the corrupt society of the eastern United States. His most important sidekick is CALAMITY JANE. Some controversy exists as to whether Deadwood Dick was based on the life of Nat Love, an African American cowboy; though Love claims the nickname, Wheeler is unlikely to have known of his existence, since no evidence suggests that Wheeler travelled in the West. EBD

Deary, Terry see *HORRIBLE HISTORIES* SERIES

Deerslayer, The see *LEATHER-STOCKING TALES*

Defoe, Daniel see *ROBINSON CRUSOE*

DeJong, Meindert 1906–91 Children's novelist. Born in the Netherlands, DeJong emigrated to the United States at the age of eight and spent most of his life in Michigan. His novels tend to describe his life in the Netherlands or on the farm in Michigan. For instance, the NEWBERY MEDAL winner, *The Wheel on the School* (1954), describes Dutch school children and the custom of placing a wheel on the roofs of buildings to attract nesting storks. He described his experiences in China during World War II in *The House of Sixty Fathers* (1956); like six others of his books, this was illustrated by MAURICE SENDAK. Many of his stories, such as his first book *The Big Goose and the Little White Duck* (1938), *Hurry Home, Candy* (1953), *The Little Cow and the Turtle* (1955) and *Along Came a Dog* (1958), focus on animals. Addressing a younger audience than the later genre of YOUNG ADULT FICTION, his stories stress the strength and integrity of his small characters, whether children or animals, dwarfed by larger forces around them. DeJong was awarded the Hans Christian Andersen Award in 1962. GRB

Delightful Nights, The see FAIRY TALES; *PUSS IN BOOTS*

DeMille, James 1836–88 Canadian author who wrote for adults and children, but whose greatest success was his *'B.O.W.C.'* (Brethren of the White Cross) series which follows the type of story popularised in England by Thomas Hughes in *TOM BROWN'S SCHOOLDAYS* (1857) and F.W. Farrar in *Eric, or Little by Little* (1858) and is somewhat similar to the *Elm Island* books of the American writer Elijah Kellog. The boy is in a self-contained world, responsible for himself, and must stand on his own merit among his peers. He must deal with personal politics of leadership, discipline and rivalry and confront moral issues such as bullying and cheating. Although these stories flourished in Britain throughout the Victorian era, DeMille's schoolboys must also learn survival skills in the wilderness, a theme uniquely familiar to his Canadian readers for whom the land takes precedence. DeMille's series began with *A Book for Boys* (1869) and continued with *The Boys of the Grand Pré School* (1870), *Fire in the Woods* (1871), *Picked Up Adrift* (1872) and *Treasure of the Sea* (1873). He also wrote a series of *Young Dodge Club* travelogue storybooks, which were based on his own tour of Europe. KSB

Demon Headmaster, The (1982–97) Series of five comic novels by GILLIAN CROSS which gained additional popularity when the series was televised in 1995. In the first novel a school is hypnotised by its headmaster; in later novels his plans become more grandiose and he embarks on a struggle to rule the country checked only by a small group of children who cannot be hypnotised. As the series progresses the headmaster's plans become grander and increasingly unscrupulous. While he plots world domination, the books question the ethics of subliminal advertising and genetic engineering. KA

Dennis the Menace see *BEANO ANNUAL*

Dennis, C(larence Michael) J(ames) 1876–1936 Australian writer, best known for his adult rhyming verse-stories, *The Sentimental Bloke* (1915) and *The Moods of Ginger Mick* (1916). His collection of humorous verse, NONSENSE RHYMES and stories, *A Book for Kids* (1921), written from a child's viewpoint, was a watershed in Australian children's poetry publishing, a welcome contrast to previous insipid or didactic offerings. Dennis's work bears strong similarities to the work of LEWIS CARROLL and EDWARD LEAR in its inventive use of language and ideas. Poems such as 'The Ant Explorer', 'The Circus', 'The Triantiwontigongolope' and 'Hist' have been republished at various times in collections, or illustrated, sometimes grandiosely, as PICTUREBOOKS, but it is the naivety and spontaneity of Dennis's original cartoon-like sketches which best retain the flavour of the verse and allow 'all good children over four and under four-and-eighty' to use their imaginations. JAP

Dennis, Wesley 1903–66 American illustrator from Massachusetts known for portrayals of horses in books for young people. Dennis illustrated dozens of stories, from *BLACK BEAUTY* by Anna Sewell to *The Small War of Sergeant Donkey* by MAUREEN DALY, but his primary claim to fame comes from having illustrated more than a dozen books by MARGUERITE HENRY, including *Justin Morgan Had a Horse* (1945, Newbery Honour Book), *Misty of Chincoteague* (1947, Newbery Honour Book), and *King of the Wind* (1948, NEWBERY MEDAL). The fluid art work by Dennis captures the spirit of the horse, an animal he knew first-hand. As a young man, he joined a cavalry unit; an avid horseman, he played polo later in life. His drawings for *Misty*, fresh as ocean breezes themselves, capture the spirit of the colt descended from Spanish horses that survived the wreck of the *Santo Cristo*. NV

Denslow, W(illiam) W(allace) 1856–1915 American illustrator of L. FRANK BAUM's *The Wonderful Wizard of Oz* (see OZ SERIES). Originally a newspaper cartoonist, Denslow met Baum in Chicago and together they created children's books, including *Father Goose: His Book* (1899) and *Dot and Tot of Merryland* (1901). Their greatest collaboration, *The Wonderful Wizard of Oz* (1900), featured innovative pictures and led the way for the later merging of ILLUSTRATION and text. Underscoring the book's motif of colours, Denslow's line drawings were printed in various colours over the words, and other full-page illustrations show characters popping out of the frame. The action, sometimes cutting from one page to the next, as well as the imaginative portrayal of the characters, added enormously to the book's appeal. His drawings were signed with his trademark 'hippocampus', a seahorse. Baum and Denslow disagreed over the rights to the *Oz* characters, and Denslow did not illustrate any of the more than a dozen sequels Baum wrote. Nevertheless, the patterns for the characters in subsequent versions were set by Denslow's pictures. He produced other books for young readers, such as *The Pearl and the Pumpkin* (1904), with Paul West. GRB

Denton, Kady MacDonald 1942– Canadian author and illustrator who has illustrated over 20 PICTUREBOOKS, FAIRY TALES and anthologies for herself and others. Denton trained at the University of Toronto, Banff Centre for Fine Art, Niagara College, and Chelsea School of Art in London. She has also designed theatrical sets and taught art. Her early works, exemplified by *Janet's Horses* (1991), were characterised by gentle Ardizzonian ink-and-pencil water colours. Recent works, such as *Would They Love a Lion?* (1998), exhibit sharply coloured, vividly animated scenes resembling in execution and effect the work of HELEN OXENBURY. Warmth, humour and joy pervade her paintings. Her ability to depict action and evoke emotions with simplicity of design, economy of line, and a minimal background make her style ideal for marginal vignettes in anthologies. Successful anthologies include the award-winning *'Til All the Stars Have Fallen: A Collection of Poems for Children* (1989), with David Booth, and *The Kingfisher Children's Bible* (1993) and *Realms of Gold: Myths and Legends From Around the World* (1993), with ANN PILLING. Denton won the prestigious Governor General's Award for her anthology *A Child's Treasury of Nursery Rhymes* in 1998. FL

see also EDWARD ARDIZZONE

Denton, Terry [Terence James] 1950– Australian illustrator whose deceptively simple but poignant images convey strong emotions, as in *Felix & Alexander* (1985), which won the CHILDREN'S BOOK COUNCIL OF AUSTRALIA BOOK OF THE YEAR AWARD (1986). *Gasp!* (1995), which is about a fish, demonstrates Denton's sense of fun. Collaborating with writers PAUL JENNINGS and TED GREENWOOD, Denton has illustrated the popular wordplays *Spooner or Later* (1992), *Duck for Cover* (1994) and *Freeze a Crowd* (1996). Denton's work has won many awards and is significant for having been selected by both adult and child judges. He helped devise the children's TELEVISION series *Lift Off*, working as designer and puppet-maker. HE

DePaola, Tomie (Thomas Anthony) 1934– American author and illustrator popular with children for his clean, bold art style and lively storytelling. First published as the illustrator for several PICTUREBOOKS, he has since written and illustrated over 180 books including original tales, FOLKTALE re-tellings and anthologies. For his body of work he was honoured with the Regina Medal from the Catholic Library Association in 1983. He was born in Meriden, Connecticut, into a family with strong Irish and Italian roots. Many of his books draw on the wealth of folktales he heard as a child, retold with amusing details. For example, *Strega Nona* (1975), which earned him the ALA's Caldecott Honour Award in 1976, is the retelling of a folktale about a magic pot that boils and boils until the proper spell is used to stop it. Drawing on his Italian heritage, DePaola sets the tale in an Italian village and the food that explodes out of the pot is pasta. Other stories draw on his childhood experiences living in a multi-generational household, such as *Nana Upstairs & Nana Downstairs* (1973), and are more realistic and serious. LAW

Deptford Mice, The Popular FANTASY trilogy by British author Robin Jarvis comprising *The Dark Portal* (1989), *The Crystal Prison* (1989) and *The Final Reckoning* (1990). The first features mice and rat characters involved in a classic Tolkienesque struggle between good and evil. Five young mice take part in a quest against the evil Jupiter and his allies, the rats. Jupiter has designs to take over the whole world but, after many underground adventures in the sewers under Deptford, he is vanquished. The other books continue with the same characters. Jarvis has subsequently written some prequels, beginning with *The Alchemist's Cat* (1991). AW

Derwent, Lavinia see *SULA* SERIES

Desai, Anita 1937– One of India's best-known contemporary writers. Her children's novels engage with some of the difficult problems of our time. *The Village by the Sea* (1982), winner of the *Guardian* Award for Children's Fiction and serialised by BBC TELEVISION in 1991, explores 'Third World' issues – the consequences of changes brought about by industrialisation, and their impact on traditional family life and values. Hari and Lila face stark choices as their small fishing village on the west coast of India is threatened by the decline of the fishing industry and an encroaching factory. The theme, sometimes didactic, is that change can be faced by learning to adapt. Hari's experience, in a Dickensian portrayal of contemporary Bombay, contrasts urban squalor and deprivation with the symbols of western capitalism. But it is in the poorest community that Hari will find support, optimism and determination to survive. In the village, where Lila is left to nurse a dying mother and cope with a drunken father and two younger sisters, the collapse of family life is cruelly highlighted by the seductive beauty of a tropical setting that draws wealthy holiday visitors from the city. Writing from the point of view of the two main characters, Desai combines stern criticism of the social inequities that threaten their existence with a sympathetic exploration of their inner lives.Two earlier children's novels, *The Peacock Garden* (1974) and *Cat on a Houseboat* (1976), also vividly evoke the atmosphere and landscape of India and the fortitude of individuals facing crises. EAG

Desperate Dan see COMICS, PERIODICALS AND MAGAZINES

Detective Comics see *BATMAN*; SUPERHEROES

detective fiction Although many young British readers' first expectations of detective fiction were formed by *Sherlock Holmes* and *Sexton Blake* stories, children's detective stories have come to constitute a subgenre of fiction whose distinguishing feature is that the child characters, alone or aided by adults, take a major part in exposing criminals. Accordingly, the detective story for children is a work in which Romantic assumptions about the child are given a new twist, the premise of children's superiority to the adult demonstrated in their solving mysteries and catching criminals while the adults bumble around helplessly. Here, children are portrayed as more observant, more energetic, and having a greater capacity for believing the unusual than the adult. The child is, moreover, not alone, but usually backed up by a gang of children who, acting as extensions of each other, have an effectiveness that the adult is unable to match: this comes through clearly, for example in Erich Kästner's *EMIL AND THE DETECTIVES* (1930). ENID BLYTON, with her *FAMOUS FIVE*, *SECRET SEVEN* and other child gangs, popularised this trope, which continues to be used (ROBERT SWINDELLS's series *The Outfit* (from 1993) faithfully adopts the format, down to the attendant dog). David Schutte's *Naitabal* series (the 'Naitabal' is defined as 'a wild species of human aged about ten') is one of the more interesting gangs, possessing their own secret language and practices.

Many of the works exist as series and fall into formulaic patterns, either specific to the genre or to that specific series. In this context, one could cite Carolyn Keene's penchant for having her heroine of the *NANCY DREW* series captured by the 'bad guys' who sneeringly 'tell all' just before her boyfriend Ned rescues her, thus conveniently providing the police with a confession; or Allan Frewin Jones's *Hunter and Moon* mysteries which, alongside their resolvable mysteries, contain an element of the unexplained/supernatural. Some of the genre's other favourite elements are secret passages, buried treasure and disguise, pointing to the fact that the children's detective tale is more frequently an ADVENTURE STORY than one strictly involving ratiocination.

The more interesting works of the genre, however, are those that rise above the morally simplified world of 'good guy' and 'bad guy' to explore more complex emotional, psychological and moral realms. Among these may be counted RUTH THOMAS's *Guilty!* (1993), whose child detectives have to contend with pain and the fear of discovering the criminal in the family; ANTONIA FOREST's *The Thuggery Affair* (1965) where Patrick Merrick, the 'detective' figure is forced to inhabit the same emotional space as the murderer and drug-smuggler, Jukie; and NINA BAWDEN's understated *The Witch's Daughter* (1966), where the relationship between Perdita and the jewel thief, Mr Smith, displays a side of the 'criminal' that subtly unbalances any tendency towards the simplistic schema.

American juvenile detective fiction began at the turn of the 20th century with EDWARD STRATEMEYER. For young children the STRATEMEYER SYNDICATE created *Honey Bunch*, the *BOBBSEY TWINS* and the *Happy Hollisters*. The syndicate produced the first action heroines for older girls: *Nancy Drew*; *Cherry Ames*; *Vicki Barr*; *Connie Blair*; and the *Dana Girls*. For boys there were the *HARDY BOYS* and *Tom Quest*. Stratemeyer stories starred super-children with unlimited freedom, having adventures and solving puzzles within a strict plot structure. Stratemeyer's formula defined juvenile detective fiction until the 1970s. *Nancy Drew* (from 1930) and the *Hardy Boys* (from 1926) continue to sell well, having been updated several times to give them a contemporary feel.

Other successful detective series include the *Judy Bolton* series (1932–67) by Margaret Sutton, and the *Trixie Belden* series (1948–86) by Julie Campbell and Kathryn Kenny. Sutton's series was unique in that the characters aged as time went by: the series begins with its heroine in high school and follows Judy through marriage and motherhood. Trixie Belden is a spunky, down-to-earth heroine, often preferred to the impossibly perfect Nancy Drew. The 1960s saw the introduction of two popular series characterised by the intelligence and professionalism of the young detectives. *Alfred Hitchcock and The Three Investigators*, by Robert Arthur, is full of appealingly eccentric characters, situations and locales. In DONALD SOBOL's series, the eponymous *Leroy 'Encyclopedia' Brown* starts his own detective agency.

Some modern American non-serial detective stories have escaped the mode's traditional formulaic structuralisation and stereotypical characterisation, incorporating humour, historical settings, and horror or SCIENCE FICTION. Three award-winning examples are E. L. KONIGSBURG's *From the Mixed-Up Files of Mrs. Basil E. Frankweiler* (1967), VIRGINIA HAMILTON's *The House of Dies Drear* (1968) and ELLEN RASKIN's *The Westing Game* (1978). Popular contemporary authors include BETSY BYARS, John Bellairs and Willo Davis Roberts.

Comparatively few detective novels from Australia and New Zealand can be said to transcend the usual formulae. Indeed, detective fiction is dominated in quantity by Australian series fiction for young readers, with examples including EMILY RODDA's *Teen Power Inc.*, HAZEL EDWARDS's *Frequent Flyer Twins*, *Skinny Mysteries* and *I Findem P.I.*. Of the remaining works that fall into this category, many are simply novels which were not successful enough to spawn series of their own. Both countries, however, have produced excellent detective novels, with the best containing strong themes or sub-plots which raise them above the exigencies of the genre. Perhaps the first of these was Len Evers's award-winner, *THE RACKETTY STREET GANG* (1961), with one of the first migrant protagonists (a German) in Australian children's fiction. This novel, like most of the others, pits a group of ordinary children against a gang of desperate criminals.

The majority of the better novels in this genre, however, appeared in the 1980s and 90s. Two which received Australian awards in the same year indicate opposite ends of the spectrum within the genre: ELIZABETH HONEY's *45 & 47 Stella Street and Everything that Happened* (1995) combines detection with humour and a colloquial style that appeals to young readers, while CATHERINE JINKS' medieval mystery, *PAGAN'S VOWS* (1995), despite a leavening of humour, deals with child sexual abuse in a monastery and the resultant blackmail and murder. More typical of the genre as a whole, however, are the New Zealand novels *Steel Riders* (1987) by KEN CATRAN, in which a gang of children break a criminal ring, and JOAN DE HAMEL's *The Third Eye* (1987), with tuatara smugglers as villains.

The corresponding Australian examples have a more obvious element of audience appeal, with computers in Claire Carmichael's *Sideswipe* (1995), an air of mild rudeness in *The Bugalugs Bum Thief* (1991) by the successful author for adults, TIM WINTON, and environmental damage in John Merson's *Jigsaw Bay* (1995), although the popular JOHN MARSDEN returned to the more traditional storyline of a group of children searching for adventure in *Looking for Trouble* (1993). BRUCE WHATLEY parodies the detective fiction genre in an amusing way in his *Detective Donut and the Wild Goose Chase* (1997), set in 1940s America. SA, JF, ELPB

Detmold, Edward [Barton] Julius 1883–1908 and **Detmold, Maurice [Charles Frederick]** 1883–1957 British illustrators, almost entirely forgotten for many years. Maurice and Edward Detmold were twin brothers, both displaying early signs of outstanding artistic gifts. Described by Edward Burne-Jones as 'geniuses', they had both exhibited work at the Royal Academy before they were 14 years old. Their early work – mostly etchings, executed both jointly and separately – was extremely successful, but in 1908 Maurice unexpectedly committed suicide at the height of his powers. His brother continued to work for many years but – disillusioned by the Depression and the outbreak of World War II – he became almost a recluse and lived for the last 25 years of his life in obscurity in Wales. Then, after almost half a century, he too took his own life. Among their early work, the Detmolds produced some outstanding etchings for RUDYARD KIPLING's *JUNGLE BOOK* (1903 in portfolio, published 1908). The illustrations for *The Second Jungle Book* began as a joint commission and were completed by Edward after his brother's death. The pictures – significantly more aggressive than the first series – appeared in black-and-white in the *Illustrated London News* and were not seen again until the Folio Society published them, recreated in colour by David Eccles in 1944. After Maurice's death, Edward illustrated a collection of *AESOP'S FABLES* (1909), *Hours of Gladness* (1912) by Maurice Maeterlinck, *THE ARABIAN NIGHTS* (1922) and a series of children's books about baby animals. A collection of illustrations – *The Fantastic Creatures of Edward Julius Detmold* – was published in 1976. VW

see also CHRISTMAS ISSUES

Dhondy, Farrukh 1944– Indian writer born in Poona whose work includes stage plays for the Black Theatre Co-operative and novels and short stories for young people. Having studied in Bombay, Cambridge and Leicester, Dhondy taught in London comprehensive schools, and this experience generated inspiration for his first book of short stories, *East End at Your Feet* (1976), which won the Other Award for its progressive representation of ethnic, social and sexual issues. Seen through the eyes of London teenagers from Asian and English families, these stories tell of life in Britain in the 1970s. The gentle compassion and gritty humour which characterises this volume is developed in the subsequent collection, *Come to Mecca* (1978), which received a similar accolade, as well as the first Samuel Beckett award for its single story 'Romance'. Dhondy's childhood experiences in India are portrayed through his witty stories of Poona life in *Poona Company* (1980), and the thriller *The Siege of Babylon* (1978) was filmed for TELEVISION. The stage play *Mama Dragon* was produced by the Unicorn Theatre for Children in 1980. Dhondy's later novel *Black Swan* (1992), a mystery, moves between contemporary and 17th-century England, taking an Elizabethan diary as its source of intrigue. This document reveals that SHAKESPEARE's plays were penned partly by Christopher Marlowe and partly by Marlowe's former black lover Lazarus, once a slave. Receiving mixed acclaim, the book explores multicultural issues and hums with literary reference. After 1984 Dhondy worked as Commissioning Editor for Multicultural Programmes at British independent television's Channel Four. CMN

Diamonds and Toads see *CONTES DE MA MÈRE L'OYE*; CHARLES PERRAULT; see also CHARLOTTE HUCK; FAIRY FANTASY

Diary of Anne Frank, The see ANNE FRANK

***Dicey's Song* series** (1981–9) Seven YOUNG ADULT NOVELS by American author CYNTHIA VOIGT. The books, many of which can be read independently of the series, are linked by their concern for the Tillerman family and their friends. The first, *Homecoming* (1981), describes how 13-year-old Dicey Tillerman resolutely marches her family from Connecticut to Maryland after their mother abandons them in a car park. Later books follow the fortunes of different members of the family and their friends. The series comes full circle with *Seventeen Against the Dealer* (1989) in which Dicey is again the heroine. Critics have speculated on the possiblity that the mysterious drifter who appears in this novel may be Dicey's father.

Dicey is an immensely resourceful and independent heroine. JOHN ROWE TOWNSEND in his book *Written for Children* (fifth edition, 1990) considers that she is 'over the top' and 'too good to be true', but she has a strong following amongst both children and adults. Her struggle to keep her family together during their long trek down Route 1 seems, despite its apparent impossibility, very plausible. Part of Dicey's attraction comes from the tempering of her strengths with blatant faults; her morality is far from absolute, for as a child she has fought and lied and she condones her younger brother's stealing when the family needs it, although she draws the line at his stealing from someone who has befriended them. Her belief in keeping her family together overrides all other considerations, and when they finally reach their initial destination Dicey is prepared to uproot them again because they cannot all be happy there.

The background to the books is made up of a series of bleak circumstances: their mother is having a nervous breakdown, their father abandoned them years ago, their fierce independence means that they have few friends, and they have no prior knowledge of the relative whom they hope will take them in. There is a prevailing ethos that they can never expect life to be easy. Despite this there is also a pervading sense of warmth and strength, generated partly by the close relationships and partly through the practical ways in which they surmount all problems.

Food plays an important part in the books. In *Homecoming* its frequent absence represents the loss of the family home. When Dicey finally arrives at her cantankerous grandmother's she is grudgingly fed on tinned spaghetti, but as the grandmother decides to let them stay she begins to can tomatoes and bake bread. Once the children have made their home at their grandmother's, family occasions are often marked by a lovingly prepared meal.

Throughout the novels the characters wrestle with the problem of combining independence with the need for a strong relationship with their families. In *A Solitary Blue* (1983) Jeff Green is able to attain his own independence only when he ignores the illusion of happiness that his manipulative mother offers. At the end of the series it is Dicey herself who has to learn that, important as her independence is to her, she still needs other people. KA

Dick Turpin see PENNY DREADFULS

Dick Whittington Nursery story based on the life of a real man, Richard Whityngton, son of a Gloucestershire landowner, who made a fortune as a mercer or cloth merchant in London. Dick Whittington, a penniless orphan, goes to London to make his fortune. He works in the kitchen of Fitzwarren, a rich merchant, whose daughter Alice befriends him. He buys a cat, a magnificent ratter, which he sends to sea on Fitzwarren's ship. Ill-treated by the cook, Dick runs away but as he leaves London he hears Bow Bells chiming 'Turn again Whityngton, Lord Mayor of London' and, returning to the merchant's house, he discovers his cat has been sold for a fortune. He marries Alice, is knighted and becomes Lord Mayor of London three times. A window in Westminster Abbey shows Dick Whittington with a cat at his feet. The real Whityngton was friendly with the kings of his day, to whom he lent money, and was Mayor of London three times. He married Alice Fitzwarren but was never knighted and history does not mention a cat. His fortune helped to build St Bartholomew's Hospital, Newgate gaol, Grey Friars library, Bow Church and the first public lavatory in London. He died in 1423. In the early 17th century, BALLADS and dramatic versions of the life of Whityngton appeared, in which his fortune was made with the help of a cat. First performed at fairs, and told in CHAPBOOKS, this story has become the most popular PANTOMIME story of the last two centuries. SD

Dickens, Charles (John Huffam) 1812–1870 Novelist and journalist of international repute, whose books, immensely popular in their day, are now better known through their many stage, film or TELEVISION adaptations. Dickens's novels attacked social evils but he also defended the value of FAIRY TALES, arguing that 'a nation without fancy, without some romance' could never be great. His best-known story, *A Christmas Carol* (1843), is a seasonal fairy tale in which the miserly, 'wicked uncle' Scrooge is transformed into a figure of exuberant, universal benevolence. Dickens wrote little specifically for children – *A Child's History of England* (1853) and *The Life of Our Lord* for his own children, and the faux-naive, purportedly child-authored *A Holiday Romance* (1868), and four short, linked stories commissioned for an American children's magazine. His popularity with all age groups, however, has rested on his novels, many of which combine sympathetic depictions of mistreated children with a packed cast of villains and grotesques. Dickens's personal identification with suffering innocence accounts for the sentimentality which often mars his works, but this was gradually modulated by an interest in more complex child–adult relationships, such as that of Dombey and his daughter (1846–8), and in the psychology of the growing boy who, like David Copperfield, or Pip in *Great Expectations* (1860–1), discovers that his values and life-defining choices have been shaped by his earliest experiences. JFB

Dickens, Monica see PONY STORIES; see also *FOLLYFOOT* SERIES

Dickinson, Emily (Elizabeth) 1830–86 American poet. Asked for her definition of poetry, Dickinson famously replied: 'If I feel so cold, no fire can ever warm me, I know it is poetry.' Original, brilliant, odd, unpredictable – such words describe both Dickinson's poetry and the character of this reclusive genius. Although the majority of her poems are in adult collections, many have found their way into anthologies for the young. *Poems for Youth* (1934) contained some of the numerous poems she wrote for her niece and nephews.

Her love of nature and childhood, her sometimes quirky childlike language and punctuation, the apparent simplicity and idiosyncrasy of some of her subject matter, give her work an affinity with thoughtful young readers. Collections include *Acts of Light* (1980), *A Brighter Garden* (1990) and *I'm Nobody! Who Are You? Poems of Emily Dickinson for Children* (1978). PDS

see also BARBARA COONEY

Dickinson, Peter 1927– British children's author and crime-writer, winner of Carnegie, Whitbread and *Guardian* awards. He is best known for THE CHANGES trilogy (1968–70), which established him as a force in children's literature. Dickinson's novels are remarkable for their huge variety of subject. Many contain an element of the fantastic, often contrasting with otherwise mundane situations, for example Davy's second sight in *The Gift* (1974). Dickinson's distinctive ability as a storyteller means he generally succeeds in mixing these elements, especially in the alternation between the remotely pre-historic and the contemporary in *A Bone from a Dry Sea* (1992), or the taut exploration of identity and responsibility in the FANTASIES *Eva* (1988) and *The Lion Tamer's Daughter* (1999). *The Kin* (1999), which follows a group of orphaned 'first human beings', is a complex, intensely written and absorbing narrative. MSed

dictionaries see INFORMATION BOOKS

Diddakoi, The (1972) Novel by RUMER GODDEN about Kizzy, a half-gypsy child who has always lived in a wagon and cannot understand Gorgio ways. She is forced to live in a house and learn about this unaccustomed way of life after the death of her beloved Grandmother. The story is, in many ways, a romantic one, with a very conventional and somewhat predictable happy ending. It is, however, also a brutal one which examines the problems of bullying at school and peer-group pressure without shrinking from descriptions of the mental and physical suffering to which Kizzy is subjected. KA

Digby, Anne see *TREBIZON* SERIES; see also SCHOOL STORIES

Dillon, Eilís 1929–1994 Irish novelist. Dillon published almost 40 books for children, a few of which are in the Irish language. Some are set in Italy, but most are firmly placed in her native west of Ireland. Dillon's love for this landscape comes across strongly but without any touch of sentimentality. She graphically, and with attention to practical details, describes the rigorous lives of those wresting a livelihood from land or sea. She catches too the cadence of western speech patterns without rendering her dialogue difficult to read. It is in this feeling of authenticity combined with a dramatic adventure, frequently in the guise of a quest, that her main strength as a writer lies.

As in an early work, *The Lost Island* (1952), her main protagonists are often teenage boys but, apart from a desire to prove their valour and resourcefulness, the usual preoccupations of adolescence do not concern them. In her later writing a deepening complexity is apparent, and girls tend to figure more in central roles. In *The Island of Ghosts* (1990) the dramatic core of the story revolves around the kidnap of two boys, their rescue instigated by their sisters, and ambiguity about the ill intent of the kidnapper. Her last novel, *Children of Bach* (1993) concerns the escape of four children from Nazi-occupied Hungary. Its conclusion, while not offering any cosy platitudes, presents the necessity of hopefulness, a constant theme in much of Dillon's writing for children. Dillon has also collaborated on a number of PICTUREBOOKS, for example *The Wise Man on the Mountain*, illustrated by Gaynor Chapman, and *The Voyage of the Mael Duin*, illustrated by Alan Howard, both published in 1969. Although much of her work was originally published in Britain with illustrations by Richard Kennedy, a number of books have been republished in Ireland. VC

Dillon, Diane (Claire) 1933– and **Dillon, Leo (Lionel John)** 1933– American husband-and-wife team who are the only illustrators to have received consecutive CALDECOTT MEDALS for their work. Leo Dillon was born in Brooklyn, New York, and educated at Parsons School of Design and the School of Visual Arts. Diane was born in Glendale, California, and attended Los Angeles City College, Skidmore College, Parsons School of Design, the American Institute of Graphic Arts and the School of Visual Arts. They began their careers as freelance artists working on book covers (see COVER ART) and illustrating articles for magazines and textbooks. The Dillons are skilful and prolific artists who work in a variety of media and genres. They received a Hugo Award from the International Science Fiction Association in 1971 for a series of jackets and the Balrog Award for their 'Lifetime contribution to Sci-Fi/Fantasy Art' in 1982. But it is their stylised ILLUSTRATIONS in children's PICTUREBOOKS that are most noteworthy. They received the Caldecott Award for their illustrations for VERNA AARDEMA's *Why Mosquitos Buzz in People's Ears: A West African Tale* (1975) and Margaret Musgrove's *Ashanti to Zulu: African Traditions* (1976). They received the Lewis Carroll Shelf Award for Aardema's *Who's in Rabbit's House?* (1977) and the CORETTA SCOTT KING AWARD for *Aida* by Leontyne Price (1991). DJH

***Dilly the Dinosaur* series** (from 1986) Series by TONY BRADMAN originally aimed at beginning readers, which reached 15 titles within ten years. An enormous commercial success, *Dilly* was animated for BBC TELEVISION's *Playdays* in 1990, leading to the publication of activity books and tapes, and the books have been widely used in schools. Billed as 'the world's naughtiest dinosaur', Dilly provides a male but fairly sexless hero with whom readers easily identify. The continuous guerrilla warfare between parents and children is conducted in acutely familiar dialogue, and sibling rivalry between Dilly and his sister provides a further point of recognition. PC

***Dimsie* series** (1920–46) Girls' SCHOOL STORIES in nine volumes, not all written in sequence, by Dorita Fairlie Bruce (1885–1970). The author was the first to develop a series which followed a key figure through schooldays to adult life and marriage, written largely between 1920 and 1927, with one retrospective novel, *Dimsie Intervenes* (1937) and a wartime story, *Dimsie Carries On* (1946).

The first, *The Senior Prefect* (1920), republished as *Dimsie Goes to School*, introduces the outspoken, candid but unerringly moral Daphne Isobel Maitland, whose mother has run off with a syndicate of cardsharps. She survives threats of opprobrium from her new schoolfellows at the Jane Willard Foundation through her cheerful good nature and breezy response to life's trials, which earn her the ultimate accolade of 'decent little kid' from the head girl.

In *Dimsie Moves Up* (1921), Dimsie and friends establish the Anti-Soppist League to discourage the juniors from 'behaving like lovelorn idiots'. This theme of distaste for sentimental, romantic schoolgirl friendships and prefect-worship is an apparent preoccupation of Bruce, who treats the phenomenon as an exasperating but passing stage of adolescent girlhood. In *Dimsie Goes Back* (1927), the adult Dimsie returns to the school, where standards have slipped, to become the headmistress's secretary, and continues the crusade to affirm a decent schoolgirl code of honour and loyalty, with no sneaking – and no cosmetics. *Dimsie Carries On* (1946) is the least successful story, the author writing less convincingly about life beyond the school, and her own conservative, even jingoistic values assert themselves uncomfortably in this wartime novel. BW

Dinan, Carolyn 1942– British illustrator who spent most of her childhood in Ireland; the Irish countryside, sea and mountain views are remembered in many of her books. She depicts them in her own story *The Seal Singer* (1996) and in *Donkey Magic* (1991) by Caroline Sutherland. A prize-winning student at Chelsea School of Art, Dinan has illustrated numerous children's books, including GENE KEMP's *TAMWORTH PIG* series and her *The Turbulent Term of Tyke Tyler*

'Let us land on one of these lovely islands.' Illustration by Carolyn Dinan for 'There's Some Sky in this Pie' by JOAN AIKEN from *A Treasury of Stories for Under Fives*, collected by Edward and Nancy BLISHEN.

(CARNEGIE MEDAL, 1979). PICTUREBOOKS include *But Martin* by June Counsel, nominated for the Best Children's Book for 1984. IW

see also *THE CRICKLEPIT COMBINED SCHOOL* SERIES

disability in children's books During the Victorian era mental disability was rarely shown in children's literature, while physical disability was frequently portrayed as a form of necessary suffering, or as a way of proving a character's essential goodness. Sometimes a temporary period of disability was used as a way of developing a child's character; in 19th-century novels the child usually became a better person as a result of his/her suffering. When Katy Carr is paralysed in *WHAT KATY DID* (1872) her cousin counsels her to learn in the 'School of Pain' and the narrator suggests that God is closer to Katy while she is suffering, for she sees 'stooping over her . . . a great beautiful Face'. When LAURA INGALLS WILDER came to write the *LITTLE HOUSE* series there had been little apparent change in attitudes towards disability; when Mary loses her sight she remains patient and optimistic and Laura comments on Mary's 'increased goodness and faith'. Mary herself says that as a child she 'wasn't really wanting to be good', whereas now her goodness comes not from thinking, but from 'just knowing. Just being sure of the goodness of God'.

In 1958 ROSEMARY SUTCLIFF's *WARRIOR SCARLET* demonstrated a different attitude to disability: Drem begins to resent his useless spear arm only when it proves an obstacle to his joining the Men's side. Throughout the book emphasis is placed not on the obstacles that the disability creates for Drem himself, but on the need for him to prove his strength to the rest of the tribe. Drem learns to live with his disability, which is seen as a challenge rather than either a necessary evil or an insurmountable obstacle. IVAN SOUTHALL's *LET THE BALLOON GO* (1968) depicts one day of freedom in the life of a 12-year-old 'spastic' boy, who escapes the over-protectiveness of his family and imposes a challenge on himself by climbing a huge tree. *'I OWN THE RACECOURSE!'* (1968) by PATRICIA WRIGHTSON, with a main protagonist who has learning difficulties, is a strong story of human relationships, rather than a treatise on disability.

During the 1970s, with the growth of the young adult genre, a number of novels were published which featured disabled children. There was a tendency for the disability to be seen as a vehicle for the teenage angst and anger that are sometimes seen as a necessary part of YOUNG ADULT FICTION. One of the more successful novels of the period was JUDY BLUME's *Deenie* (1973), in which the heroine has to wear a back brace for four years. Much of the anxiety Deenie feels seems centred upon other people's perception of her; her problems appear to be resolved when she gains a boyfriend who does not mind about her brace. In Susan Sallis's *Sweet Frannie* (1981) the heroine's disability provides a basis for the antagonism she feels towards the adult world. Like a number of other novels written at the time, this one ends sentimentally with the heroine's death. Few novels yet tackled the question of living with disability in the long term; many ended either with the deaths of the protagonists or with a simplistic solution to their problems.

Fiction written for younger children was often more pragmatic in its approach. In NINA BAWDEN's *The Witch's Daughter* (1966) Janey is blind, but adopts a matter-of-fact approach to her disability, saying, 'I don't know how people who can only see can tell what things are.' In PETER DICKINSON's *Annerton Pit* (1977) the reader has to read for a number of pages before knowing for sure that Jake is blind, and again Jake is shown to be coping with his disability, although the difficulties it presents are not belittled.

Towards the end of the 20th century there is an increasing tendency to portray disability less simplistically and with more thought for the reactions of a disabled reader, often showing how well children can cope with disability without denying the difficulty they face. GENE KEMP's *Juniper* is a noteworthy example. The heroine of MICHAEL MORPURGO's *The Ghost of Grannia O'Malley* (1996) is determined and resilient, although human enough to exaggerate the truth to her friends. Beverley Mathias's *The Spell Singer* (1989) is a collection of stories specially comissioned to describe 'the joys and pains of living with handicap'. In another anthology, *Me and My Electric* (1998), edited by ELIZABETH LAIRD, disabled children have joined with well-known authors to tell their stories. Laird's own *Red Sky in The Morning* (1988), about the relationship between an older sister and her baby brother who has hydrocephalus, shows the misery of the situation without resorting to sentimentality. Douglas, an adolescent boy, learns a great deal about himself, as well as his young autistic brother Carl, in *The October Child* (1976) by ELEANOR SPENCE. A young girl develops a more caring attitude towards others when she succeeds in teaching an intellectually disabled boy to swim in *Boss of the Pool* (1986) by ROBIN KLEIN. *Jodie's Journey* (1988) by COLIN THIELE depicts the courage of an 11-year-old girl champion horserider who develops crippling arthritis. Based on her own horrific experiences in a car accident, WENDY ORR, in *Peeling the Onion* (1996), explores the deep psychological and emotional changes in life for a young girl, Anna, permanently disfigured in an accident. In *The Flawed Glass* (1989) IAN STRACHAN successfully depicts the life of a severely handicapped girl on an isolated Scottish island. Strachan manages to show the prejudice Shona encounters without turning her into a stereotyped rebellious young adult. Science fiction has also been used as a vehicle for exploring disability. In *The Wormholers* (1996) by JAMILA GAVIN, Sophie, who spends her life imprisoned in a wheelchair, finds herself able to move freely when she is thrown into a parallel universe. Disabled children in fiction are often given special skills that compensate for their disability. In GARRY KILWORTH's *The Electric Kid* (1994) Blindboy has such acute hearing that he can hear electronic codes, and in *Adam's Ark* (1990) by Paul Stewart the autistic hero can communicate with animals in his head.

Recently, there have also been more novels about disability for a younger age group. Rachel Anderson's stories about Jessy feature a little girl who has Down's Syndrome; in *Best Friends* (1991) Jessy realises that her handicap makes friendship difficult, but nevertheless makes a new friend. Pippa Goodhart's *Pest Friends* (1997) is also about friendships, though this time it is the wheelchair-bound heroine who is in a position of strength, able to befriend the shy newcomer to the class. *Seal Surfer* (1996) by MICHAEL FOREMAN is unusual in that, in the ILLUSTRATIONS, the hero is shown sometimes with crutches and sometimes in a wheelchair, but no comment is made on his disability in the text. NAN BODSWORTH's *A Nice Walk in the Jungle* (1990) shows a child in a wheelchair as part of a class group. The fact that the small, courageous boy in Wendy Orr's *Arabella* (1998) is disabled is evident only through the illustrations, with tiny clues dotted throughout the book, whereas in *Cherry Pie* (1998) by Gretel Killeen, a young girl explores and resolves her fears about a disabled girl living next door, shown using crutches and in a wheelchair. A deaf child achieves success in *The Race* (1995) by CHRISTOBEL MATTINGLEY. There are still very few books which feature disabled parents, though Verna Wilkins *Boots for a Bridesmaid* (1995) is about a child whose mother is in a wheelchair.

A number of novels which feature disability have had only limited success in the marketplace and have therefore been taken out of print very rapidly. It is a matter for concern that books are more likely to be successful if disability is depicted melodramatically, while books that feature a child coping with disability from day to day are less likely to sell well. KA, JAP

Disher, Garry (Donald) 1949– Australian writer for adults and children. *The Bamboo Flute* (1992) – winner of the 1993 CHILDREN'S BOOK COUNCIL OF AUSTRALIA BOOK OF THE YEAR: YOUNGER READERS AWARD – draws on childhood memories and family reminiscences and is a finely crafted, lyrical novel. Set in rural Australia during the 1930s Depression, it explores themes of the loss of childhood innocence, the curative powers of music, and the debilitating effect of war on returned soldiers. Disher's versatility as an author is demonstrated with *Ratface* (1993), a suspense-filled thriller for teenage readers about a religious cult; *Ermyntrude to the Rescue* (1996), a short comic novel for early readers; *Blame The Wind* (1995), a ghost novella for teenagers; *Restless* (1995), a short story collection; *Walk Twenty, Run Twenty* (1996); and *The Apostle Bird* (1997), an evocative and compelling study of courage, honesty and prejudice.

SNJ

Disney, Walt 1901–66 American film-maker and entrepreneur. The name 'Walt Disney' not only represents the life and career of an extremely influential and in many respects controversial film-maker and head of an entertainment empire (the 'Magic Kingdom'), but has come to stand for a particular approach to family entertainment and for the commodification of world folklore and children's literature.

Disney began his career as an animator in Kansas City, Missouri, where he created cartoon advertisements shown in local movie theatres. He moved to Hollywood in 1923, and in 1928 produced *Steamboat Willie*, the cartoon that introduced his most famous and enduring creation, MICKEY MOUSE, a character who has influenced such important children's authors and illustrators as MAURICE SENDAK. In 1937 Disney produced his first feature-length animated film, *Snow White and the Seven Dwarfs*, and it was followed by other animated adaptations of folklore and children's classics, including *Pinocchio* (1940) – often considered his greatest work – *BAMBI* (1942), *CINDERELLA* (1950) and *The Jungle Book* (1967). *Fantasia* (1940), while not based on a children's story (other than the segment based on 'The Sorcerer's Apprentice'), is also an important contribution to ANIMATED FILM for children, as it has introduced a number of generations of young viewers to classical music (see MUSIC AND STORY).

From 1946 Disney also began to produce live-action films, including *Song of the South* (part live action, part animation, based on JOEL CHANDLER HARRIS's *Uncle Remus* stories), *TREASURE ISLAND* (1950), *POLLYANNA* (1960, based on Eleanor Porter's novel), and *MARY POPPINS* (1964, based on the stories by P.L. Travers), the last the most commercially and critically successful of his live-action films, and the only one to be nominated for an Academy Award for Best Picture. After Disney's death, his studio continued to produce both animated and live-action films, experiencing a renaissance in the 1980s and 1990s with a series of animated features, many with musical scores by Alan Menken. Of these, *BEAUTY AND THE BEAST* (1991) is considered the best, capturing the sweetness and magic of BEAUMONT's original literary version, yet also bringing a modern Broadway sensibility (and, some would argue, a feminist revision of the role and character of the heroine, Belle); it became the first animated film to be nominated for the Academy Award for Best Picture and was later turned into a live Broadway musical.

Disney also entered the world of TELEVISION and amusement parks in 1954 and 1955 with the television programme *Disneyland* (running intermittently to the present, with some changes in the name of the programme) and the opening of Disneyland, the amusement park in Anaheim, California (later joined by Florida's Walt Disney World/EPCOT and EuroDisney). Disney was and remains a controversial figure in the culture of childhood: to some, he was a genius, bringing a kind of magic and imagination to family entertainment and disseminating folk and literary works to a mass audience – a great educator; to others, including critics, teachers and librarians, it was precisely this popularisation and commodification of texts that made him a corrupting, anti-literary figure. It is true that many children now only know the 'Disney version' (in Richard Schickel's phrase) of traditional FAIRY TALES and children's classics and that Disney's adaptations and emendations were not always to the benefit of the original text. Arguably, his finest contribution to the culture of childhood is his creation of original cartoon characters, Mickey Mouse, Donald Duck and Goofy, rather than his appropriation of world folklore and literature. What is undeniable is the impact Disney had on several generations' familiarity with folklore and literature; for better or worse, Disney created a continuity between oral and literary traditions and the electronic age. BH

Divine Emblems see *COUNTRY RHIMES FOR CHILDREN*

Divine Songs (1715) Collection of religious poems for children by ISAAC WATTS. 'Attempted in easy language for the use of children', these didactic songs are in the tradition of BUNYAN's *COUNTRY RHIMES*, but with a gentler, more pleasurable approach to spiritual and moral education. Watts explains that: 'There is something so amusing and entertaining in rhymes and metre that will incline children to make this part of their business a diversion.' Poems such as 'How doth the little busy bee/ Improve each shining hour?' and 'The Sluggard' remained popular into the 19th century, attracting parody eventually from LEWIS CARROLL. ML

Dixon, Franklin W. see *HARDY BOYS*; ADVENTURE STORIES

Djoleto, Amu Ghanaian educationist and writer, born at Ada. Djoleto has taught many of the younger generation of writers in Ghana and is a popular novelist. He is also a well-known writer of childrens' stories, always using the story either to teach good citizenship or to draw attention to some aspect of character formation. His children's book *The Frightened Thief* (1992) tells the story of a schoolboy who is bullied by his mates into stealing. When he is caught he becomes a truant, supporting himself by selling sweets on street corners. His schoolmates search for him, but while running away from them he is hit by a speeding motorcycle, is badly hurt and sent to hospital. An earlier book, *Twins in Trouble* (1991), is about identical twins of totally different character, and shows the importance of humility. Djoleto writes in plain, well-modulated sentences which are easy to read and understand. MAs

***Doctor Dolittle* series** The figure of Doctor Dolittle was created by Hugh Lofting (1886–1947) in letters home to his children while with the Irish Guards in Flanders during the First World War. The stories were shown to an American publisher and the first book, *The Story of Dr. Dolittle*, which relates how the Doctor turned to treating animals and learning their languages, was published in 1920. Eleven sequels were to follow, three of which were published posthumously, Olga Michael (the sister of his third wife) completing what Lofting had left unfinished.

In recent years, the *Doctor Dolittle* books have come under criticism for 'political incorrectness', for supposedly proclaiming the superiority of the white man and for references to 'niggers'; Lofting has also been criticised for his representations of Africans, both in his illustrations and in his text. It has to be said in his defence that the comic style of the ILLUSTRATIONS is equally (un)kind to *all* the human characters, and it is probable that no derogation was intended. Of particular difficulty for many of today's readers is the episode in which Bumpo the black prince longs to be turned into a white prince; but it is difficult to disentangle with any certainty an authorial racist intention from the gentle comedy of Lofting's description of the prince 'strolling down the gravel-walk, humming a sad song' with a book of FAIRY TALES under his arm. Dab-Dab comments afterwards that 'he'd never be anything but ugly, no matter what colour he was made'. And the Doctor remarks, 'Still, he had a good heart . . . romantic, of course, but a good heart.' Young readers – who are often passionately anti-racist – could learn something from this about narrative complexity.

In all but this touchy area of race, however, Lofting's values – ordinary human decency and kindness to humans and animals, intolerance of bullying, etc. – are laudable ones and should be allowed to count against the other matter. It is, however, difficult to speak more specifically of the series in terms of strict adherence to any particular ideology or system of values; there are too many inconsistencies hindering this. An example is the difficulty of reconciling the doctor's feeling for animals with his apparent ease in eating meat (the film version starring Rex Harrison makes him a vegetarian).

The adventures of the Doctor and his peculiar household – Polynesia the parrot, Dab-Dab the duck, Gub-Gub the pig, Jip the dog and the two-headed Pushmi-Pullyu – are a strange mixture of the fantastic and the quotidian. One of the Doctor's problems is finding enough money to run his household, and this mundane worry finds all sorts of unusual and wonderful solutions which include the doctor's becoming a matador, writing an avian opera, composing the Puddleby Pantomime and running a circus. Against the domesticity of the house in Puddleby-on-the-Marsh we have the strange and almost mythic encounters of Doctor Dolittle with the Great Glass Snail and Mudface the antediluvian turtle. He himself occasionally takes on the resonance of a figure out of myth, as when he brings fire to the inhabitants of Spidermonkey Island.

Hugh Lofting wrote a number of stories for younger readers, including two about the 100-year-old Mrs

Tubbs and her adventures with Peter Punk the dog, Polly Ponk the duck and Patrick Pink the pig. SA

Dr Monsoon Taggert's Amazing Academy (1989) A slapstick parable by Andrew Matthews about over-eating, and a comedy of exaggeration in which everything is excessive except the moral: gluttony and greed are not the 'wise choice'. Matthews pokes fun at his cast – all outsized but recognisable types from real or FOLKTALE life – from his overfed heroine Arabella, now 'swelled up round like a pink balloon', to the eccentrics she meets on her quest 'to get down to the real you'. Just as his characters relish food, Matthews relishes wordplay, lip-smackingly spoofing their speech patterns. He invites readers to play a game – 'Throw a Six to Start' – one in which they, like Arabella, become thinner and wiser, finally learning, topsy-turvey style, to 'see things from the food's point of view'. EMH

Doctor Who TELEVISION serial for children first transmitted by the BBC on Saturday afternoons from 1964. Its SCIENCE FICTION concept, probably a new experience for young viewers at the time, gripped the audience as the series told of the mysterious and quaintly Victorian Doctor who, taking his earth-companions with him, travelled through time and space in his Tardis, which was camouflaged as a Police Telephone Box. The Doctor's main enemies were the alien Daleks, robots with mechanical voices whose war-cry was 'Exterminate! Exterminate!' William Hartnell, a popular B-movie star, played the Doctor, followed by Patrick Troughton, Jon Pertwee, Tom Baker and others. The *Doctor Who Annual* was published from 1965 until 1986. Back copies can be very valuable, especially since the Doctor developed a world-wide cult following. The *Daleks Annual* was also published from 1976 until 1979. There have been *Doctor Who* novels by Terrance Dicks, Dave Martin and several other authors, and a phenomenal number of *Doctor Who* reference books with titles like *Doctor Who: the Universal Data Bank*, *Doctor Who–Timeframe: The Illustrated History* and Peter Haining's *Doctor Who: The Time-Traveller's Guide*. DG

***Dr Xargle* books** Series of PICTUREBOOKS written by Jeanne Willis and illustrated by TONY ROSS. The first book, *Dr Xargle's Book of Earthlets*, was published in 1988. Each book is constructed in the form of a lesson, in which Dr Xargle, a teacher from outer space, takes it upon himself to explain to his class of aliens some of earth's customs, comically re-examining them for the human readers as he does so. The series looks at concepts familiar to a young child; earth weather, families, babies, cats and dogs all come under scrutiny. The combination of Willis's

Illustration by Sarah Stilwell from *Rhymes and Jingles* by Mary Mapes Dodge.

satirical descriptions and Ross's damning illustrations mocks the familiar way of life. An earth family is 'a collection of earthlings who belong together whether they like it or not', and the corresponding illustration shows a family tied together with dog leads. Earth weather comes in four different kinds, 'Too hot. Too cold. Too wet and too windy' and tiggers eat 'cowjuice, tandoori cluckbird, muckworm and old green gibble in dustbin gravy'. Tony Ross's illustrations depict comic human beings with huge red noses and tiny eyes. Owners look like their pets and are never aware of the chaos their animals are causing. Humans are divided into stereotypes: brothers and sisters are known as bothers and sulkers while grandparents have been around for as long as tyrannosaurus rex. Each lesson ends with the aliens attempting to learn some human vocabulary which they amusingly distort, before disguising themselves and setting off on a field trip to earth. KA

Dodd, Lynley see HAIRY MACLARY SERIES; see also PICTUREBOOKS; EVE SUTTON

Dodge, Mary [Elizabeth] Mapes 1831–1905 American author of *Hans Brinker; or, The Silver Skates* (1865) and editor of *ST NICHOLAS MAGAZINE* (1873–1905). Widowed in 1858, Dodge wrote *The Irvington Stories* (1864) for her two sons. Its success was followed by the bestselling *Hans Brinker*, set in Holland. She ran the children's pages of *Hearth and Home* so well that in 1873 Roswell Smith of Scribner and Company asked her to become editor of his company's ambitious new literary magazine for children, *St Nicholas*. Dodge made the magazine a 'pleasure-ground' for young readers, who could find in its pages the stories of FRANCES HODGSON BURNETT, FRANK STOCKTON, MARK TWAIN, LOUISA MAY ALCOTT and RUDYARD KIPLING; and the work of artists such as REGINALD BIRCH, JOHN BENNETT and HOWARD PYLE. Her own column, 'Jack-in-the-Pulpit', gave a friendly human touch to the influential magazine, and her serial *Donald and Dorothy* was a popular favourite. Dodge's correspondence shows she was a shrewd and sympathetic editor, skilled at showing authors how to speak to her special audience. Among her magazine's young readers over the years were such writers as Kipling, Fitzgerald, Faulkner, and E. B. WHITE. SRG

Dodgson, Charles Lutwidge see CARROLL, LEWIS

Doherty, Berlie 1943– British author who has worked as a teacher and in radio, best known for *Dear Nobody* (1991), a prize-winning and compelling account of a teenage pregnancy written in the form of the mother's letters to her unborn child. Doherty has written plays, poetry, young fiction and two adult novels as well as the recent young adult fiction for which she has won considerable acclaim. In 1987 Doherty won the CARNEGIE MEDAL for *Granny Was A Buffer Girl*, a series of linked stories which reveal a family's history. The themes of home, family life and relationships are central to much of Doherty's work. In 1998 she wrote an outstanding version of HANS CHRISTIAN ANDERSEN's heavily laden story *The Snow Queen* for Scholastic's series of paperback FAIRY TALES. KA

doll stories Early stories about dolls, like Mary Mister's *The Adventures of a Doll* (1816), are often travelogues in which the doll is passed from one owner to the next, experiencing life amongst rich and poor in a variety of places. R.H. Horne's *The Memoirs of a London Doll* (1846) and Rachel Field's *HITTY: HER FIRST HUNDRED YEARS* (1929) were popular examples, and Carol Beach York's *The Doll in the Bakeshop* (1965) continues the tradition. Although these stories may imply that girls and women are never safe from harm, the dolls frequently enjoy their adventures and take a sharply satirical view of the societies they encounter. In Anne Parrish's *Floating Island* (1930) the inhabitants of a shipwrecked doll's house experience the excitement of a desert island without being cast as victims.

Dolls may travel in time rather than in space, passed down from one generation to the next, not always with reverence: the heroine of Margaret Gatty's *Aunt Sally's Life* (1865) is reduced over 50 years to a limbless stump. Sometimes adults force girls to give away their dolls prematurely; many older stories stress the pain of losing a doll loved as a daughter, and having one's response interpreted as selfishness. In several recent stories old dolls and doll's houses are discovered by children of later generations, with the consequent unveiling of a family secret – Sylvia Cassedy's *Behind the Attic Wall* (1983), Betty Ren Wright's *The Dollhouse Murders* (1983), CORA TAYLOR's *The Doll* (1987) and Mary Downing Harm's *The Doll in the Garden* (1989).

Often when a doll stays within one family, it may be the centre of violent conflict. Boys in general, and brothers in particular, have a reputation for thoughtless, experimental or malicious abuse of dolls; but nursemaids, parents and girls themselves are often equally destructive. Many stories – for example, *The Dolls' House* (1947) by RUMER GODDEN – recognise, though, that dolls are toys, intended to be used rather than admired. Some earlier narratives include discussion of what it means to 'be of use' – Gatty's *Aunt Sally's Life* and Esther Copley's *Anna and Her Doll* (1832) are particularly interesting in this respect – and stories of all periods agree in valuing dolls that show the wear and tear of play. It is generally understood that dolls do not feel physical pain: they sometimes suffer embarrassment or humiliation, but often this proves that they were too proud in the first place. Deformity, even to the point of losing one's head, may be treated with humour: in Jean S. O'Connell's *The Dollhouse Caper* (1975), Mr. Dollhouse asks his family to remove his head in order to get the human family's attention.

In setting up the conventions of a particular story, some writers explore the boundaries between the human and the non-human. The heroine of CHARLOTTE YONGE's *The Autobiography of Patty Applecheeks* (1889) remembers being part of an apple tree, and develops human-like consciousness as she is formed into human shape. CAROLYN SHERWIN BAILEY's *Miss Hickory* (1946), on the other hand, returns to nature at the end of her doll life, grafted onto an apple tree. A common convention is that dolls can move and talk to one another when no humans are watching; sometimes they come alive only when loved. Since dolls cannot close their eyes at will, if at all, they are very observant, but often frustrated by their inability to speak. They do not mind being ignored, though, going into a kind of hibernation while waiting to be discovered by a new generation.

In more extreme forms of FANTASY, dolls can become frightening, like the tiny ebony carving that grows huge in Mark Lemon's *The Enchanted Doll* (1849), or the staring figures of Carol Beach York's *Revenge of the Dolls* (1979). Children may turn into dolls (Elizabeth Gorell's *Miss Fairitch and the Little Greenes*, 1943; William Sleator's *Among the Dolls*, 1975); in Richard Kennedy's unsettling *Amy's Eyes* (1985), Amy becomes a doll after her doll becomes human.

Generally, though, dolls are seen as companions whose usefulness needs no analysis. In Rumer Godden's *Impunity Jane* (1955) a boy and his friends soon learn the pointlessness of the dictum that 'boys do not have dolls' and a feminist mother in Sheila Greenwald's *The Secret in Miranda's Closet* (1977) has to admit that a girl who likes to play with dolls may be exercising independent thought rather than conforming to a stereotype. Almost all doll stories imply that fondness for a doll is a matter of individual preference, and that children, when free to do so, play with dolls in whatever ways suit their current needs. FEA

Domus Anguli Puensis see LATIN TRANSLATIONS

Donald Duck see WALT DISNEY; see also ANIMATED CARTOONS; COMICS, PERIODICALS AND MAGAZINES

Donkey-Skin see *CINDERELLA*

Donovan, John 1928–92 American playwright, author of children's novels, and executive director of the CBC from 1967 until 1992. As head of the non-profit-making association of United States publishers and an active member of the IBBY, Donovan was a strong advocate for an international approach to children's literature. He is perhaps best known for his groundbreaking children's novel, *I'll Get There, It Better Be Worth the Trip* (1969), the first book issued by a major American children's publisher to specifically address homosexuality (Davy, the book's lonely and isolated protagonist, has a brief sexual encounter with a fellow classmate). Response to Donovan's novel has varied widely: initial reviews interpreted the book as cautioning against homosexual behaviour but expressed concern that it could promote it; later critics have castigated the book for its depiction of homosexuality as a 'tragic flaw'; current critics typically place the book in the category of 'straight teens with gay experiences'. Donovan's subsequent novels, which examine such topics as alcoholism and death, continue to develop his central theme: the need for connection in an emotionally isolating world. JCH

see also GAY AND LESBIAN LITERATURE

Doomspell, The (2000) First volume of a proposed FANTASY thriller series by the British author Cliff McNish (1962–). Some of its darker features derive from horror fiction; others – for example, the rapturous recovery of an entire planet at the conclusion – from *THE CHRONICLES OF NARNIA*. But the writing is entirely distinctive and the storytelling is remarkable for the inventiveness of the plot, the speed of the magical transformations, and the complex psychic and physical dangers faced by its protagonists. The central evil is a witch who has destroyed or enslaved generations of children until her power is challenged by a young brother and sister strong enough and clever enough to overpower her magic. VW

Doonan, Jane see CRITICAL APPROACHES TO CHILDREN'S BOOKS

Doré, Gustave see *CONTES DE MA MÈRE L'OYE*; *THE RIME OF THE ANCIENT MARINER*

Down with Skool! see RONALD SEARLE; GEOFFREY WILLANS; see also SCHOOL STORIES

Doyle, Sir Arthur Conan see ADULT FICTION; SCIENCE FICTION

Doyle, Brian 1935– Canadian novelist for young adults. Recipient of the 1991 Vicky Metcalf Award for a distinguished body of work, Doyle was born in Ottawa, where he became a teacher in the high school he once attended. Doyle's first-person narratives – the best are set in the past – successfully combine slapstick episodes, eccentric characters and serious themes about tolerance, love and forgiveness. His finest novel, *Up to Low* (1981), winner of the CANADIAN LIBRARY ASSOCIATION BOOK OF THE YEAR AWARD, is set just after World War II. It contrasts a drunk's hilariously destructive automobile trip with a mutilated girl's healing journey to see her dying father. A brilliant fusion of TALL TALE episodes, black humour, memorable characters and religious symbols, it explores love as both an emotional and metaphysical mystery. In *Angel Square* (1984), its prequel, an actual mystery – the identity of the man who attacked a Jew – leads to explorations of the social mystery of racism, the psychological mystery of adolescent identity, and the emotional mystery of first love. *Easy Avenue* (1988), Doyle's second CLA Book of the Year winner, focuses on class and manners, tracing a post-war orphan's discovery that 'success' has social, emotional and moral meanings. REJ

Doyle, Richard 1824–83 British illustrator and painter, brought up by his painter-caricaturist father. He received no formal training, but at only 19 he was employed by *Punch*, for whom he drew a cover subsequently used by the magazine for over a century. Children knew him best for his vivid, even terrifying illustrations to *JACK THE GIANT KILLER* (1842), Ruskin's *THE KING OF THE GOLDEN RIVER* (1851) and, most memorably, *In Fairyland* (1870), with its wood-engraved glimpses of the elf-world, brilliantly printed in colour by EDMUND EVANS. Doyle, who never married, was widely loved in London social circles as a man with much charm and little malice, affectionately known as 'Delightful Dicky Doyle'. GPF

see also WOOD ENGRAVING

Doyle, Roddy 1958– Dublin-born former teacher, now novelist and playwright. His first two novels, *The Commitments* (1988) and *The Snapper* (1990), both filmed, form *The Barrytown Trilogy* together with *The Van* (1991), a Booker prize nomination. Balancing hilarity with sentimentality, they relate the highs and lows in the life of the Rabbit family in a racy conversational style that employs robust language. Winner of the 1993 Booker prize, *Paddy Clarke Ha Ha Ha* is set in 1968 Dublin. Its narrator is a ten-year-old boy whose thought processes and speech rhythms, as he struggles to express his bewilderment at the break-up of his parents' marriage, are successfully captured by Doyle. This was followed by *The Woman Who Walked into Doors* (1996), a bleak account of domestic violence. MSS

Dracula see VICTOR AMBRUS; EDWARD GOREY

Dragon Slayer (1966) Novel by the acclaimed British author ROSEMARY SUTCLIFF, originally published as *Beowulf* (1961), illustrated by CHARLES KEEPING. Sutcliff had already written several of her major books set in and before the time of the Roman occupation of Britain when she turned to the Old English poem of *Beowulf*, which tells, not of a British hero, but of the Scandinavian warrior who through his great strength and courage is able to defeat the monster Grendel, Grendel's avenging mother and, finally, a ferocious fire-dragon. Sutcliff's retelling, clearly influenced by the language and word-order of the original epic, brings out the importance of physical strength, loyalty, revenge and the place of material goods in the social order of the times. Above all, however, she fully conveys the sense of the terror that these attacking monsters bring as they creep through the darkness. JAG

Dragonwagon, Crescent [Ellen Zolotow, Ellen Parsons] 1952– American writer of children's PICTUREBOOKS and fiction. The daughter of two famous writers, Dragonwagon legally changed her name, Crescent meaning 'the Growing'. Under the pseudonym Ellen Parsons, she published her first book for children, *Rainy Day Together*, in 1970. An early book, *Wind Rose* (1976), which deals with the miracle of conception and birth, was made into a motion picture in 1983. *Half a Moon and One Whole Star* (1986), a poem written by Dragonwagon and illustrated by JERRY PINKNEY, was selected as a *Reading Rainbow* book. *Home Place* (1990), also illustrated by Pinkney, may be her most honoured book, having received the Golden Kite Award, a citation from the National Council for Christians and Jews, and an award from the National Council for the Social Studies. In the 1980s she began writing novels for children. Her first, *To Take a Dare* (1982), written with PAUL ZINDEL, was well received and earned a notable book citation from the ALA. She has published a book of poetry, *Message from the Avacadoes* (1981), and an assortment of cookbooks. JGJ

drama for children The term 'children's drama' covers a wide spectrum of activities. Unlike children's fiction and children's poetry, in which the role of the child is primarily that of reception and response, and only in a relatively minor way the actual creation of literature, children's drama includes many activities which place the child in the role of 'writer' and performer. The spectrum is accurately represented by the available meanings of the word 'play'. 'Play' refers to the earliest imaginative pretences of young children, but also to the greatest masterpieces of dramatic literature. Children's drama is concerned with the educational and experiential process by which children learn to be an appreciative and insightful audience for great drama, but it values every stage of that learning process in its own right as something of permanent value, not as a sequential development in which early and provisional competences are gradually discarded, and emphatically not as a progress from active to passive involvement. Current thinking on children's drama rests on the age-old awareness that in live theatre the audience participates along with the performers in the creation of meanings, and this achievement of simultaneous lived experience is of course something that film and TELEVISION cannot replicate. It is therefore important that 'children's drama' should include regular opportunities to experience 'children's theatre', for which other media are no substitute.

Because the spectrum of 'children's drama' is so wide, terms are needed to denote the different elements of the experience so that the relationship between them can be understood. American writers and practitioners have distinguished helpfully between 'children's theatre' and 'creative dramatics', notably in the influential collection of essays *Children's Theatre and Creative Dramatics*, edited by Geraldine

Brain Siks and Hazel Brain Dunnington (1961). Some years later Moses Goldberg, in his book *Children's Theatre: a Philosophy and a Method* (1974), added a third, intermediate term, 'recreational drama'. These three terms cover virtually all significant activity in children's drama, and are well placed to form the basic *lingua franca* of international critical discussion.

'Creative dramatics' is essentially an educational instrument drawing on the natural impulses to dramatic pretence which children display from early infancy. It channels them into activities which foster various kinds of personal development. As Goldberg notes: 'Its goal is not performance, but rather the free expression of the child's creative imagination through the discipline of an art form.' Characteristic activities may include spontaneous movement and dance in response to a musical stimulus; improvisation and acting-out of dialogues and stories; mime of everyday activities, or of natural occurrences – such as animal movements – which draw on the child's powers of observation and imitation; the creation of tableaux or 'freeze-frames' in which children physically illustrate their responses to a story or event; and 'hot-seating', in which a child answers questions while 'in role' as a historical or invented character.

The goals of creative dramatics can be multiple and varied. The teacher's or group leader's purposes may in part be social: through creative dramatics children learn to work together as a group, co-operating in a common interest. The aim may be to develop children's confidence, encouraging them to express themselves freely, both verbally and physically, in a safe, unthreatening environment. Imaginative stimulus is likely to be central to all such activities, inviting the child to live vicariously for a time, perhaps by becoming somebody other than herself, perhaps by imagining her actual self in an unfamiliar situation. Aesthetic development is also important: for example, children's appreciation of music and rhythm is likely to be enhanced through whole-body response to what they hear. A child's mastery of language may be assisted by speech improvisation, encouraging children to use, enjoy and extend their own linguistic resources, and to experiment with a range of linguistic codes and registers. Other areas of the school curriculum such as history, geography and scientific discovery can be brought to life through dramatic enactment. And of course children who are engaged in making their own plays, and formally watching those created by their peers, are learning to be an informed and appreciative theatre audience.

'Children's theatre' as defined by Goldberg is 'a formal theatrical experience in which a play is presented for an audience of children'. Children's theatre differs from theatre for adults only in its target audience and consequent selection of its repertoire. Productions draw on the full resources of the theatre, and plays are normally performed by adults – professional, or good amateur actors. Naturally there are many plays in the repertoire which include child characters. Although these parts are frequently played by adult actors and actresses who are able to assume a plausibly juvenile appearance (for example, Wendy in PETER PAN is rarely played by a young girl), they are often and increasingly played by real children. However, the basis for their appearance is not the same as for creative dramatics or 'recreational theatre' (see below). The children are often recruited from specialist stage schools, and appear on equal terms with adult players. Their position is analogous to that of cathedral choristers in relation to adult singers: the difference is one of differential skills and appropriateness, not of standards. This point is a salutary reminder that children's potential should not be underestimated, either as performers or as audiences.

Children's theatre exists mainly to entertain children by showing them enjoyable plays, and in so doing to engender a lasting pleasure in live theatre and in drama generally. It is not by definition 'educational', except in this liberal aesthetic sense. Although it inevitably 'teaches', as all art inevitably does for all audiences, this is not its raison d'être. It is not a branch of political and moral education, but an educational exemplar of life-enhancing arts. In the commercial theatre, *Peter Pan* is its founding classic text, and still dominates the repertoire. In recent decades children's theatre has merged with educational drama to produce two new kinds of company, performance and event, both of which tend to be doctrinally explicit and preoccupied in ways that 'children's theatre' proper seeks to avoid. The term Young People's Theatre is used to refer to professional theatrical performances by dedicated companies in educational venues such as schools, community centres and youth clubs, often exploring social issues. Theatre in Education (TIE) is rather different in that it involves companies of professional actor-teachers using performance in the context of other drama methods to mount drama-based learning experiences in schools. These often involve substantial student participation, and draw on features such as improvisation which are central to creative dramatics. Despite perennial shortages of money, insecure funding, and the risk of appearing to be marginal luxuries at a time of general educational cutbacks, the companies engaged in these two branches of educational theatre have done much excellent work. In terms of theatrical genre the most productive form for TIE companies has been documentary drama, with its origins in post-war classics such as Joan Littlewood's *Oh What a Lovely War*. Some of the resulting works have been politically challenging and have involved young audiences in powerful simulations and exercises in problem-solving and decision-making. Outstanding examples have included *Poverty Knocks*, about the Chartist Movement (Bolton Octagon Theatre TIE, 1973) and *Rare Earth*, a prescient environmental drama (Belgrade Theatre, Coventry TIE, 1973).

At the same time, there is always a risk that educational drama will leave children's and young people's theatre with an image which is too solemn, too problem-centred, too moralistic, and too closely linked to schools, thus deterring tomorrow's audience from straightforward pleasure in non-missionary theatre. Lowell Swortzell, writing in the excellent collection *Learning Through Theatre* (ed. Tony Jackson, 1993) notes of several plays on serious themes by important modern children's dramatists that in the United States such 'plays and authors are widely produced . . . in theatres by established companies, but not in schools by TIE teams . . . So what was once TIE's exclusive terrain is now increasingly and highly effectively encroached upon by professional companies for young people.' In so far as this entails a shift of balance from educational scripts to dramatic literature, and from task-centred to experience-centred theatre, this may well be a good thing. In Britain the shortage of dedicated children's theatres and companies means that the division between TIE and children's theatre is still sharp, with meagrely funded TIE companies concentrating on thematically serious work, while the few theatre-based companies such as Unicorn Theatre and Polka Theatre stress imaginative entertainment.

The third term, 'recreational drama', is defined by Goldberg as 'a formal theatrical presentation where the development and experience of the performers is as or more important than the aesthetic enjoyment of the audience'. It includes school plays and school or community pageants. In so far as creative dramatics is concerned with *process* and children's theatre with *product*, 'recreational drama' denotes the intermediate phases where children's mastery of process is sufficient to achieve a product, but one in which the performers' own enjoyment and learning are still paramount, and friendly audiences make allowances for work which is below (but sometimes only a little below) professional level. The most widespread and best-loved 'recreational drama' is the school nativity play, which may use a home-made script or the work of a major writer, such as TED HUGHES's *The Coming of the Kings* (1970) or CHARLES CAUSLEY's *The Gift of a Lamb* (1978).

Children's drama has a long history. Experience of theatre was a feature of education in classical Athens, and in modern Europe its origins are ecclesiastical. The dialogue between clergy and choristers which enacts the liturgy in a modern cathedral is a survival of the event which lies at the root of all modern drama, for children and adults alike. The dramatisation of the Mass during the early middle ages led from choral dialogues to short scenes, beginning a process of development which eventually produced the cycles of mystery plays which emerged in the 14th and 15th centuries. Choirboys were involved in the mystery plays as participants, and during the 15th century, as the production of the mystery play cycles became somewhat secularised and switched to the new feast of Corpus Christi, boy choristers assumed responsibility for indoor theatrical performances at Christmas and Easter.

Along with the centuries-old religious tradition, the 16th century saw the humanist educators of the Renaissance introducing dramatic performances into the grammar school curriculum, with a combination of aims, including the development of poise and confidence, which are directly analogous to those of modern teachers of creative dramatics. During the 16th century both the ecclesiastical and humanist traditions generated a public vogue for theatrical performances by children. They performed frequently at Court and in noble houses, and eventually, in the later 16th and early 17th centuries, were formed into professional companies which for several years displaced the adult companies (including SHAKESPEARE's) in popularity. Hence children as performers are essential to the origins of modern drama, and this tradition of active child involvement continues to influence modern thinking and practice, for example in the form of 'participation drama', in which the child audience becomes an agent in the stage action.

During the 18th and 19th centuries a different form of children's drama emerged. It consisted of short plays designed for performance by families as home entertainments. The key figure in this development was the French educator Mme de Genlis, a disciple of ROUSSEAU, who in 1779–80 began to publish her *Théatre à l'Usage des Jeunes Personnes*. Mme de Genlis set out to write plays which were 'moral treatises put into action'. She and her many imitators and successors over the following century produced a little-known, engaging and sometimes distinguished canon of plays for domestic theatre, especially notable because for the first time it gave a full and equal place to girls. Jonathan Levy has collected some of the best of these plays in his anthology *The Gymnasium of the Imagination* (1992), which reprints some admirable family plays from France, Britain and America.

Apart from the Christmas PANTOMIME, which had been popular in Britain and America for many decades, a commercial theatre for children did not begin until the end of the 19th century. Some of the earliest children's plays are developments from, and reactions against, pantomime. In 1901 there was a West End production of *Katawampus*, by Louis Calvert and Judge Parry, and a historically important event in the same year was Seymour Hicks's *Bluebell in Fairyland*. Described as 'A Musical Dream Play', it retained much of the apparatus of pantomime but was a true dramatic narrative with music (see also MUSIC AND STORY). Reportedly it was this play which opened J.M. BARRIE's eyes to the possibilities of dramatic FANTASY for children, and so led to the most important children's play of all time, *Peter Pan* (1904).

Peter Pan's commercial success and popularity continue into the 21st century, confounding numerous sage predictions over many decades that its days were numbered. Like many successful children's plays, it cannily offers entertainment to both child and adult, but Barrie's commercial acumen is incidental to its success. Many objections have been raised to the play, but two factors seem to override all else and fix it in the repertoire. In imaginative conception *Peter Pan* is a dramatic act of praise for the imaginative life of children. It stages archetypal childhood terrors, but tames them with laughter, child empowerment and ultimate safety. And it does so through the exuberant use of theatrical spectacle, above all the magic of flying. *Peter Pan* is total theatre for children, in ways that few of its successors have yet rivalled.

Maurice Maeterlinck's allegorical fantasy *THE BLUE BIRD* (1908) was influenced by *Peter Pan*, as was *Where the Rainbow Ends* by Clifford Mills and John Ramsey (1911), which also seems indebted to Maeterlinck. *Where the Rainbow Ends* is a dramatic quest for lost parents, but in its jingoistic patriotism, culminating in St George's defeat of the Dragon King, it seems to borrow sentiments and attitudes from *The Faerie Queene*. The play was popular in London for many years and, probably because of its nationalism, the story was reissued during World War II as a large-format storybook. More literary efforts towards a children's theatre in this period included LAURENCE HOUSMAN's 'fairy plays', *The Chinese Lantern* (1908) and *Bird in Hand* (1918), and WALTER DE LA MARE's *Crossings* (1919). Among the few other notable original plays for children in the first half of the century were Frederick Bowyer's *The Windmill Man* (1921) and A.A. MILNE's underrated three-in-one play *Make-Believe* (1918). Milne remarked feelingly, in words which many writers must have echoed: 'The difficulty in the way of writing a children's play is that Barrie was born too soon.'

These few original works apart, children's theatre was (and in large measure still is) dominated by adaptations of FAIRY TALES and well-known novels. A musical version of *ALICE IN WONDERLAND* was staged in 1886, and one of F. Anstey's *Vice Versa* in 1883, but the most important and lasting adaptations at this time were those of FRANCES HODGSON BURNETT's novels, first *LITTLE LORD FAUNTLEROY* in 1888, and most importantly *A LITTLE PRINCESS* (adapted by Hodgson Burnett from her novel *SARA CREWE*) in 1902. Some years later KENNETH GRAHAME's *THE WIND IN THE WILLOWS* was selectively and wittily dramatised by A.A. Milne as *TOAD OF TOAD HALL* (1929).

In America the dominant figure in children's theatre from the 1930s to the post-war period was CHARLOTTE CHORPENNING, for many years head of the Children's Theatre at the Goodman Theatre in Chicago. It is hard to overestimate Chorpenning's constructive influence as writer, teacher and director. Her own plays were chiefly adaptations of fairy stories, novels and historical events, such as *RUMPELSTILTSKIN* (1944) and *ROBINSON CRUSOE* (1952). Though somewhat dated in dramatic method now, they remain popular. It is a measure of Chorpenning's stature that when Siks and Dunnington recommended 25 full-length plays for children in 1961, no fewer than ten of their selection were by her.

Chorpenning's work survives not only as a set of texts but as an inspiration for later American writers and theatre directors. Several distinguished dramatists for children have emerged in the post-war years. Among the more traditional is Madge Miller, another gifted adaptor of fairy tales: her sense of their importance to child development is akin to that presented by Bruno Bettelheim in *The Uses of Enchantment*. *The Land of the Dragon* (1945) represents Miller's work at its best. The movement noted earlier towards a more thematically serious and contemporary children's theatre is particularly well represented by the work of Brian Kral, whose plays have tackled handicap and teenage suicide; by Joanna Kraus, whose outstanding play *The Ice Wolf* (1967) deals with prejudice and superstition in an Eskimo community; and by Susan Zeder, whose play *Step on a Crack* (1974) sensitively explores a young girl's relationship with her father. However, the finest of all contemporary children's dramatists is unquestionably AURAND HARRIS, whose work is characterised by its rich imagination and exuberant theatrical diversity. His version of *Androcles and the Lion* (1964) totally eclipses George Bernard Shaw's, and *Arkansaw Bear* (1980) is a major, innovative treatment of the theme of death in plays for children.

Theatrical resources, nowhere adequate except perhaps in the subsidised theatres of former communist countries, have been more parsimonious in Britain than in America. Playwrights such as DAVID WOOD and DAVID HOLMAN – both of whom have dramatised environmental themes with much responsibility and skill – have worked without the recognition customarily given to novelists and poets, and ADRIAN MITCHELL in particular has written a series of excellent adaptations and variations on traditional stories, such as *The Wild Animal Story Contest* and *Mowgli's Jungle* (1992). Particular mention should be made of Brian Way, a pioneer of modern 'participation drama' such as his play *The Mirrorman*, who has brought together children's theatre and educational method, practice and theory, with exceptional cogency and flair.

The commercial rewards of children's theatre remain very limited, and only a few successful 'adult' dramatists have engaged with it. Notable among these are ALAN AYCKBOURN, who has a rare and precious sense of community theatre, and Ann Jellicoe, whose extraordinary play *The Sport of My Mad Mother* (1958) is one of very few attempts to introduce expressionist drama into theatre for the young. Jellicoe's *3 Jelliplays* (1975) are a trio of excellent shorter works, one of which, *You'll Never Guess!*, is a version of *Rumpelstiltskin*, and shows how much theatrical originality can still be won from traditional stories. In the 1990s many gifted writers are anxious to create a new dramatic literature for children, but it cannot turn into theatrical reality without such generous sponsorship as the 1992 W.H. Smith Plays for Children Awards, which led to the production and eventual publication of the winning play, Adrian Flynn's *Burning Everest*.

Given the historical depth of children's drama, the long tradition of children's creative involvement as participants, not just spectators, the diversity of educational gains which it affords, and the omnipresence of drama in contemporary adult life, it should no longer be acceptable for children's drama to be the impoverished curricular and theatrical Cinderella which it currently is. PH

Drescher, Henrik 1955– Creator of PICTUREBOOKS. Born in Denmark, Drescher came to the United States as an adolescent and his picturebooks are known for his frenetic use of line, squiggly shapes, splotches of ink, and intricate use of detail. His books have a rough, energetic texture reminiscent of an artist's sketchbook. At the same time they are simplistic in their graphic design, looking as if the drawings might have been made by a child, but on closer inspection they are surprisingly complex. His first book, *The Strange Appearance of Howard Cranebill, Jr.* (1982), is the story of a child with a long pointy nose who mysteriously arrives on the steps of a childless couple's home, but eventually flies away. *Simon's Book* (1983) is a clever adaptation of CROCKETT JOHNSON's *Harold and the Purple Crayon* (1955), in which the child artist-protagonist finds himself trapped in one of his own sketches and must draw his way to safety. Drescher has also done a parody of DOROTHY KUNHARDT's *Pat the Bunny* (1940), entitled *Pat the Beastie, A Pull-and-Poke Book* (1993). Like LANE SMITH, Drescher is an illustrator who has brought an increasing graphic sophistication, ironic sensibility and off-beat humour to children's picturebooks. JCS

***Drina* series** Popular BALLET STORIES written by the British author Mabel Esther Allan under the pen name of Jean Estoril. The original list included *Ballet for Drina* (1957), *Drina's Dancing Year* (1958), *Drina Dances in Exile* (1959), *Drina Dances in Italy* (1962), *Drina Dances Again* (1960), and continued with her exploits in New York (1961), Paris (1962), Madeira (1963), Switzerland (1964) and on tour (1965). A new title was added 26 years later with *Drina Ballerina* (1991).

The books are limited in originality, basically following the formula established by Lorna Hill in her *SADLER'S WELLS* series begun in 1950. Andrina Adamo (luckier than most budding ballerinas and her own creator in already possessing an exotic name) is the orphaned daughter of an Italian father and the famous ballerina Elizabeth Ivory. She has to overcome many obstacles on the path to fame, such as a grandmother who is initially set against her becoming a dancer, the distractions provided by two admirers, Igor and Grant, envious rivals, Christine and Queenie, who do all they can to sabotage her and make her life a misery, and the usual accident (pulling a leg muscle) that puts a temporary halt to her dancing. This provides us with one of the more interesting interludes in the series: Drina turns to acting instead, taking the part of Margaret in J.M. BARRIE's *Dear Brutus*. Like NOEL STREATFEILD, Estoril handles description of theatre and dance production well, and this, rather than the predictable plot line, ensures the continuing popularity of the series. SA

drugs in children's books Despite the growing scale of drug use among teenagers, fiction has dealt with the issue very cautiously, perhaps because of the failure of public and political opinion on how to tackle the problem. Writers and publishers have tended to avoid this area, and many librarians and teachers, who constitute a large part of the market for teenage books, are wary of holding such controversial material. Since few people believe that teenagers cannot, or should not, read about this world, it seems likely that it is the fear of a small number of influential and articulate parents that has led to this important area being so neglected.

Teenage and younger children are usually well educated on the ups and downs of drug use through rock music, magazines, film and by word of mouth, but the books available have tended to concentrate more on the downs than the ups. Drugs and drug culture are portrayed at best obliquely, and more often symbolically. The people selling drugs are represented as beasts, the people who use them as irresponsible, and the effects of taking them as unpleasant. The *actual* experience of drug-taking and the culture in which it takes place have been more or less ignored.

That Was Then, This Is Now (1971) by S.E. HINTON is an interesting account set in the late 1960s in the United States. Two young pool hustlers lose their lifelong friendship through drugs; although the story is a good read, the portrayal of drug-takers is not convincing. The anonymous *Go Ask Alice* (1971) is an account of a 15-year-old American girl's slide to death by overdose. It is a lively story told in the first person, based on real-life diaries, but the message is so explicit that its effect is that of propaganda. *CAME BACK TO SHOW YOU I COULD FLY* (1989) by ROBIN KLEIN won a number of awards in Australia and was shortlisted for the CARNEGIE MEDAL in Britain. It is the account of a boy's relationship with an older girl, who turns out to be a junkie. *The House that Crack Built* (USA, 1992), written by Clark Taylor and illustrated by Jan Thomas Dicks, is for younger children; it is a rhyme illustrating the lines of supply from the big house at the beginning of the story to the damaged people at the end. It cleverly puts the use of crack into its social context. CYNTHIA VOIGT's *Orfe* (1993) – a strong story – is a semi-mythical tale in which drug-culture is equated with the underworld.

The Ups and Downs of Carl Davis the Third (1989) by ROSA GUY, set in the American south, chronicles a teenager's discovery of his family's involvement with drugs. *The Worm Charmers* (1989) by NICHOLAS FISK, and *Run Donny Run* (1991) by Joe Buckley, are both about groups of teenagers up against drug dealers. *Virtual Sexual Reality* (1994) by Chloë Rayban is one of the few books that depict the casual use of soft drugs. *Out of It* (1995) by MAUREEN STEWART shows a 16-year-old led into drug-taking through a love affair. *Son of Pete Flude* (1994) by Malcolm Rose has the son of a rock star kidnapped by drug dealers. *Junk* (1996) by MELVYN BURGESS is an account, based loosely on real events, of a group of teenagers squatting and eventually getting involved with heroin during the punk period in the 1980s. The controversy provoked when it won the 1996 Carnegie Medal is a measure of the concern about this issue – though the British national press was mostly favourable. MBu

Drummond, Violet Hilda 1911–2000 British illustrator. Drummond was an early recipient of the KATE GREENAWAY AWARD for *Mrs Easter and the Storks* (1957) where the scrawly, spontaneous ink drawing and splashes of limited primary colour are typical of her expressive style. There are several *Mrs Easter* titles, and another series, the *Little Laura* books (1960–3), gave rise to 18 cartoon films for the BBC. Most of her many books tell the stories of eccentrics and their engaging adventures. JAG

Du Bois, William Pène 1916–93 American author and illustrator of PICTUREBOOKS and TALL TALES. Born into a family of artists, du Bois spent six years at a French boarding school. Whilst the precision and perfectionism of his graphic style may be traced to the discipline of the Lycée Hoche, the satirical humour and wild imagination are uniquely his own. Conventional genre categories seem inadequate for his work. *The Great Geppy* (1940), for example, might be called a DETECTIVE STORY, but the detective is a red-and-white-striped talking horse. Detective story and utopia are combined in *The Three Policemen* (1938), set on imaginary Farbe Island. Du Bois's fascination with islands, utopias and inventions is also evident in his NEWBERY AWARD winner, *The Twenty-One Balloons* (1947); the narrator, a 19th-century mathematics professor, is stranded when his balloon crashes, but finds a Gourmet Government on supposedly uninhabited Krakatoa – whose total destruction, unfortunately, is only days away. Du Bois's equally original picturebooks include *Giant Otto* (1935), about a giant otter-hound; *Bear Party* (1951) and *Bear Circus* (1971), about a community of koalas; and *Lion* (1956), about the first lion created in Heaven's Animal Factory. SR

du Chaillu, Paul Belloni 1835–1903 French American author and explorer, best known for books based on his extensive travels in Africa and Scandinavia. Focusing primarily on the wildlife and birds of these areas, du Chaillu discovered and documented many species of mammals never before seen. Although much of his research was at first challenged, he redefined his data and made an immense contribution to the field of zoology. His books for children, some of which are still in print, were appealing and described his lifelong adventures and experiences as he studied gorillas and chimpanzees. The best-known of his books are *A Journey to Ashango-Land* (1867), *Stories of the Gorilla Country* (1868) and *Lost in the Jungle* (1869). Du Chaillu's study of African pygmies was documented in *The Country of the Dwarfs* (1871). Additional research concerning his journeys to Scandinavian countries inspired *The Land of the Midnight Sun* (1881) and *The Viking Age* (1889). In 1901, he began to study Russia and develop material for a book based on that area. Du Chaillu died in St Petersburg before he could complete this project. ESC

du Jardin, Rosamond 1902–63 American writer of teen romances in the style of MAUREEN DALY's *Seventeenth Summer* (1942). Though she produced several adult novels and was a prolific contributor to women's magazines such as *Cosmopolitan*, *Red Book*, *Good Housekeeping* and *McCall's*, du Jardin is remembered today for her novels about young women experiencing adolescence and young adulthood throughout the 1940s and 1950s, such as *Wait for Marcy* (1950), *Double Feature* (1953) and *Senior Prom* (1957). Set in small mid-western towns, these novels depict adolescent females learning to recognise their own values and to respect their choices. Richly laden with descriptions of proms, college weekends and weddings, du Jardin's novels remain popular. Though her characters eventually choose to marry, like Daly's heroine they also value their own educational opportunities and empowerment. College becomes a particularly transformative experience for most of du Jardin's heroines. As in *Seventeenth Summer*, the heroines may observe and learn from their older sisters' romantic predicaments. A few works have been updated since their original publication to reflect contemporary life. All of du Jardin's books have been translated and published abroad, particularly in Japan and Sweden. AKP

dual language books see MULTICULTURAL BOOKS

Duane, Diane 1952– Writer of children's books, FANTASY, SCIENCE FICTION, and popular material for all ages. Born in Manhattan, now residing in Ireland, Duane is best known for her high fantasy 'Young Wizards' series: *SO YOU WANT TO BE A WIZARD* (1983), *Deep Wizardry* (1985), *High Wizardry* (1991), and *A Wizard Abroad* (1993). Throughout the series, wizards Nita and Kit, resident advisors Tom and Carl, Fred the white hole, macaw Machu Picchu (moonlighting as one of the Powers that Be), and shark Ed'Rashtekaresket enter the eternal battle between good and evil during their conflicts with the Lone Power, who assumes forms ranging from Milton's Satan to Irish monster Balor. The poetry of language is central: in addition to suggesting universal themes of identity and maturation, the Old English flavour of the incantations reinforces the tales' epic qualities. Humour, such as Fred's hiccoughing up a Lear Jet for distraction or Nita's parents' sputtering astonishment upon realising her wizardly aptitude, provides variations in tone, while a variety of sentient objects – live helicopters, talking rocks, ravenous fire hydrants – expand the boundaries of humanity. This series provides some of the best opportunities for Coleridge's 'willing suspension of disbelief' in modern literature, and establishes Duane as a master of fantasy alongside TOLKIEN and LE GUIN. AHA

Dubosarsky, Ursula 1961– One of the most original voices in Australian writing for young people. Her works include *High Hopes* (1990), *Zizzy Zing* (1991), *The Last Week in December* (1993), *The White Guinea-Pig* (1994) and *My Father is Not a Comedian* (1999), which are all about the transition involved in the acquisition of knowledge concerning adult fallibility. In *The First Book of Samuel* (1995) Dubosarsky steers her usual dangerous course from family fragmentation to impossible, yet credible, resolution of familial discord, while capably traversing precarious obstacles – a blended family, the angst of Holocaust memories, childish misunderstanding of adult mendacity. Other works include *Bruno and the Crumhorn* (1996), *Black Sails, White Sails* (1997), the PICTUREBOOK *Honey and Bear* (1998), illustrated by RON BROOKS, and *The Strange Adventures of Isador Brown* (1998). In her use of idiosyncrasy and ambiguous whimsicality, Dubosarsky taunts the reader with suggested meanings, yet writes with warmth, wistfulness and powerful clarity. RS

Duck in the Gun, The (1984) New Zealand PICTUREBOOK written by JOY COWLEY, and originally illustrated by Edward Sorel and published in New York in 1969. Reissued in New Zealand in 1984 with watercolour illustrations by ROBYN BELTON, it established itself as a New Zealand and international classic for Belton's memorable, colourful artwork which is perfectly matched to the story. Though light-hearted, even gently sardonic in tone, the book conveys a powerful anti-war message. How can a war be conducted with a duck nesting in the gun? Both illustrator and author have further explored the unusual theme of war in picturebooks: Cowley in *Salmagundi* (1985) and Belton in *The Bantam and the Soldier* (1996). TD

Duder, Tessa 1940– New Zealand multi-award-winning writer of novels, short stories, plays for children and young adults, and non-fiction for adults and children, prominent particularly for her *ALEX QUARTET*. A trained journalist, Duder first celebrated female resourcefulness in her shortlisted novel, *Night Race to Kawau* (1982), in which 12-year-old Sam, her mother and younger sister survive a yachting ordeal. Duder then exquisitely crafted *Jellybean* (1985), allowing Geraldine (Jellybean) to discover through her cellist mother the richness of classical music and Tchaikovsky's *The Nutcracker*, before achieving her dream of conducting an orchestra. *Jellybean* was shortlisted for the adult-dominated Wattie Award, a rare achievement for a children's novel. Duder's satirical skills surface in these novels and in short story collections: *Zigzag*, edited by William Taylor (1993); *Nearly Seventeen* (1993) and *Falling in Love* (1995), edited by herself; and *Crossing*, jointly edited with Agnes Nieuwenhuizen. Her comic flair is revealed in *Mercury Beach* (1997), focusing on the foibles of a fictional New Zealand seaside community engaged in fundraising for a community hall. Four knowing 11- and 12-year-olds, including Freddy Bone from a previous short story, have personal reasons for their unconventional support. The climax is a grand parade of many groups including the local Maori gang and big-city drag queens. Duder deepens her comedy by showing the dark side of festival hype and unreality, where real people get hurt. Duder's facility with dialogue and her in-depth knowledge of the workings of TELEVISION are manifest in *The Tiggie Thompson Show* (1999), winner of the NEW ZEALAND POST AWARD, which addresses such issues as body image and society expectations when overweight 14-year-old Tiggie (Antigone) accepts a role in a soap opera. Duder's career is studded with awards such as the Choysa Bursary (1985), the 1996 Margaret Mahy Lecture Award (1996), an OBE, and national presidency of the New Zealand Society of Authors. DAH

Dugan, Michael (Gray) 1947– Australian novelist, poet, PICTUREBOOK and non-fiction writer, who has also worked with words and ideas as bookseller, literary magazine editor and generous participant in literary organisations. His NONSENSE VERSE collection *Stuff and Nonsense* (1974), with drawings by DEBORAH NILAND, was well received by children, as was *More Stuff and Nonsense* (1980), imaginatively illustrated by ROLAND HARVEY. A contemporary CAUTIONARY TALE in a picturebook, *Billy the Most Horrible Boy in the World* (1981), about a boy who comes to an untimely and gruesome end, was considered too tasteless by many adults. *Dingo Boy* (1980), *Melissa's Ghost* (1986) and *Should We Tell?* (1990) are more insightful and compassionate. HE

Dulac, Edmund 1882–1953 Dulac was born in France but came to England in 1905. He is best remembered for his full-colour ILLUSTRATIONS for GIFT BOOKS. He did, however, also produce illustrations for children's books such as M.M. Stavell's *Fairies I have Met* (1900) and *My Days with Fairies* (1913), and R.L. STEVENSON's *TREASURE ISLAND* (1927).

His painterly style exploited the new colour-printing processes which relied on the use of photographic separations being transferred to four colour-printing plates. This allowed the subtlety of his delicate colour to be reproduced on the printed page. His work was eclectic, and the elongated form of his ethereal figures looks back to late 19th-century Romantic painting rather than to the age of modernism. Persian art had a great influence on him and, because of his interest in Eastern art, he abandoned traditional European perspective in favour of a system which offered many vanishing points, exemplified by his 50 TIPPED IN illustrations for LAURENCE HOUSMAN's *Stories from The Arabian Nights* (1907). A man of many talents, he produced paintings and designs as well as illustrations. He was also a friend of W.B. Yeats, for whom he designed stage sets. AEW

Dumas, Alexandre 1802–70 French novelist and playwright, known as 'Dumas père'. One of the most prolific, versatile and popular authors of his time, best known for his great novels of action, *Les Trois Mousquetaires* and *Le Comte de Monte-Cristo*, he also wrote several charming and inventive stories for children. The best-loved in France is *Le Capitaine Pamphile* (1839), which recounts the strange adventures of the piratical Pamphile in the forests of Brazil and on the tropic voyages of the 'Roscana'. A new edition appeared in 1878, with numerous illustrations by C.A. d'Arnould Bertall. Another favourite story is *Histoire d'un casse-noisette* (1844), a free adaptation from Hoffmann, and a key source for Tchaikovsky's *Nutcracker Suite*. *La Bouille de la Comtesse Berthe* (1844) has been translated several times into English as *Countess Bertha's Honeybroth [or Honeystew] Banquet*. Another, original story was the delightful *Le Lièvre de mon grand-père* (1855), and there were several characteristic Dumas reworkings from GRIMM and ANDERSEN in a collection of 1860, *Le Père Gigogne: contes pour les enfants*. Oxford University Press published three beautifully produced titles in the 1970s, with English texts by Douglas Munro: *Captain Pamphile's Adventures*, *When Pierrot was Young*, and *The Nutcracker*. *The Three Musketeers* remains widely available in abridged versions. PR

Duncan, Lois [Lois Steinmetz Arquette] 1934– American author of suspense novels. Duncan began writing in her childhood and, during her high-school years, was a three-time winner in the magazine *Seventeen*'s short-story contest. Connections between Duncan's early life and literary development are chronicled in *Chapters: My Growth as a Writer* (1982), but most of her major works were written after the period of her life examined in this literary AUTOBIOGRAPHY. Beginning with *Ransom* (1966), Duncan established herself as a master of psychological suspense novels for young adults. The novels (which sometimes contain strong supernatural elements) begin with likeable teens who live ordinary lives in small towns, before becoming involved in a wide range of horrifying situations which they must overcome in order to succeed or even to survive. Duncan's characters are well developed, and she unfolds her plots with such skill and authority that readers are quickly drawn into the exciting narratives. She also establishes well-realised settings by including a wealth of physical detail. Two of her most popular books (*Summer of Fear*, 1976, and *Killing Mr. Griffin*, 1978) were adapted for TELEVISION, while the theatrical film *I Know What You Did Last Summer* (1973) was released in 1997. WH

Duncan, Norman 1871–1916 Canadian novelist and journalist who wrote ADVENTURE STORIES for boys. *The Adventures of Billy Topsail* (1906), *Billy Topsail and Company* (1910) and *Billy Topsail, M.D.* (1916) explore the theme of endurance in a harsh land developed by CATHARINE PARR TRAILL's *Canadian Crusoes: A Tale of the Rice Lake Plains* (1852) and JAMES MACDONALD OXLEY's *Up Among The Ice Floes* (1890). Duncan's first book tells of young Billy, a lucky survivor of a variety of pranks and hair-raising adventures set on the

Newfoundland and Labrador coast. According to Duncan: 'All Newfoundland boys have adventures; but not all Newfoundland boys survive them.' Billy does, with common sense and courage. The second book focuses on a merchant trading venture during Billy's teens, and the third on later years when he decides to become a doctor. The three volumes laud bravery, loyalty, kindness and humour. Though sometimes didactic and sentimental by today's standards, the stories give the reader a sense of what it is like to grow up on the rugged, sparsely settled Canadian coast around the turn of the 20th century. Duncan worked most of his life as a journalist in Canada, the United States and abroad, and also wrote adult novels. KSB

Duncton Chronicles, The (1980–93) Series by the bestselling British writer and former journalist William Horwood (1944–) consisting of *Duncton Wood* (1980), *Duncton Quest* (1988), *Duncton Found* (1989) and *Duncton Stone* (1993). Set in the ancient mole realm of Duncton, it narrates an epic struggle between those who are loyal to the ancient values of the Holy Books and the fanatically religious followers of the Word. Like other popular FANTASY sequences in the tradition of TOLKIEN, *The Duncton Chronicles*, together with its sequel trilogy *The Book of Silence* (1991–3), creates a complex alternative world, layered with history and mythology, as the setting for an allegory of good and evil. The landscape is based closely on actual locations in the Thames Valley, Wiltshire, and elsewhere. The bookish values of Oxford, where Horwood's grandfather was a college head, resonate in the scholar-moles who frame and narrate the vast chronicle of stories, romances, tales of war and the coming of a redeemer; this sets up a contrast between the reflective stance of the student with the active powers of the warrior. Although there are clear affinities with anthropomorphic fantasies such as *WATERSHIP DOWN* (especially in the geographical detail), Horwood's depiction of violent nature also owes much to JACK LONDON, and the mole characters lend themselves readily to themes of light and darkness, and the search for home and community. *The Duncton Chronicles* are primarily adult fantasy but attract child readers with their exciting narrative and sustained fable of a world trying to preserve and understand its own history. SG

Dungeons and Dragons Series first published in 1974 by Tactical Studies Rules (Wisconsin) as a role-playing game involving TOLKIEN-like FANTASY situations. Players build up characters of great complexity by throwing dice and entering the adventure, managed by a Dungeon-Master. The games necessitated close reading of the rule book, mathematical calculations, and written plans, grids and diagrams. They could go on for days. Magazines, for example *The White Dwarf*, and numerous accessories (including many-sided dice and model figures) became an essential part of the highly successful industry. HA

see also ADVENTURE GAME BOOKS

Dunlop, Beverley 1935– New Zealand writer of four novels in the 1980s. Dunlop first published in the *SCHOOL JOURNAL*, writing authentic, well-researched and intense stories. *Earthquake Town* (1984) is a vivid exploration of terror and loss after the 1931 Napier earthquake. In both *The Dolphin Boy* (1982) and *Spirits of the Lake* (1988), Dunlop employs mythical and spiritual elements to strengthen the linear narrative. Similarly, in *The Poetry Girl* (1983), Natalia, trapped in rural ignorance and poverty, memorises poetry to recall in emotional crises. Dunlop combines historical accuracy and mythical or literary elements to build complex, layered novels. MJH

Dunlop, Eileen 1938– Scottish novelist who uses TIME-SLIP FANTASY and legend to explore a modern child's situation. Dunlop's first novel, *Robinsheugh* (1975), contains many of the themes of her later books, as a lonely and isolated child is drawn back into the past. This idea is reversed in *Green Willow's Secret* (1993) when a figure from the past is drawn into the present through a lonely girl. Dunlop's strengths lie in her ability to use FANTASY to explore the effects of loss, bereavement and uncertainty, the realistic way her characters are portrayed, and tightly constructed plots. JEG

Dunmore, Helen 1952– British novelist and poet. Dunmore's writing uses unexpected images and evocative description to examine the strangeness in the familiar and the faces behind the masks. In her only poetry collection for children, *Secrets* (1995), which won the *SIGNAL* POETRY AWARD, a white moon presses fields with 'owl-soft heaviness / so that they yield / harvests of oak shadow'. Dunmore is fascinated by the unexplained or lost moment, the beauty and the wildness of the natural world. *Go Fox* (1996) and *Fatal Error* (1996) are novels for young readers, though most of Dunmore's work is for adults, including *A Spell in Winter*, which won the Orange Prize for Fiction in 1996. HT

Dupasquier, Philippe 1955– Illustrator and PICTUREBOOK author. Dupasquier was born in Switzerland, grew up in France, and trained in Dijon and later in London. He settled in England in 1979. His French background, with HERGÉ as a childhood idol, the cinema a childhood pleasure, and his training, have influenced his chosen graphic form – the comic strip – which he often uses without a text. *Follow that Chimp*

Down into the sewers, with the warders close behind.
"You can't catch me," says Alf. "I will never go back to prison."

Illustration by Philippe Dupasquier from *The Great Escape* © Philippe Dupasquier 1998.

(1993), which unreels like a cops' chase in a silent movie, is one example. *The Great Green Mouse Disaster* (1981), in collaboration with MARTIN WADDELL, about a hotel literally full of mice, storeys and stories to be followed, is his most complex picturebook and calls for synoptic reading. Again with Waddell, *Going West* (1984) is a moving account of an American family's pioneering experiences. Dupasquier's books address families not just children, with incidents often drawn from personal domestic observation and experience – as in *The House on the Hill* (1987), a pastoral pictorial calendar of twelve words and twelve plates, amplified by detailed strip cartoons, and *I Can't Sleep* (1989), which is expressive, allusive and paradoxical. Dupasquier has also illustrated the popular *Lenny and Jake* young reader's fiction series by Hazel Townsend. JD

Durack, Mary and Elizabeth see *THE WAY OF THE WHIRLWIND*; see also PUBLISHING AND PUBLISHERS

dustjacket design see COVER ART

Dutta, Arup Kumar 1946– Bestselling Indian writer of action-packed ADVENTURE STORIES for older children, Dutta has been widely applauded for his work by a series of awards, and in the form of translations into both foreign and Indian languages. Two of his books have been made into feature films; one has been serialised on the national TELEVISION network; and most are used in schools as supplementary readers. Already acknowledged as a classic of its genre, his first book, *The Kaziranga Trail* (1979), which focuses on rhino poaching, posits an ecological awareness and is fired by the impulse of conservation. This and its sequels, *Save the Pool* (1990) and *Oh Deer!* (1997), are set in the Kaziranga Wildlife Sanctuary of Assam and reveal an intimate knowledge of jungle terrain, flora and fauna, evidence of the painstaking research which is a prelude to every book. Believing that adventure stories are the ideal genre to invigorate young imaginations, he breaks the formula by a remarkable thematic diversity. Varied issues, such as drug peddling (*Smack*, 1987), elephant trapping (*Revenge*, 1986), mountain climbing (*The Lure of Zangrila*, 1986) and tea-growing (*A Story about Tea*, 1985), form the basis of his undertaking to create a body of juvenile literature which is distinctively Indian, with familiar Indian background and characters. MBh

see also DRUGS; ECOLOGY

Dutta, Swapna 1943– Indian fiction writer, editor and translator. Dutta started writing in school and her first poem was published when she was nine. Acutely aware of the problems of writing for children, she has been a keen critic and commentator on the scene. Dubbed the 'Indian answer to ENID BLYTON', Dutta's most popular books have been her SCHOOL STORIES for children, unabashedly based on Enid Blyton's *MALORY TOWERS* and *St Clare's* school series. The specific Indian setting and pursuits of the girls in some measure combats a frequently levelled charge of imitation. Moreover, the *Juneli* series – which includes *Juneli's First Term* (1992), *Juneli at St Avila's* (1992), *An Exciting Term* (1992) and *Summer Term at St Avila's* (1994) – is apparently based on her own school experiences with most of the characters and incidents deriving from real life. They revolve around a motherless 12-year-old girl from Bihar, whose prankish escapades at a boarding school in Ranipur form the pivot of the books. Her hilarious *Teddy* novels, *Teddy Comes to Stay* (1992) and *Teddy Makes a Friend* (1994), about two sisters and a naughty alsatian pup, have also been very popular. Apart from fiction, non-fiction and translations for children, Dutta has successfully retold Indian epics, history and folklore. MBh

Duvoisin, Roger 1904–80 Illustrator and author of children's books over a span of nearly 50 years. Best known as the illustrator of over 40 books and numerous *New Yorker* covers, he also wrote many of his own texts and worked in collaboration with his wife, Louise Fatio. Born in Switzerland, Duvoisin became a naturalised United States citizen in 1937 and lived the rest of his life in New Jersey, where he was honoured with awards. Duvoisin received numerous distinctions, including the CALDECOTT MEDAL for *White Snow, Bright Snow* (1947), written by ALVIN TRESSELT, with whom he collaborated on several highly regarded nature books. He was particularly admired for the animal personalities he created, such as Petunia, the goose; Donkey-Donkey; and the hero of the *Happy Lion* series, which won the first children's book award given in West Germany. Duvoisin also translated and illustrated medieval European FOLKTALES. His ALPHABET BOOK, *A for the Ark* (1952), is considered one of the best of its genre. Celebrated for craftsmanship and sensibility, Duvoisin is known as an artist of strong line, flat colour, simplified shapes and dramatic action, whose work promoted the international growth of the PICTUREBOOK. AL

E

Each Peach Pear Plum (1978) and PEEPO (1981) Popular and well-loved PICTUREBOOKS by JANET AND ALLAN AHLBERG, written in simple rhyming text. *Each Peach Pear Plum*, which won the GREENAWAY MEDAL, constructs an I-spy game around familiar characters from NURSERY RHYMES and FAIRY TALES. In *Peepo* the game of I-spy is enhanced by the use of die-cut holes through which the reader can see into the next page. As the baby sits watching his family the illustrations depict scenes of cosy, chaotic urban life in Britain in the 1950s, inspired by the pages of the Army and Navy Store catalogue. KA

Eager, Edward 1911–64 American writer of FANTASY in the tradition of E. NESBIT. Born and raised in Toledo, Ohio, Eager attended Harvard University. He worked in New York City as a playwright and lyricist before turning to children's books, beginning with *Red Head* in 1951 and *Mouse Manor* in 1952. Inspired by the novels of Nesbit, whom he read for the first time in adulthood, he wrote a series of magical and semi-magical stories modelled upon her fantasies. In the first two, *HALF MAGIC* (1954) and *Knight's Castle* (1956), the magic adventures of a family of boys and girls are inspired by the children's readings of Nesbit's books, and his protagonists, like hers, must learn the complexities of magical logic. Eager wrote five other stories in the same style: *Magic by the Lake* (1957), *The Time Garden* (1958), *Magic or Not?* (1959), *The Well-Wishers* (1961) and *Seven-Day Magic* (1963). His novels, which were often based on his own childhood experiences, were praised for their humour, their balance of realism and fantasy, and for the credibility of his characterisation of ordinary children. Eager should not be seen as a mere imitator of Nesbit, but rather as the best modern recreator of this kind of fantasy. DAC

Eagle Weekly boys' comic launched by the Reverend Marcus Morris in collaboration with Hulton Press, publishers of adult magazines such as *Picture Post*. *Eagle* was a post-war sensation in the world of British juvenile magazines. Its launch was on 14 April 1950. The format was a large tabloid of 20 pages, eight of them in full colour photogravure; it was priced at twopence, and the comic led off with *DAN DARE, PILOT OF THE FUTURE*, who swiftly became every boy's hero for the mid-century. Dan and Digby, his traditional and yet futuristic batman, were created by the brilliant cartoonist Frank Hampson, his first drawings for a comic. Naturally Dan Dare was also the hero of *Eagle Annual*, the first edition of which appeared in 1951. Unhappily the strip lost much of its special sci-fi appeal by being in smaller (quarto) format than the comic and by cramming about a dozen pictures into each page. Although many of the *Eagle*'s characters appeared in the ANNUAL, ranging from radio's *P.C. 49* to *Harris Tweed*, a comic detective drawn by TELEVISION's John Ryan, there were far too many text pages for readers who loved *Eagle's* accent on picture strips. The cover designs were always the same – the eagle symbol (which Hampson originally took from Morris's church lectern) plus the issue number. A compilation edited by Denis Gifford, *Best of Eagle Annual*, was published in 1989, covering the Hulton Press period before the comic endured a rival takeover. DG

Eagle of the Ninth, The (1954) The first of ROSEMARY SUTCLIFF's novels for children about Roman Britain and the Aquila family. The novel is about Marcus Aquila's attempt to find out what happened to the Ninth Hispana, his father's legion, which disappeared without trace, and to recover if he can their eagle standard which was the symbol of their honour. It bears the strong imprint of KIPLING (the phrase 'good hunting' of the *JUNGLE BOOKS* constantly returns through the work), having as one of its themes the making of British identity, although its tone is much less triumphal. *The Eagle of the Ninth* and its sequels *The Silver Branch* (1957) and *The Lantern Bearers* (1959) all have a twilight atmosphere, depicting the decline of Roman civilisation and the coming shadow of the Dark Ages. The first chapter of *The Lantern Bearers*, ends with the sentence, 'For Aquila, though he could not know it, the world had begun its falling to pieces'; and the world of *The Eagle of the Ninth* is composed of damaged things. Marcus is lamed; Esca is emotionally scarred by his slavery; the emerald in the ring which was Marcus' father's is flawed. Most poignantly, the eagle, when found, is an eagle without wings. The novel establishes a correspondence between Marcus and the Roman civilisation through the figure of the eagle, which is both symbol of Rome and tied to Marcus through his name, Aquila, which means 'eagle'. His search for the eagle is a symbolic quest to redeem both his father's honour and the honour of Rome. But the novel also suggests that identity in the end is not to be inherited or found by looking back; the reclaimed eagle does not father a new legion but is buried and put to rest; and Marcus does not return to Rome but remains in the land of his new-found allegiance.

The Eagle of the Ninth and its sequels describe a meeting of worlds. Marcus, invalided out of the legions, comes to stay with his uncle in Calleva, where he meets a British girl, Cottia, and Esca, a British gladiator whom Marcus buys and sets free. They become friends and Marcus eventually marries Cottia. Esca explains to Marcus their cultural differences:

> 'Look at the pattern embossed here on your dagger-sheath. See, here is a tight curve . . . Look now at this shield-boss. See the bulging curves that flow from each other . . . these are the curves of life . . .' He looked up at Marcus again very earnestly. 'You cannot expect the man who made this shield to live easily under the rule of the man who worked the sheath of this dagger.'

The Roman and British designs represent the tension between Apollonian rule or order and Dionysian spontaneity. The friendships and marriages within all three works symbolically attempt to resolve this tension. *The Lantern Bearers*, however, unlike *The Eagle of the Ninth*, shows that difference cannot be so easily forgotten and that unity is hard-wrought. SA

Earp, Wyatt see WYATT EARP

Earth Must Be Free, The (1984) A simply written PICTUREBOOK by Pieter W. Grobbelaar about pollution, with such characters as the Litter-Bugs and the Lazy-Bones, and Wee Willie 'who saw the looming danger'. Alida Bothman's illustrations using torn paper COLLAGE are both effective and highly appropriate. Published in both Afrikaans and English as part of a book-club programme, this was one of the earliest South African books to show an awareness of the environment. JHe

Earthfasts (1966), ***Cradlefasts*** (1995) and ***Candlefasts*** (2000) Trilogy by the acclaimed British children's writer WILLIAM MAYNE. In his early novels, Mayne had frequently represented subterranean history revealing itself to children; in *Earthfasts* the past literally walks out of the ground and into the lives of the two 20th-century friends, David and Keith, in the form of an 18th-century drummer-boy. This was followed by *Cradlefasts*, a boldly conceived narrative in which David comes to accept the death of his mother and his baby sister many years earlier by experiencing the life and death of another little girl. Finally, in *Candlefasts*, the main characters come and go freely – and dangerously – between the present and the past to resolve various issues, until the 'earthfast' standing stones are at last contentedly placed where they belong.

All three books present readers with complex challenges – gaps to fill, unexplained connections to be made, clues to observe and interpret, and Mayne's distinctive narratorial manner. For example, the entire narrative of *Cradlefasts* takes place as a flashback between two incidents separated by only a few seconds. And since time and time-travel are the themes that unite the three works, there are time-warp jokes and puzzles: for example, the drummer-boy takes back into the 18th century a 20th-century one-pound coin which is subsequently passed down as a family heirloom, eventually reaching Keith 25 years before it is minted. This trilogy exemplifies Mayne's gift of describing and suggesting landscape and place, his ability to convey the volatile and intelligent consciousness of his characters, and his experimentation with new ways of representing the interrelatedness of the two. VW

see also TIME-SLIP FANTASY

Earthsea Quartet, The Acclaimed work by the American author URSULA K. LE GUIN. For almost 20 years the Earthsea books, *A Wizard of Earthsea* (1968), *The Tombs of Atuan* (1970), *The Farthest Shore* (1971) were a trilogy, a FANTASY hero tale set uniquely in an archipelago and recounting the life and works of the Archmage Ged. In 1990 Le Guin published a fourth book, *Tehanu*, which she characterised as a revisioning of the status quo which she had created. The island nations of Earthsea are less ruled by magic than maintained by it; magic is a science, the understanding and manipulation of all matter, with its own logic, physics and chemistry, subject to Newtonian laws. For every action there is a reaction, and those who become mages and wizards undergo rigorous and lengthy training in near-monastic conditions.

A Wizard of Earthsea tells the story of Ged, known as Sparrowhawk, an arrogant and recalcitrant youth, hugely gifted but wilfully ignorant of the enormous responsibility attendant upon his gifts. Entirely unprepared to handle his powers he fatefully accepts a foolish challenge to raise the dead. He almost kills himself in the process but is redeemed at the cost of another's life, recovering to learn that he has released upon earth a shadow that haunts him. For a while he flees from it until he learns that to conquer it he must confront and name it. When he does so he addresses it by his own name, and is thus reunited with the other, darker part of himself without which he cannot be whole. The potency of true names is common to many cultures, particularly in this case that of the NATIVE AMERICAN peoples, and still survives in a diminished form in our own. Name is essence, and magic can be worked only through knowledge of the true names of all things.

The Tombs of Atuan is also deeply concerned with naming and with the image of doorways and passage through them, a theme germane to all three books but vital to this one. An obscure and malign cult of the dead is led by a priestess born, as tradition demands, at the moment of her predecessor's death. At an appointed time she loses her given name and becomes 'The Eaten One'. The rites are administered by women, eunuchs are the only men permitted in the temple demesne. The present priestess, once named Tenar, is by her teens becoming inured to human feeling, as she must, when she discovers that a whole man has broken into the labyrinth beneath the tombs. It is Ged, now a powerful Wizard, seeking the lost half of a broken amulet to restore equilibrium to the archipelago. Her duty is to kill him, but curiosity and an awakening sexual response lead her to spare his life. He persuades her to leave with him; only he can free her, only she can lead him to freedom, and they escape as an earthquake destroys the tombs. Her longing to remain with him touches Ged, but he must leave her among friends and follow his own high destiny.

The Farthest Shore takes up Ged's story in his middle age. Now Archmage, at the height of his powers, he is approached by the heir to the throne of an island kingdom with news that in the distant reaches of the archipelago magic, and people's faith in it, is failing. Wizards are losing their power and knowledge. The balance of life is profoundly threatened, and as Ged and Prince Arren discover from their guest, a renegade wizard has learned the secret of everlasting life. Without death – and this is a society with no conceptions of heaven or hell – life itself is without meaning. Ged defeats the threat but exhausts all his powers in so doing and can no longer be a mage.

Le Guin presciently ended this novel with the implication that Ged vanished into the mists of legend. Since there was no definite explanation of his fate the way was open for *Tehanu*, which resumes the story where *The Farthest Shore* leaves off, but in another place and with a different, though familiar protagonist. At the end of *The Tombs of Atuan* Ged had left Tenar with his old mentor, Ogion the wizard, but she turned her back on the powers offered by education and became a farmer's wife. In her widowhood Ged returns to her, his powers irrecoverably lost, but no more and no less than the man she has always awaited. Her adopted daughter, a child hideously abused and mutilated, emerges as Ged's natural successor, invested with the magic faculty hitherto supposed to reside only in men. In the first three books, all mages and wizards are men because men say so; since men run everything, no one has ever questioned this. Women's magic, as befits the hero tale, is a worthless thing, weak and evil. Now Earthsea can survive only if it recognises the equality of one half of its population with the other. Coming so long after the original trilogy, and demanding such a radical rethinking of the reader's expectations, it occasioned more surprise than it might have done upon more careful consideration, since the glosses are to be found in the development of feminism during the interim in which, to take the most bathetic example, the notion that women were unfit to read broadcast news bulletins was conclusively disproved. One wonders why it was ever thought otherwise, and the answers are to be found in *Tehanu*. A broader, more human book than its predecessors, it not only concludes the quartet but furnishes a useful handbook on late 20th-century thinking. JMM

East of the Sun, West of the Moon see 'Beauty and the Beast'; see also KAY NIELSEN

eco-fantasy An environmental variant of traditional FANTASY in which threats to the landscape and the natural order precipitate and exemplify the classic conflict between good and evil. EMH

ecology Since the environmental movement became a prominent scientific and social influence in the 1960s, innumerable children's books in every genre have incorporated ecological principles, emphasising the interrelationships of animals, plants, soil and weather. Modern literary ecology has roots in the didactic, pastoral, Romantic and transcendentalist traditions of the 18th and 19th centuries. Children's writers recognised the moral and spiritual benefits of appreciation of nature and kindness to animals, while magazines such as *ST NICHOLAS* assisted early conservation movements by teaching children about natural history and destructive human practices. From Victorian FANTASIES of escape from urbanisation and industrialisation to the development of more realistic ANIMAL STORIES and 20th-century novels set in cultivated gardens and real wilderness areas (by FRANCES HODGSON BURNETT and GENE STRATTON-PORTER, for example), children's literature increasingly rejected the anthropocentric, idealised pastoral concepts of ROUSSEAU and early nature writing to encourage direct observation and preservation of nature. In postcolonial societies, children's books have often depicted conflicts over land use and wilderness survival. By the late 20th century, ancient tales from many indigenous cultures were retold and reinterpreted to foster reverence for the earth and more harmonious relations among species and peoples. In Britain, as elsewhere, artists such as BRIAN WILDSMITH and RUTH BROWN transformed

Ecology: 'Jaguar.' Paper collage illustration from *V for Vanishing: An Alphabet of Endangered Animals* by PATRICIA MULLINS.

traditional folklore into PICTUREBOOKS with environmental themes.

The Lorax by DR SEUSS, published in 1971 and then animated for TELEVISION, became one of the most popular picturebook fantasies, with an explicit warning about environmental destruction caused by industry, consumerism and human greed. Lynne Cherry, director of the Center for Children's Environmental Literature, uses fantasy and history in her environmental picturebooks, such as *The Great Kapok Tree* (1990). JEAN CRAIGHEAD GEORGE has written numerous picturebooks about animal life and natural habitats, and a series of 'ecological mysteries' honouring young people who helped prove the effects of pollution in the 1960s and 70s. Her award-winning survival fiction (such as *JULIE OF THE WOLVES*, 1972), like many other modern novels, shows that the ability to think like other animals and use natural resources wisely helps young people thrive in the wilderness. In Australia, *They Found a Cave* (1948) by NAN CHAUNCY revived a commitment to environmental issues among later authors. Diana Younger's Australian *Fern Gully* stories (1992) became a popular environmental fantasy film. In New Zealand, novels by PHYL WARDELL in the 1960s and JOAN DE HAMEL in the 1970s encouraged the protection of rare species. Ecological themes also appear in SCIENCE FICTION; in *The Green Book* (1982), by JILL PATON WALSH, daring and imaginative children help their families fleeing the destroyed earth to adapt to a distant planet's unfamiliar environment.

As late 20th-century textbooks and INFORMATION BOOKS began to include more interesting writing and high-quality art, prolific science writers such as Seymour Simon, LAURENCE PRINGLE, Jim Arnosky and Gail Gibbon informed children about many ecological topics and conservation methods. Numerous environmental organisations, publications, songs, films, television programmes and games encourage children and teachers to investigate ecology first-hand in their own gardens and schoolyards, as well as studying other ecosystems such as tropical rainforests. While censors and political conservatives attack contemporary 'green' writing as a campaign to indoctrinate children with radical ideology, literary ecocritics and conservationists debate whether literature should realign the attitudes of future generations through dire warnings that the earth is in danger and children are responsible for preserving it, or by instilling aesthetic and spiritual appreciation for nature. TLH

Edgeworth, Maria 1767–1849 Anglo-Irish novelist. From the age of 15 when her family settled in the family estate at Edgeworthstown, County Longford, Edgeworth worked closely with her father, in developing his theories of education. Richard Lovell Edgeworth was noted for his humane treatment of his tenants at a time when many Irish landowners were not, and this strongly influenced the life and work of Maria. She is best known for her adult novel *Castle Rackrent* (1800), but even before its publication she had written a series of stories for children, *The Parent's Assistant; or Stories for Children* (1796). This was followed by *Early Lessons* (1801). Throughout her life she continued her interest in writing for the young. As their titles indicate, her works had a highly moral tone and featured young protagonists who, by their honesty and virtue, succeed in redressing many injustices. Her female characters in particular are also resolute and determined and not weakly sanctimonious. In the 'Rosamond' stories each tale concludes with Rosamond, a young girl, learning a lesson (frequently by doing 'the wrong thing') which adds to the development of her character. These stories appeared in various collections including *The Parent's Assistant*, *Continuation of Early Lessons* and *Rosamond: a Sequel to Early Lessons* (1821). Little of Edgeworth's writing for children bears any particular relation to Ireland. An exception to this is *Orlandino* (1848), which is an interesting reflection of Ireland at that time. VC

Editha's Burglary see SARA CREWE

Edward the Emu (1988) An extremely successful Australian PICTUREBOOK, written by Sheena Knowles, and strikingly illustrated by ROD CLEMENT. The comical story-in-verse tells of an emu who wants to be a different creature, sharing various zoo animals' cages before returning to his rightful place. There is a sequel, *Edwina the Emu* (1996). NLR

Edwards, Dorothy see *MY NAUGHTY LITTLE SISTER* SERIES; see also GHOST STORIES

Edwards, Hazel (Eileen) 1945– Australian writer with over 120 published works across a range of genres, which include adult non-fiction, and junior and adolescent fiction. She is best known for her annually reprinted PICTUREBOOK, *There's a Hippopotamus on Our Roof Eating Cake* (1980), illustrated by DEBORAH NILAND. A number of other titles involving the small girl's imaginary hippopotamus have followed. Her picturebooks, *Stickybeak* (1986), *Fish and Chips and Jaws* (1987) and *Feymouse* (1988), appeal to children's love of animals in domestic situations. In her junior novels, *So, Who's the Misfit* (1989), *Mindspaces* (1993) and *General Store* (1977), Edwards uses FANTASY, satire and humour to explore issues such as friendship and coping successfully with differences. Twice nominated for an AWGIE screenplay award, she has produced scripts, for video, TELEVISION and stage. A prolific writer, Edwards has contributed to many educational programmes and is also the author of the popular series *Frequent Flyer Twins* (1994). JAP

Edwards, Margaret A(lexander) 1902–88 American librarian who greatly influenced the field of young adult librarianship through her writing and teaching. She established a programme for young adults at the Enoch Pratt Free Library in Baltimore in 1932, and continued there for the next 30 years, while teaching and giving workshops at library schools throughout the United States and Canada. She wrote about her experiences and set forth her beliefs about library service to young adults and their reading in *The Fair Garden and the Swarm of Beasts* (1969). The title came from Jared Bean's 1773 admonishment to librarians that LIBRARIES should no more be thrown open to the general public 'than is a Fair Garden to be laid unprotected at the Mercy of a Swarm of Beasts'. Obviously, Edwards did not agree. Born in Childress, Texas, Edwards attended Trinity University in Waxahachie and received degrees in Latin and library science from Columbia University. The Margaret A. Edwards award was named in her honour in 1990 to 'give recognition to authors of YOUNG ADULT FICTION'. LH

Edwards, Monica (Le Doux) see PONY STORIES; *PUNCHBOWL* SERIES; *ROMNEY MARSH* SERIES

Edwards, Richard 1949– English poet, whose first collection *THE WORD PARTY* (1986) established his reputation for craftsmanship, inventiveness and wordplay. He has followed this with *Whispers from a Wardrobe* (1987), *A Mouse in my Roof* (1988), and *The House that Caught a Cold* (1991). In all these volumes scarcely a poem fails and hardly a word is wasted. Edwards gives voice to neglected things – a wardrobe, a carrot, Father Christmas's boots – and shows us life from unexpected points of view, like the baby's in 'Looking Upwards'. He is the celebrant of unwanted inventions and useless things: 'A hat without a head/A toaster without bread/ A riddle without a clue/ Me without you.' Edwards' tone is light, often nonsensical, but he occasionally extends his range to more serious issues, still using humour, as with famine in 'The Uninvited Guest'. Edwards' love of words and mastery of traditional forms place him deservedly in the tradition of CARROLL, DE LA MARE and CAUSLEY. That he has never won a children's poetry prize and has seen his books go quickly out of print is, therefore, astounding. His most recent collections are *Leopards on Mars* (1993) and *Teaching the Parrot* (1996). ML

***Egerton Hall* series** Young adult novels by ADÈLE GERAS. Ostensibly the stories of three girls at the end of their boarding-school careers, the novels are also modern versions of three FAIRY TALES, 'Rapunzel' (*The Tower Room*, 1990), 'Sleeping Beauty' (*Watching The Roses*, 1991) and 'Snow White' (*Pictures Of The Night*, 1992). Other stories and myths are also drawn upon, with echoes of Greek mythology (see CLASSICAL MYTHOLOGY) and medieval romance. *Watching the Roses* is most closely related to its fairy-tale background: Alice, who has been cursed at her christening by the 13th aunt, is raped at her 18th birthday party and withdraws into her own world while the furniture gathers dust and the roses which surround the house grow wild. The rape of the heroine and her obvious fear of sex make the tale particularly disturbing, but the story is resolved with a happy ending in which a kiss from her prince restores Alice to sensibility. *The Tower Room* adopts a more modern, feminist ending in which Megan decides to value her education above her lover, but in *Pictures Of The Night* Bella conforms to the fairy-tale pattern and chooses life with her boyfriend rather than further education. KA

see also SEX IN CHILDREN'S BOOKS

Eggleston, Edward 1837–1902 American regional fiction writer, clergyman, editor and historian. Eggleston was born in rural Indiana and received most of his education at home and in frontier schools. At the age of 20 he became a circuit rider, a Methodist minister who served a large rural area on horseback. He turned to writing, working as a journalist in Chicago and then as an editor of various religious publications, including the *Little Corporal*, the *National Sunday School Teacher* and *Hearth and Home*. As an editor, he often contributed stories for young people to his own publications. Many of these were issued as books, including *Mr. Blake's Walking Stick: A Christmas Story for Boys and Girls* (1870) and *The Book of Queer Stories, and Stories Told on a Cellar Door* (1871). His first novel, *The Hoosier School-Master* (1871), was based on Eggleston's own experiences in one-room schoolhouses. With its local colour and Indiana dialect, the novel was an important early piece of midwestern regional writing. The author revisited his Indiana youth in a novel for young people, *The Hoosier School-Boy* (1883). Both novels were made into films in the 1930s. Eggleston had an interest in the history of the United States, and wrote several volumes of history and HISTORICAL FICTION for children and adults. CAB

Egielski, Richard 1952– New York illustrator who creates realistic watercolours for amusing, unconventional stories with archetypal themes. Trained as a commercial artist illustrating magazines and novels, Egielski eventually recognised the PICTUREBOOK as his favourite fine art form. Early influences include cartoons, movies, narrative paintings by Rembrandt, Goya, and N.C. Wyeth; his most important teacher was MAURICE SENDAK. When publishers considered Egielski's ILLUSTRATIONS too 'wacky' for anyone's stories, Sendak recommended him to Arthur Yorinks. In their extremely successful and rare method of collaboration, writer and illustrator work closely together on innovative designs for off-beat picturebooks. Their first book, *Sid and Sol* (1977), earned critical acclaim for Egielski's black-and-white cinematic images of 'a short guy' tricking a giant to save the world. *Hey, Al* (1986), a colourful FANTASY adventure featuring a city janitor and his dog, won the CALDECOTT MEDAL. Their books attract readers of all ages with their deadpan humour, irony, dark comedy and absurd combinations of cultural allusions and anachronisms. Beginning with *The Tub People* (1989), Egielski and the writer Pam Conrad produced picturebooks popular with younger children. Egielski first wrote his own text for *Buz* (1995), in which Keystone Cop pills chase a bug through a boy's body. TLH

Egoff, Sheila A. 1918– Canadian literary critic and historian who has extended her library science background both to advocate and to criticise Canadian children's literature. Successive editions of *The Republic of Childhood: A Critical Guide to Canadian Children's Books* (from 1968) contain the thorough surveys and uncompromising assessments that characterise her approach. The three editions (edited with G.T. Stubbs and L.F. Ashley) of *Only Connect: Readings on Children's Literature* (1969–96) are compilations of thoughtful essays – including Egoff's own classic on the problem novel – which recognise trends and offer analyses. FB

Ehrlich, Amy 1942– American author for children and young adults. Born in New York, as a young adult of the 1960s she lived an alternative lifestyle of travel, communes and short-term employment, eventually finding more permanent work in publishing. Associates encouraged her to write children's books. Her first, *Zeek Silver Moon* (1972), was a *New York Times* Notable Book. Ehrlich collaborated with illustrator SUSAN JEFFERS on the retelling of several classic FAIRY TALES. *The Story of Hanukkah* (1989), illustrated by Ori Sherman, vividly tells the holiday's history to young readers and was an ALA Notable Book. In *Parents in the Pig Pen, Pigs in the Tub* (1993), illustrated by STEVEN KELLOGG, the farm animals move into the house while the family retreats to the barn to live. After the family eats a disastrous Thanksgiving dinner cooked by the pigs, life returns to normal. This zaniness contrasts with the serious young adult novel, *Where It Stops, Nobody Knows* (1988), which tells of a girl's nomadic life with her mother, ultimately revealed as her kidnapper. Ehrlich's portrayal of the girl, Nina, as she adapts to new communities, shows great compassion and a knowledge of school social structures. JRG

Eight Days of Luke (1975) Highly original modern fantasy by DIANA WYNNE JONES interwoven with elements of Norse mythology. A strange boy, Luke, erupts into David's life, and the story of a dreary holiday becomes first a quest to save Luke from his pursuers: Mr Chew, Mr Wedding, the Frys (Tyr, Odin, Frey and Freya) and to find Thor's hammer. Luke (Loki), who is linked to fire, may here be held to represent the Dionysian in both its destructive and energising aspects, and David's quest to keep him free a Promethean undertaking to steal fire from the gods for the world of men. SA

see also CLASSICAL MYTHOLOGY

Einzig, Susan 1922– British illustrator born in Berlin and educated at the Breuer School of Design. Fleeing Nazi Germany, she came to England with virtually the last Kindertransport in 1939. For the next three years she attended the Central School of Art in London. Later she worked as a technical draughtsman at the War Office. From 1946 until 1950 she taught at Camberwell School of Art, London, where she worked alongside John Minton and was influenced by his work. From 1959 Einzig taught at the Chelsea School of Art until her retirement in 1988. At Chelsea, she taught many future book illustrators, including CAROLYN DINAN, EMMA CHICHESTER CLARK and Hannah Firmin.

Early commissions included illustrations for the British periodicals *Lilliput, Picture Post* and the *Radio Times*. She has illustrated many books; those for children include GILLIAN AVERY's *In the Window Seat* (1958) and books by E. NESBIT, including *THE BASTABLES* (reissued in 1965). She won the National Book League's Best Illustrated Book award in 1946 for *Mary Belinda and the Ten Aunts*, and the CARNEGIE MEDAL with PHILIPPA PEARCE in 1958 for *Tom's Midnight Garden*. Of this book, Einzig says. 'This was very special it perfectly fitted my particular illustrator's imagination.' IW

Ekwensi, Cyprian 1921– Nigeria's most prolific writer for children, noted for social realism. Born of Igbo parents in Minna, Ekwensi's northern background is reflected in *An African Night's Entertainment* (1962) and *The Passport of Mallam Ilia* (1960), exciting tales of intrigue and vengeance, and *Juju Rock* (1960), a schoolboy ADVENTURE STORY involving a secret cult and a lost goldmine. Other juvenile novels feature a blind musician (*The Drummer Boy*, 1960), boarding-school pranks (*Trouble in Form Six*, 1962) and FANTASY adventure (*Samankwe in the Strange Forest*, 1973). Following the Nigerian Civil War, during which he ran Radio Biafra, Ekwensi described post-war recovery in *Coal Camp Boy* (1973) and new social ills in *Samankwe and the Highway Robbers* (1975) and *Motherless Baby* (1980). Recent titles include *Gone to Mecca* (1992) and *Masquerade Time* (1994). Ekwensi's early works for children also include four collections of short stories and Igbo FOLKTALES. VD

Eleanor Farjeon Award see AWARDS AND MEDALS

Elementary Spelling Book, The see *THE AMERICAN SPELLING BOOK*

Elephant and the Bad Baby, The (1969) Classic PICTUREBOOK by ELFRIDA VIPONT, illustrated by RAYMOND BRIGGS, with cumulative text and a memorable refrain, depicting a procession of irate shopkeepers chasing an elephant and a bad baby all down the road, anxious to remind them of their manners. KA

Elidor (1965) Third FANTASY novel by the British author ALAN GARNER, which began life as a short radio play and shows Garner developing a more serious concern with character and employing fantasy which does more than fuel the movement of the plot. It has parallels with *THE LION, THE WITCH AND THE WARDROBE*: four children enter a wasteland and undertake to save it from a curse. But there are important differences: Elidor is a more cheerless and empty place than Narnia and mirrors the reality of slum-clearance in Manchester. Roland and his sister and two brothers become the custodians of four treasures reminiscent of the Grail legend – a sword, a spear, a stone and a cauldron. The rest of the novel concerns their attempts to protect these objects from the enemy in Elidor who are trying to break through into their ordinary domestic life. Garner's imaginative plot-making is at its best here. He uses electricity to suggest the dangerous 'live' power of these objects. The remarkable chapter in which the family car starts without ignition, and various unplugged electrical appliances run on and on all through the night, confirmed the expectations aroused by Garner's first two novels that he was a writer committed to an uncompromising representation of fear and danger without the reassuring narratorial voice of so much children's fiction at that period. He also enhanced his reputation for achieving imaginative special effects in simple concise language. The moment when Roland discovers his sister's glove trapped in rock is chilling; '[he] peeled the turf like matting. It came in a strip, a fibrous mould of the glove below, with four neat holes. The fingers and the cuff were free, but the thumb went straight into the quartz.'

The novel is not without its faults; the dialogue of the parents is composed of clichés, and although this may be deliberately satirical it is not entirely convincing. But the bookish derivativeness of *THE WEIRDSTONE OF BRISINGAMEN* is entirely absent, and there are signs of a growing interest in psychological complexity. In the closing pages Helen, who has so far taken little part in the action, unexpectedly takes centre-stage and resolves the conflict by calming the violence of the unicorn. Garner is not content simply to borrow the traditions associating the unicorn with virginity; nor does he use the girl's power as a device for a tidy ending. Helen's victory over this great mythical beast is a complex betrayal, and her distress – and her insistence that she has 'broken it' – are indications of an authorial interest in the violent power of young sexuality which was to be worked out more fully in THE OWL SERVICE and *Red Shift*. Another feature of Garner's development as a novelist is that the four children are represented throughout as convincingly quarrelsome adolescents in the grip of passionate rivalries. Their talk is clipped, equivocal and edgy, and much is left unexplained – an indication that Garner was developing the 'riddling' narrative manner which was to characterise his later work. VW

Eliot, T.S. see *OLD POSSUM'S BOOK OF PRACTICAL CATS*; see also *THE POET'S TONGUE*

Elizabethan, The see THE YOUNG ELIZABETHAN

Ellis, Sarah 1952– Award-winning Canadian author, librarian, storyteller, lecturer and critic. In particular, her lectures and contributions to the HORN BOOK MAGAZINE invaluably promote works by Canadian writers and illustrators. As an author, her first book was *The Baby Project* (1986). Amongst her other titles are *The Next-Door Neighbours* (1989), *Pick-Up Sticks* (1991), *Back of Beyond: Stories of the Supernatural* (1997) and *The Young Writer's Companion* (1999). Ellis shows insight into the sensitivities of young people, especially girls. However serious the subject matter, her books are not without humour. Unlike much realistic writing for this age group, parents play a prominent role and closeness of family is important. PDS

Elmer (1968) Picturebook by the British illustrator DAVID MCKEE. *Elmer* is a landmark in the development of PICTUREBOOKS with a sophisticated theme, in this case of attitudes to skin colour. The patchwork elephant reappears as a *jeu d'esprit* in many of McKee's later books. The original book was revised in 1989, with simplified text and redrawn pictures, and Elmer has become a cult character, leading to *Elmer Again* (1991) and many sequels in the form of board books and bath books. PC

Eloise Series of four PICTUREBOOKS written by KAY THOMPSON and illustrated by HILARY KNIGHT: *Eloise* (1955), *Eloise in Paris* (1957), *Eloise at Christmastime* (1958) and *Eloise in Moscow* (1959). The stories are narrated by young Eloise, who lives with her Nanny at the Plaza Hotel in New York City. The texts project a genuinely child-like voice as Eloise describes her mischievous and mostly unsupervised activities at the Plaza and around Paris and Moscow. Knight's unique style of cartoon drawing captures an astonishing range of poses and feelings in elegant, flowing lines that appear to have been dashed off in the same effortless, spontaneous manner that characterises Eloise herself. The ILLUSTRATIONS depict a bewitchingly untamed child whose flyaway hair, fat belly, and impulsive antics contrast humorously with her prim outfit of Mary Janes, puff-sleeved lacy blouse, dainty hair ribbon, and pleated jumper. Unrestrained, independent, fearless and exuberantly active, Eloise was and remains a notable contrast to stereotypical portrayals of girl characters in picturebooks. Highly popular during the late 1950s and 1960s, the *Eloise* books are less well known today; however, the impish child still lives at the Plaza Hotel in the form of a large painting, and a new edition of *Eloise* was released in Britain in 2000. CV

***Elsie Dinsmore* series** (1867–1905) A series of 28 girls' books written by the American Martha Finley, under the pseudonym Martha Farquharson. *Elsie Dinsmore* and the first sequel, *Holidays at Roselands,* show the eight-year-old Elsie's attempts to win the love of her father, absent since her birth, and convert him to Christianity. Popular demand for more about Elsie led to further sequels which take Elsie through girlhood, marriage to her father's best friend, the birth of eight children, and widowhood. As a grandmother, she is matriarch of an ever-increasing clan whose activities, travels, relationships and conversations provide the content of later books. Elsie and her relatives also appear in the *Mildred Keith* series about cousins to the Dinsmores.

The *Elsie* books are criticised for their overwrought style, repetitious and excessively sentimental, lachrymose scenes, and unnatural dialogue. The most striking features of the series to modern readers are the religious didacticism and the disturbingly erotic overtones of the father–daughter relationship, as Elsie and her usually overbearing father repeatedly exchange passionate declarations of love and 'rapturous' kisses. Nevertheless, *Elsie Dinsmore* was extremely popular – second only to *LITTLE WOMEN* in copies purchased – with three generations of readers who sympathised with the virtuous, beautiful, wealthy, but often persecuted heroine. JLB

elucidaria Books of general information, primarily religious, presented as a dialogue between student and teacher. The earliest extant, a 13th-century Latin manuscript, *Elucidarium sive dialogus de summa totius Christianae Theologiae*, is attributed both to Lanfranc, Archbishop of Canterbury (c. 1005–89) and to Saint Anselm (1033–1109); there is another *Elucidarium* by Honorius of Autun (died c. 1130). Many versions exist, including one in Welsh (1346) and a Middle-English *Lucidarie* extant in two 15th-century manuscripts. There is also a French 13th-century *Elucidarium Magistri Alani*. Wynkyn de Worde printed a *Lucydarye*, possibly translated from the French by Alexander Chertsy, c. 1508. GA

Emberley, Ed(ward Randolph) 1931– American author and illustrator. Educated at the Massachusetts School of Art, where he studied painting and illustration, Emberley began focusing on children's books after short stints as sign painter and commercial artist. These early careers influenced his later work; although employing a variety of styles in his PICTUREBOOKS, his most successful efforts were those in which he used techniques of graphic design and printing. These include his two Caldecott books, *One Wide River to Cross*, an Honour Book for 1967, and *Drummer Hoff*, the 1968 award-winner, both with texts by his wife Barbara. Emberley's style in both of these books has a flat and highly stylised quality, accented and given emotion by his often bold use of colour. In the early 1970s, Emberley turned his attention to 'how-to' drawing books for children, in which simple shapes, letters and numbers could be combined to create hundreds of familiar objects. These books, beginning with *Ed Emberley's Drawing Book of Animals* (1969), earned him considerable popular appeal, although critics sometimes complained that the books taught copying rather than drawing. Emberley himself dismissed this criticism, arguing that even the greatest of artists started out by copying other artists. KS

emblem books A literary form popular throughout Europe during the Renaissance. Emblems generally took the form of an epigram or title, a symbolic picture and a brief related passage of prose or verse. The first English author to produce a collection of such emblems was Geoffrey Whitney (*A Choice of Emblemes*, 1586) who offered his work on the title page as 'both pleasant and profitable' for moral instruction. Although they were not specifically produced for a child readership, the terms within which emblem books suggested linking verbal text and image for pleasurable instruction influenced generations of writers, including Comenius (see *ORBIS SENSUALIUM PICTUS*) and JOHN LOCKE. DWh

Emecheta, Buchi 1944– Nigerian novelist, born in Lagos of Igbo parents from Ibuza, Delta State. Emecheta is known for her strong female characters and feminism (*Second Class Citizen*, 1974; *The Joys of Motherhood*, 1979). Adolescents find it easy to identify with the heroine of *The Bride Price* (1976), who defies tradition to marry the man she loves, and *The Slave Girl* (1977), who finds ways to survive enslavement. Emecheta has written specifically for a YOUNG ADULT audience in *Naira Power* (1982) and *A Kind of Marriage* (1986). Her books for younger readers concern the mystery of a new bride coming to the village (*The Moonlight Bride*, 1980) and tensions between the generations (*The Wrestling Match*, 1980). Emecheta vividly evokes traditional settings and enables readers to see events through the eyes of her characters. VD

Emil and the Detectives (1929) Acclaimed and enduring novel by Erich Kästner, a left-wing German writer and friend of Brecht. Instantly successful, it was translated into English in 1931 with an introduction by WALTER DE LA MARE. It is the first ADVENTURE STORY featuring a gang of children who finally get the better of an adult crook, in this case one who had stolen the sleeping Emil's money while he was on a train journey. The boys and girls of Berlin, some middle-class, others working already, soon rally to Emil's cause, and the story ends triumphantly with the thief safely delivered to the police. Young readers were thrilled at this flattering picture of themselves as potential members of a loyal and effective gang.

Other stories by different writers soon followed in this mode, culminating in the benign fantasies of child collective action found in ENID BLYTON's adventure stories. Kästner's follow-up story, *Emil and the Three Twins* (1935) was also successful. But it is for the first Emil story that he will chiefly be remembered. Believing that children cannot be trained too early for their role in society, Kästner concentrated on describing how they could always help each other out in any general struggle against injustice. Adult characters had a role here too, but mostly as characters in the background. The Nazis were less impressed with this message, burning some of Kästner's books publicly in 1933, although allowing the writer to live in peace until the end of the war in 1945. NT

Emil Award see KURT MASCHLER AWARD (appendix); see also AWARDS AND MEDALS

Emile see JEAN JAQUES ROUSSEAU; see also *ROBINSON CRUSOE*

Emily of New Moon (1923) First of a series by L.M. MONTGOMERY, who is better known for the *ANNE OF GREEN GABLES* series; its sequels were *Emily Climbs* (1925) and *Emily's Quest* (1927). Emily Byrd Starr is Montgomery's most autobiographical character: both love beauty passionately, live with elderly relatives, have precocious intelligence and wit, and must write. In 1923, Emily was a radically new kind of character. A strong, imperfect girl, smart and not conventionally pretty, an artist with words; gifted, ambitious and self-reflective, Emily challenged her society's assumptions about girlhood. Throughout the series, Emily struggles with and ultimately moves beyond the expectations of family and community in her journey through art, career and love. Writing is in her blood and she must defend her art against her Aunt Elizabeth's repeated attempts to prevent her from writing. She falls in love, and fights it as weakness. Her strongest ally and most dangerous enemy is herself.

As is true of Montgomery's more famous series, the first book is the strongest. *Emily of New Moon* focuses on Emily's self-discovery: her gifts and her ambition. *Emily Climbs* gives the reader more of Emily's growth as an artist, and her first tantalising glimpse of romantic passion. Yet in *Emily's Quest*, Emily's faith in herself and her work, steadfast through the first two novels, falters as she defers to the judgement of a man who sees her writing as an obstacle to his possession of her. Until Emily learns to trust herself again, the book seems hollow. In suppressing her own desire to be with the man she loves, a man who loves her and respects her work, Emily fails to demonstrate her characteristic self-knowledge. At the book's end, with Emily fully restored to herself and the reader, one only wishes there were more to follow. CEJ

Emma see CHARLOTTE, EMILY AND ANNE BRONTË; FRANCES HODGSON BURNETT

Emperor's New Clothes, The see HANS CHRISTIAN ANDERSEN; see also VIRGINIA LEE BURTON; NICHOLAS STUART GRAY; NUDITY IN CHILDREN'S BOOKS

Empire Youth Annual, The (1946–64) British children's ANNUAL distinguished by a strong commitment to the British Empire. Its ADVENTURE STORIES and information articles were written in an idealised imperial spirit reminiscent of ARTHUR MEE but adapted to the cause of world peace. In the first *Annual*, this explicit editorial commitment to peace was somewhat at odds with the stories, which were mostly about war, resulting in a strange mixture of imperialist altruism and a child-centred hope for the future – 'You will understand that much of the varied contents of this Victory Volume had to be prepared before the war with Germany and Japan was won. Indeed, it has seemed only right to me that this first Empire Youth Annual should in large part be a lasting reminder of the high courage and noble self-sacrifice of those boys and girls of another generation whose heroic efforts have thrown open the way to a new World – a World of Peace and Goodwill to all men.' The frontispiece was a picture of Field Marshal Montgomery, and there were stories about the Resistance, with information articles on such topics as the *Army Pigeon Service*, and *Stirring Deeds of Famous Regiments*. There were nature notes, and a *Floral Calendar* in which prayers and quotations from Longfellow and Demosthenes sat oddly alongside heroic articles about the blitz, spitfires and the battle of Arnhem.

The many benevolent tributes to the courage of colonial people were expressed in patriarchal terms; in one story, the Emperor Haile Selassie of Abyssinia was coolly referred to as 'the Golliwog'. An article in the 1947 *Annual* sought to establish a mythology of the British Empire by explaining that it all began when Sir Humphrey Gilbert settled Newfoundland in 1583 and the native peoples 'raised no objection . . . In this peacable fashion, a representative of Great Britain took possession of the first colony in the Empire's history.' The design of the annuals was unusual for the period, with many photographs on interleaved glossy paper, and coloured celebratory portraits of great war heroes, including Churchill and Stalin. The *Empire Youth Annual* employed no well-known writers, and the ILLUSTRATIONS were mostly undistinguished, except for the line-drawings by Anton Lock and by the unknown CHARLES KEEPING, whose work appeared regularly from 1954.

The stories and articles in the annuals reflected the confidence and optimism of the postwar period, and despite considerable historical blandness, there was a genuine idealism in the editorial desire to instruct its readers about the new United Nations and its Charter for the future peace of the world. In 1953 the title became *The Commonwealth and Empire Annual* and in 1958 simply *The Commonwealth Annual*. Later issues showed a greater interest in the arts along with historical tales and articles on industry, agriculture and geography. In 1960 the publication date was symbolically moved to Commonwealth Day, but its imperial idealism was culturally out of place and the *Annual* became a casualty of the sixties. VW

Enchanted Wood, The see ENID BLYTON; *THE MAGIC FARAWAY TREE*

encyclopaedias see INFORMATION BOOKS

***Encyclopedia Brown, Boy Detective* series** see DONALD J. SOBOL; see also DETECTIVE FICTION

Ende, Michael 1929–1995 German writer who lived for many years in Rome and has had an enormous influence on the development of post-war children's fiction in Germany. His stories and novels presented an alternative to the prevailing realism in approaching social issues, by offering an escape into FANTASY and a renewal of faith in the inner spiritual resources of the individual. The translation of his two allegorical novels – *Momo* (1984, trans. J. Maxwell Brownjohn) and *The Neverending Story* (1983, trans. Ralph Manheim) – into English and many other languages has ensured a world-wide following amongst both young people and adults. Ende's work appeals to those who have a taste for fantasy literature and who dream of metaphysical rather than political solutions to the world's problems. GL

Endpaper design for *Blackie's Children's Annual* (c. 1932).

endpapers The pages at either end of a book, glued to the inside of the front- and back-cover boards. Endpapers may be plain or coloured, and in Picturebooks they are often decorated with the artist's designs linked to the story. In the early years of the 20th century many children's books had decorated endpapers, for example *Blackie's Children's Annual*, the *Doctor Dolittle* stories and *The Secret Garden* illustrated by Charles Robinson; later it was common to use the endpaper to display a map of the story location, as in the *Swallows and Amazons* and *Lone Pine* series. JD

Engdahl, Sylvia Louise 1933– American author of thought-provoking novels of space Fantasy for young adults. Although her novels are usually designated Science Fiction, Engdahl disputes that categorisation. Rather than stressing technology and hardware, they explore philosophical issues. Born in Los Angeles, Engdahl briefly taught at elementary school before working as a computer programmer and systems specialist. In 1967 she turned to freelance writing. Of her six novels, *Journey Between Worlds* (1970), an outer-space romance, contains the most conventional elements. *Enchantress from the Stars,* which received Newbery Honor designation in 1971 and the Phoenix Award in 1990, is significantly more complex. The novel concerns the efforts of the Federation to prevent a technologically advanced culture from destroying a planet's feudal society. Engdahl offers multiple viewpoints, although the main narration is by a Federation member, Elana. Respect for different interpretations of events and the importance of non-intervention are recurring themes for Engdahl. Elana also appears in *The Far Side of Evil* (1971). Engdahl's other novels form a trilogy – *This Star Shall Abide* (1972), *Beyond the Tomorrow Mountains* (1973) and *The Doors of the Universe* (1981) – in which the protagonist challenges the conventions and values of his society on a planet colonised by scientists generations earlier. Her works reflect her underlying optimism about the future, particularly the discoveries possible through space exploration. KKP

English folktales As early as the 16th century, English storytellers from 'old wives' to wandering 'droll-tellers' had to compete with cheap printed Ballads and stories. Among the popular Chapbook texts that may derive from English folktales are *Tom Thumb* and *Jack the Giant-Killer*. From the late 18th century, translations of foreign Fairy Tales became as popular as native stories. The publication of an English translation of Grimms' fairy tales in 1823 inspired scholars to collect British folktales. While Gaelic storytelling still flourished in the 19th century (see also Scottish Folktales), English oral tradition was thought to be rapidly dying out. One of the best regional collections was Robert Hunt's *Popular Romances of the West of England* (two volumes, 1865), with its wealth of stories about giants, mermaids and fairies. Versions of English folktales were also collected among people of British descent in America and Australia.

The Australian folklorist JOSEPH JACOBS published two influential collections of English folktales (*English Fairy Tales*, 1890, *More English Fairy Tales*, 1894). In these, and in most other collections, the finest stories tend to come from the Celtic areas – Cornwall, the Isle of Man, and the Scottish and Welsh borders. Jacobs wanted his work to be enjoyed by adults and children and this tradition has been continued by some 20th-century folklorists. KATHARINE BRIGGS produced a *Dictionary of Fairies* (1976) for adults and an illustrated anthology for children, *Abbey Lubbers, Banshees and Boggarts: A Who's Who of Fairies* (1979). She also wrote two children's novels based on folklore, *Hobberdy Dick* (1955) and *Kate Crackernuts* (1963). Briggs's majestic *Dictionary of British Folk-Tales in the English Language* (four volumes, 1970–1) contains around 2,000 stories.

Some of the folktales told in English were international stories. *Tom Tit Tot* was a Suffolk variant of *Rumpelstiltskin*, and *Ashencoatie* a version of CINDERELLA. Others, such as *JACK AND THE BEANSTALK*, are distinctively English. England was particularly rich in humorous stories. Many of these mock the stupidity of the inhabitants of particular villages, such as Austwick in Yorkshire and Gotham in Nottinghamshire.

There are not many long or complex hero tales. English folk-heroes, such as ROBIN HOOD, were mainly celebrated in BALLADS (see M. Keen, *The Outlaws of Medieval Legend*, 1961). Fairies, giants and dragons are often encountered in English folktales. The term 'fairy' can include a wide range of supernatural beings. Hunt sub-divided West Country fairies into Small People, Spriggans, Piskies, Knockers and Brownies. Most English fairies were either mischievous or malevolent. Rescue of humans from the fairy realm is a common theme in folktales from all over Britain, but English stories about fairies tend to be set in the past. The tradition that the fairies were driven out of England by the sound of church bells was used by RUDYARD KIPLING in *PUCK OF POOK'S HILL* (1906). Giants were often associated with prehistoric monuments, such as stone circles. A few legendary heroes, like the East Anglian TOM HICKATHRIFT, were of unusual size and strength, but most English giants were brutal man-eaters. The giant's traditional cry of 'Fe, Fi, Fo, Fum, I smell the blood of an Englishman' dates back at least to the 16th century. Fortunately, English giants were as stupid as they were vicious and they could usually be defeated by trickery. Dragons or 'worms' are said to have plagued many parts of the country (see J. Simpson, *British Dragons*, 1980). One Sussex wood was rumoured to hide a dragon as late as the 17th century. The dragons of medieval romance were vanquished by knightly valour, but the dragons of folklore were tackled by ingenious methods involving spiked dummies, magic ointment, or sticky gingerbread. This mock-heroic tone is reflected in J.R.R. TOLKIEN's dragon and giant story, *Farmer Giles of Ham* (1949).

In 1890 Jacobs complained that English fairy tales 'have been treated in rather a step-motherly fashion'. Although there have been some good retellings for children (e.g. JAMES REEVES, *English Fables and Fairy Stories*, 1954; KEVIN CROSSLEY-HOLLAND, *The Dead Moon and Other Tales from East Anglia*, 1982, and *Small-tooth Dog*, 1988), English folktales are still comparatively neglected. Publishers may be deterred by the fact that the liveliest tales are often in broad dialect and rewriting these in standard English takes away much of their distinctive character. ALAN GARNER has included dialect tales in anthologies for children such as *The Hamish Hamilton Book of Goblins* (1969) and *A Bag of Moonshine* (1986). Garner is among the few contemporary novelists to make use of regional legends. The Cheshire tale of the 'Wizard of Alderly Edge' formed the starting point for his first novel, *THE WEIRDSTONE OF BRISINGAMEN*. Cornish folktales and legends are the inspiration for much of CHARLES CAUSLEY's poetry for children. GHP

Enid Blyton's Magazine see *SUNNY STORIES*

Enora and the Black Crane (1991) Written and illustrated by Australian Aboriginal artist Arone Raymond Meeks (1957–) as a teaching story in the Dreaming tradition of the Kokoimudji people of Northern Queensland. Enora kills a crane, and is himself changed into the crane as a consequence. But when the birds are visited with colour, Enora remains black as a caution to all. The ILLUSTRATIONS employ traditional Aboriginal art techniques (CROSSHATCHING, dots, androgynous human figures), a palette of earthy tones and richly exuberant design. SNJ

Enormous Turnip, The see MUSIC AND STORY

Enright, Elizabeth [Wright Gillham] 1909–68 American writer, critic and illustrator of children's books. The daughter of illustrators, Enright began her career with several vividly illustrated children's books: *Kees* (1930) and other books by Marian King, and her own *Kintu: A Congo Adventure* (1935). She won the NEWBERY AWARD for *Thimble Summer* (1939), the engaging story of a young girl's summer on a drought-stricken farm in Wisconsin. However, she remains best known for her two sets of fictional families: The Melendys are a family of four talented children, ably shepherded by their housekeeper and surrogate mother, Cuffy, and loosely supervised by their often-absent widowed father. In *The Saturdays* (1941), the four form a club to organise their independent weekend adventures in the city. The remaining three books in the series – *The Four-Story Mistake* (1942), *Then There Were Five* (1944) and *Spiderweb for Two: A Melendy Maze* (1951) – take place in the country, where the lively, witty and adventuresome children explore the outdoors and revel in their life together. Reflecting a secure post-war world, the *Gone-Away Lake* books (1957 and 1961) feature the Jarman and Blake children's discovery of a sunken resort lake and two eccentric but marvellously friendly old inhabitants of the deteriorating buildings facing the lake. Keenly observed and freshly written, all of Enright's stories show extraordinary insight into the delights of ordinary things seen with originality and pleasure. JDS

environmental issues see ECOLOGY

Enwonwu, Chio Nigerian writer of children's books, based in Onitsha, Eastern Nigeria. Enwonwu has drawn on her experience as a teacher and school proprietor to create modern stories of the Igbo folk hero in *Tortoise Goes to Town*, *Tortoise Returns to tile Woods*, and *Tortoise in Exile*, all published in 1992. VD

Erasmus, Desiderius 1469–1536 Dutch humanist writer whose work and contacts with scholars across Northern Europe gave new emphasis and importance to education. Erasmus spent a considerable time in England where he influenced, among others, John Colet, founder of St Paul's, one of the first English schools with a humanist curriculum. DWh

Eric, or Little by Little see SCHOOL STORIES; see also LITERATURE WITHIN CHILDREN'S LITERATURE

Erskine Clarke, Rev. J. see *CHATTERBOX*

Escape from Warsaw see *THE SILVER SWORD*; see also IAN SERRAILLIER

Estes, Eleanor 1906–88 American writer of family stories for children, including the *Moffat* series and the NEWBERY AWARD winner, *Ginger Pye* (1951). Estes was born in West Haven, Connecticut, which became the setting for her *Moffat* books, including *The Moffats* (1941), *The Middle Moffat* (1942), *Rufus M* (1943), and *The Moffat Museum* (1983). The series traces the lives of the four Moffat children and their widowed mother just prior to and during World War I. The books are episodic in structure, with each one loosely unified by the thematic thread, such as younger sister Jane's emerging independence and adaptation to life outside the family circle. Estes gives verisimilitude to the stories by allowing her characters to grow up during the course of her books. She memorably portrays small-town life in early 20th-century America, and the Moffat books have been widely praised as examples of the FAMILY STORY. *The Hundred Dresses* (1944) portrays the struggle of a Polish girl, an outsider who is the victim of ethnic prejudice. *Ginger Pye* is a light-hearted DETECTIVE STORY about a family's search for a lost dog. Estes had a talent for writing with poignancy, but without sentimentality. DLR

Esther Glenn Award see APPENDIX

Estoril, Jean see BALLET STORIES; *DRINA* SERIES

Ethel & Ernest: A True Story (1998) Strip cartoon by British PICTUREBOOK author, RAYMOND BRIGGS. Ernest, biking to work as a milkman some time in 1928, believes that Ethel, a lady's maid, is waving to him from a balcony. He waves back, and although she was in fact only shaking out a duster this eventually leads to their marriage; the book then tells of their children, middle age and finally death, both dying in 1971. Such are the bare bones of this strip cartoon BIOGRAPHY of Briggs' parents, a technical masterpiece. Appearing in ordinary book format, the contents never feel cramped and detail is always clear. Individuals are depicted with feeling, their faces or whole bodies sometimes distorted in order to make the required emotional point. Nothing is predictable: 15 frames on one page may be followed by a single illustration on the next. Characters sometimes project out of their strips, perspective constantly changes, and Briggs's hand-lettered captions occasionally break into mock capitals or heavy bold. Older readers may particularly enjoy the period detail, younger ones will learn some recent social history, and all will surely be moved by the humanity of this ordinary couple here made extraordinary by Briggs' artistry and wit. NT

Ets, Marie Hall 1893–1984 American author and illustrator of children's PICTUREBOOKS. Ets's love of the woods, lakes and countryside of her native Wisconsin is reflected in both the text and ILLUSTRATIONS of a number of her books for young children, especially *In the Forest* (1944) and *Play With Me* (1955). She became interested in art at a very young age and began studying with a group of adults when only in the first grade. Most of her life she worked both as an artist and a social worker, studying at the New York School of Fine and Applied Art, the University of Chicago, the Art Institute of Chicago and Columbia University. Her social work took her to many places, including Czechoslovakia, West Virginia and California, after which she settled in New York City.

Her first PICTUREBOOK, *Mister Penny* (1935), established her interest in FANTASY, action and simple plots. She is noted for her strong black-and-white drawings and perceptive watercolours; she always makes her animal characters appear whimsical and playful, never threatening to her young audience. In 1960 she was awarded the CALDECOTT MEDAL for *Nine Days to Christmas* (1959). Earlier, in 1956, *Play With Me* had been named a Hans Christian Andersen Honour Book. A contemporary of such picturebook artists as WANDA GÁG and ROBERT LAWSON, also noted for their back-and-while illustrations, Ets helped to define and give new dimensions to the emerging field of the American picturebook. MS

Evans, Edmund 1826–1905 Arguably the most successful British colour engraver and printer from wood in a period of huge expansion in the publishing of children's books. Evans set up a rapidly successful printing business in London when only 21. In 1865 he printed the first of his TOY BOOKS, illustrated by the youthful WALTER CRANE, whose 50 titles for children were all produced by Evans. He printed RICHARD DOYLE's delicate and magical *In Fairyland* in 1870. Evans's skill lay in a precise mastery of his craft, and a genius for detecting talent in others. He was the first to print KATE GREENAWAY, and to suggest to RANDOLPH CALDECOTT that he should illustrate for children. GPF

see also WOOD ENGRAVING

Everett-Green, Evelyn 1856–1932 British writer remembered primarily for her girls' stories; she produced books for children of both sexes and in a range of genres, some of her best work taking the form of historical romance. Educated at Bedford College and the Royal Academy of Music, Everett-Green abandoned academia for a career in nursing. In 1909 she adopted the pseudonym 'Cecil Adair', thereafter producing one Everett-Green and one Adair book annually until her death. Books by 'both' authors are characterised by their rejection of modernity and support for Victorian values. KR

Ewing [Gatty], Juliana Horatia 1841–85 Prolific British children's author. The second daughter of Mrs Margaret Gatty (1809–73), she regularly contributed to her mother's periodical *AUNT JUDY'S MAGAZINE*, despite a nomadic family life married to a soldier. Although she produced FAIRY TALES of a traditional kind, such as 'The Magic Jar', published in her *Old Fashioned Fairy Tales* (1882), *The Brownies*, a more realistic moral tale of 1870 – and the origin of the name for the junior Girl Guides (see GUIDING AND SCOUTING) – has survived longer. Mrs Ewing's poetry shows charm and observation rather than deep feeling, though the gentle lament on 'The Death of a Linnet', and the robust, comic free verse of 'The Dolls' Wash', still have some currency. But the realistic domestic stories have won most praise, notably from GILLIAN AVERY. Despite their attractive rural settings, stories like *Jackanapes* (1883) are probably too sentimental for modern tastes, while others such as *Mrs. Overtheway's Remembrances* (1869), read more like adult reminiscences of childhood than children's books. But some of her tales, for example *A Great Emergency* (1877) and *Mary's Meadow* (1886), with their lively dialogue and sense of fun, were pioneering in their tolerant depiction of real children, pointing the way forward for E. NESBIT and later writers. DB

Exeter Book A collection of Anglo-Saxon poetry compiled from earlier material and presented to Exeter Cathedral by its first bishop, Leofric (1050–71). It includes three groups of riddles by a number of hands and resembling those of Symposius (late Latin) and ALDHEM. Unlike Aldhem's title identifications, here the last line usually requests a solution; some are still debated. The book also contains the 'Precepts', a late eighth- or early ninth-century 94-line poem spoken by a father to his son, 'that he might grow up goodly'. It warns ten times against such faults as infidelity, drunkenness and anger, and advocates prudence and wisdom. GA

see also JOKES AND RIDDLES

Eyerly, Jeannette 1908– American novelist with extensive credits including magazine articles, short stories, novels and a syndicated column. When her own daughters complained that the teenage novels they were reading had unrealistically happy endings, Eyerly focused her writing efforts on the problems teens faced, offering guidance on 'real-life' situations. *More Than a Summer Love* (1962), for instance, involves the dangers of teens getting married too young without thinking about the obstacles to completing their education and finding employment. Other novels involved children dropping out of school, mental illness, suicide, crime, drug use, alcoholism and divorce. Several of her earlier novels dealt with teenage pregnancy. *He's My Baby, Now* (1977), adapted as an ABC *After School Special*, was told from the teen father's point of view. The boy takes responsibility for his child when he refuses to sign the papers putting the child up for adoption. Eyerly shows the reader the consequences of wrong decisions and lack of responsibility. The characters are strong and believeable and the stories, while seeming to lecture, are insightful and raise issues in the reader's minds. Many of her stories have been used for classroom discussions on dropping out of school, pregnancy and teenage crime. LAW

Eytinge, Sol Jr. see *THE STORY OF A BAD BOY* [illustration]

Eze Goes to School (1963) Nigerian juvenile novel by Onuora Nzekwu and Michael Crowder, the prototype for stories about a poor but brilliant village child who struggles to go to school. Eze's story, set in Igboland, is paralleled in *Sani Goes to School* (1976), a northern version by Umaru Ladan and Crowder, and *Akin Goes to School* (1978), a Yoruba version by Christe Ade Ajayi and Crowder. Eze's quest for education continues in *Eze Goes to College* (1988). VD

F

fables Short narratives in prose or verse, often accompanied by a moral. Fables are generally stories about animals, although they may also include human subjects. The classic tradition in the West derives from AESOP (sixth century BC), although, in the long history of their transmission the Aesopic fables have absorbed many innovations and additions from other traditions. Perhaps the most notable of these are from an Indian collection in Sanskrit, probably dating from the third century AD, known as the 'fables of Bidpai', which came to Europe via a Latin translation by Giovanni da Capua in the 13th century.

The majority of fables in the Aesopic tradition have animals as protagonists, although a small number figure inanimate elements, plants or trees. There are rather more which have a mixture of animal and human or purely human subjects (for example 'The Boy and the Snake' and 'The Boy who cried Wolf'). Some stories, as in *The Frogs who Asked for a King*, involve the gods.

There are striking similarities between Aesopic fables and the brief tales involving animals which have been transmitted in the oral traditions of a wide variety of traditional cultures, even though these are assumed to have grown up quite independently of each other. Animal tales from Africa, for example, often feature small, cunning beasts who trick and get the better of larger, more powerful animals. These TRICKSTERS bear an obvious parallel to the medieval REYNARD THE FOX, as well as other Aesopic creatures. As in the stories of the Aesopic tradition, the animals in African tales are associated with distinctive qualities and, though they act like humans, the incongruity created by their animal characteristics remains available as a lively source of interest and wit. These tales – again, like Aesop – can be humorous or satirical, and may teach a lesson in proverbial form, though the latter function is much less pronounced than in the more strongly didactic tradition of the Aesopic fables.

The subject matter of Aesop's fables themselves varies greatly. Some are versions of myths of origins (see CLASSICAL MYTHOLOGY), particularly related to animal species. *How the Tortoise got its Shell* and *Why the Ant is a Thief* are examples; RUDYARD KIPLING developed this story type, common in traditional cultures, in his *JUST SO STORIES*. Many fables are concerned with conditions for survival in a world perceived as harsh and dangerous. These stories deal with issues such as status, power and identity with an unsentimental clarity of vision that appears more pragmatic than idealistic. The position of the underdog or the exploited is also vividly expressed in the fables, even though it does not necessarily appear to be supported. In a number of fables, for instance, the lion is shown hunting with a loose consortium of other animals. When the time comes for the spoils to be divided the lion explains, with barbed wit and a logic yoked to the exigencies of power, that all shares should accrue to him and that he will kill any animal who disagrees. The fable appears to endorse the philosophy that 'might is right', but it is actually double-edged because it also reveals so clearly the injustice of this position. Generally fables deal with basic human instincts and desires – greed, envy, competitiveness and so on – at times providing such memorable instances of the operation of these feelings that the images (as with the fox and the 'sour grapes' or the 'dog in the manger') have become proverbial.

The link between proverbs and fables is strong. The same word is used for both in various Middle Eastern languages. Both fables and proverbs are concise and memorable, are associated with traditional kinds of wisdom, and often link a particular incident to a universal theme or sentiment. Historians have suggested connections between the origins of the fable and the earlier form of 'wisdom literature' in the Middle East; this expressed in sayings and maxims various forms of wisdom, practical as well as ethical and religious.

Given that the content of Aesopic fables seems designed more often as an appeal to common sense, cunning and the survival instinct than to ethics or spirituality, however, the tradition of attaching a moral point to each story appears somewhat incongruous. Although the practice appears from the time of the earliest surviving written collection of fables in the first century AD, the emphasis on moral instruction is distinctive to the European fable tradition and is not found so insistently within analogous stories from other cultures. It may be that the link was forged through the early association of fables with the education of the young in Roman society (see AESOP), and with the absorption of an essentially popular, oral form into high literary culture in the West. Within the European Christian culture of the Middle Ages, the practice of drawing an explicit moral point from the fables was reinforced by the exegetical tradition of interpreting sacred texts and by the extensive use of fables in sermons and preaching.

Isolated fables were incorporated into texts by authors from the time of Hesiod (eighth century BC). References to Aesop and fables attributed to him are not found until the latter part of the fifth century BC, however; thereafter, the fables appear to have been popular, examples occurring in the work of a range of authors including Aristophanes, Xenophon, Plato and Aristotle. There are references to a written collection of fables dating from around 300 BC but the first extant collection is in verse, attributed to a Roman slave called Phaedrus who lived in the first century AD. Although Phaedrus was not known to medieval Europe, his fables were transmitted via a fourth century prose collection called *Romulus* and were extremely popular. A somewhat later collection in Greek verse by Babrius was also influential. Translated into Latin elegaic verses by Avianus in the fourth century, this became the basis for standard school manuals in western Europe, where the fable stood as a central text in the study of rhetoric in the elementary phase of the curriculum.

The study of rhetoric involved both imitation and translation from model texts and this early training in retelling fables, combined with Aesop's status within the pantheon of classical writers, appears to have inspired successive generations of major authors to develop their own stories in the fable form. The first substantial collection of fables in a vernacular language in England is by Marie de France in the late 12th century. Thereafter CHAUCER, Lydgate, Henryson, Spenser, Aphra Behn, John Gay, WILLIAM GODWIN and others all tried their hand at extended literary versions of the form: most of these are of considerable artistic merit. The high point in the literary development of the fable occurred in late 17th-century France, where, in a series of dazzlingly witty and trenchant verse collections, JEAN DE LA FONTAINE made the form his own. La Fontaine published 12 books of fables – *Fables Choisies* – between 1668 and 1694. His work has been translated and rewritten many times, most notably by the great Russian fabulist Ivan Krylov, who published nine volumes between 1810 and 1820.

In England Aesop's fables were among the first books to be made available in printed form. WILLIAM CAXTON published his translation of the French version of Heinrich Steinhowel's landmark *Esopus* in 1484, with accompanying woodcut ILLUSTRATIONS. Though the woodcuts Caxton used were cruder than those in the Steinhowel edition, they retained an expressive vigour, and set the pattern for subsequent, finer printed editions of Aesop to be accompanied by illustrations, often of considerable quality. The 17th century, particularly, saw the production of a series of expensive folio editions which attempted to set themselves apart from the more run-of-the-mill school manuals and vied with each other for quality. The most important of these were John Ogilby's *The Fables of Aesop Paraphrased in Verse* (first published in 1651 but reissued frequently), Francis Barlow's polyglot edition of 1666, which was accompanied by his superb engravings, and Sir Roger L'Estrange's *Fables of Aesop and Other Eminent Mythologists; with Morals and Reflexions*, first issued in 1692. The link between fables and illustrations had always been strong: the famous Bayeux tapestry, from as early as the 11th century, included illustrations depicting nine of Aesop's fables in its borders. But from the late 17th century the role of illustrations in enhancing the appeal of fables specifically for a child readership was alluded to with increasing frequency and, in the prefaces to new editions, the issue of the most appropriate form for collections of the fables to engage children as well as adult readers was explicitly addressed and debated.

The use of fables became more politicised during the 17th century and a number of the collections, including Ogilby's and L'Estrange's, were imbued with an explicitly political agenda promoting the Royalist cause. During the course of the 18th century attempts were made by writers as diverse as John Gay, SAMUEL RICHARDSON and William Godwin both to adjust the language of fables to a register more suitable for children and to relate fables to values with consensual, rather than politically contentious, appeal. In the case of the most famous of the 18th-century collections, however, Samuel Croxall's *Fables of Aesop and Others* (1722), the strategy was to lock horns with the political concerns of his immediate predecessors, promoting an explicitly Whig agenda rather than trying to transcend the realm of the political altogether.

With the emergence of publications designed specifically for children in the latter half of the 18th century, fables became increasingly categorised as children's literature. One effect of this was greatly to reduce the massive corpus contained in the grand editions of the 17th and early 18th centuries: a much smaller selection of fables, those deemed suitable and attractive to children, increasingly found their way into slimmer editions. Another effect was to shift the creative emphasis in new productions away from the written text of the fables and towards their interpretation through the medium of illustration. While few major writers turned their attention to the fable form after the 18th century (Kipling's *Just So Stories* (1902), JAMES THURBER's *Fables of Our Time* (1940) and George Orwell's *Animal Farm* (1945), being innovative, rather un-Aesopic exceptions), the fables have attracted a wealth of talented visual artists. Following in the Caxton/Steinhowel tradition, THOMAS BEWICK (1818) and JOHN TENNIEL (1848) produced fine new WOOD ENGRAVINGS in the first half of the 19th century. Charles Henry Bennett's striking hand-coloured engravings (1857) drew on the late Victorian fashion for representing animals dressed up in contemporary costume. In addition RANDOLPH CALDECOTT (1883), WALTER CRANE (1887), ARTHUR RACKHAM (1912), Alexander Calder (1931) and EDWARD BAWDEN (1970) have all turned their creative energies to the form.

As the 20th century progressed children's writers tended to move away from the didactic tradition within which fables became embedded, particularly with regard to the accompanying morals. Some recent writers such as MARGARET CLARK (*The Best of Aesop's Fables*, 1990) have dispensed with the accompanying morals, making explicit the intention to 'dispel altogether the "preacherly" tone from the best of Aesop's shrewd and funny stories'. Others have reduced the morals to the most condensed and pithy of addenda, a far cry from the extended moral reflections of 17th- and 18th-century texts which frequently exceeded the length of the narratives themselves. Perhaps the most innovative recent intervention within the form has been by the Japanese writer/illustrator MITSUMASO ANNO. *Anno's Aesop* (1990) retells the stories from the perspective of a non-literate fox who, unable to read the original versions, reinvents them. Anno creates fascinating interplay between text and illustration and considerably extends the range of implication of the fables through this device.

Through the ages fables appear to have been able to delight and provoke thought in a whole spectrum of readers and listeners – adults as well as children, rulers as well as the enslaved, exploited and vulnerable. Although their use as a medium for communicating important ideas to adults seems to have declined in modern societies, the fable remains supremely versatile and adaptive, as is demonstrated in the vibrant new forms it takes in a range of significant writing for children. DWh

Fabula de Jemima Anate-Aquatica see LATIN TRANSLATIONS

Fabula de Petro Cuniculo see LATIN TRANSLATIONS

Fabulous Histories see *THE HISTORY OF THE ROBINS*

Factor, June 1936– What the OPIES have done for British folklore, Factor has done for Australia. She has collected vast quantities of NURSERY RHYMES, PLAYGROUND RHYMES, children's chants, taunts, parodies and RIDDLES, published under such titles as *Far Out, Brussel Sprout!* (1993), *Real Keen, Baked Bean!* (1989) and *Ladles and Jellyspoons; Favourite Riddles and Jokes of Australian Children* (1989). Factor has researched widely into such folklore, making tapes and videos and publishing *Captain Cook Chased a Chook: Children's Folklore in Australia* (1988), which includes studies of the play of Aboriginal children as well as white children in colonial times. MSax

Faerie Tale Theatre (1982–7) Cable TELEVISION series. With the growth of premium cable services, cable companies realised that, in order to be competitive with each other and with broadcast networks, they needed to produce original programming suitable for children and parents. *Faerie Tale Theatre* was one of the most creative and innovative of such programmes. Devised and produced by actress Shelley Duvall, it combined elements of such theatrical performances of FAIRY TALES as American vaudeville and burlesque and British PANTOMIME. Adaptations typically retained the genuine sense of magic and mystery that gives fairy tales their power, while at the same time often integrating contemporary, sometimes pop culture and satiric elements. In particular, Duvall made canny and sometimes surprising casting choices that added to the sense of freshness: Mick Jagger as the Emperor in Andersen's *The Nightingale*, Liza Minnelli in the title role of *The Princess and the Pea*, and Joan Collins as a very wicked witch in *Hansel and Gretel*. From 1985 to 1988, Duvall produced a second *Showtime* series, *Tall Tales*, based on legends drawn from American folklore. BH

Fairfax-Lucy, Brian see PEARCE, PHILLIPA

Fairy Books (by Andrew Lang) see 'COLOURED' *FAIRY BOOKS*

fairy fantasy The depiction of fairies and other supernatural and unnatural creatures in painting and ILLUSTRATION, especially, of the 19th and 20th centuries. Fairies have had a strong presence in the illustration of British literature ever since GEORGE CRUIKSHANK provided etchings for the first English translation of the GRIMM BROTHERS' *German Popular Stories* (1823–4). Yet from the first their purpose and value were hotly debated. Would they be used to entertain or instruct? Were they to appeal to adults or children? Such dilemmas were embodied in Cruikshank himself for, allied to the temperance cause in the early 1850s, he rewrote and reillustrated traditional FAIRY TALES as tracts (1853–4). For much of the 19th century, the fairy was the object of serious study, written about by folklore experts and painted by exhibiting artists. The potent genre of fairy painting developed out of Romanticism and responded to contemporary concerns. Its use of microscopic detail reflected aesthetic theory and scientific observation, while its depiction of exotic fairy courts mythologised nation and empire. In appealing to a desire to escape industrial reality, it not only idealised the countryside, but articulated marginalised behaviour: drug addiction (John Anster Fitzgerald), insanity (Richard Dadd), sexual liberation (John Simmons), and Roman Catholicism (Charles and RICHARD DOYLE). Yet a number of fairy painters worked simultaneously on illustrations aimed at family, and specifically juvenile, markets.

Richard Doyle so defined the range of fairy imagery for the mid-19th century, from comic through sweet to disturbing, that Austin Dobson stated that 'in Oberon's court, he would at once have been appointed sergeant-painter'. Early in his career, he wove fairies into whimsical designs for the humorous weekly *Punch* (1843–50). He marked his devotion to fairy subjects by illustrating the Grimm brothers' *The Fairy Ring* (1846) and the first, anonymous edition of John Ruskin's *THE KING OF THE GOLDEN RIVER* (1851). From the late 1860s, he exhibited haunting fairy paintings, the exquisite colour of which he attempted to match in the seminal set of published images entitled *In Fairyland* (1869).

A number of writers and illustrators provided alternatives to Doyle's rich but conventional fairy vision. EDWARD LEAR combined linguistic invention and relaxed draughtsmanship in his illustrated verse to suggest a parallel world of fabricated creatures at once comic and poignant but never threatening. Other, more intensely realised realms of the imagination seemed more menacing. Dante Gabriel Rossetti provided terrifying images for his sister's *GOBLIN MARKET* (1862) which exposed the carnality of the goblin merchants by depicting them as animals. More complex still were the characters and environments of LEWIS CARROLL's *ALICE* books (1865, 1872), especially as drawn by SIR JOHN TENNIEL. The heady mix of natural and mythic orders recreated the strangeness of existence equally recognisable to adults and children.

As the leading critic of the day, Ruskin appreciated the importance of the imagination and the power of the grotesque, and praised the artistry of Cruikshank, Doyle and the Pre-Raphaelites (a group including such striking fairy illustrators as ARTHUR HUGHES). Yet he was ambivalent about visual fantasy and increasingly favoured a further alternative 'fairy land', exemplified by the most typical work of KATE GREENAWAY. Her earliest published illustrations, for the fairy tale *Diamonds and Toads* (1871), employed full-blooded fantasy, perhaps indebted to her distant cousin, the artist Richard Dadd. But *UNDER THE WINDOW* (1879) and later books used idealised Regency settings to emphasise the innocence of childhood. Ruskin wrote in *The Art of England* (1883) that 'the fairy land she creates is not beyond the sky nor beneath the sea, but nigh you even at your doors'.

Through the later 19th century, fairy tales and fantasies were intrinsically linked to the renaissance in book production, for their subjects expressed the folk traditions promoted by the Arts and Crafts Movement and the exoticism echoed by Art Nouveau. However, fairy illustrators came fully into their own only once they had the technical means to replicate the visual richness of fairy painting. This was made possible through two phases of experimentation, in the 1860s and the 1890s.

The engraver and printer EDMUND EVANS developed a simplified method of colour woodblock printing which, from 1865, he applied to the production of children's books. He worked closely with WALTER CRANE on a series of highly decorative TOY BOOKS (1865–76), which included French and English fairy tales and eastern stories from *THE ARABIAN NIGHTS*. He collaborated similarly with RANDOLPH CALDECOTT and Kate Greenaway. However, his most important achievement in the area of fairy illustration was the production of Doyle's *In Fairyland* (1869). This large-format volume was produced and treasured for its images.

By the 1890s, photographic methods of printing were supplanting WOOD ENGRAVING, by reproducing black-and-white and colour images more economically and accurately. As a result, such volumes as Andrew Lang's 'COLOURED' FAIRY BOOKS, illustrated by H.J. Ford (1889–1901), and JOSEPH JACOBS's edition of fairy tales, illustrated by J.D. Batten (1890–5) used strong yet subtle monochrome designs to communicate the old stories to a large new readership. These were complemented by books with colour plates which could at last equal, if not surpass, the achievements of fairy painting. The finest of these, produced early in the 20th century, were the GIFT BOOKS, luxurious products aimed at adults. EDMUND DULAC, KAY NIELSEN, ARTHUR RACKHAM and the ROBINSON brothers were among the leading illustrators given an opportunity by the gift book to express their genius for sophisticated fantasy.

After World War I, fairy fantasy was dominated by the aesthetic and ideology of the nursery. In vindication of the theory of Ruskin and the practice of Greenaway, predominantly female illustrators presented the child with an idealised image of itself. Whether they chose to depict children as delicate (ANNE ANDERSON) or robust (MABEL LUCIE ATTWELL), they placed them in a clear, bright – and safe – environment such as a garden or playroom.

They employed anthropomorphism to transform animal toys into friends (HONOR APPLETON, E.H. SHEPARD), and introduced fairies to point up the charming otherness of infancy (CICELY MARY BARKER, MARGARET TARRANT).

Classic fantasy was revived through the allegories of C.S. LEWIS and, especially, those of J.R.R. TOLKIEN. Tolkien produced highly original illustrations to his own work and has since inspired some of the finest of recent illustrators, such as MICHAEL FOREMAN and ALAN LEE. Alan Lee has also worked with Brian Froud to encapsulate the entire tradition of fairy fantasy for a new generation in the phenomenally successful *Faeries*. DW

fairy tales Traditional narratives deriving mostly from oral cultures that probably had their roots in the Middle Ages, or even earlier. In the 17th and 18th centuries many such stories were taken from European folklore and adapted for publication with the genuine – or sometimes ironic – intention of making them available for children. French enthusiasts called such stories *contes des fées*, and hence they became known in English as 'fairy tales'. However, fairies rarely appear in them, and most commentators use the term as J.R.R. TOLKIEN used it, to refer to any traditional story involving magic. The 19th and 20th centuries saw the development of composed 'literary' fairy tales.

Fairy tales are centuries old. They are feudal and rural in their setting, and hierarchical in their social structures, from the king and his queen down to the seventh son of a poor miller who lives at the edge of the village. They existed in thousands of constantly changing oral versions and some have analogues in the folklore of other continents. Collections of fairy tales appeared in print for the first time during the 16th century; a collection called *Le piacevoli notti* ('The Delightful Nights') appeared in Italy in 1550/3, and in 1634/6 a Neapolitan writer called Giambattista Basile published a collection of 50 stories called *Lo cunto de li cunti* ('The Tale of Tales'). The most influential collections, however, were French. The first of MME D'AULNOY's *Contes des Fées* (which included 'The Blue Bird' and 'The Yellow Dwarf') were published in 1697, and in the same year CHARLES PERRAULT published his *Histoires ou contes du temps passé*.

From that time fairy tales rapidly became popular on the Continent. The stories of Perrault and Mmc d'Aulnoy, and MME DE BEAUMONT's 'Beauty and the Beast', were widely translated, and the climax of this French vogue was the commencement in 1785 of a series of 41 volumes of collected fairy tales, called *Le Cabinet des fées*. But Britain seems to have been slow to respond to the new taste, partly because of a deep Protestant distrust of magic and fancy. The most influential thinker of the age had given his Augustan support to this scepticism: JOHN LOCKE, in *Some Thoughts Concerning Education* (1693), had condemned the 'perfectly useless trumpery' of stories about goblins and bugbears. The taste in Britain during the 18th century was for NONSENSE books (*Dame Trot and her Cat, Old Mother Hubbard, The World Turned Upside Down*) and for bawdy doggerel (*The Pleasant History of Jack Horner, The Friar and the Boy*). A flourishing CHAPBOOK trade provided an abundance of cheap books which were not intended for children but were probably read by them. After about 1770, printers began to produce fairy-tale chapbooks specifically for children, many with traditional home-grown titles: *JACK THE GIANTKILLER, THE DEATH AND BURIAL OF COCK ROBIN, THE BABES IN THE WOOD*, and that parable of the work ethic, *DICK WHITTINGTON*. Alongside these, tales from *THE ARABIAN NIGHTS* had been translated as early as 1706, Mme d'Aulnoy's stories were translated in 1715, and Perrault's in 1729. The subtitle on Perrault's frontispiece had been 'Contes de ma Mère l'Oye' – and Mother Goose thereby made her entry into children's literature.

Perrault's collection included 'Sleeping Beauty', 'Little Red Riding Hood', 'Blue Beard', 'Puss in Boots', and 'Cinderella'. These early versions of the stories frustrate many of our modern expectations. 'Blue Beard', for example, ends by reminding its readers of the wickedness of female curiosity; following an account of male sadism, this outrageously inappropriate moral is either an expression of a ruthlessly phallocentric culture or an ironic French joke. There are other jokes, some of them not accessible to young readers; when Perrault's Sleeping Beauty wakes up to her first loving conversation with the Prince, she is, it is hinted, less embarrassed and more articulate than he is because the Good Fairy had given her some practice in the form of erotic dreams. Perrault's 'Little Red Riding Hood' also surprises modern readers, for the heroine is not rescued from the belly of the wolf; there is an implicit sexual interest in the wolf's wanting the little girl to get into bed with him, and the Moral makes this interest explicitly obvious, warning against the seductions of two-legged wolves. 'Little Red Riding Hood' is a 'knowing' story; it knows more than a young reader can fully understand. While it warns its young readers, it simultaneously entertains adults with a sophisticated parable of seduction. Whatever the source of the tale, Perrault's version is imbued with the ironic humour of the French court in the 1690s.

When the stories of the GRIMM BROTHERS were first translated into English in 1823, they spoke to a post-Romantic generation which was finding ways of welcoming children as intimates at the heart of family life. If the child was father of the man (see also *LYRICAL BALLADS*), what the child read was seen to be an issue of importance. The preface to the first English translation of the Grimms' *Kinder- und Hausmärchen* acknowledged that attitudes were changing, declaring: 'this is the age of reason, not of imagination; and the loveliest dreams of fairy innocence are considered as vain and frivolous. Much might be urged against this rigid and philosophic (or rather unphilosophic) exclusion of works of fancy and fiction. Our imagination is surely as susceptible of improvement by exercise, as our judgement or our memory.'

The connections that existed between the French stories retold by Perrault and the German versions collected by the Grimm brothers were complex. The Grimms were motivated by a strong nationalistic purpose and were seeking to identify a genuinely German folkloric literature. At a time when their country was occupied by Napoleonic forces, they seem to have done their best to disown all French sources. But their stories were in any case genuinely distinctive in their presentation of children as central and serious. In the best of their tales – 'The Frog Prince', 'Rapunzel', 'Hansel and Gretel', 'Snow White and the Seven Dwarfs', 'Rumplestiltskin', 'The Twelve Dancing Princesses' – the lives of children are essentially dramatic and important, and their perceptions profoundly moral. Many of the children are uncomplaining victims who see things with great clarity. Zohar Shavit has compared the Grimms' 'Little Red Cape' with Perrault's 'Little Red Riding Hood' and demonstrated that the Grimms' version is essentially familial and caring. Little Red Cape is admired for her good qualities, not her good looks; the Wolf in her story is just a hungry animal, not a rapist; and she is given a reassuringly happy ending, not an ironic moral warning.

It would be difficult to exaggerate the influence of the Grimms. They made FANTASY acceptable. When he realised the stories were being read by children, Wilhelm Grimm adapted subsequent editions to make them more suitable for young readers and, in doing so, confirmed the notion that fairy tales were for children, not philologists. Many of HANS CHRISTIAN ANDERSEN's stories, on the other hand, which began to appear in English translations in 1846, were vehicles for his own adult sense of alienation; his fairy tales were metaphors of unhappiness. Throughout the rest of the 19th century, there were many published collections of tales from all over the world. They were characterised by a recognition that fairy tales were international. Probably the most famous collection for children in Britain was ANDREW LANG's monumental and expensive 'COLOURED' *FAIRY BOOKS*. The *Blue Fairy Book* was published in 1889 and more than 20 titles followed in the series.

In the early years of the 20th century, several writers wrote new fairy stories for children, many of them appearing in popular publications such as *BLACKIE'S CHILDREN'S ANNUAL*. ELEANOR FARJEON, WALTER DE LA MARE, LAURENCE HOUSMAN and Compton Mackenzie all wrote fairy tales for the outstanding children's annual, *JOY STREET*. Since World War II, most young readers have encountered fairy tales in the form of separately published stories, often richly illustrated or designed as PICTUREBOOKS. More recently, the assumed centrality of the European fairy tale has been challenged by frequent publications of collected stories from other cultures. And there has been a shift towards 'alternative' retellings ironically adapted to expose or correct the gender stereotypes of many popular fairy tales. Pamela Oldfield's *The Terribly Plain Princess and Other Stories* (1977) and Jay Williams's *THE PRACTICAL PRINCESS AND OTHER LIBERATING FAIRY TALES* (1978) are examples, but the difficulty of such retellings is that they are to some extent dependent for their comic effect upon the very versions which they hope to supplant. ALISON LURIE's *Clever Gretchen and Other Forgotten Folk Tales* (1980) avoids that dependence; it is a collection of neglected stories in which girls outwit giants, answer riddles and generally show courage and resourcefulness. Some versions deliberately set out to be 'secondary'; ROALD DAHL's *REVOLTING RHYMES* work through intertextual jokes, as if 'punning' on the original stories. Recently, however, there has been a return to more traditional retellings: an example is the outstanding paperback series begun by Scholastic in 1998, each story told by a distinguished contemporary author (including ADÈLE GERAS, PHILIP PULLMAN, ANNE FINE, ALAN GARNER and HENRIETTA BRANFORD). These tellings – modern, witty, fast-moving and occasionally employing a less well-known version (for example, *Mossycoat* for *Cinderella*) – have proved very popular with children.

But stories are rarely made simply 'for children'. Once a genre is thought to be limited to such a specialised readership, all manner of adult preoccupations can be half-concealed within it. DICKENS, Thackeray, Ruskin and WILDE wrote fairy tales exposing the injustice and suffering in an acquisitive and exploitative society. With less disinterestedness, fairy tales have subsequently been purloined by advertisers, or changed into political allegories. The Nazis used them in the 1930s to instil into German children the peasant virtues of the Third Reich. It is now recognised that the great 19th-century folklorists, including the Grimms, refined and civilised their collected FOLK-TALES into coded messages about conduct and gender. In particular, many fairy tales have defined a magical but limiting version of femininity. The eponymous heroine of WALT DISNEY's *Snow-White* (1937), for example, has little ability to control her own life and tacitly acquiesces in a contract requiring her to serve men in return for their adoration; Disney saw Snow-White as Hollywood saw its filmstars. Cinderella corresponds, according to Hugh Crago, 'with the way Dorothy Dinnerstein describes adult women – inwardly fearful and self-doubting, outwardly trying hard to assume the magical "femininity" that man expects of them: "shakily posturing in the role of Goddess".' More recent versions from the Disney studios, such as *Beauty and the Beast* (1991) and *Aladdin* (1994), reflect more liberated American cultural assumptions about women and self-assertion.

Fairy tales are known narratives but with no fixed texts. There are only versions, infinitely variable but always recognisable. Each version is its own original. Roald Dahl tells his young readers that the stories they hear are the 'phoney' ones used by adults to keep the children happy. But ANGELA CARTER's erotic, sadistic and sometimes tender stories in *The Bloody Chamber* could hardly be more different. Yet Dahl's narratives of comic certitude for children and Carter's stylishly ambiguous stories for adults are evidence of the fact that from different perspectives and with different aesthetics, fairy tales continue to be turned inside-out as writers seek to expose new meanings implicit within them.

Though they are prose fictions, fairy tales have little in common with novels. There is no slow accumulation of inner and outer detail, no gradual involvement in the intricacies of subjectivity. The extraordinary narrative concentration in the opening of 'Hansel and Gretel' is a case in point: in about a dozen lines the reader is swiftly introduced to issues of life and death, love and betrayal, temptation and resistance, and parental rejection. A fairy tale is not a jumble of incident strung together according to some arbitrary rules of a lost folklore; in most of them, there is a careful artifice. 'Hansel and Gretel' almost certainly originated in realities of poverty and starvation, and images of food are used in a complex and sophisticated pattern of ironies. Its existential preoccupation is with eating. The children who are driven out of one house because there is no food find another that is made of food; the woman who intends to eat them is a reverse image of the woman who would not feed them. The children are starved by one and fattened by the other, and in its patterning of crumbs, pebbles and jewels, the story seems implicitly interested in ironies of value. This story has been poetically crafted, though whether by the Grimm brothers or by countless generations of fireside storytellers we cannot tell.

In the best-known stories, the geographical landscape is essentially a European landscape of cities, rivers, mountains and – most of all – forests. But the moral and social landscape is more equivocal; the protagonists of fairy tales have to make their way through a puzzling world of strict rules and unpredictable outcomes. There are prohibitions and taboos, bargains and promises, severe penalties for apparently well-meaning actions, and the terrible consequences of reckless wishing. Courage and honesty are an advantage, but luck and cunning are essential. A character who can understand the language of animals, or has an animal companion, or meets a donor of magical gifts, is unlikely to come to any lasting harm. In fairy tales, the wealthy have much gold but few children, while the poor often have many children but no gold; and since a poor child is likely to have golden hair, an ironic connection is implied. But such ironies are rarely made explicit. Fairy tales rarely stop to reflect, preach or analyse. They are 'naked narratives' composed only of imagery, protagonists, landscape and action. They are irreducibly implicit.

However, naked narratives may be clothed to make them more decorous, or to give them a didactic authority. A teller of fairy tales can have Cinderella's stepsisters' eyes put out to emphasise the severity of justice, or alternatively provide them with suitors to stress mercy; or he can – like Dahl – shock and amuse by letting Red Riding Hood draw a pistol from her knickers. Every version of a fairy tale will reflect the assumptions and anxieties of its age and enact in its retelling the emphases and purposes of its teller – but in almost every case the central narrative syntax remains unchanged.

The most helpful scholars of fairy tales are those whose studies lead them to textual versions, or to history – Elizabeth Cook's judicious comparisons in *The Ordinary and the Fabulous* (1969); JACK ZIPES's exhaustive analyses of the changing sociological uses to which fairy tales have been put; Max Luthi's lucid analyses of fairy-tale imagery and structure; and Hugh Crago's detailed examination of the illustrations in some contemporay versions of 'Snow-White'. One of the most innovative and distinguished contributions to the understanding of fairy tales was the publication of *The Classic Fairy Tales* (1974) by IONA and PETER OPIE, renowned collectors of early and rare books for children, in which 24 of the best-known stories were presented in the exact words of their first publication in English. Two outstanding critical commentaries were offered in the closing years of the 20th century. In *From the Beast to the Blonde* (1994) – a work of monumental scholarship and research – Marina Warner located fairy tales within a tradition of predominantly women's storytelling and argued that their extraordinary power was both symbolic and embedded in social and material circumstances. In *The Natural History of Make-Believe* (1996), John Goldthwaite provides a highly individual account of the history of fairy tales – especially with regard to HANS CHRISTIAN ANDERSEN – and explored their apparent need of a presiding muse in the form of Mother Goose or a fairy godmother, with ambivalent touches of both the pagan and the religious.

Scholars who focus on the mind of the child are on less certain ground, though A. N. Applebee's consideration of young children's expectations in *The Child's Concept of Story* is interesting and helpful, as is Maureen Crago's patient account in *SIGNAL* (no. 31) of her daughter's developing responses to 'Snow-White'. A particularly influential work in recent years has been Bruno Bettelheim's *The Uses of Enchantment* (1978). His analyses of the stories are provocative and illuminating, but his confident assertions about the therapeutic effects fairy tales can have on a young reader are questionable. How can he be sure that 'Cinderella' helps a child 'to accept sibling rivalry as a rather common fact and promises that he need not fear being destroyed by it'? Bettelheim's account is a post-Freudian version of the old didactic error: that a story 'transmits' a message and a child simply 'receives' it. Anyone studying Bettelheim would be well advised to turn for a corrective to Nicholas Tucker's generous but critical article in *Signal* (no. 43), 'Doctor Bettelheim and Enchantment'.

Every reader reads a different story. Writers who confidently tell us what fairy tales 'mean' are oversimplifying their complex, multilayered character. In 'Beauty and the Beast', for example, a child may understand the surface narrative and recognise that it concerns the moral risks of making promises. In the full version of the story, the surface narrative also has to do with class and wealth, and the obligations of hospitality. However, an adult reader might find beneath that surface a related story involving power, sex and fear, in which a girl is attracted in spite of herself by a specifically male combination of ugliness, vulnerability and masterfulness. The beast-lover motif is as old as the 'Cupid and Psyche' story, and its antiquity invites us to regard it as a true and timeless account of the sexual dynamics of young love. But the implications of 'Beauty and the Beast' do not end there, for it is also a father's story, suggesting with considerable dramatic accuracy the dilemma of the Electra complex, and a father's distress when his beloved daughter leaves him. He is left a victim of the inexorable youth/age process whereby the old parent is inevitably wrong-footed by the young lover and enfeebled by the daughter's desertion. The possibilities of implicit meaning in 'Beauty and the Beast' have tempted many artists to re-make it. There have been many storybook versions, at least two films (one by Jean Cocteau), and a full-length novel called *Beauty* by ROBIN MCKINLEY, which won the 1984 NEWBERY AWARD in the United States. More than two centuries ago SAMUEL RICHARDSON'S *PAMELA* told the 'Beauty and the Beast' story and became a controversial bestseller about sexual coercion.

Fairy tales are probably most powerful in societies ruled by strong cultural taboos. Some adult readers are troubled by the fact that many of them hint at 'forbidden' meanings which have to do with sexuality, violence, greed, and poisonous rivalry between parent (or step-parent) and child. The Frog which demands to be allowed to sleep with the Princess is uncompromisingly sexual, and the numerous stepmother murderesses hint at all manner of guiltily repressed feelings of hatred. In fact, it seems likely that fairy tales in Britain in the 19th century were popular partly *because* they provided a narrative space in which adults could encode material they were otherwise obliged to suppress. If that is so, it may partly account for the fact that in the 1990s fairy tales seemed to be in decline: a period in which media spotlights were turned upon individual, institutional or cultural taboos, there was little need for an art form that thrives on the forbidden or on secrecy. Some commentators believe this decline may be partly due to the fact that many children are now familiar with fairy tales only in the (often inspired) Disney versions. This in itself raises questions about cultural imperialism and the economics of the film and video industry.

In the face of their complexity and suggestivity, it is unwise to think of fairy tales as 'teaching' anything. A fairy tale is not a lesson, though it may be made into one. Nor is it a statement. It is an experience, and its meanings are available only in private, subjective terms. It would be a fool's game to read fairy tales to children in order to teach them not to break promises or indulge in reckless wishing. On the other hand, something is learned; the difficulty is to know precisely what it is. Fairy tales are like 'words' in the wider cultural language of recognised social and domestic predicaments. They provide a vocabulary of human possibility, a thesaurus of unapplied and dynamic meanings – approximate, ambivalent and dramatic. They have to do with hope and growth, for even the tales with sad endings offer a mysterious emotional fullness. Fairy tales have all the tricksy and absorbing magic of words; they do not contain meaning and they cannot impart meaning. They allow meanings to be made. VW

see also AFRICAN MYTHOLOGY; CLASSICAL MYTHOLOGY; FOLKTALES AND LEGENDS; IRISH MYTHOLOGY; KING ARTHUR; NATIVE AMERICAN LITERATURE; ROBIN HOOD; SUPERHEROES

Falkner, J. Meade see *MOONFLEET*; see also ADVENTURE STORIES

Family from One End Street, The (1937) The adventures of the Ruggles family by EVE GARNETT, who also illustrated the books, are told in *The Family from*

One End Street (1937), *Further Adventures of the Family from one End Street* (1956) and *Holiday at The Dew Drop Inn* (1962). The first book, a CARNEGIE MEDAL winner, was extremely popular with young readers and at the time of its publication was hailed as a long-awaited representation of the life of the working classes, though this estimation of its achievement was later modified. The books themselves are humorous and well written, but considered as a treatment of working-class life (Mr Ruggles is a dustman, his wife a washerwoman) they are superficial, and even a little (unintentionally) patronising. The names – 'Ruggles' 'Lily Rose' 'Peg' etc. – might be said to constitute a form of stereotyping, as does the depiction of the garish taste displayed in the Ruggles's wall-paper: 'a beautiful trellis-work design with bunches of pink and yellow roses'. The comic descriptions of Mr Ruggles's bad spelling and painful attempts at arithmetic are again rather crude in their assumptions about working-class levels of education and intelligence. The books betray a certain nostalgia for life in the country, which is also reflected in the romantic colouring of Garnett's illustrations of the Dew Drop Inn, an Olde Worlde thatched building. Kate fakes measles in order to be sent there, and *Holiday at the Dew Drop Inn* is an unashamed celebration of the world of flower shows and country fairs. SA

family stories A field of children's fiction that has acquired a misleading reputation for cosiness, owing in part to the rise of the nuclear family as a post-war advertising ideal. Even now, in the face of the real-life disintegration of this unit, the Norman Rockwell household continues to feature in television commercials promoting such domestic products as detergents and breakfast cereals. The first examples of children's family stories conformed to this type, being concerned as they were to reinforce parental guidance and instruction, culminating in MARY MARTHA SHERWOOD's *The History of the Fairchild Family* (1818–47). But as the moral tales metamorphosed into fiction, parents became marginalised and the focus of the narrative shifted onto siblings, with all the problems and rewards – particularly problems – attendant upon their mutual coexistence. Adults might be involved as arbiters and umpires, but primarily it was the children's relationships with each other that provided the meat of the story, as for example in the works of CHARLOTTE YONGE and JULIANA HORATIA EWING. Since it was early perceived, however misguidedly, that children with two harmonious parents were likely to have little to unsettle them, the family story as it developed through the 19th century frequently depicted children who had lost one or both parents and were reliant upon each other in their progress towards adulthood. The first of this kind is Catherine Sinclair's *HOLIDAY HOUSE* (1839), which features three motherless children living with their grandmother and uncle. The elder brother, Frank, makes few appearances; Harry and Laura are too close in age and temperament to have much effect upon one another's growth. This disadvantage was compounded by later authors who, hoping to attract readers of both sexes, fell back on the shorthand device of twins, without ever investigating the complex experience of being a twin or of having twins in the family. The clearest example of this is the American BOBBSEY TWINS series by Laura Lee Hope (1904 onwards); the twins came in two sets and possessed no personality traits whatsoever.

The family saga, in which successive books follow a group of people growing up together into adulthood, made its first appearance with LOUISA MAY ALCOTT's *LITTLE WOMEN* quartet (1868–86), but on the whole this kind of processional writing appeals more to adults who have had time to adjust to change and decay. In children's fiction it is mainly represented in school series, such as *THE CHALET SCHOOL* and the *DIMSIE* books of Dorita Fairlie Bruce. Of the three *Katy* books by SUSAN COOLIDGE, only the first, *WHAT KATY DID* (1872), is genuinely a family story. The title of *What Katy did at School* (1873) speaks for itself, and *What Katy did Next* (1886) is a fictionalised travelogue, although illuminated by some fine, funny insights. In the original book the six Carrs, children of a widowed doctor and raised by their aunt, are a convincing group of brothers and sisters, aged from four to twelve. Their natural heirs are E. NESBIT's *BASTABLES*, first encountered in *The Story of the Treasure Seekers* (1899), another family of six, desolated by the recent death of their mother and discovering that their individual assertiveness must be restrained in the interests of solidarity. Much of Nesbit's other fiction, such as *The Enchanted Castle* (1907) and the books about the Phoenix and the *PSAMMEAD*, while FANTASIES, are also rooted firmly in a family background. Nineteenth-century plotting derived as much from factual social circumstances as from authorial imperatives; an assortment of five or more surviving children with a parent dead before middle age was not unrealistic. The Woolcots, ETHEL TURNER's *SEVEN LITTLE AUSTRALIANS* (1894), have a 20-year-old stepmother and one of the few examples of a tyrannical Victorian father, a figure signally absent from Victorian fiction. The American Margaret Sidney's *FIVE LITTLE PEPPERS* (1880 onwards) were fatherless, as were the Wiggses in *MRS WIGGS OF THE CABBAGE PATCH* by Alice Caldwell Hegan (1901), but as the 20th century progressed, life expectancy rose and family numbers dropped.

By the 1930s the nuclear-family story was becoming a genre to complement the school story and the ripping yarn, furnishing a background from which children could issue collectively for holidays, adventures and education, and to which they could safely return, fortified throughout by a secure environment. Many books announced their family connections in the title: EVE GARNETT's *THE FAMILY FROM ONE END STREET* was published in 1937; KITTY BARNE's *Family Footlights* in 1939; and NOEL STREATFEILD launched *The Bell Family* in 1954. Most of Streatfeild's novels involved families, although her true subject was the performing arts. The family simply served as ballast for the activities of its various and, in her later work, frankly interchangeable members. More trenchant was Kitty Barne's *She Shall Have Music* (1938), which told the story of a gifted child's struggles to become a pianist as the youngest of a supremely unmusical family. Barne, a CARNEGIE MEDAL winner, has become an unjustly neglected writer, at once serious, informative and entertaining (see also NEGLECTED WORKS). She also allowed her adult characters to be people rather than stage props, and *Family Footlights* may have initiated the brief mid-century vogue for books about children putting on family plays. In 1950 G.B. Stern published an adult novel, *The Days of Christmas*, with a not dissimilar theme, and Judith Masefield brought out *Larking at Christmas* in which the children of a playwright attempt to write and stage a play. As the author was the daughter of JOHN MASEFIELD the book may be seen as a memoir of her own family's experience of village theatricals.

Although strictly speaking fantasies, MARY NORTON's *THE BORROWERS* series (1952–82) are also family stories. This family, aside from its height, is in any case an unusual one for fictional purposes, composed of father, mother and adolescent daughter. Their adventures and vicissitudes stem from their size and their environment, but throughout the books the three characters change and develop in themselves and in their relationships to one another. Anne-Kath Vestly published the first of her *Aurora* stories in Norway in 1966, seven years before they began to appear in the United Kingdom. Aurora's mother is a working lawyer; it is her father, a postgraduate student, who keeps house and cares for Aurora and baby Socrates. The problems faced by this secure and charming family arise not from the role reversal but from outsiders' attitudes to the situation. The books were somewhat in advance of Anglophone responses to the changing face of domestic life, but in the late 1970s two Americans, BETSY BYARS and KATHERINE PATERSON, published *The Pin-Balls* and *The Great Gilly Hopkins* respectively, each dealing with foster homes. Byars in particular has specialised in deceptively compact novellas about the fragmented family, and ANNE FINE has become a comparable authority on the same subject in the United Kingdom. Once seen as a matter for problem novels, it is a fact now so common as to be taken for granted. The notion of gay parents, which caused frenzied debate when first mooted in the Danish import *Jenny Lives with Eric and Martin* by Susanne Bösche (1981), may yet enter the mainstream (see GAY AND LESBIAN LITERATURE). It is over 30 years since RANDALL JARRELL wrote *The Animal Family* (1962), but contemporary mores are prefigured in this poetic FABLE of a hunter and a mermaid for whom, presumably, natural intercourse is impossible, and who establish a loving home for a lynx, a bear and finally a human child, with the implication that you *can* choose your relatives. A curiosity that emerges from time to time is the comedy family. The first manifestation was LUCRETIA PEABODY HALE's *The Peterkin Papers* which appeared in America in 1868, first as magazine stories and later in book form. They were followed by EDWARD LEAR's *Violet, Slingsby, Guy and Lionel* (1871) and more recently by HELEN CRESWELL's BAGTHORPES and the Fantora Family of ADÈLE GERAS.

Resourcefulness has long been the staple of American family stories. The Marches were resourceful of necessity, the Carrs needed to entertain themselves. Other enterprising siblings were the Moffats of ELEANOR ESTES (1904) and ELIZABETH ENRIGHT's Melendys (1942). In 1988 PATRICIA MACLACHLAN, best known for another family novel, *Sarah, Plain and Tall* (1986), published *The Facts and Fictions of Minna Pratt*, a tale of the dishevelled but affectionate and tolerant Pratt family, in which the daughter Minna communicates with her distracted novelist mother by writing letters from fictitious fans. Maclachlan's message is one of negotiation, harking back to the 19th-century accounts of sibling differences, only now with the adults also involved. Australian NADIA WHEATLEY's two novels of Greek family life in a Sydney suburb, *Five Times Dizzy* (1982) and *Dancing in the Anzac Deli* (1984) reintroduce the grandmother as an important figure.

Stories which use the family as their theatre of operations are written almost exclusively by women, dating from the earliest days of children's fiction when it fell to men to supply fantasy while women, fingers on the erratic pulse of domestic life, took a realistic look at their material. Men have written about families, but this has usually been a holiday interest, involving, more often than not, small boats. ARTHUR RANSOME is the most obvious example, introducing a relative who was to become indispensable in this sphere – the uncle. Ransome's Uncle Jim was known as Captain Flint. Aubrey de Selincourt weighed in with Uncle Bob in *Family Afloat* (1940) and Gilbert Hackforth Jones's *Green Sailors* were captained, in the 1950s radio plays, by Uncle George. There was a boat-owning Uncle Jacob in PETER DICKINSON's *The*

Weathermonger (1968). Uncles were less strict than fathers, less fussy than mothers, but their slightly ambiguous status has removed them from the scene. In a sense this last sub-genre illustrates the polarisation of the family story: the family as a convenient, ready-made unit of children of varying ages, versus the family as microcosm, the small universe in which children learn to be social animals and, eventually, adults. JMM

***Famine* trilogy** (1990–6) Three novels by the Irish writer, MARITA CONLON MCKENNA, set in 19th-century Ireland. *Under the Hawthorn Tree* (1990) – winner of the READING ASSOCIATION OF IRELAND AWARD – introduces three young people, Eily, Michael and Peggy. Orphaned by the Famine, they set out to find food and shelter with their great-aunts. The sights and smells of the famine-devastated countryside are described graphically, and it is the courage and resourcefulness of the children which brings them safely to their destination. In *Wildflower Girl* (1991), 13-year-old Peggy gets an assisted passage to America, where she finds work as a domestic servant in Boston. It is only her resilience which enables her to survive the horrors of the voyage and to find a future for herself in her new world. *The Fields of Home* (1996) draws to a conclusion the stories of Eily, Michael and Peggy, now grown up, and leaves the reader with the certainty that these characters will survive to build for themselves futures based on compassion, enterprise and hope. VC

Famous Five, The A series of 21 novels by ENID BLYTON, appearing annually between 1942 and 1963, apart from 1959. Though the 'Five' formula had been explicitly used before – notably in E. NESBIT's *Five Children and It* and FRANK RICHARDS' 'Famous Five' of the Remove – Blyton's Five are distinctive. They comprise three siblings, Julian, Dick and Anne, their cousin Georgina, a tomboy who insists on being called George, and, most unusually, her mongrel dog, Timothy. They meet in the first novel, and one of the best in the series, *Five on a Treasure Island* (1942). George's power is cultivated from the outset, in her anticipated but delayed appearance. Thereafter she dominates the book, outshining the boys in various activities. At the climax, when the crooks have unsuccessfully tried to take over George's island, she is seen wielding an axe and wrecking their boat. There are clearly parallels with the British at war, when King George's people – on St George's 'sceptred isle' – were seeking to defend themselves from 'wicked men'. Churchill himself had spoken of 'This wicked man . . . resolved to break our famous island race.'

More generally, this first book shows how a fiercely independent girl relinquishes some of her autonomy in exchange for friendship. The price to pay, though, is entry into a patriarchal world. Though many critics accuse the books of being sexist, it seems that Blyton frequently problematises the whole notion of sexism. Throughout the series the unfairness of traditional gender roles is exposed, mainly through George. Anne is certainly a much more traditional, domesticated girl, but she thereby serves as a foil to George's subversiveness. As for George being nothing more than a token boy, it is worth noting that she is also the most passionate of the Five, whether angry, tearful, or expressing her love for Timmy. In a recent survey of Blyton's appeal, not only was the Five by far the most popular series, but George was overall Blyton's most popular character, particularly amongst girls, many of whom saw her as a proto-feminist; less predictably, George was also more popular with male readers than either of the boy characters.

Whilst there are many individual favourites, *Five Go to Smuggler's Top* is one that most regard as exemplary, with its secret passages, tunnels, marshes, mists, false leads and enigmatic crooks. It also features another memorable character in the series – George's father, Quentin: an eccentric scientist, as irascible as his daughter, and often as childish. He exemplifies the capriciousness of adults and often suffers the consequences, being clubbed, drugged, imprisoned, and even locked up with a snake on one occasion. Besides a stage play, the Five have attracted attention from other media, having been filmed three times, the latest series by Zenith Films (1994) who attempt to recapture the period feel whilst updating the social attitudes. The Five have also been much parodied, most famously by the Comic Strip in *Five Go Mad in Dorset* (1982), in which the apocryphal phrase 'lashings of ginger beer' originated. DR

Famous Tommy Thumb's Little Story-Book, The see NURSERY RHYMES

Fantasia see WALT DISNEY; MUSIC AND STORY; KAY NIELSEN; see also NUDITY IN CHILDREN'S BOOKS

fantasy A modern, extended fictional form, belonging to the age of the novel. MYTH, LEGEND and FAIRY TALE will not be discussed here as subjects in themselves, though it must be emphasised that modern fantasy continually draws upon and is enriched by them.

The establishment of the novel as a major form dates from the 18th century. The children's book, defined as a recreational work produced specially for children, also dates from that century. The pioneers of children's publishing did not, however, publish fantasy. In the Age of Reason, imagination was at a discount among writers who addressed themselves to children. Fairy tales were despised: 'People stuff Children's Heads with Stories of Ghosts, Fairies, Witches, and such Nonsense when they are young', complained the author of *Little Goody Two-Shoes*, 'and so they continue Fools all their Days'. Edifying works of humourless realism, showing naughty or careless children bringing disaster upon themselves and serving as a warning to their readers, were characteristic of the late 18th century.

Yet, in a tentative way, fantasy began to raise its head. Stories of humanised animals and objects were early examples. DOROTHY KILNER, in 1783, wrote *The Life and Perambulations of a Mouse*, in which a mouse, with 'a little squeaky voice', tells its story to a gathering of children, and in which a family of four small mice are called Nimble, Longtail, Softdown and Brighteyes. SARAH TRIMMER, a formidable and conservative educationist, wrote three years later the somewhat similar *HISTORY OF THE ROBINS*, in which 'the sentiments and affections of a good father and mother and a family of children are supposed to be possessed by a nest of redbreasts.' But Trimmer was at pains to point out that *The Robins* did not record the real conversations of birds, which 'it is impossible we should ever understand', but was 'a series of FABLES intended to convey moral instruction'.

The best of these anthropomorphic forerunners of fantasy came some years later with Richard Henry Horne's *Memoirs of a London Doll*, published in 1846. By this time, however, attitudes to imaginative fiction and views on what was good for children had altered. The great change came in the early 19th century, and in a wider cultural context may be linked with the rise of the Romantic movement and the replacement of classical by Gothic influences. In children's literature the change was marked by the rehabilitation of the fairy tale and by successive publication in England of PERRAULT, the GRIMM BROTHERS and ANDERSEN. Early works of fantasy such as John Ruskin's *KING OF THE GOLDEN RIVER* (written in 1841, published in 1851), F. E. Paget's *Hope of the Katzekopfs* (1844) and W. M. Thackeray's extravaganza *THE ROSE AND THE RING* (1855) may all be said to arise out of the fairy-tale tradition. The decade in which fantasy took flight on its own wings was the 1860s, when the two *Alice* books were published. *ALICE'S ADVENTURES IN WONDERLAND* (1865) and *Through the Looking-Glass* (1871) were the first, and some would say still the greatest, of the major English fantasies. They had no predecessors of their own kind; they had no lessons to teach. They promoted the child: instead of being a receptacle for adult wisdom, Alice is the wise child in a crazy world, opposing absurd logic with homely common sense. When, at the end of *Wonderland*, she confronts the assembled royalty and court of law with the words 'Who cares for you? You're nothing but a pack of cards!' the implication is subversive: is she perhaps putting the adult world in its place? The books combine memorable verse with memorable dialogue; like *Hamlet*, they now appear to be composed largely of quotations, and, like *WINNIE-THE-POOH* (1926) and *THE WIND IN THE WILLOWS* (1908) but no other children's book, they feature characters instantly recognised by every literate adult. One hears frequently of children who do not take to them, but sooner or later they must be read by anyone who wants to take part in civilised conversation.

The *Alice* books had imitators but no real heirs in their own time. The other major fantasy of the sixties, CHARLES KINGSLEY'S *WATER BABIES* (1863), had a social, moral and religious purpose, water babies being all the children who 'come to grief by ill-usage or ignorance or neglect'. The book itself, long, confused, and often avuncularly didactic in tone, now survives mainly as a familiar name, but its combination of fantasy with social and religious concern may be seen again in GEORGE MACDONALD'S *At the Back of the North Wind* (1871), in which little Diamond's harsh life in working-class London runs in parallel with another life in a dream world. MacDonald, a powerful and productive writer, was the author of *The Princess and the Goblin*, published in 1872 and still read, which has a fairy-tale ambience and which can be mined for psychological symbolisms but is in fact a religious allegory. Its successor, *The Princess and Curdie* (1883), which is equally powerful, has a dark and disturbing conclusion.

E. NESBIT wrote both fantasies and family stories, and combined them in *Five Children and It* (1902) and *The Phoenix and the Carpet* (1904), featuring respectively the bad-tempered but magical Psammead and the vain Phoenix. A third book about the same family, *The Story of the Amulet* (1906), is of special interest, as introducing to children's literature a new sub-genre, the TIME-SLIP FANTASY. The inspiration clearly was H. G. Wells's *The Time Machine* (1895). RUDYARD KIPLING'S *PUCK OF POOK'S HILL* (1906) and *Rewards and Fairies* (1910) also engage with time, bringing figures from the past into the present; but Kipling had already made his primary contribution to fantasy with the Mowgli stories in the two *JUNGLE BOOKS* (1894–95) which, insofar as they can be categorised, are in the talking-animal tradition. KENNETH GRAHAME'S *Wind in the Willows* (1908) is also in this tradition, although in the very different context of quiet English countryside.

British writers of fantasy had an inheritance of folklore and story that did not fully transplant into newer lands and cultures. *The Wizard of Oz*, by L. FRANK BAUM (1900) has been described as 'the first distinctive attempt to construct a fairyland out of American materials'. The Scarecrow, who wants a brain instead of straw, the Tin Woodman, who needs a heart, and the Cowardly Lion, who lacks courage, are ingenious creations and – like Dorothy, who says she has something better than royal blood: she comes from Kansas – are as American as their midwestern author. There were too many Oz books in the end, but the early ones were rich in inventions and ideas.

Norman Lindsay's boisterous *The Magic Pudding* (1918), was as thoroughly Australian as Baum's book was American. Bunyip Bluegum and his friends, Barnacle Bill the sailor and Sam Sawnoff the penguin, defend the cut-and-come-again pudding against the repeated attacks of pudding snatchers. 'Roughly stated', according to Lindsay himself, 'the theme is eating and fighting, which is child psychology at its simplest'.

Hugh Lofting's *Doctor Dolittle* books in the 1920s and 1930s continued the talking-animal strain – though the innocent, almost saintly Doctor himself is the central figure, rather than his friends Dab-Dab the duck housekeeper, Polynesia the parrot, and the Pushmi-Pullyu with a head at each end. The hugely-successful *Winnie-the-Pooh* books of the 1920s, still selling immensely and producing profitable spin-offs seventy years later, feature humanised toys rather than animals; and among other toy stories that survived for many years alongside them were *The Velveteen Rabbit* (1922) and *Poor Cecco* (1925), by Margery Williams Bianco.

At the opposite pole from toy fantasies were John Masefield's *The Midnight Folk* (1927) and *The Box of Delights* (1935), full-blooded adventure stories which made uninhibited use of magic as an ingredient. The little box in the latter book enables Kay Harker to move into the past, and a visit to an ancient farmhouse gives similar access to a girl called Penelope in Alison Uttley's *A Traveller in Time* (1939).

The most remarkable fantasy of the 1930s in terms of influence on the genre's development in the post-war years was J.R.R. Tolkien's *The Hobbit* (1937). In conjunction with Tolkien's later trilogy on the adult list, *The Lord of the Rings* (1954–5), it was to initiate what has been called high fantasy: a form which almost invariably draws on ancient legend and frequently involves the creation of secondary worlds, such as Tolkien's own Middle-Earth. Tolkien's friend and colleague C.S. Lewis invented such a world with the hugely successful *Chronicles of Narnia* books (1949–56). Several writers developed similar concepts with greater intensity: Alan Garner, regarded by many as the leading talent of his day, in his early books created magical worlds that were in and around the real one, and *The Owl Service* (1967) showed legend still being re-enacted in the present. *Red Shift* (1973) explored the interaction of time and space in the light of relativity. Lloyd Alexander's five *Chronicles of Prydain*, beginning with *The Book of Three* in 1964, were inspired by Wales and its legends, but Prydain was none the less imaginary, and Alexander dipped freely into what he called the ever-simmering cauldron of story. Susan Cooper's *Dark is Rising* quintet (1965–76) had as its background a cosmic struggle between good and evil forces; Diana Wynne Jones devised several ingenious worlds of her own; and the number of lesser writers whose work could be described as post-Tolkien was wearyingly large. Most impressive of all the imagined lands in its depth and complexity was Ursula Le Guin's Earthsea in *A Wizard of Earthsea* (1968) and its three successors (see *The Earthsea Quartet*). And most ambitious in its aims was Patricia Wrightson's epic trilogy *The Book of Wirrun* (1977–82) (see *Wirrun* Trilogy), in which she turned away from European 'elves and dragons and unicorns' to explore a kind of magic intrinsic to Australia: that of its original inhabitants.

Anthropomorphic fantasy, an enduring form, continued to flourish, producing among much else E.B. White's *Charlotte's Web* (1952), long acknowledged as one of the world's great children's books. Russell Hoban's *The Mouse and his Child* (1967), of which the background is clearly North American, was seen by many in Britain as a masterpiece, but was less highly esteemed in the United States. To follow, among many other works, were Robert C. O'Brien's *Mrs Frisby and the Rats of NIMH* (1971), Richard Adams's *Watership Down* (1972), and a long line of humanised-animal stories by Dick King-Smith.

The border between reality and fantasy is not necessarily clear-cut, and some distinguished modern books have left it intriguingly in doubt. In the first two of Lucy Boston's *Green Knowe* books (1954 and 1958), a small boy called Tolly seems to meet children who lived in an ancient house in earlier centuries: but does he 'really' meet them or does he imagine it? Does Barney in Clive King's *Stig of the Dump* (1963) 'really' find a cave-boy living in a tip? Readers can believe or disbelieve, or both at once. Philippa Pearce's unparalleled *Tom's Midnight Garden* (1958) is a haunting time-slip fantasy, yet much of its strength comes from its precise and realistic portrayal of place and people. In another exceptional fantasy, Natalie Babbitt's *Tuck Everlasting* (1975), everything follows naturally from a single displacement of natural laws: the notion that drinking from a particular spring could confer immortality.

Stories combining magic and comedy are common, but outstanding ones are rare. Penelope Lively's *The Ghost of Thomas Kempe* (1975), in which an old rogue of an apothecary emerges from a bottle to make trouble, and Joan Aiken's riotous *James III* 'unhistorical' novels are exceptions; Joan Aiken is also probably the most brilliant exponent of the modern fairy tale, for example in *A Necklace of Raindrops* (1968). Finally, mention should be made of ROALD DAHL, a writer of endless, uninhibited invention, loved by children and loathed by many of their elders. There are many more fantasy writers of excellence or interest; at the start of the 21st century, the genre seems in good health and as well set for survival as any other branch of children's literature. JRT

see also FAIRY FANTASY; PICTUREBOOKS

Far-Distant Oxus, The (1937), ***Escape to Persia*** (1938) and ***Oxus in Summer*** (1939). Three novels by Pamela Whitlock and Katharine Hull, the first written when they were 15 and 16 years old respectively and published by Cape with an introduction by ARTHUR RANSOME. The two CHILD AUTHORS employed the narrative characteristics of Ransome to produce stories of camping and exploring with, cleverly, the additional interest of ponies. The books were published in a format identical to that of *SWALLOWS AND AMAZONS*, but in a different colour. Their characters' imaginative renaming of the Devon landscape was based on Matthew Arnold's *Sohrab and Rustum*. The novels are as absorbing as Ransome at his best, with liveliness, a fast plot and frequent touches of lyrical descriptive prose, but without the adult writer's greater psychological depth. VW

see also CAMPING AND TRAMPING FICTION; NUDITY IN CHILDREN'S BOOKS; NEGLECTED WORKS

Farjeon, Eleanor 1881–1965 British author who never forgot the child she once was. From the age of six, Farjeon filled small notebooks with stories, and later she followed the advice she offered would-be writers in 1935: 'Don't "write down" to children; don't try to be on their level . . . don't be afraid of words or things you think children can't yet grasp . . . when you write for children be yourself.' A shy bespectacled child, happiest in her author father's dusty bookroom, she learned, like CHARLES LAMB, to read anything that could be called a book. Governess-educated, she was captured by her eldest brother's intense play-acting game, TAR. Although this imaginative play replaced reality for too long, delaying adolescence into her late 20s, she said: 'I owe to TAR . . . that flow of ease that makes writing a delight.'

Her first published work was derivative verse for adults (1908), but during World War I she found her forte in topical verses for the *Daily Herald*, and in rhymes on place-names, first for *Punch*, later published as *Nursery Rhymes for London Town* (1916/17). The word-play retains a period charm, and a 1996 facsimile edition proclaims again: 'Wormwood scrubs the city streets . . . Earls court with knees bent low', while lazy Kensal is warned, 'Get up, Kensal! Kensal . . . rise!' Forjeon's deep, unrequited love for the poet EDWARD THOMAS, killed at Arras in 1917, was a turning-point; now part of an artistic Bohemian circle, her personality and writing developed. From 1920 she shared cottages in Hampstead and Sussex with George Earle, a literature teacher, and the latter became the setting for *Martin Pippin in the Apple Orchard* (1921), which established her reputation.

As EILEEN COLWELL noted, 'that it is in the short story in which she is happiest says much for her skill'. All Farjeon's stories can stand alone, and are included separately in anthologies. Her own favourite, *Elsie Piddock Skips in her Sleep*, is a masterpiece of storytelling (reissued 1997, and in 2000 illustrated by CHARLOTTE VOAKE). Her 'Tom Cobble' was the opening story in the first issue of the new annual children's publication, *JOY STREET* (1923), and – along with WALTER DE LA MARE, ROSE FYLEMAN, HILAIRE BELLOC and Edith Sitwell – she continued to be a regular contributor. She was also a contributor to the *PLAY-HOUR BOOK*, another ANNUAL of the period. The alphabet device pleased Farjeon, and *Alphabets of Magic*, *Town and Country Child* and *Sussex* were among her poetry books in the 1920s. Although her work was always well crafted the conception could be inhibiting, leading to slight, tripping verse. Her poetic output over 50 years – poems reappearing inside different covers – is hard to assess, but she made her own choice in *Silver Sand and Snow* (1951) and *The Children's Bells* (1957). Although her work is still popularly anthologised, no collection now remains in print. Those who pronounce her 'dated' have missed the timeless qualities of her work, the variety of verse forms and ideas, and her down-to-earth and bubbling humour.

A renowned cat-lover, she immortalised her favourite in 'The Golden Cat' – 'Lovely as yellow mackerel skies / In moonlight, or a speckled trout. / Clear as swung honey were his eyes.' And she herself must have been Mrs Malone, welcoming stray sparrow, cat, vixen, donkey and bear, with the refrain: 'There's room for another one.' One of her best poems, 'It Was Long Ago', opens with the words 'I'll tell you, shall I, something I remember', and a childhood memory, rich in taste, smell and sight unfolds, ending: 'It won't mean much to you, it does to me, / Then I grew up, you see.' Farjeon believed that 'childhood is one of the states of eternity'.

Some highly successful writing was produced in collaboration with her brother, the drama critic Herbert. They wrote stage musicals, among them *The Glass Slipper* (1944), and the witty verses *Kings and Queens*. Official recognition came in the 1950s, when her own compilation, *THE LITTLE BOOKROOM* (1955), won the CARNEGIE MEDAL and the HANS CHRISTIAN ANDERSEN AWARD. These 27 original stories set in places as diverse as Egypt, Connemara, Paradise, and a Fairyland boasting tramps and detectives, though unobtainable for many years, justify EDWARD ARDIZZONE's description of Farjeon as the 'Perfect Storyteller'. For Ardizzone, her favourite illustrator, her work had ageless appeal.

Children still recite 'Cats Sleep Anywhere' and sing 'Morning has Broken', and, if she has slipped from her exalted position of the 1940s and 50s, there have been signs of revival. She is widely translated and, in Japan especially, revered. She completed her final work, a moving introduction to *The Green Roads* (1965), her selection of Edward Thomas's poems for young readers, the day before her 84th birthday. The Children's Book Circle give the Eleanor Farjeon Award annually for Distinguished Services to Children's Literature. AHa

see also *MARTIN PIPPIN IN THE APPLE ORCHARD*

Farmer Giles of Ham see J. R. R. TOLKIEN

Farmer, Penelope 1939– British author mostly of FANTASY stories. Farmer's best-known work, *Charlotte Sometimes* (1969), describes the meeting of one girl with another born in a different time. Like many of Farmer's works, it draws upon her experience as an identical twin – someone who is both separate from the other but at other times almost the same person. *A Castle of Bone* (1972) also describes time-changes, this time when a boy finds out more about himself by travelling to the past. *Penelope* (1994) is a rich story with a strong historical dimension. An elegant stylist with a distinctively individual voice, Farmer also writes for adults. NT

Farrar, F.W. see *THE FIFTH FORM AT ST DOMINIC'S*; see also GAY AND LESBIAN LITERATURE; SCHOOL STORIES

***Farthing Wood* series** see *THE ANIMALS OF FARTHING WOOD* SERIES

Fat Man, The (1994) Controversial New Zealand children's novel by MAURICE GEE which unflinchingly confronts bullying. During the Depression, a warped adult returns home to wreak revenge on those who bullied him in childhood, especially Colin's parents. He embroils Colin and Verna in his horrible convoluted games. Compellingly told from Colin's perspective, the story balances staccato and parenthetically complex sentences with death images sustaining the dark mood. A sudden conclusion sees a type of natural justice done. The novel won the 1995 ESTHER GLEN MEDAL and the Junior Fiction and Supreme Book of the Year Awards, provoking debate over its suitability for juniors. DAH

Fatchen, Max 1920– Engrossing Australian storyteller, who has an eye and ear for detail, honed by his career as a journalist. Evocation of landscape, characterisation and historical adventuring make Fatchen's novels highly filmic; his novel *The River Kings* (1966) became a telemovie. The effects of landscape are explored in *The Spirit Wind* (1973), a tale of square rigger days set in South Australia's last windjammer port. His verse collections, such as *Wry Rhymes for Troublesome Times* (1983) and *Tea for Three* (1994), the latter with COLIN THIELE, indicate his characteristic irreverence. Fatchen received an Order of Australia in 1980. HE

Father Christmas (1973) PICTUREBOOK by RAYMOND BRIGGS. Though not strictly a wordless picturebook there is little conveyed through the speech bubbles other than the character's irascibility and his fondness for food, comfort and his animals. It is the pictures that build the narrative and move it forward. These depict, in hard-edged rectangular frames, Father Christmas's preparations, his delivery of gifts, and his grateful return home to a hot bath and Christmas dinner. Much of the book's appeal lies in its subversion of the stereotype of a wholly benign Father Christmas – Briggs's character frowns a great deal, curses the weather and bemoans having to climb down chimneys and up stairs. The book also successfully integrates MYTH and FANTASY with a down-to-earth, working-class realism. Father Christmas lives in an unconverted terraced house with an outside toilet and an old-fashioned stove. Without the beard he could easily pass for a stoical elderly postman longing for retirement (Briggs's milkman father was a model). *Father Christmas* won for Briggs a second KATE GREENAWAY MEDAL and was followed by the sequels, *Father Christmas Goes on Holiday* (1975) and *Father Christmas Having a Wonderful Time* (1993). DL

Fatima, Pam Nigerian author of books for young children. Her best-known work is *Amina the Milkmaid* (1988), a PICTUREBOOK colourfully illustrated by K. Afori Pani. It tells the story of a young girl kidnapped into slavery, whose goodness wins her favour and freedom. VD

Faulknor, Clifford 1913–98 Canadian author of several books about Native American tribes in western Canada, both in historical and contemporary settings. Sympathetic to the Native American plight without being sentimental, Faulknor won several awards, including the Vicky Metcalf Award in 1979 for his work as a whole. *The White Calf* (1965), the first of a trilogy of books about Eagle Child, the son of a Blackfoot chief, attracted particular notice; it not only received the Little, Brown Award for Children's Books but also became a TELEVISION musical and was translated into Russian. Faulknor's novels make use of

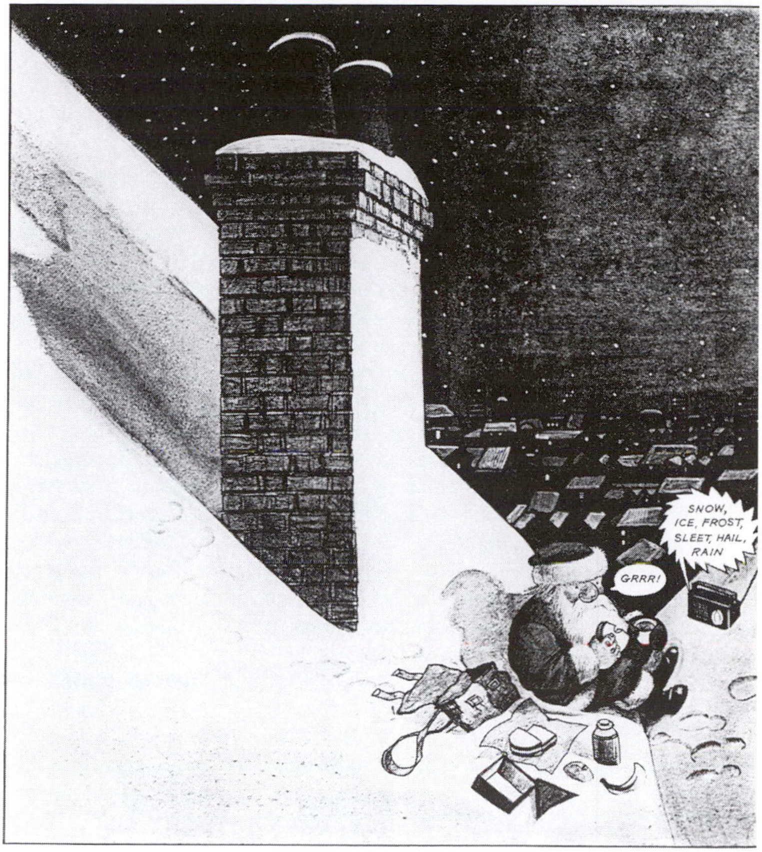

Illustration from *Father Christmas* by RAYMOND BRIGGS.

more carefully researched historical detail than many other novels about Native Americans authored by non-Natives; unfortunately, this effort is too often lost in his uncomfortably stilted dialogue. KS

Faville, Barry 1939– New Zealand writer of teen novels. In *The Keeper* (1986), Faville investigates mass hysteria, violence and lasting love through the travails of survivors of nuclear and volcanic disasters. The plot is tense, the resolutions logical if somewhat optimistic, but the characters are stereotypical rather than emotionally developed. However, *The Return* (1987) shows an increasing richness of characterisation. This novel is a gentle mix of SCIENCE FICTION and domesticity incorporating an exploration of intergenerational friendship. In *Stanley's Aquarium* (1989), Faville shows further psychological insight and his emotionally generous narrator displays a wide-ranging intellectual life. Faville writes faultless prose and memorable dialogue. MJH

Federation of Children's Book Groups see AWARDS AND MEDALS; see also *CAROUSEL*; CHILDREN'S BOOK AWARD (appendix)

Feelings, Muriel (Grey) 1938– American author of children's PICTUREBOOKS. Feelings was born in Philadelphia, Pennsylvania, and studied at the Philadelphia Museum School of Art. In the 1960s she travelled to Uganda, where she taught art in a boys' secondary school. Her interest in and respect for East African culture led to picturebooks meant to teach black children about their heritage: *Zamani Goes to Market* (1970), *Moja Means One: Swahili Counting Book* (1971) and *Jambo Means Hello: Swahili Alphabet Book* (1974). These highly regarded books, which present a view of East Africa that is informed and admiring, but never cloying, were illustrated by TOM FEELINGS, who was then the author's husband. CAB

see also ALPHABET BOOKS; COUNTING BOOKS

Feelings, Tom 1933– Brooklyn-born writer and illustrator of over 20 books, including seven for children. First as a comic strip illustrator and later as a writer and illustrator, Feelings has made it a central concern of his work to discover the depth and significance of African American history and communicate it to his audience. Feelings has received the CALDECOTT AWARD twice as a children's book illustrator. He first illustrated *To Be A Slave* (1968) and *Black Folk Tales* (1969), written by JULIUS LESTER. With his wife, MURIEL FEELINGS, he produced *Moja Means One: Swahili Counting Book* (1971) and *Jambo Means Hello: Swahili Alphabet Book* (1974). He collaborated with Maya Angelou on *Now Sheba Sings the Song* (1987) and he received his second CORETTA SCOTT KING AWARD for *Soul Looks Back in Wonder* (1993). Feelings's most recent work, *Middle Passage: White Ships, Black Cargo* (1995), is a wordless PICTUREBOOK of 60 black-and-white ILLUSTRATIONS. In it, Feelings documents the suffering and tragedy experienced by the millions of people taken from Africa and sold as slaves in the West Indies and the Americas. Feelings's success as an artist comes from his ability to depict both the terror and the beauty of the African-American experience. JZo

see also AFRICAN AMERICAN LITERATURE

Felix, Monique 1950– Swiss creator of a range of small, intriguing, metafictive wordless PICTUREBOOKS. Best known are *A Story of a Little Mouse Trapped in a Book* (1981), republished as *The Plane*, and a second *Little Mouse* story republished as *The Boat* (1983). *Tuba Lessons* (1997) plays with a musical theme. AR

Felstead, Cathy see *A CARIBBEAN DOZEN*

***Feluda* series** (1961–1992) Thirty-five stories by SATYAJIT RAY, originally written in Bengali. Subsequently translated ably by Gopa Majumdar over a number of years, this body of DETECTIVE FICTION has proved the most popular of Ray's works, centring around Feluda, a quiet, keenly observant, ambidextrous man of many talents and interests. He travels extensively, each of his adventures being set in a new land, information about which is ingeniously and creatively woven into the simple plot. Cinematically captured in words, the setting is then peopled by local characters such as the sinister boatman from Benares. Yet the most endearing quality of this extremely intelligent man is the generosity of spirit exhibited in his willingness to share his knowledge, and his gentle, protective affection for the teenage narrator. The stories are rich with the humour born of Feluda's irrepressible wit and his interaction with naive, gullible Lalmohan Babu, a writer of cheap thrillers. MBh

Fenian Cycle, The see IRISH MYTHOLOGY AND FOLKLORE; SCOTTISH FOLKTALES

Fenn, Lady Eleanor [née Frere] 1743–1813 Popular and influential British author of many children's books. She wrote entertainingly and with affection, endeavouring to amuse her readers as well as to instruct. She used the pseudonyms 'Mrs Teachwell', 'Mrs Lovechild' and 'Solomon Lovechild'. Her 'reading' book *Cobwebs to Catch Flies* (c. 1783) contained gentle advice and charming woodcuts, and *The Rational Dame, or, Hints towards supplying prattle for children* (c. 1790) used simple language and good common sense. She also wrote *The Fairy Spectator* (1789) and several books for girls. Although she had no children of her own She started Sunday schools near her Norfolk home, and with her publisher JOHN MARSHALL devised original ways to educate children. SD

Ferguson, Ruby see *JILL* SERIES; PONY STORIES

Fib and Other Stories; The (1975) Stories based on the early experiences of British author/scriptwriter GEORGE LAYTON, which narrate with wry humour and in direct vernacular dialogue the hardships and small triumphs of a northern childhood and adolescence. Home and school issues are perceptively revealed through comic and poignant situations. The stories are excellent for reading aloud and are particularly popular with teachers in the middle years of schooling. CMN

Field, Eugene 1850–95 American journalist and poet recognised as the 'poet of childhood'. He was born in St Louis, Missouri, and died in Chicago, Illinois. Though he attended several colleges and a university, he never graduated. He took a job as a journalist for newspapers in Missouri and Colorado and wrote the column 'Sharps and Flats' for the *Chicago Morning News* (renamed *Chicago Record* in 1890) from 1883 to 1895. He loved children and, after marrying Julia Sutherland Comstock in 1873, had eight children of his own. He is best known for his volumes of poetry, most notably those for children. Many have been reprinted or reissued since first appearing in the late 19th century. Some of his poems, such as 'Wynken, Blynken, and Nod' from *Wynken, Blinken, and Nod, and Other Child Verses* (1925), have been illustrated by modern artists such as BARBARA COONEY. His children's poetry has a quick cadence, resolving some action in two or four lines. An example from *The Sugar Plum Tree and Other Verses* (1930) shows his childlike appeal: 'The stock was of pine and the barrel of tin / The 'bang' it came out where the bullet went in'. LAW

Field, Rachel (Lyman) 1894–1942 American author of plays, poetry and HISTORICAL FICTION. Already a brilliant contributor to the *ST NICHOLAS* League in her teens, Field was one of America's most respected children's writers by the early 1930s. Many of the poems from *The Pointed People* (1924) and *Taxis and Toadstools* (1926) – on subjects ranging from elves to skyscrapers – are still anthologised. Her Newbery winner *HITTY* (1929), and her historical novels for older girls, *Calico*

Bush (1931) and *Hepatica Hawks* (1932), are notable for their strong female characterisations, finely observed detail and New England flavour. SR

Fielding, Sarah 1710–1768 British novelist and author of *The Governess, or Little Female Academy* (1749), in which Mrs Teachum's nine lively, quarrelsome pupils relate their faults and respond to FAIRY TALES and FABLES recounted for their 'Entertainment and Instruction'. For an account of the book's long popularity and influence, see the edition by Jill E. Grey (1968). JFB

Fienberg, Anna 1956– British-born Australian writer of PICTUREBOOKS and novels, whose very popular, action-packed stories combine humour, magic and FANTASY with strong, resourceful child characters in exciting and believable adventures. *Wiggy and Boa* (1988) and its sequel, *Dead Sailors Don't Bite* (1996), with their swashbuckling nautical dialogue, follow the adventures of incorrigible Boa(dicea), and her serious schoolfriend Ludwig (Wiggy) as they tame evil but slow-witted pirates invoked from the past. Characters and motifs in *The Magnificent Nose and Other Marvels* (1991), winner of the 1992 CHILDREN'S BOOK COUNCIL OF AUSTRALIA BOOK OF THE YEAR AWARD in the Younger Readers category, come in imaginative new guises based on folktale traditions. Lindylou, for example, is born with a golden hammer and golden nail, and her first word is 'wood'; and Hector in *The Hottest Boy Who Ever Lived* (1993) manages to put his excessive heat to practical use – instant hot water, fried eggs, and bringing a frozen baby back to life. Fienberg enters into a child's STORYTELLING world with zest in *Tashi* (1995), *Tashi and the Giants* (1995) and *Tashi and the Ghosts* (1997), co-authored with her mother, Barbara. A more dramatic story is told in the novel *Power to Burn* (1995), which manages to combine successfully fantasy and humour with mystery and adventure. JAP

The Fifth Form at St Dominic's; The (1887) Boys' public-school story by TALBOT BAINES REED, featuring not only the adventures of the hero, Oliver Greenfield, and his friends in the Fifth, but also those of his younger brother in the Fourth Junior. The unwary reader may misconceive it as only one of thousands of cloned SCHOOL STORIES in its depiction of stereotypical events, but it was an innovation in its day, freeing school fiction from the moralising of F. W. Farrar and THOMAS HUGHES, outclassing subsequent imitations and remaining an enjoyable read with lively dialogue and sympathetic characters. JMM

Figgie Hobbin (1970) Poems by British poet CHARLES CAUSLEY. Such is the distinction of Causley's first collection for children that it was reissued 20 years later with some extra poems, illustrated by GERALD ROSE. It launched Causley to a central place in children's poetry with its mesmerising BALLADS, narratives of extraordinary characters, playfulness, folklore and social comment – all delivered in verse that is essentially musical. MCCS

figure In PICTUREBOOKS or ILLUSTRATION the shape or object portrayed as distinct from the (back)ground against which it is set. The terms *figure* and *ground* go together, and can be relative and changing within the same picture. For example, a depicted character may be framed by a door which acts as its background, but the depicted character and door together can be seen as the figure against the background of a wall into which the door is set. JD

see also FRAME

Film Fun see ANNUALS; COMICS, PERIODICALS AND MAGAZINES

film see ANIMATED CARTOONS

Fine, Anne 1947– One of Britain's most distinctive literary voices, whose subject, particularly in her novels for young adults, is the politics of family and school. In an award-winning body of work that spans all ages, from PICTUREBOOK to adult novel, Fine's underlying interests are in the dark side of life, moral conflicts and what happens when personal and political responsibilities meet, merge and clash. Her singularity lies in the sparkling comic invention – sometimes black, sometimes playful – and the acute accuracy and emotional truth with which she invests these matters.

Born in Leicester, Fine read History and Politics at the University of Warwick, taught, worked for a famine relief charity, married and moved to America before returning to Edinburgh, where she wrote her first novel, *The Summer House Loon*, in 1978. It is a domestic comedy concerning a teenager's puzzled perceptions of the romantic entanglements of her adult friends. While family tensions underpin her early novels, the family as battleground emerged in *The Granny Project* (1983), in which four children decide to fight their parents' decision to put their ageing, demanding grandmother into care. Family warfare fuels *MADAME DOUBTFIRE* (1987), *GOGGLE-EYES* (1989) and *The Book of the Banshee* (1991). Fine's characters are noisily eccentric, bright and articulate; their outward lack of conventionality takes many forms, and they often remain stubbornly untamed yet capable of growth. Fine broadens her social canvas with fatherless, semi-delinquent, unmotivated Simon Martin in *Flour Babies* (1992) – whose awareness about self and his absent parent springs from a science project on parenting which involves caring for flour sacks as if they were babies – and disturbed, dangerous Tulip in *The Tulip Touch* (1996) – a study of 'evil' explored through the friendship between Tulip, a victim turned victimiser, and outsider Natalie. The rich but serious black humour and open endings of her earlier work are notably absent in her tale of Tulip, arsonist and potential murderer. In *Bad Dreams* (2000) – a novel about the difficulties of possessing second sight – Fine returns to her own childhood and the importance to her of books and reading.

A moralist, Fine demonstrates this characteristic more overtly in her fiction for younger readers. From the hilarious reversal of parent/child roles in *Crummy, Mummy and Me* (1988), and of gender roles in the feminist *BILL'S NEW FROCK* (1989), to bullying in *The Angel of Nitshill Road* (1991) and animal rights in *The Chicken Gave it to Me* (1992), Fine uses humour to help her readers read the world afresh. This characteristic is also much in evidence in her retelling of *The Twelve Dancing Princesses* for Scholastic's series of FAIRY TALES (1998). EMH

Finetta the Cinder-Girl see *CINDERELLA*

Finn Family Moomintroll see *MOOMIN* SERIES

Fir Tree, The see HANS CHRISTIAN ANDERSEN; see also NANCY EKHOLM BURKERT

Fire and Hemlock (1985) A complex work by the British author DIANA WYNNE JONES, which uses the TAM LIN and Thomas the Rhymer legends as its basic structure. However, it reworks them in modern idiom and weaves them into the narrative of Polly's broken home to produce a dense work that functions on many levels. It is, apart from anything else, a book about growing up, and the relationship between Polly and Thomas Lynn is the most fascinating part of the book, as he shifts from his role as surrogate parent, friend and co-hero in the epic they compose together, to lover at the end. SA

Firebird, The see MUSIC AND STORY; see also SELINA HASTINGS

Fireweed (1969) Acclaimed novel by JILL PATON WALSH, set in the London Blitz of 1940 and telling the story of two adolescents who meet after evading attempts to evacuate them. The excitement of freedom grows as they survive together and share the feeling of solidarity with others in the city, but the dangers of war are always present. Bill and Julie set up house with a lost child in the basement of a bombed house, but this FANTASY family life is not meant to be; Bill is firmly shut out from Julie's life when she returns to her family. The telling of his story many years later arises from his feelings of hurt and betrayal. EA

see also WAR STORIES

Firmin, Peter see OLIVER POSTGATE AND PETER FIRMIN; see also *NOGGIN THE NOG* SERIES

Firth, Barbara 1928– British illustrator who came to the ILLUSTRATION of children's books late in life after a career creating sewing and knitting patterns. Her work with the PICTUREBOOK text-writer MARTIN WADDELL is well known, but she has several other titles to her name, including *'Quack!' said the billy-goat* (CHARLES CAUSLEY, 1997), *The Grumpalump* (Sarah Hayes, 1991) and *A Song For Little Toad* (Vivien French, 1995). She will be remembered, however, for the expressive work in Waddell's *The Park in the Dark* (1989) and his *Little Bear* books, the first of which – *Can't You Sleep Little Bear?* (1988) – won the KATE GREENAWAY and SMARTIES awards and was described by a reviewer (Molly Keane in *The Sunday Times*) as 'the most perfect children's book ever written or illustrated'. Fine line drawing, delicate watercolour, sensitive characterisation in the bears and the toys, great drama in the composition, and always the slight suggestion of peril in the dark depths of a cave or in an urban park or lonely snow-filled forest, make these books favourites with their readers and worthy of their awards. JAG

Fisher, Aileen (Lucia) 1906– American poet, author and playwright whose verse, from *The Coffee-Pot* (1933) onwards, has dealt mainly with childhood remembrances and nature. Fisher has published over 100 works in collaboration with well-known illustrators, including single-poem PICTUREBOOKS such as *Listen, Rabbit* (1964) and *In the Middle of the Night* (1965). PDS

Fisher, Catherine Welsh novelist and poet who has in recent years established herself as a major contemporary writer of FANTASY. She is fascinated by myths (see CLASSICAL MYTHOLOGY) and folklore, by what she calls the 'dangerous territories of the imagination'. She has written a number of single novels, including *The Candle Man* (1994) – a haunting fantasy set on the Gwent Levels, winner of the *Tir Na n'Og* award – and *The Lammas Field* (1999) – a compelling story of a boy's obsession with music and possession by fairy-craft.

However, Catherine Fisher is best known for two fantasy sequences, each consisting of three novels to date. In the *Snow-Walker* sequence (*The Snow-Walker's Son*, 1993; *The Empty Hand*, 1995; *The Soul Thieves*, 1996), the setting, language and mythology have a bleak and highly charged Norse quality. The *Book of the Crow* sequence (*The Relic Master*, 1998; *The Interrex*, 1999; *Flain's Coronet*, 2000), though resembling SCIENCE FICTION in its narrative basis, is experienced more as a fantasy set on a different planet with seven moons, its own mythology, and its own struggles between good and evil. A particularly appealing feature are the Sekoi, tall, intelligent catlike creatures. Fisher is an inventive and highly skilled storyteller and an unusually gifted wordsmith: her language is rich and evocative, capable of representing moments of horror or great beauty with rare precision. VW

Fisher, Dorothy (Frances) Canfield 1879–1958 Influential American novelist who incorporated her interest in childhood and child-rearing practice into her writing for adults as well as for children. In 1912 Fisher visited Marie Montessori's school in Rome. Impressed by the happy self-reliance of the children, she introduced Montessori principles to American parents in the much-discussed *A Montessori Mother* (1912) and *Mothers and Children* (1914); several of her best-selling novels, including *The Bent Twig* (1915) and *The Home-Maker* (1924), and her short story collection *Fables for Parents* (1937), expressed these convictions in fictional form. Her first children's book, *Understood Betsy* (1917), was also Montessori-inspired; Betsy, a timid, sickly child, grows into a model of health, happiness, and self-reliance on her cousins' Vermont farm. Despite its didacticism, *Betsy*'s theme and heroine still appeal to young readers. More subtly Montessorian were the highly original *Made-to-Order Stories* (1925), in which Jimmy chooses the collections of unrelated objects around which his obliging mother spins unlikely tales. Fisher was among the first writers to contribute to Random House's *Landmark Books*, with *Paul Revere and the Minute Men* (1950) and *Our Independence and the Constitution* (1950). SR

Fisher, Leonard Everett 1924– American author and illustrator who once described himself as 'the best-known unknown in children's books'. With countless books, both fiction and non-fiction, to his credit, he is one of today's most prolific contributors to children's literature. Much of his work concentrates on historical themes and requires specialised research. He is best known for his scratch-board ILLUSTRATIONS, which form an integral part of two of his series: *Colonial Americans* (1964–76) and *19th-Century America* (1979–83). Four books on the history of 13 different alphabets, number systems, symbols and calendars from around the world are also illustrated with scratch-board. He turned to acrylics for his books on famous historical places, including *The Great Wall of China* (1986), *The Alamo* (1987) and *The Wailing Wall* (1989). A more recent title is a BIOGRAPHY, *Alexander Graham Bell* (1999). He collaborated with the poet, MYRA COHN LIVINGSTON, to produce seven outstanding books of poetry and paintings, for example *A Circle of Seasons* (1982) and *Space Songs* (1988). PDS

Fisher, Margery 1913–92 British critic and teacher, married to the naturalist James Fisher, and mother of six children. Her passion for children and their reading material coincided with the renaissance of excellence in children's literature after World War II. Her review columns in *Good Housekeeping* and *The Sunday Times* prompted the Brockhampton Press to commission longer works from Fisher. *Intent upon Reading* (1961), an appraisal of the many genres of children's fiction, was the result; this was followed by *Matters of Fact* (1972), a highly critical look at information books. In 1986 *The Bright Face of Danger* appeared, an exploration of the ADVENTURE STORY; and the same year saw Fisher's forthright analysis of classic fiction in *Classics for Children and Young People*. *Who's Who in Children's Books* (1976), a monumental 'treasury of the familiar characters of childhood', has all the Fisher hallmarks: energy, liveliness, acuity and the will-power to see a formidable task through. Her books are milestones in the appreciation of children's literature. It is almost impossible to believe that from 1962 until the last year of her life Fisher was simultaneously writing books and publishing her review magazine, *GROWING POINT*. EM

Fisher, Suzanne Staples see *DAUGHTERS OF THE WIND*

Fisherman and the Theefyspray, The (1994) Written by PAUL JENNINGS and illustrated by JANE TANNER, this poignant, environmentally concerned and visually striking Australian PICTUREBOOK tells of the last two 'theefysprays' (an imaginary fish species) in the ocean – a mother and child – and a fisherman who, catching the baby fish, chooses to return it to the sea. NLR

Fisk, Nicholas [David Higginbottom] 1923– British novelist, best known for stories only obliquely categorised as SCIENCE FICTION. After RAF war service and a career as musician, journalist and publisher, Fisk started writing in the 1960s. The years 1939 to 1941, up to his enlistment, are chronicled in the autobiographical *Pig Ignorant* (1992). This period, important to him, is evoked in his masterpiece, *A Rag, A Bone and a Hank of Hair* (1980), a moving novel rehearsing many pervasive themes: the Blitz of the 'reborn' children is contrasted with Brin's anodyne, dying, future world. Children are more far-sighted than corrupted adults; technology has almost limitless, untrustworthy power; human values survive through adversity, which is a condition of freedom.

The ever-popular *Grinny* (1974) and its sequel *You Remember Me* (1987) revitalise the science-fiction theme of the high-technology extra-terrestrial threat: Tim and Beth's youthful insight enables them alone to understand alien wiles behind, first Grinny, then Lisa Treadgold and 'The Rollers', which unnervingly reflect contemporary human tendencies. *Trillions* (1973), *Antigrav* (1978), *Monster Maker* (1979, subsequently filmed), *The Worm Charmers* (1989) and the short-story collection *Sweets From a Stranger* (1982) are a few examples from this ingenious, original and immensely readable novelist's prolific output. DCH

Fitch Perkins, Lucy see TWINS SERIES

Fitzgerald, John D(ennis) 1906/7?–88 American author who wrote *The Great Brain* (1967) and six other titles in the same series, all illustrated by MERCER MAYER. Partly autobiographical, the books centre upon the three brothers in the Fitzgerald family living in Southern Utah at the end of the 19th century. The eldest, Tom, a conniver and schemer, is the 'Great Brain', always looking to turn a profit. His brother, 'JD', the narrator, is Tom's accomplice and often his victim. Readership has remained strong for middle-grade children. PDS

Fitzhugh, Louise 1928–74 An American writer of children's fiction best remembered for *HARRIET THE SPY* (1964) and *NOBODY'S FAMILY IS GOING TO CHANGE* (1974). Louise Fitzhugh was born into a wealthy Tennessee family, but despite this genteel background her childhood was marked by a great deal of strife. Her parents divorced and a fierce custody battle ensued over Louise. Her mother, the social inferior of her father, never stood a chance against the social power of her former husband and his family. Louise was left to be raised mainly by her grandparents, who provided their granddaughter with financial security, but little warmth and affection. In this rarefied atmosphere, Louise was out of place; she hated the racism of the South and felt ill at ease with expressing her lesbianism.

Seeking the freedom that eluded her in Tennessee, Fitzhugh moved away to attend college. Southern College in Florida failed to offer her the environment she desired; therefore, she enrolled in Bard College and, later, the School of Education at New York University. In New York City, she discovered the freedom for which she hungered. In the bohemian atmosphere of Greenwich Village, Fitzhugh found support and encouragement to become both an author and an artist. She was successful in both fields.

Her career as a writer of children's books began with *Suzuki Bean* (1961), a PICTUREBOOK that she co-authored with Sandra Scoppettone. But it was only with the publication of her first full-length novel, *Harriet the Spy*, an often cynical portrait of adult society as seen through the eyes of Harriet – a young girl who spies on her neighbours and records her often biting comments about their actions – that she gained the national and international fame that helped establish her as an important voice in children's literature of the late 1960s. Fitzhugh's second novel, *The Long Secret* (1965), was also popular with children, but most critics viewed it as less successful than *Harriet the Spy*.

After her tremendous early success, Fitzhugh seemed poised to become a major contributor to children's literature, but her productivity was limited, perhaps because her father died in 1965, leaving her an heiress to his large estate. She did publish *Bang, Bang, You're Dead* (1969), another picturebook which she co-wrote with Scoppettone. Slightly later Fitzhugh wrote another novel, *Nobody's Family Is Going to Change*, a work that marked the tragic end of her short career, as she died of an aneurysm in 1974. After her death, a few pieces of Fitzhugh's work were published, including the novel *Sport* (1979) and the picturebooks *I Am Three* (1982), *I Am Four* (1982) and *I Am Five* (1978). These posthumous works, however, failed to show the same power as *Harriet the Spy*. But for *Harriet the Spy* and *Nobody's Family Is Going to Change* alone Fitzhugh would deserve an important place in the history of children's literature. SAI

Fitzpatrick, Marie-Louise Irish author and illustrator whose first book was *An Chanáil* (1988), an Irish-language PICTUREBOOK. *The Sleeping Giant* (1991) is a modern story based on a legend in which a giant-shaped island off the Kerry coast comes to life. *The Long March* (1998) is a picturebook for older readers, in which the march of the Choctaw tribe across the plains of America is illustrated by black-and-white pencil drawings. This is the most powerful of Fitzpatrick's books to date. With *Izzy and Skunk* (2000) she returns to the watercolours of her earlier work. VC

FitzPatrick, Percy see *JOCK OF THE BUSHVELDT*

***Five Children and It* series** see *PSAMMEAD* SERIES; see also FANTASY; see also ILLUSTRATION IN CHILDREN'S BOOKS

***Five Little Peppers* series** (1881–1916) Twelve FAMILY STORIES by the American author Margaret Sidney [Harriet M. Lothrop] (1844–1924). The Pepper family first appeared in short stories for *Wide Awake* magazine in 1878. *The Five Little Peppers and How They Grew* (1881) showed the fatherless family living in their little brown house in the country. The mission of the five children is to help their hard-working mother, who struggles to feed, clothe and educate her family.

The Peppers' mutual affection and enjoyment of life impress a wealthy boy and his father, who persuade the Peppers to live with them in the city. In the sequels demanded by eager readers, the Peppers live affluently, but idealise the times of poverty they shared in the little brown house. The novels, written for both boys and girls, present episodic stories of the children's adventures at home, school, work and abroad. Maintaining the virtues taught in the little brown house, the boys establish themselves in respectable professions and the girls marry well. Despite the occasional sentimentality of Sidney's stories, the Peppers' close family relationships and triumphs over misfortune have kept *The Five Little Peppers* in print and enjoyed by children for over a century. JLB

Five on a Treasure Island see THE FAMOUS FIVE

Flack, Marjorie 1897–1958 American writer and illustrator of PICTUREBOOKS for young children. Her books integrate design, story and ILLUSTRATION and show a sensitive awareness of the child reader. Flack is best-known for *The Story About Ping* (1933), illustrated by KURT WIESE, an enduring tale of a Chinese duck attempting to avoid punishment. Like all of Flack's work, this story addresses the feelings of young children in lively prose, and adds drama to everyday subjects. Flack also wrote and illustrated a series of books (1933–5) about the scottish terrier Angus, who undergoes many of the tribulations young children do, such as jealousy of a new member of the household. MDK

***Flambards* series** Originally a trilogy comprising *Flambards* (1967), *The Edge of the Cloud* (1969) and *Flambards in Summer* (1969), the series by British writer K.M. Peyton later expanded to include a fourth book; *Flambards Divided*, which was published 12 years after the trilogy had supposedly ended, is the least satisfying of the novels. The works centre around the figure of Christina Parsons, an orphan who comes to stay with her uncle and cousins, Mark and Will, at their home, Flambards; the setting at the start of the series is Essex in the period before World War I. The first three novels form a tight structural unit; together, they depict the transition between cultures as the world of the landed gentry, represented by the activities of hunting and riding, yields to the age of the machine, the motorcar and aeroplane. The relative serenity of the traditional ways of life is disrupted with the coming of war: male dominion succumbs to female rule, the 'aristocratic' structure of inheritance gives place to a new 'bourgeois' system based on finance. This last is seen in *Flambards in Summer* when Mark, who as Uncle Russell's heir should own Flambards, sells the place to Christina and marries a girl who 'owns a house – a hotel – in Northamptonshire' from which she intends to make a living after the war. The movement from 'house' to 'hotel' is a telling one.

Flambards begins by establishing the terms of the old patriarchal order; Uncle Russell is presented as a tyrant whose thinking belongs to the Middle Ages: his plan is to wed Christina and her money to Mark, who will inherit Flambards. But Christina and Will, the younger son, rebel against this. Hurt in a hunting accident, Will deliberately works to keep the leg maimed and thereby prevent his being able to ride again, symbolically refusing to participate in the value system represented by his family. Finally, the two elope in a motorcar while Mark chases them on his horse Woodpigeon.

The Edge of the Cloud, which won the CARNEGIE MEDAL, takes place away from Flambards and is concerned with the coming new order. Will is engaged in his flying, and Christina embarks on a very different kind of life where she has to earn a living and live away from home. In *Flambards in Summer*, after Will has been shot down in his aeroplane, Christina falls in love with Dick, the erstwhile stableboy, who has returned to Flambards. The trilogy thus ends by affirming the beginning of a new social order: marriage is countenanced between the representatives of different classes, something which would have been socially impossible under the old dispensation. However, though the values of that older order are presented as questionable, one may sense a residual sense of lament for that which was gracious and which has passed away. The series was adapted for TELEVISION by Yorkshire Television. SA

Flanagan, Joan 1931– Australian writer of bizarre domestic and social comedies for children. In *The Dingbat Spies* (1984) toasters talk and computers spew out impossible information, and in *Sister* (1988) an imaginary playmate materialises to cause mayhem in a contemporary Australian household. Flanagan's zany humour led her to quasi SCIENCE FICTION in *The Squealies* (1987) and *Musclenut and Brainbox* (1989), both of which ironically and playfully mock serious speculation about extra-terrestrial life. But Flanagan also brings tenderness and romance to her FANTASIES *Rose Terrace* (1986) and *The Ghost in the Gazebo* (1987), both of which hint at the fascinating possibilities of the power of the unconscious. MSax

flap-books see ROD CAMPBELL; MOVABLE BOOKS; PUBLISHING AND PUBLISHERS

Flash Gordon see COMICS, PERIODICALS AND MAGAZINES

***Flat Stanley* series** (from 1964) CHAPTER BOOKS by Jeff Brown. The first book, *Flat Stanley*, with illustrations by TOMI UNGERER, is deservedly the best known and most popular, having become a modern classic. Stanley's family wakes up one morning to discover that he has been squashed by a bulletin board. His parents take this apparent calamity in their stride and remain firmly concerned with manners and polite behaviour at all times. Later novels follow a formula in which Stanley, no longer flat, discovers other useful talents. These do not have as original an appeal for the audience, but nevertheless make entertaining reading. KA

Flegg, Aubrey 1938– Irish author whose first novel, *Katie's War* (1997), winner of the IBBY Sweden's Peter Pan Prize, addresses the inter-family tension arising during the Irish Civil War. *The Cinnamon Tree* (2000) also deals with conflict, this time in an African country. VC

Fleischman, Paul 1952– American author of more than 20 widely acclaimed books, including distinctive fiction, poetry and PICTUREBOOKS known for their precise, lyrical language. Born in California, Fleischman finished college at the University of New Mexico. He sampled various regions of the United States, many of which become historical and contemporary settings in his books, before circling back to settle in Pacific Grove, California, with his family. Fleischman's works increasingly incorporate participative, provocative and multifaceted experiences for young readers. In earlier works, exemplified by the Newbery Honour Book *Graven Images* (1982), Fleischman establishes an abiding standard for tantalising tales. With his poems for two voices, *I Am A Phoenix* (1985) and NEWBERY MEDAL winner *Joyful Noise* (1988), he makes communal reading essential to the whirring stories of winged creatures. A slim but powerful historical novel, *Bull Run* (1993), and the contemporary community saga *Seedfolks* (1997), each told from more than a dozen carefully orchestrated perspectives, strongly suggest readers' theatre. Blending joy and sorrow, Fleischman examines human nature across centuries in *Dateline: Troy* (1996); within family history in *The Borning Room* (1991); through a teenager's personal trauma in *Whirligig* (1998); and, in *Weslandia* (1999), through the rich imaginative life of a rejected boy who creates an alternative civilisation in his garden. (*Weslandia* was shortlisted for the 1999 KATE GREENAWAY AWARD for Kevin Hawkes's illustrations.) Paul and SID FLEISCHMAN, admirers of one another, are the only father-and-son couple who have both won Newbery awards. ETD

Fleischman, Sid 1920– American writer of children's books, professional magician and screenwriter. Sid Fleischman was born in Brooklyn, New York, but has lived most of his life in Southern California. He became a professional magician while still a teenager. After serving in the Naval Reserve during World War II, Fleischman worked as a reporter, a novelist and a screenwriter. *Mr. Mysterious and Company* (1962), Fleischman's first children's book, was written primarily for his own children, but critical acclaim ushered in a new career. Today he has more than 35 children's books to his name, including the popular *McBroom* series, which recounts the TALL TALES of an Iowa farmer. The sleight-of-hand that Fleischman practised in his magic is also a trademark of his fiction. His abundant use of metaphor, colourful expressions and humour have delighted children for three decades. Among numerous other awards and honours, *Humbug Mountain* (1979) received the BOSTON GLOBE-HORN BOOK AWARD FOR FICTION, and *The Whipping Boy* (1987) was awarded the NEWBERY MEDAL. Fleischman's life is vividly portrayed in his AUTOBIOGRAPHY, *The Abracadabra Kid* (1996). His son, PAUL FLEISCHMAN, is also a children's writer and Newbery Medal recipient for *Joyful Noise*. EB

Fleming, Ian see *CHITTY CHITTY BANG BANG*; see also HAIKU; ADULT FICTION

Fletcher, Claire Illustrator born in Leicester, England, and a Royal College of Art graduate. Fletcher won the MOTHER GOOSE AWARD with *The Seashell Song* (Susie Jenkin-Pearce, 1993). Unusually for a children's book illustrator, she works in acrylic paint applied thickly and with visible brush strokes, thereby achieving an enhanced sense of movement and reality. *The Snow Angel* and *The Wind Garden* (Angela McAllister, 1993, 1994) have followed in the same style. The ebullience of the rich pictures suits the wild story lines. JAG

Flock of Words, A (1969) Collection of poetry edited by David Mackay. It grew out of an enthusiast's reaction against what he called 'whimsical ineffectual school books'. In the tradition of *COME HITHER*, *THE POET'S TONGUE*, and more recently, *THE RATTLE BAG*, it widens the definition of poetry for children. The book is so arranged that one poem strikes sparks off those around it. Strong on verse from other cultures, innovative, creative and knowledgeable, Mackay set a high standard for later anthologists, though his inclusivity does not extend to women poets. FRBS

***Flower Fairy* series** (from 1923) Collections of verse, written and illustrated by Cicely Mary Barker (1895–1973). The series began in the 1920s with *Flower Fairies of the Spring*. After Barker ran out of seasons (*Flower Fairies of the Winter* being posthumously published in 1985), the series moved on to distinguish between wild and cultivated plants (*Garden* and *Wayside*). The verse deals with botanical matters and plant lore and may be described as pedestrian, but the illustrations – detailed and imaginative personifications of the flowers romantically rendered – are of more merit and have ensured the books' continuing popularity, especially with adult collectors. SA

Folkard, Charles (James) 1878–1963 British writer and illustrator. Folkard left an apprenticeship with a firm of designers to become a conjuror, and discovered his ability to draw while designing programmes for his shows. He studied at various institutions, including St John's Wood School of Art and Goldsmiths' College, and then turned to ILLUSTRATION, while also writing children's plays and PANTOMIMES. He developed under the inevitable influence of ARTHUR RACKHAM and, before World War I, produced a number of true GIFT BOOKS for A. & C. Black, including GRIMMS' *FAIRY TALES* (1911) and AESOP'S *FABLES* (1912). Yet he immediately established his own wide range, and could move easily beyond FANTASY to naturalism, as in *THE SWISS FAMILY ROBINSON* (1910). In 1915, as staff artist on the *Daily Mail*, he invented *TEDDY TAIL*, the first ever British newspaper strip, which encouraged the rival creation of *RUPERT BEAR* in the *Daily Express*. In charting the comical adventures of a mouse, the strip confirmed the talent for humour that Folkard had already revealed in illustrations and would extend in later books, usually published by J.M. Dent. Working confidently in both black-and-white and colour, he compensated for any loss of subtlety by appealing directly to children through visual clarity and down-to-earth humanity. DW

folktales and legends Stories of great antiquity; both originate in oral stories, but whereas folktales were probably first told by ordinary working people, often women, legends were probably first told by people whose job it was to entertain others – minstrels, singers, skalds, shanachies and troubadours. Folktales tell of ordinary people's experience; legends tell of heroes. Like myths (see CLASSICAL MYTHOLOGY), these stories were not created with children in mind. They arose as part of the community's way of making its mark, of entertaining but instructing at the same time, and of making public and celebrating the strengths and talents of the group.

Part of the magic and mystery of folktales and legends is that the same story can appear in different guises throughout the world. There is a version of *CINDERELLA* told by the Algonquin nation of North America – indeed there are more than 350 different versions of that story; the Scottish ballad *The Barring of the Door* appears in Turkey, Sri Lanka, Venice, Kashmir, the Middle East, Sicily and no doubt in other places too. There are often references to tales in other stories – SHAKESPEARE'S Ophelia recalls the *Owl Who Was a Baker's Daughter*. Gradually, in communities throughout the world, many traditional tales were collected in writing: the *Panchatantra*, the far-Eastern collection of stories for the education of Indian Princes; the Jataka Buddhist birth stories; the *THOUSAND AND ONE NIGHTS*; the Mabinogion from Wales; the teaching stories of the Dervishes and collections of Eastern and European tales by Boccaccio and CHAUCER, the brothers GRIMM and Tolstoy.

As with myth and FAIRY TALE there is a problem of terminology in writing about folktales and legends together. While they share certain common characteristics, there are significant differences. Both tend to include stories of people carrying out impressive feats often against the odds; both often deal with real and metaphorical journeys; both often include magic. Every culture seems to value the underdog who can outwit the rich and powerful, and both folktales and legends record victories of the (relatively) weak against the strong and dominant figure. But here the common features begin to diverge. Where folktales often celebrate the cunning of the ordinary man or woman, boy or girl, legends tend to cluster around heroes (less frequently, heroines) – those who are seen as possessing extraordinary characteristics even before they begin their adventures. The central characters of folktales, may, of course, become heroic as the tales unfold, even though they began as humble and unnoticed folk. This raises another problem of terminology: just what is a hero (see also SUPERHEROES)?

WILLIAM MAYNE has suggested that heroes have to be not only larger than life but also larger than death, because as stories are told about them they become greater than they were in life. 'They even have added to them stories that were nothing to do with them at all, tales of deeds that they did not accomplish themselves, of actions in places they never saw in ages in which they did not live.' Mayne's words reflect what folktales and legends do; they merge and weave history and make-believe. Some tales of heroic figures, for example *Cap o' Rushes* or *Beowulf*, paint a picture of virtues – of determination, moral strength, compassion, self-sacrifice – but other tales recount acts of vengeance, jealousy and rough justice, as in the legends of Cuchulain. These ambiguous qualities demand from the audience some participation in deciding what meanings can be taken from the tales. They offer a bridge by which to cross from questions about the everyday realities of fallible human nature to ways of transcending or resolving those questions.

Through stories people keep community experience alive, pass on wisdom or the morality of the group, raise hopes, sustain determination, record historical events, amuse, terrify, criticise, and perhaps most significantly, subvert. Weaving the spell of story carries power – the power to transform and transmute everyday reality into something which goes beyond the mundane; the power to warn, to reprimand or to overcome fears by making them into art. Stories change experience, and retelling stories in turn changes the stories. While there are recognisable conventions and patterns to traditional stories – cycles of time and the seasons, events happening in threes – they are nevertheless open to change and adaptation. Over the years and across the world, stories have been adopted and adapted to suit the historical and cultural contexts of their telling.

In telling of journeys and feats against the odds, folktales and legends are subversive. They carry messages about the poor, defenceless, weak members of the population; heroes defend the rights of the disadvantaged, become guerrilla fighters like ROBIN HOOD, work on behalf of widows and orphans who are being oppressed by the rich landowning classes. Existing law is often evaded; the TRICKSTER – Till Eulenspiegel, ANANCY, the Hodja – fools the community's dignitaries and the poor widow's third son carries off the treasure from the dragon, the ogre, the false friend. The material status of the rich is often depicted as an affliction, or they have riches but not happiness, health or peace of mind. The subversive nature of these tales places them firmly at the centre of orally transmitted cultures; they were the property of working folk, not the educated classes. The moment the tales became captured in print they were considered dangerous to young minds and were adapted, edited and further changed – as is the nature of stories – to fit the sense of decorum considered appropriate by the adults who mediated the stories. Nevertheless, folktales and legends have developed strong muscles over the years of their honing, reshaping and embellishment, and despite the attempts to curb their force, they are still stories of hope for those who presently cannot wield power. Perhaps that is one reason why they have become such an important strand of literature for children.

Another reason may be that whilst being deeply disruptive of social order in one sense, folktales and legends are also fundamentally conservative in another aspect – the value given to family and to belonging to a stable community group. They often begin with a description of the family structure 'Once upon a time there lived a widow with two daughters . . .' and they often end with the establishment of a new family '. . . and they lived happily ever after'. In between there are tests of fitness – three impossible feats, solving the riddle, making the princess laugh, spinning corn into gold – before the protagonist is accepted as part of the new family structure, a shift which is often one of upward social mobility. These feats are required of female and male characters alike. Whilst critics have analysed folktales and legends as being largely to do with men and their power over women, there are many stories which record the strength of mind, astuteness and courage of female characters. Scheherazade herself is a striking example. ALISON LURIE's collection *Clever Gretchen and Other Forgotten Folktales* (1980) offers a selection of these, strongly suggesting that there are many others in traditions throughout the world, but that when editors began to anthologise folktales in the West, stories about strong women and girls were considered unfit for young readers and were omitted from books for the young.

Another characteristic of folktales and legends is their stark truthfulness. Some stories end in disaster; versions of *Baba Yaga*, the metal-toothed ogress of Russian tales, and of the selkie, the seal-woman, told throughout northern islands – Ireland, Scotland, Iceland and beyond – end in death or desolation. Tales about human attempts to live forever offer no hope of immortality, as in the Turkish tale *Youth Without Age and Life Without Death*. Whilst celebrating the human capacity to take on just about anything that life presents, folktales and legends keep their feet firmly on the ground. Till Eulenspiegel perishes, even if his spirit remains to mock authority.

Despite the changes and editors' whims, folktales and legends remain in favour. They are shape-shifters who escape their captors and live in the free air of social pleasure. Their insouciance is captured in collections like ALAN GARNER's *A Bag of Moonshine* (1986) or Grace Hallworth's *Mouth Open, Story Jump Out* (1984); their richness and variety are represented by such impressive collections as JANE YOLEN's *Favourite Folktales from Around the World* (1986) and Idries Shah's *World Tales* (1979). Even where the tales have not been specifically retold for children, as in Magnus Magnusson's version of the Icelandic epic *Njal's Saga* (1960) or Marie Heaney's retelling of the Irish legends in *Over Nine Waves* (1994), the tales can still bind the hearer or reader with spells. In joining in with stories, as they hear or read them, anticipating events, inwardly comparing experiences, using the stories to rehearse possibilities, young readers have the chance to stand both within and outside themselves. They can practise the kinds of understanding which are uniquely offered by traditional stories drawn from other times and other places and draw strength from the vigour of the tales. ECB

See also ABORIGINAL CULTURE; AFRICAN MYTHOLOGY; CLASSICAL MYTHOLOGY; FAIRY TALES; IRISH MYTHOLOGY; KING ARTHUR; MAORI WRITING; NATIVE AMERICAN LITERATURE; ROBIN HOOD; SUPERHEROES

Follen, Elisa Lee (Cabot) 1787–1860 American editor and writer for the periodical *The Child's Friend*

(1843–58). She also compiled young children's collections, including *Little Songs for Little Girls and Boys* (1833) and *Home Drama for Young People* (1859). Follen popularised, but is often incorrectly ascribed authorship of, the traditional poem *Three Little Kittens*, illustrated by Marjorie Cooper. SCWA

***Follyfoot* series** (1971–6) Five children's novels by Monica Dickens (1915–89) about a home for ill-treated horses, popularised by the TELEVISON series *Follyfoot*. The stories originated in the writer's crusading adult novel, *Cobbler's Dream* (1963), about cruelty to horses, inspired by the author's work with the RSPCA. Yorkshire Television adapted it for children and Dickens wrote five 'original' stories based on the series. Though superior to the Television version, the books suffer from being too episodic, really a series of case studies. But the compassionate treatment of an emotive subject made both the Television series and the books popular world-wide. ARH

Forbes, Esther 1891–1967 American historical novelist whose reputation as a children's author is based on her only novel for young adults – *Johnny Tremain* (1943). This novel earned her the NEWBERY MEDAL in 1944 and the Metro-Goldwyn-Mayer Novel Award in 1948 when it was adapted for film. She also won the Pulitzer Prize in 1942 for *Paul Revere and the World He lived In* (1942), a BIOGRAPHY for adults. While researching this book she became interested in the lives of colonial apprentices, the basis for *Johnny Tremain*. The story is about a young apprentice silversmith who becomes involved in the Revolutionary movement in Boston. It is considered a classic example of American HISTORICAL FICTION for young people, praised for its blend of storytelling with factual accuracy. Forbes was born in Westborough, Massachusetts. Her father was a judge and her mother an historian. After graduating from Bradford Junior College in 1912 Forbes took courses at the University of Wisconsin before pursuing a career in publishing. She also wrote six historical novels and four non-fiction books for adults. Besides *Johnny Tremain*, she wrote only one other book for children, a biography entitled *America's Paul Revere* (1948). LAW

Forbidden Marriage, The (1998) Primary-school story by Ugandan author Paul Palia Kiapi, written to stimulate reading skills, develop and sustain reading habits and impart cultural values. It tells the story of a daughter and a son from two families which have not been on talking terms for years. The young lovers decide to leave the village. They get married and raise a family. After many years, there is famine in their original home, and, as the population wanders around looking for food, the young married couple forgive their parents and the relationship between the two families is normalised. ABO

Illustration from *War Boy* by Michael Foreman.

Foreman, Michael 1938– Born in Pakefield, England, Michael Foreman lived with his mother, who ran a corner shop, and his two older brothers. His father died one month before he was born. War-time brought to his village many soldiers and sailors, and many adventures. This period of his life is graphically brought to life in *War Boy* (1989). Later – and this he describes in *After the War Was Over* (1995) – he studied at Lowestoft School of Art, St Martin's School of Art and the Royal College of Art, where he also taught and from where he won a scholarship to the United States in 1963. He has had many jobs, including a spell as Art Director of *Playboy* (which he found boring) and of two other magazines. He publishes artwork in magazines and has had exhibitions in Europe, America and Japan. He designed the British 1987 Christmas stamps.

It is as an illustrator and as a writer/illustrator, however, that Foreman is best known. He has contributed illustrations to more than 70 books, suitable for all ages and covering a wide range: FOLK and FAIRY TALES, classics, poetry, PICTUREBOOKS, children's novels and a type of INFORMATION BOOK which is peculiar to him – 'history as a compulsive read' (*BOOKS FOR KEEPS*).

In his own picturebooks, of which he has created approximately two dozen, he demonstrates a concern for our fragile environment and the evils of war, and he frequently returns to questions of identity, imagination and freedom. His distinctive illustrative style lies in his use of quite rough-textured cartridge paper, colour washes of great luminosity and boldness (his liking for the colour blue is evident) and fine line drawing giving detail when required. He is equally successful at empty, suggestive expanses and at bustling crowd scenes. He responds sensitively to language, mood and location in others' texts: his illustrations range, as required, from humorous (as for TERRY JONES's texts or in his own *MOTHER GOOSE*, 1991) to romantic, magical or mysterious (as in many of the traditional tales), tender (as in his additions to Saint Exupéry's *THE LITTLE PRINCE*, 1995), grotesque or menacing (in ALAN GARFIELD's *Shakespeare Stories*, 1984/5, for instance), or haunting (as in Daphne du Maurier's *Classics of the Macabre*, 1987). Another illustrator, QUENTIN BLAKE, says he has 'a flair for turning a book into a special occasion.'

It is possible to identify many locations in his books: Cornwall, London and Suffolk feature often. In a book such as *Cat and Canary* (1984), the buildings of New York are dramatically painted from the perspective of a kite-borne cat, and in the *Panda* books (1977/81) Foreman's travels provide atmospheric paintings from the Far East and Australia. For *The Boy Who Sailed with Columbus* (1991), Foreman himself sailed in the Caribbean and made trips to Spain and the United States. It was inevitable that he would make a collection, *World of Fairy Tales* (1990), which as well as being illustrated appropriately for the cultures from which the stories are taken, is decorated with fine, painted sketches done on location. Foreman also makes use of more private locations and personal connections: he uses his London home in several books including *PETER PAN AND WENDY* (1988). The 'Ben' and 'Jack' books (1986/87/92), as well as *One World* (1990), were prompted by his sons; the idea for *Grandfather's Pencil and the Room of Stories* (1993) came from a child in a classroom he was visiting who produced a stub of a pencil from his pocket; and Scrooge's office in *A Christmas Carol* is his mother's filing system. The three war books are the most personal, recalling his childhood and youth and recreating in *War Game* (1993) World War I in which four of his uncles died. More recently, Foreman has collaborated with MICHAEL MORPURGO on four distinguished historical works, *Robin of Sherwood* (1996), *Farm Boy* (1997), *Arthur, High King of Britain* (1998) and *Joan of Arc* (1998). Foreman's books have been awarded many prizes. They also appear in several foreign editions and some have been adapted for TELEVISION and radio. JAG

Forest, Antonia A Londoner of mixed Irish and Russian descent, Antonia Forest is the author of 13 books for children. Ten of these form the *MARLOW* sequence; *The Player's Boy* (1970) and *The Players and the Rebels* (1971) may be thought of as extensions of the series, as they trace the adventures of an Elizabethan ancestor of the Marlows. *The Thursday Kidnapping* (1963), not related to the series, is a novel set in modern-day Hampstead. Forest's work is marked by an extraordinary richness and complexity of characterisation, sensitive treatment of difficult situations, and a deep love of history and literature. SA

see also NEGLECTED AUTHORS

Forester, C.S. see ROALD DAHL; see also ADULT FICTION; LITERATURE WITHIN CHILDREN'S LITERATURE

Forever see JUDY BLUME; see also NUDITY IN CHILDREN'S BOOKS

Forrestal, Elaine 1941– Award-winning Australian writer of fiction for younger readers, which includes the titles *Straggler's Reef* (1999), *Graffiti on the Fence* (1999) and *Someone Like Me* (1997). Her settings are quintessentially Australian, yet the themes of growing up and all it entails are universal. RTh

Forrester, Helen 1919– Canadian writer of non-fiction and fiction. Born in Hoylake, Cheshire, England, Forrester grew up in Manchester and Liverpool, and has lived in Edmonton, Alberta, since 1953. Forrester's first novel, *The Latchkey Kid* (1971), about parental neglect, was followed by her four autobiographical novels collected in *The Helen Forrester Omnibus*. *Twopence to Cross the Mersey* (1974), *Liverpool Miss* (1979), *By the Waters of Liverpool* (1981) and *Lime Street at Two* (1985) are based upon memories of the extreme poverty Forrester and her family endured following the Great Depression and World War II.These novels, marketed for adults, are popular with children. Forrester has published almost 20 novels and her most recent, *Morning Dove* (1996), was nominated for the Commonwealth Prize. Forrester has also been honoured by the City of Edmonton for her distinguished contribution to the literature and life of that city. She has also received the Government of Alberta Achievement Award for Literature (1979), Alberta's Award for non-fiction for *Lime Street at Two* in 1986, and an honorary Doctor of Literature degree from the University of Liverpool in 1988. MRS

Fortunes of Philippa, The see ANGELA BRAZIL; see also SCHOOL STORIES

45 & 47 Stella Street: and everything that happened see ELIZABETH HONEY; see also DETECTIVE FICTION

Foster, Genevieve 1893–1979 American author of biography and HISTORICAL FICTION for children. She is best known for her series of *World* books, including *George Washington's World* (1941), *Abraham Lincoln's World* (1944) – both of which were Newbery Honour Books – *Augustus Caesar's World* (1947) and *The World of Captain John Smith, 1580–1631* (1959), all written for children in the middle years. Her goal was to write history that would provide readers with a cross-section of the historical period, what she called 'horizontal history'. Thus a reader would get the complete flavour of a historical period, not just the politics, but the art, music, science, exploration and social movements as well. She was also interested in incorporating events from across the world so her histories have a multicultural flavour about them. Foster also wrote an acclaimed series of BIOGRAPHIES, which she called 'Initial Biographies', for younger children, including Newbery Honour Book *George Washington* (1949), *Abraham Lincoln* (1950), *Andrew Jackson* (1951) and *Theodore Roosevelt* (1954). *Birthdays of Freedom, Vol. I* (1952) also was named a Newbery Honour Book. She illustrated many of her own books with charts, diagrams and cross-sections, adding to their clarity and liveliness. Her works, widely praised as original and stimulating, were translated into at least 15 languages. DLR

Foster, John 1941– British anthologist, the most prolific published collector of poems for children. His *First, Second, Third* and *Fourth Poetry Books*, ubiquitous in schools, have the virtue of demystifying poetry in the classroom while retaining some of its magic. FRBS

Four and Twenty Lamingtons (1988) Anthology of Australian NURSERY RHYMES, compiled by Jane Covernton and illustrated with humorous cameo images in warm colours by Jenny Rendall. This well-designed book introduces young children to simple verse by such established poets as Mary Gilmore, C.J. DENNIS, A.B. PATERSON and D.H. Souter; contemporary poets, including MICHAEL DUGAN, DOUG MACLEOD, Irene Gough and MAX FATCHEN; as well as some anonymous verse. Ranging from the humourous to the lyrical, the strongly rhythmical verses, many using alliteration, onomatopoeia, assonance and rhyme, reflect young children's fascination with language play, and introduce them to many Australian animals, places and expressions. JAP

Fowler, Thurley 1925– Australian writer whose novels are popular with junior readers for their credible child characters, and the way they cope with growing up in ordinary families, both present and past. Often using humour, and drawing with assurance on her own life experiences, Fowler has a growing list of novels. Her first, *Wait for Me! Wait for Me!* (1981), shortlisted for the 1982 Children's Book Council of Australia Book of the Year Awards, shows Robert, the puny weakling of his family, becoming a hero, while in *The Green Wind* (1985), set in 1948, 11-year-old Jennifer copes with her final year of primary school as she searches for true friendship. It won the CHILDREN'S BOOK COUNCIL OF AUSTRALIA BOOK OF THE YEAR AWARD (1986). Its sequel, *The Wind is Silver* (1991), shows the irrepressible Jennifer four years later, coping with tragedy and romance. Fowler shifts from female to male protagonists with ease; her characters include Greg, in *A Hippo Doing Backstroke* (1988), who suffers greatly from being overweight; Roger, who is obsessed with flying, in *The Kid From Licorice Hill* (1988); Rebecca, in *There's a Bushranger in my Bedroom* (1990), a light-hearted mystery; and Annie, 'an ant with attitude', in *A Brat called Annie* (1997). Other titles include *The Caretakers* (1994); *Not Again, Dad* (1994) and *Journey to a Dream* (1994). JAP

***Fox* Series** (1983–99) Six titles by the Irish author TOM MCCAUGHREN in which he has created a community of foxes who, although able to think and communicate in the manner of humans, never lose their essential animal characteristics or dignity. Each book, beginning with *Run With the Wind* (1983), describes the foxes battling with mankind's efforts to desecrate the countryside. The series continues to grow in popularity with each new title owing to McCaughren's empathy with wildlife, his knowledge of environmental matters and a growing stylistic assurance and complexity. The other titles in the series are *Run to Earth* (1984), *Run Swift, Run Free* (1986), *Run to the Ark* (1992), *Run to the Wild Wood* (1996) and *Run for Cover* (1999). VC

Fox's Book of Martyrs see BIOGRAPHY AND AUTOBIOGRAPHY

Fox, Carol see CRITICAL APPROACHES TO CHILDREN'S BOOKS

Fox, Geoff see CHILDIST CRITICISM; CRITICAL APPROACHES TO CHILDREN'S LITERATURE

Fox, Mem [Merrion Frances] 1946– Exuberant Australian storyteller, best known for her enormously successful PICTUREBOOK, *POSSUM MAGIC* (1983). Mutual respect between the old and the young are dominant themes in many of Fox's picturebooks: in

Wilfrid Gordon McDonald Donald Partridge (1984), illustrated by JULIE VIVAS, there is a sensitive portrayal of relationships, a child offering memorable gifts to an old woman who is losing her memory; in *Sophie* (1989), illustrated by CRAIG SMITH, Sophie's grief over her Grandpa's death is resolved with the birth of her first child; and Lilly Laceby, dreaming of her childhood in *Night Noises* (1989), has a special surprise 80th birthday party. Fox has a keen ear for rhyme and rhythm, and often employs cumulative sequences or repetition in books, as in *Shoes From Grandpa* (1989), *Koala Lou* (1988), *Hattie and the Fox* (1986) and *Sleepy Bears* (1999), all of which lend themselves particularly well to being read aloud. Other titles include *Tough Boris* (1998). Fox is a former university lecturer and a passionate International Reading Association conference speaker. Her autobiography *Mem's the Word* (1990) explores her motivations for writing and teaching. Many of her books have been translated, and in 1990 she was awarded the Dromkeen Medal. HE

Fox, Paula 1923– American novelist, born in New York City and educated at Columbia University and the Julliard School of Music. Among the most praised and honoured realistic novels for young readers, receiving the NEWBERY MEDAL, the BOSTON GLOBE-HORN BOOK AWARDS and the HANS CHRISTIAN ANDERSEN AWARD, Fox's fiction is marked by the complex and difficult situations in which her protagonists undergo character development and individuation, whether it be the historically distant world of 18th-century slave ships of *The Slave Dancer* (1974) or her more characteristic contemporary urban and seascapes, in such novels as *Monkey Island* (1991) and *The Village by the Sea* (1988).

Her best-known novel is *The Slave Dancer*, which follows the adventures of Jesse Bollier, a young man kidnapped from his family in New Orleans and forced to serve as a 'slave dancer' on a ship, playing the flute to exercise the cargo of slaves, thus keeping them alive as valuable property for their enslavers. The novel's reception ranged from high praise (including the award of the Newbery Medal) to sharp attack by some critics for what they saw as the novel's distortion of history in its depiction of the role of blacks in their own enslavement. Whatever the estimation of her novels' politics and historical accuracy, most critics praise Fox for her writing style and for her insights into the psychology of young people. BH

see also HISTORICAL FICTION

Foxspell (1994) Novel by the Australian author GILLIAN RUBINSTEIN. Frustrated by a disintegrating family life, bullied by a graffiti gang and bored at school, Tod (12) finds refuge in a quarry, home to the foxes which fascinate and then 'adopt' him. Tod becomes a fox in a remarkably convincing transformation of the body and senses. He must then choose between human existence or life as a fox. Rubinstein espouses acceptance of the 'grim but hilarious' reality of life, but her dramatic finale is open-ended. The book explores loss of innocence, both literally – in Tod – and metaphorically, through the transformations Europeans have inflicted on Australian landscape and fauna. NLR

frame In PICTUREBOOKS illustrations may be framed by decorative borders, by ruled or free-hand drawn lines of varying thickness and style, or by the unworked page space on which an image, is set (air frame). The type of frame affects the meaning of what it surrounds: heavy frames tend to contain events, whilst lighter free-hand ones appear less formal and allow for a livelier effect; air frames isolate, or allow depicted participants to move freely across the page opening. Within, the picture itself, participants may be framed by objects, architectural elements, colour, and so on. Whether a single picture frame, or frames within frames, this device acts like pauses in speech – brief or protracted – with bolder or lighter framing giving corresponding significance to the enclosed or partly enclosed episode. JD

François, André [André Farkas] 1915– Illustrator and writer of juvenile books. Born in Romania, Farkas studied art in France, changing his name to François when he took French citizenship in the 1930s. He began his career as a commercial artist, drawing advertisements for companies like Olivetti and Perrier, but has worked on theatre design, paintings and political cartoons as well as children's books. Citing the influence of George Grosz, Paul Klee and the French poster painter, Cassandre, under whom he studied, François's first American ILLUSTRATION was for Isobel Harris's award-winning *Little Boy Brown* (1949). Here, François assisted in the telling of the story by drawing scenes in pen-and-ink and using a warm brown wash. Studying with Picasso in the 1950s, François experimented with multiple design, dissected action and distinctive line. In his later work his illustrations are more cartoonish, but with an air of sophistication due to their wit and invention. He has illustrated many of John Symonds's books, including *William Waste* (1946), *Tom and Tabby* (1964) and *The Magic Currant Bun* (1952), for which François won awards. He has also written and illustrated his own books, including *Crocodile Tears* (1956) and *You Are Ri-di-cu-lous* (1970), absurd cartoons which appeal to knowing juveniles. SCWA

Frank Leslie's Boy's and Girl's Weekly (1866–84) Popular illustrated periodical edited and published in

New York by 'Frank Leslie' [Henry Carter]. Originally for younger children, *Frank Leslie's Boy's and Girl's Weekly: An Illustrated Journal of Amusement, Adventure and Instruction* met with such an enthusiastic initial response from readers that it was soon expanded and directed to a general audience of young people. Leslie's sense of what his audience wanted, the economies offered by an extensive distribution network, and technological innovations in the reproduction of engravings made the *Weekly* a huge financial success. But critics complained of the magazine's sensationalism, and despite Leslie's initial claims that it would be a repository of varied instruction and amusement for a family audience, his *Boy's and Girl's Weekly* was aggressively promoted to a mass market more interested in its many sensational stories and eye-catching, if somewhat lurid, pictures. Among the more memorable series presented were the *Jack Harkaway Stories* by Samuel Bracebridge Hemyng and W. O. Stoddard's stories about the Indians of the West. After Leslie's death in 1880 his company no longer saw the magazine as a high priority, and it ceased publication. SRG

see also WOOD ENGRAVING

***Frank Reade* series** see SCIENCE FICTION

Frank, Anne(liese Marie) 1929–1945 Born in Frankfurt, Germany, Anne Frank is known throughout the world for her diaries, kept during two years in hiding in her father's factory in Nazi-occupied Amsterdam. In August 1944 the Frank family and friends were arrested and sent to Westerbork Concentration Camp. From there Anne's family was taken to Auschwitz-Birkenau, Poland; she and her sister Margot were transferred to Bergen-Belsen, Germany, where both died from typhus fever. Anne's diaries, however, were saved and Otto Frank, Anne's father, the only member of her immediate family to survive, carried out her wishes and published them. *The Diary of Anne Frank* (1947), translated into over 50 languages and with more than 20 million copies sold, is considered by many to be a key text of European literature, both for its content and the quality of the writing. It provides a remarkable record of a young girl's innermost thoughts and aspirations, her observations of others and of the circumstances and events which determined their day-to-day existence. In 1995 a new translation was published, *The Diary of a Young Girl: Anne Frank, The Definitive Edition*, including further material from Anne's original manuscripts. The full texts of these manuscripts are included in the scholarly work *The Diary of Anne Frank: The Critical Edition* (1989), prepared by the Netherlands State Institute for War Documentation. Anne Frank has become a symbol for all Jews who died in the Holocaust, inspiring exhibitions, plays, films and biographical texts. Anne's stories, written in an accounts book, have also been published, in *Tales From the Secret Annexe* (1983). MSut

Frasconi, Antonio 1919– Artist, illustrator and author, internationally known for his woodcuts. Frasconi was born in Buenos Aires, Argentina, to Italian parents. He spent his childhood and early adult years in Montevideo, Uruguay, where he studied at the Circulo de Bellas Artes. In 1945 he won a Guggenheim Foundation fellowship to the Art Students League in New York City, and subsequently lived in the United States. Perhaps more widely known as an artist than as an author and illustrator of children's books, Frasconi has received numerous awards and honours and his art may be found in the world's major museums. He illustrated *Twelve Fables of Aesop* in 1954, and *See and Say* followed in 1955, written at the suggestion of MARGARET MCELDERRY. Its text consists of definitions in English, Spanish, Italian and French. He followed this in 1958 with *The House that Jack Built* and in 1964 with *See Again, Say Again*, also in four languages. Frasconi wrote that he wanted a book 'that would show there are different ways to say the same thing, that there is more than one nation in the world, that there are many other countries where people speak different languages'. Since then he has written and illustrated several highly acclaimed children's books and illustrated many more for both children and adults. His recent work, especially, is known for his remarkable sense of colour. LH

Fraser, Antonia see KING ARTHUR

Freaky Friday (1972) Novel by Mary Rodgers, one of the first modern adolescent novels (see also YOUNG ADULT FICTION) that deal with difficult transitional periods in parent/child and body/self relations, creating a delightfully funny situation which begins with the promising line: 'When I woke up this morning I found I'd turned into my mother.' Thirteen-year-old Annabel is then plunged into a hectic day, dealing with children, husband, the cleaning-lady and her own schoolteachers, until near disaster is reached. In the process of learning how others see her, Annabel realises what is good about herself and what she has to give to those around her – including her mother. EA

***Freddy the Pig* series** (1927–58) Popular American series of some two dozen humorous animal FANTASIES by Walter R. Brooks (1886–1958). The first of these, *To and Again*, in which a group of farm animals from New York State takes a vacation trip to Florida, was written with no sequel and no main character in mind. By the third book, however, Freddy the Pig had emerged as a natural leader and a favourite with children; *To and*

Again was eventually reissued as *Freddy Goes to Florida* (1964). Freddy's endless experimentation with new roles – as poet, editor, magician, detective, politician, pilot, even cowboy – seems the logical outcome of his restless intelligence and thirst for experience; as a character, he is genuinely complex as well as simply funny. In some respects the Freddy books resemble the DOCTOR DOLITTLE series; Brooks and Lofting share an interest in the organisation of social institutions, a concern with political issues, and a vein of wry social satire. *Wiggins for President* (1939), reissued in 1948 as *Freddy the Politician*, is one of the most politically sophisticated stories in American children's literature, detailing the rise of a dictatorship on the Bean Farm with chilling particularity. SR

Frederick Warne see PUBLISHING AND PUBLISHERS; see also WALTER CRANE

Freedman, Russell 1929– Distinguished American writer of INFORMATION BOOKS which incorporate extensive visuals. Initially a journalist Freedman published his first book in 1961: *Teenagers Who Made History* is a compelling collection of BIOGRAPHIES including that of the 15-year-old Louis Braille who developed the alphabet for the blind. Freedman prefers the term 'informational' over 'non-fiction' because he wants his books to be as pleasurable to read as fiction. Since 1980 Freedman has primarily written biographies and books dealing with historical periods, attempting to make history more accurate and accessible to younger readers. With JEAN FRITZ and MILTON MELTZER, Freedman has introduced historical revisionism to children's literature, a reaction against the Parson Mason Weems theory of sanitised, sugar-coated history exemplified in the fifth edition of *Life of George Washington* (1806), in which Weems invented the story of Washington and the cherry tree. Freedman has led the way to greater use of graphics and historical documents in informational books. Photographs are an essential aspect of his volumes and are used effectively in *Lincoln: A Photobiography* (1987), which won the NEWBERY MEDAL. This work examines the man behind the myth and shows Lincoln to be a highly complex and paradoxical figure who is vastly more interesting than the legendary Lincoln. JCS

Freeman, Don 1908–78 An American author and illustrator of popular PICTUREBOOKS, as well as an illustrator for numerous other works of literature. Starting with *Chuggy and the Blue Caboose* (1951), Freemen's career as a children's writer spanned more than 25 years and produced a number of important works that demonstrated his ability to combine words and pictures to create deceptively simple stories with hidden depths. His books often contain subtle messages that mock the social conventions of American society. In *Dandelion* (1964), a lion discovers how ridiculous fashion can be when he dresses as a stylish dandy to impress a friend who has invited him to a party. She fails to recognise him, and only does so when he loses his finery. In *Norman the Doorman* (1972), a mouse enters a sculpture in an art show and wins first prize, turning out to be a better artist than any human being. One of Freeman's best-known works is *Corduroy* (1968), a tale about a lonely teddy bear in a shop who finds love when a small girl purchases him. SAI

French, Fiona 1944– British picturebook author. French studied Design, Painting and Lithography, specialising in Printmaking. She has published brilliantly coloured and imaginatively conceived PICTUREBOOKS of Bible STORIES and traditional tales from around the world, beginning with *Jack of Hearts* (1968). Subject matter is matched with an appropriate style and medium, painterly or graphic, whether 'set' in stained glass as in *City of Gold* (1974); in a rural, ritual-bound past as in *John Barleycorn* (1982); in Vermeer's Amsterdam as in *Hunt the Thimble* (1978); an African village as in *King of Another Country* (1992); or in 1930s gangland, as in *Snow White in New York* (1986). The last-named book was winner of the KATE GREENAWAY MEDAL. JD

French, Jackie 1953– Australian author, non-fiction writer, gardening columnist and TELEVISION presenter, who lives with her family and a menagerie of animals on a hobby farm in the bush. French has described creating stories as 'a bit like making compost', and the manuscript of one of her earliest children's books, *Rainstones* (1991), was smudged so badly with wombat droppings the publishers deemed it the messiest they had ever received. French's inspiration for most of her books comes from her love of the Australian bush as well as her desire to bring Australian history to life through her characters. Her tales are finely and distinctively woven with sights, smells, flavours, landscapes, native flora and fauna, and the ghosts and legends of the Australian past. *Somewhere Around the Corner* (1994), a book in which the heroine slips through time back to the 1930s Depression years, was a 1995 CHILDREN'S BOOK COUNCIL OF AUSTRALIA BOOK OF THE YEAR Honour Book. French is a prominent, highly successful author and has been the recipient of two Commonwealth Literary Awards. REVIEWERS have called her 'exuberantly witty', 'full of wisdom' and 'one of the most perceptive and versatile writers for children'. She has also written books for younger children, short stories, and novels for older children. AT

see also THE BUSH

French, Simon 1957– Australian writer and schoolteacher, who draws upon his first-hand observation of children's lives and writes sensitively from the outsider's point of view, about respect for all people. His first novel, *Hey Phantom Singlet* (1975), written at the age of 15 to amuse classmates, was published two years later. In *Cannily, Cannily* (1981) Trevor Huon, an outsider at a new school in a small country town, attempts to use sport to fit in but is persecuted by a bullying teacher/coach. *All We Know* (1986), winner of the 1987 CHILDREN'S BOOK COUNCIL OF AUSTRALIA BOOK OF THE YEAR AWARD for older readers, is an introspective story of Arkie's last year of primary school, in which her step-father's gift of a camera provides a literary device for Arkie to reflect upon her past, present and future. SNJ

see also CHILD AUTHORS

Friel, Maeve 1950– Irish novelist whose first children's book is *The Deerstone* (1992), a TIME-SLIP novel in which the present-day hero travels back to monastic Ireland. Each of her works shows a growth in mastery of plot and of characterisation. *Charlie's Story* (1993) catches the anguish felt by a teenage girl from a troubled background who falls victim to school bullies. *Distant Voices* (1994) is also a time-slip novel, but with the added dimension of the young teenage heroine's gently nuanced attraction to the Viking boy who calls her back to his time, giving greater depth to a well-told story. *The Lantern Moon* (1996) is a powerful novel with strong moral undertones in its depiction of social inequality in 18th-century England and Australia. VC

Fritz, Jean 1915– American writer best known for her children's BIOGRAPHIES of famous historical figures. She is unique in presenting subjects such as Patrick Henry, Ben Franklin and Christopher Columbus in a familiar, humorous manner, yet with great accuracy and skill. Her humour begins with the titles: *And Then What Happened, Paul Revere?* (1973) or *Bully for You, Teddy Roosevelt!* (1991).

In *Homesick: My Own Story* (1982) she writes about growing up in Hankow, China, where she was born and lived for 13 years. Her missionary parents often told her about their former life in the United States and described the leaders who had shaped the country. Those early years gave her a deep sense of the past, and a special appreciation for American history, which later led her to write about her country. She told about the struggles faced by the men who wrote the Declaration of Independence in *Will You Sign Here, John Hancock* (1976). In *You Want Women to Vote, Lizzie Stanton?* (1995), Fritz describes the life of Elizabeth Cady Stanton who spoke at the first Woman's Rights Convention in Seneca Falls, New York, in 1848, and continued writing and speaking to groups for the next 50 years. As she does with all her subjects, Fritz brings Stanton and Hancock vividly to life in slim volumes.

In addition to her biographies she has written HISTORICAL FICTION about the American Revolution or the days before the Civil War. She based a story on her great-great-grandmother's experiences in *The Cabin Faced West* (1958), telling of a young girl who moves with her family from Gettysburg across the Allegheny Mountains into the barren wilderness of Western Pennsylvania in the 1780s. Ann Hamilton was a lonely child who kept a journal describing her emotional feelings about the journey and the difficulties of her new life. One highlight occurs when George Washington stops to share a meal with her family at Hamilton Hill.

Jean Fritz makes the study of history enjoyable for her young readers because she uncovers the human qualities of her subjects, acting, as she put it, as 'a detective, a treasure hunter, an eavesdropper'. Her portraits are based on solid research, but she does not present dry dates and facts. She gives her readers the essence of her subjects, always selecting their authentic dialogue and intriguing quirks. She once said, 'I eavesdrop on the past to satisfy my own curiosity, but if I can surprise children into believing history, I will be happy, especially if they find, as I do, that truth is stranger (and often funnier) than fiction.'

Fritz has received numerous awards: in 1978 she was presented the Children's Book Guild's Honour Award for Nonfiction for the 'body of her creative writing'; in 1983 she won the Newbery Honour Book Award, American Book Award, and Boston Globe-Horn Book Honour Book Award, all for *Homesick: My Own Story*. The following year she received the Boston Globe-Horn Book Nonfiction Award for *The Double Life of Pocahontas*. BG

***Frog and Toad* series** *I Can Read* Books for beginning readers written and illustrated by American ARNOLD LOBEL. These refreshing books detail events in the daily lives of two friends who, although they are animals, are remarkably lifelike and human. Lobel was a genius at this genre. He had the ability to convey simple human emotions with humour and grace. His accompanying ILLUSTRATIONS – done in two colours of brown and green with black line drawings – add to the enjoyment. The books invite children to enjoy simple things like planting a garden or baking cookies; to explore and overcome feelings like being afraid; and to learn how to be a better friend. Although marketed by the publisher as books for beginning readers, the series contains complex concepts and difficult words, and each book is divided into short chapters. Books in the series include *Frog and Toad All Year* (1976); *Frog and Toad are Friends* (1970), a Caldecott Honour Book; *Days with Frog and Toad* (1979);

Original design for *The Frog Prince* by JAN ORMEROD.

and *Frog and Toad Together* (1973), a Newbery Honour Book. In 1978 the series received the Children's Books Recognition of Merit Award. DJH

Frog Prince, The (1990) FAIRY TALE retold by David Lloyd and illustrated by JAN ORMEROD. The older version by the GRIMM BROTHERS is as stern as its title suggests: *Der Froschkönig: oder der eiserne Heinrich Nr 1* [*The Frog-King, or Iron Henry*] was translated by Brian Alderson in 1978. The Everyman edition (1906) is more bland and ARTHUR RACKHAM's ILLUSTRATIONS evoke the mythical past of FAIRY TALE princesses. David Lloyd's text is admirably spare. Ormerod's illustrations, like the princess's world, are at the same time everyday and suggestively magical. The girl is a contemporary teenage girl. On her bed in her white nightshirt, with the frog a small nonchalant stain on the pillow, she might be from one of Ormerod's books about family life. Her family wear fairy-tale medieval clothes, the queen in passionate red. Her surroundings, otherwise unplaced in time, are filled with slithery images of water-creatures and foliage which are repeated in the elaborate borders. The subject of the story, the sexual awakening of an adolescent girl, permeates every page. Only at the end, in crown and regalia, is the princess a little girl in a fairy story, her young sister now holding the magical golden globe which has passed through every illustration. RC

see also NIGEL GRAY

Frost, A(rthur) B(urnett) 1851–1928 American illustrator and cartoonist. His work in children's books includes artwork for *Uncle Remus: His Songs and his Sayings* (1881), *Nights with Uncle Remus* (1883) and *Uncle Remus and His Friends* (1892), all by JOEL CHANDLER HARRIS. Frost's strong sense of humour was especially appropriate to Harris's stories, most of which are talking-beast tales of African origin, and to *Rhyme? and Reason?* (1883), a selection of the poems of LEWIS CARROLL. Other works include ILLUSTRATIONS for adult books. Frost was one of many contributors to the highly literary magazine *ST NICHOLAS*. KSB

Frost, Robert 1874–1963 Quintessentially American poet who immortalised the New England landscape and character. The apparent simplicity of some of Frost's poetry makes it accessible to children, while his work is also eminently suitable for study by young adults. Although Frost disliked free verse and believed in the discipline of conventional form, rhyme and regular metre, it is the conversational quality of his particular voice that readers often comment on. Nature is a major theme in his poetry and rural settings and subjects abound: a butterfly, a calf, trees and paths, a wood-pile, even a wall that needs mending. The poem most closely associated with young readers is 'Stopping by Woods on a Snowy Evening'; the mixture of mystery, lyricism and longing moves children as young as six, while it remains one of his best-loved poems for adults. *You Come Too: Favourite Poems for Young Readers* (1959) includes Frost's most anthologised poems for children, some of which have been made into PICTUREBOOKS. Frost received many awards in a distinguished career, which included Pulitzer prizes, honorary degrees and the performance of his poem, 'The Gift Outright', at J.F. Kennedy's inauguration. Throughout his work, Frost celebrated the transitory nature of life and the preciousness of the moment.

NV, MCCS

Frye, Northrop see CRITICAL APPROACHES TO CHILDREN'S LITERATURE

Fulani, Dan Nigerian writer of fast-paced DETECTIVE FICTION and other novels dealing with socio-ethical issues in a northern Nigerian setting. His works include four books (1981–6) featuring Sauna, a boy detective who defeats bank robbers, arms-smugglers, crooked businessmen and drug peddlers. Special agent Pius Shale and his partner track down similar villains in *No Condition Is Permanent* (1981) and three other novels. Unscrupulous international business interests bring harm in the form of dangerous pesticides (*The Price of Liberty*, 1981) and powdered baby

'Make veal of that pretty creature! 'Tis a shame!' says the Human man. 'I will buy him and take him home to the children.' Illustration by A.B. Frost for *Uncle Remus: His Sayings* by JOEL CHANDLER HARRIS.

milk (*The Fight for Life*, 1982). His book for younger readers, *The Angel Who Wore Shoes* (1993), takes up another Fulani theme, the misuse of religion to perpetuate fraud. VD

Fuller, Roy (Broadbent) 1912–91 Award-winning British poet whose books *Seen Grandpa Lately?* (1972), *Poor Roy* (1977) and *Upright, Downfall* (1983) form his collected children's poems, *The World Through the Window* (1989). Fuller is never condescending and his readers are offered adult preoccupations, tongue-in-cheek humour, well-crafted poems – funny, dry, often gloomy. 'In the Restaurant' reveals a clever punster – the bald man orders 'hare', the actor a 'roll', the cleric some 'sole'. 'How unmemorable to meet Mr Fuller', he wrote, parodying EDWARD LEAR, but his poetry has much to offer young readers with stamina. AHa

Fun with Mrs. Thumb see NICOLA BAYLEY; JAN MARK

Fyleman, Rose 1877–1957 British author of the poem with the classic opening line, 'There are fairies at the bottom of our garden!' Fyleman was a contemporary of E. NESBIT. She was admired and emulated by ENID BLYTON and ETHEL TALBOT. The poems in her collections *Fairies and Chimneys* (1918) and *The Fairy Green* (1919) were originally published in *Punch*. They reflect a bygone view of childhood in a sentimental tone ('Please be careful where you tread/The fairies are about'). Her poems are not for later generations of more streetwise kids, nor for politically correct anthologists, yet she was exhaustively anthologised over a 70-year period and was a regular contributor to *JOY STREET*, a distinguished contemporary children's ANNUAL. EAG

G

Illustration by Wanda Gág for *Three Gay Tales* from the GRIMM BROTHERS

Gaarder, Jostein 1952– Norwegian philosophy teacher and author of the international bestseller *Sophie's World* (trans. Paulette Møller, 1994). Gaarder's awareness of the natural tendency of the young to pose anew life's eternal moral and spiritual questions inspired his presentation of an absorbing overview of the history of philosophy within a narrative framework. Fourteen-year-old Sophie Amundsen, the central character, has to apply her knowledge of philosophy in order to solve puzzles and answer metaphysical questions with the assistance of a mysterious teacher. Promoted and sold as a children's book in Scandinavia and Germany, it is interesting to note that *Sophie's World* has been marketed in Britain for adults, perhaps because of the complex postmodernist structure of its plot. However, a number of subsequent works specifically for children have been translated: *The Christmas Mystery* (1996), *The Solitaire Mystery* (1996), *Hello? Is Anybody There? (A Story for Children Everywhere)* (1997) and *Through a Glass, Darkly* (1998). GL

Gaffer Samson's Luck (1984) Powerful and moving novel by JILL PATON WALSH, dealing with several themes common in children's literature: James's family has moved to an apparently boring place in the English Fens where the local children are hostile, but through the friendship of Gaffer Samson, an elderly neighbour, and Angey, the tinker, he eventually manages to confront his situation. The story is made memorable through Walsh's stirring description of the landscape and, in particular, by the moment in which the boys cross a dangerous weir. As James, an extremely empathetic character, begins to find beauty in the flat fenlands he also begins to understand the meaning of luck, friendship and death. EA

Gág, Wanda 1893–1946 American author and illustrator. Best known for *Millions of Cats* (1928), Gág stands as one of the first and foremost illustrators of American PICTUREBOOKS. She was born in New Ulm, Minnesota, the oldest child of German parents. As a child, Gág read GRIMMS' FAIRY TALES intensively, and she began writing and illustrating her own stories in elementary school. When her father died, 15-year-old Wanda assumed financial responsibility for her family and began selling her drawings to support her mother and six siblings. Determined to be an artist, she pursued her studies at several art schools in Minneapolis-St Paul, and then moved to New York as a commercial artist.

In 1928 Ernestine Evans, an editor at the new publishing company Coward-McGann, was looking for artists to meet the rising demand for quality children's books. Impressed by Gág's work in an exhibition, Evans asked her to create a children's book. Gág offered a manuscript which had been in her rejection box since 1921. This story became *Millions of Cats*, a humorous original fairy tale closely modelled on the European tales Gág had loved as a child. The book featured several significant technical innovations: the use of double-spread ILLUSTRATIONS, a consistent left-to-right movement to suggest the old man's journey, and hand-lettered text. Gág's black-and-white illustrations use strong lines well-suited to delineating the peasant characters; through these innovations, she achieved the perfect symbiosis between illustration and text which has led to the book's recognition as one of the first true American picturebooks. It was a Newbery Honour Book in 1929, and it remains popular today for its humorous plot, active older characters and irresistible refrain: 'Hundreds of cats,/Thousands of cats,/Millions and billions and trillions of cats.'

Gág produced several other important children's books. *The ABC Bunny* (1933), also a Newbery Honour Book, offered significant innovations to the ALPHA-

BET BOOK genre, telling a story – about a rabbit in its natural habitat – rather than depicting unrelated objects in alphabetical order, and Gág designed it in a large format and illustrated it with lithographs. Gág's other books include *The Funny Thing* (1929), *Snippy and Snappy* (1931), *Wanda Gág's Story Book* (1932), *Gone is Gone: The Story of a Man Who Wanted to Do Housework* (1935) and *Growing Pains* (1940), an autobiographical book based on the diary she had kept as a teenager. *Nothing at All* (1941) and *Snow White and the Seven Dwarfs* (1938) were Caldecott Honour Books; Gág intended the latter to counter the sugary DISNEY film version released in 1937. It was one of her highly praised illustrated translations of Grimms' tales, which also included *Tales from Grimm* (1936), *Three Gay Tales from Grimm* (1943) and the posthumous *More Tales from Grimm* (1947). KK

see also LITHOGRAPHY

Gaiman, Neil see GRAPHIC NOVELS

Galdone, Paul 1914–86 American illustrator and author/reteller. Born in Hungary, Paul Galdone immigrated to the United States as a youth and remained in New York and Vermont until his death. After attending the New York School of Industrial Design, Galdone worked in the art department of Doubleday and Co. for four years before going freelance in the 1950s. Galdone illustrated nearly 200 books over the course of his long career. His early successes included the illustrations for Ellen MacGregor's *Miss Pickerell* series. Galdone also illustrated several books by Eve Titus, including *Anatole* (1956) and *Anatole and the Cat* (1967), both Caldecott Honour Books, and her short novels starring the great mouse detective Basil, starting with *Basil of Baker Street* (1957). Galdone is best remembered, however, for the dozens of FOLKTALES and NURSERY RHYMES he illustrated, many of which he also wrote or retold. Galdone's style is gentle and cartoon-like, with large characters, intricate details and, for the times, rich colours, done in pen-and-ink and wash. Critics applauded the whimsical bent of his work and his bold, distinctive style. A landscape painter as well, Galdone often drew his inspiration for his art from nature. MPH

Galland, Antoine see *THE ARABIAN NIGHTS' ENTERTAINMENTS*

Gallico, Paul (William) 1897–1976 American author, born in New York, of Italian and Austrian parentage. After working for many years with a New York newspaper, he moved to England and later to Monaco, becoming a full-time writer. He was the author of over 40 books, a good number of these generally managing to defy the usual adult/child classification. The adult works are written with an extreme lucidity and simplicity of style, and there is a FAIRY TALE quality about such works as the *Mrs. Harris* books, *The Snow Goose* (1941) and *The Zoo Gang* (1971) which renders them easily accessible to the child. His writing is strongly marked by a wholesomeness, a sense of traditional values; he is unafraid of using words like 'kindness', 'honour', and 'honesty'. His character Hiram Holliday is a man inspired to heroic action by an old-fashioned sense of romanticism in a world which is no longer comfortable with it.

Gallico's works for children are equally robust if marginally less interesting. The *Jean-Pierre* books, about an Abyssinian guinea-pig, take the opportunity to be informative and are consequently a little plodding. In *The Day Jean-Pierre Went Round the World* (1965) Cecily Durand, following the travels of her guinea-pig, learns about the different places visited. Of much greater merit is *Manxmouse* (1968), about a blue porcelain mouse without a tail who comes to life. His adventures are both funny and heart-warming, and the allegorical element is understated but powerful. SA

Illustration by Kim Gamble from *Tashi and the Baba Yaga*, by A. and B. FIENBERG.

Gamble, Kim Australian illustrator, whose cartoon style of drawing and gentle use of watercolours have established him as one of the country's most recognisable and sensitive artists. His use of tonal pencil drawings to portray the engaging eponymous Tashi in ANNA FIENBERG's series shows clearly his ability to interpret a text and to convey mood through a deft use of line. Other Fienberg books he has illustrated include *The Hottest Boy Who Ever Lived* (1993) and *The Magnificent Nose and Other Marvels* (1991), winner of the 1992 CHILDREN'S BOOK COUNCIL OF AUSTRALIA BOOK OF THE YEAR AWARD. In *Minton Goes Sailing* (1998), and *Minton Goes Flying* (1988), also by Anna

Fienberg, Gamble uses cheerful colours to depict Minton, a resourceful and adventurous beachcombing salamander. The changing moods of the sea are skilfully conveyed in the swirling watercolour illustrations for *Arabella* (1998) by WENDY ORR – a PICTUREBOOK which shows Gamble in full control of his medium – and in his use of powerful symbols. *First Day* (1998) by MARGARET WILD is an excellent showcase for Gamble's characters, with their tiny upturned or rounded snub noses, and skinny limbs. COVER ART is another aspect of Gamble's versatility: he has designed covers for MORRIS GLEITZMAN's novels and Michael Stephens's *Titans* (1993). JAP

Gammell, Stephen 1943– American illustrator whose work is consistently honest, exhilarating, spontaneous and playful. Gammell began illustrating books in 1973 and has won numerous honours and awards. He received the CALDECOTT MEDAL for his ingenious ILLUSTRATIONS for Karen Ackerman's *Song and Dance Man* (1988), a charming story of an elderly man recapturing his early days in vaudeville. Gammell presents a younger, more energetic Grandpa through shadows, silhouettes and bursts of colour. Both Olaf Baker's *Where the Buffaloes Begin* (1981) and CYNTHIA RYLANT's *The Relatives Came* (1985) were Caldecott Honour Books. Gammell's trademark rainbow colours and witty style are the perfect complement to the humorous text of *The Relatives Came*, a nostalgic look back at the love and laughter of family reunions in rural Appalachia. His illustrations demonstrate his conviction that 'you can have fun with people without making fun of them'. Gammell began writing his own texts with *Once Upon MacDonald's Farm* (1981), a whimsical version of a classic. *Is That You, Winter: A Story* (1997) is the story of grumpy Old Man Winter, captivatingly illustrated in pastel, pencil and watercolour. Children and adults alike smile when they encounter the somewhat eccentric protagonist and his rickety truck. JAT

Gannett, Ruth Stiles 1923– American author who, with her stepmother Ruth Chrisman Gannett as illustrator, wrote *My Father's Dragon* (1948), a Newbery Honour Book in which nine-year-old Elmer Elevator journeys to a distant land to free a baby dragon. *Elmer and the Dragon* (1950) and *The Dragons of Blueland* (1961) complete the series. The trilogy was reissued as *Three Tales of My Father's Dragon* (1997). PDS

Gardam, Jane 1928– British author. Born in Coatham, on the coast of northeast Yorkshire, England, she spent her childhood there and on a farm in Cumbria, two landscapes evoked with powerful effect in her writing. Gardam's fame as an adult novelist came after critical acknowledgement of her early books about childhood and adolescence. *A Few Fair Days* (1971, 1998) recalls her childhood in the 30s, overshadowed by approaching war; *A LONG WAY FROM VERONA* (1971) is a teenager's account of school, growing independence and self-awareness. In *THE SUMMER AFTER THE FUNERAL* (1973), bereavement, homelessness and seriocomic encounters align the heroine's literary fantasies with other realities. Of *BILGEWATER* (1976) Gardam says 'it is the choice that has to be made between the creative and the critical or academic life'. It is also her most seriously funny book. The cramping social worlds of these clever girls have almost disappeared, but their creator's skill encourages rereadings and different interpretations of the details, hence the appearance of new editions on adult lists. In terms of textuality, the novels have much in common with those of WILLIAM MAYNE. They also represent the beginning of a second post-war flowering of classical storytelling.

There are new editions of Gardam's books for younger children, as if to suggest that later readers have grown into them more quickly than the first. *The Hollow Land* (1981) (a WHITBREAD AWARD winner) and *Bridget and William* (1981) are set in Cumbria, where insiders and incomers learn each other's ways. Young males explore history in the landscape and in oral stories. *Horse* (1982) is ideal for beginning readers with its well-paced telling. In *Kit* (1983) and *Kit in Boots* (1986) Gardam's youngest readers experience the contrast between what the storyteller thinks has to be exactly recorded and what the reader has to infer. *Tufty Bear* (1996) for the youngest in the next generation seems weaker. A FANTASY metafiction, *Through the Dolls' House Door* (1987) shifts between the great legends told to each other by the abandoned dolls and their owners' outgrowing of childhood imagination; an intertext for bookish insiders. MM

Garden, Nancy 1938– An American author of YOUNG ADULT FICTION whose work has been acclaimed for its sensitive portraits of the difficulties confronting lesbians. Garden was brought to national attention by the many attempts to censor *Annie on My Mind* (1982), a novel that focuses on the lesbian relationship between teenagers Lisa and Annie and the social pressures that they face when their lesbianism is made public. Although not the first juvenile book to address lesbianism, Garden's book is one of the most sensitive. Despite the critical acclaim the book has received, it has been widely censored by educators and parents across the United States, even being burned in one notorious case. The censorship does not prevent Garden from continuing to make lesbianism a central concern in many of her later books, including *Lark in the Morning* (1991) and *Good Moon Rising* (1996). Garden also addresses many other social problems in her realist novels, including child abuse and runaway children, but her chief fame is her ability to talk honestly about lesbianism, a controversial issue that is seldom discussed in children's literature. She strives to present positive depictions of lesbianism to young people who might only have received negative portraits. SAI

see also GAY AND LESBIAN LITERATURE

Garfield, Leon 1921–96 The most flamboyantly brilliant British children's author of his time, Garfield was born and brought up in Brighton. He broke away from his strictly Jewish family when he married VIVIEN ALCOCK, later to become a distinguished author herself. The theme of father–son conflict was subsequently never far away in many of Garfield's novels. His war service was spent in the Medical Corps, where one of his duties was disinterring concentration camp victims. This personal experience of evil was also to work its way into his stories.

His first published work, *JACK HOLBORN* (1964), immediately picked Garfield out as a writer of rare distinction. His feeling for odd, archaic language, assisted at times by Eric Partridge's monumental *A Dictionary of The Underworld* (1950), was linked to an action-packed ADVENTURE STORY format dating back to ROBERT LOUIS STEVENSON. There was also a black sense of humour plus an exuberant use of metaphors owing much to DICKENS, whose own unfinished *The Mystery of Edwin Drood* was completed by Garfield in 1980, so expertly that it is almost impossible to spot the join. Had Garfield been writing a hundred years ago, his books would surely have been read by all ages at a time when adventure stories enjoyed universal popularity. The decision in 1964 to publish him as a children's author was probably inevitable, although children themselves sometimes found his language opaque and his plots convoluted. Those who persevered, however, were well rewarded by unforgettable characters and melodramatic climaxes of rare excitement. There was also a strong moral tone to his work. A typical young Garfield hero or heroine usually has to learn that appearances can deceive, with handsome, outwardly philanthropic characters often far more dangerous than those whose unprepossessing looks sometimes conceal a noble inner spirit.

Garfield's strong sense of social justice is also never absent. Skilled in describing poverty and squalor in all their various manifestations, he always condemned cruelty and neglect for what it was. This was achieved without preaching and with a firm sense of the possibility of redemption. Even the worst Garfield villain is usually offered – and sometimes accepts – a last chance to change. Consistently outstanding in everything he did, high points in his large output include *BLACK JACK* (1968), and *Smith* (1967), the story of a young pickpocket. *The Strange Affair of Adelaide Harris* (1971) shows Garfield in a more light-hearted vein than usual telling the story of a kidnapping with a happy ending. *The Sound of Coaches* (1974) unforgettably describes the struggle of an adopted boy choosing between his glamorous but corrupt natural parent and his hard-working, less romantic adoptive father. Garfield also expertly adapted SHAKESPEARE's plays for ANIMATED films on television, and many of these were also published in special editions aimed at children in a daring and often brilliant attempt to emulate the success of CHARLES and MARY LAMB's original *TALES FROM SHAKESPEAR* (1807). He and his great friend EDWARD BLISHEN won the CARNEGIE MEDAL for their retelling of Greek myths (see CLASSICAL MYTHOLOGY) in *THE GOD BENEATH THE SEA* (1970). NT

Gargling With Jelly (1985) The first of several successful collections for children, in which the British poet BRIAN PATTEN combines amusing verse about weird characters, disgusting predicaments and crazy scenarios with serious poetry dealing with urban deprivation and pollution. His humour is too robust for some adults, but he is extremely popular with children. JL

Garland, Sarah 1944– Garland is noted for her PICTUREBOOKS, such as *Going Shopping* (1982), *Doing the Washing* (1983), *Having a Picnic* (1984) and *Oh, No!* (1989) which, with perception, humour and a fluent drawn line, reflect the world of the young child, complete, frequently, with harassed mother and domestic chaos. She has also written 'junior novels' with ILLUSTRATIONS, such as *The Survival of Arno Mostyn* (1996). JAG

garlands see MISCELLANIES

Garner, Alan 1934– British writer for children and adults, whose ambitiously innovative work has won many prizes. Born in Cheshire into a family with a long history of craftworking, he has lived most of his life in the vicinity of Alderley Edge, which forms both the outer and inner landscape for all his work, most explicitly in the *STONE BOOK QUARTET* (1976/8). Formative experiences include childhood illness, an education in classical languages and archaeology at Manchester Grammar School and Oxford University, which separated him from his working-class family, and a history of recurring depression, all described in the essay collection *The Voice that Thunders* (1997).

After serving briefly in the army Garner dedicated himself to writing, using extensive research on Celtic mythology, local folklore and scientific theory as the springboard to explore the interconnection of real and magic worlds, past and present, time and place. *THE*

WEIRDSTONE OF BRISINGAMEN (1960), its sequel *The Moon of Gomrath* (1963) and *ELIDOR* (1965) are vividly told FANTASIES in a Cheshire setting, written for younger readers, whilst *THE OWL SERVICE* (1967) and *Red Shift* (1973) experiment controversially with dialogue and structure to treat adolescent sexuality, class and violence.

Garner has also written a locally set nativity play, *Holly from the Bongs* (1974), librettos, screenplays for films and TELEVISION documentaries, radio drama, poetry, and critical and historical essays, and retold folk and FAIRY STORIES in collections such as *Fairy Tales of Gold* (1980) and *A Bag of Moonshine* (1993). His first novel for adults, *Strandloper* (1996), links the rituals of 19th-century Cheshire with those of Australian Aboriginals. He was awarded the O.B.E. in 2001. SG

Garnett, Eve 1900–91 Author and illustrator, Garnett wrote the first 20th-century bestseller for children peopled entirely by working-class characters. *THE FAMILY FROM ONE END STREET* (1937) won the CARNEGIE MEDAL for that year, beating J.R.R. TOLKIEN'S *THE HOBBIT* on the way, and was also widely translated. Garnett treats her dustman character Mr Ruggles and his large, cheerful family with some condescension, but each child's particular adventures are well described, beautifully illustrated and often very funny. Other books followed, but none as successful as this minor but pleasing work, partially set in Lewes where the author lived most of her life. Garnett also illustrated *A CHILD'S GARDEN OF VERSES* for Puffin in 1948, as well as editing and illustrating an anthology of her own, *A Book of the Seasons*, in 1952. NT

Gaskin, Chris 1957– New Zealand's best-known illustrator of children's books who has worked closely with writers such as RON BACON (*The Clay Boy*, 1989), GAELYN GORDON (*Duckat*, 1991) and CAROLINE MACDONALD (*Joseph's Boat*, 1987). Gaskin works in a range of media and styles and his art reflects his intense interest in the natural living world. In *Joseph's Boat* he uses colour pencil on paper to capture the beauty of a New Zealand island landscape, while in a series written by Philip Temple – which includes *Beak of the Moon* (1981), *Moa, The Story of a Fabulous Bird* (1985) and *Kotuku: the Flight of the White Heron* (1994) – he combines realistic depiction with lyrical and evocative settings. In *A Walk to the Beach* (1988), one of four titles Gaskin has written and illustrated, the reader is invited to explore the New Zealand environment in a series of carefully crafted realistic scenes. He has been awarded the RUSSELL CLARK AWARD for children's book ILLUSTRATION three times, twice in consecutive years. In addition to children's fiction, Gaskin, in *Picture Magic: Illustrating a Picturebook* (1992), describes the collaborative process involved in illustrating the PICTUREBOOK *Duckat* while *Picturebook Magic* (1996) reflects the dreams and visions of nine prominent New Zealand illustrators. LL

Gates, Doris 1901–87 Librarian, storyteller and author of children's books. Born in Mountain View, California, Gates spent most of her life in that state, the setting for many of her books. In 1940, her second novel, *Blue Willow*, earned widespread attention for its sensitive portrayal of migrant workers in the San Joaquin Valley. This pioneering work of social realism, runner-up for the NEWBERY MEDAL, was based in part on Gates's experiences as a Fresno children's librarian. The sympathic portrayal of various ethnic and racial groups occurs in other novels, notably *Little Vic* (1951). Pony Rivers, a black boy, encounters prejudice, but his devotion to the horse Little Vic leads to his winning ride as a jockey.

An advocate of children's reading, Gates contributed to the series of Ginn readers. Her interest in classics resulted in her six-volume retelling of Greek myths. However, the influence of her dozen novels, especially *Blue Willow*, remains her most important legacy. Janey Larkin's hope and courage in the face of daunting poverty continue to ring true more than 50 years after the novel's publication. KKP

see also CLASSICAL MYTHOLOGY

Gatty, Margaret see JULIANA HORATIA EWING; see also *AUNT JUDY'S MAGAZINE*; DOLL STORIES; PUBLISHING AND PUBLISHERS

Gavin, Jamila 1941– Anglo-Indian author whose novels reflect her own childhood, which was divided between India and England. Many of her books are about friendships between British and Indian children. *Kamla and Kate* (1983) shows how an Indian girl and her white neighbour each find the other's lifestyle strange, but enticing. *Wheel of Surya* (1992) is the first of a thought-provoking trilogy for young adults which opens in India before partition. Gavin does not shirk from describing violent and horrific situations, but her novels remain both warm and optimistic. *Coram Boy* (2000) won the Whitbread Children's Book of the Year Award. KA

Gawain, Sir see also KING ARTHUR; SELINA HASTINGS; JOANNA TROUGHTON; JUAN WIJNGAARD

Gay, John see FABLES

Gay, Marie-Louise 1952– Canadian illustrator and author. Born in Quebec City, Gay lived in British Columbia and Ontario and studied at the Montreal Institute of Graphic Arts. After publishing her first illustrated book, Bertrand Gauthier's *Hou Ilva* (1976), she also attended the Academy of Art College in San Francisco before working for the Montreal children's book publisher La Courte Echelle. In addition to illustrating the work of prominent poets and writers, such as TIM WYNNE-JONES's *The Last Piece of Sky* (1993) and Susan Musgrave's *Dreams are More Real than Bathtubs* (1998), she illustrates her own texts. Her exuberant pen-and-ink graphics washed by ink dyes are distinctive and sophisticated. In 1984 she won the Prix Alvin Bélisle for her own title, *La Soeur de Robert*, as well as the Canada Council for Children's Literature Prize for French illustration for her *Drôle d'école* and the equivalent English prize for DENNIS LEE's *Lizzy's Lion*. In 1987 she received two Amelia Frances Howard-Gibbon illustration awards for her own titles, *Moonbeam on a Cat's Ear* and *Rainy Day Magic*, which also won the Governor General's Award for English illustration. In 1997 she was nominated for the same award for *Rumplestiltskin*. MB

gay and lesbian literature for children and young adults While books with explicitly gay and lesbian content have appeared only in the last several decades, many Anglo-American classics are fundamentally homosocial, or concerned with same-sex friendships and family bonds. The public-school story, for instance, championed passionate and arguably erotic friendships among boys; Thomas Hughes' *TOM BROWN'S SCHOOLDAYS* (1857) and F.W. Farrar's *Eric, or Little By Little* (1858) are representative. KENNETH GRAHAME's *WIND IN THE WILLOWS* (1908) portrays a similar fraternal enclave. Romantic friendship drives LUCY MAUD MONTGOMERY's *ANNE OF GREEN GABLES* (1908); Anne and Diana pledge eternal love and enact courtship rituals lifted from romance novels. Like Anne, tomboy Jo March in LOUISA MAY ALCOTT's *LITTLE WOMEN* (1868) yields to compulsory heterosexuality, but not before some spirited gender-bending and 'queer performances'. Victorian and Edwardian periodical serials also idealised the homosocial, innocent world of chums, even as the medicalisation of homosexuality was well underway.

Some genres offer protective but expressive cover for fairly specific homosexual experience. Oscar Wilde's heart-breaking FAIRY TALES in *THE HAPPY PRINCE* (1888) – written for his own children – blend Victorian Protestant pathos with homoerotic imagery, emphasising physical and moral anguish. Ann Weil's ADVENTURE STORY and Newbery Honour Book *Red Sails to Capri* (1953) features three dashing male characters powerfully reminiscent of the famous homosexual artists and writers who fled Europe in the 19th century and turned Capri into a sub-cultural paradise. Michele, the young protagonist, falls in love with the three aesthetes and their flaming red sails. Both L. FRANK BAUM's *The Wonderful Wizard of Oz* (1900) (see OZ SERIES) and J. M. BARRIE's *PETER PAN* (1911) celebrate alternative families in a utopian/dystopian landscape; MGM's 1939 film *The Wizard of Oz* has become a gay male touchstone, as such coded phrases as 'friends of Dorothy' and 'I have the feeling we're not in Kansas any more' attest.

Homosexuality made its official début in a young adult 'problem novel', JOHN DONOVAN's *I'll Get There. It Better Be Worth the Trip*, published in 1969, the year of the Stonewall Riots. Thirteen-year-old Davy has a brief sexual encounter with classmate Altschuler, which reviewers found groundbreaking. Around 90 novels with gay and/or lesbian content have since been published for adolescents in the United States and Britain. As Christine Jenkins has noted, many feature white, middle-class protagonists, affirm homophobic stereotypes, and end in violence and death. In Sandra Scoppettone's *Trying Hard to Hear You* (1974), Jeff is beaten up, and his lover, Phil, reacts by getting drunk and driving his car into a tree, killing himself and a female passenger. In *Dance On My Grave* (1982), AIDAN CHAMBERS attacks sexual obsession and homophobia, rather than homosexuality, but sadly Hal's lover Barry is sacrificed to illustrate the point. The first young adult novels about AIDS, M.E. KERR's *Night Kites* (1986) and Gloria Miklowitz's *Goodbye, Tomorrow* (1987), emphasise homophobia and AIDS-phobia as social problems but still affirm stereotypes.

The 'problem' mode has given way to the coming-out novel. Deborah Hautzig's *HEY, DOLLFACE* (1978) and Elizabeth Levy's *Come Out Smiling* (1981) provide fairly objective information about teen lesbianism; NANCY GARDEN's *Annie On My Mind* (1982) and *Good Moon Rising* (1996) emphasise the importance of achieving a lesbian-positive identity. Writers working in the information or coming-out tradition include Keith Hale, A.M. Homes, M.E. KERR, NORMA KLEIN, Ron Koertge, Isabel Miller and DAVID REES. Inspired partly by postmodernism, some authors even question the personal and political efficacy of gay/lesbian identity, musing instead on the elusive weirdness of life and love. Francesca Lia Block's metafictional Weetzie Bat series (see *DANGEROUS ANGELS* SERIES) chronicles the love of Dirk and Duck in multicultural Los Angeles; in *Baby Be-Bop* (1995), Dirk becomes infatuated with his best friend Pup, and admits this to himself and to the ghost of his surfer dad. Stacey Donovan's innovative *Dive* (1996) describes both the sexual awakening of its protagonist Virginia and her resistance to conventional patterns of thought. Theresa Nelson's *Earthshine* (1996) is a sophisticated meditation on AIDS, family and community, which often alludes to *The Wizard of Oz*. In such works, same-sex desire is respected but not always assigned a consistent 'identity'; storytelling, rather than sexuality, tends to be foregrounded.

While contemporary gay and lesbian identity seems largely an American idiom, with roots in the Puritan fetish of evangelical conversion, young adult novels with lesbian and gay themes are now appearing in countries outside the United States and Britain (often former colonies). Australian texts include NADIA WHEATLEY'S *The Blooding* (1987) and MORRIS GLEITZMAN'S *TWO WEEKS WITH THE QUEEN* (1989), both about boys, and JENNY PAUSACKER'S terrific *What Are Ya* (1987), which addresses lesbian sexuality and identity. *Skin Deep*, by the South African writer Toeckey Jones, likens homophobia to racism, situating the text in a long tradition of resistance literature. Some excellent work has also appeared in New Zealand and Canada. In the United States, two useful anthologies of young adult lesbian/gay fiction were published in 1994, which emphasise the complexities of class, race and geography as well as sexual orientation: *Not the Only One*, edited by Tony Grima, and *Am I Blue?*, edited by Marion Dane Bauer.

In the late 1980s the establishment of the Alyson Wonderland series by the lesbian/gay publishing house Alyson Publications introduced PICTUREBOOKS about lesbian/gay families, which in turn inspired controversy and censorship. Leslea Newman's *Heather Has Two Mommies* (1989) and Michael Willhoite's *Daddy's Roommate* (1991), which do little more than depict children with lesbian/gay parents, have been consistently removed from school and public LIBRARIES. Nevertheless, these and later titles (now close to 20 in all) have been praised for their positive images of same-sex parents; sexuality is downplayed in favour of a normalising rhetoric of family values. In picturebooks about AIDS, such as Mary Kate Jordan's *Losing Uncle Tim* (1989), the gay male body is typically absent or implied. Adults are invited to read between the lines. Still to appear is a picturebook about a young gay or lesbian child, despite the existence of such self-aware children and the example of foreign films such as *Du er kanne alene*, *Voor een verloren soldaat* and *Ma vie en rose* (the last of which tells the story of a transgendered 'boy'). This gap is due both to the general reticence about SEX IN CHILDREN'S BOOKS, and to the lingering belief that homosexuality is incompatible with (even antithetical to) childhood and its culture. KBK

Gay Neck: The Story of a Pigeon see BORIS ARTZYBASHEFF; DHAN GOPAL MUKERJI; see also ANIMALS IN FICTION

Gee, Maurice 1931– International award-winning New Zealand writer of FANTASY/SCIENCE FICTION for children. In *Under the Mountain* (1979), telepathic twins harness Auckland's volcanic energy to overcome huge, voracious cosmic slugs. In *The World Around the Corner*, illustrated by Gary Hebley (1980), Caroline helps Moongirl battle against a poison-spewing dragon. In the *World of O* series – *The Halfmen of O* (1982), *The Priests of Ferris* (1984) and *Motherstone* (1985) – Susan and Nick battle against political, religious, and military tyrannies. They defeat Otis Claw by placing both stone Halves of Evil and Good on the Motherstone; they overturn the High Priest's rule; they nullify the Weapons by re-placing the Halves on the Motherstone and returning O to palaeolithic time. The outstanding character is the raw-humoured go-between, Jimmy Jaspers.

Subsequently, in uncompromising realistic novels set in New Zealand's past, Gee has exposed community prejudice, racism, cowardice, heroism, and the long-term damage caused by abuse and bullying. In *The Fire Raiser* (1986), set during World War I, two boys and two girls finally identify the middle-aged arsonist whose still-grieving mother blames him for his little sister's drowning. In *The Champion* (1989), set during World War II, Gee explores the relationship between three children – Kiwi Rex, part-Maori Dawn, Dalmatian Leo – and a war-shocked black American billeted with Rex's family for recuperation. These two novels made powerful TELEVISION films. In his multi-award-winner, *THE FAT MAN* (1994), Gee confronts bullying, while *The Hostel Girl* (1999) – a novel set in the 1950s – shows 14-year-old Ailsa and her friend Callum confronting a stalker. Gee's awards also include several shortlistings, the NEW ZEALAND BOOK OF THE YEAR for *The Halfmen of O*, and the ESTHER GLEN MEDAL for *Motherstone*. DAH

Gem, The see *'THE BIG FIVE'*; see also ANNUALS; *GREYFRIARS HOLIDAY ANNUALS*; SCHOOL STORIES

***Gemma* series** (from 1968–9) Novels by NOEL STREATFEILD which began with *Gemma* and continued through another three books: *Gemma and Sisters* (1968), *Gemma Alone* (1969) and *Goodbye Gemma* (1969). The series follows the doings of Gemma Bow and her cousins. Gemma, child of a divorced actress and herself a once-famous child-star, comes to live with her aunt's family in Headstone. The series, while focusing mainly on the stage and recording activities of the children (who all turn out to be highly talented), is also loosely structured around the development of Gemma, though as in most of Streatfeild's other work, this 'development' is only lightly or superficially treated. From being thoroughly selfish and self-centred, Gemma comes to comprehend the idea of being part of a family, and through the roles she takes in plays emerges with understanding of other emotional realities than her own.

Mary Cadogan and Patricia Craig in *You're a Brick, Angela* (1976) describe the *Gemma* books as vulgar and pedestrian, complaining that in 'the four books there is hardly a memorable episode'. The *Gemma* series certainly has its share of literary cliché, but does not deserve the degree of dismissiveness with which Cadogan and Craig treat it. If they do not represent a departure in a new direction, the books at least display Streatfeild's usual strengths, which include the ability to pace the action well, to discuss the theatre and to use other literary work (e.g. *REBECCA OF SUNNYBROOK FARM* and *Romeo and Juliet*) interestingly. SA

Geoffrey of Monmouth ?–1155 Author of the *Historia Regum Britanniae* (c. 1136), a romanticised history of the kings of Britain from its founding after the Trojan War (c. 1115 BC) to the last British king, Cadwallader (d. 689 AD). The book is based on lost Welsh chronicles, historians such as Nennius (c. 800), oral material, and Geoffrey's own imagination. He turned chronicle into literary history, and is the source for such characters as Hudibras, King Lear, Cymbeline, King Cole and, above all, Merlin, KING ARTHUR, Guinevere, Gawain and Mordred. His work, immediately popular, generated later Arthurian material in English, Welsh and French, and much that has formed an important part of children's culture. GA

Geography Made Easy (1784) An early American geography book by Jedediah Morse. For the most part it contained descriptions of America and became one of the most popular works of its kind. It also contained unusual features, such as the characterisation of the residents of Connecticut as being intemperately fond of law suits and petty arbitrations. Morse followed a practice begun in England with the publication of *The Geography of Children; or a short and easy method of teaching or learning geography* (1737), translated from a French work by Abbé Nicolas Lenghet du Fresnoy; THOMAS BOREMAN's *Gigantick Histories* (1740); and JOHN NEWBERY's *Circle of the Sciences* (1745). KSB

George, Jean Craighead 1919– American writer and illustrator. Born in Washington DC, George, having worked as a reporter, artist, teacher and editor, has written (and illustrated some of her own) PICTUREBOOKS, juvenile novels, a wide variety of non-fiction (both single books and series on nature), information guides, articles on natural history and children's literature, and an autobiography, *Journey Inward* (1982). George's first novel, *Vulpes, the Red Fox* (1948), was written in collaboration with her husband, John George. Her first book written under her own name, *My Side of the Mountain* (1959), adapted as a film in 1969, is a survival story about Sam, a teenage boy who runs away from his New York City home and lives alone in the Catskill Mountains for a year. In 1990, George's sequel to this novel, *On The Far Side of the Mountain*, takes teenage Sam out again upon an adventure journey into the wilderness in search of his missing sister and pet falcon. George's books often deal with survival and journeys leading toward self-discovery.

As a naturalist, George's work is realistic with no attempt made to humanise the wildlife she writes about. George observes and reports upon animals' behaviour, their habits and habitats, in a distanced, scientific way. She draws upon her own reading, research and actual study of animals in the wilderness. Her carefully researched and varied material appears in many different formats, both fiction and non-fiction, including her juvenile series *Thirteen Moons* and *One Day*, cookbooks, nature maps, trail guides and 'how-to' books directly involved with her subject of nature, wildlife and the environment. Some of her books have been re-released with new ILLUSTRATIONS for her current readers of all ages.

George's effective use of her material is due in large part to her skill and expertise as a storyteller. Her NEWBERY AWARD winner *Julie of the Wolves* (1972) was followed by a sequel, *Water Sky* (1987). In this novel, George focuses upon the ancient Eskimo ritual of carving up the bowhead whale to be shared amongst their people. This novel also deals with the tension between the native people and the environmentalists, noting the fact that it was white whalers who led to the gradual decimation of the whale population which is so important to the history, religion, culture and food supply of the Inuit people. George has won many awards for her writing and world-wide public and scientific recognition for her work. MRS

see also ANIMALS IN FICTION; ECOLOGY; NATIVE AMERICANS IN CHILDREN'S LITERATURE; KATHERINE PATERSON; ROBINSONNADES

Geras, Adèle 1944– British novelist and poet, Born in Jerusalem and living in Manchester. Her Oxford student days are recounted in the autobiographical *Yesterday* (1992). Formerly actress and teacher, she writes prolifically for all age groups. Her stories for the young often show the magic of objects – patchwork quilts in *Apricots at Midnight* (1977), Russian dolls in *Nina's Magic* (1990) – and humour in inimitable eccentricity, as in *The Fabulous Fantoras, Book One: Family Files* (1988) and *The Fabulous Fantoras, Book Two: Family Photographs* (1993). Jewish culture and history influence the novels *The Girls in the Velvet Frame* (1978) and *Voyage* (1983) – a moving narrative set on an emigrant ship to America – the retellings in *My Grandmother's Stories* (1990) and the story collection *Golden Windows* (1993). Her *Beauty and the Beast and other stories* (1996) was illustrated by LOUISE BRIERLEY, and in 1998 she wrote *The Six Swan Brothers* for Scholastic's series of paperback

FAIRY TALES. Her atmospheric supernatural stories include *Letters of Fire* (1984), containing the memorable 'The Graveyard Ghost', and haunting Manchester-based narratives in *A Lane to the Land of the Dead* (1994). Geras's strong depiction of the trials of adolescent feeling is evinced in the EGERTON HALL trilogy, the stories in *The Green Behind the Glass* (1982), *Happy Endings* (1986), in which a production of Chekhov's *Three Sisters* subtly mirrors the characters' developing relationships, and *Stagestruck* (1999), also dealing with the theatre. The monumental *Troy* (2000) is her most complete achievement to date. DCH

Gerrard, Roy 1935–97 After Salford School of Art, Gerrard was both a teacher and a painter before turning to children's books. By the time of his death, he had completed a dozen books, each instantly recognisable through his three trademarks: sprightly, comical, rhyming verse; rotund, squat characters; and highly finished, impeccably researched, richly detailed and decorated pictures. Heroic action was his favourite subject, whether that of famous historical characters, as in *Sir Francis Drake, His Daring Deeds* (1988), or that of unknown children, as in *Croco'nile* (1994). *Sir Cedric* (1983) was voted one of the top ten books of the year by the New York Times. JAG

Gesta Romanorum [*Deeds of the Romans*] (c. 1290) A collection in simple Latin of tales, LEGENDS, FABLES and saints' lives, with allegorical morals, presented as history and set in the time of a Roman emperor. The tales have multiple sources, including eastern and classical. Perhaps intended as sermon exempla, they were early appropriated for children and provided material for such writers as CHAUCER, SHAKESPEARE and Schiller. There are many versions; the earliest extant manuscript is dated 1326, the first printed edition (Dutch) appeared in 1481, and the first English edition was published by Wynkyn de Worde c. 1517. GA

Getting of Wisdom, The (1910) Novel by the Australian writer, Henry Handel Richardson (Ethel Florence Lindesay Richardson, 1870–1946). Described by H.G. Wells as the best SCHOOL STORY he knew, it traces the progress of Laura Rambotham at a Ladies College in Melbourne. Richardson's autobiography *Myself When Young*, left unfinished on her death, suggests an identification with Laura, and the work draws on the author's own life. It ironically juxtaposes the quest for knowledge (the overt point of Laura's being at school), and the 'getting of wisdom', which is both a slightly cynical schooling in the ways of the world and people, and a more profound and growing understanding of herself.

Where a good many school stories are structured around the integration of individuals into a group, *The Getting of Wisdom* is unusual in that, while on the one hand charting the ways in which Laura does her best to be accepted and liked by a community which she in fact rather despises, it also affirms her basic non-conformity and difference, her essential and interior alienation from the group. 'She went out from school with the uncomfortable sense of being a square peg, which fitted into none of the round holes of her world; the wisdom she had got, the experience she was richer by, had, in the process of equipping her for life, merely seemed to disclose her unfitness. She could not then know that, even for the squarest peg, the right hole may ultimately be found; seeming unfitness prove to be only another aspect of a peculiar and special fitness.'

What the novel also traces is the making of the artist. It moves from Laura's inventing of stories for her siblings – stories which despite their derivative and clichéd language show the mind and consciousness at work in the process of creation – to her neo-gothic efforts with Doges and black-cloaked assassins, and eventually, it may be presumed, to the kind of novel which *The Getting of Wisdom* itself is: profound and insightful, compassionate and wry. SA

ghost stories Stories of the supernatural which play upon the desire of many children (as also some adults) to be pleasurably frightened, even terrified. Originally orally transmitted, FOLKTALES and LEGENDS, including the ghostly, were for audiences of all ages. In SHAKEPEARE's *The Winter's Tale*, Queen Hermione begs her little son 'to do your best/To fright me with your sprites'. He 'will do it softly' and begins at once: 'There was a man . . . dwelt by a churchyard . . .' Children have also frightened each other in ancient games and rituals which are half-acted stories. In one such the children sit in a circle in eerie half-light; they provide a dismal groaning refrain to the narrator's low-voiced churchyard tale, which ends with an explosive ghostly screech, followed by semi-hysterical laughter all round.

Traditional stories of the supernatural appeared in children's books throughout the 20th century. And in that century original ghost fiction for children began to establish itself. Some was still based on STORYTELLING: M.R. James (1862–1936), master of the genre for adults, also told two ghost stories to children – *A School Story* and *Wailing Well* – which were later included (probably after some adaptation) in his adult collections. His friend, A.C. Benson, produced two volumes of original stories told to Eton schoolboys. These and similar work were, however, not in the mainstream of writing for children. Professional children's writers, such as ELEANOR FARJEON and LAURENCE HOUSMAN, wrote only the occasional, mild-mannered ghost story for children's miscellanies such as *JOY STREET*.

Change came towards the middle of the century. Christopher Woodforde's *A Pad in the Straw* (1952) – an otherwise rather undistinguished collection – was hailed by the Oxford critic, Lord David Cecil, as 'breaking new ground. Stories for the young, except FAIRY TALES and FANTASIES, belong to the same categories as stories for grown up people; only they are, as it were, transposed into a treble key. We have seen this process applied to thrillers, historical romances, detective stories and stories of domestic life. Dr Woodforde is the first writer I know of to have applied it to the ghost story.'

There was a ready-made readership, extending even to the very young, for whom (it was felt) the fearfulness had to be tempered. From the mid-40s onward Robert Bright (1902–88) was producing simple, illustrated story-books about a cheery little ghost, Georgie, who 'never scared anybody, he was much too shy for that'. Most stories, however, were for older children, and took a tougher line. The genre became popular, and there cannot be many British writers for children who have not tried their hand at it. JOAN AIKEN has been particularly prolific, with collections such as *A Fit of Shivers* (1990). Most ghost stories are short and tend to focus on the trigger of fear, wonder or awe. Even so, the supernatural often allows for a projection of character or situation not otherwise possible. Longer stories have room for developed comedy – as in *The Ghost of Thomas Kempe* (1973) by PENELOPE LIVELY – or for metaphysical and moral analysis – as in *The Ghost Downstairs* (1972) by LEON GARFIELD.

As well as retold traditional ghost stories and modern stories specifically written for children, editors have trawled through old publications for tales originally thought suitable only for adults, with a view to re-presenting them for children. Examples are *The Monkey's Paw* by W.W. Jacobs and tales by M.R. James other than the two he himself meant for young listeners. Anthologists using such material have themselves often been writers of ghost fiction for children; they include, for instance, ROBERT WESTALL and AIDAN CHAMBERS.

In the world of children's ghost fiction written in the English language, the British themselves so far seem to have led in quantity, if not always in quality. Among the best known (besides those already mentioned) are JAN MARK, JOHN GORDON, GEORGE MACKAY BROWN, VIVIEN ALCOCK, HUGH SCOTT, DOROTHY EDWARDS, SUSAN PRICE and GILLIAN CROSS. In the United States such writers include VIRGINIA HAMILTON and Alvin Schwartz; in Canada, Paul Yee and TIM WYNNE-JONES; in India, RUSKIN BOND; in Australia, GILLIAN RUBINSTEIN and PAUL JENNINGS; in New Zealand, MARGARET MAHY.

The suitability of ghost stories for children is debated by concerned adults. Stories are generally found acceptable in which the supernatural verges on fantasy, or where fear is almost replaced by wistfulness, whimsicality or outright comedy. (The supernatural can also take a different, darker direction, towards horror. Horror stories – popular with many children – form a separate genre, not considered here.) To what extent should young readers be encouraged to experience fear – even at their own wish, even safe fear? To this question must always be added the doubts of the sceptics and rationalists – although it is certainly not necessary to believe in ghosts to enjoy ghost stories. Finally, there are theological objections, particularly among certain religious groups, to a literature which features the supernatural – ghosts and ghouls, spectres and spirits, wraiths and apparitions, poltergeists and *doppelgängers*. In defence of such literature for children, it can be argued that the stories stretch the imagination in ways otherwise impossible, and that the fear engendered is often akin to awe – a not unhealthy attitude towards the unknown or the unknowable. PP

Giant Golden Books see *GOLDEN BOOKS*

Gibbs, May [Kelly, Cecilia May Ossoli] 1877–1969 Australian author and illustrator. Gibbs's Gumnut, Wattle and other bushland babies have become icons of the mystery and magic of the Australian BUSH. Other images, such as her bold bad Banksia men, symbolise the threat that can be seen as inherent in that same landscape. While earlier writers and illustrators either etherealised the bush or saw it through English eyes, Gibbs created a FANTASY that grew out of her love of the native flora and fauna. More than any other children's writer in Australia, Gibbs became a household friend through her comic strips and some 20 publications which, even in her lifetime, were accompanied by cards, posters and other merchandise. In 1986 a vigorous campaign was mounted across Australia to preserve 'Nutcote', the home of May Gibbs, for posterity. As a result it is now a museum and educational centre, a shrine to Australia's first writer-illustrator to gain widespread critical acclaim and to become a 'popular' figure. Her most famous book, *SNUGGLEPOT AND CUDDLEPIE* (1918) has never been out of print. Gibbs's homely stories of animals and bush creatures are based on the perpetual battle between those who are 'on the side of the angels', and their enemies. She was a conservationist and believed in the primacy of story told in simple but measured language. She provided an early literary experience for countless Australian children. Many expressions used by her characters – 'quicksticks', 'deadibones', 'silly sooted cinder that I am' – have quickened the language of young readers and some have passed into Australian common usage. MSax

Giblin, James Cross 1933– American writer, and long-time editor with Clarion whose INFORMATION BOOKS are credited with having brought non-fiction for children to a new level. His books blend fact with intriguing presentation of unusual subjects such as milk, chimney sweeps, windows and eating utensils. In today's multimedia world where facts and visuals need to seize a reader's attention or risk losing it, his books are exceptionally popular. He has discovered a sequence that works, beginning with attention-grabbing titles such as *From Hand to Mouth* (1987), a history of utensils, and *Let there be Light: A Book about Windows* (1988). The books then take the reader from the subject's earliest history through to present-day use. Born in Cleveland, Ohio, he is the son of a lawyer and a teacher. Described as a shy, bookish child, he discovered the joys of editing in junior high school while serving on the school newspaper. In high school he discovered community theatre and soon developed a desire to write and direct plays. He earned his MFA as a playwright from Columbia University in New York. LAW

gift books Luxurious publications from the first two decades of the 20th century marking the climax of FAIRY FANTASY illustration. Fine examples of coloured fairy ILLUSTRATIONS had been available since the experimental printer EDMUND EVANS produced WALTER CRANE'S TOY BOOKS (1865–76) and RICHARD DOYLE'S *In Fairyland* (1869). However, the perfection of the photographic methods of three- and four-colour printing enabled the accurate reproduction of sophisticated images at a more reasonable cost. This was initially demonstrated in the largely topographic series of colour plate books published by A. & C. Black (from 1901). In 1905 Heinemann issued an edition of *Rip Van Winkle*, with illustrations by ARTHUR RACKHAM, which emulated those handsome volumes and set the pattern for subsequent gift books.

These small, fat quartos of classic tales of wonder were beautifully bound and extensively illustrated in colour; each plate was tipped in (see TIPPING IN) to a light card mount and protected with tissue printed with the picture caption. Deluxe limited editions were printed on handmade paper, bound in vellum tied with silk ribbons, and signed by the illustrator. Such an approach to presentation betrayed the fact that the gift book was a fine-art product exploited by commercial galleries, which would regularly exhibit the artwork for gift books prior to publication. The gift book soon became an essential feature of the Christmas market, encouraging rivalry between publishers, with Rackham often representing Heinemann, and EDMUND DULAC and KAY NIELSEN representing Hodder & Stoughton. World War I brought restrictions of paper and production, which hampered the publication of gift books and created a change of atmosphere which undermined attempts to revive them. DW

Gigantick Histories see THOMAS BOREMAN; see also *GEOGRAPHY MADE EASY*

Gilchrist, Jan Spivey 1949– African American illustrator and writer, born in Chicago and educated at Eastern Illinois University and the University of Northern Iowa. Gilchrist is the daughter of a minister who encouraged her to sketch from the family Bible using a no.2 pencil. Later, while teaching art, she worked as a freelance painter, but it was not until she met the poet ELOISE GREENFIELD that she was encouraged to try her hand at illustrating books. Her first assignment was *Children of Long Ago* (1983), a book by Greenfield's mother, Lessie Jones Little. The pastels for this book were so successful that it received a Parent's Choice Award. Now comfortable in many media, Gilchrist won acclaim for her ability to depict warm family scenes and to use light and dark effectively. In 1988 she illustrated *Nathaniel Talking*, a book of poetry by her mentor, Greenfield, which discusses growing up from the vantage-point of a nine-year-old narrator, Nathaniel B. Free. Rendered in black-and-white, the illustrations were cited for their vitality and dynamism, and won for Gilchrist the CORETTA SCOTT KING AWARD for ILLUSTRATION as well as the ALA's Social Responsibilities Round Table Award (1990). She later received the Coretta Scott King Honor Award for *Night on Neighborhood Street* (1992), a collection of poems by Greenfield about the different people who live in a community. After illustrating over ten books by Greenfield and others, Gilchrist wrote and illustrated her own *Indigo and Moonlight Gold* (1993), a PICTUREBOOK that explores the bond between mother and child. *Madelia* (1997) is about the tension between a young girl who wants to stay home and use her new watercolour set instead of accompanying her father, a minister, to his church on Sunday. Whatever her medium, Gilchrist's illustrations convey her pride in her African American heritage and her strong sense of community and family life. DJH

see also AFRICAN AMERICAN LITERATURE

Gill, Margery 1925– Although originally an engraver and etcher, Gill turned to illustrating children's books in pen-and-ink and found a ready market for her fluent sketches which can be found in numerous children's titles from the 1950s onwards, including *A Day without Wind* (WILLIAM MAYNE, 1964), *The Castle of Yew* (LUCY BOSTON, 1965), *Over Sea, Under Stone* (SUSAN COOPER, 1965) and several titles by MARGARET MAHY, NOEL STREATFIELD and HELEN

CRESSWELL. At a time when many illustrators were working in a similar field, Gill's drawings are instantly recognisable, popular with children and successful in their rôle of supporting and illuminating the narrative. JAG

Gimore, Mary see *FOUR AND TWENTY LAMINGTONS*

Gilmoure, Margaret see *AMELIARANNE* SERIES

gilt covers Children's GIFT BOOKS and ANNUALS from about 1870 to the 1920s were generally offered in pictorial covers with a design BLOCKED with gold foil, continuing a tradition that had started with early Victorian keepsakes. The best were designed by the illustrator of the book as part of an integrated design. GCB

Giltspur Trilogy comprising *The Battle Below Giltspur* (1988), *Dance of the Midnight Fire* (1989) and *Lightning Over Giltspur* (1991), in which Cormac MacRaois creates a landscape, firmly identified as County Wicklow, in which ancient forces of good and evil battle. The three young protagonists in these novels are modern-day children and share the preoccupations and interests of their peers. When spring comes, however, and the old powers of Bealtaine stir, they are hurled into a conflict which echoes back to the pre-history of Ireland as the terrible Morrigan, Formorians, Fir Bolgs and a cast of other characters from IRISH MYTHOLOGY rise up once more. Jeanette Dunne's pen-and-ink illustrations complement the text in catching the blurred worlds of FANTASY and reality. VC

Ging Gang Goolie, It's an Alien (1988) A SCIENCE FICTION farce in which British author Bob Wilson's deadpan text recounts how the course of interplanetary conquest is changed by the unexpected meeting of an alien Grobblewockian spaceman and the 3rd Balsawood Scout Troop. Wilson's inventive interlacing of comic-book literacies, TELEVISION-type narrative, line drawings, diagrams, handwritten and printed notes, and running jokes begun verbally and finished pictorially, captures several points of view in this encounter of two cultures and languages. Using familiar conventions, Wilson intriguingly offers language and form to young readers as playthings with which to explore the question 'What if?' EMH

Ginger Meggs Australian archetypal child larrikin and central character of the humorous newspaper comic strip (and film) of the same name, although first appearing in the cartoon strip 'Us Fellers' (1921) in the Sydney newspaper *Sunday Sun*. The work of J.C. Bancks and several successors, the strip continues today. Ginger always tries to get out of work, to bait the neighbourhood bully, and to impress those around him, especially his girlfriend, Minnie. A character of action, he is surprisingly philosophical about life, because he realises that, although he sometimes is not punished when guilty of a 'crime', he can be punished when innocent, and that this is the way of the world. JF

Giovanni, Nikki 1943– American poet for children and adults. Born in Tennessee, she became popular as a black revolutionary poet in the 1960s. Her first book for children was *Spin a Soft Black Song* (1971), depicting the experiences of urban black children in their neighbourhoods. The collection *Ego-Tripping and Other Poems for Young People* (1973) is more wide-ranging, celebrating the pride and energy of black children. Giovanni has always believed that poetry and politics go together, as demonstrated in her introduction to EVE MERRIAM's *The Inner City Mother Goose* (1996) and her own *Shimmy Shimmy Shimmy Like My Sister Kate: Looking at the Harlem Renaissance through Poems* (1996). CAB

Girl Weekly 'sister paper to the *EAGLE*' and companion to *SWIFT* and *ROBIN*. *Girl* was the first new post-war comic designed specifically for girls, first appearing in November 1951. It was founded by Revd Marcus Morris and published by Hulton. Combining the Amalgamated Press ethos of entertaining schoolgirl fiction with the less popular, high-minded respectability of the *GIRL'S OWN* approved by many parents, *Girl* aimed to attract the 10-to-16-year-old reader with information on careers (as nurses rather than doctors, kennel-maids but not vets, air-hostesses but never airline pilots) and instruction on horseriding and dog grooming, copious but lively fiction, and uplifting accounts of the lives of honourable women (contributed by Revd Chad Varah). Reflecting the early post-war era, and marking a modest break from the conventional fare of girls' papers, the first of the paper's heroines was air-ace Kitty Hawke (a female parallel to *Eagle*'s DAN DARE), whose adventures were soon to be replaced by more popular and enduring story strips such as 'Belle of the Ballet', 'Lettice Leafe' ('the greenest girl in the school') and the nursing serial, 'Susan of St. Brides'. *Girl* was printed on good paper with full-colour photogravure, and its high-quality artwork, instantly recognisable logo and ILLUSTRATIONS were its distinctive features.

While it did little to challenge traditional gender roles, *Girl* resisted the advertising and consumerism of the newly developing teenage market until 1960, when it changed in both quality and content in the editorial hands of Clifford Makins, under its new publisher, Longacre Press. Containing features on personal problems, teenage fashion and beauty (with an

'Am I a lily growing?' Illustration from *The Girl's Own Paper.*

emphasis on 'the natural look'), and popular stars such as Elvis Presley and Cliff Richard, *Girl* cast about to redefine and expand its readership. Failing to find approval with the younger end of the teenage market, it incorporated IPC's *Princess* in 1964, and ceased production in 1969. The title was relaunched in 1982 in a new, almost unrecognisable guise as a Fleetway publication, heralded as 'your very best friend', containing 'exciting stories, smashing pin-ups and lots of fun', and surviving until 1990, though without ever regaining the integrity or popularity of its origins.

Between 1953 and 1965, 13 volumes of *Girl Annual*, aimed at the Christmas market, were also published, reflecting the changing content and focus of the paper as it attempted to cater to the increasingly sophisticated and consumer-led interests of the teenager. Both the paper and the ANNUAL attracted well-known children's writers, including ELIZABETH BERESFORD, NOEL STREATFEILD and ROSEMARY SUTCLIFF; Barbara Woodhouse contributed articles on dogs. According to Mary Cadogan and Patricia Craig in *You're a brick, Angela* (1976), *Girl* 'never had the addictive quality of the cheaper papers'; nevertheless, it broke new ground in establishing a high-quality publication for girls whose lively and varied content has yet to be matched. BW

Girl's Own Paper, The Periodical which began as a pioneer RELIGIOUS TRACT SOCIETY penny weekly 'for girls of all classes' in 1880, edited by Charles Peters until 1907, after which it became a monthly magazine under the long-lived editorship of Flora Klickmann. The paper combined with *Woman's Magazine* in the 1920s, but it was redefined in 1931, on Klickmann's retirement, as a periodical for schoolgirls (but not young workers) aged 12 to 18. It combined with *Heiress* in the 1940s and, failing to respond to changing juvenile tastes, ceased publication in 1956.

Publishing fiction, articles and guidance on spiritual and domestic matters, education and employment, as well as a comprehensive advice column, from its inception the paper attracted notable women writers and journalists of the day, including MRS MOLESWORTH, Mrs de Horne Vaisey, Annie Swan, and E. NESBIT. Among its illustrators were WALTER CRANE and KATE GREENAWAY. While its pre-war outlook was essentially conservative and readers were encouraged to be dutiful and attentive to household matters, its advice on the need for training for employment was shrewd and radical in its time. It demonstrated patriotic worth during the World War II but always lacked the broader appeal and vitality of the other schoolgirl papers. BW

Girls' Crystal Periodical for young readers owing its origins to one of the Amalgamated Press weekly schoolgirl story papers, *The Crystal* (1935). It incorporated *The Schoolgirls' Weekly* within the same year (and *The Schoolgirl* in 1940), and from then on survived as *Girls' Crystal* until 1963. Story papers for elementary-schoolgirls had their heyday in the inter-war years, selling around 350,000 copies per week in the 1930s. Committed to a diet of entertainment rather than instruction, most girls' story papers were edited at one time or another by the legendary R.T. Eves, who fostered teams of male writers in the belief that women were unable to produce exhilarating and lively stories for girls. Each issue of *Girls' Crystal* contained a 20,000-word SCHOOL STORY, together with subsidiary fiction about girl sleuths and racing drivers, CAMPING, GUIDING, and circus adventures. While it catered for elementary-school girls, *Girls' Crystal* fiction rarely reflected the educational experience of these readers, focusing instead on exclusive boarding schools and scholarship girls from modest backgrounds. The only girls' story paper to survive the war years, it was transformed into a comic with a picture-strip format in the 1950s, increasingly attracting a younger schoolgirl readership and sustained by its membership club. The ANNUAL, published from 1942 to 1976, enjoyed a longer life, a tribute to its readership's lingering loyalty to a paper whose content was increasingly beyond its day. BW

Girl of the Limberlost, A see GENE STRATTON PORTER; see also ANIMALS IN FICTION

Gleeson, Libby (Elizabeth) 1950– Australian author of novels, short stories and PICTUREBOOKS, and activist on behalf of authors' rights. Gleeson worked as a teacher before becoming a full-time writer. Initially she wrote chiefly for younger teenagers: the warm, pared-down stories of pre-adolescent loneliness and self-discovery, *Eleanor, Elizabeth* (1984) and *I am Susannah* (1987). She (somewhat unusually) deals sympathetically with both adolescent and adult characters, as evidenced in *Dodger* (1990), which tells of a difficult boy coming to terms with parental abandonment through a teacher's intervention and a role in his school's production of the musical *Oliver*, and the linked short stories *Love Me, Love Me Not* (1993), detailing with restraint the stumbling minutiae of early adolescent romance. More recently, Gleeson has become one of Australia's most adventurous PICTUREBOOK writers – especially in creative partnership with Brisbane illustrator ARMIN GREDER. In *Uncle David* (1992) and *The Princess and the Perfect Dish* (1995) they explore perceptions of generic FAIRY TALE characters – the giant and the princess, while *The Great Bear* (1999) is an intensely powerful story of a dancing bear who finds freedom. *Where's Mum?* (1992), illustrated by CRAIG SMITH, also involves traditional fairy tale and NURSERY RHYME characters. Gleeson has written the engaging junior novel *Skating On Sand* (1994) and its sequels *Hannah + 1* (1996) and *Hannah and the Tomorrow Room* (1999), illustrated by ANN JAMES. NLR

Gleitzman, Morris 1953– British-born Australian novelist, screenwriter and journalist, best known for the novel *TWO WEEKS WITH THE QUEEN*. This moving book typifies Gleitzman's unsentimental blend of comedy and pathos – and also his formulaic plotline, in which a determined 11- or 12-year-old child goes to absurd lengths to resolve desperately serious family problems, simultaneously confronting social issues. Titles include the trilogy *Misery Guts* (1991), *Worry Warts* (1991) and *Puppy Fat* (1994), in which Keith struggles to cheer up his gloomy parents; and *Blabber Mouth* (1992), *Sticky Beak* (1993) and *Gift of the Gab* (1999), which tell of voiceless Rowena's difficulties with her loud father, stepmother and rude cockatoo. *Bumface* (1999) employs a similar mixture of burlesque and seriousness to address the issues of arranged marriages and the power of parents. NLR

Glen, Esther 1881–1940 New Zealand children's writer, journalist and philanthropist, best remembered for *Six Little New Zealanders* (1917), an account of family life on a sheep station, which was significant for its unusually light-hearted style and realistic characters. It was followed by *Twinkles on the Mountain* (1920), *Uncles Three at Kamahi* (1926) – sequel to *Six Little New Zealanders* – and *Robin of Maoriland* (1929). From 1925 Glen ran the children's pages in the Christchurch newspapers *The Sun* and later *The Press*. The annual ESTHER GLEN AWARD for a children's novel commemorates her huge contribution to promoting children's literature. LO

Go Well, Stay Well (1979) By Toeckey Jones, the earliest South African YOUNG ADULT novel to deal with the uprising of school pupils against apartheid in June 1976 and the irreversible changes which followed. (See also *THE SOUND OF THE GORA* by Ann Harries.) Through the courageous friendship between a white girl and a black girl, the white girl learns about the lives of black people and comes to see them in a new light, at the same time showing up the prejudices of her so-called liberal parents. A courageous work for its time, the novel is cautious on racial matters: everything is seen from the viewpoint of the white girl, and the author is patronising as well as stereotypical in her portrayal of an African manservant and her pop psychology about the attraction white boys feel for black girls. The book ends presciently with the thoughts of the protagonist about the future of the country and the value of personal commitment: 'But she was afraid to be too optimistic. There was a long, long way to go yet, and she had a feeling that time was running out. All the same, she told herself, simply to have started was something; at least there was hope in that.' ERJ

see also BIAS IN CHILDREN'S BOOKS

Goalkeeper's Revenge, The see BILL NAUGHTON

Gobbolino the Witch's Cat see URSULA MORAY WILLIAMS

Goble, Paul 1933– English-born American author and illustrator. Fascinated by American Indians from a young age, Goble read extensively on the subject and published his first children's book, *Red Hawk's Account of Custer's Last Battle*, in 1969. Throughout his career Goble has emphasised the humanity of Native Americans and their history, as told by them and not by outsiders. He has lived among Plains Indian tribes and been adopted by two of them, an indication of how well he understands Native culture and is trusted by those about whom he writes.

Goble won the CALDECOTT AWARD in 1979 for *The Girl Who Loved Wild Horses*. The ink and watercolour ILLUSTRATIONS accurately reflect Plains Indian culture, particularly in the importance paid to tipi placement and decoration. Another book based upon traditional narrative is *Iktomi and the Boulder: A Plains*

Indian Story (1989), a TRICKSTER tale. Here Goble's illustrations make use of extensive white space, boldly coloured figures, large black print for the narrative, grey italic for the narrator's comments to the audience, and small print for the trickster's comments upon the action, thus visually recreating the oral complexity of Native STORYTELLING techniques. He is widely considered to be the foremost interpreter of Native folklore for young people today. MDK

see also GEORGE ARMSTRONG CUSTER; NATIVE AMERICANS

Goble, Warwick 1862–1943 British illustrator of children's books. Two influences on Goble's work were his initial training as a printer specialising in chromolithography and his extensive travels through the Orient. He favoured soft, flowing watercolours with an oriental flavour which suited the atmosphere of the FAIRY TALES and mystical settings in which he specialised. His understanding of design and the reproduction of colour is evident in his work, for example in his series of colour plates for *Stories from the Pentamerone* by Giambattista Basile (1911). His watercolours were also published in GIFT BOOKS and exhibited at the Royal Academy. SM

see also LITHOGRAPHY

Goblin Market (1862) A powerful narrative poem of the Pre-Raphaelite period by CHRISTINA ROSSETTI. The morality of its plot is explicit: Lizzie, pure and invulnerable, saves her sister Laura from the wiles of the goblins who try to spirit the passionate girl away to a life of dissipation. But the richness of the language is erotic, particularly when the goblins attempt to squeeze the sinful fruit into Lizzie's mouth. Dante Gabriel Rossetti's line-drawings in the first edition highlight the sensuousness of the poem. It has been issued in several illustrated versions. HA

God Beneath the Sea, The (1970) and ***The Golden Shadow*** (1973) Celebrated retellings of Greek myth by LEON GARFIELD and EDWARD BLISHEN. Both books were distinctively illustrated by CHARLES KEEPING and both were worked as continuous narrative rather than presented as separate myths. *The God Beneath the Sea* is unified by the figure of Hephaestus who is told the tales of the pantheon by Thetis. Thetis rescues him when he is hurled from Olympus, the fall being a repeated motif which concludes the work. SA

see also CLASSICAL MYTHOLOGY

Godden, (Margaret) Rumer 1907–98 British author of novels written for adults, many of whom are quasi-autobiographical. Born in Sussex, she spent her early years in India where she returned again in 1929 to set up a dancing school; her interest in dance surfaces in both her adult and juvenile novels, *A Candle for St. Jude* (1948), *Thursday's Children* (1984), *Listen to the Nightingale* (1992), and in one of her last works, *Pippa Passes* (1994). After her first marriage to Lawrence Sinclair Foster in 1934 ended with his desertion – this period fictionalised in *Kingfishers Catch Fire* (1953) – and subsequent death, she remarried and settled in Scotland.

Godden's works for older readers, such as *THE GREENGAGE SUMMER* (1958) and *THE PEACOCK SPRING* (1975), present the world as emotionally complex and fragile; in this world, adults are as helpless and puzzled as the children. Her books for younger children, however, tend to affirm it as protective and loving – the possible exception to this rule being *The Doll's House* (1947), where domestic tragedy is permitted to erupt within the space assigned to play. *Miss Happiness and Miss Flower* (1961), for example, uses the construction and furnishing of a doll's house for two Japanese dolls as a powerful metaphor corresponding to the child Nona's gradual assimilation into her new household. Unlike in *The Greengage Summer*, the grown-ups in this book and its sequel, *Little Plum* (1963), are powerful and reassuring, able to make things come right. SA

see also DOLL STORIES

Godwin, William 1756–1836 British philosopher and author. Best known as the author of politically radical philosophy and fiction, Godwin also participated with his second wife Mary Clairmont in a business publishing children's books, started in 1805. Worried about the effect of Godwin's political reputation, the couple published under the name of their manager, Thomas Hodgkins, and Godwin himself wrote under various pseudonyms. The most important of Godwin's own works for children was probably *Fables Ancient and Modern* (1805). The firm also published other writing, including nearly all the children's books of CHARLES and MARY LAMB (most famously *TALES FROM SHAKESPEAR*, 1807). DWh

Goffstein, M(arilyn) B(rooke) 1940– American illustrator and writer of children's and YOUNG ADULT FICTION, known especially for the simplicity and clarity of her writing and drawing. Trained as an artist, M.B. Goffstein has written and illustrated more than 20 books, most notably the hauntingly poignant *Goldie the Dollmaker* (1969) and the related *Two Piano Tuners* (1970), both of which can be described as FAIRY TALES or FOLKTALES for our own time. Concerned with what constitutes human fulfillment, both stories explore, through careful, minimalist drawing and precise, simple text, the essence of what it means to be an artist and a craftsman. Fragile pen-and-ink and watercolour wash ILLUSTRATIONS combine with spare, surprisingly strong words, to create the atmosphere of a

GRIMMS' fairy tale. In her best work, Goffstein combines a keen miniaturism with a disarming delicacy, making the reader receptive to her point. Evincing a Jewish reverence for life, she explores themes such as those of vocation, creativity, the importance of ritual, and familial love. Yet it is in her precise characterisations of Goldie Rosenzweig and Debbie Weinstock that Goffstein finally achieves a sense of the wonder and the holiness of life and art. JCA

Goggle-Eyes (1989) Novel by ANNE FINE which belongs superficially to the sub-genre of the teenage 'problem novel'. The narrator is Kitty Killin who tells the story of how her initial dislike of her mother's new boyfriend (nicknamed 'Goggle-Eyes') gradually changes. Her listener is a distraught classmate in similar straits. However, unlike most other works dealing with broken homes and connected issues, *Goggle-Eyes* is written with a humour that not only energises and lightens but possesses the potential to change the situational dynamics which are at the heart of the book; Kitty feels the first smatterings of liking for Goggle-Eyes when she finds herself responding to his caustic wit. The book might in fact be said to be about transformation, for not only does Goggle-Eyes undergo a transformation in Kitty's perception from frog to prince, but the household under his supervision becomes more ordered and stable. Negative feelings are transformed into creative energy, as Kitty's writings for her English teacher (e.g. 'Ode to an Unwelcome Guest', 'Will She, Won't She Marry Him?' and 'Tales from a Once Happy Home') make clear, rather than being allowed to fester. *Goggle-Eyes* won both the GUARDIAN CHILDREN'S FICTION AWARD and the CARNEGIE MEDAL and was later adapted for British TELEVISION in four parts. SA

Golden Age, The (1895) Work by KENNETH GRAHAME which, along with its sequel, *Dream Days* (1898), is one of several books, also including *BEVIS* and *THE CATCHER IN THE RYE*, which, although intended for adults, have been highly influential for children's literature. *The Golden Age* is a first-person account of childhood in a closely knit Victorian family, much of the humour deriving from the ironically elevated tone of an adult observing children. Swinburne called it 'well-nigh too praiseworthy for praise', and it established Grahame's reputation. E. NESBIT's *BASTABLE* STORIES use a similar situation, but with a child-focused child narrator. PLH

Golden Books (from 1942) Inexpensive, brightly coloured American PICTUREBOOKS. Influenced by European models, especially the widely disseminated pamphlet-like books of the Soviet Union in the 1930s, *Golden Books* were printed with cardboard covers and a distinctive gold foil spine. Issued during the war-time paper rationing, the first dozen titles were strong on NURSERY RHYMES and traditional stories, such as *Three Little Kittens*, *MOTHER GOOSE*, *The Little Red Hen* and *Prayers for Children*. Originally costing a quarter, they were sold in grocery and drugstores as well as traditional venues. The lively pictures took precedence over the words, and Europeans were some of the most distinctive illustrators, including FEODOR ROJANKOVSKY, Tibor Gergely and Gustaf Tenggren. Other artists, such as GARTH WILLIAMS, RICHARD SCARRY and Eloise Wilkin, also produced notable works. Smaller series were also offered, such as the *Bank Street Books*, WALT DISNEY and *SESAME STREET* stories, as well as *Big Golden Books*, and *Giant Golden Books*. Having sold 300 million copies in 200 titles in their first dozen years, the Golden Books led the way for the proliferation of elaborate picturebooks of the 1950s in America and are still popular. GRB

Golden Compass, The see *HIS DARK MATERIALS*

'Golden Gorse' see *MOORLAND MOUSIE*; see also ANIMALS IN FICTION

Golden Shadow, The see EDWARD BLISHEN; *GOD BENEATH THE SEA, THE*; see also CLASSICAL MYTHOLOGY

Goldie [King], Fay 1905–93 Prolific South African writer of non-fiction and some fiction. She contributed a few children's books to the small output of children's literature in English in South Africa in the 1950s and 60s. (See also W.M. LEVICK, JULIET MARAIS LOUW and MARY PHILLIPS.) She mixed themes typical of 19th-century stories set in South Africa with more innovative ones, such as making a black boy the protagonist of *Zulu Boy* (1968). *Friends of the Bushveld* (1954) is her most enterprising and complex novel. Goldie's books lack strong characterisation, and are marred by inaccuracies. Her complacent, patronising racial attitudes were typical of white writers of the period. ERJ

Goldilocks and the Three Bears Familiar nursery tale, for a time thought to have been written by Robert Southey, who rendered it widely known by publishing it in *The Doctor* in 1837. However, a metrical manuscript written by Eleanor Muir (1831) exists in the Osborne Collection, and JOSEPH JACOBS, in *More English Fairy Tales* (1894), published what he believed was likely to be a much earlier version of the tale, 'Scrapefoot', the story of a fox and three bears. In Southey's version, an old woman, 'who could not have been a good, honest old Woman', enters the house of three bears, one a 'Great, Huge Bear', one 'Middle-sized' and one a 'Little, Small, wee Bear', and tastes the porridge which has been left to cool. She then tries out each of their chairs and beds in turn until she finally falls asleep, replete and comfortable, in the smallest bear's bed. On their return the bears discover the intruder and in fear of her life the old woman leaps through the open window, to an uncertain fate. Subsequent retellings have brought about certain changes, the most notable being the transformation of the old woman into a young girl, whose name was altered from Silver-hair to Silver Locks, and then to Little Golden-Hair before writers settled on the now familiar Goldilocks, towards the end of the 19th century. The rhythmical refrains of the bears – 'Who's been eating my porridge?' – in their 'Great, Huge', 'Middle-sized' and 'Little, Small, wee' voices have, however, survived. MSut

Golding, William see *LORD OF THE FLIES*; see also ADVENTURE STORIES; see also ROBINSONNADES

Goldsmith, Oliver ?1730–74 Irish writer, the son of an Anglican clergyman, who in later life settled in London. Goldsmith formed a highly productive friendship with the publisher JOHN NEWBERY, whose firm published much of his most important work – *The Vicar of Wakefield* (1766), *The Traveller* (1764) and *She Stoops to Conquer* (1773). Goldsmith wrote only one book strictly for the older children's market, *An History of England, in a Series of Letters from a Nobleman to his Son* (1764). He is believed by some scholars to have influenced or contributed to a number of Newbery's children's books, and the genial humour of his adult work (including lighter poems such as *Elegy on the Death of a Mad Dog*, adapted as a PICTUREBOOK a century later by RANDOLPH CALDECOTT) won an audience among generations of younger readers. DWh

Goldthwaite, John see CRITICAL APPROACHES TO CHILDREN'S BOOKS

***Golliwogg* series** (1895–1909) Anglo-American series produced by Florence K. and Bertha Upton. Florence Upton (1873–1922), though born in America, lived and worked in England, where the series was more important; Bertha (1849–1912) lived in America, but was English by birth. Beginning with *The Adventures of Two Dutch Dolls – and a 'Golliwogg'* in 1895, 13 *Golliwogg* books were offered for the Christmas market, ending with *Golliwogg in the African Jungle* in 1909. By then, the exuberant Golliwogg and five wooden dolls had discovered the North Pole, conquered automobile, bicycle and balloon travel, fought a war, and otherwise humorously participated in the topical, technological and social adventures of their era.

Florence K. Upton created the characters and illustrated the oblong, approximately 60-page books; her mother, Bertha, then wrote the rollicking verses. The books were enormously popular; thousands of (unlicensed) Golliwogg spin-off items were sold. Although the Upton Golliwogg was a beloved role model, the ILLUSTRATIONS depict minstrel-show facial features. The books have been accused of racism in our time (which five of the books deserve). The question of the Golliwogg in relation to race, however, is complex and depends, in part, on the fin-de-siècle *Zeitgeist*. The Uptons were surprising and transgressive in their own time and still are in ours. In its use of a black hero, naked white female dolls, irreverence about the American flag and president, criticism of war, and gentle satire on social customs, the series was and is unusual. MSO

Gondal and Angria see LITERATURE IN CHILDREN'S LITERATURE; see also *MARLOW* SERIES

Good Words for the Young see GEORGE MACDONALD; see also PUBLISHING AND PUBLISHERS; WILLIAM BRIGHTY RANDS

Goodall, John S. 1908–96 British illustrator. Goodall is known for his wordless texts and for his imaginative use of the alternating half-page to advance the narrative. The first of the *Paddy Pork* series, *The Adventures of Paddy Pork*, won the BOSTON GLOBE-HORN BOOK AWARD in 1969. The split-page technique is also used successfully to chart the changes wrought by time in such books as *The Story of an English Village* (1978), *The Story of a Castle* (1986) and *Great Days of a Country House* (1992). Goodall's conscientious research is evident in his finely detailed drawing. JAG

Goodbye Dove Square see *THE BATTLE OF ST. GEORGE WITHOUT*

Goode, Diane 1949– Illustrator born in America of European descent. Goode won a Caldecott Honor Medal for CYNTHIA RYLANT's rural memoir *When I Was Young in the Mountains* (1982). Riki Levinson's *I Go With My Family to Grandma's* (1986) gives ample scope to Goode's round and cheerful cartoon characters as they converge on their grandmother from all quarters of New York. *The Andersen Book of American Folk Tales and Songs* (1989) shows Goode at her most versatile, and *Where's Our Mama?* (1992) and *Mama's Perfect Present* (1996) reveal Goode confidently able to create her own ingeniously juxtaposed ILLUSTRATIONS and texts. JAG

Goodman, Vivienne 1961– Australian illustrator, born in Christchurch, New Zealand. Goodman's first PICTUREBOOK, *Oodoolay* (1983), was begun in her final year of study in South Australia. She then completed the complex *Guess What?* (1988), in her distinctive, minutely detailed medium. She has since become one of Australia's most noted cover artists. Using a size 000 sable brush she executes photo-realistic images which are painstakingly detailed and instantly recognisable. She has completed further picturebooks, such as *Where the Whales Sing* (1994) with text by VICTOR KELLEHER, and continues to produce covers which are both memorably beautiful and faithful to her subjects. RS

see also COVER ART

Goodnight Mister Tom (1981) Acclaimed first novel by the British author MICHELLE MAGORIAN, winner of the GUARDIAN AWARD. During World War II Willie Beech is evacuated to stay with Mister Tom Oakley. He arrives bruised and battered, sewn into his underwear for the winter, and with instructions that he must live near a church. Mister Tom has shut himself away from the world since the death of his wife and child and hates the idea of sheltering an evacuee. He comes to love Willie, however, and eventually adopts him after the suicide of the boy's mother. Although some adults have criticised the novel for being too long, few children find its length a problem. The novel does not shrink from brutal depictions of the cruelty Willie endures at the hands of his mother; in the bleakest episode of the novel Willie returns to London where his mother locks him into a cupboard with his baby sister. He is eventually found trying to nurse the dead child. Although its suitability for children has been questioned because of this episode, the novel is widely taught in schools, both for its convincing depiction of World War II and because of the strength of its writing, plot and characterisation. KA

see also WAR STORIES

Goodnight Moon (1947) Best-known PICTUREBOOK by MARGARET WISE BROWN, illustrated by CLEMENT HURD. The book records a rabbit child ritualistically saying goodnight to the various objects in its bedroom as it prepares to go to sleep. It is the sequel to *The Runaway Bunny* (1942), also illustrated by Hurd. The comforting and soothing text is complemented by the gradually darkening ILLUSTRATIONS. It has become a classic bedtime book for young children. JCS

Goodnight, Prof, Love (1970) Novel by the British author JOHN ROWE TOWNSEND, consisting mainly of dialogue, most of which takes place in the head of 16-year-old Graham Hollis as he struggles to make sense of the conflict between loyalty to family ties and the desire for independence. As he runs away from the conventional future that awaits him in his father's accountancy firm in small-town Crimley, he tries to answer the question of whether Lynn, subject to bad moods and seemingly unworried about the future, is indeed the girl of his dreams. The author skilfuly presents readers with a humorous but realistic portrait of first love. EA

Goodrich, Samuel Griswold 1793–1860 Prolific American author and publisher known especially for his instructional 'Peter Parley' stories – chatty, improving, fact-filled narratives that became international bestsellers and were widely imitated. Goodrich also founded *Parley's Magazine* (not connected with the British *Peter Parley's Magazine*) and *MERRY'S MUSEUM*. SRG

see also *PETER PARLEY'S ANNUAL*

Goody Two Shoes see JOHN NEWBERY; see also ILLUSTRATION IN CHILDREN'S BOOKS; SCHOOL STORIES; ISAIAH THOMAS

***Goosebumps* series** Immensely popular and controversial series of scary books for middle-school readers, written by the American author R.L. Stine (1943–), beginning with *Welcome to the Dead House* (1992). Horror fiction became the most popular genre for adolescent readers during the 1990s, and Stine has been the most successful author to adapt the genre for slightly younger readers aged 8 to 12. *Goosebumps* are significantly different from the violent and sexually suggestive adolescent horror fiction, including Stine's own popular *Fear Street* series, in that the books combine equal parts humour – particularly gross humour – and fright. Almost every *Goosebumps* has an episode involving a character eating something disgusting like a bug or a worm. *Goosebumps* stories involve surprise and cliff-hanging chapter endings rather than horror or shock. There are numerous references to contemporary youth culture and characters speak in the slang of the day. *Goosebumps* merchandise has been extensively marketed and the books have been made into a popular TELEVISION series. JCS

Gordon, Gaelyn 1939–97 One of New Zealand's most versatile and prolific writers for children, young adults and adults. Born in Hawera, educated at Canterbury University, Gordon worked as a teacher, actor and theatre director before becoming a full-time writer in 1987. Her first novel, *Stonelight* (1988), established her as a writer of unusual gifts prepared to challenge the boundaries between FANTASY and realism. These features, along with a deep love of language and myth, were evident in the books which completed the *Stonelight* trilogy, *Mindfire* (1991) and *Riversong* (1995), but were perhaps most fully realised in two studies on the abuse of power, *Prudence M. Muggeridge, Damp Rat* (1991) and *Tripswitch* (1992). Of a number of PICTUREBOOKS, her best known is *Duckat* (1992), illustrated by CHRIS GASKIN, a wryly comic tale of a duck having an identity crisis. She was also known as the writer of five adult novels and as an eloquent speaker on children's literature. TD

Gordon, John 1925– British novelist, best known for young adult stories with strong FANTASY elements. Born in Jarrow, Gordon recounted his Navy service in *Ordinary Seaman* (1992). He was a journalist in Plymouth and East Anglia, which provide the backdrop to most of his narratives. Gordon's fantasy springs from a solidly evoked world from which magic is never far. He is honest and direct in portraying strong feeling, especially adolescent sexual tension. In *Giant Under the Snow* (1968), Norwich children enter an ancient magic world of witches and the disturbing Leathermen. A tremendous climax shows the prehistoric giant rising for an even older magic to prevail. *House on the Brink* (1970), a psychological, supernatural thriller, involves Dick and Helen's burgeoning relationship and the haunting of Mrs Knowles by the black shape – mere log or cursed prehistoric body? – rising from the River Nene. *The Ghost on the Hill* (1976), *The Edge of the World* (1983), *The Quelling Eye* (1986), *The Grasshopper* (1987) and *The Midwinter Watch* (1999) develop these themes, as do Gordon's short stories, especially in *Catch Your Death* (1984) and *The Burning Baby* (1992). The sheer imaginative scope of *Gilray's Ghost* (1995) reveals new levels of complexity and power from this meticulous author, as do *The Flesh Eater* (1998) and *The Midwinter Watch* (1998). DCH

Gordon, Margaret 1939–90 British illustrator. The publication in 1968 of *The Wombles* (ELIZABETH BERESFORD) gave rise to a hugely popular series broadcast on British TELEVISION, though the bear-like creatures that were originally and precisely drawn by Gordon in the numerous *Wombles* books were somewhat changed. Gordon created other memorable characters such as the bear Wilberforce who first appeared in *Wilberforce Goes on a Picnic* (1982). Here, and in *The Supermarket Mice* (1984), Gordon's fine, detailed, expressive illustrations extend and exploit her deadpan texts, and in *Mousetale* (1988) she demonstrates unrestrained visual and verbal inventiveness. She also illustrated books by KEVIN CROSSLEY-HOLLAND and HELEN CRESSWELL. JAG

Gorey, Edward 1925–2000 Artist, illustrator and author of PICTUREBOOKS, especially ALPHABET BOOKS. Born in Chicago and trained at the Art Institute and Harvard, Gorey specialises in macabre gothic stories, in self-illustrated books such as *The Unstrung Harp* (1953), *The Hapless Child* (1961) and *The Beastly Baby* (1962). He began as an artist and designer for Doubleday, and early produced books which are clearly for children, such as FLORENCE P. HEIDE's *The Shrinking of Treehorn* (1971) and *Donald & the . . .* (1970), with Peter F. Neumeyer. His books – including his many alphabets – satirise the conventions of didactic books. For example, *The Gashlycrumb Tinies or After the Outing* (1963) ghoulishly describes the deaths of 26 children, in alphabetical order: 'I is for Ida who drowned in a lake/ J is for James who took lye by mistake.' His picturebooks, illustrated in black-and-white ink drawings with heavy HATCHING, blur the boundaries between books for children and for adults. His work has been collected in a number of anthologies, including *Amphigorey* (1972), *Amphigorey, Too* (1975), and *Amphigorey Also* (1983). Gorey won the Tony Award for his costume and set designs for the 1977 Broadway production of *Dracula*. GRB

see also ALPHABET BOOKS

Gorilla (1983) PICTUREBOOK by the British illustrator ANTHONY BROWNE and winner of the KURT MASCHLER AWARD. Browne's fascination with the larger primates is here given focus in a satisfying tale of a little girl's disappointment and loneliness resolved through FANTASY and the rediscovery of parental love. Hannah wants a gorilla for her birthday but is disappointed with the tiny toy given to her by her father. During the night the toy is transformed, according to her desires, into a real gorilla and she is entertained by the huge creature, who dresses in her father's coat and hat and takes her to the zoo. Browne's fondness for visual puns and surreal juxtapositions is here kept firmly in the service of the narrative, Hannah's obsession being cleverly conveyed in the way gorilla imagery seeps into embedded pictures such as the framed prints hanging on the walls. Browne also uses colour, point of view and contrasts of light and dark to underline Hannah's loneliness and isolation. As always, his style tends towards the flattened and the stylised, but his portraits of the primates in the zoo are rounded, realistic images that contrast touchingly with the fantastic scenes that surround them. DL

Goudge, Elizabeth (De Beauchamp) 1900–84 British novelist whose upbringing in the cathedral environs of Wells and Ely accounts for the importance of ancient buildings and secret places in her books. These appeal to the desire for security and a place of one's own. Although vulnerable to accusations of sentimentality, Goudge's best works, such as *Henrietta's House* (1942) – called *The Blue Hills* in the United States – and *The Little White Horse* (1946), are largely successful in combining FAIRY TALE elements with the comic and mundane. The latter work, awarded the CARNEGIE MEDAL, also draws effectively on an older symbolism of darkness and light. JFB

Illustration by Peter Gouldthorpe from *First Light* by Gary Crew.

Gouldthorpe, Peter (James) 1954– Australian painter, illustrator, printmaker and writer. Gouldthorpe uses fine, hand-coloured linocuts in *Jonah and the Manly Ferry* (1983); *Hist!* (1991), a poem by C.J. Dennis; and *The Wonder Thing* (1995) by Libby Hathorn. His luminous illustrations for Jack Bedson's *Don't Get Burnt!* (1985) are amongst the finest evocations of summer and the Australian beach. *Walking to School* (1988), *Sheep Dogs* (1990), *Grandad's Gifts* (1991) and the winner of the 1994 Children's Book Council of Australia Picturebook of the Year Award, *First Light* (1993), all display Gouldthorpe's skill in capturing mood and atmosphere through tonal qualities of light and shade, a subtle, rich palette and a broad range of styles and techniques. *The Lost Diamonds of Killiecrankie* (1995) exemplifies Gouldthorpe's fine draftsmanship. SNJ

Governess, The, or Little Female Academy see Sarah Fielding; see also school stories

Gowar, Mick 1951– British author of poetry, fiction and picturebooks. His poems for teenagers in particular combine a sensitive ear for this age group with an awareness of modern sub-cultures. Collections like *Swings and Roundabouts* (1981) and *Third Time Lucky* (1992) capture the detail of modern, urban family life with humour and sensitivity for younger readers. Influenced by the music of Saint-Saëns, his poems in *Carnival of the Animals* (1992) are beautifully observed:

the swan, for example, 'too perfect/For a thing of flesh and feathers'. In 1995 Gowar wrote the words for a musical drama based on a dark Suffolk FOLKTALE, which in 1998 was adapted and published as *Yallery Brown* in Scholastic's series of paperback FAIRY TALES. FRBS

Grace (1991) Acclaimed novel by British author JILL PATON WALSH recounting not only the famous rescue of the survivors wrecked off the Northumbrian coast in 1838, but also the consequences it brought for Grace Darling and her family. The honours showered upon the young woman kindle the resentment of the locals and her peace of mind is so disturbed that, as her body grows weak with consumption, she begins to doubt her own motives. Using historical details and a profound understanding of her character, Walsh describes the events surrounding the rescue and draws an empathetic portrait of Grace, whose isolated life was shattered by publicity and irrevocably changed. EA

Grace, Patricia 1937– Major New Zealand novelist who has written a number of PICTUREBOOKS for children, including the award-winning *The Kuia and the Spider* (1981), and a long-time favourite, *Watercress Tuna and the Children of Champion Street* (1985). Both, like several others, were illustrated by ROBYN KAHUKIWA. Grace seeks to give expression to Maori values. Two recent books deal with family experience, although in notably different ways. In *The Trolley* (1993) Grace plays delicately with the anxieties of the disadvantaged, as a single mother imaginatively compensates for her poverty; *Areta and the Kahawai* (1994), on the other hand, fantastically celebrates the familiar Maori extended family while also acknowledging its tensions. Grace is unusually important as a writer of children's fiction, in that many of her adult short stories and novels have proved immensely attractive to adolescent audiences and their teachers, partly because of their emphatic representation of Maori culture and perspectives, and partly because of their lucid, suggestive economy. CM

see also MAORI WRITING FOR CHILDREN

Graham, Bob (Robert Donald) 1942– Australian PICTUREBOOK author and illustrator, best known internationally for the popular *Les Aventures de Charlotte et Henri*, a six-page comic strip in the French children's magazine *Les Belles Histoires*. Sympathetically translated into French by Bernadette Garreta, the characters have retained their distinct personalities, which Graham claims are based on opposing natures found within himself and his extended human and animal family. Pets feature strongly in Graham's apparently spontaneous cartoon-style illustrations, done with watercolours, inks and crayons. *First There Was Frances* (1985), *Greetings from Sandy Beach* (1990) – which captures the essence of family beach holidays – *Crusher is Coming!* (1987), *Grandad's Magic* (1989) and *Zoltan the Magnificent* (1994) all draw on foibles of family relationships.

Graham's strength is his ability to portray realistic and humorous reactions to absurd problems or personalities. He inverts stereotypes like 'bikies' or 'bullies', and with gentle satire challenges readers to question their assumptions. There is an essential reassurance in Graham's stories that, despite problems, good nature will prevail, a characteristic exemplified by his comic picturebook *Brand New Baby* (1992). *Rose Meets Mr Wintergarten* (1992), a modern FAIRY TALE, shows the reclusive, despondent Mr Wintergarten's life being turned around by a small girl's friendliness. Graham's move to England in 1995 is reflected in the settings of the zany *Queenie the Bantam* (1997). *Buffy: An Adventure Story* (1999) is the tale of a magician's dog, kicked out of the theatre, who eventually finds warmth and security. *Max* (2000) winner of the SMARTIES BOOK PRIZE tells the story of a young SUPERHERO unable to fly like his parents, characters who first appeared in the French magazine *Pomme D'Api*. Graham has received numerous awards, including the CHILDREN'S BOOK COUNCIL OF AUSTRALIA PICTUREBOOK OF THE YEAR AWARD in 1988, 1991 and 1993. HE

Graham, Eleanor 1896–1984 First editor of Puffin Books, a post she held from 1941 to 1961, and author of four children's books, including *The Story of Jesus* (1959), illustrated by BRIAN WILDSMITH. Prior to her editorship at Puffin, Graham ran the influential Children's Room at Bumpus' Bookshop and reviewed for the *Sunday Times* and *The Junior Bookshelf*. This background enabled her rapidly to establish Puffin as a quality list at a time when paperback publishing for children was regarded with considerable suspicion. She received the Eleanor Farjeon Award in 1973. KR

see also REVIEWING; *THE CHILDREN WHO LIVED IN A BARN*

Graham, Harry 1874–1936 One of the wittiest exponents of English light verse. Of his many publications the dark, cruel humour of *Ruthless Rhymes* (1899) appeals most to children, as in:

> Sam had spirits nought could check,
> And today at breakfast, he
> Broke his baby sister's neck,
> So he shan't have jam for tea!

AHa

Graham, Lorenz (Bell) 1902–89 American writer of children's books. Born in New Orleans, the son of a pastor, Graham worked as a missionary teacher in

Illustration by Bob Graham from *Buffy*.

Liberia from 1924 to 1928. He put a new perspective on religion for children by producing *How God Fix Jonah* (1946), a collection of BIBLE STORIES rewritten in Liberian pidgin English. Many of these stories were published separately, including *Every Man Heart Lay Down* (1970), illustrated by Colleen Browing, *David He No Fear* (1971), illustrated by Ann Grifalconi, and *God Wash the World and Start Again* (1971), illustrated by Clare Romano Ross, which tell the stories of the Nativity, David and Goliath, and Noah respectively. In 1955/6, he adapted *The Story of Jesus* and *The Ten Commandments* into a popular comic-book format. He has also written stories about children in Liberia, including *Tales of Momolu* (1946) and *I, Momolu* (1966). In his award-winning *Town* series of novels, including *South Town* (1958) and *Whose Town?* (1969), he deals with issues of racism in various parts of the United States. Graham has been awarded honours by both African American and religious associations for his work in enhancing the value of African American culture. SCWA

see also AFRICAN AMERICAN LITERATURE; BIBLE STORIES

Graham-Sutherland, Efua (Theodora) 1924– Ghanaian academic, dramaturgist and writer, best known for her research and experimentation with traditional dramatic forms and theatre. Generally interested in the oral traditions, she has also been studying children's games which include words, drama and song, and has based her children's books on those sources. A good example of her writing for children is *Fafanto (Butterflies)* (1972), which exploits the alliterative and descriptive capabilities of the Fanti language and the ease of blending it with the English language. This makes her children's books exceptionally suited for both reading and performance. MAs

see also DRAMA FOR CHILDREN

Grahame, Eleanor see REVIEWING AND REVIEWERS

Grahame, Kenneth 1859–1932 British author, and a curious major figure in children's literature, as it could be cogently argued that he never wrote a children's book. *Dream Days* (1895) and *THE GOLDEN AGE* (1898) are *about* childhood, while *THE WIND IN THE*

WILLOWS, for all its status as a major children's classic, can be read as an allegory of Grahame's own personal and political preoccupations.

Peter Green's definitive biography (1959) points out how closely Grahame's literary sub-texts can be related to his life. He was born in Scotland, but after his mother's death when he was five, he went to live with his grandmother at Cookham Dene on the River Thames. His father left the family in 1867, and Kenneth's ambition of attending Oxford University remained unfulfilled. He joined the Bank of England (as 'gentleman clerk') in 1879 and rose to be one of its youngest top officials, Secretary, in 1898.

Grahame was influenced by the fashionable neo-pagan and 'bohemian' fin-de-siècle literary movements of his day, and was friends with F.J. Furnivall and W.E. Henley. This was a 'man's world', and Grahame spent weekends of hearty walking and eating in the country. In this period, the women's liberation movement was established, the motor car and suburban railways were encroaching on the countryside, and socialism was becoming a significant force. All his books reflect these changes in the traditional way of life and are chracterised by nostalgia, male society and the search for a father-figure.

Grahame's first collection of short pieces, *Pagan Papers* (1893), previously published in Henley's *National Observer*, was thought at the time to be imitative of R.L. STEVENSON, and it has been suggested that he may have been influenced by RICHARD JEFFERIES. They broadly extol a 'simple', quasi-mystic, pseudo-rural lifestyle. His two nostalgic and witty portraits of childhood, *The Golden Age* and *Dream Days*, made his name internationally.

In 1899 Grahame married Elspeth Thompson. The marriage does not seem to have been a happy one; the couple had one son, Alastair, for whom Grahame began what was to be *The Wind in the Willows* in a series of letters in 1907. The letters, written when the Grahames were *de facto* living apart, became progressively less related to the child. In 1908, Grahame retired from the Bank of England, and, after some rejections, *The Wind in the Willows* was published. The book gradually became successful, partly because of its endorsement by the United States President Theodore Roosevelt. Its combination of hearty farce, rural nostalgia, ingenious language and archetypal characters has maintained its popularity to the point at which it has become a cultural icon – despite its essentially repressed and repressive themes and its deep, male-centred conservatism.

Describing himself as 'a spring, not a pump', Grahame wrote little else, although Elspeth published *First Whispers of The Wind in the Willows* containing some early materials, in 1944. Alastair was killed (probably a suicide) in 1920, and the Grahames, deeply affected, then divided their time between the Thames Valley and Italy, until Kenneth's death. PLH

Grail stories see KING ARTHUR; see also ELIDOR

Gramatky, Hardie 1907–69 American author-illustrator of children's PICTUREBOOKS. Most notable among them are *Little Toot* (1939) – the tale of a little tugboat which in a crisis, proves itself through determination and courage – and *Hercules* (1940) – about a cranky horse-drawn fire engine forced into retirement by a motorised vehicle. Gramatky was a pioneer in the writing of children's stories about anthropomorphic machines; these include *Sparky: The Story of a Little Trolley Car* (1952), *Homer and the Circus Train* (1957) – about a caboose – and five sequels to *Little Toot*. He typically focuses on the character's need to acquire self-knowledge and confidence, and his best ILLUSTRATIONS are spirited and boldly drawn cartoons. DLR

Grange Hill (1978–) British TELEVISION series transmitted by the BBC, about a London comprehensive school. The programme has revived and democratised the SCHOOL STORY genre. Unlike its literary predecessors, *Grange Hill* portrays a mixed rather than single-sex community, with an annual turnover of pupils who visibly age as they progress through school. Its initial success led to a yearly series and an increase from 9 to 18 episodes. However, the depiction of pupils' unruly classroom behaviour provoked fierce attacks from many parents and teachers who deplored the model of schooling being offered. Scenes of violent bullying, they argued, seriously alarmed children moving into secondary school, and teachers in a real school would never be so lax and ineffectual. Unfortunately, debates about the programme's realism and 'authenticity' were often confused by a tendency to use 'realism' either to refer to the text's adoption of a realist aesthetic, or to notions of typicality and the perceived verisimilitude of its representation of school life.

Not all critical responses to *Grange Hill* were negative. Supporters pointed to the narrative centrality of the child, reflected through the positioning of the camera at the pupils' level. Also, as an inner-city comprehensive based within the wider framework of the community, *Grange Hill* escaped the limitations of boarding-school stories (which rarely moved outside the school) and demonstrated the importance of the home and local environment in children's lives.

The programme attracted most attention for its powerful and sensitive dramatisation of controversial issues like racism, teenage pregnancy and drug addiction. While there may be some truth in accusations of tokenism (that black faces, for example, only had a strong, visible presence when racist themes were being explored), the series undoubtedly adopted a liberal or progressive standpoint on a range of issues. Given the 25-minute duration of episodes and the multiple characters and plot strands, there has inevitably been some 'magical' resolution of complex topics, but this has often resulted in dramatic climaxes that are emotionally and aesthetically satisfying. For example, one series concluded with a moving scene in which black pupils defended a gay teacher because they recognised they were both victims of prejudice. *Grange Hill* has also given its young audience insights into school politics, showing tensions among staff, and a headteacher who welcomes student representation on the School Council (as a PR exercise) and then undermines it for her own ends.

With its interweaving plot strands, large number of characters, and matching of dramatic and chronological time, *Grange Hill*'s narrative construction closely resembles that of SOAP-OPERA. Its creator, Phil Redmond, was also responsible for the soap-opera *Brookside*, and several actors from the children's series have graduated to major roles in another British soap, *EastEnders*. When Redmond offered Collins the fiction rights to *Grange Hill*, ROBERT LEESON was invited to write a series of novels based on the television series. Leeson, who was determined to create new stories and avoid 'novelisation', produced five books, four involving main characters from the television series and a fifth based on *Tucker's Luck*, a spin-off series from *Grange Hill*.

The programme's continuing popularity and growing critical recognition (a British Academy Award in 1986 for best children's drama series) owes much to its progenitor's influence, and to talented scriptwriters and directors. Though they borrowed many of the familiar school-story motifs, such as inter-school rivalries and bullying, they took the genre in new directions, using the programme as a radical forum for debates about children's education. DJ

see also ROBERT LEESON; DRUGS IN CHILDREN'S BOOKS; TELEVISION

Granny's Wonderful Chair Popular collection of linked FAIRY TALES by the blind Irish writer, Frances Browne, written in 1857 when – according to JOHN ROWE TOWNSEND – there was a nostalgia 'for a land fit for fairies to live in'. The tales dramatise the traditional contrasts between greed and kindness, wealth and poverty, in a vivid setting of mountains, forests and moors. In 1904 the stories were reissued with a preface by FRANCES HODGSON BURNETT, in which she applied Emerson's Law of Compensation to the blind writer: 'To her was given the inward eye of imagination and the mind.' VW

Granpa (1984) PICTUREBOOK by JOHN BURNINGHAM concerning the relationship between a young girl and her grandfather. The grandfather dies in the closing pages, leaving the child gazing unhappily at his empty armchair. Because of its lack of a clearly told story, *Granpa* has challenged many assumptions about how children read. Its design assumes an interactive view of reading which tolerates uncertainties and gives free rein to the child's readiness to question and speculate. Burningham has used the page-openings to suggest rather than to explain a series of dynamic situations. On one right-hand page, for example, there is a richly coloured ILLUSTRATION showing Granpa's house in heavy rain. (It is almost identical to the house in *MR GUMPY'S OUTING* – an intertextual detail appreciated by observant young readers.) On the opposite page are two sentences in different type-faces, one supposedly Granpa telling the story of Noah, the other his granddaughter asking if there is any danger of their house floating away. Below, on the left-hand page, is an uncoloured sketch of a garden pond. Nothing is explicitly told; the speeches are not attributed, and the relationship of the pond-sketch to the rest is not explained. The 'reading rules' change from one opening to the next. Burningham had earlier used this technique – of different kinds of illustration obliquely related to one another – in his two *SHIRLEY* books, but in *Granpa* the obliqueness leaves even more for young readers to do. This is why it cannot simply be read aloud. In another – now famous – page-opening, there is a sketch of the old man and the young girl with their backs to one another, their faces and body-language eloquently suggesting anger and hurt; the only words are: 'That was not a nice thing to say to Granpa.' The text gives no indication of what she has said; it trusts its young readers to fill the gap from their own experience. This fragmentation of expected narrative patterns has been defended by Peter Hunt, who argues that 'its very complexity, together with the relinquishing of any authorial control in the verbal text, makes *Granpa* closer to the comprehension patterns of an orally based reader than the vast majority of texts that set out to be "for children"'.

The death of the grandfather has led some adults to question the book's suitability for young readers. But *Granpa* is to be found in many primary classrooms, and teachers have used it to develop children's understanding of bereavement. In 1989 a film of *Granpa* was made for TVS and Channel Four. It was visually very appealing and its rather operatic treatment was true to the theme that has been explored in many of Burningham's picturebooks – the versatility and intelligence of the individual imagination. But to expand a picturebook of 16 page-openings into a 30-minute film required so much additional material that much of the mysteriously implicit quality of the original book was lost. In 1990 *The Book of the Film* was published, a royalty on all its sales pledged to UNICEF. VW

graphic novel Long story in comic-strip format, printed in a single volume. Such works had long been familiar to readers in France and Belgium, and in translation to English readers (ASTÉRIX and TINTIN principally), without needing a special name, but it was the appearance of works with adult themes during the 1970s and 80s that seemed to make a more grown-up designation than 'comic' necessary. The first work to call itself a graphic novel was Will Eisner's *A Contract with God* (1978), which was anything but a work for children, and the first to make a commercial impact was Frank Miller's *Batman: The Dark Knight Returns* (1986). This was a work whose complexity of style and psychological darkness of subject matter appealed more to adults, or at least to teenagers with a sophisticated understanding of the possibilities of the form.

During the 1980s several mainstream British publishers tried to find a readership for works of this kind, with varying success. Part of the problem lay with booksellers' uncertainty as to who was likely to read them: were they for children (because they were full of pictures) or adults (because of their subject-matter)? Underlying that was the difference between British and European traditions of comic productions. Whereas British publishers had specialised in weekly issues containing complete short funny stories (for example, BEANO), European creators from Hergé onward were able to work towards a full-length story published first serially in a magazine and then, when complete, in book form. There has never been a British counterpart of *Tintin*, nor is there likely to be. Whether or not the most characteristic examples of the form are truly works for children is another question, but personal observation suggests that they do speak to adolescent readers in a way that word-based literature sometimes fails to do.

The field is so vast that it is not possible to do more than indicate some of the most significant works. Foremost among them is Art Spiegelman's *Maus*, Parts I and II (1987/92). This astonishing work tells the story of the writer's father and how he survived Auschwitz. It depicts Jews as mice, Germans as cats, Poles as pigs, and so on – a risky strategy which comes off because of Spiegelman's tact and emotional truthfulness. *Watchmen* (1987), by Alan Moore and Dave Gibbons, is both a dark, dystopian adventure and a complex meditation on the nature of STORYTELLING itself. RAYMOND BRIGGS's *When the Wind Blows* (1982) shows a master of the PICTUREBOOK engaging with the form and producing a work full of horror and pity. Neil Gaiman's *Sandman* series (1991 onwards) is perhaps the most accomplished work of pure FANTASY the form has yet produced; complex, dream-filled and demanding, it represents the point at which the form probably leaves most young readers behind. PNP

Graves, Robert (von Ranks) 1895–1985 British writer and poet. His prodigious output includes some writing specifically for children. *Greek Gods and Heroes* (1960) clarified the old CLASSICAL MYTHOLOGY, and *The Green Book* (1962), illustrated by MAURICE SENDAK, is a quirky tale of magic. Two poetry books, illustrated by EDWARD ARDIZZONE, are collectable: *The Penny Fiddle* (1960) and *Ann at Highwood Hall* (1964) contain popular poems from Graves's adult collections, like 'Warning to Children' and 'A Boy in Church', as well as delightful poems like 'Allie' – 'Allie, call the birds home, / The birds from the sky.' *The Poor Boy Who Followed his Star* (1986) contains a story and three poems, one on himself. AHa

Gray, Elizabeth Janet (Elizabeth Gray Vining) 1902–99 American author of HISTORICAL FICTION. Although her stories of contemporary teenage girls – especially *The Fair Adventure* (1940) and *Sandy* (1945) – are characterised by intelligence, humour and vitality, Gray is best known for her story BIOGRAPHIES *Young Walter Scott* (1935) and *Penn* (1938), and such excellent historical novels as *Meggy MacIntosh* (1929), *Beppy Marlowe of Charles Town* (1936) and the NEWBERY AWARD winner, *Adam of the Road* (1942). As a prominent Quaker, she was appointed tutor of Japan's Crown Prince after World War II; *The Cheerful Heart* (1959) shares with children her knowledge of post-war Japan. SR

Gray, Nicholas Stuart 1922–81 British dramatist, novelist and writer of short stories. Gray was a man of the theatre, who directed and acted in productions of his own plays for children. In the last ten years of his life Gray concentrated on prose fiction, but it is his practical and imaginative commitment to children's theatre in the 1950s and 60s which makes him an important figure in post-war children's writing. Most of his plays are adaptations of traditional FAIRY TALES, which he treated with wit and inventiveness, giving subtle, delicate intimations of the serious themes underlying comic FANTASY. He was particularly attracted to HANS CHRISTIAN ANDERSEN, and produced highly actable versions of *The Tinder-Box*, *The Imperial Nightingale*, and *New Clothes for the Emperor*. In these and other plays based on well-known stories he demonstrated his ability to defamiliarise the traditional, using mischievous and irreverent playfulness as a means to being serious. The original plots of his own stories and novels sustain his characteristic blend of comedy and magic, but also show his concern for

Illustration by Armin Greder from *The Princess and the Perfect Dish* by LIBBY GLEESON.

the natural world. The novel *The Wardens of the Weir* (1978) is a striking conservationist FABLE, in which children aid a mysterious other-worldly figure to rescue the earth's doomed species, who include dinosaurs, the unicorn, the yeti, and finally humankind itself. PH

Gray, Nigel 1941– Irish-born, award-winnning Australian writer, editor, teacher and photographer who has produced over 50 books for children and adults, many published internationally. His PICTUREBOOK, *I'll Take You to Mrs Cole* (1985), illustrated by MICHAEL FOREMAN, provides a delicious slice of English home life in both the words and the pictures, as a lonely latch-key boy runs away from home, overcomes his fears and discovers warmth and family fun with homely neighbour, Mrs Cole. *Running Away From Home* (1995), set in Australia, with its realistic crayon illustrations by GREGORY ROGERS, is about Sam who, feeling left out, leaves his comfortable home – and gets as far as under the front verandah. Gray uses humour to advantage in *The Grocer's Daughter* (1994), a CAUTIONARY rhyming tale; *THE FROG PRINCE* (1995), an elegant variation on the traditional tale; and *The Dog Show* (1996), which is judged by a cat. A well-paced YOUNG ADULT novel, set in contemporary Australia, *Night Music* (1992) shows Gray drawing on his Irish background for his characters and plot, in a tale of romance, fear and courage. JAP

see also JANE RAY

Great Smile Robbery, The (1982) A spoof adventure as engaging for the surreal twist which ROGER MCGOUGH and illustrator Tony Blundell add to a tale of stock villainy (theft of a cupboard full of smiles by the Stinker Gang to win a National Smile competition) as for its unconventional form. An inventive precursor of *Jets*, an innovative and influential multimedia-inspired early reading series (from 1988), it plays to the verbal wit and streetwise culture of readers raised on comic and televisual literacies. Absurd plot, language and pictures are mischievously interleaved with visual jokes, wordplay, puns, jingles, parody, authorial asides and some orthodox narrative en route to the Stinkers' inevitable demise. EMH

Greder, Armin 1942– Swiss-German illustrator, who lives and lectures in Queensland, Australia. His works, such as *Big Dog* (1991), though not overtly multicultural, are quietly inclusive of culture and gender. They demonstrate his precise observation of children, his drawing abilities and intelligent wit. He is adept in creating the refracted FAIRY TALE, such as *Uncle David* (1992) and *The Princess and the Perfect Dish* (1995), both written by LIBBY GLEESON. His ILLUSTRATIONS for Gleeson's *The Great Bear* (1999) are potent with metaphor. Works for very young children, such as *Sleep Time* (1993) and *Danny and the Toybox* (1990) are masterly, visually spare texts. The subtle expressiveness of limb and facial feature in this work is in itself a lesson in artistic technique. RS

Greek mythology see CLASSICAL MYTHOLOGY

***Green Knowe* series** (1954–76) Six novels by L. M. BOSTON, the first five published between 1954 and 1964, and a sixth, *The Stones of Green Knowe*, added in 1976. The novels are linked by a common setting, a 12th-century manor house near Cambridge, England. The fictional 'Green Knowe' is a real place, the Manor at Hemingford Grey in Cambridgeshire, which Lucy Boston bought just before World War II and subsequently restored, and which since her death has been open to the public (by appointment). The house, its gardens, moat and riverside setting alongside the Great Ouse are faithfully reflected in the stories. All

Illustration by Peter Boston for *A Stranger at Green Knowe* by L.M. BOSTON.

the *Green Knowe* books are illustrated by Peter Boston, the author's son (1918–99). His drawings are integral with the stories in their amused celebration of the play, exploration and wonderment which the house and its surroundings excite in child characters. It was, as Lucy Boston said, 'a most happy partnership'.

Her actual experience as owner, restorer and occupier of the ancient house is thematically important in the books, three factors being especially prominent. Chief of these is her consciousness of the manor's long history: it has been claimed to be the oldest inhabited house in England. In Boston's imagination the house is a conduit for the lives it has contained in former generations, all of which survive not only in a linear history but in a kind of continuous present. Children of different historical periods can perceive and speak with each other through the intuitive consciousness for which the house and gardens are a catalyst. Therefore the series is an early, innovative and original example of the TIME-SLIP story which has flourished in post-war children's fiction. Inter-generational time travel amongst successive generations of the Oldknow family, who have occupied the house since its foundation, is important in the first two stories, *The Children of Green Knowe* (1954) and *The Chimneys of Green Knowe* (1958), and above all in the last, *The Stones of Green Knowe* (1976). Time travel of a vaster, more exuberantly fantastical kind is also the subject of the third story, *The River at Green Knowe* (1959), the only book in the series which entirely excludes the Oldknow family.

The second major theme derived from Lucy Boston's own experiences is that of hospitality and displacement. During World War II Lucy Boston regularly extended hospitality to military personnel stationed at bases near the Manor. Records were played in the Music Room (the 'Knight's Hall' of the stories), and those who came enjoyed a break from their impersonal service life. In later years she was always willing to show the house and gardens to interested visitors. In the stories she depicts Green Knowe itself as a hospitable place, inclusive and welcoming towards those who wish it well or need it as a refuge.

This preoccupation is magnified in the books into a thematic concern with 'displacement'. The 'spirit of place' dominates the stories, and for successive Oldknow generations it is vital to their well-being to know that the house survives as a dependable home and centre. To be 'displaced' is a human catastrophe. The term 'displaced person', denoting refugees and homeless victims of war, has a deeper than usual resonance for Lucy Boston. The theme is present in a minor key in the first two books. Seven-year-old Tolly, in *The Children of Green Knowe*, is the great-grandson of the house's current owner. Without her and the house he would be obliged to spend his holidays at school, his mother being dead and his remarried father overseas. In *Chimneys* Green Knowe welcomes Jacob, a black West Indian boy who is rescued from slavery and given a home by the seafaring Captain Oldknow in the 18th century.

The house's ethnic receptiveness is developed as a dominant theme in *The River at Green Knowe*, where Polish Oskar and Chinese Ping from Burma, both displaced children, spend a magical summer at the house. In this wild, ingenious story the term 'displacement' is overt, insistent, all-embracing. It is carried forward into the fourth book, *A Stranger at Green Knowe*, which was awarded the CARNEGIE MEDAL in 1961 and is surely Lucy Boston's masterpiece. In this story the house's hospitality extends to include other species. Hanno, a gorilla who has escaped from London Zoo, takes refuge in the Thicket at Green Knowe which includes an area of bamboo. There he is found by Ping, who has returned to the house for a second, very different summer, and between displaced boy and displaced gorilla there develops a brief and moving intimacy which is broken only by a brutal intrusion of the outside world. However improbable the story, it is a major, ever more urgent statement for children about relations between humankind and the animal world.

The invasion by officials and marksmen which ends Ping's brief idyll with Hanno is a pointer to the third key element in Lucy Boston's own experience at Hemingford Grey. From the outset she was conscious that so old a house, so unlikely a survival through the centuries, was vulnerable not only to natural decay but to the modern world. In later years her anxiety was sharpened by parochial conflicts, as urban developments such as playing fields encroached ever more threateningly on the house's fragile seclusion. The outside world contains not only refugees but vandals and destroyers. In the conclusion of *A Stranger at Green Knowe* they are perceived as hostile, and in *An Enemy at Green Knowe* (1964), the fifth book, the hostility is intensified and personified in the witch-like form of Dr Melanie Powers, who mounts a supernatural attack on the house and its ancient pieties. She is finally defeated only by a tremendous invocation of superior protective forces.

Green Knowe, then, is increasingly embattled as the series progresses. The mood darkens, and the age of the implied child reader, like that of the child characters, appears to rise. The narratives become less episodic and more complex. The series noticeably changes and evolves over the years, and the late addition of *The Stones of Green Knowe* forms an elegiac coda, lovingly celebrating the house, yet sadly accepting the truth of a moment in *The River at Green Knowe*, where the children experience an 'agonising second of revelation that ALL passes'. PH

Green, Hannah [Joanne Greenberg] 1932– American writer. When she wrote *I Never Promised You a Rose Garden* (1964), Joanne Greenberg adopted a pseudonym designed to protect her sons in their youth from the stigma that their mother was once hospitalised with mental illness. A story of schizophrenia, Greenberg's book details the intense work between patient and therapist; it begins when Jacob and Esther Blau commit their daughter Deborah to the care of doctors. At 16, Deborah lives partly in the Kingdom of Yr, her own invention. Although she experienced sibling rivalry when her sister, Suzy, was born, Deborah's problems go far deeper than competition, and she attempts suicide. Doctor Clara Fried works to uncover the health within Deborah; encouraged by the wise doctor, Deborah courageously ventures away from Yr toward life in reality where there is, as her physician promises, no rose garden. Nevertheless, the teenager battles for recovery. A filmed version of the book appeared in the 1970s (New World Pictures). Other titles by Greenberg include *The King's Persons* (1963, winning two awards from the National Jewish Welfare Board), *The Monday Voices* (1965) and *In This Sign* (1968, winner of the Christopher Award). From the American Academy of Psychoanalysis Greenberg received the Frieda Fromm-Reichmann award. NV

Green, Roger (Gilbert) Lancelyn 1918–87 British actor and distinguished historian, biographer, editor, children's author, and writer of one of the earliest serious studies of children's writers, *Tellers of Tales* (1946). He edited a number of poetry anthologies for

'The cowslip children.' Early illustration by Kate Greenaway for *Little Folks* (1880).

children but is best known for his collections and retellings of traditional stories, including tales from CLASSICAL MYTHOLOGY, FAIRY TALES, SHAKESPEARE, the KING ARTHUR cycle, and ancient Israel. Most young British readers in the 1970s knew his work through the collections of stories he edited for Hamish Hamilton: *The Hamish Hamilton Book of Dragons* (1970), *Magicians* (1973) and *Other Worlds* (1976).

Before Green became an editor he had written a number of works which, though not strictly speaking novels, made the somewhat intractable matter of mythology accessible to young readers by presenting the stories in a form resembling one with which they were familiar. He was a careful stylist, employing language that was simultaneously dignified, austere, unpretentious and sometimes melodious. ('Away sailed Odysseus from the fair Aegaean isle and came to the White Rock and the Poplars of Persephone.') Several of these works were published by Puffin Books at a time when this ensured a wide readership. They included *King Arthur and His Knights of the Round Table* (1953), *Robin Hood* (1956), *Tales of the Greek Heroes* (1958), *The Tale of Troy* (1958) and *The Saga of Asgard* (1960). In these, as in his better-known *The Luck of Troy* (1961), mythology was neither debunked nor deconstructed as alternative comedy; it was represented as serious, sometimes tragic and always romantic (' "Percivale", she answered gently, "I have seen you only in dreams . . . and my heart has gone out to you across the darkness." ').

The number of distinguished artists who illustrated his works is a mark of Green's standing; they include MARGERY GILL, Rene Cloke, SHIRLEY HUGHES, BRIAN WILDSMITH, CHARLES FOLKARD and CHARLES KEEPING. VW

Green, Winifred (active 1892–99) British illustrator who played a small but distinctive role in Birmingham's major contribution to the Arts and Crafts Movement. She aligned herself with the GREENAWAY manner, working with Greenaway's printer EDMUND EVANS and giving her Regency imagery an Art Nouveau twist. Her first children's books included *Children's Singing Games* (1894) and *Nursery Rhymes and Songs of England* (1895). In 1898 she illustrated an edition of CHARLES and MARY LAMB's *Poetry for Children* with elegant, understated full-page illustrations. *MRS LEICESTER'S SCHOOL*, which appeared in the following year, made a perfect companion volume. DW

Greenaway, Kate 1846–1901 Illustrator and author of children's books, predominant, along with RANDOLPH CALDECOTT and WALTER CRANE, in the creation of a new style of nursery PICTUREBOOK in the late 19th century. Daughter of an engraver for the *Illustrated London News*, she was encouraged to draw from an early age, and proceeded to formal art-school training. Following her studies she first designed for the new greetings card industry, especially valentine cards, and worked as a freelance illustrator of calendars and books, including FAIRY STORIES and the popular magazine *LITTLE FOLKS*. She later designed frontispieces and title-pages for the *GIRL'S OWN ANNUAL*.

The growth of the children's market in PUBLISHING and the development of colour printing, provided a context for the huge commercial success which met her first venture into writing and illustrating books under her own name. EDMUND EVANS, her printer and publisher, produced 100,000 copies of *UNDER THE WINDOW* (1878), including French and German editions, and *Kate Greenaway's Birthday Book* (1880) ran to 150,000 copies. She designed an edition of *Mother Goose* in 1881, and in that year was featured three times in *Punch* magazine, an unprecedented recognition for a children's illustrator. Though increasingly disinclined to illustrate other writers' work, she produced an edition of *Little Ann and Other Poems* (1883) by ANN and JANE TAYLOR, favourite reading from her own childhood.

Flowers were a speciality in her drawing from nature, and the *Language of Flowers* (1884) describes their symbolism. In the *MARIGOLD GARDEN* (1885), a second collection of her own verse, neat gardens of well-trimmed hedges and lawns, abundant roses, lilies and sunflowers, and fruit trees in perennial blossom surround gabled houses with red-tiled and white-washed walls. This subject matter and drawing style exhibit the values of the Aesthetic Movement in architecture and design of the 1870s. It is the quintessential Greenaway setting in which playful rhymes capture the innocent spirit of childhood, an idealised perception of the young embraced by middle-class adults in the closing decades of Victoria's reign. In *A APPLE PIE* (1886) sadness and squabbles only briefly interrupt the charming scenes of joyful leisure and play. Her observation of nature and her fondness for children earned her the approbation of John Ruskin, who particularly admired her *Annual Almanacks* which appeared continuously from 1883 to 1895. Two bestsellers of enduring quality which kept her illustrations in the public eye are *The Queen of the Pirate Isle* (1886) and *THE PIED PIPER OF HAMELIN* (1888).

The old-world costumes of her characters, drawing loosely on Georgian and Regency styles of dress, caught the public imagination and were imitated by the fashion-conscious, especially in France where 'Greenawisme' took hold. Her publications set new standards of quality in children's books. Page designs are uncluttered to let the neatly typeset verses breathe, yet they are full of invention and variety, and printed on heavy paper in sturdy, decorative bindings. PC

Greene, Bette 1934– American writer best known for *Summer of My German Soldier* (1973), which caused much controversy. Born in Memphis, Tennessee, and raised in a small town in Arkansas, Greene depicts southern life and ideals through first-person narrations seasoned with strong emotional appeal. Her books have won several awards including Parent's Choice, Children's Choice, and ALA Notables. Her Newbery Honour Book was *Philip Hall Likes Me, I Reckon Maybe* (1974), though this honour is often mistakenly assumed to be for *Summer of My German Soldier*, which is about a 12-year-old Jewish girl who hides an escaped German POW. The novel confronts violence and anti-Semitism, and the writing is intense, possibly autobiographical. It is perhaps not surprising that it was rejected by 18 publishers before it was finally issued. LAW

see also WAR STORIES

Greene, (Henry) Graham 1904–91 English novelist whose fiction for adults is characterised by a shadowy world of Catholicism, political ideology and difficult moral choices, described in spare and elegant prose. His series of four stories for young children is surprisingly different: *The Little Train* (1946), *The Little Fire Engine* (1950), *The Little Horse Bus* (1952) and *The Little Steam Roller* (1953), originally illustrated by Dorothy Craigie and reissued in 1973 and 1974 with illustrations by EDWARD ARDIZZONE. The world of these stories, is comfortable and familiar, with a suggestion of menace avoided on the way to a reassuringly safe conclusion.

Greene divided his fiction for adults into 'entertainments' and 'novels', considering the former to be less serious. *The Third Man* (1950) is a short story taken from his screenplay for the film (1949). The hero of the novel *Brighton Rock* (1938) is Pinky, a teenager and a Catholic who might be seen as dangerously disturbed but is here presented as evil or damned. Even this is seen as a kind of grace, Greene's revelation of a world beyond the merely physical. The occasional and casual anti-Semitism was unremarkable for its period but will be noticeable to modern readers. RC

Greenfield, Eloise 1929– AFRICAN AMERICAN author of poetry, PICTUREBOOKS, BIOGRAPHY, board books and fiction for children. Greenfield's birth in Parmele, North Carolina and her family's move soon after to Washington DC are discussed in *Childtimes: A Three-Generation Memoir* (1979). Co-authored with her mother, Lessie Jones Little, the memoir sketches the respective 'childtimes' (historical era and childhood) of Greenfield, Little, and Little's mother. Believing that all art is political, Greenfield stresses self-respect, the power of love, and the strength that comes from pride in one's heritage. In 1971 Greenfield joined the District of Columbia Black Writers Workshop, which led to her writing the first of her award-winning books, the biography *Rosa Parks* (1973). Its evocative text foreshadows the poetic language in such picturebooks as *Africa Dream* (1977) – a winner of the CORETTA SCOTT KING AWARD – and *Grandpa's Face* (1988). Convincing child personae voice the poems in *Honey, I Love, and Other Poems* (1978) and *Nathaniel Talking* (1988), while the poems in *Night on Neighborhood Street* (1991) recall the city children brought to life by Gwendolyn Brooks in *BRONZEVILLE BOYS AND GIRLS*. The importance of family, of childhood itself, and of black people's struggle to live fully despite racism resonate throughout Greenfield's estimable body of work. JMA

Greengage Summer, The (1958) Novel by the British author RUMER GODDEN, which, like much of her other work, is about the growth of consciousness. The events relating to the Grey family one summer in

Illustration by Ted Greenwood from *Ginnie*.

France are narrated by one of its members, Cecil, who, as a 13-year-old girl, is situated in the awkward space between childhood and adulthood. Her tone is one of bewilderment and alienation at no longer being able to see things innocently nor yet able to understand the full import of what it is she sees and describes for us; at the same time there is also a wonder at the world that is being unveiled. The narrative gropes for language with which to articulate and understand new experiences (these ranging from new kinds of food to adult emotions and physical change), reflecting the search for being and identity that is the novel's main theme. The novel, however, suggests that this is an ongoing process; to be adult is not necessarily to have reached a final or settled state of self, for the adult can revert to childhood even as the child reaches towards adulthood. SA

Greenwood, Barbara 1940– Canadian writer of short stories, HISTORICAL FICTION, reference books and BIOGRAPHIES. Her first novel, *A Question of Loyalty* (1984), describes the personal anguish and humanitarian emotions aroused during the War of 1812, especially between young adults, and their families and neighbours. Greenwood's second novel, *Spy in the Shadows* (1990), which describes the Fenian Raids of 1866, became the 1992 White Ravens Selection of the International Youth Library in Munich. Greenwood also received the 1995 Information Book Award given by the Children's Literature Roundtable of Canada. Her non-fiction includes three biographies and *A Pioneer Story: The Daily Life of a Canadian Family in 1840*, re-titled as *A Pioneer Sample* (1995). This well-researched book, illustrated by HEATHER COLLINS, won the Mr. Christie Book Award and the Ruth Schwartz Award. Greenwood and Collins followed with *Pioneer Crafts* (1997), which contains ILLUSTRATIONS accompanied by craft instructions designed especially for children who want to do things the pioneer way. The most significant aspect of Greenwood's work is her ability to involve readers in the lives of real and fictional people of the past. MRS

Greenwood, Ted (Edward Alister) 1930–99 Australian illustrator and writer, whose illustrations for IVAN SOUTHALL's *Sly Old Wardrobe* (1968) won him the Children's Book Council of Australia Picturebook of the Year award, and helped establish the modern Australian PICTUREBOOK. His award-winning books – such as *Obstreperous* (1969), about a kite which has a life of its own – broke new ground in their use of poster art and the manipulation of lines, shapes, letters and patterns to suggest vigorous action. *V.I.P.: Very Important Plant* (1971) and *Everlasting Circle* (1981), through dramatic images (such as a chain-saw or a box of matches), make a strong statement about conservation and the environment. MSax

Gretz, Susanna 1937– British illustrator and author. Gretz has made her mark with her series of titles about a family of pigs, first among them the obsessive, sulky and obstinate Roger. *It's your turn Roger!* (1985) has characteristic accurate observation, inventive page design and fine, spirited line-drawing. For slightly younger children, Gretz has produced a series featuring a teddy-bear family. Gretz has also contributed black-and-white ILLUSTRATIONS for *I Din Do Nuttin* (JOHN AGARD, 1984). JAG

Grey Owl (Washaguonasin) [Archibald Stansfeld Belaney] 1888–1938 Author, film-maker and conservationist. Born in England, Belaney emigrated to Canada, where he spent some time hunting and trapping in Ontario. Finally repulsed by the cruelty of the steel-jaw trap, the rifle and poison, Belaney denounced the profession and set up his own beaver sanctuary in an attempt to right some of the wrongs he had seen done to animals. To support his family, he turned to writing, his stories being especially well received in England. His only children's book, *The Adventures of Sajo and Her Beaver People* (1935), covers a year in the lives of two beaver kittens rescued by an Indian and given to his motherless daughter Sajo. Two other novels, *Men of the Last Frontier* (1931) and *Tales of an Empty Cabin* (1936), appeal to all ages. His films and novels are realistic ADVENTURE STORIES which focus on the wilderness, the true nature of animals and man's interaction with both. He took the pseudonym of Grey Owl when he was adopted as a blood brother by the Ojibwa Indian tribe in 1920. He wrote his AUTOBIOGRAPHY, *Pilgrims of the Wild,* in 1934. KSB

Grey Rabbit see *LITTLE GREY RABBIT*

Greyfriars Fictional school created by 'Frank Richards', one of the many pen-names used by CHARLES HAMILTON (1876–1971), who is perhaps the most prolific and certainly the widest-read and best-loved of all British writers of SCHOOL STORIES for boys. He had been writing stories for boys' weeklies and COMICS since 1894, but it was not until 1906, when he created St Jim's College for *The Gem*, that he became fully established. His adventures of *Tom Merry and Co* were so popular that he was asked to write a second series for a new weekly, *Magnet* (1908). This, based at Greyfriars College, was his masterpiece, starring Harry Wharton, leader of the Famous Five, and Billy Bunter, the fattest, greediest pupil of the Remove, if not the fattest 'on earth', as he was later branded. *Magnet* ran until 1940 when it was killed by wartime paper shortage, but Bunter survived as a comic strip by Frank Minnitt in *Knockout*. *GREYFRIARS HOLIDAY ANNUAL* was a huge 'bumper book' running from 1920 to 1941, and after the war Hamilton – still as 'Frank Richards' – wrote a large a number of *Greyfriars* novels in hardback. He also wrote a series for BBC TELEVISION, which starred Gerald Campion as Bunter in *Billy Bunter of Greyfriars School*. DG

Greyfriars Holiday Annual for Boys and Girls, The (from 1920) An immensely popular publication chiefly featuring boarding-school stories which had originated in the weeklies, *The Magnet* and *The Gem*. The satisfyingly thick volumes, with their high-spirited ILLUSTRATIONS, appeared each year from 1920 until wartime shortages brought the series to an end in 1941. Largely written by the prolific CHARLES HAMILTON under his many pseudonyms, they chronicled the exploits of such heroes as Billy Bunter and Harry Wharton and his chums. Fellows' sisters were welcomed as readers of these boys' stories. Reprints of the annuals, published by Howard Baker from the 1970s, found an enthusiastic readership. GPF

Grice, Frederick see *BONNIE PIT LADDIE, THE*

Wood engraving by GUSTAVE DORÉ for 'Little Red-Cap' by the Grimm Brothers.

Grimm brothers, Jacob Ludwig Carl 1785–1863 and **Wilhelm Carl** 1786–1859 German folklorists, philologists and editors, the Grimm brothers were born in Hannau, a small town set in the independent state of Hesse. Their lawyer father died in 1796, leaving a wife and six children with just enough to live on. Jacob and Wilhelm began studying law at university before becoming engaged in the study of poetry. Intensely nationalistic, the brothers saw folk songs and stories in particular as evidence for an ancient Teutonic culture which they hoped would one day form the basis for a new, united Germany.

In 1805 two friends, Achim von Arnim and Clemens Brentano, published some traditional folk songs under the title *Des Knaben Wunderhorn*, much later set to music by Gustav Mahler. Spurred on by this example, the brothers also began collecting traditional titles in the following year. Domestic troubles then intervened. In 1808 the Grimms' mother died, leaving Jacob in charge of the family. Wilhelm was now in poor health, unable to work full-time. But the brothers persisted in their collecting, with the dream of one day producing a history of the whole of German literature. Living and working in the same house, their relationship stayed as close as it had always been in childhood. In 1812 they decided to go ahead with publishing the FOLKTALES they had so far assembled. That Christmas the first volume of their famous

Kinder- und Hausmärchen appeared. It was an immediate success, and a second volume came out in 1814.

Jacob then returned to the study of German philology, producing his great *Deutsche Grammatik* in 1819. This brilliant scientific analysis of language was another step forward in the brothers' determination to raise general consciousness about German culture. Years later they started on a new German dictionary. Wilhelm was now married with three children; his bride was a former neighbour from whom the brothers had collected three of their stories. By the time the dictionary had reached the letter D, Wilhelm died. Four years later Jacob also died with the dictionary now on F; another hundred years were to pass before it was finally completed.

The brothers' most enduring work was always their FAIRY TALE collection. Although the first edition was unillustrated and carried a scholarly introduction and accompanying notes, it was neverthless popular with those few children to whom the Grimms presented copies. Stories like 'The Frog Prince', 'Rapunzel', 'Rumplestiltskin' and 'Snow White and the Seven Dwarfs' are, after all, some of the best in the world, still capturing children's imaginations wherever they are heard. Later editions of the tales dropped a few stories that were thought too cruel or indelicate for the young and also left out the scholarly footnotes, while adding illustrations. By the time of the seventh edition in 1856 many of the tales were much longer than in the original volume, padded out with extra detail, moralising passages and literary phrases like 'Once upon a time'.

Such rewriting, easily accepted at the time, has since become a source of controversy. Some of the changes the Grimms made seem to go in the direction of particular ideologies now more open to criticism. Changing the wicked mother to a stepmother in 'Hansel and Gretel' is seen by some as an attempt to deny that any harm could ever come to children at the hand of a blood relative. To admit otherwise might seem to damage the Grimms' general claims for the nobility and purity of the particular Teutonic culture supposedly enshrined in these stories. Exalting the woodcutter father in the same tale, with succeeding editions describing him far more favourably than he appears in the original version, also comes over as an endorsement of patriarchal values at the expense of women, represented here by the cruel stepmother and the witch. A closer look at the tales' sources also reveals that the brothers were not always straightforward when it came to describing their research. The original notion they put about was that they collected stories chiefly from the mouths of simple peasants, typified by their most famous source Katharina Viehmann, a tailor's wife living in a local village. But subsequent analysis reveals that in many cases the brothers often relied instead upon middle-class friends and family for their stories. In this way, French fairy tales were sometimes unwittingly fed back to them, originally taken from Perrault but since transferred into the German language. It was important for the Grimms to emphasise the tales as an intrinsic part of the oral Teutonic culture in which they believed so ardently. But this belief caused them to exaggerate the claims they made about the tales' origins, and may also have led them to reshape some of the same stories in line with the values they held.

Such criticisms, however, should not be taken too far. In the original versions published by the Grimms, many of the stories were very brief and unsatisfactory, concentrating on a rush of incident at the expense of general atmosphere and characterisation. By polishing and adding to these tales, the brothers greatly enhanced the readability of their material. Proof of this can be found in the success of these stories worldwide. Translated into English by Edgar Taylor in 1823, the collection was never since out of print and formed the basis for the hosts of illustrated books and films still to come. Many other countries also took eagerly to these tales. The Grimms were not the only folklorists to reshape the stories they collected. They were certainly among the very best when it came to making their material accessible to the huge audience which has so greatly enjoyed it ever since. Bruno Bettelheim in his psychoanalytic study *The Uses of Enchantment; the Meaning and Importance of Fairy Tales* (1976) also claims that reading these stories helps children to understand themselves and their own emotions at a deep level of the unconscious. NT

Gross, Philip 1952– English poet and novelist, born in Cornwall. His collections include *Manifold Manor* (1989), *THE ALL-NITE CAFE* (1993) and *Scratch City* (1995). Often amusing, Gross has a surreal imagination. His distinctive, well-crafted poetry is located in moody, atmospheric settings, sometimes peopled by strange characters, but Gross always has something interesting to say about contemporary life, especially for older readers. *Transformer* (1996) was the first Point Horror novel (see POINT SERIES) by a British author. HT

Growing Point (1962–92) British review journal of books 'for growing families . . . and for parents, teachers, librarians and other guardians', written, published and mailed (in hand-addressed envelopes) by the phenomenal British critic MARGERY FISHER for 30 years (nine issues per annum until 1977, six thereafter). Its consistently high standard makes it an invaluable resource for the study of children's literature. Eclectic, perceptive and generous, Fisher believed that children must come to the book, not the other way round. She covered new books in every genre including occasional adult novels, bibliographies and reminders of books past. Where necessary, specialist reviewers were invited to contribute. EM

Guardian **Award for Children's Fiction** see APPENDIX

Guardian Circle, The see MARGARET BUFFIE

Guess How Much I Love You (1994) PICTUREBOOK written by the Irish writer SAM MCBRATNEY and illustrated by ANITA JERAM. It is a robust story full of surprises – in the relationship at the heart of the story; the initiator of the guess; the unpredictability of the text and, above all, the book's unsentimentality. A conversation turns into play, precipitating a rough-and-tumble crescendo succeeded by the wind-down into sleep. Throughout, the seriousness and playfulness, boisterousness and tenderness of family love are all revealed. Most of all we see the total security that makes the issue not 'do you love me?' but 'how much I love you!' AMN

Illustration by Tapas Guha.

Guha, Tapas 1963– The self-taught Indian illustrator Tapas Guha invests his ILLUSTRATIONS with a deep literary understanding and humanity, as the emotional appeal of his illustrations to SIGRUN SRIVASTAV's *A Moment of Truth* (1991) reveals. Never one to shirk experimentation, he emerges as a versatile artist who varies his style, medium and texture according to the demands of the text. His style is naturalistic, born out of a keen observation of life and an ability to visualise cinematically. His illustrations, backed by intensive research, are meticulous in their detail. Guha started his career with illustrations for his own SCIENCE FICTION story *Roop and the Aliens from Space* (1982), published in the popular children's magazine, *Children's World*. He prefers illustrating funny stories, his forte being comic-book illustration. He uses pencil colours, watercolours, photo-colours or pen-and-ink, depending on the paper he is using and the effect he wishes to produce. The illustrator EDMUND DULAC has been a 'kind of ideal' for Guha. MBh

Guiding and Scouting fiction Since the birth of the Scout and Guide Movements in 1907 and 1910 huge numbers of children's books have been published directly or indirectly featuring Scouts and Guides. The founder of both Movements, Lord Robert Baden-Powell (1857–1941), wrote fictional stories to liven up the educational text of the first Scout handbook, *Scouting for Boys* (1908), and to illustrate the ethos of Scouting – that of training character and instilling a sense of good. First published in fortnightly parts, this book has remained in print and is among the world's most translated bestsellers along with the Bible and the Koran. Baden-Powell's first work for the Girl Guides was written jointly with his sister Agnes Baden-Powell – *How Girls Can Help Build up the Empire, a Handbook for Girl Guides* (1912), a training manual explaining what was expected of Guides. Chapters with titles like 'Pursuits', 'Patriotism' and 'Home and Frontier Life' included true stories of prominent people, such as CHARLES DICKENS, Florence Nightingale and Queen Mary, in order to instil the idea of high principals and good qualities into its girl readers.

The Jungle Books by RUDYARD KIPLING were used to give an attractive background setting to the Scout Movement's junior branch for 8- to 11-year-olds, the Wolf Cubs, when it was formed in 1916. The story of Mowgli, a boy brought up by wolves in the jungle, caught the imagination of younger boys and provided inspiration for the Wolf Cub programme, its terminology, leaders' names and mascots. Today some of this still lives on in the section now called Cub Scouts. Kipling later wrote *Land and Sea Tales for Scouts and Guides* (1923) specifically for the Scout and Guide market, such was his admiration for Baden-Powell and his fledgling organisations. The book contains stories of heroism and adventure, interspersed with poems. When introducing the younger section of the Girl Guides, the Brownies, in 1914, Baden-Powell adapted *The Brownies* from JULIANA HORATIA

EWING's book *The Brownies and Other Tales* (1870); the two lazy characters in the story, Johnnie and Tommy, are changed to Betty and Tommy, the 'brownies' who learn the importance of hard work and helpfulness.

Numerous children's authors have written Scout fiction. PERCY WESTERMAN wrote over 14 Scout novels between 1914 and 1955, of which *Sea Scouts of the Petrel* (1914) and *Sea Scouts of the Kestrel* (1930) were among the most popular. The most prolific author was F. Haydn Dimmock (1895–1955), who as well as being editor of *The Scout* from 1919 to 1954 wrote at least 16 Scout novels in these years and countless other tales in the pages of his magazine. Scouting has also played its part in providing a background or inspiration for other children's writers, as in Richmal Crompton's *More William* (1922) (see *JUST WILLIAM*), which features a chapter in which the notorious William Brown is a Scout.

Similarly, around 100 authors have written lively, informative, adventurous HISTORICAL FICTION and non-fiction works associated specifically with Guiding. The first British author to write Girl Guide novels was Dorothea Moore, beginning with *Terry the Girl Guide* (1912). Other authors followed, such as Dorothy Osborn Hann and Frances Nash, who wrote of their experiences in the Movement. Hann's *Peg* series followed its heroine through her time as a Brownie in *Peg Junior* (1931), and as a Guide in *Peg's Patrol* (1924), *Captain Peg* (1928) and finally *What Happened to Peg* (1932). Frances Nash wrote the *Audrey* series, beginning with *How Audrey Became a Guide* (1922). In 1924 she also wrote a story for the Brownies, *Some Brownies and a Boggart*; since in books bad children are much more exciting than good ones, the real heroine until almost the end of the story is Victoria Grice-Budden, the boggart. Guides have often appeared in the *RUPERT BEAR* stories serialised in the *Daily Express* and the *Rupert Annuals*; and in no. 49 of the *Rupert Adventure Series* (1963), Rupert and his friend Edward visit the Guides in camp.

The Scout Movement's magazine, *The Scout*, which appeared weekly from 1908 to 1966, was dominated by fictional tales which, together with news and other educational material, fed the appetites of the growing army of eager boy readers. Saving lives, catching horse thieves and stopping runaway trains and horses exemplified the central philosophy of 'doing a good turn' and emphasised the ideology of honesty, gallantry and clean living that made Scouting so acceptable to the society of the time. Boys looking for role models needed to look no further than their fictional heroes and their peers. For a short period the Wolf Cubs also had their own magazine, *The Wolf Cub* (1917–19), which mixed fiction and non-fiction. The magazines have ceased, but the *Scout Annual* (1930–93), the *Wolf Cub Annual* (1935–66), the *The Cub Scout Annual* (1966–), the *Sixer's Annual* (1961–79) the *Scout Pathfinder Annual* (1963–79) and the *Beaver Scout Annual* (1985–) have all continued to carry fictional tales of daring deeds performed by boys no older than the readers.

Similarly, periodicals published by the movement played a large part in the Guiding lives of the membership, supplying them with serialised stories by new authors, ideas to practise with their units, information about changes to the rules and uniform, as well as articles of everyday interest. *Guiding* (formerly *The Guider* and *Girl Guide Gazette*) has been continually published since 1914 for the adult section, while *Guide Patrol* (formerly *Today's Guide* and before that *The Guide*) ran from 1924 until 1994, primarily for girls of Guide age; the *Brownie* magazine, published since 1962, is especially for the 7- to 10-year-old membership. A periodical for Rangers ran from 1947 until 1974. Guides have also had their own ANNUALS: in 1951 *The Girl Guide Annual* was introduced, followed by *The Brownie* in 1958. With a tendency for annuals to be more popular with the younger girls, *The Girl Guide Annual* was discontinued in 1993 and *The Rainbow Annual* introduced in 1992 for the Rainbow Section (5- to 7-year-olds). MC, PM

see also CAMPING AND TRAMPING FICTION

Guinness Book of Records see INFORMATION BOOKS

Gulliver's Travels (1726) Satire by Jonathan Swift (1667–1745), first published in London by Benjamin Motte. This edition was revised several times by Swift; the edition published in 1735 in Dublin by George Faulkner is usually preferred by modern editors. It recounts in four parts the adventures in exotic lands of Lemuel Gulliver, a ship's surgeon. Originally written as a satirical comment on 18th-century Britain, it has been widely read by children. The many adaptations and retellings for children usually feature only parts one and two, *A Voyage to Lilliput* and *A Voyage to Brobdingnag*. Many of these adaptations are poor, both in the quality of the text and in the presentation. Earlier editions include one illustrated in colour by ARTHUR RACKHAM (1909), and PADRAIC COLUM's edition illustrated by WILLY POGANY (1917). More recent editions of note include ELAINE MOSS's adaptation, illustrated by Hans Balthazar (1961). James Riordan's adaptation (1992) is skilful and VICTOR G. AMBRUS's accompanying illustrations capture the humour of the story. It is enlivened too by the inclusion of Gulliver's need to relieve himself, following his shipwreck in Lilliput. This, and other incidents of an earthy nature have been bowdlerised from many editions. Ann Keay Beneduce's retelling (1994) is somewhat static but Gennady Spirin's accompanying illustrations in the style of 18th-century paintings create a highly decorative edition. VC

see also ABRIDGEMENT

Gumble's Yard (1961) The first novel by the British novelist JOHN ROWE TOWNSEND, in which a deserted warehouse by a canal is used as a hiding-place for various characters. In this story, it becomes home to four children left to fend for themselves by the adults who looked after them. Fearing they will be separated by the authorities, they move into Gumble's Yard, only to stumble upon a dangerous criminal plot. Sandra and Kevin are tough and work hard to stay together, their strong ties of affection for the younger children providing a moving contrast to the selfish actions of the grown-ups. The book has been accused of employing class and gender stereoypes, as the run-down district in Cobchester is populated by seedy working-class characters and the children's roles are determined by their sex. Despite this, the book was seminal in its attempt to portray the adventures of a group of children within a realistic context of urban poverty. EA

***Gumbles* series** see *BOTTERSNIKES AND GUMBLES*

***Gumdrop* series** Sequence of (to date) nine stories by the British illustrator Biro (1921–). Val Biro is a prolific illustrator in many fields. In 1966 he wrote and illustrated his first story for Brockhampton Press about his own vintage car – a 1926 Austin Clifton Twelve-Four – and started an appetite for 'the adventures of a vintage car' stories which resulted in a series continuing into the 1990s. Surprisingly for a car which has lasted so long, the first story, *Gumdrop, The Adventures of a Vintage Car* (1966), begins with the slow, sad dismantling of Gumdrop. A young enthusiast (who is surely Biro himself) arrives and is determined to reassemble the car and so the hunt is on for its far-flung parts. There is an immensely satisfying ending when, at a rally, the restored Gumdrop wins first prize, presented by the old owner who hands over the last missing piece – Gumdrop's shiny brass horn. Informal language, authentic detail (the ENDPAPERS show detailed, labelled cross-sections of the car), high drama with a full complement of villainy, absurd coincidence and pleasing resolutions characterise these stories. The illustrations have become more sophisticated over 30 years, but Biro's line, used to create his characters, remains lively, and each self-contained story retains the classical and pleasing shape of Gumdrop's first adventure. JAG

Gun Law see COMICS, PERIODICALS AND MAGAZINES

Gunn, Mrs Aeneas (Jeannie) 1870–1961 Australian writer. Affectionately known in Australia as the 'Little Missus', Mrs Gunn drew on her experiences as 'boss' of a large cattle station in the Northern Territory to write one of the first sympathetic and amusing stories (albeit now regarded as somewhat paternalistic) of Aboriginal life. Bett-Bett, the eponymous *Little Black Princess* (1905), endeared herself to generations of Australian readers because in spite of racial differences she embodies universal traits of childhood, especially an exuberant sense of fun. *We of the Never-Never* (1908) recreates a way of life that was isolated and demanding, but sustained by the endurance and good humour of the characters who supported the 'Little Missus'. MSax

gutter In PICTUREBOOKS, the space of inner margin where two pages meet at the binding. Since there is a slight loss of picture area where the pages are stitched or glued together, a double-spread illustration presents a compositional challenge to the artist. JD

Guy, Rosa 1928– Author of 15 books for children or young adults, often about orphaned children of West Indian heritage growing up in Harlem. Born in Trinidad, Guy has lived in New York City since she was seven. Orphaned at an early age, she quit school by the age of 14 and took a factory job, very much like one of her best-drawn characters, Edith Jackson. Later she became a social activist, involved with labour unions and the civil rights movement. She helped to found the Harlem Writers' Guild and aspired to be a playwright. Finally, in 1990, her novel *My Love, My Love*, about class conflicts facing a peasant girl in the French Antilles, was staged as a Broadway musical.

Rosa Guy's long career began in the 1950s; by the early 1970s she had published what would become her most famous–and best–children's book, *The Friends* (1973), the story of 14-year-old Phyllisia Cathy, newly arrived from the West Indies in New York. Phyllisia's friendship with brave, outspoken Edith Jackson, and her trials – with bullies and a bigoted teacher at school and at home with a tyrannical father, Calvin, and a mother who is dying – provided the potential for two sequels. In the second book, *Ruby* (1976), Guy focused on Phyllisia's older sister, who works through a debilitating Electra complex by entering, for a time, into a lesbian relationship with Daphne, a precocious 14-year-old. In *Edith Jackson* (1978), Guy focused on the plight of black orphans in foster care and interracial social conflicts.

A second YOUNG ADULT trilogy – *The Disappearance* (1979), *New Guys Around the Block* (1983), *And I Heard a Bird Sing* (1987) – features a male protagonist; in two teen romances, *Mirror of Her Own* (1981) and *The Music of Summer* (1992), she explores intra-racial class differences; a PICTUREBOOK, *Billy the Great* (1992), explores interracial, cross-age friendship, as does *The Ups and Downs of Carl Davis III* (1989), a multilayered, richly textured novel for middle-grade readers; and *Mother Crocodile*, a Caribbean FOLKTALE retelling, illustrated by JOHN STEPTOE, won the 1982 CORETTA SCOTT KING AWARD.

Guy's special talent rests in the ability to create a multi-voiced cast of engaging, empathetic characters. Many of these (Edith, Daphne, Carl) convey her strong convictions about social inequities in America, whereas others, like Calvin Cathy, because of human foibles or conflicting social customs, constitute humorous and captivating adult portraits. It is perhaps not surprising that Guy, in 1995, the year of her son's death, would produce at the age of 67 her best work yet. *The Sun, the Sea, a Touch of the Wind* is a novel about an artist, not unlike herself, an orphan in New York City since childhood, and an outspoken feminist, who travels to Haiti in search of new ways to define herself. NM

***Gwydion* sequence** A FANTASY by the popular Welsh writer Jenny Sullivan. In the first of the sequence, *The Magic Apostrophe* (1994), a contemporary schoolgirl discovers at the age of 13 that, by using an apostrophe in her name (Tan'ith), she can come into her full power as a witch alongside her mother and aunts. In this and the two sequels – *The Island of Summer* (1996) and *Dragonson* (1997) – she and her best friend are thrown dramatically into a series of conflicts involving landscape and characters from Welsh mythology, especially Gwydion and TALIESIN. The bright and streetwise narrator is engaging and convincing, though her relentlessly cheerful narrative voice works rather against the brooding and dark character of traditional WELSH MYTHOLOGY. A particularly attractive feature is the treatment of Tan'ith's Aunt Fliss, who has dementia – except when she reverts to being a witch; in the second narrative, she sidesteps her condition by staying behind in Ynys Haf. VW

Gwynne, Phillip 1958– Australian writer whose first novel, *Deadly, Unna?* (1998) won the Children's Book Council of Australia Book of the Year Award: Older Readers. His second book, *The Worst Team Ever* (1999), was chosen as a Notable Book for that year. Gwynne is a master of realistic dialogue and interior monologue; the characters he creates are complex and reflect Gwynne's compassionate insight into life and humanity and his capacity to see the humour in it. An obvious fan of Australian Rules football, Gwynne uses the game as a backdrop for much of the action. But the focus is always on the people – their lives, prejudices, loves, malice and growth in a society which still has a long way to go to reach maturity. RTh

Gypsy Breynton (1866) First in a series of four volumes by the American author Elizabeth Stuart Phelps Ward (1844–1911), who wrote the books under her maiden name Elizabeth Stuart Phelps. *Gypsy Breynton* (1866) was followed by *Gypsy's Cousin Joy* (1866), *Gypsy's Sowing and Reaping* (1866), and *Gypsy's year at the Golden Crescent* (1867). The heroine of the series is a lively 12-year-old, adventurous and devoid of stereotypically feminine characteristics. 'There was not a trout-brook for miles she had not fished. There was hardly a tree she had not climbed . . . Gypsy could row and skate and swim, and play ball and make kites, and coast and race and drive and chop wood.' Best of all, her brother Tom identifies her as uncharacteristic of the worst of her gender: 'I don't believe Gypsy cries four times a year . . . with all of her faults there's none of your girl's nonsense about her.' The last book of the four deals with Gypsy's year at boarding school. The series features pleasant, humorous tales of Gypsy's life and antics as a charming, mildly tomboyish girl. KSB

H

Habberton, John 1842–1921 American writer best known for *Helen's Babies* (1876), a humorous account of a young bachelor's experiences when left in charge of two lively nephews. Habberton was born in Brooklyn, New York, and after serving in the Civil War worked on the editorial staff of various periodicals. *Helen's Babies,* his first book, was very successful, adult and child readers alike enjoying the small boys' ingenious mischief that constantly interrupts their uncle's romantic endeavours. *Other People's Children* (1877) and *Budge and Toddie* (1908) followed as sequels, but like Habberton's other writings were less popular. FEA

Hader, Elmer (Stanley) 1889–1973 and **Hader, Berta [Hoerner]** 1890–1976 Authors and illustrators of over 100 PICTUREBOOKS from the 1920s through to the 1960s. Berta was born in San Pedro, Coahuila, Mexico, and Elmer in Pajaro, California. They married in New York in 1919, and began illustrating and writing children's books together. The Haders built their home, Willow Farm, overlooking the Hudson River near Nyack, New York, and wrote about the experience in *The Little Stone House* (1944). Many of their subsequent books were set in the rural surroundings of their home, including the 1949 CALDECOTT AWARD winner *The Big Snow.* This beautifully designed book with snowflake-patterned ENDPAPERS combines luminous watercolour ILLUSTRATIONS with detailed drawings of the woodland birds and animals, reflecting the Haders' lifelong interest in nature. In this book people are important only in their connection to the animals, and appear in only three of the pictures. In *The Cat and the Kitten* (1940) humans are also peripheral to the adventures of the cat Minnie and her kitten Timmy, who spends a harrowing winter alone when accidentally left at the family's country house. In the 1980s and 1990s some of the Haders' earlier works, mainly illustrations of NURSERY RHYMES and FOLKTALES, were reissued. LH

see also ANIMALS IN FICTION

Haggard, Sir (Henry) Rider 1856–1925 British colonial administrator, prolific novelist and agricultural reformer. Born in Norfolk, Haggard spent five formative years in southern Africa, where he was involved in the annexation of the Transvaal in 1877. He loved the country and admired the Zulu people. Soon after returning to England in 1881, he began to write to earn a living, publishing the highly successful *KING SOLOMON'S MINES* in 1885. He repeated the formula in *Allan Quatermain* (1887), adding a sexual and mystical dimension to extend his appeal, something he developed further in *She* (1887). She, or Ayesha, She-Who-Must-Be-Obeyed, was the supposedly immortal white queen of the hidden cavern-city of Kor, a civilisation partly suggested by the Zimbabwe ruins.

Haggard wrote nearly 60 novels, which formed the basis of 28 films. Of his many settings, including the ancient Egyptian and Aztec civilisations, those in Africa are the most fully achieved, an arena in which idealised male protagonists search for unattainable beauty and the heroic life. Haggard's ADVENTURE STORIES feature a struggle between good and evil within vividly imagined landscapes. His version of imperialism, like that of his friend RUDYARD KIPLING, is surprisingly complex, often critical of western values and appreciative of the qualities of non-European societies. PR

Haig-Brown, Roderick (Langmere) 1908–76 Canadian author highly regarded for his realistic fiction, ANIMAL STORIES, HISTORICAL FICTION and BIOGRAPHIES for children. He won the Canadian Library Association's Children's Book of the Year Award for *Starbuck Valley Winter* (1944) and *The Whale People* (1962). Born in Lancaster, England, he emigrated to Canada in 1926. In addition to serving in the Canadian Army he worked as a logger, trapper, fisherman and guide on the Canadian and United States western coast. His love for the wilderness is evident in his storytelling. His main characters, whether animal or human, either possess or develop an intimate understanding and reverence for the land. In *Starbuck Valley Winter* the main character struggles to succeed at trapping in order to earn money for a boat, and in doing so learns to overcome his insecurities and fears. *The Whale People* describes the ritual steps necessary for a native boy to succeed his father as chieftain while also emphasising the wisdom needed in being a true leader. *Ki-yu* (1934) is a unique and suspenseful novel from the perspective of a panther pursued by a professional hunter. LAW

haiku Poetic form which originated in Japan, consisting of 17 syllables, usually arranged in three lines of five, seven and five syllables. The master of the form was Matsuo Basho (1644–94), one of whose lines gave Ian Fleming the title for the novel *You Only Live Twice*. In its pure form the haiku contains some kind of contrast, direct imagery, explicit or implicit reference to a season, and words which mean more than they say. The brevity, simplicity and directness of the haiku make it appealing to children, who are often invited to write their own versions in classrooms. FRBS

***Hairy Maclary* series** (1983–97) PICTUREBOOKS by New Zealand author-illustrator Lynley Dodd, who also illustrated EVE SUTTON's classic *My Cat Likes to Hide in Boxes* (1973). The books portray the adventures of the eponymous scruffy little black dog, but there are other canine and feline characters as well. The success of the stories lies mainly in Dodd's succinct yet flamboyant rhymes, which, always effortless, make the books a delight to read aloud. The illustrations are also strong, comically depicting the individual personalities of the animals. KA

Hale, Edward Everett 1822–1909 American clergyman, writer and public figure. Among his many publications are several biographical and historical books for children, the *Family Flight* series being co-authored with his sister, Susan Hale. His best-known work, *The Man Without a Country* (1863), is about a young man being tried for treason who angrily declares that he never wants to hear the name of the United States again. He is sentenced to have his wish granted, and to spend his life in exile at sea, deprived of all information about his homeland. The story became required reading in many schoolrooms. FEA

Hale, Kathleen 1898–2000 Scottish author, born in Lanarkshire. Hale's childhood was often unhappy; her father died when she was five and she was brought up largely apart from her mother. However, she believed that without these early hardships she would have been 'less adventurous'. A rebel at school, Hale blossomed in the more vital atmosphere of art school and later at Reading University. She was introduced to London's artistic society and worked as a Land Army girl in World War I. A succession of temporary jobs followed until the security of a job as secretary to the artist Augustus John enabled her to earn a living from her own painting. In 1926 she married a young artist, Douglas McClean, and they bought a large house in Hertfordshire in which to raise their two sons and many pets. It was here that she began the *ORLANDO* stories for the amusement of her own children. Hale was awarded the OBE in 1976 and published her autobiography, *A Slender Reputation*, in 1995. HCE

Hale, Keith see GAY AND LESBIAN LITERATURE

Hale, Lucretia P(eabody) 1820–1900 Often cited as the first American author of nonsense for children. Born in Boston to a literary family, Hale is best known for *The Peterkin Papers* (1880) and *The Last of the Peterkins, With Others of Their Kin* (1886). Like traditional simpletons, the Peterkins lack common sense, but their misadventures stem from the entanglements of family life and skewed Yankee ingenuity. Hale frequently collaborated with her brother, EDWARD EVERETT HALE (author of *The Man Without a Country*), on projects such as *The New Harry and Lucy: A Story of Boston in the Summer of 1891* (1892), a revision of MARIA EDGEWORTH's *Harry and Lucy* stories. Only the *Peterkin* titles still claim attention today. JMA

Hale, Mrs Sarah (Josepha) (Buell) 1788–1879 Boston editor, author and advocate of children's literature. She edited the American periodical *Juvenile Miscellany* in 1830 and included her own poem 'Mary Had a Little Lamb', a sentimental favourite of children even today. It also appeared in Hale's own collection, *Poems for Our Children Designed for Families, Sabbath Schools and Infant Schools* (also 1830), was set to music two years later, and is frequently included – without attribution – in anthologies of NURSERY RHYMES. She later edited *Godey's Lady's Book*. Mrs Hale was the first editor to print stories by FRANCES HODGSON BURNETT. In addition to poems, she wrote novels and books of short stories. KSB

Haley, Gail 1939– American artist and author of PICTUREBOOKS filled with dynamic and original artistic techniques, including woodcuts, block prints, painted wood, and vibrant paintings. Haley's CALDECOTT AWARD winner, *A Story, A Story* (1970), captures perfectly the folk language and rhythms of the African legend she is retelling. Her travel to the Caribbean and study of African dance produced words as striking as the vivid figures and motifs in the colourful woodcuts. Living in England from 1973 to 1980, Haley produced *The Post Office Cat* (1976), which won the KATE GREENAWAY MEDAL; *Go Away, Stay Away* (1977), a folk FANTASY that took her to Switzerland and Cornwall to investigate spring festivals; and *The Green Man* (1979), her own story of the legendary vegetation god. In the 1980s, Haley produced *Jack and the Bean Tree* (1986) and *Jack and the Fire Dragon* (1998), both about Appalachian Jack, a TRICKSTER American 'cousin' of the English Green Man. NM

see also AFRICAN MYTHOLOGY AND FOLKTALES

***Half Magic* series** Sequence of novels by the American author EDWARD EAGER. *Half Magic* (1954), *Magic by the Lake* (1957), *Knight's Castle* (1956) and *The*

Time Garden (1959) may best be described as comic FANTASIES modelled upon E. NESBIT's stories. However, Eager's work is always light-heartedly aware of its literary debts and uses its borrowings creatively rather than derivatively. *Knight's Castle*, for example, is a happy pastiche of Nesbit's *The Magic City* (1910), SCOTT's *Ivanhoe* and the genre of doll's house fiction; the city which the children build in the spirit of Nesbit's book comes alive around the toy castle of Torquilstone (the doll's house becomes the giant's lair) and the mixture of idiom that results (knights on motorcycles, Ivanhoe reading SCIENCE FICTION etc.) is very funny. Other people's books are used, but (re)presented and rewritten as the children – and doubtless the author – would have liked to read them (in Eager's 'version' of *Ivanhoe*, Ivanhoe marries Rebecca). Moreover, his literary loans are repaid with interest and his work breathes life back into the modes or genres borrowed from; this is exemplified in *The Time Garden* when the children, visiting the March sisters, inspire in Jo the idea of writing *LITTLE WOMEN*. SA

see also DOLL STORIES; LITERATURE IN CHILDREN'S LITERATURE

half-tone process In order to reproduce tone using only black and white it is necessary to trick the eye into believing that a range of greys have been printed. This is achieved when making the process block (see PROCESS ENGRAVING) by interposing between the image to be reproduced and the negative a screen with a grid of fine diagonal lines. The original image, passing through the lens, is broken up into a pattern of dots of different sizes. Variations in the size of the dots have the effect of printing all the shades of grey, although the dots are black and the space between them white. GCB

Hall, Donald 1928– One of America's most respected poets, essayists and editors as well as a distinguished contributor to children's literature. In 1975 Hall abandoned his career as a professor at the University of Michigan and moved to the New Hampshire farm that had belonged to his family for generations and where he has made his living entirely as a writer. Foremost among his works for children is the nostalgic PICTUREBOOK *Ox-Cart Man* (1979) which was awarded the CALDECOTT MEDAL for BARBARA COONEY's illustrations. Based on a poem by Hall that had appeared in his collection *Kicking the Leaves* (1978), it tells the true story of a man who would walk to Portsmouth market every fall to sell everything he and his family had made or grown during the preceding year, including the ox-cart and the ox. Hall's mother is the central character in *Lucy's Christmas* (1994) and *Lucy's Summer* (1995), picturebooks illustrated by Michael McCurdy and featuring the happenings in Hall's ancestral home around the year 1910. *The Oxford Book of Children's Verse in America*, which Hall edited in 1985, is an important demonstration of the vitality of the American tradition of poetry for children. JS

Hall, Willis 1929– Popular British writer whose association with children's fiction began with his creation of children's radio plays. He is credited with a satirical eye and said to be attuned to the quality of everyday speech, talents which are evident in *The Summer of the Dinosaur* (1977). In this children's novel the story is carried by the young Henry, who injects confusion into the conventional lives of his parents, Albert Hollins and his benevolent wife Emily, upon his discovery of a dinosaur egg. Henry's struggle in the face of adult scorn is well documented, until finally Hall allows their preoccupation with what is real to give in to the element of FANTASY encouraged by the existence of the dinosaur. GD

see also DRAMA FOR CHILDREN

Halliwell, James Orchard see NURSERY RHYMES; MOTHER GOOSE

Hallworth, Grace see FOLKTALES AND LEGENDS

Hamanaka, Sheila 1949– American author and illustrator for children. Hamanaka grew up in New York City and continued to live there as an adult. She is best known for *The Journey* (1990), which focuses on the internment of Japanese Americans during World War II. To illustrate this book Hamanaka painted a 25-foot mural depicting the history of Japanese immigrants to America and used photographs of various sections to accompany the text. She also explores the intersection of Japanese and American cultures in *Peace Crane* (1995), in which a young African American girl is inspired by the story of an atomic bomb survivor who folded a thousand paper cranes to promote peace. The historical and the contemporary are blended in this compelling story. She has also delved into folklore with *Screen of Frogs* (1993), the story of a wealthy but lazy man who finds contentment after changing his ways. The story is beautifully complemented with acrylic and coloured pencil on decorated paper. In addition, Hamanaka has illustrated other people's texts, including several books of poetry by EVE MERRIAM. She uses oil on canvas, coloured pencil, acrylics and COLLAGE, and her styles and media are as diverse as the characters and contexts she depicts. EB

see also AFRICAN AMERICAN LITERATURE

Hamilton, Charles Harold St John 1876–1961 Star-writer of British boys' weeklies, who produced over 72 million words under more than 20 different pennames. Writing as Frank Richards, he introduced Billy Bunter and Harry Wharton of GREYFRIARS School in the first issue of *The Magnet* in February 1908. Pace without sensationalism, conflict without violence, combined with a strict adherence to the ethic that 'cheats never prosper', earned his boys' school stories a loyal readership. Hamilton was less successful in writing as Hilda Richards, originator of the Cliff House girls' school stories, featuring Bunter's sister, Bessie, although the *SCHOOL FRIEND* series flourished in other hands. BW

see also COMICS, PERIODICALS AND MAGAZINES; SCHOOL STORIES; 'THE BIG FIVE'

Hamilton, Virginia 1936– American author residing in Yellow Springs, Ohio. Her productivity (36 books in 33 years), variety of literary output (nearly every genre possible and many cross-genre works), and extent of critical recognition (she has been the recipient of every major award in the field) place Hamilton among the best and the most important of children's and young adults' authors. Her trademark is the use of language to produce new meanings and ideas. Challenging and thought-provoking, she is a symbolist, playing with conventional words and phrases to create new ways of seeing. Her invented term 'parallel cultures' (denoting equal lines or ethnicities running across the contours of a dominant culture) promises to make terms like 'minority' and 'non-mainstream' obsolete. Her phrase 'Great American Hopescape' has been similarly provocative.

Hamilton is in many ways a postmodernist writer who deconstructs the notion of a distinction between realism and FANTASY. A recent work, *Jaguarundi* (1995), is not just a fantasy in the African folklore tradition of animals who talk; it is also a realistic information book about endangered animals, a rainforest science book, a book that resonates with historical references to slavery, African American and African life, and a MULTICULTURAL BOOK, focusing as it does on creatures of different colour and background learning to live together and to respect one another's ways of thinking and living.

Hamilton works at times in the area of 'magic realism', producing, like Toni Morrison, variations on the theme of the ancestral ghost and the legend of the flying African. *Sweet Whispers, Brother Rush* (1982) is neither fantasy nor realism but psychic realism in which a young girl, Teresa (nicknamed 'Tree'), is endowed with the same power the slaves brought with them from Africa – the magical ability to see into her family past. (Morrison's *Beloved* explores similar abilities.) Tree's 'self' is a family tree: the 'rings' of self cannot be separated from the heartwood or centre of her family history.

Like many postmodernist writers, Hamilton reveals the propensity to entertain conflicting points of view. As a children's novelist, this ability works especially well to soften didacticism and allay sentimentality, overly idealised characters or value-judgements. Readers can view a neglectful mother in *Plain City* (1993), or even an abusive one in *Sweet Whispers*, with greater understanding, the result of Hamilton's maintaining a sympathetic vantage-point for all her characters. Yet Hamilton, who describes herself as a moral realist, never deprives her books of an ethical centre; most often this is the child protagonist, who may be wrestling with the failures and weaknesses of adults but who never loses empathy with them.

Hamilton produces a variety of narrative voices in her fiction. There is always the dialogic interplay of characters who are telling stories to themselves and to one another to make sense of the world (the 'big' picture) as well as a smaller, more personal world of heritage and ancestry. Several books reveal metafictional techniques of storytelling, especially in *Arilla Sun Down* (1976) and *A White Romance* (1987). In *A Little Love* (1984) and *Plain City*, she devised an intricate interplay of narrative voices to fuse narrator's story and protagonist's storying.

The way characters tell stories to one another and to themselves in these books – and most especially in *The Magical Adventures of Pretty Pearl* (1983) – enables Hamilton to produce a richly textured story and her characters to grow into stronger awareness of the world and their place in it. Very few, if any, writers in the field use embedded stories to the extent that Hamilton does.

Hamilton most often writes YOUNG ADULT FICTION for readers of around 12–15 years of age, although some books – for example *Cousins* (1990) – are accessible to slightly younger readers. The realism can embrace history, BIOGRAPHY and folklore, as it does in *Anthony Burns* (1988), or time-travel, FANTASY and SCIENCE FICTION, as it does in the *JUSTICE TRILOGY* (*Justice and Her Brothers*, *Dustland* and *The Gathering*, 1980–1); and the fantasy can embrace history, folklore and time-travel, as it does in *Magical Adventures*. Since Hamilton has a deep interest in African American history and cultural traditions, as well as in exploring the African American female quest for self, she is an important multiculturist, as seen in her novella *Bluish* (1999) – the story of three children of African American and mixed ethnic backgrounds – and an inventive ethnic feminist, as revealed in many of her books, from *Arilla Sun Down* to *Second Cousins* (1998).

But even though Hamilton writes most eloquently about her own experiences of growing up as an African American, her work has far-reaching implications for young adults of all times and places in

America, who are struggling to define themselves in an often confusing and endangered world. Most of her novels are coming-of-age stories.

In male coming-of-age stories (*The Planet of Junior Brown*, 1971; *M.C. Higgins the Great*, 1974; and *Junius Over Far*, 1985), the hero rebels openly and aggressively against a male authority-figure in order to attain a separate identity. In female coming-of-age stories (*Zeely*, 1967; *Arilla Sun Down*; *Willie Bea and the Time the Martians Landed*, 1983; *A Little Love*; *A White Romance*; and *Plain City*), heroines escape constricting circumstances through the power of the imagination (or through psychic power, like Tree's in *Sweet Whispers*). In Hamilton's view this is the only way African American females, from slavery days to the present, have had of attaining freedom of self-expression. Those who are most oppressed ultimately develop heightened imaginative capabilities. Some books, like *The Magical Adventures of Pretty Pearl*, are both coming-of-age stories and what Hamilton calls 'liberation literature', or stories of a people's suffering and growing awareness of self in the pursuit of freedom, for example *Anthony Burns, the Defeat and Triumph of a Fugitive Slave* or the collection of historical sketches in *Many Thousand Gone* (1992).

Hamilton's collections showcase her talent for creating folk 'tellings' of stories she takes from both the African American tradition (*The People Could Fly*, 1985, and *Her Stories*, 1995) and from stories world-wide (*In the Beginning; Creation Stories from Around the World*, 1988; *The Dark Way: Stories from the Spirit World*, 1990; and *A Ring of Tricksters: Animal Tales from America, the West Indies, and Africa*, 1997). She recasts these stories in the language and cadence of her own narrative voice. *Her Stories* is a magical celebration of strong-willed African American heroines. NM

see also AFRICAN AMERICAN LITERATURE

Hamley, Dennis 1935– British author of *HARE'S CHOICE*, which was selected by the International Reading Association as 'Favorite Paperback of 1994'. After a career in education – much of which was devoted to encouraging the creativity of both children and teachers – Hamley turned to full-time writing. He began with GHOST STORIES (*The Shirt off a Hanged Man's Back*, 1984; *The Railway Phantoms*, 1995; *The Ghosts Who Waited*, 1997) and wrote a successful WAR STORY (*The War and Freddy*, 1995, shortlisted for the SMARTIES PRIZE). His style is direct and accessible to young readers, his theme almost always the making, or recovering, of stories. In *The Fourth Plane at the Flypast* (1985), for example, two children watching an air display see a shattered Wellington bomber which nobody else sees; this supernatural element in a gripping story leads to the uncovering of a tragic story their mother has repressed.

Hamley subsequently moved into writing murder mysteries for the Point crime series (*Death Penalty*, 1994). In 1998 he wrote the first of a series of six medieval crime novels, the *Joslin de Lay Mysteries*, set in the 14th century. He has been widely translated and has written short stories appearing in numerous anthologies. He has also produced a retelling for schools of Bram Stoker's *Dracula* (1999), and *Spilling the Beans on William Shakespeare and other Elizabethans from around the Globe* (2000), the last a highly original and quirky WILLIAM SHAKESPEARE 'biography' for today's young readers, with comic-style ILLUSTRATIONS by Mike Mosedale. VW

see also DETECTIVE FICTION; GHOST STORIES; POINT SERIES

Hammill, Elizabeth see REVIEWING AND REVIEWERS; see also CENTRE FOR THE CHILDREN'S BOOK; CHILD AUTHORS

Hampson, Frank see ANNUALS; *DAN DARE*; *EAGLE ANNUAL*

Handford, Martin see *WHERE'S WALLY?* SERIES

Hanna, Bill see *TOM AND JERRY*; see also ANIMATED CARTOONS

Hans Christian Andersen Medal see APPENDIX

'Hansel and Gretel' see GRIMM BROTHERS; see also ANTHONY BROWNE; FAERIE TALE THEATRE; *HOP O' MY THUMB*; MUSIC AND STORY; KAY NIELSEN; IAN WALLACE; PAUL ZELINSKY; LISBETH ZWERGER

Hansen, Joyce 1942– African American writer of children's fiction, specialising in sensitive portraits of children living in present-day urban, underclass neighbourhoods or in slavery times. *The Gift-Giver* (1980), its sequel, *Yellow Bird and Me* (1986), and *Home Boy* (1982), are all set in the New York City Bronx neighbourhood, where Hansen, as a public-school teacher, observed closely the black vernacular language patterns that she uses to produce realistic dialogue and naturalistic scene-building. Here children survive societal inequities of race and class through hope, determination and belief in themselves, the result of strong extended-family relationships and friends who become part of their extended 'family'. In *Home Boy* Hansen also uses the device of flashback to dramatise the cross-cultural conflict of the young adult Caribbean American character, a recent immigrant to America.

Hansen's historical novels are survival stories involving the quest for freedom. In her Civil War trilogy – *Which Way Freedom* (1986), a Coretta Scott King Honour Book, *Out From This Place* (1988) and *The Heart Calls Home* (1999) – the slave-children Obi and his friend Easter become runaways, with Obi joining the Union forces and Easter travelling to the Sea Islands where she faces the evils of reconstruction times in America. In *The Captive* (1994), Kofi, an African Prince, is kidnapped into slavery in 1788 and taken to Massachusetts, where the spiritual strength that unites all of Hansen's separated people never fails him. NM

see also AFRICAN AMERICAN LITERATURE; HISTORICAL FICTION

***Happy Families* series** (1980s and 90s) A highly entertaining series, that has brought and continues to bring great enjoyment to children, comprising, 18 single story books to date, all written by the British author ALLAN AHLBERG. Whilst he remains solely responsible for the text, a range of illustrators have contributed to his work, JANET AHLBERG and ANDRÉ AMSTUTZ proving popular choices. The characters of the series are given wonderfully alliterative names – Miss Dose the Doctor's Daughter, for example – which serve to outline their nature or profession. Although individual stories refer to a single character, there is evident an interrelatedness between the families: Mr Biff is Bertie Bun's uncle and several other characters can be found in stories which are not their own. This helps to engender and sustain an interest in the series, aided by the characteristic use of the phrase 'but that's another story'. The language employed is repetitive (echoed by the speech bubbles adorning the ILLUSTRATIONS) and simple, mostly comprising short sentences. The series is easily accessible to inexperienced readers. Published during the 1980s and 1990s, some stories appeared as recently as 1996. Although these later works reflect more contemporary concerns, Ahlberg chooses to tackle such issues as single parenthood and divorce in a light-hearted manner. GD

***Happy Orpheline, The* series** see NATALIE SAVAGE CARLSON

Happy Prince and other Tales, The (1888) Oscar Wilde's first collection was illustrated by WALTER CRANE and Jacomb Hood. The other tales were 'The Nightingale and the Rose', 'The Selfish Giant', 'The Devoted Friend' and 'The Remarkable Rocket', and all explore the price paid in human suffering for beauty, art, power and wealth, and the corresponding salvation offered by selfless love. In the title story, the statue of the Happy Prince gives away his jewels and gold-leaf to help the poor children, while his friend the Swallow stays in the north to keep him company and dies of cold, in sharp contrast to the insensitivity of the human characters. Wilde's two sons were born in 1885 and 1886, and the direct tone he uses strongly reflects the oral tradition of STORYTELLING, whilst the skilful economy of form and the sharp inflections of the language indicate the more sophisticated, 'adult' meanings of literary FAIRY TALES. In the context of Wilde's own life, 'The Selfish Giant', with its motifs of the Giant's selfishness, his secret garden, and the wounded little boy he learned to love, has a poignant resonance which was effectively used in Julian Mitchell's screenplay for the 1997 film *Wilde*. PR

Hardcastle, Michael 1933– Popular and prolific British author, mainly of action-packed sports stories. His first book was published in 1966, since when he has written over 100 other works, including a series, *Goal Kings* (from 1998). The stories, which present positive role models, deal with issues of confidence, positive competitiveness, good team spirit and, especially, good sportsmanship. These fast-moving stories are full of exciting cliff-hanger games with enough match detail, analysis and running commentary to delight any sports-mad reader. Hardcastle has also written a few books on more serious social issues and in 1998 he was awarded an MBE for services to children's books. JSW

***Hardy Boys* series** American mystery series originally produced by the STRATEMEYER SYNDICATE. Along with the *NANCY DREW* books, the *Hardy Boys* books were one of the most popular of the Syndicate's numerous series, containing over 100 books that track the adventures of Frank and Joe, the teenage sons of world-famous detective Fenton Hardy. Written by EDWARD STRATEMEYER, Leslie McFarlane and other ghost writers – all writing as F.W. Dixon – the formulaic books recount the adventures of the brothers and their pals, Chet Morton, 'Biff' Hooper, Phil Cohen and Tony Prito. The first book of the series, *The Tower Treasure* (1927), contains many of the elements that appear in subsequent volumes. The boys discover a mystery that baffles the police but – after a number of false leads – is solved by Frank and Joe. The boys' adventures are glamorous and exciting, especially since they are able to travel anywhere around the globe without their father questioning their activities. *The Hardy Boys* have been so successful that their current publisher spun off the *Hardy Boys Casefiles* and the *Nancy Drew/Hardy Boys Super Mysteries*, new series that track the adventures of a more sophisticated Frank and Joe. SAI

Hardy, Thomas see *OUR EXPLOITS AT WEST POLEY*

Hare and the Tortoise, The see ABRIDGEMENT; CD-ROMS

***Hare's Choice* trilogy** Sequence of short novels by British author DENNIS HAMLEY. *Hare's Choice* (1988), *Badger's Fate* (1992) and *Hawk's Vision* (1993), like a good deal of classical children's fiction, combine a surface simplicity with a deeply felt complexity. At one level the trilogy tells the story of a small village school in England in the 1980s, presided over by a wise head-teacher with faith in his pupils. Each narrative, enhanced by Meg Rutherford's superb ILLUSTRATIONS, is also an animal story involving naturalistic accounts of animal behaviour. The children come to terms with the ill-treatment and death of animals by composing collaborative stories about them.

The novels also explore what happens to animals when they become part of the stories we tell. There are readerly games to be played here, as Hamley posits an alternative after-life for fictional animals – where Hare meets rabbits called Peter and Hazel, a water rat, a mole, various pigs, and so on. A more subtle intertextuality is to be found in the light literary allusiveness of the writing – especially to the poetry of TED HUGHES.

Because the stories are by a community of children and about a community of animals, this complex trilogy is also an exploration of the nature of communal narratives – how we compose them and why we need them. This becomes particularly apparent in the moving final section, when the children – aware that the school is to close and they will be transported to a nearby town – compose a story about a hawk whose 'vision' can hold together two distant communities. Like WILLIAM MAYNE's *No More School*, children are at the heart of this trilogy with their concern for threatened wildlife, but also their need to transform animals into symbols. For adult readers aware of recent changes in British primary schools, the trilogy will read a little like an elegy. VW

see also ANIMALS IN CHILDREN'S FICTION

Hargreaves, Roger see *MR MEN* SERIES

Harlen, Jonathan 1963– Australian author who writes across the age range of children's literature. Born in Christchurch, New Zealand, Harlen is perhaps best known for the novel *The Lion and The Lamb* (1992), a spare, hopeful FABLE about Nicaraguan immigrants, a violent father and pacifist son, living in Sydney. Harlen also deals with migrant experiences in the adolescent novel *Fracture Zone* (1994). His writing has become harder-edged with the violent short book *Blackeye* (1995), and the explicitly sexual *Fireflies* (1996). He has written three junior books, and the verse PICTUREBOOK *The Dream of the Dusky Dolphin* (1995), illustrated by PATRICIA MULLINS. NLR

harlequinade see PANTOMIME; see also MOTHER GOOSE; MOVABLE BOOKS

Harnett, Cynthia Mary 1893–1981 British writer of historical works for children. The best-known of these are *The Great House* (1949), *The Wool Pack* (1951), *Ring Out Bow Bells* (1953) – a novel about the real DICK WHITTINGTON – and *The Load of Unicorn* (1959). Her writing tends towards detail, and the woodcut-style ILLUSTRATIONS which she did herself indicate not only the degree of research which went into her work, but also an intention of (factually) educating the reader. The style and dialogue are lively and unfreighted with archaisms and her books, though no longer universally popular, have on the whole worn well. SA

Haroun and the Sea of Stories (1990) Novel by Salman Rushdie. Though written, as we know from an interview given by the author in 1991, with his child's enjoyment in mind, is only superficially a children's book. Its issues are adult, literary and political: the freedom of speech, the relation of modern fiction to older, traditional literature, and the life of the imagination in a world which does not sufficiently value it. It is an extremely self-conscious work, one which uses the metaphors of writing and story-telling to tell its own tale. It draws upon the Sanskrit *Kathāsaritsāgara:* the Ocean of the Sea of Story, the mother lode of the world's tales; and it also builds upon the *ALICE* and *OZ* books, DICKENS, KIPLING and countless other writers in order both to create itself and to recreate these other works, thereby keeping them alive. Written in a mode which deliberately invokes the *ARABIAN NIGHTS* (the Ocean, for example, is 'made up of a thousand thousand thousand and one different currents'), the work is structured as a quest FANTASY, in which Haroun searches for a way to stop the pollution of the old tales in the Sea of Stories and bring back his father's gift of storytelling. SA

Harper's Young People: An Illustrated Weekly An ambitious American children's magazine published by Harper Brothers of New York (1879–99), similar in standards to their magazines for adults, including *Harper's Monthly*. Influenced by its rival, the monthly *ST NICHOLAS*, *Harper's Young People* sought to provide entertainment and instruction to an upscale family audience. Founding editor Kirk Munroe noted in the fourth issue that he meant 'to make *Young People* the very best weekly in the world'. The magazine was to provide children aged from 'six to sixteen a weekly treat in the way of entertaining stories, poems, historical sketches . . . with profuse and beautiful ILLUSTRATIONS'. The magazine avoided sensationalism, aiming to 'harmonise with the moral atmosphere which pervades every cultivated Christian household'. The editors pledged to seek the best writers and artists 'so that fiction shall appear in bright and innocent colours, sober facts assume such a holiday dress as to be no longer dry or dull, and mental exercise, in the solution of puzzles, problems, and other devices, become a delight'. Among the contributors were J.T. TROWBRIDGE, Sophie Swett, LOUISA MAY ALCOTT and William Dean Howells. SRG

Harriet the Spy (1964) Novel by the American author LOUISE FITZHUGH about an unconventional heroine, Harriet M. Welsch, an 11-year-old spy and aspiring writer who records her observations of the often quirky behaviour of the people she encounters. Although Fitzhugh previously published the idiosyncratic PICTUREBOOK *Suzuki Beane* (1961), which she co-wrote with Sandra Scoppettone, *Harriet the Spy* was her first full-length novel. The book established its author as a major voice in children's literature and quickly gained broad critical acclaim, although some critics worried that the often sharply satirical novel was inappropriate for children since it portrayed a bleak vision of the adult world. Today, the book is regarded by most critics as a masterpiece of psychological realism. Along with its sequel *The Long Secret* (1965) *Harriet the Spy* marked a turning-point in children's literature, which has subsequently been influenced by Fitzhugh's realism and her recognition that children can handle concerns that were previously perceived as the province of adults.

The novel records Harriet's often biting comments about the people she observes, whether strangers or friends. In her standard block lettering, all in capitals, she records her thoughts: 'IF MARION HAWTHORNE DOESN'T WATCH OUT SHE'S GOING TO GROW UP INTO A LADY HITLER', or 'SOMETIMES I CAN'T STAND SPORT. WITH HIS WORRYING ALL THE TIME AND FUSSING OVER HIS FATHER, SOMETIMES HE'S LIKE A LITTLE OLD WOMAN', or 'THE REASON SPORT DRESSES SO FUNNY IS THAT HIS FATHER WON'T BUY HIM ANYTHING TO WEAR BECAUSE HIS MOTHER HAS ALL THE MONEY.' Through Harriet's spying and writing, readers are able to visualise the memorable, odd characters that are an essential part of Fitzhugh's unique cosmos, such as Joe Curry, who appears to engage in non-stop eating; the Robinsons, who are consumed by the passion to buy possessions and show them off; Harrison Withers, who loves cats and builds delicate, beautiful birdcages; and Mrs. Plumber, an eccentric woman who spends most of her time in bed, chatting endlessly on the telephone. Harriet's sharp observations bring these characters and others to life, exposing all of their foibles. She is just as brutally honest about her best friends: Sport, who cleans house and cooks for his father, while worrying incessantly about their poor financial situation, and Janie, who plots to be a mad scientist and whom Harriet fears might blow up the world.

Harriet's observations about these characters and others are often frank and unkind, which becomes a problem when they discover what she has written in the secret notebooks she carries everywhere. After this discovery, her friends ostracise her, a painful experience that results in Harriet's slow and painful gaining of empathy for others. Although the book has been repeatedly censured for Harriet's cynicism, what critics sometimes ignore is that the book is essentially about her growing recognition that other people are worthy of consideration and kindness. SAI

Harris, Aurand 1915– American playwright, born in Jamesport, Missouri. Harris has been cited by Coleman Jennings as 'America's most-produced children's theatre playwright'. His children's plays run the gamut of dramatic forms from *commedia dell'arte* (*Androcles and the Lion*) to melodrama (*Rags to Riches*, based on HORATIO ALGER's *Ragged Dick* and *Mark the Match Boy*) to historical chronicle and musical revue (*YANKEE DOODLE*). Many of his plays use traditional FOLK and FAIRY TALES as the basis of their plot. BH

Harris, Benjamin see *NEW ENGLAND PRIMER, THE*

Harris, Christie 1907– Canadian children's author, counting among her honours the Vicky Metcalf Award for a distinguished body of work (1973) and membership of the Order of Canada (1981). Born in Newark, New Jersey, but raised in British Columbia, Harris worked as a teacher, scriptwriter and journalist before becoming a children's writer. She produced work in various genres, from HISTORICAL FICTION to SCIENCE FICTION, but her only notable early work is *Raven's Cry* (1966), a CANADIAN LIBRARY ASSOCIATION BOOK OF THE YEAR MEDAL winner that movingly traces the destruction of the Haida nation. Harris achieved both popularity and critical respect through publication of seven volumes retelling Northwest Coast Indian tales: she won her second CLA medal for *Mouse Woman and the Vanished Princesses* (1976) and the Canada Council Children's Literature Prize for *The Trouble with Princesses* (1980). Believing that non-native readers would undertand them only if she altered the tales, Harris combined versions and imposed narrative patterns and motifs from European CAUTIONARY and FAIRY TALES. Although the resulting tales support a theme Harris derived from native culture – the need to respect nature and its balance – some critics now regard her collections as examples of inappropriate cultural appropriation. REJ

see also NATIVE AMERICANS IN CHILDREN'S LITERATURE

Harris, Christine 1955– Australian writer whose novels and short stories such as *Fortune Cookies* (1998), attempt to reflect an increasingly multicultural society. Her characters are usually to be found in ordinary settings such as the school and home, yet they often have very extraordinary and dramatic stories to tell, like coming to the country as refugees on a rickety raft in perilous seas. Harris is not afraid to expose the prejudices still lurking within many people towards foreigners, and often her characters have to endure persecution at the hands of their Australian contemporaries. Her *Vibes* series (1998), which appeals mainly to girls, exemplifies responsible popular novels, with plot and character superior to that of much lightweight fiction. *Foreign Devil* (1999) is a partly historical novel set in China. RTh

Harris, David 1942– Australian writer whose books appeal especially to boys, a frequently neglected readership. His *Cliffhanger* series (1999), which includes the titles *Devil's Island*, *Fortress*, *Firebug* and *Dead Silence*, has realistic male protagonists who undergo credible struggles with family, society and themselves. It is evident that Harris draws on the way young people actually speak to create his dialogue. Rather than being action heroes, these characters are flawed and essentially very human. The adventures are believable and very Australian in setting and context. RTh

Harris, Joel Chandler 1848–1908 American author, from Eatonton, Georgia, who produced eight volumes of animal tales known as the *Uncle Remus* stories. As a boy of 14, Harris worked as a printer's assistant for Joseph Turner, who published a literary journal on the site of his plantation. For four years, Harris listened to slaves telling the talking animal stories that he would later bring to the attention of the American literary establishment in his own creative retellings.

Living at the Turnwold Plantation led Harris down two paths in his adult life. One made him famous with adults: the pieces he would write for the *Atlanta Constitution* about an old slave named Uncle Remus, an invented persona who entertained white readers with obsequious, ignorant and bigoted sayings that reflected more the feelings of his audience than those of any black person ('No use talkin' boss – Put a spelling book in a nigger's han's, en right den en ear' you loozes a plow-hand'). The other made him famous with children: the animal tales that Remus told to a little white boy in Harris's books. There are 185 tales in all, of literary and historical importance for the moral and social viewpoints they directly and indirectly express, for the framing device of the old man's comments and the young boy's questions, for the humour and picturesque language, and above all, for the continuously intriguing question of whether or not Harris was able to deal with another race in literary terms.

Illustration by Frederick S. Church with James Moser from *Uncle Remus and His sayings* by Joel Chandler Harris.

Thematically, the tales set forth a rural, Southern mythology, a code of behaviour for the underdog, in which cunning and subterfuge replace open resistance, neither debate nor compromise being a possibility within the master-slave relationship. The underdog TRICKSTER who survives and triumphs is most often the rabbit, as is often the case in both Indian and African tales. 'It needs no scientific investigation', said Harris, in his introduction to the first book, 'to show why he (the black person) selects as his hero the weakest, the most harmless of all animals, and brings him out victorious in contests with the bear, the wolf, and the fox. It is not virtue that triumphs, but helplessness; it is not malice but mischievousness.' Neither superhuman nor possessing magic powers, Brer Rabbit is quite frequently all too human, guilty at times of foolish and prideful actions, at other times of illegal or amoral ones. Yet always he survives, for small and defenceless as he is, his more powerful opponent invariably exercises less intelligence.

Harris was diligent as a folklorist, anxious to preserve the stories as he had heard them, and he did manage to preserve the tales at a time when black tellers were not being encouraged to read and write, and certainly not to publish. But the dialect he created makes them both difficult to read today and stereotypical of black speech patterns, and the fact that a black teller was transmitting (and preserving) the tales for a white child has been particularly troubling for African Americans. NM

see also AFRICAN MYTHOLOGY AND FOLKTALES; INDIAN MYTHS, LEGENDS AND FOLKTALES

Harris, John 1756–1846 British publisher who inherited one of the most successful 18th-century businesses producing children's books from Elizabeth Newbery, widow of the seminal children's book publisher JOHN NEWBERY. Harris took over the business, which he had previously managed for Elizabeth Newbery, in 1801–2. One of the firm's most notable publications was *THE BUTTERFLY'S BALL* (1807), a poem by WILLIAM ROSCOE which set a new fashion – and standard – in humorous verse for children and was followed by many successors, a number of which Harris himself published. John Harris's son (also called John) took over the firm in 1824 when his father retired. DWh

Harris, Ruth Elwyn 1935– British author of a series of novels set between 1910 and the 1930s and known collectively as the *Quantocks Quartet*. The action of the four novels overlaps, though each is told from the viewpoint of a different sister, allowing the author to explore different aspects of the same situation. There is a strong sense of the permanence of their Somerset home set against the changes brought by World War I. Social changes bring considerable freedom for the sisters, whose artistic lifestyle is often in marked contrast with the more sedate lives of their contemporaries. KA

Harrold, John see *RUPERT BEAR*

Harry Potter Eponymous hero of a series of phenomenally popular prize-winning novels written by J. K. Rowling (1970–). The series – which begins with *Harry Potter and the Philosopher's Stone* (1997) and *Harry Potter and the Chamber of Secrets* (1998) – was conceived from the start as a series of seven novels covering the seven years Harry spends as a pupil at the Hogwarts School of Witchcraft and Wizardry, and among its many themes the series examines the development of identity during adolescence. The books draw heavily upon the conventions of children's literature, their success being in part attributable to the powerful blend of SCHOOL STORY, ADVENTURE STORY and FANTASY. Harry is removed from an orphaned and miserable childhood into a magical version of the traditional boarding school where he learns the craft of wizardry. The books chronicle a struggle between the forces of good and evil in which Harry's task is to preserve the world from the forces of evil embodied by the Satanic wizard Voldemort. While the abstract concepts of good and evil remain clearly defined, the central characters are depicted as complex, multifaceted beings who embody the capacity for both good and evil. As the series progresses the danger to Harry's inner self becomes visibly greater; the 'dementors' of the third novel – *Harry Potter and the Prisoner of Azkaban* (1999) – represent not only the physical threat of imprisonment (they chase an escaped prisoner) but also the mental threat of depression.

The *Harry Potter* series has attained unprecedented popularity with adults as well as children, and first editions of the early books quickly became extremely valuable. However, by the publication of the fourth in the series, *Harry Potter and the Goblet of Fire* (2000), there were signs of a critical backlash. Much of this was directed against the unprecedented pre-publication publicity, though Anthony Holden, writing in *The Observer*, went further, referring contemptuously to 'Billy Bunter on broomsticks' and complaining that the minds of Rowling's readers would be 'unstretched by any reflective pauses in the breathless narrative'. This judgement, however, is wide of the mark; a criticism that might justly be made of *Goblet of Fire* is that the opening chapters might have been shortened – though the fact that thousands of young readers (some as young as seven) are willing to tackle a novel of 636 pages is a refreshing challenge to the long-held assumption that they can cope only with slim books. The author's inventiveness and wit are undiminished in this fourth work, and the main characters mature convincingly in a narrative which is uncompromisingly darker and more complex, and which has also successfully sustained the enthusiastic interest of adult readers.

Young readers are probably indifferent to the furore aroused by the doubts and irritation of a few adult commentators; they remain passionately loyal to J. K. Rowling and Hogwarts, and – astonishingly – many have written to national newspapers in defence of her work. On the morning of publication of *Goblet of Fire*, thousands of children were queuing outside bookshops as early as 7.00 a.m. to buy copies. This enthusiasm is an entirely new – and an extremely exciting – development in children's book publishing. KA, VW

Harte, Bret see MARK TWAIN; see also WESTERNS

Hartnett, Sonya 1968– One of Australia's most exciting and controversial new writers for older teenagers. Her first novel, *Trouble All the Way,* was published in 1984, but despite her youth she was described by her publisher as a 'veteran' writer. Most recently she has been acclaimed for *Wilful Blue* (1994) and *Sleeping Dogs* (1995) – inaugural winner of Australia's Victorian Premier's Young Adult Fiction Award – and *The Devil Latch* (1996), her sixth novel. *Black Foxes* (1996) was released as an adult work. *Stripes of the Sidestep Wolf* (1999) is a serious novel inviting reflection on Australian family and community life. Her works are about fear and decay, evil and innocence, and they ask questions about life and art. Her refusal to consign to adult literature subjects such as incest and psychological violence has been challenged by those craving happy endings for young readers. RS

Harvey, Amanda British illustrator. Three picture books of her own, *A Close Call* (1990), *Stormy Weather* (1991) and *The Iron Needle* (1994), full-colour ILLUSTRATIONS to Judith Gorog's *Zilla Sasparilla and the Mud Baby* (1995) and line illustrations to FIONA WATERS's poetry collection *Glitter When You Jump* (1996) are Harvey's major achievements since she won the Macmillan Prize for a Children's Picture Book in 1989. She won THE MOTHER GOOSE AWARD in 1991 for *A Close Call*, an enigmatic story of the theft and rescue of a baby, told economically in rhythmic words and delicate line and colour-wash pictures, which move into sepia for a 'time-past' sequence. JAG

Harvey, Anne 1933– British anthologist and actress. Harvey's anthologies of poems, including *Poets in Hand* (1985), *Six of the Best* (1989), *Shades of Green* (1991) and *He said, She said, They said* (1993), betray a passion for poetry (for both adults and children), an exhaustive knowledge, and an exemplary scholarly fastidiousness. FRBS

Harvey, Roland 1945– Australian illustrator. Casting an analytical and ironic eye over Australia, past and present, Harvey has illustrated some 20 titles, all in his own idiosyncratic manner. His outlined watercolour drawings for Alan Boardman's historical studies such as *The First Fleet* (1982) and *The Crossing of the Blue Mountains* (1984), and especially for his own *Burke and Wills* (1985), not only give life to the history in the text, but invest it with humour that has an underlying pathos. Harvey's hallmark is that of country or harbourside landscapes often swarming with Bosch-like figures that demand close and detailed study for their wry comment on the action. MSax

Haskins, James [Jim] 1941– American writer of juvenile histories and BIOGRAPHIES. Born in Montgomery, Alabama, Haskins pursued his graduate studies in New York City and has since worked as an educator and member of numerous committees. His first book, *Diary of a Harlem Schoolteacher* (1969), tells of his own experiences as a special education teacher. Haskins covers current events and African American history, producing biographies of key figures from Rosa Parks to Colin Powell. He describes people's lives, but also indicates the historical, political and social perspectives of the civil rights movement impacting on such lives. With more than 80 books to his credit, his topics range from politics to education, and from sports to music. Many have won awards, including *Social Education* (1971), *Profiles in Black Power* (1972), *The Story of Stevie Wonder* (1977) and *James Van DerZee: the Picture Takin' Man* (1980). He has also written a series of books teaching children to count in different lanquages and telling them about the geography, history and culture of such places as Greece, Israel, Brazil and Japan. His writings are both sensitive and honest, providing the African American community with positive self-images and serving to lessen the negative stereotypes of the past. SCWA

Hassall, Joan 1906–88 Distinguished British illustrator, believed by many to be the most accomplished wood engraver since THOMAS BEWICK. She illustrated many commercial and private press books and bookplates during her long career. Hassall began her studies at the Royal Academy Schools and at an evening class in engraving at the London County Council School of Photo-Engraving, which she attended from 1931 to 1934. This was her first encounter with the discipline of WOOD ENGRAVING, despite being the daughter of JOHN HASSALL the poster artist, but she found that it came naturally to her. She reports that 'it was very much more like remembering than learning'. Joan Hassall's subjects range from nature scenes, such as *Portrait of a Village* (1937) to costume books such as *Cranford* (1940). She had the ability to combine her skills with the author's intentions so that the engravings were in complete harmony with the subjects of the books. In 1955 she collaborated with PETER and IONA OPIE to produce 150 engravings for the *Oxford Book of Nursery Rhymes*. The VIGNETTES she created to illustrate individual rhymes exemplify this harmony – for example 'The man in the moon' and 'Georgie Porgie, pudding and pie'. SM

Hassall, John 1868–1948 Illustrator of children's books, posters, COMICS and magazines from the turn of the 20th century to the 1940s. Hassall began his artistic career studying under Professor Van Havermaet at the Antwerp Academy and then at the Academie Julien, Paris, under Bougeureau and Ferrier. Following this, he developed his distinctive styles of watercolour and line drawing, which show the influence of the painter Mucha. In 1909 he illustrated Walter Jerrold's edition of *Mother Goose's Nursery Rhymes* for Blackie and Sons, containing coloured and black-and-white illustrations. The full-plate illustrations offer bold blocks of colour, often without any shadow around the figures, in contrast to the black-and-white drawings which have a sketchy, evocative quality. Hassall was commissioned by George Newnes to design a cover for *The Captain: a magazine for boys and 'old boys'*. He illustrated many boys' ADVENTURE STORIES which appeared in popular magazines such as *The Captain, The Graphic* and the *Illustrated London News*. He was elected a member of the Royal Institute of Painters in Watercolours and the Royal Miniature Society in 1901. His daughter was JOAN HASSALL, the prominent wood engraver. SM

see also WOOD ENGRAVING; ILLUSTRATION

Hastings, Selina 1945– Author of a number of books retelling popular stories, including *The Firebird* (1993), *REYNARD THE FOX* (1990) and *Peter and the Wolf* (1987). She is well known for her lively translations of medieval works – *The Canterbury Tales* (1988), *Sir Gawain and the Green Knight* (1981) and *Sir Gawain and the Loathly Lady*, which won the 1985 KATE GREENAWAY MEDAL. Her writing is very readable while remaining true to the original stories and texts. Hastings is a regular book reviewer and feature writer and has also published biographies of Evelyn Waugh and Nancy Mitford. HCE

Hathorn, Libby (Elizabeth) 1943– Australian author of PICTUREBOOKS and of novels for older readers, with a long and growing list of works, dealing with contemporary social issues, which have proved both critically and commercially successful. Her picturebooks reveal the bright and dark sides of city life. *The Tram To Bondi Beach* (1981), illustrated by JULIE VIVAS, recreates the resilience of a young boy selling newspapers to tram passengers during the 1930s. *WAY HOME* (1994), illustrated by GREGORY ROGERS (KATE GREENAWAY MEDAL, 1995), the story of a lonely urban runaway, is a darkly poignant narrative. In *The Wonder Thing* (1995), illustrated by PETER GOULDTHORPE, Hathorn makes a plea, using a minimal poetic text, for the defence of the rainforest and the survival of the trees, mountains and rivers.

For younger readers her works provide opportunities to observe humankind with sympathy, growing understanding and humour. *All About Anna and Harriet and Christopher and Me* (1986) depicts family life with its energetic mix of aunts, uncles and cousins, friendships, play and childhood accidents. *Looking out for Sampson* (1987) presents the unbearably boastful Cheryl, yet gives her redeeming features (see also FAMILY STORIES). The pleasures of secrets, of friendships and of cats are featured in *Paola's Secret* (1985). Extraordinary children, supra-normal abilities, magic and individual success are celebrated in *Extraordinary Magics of Emma McDade* (1989).

Her novels for older readers explore the demands of adolescence and family, as well as revealing her concerns about poverty, homelessness and the environment – urgent political and social matters. *Love Me Tender* (1992) revisits 20 years of Sydney life between 1945 and 1965, richly evoking aunts, uncles, cousins, restaurants and music. Contemporary urban poverty and homelessness and the need for trusted companionship (paralleling aspects of *Way Home*) are poignantly presented in *Feral Child* (1994). *Thunderwith* (1989), where the companionship of a dog is central, and its sequel *Chrysalis* (1997), capture adolescent needs for love. It is a theme examined again in *Valley Under the Rock* (1993). *The Climb* (1996), with its incipiently totalitarian setting, weaves the personal and political together, while showing a way of gaining personal and altruistic independence. The novels *Rift* and *Dear Venny, Dear Saffron*, co-authored with GARY CREW, were both published in 1998. Hathorn also writes in other genres: verse for primary readers in *Talks with My Skateboard* (1991) and short stories in *Who?* (1992), dealing with love, friendship, ghosts and mysteries. Despite her usual focus on contemporary social issues her novels are never overtly didactic. Her work shows a continuing desire to explore the complex art of narrative and the ways it engenders and engages moral reflection. CH, HMcC

Haunting, The (1983) New Zealand novel, in which Barney's conviction that he is 'about to be haunted again' heralds a book dealing with familiar MARGARET MAHY material – familial relations, sibling tensions, skeletons in cupboards and the search for individual identity by means of a magical scenario. Though Barney's 'ghost' is his great-uncle Cole, he fails to recognise that he himself has 'special' qualities, and that the rest of the family hold the key to the secret. Told in the deliciously ambiguous turn of phrase which is Mahy's forte, this was her first full-length novel and a deserved winner of the 1982 CARNEGIE MEDAL. RS

Hautzig, Deborah see *HEY, DOLLFACE*

Hautzig, Esther 1930– Polish-born American writer. In 1941, ten-year-old Esther was deported with her family by invading Russian soldiers and spent the next five years in Siberia, an experience which formed the basis for nearly all of her writings–not only the much-honoured *The Endless Steppe: Growing Up in Siberia* (1968), but also the craft and cooking books for children and the PICTUREBOOKS she produced with text in many languages. Hautzig's *Four Languages* books were among the first in the United States to offer basic vocabulary words in English and three other languages as well. A vivid account of harrowing years spent in harsh conditions with her mother and grandmother, *The Endless Steppe* portrays a loving family whose sustaining relationships endure in spite of the trials of poverty and deportation. It has received many honours, among them the Jane Addams Children's Book Award (1969) and the Lewis Carroll Shelf Award (1971). MJKP

Haviland, Virginia 1911–88 American writer and critic of children's books. Born in Rochester, New York, Haviland started her career as a children's librarian in Boston in 1934 and later moved to Washington DC. She began writing critical pieces on children's literature and by the 1950s had developed a keen interest in editing and compiling FAIRY TALES and FOLKTALES for young children from all around the world, contributing 16 titles to Little, Brown's *Favorite Fairy Tale* series. She produced a number of excellent children's literature resources, including reference guides and collections of articles and interviews, such as *Children and Literature: Views and Reviews* (1973) and *The Openhearted Audience: Ten Authors Talking About Writing for Children* (1980). She also worked as an associate editor for *Horn Book* for ten years. A member of numerous committees and panels, including the Children's Book Section with the Library of Congress, the Newbery-Caldecott Award Committee, and the executive board of the IBBY, Haviland spent much of her life promoting and improving juvenile literature. For her overall contribution to children's literature she received the Catholic Library Association's Regina Medal and an award from Grolier Publishing. SCWA

Hawkins, Colin 1945– and **Hawkins, Jacqui** 1945– English partnership writing and illustrating children's books in the 1990s. Appealing to adults and children alike, their books are witty and beautifully illustrated, making learning fun. Aiming their work primarily at young children, they have written various series including the *Foxy* series for Collins' *Toddler* range, and Walker Books' character series of *Spooks, Vampires, Pirates, Monsters* and *Witches,* where the Hawkins' characters are offbeat, weird and wonderful. Easy words, humour and bold-coloured pictures are recognised as their trademark. SET

Hawthorne, Nathaniel 1804–64 First major American author to focus literary attention on the child and to write for the young. Published from 1835 to 1853, Hawthorne's juvenile writing, including essays and six books in a series of history, BIOGRAPHY and MYTH, spans the two decades of his evolution into a major literary artist and reflects radical changes in how adults conceived of childhood. Romantic ideas about the child's divine innocence permeated transcendentalist thought, educational reforms, the Sunday school movement, the growth of pediatrics, and the spawning of new secular works for and about children. As the Calvinist notion of infant damnation was discarded, gentler discipline was advocated in the child-rearing manuals, now addressed to mothers, which proliferated after 1830. Adults in Hawthorne's boyhood, however, had no such confidence in childhood purity or maternal power.

Hawthorne's pragmatic uncle Robert Manning, who, after his father's death, supervised Nathaniel's schooling in Salem, seems to have imparted to his nephew the suspicion that the artistic side of his nature was morally weak and indolent. Early letters indicate that the boy felt chastised by his aunts and that he deeply missed his mother, who remained at the family home in Raymond, Maine. After visits there, he always looked back on this northern frontier as a paradise. At 16 he penned the elegiac 'Days of My Youth', which forecast his need to remain at home in his 'natal spot' of Salem with his mother and two sisters for 'twelve dark years' after graduating from Bowdoin College.

Collaborations with his sister Elizabeth on the *Universal History* (1837) for SAMUEL GOODRICH's *Peter Parley* series reflect Hawthorne's financial struggles and a willingness to accommodate himself to an established market. His career as an independent writer for children was launched in 1841 when *The Whole History of Grandfather's Chair* (1851) was first published by his future sister-in-law, Elizabeth Peabody, as a series: *Grandfather's Chair, Famous Old People* and *Liberty Tree.* Framed by a story in which Grandfather tells four children the adventures of the old English chair on which he sits, this historical non-fiction traces the founding of Massachusetts from the Puritan settlement of Salem and Boston through the Revolutionary era. The 'substantial and homely reality' of a fireside chair unifies these 'true stories' and valorises oral transmission of culture from old to young. Exemplifying the home-centred learning advocated by domestic manuals, the frame manifests Hawthorne's canny awareness of his dual audience as well as the mediating space American boys and girls required to see themselves as part of history. Peabody also arranged for the publication of *Biographical Stories* (1842), in which a boy confined to a darkened room because of an eye ailment listens to his father recount incidents in the childhoods of 'eminent personages of times gone by'. This non-sectarian non-school book is characteristic not only in its implied audience of young and mature listeners, but also in the contradictory attitudes toward childhood conveyed by the precocious behaviours of Benjamin West, Isaac Newton, Samuel Johnson, Oliver Cromwell, Benjamin Franklin and Queen Christina of Sweden. The interplay of child and adult points of view within a metafiction about going blind becomes darkly ironic in 'Samuel Johnson', an account of the great writer's penance to his father at Uttoxeter market.

Hawthorne's own sense of early displacement helps explain his literary focus on children, origins and the past. His child figures, among the first to speak in American fiction, are strikingly voluble in lifelike talk and inscrutable outbursts. The wild and prescient Pearl in *The Scarlet Letter* (1850), based on Hawthorne's observations of his daughter Una, illustrates the ambiguity of his view. The protean child, whether 'elfin or angelic', was for him like Emerson's Nature, 'a mere mirror' which 'shows to each man only his own quality'. In 'The Gentle Boy', a Quaker child abandoned and martyred is a tragic projection of the artistic sensibility, while in 'Little Annie's Ramble', published in *Youth's Keepsake* (1835), Hawthorne initiated his lifelong pattern of renewing himself through young female characters. The first audience of *A Wonder-Book* (1851) and *Tanglewood Tales* (1852), still in paperback today, were his own children.

This final and most famous of Hawthorne's series was conceived in 1838 when he wrote to HENRY WADSWORTH LONGFELLOW, a Bowdoin friend, about collaborating on 'a book of fairy tales' which might 'revolutionise the whole system of juvenile literature'. But the actual writing of such stories, taken 'out of the cold moonshine of classical mythology' and 'modernised, or perhaps gothicised', awaited the writer's marriage, financial success, and settlement in Lenox. Adapted freely from Anton's *Classical Dictionary* (1842), the first volume features legends of Perseus, Midas, Pandora, Hercules, Baucis and Philemon, and the Chimaera, linked by an idyll of seasonal expeditions in the Berkshires. Framing scenes include discourse on the 'sophomoric erudition' of the storyteller, Eustace Bright, a freshman at Williams College, whose 'vagrant audacity of imagination' is critiqued by old Mr Pringle, a classical scholar and parent. Dispensing with the frame in the sequel, Hawthorne introduces himself as Bright's editor and claims that the original 'purity' of tales involving murder, cannibalism, rape and incest has now been restored from encrustations of history. Bright's child-centered revision of the Minotaur, the Pygmies, the Dragon's Teeth, Circe's Palace, the Pomegranate Seeds and the Golden Fleece is thus aligned with the romantic warmth and joy of an idealised American childhood and with the golden age of the Earth, the source of these 'nursery-tales'. In the preface to *A Wonder Book*, Hawthorne did not express pride, as he might have, in being the first to adapt CLASSICAL MYTHOLOGY in English for the young. Rather he expressed pleasure in having avoided writing 'downward' to children, affirming his belief that they 'possess an unestimated sensibility to whatever is deep or high, in imagination or feeling'. He confessed to WASHINGTON IRVING in 1852: '*The Wonder Book* ... being meant for children ... seemed to reach a higher point, in its own way, than anything I had written for grown people.' EG

Hayes, John F(rancis) 1901–80 Canadian writer of historical adventures. Born in Ontario, Canada, Hayes worked in the publishing industry. He produced 11 juvenile novels that covered the panorama of Canadian history, three of which won awards. *A Land Divided* (1951) recounts events in 1755 surrounding the removal of Acadians by the British from what is present-day Nova Scotia and New Brunswick. The 1837 Mackenzie Rebellion in Toronto is the subject of *Rebels Ride at Night* (1953). Seventeenth-century Newfoundland is the locale of *The Dangerous Cove* (1957), during the struggle between settlers and Devon fisherman over control of ports. Hayes's novels are fast-paced and focus their action on the struggles of resourceful young heroes who are deeply involved in the events of their time. Although considered historically authentic, his books have been criticised for offering facile interpretations of tragedies such as the Acadian Deportation. For young readers his adventures have breathed life and excitement into the dry facts of Canadian history. DAC

see also HISTORICAL FICTION

Haywood, Carolyn 1898– American author, portrait painter and illustrator. Born in Philadelphia, she attended the Pennsylvania Academy of the Fine Arts and calls herself the 'grand-pupil' of the great American illustrator HOWARD PYLE, having studied under three of his famous students, Elizabeth Shippen Elliott, Violet Oakley and JESSIE WILCOX SMITH. Haywood is best known for her *Betsy* and *Eddie* books, mostly illustrated by herself. Early titles include *B is for Betsy* (1939) and *Little Eddie* (1947). Haywood has also designed murals for the State Capitol at Harrisburg, Pennsylvania, and her work is represented in the Pennsylvania Academy of Fine Arts permanent collection. KSB

Hazard, Paul 1878–1944 French literary critic and historian. An eminent scholar of comparative literature Hazard, taught at the Sorbonne and at the Collège de

France. He wrote several important histories of European thought and travelled widely in Europe and in the Americas. He visited the United States regularly to teach at Columbia University. His *Les Livres, les enfants et les hommes* (1932), translated as *Books, Children and Men* (1944), was an influential analysis of children's reading in its psychological and philosophical context from an historical and comparative viewpoint. His study of the relations between values and ideas in the development of children's literature has influenced numerous scholars and critics in the field. DAC

headpiece A small illustration or decoration at the start of a chapter or poem, often used by an illustrator to provide a witty comment on the text. GCB

Heale, Jay see BOOKCHAT

Heale, Jonathan 1949– British illustrator who came to attention with his sophisticated, framed woodcuts which accompany and match ADRIAN MITCHELL's lyrical, multi-levelled retelling of *The Ugly Duckling* (1994). He went on to win the KURT MASCHLER AWARD in 1997 for *Lady Muck* (WILLIAM MAYNE) in which the full-bellied pigs come to life in pencil and wash ILLUSTRATIONS as well as in his classic woodcuts. JAG

Heaney, Seamus 1939– Northern Irish poet, born in County Derry. Winner of the Nobel Prize for Literature (1995) and Oxford Professor of Poetry from 1989 until 1992, Heaney is one of the most distinguished poets in the world. Collections like *Death of a Naturalist* (1966) are regularly used in secondary schools, recapturing the intense experience of childhood where a trout 'slips like butter down / the throat of the river'. Heaney has co-edited (with TED HUGHES) two anthologies for the young – the inspired *RATTLE BAG* (1982) and the less successful *School Bag* (1997). His *Beowulf* won the 1999 WHITBREAD AWARD. HT

Hearn, Lafcadio 1850–1904 Journalist and author whose Japanese name is Yakumo Koisumi. Hearn was one of the first westerners to collect and interpret Japanese folk culture, taking HANS CHRISTIAN ANDERSEN as his model. Born in Greece, Hearn was raised in Dublin by his mother and great-aunt, who gave him his lifelong fascination with GHOST STORIES, FOLKTALES, LEGENDS and MYTHS (see CLASSICAL MYTHOLOGY). In 1869 Hearn left Ireland for America; he lived in Cincinnati and New Orleans and became a journalist, well-known for his coverage of shocking events and his essays on African American and Creole cultures. His first story collection was *Stray Leaves from Strange Literature* (1884). Hearn moved to Japan in 1890, becoming a Japanese citizen in 1895. His technique of interviewing people for their cultural stories and immersing himself in multiple versions of stories before allowing his imagination free rein found a special outlet in Japan. Other published story collections include *Japanese Fairy Tales* (1898–1922) and *In Ghostly Japan* (1899). Hearn was a gifted teacher and a sensuous writer, possessing a talent for combining vivid, detailed description and a culture's lore with his own personal narrative. Jonathan Cott's *Wandering Ghost* (1991) gives an accurate, informative account of Hearn. ELPB

Hearne, Betsy (Gould) 1942– American author for children, and children's literature critic and teacher. After a peripatetic southern childhood, Hearne settled in the Midwest, receiving her PhD in Library Science from the University of Chicago. Achieving the unusual distinction of editorial status at two major review periodicals (*Booklist* for 12 years and *The Bulletin of the Center for Children's Books* for seven), Hearne has also written extensively on children's books in both the mainstream and professional/academic press, and has served on several major awards committees. Her *Choosing Books for Children: A Commonsense Guide* (1980) received a Parent's Choice Award, and her *Beauty and the Beast: Visions and Revisions of an Old Tale* (1989) focuses on one of her main areas of critical concern, folklore and its adaptations. In addition, Hearne has written several novels for young people, often using real-life events as a basis for her fiction; she has also produced two volumes of poetry for young adults, *Love Lines: Poetry in Person* (1987) and *Polaroid and Other Poems of View* (1991), as well as a PICTUREBOOK based on her family history, *Seven Brave Women* (1997). DS

Heath, Shirley Brice see CHILDIST CRITICISM; CRITICAL APPROACHES TO CHILDREN'S LITERATURE

Hedderwick, Mairi 1939– After training at Edinburgh College of Art, the Scottish author Mairi Hedderwick lived on Coll, a Hebridean island, which is the setting for her *KATIE MORAG* books. *Katie Morag Delivers the Mail* was the first of a series, started in 1984. Not only do the books capture the special quality of rural island life but they also convey the robust nature of Katie Morag and her complex, full-blooded family and island relationships. Fluent line-and-wash illustrations supply extra and delightful detail. Hedderwick has also illustrated RUMER GODDEN's *The Old Woman who Lived in a Vinegar Bottle* (1972) and Jane Duncan's *Janet Reachfar* books (1975–8). JAG

Heide, Florence Parry [Jamie McDonald; Alex B. Allen] 1919– Versatile American author who grew up in Punxsutawney, Pennsylvania, surrounded by cousins, aunts, uncles and grandparents in a spacious old family home, and also in Pittsburgh where her actress-writer mother established a successful photographic studio. After graduating from the University of California at Los Angeles, Heide worked in advertising in New York City for a few years before marrying, moving to Kenosha, Wisconsin, and raising five children. Her earliest books were written in collaboration with another young mother, Sylvia Van Clief. She found writing for children an 'unexpected delight' through which she could reach her 'child-self (never long away or far from me)' and the lives of other children. Later she wrote mystery stories in collaboration with her daughter Roxanne, and PICTUREBOOKS in collaboration with Roxanne's twin, Judith Heide Gilliland, who lived in the Middle East. *The Day of Ahmed's Secret* (1990), set in Cairo, and *Sami in the Time of Troubles* (1992), set in war-torn Beirut, are both illustrated by Ted Lewin. But the Heide work that seems destined to become a classic is the *Treehorn* trilogy, darkly humorous tales about a child who is ignored by adults, that are perfectly accompanied by EDWARD GOREY's macabre drawings: *The Shrinking of Treehorn* (1971), *Treehorn's Treasure* (1981) and *Treehorn's Wish* (1984). LH

Heidi (1882) Popular and enduring novel by Swiss writer Johanna Spyri (1827–1901). As the novel opens Heidi is already a damaged child, an orphan living with a second reluctant stepmother. When visiting her elderly grandfather in the alps, Heidi discovers the healing powers of nature and the friendship of Peter, a young goatherd. The process of spiritual and physical restoration is interrupted when she is sent to Frankfurt as companion to the disabled Clara. In the confining and unhealthy atmosphere of Frankfurt, Heidi suffers from depression and bouts of sleepwalking which are cured only when she returns to the alps. Spyri appears to be ahead of her time in the acute psychological insight demonstrated in the Frankfurt scenes. These perceptive interpretations of behaviour are contained, however, within a framework of conservative Christian morality: Heidi persuades her grandfather that even her 'time in the wilderness' of Frankfurt had been perfectly arranged by God. It would appear that spiritual healing can take place only in the mountains, a message which is reinforced on the physical plane when Clara miraculously learns to walk again during her stay in the alps. *Heidi*'s success as a girls' classic owes much to its sentimentality of tone, to its satisfying conclusion in accordance with natural justice and to an idealised view of alpine peasant life. The book's continued popularity has inspired many film and TELEVISION versions as well as sequels written by Charles Tritten: *Heidi Grows Up* (1961) and *Heidi's Children* (1967) GL

Heinlein, Robert A(nson) 1907–88 Writer of SCIENCE FICTION stories and novels for children and adults. Many credit Heinlein with renewing interest in juvenile science fiction with the 1947 publication of *Rocket Ship Galileo*. Twelve other novels for juveniles followed. Prior to Heinlein's career as a writer, he graduated from the US Naval Academy and served as a Naval engineer until contracting tuberculosis forced him to retire. He used his engineering background and experience to knowledgeably describe future technology. Heinlein's books for juveniles are in the *Bildungsroman* tradition. He wrote them with an audience of teenage boys and young men in mind and, unsurprisingly, had – with the exception of *Podkayne of Mars* (1963) – teenage boys as protagonists. Yet Heinlein's female characters are often quite capable and appear in such non-traditional roles, for science fiction in the 1950s and 1960s, as spaceship captains, soldiers and engineers. His works have strong elements of sociology, political science, parapsychology and anthropology, emphasise self-reliance, and support a vigorous education and respect for older, and usually wiser, adults. MF

Heins, Paul and Ethel see REVIEWING AND REVIEWERS

Helen's Babies see JOHN HABBERTON

Hemans, Felicia Dorothea [née Browne] 1793–1835 English poet who published her first collection when she was 13. This well-read woman, whose poetry titles include *Lays of Many Lands* and *Records of Woman*, brought up five sons alone, writing tirelessly to support the family. *Hymns for Childhood* (1834) is no longer remembered, but the much parodied 'Casabianca' ('The boy stood on the burning deck . . .') is worthy of respect for that rare thing – a child given heroic status. MCCS

Hendry, Frances Mary 1941– Scottish writer of novels for young adults. In her *Quest for a Queen* trilogy – *The Falcon* (1989), *The Lark* (1992) and *The Jackdaw* (1993) – ordinary young people are caught up in critical events in the life of Mary Queen of Scots. Two other *Quest* novels are set in earlier periods, and *Quest for a Kelpie* (1986) during the 1745 Rebellion. She creates a dense, historically accurate sense of culture, place and time for her fast-moving plots and adventurous heroines. Recently published is *Chandra* (1995), set in India, and *Atlantis* (1997) in an Antarctic FANTASY world. VCH

Henkes, Kevin 1960– American author and illustrator whose *A Weekend with Wendell* (1986) was his first PICTUREBOOK, using mouse characters as substitutes for humans. It was *Chester's Way* (1988) that introduced his now famous Lilly with the red cowboy boots. *Julius, the Baby of the World* (1990) presented Lilly with a new brother and new problems. *Lilly's Purple Plastic Purse* (1996) creates difficulties between Lilly and her favourite teacher. Using pen-and-ink and watercolours, Henkes portrays characteristic human predicaments which young children experience, such as bossiness, boastfulness, sibling jealousy, and in *Owen* (1993), a Caldecott Honour Book, the need to give up a fuzzy blanket. In *Jessica* (1989) and the curiously named *Chrysanthemum* (1991), two small girls overcome hurdles with satisfying results. *Oh!* (1999) is a more recent picturebook. Henkes has also written novels for middle-grade children including *Words of Stone* (1992), *Sun and Spoon* (1997) – in which a boy must find some remembrance of his Gram who has recently died – and *The Birthday Room* (1999). PDS

Henri, Adrian 1932–2000 English poet and painter. Henri was published as one of the Liverpool Poets in the adult collection *The Mersey Sound* (1967), along with ROGER MCGOUGH and BRIAN PATTEN, and quite frequently published and performed with them. His first children's collection was *The Phantom Lollipop Lady* (1986) and his latest is *Robocat* (1998). A new selection of poems, *The World's Your Lobster* (1998), has deservedly brought back into print poems such as 'Rhinestone Rhino' and 'Sammy the Flying Piglet', which have the dynamism of performance poetry and popular music, along with quieter poems such as 'Autumn', which deal with the 'small things' that children notice. ML

Henry, Marguerite [Breithaupt] 1902–97 America's premier writer of HORSE STORIES. Henry wrote over 30 novels featuring horses and emphasising the bond between horses and their masters. Two of these, *Justin Morgan Had a Horse* (1945) and *Misty of Chincoteague* (1947), were Newbery Honour Books, and *King of the Wind* (1948) won the NEWBERY MEDAL. Henry's works are especially notable for the author's meticulous research; many of her best books portray horses who actually lived, and their historical settings are captured in vivid detail. *Justin Morgan*, for example, portrays the famous foundation sire of the Morgan breed and accurately represents the rural Vermont of an earlier era. *King of the Wind* is an historical novel, depicting the Godolphin Arabian, progenitor of the thoroughbred racehorse. Local colour predominates in *Misty of Chincoteague*, a tale of the annual round-up of wild ponies on a small Virginia island. Human characters, such as Justin Morgan, the mute Agba – groom of Sham, the Goldolphin Arabian – and the children who adopt Misty and his mother, are realistically and sympathetically portrayed. With her longtime illustrator and collaborator WESLEY DENNIS, Henry left a rich legacy for horse-loving readers. JB, NV

see also PONY STORIES

Henryson, Robert see FABLES; see also ANIMALS IN FICTION

Henson, Jim 1936–90 Puppeteer, TELEVISION programme and film-maker. The uplifting entertainment worlds Henson created (*SESAME STREET*, *THE MUPPETS*) contrast with the feel-good empires of DISNEY. Both celebrate innocence, zaniness and the power of positive thinking, but while Disney mass-produced escapist and glossy entertainment, reassuring for its conventionality, Henson's fantasies promoted these American values with added bite and a lovable unpretentiousness. His genuine optimism comes with a caustic undertow; the real world is part of the magic. Decency and innocence are packed with deconstruction, parody and wit. Sharp, multilayered storytelling – absurd, affectionate and socially concerned – uses everything from modern media genres to FOLKTALE, playing to an intelligent audience. Genuine idealist and businessman, Henson built hard-working collaborative teams extending the limits of the possible, narratively and technically. Later work explored darker themes (*Labyrinth*), with *The Storyteller* a highpoint in his imaginative blend of stunning technology and compassionate narration of traditional stories. His approach survives him in the special effects company Jim Henson Creature Shop, which has contributed to numerous children's films for cinema and television, such as the BBC production of *THE ARABIAN NIGHTS* (2000). CMP

Henty, G(eorge) A(lfred) 1832–1902 British journalist and writer, remembered for his series of historical ADVENTURE STORIES. Henty's output was prodigious – in excess of 200 titles, 90 of which are boys' stories. A distinguished war correspondent, Henty transferred to his fiction his experience of being present at historic moments. His boy heroes also experience history in the making at first hand, whether it be *With Clive in India* (1884), *With Lee in Virginia* (1890) or *With Kitchener in the Soudan* (1903). Despite the rapidity with which he worked and the breadth of his historical coverage, Henty was known for the accuracy of his history. Indeed, portions of some texts are heavily indebted to accounts of military campaigns and established histories.

There is a recognisable Henty formula at work in most of his books: a plucky youngster gets caught up in a military career through which he achieves recognition and an appropriate reward. Henty's heroes are uncomplicated young men (usually accompanied by a comic side-kick). They believe that boxing sharpens the wits better than books, and are fiercely patriotic, assuming that, as muscular English gentlemen, they are capable of administering a 'thoroughly sound and manly thrashing' to any number of ruffians. This belief system encompasses most kinds of chauvinism: Henty's books promulgate the idea that pluck and fighting power (rightly) made the British masters of all colonised peoples, and the British gentleman the master of all. However, he was surprisingly alert to the capabilities of women. Many girls read his novels, and he not only corresponded with them but also exhorted his boy readers to recognise their qualities. He wrote in the preface to *One of the 28th*: 'Boys are apt to think, mistakenly, that their sex has a monopoly of courage, but I believe that in moments of great peril, women are to the full as brave and collected as men.'

In addition to his juvenile novels, Henty also wrote for periodicals and edited *The Union Jack*. The definitive Henty bibliography was published in 1997: *G.A. Henty 1832 –1902: A Bibliographical Study,* by Peter Newbolt. KR

Hergé see TINTIN SERIES; see also SCIENCE FICTION

Heroes, The see CHARLES KINGSLEY; see also CLASSICAL MYTHOLOGY

Herrick, Steven One of Australia's most popular performance poets for young people, Herrick writes for two main age groups: upper primary and young adult, using predominantly the verse-novel genre so that his characters are real for readers. He writes with honesty and empathy about subjects and issues close to children's hearts – school, parents, family breakdown, first-love, acne and death. His free-verse form is accessible to young readers who might otherwise reject the genre. Herrick skilfully combines humour and pathos within the same novel, reflecting most people's lives. Titles include *Love Ghosts and Nose Hair* (1996), *Poetry to the Rescue* (1998), *A Place like This* (1998) and *The Spangled Drongo* (1999). RTh

Herriot, James 1916–95 British author, born in Scotland, who based his highly popular series, beginning with *All Creatures Great and Small* (1975), on his life as a vet in North Yorkshire. The stories are full of humorous anecdotes about the eccentricities of people and beasts alike, in particular his fellow vets Siegfried and Tristan Farnon. The books are popular with both children and adults. *All Creatures Great and Small* was made into a feature film and later stories in the sequence were serialised on British TELEVISION shortly after publication. Herriot later wrote a number of PICTUREBOOKS for younger readers. *Bonny's Big Day* (1991) is an expansion of a chapter from *It Shouldn't Happen to a Vet* (1972) and tells the story of a lonely old farmer who is persuaded by Herriot to enter his beloved retired carthorse Bonny in the Darroby Show Family Pets class. She is, of course, awarded the winning rosette. *The Christmas Day Kitten* (1986), also a vignette from a previous book and illustrated by RUTH BROWN, is a poignant story about a dying stray cat bringing her kitten to a kind lady's house on Christmas Day. The kitten is adopted and becomes a much-loved Christmas present. HCE

Hesse, Karen 1952– American writer and poet whose book, *Out of the Dust* (1997), won the NEWBERY MEDAL. Written in free verse and organised as a diary, it is the story of a farming family's struggle and endurance in the face of tragedy in the Oklahoma dust bowl during the Depression. Hesse's HISTORICAL FICTION is well-researched and convincingly lifelike: *Letters From Rifka* (1992) is based on the experiences of a family member escaping Jewish persecution in Russia in 1919. Other titles by Hesse include *Phoenix Rising* (1994) and *The Music of Dolphins* (1996). *A Light in the Storm: The Civil War Diary of Amelia Martin* (1999) and a PICTUREBOOK, *Come On, Rain!* (1999), are recent titles. PDS

Heward, Constance see *AMELIARANNE* SERIES

Hewins, Caroline M. 1846–1926 Pioneer American women's library director and author. Born in Roxbury, Massachusetts, the eldest of nine children, Hewins became librarian of a subscription library that became the Hartford, Connecticut, Public Library, where she served for 50 years. Active in her involvement in professional associations, Hewins was one of the first women to address the fledgling ALA and to survey their work in encouraging 'a love of good reading in boys and girls'. While not a children's librarian, she made the cause of children's reading and library service for children a primary concern. Noted as a bibliographer, she published the first selective guide on books for children, *Books for the Young: A Guide for Parents and Children* (1882). Hewins also wrote a regular column, 'Literature for the Young', in *Library Journal* and reflected on her own childhood reading in her autobiography, *A Mid-Century Child and Her Books* (1926). Hewins was a close ally of children's librarians, the most distinguished of whom was ANNE CARROLL MOORE, the legendary director of children's work for the New York Public Library who helped to shape children's literature in the early 20th century. AL

see also LIBRARIES

Hey, Dollface (1979) A persuasive and convincing novel by Deborah Hautzig, pitched at young adults, and providing a sensitive and amusing exploration of the dawning of sexual attraction. The story focuses upon the intimacy developed between Val Hoffman and Chloe Fox, misfits at a society school, who are drawn together by shared experience. Hautzig writes with great perception as Val tries to make sense of her feelings for Chloe. The confusion of adolescence is captured, heightened by Val's fears of homosexuality. Ultimately the resolution teaches that we may not fit into any of the slots the world designates for us, and so Val and Chloe learn that it is their experience alone which is important. GD

see also GAY AND LESBIAN LITERATURE; SEX IN CHILDREN'S BOOKS

Heyer, Georgette see ADULT FICTION

Hiawatha see *THE SONG OF HIAWATHA*; see also ERROL LE CAIN

Hickok, James Butler [Wild Bill] see WILD BILL HICKOK

Hickson, Joan see *POSTMAN PAT*

Highlights for Children (1946–) American magazine for children from pre-school to upper elementary grade. Its mantra is 'fun with a purpose'. Monthly issues include regular special features such as the science corner and Timbertoes. Articles are of interest to both the very young and the older child. Each issue's contents page has a parent-teacher guide that codes three focuses: reading, creative thinking, and traditional moral values stories. The magazine regularly includes contributions from children, who send in riddles, jokes or drawings. For parents who want a 'safe' magazine that provides recreational and educational benefits, *Highlights* is ideally suited. ALW

see also COMICS, PERIODICALS AND MAGAZINES

Highwater, Jamake (Mamake, Jay Marks, J. Marks, J. Marks-Highwater) 1942?– Controversial American author and storyteller. Since Highwater was adopted at around the age of seven by Alexander and Marcia Marks, his exact birth date and the location and culture of his birth parents are unknown. Highwater claims to have been born in Glacier County, Montana, and has an affidavit from his adopted mother stating that his birth parents were Native Americans.

Most of his fictional works for young people deal with themes of alienation, the search for the old ways and the classic hero journey. *Anpao: An American Indian Odyssey* (1977) weaves several stories from different Native American peoples together to retell the Blood/Blackfoot legend of Scarface. The pacing and language were reminiscent of a storyteller. It was designated a Newbery Honour Book by the ALA, as well as a Boston-Horn Book Honour Book; *Many Smokes, Many Moons* (1979), which explores Native art from 3500 BCE to modern times, won the Jane Addams Children's Book Award in 1979. In addition to several films for the Public Broadcasting Service, Highwater is the author of the *Ghost Horse Cycle* which consists of *Legend Days* (1984), *The Ceremony of Innocence* (1984) and *I Wear the Morning Star* (1986), a multi-generational trilogy dealing with the destruction caused by encounters between Native and white civilisations. DJH

see also NATIVE AMERICANS IN CHILDREN'S LITERATURE; STORYTELLING

Highwayman, The First published as part of Alfred Noyes's collected works in 1913, this work remains the best-known poem by a largely forgotten British writer. It is a swash-buckling narrative BALLAD, telling how Bess, the landlord's 'black-eyed, red-lipped' daughter, died for her love, the highwayman, at the hands of King George's red-coat men. Its visual and auditory images are strikingly dramatic, and the six-line stanza pattern, with its short penultimate line, enables haunting repetition to work to full effect:

> And he kissed its waves in the moonlight,
> (Oh, sweet black waves in the moonlight!)

The Highwayman was successfully republished in 1981, enhanced by illustrations by CHARLES KEEPING. HA

Hilder, Rowland see *THE MIDNIGHT FOLK*; see also *LADYBIRD BOOKS*

Hildick, E(dmund) W(allace) 1925 – British children's author remembered more as a successful entertainer than a challenging writer. Because he was prepared to accept the formulaic constraints of series fiction, his stories tend to explore situations in a light-hearted way and, despite their limited emotional range, are invariably well constructed and amusing. His first book, *Jim Starling* (1958) introduced a new democratic strain to the SCHOOL STORY genre by focusing on tough, working-class boys in a secondary modern school. Hildick drew upon his own experience as a secondary modern teacher to create realistic characters and setting, and by 1963, six more *Jim Starling* books had appeared. *Louie's Lot* (1965), which spawned a series about Louie, a milkman famed for his efficiency and resourcefulness, typified the construction and style of much of Hildick's fiction: a simple plot with ingenious variations on a theme (*Louie's Lot* revolves around the various tests Louie sets young job applicants); short, staccato sentences; lively characterisation; and extremely funny dialogue. This format appealed to reluctant, as well as more sophisticated, readers. *Meet Lemon Kelly*, *Birdy Jones* (both 1963) and *The*

Questors (1966) generated further series and established Hildick as a writer capable of employing formulaic conventions with wit and imagination. DJ

Hill, Anthony 1942– Australian writer and journalist, who has written a number of novels for adolescent readers. His first, *Birdsong* (1988), described by Maurice Saxby as 'a curious, oddity of a novel', is an improbable detective story with a difference – Samuel unmasks a bird-smuggling ring with the help of a loquacious wild cockatoo. By contrast, the acclaimed *The Burnt Stick* (1994), sensitively illustrated by Mark Sofilas, is based upon actual events told to Hill by an Aboriginal man. This is an emotionally powerful story of the pain and disregard for human rights inflicted by the Australian Government policy, when, until as late as the 1960s, Aboriginal children were removed from their families and placed in institutions or white foster homes. The 'burnt stick' refers to the charcoal used by Aborigines to rub into children's skin to hide the fact that they were of mixed blood. Loss and grief are also the theme of *Spindrift* (1996), in which Elizabeth experiences the death of her grandmother. Sofilas's charcoal and graphite illustrations embrace the closeness of personal grief and give an added intensity to Hill's elegant understated prose. JAP

Hill, David 1942– New Zealand writer and playwright who, before becoming a full-time writer, reviewer and journalist in 1982, had worked as a secondary school teacher, soldier, van driver and barman. Hill achieved early success as a playwright with *Ours But To Do* (1986), *A Time to Laugh* (1990) and *Branches* (1993), and as a short-story writer, especially for radio and the *SCHOOL JOURNAL*. His first young adult novel, *See Ya, Simon* (1992), is a moving portrayal of a teenage boy's losing battle with muscular dystrophy, told through the eyes of a friend, and skilfully avoids the sentimentality and didacticism often associated with books about illness written for teenagers. *Take It Easy* (1995) and *Cold Comfort* (1996) are well-crafted ADVENTURE STORIES, reflecting his love of tramping and the New Zealand bush, while *Comes Naturally* (1998) addresses important environmental issues in a realistic yet engaging manner. *Just Looking Thanks*, a detective mystery with elements of both FANTASY and social realism was published in 1999. Hill is also known as a travel and sports writer, book reviewer and columnist and speaker on children's literature. TD

Hill, Douglas 1935– Canadian-born novelist living in Britain, best known for his SCIENCE FICTION for older readers. In 1979 he published *Galactic Warlord*, first in the *Lost Legionary Quintet*. Notable titles are the *Warriors of the Wasteland* and *Colsec* trilogies (1982, 1984), *World of the Stiks* (1994) and the *Cade* trilogy (1996). Packed with action, they deal with serious themes – colonisation in the *Colsec* trilogy, exploitation and corruption in *World of the Stiks*, inspired by the experience of Native Americans. Works for younger children include *The Dragon Charmer* (1997) and *Melleron's Monsters* (2000). Hill also writes non-fiction: *The Young Green Consumer Guide* (1990) won the Earthworm Award. DCH

Hill, Elizabeth Starr 1925– American writer of juvenile fiction, born in Florida. Many of Hill's novels deal directly with adolescent concerns, including her award-winning *Evan's Corner* (1967), which explores a young boy's need for a space of his own, and *When Christmas Comes* (1989), which looks at a daughter coping with her father's remarriage. Other stories have a more magical surface, yet continue to deal with realistic issues, such as *Pardon My Fangs* (1968), revised as *Fangs Aren't Everything* (1985), where a young man becomes a werewolf, but the story's emphasis is on how he hides this secret from his friends. Hill's own performing experience gave her a love of the theatre which is reflected in a more recent series of stories about the Dales, a show-biz family, including *The Street Dancers* (1991), *The Banjo Player* (1993) and the award-winning *Broadway Chances* (1992). These stories effectively combine an insider's look at show business with elements of mystery and suspense. SCWA

Hill, Eric see *SPOT* SERIES

Hill, Lorna see *SADLER'S WELLS* SERIES; see also *DRINA* SERIES; BALLET STORIES

Hill, Susan 1942– Writer, editor, critic and radio dramatist born in Scarborough, England. Her recurrent theme is childhood, real or recollected, about which she writes unflinchingly, making her readers face what they may fear. Award-winning adult fiction – *The Albatross and other stories* (1970), *The Bird of Night* (1972), *I'm the King of the Castle* (1981), which is a searing study of bullying, and *Strange Meeting* (1971), about World War I – combine Hardy-like descriptions of surroundings with pellucid introverted characters at odds with life. These are now teenage study texts. Later PICTUREBOOKS pinpoint incidents of childhood frustration and apprehension: *Suzy's Shoes* (1980), *One Night at a Time* (1984), *Mother's Magic* (1986), *I Don't Want to Go There Again* (1990), *Pirate Doll* (1992) and *Septimus Honeydew* (1996). The most successful partnership is with ANGELA BARRET, in *Beware, Beware* (1993). Four stories and a verse narrative of the Nativity, *Can It Be True?* (1988 SMARTIES PRIZE) are brought together as *The Christmas Collection* (1994), comforting folk-memory edged with tragedy. A distinctive anthology of GHOST STORIES also reveals the painful deep structures of all her work. MM

Hilton, Nette (Margaret Lynette) 1946– Australian author of PICTUREBOOKS, novels and adult fiction, winner of two Children's Book Council of Australia Honour Book awards, whose convincing, often humorous, and frequently poignant stories show the realities for children growing up, sometimes in stressful situations, while affirming the importance of family values and continuity. Hilton defines family expansively – Emmaline in *The Belonging of Emmaline Harris* (1994) has to adjust to a new stepfather and stepsisters, while Jenny in *The Web* (1991) shares a special relationship with her dying great-grandmother. In *A Ghost of a Chance* (1998) Anne-Marie overcomes homesickness while living in England for a year. Her PICTUREBOOKS – *The Long Red Scarf* (1987), *Dirty Dave the Bushranger* (1988) and *Prince Lachlan* (1989) – and junior novels such as *A Frilling Time* (1993) humorously question conventional gender stereotypes of behaviour and dress, with such characters as a knitting grandfather and a sewing bushranger, while still retaining a central core of family relationships. Hilton's writing is at its most powerful in her books for young adults, *Square Pegs* (1991) and *Hothouse Flowers* (1997), where she tackles such emotive subjects as teenage relationships, mental illness and teenage suicide, with sensitivity and compassion. Hilton faces squarely the complexities of contemporary lifestyles, especially from a child's perspective. JAP

Himler, Ronald [Norbert] 1937– American illustrator of books for children, born in Cleveland, Ohio, and educated at the Cleveland Institute of Art, Cranbrook Academy of Art in Bloomfield Hills, Michigan, New York University and Hunter College in New York City. Himler worked as a technical sculptor for General Motors, a toy designer, and a commercial artist before becoming an illustrator. His gentle, sensitive portrayal of emotions, fine attention to detail, historical research into Native American costumes, and skilled use of shadow have made him a successful illustrator for authors as varied as ARNOLD ADOFF, EVE BUNTING, Byrd Baylor, ANN TURNER and Virginia Driving Hawk Sneve. He has received numerous awards for his work, including the Award for Graphic Excellence from the American Institute of Graphic Arts for his book *Baby* (1972), and the Notable Book Citation from the ALA for *Dakota Dugout* (1986) by Ann Turner. He is also the illustrator of Marjorie Weinman Sharmat's *Morris Brookside* series and Virginia Driving Hawk Sneve's *Native American* series. DJH

Hines, Barry see *KES*

Hinton, Nigel Highly acclaimed British writer producing works of fiction for young adults and children. *Buddy* (1982) – perhaps his most significant book – was chosen as a 'Top Teen Read' and nominated for the CARNEGIE MEDAL. The story centres upon the sensitive and intelligent Buddy Clark, exposing the inner turmoil he experiences, struggling with the confusions and contradictions that accompany adult life. Hinton also successfully adapted the book for TELEVISION. *Buddy's Song* (1987) concludes the story with Buddy achieving fame in a rock group. This is augmented by his resolution of the conflicts played out in the original book. *Getting Free* (1978) and *Collision Course* (1976) are further examples of socially realistic novels, again representative of the troubled journey to adulthood. *Getting Free* discusses the possibility of sanctuary from a rule-driven society and *Collision Course* teaches the need to accept the consequences of one's actions. Both these books have been translated into different languages with *Collision Course* winning the Dutch Silver Pen Award. Hinton has also produced a trilogy for younger children comprising *Beaver Towers* (1980), *The Witches' Revenge* (1981) and *Run to Beaver Towers* (1989). The tales are of humour, magic and adventure, demonstrating Hinton's ability to provide for both older and less mature readers. GD

Hinton, S(usan) E(loise) 1950– American author credited with writing the first genuine young adult novel. Her novels are realistic, portraying contemporary male teens in troubling situations and their growth in overcoming these adverse circumstances. The plots are fast-moving and involve violence and delinquent behaviour, yet the narrative uses simple language. For this reason they are especially popular with reluctant readers. In 1987 Hinton received the first Margaret A. Edwards Lifetime Achievement Award from the ALA and *School Library Journal*. Four of her novels have been made into motion pictures as popular as her books.

Hinton was born in Tulsa, Oklahoma in 1950. An introverted and deeply feeling young woman, she was outraged by the social injustice and groundless violence occurring between two gangs of teens of opposite social class – the lower-class greasers and the upper-class socialites or 'socs'. She began writing a novel based on this conflict, embellishing upon events she saw take place among her own friends and classmates. She completed this first novel while still in high school and kept re-working it. *The Outsiders* (1967) was published when she was 17 years old. Since the story centred on male characters and contained violence, her initials were used on the book to hide her female identity. The novel was such a success among teens and critics it sold over four million copies, enabling her to attend the University of Tulsa where she majored in education. Her startling success caused writer's block and it was only with the encouragement of her future husband that she painstakenly wrote her second novel *That was Then, This is Now* (1971), about friendship and betrayal.

Her voice is realistic and her characters, though outwardly tough, using hard language and facing hard choices, are inwardly sensitive young men longing to be accepted by both family and society, and desperately trying to establish an identity. *Rumble Fish* (1975), about a boy trying to acquire a tough reputation, and *Tex* (1979), about two brothers left in each other's care while their father rambles about, continue her tradition of first-person narrative. All four novels are nearly void of adult characters, forcing the protagonists to make their own decisions and pay the often violent consequences.

During the 1980s Hinton's career focused on adapting her novels for film. *Tex* was the first to be filmed by WALT DISNEY Productions, in 1982. Hinton was involved in the casting, scriptwriting and directing. While this was taking place a group of teens in California petitioned Francis Ford Coppola to make a movie of *The Outsiders*. Hinton was also involved in this project, working with Coppola on the screenplay for it and *Rumble Fish*.

Hinton returned to novel-writing with the publication of *Taming the Star Runner* (1988). Told in the third person, it is about a young man writing and publishing a novel while still a teen. This novel demonstrated that Hinton remained in touch with the emotions, pressures and internal conflict of adolescents. LAW

see also YOUNG ADULT FICTION; CHILD AUTHORS

Hirsch, Odo Australian author and doctor living in London, whose writing is characterised by gentle exaggeration, quirky characters and understated humour, reminiscent of A.A. MILNE. Bartlett, in *Bartlett and the Ice Voyage* (1998) and *Bartlett and the City of Flames* (1999), is a hero of the old tradition, with all the great qualities of 'Perseverance, Desperation and Inventiveness', and his adventures are unique rather than swashbuckling. The eponymous heroine of *Hazel Green* (1999) and *Something Fishy, Hazel Green* (2000) is a feisty girl, whose tenacity and imagination inspire the people around her. Hirsch usually sets his stories in imaginary or unidentifiable locations, giving them an exotic, timeless appeal, and through his characters he makes wonderfully perceptive comments about human nature. RTh

His Dark Materials (1995–2000) prose trilogy of epic scale by the British author, PHILIP PULLMAN. *Northern Light*, the first book, won the *Guardian* Fiction Award and the CARNEGIE MEDAL. In the USA, the book (titled *The Golden Compass*) was published in an initial print-run of 100,000 copies, appeared on eight award lists, and was a best-seller for both adult and young readers. The second book, *The Subtle Knife* (1997), won the United Kingdom Reading Award. The publication in November 2000 of *The Amber Spyglass* completed the work.

The title of the trilogy is drawn from Book I of Milton's *Paradise Lost*, and Pullman's argument also concerns a Fall. Good and evil are redefined in his theology, however: 'Every little increase in human freedom has been fought over ferociously between those who want to know more and be wiser and stronger, and those who want us to obey and be humble and submit.' That struggle is embodied in a narrative which is, over some 1500 pages, brilliantly exciting. It is remarkable to find children as young as eight utterly absorbed in a text which invites a mature reader to pause over a re-interpretation of the nature of the soul and the afterlife. Yet so insistent is the power of the narrative that adults often report that on their first reading they trusted their sense that the great themes at the core of the books have been consistently worked through – things hold together – and surrendered themselves to childlike headlong reading. Pullman's Eve and Adam figures – the resilient, passionate Lyra and her determined companion Will – have decisive roles to play as the multiple narratives take us into the land of the dead, towards a cataclysmic war and, as in the Eden of Genesis and Milton, to a single, agonising choice where the stake is no less that the future of the universe. It is extraordinary that Pullman compels readers to absolute belief in such a moment – and to be powerfully moved by the decision that is made. Pullman is especially good at action on a grand canvas: a fortress under siege from huge invading armies or the slow movement of hosts of the dead across the wasteland of their terrible world. The ingenuity of his creations is endlessly engaging: armoured bears with the power and courage of saga heroes, spies no bigger than a handspan armed with lethal spurs, or the gentle 'muletha' spinning along hardened lava roads on wheels fashioned from the fruit of great trees.

In the end, though, the seriousness of Pullman's assault upon the forces of ritual, control and authority – and his attack is fierce and sustained – is carried by the human characters. Here, he transcends the simplification of personality common in FANTASY literature, and indeed it would be misleading to limit the trilogy to that genre. His human beings have the courage, the duplicity, the wisdom, the cruelty, the electric sexuality, the ambiguities, and, finally, the complex capacity to love, which mark a great work of fiction. *His Dark Materials* will surely be valued as one of the most distinguished literary achievements of the 20th century. GPF

Hissey, Jane 1952– British PICTUREBOOK author and illustrator whose stories, based on her own soft toys, are set in a warm, cosy, unchanging world. The toys are always kind to one another; they take in strangers without a second thought and when a toy dog turns up they look after him, giving him seven birthdays and inviting him to stay with them, even though his barking and leaping around clearly disquiet them. The brightly coloured pencil-crayon illustrations are almost tangible, depicting a world where the toys make whatever they need from scraps and where the children who own them never appear. KA

historical fiction A historical novel is not merely a story set in the past but a story which attempts, with the aid of scholarly research, to reconstruct and bring to life the events, culture and *Zeitgeist* of the period. Generally, historical novelists for children are less concerned with depicting major historical events and figures than those who write for adults; more frequently, they emphasise what it was like to live and grow up in another era, the cultural differences between past and present, and the living continuity between them. Sometimes well-known historical figures will make an appearance, but they are rarely the central characters. Mary, Queen of Scots appears briefly in ALISON UTTLEY's *A TRAVELLER IN TIME* (1939) and Elizabeth I in CYNTHIA HARNETT's *Stars of Fortune* (1956), but the main concerns of both books are with the ordinary lives of people at the time. JILL PATON WALSH's *GRACE* (1991) takes a well-known figure, Grace Darling, and re-examines her story to show how history has mistreated her.

Many of the classics of children's literature, from *KIDNAPPED* to the *LITTLE HOUSE* books, have been historical novels, and the genre has continued to attract such distinguished writers as JOAN AIKEN, GILLIAN AVERY, BARBARA COONEY, PETER DICKINSON, LEON GARFIELD, Erik Christian Haugaard, SCOTT O'DELL, KATHERINE PATERSON, K.M. PEYTON, ROSEMARY SUTCLIFF, MILDRED D. TAYLOR, FRANCES TEMPLE, Jill Paton Walsh, ROBERT WESTALL and BARBARA WILLARD.

SIR WALTER SCOTT invented the historical novel in the process of writing *Waverley, or 'Tis Sixty Years Since* (1814). His *Ivanhoe* (1819) and *The Talisman* (1825) were read enthusiastically by young people throughout the 19th century. Although sporadic attempts were made to adapt the new genre for children – most notably HARRIET MARTINEAU's *The Settlers at Home* (1841) and FREDERICK MARRYAT's *The Children of the New Forest* (1847) – CHARLOTTE YONGE first succeeded in radically rethinking it, re-orienting historical perspective in such a way that in *The Little Duke* (1854) and *The Dove in the Eagle's Nest* (1866) a small boy or a teenage girl might occupy its centre. Towards the end of the century, ROBERT LOUIS STEVENSON and RUDYARD KIPLING raised the children's historical novel to classic stature, while Kipling and E. NESBIT infused it with magic to create the first TIME-SLIP FANTASIES. G.A. HENTY's 70-odd volumes delighted boy readers – and girls too, probably – while introducing them to the major military campaigns of history and the concept of Empire. Historical novels by American authors of this period – such as JOHN BENNETT and HOWARD PYLE – often followed British models or, as with MARK TWAIN's *The Prince and the Pauper* (1882), sought consciously to counteract their influence.

In Britain in the middle of the 20th century, the innovations of GEOFFREY TREASE introduced a fresh, modern style and a democratic point of view to a genre that had become fossilised. In his *Thunder of Valmy* (in America, *Victory at Valmy*) (1960), for example, the French Revolution is viewed from the perspective of a peasant boy rather than the usual gallant aristocrat. As early as 1934, when he wrote *Bows Against the Barons*, a retelling of the *ROBIN HOOD* story, he was determined also to show not the glamour of its hero, but the brutal conditions in which the peasants lived. This represented a marked change in the outlook of children's historical fiction, which in the 19th century had worked on the assumption that a middle-class readership would be primarily interested in the lives of the aristocracy. In *The Children of the New Forest*, for example, Marryat had assumed that the reader would share the royalist sympathies of the four children and pity them when they have to leave their mansion and live as ordinary people. In America during the 1920s and 1930s, a group of women writers including ELIZABETH COATSWORTH, RACHEL FIELD, ELIZABETH JANET GRAY, CORNELIA MEIGS and LAURA INGALLS WILDER discovered a new potential in American history and the everyday lives of women and girls. The consequence was that, from the early 1940s to the mid-1960s, historical fiction for children in both Britain and the United States enjoyed a 'golden age', with such writers as Geoffrey Trease, Rosemary Sutcliff, CYNTHIA HARNETT, HESTER BURTON, Stephanie Plowman, HENRY TREECE, ESTHER FORBES, MARGUERITE HENRY, Maud Hart Lovelace, ELOISE JARVIS MCGRAW and ELIZABETH GEORGE SPEARE all at the height of their powers. At about the same time, Laura Ingalls Wilder's autobiographical *Little House* series about the author's own childhood in a pioneer family moving west across the States during the second half of the 19th century tells the reader much about the history of America. In *Little Town On The Prairie* (1941) considerable emphasis is placed on the creation of the United States and Laura has to recite at the School Exhibition a long account of the country's history up to 1825 – thus avoiding the difficult issue of the Civil War.

Although the genre suffered from the anti-historical bias of the 1960s and its popularity subsequently declined, there was a revival in the late 1980s and 1990s, when stories with World War II or 19th-century settings, stories with a frame of family history connecting past and present – such as KATHRYN LASKY's *The Night Journey* and BERLIE DOHERTY's *Granny Was a Buffer Girl* (1986) – and time-slip fantasies such as RUTH PARK's *PLAYING BEATIE BOW* (1980) proved to have wide appeal. In addition, historical novels frequently became a means of illuminating those aspects of history formerly unexplored or forgotten – the lives of servants in an Edwardian household (*Granny Was a Buffer Girl*), factory girls in New England (Katherine Paterson's *Lyddie*, 1991) Chinese immigrants in 1905 San Francisco (LAURENCE YEP's *Dragonwings*, 1975), a 16th-century Cherokee village ravaged by smallpox (Joyce Rockwood's *To Spoil the Sun*, 1976), or a Japanese-American family in a World War II internment camp (YOSHIKO UCHIDA's *Journey to Topaz*, 1971).

It is not surprising, therefore, that authors of historical fiction in the 20th century were at pains to point out that the historical novel is more than just 'costume drama'. Its author seeks 'not only authenticity of fact but . . . a faithful recreation of minds and motives' (*CHILDREN'S LITERATURE IN EDUCATION*, no. 7, 1972). Accordingly, many historical novels have been actively and explicitly concerned with the injustices of history, drawing attention to inhumane customs and unfair practices. Hester Burton rarely shrinks from depicting the cruelty of past times, stating emphatically that 'history is not pretty' and admitting that 'the brutality of times past may shock the over-sensitive' (*HORN BOOK MAGAZINE*, 1969). Her novel *Thomas* (1969), set after the English Civil War, graphically describes the persecution of the Quakers and the horrors of the plague, while *Castors Away* (1972) shows the violence of Navy life in the early 19th century. More recently THERESA TOMLINSON's novels depict a world in which life is dangerous and difficult for the working class, and disease and childbirth bring early deaths to much of the population.

The evils of slavery have been written about by many writers, both British and American. Scott O'Dell's *My Name is Not Angelica* (1989) shows the masters' attempts to control the inner lives of the slaves; JULIUS LESTER's *To Be A Slave* (1968) contains accounts taken from true stories of life as a slave; and PAULA FOX's *The Slave Dancer* (1973) shows how slavery degrades master and slave alike. In MARJORIE DARKE's *The First of Midnight* (1977) parallels are drawn between the life of a slave in England after legislation abolishing slavery, and that of a servant-girl who is bought and sold like a chattel. The aftermath of slavery in America was the subject of MILDRED D. TAYLOR's *ROLL OF THUNDER, HEAR MY CRY* (1976), a moving account of a black family in Mississippi in the 1930s. CYNTHIA VOIGT's *The Runner* (1985) was concerned with the continuing oppression of black Americans in the 1960s.

In Australia, SALLY MORGAN with her autobiographical account, *My Place* (1987) and subsequent retellings of her family's ancestral stories, set the scene for Aboriginal authors to tell of their abduction by welfare officers and exploitation at the hands of an ignorant society, helping to give rise to reconciliation movements, land-rights treaties and a general raising of awareness. ANTHONY HILL provides a moving account of how Aboriginal babies were wrenched from their mothers in *The Burnt Stick* (1994). Australian authors came to acknowledge the disgrace of the treatment of indigenous Australians as something that must be written about with honesty and integrity. *The Rabbits* (1998) by JOHN MARSDEN, illustrated by SHAUN TAN, makes a powerful statement about the brutality of invading colonists towards the aboriginal people and the native environment.

Two distinguished writers of the post-war heyday of historical fiction for children in the United Kingdom were RONALD WELCH and HENRY TREECE, who wrote about Britain, often concentrating with uncompromising realism on its military history. Welch's *Bowman Of Crecy* (1973) describes the deadly effect of the long-bow at the famous battle, while Treece writes of the Vikings' fierce warfare in his *VIKING SAGA* trilogy (1955–60). Best known of writers about early Britain is ROSEMARY SUTCLIFF; her novels cover a wide time-span, from the Bronze Age of *WARRIOR SCARLET* (1958) to the 18th century of *Flame Coloured Taffeta* (1986). JOHN ROWE TOWNSEND has noted that the body of Sutcliff's work has as its subject 'the making of Britain' (*Written For Children*, 5th edition, 1990), showing the gradual integration of the many different races who make up the country's population.

However, not all historical fiction seeks to represent the brutality and injustice of the past. Many authors describe a past in which the difficulties of life without modern conveniences are minimised and the past is portrayed optimistically. The two World Wars in particular have appealed to such writers of historical fiction. RUTH ELWYN HARRIS in *The Dividing Sea* (1989) and MARJORIE DARKE in *A Rose From Blighty* (1990) both show the dreadful injuries witnessed by nurses at the front during World War I, but the overall impression left by both novels is not of the inhumanity of war, but rather of the hope and human feeling that can arise out of tragedy. MICHELLE MAGORIAN's *A Little Love Song* (1991), though set within the realities of the World War II, also describes the liberation which the war brought to two young girls who were able to escape the restrictions of adult authority for the first time. Robert Westall, who set many of his novels during the World War II, presents the period as one of opportunity as well as tragedy; in *The Machine Gunners* (1975) Chas and his friends use the spoils of war to create a world which, like Magorian's, is free, initially at least, from adult supervision.

However, there were also many children's novels about World War II which depicted the terrible impact that the war had upon the lives of children. Judith Kerr's autobiographical trilogy *Out Of The Hitler Time* (1971–8) describes the life of a young Jewish girl who has to flee Nazi Germany. Despite its subject matter, the novels remain optimistic and cheerful, suggesting that children adapt better to such changes than their parents. *Rose Blanche* (1985) by Roberto Innocenti and Christopher Gallaz paints a much bleaker picture; this moving picturebook shows a child who discovers a concentration camp and dies in the attempt to help its inmates. Myron Levoy's *Alan and Naomi* (1977) shows a Jewish girl permanently traumatised by her experience of the Holocaust. *Hiroshima No Pika* (1980) by Toshi Maruki provides in words and pictures a horrifying child's-eye-view of the devastation wrought by the atomic bomb.

In Australia children's writers after World War II reflected a more pluralist society than that represented by earlier writers such as Ethel Turner and Mary Grant Bruce, and gave due consideration to Australia's place in the world community. Ruth Park, David McRobbie, Roland Harvey and Anthony Hill have highlighted the importance of a historical perspective in Australia's move towards self-determination as a nation; this has been particularly true of historical fiction about both World War II and more recent conflicts. Jackie French sets several of her stories in alternating modern and historical settings; *Hitler's Daughter* (1999) moves between modern rural Australia and Germany during the Third Reich, while *Daughter of the Regiment* (1998) maintains the same physical setting, but shifts between contemporary and 19th-century time-frames, a format reminiscent of Park's *Playing Beatie Bow* (1983). Gary Crew's *Mama's Babies* (1998) is also set during Hitler's fascist regime and raises some chilling questions about the nature of human life and the misuse of science. Christobel Mattingley's *Cockawun and Cockatoo* (1999) was inspired by the true story of a man's lifelong friendship with his pet cockatoo in the early part of this century, whereas her *Asmir* series reflects the turmoil in Bosnia in the 1990s. *Captain Mack* (1999) by James Roy, although set in modern suburbia, has the elderly Captain Mack telling Dan about his time as a prisoner of war in Burma during World War II, and these stories still have a place of honour in Australian society, providing another foundation for the Anzac tradition of 'Lest We Forget'. War is also the theme of *Memorial* (1999), a profoundly evocative picturebook suitable for all ages; written by Gary Crew and illustrated by Shaun Tan, this book covers the war experience of four generations of the same family and the significance of the memorials erected to remember the tragedy of conflict.

Australian historical fiction has not confined itself to war stories; growing up in years past has been perceptively captured by Robin Klein, with her 1940s evocations in her series about the Melling sisters, while Anthony Hill's *Growing Up* (1999) gives us windows into the world-views and social mores in Australia in the 1950s, allowing readers to draw comparisons with their own realities in much the same gentle way that Albert Facey and Colin Thiele did a generation before. Nadia Wheatley drew on a true incident for her gripping novel, *The House that was Eureka* (1985), set in the 1930s Depression in Sydney. Wheatley broke new ground with the historical picturebook *My Place* (1987), illustrated by Donna Rawlins, which repeated the same urban streetscape, but moved back a decade on each double-page spread, vividly depicting the social, cultural and physical changes. Other picturebooks also present images of Australia's past, from the extremely accurate and enticing renditions of an Australian corner shop in Ian Edward's *Papa and the Olden Days* (1989) illustrated by Rachel Tonkin, to the always humorously illustrated account of historical events by Roland Harvey in titles such as *Eureka Stockade* (1981) and *The First Fleet* (1982), both written by Alan Boardman.

Many historical novels seek to suggest a continuity between the contemporary reader and the historical characters and achieve this partly by placing a strong emphasis on the physical landscape in which the novel is set, perhaps because landscape changes little over the centuries. *Sarah, Plain And Tall* (1985) by the American author Patricia MacLachlan contrasts the wide prairie landscape with the Maine coast which Sarah herself loves. Rosemary Sutcliff wrote about the 'white horse' that can still be seen on the hillside at Uffington, England, and when Cynthia Harnett wrote about medieval London she described places that can still be found there. Continuity between past and present is also created when historical characters are shown to have been beset by the same worries and preoccupied with the same issues as we are today. Geoffrey Trease explains this as the coming together of two themes; while the first theme is historical, 'the second theme can be modern and highly topical, but suitably transmuted and transferred to another period it helps to give the emotional vitality the story needs.' Hester Burton has described how the emotions she recalled from the summer of 1941 were the same that her characters in *Castors Away* must have experienced at the time of the battle of Trafalgar.

In the late 1990s Australian writers achieved this continuity by using specific historical and geographical settings. *The Stinking Great Lie* (1999) by CATHERINE JINKS, creator of the celebrated *PAGAN* series, is a wonderfully quirky story of a rebellious girl in medieval Italy; however, it addresses human rights and particularly women's rights regarding arranged marriages. David McRobbie's novel *Tyro* (1999) is set in a Scottish dockyard in the 1950s and the language used and customs depicted are true to the times, yet the themes of bullying, unjust working conditions and class distinction are timeless. ALLAN BAILLIE has set many of his books in Southeast Asia, reflecting Australia's place in that region and drawing children's attention to modern events having an impact on people's lives in countries close by. VICTOR KELLEHER's *The Ivory Trail* (1999) alternates between past and present via the channelling quests of young Jamie Hassan which take him into different historical and social contexts and introduce readers to times and worlds they would be unlikely to experience.

Despite the adverse conditions in which their characters may live, some writers take care to ensure that their novels retain a strong sense of humour in order to avoid the charge of didacticism. LEON GARFIELD used the 18th century as a setting for his highly entertaining novels which, below their humorous surface, often examine philosophical issues about the nature of good and evil. The *APPRENTICES* sequence (1976–8) makes particular use of biblical stories and images. KAREN CUSHMAN's *Catherine Called Birdy* (1994) uses the format of a teenager's diary to produce an entertaining account of life in the Middle Ages.

One of the greatest difficulties for the historical novel is that it must convey an authentic sense of period without allowing the plot to be overwhelmed by a mass of detail. A general impression may be given through descriptions of clothing, food and daily routines. GILLIAN AVERY's novels recreate the opppressive and monotonous atmosphere of the Victorian age without describing the setting in minute detail. Many children's authors research their period meticulously to ensure that even inconsequential details are reproduced as accurately as possible. Dialogue can prove a particular obstacle for the author of a historical novel since it must recreate the period convincingly but be intelligible to a contemporary reader. Some writers invert word order to create an archaic yet understandable impression of the past: 'Who's he you're with? Your father? . . . There's none of his ugly mug in you.' (GERALDINE MCCAUGHREAN, *A Little Lower than the Angels*, 1987). Sentences may also be longer and more formal than in a contemporary conversation; 'Could you of your goodness direct me to the house of one master Simon Leach?' a character asks in Cynthia Harnett's *The Wool Pack* (1951). In Barbara Willard's *MANTLEMASS* series, language is used to create a sense of place as well as period. When Cecily arrives in the Sussex Weald she cannot understand the conversation she overhears: 'I come my way by Salehurst . . . and I doddled a bit where they make a goodish warren on stoachy ground.' The reader, like Cecily, is initially bewildered by the strangeness, but grows in understanding of both language and customs as the novel continues.

In 1961 Marion Lochhead wrote: 'History . . . must answer two questions: "What happened then?" and "What were they like?" – the kings and queens, the leaders and warriors, the great and the common folk, old and young in this century or that: the people who caused or witnessed events. Historical fiction should perhaps answer the second question even more fully than the first.' Throughout the English-speaking world and from a variety of shifting ideological perspectives, historical fiction for children continues to address both questions. KA, SR, RTh

see also WAR STORIES

History of Little Jack who was suckled by a goat, The (1787) Story by the English author THOMAS DAY, written in CHAPBOOK style but inspired by ROUSSEAU. Hardiness, versatility and steadfastness are held up as desirable qualities for the young male reader. Despite his deprived upbringing, Little Jack eventually 'makes good' through his cheerful acceptance of adversity. CWB

see also *THE HISTORY OF SANDFORD AND MERTON*

History of Sandford and Merton, The Didactic moral tale by THOMAS DAY first published in three parts in 1783, 1786, and 1789. Day (1748–89) admired ROUSSEAU's educational work *Émile* (1762), and wrote his version of Rousseau's treatise in the form of a book for children. *Sandford and Merton* in fact really consists of a collection of stories woven round two boys, Harry Sandford, an honest farmer's son, and Tommy Merton, the spoiled son of a rich merchant. When Mr. Merton sees what a fine boy Harry is, he sends Tommy to the same tutor, Mr Barlow. Tommy's character then develops through a variety of practical activities, such as when he learns to garden, as well as hearing such stories as *ANDROCLES AND THE LION*, which are then discussed with Mr. Barlow and Harry. Thus Tommy makes moral progress, and finally learns 'how much better it is to be useful than to be rich; how much more amiable to be good than to be great'. Though sometimes criticised for its lack of realism the book was immensely popular throughout the 19th century, and influenced the work of such writers as MARIA EDGEWORTH, whose father was a friend of Day. DB

History of Sixteen Wonderful Old Women see ANECDOTES AND ADVENTURES OF FIFTEEN GENTLEMEN

History of the Fairchild Family, The see MRS SHERWOOD; see also FAMILY STORIES

History of the Robins, The (also variously entitled *The Story of the Robins* or simply *The Robins*), originally *Fabulous Histories* (1786). The most popular work of SARAH TRIMMER, which remained in print throughout the 19th century. Later editions were adorned with exquisite and sometimes coloured engravings, or issued as simplified school versions with monosyllabic texts and large type. In *Fabulous Histories*, subtitled: '*Designed For The Instruction Of Children, Respecting Their Treatment Of Animals*', Mrs Benson instructed her children on 'the welfare of inferior creatures', according to 'the divine principle of general benevolence'. But the robins' own values and domestic economy are recorded through their eyes and this aspect predominates in the posthumous editions. PC

Hitchcock, Alfred see DETECTIVE FICTION

Hitty – Her First Hundred Years (1929) Combined HISTORICAL NOVEL and DOLL STORY by RACHEL FIELD which won the Newbery award. Carved from a six-inch piece of mountain-ash wood in the 1830s, Hitty recounts a life filled with change, incident and peril. Shipwrecked on a whaling voyage; serving as goddess on a Pacific island, snake charmer's fetish in India, and artist's model in New England; dropped at the feet of CHARLES DICKENS; and flung by a conscience-stricken child into the Mississippi, Hitty never loses her calm self-possession or her pleasant expression. Her strong personality and the interestingly varied characters of her girl-owners centre 100 years of cultural and social history firmly within a child's (or doll's) perspective. The real-life Hitty was discovered in an antique shop by Field and her friend DOROTHY P. LATHROP, who collaborated in planning her adventures; Lathrop's ILLUSTRATIONS for the story were among her finest. SR

Hoban, Lillian 1925–98 American writer and illustrator of children's books, known especially for her collaborative work with her former husband, RUSSELL HOBAN, particularly the *Frances* series of books about an anthropomorphic badger family. Born in Philadelphia and trained as an artist, Hoban began her artisitic career in 1961, illustrating *Herman the Loser* and *The Song in My Drum*, both written by Russell Hoban. She went on to illustrate more than 20 of his titles, including *THE MOUSE AND HIS CHILD* (1967), which was an ALA Notable Children's Book. In addition to the more than 70 titles she illustrated for others, Hoban wrote and illustrated over 20 of her own, including the *Arthur* series, centring on Arthur, the chimpanzee, and his little sister, Violet. In the *Frances* books, as well as others, she uses black-and-white pencil drawings and pen-and-ink wash to make the animals shine with the vibrancy of human life. In *The Mouse and His Child*, her black-and-white ILLUSTRATIONS vigorously and sensitively depict the toy wind-ups, making them come alive as they complete their arduous, existential journey toward self-windingness. Through stories about animals and talking toys, Hoban continued to explore the human condition in all its delight and poignancy. JCA

Hoban, Russell (Conwell) 1925– Prolific American writer of experimental fiction for both adults and children, with a cult following of readers crossing the generation gap. Born in Pennsylvania, he trained as an artist. After war service in the US Army in Italy, his work included films, TELEVISION directing, freelance journalism and advertisement copy-writing. In the 1960s, his early books for young children, illustrated by his wife Lillian and known as the *Frances* series (after the little girl-badger heroine), are shrewd, realistic observations of child behaviour of the kind found only in children's books. Frances learns acceptance of how the social world works – bedtime, sisters, family meals and friends – as the animal-adults balance freedom and control. The books provide comforting lessons for young readers in witty, simple sentences and beguiling pictures.

After the appearance and success of *THE MOUSE AND HIS CHILD* (1967), now regarded as his most significant book (not only for the young), Hoban moved to London to be a full-time writer. His recurrent theme is the interchangeability of the real and the imagined, not only in the conventions of fiction – although in storytelling each can stand the other on its head – but as something to be explored in life. In his adult novel *The Turtle Diary* (1975), the heroine, a writer of narrative INFORMATION BOOKS for children, says: 'People write books for children and other people write about the books written for children, but I don't think it's for the children at all. I think that all the people who worry so much about children are really worrying about themselves, about keeping their world together and getting the children to help them do it, getting the children to agree that it is indeed a world.'

Hoban's best PICTUREBOOK texts arise from collaborations with illustrators whom he has inspired to unfold the worlds he imagines. QUENTIN BLAKE suits his cast of mind best. Challenged by the linguistic inventions and the satirical, anti-adult plot of *How Tom Beat Captain Najork and his Hired Sportsmen* (1975) to illustrate the zany 'fooling around' of the TRICKSTER hero, the social background of Aunt Fidget Wonkham-Strong and Captain Najork, and the games of womble, much and sneedball, Blake extends the display of tomfoolery into what is, virtually, a story of its own. Thus Hoban's satire on CAUTIONARY TALES is linked to Blake's version of BELLOC's poems. Hoban's sequel, *A Near Thing for Captain Najork*, appeared a year later but is less well-known. This successful partnership includes, among others, *The Twenty Elephant Restaurant* (1978) and *Ace Dragon Ltd* (1980). The subtleties of *The Rain Door* (1986) – evocations of a heat-wave, depictive success with Hoban's rag-and-bone man and his horse, Lightning, a scrap-heap dinosaur and a rampant, roaring lion – make a visible-audible metaphor for a thunderstorm. In *Monsters*, the postmodernist hero who obsessively draws the monsters gives Blake scope to run the gamut of pictorial monstrosity, while the storyteller and the reader explore the imaginative possibilities of art and literature, the 'what if' which noetic school-learning ignores. In another vein, *M.O.L.E. Much Overworked Little Earthmover* (1993), illustrated by JAN PIEŃKOWSKI, is a teleological sequence which displays both the tough and the tender aspects of Hoban's vision of the history of the world.

It is difficult to catch the essence of Hoban's writing. It slips between powerful insights and experimental voiceovers that link him with Samuel Beckett. He is also preoccupied with small things: artefacts like the clockwork mice in search of a home, and the field-mouse who 'holds the small purse of his life' in the collection of poems *The Pedalling Man* (1969). We see the extraordinary and continuing variety of his work in the powerful adult novel *Ridley Walker* (1980), where children live with dragons and monsters, and *The Trokeville Way* (1996), a story in the rich tradition of maze and wardrobe FANTASIES, where the adolescent hero debates with himself the nature of the real and the imagined in a textual process described by the critic Valentine Cunningham as 'lexical leaks'. *The Last of the Wallendas and other poems* (1997) contains characteristic secrets, mirror images and musings. 'What the Fairy Said to the Bibliophile' sets the 'elderly hero of Anatole France's *The Crime of Sylvestre Bonnard* wondering if the pink-stockinged fairy is really there':

> 'Nothing is real,' she said, (and here's the twist)
> 'except what is imagined; therefore I exist.'

This reiterates Hoban's conviction: 'I know she really is imaginary – that's why she's real.' A comprehensive study of Hoban's work is yet to be written. MM

Hoban, Tana Photographer and author who established standards for excellence in photographic children's books with pioneering publications in the early 1970s. Her books introduce concepts such as dimension, shape, colour, number and currency with gloriously photographed real-life examples. She reveals layers of arrangement, texture and relationships geared to her young readers' cognitive development. Hoban's photographs are usually snapped on the streets of Paris, where she now lives.

A self-supporting artist since 1939, Hoban has published scores of books; many remain in print. She writes the text herself, usually as reinforcement of the abstractions she depicts as opposed to narrative. There are occasional collaborations: *The Wonder of Hands* with Edith Bauer, reissued as a 25th anniversary hardback, and *The Moon Was the Best* with CHARLOTTE ZOLOTOW's poetic prose describing Paris's scenic richness, and several books with her daughter, Miela. In 1992–3, a representative year with long-term publisher Greenwillow, Hoban produced *Spirals, Curves, Fantails, and Lines*, *Look Up, Look Down* and *The Moon Was the Best*. For the first, at a Paris street market she photographed a cockatiel's crest, scallops, loaves of bread, a ferris wheel, and a French horn. In *Look Up, Look Down* she photographed weeds, clothes-lines, birds and other wonders usually above and below our horizontal awareness. These stimulating books have been very popular for decades. AA

Hobberdy Dick see ENGLISH FOLKTALES; K.M. BRIGGS

Hobbit, The (1937) and ***The Lord of the Rings*** (1954–6) Related novels by J.R.R. Tolkien. *The Hobbit* is one of the most original and enjoyable works of FANTASY written for children this century. Middle-Earth contains many types (elves, dwarfs, etc.) commonly found in folklore and MYTHOLOGY, but hobbits, 'a little people, about half our height' without beards and who go unshod on their furry feet, were Tolkien's own brainchild.

The Hobbit recounts the adventures of Bilbo Baggins who is whisked off by 13 dwarves and one wizard to burgle the dragon Smaug. It is a very different kind of work from *The Lord of the Rings* (1954–6), to which it is generally considered a pendant. The work was written for Tolkien's children, and though it is possible especially with the benefit of hindsight to comment on how the shadow of *The Lord of the Rings* is prefigured in the earlier work, the idiom, style, mood and (arguably) structural meaning of *The Hobbit* are in fact reflective or conscious of this younger readership. For *The Hobbit* is a lighter-hearted and more hopeful work, one governed by an ethos of protection which operates on many levels, though this is never made too obvious. Aragorn in *The Lord of the Rings* says, '"Strider" I am to one fat man who lives within a day's march of foes that would freeze his heart, or lay his little town in ruin, if he were not guarded ceaselessly. Yet we would not have it otherwise. If simple folk are free from care and fear, simple they will be, and we must be secret to keep them so.' And while *The Lord of the Rings* reluctantly permits the death of such innocence, *The Hobbit*, like Aragorn, struggles to maintain the simplicity of childhood. The subtitle *There and Back Again* implies a return to the place of beginning. Doubtless, Bilbo changes somewhat during the course of his adventures; from an unimaginative and stodgy hobbit dismayed by the absence of a pocket handkerchief, Bilbo gains in heroic stature as he engages in the riddle game with Gollum, burgles from Smaug and gives up his share of the treasure to Bard and his men. At the end, we are told that he 'took to writing poetry and visiting the elves', this signalling the emergence of a new creativity and imaginative life. But it is also true that the world Bilbo returns to remains essentially tranquil and unaltered; in comparison to the grimness that greets the returning hobbits at the end of *The Lord of the Rings*, the sale of effects that Bilbo comes home to is a brief and minor disruption. The proposed title to Bilbo's own writing of the story: *There and Back Again, a Hobbit's Holiday*, further suggests that Bilbo himself thinks of the Shire as the primary reality and the dark and dangerous world beyond merely as a change of scene. The hobbit/child can always return to the safety of the Shire/home which remains a stable point of reference throughout.

The narrative style also betrays its constant awareness of the child. The voice of the author intrudes every so often, for example, 'Now certainly Bilbo was in what is called a tight place. But you must remember it was not quite so tight for him as it would have been for me or for you.' The direct, relaxed, speaking of adult author to child reader places this within a different register from the mode of high fantasy which marks *The Lord of the Rings*. The author's voice remarks, 'You would have laughed (from a safe distance), if you had seen the dwarfs sitting in the trees', itself establishing that 'safe distance', by the intrusions which serve to remind the reader of the fictionality of the work. The author's voice thus reinforces the safety wards between the child and the dangers of the wargs and would-be cannibals. Gandalf may perhaps be read as the figure of the adult/author within the text, occasionally withdrawing from the action to allow the hobbit/child to learn independence, but returning promptly when there is serious danger.

The songs in the text, even those sung by the evil creatures, are characterised by a certain light humour; their metre and mode is uniformly that of folk BALLAD or NURSERY RHYME, whereas in *The Lord of the Rings* the verse is graver, grander, its style and rhythms reminiscent of Middle English verse and early sagas. The elves, who in *The Lord of the Rings* are creatures of high fantasy, their separate language pointing to their difference, are, in *The Hobbit*, less stately and more playful. Rivendell – later to figure as a citadel against the Black Riders – is here simply a 'homely house'. The world of *The Hobbit,* despite its trolls, spiders and goblins, is thus essentially safe, familiar and English.

The Hobbit is about winning a treasure; *The Lord of the Rings* – written 17 years later for an older audience – is about destroying one, to stop the One Ring, which conveys absolute power to its wielder, from falling again into Sauron's hands. Though Tolkien himself denied it, it is hard not to read the work as a mythologisation of the World Wars. *The Lord of the Rings* has been criticised for the simplicity of its moral scheme, but its power in fact comes from the potential of its characters for both good and evil, the capacity for fall giving point to the moral struggle and choices that the characters have to make. Frodo, the hero of the novel, in fact fails at the crucial moment, and the ring's destruction is accomplished not by him, but by the creature Gollum. The work became a cult book of the fifties and its popularity is as high today as it was when published. The first two volumes were made into an animated film in the 1980s, and the novel has become an archetypal work of the FANTASY genre. SA

Hobbs, Will see NATIVE AMERICANS IN CHILDREN'S LITERATURE

Hoberman, Mary Ann 1930– American writer of over 20 books of children's verse. Her work reflects not only the everyday lives of children but their interests as well. Her verses are usually informative as well as humorous, many through rhythmic wordplay. In *A House is a House for Me* (1978), probably her best-known work, the reader discovers the dwelling-places of humans, animals and objects. More recent titles are *The Seven Silly Eaters* (1997) and *The Llama Who Had No Pajama* (1998), the latter title celebrating 40 years of Hoberman's verse. PDS

Hodges, C(yril) Walter 1909– British illustrator and author, who mostly uses pen-and-ink for his drawings. He is known particularly for his immense scholarship about the Elizabethan stage, winning the KATE GREENAWAY MEDAL in 1964 for his superbly illustrated *Shakespeare's Theatre*. He also chooses historical themes when writing children's stories. These include his fine sequence about Alfred the Great, *The Namesake* (1964) and *The Marsh King* (1967). *The Overland Launch* (1969) tells the true story of how a lifeboat was dragged over a steep hill during a terrible storm last century. Hodges has also illustrated the works of other authors, including ROSEMARY SUTCLIFF and GEOFFREY TREASE. NT

Hodges, Margaret (Moore) 1911– American writer best known for her retellings of FOLKTALES, LEGENDS and classic stories. The Japanese folktale *The Wave* (1965), illustrated by BLAIR LENT, *St George and the Dragon* (1984) and The *Kitchen Knight: A Tale of King Arthur* (1990), both illustrated by TRINA SCHART HYMAN, brought her praise for introducing these and other tales to younger readers. Hodges has produced over 30 books for children. Her retellings of *The Hero of Bremen* (1993), *Gulliver in Lilliput* (1995) and *The True Tale of Johnny Appleseed* (1997) continue to enhance her reputation as a gifted storyteller. PDS

***Hodja* stories** see FOLKTALES AND LEGENDS

Hoff, Syd(ney) 1912– American author and illustrator whose characters, both animal and human, exist side-by-side in situations to which children can relate. He is recognisable by his simple texts and humorous cartoon-style drawings in *Danny and the Dinosaur* (1958), *The Horse in Harry's Room* (1970) and numerous other works for beginning readers. PDS

Hoffman, E.T.A. see ROBERTO INNOCENTI; LISBETH ZWERGER

Hoffman, Mary (Margaret) 1945– British writer born in Hampshire. Though she has also written for adults she is mainly known for some 22 works of children's fiction and her non-fiction *Animals in the Wild* series, of which there are 18 titles. Stressing the uniqueness of each species, these books are what the author calls 'sharply conservationist', and she declares herself a vegetarian who 'cares very much about the way people treat animals'. Each book presents a realistic picture of the creature's place in its wild kingdom, and her canon includes such titles as *Tiger* (1983), *Monkey* (1983), *Elephant* (1983), *Panda* (1983), and *Lion* (1985). Her fictional titles include *Dog Powder* (1989), *Mermaid and Chips* (1989), *Min's First Jump* (1989), *All About Lucy* (1989), *Dracula's Daughter* (1988), and *My Grandma Has Black Hair* (1988), the latter intended to update contemporary thinking about ageing. Hoffman's *Nancy No-Size* was shortlisted for the SMARTIES PRIZE in 1987 and she has served as reading consultant for the BBC school TELEVISION series *Look and Read* since 1977. KSB

Hoffmann, Heinrich 1809–94 German doctor and lunatic asylum superintendent, best-remembered as the author of *Lustige Gesichten und drollige Bilder*, [Merry stories and funny pictures] (1845), published in an anonymous English translation in 1848 as *STRUWWELPETER*, a popular book of CAUTIONARY VERSE, both unintentionally funny and horrifying. ML

Hofmeyr, Dianne 1947– Writer of youth novels and books for young children that are intensely South African in setting and theme while feelingly portraying the angst of growing up. *When Whales Go Free* (1988) takes a conservationist view of whaling at the Cape a hundred years ago through the dilemma of a sensitive boy who discovers the brutality of his family's occupation as whalers. *A Red Kite in a Pale Sky* (1990) is an unsentimental, bleak story featuring a little boy in a flood. *A Sudden Summer* (1987), about a white girl learning to empathise with the sufferings of people of other races, enjoys continued popularity with young teenage girls, probably because it is also a good love story. Two others are written as the diaries of teenagers in inner-city Johannesburg. *Blue Train to the Moon* (1993), a predictable story of a girl facing the possibilities of pregnancy and AIDS, had a good reception. In its highly skilled successor, *Boikie You Better Believe It* (1994), which won the M-Net Prize, Hofmeyr balances the humour of a boy and his eccentric father and friends with the ghastliness of urban terrorism. Her charming PICTUREBOOKS, such as *The Magical Mulberry Blanket* (1991), feature African children in humorous plots which carry a reassuring lesson. ERJ

Hogarth, Anne see *MUFFIN THE MULE*

Hogrogian, Nonny 1932– American author-illustrator of children's PICTUREBOOKS. She won the CALDECOTT MEDAL for *Always Room for One More* (1965), a story by SORCHE NIC LEODHAS, and for *One Fine Day* (1971), her own retelling of an old FOLKTALE. She also received a Caldecott Honour citation for *The Contest* (1976), also based on a folktale. A prolific illustrator, she has collaborated with her husband, David Kherdian, also a writer, on numerous books, and she is especially attracted to the folktale. Her ILLUSTRATIONS, typically watercolours, are noted for their quiet beauty and their assiduous attention to detail. DLR

Holbrook, David see *CHRONICLES OF NARNIA*; see also CHILD AUTHORS

Holcroft, Anthony 1932– New Zealand writer who in his first collection of stories, *Tales of the Mist* (1987), introduced New Zealand children to a literary, elegant combination of traditional western FAIRY TALE motifs and archetypes (such as goblins and making wishes), and local landscapes. This approach is already evident in his first PICTUREBOOK, *The Old Man and the Cat* (1984), which is about the importance of living in harmony with nature – a prevailing theme in Holcroft's work. *Chen Li and the River Spirit* (1990), about a man who plants trees and saves his valley, won Holcroft the International Reading Association's Paul

Illustration by Quentin Hole from *Dancing Phoebe and the Famous Mumblegum Piano.*

A. Witty Award. A later collection, *The White Bird and Other Stories* (1995) is a mixed success; adult and children's stories sit uneasily side by side, while the folktale elegance gives way at times to a more prolix style. BN

Hole, Quentin 1923–99 Australian illustrator whose work for the theatre as a costume and set designer made him an admirable choice as illustrator for A. B. (Banjo) Paterson's bush ballads, *The Man from Ironbark* (1974) – for which he was awarded the Children's Book Council of Australia Picture Book of the Year – and *A Bush Christening* (1976). Hole fleshes out the story line with authentic period costume and detail and strong characterisation. For his own text, *How to Demolish a Monster* (1981), he recreates a lush Queensland landscape in which two youths enter Bunyip territory, but returns with gusto to a period setting for his tall story, *Dancing Phoebe and the Famous Mumblegum Piano* (1987). MSax

Holes (US, 1998; UK, 2000) Novel by the popular American author Louis Sachar (1954–). *Holes* begins as a realistic account of a boy wrongly sentenced to a spell in a correction centre in Texas. Like Stanley Yelnats's palindromic name, the narrative moves back into the past as it moves forward. The punishment imposed requires each boy to dig a single hole five feet deep and five feet across in the floor of a dried-up lake – and to report any unusual find. The uncompromising account of the brutal life at the centre is undercut by accounts of Stanley's forebears, especially a curse placed upon the family because of the conduct of a 'no-good-dirty-rotten-pig-stealing-great-great-grandfather'. However, the narrative turns into a fast-paced thriller as the sinister purpose of the jailers is gradually realised. He and his friend, Zero – believed to be innumerate and illiterate and named 'because there's nothing inside his head' – escape into the desert where Stanley's humble and unselfconscious heroism at last cancels the family curse. Narrative strands from American history, family folklore and Stanley's own experience are brilliantly brought together to conclude this complex novel about social justice, friendship and redemption.

Sachar is the author of a number of other works extremely popular with younger readers, notably the *Marvin Redpost* stories and *Wayside School* stories. In the first of the latter, *Sideways Stories from Wayside School* (1978), 30 zany stories are told about the children on the top floor of a 30-storey school; the stories are short, funny, full of puns, weird magic and eccentric children – and the last story is about Louis the yard teacher, narrator (and author?). In *Dogs Don't Tell Jokes* (1978) the hero – an inveterate and irritating joker – achieves his ambition of winning a school contest as a stand-up comedian. *There's a Boy in the Girl's Bathroom* (1987) addresses with characteristic humour the difficulties of a school misfit and his relationship with a school counsellor. VW

see also School Stories

Holiday House (1839) Moral tale by Catherine Sinclair (1800–64). Written, the preface says, in protest against the prevalence of utilitarian children's books, *Holiday House* is about the Graham children. After their mother's death, their father is ordered abroad, and Frank, Lucy and Harry are left in the care of their grandmother and uncle David. When Harry and Lucy get into various scrapes – Lucy cuts off her ringlets and Harry sets the nursery on fire – they are not punished but treated with a degree of forgiveness unusual for the time. The turning-point comes when, after Harry has locked himself in a room and broken the key, their uncle David tells the children a nonsensical story about Giants and Fairies. Though the tale is humorously told, it makes a moral point, and from then on the book becomes increasingly religious, as the children learn of war and poverty, and witness the fatal illness of brother Frank. The story was extremely popular, and J. Harvey Darton (3rd edition, 1982) called it 'the best original children's book published up to that time' Though *Holiday House* is a didactic tale, it is often light-hearted, with the children's mischief realistically portrayed, and treated with unusual tolerance for the period. DB

Holkham Bible Picture Book (c. 1325–30) A unique manuscript in the British Museum. It is a GRAPHIC TEXT composed of stories from the Bible and including much apocryphal material, particularly about the childhood of Christ. Commissioned by a Dominican, from a teaching order active among the London guilds, it was probably paid for by a wealthy Londoner in the building trade. The sketchy, simple Anglo-Norman text, which runs in several lines above the top of each of the 40 pictures, indicates that the book was intended for a semi-literate audience, presumably including children. The Dropmore Press published a printed facsimile in 1954. GA

Holland, Isabelle 1920– American novelist, born in Basle, Switzerland. While Isabelle Holland has written novels for various ages and about a number of different historical periods, she is best known as one of the most prolific and challenging writers of YOUNG ADULT FICTION. Her novels address some of the typical major issues of the problem novel of the last few decades (such as alcoholism, homosexuality and eating disorders), yet, as critics have pointed out, she rarely deals with such issues simplistically and the 'problem' in each novel is always subordinate to her concern for realistic characterisations and complex, often unresolved plots.

Her use of characters and settings as symbols – the disfiguration of the titular *Man Without a Face* (1972) as a Hawthornean 'black veil' for the disgraced homosexual, a school production of *Antigone* as a text of the conflicting parental loyalties Melissa experiences in *Heads You Win, Tails You Lose* (1973), and a decaying Italy as metaphor for Meg's dying mother in *Of Love and Death and Other Journeys* (1975) – are often rather heavy-handed for adult readers; for the yong adult, they seem appropriate introductions to the idea that texts may possess possibilities beyond the literal.

Holland typically chooses a first-person narrator for her novels, and, while these narrators sometimes seem to possess a vocabulary and a frame of cultural allusions beyond the typical young adult reader, their emotions and psychology feel authentically adolescent: the reader will either identify with outsider storytellers or gain empathy for their situation. Her heroes – while often caught in difficult situations not of their own making (for example, Meg's mother is dying in *Of Love and Death and Other Journeys*, Charles's parents have separated long before the novel begins in *Man Without a Face*, and Melissa's mother's history as an alcoholic in *Heads You Win, Tails You Lose*) – never abdicate their own responsibility for their actions and for creating their own happiness and their own futures. *The Man Without a Face* was made into a feature film two decades after its publication, directed by actor Mel Gibson and starring him as the disfigured Justin McLeod of the title; unfortunately, all mention or suggestion of McLeod's homosexuality and his brief sexual relationship with teenage Charles, the novel's narrator, was omitted. While it is true that Holland's novel is first and foremost a story about the rite-of-passage from childhood to adult of a troubled youth with the help of a difficult, but ultimately loving adult, and not a story of child molestation, the movie ultimately lacks the courage of Holland's novel. BH

see also GAY AND LESBIAN LITERATURE

Hollindale, Peter see CHILDNESS; see also CHILDIST CRITICISM; CRITICAL APPROACHES TO CHILDREN'S LITERATURE

Holloway, David see REVIEWING AND REVIEWERS

Holloway, Stanley see ANIMATED CARTOONS; *THE LION AND ALBERT*

Holm, Ann see *I AM DAVID*; ADVENTURE STORIES; WAR STORIES

Holman, David British dramatist who has specialised in work for the Young People's Theatre and Theatre in Education companies. Holman's work has always been thematically strong and issue-based, and he is committed to engaging children's interest in international political and moral conflicts. *No Pasaran*, first performed in 1977, is typical of his earlier work. An anti-fascist play, it enacts the life of a Jewish boxer whose ambition to fight at the 1936 Olympics is thwarted by the Nazis. Some of Holman's more recent plays have dealt with ecological and conservationist concerns. They include *Whale*, based on the 1988 rescue of grey whales trapped under the Arctic icecap, and *Solomon's Cat*, about the plight of leopards in Tanzania. PH

Holman, Felice 1919– American author of stories and poetry, best known for her stories of children surviving despite momentous obstacles. Though her novels deal with situations alien to her readers, the characters share goals common to the reader in their struggles to grow up and live peacefully. Her most popular novels are *Slake's Limbo* (1974) and *Secret City, USA* (1990), focusing on homeless children, and *The Wild Children* (1983), about wandering gangs of homeless children in the early days of the Soviet Union. Characters, and readers, learn how crucial family is, even family found in an alternative close-knit community. LAW

Holub, Miroslav 1923–98 Celebrated Czech poet, some of whose uncompromising poems first appeared for British readers in Geoffrey Summerfield's *JUNIOR VOICES*. Several poems by Holub are regularly anthologised, especially 'A Boy's Head' and 'The Door', encouraging children to observe their relations with their environment, and to write with a due and scrupulous weirdness. Holub, the poet-scientist, understands that both poetry and science begin in intense looking. He observes until it hurts, and his poetry is, in the profoundest sense, a liberating teacher: a 'day . . . so bright / that even birdcages flew open' ('A Dog in the Quarry'). FRBS

Holy Grail see KING ARTHUR; see also *ELIDOR*

Homer, Winslow 1836–1910 One of the greatest 19th-century American artists and illustrators. As a young man he was apprenticed briefly to a Boston lithographer and then became a freelance illustrator for periodicals in Boston and New York. Many of his early ILLUSTRATIONS for young people were contributions to children's books and periodicals published as part of the boom in publishing for children that arose with the Sunday School movement. These publications, though sometimes heavy-handed in their didactic moralism, were loved by children and contributed greatly to the development of the audience for children's books in America. Homer's pictures for such books as *The Eventful History of Three Little Mice and How They Became Blind* (1858, 1996) showed his wit and lively line to good advantage. Homer's illustrations for luxury collections of poetry were also among his most influential works. Particularly notable are his pictures for LONGFELLOW's *Excelsior* (1877) and Lowell's *The Courtin'* (1874). Such poetry-collection illustrations helped fuel the American desire for relatively inexpensive, luxuriously illustrated books that has persisted in the children's PICTUREBOOK market to the present time. Although Homer later abandoned illustration work, his depictions of children at play and at school in paintings such as *Snap the Whip* have become classic images, much reproduced and imitated in children's literature, especially his barefoot boys. JS

Honey [Clarke], Elizabeth (Madden) 1947– Australian illustrator and author of PICTUREBOOKS and novels, known for her versatility of styles in information texts, and for her early illustrations for writers MORRIS LURIE and CHRISTOBEL MATTINGLEY. Honey's first picturebook, the colourful *Princess Beatrice and the Rotten Robber* (1988), is about a pint-sized, jewel-bedecked, tough heroine who outwits her slow-witted, brawny kidnapper. The princess finds a contemporary new image in Honey's resourceful 'princess in a Sydney penthouse' character, Bean, in *What Do You Think, Feezal?* (1997), the third of Honey's junior novels. As with her two Children's Book Council of Australia Honour Books, *45 & 47 Stella Street: and everything that happened* (1995), and *Don't Pat the Wombat* (1996), beneath the zany characters, the slapstick style, the contemporary idiom and the handwritten annotations there are deeper, sometimes sinister aspects of people and their behaviour. The former title won Honey the Italian Premio Cento Award in 1998, and the Stella Street gang reappeared in *Fiddleback* (1998), with the indomitable narrator, Henni, leading a battle to stop the milling of rainforest timber. The 1997 Children's Book Council of Australia Picture Book of the Year Award for *Not a Nibble* (1996) is a confirmation of Honey's ability to capture what is important to children. JAP

Hood, Thomas 1799–1845 English poet and journalist. His poems are humorous and satirical, making ingenious use of puns. His much-anthologised poems for children were collected posthumously in *Fairy Land* (1861). He is best known for 'I remember, I remember', 'November', and his parody of ANN TAYLOR's 'My Mother'. ML

Hook see STEVEN SPIELBERG; see also *PETER PAN*

Hop o' my Thumb FAIRY TALE included in *Histoires ou contes du temps passé* (1697) (see CONTES DE MA MÈRE L'OYE) by CHARLES PERRAULT, originally entitled 'Le Petit Poucet'. It is the story of the youngest son of seven, Hop, who saves his brothers from getting lost in the woods by leaving a trail as well as saving them all from an ogre by tricking him into killing his seven ogress daughters instead. Hop steals the ogre's seven-league boots and makes his fortune. The term Hop o' my Thumb (hop on my thumb) was common in the 16th century but was used as the title to this story only in the 19th century; until then the story was known as 'Little Poucet' or 'Little Thumb'. There are parallels with *Hansel and Gretel* (see also the GRIMM BROTHERS) as well as with the 16th-century story 'Schwankbücher'. JHD

Hope, Anthony see ADULT FICTION; see also *THE LOST PRINCE*

Hope, Laura Lee see *BOBBSEY TWINS* SERIES; see also FAMILY STORIES

Horder, Margaret (L'Anson) 1903–78 Australian illustrator. After gaining experience as an illustrator of children's books with Oxford University Press in London, Horder returned to Australia and quickly made a reputation as a careful and meticulous artist. Her ability to draw children in their many moods, and her feel for the Australian landscape, made her the ideal illustator for the early novels of NAN CHAUNCY, JOAN PHIPSON and PATRICIA WRIGHTSON. Her delicate yet firm drawings of country children and all manner of animal life, and her ability to draw places such as Sydney's Rocks area, along with her knowledge of book design, helped give elegance to the emerging Australian children's novel in the 1950s and 60s. MSax

Horn Book Magazine, The 1924– Bimonthly journal for professionals working with children, published in Boston, Massachusetts, since 1924. The founder and first editor, BERTHA MAHONY MILLER, wrote in her first issue, 'We are publishing this sheet to blow the horn for fine books for boys and girls–their authors, their illustrators, and their publishers.' The name is also a tribute to the historic ALPHABET BOOKS created by educators for children to use. Acknowledged as the venerable first professional journal on children's books and reading, the *Horn Book* arose from a newsletter written for Miller's bookstore, 'The Bookshop for Boys and Girls', located near the Public Garden in Boston. The magazine is primarily a reviewing journal of recommended titles, with additional essays, news and information on children's literature. Subseqent editors have maintained the initial commitment to good literature. Since 1967, the magazine has co-sponsored THE BOSTON GLOBE-HORN BOOK AWARDS for excellence in children's literature, covering fiction, non-fiction, and PICTUREBOOKS. In 1990, the magazine launched a second publication, *The Horn Book Guide,* a semi-annual review of most hardcover trade books published in the United States for children and young adults. AL

Hornblower NOVELS see LITERATURE WITHIN CHILDREN'S LITERATURE; see also ADULT FICTION

hornbooks and battledores The hornbook was amongst the earliest tools in the teaching of reading from at least the 16th century. It was usually a paddle-shaped piece of wood with a handle, often containing a hole for twine or ribbon. To the paddle was attached a letterpress sheet on which was printed the alphabet, in both upper and lower case, and the five vowels, followed by a short syllabarium and the Lord's Prayer. It might also contain the nine digits. The paper was covered by a thin sheet of horn. The alphabet was usually preceded by a cross, and this came to be known as the Criss-Cross Row. The hornbook's shape was convenient for patting objects from one inattentive scholar to another, and thus it was often called a 'battledore', a name transferred to a modification of the hornbook, invented by Salisbury publisher Benjamin Collins; this was an oblong piece of card approximately 13 x 20 cms folded into three leaves, the third leaf being half the width of the other two. Printed on both sides, it contained an alphabet, and often a syllabarium, one or more sentences or rhyming couplets, and was illustrated with cuts. Collins printed 100,000 between 1771 and 1780. Their popularity led to other provincial publishers following his lead. PG

Horne, Richard Henry see DOLL STORIES; FANTASY; NEGLECTED WORKS

Horowitz, Anthony 1955– English author of TELEVISION and radio programmes and books for children. *Groosham Grange* (1988) (Lancashire Book Award, 1990, and Prix Européen), *Granny* (1994) and *The Switch* (1996) are gruesomely funny accounts of what he describes as the deprivations of his affluent childhood. *The Falcon's Malteser* (1986), *Public Enemy Number 2* (1987), and *South by South East* (1991) are a series of self-deprecatingly British parodies of hard-boiled American DETECTIVE FICTION, set in unglamorous South London and narrated by a 13-year-old schoolboy. The narrative is sharp and witty, the plots are complex and exciting, and there are some memorable one-liners. RC

Horrible Histories (from 1993) Popular British series of INFORMATION BOOKS by Terry Deary et al. Books in this unusual series (e.g. *Awesome Egyptians, Terrible Tudors, Rotten Romans*) not only give the gory facts missing from most history lessons but also give a flavour of what life was like for ordinary people – the food, clothes, education – together with the major events and personalities of the periods covered. Through jokes and puzzles children can compare their lives with those of their historical counterparts. They are encouraged to weigh evidence, differentiate between fact and legend and make up their own minds as to what really happened. Throughout, children are encouraged to see that they, just like the adult professionals, are historians too. AMN

horse stories The American horse story developed in the 1930s as a distinctive type of animal story, achieving great popularity in the 1940s and 50s. The protagonist may be either a horse – often wild – or, more commonly, a human being whose relationship with a horse is the main focus of the story. These fictional horses are not endowed with speech or anthropomorphic thought-processes. After Will James's pioneering NEWBERY MEDAL winner, *SMOKY, THE COWHORSE* (1926), came STEPHEN MEADER's *Red Horse Hill* (1930), the first story to develop the 'boy and his horse' theme, and Colonel S.P. Meek's *Frog: The Horse That Knew No Master* (1933), the first to feature an outlaw horse tamed by love and patience into a friend. The numerous authors of the 1940s and 50s included C.W. ANDERSON, Paul Brown, Glenn Balch, Fairfax Downey, Walter Farley, MARGUERITE HENRY, Dorothy Lyons, and MARY O'HARA, author of the *Flicka* trilogy. Horse stories were often crossbred with regional or HISTORICAL FICTION, as with Henry's *Misty of Chincoteague* (1947) and *King of the Wind* (1948). The horse story's popularity collapsed in the 1960s, although a writer such as Lynn Hall can still evoke its strong emotional potential, and such paperback series as *The Saddle Club* still attract many girl readers. SR

see also PONY STORIES; ANIMALS IN CHILDREN'S FICTION

Horwood, William see *DUNCTON CHRONICLES*

Hotspur see *'THE BIG FIVE'*

Hounds of The Morrigan, The (1985) Children's FANTASY by Pat O'Shea (1931–) entwining figures from IRISH MYTHOLOGY AND FOLKLORE with modern characters. In some ways similar to Jenny Nimmo's *SNOW SPIDER* TRILOGY and ALAN GARNER'S *WEIRDSTONE OF BRISINGAMEN*, the story revolves around Patrick Joseph ('Pidge', a corruption of 'P.J.') and his sister Bridget. He discovers an old manuscript in his town bookshop and this magical book moves the characters into a world which alternates between dreams and reality, with witch-like villains, talking frogs and the Hounds which can resemble people. SET

House at Pooh Corner see *WINNIE-THE-POOH*

House in Norham Gardens, The (1974) Novel by PENELOPE LIVELY about the links between an Oxford house and a tribe in New Guinea, based around a ceremonial shield which had once belonged to the tribe but was brought back to England by Clare's great-grandfather, an anthropologist. Most of the book is set firmly in North Oxford in the early 1970s, but there are also dream passages showing the life of the tribe and its gradual westernisation. The cold greyness of wintertime Oxford forms a marked contrast with the vitality of New Guinea which gradually seems to infuse the house in Norham Gardens. KA

House Like a Lotus, A see *WRINKLE IN TIME, A*

House that Jack Built, The Cumulative NURSERY RHYME which was first published, in CHAPBOOK form, by JOHN NEWBERY, in the mid-18th century. The rhyme has remained popular as successive generations of writers and illustrators have sought to parody and redefine it in terms appropriate to their times. Among the most recent are PICTUREBOOK interpretations by Jenny Stow (1992) – a Caribbean version – and John Yeoman and QUENTIN BLAKE's *The Do-it-Yourself House that Jack Built* (1994), which exploit the potential for counterpoint between text and ILLUSTRATIONS in humorous and inventive ways. In this they are following in the tradition of RANDOLPH CALDECOTT, whose outstanding Shilling Book version, published in 1878, was one of the series of picturebooks he created for EDMUND EVANS which influenced the development of the form so significantly. The rhythm and cumulative nature of the rhyme have prompted picturebooks on a range of themes: for instance, *The World that Jack Built* (RUTH BROWN, 1990), *This is the Bear* (Sarah Hayes and Helen Craig, 1986), *The House that Jack Built* (COLIN AND JACQUI HAWKINS, 1990) and *BRINGING THE RAIN TO KAPITI PLAIN* (VERNA AARDEMA and Beatris Vidal, 1986). Their numerous antecedents, which include political and topical parodies, are listed by IONA AND PETER OPIE in *The Oxford Dictionary of Nursery Rhymes* (1951). The view that the rhyme derives from a Hebrew chant, *Had Gadyo*, first published in 1590, has been disputed by the Opies although they do not doubt its age; European equivalents substantiate claims for its antiquity. MSut

Household, Geoffrey see *SPANISH CAVE, THE*

Housman, Laurence 1865–1959 British writer, illustrator and painter. Housman designed books with great care to unify word and image, and through them revived the style of wood-engraved illustration of the 1860s. He made his name with intense, claustrophobic designs for CHRISTINA ROSSETTI's *GOBLIN MARKET* (1893), which were presented in a long, slim format which would typify the Art Nouveau book. From 1894 he decorated a number of his own stories, beginning with *A Farm in Fairyland*, and gradually abandoned art for writing. His later illustrative work included

MACDONALD's *At the Back of the North Wind* and *The Princess and the Goblin* (both 1900). DW

see also WOOD ENGRAVING

Houston, James A. 1921– Canadian writer and illustrator. Born in Toronto, Houston received special instruction at the Toronto Art Gallery and after studies in Canada and abroad began a commercial art business in Quebec. In 1948 a chance trip to a remote native community near Hudson Bay turned into his life's adventure. For the next 14 years the Inuit taught him survival skills and demonstrated their carving artistry, which Houston exhibited and marketed in Canadian cities. He also promoted the creation of government-subsidised workshops to develop native art as a cottage industry. Houston served as a government administrator on West Baffin Island over widely spread Inuit camps, where he observed STORYTELLING performances of adventures and LEGENDS that would be the substance of his fiction. In 1962 he left the Arctic to work in design for the Steuben Glass company and also began to write and illustrate children's stories that were based on native lore that he had gathered in the north and across Canada.

Many of Houston's 15 books were award-winners. His first work, *Tikta'liktak* (1965), sets the pattern for a group of books that are essentially mythic interpretations of real adventures. The narrative focuses on an adolescent hero who embarks on a quest that is of crucial importance to the survival of his family or community and that also tests the protagonist's readiness to take his place as an adult provider in the group. Four other books about ordeals in the Arctic – *The White Archer* (1967), *Akavak* (1968), *Wolf Run* (1971) and *Long Claws* (1981) – include tests of moral courage that arise in man's relationships with his fellows, or portrayals of how men and animals offer each other mutual support to overcome a harsh environment. Houston's adventures about Indian life – *Eagle Mask* (1966) and *Ghost Paddle* (1972) – explore the climate of rival hatred among coastal tribes of British Columbia in times past and offer a message of brotherhood and peace as a recourse of spiritual and moral survival. In the mid-1970s, in several young adult novels, he tackled the problem of cross-cultural interaction. The books were thematically and structurally patterned on a similar concept, that of the growth of mutual understanding between a native teenager and a white youth from southern Canada. A trilogy of novels – *The Frozen Fire* (1977) and its two sequels, *Black Diamonds* (1982) and *Ice* Swords (1985) – uses a contemporary context to examine the impact of modem technology on Inuit culture. *River Runners* (1979), set in the 1940s, explores economic exploitation in trade relations between natives and whites.

Houston's books have revitalised the Canadian survival story through his informative, terse style and his unique treatment of original sources. His ILLUSTRATIONS evoke the immediacy and intensity of Eskimo sculpture. The value of his work, beyond its artistic and literary qualities, lies in its impact as a cultural bridge between two worlds with very different sets of values. DAC

see also NATIVE AMERICANS IN CHILDREN'S LITERATURE; YOUNG ADULT FICTION

Houston, Libby 1941– English poet who has published both adult poems and an accomplished children's collection, *All Change!* (1993). Many of these carefully crafted poems were written for schools radio and contain a wide variety of different moods, voices and forms, including songs, long narrative poems, nonsense and JOKES. Houston often draws on myths and legends for inspiration. Poems such as the title piece, 'All Change!', and 'Black Dot', a 'catalogue' of what makes a frog, written entirely in kennings, have become deservedly popular anthology pieces. ML

see also CLASSICAL MYTHOLOGY; FOLKTALES AND LEGENDS

Howarth, Lesley Prize-winning British novelist whose first book, *The Flower King* (1993), met with immediate critical acclaim. Many of her books, although set in a recognisable world, contrast the clear-cut world of SCIENCE FICTION with the emotional complexities of human life. Her work, which takes a humorous look at human foibles, shows people being preoccupied with the same concerns, wherever and whenever they live. In *Maphead* (1994) – winner of the *GUARDIAN* AWARD – a boy from another planet struggles to understand human feelings, while *Weather Eye* (1995), a powerful novel about the millennium, stresses the importance of friendship and trust between teenagers working together to combat global warming. *Paulina* (1999) is a GHOST STORY written with Howarth's characteristic chilling precision. KA

Howe, James 1946– American author. Howe cowrote *Bunnicula: A Rabbit Tale of Mystery* (1979) with his late wife, Deborah. This title and its sequels continue to be in demand. Howe is also the author of a series of books for younger children, *Pinkie and Rex* (from 1990), which deals humorously with the ups and downs of friendship. His mysteries for older readers are as popular as his PICTUREBOOKS, including *There's a Monster Under My Bed* (1986). His non-fiction includes *The Hospital Book* (1981), which continues to be a valuable resource in preparing children for a hospital experience. PDS

Howitt, Mary 1799–1888 Prolific English writer who often collaborated in publishing with her husband, William. She was highly regarded in literary circles in her day and was a friend of CHRISTINA ROSSETTI. She was largely responsible for bringing HANS CHRISTIAN ANDERSEN to London shortly after the publication of his FAIRY TALES. Howitt wrote a great number of books for children. Her verse often focuses on nature and her most famous poem, 'The Spider and the Fly' appeared in a collection entitled, *Sketches from Natural History* (1834). MCCS

Howker, Janni 1957– British author, widely acclaimed as a rising star on the appearance of her first book. Howker was brought up and still lives in northern England. All her work is strongly regional. After doing various jobs, she took an MA in creative writing and in 1984 published *BADGER ON THE BARGE*, a collection of short stories. This and a novel, *THE NATURE OF THE BEAST* (1985), won numerous awards and had TELEVISION and film adaptations respectively, but her sombre third and fourth books, *Isaac Campion* (1986) and *Martin Farrell* (1994), suggest that she might be moving away from the children's list. JRT

Huck, Charlotte 1922– Noted American scholar of children's literature whose textbook *Children's Literature in the Elementary School* has been respected since the 1960s. During her 30-year career at Ohio State University, Huck received many honours and awards, including the first endowed professorship in children's literature in the United States. Huck made her mark as a children's book writer with an elegant retelling of *Princess Furball* (1989), a variant of the CINDERELLA story with a strong female protagonist. *Toads and Diamonds* (1996), Huck's crisp re-telling of PERRAULT's *The Fairies* presents another spirited female in the younger sister, Renee. Both stories were illustrated by ANITA LOBEL. Huck is the recipient of the Arbuthnot Award for excellence in teaching children's literature. JAT

Huckleberry Finn see *ADVENTURES OF TOM SAWYER, THE*

Huckleberry Hound see *TOM AND JERRY*

Hughes, Arthur 1832–1915 British painter and illustrator influenced by the Pre-Raphaelites and popular for his tender depiction of children. He illustrated the work of authors whose acquaintance he made through Christian Socialist connections. In Thomas Hughes's *TOM BROWN'S SCHOOLDAYS* (1869 edition), expressive pose, dense composition and dramatic lighting lend emotional intensity to the scenes. His debt to Dante Gabriel Rossetti is evident in the swirling tresses of North Wind in GEORGE MACDONALD's *At the Back of the North Wind* (1871) and his drawings for CHRISTINA ROSSETTI's *SING-SONG* (1872) combine detailed observation from nature with sentimental simplicity in the human figure. PC

Hughes, Langston 1902–67 African American poet, fiction writer, playwright, anthologist and essayist. Hughes's first fame was as a Harlem Renaissance poet. Although he wrote only one book of poetry specifically for young readers, *The Dream Keeper* (1932), much of his poetry appeals to children, as the posthumous collection *Don't Turn Back* (1969) attests. Most of Hughes's books for children were histories. Only *Popo and Fifina: Children of Haiti* (1932), a tale co-authored with ARNA BONTEMPS, and the posthumous book of aphorisms, *Black Misery* (1969), belong to other genres. The best of his historical work are BIOGRAPHIES of famous African Americans – *Famous American Negroes* (1954) and *The First Book of Negroes* (1952) – and introductions to African American music, *Negro Music Makers* (1955) and *The First Book of Jazz* (1955). These works, written during the civil rights era, aimed to provide African Americans with history, heritage and role models. Hughes's most enduring work for children, however, is his poetry. Because of his simple diction and musical rhythms, most of his poems appeal equally to children and adults. DWR

Hughes, Monica 1925– One of Canada's most distinguished authors, best known for her SCIENCE FICTION. Hughes was born in Liverpool and educated in England and Scotland, having spent her first six years in Egypt. She settled in Canada in 1952 and subsequently developed a reputation for skilfully paced narratives and a distinctively lucid and contemplative prose.

Perhaps informed by the Canadian pioneering consciousness, Hughes's fiction explores the many aspects of isolation and alienation in vast wilderness landscapes (the ADVENTURES STORY *Hunter in the Dark*, 1982); conflicts between traditional and technological cultures (*Ring-Rise, Ring-Set*, 1982); futuristic dystopian and utopian societies (*Beyond the Dark River*, 1979, and *Invitation to the Game*, 1990); the consequences of environmental recklessness (*The Crystal Drop*, 1992); the dangers of totalitarianism (*The Tomorrow City*, 1978) and the ethical implications of plundering the resources of another planet for the needs of Earth (*The Golden Aquarius*, 1995).

Hughes is best known for two sequences: the *Isis* trilogy (*The Keeper of the Isis Light*, 1980, *The Guardian of Isis*, 1981, *The Isis Pedlar* 1982); and *Devil on My Back* (1984) and its sequel *The Dream Catcher* (1986). In these, Hughes explores her favourite themes – social isolation and prejudice; cultural differences; and the courage, idealism and good sense of young people and their capacity for friendship. Her stories are never mechanistic, her characters are well-rounded and

Illustration from *Enchantment in the Garden* by Shirley Hughes.

engaging, and her surface realism is often enriched by an underlying symbolism. VW

Hughes, Richard (Arthur Warren) 1900–74 A novelist who occasionally wrote for children, Hughes's best known work, *A High Wind in Jamaica* (1929) is about rather than for the young. But *The Spider's Palace and Other Stories* (1931), a collection of 20 magical tales, has some of the quirky appeal later found in the fantasies of ROALD DAHL. *Don't Blame Me* (1940) is another collection of tales, arising from stories Hughes told young evacuees billeted on the family home during the war. Never predictable and always retaining a power to disturb, everything Hughes writes is of interest, whether for children or adults. NT

Hughes, Shirley 1927– Distinguished British illustrator and picturebook author. Hughes was born and grew up in the north of England and trained at Liverpool Art School and at the Ruskin School of Art, Oxford. Her long career began in the early 1950s, since when she has illustrated over 200 titles. These include ILLUSTRATION of children's fiction by writers such as Dorothy Edwards (see *MY NAUGHTY LITTLE SISTER*), WILLIAM MAYNE, NOEL STREATFEILD, NINA BAWDEN and MARGARET MAHY; in more recent years Shirley Hughes has concentrated upon her own PICTUREBOOKS.

Hughes's illustrative style is distinctive, bearing a sketchbook immediacy with its expressive sepia or black line, free brush-work in water paints, and modelling through tone. Her ability to animate the visual narrative by various autographic means, and by page design, is outstanding. Hughes's range as a picturebook maker encompasses the youngest viewer, the apprentice reader, and the more skilled and reflective audience. *UP AND UP* (1979) a wordless picturebook in strip-cartoon format, is not tethered to age-limits.

Hughes's picture story-books for the very young, introduced by *Lucy and Tom's Day* (1960), are affectionate and reassuring in concept and content, drawing upon the dramas of everyday life and featuring robust, endearing participants. The *ALFIE* SERIES began in 1981 and still continues. Hughes won The Other Award for *Helpers* (1975), followed by the KATE GREENAWAY MEDAL for *Dogger* (1977); the latter is about a small boy who temporarily loses his favourite toy. The layout creates continuous and simultaneous action punctuated by reflective pauses, and the vigorous line is complemented by warm hues, impressionistic dappling of pigment and strong tonal effects. *Out and About through the year* (1988) brings together simple poems and lyrical pictures.

Innovative ways of accommodating narrative fiction with visual action continue and develop in *Chips and Jessie* (1985), a collection of stories intended for a more experienced audience. The pages of this metafictive book invite linear and synoptic readings, with information coming in text, speech and thought-bubbles from human and animal sources, framed and unframed ILLUSTRATIONS, strips, and from tales within tales within tales. *Stories by Firelight* (1993) encompasses poems, multilayered narratives and wordless strip dream-drama, and carries intertextual references to FOLKTALE, myth, medieval art and the Bible.

Hughes's sketchbooks of holidays spent in Italy are the visual inspiration for *Enchantment in the Garden* (1996). Set in the 1920s, the story of how a lonely young girl brings to life the statue of a young sea god combines Christian, pagan and magical elements, and the stirrings of an ecological theme. Musical and theatrical analogies, particularly to opera, suggest themselves as the pages turn. Tall upright panels which carry the text structure the visual rhythms of each opening. The painterly illustrations in sensuous colour expand or contract to intensify or lull the action. The ending – showing a clash of light upon water – is left open for the audience to determine.

In 1984 Hughes was awarded the ELEANOR FARJEON AWARD for Services to Children's Literature, and in 1997 was UK nominee for the HANS CHRISTIAN ANDERSEN AWARD. In 1999 she was awarded the OBE and she was made a Fellow of the Royal Society of Literature in 2000. She is published widely in other countries and has total sales of over seven million. JD

Hughes, Ted [Edward] (James) 1930–98 British Poet Laureate and children's writer. Hughes was born in Yorkshire, England, where his childhood and the lure of the countryside are documented in *POETRY IN THE MAKING* (1967). It was, however, the vision of the burnt fox in his Cambridge room – memorably captured in *The Thought Fox* – which was the turning-point. The maimed creature's bloody pawprint on the unfinished essay, its words 'Stop this – you are destroying us', released energies which were the making of a writer. His sequence of 'family' poems, *MEET MY FOLKS* (1961), was followed by the prose FABLES *How The Whale Became* (1963, reissued in 2000 with illustrations by Jackie Morris) and *THE IRON MAN* (1968), both dedicated to the children of his first marriage to Sylvia Plath and written alongside the darker adult poetry which followed her death in 1963. *Birthday Letters* (1998), which received widespread critical acclaim, explores the same ground in much more positive poetry.

An immediate child audience is a huge impetus to writing but it is the survival of the child within the man which Hughes himself stresses: 'I find a common wavelength . . . between the self I was then and the self I am now.' *WHAT IS THE TRUTH?* (1984), arguably Hughes's greatest children's work, was written for the Farms for City Children Scheme. It was reissued in paperback by Faber in 1995 as part of a quartet of Hughes's poetry for younger readers, along with *The Iron Wolf*, *The Thought Fox* and *A March Calf*. Hughes's spare cadences draw younger children into the natural world, which remained his greatest inspiration. Hughes's work for children is extensive and serious. In his own words: 'They will accept plastic toys, if that's all they're given, but their true driving passion is to get possession of the codes of adult reality – of the real world.' JP

Hughes, Thomas see *TOM BROWN'S SCHOOLDAYS*; see also SCHOOL STORIES

Hull, Katharine see CHILD AUTHORS; *FAR DISTANT OXUS, THE*; see also NEGLECTED WORKS

Hulme, Beaman S.G. see *TOYTOWN* SERIES

Humpty Dumpty Magazine see ALVIN TRESSELT

Hundred Million Francs, A (1957) Novel by French author Paul Berna, the first of a series of nine books about Gaby and his gang. The headless toy horse, the gang's most treasured plaything, becomes the focus of the action when a thief, about to be caught, throws into the body of the horse the key to the warehouse where the loot is. The children, while ultimately the agents who restore order and solve the crime, also suggest the creative and energetic forces of the Dionysian as they run rampant, together with Marion's dogs, through the staid adult world. SA

Hunt, Irene 1907– American author of HISTORICAL FICTION widely praised for giving a human dimension to history. As a teacher for well over three decades, Hunt recognised that traditional history books did not catch and hold her students' attention. In her novels Hunt thus sought to recreate history in such a way as to hold her reader's attention by telling lively, engaging stories about young characters living through times of great historical change, whether the Civil War or the Depression. Her first novel, *Across Five Aprils* (1964), explores the Civil War as seen through the eyes of nine-year-old Jethro Creighton, who comes to the painful recognition that the war has torn apart his friends and his country. For its vivid depiction of wartime life, Hunt's novel was a 1965 Newbery Honour Book. Also noteworthy is her *Up a Road Slowly* (1966), the recipient of the 1967 NEWBERY MEDAL, which recounts the story of young Julie Trelling's maturation during the 1930s, a period of great social upheaval. Although Hunt wrote a number of other well-crafted historical novels, these two books are the most memorable. SAI

Hunt, Nan [N.L. Ray] 1918– Australian writer, best known for the texts of her PICTUREBOOKS, especially *Whistle Up the Chimney* (1981), a FANTASY which has a locomotive hurtling down the chimney and through the house while Mrs Millie Mack sits excitedly knitting by the fire. Hunt is a prolific and versatile writer:

of magic realism as in *Roma Mercedes and Fred* (1981), about a flying horse; thrillers, such as *Nightmare to Nowhere* (1980); SCIENCE FICTION, in *There Was This Man Running . . .* (1979); and psychological drama, in *Never Tomorrow* (1989). Hunt has high ethical principles and constantly explores ideas about the human condition, always affirming those values that give dignity to life. MSax

Hunt, Peter see CHILDIST CRITICISM; CRITICAL APPROACHES TO CHILDREN'S LITERATURE; see also *GRANPA*

Hunter, Bernice Thurman 1922– Canadian writer of the popular *Booky* trilogy, comprising *That Scatterbrain Booky* (1981), *With Love from Booky* (1983) and *As Ever, Booky* (1985). This trilogy and a later novel, *Amy's Promise* (1995), are drawn from Hunter's own memories about what it was like growing up as a young child and a teenager during the Depression of the 1930s in Toronto. Hunter's second series – *A Place For Margaret* (1984), *Margaret In The Middle* (1986) and *Margaret On Her Way* (1988) – provide another convincing description of life in rural Ontario during the 1920s. Hunter's other HISTORICAL FICTION – *Lamplighter* (1987), *The Railroader* (1990), *The Firefighter* (1991) and *Hawk and Stretch* (1993) – was based upon her research and also upon family memories passed down to her. Hunter's work – both her coming-of-age fiction and her non-fiction – deals with poverty, family disunity, displacement, unemployment and humiliation, balanced by emotional sensitivity, deeply ingrained family loyalty, affection and courage. She received the 1981 IODE Book Award for *That Scatterbrain Booky* and the 1990 Vicky Metcalf Award for a body of work. MRS

Hunter, Kristin 1931– African American writer. Born in Philadelphia, Pennsylvania, Hunter wrote a column for the *Pittsburgh Courier* when she was a teenager, addressing such issues as segregated swimming pools. Her awareness of injustices is incorporated in her fiction set during the Civil Rights movement. In *The Soul Brothers and Sister Lou* (1968), Hunter describes 14-year-old Louretta Hawkins's anger and frustration with socio-economic and racial disparities. Hunter realistically portrays inner-city culture, emphasising themes of family, optimism and survival. Her characters are intelligent, resourceful and ambitious, seeking financial security and weighing up the value of education versus profitable jobs. Lou aspires to attend college but gains instantaneous fame and prosperity with her music. In the sequel, *Lou In the Limelight* (1981), she discovers the perils, such as gambling and addictions, that often accompany success. Hunter's short-story collection, *Guests in the Promised Land* (1968), explores how African American teenagers comprehend their role in a predominantly white society and protect their identity and racial pride. Through distinctive, authentic voices, Hunter reveals the violence and despair faced by many impoverished urban children while stressing the resilience of the African American community. She received the Council on Interracial Books for Children Award. Hunter also wrote *Boss Cat* (1971), *The Pool Table War* (1972) and *Uncle Daniel and the Raccoon* (1972). EDS

see also AFRICAN AMERICAN LITERATURE

Hunter, Mollie 1922– One of Scotland's most distinguished children's writers. Mollie Hunter's awareness of her Scottish-Irish ancestry inspires and informs the content and craft of her writing. Her books fall into four categories: PICTUREBOOKS, FANTASY, historical adventure, and realistic novels for young adults. Her most celebrated work, *The Stronghold* (1974), set on an Orkney island in the Bronze Age, won the CARNEGIE MEDAL, and other recognition included the Scottish Arts Council Literary Award in 1972 and 1977. Typically, her writing recreates and celebrates aspects of Scottish history, culture and folklore. HISTORICAL FICTION includes romances such as *The Lothian Run* (1970) and the more authentically researched *A Pistol in Greenyards* (1965), set in the troubled times of the Highland Clearances. Themes of courage and conscience motivate Hunter's protagonists to behave in reckless, daring ways. In FANTASY novels such as *The Haunted Mountain* (1972) and *A Stranger Came Ashore* (1975), the fateful conflict between good and evil is represented by human characters who challenge powerful supernatural forces. Hunter's childhood struggles and her emergence as a writer are conveyed in the acclaimed semi-autobiographical novel *The Sound of Chariots* (1972). In the collection of essays *Talent is Not Enough* (1976) she considers her role and responsibility as a children's writer. CMN

Hunter, Norman (George Lorimer) see *PROFESSOR BRANESTAWM* SERIES; see also FRITZ WEGNER

Hunting of the Snark, The (1876) Long nonsense BALLAD by LEWIS CARROLL, subtitled 'An Agony in Eight Fits', which first appeared with surreal ILLUSTRATIONS by Henry Holiday and has since been attempted by many distinguished artists. Carroll suggested that the poem 'is to some extent connected with the lay of the Jabberwock', and some of the earlier poem's portmanteau words like 'beamish' and 'outgrabe', as well as creatures such as the Jubjub bird and Bandersnatch, reappear. 'Snark' itself may be a packing-together of 'shark' and 'snake' or 'snail', as well as 'snarl' and 'bark'. However, the mood of this later narrative poem is quite different: there is less exuberance in the wordplay and much more adult fear and anxiety throughout. The poem itself became a prey to allegory-hunters within Carroll's lifetime, despite his insistence that he 'didn't know' what it meant. The pursuit of the snark has variously been seen as the quest for happiness, wealth or social success, and as an example of existentialist absurdity. Carroll himself had to admit that 'some children are puzzled with it', but the poem has continued to attract a small cult following of adult readers. ML

Hurd, Clement 1908–88 American illustrator. Born and raised in New York City and a graduate of Yale, Hurd began his career as a modernist painter, studying in Europe for several years, notably with Fernand Léger, whose influence helped him to discover the compelling advantages of the use of flatly painted primary and secondary colours in combination with simplified representational forms. MARGARET WISE BROWN, in her double role as author and editor, enlisted Hurd in the cause of illustrating children's books. His wonderful pictures for Brown's *Runaway Bunny* (1942) and *GOODNIGHT MOON* (1947) remain his most famous works, but he went on to have a long career in book ILLUSTRATION, usually collaborating with his wife, Edith Thatcher Hurd. Though the Hurds produced numerous delightfully humorous PICTUREBOOKS – such as *Last One Home is a Green Pig* (1959) and *Hurry, Hurry* (1960) – it is their lyrical non-fiction series on motherhood in the animal kingdom that best displays Clement's artistic genius. For this series – which includes *The Mother Beaver* (1971), *The Mother Deer* (1972), *The Mother Whale* (1973) and several others – Hurd used three-colour woodblock printing from blocks of heavily weathered wood to make the swirls and grains of the wood suggestive of the textures, patterns and moods of sky, water and forest. These lovely, understated books are among the best American demonstrations that children's picturebooks can be distinctive as works of art. JS

see also WOOD ENGRAVING

Hurd, Edith Thatcher see PICTUREBOOKS; see also CLEMENT HURD

Hurricane (1964) First and best-known title in a quartet of novels by the West Indian author Andrew Salkey (1928–95), a founder member of the Caribbean Artists' Movement and winner of a number of awards for adult poetry. *Hurricane* was followed by *Earthquake* (1965) – an oral account of the great quake of 1907 – *Drought* (1966) and *Riot* (1967). The four stories are told in unpretentious and sparse prose through the eyes of Kingston children experiencing the troubles of Jamaica, simultaneously communicating to the reader a rich sense of their family and cutural lives. Salkey also wrote stories about ANANCY. VW

Illustration by Pat Hutchins from *Changes, Changes.*

Hutchins, Pat 1944– British PICTUREBOOK maker and writer. Hutchins specialised in illustration at Leeds College of Art, after which she worked in an advertising agency in London, where she met her husband Laurence. After their marriage in 1966 they lived for a period in New York where her first picture book, *ROSIE'S WALK* (1968), was published. They then returned to London, and subsequently had two sons who have influenced her work; she has written for them, and of them, in fictional form.

Hutchins entertains and involves her young beholders and emergent readers with great skill by writing simply and developing a key idea in each book, encouraging participation in verbal play and prediction, and exploring relevant themes. She draws fluently and is an adventurous colourist. For the very young, *Goodnight Owl* (1972) has the illustration on the left-hand page and text on the right, giving first place to the owl being kept awake by a succession of noisy fellow creatures; a child beholder can mimic the noises via object recognition without needing the brief text at all. *The Wind Blew* (1974), winner of the KATE GREENAWAY MEDAL, invites the reader to predict from the pictures which item will blow away next. Clean outlines, earthy autumnal colours and a frieze of increasing numbers of characters and swirling objects carry the tale.

Growth is the key idea in the *Titch* books, based on her first son's experience with older children when he was small. *Titch* (1972) records the triumph of the underdog, the smallest of a trio of children, who grows a huge plant from a tiny seed; and *You'll Soon Grow into Them, Titch* (1983) offers a humorous view on hand-me-downs. Small young readers empathise with the hero of *Happy Birthday, Sam* (1978), who carries a little chair around so that he can reach things. This book is perfectly focused: the sturdy figures, a low eye-level, and a palette of cool green, lemon, ochre and cobalt blue, evoke a sense of quiet determination. A different emotional tone, in saturated day-glo yellow and singing pink and purple, is achieved in *The Doorbell Rang* (1986), which exemplifies generosity, as a little family with one plate of cookies experiences a constant stream of hungry visitors.

Some of Hutchins's most popular picturebooks feature the Monster family, whose green-nosed, long-eared and clawed appearance is softened and offset in translucent watercolour. Their emotions are all too human. Jealousy besets Hazel, the Monster daughter – in her Liberty print dress – in *The Very Worst Monster* (1985), though she secretly enjoys the mayhem her baby brother causes in *Where's the Baby?* (1988) and draws us in with a colluding glance.

As her children grew older, Hutchins began to write fiction, illustrated by Laurence Hutchins. *The House that Sailed Away* (1976) and *The Curse of the Egyptian Mummy* (1983) are two of their successful collaborations. JD

Hutton, Warwick 1939–94 Son of the British glass engraver John Hutton, Warwick Hutton first started his working life as a portrait painter with the support of John Nash. After a period working as an illustrator for Independent Television News he started a freelance career. The American publisher Margaret K. McElderry, while on a visit to London in 1976, agreed to publish *Noah and the Great Flood* (1977). He brought together his drawing and STORYTELLING skills in order to retell a series of classic stories. A highly respected teacher, he taught drawing, illustration and printmaking at the School of Art in Cambridge. AEW

Hyman, Trina Schart 1939– Award-winning American author/illustrator of over 130 books, especially known for her vibrant, romantic illustrations of FOLKTALES. Hyman was born in Philadelphia; she studied at the Philadelphia Museum College of Fine Arts, the Boston Museum School of the Arts, and the Konstfackskolan, Stockholm. From 1972 to 1979 she was the art director of *CRICKET MAGAZINE*. *Saint George and the Dragon* (1984) – adapted from Edmund Spenser's *The Faerie Queene* by MARGARET HODGES – won the CALDECOTT MEDAL in 1985. Its light-filled landscapes decorated with borders of flowers and herbs are framed with window-like constructions that place the viewer in intimate relationship to the scenes depicted. However, many consider Hyman's dramatic and intensely emotional illustrations for Paul Heins's translation of *Snow White* (1974) to be her best work. Her versions of *SLEEPING BEAUTY* (1977), with its arches and colonnades framing the scenes, and *LITTLE RED RIDING HOOD* (1983), with its richly detailed folk-art borders, have also become classics. Hyman has sometimes been criticised for over-illustrating her stories and for her sensual, sometimes scantilly clad queens and princesses. Her *Self-Portrait: Trina Schart Hyman* (1981) is a fascinating PICTUREBOOK account of her life, told and illustrated in the manner of her folktales. LH

Hymns for the Amusement of Children see SMART, CHRISTOPHER; see also *HYMNS FOR CHILDREN*

Hymns in Prose for Children (1781) Collection by ANNA BARBAULD, highly regarded British poet and educationalist. The collection is the nearest Barbauld came to writing verse for children, though she wrote lesson books a-plenty. Despite emphasising the limited capacities of children in her preface, she challenged young readers with these lyrical prose poems which equated religious feeling with freedom in nature long before the Romantic poets. MCCS

I

I Am David (1965) First published in Denmark as *David* in 1963, this novel by Anne Holm (1922–98) charts a boy's solitary journey from an Eastern European concentration camp to his homeland of Denmark. A generous measure of piety pervades the narrative, which explores themes of displacement and the search for identity within the quest structure. An allegorical dimension is imparted through the physical challenges and human encounters which test David's endurance. As the principles and complexities of human behaviour elucidate his own soul-searching, uplifting words of David the psalmist resonate as a mantra to fortify his spirit and sustain his resolve. CMN

see also WAR STORIES

***I Can Read* series** see ELSE MINARIK; see also ILLUSTRATION IN CHILDREN'S BOOKS; ARNOLD LOBEL

I Capture the Castle (1949) Outstanding novel by British author DODIE SMITH, for many years popular with young adult readers and still in print. The narrative is the private journal of 17-year-old Cassandra Mortmain, who lives with her eccentric family in a partly ruined castle in Suffolk, and who wishes to 'capture' in words the unique quality of her family and personal life. Although it is partly a love story and the subject matter invites cliché at every point, it is distinguished by the firm and intelligent personal voice of the young fictional narrator – impassioned, honest, generous and ruefully aware of her shortcomings in dealing with the complexities of first love. The subtleties and naivety of her character, and her developing self-awareness, are convincingly and directly represented without authorial archness or irony, and with an absolute sincerity which is for the writer a triumph of style. Dodie Smith also successfully captures the sharp and dramatic immediacy characteristic of the true journal written without a foreknowledge of outcomes. There is nothing hackneyed or derivative about this fictional narrator, and no embarrassment about her interest in art, poetry and music, or her determined attempt to be honest and true to herself. VW

see also ONE HUNDRED AND ONE DALMATIANS, THE

I Hate My Teddy Bear (UK, 1982; USA, 1984) British picturebook author DAVID MCKEE engulfs Brenda and John and their teddy bears in strange incidents and ambiguous spaces. Ignored by their mothers, like Bernard in *NOT NOW, BERNARD*, the children project that cruel indifference onto their own teddies. Pink Teddy and Blue Teddy, the only sympathetic characters in the drama with their wry smiles and knowing looks, see through the children's guile. Adults come and go, engaged in bizarre occupations which are only partially explained at the end. Young readers can ignore McKee's sophisticated cultural references, and enjoy the delightful absurdity of the visual narrative. PC

I Like That Stuff (1984) Groundbreaking anthology of poems from many cultures, selected by Morag Styles for 8- to 13-year-olds, ranging from songs and HAIKU from Zimbabwe and Japan to poems from India and the Caribbean. The collection is also notable for the introduction and the 'Initiation' poem written by Edward Kamau Brathwaite, and for its strong representation of black British voices. HT

I Like This Poem (1979) This innovative collection of poems edited by KAYE WEBB was chosen and annotated by children aged from 6 to 15. Their choices show their love of onomatopoeia, their early awareness of strong rhythm and wordplay, and a sense of their mixed feelings about life, for example: 'It makes me feel both happy and sad, because it is funny and full of nasty things.' HA

'I Own the Racecourse!' (1968) Novel in which the distinguished Australian writer PATRICIA WRIGHTSON created disabled Andy Hoddell, who naïvely believes that he has 'bought' the local racetrack from a drunk after overhearing inner-city children playing a game in which they 'own' and swap properties. Andy lives 'behind a closed window'. 'When he smiled his warm smile and spoke a little too loudly, it was as if he was speaking through the glass.' Thus the dilemma that confronts his mates, when Andy's proprietorial actions threaten to blow up in his face, is how to extricate him from an embarrassing situation without damaging his self-esteem. Wrightson's solution is sensitive and convincing. MSax

I Saw Esau, Traditional Rhymes of Youth (1947) As the first editorial venture of the British scholars and collectors IONA AND PETER OPIE this collection staked out the ground for the extraordinary riches of their subsequent studies of children's literature and language. Despite its modest post-war appearance, this unique collection marks the distinction between the traditional NURSERY RHYMES of the Opies' great *Dictionary*, those that adults recite to children, and these verses, callings, jeers, taunts, jokes and superstitions, that children bandy about with rumbustious illocutionary force. ('I beg your pardon, Grant your grace; I hope the cows Will spit in your face.') The editors' notes display the blend of scrupulous research and enlivening humour of all their later works. Despite appreciative reviews, the book was remaindered in 1953, but a single Opie copy survived to be re-edited in 1992. Some American verses were substituted for the mnemonics of English, Latin and Greek grammar. Transformed in appearance by Walker Books and the illustrative genius of MAURICE SENDAK, it became *The School Child's Pocket Book*. In her introduction Iona Opie says, 'It is more than ever a child's brave defiance in the face of daunting odds.' Sendak's unbuttoned drawings, his colours and characterisations, fill the small pages with new narrative dimensions, subtle overplays of nonsense and serious self-reflection. Childhood joys of excess and surprise spill over into the revised notes. The book has now taken its important place as the link between the oral tradition and written literature to make plain to all its readers the continuity of childhood in both. MM

see also PLAYGROUND RHYMES; RIDDLES AND JOKES

I Want My Potty (1986) British PICTUREBOOK about a small princess who is being potty-trained, written and illustrated by TONY ROSS, in the tradition of books which deal with situations young children experience. The simple style incorporates repetition of phrases typical of traditional children's stories and demands to be read aloud – very loudly in places – with character voices and pauses. Ross's deceptively childlike illustrations are also full of comedic detail. There are stock FAIRY TALE characters, together with an everyday familiarity for young children, providing a humorous balance between the traditional and the modern. Further books include *I Want to Be* (1993), *I Want My Dinner* (1995) and *I Want a Sister* (1999). AW

I-Spy Books Series of books which had their origin in a column in the British *News Chronicle* and flourished in the 1950s and 60s. Readers, or 'redskins', were encouraged to search the environment for sights 'worth seeing'. Big Chief I-Spy rewarded the vigilant with a prize based on points scored: successful redskins moved up a place at the Council fire and claimed a rank. The Chief's classificatory system entailed a hierarchy in which distinctive British sights such as organ-grinders, market-crosses, rood screens and schoolboys with straw hats scored highly. The system of values the books promoted and rewarded was thus consistent with those emerging in the concept of a national heritage in the 50s and 60s. The series' first ANNUAL was issued in 1954.

Since 1991 the books have been published by Michelin, and the tribe of redskins has disappeared, but the notion of scores and rewards for seeing appropriately has been retained. In the light of the early volumes' privileging of the auratic and rare it is worth noting that *I-Spy Stonehenge* (1995) bears the imprint of English Heritage. Stonehenge is a place built, according to the book's somewhat disingenuous claim, by 'people who looked and felt as we do'. It seems that the I-Spy spirit is an adaptable survivor. VK

Ibbotson, Eva 1925– A writer of parodies which satirise human and folklore behaviour and mores. Born in Vienna, Ibbotson was educated at Dartington Hall and London University, and was engaged in research at Cambridge University before marrying and raising a family. A writer of short stories and adult historical novels, Ibbotson's *The Great Ghost Rescue* (1975) established her irreverent tongue-in-cheek voice which here obliquely explores environmental issues through the plight of a group of dispossessed ghosts needing sanctuary, a theme pursued in *The Haunting of Hiram* (1987) and *Dial a Ghost* (1996). In *Which Witch?* (1979), runner-up for the CARNEGIE AWARD, her target is beauty contests, a wizard using a spell-casting competition to find a suitable witch spouse. Antic invention and deft comic pacing characterise these contemporary tales in which traditional expectations are overturned. EMH

Icelandic saga see CLASSICAL MYTHOLOGY; FOLKTALES AND LEGENDS

Igbo folktales see *THE MAGIC APPLE TREE*; see also CYPRIAN EKWENSI; CHIO ENWONWU; TERESA E. MENIRU

Ihimaera, Witi 1944– Major New Zealand novelist and editor of modern MAORI WRITING. His stories for children include *The Whale Rider* (1987),which, like his collection of stories *Pounamu, Pounamu* (1972), is widely studied in New Zealand schools. In *Te Ara O Te Hau* (1994), an anthology of Maori children's litera-

Illustration in children's books: 'William Cobbett's School.' Illustration by HOWARD PYLE for *Harper's New Monthly Magazine* (1881).

ture, Ihimaera observes that it is often difficult to separate stories written for children from those written about them. His own writing bears this out. *The Pupu Pool* for instance, which melds childhood reminiscence to a haunting devotion to the land, appeared first in the *SCHOOL JOURNAL*, before being republished in Ihimaera's adult collection *The New Net Goes Fishing* (1977).

The Whale Rider, the most notable of the very few pieces of Maori fiction that includes the older child in its readership, is a remarkable fusion of myth and history, old ways and modern society, realism and symbol. The mythical history of Paikea, the whale rider, is repeated in the amazing career of his descendant Kahu, clearly chosen, despite her patriarchal grandfather's resistance, to re-found her tribe by reenacting Paikea's heroic relationship with the ancient whale. The novel becomes, therefore, a powerful and moving demand for inclusion of women in the political organisation of Maori society. There is immense appeal in the admission of the girl child to the ranks of the heroes; but what will perhaps most impress contemporary readers is the potent magic realism, which always does justice to Ihimaera's tribal heritage. CM

Iliad see ABRIDGEMENT; CLASSICAL MYTHOLOGY; see also ILLUSTRATION IN CHILDREN'S BOOKS

Ill-Made Knight, The see *THE ONCE AND FUTURE KING*

Illustrated Chips see COMICS, PERIODICALS AND MAGAZINES

illustration in children's books Few children will have had access to the earliest illustrated books, the handwritten illuminated manuscipt that circulated before the invention of the printing press; and in any case, the content was not intended for them. When printing arrived, although books were illustrated right from the beginning (though without the colour, page design and individuality of earlier hand-made books), there was still little sense of children as audience. CAXTON's *The Fables of Aesop* (1484), illustrated with woodcuts, was intended for adults. However, it undoubtedly pleased children in much the same way as later 'adult' texts would: *THE PILGRIM'S PROGRESS* (1678), *ROBINSON CRUSOE* (1719) and *GULLIVER'S TRAVELS* (1726) found child audiences who were drawn to their illustrated engraved frontispieces and woodcuts placed at key narrative points.

Children were also drawn to the relative excitement of these texts. On the whole, reading for children was not intended to entertain but to instruct and indoctrinate. In such circumstances, early didactic books, such as EMBLEM BOOKS deriving from medieval hand-created bestiaries, were made a great deal more attractive to children by the number of illustrations they carried. In the *ORBIS SENSUALIUM PICTUS* of Comenius, published in 1658 in Nuremberg with woodcuts, and in an English translation a year later with copperplate engravings, 150 small pictures illustrate the whole of the 'visible world'. This book was a most comprehensive pictorial encyclopaedia for children and remains a milestone in the history of illustrated children's books. By 1693, JOHN LOCKE was echoing Comenius' belief in the use of pictures for children and recommending that children be given pictures 'to encourage enquiry and knowledge'. The way was clear for the growth of illustrated books in the 18th century.

The year 1744 saw the publication in Britain of two significant children's illustrated books. Mary Cooper published *TOMMY THUMB'S POCKET SONG BOOK* with engraved text and pictures, and JOHN NEWBERY published *A Little Pretty Pocket Book* with woodcuts. These two books share the distinction of being considered the first entertaining illustrated books for children. In both, the pictures were unattributed, as was frequently the case in the early days of illustration. Where illustration was attributed, there is reason to be suspicious – as in Newbery's claim that the cuts in *The History of Little Goody Two Shoes* (1765) were by Michael Angelo of Rome.

The 18th century also saw the expansion of CHAPBOOKS, cheap, cheerful, frequently sensational publications, illustrated with woodcuts and sold by pedlars. Although the woodcuts sometimes bore little relation to the content of the written text and reproduction was poor as the cuts became more and more worn, chapbooks were read avidly by children and a market for cheap juvenile literature was created. For some time to come, the market was flooded with inferior stories and recycled woodcuts.

At the end of the 18th century, there were some exceptional illustrated books from William Blake. His copper-engraved, hand-tinted illuminated poems, *Songs of Innocence* (1789) and *SONGS OF INNOCENCE AND EXPERIENCE* (1794), in which text and image were designed together as a unified whole, were unique at this time. But the laborious process of production meant that copies were few. Even fewer found a child readership.

Illustration, tailor-made, attributed, imaginative, and precisely and commercially printed had to wait until the arrival of the great illustrator THOMAS BEWICK, whose refined WOOD ENGRAVINGS, in such books as *Aesop's Fables* (1818), influenced future generations of illustrators. Even the tiny VIGNETTES in his natural history books managed to introduce narrative and humour. GEORGE CRUIKSHANK, the first illustrator of GRIMMS' tales in this country (1823), RICHARD DOYLE who illustrated John Ruskin's *THE KING OF THE GOLDEN RIVER* (1851) with his graceful line, JOHN TENNIEL, linked forever with LEWIS CARROLL'S *ALICE* books (1865, 1871) and ARTHUR HUGHES with his romantic drawings for GEORGE MACDONALD'S *At the Back of the North Wind* (1871) all owe something to Bewick's example and to his involvement in and monitoring of the printing process to ensure clearer printing of the original image. The DALZIEL BROTHERS were the engravers chiefly credited with bringing these and other illustrators' work onto the page so accurately.

Colour, where it was used in children's books up to this point, was usually applied by hand (often by teams of children) after the printing in black-and-white had taken place, and many of the finest illustrators were quite happy to achieve their effects without it. However, in the second half of the century printed colour began to appear in more and more children's books. EDWARD LEAR'S entertaining *BOOK OF NONSENSE,* which had appeared in 1845, was reissued in colour in 1875. EDMUND EVANS, who had printed Richard Doyle's pictures for WILLIAM ALLINGHAM'S poem *IN FAIRYLAND* in a range of subtle colours in 1870, was the key figure to whom the trio of great illustrators of the end of the century, WALTER CRANE, KATE GREENAWAY and RANDOLPH CALDECOTT, owed recognition, encouragement and brilliant colour reproduction. Crane's life-long concern with design and decoration is evident in a book such as *Beauty and the Beast and Other Tales* (1875), and he was probably the first illustrator to control the look of the whole book, including each double-page spread. Kate Greenaway was also served well by Evans when he printed her first book, *UNDER THE WINDOW* (1879), which established her instantly as a PICTUREBOOK star. Randolph Caldecott, with economy and wit, could be said to have been the first to show what was possible in terms of allowing pictures to carry a narrative line quite other than the written text. His 16 TOY BOOKS (1878–86), in which he illustrates and extends traditional rhymes, established a reputation that still stands.

As the 19th century came to an end, one could point to the utmost variety in the illustrator's art. Amongst the illustrated books that fortunate British children could have seen or owned might have been ANDREW LANG'S 'COLOURED' *FAIRY BOOKS*, illustrated with intricate detail by Henry Ford, Florence Upton's pleasingly uncluttered pictures for *ADVENTURES OF TWO DUTCH DOLLS AND A 'GOLLIWOGG'* (1895), R.L. STEVENSON'S *A CHILD'S GARDEN OF VERSES* with CHARLES ROBINSON'S Art Nouveau black-and-white illustrations (1895/6), WILLIAM NICHOLSON'S graphically dramatic woodcuts in *An Alphabet* (1898), *Two Well-Worn Shoe Stories* cheerfully illustrated by JOHN HASSALL and Cecil Aldin (1899), FRANCIS BEDFORD'S elegant *The Book of Shops* (1899) and Helen Bannerman's *THE STORY OF LITTLE BLACK SAMBO* (1899). If their parents had been adventurous, these hypothetical children could also have had M. Boutet de Monvel's heroic *Joan of Arc* (1896) in French (see below), L. FRANK BAUM's *Mother Goose in Prose*, illustrated in America by MAXFIELD PARRISH in his distinctive polished style (1897) (see below), IVAN BILIBIN's *Ivan the Crown Prince* (Pushkin, 1899), full of Russian exuberance, and the affectionate domestic record kept by the Swedish Carl Larsson in *A Home* (1899). They might also have had access to the numerous ANNUALS to which many fine illustrators contributed.

After the turn of the century there was as much variety again. In Britain the vogue was for elaborate GIFT BOOKS, usually of FAIRY TALES and often produced at Christmas time, which had four-colour 'process' plates, protected by TISSUE GUARDS or bound into the book all together at the back. ARTHUR RACKHAM is particularly associated with the gift book, as are EDMUND DULAC, the three Robinson brothers and the Copenhagen-born KAY NIELSEN. In very different mode, one of the Robinson brothers, WILLIAM HEATH ROBINSON, inventively line-illustrated his own story, *The Adventures of Uncle Lubin*, in 1902. At the same time, BEATRIX POTTER started her hugely significant series of animal tales, for which she wrote her own texts. L. LESLIE BROOKE, whom we could have encountered before the turn of the century as a line illustrator for writers such as MRS MOLESWORTH, entertains his readers with picturebooks, such as *Johnny Crow's Garden* in 1903. In 1903 also, LOUIS WAIN's 'cat' books would have been everywhere and MABEL LUCIE ATTWELL's work would have started to be recognised. The well-known line illustrators H.R. MILLAR and C.E. BROCK would have been enjoyed by children reading E. NESBIT's *Five Children and It* (1902) and *THE RAILWAY CHILDREN* (1906). Millicent Sowerby's illustrations for Stevenson's *A Child's Garden of Verses* (1908) would have been available to put alongside the first illustrated version that had come from Charles Robinson, or there was Jessie Willcox Smith's edition, from America (1905), with its romantic watercolour plates in addition to numerous line drawings.

Such reillustrating of certain works was to become well established from this period onwards. PERRAULT, Grimm and Andersen fairy tales, legends, such as *ROBIN HOOD*, and NURSERY RHYMES had all appeared illustrated by many hands, frequently unacknowledged, in the early days. In the 20th century, 'classics' such as *ALICE'S ADVENTURES IN WONDERLAND* (1865), several of GEORGE MACDONALD's titles, CHARLES DICKENS's *A Christmas Carol* (1843), CHARLES KINGSLEY's *THE WATER-BABIES* (1863), R. L. Stevenson's *TREASURE ISLAND* (1883), Carlo Collodi's *PINOCCHIO* (1883), *THE WIND IN THE WILLOWS* (1908), FRANCES HODGSON BURNETT's *THE SECRET GARDEN* (1911) or suites of poems such as WALTER DE LA MARE's *PEACOCK PIE*

Illustration by Linley Sambourne for *THE WATER-BABIES* by CHARLES KINGSLEY. (1885).

(1913), were all to draw many illustrators to their impelling texts. For instance, to the three interpretations of Stevenson's *A Child's Garden of Verses* which have already been mentioned can be added versions by, among others: Ruth Mary Hallock (1919), Kate Elizabeth Olver (1927), Clara M. Burd (1930), H. Willebeek le Mair (1931), EVE GARNETT (1938), MARGERY GILL (1946), JOAN HASSALL (1947), BRIAN WILDSMITH (1966) and MICHAEL FOREMAN (1986). There are in fact very few important illustrators in the 20th century who have not turned to an already illustrated text to add their vision of it. BEATRIX POTTER is perhaps a key exception.

WILLIAM NICHOLSON and EDWARD ARDIZZONE joined Beatrix Potter as illustrators in the first half of the 20th century notable for writing their own texts. Though he had wood-cut *An Alphabet* in 1898, Nicholson used offset colour lithography, an oblong format, limited colour and a hand-lettered text to produce two children's picturebook stories, *Clever Bill* (1926) and *The Pirate Twins* (1929), in which a unity and balance in story and line returned after a long period where decoration, pattern and full colour were the order of the day. In this respect, these two books are seen by many as heralding the start of the modern picturebook. Ardizzone also used the advantages offered by offset lithography to create his first picturebooks

'Opussum: "What is new in Winter styles?"
Hare: "Ears and hind legs are to be worn long – tails short."' Illustration by Peter Sheaf Newell from *St Nicholas Magazine* (1892).

and, with *Little Tim and the Brave Sea Captain* (1936), he began his *Little Tim* books. With their colour-wash pictures alternating with black-and-white, distinctive speech bubbles, highly dramatic stories and heroic main character, they are among the most memorable picturebooks of the middle of the century. Only Kathleen Hale's *Orlando* books could compete with them at the time. Ardizzone not only created his own picturebooks; he also contributed line illustrations to the work of many distinguished writers, including de la Mare's *Peacock Pie* (1946), James Reeve's *Blackbird in the Lilac* (1952), Eleanor Farjeon's *The Little Bookroom* (1955), Philippa Pearce's *The Minnow on the Say* (1955) and Clive King's *Stig of the Dump* (1963). In each of these very different books, and in many others, his drawings reflect, and indeed help create, the atmosphere of the books and yet remain instantly identifiable as Ardizzone.

Ardizzone continued to illustrate others' stories as well as his own until his death in 1979. This is a pattern which is repeated in many other illustrators of the later 20th century. Although such illustrators as Charles Keeping, Quentin Blake, Shirley Hughes, Raymond Briggs, Michael Foreman and Brian Wildsmith are principally known for their picturebooks, all have contributed countless drawings to fiction, and not only in the early days of their careers, although that is more common. If one looks through the work of children's authors, such as Rosemary Sutcliff, Geoffrey Trease, Kevin Crossley-Holland, Leon Garfield, Frederic Grice, Joan Aiken, Betsy Byars and Margaret Mahy, the line drawings of these illustrators crop up again and again, supporting the reader's visualisation of scene and character, encouraging prediction, aiding recollection or clinching atmosphere and era.

Picturebooks in the late 20th century have a much higher profile and the labour involved in their production is no longer immense, as almost any artwork can now be reproduced relatively accurately and relatively easily; nevertheless it is interesting to note that some of the above illustrators still make opportunities to illustrate fiction, even occasionally without the use of colour. Thus, we find Keeping at the end of his life illustrating Anna Sewell's *Black Beauty* (1988); Quentin Blake working vigorously for Roald Dahl, Michael Rosen, John Yeoman, Margaret Mahy and Joan Aiken, as well as on Dickens; Shirley Hughes giving her sensitive interpretation of F.H. Burnett's *The Secret Garden* (1988) and Michael Foreman illustrating Alan Garner's *The Stone Book Quartet* (1976–8) as readily as Terry Jones does humorous fiction and countless classics and collections of poetry. It is true that Raymond Briggs and Brian Wildsmith appear to have moved exclusively into the picturebook world – perhaps because each has found so distinctive a style and niche, Briggs with his strip cartoon and Wildsmith with his exuberant paintings. Both these illustrators, however, served long apprenticeships as line draughtsmen for fiction in their early careers.

There are several notable British illustrators in the 20th century whose careers are exclusively as line illustrators of the fiction and poetry of others. E. H. SHEPARD's economical, affectionate pen-and-ink drawings graced the work of A.A. MILNE and KENNETH GRAHAME in the late 1920s and early 1930s, but Shepard never moved into writing his own texts nor into a picturebook career. Into this category come also LYNTON LAMB, Margery Gill, Peggy Fortnum, PAULINE BAYNES, ROBIN JACQUES, FAITH JAQUES, ANTHONY MAITLAND, PATRICIA MARRIOTT, DIANA STANLEY and FRITZ WEGNER, who between them have contributed line drawings, colour illustrations and sometimes cover illustrations to all the major 20th-century children's fiction writers. Sometimes, as in the case of Anthony Maitland, a writer is linked with one illustrator in particular: LEON GARFIELD and Maitland have a partnership in Garfield's HISTORICAL FICTION which it seems no other illustrator could usurp, just as there seems no possibility of separating C.S. LEWIS's *NARNIA* books from PAULINE BAYNES. Sometimes, quite the reverse situation occurs: the writer WILLIAM MAYNE, for example, numbers at least 20 top illustrators in his books. With more than 80 books to his name that is perhaps not so surprising, but even Philippa Pearce, with far fewer titles, is associated with a dozen different illustrators. Sometimes the fear is voiced that the days of the line illustrator are numbered. It is true that line illustrators today are not so instantly recognised for their contribution as were their precursors, such as John Tenniel and E.H. Shepard, but there is no doubt that the images created by fiction illustrators are important to their readers and are long remembered. The recent success of a book such as PHILIP PULLMAN's *The Firework-Maker's Daughter* (1995), winner of the SMARTIES AWARD, owes not a little to Nick Harris's exuberant black-and-white drawings.

It is interesting to note, however, that even those illustrators such as ANTHONY BROWNE, JOHN BURNINGHAM and JAN ORMEROD whose new picturebooks are eagerly awaited by adults and children alike have occasionally branched out into different worlds: Browne has illustrated *Alice's Adventures in Wonderland* (1988) and the story of *King Kong* (1994), both in full colour, and *Trail of Stones* (1990), a collection of poems by Gwen Strauss, in black-and-white; Burningham in 1983 took on the challenge of reillustrating *The Wind in the Willows* with his delicate line drawings and pastel colour plates; Ormerod has illustrated J. M. BARRIE's *PETER PAN* (1988), using the traditional combination of colour plates and black-and-white drawings, and Charles Kingsley's *The Waterbabies* (1996), in which she uses colour throughout for plates, headers and spots.

Other illustrators deserving special mention include VICTOR AMBRUS, who has been hugely successful in many fields, including fine line work for fiction, award-winning picturebooks, classic tales, folk tales and non-fiction. His recent work for *The Odyssey* (1993) and *The Iliad* (1997) fully demonstrates his talent, with full-colour, dramatic, realistic, historically convincing illustrations, as well as imaginatively conceived page design. JAN PIEŃKOWSKI is equally prolific and equally hard to pin down: he is the designer and illustrator of Helen Nicholl's cheerful *MEG AND MOG* books for the very young child (from 1972), the inventive pop-up creator of *Haunted House* (1979) and *Robot* (1981), the silhouette illustrator for JOAN AIKEN's short stories and for his own *Christmas* (1984) and *Easter* (1989), and the collaborator with RUSSELL HOBAN on *M.O.L.E.* (1993) which is surely the only picturebook to have corrugated brown paper for its endpapers.

America has its own history of illustrations for children. In colonial America the Puritan settlers were determined to protect their children from Original Sin by means of unrelenting education. *THE NEW-ENGLAND PRIMER* (published in various versions from the 1680s to the early 19th century), and a strong tradition of Sunday School publications, were among the means to that end. Educational fervour reinforced an expectation that American books for children should communicate compellingly; therefore, despite the Puritan bias against painterly frivolities, illustrations (at first primarily woodcuts but later copper ENGRAVINGS) quickly became essential ingredients of American books for children. Although many of the early images were derived from British plates, an American illustrator with verve and vigour emerged in the 1840s when F. O. C. DARLEY produced popular illustrations for stories by WASHINGTON IRVING and others.

America's ambition that all citizens should read provided fertile ground for the development of periodicals for all ages. From the middle of the 19th century, such magazines for children as *OUR YOUNG FOLKS*, *ST NICHOLAS* and *THE RIVERSIDE MAGAZINE* became important vehicles for illustrated works. At the same time the proliferation of cheap chapbook publications excited broad audiences and demonstrated that even crude pictures can ignite interest in books.

WINSLOW HOMER was an important innovator in American illustration. His most distinctive illustations tended to be for volumes of poetry such as James Lowell's *The Courtin'* (1874) and LONGFELLOW's *Excelsior* (1877). In a similar vein, E.W. Kemble's depictions of the quintessenial Bad Boy in MARK TWAIN's *Huckleberry Finn* (1884) (see *THE ADVENTURES OF TOM SAWYER*) gave vivid life to distinctively American images appealing to readers of all ages. Also drawing for a double audience, A. B. FROST was one of the first

Illustration by E.W. Kemble from *The Adventures of Huckleberry Finn* by MARK TWAIN (1901).

of many American illustators to bridge the gap between journalistic comics (his infamous sequence 'Our Cat Eats Rat Poison' of 1881 is a ferocious classic of the form) and book illustration. Frost's best-remembered illustrations are for volumes of JOEL CHANDLER HARRIS's *Uncle Remus* tales published in 1892 and 1895; these classic pictures provide deft caricatures of the very human nature of certain animals amidst affectionate renderings of the American countryside.

HOWARD PYLE, whose personality was expressed in both his illustrations and his teaching, is often referred to as the father of American children's book illustration. Pyle was an enthusiatic medievalist, whose best-known books included *The Merry Adventures of Robin Hood* (1883), *Pepper and Salt* (1886), *The Wonder Clock* (1888) and *Otto of the Silver Hand* (1888). The sturdy linear designs of Pyle's early books played more to his strengths than did his later works that relied upon TIPPED IN HALF-TONE plates. The most renowned of Pyle's Brandywine Valley students, N.C. WYETH, was more in tune with the advantages of tipped-in colour pictures, although recent photographic techniques of reproduction reveal more fully the glories of Wyeth's paintings for Scribner's editions of such classics as Robert Louis Stevenson's *Treasure Island* (1911) than did the original plates. Special design innovations of the Pyle/Wyeth tradition included a tendency to fill the page with human figures so that their heads often touch, or almost touch, the tops of the picture – thereby dispensing with background atmospherics to concentrate on illustrating the action. Another of Pyle's star pupils, JESSIE WILCOX SMITH, illustrated such classics as *LITTLE WOMEN* (1915). She was at her best in capturing children at odd moments of play and reflection, and she also had a knack for rendering, without sentimentality, occasions of tenderness between parents and children.

An unwavering confidence in the potential of children's book illustration is Pyle's most enduring legacy to America's illustrators. Such Brandywine-influenced artists as MAXFIELD PARRISH shared Pyle's conviction that illustrations could aspire toward artistic greatness. Parrish's particular contributions to the form included his innovative use of photography for the derivation of images and his fabulous employments of bright colour. His wonderful use of blue may derive from the works of N.C. Wyeth, but no one did more than Parrish to develop and demonstrate the expressive and decorative potential of vivid colour in book and poster art. Parrish's works for children included EUGENE FIELD's *Poems of Childhood* (1904) and L. FRANK BAUM's *Mother Goose in Prose* (1897).

An illustrator even more famously associated with the works of Frank Baum is W.W. DENSLOW. His pictures for the first *WIZARD OF OZ* book (1900) established the definitive look for one of the world's favourite American fantasies and showed that poster-like forms could add excitement and verve to the illustrated book for children. But Denslow was not the only one demonstrating the potential of new 'mass culture' forms. The baroque sophistication and dream-obsessed imagery of the comic strip and cartoon works of WINSOR MCCAY, such as his *Nemo in Slumberland* (from 1906), showed American book illustrators that there was much they could learn from the comics. Similarly, the bizarrely numerous brownies in PALMER COX's line drawings beginning in the 1880s drew satirical energy from editorial cartooning and laid the groundwork for the 'find-me' genres of more recent times.

At the turn of the century the French artist M. Boutet de Monvel accomplished the magic trick of fitting history paintings into the illustrated-book mode. His illustrations accommodate heavily populated and complexly composed scenes while answering the need for elegant simplification. His *Jeanne d'Arc* (1896) created a sensation in America both before and after it was translated into English. Monvel's success with delicate line drawing and ukiyo-print-like colourations marvellously fitted grandeurs and spectaculars into modestly-sized pages. The American artist who best realised the potential of such strategies was the French-trained E. Boyd Smith, whose masterworks included *The Story of Noah's Ark* (1905), *The Story of Pocahontas and Captain John Smith* (1906) and *Chicken World* (1910). Another artist, PETER NEWELL, distinctively applied Monvel's technique of drawing in half-tone washes to the business of making humorous books for a broad audience. He famously added furious action to his tonal drawings by such devices as making a hole go all through the book (to follow the remarkable career of a stray bullet) in his *The Hole Book* of 1908.

The works of WANDA GÁG, one the most influential of the illustrators who began working in the late 1920s, were graphically experimental in their exciting display of the double-page spread to combine storytelling with story showing, but the overall feel of her drawings was archaic and old-world. *Millions of Cats* (1928) was her first and her best book. Gág's work demonstrated that freshly imagined illustrated works could become instantly classic, but the old-fashioned feel of her pictures seemed to support the continuing popularity of European folklore as a source of imagery for children.

By the 1930s a huge audience for children's books had developed in America. Although a preference for illustrations by foreign artists and writers persisted for many years, America had become the centre of a huge children's book industry. The development of children's departments in American public LIBRARIES and the slightly later development of departments for children's literature in American PUBLISHING houses created institutional contexts that enabled illustrated children's books to thrive. The expansion of the mass market also meant that distinguished artists and writers could expect significant financial rewards from success in this field and thus made possible the recruitment of some of the best emerging talent.

Among the key imported talents from European regions were BORIS ARTZYBASHEFF (*The Seven Simeons*, 1937), Miska Petersham (*Miki*, 1929), FEODOR ROJANKOVSKY (*The Tall Book of Mother Goose*, 1942), Ludwig Bemelmans (*MADELINE*, 1939), JEAN CHARLOT (*Two Little Trains*, 1949) and ROGER DUVOISIN (*Petunia*, 1950). All of these masters had reached America by the 1930s and remained there for most of the rest of their careers.

Although the popularity of European-born artists may have been inspired, in part, by a view prevalent in library and school circles that illustrated books could fill an important need by providing children with windows onto the international scene, some of the imported talents also became associated with

'Yes, that will be a nice game.' Illustration by HONOR APPLETON for *Josephine is Busy* by H.C. Cradock (1918).

American subjects. This was the case with Ingri and EDGAR D'AULAIRES whose deftly designed colour LITHOGRAPHS graced biographies of such figures as *George Washington* (1936) and *Abaham Lincoln* (1939) as well as books on Norwegian lore and other European topics.

By the 1930s there were many reworkings of traditional fairy tales. MARCIA BROWN, who had her start in the New York Public Library's storytelling programme, eventually emerged as one of the best of the fairy-tale illustrators in such books as *Cinderella or the Little Glass Slipper* (1954). URI SHULEVITZ's illustrations for such folk-tale books as *The Fool of the World and the Flying Ship* (1968) have a freshness and wit that make the pictures lively partners to the spirited incidents of the stories. In recent years the improved quality of full-colour printing has allowed a new generation of fairy-tale illustrators, such as PAUL ZELINSKY (*Rumplestiltskin*, 1986), to concentrate on painting without worries about printing logistics. Richer possibilities for colour printing have also opened up new prospects for such veteran artists of the fairy-tale picture as NANCY EKHOLM BURKERT (*Valentine & Orson*, 1989) and TRINA SCHART HYMAN (*Little Red Riding Hood*, 1983).

SHIRLEY HUGHES's much-loved character, Alfie.

In the same period 'here-and-now' story books became popular, influenced by progressive views on education. Among the best artists associated with this trend were the various talents who illustrated the books of MARGARET WISE BROWN – including LEONARD WEISGARD (*The Noisy Book*, 1939), CLEMENT HURD (*Goodnight Moon*, 1947) and ESPHYR SLOBODKINA (*The Little Fireman*, 1938). An artist who later richly realised the narrative potential of the urban-scene aspect of the trend was EZRA JACK KEATS, for example in *Whistle for Willie* (1964).

Although full-colour printing offered some obvious advantages for certain kinds of artists, technical constraints and the related limitation of numbers of colours sometimes led to special sorts of excellences. KURT WIESE, in his pictures for such books as the *The Story about Ping* (1933) and *Five Chinese Brothers* (1938), showed how much could be done with very little colour. Likewise, in the 1970s, ARNOLD LOBEL in his *FROG AND TOAD* SERIES – and many other books for Harper's *I Can Read* series – made lyrical use of a limited palette.

In the midst of the other trends an interest in nostalgic renderings of the lore and local colour of small towns, western landscapes, and other essentially American places held steady. Perhaps because of the inspirational example of the lively lines of Frederick Remington, a tradition of eloquent drawing became associated with Americanist topics in the illustrations of such masters as GARTH WILLIAMS (*The Little House in the Big Woods*, 1932), JAMES DAUGHERTY (*Daniel Boone*, 1939), ROBERT LAWSON (*Ben and Me*, 1939), GLEN ROUNDS (*The Blind Colt*, 1941), ROBERT MCCLOSKEY (*Make Way for the Ducklings*, 1941), VIRGINIA LEE BURTON (*The Little House*, 1942), ALICE AND MARTIN PROVENSEN (*The Fireside Book of Folksongs*, 1947), LYND WARD (*The Biggest Bear*, 1952) and BARBARA COONEY (*Ox-Cart Man*, 1978). Some more recent American works, however, such as those of THOMAS LOCKER (*Where the River Begins*, 1993), depart from the linear and take a painterly approach. Locker's style is a surprising return to some of the tendencies of the 19th-century Hudson River School of landscape painting.

Since at least the 1960s America's ethnic traditions, legends and histories have become a primary focus for the illustrated book. Related to the long-standing internationalist (window-on-the-world) preoccupation, the new interest in diverse cultural traditions reflects America's increasing self-consciousness about its own internal diversity. Books designed to satisfy the demand for multicultural materials have been among the bestselling and most honoured of recent illustrated books. LEO POLITO (*Pedro, the Angel of Olivera Street*, 1946) was among the pioneers of this movement. Other much-praised illustrators of multicultural topics are TOM FEELINGS (*To Be a Slave*, 1968), JOHN STEPTOE (*Stevie*, 1969), GERALD MCDERMOTT (*Arrow to the Sun*, 1974), TOMIE DE PAOLA (*Strega Nona*, 1975), PAUL GOBLE (*The Girl Who Loved Wild Horses*, 1978), LEO and DIANE DILLON (*The People Could Fly*, 1985), JERRY PINKNEY (*The Patchwork Quilt*, 1985), Ed Young (*Lon Po Po*, 1989), ALLAN SAY (*The Grandfather's Journey*, 1993) and David Diaz (*Smokey Night*, 1995).

Visual FANTASY had been prominent in American illustration even before Denslow and Baum. From the middle of the 20th century various tradition of fantasy began to combine forces. In particular, the fine-arts tradition of surrealism began to intermix with images out of books of NONSENSE, mystery and horror. Comic-book, comic-strip and advertising-graphics motifs fuelled experiments by fine-arts-trained illustrators. WILLIAM PENE DU BOIS (*The Twenty-One Balloons*, 1947), EDWARD GOREY (*The Unstrung Harp*, 1953), CROCKETT JOHNSON (*Harold and the Purple Crayon*, 1955), DR SEUSS (*The Cat in the Hat*, 1957) and TOMI UNGERER (*Moon Man*, 1967) are among the pioneers of the enhanced bizarre. RICHARD EGIELSKI (*Louis the Fish*, 1980), CHRIS VAN ALLSBURG (*Jumanji*, 1981), William Joyce (*George Shrinks*, 1985), JON SCIESZKA (*The True Story of the Three Little Pigs*, 1989), DAVID WIESNER (*Tuesday*, 1991) and PETER SÍS (*The Three Golden Keys*, 1994) belong to a new generation of fabulists.

Among the most important underlying forces in American illustration has been the playing out of the implication of Howard Pyle's notion that illustration can be fine art. In a class by himself in his mastery of most traditions and styles of American illustration is MAURICE SENDAK, who is sometimes referred to as the 'Picasso of picturebooks'. Sendak is the best example of an illustrator who has earned a status so high that it transcends whatever boundaries might be thought to exist between fine and popular arts. *IN THE NIGHT KITCHEN* (1970) is a masterwork of American art that just happens to be an illustrated book.

In Australia, the publication of *Gum Nut Babies* (1916) by author-illustrator MAY GIBBS is considered a turning-point in children's book illustration. Gibbs, and her contemporaries, IDA RENTOUL OUTHWAITE, DOROTHY WALL and NORMAN LINDSAY all wrote and illustrated books redolent with Australian fauna and flora, both real and imaginary. There was in many of these books a propensity for dainty Art Nouveau elves and fairies, although Lindsay's drawings for his classic, *THE MAGIC PUDDING* (1918), were bold black-and-white caricatures. Mary and Elizabeth Durack's book *THE WAY OF THE WHIRLWIND* (1941), another watershed in Australian picturebook illustration, has been described as 'one of the most lavishly illustrated children's books ever to be produced' (Saxby, 1998), with vibrant coloured plates, together with black-and-white drawings. Paper rationing during World War II and right up until the 1960s meant that children's book production was mainly handled by printers, rather than publishers, resulting in quantities of cheap, board-covered picture-story books, many of dubious quality. One notable illustrator of this period, however, was WALTER CUNNINGHAM. A staff artist for the John Sands printers, Cunningham became one of their foremost illustrators, with his innovative designs and layout for LESLIE REES's *Digit Dick* series. Australian picturebook production declined from the 1950s, with the importation of books from England, and the focus moved to junior fiction, bringing illustrators such as MARGARET HORDER, ASTRA LACIS, Margaret Paice, Margaret Senior, ANNETTE MACARTHUR-ONSLOW and Walter Stackpool into the limelight. There was a renewed interest and increase in picturebook publication in the 1970s, spurred on by a growth in opportunities for training for artists, more sophisticated production techniques, as well as a demand for Australian books by pre-school and kindergarten educators. Illustrators were able to experiment with a wider range of media, knowing that their artwork could now be reproduced (most of the time) more authentically. DICK ROUGHSEY captured the essence of the Australian landscape and lifestyle using flat acrylic colours and elongated figures in *The Giant Devil Dingo* (1973), while RON BROOKS achieved mysteriousness with the use of coloured inks and cross-hatching in *The Bunyip of Berkeley's Creek* (1973). Other illustrators who began their careers in the 1970s and 1980s, and whose work continues to remain popular with children, include TED GREENWOOD, QUENTIN HOLE, ROBERT INGPEN, ELIZABETH HONEY, JUDITH CRABTREE, RODNEY MCRAE, BOB GRAHAM, GRAEME BASE, CRAIG SMITH, NOELA YOUNG, PATRICIA MULLINS, and DEBORAH and KILMENY NILAND. While many of these illustrators have achieved international standing, JEANNIE BAKER's intricate collages of Australia have done much to promote knowledge of that country's natural heritage, as has SHAUN TAN's *The Rabbits* (1998).

Illustrators are moving beyond the more traditional media of oils, pastels, watercolour and sketch, to experiment with silk painting, paper sculpture, collage, photo-realism and surrealist or impressionist styles, as in NADIA WHEATLEY's *Luke's Way of Looking* (1999), illustrated by Matt Ottley, which attempts to break down conservative assumptions about the way children see the world. ANN JAMES's illustrations for ROBIN KLEIN's *PENNY POLLARD* series makes use of a collection of scraps – pinboard notes, emails, notes passed in class on paper bags, tickets and little scribbles. There is now a growing awareness that children can, and do, recognise abstract concepts and appreciate them in various representations. ENDPAPERS, too, are deemed more significant, and illustrators often use colour and design to reflect the theme of the book itself. An example of this has been achieved by ARMIN GREDER in *The Great Bear* (1999), which has endpapers full of astronomical symbols, signifying the metaphysical world to which the savagely treated circus bears of Eastern Europe aspire in an effort to escape their physical lives. Australian editors now recognise the place of symbolism achievable through the marriage of literary and visual text. Increasingly, one text is complementing the other, rather than merely duplicating, so that at least two perspectives are at work simultaneously. JUNKO MORIMOTO, PETER GOULDTHORPE, ROD CLEMENT, JANE TANNER, Ann Spudvilas, GREGORY ROGERS, PAMELA ALLEN, DAVID COX, TERRY DENTON, BRONWYN BANCROFT, COLIN THOMPSON and BRUCE WHATLEY are among illustrators who provide stimulating and idiosyncratic interpretations of texts. Since illustrating the very popular *POSSUM MAGIC* (1983) by MEM FOX, JULIE VIVAS has continued to employ her distinctive watercolour style, but always manages to give each new text an extra dimension, as in *Hello Baby* (1999), an emotionally charged interpretation of a baby being born.

JOHN LOCKE wrote in 1693 that, for the young child, 'as many pictures of animals should be got him as can be found, with the printed names to them, which at the same time will invite him to read, and afford him matter of enquiry and knowledge.' Undoubtedly he was correct in his utilitarian view of the role of pictures. What he was not able to assess, because it was so far from the view held of children and their literacy needs in those times, was the affective role of pictures in narrative texts and the significant part they could play in fleshing out and counterpointing story, character, setting, mood and theme. He could never have foreseen how, for instance, even the single illustration on a cover could create anticipation and be continually returned to for confirmation. In the three centuries since Locke wrote those words, thousands, probably millions of illustrated books have been published. Their contribution to children's delight in, persistence with, understanding of and affection for books cannot be underestimated. JAG, IW, JS, JAP, RTh

Impey, Rose 1947– British teacher and author. Rose Impey's writing reveals understanding of what attracts and keeps a reader's attention. She is known for well-constructed, fast-paced stories, often involving magic and scary situations, modern believable characters and satisfying resolutions. Inventive use of talk-bubbles, lists and other devices break up the text for the newly independent reader. Above all, Impey creates reading appetite through her series books, *Jets*, –among them her satisfying *Desperate for a Dog* (1988, with Jolyne Knox) – *Banana* books, the *Potbelly* series, the *Sleepover Club* series, marketed as 'definitely not for boys', and *Animal Crackers*, which are stories based on real-life animal record-breakers. JAG

In Fairyland see WILLIAM ALLINGHAM; RICHARD DOYLE; EDMUND EVANS; FAIRY FANTASY; GIFT BOOKS; ILLUSTRATION IN CHILDREN'S BOOKS; WOOD ENGRAVING

In The Night Kitchen (1970) Picturebook by the acclaimed American illustrator MAURICE SENDAK, the second of his PICTUREBOOK trilogy. *In the Night Kitchen* is a complex work, capable of being appreciated on many levels – taken simply as a comic-book hero's FANTASY adventure in dream form; or as a celebration and candid acceptance of the sensuality and sexuality of children, an exploration of the relationships between dreams and the psyche; or interpreted as a mythic journey into the underworld where potentially annihilating forces are defeated by the hero's bravery and creativity. A small boy, Mickey, falls out of bed and drops naked into a bowl of batter in a bakery presided over by a trio of Oliver Hardy lookalikes. They mix him into a cake and put him in the oven; it looks like the end of Mickey. But Mickey rises, phoenix-like, kneads himself a dough-plane, flies over the Milky Way to get milk for the bakers, and after a climactic cry of 'Cock a Doodle Doo!' finds himself back in bed. WINSOR MCCAY's comic strip *Little Nemo in Slumberland* was a major source of inspiration. Sendak's pictorial style is flat and fat, with comically squat characters and rotund forms drawn in magic marker outline. Colour is muted and warm, and the layout enables the action to flow with cinematic ease. The picturebook, replete with authentic 1930s period details, is a tribute to the artist's childhood, with visual references to his personal life, and influenced by popular culture, especially comic-books, and the films of WALT DISNEY and Busby Berkeley. JD

Incredible Journey, The (1961) Novel by Sheila Burnford, based upon Burnford's fascination with the communication that exists between animals. Set in Northern Ontario, the novel describes the dangerous wilderness journey undertaken by three family pets – two dogs and a cat – who have been left in the care of a friend while their owners are away on a trip to Europe. The 'incredible journey' begins when the animals set off together in search of the new home of their owners. Burnford's award-winning novel has been translated into over 25 languages and made into a film. The theme of the balance between individual personalities and particular strengths is emphasised by the animals' deep affection and loyalty toward one another, and their mutual determination to reach their goal. Burnford's novel, which depicts animals anthropomorphically expressing human emotions, falls outside the realistic tradition of the American JEAN CRAIGHEAD GEORGE and the Canadian authors and naturalists ERNEST THOMPSON SETON, CHARLES G. D. ROBERTS and FARLEY MOWAT. MRS
see also ANIMALS IN CHILDREN'S FICTION

***Indian in the Cupboard* series** (from 1980) Series of five (to date) FANTASY novels by British novelist LYNNE REID BANKS. Combining two different traditions in children's literature, that of Lilliputian races and that of toys that come to life, *The Indian in the Cupboard* tells the story of a boy, Omri, whose magic cupboard has the power to change his plastic toys into real (though tiny) people with real histories. Initially, Omri views the magic with delight, but as his tiny people become more demanding and less satisfied with living in a world of giants, the responsibilities of caring for his cupboard's creations begin to weigh on him. The book and its four sequels detail Omri's continuing struggle between pleasure and responsibility as he not only brings more plastic people to life, but visits the past as well. In the tradition of E. NESBIT, Banks sets her fantasies in a middle-class, modern-day England, and Omri and his friend Patrick must deal with contemporary issues such as divorce, gangs and a highly mobile society. This combination of real-life problems with vivid fantasy has won the books several awards, particularly in the United States. However, despite Banks's attempts at including Native American history, the books have also raised controversy over the portrayal of the title character, Omri's plastic Indian. The controversy only increased with the release of the 1994 film version of the book, which moved the setting from England to America but otherwise did not stray far from the themes and content of the original novel. KS

Indian myths, legends and folktales India is the ancient home of the tale and the teller. Endowed with one of the longest histories of both oral and written fiction, India boasts a vast, vibrant storehouse of myths, FOLKTALES AND LEGENDS which are characterised by a protean, chimerical bond between the tale, the teller and the listener. Nestling in the crook of a grandmother's arms, listening in rapt attention to her yarns, the child grows up in a social milieu where stories are an integral part of everyday life as a familiar cultural ingredient. This dynamic environment keeps the magic realm of gods, fairies, demons, heroes, heroines and animals alive, which in turn actively shapes the world-view of the child.

The peculiar multilingual character of the Indian subcontinent shows itself in various versions of myths, folktales and legends that are constantly adapted to changing circumstances. As elsewhere, myths originally made to explain the unknown have been elevated through time to the level of religion. The beginning of all myths is to be found in the grand Puranic myth of Creation by Brahma the Creator, the first of the Hindu Trinity which is completed by the most popular gods of the Hindu pantheon, Vishnu the Preserver, and Mahesh (Shiva) the Destroyer. Vishnu, a favourite in his benignity, has apparently appeared in nine incarnations paralleling successive stages of evolution, starting from the matsya (fish) and culminating in the village king Rama, the town king Krishna and the Buddha. The exploits of the seventh and eighth incarnations of Rama and Krishna form the substance of the popular tales in the two premier epics of Hindu India, the *Ramayana* and the *Mahabharata*. To various extents, every Hindu, whatever the antecedents, is familiar with the story of these sacred texts that dramatise the conjoining of gods and humans in the concerted archetypal conflict between good and evil.

The *Ramayana*, uncertainly and speculatively dated between 1500 and 400 BC, was originally composed by Valmiki in Sanskrit with 24,000 stanzas. With an impressive array of characters, this literary composition contains an enduring philosophy and is the largest source of inspiration for creative writers. It narrates the story of Rama, the brave and righteous ruler of Ayodhya, revered as the original paragon of steadfast moral virtues. It details his brave exploits as a child and as a young man, highlighting the circumstances of his marriage to the beautiful Sita. Following him through a 14-year banishment by his father at the behest of an ill-meaning stepmother, the narrative climaxes in a battle against Ravana, the demon-king of Lanka, who has spirited Sita away by deceit and cunning.

The drama of the war between the forces of good and evil is also played out in the confrontation between the five virtuous Pandavas backed by the attractive God-King Krishna, and the hundred Kauravas in the *Mahabharata* of Vyasa. This longest extant epic – retold in *Mahabharata: A Retelling of the Great Story of India* (2000) by Margaret Simpson – includes the teachings of Krishna to a wavering Arjuna, third of the five Pandavas, in the holy *Bhagvad Gita*, which contains the essence of Hindu philosophy and religion.

The Buddhist *Jataka* or Birth stories, originally appearing in the Pali language, deal with episodes from the previous births of the Buddha in which he is known as the Boddhisattva. He appears in many guises: as a prince, as a merchant, or even as an animal. The earliest of these sage, persuasive and avowedly didactic stories, goes back to the third century BC. They are lucid, expressive and tinged with a bald, understated humour. Common human follies and foibles – like the dangers of garrulity, or trusting foolish friends – are wittily exposed without wounding the audience. These timeless alluring fabular animal tales of common folklore (see also ANIMALS IN CHILDREN'S FICTION) are extant in several versions, having passed into widespread currency with their appearance in tales like those in Boccaccio's *Decameron* and CHAUCER's *Canterbury Tales*. Popular fare for both the young and old, these amenably preach of the need for the development of the faculties of intelligence and virtue in dealing with the sordid side of life.

By far the most popular primary stories for children are the tales of the *Panchatantra* (5th century BC). These didactic tales, usually focusing on small animals which outsmart the tyranny of bigger animals, deal with the common politics of power. They identify wit and cunning as the retaliatory weapons of the weak: powerful tigers are outwitted by the little rabbit; the deceitful crocodile is hoodwinked by the quick-thinking monkey. Sedition, perfidy and swindling are regular themes. These supposed precursors of the later AESOP'S FABLES have entered regular Indian parlance by supplying images and comparisons.

The *Kathāsaritsāga* or the *Ocean of Stories* (11th century AD) by Somadeva has a tremendous variety of character and situation, the collection of tales being the largest, twice that of the *Iliad* and the *Odyssey*. Paralleling the *ARABIAN NIGHTS* cycle, the mighty ocean includes the various elements of myth, mystery, fact, fancy, legend, tradition and romance. These are recalled directly as an inspirational beginning for Salman Rushdie's *Haroun and the Sea of Stories*.

Children's literature in any language in India cannot emerge untouched by this inheritance of myths and legends. The many attempts to retell the epics for children, eliciting the finest inputs from writers and illustrators, bear witness to this early imaginative introduction to the universal human condition. MBh

Infant's Magazine, The see American Sunday School Union

information books A wide category of texts specifically designed in print, graphics and illustrations to interest, inform, instruct and thus extend the knowledge of young people about subjects, events and ideas they encounter during their years of formal education. In publishing terms they differ from textbooks, the traditional material of school lessons written in the conventional subject discourse and organised as a linear programme of study. The common description of information books as non-fiction, or as collections of facts, commends them to parents and teachers as sources for children's learning. Conventional books of reference – dictionaries, atlases and encyclopedias, now more swiftly updated – are simplified in content and structure for young learners according to adult perceptions of children's need for learning tools to acquire competence in study skills. Encyclopedias vary from single compendia – books of 'knowledge' and the *Guinness Book of Records* – to prestigious volumes like the *Oxford Children's Encyclopedia*, large investments for both publisher and purchaser. For inexperienced users, looking something up in multi-volumed sources is rarely straightforward. (For example, Morse code may appear under telegraph and not under codes and ciphers.)

In contrast, contemporary topic books are part of information 'resources'. Shorter, with eye-catching covers, graphics and photography, they are designed to attract young readers into browsing through a number of illustrated pages for something that fits into a unit of school work. Cheaper productions are usually recognisable in series, varied in content but uniform in design. Readers expect topic books to be as interesting, attractive and up-to-date as television and video presentations, and as user-friendly as electronic technologies which are now the prime sources for immediate information retrieval. A short book about rainforests may serve a nine-year-old as an introduction to thinking and writing about an area of interest first encountered as a television documentary. Data hitherto unavailable, or information once considered unsuitable for young learners, now appear in illustrated books for primary schools.

Individual authors of information books are usually enthusiasts who communicate the passion of their interest as well as the details of their subject. They address their readers as apprentices or young experts. Most books that offer segments of topic information are compilations by editorial teams working to a familiar blueprint of generalisation and examples. The success in packaging information of the publishers Dorling Kindersley comes from skilled topic editing, distinctive photography of authentic sources, significant page design and good marketing. Young learners appreciate the modern appearance of these books with their distinctive format and house style, and this helps them to become confident enough to engage with a wider range of subject matter. Clarity of topic presentation holds the readers' attention just long enough to take in the short explanatory paragraphs and captions. In most current topic books, print fills no more than a quarter of a page. Some page designs now replicate Internet screens and are spiral-bound as files instead of chapters. The reader is encouraged to log on to sub-title tabs so as to move directly to divisions of the database: photos, notes, index or references, as if the book were an electronic note-pad. The challenge of visual presentations in the world outside school has produced in books a much greater flexibility and variety of texts adjusted to curriculum topics, to readers' purposes and to their information needs. Nevertheless, in Britain at least, information books for young people still suffer from a lack of sustained, critical reading by interested and well-informed adults, such as have influenced other areas of children's literature. Few journals other than *Books for Keeps* and *The School Librarian* undertake regular reviewing. The *Times Educational Supplement* Information Book Award and the Rhone-Poulenc Science Book Prize excite much less general interest than they deserve.

The common assumption that boys are more interested in 'non-fiction' than in imaginative literature is a comment on their perceived reading habits; they read in shorter bursts, and seem to prefer magazine-type texts to continuous prose. Girls are regarded as better readers, but their noted preference for novels results in a disregard for their needs as readers of information. Another common fallacy – that in order to promote knowledge information books should not be written as narratives – ignores the 'facts' that lie behind every story ever told. A more important version of this concern is that, to be competently literate in the handling of sources of information which they will read and understand, young people need books and texts which give them experience of a wide range of discourses, the different ways of writing about modern subject matters as these evolve and become part of general knowledge.

Information books for children in America have a long and distinguished history. Evelyn Wenzel, in Jo Carr's *Beyond Fact* (1982), briefly sketches their history, beginning in the 19th century with the travel books of SAMUEL GOODRICH, Jacob Abbot and others, followed by history and science books, such as T.W. Higginson's *Young Folks' History of the United States* (1875) and Arabella B. Buckley's *The Fairy-Land of Science* (1879). In the early 20th century advances in technology enabled information books to combine illustrations more effectively with texts, resulting in books like E. Boyd Smith's *The Farm Book* (1910). HENDRIK VAN LOON's non-fiction *The Story of Mankind* was the winner of the first NEWBERY MEDAL in 1922.

In the 1920s LUCY SPRAGUE MITCHELL's 'here and now' philosophy helped focus the attention of writers, teachers and children on realistic stories and non-fiction depictions of the real world. In addition to such fanciful stories about machines as Virginia Lee Burton's *Mike Mulligan and His Steam Shovel* (1939), many non-fiction books, such as *How the Derrick Works* (1931) by Wilfred Jones, featured machines and technology. Barbara Bader in *American Picturebooks* (1976) points out the influence of Russian books and illustrators on non-fiction picturebooks and discusses the work of Maud and Miska Petersham, Dorothy Waugh, and Herbert Zim, Millicent Selsam, CROCKETT JOHNSON, Holling Clancy Holling, ALIKI, and others.

Federal funding for science education in the 1960s resulted in a great increase in numbers of information books in the United States, followed by a decline in the 1970s. But the early 1980s saw a renaissance, with the publication of new, more colourful and livelier information books to replace outdated works. Among outstanding American authors of information books beginning in the 1970s are JEAN CRAIGHEAD GEORGE, Patricia Lauber, LAURENCE PRINGLE and SEYMOUR SIMON for science writing; and Rhoda Blumberg, RUSSELL FREEDMAN, JEAN FRITZ, JAMES CROSS GIBLIN, KATHRYN LASKY, PATRICIA and FREDRICK MCKISSACK, MILTON MELTZER and JUDITH ST. GEORGE for BIOGRAPHY, history and social issues.

Awareness of nonfiction as literature was sparked by Milton Meltzer's 'Where Do All the Prizes Go?: The Case for Nonfiction' (HORN BOOK, February 1976). Meltzer argued that the best of non-fiction involves 'imagination, invention, selection, language, and form' as much as any work of fiction. As a result more attention began to be paid to information books, several became Newbery Honour Books, and THE BOSTON GLOBE-HORN BOOK AWARD established an award category for non-fiction. Jo Carr in the introduction to *Beyond Fact* (1982) states that the non-fiction writer ought to combine the qualities of the teacher and the artist, and that writing 'the literature of fact' must involve emotions, passion, imagination and artistry as well as facts. 'Good non-fiction writers, like all teachers who know their subject well, distill from their knowledge a significant view of the world. But it is how the author communicates this insight that is crucial. In literature of fact the teacher's insight is vividly illuminated by the writer's art.'

Beverly Kobrin, who reviews information books in the *Kobrin Letter*, outlines her criteria for judging non-fiction in the chapter in *Eyeopeners!* (1988) entitled 'How to Judge a Book By Its Cover – and Nine Other Clues'. Criteria include: (1) attractiveness, (2) accuracy, (3) authority, (4) appropriateness, (5) rhetoric, (6) stereotypes, (7) tone, (8) cautions, (9) format and (10) book design. Readers may quickly check any information book for the qualifications of the author, authorities consulted, acknowledgement of sources, the existence of a bibliography or references, an index, a table of contents and a glossary. Illustrations and graphics should be appropriate, accurate and well captioned.

Information books for children are currently in the midst of rapid changes influenced by television and computer technology combined with changes in society and its perceptions of childhood. The boundaries between fiction and non-fiction, and between childhood and adulthood, are more slippery than ever. (See Eliza T. Dresang's *Radical Change: Literature for Youth in an Electronic Age*, 1998.) Books like the popular *Magic School Bus* series by JOANNA COLE and Bruce Degen combine fact and fiction in comic-style formats, while a picture story-book such as BETSY JAMES's *Mary Ann* (1995) concludes with an information note about praying mantises. DAVID MACAULAY, whose stunning architectural books – beginning with *Cathedral* (1973) – are works of fiction based on architectural facts, also produced the encyclopedic *The Way Things Work* (1988), combining information with humourous cartoons and CAUTIONARY TALES. This book is now also available as a CD-ROM that can be manipulated. In *Rome-Antics* (1997) Macaulay has combined story with a dizzying architectural tour of Rome as seen from a pigeon's perspective. *It's Perfectly Normal* (1994), written by Robie H. Harris and illustrated by Michael Emberley, has won numerous awards and been acclaimed by countless critics, yet its explicit text and detailed cartoon-like drawings explaining puberty and sexuality made it one of the most censored books of 1996 (see also CENSORSHIP). In the realm of historical and social issues, Jill Krementz has continued to produce photo essays such as *How It Feels When a Parent Dies* (1991), and Susan Kuklin has published *Speaking Out: Teenagers Talk on Race, Sex, and Identity* (1993), and *Irrepressible Spirits: Conversations with Human Rights Activists* (1996). TOM FEELINGS published his powerful, visually stunning *The Middle*

Passage in 1995, and Patricia and Fredrick McKissack their painstakingly researched *Rebels Against Slavery* in 1996.

American information books for children were also strongly influenced in the 1980s and 90s by the books of innovative British publishers, Usborne and Dorling Kindersley. Information books now include elaborate pop-up book formats (see MOVABLE BOOKS). At least one book, *Tie Your Shoes* (1997), a how-to guide, comes with real shoelaces to tie in the book's shoe. Robert Sabuda's *Cookie Count* (1997) reinforces counting concepts while presenting three-dimensional versions of several kinds of cookies through ingenious paper engineering. ANN TURNER's and Wendell Minor's *Shaker Hearts* (1997) is an information picturebook written in poetry. *The Etcher's Studio* (1997) by Arthur Geisert describes the process of etching in a book created with etchings, shows examples of various etching styles in close-up and at the same time tells a story. CHRIS RASCHKA's *Mysterious Thelonious* (1997) presents the music of jazz musician Thelonious Monk in an innovative picturebook format using colours to represent musical tones. Ruth Heller's *Mine, All Mine* (1997) is a vividly coloured picturebook about pronouns. Ed Young in *Voices of the Heart* (1997) translates Chinese characters into Western symbols, expanding the reader's perceptions of ways in which language works. PAUL FLEISCHMAN's *Dateline: Troy* (1996), although technically classified as fiction, defies categorisation with its retelling of the Trojan War juxtaposed with collages based on photocopies of 20th-century newspaper clippings. Walter Wick offers stunning photographs of water in all its forms in *A Drop of Water* (1997), and acknowledges that his work was inspired by Arabella B. Buckley, one of the earliest American authors of science books for children.

Australia's first locally published book was really an information book. Entitled *A MOTHER'S OFFERING TO HER CHILDREN BY A LADY LONG RESIDENT IN NEW SOUTH WALES* (1841) by Charlotte Barton, it reflected the current attitudes to the instruction and moral development of children. Other early landmark information books were Walter G. Mason's *The Australian Picture Pleasure Book* (1857), Louisa Anne Meredith's *Tasmanian Friends and Foes: Feathered, Furred and Finned* (1880) and Mary Anne Fitzgerald's *Australian Furs and Feathers* (1889). For the first half of the 20th century a British-based school curriculum model, combined with the greater technological strength of British publishing, created an extensive market for British information books in Australia. Since World War II, the balance of cultural dominance has tipped towards the United States, most notable today in educational computer software and CD-ROMs. Though there has been publication of Australian information books throughout this century, it has only been in the last 20 years that the Australian identity has asserted itself fully in an expansion of information book publishing. The strong influence of the CHILDREN'S BOOK COUNCIL OF AUSTRALIA BOOK OF THE YEAR AWARDS has now been extended with the Eve Pownall Award for Information Books, established in 1993. This is for 'outstanding books . . . documenting factual material . . . with imaginative presentation, interpretation and variation of style.' Some winners are Kathie Atkinson's *Life in a Rotten Log* (1993) and John Nicholson's *The First Fleet: A New Beginning in an Old Land* (1995).

More sophisticated printing techniques have facilitated the growth of information PICTUREBOOKS. Striking examples are JEANNIE BAKER's *WHERE THE FOREST MEETS THE SEA* (1987) and *Window* (1991); NARELLE OLIVER's *The Best Beak in Boonaroo Bay* (1993) and Christopher Cheng's *One Child* (1997). Single titles with longer connected discourse and strong factual content include Wendy Macdonald's *The Voyage of the Endeavour* (1995), Eleanor Stodart's *The Australian Echidna* (1989) and Denise Burt's *The Birth of a Koala* (1987). *Killer Plants: And How to Grow Them* (1996) by Gordon Cheers and Julie Silk, winner of the Eve Pownall Award in 1997, and Monnie Fenner's *Keeping Silkworms* (1992) are in a magazine format with small blocks of text interspersed among captioned illustrations, a format popular in the many non-fiction series developed in recent years. Among a number of excellent current series are the comprehensive Kondinin Group's 'Workboot' books on *Wheat* (1994), *Wool* (1995), *Dairying* (1995) and *Cotton* (1997) and the Allen and Unwin 'Discoveries' series on topics such as *Reptiles* (1996), *Flight* (1995) and *Great Inventions* (1995). Densey Clyne's 'Small Worlds' series and Eleanor Stodart's 'Australian Junior Field Guides' cover Australian fauna. Fictionalised information books (faction) provide an added dimension to bare facts. NADIA WHEATLEY's *MY PLACE* (1988) opens up a vista of Australian history from 1788 to 1988. Gerald and Guundie Kuching's books (1996–7) are about *Yakkinn the Swamp Tortoise*; Richard Scott-Child's *Pirates Don't Pick Flowers* (1996) concerns his ancestor William Dampier. A valuable and relatively recent development has been the publication of books by Aboriginal Australians and the establishment of an indigenous publishing house, Magabala Books (1987). The autobiographical *Stradbroke Dreamtime* by OODGEROO NOONUCAL (1972) was reissued in 1993 with brilliant illustrations by BRONWYN BANCROFT (1993), who has also illustrated Roland Robinson's retelling of Percy Mumbulla's *The Whalers* (1995). *Tjarany Roughtail: The Dreaming of the Roughtail Lizard and Other Stories* (1992), told by the Kukatja people of Western and Southern Australia, won the Eve Pownall Award for Information Books in 1993, while Ian Abdulla's *Tucker* (1994) was shortlisted for the award.

'The Poppykettle' from *The Encyclopaedia of Things that Never Were* by Robert Ingpen and Michael Page.

While New Zealand publishers have for many years produced information books aimed at the school market, general non-fiction is only now coming of age. Awards for this category have helped in its development. The Library and Information Association established the first specific award for non-fiction in 1987. It went to *Gaijin: Foreign Children in Japan* (1986), a very personal and engaging account written by Olive and Ngaio Hill. The AIM and *NEW ZEALAND POST* AWARDS further encouraged publication in this area although judges for the 1998 awards commented in their report: 'In New Zealand many of the children's non-fiction books published are either clearly aimed at curriculum support or for a wide-level audience, books to be used by both adults and children alike. There are few books produced that are targeted purely at a child's pleasure.' The report went on to ask why such a narrow range of topics was covered, mainly flora and fauna: 'Where are the books that we need of New Zealand history and biography – where are those small tales of human endeavour that have shaped our country . . .?' However, books such as *It's OK to be You: Feeling Good About Growing Up* (1988) and *The Know, Sow and Grow Kids' Book of Plants* (1997) are very child-centred, while titles such as ELSIE LOCKE's *Two Peoples, One Land: A History of Aotearoa/New Zealand Especially for Young Readers* (1992) and *Joe's Ruby* (1995) give children a sense of both national and individual endeavour. MM, JZ, BN, LH

***Ingary* series** A set of two (to date) novels by DIANA WYNNE JONES. Ingary, an idealised pre-industrial England, is the setting for *Howl's Moving Castle* (1986) and part of its sequel, *Castle in the Air* (1991), which also takes place in Rashpuht, an eastern kingdom like Calormen (see *CHRONICLES OF NARNIA*). The two form a magical world incorporating elements from North European FAIRY TALE and from the *ARABIAN NIGHTS*, such as witches, enchanters, djinns and the power of three. Wynne Jones inverts many conventions from these stories in creating her characteristic blend of powerful female characters, inept and irresponsible males, magic and comedy. JEG

Ingelow, Jean see *MOPSA THE FAIRY*; see also ALICE IMITATIONS

Ingpen, Robert (Roger) 1936– The only Australian illustrator to have won the HANS CHRISTIAN ANDERSEN MEDAL (in 1986). While he expresses through his paintings and ILLUSTRATIONS his own feeling for the environment, and the Australian landscape in particular, Ingpen also perceives a hidden history which he has expressed in words and paintings in books like *The Voyage of the Poppykettle* (1980) and *The Unchosen Land* (1981), in which an expedition of Hairy Peruvian gnomes sails to Australia in a Poppy Kettle and on arrival, led by Don Avante, explores the land. Ingpen's vision not only enables him to represent assorted Australian gnomes and explore secret landscapes but it also gives him access to the ruminations of teddy bears in *The Idle Bear* (1986) and *The Age of Acorns* (1988), and in *The Dreamkeeper* (1995) to tell of that being who 'lives in the world just around the corner . . . where reality is an intruder and dreams, both good and bad, come true.' That Dreamkeeper illuminates all of Ingpen's art from COLIN THIELE's *STORM BOY* (1974) to Philip Wilkinson's *The*

Encyclopedia of Events That Changed the World (1991) and Ted Egan's *The Drover's Boy* (1998). In *Once Upon a Place* (1999) Ingpen's paintings and notes bring to life many imaginary places drawn from literature. MSax

Inkpen, Mick 1952– British PICTUREBOOK author and illustrator. After studying graphic design Inkpen worked with Nick Butterworth (see PERCY SERIES) but is now best known for the work he has done on his own. *The Blue Balloon* (1989) is the story of a boy and his dog, Kipper, who together find a soggy balloon which grows bigger and bigger. Kipper has since become the subject of a series of picturebooks which feature the dog continually trying to put things right and never quite managing it. The ILLUSTRATIONS are clear and simple, outlined in black and drawn from a small child's perspective. Kipper's owner does not reappear and Kipper clearly thinks – and writes – like a small child. Other characters adopt the adult roles, explaining things and tempering Kipper's bouncy enthusiasm. The same apparently simple style of illustration coupled with a novelty format is used to particular effect in *Threadbear* (1990), *Penguin Small* (1992) and *The Great Pet Sale* (1999). With *Nothing* (1995) Inkpen adopted a more subtle style. The book is intended for an older age group and does not use novelty devices. Instead the illustrations progress from sombre grey colours to become lighter and brighter as the 'little thing' becomes confident in a new-found identity. KA

Inky Pinky Ponky: Children's Playground Rhymes (1982) Anthology collected by the British poet MICHAEL ROSEN and Susanna Steele, illustrated by Dan Jones. These contemporary versions of children's traditional jingles, jeers, songs and repartee, reclaimed from scholarly anthologies, are overprinted as graffiti on lively scenes of London's multicultural East End to make a statement about popular art and cultural heritage. MM

see also PLAYGROUND RHYMES; RIDDLES AND JOKES

Innocenti, Roberto 1940– Italian artist. After animation work in Rome Innocenti returned to his birthplace, Florence, to design and eventually to illustrate books. He has illustrated IAN MCEWAN's retelling of the poignant war-time story *Rose Blanche* (1985), Carlo Collodi's PINOCCHIO (1988), DICKENS's *A Christmas Carol* (1990) and E.T.A. Hoffman's *The Nutcracker* (1996). His realistic paintings, dominated by browns and greys, are carefully crafted, providing much period detail. JAG

International Board on Books for Young People (IBBY) Organisation founded in October 1953 in Zurich, Switzerland, by JELLA LEPMAN, a German Jew who had been forced to flee Germany with her two children in 1938. Lepman returned after World War II, eager to promote understanding among the world's children, believing they were the hope for a peaceful future. Partly sponsored during its formation by the Rockefeller Foundation and later under the aegis of UNESCO, IBBY now comprises members from more than 65 countries. The Board's stated purpose is 'to support and unify those forces in all countries connected with children's book work: to encourage the production and distribution of good children's books, especially in the developing countries.' IBBY also supervises an IBBY Honour List, consisting of two books (one for text and one for illustration) from each of its national sections. These are chosen as representative of the best in children's literature from each country and are considered suitable for publication throughout the world. MS

International Research Society for Children's Literature An organisation founded by seven specialists in literature for children and young people. The Society held its first biennial symposium in 1971. Eighteen countries and 50 scholars made up the membership rolls; in 1997 230 members from 39 countries participated in the Society. From the beginning the IRSCL has considered serious cultural, historical and political questions in terms of children's literature, including gender stereotyping in texts for children, problems of translation, the history of children's literature, the application of critical theory to children's literature, and multiculturalism in children's literature. The IRSCL exchanges professional information, initiates the discussion of theoretical questions, and helps to co-ordinate research from different academic disciplines. JZo

International Youth Library Unique library dedicated to children's and youth literature, working to foster knowledge and international understanding. The International Youth Library was founded in 1948 in Munich, Germany, by JELLA LEPMAN, a political activist and children's advocate. In 1953 it became an associated project of UNESCO. During its first years of existence, stress was laid upon activities with children, and later it also became a research library. This special library now includes a total of approximately 460,000 books, photographs, tape recordings, manuscript collections and professional literature in more than 65 languages. Scholars may use its more than 300 professional periodicals and 20 national biographies. Housed in the 15th-century Blutenberg Castle, the library receives copies of new titles from over 100 publishers each year. In addition to its research mission, the library continues the tradition established by Lepman, maintaining a public lending library, presenting frequent children's programmes, organising travelling exhibitions and offering language courses throughout the year. MS

see also COLLECTIONS OF CHILDREN'S BOOKS

internet A global network of linked computers, operated by organisations, institutions and individuals, primarily accessed through a graphical interface called the World Wide Web. Several pieces of hardware – a personal computer, a modem and a phone-line – combined with appropriate software, are required to enable the individual to converse with users all over the world. The pedagogic potential of the internet is enormous, providing parents and teachers with a massive supply of teaching resources. It also furnishes children, who are frequently more computer-literate than their elders, with unlimited access to world-wide reservoirs of information. Indeed, the internet is a highly democratic medium, allowing entry to anyone and thus making regulation difficult.

Clearly, children require protection from inherently harmful material and consequently several internet censor programmes have been developed; *Net Nanny* (Leaf Distribution), for example, closes applications containing forbidden keywords, while *Cyber Patrol* (Microsystems Software) refuses admittance to certain internet sites.

As a literary resource, the internet is remarkably dynamic, allowing the user to function variously as researcher, reader, critic or author. General subject searches provide access to children's publishers, libraries or museums, while more specific keyword searches reveal biographical information on such authors as BEATRIX POTTER and ROALD DAHL, or fanatical tributes to such popular characters as the MOOMINS or ASTERIX.

A large amount of fiction written by children (see also CHILD AUTHORS) is published on the internet, from short stories and poems, to animated comic strips; children are encouraged to express themselves both through literary genres and popular media. Users are frequently invited to review the work of young authors, or even enter into a discussion with them via email; children are thus given a voice in the field of children's literature, which in other cases is primarily written, produced and disseminated by adults.

Commercial fiction is also available, although rather than replacing extant printed works, it largely complements them. For example, the full text of COOLIDGE's *What Katy Did Next* (1886) is useful for online research; keyword searches take the reader to specific lines, though phone bills and printing costs make it an impractical replacement for a cheap edition of the book. PICTUREBOOKS can also be found; for example, the DISNEY site contains a picturebook based on the 1996 film version of *James and the Giant Peach* (1961). However, while its graphics are impressive, their appearance on screen entails a tedious and expensive wait. A resolution to this type of problem possibly lies in the union of multimedia CD-ROMs – currently the most viable platform for electronic literature – and the internet. Multimedia is costly to develop in CD-ROM, while the combined media of the internet significantly reduce these expenses. Additionally, while video, sound and graphics are extremely slow to download from the internet, the CD-ROM can hold vast amounts of digitised information. Accordingly, Dorling Kindersley and Microsoft, the most influential publishers of multimedia, are developing links between the Web and CD-ROM, thus extending the dimensions of the literary arena. LS

intertextuality see LITERATURE WITHIN CHILDREN'S LITERATURE

Intruder, The (1969) Novel by the British author JOHN ROWE TOWNSEND which, like many of his works, is about a young man's painful process of questioning both his future and his identity. It is set in the economically stagnating village of Skirlston where Arnold Haithwaite has learnt to guide people across the precarious sands of the bay. The unexpected arrival of a stranger who claims to have his own name and to be his only family connection causes Arnold to retreat into solitary resignation, and he rejects even his friends' attempts to help. There are no easy anwers, but the harsh landscape holds the key to his future and also his survival. EA

Invisible Dick see COMICS, PERIODICALS AND MAGAZINES

Ireson, Barbara British anthologist of stories and poems. Her *Faber Book of Nursery Verse* (1958) reflects Ireson's conviction that children are capable of enjoying 'poetry of surprising variety'. Her eclectic collection avoids sentimentality and displays both a sure judgement of what appeals to the young reader and a wide knowledge of poetry. French NURSERY RHYMES, the Chinese MOTHER GOOSE, poets such as JAMES REEVES and A.A. MILNE: all these, as well as various inspired Anons, are creatively juxtaposed. FRBS

Irish Children's Book Trust Founded in 1989, its aims were to encourage Irish writing for children and to promote books and reading. It administered the CBI BISTO BOOK OF THE YEAR AWARD, published two guides to Irish children's books and developed a library and information centre. In 1996 it merged with the CHILDREN'S LITERATURE ASSOCIATION OF IRELAND, to form CHILDREN'S BOOKS IRELAND. VC

Irish mythology and folklore Twentieth-century children's literature in Ireland has drawn considerably from Irish mythology and folklore and continues to do so. There are two main wellsprings of this material: literary tradition and oral tradition. In ancient Ireland there were many varieties of storytellers, from the unlearned spinner of yarns to the learned poet and master of history, genealogy and local lore. In the 12th century tales were divided into lists of prím-scéla and fo-scéla, main tales and susbsidiary tales. Today, modern scholars have categorised the tales in four main cycles: the Mythological Cycle, the Ulster Cycle, the Fenian Cycle and the Cycles of the Kings.

In tales of the Mythological Cycle the Tuatha Dé Danann are the principal characters. Their chief opponents are the Fir Bolg, the Fomoiri and latterly Clanna Míleadh. The tales and traditions surrounding the pantheon of mythological figures in early Irish literature are to be found in the compilation known as *Lebor Gabála Érenn* [*The Book of Conquests*]. It has been accepted by scholars that this is a deliberate work of fiction. Otherworldly characters, gods of pagan Ireland and their descendants people this cycle. They are characterised as highly skilled, clever, wily and very adroit, and surrounded by an aura of marvellous mystery and wonder, with many strange deeds, and great contrasts of beauty and terror.

The Ulster Cycle has Cúchulainn at its centre. It comprises a large collection of heroic tales, based on the Ulaidh, an ancient tribe which subsequently gave its name to the province. The Ulaidh resided in Rudhraighe, and are often called Clann Rudhraighe (the family or tribe of Rudhraighe). The Ulster Cycle is often called *Rudhraigheacht* as a result, and a loose translation of this has led to its being erroneously named as stories of the Red Branch Knights. The characters are valiant, courageous, steadfast heroes who take on challenges, undergo adventures and endure horrific physical tests in the name of honour and glory. Many of the stories are concerned with the long-standing animosity between the provinces of Ulster and Connacht, and its principal tale is the well-known lengthy saga *Táin Bó Cuailgne* (*The Cattle Raid of Cuailgne*) which epitomises the intensity of their hostility at the time when King Conor Mac Nessa was king of Ulster, Queen Maeve reigned in Connacht, and Cú Chulainn defended Ulster against all of Maeve's warriors. The traditional date for these tales is the beginning of the Christian era.

The Fenian Cycle is somewhat later, set during Cormac Mac Airt's reign, which is generally supposed to be in the third century. Fionn, Oisín, Diarmaid, Caoilte, Oscar, Goll and Conán Mac Mórna are the main characters, though the Tuatha Dé Danann exercise a considerable influence on events. There is a strong sense of place in Fenian literature, with locations and place-name lore adding proofs of authenticity to the events. Coupled with this, however, is the ethereal presence of the otherworld, which both beckons and threatens Fenian heroes. There is also an interesting undercurrent of conflict between the ancient pagan beliefs and practices and those of the newer Christian religion.

The Cycles of the Kings, also known as the Historical Cycle, contains about 70 tales, some about legendary kings, others about historical characters of note. The heroic tales of Ulster celebrate individual heroes' feats; tales in the Cycles of the Kings, however, pay homage to important aspects of the community and society. They contain lore about the origins of important dynasties, as well as interesting and illuminating stories about particular kings, accounts of battles which altered the course of history, or events which seek to explain a certain custom. Tales of King Niall (of the Nine Hostages), Cormac Mac Airt, Eoghan Mór of Munster, Rónán, and many others are to be found in this cycle.

Writers such as Crofton Croker, Lady Gregory, W.B. Yeats, EILEEN O FAOLAIN, PATRICIA LYNCH, LIAM MAC UISTÍN, CORMAC MAC RAOIS, Mary Regan, Eddie Lenihan, Una Leavy, MICHAEL SCOTT, Niamh Sharkey are among the many who have used these sources to present some of the corpus of ancient Irish tales in a new light to children of the 20th century.

The second major source for modern writers to draw upon is the oral tradition of STORYTELLING, which encompasses the märchen, heroic and adventure tales, explanatory tales, local legends, animal stories, exempla and apologues, and formula tales. However, the wonder-tale or märchen and the legend have been the most commonly used sources from this list. The *dramatis personae* of these tales include the hero who sets out to make his fortune and embarks on a fabulous adventure where the real and the surreal become indivisible. Fairy helpers, talking animals and birds, evil ogres, shapeshifters of great cunning, princesses, witches and monsters are familiar to devotees of these tales. Writers such as JAMES STEPHENS, Edmund Leamy, PADRAIC COLUM, Eileen Ó Faoláin, Brendan Behan, Bryan Mac Mahon and Kevin Danaher, have all drawn from this source. MUíM

Iroaganachi, John 1928– Nigerian educator born in Umuahia, Abia State. His works include one of the first and most outstanding Nigerian PICTUREBOOKS, *How the Leopard Got Its Claws* (1972), written with CHINUA ACHEBE and illustrated by Adrienne Kennaway. Other traditional tales for young readers are *Night and Day* (1975), *The Sunbird's Drum* (1976) and *A Fight for Honey* (1977). VD

Iroh, Eddie see *WITHOUT A SILVER SPOON*

Iron Giant, The see THE IRON MAN

Iron Man, The (1968) A modern myth 'in five nights' by the former British poet laureate TED HUGHES, written 'with some sort of educational purpose'. (In America the book is called *The Iron Giant* to distinguish it from comic-book stories about another iron man.) Young readers respond with pleasure to the compelling pace of the story and the awesome clarity of the details. Critics seeking to define children's literature are confronted by a paradigmatic instance of its complexity. In an unprecedented narrative opening, the gigantic steel hero appears, alone and from nowhere, falls over a cliff edge and crashes, noisily, to complete demolition on a beach. To recreate his strength, he slowly fits himself together, beginning with one hand and one eye, then walks into the sea. The dramatic description of the Iron Man's reconstruction implies that earlier types of heroes, those endowed with superhuman strength (Goliath, Hercules), or magically armed (St George, KING ARTHUR), have been superseded by a technological personification of cosmic energy. Consequently, in this metaphoric FABLE the rules of engagement are also changed. When the Iron Man reappears, he is lured by Hogarth, the intelligent boy-hero, into a deep but useless trap dug by farmers whose machinery the Iron Man has eaten and who see his elimination as essential. But Hogarth saves him; he recognises the giant's virtue – eating scrap metal – and they become friendly collaborators. When a monster from outer space menaces the whole world population, Hogarth knows that only the Iron Man is a match for it. The apocalyptic climax, a trial by fire, is not simply the Iron Man's great triumph, but also the revelation of the monster's power to restart the music of the spheres. The transformation of two gigantic threats to world order into beneficent organisers of its peaceful continuance is detached from any narrative convention of realism; this is pure make-believe. Hughes's mythopoeic imagery, the strength and beauty of his metaphors, stretch the reader's insight. In this story, FANTASY takes on new dimensions. The spellbinding narration has the pace, emphasis, sound effects and rhetorical devices of oral storytelling.

In a conference paper on myth and education published in the first issue of *CHILDREN'S LITERATURE IN EDUCATION* (1970), Hughes analysed his story in detail. Later versions of the essay omit this part and include instead extended discussion of the idea, mirrored in the tale, that imagination is central to education. Hughes argues that, as in Plato, myths and legends 'can be seen as large-scale accounts of negotiations between the powers of the inner world and the stubborn conditions of the outer world, under which ordinary men and women have to live.' The first edition and subsequent reprintings of the book have illustrations by George Adamson. Advances in technology and children's awareness of these contribute to ANDREW DAVIDSON's pictures for the 1985 edition. In 1972 a film appeared on the BBC's *JACKANORY* programme where the author's words were only in the dialogue, a significant point for discussions of children's reading. Although there is no direct reference to the nuclear threat of the Cold War, this was the climate in which the book first appeared.

The Iron Woman (1993), also a text for its time and addressed to more experienced readers, is about environmental pollution brought about by waste disposal. The incidents in the narrative are impelled by social awareness of exploitation of natural resources. Gender issues lurk in the characterisation of both heroines, Lucy and the Iron Woman, who never quite reach the easy friendship of Hogarth and the original Iron Man. From her first rising from a marsh, 'a truly colossal man-shaped statue of black mud' to the spring-flowered conclusion, the Iron Woman conveys distress, even hysteria. Her initial power lies in making humans hear the intolerable primeval screaming of threatened species. In order to change more than the words and intentions of those who profit from waste, mess and greed, she has advice from the Iron Man, and the power of the Space-Bat-Angel-Dragon (his one-time opponent), to convert all males into creatures that can stay alive only in water; in the domestic setting, bathwater, so that for a short time women are in control of things. In the coda of successful retroversions, rubbish is turned into fuel. The most vivid scenes are metamorphoses of a distinctly Ovidian kind, which link this text with Hughes's translations of the Latin tales. Shot through with transformative imagery, these episodes extend the readers' imaginative understanding of what happens when the natural world is unremittingly exploited and manhandled. As a poet's contribution to an important and disturbing general problem, one that needs action as well as thought, the text has most power when it addresses the plight of creatures in the wild. The distinctive Hughes metaphors and descriptions are mirrored in Andrew Davidson's carefully realised ILLUSTRATIONS. But as a mainspring of what happens, the central character evokes more pity than admiration. MM

see also SUPERHEROES

Iron Wolf, The see; *COLLECTED ANIMAL POEMS*; TED HUGHES

Iron Woman, *THE* see *THE IRON MAN*

Irving, Washington 1783–1859 American author of over 20 books, including the groundbreaking *The*

Illustration by Charles S. Reinhart from *Rip Van Winkle* by WASHINGTON IRVING, published in *Harper's New Monthly Magazine* (1886).

Sketch Book of Geoffrey Crayon, Gent. (1819), a slim pamphlet of 93 pages, containing five sketches, including 'Rip Van Winkle' and 'The Legend of Sleepy Hollow'. Published in seven instalments, over a two-year period, *The Sketch Book*, later illustrated by RANDOLPH CALDECOTT, became an influential work in Britain and America. Although indebted to German sources for their atmosphere and Gothicism, the two main stories demonstrate Irving's keen interest in indigenous American folklore. In his hands, the two tales become American parables mined from both New World and Old World lodes. Irving, though fascinated by the long European past, awakens within the still-new American consciousness a child's sense of wonder and awe, of play and possibility. Indeed, in his characterisation of Rip Van Winkle, a man who resists growing up and responsibility, and Ichabod Crane, a superstitious Yankee pedagogue, pitted against a robust frontiersman in Brom Bones, he creates American 'types'. It is intriguing that both these characters enjoy children's play more than work, and both are given to flights of fancy. Both were to prove enduring and highly imitable, as evinced by such 'eternal' boys as MARK TWAIN's Huck Finn and such 'boy-men' as Ernest Hemingway's Francis Macomber. JCA

Isaacs, Anne 1949– American author of children's PICTUREBOOKS and poetry. Born in Buffalo, New York, Isaacs is best known for *Swamp Angel* (1994), a witty TALL TALE whose heroine is Angelica Longrider. She is a big girl with great physical abilities; the comparison with the American legendary folk hero Paul Bunyan is unavoidable. The story is great fun and beautifully illustrated by PAUL ZELINSKY. The primitive style of painted wood veneers is a perfect complement to Isaacs's text evoking a young girl who is quite capable of handling any situation that comes her way. *Swamp Angel* was named a 1994 Caldecott Honour Book in addition to receiving many other American awards.

Isaacs's other books include *Treehouse Tales* (1997) and *Cat Up a Tree* (1998). Her imaginative flair with language makes Anne Isaacs a fresh voice in children's literature. ESC

Isadora, Rachel 1953– American author and illustrator of children's books, and ballet dancer. Isadora was born in New York City. She trained professionally as a dancer and was a member of the Boston Ballet Company until an injury cut short her dancing career. Her first book, *Max* (1976), tells the story of a boy who learns that ballet exercises can help him become a better athlete. Max was well received for its ILLUSTRATIONS and style as well as for its non-sexist storyline. Isadora's books generally convey her love for and knowledge of the performing arts. *Swan Lake* (1989), for example, is a beautifully rendered PICTUREBOOK adaptation of Tchaikovsky's ballet. She is especially adept at conveying body movements in her illustrations. *Ben's Trumpet* (1979), which was lauded as both a Caldecott Honour Book and the BOSTON GLOBE-HORN BOOK AWARD winner, takes place in the 1920s and utilises a jazz theme and an art-deco style reminiscent of the era. She has also authored two picturebooks set in apartheid South Africa, *At the Crossroads* (1991) and *Over the Green Hills* (1992). In addition, Isadora has illustrated books written by other authors, including PATRICIA MCKISSACK'S *Flossie and the Fox* (1986). EB

see also MUSIC AND STORY; BALLET STORIES

Island of the Blue Dolphins (1960) Novel by the American author, SCOTT O'DELL. Winner of the NEWBERY AWARD, this novel is based on the true story of a young native girl stranded on an island off the California coast in the early 1800s and her survival on that island for 18 years. The story is a variation of the ROBINSONNADE in which the heroine, Karana, instead of subduing nature as does Robinson Crusoe, learns to co-exist with nature and become an integral part of the world around her. Karana tells her own story and the reader sees her indomitable spirit overcome both tremendous physical obstacles and profound loneliness. O'Dell's skilful combination of the day-to-day details of survival with episodes of high adventure helps to maintain the story's pace. The book is generally regarded as a modern classic and its influence can be seen in virtually all succeeding survival stories for children. DLR

It's My Life (1981–90) Trilogy by the British author ROBERT LEESON, comprising *It's My Life* (1981), *Jan Alone* (1989) and *Coming Home* (1990). *It's My Life* appeared first as as a one-off novel. Jan Whitfield, sixteen, attending a north-country comprehensive, is attracted to fellow student Peter Carey. Her mother, without apparent reason, walks out, shattering normal family life. Jan tries to accept this disaster, trapped into responsibilities compromising her natural expectations. This perceptive, convincing novel proved very popular and the need to chart Jan's subsequent progress became pressing. In the 1989 sequel Jan makes her own luck in a male-dominated world of work, encountering men in many guises – dependants, colleagues, exploiters. Peter remains a constant friend but circumstances prevent the relationship from running smoothly. The book shows Jan developing towards responsibility, understanding both of self and others, and adulthood, and she finally commits herself to Peter. The mother's disappearance was a given: 'it had everything to do with what happened to Jan'. At the end, the mother, in a superbly realised episode, returns with the question 'Why should I have to do the unforgivable to get away from the unbearable?' – which seals the overarching structure of this masterpiece of realist fiction. DCH

Itsekiri folktales see NEVILLE UKOLI

Ivanhoe see SIR WALTER SCOTT; see also HISTORICAL FICTION

Ivor the Engine (from 1959) Saga of a Welsh railway engine by OLIVER POSTGATE and PETER FIRMIN, in a series produced by Oliver Postgate's Smallfilms company for the BBC children's TELEVISION department. Ivor works for the Merioneth and Llantisilly Rail Traction Company Limited, a small railway line in 'the top corner of Wales'. Ivor's driver is Jones the Steam, and other friends are Owen the Signal and Dai Station. In one story, Ivor manages to be a part of the Grumbly choral society when Jones fits him up with old organ pipes from a roundabout. Books include *Ivor the Engine* (1962), *Ivor's Outing* (1967), *Ivor's Birthday* (1984) and *Ivor the Engine Red Story Book* (1986). The first episode was shot in black-and-white in 1959 in Peter Firmin's cowshed, and remade in colour in the 1970s; in 2000, all 26 episodes in colour were released on video. SET

J

Jabberwocky see LEWIS CARROL; see also GRAEME BASE; *THE HUNTING OF THE SNARK;* NONSENSE VERSE

Jack and Gill see JAMES CATNACH

Jack and Jill (1938–) American magazine primarily for children aged six to eight. *Jack and Jill* is published by Children's Better Health Institute in Indianapolis and contains poetry, stories, jokes and puzzles. Nonfiction, regular columns, and series enhance a publication which has been popular with generations of young subscribers. NV

see also COMICS, PERIODICALS AND MAGAZINES; *ST. NICHOLAS MAGAZINE*

Jack and the Beanstalk Traditional tale, often regarded as quintessentially English. Jack, a lazy boy, exchanges his widowed mother's only cow for five beans and subsequently climbs the enormous beanstalk which grows from one of them to a land in the sky. Making three visits to the castle of the giant who lives there, Jack, protected by the giant's wife, steals the giant's treasures: a hen which lays golden eggs, sacks of money, and a magic harp. On each occasion he narrowly escapes with his life and the tale ends with the death of the giant and a prosperous future for Jack and his mother. The story's motifs are found in numerous other tales: for instance, the beanstalk ascending to the sky finds echoes in the world-tree Yggdrasill in the prose *Edda*, and in Jacob's Ladder of the Old Testament; the giant's chant 'Fee-fi-fo-fum . . .' appears in several giant stories, including *Molly Whuppie* and *JACK THE GIANT-KILLER*. While there is disagreement about the origins of the tale, which first appeared in print in the early 19th century, evidence that the story existed much earlier, and was popular, is provided in the skit upon the telling of the tale in *Round about our Coal-Fire: or Christmas Entertainments* (1734 edition). Most modern retellings, including PICTUREBOOK versions such as those by John Howe (1989) and ALAN GARNER (1992) – the latter particularly reflects the oral origins of the tale – derive principally from that of Tabart's 1807 CHAPBOOK edition, albeit usually without the moralising fairy urging Jack to avenge his father. MSut

Jack Holborn (1964) LEON GARFIELD's first novel, originally sent to Constable's adult fiction section. Grace Hogarth, a leading children's literature editor, saw its potential as a book for older children. After the author had been persuaded to make some cuts in what was always a somewhat rambling plot, the book finally appeared, to instant acclaim. Jack himself is an 18th-century orphan taking his surname from the London parish where he was originally discovered. He goes to sea, becomes involved with some realistically murderous pirates, and after adventures in the African jungle returns at last to a more optimistic future. NT

Jack the Giant Killer A FAIRY TALE featured in CHAPBOOKS, Eddows and Cotton's version (c. 1761) being the best-known. It is the story of Jack, who lives in the reign of KING ARTHUR and becomes renowned for his killing of giants, including Blunderboar and the two-headed Welsh giant. He eventually becomes one of the knights of the round table. The earliest edition of this tale was printed by J. White of Newcastle (1711). This was one of the most popular chapbook stories, with numerous penny and twopenny editions. The humorous scene in which, following a giant's attempt to beat Jack to death in the night, Jack complains that he felt a rat strike him with his tale, has many equivalents. In the Swedish tale of 'The Herd-boy and the Giant' the boy says he felt himself being bitten by a flea when the giant believes that he has clubbed him to death. Jack's cloak of invisibility, cap of knowledge, shoes of swiftness and sword of sharpness are gifts which first appeared in Northern mythology (see CLASSICAL MYTHOLOGY) and can also be found in *TOM THUMB*. This story includes the words 'fe, fi, fo, fum' although spelling and ordering differ from version to version. JOHN NEWBERY'S *A Little Pretty Pocket Book* contains make-believe letters from Jack. JHD

Jackanory Distinguished and highly successful STORYTELLING series created by British television producer Joy Whitby for the BBC, starting on 13 December 1965, and designed to revive the art of storytelling directly 'out of screen' to the individual young viewer. Running-time was 15 minutes and the programme was transmitted five days a week, Monday to Friday. A phenomenal number of novels was serialised over the years. Storytellers were usually well-known actors, the first being Lee Montague, followed by Dame Wendy Hiller and film star Mai Zetterling. Sir Compton Mackenzie narrated *The Legend of Perseus*. DG

Jackson, Garnet Nelson 1944– American biographer. Unable to find suitable ethnic BIOGRAPHIES for young children when teaching first grade in Michigan, Jackson wrote her own. Using easy-to-read prose or rhyming texts, her stories – including *Garrett Morgan, Inventor* (1993), *Mae Jemison, Astronaut* (1994), *Charles Drew, Doctor* (1994), and *Phyllis Wheatley, Poet* (1993) – introduce children to African American contributions to both science and art. Her short books depict African American role models not often discussed, promoting self-esteem and cultural awareness. She has received awards from the National Association for the Advancement of Coloured People and city councils for her writing and contributions to the community. SCWA

see also AFRICAN AMERICAN LITERATURE

Jackson, Helen Hunt 1830–85 American poet and novelist. Jackson was considered by her contemporaries a 'graceful' and 'colourful' writer who achieved great maturity in her later career, in particular in her western regional work. She was a prolific author and produced numerous novels, essays and reviews. It was thought at the time that she would be remembered for her poetry, which is now, however, considered overly sentimental and moralistic. Although Jackson was primarily known as an author of ADULT FICTION, she was also a frequent contributor to juvenile periodicals, including *ST NICHOLAS* and *THE RIVERSIDE MAGAZINE FOR YOUNG PEOPLE*. Collections of these pieces were published as *Bits of Talk, in Verse and Prose, for Young Folks* (1876). *Nelly's Silver Mine* (1878), a juvenile novel, was praised by contemporary critics for its emphasis on family life and the scenic descriptions of Colorado; modern readers applaud her independent female protagonist. After her death, two collections of previously published children's stories were issued: *Pansy Billings and Popsy* (1898) and *Cat Stories* (1898). Jackson is now remembered for her works on the American Indian: the factual history *Century of Dishonor* (1881) and the fictionalised romance *Ramona* (1884). JKB

Jackson, Holbrook see *COMPLETE NONSENSE*; NONSENSE VERSE

Jackson, Jesse 1908–83 African American writer of books for children in the middle years and older, noted particularly for *Call Me Charley* (1945), one of the first novels portraying an African American protago-

He soon found the edge of his blade,
Became a most humble suppliant;
And, while he complained of the pain,
Jack took off the head of the giant.

Jack threatens,—all braggarts beware!
And coward poltroons he makes pliant;
And thus all vain-glorious puffs
Are silenced as Jack served the giant.

From J.G. RUSHER's chapbook *Jack the Giant Killer – A Hero.*

nist. Jackson's early work reveals the influence of the assimilationist theory of racial harmony, which believed that minority groups must learn to adapt to the majority society, assume their attitudes and mores. Consequently, Charley, the only African American in a middle-class white school, essentially succeeds because, as well as being intelligent and articulate, he is willing to adopt the white culture. Jackson, however, wrote throughout the period of civil rights reform and the emergence of the Black Pride movement. As a result, his works underwent a dramatic change as he began to portray the grimmer side of racism. In books like *Tessie* (1968) and *The Fourteenth Cadillac* (1972) he describes the pervasiveness of racism and explores its psychological impact on individuals. Although his books seem dated and at times didactic, he is important as a pioneering figure in African American literature for children. DLR

see also AFRICAN AMERICAN LITERATURE

***Jacob Two-Two* series** see MORDECAI RICHLER; see also FRITZ WEGNER

Jacobs, Helen (Mary) 1888–1970 British illustrator and painter. Jacobs contributed images of FAIRY FANTASY to ANNUALS such as *LITTLE FOLKS*, *PLAYBOX* and *Rainbow*, and soon received commissions from several major publishers. Her work included frequent collaborations with her friend Stella Mead, and a series of drawings of species of moth for the entomologist Lord Rothschild. In later years, she taught at a primary school in Stoke Newington and produced school books and primers, including *The Open Road* (1952). This pedagogic material led her to move away from the delicate beauty of her best early watercolours to work in a brighter, bolder graphic style. However, she retained the use of fine detail in her naturalistic pen-and-ink drawing, as in the figures and interiors for *Let's Paint Pictures of China* (1947). DW

Jacobs, Joseph 1854–1916 Born in Australia, Jacobs came to England to study at Cambridge University. Later a distinguished historian, he also edited the British journal *Folk-Lore*. In 1890 he put together *English Fairy Tales*, which was an immediate success, followed four years later by *More English Fairy Tales*. In these important volumes, much drawn upon by later anthologists, Jacobs rewrote traditional stories in child-friendly language from sources originally known to him in dialect or BALLAD form. They included famous tales like *DICK WHITTINGTON* and *THE THREE LITTLE PIGS*. Jacobs also edited *Celtic Fairy Tales* and *Indian Fairy Tales*, both published in 1892. NT

Jacques, Brian see *REDWALL* SERIES; see also ANIMALS IN FICTION; COVER ART

Jacques, Robin 1920–95 British illustrator. Jacques taught himself to illustrate books during World War II in quiet moments of his army service. He then established himself as a distinct talent with regular contributions to the *Radio Times* and *The Listener*. He proved an ideal illustrator of both 19th-century fiction and modern classics, but worked more extensively on children's books, especially with RUTH MANNING-SANDERS on the series beginning with *The Book of Giants* (1962). Jacques communicated much of his knowledge and experience of ILLUSTRATION by teaching and by publishing *Illustrators at Work* (1963). His meticulous pen-work long continued to reveal the influence of a tradition of wood-engraved illustration. DW

see also WOOD ENGRAVING

Jaffrey, Madhur Born near Delhi, Jaffrey was already well known as an actress, television presenter and cookery writer before she wrote *Seasons of Splendour* (1985), a children's book of the Indian mythological tales which she was told as a child. The stories are retold with vitality and a strong feeling for the spoken form in which they originated. The collection, illustrated by MICHAEL FOREMAN, was well received in Britain and the United States. HCE

see also INDIAN MYTHS, LEGENDS AND FOLK-TALES

***James III* series** Sequence of novels by the British author JOAN AIKEN, which began in 1962, appeared at intervals over a third of a century and reached its ninth title in 1999. It occupies a realm of its own, that of historical, or better, unhistorical FANTASY. The underlying notion is that the Hanoverian succession of 1714 never happened; in the early books King James III is on the British throne, to be followed later by Richard IV. Clearly, in a time that never was, anything can happen; Joan Aiken has written herself an open licence, and although in this series she rarely uses the traditional trappings of fantasy, she makes free use of wild improbability, with frequent excursions into the downright impossible. She can also be extremely funny.

The first book, *The Wolves of Willoughby Chase* (1962) sets the period: it is soon after James III's accession in 1832. The Channel Tunnel has just been opened – in characteristic defiance of chronology – and a great many wolves, driven by severe winters in Europe, have migrated through it into Britain. The story is of two small girls in a stately home who are left in the care of a wicked governess and are consigned by her to a hideous poor-farm. They are rescued, in the teeth of marauding wolves and other hazards, by a boy goose-keeper, Simon, the first of several characters who recur at intervals through the series. The second book, with the splendid title of *Black Hearts in Battersea* (1964), introduces the main theme of Hanoverian plotting, on behalf of Bonnie Prince Georgie:

> My Bonnie lies over the North Sea,
> My Bonnie lies over in Hanover,
> My Bonnie lies over the North Sea,
> Oh why won't they bring that young man over?

A tale of wild and whirling action culminates in a voyage by air balloon to rescue King James and the Duke and Duchess of Battersea from Battersea Castle. Simon the ex-goose-boy turns out to be heir to the dukedom, and Sophie the Duchess's maid is found to be his long-lost sister: 'My own dear husband's dead brother's long-lost child!' exclaims the Duchess. But the scene-stealer is the skinny, shrewish Cockney waif Dido Twite, who was to dominate the series.

And so it goes on through the succeeding books: more deep, dark plotting and ever more amazing escapes from ever more bizarre perils. In *Night Birds on Nantucket* (1966) the Hanoverians have engaged innocent Professor Breadno to fire across the Atlantic from that island his newly invented monster cannon that will blow up St James's Palace. In *The Cuckoo Tree* (1971), Good King James has gone to his rest and Dido, arriving on an elephant, helps to thwart a villainous scheme to do away with Richard IV at his Coronation; in *The Stolen Lake* (1981) she is off on a mission to Roman America, where the peasants speak Latin, to answer an appeal from New Cumbria, Britain's oldest ally. In *Dido and Pa* (1986), the Hanoverians, masterminded by the sinister Margrave of Nordmarck, are thwarted yet again and Dido's shady Pa Twite, who has combined nefarious deeds with being the Margrave's court composer, comes to a gruesome end, eaten alive by wolves.

Joan Aiken's imagination seems inexhaustible; she will squander in a dozen pages enough ideas to serve other writers for a decade. Her ability to keep a story racing along at breakneck pace is unrivalled; her style has a matching exuberance and she can turn a neat verse. Obviously the demands of non-stop action must conflict with the exploration of moral issues and with the subtle development of character. The Aiken world is a moral world, but a fairly simple one. There are goodies and baddies, and from wicked governess to scheming Margrave there is no mistaking who are the baddies. 'Our' side are naturally the goodies. It could be objected that such divisions are psychologically as well as morally simplistic; in real life there are few outright heroes and villains and a great many variations in between. But these are books for children (and for older readers who have the fortunate gift of being able to read as children read) rather than for questing adolescents and adults; they offer a clear concept of right and wrong, rather than a struggle with complex moral perceptions. For similar reasons, they recognise love but do not feature sexuality.

Joan Aiken's characters are clearly and vigorously drawn, usually in a few strokes. King James himself makes an appearance in *Black Hearts* as 'a little, dapper, elderly Scottish gentleman', and addresses the Duke of Battersea: 'Och, weel, noo, Battersea . . . how's your gude lady?' Some, like Mrs Brisket, who runs the orphanage in *The Wolves of Willoughby Chase*, have a high Dickensian colour. There are elements of caricature and burlesque: Captain Casket in *Night Birds on Nantucket*, obsessed with the pursuit of the pink whale Rosie, is an obvious skit on Captain Ahab in *Moby Dick*. *The Stolen Lake* revives KING ARTHUR, always a rash enterprise. The most memorable characters however are the pawky, resourceful Dido Twite and her devious Pa, who was, as Dido admits, 'a real bad lot', but will be missed for his musical talent.

The first two books – *Wolves* and *Black Hearts* – are the best-known and probably the best of the series; both have become modern classics and have been made into major films. The next four, featuring Dido, kept up the standard, although they no longer seemed quite so astonishing. In the seventh and eighth books, *Is* (1992) and *Cold Shoulder Road* (1995), Dido is succeeded as central character by her younger sister Is, who is however, indistinguishable from Dido. Though events come as thick and fast as ever, and invention could hardly be said to flag, the action begins to seem mechanical and to invite the comment: 'More of the same.' No series can go on forever, and it was possible to feel it was now time to stop, though another title, *Limbo Lodge* (1999), added a fresh story about Dido Twite – characteristically fast-moving and complex – to an earlier narrative space when the young heroine was on her way back to England via the Pacific Ocean.

JRT

Illustration from *Rockhopper* by Ann James.

James, Ann (Catherine Stewart) 1952– Innovative Australian illustrator and author, who designed and illustrated ROBIN KLEIN'S *PENNY POLLARD* series (1983–9) in a child-centred scrapbook style. James's most popular ILLUSTRATIONS were made for MAX DANN'S *Bernice Knows Best* (1983) and GILLIAN RUBINSTEIN'S *Dog In, Cat Out* (1991). James also wrote and illustrated the deceptively casual *One Day: A Very First Dictionary* (1989). She uses a range of media, from the exuberant pen-and-wash drawings in *Skating on Sand* (1994), with text by LIBBY GLEESON, to vibrant pastels in *The Midnight Gang* (1996), by MARGARET WILD. In 1988, James and partner Ann Haddon established the now influential Melbourne Books Illustrated, a gallery which displays high quality children's book illustrations.

HE

James, Betsy 1948– Versatile American author of two coming-of-age novels for young adults, *Long Night Dance* (1989) and *Dark Heart* (1992), and several PICTUREBOOKS, including *The Dream Stair* (1990) illustrated by Richard Jesse Watson, *The Mud Family* (1994) illustrated

Illustration by Faith Jaques for the Puffin edition of *The Railway Children* by E. NESBIT.

by Paul Morin, and *Blow Away Soon* (1995) illustrated by Anna Vojtech. She has both written and illustrated *The Red Cloak* (1989), a retelling of the *TAM LIN* legend, and *Mary Ann* (1995), a story of friendship and praying mantises. James's love of nature, and her close relationships with Native Americans and other peoples of the Southwest among whom she has lived and worked, are evident in many of her books. LH

James, Jesse 1847–1882 Raider, robber and gang leader immortalised in American folk history. A resident of Missouri, he concentrated his illegal activities in the neighbouring central states. He began as a member of the pro-Confederate Quantrill raiders in the 1860s and then formed his own gang to rob both banks and railroads. He was perceived as a cowboy ROBIN HOOD by an indulgent public which celebrated the mythic West, and he was widely read about by children in the ADVENTURE STORIES known as DIME NOVELS. He was featured in Hollywood movies, including *Jesse James* (1939), starring Tyrone Power and Henry Fonda. JRG

James, M.R. see GHOST STORIES

James, Simon 1961– British line and colour-wash artist in the understated tradition of the later JOHN BURNINGHAM. James has created PICTUREBOOKS distinguished for their convincing portrayal of childhood experience. Many also express quiet concern for the environment. *My Friend Whale* (1990), *Dear Greenpeace* (1991), *Sally and the Limpet* (1991), *The Wild Woods* (1993) and *Leon and Bob* (1997) are all touching stories told with restraint and gentle humour. JAG

James, Will see *SMOKY, THE COWHORSE*; see also ANIMALS IN FICTION; HORSE STORIES

Jane Eyre see CHARLOTTE, EMILY AND ANNE BRONTË; see also LITERATURE WITHIN CHILDREN'S LITERATURE

Janeczko, Paul (Bryan) 1945– American anthologist and poet whose name has become synonymous with poetry for young adults. His anthologies, rich in their selection of contemporary poets, are thoughtfully compiled, geared toward the interests and needs of young people. A former teacher, he recognised the lack of poetry appropriate for teenagers. In *Poetspeak* (1983) and *The Place My Words Are Looking For* (1990), the poets represented also discuss their work. *Pocket Poems: Selected for a Journey* (1985), a pocket-sized volume, is for 'travellers on the move'. *Preposterous* (1991) reflects the pleasure and pain of growing up; *Looking For Your Name* (1993) explores current issues faced by young adults in contemporary American life. Janeczko has compiled over 15 anthologies and was compared to ROBERT FROST with *Bridges to Cross* (1989), a volume of his own poems. A recent anthology is *Stone Bench in an Empty Park* (2000). PDS

Janet and John see READING SCHEMES

Janeway, James see *TOKEN FOR CHILDREN, A*; see also BIOGRAPHY AND AUTOBIOGRAPHY

Jansson, Tove see *MOOMIN* SERIES

Jaques, Faith 1923–97 British illustrator, born in Leicester, where she first studied art. Her pen-and-ink drawings have been used mainly to illustrate children's books such as the very popular *LIZZIE DRIPPING* series by HELEN CRESSWELL, first published in 1974. She has also illustrated ROALD DAHL's work, including *CHARLIE AND THE CHOCOLATE FACTORY* (1967) and *Charlie and the Great Glass Elevator* (1973). In 1972 she illustrated PHILIPPA PEARCE'S *WHAT THE NEIGHBOURS DID AND OTHER STORIES*. Her strongly structured and highly detailed drawings apply a realist style which uses line, tone and space to advantage. AEW

Jarrell, Randall 1914–65 American poet, critic, novelist and writer for children. Well-known as a writer for adults, Jarrell did not begin writing for children until 1962. After translating tales by the GRIMM BROTHERS and Ludwig Bechstein, Jarrell began to write his now-classic children's books at the suggestion of his editor, MICHAEL DI CAPUA. *The Gingerbread Rabbit* (1964) is notable for introducing the theme of the family romance common to Jarrell's children's stories and for the charming ILLUSTRATIONS by GARTH WILLIAMS. For his subsequent books, Jarrell collaborated with MAURICE SENDAK. *The Bat-Poet* (1964) explores the family romance in terms of poet and audience, showing the reader (better than any textbook) what poems and poets are like. Sendak's cross-hatched marginal drawings of bats and his evocative double-page spreads are themselves visual poetry. Likewise, Sendak's chapter decorations for *The Animal Family* (1965) are as haunting as the tale about an odd family consisting of a hunter, mermaid, lynx, bear and boy. After Jarrell was struck by a car and killed on 14 October 1965, it took Sendak over 10 years before he could illustrate *Fly By Night* (1976) – the story of lonely David who turns to dream-work to invent the family he lacks. Though Jarrell wrote only four children's books, they have endured for over 30 years. RF

Jarvis, Robin see *DEPTFORD MICE* TRILOGY; *WHITBY* TRILOGY

***Jataka* stories** see AFRICAN MYTHOLOGY AND FOLKTALES; FOLKTALES AND LEGENDS; INDIAN MYTHS, LEGENDS AND FOLKTALES

Jefferies, Richard see *TARKA THE OTTER*; *WOOD MAGIC*; see also adventure stories

Jeffers, Susan 1942– American writer and illustrator of children's books. Jeffers graduated from Pratt Institute in Brooklyn, New York, and began her career working in the art departments of several publishers of children's books. Her first book, *Buried Moon* (1969), is one of several she has produced using the English FOLKTALES of JOSEPH JACOBS. *Three Jovial Huntsmen* was a Caldecott Honour Book (1974). Jeffers has illustrated several retellings of HANS CHRISTIAN ANDERSEN's stories with AMY EHRLICH. *Brother Eagle, Sister Sky* (1991) exemplifies Jeffers's deep love for nature; cross-hatched renderings help relate Chief Seattle's concern for preserving the environment for future generations. Unusually detailed pen-and-ink ILLUSTRATIONS allow her to simultaneously highlight the real and FANTASY worlds. The reader is treated to exquisite drawings of trees in which each piece of bark seems accounted for, and animals where one can almost feel the fur, while washes and dyes allow the imagination to fantasise. Likewise, Jeffers's collaboration with Reeve Lindburgh on *The Midnight Farm* (1987) draws the child to the seen and unseen world of the barn. Jeffers chooses strong stories that deal with a child's experience with family and animals, and the conflict of making choices resulting in courage, hope and despair. JRG

Jefferson, Thomas see *MCGUFFEY ECLECTIC READERS*

Jellett, Celia see *SOMEONE IS FLYING BALLOONS*

***Jennings* series** The British author Anthony Buckeridge's 25 Jennings books were bestsellers from 1950 to the mid-1970s. First heard as a radio broadcast on BBC Children's Hour in 1948 to immediate popularity, Jennings stories in book form soon followed. Translated subsequently into 13 different languages and with sales exceeding 6 million copies, they are set in an imaginary prep school in the south of England populated by a lively group of pre-teenage boarders. The two main characters, Jennings and his friend Darbishire, get into innumerable scrapes either from misplaced efforts to help or following from an initially small mistake such as forgetting to get off a train at the correct station.

The prevailing mood throughout is consistently good-humoured; the headmaster and the two long-suffering teachers Mr Carter and Mr Wilkins may occasionally become irritated, but punishment is never severe and more often than not does not occur at all. A constant delight is the boys' stream of outlandish argot, invented by Buckeridge himself after he realised how quickly current slang dates in a story. 'Fossilised fish-hooks', one of Jennings's favourites, is typical of this talent for humorous creation. The author, a teacher himself, also had a keen ear for juvenile dialogue; some of the wonderfully amusing conversations and arguments in these books are based on former memories of the real thing. Updated in later years with old money converted to decimal currency and changes in some of the pupils' more dated references, the books finally went out of print in the 1990s. NT

Jennings, Elizabeth 1926– British poet and critic who excels at crafting her thought on relationships, childhood, the arts, animals and religion into subtly understated poetry. She wrote directly for young readers in *Let's Have Some Poetry* (1960) and some of her adult poems also appeal to teenagers. For a younger age-group are *The Secret Brother* (1966), *After the Ark*

(1978) and most notably *A Spell of Words* (1997) – which contains the poem 'A Classroom', in which she recalls the school poetry lesson that caught her up, 'excited, charged and changed . . . / Locked into language with a golden key.' AHa

Jennings, Paul 1943– Australia's bestselling children's author, with over 2.7 million sales worldwide. British-born Jennings moved to Australia at the age of six and as an adult worked as a teacher and academic. Jennings has said that 'the biggest sin in writing for children is to be boring . . . I only want to write the sorts of things that I think kids want to read.' His form is the short story – bizarre, rude, supernatural, surprising – his writing colourful but accessible, and moralistic in that wrongdoers are invariably punished. The first of his many collections was *Unreal!* (1985). *The Paw Thing* (1989) and *The Gismo* (1994) are amongst his junior novels, and Jennings's picturebooks include the chilling *Grandad's Gifts* (1992), illustrated by Peter Gouldthorpe, and *The Fisherman and the Theefyspray* (1994), perhaps Jennings's gentlest tale. He co-wrote the television series *Round the Twist*, and his 1992 collaboration with Ted Greenwood, *Spooner or Later*, a collection of spoonerisms illustrated by Terry Denton, is exceptional in design and comic content. Sequels are *Duck for Cover* (1994) a joke and puzzle book, and *Freeze a Crowd* (1996), full of visual puns, riddles and conundrums.

In Australia, Jennings's name often arises amidst controversy: he constantly features in children's choice book awards, but has never won the prestigious Children's Book Council of Australia Book of the Year Award (although *Grandad's Gifts* and *Duck for Cover* have been shortlisted). While the Council insists the award is for quality rather than popularity, critics (often journalists with an eye for controversy) declare that Jennings's achievement in bringing children and books together is worthy of an award. NLR

Jeram, Anita Best known as the illustrator of Sam McBratney's *Guess How Much I Love You* (1994) which, shortlisted for the Kurt Maschler Award and the British Book Awards for 1994, went on to become a cult book and sold in millions in Britain and America. Fine, expressive drawing in pen-and-ink and gentle colour-wash are her hallmark both here and in her other books, where her affection and eye for capturing the movement of animals is evident. JAG

Jill A series of nine pony stories by the British author Ruby Ferguson (1899–1966), starting with *Jill's Gymkhana*, published between 1949 and 1962. Archetypal pony heroine Jill Crewe writes about her adventures with her two ponies and her friends. Told in a breathless first-person narrative, combining aspects of E. Nesbit and Joanna Cannan, these adventures never rise above the commonplace – gymkhanas, pony treks, running stables – though they contain much simple information about riding, laced with knockabout humour and the misfortunes of stuck-up girls. Despite the dated slang and attitudes, they remain extremely popular and are all still in print. ARH

Jinks, Catherine (Claire) 1963– Australian writer who was born in Queensland and grew up in Papua New Guinea. A graduate in medieval history, Jinks gained critical success with the Pagan series (1991–6) set amidst the Crusades of the 12th and 13th centuries in Palestine and France. Though distancing readers in time, the language, characters and stories make the past accessible to contemporary readers without didactic impediments. Pagan's life, while set in a well-documented past, shares many of the emotional challenges of loyalty and courage of today. Her first work for young readers, *This Way Out* (1991), focuses on a 15-year-old girl's dissatisfaction with her life as she pursues a modelling career. *Witch Bank* (1995) explores a shy, self-effacing teenager's transformation through magical intervention as she learns to understands office politics. *Eye To Eye* (1997), a science fiction novel which examines moral differences between human and robotic beings, was winner of the Children's Book Council of Australia Book of the Year Award in 1998. Jinks has written another science fiction novel, *Piggy in the Middle* (1998) and, in contrast, *The Stinking Great Lie* (1999), a witty story full of scatological imagery. Her stories present sharp strong language, believable characters and fast moving events which support and elicit moral reflections. CH, HMcC

***Jinny* series** Twelve pony stories by Patricia Leitch (1933–), covering three years in the life of Jinny (Jennifer) Manders and the wild circus-horse she rescues. The series started with *For Love of a Horse* in 1976 and was completed in 1988, when the genre was in decline. The books are written with unusual intensity, combining realistic family relationships and robust adventures arising from the Scottish Highland setting, with a strong underlying mysticism. What lifts them above the ordinary is Jinny's growth in maturity as she faces difficult emotional and moral situations, and the overt links between an adolescent love of horses and the libido. The titles are all still in print. ARH

Jo's Boys see *Little Women*

Jock of the Bushveld (1907) Novel by Sir Percy FitzPatrick (1862–1931), South Africa's best-known children's book and a world classic among animal stories. It began in the form of stories told to the author's children, which his friend RUDYARD KIPLING persuaded him to write down. The appeal of the book is heightened by the many attractive full-page and marginal illustrations by Edmund Caldwell. It has never been out of print and has also appeared in many translations and condensed and simplified versions. It tells of the author's adventures, most of them with his courageous bull-terrier Jock, in Portuguese territory and the Eastern Transvaal in 1884/5. The quality of the prose, its descriptive power, and the vigour, self-confidence and grand scale remain unmatched in South African literature to this day. Particularly appealing is the bond between Jock and his master, 'the friendly wagging of that stumpy tail, a splashy lick, a soft upward look, and a wider split of the mouth that was a laugh as plain as if one heard it.' Depicting the growth to maturity of a greenhorn among pioneering types, the book embodies typical colonial values of manliness, and the author's handling of racial issues and the frequent gory descriptions of hunting are typical of their time. ERJ

see also ANIMALS IN CHILDREN'S FICTION

John Brown, Rose and the Midnight Cat (1977) Acclaimed Australian picturebook in which the finely cross-hatched ILLUSTRATIONS of RON BROOKS perfectly complement JENNY WAGNER's story of Rose, an elderly widow, who lives comfortably with her dog, John Brown, until the midnight cat, with eyes 'like lamps', threatens John Brown's companionable role. The seemingly simple story of the battle between Rose and John Brown can be interpreted as a metaphor of the games that people play to gain ascendency, and the cat has been variously interpreted as a symbol of death (for which Rose is ready) or of those innate responses that strengthen humans as the end of life approaches. MSax

John Gilpin see GEORGE CRUIKSHANK; see also WILLIAM COWPER

John Newbery Medal see NEWBERY MEDAL (appendix); see also AWARDS AND MEDALS

John of Garland c.1195–1272 English scholar who taught at the University of Toulouse. Among his other works he compiled a *Dictionarius* (c. 1225), the first use – according to the *Oxford English Dictionary* – of that word. Written to help young students with everyday colloquial Latin, it is not a dictionary in the modern sense. After describing the parts of the male and female body, it presents a series of scenes from daily life in and around Paris, followed by notes on the various words with some French equivalents. The work provides a fund of information about such topics as clothing, furnishings, cooking and warfare. GA

Johns, Captain W(illiam) E(arle) see *BIGGLES* and *WORRALS* SERIES; see also ADVENTURE STORIES; BIAS IN CHILDREN'S BOOKS; COMICS, PERIODICALS AND MAGAZINES; TELEVISION

Johnson, Annie Fellows see *LITTLE COLONEL* SERIES

Johnson, Crockett (David Johnson Leisk) 1906–75 American cartoonist, painter, art editor and illustrator best known for *Harold and the Purple Crayon* (1955) and its sequels. He first won fame as the creator of the popular cartoon *Barnaby* (1941–62), featuring a boy and his guardian angel. Born in New York, Johnson married the writer RUTH KRAUSS in 1940 and illustrated his first children's book with her, *The Carrot Seed* (1945). There are seven *Harold* books, and like all Johnson's main characters, Harold is a round-headed boy drawn in profile with simple line, who sketches his scenery with his crayon and goes travelling in a world of his own imagining. GRB

Johnson, Edgar 1912–90 and **Johnson, Annabel** 1921– American co-writers of HISTORICAL FICTION, contemporary stories and SCIENCE FICTION. Hoping to share with urban young people their fascination with the American West and its history, the couple spent 12 years travelling in a small camping trailer, researching their stories on location and holing up in the woods to write. Each of their well-crafted historical novels deals with some aspect of the frontier period, from fur-trapping and gold-panning to the unionisation of the Montana coal mines. *Torrie* (1960), *Wilderness Bride* (1962) and *A Peculiar Magic* (1965), which focus on young women's lives, are as vigorous and exciting as the stories with male protagonists. Their most popular story, however, has been *The Grizzly* (1964), the hair-raising adventure of a contemporary boy, his long-estranged father, and a maddened mother bear. In the late 1960s, increasingly concerned about the confusing problems facing young people, the Johnsons turned to contemporary stories and finally to science fiction. *The Danger Quotient* (1984), *Prisoners of Psi* (1985) and *A Memory of Dragons* (1986) use time travel and extra-sensory powers to look at such issues as nuclear destruction, alienation and the breakdown of community. SRI

see also TIME-SLIP FANTASY

Johnson, Jane 1707–59 Wife of a British clergyman, who produced a remarkable range of hand-made teaching materials for her own children, including card games, rhymes, learning activities, mobiles and little books, most of which are kept in the Lilly Library of Indiana University. In 1994 a single FAIRY TALE came to light, *A very pretty Story to tell Children when they are about five or six years of age*, written by Johnson in 1744, and currently kept in the Bodleian Library, Oxford.

Johnson's writing for her children – several years before there was an established published literature for children – is characterised by her uniquely loving voice and the kindly humour with which she tempered her consistent concern for their moral well-being. The discovery of her work has thrown light on the role of 18th-century mothers in the education of their children. It now seems likely that there was an abiding parental provision for the moral and social well-being of children, and an unrecorded tradition of adults writing for their children that may go back centuries and involved the oral sharing of a wide range of what later came to be called NURSERY RHYMES. Jane Johnson's work raises the possibility that what occurred in the 18th century was not the 'beginning' of children's literature but the emergence into print of a domestic nursery-culture, undervalued, orally transmitted from one generation to the next, and mostly sustained by mothers, from which JOHN NEWBERY and other early producers of children's books drew much of their material. VW

Johnson, Jane 1951– British writer and illustrator of children's books. Her first book, *Sybil and the Blue Rabbit* (1980) won the Japanese Owl Prize and was runner-up for the MOTHER GOOSE AWARD. The success of her second book, *Bertie on the Beach* (1981), enabled her to become a full-time illustrator. Her attention to detail and her stylistic versatility have helped her encourage children to consider the historical past as just as absorbing as any fairyland. This interest has been sustained in the text and images of *The Princess and the Painter* (1995), which together recreate the world of Velasquez. DW

Johnson, Owen (McMahon) 1878–1952 American novelist. With *Stover at Yale* (1911), Owen Johnson, son of the poet R. U. Johnson, wrote a classic college novel: at Yale, Dink Stover encounters many challenges, beginning with Jean Story, who considers him a naive freshman. Caught between peer pressure and individualism, Dink has an identity crisis and eventually relinquishes his chance at being football captain to Tom Regan, a good friend. Set in a single-sex Ivy League institution, the book ends with Dink's tapping for Skull and Bones, a secret society for seniors. Dink entered Yale a boy from Lawrenceville; he emerges a man, having won Jean's heart. NV

Johnson, (E.) Pauline [Tekahionwakei] 1861–1913 Canadian writer and stage performer. Born at the Six Nations Reserve in Ontario, Canada, Johnson was the daughter of a Mohawk chief and an Englishwoman. Her informal education included an appreciation of English Romantic poetry from her mother, and a love of nature and fund of Indian lore acquired from tribal elders. She wrote poetry in her girlhood but earned her greatest fame and fortune later in life through stage performances across North America and abroad; in these tours, dressed as an Indian princess, she recited original poetry and told stories that celebrated her Indian heritage. Her first book of verse, *The White Wampum* (1895), contained several famous poems later anthologised in Canadian schoolbooks, particularly 'The Song My Paddle Sings'. Other poetry collections include *Canadian Born* (1903) and *Flint and Feather* (1912). Her *Legends of Vancouver* (1911), stories she heard from a Squamish chief, is Canada's first non-anthropological collection of aboriginal oral literature. Two posthumous books of stories, *The Moccasin Maker* (1913) and *The Shagganappi* (1913), include previously published boys' ADVENTURE STORIES. Although Johnson's work was not specifically written for children and now appears dated by its sentimentality, it endured as a unique gateway for the young into unfamiliar cultural terrain in Canada. It is historically significant as Canada's first form of literary mediation between aboriginal and white worlds. DAC

see also NATIVE AMERICANS IN CHILDREN'S LITERATURE

Johnson, Richard see *TOM THUMB*

Johnston, Annie Fellows see *LITTLE COLONEL SERIES*

Johnston, Phyllis 1935– New Zealand writer, the eighth child in a family of nine, who spent her younger years on a farm in the Waikato. Her parents and extended family often recounted stories of their own childhoods, which provided Johnston with the inspiration and raw material for her historical novels. *No-one Went to Town* (1980) describes the struggles of a pioneer family in the backblocks (remote lands) of Taranaki at the turn of the century. *Black Boots and Buttonhooks* (1984) continues the family's story on their farm in the King Country. Four more novels followed, with *No Lily-Livered Girl* being published in 1992. Johnston's authentic historical detail provides contemporary children with valuable insights into the harsh lives of the New Zealand pioneers, but it is the warmth, courage and determination of the characters as they go about the business of simply staying alive that gives these novels an enduring quality. LO

jokes see RIDDLES AND JOKES

Jolly Pocket Postman, The see *THE JOLLY POSTMAN AND OTHER PEOPLE'S LETTERS, THE*; see also ALLAN AND JANET AHLBERG

Jolly Postman, The, or Other People's Letters (1986) Interactive PICTUREBOOK by JANET and ALLAN AHLBERG regarded by many as a key work that synthesised many of the Ahlbergs' abiding concerns with some enduring picturebook traditions. Like *EACH PEACH PEAR PLUM* and *Jeremiah in the Dark Woods,* the book is built around intertextual reference to familiar western FAIRY TALES and NURSERY RHYMES, the eponymous postman delivering mail to characters such as Mr and Mrs Bear of the Three Bears, the Wicked Witch in her Gingerbread Cottage, and the Wolf from *LITTLE RED RIDING HOOD*. So intertwined are the references and allusions, however, that characters such as the wolf are assumed to have played roles in other well-known tales. The structure of the story is simple and circular. The first letter to be delivered – an apology from GOLDILOCKS for having eaten baby bear's porridge and broken his chair – ends with an invitation for baby bear to Goldilocks's birthday party. The reader, along with baby bear, arrives at the party itself at the end of the book when the final delivery is made: a birthday card containing a pound note.

The postman's route is described in a light, carefully constructed verse but it is the half-page illustrations and VIGNETTES that really tell us what is happening. As in the earlier *Each Peach Pear Plum* there is a game-like quality to the book which encourages the reader to search the pictures for significant detail. For example, while the wicked witch reads her advertising flyer from Hobgoblin Supplies Ltd the postman reads the Mirror Mirror newspaper, on the back of which is visible an article about a stolen pig and on the front a story concerning the return home of a honeymoon couple who, later in the book, turn out to be CINDERELLA and her Prince Charming. The letters themselves are extraordinarily varied and range from a holiday postcard (from Jack to the Giant) to a formal letter of complaint from a firm of solicitors (addressed to Mr B.B. Wolf). The provenance and contents of the letters further enrich the intertextual mixture and collectively they endow the book with a novel-like density and depth.

The real pleasure of the work, however, especially for young readers, arises from the incorporation of free-standing letters within the body of the book. In requiring readers to withdraw the contents of the envelopes physically, the Ahlbergs generate an imaginative re-enactment of a commonplace literary event – the opening and reading of mail. Fantasy, play and everyday reading and writing are thus inextricably intertwined. In *The Jolly Postman*, and in its sequels *The Jolly Christmas Postman* (1991) and the *Jolly Pocket Postman* (1995), Janet and Allan Ahlberg make brilliant use of an interactive device that in other hands might have been little more than a gimmick, and in so doing they helped to revitalise the Victorian tradition of the book that can be played with. DL

see also MOVABLE BOOKS

Jones, Dan see *INKY PINKY PONKY*; *CHILDREN'S PLAYGROUND RHYMES*

Jones, Diana Wynne 1934– British author born in London. She was educated at St Anne's, Oxford,where she attended lectures by C.S. LEWIS and J.R.R. TOLKIEN. Jones started working as a full-time author in 1965. She is married to the medievalist J.A. Burrow, and lives in Bristol. While most of her work comes under the heading of FANTASY, she avoids the usual topoi and conventions of fantasy, or employs them only to undercut them, usually with startling (and comic) effect, as in *Howl's Moving Castle* (1986) and *Dark Lord of Derkholm* (1998). *The Tough Guide to Fantasyland* (1996) also offers a brilliant parody of these conventions.

Underneath a deceptively simple style which treats the quotidian and the magical with equal matter-of-factness lies a density of meaning; operating together with the fantastical narrative one may generally find another narrative which, with restraint and understatement, examines the often complex dynamics of family relationships, as in *Charmed Life* (1977) and *EIGHT DAYS OF LUKE* (1975), or personal relationships, as in *Deep Secret* (1997).

With more than 25 full-length novels for children and adults, as well as collections of short stories and many works for younger readers to her credit, Jones is one of the most prolific writers of fantasy in Britain. She is also perhaps the most original and inventive: her plots never repeat, and are always elegantly complex. The number of AWARDS and commendations which her work has garnered testifies to this: *Charmed Life* won both the GUARDIAN AWARD (1978) and a Carnegie Commendation; *Archer's Goon* (1984) and *Howl's Moving Castle* were both BOSTON GLOBE-HORN Honour Books; *Dogsbody* (1975) and *The Lives of Christopher Chant* (1988) won CARNEGIE commendations and *Power of Three* a Guardian commendation. More recently, *Dark Lord of Derkholm* won the Mythopoeic Fantasy Award for Children's Literature, and in 1999 Diana Wynne Jones was given the British Fantasy Society's special award: the Karl Edward Wagner Award. Her most recent work, *Year of the Griffin*, scheduled to appear in 2000, is a sequel to *Dark Lord of Derkholm*. SA

see also *CHRESTOMANCI SERIES*; *INGARY SERIES*

Illustration by Harold Jones for Kathleen Lines's *Lavender's Blue: A Book of Old Nursery Rhymes.*

Jones, Harold 1904–92 British artist, illustrator and writer of children's books. Though Jones abandoned his early idea of becoming a farmer, he carried his profound experience of the natural world into his work as an illustrator. He established his reputation in 1937 with *This Year: Next Year*, a PICTUREBOOK of lithographed rural and domestic scenes, with verses by WALTER DE LA MARE. Its traditional qualities of muted colour and delicate line are revitalised, or perhaps undermined, by many haunting details. Jones subsequently produced a number of children's books and illustrated some classics. His most acclaimed book was *Lavender Blue* (1954), the classic collection of NURSERY RHYMES compiled by Kathleen Lines; it was given an honourable mention by the HANS CHRISTIAN ANDERSEN AWARD and received the American Library Association Award. Brian Alderson has called Jones 'perhaps the most original children's book illustrator of the period'. DW

see also LITHOGRAPHY

Jones, Terry 1942– British writer and film director. Born in North Wales, Jones read English at Oxford University, then worked in TELEVISION, collaborating with Oxbridge contemporaries to create the influential BBC comedy series *Monty Python's Flying Circus*. He directed two *Python* feature films, and a version of *THE WIND IN THE WILLOWS* (1996) with human actors, in addition to his own *Eric the Viking* (1989). His children's books include Tolkienesque catalogues of goblins and fairies, and variations on traditional forms such as *Fairy Tales* (1981), *Nicobobinus* (1985) and *Fantastic Tales* (1992), which all exibit the zany, often violent humour associated with *Monty Python*. SG

Jordan, June 1936– American poet, novelist and educator, born in New York City, the child of Jamaican immigrants. She attended a girls' prep school in Massachusetts, where she was encouraged to develop her skills as a poet. Her experiences as a black woman in a largely white world, as a mother, and as a child in a violent household became important themes in her writing. Although she is best known as a poet for adults, Jordan's first book was a long illustrated poem in free verse for children, *Who Look at Me* (1969). The poem examines the relationships between blacks and whites by depicting an exchange of glances between two people. Jordan has also edited important anthologies, including *Soulscript: Afro-American Poetry* (1970), which includes some of her own poems, and *The Voice of Children* (1970), which grew out of a writing workshop she co-founded and taught. Jordan has found writing poetry a strengthening experience, and has remained committed to sharing the experience with children. Her other works for young people include *His Own Where* (1971), a celebration of Black English and the right to speak it, *Dry Victories* (1972), a history, and *Kimako's Story* (1981), a children's book about a single mother and her daughter. CAB

Jordan, Sherryl 1949– One of New Zealand's best-known and most widely published authors of young adult FANTASY. Jordan was already an accomplished illustrator before her first novel, *Rocco*, was published in 1990. Sometimes her work is encumbered by inflated prose and pointed Christian symbolism, as in *Sign of the Lion* (1995), a story about 12-year-old Minstrel, who, with the guidance and support of her winged guardian angel, Elmo, is instrumental in helping a king to win a war. However, Jordan's books are noteworthy for their soaring, epic-like narratives, grounded by likeable, affirmative characters. In *Secret Sacrament* (1996) the author has crafted a compelling quest novel which, while no less symbolic or idealistic than *Sign of the Lion*, is a convincing and absorbing tale in which Jordan's vision becomes the reader's as well. *The Raging Quiet* (1999) is a quasi-historical romance, fast-paced and absorbing. BN

***Josephine and Her Dolls* series** see APPLETON, HONOR C.

***Josephine* series** see STÉPHANE POULIN

Joshi, Jagdish 1937– Indian illustrator. A graduate from the Calcutta School of Art, Joshi began his career in 1970. He has illustrated more than 150 books and won many awards, including the prestigious Noma Concours by UNESCO in 1983 for his simple, colourful PICTUREBOOK, *One Day* (1983). The abiding appeal of his wide-ranging work lies in the happy mix of the traditional and the spontaneously playful. In his effort to portray a text faithfully, he tries to find a suitable style, making realism his guiding principle. It was under his mentor Shankar's umbrella that Joshi found his artistic feet (see KESHAV SHANKAR PILLAI). The poetry of his soft, sensuous, sepia-tinged ILLUSTRATIONS to Shankar's retelling of classic romantic tales exudes an aura of mystery and charm that etched the names of his fine, chiselled heroines in Indian illustrating history. The hallmark of his simple yet innovative illustrations is an unmistakable Indianness. His strength lies in the creation of figures and animals best seen in books like ARUP KUMAR DUTTA's *The Kaziranga Trail* (1979). His successful and exquisitely executed picturebooks, *How Munia Found Gold* (1984) and *A Voice in the Jungle* (1986), communicate a positive message on the environment. He was nominated for the 1998 HANS CHRISTIAN ANDERSEN AWARD for illustration. MBh

Journey to Topaz see HISTORICAL FICTION; see also YOSHIKO UCHIDA

Joy Street British miscellany for children published by Basil Blackwell (Oxford) in the 20s and 30s, unusual for its editors' commitment to high standards of design, printing and bookbinding, and for its policy of publishing stories and poems by the best-known children's writers of the period. At a time when most children's annuals published work by unknown writers, *Number One Joy Street* (1923) contained original work by WALTER DE LA MARE, ELEANOR FARJEON, HILAIRE BELLOC, Laurence Housman, Edith Sitwell and ROSE FYLEMAN. Contributors to subsequent issues included G. K. Chesterton, A.A. MILNE, and Compton Mackenzie. There were few ADVENTURE STORIES, few SCHOOL STORIES, and no non-fiction articles; the emphasis was on FANTASY, magic, humour and poetry. What helped to make *Joy Street* distinctive was the unusually high standard of artwork; in the early issues, the colour plates were TIPPED IN on special paper, and the black-and-white drawings were of a very high quality, providing young readers of the day with an alternative to the poorly designed but less expensive annuals such as *CHATTERBOX*. Although the 13th issue was superstitiously entitled *Number 12a Joy Street*, publication unluckily came to an end in the early 1940s. VW

'She was sitting in the boughs of a tall tree.' Illustration by Marion Allen for *Number Nine Joy Street*.

Joy, Margaret see *ALLOTMENT LANE* SERIES

Joyce, William see BIOGRAPHY AND AUTOBIOGRAPHY; ILLUSTRATION IN CHILDREN'S BOOKS

Judge Dredd see ANNUALS; see also SUPERHEROES

Judy see COMICS, PERIODICALS AND MAGAZINES

***Julia Redfern* series** see ELEANOR CAMERON

Julian Stories Series of stories by Ann Cameron (1943–) about Julian and his brother Huey. *The Julian Stories* (published in the United States as *The Stories Julian Tells Us*) (1981) is illustrated by Ann Strugnell, as are *More Stories Julian Tells* (1986) and *Julian's Glorious Summer* (1988). Liz Toft provides the illustrations for *Julian, Secret Agent* (1988), *Julian, Dream Doctor* (1992) and *The Stories Huey Tells Us* (1995), which turns its focus on the younger brother. Cameron's first-person narrations are totally absorbing in their combination of a compelling characterisation of the naive child and accessible, delicately poetic language. JHD

Julie of the Wolves (1972) An outdoor survival story by JEAN CRAIGHEAD GEORGE set in the Alaskan wilderness. Miyax, whose American name is Julie, is torn between Eskimo and American cultures. Following the death of her parents, Miyax rebels when an Eskimo 'child marriage' custom is forced upon her, and escapes into the Alaskan wilderness, determined to find her way to her pen pal in San Francisco. Miyax becomes 'Julie of the Wolves', but it is as Miyax that she survives, because of the wilderness skills she has acquired from her Eskimo father. Julie's journey into the wilderness reaffirms her own identity, and her loyalty to and deep respect for her people. Her acceptance by a pack of Arctic wolves transforms the northern wilderness into a place of healing and emotional power which confirms Julie's sense of identity and belonging within her own culture. *Julie of the Wolves* was a winner of the NEWBERY MEDAL. MRS

Juliet's Story (1991) The British author William Trevor's only children's book. Juliet's journey from Ireland to France with Grandmamma is enlivened by tales told by the old lady. These deepen Juliet's understanding and bring her to an appreciation of the art of STORYTELLING and of the stories she has within herself. VC

Jumblies, The see EDWARD LEAR; see also NONSENSE VERSE

Jungle Book, The (1894) and ***The Second Jungle Book*** (1895) Collections of stories by the British author RUDYARD KIPLING, some of which are centred upon Mowgli, the child brought up among the wolves, and others upon various animal protagonists. One may read the tales on many levels, for example as refractions of history (the chapter 'Red Dog' might possibly be read in terms of the Indian mutiny and the vengeance taken for it) or as social critique, where the values of the jungle and village become mutually interrogative.

The *Jungle Books* contain strong mythic overtones, though Kipling's tales generally twist myth into new forms. 'The King's Ankh', where Mowgli meets the White Cobra in the Cold Lairs, for example, recalls the temptation of Eve and the release of evil into the world, though in the end Mowgli flings the ankh back at the snake, symbolically penning evil up again. In 'Mowgli's Brothers', the bringing of fire (the 'red flower') to the jungle is not a Promethean bringing of wisdom to the animals but an establishment of mastery over them. The tales are not mere reworkings, however, but have a certain primal quality that establishes them as mythic in their own right. *The Jungle Book* and its sequel have enjoyed a lasting popularity ever since their publication and their influence may be seen in the works of E. NESBIT, ROSEMARY SUTCLIFF, JEAN LITTLE and many other writers for children. SA

see also EDWARD AND MAURICE DETMOLD

Junior Bookshelf see REVIEWING AND REVIEWERS; see also ELEANOR GRAHAM

Junior Education see REVIEWING AND REVIEWERS

Junior Voices (1970) Edited by Geoffrey Summerfield, this four-volume poetry anthology typifies Penguin Education's innovative publishing. It contains many traditional rhymes from international sources. Summerfield, a teacher and academic, made no compromises for younger readers: the multicultural poems and ILLUSTRATIONS are often tough and always unsentimental, as seen in the final poem by Carl Sandburg, 'You Can Go Now': 'And from here if you choose you send up rockets, you let down buckets. Here then for you is the centre of things.' HA

Junk see MELVYN BURGESS; see also DRUGS IN CHILDREN'S BOOKS; SEX IN CHILDREN'S BOOKS; YOUNG ADULT FICTION

Just Jane (1928) First in a series of 10 novels by 'Evadne Price' (Helen Zenna Smith 1896–1985), concluding with *Jane At War* (1947). Critics have seen the incorrigible Jane Turpin as the female counterpart to Richmal Crompton's William Brown (see *JUST WILLIAM* SERIES), though her creator rejected any notion of imitation. Nevertheless, the books echo the William series in content, illustration, format and even their titles. Jane's Home Counties village is dominated by middle-class adults of varying degrees of pettiness, snobbery or eccentricity, sustained by long-suffering nannies, cooks and gardeners. Life in Little Duppery is marked by fêtes, amateur dramatics, fancy dress parties (with magicians) and weddings. Without malice or even intent, Jane invariably wrecks these activities, to the embarrassment of her status-conscious mother and older sister. Her most trusted lieutenants, Chaw Smith and Pug Washington, would cheerfully be accepted by William's Outlaws. Her arch enemy, and one of Evadne Price's most successful creations, is the sanctimonious daughter of the vicar, Amelia Tweeddale or 'Soppy 'Melia'. Jane never matched William's popularity. The humour is less benevolent and the plotting less sure. Mary Cadogan and Patricia Craig speculate that, in the pre-war years, 'there was a subconscious reluctance to accept in a girl behaviour which seemed normal in a boy'. GPF

Just So Stories for Little Children (1902) Collection of twelve FABLES and stories by RUDYARD KIPLING, first published as magazine stories between 1897 and

1902 and collected together in a first edition with poems and drawings by Kipling himself. The drawings have their own written and pictorial text which elaborates on and adds to the theme of the stories so that they form an essential part of the narrative background. Just as the stories are intended to be read aloud and shared at many levels through the use of rhyme, assonance, cadence and pun, so too the drawings, in art-deco style, carry multilayered messages. The interspersed poems offer a further commentary but, unlike some of the poems in the later *PUCK OF POOK'S HILL* and *Rewards and Fairies*, which add a deeper layer of meaning to the prose, they are short, sometimes encoded for fun and clearly written for a young audience.

The first seven stories are a gentle Darwinian joke about evolutionary adaptation – the whale's throat, the camel's hump, the rhinoceros's skin, the leopard's spots, the elephant's trunk, the kangaroo's legs and the scales of the armadillo. Human beings in these stories, like djinns and gods, appear as the animals' equals, appropriately inhabiting the same finely drawn and specific environments. The animals' personalities are based on a mixture of natural observation and anthropomorphism, but so strong is Kipling's influence on contemporary understanding of the same animals that readers today expect rhinos to be short-tempered almost because of the cake-crumbs. Kipling's descriptions and use of language in the *Just So Stories* permeates our own until all tropical rivers are 'great, grey-green and greasy' like the Limpopo in 'The Elephant's Child'. Adult words like 'sclusively' and 'fulvous' in 'How the Leopard got his Spots' entered children's language like 'soporific' in THE TALE OF PETER RABBIT.

Of the later five stories, one, 'How the Alphabet was Made', was first published in the collection as a sequel to 'How the First Letter was Written' in which the central characters are human. Here Kipling indulges his passion for archaic detail but the jokes are recondite and the barely suppressed anguish about his beloved daughter Josephine (who died in 1899) makes the relationship between father and daughter sentimental instead of endearing. The same sentimentality creeps into the adult relationship between Solomon and Balkis in 'The Butterfly that Stamped'. Both the 'Butterfly' and 'The Crab that Played with the Sea' have a magical eastern setting that harks back to Kipling's own early experience of the *ARABIAN NIGHTS*. Probably the most successful of the final stories is 'The Cat that Walked by Himself', though here the human beings attempt to dominate the Cat which with true Kiplingesque (and catlike) subversiveness both wins and loses the contest. The *Just So Stories* are now the most widely read of Kipling's books for children, although the *JUNGLE BOOK* characters are probably more widely known. KP

***Just William* series** (1922–70) Popular stories by British writer Richmal Crompton (1890–1969), comprising more than 40 titles. The large numbers of reprints are a rich testimony to the enduring quality of this very English anti-hero. In the comfortable, almost stifling atmosphere of late Edwardian England, William Brown marauds through the sensibilities and conformities of 'middle England' with a youthful zeal which has lost none of its appeal over time. William first appeared in the magazine *Home* in 1919, intended for adult readers. Crompton claimed that he was an original creation, but it has been observed that he is remarkably similar to the eponymous hero of the *PENROD* series, an American fictional character from the stories of BOOTH TARKINGTON, published in England in 1914.

The product of a very typical middle-class upbringing, Richmal Crompton read classics at Royal Holloway College. Her deep love of Homer might be a clue to her storytelling ability. She came from an ecclesiastical family, having an older sister and younger brother. She taught classics until an attack of poliomyelitis left her seriously weakened and unable to continue her teaching career. Instead, she turned to writing and William evolved from the magazine character. Although she wrote adult fiction too, it is for the William books that she is most remembered and appreciated.

William is forever young; caught in a world which constantly shapes, confines and controls, he alone asserts his individuality with exuberance and irreverence, helped by the gang, Ginger, Henry and Douglas – and sometimes the unwelcome and lisping Violet Elizabeth Bott. There is nothing malicious in William; he brings a childlike logic to his thinking which utterly confounds adult ways of behaving. His contempt for academics, love matches and 'do-gooders' is matched only by his misplaced ingenuity and his capacity for great schemes doomed to failure. William lives by what he loves, his freedom to roam the countryside, his gang, Jumble the dog, and a sense of heroism and valour. He strives to do what is right and make some small amount of money in the process (usually in order to buy either food or a much-desired object). Inevitably something goes wrong and his motives are misconstrued, although usually everything works out satisfactorily, and his mother's trust in him does not always prove misplaced.

William is guaranteed future interest as a result of the very successful BBC screening in the early 1990s. A number of series were made with careful attention to detail and excellent casting. The playfulness of the stories and the family audience appeal resulted in renewed reading of the William books – a good example of popular culture encouraging literacy. JDan

see also *JUST JANE*

Juster, Norton see *PHANTOM TOLBOOTH, THE*

Justice League of America see SUPERHEROES; see also MARVEL COMICS GROUP

Justice Trilogy, The (1980–1) Virginia Hamilton's science FANTASY sequence, including *Justice and Her Brothers*, *Dustland* and *The Gathering*. The protagonists are 11-year-old Justice Douglass and her twin brothers, Thomas and Levi, aged 13. Because of her own genetic disposition and extra-sensory gifts (as an African American child, the descendant of slaves endowed with survival power), Justice becomes 'pregnant' with a psychic power called the Watcher, which she must 'deliver' to future generations in the world of Dustland (Earth in the future).

The books comprise a coming-of-age story for Justice. And it is a specifically *female* coming-of-age story, since the Watcher gift is embedded in a female child in the first book of the sequence, when she most needs it because she is being mistreated by a jealous older brother. In the next two books, the Watcher continues to grow and illuminate the nature of female power and how Justice must learn to live with it and keep it in balance. Endowed with this extra-sensory strength, the 'unit' – consisting of Justice, her brothers and their companions – is able to 'mind-jump' to the future. However, they must imagine the future before they can create or recreate it – in fact, the faith that *everything that can be imagined is possible* is an important theme running through all of Hamilton's work. By the end of the third book, the children have learned the history of the earth after their time from the cyborg Celester – how an ultimate catastrophe occurred in which advanced technologies usurped natural resources, and how thermo-nuclear accidents transformed the earth into a dustland filled with poisonous ash, causing genetic mutations to occur among human survivors. In fulfilling their quest to deliver the crucial Watcher power, the children of the present succeed in starting what the original 'Starters' left undone – saving the earth. NM

Juvenile Miscellany, The: For the Instruction and Amusement of Youth One of the best-known American periodicals for children of its time, edited first by LYDIA MARIA CHILD (1826–34) and then by SARAH JOSEPHA HALE (1834–6). Founded by Child as a bimonthly publication, the magazine attracted a number of prominent women writers including Lydia Sigourney, and Hale. The contents included fiction, FABLES, dialogues and puzzles. Non-fiction included BIOGRAPHY, science, travel, history and conduct-of-life. There was a strong religious focus and articles on scripture study. The first piece in an issue was often a serialised domestic story focusing on moral values. When in 1833 Child published her essay 'An Appeal in Favor of That Class of Americans called Africans', supporting the abolition of slavery, subscribers withdrew their support and Child resigned as editor in favour of Hale, who undertook an ambitious monthly publication schedule. Hale added an editorial column, and her contributors included FELICIA HEMANS, Emma Willard, and MARY HOWITT. However, the *Miscellany* ceased publication in 1836. SRG

K

Kahukiwa, Robyn 1940– Notable New Zealand painter and leading illustrator and writer of children's PICTUREBOOKS. Kahukiwa first illustrated *The Kuia and the Spider* (1981), written by PATRICIA GRACE. More recently she has composed and illustrated her own stories, including the award-winning *Taniwha* (1986) New Zealand Picturebook of the Year, 1987, *Paikea* (1993), *The Koroua and the Maori Stone* (1994) and *Kehua* (1996).

Kahukiwa has said that she is interested in making books for Maori children that deal in their own experience and communicate Maori traditions and culture. Her stories are kept extremely simple, but often possess the rhetorical power of chant and resonate by virtue of their affiliations with MYTH and LEGEND. In *Taniwha*, a characteristic Maori sense of a natural cosmos infused with spiritual force is strongly communicated, as a young boy makes friends with the familiar Maori water monster.

Kahukiwa's ILLUSTRATIONS tend to be boldly stylised, often adapting decorative and figural patterns derived from Maori carving, perhaps nowhere more effectively than in her recent book, *Paikea*. This tale tells the history of the eponymous hero of the Ngati Porou, saved from his jealous brother by a whale that carried him from Hawaiki to Aotearoa, where he takes several wives and begins several family lines. The elemental force of the story is supported by highly patterned illustrations that convey its broad, foundational significance. CM

Kalman, Maira 1949– American illustrator and writer. Kalman's baroque imagination, fuelled by an integrated knowledge of high culture, has made her sophisticated dog character Max Stravinsky the star of a series of books, including the witty and urbane 1991 *New York Times* Best Illustrated Book, *Ooh-la-la (Max in Love)*, which took him to Paris for a stylish stay and a chance at romance. Born in Tel Aviv, Kalman grew up in New York City in a cultured family that valued the arts, especially music. She studied piano through high school, majored in literature at New York University, and then became an illustrator. In 1986 she combined her interests in her first PICTUREBOOK, *Stay Up Late*, with text by musician David Byrne. The highly successful *Max* series, like all her books, with their energetic and wacky texts, surreal images, and culture-dropping references, appeal intentionally to adults as well as children. Kalman says, 'Good writing, like good music, good art, good anything, takes you out of the mundane, to an extremely inspiring and creative level.' MMG

Kantey, Mike see *SOME OF US ARE LEOPARDS, SOME OF US ARE LIONS*

Kästner, Erich see *EMIL AND THE DETECTIVES*; see also ADVENTURE STORIES

Kate Crackernuts see ENGLISH FOLKTALES; K.M. BRIGGS

Kate Greenaway Medal see APPENDIX

Kathasaritsagar, The see *HAROUN AND THE SEA OF STORIES*; see also INDIAN MYTHS, LEGENDS AND FOLKTALES

***Katie Morag* series** Contemporary PICTUREBOOKS by Scottish author MAIRI HEDDERWICK. The cheerful stories set on a Hebridean island construct a complete world around the lives of Katie Morag and her family. Katie Morag herself is a sturdy and determined little girl, dressed always in wellington boots and well-known by everyone on the island. The ILLUSTRATIONS show a cheerful and chaotic household packed with tiny details: Katie Morag is often to be seen reading one of the earlier books in the series, the shop sells Grannie Island's potatoes and displays posters advertising the annual show. A strict time-scale is observed in the books so that Katie Morag is one of the few picturebook heroines who grows older as the stories continue. Throughout the series the gentle rivalry between Grannie Island, who wears dungarees and drives a tractor, and Grandma Mainland, who arrives with a suitcase full of smart clothes, provides a focus for the contrast between life on the island and that on the mainland. The encroachment of the modern world is central to the fifth book, *Katie Morag and the New Pier* (1993). The opening ENDPAPERS show the island before the new pier, isolated and with few facilities; those at the end show the changes brought by tourism, with a new bistro, craft shop and tea-rooms. Only Grannie Island is pessimistic, convinced that the old ways will be forgotten, but even she can see that some concession to the new way of life is inevitable. KA

***Katy* series** see *WHAT KATY DID*

Katz, Welwyn 1948– Canadian writer of myth, FANTASY, magic and historically based fiction. Her first book was *The Prophecy of Tau Ridoo* (1983), followed by *False Face* (1987), *The Third Magic* (1990), *Witchery Hill* (1990), *Sun God, Moon Witch* (1990), *Whale-singer* (1990), *Come Like Shadows* (1993), *Time Ghost* (1994) and *Out of the Dark* (1995). In *False Face*, Katz writes about the supernatural invading the world of reality. The intensity of her work derives from emotional and psychological conflicts such as power struggles within mother–daughter relationships, family stresses due to divorce, ethnic differences and racial antagonisms. Katz won the 1987 International Children's Fiction Contest for *False Face*, for which she also received the Max and Gretel Ebel Memorial Award for Children's Writing. In 1988 she won the Governor General Literary Award for *The Third Magic*, and in 1994 the Vicky Metcalf Award for her body of work and the Ruth Schwartz Award for *Out of the Dark*. MRS

Katzenjammer Kids A comic strip by Rudolph Dirks, first appearing in 1897 in the comic weekly *The American Humorist of the New York Journal*. The series featured the raucous behaviour of two boys, Hans and Fritz, and adult counterparts Der Inspector, Der Captain and Mama. At the suggestion of the editor Rudolph Block and publisher William Randolph Hearst, Dirks based the strip, at first without dialogue, on the German *Max und Moritz* by Wilhelm Busch, in which two mischievous boys engage in pranks and slapstick. 'Katzenjammer' is German slang for 'hangover' and literally means 'howling cats'. H. H. Kneer continued the series after 1913. KSB

Kay, Jackie 1961– Scottish poet who writes about growing up in Glasgow as an adopted black child in her collections *TWO'S COMPANY* (1992) and *Three Has Gone* (1994). Her interest in drama and song is reflected in her use of monologue and in the speech rhythms of her free verse. *Two's Company* deservedly won the *SIGNAL* AWARD. ML

Kaye, Geraldine 1925– British author many of whose novels reflect the time she has spent living abroad. They often concern relationships across cultures and traditions, as in *COMFORT HERSELF* or *A Breath of Fresh Air* (1987), in which a contemporary Bristol schoolgirl travels back in time to the Jamaican plantations and experiences the horrors of slavery at first hand. In Kaye's novels for younger readers cultural differences provide interest but are no obstacle to friendship; the *Small Street* series features a street where 'the houses are the same and all the people are different'. *My Second-Best Friend* (1998) deals with the realities of itinerant people and attitudes towards them. Kaye lives near Bristol and the city and its history form a backdrop for much of her work. KA

Kaye, M. M. see *ORDINARY PRINCESS, THE*

Keats, Ezra Jack 1916–83 American artist and creator of 24 distinguished PICTUREBOOKS, who lived and worked in New York City. Keats's world is a bright, sprawling, multi-ethnic, inner-city neighbourhood filled with puppet shows, birthday parties, snowy days and Hallowe'en nights, a place where pets live and sometimes die, where big boys tease, little sisters are bothersome, and dogs can go roller-skating. It is a world no child can easily resist, especially when the techniques that have become Keats's trademarks – fabric and paper COLLAGE and marbled paper – endow the characters and backgrounds of the pictures with a vibrant, touchable quality and make the water, sky and dreams of these stories seem, to children, quite real.

Keats had made books for every season and holiday, as well as a COUNTING BOOK, a Christmas carol, the legend of John Henry, three wordless PICTUREBOOKS, and even a bilingual story for Spanish-speaking children. But his fame rests most securely on the CALDECOTT MEDAL winner, the picturebook *The Snowy Day* (1962), about the delight a child has playing in the first snow of the year, an experience Keats remembered vividly from his own childhood. That he painted a black child caused a stir at the time, since Peter was the first protagonist of colour to appear in full colour in an American picturebook.

Keats went on to produce six more books in which this appealing character grew a little taller through the years: *Whistle for Willie* (1964), *Peter's Chair* (1967), *A Letter to Amy* (1968), *Goggles* (1969), *Hi, Cat!* (1970) and *Pet Show!* (1972). Each book explores a small but significant problem or preoccupation of childhood (a special snowball melting, learning to whistle, a new baby in the family, a mix-up in communication, out-smarting the big boys, and the unpredictability of pets). Also significant in the Keats canon are the stories in which Louie, a shy Hispanic child, takes centre-stage: *Louie* (1975), *The Trip* (1978), *Louie's Search* (1980) and *Regards to the Man in the Moon* (1981). In *Dreams* (1974) Roberto is joined on stage by Peter's friends Amy and Archie, of *Goggles* fame, and even Archie's cat of *Hi, Cat!* and *Pet Show!*. The cat is saved by Roberto's paper mouse, a character who, like so many of Keats's story-children,

An early illustration by Charles Keeping for *The Commonwealth and Empire Annual.*

takes on a life of his own once Roberto sets him in 'motion'. NM

Keats, John 1795–1821 English Romantic poet who died of tuberculosis at 25. He wrote some light and comic verse for young children, but his work more often appeals to young readers because of its poignantly intense portrayal of the yearnings, joys and pains of adolescence and romantic love: 'La Belle Dame Sans Merci', 'Ode to a Nightingale', and 'Bright star, would I were as steadfast as thou art' (1820). The verse is richly sensuous and pictorial. The longer narrative poems – *The Eve of St Agnes* (1820) and others – use imagery and techniques of storytelling in ways which might now be described as cinematic. RC

Keene, Carolyn see NANCY DREW SERIES; ADVENTURE STORIES; see also STRATEMEYER SYNDICATE

Keeping, Charles (William) 1920–88 One of the leading British illustrators of his time, Keeping was born in Lambeth. He remained committed to inner-city London all his life, frequently featuring typical urban scenes in his work. Leaving school at 14, his first commission in 1956 was to illustrate some stories by ROSEMARY SUTCLIFF for Oxford University Press, the publisher with whom he subsequently did most of his best work. Starting with his characteristically swirling line illustrations, he later moved to colour. In 1967 he won the KATE GREENAWAY MEDAL for *Charley, Charlotte and the Golden Canary*. He then moved away from ILLUSTRATION simply as a record of character or incident, deciding instead to make his artwork more evocative of a general mood. There followed some remarkable PICTUREBOOKS composed entirely by himself. *Joseph's Yard* (1969) is less a story than a series of snapshots of what a small boy sees going on down below, closely based on Keeping's own childhood memories of playing in the family yard next to a stable housing a cart-horse. *Through the Window* (1970) is another dream-like recording of a street accident, again witnessed by a small boy. *Inter-City* (1977) wordlessly describes a railway journey seen through a train window. Some critics complained that children might not always understand these books. But other illustrators were also beginning to produce work which demanded more of readers, requiring them to fill in gaps in the narrative for themselves in order to make up their own minds about what was really happening. This growing sophistication of young readers allowed picturebooks to become more ambitious, and few were more adventurous during this time than Keeping's own brilliant contributions.

Also controversial were the occasional violence and horror in Keeping's work. As someone who had served in the navy during the war, he knew about these topics from first hand and did not believe that modern children should always be protected from such knowledge. His illustrations for *THE GOD BENEATH THE SEA* (1970) bring out the savagery as well as the beauty inherent in Greek mythology. In *THE HIGHWAYMAN* (1981, reissued 1999), another Kate Greenaway Medal winner, Keeping portrays death in what some saw as shocking detail. Alfred Noyes's romantic poem describes the taking of a beautiful young woman as hostage in the expectation that her highwayman lover will come to her. The cruelty on the soldiers' faces holding the girl captive and her own suicide are both pictured unforgettably, as is the subsequent ghost of the highwayman. This book also marked a return to drawings done in brown and black after experiments with colour which Keeping himself described as sometimes leading to 'a fruit salad effect'. Yet in everything this gifted artist did, his fine artistic line, passionate commitment to telling the truth and vivid recollection of a child's perception of the world constantly picked him out as a rare talent. NT

Keith, Harold 1903– American writer of juvenile fiction. An Oklahoman, Keith grew up near the Cherokee county setting of *Rifles for Watie* (1957), a Civil War story and winner of the NEWBERY MEDAL. Keith's award-winning HISTORICAL FICTION – including *Komantcia* (1965), *Susy's Scoundrel* (1974) and *The Obstinate Land* (1977) – is noted for its accuracy and attention to detail. As sports publicity director at the University of Oklahoma for 40 years, he also wrote sports histories and inspirational books showing children striving against preconceived stereotypes to take part in team sports, including *Brief Garland* (1971) and *Go, Red, Go!* (1972). SCWA

Kelleher, Victor 1939– Australian novelist, born in London, who took up full-time writing in 1987 after a career as an academic in universities in Africa, New Zealand and Australia. After living in Africa for 20 years, Kelleher moved to New Zealand, and whilst there was desperately homesick for Africa. His first book for young people, *Forbidden Paths of Thual* (1979), was written during this time, and it was this nostalgia which prompted him to begin writing. It was, as he says, 'as difficult to write as my first adult novel . . . It was that difficulty which I found attractive and which tempted me to tackle further books.'

Kelleher writes for both adults and young people and embraces a number of genres from FANTASY to psychological realism, SCIENCE FICTION, HISTORICAL FICTION and DETECTIVE FICTION. Similar themes recur in his works: colonisation and the fate of indigenous peoples in *Em's Story* (1988), *Earthsong* (1995) and *Baily's Bones* (1988); horror in *The Hunting of Shadroth* (1981) and *The Green Piper* (1984); and life after some form of cataclysmic event in *Parkland* (1994) and TARONGA (1986). *The Ivory Trail* was published in 1999. Notions of the interconnectedness of humanity with other creatures is an underpinning in both *Parkland* and *Earthsong*. *Johnny Wombat* (1996), a humorous PICTUREBOOK, with ILLUSTRATIONS by CRAIG SMITH, has a message for adults concerning the way they handle children's fantasies.

Many of Kelleher's works feature young people on hazardous journeys, symbolic of their inner search for self and the journey toward maturity. Kelleher's worlds are richly mythological, dealing with timeless issues such as the importance of overcoming hate, evil, guilt, violence and desire. He masterfully weaves psychological truths into storylines which are at once magical, fantastical, suspenseful, frightening and full of fast-paced action. He has explained that many of his ideas stem from his dreams and his attempt to exorcise his own personal demons. The moral and ethical issues he questions include such issues as genetic engineering and biological diversity, and in *Slow Burn* (1998) he confronts green politics. All of his books, in their individual ways, provide excellent yet disturbing and taxing reading.

Evidence of the quality and popularity of his work can be found in the impressive list of awards his works have received, including: CHILDREN'S BOOK COUNCIL OF AUSTRALIA Book of the Year; Children's Literature Peace Prize; Hoffman Award; Australian Science Fiction Achievement Award, and various children's choice awards. SAM

Kellogg, Steven 1941– American illustrator and author whose PICTUREBOOKS, almost 100 in number, appeal to the imagination of all ages. *Pinkerton, Behave!* (1979) was the first of four books about his obstreperous Great Dane. Prior to these, he wrote and illustrated several books such as *The Island of the Skog* (1973) and *The Mysterious Tadpole* (1977), both still popular today. A series of TALL TALES began with *Paul Bunyan* (1984), introducing children to the heroes and heroines of that genre. Among his FOLKTALES are *Chicken Little* (1985), *JACK AND THE BEANSTALK* (1991), *THE THREE LITTLE PIGS* (1997) and *The Three Sillies* (1999). ILLUSTRATIONS for other authors include MARGARET MAHY's *The Boy Who Was Followed Home* (1975), David M. Schwartz's *How Much Is a Million?* (1985) and JAMES THURBER's *The Great Quillow* (1994). Kellogg's illustrations, usually pen-and-ink with full-colour wash, are always recognisable: the exuberance and movement that covers the page; the abundance of detail, often including tiny visual sub-plots; the exaggerated expressions of the characters; and light-heartedness and humour. PDS

Kelly, Eric P(hilbrook) 1884–1960 American author best known for his first novel, the NEWBERY AWARD winner *The Trumpeter of Krakow* (1928). Kelly was born in Amesbury, Massachusetts and educated at Dartmouth College. He worked as a newspaper reporter in Massachusetts and New Jersey, and taught English and journalism at Dartmouth from the 1920s to the 1950s. In 1925/6 he was a Kosciuszko Foundation scholar and lecturer at the University of Krakow. Set in Krakow, Poland, a place Kelly knew well, *The Trumpeter of Krakow* vividly depicts the historical setting of the church of St Mary the Virgin, the castle on Wawel Hill and Krakow University as they might have been in the 15th century. His language is poetic and his story action-packed and thrilling, full of intrigue, alchemy, superstition, patriotism and adventure. Kelly followed the success of his first novel with two other historical novels with Polish settings: *The Blacksmith of Vilno* (1930) and *The Golden Star of*

Halich (1931). He continued to write romantic, optimistic books in the 1930s, but with the coming of World War II his life changed. Temporarily leaving his teaching position at Dartmouth he worked helping to settle Polish refugees in Mexico. For Kelly, the loss of Polish independence after the war was heartbreaking. LH

See also HISTORICAL FICTION

Kemp, Gene 1926– British children's author most famous for the *CRICKLEPIT COMBINED SCHOOL* series. She was born and brought up in a small village near Tamworth, which inspired her first series of children's tales, the *Tamworth Pig* stories. After reading English she began teaching in primary and secondary schools in the Exmoor area and was later awarded an MA by the University of Exeter in recognition of her work for children.

The four works beginning with *The Prime of Tamworth Pig* (1972) illustrate both her strengths and weaknesses as a writer. The vibrant and anarchic lifestyle of Thomas, the young hero of these stories, is captured with realistic detail and wit, whilst the talking pig of the title gives a rich FANTASY element to which young readers respond. The stereotypical portrayal of many characters, particularly those with minor roles, and the overtly sexist attitudes explicitly conveyed by the main characters and implicit within the narratives and structure, are elements which were to recur in the author's later work.

Many of her other stories are lively tales of school and home life told from the child's point of view. There is an honesty about her main protagonists which makes the reader care about what happens to them even when they are seemingly unlovable. One of her protagonists announces: 'I don't want to be liked, I don't want to be good, I don't want to be in the football team, or a useful member of anything, I don't want to know. I don't care' (*Gowie Corby Plays Chicken*). Throughout her novels there is an authentic playground humour, whether in the somewhat cruel name-calling, the sarcastic one-liners, or the excruciating puns and jokes which open many of the chapters in her SCHOOL STORIES.

Kemp has also written novels for adolescent teenagers, and these reveal an ability to tackle issues such as abuse and neglect with sensitivity and understanding. As with the rest of her work, they are mostly first-person narratives and accurately capture the speech patterns and nuances which can be heard in British playgrounds and youth clubs. PJR

Kendall, Carol 1917– American writer, author of *The Gammage Cup* (1959), a Newbery Honour Book about the mock-heroic struggle between the Minnipins and the Mushrooms. In *The Gammage Cup* Kendall creates a utopian society of diminutive characters living a peaceful but too complacent existence in their isolated valley. Nonconformists, who are the society's poets, artists and philosophers, are seen by the rest of the community as threatening and are exiled. But ultimately they are the ones who recognise imminent danger from an old enemy and orchestrate the Minnipins' triumph over the Mushrooms. A product of the Cold War era of the 1950s, the book's anti-totalitarian message and its attack on mindless conformity constitute thinly-veiled didacticism, but it is admirably softened by Kendall's charming characterisation, gentle humour and inventive use of language. Her other works include *The Big Splash* (1960), a realistic novel, and *The Whisper of Glocken* (1965), which returns to the FANTASY of the Minnipins. Kendall has also collaborated with Yao-wen Li, a native of Canton, China, on *Sweet and Sour: Tales from China*. NV

Who will be the clerk?
I, said the Lark,
If 'tis not in the dark,
And I will be the clerk.
AMEN

From James Kendrew's chapbook *The Death and Burial of Cock Robin.*

Kendrew, James c.1770–1841 Important publisher of Colliergate, York, England, who printed popular literature, songs, lives of famous people, dying speeches, school books, and the children's CHAPBOOKS for which he is best remembered. These came in two different one-penny series, and a halfpenny series. They were of a higher standard than those of many other provincial printers. Carefully printed and illustrated, some of the woodcuts were engraved by the York printer M.W. Carrall. Kendrew's five daughters are thought to have assisted in hand-colouring the ILLUSTRATIONS after school. One of his children's chapbooks was a slightly adapted – and unacknowledged – version of WILLIAM WORDSWORTH's poem 'We Are Seven'. SD

see also WOOD ENGRAVING

Kenmuir, Dale 1945– A modern, conservation-conscious successor to the 19th-century writers of African hunting adventures. A South African, he draws on his experiences and research as a game warden and scientist to write stories set in the African bush or on the Namibian coast. Of his four books featuring Tom Finnaughty, the two about his boyhood, *Dry Bones Rattling* (1990) and *Ol' Tangletooth* (1990), are more intended for younger readers than are the two about his adult life as a ranger, *The Tusks and the Talisman* (1987) and *Sing of Black Gold* (1991). These novels about battles against poachers argue for conservation which realistically takes into account the contending needs of local tribespeople, economic development and tourism. *The Catch* (1993) combines the excitement of a fishing competition with the internal struggles of a teenager over questions of honesty and trust in his father. *Song of the Surf* (1988), untypically, is the haunting study of a sensitive, lonely little boy who resents his rugged father's role in the slaughter of seals on the Namibian coast. Kenmuir's exuberant prose evokes superbly the sights, sounds and smells of the bush and sea, but becomes melodramatic in the action sequences and dialogue. ERJ

Kennedy, (Jerome) Richard 1932– American writer of FANTASY and poetry for children. Lucid writing, elegant narrative construction and an encyclopaedic imagination characterise Kennedy's 17 works of fiction and two books of poetry. Kennedy employs a wide range of devices and expressive styles inspired by folklore, FAIRY TALE and literary fantasy, and he is equally skilled at evoking the pithy speech of a peasant, the menacing growl of a villain, and the nuanced, romantic musings of a young girl in love. He is a master of the striking, well-turned phrase, the unforgettable image, and the ingenious plot twist. His writing is clear and lively enough for young readers while providing a level of poetic imagery and symbolic complexity that is satisfying to the most sophisticated adult reader. *Amy's Eyes* (1985) is Kennedy's masterpiece – a story of magical transformations, obsession, greed and love that features living dolls who journey across the sea to seek a lost father. NURSERY RHYMES, high adventure, slapstick comedy and romance are ingeniously integrated. *Collected Stories* (1987) demonstrates Kennedy's versatility in works such as the surreal and poignant 'Oliver Hyde's Dishcloth Concert', and 'The Dark Princess', one of the most romantic stories ever written. CV

Kennedy, Lisa see *LIELLE'S SPIRIT BIRD*

Kennedy, X.J. [Joseph Charles] 1929– American children's poet, novelist and anthologist, a former college professor and winner of numerous poetry prizes, including the Lamont Award. Kennedy, born in Dover, New Jersey, has compiled a number of poetry anthologies together with his wife, D. M. Kennedy, including *Knock at a Star: A Child's Introduction to Poetry* (1982) and *Talking Like the Rain: A First Book of Poems* (1992), which received ten notable book citations and an ABC Children's Book Sellers Choice Award.

It is clear from his work that Kennedy understands the love of language, particularly rhythm and rhyme, inherent in young children, and he refuses to underestimate the intelligence of his audience. By the time he published his first book of children's poems, *One Winter Night in August and Other Nonsense Jingles* illustrated by David McPhail, in 1975, he was already recognised and had received much critical acclaim as a poet for adults. Other collections of award-winning children's NONSENSE VERSE followed, including *Brats* (1986), *Fresh Brats* (1990) and *Drat These Brats!* (1993). In 1983, he published his first children's novel, *The Owlstone Crown*, which received a Best Book Citation from the Library of Congress, and a Finest Fantasy award from Ethical Culture School. JGJ

Kent, Rockwell 1882–1971 American illustrator, writer and painter of ADVENTURE STORIES and scenes. A powerful talent for adventure defines Kent's life, and he intended his illustrated books to appeal to adults as well as to the young. Born in Tarrytown Heights, New York, he was a rebellious student who attended a series of schools, then spent ten years travelling and painting. He financed a 1916 trip to Alaska by incorporating himself and selling shares; the resulting paintings sold well enough to pay a 20 per cent return. He worked in woodcut, LITHOGRAPHY, painting and drawing, at times combining them. In *Salarnina* (1935) chapter openings have small woodcuts of Greenland landscapes, while full-page sepia-tone lithographs illustrate characters and events. His vigorous, unequivocal images, often of solitary figures battling against the wild forces of nature and of life, strike with moral as well as graphic force. He was once described as an 'athlete of the brush'. Kent's advocacy of socialist ideas resulted in a Communist label from the House Un-American Committee in the 1950s. He believed that 'the real art of living consists in keeping alive the conscience we had when we were young'.

MMG

Ker Wilson, Barbara see WILSON, BARBARA KER

Kerr, Bob 1951– New Zealand illustrator and writer whose exceedingly popular work has grown out of the comic idiom. Popular success came with his ILLUSTRATIONS for *Terry and the Gunrunners* (1981), a series written by Stephen Ballantyne. *Lucy Loops the Loop* (1979), a simple PICTUREBOOK wherein the hero,

Lucy, invents machines, is a precursor to Kerr's *Mechanical Harry* (1997), which won the inaugural *New Zealand Post* Children's Choice Award. The Heath-Robinson tour through Harry's day, is simultaneously a lesson in Newton's laws of motion and a fond reference to TINTIN and *Wallace and Gromit*. It is a triumph – what children want, not what adults want for them. MJH

Kerr, Judith 1923– Writer who was born in Germany and came to England in the 1930s. Well known for her autobiographical novels, Kerr is also the author/illustrator of the well-paced and satisfying *The Tiger who Came to Tea*, which has been continuously in print since it was published in 1968. Her exasperating, endearing cat character, Mog, first appeared in *Mog, the Forgetful Cat* (1970) and there have been several sequels; all these titles remain popular. Kerr's uncluttered, literal illustrations are readily appreciated by young children. JAG

see also OUT OF THE HITLER TIME

Kerr, M.E. [Marijane Meaker] 1927– American writer of YOUNG ADULT FICTION, often dealing with social problems. Born in New York, Meaker was already a writer of adult novels before she established herself as a writer of juvenile problem novels. With the publication of *Dinky Hocker Shoots Smack!* (1972), Kerr earned a reputation as an author who writes about the trials and tribulations of outsiders to society, often young people who must struggle to find love and understanding even though society spurns them. Kerr is not afraid to address controversial issues. Her novel *Is That You, Miss Blue?* (1975) focuses on the effects of a painful divorce on children; *Night Kites* (1986) is the first American young adult novel to deal with AIDS; *Linger* (1993) discusses the impact of the Persian Gulf War on life in the United States; and *Deliver Us from Evie* (1994) addresses the hatred experienced by a young lesbian couple growing up in the South. In all her novels, Kerr deals openly and honestly with troubling social issues, never talking down to her young readers or concealing factual information about the most difficult topics, one of the reasons for her books' popularity over more than two decades. SAI

see also GAY AND LESBIAN LITERATURE

Kes Popular and controversial novel by British author Barry Hines, first published in 1968 as *A Kestrel for a Knave*. In keeping with so-called 'kitchen sink' drama at the time, Hines shocked readers with his story of Billy Casper's family life in a working-class northern town. The novel explores the brutality and harsh conditions, both material and emotional, experienced by Billy as he struggles to make sense of his life. Hines challenges directly any Romantic assumptions of childhood: Billy has to learn to survive a neglectful and self-obssessed mother, a bullying brother, and an education system which will clearly fail him.

Kes is the name he gives to a kestrel which he takes from the nest and trains. The bird becomes a focus for Billy's emotional needs and provides an opportunity for learning, excitement and growth. The soaring kestrel stands in stark contrast to the narrow and cruel existence to which Billy is condemned. The climax of the novel is uncompromising and painful, exposing the awfulness of early childhood for large numbers of working-class children in Britain in the 1960s. Hines condemns family life, the education system and the state, accusing them of neglect and indifference. The bleakness of the novel caused outrage at the time, but it resonates in a disturbing manner through the decades. JDan

Kestrel for a Knave, A see KES

***Kevin and Sadie* series** (1972–7) Five books by Scottish author JOAN LINGARD. The first two books in the series are set against the background of the troubles in Belfast in the late 1960s and describe the growing relationship between a Catholic boy and a Protestant girl. Initially sworn enemies, they become friends and are driven away from Belfast by the murder of a kindly old teacher who had befriended them. Throughout the novels Lingard does not shy away from the horrors of the situation in Belfast. Even after Kevin and Sadie have left Ireland they hear of the tarring and feathering of one of Kevin's old girlfriends. Unusually for a children's series, the novels continue after their marriage, the later novels describing the problems of their early married life in England. Both Kevin and Sadie are strong and determined characters whose initial hostility is as forceful as their eventual relationship. They are resolute in their refusal to accept that the religious divide should affect their friendship despite the considerable opposition they face. In *Across the Barricades* (1972) the second and strongest novel in the series, the two begin to go out with each other, despite the antagonism of friends and family. As a direct result of this Kevin gets beaten up and they are both nearly killed when their car is tampered with. There are few children's novels that deal with the troubles in Northern Ireland, and this series is widely read in schools. KA

Kewpies Cupid-like figures with a curl of hair at the top of their heads, invented by American Rose O'Neill (1874–1944), who explained that Cupids got people into trouble, and Kewpies (spelled with a k 'because it seemed funnier') got them out. O'Neill's illustrated stories about Kewpies appeared first in the *Ladies'*

Home Journal of 1909, and Kewpie dolls soon became popular. All Kewpies were male – Scootles, the 'Baby Tourist', is the only girl in Kewpieville – but they are androgynous in appearance and behaviour, donning frilly aprons, for instance, to carry a flag proclaiming 'Votes for Women'. FEA

Khalsa, Dayal Kaur 1943–89 Canadian writer and illustrator of PICTUREBOOKS. Born Marcia Schoenfeld in Queens, New York, Khalsa attended City College, travelled during the 1960s, and made Canada her home in 1970. She later became a Sikh. Montreal publisher May Cutler of Tundra Books, impressed by Khalsa's unconventional colour sense, engaged the self-taught artist to design the innovative *Baabee Books* (1989–94). Khalsa is best known for an untitled picturebook series based on her Jewish childhood in Queens, starring a little girl called May (named after Cutler). Beginning with *Tales of a Gambling Grandma* (1986), which celebrates life with her grandmother, these stories are funny, poignant and full of 1950s detail. Her naive acrylics pay playful homage to favourite painters such as Seurat, Hopper and Van Gogh. Barely launched on her career, Khalsa learned she had cancer. This spurred her to produce seven more books in three years – while undergoing debilitating cancer treatment. *I Want a Dog* (1987), *My Family Vacation* and *Sleepers* (both 1988), *How Pizza Came to Our Town* (1989) and – posthumously – *Julian* (1989), *Cowboy Dreams* (1990) and *The Snow Cat* (1992) all testify to Khalsa's affection for dogs, family, friends and especially cowboys. Her unique talent was recognised with 18 major honours in Canada and the United States, as well as a 1999 retrospective at the National Gallery of Canada. AG

Kiapi, Paul Palia see *THE FORBIDDEN MARRIAGE*

Kidd, Diana (Celene) 1933– Australian writer whose short novels make both humorous and poignant comment on the mix that now makes up Australian society: Italian migrants, Boat People, Aborigines and street kids. Kidd varies her point of view and narrative stance to suit her subject matter: a pertly humorous diary in *The Day Grandma Came to Stay (and Spoiled My Life)* (1988); letters in the tender *Onion Tears* (1989), in which a displaced little girl writes to her canary left behind in her homeland; an Aboriginal boy's first-person rumination in *The Fat and Juicy Place* (1992); and verse, grafitti and narrative in *Spider and King* (1994). MSax

Kiddell-Monroe, J. see CAMPING AND TRAMPING FICTION; *THE SONG OF HIAWATHA*

Kidnapped (1886) Romantic Scottish historical adventure tale by ROBERT LOUIS STEVENSON written in Bournemouth during a period of convalescence and nostalgic exile. First published serially in *Young Folks* – in the same year as *The Strange Case of Dr Jekyll and Mr Hyde* – the novel confirmed Stevenson's reputation as an innovative storyteller and the creator of memorable, complex characters. The story combines actual, localised historical events of the period after the 1795 Jacobite rebellion with two strongly contrasted protagonists, seen by biographers as reflecting dualities in Stevenson himself. Alan Breck Stewart, an attractive, swashbuckling Highlander, collects rents for Scots in exile on the Continent and is in constant flight from his enemies. David Balfour, the narrator, is the sententious Presbyterian Lowlander – he cannot wield a sword – whose increasing admiration for Alan is one of the subtlest strands of the tale. His kidnapping, followed by a shipwreck, a historically attested murder and a flight across the Highlands, are set pieces of pace and clarity. The book satisfied young Victorian readers in search of heroic deeds, and their fathers reliving imagined or recollected youthful adventures – a dual readership no longer common. There is evidence, however, that quite young readers are attracted by the narrative swiftness, elements of constant surprise, witty dialogue and moral ambiguity, which first appeared in *Treasure Island* (1883). The self-referencing of the author engages other admirers of the novel who include Henry James, GRAHAM GREENE and Jorge Luis Borges. The sequel, *Catriona* (1893) written in Samoa near the end of Stevenson's life, continues with David's romantic attachment to the heroine and the author's rootedness in the history of his birthplace. MM

Kildare Place Society Popular name for the Society for Promoting the Education of the Poor in Ireland, founded in Dublin in 1811 by philanthropic businessmen. In the earlier part of the 19th century, the Society published a series of books, fiction and non-fiction, designed for use in the schools supported by the Society. VC

Kilner, Dorothy 1755–1836 Prolific English writer for children who, with her sister Mary-Ann, was popular in the latter part of the 18th century. Most of her books – which take the form of stories, poems, lectures, history and letters, mostly on moral and religious topics – fall into the category of didactic literature for the young, but *The Life and Perambulations of a Mouse* (2 volumes, 1783/3) promised what F.J. HARVEY DARTON calls 'a freshness hardly seen until Alice appeared'. *Poems on Various Subjects for the Amusement of Youth* (1783) contains a few gems, such as 'The Retort to Master Richard', which gives a nod in the direction of the CAUTIONARY TALE, rather than the more familiar and tedious moral tale in verse. MCCS

Kilworth, Garry 1941– British author whose work moves through the futuristic, with *The Electric Kid* (1994), the historical, with *The Drowners* (1991), the contemporary, with *The Third Dragon* (1991) and *The Brontë Girls* (1995), and the comic, with *Billy Pink's Private Detective Agency* (1993). His tightly-plotted novels make use of the exotic and the strange to explore the nature of good and evil. Strong and carefully drawn characters ensure that there are no easy answers in the worlds that he creates, making the dilemmas in which his protagonists find themselves all the more powerful. JEG

Kim (1901) Story set in India by RUDYARD KIPLING. Kim is a British orphan, a street child, The Little Friend of all the World. He encounters a Lama who is following the Buddhist Way on a quest to find the River of Healing. Drawn into the Lama's quest Kim discovers his own British roots and is recruited into the British espionage network – The Great Game. The Lama represents wisdom without experience, Kim the reverse. The book pursues the quest and the Game which offer moral choices to the Lama and Kim, who are bound together by an affection and mutual kindness which temporarily prompts in those they encounter an equal, if unwonted, generosity. Kim, the orphan of the streets, is foreshadowed by the orphaned Mowgli of *THE JUNGLE BOOKS* but, unlike Mowgli, Kim does not fully grow up and his fate is unresolved. The book's lasting charm lies not only in the two main characters but in Kipling's nostalgic, tenderly drawn images of Indian life on the Great Trunk Road, in the teeming urban wards and in the Hills. Seen by many as Kipling's masterpiece, *Kim* is not specifically a children's book just as Kim himself is not wholly a child. KP

Kimenye, Barbara One of the most prominent children's writers in East Africa, Kimenye is a Ugandan citizen who has lived in Kenya for years. She has written many stories in the *Moses* series. *Moses and the Penpal* (1981) is one of the most popular books in this series and has been reprinted repeatedly. It is is an ADVENTURE STORY set in Uganda and written for the Oxford Library for East Africa. *Moses and the Kidnappers* (1970) has also been reprinted many times by the Oxford University Press. Kimenye has also written several books for adolescent readers. ABO

Kind of Wild Justice, A (1978) Written with all the taut tension of an adult thriller, this is one of British author BERNARD ASHLEY's most gripping books. It also takes an unflinching look at child neglect. Ronnie's alcoholic father is involved as a driver for some vicious criminals. But Ronnie seems unintentionally to have given his father away after a previous crime, and he is arrested. Ronnie's mother – the real culprit – promptly decamps from home. Ronnie then takes up with a friendly coach-driver but he too is unwillingly involved with the same gang, this time smuggling in illegal Indian immigrants. NT

Kinder- und Hausmärchen see GRIMM BROTHERS; see also FAIRY TALES

King Alfred see C. WALTER HODGES

King Arthur It is not known for certain whether Arthur really existed, or exactly how the Arthurian legend began, for the medieval authors who handed down the stories had little understanding of historical authenticity. One theory is that Arthur was a fifth-century war-leader who resisted the invading Saxons after the Roman occupation of Britain: Arthur is the Welsh form of a Roman name, Artorius. He is first mentioned in a poem of about 600, written in Welsh, and referred to in the ninth-century *Historia Brittonum* ascribed to Nennius. His story is continued in the tenth-century *Annales Cambriae*, in the *Black Book of Carmarthen* and in the ancient Welsh romance *Kilhwch and Olwen*. In the 11th-century *Mabinogion*, he is portrayed as a powerful and successful war-leader. GEOFFREY OF MONMOUTH in his 12th century *Historia Regum Britanniae* is the main source of Arthur's story as we know it today.

In the middle ages the stories of King Arthur were immensely popular all over Europe, eventually becoming known as the 'Matter of Britain'. In France authors such as Chrétien de Troyes and in Germany Wolfram von Eschenbach and Gottfried von Strassburg, besides many others known and unknown, added new characters, episodes and tales.

At the end of the 15th century SIR THOMAS MALORY, a 'knight prisoner', gathered together and translated into contemporary English a large number of the Arthurian stories from earlier English or French originals: his great work, *Le Morte Darthur*, was printed by WILLIAM CAXTON in 1485. In the course of time, although the stories continued to be known, interest in them waned, but eventually *Le Morte Darthur* was virtually rediscovered after new editions were published in 1816 and 1817. Most 19th-century retellings of the story were based on Malory. The ideal of chivalry represented by the oath which Arthur's knights took and renewed each year at Pentecost made Malory's stories appear an admirable source of inspiring material to the Victorians, but writers were faced with two major problems: first, how to deal with the sexual encounters within the story, which were unacceptable to contemporary morality; and secondly, whether they should modernise the language of their original.

Arthurian children's books really begin with Sir J. Knowles's *Story of King Arthur and his Knights of the Round*

Table (1862), soon to be followed by a sequence of very similar titles by authors such as SYDNEY LANIER (1880), Henry Frith (1884), Mary McCleod (1900) and B. Clay (1901). HOWARD PYLE's *Story of King Arthur and His Knights* (1903) filled four volumes and was followed by V.W. Cutler's book of the same title (1905) and Norley Chester's *Knights of the Grail* (1907). Cutler's declared aim, to remove what was 'so crude in taste and morals as to seem unworthy of the really high-minded author of 500 years ago' speaks for them all. The intention was to inculcate the ideals of loyalty, courage and courtesy, and to provide a 'model for the pure of heart'. Baden-Powell, influenced by the American movement the Knights of King Arthur, actively promoted the chivalric ideal celebrated in these books in his *Yarns for Boy Scouts Told Round the Camp Fire* (1909). He linked Scouts and Guides (see GUIDING AND SCOUTING FICTION) in the fellowship of King Arthur and the Round Table with the object of reviving 'the spirit of chivalry, courtesy, deference to womanhood', and so forth.

After World War I enthusiasm for chivalry waned, and although some new children's versions of *Le Morte Darthur* were published, new trends soon became apparent. JOHN MASEFIELD, for example, introduced an Arthurian sequence into *THE MIDNIGHT FOLK* (1927) when Kay Harker – a 20th-century boy – meets members of Arthur's court in the course of his nocturnal adventures.

T.H. WHITE's remarkable FANTASY *The Sword in the Stone* (1938), which deals with Arthur's (or the Wart's) childhood, is the first part of *THE ONCE AND FUTURE KING* (1958). White's admiration for Masefield's *Midnight Folk* prompted him to write an Arthurian story in somewhat the same mode, specifically for children; but as he dealt with Arthur's adult life in the subsequent parts, *The Once and Future King* ceased to be a children's book as the tragedy unfolded. In the *Sword in the Stone*, however, with Merlin as his tutor the Wart has a carefree boyhood in the realm of Grammarye, experiencing magical transformations into other modes of being as a fish, an ant and a goose, ending with his coronation. White brilliantly blends comedy with serious political concerns and displays his lifelong interest in the natural world in the course of this ebullient work which is nevertheless firmly based on Malory – and in turn forms the basis of WALT DISNEY's *Sword in the Stone*.

In *King Arthur and His Knights* (1953) and *Sir Lancelot of the Lake* (1966) ROGER LANCELYN GREEN tells the stories afresh from *Le Morte Darthur* and other medieval sources. Admirably close to the originals, he avoids archaism for the most part and conforms with earlier convention in his delicate handling of illicit love. Barbara Leonie Picard's *Stories of King Arthur and His Knights* (1955) is in the same mode, a traditional retelling based on Malory with rather archaic language. Antonia Fraser's *King Arthur and the Knights of the Round Table* (1954) adopts the inconsistency of medieval romance: at the beginning of the book Mordred as Morgan Le Fay's husband fights the young Arthur, while at the end as Morgan's son he fights the aged king in the traditional Last Battle.

By contrast, HENRY TREECE's *The Eagles Have Flown* (1954) is set in the Romano-British period, depicting Artos the Bear as a ruthless and half-barbaric Celt. Treece portrays the savagery of primitive warfare, balanced to some extent by the values of loyalty and compassion. He rejects magic except for Merlin's prophecies, suggesting that the legends grew from actual incidents: Artos in a trial of strength with Medrodus draws a sword embedded in a great oak-tree trunk, for example. ROSEMARY SUTCLIFF's *The Lantern Bearers* (1959) is also set in this period and describes the struggle of Vortigern and Ambrosius. Though it centres on Aquila, a Roman-British youth, Artorius the bastard son of Utha is introduced as a boy growing up to be a great leader whose destiny is to drive the Sea Wolves back into the sea. In her distinguished trilogy *The Light Beyond the Forest: Quest for the Holy Grail* (1979); *The Sword and the Circle* (1981); and *The Road to Camlann* (1981) Sutcliff has also taken *Le Morte Darthur* as her main source. She has a strong sense of a good story, and brings the episodes to life with dialogue and background detail while ensuring that Malory's idealism subtly pervades the series.

Instead of retelling *Le Morte Darthur*, modern writers often incorporate motifs or characters from the legends into contemporary fantasies, a trend apparent in adult Arthurian fiction earlier in the century in such works as Charles Williams's *War in Heaven* (1930). SUSAN COOPER, in *Over Sea, Under Stone* (1965), *THE DARK IS RISING* (1973), *Greenwitch* (1974), *The Grey King* (1975) and *The Silver Tree* (1977), introduces motifs drawn from Celtic and Arthurian legend such as the grail, the quest and the Pendragon's sword. Arthurian characters, Merlin in the shape of Merriman or Great Uncle Merry, and Bran, son of Arthur and Guenevere, also appear in this sequence set in modern Britain. The mysterious evil power, the Dark, must be combated by Will Stanton, last-born of the Old Ones, with his friends' help. Time is also transcended in WILLIAM MAYNE's *Earthfasts* (1966) (see *EARTHFASTS* TRILOGY) in which a drummer-boy who had marched into a hillside in 1742 in search of King Arthur's burial-place meets two 20th-century boys. The king appears only briefly at the end, to be returned to his rest by one of the boys.

ALAN GARNER's *WEIRDSTONE OF BRISINGAMEN* (1960) and *The Moon of Gomrath* (1963) also allude to the legend of the king who sleeps with his warriors in a cave and is discovered by two modern children, and involve a struggle against the forces of evil. Similarly set in modern times, *ELIDOR* (1965) includes the motif of the Wasteland and of the Fisher King from the Grail story, while *THE OWL SERVICE* (1967) draws on the *Mabinogion*. In PENELOPE LIVELY's *Whispering Knights* (1970) present-day children come into confrontation with Morgan le Fay and her magic.

Merlin gives trouble in PETER DICKINSON's *The Weathermonger* (1968) (see *CHANGES* TRILOGY). England under his influence has reverted to the Dark Ages, rejecting all forms of machinery and all modern devices. He has been awakened from his long sleep by a chemist who then tries to drug him into quiescence, but he is persuaded to sleep again by the children. He reappears in Dickinson's *Merlin Dreams* (1988) illustrated by ALAN LEE. Still imprisoned beneath the stone by Nenyve, he wakes from his enchanted sleep and recalls images from his past life which are then transmuted into a brilliantly imaginative series of tales, set in the never-never land of medieval romance. JANE YOLEN's *Young Merlin* trilogy tells the story of the early life of Merlin: *Passager* (1996), *Hobby* (1996) and *Merlin* (1997). In GERALDINE MCCAUGHREAN's *King Arthur and the Round Table* (1988), illustrated by ALAN MARKS, magical happenings are both subtly and vividly represented. In this retelling the traditional stories are freely handled, making Morgan the explicit source of all the evil.

Many authors now allow an Arthurian character to tell his own story: in MICHAEL MORPURGO's *Arthur High King of Britain*, illustrated by MICHAEL FOREMAN (1994), Arthur (in Lyonesse) explains 'how it really happened' to his young 20th-century listener, so that 'people can know the truth'. The idiosyncratic variations on the traditional narrative enhance the sensitivity of this retelling. Merlin gives his account, somewhat similarly, in Robin Lister's *Story of King Arthur* (1988), beginning with the reign of Vortigern and ending with the Last Battle, while in Neil Philip's *The Tale of Sir Gawain* (1987), illustrated by CHARLES KEEPING, the mortally wounded Gawain tells his own tale. This draws together diverse adventures from various sources. They include the 14th-century alliterative poem *Sir Gawain and the Green Knight* and also *Sir Gawain and the Loathly Lady*. Elsewhere, both tales are well retold on their own, the former by IAN SERRAILLIER in *The Challenge of the Green Knight* (1966), while SELINA HASTING's *Sir Gawain and the Loathly Lady* (1985) has 'medieval' illuminations and illustrations by JUAN WIJNGAARD. Other writers have often incorporated these quite separate Gawain stories into their retellings of *Le Morte Darthur* (for example, James Riordan in his excellent *King Arthur* (1998), illustrated by VICTOR G. AMBRUS). Chrétien's tale of *Yvain* in John Howe's *The Knight with the Lion* (1996) is accompanied by fine illustrations.

MARCIA WILLIAM's *King Arthur and the Knights of the Round Table* (1996) represents a new approach: the text succinctly tells the traditional stories with special emphasis on the Grail quest while strip cartoons amusingly fill in the details. A quite different approach is adopted by KEVIN CROSSLEY-HOLLAND in *THE SEEING STONE* (2000), which tells the Arthurian story through the eyes of a historical boy – also called Arthur – living in England in 1199. LEB

see also WELSH MYTHOLOGY AND FOLKLORE

King, (David) Clive 1924– British writer and editor of children's books, whose work as a language teacher with the British Council took him all over the world. Born in Richmond, Surrey, he moved as a baby to Ash near Sevenoaks, Kent. Here Oliver's Farm, with its chalk pit, became the setting for his best-known novel, *STIG OF THE DUMP* (1963). According to the author, inspiration for this tale of a caveman owed much to stories of the Stone Age heard as a child, and to the time-warp in KIPLING's *PUCK OF POOK'S HILL*. In it are reflected some of the author's interests: an ardent linguist, he graphically portrays the difficulties Barney experiences in communicating with the caveman, Stig, while King's enthusiasm for DIY is shown in the way household items are improvised from rubbish found in the dump. *The Twenty-Two Letters* (1966) was followed by *The Night the Water Came* (1973) about a relief operation on an island hit by a cyclone. *Me and My Million* (1979) tells the adventure of Ringo, asked to deliver a bag of laundry which in reality contains a picture worth a million pounds. King's most recent book is *A Touch of Class* (1997). MSS

King, John Anthony 1949– Australian illustrator of historical PICTUREBOOKS. *An Uncommonly Fine Day* (1988) describes the first white people's landing at Botany Bay. King's paintings enrich the ironies of the original diary text which provides the narrative of the book. His ILLUSTRATIONS for traditional works by Henry Lawson, *Andy's Gone With Cattle* (1984), *Farewell to Old England Forever* (1984), *Wild Colonial Boy* (1985), *Teams* (1986) and *Mary Called Him Mister* (1991) are invested with life, colour and a sense of history. Other works include *Lobster Quadrille* (1989) and *The Days When We Went Swimming* (1992), as well as TELEVISION scripts. RS

King Cole see GEOFFREY OF MONMOUTH

King of the Golden River, The (1841) FAIRY TALE in five chapters written by John Ruskin and illustrated by RICHARD DOYLE. Hans, Schwartz and Gluck set out to pour three drops of holy water into the Golden River in order that their valley might become productive again. Gluck succeeds where his brothers fail, his mercy to those he encounters along his way sanctifying the dew which he finally casts in, where his brothers' selfishness with their store of water renders the water impure, earning them the punishment of an eternal existence as TWO BLACK STONES, 'still called by the people of the valley THE BLACK BROTHERS'. A new edition with illustrations by JUAN WIJNGAARD was published in 2000. SA

King-Smith, Dick 1922– Popular and respected British writer whose sales are thought to have been exceeded only by ENID BLYTON and ROALD DAHL. King-Smith began writing late in life, having been a soldier in World War II in the Grenadier Guards, a primary-school teacher and a farmer. All these aspects of his life feature in his books. He is a prolific writer, having written more than 50 books, and is widely known for his humorous animal stories combining adventure and witty dialogue. His first book was *The Fox Busters* (1978), an amusing tale of three young female pullets who develop the ability to lay hard-boiled eggs in flight, aiming them directly at the enemy, the dreaded 'long-noses' (foxes). Part of the training of the pullets is to aim the eggs into a tyre floating in a nearby pond, reminiscent of the film *The Dam Busters*. The novel was praised for its originality, technical skill and characterisation. In *Daggie Dogfoot* (1980; *Pigs Might Fly* in US) female sows called Mrs Barleylove, Mrs Maizemund and Mrs Gobblespud all speak in a Gloucester dialect. Although his fictional animals are presented anthropomorphically, the realities of farming are not overlooked: in *THE SHEEP-PIG* (1983), his prize-winning novel, Babe is brought home to be eaten eventually for Christmas dinner, and in *Martin's Mice* (1988) the cat Martin is seen to be odd because he dislikes killing mice. Throughout most of King-Smith's books there is a strong didactic element: in *Saddlebottom* (1985) the readers learn that a deformity can be turned into something positive; in *Martin's Mice* gentle lessons are given on pets' need for freedom; politeness is explored in *The Sheep-Pig* and unselfishness in *The Queen's Nose* (1983). Weaker or unusual animals usually come out on top.

King-Smith has also written a series of books about Sophie (see the *SOPHIE* series), a tough young girl who wants to be a farmer. And because of his love of animals, especially pigs, he has written several INFORMATION BOOKS, one of which, in the 'Read and Wonder' series, is entitled *All Pigs Are Beautiful*, an appealing book with thoughtful, humorous illustrations by ANITA JERAM.

King-Smith has also written a number of historical novels. The irreverent and humorous *Noah's Brother* (1986) explains several unanswered questions about Noah's ark, such as why the flood did not wash away all the evil in the world, and how the animals were actually gathered together. *Lady Daisy* (1992) is a well-constructed novel about a Victorian doll who can speak. Other historical novels are *The Toby Man* (1989) and *The Swoose* (1993). In 1996 Dick King-Smith moved away from the younger market with *Goldhanger*, a book for adolescent readers, set in the vicious world of a country wood where animals fear the cruel gamekeeper and are watched over constantly by Skymaster, a bird respected by all other creatures. In 1998, with *Mrs Jolly's Brolly*, illustrated by Frank Rodgers, he returned to younger readers with an enchanting picturebook about an eccentric witch winning a balloon race. FMC

see also ANIMALS IN FICTION

King Solomon's Mines (1885) This boys' romance by the British author RIDER HAGGARD, inspired by *TREASURE ISLAND*, coincided topically with the Berlin Africa Conference. Allan Quatermain, Sir Henry Curtis, Captain Good R.N. and the majestic Zulu Umbopa set off, map in hand, to search for Sir Henry's missing brother and fabulous treasure. They journey arduously through the desert and over mountains to the 'lost' country of the Kukuanas, where they encounter the usurping king Tuala and the evil witch Gagool. In the ensuing civil war Umbopa triumphs, while the Europeans narrowly escape from Gagool's clutches. The country is sealed off, to preserve it from contamination. PR

Kingsley, Charles 1819–75 English clergyman, popular writer and enthusiastic teacher. Born in Devonshire, the son of an Anglican clergyman, he became rector of Eversley, Hampshire, in 1844, and was later Regius Professor of Modern History at Cambridge. He wrote two controversial novels with social themes, *Yeast* (1848) and *Alton Locke* (1850). Historical adventure novels such as *Westward Ho!* (1855) and *Hereward the Wake* (1865) brought him a wide audience with adults and children. *The Heroes* – lively, lucid 'Greek Fairy Tales for my children' – was published in 1856, with his own illustrations, *THE WATER BABIES* in 1863, and *Madam How and Lady Why* in 1869. PR

Kingston, W(illiam) H(enry) G(iles) 1814–80 Prolific British author of ADVENTURE STORIES. After writing adult novels, Kingston produced his first boys' story, *Peter the Whaler*, in 1851. Its success led to many other tales, often of the sea, describing battles and storms, such as *The Three Midshipmen* (1873) and its sequels. Kingston also edited *Kingston's Magazine for Boys* (1859–63) and *The Union Jack* (1880), which often serialised his stories. Voted second only to Dickens in a boys' poll of 1884, perhaps because of the high spirits of his young heroes and the exuberance of his naval descriptions, Kingston's works moved away from a religious note in the early stories to the breezy and imperialistic tone of the middle novels, before showing a return to religion in the later tales. But, although Kingston's books are interesting historically, they seem unlikely to regain their great popularity today. DB

Kipling, Rudyard 1865–1936 British novelist, poet and writer of short stories for both children and adults. Kipling's father, Lockwood, was a museum curator in India, and Kipling's early years there and his time as a journalist in Lahore and Allahabad between 1882 and 1889 provided the background for his early stories for adults, such as *Plain Tales From the Hills* (1886), and his most famous children's books, *The Jungle Books* (1894, 1895) and *Kim* (1901). At the age of six Kipling returned to England where he and his sister boarded with a repressive landlady, an experience fictionalised in *Baa, Baa, Black Sheep* (1888). During this period he met his mother's family, notably Edward Burne-Jones and his circle, which had a lasting effect on Kipling's own drawings, best seen in the *Just So Stories* (1902). Between 1878 and 1882 he attended the United Services College immortalised in *Stalky & Co* (1899). The Headmaster, 'Crom' Price, encouraged Kipling, a precocious, romantic schoolboy, the 'egregious Beetle' of the *Stalky* stories, towards a literary career. 'Stalky' – Major-General Dunsterville – and 'Crom' Price had reservations about this evocation of his schooldays, and the book reveals Kipling's admiration for the man of action, his innate anti-intellectualism and more than a streak of sadism in the cat-killing and bullying episodes. Coupled with the mawkish patriotism and sentimentality that later produced 'If', *Stalky & Co* distills the side of Kipling most disliked by modern readers. However, it also contains the thread of subversion so characteristic and engaging throughout Kipling's children's books – the triumph of the underdog through cunning and knowledge gained through experience.

In *The Jungle Books* this subversion is characterised by Mowgli, the naked mancub, who learns the Jungle Law in order to master first himself and then the Law-Makers. Mowgli and Kim, the young and beautiful, have been seen as the epitome of a repressed homosexuality which possibly surfaced in Kipling's close friendship with the American Wolcott Balestier, whose redoubtable sister Carrie he married in 1892, shortly after Balestier's death. Famous, but poverty-stricken by a bank collapse, the Kiplings moved to America where their daughters Josephine (Kipling's 'best-beloved') and Elsie were born, *Kim* was started and the *Jungle Books* published. Family quarrels drove them back to England in 1896 and, following John's birth and Josephine's death, and a brief stay in South Africa between 1900 and 1905, the Kiplings settled at Bateman's in Sussex where they lived until Kipling's death in 1936. African settings appear in two *Just So Stories*, 'The Elephant's Child' and 'The Leopard', but Sussex forms the heartland of Kipling's own favourite books, *Puck of Pook's Hill* (1906) and *Rewards and Fairies* (1910). In both books Kipling felt 'inspired by his Daemon' and his characters, from kings to gypsies, reflect his long-term preoccupations with power, action, craftsmanship and time passing. Later authors like Rosemary Sutcliff are visibly steeped in Kipling's evocation of this past, deepened by some of his most lyric poetry.

Kipling's poetry for children lies interleaved in his five books of stories for children. In the two *Jungle Books* he uses his verses either to enhance a theme like 'The Law of the Jungle', or an emotion unexplored in the tale, such as fear in 'The Song of the Little Hunter', or to provide additional characterisation as in the 'Road-Song of the *Bandar-Log*'. The verses range from Kipling at his most sinister in 'A Ripple Song', where death lurks beneath the water, to the lyrical lullaby 'Shiv and the Grasshopper'. A similar contrast is found in *Puck of Pook's Hill* and *Rewards and Fairies*, encapsulated in the poem 'A St Helena Lullaby'. Kipling wrote in his autobiography *Something of Myself* (1937) that in these later books he 'put in three of four really good sets of verse' including 'If', which by 1937 was 'anthologised to weariness'. Again the poems serve to echo the deeper themes of the stories without interrupting the narrative but, unlike those in the *Jungle Books*, these can stand alone; the insistence on self-reliance in 'If' does not depend on the story of 'Brother Square-Toes', nor does the 'The Way Through the Woods', with its elegiac sense of the past, directly refer to the doomed Philadelphia in 'Marklake Witches'. From the opening of 'Puck's Song' – 'She is not any Common Earth' – to the final 'Children's Song' – 'Land of Our Birth' – the verse in *Puck of Pook's Hill* expresses Kipling's obsession with people and place. Only in the *Just So Stories* did Kipling write children's verse, relying on puns and wordplay to produce memorable doggerel like 'the cameelious hump'; his later poems, despite their context, are for adults.

After his son's death in 1915 Kipling wrote no more books for children. 'If' was found to be the best-loved British poem of 1996 in the UK. KP

Kirkup, James 1918– English poet who called his autobiographical essays *A Child of the Tyne* and stayed emotionally close to his roots in the Northeast while travelling all over the world as a poet, translator and scholar. Kirkup was particularly renowned for his work on Japanese poetry, and his translations and anthologies reached many British classrooms in the middle of the 20th century. *Look at it This Way (Poems for*

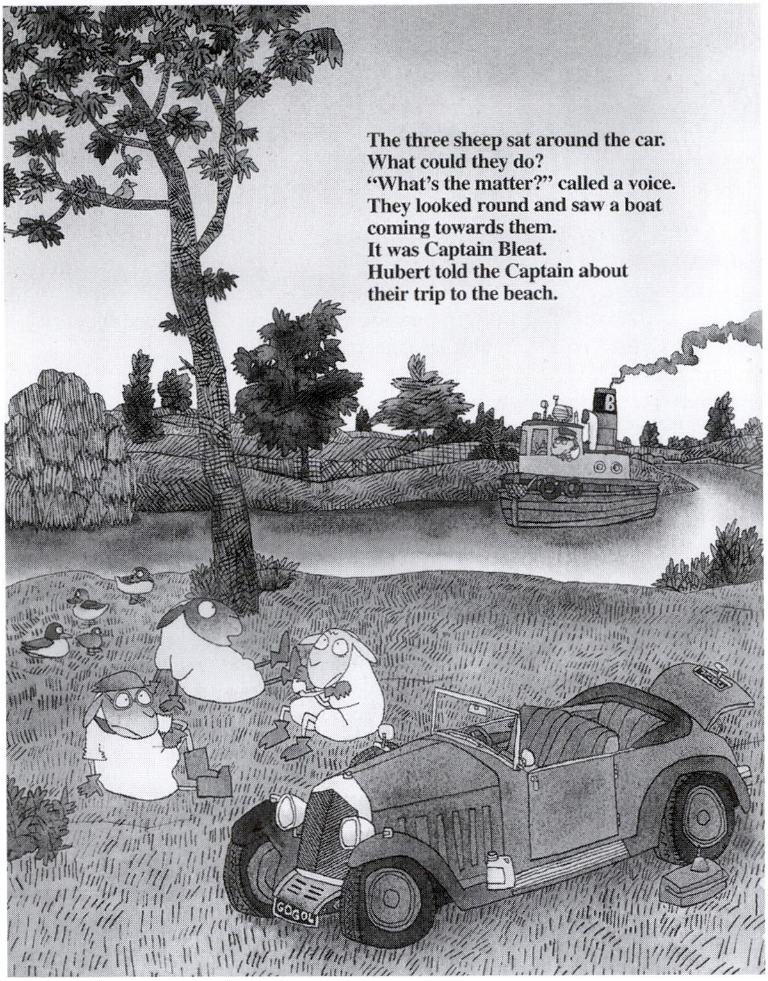

The three sheep sat around the car.
What could they do?
"What's the matter?" called a voice.
They looked round and saw a boat
coming towards them.
It was Captain Bleat.
Hubert told the Captain about
their trip to the beach.
GOGOL

Illustration from *Sheep in Wolves' Clothing* by Satoshi Kitamura.

Young People) was published in 1992. He also wrote two novels for children, *Insect Summer* (1971) and *The Magic Drum* (1973). 'Imagination is what distinguishes us from the dead', he wrote. MCCS

Kit's Wilderness see DAVID ALMOND

Kitamura, Satoshi 1956– Kitamura was born in Tokyo and worked initially as a commercial artist on posters and greetings cards in both Japan and Britain, where he moved in 1979. His first major commission was for Andersen Press, visualising HIAWYN ORAM's *ANGRY ARTHUR*. This won for Satoshi Kitamura both The MOTHER GOOSE AWARD for most exciting newcomer in 1982 and the Japanese Picturebook Award. His work displays a sure, bold use of line, rich, subtle colour and a good sense of movement. His partnership with Hiawyn Oram continued with such books as *Ned and the Joybaloo* (1983) and *A Boy Wants a Dinosaur* (1990). At the same time he created and illustrated his own books, including *WHEN SHEEP CANNOT SLEEP* (1986), *UFO Diary* (1989), shortlisted for the SMARTIES PRIZE, *From Acorn to Zoo* (1992), *SHEEP IN WOLVES' CLOTHING* (1995), *Goldfish Hide and Seek* (1997) and *Me and My Cat* (1999). AR

see also *LILY TAKES A WALK*

Klein, Norma 1938–89 American writer for adults and children, best known as an author of YOUNG ADULT FICTION. After growing up in New York City and studying at Columbia University, Klein recognised in her 20s that she wished to pursue a career as a writer. A prolific author, she had over 60 short stories for adults published by the time she was 30. As a children's writer she is best remembered for *Mom, the Wolf Man, and Me* (1972), a groundbreaking work that depicted life for an 11-year-old girl living in a non-traditional family. Klein also wrote the PICTUREBOOK

Girls Can Be Anything (1973), an early work that championed girls' rights. She wrote a number of other young adult novels, including *Taking Sides* (1974), *Hiding* (1976) and *Breaking Up* (1980) that focused on social issues, including divorce, homosexuality and teenage sexuality. Although better known for the issues they addressed than for their characterisation, Klein's novels are an important addition to the development of the juvenile social problem novel. Particularly noteworthy is her emphasis on creating strong young women characters. SAI

Klein, Robin 1936– Popular Australian author of more than 50 novels, PICTUREBOOKS, short-story and verse collections, frequently honoured in CHILDREN'S BOOK COUNCIL OF AUSTRALIA BOOK OF THE YEAR AWARDS, and 1991 Dromkeen Medal winner for her contribution to Australian children's literature. Klein's first picturebook, *The Giraffe in Pepperell Street* (1978), established her trademark use of quirky humour, the unexpected, verse and wordplay, in her work for younger readers. In *Oodoolay* (1983), country townspeople utilise their station-master's love of opera to motivate improvements in his work performance. *The Princess Who Hated It* (1986), a female version of the *PRINCE AND THE PAUPER* story, challenges and confirms stereotypes about princesses. It has pastel illustrations by ALISON LESTER, who also illustrated Klein's *Thing* series, and *Birk the Beserker* (1987), in which another of Klein's heroes, a timid Viking, does not live up to the stereotypes.

Klein returns to themes of family, friendship between the young and the elderly, peer-group manipulation, female stereotypes and the treatment of outsiders in her fiction for older readers, such as *Honoured Guest* (1979), the cultish *PENNY POLLARD* series (1982–89), *The Enemies* (1985), *Laurie Loved Me Best* (1988) and *Seeing Things* (1993). The hugely popular *Hating Alison Ashley* (1984), a working-class SCHOOL STORY exploring themes of friendship, confidence and self-worth, highlights Klein at her comic best – acutely observant of human nature, with a strong control of language, speaking with veracity to her pre-teen audience, and with a glinting, ironic sense of humour. In *People Might Hear You* (1983), a suspenseful, almost claustrophobic atmosphere is created through the use of strong characterisation and descriptive language, in an emotive account of life within a reclusive, joyless, repressive religious sect. *Boss of the Pool* (1986) addresses the ignorance, fears and prejudices with which people marginalise those 'not like us'. *CAME BACK TO SHOW YOU I COULD FLY* (1989), which treats themes of drug-dependency, is very personal, and the most literary of Klein's works.

Girls on the brink of puberty, frequently outsiders, struggling under adverse conditions to make sense of themselves and their world, are a recurring concern in Klein's work. In *The Listmaker* (1997), Sarah compulsively makes lists to structure her world, as she yearns to be reunited as a family with her father and his new wife. A sequence of novels, set in late-1940s Australia, chronicles the growing up of the Mellings girls. *All In The Blue Unclouded Weather* (1992) introduces Grace, Heather, Vivienne, Cathy and cousin Isobel in a rural Victorian town, beneath endless summer skies. *Dresses of Red and Gold* (1993) continues these stories through the autumn, concluding with the hard times of life in the city and winter in *The Sky in Silver Lace* (1995). Klein's penetration of the facades of her feisty characters, her deep understanding of her audience, her ironic humour, love of language and STORYTELLING ability ensure that her works combine popular appeal with literary quality in explorations of issues which are important to young readers. SNJ

see also DRUGS IN CHILDREN'S BOOKS

Klickman, Flora see *GIRL'S OWN PAPER*

Knight, Hilary 1926– American illustrator and author who acknowledges the influence of French illustrator Maurice Boutet de Monvel's works for children as having a direct influence on his own. His love of zoos is reflected in *Where's Wallace?* (1964), the story of a little orangutan who escapes to some of the most interesting places in town, including the department store, museum, ballpark and beach. Pictures encourage readers to track down Wallace and other comic figures on each page. This book was no doubt an inspiration to many later books of a similar type. Knight has illustrated over 50 books for children including the *ELOISE* books by KAY THOMPSON, works by Betty MacDonald, CHARLOTTE ZOLOTOW, OGDEN NASH and others, as well as poetry books and classic FAIRY TALES. PDS

Knockout Fun Book, The see ANNUALS

Knockout see COMICS, PERIODICALS AND MAGAZINES; see also *GREYFRIARS*

Kobie and the Military Road (1987) Novel by Peter Younghusband, published at the height of the final struggle against apartheid in South Africa. Of the juvenile novels that dealt with the political issues of the time it is remarkable for being addressed to preteens and being almost the only one that uses satire and humour. This tone ameliorates the grim background to the story: Kobie, a white boy, has been crippled in a landmine explosion that killed his parents, and the road which he opposes because it threatens a wildlife sanctuary is being built to transport soldiers. ERJ

Koch, Kenneth 1925– American poet and poetry teacher. *Wishes, Lies, and Dreams* (1970) is an anthology of poems by Koch's pupils, with an account of his approach. This involves offering children simple, non-rhyming structures in which to address themes such as those in the book's title, and encouraging collaborative authorship. Koch also uses poems like Blake's 'Tyger' as models for children's poetry writing, conveying the poem's method in terms accessible to children ('imagine you could ask an animal questions'). *Rose, Where Did You Get That Red?* (1973) is an anthology of the 'great poems' Koch recommends, with sample lessons. ML

see also CHILD AUTHORS; *SONGS OF INNOCENCE*

Koin, Nyengi Nigerian writer and TELEVISION producer from Rivers State, a long-time resident of Lagos, the main setting of her novels. Koin has written three novels for YOUNG ADULTS on the theme of love overcoming differences. *Time Changes Yesterday* (1982) sensitively portrays love the second time around and the struggle of an adolescent girl to come to terms with her widowed father's new love and a new family. *The Second Chance* (1986) and *All You Need Is Love* (1987) explore the obstacles posed by parental opposition and differences in class and culture. VD

Kola, Pamela Kenyan author of three books for children, *East African Why Stories* (1966), *East African How Stories* (1966) and *East African When Stories* (1986). The books are designed to encourage reading for pleasure and to improve written and spoken English. These are FOLKTALES told to the author by her grandmother. ABO

Konigsburg, E(laine) L(obl) 1930– American author and sometime illustrator, most known for novels aimed at children aged between 8 and 14, whom she terms the 'middle-aged child'. Educated as a chemist at Carnegie-Mellon University and at the University of Pittsburgh, Konigsburg began writing while living in the New York City area after her three children began school. She is the only writer ever to win the NEWBERY MEDAL and Newbery Honour award the same year; in 1968, her second book, *From the Mixed-up Files of Mrs. Basil E. Frankweiler* (1967), won the Newbery, and her first, *Jennifer, Hecate, Macbeth, William McKinley, and Me, Elizabeth* (1967) was the runner-up. Konigsburg made further Newbery history in 1997 by winning a second medal nearly 30 years after the first with *The View from Saturday* (1996). While *Mrs. Frankweiler* remains her best-known work, Konigsburg has published many works, including HISTORICAL FICTION about Eleanor of Aquitaine (*A Proud Taste for Scarlet and Miniver*, 1973) and Leonardo da Vinci (*The Second Mrs. Giaconda*, 1975), and has illustrated several of them. Additionally, she has published short-story collections, a number of PICTUREBOOKS and a collection of her speeches (*Talk Talk*, 1995).

Konigsburg's novels typically focus on highly intelligent suburban children in search of identity, surrounded by a wide range of unusual supporting characters: a father who owns a camel in *Journey to an 800 Number* (1982), the restless spirit of a dead actress in *Up from Jericho Tel* (1986), the manifestation of what may be the main character's schizophrenia in *(George)* (1970). The protagonists' development frequently results from interactions with a wise older person, relationships that often benefit the older person as well, such as Mrs Frankweiler, Tallulah in *Up from Jericho Tel*, and Mrs Olinski in *The View from Saturday*. Konigsburg also values the connections between young people: Claudia's brother Jamie (*Mrs. Frankweiler*) and Malcolm Soo (*Jericho Tel*), both well-drawn characters in their own right, also challenge and complement the female protagonists; and the four disparate sixth-graders who comprise the Academic Bowl team in *The View from Saturday* enhance one another's development while enriching the life of their teacher-advisor. As befits the theme of search, many of Konigsburg's plots involve searches or mysteries in which the characters puzzle out situations outside themselves and inside themselves at the same time.

Konigsburg's reach for the unusual occasionally exceeds her grasp; in particular, critics have pointed out speech and character anachronisms in her two historical fictions. However, a wide range of subject matter and her ever-present wit make her work engaging to intellectually curious readers. At its best, Konigsburg's art achieves the Renaissance quality she so values, *sprezzatura*: possessing excellence and substance, but with the outward appearance of lightness. Further, her experience as a chemist-turned-writer – that is, her own search for identity – appears in her work, which demonstrates a multitude of ways in which young people may come to terms with who they are, a multitude of possibilities as to what human beings can be. CD

Korky the Cat see ANNUALS; COMICS, PERIODICALS AND MAGAZINES

Korman, Gordon 1963– Contemporary writer of SCHOOL STORIES. Born in Montreal, Korman attended New York University. He sold his first novel, *This Can't be Happening at McDonald Hall!* (1978) when he was 14. The second novel in his *Bruno and Boots* series, *Go Jump in the Pool* (1979), was followed by *Beware the Fish* (1980) and *The War with Mr. Wizzle* (1982). In *I Want to Go Home* (1981), the theme is opposition to the conformity imposed by strict regulations. The theme in

Who is Bugs Potter? (1980) and its sequel *Bugs Potter Live at Nickaninny* (1983) is student obsession with rock-and-roll and adult irritation. In 1995, Korman returned to his original setting in *Something Fishy at McDonald Hall*. Korman's formulaic stories, predictable and farcical, are exemplified in his latest middle-school comedy, *The Chicken Doesn't Skate* (1996). His settings are boys' boarding schools where practical jokers break school rules and thwart or outwit authority figures. Order is often restored only after physical destruction. Korman was one of the 1997 nominees for the American Rebecca Caudill Young Readers' Book Award, for his novel *Toilet Paper Tigers*. MRS

Krasilovsky, Phyllis (Manning) 1926– American author of children's PICTUREBOOKS, chapter books and an autobiographical young adult novel, *L.C. Is the Greatest* (1975). Krasilovsky grew up with her mother and two sisters in Brooklyn, New York, product of a broken home. She credits her mother with encouraging her interests in reading and writing during her early years. After graduating from high school, she went to work, attending classes at Brooklyn College in the evenings. Married at 19, she again attended classes at Cornell University while her husband went to law school. Her first book, *The Man Who Didn't Wash His Dishes* (1950), was also the first in a series of 'little man' books. She claims 'the little man must be inside me someplace', and wrote this book specifically for a little boy who was dying of cancer. In each of these books, the main character leaves his everyday existence, has an adventure, and returns home again to safety, but with an increased self-knowledge. An inveterate world traveller, Krasilovsky was inspired by a trip to Holland to write two books, *The Cow Who Fell in the Canal* (1957) and *The First Tulips in Holland* (1982). Her chapter book *Popular Girls Club* (1972) examines false friendships and girls' cliques. A series of 'little girl' stories includes *The Shy Little Girl* (1970), written about one of her daughters and also, she claims, her favourite book. Krasilovsky's illustrators have included such notables as BARBARA COONEY, TRINA SCHART HYMAN, PETER SPIER and S.D. Schindler. MS

Krauss, Ruth 1911– American author of children's PICTUREBOOKS. Krauss was trained in music and art, but turned early to children's stories. Her lyrical stories with their appealing humour tend to be brief and simple, aimed at very young children. One of her early illustrators was her husband, the noted illustrator CROCKETT JOHNSON. *The Carrot Seed* (1946), the couple's first collaborative venture, remained popular for many years. *The Backwards Day* (1950), illustrated by MARC SIMONT, is a charming work that reveals Krauss's understanding of the child's mind and of children's humour. In addition to Simont and Johnson, her stories attracted several other talented illustrators, most notably MAURICE SENDAK, who illustrated numerous Krauss books in his early career, among them *A Hole Is to Dig: A First Book of Definitions* (1952), *Charlotte and the White Horse* (1955) and *Somebody Else's Nut Tree, and Other Tales from Children* (1958). JAN BRETT, Remy Charlip and ELLEN RASKIN illustrated her works as well, and Krauss occasionally illustrated her own books. Her success can be attributed to her deft use of language and her keen understanding of a child's imagination. DLR

Krindlekrax (1991) Third children's novel by the British author Philip Ridley, which mixes elements of traditional stories with modern urban life. Ruskin Splinter, who lives with his toast-obsessed mother and nervous father, characters portrayed in the comic style that has become Ridley's trademark, wants to play the hero in the school play and in life. But to do so he must face the local bully, Elvis Cave, his own lack of confidence, and the threat, unrecognised by other inhabitants of Lizard Street, from Krindlekrax, a crocodile/dragon from the sewers. Ruskin finds the courage to fulfil his ambition in an ending that combines both elements of the story. JEG

Krumgold, Joseph Quincy 1908–80 American author of children's books, the first to win the NEWBERY MEDAL twice, first for ... *And Now Miguel* (1953) and second for *Onion John* (1959). The first of these is perhaps Krumgold's finest work, the story of an Hispanic boy in New Mexico coming of age through his experiences herding sheep with his family. It is a sensitive and moving story and important in several respects. Among Newbery winners from 1922 to 1969, only two other books include minority characters, and the book pre-dates interest in multiculturalism and Hispanic literature in general by some 20 years. The young Miguel tells his own story, and tells it in Spanish-flavoured English. *Onion John* seems entirely different, focusing on the triangular relationship between a young protagonist, his father, and an East European hobo. But like all of Krumgold's work, this novel centres on the struggle for identity and the struggle towards adulthood ... *And Now Miguel* opens with a simple assertion of identity, 'I am Miguel', the kind of assertion all of his young protagonists are trying to attain. MDK

Kühne, Klaus 1953– South African writer. Son of the popular Afrikaans writer for children, W.O. Kühne, Klaus works as an Anglican priest in Johannesburg. He has written a number of light-hearted children's books which have a quiet point to make behind the brisk adventure. For example, *The Secret of Big Toe Mountain* (1987) has a 'hidden treasure' which turns out to be a rare, threatened species of protea flower. JHe

Kuia and the Spider, The (1981) PICTUREBOOK written by PATRICIA GRACE, and winner of the New Zealand Picturebook of the Year Award, 1982. Its narrative subject makes it exemplary as a work of Maori children's fiction – a contest between a grandmother, the kuia of the title, and a spider, to settle who is most skilled at weaving. The judges, their grandchildren, prove less interested in the grandparents' concerns than in what they gain from their handiwork. The story is simply told, but speaks volumes concerning the special position of the grandmother in Maori society, even now. It exemplifies the brilliant success with which many Maori writers have employed the combination of text and ILLUSTRATION. More particularly, it demonstrates the sympathetic collaboration between Grace and the illustrator, ROBYN KAHUKIWA, whose slightly naive style here responds admirably to the double anchoring of the tale in everyday reality and FANTASY. CM

Kunhardt, Dorothy 1901–79 American author and designer of *Pat the Bunny* (1942), the tactile book which encourages young readers to interact with the characters Paul and Judy. Clever design allows the child to 'pat the bunny' by touching the white cotton behind the cut-out of the rabbit figure, or feel Daddy's scratchy face where the ILLUSTRATION has a piece of sandpaper, or view themselves in a mirror. Kunhardt created a sequel tactile book, *The Telephone Book* (1942), and her daughter, Edith Kunhardt, created *Pat the Cat* (1984). These books blur the distinction between book and toy. JCS

Kurelek, William 1927–77 Canadian painter and PICTUREBOOK illustrator and author. Born in Whitford, Alberta, William Kurelek overcame a difficult childhood, spent mainly in rural Alberta and Manitoba, as well as several years in a psychiatric hospital in England for depression, to become a widely respected Canadian painter whose work appears in the Montreal Museum of Fine Arts, New York City's Museum of Modern Art, and Queen Elizabeth II's personal collection. Kurelek's work, which has been compared to that of Bosch and Brueghel, frequently features landscapes or religious subjects, as in the case of a series of paintings, *The Passion of Matthew*, which hangs in the Niagara Falls Gallery and Art Museum. Eventually, Kurelek discovered the children's picturebook as a forum for his work, producing several award-winning books. These include *Lumberjack* (1974) – inspired by his experiences in Canadian logging camps – and the autobiographical *A Prairie Boy's Winter* (1973) and *A Prairie Boy's Summer* (1975) – both recipients of the CANADIAN LIBRARY ASSOCIATION BEST ILLUSTRATED BOOK FOR CHILDREN AWARD – which represent Canadian prairie life in a series of vignettes. Kurelek's conversion to Roman Catholicism and spirituality is reflected in *A Northern Nativity* (1976), depicting the Nativity in a variety of contemporary settings. JDC

Kurt Maschler Award see APPENDIX

Kushner, Donn 1929– Canadian writer of fiction. Born in Louisiana, Kushner is a microbiologist who taught at the University of Ottawa from 1965, an author of science articles, a musician, storyteller and children's novelist. *The Violin-Maker's Gift* (1980), which won the CANADIAN LIBRARY ASSOCIATION BOOK OF THE YEAR FOR CHILDREN AWARD, *Uncle Jacob's Ghost Story* (1985), *A Book Dragon* (1987) and *A Thief Among Statues* (1993) are written in the style of traditional FOLKTALES supported by strong characterisations, mysticism and rich symbolism. *A Book Dragon* is a satirical FANTASY, based on a dragon immortalised in a monk's drawings for a medieval *Book of Hours*.

Kushner's novels contain a mix of ordinary everyday people and events caught up inside the magical. The underlying theme of his work is that gifts and giving open up communication between individuals and nations while the act of withholding creates a climate of repression and alienation toward oneself and others, allowing misery and evil to flourish. Kushner's later contemporary novel, *The Night Voyagers* (1995), concerns a boy from Central America who escapes to Canada pursued by immigration officers, his father's spirit and legendary Mayan figures. The book deals with human rights abuse but also combines history, myth and the supernatural. MRS

Kuznet, Lois see CRITICAL APPROACHES TO CHILDREN'S LITERATURE

L

Lacis, Astra 1937– Australian illustrator born in Latvia, who works mainly in line and wash and has illustrated numerous short stories, INFORMATION BOOKS and picture stories including CHRISTOBEL MATTINGLEY's *The Angel with a Mouth-Organ* (1984) which in many ways parallels Astra's own experience as a refugee in World War II. MSax

Lady of Shalott, The (1832) Well-known narrative poem by ALFRED, LORD TENNYSON, which combines a hypnotic refrain with vivid and haunting imagery to contrast the shadowy world of the cursed Lady of Shalott with the vital, active world of Camelot. The Lady weaves a tapestry of the shadows of real life she sees only in her mirror. Splendid Sir Lancelot flashes by; she looks out and is doomed. A boat bears her down the river to Camelot where she dies and is blessed by Lancelot, who is unaware of the part he has played in her tragedy. This dramatic poetic tale is still regularly anthologised for children, most notably illustrated by CHARLES KEEPING. HT

Ladybird Books British book imprint, first published by Wills and Hepworth in 1915. In World War II, they became the first standardised pocketsize series and the first with colour at every page opening. In 1952, the first non-fiction series were published. The prose was plain and economical; the original ILLUSTRATIONS were literal, informative and well composed. Commissioned artists included C.J. Tunnicliffe and Rowland Hilder. The *Ladybird Key Words Reading Scheme* was introduced in 1964. When the imprint came to an end in 1999 there were more than 100 fiction and non-fiction series in 60 languages and a variety of formats, as well as cassettes, activity packs and posters. RC

see also READING SCHEMES

Ladybug see CRICKET MAGAZINE

La Fontaine, Jean de see DE LA FONTAINE

Lagerlöf, Selma see *THE WONDERFUL ADVENTURES OF NILS*

Laird, Elizabeth 1943– Novelist born in New Zealand, now living in England, who won the 1992 Children's Book Award for *Kiss the Dust*, the story of a family of Kurdish refugees and their flight from Iraq. All her stories for the 9–12 age-group are concerned with a central theme of loss. In *Red Sky in the Morning* (1988) she writes movingly of a sister's relationship with her brother born with hydrocephalus. The theme of the pleasures and difficulties of family life and close friendships runs through Laird's fiction, much of which is concerned with the breakdown of these relationships. KA

Lake at the End of the World, The (1989) SCIENCE FICTION story by the Australian author CAROLINE MACDONALD. Set in the mountains and forests of New Zealand, in a future depopulated by an unspecified disaster, Diana and Hector, unknown to each other, live by a lake unsullied by change, with adults distracted by the collapse of society. Diana and Hector relate alternately how each comes to discover the other's existence. Macdonald characteristically blends skilful narrative with keen word choice and an insight into motivation. The novel was an Honour Book for the CHILDREN'S BOOK COUNCIL OF AUSTRALIA BOOK OF THE YEAR AWARD (1989) and was a runner-up for the *GUARDIAN* AWARD (1990). MN

Lamb, Charles 1775–1834 British author best known for the 'Elia' essays, who wrote several works for the Juvenile Library of WILLIAM GODWIN. Of these the *TALES FROM SHAKESPEAR* (1807), written with MARY, were immediately successful and lastingly influential. Lamb believed strongly in the value of a literature which stimulated the imagination of children, and railed against the trend toward moralising and censorship, though 'The Witch Aunt', a story he wrote for *MRS LEICESTER'S SCHOOL*, is a vivid account of childhood terrors inspired by reading. His own best, because least constrained, work is the lively and vigorous *Adventures of Ulysses* (1808). JFB

Lamb, Lynton Harold 1907–77 British painter, printmaker, illustrator and designer. He worked during a period in Britain when there was no need to make a distinction between these practices. From 1950 to the early seventies he was a lecturer at the Slade and the Royal College of Art. His illustrations were mainly

Illustration by Lynton Lamb from *A Grass Rope* by WILLIAM MAYNE.

for classic works of fiction written by CHARLES DICKENS, Thomas Hardy and CHARLOTTE BRONTË. Among his best known work for children's books is E. NESBIT'S *THE RAILWAY CHILDREN* (1957). There is a great strength of drawing evident in his ILLUSTRATION work with its impressionistic style of fragmented pen-and-ink lines, dots and dashes. AEW

Lamb, Mary (Anne) 1764–1847 Author of the influential *TALES FROM SHAKESPEAR* (1807), and other stories and poetry for children, in collaboration with her brother CHARLES. Born into the upper-servant class – her father was manservant to the lawyer and MP, Samuel Salt – Mary Lamb received little schooling, though access to Salt's library stimulated in her a life-long passion for reading. She became a seamstress, commenting later, in a shrewd analysis of the economic position of women, that 'needlework and intellectual improvement are naturally in a state of warfare', and though she taught herself Latin and other languages in an effort to acquire a 'correct style', she never felt that confidence in her abilities which her intelligence and scholarship warranted. Her life changed dramatically in 1796, when she killed her mother in an attack of the manic-depressive illness incident to the Lamb family. A coroner's verdict of lunacy allowed Charles to take formal responsibility for her, and she became his housekeeper and close companion, participating fully in the literary gatherings which developed around him, except when exhaustion or stress precipitated another breakdown. These traumatic events could therefore be said to have freed her to become a writer, though the extent to which they also limited her ability to write can only be guessed. It was also, perhaps, a consciousness of her own emotional insecurity and socially anomalous position which gave her an unusual empathy with the fears and worries of children, particularly girls. Years later Mary Cowden Clarke was to pay tribute to her ability to 'take an estimate of things so entirely from *their* point of view' with a 'tact and skill quite surprising'.

The knowledge that other women, such as Mary Wollstonecraft (see *ORIGINAL STORIES FROM REAL LIFE*) and MARIA EDGEWORTH, were creating a new field of literature for children may have helped Mary Lamb overcome her diffidence. The *Tales from Shakespear*, commissioned for the Godwins' Juvenile Library, appears originally to have been her project, and though she spoke deprecatingly of her 'poor little baby-stories' she was sufficiently pleased with them to embark almost immediately on a new work, *MRS LEICESTER'S SCHOOL*. Another breakdown during this period perhaps accounts for Charles having to contribute three of the last four stories to this collection, but it was quickly followed by two volumes of *Poetry for Children* (1809), probably modelled on the success of ANN and JANE TAYLOR. Mary wrote two-thirds of these poems, many of them dialogues between a brother and sister, or showing a shrewd observation of child behaviour. Though predominantly didactic they have a range and variety which may easily be overlooked. The poems were not the success that had been hoped for, but both the *Tales* and *Mrs Leicester's School* went through many editions within the Lambs' lifetime. The convincing use of children's narrative voices in the latter was recognised by many as something entirely new, and COLERIDGE described the book as 'a rich jewel in the treasury of our permanent English literature'. JFB

Lambert, Janet 1894–1973 Indiana-born writer of domestic fiction, predominantly about American military families – *Penny Parrish* series (1941–50), *Tippy Parrish* series (1948–56), *Candy Cane* series (1945–65), *Christie Drayton* series (1948–49), and so on. Based on her experiences both as an actress and as an army wife living on bases around the world, Lambert's work celebrates strong family ties. Like MADELEINE L'ENGLE, Lambert invents connections between characters in different series: Tippy Parrish marries Peter Jordan, Alcie Jordan marries Jonathan Drayton. Though they are unabashedly romantic, these books also contain complex depictions of American family life, particularly of families involved with the military, from the 1930s to the 1960s. Army customs are prominently depicted throughout these novels. Male characters attend West Point and fight in Europe, Korea and Vietnam; female characters follow their families and fight their own battles. Though young women in these books occasionally choose marriage over careers, others, such as Penny Parrish, establish successful careers in addition to marriage and motherhood. Lambert's novels are not merely light romances; they provide well-developed representations of American history and culture: men die in combat, women must rebuild their lives, a child in the Parrish series contracts polio and must learn to live with its effects. AKP

Lamplighter, The (1854) A novel by American writer Maria Susanna Cummins (1827–66) that achieved rapid success, selling 100,000 copies in its first year and remaining in print into the next century. Although the novel was written for an adult audience, its opening chapters in particular, which introduce the small abused orphan Gerty, were appealing to younger readers. Gerty loves to watch the lamplighter Trueman Flint on his evening rounds, and when she finds herself homeless Flint cares for her. After his death she is taken into the home of Mr Graham and his blind daughter Emily, whose uncomplaining endurance is a constant inspiration to the hot-tempered Gerty. Throughout most of the novel Gerty, and indeed all the female characters, are in a position of financial dependence on men, and Cummins explores the conflicts of duty caused by this dependence. When Gerty decides to leave the Graham household in order to help the needy Mrs Sullivan and her father, for instance, Mr Graham accuses her of ingratitude; he refuses to acknowledge that sincere generosity does not impose obligations on the recipient. Gerty's own generosity nearly leads to her death, but the story has a happy conclusion. FEA

Lancelot of the Lake see KING ARTHUR

Land of Green Ginger, The (1966) Novel by Noel Langley, illustrated by EDWARD ARDIZZONE, first published as *The Tale of the Land of Green Ginger* in 1937. It follows the adventures of Abu Ali, son of Aladdin, as he sets out to win Silver Bud and to free a magician who has inadvertently turned himself into a Button-Nosed Tortoise, accompanied by Boomalakka Wee, the son of the genie of the lamp. The story is told rather in the manner of A.A. MILNE's *Once on a Time*, its humour deriving from its send-up of FAIRY TALE conventions and its refusal to take itself seriously. SA

Lang, Andrew see *THE BLUE FAIRY BOOK*; 'COLOURED' *FAIRY BOOKS*; see also CLASSICAL MYTHOLOGY; FAIRY FANTASY; ILLUSTRATION IN CHILDREN'S BOOKS; ANTONY MAITLAND; CHARLES PERRAULT; *TAM LIN*

Langley, Noel see *LAND OF GREEN GINGER, THE*

Langton, Jane 1922– American author best known for *The Fledgling* (1980), a 1981 Newbery Honour Book and a 2000 Phoenix Award Honour Book, *The Fragile Flag* (1984), an anti-nuclear war novel, and for her mysteries for adults. Transcendentalist ideas figure heavily in her work. Born in Boston, Massachusetts, Langton studied astronomy at Wellesley College and the University of Michigan and did graduate work in art history at the University of Michigan and Radcliffe College. In 1961 she published her first YOUNG ADULT novel, *Majesty of Grace*.

She has published 11 young adult novels. Several centre on the escapades of the Hall family, including *The Diamond in the Window* (1962), *The Swing in the Summerhouse* (1967) and *The Astonishing Stereoscope* (1971). *The Fledgling* is a touching story about young Georgie Hall's growth and self-realisation process. In *The Fragile Flag* nine-year-old Georgie leads a children's march to Washington to protest against the President's nuclear 'Peace Missile', using the American flag as a symbol of peace and global friendship. Langton has most recently retold FOLKTALES, among them *Salt: From a Russian Folktale* (1992) and *The Queen's Necklace: A Swedish Folktale* (1994). She has also written essays on children's literature and DETECTIVE FICTION. ELPB

Lanier, Sidney 1842–81 American author, poet and musician from Georgia. Hampered by the tuberculosis he had contracted as a confederate solider during the Civil War, Lanier struggled to support his family with his artistic pursuits. In one attempt to earn money, he edited what he considered to be four juvenile potboilers: *The Boy's Froissart* (1879), *The Boy's King Arthur* (1880), *The Boy's Mabinogion* (1881) and *The Boy's Percy* (1882). In his introductions to these volumes Lanier stated that he had remained faithful to the original texts, with deletions only to tie the narratives together more tightly and to censor inappropriate passages. In truth, Lanier changed and edited the texts more freely than he perhaps admitted to himself. He intended, however, for the books to inspire boys with an idealised chivalric code of behaviour. Lanier now remains known today, however, for his poetry and his role as literary critic and theorist. JKB

Lantern Bearers, The see *EAGLE OF THE NINTH, THE*

Larcom, Lucy 1824–93 American author and poet whose autobiographical writings included *A New England Girlhood* (1889). She became a teacher and editor of the magazine, *OUR YOUNG FOLKS*. Her own verses appeared in the *ST NICHOLAS MAGAZINE* and *THE YOUTH'S COMPANION*. Her children's poems are collected in *Childhood Songs* (1875) with illustrations by WINSLOW HOMER and others. PDS

Larrick, Nancy 1910– Virginia writer and editor, who precipitated changes in children's literature in

America. She collected and published *A Parent's Guide to Children's Reading* (1964, 1975, 1982) and *A Teacher's Guide to Children's Books* (1960). Her essay 'The All-White World of Children's Books' (*Saturday Review*, September 1965) questioned the racial imbalance in children's books. By means of surveys with editors, librarians and parents, she demonstrated the disproportionate use of the white child, in text and ILLUSTRATION, as representative of the entire world of children, specifically the stereotypical representation – or total absence – of the African-American child in American books. Among her concerns was the poetry available for young people. Larrick published *Piping Down the Valleys Wild: Poetry for the Young of All Ages* (1968), an anthology of poems grouped in 16 parts, each devoted to a particular subject such as animals, seasons, holidays or people. This collection was followed by *I Heard a Scream in the Street: Poetry by Young People in the City* (1970), *Crazy to be Alive in Such a Strange World: Poems About People* (1977), and 'in celebration of the 25th Anniversary of *Reading is Fundamental*' – a reading motivation programme – *To Ride a Butterfly: Original Pictures, Stories, Poems and Songs for Children* (1991). KSB

Larry the Lamb see COMICS, PERIODICALS AND MAGAZINES; see also TELEVISION; *TOYTOWN SERIES*

Lasenby, Jack 1931– New Zealand award-winning novelist, whose superbly crafted books reflect his knowledge and love of the land and people of New Zealand, as well as a fascination with the English language. Best-known titles are *The Lake* (1987), *The Mangrove Summer* (1990), *The Conjuror* (1992) and a trilogy (*Dead Man's Head* (1994), *The Waterfall* (1995), and *The Battle of Pook Hill* (1996)) set in rural New Zealand between the two World Wars. Lasenby's strength as a storyteller is evident in his story collections, the *Uncle Trev* volumes, humorous tales of family relationships in country life in New Zealand. Although Lasenby's settings are the New Zealand of his readers' grandparents, his explicit descriptions and timeless themes of adventure and friendship make them accessible to, and loved by, contemporary children. He has also written extensively for the New Zealand *SCHOOL JOURNAL*. LL

Lasky, Kathryn 1944– Versatile American writer of fiction and non-fiction for all ages. Known as one of the best realistic writers for children, Lasky is a sound researcher. One of her major interests is nature; another is travel. Author of a dinosaur trilogy, she introduces CUSTER and Black Elk in *The Bone Wars*, a story of two young adults, the American Thaddeus Longsworth and the British Julian DeMott, who discover a triceratops in the Badlands. Lasky modelled Thaddeus in part on Charles H. Sternberg, the eminent fossil collector. *Traces of Life: The Origins of Humankind* (1989) is a sweeping paleoanthropological study. Lasky married the photographer Christopher G. Knight and he has collaborated on some volumes. Her son Max appears in *Dinosaur Dig* (1990), the third of the dinosaur books, and her daughter Meribah co-authored *Searching for Laura Ingalls: A Reader's Journal* (1993). Lasky's Jewish roots in Russia inspired *The Night Journey* (1986), Nana Sachie's story told to the teenager, Rachel. Here, as elsewhere in Lasky's work, family is an important theme. She does not hesitate to tackle hard issues such as intellectual freedom and CENSORSHIP (*Memoirs of a Bookbat*, 1994) and a sense of awe at the universe pervades her books. NV

Lassie Come-Home (1940) Only juvenile novel by the Anglo-American author Eric (Mowbray) Knight (1897–1943). The story depicts the devotion between a faithful collie dog (Lassie) and her 12-year-old master (Joe). To his impoverished mining village in the north of England, Lassie seems to symbolise the pride of its inhabitants, but the Duke of Rudling eventually persuades Mr. Carraclough, Joe's father, to let him purchase Lassie and take her to northern Scotland. Lassie's escape and arduous journey back to the Carraclough farm constitutes the novel's plot. Knight, born and raised in Yorkshire himself, was very familiar with poverty, class distinctions and working-class dialects, all of which he uses to advantage in the story. In addition, his depiction of the true intelligence of the collie breed makes the story believable to the reader. Considered one of the best dog stories ever written, the book has been published in various editions and Lassie has been portrayed by various illustrators, including ROSEMARY WELLS in a 1995 PICTUREBOOK adaptation. The novel was the basis for eight films and six TELEVISION series, but its most memorable adaptation is probably the 1943 film starring Elizabeth Taylor and Roddy McDowell. MS

see also ANIMALS IN CHILDREN'S FICTION

Last of the Mohicans, The see *LEATHER-STOCKING TALES*

Last of the Wallendas, The (1997) Collection of poems by the American author, RUSSELL HOBAN, with well-matched drawings by PATRICK BENSON. Hoban writes throughout the collection about dragons and fabulous beasts of different kinds, culminating in the moving 'My Last Dragon':

> I left him when at childhood's end
> I waved to him as round the bend
> of time he grew quite small.

Alongside these go reflections on the everyday, pigeons and the London underground, and celebrations of real historical people, as in the title piece about a high-wire team. The poems display Hoban's quirky humour and idiosyncratic imagination, along with his instinctive feel for rhythm and rhyme. The poems in Hoban's much earlier collection *The Pedalling Man* (1969) are more homogenous, often about the natural world and his own children's fantasies. ML

Latham, Jean Lee 1902–95 Prolific and versatile American author of novels, poetry, plays and BIOGRAPHIES for children and young adults. She received special recognition with *Carry On, Mr. Bodwitch* (1955), a biography of the famed astronomer, which was awarded the NEWBERY MEDAL. Latham demonstrates an ability to fluidly convey the technical information surrounding the life of her biography subjects – doctors, inventors, mathematicians and scientists. She was born in Buckhannon, West Virginia, in 1902. From an early age she wove tales and wrote plays. After completing her masters degree at Cornell in 1930, she became editor-in-chief of Dramatic Publishing Company in Chicago. In 1945 she pursued a freelance writing career, switching from plays to narratives, especially biographies. Though it is evident these works were carefully researched, by today's standards they are considered fictionalised biographies. Throughout their childhoods, the main characters retain a clear focus on the life-goal they will carry into their adult lives. The narrative moves forward using elements of fiction – added scenes and characters, dialogue, and interior thoughts of the main character – each unsupported by historical documents. Most of Latham's books focus on male subjects and are especially appealling to boys. LAW

Lathrop, Dorothy (Pulis) 1891–1980 One of America's best-known illustrators during the 1920s and 1930s; author-illustrator of 17 PICTUREBOOKS. Lathrop's exquisite ILLUSTRATIONS, influenced by Art Nouveau, appeared in such outstanding children's books as WALTER DE LA MARE's *The Three Mulla-Mulgars* (1919), DOROTHY CANFIELD FISHER's *Made-to-Order Stories* (1925), and RACHEL FIELD's *HITTY* (1929). *Animals of the Bible* (compiled by Helen Dean Fish) won the first CALDECOTT AWARD in 1938. Lathrop's own animal stories include both FANTASY (from *The Fairy Circus*, 1931, to *The Dog in the Tapestry Garden*, 1962) and realistic stories of wild creatures and pets. SR

see also ANIMALS IN CHILDREN'S FICTION

Latin lessons and Latin masters 'Latin is a language, as dead as dead can be. It killed the ancient Romans and now it's killing me.' This was the traditional view of Latin, expressed by J.C.T. Jennings in *Jennings Follows a Clue* (1951) (see JENNINGS series). Over the past 50 years, Classics has declined steeply in British schools and the present generation of school fiction writers reflect this by rarely featuring the subject in their stories. However, for almost a century after *TOM BROWN'S SCHOOLDAYS* (1857), in which the daily task of the pupils at Arnold's Rugby is 'with dictionary and grammar to hammer out their twenty lines of Virgil and Euripides', there is barely a fictional lesson that is not of a classical nature. Latin and Greek classes are, as the Mock Turtle remembers in *ALICE'S ADVENTURES IN WONDERLAND* (1865), occasions for both 'Laughing and Grief'. And Billy Bunter's translation of the Latin 'o dea' as 'oh, dear' provoked much merriment in the GREYFRIARS Remove, but resulted in a beating for the luckless Owl. Latin, in the form of a book of Virgil to copy out, is often used as a means of punishing adolescent misdemeanours. But occasionally the tables are turned and Latin is employed by pupils to avenge themselves on unpleasant teachers: the young protagonist of RUDYARD KIPLING's *STALKY & CO.* (1899) deliberately produces an awful translation of a passage of Horace to torture the master who has to read it. Fictional public schoolboys can also assert their superiority over those outside their own community by using Latin. This may be via classical quips, such as P.G. WODEHOUSE's 'what the sherry said to the man about to drink it: nemo me impune lacessit' in *The Head of St. Kay's* (1905), or by the manipulation of Latin as a sort of secret language. Consequently, both boys and masters in the fictional school define themselves and the particular social sphere in which they dwell via the use of classics.

The antiquity of the subject seems all too easily transferable to the pedagogues who teach it; GEOFFREY WILLANS's and RONALD SEARLES's Molesworth remarks 'Everything in lat. hapned a long time ago. Latin masters therefore are always old and bent with age.' Mellish in Wodehouse's *Tales of St. Austin's* (1903), who glories in a name that sounds like 'Hellish' and who has a perverse penchant for 'picking out untranslatable passages', is perhaps the archetypal sadistic Classics master. One fictional Classics teacher who confounds the stereotype of the adult classicist as an elderly, dull, white middle-class male is ARTHUR RANSOME's eponymous *Missee Lee* (1941), a female Chinese Pirate who threatens walking the plank rather than a conventional beating as an ultimate sanction for any member of the captured *SWALLOWS AND AMAZONS* who slacks in class. She is the antithesis of the seemingly familiar and 'safe' world of a classical education. This world shaped generations of English public schoolboys. It is important to understand it if one is to appreciate the huge appeal of this fictional public-school universe to thousands of young readers who had no experience of independent schooling but whose grammar-school education enabled them to enjoy the Latin jokes. JC

Latin versions Nonnulli libri bene noti ad usum liberorum scripti in linguam Latinam conversi sunt. Quamquam homo quidam qui libros typis exscibendos curabat ad Alexandrum Lenard scripsit talem laborem esse irritum, quod liberi Latine nescirent, adulti libros ad usum liberorum scriptos non legerent, tamen fabulae de *Pooh Bear* ab A.A. MILNE Anglice scriptae et Latine ab eodem Alexandro Lenard redditae multis in terris per mundum universum editae sunt.

Equibus prima erat *Winnie ille Pu* (1958), et paucos post annos apparuit *Domus Anguli Puensis, liber alter de Urso Puo de anglico sermone in Latinum conversus auctore Briano Staplesio* (1980).

Praeterea duo e libris Beatricis Potter optime notis Latine sunt redditi, *Fabula de Petro Cuniculo; liber omnibus notus B. Potter in Latinum conversus est auctore E.P. Walker* (1962), et *Fabula de Jemima Anate-Aquatica* (1965) conversus est auctore Jonathan Musgrave.

Fabulae autem de Alicia a Ludovico Carroll scriptae maiora impedimenta afferebant interpretibus illis qui volebant eas Latine exprimere. Nihilominus anno 1964 apparuit *Alicia in Terra Mirabili, Latine redditus ab eius fautore vetere gratoque C.H. Carruthers*, et paulo post (1966) *Alicia per Speculum Transitus Latine Redditus*. JTh

vide *ALICE'S ADVENTURES IN WONDERLAND*; *THE TALE OF PETER RABBIT*; *WINNIE-THE-POOH*

Lattimore, Eleanor Frances 1904–86 American writer of fiction for younger children. Lattimore was born and brought up mostly in China, one of the five children of an American professor. Returning to the United States in 1920, she attended art school, and in 1930 published her first book, *Little Pear*: 'I started writing in order to have something to illustrate.' Her drawings are unremarkable, except for their Chinese authenticity. The writing is direct and simple, her Chinese stories always the most vivid. *The Chinese Daughter* (1947) tells of a little girl, adopted by missionaries, who has to choose between her American and her Chinese families. PP

Laurence, (Jean) Margaret (Wemyss) 1926–87 Canadian novelist. Born and educated in Manitoba, Canada, Laurence worked as a reporter in Winnipeg, then lived abroad in Somalia and England before returning to Canada. She began to write children's books late in her career when she was already an award-winning author, and her juvenile books often reiterate the themes and narrative techniques of her adult fiction. *Jason's Quest* (1970) is a social allegory that uses the structure of the romantic quest to describe a mole's discovery of wisdom and self-esteem as he journeys in search of a cure for the social paralysis that plagues his city, Molarium. *The Olden Days Coat* (1979) is a TIME-SLIP FANTASY that explores both the relationship of the past to the present and the bridge between generations, through a magic Christmas gift. Along with her two other children's stories, *Six Darn Cows* (1979) and *A Christmas Birthday Story* (1980), these books, like much of Laurence's literary work, present a modern, liberating outlook through a focus on the psychology of characters and a stress on humane values and the capacity for self-awareness. DAC

Lavelle, Sheila 1939– Born in Gateshead, County Durham, England, Lavelle has written many books for younger readers, including the *Ursula* stories in which the heroine is able to turn herself into a bear. She is best known for her series of humorous books about *My Best Fiend* (1979) in which the angelic-looking 'fiend' Angela gets Charlie Ellis, the narrator of the stories, into endless scrapes, usually at school or at home. The stories are aimed at confident junior readers. HCE

Laverty, Maura 1907–66 Irish playwright and author of novels for adults and children. Her children's books, which include *The Cottage in the Bog* (1946), are set in rural Ireland. *The Queen of Aran's Daughter* (1995), illustrated by her daughter Barry Castle, is a collection of seven FAIRY TALES. VC

Lawrence, Ann 1942–87 British writer. Owing to her tragically early death, the corpus of Ann Lawrence's work is a small one. It is, however, varied in type – the *Oggy the Hedgehog* books are animal tales for younger children, *Mr Robertson's Hundred Pounds* (1976) and *Between the Forest and the Hills* (1977) are historical novels, and the others may be classed as FANTASIES – and the writing is of uniformly high quality. Of her books, *Tom Ass* (1972), a FAIRY TALE which tells the story of an idle boy turned into an ass by a fairy, is perhaps the best known and loved. SA

Lawrence, John 1933– British illustrator. After study at Hastings and the Central School of Arts and Crafts, Lawrence taught at several colleges of art, developing his art of WOOD-ENGRAVING. His engravings for IAN SERRAILLIER's *The Road to Canterbury* (1979) are typical: a packed, engraved frontispiece from which he extracts and enlarges details for use throughout the book. Occasionally his wood-engravings are tinted as in *A Pair of Sinners* (1980) where they joyfully capture the spirit of ALLAN AHLBERG's verses. He also uses line, hatching and wash as in his *TREASURE ISLAND* (ROBERT LOUIS STEVENSON, 1990) and SUSAN HILL's touching Christmas story *King of Kings* (1993). Lawrence has illustrated over 100 books, including the work of PHILIPPA PEARCE, GILLIAN AVERY, ROSEMARY SUTCLIFF, LEON GARFIELD, KEVIN CROSSLEY-HOLLAND, CHARLES

CAUSLEY and ROALD DAHL. He has twice been a recipient of the Francis Williams Illustration Award. JAG

Lawrence, Louise Pen-name under which British author Elizabeth Rhoda Wintle Holden (1943–) writes, her work dividing equally between SCIENCE FICTION and FANTASY. Her first novel, *Andra* (1971), a dystopian fiction recalling E.M. Forster's 'The Machine Stops' and Aldous Huxley's *Brave New World*, ponders issues of free will, moral responsibility and the shaping of society, issues which also arise in her later work, such as the *Llandor* novels. In these issues, and in the bias towards the natural and the pre-industrial, one may perhaps discern in Lawrence a latter-day Romanticism. A certain shapelessness to the narrative lines, however, handicaps otherwise good and interesting work. SA

Lawson, Robert 1892–1957 Prolific American writer and illustrator for children, the only individual to have won both a Caldecott and a Newbery Medal. A master draughtsman, Lawson illustrated both his own and other writers' stories with strong, knife-sharp images in black-and-white that exude action, robust humour and confidence. *They Were Strong and Good*, an illustrated BIOGRAPHY of his ancestors, won the Caldecott Award in 1940. As a writer, Lawson is the quintessential Yankee, celebrating both in content and style the values and traditions of American history as it was conceived during his lifetime. His four historical fantasies, beginning with *Ben and Me* (1939), describe the adventures of Ben Franklin, Christopher Columbus, Captain Kidd and Paul Revere, as revealed in a comic manner by their animal companions. *Rabbit Hill* (1944), for which Lawson won the Newbery Medal, tells the story of an animal community achieving prosperity after a period of hardship. Integrating brilliant comic characterisations with lyrical passages that voice a deep love of nature and boundless faith in the prosperity and happiness that can be achieved through community co-operation, *Rabbit Hill* is an eloquent expression of post-World-War-II American idealism. CV

Layton, George 1943– British actor and scriptwriter. Layton published his first story collection (originally written for broadcasting) in 1975, *The Balaclava Story and Other Stories*, followed by THE FIB AND OTHER STORIES (1978) and *The Swap and Other Stories* (1997). The stories, told in the first person, while dealing specifically with the lives of children growing up in the 1950s, yet have a universal and timeless appeal, evoking immediate empathetic responses as they explore familiar feelings and problems – bullying, victimisation, poverty, lying, stealing, disadvantage and isolation. The lively story lines, sympathetic humour and colloquial language reflect Layton's scriptwriting skills. JSW

Le Cain, Errol 1941–89 British author and illustrator of three PICTUREBOOKS early in his career (notably *The Cabbage Princess* 1969), but most successful as an illustrator in collaboration with other writers. His work for Antonia Barber's *The Enchanter's Daughter* (1987) and for traditional tales such as the GRIMMS' *Thorn Rose* (1975) and *Twelve Dancing Princesses* (1978) depicts remote lands peopled by fantastic swirling figures. His colours are exotically brilliant and his page designs, with their intricately patterned borders, are reminiscent of the Russian artist, Bilabin. Le Cain won the 1985 KATE GREENAWAY AWARD with the atmospheric *Hiawatha's Childhood*, evoking the mysterious but harmonious life of the wild forests of North America. GPF

Le Guin, Ursula K(roeber) 1929– Acclaimed American author, born in Berkeley, California. In a writing career spanning 30 years Le Guin has won distinction and honours as a writer of SCIENCE FICTION, fiction and poetry for adults, and as the creator of the *EARTHSEA QUARTET* (1968–90), which was published for young adults in the United States and Britain. However, she is a writer whose work is compartmentalised only with difficulty and some artifice. Much of the science fiction, such as *The Beginning Place* (1980), is accessible to a younger reader while the *Earthsea* books offer sufficient intellectual challenge to invite serious adult interest. Her supreme gift, manifest in all her works of FANTASY, is perhaps that of creating and developing entire cultures complete with myth, legend, history, language, many of which induce the reader to question contemporary attitudes and to recognise the residual myths and beliefs that inform contemporary thinking – less fantasy, in fact, than anthropology: the massive *Always Coming Home* (1985), *The Left Hand of Darkness* (1969) and, after 20 years, *Tehanu* (1990), the book that 'revisioned' the world posited in what had been the *Earthsea Trilogy*. Less well-known to British readers are her PICTUREBOOKS, such as *Leese Webster* (1988), the *Catwings* (1988) – stories about flying cats – and the novella *Very Far Away from Anywhere Else* (1976), in which two teenage friends rebel not merely against the conventional Middle-American expectations of their society but also, implicitly, against the kind of YOUNG ADULT FICTION which equally precisely prescribes accepted attitudes of rebellion and disaffection. Le Guin slyly undermines the abdication of responsibility promoted by writers who suggest that the miseries of adolescents are inflicted upon them by adults.

Whether creating a small village or a whole planetary system, Le Guin brings her environments to life as surely as her characters: the Pacific Northwest of *Searoad* (1991), the Europe of the Soviet Bloc in *Orsinian Tales* (1976), the far-flung archipelago of *Earthsea*. Communities are rarely static, being caught at moments of religious, political or moral upheaval. In many of her fictions Le Guin has explored the burden of moral responsibility, most notably in her short story, 'The Ones Who Walk Away From Omelas', in which the success and well-being of a society rests upon the unimaginable misery of an appointed sacrifice, and the marginalisation of women in societies where masculine superiority obtains through the collusion of oppressors and oppressed. In her younger fiction this is examined in *Tehanu* in which the hero-figure of Ged can be seen to have traded his sexual manhood for his power as a mage, and having lost the latter must rediscover himself as a human being neither better nor greater than the woman to whom he turns. An exposition of the thinking that occasioned this return to Earthsea is found in *Earthsea Revisioned* (1993). In antic mood there is also a book of *Bunditsu*, a delightful small-press publication (undated) devoted to the esoteric art of cat arranging. JMM

Le Sueur, Meridel 1900–96 American social activist and prolific author of fiction and non-fiction. Born in Murray, Iowa, she grew up in a household devoted to championing the working class. After quitting high school, she acted and did stunt work until the late 1920s. Her writing was widely recognised in the 1930s and, although she was blacklisted after World War II, Knopf continued to publish her children's books. In 1947 her first, *Little Brother of the Wilderness: The Story of Johnny Appleseed*, blended fact and folklore, incorporating tales from 'my grandmother'. Le Sueur employed a similar style for books about DAVY CROCKETT and Nancy Hanks. *The River Road: A Story of Abraham Lincoln* (1954) concentrates on young Lincoln's growing awareness of injustices against poor whites and slaves. The victimisation of the defenceless is a common theme for Le Sueur. *Sparrow Hawk* (1950) recounts the futile attempt of a Sauk Indian and his white friend to develop more productive corn to help avert war. Le Sueur includes both good and bad whites and Indians in a remarkably even-handed treatment. Feminist scholarship led to renewed interest in her work in the 1970s. The *Wilderness Road* books were republished between 1987 and 1991. KKP

le Mair, H. Willebeek see ILLUSTRATION IN CHILDREN'S BOOKS; see also *A CHILD'S GARDEN OF VERSES*

Leach, Sheryl see *BARNEY AND FRIENDS*

Leaf, (Wilbur) Munro (John Calvert; Mun) 1905–76 American illustrator and author of PICTUREBOOKS, fiction and non-fiction for children. Born near Baltimore, Maryland, and educated at the University of Maryland and Harvard University, Leaf worked as a teacher, journalist and director of a publishing company, and also wrote under the names Mun and John Calvert. He is best known for *The Story of Ferdinand* (1936), a bull who refused to fight, which he 'dashed off in 25 minutes' for ROBERT LAWSON to illustrate. The Leaf-Lawson team produced three other successful books: *Wee Gills* (1938), which received the Caldecott Honor Award; *The Story of Simpson and Sampson* (1941); and *Aesop's Fables* (1941). Leaf also collaborated with Ludwig Bemelmans on *Noodle* (1937), about a dachshund who gets his wish to be something else but learns a lesson in the process. Leaf self-illustrated a series which included *Grammar Can Be Fun* (1934); *Health Can Be Fun* (1943); *Arithmetic Can Be Fun* (1949); *History Can Be Fun* (1950); *Geography can Be Fun* (1951); *Reading Can Be Fun* (1953); *Science Can Be Fun* (1958); *Being an American Can Be Fun* (1964) and *Metrics Can Be Fun!* (1976). For over 20 years he wrote the 'Watchbirds' column for *Ladies Home Journal* about raising children. These were later collected into *3 and 30 Watchbirds* (1944) and *Flock of Watchbirds* (1946). DJH

Lear, Edward 1812–88 English artist and poet, best known for writing and illustrating NONSENSE VERSE. Lear, born the 20th child of a family of 21, had a lonely and unhappy childhood, haunted by ill health, epilepsy and depression. Always sensitive about his own appearance, he later described himself as being 'half-blind', with a 'singularly long' neck and 'a most elephantine nose', characteristics which often appear in the nonsense drawings and poems (see 'How Pleasant to know Mr Lear'). Lear earned a precarious living as a 'nartist', as he put it, drawing birds, animals and then, as his eyesight worsened, painting landscapes. He travelled widely from 1837 onwards and settled in Italy from 1871 until his death.

Throughout his life, Lear despised idleness, valued friendship and loved wordplay. These were qualities he also found in children, and writing for them provided a release from his frequent feelings of alienation from adult society and its values. He began writing LIMERICKS in the 1830s for the children of his then patron, developing the form invented by Richard Scrafton Sharpe (1775–1852) in *ANECDOTES AND ADVENTURES OF FIFTEEN GENTLEMEN* (1822), and eventually publishing *A BOOK OF NONSENSE* (1846), enlarged in 1861, and *More Nonsense* (1872). The limericks are carefully crafted in their use of rhyme and metre and usually light and inconsequential, sometimes self-mocking. Occasionally, though, they are disturbing in the violence, disgust and despair presented through the verbal and visual humour (characters are 'smashed', 'knocked about', live up trees, kill themselves). In the accompanying nonsense drawings, Lear, a skilful draughtsman, deliberately distorts the human figure, putting huge, bird-like heads on tiny bodies; animals, by contrast are drawn naturalistically. Lear's distorted drawings, as well as his distortions of spelling and meaning, attracted condemnation from some contemporaries as unsuitable for young readers. Children, however, responded with 'uproarious delight and welcome', Lear was pleased to discover.

Lear's later narrative poems were collected in NONSENSE SONGS (1871) and *Laughable Lyrics* (1877). In these longer pieces, there is an obvious delight in sound-patterning and in musical and dance-like rhythms in particular, often incorporating extended dialogue ('The Owl and The Pussy-Cat'). There is also a greater imaginative richness in the creation of a FANTASY world of characters and places which is carried over from poem to poem. The story poems also have pathos and melancholy: there are flights to faraway places and wanderings in exotic lands ('The Daddy Long-legs and the Fly', 'The Jumblies'), tales of loneliness and unrequited love ('The Dong with a Luminous Nose') and of loss and mutilation ('Calico Pie', 'The Pobble who has no Toes'). Presenting these often personal feelings in the genre of nonsense poetry allowed Lear a detachment and humour which gave the poems their unique blend of innocence and experience, which has helped them endure for adult as well as child readers. Fittingly, Lear wrote his own obituary in his final nonsense poem, 'Incidents in the Life of My Uncle Arly'. ML

Leather-Stocking Tales A series of five novels by James Fenimore Cooper (1789–1851) tracing the life of Nathaniel Bumppo, a character based on DANIEL BOONE. *The Pioneers* (1823) establishes the major theme that permeates the series – the corruption of civilisation in contrast to the morally pristine wilderness – by opposing the 70-year-old Natty Bumppo to the forces and laws of civilisation. In *The Last of the Mohicans* (1826), Natty Bumppo as a much younger man twice rescues the daughters of a British officer from kidnapping by Delaware Indians. In *The Prairie* (1827) Natty Bumppo leads a settlement party across the prairie and dies at the end of the novel. *The Pathfinder* (1840) and *The Deerslayer* (1841) record the hunting and wilderness adventures of the young Natty Bumppo. The series initiated many of the frontier and adventure motifs that characterised much popular American literature written for boys, including woodlore, Indian-fighting, chase and rescue, wilderness survival, hunting and marksmanship, landscape, and the pleasures and freedom of individualism. The series also influenced the subsequent portrayals of Native Americans: Cooper developed the stereotypes of the noble and the blood-thirsty savage. EBD

Lee, Alan 1947– British illustrator. Lee achieved early and spectacular success with his FANTASY illustrations to Brian Froud's *Faeries* (1978). *The Mirrorstone* (Michael Palin and R. Seymour, 1986), in which Lee introduced holograms into his illustrations, was a joint winner of the 1986 Smarties Innovation Prize. *The Moon's Revenge* (JOAN AIKEN, 1987) exhibits his muted, mystical paintings at their best. In 1991, he illustrated the Centenary Edition of J.R.R. TOLKIEN's *The Lord of the Rings*. *Black Ships before Troy* (ROSEMARY SUTCLIFF, 1993), winner of the KATE GREENAWAY MEDAL, was followed by the equally effective *The Wanderings of Odysseus* (Rosemary Sutcliff, 1995). JAG

Lee, Dennis (Beynon) 1939– Canadian poet whose award-winning light NONSENSE VERSE and CAUTIONARY TALES invite comparisons with R.L. STEVENSON, MILNE and HEINRICH HOFFMANN. Humour abounds in his contemporary landscapes and depictions of everyday life, the focus of his *Mother Goose*-like rhymes. His works include *Alligator Pie* (1974), *Garbage Delight* (1977), *Jelly Belly* (1983) and *Dinosaur Dinner: With a Slice of Alligator Pie* (1997). PDS

Lee, Harper see *TO KILL A MOCKINGBIRD*

Lee, Laurie see *CIDER WITH ROSIE*

Lee, Tanith 1947– Prolific and original British author of FANTASY novels for children and adults. Born in London, she originally studied art before becoming a librarian. Her first short stories appeared in print in 1968, followed by *The Dragon Hoard* in 1971. Though they are marketed for young readers, Lee says she does not intend her works for any particular age group. Series for adults, such as *Secret Books of Paradys* – which includes *The Book of the Damned* (1988), *The Book of the Beast* (1988), *The Book of the Dead* (1991), and *The Book of the Mad* (1993) – and *Tales from the Flat Earth* – which includes *Night's Master* (1978), *Death's Master* (1979), *Delusion's Master* (1981), *Delirium's Mistress* (1986), *Night's Sorceries* (1987) and *Night's Daughter* (1987) – are also enjoyed by young adult readers. Her short-story collections – especially *Cyrion* (1982), *Red as Blood* (1983) and *Tamastara* (1984) – have also become popular among young adults. She uniquely blends elements of SCIENCE FICTION, FAIRY TALES and FANTASY in tales where the main character searches for identity and explores the balance between good and evil, destiny and free will. *Black Unicorn* (1991) is a coming-of-age story in which Tanaquil, an adolescent, finds her strength and own special magic. Her story continues in

Gold Unicorn (1994) and *Red Unicorn* (1998), part of the *Dragonflight* series. Lee has been praised for her highly descriptive writing, well-formed, engaging characters, and plots involving quests usually containing some element of magic. Her fairy-tale collections reveal a darker side to human nature and a sinister irrationality in which princes marry witches (*Princess Hynchatti and Some Other Surprises*, 1972), heroines struggle against madness, and heroes almost surrender to evil (*Companions on the Road*, 1977, and *Shon the Taken*, 1979). Since 1975 she has produced on average two novels or story collections per year. LAW

Leeson, Robert (Arthur) 1928– British novelist, dramatist, critic and social historian, best known for his many books for children and young adults. A tireless advocate for children's literature, his consistent attitude to children, literature and society is stated in *Reading and Righting* (1985). This polemic text identifies books as means of human – mainly children's – liberation and empowerment in a society which denies voices to many members. Books are both symbols of a restrictive culture and potent agents of change uniquely adaptable to an ever-shifting society. This tension goes a long way towards explaining the variety and energy of Leeson's work. His narratives are suffused with both understanding of and discontent with the literary tradition: his characters, through social position, ethnic origin or gender, are not customarily seen taking central roles.

Leeson's childhood was spent in Barnton, Cheshire. After army service he became a journalist on the former *Daily Worker*. His earliest works were working-class histories in the tradition of E.P. Thompson, culminating with *Travelling Brothers* (1979). His first children's books were the historical *Maroon Boy*, *Bess* and *The White Horse*, (1974–6) about the Cimaroons, a historical episode of rebellion rarely acknowledged in established accounts. Thereafter, he wrote prolifically for all age groups. His first popular successes were *The Demon Bike Rider* (1976) and, especially, *The Third-class Genie* (1975), which led to the sequels *Genie on the Loose* (1984) and *The Last Genie* (1993). Good-naturedly humorous, the *Genie* stories rework a traditional convention for contemporary effect. Using traditional tales to new effect is consistent with his attitudes to literature and society; *Never Kiss Frogs!* (1988) is one hilarious example among many. Recent examples are *Idle Jack* (1995), *Smart Girls* (1994, shortlisted for the GUARDIAN AWARD) and *Smart Girls Forever* (1996), both showing strong female characters in traditional tales from many cultures.

Another aspect of Leeson's affectionate questioning of received notions of the literary heritage lies in his 'sequels' to classics. Typical are *Karlo's Tale* (1992), where Browning's *THE PIED PIPER* is given an unexpected twist, and the ambitious *Silver's Revenge* (1978), a subversive, wrily humorous continuation of *TREASURE ISLAND*. Leeson's best-known works are his five *GRANGE HILL* novels (1980–3). His central achievements are his novels for young adults, especially the *IT'S MY LIFE* trilogy, *Candy For King* (1981), *Time Rope* (1986), *Slambash Wangs of a Compo Gormer* (1987), *Red, White and Blue* (1995) and *Liar* (1999).

The picaresque *Candy For King* follows the unwitting trail of disaster left through the army by Kitchener Candeford, gentle innocent giant, like Candide the possessor of a nobility the world is unready for. The *Time Rope* quartet, using SCIENCE FICTION conventions, pits underprivileged young people against a disturbing future society. *Slambash Wangs*, an imaginative *tour de force*, humorously merges realism with FANTASY. More seriously, the typographically innovative *Red, White and Blue* uses comparable narrative techniques, as Wain finds the truth about both himself and his father who is missing in the Falklands. In *Liar*, Mack's search for a missing friend uncovers his own reality.

Leeson's achievement and influence were recognised in 1986 with the Eleanor Farjeon award. DCH

LeGallienne, Eva 1899–1991 American actress, playwright, novelist and director-producer, born in London, England. She is best known for her work as an actress, particularly in the plays of Henrik Ibsen, some of which she translated into English. She made three notable contributions to children's literature and children's theatre. In 1932, she adapted for the stage (with fellow actress Florida Freibus) LEWIS CARROLL'S *ALICE'S ADVENTURES IN WONDERLAND* and *Through the Looking-Glass* in a single play. Entitled simply *Alice in Wonderland*, the play was produced three times on Broadway, each time featuring LeGallienne in the role of the White Queen. In 1949 she published *Flossie and Bossie*, an animal story about two hens. Critics have suggested that the novel, which has as much appeal for adults as for children, is semi-autobiographical, based on her own household relationships; the title characters are named after two hens LeGallienne owned and observed. Between 1965 and 1985, she translated a number of HANS CHRISTIAN ANDERSEN'S FAIRY TALES; an anthology of them, *Seven Tales* (1959), includes both familiar and less familiar tales, with ILLUSTRATIONS by MAURICE SENDAK, and two volumes are devoted to individual tales, *The Nightingale* (1965) and *The Snow Queen* (1985). BH

legends see FOLKTALES AND LEGENDS

legends, Aboriginal see ABORIGINAL CULTURE IN CHILDREN'S BOOKS

Leitch, Patricia see *JINNY* SERIES; see also PONY STORIES

Lemieux, Michele 1955– Canadian author and illustrator, born in Quebec City. Lemieux has held exhibitions in North America, Europe and Japan, and her books have been published in English, French and other languages. A meticulous technician, Lemieux conducts thorough research and makes many small drawings and rough sketches before working on her final paintings. She is a versatile artist, experimenting with different media, including watercolour, gouache, acrylics, oils and COLLAGE. Her style, in keeping with the mood of her stories, ranges from the sombre, as in *A Gift from Saint Francis: The First Creche* (1989), to the whimsical, as in *There Was an Old Man: A Gallery of Nonsense Rhymes* (1994). *Amahl and the Night Visitors* (1991), *Peter and the Wolf* (1991) and *The Pied Piper of Hamelin* (1993) exemplify her ability to create high drama, strong ethnic flavour, and distinctive personalities by means of bold palettes, intriguing perspectives, and details of architecture, costume and facial type. The ILLUSTRATIONS for her award-winning *Voices on the Wind: Poems for All Seasons* (1990) existed before the text, which David Booth selected under commission to match Lemieux's beautiful artwork. FL

L'Engle, Madeleine 1918– American author of children's and YOUNG ADULT FICTION. Born in New York City to drama critic Charles Wadsworth Camp and pianist Madeleine Barnett Camp, L'Engle spent much of her childhood alone with books such as L. M. MONTGOMERY's *Emily of New Moon* series, E. NESBIT's *Bastable* series, and GEORGE MACDONALD's fantasies. To her chagrin, her parents enrolled her in private schools and, later, European boarding schools. Her father, who had been subjected to mustard gas in the first World War, died when she was 17. She attended Smith College, graduating *cum laude* in 1941. After graduation, she moved to New York, where she acted on Broadway, and published her first novel, *Ilsa* (1946). There she met and married actor Hugh Franklin.

L'Engle's writing for children spans different genres. Her fantasies, including *A WRINKLE IN TIME* (1962), *A Swiftly Tilting Planet* (1978) and *An Acceptable Time* (1989), combine FANTASY, science and theology. They commonly use time travel and incorporate the scientific theories of Einstein and Planck. Her espionage thrillers include *The Arm of the Starfish* (1965), *Dragons in the Waters* (1976) and *Troubling a Star* (1994); they frequently focus on exploitation of the third world and the potential misuse of technology. Her domestic fiction, including the *AUSTIN* SERIES and others, commonly features adolescent female protagonists who desire to establish themselves as individuals outside their close, loving family circles or to develop their artistic talents despite the limitations of their conventional schooling. She has also written *The Journey with Jonah* (1967) and *Dance in the Desert* (1969), fictional vignettes based on the life of Christ. All of her works address perennial metaphysical concerns such as the meaning of evil and the place of humanity in the universe. She has been criticised for creating unbelievable characters such as Polyhymnia O'Keefe, who speaks six languages by the time she is a teenager, or Meg Murry's mother, who is a Nobel prize-winning physicist. The Christian aspect of her work has also been the subject of controversy: in particular, conservative religious groups have challenged *A Wrinkle in Time* for its depiction of magic and 'witches'. Other critics perceive what they describe as overtly Christian themes of love and redemption in her work. Nonetheless, L'Engle has been praised for challenging adolescent readers with her sophisticated plots and characterisations. She has received many awards, including the NEWBERY MEDAL for *A Wrinkle in Time*, the American Book Award for *A Swiftly Tilting Planet*, and a Newbery Honour Award for *A Ring of Endless Light*, in addition to the University of Southern Mississippi Medallion in 1978 and the Regina Medal in 1984.

L'Engle's autobiographical works include the *Crosswicks* Trilogy – *A Circle of Quiet* (1972), *Summer of the Great-Grandmother* (1974) and *The Irrational Season* (1977) – as well as *Two-Part Invention* (1988). AKP

Lenski, Lois 1893–1974 American author and illustrator of fiction, PICTUREBOOKS and non-fiction for children. Lenski was born in Springfield, Ohio, and spent most of her youth in rural Ohio. Her father was a Lutheran minister who instilled a strong sense of duty in her. She was educated at Ohio State University, where she earned a degree in education, but later she studied art at the Art Students League in New York City. Lenski lived most of her married life in the rural Connecticut area which formed the backdrop for two of her HISTORICAL FICTION works, *Skipping Village* (1927) and *A Little Girl of 1900* (1928), but *Indian Captive* (1941), the story of Mary Jeminson, is the best-remembered. The nearly 150 books she illustrated encompass picturebooks for young children, historical fiction, music, poetry and her autobiography, *Journey into Childhood* (1972), but her accurate and realistic depiction of different classes of children in her regional series and *Round About America* series are her main contribution to American children's literature. Lenski received the NEWBERY AWARD for one of these books, *Strawberry Girl* (1945) – the story of migrant labourers – and the Silver Medallion from the University of Southern Mississippi 'for distinguished service to children's literature'. DJH

'The campfire.' Illustration by Alison Lester from *My Farm*.

Lent, Blair 1930– Award-winning American author and illustrator best known for his use of cardboard cuts in ILLUSTRATIONS. *The Wave* (1964), a Japanese FOLKTALE retold by MARGARET HODGES, won the first of several Caldecott Honour Book Awards for Lent. He turned to painting for *Tikki Tikki Tembo* (1968), a Chinese folktale, and *The Funny Little Woman* (1972), a Japanese tale, both re-told by Arlene Mosel. These two are probably his most popular works, the former winning the BOSTON GLOBE-HORN BOOK AWARD for Illustration and the latter, the CALDECOTT MEDAL. He retold and illustrated *John Tabor's Ride* and *Baba Yaga*, both in 1966, attributing the retelling to Ernest Small, his pseudonym. PDS

Leodhas, Sorche Nic see NIC LEODHAS, SORCHE

Lepman, Jella see *BOOKBIRD*

Lester, Alison (Jean Hume) 1952– Award-winning Australian illustrator and author. Lester initially illustrated other writers' works, such as ROBIN KLEIN'S *Thing* (1982), before producing her own PICTUREBOOK, *Clive Eats Alligators* (1985), the first of a series which includes *Rosie Sips Spiders* (1988), *Tessa Snaps Snakes* (1990) and *When Frank was Four* (1994). In these, Lester perceptively captures the daily lives of six distinctive but recognisable contemporary preschool children with whimsical humour, using soft, fluid pencil drawings, with muted watercolour and rhythmic apposite caption-style texts. *The Australian Baby Books* (1989), a series of four small, heavy card books with titles like *Bumping & Bouncing* and *Crashing & Splashing*, have achieved great success internationally. Children's curiosity about the world, their imagination, their control of the fine line between reality and FANTASY, and especially their hunger for adventure, are celebrated in *Ruby* (1987), *The Journey Home* (1989), *Imagine* (1989), *Magic Beach* (1990) and *Isabella's Bed* (1991), where children engaged in everyday happenings, such as digging a hole in the sandpit, or playing on the beach, are transported to magical worlds, to kingdoms under the sea, to the North Pole, and beyond. Lester's first novel, *The Quicksand Pony* (1997), a well-conceived ADVENTURE STORY, is strongly evocative of the Gippsland region, Lester's home ground. HE

Lester, Julius 1939– American author, civil rights activist, musician, radio talk-show host, and professor of Judaic studies. Lester was born in St Louis, Missouri. He has written poetry, fiction, folklore, nonfiction and autobiography. *To Be a Slave* (1968), a collection of slave narratives and commentaries, was a Newbery Honour Book and established Lester's reputation as both an author for young adults and a teller of African American history. Much of his writing focuses on the southern Black experience and combines realism with a refined STORYTELLING ability. *Long Journey Home* (1972) and *This Strange Feeling* (1982) both recount powerful stories drawn from the African American experience previously absent from literature for children. Lester has also compiled several collections of FOLKTALES, including a series in which he retells the *Uncle Remus* stories (see JOEL CHANDLER HARRIS). In another retelling, *Sam and the Tigers* (1997), he manages to keep the humour and imaginative qualities of the TRICKSTER tale *LITTLE BLACK SAMBO* without the racist and stereotypical elements of Helen Bannerman's version. Some of Lester's books have also dealt with Black–Jewish relations. His personal connection with this issue and his conversion to Judaism are portrayed in the autobiographical *Lovesong* (1988). EB

see also AFRICAN AMERICAN LITERATURE; BIOGRAPHY AND AUTOBIOGRAPHY

L'Estrange, Sir Roger see FABLES

Let The Balloon Go (1968) Australian novel by IVAN SOUTHALL which explores the physical and interior life of John Clement Sumner, a boy with cerebral palsy who is persistently seeking independence. He refuses 'to be handled like a broken egg'. Inside the body 'that shook and jerked and smudged his pages' is someone who can celebrate moments of victory. Readers gain some sense of what it is like to live with a DISABILITY. It shows how John sees the world, and how the world sees him. This shifting point of view creates a great deal of tension. The reader is led to understand how everyone uniquely understands, and distorts, the world. CH, HMcC

Let The Celebrations Begin! (1991) Australian PICTUREBOOK by MARGARET WILD and JULIE VIVAS. It is a fictitious story – though based on an actual event in the Nazi concentration camp in Belsen – in which the narrator, Miriam, tells how she and the older women prepare for a children's party after liberation, when they will give toys improvised from scavenged cloth to the children in the camp. Wild's words combined with Vivas's illustrations show how, amidst unimaginable loss, individuals care for each other. The faded colours combined with generous white backgrounds emphasise the light, a hope against the horror. CH, HMcC

Letters from the Inside (1987) Controversial epistolary novel by Australian, JOHN MARSDEN, in which two 16-year-old girls make contact via a pen-pal advertisement. Mandy lives a normal suburban life – except for the increasingly threatening violence of her older brother – but Tracey is mysterious. Eventually Tracey's grandiose lies peel away, and she is gradually revealed as a murderer, incarcerated in a girl's prison. This intense book has drawn hostile responses from adults objecting to the grim implied ending, in which Mandy's brother has massacred her family, and Tracey is in psychological collapse. Undeniably a study of violence, it also sensitively explores the benefits and limitations of supportive friendship. NLR

Levick, W. M. Author of two popular South African stories, *Dry River Farm* (1955) and its sequel, *River Camp* (1960), which are typical of the period. They portray in mundane detail the lives of children and adults on an Eastern Cape farm and on holiday. The white people live out their traditional settler lives surrounded by African servants and farm labourers. Everyone is unfailingly good-humoured in a feudal community which is not threatened by the friendship of young Robin and Fikili, son of a labourer, since it is accepted that when Robin goes off to school Fikili will join the contented labourers on the farm. ERJ

Lewis, C(ecil) Day see *THE OTTERBURY INCIDENT*

Lewis, C(live) S(taples) 1898–1963 British author born in Belfast, the second son of Albert James Lewis and Flora Hamilton. As a young child, Lewis was known as Jack or Jacksie to his family and was already displaying the creativity and imagination which would produce the *Narnia* books; in the attic of their home at Little Lea, Lewis would write and illustrate stories set in the land of Boxen around a range of animal characters, while his brother Warren listened. His mother dying of cancer when he was ten, C.S. Lewis was sent away to Wynyard school in Hertfordshire, from which he later moved to Malvern; he spent two years studying with W.T. Kirkpatrick, his father's old headmaster, and after the war he went to Oxford University, where he read Greats. His first book, *Spirits in Bondage* (1919), a collection of lyrics, was published during his first year there. Lewis read for a second degree in English language and literature in 1923, after which he took up a fellowship at Magdalen College. He was to remain in Oxford for another 30 years, and it was during this period that he became friends with Charles Williams and J.R.R. TOLKIEN, and a member of the Inklings. Not only was their work to be mutually shaping, but, partly as a result of Tolkien's influence, Lewis would regain his abandoned Christianity. Although he described himself in *Surprised by Joy* (1955) as 'perhaps the most dejected and reluctant convert in all England', his writings all bear the stamp of a steadily professed faith and he may perhaps be described as one of the most influential Christian writers of the 20th century. Lewis later continued his academic career in Cambridge as Professor of Medieval and Renaissance English (1954).

He was married in 1956 to Joy Gresham (née Davidman), an American divorcee, who was, sadly, to die of cancer four years later (see *THE WIND ON FIRE*). Lewis himself died on 22 November 1963 as a result of kidney disease, at his home in Oxford.

Though perhaps best remembered for the *CHRONICLES OF NARNIA*, he was also the author of many academic and theological works; among the best-known of these are *The Pilgrim's Regress* (1933), *The Allegory of Love* (1936), *The Problem of Pain* (1940), *The Screwtape Letters* (1942), *Studies in Words* (1960) and *The Discarded Image* (1964). *Till We Have Faces* (1957) is a powerful version of the Cupid and Psyche myth, a contemplation of the many faces of love, and is readable, as are his other fictional works, as allegory. Lewis's other three novels, *Out of the Silent Planet*, (1938), *Perelandra* (1943) and *That Hideous Strength* (1945), are popularly thought of as belonging to the genre of SCIENCE FICTION, although there are elements of the fantastic and Arthurian legend present in them as well. They are, however, slightly uneven as a trilogy:

while each is powerful in its own way – *That Hideous Strength* in particular has terrifying moments – there is no truly overarching narrative structure which the three together work towards. Again, as with his other works of fiction, the trilogy is also significant on the level of Christian allegory. SA

Lewis, Hilda see NEGLECTED WORKS; see also TIME-SLIP FANTASY

Lewis, Naomi British critic and broadcaster, and historian of children's literature. Naomi Lewis is also an inspired writer and anthologist. Her own delicate conversation poem, *A Footprint in the Air*, is also the title poem of her telling selection of nature verse (1983). *Messages* (1985) is a classic of old and new poetry, and both books are enhanced by her introductions – original, memorable, accessible, entirely individual. Her translations (1981) of 12 of HANS CHRISTIAN ANDERSEN's stories are the best available, and her collection of DOLL STORIES, *The Silent Playmate* (1979), perfectly illustrated by HAROLD JONES, is full of treasures. The witty poems she wrote to complement Paul Stagg's cat paintings in *The Mardi Gras Cat* (1993) include the Ballet Cat – who insists 'none can outmatch my entrechat, pas de chat' – and the Convent Cat who sings the Magnificat. Lewis is a Fellow of the Royal Society of Literature and has won the ELEANOR FARJEON AWARD for her notable contribution to children's literature. AHa

see also PUBLISHING AND PUBLISHERS; REVIEWING AND REVIEWERS

Lewis, Shari 1934–98 Popular American entertainer and writer. Creator of Lamb Chop, the beloved woolly sock puppet with a pert if not saucy manner, Shari Lewis entertained generations. Lewis and Lamb Chop entered children's TELEVISION on 'The Captain Kangaroo Show'. Like Buffalo Bob and Howdy Doody, they delighted their audiences. Among Lamb Chop's friends were Charlie Horse and Hush Puppy. Master of magic and conductor of orchestras, the versatile Lewis hosted television shows including 'Shariland' and 'Lamb Chop's Play-Along'. She authored numerous books, such as the *Kids-Only Club Series*, and also wrote 'One-minute' series books such as the *One-Minute Bible Stories* (Old Testament). She also wrote books for young people about the Jewish heritage. An enthusiastic advocate of education, Lewis was a charismatic, generous and effervescent person who won numerous awards for her television performances, including Emmys. NV

Li'l Abner A comic strip originated by Al Capp [Alfred G. Caplin] in 1934, featuring Abner and Mammy and Pappy Yokum (from 'yokel' and 'hokum'). The adventures of bumpkins in Dogpatch and Lower Slobovia, *Li'l Abner* contains a secondary cast of characters such as Southern Senator Jack S. Phogbound and Bostonian Henry Cabbage Cod. The strip contributed three symbols to American mythology – Kickapoo Joy Juice with almost magical power, the Kigmy who enjoys being kicked, and the lovable, but controversial Schmoo. *Li'l Abner* is often read as a satire on American pretensions. It was filmed and made into a Broadway musical. KSB

see also COMICS, PERIODICALS AND MAGAZINES

libraries In North America children's services in libraries began first through the schools. Baskets of books, lectures and special instruction sessions were held in public libraries, with materials collected from the adult sections. Among the early librarians who worked to institute services for children were CAROLINE HEWINS, Samuel Green, Lutie Stearns and Minerva Sanders. As libraries opened their doors to children in the 1890s, books were set aside for their use, on a shelf, an alcove, and finally in a room of their own. The first children's rooms appeared in Brooklyn, Boston, Buffalo, Denver, Milwaukee, Minneapolis and Pittsburgh. After the turn of the century, the first children's librarians began to shape the field. The most famous was ANNE CARROLL MOORE, who served the first specially designed children's room at Pratt Institute, Brooklyn. Moore directed children's services for the New York Public Library (1906–41) and mentored many librarians, editors and writers in the making of American and Canadian children's literature and in the provision of services for children. LILLIAN SMITH learned her craft under Moore and became the most important pioneer in children's services in Canada. Moore's motto – 'the right book into the hands of the right child at the right time' – stresses the importance of book collections and library provision.

In England and Wales public library services for children were established following the 1850 Public Libraries Act. Manchester led the way in 1862 with its special reading room for boys, although initially this was established only because they 'caused so much inconvenience to grown-up readers'. Moral, educational and social improvement were the early leading motives for library authorities, but by 1914 leisure reading needs were more fully acknowledged and open access became common. Separate provision from adults increased steadily from then until the 1960s, when a Library Association survey identified 1,227 children's libraries. Today, every library authority provides a service for children. Developments in Scotland were particularly rapid during the 1960s, and by 1971 several library authorities had appointed specialist children's librarians, as had already happened elsewhere in the United Kingdom. School library services, provided by the public library as agents for the local education authority, were also important in supporting children's access to books and other materials. During the 1980s and 90s there were further developments, but also some setbacks in provision. Audio-visual materials and computers are now commonly available, and services to teenagers (as in Bradford and Renfrew) seek to redress reading reluctance. Promotional programmes are a standard feature, and issues of children's books have risen compared with those for adult readers. However, funding constraints have meant fewer children's specialists and diminished book budgets, even the closing of some specialist libraries. The impact of the 1988 Education Reform Act has also meant the demise or curtailment of several school library services.

Since the early 1940s the New Zealand School Library Service has supported the development of the country's school libraries in a number of ways, most recently in its School Library Development Programme (1994). The programme involves advisers working with schools to develop plans for their school library. Teacher-Librarianship training began in 1986 and over 10,000 teachers have studied the information literacy component of that training. While public library service to children began early in the 20th century, the resources of smaller libraries are understandably not always as current or varied as those in larger metropolitan areas. Larger libraries usually have separate children's areas and their materials are sourced from Britain, the United States, Canada, Australia and elsewhere. In general, the book stock of libraries of any size has tended to be less parochial than that encountered in the libraries of their northern-hemisphere counterparts. In 1995 the Library and Information Association of New Zealand Aotearoa adopted a Policy on Library Services to Children and Young People which stated that 'the curriculum needs of students are the chief focus and responsibility of the school library', to be 'supplemented by the more general resources of the public library'.

The first public library provision for children in Australia was the Children's Library which opened in Adelaide in 1915, and the first youth library service began in Adelaide in 1957. Prior to both, the first Mechanic's Institute or School of Arts to have a children's room was that at Port Adelaide in 1902. In the 19th century, expensive private schools included libraries in the advantages they offered. For the majority of Australian children the libraries of Sunday schools were important sources of leisure-time reading. Sunday school libraries remained influential well into the 20th century. The second half of the 20th century saw a steady expansion of children's services in the public library system. However, the single most important development in the last few decades has been the growth of school libraries. In the late 1960s, the Federal Government designated funds to achieve the goal of a substantial library in every school. Today most Australian children access their major library service from one of the nation's 10,000 school libraries

ME, MN, AL, BN, GG

Library and Information Association of New Zealand Aotearoa (LIANZA) Young People's Non Fiction Award see APPENDIX

Library of Congress see COLLECTIONS OF CHILDREN'S BOOKS

Liddell, Alice see *ALICE'S ADVENTURES IN WONDERLAND*; LEWIS CARROLL

Lielle's Spirit Bird (1995) PICTUREBOOK by Australian Aboriginal artist, Lisa Kennedy, whose poetic text and luminous pastel artworks, which mix traditional and contemporary indigenous techniques, trace the night time flight of Lielle, a young girl, with Tarrina the Albatross, her spirit bird, back in time and place, where she learns from her great-great-grandfather, Manalargenna, 'to share wisdom and spirit with the people with whom you live'. Set in Tasmania, the home of Kennedy's ancestors, this is a gentle and uplifting 'healing' story, in the tradition of those handed down over generations. JAP

lift-the-flap books see MOVABLE BOOKS; see also PUBLISHING AND PUBLISHERS

Light Beyond the Forest, The see KING ARTHUR; ROSEMARY SUTCLIFF

Light on Dum-y-at (1982) Adventure novel by Rennie McOwan. Gavin, an English boy, holidays with his Scottish uncle and aunt near Stirling in view of Dum-y-at, part of the Ochill Hills. Together with three young members of the Stewart clan, he foils an attempt by crooks to steal ancient silver treasures from his uncle. With information about survival in the wild, woodland lore, clan systems and even Pictish history, McOwan's style is sometimes intrusively didactic, while its main characters enjoy an alarming freedom from adult supervision. The adventures of the four friends continue in *The White Stag Adventure* (1986) and *The Day the Mountain Moved* (1994). MSS

Light Princess, The see GEORGE MACDONALD; see also PUBLISHING AND PUBLISHERS

Lightburn, Ron 1954– Canadian illustrator, born in Cobourg, Ontario, raised in (West) Vancouver, and educated at the Alberta College of Art. As a child, he produced and sold his own comic books. His favourite medium is coloured pencils on coloured paper, and his photographic style is realistic and atmospheric, emphasising the play of light and shadow. His first PICTUREBOOK project, ILLUSTRATIONS for Sheryl McFarlane's *Waiting for the Whales* (1991), received the 'triple crown': the Amelia Francis Howard-Gibbon Illustrator's Award, the Elizabeth Mrazik-Cleaver Canadian Picturebook Award and the Governor General's Literary Award for children's book illustration. Other picturebooks illustrated by Lightburn include Patti Farmer's *I Can't Sleep* (1992), Sheryl McFarlane's *Eagle Dreams* (1994) and Nan Gregory's *How Smudge Came* (1995), a Christmas story which won both the Sheila A. Egoff Children's Book Prize and the Mr Christie's Book Award and also became a TELEVISION film. *Driftwood Cove* (1998), written by his wife, Sandra Lightburn, featured another West Coast setting. He has designed more than two dozen book covers (see also COVER ART), including one for KIT PEARSON's award-winning *Awake and Dreaming* (1997) and several SCIENCE FICTION anthologies. MB

Lily Takes A Walk (1987) PICTUREBOOK by SATOSHI KITAMURA. Lily walks home in the dusk, oblivious of the transformed inanimate objects which threaten her, but protected by her watchful dog, Nicky. The 'threats' all explore ways of seeing and illustrate Kitamura's inventiveness in transformation and in playing the human game of anthropomorphising everything. The detailed unframed doublespreads repay careful reading for their observation and humour. There is a delightful touch near the end when Lily tells of her uneventful stroll home while Nicky recounts the real story in picture speech/bark balloons. AR

limerick A popular, five-line verse form with a regular rhythm and simple rhyme pattern (aabba), used in various ways to entertain and amuse young readers, and immortalised in EDWARD LEAR's *A BOOK OF NONSENSE* (1846). Lear, whose precursor was Richard Scrafton Sharpe (see *ANECDOTES AND ADVENTURES OF FIFTEEN GENTLEMEN*), wrote limericks which can appear rather tame today, as his tendency to more or less repeat first and last lines produced a flattening effect. Delivering a surprise or joke in the final line has now become customary. Limericks contain many features peculiar to comic verse in general: an emphasis on how words sound; tongue-twisters; bizarre occurrences; inventive language; and a zest for playing with the quirks and oddities of English spelling and pronunciation. JL

Linde, Friede see *THE SINGING GRASS*

Lindgren, Astrid see *PIPPI LONGSTOCKING* SERIES

Lindsay, Norman see *MAGIC PUDDING, THE*; see also A.B. PATERSON

Lindsay, (Nicholas) Vachel 1879–1931 American poet born in Springfield, Illinois. He travelled America, bringing poetry to the people and trading readings for bed and board, until he found wider literary recognition in 1913 with the publication of 'General William Booth Enters into Heaven'. He toured the professional recitation circuit in both the United States and Britain, where he received encouragement from W.B. Yeats. Believing strongly in the social function of poetry and the importance of appealing to all classes, Lindsay developed a form of verse which he called 'the Higher Vaudeville', intended for 'vocalisation' or chanting, and employing repetition, and a variety of incantatory, syncopated or melodic rhythms. He also lectured on the relation of poetry and art, and wrote an analysis of film as an educative medium, *The Art of the Moving Picture* (1915).

Lindsay was keen to encourage children's interest in poetry. In *Every Soul Is a Circus* (1929) he described the way he taught children through Poem Games, such as 'The Potato's Dance', using 'drumming, thumping and musical notation' which modulated into verbal expressiveness, 'reading that comes to the edge of chant' without losing its literary meaning. Other poems for children include 'The Ghost of the Buffaloes' and 'The Sea Serpent Chantey'. JFB

Lines, Kathleen see HAROLD JONES; see also CLASSICAL MYTHOLOGY; NURSERY RHYMES

Lingard, Joan (Amelia) Distinguished contemporary Scottish novelist best known for her *KEVIN AND SADIE* series of young adult novels. Working-class family life often forms the background to Lingard's novels, many of which are set in Scotland. Her central characters tend to be tough survivors, often given to provoking family rows but always loyal to one another. Her heroines are strong and spirited, generally with a sharp sense of humour. Maggie, Glaswegian heroine of the four *Maggie* novels, is tough and independent, determined to start her family on their own plumbing business yet but not to be drawn into it herself, so that she would have to give up her dream of a university education. Her background is in marked contrast to the family life of her Edinburgh boyfriend James Fraser. Although in some respects Maggie is seen to have more in common with James's parents than with her own, the relationship does not survive Maggie's fierce need for independence. Maggie's tough grandmother and her ancestors who lived during the time of the Clearances provide forceful role models. *Tug of War* (1989) and its sequel *Between Two Worlds* (1991) also feature a strong family, this time escaping from Latvia during the Second World War. The powerful story is based on Lingard's husband's family history. Other novels deal with more conventional teenage problems – the affect of divorce and stepfamilies in *Strangers in the House* (1981), not having a boyfriend in *The Gooseberry* (1978), or meeting a birth-father in *Lizzie's Leaving* (1995). Joan Lingard was awarded an MBE for services to literature in 1998. KA

Lingstrom, Freda see TELEVISION; see also *WATCH WITH MOTHER*

Linklater, Eric 1899–1974 A prolific British author of adult texts, Linklater wrote three children's novels, *The Wind on the Moon* (1944), *The Pirates in the Deep Green Sea* (1949) and *Karina With Love* (1958). The first of these is the best-known and was awarded the CARNEGIE MEDAL. It is about two sisters, Dinah and Dorinda, whose adventures include becoming kangaroos and rescuing their father from a Hitlerian tyrant, enlisting the anthropomorphic help of a puma and a falcon. The book evolved from a story which Linklater told his daughters whilst trying to entertain them. The novel shows great imagination and STORY-TELLING skill, whilst exploring the more profound themes of imprisonment and freedom. *The Wind on the Moon* and *The Pirates in the Deep Green Sea* were reissued in 2000 by Jane Nissen Books, an imprint dedicated to bringing back a number of children's books which have been out of print for many years. HR

Lion and Albert, The (1933) Verse monologue by Marriott Edgar (1880–1951), a British music-hall actor and writer, which was popularised by Stanley Holloway's famous performances. The story of a tragicomic visit to Blackpool Zoo by the Ramsbottom family is narrated with droll humour in a Northern accent. It contains echoes of HILAIRE BELLOC's 'Jim' who is eaten by a lion in *THE BAD CHILD'S BOOK OF BEASTS*. *Albert Comes Back* was written as a sequel. ML

Lion and the Unicorn, The (1977–) American critical and scholarly journal aiming to fill the need for further evaluation in the field of children's literature. Published three times a year by The Johns Hopkins University Press, it features essays in one thematic and two general issues. In the past, contributors have focused on such topics as BIOGRAPHY AND AUTOBIOGRAPHY for children, poetry by and for children, the FAIRY TALE, the child hero, the state of criticism, the junior novel, humour in children's books, and current trends. The journal also features reviews of recent critical and educational works and discussions of forgotten classics that 'deserve renewed attention'. KSB

Lion, The Witch and the Wardrobe, The see *CHRONICLES OF NARNIA SERIES*

Lionni, Leo 1910–99 American author of over 30 PICTUREBOOKS, utilising COLLAGE, marbling, and vibrant, colourful designs, all of which denote his professional career as a graphic artist. Born in Holland, Lionni travelled to the United States in the late 1930s, where he became a distinguished graphic artist, and the ideas and major themes emanating from his books may reflect his own struggles in the professional world to maintain a separate vision in the face of those who demand conformity. Lionni's characters are always animals – often mice – who teach subtle lessons about finding one's place in the world, needing others, finding contentment in nature, following one's dreams, belief in oneself as the 'magic' that grants wishes, risk-taking and danger as the price of freedom, and unity in strength. Several of his modern FABLES are Caldecott Honour Books: *Inch by Inch* (1960), *Swimmy* (1963), *Frederick* (1967), and *Alexander and the Wind-Up Mouse* (1969). Sometimes his characters are outsiders like Alexander, who wish or hope for acceptance; sometimes they are insiders like Frederick, who are introducing others to new and controversial ideas like the value and need of the artist in society. Often, like Swimmy, a tiny black fish who outsmarts the big tuna, they are heroes. NM

Lippincott, Joseph Wharton 1887–1976 American publisher and author of wildlife stories. A member of the Lippincott publishing family, he served as president and board chair of J.B. Lippincott for over 30 years, where he encouraged the production of a number of notable children's books. He was an avid sportsman, world traveller, and amateur naturalist, who collected wild animals for museums and eventually came to respect the creatures he had hunted. It was his love of the untamed environment that gave rise to his own stories for young readers, all realistic animal books. His *Wilderness Champion* (1944) is about a pup who is raised by a Canadian wolf and suffers from divided loyalties when he is brought back from the wild by his master. In *The Wahoo Bobcat* (1950), he describes the friendship between a young boy and a wild bobcat. *Old Bill, the Whooping Crane* (1958) combines the description of the habits of a whooping crane with a plea for wildlife conservation. His works, 17 books in all, were well received in their day and frequently praised for their lively style and scientific accuracy. DLR

see also ANIMALS IN CHILDREN'S FICTION

Lipsyte, Robert 1938– Columnist and writer of fiction. A New Yorker, Lipsyte has written for *The New York Times* and won an Emmy for his talk show on PBS

TELEVISION. His first novel was a boxing story, *The Contender* (1967), in which a fatherless young man, Alfred Brooks, trains diligently in a Harlem gym modelled upon that of Cus D'Amato. Along the way he resists gang pressure and develops a sense of responsibility, especially when one of his friends lands in jail. Ultimately, Alfred finds the challenge of helping others in the inner city a greater one than winning matches, but boxing has taught him that to be a sports champion one must first be a contender, and that success is a journey, not a destination. Another well-known title is *One Fat Summer* (1977), the story of an overweight boy, Bobby Marks, who mows yards and sheds both excess emotional baggage and excess weight in the process. *Free To Be Muhammad Ali* (1978) is one of Lipsyte's many sports BIOGRAPHIES. NV

Listen with Mother BBC radio programme devised in 1950 for those too young for *Children's Hour*, on the model of the Australian *Kindergarten of the Air*, and transmitted every weekday for 32 years. Post-war concern to re-establish traditional female roles, and new ideas about child development both contributed to the programme's format. Its soothing diet of songs, stories and NURSERY RHYMES was written and presented mainly by women, and its policy of repetition was based on educational theories about how young children best learn and enjoy. Certain series of stories, for example *My Naughty Little Sister*, were transmitted frequently over the years, and anthologies were published with introductions by radio celebrities such as Harry Secombe. Although it rapidly became a national institution (at least in middle-class households), as did its catchphrase, 'Are you sitting comfortably? Then I'll begin,' it increasingly lost audience to TELEVISION, first to *Watch with Mother*, which had been launched in the same year, and to commercial channels from 1955. Once its regular slot was abandoned in the 70s the number of listeners declined still further and it finally went off air in 1982, replaced for a time by a five-minute *Listening Corner*. SG

literary theory and children's books see CRITICAL APPROACHES TO CHILDREN'S BOOKS

literature within children's literature Some of the most interesting writing for children is marked by the opening up of a creative dialogue between what might be called a 'host' work and the works that come to 'guest' within it. At the most basic level, the dialogue works to create a sense of extra-dimensionality in the host text. Knowing what fictional characters read amplifies them for the real reader, informing us not just of their nature or their tastes but also of what they might become through their interaction with the guest work(s). In *LITTLE WOMEN* Jo March's fondness for the works of de la Motte Fouqué, *Sintram*, *Undine* and *Aslauga's Knight*, mark her as a Romantic, and we may trace the influence of her reading in her early writings: 'The Phantom Hand' obviously denotes the gothic/fantastic.

Guest works may also illuminate their hosts in more subtle ways, by suggesting parallels between situations in both works. For instance, Jane Eyre's favourite reading, *GULLIVER'S TRAVELS*, points the theme of the outsider (the midget in the giant's world and vice versa); both Jane's sense of alienation and her helplessness as a child in a world ruled by adults are forcefully brought home to the reader by means of the literature in which she is absorbed.

Literature within children's literature may enable the comprehension not just of self, but also of otherness. In NOEL STREATFEILD'S *BALLET SHOES*, Petrova, acting the part of Myltyl in Maeterlinck's *BLUE BIRD*, learns from inhabiting the part what it is to be hungry and poor. Alternatively, a guest work may aid the reader-figure within the host work to comprehend and cope with her/his own situation through detecting the correspondences or differences between the situation in the text-within-the-text and the fictional reader's own situation. In JEAN LITTLE'S *Mama's Going to Buy You a Mockingbird*, the protagonist's dying father wants him to read KIPLING'S *KIM*, an insistence which the child cannot understand. Little wisely leaves the meaning of the guest text unexplicated, understatement both leaving room for manoeuvre and protecting the integrity of the guest text in its refusal to simplify its meaning by reducing it to therapeutic formula. We may perhaps infer, however, that a part of what the dying man wishes to give his son as legacy through *Kim* is the understanding that to be fatherless is not necessarily to be helpless and that self, in the end, is not an inheritance but a construction. In ANTONIA FOREST'S *The Readymade Family* (see *MARLOW* series), Nicola Marlow reads the emotional dynamics of her family situation into Austen's *Persuasion*, and *Persuasion* into the complexities of that situation, demonstrating the symbiotic nature of guest and host texts.

Further examples of literature within children's literature may be found in NOEL STREATFEILD'S *The Painted Garden*, which engages with FRANCES HODGSON BURNETT'S *THE SECRET GARDEN*, and Antonia Forest's *Peter's Room* which hosts the BRONTË siblings' tales of Gondal and Angria. (The Brontës themselves, interestingly, are more often referred to in children's literature than are their works, inspiring not only *Peter's Room* but also JANE GARDAM'S *THE SUMMER AFTER THE FUNERAL*, GARY KILWORTH'S *The Brontë Girls*, and PAULINE CLARKE'S *The Twelve and the Genii*.) Forest's entire Marlow series introduces a whole host of other books, such as Mary Renault's *The*

Mask of Apollo, Dudley Pope's books on Lord Ramage, C.S. Forester's *Hornblower* series, GODDEN's *THE GREENGAGE SUMMER*, Baroness Orczy's *SCARLET PIMPERNEL*, D.K. Broster's *The Flight of the Heron*, MARK TWAIN's *The Prince and the Pauper*, *WORZEL GUMMIDGE*, and works by TOLKIEN and SAYERS. Jo Bettany of ELINOR M. BRENT-DYER's *CHALET SCHOOL* series is a serious reader, perhaps not surprisingly since she later becomes a writer herself, and the series is filled with references to other books and writers, including the *ELSIE DINSMORE* series, the poetry of Alfred Noyes and ELEANOR FARJEON's *MARTIN PIPPIN* books. Laura Rambotham, in Henry Handel Richardson's *The Getting of Wisdom*, struggles to make sense of Ibsen's *Doll's House*. KIPLING uses Farrar's *Eric: or Little by Little* as a 'negative paradigm' in *STALKY & CO.*, and NESBIT's fictional children in turn refer, though much more favourably, to Kipling's work, less so to *Ministering Children* and other pious 19th-century writings for children. Continuing the web of cross-referencing, EDWARD EAGER and C.S. LEWIS refer in their books overtly and covertly to Nesbit's work, which indeed is one of the most popular bodies of writing referred to in children's fiction. SA

lithography A printing process in which an image is drawn on a porous surface, originally limestone, with a wax crayon or pencil. The surface is wetted and oil-based ink applied. The wet surface repels the ink, which sticks only to the areas marked by the crayon, and prints can be taken. The main advantage of lithography is that it is a cheap medium for reproducing colour. The term chromolithography refers to the process by which an artist's original is redrawn on a number of lithographic plates by the printer, one for each colour. The colours may be printed over a black outline from a PROCESS ENGRAVING. European book ILLUSTRATION was influenced by widespread use of the technique in Russian mass-produced books for children in the 1920s and 30s. Successful examples in England included EDWARD ARDIZZONE's *LITTLE TIM* books, CATHERINE HALE's *ORLANDO* series and most importantly the *PUFFIN PICTURE BOOKS* in Britain and the *GOLDEN BOOKS* in the US. GCB

Little, Jean 1932– Canadian author, born in Taiwan. Little attended the University of Toronto and, prior to becoming a full-time writer, was a special-education teacher. The author of more than 20 books for children, her first novel, *Mine for Keeps* (1962), was followed by *Home from Far* (1965), about a child who must adapt to physical problems. Little's work includes PICTUREBOOKS, novels, poetry, BIOGRAPHY AND AUTOBIOGRAPHY. Her themes include family displacement, physical and emotional problems, disruption and alienation. Little admits to being intrigued with the subject of orphaned, unwanted and foster children. *The Belonging Place* (1997) describes a Scottish orphan's search for a place to belong. The Gordon clan and Elspet set out on a journey to Upper Canada where they clear a homestead – which later becomes Little's historic home in Elora, Ontario. Little has won many awards, including the Canada Council's Children's Literature Prize in 1977; her autobiography *Little by Little* (1987) was chosen as a 1988 Boston Globe-Horn Book Honour Book. Jean Little and the illustrator Johnny Wales were shortlisted for Mr Christie's Book Award for *Gruntle Pig Takes Off* (1997). The ILLUSTRATIONS were also shortlisted for the Governor General's Award. MRS

***Little Bear* series** see ELSE MINARIK; URSULA NORDSTROM; see also ANIMALS IN FICTION

Little Black Sambo, The Story of (1899) Written and illustrated by Helen Bannerman (1862–1946), this miniature PICTUREBOOK tells how the hero of the title set off one day into the jungle carrying a green umbrella and wearing blue trousers, purple shoes and a red coat. He soon loses all these to some tigers he meets, each of which has to be bought off with a gift. The tigers start quarrelling among themselves about who looks the smartest, finally chasing each other round a tree so fast they melt into butter. Little Black Sambo scoops this into a pot and returning home gives it to his mother Black Mumbo. She uses it to make 169 pancakes for her son, all of which he consumes. Sequels to this story followed. *Little Black Mingo* (1901), *Little Black Quibba* (1902), *Little Black Quasha* (1908) and *Little Black Bobtail* (1910). On the author's death, *Little White Squibba* was found among her papers and finally published in 1966. But it was always *Little Black Sambo* that proved the most popular, and this story eventually came under attack in the 1970s. Librarians complained that parents from the New Commonwealth detested the name Sambo, often used for racial insults. Other critics disliked the hero's exaggerated Negroid features, which they saw as close to insulting caricature. While older readers rallied to its defence, many libraries and bookshops gradually stopped stocking this book because of the controversy it continued to raise so long as it was widely available. NT

Little Book-Room, The (1955) Collection of 27 short stories by ELEANOR FARJEON which won both the CARNEGIE and ANDERSEN AWARDS. As with most of Farjeon's work, one senses here a kindness and affection for children manifest in the care shown to them in the stories. The tales, simply written, contain an unobtrusive and understated wisdom, a principle which becomes a theme in 'The Tims', in which a farmer with gypsies in his barn goes to seek the advice of a family known for its wisdom and is referred to the baby who says nothing, which 'advice' he follows to his benefit. SA

'Little Briar Rose' see 'SLEEPING BEAUTY'

Little Brown Mouse stories, The (from 1950) Series of 14 stories for young readers by ALISON UTTLEY, mainly about the adventures of Snug and Serena, who live at the 'Rose and Crown' – a tiny inn 'down the lane, sheltered by a wild rose bush [and] hidden in the bank'. The books are similar in design to the *LITTLE GREY RABBIT* series, but illustrated by Katherine Wigglesworth. They demonstrate the author's extraordinary capacity for recycling her favourite characters and ideas (gypsy hedgehogs, robin redbreast the postman, cowslip-picking) which she more successfully realised in *THE LITTLE GREY RABBIT* series. VW

***Little Colonel* series** A series of 12 girls' stories by Annie Fellows Johnston (1863–1931), which chronicles the lives of a Kentucky girl and her friends. In *The Little Colonel* (1895) Lloyd Sherman, the small daughter of a Southern lady and a Yankee officer, seems to represent a post-Civil-War reconciliation of North and South, whether she is playing with (properly subordinate) 'little darkies' or reuniting her parents with the long-estranged Old Colonel, her crusty Kentucky grandfather. As the series proceeds, however, the hot-tempered tyke swiftly metamorphoses into a model of Southern girlhood. Lloyd is married off at the end of *The Little Colonel's Knight Comes Riding* (1907), though the series continues with three books about 'the Little Colonel's chum', Mary Ware. In her day, many considered Johnston the successor to LOUISA MAY ALCOTT; the series was enormously popular, and thousands of girls aspired to be like the beautiful, noble, high-spirited Little Colonel. A generation later, the 1935 film of *The Little Colonel* gave Shirley Temple one of her best roles. SR

Little Engine That Could, The A story known to generations of Americans about a formidable little engine and her famous lines, 'I think I can' and 'I thought I could', which continues to evoke recognition and delight in children and adults alike.

However, the source of the story remains a mystery. Some believe it to have originated in 19th-century Germany; indeed, the phrases 'I think I can' and 'I knew I could' are found in the opera-singer Lotte Lehmann's autobiography (1938), referring to a story told her in the early 1890s when she was a little girl. In America, two READING SCHEMES of the 1890s were said to include *The Little Steam Engine* and early in the 1900s the story's theme of perseverance was used in lectures, graduation speeches and political rallies. The story appeared in print in 1910: *The Pony Engine* by Mary C. Jacobs was published in *The Kindergarten Review* in September, telling of a little freight car filled with coal waiting to be pulled over the hill to keep the people in the valley warm during the winter. The stalwart little engine was accompanied by the lines 'I think I can' and 'I thought I could'. In 1912 there appeared *The Little Switch Engine* by Frances M. Ford and in 1914 *The Royal Engine* by J.T. Stocking, both with similar themes and repetitive phrases.

In 1916 Mabel C. Bragg retold *The Pony Engine* for a magazine she edited, called *Something To Do*; it was later published in volume I of *My Bookhouse: In the Nursery* (1920), edited by Olive Beaupré Miller, as *The Little Engine That Could*. Bragg had never claimed to be the original author; she believed the story might have come from WILLIAM DEAN HOWELLS's *The Pony Engine and the Pacific Express* (1882), which certainly told of a high-spirited little engine, though there the similarity ends.

In the 1920s the publishers Platt and Munk purchased the story from George H. Doran and tried unsuccessfully to find the author. In 1930 they published *The Little Engine That Could* with illustrations by LOIS LENSKI and with a house pseudonym, Watty Piper, as its author. The fictitious Piper continues as the author today, with Mabel C. Bragg's name included with the copyright information, in small print. The text had been changed slightly: Bragg's story takes place at Christmas and the 'Train-of-Cars' carries only toys, whereas the 1930 version dropped the holiday setting, described the toys and added healthy foods for the 'good little boys and girls on the other side of the mountain'. The 'chugs', 'puffs' and 'ding-dongs' along with 'I think I can' and 'I thought I could' were as they remain today.

In October 1953 *Time Magazine* announced that the original author had been found. It was the same Frances M. Ford – now aged 100 – who had written *The Little Switch Engine* in 1912. The publishers Grosset and Dunlap (who had acquired the Platt and Munk imprint) signed a contract with her and it was to be published in 1954. However, Mrs Ford remained fairly silent as her relatives persisted with vigour to gain recognition for her. She had indeed written the story of a little switch engine as 'Uncle Nat' for a children's newsletter. Curiously, the promised publication never took place.

Platt and Munk brought out a new edition of their book in 1954, illustrated by George and Doris Hauman, and in 1955 they announced a reward of $1,000 to be paid to 'anyone who can furnish authentic proof conclusively establishing the identity of the original author and creator of the underlying story' upon which *The Little Engine That Could* was based. A trio of professionals was named as 'the little jury that will', and many letters were received. However, by February, 1956, 'proof of ultimate authorship' had not been provided and the money was divided among three people: Mary C. Jacobs, who had submitted an original page from her 1910 story; a librarian, who had sent in a copy of the same story; and a person who provided a Sunday school publication of 1910, with the story *Thinking One Can*.

The 60th anniversary of the book was celebrated in 1990 following the sale of millions of copies over the years. Along with the several editions of the original story in various formats are new sequels, an *ABC* and a COUNTING BOOK, as well as records, tapes and videos. The story maintains its popularity and the mystery of its authorship continues. PDS

Little Fire Engine, The see EDWARD ARDIZZONE; see also GRAHAM GREENE

Little Folks Immensely popular and long-lived British children's magazine, issued monthly from 1875 until 1933, also sold twice-yearly in a total of 117 bound volumes. Many young readers had their collections bound inexpensively, but those bound in the publishers' special pictorial boards – often with an additional coloured frontispiece – are particularly valued today by collectors. These covers vary in style from Victorian opulence in gold and deep colour to beautiful Art Nouveau designs, and eventually to bright comical pictures by LAWSON WOOD. Fewer summer volumes survive, which suggests that additional winter issues were produced for Christmas. *Little Folks* had regular contributions by some of the best illustrators of the period, including S.B. Pearse (see *AMELIARANNE*), ARTHUR RACKHAM, Harry Rountree, WALTER CRANE, Gordon Browne, MABEL LUCY ATTWELL and Ernest Aris. Among its writers were Elsie J. Oxenham, MRS MOLESWORTH and Bessie Marchant. During the Victorian period a separate *Little Folks Annual*, with different contents, was published in time for Christmas.

Despite its title, the ages of the children whose letters were published indicate that it appealed mostly to readers aged 8–15. Its regular features included a letters page, answers to readers' questions, and special items in a larger font for 'Very Little Folk'. Many issues included a classical 'Novel in a Nutshell'. There were ADVENTURE and SCHOOL STORIES, poems, information articles, puzzle pages and competitions. There were amusing surprises: some volumes, for example, had sequences of RUNNING STORIES in tiny cartoons placed in the bottom corner of the right-hand pages. Throughout the 1930s there were up-to-date features

'A four-in-hand.' Illustration from *Little Folks* (1892).

on 'Films of the Month', with retold plots supported by black-and-white stills. In 1882 the magazine founded the Little Folks Humane Society 'for the purpose of inculcating Kindness towards Animals'; by 1884, there were 50,000 young members. Readers of the magazine also endowed money to maintain a number of cots at the East London Hospital for Children, and regularly donated money and gifts to the Little Folks Home at Bexhill-on-Sea.

Little Folks was distinguished by a genuine editorial commitment to provide interest, variety and high standards for young readers, and is unusual among children's periodicals in that it maintained its high quality even in its last few issues. The editorial tone completely avoided the heavy moralising associated with some other Victorian and Edwardian periodicals for the young, and – especially during the editorship of H. Darkin Williams in its final years – both the magazine and the bound volumes had a distinctively vigorous and jazzy appeal. VW

Little Goody Two Shoes see JOHN NEWBERY; see also ILLUSTRATION IN CHILDREN'S BOOKS; SCHOOL STORIES; ISAIAH THOMAS

Little Grey Men, The (1942) and its sequel *Down the Bright Stream* (1948) were written and illustrated by the

British author 'B.B.' [D.J.Watkins-Pitchford] and were popular with young readers for more than 20 years. The first tells the story of three gnomes – the last gnomes left in Britain – who set off on a quest to find their missing brother. Although their adventures are recounted in an engaging and sometimes gripping manner, what really interested the writer were his descriptions of wildlife in an English landscape. The novel owes a good deal to *THE WIND IN THE WILLOWS* and indeed makes a better use of the god Pan than KENNETH GRAHAME did in his chapter 'The Piper at the gates of Dawn', for B.B.'s Pan – who makes it clear that he has 'come back once more' before leaving England for good – makes a crucial contribution to the narrative. In *Down the Bright Stream* these valedictory hints become more explicit: the gnomes, having decided that the beauty of Britain is being destroyed by Mortals, set off on a journey to Ireland, where little people are welcomed. However, B.B.'s messages about the environment are mixed, rooted in a conservative hunting-and-fishing ethos that many contemporary young environmentally-aware readers would find unacceptable. VW

Little Grey Rabbit A series of 34 stories (and four play-scripts) by ALISON UTTLEY. The first, *The Squirrel, the Hare and the Little Grey Rabbit*, was published in 1929 and the last, *Hare and the Rainbow*, in 1975. The books are for very young readers and were for many years as popular as stories by BEATRIX POTTER. They are still being reissued in various formats and in 2000 a children's TELEVISION series was devoted to them. They were illustrated by MARGARET TEMPEST until 1967, when Katherine Wigglesworth took over for the last five titles. The books were in hard covers with the text in blue ink. Every story had the same ENDPAPER design, an illustration of Little Grey Rabbit's steep-roofed cottage at the edge of the forest, with its square of garden, washing blowing on the line, and windows open to the fresh air. Margaret Tempest's ILLUSTRATIONS used mostly conventional square or round frames; her colouring was especially good at suggesting the open-air quality of weather and season, and in her representations of anthropomorphic characters she used posture and gesture to great effect to suggest feeling and comedy in this miniature world of imagined animal life.

The early stories have a dark quality. The first opens with the words: 'A long time ago there lived in a little house on the edge of the wood, a Hare, a Squirrel, and a little Grey Rabbit. The Hare, who wore a blue coat on weekdays and a red coat on Sundays, was a conceited fellow. The Squirrel, who wore a brown dress on weekdays, and a yellow dress on Sundays, was proud.' Little Grey Rabbit, however, is kind, clever and brave. She does the housework and shopping for her lazy companions, but when they are captured by the Weasel and she rescues them, they are so grateful that they promise to reform. Little Grey Rabbit, in seeking advice from Wise Owl, is obliged to let him bite off her tail – painfully – for use as a doorknocker. Such rather startling and inconsequential savagery is reminiscent of Beatrix Potter, and it was a feature of the next two stories, especially *The Great Adventure of Hare* (1931), a grimly comic tale of Hare's capture by Mr Fox. Several incidents in the later stories, and even some of the phrasing, were adapted from Uttley's famous autobiographical novel, *THE COUNTRY CHILD*. Throughout the series, her economical prose and Margaret Tempest's clear pastoral illustrations perfectly combine to evoke a simultaneously recognisable and mysterious 'other-world' of secure cosiness surrounded by a country-side full of surprise and danger. After Hare's escape from the Fox's tumbledown den, for example, he races in a state of terror through the wood and the story ends on a lyrical note of homecoming and safe arrival: 'as he ran out of the trees he saw a candle burning in the window of the little house, and he shouted for joy'. This unpretentious language is matched by a simple framed illustration of the distant cottage, its windows shining in the darkness under a sky full of stars.

As new stories were written, the series became less like the Beatrix Potter tales and more like the imaginative world of *THE WIND IN THE WILLOWS*. Uttley created an entire animal community, with Hedgehog the Milkman, Moldy Warp the Mole, Robin Redbreast the Postman, Water Rat, Wise Owl, Badger, and a host of other characters, many of whom have an entire story devoted to them. The social order is kindly but hierarchical and conservative, and the animals have the characteristics traditionally associated with them: the Fox is cunning, the Owl is wise, and the Badger is an eccentric historian. At the centre of the stories are Squirrel (wild, brave and determined), Hare (well-intentioned and foolish) and Little Grey Rabbit (kind-hearted, hard-working and dependable). As the series progressed, the domestic and pastoral atmosphere was sustained but humour and nostalgia came to predominate over danger. There was a sharp moral sense in some: when Rat burgles their house, Squirrel ties a knot in his tail as a punishment, and this knot drags heavily behind him until, in *The Knot Squirrel Tied* (1937), Wise Owl gives him a severe lesson in its meaning and it gradually lightens as the Rat turns over a new leaf and turns to work instead of thieving. Many of the tales have an evocative dreamlike appeal in which the magic of life in the country has a hint of strangeness or an edge of danger. In *Little Grey Rabbit's Christmas* (1940), for example, Hare goes sledging at midnight but runs away in terror, frightened by his own moon-shadow. In *Hare Joins the Home Guard* (1941), the animal community has to defend itself against invasion by an army of weasels. When the enemy is defeated, the story ends with Grey Rabbit carving COURAGE! FIGHT FOR FREEDOM on 'the great oak tree which grew by the Roman Road, so that they would always remember' – an unobtrusive clustering of images and ideas expressing for very young readers the ideology and patriotic symbolism of wartime Britain.

Because the series was written over almost half a century, the contemporary setting of the early titles eventually became a historical one. Margaret Tempest's illustrations of cottage interiors were based on authentic country life of the 1920s and 1930s, with an open fire in the grate, a dresser against the wall, a blue enamel bread-bin, gingham curtains and potted geraniums on the window-sill. In the later stories a rather self-conscious foreword explained to a generation of incredulous readers that in Grey Rabbit's house there was no electricity or gas, and that water came from an outside spring. The emphasis now was on old country traditions such as lacemaking and May Day processions. But it would be misleading to suggest that the appeal of these stories lies only in a nostalgic evocation of a lost rural community life. Alison Uttley's STORYTELLING was spare, disciplined and capable of subtle effects of surprise, comedy and fear, and was precisely complemented by the illustrations of Margaret Tempest. VW

***Little House* series** Nine novels by LAURA INGALLS WILDER, published in the United States between 1932 and 1943 (UK, 1956–65), and further sequels. *Little House in the Big Woods* (1932/56) establishes Pa, Laura's father, as the central character, a place that he retains until usurped by Laura in *These Happy Golden Years*. Pa stands for home and security; without Pa and his fiddle-playing Laura's world is empty and potentially life-threatening. The novel covers a single year, and this structure provides a safe and enclosed setting for the events. Between descriptions of everyday life are interspersed the stories told by Pa of his boyhood. These are mostly moral tales for children but they also establish a clear picture of male dominance. *Farmer Boy* (1933/65), the story of Laura's husband Almanzo's boyhood in New York State, has a similar closed structure, but describes a life of plenty in stark contrast to Laura's childhood. The theme of growing up which underlies the entire series is established in this book. As in *Little House in the Big Woods*, the importance of home and family is continually stressed.

The physical journeys of Laura's childhood begin in *Little House on the Prairie* (1935/57). The family moves from the security of the Big Woods into Indian Territory. The home, whether it be the covered wagon, log house, dugout or town store, now becomes the focal point around which the characters move. Without Pa there is no home, but it is Ma who makes the home a place of happiness and industry through the symbolic placing of the china shepherdess on the mantelpiece. *Little House on the Prairie* also deals with a larger concept – the American dealings with the Native Americans. It is this aspect of the book that has led critics to regard it as Wilder's best. *On the Banks of Plum Creek* (1937/58) sees the family settling on a new and promising piece of land with the prospect of a good harvest. Laura and her sister Mary make their first excursions into social life. Wilder is torn between depicting the traditional ideal of womanhood as characterised by Ma, and the ideal of the new independent woman with whom she clearly identifies. When a plague of grasshoppers destroys their crops, Pa leaves home to find work and immediately the family is depressed and lonely and it is only his return that brings happiness back to them.

By the Shores of Silver Lake (1939/61) opens with the darkest period of the entire series. A series of misfortunes results in debt, and illness leaves Mary blind. The country is also described as worn out, as the many new settlers have driven the game away. Both Pa and Laura feel a strong affinity with the land which itself battles against man to assert its individuality, a quality much admired by Wilder. In this book, man is beginning to tame the hostile forces of nature through the building of railways and the subsequent settling of the land. Laura gains in maturity and awareness of the advantages and disadvantages of this inevitable process. It is at this point that the theme of becoming separate and alone becomes important, a change that will come inevitably to all but is thrust upon Mary by the fact of her blindness. Nature again intervenes in the lives of the family in *The Long Winter* (1940/62). Laura now leaves her childhood behind and takes on a more adult role within the family as she begins to see their situation in a wider context. She resolves to become a schoolteacher to gain independence for herself and for Mary. The family almost starves to death and it is only the resourcefulness of Pa and Ma, and their attitude of grim determination, that enables the family to survive. Laura's future husband Almanzo is introduced as an adult in this book and his character and attributes are quickly established, as he gradually replaces Pa as the idealised male role model.

The remaining two books, *Little Town on the Prairie* (1941/63) and *These Happy Golden Years* (1943/64) are much lighter in tone. Although nature still occasionally asserts itself, it is no longer the powerful force that it was in the earlier books: the emphasis is now on the problems associated with social interaction. Laura has to deal with a variety of social situations, including conflict with the schoolteacher Miss Eliza Wilder and the jealous Nellie Oleson. She also begins her courtship with Almanzo. The book ends with Laura becoming a schoolteacher herself, a sign of her passing from child to adult as she achieves independence and responsibility. *These Happy Golden Years* affirms Laura's ability to survive both physical and emotional hardship. She returns to the family home for reassurance, but home is no longer the centre of her life. The friendship between Laura and Almanzo blossoms into love and the series ends with Laura's marriage and the final departure from the family home.

The First Four Years (1971/73) accurately describes the first years of Laura's married life. It was a time of considerable hardship and loss, including the death of her infant son, continual crop failure and consequent debts, debilitating illness and a fire which destroyed their home. The tone of the book, which is increasingly pessimistic, reflects this and is therefore very different from that of the previous books. The character of Laura appears significantly changed, from a person who is excited by life's challenges to one who is angrily ready to give in when faced with overwhelming unfairness. The book was published posthumously, though without any revision or input from her daughter Rose, and this may also account for some of its noticeable difference from the rest of the series. After seeing *The First Four Years* through the press, Roger Lea MacBride, Laura's executor, went on to write four novels about Rose, beginning with *Little House on Rocky Ridge* (1993). These books are accurate in their description of biographical events and MacBride makes a commendable effort to match Laura's tone and style. In contrast *Little House in Brookfield*, (1996) by Maria D. Wilkes, which describes the early life of Laura's mother, Caroline Quiner, fails stylistically and the book comes over as flat and episodic. ASTH

Little Lord Fauntleroy Novel by FRANCES HODGSON BURNETT, first serialised in *ST NICHOLAS MAGAZINE* and then published in book form in 1886. Cedric Errol, a young boy living on the edge of poverty in New York, suddenly learns that he is the heir to an English Earl. Travelling to his grandfather's castle, Cedric shows his trusting and democratic nature in his dealing with servants and farmers, and begins to win the love of his proud and unfeeling grandfather before the appearance of an unexpected rival claimant brings the story to a dramatic climax. The book became immensely popular, particularly after a stage version was produced, and illustrations of the hero (by REGINALD BIRCH) inspired a mania for dressing children in Fauntleroy suits of black velvet with lace collars all over America and Europe. The story has been frequently filmed, and its worldwide and enduring popularity has made it a cultural phenomenon. Although her sentimentality and use of coincidences may be criticised, Mrs Burnett handles the elements of popular fiction with considerable skill, particularly the relationship between Cedric and his grandfather. In Marghanita Laski's words, *Little Lord Fauntleroy* is 'the best version of the CINDERELLA story in modern idiom that exists'. DB

***Little Maid* series** An American series of historical novels by Alice Turner Curtis (1860–1958) written between the 1910s and the early 1930s. Intended for girls between 7 and 12, the *Little Maid* stories take place during the American Revolution, in settings ranging from Maine to New Orleans. Each story, according to the jacket copy, 'relates the adventures of a quick-witted, resourceful American girl at a critical time in the history of our country'. In *A Little Maid of Old Philadelphia* (1919), for example, Ruth Pennell ventures into the headquarters of the occupying British army in search of her lost dog, meets Major André, and overhears some important information to pass on to General Lafayette. Girl readers enjoyed the mixture of heroic exploits not beyond their reach with cosy details of daily life and quaint Colonial customs – very similar to that of the *AMERICAN GIRLS* SERIES today. The series' success also attests to the influence of the Colonial Revival (then at its peak) on HISTORICAL FICTION for children; while Curtis also wrote a *Frontier Girl* series and a *Yankee Girl Civil War* series, the two dozen *Little Maids* were more numerous and much more popular. SRI

Little Nemo see WINSOR MCCAY; see also ILLUSTRATION IN CHILDREN'S BOOKS; *IN THE NIGHT KITCHEN*

'Little Orphan Annie' see JAMES WHITCOMB RILEY

Little Orphan Annie A comic strip by Harold Gray, originating in the *Chicago Tribune* (1924). Annie with her blank eyes is accompanied by her highly intelligent dog Sandy. Her protectors are Daddy Warbucks, richest man in the world, and his assistant, an oriental giant, but they are often unavailable. Annie's scrapes range from murder plots in the countryside to city warfare, but her presence gives the advantage to the virtuous and courageous. Probably the most famous of comic–strip tykes, Annie defeats unbelievably evil villains and finds unbelievably good friends. The story became the stage and film musical *Annie*. KSB

Little Pretty Pocket-Book, A see JOHN NEWBERY; see also ILLUSTRATION IN CHILDREN'S BOOKS; *JACK THE GIANT KILLER*; PUBLISHING AND PUBLISHERS; ISAIAH THOMAS

Little Prince, The (1943) Much-loved story written and illustrated by the French aviator and existentialist writer Antoine de Saint-Exupéry (1900–44). *Le Petit Prince* has been translated into many languages, the first English translation – by Katherine Woods – appearing in 1945. The narrator, an aviator whose plane has crashed in the Sahara desert, meets the Little Prince, who greets him with a request for a drawing of a sheep. The Little Prince is the ruler and only occupant of a tiny asteroid the size of a house, on which he has a beloved flower in danger of being overwhelmed by invasive baobab trees; he needs the sheep to graze the baobab seedlings (but not to eat the flower). In the conversation that follows, the Little Prince tells of his travels to six other small planets, and of his encounters with a Fox and a Snake. It is the fox who tells him what lovers of Saint-Exupéry regard as the central great secret: 'It is only with the heart that one can see rightly. What is essential is invisible to the eye.' This conviction underlies the Romantic philosophy implicit in the work, along with frequent disparaging comments on the 'great people' who are incapable of understanding it in the way that children can. The Prince's final disappearance – falling soundlessly onto the sand – remains a mystery: has he died or returned to his asteroid? *The Little Prince* has been adapted for stage and film and has a number of websites. A new translation by Alan Wakeman appeared in 1995, illustrated by MICHAEL FOREMAN. VW

Little Princess, A (1905) Acclaimed novel by FRANCES HODGSON BURNETT which originally saw life in book form as *SARA CREWE, OR WHAT HAPPENED AT MISS MINCHIN'S*. It had first been written by Hodgson Burnett as a play, and was produced in 1902, originally entitled *A Little Unfairy Princess*. While at school, Sara Crewe, a rich pupil, suddenly finds herself destitute upon her father's death and is made to drudge for Miss Minchin, her erstwhile schoolmistress. The power of her imagination, however, enables her to transcend the unpleasant conditions of her life, and the development of her inner, imaginal, identity as a princess helps her shape a resistance to Miss Minchin's attempt to break her. Eventually, it is discovered that Sara is an heiress to a considerable fortune and she is adopted by a friend of her father. While the imagination and inner life are presented as valuable throughout the text, it is also true that they seem to gain in force and intensity when material goods are in abeyance; in other words they function as substitutes for absent things. If this is so, then the restitution of the material at the end of the text would displace the imagination from the central position it has enjoyed, as its substitutive function has now become unnecessary. Nonetheless, the values espoused in *A Little Princess* are good ones: the social aspect of the work is particularly interesting, the heroine not merely shown as benevolently distributing charity to the poor, but as having experienced poverty and misery at first hand. SA

Illustration by MARGERY GILL for the Puffin edition of *A Little Princess* by Frances Hodgson Burnett.

'Little Red Cape' see 'LITTLE RED RIDING HOOD'

Little Red Hen, The see MUSIC AND STORY; see also *GOLDEN BOOKS*

'Little Red Riding Hood' One of the most enduring traditional tales, which continues to fascinate young children and academics alike. The story exists in countless illustrated editions – Red Riding Hood may well be the world's most published heroine. She appears on records, in advertisements, greeting cards, political cartoons, as a collectible piece of Staffordshire pottery, and on CD-ROM. The plot varies. Sometimes the little girl joins her grandmother in the wolf's stomach and the tale is done; the first printed version (CHARLES PERRAULT, 1697) stopped there, apart from a moral verse warning of men whose pleasing appearances conceal their wolvish natures. In other versions, a woodcutter comes to the rescue; the wolf has stones stitched into his belly; a second wolf calls and is summarily drowned; or blue-tits and an old watercress-seller play a part in the rescue. In a Chinese tale, three daughters are almost tricked by a wolf in their own home while Mother is away visiting Grandmother. In his brilliant *The Trials and Tribulations of Little Red Riding Hood* (1993), which includes 35 variations, Jack Zipes argues that the oral tale told by peasants has been appropriated by men and turned into a story which does violence to women in several respects. Certainly, different cultures have reworked the tale to exemplify their own values; but some recent versions, from Russia to Brazil, reflect DISNEY's trivialising sentimentality or obscure the power of the story beneath slick humour or parody. GPF

see also FAIRY TALES

Little Thumb see *HOP O' MY THUMB*

***Little Tim* series** The first book in the series by the British illustrator EDWARD ARDIZZONE, and his own first children's book, was *Little Tim and the Brave Sea Captain* (1936). Ardizzone wrote as though for his own children, then aged five and six. It was published in New York, and contained 40 drawings in pen and colourwash, with a text hand-lettered by Grace Hogarth. This was followed by *Lucy Brown and Mr Grimes* (1937), a story which alarmed American librarians by implying that it was acceptable for a young girl to talk to an unknown old man in a public park, a scenario changed in later editions by making Mr Grimes a family friend. The two characters Tim and Lucy were then brought together in *Tim and Lucy go to Sea* (1938). The three volumes looked like sketch-books. They were printed on one side of the paper only, and the illustrations were reproduced by offset LITHOGRAPHY.

After the Second World War, Ardizzone resumed the series with *Tim to the Rescue* (1949). With a sequence of pen drawings supplementing the colour pictures, and the addition of speech bubbles, this volume served as a model both for subsequent *Tim* books, and for the first three stories which were rewritten and redrawn for the revised format. *Tim to the Rescue* expands the range of children's characters through the first ship's boy Ginger, whose lively, slightly obstreporous nature provides a foil for the more orthodox, though amazingly adventurous, Tim. The ship's cat, too, makes a memorable first appearance. *Tim and Charlotte* (1951) and *Tim in Danger* (1953) were followed by *Tim All Alone*, the 1956 first winner of the KATE GREENAWAY AWARD. This story, in which Tim is separated from his parents, has a more serious tone, and Tim has to survive a hard time from an unsympathetic crew, with only the cat for a friend. After a six-year gap, the series continued with *Tim's Friend Towser* (1962) – Tim and Ginger serve as cabin boys under a captain who loves cats but hates dogs. Two more localised coastal stories were *Tim and Ginger* (1965) and *Tim to the Lighthouse* (1968), in which Tim, Ginger, Charlotte and Captain McFee (the original brave sea captain) combine to thwart a gang of wreckers. The sequence seemed to be closed in *Tim's Last Voyage* (1972) – Tim's parents were becoming anxious about the dangers of life at sea – but Ardizzone relented with *Ship's Cook Ginger* (1977).

As stories, perhaps *Tim in Danger* and *Tim All Alone* stand out, but the quality of the ILLUSTRATIONS is uniformly high throughout the series. Ardizzone never condescends, in text or picture. The children come across as autonomous individuals in a world which is sometimes harsh, sometimes kind, but always realistic. The varied life of ports is conveyed with subtlety and humour. Each ship provides a microcosm of the world, and the device of a sea voyage transports Tim – and reader – from known to unknown, and, eventually, safely back.

Tim and Lucy Go to Sea was reissued in 1958 with a revised text and illustrations by Ardizzone, and in 1999 Scholastic began a programme of reissuing the entire series. PR

Little White Duck see MUSIC AND STORY

Little Women (1868) First of a quartet of books by LOUISA MAY ALCOTT, detailing the progress of the March family over 30 years, from their early struggles during the American Civil War to success and affluence. *Little Women*, the most overtly autobiographical, opens with the mother, Marmee, and her four daughters coping at home – in recently reduced circumstances – after Father has joined the Union Army as a chaplain. To aid their struggles in the year ahead Marmee suggests that the girls resume their childhood game based upon *THE PILGRIM'S PROGRESS* and the novel is constructed around this device. Meg, the eldest, falls victim to the temptations of Vanity Fair, Jo, Alcott's alter ego, battles with a vile temper (Apollyon), Beth, pathologically shy and a pattern of passive domesticity, is Little Faithful while the youngest, Amy, suffers for her pride and conceit in the Valley of Humiliation. This apparently disastrous recipe does not result in a sermon, however, but in an attractive, sympathetic story of four intelligent sisters often at odds with each other and with much to discontent them, learning to pull together. When Jo strikes up a friendship with Laurie, grandson of the rich businessman next door, their social and cultural horizons expand. Adversity comes in the shapes of Marmee's departure for Washington when Mr March falls ill, and Beth's near-fatal bout of scarlet fever, caught while ministering to an impoverished immigrant family. The action of the novel runs from one Christmas to the next and ends with Beth's recovery and Mr March's return. The characters of the girls are carefully differentiated and they are not static stereotypes. They are adolescents, growing up with both eagerness and reluctance.

Little Women Part II (1869), always known in Britain as *Good Wives*, develops into a more complex work altogether, examining loss, disappointment and compromise. It takes up the story three years later with Meg about to discover the setbacks to marriage on a shoestring with the honourable but unexciting John

Brooke. Laurie is at Harvard while Amy tries to better herself socially and artistically. Beth is succumbing to the after-effects of her illness and Jo helps her mother. Mr March languishes in his study for months at a time, largely forgotten by his author. Jo still has hopes of a literary career but her rebarbative behaviour costs her a trip to Europe which Amy takes instead. Jo remains at home to refuse Laurie's proposal of marriage, abandoning literary dreams to earn good money writing sensational stories, as did Alcott herself. Laurie, finally accepting Jo's rejection, settled for second-best with Amy whose exposure to great European art has convinced her that her own talents are inadequate to her ambition. Jo, having nursed Beth through her last illness, sees for herself, at 26, a lonely and loveless future. She ultimately finds love and comradeship with Professor Bhaer, an émigré German intellectual, and marries him. The book ends with the realisation of their joint dream of opening a progressive school which will give room to Bhaer's theories on education.

Little Men (1871) begins virtually where *Good Wives* leaves off. As well as being a lively novel, following the fortune of one pupil, Nat, a promising violinist rescued from street life by Laurie, and Nat's louche friend Dan, it allowed Alcott to suggest how her own father's educational theories might have succeeded had he ever had the opportunity to put them fully into practice. Apart from Meg's twins and Jo's own two small sons, the boys – and later girls – are all in some way mentally, physically or socially damaged and there is more than conventional education at stake. A 15-year gap intervened between the publication of *Little Men* and that of the final book, *Jo's Boys* (1886), condensed into ten years in the sequence. Many changes have occurred. The school, Plumfield, has expanded into a co-educational college founded by Laurie, now a wealthy benefactor. The children of Jo, Meg and Amy are teenagers, the schoolboys young men. The book is principally concerned with the fortunes of three of them, Nat, the violinist, Emil, the professor's nephew, now following a career at sea, and the enigmatic Dan who has taken Jo's place at centre stage. Dan is a rover and unlike any of the other men in the book, dangerous, being sexually active and attractive. The three are glimpsed at crisis points in their adventures while at home the adolescents learn, play, squabble and set foot on the first rungs of their career ladders. Also memorable is Nan, a raucous small girl in *Little Men*, now a dedicated medical student plagued by the attentions of her childhood sweetheart who believes that all she truly wants is the love of a good man.

As always, with Alcott, there is polemic: feminism, suffragism, education and good housekeeping; there is also sardonic self-reference, for Jo has become a famous children's author, distracted by her besotted fans. Realism overrides many romantic expectations, as usual. The artistic aspirant will achieve success through hard work, not luck or genius. Nat will never be a virtuoso, but a front-desk orchestral player; Dan will not win the love of his life and Jo, clearly, has not become the great writer she once dreamed of being. Alcott's note of exasperation at the close, where she mutters sullenly of concluding the saga with an earthquake, has been taken to indicate her distaste for the whole enterprise which, indeed, began with her reluctance to write a story for girls. But, a true professional, she never sold her readers short, developed her characters credibly and made them into likeable, interesting people. The threat of an earthquake was a warning to her insatiable readers who would have continued willingly with the family that had become so vividly real to them. It was, one might say, Alcott's Reichenbach Falls. JMM

Littlewood, Joan see DRAMA FOR CHILDREN; see also NATIONAL YOUTH THEATRE

Lively, Penelope 1935– British prize-winning writer of fiction for children and adults. Although in recent years she has been better known for her novels for adults, her children's fiction was particularly popular during the 1970s and is still in print today. She won the CARNEGIE MEDAL for *The Ghost of Thomas Kempe* (1973) – arguably her most popular children's novel – and the WHITBREAD AWARD for *A Stitch in Time* (1976). Both novels deal with a theme common to much of Lively's work, the passage of time and the layers of history hidden behind a particular place. In *A Stitch in Time* an only child finds companionship through an old sampler that takes her back in time. As in *THE HOUSE IN NORHAM GARDENS*, the isolated only child's involvement with the historical world around her and her gradual incorporation into the modern world are convincingly described. The hero of *The Ghost of Thomas Kempe* is haunted by a poltergeist who had lived in the house centuries earlier. The past is seen to linger not only in buildings, but also in landscape; in *The Wild Hunt Of Hagworthy* (1971) and *The Whispering Knights* (1971) history and folk customs have become part of the landscape, being re-enacted in the present day world. This theme is dealt with most fully in *The Driftway* (1972), a complex novel about the presence of history on a particular old road. KA

Livingston, Myra Cohn 1926–96 American poet and anthologist whose desire to bring poetry to young people resulted in the production of numerous books of award-winning poems. Her first book, *Whispers and Other Poems* (1958), reflected her own everyday experiences of childhood. With *The Malibu and Other Poems* (1974) she began to take a more contemporary view of young people. Trained as a traditionalist in poetry, she learned the importance of order imposed by fixed forms, metre and rhyme. Writing in free verse, and complemented by Leonard Everett Fisher's paintings, she explored the seasons, sky, sea, earth and space in a series of books. Music was of great importance – she was an exceptional French horn player – and constantly enhanced her poetic skills. *A Tune Beyond Us* (1968) was the first of her 35 thoughtfully edited anthologies, for which she chose poets of different ages and cultures as well as various subjects. She also edited collections of EDWARD LEAR and LEWIS CARROLL, both of whom she greatly admired. Her impact on children's literature was significant in the United States both through her books and through her teaching in schools and universities. She wrote several critical texts, including *The Child as Poet: Myth or Reality?* (1984). PDS

Livingstone, Ian see ADVENTURE GAME BOOKS; ADVENTURE STORIES

***Lizzie Dripping* series** Commissioned by BBC TELEVISION as a pilot programme for the *JACKANORY* Playhouse in 1972, the popularity of the first story, *Lizzie Dripping and the Orphans* by HELEN CRESSWELL, inspired two popular television drama series in 1973 and 1975 which were filmed on location in the author's Nottinghamshire village. Four collections of the *Lizzie Dripping* stories, from which the screenplays were adapted, were published in tandem with the series. Denied the visual conviction of setting and character representation, these stories nevertheless retain the distinctive flavour of the highly acclaimed television series. A stage version of *Lizzie Dripping and the Witch* was produced at the Unicorn Theatre in 1977.

Lizzie, 'dreamy and daring at the same time', has a reputation within her family and the village of Little Hemlock for 'turning thing upside down and inside out'. Reality and FANTASY sit easily within her imagination and the fibs she tells are manifestations of her talent for invention. Lizzie's most consistent creation is the mischievous witch who knits in the graveyard and who represents needy companionship but also the capacity for adult irresponsibility. At home, caught in the confusing time between childhood and adolescence, Lizzie unwittingly tests the nature of adult patience and parental love as her misjudged or fanciful efforts to please cause minor domestic upheaval and temporary discord. Cresswell's acute depictions of the solid adults who people Lizzie's world are supplemented by their observation through the subversive filter of Lizzie's thoughts. Authentic characterisation, vivid dialogue and gently expressive language have distinguished this successful series. CMN

Lloyd, David see *THE FROG PRINCE*

Llywelyn, Morgan 1937– Texas-born writer living in Ireland. Using a meticulously researched scaffold of period detail, she focuses on two dynamic characters in Irish history in *Brian Boru* (1990) and *Strongbow* (1992). *Strongbow*, narrated from the different perspectives of Richard de Clare (Strongbow) and his wife, Aoife, frames a troubled time in 12th-century Ireland in an understated love story. *Star Dancer* (1993) and *Cold Places* (1995) are centred on contemporary young people, but she again shifts to the past in *17 Railway Street* (1996), jointly written with MICHAEL SCOTT, and in the semi-fictionalised *The Vikings in Ireland* (1996). Her prose is crisp and concise and her historical novels convey to the reader her enthusiasm for the past. VC

Lobel, Anita [Kempler] 1934–98 Writer and illustrator of children's books. Born in Poland, Anita Lobel was incarcerated in a Nazi concentration camp as a child. She creates buoyant and colourful ILLUSTRATIONS in spite of her own harsh childhood. It was the editor for her husband, children's author and illustrator ARNOLD LOBEL, who encouraged her to create her own book. The result, *Sven's Bride*, was named among the best-illustrated PICTUREBOOKS of 1965 by *The New York Times*. Anita Lobel went on to write and illustrate many of her own books, as well as illustrating the work of other authors. She uses bright oranges, greens and pinks, with elaborate floral patterns and clothes on her voluptuous characters. The designs and motifs of her native Poland influence her work, as does her love of the stage. She often blocks out her books as though staging a play. Although they were initially reluctant to work togther, Arnold Lobel wrote several books specifically for his wife to illustrate, such as *A Treeful of Pigs* (1979), and they collaborated on the 1982 Caldecott Honour Book *On Market Street*. Lobel's fondness for FAIRY TALE motifs can still be seen in her more recent illustrations, such as those for *Princess Furball* (1989) by CHARLOTTE HUCK. EHI

Lobel, Arnold (Stark) 1933–87 American illustrator of poetry, fiction and non-fiction, best known for his *I Can Read* books, which have limited or controlled vocabularies, his *FROG AND TOAD* series, and his ability to convey humour and emotion in his use of colour and line drawings. Born in Los Angeles, California, Lobel grew up in Schenectady, New York, and was educated at the Pratt Institute where he met and married fellow student and author-illustrator ANITA KEMPLER LOBEL. A prolific artist, Lobel wrote and/or illustrated over 100 books for children during his distinguished career. In 1981 he received the CALDECOTT AWARD for *Fables* (1980), 20 original FABLES exemplifying Lobel's playful inventiveness and humour. He received numerous other awards including Caldecott Honour Awards for *Frog and Toad are Friends* (1970) and *Hildilid's Night* (1971); a Christopher Award for *On the Day Peter Stuyvesant Sailed into Town* (1971); Newbery Honor Award for *Frog and Toad Together* (1972); and American Book Award nominations for *Frog and Toad are Friends* and *On Market Street* (1982). In 1985 he received the University of Southern Mississippi Silver Medallion for 'distinguished service to children's literature'; in 1986 a Laura Ingalls Wilder Medal nomination for 'distinguished, enduring contribution to children's literature'; and in 1987 the Society of Children's Book Writers awarded him its 1987 Golden Kite Award for *The Devil and Mother Crump*. DJH

Locke, Elsie (Violet) 1912– New Zealand award-winning pioneer writer, whose imaginative and lively novels for children draw on profound historical knowledge and a commitment to world peace and environmental conservation. *THE RUNAWAY SETTLERS* (1965), *The End of the Harbour* (1968), *Journey Under Warning* (1983) and *A Canoe in the Mist* (1984) are stories set in early New Zealand. They demonstrate Locke's attention to authentic historical and geographical details, while *The Boy with the Snowgrass Hair* (1976), co-authored with Ken Dawson, and *Explorer Zach* (1978) reflect her deep love and concern for the environment. In 1996 Locke was awarded the New Zealand Children's Honour Book Award for non-fiction for *Joe's Ruby* (1995), a true story of a rook raised in a man's home. LL

Locke, John 1632–1704 English philosopher whose most important work, *Essay Concerning Human Understanding* (1690), rejected the proposition that human ideas are innate. Instead, Locke stressed the degree to which human beings learn from experience. This emphasis underpinned *Some Thoughts Concerning Education* (1693), which exercised considerable influence on ideas about children and learning during the 18th century. Locke's clear, seemingly common-sense rationalism was immensely persuasive and helped steer succeeding generations towards a more responsive attitude to child development and tutelage. Locke laid particular stress on sense experience, promoting the view that ILLUSTRATION and example should accompany learning from texts. DWh

see also 'SOME EASY PLEASANT BOOK'

Locker, Thomas 1937– American author and illustrator of children's books, born in New York. Locker writes: 'After a long career in gallery painting, I discovered the art form of the picturebook while reading to my five sons . . . I see my books as a kind of bridge between generations and a way to bring fine art to the young mind.' A landscape painter whose works are reminiscent of the earlier Hudson River School style, Locker, a college art professor, left the academic world in the mid-1970s to become a freelance author and illustrator. His *Where the River Begins* (1984) was chosen as one of the *New York Times* Best Illustrated Books of the Year, as well as winning other awards. Locker is probably best known for his adaptation of WASHINGTON IRVING'S *RIP VAN WINKLE* (1988) and his ILLUSTRATIONS for JEAN CRAIGHEAD GEORGE'S *The First Thanksgiving* (1993). Other works he has both written and illustrated include *The Mare on the Hill* (1985), *Sailing with the Wind* (1986), *Family Farm* (1988) and *The Young Artist* (1988). The particularly stunning and rich oil paintings that distinguish his books present accurate panoramas of life in early, rural America, demonstrating an obvious love for America's impressive and legendary past, and a devotion to nature. Locker brings fine art and a deep respect for the child to the PICTUREBOOK genre. MS

Lofting, Hugh (John) see *DOCTOR DOLITTLE SERIES*; see also BIAS IN CHILDREN'S BOOKS

London, Jack 1876–1916 American novelist, short-story writer and socialist, most remembered for his ADVENTURE STORIES in which men are tested in harsh conditions. The animal stories set in the Klondike – of which the novels *White Fang* (1906) and *The Call of the Wild* (1903) are the most famous examples – have been particularly popular. Jack London was born in San Francisco into a family who often lived on the brink of poverty. Though he read voraciously as a child, lack of money meant that he was able to continue his formal education only spasmodically. He worked from the age of 15 in a variety of manual jobs – including factory work and being an oyster pirate – and travelled widely, both as a seaman and a tramp, spending a memorable year in the Klondike prospecting for gold. He drew on many of these experiences in his fictional writing. From 1894 he was increasingly involved in the socialist movement, and although his relationship with the movement became more strained in his later years, when his popularity as a novelist had made him very rich, much of his major fiction drew, often in contradictory ways, on socialist ideas.

Jack London's first full-length novel *The Son of the Wolf*, was published in 1900. The figure of the wolf – related to the dog, working within the collective social form of the pack, yet wild – recurs in his fiction (most notably in *The Call of the Wild*, *The Sea Wolf* (1904) and

Lone Pine: 'Peter grabbed at the horse's head.' Illustration by Bertram Prance from *Seven White Gates* by Malcolm Saville.

White Fang), embodying some of his central concerns about forces straining against each other within civilisation. Most of his major fiction deals with forces which oppose the individual's will to power or self-fulfillment, often threatening to destroy him altogether. In the most overtly political stories, such as *The Iron Heel* (1907), these forces are clearly identified as the conditions of inequality and alienation brought about by capitalism. In others, such as *The Sea Wolf* or *Martin Eden* (1908), it is the self-destructive potential of the heroes which is examined. Jack London held racist views about 'white' superiority and was strongly influenced by both social Darwinism and aspects of Nietzschian philosophy. In his best fiction his attempts to squarc this seemingly fraught amalgam with conflicting socialist ideals can produce powerful and fascinating tensions. Most young readers are not aware of the philosophical contradictions underlying the stories, but are captivated by the spirit of heroism, endurance and adventure that enthralled London throughout his life and which he communicates with vivid, lyrical directness. Jack London did not write specifically for young readers, but his clear, forceful prose style and his original development of the genres of animal story and adventure writing have won him a regular readership amongst children. Though he has remained a popular writer, with several of his novels having been made into successful films, his critical reputation has fluctuated. His best work engages graphically with a range of ideas concerning social values, human drives and destiny while offering all the virtues of a well-told story. DWh

***Lone Pine* series** (1943–78) An unjustly overlooked series of 20 ADVENTURE STORIES by MALCOLM SAVILLE. The books are set in real locations, involving members of a club founded at a solitary pine tree in a small valley of the Long Mynd in Shropshire. The rules of the Lone Pine club are buried in a sardine tin beneath the pine tree at Witchend, an isolated farmhouse, where the members have sworn an oath 'to be true to each other' before signing the grubby 'dokkerment' in blood. The club's aims – explained in *Mystery at Witchend* – reflected Saville's interest in and concern for the countryside. He later established a branch of the club which his readers could join. They received a membership card, stickers, a code and coveted badges. The club, formed when the original members were evacuated to Shropshire during World War II, continued through 19 adventures over the next 25 years, during which time the members aged only slightly, in accordance with readers' requests. They continued to epitomise integrity and loyalty, and displayed such credible qualities that all readers could recognise a part of themselves or their friends within the characters' behaviour and conversations.

The first book in the series was written while Saville was carrying out duties as an Air Raid Precautions night warden. As each chapter was finished it was sent to his wife and four children, who had evacuated to Shropshire. He wrote about areas he loved and had explored with his family, encouraging his readers in detailed forewords and maps to visit these 'real' locations. Saville was initially inspired by ARTHUR RANSOME, and this is reflected in his choice of real locations and the provision of sketch-maps for readers to follow the Lone Piners in their adventures. The first eight books in the series are enhanced by the apt and sensitive illustrations of Bertram Prance. His drawings are well-observed and characterised, and work in harmony with the text to accurately depict emotions and incidents relevant to the story. Charles Wood displayed a similar sensitivity in his beautiful dust jackets for some of the later books in the series. Malcolm Saville's individual style is identified through his genuine sympathy and respect for children, both his readers and those depicted in his books. Particularly prevalent in the Shropshire books are the night adventures and tit-bits of folklore, history and LEGEND that are woven into the narratives. Readers are captivated by age-old tales relevant to the feeling and mood of his characters and their surroundings. His sensitivity to the setting of his stories is a key factor throughout.

Later editions of the Lone Pine books omitted much of Saville's descriptive narrative and the childish chit-chat of the twins in an effort to cater for what the publishers believed to be the tastes of the modern child. But it is his attention to detail and his feeling for the landscape, be it The Mynd, Rye, Romney Marsh, the Yorkshire Dales, East Anglia or Old London, as well as his ability to relate a gripping and stimulating tale, that is the distinguishing quality of his writing. LW

Long Way from Verona, A (1971) First full-length novel by British author JANE GARDAM, about the transition from childhood to adolescence, set in a seaside town in wartime North Yorkshire. The heroine, Jessica Vye, is 13; lively, imaginative, awkward, tormented by intuitive awareness of what others think of her and acutely bound to tell the truth. Her narration of a schoolgirl's determination to shake off the confinements of her social life includes encounters that make adults uneasy: a maniac in a forbidden wood, a snobbish children's houseparty, a boy, the crushing indignities of school, the terror of an air-raid. Jessica's telling includes counterpoint conversations with her left-wing parents, interior monologues, letters and passages of mild hallucination reported in tones of mock-heroic adolescent irony, often witty and sometimes very moving. Jessica finds adults plainly absurd.

Gardam's skill in capturing the layered complexity of what, at first, seems a localised 'domestic' novel, is displayed in the underlying theme of Jessica's determination to become a writer. The textual variety of close descriptions, shifting viewpoints, allusions, half-utterances, where what is said is set against what is left out, creates suspense as the reader becomes aware of duplicity in the adults who think they are behaving for the best. Jessica's English teacher tells her she should destroy what she has written if she thinks it good, so that she will not be ashamed of it later. Literature comes to her rescue, though not simply and not entirely. When this book appeared, it brought a new way of reading adolescence, not simply reading 'about' it, which enlarged both understanding and readership. MM

Longfellow, Henry Wadsworth 1807–82 American poet, still frequently anthologised for children. Along with *Evangeline*, HIAWATHA and *The Courtship of Miles Standish*, Longfellow's *Paul Revere's Ride* (1863) lives as an icon of young America. Longfellow helped popularise poetry, and his narrative poetry was highly regarded in the 19th century, though less so in the 20th, especially after the Great Depression. A master of metre, Longfellow composed such memorable lines as: 'Listen, my children, and you shall hear/Of the midnight ride of Paul Revere.' A college classmate of NATHANIEL HAWTHORNE, Longfellow modelled *Tales of a Wayside Inn*, one of which is *Paul Revere's Ride*, on CHAUCER's *The Canterbury Tales*. NV

Looking for Alibrandi (1992) Contemporary Australian 'rites-of-passage' novel by Melina Marchetta about a 17-year-old Italian Australian in her final year of high school in Sydney. The book's appeal lies in the main character, Josephine, who is by turns strong, vulnerable, out-spoken, difficult, lovable and exasperating, and in her relationship with her mother and grandmother, who are also strong female characters. The resolution satisfyingly avoids the glibness which can mar such novels. The book has won numerous awards including that for the CHILDREN'S BOOK COUNCIL OF AUSTRALIA BOOK OF THE YEAR (Older Readers, 1993), and the Australian Multicultural Children's Literature Award, and was subsequently released in an adult edition. MLH

Looking Glass, The see COMICS, PERIODICALS AND MAGAZINES

Looney Tunes see ANIMATED CARTOONS

Lord, Bette Bao 1938– American author of books for children and adults. Born in Shanghai, China, Lord immigrated with her family to the United States in 1946. In 1963 she married Winston Lord, future US Ambassador to the People's Republic of China. Her first book, *Eighth Moon: The True Story of a Young Girl's Life in Communist China* (1964), is based on the experiences of her sister, who was left behind in China when her family emigrated. *Spring Moon* (1981), Lord's first novel, chronicles a woman's life in China from childhood to old age. Lord is the author of two other books for adults: *Legacies: A Chinese Mosaic* (1990), a collection of Chinese oral histories, and *The Middle Heart* (1996), a novel about three friends in World War II China. *In the Year of the Boar and Jackie Robinson* (1984) is Lord's only book for children. This semi-autobiographical story, set in 1947 New York City, narrates a Chinese girl's immigration to the United States and her adjustment to American culture through baseball. Illustrated effectively by MARC SIMONT, the book offers a convincing look at the immigrant experience from a child's perspective. It is one of the few books about Asian Americans for middle-grade readers. EAM

see also BIOGRAPHY AND AUTOBIOGRAPHY

Lord of the Flies (1954) Adult story by the British novelist William Golding which has often also attracted young readers. It reverses the romantic

ROBINSONNADE type of FANTASY started by Defoe's classic and continued in R.M. BALLANTYNE'S *The Coral Island* (1858). Instead of showing how well children on their own cope with living on a desert island, Golding traces the quick disintegration of a marooned group of contemporary pre-teenage boys. Initially excited by their island, and recalling fictional adventures with the same type of setting, the children's elected leader, Ralph, is unable to counter the growing aggression of the leading hunter, Jack. When Piggy, an intelligent but over-weight, unathletic child, is killed by what is now a murderous mob, Ralph flees for his life. He is rescued by a visiting naval officer just in time. This deeply pessimistic story, with its central notion of original sin, has remained a popular text. NT

see also ADVENTURE STORIES

Lord of the Rings, The see *THE HOBBIT*; J. J. R. TOLKIEN; see also PAULINE BAYNES

Lore and Language of Schoolchildren, The (1959) A collection by IONA AND PETER OPIE from their decade-long ethnographic study, unprecedented at that time, of the traditional verbal play that schoolchildren indulge in to order their games and social life. Questionnaires, direct observations and reports from 5,000 pupils produced rhymes, quips, RIDDLES, paradoxes, rules and bamboozling jokes, sampled earlier in *I SAW ESAU* (1947). The Opies' scholarly editing, always tempered with glee, reveals how traditional verses are updated in each generation as subversive commentaries on current events. Adults are aware of these verbal exuberances but play no part in their transmission. What emerges is a distinctive oral literature and a rich tapestry of childhood at a time when TELEVISION was still new. MM

Lost Diamonds of Killiecrankie, The (1995) Australian PICTUREBOOK, written by GARY CREW and illustrated by PETER GOULDTHORPE, ostensibly comprising a collection of found objects and documents, with a narrative 'as told' to Crew by an aging landscape artist. In fact, the book mingles historical fact with a fictional story; it is at once a straightforward adventure – an examination of the fate of Tasmania's Aborigines – and a statement about the exploitative nature of colonisation. ILLUSTRATIONS include historical documents, photos, maps and paintings. It is unusual in that it is published in picturebook format, but with a lengthy text and an implied teenage readership. NLR

Lost Prince, The (1915) Novel by FRANCES HODGSON BURNETT. Its lineaments are roughly those of a child's ADVENTURE STORY and would appear to owe something of its flavour to Anthony Hope's *Zenda* novels. Its protagonist Marco Loristan, a young Samavian exile, with his crippled friend the 'Rat', travels through Europe to signal the beginning of an uprising that results in the restoring of the 'Lost Prince' of Samavian legend; it turns out that his father is the latest inheritor of that 'title'. There are similarities with Burnett's other, more famous, works for children. For example, both Marco Loristan and Sara Crewe (*A LITTLE PRINCESS*) bear themselves in adversity with dignity and a sense of care for the feelings of those even less fortunate – and both are, in the end, restored to their 'proper' estate.

Child protagonists in Burnett's novels tend either to be brats (eventually reformed) or idealised children. *The Lost Prince* is an interesting work in this regard as it plays off one type against the other. Marco – noble, brave, well-born, physically attractive – is paired with the 'Rat' who is crippled, from a dissolute household, and with a propensity to violence. Certainly, Burnett is not innocent of a degree of stereotyping, but it must be noted that it is in the 'Rat' rather than in Marco that we find the work's greatest interest. Like Colin of *THE SECRET GARDEN*, he is crippled and struggles against this; like Sara Crewe, he possesses a deep imaginative life (it is his imaginings that shape the poor children of the streets into something more visionary and purposeful); his intellect is one which demands respect, and even his jealousy and anger find honest expression. While Marco remains the text's avowed protagonist, the 'Rat' has the greater depth. SA

Lothrop, Harriet M(ulford) see *FIVE PEPPERS* SERIES

Louw [Koenig], Juliet Marais 1910– The only South African children's writer to be awarded the Gold Medal of the English Academy of Southern Africa. As a writer of fiction and non-fiction, poet, broadcaster, historian and anthologist, she introduced generations of children to the stories, poetry and peoples of their land, conveying a strong message of interracial respect and understanding, such as in *Sipho and the Yellow Plastic Purse* (1977), which broke with the tradition of sentimental patronising in its portrayal of a black boy in Soweto. Among her verse, *Fugitive Child* (1945) was written in honour of the children of the Holocaust, and *South Wind* (1943) is considered a classic. In 'Midway' she wrote what could be her own epitaph:

> And though I be grey and weary,
> The core of my spirit shall be
> A barefooted child forever,
> Where sands are awash with the sea.

ERJ

Lovelace, Maud Hart see *BETSY-TACY*; see also HISTORICAL FICTION; NEGLECTED WORKS; SCHOOL STORIES

Lowrey, Janette Sebring 1892–1986 American author of children's books and short stories. Born in Orange, Texas, Lowrey is best known for *The Poky Little Puppy* (1942), a book for pre-schoolers about a rascally little puppy that gets into mischief. This book was still listed by the *Publishers Weekly* (1996) as the bestselling American children's book of all time. She also wrote *Margaret* (1950), an autobiographical novel for middle-grade readers, which was made into a DISNEY movie and later a series for TELEVISION. The sequel, *Love, Bid Me Welcome* (1964), was also an award-winner. A high-school English teacher, Lowrey's strength was her skill with vocabulary and word play. She sensed the importance of the sound each word makes and the images it could evoke. Lowrey produced historical non-fiction in *Six Silver Spoons* (1971) and retold BIBLE STORIES and Greek myths (see CLASSICAL MYTHOLOGY) in *In the Morning of the World* (1944). ESC

see also BIOGRAPHY AND AUTOBIOGRAPHY; PICTUREBOOKS

Lowry, Lois 1937– Award-winning American author of humorous, historical and problem fiction. Born in Honolulu, Hawaii, to a military dentist, Lowry lived as a child in such diverse locations as Brooklyn, New York; Carlisle, Pennsylvania; and Tokyo, Japan. She began her writing career by producing freelance articles and taking photographs for a variety of publications, including *Down East* and *The New York Times*. At the invitation of an editor from Houghton Mifflin, who had read a short story she had written, Lowry wrote *A Summer to Die* (1977), a fictionalised account of her relationship with her older sister who had died of cancer. *A Summer to Die* was widely praised and received the International Reading Association Children's Book Award, launching Lowry's career as a children's writer. Most of Lowry's early novels, including *Find a Stranger, Say Good-Bye* (1978) – the story of a teenager searching for her birth-mother – and *Autumn Street* (1980) – based on her own childhood during World War II – appeal to older young adults.

In 1979, Lowry created her most popular character, Anastasia Krupnik, a precocious young Boston girl who deals with both the humour and tragedy of everyday life. The popularity of Anastasia prompted Lowry to create nine novels about her, including *ANASTASIA KRUPNIK* (1979), *Anastasia Again!* (1981), *Anastasia at Your Service* (1987), *Anastasia on Her Own* (1985) and *Anastasia, Absolutely* (1995). Prompted by requests from fans, Lowry wrote a story for younger readers featuring Anastasia's younger brother, Sam, as a protagonist. The result was *All About Sam* (1988), *Attaboy, Sam!* (1992) and *See You Around, Sam* (1996). All of the Krupnik books are set in Cambridge and Boston, Massachusetts, where Lowry lived for many years. The *Anastasia* series – along with three humorous novels about Caroline Tate (a budding paleontologist) and her computer-whiz brother, J. P., who first appeared in *The One Hundredth Thing About Caroline* (1983) – has prompted critics to compare Lowry to writers such as BEVERLY CLEARY, BETSY BYARS and PAULA DANZIGER. Lowry's humorous novels, however, are deceptively simple and treat such important themes as the misleading nature of appearances and the value of memory.

Lowry's willingness to experiment has resulted in her three most critically acclaimed novels, *Rabble Starkey* (1987), *Number the Stars* (1988) and *The Giver* (1993). *Rabble Starkey*, set in rural Virginia, focuses on a young girl born to a single teenage mother, and her quest for a family. *Rabble Starkey*, which received the BOSTON-GLOBE HORN BOOK AWARD and a Golden Kite Award, was followed by *Number the Stars*, which earned Lowry her first NEWBERY MEDAL. Set in Denmark during World War II, the novel introduces young readers to the issues surrounding the Holocaust, while exploring the nature of true friendship and bravery. In 1993, Lowry published her second Newbery Award winner, *The Giver*, a dystopian novel about a futuristic society called the 'community' and a young boy's attempt to break free from a world which has no colours, memories or real individuality. JDC

Lucas, E(dward) V(errall) 1868–1938 English journalist, essayist, critic and man of letters who contributed regularly to *Punch* and was Chair of Methuen from 1924 to 1936. In that position he famously introduced A.A. MILNE to ERNEST SHEPARD. Lucas published one of the earliest appreciative essays on children's literature, 'Some Notes on Poetry for Children' (1896), and produced two excellent anthologies for children. MCCS

see also *A BOOK OF VERSES FOR CHILDREN*

Lucidarie see ELUCIDARIA

lullabies The first part of the word 'lullabye' is of ancient origin: IONA and PETER OPIE quote a Roman lullaby beginning 'Lalla, lalla, aut dormi, aut lacte . . .', while the syllable 'bye' is associated with sleep, as in the infant expression 'bye-byes'. Repeated and improvised upon by generations of forgotten mothers and carers, lullabies constitute an ancient and abiding mass of folk poetry and song, most of it unrecorded and unvalued. Many major poets have added to the traditional material by composing lullabies of their own.

Like NURSERY RHYMES, many lullabies known today first appeared in print in the 18th and 19th centuries, though they are probably much older. One of the earliest, from the 15th-century Coventry Plays, is what has come to be known as the 'Coventry Carol', which begins with the words: 'Lully, lullay, thow litell tine child', sung by the mothers of Jersualem before the Massacre of the Innocents. In Christian cultures, the childhood of Christ is often implicitly or explicitly present, either because the infant invokes thoughts of the baby Jesus, or because the child's crying is seen as anticipating the sorrow and suffering ordained for all human sinners – as here, in this 14th-century lullaby quoted by the Opies:

Lollai, lollai, litil child,
Why wepistou so sore?
Nedis mostou wepe,
Hit was iyarkid the yore.

Defined by most dictionaries as songs for lulling children to sleep, lullabies are in fact more complex and more ambivalent than that definition suggests. While the melody, tone and rhythm may have a soothing effect upon a restless infant – together with the rocking of a cradle or swaying the baby in a parent's arms – the words convey meanings which are sometimes far from reassuring and which arise directly from strong parental fears and powerful cultural factors. 'Hush [Rock]-abye, baby, on the tree top' – probably the best-known lullaby in the English-speaking world – ends with a puzzling warning of danger. It has been suggested that it was composed by a Pilgrim newly arrived on the American continent and struck by the Native American practice of hanging a birchwood cradle in a tree. Or it may, as the Opies suggest, simply indicate that 'long ago . . . cradles were rocked by wind power'.

Marina Warner believes that, in addition to soothing the baby, lullabies also calm and assist the mother. They tell of the hard life of the parents ('Bye, Baby Bunting'), comment on the frailty of human life, and call up bogeymen – Cromwell, Napoleon, Hitler – to warn babies into being quiet.

Baby, baby, naughty baby,
Hush, you squalling thing, I say.
Peace this moment, peace, or maybe
Bonaparte will pass this way.

Sometimes a simple irony is enjoyed as the situation allows the mother to lull and reassure her baby through tone or melody while simultaneously venting her tiredness ('Dance a baby, diddy; What can mammy do wid 'e?'), or her sense of social injustice.

Bye, O my baby,
When I was a lady,
O then my baby didn't cry;
But my baby is weeping,
For want of good keeping,
O I fear my poor baby will die.

An extreme example of this is to be found in the traditional American lullaby 'All the Pretty Li'l Horses', where the second verse is unequivocally bitter:

Hush-a-bye don't you cry, go to sleep you little baby
Way down yonder in the meadow lays a poor little lambie
The bees and the butterflies pecking out his eyes
The poor little thing cries 'Mammy'.

– possibly sung by a black foster-mother to a white baby while her own child dies of neglect. Whatever the precise application of the dying lamb, the verse is omitted from many published versions of the lullaby, including the version in one of the most beautiful books ever produced for small children, *Lullabies and Night Songs* (1965), with verses set to music by Alec Wilder and illustrated by MAURICE SENDAK.

For poets, the composed lullaby offers a particular challenge: how to retain simplicity whilst avoiding banality. But many have accepted the challenge, including male poets like George Withers, who wrote 'Rocking Hymn' in the 17th century ('Sweet baby, then, forbear to weep; /Be still, my babe, sweet baby, sleep.'). ISAAC WATTS's 'A Cradle Hymn' provides a tender moment in his morally uplifting *DIVINE SONGS* (1715); Charles Wesley writes of Jesus as a baby in *Hymns for Children* (1763) ('Gentle Jesus, meek and mild, / Look upon a little child . . .'); and Blake's *SONGS OF INNOCENCE* (1789) includes extraordinarily simple nursery verse, particularly 'A Cradle Song', though Blake's intentions were more complex and ambitious than soothing babies. One of Samuel Taylor Coleridge's finest poems, 'Frost at Midnight', almost contains a lullaby as the poet memorably addresses his infant son, 'Dear Babe, that sleepest cradled by my side'.

Some hold that it is women we must look to for the soul of lullabies, writing out of personal experience as they do. Yet the women who wrote the most memorable were childless. JANE and ANN TAYLOR were unmarried teenage girls when they included lullabies in *ORIGINAL POEMS FOR INFANT MINDS* (1804) and *Rhymes for the Nursery* (1807); these were seminal texts in a more loving and gentle treatment of children by authors writing for the young in the early dawn of the Romantic period. Although DOROTHY WORDSWORTH's 'The Cottager to her Infant' (1835) was not strictly a lullaby, nor written for a public audience, in its concern to soothe a fretful baby and its simple, child-centred language, it has all the hallmarks of the mother/baby address. It is also an example of Dorothy Wordsworth's empathy with both the poor and the young.

The person who developed the lullaby as pure poetry is CHRISTINA ROSSETTI. Surprisingly, the fact that she wrote convincing love poems for babies in the voice of a mother, despite minimal personal experience of babies or mothering, has rarely been commented on. The physicality and musicality of many poems in *SING-SONG* (1872) make it a unique collection.

Mother's arms under you,
Her eyes above you.
Sing it high, sing it low.
Love me, – I love you.

Different from but related to lullabies are bedtime prayers, the most famous of which is perhaps A. A. MILNE's 'Vespers', or the anonymous rhyme which first appeared in print in the 17th century:

Matthew, Mark, Luke and John
Guard the bed that I lie on.
Four corners to my bed,
Four angels round my head.
One to watch and one to pray,
And two to bear my soul away.

MCCS, VW

Lumsden, Glenn see *ROUND THE TWIST*

Lunn, Janet 1928– Canadian author of PICTUREBOOKS, non-fiction and HISTORICAL FICTION. Born in Dallas, Texas, Lunn attended Queen's University in Kingston, Ontario. The themes in her work include a search for self provoked by a sense of alienation, family history, the necessary and acquired realisation of the effect the past has upon the present, and the need for the freeing power of forgiveness and reconciliation. Lunn says she writes about 'never quite belonging, never being sure'. Her work includes *Larger than Life* (1979), *Twelve Dancing Princesses* (1979), *The Root Cellar* (1981) – based upon the American Civil War – and *Double Spell* (1983). Lunn has won many literary awards for her work. Her first picturebook, *Amos' Sweater* (1988), illustrated by Kim LaFave, won the Ruth Schwartz Foundation Award for Best Children's Book and the Governor-General's Children's Book Award for ILLUSTRATIONS. *Shadow in Hawthorn Bay* (1986), a historical novel with overtones of FANTASY, won the Canada Council Award for Children's Literature, the CANADIAN LIBRARY ASSOCIATION BOOK OF THE YEAR AWARD, the National IODE Children's Book Award and the Saskatchewan Library Association Young Adult Book Award.

MRS

Lurie, Alison 1926– Professor of English (folklore and children's literature) at Cornell University. The social wit and irony characteristic of her adult novels extend to her essays about the subversive nature of children's literature in *Don't Tell the Grown-ups* (1990). The power of narrative make-believe is the theme of her feminist anthology, *Clever Gretchen and Other Forgotten Folktales* (1991), and of *The Oxford Book of Modern Fairy Tales* (1993) and two collections of original fables, *The Heavenly Zoo* (1979) and *Fabulous Beasts* (1981). The heroine of her Pulitzer Prize novel, *Foreign Affairs* (1985), is a children's literature expert.

MM

Lurie, Morris 1938– Award-winning Australian journalist and writer of books for adults and children. Lurie combines a joyful and innovative use of language with a vivid imagination. His first children's book, *The 27th Annual African Hippopotamus Race* (1969), reissued as a paperback in 1977 with illustrations by ELIZABETH HONEY, is still a bestseller; it received a YABBA award in 1986. *Toby's Millions* (1982) takes a satirical look at suburban England, as Toby, a considerate, serious child, uses the proceeds of buried pirate treasure in surprising ways. *What's That Noise? What's That Sound?* (1991), a PICTUREBOOK which evolved over seven years while working with the illustrator TERRY DENTON, is an engaging FANTASY with a strongly rhythmical text and a magical ending. Rich imagery and a poetical use of language underpin *Racing the Moon* (1993), a picturebook for older readers, and *Boy in a Storm at Sea* (1997), a junior novel which shifts between reality and fantasy as a young boy, Peter Partridge, is trapped into writing a story.

JAP

Lynch, Chris 1962– Novelist, born in the United States and now living in Ireland. Author of sinewy novels concerning adolescent development, Lynch has said, 'I have made a commitment that when I write I'm going to write as hard and as tough and as raw as I can about real emotions.' He views the search for identity as a common thread running through all of his characters. Mainly male and in their teen years, we watch them as Lynch peels away their protective carapaces, and then rebuilds them, no less tough, but with an awareness which allows for a recognition of their own vulnerability and that of other people. *Shadow Boxer* (1993), *Iceman* (1994) and *Slot Machine* (1995) confront machismo attitudes in sport, seen through the eyes of protagonists who range from a supremo at ice-hockey to a worldly-wise 'overweight sports incompetent'. Family issues intertwine in these and all of his novels, but while adolescent frustrations and anger are conveyed, so too are the viewpoints of the adults. *Gypsy Davey* (1994) is a heart-wrenching account of Davey, neglected, rather slow and on the brink of adolescence. The story of Davey unfolds, told from alternating first and third-person perspectives, allowing the reader to witness how much better is his ability to cope than that of those who are older and supposedly wiser. Sibling rivalry is the driving force for the *Blue-Eyed Son* trilogy, while the focus shifts to an inter-generational relationship in *Political Timber* (1996). Here Gordie, 18, is torpedoed into running for mayor by his grandfather, who regards the office as belonging to him and his family. Gordie's eventual realisation that he must make his own decisions, no matter how imperfect they may be, is typical of many of Lynch's characters.

VC

Lynch, P(atrick) J(ames) 1962– Belfast-born PICTUREBOOK artist. P.J. Lynch studied at Brighton College of Art; although not initially intending to pursue a career as an illustrator, he entered work in a student exhibition which resulted in a collaboration with ALAN GARNER on *A Bag of Moonshine* (1986). Subsequently this won the MOTHER GOOSE AWARD and set Lynch on his path as a picturebook artist. Stylistically very much a traditionalist, Lynch readily acknowledges his influences: RACKHAM, DULAC and more recently MAXFIELD PARRISH and Norman Rockwell.

Selective in what he chooses to illustrate, he can take up to a year to complete a work. Before starting on a book, he engages in meticulous research, studying photographs and visiting museums to look at costumes and absorb period details. For *East o' the Sun and West o' the Moon* (1991), a Norwegian FOLKTALE, he visited Norway to study the architecture, fishing boats and carvings of the country. He works from photographs of models costumed appropriately, which gives him the flexibility to experiment with a variety of angles and groupings, heightening the dramatic sense of his pictures.

Much of Lynch's work is set in a FANTASY or FAIRYTALE landscape and he believes that by first creating an accurate infrastructure, he can then impose upon it fantastical occurrences. This sense of the fantastic, of 'otherness' is what breathes life into his work. The onlooker is not confined to what appears on the page: there is also a sense of something unseen but present. Occasionally, this may be visible, as in *Catkin* (1994), where close viewing of the opening sequences will show the fairy people, dimly outlined in the hedges, as they observe the farmers whose child they steal. Lynch's medium is watercolour and gouache. His palette is distinctive, and his work is also distinguished by the perspectives with which he chooses to illuminate a text; often viewing a scene from above, or from an unexpected angle, he adds an extra dimension and heightens the tensions of the narrative, as in *The Steadfast Tin Soldier* (1991) when the tin man falls from a height onto the street. *The Christmas Miracle of Jonathan Toomey* (1995) (text by Susan Wojciechowski) brings a change of pictorial style, but a feeling for the numinous is still conveyed as the heart of an embittered woodcarver is melted by a young widow and her son. This won for Lynch the KATE GREENAWAY MEDAL and the CBI/BISTO BOOK AWARD in 1996 and consolidated his reputation. He returned to pen-and-ink drawings for MERVYN PEAKE's *Boy in Darkness* (1996). This was followed by another picturebook, *When Jessie Came Across the Sea* (1997) (text by Amy Hest), telling the story of a young Jewish girl's journey from Europe to the United States in the early years of the 20th century, and her subsequent life in New York. This book also won the Greenaway Medal. In *Grandad's Prayers of the Earth* (1999) (text by Douglas Wood) he conveys the close relationship between an ageing man and a young boy. *The Names Upon the Harp* (2000) sees Lynch's return to illustrating a mythological world in Marie Heaney's retelling of old Irish tales.

Lynch has illustrated the work of many authors, including HANS CHRISTIAN ANDERSEN, OSCAR WILDE, W.B. Yeats, Brendan Behan, E. NESBIT and Antonia Barber. VC

Lynch, Patricia (Nora) 1894–1972 Irish novelist, once Ireland's best-known and, arguably, best-loved children's writer. Her popularity has now waned, perhaps owing to the apparent artifice, to present-day ears, in the speech-patterns of many of her characters. She should not, however, be dismissed, as her writing spans an era of great change in Irish society. Her first book, *The Green Dragon*, was published in 1925, her last, *The Kerry Caravan*, in 1967, and in between she published over 40 titles, including some retellings of Irish legends. Her best-known books, *The Turf-Cutter's Donkey* (1934), its sequels, and the *Brogeen* series, are typical of much of Lynch's writing in the juxtapositioning of reality with supernatural events which have overtones of IRISH MYTHOLOGY and FOLKTALES.

Fiddler's Quest (1943) and *The Mad O'Haras* (1948) have no supernatural aspects. The latter is a FAMILY STORY, and in the former, as in many of Lynch's works, a quest is the central motif. Interwoven with this, however, is a theme related to Irish nationalism, which was also unusual for Lynch, who mostly ignored in her writing the social and political upheavals of her time, although her account of events in Dublin following the Easter 1916 Rising was published in a suffragette newspaper in Britain.

The Bookshop on the Quay (1956), partly set in Dublin, is a realistic story except for one section in which a puppet comes to life and the ghost of Dean Swift appears. The characters are typical Lynch protagonists: Shane, the young hero, though in poor circumstances, is thoroughly honest and decent; the adults, while eccentric, are kindly and well-motivated. Even Shane's vagabond Uncle Tim, in a coincidence which must strain the imagination of even the most credulous reader, turns out to be a hero.

Lynch gives a somewhat fictionalised account of her early years in *A Storyteller's Childhood* (1947). A number of of her books were illustrated in the original editions by well-known Irish artists including JACK B. YEATS, Sean Keating and Harry Kernoff. VC

Lyon, Elinor 1921– Postwar British author, the daughter of a former headmaster of Rugby School, whose novels for children were successful in both

Britain and the United States. Elinor Lyon turned to writing after serving as a radar operator in World War II. *Wishing Water-Gate* (1949), her second novel, was admired by WALTER DE LA MARE, in particular for its 'lively English'. Most of her 20 children's books were set either in Wales or in Scotland, usually in a coastal, mountainous landscape; in *Echo Valley* (1965), for example, the story of four children who uncover a sad personal secret is placed in an atmospheric and vividly realised setting on the west coast of Wales. *The House in Hiding* (1950) was the first of a series of eight Scottish novels mostly about three children – Sovra and Ian and their orphan friend Cathie – living more or less unsupervised and experiencing holiday adventures in the remote and beautiful mountains and lochs west of Fort William; two later titles were added to the series dealing with their children, *The King of Grey Corrie* (1975) and *The Floodmakers* (1976). Throughout the series – which includes *We Daren't Go A'Hunting* (1951), *Cathie Runs Wild* (1960), *The Dream Hunters* (1966) and *Strangers at the Door* (1967) – there is a sustained authorial interest in characterisation that sets the series apart from the run-of-the-mill CAMPING AND TRAMPING FICTION of the period. What most distinguishes Lyon's Scottish novels is the intensely realised but understated relationship of the three children, both with each other and with the landscape. Most of these works were illustrated by Mary Dinsdale, whose line drawings subtly intensify the author's accounts of thoughtful, independent and sometimes passionate children in a romantic landscape of mountains and sea. VW

see also NEGLECTED WORKS

Lyrical Ballads Collection of poems by William Wordsworth and Samuel Taylor Coleridge, first published in 1798. The four poems by Coleridge in the first edition included *THE RIME OF THE ANCIENT MARINER*, frequently anthologised for children. Although the remainder were not intended as poems for children, many were concerned with childhood and parenthood, implying a rejection of 18th-century assumptions and positing an alternative view of the significance of childhood in the developing life of an individual.

Wordsworth's ideas on the nature and significance of infancy and childhood were to be worked out more fully in *The Prelude* and other works, and his conceptually suggestive and cryptic reversal: 'The child is father of the man' was to appear later (1802). In *Lyrical Ballads* he emphasised the mutual and vital responsiveness of all creatures in a living universe. In 'Anecdote for Fathers', the child's thinking is less responsive to his father's reason than to the immediacy of happenings around him; in 'The Mad Mother', the mother – healed and soothed by her sucking baby – utters a rhapsodic account of maternal love; and in 'The Idiot Boy', a tight verbal and formal structure enacts the idyllic pastoral unity of the boy's envisioned world.

One of the ballads became an actual children's book. 'We Are Seven' – in which the persistent adult fails to make any progress in seeking to change the little girl's intuitive and holistic view of life and death – was transformed by JAMES KENDREW, the York printer, into a book for children; he issued it, without acknowledgement, as a 16-page CHAPBOOK story for children, with woodcut illustrations. VW

M

Illustration from *Trim* by Annette Macarthur-Onslow.

Mabetoa, Maria Author of two simple PICTURE-BOOKS for South African children, *Our Village Bus* (1985) and *A Visit to my Grandfather's Farm* (1988). Both were strikingly illustrated in colour by Mzwakhe in a bold style, reminiscent of African wood-carving, which did not find much favour among European reviewers. Created by a black author and illustrator for black children, the books proved immensely popular and were used by the READ organisation as the basis for literacy worksheets. JHe

Mabinogion, The see WELSH MYTHOLOGY AND FOLKLORE; see also *THE CHRONICLES OF PRYDAIN*; KEVIN CROSSLEY-HOLLAND; FOLKTALES AND LEGENDS; KING ARTHUR; SIDNEY LANIER; *THE SNOW-SPIDER*

Mac Uistin, Liam Irish author of novels in both English and Irish. His most notable works for children are *The Tain* (1989), *Celtic Magic Tales* (1993) and *The Hunt for Diarmaid and Grainne* (1996), retellings of Celtic legends in an accessible and lively form which does not make sacrifices to accuracy. VC

Macarthur-Onslow, Annette 1933– Australian writer and illustrator, best known for her PICTURE-BOOK *Uhu* (1969) (CHILDREN'S BOOK COUNCIL OF AUSTRALIA BOOK OF THE YEAR AWARD, 1970). The story is based on an attempt to rear an English baby owl whose short but eventful life is conveyed with great feeling in soft pencil drawings and a fluid impressionistic use of watercolour and gouache. Macarthur-Onslow's affinity with animals is also evident in two books featuring cats, *Minnie* (1971) and *Trim* (1977), based on an essay by explorer, Matthew Flinders, about his faithful shipboard cat. Her vigorous but spare black-and-white line drawings in numerous works of both English and Australian writers, such as RUTH MANNING-SANDERS, NAN CHAUNCY, HESBA BRINSMEAD and ELYNE MITCHELL capture evocatively such episodes as the movement and excitement of the rounding-up of cattle or the soaring cliff of a surf wave. Using layered watercolour images, Macarthur-Onslow is especially successful with her interpretation of A.B. PATERSON's ballad, *The Man from Snowy River* (1977). JAP

Macaulay, David 1946– American author and illustrator born in Burton-on-Trent, England, where he lived until he was 11, when his parents moved to New Jersey. Macaulay studied architecture at the Rhode Island School of Design, taught junior high-school art, and worked in interior design. His first book, *Cathedral: The Story of Its Construction* (1973), with its detailed black-and-white drawings, was an immediate success, winning numerous awards, including a Caldecott Honour Medal. This was followed by a number of similarly successful books including *City: A Story of Roman Planning and Construction* (1974), *Pyramid* (1975), *Underground* (1976), *Castle* (1978), also a Caldecott Honour Book, *Unbuilding* (1980), in which the Empire State Building is taken apart, and *Mill* (1983), which traces the development of a 19th-century New England mill. In 1989 Macaulay published *The Way Things Work* a massive compilation of detailed drawings and explanations of everything from 'hologram to hovercraft, parachute to parking meter'. Yet another strand in Macaulay's work is his whimsical, humorous and satirical PICTUREBOOKS, such as *Motel of the Mysteries* (1979), a parody of archaeologists; *Baaa* (1985), a FABLE on the future of the human race; and the CALDECOTT AWARD winner *Black and White* (1989), a brilliant, multilayered, non-linear exploration that extends the picturebook form and may contain 'a number of stories' or possibly 'only one'. LH

McBratney, Sam 1943– Irish novelist who has written a series of humorous novels for emerging readers, such as *Jimmy Zest* (1982). While these are competent and entertaining they do not match the depth and complexity of *The Chieftain's Daughter* (1993) and his other novels for older readers.

The Chieftain's Daughter is set in an early Irish landscape in which the old pagan religions meet the new. It is also a story of young love, achingly described in prose which is spare but unsparing in conveying the hurt felt by the young Dinn Keene as he is teased and mocked by Frann, the eponymous chieftain's daughter. Told from the perspective of the old chief, Dinn Keene, it shifts in and out from a first-person to a third-person narrative and makes demands of the reader which are amply repaid, but also explain why it has not gained greater popularity. *Put a Saddle on the Pig* (1992) is set in McBratney's native Northern Ireland during the time of the 'troubles'. While these are present in the background they are not the focus of the novel; instead, the theme is change as it affects both older and younger adults. Laura, nearly 17, wryly observes her opera-loving widowed mother's growing affection for a pig farmer. Their impending house move resulting from this symbolises for Laura a major change of the sort which 'can plunge your whole life into darkness, uncertainty and despair'. McBratney has also written text for PICTUREBOOKS. Whether conveying the love between the hares in *GUESS HOW MUCH I LOVE YOU* (1995) or the bravado of the young mice in *The Dark at the Top of the Stairs* (1996), his touch is light and his words tightly controlled. VC

McCaffrey, Anne [Inez] 1926– American author of several series of science FANTASY novels, the most famous of which is set in the imaginary world of Pern. *The Dragonriders of Pern* series presents a male-dominated feudal society, beset by 'Thread', spores from a neighbouring planet that destroy all life in their path. Pern's inhabitants are protected from Thread by the dragonriders, men and women who telepathically bond for life with dragons that can incinerate the Thread in mid-air. McCaffrey has written two major Pern trilogies and a number of other novels set there; the *Harper Hall* trilogy – *Dragonsong* (1976), *Dragonsinger* (1977) and *Dragondrums* (1979) – is more commonly read by adolescents. It omits the sex-scenes found in the adult novels and it draws heavily on McCaffrey's experience as a musician. McCaffrey's protagonists are usually women or children, outsiders in a traditional society beginning to undergo change. They search for their place in society, a position based on their talents rather than blind acceptance of traditional roles. McCaffrey's strong protagonists experience and find solutions to common adolescent dilemmas; she has a gift for creating memorable minor characters also, all in a fully realised fantasy world with a strong SCIENCE FICTION background. KK

McCarthy, Maureen 1953– Australian writer of realistic fiction for older teenagers. Born in rural Victoria, McCarthy attracted attention as a fiction writer in the late 1980s with the novelisation of her TELEVISION scripts for the *In Between* series. McCarthy wanted young people of diverse ethnic origins to find themselves represented in current writing. *Ganglands* (1991) presents clashes and tensions between Greeks and Australians but also between public and private school students. Romance finally brings the cultures together. McCarthy's next two expansive books, widely read by adults and young adults, propelled her into the mainstream and proved that young people will read long books if they are provided with strong stories and characters. McCarthy considers *Cross My Heart* (1993) her homage to the Australian outback and the spirit of those who make a life there. A pregnant teenager escapes small-town country life and accepts a lift from a young man just out of gaol. From this inauspicious start McCarthy builds a tough, but promising future for the two. In *Queen Kat, Carmel and St Jude Get a Life* (1995), McCarthy powerfully mingles country and city events, politics, music and rites of passage. Three young women from diverse social and educational backgrounds share a house in their first year of university. They fight, compete, make friends and fall in and out of love. Carmel finds her voice through music and Jude believes she has found, living in Melbourne, her father's torturer from the time of political turmoil in Chile. This forms the most gripping and challenging aspect of the novel, particularly as few Australian children's writers focus on politics and public issues. AN

McCaughrean, Geraldine 1951– British writer who was born in London and took a degree in education at Christ Church, Canterbury. She never taught, but instead began a career in publishing and subsequently turned to writing on a full-time basis, for both adults and children. Many of her works have won awards: her first children's novel, *A Little Lower than the Angels* was the 1987 WHITBREAD CHILDREN'S BOOK OF THE YEAR; *A Pack of Lies* (1988) won both the CARNEGIE MEDAL and the *GUARDIAN* CHILDREN'S FICTION AWARD, and *Gold Dust* (1993) the Beefeater Children's Novel Award. Her adult work has won equal acclaim. Her writing is vibrant, the language alive, and her plots and settings vary widely: *A Little Lower than the Angels* is set in the Middle Ages; *Plundering Paradise* (1996) is a tale about pirates; *Forever X* (1997) is about a hotel in which Christmas is a perpetual event. Her most recent works are *Cowboy Jess Saddles Up* (1998), for younger readers, and *The Stones are Hatching* (2000), a FANTASY about a boy's quest to stop the Worm waking. Especially noticeable in McCaughrean's work is the value placed on literature and the imagination. In *A Little Lower than the Angels* one of the most urgently felt things is Monsieur Lucie's need to pass on the 'Words' (that is, the text of the Mysteries) intact, to ensure their continuance. These issues are, however, most marked in *A Pack of Lies*, where the relationship between literature and the marketplace, between reading and writing, the status and worth of fiction, are humorously examined. Her retelling of JOHN BUNYAN'S *Pilgrim's Progress* (2000) won the inaugural *BLUE PETER* Award. SA

McCaughren, Tom 1936– Irish author and broadcaster. His ability as a communicator is evident in his writing for children which flows easily yet informatively. He has written a number of ADVENTURE STORIES which are of interest for their particularly Irish settings. The sense of place is also evident in the *Fox* series but matched with a more reflective text. With *Rainbows of the Moon* (1989) he endeavoured to show something of the Northern Ireland conflict through the eyes of two boys from opposing traditions who are caught up together in what is ultimately another adventure yarn. The historical distancing of *In Search of the Liberty Tree* (1994) and *Ride a Pale Horse* (1998), both stories of the 1798 Rebellion, allows him to be bolder in his presentation of conflict. Again with a focus on two boys, the violence of the times and its effect on a small community is described in controlled prose which serves to heighten the tensions and horrors contained within the plot. VC

McCay, Winsor 1867?–1934 American COMIC-strip artist and ANIMATED FILM pioneer. He gained early graphic experience as a poster artist but his first real success came in New York when he created *The Dream of the Rarebit Fiend* for the *New York Evening Telegram*. His best-known and longest-running invention was *Little Nemo In Slumberland*, a full-page colour comic-strip which he drew for the *Sunday New York Herald*. Little Nemo's adventures continued there from October 1905 to July 1911, when McCay transferred to Randolph Hearst's *New York American*, renaming the strip *In the Land of Wonderful Dreams*.

Little Nemo is a child of about six and each strip recounts a dream, always bizarre and often frightening. *Nemo* is Latin for 'nobody', and this is appropriate for a child with no character and no purpose. He does, however, have feelings, often fear or distress. The final frame of each strip shows the serious and often confused little boy waking back into the real world. In creating Little Nemo's dreams and nightmares of giants and monsters, McCay used a visual language he had learned drawing carnival posters as a student, recalling the idiosyncratic people he met in the music halls and the travelling circus. He was also influenced by Art Nouveau graphics. He was a consummate draughtsman, often playing with perspective and changes of scale to challenge the reader and to create a powerful sense of movement. He was innovative in the framing of the strip, for example by stretching a frame horizontally in order to detail the context of an incident or allowing characters to break out of their frames. MAURICE SENDAK, whose own book *IN THE NIGHT KITCHEN* is a homage to popular culture in general and McCay in particular, gives him high praise when he suggests that McCay is 'in league with LEWIS CARROLL and GEORGE MACDONALD'. AR

McCloskey, Robert 1914– American author and illustrator best known for his *Make Way for Ducklings* (1941), awarded the CALDECOTT MEDAL, and for *Homer Price* (1943), his only novel for older readers. Born in Hamilton, Ohio, McCloskey pursued an art career during the depression years, winning the prestigious Prix de Rome in 1939. Though he refers to each of his PICTUREBOOKS as 'a book of drawings', McCloskey has proven he is as adept at putting down a line of prose as he is a line of ink. His books are still praised today for providing a glimpse into the small-town life of yesteryear. McCloskey draws on family experiences for his stories. Homer Price, innocently accident-prone, is much like McCloskey who was himself a tinkerer, an inventor and a would-be musician. The stories are embellished with TALL TALE humour. His *Lentil* (1940) character reflects McCloskey's experience in learning to play the harmonica. His later books are based on situations with his own two daughters, who were also used as models for such books as *One Morning in Maine* (1952) and *Blueberries for Sale* (1948). LAW

McClung, Nellie Letitia 1873–1951 Canadian feminist, social activist, speaker and writer. Currently remembered for her political activities, McClung wrote several popular children's books, notably *Sowing*

Seeds in Danny (1908) and its sequels *The Second Chance* (1910) and *Purple Springs* (1921). The central figure is Pearl Watson, oldest in a large family struggling to make a living in rural Manitoba. Pearl has an optimistic and outspoken naivety that often disrupts adult complacency, and she develops into a powerfully satiric speaker. While McClung makes serious points, especially about the abuse of alcohol, her books are full of lively humour. FEA

McClure, Gillian 1948– British author and illustrator who has helped to promote children's books by giving numerous workshops in schools and libraries in England. Her first book, *The Emperor's Singing Bird*, was published in 1974. In *What's The Time, Rory Wolf?* (1982), the pictures are full of action, the drama partly unfolding through a freeze-frame technique. Also among her earlier books are *Witch Watch* (1989) and *Tog the Ribber, or Granny's Tale* (1985), both based on unusual and somewhat grim dialect poems by her father, Paul Coltman, and both centring upon a child's highly charged, irrational fears. The pictures in *Witch Watch*, with their references to the Russian tale of *Baba-Yaga*, make use of an interesting range of colours, a misty lack of definition, subtlety of expression and slightly stylised human forms to enhance the mystery of the poem. *Tog the Ribber* was shortlisted for both the SMARTIES PRIZE and the KATE GREENAWAY AWARD. McClure's distinctive use of illuminated letters and borders evokes and intensifies the nightmarish emotions felt by a child fleeing in panic from Tog's ghost.

In *The Little White Hen* (1996), a charming story by PHILIPPA PEARCE, the contrast between the gaudy cockerel and the soft, delicate white hen, and the expressions on the animals' faces, greatly enrich the text. In *Selkie* (1999), written and illustrated by McClure and based on legends of seals who can become human when they shed their skins, the stunning use of colour – particularly greens and blues – is again evident, and the sea- and sky-scapes are full of movement and light. JSW

McCord, David (Thompson Watson) 1897–1997 American author who wrote or edited over 40 books of poetry, essays and light verse for children and adults, but was most highly regarded for his children's poems. Born in New York City, he grew up on Long Island, in Princeton, New Jersey, and in Oregon. A graduate of Harvard, he was the executive director of the Harvard Fund Council and an editor of the Harvard Alumni Bulletin. He was the first recipient of the NCTE Award for Excellence in Poetry for Children in 1977, and received many other honours and honorary degrees. His first book of poetry for children, *Far and Few: Rhymes of Never Was and Always Is* (1952), was followed by *Take Sky* (1962). *One at a Time: Collected Poems for the Young* (1977) features poems from seven earlier volumes. McCord has been called an acrobat with language, and most of his poems involve wordplay. Among his best-known are the rollicking chant 'The Pickety Fence', 'Books Fall Open' and 'This Is My Rock'. McCord wrote that 'Poetry, like rain, should fall with elemental music, and poetry for children should catch the eye as well as the ear and the mind. It should delight, it really *has* to delight.' LH

McCully, Emily Arnold 1939– American author and illustrator of books for children and occasional writer of fiction for adults. Born in Illinois, McCully eventually headed east, eschewing the art-school route and instead obtaining an MA in Art History from Columbia University in New York. A prolific illustrator, she provided the artwork for MEINDERT DEJONG's *Journey from Peppermint Street* (1968), the first children's book to win a National Book Award, as well as contributing ILLUSTRATIONS for dozens of other books by authors such as JANE YOLEN, ARNOLD ADOFF and Lee Bennett Hopkins – as well as Sylvia Plath and Arthur Miller. She first soloed in the wordless *Picnic* (1984), then became author-illustrator of books such as *The Grandma Mixup* (1988) and its lighthearted easy-reader sequels. *Mirette on the High Wire* (1992) – the story of a famous high-wire artist who has lost his nerve and is helped by a little girl to make a triumphant comeback – marked a departure from her previous illustrative style of casual pen-and-ink or line and wash, and it was awarded the CALDECOTT MEDAL. McCully illustrated her saga of the young tightrope walker in turn-of-the-century Paris with rich, painterly watercolours highlighted by pastel, which gives the wish-fulfilling 'child to the rescue' plot a glamorous allure. A sequel, *Starring Mirette and Bellini*, appeared in 1997. McCully has described the story of Mirette as 'a metaphor for artistic transformation and an actual artistic leap'. Though less effective than *Mirette*, her other historical PICTUREBOOKS have similarly offered appealing and youthful protagonists in unusual adventures. McCully has also written short stories and *A Craving* (1982), a well-received novel for adults. DS, LH

McDermott, Gerald (Edward) 1941– American illustrator, reteller of FOLKTALES, film-maker and graphic designer. McDermott was born in Detroit, Michigan, where he began his art education at the age of four when his parents enrolled him in a special programme at the Detroit Institute of Arts. He was educated at the Pratt Institute and began his career as a graphic designer and maker of animated films. His first film was *Stonecutter*, based upon a Japanese folktale he remembered from his childhood. In his most

Illustration by Arthur Hughes from *At the Back of the North Wind* by George MacDonald.

successful works, McDermott combines his extensive knowledge of folklore and hero tales with a highly developed sense of graphic design which incorporates colour, texture and pattern to create powerful tales with strong visual narrative lines. He won the Caldecott Honor Award for his first children's PICTUREBOOK, which was an adaptation of his film, *Anansi the Spider* (1972) (see ANANCY). He also received a Boston Horn Book Honor Citation for *The Magic Tree* (1973); the CALDECOTT MEDAL for *Arrow to the Sun* (1975); and a Caldecott Honour Award for *Raven* (1994). Ever since his association with mythologist Joseph Campbell, who served as a consultant on several of his early films, McDermott has been interested in the different stages and cycles of hero and TRICKSTER tales. His trickster tales collection includes *Anansi* (1972), *Papagayo* (1978), *Zomo* (1992), *Raven* (1994) and *Coyote* (1997). DJH

MacDonald, Betty see *MRS PIGGLE WIGGLE* SERIES; see also HILARY KNIGHT

Macdonald, Caroline 1948–97 Popular Australian writer of adolescent fiction, renowned for her exploration of new ideas in varied settings and genres which include, and in some cases blend, SCIENCE FICTION and FANTASY. Macdonald's early award-winning books, *Visitors* (1984) and *THE LAKE AT THE END OF THE WORLD* (1988), are characterised by questions posed about the place of human beings in the universe. In later titles her strong characters, often in striking landscapes, continue to ask questions and play roles in narratives leading to unusual resolutions. Her sometimes eccentric characters fall just within the bounds of reality. *The Eye Witness* (1991), a murder mystery set in the year 2046, in a very controlled world, is particularly absorbing for young readers. *SPEAKING TO MIRANDA* (1990) depicts Ruby in a search for her identity. The intriguing idea of 'colonising' – where one family takes over another – is played out by a group of entirely believable dysfunctional characters in *Spider Mansion* (1994). Many of Macdonald's later titles could best be described as psychological thrillers. Her compelling narratives, all of which address relevant life issues, are written with assurance and conviction, and confirm her reputation as a significant writer for young people. FK

MacDonald, George 1824–1905 Perhaps the most important of the Victorian fantasists, MacDonald was born into a farming family in Aberdeen, Scotland. He was brought up as a Calvinist, and entered a theological college in 1848, though he later resigned his ministry in Arundel, Sussex, because of doctrinal disagreements with his congregation. Though struggling for a time with financial hardship (his marriage to Louisa Powell in 1851 produced a large family of eleven children to bring up), his career as a writer was eventually to bring him both fame and a steady income. He was accepted into the best literary circles of the day, his friends including John Ruskin and LEWIS CARROLL; he met the latter in 1862 while both were undergoing speech therapy with James Hunt. The MacDonald family were in fact responsible for encouraging Carroll to publish *ALICE'S ADVENTURES IN WONDERLAND*. He took up a professorship at Bedford College in 1859, later moving to Italy in 1881. The MacDonalds returned to England in 1900, and he died five years later.

His first published work was the poetic drama *Within and Without* (1855), but the first of his major works for children, *At the Back of the North Wind*, was not published until 1871 when MacDonald was 47. The year before this he had become the editor of the magazine *Good Words for the Young* in which the two books about Princess Irene and Curdie the miner's son, *The Princess and the Goblin* (1872) and *The Princess and Curdie* (1883), were first published in serial form. Though MacDonald's achievement in children's literature is today mainly discussed in terms of the three novels mentioned above, his FAIRY TALES are also minor masterpieces, *The Light Princess* being perhaps the most frequently anthologised of these.

MacDonald's writing has often been described as mystical and allegorical, though it is not always easy to say exactly how the allegories are to be read. One of the characteristics of MacDonald's work is its double vision: its insistence that behind the tangible and material world lies another reality, which is often apprehendable only through faith. In the *The Princess and Curdie*, for example, Curdie begins to be able to discern the rich reality surrounding the existence of old Princess Irene, which he could formerly only perceive as a 'bare garret, a heap of musty straw, a sunbeam and a withered apple'. He also learns that the 'truths' of flesh are not necessarily ultimate truths: men's bodies may hide a bestial spirit, the monster's paw a child's hand. Unlike the playfulness of the *Alice* books, MacDonald's fantasies are sombre pieces of writing, whose strong and occasionally frightening images underline the seriousness of the moral and spiritual dimension of the stories; for example, the old princess's rose-fire, into which Curdie has to plunge his hands, constitutes a beautiful but fierce reminder of the price one pays in pain for spiritual cleansing. The influence of Macdonald's work may be traced in that of C. S. LEWIS and J. R. R. TOLKIEN. SA

McDonald, Meme 1954– and **Pryor, (Monty) Boori** 1950– The creative partnership of these two indigenous Australians has produced poignant and beautifully crafted semi-autobiographical work which is lauded in Australian literary circles. McDonald and Monty Pryor travel the country, celebrating both aboriginal culture and common humanity with groups of young people through music and STORYTELLING. The award-winning *My Girragundji* (1998) and *The Binna Binna Man* (1999) are powerful novels about a boy growing up in two cultures and attempting to define himself. The authors employ language true to the oral tradition to draw readers into a world of tragedy, comedy, prejudice, spirituality and the love of an extended family. The stories show great respect for traditional custom and acknowledge the part played by heritage in creating an identity. Ultimately, though, they are about belonging, so that the stories are not so much exclusively indigenous as simply human. RTh

Macdonald, Shelagh see NEGLECTED WORKS; see also NUDITY IN CHILDREN'S BOOKS

McEwan, Ian 1948– British novelist born in Aldershot who began writing in 1970. Probably his best-known work, *The Child in Time* (1987) won the Whitbread Prize for Fiction and its chapters painfully convey the emotional devastation which follows the abduction of a child. The novel explores and charts how the passage of time, the process of grief and the nature of human love can effect a slow recovery from such anguish. McEwan's only book for children, *The Daydreamer* (1996), examines the possibilities and consequences of transformation. In these seven short stories Peter, whose idiosyncratic ways and inclination to live within his FANTASIES identify him as the 'difficult' daydreaming child of the title, observes his own daily life from a variety of metamorphosed perspectives. Distinctively illustrated by ANTHONY BROWNE, the book's current of black humour flowing through the lucid prose pulls in the adult alongside the child reader. McEwan wrote the text for the British publication of the controversial PICTUREBOOK *Rose Blanche* (1985). Based on fact – via a story by Christophe Gallaz – without overt comment or judgement, the quiet, understated text chronicles the experiences of a German child through the Winter of 1944/5. The eloquence of McEwan's language is complemented by the compelling poignance of ROBERTO INNOCENTI's illustrations. CMN

McFarlane, Leslie see *HARDY BOYS*

McFarlane, Peter 1940– Australian poet, anthologist, performance poet, short-story writer and novelist. During many years as a secondary-school teacher McFarlane was active in promoting drama and poetry, both in his home state of South Australia and nationally. A partly autobiographical novel, *The Tin House* (1989), followed several notable poetry anthologies and texts that included his own work. Two collections, *The Flea and Other Stories* (1992) and *Lovebird* (1993), established McFarlane's ability to capture the interests, concerns, spirit and voices of Australian young adults.

The Enemy You Killed (1996) is a portrait of obsession and of young people looking for meaning, love, excitement and danger. Now a full-time writer, McFarlane drew on his teaching experiences to tell the story of teenagers who regularly play war games, sometimes with real bullets, in the Adelaide Hills. For some these games are a chance to escape and show off to their peers and girlfriends. For others, such as the psychologically disturbed Wade, real-life needs and emotions become confused. Popular with many readers, who admire its gritty honesty and realism, the book proved too confrontational for some adults.

McFarlane continues to work on poetry books and is in demand as a speaker, performance poet and workshop leader. He can captivate and involve even large groups of apparently disaffected young people, as well as professionals. Twenty-year-old Tammy, a loyal supporter of a football team, is the narrator in *More Than a Game* (1998); despite some intellectual disability, Tammy has grit and determination, especially when it involves her football team. McFarlane is versatile, revealing a lighter and brighter side in the series of romps for younger readers, which include *Rebecca the Wrecker* (1995), *Bruce the Goose* (1996) and *Max the Mountain Man* (1997) AN

McGillis, Roderick see CRITICAL APPROACHES TO CHILDREN'S LITERATURE

McGinley, Phyllis 1905–78 American poet and essayist for children and adults. Born in Ontario, Oregon, McGinley was raised in the Colorado 'wild west'. The nearest school was four miles away and the nearest library was much farther, but McGinley was an avid reader. She wrote her first poem when she was six years old, and discovered her vocation. After graduating from the University of Utah she spent four years working as an English teacher. Later she married, had two daughters, and was glad to stay at home with them and write when she could do so without compromising her family responsibilities. In 1944 she published her first children's book, *The Horse Who Lived Upstairs*, a story in verse. This was followed by nearly two dozen more children's books, including *All Around the Town* (1948) and *The Most Wonderful Doll in the World* (1950), both named Caldecott Honour Books. McGinley believed strongly that children deserve excellent books that do not talk down to them. Her own books are rich in difficult and mysterious words and complicated imagery. In addition to children's books, McGinley wrote volumes of humorous essays and more than a dozen books of poetry for adults, including the Pulitzer Prize-winner, *Times Three: Selected Verse from Three Decades* (1961). CAB

see also DOLL STORIES

McGough, Roger 1937– English poet and anthologist. McGough made his name as a member of the pop group 'The Scaffold', and as one of the 'Mersey Sound' poets along with BRIAN PATTEN and ADRIAN HENRI in 1960s Liverpool. The inspiration of his young son, Finn, lay behind McGough's first collection for children, *Mr Noselighter* (1976). The wordplay evident in these poems has become McGough's hallmark in his many subsequent children's collections, including the SIGNAL AWARD winner *SKY IN THE PIE* (1983). McGough's highly individual brand of nonsense is counterbalanced by the dark shadows which lurk within his best poems, a disquieting reality on which the humour casts an oblique light. In the joint collection with MICHAEL ROSEN, *You Tell Me* (1979), for instance, 'Snipers' deals with Uncle Tom's delayed wartime shock from a child's point of view, with sympathetic humour but underlying seriousness: 'He knows damn well he's still at war,/just that the snipers aren't Japs anymore.' 'Streemin', in the same collection, sees school groupings in a mordant light: 'look at the cemetery/no streemin there'. McGough has published many other collections and selections of his poems, including *Nailing the Shadow* (1987) and *An Imaginary Menagerie* (1988); and for a younger audience, *Pillow Talk* (1990) and his latest *Bad, Bad Cats* (1997). He is also the editor of anthologies of comic verse and love poems. He is a regular performer of his own poetry, with a characteristic deadpan manner. ML

McGraw, Eloise Jarvis 1915–2000 American author of HISTORICAL FICTION, contemporary stories and FANTASY. Formerly a professional artist, McGraw married journalist William Corbin [McGraw]; both became successful children's writers. McGraw's early contemporary stories were notable for compelling storytelling, unusual backgrounds – a circus (*Sawdust in His Shoes*, 1950) and a logging camp (*Crown Fire*, 1951) – and semi-civilised but appealing adolescent heroes. While her first historical novel, *Moccasin Trail* (1952), featured a similar hero in a conventional frontier setting, its successors ranged from a vividly realised ancient Egypt (*Mara: Daughter of the Nile*, 1953; *The Golden Goblet*, 1961, a Newbery Honour Book), to London during the Great Fire of 1666 (*Master Cornhill*, 1973) and England in 1066 (*The Striped Ships*, 1991). McGraw returned to contemporary stories with *Greensleeves* (1968), which depicts with unerring accuracy an adolescent identity-crisis of the mid-1960s. Entranced by the OZ books as a child, she contributed two well-received volumes to the series, in collaboration with her daughter Lauren. *The Moorchild* (1996), another venture into fantasy and a Newbery Honour Book, poignantly comments through the changeling legend on the situation of any child who is rejected by a community for being 'different'. SR

McGraw, Sheila see ROBERT MUNSCH

McGuffey Eclectic Readers, The School texts first developed in 1836 by William Holmes McGuffey, a Presbyterian minister and Professor of Moral Philosophy and Ancient Languages at Miami University, Ohio. They were the most widely circulated school texts sold in the United States during the second half of the 19th century. The McGuffey texts were a series of readers graded in levels of increasing difficulty that were also intended to teach moral precepts. McGuffey compiled the series at the request of the Cincinnati publishing firm, Truman and Smith, who were eager to produce material for the influx of new immigrants and the burgeoning mid-west book market. The *Eclectic First Reader* and the *Eclectic Second Reader* first appeared in 1836, and the *Third* and *Fourth* readers in 1837. McGuffey's brother, Alexander, produced the *Fifth Reader* in 1844, a spelling book in 1846, and the *Sixth Reader* in 1857 (although credit for these volumes is often mistakenly given to William).

In preparation for the first two readers, McGuffey gathered a group of young children in his house to determine the material appropriate to their ages and interests. As he created his series, he compiled excerpts from a variety of existing textbooks. Although this was a common editorial practice at the time, it resulted in a lawsuit from a competing publisher; the case was later dismissed.

The books consisted of extracts of stories, poems, essays and speeches from a variety of English and American sources. Selections from British literature included WILLIAM SHAKESPEARE, John Milton, SIR WALTER SCOTT, CHARLES DICKENS, LORD BYRON and MARIA EDGEWORTH. American authors included SARA JOSEPHA HALE, S. G. GOODRICH, Harriet Beecher Stowe, WASHINGTON IRVING, NATHANIEL HAWTHORNE and JOHN GREENLEAF WHITTIER. Several prominent political theorists, such as Noah Webster, Thomas Jefferson, JEAN JACQUES ROUSSEAU and William Blackwood were also represented. The readers also included guides for pronunciation, elocution and syllabication, as well as new vocabulary and questions to test reading comprehension. The readings themselves emphasised independence, industry, compassion to the poor, temperance and a strict Calvinist sense of piety. Truman and Smith chose the title 'eclectic' to describe both the content of the volumes and a new form of pedagogy supposedly developed by companions of Pestalozzi.

During the Civil War, the Methodist Book Concern of Chattanooga, Tennessee, began to publish the McGuffey Readers in the southern states. The books passed through a series of publishers and seven distinct editions. During these revisions, much of the original emphasis on Calvinist doctrine was replaced by a more secularised civil morality. McGuffey himself was not, however, responsible for any of the revisions or new editions. Indeed, while the first editions sold over seven million copies, McGuffey received an initial payment of only 1,000 dollars (although McGuffey lore adds that he was sent, in recompense, a barrel of hams each Christmas). Over 122 million copies of the readers were eventually sold between 1836 and 1920. The books are still in print and continue to be used to this day in some school districts. JKB

Machine Gunners, The (1975) Novel by the British author ROBERT WESTALL and winner of the CARNEGIE MEDAL. It describes the life of a group of children living in Westall's fictional Garmouth during World War II. Chas McGill, who also appears in a short story, *The Haunting of Chas McGill* (1983), is intent on creating a prize collection of war-time souvenirs. He and his friends build a professional encampment around a machine gun. The children, like those in many of Westall's novels, form a unit which is almost self-sufficient, looking after themselves competently in the camp. They take a German pilot prisoner, enlisting his help to make the gun work; he comes to care for them but questions the wisdom of giving a gun to children and as he does so the adult world starts to impinge for the first time. When adults do finally discover the camp their arrival clearly brings tragedy for the children, who are never to be together again. A sequel, *Fathom Five* (1979), returns to the same setting where Chas and a couple of his friends, now older and distanced from adult rules, are intent on catching a spy. The story is less compelling than the first book, but nevertheless retains many of its strengths. KA

Mackay, Claire 1930– Canadian writer of fiction and non-fiction. Born and raised in Toronto, Mackay worked as a social worker and raised a family of three boys. Her first novel, *Mini-Bike Hero* (1974), was followed by two sequels, *Mini-Bike Racer* (1975) and *Mini-Bike Rescue* (1982). *Exit Barney McGee* (1979) is one of her popular ADVENTURE STORIES for middle-grade readers. *One Proud Summer* (1981) is about the 1946 Valleyfield Textile Workers' Strike in Quebec. *Pay Cheques and Picket Lines* (1987) further reflects Mackay's interest in the Labour Movement. *The Minerva Program* (1984) is about computers. Mackay's non-fiction also deals with geography, history, sports and computers. Her fiction concentrates on the conflicts and problems faced by adolescents, who learn to identify with adults and acquire a greater awareness of the trouble adults must face. Mackay won the Ruth Schwartz Book Award in 1981 and Honourable Mention in the 1982 Canada Council Children's Literature Prize and The Vicky Metcalf Award for a Body of Work for Children in 1983. A short story, 'Marvin and Me and the Flies' published in *Canadian Children's Annual* no. 11 (1987), won the Vicky Metcalf Short Story Award in 1988. MRS

Mackay, David see *FLOCK OF WORDS, A*

McKee, David (John), 1935– British author and illustrator, celebrated for a number of classic PICTUREBOOKS and popular series from the later 1960s onwards. He helped to pioneer the genre of highly sophisticated pictorial narratives which can appeal on different but overlapping planes both to very young children and to adults. *Two Can Toucan* (1965, revised edition 1989) broached his continuing concern with individual difference and isolation, and the funny ways in which it can be resolved. This powerful theme ran through the classic ELMER (1968) to the more recent *Isabel's Noisy Tummy* (1994). Wider overtones of racial conflict and resolution were evident in *Tusk Tusk* (1978). Most successful of McKee's series have been *Mr Benn* (1967 onwards) and *King Rollo* (1979 onwards), a witty metaphor of the nursery, in which McKee's empathy with small children is convincing and funny. That empathy informs *NOT NOW, BERNARD* (1980) and *I HATE MY TEDDY BEAR* (UK, 1982; USA, 1984) which explore serious childhood emotions in a very humorous vein. *Who's a Clever Baby, Then?* (1988) (USA: *Who's a Clever Baby?*) and *The Monster and the Teddy Bear* (1989) continue to portray aspects of the communication gap between adults and children. McKee has been a regular illustrator of other major authors, including Forrest Wilson (*SUPER GRAN* series, 1978 onwards) and URSULA MORAY WILLIAMS (*Jeffy, the Burglar's Cat*, 1981) and has illustrated editions of *THE WIZARD OF OZ* and *The Marvellous Land of Oz*. PC

Macken, Walter 1915–67 Irish novelist and dramatist. Mainly a writer for adults, he produced two adventure stories for children, *The Island of the Great Yellow Ox* (1966) and *The Flight of the Doves* (1967). VC

Mackenzie, Sir Compton see FAIRY TALES

McKinley, (Jennifer Carolyn) Robin 1952– American author of nearly 20 books for children and young adults, known especially for her high FANTASY and personalised adaptations of FAIRY TALES. In her first novel *Beauty: A Retelling of the Story of Beauty and the Beast* (1978), she uses a first-person voice, that of Honour, the renamed heroine of the tale. Like the female protagonists of her other books, especially those who appear in the *Damarian Cycle*, Honour starts out as an unlikely hero but becomes one of the 'girls who do things' – a focus for much of McKinley's writing. In both *The Blue Sword* (1982) and the sequel, NEWBERY AWARD winner *The Hero and the Crown* (1984), McKinley develops the realm of Damar, a pseudo-Victorian world reminiscent of KIPLING's India. Here she skillfully combines fantasy and romance with strong, feisty heroines like Harry Crewe and Aerin, the legendary Damarian king's daughter. In these books, and in later ones such as *The Outlaws of Sherwood* (1988) and *Deerskin* (1993), McKinley is careful to make her feminist point while blending the magical and the mundane, the fantastic and the real. JCA

McKissack, Fredrick 1939– and **McKissack, Patricia** 1944– American authors of books for children. Fredrick McKissack and Patricia Carwell were born in Nashville, Tennessee, and have known each other since their teens. They both received degrees from Tennessee State University and were married in 1964. Fred then worked as a general contractor, and Patricia became a teacher and educational consultant. Patricia began writing for children while a teacher. Confronted with an absence of materials for children on African American history, she wrote her first book, a BIOGRAPHY of Paul Lawrence Dunbar in 1984. She has since written prolifically, producing non-fiction, PICTUREBOOKS and novels, as well as retelling FOLKTALES. *Flossie and the Fox* (1986) and *Mirandy and Brother Wind* (1988) are both Caldecott Honour Books, and the latter received a CORETTA SCOTT KING AWARD. She has also compiled a collection of folktales, *The Dark-Thirty* (1993), which was a Newbery Honour Book. Her folktales employ a distinctive rural, southern African American dialect. Fredrick has also written several books, including a biography of Frederick Douglas and *The History of the Civil Rights Movement* (1986).

However, the McKissacks are best known for their co-authored books. They published their first book together in 1984 and have collaborated on more than 50 books since. Many of these texts have been biographies, including those published in the *Great African American* series. *Sojourner Truth: Ain't I a Woman* (1993) received the BOSTON GLOBE-HORN BOOK AWARD for non-fiction and was also a Coretta Scott King Honour Book. In addition to their biographical accounts, the McKissacks have authored non-fiction books which are known for being detailed and meticulously researched. These books have focused on diverse aspects of African American history. *A Long Hard Journey: The Story of the Pullman Porter* (1990), which looks at the labour movement and the creation of the sleeping car porters, is a Coretta Scott King Award recipient. *Rebels Against Slavery* (1996) examines various forms of struggle against enslavement. In *The Royal Kingdoms of Ghana, Mali and Songhay: Life in Medieval Africa* (1994) the McKissacks reach back even further in time to examine three West African kingdoms during medieval times. *African-American Scientists* (1994) and *African-American Inventors* (1994) are testaments to the achievements and contributions of African Americans in science from colonial times to the present. These books profile well-known scientists – Benjamin Banniker and George Washington Carver – as well as virtually unknown scientists. In each of these non-fiction books, archival documents, photos and ILLUSTRATIONS supplement the text.

The husband-and-wife team has also retold folktales and authored original fiction. Their picturebook *Christmas in the Big House, Christmas in the Quarters* (1994), which contrasts the lives of the enslaved people with those of the landowners, was a recipient of both the Coretta Scott King Award and the Boston Globe-Horn Book Award. The McKissacks have three children, one of whom, Fredrick McKissack Jr., collaborated with his mother to produce *Black Diamond* (1994), a non-fiction book about the Negro Baseball League. EB

see also AFRICAN AMERICAN LITERATURE

MacLachlan, Patricia 1938– American author of fiction and PICTUREBOOKS best known for her NEWBERY MEDAL winner, *Sarah Plain and Tall* (1985), which was made into a film. Based on an episode in family history, the book tells the story of a farmer who advertises for a companion to look after himself and his children. Sarah, who describes herself as 'plain and tall', answers the advertisement and comes to live with the family. The story is a simple and slow-paced one; while the children dream of having Sarah for a second mother, events move so slowly that at times they become convinced that they will lose her. This strong and uncomplicated relationship between Sarah and her stepchildren is unusual in contemporary fiction, which tends to represent such relationships as problematic. The book is lyrically written and compresses strong emotions into few words, creating a short but very powerful novel. It is fused with a sense of the vastness of the prairie landscape that surrounds the family, a setting which is in marked contrast to Sarah's beloved Maine coast. There is a strong sense of family unity and mutual support while the isolation of the family in the wide prairie landscape is reminiscent of LAURA INGALLS WILDER's *LITTLE HOUSE* series. In the sequel, *Skylark* (1994), the family's livelihood is threatened by the drought on the prairie and Sarah and the children have to leave their home. Much as the children enjoy their new life in Maine they fear that they will never see their father again and that their precious family will be destroyed. However the reader gradually realises that Sarah is pregnant and the news of the impending baby restores the children's belief in their family.

MacLachlan's picturebook *All The Places To Love* (1994) also examines the importance of home and the special places a small child comes to love, showing the link that the family home provides across the generations. Two later novels, *Journey* (1991) and *Baby* (1993), are both written in the same sparse but lyrical style. Again the family unit provides the main theme, though these novels begin with a broken family and it is the attempt to make it whole again which forms their centre. In *Journey* the hero struggles to understand why his mother should have left them while his grandfather tries to recreate a family by taking endless family photographs. In *Baby* a family take in an abandoned baby and grow to love her, although they know that one day they will lose her; only when the child returns to her mother can they begin to talk about their own baby son who died. Language is shown to have healing properties; Papa tells Mama that they need 'Words . . . Not painting. Not dancing. *Words*.' Once they give the dead baby a name they can begin to mourn him properly. As with all Maclachlan's novels, the reader is always conscious of the fragile nature of happiness, although misery is again held at bay by the strength of the family. KA

McLean, Andrew 1946– and **McLean, Janet (Neilson)** 1946– Australian husband-and-wife team, who have collaborated on a number of successful PICTUREBOOKS. *The Riverboat Crew* (1978), *The Steam Train Crew* (1981) and the later *Fire-Engine Lil* (1989) are humorous, well-structured stories which, while commemorating the excitement of early forms of transport, also highlight with an economical use of words the universality of human foibles. Andrew's early intense and regular CROSS HATCHING style was followed by a more fluid use of soft crayon and ink, as in *Hector and Maggie* (1990), a CHILDREN'S BOOK COUNCIL OF AUSTRALIA Honour Book (1991), where words and pictures form an inseparable text in this tale of a bossy rooster put in his place by a shy sheepdog. Animals also feature in *Oh, Kipper* (1991) – a deceptively simple and tender story of the need for humans (and dogs) to belong – in *Dog Tales* (1992), another Children's Book Council of Australia Honour Book (1994), and in *Cat Goes to Sea* (1994). JAP

MacLeod, Anne Scot see CRITICAL APPROACHES TO CHILDREN'S LITERATURE

Macleod, Doug 1959– Australian poet, writer and scriptwriter who published his first book, *Hippopotabus* in 1976, while still a teenager. Humorous poetry books include *In the Garden of Badthings* (1982), and *Fed-Up Family Album* (1983). An inventive absent-minded professor features in *Tales of Tuttle* (1980), and *Frank Boulderbuster* (1985) is a satirical collection of outback ADVENTURE STORIES. His riotous, irreverent *Sister Madge's Book of Nuns* (1986) and its sequel earned him both accolades and some notoriety. A picturebook, *Ten Monster Islands* (1987), was one of his later works. In later years he concentrated on his work as editor and scriptwriter of significant TELEVISION comedy programmes. RS

McMurtry, Larry see *BILLY THE KID*; see also *CALAMITY JANE*

McNaughton, Colin 1951– British illustrator and writer. *Have You Seen Who's Just Moved In Next Door To Us?* (1990) was winner of the KURT MASCHLER AWARD in 1991. In *Making Friends with Frankenstein* (1993), *There's an Awful Lot of Weirdos in Our Neighbourhood* (1987) and *Who's Been Sleeping in my Porridge* (1990), McNaughton spoofs NURSERY RHYMES and familiar characters from FAIRY TALES and popular culture, or creates his own endearing monsters and animal/human mutations, at the same time as managing to address issues of difference and prejudice. McNaughton was influenced by comics, and also by the work of EDWARD ARDIZZONE and MERVYN PEAKE. As a trained graphic designer he is responsible for the overall design of his books. His colourful, bold and expressive ILLUSTRATIONS exaggerate and heighten absurdity, weirdness and, in particular, the disgusting details of some of his characters' behaviour, many of whom – for example the eccentric sailors from *Captain Abdul's Pirate School* (1994) – make frequent appearances in his books. Playfulness with traditional narrative is also evident in prose stories featuring the adventures of Preston Pig and the Big Bad Wolf, such as *Suddenly* (1994) – shortlisted for the SMARTIES PRIZE – *Boo!* (1995) and *Oops!* (1996), winner of the Smarties Prize. JL

McNeill, Janet 1907–94 Dublin-born novelist and dramatist. McNeill was a prolific and popular writer for children and adults during the 1950s, 60s and 70s. In *My Friend Specs McCann* (1955) the exploits of schoolboy Specs are narrated by his friend Curtis in a direct, somewhat idiosyncratic manner, giving them a gentle charm as reality, at times, blurs into mild FANTASY. The first *Specs* book was followed by others, all illustrated by Rowel Friers in the original editions. In her later writings, and in particular in the *Dove Square* books (see *THE BATTLE OF ST. GEORGE WITHOUT*), McNeill displays considerably more subtlety. She also contributed to the *Nipper* reading series. VC

McNish, Cliff see *THE DOOMSPELL*

McOwan, Rennie see *LIGHT ON DUM-Y-YAT*

McPhail, David see X. J. KENNEDY

McRae, Rodney (John) 1958– New Zealand-born Australian illustrator and writer, whose experiences as a graphic designer, animator and erstwhile taxidermist are evident influences on his approaches to ILLUSTRATION. With over 60 published works, his illustrations range from realistic images in coloured pencil in his first book, *The Terrible Taniwha of Timber Ditch* (1982), written by JOY COWLEY, to the decorative, geometrically patterned symbolic images exploring Australian architecture, politics and social structures for W.A. Cawthorne's original (c. 1870) poem, *Who Killed Cockatoo?* (1988). McRae's own PICTUREBOOKS include *Why Doesn't Anyone Like Me?* (1984), *The Trouble with Heathrow* (1986), and his own favourite, *Cry Me a River* (1991), with its more serious ecological theme. *Aesop's Fables* (1992) is a fine showcase of McRae's versatility and talent in which he adopts his techniques to present different cultural styles and media, ranging across line-and-wash, acrylic paint, woodcut and block prints, while at the same time tracing the chronological history of art. JAP

MacRaois, Cormac see *GILTSPUR* TRILOGY

McSkimming, Geoffrey 1962– Australian actor, editor and author of the comic-adventure *CAIRO JIM* series, published since 1991. McSkimming has built up an avid audience – over 3,000 children have joined the Cairo Jim Club, which was formed in 1995 – but, perhaps because of his chosen genre, his writing has received little critical attention. NLR

Mad Magazine (1953–) American comic monthly, published by William Gaines. Part of his E-C Comics empire, *Mad* quickly evolved from a satire on other comic books into an enormously popular magazine of irreverent, sometimes sophomoric, commentary on America's changing culture. Featuring the cartoons and writing of the brilliant, self-named 'usual gang of idiots' – now in its second generation – *Mad* continues even-handedly to deflate politicians, celebrities, relationships, media, religion, and more. Its best-known character, the gap-toothed Alfred E. Newman, and his motto 'What, Me Worry?' also appear in scores of *Mad* series books and was humorously run for President in 1972. AA

Madame Doubtfire (1987) (US: *Alias Madame Doubtfire*) Perceptive comic novel by the British author ANNE FINE about the aftermath of divorce, adapted into the American hit movie *Mrs Doubtfire* (1993). An unemployed father sees more of his children by impersonating a respectable older woman, appointed nanny by his hostile ex-wife. The inventive rantings of the angry father entertainingly recount the adult-inflicted cruelties, while the children plod stoically on. Comic tension coaxes the reader through the battered feelings of everyone. As the impeccable and indispensable nanny the father gains a fresh vantage point, but thankfully there are no concessions to glib endings. CMP

Madeline Series of award-winning PICTUREBOOKS by the Austrian-born American author-illustrator Ludwig Bemelmans (1898–1962), published between 1939 and 1961. The stories, which are written in rhyming couplets and illustrated in deceptively simple style, are about a group of French convent-school girls of whom the smallest and bravest is Madeline. The books have become household favourites, still in print in Britain, France and America. The first, conceived while the author was on holiday on a French island, is set against a Parisian background featuring familiar landmarks. Later stories take the 'twelve little girls in two straight lines' around France and as far as London. KA

Maeterlinck, Maurice see *BLUE BIRD, THE*; see also DRAMA FOR CHILDREN

magazines see COMICS, PERIODICALS AND MAGAZINES; see also ANNUALS; PUBLISHING AND PUBLISHERS

Magee, Wes 1939– British educationalist, anthologist and poet. Sometimes his own poetry hits the right tone with astonishing sensitivity and precision – see especially 'Tracey's Tree', which is about a schoolgirl killed in a road accident, and 'Good Questions Bad Answers', which is a remarkable exercise in nostalgia. His edited poetry volumes for children include *A Christmas Stocking* (1988) and *A Big Poetry Book* (1989). His inventive and amusing *Scumbagg School* stories (from 1993) are enormously successful. FRS

Magic see ANNUALS; COMICS, PERIODICALS AND MAGAZINE

Magic Apple Tree, The (1980) Nigerian folktale retold by Ogbonne Alor, with striking abstract pen-and-ink drawings by artist Chika Aniakor. Evoking the narrative style of Igbo storytelling, it relates how an orphan boy receives bountiful fruit from his dead mother and wins out over his tormentors. VD

Magic Bedknob, The see *BEDKNOB AND BROOMSTICK*; see also NUDITY IN CHILDREN'S BOOKS

Magic Faraway Tree, The (1943) A novel by ENID BLYTON about four children – Jo, Fanny, Bessie and Dick – and their adventures in the different FANTASY lands reached via a huge tree inhabited by a variety of fantasy beings such as Moon-Face and the Saucepan Man. The initial idea probably came from the tree of Norse mythology, Yggdrasill, which also has a squirrel running errands, and, likewise, has its roots attacked (see CLASSICAL MYTHOLOGY). Altogether there are four Faraway Tree books, beginning with *The Enchanted Wood* (1939); *The Folk of the Faraway Tree* (1946) eventually followed and the last was *Up the Faraway Tree* (1951), which was in picture format and illustrated by Dorothy M. Wheeler. The books seem to have provided the springboard for innumerable fantasies amongst tree-climbing readers worldwide. DR

Magic Gourd, The (1985) Story by Kenyan author Kurji Naya, one of the few Kenyans of Indian origin who has written a story for Kenyan children. It concerns a polygamous home and the normal problems which face most of the members, such as jealousies among the wives, and the use of witchdoctors and herbal medicines. The story includes a variety of incidents especially appealing to the enquiring minds of children. ABO

Magic Listening Cap, The: More Folk Tales from Japan see YOSHIKO UCHIDA

Magic Mirror (1985) First collection of poems by JUDITH NICHOLLS, which, with its rich variety of themes and forms, including HAIKU and shape poems, demonstrates Nicholls's versatility and characteristically gentle humour. Her continuing concern for and sense of wonder at all aspects of the natural universe also comes through strongly. Nicholls's earlier career as a primary-school teacher positively informs her work. ML

Magic Pudding, The: Being the Adventures of Bunyip Bluegum and His Friends Bill Barnacle and Sam Sawnoff (1918) Written and illustrated by Australian artist Norman Lindsay (1879–1969), who believed that a funny story about food would interest every child, this story has become a classic. Albert, the pudding with personality, is fought over by the rightful Pudding Owners (Bunyip BlueGum, a koala in a porkpie hat, Sam Sawnoff the penguin, and Bill Barnacle, a sailor) and the Pudding Thieves, Possum and Wombat. The story is fast-paced and written in a rumbustious style. Much of the slang is dated. Lindsay's sketches decorating the prose and comic verse are probably better known today than his story, despite constant reprints. It is Lindsay's only memorable children's book. HE

Magic Roundabout, The Long-running series of five-minute films made for British TELEVISION, starting on 18 October 1965, at 5.50 pm on BBC, a time assumed to be just before bedtime for very young viewers. Adults soon became hooked too, and the series quickly assumed cult status. Having been created in France by Serge Danot, the programmes were anglicised by Eric Thompson. Episode 1 was entitled 'Mr Rusty Meets Zebedee', and other favourite characters included Ermentrude the cow, Brian the snail, and Dougal, a somewhat unlikely Scots terrier. A cartoon-strip adaptation ran in the COMIC *T.V. Toyland* (1966). DG

Magician's House Quartet, The see WILLIAM CORLETT

Magnet see COMICS, PERIODICALS AND MAGAZINES; *'THE BIG FIVE'*; see also ANNUALS; *GREYFRIARS HOLIDAY ANNUAL*; CHARLES HAMILTON; SCHOOL STORIES

Magorian, Michelle 1947– British author, best known for her YOUNG ADULT FICTION, who won widespread acclaim for *GOODNIGHT MISTER TOM*. The novels are set during the 1940s and examine how people coped with the many difficulties of the period. Parents are often depicted as absent or very strict, and sometimes brutal. The heroes and heroines are not afraid to query the judgement of their elders; in *A Little Love Song* (1991) Diana is resolute in her defence of an unmarried pregnant girl, and in *Cuckoo in the Nest* (1994) Tom is determined to work in the theatre, despite his father's opposition. KA

Magpies (1986–) Australian magazine reviewing children's books, both fiction and information, with a special emphasis on Australian material. It also publishes profiles of leading authors, illustrators and 'book people' along with articles and papers (many of which originated at *Magpies* seminars), by leading Australian writers and critics. MSax

Maguire, Gregory 1954– American writer for children and adults, teacher, and commentator on children's books. Maguire's early work, beginning with *The Lightning Time* (1978), established his reputation as a writer of FANTASY. Since then he has shown himself to be a versatile storyteller, ranging from the intensity of *I Feel Like the Morning Star* (1989), set in a fall-out shelter in the future, to the nonsense world of *Seven Spiders Spinning* (1994). Strong characterisation is the hallmark of *The Good Liar* (1995), set in Nazi-occupied France. Maguire's ability to depict a terrible time in a manner appropriate to his readers but without pulling punches is evident here. His lightness of touch is apparent in *Lucas Fishbone* (1990), a PICTUREBOOK on the theme of death and regeneration. VC

Mahabharata see INDIAN MYTHS, LEGENDS AND FOLKTALES; see also SHANTA RAMESHWAR RAO

Mahy, Margaret 1936– Prolific New Zealand writer of over 150 PICTUREBOOKS, short-story collections, and novels ranging from beginner to young adult levels of readership. Mahy's international career began in 1969 with the publication of five picturebooks, their texts previously published in the New Zealand *School Journal*. In these early picturebooks, notably *A Lion in the Meadow*, illustrated by Jenny Williams, Mahy deals with opposing concepts of reality and illusion, truth and imagination – concepts which become a constant preoccupation in her fiction. The energetic and exuberant sense of humour which characterises her stories enlivens even the most serious, from the antics of a supposedly wicked uncle in *The Pirate Uncle* (1977), and the 'Doom and Destiny' squawks of a 'psitticotic critic' of a parrot in the rollicking spoof, *The Pirates' Mixed-Up Voyage* (1983), to the illogical twists in old Sophie's demented perceptions in *MEMORY* (1987), or the adventures of the hero of *Simply Delicious* (1999) as he saves his ice-cream from a variety of hungry predators.

Much of Mahy's structure and imagery comes from European FOLKTALES AND LEGENDS. Throughout her many stories stalk strong, individualistic, often female characters, including witches, wizards, clowns and pirates, whom she herself has called forms of anarchic energies, challenging the commonplace and the respectable. Her picturebooks are illustrated by either European or American illustrators, which emphasises the universal aspects of her stories, but often obscures New Zealand idiom, such as 'quick as a cockabully' in *The Witch in the Cherry Tree* (1974), illustrated by Jenny Williams.

Mahy's later novels, however, are more obviously set in New Zealand, both implicitly and explicitly. They merge FANTASY and wonder variously with the daily reality of family life, increasingly involving Maori-Pakeha destinies, as in *Aliens in the Family* (1986) and *Memory* (see also MAORI WRITING FOR CHILDREN). However solitary Mahy's teenage protagonists might feel in navigating their problems or ordeals, they constantly assess their links with family and close friends, as in *THE CATALOGUE OF THE UNIVERSE* (1985). *A Villain's Night Out* (1999) is a comic and complex masterpiece about story-making. *The Other Side of Silence* (1997) is about a heroine called Hero, who elects not to talk in a complex family situation in which 'words flow away like wasting water'. Above all, Mahy conveys her empathy for the foibles, frailties and follies of human beings, and also her belief in the power of love and the power of the imagination to enhance and redeem our world. Mahy's international awards include the CARNEGIE MEDAL for *THE HAUNTING* (1982) and *THE CHANGEOVER* (1984), the IBBY Honour Award for *The Changeover*, the Young Observer Award for Teenage Fiction for *Memory*, runner-up for the Carnegie Medal with *Memory*, and a shortlisting for the Observer Award with *THE TRICKSTERS* (1986). These titles are also represented on the Australian Library Association lists of the year's best books. Mahy has received the New Zealand Library Association's ESTHER GLEN AWARD five times. Her achievements have lifted her to the restricted ranks of the Order of New Zealand, and the annual Children's Book Foundation Lecture Award carries her name in her honour. DAH

Main, Neville see *MUFFIN THE MULE*

Maitland, Antony 1932– British illustrator. After winning the KATE GREENAWAY AWARD with a combination of line and wash ILLUSTRATIONS for his first book, *Mrs Cockle's Cat* (PHILIPPA PEARCE, 1961), Maitland went on to illustrate a second Pearce story, *A Dog so Small* (1962), and then began a long association with LEON GARFIELD to produce *Jack Holborn* (1964), *Smith* (1967), *BLACK JACK* (1968), *John Diamond* (1968),

The Ghost Downstairs (1972) and some of *The Apprentices* (1976–8). The dark, cross-hatched and stippled drawings reveal Maitland's immersion in Garfield's 18th-century world. He also reillustrated *The Green Fairy Book* (Andrew Lang, edited by Brian Alderson, 1978) and contributed illustrations to work by BARBARA WILLARD, PENELOPE LIVELY and ELEANOR FARJEON. JAG

Major, Kevin 1949– Canadian novelist awarded the 1991 Vicky Metcalf Award for a distinguished body of work. With each book, Major has said, he re-invents himself as an author, maintaining his own and his readers' interest by changing his narrative method or subject matter. Born in Stephenville, Newfoundland, Major graduated from Memorial University and began teaching in an outport high school. Realising that his students had no books reflecting their lives, he wrote *Hold Fast* (1978), a first-person narrative about Michael, a teenager sent to live with relatives after his parents are killed. Its local colour is thematic, not decorative, contrasting traditional values in Michael's idyllic outport home with the materialism of contemporary cities. An honest portrait of alienation, *Hold Fast* won the Canada Council Award, the CANADIAN LIBRARY ASSOCIATION BOOK OF THE YEAR AWARD, and The Ruth Schwartz Award.

In his next three books, Major injected narrative variety into conventional problem novels. *Far from Shore* (1979), winner of the Canadian Library Association Young Adult Book Award, uses several first-person narrators to provide multiple perspectives of a boy who gets into legal trouble after his father leaves home to search for work. It suggests that unemployment and alcoholism are destroying traditional Newfoundland family life. Predictable plots weaken Major's other problem novels, but both employ interesting narrative strategies. *Thirty-six Exposures* (1984) uses 36 snapshot-like vignettes, and *Dear Bruce Springsteen* (1987), his first book without a Newfoundland setting, employs letters a teenager addresses to the famous singer. Although critics praised Major for his realism and narrative experimentation, some school boards and libraries banned his novels because of scenes involving swearing, alcohol, DRUGS or SEX.

After his fourth book, Major abandoned what he calls the 'high realism' of problem fiction. He still explored the familiar problems of adolescents seeking love and meaningful identities, but he did so within the context of history, FANTASY or humour. Daringly, *Blood Red Ochre* (1989) combines a disappointing, unresolved third-person narrative about a boy trying to understand both his personal history and a mysterious girl, a first-person historical account by the last Beothuk Indian, and a TIME-SLIP FANTASY that links the two. In *Eating Between the Lines* (1991), winner of the Canadian Library Association Book of the Year Award, Major revealed a previously unexpressed comedic talent. This fantasy describes the rollicking adventures of a teenager who magically enters scenes described in books, gaining the experience to solve problems at school, to win the heart of a girl, and to save his parents' marriage. Given Princess Diana's unfortunate death, the premise of *Diana: My Autobiography* (1993) no longer seems amusing; nevertheless, this novel about an egocentric eleven-year-old whose reading of Andrew Morton's BIOGRAPHY of Princess Diana convinces her that she has royal parents cleverly combines identity themes and a satire of manners.

Arguably Canada's most original writer for young adults, Major has recently re-invented himself once again, publishing two adult novels about Newfoundlanders, *No Man's Land* (1995) and *Gaffer* (1997). REJ

Majumdar, Gopa see *FELUDA* SERIES

***Malory Towers* series** (1946–51) Six novels by the British author ENID BLYTON. This was Blyton's last and best foray into the schoolgirl story, featuring an artistically-inclined protagonist called Darrell Rivers, who learns to control her temper over her years at school. The usual SCHOOL STORY incidents feature, as in ANGELA BRAZIL and ELINOR M. BRENT-DYER – midnight feasts, practical jokes and changing alliances – but Blyton's investment in her main character gives the books an extra appeal, making Darrell the most popular of Blyton's female characters with the exception of George in the *FAMOUS FIVE*. (Blyton herself was Mrs Darrell Waters, and her husband, like the fictional Darrell's father, was a surgeon – also with a fiery temper.)

The main appeal of Malory Towers lies in the magical space it opens for girls, one that alluringly combines the secure and the daring, mirroring a growing child's own experiences. Malory obviously has romantic associations with the world of KING ARTHUR, which had its own magic centre at Camelot. Malory is also likened to a castle, set against the Cornish sea. It is also very much a female realm, its description reminiscent of courtly symbolism with its sunken rose garden and enclosed pool, periodically cleansed by the sea. However, the passive image of a princess, to which Gwendoline and some others aspire, is quickly dispelled. This is a realm where girls must be more active, the pool itself often being the testing ground. Here the girls are stripped of any pretensions. Outward appearance is seen as far less important than inner development, although Blyton's ability to depict the latter is limited. However, there are some memorable types (rather than individualised characters): the clever but cold Alicia, the 'mannish' Miss Peters, who wears breeches with bravado, the tomboy Wilhelmina, or 'Bill', and the pointedly obnoxious and lazy Gwendoline. It is significant that only the last aspires to go to finishing school, whereas many of the other characters want to be women on their own terms. Although it can be argued that the whole Malory experience should result in more biddable women – 'women the world can lean on', as the Head puts it – for most readers it is the subversion of this rather rigid, hierarchical system that provides the pleasure: the feasts and pranks. As Alicia puts it, seeking to ward off an impending adulthood, 'Long live our appetites!' DR

Malory, Sir Thomas 1405–71? Author of the MORTE DARTHUR, a long prose reworking of earlier Arthurian material which became the principal source for most subsequent retellings of these stories in English. One of the first books to be printed by WILLIAM CAXTON, it was later criticised by the humanist ROGER ASCHAM as unsuitable for children since 'the whole pleasure . . . standeth . . . in open manslaughter and bold bawdry'. However it became a key text in the 19th-century revival of interest in chivalry, popularised particularly by TENNYSON, and many 20th-century children's versions have been based substantially on sections of Malory's book. DWh

see also KING ARTHUR

Maltby, Peg [Agnes Newberry] 1899–1984 Australian artist whose fairies and idealised Aboriginal children were extremely popular for many years. Maltby was born in England and settled in Melbourne in 1924, where she studied at the National Gallery School. Her first book, *Peg's Fairy Book* (1944), was the result of an exhibition. Its success led to *Nursery Rhymes* (1945) and a number of retellings of FAIRY TALES, including *LITTLE RED RIDING HOOD* (1950), *THE SLEEPING BEAUTY* (1951) and *Little Thumbeline* (1951). The *Ben and Bella* series began in 1947, and her other fairy character, Nutchen, appeared in *Nutchen of the Forest* (1945) and *Nutchen and the Golden Key* (1948). She wrote the *Pip and Pepita* series (from 1944) under her pseudonym. VW

Mandara, Jedida Kivali see *STORIES BY THE FIRESIDE*

Mandela, Zinziswa see *POETRY JUMP UP*

Mandu and the Forest Guardian (1987) Fictional story of pygmies in Central Africa by Mitzi Margoles and Sheila Hoffenberg, illustrated by Joan Rankin with haunting, dark scraperboard pictures in the days when colour printing was beyond the budget of most South African publishers for children. One of the earliest conservation works in South African youth literature, it tells the story of a boy wanting to prove himself more grown-up and flinching from killing the strange creature that he finds, so that the okapi lives again. JHe

Mangut, Joseph 1955– Nigerian novelist for young adults, born in Gwande, Plateau State. His novels, all set in the North, focus on urban low-life and consider moral ambiguities. *Have Mercy* (1982) questions whether stealing can be justified, while *The Blackmailers* (1982) asks whether the hero's downfall was due to moral weakness or the inequities of society. The main character of *The Blackmailers* picks up his life after prison in Mangut's third novel, *Women for Sale* (1984). VD

Manning, Rosemary 1911–88 British teacher and author. In *Green Smoke* (1957) R. Dragon, a 1500-year-old, toothless, sardonic storyteller (herself in disguise) flies, with Sue aboard, to Tintagel and other legendary sites. It uses the story-within-the-story technique with great aplomb, and was published on the prestigious new Young Constable list. It and its less compelling but popular sequels, *Dragon in Danger* (1959) and *The Dragon's Quest* (1962), were brought back into print by Puffin (1967–74). *Dragon in the Harbour* (Kestrel) followed in 1980. Manning's historical novel for teenagers, *Arripay* (1969), bears comparison with the best of the then critically acclaimed genre. Set in medieval Dorset it tells the story of Adam for whom neither the monastery nor privateering holds any attraction. Its theme is the courage to be yourself, a theme that also characterises Manning's adult fiction. EM

see also HISTORICAL FICTION

Manning-Sanders, Ruth 1895–1988 Welsh author, born in Swansea, best-known for her prolific retellings of FOLKTALES. Folk themes also appear in her original stories. She produced an extensive series on magical themes – *A Book of Wizards*, *A Book of Dragons* – and other stories about witches, magic horses, charms and changelings, and devils and demons. Manning-Sanders also wrote historical novels, such as *The Smugglers* (1962), set in Cornwall, in which the charismatic Zach and the squire's son, Ned, are the smuggler heroes. *The Extraordinary Margaret Catchpole* (1966) tells the real-life story of a Suffolk girl who was condemned to death and eventually transported. *Circus Boy* (1960) is a story about the life of travelling showmen in Victorian times. The author herself had travelled for two years with a circus. Manning-Sanders received the Blindman International Poetry Prize in 1926. HCE

***Mantlemass* series** (1970–80) Historical novels by the British author Barbara Willard. The eight novels are set around a family house in the Sussex Weald and cover a period of English history from the Battle of Bosworth to the Civil War. A further collection of short stories, *The Keys of Mantlemass* (1981) begins with the building of the house and ends with a present-day descendant. The books tell the stories of two related families, the Mallorys and the Medleys, who live through turbulent, war-torn times which test both family and political loyalties. The five books written between 1970 and 1975 describe key episodes in family history, while later – arguably less successful – books overlap in time with the earlier novels and tell connected stories. The Medleys are descended from the last Plantaganet King and proudly pass down a book that he once owned from one generation to the next. Richard III's hunched back is inherited by some of his descendants and those who suffer it are taught to think of the DISABILITY as a badge of honour; in *The Iron Lily* (1973) it also becomes an important symbol of kinship. This transformation of adversity into strength becomes a pattern that is repeated through the series as characters struggle to survive difficult physical and political conditions.

The first book, *The Lark and the Laurel*, opens in 1485 at the beginning of a new era in British history. The heroine, Cecily Jolland, is a feeble London girl who gradually learns common sense and the country ways and becomes the first of a line of strong women dominating the novels, holding the family and house together in adverse circumstances. Throughout the series the women are determined to protect the family home without jeopardising their own integrity or sacrificing their family.

The theme of family loyalty is central to all the novels. The lark and the laurel of the first book, and the sprig of broom of the second, provide important family emblems which link the generations together. The wars, and the conflict between the developing iron industry and the traditional way of life, cause a rift in the family which distresses characters through the generations until it is finally healed in *Harrow and Harvest* (1974); the wheel comes full circle as the English Civil War finally reunites the family and brings Richard Plantaganet's book back to the Sussex Weald. Willard did not tell the full story behind the family quarrel in the original series, but came back to the theme later in *The Eldest Son* (1977).

In the first book Cecily's progress from delicate, fussy child to strong adult is marked by her growing understanding of the countryside around her and the people who live there, an understanding which is reflected in her adoption of the 'foresty' way of talking. Later generations are happy to swap between local idiom and standard English. The continuing use of the idiom, together with the physical presence of the house itself, provides a sense of continuity across the generations. KA

'Jacka teases Luck.' Illustration by ANNETTE MACARTHUR-ONSLOW from *Animal Stories* by Ruth Manning-Sanders.

Maori writing for children This corpus of work has had to clear itself of a double burden. It has had to deal firstly with the imaginative orientations and ideological imperatives of the immensely rich tradition of European children's literature; the scale of this burden is emphatically evident in a critical history like Betty Gilderdale's *A Sea Change: 145 Years of New Zealand Junior Fiction* (1982). Secondly, it has had to negotiate a relationship with Maori culture itself, given its unsurpassed traditions of STORYTELLING, song and performance. This culture is largely oral, and by no means segmented into child and adult fields. In consequence the history of Maori publications is very recent, very political and still concerned with primary issues like the preservation of Maori language and the traditional corpus of myth and legend.

A great deal has been produced in the last two decades, mostly PICTUREBOOKS for the very young or for readers making their way into literacy as users of Maori; many of these books have been published in parallel with Maori-language editions, or with parallel Maori texts. A notable feature of this modern tradition of Maori children's literature is the extensive involvement of women writers, especially since the 1970s, beginning with significant figures like Katarina Mataira and Moehau Reedy, determined to ensure that a literature developed which upheld Maori language and kept alive cultural concepts and cultural practices. In effect, the dominant role of women, already well established in the oral tradition – with their responsibility for preserving the stories and histories, as well as the waiata and karanga (teaching songs, laments, and love songs) – has been transferred to literary publication.

One point of connection between this new literature and the children's culture of the past is the traditional tale. A high proportion of recently published books offer versions of stories from a familiar corpus. Most commonly these tales are told singly, as in ROBYN KAHUKIWA's *Paikea*, but not infrequently they are incorporated with greater or lesser connectedness into anthologies. Collections of such material featured prominently, in fact, among the earliest publications of Maori writers, such as Alistair Campbell's *Maori Legends: Some Myths and Legends of the Maori People* (1969); and Katarina Mataira's *Maori Legends for Young New Zealanders* (1975). An interesting recent addition is the volume of tales retold by Kiri Te Kanawa, *The Land of the Long White Cloud* (1989), splendidly illustrated by MICHAEL FOREMAN. Other modern anthologies include Bradford Haami's *Traditional Maori Love Stories* (1997), which is lightly illustrated, but in the sophistication of its language, and in its interest in SEX and in genealogies, seems written for older children. A favourite legendary love story told for young children, and a fine instance of her work, is Hepora Young's picturebook *Hinemoa and Tutanekau* (1995). It tells of Hinemoa's forbidden passion, driven by which she triumphs over the elements and her father's will, in swimming across Lake Rotorua to join her lover.

Such tales consistently imply the traditional taleteller. Perhaps most popular in these terms are tales that re-present incidents in the life of the TRICKSTER-hero, Maui. Katarina Mataira's *Maui and the Big Fish* (1972) is an important, early and distinctive example of the modern picturebook development of this genre, in its dynamic combination of vigorous storytelling and vivid illustration. Among the most recent examples is *Maui. Legends of the Outcast* (1996), produced by Chris Slane and Robert Sullivan, which connects several of the major incidents in the cycle of Maui tales, including his extraordinary birth and equally extraordinary death, but presents them not as oral culture could ever imagine them, even in a print society, but rather according to the demands of pop-video culture. It is, in fact, a GRAPHIC NOVEL, working within the conventions of contemporary adolescent gothic FANTASY. The brutal illustrations create a scene that is not so much darkly brooding as paranoiac. If it seems laden with postmodern obsessions, it also speaks of a disturbing cultural malaise, treading the fine line between alienation and violence.

A less disturbing, indeed richly comic updating of the trickster-cycle is to be found in James Waera's engaging *Pukunui* picturebooks, full of unexpected adventures, canny parallels and illustrative delights. Equally familiar are the stories that convert the stuff of daily experience, especially the daily experience of rural Maori, through reminiscence into narrative; since they deal with childhood, they readily become stories for children. Miriam Smith's *Annie and Moon* (New Zealand Picturebook Award, 1990) brilliantly reworks this pattern in tracing the sense of dislocation and loss suffered by a child who, with her mother, in a familiar history, must leave her home in the country for a new home in the city. The tale is imaginatively graced by giving centre-stage to Annie's cat, Moon. Significantly, in a move that can be found many times over, home is finally found once more with the child's grandmother. Smith has said that she hopes that in her picturebooks there is always something for anybody to take away, but that she is concerned in them to reflect Maori values: 'They tell of relationships between the young and the very old and how we are all of the earth.'

This defines a constant concern in modern Maori children's fiction. Again the history of such writing is longer than might at first appear, since it has important precedents in articles and quasi-factual stories published in the major educational publication, the *School Journal*. If this publication of 'faction-literature' has seemed in some measure the instrument of a patronising colonialist education system, it has also provided an opportunity for many writers, including major figures like PATRICIA GRACE and WITI IHIMAERA, to develop their art as storytellers. The modern tradition of this kind of writing, much of it published in this and other magazines, gives narrative expression to an identifiable Maori experience, often located in rural areas where iwi or tribal consciousness dominates, but also among urban Maori whose social experience, on the other hand, is all too often that of the disadvantaged. The objective particularity of much of this writing testifies to the cultural pride that has spread with what is sometimes known as the Maori renaissance, but also contributes markedly to the educationist's interest in stitching together a nation that acknowledges its racial, cultural and social differences. CM

Map of Nowhere, A (1988) Novel by the British author GILLIAN CROSS which sets out to challenge comfortable certainties. FANTASY and reality become disturbingly confused when the familiar rules of the role-playing adventure game take on a parallel dimension in real life. Set in a featureless fen, the narrative recounts how the protagonist struggles to construct a map that will take him from the secure certainties of childhood into the uncharted territory of adult relationships. The tightly constructed plot has chilling moments, threatening scenarios and stark contrasts. The novel portrays some of the unrelenting questions that face adolescents. The author's taut style is particularly effective in maintaining the tension and uncertainty. EAG

Marchant, Bessie see *LITTLE FOLKS*

märchen see SCOTTISH FOLKTALES

Marchetta, Melina see *LOOKING FOR ALIBRANDI*; see also YOUNG ADULT FICTION

Margaret Mahy Lecture Award see THE NEW ZEALAND CHILDREN'S BOOK FOUNDATION

Margoles, Mitzi see *MANDU AND THE FOREST GUARDIAN*

Marianne Dreams (1958) Popular and almost canonical FANTASY by the British author CATHERINE STORR, well-known for her *CLEVER POLLY* stories. At a time when fantasy was in the ascendancy in Britain – and in the same year in which PHILIPPA PEARCE'S *Tom's Midnight Garden* was published – *Marianne Dreams* made an enormous impact on children's books in Britain. It is a study of two children in the difficult period of convalescence after serious illnesses. They never actually meet but encounter one another in a strange and menacing dreamworld controlled by the pictures drawn by Marianne with a magic pencil found in an old workbox. Their relationship is at first difficult, developing through bad temper and moodiness into a sturdy friendship. What makes the story so compelling is the carefully paced narrative, with episodes in Marianne's everyday sick-bed reality alternating with her dreams in an increasingly sinister atmosphere of excitement and urgency. There is nothing formulaic in this novel: the fantasy reflects and shapes psychological reality in ways which are neither entirely understandable nor predictable.

In 1960 the author published a sequel, *Marianne and Mark*, a kind of anti-romance in which the two protagonists, a few years older, meet by chance in Brighton. This was so different from readers' expectations that it was less successful than its predecessors. There was no fantasy and, although it was again a story of friendship, there were elements of class BIAS. It was not accepted by the publisher of *Marianne Dreams* (Puffin Books). VW

Marigold Garden (1885) Collection of pictures and rhymes, the second major triumph of the British artist KATE GREENAWAY, close in style to her earlier *UNDER THE WINDOW*. By this time she was at the peak of her success, and her popularity now becoming world-wide, this volume and subsequent works sold even more in the United States than in Britain. The verses have become a little more inventive and sophisticated, with occasionally a more stately metre and more reflective mood than in the earlier volume. A celebration of conventional femininity, of motherhood and babies, but also of children's wondering minds, pervades this volume. PC

Mark, Jan(et Marjorie) 1943– British author with several award-winning books to her credit, nominated for the HANS ANDERSEN AWARD in 1984. Born in Welwyn, Hertfordshire, Mark was educated in Ashford, Kent, and having completed a National Diploma in Design course at Canterbury College of Art she taught Art and English at Southfields School, Gravesend. Since 1975 Mark has published books for children, fiction for adults, reviews and articles for education journals. She has contributed specialist chapters in books on the history of children's literature and has edited collections of short stories, including *The Oxford Book of Children's Stories*. Mark frequently works with teachers of English, visiting schools, libraries and colleges throughout Britain and abroad, giving talks, lectures and readings, and providing writing workshops for children, students and teachers. Mark also enjoyed a period as Writer in Residence at Oxford Polytechnic (now Oxford Brookes University) and is a tutor for the Arvon Foundation.

Her first, highly acclaimed novel, *THUNDER AND LIGHTNINGS* (1974), for which she received the Penguin/Guardian Award and the CARNEGIE MEDAL, established her as a writer with a distinctive voice. Mark's range of books for children now includes PICTUREBOOKS such as *Out of the Oven* (1986), *Fun* (1987), *Strat and Chatto* (1989), *Carrot Tops and Cotton Tails* (1993) and *The Tale of Tobias* (1995); stories for newly independent readers such as *The Dead Letter Box* (1982), *The Twig Thing* (1988), *All the Kings and Queens* (1993), *A Worm's Eye View* (1994) and *Lady Long-Legs* (1999); and novels such as *Handles* (1983), *TROUBLE HALF-WAY* (1985), *Dream House* (1987), *The Hillingdon Fox* (1991), *They Do Things Differently Here* (1994), *A Fine Summer Knight* (1995) and *The Sighting* (1997).

Never patronising or underestimating her readers, Mark demonstrates a serious concern for the way in which language is used; stylistically, her work has been likened to that of WILLIAM MAYNE. The integrity of her writing is matched by the integrity of her depiction of the realities of life, and readers respond to the truthfulness of the worlds she creates. Mark reflects on the real concerns of childhood with perceptive accuracy and wry humour; scrupulous observation and penetrating analysis of human nature characterise her writing. Friendship and the sometimes harsh realities of life are two of Mark's recurring themes, the naturalistic situations of home and school providing the settings for much of her work, with the notable exceptions of what she has called her 'speculative novels': *The Ennead* (1978), *Divide and Rule* (1978), *Aquarius* (1982) and *The Eclipse of the Century* (1999).

It is perhaps her work as a creator of short stories for which she is most highly regarded, however, and in which her writing has been most finely honed as she has responded to the demands of the form. In collections such as NOTHING TO BE AFRAID OF (1980), *Hairs in the Palm of the Hand* (1981) and *Feet* (1983) Mark skilfully interweaves the essential elements of her stories, achieving a satisfying unity of language, content and form. In *God's Story* (1997) she retells the stories of the Old Testament with characteristic clarity. MSut

marketing see PUBLISHERS AND PUBLISHING

Markoosie 1942– Canadian (Eskimo) writer. Markoosie is the author of *Harpoon of the Hunter* (1970), the first novel to be published in Eskimo. It was originally published in a syllabic-symbol system invented by missionaries in the publication *Inuttittut* (*Eskimo Way*); it was then translated into English. The novel concerns the initiation of an Eskimo boy, Kamik, into the harsh life of the hunters of the Arctic circle. Stylistically, the novel has many of the rhythms of the oral tradition from which it came; at the same time, like much modern fiction, it enters into the inner lives of its characters. BH

Marks, Alan 1956– British illustrator. After a childhood in London and study at Bath College of Art, Marks went straight into freelancing, working mostly in black-and-white. His first colour work, modest but appropriate, was for KEVIN CROSSLEY-HOLLAND'S CARNEGIE AWARD winner, *Storm* (1985). Since then he has worked with Crossley-Holland again in *The Green Children* (1994), where the illustrations play a major part in establishing mood and period. He has contributed illustrations to work by JILL PATON WALSH, JOAN AIKEN, DICKENS and Jenny Nimmo, and to several collections of poetry and NURSERY RHYMES. He demonstrates a sensitive response to different authors' words whilst always retaining his own distinct style, which is grounded in fine line-drawing, spectacular composition and free-flowing watercolour washes. JAG

***Marlow* series** (1948–80) Sequence of works by ANTONIA FOREST beginning with *Autumn Term*; this was followed by nine sequels over a period of 32 years. This time lag has resulted in one notable peculiarity; as she herself says in the note which heads *The Thuggery Affair* (1965): 'The first story about the Marlows was written in 1947 – that is to say . . . seventeen years ago. . . . On the other hand, the fictional time which has passed in the six books written about the Marlow family is just on eighteen months. Since it would be a bore, to me as well as everyone else, to keep strictly to period time . . . each story has been given a background more or less consistent with the year in which it was written . . . the only way of coping with (the resulting inconsistencies) seems to be to say that the fictional time in which the Marlows exist is in the period Since The War; and that anything true during that time can be true and happening "now" in the books I write about them.'

This allows the Marlows to exist in a fictional space within which the usual rules pertaining to time have been suspended; we would normally call a work so described 'fantastic', and yet nothing could be more inappropriate to the spirit of Antonia Forest's works, whose characters are some of the most real and believable that children's literature has to offer.

Though unified in terms of the (realist) mode of their writing, the Marlow books do not conform to a single genre. It is, indeed, difficult to speak of Forest's works in terms of genre at all. For while *Autumn Term* and *End of Term* (1959), *The Cricket Term* (1974) and *The Attic Term* (1976) might bear classification as SCHOOL STORIES, *The Marlows and the Traitor* (1953), *The Thuggery Affair* (1965) and *Run Away Home* (1982) as ADVENTURE STORIES, *Falconer's Lure* (1957) and *Peter's Room* (1961) as holiday tales and *The Ready-Made Family* (1967) as a 'problem novel', the concept of genre is roughly predicated upon the idea of formula and the presence of set elements, and the Marlow books tend to combine several of these literary formulae and twist them, rendering classification by genre an exercise in reductivism. *Peter's Room*, for instance, contains within its realist holiday story a FANTASY adventure woven by the characters along Gondalian lines. *The Thuggery Affair*, while apparently an ADVENTURE STORY, is at another level about DRUGS and the underprivileged, and could be considered a 'problem novel'. Forest's books are always aware of literary cliché and sidestep it. In *End of Term*, watching a netball match from which Nicola Marlow has been excluded, her friend Tim says:

> 'Now in a book, about ten minutes from time someone would sprain their ankle and you'd rush on and win the game in one magnificent burst. Wouldn't you, Miss Marlow?'
> 'I wouldn't. Because all the subs are here.'
> 'In a book, I said. You are a clot, sometimes.'

Forest's characters must surely rank among the most intelligent and literate in children's literature. Through the close interaction of the series with the world of literature at large, the author not only increases the density of her characters but also uses what is being read to amplify the situations within her books, as in *The Ready-Made Family*. Here, the emotional dynamics of the situation which ensues when Karen leaves Oxford to marry a widower with three children are read and filtered through Nicola's reading of *Persuasion*. Nicola, especially, emerges as an individual through her reading; she is interested in Nelson and the navy (Dudley Pope's *Ramage* books), history and literature (Mary Renault's *Mask of Apollo*, Austen's *Persuasion*, and a good deal of Thackeray, DICKENS and the BRONTËS), crime fiction (Dorothy L. Sayers's *The Nine Tailors*), and children's books (*Sara Crewe*).

The most interesting of the series to anyone interested in the interaction of literature with other literature is *Peter's Room*. During the Christmas vacation, Ginty introduces the Brontë-created worlds of Gondal and Angria to her siblings and their friend Patrick Merrick. Taken by the idea of creating their own narrative and acting it out, Patrick and the younger Marlows 'Gondal' in private, their shared fantasy world occasionally threatening to overwhelm the real one, the characters they create coming to have a life and inevitability of their own. Patrick and Ginty, who establish a relationship in their fictional world, find this beginning to influence their real feelings for each other. The Marlows and Patrick use these characters to explore their own darker potentialities – those for cowardice and betrayal, for example – and in this way emerge with greater self-awareness. However, while the work thus argues for the value of literature in bringing about awareness of self and of 'otherness', it also subtly suggests the danger of erasing the line between fiction and reality: Patrick, who in the 'Gondal' narrative has become a traitor, attempts to shoot himself; the antique pistol he is using turns out to have a real bullet in it that almost kills him.

The underlying theme of the series is the attempt to be 'enough' – that is, to possess sufficient self-awareness, selfhood and integrity to maintain oneself unchanged in the world. Of the Marlows, Nicola is most seen to possess and acquire 'enoughness'; she stands in contrast to Ginty who is described by Lawrie as a 'chameleon' and by Ann as bringing to mind Orsino 'the one who wore changeable taffeta because his mind was a very opal'. Patrick's father says:

> 'I don't dislike her – I think its evens whether she goes to the good or to the bad. But I doubt if it'll be very spectacular either way.'
> 'How devastating,' said Patrick, after a moment.
> 'It wasn't meant to be.'
> 'It sounds like the souls who can't be ferried over the Styx because they've never been enough –'

Though the strengths of the Marlow books lie mainly in their complex psychology and their depiction of the subtle shifts that occur in relationships, they are most memorable for the absolute and uncompromising honesty with which the author treats her characters, baring their souls to us and to themselves.

Despite the outstanding quality of the writing, the Marlow books have suffered neglect in recent years. The perceived datedness of certain of the works in the series may be in part responsible for this; *The Marlows and the Traitor*, which at the narrative level is about espionage in the period directly after World War II, and *The Thuggery Affair*, which is steeped in the 'Ted' and drug culture of the sixties, are the most susceptible to criticism in this respect. It is also possible that the series has been the victim of a form of narrow-minded 'political correctness' that refuses to countenance books about children who, as Jukie, a Teddy-boy in *The Thuggery Affair* says, have 'cars 'n hosses 'n butlers 'n a rafty great house and loot stacked in the vaults.' In any case this perception is a flawed one, for Lawrie and Nicola have to wear out their elder sisters' school uniforms for reasons of economy. The entire series was out of print for most of the 1990s, a consequence partly of the complex relationships of its two publishers, Puffin and Faber. It is to be hoped that none of these reasons will be allowed to stand in the way of the Marlow books being eventually reissued as a series, for the quality of Forest's writing places them among the best in the language. Their being unavailable to contemporary young readers for so long is a challenge to those who believe that excellence in children's books is immune to the misfortunes of market forces. SA

see also NEGLECTED WORKS; LITERATURE WITHIN CHILDREN'S LITERATURE

Marmalade Atkins Series of stories about Marmalade Atkins, 'the worst girl in the world', amounting to an update of the rebellious schoolgirls of St. Trinian's. Constantly in scrapes, in combat with teachers, she is every parents' nightmare. The *Marmalade* books are written by ANDREW DAVIES, the well-known British TELEVISION scriptwriter. When televised on ITV, Marmalade was played by Charlotte Coleman (later to take the leading role in *Oranges are Not the Only Fruit*). There are several Marmalade titles, including *Marmalade Atkins' Dreadful Deeds* (1979), *Educating Marmalade* (1983), *Marmalade Hits the Big Time* (1984), *Marmalade Atkins in Space* (1986), and *Marmalade Atkins on the Ball* (1995). SET

Marriott, Edgar see *THE LION AND ALBERT*

Marriott, Janice 1947– English-born New Zealand writer of novels for children and young adults. Marriott, best known for her humorous and imaginative writing, always creates a strong sense of place and character, developed through the use of convincing dialogue, colloquial language and internal monologues. *Letters to Lesley* (1989), *Brain Drain* (1993) and *Kissing Fish* (1997) feature a lovable budding adolescent, Henry Jollifer, his difficulties with his mother, and his problematic pubescence. Marriott's understanding of adolescent concerns and the realities of growing up in contemporary real-life families, with all their complexities, is evident in *I'm Not a Compost Heap* and *Hope's Rainbow* (both 1995). A more serious book, *Crossroads* (1995), deals with sensitive issues such as teenage driving. Winner of the New Zealand Post Senior Fiction Award and overall winner of the Aim Awards, and the ESTHER GLEN AWARD in 1996, Marriott's writing, without being pedantic, is firmly placed in the teenager's world. LL

Marriott, Pat 1920– British illustrator who studied at Westminster and Chelsea Schools of Art. Known particularly for her lively pen drawings in JOAN AIKEN's children's novels, she has also contributed illustrations to the fiction of IAN SERRAILLIER, NOEL STREATFEILD and ELFRIDA VIPONT, amongst others. Her success lies in her ability to capture the writer's intent. JAG

Marryat, Captain Frederick 1792–1848 Pioneer of British ADVENTURE STORIES. After an illustrious naval career, Marryat achieved success with novels such as *The Naval Officer* (1829). DANIEL DEFOE and JONATHAN SWIFT had produced sea stories in the 18th century which children 'adopted', but Marryat now began to write adventure stories specifically for them. He produced a ROBINSONNADE in *Masterman Ready* (1841–2), an account of life on the frontier in *The Settlers in Canada* (1844), and then in 1847 his near masterpiece *The Children of The New Forest*, a story of the Civil War, the first historical tale for children to remain popular up to the present day. DB

see also HISTORICAL FICTION

Marsden, John 1950– Australian novelist whose first book *SO MUCH TO TELL YOU* (1987) won several prizes. Now a major figure in Australian youth literature, Marsden writes convincing, accessible first-person narratives about contemporary teenagers, and has earned popularity, high sales figures and a mixed critical reception – the latter often in response to his social realism. Marsden has said: 'To shrink from some topics because they are seen as too shocking, too depressing, too realistic, is to continue the repression of the young, to prolong their ignorance and therefore their impotence' (Agnes Nieuwenhuizen). *So Much To Tell You*, *LETTERS FROM THE INSIDE*, the series of seven works beginning with *TOMORROW, WHEN THE WAR BEGAN* and *Checkers* (1996) deal, with some amount of structural repetition, with teenagers in traumatic, often institutionalised, situations. Marsden takes an interest in (and speaks of the need for) coming-of-age rituals, especially in *The Journey* (1988), an allegorical FANTASY in which a boy undertakes a spiritual and physical journey, learning to tell seven tales and thereby earn adulthood. His only other novel with fantasy elements is *Out of Time* (1990), a rather confusing tale of time travel, missing persons and grief. Marsden also writes humorous fiction, including the SCHOOL STORIES *The Great Gatenby* (1989) and *Staying Alive in Year Five* (1989), and the light-hearted adventure *Looking For Trouble* (1993), the latter two for younger readers. Recently, he has published the comical choose-your-own-adventure books, *Cool School* (1995) and *Creep Street* (1996). NLR

Marsh Award see AWARDS AND MEDALS

Marshall, James (Edward) [Edward Marshall] 1942–92 A self-taught American illustrator, writer and reteller of FOLKTALES, best known for his seven titles in the *George and Martha* series about two hippopotamuses, and the four titles in the *Stupids* series. Marshall was born in San Antonio, Texas, and educated at the New England Conservatory of Music in Boston and Southern Connecticut State College. He worked as a high-school teacher until his skills as an illustrator emerged. In 1971 he illustrated his first book, *Plink, Plink, Plink* by Byrd Baylor. During his career he illustrated over 75 books including the *I Can Read Fox* series, which he wrote as Edward Marshall. Marshall's work was marked by his page design, ability to capture the personality of characters, his deceptively simple line drawings and his gift for portraying the most humorous situations with a kind of dead-pan seriousness that delighted children. The family in *The Stupids Die* (1981) believe they are dead because the lights have gone out. In *Miss Nelson is Missing!* (1977) the sweet but ineffectual Miss Nelson is replaced by an evil substitute teacher named Viola Swamp. He also illustrated folktales such as *LITTLE RED RIDING HOOD* (1987), *THE THREE LITTLE PIGS* (1989) and *CINDERELLA* (1989). His ILLUSTRATIONS for *GOLDILOCKS AND THE THREE BEARS* (1988) received the Caldecott Honour Award. DJH

Marshall, John 1756–1823. A prolific printer and publisher of children's books at Aldermary Churchyard, and Queen Street in London from 1780 until 1807, when he moved to Fleet Street. Marshall inherited his father's CHAPBOOK business in 1779 but decided to concentrate on producing entertaining and educative children's books. He entered his first book at the Stationer's Company, *The Imperial Spelling Book*, in 1782. During the next 40 years he published over 100 books by some of the best-known authors of the day, including MRS TRIMMER, LADY FENN and DOROTHY and MARY ANN KILNER. He was chosen by HANNAH MORE, the reformer, to print her *CHEAP REPOSITORY TRACTS* in 1795, but she found him tricksy and difficult, and the arrangement did not last long. A keen businessman, Marshall published much 'improving' literature, but he also printed popular tales regarded suspiciously by many respectable parents and much loved by children. He devised new ways to teach children to read and count, with pictures, sets of cards, and counting beans. He published two magazines for children, and in 1800 was probably the first to publish children's 'Libraries', or collections of little books in boxes for children. SD

Marshall, Richard see *COCK ROBIN*; see also *SIMPLE SIMON*

Marshall, Simkin see *PETER PARLEY'S ANNUAL*

Martchenko, Michael 1942– Canadian illustrator of PICTUREBOOKS. Born in Carcassone, France, Martchenko grew up amidst the 'rubble and rubbish' of World War II. His father was presumed lost in battle, and Martchenko, aged seven, moved to Canada with his mother and sister. Unable to speak English, he delighted in the communication he could achieve through a box of crayons given to him at school. Upon graduation from the Ontario College of Art, he worked in advertising for the next 20 years. The author ROBERT MUNSCH happened to see a company exhibition featuring a Martchenko painting as a 'filler' piece. Martchenko's ILLUSTRATION and animation career was launched with Munsch's *The Paper Bag Princess* (1980).

Over 20 Munsch stories have been illustrated by Martchenko with humorous cartoon-like characters. He has illustrated around 50 children's books, including titles in the *Matthew* series (from 1984) by Allen Morgan. In addition to advertising awards, Martchenko has won the Ruth Schwartz Children's Book Award for *Thomas' Snowsuit* (Munsch, 1986). His interest in World War II aviation and his skill at realistically capturing times past are evident in his detailed illustrative work in Morgan's *Jessica Moffat's Silver Locket* (1994) and *High Flight: A Story of World War II* (1999), a picturebook BIOGRAPHY by Linda Granfield. LG

Martel, Suzanne 1924– French Canadian writer of HISTORICAL FICTION, SCIENCE FICTION, ADVENTURE STORIES, FANTASY and sports fiction. In her action-filled stories Martel deals with self-discovery and the human need for love, understanding, friendship and connection with others. She wrote a sports novel entitled *Pee Wee* (1982); and her historical novels include *The King's Daughter* (1980), which was reprinted in 1994 having won the Ruth Schwartz Children's Book Award in 1981. Martel won The Canada Council Children's Literature Prize for *Nos Amis Robots*. *Surreal 3000* – translated into English as *The City Underground* (1964/94) – deals with the possible aftermath of an atomic attack, one that divides society into two groups, the underground society, fearful of radiation effects, and a more 'primitive society' above ground that struggles against almost overwhelming odds to survive. Martel's earlier awards include the 1976 Vicky Metcalf Award for a body of work and the Prix Alvine-Belise for the best French Canadian children's book, for *Jeanne, Fils du Roi* (1974). MRS

Martin Pippin in the Apple Orchard (1921) Romance which established the British author ELEANOR FARJEON's reputation. Based on an old singing-game, this Arcadian tale of a wandering minstrel and the lovely Gillian, imprisoned with six milkmaid companions, was intended for adults but appealed to young readers. It now seems unfashionably whimsical, but is noteworthy for being Farjeon's first linking of stories around a central storyteller. The same structure served for *Italian Peepshow* (1926), *Kaleidoscope* (1928), *Jim at the Corner* (1934) and *The Old Nurse's Stocking Basket* (1931). Here Farjeon identifies with the darning, storytelling old Nurse – the larger the stocking hole, the longer the tale. Martin Pippin reappeared in *Martin Pippin in the Daisy Field* (1937) for younger readers (though it should be noted that Farjeon deplored age-grouping). Six precocious small girls (dream daughters of the milkmaids?) hear fresh, original Sussex stories. AHa

Martin, Bill, Jr 1916– American author best known for *Brown Bear, Brown Bear, What Do You See?* (1983), illustrated by ERIC CARLE, which first appeared in an educational READING SCHEME. Young children revel in its uncomplicated, rhythmic text. In 1989 John Archambault, a poet and storyteller, collaborated with Martin on an ALPHABET BOOK, *Chicka Chick Boom Boom* (1989), illustrated by Louis Ehlert, creating a similar kind of rhythmic and visual pleasure. Martin and Archambault have written other books together, including *The Ghost-Eye Tree* (1985) and *Knots on a Counting Rope* (1987), both illustrated by Ted Rand. PDS

Martin, Reverend J(ohn) P(ercival) 1880–1966 British Methodist minister and author of the six *Uncle* fantasies, illustrated by the Children's Laureate, QUENTIN BLAKE. The first book, *Uncle* (1964), and the second were published in the author's lifetime; the rest, ending with *Uncle and the Battle for Badgertown* (1973), were assembled from his papers. The tales, which are all adapted from stories Martin told to his children and grandchildren, centre on Uncle, a near-omnipotent millionaire elephant in a purple dressing-gown – a little like an old-style squire. Uncle's unusual retinue, his projects and particularly his constant skirmishing with the outrageous Badfort crowd, are described with surrealist comic verve. PP

Martin, Patricia Miles [Jerry Lane, Miska Miles] 1899–1986 Prolific American writer, who was born in Cherokee, Kansas, and began writing fiction, INFORMATION BOOKS, BIOGRAPHIES and PICTUREBOOKS for children while taking a course in creative writing at the College of San Mateo in California. She wrote over 100 books dealing primarily with native Americans, the American Midwest and animals. Her favourite themes were the importance of friendship and the need for honesty. Her biographies include works on historical and contemporary figures, such as *Pocohontas* (1964), *Daniel Boone* (1965) and *Jacqueline Kennedy Onassis* (1969). Picturebooks written by her were illustrated by some of the most respected American illustrators of her day: *The Rice Bowl* (1962) by EZRA JACK KEATS, *Rabbit Garden* (1967) by JOHN SCHOENHERR, who illustrated a total of nine of her works, and *Gertrude's Pocket* (1970), illustrated by EMILY MCCULLY. *Apricot ABC* (1969) was illustrated by Peter Parnall, as was her Newbery Honour Book, *Annie and the Old One* (1971), the touching story of Annie and her grandmother, who tells her simply that when Annie's mother is done weaving her rug the grandmother will 'go to Mother Earth'. Parnell's full-colour ILLUSTRATIONS underscored and enhanced this dignified story of contemporary Navajo life. Martin's manuscripts are at the deGrummond Collection at the University of Southern Mississippi and the Kerlan Collection of the University of Minnesota. DJH

see also COLLECTIONS OF CHILDREN'S BOOKS; NATIVE AMERICANS IN CHILDREN'S LITERATURE

Martineau, Harriet see *TOM BROWN'S SCHOOLDAYS*; see also HISTORICAL FICTION; SCHOOL STORIES

Maruki, Toshi 1912– Artist and author. In the United States Maruki is most famous for her controversial PICTUREBOOK *Hiroshima No Pika* (1980). Born in Hokkaido, Japan, Maruki studied western art for four years in Japan. In 1941 she married fellow artist Iri Maruki. After the United States dropped the atomic bomb on Hiroshima, Maruki and her husband travelled there to assist the survivors. This experience had a profound effect on the Marukis's lives and work. The couple collaborated on many works depicting World War II experiences, the most famous of which are *The Hiroshima Panels*, exhibited world-wide. In 1953 the couple received a prize from the World Peace Council for their artwork. *Hiroshima No Pika* is the story of a seven-year-old girl, Mii, and her family on and after 6 August 1945. It has been translated into many languages and has won several awards world-wide, including in 1983 the Mildred L. Batchelder Award and the Jane Addams Children's Book Award. The book is painfully truthful, haunting and beautiful, with sweeping, brilliantly coloured, graphically detailed ILLUSTRATIONS and spare text. It has received much criticism for brutally portraying such a subject in a picturebook format and for that format's uncontextualised use. ELPB

Marvel Comics Group (now Marvel Entertainment Group) American publisher of comic books which began in 1939 as Timely Comics. For the first two decades of production, COMICS were crude, following trends set by TELEVISION and film. In 1948 Marvel introduced its comics code, following the national code regulations on sex, violence and language. In the 1960s comics became serious business. Better-quality comics were produced, with more depth and complexity in artistry, plot and character. First created were *The Fantastic Four* (The Thing, Mr Fantastic, Human Torch, and Invisible Girl), modelled on National Comics' successful *Justice League of America*. The resulting success led to the creation of The Incredible Hulk, Dr Strange, and Thor. With *SPIDER-MAN* Marvel Comics broke new ground, publishing a mainstream comic without comic code approval, and thereby forcing code updates. Comics had evolved: there were characters who were humans who happened also to be SUPERHEROES; romance was treated seriously; dialogue and art became more realistic and sharply satirical. Cross-pollination among comics became common. In the 1970s superheroes became less popular, and comics adopted sword and sorcery, SCIENCE FICTION and horror modes. Marketing practices also changed; comics catered more for adults. Today Marvel has a strong INTERNET presence and features early famous characters along with over 40 other characters. ELPB

Marvelman see COMICS, PERIODICALS AND MAGAZINES

'Mary had a little lamb' (1830) NURSERY RHYME by American writer, SARA JOSEPHA HALE (1788–1879), described by E.V. LUCAS as starting with the best-known four lines in the English language, and partly based, as the OPIES tell us, on a true story. Hale was the editor of *The Boston Ladies' Magazine* (1828–37) and also wrote stories for children. MCCS

***Mary Plain* series** (1930–65) Series of CHAPTER BOOKS for young readers written by Gwynedd Rae (1892–1977). The heroine is a small bear from the bear pits at Berne who goes to stay with her special friends the Owl Man and the Fur Coat Lady. The irascible and entertaining cub, who takes things very literally, has been a favourite for many years. First published in the 1930s, they were reissued with illustrations by Joanna

Ede in the 1970s. To a contemporary publisher they present problems of political correctness and therefore only two titles are currently in print. KA

***Mary Poppins* series** (1934–88) By the British author P.L. Travers, originally comprising *Mary Poppins* (1934), *Mary Poppins Comes Back* (1935), *Mary Poppins Opens the Door* (1943) and *Mary Poppins in the Park* (1952), later expanded to include three shorter works, *Mary Poppins in the Kitchen* (1975), *Mary Poppins in Cherry Tree Lane* (1982) and *Mary Poppins and the House Next Door* (1988). Mary Poppins is the magical nanny to the Banks family, coming and going as she pleases without a moment's notice, blown in and away by the wind, arriving by kite or rocket and leaving by Merry-Go-Round. While her prim and priggish behaviour conveys the impression of orthodoxy and correctness, this is at variance with the manner of her exits and entrances which suggest a refusal to take the forms governing Proper Behaviour too seriously. In the presence of Mary Poppins the line separating the real and the quotidian from the magical and the imaginary blurs: statues jump off pedestals; characters emerge from books to pass the time with the Banks family; and the paper stars on their pieces of gingerbread are pasted onto, and become, the stars in the sky. The encounters of the Banks children with Mary Poppins's relatives allows them to see life from the air ('Laughing Gas'), upside down ('Topsy Turvy'), or from the height of a few inches ('The Park in the Park'). Thus, the perspective from which the children view the world is never permitted to remain static or 'normative', but instead is continually refreshed. The film version of *Mary Poppins* starring Julie Andrews and Dick Van Dyke contained a good deal of charm but removed much of Mary Poppins's acerbity and tartness. SA

Maschler, Kurt see AWARDS AND MEDALS; see also KURT MASCHLER AWARD (appendix)

Maschler, Tom see PUBLISHERS AND PUBLISHING; see also NICOLA BAYLEY

Masefield, John 1878–1967 British poet, novelist, dramatist and essayist. In his autobiography, *So Long to Learn* (1952), he declared that 'the finding, framing and telling of stories, in verse and prose' is 'the law of my being'. His style of writing was a departure from the 'poetic perfection' of TENNYSON and Swinburne, using language and subject matter that made few concessions to conventional ideas of what was suitable for poetry. He wrote for, and about, everyone, and his gift for striking universal chords ensured that he was read by a wide audience, not just the poetry-reading public.

Born in Ledbury, Herefordshire, his childhood until the death of his mother (when he was six), was a 'paradise' of rural pursuits. A move to his grandfather's house gave him access to a large library which fed his imagination until his father died in 1891. He and three brothers and two sisters were then brought up by his childless aunt and uncle. His Aunt Kate, an advocate of 'muscular Christianity', disliked his interest in books and the arts, and at 13, to toughen him up, he was sent for merchant ship training to HMS Conway on the Mersey. Constant bouts of seasickness forced his discharge in 1894, but on the insistence of his aunt he returned to sea – only to desert on the way to New York. After spending time as a vagrant in America, doing odd jobs in bars and a carpet factory, ill health forced him back to London, 'with about six pounds and a revolver', and there he became a clerk.

From the age of ten Masefield had been writing poems, and in his teenage years he was much influenced by CHAUCER, William Morris, the Pre-Raphaelites, KEATS and W.B. Yeats, with whom he became acquainted in 1901. *SALT WATER BALLADS* was published in 1902, but it was not until his narrative poem *The Everlasting Mercy* was published in 1911 that he became a public figure. A prolific writer in other areas, his subjects ranged from the rigging of model ships to the Gallipoli campaign. In 1919 he moved with his wife Constance and their two children to Boars Hill in Oxfordshire, where he started a theatre company for local people, the Oxford Recitations – annual verse-speaking contests – and wrote *REYNARD THE FOX* (1919), *Sard Harker* (1924) and *THE MIDNIGHT FOLK* (1927). In 1930 he succeeded Robert Bridges as Poet Laureate, the first without a university education. *The Box of Delights* was published in 1935, the same year he received The Order of Merit. A master storyteller and chronicler of English life, Masefield was one of the most active and popular Poets Laureate England had seen for many years. HT

Mason, Cyrus see *AUSTRALIAN CHRISTMAS STORY BOOK, THE*

Massee, May 1883–1966 Influential American editor of children's books. May Massee was a generous, inspirational pioneering force. Originally a librarian, she had high standards, and in 1922 she established the first juvenile department at Doubleday, Page, which was soon second only to Louise Seaman's department at Macmillan. In the 1930s she started Viking's juvenile department. The May Massee Collection in the William Allen White Library at Emporia State University in Kansas contains ILLUSTRATIONS for ROBERT MCCLOSKEY's *Make Way for Ducklings* and KATE SEREDY's NEWBERY MEDAL for *The White Stag*. The American Institute of Graphic Arts awarded Massee a gold medal. NV

Masson, Sophie (Veronique) 1959– Australian novelist, born in Indonesia of French parents and living in Australia since the age of four. Masson writes stories for young, adolescent and adult readers. Her interests are wide-ranging: using family settings to explore racial tensions in *Sooner or Later* (1991), cultural differences in *The Cousin From France* (1993), ethnic differences in *The Sun is Rising* (1996), religious differences and constraints in *The First Day* (1995), and growing up in situations which do not give support in *The Troublemaker* (1997). Her works include explorations of FANTASY possibilities, such as the reworking of *PUSS IN BOOTS* in *Carabas* (1996), and an imaginative exploration of the differences between Roman and Celtic culture in *The Gifting* (1996). *Lucky Break* (1996) explores in three interconnected short stories how nothing is simple in family living when big changes unexpectedly occur. *Cold Iron* (1998) is set in Elizabethan times. One of the attractions of Masson's writing is that she focuses attention on characters out of the mainstream. CH, HMcC

see also FAMILY STORIES

Masterman Ready see CAPTAIN FREDERICK MARRYAT; see also ADVENTURE STORIES

Matas, Carol 1949– Winnipeg-born Canadian children's author who started out as an actor. While expecting her first child, she turned to writing as a creative outlet. Matas writes SCIENCE FICTION and contemporary fiction for children and young adults, but it is her HISTORICAL FICTION for which she has received critical acclaim. Award-winning *Lisa* (1987) tells the heroic story of the escape of the Danish Jews during World War II. The sequel, *Jesper* (US title: *Code Name Kris*) (1989) focuses on the Danish resistance to the Nazi occupation. Matas's interest in the experience of European Jews during and after the war continues in *Daniel's Story* (1993), which is about a survivor of concentration camps who remembers his life through a series of mental 'snap-shots', and in *After the War* (1996), the story of Ruth Mendenberg, a Polish Jewish survivor who joins a group of young people travelling illegally to Palestine. *The Garden* (1997) continues Ruth's journey and tells of the struggle to found the State of Israel. Her novels are dramatic and emotional, if not highly literary. A thorough researcher, Matas fills her stories with accurate detail. Her theatrical training is in evidence in her novels, with their first-person narratives, natural dialogue and excellent pacing. An actor still, Matas's dramatic school and public readings leave her listeners spellbound. TH

Mather, Cotton 1663–1728 American Puritan minister, infamously associated with the Salem witchcraft trials of 1692, author of 445 works printed in his lifetime. Born in Boston, he joined his father at the Old North Church after graduation from Harvard College. Important works include *The Wonders of the Invisible World* (1693), on Salem witchcraft, *Magnali Christi Americana* (1701), a history of New England, and *Bonifacius: an Essay upon the Good* (1710), which influenced Benjamin Franklin. Mather wrote many works for children, including BIOGRAPHIES, catechisms, hymns, poetry, sermons and moral guides. His most important children's work is *A Token, for the Children of New-England* (1701), which tells of the illnesses and deaths of seven pious children. DHW

Mathis, Sharon Bell 1937– AFRICAN AMERICAN writer for children and adolescents born in Atlantic City, New Jersey. Mathis established her reputation during the 1970s, when she published seven books in eight years, founded the children's literature division of the Washington DC Black Writers Workshop, and began writing a monthly column for *Ebony Jr!* (1972–85). *Sidewalk Story* (1971), the first of her major prize-winning books, elicited Toni Morrison's praise for its portrayal of a realistic and strong-willed nine-year-old. More upbeat than most of Mathis's fiction, the novel concerns Lilly Etta's successful mobilisation of support for a friend's family when they are evicted from their apartment. Mathis's fiction testifies to her profound respect for the African American children and teenagers for whom she writes. Her other young protagonists grapple with the loss or diminishment of loved ones and face harsh circumstances without falling prey to the self-destructive coping mechanisms of DRUG addiction (*Teacup Full of Roses*, 1972), alcohol (*Listen for the Fig Tree*, 1974), and deadened emotions (*The Hundred Penny Box*, 1975) that disable their parents or siblings. Similarly, the BIOGRAPHY *Ray Charles* (1973) focuses on struggles overcome. JMA

Matilda (1988) British writer ROALD DAHL's last major, and very characteristic work, a mixture of comedy, farce, bathos and polemic. Although the published version was only the second draft (Dahl had quarrelled with his editor, Stephen Roxborough) and is very uneven in pace and tone, the book was a huge success, breaking paperback sales records. Matilda is an engagingly innocent but super-intelligent heroine, who achieves justice for the mild Miss Honey at the expense of the gross PANTOMIME figure of Miss Trunchball. In his last interview, Dahl said that *Matilda* was based on the theory that parents and teachers are the enemy: 'There are foul parents and a disgusting barbaric teacher. Children absolutely warm to this. They think, "Well, Christ! He's one of us." I don't think you'll find many chaps . . . in their mid-seventies who think as I do and joke and fart around.

They usually get pompous, and pomposity is the enemy of children's writing.' Danny de Vito's film of the book (1996) concentrates on the magical and farcical elements. PLH

Matindi, Ann Kenyan author for children and also a nurse by profession. She has written two storybooks for young children. *The Kasiwes and their Animals* (1993) is a collection of seven stories which emphasise friendship and the importance of keeping promises and being kind to animals. Her other work, *The Sun and The Wind* (1967), also consists of stories based on traditional tales and these have proved especially popular with young children. ABO

Matters of Fact see MARGERY FISHER; see also BIOGRAPHY AND AUTOBIOGRAPHY

Matthews, Andrew see *DR MONSOON TAGGART'S AMAZING FINISHING ACADEMY*

Matthews, Rodney 1945– From influences as diverse as ARTHUR RACKHAM and WALT DISNEY, the British illustrator Rodney Matthews has fashioned an illustrative style highly suited to his favourite material, FANTASY and SCIENCE FICTION. Painting in coloured inks and gouache, he produces imaginative and detailed work, especially suited to covers but also to be found in *Greek Myths and Legends* (1986) and *Norse Myths And Legends* (1986). JAG

Mattingley, Christobel (Rosemary) 1931– Australian writer and former librarian, who has also written for radio and TELEVISION. Mattingley, a highly respected author, frequently deals with social issues. A number of books involve characters who must confront fear or loneliness; Pete, in *Brave with Ben* (1982), overcomes his fear of his grandmother's wild garden; concern for nature is explored in books such as *Lizard Log* (1975); the problems of being different are dealt with in *New Patches for Old* (1977) and *Rummage* (1981). The novels, *The Sack* (1993) and its continuation *Work Wanted* (1998), tackle the impact of unemployment on a family. The *ASMIR* SERIES, set in Bosnia, are true stories showing how war affects an ordinary family, a theme previously explored fictionally in *The Angel with a Mouth Organ* (1984) and *The Miracle Tree* (1985). Much of Mattingley's writing has been directly influenced by her own experiences; working in the Department of Immigration in Hobart in 1951 gave her an affinity with refugees, and her time living in Europe with her own children can be seen as the genesis of *The Magic Saddle* (1983), illustrated by ASTRA LACIS. Her books have won numerous awards, and she was made a Doctor of the University of South Australia in 1995. MLH

Maui tales see MAORI WRITING IN CHILDREN'S BOOKS

May, Kara see *EMILY* SERIES

May, Sophie [Rebecca Sophia Clarke] 1833–1906 American author of girls' stories. After a brief teaching career in Indiana, she retired because of hearing impairment, returning home to Maine. There she wrote some 40 books for children. Most popular are her series *Little Prudy* (from 1864), *Dotty Dimple* (from 1865) and *Flaxie Frizzle* (c. 1877). She also wrote the *Quinnebasset* (or *Maidenhood*) series for teenage girls (c. 1877). May is praised for her mischievous, natural child characters, known for their quaint sayings and mispronounced words. Her plots are episodic, detailing daily life and adventures within a close community of family and friends. Moral instruction is woven unobtrusively through the stories. JLB

Maybury, Ged 1953– New Zealand writer whose earlier books took as their starting point familiar, albeit disguised local landscapes, peopled with lively contemporary characters. His first children's novel, *Time Twister* (1986), is a fast-moving time-travel tale in which Jason, Helena and Troy meet their future selves. In the thoughtful *StarTroopers: The Final Episode* (1991), characters from a series of SCIENCE FICTION stories take on an unexpected reality, involving Spencer and Rebecca in a historical conflict, which echoes New Zealand's own troubled colonial past. *The Seventh Robe* (1993) and its sequel *The Rebel Masters* (1995) are full-blooded science fantasy novels which present the reader with a matriarchal society on a planet colonised from Earth; despite their inventiveness, they come across as somewhat impersonal. *Hive of the Star Bees: the First StarTroopers* (1995) is a straightforward science fiction prequel to *StarTroopers*, and is a more successful blend of Maybury's characteristic down-to-earth humour and curiosity about the ways in which societies work. *Horse Apples* (1998) is a humorous contemporary novel. Maybury has also published several stories on the INTERNET. BN

Mayer, Marianna 1945– American illustrator and writer of elementary and young juvenile books. Born in New York City, she started her career as an artist and found herself drawn to children's books. Together with her former husband, MERCER MAYER, she produced works including *Mine* (1970) and the award-winning *A Boy, a Dog, a Frog, and a Friend* (1971). Mayer is best known for her adaptations of FOLK and FAIRY TALES. Her interpretations preserve the original elements of a tale intact, fleshing out characters to make such tales her own, as in *BEAUTY AND THE BEAST* (1978), where she depicts the Beast as an unmaned lion whose true identity is made evident to everyone (except Beauty) through dream sequences. Mayer's retold stories come from all around the world, and include *Aladdin and the Enchanted Lamp* (1985), *Iduna and the Magic Apples* (1988), *Noble-Hearted Kate: A Celtic Tale* (1990), and *Baba Yaga and Vasilisa the Brave* (1994). Mayer has also produced ALPHABET and COUNTING BOOKS, such as *Alley Oop!* (1985) and the *Brambleberry* series, illustrated by GERALD MCDERMOTT. Her original tales include the award-winning *The Unicorn and the Lake* (1982), illustrated by Michael Hague. SCWA

Mayer, Mercer 1943– American author and illustrator for children. He was born in Little Rock, Arkansas, and grew up in Hawaii. He attended the Honolulu Academy of Arts and the Art Students League in New York City and settled in Connecticut. Mayer's first publication was a wordless book for preschool children, *A Boy, A Dog and a Frog* (1967), followed by *There's a Nightmare in My Closet* (1968). Both books were autobiographical. *A Boy, A Dog, A Frog and A Friend* followed in 1971. *Nightmare in My Closet* is regarded as a children's classic, and the *Los Angeles Times* selected it as one of ten books which enrich a child's life. *There's an Alligator Under My Bed* (1987) and *There's Something in My Attic* (1988) are kindergarten favourites. In each the anxious young protagonist finds courage within himself to overcome his fears. In 1977, Mayer's collaboration with writer Jay Williams on *Everyone Knows What a Dragon Looks Like* received both a *New York Times* Citation for Best Illustrated Children's Book of the Year and the Irma Simonton Black Award. Mayer's *Lisa Lou and the Great Yeller Belly Swamp* (1976) won the 1983 California Young Reader Medal. JRG

Mayhew, James British PICTUREBOOK author. After graduation from Maidstone College of Art in 1987, Mayhew turned to illustrating and writing children's picturebooks. His expressive ink line, complemented by deep, rich watercolour, can be seen at its most effective in *Koshka's Tale: Stories from Russia* (1993) and *The Boy and the Cloth of Dreams* (by Jenny Koralek, 1994) where the visual response to strange happenings and powerful language is intense and exciting. In *Katie and the Mona Lisa* (1998), *Katie's Picture Show* (1993) and *Katie Meets the Impressionists* (1998), Mayhew introduces very young readers to the great artists; in the first, for example, the Mona Lisa steps out of her painting and she and Katie meet – among others – Raphael's St George and Flora in Botticelli's 'Primavera', his own art perfectly integrated with reproductions of the original works. JAG

see also CATHERINE and LAURENCE ANHOLT; POSY SIMMONDS

Mayne, William 1928– Prize-winning British author who has been writing prolifically since the early 1950s. Although Mayne's books have received considerable critical acclaim, he has never achieved widespread popularity nor bestselling status. Best known for his fiction for the 10–13 age-group, and in particular his *CHOIR SCHOOL* series, Mayne has also written books for younger readers and PICTUREBOOK texts.

Mayne is widely regarded as a difficult writer, mainly because the language he uses is unusually precise and economical. It requires careful reading; few explanations are provided and the inattentive or inexperienced reader may well have difficulty in understanding what is happening, particularly as past and present, reality and FANTASY, often run into one another. Even for a diligent reader some things will become clear only on a second reading. However, the language rewards persistence; frequently monosyllabic, and often onomatopoeic, it conveys a strong sense of the physical reality it describes, often forcing the reader to proceed at a slow pace, as when Antar in *Antar And The Eagles* (1989) takes his first walk in new boots: 'clump over the doorstone, crunch across the gravelly path outside, and then quiet but heavy across the green.'

Mayne often makes use of local dialect and this too can make the text appear difficult. When the drummer boy first marches out of the hill in *Earthfasts* (1966) (see *EARTHFASTS* TRILOGY) even the local boys have difficulty in understanding his historical version of the dialect. Dialogue rarely takes the form of informative conversation, particularly between parent and child where each often seems preoccupied with private concerns and oblivious to the comments of the other. Speech is rarely reported with any phrase other than the basic 'said . . .' so that emotions can appear muted to the inexperienced reader.

The concerns of parents and children are often shown to be very different. While parents are preoccupied with mundane, everyday matters, children have a strong belief in magic and the supernatural, which is often supported in the narrative by the existence of tangible objects whose presence is explained by magical events. In the CARNEGIE MEDAL winner *A Grass Rope* (1958) Mary uses a magical local legend to find hidden treasure, and although the adults can provide a rational explanation for Mary's discovery, the presence of a unicorn's skull supports her belief.

In the *The Book of Hob Stories* (first published in 1984 in four separate volumes, illustrated by PATRICK BENSON) adults are again excluded from the world of magic; the children know that Hob lives in a cutch (cupboard) in the stairs and emerges at night to tackle the disorder in the human home, but the adults resolutely refuse to acknowledge his existence, even when the children produce a blurred image on a photograph. The father not only questions his existence, but declares, 'If there was such a person as Hob he would have to go' – clearly demonstrating his ignorance of the debt he owes Hob. The language used throughout is deceptively simple, predominantly monosyllabic, with generic names used in place of specific ones; the inhabitants of the house are known as 'Girl, Boy, Baby, Mr, Mrs' and dialogue and narrative voice often merge into one:

> Who lit a twiggy fire in the ashes of the hearth and filled the house with smoke in the middle of the night? Mr asks the question. Mr wants to know.

Mayne uses settings as diverse as Australia, New Zealand and Eastern Europe as well as his familiar Yorkshire, but local legend and landscape are always central. For example, *Low Tide* (1992), winner of THE GUARDIAN CHILDREN'S FICTION AWARD, is set in New Zealand in the aftermath of a tidal wave at the turn of the century. Three children know that they will only be able to survive because of a MAORI LEGEND, but again the adults, reappearing at the end of the story once the children are out of danger, question the children's belief in the magic they have witnessed. Their domineering attitude toward the children who have survived potential catastrophe without adult help emphasises the size of the gulf between the world of the children and that of the adults. Mama has clearly been upset, but all Papa says is: 'If you can't tell the truth you might as well go away again.' In *Earthfasts* legend and landscape are interwoven when the drummer boy uses the natural crevices found in the dales to travel across time. There is a strong sense in this trilogy, as in much of Mayne's work, of the landscape's history beneath its surface.

Mayne is particularly good at describing the continual struggle between humans and the elements. In *The Rolling Season* (1960) the community comes together to battle against a seemingly endless drought, while in *Over The Hills and Far Away* (1968) the children travel through a thick mist:

> It was like going along a tunnel and being enclosed in a bubble. The skin of the bubble was as far as they could see, and the occasional glimpses of the walls on either side were like the tunnel itself.

This acute awareness of the world around is common to all Mayne's novels. Senses are often fused together so that Hob 'hears the milk go sour . . . hears the bread go mouldy'. *The Twelve Dancers* (1962) opens with a colourful description of the outside world, but the world inside becomes suddenly vivid with the description of Marlene's foot, so cold that Marlene feels it like a bitter taste: 'There was a foot out of bed. Marlene brought it in and put it bitter behind the other leg's warm knee.'

Walker Books reissued *The Book of Hob Stories* in 1997, while Hodder reissued *Earthfasts* and published two sequels, *Cradlefasts* in 1996 and *Candlefasts* in 2000. Perhaps this signals a deserved revival of interest in Mayne's writings. KA

Mazer, Harry 1925– American author of YOUNG ADULT FICTION. Following service in World War II, Mazer held a variety of jobs before becoming a writer. Several of his works have been included on various 'best books lists', including *Snow Bound* (1973), *The Dollar Man* (1974) and *The War on Villa Street* (1978). He is probably best known for his partly autobiographcal work, *The Last Mission* (1979), the story of a 15-year-old Jewish boy who joins the Forces to fight the Nazis. It is a powerful and moving account of the futility of war. *The Cave Under the City* (1986) describes the hardships in the lives of one family during the Depression – not unlike those faced by today's homeless. Mazer's most recent title to receive high praise is *The Wild Kid* (1998), the story of a teenage runaway holding captive a young boy with Down's syndrome. Strong characterisation, suspense and powerful survival instincts are prominent features in all Mazer's work. He has also collaborated with his wife, NORMA FOX MAZER, to write for adolescent readers. PDS

Mazer, Norma Fox 1931– American writer of children's books. Growing up in a small town with poor parents who frequently moved house left Mazer feeling like an outsider, even in her own family. Her ability to translate the confused, isolated feelings of that time into fiction has undoubtedly contributed to her success. It was not until after her marriage to author HARRY MAZER that the two decided they wanted to write for a living. They began writing for women's romance magazines, and Mazer finished her first novel *I, Trissy*, in 1970. Most of her novels deal with such issues as drunk driving, parental kidnapping and family violence. In *The Taking of Terri Mueller* (1981), which won the Edgar Award from the Mystery Writers of America, Terri realises her beloved father kidnapped her as an infant. Izzy, the heroine of *After the Rain* (1987), a Newbery Honour Book, faces the death of a grandfather she has just come to know. In her 20 novels and two short-story collections, Mazer has created strong characters who in learning to cope with the unpleasant aspects of family and the outside world become more mature and sure of themselves. EHI

Mbatha, Mdidiyela see *MSINGA* SERIES

Meade, L.T. (Elizabeth 'Lillie' Thomasina) 1854–1914 Irish author born in County Cork and later living in London. She wrote over 250 books but is now mainly remembered for her SCHOOL STORIES for girls, which helped to shape the subsequent development of the genre. Most of her novels were set in England, and those set in Ireland or featuring Irish characters tend to focus on 'a wild Irish girl' who is in conflict with the more orderly English society portrayed by Meade. She also co-edited a magazine for girls and young women, *Atalanta*, for six years. VC

Meader, Stephen W(arren) 1892–1977 American author of numerous boys' stories. Beginning with *The Black Buccaneer* (1920), Meader alternated HISTORICAL FICTION – mostly set on the American frontier – with contemporary stories. The latter include his fine New Hampshire HORSE STORY, *Red Horse Hill* (1930), and several career stories, in which a boy transforms an unpromising asset – an abandoned bulldozer in *Bulldozer* (1951), a barren mountainside in *Snow on Blueberry Mountain* (1961) – into much-needed family income. Meader's likeable protagonists suggest to young readers that self-reliance, integrity and ingenuity enable a young man to make his way in any era. SR

Means, Florence Crannell 1891–1980 The first American author to specialise in fiction dealing with ethnic minorities. A minister's daughter, from a home where many races mingled freely, Means began her long and prolific career with a pioneer story based on her mother's girlhood, *Candle in the Mist* (1931), but was soon experimenting with novels whose teenage heroines were Navajo, Hopi, African-American and Hispanic. Fascinated by what she called the 'American mosaic' of ethnic groups, Means hoped to foster mutual understanding and appreciation. Harriet Freeman of *Shuttered Windows* (1938), for example, is a proud, intelligent and attractive black heroine in whom black girl readers can enjoy seeing themselves and with whom white girl readers will also identify. Means's most courageous novel, and a Newbery Honour Book, was *The Moved-Outers* (1945). The story of a Japanese-American family forced into an internment camp during World War II, it was published in wartime, while anti-Japanese feeling was at its height. Through its protagonist, Sue Ohara, Means enabled young readers to feel the impact of racial prejudice, the pain of losing home and friends, and the deadening, long-term effects of imprisonment. SR

Mee, Sir Arthur 1875–1943 Children's book and journal editor. Son of a Nottingham railway fireman, Mee worked as a local journalist before moving to London. He eventually became literary editor of the *Daily Mail* as well as supplying a daily column drawing on his by now vast general knowledge backed up by thousands of press cuttings. In 1905 he compiled *The Harmondsworth Self-Educator*, which in turn led to THE CHILDREN'S ENCYCLOPEDIA (1908). The success of this work, still in print during the 1950s and widely translated, led to the publication of *The Children's Newspaper*, published from 1919 to 1965 and edited by Mee up to his death.

This 12-page journal, later expanded in size, quickly turned Mee into a household name. Contents were easy to read and copiously illustrated. Stories, jokes and verse were interspersed with non-fiction which frequently celebrated the heroic achievements of the day. Popular with parents who wanted to see their children reading something educational, *The Children's Newspaper* in later years came to seem old-fashioned and too worthy for its own good. But at its best it provided quantities of information in a way that was unusually child-friendly for its time. Other edited books are testament to Mee's hard work and strong commitment to young people: *The Children's Bible* (1924), *The Children's Shakespeare* (1926) and *One Thousand Famous Things* (1937). Mee's fierce patriotism was also evident in titles like *Arthur Mee's Book of the Flag* (1941), and 37 travel books under the general title *The King's England*. NT

Meek, Margaret (Mrs Margaret Spencer) Leading British theorist on the relationship between childhood, literature and literacy. Meek is part of an academic movement which focuses as much critical attention on the experience of the reader as on author or topic. Working in the London Institute of Education since 1968, she was for 21 years Reviews Editor of *The School Librarian*, winning the Eleanor Farjeon Award in 1970 for her outstanding contribution. Many publications followed, including THE COOL WEB (1977), co-authored with Aidan Warlow and Griselda Barton, *Learning to Read* (1982), *How Texts Teach What Readers Learn* (1988), *On Being Literate* (1991) and *Information and Book Learning* (1996).

In all her writing, Meek asks important questions all too easily ignored when talking about children and literature. What, for example, do children actually get out of reading? Do they all profit equally? How do children's perceptions of story differ from those of adults? What, putting it most bluntly, is reading actually for? The questing intelligence and wide cultural range she brings to such issues have made her widely sought-after at conferences or as a contributor of prefaces, epilogues or chapters to books edited by others, including a number by her former students. The deserved winner of honorary degrees from other universities, Meek's overall contribution to the study and discussion of children's literature has been of great importance and still shows no sign of diminishing. NT see also CHILDIST CRITICISM; *COOL WEB, THE*; CRITICAL APPROACHES TO CHILDREN'S LITERATURE

Meeks, Arone Raymond see *ENORA AND THE BLACK CRANE*

Meet My Folks! (1961) A poetic celebration of his extraordinary family by the British poet TED HUGHES. The exuberant surrealism of poems like 'My Sister Jane' and 'My Aunt Flo' irresistibly draws attention to our own eccentricities and puts the human predicament into a humorous perspective, softened always by affection. JP

Meeting Midnight (1999) First collection for children by the distinguished British poet, Carol Ann Duffy. She is well known for the wit, irreverence, gender politics and technical mastery of her adult work, and these are also features of her poetry for young readers, leavened by a quirky sense of fun. The subject matter is often unusual and Duffy's unique voice is likely to appeal to discerning young readers. She has also produced two anthologies for young adults, *I Wouldn't Thank You for a Valentine* (1994) and *Stopping for Death* (1996). MS

Meg and Mog (from 1972) British series of 16 stories by JAN PIEŃKOWSKI and Helen Nicoll. Meg is a witch who is happiest when in her witch's outfit but, although she looks the part, her spells do not always turn out the way she intended. The stories are funny: does she tread on Mog's tail every night to wake him up or is it just an accident? The ILLUSTRATIONS include speech bubbles and sound words which children can say while the stories are read to them. The strong, bright colours that are used make it a very safe magical world. The illustrations are deceptive, looking at first glance like drawings by children themselves but actually conveying much of the humour of these amusing books. AMN

Meggendorfer, Lothar see MOVABLE BOOKS; PICTUREBOOKS

Meigs, Cornelia (Lynde) 1884–1973 American author of HISTORICAL FICTION and other books for children. Between 1920 and 1940 no American children's author was more respected. *Master Simon's Garden* (1916) was considered a landmark for its ambitious scope – covering three generations of New England history – and for its idealistic theme: the flower garden planted by Master Simon and tended by his descendants symbolises qualities of beauty, love and tolerance that must be nurtured in a harsh new land. Meigs's tendency to develop ideas rather than characters, however, and her less than sparkling style, limited the life-span of her novels for older readers; her simpler stories for children aged 9–12 – *Wind in the Chimney* (1934), *The Covered Bridge* (1936), *The Dutch Colt* (1953) – have retained their quiet charm. Her BIOGRAPHY of LOUISA MAY ALCOTT, *Invincible Louisa* (1933), was the first of its genre to win the NEWBERY AWARD. She also conceived, edited and wrote the initial section of *A Critical History of Children's Literature* (1953; revised 1969), the first comprehensive history encompassing both British and American children's literature; here she argued the power of children's preferences in shaping a literature with 'its own characteristics, its own individuality and its own greatness'. SR

Melling, Orla Irish author who has spent a number of years in Canada, writer of three distinctive FANTASIES in which contemporary young adult characters are embroiled in aspects of IRISH MYTHOLOGY AND FOLKLORE. Mythological 'history' is represented as existing both in the past and alongside the present in an alternative world into which it is possible to cross by using the ancient historical sites of Ireland as a magical threshold. *The Druid's Tune* (1983) takes two teenagers into the mythical world of Cúchulainn and Maeve and the *Táin Bó Cuailgne* (*The Cattle Raid of Cuailgne*). *The Singing Stone* (1986) goes further back into Ireland's mythical past, taking a lonely and rootless teenage girl to the last days of the Tuatha Dé Danann. In both novels, the attempt to reconcile well-meaning contemporary liberalism with the savagery of the mythical material is sometimes a little awkward. However, Orla Melling is a powerful storyteller with a strong sense of style, especially in descriptions of landscape and faery experience, and the simultaneity of modern Ireland alongside mythical Ireland is entirely convincing. These characteristics are especially apparent in her best work, *The Hunter's Moon* (1993), winner of the 1994 Ruth Schwartz Children's Literature Award. Here two teenage girls are caught up in the ecstatic excitement and dangerous rules of Ireland's stories of faery. Implicit in all three novels is a strong but unobtrusive spiritual sense of the wholeness of all created life. VW

Meltzer, Milton 1915– American writer of nonfiction. The son of Jewish Austrian parents, Meltzer grew up in Worcester, Massachusetts. His first book was a collaboration with the poet LANGSTON HUGHES, *A Pictorial History of the Negro in America* (1956), reprinted in 1983 as *A Pictorial History of Black Americans*. Discouraged by the quality of history texts available to children, Meltzer began to write historical non-fiction for young readers, eventually producing more than 70 books. A vigorous proponent of multiculturalism, Meltzer wrote, in *Remember the Days: A*

Short History of the Jewish American (1974), that 'all voices should not be expected to sing in unison the old Anglo-Saxon theme of "America." What is much better is the orchestration of the many rich and different voices that express the life of each ethnic group.'

He has celebrated those voices in a series of young people's history books about Jewish Americans, Hispanic Americans, Chinese Americans and Black Americans, all subtitled *A History in Their Own Words*. In these works, and others, Meltzer's writing continually reveals a strong faith in his young readers, and a conviction that they are not only worthy of, but entitled to, an exposure to history which is neither dry to the point of stultification, nor sugar-coated.

Meltzer's greatest contribution to children's literature may be his preference for primary sources. His writings were among the first to give youngsters access to records often otherwise unavailable to them, thus providing a vivid immediacy and accuracy. As he explains in *The American Revolutionaries* (1987 ALA Best Book for Young Adults): 'The focus . . . is not so much on official papers as on the experiences of ordinary Americans, men or women, young and old. They speak in their own words.' In each of his works, Meltzer characteristically provides a carefully constructed context for his readers which places these citations within an understandable framework.

Meltzer's writings include many BIOGRAPHIES, all of which reflect his strong interest in human rights and political activism. In *Starting from Home: A Writer's Beginnings* (1988), Meltzer discusses his own childhood and the roots of his craft. His *Never to Forget: Jews of the Holocaust* (1977), which won the National Jewish Book Award in 1978 and a Jane Addams Children's Book Award in 1977, is probably his most honoured book, but Meltzer has won innumerable other awards and honours, including another Jane Addams Children's Book Award for *Ain't Gonna Study War No More: The Story of America's Peace Seekers* (1986).

Other honours have included two Christopher Awards, for *All Times, All Peoples: A World History of Slavery* (1981) and for *Brother, Can You Spare a Dime? The Great Depression, 1929–1933* (1970). *The Jewish Americans: A History in Their Own Words 1650–1950* was given a 1983 BOSTON GLOBE-HORN BOOK AWARD for non-fiction and was also named a 1982 Notable Children's Book. *The Black Americans: A History in Their Own Words* also won a 1984 Notable Children's Book Award. Meltzer won a Golden Kite Award in 1986 for *Poverty in America* and the Catholic Library association's Regina Medal in 2000. MJKP

see also INFORMATION BOOKS; MULTICULTURAL BOOKS

Melwood, Mary British dramatist and novelist, whose output of published and performed works is small but distinguished. Over a 30-year period Melwood's work for children consisted only of four plays and two novels, but one of the plays is a classic of modern children's theatre. *The Tingalary Bird* was first produced in England by Caryl Jenner in 1964, and received an Arts Council Award. This extraordinary work is an absurdist drama for children. Its chief characters are an old man and an old woman who keep a ramshackle inn at the edge of a forest. Their lives have fallen into a stalemate of mutual antagonism and mutual need, their polarised condition represented by the old man's desire to welcome customers and the old woman's urge to repel them. The arrival of a huge and magical bird in the inn's main room precipitates a night of strange events which drastically alters their relationship. Bizarre comedy, and active participation by the child audience, make major children's theatre from material which seems deterrently arcane, disturbing and adult. Melwood's next play, *Five Minutes to Morning* (1965), again shows the decisive upheavals of a single traumatic night changing the direction of a character's life. These are highly original and brilliantly theatrical plays, which have won more attention in the United States than in England. Melwood's fiction is more conventional, but her novel *The Watcher Bee* (1982), the story of a girl's gradual emergence from romantic day-dream and watchful detachment into vigorous independence, is a remarkable and underrated work, reminiscent in some ways of Alain-Fournier's masterpiece, *Le Grand Meaulnes*. PH

Memoirs of a London Doll see DOLL STORIES; FANTASY; NEGLECTED WORKS

Memory (1987) New Zealand novel by MARGARET MAHY, in which the words 'Are you the One?' signal the mythical quality of this modern parable. Jonny Dart, half-drunk and lost in an inner-city subdivision, chances upon an old lady surrealistically pushing a shopping trolley through the early morning gloom. He escorts her home, finds a sad picture of neglect and madness, but also wisdom and a capacity for love, which he has never known before. This is one of Mahy's many triumphs; she elevates the human capacity for muddle-headedness and misguided behaviour into a search for spiritual identity. RS

Meniru, Teresa E. 1931–94 Nigerian children's author and educationist, born in Ozubulu, Anambra State, best known for her spirited heroines. The heroine of *Unoma* (1976), one of the few girls of her generation to go to school, survives various mishaps and goes on to more adventures in *Unoma at College* (1981). Nnenne in *The Drums of Joy* (1982) is kidnapped by slavers but escapes to find a new and exciting life in a missionary school. Her story has its parallel in

Footsteps in the Dark (1982), where an abused street boy faces great danger before finding a secure home. The courage and alertness of the hero of *Ibe the Cannon Boy* (1987) saves his village from enemy attack. Meniru's earliest works, published in 1971, were three books of Igbo FOLKTALES. Her last book, *The Mysterious Dancer* (1996), returns to folkloric themes with a down-to-earth Igbo rendition of the CINDERELLA story. VD

***Mennyms, The* series** Novels by Sylvia Waugh about a family of rag dolls living human lives. The first, *The Mennyms* (1993), won the GUARDIAN CHILDREN'S FICTION AWARD and is already viewed as a classic, being popular with children and adults alike. It examines the practical questions of how to survive as rag dolls, who never grow older and are potentially under threat from everyone around them. The dolls are shown to cope only by means of complex games through which they can pretend to be human. Later novels deal with philosophical questions about the nature of life. In the third book, *Mennyms Under Siege* (1995) Appleby Mennym, the doll who has been a truculent teenager for over 40 years, dares to open the forbidden door of the attic, unleashing allegorical and literal 'powers of destruction' upon the Mennym family; the door which had been 'promising paradise' threatens hell-fire instead while the narrator steps back from her characters and reminds the reader of earlier tragic falls in literature from Adam and Eve to the Lady of Shallott. They are able to shut the door only with the aid of what appears to be divine intervention, and by then it is too late for Appleby, who becomes the first rag doll to die. After her death the whole family is conscious of its fall and potential mortality, recovering only when they move away from their original home to a new one in a place that is likened to paradise. KA

Merriam, Eve 1916–92 American writer of poetry, fiction, non-fiction and plays for children. Born in Philadelphia, Merriam joked that the reason her parents owned women's dress shops was that it was the only way of affording to clothe three girls. Her non-fiction work includes *Figleaf: The Business of Being in Fashion* (1960). However, poetry remained her passion. She began her career auspiciously by winning the prestigious Yale Younger Poets Prize for *Family Circle* (1946) and having it published by her idol, Archibald MacLeish. Her first book of children's poetry, *There Is No Rhyme for Silver* (1962), led to numerous books variously praised for skilful metered verse, free verse, NONSENSE VERSE and fierce social conscience. In 1981 the National Council of Teachers of English Award for Excellence in Poetry for Children recognised this unofficial poet laureate. Her advice to adults reflects her gusto for poetry: 'Eat it, drink it, enjoy it, and share it.' And 'How to Eat a Poem' (from her 1964 collection *It Doesn't Always Have to Rhyme*) convinces children just to have fun and 'bite into' poetry: 'Pick it up with your fingers and lick the juice that may run down your chin. / It is ready and ripe now, whenever you are.' LMZ

Merry's Museum (1841–72) Long-lived American children's periodical founded by SAMUEL GRISWOLD GOODRICH in 1841. It was edited by, among others, Goodrich (1841–50), Stephen T. Allen (1850–7), John N. Stearns (1858–66) and, perhaps most notably, LOUISA MAY ALCOTT (1868–70). The magazine began as *Robert Merry's Museum*, featuring as editorial persona a kindly old gentleman resembling Goodrich's better-known character Peter Parley. Under various editors, the magazine became an improving and educational MISCELLANY of short articles about natural phenomena, history and BIOGRAPHY, though there was a rare excursion into FANTASY with some HANS CHRISTIAN ANDERSEN stories in the 1840s, and a long-running and very popular letter department – 'Merry's Monthly Chat with his Readers'. Just around the time that she was invited to write *LITTLE WOMEN* for Thomas Niles of Roberts Brothers, publisher Horace Fuller also asked Alcott to edit *Merry's Museum*. Alcott worked hard, writing much of her own material, including a series of nature sketches called *Will's Wonder-Book* and her novel *An Old Fashioned Girl*, serialised in 1869. However, since many new doors were now open to the author of *Little Women*, Alcott resigned in 1870 and in 1872 the magazine ceased publication. SRG

Merryll of the Stones (1989) Australian novel by BRIAN CASWELL, his first published, set in Australia and Wales, in the present and in the legendary Welsh past. Megan Ellison discovers she has the extra-sensory powers of the Old Ones and can slip between times from suburban Sydney to ancient Wales, where, as the Lady Merryll, she fights to prevent the extermination of her people. Through her experiences Caswell conveys a powerful sense of atmosphere and history, combining adventure with FANTASY, historical and romance genres. SNJ

see also WELSH MYTHOLOGY AND FOLKLORE; TIME-SLIP FANTASY

Metzenthen, David 1958– Australian writer, a champion of the underdog and of the value of (often physical) work in creating confident and independent young people. Metzenthen, who abandoned a career in writing advertising copy, has a laconic voice infused with compassion and humour. In *Danger Wave* (1990) a windsurfing competition allows a teenager in trouble to prove himself. *Lee Spain* (1991) throws together a hurt and angry boy escaping his damaged Vietnam veteran father, and a woman also facing a crisis. Metzenthen uses this unlikely scenario, presented from alternating perspectives, to weave an engaging and healing story. Shorter works include *Roadie* (1995) and *Animal Instincts* (1996) and the popular *Brocky's Bananagram* (1994), with the inventive notion of two friends on a banana plantation dispatching messages on bananas. The result encompasses changing attitudes to city folk and those from other cultures. A major work, *Johnny Hart's Heroes* (1996), features a larger-than-life drover, bent on saving 2000 scrawny sheep from drought. Desperate for work, Lal and her ex-boxer Aboriginal friend, Ralph, join Johnny and find meaning in their many adventures. Never sentimental or didactic, Metzenthen's books celebrate landscape and friendship, and allow their characters to overcome odds. In *Finn and the Big Guy* (1997) a country boy unearths crime and mystery but also finds fulfilment in his desired work as a horse strapper. *Gilbert's Ghost Train* (1997) is a subtle and gentle portrayal of a family living through the death of a boy from leukaemia. The mysterious daily appearance of Gilbert Royden Cutler cleverly highlights the transformational power of STORYTELLING and of understanding the past. *Falling Forward* (1998) again places marginalised youth in situations where, with some sympathy, trust and support, they can prove their worth. AN

Meyer, Renate 1930– Author-illustrator born in Germany, later a naturalised British subject. Meyer trained to be a painter at the Regent Street Polytechnic (now defunct). Her first book, *Vicki* (1968), with its story conveyed solely through monoprint images, is the first British wordless PICTUREBOOK. She followed this with *Hide and Seek* (1969), which has the same narrative structure. Her last book, *Knittle and Threadle* (1970) reflected her increasing interest in textiles and her experiences of cultural differences between the German Jewish family life from which she came and the strongly Cockney culture of her husband, CHARLES KEEPING. JD

Mezie the Ogbanje Boy (1984) Nigerian juvenile novel by Nathan Nkala, which weaves a story around the popular traditional belief in children who torment their parents by repeatedly dying and coming back. The hero finds the courage to free himself from the Ogbanje spirits and grow into a normal boy. VD

Mhlophe, Gcina 1958– South African storyteller. 'Almost single-handedly, Gcina Mhlophe has revived the art of STORYTELLING in this country. Today her name is synonymous with storytelling. Her vibrant personality, powerful voice and love of story combine to make her sessions unforgettable.' That citation for Mhlophe's winning of the Carl Lohann Award in 1996 sums up her contribution to the culture of South Africa. For some time a director of the Market Theatre in Johannesburg, she has published many of her stories in *The Snake with Seven Heads* (1989), *Queen of the Tortoises* (1990) and *The Singing Dog* (1992). JHe

Michael, Olga see *DOCTOR DOLITTLE* SERIES

Mickey Mouse Cartoon character created by WALT DISNEY. Mickey made his first appearance in the theatrical short *Plane Crazy*, and his first talking picture appearance in *Steamboat Willie* (both 1928). Perhaps the most famous and best-loved cartoon character in the history of animation, Mickey Mouse was born out of a legal entanglement: Disney learned, early in 1928, that the rights to his already successful animated series of short subjects featuring the character of Oswald the Lucky Rabbit had been acquired by its distributor, Charles Mintz. Out of financial desperation, Disney quickly transformed Oswald from a rabbit into a mouse. The mouse was originally named Mortimer; Disney's wife Lillian insisted that it be changed to Mickey. In later years, Disney was fond of saying that his empire (and the entire Disney ethos) was built upon this mouse.

In his earliest appearances, Mickey was a thin and angular creature, and was prone to some of the violent and mischievous behaviour of the TRICKSTER figure. However, by the end of the 1930s Mickey had changed in shape and personality to the rounder, softer and more genial figure familiar to contemporary audiences. Indeed, much of Mickey's appeal rests in the ways in which he stands as an 'Everymouse' – friendly and generally harmless, more acted upon than acting, and a stand-in for the ideal of who we might like to be. While he is clearly depicted as an adult, he possesses a childlike innocence that makes him appeal to young and old audiences alike. Mickey quickly became the hub of the Disney animated universe, accompanied by his girlfriend Minnie, bedevilled by his nemesis Donald Duck, and joined in his adventures by his friend Goofy and his dog Pluto.

In addition to playing himself, Mickey has been cast from time to time in roles taken from children's literature and world folklore; examples include the Bob Cratchit role in Disney's adaptation of the perennial favourite, from DICKENS *Mickey's Christmas Carol*, as well as the central role in *Mickey and the Beanstalk*, *The Brave Little Tailor*, *Thru the Mirror* (playing himself, but in a tale clearly inspired by LEWIS CARROLL'S *ALICE* books) and, perhaps most memorably, in the segment in *Fantasia* inspired by Paul Dukas's tone poem of the FOLKTALE *The Sorcerer's Apprentice*.

Mickey has also made his way into COMICS, PERIODICALS AND MAGAZINES as well as serious art, and has become a famous cultural icon (Mickey Mouse wristwatches). He was the host and star of a TELEVISION series for children, *The Mickey Mouse Club*, which ran for several seasons in the 1950s, and has even entered the lexicon of American slang ('Mickey Mouse' is a term – usually derogatory – for any task, issue or achievement considered too trivial or easy to merit serious attention). MAURICE SENDAK acknowledges Mickey Mouse as one of the most important influences in his childhood. BH

Mickey Mouse Annual The famous animated creation by WALT DISNEY was first seen in the early talkie short *Steamboat Willie* (1928). Mickey achieved worldwide popularity so swiftly that in the Autumn of 1931 the first *Mickey Mouse Annual* was published. This thick 128-page book of comic strips starring Mickey, Minnie and Pluto the Pup, was entirely British and drawn by Wilfred Haughton, who illustrated every page except the cover. Originally priced at 2s.6d. (12.5 pence), this edition is now valued in excess of £500, particularly as no copy was preserved in the British Library. Published by Dean, the ANNUAL ran until 1965, and was unrelated to *Mickey Mouse Weekly*, the tabloid photogravure COMIC published by Odhams from 8 February 1936, to 18 December 1957 (920 issues). Haughton drew and painted the covers of the comic for the first three years. DG

Midnight Folk, The (1927) Novel by JOHN MASEFIELD. A fast-moving children's story, told from the child's point of view, skilfully blending FANTASY and realism, black comedy and English rural life, to produce one of the classic children's novels of this period, memorably illustrated by Rowland Hilder. Kay Harker, an orphan, has an unpleasant governess, Sylvia Daisy Pouncer (modelled on Masefield's own hated governess, Mrs Broers) and an ineffectual guardian, Sir Theopompus. His days are spent conjugating Latin verbs, being told off by Mrs Pouncer or frightened by the kitchen-maid's stories of smugglers and murders: 'stabbed right through the skull . . . which shows you the force that must have been used'.

Kay is soon caught up in the world of the Midnight Folk and his matter-of-fact approach to events as they unfold is part of the charm of the story. Adventures and discoveries come thick and fast; Kay's cats talk and dabble in magic, his toys have gone off in search of the Harker treasure, and his house is the centre for the Pouncer Seven, a coven of witches led by his governess and the ruthless Abner Brown (both of whom later appear in the sequel, *The Box of Delights*, in 1935). The story, peppered with Masefield's verse, races on with pictures coming to life, journeys through the night

Illustration by Rowland Hilder from *The Midnight Folk* by John Masefield.

with bats, Blink the owl and Bitem the fox; 49-league boots 'secured down to keep them still', invisible mixture, mermaids and flying brooms all help Kay to find the treasure, outwit Mrs Pouncer and find a new guardian. HT

***Miffy* stories** see DICK BRUNA

Mighty Mouse Cartoon character in theatrical and televised films, beginning in 1942 and continuing, off and on, until 1987. Created by Paul Terry for his Terrytoon Studios, Mighty Mouse was a caped SUPERHERO, similar to Superman (his original name was Super Mouse). In the late 1940s, Terry did a Mighty Mouse cartoon spoofing operetta and melodrama, and this became the standard convention for all future *Mighty Mouse* cartoons, as he battled villains to preserve the honour of his sweetheart Pearl Pureheart. Mighty Mouse became the source of some controversy when on *Mighty Mouse: The New Adventures*, one of a number of Saturday morning series on which he appeared, he sniffed some flower petals, causing some conservative critics to accuse the series of promoting DRUG use. BH

Mikolaycak, Charles 1937–93 American illustrator, designer and author. Mikolaycak graduated from the Pratt Institute in 1958, and began a career in graphic design. He enjoyed illustrating children's books, where his loves of ILLUSTRATION and design naturally converged. He designed many of the books he illustrated, blending art and text, expanding text with art. Characteristically vivid and colourful, Mikolaycak's art fills the page and crosses its borders. His multilayered illustrations incorporate many textual and sub-textual elements; he chooses to illustrate tiny details from the story's text, culture or history. He gravitated toward myths, FOLKTALES and religious stories, enjoying the challenge of developing new interpretations of familiar tales. His respect for the stories' integrity and his resistance to stereotyping helped him to meet that challenge. Mikolaycak never condescended to his audience or censored his work. In *I Am Joseph* (1980), written by Barbara Cohen, a four-chapter, first-person retelling of the biblical Joseph story, and *Orpheus* (1992), an intimate recounting of the Greco-Roman myth, Mikolaycak refused to shy away from NUDITY and violence, remaining true to the story he had to tell. CEJ

see also CLASSICAL MYTHOLOGY

Mildred L. Batchelder Award see AWARDS AND MEDALS

Milk for Babes. Drawn Out of the Breasts of Both Testaments (1646) Catechism by John Cotton (1584–1652). Cotton, the teacher of Boston's First Church, probably wrote the catechism in response to a request from the Massachusetts General Court in 1641. The intent was to create a standard work of sound Puritan doctrine for young children at a time of religious controversy in New England. It was probably published in Cambridge, Massachusetts, between 1641 and 1645, but the 1646 English edition is the earliest surviving copy. American editions of 1656, 1657, 1684 and 1690 are titled *Spiritual Milk for Boston Babes,* and from 1701 it was included in hundreds of editions of *THE NEW-ENGLAND PRIMER*, often under that title. Native American language editions appeared in 1701 and 1720. Cotton's catechism served children not ready for the lengthy 'Shorter Catechism' of the Westminster Assembly of Divines, replacing its 107 questions with 61 in simpler language, and with short answers, such as: 'Q. *What are the wages of sin?* A. Death and Damnation.' Cotton Mather wrote in 1702 that *Milk for Babes* 'will be valued and studied and improved until New England cease to be New England.' DHW

Millar, C.M. see *BLACKIE'S CHILDREN'S ANNUAL*

Millar, Harold Robert 1869–c. 1940 British illustrator. Millar's greatest contribution to children's literature was as the illustrator for E. NESBIT's stories. Their first collaboration was *The Book of Beasts* published in *The Strand* (1899). Following this he executed remarkable illustrations of Nesbit's FANTASY creations, such as the Psammead in *Five Children and It* and the Phoenix in *The Phoenix and the Carpet*. He so successfully captured the essence of Nesbit's imagination in his evocative black-and-white drawings that she suggested he must have telepathic powers. Millar disagreed, preferring to think that his skills as an illustrator were responsible for their success. SM

Millay, Edna St Vincent 1892–1950 American poet and winner of the Pulitzer Prize for the *The Harp Weaver and Other Poems* in 1923. She began publishing in her teens with contributions to the *ST NICHOLAS MAGAZINE*. Her love of nature was a source of literary inspiration, as were FAIRY TALES. Millay's 'Dirge Without Music' figures prominently in PATRICIA MACLACHLAN's *Baby* (1993). PDS

Miller, Bertha Mahony 1882–1969 Founder of the first bookstore for children in the United States, the first professional children's literature journal, *THE HORN BOOK MAGAZINE*, and author of books about children's literature. Born in Rockport, Massachusetts, Miller was a member of the first class to attend Simmons College in Boston. In her work with the Women's Educational and Industrial Union, Miller conceived of the idea of a bookstore for children, begun in 1916. In 'The Bookshop for Boys and Girls', she and her staff prepared booklists on many subjects, which inspired the establishment in 1924 of *The Horn Book Magazine*, devoted to the selection and criticism of children's literature, which she edited until 1950. Miller co-edited a number of books about children's literature – *Realms of Gold in Children's Books* (1929); two volumes on *Illustrators of Children's Books* (1947, 1958); and works on *Newbery Medal Books* (1955) and *Caldecott Medal Books* (1957). Miller was also instrumental in publishing through Horn Book, Inc. other such works, including PAUL HAZARD's *Children and Men* (1944). Mahony's prodigious influence and accomplishments are chronicled in her biography, *The Spirited Life: Bertha Mahony Miller and Children's Books* (1973) by Eulalie S. Ross. AL

Milligan, Spike 1919– British humorist, nonsense writer, musician, actor, scriptwriter, novelist and one of the key figures behind the extremely popular BBC Radio programme, *The Goon Show*. Milligan has written many books of comic verse which are bestsellers for children. *Silly Verse for Kids* (1968) was the first, followed by *Unspun Socks from a Chicken's Laundry* (1981) and his best, *Startling Verse for all the Family* (1987). Like LEAR, he uses his idiosyncratic ILLUSTRATIONS to heighten the sense of the ridiculous in his verse. Lacking the fluency and musicality of his master, Milligan's verse, though invariably funny, can sometimes descend to doggerel and has elements of racism.

JL

see also NONSENSE VERSE

Millions of Cats see WANDA GÁG

Mills, Annette see *MUFFIN THE MULE*

Mills, Clifford see DRAMA FOR CHILDREN

Mills, Lauren 1957– American writer and illustrator who began her career by illustrating children's classics, *At the Back of the North Wind* (1988) and *ANNE OF GREEN GABLES* (1989). Romantic and realistic, Mills's richly detailed watercolours and lively text reveal her 'sense of wonder for the past'. Her first original story, *The Rag Coat* (1991), has been performed as a ballet and a play, and has been told over the radio. Her ILLUSTRATIONS in *Tatterhood and the Hobgoblins: A Norwegian Folktale* (1993), New England Book Design Award winner, have been favourably compared with the work of ARTHUR RACKHAM and with Pre-Raphaelite painting.

JAT

***Milly-Molly-Mandy* series** (1928–67) Six collections of short stories (some first appeared in *The Christian Science Monitor*) written and illustrated by Joyce Lankester Brisley. The stories chronicle the everyday experiences of a small girl who lives with her benevolently responsive parents, grandparents, uncle and aunt 'in a nice white cottage with a thatched roof'.This model of communal fellowship finds reflection in the solemn virtue and impetuous generosity of Milly-Molly-Mandy, whose wholesome childhood in a bygone, romanticised era these stories celebrate. The somewhat condescending texts, expanded by the author's detailed line drawings, continue to appeal.

CMN

Milne, A(lan) A(lexander) 1882–1956 British playwright, novelist and poet. The great irony of his life was that although he was not close to children or childhood, and did not consider himself a writer for children, he was, and has remained, most famous for four children's books, *WHEN WE WERE VERY YOUNG* (1924), *WINNIE-THE-POOH* (1926), *Now We Are Six* (1927) and *The House at Pooh Corner* (1928).

Milne began as a freelance writer, becoming assistant editor of *Punch* in 1906; during World War I (what he called 'that nightmare of mental and moral degradation') he was a signals officer; throughout the 1920s he was one of Britain's most successful playwrights, and a force on Broadway. *Mr Pim Passes By* (1919) and *The Truth About Blaydes* (1921) were typical, although modern critics regard his plays as whimsical and strained. He wrote nearly 30 plays – several were filmed – and seven novels, including a well-regarded detective story, *The Red House Mystery* (1922), three books of verse, several volumes of essays, pacifist tracts, and even a reader's guide, *Books for Children* (1948). He also wrote a robust stage version of KENNETH GRAHAME'S *THE WIND IN THE WILLOWS*, *TOAD OF TOAD HALL* (1929) which, he explained – in a characteristically acute preface – did not attempt to preserve 'the best parts of the book, and for that, if he has any knowledge of the theatre, Mr Grahame will thank me.' His last three plays were failures, and by 1938 a man who had always regarded himself as lucky in his public found himself 'out of fashion': his public had deserted him.

But in 1922 he had been asked by ROSE FYLEMAN, herself a very popular writer of sentimental light verse for and about children, to contribute to a new magazine for children, *Merry-Go-Round*. 'The Dormouse and the Doctor' led to *When We Were Very Young*, verses, as Milne said, 'some *for* children, some *about* children, some by, with or from children'. In his autobiography, *It's Too Late Now* (1939), he called them 'the work of a light-verse writer taking his job seriously even though he is taking it into the nursery'. Despite their fame, his verses are virtually indistinguishable from many other contemporary collections (often also illustrated by E. H. SHEPARD, or illustrators in the same style).

Pooh Bear first appeared in a Christmas-Eve story in the *Evening News* in 1925; the 'Pooh' books were immediate successes both in Britain and in the United States and remain bestsellers and cultural icons. In 1929 Milne wrote: 'in the main, writing is just thrill; the thrill of exploring. The more difficult the country, the more untraversed by the writer, the greater (to me, anyhow) the thrill. Well, I have had my thrill out of children's books, and know that I shall never recapture it.' Although Milne would have preferred to be remembered for his plays, it is his children's books which have brought him lasting fame.

PLH

Minarik, Else Holmelund 1920– Teacher and author of PICTUREBOOKS for small children. Born in Denmark, Minarik came to the United States when she was four. As an elementary-school teacher, she found a lack of books for children learning to read. Her first book, *Little Bear* (1957), was published by Harper in its *I Can Read* series, similar to Random House's *Beginner Books* but for slightly older readers. Illustrated by MAURICE SENDAK, this brought her first success and led to four other books about the same characters, including *Father Bear Comes Home* (1959) and ending with *A Kiss for Little Bear* (1968), all with ILLUSTRATIONS by Sendak. Other works include her second, *No Biting, No Fighting!* (1958), also with pictures by Sendak, *The Little Giant Girl and the Elf Boy* (1963) illustrated by GARTH WILLIAMS, *Percy and the Five Houses* (1989) illustrated by JAMES STEVENSON, and *Am I Beautiful?* (1992). Her stories often focus upon a small animal and his close and loving relationship with his mother and family. GRB

Mind Your Own Business (1974) First collection of poems by MICHAEL ROSEN. The design suggests a radical new approach: no titles, poems at the foot of pages and QUENTIN BLAKE's drawings spilling across them. Rosen's originality lies in conveying childhood experience in what appears to be children's own thoughts and words. He writes about familiar daily events, putting on shoes or sharing a bedroom, using free verse inventively. Blake's ILLUSTRATIONS match the poems' expansive, apparently artless sprawl. But the collection overall has a range of moods and forms. There are shorter poems, some lyrical and reflective, some nonsense, using rhyme, repetition and metaphor. ML

Minghella, Anthony see *THE STORYTELLER*

miscellanies Anthologies of stories, poems and pictures for children, popular throughout the 19th and early 20th centuries as gifts, especially at Christmas. JOHN NEWBERY was the first to produce children's miscellanies. Although often issued annually, they differed from most ANNUALS in that they were not necessarily associated with weekly or monthly magazines. In the 1920s and 30s they were often called *treasuries*, *budgets* or *garlands*. Titles such as *The Child's Companion* or *The Infant's Friend* usually signified a collection of improving material suitable for Sunday reading. Twentieth-century miscellanies were often badly designed and cheap, but their role in bringing fiction and poetry to children whose families could not afford more expensive books should not be underestimated. VW

***Miss Bianca* series** Stories by the British author Margery Sharp (1905–91), about the adventures of the white mouse Miss Bianca and her sturdy companion Bernard. The series began with *THE RESCUERS* (1959) and continued through more than ten books. In the first book Miss Bianca is enlisted by the Prisoners' Aid Society to contact the bravest mouse in Norway to help a young Norwegian poet escape from the Black Castle where he is held captive. The real villain of the piece is not, however, the jailer but Marmalouk the cat, who is rather taken aback by Miss Bianca's failure to realise that cats are the natural enemies of mice and her coming out to talk to him. The comedy of the book is in large part due to the gentle irony with which the author treats her characters, and also to the parodying of the heroic adventure thriller. Miss Bianca is the archetypal (unconsciously self-imaged) Romantic heroine, a poetess (the angle which the Society uses to persuade her to help the prisoner) who writes sentimental verse to her Boy, and works out in her imagination Romantic scenarios involving Bernard (who takes her at her own valuation). Her final farewell to Bernard, when she at last returns to the embassy and her Boy, is another Romantic set-piece faintly reminiscent of the ending of *The Prisoner of Zenda*. The series retains the charm of the first book though there is little development in the characters or situations. SA

Miss Tafferty's Cats (1993) Storybook by British illustrator Liz Underhill. The work has beautifully crafted ILLUSTRATIONS with cut-out windows which invite the reader to look in and out as the pages turn, revealing Miss Tafferty's house and her cats. The story, sensitively told, tells of her ultimate integration into the community. JAG

Mister Rabbit and the Lovely Present see MAURICE SENDAK; see also CHARLOTTE ZOLOTOW

Mistress Masham's Repose (1946) The only work by the British author T.H. WHITE that could genuinely be classed as a children's book, written for the daughter of a friend. The fantastical narrative, suspenseful and funny, concerns the orphan Maria, victim of cruel guardians and a prisoner in a crumbling historic mansion, who stumbles upon the descendants of Lilliput inhabiting the grounds. It contains much erudition and philosophy to challenge the adult reader; the significance of *GULLIVER'S TRAVELS*, relationships between human races and between culture and nature are discussed. White caricatures himself as the Professor and anticipates ROALD DAHL's darker treatment of adult/child relationships. *Mistress Masham's Repose* was reissued in 1998, beautifully illustrated by Martin Hargreaves. PC

see also KING ARTHUR

Mitchell, Adrian 1932– British poet, playwright and novelist, and one of the leaders of the revival in oral poetry in the 1960s, writing poetry to protest against war, social injustice and complacency. *Heart on the Left: Poems 1953–1984* and *Blue Coffee* (1996) collect his poems for adults. His first poetry collection for children was *NOTHINGMAS DAY* (1984). His writing is influenced by music, and his hero, William Blake (see *SONGS OF INNOCENCE*), was the subject of one of his many plays, *Tyger* (1971). His poetry features JOKES and wordplay but often reverts to serious themes, tackling racism, the environment, and his hopes and dreams for the future. It also shows an instinctive understanding of a child's concerns and interests. Most of these poems are collected in *Balloon Lagoon* (1997). Books for children include retellings of the BARON *MÜNCHAUSEN* stories and HANS CHRISTIAN ANDERSEN classics. The *Our Mammoth* series and *Maudie and the Green Children* (1996) mix the everyday and the unexpected, basing the story-line firmly in the real and unreal world of the child. In 1997 he published *The Adventures of Robin Hood and Marian*, illustrated by EMMA CHICHESTER CLARK, a retelling of the famous stories combining the traditional elements with new child-characters of Mitchell's own invention. *Nobody Rides the Unicorn* (2000) is a FAIRY TALE illustrated by Stephen Lambert. Mitchell always accompanies his signature with a drawing of an elephant, representing strength, gentleness and peace. HT

Mitchell, (Sibyl) Elyne (Keith) 1913– Australian writer for adults and children, best known for her novels usually referred to as *THE SILVER BRUMBY* SERIES, about the wild horses which live in the high country of the Australian alps. Her intimate knowledge and great love of this region, her passion for horses, especially brumbies, and her enjoyment of a physically active life are central to her stories, but her enthusiasm at times leads to an extravagance of imagery. Other books include *Kingfisher Feather* (1962); *Jinki, Dingo of the Snows* (1970) – about a dingo pup and an Aboriginal boy who befriends him – and a mystery thriller, *Winged Skis* (1964), as well as a series of other brumby stories, told from a human perspective. Mitchell also wrote the screenplay for the film *The Man from Snowy River* (1982), loosely based on the poem by A.B. PATERSON. JAP

Mitchell, Jane 1965– Irish novelist who has written an Irish-language PICTUREBOOK and novels for younger readers, but whose most significant work consists of her two novels for older readers. The central theme of both *When Stars Stop Spinning* (1993) – winner of the CBI/BISTO BOOK OF THE YEAR AWARD – and *Different Lives* (1996) is the emotional growth of her central characters. VC

Mitchell, Lucy Sprague (1878–1967) Founder of the Bank Street School in New York City, which became a laboratory for the development of 'here-and-now' books that emphasised the everyday experiences of children (often in urban settings) and featured language patterns and concepts resembling those used by actual children. Stories developed at Mitchell's school were often experimentally tried out on children with the author and illustrator on hand to observe the results and take notes toward revisions. MARGARET WISE BROWN and RUTH KRAUSS were among the authors influenced by Mitchell's experience-based model. To demonstrate the kinds of stories she advocated and to provide a tool for progressive teachers and parents, Mitchell developed (and wrote many of the stories for) the *Here and Now Story Book* (1921) and *Another Here and Now Story Book* (1937). Among the most widely read of her tales is the amusing 'Golden Book', *The Taxi That Hurried* (1933), illustrated with lively pictures of downtown Manhattan traffic by Tibor Gergely. The most admired of her urban here-and-now books was *Skyscraper* (c. 1946), an innovative photographic book that juxtaposed remarkable Lewis Hine photographs of the construction of the Empire State Building with her own poetic commentaries. JS

see also *GOLDEN BOOKS*

Mitton, Tony see PLUM

Mohr, Nicholasa 1935– Illustrator and writer of juvenile novels and short stories. Mohr was born in New York City. She went to art school and began her career as a graphic artist, having work exhibited in New York and Puerto Rico, before deciding to write full-time. Her first book, *Nilda* (1973), won awards both for the writing and for her ILLUSTRATIONS, which combined representational art, symbols and words to suggest the nature of the interrelationships of her characters. Mohr is concerned with the plight of Puerto Ricans on the mainland and tries through her fiction to bring this sub-culture greater recognition stressing its positive aspects as much as its difficulties. Her writing, which includes short-story collections – such as *El Bronx Remembered* (1975) or the award-winning *In Nueva York* (1977) – and novels such as *Felita* (1979), illustrated by Ray Cruz, evokes with colourful, humorous and realistic detail the Spanish Harlem in which she was raised. SCWA

Mole, John 1941– British poet, teacher and jazz musician. Mole was winner of the *SIGNAL* AWARD FOR POETRY for *Boo to a Goose* (1987), which was illustrated by his wife, Mary Norman. This was followed by *The Mad Parrot's Countdown* (1990), and the two collections comprising *Back By Midnight* (1994). Mole's poetry makes few concessions to young readers. The quality of his language and the mastery of technique are two hallmarks of his verse, which favours wit and humour but is sometimes accompanied by underlying darkness. For example, in 'September' (from *Hot Air*, 1996) unease pervades apparently safe and familiar territory. Toulouse Lautrec, Plato, CINDERELLA, Montaigne, Wordsworth, Sherlock Holmes and MICKEY MOUSE are amongst the personalities woven into the poems, and surprisingly – 'Marcel Proust's my hero / Marcel Proust's my man'. These poems do not finish on the page but continue to work in the mind of the reader. AHa

Molesworth see RONALD SEARLE; GEOFFREY WILLANS; see also LATIN MASTERS AND LATIN LESSONS; SCHOOL STORIES

Molesworth, Mrs (Mary Louisa) (née Stewart) 1839–1921 British writer remembered today mainly for *THE CUCKOO CLOCK* (1877), a story about a little girl who finds her way into a cuckoo clock whose resident cuckoo is a fairy. Her output, both as Mrs Molesworth and as Ennis Graham, in fact included many more works. The unsatisfactoriness of her marriage to Major Richard Molesworth (from whom she was later separated) found utterance in her early works for adults, and even her works for children bear some imprint of her unhappiness, though this is generally expressed in terms of loneliness or alienation which her child protagonists experience. It is possible to detect an escapist tendency in works like *The Cuckoo Clock*, *The Tapestry Room* (1879) and *The Carved Lions* (1895), the element of magic in the first two enabling the child to escape into another environment where it can forget its loneliness, and in *The Carved Lions*, the protagonist Geraldine runs away from school to hide in the shop where the lions are. Despite the rather cloying representations of baby-talk found in works like *Carrots* (1876), Molesworth's writing is mostly unsentimental; her fairies are acerbic and her children are down-to-earth and believable. SA

Moloney, James (Francis) 1954– Award-winning Australian novelist who drew on his teaching experiences in outback Cunamulla in Queensland for his books for adolescent readers. *Dougy* (1993), *Gracey* (1994) and *Angela* (1998) form a trilogy in which Moloney follows the lives of Dougy and his family, who live near the fictitious far-north Queensland town of Cunningham. In the first book, Dougy, the narrator, unfolds for the reader a poignant depiction of relations between the Aboriginal and the white inhabitants of Cunningham. In *Gracey* (1994), Moloney writes with an authentic voice as he relates through the eyes of his characters the suspicion and jealousy that exist between groups of people in a small country town, and the tension this causes. In *The House on River Terrace* (1994), Moloney addresses issues of parent/child conflict, the power of the media, and homelessness, in a readable and thought-provoking novel about the history of a Brisbane house, 'Gwendolyn', and its past and present inhabitants. SAM

Monjo, F(erdinand) N(icholas, III) 1924–78 American historical novelist for children, and children's books editor with Harper and Row and other New York publishing houses. Monjo's books demystify famous people and personalise history by using young eyewitnesses. Sometimes the texts employ invented diaries, as in *The One Bad Thing About Father* (1970), in which Quintin complains about his father Theodore Roosevelt; letters, as in *Letters to Horseface: Wolfgang Amadeus Mozart's Journey to Italy 1769–1770* (1975); or journals, as in *The Porcelain Pagoda* (1976), a 19th-century voyage to China. He is known principally for *The Drinking Gourd* (1970) in which children are involved in helping escaped slaves on a station of the Underground Railroad; *Poor Richard in France* (1973), a portrait of Benjamin Franklin; and his first book, *Indian Summer* (1968), which has been criticised for its portrayal of Indians as cruel, unfeeling and cowardly. Other titles include *Jezebel Wolf* (1971), *Me and Willie and Pa: The Story of Abraham Lincoln and His Son Tad* (1973), *Grand Papa and Ellen Aroon* (1974), *King George's Head Was Made of Lead* (1974), *Gettysburg: Tad Lincoln's Story* (1976), *The House on Stink Alley* (1977) and *A Namesake for Nathan: Being an Account of Captain Nathan Hale by His Twelve-Year-Old Sister, Joanna* (1977). KSB

montage In PICTUREBOOK illustration, a collection of interconnected images, or depicted fragments of interrelated episodes, arranged as a single composition; as a term, 'montage' overlaps with COLLAGE. JD

Montgomery, L(ucy) M(aud) 1874–1942 Canadian novelist who created such notable characters as Anne Shirley (*ANNE OF GREEN GABLES*) and Emily Byrd Starr (*EMILY OF NEW MOON*). Montgomery was born in Clifton (now New London), Prince Edward Island, Canada. Her mother died before Maud was two years old, and her father soon left the Island, leaving Maud with her elderly maternal grandparents who cared little for her sensitive nature or literary ambition. She keenly felt the loss of her father and incorporated his iconographic presence in her life in almost every novel she wrote, especially as Douglas Starr, Emily's father.

Despite her rigid upbringing, Maud Montgomery was a passionate, emotional child, rejoicing in the beauty of the world around her and marking the eccentricities of the people she encountered, hoarding everything for poems and stories. Montgomery loved writing and employed it as her chief method of self-expression from her earliest years – poems, sketches, journals, stories – using words as an outlet for the continuous battle between what she called her 'passionate Montgomery blood and [her] Puritan Macneill conscience'. She began publishing poems and stories when she was 16, and continued to do so after she had established herself as a novelist. After her grandfather's death in 1898, Maud's 'puritan conscience' tied her to her grandmother's household, where she assumed all the duties of housekeeper and hostess and was expected to subordinate her own needs and desires, including her writing career, to her family's expectations. Her grandmother died in 1911, when

Maud was 36 and already the enormously popular author of *Anne of Green Gables* (1908), *Anne of Avonlea* (1909), *Kilmeny of the Orchard* (1910) and *The Story Girl* (1911).

In July 1911, Montgomery married Ewan Macdonald, a Presbyterian minister, and left the beloved island of her birth. The couple settled in Leaskdale, Ontario, moved to Norval, Ontario in 1925, and retired to Toronto in 1935. They had three sons, one of whom was stillborn. Reverend Macdonald suffered from depression, which Montgomery could define only as religious melancholia, and she did all she could to hide the nature and severity of his illness from their congregations, friends and family. This subterfuge, as well as the reliance of the family on her literary income, took a toll on her own mental and emotional stability. Her husband never expressed interest in her work as an author, and never acknowledged the family's dependence on her income. His indifference hurt Montgomery deeply; for anyone to ignore her as a writer was to ignore her true calling.

Despite the decidedly constricted circumstances of her own life, Montgomery created vital, engaging and memorable novels. Her heroines are introduced as outsiders who speak their hearts and minds, making outrageous statements that challenge their small communities to soften hard hearts and open long-closed minds. She juxtaposes potentially subversive ideas and themes (strong, independent, ambitious girls) with themes of feminine domesticity, more socially acceptable for her times. Contemporary critics generally praise the first novels of her series, and lament the weakening of her vibrant young heroines as they become women who must ultimately shrink to meet society's expectations of hearth, husband and home. Critics also take issue with Montgomery's tendency to marry off her heroines, and, while Montgomery herself occasionally lamented that necessity, and continued to write the happily-ever-after endings that guaranteed commercial success, she stretched the traditional marriage formula, proffering the idea that women deserve full, happy lives, uniting career with companionship, art with domestic joy.

The *Anne* books have been adapted for stage and screen internationally, and the 1986 WonderWorks production of *Anne of Green Gables* renewed public interest in all of Montgomery's work, particularly in the United States. Her journals have been published as *The Selected Journals of L. M. Montgomery* (1985, 1987, 1992, 1998). Five volumes are projected. CEJ

Montgomery, Rutherford George [Al Avery; Everitt Proctor] 1894/6?–1985 American writer of juvenile fiction. Under his own name and pseudonyms, Montgomery wrote over 70 ADVENTURE STORIES, specialising in animal, western and aviation themes, and more than 500 short stories for children's magazines. Born in North Dakota, he later moved to California, winning a NEWBERY AWARD for *Kildee House* (1950), and awards for *Wapiti the Elk* (1952) and *Beaver Water* (1956). Montgomery specialised in family-oriented sagas, and it is unsurprising that he also wrote screenplays for WALT DISNEY productions, including *Flash the Teenaged Otter* (1960) and *Killers of the High Country* (1964). SCWA

Montresor, Beni 1926– Italian author and illustrator who was born in Bussolengo, Italy, and studied at the Liceo Artistico, Verona, the Academia di Belle Arti, Venice, and the Centro Sperimentale di Cinematografia, Rome. He came to the United States in 1960, after working as a set and costume designer with film directors such as Fellini, Rossellini and de Sica. He designed sets and costumes for the Metropolitan Opera and the New York City Ballet, and at the same time discovered children's books, something he had never seen as a child or paid attention to as an adult. His highly original books were immediately successful. *House of Flowers, House of Stars* (1962) describes and depicts all kinds of houses, both real and imaginary, for good children and bad, for example a house of stars for a little boy who died and a house of cheese built by a 'pompous mouse'. His ILLUSTRATIONS for BEATRICE SCHENK DE REGNIER's *May I Bring a Friend?* (1964) won the CALDECOTT MEDAL. Montresor has claimed that editors have found the subject matter of some of his more recent books too disturbing to publish. His LITTLE RED RIDING HOOD (1991), a book of stunning design and originality, has attracted disapproval because it shows Little Red Riding Hood actually being devoured and then floating peacefully, arms extended, inside the belly of the wolf. LH

Moomins, The 1945–77 Series by Tove Jansson, a Swedish-speaking Finn who was born in Helsinki in 1914 to parents who were both artists. The first book, *The Little Trolls and the Great Flood* (1945) was never published in Britain, but all of the subsequent 11 have been, of which three are PICTUREBOOKS for younger children – *The Book about Moomin, Mymble and Little My* (1952), *Who Will Comfort Toffle?* (1960) and *The Dangerous Journey* (1977).

Moominvalley is an idyllic FANTASY land somewhere along the coast of Finland, and the Scandinavian context is integral to many of the stories. The long, dark, inhospitable winter of *Moominland Midwinter* (1957), for instance, enhances the mood. The unknown plays an important part in this extended fantasy and there is something mysterious and unrevealed about Moominvalley, an element which adds to the magic and stimulates the reader's imagination. This was important to Jansson in the writing of the books: 'In a children's book there must be a path where the author stands still and the child walks on. A threat or a wonder that is never explained. A face that never shows itself entire.' Jansson's descriptions of the valley are evocative, often with a sense of beauty and melancholy creating a serene atmosphere. Although a new world and mythology have been devised (e.g. The Protector of all Small Beasts), influences of Scandinavian folklore are also apparent, such as the importance of weather and seasons, and magical dates such as midwinter and midsummer when huge bonfires are lit and strange creatures come briefly out of hiding.

The first of the novels, *Comet in Moominland* (1946), contains many classic elements of fantasy: the calm and tranquillity of Moominvalley is threatened by a comet on a collision course with the Earth. The central figures, Moomintroll and Sniff, go on a quest to find out more about the comet, in order to save themselves and their family from destruction while meeting many other characters along the way. The other early books in the series contain further fantastical adventures, such as discovering life on a floating theatre in *Moominsummer Madness* (1954), and experiencing the magic of the hobgoblin and fear of the Groke in *Finn Family Moomintroll* (1948). *The Exploits of Moominpappa* (1950) details a sequence of adventures involving life at sea and on a haunted island in Moominpappa's youth.

Later books in the series adhere less to the traditional fantasy structure and the tone of the books changes. In *Moominland Midwinter* the valley is not the secure place it has been previously. It is a cold and unfamiliar place, and Moomintroll is disturbed by it and spends much of the winter unhappy. It is as much a story of his longing and self-discovery as of the winter life in the valley. In this way the books become progressively more like psychological novels than adventure stories for children. It is this added depth that has helped the Moomins to appeal to a wide age-range. At the heart of these books there are still stories to be enjoyed by children, such as voyages across the sea to a new, mysterious island (*Moominpappa at Sea*, 1965), but much more time is also spent with the characters and how they perceive the world and their interpersonal relationships. With the possible exception of the Mymble, all the characters in *Moominvalley in November* (1970) have worries and self-doubts. The collection of short stories *Tales From Moominvalley* (1962) contains both exciting episodes such as 'The Filijonk Who Believed in Disasters' and more introspective tales like 'The Spring Tune', which has been described by K. Helakisa as 'perhaps the most complete description of the creative process in the entire world of literature'.

As well as providing adventures for the characters to embark upon, the books can also be interpreted on other levels. The many different characters represent different philosophies of life. As Too-ticky says in *Moominland Midwinter*: 'All things are so very uncertain, and that's exactly what makes me feel reassured.' This sense of uncertainty is reflected through the representation of many different philosophies, which often exist in opposition to one another. The lifestyles of Snufkin, the anti-materialistic and anti-authoritarian traveller, and the conventional and materialistic Filijonk, can be seen to be in direct conflict with each other. By presenting these elements within stories Jansson enables the young reader to make judgements about which lifestyle is preferable. However, the tone is not a moralising one, as none of the lifestyles is condemned and each character is still able to find happiness in some way.

It is, in part, the development of the narrative style through the series that enables the Moomins to maintain a freshness and originality. The tried and tested formula of fantasy is not over used, and familiar Moomin characters appear but are allowed quite different experiences to create fresh tales which are full of thoughtfulness without losing their engaging appeal to children. TM

Moon of Gomrath, The see THE WEIRDSTONE OF BRISINGAMEN

Moon, Grace see ADVENTURE STORIES

Moonfleet (1898) Adventure story by J(ohn) Meade Falkner (1858–1932), set in 18th-century Dorset. Its 15-year-old hero John Trenchard begins as a smuggler but is forced to flee to Holland with a price on his head, undergoing ten years of slave labour before he finally reaches home again. SA

Moore, Anne Carroll [Annie Carroll Moore] 1871–1961 American librarian, reviewer, author and pioneer in the establishment of library services to children. Born in Limerick, Maine, and educated at the Pratt Free Institute Library School in Brooklyn, New York, she was the first President of the ALA's children's services section; York Public Library's first supervisor of children's work, a post she held for 35 years; and the first children's book reviewer for *The Bookman*. She later wrote 'The Three Owls' column for the *New York Herald Tribune Books*. Her essays include *Roads to Childhood* (1920), *New Roads to Childhood* (1923) and *Crossroads to Childhood* (1926). Her juvenile novels are *Nicholas: A Manhattan Christmas* (1924) and *Nicholas and the Golden Goose* (1932). DJH

see also REVIEWERS AND REVIEWING

Moore, Clement Clarke see *A VISIT FROM ST NICHOLAS*

Moore, Lilian 1909– American author, poet and teacher whose easy-to-read fiction and poetry include *I'll Meet You at the Cucumbers* (1988), *Don't Be Afraid, Amanda* (1992) and *Adam Mouse's Book of Poems* (1992). Her poetry reflects a love of city and countryside, nature and childhood. Poems of six early books are collected in *Something New Begins* (1982). PDS

Moorland Mousie (1929) Seminal story of an Exmoor pony by Golden Gorse, pseudonym of Muriel Wace (1881–1968), which started the trend for anthropomorphised PONY STORIES. Heavily influenced by *BLACK BEAUTY*, it is a type of animal Pilgrim's Progress, with characters called Flabber, Mr Gammon, and Patience, the saintly heroine. Written with grave charm, it is a didactic book which preaches that there are no bad horses, only bad owners. The writer's knowledge and love of native ponies and rural life, and original ILLUSTRATIONS by Lionel Edwards, have ensured its lasting popularity. It has a less satisfying sequel, *Older Mousie* (1932). ARH

Mopsa The Fairy (1869) Written by the popular Victorian poet, Jean Ingelow (1820–97), and probably inspired by *ALICE'S ADVENTURES IN WONDERLAND*, this is a FANTASY woven around the adventures of its protagonist, Jack, who finds a nest of fairies, one of whom he looks after till she grows into the Fairy Queen. SA

More, Hannah 1745–1833 Influential British writer, extremely successful in a range of literary and discursive genres. Her major contribution to writing involving children was *THE CHEAP REPOSITORY TRACTS* (1795–8). In these tracts she adapted the clear, popular style of the CHAPBOOKS to an educational project designed particularly to secure the labouring poor in their traditional roles and prevent the spread of radicalism. Hannah More was also partly responsible for developing the Sunday school movement in England. An Evangelical Anglican, and politically conservative, her views on the education of women nevertheless share common ground with radical thinkers such as MARY WOLLSTONECRAFT. DWh

Morey, Walt(er Nelson) 1907–92 American writer of juvenile fiction. Born in Washington, Morey began by writing stories for pulp magazines, where he developed his concise, action-packed style. Later, he turned to writing animal stories for children, mostly set in the wilds of Alaska and largely based on people and animals he knew. These included his award-winning *Gentle Ben* (1965), which became a film and a TELEVISION series, and *Kavik, the Wolf Dog*, (1968), also made into a film. Morey wrote about endangered species and the wildernesses in which they lived, partly as a means of preserving their memory. He was honoured by the Oregon Library Association for his contributions to children's literature. SCWA

see also ANIMALS IN FICTION

Morgan le Fay see KING ARTHUR

Morgan, Sally (Jane) 1951– Australian writer and artist, whose moving autobiography, the critically acclaimed *My Place* (1987), winner of the inaugural 1987 Human Rights Award for Literature, did much to raise the public consciousness of what it means to be Aboriginal. A version for younger readers in three parts, *My Place for Young Readers* (1990), was edited by BARBARA KER WILSON, with new cover ILLUSTRATIONS by Morgan. Collaborating with illustrator BRONWYN BANCROFT, Morgan has written *Dan's Grandpa* (1996), a strongly spiritual story of Dan coming to terms with his Grandpa's death; *Just a Little Brown Dog* (1997), a universal story of a child wanting a pet, and *In Your Dreams* (1997), a story in a more western style. She has also written *Hurry Up, Oscar* (1993), illustrated by Bettina Guthridge. *The Flying Emu and Other Australian stories* (1992) is a collection of imaginative, humorous stories, written by Morgan and richly illustrated with her vibrant paintings. JAP

Morgenstern, Christian 1871–1914 German poet and journalist born in Munich, and best known for *Kindergedichte & Galgenlieder*. Like CARROLL and LEAR, his NONSENSE VERSE sometimes has a dark undertone or a point to make about the human condition. A recent edition, *Lullabies, Lyrics and Gallows Songs: selected poetry of Christian Morgenstern* (1992) is finely translated by Anthea Bell and superbly illustrated by LISBETH ZWERGER. This outstanding text in PICTUREBOOK format makes the work of the German poet available to children. For some time, discerning editors have selected Morgenstern in anthologies for younger readers. He writes strange, haunting, almost surreal nonsense-type poems which appeal to many children as well as adults. Here he is vividly brought to life by the prize-winning illustrator, whose odd, dramatic, charming and arresting pictures in radiant colour perfectly match Morgenstern's voice. This is an exquisite book in every way: the choice of paper, fonts, print, layout, design and binding make it a text with lasting qualities. MCCS

Morimoto, Junko 1932– Born in Hiroshima, the young Morimoto trained in fine arts at Kyoto University. She settled in Australia in 1982, and in 1983 illustrated *The White Crane*, an adaptation of a Japanese folktale, the first of a series of such PICTUREBOOKS. They include *Kojuro and the Bears* (1985), the working

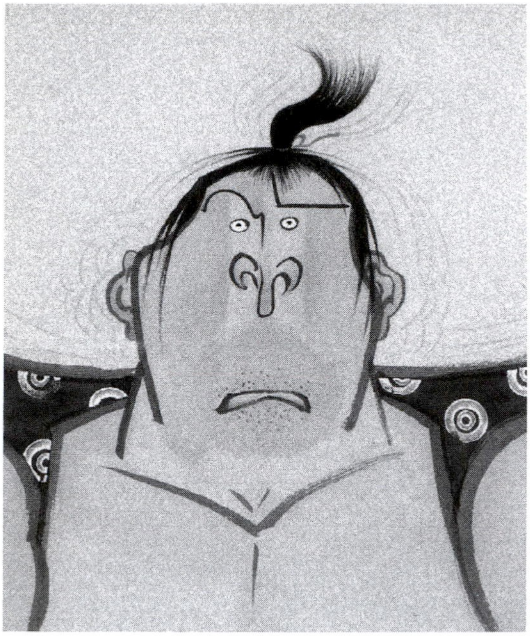

Illustration by Junko Morimoto from *The Two Bullies*.

out of karma in the life of a hunter, and *Kenju's Forest* (1989), which employs a metaphor enshrining the principle of conservation. Nowhere are Morimoto's versatility with line and colour, her passion and her range of emotional register more striking than in *My Hiroshima* (1987), a graphic record of the tragedy that Morimoto witnessed as a child. MSax

Morpurgo, Michael British prize-winning author and editor who also runs the charity 'Farms for City Children' from his farm in Devon. A number of Morpurgo's books reflect this interest in farming, either in their central theme, as in *Peter's Duck* (1996), a story about a child who visited his farm, and *My Friend Walter* (1988), in which the ghost of Sir Walter Raleigh helps a family to save their farming livelihood, or in the background setting, as in *Waiting for Anya* (1990). This tragic story about a group of resistance workers during the war began in a conversation Morpurgo had with a group of French farmers while on holiday. In *The Butterfly Lion* (1996) the old lady who is telling the story says to the young listener, 'true stories do not end just as we would wish them to. Would you like to hear the truth of what happened or shall I make up something just to keep you happy?' Morpurgo does not shrink from unhappy endings, though he often leaves room for hope. Recent work has included a number of collaborations with MICHAEL FOREMAN and the editing of short-story collections, as well as the acclaimed ROBINSONNADE, *Kensuke's Kingdom* (1999) – winner of the CHILDREN'S BOOK AWARD – and *Wombat Goes Walkabout* (1999) which was shortlisted for the 1999 KATE GREENAWAY AWARD for CHRISTIAN BIRMINGHAM's illustrations. KA

Morris, Jill 1936– Australian author, scriptwriter and producer, best known for her books about nature. *Australian Bats* (1992), *Australian Owls, Frogmouths and Nightjars* (1993) and *Australian Frogs: Amazing Amphibians* (1995) are inspired by her Queensland rainforest home. Lynne Tracey's detailed, realistic ILLUSTRATIONS in this informational rainforest series are a *tour de force*. Morris's first books, a number of Australian animal stories published in the 1970s, were followed by *The Boy Who Painted the Sun* (1983), illustrated by Geoff Hocking, about a small country boy's adjustment to city life. A prolific writer of books and articles, Morris also wrote, produced and directed the stage play *The Ark of Oz* (1988), and 65 episodes of the radio serial *Bangotcher Junction* (1985). HE

Morris, Revd Marcus see *EAGLE*; *GIRL*; *ROBIN*; *SWIFT*; see also COMICS, PERIODICALS AND MAGAZINES

Morse, Jedediah see *GEOGRAPHY MADE EASY*

Morte Darthur, Le see KING ARTHUR

Morton-Sale, John 1901–90 and **Morton-Sale, Isobel** 1904–92 British illustrators and founders of the Parnassus Gallery. John Morton-Sale and Isobel Lucas studied together at the Central School of Art and developed complementary approaches to ILLUSTRATION. A decade after their marriage in 1924, they made the first of a number of collaborations, jointly illustrating Mary Griggs's *The Yellow Cat* (1936). The great success of their illustrations to ELEANOR FARJEON's *MARTIN PIPPIN IN THE DAISY FIELD* (1937) made them essential members of her circle. Inspired by Neo-Romantic trends, they used their loose, confident handling of media to present children as creatures of nature. This is revealed most forcibly in their last collaboration, *Something Particular* (1955), which records 'a venture by children in mime, music and dance' devised by Rosalind Ramirez, an educationalist and royal tutor. DW

Moser, Barry 1940– American illustrator born in Chattanooga, Tennessee, and known for his mastery of WOOD ENGRAVING. Moser's early drawings in the margins of his military-school textbooks won him punishment, not praise, but he nevertheless succeeded in becoming one of the most prolific of artists. He has illustrated over 80 books and there have been more than 100 exhibitions of his impeccable drawings, watercolours and engravings. He credits his late intellectual awakening with allowing him an often startlingly fresh direction – even with such familiar classics as *Moby Dick* or *ALICE'S ADVENTURES IN WONDERLAND*: 'Four years of college and I never read a book. I had no intellectual curiosity until I was 25.'

Graduate studies in painting took him out of the South to Massachusetts, where he met Leonard Baskin, an important influence and teacher. In 1968 Moser founded the Pennyroyal Press and began making wood engravings to illustrate Pennyroyal's hand-printed editions. For him the creation of ILLUSTRATIONS means merging 'the theoretical and the practical'. His meticulous command of tools and materials and his thorough knowledge of book production give his work the sense of mastery that has won him numerous awards, including the *New York Times* Best Illustrated Book Award (for *Jump Again*) in 1987, and the IBBY Award in 1992. MMG

Moshi, E.A. Tanzanian author of the PICTUREBOOK *Let's Read ABC* (1996), written as part of the Children's Book Project for Tanzania. The book teaches the basic vocabulary of objects with which children are familiar in their surroundings. He also wrote the *English Picturebook for Children*, which is also for beginners. Tanzania uses Kiswahili as its official language and there are many children's books in Kiswahili, but Moshi's works are some of the very few children's books in English written by a Tanzanian. ABO

Moss, Elaine 1924– Influential British children's librarian, writer and reviewer whose efforts significantly affected the range, quality and appearance of juvenile publishing. Before becoming a librarian, Moss trained and worked as a teacher. In the 1960s she began working with American Grace Hogarth, subsequently one of the foremost children's editors in England. An active supporter of *SIGNAL* from its inception, she reviewed children's books in the press and on radio; in 1970 she assumed responsibility for *Children's Books of the Year*. Moss worked as a children's librarian in a large, culturally diverse school in London, where she gained first-hand knowledge of children's reading likes, dislikes and needs. KR

see also PUBLISHING AND PUBLISHERS; REVIEWING

Mother Bunch see COMTESSE D'AULNOY

Mother Goose A nursery character featured in innumerable books of NURSERY RHYMES and FAIRY TALES, and in PANTOMIMES. In the United States 'Mother Goose rhyme' is synonymous with 'nursery rhyme'. The name probably originated in the words 'CONTES DE MA MÈRE L'OYE' – 'Mother Goose's Tales' – which appeared in a panel in the frontispiece of CHARLES PERRAULT'S *Histoires ou contes du temps passé* (1697). The frontispiece shows Mother Goose as an old woman telling tales to children by the fireside. Perrault's FAIRY TALES were translated into English as *Histories, or Tales of Past Times* in 1729, and in the 1760s JOHN NEWBERY'S son Francis and his stepson THOMAS CARNAN issued a version under the title *Mother Goose's Tales*. Later they published a book of traditional nursery rhymes, *MOTHER GOOSE'S MELODY*, re-using 'Mother Goose' as the fireside source along with others such as TOMMY THUMB and Nurse Lovechild, which were also used as figures of nursery authorship. In 19th-century America, a lady from a family named Goose, or Vergoose, of Boston in the mid-17th century was believed to have been the source of the earlier collection of Mother Goose rhymes, though no proof of this has ever come to light.

By the end of the 18th century, many titles for children attributed to Mother Goose had been issued and her popularity as a nursery character led to her adaptation in pantomime. The immensely successful pantomime *Harlequin and Mother Goose; or, the Golden Egg* was performed at the Theatre Royal, London, in 1806. Mother Goose, a drag role, was played comically as an ancient hag with a conical hat and a hooked nose and chin. Her features were shared by other nursery characters of the time, such as OLD MOTHER HUBBARD, Old Dame Trot and Dame Wiggins of Lee. She was represented as a fairy godmother who helped the young suitor and the maiden with her wisdom and her magic powers, which included raising a storm and a ghost, and flying on a gander. Her combined image as storyteller and fairy godmother or magic old woman has been seen ever since in illustrated books. Soon a rhyme based on the pantomime began to appear in CHAPBOOKS. The type was established by J.E. Evans's *Old Mother Goose; or, the Golden Egg* (c. 1820), which began:

> Old Mother Goose, when
> She wanted to wander,
> Would ride thro' the air
> On a very fine gander.

The accompanying woodblock showed her thus flying. In the 19th century, many chapbooks and children's books, and James Orchard Halliwell's more official nursery rhyme book, *The Nursery Rhymes of England*, adopted Evans's poem, and it is included in many current nursery rhyme collections. In the 20th century, Mother Goose has continued to appear in children's books. In ARTHUR RACKHAM'S *Mother Goose: The Old Nursery Rhymes* (1913), she was portrayed as a haggard old witch, while in the mid-century, in RAYMOND BRIGGS'S *The Mother Goose Treasury* (1966), she is an amiable, grandmotherly figure in contemporary dress flying on a gander. She was depicted regularly in the ENDPAPERS of *BLACKIE'S CHILDREN'S ANNUAL* between 1910 and 1914, perhaps most originally piloting an air-ship full of children delivering copies of the annual to the star fairies. In productions of the pantomime since the beginning of the century, Mother Goose has been presented as an old woman willing to sacrifice everything to gain beauty. RT

Mother Goose Award see appendix; see also AWARDS AND MEDALS

Mother Goose in Prose see ILLUSTRATION IN CHILDREN'S BOOKS; see also L. FRANK BAUM; MAXFIELD PARRISH

Mother Goose or the The Old Nursery Rhymes see NURSERY RHYMES

***Mother Goose* rhymes** see MOTHER GOOSE; NURSERY RHYMES; see also MABEL LUCIE ATTWELL

Mother Goose's Melody (1760) One of the earliest and most charming anthologies of poetry for children, featuring NURSERY RHYMES (many of which are still well known today) and extracts from SHAKESPEARE. The anonymous editor is widely suspected to be the poet OLIVER GOLDSMITH. Whoever it was showed great wisdom: 'Singing these songs and lullabies to children is of great antiquity . . . the custom of making Nonsense Verses in our schools was borrowed from the practice among the old British nurses . . . (who) may be considered as the great-grandmothers of science and knowledge.' MCCS

Mother Goose's Quarto, or Melodies Complete see PUBLISHING AND PUBLISHERS

Mother Hubbard see *COMIC ADVENTURES OF OLD MOTHER HUBBARD AND HER DOG*; see also PICTUREBOOKS

Mother's Offering to Her Children, A (1841) The first children's book to be written and published in Australia. The author, Charlotte Barton (1797–1862), was a governess. It is written in the catechistic question-and-answer style (a colloquy between a Mrs Saville and her children) and is highly didactic and moralistic, but bursts into life with its descriptions of shipwreck and massacre in the Torres Straits. MSax

Mouse and His Child, The (1967) A closely wrought metaphorical FABLE by RUSSELL HOBAN, his best-known story for young readers and a biting social satire cast as a picaresque tale. The protagonists are joined clockwork toy mice; wound up, they dance in a circle. Existentially they are humans, with human longings for a home, independence ('self-winding') and a future, but without human counterparts. Smashed by accident and then discarded, the toy is roughly mended by a tramp, so that the father moves unsteadily forward, pushing the child before him into threatening encounters and situations of muddle and menace. The innocence of the mice outrages and fascinates Manny Rat, a villain in the satanic tradition, entrepreneurial junkyard owner, deceiver and destroyer, with 'a look of tenure'.

Hoban's claim that 'FANTASY isn't separate from reality; it is a vital approach to the essence of it' is justified in his illusion-making. Young readers, intrigued by events and memorable characters, are surprised by the disjunction of their imagined vision of the great length of the journey and the map illustrating a small locality. They respond in part to what adults see more clearly in the image of the ill-fitting jointure of the toys, the layered mimicries of a Beckett play ('The Caws of Art'), academic mathematics, witty journalistic slogans, overtones of fortune-telling, and the repeated injunction 'be happy' in the melancholy, near-black humour and violence of the whole. JOHN ROWE TOWNSEND (1996) reports that 'the background of the tale is clearly North American', where one might expect the author to be linked with E. B. WHITE, but 'it has never been esteemed as highly in the United States as in Britain, where it is regarded by many, including myself, as a classic.' MM

Mousehole Cat, The see NICOLA BAYLEY; see also MUSIC AND STORY

movable books Texts in which the reader lifts flaps, spins revolving discs or 'volvelles', pulls tabs to work sections of the page, or effects 'transformations' when moving discs or slats create new images. The field of movable books is little visited by critics or historians; yet it is a thriving and lucrative area of publishing and the story of its development is intriguing.

It is uncertain when the first movable books were made. The American bibliographer, Ann Montanaro, cites the use of a revolving disc in a philosophy text by the 13th-century Majorcan poet and mystic Ramon Llull, as one of the earliest known examples. In the 14th century, volvelles were used to tell fortunes and create secret codes; while flaps were lifted in anatomical textbooks to reveal the workings of the human body, much as they were in some fine INFORMATION BOOKS for children in the 1980s. Astronomical treatises in the 16th century used overlaying revolves to determine the movement of the planets.

Children probably enjoyed the 15 'metamorphoses' produced by Robert Sayer in London between 1766 and 1772. Several of these texts, much imitated by other publishers, recorded the adventures of Harlequin and came to be known as 'harlequinades'. They depended for their effects upon the movement of hinged folds in a page cut horizontally across the centre. As a section was folded over, a new picture was created.

The first movable books for young readers – for instruction rather than delight – were the 'Toilet' books of the 1820s, produced by the Grimaldis (father and son). At 3 shillings plain or 4 shillings and sixpence coloured, they were directed towards the children of the affluent. The books were sustained conceits based on items furnishing a dressing table – each teaching a moral virtue:

> My lovely Girls, I write for you
> And pray believe the TOILET true;
> 'Twill form your mind to every grace,
> 'Twill add new beauties to your face.

The hinged oval glass of 'the enchanting mirror' folds down to reveal the word 'Humility'; seven lines of verse on the following page offer stern advice to 'an unlessoned girl'. Cheerfulness (in a jar of 'fine lip salve') and all the other virtues are revealed in the subsequent pages.

Dean & Son, established before 1800 in London, claimed to be the originators of the first movable books for children. Between 1860 and the end of the century, they produced some 50 titles. The pages were manipulated by the pull of a flap, a piece of tape or even thin copper wire. Deans first published *Little Red Riding Hood* in this form followed by versions of *Robinson Crusoe*, *Cinderella* and *Aladdin*. They produced movable books for well over a century – and the name (by then owned by Paul Hamlyn) was still in use in the 1980s for such titles as *The Royal Family Pop-Up Book* ('Call it a souvenir or a memento, here is a fascinating record of one of the most exciting periods in the lives of the Royal Family').

Deans were one of three elements in what enthusiasts term the first golden age of the movable book – the late 19th century. The others, Ernest Nister and Lothar Meggendorfer, were both based in Germany, which led the world in printing technology. Nister was originally a printer; his elegantly made movable books usually showed idealised, plump children enjoying the pleasures of garden and countryside. He used transformation slats and rotating 'dissolves' by which the reader created one picture out of another; and he also devised figures which lifted from the page – the models were connected to each other and the base page by paper guides. Nister shrewdly established an office in London, where he was very successful, and an effective partnership with the New York firm of E.P. Dutton, who distributed the Nister titles in the United States.

Where the subjects of Nister's artists were pastoral in mood, the work of Meggendorfer (1847–1925) was charged with ingenious, even streetwise mischief. Meggendorfer had been a satirical cartoonist, and there is an energetic humour about both his drawings and the means by which they are activated. Some of his most famous works are extensive tableaux/panoramas; his *International Circus* (1899) contains some 450 separate figures against a backdrop of the circus crowd. The characters in his books move by means of minute levers, coiled wire and pivots, hidden between pages glued together at the edges. Frequently, the pompous are chopped down to size through the movement within the picture. In America meanwhile, the firm of McLoughlin Brothers reprinted work which originated in Germany; some 50 years later, they were to become highly successful with their own *Jolly Jump-Up* series of movables.

Inevitably, World War I curtailed the sale of German books in Britain and America – probably for reasons of austerity as well as patriotism. Towards the end of the 1920s, in modest enough circumstances, the pop-up book as we know it now was conceived. S. Louis Giraud was employed in the promotions department of *The Daily Express*, responsibile for the production of the paper's children's annuals. Using an idea submitted to *The Express* by a designer, Theodore Brown, Giraud created in the Annuals the first self-supporting models which sprung from the centre of a double page as the book was opened. Each annual contained at least five models, and one of the earliest (1929) was a rather crop-eared, grimacing Rupert Bear. By 1934, Giraud had left *The Express* and set up business in what had been his own home in Finchley. For 16 years, including the period of the war, he produced the *Bookano* books – an annual each year – and other occasional publications, such as *The Story of Jesus* (1937). The models were assembled by outworkers to Giraud's designs, and then glued into the books by a production line of some 50 temporary women workers. Despite Giraud's attempt to copyright the process internationally, his techniques were inevitably imitated, notably in Harold Lentz's *Blue Ribbon* series, published in New York in the 1930s. The models echoed some of Giraud's, and surpassed them in aesthetic quality. Lentz is usually credited with coining the term 'pop-up'.

The art of cutting and folding paper had been traditionally practised in Eastern Europe, and the influence of the region is evident in the post-war development of the form. In America, for example, the immigrant Julian Wehr devised some 30 technically excellent books. The most influential paper engineer of the period, however, was Vojtech Kubasta, a Czech artist whose work was 'discovered' and brought to the West by Leopold Schliesser, a Jewish banker from Prague who had fled to London in 1938.

By the early 1950s, Schliesser had become the owner of Bancroft and Co., a firm trading in fancy goods.

Visiting his native city in search of cheap products for his firm, Schliesser contacted Artia, the state-owned import/export business established to trade with non-communist countries. Through Artia, Schliesser discovered some card-backed versions of traditional tales devised by Kubasta, with models which spring off the page by a system of cut-outs and folds. Kubasta's illustrations are not exceptional – but the sheer wit and animation generated by the movement of the folded figures, along with those operated by the reader pulling tabs, have something of the spirit of Meggendorfer. Kubasta worked until his death in 1992, creating some 70 titles; Artia sold around 30 million copies of his books, translated into 70 or more languages. Yet, like almost all creators of movable books, he has received little critical attention, although early Kubastas in good condition now attract increasing interest among collectors.

Curiously, it was the failure of an American businessman to secure Kubasta's books for his home market which initiated a transformation in the production and artistic development of movable books. Waldo ('Wally') Hunt was a Los Angeles advertising man based in New York City. In the 1960s, he saw Kubasta's work in London and, so the story goes, attempted to buy a quarter of a million copies of each of four titles through Bancrofts. The initiative collapsed when the manufacturing plant in Prague declined the order; it was not in their five-year plan.

Hunt's response was to set up the business which eventually became Intervisual Books Incorporated, driven not only by Hunt's acumen but by his personal enthusiasm for movables. As a 'packager', his firm coordinates authors, illustrators, designers, paper engineers, printers and those who physically assemble the books. Brian Wildsmith, author of the superb movable, *The Creation* (1995), has described how he makes a rough model and sends it to Intervisual who liaise with appropriate paper engineers. After many negotiations about what is feasible within the models, the shapes are produced for Wildsmith to paint. The packager may also negotiate deals with numerous publishers – initial print runs can be as high as 200,000 in different languages and countries. Eventually, the separate shapes are sent to an assembly line – in Wildsmith's case, this was to the area first used by Hunt, near Cali, Colombia. Here some 500 women might be at work – a single book can have as many as 200 glue points. This labour-intensive stage of production, not surprisingly, is always sited in less developed countries: China, Thailand, Ecuador, Mexico and Tunisia, for example.

Mainstream publishers – and well-known illustrators – could not ignore so rewarding a field. In Britain, Kestrel published Robert Crowther's *The Most Amazing Hide and Seek Alphabet Book* (1977). It has sold over 200,000 copies. The children's literature establishment recognised the movable format in awarding the Kate Greenaway Medal to *Haunted House* (1979), which has sold over a million copies. Its chief creator, Jan Pieñkowski, another artist with East European roots, was already widely praised as a 'flat book' illustrator. In North America, some of the finest work is created by Robert Sabuda, who is unusually both illustrator and paper engineer. His superlative *The Christmas Alphabet* (1994) balances artistic restraint and exuberant celebration.

All large bookshops now devote a section exclusively to movable books. *Haunted House* has had many imitators, since surprise is the essence of the form. There are excellent information books and packs. *The Human Body* (1983) and *The Facts of Life* (1984) by Jonathan Miller and David Pelham are classics of their kind, and major publishers such as National Geographic regularly produce movable books. One of the most inventive workers in this field, the English-based Ron van der Meer (creator of intricate teaching packs on *Maths, Music* and *Art*) cites research which shows that handling the three dimensional material leads to far greater retention than that achieved by studying textbooks.

Most of the classic children's stories have appeared in pop-up format – not very satisfactorily, for the nature of a movable book means that there is little space for the printed word. More satisfying are stories, sometimes based on conventional picturebooks, in which the movement is integral to the plot itself (as Kubasta had realised). *Dinner with Fox* (1990), by Korky Paul and Stephen Wyllie, and Hans de Beer's *Ahoy There Little Bear* (1995) are excellent examples.

There seems to be no limit to the ingenuity of the makers of movable books. Larousse's *What the Painter Sees* shows how perspective works, includes a 50-centimetre-long fold-out 'Guernica', and uses a tubular silver paper mirror to reveal an anamorphosis. Jay Young's *The Most Amazing Pop-Up Science Book* includes a rotating record (with needle) of Edison's first message, a kaleidoscope, a sundial, a microscope, a camera obscura, and a periscope. *Monet's Garden* opens out into a tableau of Giverny with the painter at his easel by the water lilies. If this is not to the reader's taste, there are movable versions of sandwiches and burger buns, bursting with lettuce and resident caterpillars. The frontiers of the form are still being explored. GPF

Mowat, Farley 1921– Canadian environmental activist and writer, born in Belleville, Ontario, and raised in Saskatoon. Mowat served in the Canadian army during World War II, studied biology at the University of Toronto, and worked as a wildlife researcher for the Canadian government. Mowat's novels, both for children and adults, feature humour, adventure, survival in the Arctic, and both domesticated and wild animals; they are informed by history, ecology and anthropology. His themes are individual growth through self-discovery, reliance upon others, and the need to protect the resources of the Arctic. His first book, *People of the Deer* (1952), was followed by *Lost in the Barrens* (1956), *Never Cry Wolf* (1963), *The Curse of the Viking Grave* (1966), *A Whale for the Killing* (1972) and *Sea of Slaughter* (1984). The success of Mowat's work can be attributed to his gentle humour and ability to speak with compassion about the plight of the Inuit and the necessity of preserving the natural world. MRS

Mowgli STORIES see *THE JUNGLE BOOKS*

Mphahlele, Es'kia [Ezekiel] 1919– Probably the best-known and most respected African novelist and literary critic of South Africa. His classic account of his childhood, *Down Second Avenue* (1959), is suitable for young readers. In his youth novel, *Father, Come Home* (1984), the plot is episodic and interrupted by frequent didactic digressions on tribal customs and the bitter history of African people under white domination, with dialogue in a heavily indigenised style. The short story for children, *The Dream of Our Time* (1991), bears a message of racial harmony and upliftment for his people. ERJ

Mr Fox (1982) New Zealand PICTUREBOOK by GAVIN BISHOP. This is a rich retelling of a traditional story, a genre in which Bishop excels. As ever with Bishop, while the text is clear and unambiguous, every picture tells a further story with layers of references and reminders for young readers. Specific details, in both landscapes and interiors, are rendered with surreal clarity. Things become observers as the inanimate takes on life: dark clouds behind a lolly-pink house seem to threaten the Fox, and possibly the reader. Bishop's powerful brush work insinuates insecurity, while conversely the domestic detail denotes a solid, comfortable sense of place. MJH

Mr Gumpy's Outing (1970) Picturebook for which author-illustrator JOHN BURNINGHAM won the GREENAWAY AWARD. The book, which has become a classic, tells the story of a day's outing on the river. In simple, almost monosyllabic, language the text invites the reader to explore the picures. The book opens and closes with a picture of Mr Gumpy's house. The opening picture, on the right-hand side of the page, is in colour with pen CROSSHATCHING in different colours, the pale yellow suggesting a sunny morning. The closing picture, on the left hand side of the page, is sketched in black and white with closed crosshatching to show that it is now night-time. The illustrations follow a repeated pattern whereby the right-hand side of the page is in colour, depicting the animal who wants to join in, while on the left-hand side there is a sepia sketch of the boat and its occupants, which allows the experienced reader to anticipate the inevitable disaster. The pattern changes only at the point of disaster when a double-page colour spread depicts everyone splashing in the water. A corresponding spread in which the characters sit around a table eating tea repairs the happy mood of the day. KA

***Mr Men* series** (1971) Written by Roger Hargreaves (1934–1988), previously a creative director in advertising, the *Mr Men* series is one of the most marketable. It is popular with both adults and children, mainly because of the simply drawn characters, each a personification of a human trait or movement (for example, Mr Muddle who muddles everything). Apart from the 43 books, there is a club, a comic, stickers, badges, jigsaws and other merchandise. There is a also sister series, *Little Miss* which comprises 30 titles and first appeared in 1981. The *Mr Men* characters were later used for advertising rail travel. SET

Mrs Doubtfire see *MADAME DOUBTFIRE*

Mrs Frisby and the Rats of NIMH (1971) Acclaimed animal FANTASY and winner of the NEWBERY AWARD, by the American author ROBERT C. O'BRIEN. Mrs Frisby, a widowed fieldmouse, is befriended by a group of super-intelligent rats, escapees from a secret governmental laboratory. As it unfolds the rats' plans to create a self-sufficient society free from human influence, the story develops themes of social responsibility, individual resourcefulness and cooperation. Praised by critics for its successful imaginative integration of animal habits with human aspirations, the book's fast-paced action and lively and sympathetic characterisations have contributed to its enduring popularity on both sides of the Atlantic. CV

Mrs Leicester's School (1809) A collection of stories by MARY and CHARLES LAMB. 'M.B.', a young teacher new to the school, encourages a group of sad and lonely pupils to share their life-stories with each other, becoming, herself, their amanuensis. Although modelled on SARAH FIELDING's *The Governess*, the book is remarkable for its period in not being didactic: the girls' emotions are both complex and psychologically convincing, and their troubles reflect more upon adult society than themselves. Described by an early reviewer as 'simple and exquisitely told', the best of these stories read as freshly today as ever. JFB

***Mrs Pepperpot* series** Six immensely popular collections of stories by Alf Prøysen (1914–70), published in English translation (trans. Marianne Helweg)

between 1959 and 1973. Mrs. Pepperpot shrinks to the size of a pepperpot at the most inconvenient and unexpected moments. Amusing adventures regularly befall this resourceful and determined countrywoman as she uses her changing size to outwit enemies and trick friends. Prøysen is a true storyteller who confides in his audience and whose stories are ideal for reading aloud. The setting of these tales is the Norwegian countryside, with its customs and rhythms dictated by the changing seasons. GL

***Mrs Piggle-Wiggle* series** (1947–57) Four books for young readers by American author, Betty MacDonald (1908–58). The books consist of self-contained chapters, each a humorous story of how the kind and clever Mrs Piggle-Wiggle cures a child of some common fault such as being a 'Thought-You Saider', a 'Waddle-I-Doer', or a 'Slow-Eater-Tiny-Bite-Taker'. In *Mrs Piggle Wiggle* (1947) children are allowed to indulge in problem behaviours until absurdly exaggerated natural consequences, such as radishes growing from unwashed skin, become unendurable. *Mrs Piggle-Wiggle's Magic* (1949) and *Hello, Mrs Piggle-Wiggle* (1957) introduce magical medicines, such as pills that cause big black clouds with furry black tails hanging down to spring out of the mouths of tattle-tales. The cures in *Mrs Piggle-Wiggle's Farm* (1954) are based on work therapy, as Mrs Piggle-Wiggle devises various farmyard challenges that are uniquely suited to helping each child overcome his or her problem. Whether absurd, magical or realistic, the cures are psychologically credible and comically appropriate for the faults for which they are prescribed. The *Mrs Piggle-Wiggle* books have remained popular staples of childhood reading ever since their first publication. CV

Mrs Wiggs of the Cabbage Patch (1901) An American novel by Alice Caldwell Hegan (later Alice Hegan Rice) about the adventures of Mrs Wiggs and her family, which enjoyed a vogue in the early years of the 20th century. The book revolves around the trials and tribulations faced by the poverty-stricken Wiggs family, including insufficient money for rent and the death of a child. Despite confronting these problems and others, Mrs Wiggs remains generous, kind and optimistic, continuing to dispense the homespun folk wisdom for which she is famous. Mrs Wiggs also spreads her philosophy in *Lovey Mary* (1903). SAI

Msinga Title of a projected series from Ravan Books in Johannesburg to be created as autobiographies of actual children. *The Story of Mboma* (1979) by Mboma Dladla as told to Kathy Bond, illustrated by Mboma and his friend Mdidiyela, tells how the children's family in Natal, South Africa, were ordered by the farmer to move off his land. 'We could not move because we had no homes to go to. The farmer was angry and the police burned our homes down.' Such blunt criticism of the regime and the apartheid system was not encouraged, and the series never went beyond its first title. JHe

Muddle-Headed Wombat, The Long-running Australian children's serial written by RUTH PARK, which was initially broadcast on the ABC children's radio programme *The Argonauts*. The likeable but not very bright Wombat – and his distinctive friends Tabby Cat and Mouse with the odd voice – endeared himself to very young listeners and readers. It was originally called *The Wide-Awake Bunyip*, but Park changed the major character to a wombat. Fancifully illustrated by NOELA YOUNG, *The Muddle-Headed Wombat* was first published as a book in 1962 with further adventures published in 1964 and 1976. HE

Muffin the Mule First television character to become truly a children's favourite in Britain, making his small-screen début on 4 August 1946. Muffin the Mule was a wooden puppet animated by Anne Hogarth on top of the grand piano played by Annette Mills. Miss Mills, sister of the film actor John Mills, was a composer herself and wrote the still-remembered signature tune 'We want Muffin the Mule, dear old Muffin playing the fool.' Almost as popular was Muffin's other main protagonist, Peregrine Penguin, a grumpy, beak-clacking bird. There were many small individual *Muffin* books, and he starred on the front page of the first British comic based on television, *T.V. Comic* (9 November 1951). He was drawn by Neville Main, and Peregrine had a separate strip inside the comic, by Ron Murdoch. Muffin and Miss Mills were awarded the Television Society's Silver Medal in 1950. DG

Mukerji, Dhan Gopal 1890–1936 The only Indian author to have won the NEWBERY MEDAL for an outstanding literary work for children. Born in Calcutta in a Brahmin family, he migrated to America at the age of 19 and spent the rest of his life there. He brought with him the lore and the religion of India which he wove into his books in the creation of pictures of his own boyhood and of the life he had seen around him. He articulately interpreted India for American readers in his *Kari, the Elephant* (1922), *Jungle Beasts and Men* (1923), *Hari, the Jungle Lad* (1924), *Ghond, the Hunter* (1928), *The Chief of the Herd* (1929) and *Fierce-Face: The Story of a Tiger* (1936), even though he was often troubled by the dislocation of cultural setting. He won the Newbery Award in 1928 for *Gayneck: The Story of a Pigeon* (1927). It is a touching story of the training of a carrier pigeon bearing the message of courage and love, and

Collage and linocut illustration from *One Horse Waiting For Me* by Patricia Mullins.

its service during World War I. It follows the bird's courageous and spirited adventures over the housetops of an Indian village in the Himalayan Mountains, and on the French battlefield. Mukerji has always respected the capacity of children to understand. MBh

Mullen, Michael 1937– Irish novelist who has written extensively for children and adults. His first children's book, *Magus the Lollipop Man* (1981), a FANTASY, displays a flair for wryly comic writing. He has subsequently, however, chosen to concentrate on the more serious HISTORICAL FICTION which makes up most of his output. *Sea Wolves from the North* (1982) and *The Viking Princess* (1988) are both stories of Viking times in Ireland. Five novels set in 17th-century Ireland followed. More recently Mullen has turned his attention to Michelangelo, the Spanish Inquisition and tsarist Russia. These are carefully crafted books, demonstrating Mullen's regard for the past and his desire to impart this to his readers. While set in modern times, *The Caravan* (1990) also looks to the ways and values of previous days, again emphasising his belief that these are worth preserving. VC

Mullins, Patricia 1952– Australian illustrator who used COLLAGE, photographs and lino cuts to portray unusual textures in ILLUSTRATIONS for CHRISTOBEL MATTINGLEY'S *Rummage* (1981), which won the CHILDREN'S BOOK COUNCIL OF AUSTRALIA Junior Book of the Year Award in 1982, and *The Magic Saddle* (1983). An early paper collage for MEM FOX'S *Hattie and the Fox* (1986) shows skills which were later honed in the complex, multi-award-winning *V for Vanishing: An Alphabet of Endangered Animals* (1993), with its accurate depiction of scales, skin and fur using textured papers, rubbings and lino cuts. In *One Horse Waiting for Me* (1997), a counting book of both real and imaginary horses, an ethereal effect is achieved with the use of coloured Japanese rice and tissue papers. HE

multicultural books A subject genre focusing on the social realities of cultural groups, based on ethnic, religious or national heritage. What the culture is, in relation to traditions, beliefs and worldview, plays a significant part in the work. Often the cultural group is under-represented and unassimilated, as opposed to Euro-American groups.

In North America the term 'multicultural' usually means 'multi-ethnic', as in the poetry and fiction of Mexican American writer GARY SOTO and Native American writer JOSEPH BRUCHAC; the FOLK TALE collections and fiction of African American VIRGINIA HAMILTON and Chinese American LAURENCE YEP; the PICTUREBOOKS of Japanese American ALLEN SAY; and the coming-of-age novels of Korean American SOOK NYUL CHOI. However, 'multicultural' can also mean 'cross-cultural'; many children of various cultures and ethnicities are immigrants, refugees and travellers, as with Sook Choi's characters. Sometimes authors like Nava Semel and URI ORLEV from Israel, Rafik Schami from Syria, and Tormod Haugen from Norway cross cultures when their work appears in translation. And sometimes authors collect stories that have crossed cultures: In *A Ring of Tricksters; Animal tales from America, the West Indies, and Africa* (1997), Virginia Hamilton shows how African culture migrated to America through the Caribbean Islands, when slaves brought their stories with them.

How the writer enables readers to cross into a particular culture is an individual matter. There is no single way to create a multicultural book. Virginia Hamilton, in her fiction, weaves a universal situation about the child's growing-up time (an absentee parent, a coming-of-age identity conflict, sibling rivalry) into richly textured accounts of African American voices, traditions, values, beliefs, idioms, concerns, social classes and regional settings. In her folk collections, she introduces characters like TRICKSTERS, runaway slaves or clever females, who travel through or across cultures to escape constricting circumstances. FAITH RINGGOLD places readers in the situation of an African American child. TOM FEELINGS has a strong commitment to helping others into and through the same emotional 'passage' as that of his fictional characters: in *The Middle Passage: White Ships/Black Cargo* (1995), he aligns reader and character, one inside the other, in order to achieve a total emotional response to a painful human experience. Laurence Yep reverses the usual convention of putting foreign words in italics, with the remainder – or the majority – of the text in conventional print. His bilingual mode of presentation elevates the Asian American language in importance in order to place the mono-cultural reader into the bi-cultural character's shoes. At first Yep's positioning of readers is disorienting, but most readers eventually realise how disorienting it is to be a foreign speaker in an unfamiliar cultural setting.

When large immigrant populations were flooding into early 20th-century America, multicultural writers emphasised people of different colour and background learning to live together with mutual respect. Many books were written by outsiders, and critics, reviewers and educators could find no fault with their work. RUTH SAWYER's *Roller Skates*, set in the 1900s, shows what an American multicultural book looked like in 1936.

However, since the 1960s, when many African Americans began telling their own cultural stories, publishers began to recruit more insider writers, the result of political pressures during the Civil Rights movement. Consequently multicultural books came to be painted less in terms of cultural pluralism (focusing on transcendence of cultural boundaries) than in terms of emphasised diversity. When large numbers of immigrants from Viet Nam and the Caribbean began arriving in America during the last three decades, publishers cultivated writers from these cultures for their lists.

New writers are continually coming to the United States as representatives of other nations, imbuing the field of children's literature with a fresh sense of the cultural identities of various nations. For instance, Baba Wagué Diakité is a West African writer and illustrator who recently immigrated; his first book, *The Hunterman and the Crocodiles* (1997), is an African FOLK TALE that represents his cultural heritage. As a United States resident, his work may soon reflect a growing understanding of what it means to become an African American, like many immigrant writers who have since become 'American' writers. Recently Latoya Hunter, a Caribbean American child living in the Bronx, produced a book about her new life in America (*The Diary of Latoya Hunter*, 1992). LENSEY NAMIOKA, who was born in China, moved to the United States in World War II and later began to write children's books which drew upon her Asian heritage, beginning with *White Serpent Castle* (1976). She later wrote about her Asian American experience in such books as *Who's Hu?* (1981) and *Yang the Youngest and his Terrible Ear* (1992). Naomi Shihab Nye, who has been instrumental in exposing American children to the poetry of cultures around the world with anthologies like *This Same Sky* (1992), has presented her own experience as a Palestinian American, especially in her novel *Habibi* (1998). The prolific Czech writer and illustrator PETER SÍS has been a prominent figure among the growing community of Slavic American illustrators that includes the Russian American Gennady Spirin (*The Sea King's Daughter*, 1997) and Vladimir Radunsky (*Telephone*, 1996), Czech-American Anna Vojtech (*Murashka and the Month Brothers*, 1996), and Polish-American Tomek Bogacki (*I Hate You! I Like You!*, 1997). Sís's own autobiographical picturebook *Three Golden Keys* (1994) tells a touching story from his childhood in Prague and provides insight into his Czech American experience.

There is an authentic literature of cultural pluralism produced by writers and illustrators of Euro-American background like ARNOLD ADOFF, RACHEL ISADORA, Jill Krementz, ELAINE KONIGSBURG and Sharon Wyeth. Krementz's *A Black Girl Growing up in the Rural South* (1969), a photographic picturebook featuring a nine-year-old girl living in a large family in Alabama, is a rare achievement and an important historical document. Isadora's picturebook *Ben's Trumpet* (1979) is an outstanding work of art. Wyeth's novel, *The World of Daughter McGuire* (1994), explores the multifaceted heritage of 11-year-old Daughter, a polyethnic child (African-Italian-Irish-Jewish-Russian American), who is growing up to see that she is a citizen of the world. Adoff's poetry, in which he incorporates authentic experiences of his own family life, shows children growing up in bi-cultural families like his own. Children in his poem-storybooks reflect on their bi-cultural identities, on race, prejudice, being different and being loved. Cultural backgrounds are bridged by the concept of family or school activities, in terms of the children's own ethnic backgrounds.

Elaine Konigsburg's latest Newbery winner, *A View From Saturday* (1996), brings together – as friends – nearly every possible contender for multicultural status in America: a child of rural farming parents, a Jewish American child, a child of East Indian heritage, a child of divorce, and a disabled, handicapped female as their teacher. The book becomes a warm, humorous send-up of political correctness at a time when special-interest groups and mono-cultural, cross-cultural, poly-cultural and multi-ethnic heritages are all competing for the attention of readers.

In Britain since the early 1960s teachers and librarians moved away from concentrating on assimilation of immigrant children and focusing narrowly on the national heritage, towards cultural pluralism, and the recognition of and respect for children's cultures and countries of origin,while at the same time seeking to widen the perspectives and understanding of all children in a developing multicultural society. In the United States the context is significantly different, for the heritage itself is more multicultural and immigration is itself part of the heritage.

In Britain the category 'multicultural books' includes: literature from diverse countries and cultures; a range of fiction of immediate relevance to 'minority group' children growing up in Britain – for instance, from black and Asian writers in Britain such as MALORIE BLACKMAN, FARRUKH DHONDY, JAMILA GAVIN, Errol Lloyd, Jacqueline Roy and Rukshana Smith; and fiction which relates in more subtle ways to their experience, for example through FANTASY and through distancing in time and place. ROSEMARY SUTCLIFF's *EAGLE OF THE NINTH* is set in Roman Britain and takes on a new significance for those children who are themselves trying to settle in an alien and confusing culture. Multicultural fiction in Britain also includes efforts by children's writers to recognise the composition of their readership and even to allot 'minority group' children leading roles – although there is a danger of portraying such children as victims, as in BERNARD ASHLEY's *THE TROUBLE WITH DONOVAN CROFT* (1980).

Multicultural literature is world literature, but for expediency examples here are limited to books that have proved rewarding from the first two major areas of immigration into the United Kingdom: the Caribbean and the Indian subcontinent. In spite of the remarkable output of creative writing in the Caribbean in the fifties and sixties little was published specifically for children, apart from retellings of oral literature. Vic Reid's stories of the breakaway Maroons in Jamaica (*The Young Warriors*, 1967, for example) are popular as ADVENTURE STORIES, and as part of Jamaica's history. Merle Hodge's novels deal with children shuttled between two strands of extended families with conflicting values. *Crick Crack Monkey* (1970) examines the pain and confusion and eventual doubting of her own values experienced by a girl in her teens when she is removed from the warm-hearted, down-to-earth family of one aunt to the black, middle-class, socially aspiring family of another. *Life For Laetitia* (1995), for younger children, also reflects the fragmented lives of many children, but is less complex. Hodge captures the strength, warmth and wisdom of the proverbial Caribbean grandmother; and the account of Laetitia's recovery from a breakdown is memorable.

Jacob Ross's *Song For Simone* (1986) is a wonderfully varied collection of stories about, or seen through the eyes of, young people, and is set in Grenada. They powerfully evoke a sense of Caribbean childhood and landscape, and are informed by a respect for women and an awareness of the potential for tenderness in men. Several stories are set in recent times, against the backdrop of the struggle of Grenada's revolution, and the American invasion of 1979. Anne Walmsley broke new ground with *The Sun's Eye* (1968, updated in 1989), an anthology of stories, extracts and poems drawn mainly from adult writing but selected for secondary children. This served also as a stimulating introduction to the adult literature that was emerging.

The Caribbean is rich in novels about young people growing up. Olive Senior's stories in *Summer Lightning* (1986) are set in the rural Jamaica of her childhood. Several have a girl as the central character, with similar characteristics: bright, rebellious and outspoken, but also private in her thinking and imagining as she tries to make sense of the adult world around her. Senior captures the immediacy of oral STORYTELLING in diverse ways – from third-person narration in Standard English to the authentic creole voice of the final story, 'Ballad', where the narrative unfolds through the complex route of the child's own puzzled reflection and piecing together.

Since the population of Trinidad has almost equal numbers of people originating from Africa and India, as well as many from China and other countries, there is much reflection in its literature on the multicultural society. In Michael Anthony's *Green Days By The River* (1967) 15-year-old Shell, a Trinidadian of African origin, moves with his mother and dying father to a new village. We see him trying to find himself in the new community: he is responsible for his family, but is tentatively exploring relationships with girls, and being accepted as one of the boys, working on the land with Mr Ghidaree, a farmer of Indian origin who in part takes over the role of his father. As in all of Michael Anthony's books there is much exploration of feeling, and a sensitive evocation of background. In the end events overtake Shell. Mr Ghidaree takes charge and Shell is under pressure to marry his daughter. How much responsibility Shell has for the shaping of his destiny, and his acceptance of it, are preoccupying questions for the young reader.

Samuel Selvon's first novel, *A Brighter Sun* (1952), set in Trinidad during World War II, holds a similar kind of interest for the young reader, but deals more specifically with identity and other issues of the multicultural society. Tiger, a Trinidadian of Indian origin, has an arranged Hindu marriage at 16 and has to take on an adult's responsibilities in a strange village with his unknown wife. Not only is Tiger trying to find a place as a man in a new community, but he is also questioning his allegiance to the old Indian traditions his family clings to, while at the same time respecting the wisdom of Sookdeo, an elderly Indian in the village. He and his wife slowly build a workaday and eventually enduring relationship with their neighbours; and in a wider sense, as he yearns to make sense of his young life, he searches for his identity as a Trinidadian. Selvon breaks new ground with the language of this novel: it is related in Standard English, with the dialogue in appropriate creoles of Trinidad, but at times he uses an interesting convergence of the two in the narration so that the reader enters more easily into Tiger's thinking.

From the Indian subcontinent many attractively produced retellings of epics, legends, tales and FABLES are available for younger children, but there are few published children's writers. Two in particular stand out. RUSKIN BOND engages children of about nine upwards with his quietly written, deceptively simple books set in his homeland, the isolated villages and towns of the foothills of the Himalayas, with stories woven around children facing, in their everyday lives, natural and man-made disasters – forest fires, drought, flooding, deforestation, and also encounters with animals that command both respect and fear. *Angry River* (1972), which portrays a young girl stranded in monsoon floods, is the most fully realised of the stories, and makes subtle hints to the reader that the boy who rescues her may be the god Krishna. ANITA DESAI's *Peacock Garden* (1979) has a FAIRY-TALE quality, although it is in fact a sensitive introduction to partition in India. A young child, Zuni, is woken in the dark, and with her Muslim family escapes from the burning and killing in her Hindu village, but instead of fleeing to Pakistan they take refuge in a mosque garden, with its contrasting tranquility. It is a time of enchantment for Zuni as they make their temporary home there, but also one of loneliness. When it is safe to visit the village the reader now sees it in daylight for the first time – and through Zuni's eager eyes as she is re-united with her Hindu friends. *The Village by The Sea* (1982), for older readers, tells of a brother, Hari (12), and sister, Lila (13), who take responsibility for their poverty-stricken family in a village where the traditional way of life – farming and fishing – and the environment are threatened by plans for a huge chemical fertiliser complex. In despair at his inadequacy Hari leaves for Bombay to seek work while Lila holds the family together. Conditions in Bombay are even harsher, but this wider experience equips Hari to return to his family in a spirit of optimism, ready to adapt and compromise.

Vedi (1982) by Ved Mehta vividly describes five years of the blind Indian journalist's childhood. Born in Lahore into a large, middle-class Hindu family, he was transported at four to an orphanage for the blind in Bombay to be educated. Teenage readers are attracted to the way he 'sees' so much through his blindness, and to his resilience, courage and humour. He portrays so well the private feelings of a child, the lonely knowledge and understanding he has of each of his cultures – including class – and his reluctance to betray either to members of the other. Similarly he is exposed to differences of religions and language. Older and more mature readers may go on to *Face to Face* (1957), which tells the whole of Mehta's story up to the age of 20, with a more detailed portrayal of the India he grew up in, the problems of partition, and his own growing political awareness.

In the 1990s the range widened yet again as teachers and librarians in Britain sought out books which reflected the cultures and countries of origin of refugee children – from Kurdistan, Somalia, Bosnia and other areas of war and conflict. Later, at a time when asylum seekers were a subject of bitter political debate in Britain, *Girl in Red* (2000) by Gaye Hiçyilmaz addressed the issue in a beautifully written and not entirely pessimistic novel. JG, ARTL, NM

see also HISTORICAL FICTION; WAR STORIES

multilayered text A term used loosely to refer to any narrative or poem with different levels of meaning. More specifically, however, it is linked to the practice of re-reading and applied to any narrative which enables a reader to find new pleasures or understanding on subsequent readings. Its use acknowledges that all readings are personal and unique, and that no one reads the same text in precisely the same way on subsequent occasions. Together with a related term, *the multilayered reader*, it implies that becoming a reader is an unfolding process inseparable from other aspects of a child's developing life. VW

Münchausen, Baron see BARON MÜNCHAUSEN

Munoz, Claudio 1945– Born and brought up in Chile, Munoz has established himself in Britain as a distinctive illustrator. His fluid line, which readily conveys movement and facial expression, works as well for the dotty stories of Ivor Cutler (*Doris the Hen*, 1992; *The New Dress*, 1995) as it does for the poignant *Come Back, Grandma!* (Sue Limb, 1993) or the perceptive *Horrible Crocodile* (Jonathan Shipton, 1995) and *Nobody Like Me!* (Fay Weldon, 1997). He enjoys supplying telling visual details and clues to interpretation. JAG

Munsch, Robert 1945– Canadian storyteller and PICTUREBOOK author. Munsch, who won the 1987 Vicky Metcalf Award, was born in Pittsburgh, Pennsylvania, and emigrated to Canada in 1976. Most of Munsch's enormously popular books are entertaining farces in which children triumph over incompetent adults. Avoiding didacticism, they often conclude with a joke or ironic twist. Munsch's stories begin as oral performances; he revises them constantly before commiting them to paper. This oral heritage is most evident in their dependence on repeated sounds, phrases and situations. Typical is *Thomas' Snowsuit* (1985), illustrated by MICHAEL MARTCHENKO, a raucous tale about the futile efforts of a female teacher and a male principal to get stubborn Thomas into his snowsuit: it ends with the flustered adults wearing each other's clothes. Munsch's best book is undoubtedly *The Paper Bag Princess* (1980), illustrated by Martchenko, a feminist parody of traditional tales, in which a clever princess rescues a vain prince from a dragon. She then rejects him as a marriage partner because he shows concern only for her appearance. Munsch's most popular book, however, lacks his characteristic humour: *Love You Forever* (1986), illustrated by Sheila McGraw, is a sentimental celebration of the enduring power of parental love. REJ

see also FAIRY TALES

Muppets Ensemble of hand puppets created by JIM HENSON. The Muppets first appeared on a five-minute children's TELEVISION series, *Sam and Friends*, in 1955, and they also appeared in commercials and on variety shows during the 1950s and 60s. From 1969 they appeared on the television series *SESAME STREET*, on their own variety series, *The Muppet Show* (1976–81), and later on a Saturday morning cartoon series, *Muppet Babies*. They also starred in a number of feature films, along with human actors, including adaptations of such children's classics as *A Christmas Carol* and *TREASURE ISLAND*. The Muppets include such now iconic figures as Kermit, Big Bird, Miss Piggy, Cookie Monster, and Bert and Ernie, all of whom have entered the pantheon of beloved children's characters. BH

Murphy, Jill 1949– As well as the books in her *WORST WITCH* series, Murphy is known for her PICTUREBOOKS, particularly those which examine the domestic mayhem in the family life of the Large family: *Five Minutes' Peace* (1986), *All in One Piece* (1987), *A Piece of Cake* (1989) and *A Quiet Night In* (1993). Convincing domestic incidents in this family of elephants are handled with humour in both words and pictures. The four stories were reissued as *The Large Family Collection* in 2000. JAG

Museum of Childhood, Bethnal Green, London see COLLECTIONS OF CHILDREN'S BOOKS

Museum of Childhood, Edinburgh see COLLECTIONS OF CHILDREN'S BOOKS

music and story Children's stories have often been employed as the basis of musical composition. Stories have been set to music as through-composed orchestral or piano pieces where the narration introduces the music or is spoken simultaneously over the music. Other forms where the story forms the lyric basis include opera, music theatre pieces, musical plays, musicals, secular cantatas, and simple story-songs.

Prokofiev's *Peter and the Wolf* (1936) is one of the first examples of an orchestral piece with spoken narration. The composer collaborated with Natalie Satz, Director of the Moscow Children's Theatre, to produce a 'symphonic fairy tale' designed to introduce children to the instruments of the orchestra. Characters in the story are represented by individual instruments and musical motifs; Peter, for example, is represented by a jaunty motif played by the string section of the orchestra, the wolf by a menacing motif played by three french horns. A narrator guides the listener through the story and the musical associations. In Poulenc's *L'Histoire de Babar le petit éléphant* (1940) the story, adapted by Jean de Brunhoff (English version by Nelly Rien), is narrated with piano accompaniment (orchestral arrangement by Jean Françaix). A series of distinctive stylistic set pieces interpolate the text to include, for example, a LULLABY and a lilting tea-waltz. In the final section the fusion of narrative and music is at its most effective when the words are spoken over the music, feeding the images without breaking the musical texture.

In the tradition of opera, Humperdinck (1893) set the FAIRY TALE *Hansel and Gretel* as a large-scale opera in three acts to the libretto written by Adelhaid Wette. Janáček's operatic setting of *The Cunning Little Vixen* (1921–3) transformed a simple Moravian story to a symbolic level, elements of which appeal to both child and adult audiences. In Ravel's opera *L'Enfant et les sortilèges* (*The Child and the Magic*, 1925), with text by Colette, a similar duality between parody and FANTASY is achieved. This tradition is continued in the work of John McCabe's operatic setting of C.S. LEWIS's story *The Lion, the Witch and the Wardrobe* (see *CHRONICLES OF NARNIA*). In collaboration with the children's author MAURICE SENDAK, the composer Oliver Knussen produced two one-act fantasy operas, *WHERE THE WILD THINGS ARE* (1979/83) and *Higglety-Pigglety Pop!* (1984/90). The former was commissioned by the Opéra National, Brussels, and the latter for Glyndebourne by the BBC. Knussen has also composed *Hums and Songs of Winnie the Pooh* (1970–83) for soprano and chamber ensemble to texts selected from the work of A.A. MILNE.

Children's stories have also been set to music in the genre of music theatre. Examples include Alun Hoddinott's *What the Old Man Does is Always Right* (1977) as a setting of a HANS CHRISTIAN ANDERSEN fairy tale (libretto by Myfanwy Piper). Michael Berkeley produced a music-theatre piece in three acts, called *Baa Baa Black Sheep* (1993), based on RUDYARD KIPLING's classic *JUNGLE BOOKS* and using a libretto by David Malouf. ROALD DAHL's retelling of the fairy tale *Snow White and the Seven Dwarfs* has been adapted by Donald Sturrock to form the basis of the one-act music theatre piece called *Snow White* by the composer Eleanor Alberga (1994).

In the world of entertainment, children's radio has contributed significantly to the setting of music and story since the 1950s. One of the most famous programmes was the BBC's request spot 'Children's Favourites', hosted by the presenter Derek McCulloch, known as Uncle Mac. Narrated stories, such as *Sparky's Magic Piano*, *Sparky and the Magic Train* and *Tubby the Tuba* (Danny Kaye), were written to include musical sound effects, narrated sections with music and songs. Frank Luther's interpretation for voice and electric organ of the traditional children's story *THREE BILLY GOATS GRUFF* became a classic, with such memorable songs as 'I'm a troll, fol-de-rol' and 'Trip, trap, hop and skip'. Other classic narrated song-stories included *The King's New Clothes*, *Little White Duck* and *The Ugly Duckling*.

This tradition continues in contemporary musical settings of children's stories. Roald Dahl's retelling of *LITTLE RED RIDING HOOD* is narrated with music by the composer Paul Patterson. MICHAEL BOND's *Paddington Bear's First Concert* exists as a narrated story for full orchestra or piano arranged by the composer Herbert Chappell. Keith Amos's narrated version for piano and orchestra of Hans Christian Andersen's story *The Steadfast Tin Soldier* (1993) was commissioned by Mari Markus Gomori Children's Concerts Ltd, and *THE SNOWMAN* by RAYMOND BRIGGS (1978) has been set to music by Howard Blake. It also exists as an animated film and for concert performance, and includes the well-known song 'We're walking in the Air'. *The Mousehole Cat* (1990), based on the Cornish legend told by Antonia Barber and NICOLA BAYLEY, has been produced as an animated film version. The music, composed by Ian Hughes, derives from the film source, and exists in its own right as an orchestral concert version and as a vocal/piano score. It was premiered in the Barbican, London, in 1994. The tradition of animated film versions of children's stories includes classics such as WALT DISNEY's *Fantasia*, *Cinderella* and *The Lion King*.

Stage musical plays and musicals use children's stories as the basis for dramatic action with songs and accompaniments. Examples include John Rutter's settings of KENNETH GRAHAME's stories *The Reluctant Dragon* (1985) and *THE WIND IN THE WILLOWS* (1996). *THE PRINCE AND THE PAUPER* and *THE ADVENTUES OF TOM SAWYER* are musical plays based on the MARK TWAIN stories, set to music by Gwendolyn Skeens. Two Hans Christian Andersen tales, *The Snow Queen* and *The Little Match Girl*, are combined in Susan and Philip Kern's musical adaptation called *The Christmas of the Snow Queen*. Many versions of *THE PIED PIPER OF HAMELIN* exist in the form of musical plays – for example, *Rats*, with music by Nigel Hess and lyrics by Jeremy Browne; *Rattrap*, with lyrics by Douglas Waft and music by John Parkes; and *The Pied Piper* by Karen Sturges. New stories which have been created as the basis for children's musical plays and cantatas are many and various. Examples are BBC award-winner Michael Plaskett's musical play *Dream-Maker* and Debbie Campbell's secular cantata series published in association with the World Wide Fund for Nature to include *Big Mama*, *Bumblesnouts Save the World* and *The Emerald Crown*.

Children's singing books also use children's story as the basis for simple story-songs with accompaniments, and as stimuli for musical composition and musical education activities. An example in this genre is Kaye Umansky's volume *Three Singing Pigs* (1994), which employs a range of well-known stories, such as *Little Red Hen*, *TREASURE ISLAND*, *JACK AND THE BEANSTALK*, *The Awongalema Tree* and *The Enormous Turnip*.

Finally, a number of novelists have featured musical children in their work, notably NOEL STREATFEILD, KITTY BARNE, ANTONIA FOREST and ELFRIDA VIPONT. EJM

Mvurungi, Martha see *YASIN IN TROUBLE*

Mwije, Tumusiime see *WHY THE SUN LIVES IN THE SKY*

My Naughty Little Sister Popular series of CHAPTER BOOKS written by Dorothy Edwards between 1951 and 1974 about a nameless little sister who is often up to gentle – frequently well-intentioned – mischief. The stories, written as if by a benevolent older sister, were first read aloud on the BBC's *LISTEN WITH MOTHER*. Although first published with a number of different illustrators, the stories are now illustrated by SHIRLEY HUGHES. They are set in a middle-class world in the 1950s and peopled by kindly adults who look after the small child. Her 'naughtiness' never consists of anything truly dreadful and there is always a clear line drawn between wilful disobedience and accidents or misunderstandings. KA

My Place (1987) A highly successful, innovative PICTUREBOOK history of Australia by NADIA WHEATLEY and DONNA RAWLINS. Starting in urban Sydney in 1988 (the controversial bicentenary of European colonisation of Australia), it jumps ten years backwards with each double-spread, but remains focused on the same site. In each period a child describes his/her life – variously in a house, saddlery, farm and bush camp – draws a map of the local area, and reveals much about family, social and economic structures. This is 'bottom-up' history; most characters are Aborigines, convicts, migrants and working people. The result is both complex and accessible. NLR

see also ABORIGINAL CULTURE IN CHILDREN'S BOOKS

Myers, Mitzi see CRITICAL APPROACHES TO CHILDREN'S LITERATURE

Myers, Walter Dean 1937– American writer of over 50 books for children in diverse genres, including poetry, PICTUREBOOKS, FANTASY, ADVENTURE STORIES, HISTORICAL FICTION and non-fiction trade books (see INFORMATION BOOKS). Myers is best known for his novels depicting urban African American youth. Born in Martinsburg, West Virginia, he was adopted and spent most of his youth with his new family in Harlem. He attempted his first children's fiction in 1969 for a picturebook contest sponsored by the Council on Inter-racial Books for Children. Myers's text, *Where Does the Day Go?*, won the contest and was published. Spurred on by his success, Myers published three more picturebooks in the early 1970s. He also took an editorial position at Bobbs-Merrill and worked in publishing for seven years until determining that he could make a living as a full-time writer. With *Fast Sam, Cool Clyde, and Stuff* (1975) and *Mojo and the Russians* (1977), Myers gained a reputation as a young adult novelist. Among his numerous achievements, Myers received a Newbery Honour for *Scorpions* (1988), and several of his novels have received the distinction of being CORETTA SCOTT KING Honour Books, including *Monster* (2000), which was also the recipient of the first Michael L. Printz Award for excellence in YOUNG ADULT FICTION. EB

see also AFRICAN AMERICAN LITERATURE

mystery plays see DRAMA FOR CHILDREN

Mythological Cycle, The see IRISH MYTHOLOGY AND FOLKLORE

mythology see CLASSICAL MYTHOLOGY; see also ABORIGINAL CULTURE IN CHILDREN'S BOOKS; AFRICAN MYTHOLOGY; INDIAN MYTHS, LEGENDS AND FOLKTALES; IRISH MYTHOLOGY AND FOLKLORE; MAORI WRITING IN CHILDREN'S BOOKS; NATIVE AMERICAN LITERATURE; WELSH MYTHOLOGY AND FOLKLORE

N

Naidoo, Beverley South African writer. Born into an apartheid-ruled country, Naidoo left to study and teach in England. There she published *Censoring Reality*, a study of children's non-fiction books about South Africa. Then came the children's novel for which she is best known, *Journey to Jo'burg* (1985). Banned in South Africa for many years, this tells of two children journeying to Johannesburg to find their mother but lacking the vital Pass without which no black people could leave their designated area. Later came a sequel, *Chain of Fire* (1989), which deals with forced removal to a barren 'homeland', and *No Turning Back* (1995), about children living on the streets of Johannesburg. JHe

Namioka, Lensey 1929– Chinese American author of historical and contemporary novels. Born in Beijing, Namioka came to America with her family during World War II. Although she majored in mathematics, did doctoral work in topology, and taught at Cornell University, she eventually realised that she would never become a creative mathematician and turned to writing HISTORICAL NOVELS. *White Serpent Castle* (1976) was inspired by the traditional Chinese martial arts novels she had loved as a child, but set in her husband's native Japan. It was the first of six swashbuckling mystery ADVENTURE STORIES to feature Zenta and Matsuzo, two masterless samurai. The Chinese American protagonists of Namioka's contemporary stories face both distinctively ethnic and universal problems. In *Who's Hu?* (1980), for example, a teenage girl of the 1950s must resolve both her identity as a Chinese American and her 'unfeminine' gift for mathematics, while the nine-year-old narrator of *Yang the Youngest and His Terrible Ear* (1992) is the only untalented member of an immigrant family of musicians. Zest and humour pervade Namioka's work, mitigating the grimness of a violent feudal society in her samurai novels and creating scenes of high comedy in her Chinese American stories. SR

see also MULTICULTURAL BOOKS

***Nancy Drew* series** Popular 20th-century American girls' series. Since its beginnings in 1930 with *The Secret of the Old Clock*, the series originated by the STRATEMEYER SYNDICATE has sold well over 80 million copies, and Nancy has become an icon of American girlhood. Originally, Nancy was the brainchild of EDWARD STRATEMEYER, a prolific writer who wrote dozens of juvenile books for boys and girls and ran a literary syndicate that published many different series. Nancy's originator died before he could see the phenomenal success of the *Nancy Drew* books, which were continued by Harriet Stratemeyer Adams, who ran the Syndicate for half a century after her father's death. Along with a host of ghost writers, including Mildred Wirt Benson and Walter Karig, Harriet Adams produced the Nancy Drew books, always using the pseudonym 'Carolyn Keene', a name that became so linked to the *Nancy Drew* series that many readers assume there actually is a Carolyn Keene. After Harriet Adams's death in 1982, the Syndicate was sold in 1984 to Simon & Schuster, the company that continues to publish the *Nancy Drew* books today.

Although the Syndicate introduced numerous other mystery-solving heroines, including Ruth Fielding, Betty Cordon, Judy Bolton, Trixie Belden, Cherry Ames and Kay Tracey, none proved as enduring and popular as Nancy Drew. The reasons for her appeal are many. With no mother and a lawyer father who delights in her sleuthing exploits, Nancy has a tremendous amount of physical freedom that young readers rarely share. Driving her latest shiny new sportscar, Nancy is prepared to take on even the most devious crooks and solve the most baffling mysteries, whether in *The Mystery at Lilac Inn*, *The Clue in the Diary*, *The Clue in the Jewel Box*, *The Emerald-Eyed Cat Mystery*, or the hundred-plus other volumes that feature her exploits.

Conveniently, Ned Nickerson, Nancy's boyfriend through much of the series, is almost as invisible as her father, allowing her greater autonomy. But, despite Nancy's freedom, it is always clear that she and her crime-solving chums, George Fayne and Bess Marvin, are 'nice' girls. Although she can solve crimes that baffle adults and is always one step ahead of her cohorts, Nancy is also polite, modest and considerate – the perfect girl-next-door. From this paragon, girl readers might learn independence, but also the kind of behaviour expected for middle-class girls, making the series appealing to both children and adults. Another reason for her lasting fame is that

Nancy, despite her good manners and social graces, is not old-fashioned. She has kept up with the times, becoming a thoroughly modern teenager who now solves computer crimes and uses modern technology. For over 60 years Nancy has managed to keep up with the times, and she seems ready to survive and thrive in the 21st century. SAI

Narayan, R.K. see *SWAMI AND FRIENDS*

Nargun and the Stars, The see *WIRRUN TRILOGY*; see also PATRICIA WRIGHTSON

Narnia see *CHRONICLES OF NARNIA*

narrative verse see BALLADS

narratology see CRITICAL APPROACHES TO CHILDREN'S BOOKS

Nash, Ogden 1902–71 American writer of comic poetry which examined the foibles of daily life and derived its humour, in part, from uneven lines and quirky, unexpected rhyme. A number of his poems were made into PICTUREBOOKS for children, including *Custard the Dragon* (1959) and *The Adventures of Isabel* (1963). GRB

Nast, Thomas see HORACE ELISHA SCUDDER; see also *THE RIVERSIDE MAGAZINE*; *A VISIT FROM ST NICHOLAS*

National Book Award see AWARDS AND MEDALS

National Book League see REVIEWING AND REVIEWERS

National Centre for Children's Literature (India) see PARO ANAND

national curriculum (UK) see PUBLISHING AND PUBLISHERS

National Library of Scotland see COLLECTIONS OF CHILDREN'S BOOKS

National Library of Wales see COLLECTIONS OF CHILDREN'S BOOKS

National Velvet see ADULT FICTION; ANIMALS IN FICTION; PONY STORIES

National Youth Theatre Organisation founded in Britain in 1956 by Michael Croft, a former actor who taught English at Alleyn's School, Dulwich, England. Based originally at Croft's own school in partnership with Dulwich College, it has expanded to become a national organisation. The NYT is highly selective, and offers advanced theatrical experience to students between the ages of 14 and 21, not only as actors but in all branches of theatre expertise. Two or three productions take place over the school holiday period each summer. Croft's original emphasis was on SHAKESPEARE – the initial production was *Henry V* – but modern plays were introduced in 1965 with David Halliwell's *Little Malcolm and his Struggle Against the Eunuchs*.

Over the years the NYT has commissioned and produced a number of distinguished plays for young actors, usually with large casts which would not be viable in commercial theatre, and often with controversial social and political content. Notable among these are Peter Terson's *Zigger-Zagger* (1967) and *The Apprentices* (1968), and Paul Thompson's *The Children's Crusade* (1973) and *By Common Consent* (1975). The NYT now has a permanent base at the Bloomsbury Theatre in London. One of its annual productions is always a Shakespeare play, and the Company retains its commitment to modern political drama, for example in its 1994 revival of Joan Littlewood's *Oh What a Lovely War*. PH

Native Americans in children's books Although some authors perpetuate stereotypes or emphasise general traits that Native characters share with all readers, increasing numbers of PICTUREBOOKS, FOLKTALE collections and novels accurately depict the uniqueness of specific Native groups.

Many traditional oral stories that presented children with examples of positive and negative behaviour have been adapted for non-Native readers. The hero of *SONG OF HIAWATHA*, HENRY WADSWORTH LONGFELLOW's 1855 adaptation of Ojibway legends, was often stereotyped as nature's child or a noble savage in children's versions. Siouxan author Arthur Eastman's *Wigwam Evenings: Sioux Folk Tales Retold* (1909) sought to help non-Native readers understand the cultural significance of stories that 'teach us the way of life'. In the 20th century, most traditonal stories have been adapted, with varying degrees of accuracy, by non-Native writers and artists. Whereas in *Rainbow Warrior's Bride* (1981), Marcus Crouch's adaptation of an east-coast Algonquin tale, William Stobbs's (1914–2000) ILLUSTRATIONS include west coast, plains and Atlantic coast artifacts, in GERALD MCDERMOTT's in *Arrow to the Sun* (1974), an Acoma Pueblo tale, and PAUL GOBLE's *Buffalo Woman* (1984), a Sioux transformation myth, physically accurate illustrations embody the narratives' cultural symbolism.

Recently, Native peoples' own adaptations have received wider distribution. Haida Bill Reid in *The Raven Steals the Light* (1980), Mohawk C. J. Taylor in *How*

Two-Feathers Was Saved from Loneliness (1990) and Navajo Shonto Begay in *Ma'ii and Cousin Horned Toad* (1992) present central figures of their cultures' mythologies. Gayle Ross's *How Rabbit Tricked Otter and Other Cherokee Trickster Stories* (1994), *Iroquois Stories: Heroes and Heroines; Monster and Magic* (1985), by JOSEPH BRUCHAC; and Basil H. Johnson's *Tales the Elders Told: Ojibway Legends* (1981) are collections for non-Native, as well as Native children.

Non-Native writers' novels that helped to overcome negative stereotypes fostered by 19th-century boys' ADVENTURE STORIES, COMICS and motion pictures include LOIS LENSKI's *Indian Captive: The Story of Mary Jameson* (1941), SCOTT O'DELL's *ISLAND OF THE BLUE DOLPHINS* (1960), and JEAN GEORGE's *JULIE OF THE WOLVES* (1972). In each, the characters' survival struggles are related to the values of their cultures. In JOAN BLOS's *Brothers of the Heart* (1985), Kristiana Gregory's *The Legend of Jimmy Spoon* (1990) and James Houston's *Frozen Fire* (1977) white boys encounter Native cultures. In Will Hobbs's *Bearstone* (1989), ROBERT LIPSYTE's *The Brave* (1991) and Margaret A. Robinson's *A Woman of Her Tribe* (1990), Native characters experience difficulties entering the white world.

Native novelists have also addressed Native–white contacts and conflicts. Michael Dorris's *Morning Girl* (1992) and *Guests* (1995) recount young people's reactions to the arrivals of Columbus and the Pilgrims respectively. Janet Hale's *The Owl's Song* (1974) and Beatrice Culleton's *In Search of April Raintree* (1983) present characters' tragic encounters with the urban world. In Natchee Scott Momaday's *Owl in the Cedar Tree* (1965), an artistic Navaho faces the differing expectations of parents and a white teacher. JCSt

nativity plays see DRAMA FOR CHILDREN

Nativity, The (1986) Innovative and original Australian PICTUREBOOK, in which JULIE VIVAS illustrates the traditional King James Bible text describing the birth of Christ. The book has many surprises – from the symbolic red cover with arched frame surrounding the figures of Mary and Joseph, to the unusual portrayal of Mary in swaddling garments which accentuate rather than camouflage her pregnancy. Vivas solves design puzzles, such as the depiction of the birth, in innovative and expressive ways, and refuses to couch the story in banal conventional imagery, thus investing it with new emotional power. This is one of Australia's publishing classics; sadly many considered the book irreverent, failing to recognise its humanity. RS

Nature of the Beast, The (1985) Novel by JANNI HOWKER, her second, which strengthened the impression given by *BADGER ON THE BARGE* that hers was a major new talent. The story, about a working-class boy, his father and his grandfather, living in a northern industrial town with country on its doorstep, has the gritty authenticity of an account based on knowledge from inside. The mill on which the town depends closes; at the same time as the rumoured Haverstock Beast prowls around, savaging farmers' stock, the 'beast' of unemployment (or 'the system'?) savages people. Bill Coward's dad leaves town to find work; Bill, sick of being 'just another kid whose old feller and grandad got pushed around, and who would get pushed around himself in the end', goes out with his air-rifle to hunt the Beast, and perhaps sees it die, though perhaps not. There is a brilliant late switch of viewpoint in which the reader suddenly sees through a social worker's eyes the loving-but-squalid home the boy now shares with his grandfather. It seems that even this shaky remnant of family life must be destroyed. In the end, the Beast – if it existed – lives on inside the boy: 'I'm going to take over where the Beast left off. They've not seen nothing yet!' Anger is the driving force of this dark but powerful novel. The picture of 'old' working-class lives and attitudes has begun to seem dated, but the vividness and vigour are undiminished. JRT

Naughton, Bill 1910–92 Writer of short stories, novels, autobiographies and plays. Born in County Mayo, Ireland, Norton grew up in Bolton, Lancashire, where most of his work is set. Though his books regularly feature in British classrooms, they are frequently neglected in discussions of children's literature. This is partly because much of his work is unclassifiable as specifically children's or adults' literature, frequently exploring the rites of passage between the two worlds. Naughton is also neglected because he writes predominantly about an all-male working-class world. But the strength of his work lies in showing the humanity and tenderness beneath its macho surface. In the close-knit cobbled streets, friendship, or 'pals', is what matters. Many of his works, like *A Dog Called Nelson* (1976) and *My Pal Spadger* (1977), vividly and humorously capture this 1920s street-corner life, peopled by laconically delineated characters, and giving insights into such things as tin-can football and the work of the night-soilman. His work has its weaknesses – occasionally sentimental, with some contrived endings and beatified protagonists – but at its best, as in the much-anthologised 'Spit Nolan' in *The Goalkeeper's Revenge* (1961), this is outweighed by an exacting, sinewy prose. DR

Naya, Kurji see *THE MAGIC GOURD*

Naylor, Phyllis Reynolds 1933– American fiction and non-fiction writer. Born in Indiana, Phyllis

Reynolds lived in several midwestern states before settling in Maryland. Though she earned a degree in psychology and taught school, she always saw herself as a writer, even at the age of 10 when she made small books to lend to friends. Her first book, *The Galloping Goat and Other Stories*, came out in 1965; her 64th, *Shiloh* (1991), won the NEWBERY AWARD and was followed by 24 additional titles, with more in progress. Naylor's popularity stems from her ability to pull readers immediately into a story, entertaining them with on-target humour and believable characters while subtly imparting an appropriate truth. Energised by variety, she has published over 2,000 articles and five books for adults, but mainly she writes for children, bouncing happily from a young adult suspense novel like *Night Cry* (1985), winner of the Edgar Allan Poe Award for Best Juvenile Mystery, to FANTASY for middle-grade readers, as in *The Grand Escape* (1993), and on to a PICTUREBOOK such as *I Can't Take You Anywhere* (1997), about Amy Audrey, 'sort of a klutz'.

Based on midwestern ethics inherited from her Sunday-school-teaching mother and minister grandfather, Naylor's YOUNG ADULT FICTION shows teenagers confronting life's tougher obstacles. In *A String of Chances* (1982), Evie Hutchins wrestles with religious doubt, as did Naylor herself. *The Year of the Gopher* (1987) and *Send No Blessings* (1991) feature characters struggling for self-acceptance and self-esteem. In novels for younger readers, Naylor's wit predominates, as in *Beetles, Lightly Toasted* (1987), about Andy Moller, who would do almost anything to get his picture in the paper. Always with respect for her readers' intelligence, Naylor offers them 'high camp' satire in the Bessledorf mystery series that began in 1983 with *The Mad Gasser of Bessledorf Street*; spooky humour in a series beginning in 1975 with *Witch's Sister*; and warm, light-hearted realism in a multi-award-winning series that began in 1985 with *The Agony of Alice* and continues in 1997 with *Outrageously Alice*. Of the nine *Alice* books women often say, 'How I wish I'd had those books when *I* was growing up!'

Naylor received the Newbery Award for *Shiloh* (1991), the story of an abused runaway dog, based on an actual stray beagle. Though leavened with humour, this story is charged with tension throughout as Marty struggles to keep his beloved Shiloh rather than return him to the rightful, vicious owner, Judd Travers. Told in West Virginia dialect in the present tense, Marty's story frames a compelling moral question well within childhood's province. Already it has won 24 statewide readers' choice awards. Because, as Naylor said, 'I hadn't finished with Judd Travers yet', two sequels followed: *Shiloh Season* (1996) and *Saving Shiloh* (1997). Very possibly, Phyllis Naylor—who has now published over 100 books – has the widest, most loyal readership of any American children's author working today. JEDC

Neckam [or Nequam], Alexander 1157–1217 Foster-brother of King Richard I, Neckam began teaching at Dunstable and ended as Abbott of Cirencester. While studying and teaching in Paris, he wrote *De Utensilibus* ('About Tools'), c. 1178, a descriptive vocabulary designed to help students with colloquial Latin; it includes Anglo-Norman and Middle-English glosses. It consists of long paragraphs about the kitchen, cooking methods, houses, clothing, servants, castles, war, arms, the farm, agriculture, weaving, home-building, navigation, urban trades, scribes, and ecclesiastical furniture – a goldmine of information about 12th-century life much-consulted by historians. Neckam also adapted Avianus' Aesopic *Fables* for students. GA

see also AESOP'S FABLES

Needham, (Amy) Violet 1876–1967 British author of 19 novels, mostly historical romances for children, published between 1939 and 1957. Typical of many is *The Changeling of Monte Lucio* (1946), in which the forceful and intelligent, but inexperienced and unconciliatory young Count of a fictional Renaissance principality searches for a way through adult conspiracies and his own inner conflicts. Lightly sketched 'period' detail provides a convincing background to fast-moving stories of courage and ingenuity on the part of the young protagonists, but the moral dilemmas which confront them are genuinely complex and not fully answered even by the resolution of the narrative. JFB

Needle, Jan 1943– Versatile British writer whose work is characterised by a strong narrative drive and a passionate concern for victims of social injustice and bigotry. *My Mate Shofiq* (1978) and *Piggy in the Middle* (1982), for example, explore racial prejudice, with the white protagonists drawn, almost unwillingly, into defending their local Pakistani communities against individual and institutional racism. In *Wild Wood* (1981) – Needle's playful response to *THE WIND IN THE WILLOWS* – the oppressed denizens of the Wood rebel against Toad and his capitalist cronies. Class oppression is also explored (though in a different genre and tone) in the bleak, disturbing *A Fine Boy for the Killing* (1979), where a young midshipman finally acknowledges, and condemns, the dehumanising cruelty of his uncle (the captain) towards sailors press-ganged into service. Michael, a vicious young xenophobe in *A Game of Soldiers* (1985), undergoes a similar moral regeneration in the Falklands War, finding that the initial impulse to kill a wounded Argentinian soldier, changes to a compassionate regard for a boy only two years older than himself. Needle's strength as a writer lies in his sensitive, finely balanced treatment of ethical and social problems; eschewing easy solutions to those problems, his books are polemical in the way that all good books are polemical. DJ

neglected works There are hundreds of children's writers whose works are now largely forgotten; a book's excellence is no guarantee of its survival. Though many such 'lost' books are competent but undistinguished, there are others which ought to have been kept alive and in print, either to serve the interests of literary and publishing history or because they might still appeal to young readers. Clearly, economic and cultural factors are involved in this casual culling of titles, but arbitrary publishing decisions – not necessarily connected with poor sales – have a lot to answer for. An outrageous example of this is the fact that the entire *œuvre* of one of the best British children's writers of the 20th century, Antonia Forest, was out of print for so long that two generations of readers had never heard of the *Marlow* series until the first was finally reissued in 2000. A similar writer, Jenny Overton, is also neglected. It seems that the best interests of young readers have rarely been decisive.

Works may fall into neglect because of poor promotion, or changes in publishing structure or personnel whilst a book is in publication; an unwillingness on the part of the artist to engage with the promotional circuit; an inability amongst critical circles to engage with the artist's work because of its innovative or challenging nature; or perhaps because the work appeals only to a discrete and selective audience. In Australia, some commentators believe that the Children's Book Council now has so much influence that many of the books not shortlisted for annual awards simply disappear from the market – remaindered early because of limited institutional demand.

During the unadventurous middle years of the 20th century there existed British writers whose approach to children's fiction was perhaps too nonconformist to admit them to the mainstream. In *Caterpillar Hall* (1950) Anne Barrett makes a haunting dreamscape of bombed-out London, recounting the story of Penelope who, by means of magic and intuition, discovers the childhood disappointments that have shaped the lives of the adults who surround her. Judith Masefield's *Larking at Christmas* (1953), the second of her four novels, typically contains candid portrayals of the lower orders that would render it unpublishable today, but her ear for dialogue was phenomenal and the book affords many allusions to her father's classic, *The Midnight Folk*. A real curiosity, *King Purple's Jester* (1947) by D.H. Chapman, is an eccentric comedy thriller with a plot that combines elements of *King Lear* with the Ruritanian yarns of Anthony Hope. It features Leo, the world's last court jester, attached to the endearingly moth-eaten Royal Family of Patria, whose citizens bear more than a passing resemblance to those of Britain enduring post-war austerity.

In Britain, the extraordinary output and popularity of Enid Blyton in the 1940s and 1950s seems to have had the effect of retrospectively obscuring the contribution of other authors of her time, so that writers like Garry Hogg, M.E. Atkinson and David Severn – all considerably better writers than Blyton – are now largely forgotten, along with Kitty Barne, a writer whose work is as interesting and varied as that of Noel Streatfeild, to whom she dedicated her biography of Elizabeth Fry. Blyton's massive production of fiction had the effect of defining for the general public what 'children's literature' was supposed to be – accessible, easy, formulaic, reassuring and often banal. In such an atmosphere, writers who sought to use language which was more evocative, contemplative or literary, or who tackled difficult or challenging subjects, were less likely to achieve the sales figures Blyton regularly won and more likely to find their titles discontinued. In 1947 Katharine Hull and Pamela Whitlock collaborated on *Crowns*, a strange but compelling novel about a fantasy world dreamed up and shared by a group of young friends. It would probably not appeal to readers today, but it deserves to be better known by scholars if only because it strikes out in a different direction from that dictated by the tyranny of Blyton's overwhelming output.

An early casualty was Hilda Lewis's *The Ship that Flew* (1939), a minor classic of the time-slip fantasy novel, in which four children, in the tradition of E. Nesbit, are taken back into history in a magical Viking ship. Elinor Lyon is another entirely forgotten writer whose work deserves to have stayed in print; her Scottish series – about three close friends on the west coast of Scotland – is distinguished by a combination of fast action and thoughtful romanticism. *My Friend Mr Leaky* (1937), by the Cambridge geneticist J.B.S. Haldane – a wonderfully inventive story of comical magic, with touches of *Doctor Dolittle* but with the addition of science – ought also to be available for modern readers. Another work which deserves to be valued and read is Malcolm Saville's *Jane's Country Year* (1946), a beautifully designed book with illustrations – tinted in some early editions – by Bernard Bowerman; it is an unhurried narrative, partly fiction and partly nature study, with one chapter celebrating each month of the year. Much more in keeping with the tastes of today's young readers would be David Severn's *The Future Took Us* (1957) – a thrilling futuristic fantasy adventure story quite unlike the leisurely pastoral narratives of his countryside series. *No Way of Telling* (1972), by Emma Smith, is an outstanding thriller crime story set in Wales and remarkable for the way in which it persuasively represents a highly intelligent schoolgirl at the centre of a potentially violent hostage crisis. Her earlier work, *Out of Hand* (1963), is an excellent and thoughtful novel in the Arthur Ransome mode. Another work – also concerning an intelligent and thoughtful schoolgirl – is

Shelagh MacDonald's *No End to Yesterday*, though here the style and wit are both subversive and challenging (see also NUDITY IN CHILDREN'S BOOKS).

Other excellent 19th- and early 20th-century British works – from Richard Henry Horne's amusing *Memoirs of a London Doll* (1846) to Flora Shaw's passionate *Castle Blair* (1882), LAURENCE HOUSMAN's *fin de siècle* FAIRY TALES (from 1894), and WALTER DE LA MARE's poetic FANTASY *The Three Mulla-Mulgars* (1918) – are unknown to children who might enjoy them today. The same holds true in America. Old volumes of *ST NICHOLAS MAGAZINE* reveal a treasure trove of children's authors whose very names – JOHN T. TROWBRIDGE, Sophie Swett, Tudor Jenks, Rossiter Johnson – are forgotten.

Little remains in print of American children's literature from the first decades of the 20th century. Although much was of mediocre quality, it is regrettable to miss so may of the interesting historical and ethnic novels written by women during this period. Caroline Snedeker's *The Perilous Seat* (1923), CORNELIA MEIG's *Wind in the Chimney* (1934), Lucile Morrison's *The Lost Queen of Egypt* (1936), ELIZABETH JANET GRAY's *Beppy Marlowe of Charles Town* (1936), and FLORENCE CRANNELL MEANS's *Shuttered Windows* (1938) are all well worth recovering. Other authors survive, so to speak, in a single book – and not necessarily their best: we still know DOROTHY CANFIELD's *Understood Betsy* (1917), but not her more experimental *Made-to-Order Stories* (1925); KATE DOUGLAS WIGGINS's *Rebecca of Sunnybrook Farm* (1902), but not *Poor Oliver's Problem* (1893); Margery Williams Bianco's *VELVETEEN RABBIT* (1922) but not *Poor Cecco* (1925); RACHEL FIELD's *HITTY* (1929), but not *Hepatica Hawkes* (1932). While the NEWBERY and CALDECOTT AWARDS have enabled some older titles to stay in print, equally fine books by the same author have generally been ignored. Textbooks have exacerbated the situation by refusing to recommend to teachers and librarians any book which is not in print.

The work of illustrators is even more likely to be unjustly neglected. The number of gifted illustrators (mostly women) who are given scant or no mention in the standard works of reference is legion. The reasons are many but, principally, it is because scholarship in this area is still only nascent. Some artists appear to have contributed only to ANNUALS and MAGAZINES, Mollie Bailie being a notable example – *Boys' and Girls' Wonder Book* (1934), *Collins' Children's Annual* (1927) and *The Playtime and Wonderland Annual* (1927). The careers of the illustrators of the splendid *The Merry-Go-Round* magazine (around 1923) are equally fugitive: Mary E. Bennett, Matthew Mole, Tinker Taylor, Audrey Teago and Frank Rogers (Frances Clare Rogers, who illustrated at least 23 titles between 1927 and 1948). Another notable absentee is Anne Rochester.

For the researcher, many illustrators have in common the problem that, though their name generally appears on the title-pages, this detail is often omitted from British Library Catalogue entries. There are, in addition, curious omissions from works of reference – in particular MAURICE AND EDWARD DETMOLD, Phyllis Bray, Joyce Dennys, Nora Fry/Lavrin, and, amazingly, Astrid Walford, given the quality of her work and her 30 titles (including those in the *Little Miss Pink* series produced in partnership with Rodney Bennett). Strange, too, is the omission of an illustrator of 43 children's books, Helen Haywood, great-niece of TENNIEL.

It is unlikely that future writers or illustrators will be any more safe from the arbitrary misfortunes of publishing decisions, but the INTERNET may provide ways of rescuing neglected works from the past. Antonia Forest has a website, and it may be only a matter of time before whole texts of out-of-print works appear. One encouraging trend in American publishing has been the reissuing (usually in paperback) of books and series from the rich period between 1940 and 1965; Maud Hart Lovelace, JOHN R. TUNIS, ELIZABETH ENRIGHT, ELIZABETH MARIE POPE, Walter R. Brooks and ELOISE JARVIS MCGRAW are all being discovered by a new generation of readers.

VW, JMM, RS, SR, WC

Nelson, Claudia see CRITICAL APPROACHES TO CHILDREN'S LITERATURE

Nemo in Slumberland see ILLUSTRATION IN CHILDREN'S BOOKS; *IN THE NIGHT KITCHEN*; WINSOR MCCAY

Nesbit, E(dith) 1858–1924 British author who embarked on her writing career in the 1880s in order to support a highly unconventional household, which included her husband's children by her companion and housekeeper Alice Hoatson. Though a prolific writer of (second-rate) poetry and suspense or horror fiction for adults (some of this produced under the pen-names Fabian Bland and E. Bland), it is for her children's books that Edith Nesbit is remembered today. Her work borrowed some of its ideas from F. Anstey and MRS MOLESWORTH, inspiring in turn many other writers, the most notable of which perhaps being EDWARD EAGER – whose *Knight's Castle* (1956) acknowledges a debt to *The Magic City* (1910) – and JOAN AIKEN, whose short stories share with Nesbit's the flavour of the witty and unexpected. Many of Nesbit's works have been filmed or televised, including *THE RAILWAY CHILDREN*, *The Enchanted Castle* and the *PSAMMEAD* SERIES.

Nesbit, her first husband Hubert Bland, George Bernard Shaw and H.G. WELLS were founding members of the Fabian Society in 1884, and a strong vein of socialism may be detected in both her FANTASY and non-fantasy work for children. The living conditions of the less fortunate are touched on in *The Story of the Amulet* (1906), where the different societies visited through the time-travelling of the four children serve as comparisons to, and critiques of, early 20th-century English society. Nesbit's desire for social improvement may also be seen in *Harding's Luck* (1909) – a companion volume to *The House of Arden* (1908) – which sees the rehabilitation of Beale, a burglar, tramp and cadger, through the agency of a lame orphan, Dickie Harding, who teaches him the value of honest work.

The stories on one level appear to be formulaic and repetitive, the non-fantasies working the idea of escapades or well-intentioned enterprises that tend to go wrong, the fantasies often using the same idea with a magic component to the plot. However, Nesbit's work is redeemed from sameness and brought to glorious life by the humour of the writing and the creative energy displayed by her child protagonists. The humour is partly situational and partly an effect of style, generated by the discrepancies between child and adult points of view, between reader and narrator awareness. Some of the humour may, however, be lost on the modern reader, especially that portion of it dependent upon literary consciousness – that is, the reader's acquaintance with the works Nesbit may be parodying. The children in Nesbit's books are played off against child types in other works of the period, and themselves self-consciously behave (or refuse to behave) according to the conventions of literature. In *The Phoenix and the Carpet* (1904), Jane, encountering a burglar, 'knows' from her reading that 'no burglar will ever hurt a little girl if he meets her when burgling' but wonders worriedly if she can bring herself to lisp childishly and say 'What's 'oo doing here, Mihter Wobber?' However, Nesbit's work has on the whole tended to wear well. SA

Ness, Evaline 1911–86 American artist, author and illustrator. Ness won the CALDECOTT MEDAL for *Sam, Bangs and Moonshine* (1966) and also received three Caldecott honour awards. Born in Ohio, Ness grew up in Pontiac, Michigan, where her father worked on an automobile assembly line. She worked in fashion advertising while studying first at the Art Institute of Chicago and later at the Corcoran Gallery in Washington DC and the Accademia di Belle Arti in Rome. Married for 12 years to Eliot Ness, famous for his exploits in capturing Al Capone, she also had a highly successful career in fashion and commercial art. She illustrated her first children's books in 1960, and soon also began to write. Her ILLUSTRATIONS were original, strong in design, and often experimental in technique. The endnote for *Do You Have Time Lydia?* (1971) states that the illustrations were created with 'a small wooden dowel, sharpened and dipped in ink, for the drawings on heavy rice paper. The shading was done with a pencil and a lithographic crayon. The textures were applied and pressed down on the art.' Her texts often featured strong, vividly characterised young girls, and have been praised for their 'economical language, sprightly storytelling, and skillful interweaving of art and words'. LH

Neville, Emily Cheney 1919– American novelist, born in Manchester, Connecticut, and educated at Bryn Mawr College, originally a journalist and later a lawyer. Her best-known and most acclaimed novel is *It's Like This, Cat* (1964, NEWBERY MEDAL and Jane Addams Children's Book Award). Of this novel, Neville has claimed that it was the first 'boy-and-his cat' novel, as opposed to the scores of 'boy-and-his-dog' books. Like the cat, its hero, Dave Mitchell, an urban boy on the brink of adolescence, is somewhat disaffected and alienated from his world. His closest companion is Cat, the nameless tomcat he adopts in the first chapter of the novel. Dave is no 'troubled youth', except insofar as all adolescents feel the need to separate from their parents. The novel is episodic and depicts Dave's encounters with a number of New York City types: Tom, a high school drop-out and thief; Kate Carmichael, 'cat woman' and eccentric; and Mary, Dave's first girlfriend, a spirited, bright and independent young woman. While the novel, like many topical works, feels dated in its language and its specific details, it still captures the malaise of middle-class youth. Neville also wrote a well-received novel two years later, *Berries Goodman* (1966), which dealt with anti-Semitism and the problems of suburbia. Neville went back to school and earned a law degree in 1976; her literary output since then has been minimal. BH

New-England Primer, The (1689?) Children's PRIMER, including alphabets, word lists, a picture alphabet, biblical extracts, prayers, pious poetry, and dialogues, usually printed with John Cotton's *Spiritual Milk for American Babes* and the Westminster Assembly's 'Shorter Catechism'. The first surviving American copy is dated 1727, but the *Primer* was probably printed by Benjamin Harris in Boston in 1689, with a second edition advertised in 1690. Harris was a protestant dissenter who fled persecution in England to set up his press in Boston. The *Primer* embodies the religious doctrines and pedagogical theories of English dissenters and New England Puritans. Harris assembled materials from horn-books (see HORN-BOOKS AND BATTLEDORES), other primers, collections of poetry and prayers for children, and his own writings. Portions of the *Primer* appeared earlier in Harris's English primer, *The Protestant Tutor* (1679).

The *Primer* begins with lists of letters, syllables and words of one to six syllables, and then presents increasingly complicated texts. All was to be memorised, but the text reflected new ideas of pedagogy by associating words with things, in ILLUSTRATIONS, to aid memory, and by fitting the sequence of texts to the capacities of children of various ages and skill levels. In the 18th century the title *The New-England Primer Enlarged, For the more easy attaining the true Reading of English* indicates the inclusion of prayers and such poems as 'A Dialogue between Christ, Youth, and the Devil' and John Rogers's 'Exhortation to his children'. From 1744, editions titled *The New-England Primer Improved* signalled to parents the presence of ISAAC WATTS's 'Cradle Hymn', pious revisions of the picture alphabet, and short moral tales. The core texts of each of the *Primers* are the picture alphabet, with its primitive woodcuts and simple rhymes ('In Adam's Fall / We sinned all', 'Whales in the Sea, / GOD's Voice obey'), word lists, poems, prayers, the 'Dialog', and Rogers's 'Exhortation', accompanied by a woodcut of John Rogers burning at the stake in front of his wife and ten children, and a catechism. Given New England's reputation for literacy and piety, the *Primer* was marketed throughout America in hundreds of editions totalling 5–7 million copies in the 1700s and early 1800s. However, after the American Revolution, more secular texts, including Noah Webster's famous 'Blue-Backed Speller', *A Grammatical Institute of the English Language* (1783), quickly replaced the *Primer* as the preferred text of school teachers and parents.

The *Primer's* emphasis on childhood mortality was in its day a prod to early literacy and a reminder of the original sin of disobedience which brought death to Adam and Eve and all their children. Children read, 'While Youth do cheer, Death may be near', and 'I in the burying place may see / Graves shorter there than I', as well as the Bible story of bears tearing disrespectful children to pieces. Nevertheless, many adults, such as LOUISA MAY ALCOTT in *LITTLE WOMEN*, remembered the *Primer* with affection. The 1737 edition contains the first printing of 'Now I lay me down to sleep', which has become one of the most popular children's bedtime prayers in America. DHW

New Kid on the Block, The (1986) Arguably the best collection of poetry by JACK PRELUTSKY, skilfully illustrated by JAMES STEPHENS, whose images perfectly match the cheeky wit of the words. Playfulness abounds – wordplay, cautionary verse, 'over-the-top' comic creatures – and the tough, street-wise 'new kid' of the title poem is a girl. SILVERSTEIN apart, Prelutsky is, perhaps, the American poet who comes closest to the genre most popular in Britain today (JOHN ROWE TOWNSEND has characterised it as 'urchin verse'), which is irreverent and informal, favours the vernacular, and moves the location for children's poetry firmly out of the metaphorical garden onto the street or sidewalk. MCCS

New Treasure Seekers see *BASTABLES* SERIES

New Zealand Children's Book Foundation Organisation established in 1990 as a national clearing-house for individuals and organisations in New Zealand concerned with children's literature and literacy. It has established the MARGARET MAHY Lecture Award which is awarded annually to a person who has made an especially distinguished and significant contribution to children's literature, publishing or literacy, and the Tom Fitzgibbon Award for a work of fiction for children by a previously unpublished writer. The Children's Book Foundation also co-ordinates the Storylines New Zealand Children's Writers and Illustrators Festival and sponsors an annual Spring Lecture series. FP

Newbery, John 1713–67 Pioneer publisher of books for children. The son of a Berkshire farmer, Newbery worked for a printer in Reading, married his employer's widow, and took over the business. In 1744 he moved to London and published the *Little Pretty Pocket-Book*, a collection of rhymes and pictures which was the first of more than 20 pocket-sized books for 'Little Masters and Misses' or 'Young Ladies and Gentlemen'. The best known is *Little Goody Two-Shoes* (1765). This is often attributed to OLIVER GOLDSMITH, but from available indications it seems more likely that Newbery wrote it himself. JRT

Newbery, Linda see *SOME OTHER WAR* SERIES

Newbery Medal see appendix; see also AWARDS AND MEDALS; BERTHA MAHONEY MILLER; PUBLISHING AND PUBLISHERS

Newell, Peter Sheaf 1862–1924 American illustrator whose nonsense books challenged the traditional book format. His ILLUSTRATIONS for LEWIS CARROLL's *ALICE'S ADVENTURES IN WONDERLAND* (1901) and *Through the Looking-Glass* (1902) – drawn after the copyright expired – are some of the most original interpretations of these books. *Topsys & Turvys* (1893) is a series of illustrations that can be turned upside down for humorous results. *The Hole Book* (1908) features a hole made by an 'accidental gunshot' which is punched in the text so that the reader can follow the chaos it creates in subsequent illustrations. This playful design is repeated in *The Rocket Book* (1912). *The Slant Book* (1910) is designed so that it sits on an angle causing characters to slide down the page. JCS

see also MOVABLE BOOKS

Peter Sheaf Newell's *The Hole Book*, showing the hole itself.

Nic Leodhas, Sorche [Leclaire Gowans Alger] 1898–1969 American writer, whose invented Gaelic pseudonym stands for 'Claire, daughter of Louis'. Her family claimed Highland descent, and Nic Leodhas specialised in retellings, as in *Thistle and Thyme* (1962), of traditional Scottish stories still extant in the United States. 'They may be found in big clan gatherings, at Gaelic Club meetings, at Ceilidhs, big and little. I've found stories along the docks of the East River, in New York . . . in the engine room of an old coastwise steamer; in a cabin on a Pennsylvanian hillside; in the kitchen of a Nova Scotia farmhouse.' PP

Nicholls, Judith 1941– English poet and anthologist. Born in Lincolnshire, she was a teacher before making her début as a writer with *Magic Mirror* (1985). She has produced five collections, characterised by humour and a fascination with words, developing a variety of forms for a wide age-range. Thc first of her deservedly popular anthologies was *Wordspells* (1988). ML

Nichols, Grace 1950– British Guyanese author who has lived in England since 1977. In poetry and prose for adults and children, Nichols's inspiration comes in part from her Guyanese childhood: 'I was awakened by tropical things.' Her poetry for young readers revels in observations of character and environment – sights, sounds and STORYTELLING. Writing both in standard English and modified Creole, she has catered for the young in *A CARIBBEAN DOZEN* (1994), *No Hickory No Dickory No Dock* (1991), a collection of Caribbean NURSERY RHYMES (both in collaboration with her partner, fellow poet JOHN AGARD). A typical poem, 'Baby-K Rap Rhyme' is a deceptively simple bouncing-song for a baby which brings together many of Nichols's talents – warmth, irrepressible humour, musical rhythms and a concern for the environment. *COME ON INTO MY TROPICAL GARDEN* (1988) and *Give Yourself a Hug* (1994) are poetry collections for readers of 7 to 11, an age-group to which her novel *Whole of a Morning Sky* (1986) also appeals. She is a gifted anthologist, promoting poetry from 'Black, Asian and American Indian cultures' in *POETRY JUMP-UP* (1988) and *Can I Bring You a Slice of the Sky?* (1991) HT

Nichols, Ruth [Joanna] 1948– Canadian writer. Born in Toronto, Nichols received a BA in Religious Studies from the University of Columbia in 1969 and a PhD from McMaster University in 1977. Nichols has published four novels for children and young adults. The first two, *A Walk Out of the World* (1969) and *The Marrow of the World* (1972), are considered among the best Canadian fantasies for children. Somewhat derivative of TOLKIEN, LEWIS and MACDONALD, they nonetheless show Nichols's trademark concern with a sense of self and her ability to create compelling plots, profoundly symbolic settings and powerful female characters. Her YOUNG ADULT FICTION, *Song of the Pearl* (1976) and *The Left-Handed Spirit* (1978), depart from classic FANTASY and deal more obviously with the spiritual needs and development of young women while continuing to demonstrate her strengths with plot, setting and character. They also display Nichols's fascination with the life and social manners of the past and her ability to create convincing historical settings (China in the former, the Silk Road in the latter). More recently, she has published adult historical novels. TR

Nicholson, Sir William (Newzam Prior) 1872–1949 British artist, illustrator and writer. The multi-talented Nicholson made a great impact on the development of the PICTUREBOOK through a small body of work. Studying at the Académie Julian, Paris, in the late 1880s, he and his brother-in-law James Pryde were jointly inspired by the Art Nouveau poster to produce their own influential posters under the name of The Beggarstaff Brothers. Nicholson also created a number of books which synthesised French design and the native CHAPBOOK through their minimal texts and spare, bold images. Some even had texts cut in wood, though they were reprinted lithographically for the mass market. *An Alphabet* (1898) and *The Square Book of*

Animals (1900) were partly aimed at children. In this early period, he also designed the sets for the first production of PETER PAN (1904). Though his later career was almost entirely devoted to painting, he was encouraged by the presence of his grandchildren to illustrate Margery Williams's classic *THE VELVETEEN RABBIT* (1922) and publish two further picturebooks: *Clever Bill* (1926) and *The Pirate Twins* (1929). Their jaunty lithographed illustrations and economical handwritten scripts helped provide a real fusion of word and image, becoming a model for others on both sides of the Atlantic. MAURICE SENDAK has written that 'Clever Bill . . . is among the few perfect picturebooks ever created for children.' DW

see also LITHOGRAPHY; WOOD ENGRAVING

Nick Carter DIME NOVELS (from 1889) Inexpensive serial publications featuring a popular fictional detective. Nick Carter made his début in a serialised story that ran from 18 September to 11 December, 1886, in *Street & Smith's New York Weekly*. Written by John Russell Coryell, the story was republished in book form as *The Old Detective's Pupil* (1889), no. 17 in Street and Smith's *Secret Service* series. Despite its 25-cent cover price, this book can be considered the first *Nick Carter* dime novel. The first *Nick Carter* dime novel for boys was *Nick Carter, Detective* (1891), no. 1 in the *Nick Carter Detective Library*, a nickel-weekly series. The book was signed 'by A Celebrated Author', actually Frederic Van Rensselaer Dey. Street and Smith inaugurated the series with this statement: 'We feel that there is a demand on the part of the boys for a first-class five cent detective library.' Published in both pamphlet and thick-book formats, *Nick Carter* dime novels all had cover prices of between 5 and 25 cents. They appeared in various Street and Smith series, including *Nick Carter Weekly* and *Magnet Detective Library*. Though at least 30 writers used the Nick/Nicholas Carter pseudonym, Dey and Frederick William Davis were the most prolific. Dey published at least 500 stories under that pseudonym. As a character, Nick Carter was young, athletic and American – a new paradigm in detective fiction. He revelled in disguises and relied more on material clues than cerebral deduction. JRC, EAM

The first Nick Carter dime novel, 1891.

Nicolajeva, Maria see CRITICAL APPROACHES TO CHILDREN'S BOOKS

Nicoll, Helen see *MEG AND MOG* SERIES; JAN PIEŃKOWSKI

Nielsen, Kay (Rasmus) 1886–1957 One of the last great illustrators of the English GIFT BOOK. Nielsen was a Danish artist born in Copenhagen, son of the director of the Dagmartheater. He studied in Paris, at the Académies Julian and Colarossi, and was influenced by Art Nouveau, by its Oriental sources and by English artists that it inspired, such as Aubrey Beardsley. The illustrations for a projected 'Book of Death' that Nielsen exhibited in 1912, at London's Dowdeswell Galleries, attracted the attention of Hodder and Stoughton publishers. As a result, he was commissioned to produce the four books of FAIRY TALES on which his reputation rests: In *Powder and Crinoline*, retold by Quiller Couch (1913), *East of the Sun, West of the Moon*, retold by Asbjørnsen and Moe (1914), HANS ANDERSEN's *Fairy Tales* (1924) and *Hansel and Gretel* by the GRIMM BROTHERS (1925). His illustrations combine a sinuosity of line with brilliant washes, so resulting in bejewelled surfaces with often sinister details. During World War I, he produced some spectacular sets and costumes for the Royal Danish Theatre. From 1929 he lived in Hollywood, where he worked with WALT DISNEY on *Fantasia*. However, he had been virtually forgotten by the end of his life. DW

Night Before Christmas, The see *A VISIT FROM ST NICHOLAS*

Nightingale, The see HANS CHRISTIAN ANDERSEN; NICHOLAS STUART GRAY; *FAERIE TALE THEATRE*; see also NANCY EKHOLM BURKERT; EVA LEGALLIENNE

Niland, Deborah 1952– Award-winning prolific Australian illustrator, whose best-known work is the popular *Hippopotamus* series by HAZEL EDWARDS, which began with *There's a Hippopotamus on Our Roof Eating Cake* (1980). Niland draws whimsical animals and comical, stylised people, reminiscent of European traditions, in *The Sugar Plum Christmas Book: a Book for Christmas and All the Days of the Year* (1977) and in other anthologies compiled by JEAN CHAPMAN. Self-authored illustrated texts include *ABC of Monsters* (1976) and *Old Macdonald Had an Emu* (1986).

Niland is a twin sister of KILMENY NILAND and daughter of RUTH PARK, for whom she and Kilmeny have illustrated many PICTUREBOOKS, including *The Gigantic Balloon* (1975) and *Roger Bandy* (1977, 1992). On her own she illustrated Park's *When the Wind Changed* (1980) and *James* (1991). The Nilands' collaborative rendition of *Mulga Bill's Bicycle* (1973), the humorous rhyming BALLAD by A.B. PATERSON, won them the CHILDREN'S BOOK COUNCIL OF AUSTRALIA Picturebook of the Year and established a turning-point in the style of children's book illustration, with its use of caricatured images. The ink-and-watercolour drawings of the lanky figure of 'Mulga Bill from Eaglehawk' and his impressive handlebar moustache, as he attempts to ride a penny-farthing bicycle through the countryside, resonate with energy, and mirth. JAP

Niland, Kilmeny 1952– Australian writer and illustrator whose love of Australian native fauna is evident in several of her works, but particularly in an INFORMATION BOOK, *Feathers, Furs and Frills* (1980), which was based on detailed realistic paintings which Niland completed for an exhibition. *A Bellbird in a Flame Tree* (1989), an Australian version of *The Twelve Days of Christmas*, is an exuberant and colourful celebration of fauna and flora. Her PICTUREBOOKS include *Fey Mouse* (1988) by HAZEL EDWARDS; *My Brother John* (1990) by Kristine Church; *Just Like That* (1986) by MEM FOX; and *The Window Book* by SALLY ODGERS. Using water-colour and coloured pencils, Niland depicts young children with warmth and humour. Her pictures have a timeless, FAIRY-TALE quality, and an affinity for the geography of a child's world. For her mother, RUTH PARK, she has illustrated a number of works, including *Callie's Castle* (1974) and *Callie's Family* (1989). She also illustrated *Pancakes and Painted Eggs* (1981) and other anthologies by JEAN CHAPMAN. In collaboration with her sister, DEBORAH NILAND, she illustrated *Mulga Bill's Bicycle* (1973), for which they won several awards. JAP

Nils Holgersson see *THE WONDERFUL ADVENTURES OF NILS*

Nilsson, Eleanor 1939– Scottish-born writer who came to Australia at the age of 12. Nilsson's first work was a PICTUREBOOK, *Parrot Fashion* (1983), illustrated by CRAIG SMITH. Her later stories and junior novels embrace animal themes, often with an unexpected twist in the plot. Her focus on local seasonal settings is a mark of her work. *The House Guest* (1991), Nilsson's first, and very popular, adolescent novel is about a young gang of house-breakers. Two novellas for adolescent readers, *Graffiti Dog* (1995) and *The Experiment* (1996), and a second novel, *Outside Permission* (1997), continue to show Nilsson's skill at developing contrasting characters in problematic situations. Her books have received Australian awards and are published internationally. FK

Nimmo, Jenny see ALAN MARKS; *SNOW SPIDER TRILOGY*

***Nineteenth-Century America* series** see LEONARD EVERETT FISHER

Nineteenth Century Children see CRITICAL APPROACHES TO CHILDREN'S BOOKS

Ninja Turtles see *TEENAGE MUTANT NINJA TURTLES*; see also TELEVISION

Nintendo see VIDEO GAMES

Nister, Ernest 1842–1909 Distinguished and innovative publisher of a range of PICTUREBOOKS, puzzles, calendars, greetings cards and in particular MOVABLE BOOKS for children. Born in Oberkirkligen, Bavaria, the only son of a protestant pastor, Nister purchased in 1877 a small chromolithographic printing shop (see also LITHOGRAPHY) from Heinrich Scroeder in Nuremberg, Germany. He moved to London and in 1888 became a publisher with offices in St Bride's Street, London. Under the directorship of Robert Ellice Mack, material was selected and edited for publication in Britain and America, the New York connection being E.P. Dutton. By 1900 the Ernest Nister company's output was considerable and it employed over 600 workers. Nister personally supervised his firm's productions and began to produce his moving picturebooks. These were mainly in the form of pop-ups, revolving pictures, and slats that moved one picture over another at the pull of a tab. One of his finest was *Peeps into Fairyland* written by E. NESBIT and illustrated by Eveline Stuart Hardy. This was in the form of a 'grotto': when the book was opened, linen tabs attached on the inside margins pulled the scene up so that the reader could look into a three-dimensional stage. His first 'magic book' was *Nister's Panorama Pictures* (1890), a pop-up book, and this was followed by *The Magic Toy Book*, the 'Nister sensation' of 1891, in which the pictures had a hidden scene revealed only when the book was held in front of a bright light. Nister was not the first to publish movable books but – with writers like E. Nesbit, Clifton Bingham and F.E. Weatherly, and illustrators who included LOUIS WAIN, Helena Maguire and William Foster – he was certainly one of the most distinguished. After his death his thriving business continued to operate through the London office until 1916 and the Nuremberg office survived until 1927. JHu

see also PAPER ENGINEERING

Nix, Garth 1963– A major Australian writer of SCIENCE FICTION and FANTASY. Nix made history in Australia by winning both the adult and young adult sections of the inaugural Aurealis Awards with his second novel, *Sabriel* (1995). In a powerful, fast-paced, intricate adventure featuring a feisty female protagonist, Nix creates a complex, believable world where, in true high-fantasy mode, the forces of good and evil struggle for dominance. Nix manages to create high art and entertainment from the gloomy mysteries of necromancy. *Sabriel* and its companion, *Daughter of the Clayr* (1998), achieved wide publication and praise in the United States as did the science fiction work, *Shade's Children* (1997). This is set in a future world of holograms and artificial intelligences where marginalised youth, living precariously among ruins, battles with horrific creatures masterminded by the pitiless Overlords. Nix conjures a frightening world where young people's brains are cannibalised in a 'Meat Factory'. These works show how far Nix has travelled since his first fantasy, *Ragwitch* (1991). His versatility is reflected in some tiny, charming, witty books for babies and in his short stories and articles. Nix is one of a new breed of talented young writers who insist on being actively involved, locally and internationally, in all aspects of the production and marketing of their works. AN

Nixon, Joan Lowery 1927– American writer of fiction, non-fiction and PICTUREBOOKS for children and young adults. Born in Los Angeles, California, Nixon was so interested in books she began to teach herself to read when she was only three. Her works are most popular with 8-to-12-year-olds, and they range from mysteries to HISTORICAL FICTION and non-fiction. Nixon has earned Edgar Allen Poe Awards for *The Kidnapping of Christina Lattimore* (1979), *The Seance* (1980) and *The Other Side of Dark* (1986), one of her most honoured books. She has also created a series of holiday mysteries for early readers, including *The Thanksgiving Mystery* (1980) and *The Christmas Eve Mystery* (1981) illustrated by Jim Cummins. Her most popular historical fiction, the *Orphan Train* series, has earned her high praise as well as the Golden Spur, Western Writers of America, and Virginia Young Adult Silver Cup awards. In addition, she has done a great deal of informational and textbook writing, winning awards, along with co-author H. Nixon, from the Science Trade Book, the National Science Teachers Associations and the Children's Book Council, for *Volcanoes: Nature's Fireworks* (1978), *Glaciers: Nature's Frozen Rivers* (1980) and *Earthquakes: Nature in Motion* (1981). JGJ

see also INFORMATION BOOKS

Njal's Saga see FOLKTALES AND LEGENDS

Nkala, Nathan see *MEZIE THE OGBANJE BOY*

Nobody's Family Is Going to Change (1974) LOUISE FITZHUGH's third novel, published only a few days after her untimely death. This satirical novel features an upper-middle-class black family, the Sheridans, living in New York City. The two privileged Sheridan children (they attend private school and have a white maid), Emma and Willie, are growing up to be everything their parents do not want them to be. Emma wants to be a lawyer and Willie wants to be a dancer, while their father despises both male dancers and women lawyers, and their mother weakly acquiesces. The clash between children and parents occupies much of the book, which is narrated by Willie and Emma, a technique that allows readers two very different perspectives on the Sheridan family. Emma's thoughts predominate. She is full of anger, a young girl who despises herself and the hypocrisy of the adult world. Emma is a more cynical version of Harriet M. Welsch, the star of *HARRIET THE SPY*. Both characters are honest, blunt and straightforward, but Emma is also filled with rage at a social system that often seems unjust. Ultimately, the book's message about the possibility for change is ambivalent. At the book's conclusion, Emma is still set on her career goal, but her father refuses to listen to her. It seems evident that nobody's family is going to change, as the title suggests. Although this novel has been overshadowed in the United States by the author's more successful and famous first two novels (*Harriet the-Spy* and *The Long Secret*, 1965), Fitzhugh's third novel has been especially valued in Britain for its questioning of gender stereotypes and its insistence on the importance of self-determination for children. SAI

Noddy A wooden doll with a spring-mounted head, conceived by ENID BLYTON. He features in more of her works than any other character. There are 24 books in the original Sampson Low, Marston series (1949–64), but Blyton wrote over a hundred other 'Noddy' titles. Like Pinocchio, Noddy flees his creator. He ends up in Toyland, a very materialistic place, where the

Illustration by Peter Firmin from *Noggin the Nog*.

emphasis is on paying your way and protecting your possessions from theft. Noddy is an immature and naive character: not only can children relate to him; they can also feel a sense of superiority. He also has an enviable autonomy, with his 'House-for-One' and car. Parental figures like Big-Ears and Mr Plod, though they monitor his behaviour, generally end up singing his praises.

The books have been criticised for their supposed racism. *Here Comes Noddy Again!* (1951) is the main offender, which shows Noddy being mugged by golliwogs, who steal his car and clothes. Generally, though, the Toyland golliwogs are well-behaved and agreeable. Nevertheless, a revised edition of the series, launched in 1990, replaced them with goblins. The Sampson Low, Marston series was exceptionally well produced for its time, with full-colour illustrations on every page, beautifully rendered by the Dutch artist, Harmsen van der Beek, who died after the first seven books. The series topped world-wide sales of 100 million in 1992; there has also been extensive merchandising, a highly successful Christmas play, *Noddy in Toyland* (1955), plus others using the Noddy characters, and three TELEVISION series, in the 1950s, 70s and 90s. DR

Nodelman, Perry see CHILDIST CRITICISM; CRITICAL APPROACHES TO CHILDREN'S LITERATURE

***Noggin the Nog* series** (from 1965) Twelve stories, first accepted by the BBC, by the writer-illustrators OLIVER POSTGATE and PETER FIRMIN. They relate, in simplified saga form, the exploits of Noggin, a gentle, friendly Viking king, champion of the just but downtrodden, who is pitted against the forces of evil, led by the classically wicked uncle, Nogbad. In the inventive story lines Nogbad is constantly thwarted, in the nick of time, by Noggin, aided by Queen Nooka, Prince Knut and other eccentric characters, such as Olaf, the court inventor, Graculus, a great green bird, and other magical forces. There is confrontation, attack and defeat, but all is told with a light, humorous touch, in which there is no real violence or threat. The black-and-white, tinted ILLUSTRATIONS have a vigorous cartoon-like character. The ENDPAPERS show detailed, fascinating pictorial maps of Noggin's world. A parallel *Starting to Read* series was written about the same characters. JSW

non-fiction books see INFORMATION BOOKS

Nonsense Songs and Stories (1871) At the height of his powers, EDWARD LEAR produced these wonderfully surreal, crazy narratives and memorable characters in delightful musical language – 'The Jumblies' and 'The Quangle Wangle Quee' who lived in a Crumpetty Tree, Chankly Bore or the Torrible Zone. Deservedly still popular today, this NONSENSE VERSE ranks with the best of LEWIS CARROLL's. Many illustrators have tried their hand at poems from this collection, but Lear's own drawings are hard to beat. One of the best attempts is HELEN OXENBURY's PICTUREBOOK version of *The Quangle-Wangle's Hat* (1969). JL

nonsense verse A centuries-old tradition that delights in the implausible or incongruous, in some cases the complete abandonment of sense, and in playing with language itself. In the 19th century LEWIS CARROLL and EDWARD LEAR effectively established the rich and complex nature of contemporary nonsense, as seen today in the works of MERVYN PEAKE, SPIKE MILLIGAN, OGDEN NASH, ROALD DAHL and SHEL SILVERSTEIN. The poetry of these two Victorians fused the central elements of nonsense verse: the incongruous, like Lear's Jumblies setting out to sea in a sieve; the bizarre, like the marriage of the Owl and the Pussy Cat; the practice of changing or inventing words as exemplified in Carroll's 'Jabberwocky' – ''Twas brillig, and the slithy toves / Did gyre and gimble in the wabe' – and finally a natural, song-like quality and fluency, plus a relish for word sounds that make the reader want to recite them aloud.

Lear is generally seen as the laureate of nonsense: his LIMERICKS; his nonsense alphabets, geography, natural history, botany, anthropology; his word-making and games with phonetic spelling and pronunciations, defined the whole nonsense repertoire. This has been continued and developed today in the work of Silverstein and COLIN MCNAUGHTON who, like Lear, utilise ILLUSTRATION to accentuate the nonsense of their verse. Like today's exponents, Lear and Carroll were also popular with adults as well as children, and were interested in parodying or challenging social conventions of their time – snobbery, self-importance, and the didactic and rather limited nature of a lot of writing for children.

HILAIRE BELLOC, writing at the turn of the century, openly satirised social attitudes and behaviour and, like Dahl, he excelled at what QUENTIN BLAKE, in his introduction to Belloc's *Cautionary Verses*, describes as 'the level-voiced assertion of facts that we all know are untrue'. He tells us, for instance . . . that the tiger (like the yak) is just the thing as a companion for children. In the introduction to his *Complete Book of Nonsense* (1994) Blake says: 'The rhymes, the metre, the verse forms are just as regular as . . . those of more serious poems . . . [and because] at first they might appear to be serious . . . it allows them, sometimes, to have their own mysterious poetry and atmosphere, so that they are funny and serious at the same time.'

Nonsense verse is about breaking laws. It challenges accepted but inherently narrow rules for writing, and can, in turn, question codes of behaviour that underpin society. As Holbrook Jackson explains in his introduction to Lear's *Complete Nonsense*, it 'begins with fun [and] ends in the extension of the boundaries of expression'. JL

Noonan, Diana 1960– Versatile New Zealand writer of PICTUREBOOKS and novels for children and young adults. *The Best-Loved Bear Competition* (1994), winner of the 1995 *New Zealand Post* Picturebook Award, recognises that love and caring are qualities deserving first place in a teddy-bear contest. Noonan's novels have strong themes. The preservation of forests and places which hold special memories of the land are central to her first novel, *The Silent People* (1990), set in an isolated part of the South Island of New Zealand. *The Last Steam Train* (1992) evocatively describes the passing of an era of early New Zealand. In *Sonnet for the City* (1992) Noonan explores the tensions and difficulties experienced by a country-born 16-year-old going to university in the city, whilst *The Whaler's Garden* (1995) embraces a spiritual dimension. Noonan writes powerfully about real people dealing with everyday problems. Other titles include *Goodbye Toss* (1993), *A Dolphin in the Bay* (1993) and *Hercules* (1996). Diana Noonan has written extensively for educational publications, and is currently editor of the New Zealand SCHOOL JOURNAL. LL

Noonuccal, Oodgeroo 1920–93 Aboriginal Australian poet and activist, born Kathleen Ruska, on North Stradbroke Island, Queensland. *We Are Going* (1967) was the first published Aboriginal poetry book. *The Dawn Is at Hand* (1996) was followed by *Stradbroke Dreamtime* (1967), reissued in 1993 with ILLUSTRATIONS by BRONWYN BANCROFT – a unique coverage of an Aboriginal life told via traditional stories and individual life recollections. *Father Sky and Mother Earth* was published in 1981.

Known as Kath Walker after her marriage, she was active in bringing about a referendum which gave Aboriginal people the vote. She returned her 1970 MBE in protest in 1988, and became Oodgeroo of the tribe Noonuccal, Custodian of the Land Menjerribah. She spent much of her life on Stradbroke Island and her home there – Menjerribah – is being maintained in her memory. Recipient of many awards and honorary doctorates from Australian Universities, she also sat on many committees and was an international delegate, winning a Fulbright Fellowship to the United States in 1978/9. She travelled as an official visitor to China in 1985, and her poems were the first Aboriginal text co-published by Australian and Chinese publishing houses. Prior to her death her life was dramatised by the Queensland Theatre Company in *One Woman's Song* (1993). RS

see also ABORIGINAL CULTURE IN CHILDREN'S BOOKS

Norcliffe, James 1946– New Zealand writer, whose first children's novel, *Under the Rotunda* (1992), features a wicked magician, who reduces a brass band to leprechaun size. It is a fast-paced combination of mystery and FANTASY, made convincing by its contemporary idiom. In this story, as in subsequent ones, Norcliffe uses local landmarks and settings, such as a band rotunda and the Christchurch Botanic Gardens. Despite a somewhat slow narrative style in subsequent books, Norcliffe offers readers literate stories that puzzle and intrigue, twisting the very familiar into, at times, fantastic shapes. BN

Nordstrom, Ursula [Marie] 1910–88 American author and editor of books for young people. As director of Harper's Department of Books for Boys and Girls from 1940 to 1973, Nordstrom exercised a protean influence over virtually every aspect of her field. An iconoclast as well as a perfectionist by nature, she championed books that, with unprecedented candour, validated young people's complex emotional lives while providing them with aesthetic experiences of the highest order. The long roster of genre-bending classics Nordstrom published runs the gamut from PICTUREBOOKS – MARGARET WISE BROWN'S *GOODNIGHT MOON* (1947), CROCKETT JOHNSON'S *Harold and the Purple Crayon* (1955), MAURICE SENDAK'S *WHERE THE WILD THINGS ARE* (1963) and *William's Doll* by CHARLOTTE ZOLOTOW – to middle-grade fiction by E.B. WHITE, MEINDERT DEJONG, and Mary Rodgers, to young adult fiction by MARY STOLZ, JOHN DONOVAN and M.E. KERR. With the publication in 1957 of HOLMELUND MINARIK'S *Little Bear*, Nordstrom also pioneered the genre of books for the beginning reader. A tireless cheerleader on behalf of her authors' varied talents, Nordstrom produced a vast and brilliantly witty professional correspondence, but wrote only one book of her own. The semi-autobiographical *The Secret Language* (1960) recalls boarding-school life for two pre-teen girls who, in typical maverick fashion, learn more from each other than they do from their teachers or texts. LSM

Norman, Lilith 1927– Australian writer, a former librarian and editor of the New South Wales *SCHOOL MAGAZINE*. Her first book, *Climb a Lonely Hill* (1970), was among the first to represent adult weakness in children's fiction. Fourteen-year-old Jack, surviving for 11 days in the bush after a car crash, comes to realise his own inner strength compared with that of his alcoholic father. *The Shape of Three* (1971) finds teenage boys discovering their birth mix-up and is almost a social documentary. Two novels with FANTASY elements are *The Flame Takers* (1973), which shows a dark side to the city of Sydney, and *A Dream of Seas* (1978), which flows elegantly and lyrically between realism and fantasy, as a boy's life is paralleled with that of a male seal. In 1997 six of Norman's titles were reissued, although contemporary readers used to more complex narratives may consider them old-fashioned. Norman has also written a number of books for younger readers, including the PICTUREBOOKS *The Paddock* (1992) and *Aphanasy* (1994), a retelling of a Russian folktale. JAP

Norriss, Andrew 1947– Educated at Trinity College, Dublin, Andrew Norriss was a teacher before turning to full-time writing in 1982. *Aquila* (WHITBREAD AWARD, 1997) and *Bernard's Watch* (1999) both play with time, *Aquila* with time travel, and *Bernard's Watch* with a watch that can stop time. *Matt's Million* (1995) is about a boy who suddenly finds himself a millionaire. While all three works display a marked sense of fun and understanding of what children enjoy, Norriss's work is also concerned (although this is quietly understated) with the development of self-confidence and wisdom in children, and the need for them to develop at their own pace. He has also written the *Woof!* books, and *The Unluckiest Boy in the World* is scheduled for publication in 2001. SA

Norse mythology see CLASSICAL MYTHOLOGY; see also RODNEY MATTHEWS

North to Freedom see *I AM DAVID*

Northern Lights see *HIS DARK MATERIALS*

Norton, Andre [Alice Mary Norton] 1912– American writer of juvenile and adult SCIENCE FICTION and FANTASY. The prolific author (who legally changed her name from her birth name) has written over 90 science-fiction and 20 other books. Along with Marion Zimmer Bradley and ANNE MCCAFFREY, Norton has established herself as an important writer of young adult fantasy, particularly in the volumes of her *Witch World* series, which includes *Galactic Derelict* (1959), *Witch World* (1964), *Web of the Witch World* (1964) and *The Gate of the Cat* (1987). Norton is even better known as a science-fiction writer who explores an unusually wide range of issues in her books. *Star Rangers* (1953), *Moon of the Three Rings* (1966), *The X Factor* (1965) and *The Zero Stone* (1968) are typical of Norton's œuvre in that they include an eclectic combination of diverse worlds, technologies, characters, plots and themes. In many of her works, Norton includes a rite of passage that her hero needs to undergo, one of the reasons her works are popular with young people. Along with ROBERT A. HEINLEIN, Norton is one of the most prolific and popular writers of juvenile science fiction of the 20th century. SAI

Norton, Mary 1903–92 Distinguished and popular British author. Norton was born in London, educated at St Margaret's Convent in Sussex, and was an actress at the Old Vic before turning to writing as a career. Her marriage to Robert Norton in 1927 produced four children; her second marriage, to Lionel Bonsey, took place in 1970.

The Magic Bed-Knob (1943) and *Bonfires and Broomsticks* (1947), her two earliest works, were eventually conflated, becoming *Bedknob and Broomstick* (1957). As in Hilda Lewis's *The Ship that Flew* (1939), the children in the story travel magically (by turning the eponymous bedknob), and have various adventures. Norton is perhaps best known, however, for the series which commenced with *THE BORROWERS* (1952). The series focuses on Homily, Arriety and Pod, a family of tiny people who 'borrow' things from their human hosts (a lovely explanation for vanished safety pins etc.), and their travels 'aloft', 'afloat' and 'afield'. Both *The Borrowers* and *Bedknob* have been filmed. Her other work, *Are All the Giants Dead?* (1975), looks at certain FAIRY TALE characters after the ritual 'happily ever after' has ended the narrative. Mary Norton was the recipient of both the CARNEGIE MEDAL and the Lewis Carroll Shelf Award. SA

Nöstlinger, Christine see WAR STORIES

Not Now, Bernard (1980) DAVID MCKEE'S PICTUREBOOK exploration of adult neglect, renowned for its macabre humour and sophisticated visual representation. Unable to gain his parents' attention, Bernard disappears, consumed by a monster. The frisson of fear this provokes is overshadowed by the truly horrific indifference of Bernard's mum and dad. Their expressionless faces are animated only by irritation at Bernard's (and the monster's) interruptions of their routines. The funny side is the monster's hurt astonishment at not being recognised for what he is. Flattened space, vivid colour and humorous details extend the narrative in this masterpiece of pictorial storytelling. PC

Nothing to be Afraid of (1980). Short-story collection by JAN MARK, establishing her mastery of what she has called a 'virtuoso' form. The ten stories, some set in the fifties, contain wit, satisfyingly accurate dialogue and warm, sympathetic humour. Some read like childhood reminiscences. All have classic short-story twists, which spring from sharp observation and profound knowledge of children and their powers of imagination. 'William's Version' has become a reference point for describing the nature of children's responses and understanding. The delicately disturbing suggestion of the supernatural in 'Nule' presages a strong element in Mark's subsequent work. DCH

Nothingmas Day (1984) ADRIAN MITCHELL'S first collection of poems for children has subsequently fallen out of print, but most are included in *Balloon Lagoon* (1997). All the qualities which distinguish Mitchell's work are here – wit, wisdom, wordplay, compassion, music, and sometimes rage. Affirmation of life, faith in the child, and concern for how adults can abuse children, are constant themes. 'A Child is Singing' deals with loss of innocence, while 'Stufferation' keeps the beat going. HT

Now We are Six see A.A. MILNE; *WHEN WE WERE VERY YOUNG*

Noyes, Alfred see *HIGHWAYMAN, THE*; see also CHARLES KEEPING; LITERATURE IN CHILDREN'S LITERATURE

nudity in children's books Although naked children are a fact in the lives of families, powerful taboos have ensured that nudity, even of babies and small children, is an embarrassment in children's books. Writers and illustrators have generally reflected prevailing social attitudes towards nudity, but a few rare individual writers have challenged these norms. CYNTHIA VOIGT, in *Homecoming* (USA, 1981; UK, 1983), communicated with considerable tact a grown-up sister's affectionate appreciation of her baby brother's naked body: 'Dicey could still remember his short, plump little body, sturdy legs and round blond head, and his tiny penis that bobbled up and down as he ran.' Voigt carefully represented the naked child in the context of a loving family group, but this was nevertheless bold writing in defiance of some strong cultural prejudices.

In the many FAMILY STORIES of the 1930s, 40s and 50s, there were few narratorial references to naked children. However, MARY NORTON, in *The Magic Bedknob* (1947), delicately employed the subject of mixed bathing to make a point about prudery: although the prim Miss Price forbids bathing, 'They were hot and tired, so, in spite of Miss Price, they threw off their pyjamas and bathed.' The author's implication is clear: children are uninhibited about nakedness, and prudery is an adult problem. In *Paul's Tale* (1994) she again used the idea of nakedness, but here it was to highlight the troublesome dynamics between an adult storyteller and a child listener. Aunt Isobel dresses her fairy hero in 'a little red jerkin and a dear little cap made out of a foxglove.' But this is not what the young Paul has in mind. 'He didn't have any clothes . . . He was quite bare . . . He had thick skin, like a twig.' A little later we are told that Aunt Isobel 'didn't like the little naked man nearly as much as the little clothed man: she was trying to get used to him.'

The two CHILD AUTHORS, Katharine Hull and Pamela Whitlock, in their novel *THE FAR DISTANT OXUS* (1937), had no inhibitions about describing their rather idealised boy-hero swimming by a waterfall and letting 'the water shower down on to his naked body'. They also showed themselves fully alert to the comic embarrassments of nakedness when another of their characters decides 'that the owners of the hideous house might be unduly shocked if they looked out of their window and saw a nude boy propelling himself across the lake.'

Perhaps the most compelling use of nudity is in PHILIPPA PEARCE'S *The Way to Sattin Shore* (1983). This is a narrative composed of secrets and conspiracies and so, when Kate sees her unknown and long-lost father for the first time, it is a significant moment of unequivocal recognition: 'He had been swimming naked, as the place was deserted; and so Kate saw her father as Eve saw Adam, newly created, in the Garden of Eden.' Nakedness here is not intimacy, but knowledge,

'She laid him upon the warm sand.' Illustration by Helen Stratton for HANS CHRISTIAN ANDERSEN's *Fairy Tales.*

double-edged and – like Kate's father – slightly troublesome.

Writing about early adolescence and the sexual curiosity that may accompany it is a more complex matter. The cultural factors which left most western teenagers until the 1960s largely ignorant about the bodies of the opposite sex prevented children's writers from referring to nakedness at all. JOHN ROWE TOWNSEND noted of the *SWALLOWS AND AMAZONS* series that the 'sexless comradeship' of the older children 'does not quite accord with the facts of adolescence' – a point that could be made about all children's fiction of the period. Much later, in 1977, Shelagh MacDonald's novel *No End to Yesterday* – winner of the 1977 WHITBREAD AWARD – took a bolder line; in an exchange between Marjorie and her cousin Teddy, embarrassment and sexual ignorance are combined for comic effect:

> Uncle Bertie planting a seed in Auntie Flora with his Thing, it was hilarious, ludicrous, how could they, but it was strange too, did everyone? Stop fiddling with yourself, Teddy, she stopped laughing, you know Auntie Flora says it's bad for you. Look at mine, Marj, I bet you never saw one like that before. Teddy! What've you done to it? It's gone all – oh, your Mum will be cross!

From the 1970s onwards, the treatment of nudity became inseparable from the treatment of SEX in books for young adults. JUDY BLUME's *Forever* (1975) was notorious for its explicitness; but her account of two young lovers' discovery of their bodies, though sympathetic, is more explanatory than dramatic, and many inquisitive young readers have read it in that spirit. AIDAN CHAMBERS attempted something more complex and evocative in *BREAKTIME* (1978), where the hero's discovery of the naked female body is unashamedly sexual and celebratory.

For most English-speaking readers, nudity invokes centuries of Judaic and Christian culture, but its significance in non-European stories is likely to be different. James Vance Marshall's *Walkabout* (first issued as *The Children*, 1959) is an exploration from a narrow European standpoint of precisely that difference. A white girl, lost in the Australian desert, finds the nakedness of an Aboriginal boy 'shockingly and indecently wrong'. Edward Bond's screenplay adaptation transformed the work into an adolescent idyll in which the camera focused lovingly on Jenny Agutter's body and unselfconscious nakedness was seen to cut triumphantly through all cultural difference to unite the children in innocence – reversing the thrust of Marshall's original novel, in which the girl's fear of nakedness is at the centre of the children's failure to understand one another.

This awareness of nakedness in different cultural settings is also reflected in Carolyn Logan's *Riverchild* (1995), where an orphaned 16-year old English girl, Sarah, an 1820s migrant to Perth in Western Australia, builds a relationship with an Aboriginal woman, Bilu, and her son, Warlu. In a dream-like sequence Sarah is undressed by Bilu and, together with Warlu, is led naked into the river. Sarah covers her breasts with her hands to avoid English sailors on the far side of the river seeing her nakedness. The stroking of her body by Bilu, and her immersion in the river, enable Sarah to cleanse herself of her childhood beatings.

Illustrators have different problems. *THE EMPEROR'S NEW CLOTHES* is something of a touchstone since it could be said to provide artists with an opportunity to confront the comic potential of revealed grown-up nakedness. But in fact most illustrators have avoided the issue. EDWARD ARDIZZONE depicted the emperor parading in his longjohns. ERNEST SHEPARD displayed the Emperor in his underclothes – but, in an odd transference, the little boy who points out the Emperor's nakedness has a bare behind. MICHAEL FOREMAN, whose Emperor is naked, pear-shaped and viewed from behind, and Rex Whistler, whose Emperor is a Restoration monarch in his underclothes, both concentrate the reader's attention on the faces of the crowd. This is dramatically appropriate – but disappointing to inquisitive young readers. *THE WATER BABIES* offers illustrators a different challenge, but here too most artists have contrived to suggest nakedness without depicting it fully. In Linley Sambourne's illustrations (1885) there is a coyness about Tom's nakedness which sits oddly alongside the stylised use of adult female nudity. Anne Anderson, a popular illustrator of the 1920s and 30s, 'dressed' Tom in fish scales.

At this period there was a fashion in children's books for the representation of chubby naked toddlers, probably associated with government publicity suggesting that healthy babies were fat babies. A popular Australian writer-illustrator in this mode was MAY GIBBS, whose gumnut babies were shown in a variety of amusing situations, though only the girl gumnuts were shown in full-frontal nudity. There was a vigour and comedy in May Gibbs's illustrations which rescued them from sentimentality, but the same cannot be said for MABEL LUCIE ATTWELL's illustrations for *PETER PAN AND WENDY*. The motif of cute bottoms was taken up later by WALT DISNEY in *Fantasia*, in which a naked girl-cherub presents the audience with a view of her bare and rosy behind, which then turns into a pink love-heart. The Freudian implications of this transformation were presumably lost upon the Disney animators.

The naked adult body was rarely represented by Victorian artists except in the depiction of mermaids – presumably because a clothed mermaid would be ridiculous (though a century later Disney dressed the *Little Mermaid* in a bikini-top). A.W. Bayes dealt with the difficulty in a rather statuesque but directly sexual manner in his illustration (engraved by the Dalziel brothers) for Andersen's *The Little Sea Maid*. Around the turn of the century hints of female nakedness were allowed, but only in a Pre-Raphaelite manner suggestive of 'high art'. Artists were allowed to represent nakedness provided it was transparently draped or in miniature form. The Pre-Raphaelite love of loose drapery provided endless suggestive opportunities, and if a breast was revealed at all, it was small and lightly contoured. H.J. Ford, the chief illustrator of Andrew Lang's *FAIRY BOOKS*, excelled at this type of depiction. The gender implications of this incomplete undressing of the female body while the male remained resolutely covered – often in armour – are considerable. It seems that the representation of the naked female body – even in children's FAIRY TALES – was employed to define a culture of the male. However, such conventions were not the exclusive practice of male illustrators: several years later, Helen Stratton's illustration of the Little Mermaid suggested a delicate mixture of young tenderness and passion.

In spite of such cautious stepping around the edges of the forbidden, some more recent children's illustrators have boldly exploited the direct dramatic power of nakedness. ARTHUR RACKHAM's work was notable in the 1920s; a more recent example is ANTHONY MAITLAND's illustration of the imprisoned and abused Belle at the moment she is discovered by her friend Tolly in LEON GARFIELD's *BLACK JACK* (1968). CHARLES KEEPING, collaborating with EDWARD BLISHEN and Garfield in their retelling of the Greek myths (see CLASSICAL MYTHOLOGY), was uncompromising in his use of the highly charged dramatic power of nudity, exploiting both the vulnerability, and the sexual and symbolic appeal, of the naked human body.

MAURICE SENDAK's depiction of a naked boy in *IN THE NIGHT KITCHEN* (1970) evoked some hostile reactions, as did KATHY STINSON's *The Bare Naked Book* (1986) with its frank exploration of the human body. More recently, a child's pleasure in being naked is evident in Barbara Giles's *Jack in the Bush* (1983), in which Betty Greenhatch's realistic pencil illustrations show a carefree and bold young Jack, wearing only his boots, as he romps with the nocturnal animals in the Australian bush. A current convention is to represent nakedness in cartoon form; BABETTE COLE's *MUMMY LAID AN EGG* (1993) and *Hair in Funny Places* (1999), TONY ROSS's *I WANT MY POTTY* (1986) and his illustrations for Jeanne Willis's *DR XARGLE'S BOOK OF EARTHLETS* (1988) make use of cartoon nakedness, as do TERRY DENTON in *Flying Man*, and PAMELA ALLEN in *Mr Archimedes' Bath* (1980), both of whom humorously depict naked adult males.

In children's fiction – but not for some reason in INFORMATION BOOKS – there are still powerful embarrassments and anxieties about nudity, and these have become more acute in a culture still coming to terms with the realities of child abuse. An earlier age was afraid that depictions of naked adults might corrupt the minds of young readers; the contemporary fear is that depictions of naked children might arouse the interest of corrupted adults. VW, JAP

***Nurse Matilda* stories** (from 1964) Written by Christianna Brand and illustrated by EDWARD ARDIZZONE, the three *Nurse Matilda* books are lightly humorous works about a large family of children and their nurse whose magic stick, when thumped, causes whatever naughty enterprise the children may be engaged on (and these are both legion and, in their own way, creative) to continue until they tire of it and she allows them to stop. All three works share the same narrative pattern, Nurse Matilda – like P.L. Travers's MARY POPPINS – leaving at the end of the story, after the children have been, for the time being, cured of their naughtiness. SA

Nurse Truelove's New Year's Gift see ISAIAH THOMAS

Nursery rhymes: 'Tom, Tom, the piper's son.' Illustration by Katherine Robertson for ST NICHOLAS MAGAZINE (1892).

Nursery 'Alice', The see *ALICE'S ADVENTURES IN WONDERLAND*; LEWIS CARROLL

nursery rhymes or **Mother Goose** RHYMES Short poems or songs, often of great antiquity, traditionally for very young children and sometimes involving interactive play. They include counting rhymes, bouncing rhymes, clapping rhymes, LULLABIES, BALLADS, proverbs, RIDDLES, and short nonsense narratives.

The history of nursery rhymes is complex and not without controversy. While it is certain that many are several centuries old and are recorded or referred to in medieval and renaissance texts, and that some of the oldest have their equivalents in other European languages, it is not known how many genuinely derive from an oral folk culture. Many of them originally had little to do with children; some refer to historical events, others were satires or popular ballads, and in the 17th and 18th centuries some existed as extended bawdy narratives. According to IONA and PETER OPIE, the first recorded use of the term 'nursery rhyme' was in 1824, but there had been a developing interest in them throughout the previous century, when they were usually called 'songs' or 'ditties'. The dating of children's books in this period is problematical, but it seems likely that Mary Cooper's *TOMMY THUMB'S PRETTY SONG BOOK* was published in 1744, and a few years later S. Crowder issued *The Famous Tommy Thumb's Little Story-Book* containing nine rhymes. The most complete collection of children's rhymes of the period was JOHN NEWBERY's *MOTHER GOOSE'S MELODY, OR SONNETS FOR THE CRADLE*, probably published in 1766. Newbery's *Mother Goose* and other collections in Britain were reproduced in New England, leading to a flourishing and independent nursery-rhyme tradition in America, as well as a belief that the original MOTHER GOOSE was American. There is some evidence to suggest that, alongside such published rhymes, there was in the 18th century – and probably in much earlier times – a traditional oral nursery culture, transmitted and sustained almost exclusively by women in their child-rearing role, and that an aspect of this culture was the sharing of ancient lullabies, counting rhymes, finger-games, lap-rhymes and rhyming alphabets (see also ALPHABET BOOKS) composed and improvised upon specifically for children. We know from the surviving records of JANE JOHNSON that women in the 18th century used popular published material, adapting it to suit the needs of their children. This practice was probably widespread, but the evidence is at present fragmentary. However, it is clear that by the second half of the 18th century there was a substantial and varied body of nursery lore, a flexible and shifting literature combining traditional rhymes for children with adult verses or songs adapted to suit their needs.

In the early 19th century, when cheap children's CHAPBOOKS were popular, several of them were devoted to a single rhyming narrative (for example, *COCK ROBIN*, or *MOTHER HUBBARD*) or issued as tiny 16-page anthologies (such as *Nursery Rhymes from the Royal Collections*, published by J.G. RUSHER of Banbury, the publisher who put his home town into some popular rhymes). There were more extensive collections, too, such as Robert Chambers's *Popular Rhymes of Scotland* in 1826, and in America *Mother Goose's Melodies* published in Massachusetts in 1833.

By the middle of the 19th century published nursery rhymes were established and valued as traditional literature for very young children. In 1881 the publisher EDMUND EVANS, who had developed techniques for inexpensive, high-quality colour reproduction, published KATE GREENAWAY's *Mother Goose or the Old Nursery Rhymes*, but his most outstanding success was a series of PICTUREBOOKS or TOY BOOKS, illustrated by

RANDOLPH CALDECOTT, each entirely devoted to a single nursery rhyme and transformed through careful design and artwork into an extended picturebook narrative.

Nursery rhyme literature has been continually added to: several composed poems have been anthologised (often without acknowledgement) as nursery rhymes – for example, 'The Spider and the Fly' by MARY HOWITT, JANE TAYLOR's 'Twinkle, Twinkle, Little Star' and 'MARY HAD A LITTLE LAMB' by SARA HALE of New England. The wisdom of generations of mothers in sustaining the use of nursery rhymes has been vindicated by a considerable body of research indicating that an early familiarity with the alliteration and rhyming of nursery rhymes is a great help to children learning to read.

Nursery rhymes have traditionally been associated with song, and there have been many collections for young children in which the musical score has been included. One of the best of these was *National Nursery Rhymes Set to Music* edited by J.W. Elliott and illustrated with engravings by the DALZIEL BROTHERS. Another was WALTER CRANE's *The Baby's Opera* (1877) (see BABY BOOKS), which was a nursery rhyme-book, a picturebook and a songbook all in one. A more recent publication in the same tradition was the stunning *Lullabies and Night Songs* (1965), illustrated by MAURICE SENDAK. Musical versions of nursery rhymes have in recent times become increasingly popular as numerous audiotape collections have become available.

Nursery rhymes seem more able to endure through several generations than other genres of children's literature, perhaps because they are so readily memorable. Adults genuinely remember them from their own childhood, and pass them on to their children, either orally or through the many published versions which are currently available. These include collections illustrated by HELEN OXENBURY, NICOLA BAYLEY, IAN BECK, MICHAEL FOREMAN and RAYMOND BRIGGS. One of the best nursery-rhyme anthologies – containing over 300 rhymes illustrated in an Art Nouveau manner by Blanche Fisher Wright – is *The Real Mother Goose*, first published in the United States in 1916 and still being reprinted. Another distinguished collection is Kathleen Lines's *Lavender's Blue* (1954), illustrated by HAROLD JONES. Collectors will pay up to £200 for a surviving copy of the sumptuous Volland edition of *Mother Goose*, published in Chicago in 1915.

The first person to take a scholarly interest in the history and provenance of nursery rhymes was James Orchard Halliwell, who published *The Nursery Rhymes of England* in 1842. This was an annotated collection, and Halliwell followed it in 1849 with *Popular Rhymes and Nursery Tales*. Halliwell's claims were not entirely reliable and little serious and systematic scholarship

'Mary, Mary, Quite Contrary' by unknown illustrator.

was available until, in 1951, Iona and Peter Opie published *The Oxford Dictionary of Nursery Rhymes*, which – with their other work – remains the most informed and entertaining source for any reader wishing to learn more about the history of individual rhymes. Iona Opie, in a preface to her anthology, *My Very First Mother Goose* (1996), illustrated by ROSEMARY WELLS, described nursery rhymes as 'astonishing, beautiful, capricious, dancy, eccentric, funny, goluptious, haphazard, intertwingled, joyous, kindly, loving, melodious, naughty, outrageous, pomsidillious, querimonious, romantic, silly, tremendous, unexpected, vertiginous, wonderful, x-citing, yo-heave-ho-ish and zany'. VW

Nutcracker, The see BALLET STORIES; TESSA DUDER; ALEXANDRE DUMAS; ROBERTO INNOCENTI; MUSIC AND STORY

Nwankwo, Nkem 1936– Nigerian novelist, teacher and journalist, born in Nawfia, Anambra State. In addition to novels for adults (*Danda, My Mercedes Is Bigger Than Yours*), Nwankwo has written two much-read children's books: *Tales out of School* (1963) is a typical boarding-school saga, while in *More Tales out of School* (1965) the same boys solve a kidnapping case. VD

Nwapa, Flora (Nwanzuruahal) 1931–94 Nigeria's first female novelist (*Efuru*, 1966; *One is Enough*, 1981), born in Oguta, Imo State. In 1978 Nwapa set up a publishing company specialising in PICTUREBOOKS. Her best-known children's books are *Mammy Water* and its sequel *The Adventure of Deke* (1977), both illustrated by artist Obiora Udechukwu, FANTASY tales based on the mythological figure of the mermaid. Others include *Journey to Space* (1980), *The Miracle Kittens* (1981) and *Emeka, Driver's Guard* (1972). VD

Nzekwu, Onuora see *EZE GOES TO SCHOOL*

O

O'Brien, Robert C. [Robert Leslie Conly] 1918–73 American writer, best known for *Mrs Frisby and the Rats of NIMH* (1971), winner of the Newbery Award. O'Brien worked as a journalist for most of his life. His three children's books use fantasy or science fiction devices to portray the conflict between corrupt social forces and individuals who are struggling for physical survival while retaining their ethical integrity. Technological pessimism and distrust of big government combine with ingenious fantasy elements and a strong faith in individual resourcefulness to give these books their distinctive appeal. *The Silver Crown* (1968) features a modern urban girl who journeys to a dystopic dark forest kingdom, where she encounters a black-crowned king and the evil Hieronymus Machine that brainwashes its captives. *Mrs Frisby and the Rats of NIMH* has a more utopian emphasis, as it recounts the efforts of a group of super-intelligent rats to build a self-sufficient and ethical society. *Z is for Zachariah* (1974) follows a girl's passage from adolescence to adulthood in a post-nuclear world. It was completed posthumously by O'Brien's daughter, Jane Leslie Conly, who also wrote sequels to *Mrs Frisby and the Rats of NIMH*. CV

O'Dell, Scott 1898–1989 American writer of children's historical fiction. A native of California, he was born Odell Gabriel Scott and changed his name when he turned to writing. A lifelong writer, he achieved fame only in 1960 with *Island of the Blue Dolphin*, a survival novel and his first children's book. It received the Newbery Medal and O'Dell turned permanently to writing for young readers. Many of his works are set in his beloved Southwest or on the sea. Both *The King's Fifth* (1966), the story of a young cartographer at the time of Coronado in the American Southwest, and *The Black Pearl* (1967), an allegorical tale of good and evil set in Mexico, were selected as Newbery Honour Books, as was *Sing Down the Moon* (1971), based on the true story of the oppression of the Najavos by the American Army. Many of his books describe the plight of the Native Americans at the hands of the European explorers and settlers. He also wrote of people and events in other times and places – the Bible translator William Tyndale in *The Hawk That Dare Not Hunt by Day* (1975), the American Civil War in *The 290* (1986) and St Francis of Assisi in *The Road to Damietta* (1985). In all his works, including his contemporary fiction, O'Dell writes with a firm moral purpose attacking human greed, arrogance and lust for power. His best works have exciting plots and vividly drawn characters, and he is particularly noted for portraying strong females. O'Dell received, in 1972, the prestigious Hans Christian Andersen Award, and in 1984 he established the Scott O'Dell Award for Historical Fiction, which is still awarded annually. The popularity of his works significantly contributed to the revitalisation of historical fiction for young readers in the last half of the 20th century.
DLR

O'Faolain, Eileen 1902–88 Irish author. O'Faolain wrote a number of novels for children, all of which have a strong element of fantasy and folktale, such as *The Little Black Hen* (1940) and the *Miss Pennyfeather* books. Her lucid retellings of Irish legends (see Irish mythology and folklore), *Irish Sagas and Folktales* (1954) and *Children of the Salmon and Other Irish Folktales* (1965), made these stories accessible to contemporary readers. VC

O'Hara, Elizabeth see *Sally* series

O'Hara, Mary (Alsop) 1885–1980 American novelist and screen writer. Born in New Jersey, O'Hara grew up in Brooklyn Heights, New York, and was educated privately in the United States and studied languages and music in Europe. She moved to California to become a screen writer in the 1920s, working on *The Prisoner of Zenda*, *Black Oxen*, Dorothy Canfield's *Homemaker*, *Peg 'o My Heart*, *Turn to the Right* and Cecil B. DeMille's *Braveheart*. Her life in Wyoming yielded material for her novels, first exposed to readers in a summer extension class from Columbia University in New York under Whit Burnett, editor of *Story* magazine. He encouraged her to mine her western experience for young readers in her novels *My Friend Flicka* (1941), *Thunderhead* (1943), *Green Grass of Wyoming* (1946), *The Son of Adam Wyngate* (1952), and *Wyoming Summer* (1963). *My Friend Flicka* was filmed by 20th Century Fox in 1943 and was followed by the sequel *Thunderhead: Son of Flicka* in 1945 and *Green Grass of Wyoming* in 1948. An

Illustration by Pixie O'Harris for her poem 'Brownies'.

ABC TELEVISION series was based on *My Friend Flicka* in 1957. In her autobiography, *Novel-in-the-Making*, she calls herself 'a dramatic writer, not only by nature, but by training'. KSB

O'Harris [Pratt], Pixie [Rhona Olive] 1903–91 Australian illustrator, author and poet, born in Wales, who emigrated in 1920. Her ILLUSTRATIONS first appeared in *Cinderella's Birthday* (1923), but the first book she both wrote and illustrated was *Pearl Pinkie and Sea Greenie* (1935). She illustrated numerous works by other writers and produced 24 of her own, most notably the SCHOOL STORY *The Fortunes of Poppy Treloar* (1941). Her last book was published in 1988. Her FAIRY STORIES, especially, were criticised for their saccharine, usually brightly coloured illustrations and pedestrian texts. However, children enjoyed aspects of her work, especially the Australian settings. She received an award for decorating children's hospitals with murals. JF

O'Keefe, Adelaide see *ORIGINAL POEMS*; see also ANN AND JANE TAYLOR

O'Shea, Pat see *HOUNDS OF THE MORRIGAN, THE*

Oakley, Graham see *CHURCH MICE* SERIES

Obele, Cheryl Ann Nigerian author of juvenile fiction conveying children's concerns with sympathy and humour. *Nwogo the Witch* (1987) discredits the prejudices and fears occasioned by a girl's unusual facial mark as the heroine overcomes her insecurities. *Stepping Out* (1988) concerns a boy's successful effort to withstand pressures to follow prestigious career paths rather than his natural talents. VD

Obernewtyn Chronicles, The Series of four novels by Australian ISOBELLE CARMODY, comprising *Obernewtyn* (1987), *The Farseekers* (1990), *Ashling* (1995) and *The Keeping Place* (1999). These SCIENCE FICTION novels tell of a time following a holocaust, when life, in terms of technology at least, resembles the far simpler times of our ancestors, but where some of the inhabitants, 'The Misfits', figures of mistrust and hatred, have developed mindpowers, such as 'beast-speaking', 'deep probing', and 'techno-empathy', which set them apart. One of these Misfits, Elspeth Gordie, travels to Obernewtyn in a sinister mountain region, originally set up as an institution for experimental work on Misfits. Through the course of the *Chronicles*, Elspeth is involved in numerous situations, which see her pitting her wit and powers and those of her other Misfit friends, against the evil power of the Council and its minions.

Carmody's series explores a society in which being different is dangerous, where 'Misfits' are hated and expelled. Life for a Misfit is cloaked in shadows of menace. Performing noble deeds and rising to defend difference are subtexts underlying this richly mythological story. The great quest of Elspeth is a call for a society in which, according to Carmody herself, 'even a misfit might become a hero'. SKS

Ocean of Stories, The see INDIAN MYTHS, LEGENDS AND FOLKTALES

Odaga, Asenath Bole Kenyan author who has written more than 40 books for children and adults in both English and Luo, her mother tongue. She is a teacher, and has studied history, education and literature at both graduate and postgraduate levels. Some of her books have been translated into Kiswahili (the official language of Tanzania) and other languages. *The Secret of the Monkey Rock* (1966), one of her earliest children's books, tells of a girl, Jumamosi, who goes to look for firewood and returns with a piece of wood from which she can get anything she and members of her family wish to have.

Jande's Ambition (1966), which has been reprinted many times, is the story of a girl keen to go to school at a time when most parents did not allow their daughters to have any education and would rather marry them off early for a dowry. Because of her determination she does well at school and finally becomes a teacher. The story gives inspiration to young people in general and to girls in particular.

In *The Villagers' Son*, written for adolescent readers, a young Kenyan living at the cross-roads between tradition and modernity – where values, hopes and possibilities often conflict – is caught in the dilemma of whether or not to send his son Jako to school. He does so, believing that education is good in itself, and Jako does well. However, Jako refuses to leave school to marry a girl he does not love. He eventually finds his own girlfriend and threatens to commit suicide if the parents and family members impose their choice on him. His wish is granted.

The Diamond Ring (1968) has been reprinted several times. Written for the *Basic English Readers Series*, it tells how Rapemo sets out on an adventure to visit his grandfather. On his way he comes across a thick forest in which there is a beautiful city. There he saves the life of the chief's son, for which the chief's daughter gives him a diamond ring so that they may marry. But Rapemo escapes and returns home where he becomes a great leader of his people.

Odaga has also written *The Hare's Blanket and Other Stories* (1967), three short narratives retelling tales from the oral tradition, suitable for young readers from both urban and rural backgrounds. *Kip Goes to the City* (1977) and *Kip At the Coast* were written for Evans Brothers Ltd, in their *English Readers* series, whose aim is to teach basic vocabulary and develop reading skills.

Odenigbo (1978) Nigerian children's novel by Thomas Chigbo, which looks at the interplay of old and new in colonial society. The hero runs foul of the corrupted traditional leadership and flees to the town, where he has humorous confrontations with strange food, English names and modern technology. VD

Odgers, Sally (Patricia) Farrell 1957– Versatile Australian author who writes across the media, with TELEVISION storylines, novelisations, verse and non-fiction, in addition to children's and adult fiction. *Kingdom for a Pony* (1977), Odgers's first novel, published when she was 20, drew heavily on her familiarity with the rural settings of Tasmania, her birthplace. *Dreadful David* (1984), a PICTUREBOOK, illustrated by CRAIG SMITH, relates in lively humorous verse how high-spirited David spends his day with his grandmother. *Shadowdancers* (1994) demonstrates Odgers's ability to develop complexity of plot in a science FANTASY. As Sally Darrol, she has written BLINKY BILL tie-ins for Yoram Gross Film Studios. Because she is prolific, and writes across a wide range of genres, using a variety of pseudonyms, Odgers' literary output has often been unfairly underrated. HE

Odyssey see CLASSICAL MYTHOLOGY; see also ILLUSTRATION IN CHILDREN'S BOOKS

Ofurum, Helen 1941– Nigerian author of juvenile fiction, born in Scotland of a British mother and Nigerian father. Ofurum's work is part of a trend towards diverse themes of everyday life in the Nigerian children's literature of the 1980s. Her works include *Ihuoma Comes to Stay* (1982), the story of a baby abandoned by her mentally ill mother, and *A Welcome for Chijioke* (1983), in which a boy's search for his long-lost father gains him a new family. VD

Ogoni folktales see KEN SARO-WIWA

Ohu, Charles 1941– Nigerian illustrator of children's books, born in Bukuru, Plateau State. His folk art ILLUSTRATIONS in a colourful PICTUREBOOK on traditional occupations (*Ise Awon Iya ati Baba Nla Wa*, by Agbeke Johnston, 1982) won national and international prizes. Ohu's black-and-white drawings illustrate *One Week, One Trouble*, *Akin Goes to School* and other books. VD

Ohuka, Chukwuemeka Nigerian author for young readers. Ohuka's first two novels, both set in traditional Igbo society, concern the struggle of the rightful heir to regain his father's throne (*The Return of Ikenga*, 1980) and the rescue of the village beauty from a neighbouring chief (*A Bride for the Brave*, 1985). Ohuka's third novel, *The Intruder* (1985), turns to urban crime and the struggle for justice in a modern setting. VD

Okoro, Anezi 1929– Nigerian professor of dermatology and children's writer of SCHOOL STORIES and ADVENTURE STORIES, born in Arondisiogu, Imo State. The colonial era of the 1930s is depicted in *The Village School* (1966) and its sequel *New Broom at Amanzu* (1967). *One Week, One Trouble* (1975) and *Double Trouble* (1986) centre upon the hero's chequered career in secondary school. Four daring children explore fearsome caves in *Febechi in Cave Adventure* (1971) and embark on a dangerous canoe trip in *Febechi Down the Niger* (1975). Okoro has also written a PICTUREBOOK (*Education Is Great*, 1987) and two collections of poetry. VD

Okoye, Ifeoma Nigerian author and educator from Eastern Nigeria. Her three adult novels on such themes as a young woman's coming to terms with illegitimacy (for example, *Chimere*, 1992) are popular with adolescents. Her juvenile novel, *Village Boy!* (1981), describes a rural boy's struggle for academic and social success in a sophisticated urban school. Her most popular PICTUREBOOKS feature Eze, a small boy who learns the benefits of sensible behaviour in *Only Bread for Eze*, *No Supper for Eze*, and *No School for Eze* (1980).

Illustration by Narelle Oliver from *Leaf Tail*.

Everyday experiences are also portrayed in *Adventures of Tulu the Little Monkey* (1980) and other recent titles for beginning readers. VD

Okoye, Mary Author of juvenile DETECTIVE FICTION, British by birth and Nigerian by marriage. Her books feature the Secret Council, a group of six friends who uncover the villain blocking progress on the community's girls' secondary school (*Kukoro-Koo*, 1982), and help bring a gang of robbers to book while assisting an injured palm-wine tapper (*Nwankwo and the Secret Council*, 1986). VD

Okpi, Kalu 1947– Nigerian novelist and broadcaster, born in Abam, Imo State, best known for his DETECTIVE FICTION for young adults. His earliest novels (*The Smugglers* and *On the Road*) look at the criminal underworld, as does his ninth novel, *The Oil Conspiracy* (1988). Political intriguc is the subject of *Coup!* (1982) and *The South African Affair* (1982). *The Politician* (1983) presents a man obsessed with gaining power at any cost. More recently Okpi has turned to the theme of love in *Love Changes Everything*. VD

Old Possum's Book of Practical Cats (1939) Poems by T.S. Eliot, the only volume of Eliot's poetry accessible to the young. Eliot was fascinated by the manners and habits of cats – Ezra Pound had given him the affectionate nickname, Old Possum. Eliot created some truly memorable and amusing feline characters including Macavity, the master criminal, and Skimbleshanks, the railway cat, in amusing, well-crafted poems. He was lucky in two early illustrators, Nicholas Bentley and EDWARD GOREY. Andrew Lloyd Webber adapted the poems for his musical *Cats*, one of the most successful West End shows of the 1980s. MCCS

Oldfield, Jenny see *ANIMAL ARK* SERIES

Oliver, Narelle 1960– Australian author-illustrator, whose love of the natural environment is reflected in her PICTUREBOOKS, which depict a fascinating variety of less well-known wildlife species going about their real-life activities in real-life settings. Oliver's command of her preferred medium, linocuts, is evident in *Leaf Tail* (1989), *High Above the Sea* (1991), *The Best Beak in Boonaroo Bay* (1993) and *The Hunt* (1995), winner of the 1996 AUSTRALIAN CHILDREN'S BOOK COUNCIL Picturebook of the Year Award, in which a Tawny Frogmouth owl, hunting for food for her hungry chicks, becomes the hunted. *Sand Swimmers: The Secret Life of Australia'a Dead Heart* (1999) is an in-depth work embracing the natural, indigenous and European histories of Central Australia, illustrated with Oliver's superb linocuts in soft earth tones. Oliver bases her work on close observation, and uses scientifically accurate names for the animals and plants. She has also illustrated GARY CREW'S *The Well* (1996), and is featured in the anthologies, *The Bunyip and the Night* (1994) and *Swamp Soup* (1995). SAM

Omolo, Leo Odera Kenyan writer and journalist. He is the author of *Triumph* (1968), about his school days from the age of seven, and of *The Talking Devil* (1969), a delightful collection of African tales for children in mid-primary school. ABO

On the Edge (1985) Novel by GILLIAN CROSS offering its readers no comforting solutions.The young protagonist in this novel is kidnapped by a bizarre pressure group wanting to get at his mother, a public figure whose beliefs they oppose. Exposed to their brutal psychological tactics, he is forced to confront his own identity and beliefs. Stereotypes are challenged and opposing ideologies conflict in a tense narrative that deliberately confounds reassuring expectations and explores the possibility of coping in an adult world which is revealed as anarchic and unstable. Although the protagonist is male, a young woman is crucial to the resolution of the drama. EAG

Onadipe, Kola 1923–89 Nigerian author of children's books, born in Western Nigeria. His experience as a school principal led to later careers in writing and publishing for children. Onadipe's many books are varied and popular with children. *The Adventures of Souza* (1963) portrays boyish pranks in a rural setting. Nineteenth-century slavery in Northern Nigeria is the subject of *The Boy Slave* (1966) and its sequel *The Return of Shettima* (1972). Onadipe's early books for younger readers address traditional beliefs in heart-warming stories of an abandoned twin baby saved by a childless woman (*Koku Baboni*, 1965) and a lost girl rescued by a presumed witch (*Sugar Girl*, 1964). *The Magic Land of the Shadows* (1970) is a FANTASY based on the orphan theme. In 1980 Onadipe began writing a number of modern stories with familial themes and a strong moral tone (*Sunny Boy*, *The Pot of Gold*, *Sweet Mother*, all in 1980, *Beloved Daughters*, 1985, *The Mysterious Twins*, 1986). Onadipe is also the author of plays, short stories, biographical sketches and a fictional travelogue of Nigeria. VD

Once And Future King, The (1958) Historical fantasy by T.H. WHITE which combines three earlier books, *The Sword In The Stone* (1938), *The Queen Of Air and Darkness* (originally *The Witch In The Wood*, USA, 1939; UK, 1940) and *The Ill-Made Knight* (USA, 1940; UK, 1941), with a fourth story *The Candle In The Wind*. A 20th-century retelling of the legends of ARTHUR, its status as a children's book is dubious, resting perhaps on the fantastic and often light-hearted treatment of Arthur's childhood in the first book, with debts to LEWIS CARROLL and KENNETH GRAHAME. A distinctive mélange of folklore, natural history and country sports, with intricate details of hunting, jousting and archery, colours this account. The subsequent three books become steadily gloomier in their treatment of politics, war, psychology and sexuality. An apparent attraction for children may be the vividly pictorial medieval setting; yet White's romantic descriptions are punctured time and again by irony and scepticism. Sanitised versions of the text were the musical *Camelot* (1960) and a DISNEY cartoon of *The Sword In The Stone* (1963). White originally planned a conclusion to this work, *The Book Of Merlyn*, posthumously published in 1977. PC

One Hundred and One Dalmatians (1956) Picaresque ANIMAL STORY by DODIE SMITH set in London and Suffolk. Pongo and his wife, Missus, a pair of human-owning dalmatians, realise the aptly named and fur-obsessed Cruella de Vil is behind the theft of their first litter of sixteen puppies. In order to 'make England safe for dalmatians' they journey to Hell Hall in Suffolk to rescue their offspring and pause on their return, accompanied by 81 extra dalmatian puppies, to destroy Cruella financially. That the book has been filmed twice by DISNEY is a measure of its appeal, but it is difficult to capture on film the novel's full humour. This is created through the wry observations of the author and some appalling puns, as well as the more obvious comic situations and slapstick. The comedy is balanced by serious moments as when Pongo and Missus are mistaken for ghosts, and the Dearlys, the dalmatians' beloved human pets, anxiously await their return on Christmas Eve. Part of the book's appeal lies in the way in which, on one level, all the animals live in a realistic, if somewhat idealised world and yet manage to live a secret life, something most pet-owners find believable. JEG

Oneal, Zibby (Elizabeth) 1934– American writer of critically acclaimed novels for young adults. Growing up in her birthplace, Omaha, Nebraska, Oneal developed interests in writing and painting. She took creative-writing classes in college but began publishing only after creating stories for her own children. A suspense novel and two PICTUREBOOKS preceded her best-known works. The publication of *The Language of Goldfish* (1980), an exploration of 13-year-old Carrie Stokes's mental illness and suicide attempt, earned praise for its perceptive portrayal of emotional turmoil. *A Formal Feeling* (1982) handles with equal sensitivity the struggles of 16-year-old Anne Cameron to accept her mother's sudden death and father's remarriage. *In Summer Light* (1985) explores 17-year-old Kate Brewer's need to forge her own future as an artist rather than remain in the shadow of her painter father. This work, which won the BOSTON GLOBE-HORN BOOK AWARD, evokes the light and colour of summer on a Massachusetts island. In all three novels, Oneal examines the difficult transition from childhood to adulthood that requires changes in family relationships. Although Oneal has written works of fiction and non-fiction for younger readers, her reputation rests on her finely crafted YOUNG ADULT FICTION. KKP

Onobrakpeya, Bruce 1932– Distinguished Nigerian artist and award-winning illustrator of children's books. He has used pen-and-ink drawings and block engraving to illustrate three titles by CYPRIAN EKWENSI, as well as *Sugar Girl* (1964) and *The Magic Land of the Shadows* (1970) by KOLA ONADIPE, and *Akpan and the Smugglers* (1965) by ROSEMARY UWEMEDIMO. VD

Opie Collection see COLLECTIONS OF CHILDREN'S BOOKS

Opie, Peter [Mason] 1918–82 and **Opie, Iona [Margaret Balfour]** 1923– Eminent British collectors of early and rare books, toys and games for children. Their scholarly partnership of over 40 years established, in their edited anthologies, new standards for the study of children's literature and the social history of childhood. *I SAW ESAU* (1947) distinguished the children's own tradition from the adult-transmitted verses in the authoritative *Oxford Dictionary of Nursery Rhymes* (1951), the foundation volume of the Opies' reputation. In contrast, *The Oxford Nursery Rhyme Book* (1955), with its 800 'rhymes and ditties' was deliberately designed with WOOD ENGRAVINGS for adults and children to read and recite together. The most popular anthology, *The Puffin Book of Nursery Rhymes* (1963), has both traditional favourites and less commonly known verses. When it appeared as the first result of a ten-year study, *THE LORE AND LANGUAGE OF SCHOOLCHILDREN* (1959) stirred up incredulity about the provenance and persistence of this subversive literature, but *Children's Games in Street and Playground* (1969) and *The Singing Game* (1985) confirmed its oral transmission. To underwrite these studies and other acquisitions, the Opies edited a number of anthologies for Oxford University Press, including *THE OXFORD BOOK OF CHILDREN'S VERSE* (1973) and *The Classic Fairy Tales* (1974), and exhibited selected treasures from their unrivalled archive.

After Peter Opie's death, a public appeal, which included the publication of *Tail Feathers from Mother Goose* (1988), secured the book collection for the Bodleian Library. Iona's distinctive work continues, adapted to the more informal reading of a wider public. *The People in the Playground* (1993) is a masterpiece of observation; *My Very First Mother Goose*, (1996) with pictures by Rosemary Wells, pays tribute to children's resilience. The triumph of the insights and innovative scholarship of the Opies lies in their transformation of what had long been thought of as the least part of children's language into treasuries of pleasure and enlightenment. MM

see also NURSERY RHYMES

Opio, Janet Ugandan writer of children's stories in English suitable for use in urban and rural primary schools. They develop comprehension and teach cultural and moral values. Both *The Hare and His Disco Dance* and *The Witch and Her Daughter* are interesting books, the former a modernised version of an ancient traditional tale. ABO

Optic, Oliver [William Taylor Adams] 1822–97 American writer of over 125 books under various pseudonyms. Born and brought up in Massachusetts, he spent some years as a teacher before achieving success with *The Boat Club* (1855), a story about boys learning the value of discipline as members of a rowing team, in contrast with some 'unruly fellows' who remain incorrigible. Optic often grouped six books together into a series, such as the *Blue and Grey* series and the *Young America Abroad* series. Although often criticised for their stilted language and sensationalism, his books achieved wide popularity. FEA

Oram, Hiawyn Born in Johannesburg, Oram moved to London. She is the author of numerous PICTUREBOOKS, the best-known being *ANGRY ARTHUR* (1982), illustrated by SATOSHI KITAMURA. Other books created in collaboration with this illustrator are *In The Attic* (1984) and *A Boy Wants a Dinosaur* (1990). TONY ROSS provides the illustrations for, amongst others, *Reckless Ruby* (1992) and *The Second Princess* (1994). Whilst her earlier books create witty stories around imaginative, often naughty children, her latest work is packed with animal characters such as in the three works illustrated by SUSAN VARLEY, *Badger's Bad Mood* (1997), *Mole's Moon* (1997) and *Princess Camomile Gets Her Way* (1998). RUTH BROWN was the illustrator for *The Wise Doll* (1997), an excellent Baba Yaga tale. Her stories provide irony for the adult reader and pure pleasure for the child. JHD

Orbis Sensualium Pictus (1658) Written by the Czech philosopher, teacher and educational theorist John Amos Comenius, this was one of the earliest PICTUREBOOKS especially designed for children. It consists of a series of ILLUSTRATIONS depicting various aspects of the natural world, human industry and endeavour, each with a brief parallel explanatory text in Latin and a vernacular language. The book was first printed in Nuremberg, an English language translation being published a year later by the grammar-school teacher John Hoole. In the English version the original Kreutzberger woodcuts were reproduced as metal engravings, allowing finer detail and greater clarity in design to be incorporated. The book, whose production costs made it initially very expensive, was used in schools and in some noble households largely as a practical and effective aid to learning Latin. Comenius designed the book as part of a much wider, idealistic enterprise, whose goal was a universal system of education, 'pansophy', which would profoundly reform the whole of society. The pictures were incorporated, not just as a pleasant aid to reading, but as the cornerstone of a programme meant to revolutionise teaching by relating all learning, from infancy onwards, to its basis in sense experience. DWh

Orczy, Baroness (Emma Magdalena Rosalia Marie Josepha Barbara) see *SCARLET PIMPERNEL* SERIES; see also ADULT FICTION; LITERATURE WITHIN CHILDREN'S LITERATURE

Ordinary Princess, The (1980) Original story by the British writer, M.M. Kaye. Told in a self-consciously FAIRY TALE style, this is the story of what happens when one is rash enough to invite fairies to be godmothers. Princess Amethyst is the perfect royal baby until a bad-tempered fairy gives her an unusual christening present: the gift of being ordinary. Although one of its consequences is that she is too plain ever to be considered a proper princess, she enjoys her gift and the fun it brings. The requisite happy ending manages to show that even ugly ducklings who never become swans may find love and happiness. AMN

Oriental Moralist, The, or Beauties of the Arabian Nights Entertainments see *ARABIAN NIGHTS' ENTERTAINMENTS*; see also ABRIDGEMENT

Original Ditties from the Nursery see *TWEEDLEDUM AND TWEEDLEDEE*

Original Poems for Infant Minds (1804) Collection of poetry by ANN and JANE TAYLOR and 'other young persons', who included their brother, Isaac, and Adelaide O'Keefe, writer of jaunty verse of the cautionary type. *Rhymes for the Nursery* (1806) and its precursor were the most influential collections of verse for children in the first half of the 19th century. Its many imitators included CHARLES and MARY LAMB's *POETRY FOR CHILDREN* (1809). The Taylors were typical of their period in producing moral tales in verse, though their messages were less didactic and kinder than their predecessors'. Their range included tender cradle songs and joyful nature poetry. Best known is 'The Star' (Jane Taylor), an exquisitely simple rhyme. MCCS

Original Stories from Real Life (1788) Moral treatise for children by MARY WOLLSTONECRAFT, judiciously spliced with brief exemplary stories. The book depicts two 'shamefully ignorant' young girls, Mary and Caroline, whose faults, by modern standards, seem venial. They are placed in the charge of the severe yet apparently inspiring Mrs Mason, a paragon of virtue herself, who uses reason and example to direct her charges towards values which will harness their best selves. Mrs Mason's lessons are taken from life experience and stories, often with grim and tragic outcomes ameliorated only by personal intervention and charity. Though her stories encompass joy in understanding the nature of the God-given world, their more stringent purpose is to move young minds away from selfish impulses and enable them to cope rationally with suffering and injustice. The stories stop short of the political perspectives developed in Wollstonecraft's later work but the morality expressed is progressive, though severe, and themes of social oppression figure strongly. William Blake responded sympathetically to the stories, and the 1791 edition, reissued by Joseph Johnson, contains illustrations by him which considerably enhance the work. Despite similarities with conventional moral tales, the *Original Stories* are, as Harvey Darton judged, 'most determinedly original'. DWh

see also *SONGS OF INNOCENCE*

Orlando: illustration by Kathleen Hale.

***Orlando, the Marmalade Cat* series** Created by author-illustrator KATHLEEN HALE in 1938, Orlando must be the best-known cat in children's literature. With his wife Grace and the three kittens Pansy, Blanche and Tinkle, he appeared in 18 PICTUREBOOKS setting new standards for draughtsmanship and colour reproduction. The world this happy family lives in is an amiable amalgam of animals and humans, where horses wear pyjamas at night but get on with orthodox ploughing and carting during the day. Plots vary from the lovingly mundane – working on a farm, going on a seaside camping holiday – to trips to the moon. The giant format of the early books was another striking feature. Huge double-page spreads presented children with a feast of individual, humorous detail which gradually came together into an integrated whole after repeated viewing. Sometimes characters are hidden away, with a kitten merging into a sack of onions or only discernible as a pair of eyes. There are also constant changes in perspective. Some stories take a cat's-eye view of human feet and legs pounding along a pavement. Turn a page, and readers are now in the position of a bird looking down on what is happening below.

Most of these books were critical rather than popular successes. The early giant format, however popular with children, made them difficult for libraries or bookshops to stock. Some of the references (parents called 'Pater' and 'Mater'), were socially exclusive, and the written texts occasionally ramble inconclusively away from a well-ordered story-line. But their restless energy and generous swirling colours can still make an almost physical impact on young readers. Originally composed in seven different colours, the first book, *Orlando (The Marmalade Cat): A Camping Holiday*, ran into problems with its publisher. All the diminutive, accompanying character – rabbits, snails, beetles and grasshoppers – had so pushed up printing costs that Hale was told they would have to go. As she writes in her autobiography *A Slender Reputation* (1994), 'I refused to allow this, because I knew how much children love detail.' Instead she learned how to manage lithographic techniques for herself, retaining both colour and detail. The amount of work entailed, however, was enormous: it took four to five months working seven hours a day, seven days a week, to produce the 128 plates needed for a 32-page book. A number of these titles remain in print today. The image they convey of a traditional rural countryside, with chickens wandering around every farmyard, is full of nostalgia for lost times still existing within living memory. Orlando himself, although an admirably conscientious husband and father, now seems rather over-dominant, particularly where his wife Grace is concerned. But elsewhere swaggering gypsies, red-faced market traders and immaculate fashion models make up a fascinating human cast in these books. Such characters are often balanced by incidental drawings of outsize insects shown crawling over the bottom edges of pages, happily out of perspective and all part of the infectious unpredictability of these cheerfully inventive and utterly original picturebooks. NT

see also LITHOGRAPHY

Orlev, Uri (Jerzy Orlowski) 1931– Prize-winning Israeli author of realistic juvenile novels. Orlev was born into a well-to-do and assimilated Warsaw family but considers the Holocaust his childhood. Interned in Bergen-Belsen from 1943 to 1945, Orlev survived by reading, writing poetry and telling stories. Since the war, he has made his home in Israel, where he completed his schooling and is now married and the father of four children. Finding he could no longer write poetry, he turned to fiction, including 25 juvenile books, and has received the most prestigious international prizes for literature: three Mildred Batchelder awards and the 1985 Honour Award of the Jane Addams Peace Association. In 1996, he received the HANS CHRISTIAN ANDERSEN AWARD in recognition of his entire body of work. Though he now writes only in Hebrew, his novels have been translated into English, most notably by Hillel Halkin, and are published world-wide. In his earliest biographical novel, *The Lead Soldiers* (1956), Orlev returns to his childhood in the Holocaust, describing how two young protagonists respond to the horrendous events around them by escaping into imagination through games and stories. *The Island on Bird Street* (1984) is the story of a boy's survival. *The Man from the Other Side* (1991) is the memoir of a boy who lives through the Warsaw ghetto uprising, but unlike some of Orlev's earlier titles, it is a story of character and moral conflict as well as action. *Lydia, Queen of Palestine* (1993) describes a 10-year-old's attempts to understand her parents' divorce amid the chaos of war. *The Lady with the Hat* (1995) is concerned with Jewish post-war settlement in Palestine and the effects of the war on a group of teenage survivors. In spite of his own hardships and those of his characters, Orlev is able to retain a basically optimistic view of humanity both in life and story. MS

see also WAR STORIES

Orme, David 1948– English poet and anthologist. Orme has published poetry collections such as *Heroes and Villains* (1995) and edited many anthologies, appealing particularly to reluctant boy readers, on themes such as soccer (*Ere We Go!*, 1993), rap (*Doin Me Ed In*, 1993) and city life (*Toughie Toffee*, 1989). ML

Ormerod, Jan 1946– Illustrator and author of more than 60 books for children. As a child in Australia, Jan Ormerod drew compulsively and learnt from the draughtsmanship in English girl's ANNUALS and American comic books.

Her first published book was *Sunshine* (1981) which won the MOTHER GOOSE AWARD in 1982. The inspiration and the subject of this and much of her work is the emotional closeness of parents and children in the unremarkable events of everyday family life. Without text, it depicts the early morning in the life of a young girl and her parents. The girl wakes up. She goes to her sleeping father in bed. He gets up, makes her breakfast and burns the toast. They take tea to the sleeping mother. The father reads the paper. The girl brushes her teeth and goes to the lavatory. Over four pages, she gets dressed. Her mother and father realise it is late, get up and hurriedly dress. She leaves for school with her mother. The events, so described, are commonplace. What makes them compelling and moving is the care with which they are chosen, the accuracy with which they are observed, the simplicity with which they are drawn and the precision with which they are structured and placed on the page: a process of observation, recording and editing. These – the subject and the method – are features which characterise all of Ormerod's work (except where unsympathetic editors, one suspects, have interfered with it). *101 Things To Do*

With A Baby (1984) is illustrated in watercolour and brush line and depicts in the same way the activities, from morning until bedtime, of a baby and his older sister.

Ormerod has also illustrated the work of contemporary authors. *Two Bears And Joe* (1995), by PENELOPE LIVELY, is drawn in pen-and-ink with heavy CROSS-HATCHING and near-monochrome watercolour and depicts a day in the life of a small boy who wakes to find two bear cubs in his bedroom. *Sky Dancer* (1996), with Jack Bushnell, is set in the countryside of New England in winter and tells of the relationship between a young girl and a wild hawk. The subjects are fantasies. The ILLUSTRATIONS of the characters and settings are more elaborate. They are based, though, on the same close observation. Underlying them is the same simplicity, sense of space and design. Because of this, they retain the same credibility as the everyday domestic stories: a fantastic situation peopled by recognisable children and adults. Here, as in all her work, Ormerod shows the difference between what is real and what is merely literal. Her illustrations of traditional stories and FAIRY TALES show the same qualities: *THE STORY OF CHICKEN LICKEN* (1985), *PETER PAN* (1987), *THE FROG PRINCE* (1990). In *To Baby With Love, Rhymes For Babies* (1994), the illustrations are broader (gouache rather than watercolour) and the colours are brighter. The observation and characterisation are as acute as ever. In 1997, Ormerod produced *Rock-A-Baby*, a pop-up book. RC

see also *BABY SERIES*

Orr, Wendy (Ann) 1953– Canadian-born Australian writer of over 20 PICTUREBOOKS, junior and young adult novels, many published internationally. Since her first picturebook, *Amanda's Dinosaur* (1988), Orr's writing has developed in its eloquence and power, especially since she took up full-time writing after a serious car accident, an experience she drew on for *Peeling the Onion* (1996), Honour Book in the CHILDREN'S BOOK COUNCIL OF AUSTRALIA Book of the Year Awards (1997). Anna, on the threshold of independence, is permanently impaired in a car accident and has to deal not only with pain, but with a new identity of self – 'The blackness is swallowing me and I know that if I can't fight it the me will be gone and the blackness will go on without end.' Through a series of 'onion' poems, the reader shares in Anna's courage and growth.

A keen observer, Orr creates unique, memorable, well-rounded contemporary characters in her realistic novels, such as tough Mrs Pugh, fiercely independent in old age, who is set alongside the young Linda, in *Leaving it to You* (1992). Touches of FANTASY ripple through *Ark in the Park* (1994), winner of the Children's Book Council of Australia Book of the Year: Younger Readers Award (1995), as lonely Sophie befriends the warm-hearted Noahs in their aptly designed pet shop in the park. Kerry Millard's lively black-and-white cartoon illustrations add to the humour. The special relationship between a boy and his grandpa is exquisitely depicted in the PICTUREBOOK *Arabella* (1998), with its lyrical spare text and KIM GAMBLE's haunting watercolour illustrations. Other titles include *Mind Blowing* (1994), *Yasou Nikki* (1995), *Dirtbikes* (1995) and *Paradise Palace* (1997). JAP

Orwell, George see ANIMALS IN FICTION; *'THE BIG FIVE'*; see also FABLES; SCHOOL STORIES

Orwin, Joanna 1944– New Zealand writer, whose small output disguises her importance. Orwin's first two novels, *Ihaka and the Summer Wandering* (1982) and *Ihaka and the Prophecy* (1984), are among the few to be located in the earliest period of New Zealand's settled history, around 900 years ago. Showing a rare depth of scholarship and empathy with the time, as well as telling interesting and relevant stories, the books follow the maturing of Ihaka from child to apprentice stone-worker to *tohunga* (skilled expert). Hunting, adze-making, tree-felling, ritual ceremony, and the pattern of lives lived close to the natural and spiritual worlds, are combined to create a satisfying and believable world picture. *The Guardian of the Land* (1985), which won the New Zealand Children's Book of the Year Award, moves between the present and the past as new friends, David and Rua, seek a lost pendant and in the process forge closer bonds between Maori and pakeha. Time shifts in a similar way in *Watcher in the Forest* (1987) when, during a tramping trip, Jen is chosen to find and replace a sacred piece of greenstone. BN

Osborne Collection see COLLECTIONS OF CHILDREN'S BOOKS; see also LILLIAN H. SMITH

O'Sullivan, Mark 1954– Irish writer whose first novel, *Melody for Nora* (1994), is set during the Irish Civil War. His writing career has latterly focused on books for young adults, most notably *White Lies* (1997) and *Angels Without Wings* (1997), both winners of READING ASSOCIATION OF IRELAND AWARDS. *SILENT STONES* won the CBI/ BISTO BOOK AWARD (1999/2000). VC

Other Award see AWARDS AND MEDALS; BIAS IN CHILDREN'S BOOKS; see also CRITICAL APPROACHES TO CHILDREN'S LITERATURE

Otis, James (James Otis Kaler) 1848–1912 American writer of boys' stories. Born in Maine, Otis began his writing career as a reporter for the *Boston*

Illustration by W.A. Rogers from *Toby Tyler; or Ten Weeks with the Circus* by James Otis.

Journal. He used his early experiences as a publicity man for a circus to write his first and best-known children's book, *Toby Tyler, or, Ten Weeks with a Circus* (1881). He was a prolific contributor of stories and serials to major children's periodicals such as *HARPER'S YOUNG PEOPLE* and *ST NICHOLAS*. He worked for *FRANK LESLIE'S BOYS' AND GIRLS' WEEKLY*, known for its sensationalised, moralistic fiction, and wrote over 100 books of historical and war adventures. These have now fallen into obscurity, but *Toby Tyler* went through 30 editions and remains in print. Dubbed an American *Pinocchio*, the book succeeded by combining a grimly realistic portrait of circus life with a CAUTIONARY TALE on rejecting the simple life and safety of home. Much of the book's appeal for children springs from the pathos surrounding Mr Stubbs, Toby's monkey companion. Otis's work is historically significant as a representation of the moralism and didacticism that American culture transmitted to its youth at the turn of the 19th century. DAC

Otterbury Incident, The, (1948/58) Novel by C. Day Lewis, illustrated by EDWARD ARDIZZONE and based on the plot of a French film, *Nous les Gosses*, shown in Britain as *Us Kids*. The eponymous 'Incident' is a bomb-site, from where two gangs of boys foil a robbery and earn the praise of their headmaster when their dogged detective work leads to the capture of the villains. Despite Lewis's ignorance of working-class speech, it was one of the best of the many post-war stories representing children as heroic defenders of the law and using their 'street wisdom' to assist a grateful police force. VW

Our Exploits at West Poley (1952) Thomas Hardy's only attempt to write for children, published in book form nearly 70 years after its original submission for serial publication. Set in the Mendip Hills and adhering to the 19th-century ADVENTURE STORY genre, this tale recounts the exploits of the youthful narrator and his companions who struggle to rectify complications that arise after they divert an underground water course from one community to another. Such disruption of natural elements threatens local livelihoods and Hardy's 'sufficiently apparent moral' is evident as the resultant physical and philosophical dilemmas are confronted and reconciled. CMN

Our Young Folks: An Illustrated Magazine for Boys and Girls (1865–74) American children's periodical. It was edited by JOHN TOWNSEND TROWBRIDGE, Gail Hamilton [Mary Abigail Dodge] and LUCY LARCOM (Hamilton resigned in 1868). The magazine reflected its New England origins, being frankly pro-Union and anti-slavery in its sympathies. Readers were encouraged to be honest, brave, hardworking, charitable and cheerful. The standard of writing was high, contributors including Thomas Bailey Aldrich, Harriet Beecher Stowe, JOHN GREENLEAF WHITTIER, LOUISA MAY ALCOTT, MAYNE REID, HENRY WADSWORTH LONGFELLOW and CHARLES DICKENS, whose 'The Magic Fishbone' was published in 1868. Among the illustrators was WINSLOW HOMER. Young readers eagerly participated in many interactive departments including a 'Letter Box', a 'Young Competitors' feature, and a 'Mutual Improvement Corner'. Trowbridge contributed a number of highly readable and enormously popular serials, including *Jack Hazard and his Fortunes*. In 1874, much to Trowbridge's regret, *Our Young Folks* was sold to Scribner and Company, and merged with their distinguished new periodical for children, *ST NICHOLAS*. Happily, Trowbridge and many of the best writers who had appeared in *Our Young Folks* continued to write for the new magazine. SRG

Out of The Hitler Time (1971–8) Trilogy of autobiographical novels written by Judith Kerr, author of the popular *Mog* PICTUREBOOKS, which describe life for a German Jewish family from the early 1930s onwards.

The first and best-known novel, *When Hitler Stole Pink Rabbit* (1971), describes the life of Anna and her family as the Nazis come to power in Germany in the 1930s. Anna's father is a famous Jewish writer and when the Nazi regime announces a price on his head the family have to flee Germany, leaving behind Anna's beloved pink rabbit. Later novels tell of the family's subsequent life, first in France and then in England, where Anna herself thrives, although her parents find the transition difficult and her brother is rounded up as an enemy alien. The second novel, *The Other Way Round* (1975), describes the teenage Anna's changing relationship with her parents as she gains independence while they struggle with the new language and customs. The third novel, *A Small Person Far Away* (1978), moves forward in time; Anna's father is now dead and Anna herself is married. She returns to Germany in the middle of the Suez crisis to visit her mother who has tried to kill herself. The book re-establishes the strong sense of family found in the earlier novels, ending with Anna looking forward to the birth of her own child. Anna's changing perspective as she grows older is shown gradually and convincingly so that younger readers can understand the problems she faces in the later novels. The books can be read by a child who has no previous knowledge of the Holocaust since Anna herself is only nine when the books begin and has no understanding of the possible ramifications of the Third Reich's rise to power. Throughout the series complex situations are described in simple language which can be read at different levels as the reader grows older. However, to a reader familiar with the history of Germany during the 1930s, the family's inevitable need to escape Germany is rendered all the more potent by Anna's ignorance of the horrors in store for the German Jews.

Anna's own strength of character and the strength of the entire family unit, even in these terrible conditions, help to give the trilogy unity over the different settings and the long time-gap between the first and last novel. In the second novel Anna faces separation from her parents for the first time and declares, 'I've never minded being a refugee before. In fact I've loved it... But now I'm so terribly frightened... that I might really feel like one.' The poverty and hardship in which the family find themselves throughout Anna's childhood are lessened by their courage, optimism and humour in the face of both major national disaster and minor personal difficulties. It seems hardly surprising, therefore, that by the final book Anna herself should be about to take on the strong parental role for which the second novel had prepared her. KA

see also WAR STORIES

Outfit, The Series by ROBERT SWINDELLS, including *The Secret of Weeping Wood* (1993), *We Didn't Mean To, Honest* (1994), *Kidnap at Denton Farm* (1995), *The Ghosts of Givenham Keep* (1996), *A Peril in the Mist* (1997) and *The Strange Tale of Ragger Bill* (1998). Group ADVENTURE STORIES with four children and a dog – Jillo (nine) and sister Titch (seven), farmer's daughters; Shaz (nine), a Pakistani boy living with his grandfather; Mickey (ten) and Raider, living in a caravan with their father frequently absent. Cliché is avoided through the representation of responsible adults, the realistic depiction of children's resourcefulness, unstereotyped gender roles, multi-ethnicity and an undogmatic ecological emphasis. Vivid dialogue, tight plotting and short chapters make them good first novels for under-tens. DCH

Outhwaite, Ida Rentoul 1888–1960 Australian illustrator and author, whose reputation rests largely on two of her dozen works, *Elves and Fairies* (1916), written by her sister Annie, and *The Enchanted Forest* (1921), a collaboration with her husband, Grenbry. Criticised for not using recognisably Australian settings and creatures, Outhwaite, instead created her own idealised and romantic world, gave it an obvious Art Nouveau flavour, and filled it with beautiful young fairies and an array of animals, most of which were European. Less successful than her illustrations were her accompanying texts, which tended towards the sentimental. JF

Outside Over There (1981) The third and most complex of MAURICE SENDAK'S PICTUREBOOK trilogy, and what he calls his symbolic portrait of Mozart's life. Ida goes 'outside over there' to rescue her baby sister from sinister faceless goblins who have kidnapped her. Ida's adventure includes an Orphic descent into underworld caverns, where she outwits and transforms the goblins into a harmless dancing stream, and culminates in her recognition of how much she loves her sister. The kidnap and quest may be understood as a day-dream, Ida's interior journey to overcome her own destructive feelings of sibling antagonism, jealousy, desire for her father, and resentment. The expiation of her guilt, and hard-won acceptance of her lot as the older child, are accomplished through the music Ida plays on her wonder horn, or hears from her father's song, accompanied by Mozart's clavichord. The prime literary source is probably the GRIMM BROTHERS tale, *The Goblins*. To complement the country of source, and the historical period of Mozart's life, Sendak adopts the visionary style and iconography of the Northern Romantic artists of the late 18th century, especially Philipp Otto Runge and Caspar David Friedrich. William Blake (see *THE SONGS OF INNOCENCE*) is another major influence. Sendak creates for Ida a dream-world that is both real and intensely surreal, in finely painted naturalistic detailing, through an innovative use of perspective and the disconcerting effect of playing with the scale of figures so as to destroy their natural relationships. JD

see also IN THE NIGHT KITCHEN; WHERE THE WILD THINGS ARE

Outsiders, The see S. E. HINTON

Ovbiagele, Helen Nigerian writer of YOUNG ADULT FICTION born in the 1940s in Benin City. Her novels explore love and the often troubled relationships between women and men. *A Fresh Start* (1982) concerns the misunderstandings brought about by differences in class. The heroine of *Evbu My Love* (1980) loses one boyfriend when she becomes a call-girl to fund her education, but then finds a more understanding one. *You Never Know* (1982) describes an idyllic love relationship gone wrong in middle age. Ovbiagele's later novels include *Forever Yours* and *Schemers*. VD

Over The Water (1987) Novel set in Ireland, by Irish author Maude Casey. An English girl from an Irish family goes home to Ireland for the holidays. The death of her grandfather and her own adolescence encourage Mary to re-examine family relationships in the light of political and familial history. KA

Overton, Jenny 1942– British author born in Surrey, England, and educated at the Guildford County Grammar School and at Girton College, Cambridge. Most of her working life was spent in the field of publishing, and it was while with Macmillan that she began writing her first book for children. Overton's output is small but of a uniformly high quality. Her four books all demonstrate an interest in history and literature. *Creed Country* (1969) and its sequel *The Nightwatch Winter* (1973) examine the complex dynamics of being part of a huge family and establishing relationships outside that circle. This examination is intertwined with the discovery of old letters in the first book, and with the putting together of a cycle of old Mystery plays in the sequel. *The Thirteen Days of Christmas* (1972) and *The Ship from Simnel Street* (1986), both written in a simpler style, are set in the 17th and 18th centuries respectively. Overton weaves story around the bones of old songs and NURSERY RHYME, and these works speak both about the endurance of traditions as well as the making of them. SA

see also NEGLECTED WORKS

Owen, Gareth 1936– English poet, novelist and dramatist. Raised in Lancashire and eventually becoming a teacher, he is best known for his four collections of poetry, including *SALFORD ROAD* (1979) and *Song of the City* (1985), a *SIGNAL* POETRY AWARD winner. His poems characteristically use children's voices to recreate childhood experiences. ML

Owen, Wilfred see *THE RATTLE BAG*

Owl and the Pussy-Cat, The see EDWARD LEAR; see also NONSENSE VERSE

Owl Magazine (from 1976) A science and nature magazine for children. Founded by Canadian publisher Annabel Slaight, *Owl* features articles, puzzles, jokes, comics and science experiments for children. Its mission is to educate young readers, aged 8 to 12, about their environment. Winner of numerous awards, including Canada's Magazine of the Year Award, *Owl* has set the standard for child-centred nature and science publications. *Hibou* and *L'Orsa* are the French- and Italian-language versions of the magazine. Related publications include *Chirp* for preschoolers, *Chickadee* for 3- to 8-year-old children, and *Family* for parents. *Owlkids Online* is an INTERNET site that supplements and promotes the print publications. EAM

Owl Moon see JANE YOLEN; JOHN SCHOENHERR

Owl Service, The (1967) and ***Red Shift*** (1975) Critically acclaimed novels by ALAN GARNER, the first awarded both the CARNEGIE MEDAL and the *GUARDIAN* AWARD, and recognised immediately as a work which fulfilled the promise of Garner's earlier writing. However, the excitement that greeted *The Owl Service* was mixed with some uncertainty about the intended readership: junior school teachers who seized upon it as another compelling FANTASY for young readers found themselves dealing with a work about the violent emotions of adolescence. While some REVIEWERS claimed that Garner had demonstrated that a children's novel might be a great novel for all ages, others suspected that he was losing interest in young readers. Their fears seemed justified when *Red Shift* was published: there was angry controversy, some critics claiming that this work extended the boundaries of literature for older readers, others that it was not a children's book at all. *Red Shift* is not a sequel to *The Owl Service*, but the two works are thematically and structurally linked, focusing dramatically and closely on the theme briefly hinted at in the closing chapter of *ELIDOR* – the ambiguous power of young femininity both to destroy and to heal.

The Owl Service concerns the tense relationship between three teenagers spending the summer in a Welsh valley. It is a fantasy in that the main characters' emotions are both their own and at the same time a cyclical re-enactment of the Celtic story of Blodeuwedd, a tale of violence, passion and betrayal. A further complication is that the youngsters discover that a generation earlier their parents had been caught up in a similar cycle of events, with tragic consequences. *Red Shift*, too, is concerned with contemporary teenage lovers, and their story is also linked with two others – one set at the end of the Roman occupation of Britain, the other at the time of the Civil War. The three stories are enmeshed with one another by means of talismanic objects and a sense of place. Garner's interest in both novels focuses on the three-way dynamics that occur when one girl is torn between two boys, or a woman between two men. In these two novels he has explored this conflict six times, uniting myth, history and modern realism with an extraordinary narrative control. In each case, one of the males is a dreamer – wayward, passionate and desperate – while the other is a pragmatic realist who knows how to deal with life as he finds it, brutally if necessary. The imaginative focus is always on the girl or young woman who is drawn towards both kinds of maleness, and can make the world safe for the vulnerable one only by colluding with the other. Another feature of the narratives is the mother who has crippled her son's capacity for sexual relationships. In *The Owl Service* these mythic and inevitable conflicts occur in the context of class envy, public-school snobbery, and the mutual suspicion between a local Welsh boy and an English land owner. In *Red Shift* it is openly sexual and – in two of its three narratives – it is set in a historical context of rape and butchery. There is nothing formulaic or schematic in these six narratives; the drama in each case is determined by historical and cultural context, and only the basic mythic pattern is constant.

Garner makes no concessions for young readers. He provides no authorial explanations and frustrates at a stroke the traditional expectation that the authorial voice should provide constant reassurance. The plots are driven by anxiety or fear, and the only explanations the reader is given are those of the puzzled characters themselves. Nor do his endings provide clear resolutions: they are ambiguous and controversial. Another new development is his use of long episodes of unattributed dialogue composed of utterances which follow on from one another psychologically rather than logically; this makes for difficult reading but has the effect of removing the sense of an author's shaping control and of miming the uncertainty of actual speech. Both novels demand to be re-read – studied, in fact – because there are clues in the narratives which cannot be understood by a first-time reader. At critical moments in *The Owl Service*, for example, the sound of a distant motor-cycle is heard – but this can mean nothing to a reader until chapter 24. These two novels require a different kind of reading; Garner obliges his readers to become initiates in the hunt for clues. Here, for example, a significant action is 'hidden' in dialogue:

> 'Bikini!'
> 'I love you.'
> 'Bikini!'
> 'It's hurting you too much,' said Jan. 'I'll get rid of it.'
> 'Have you caught up?' said Jan.
> 'Don't.'
> 'I only want to know.'

When Jan asks Tom if he has 'caught up', they have made love for the first time; but readers might be forgiven for not appreciating this significant moment and will do so only if they have attentively remembered that earlier – when Tom learned that Jan was not a virgin – he said he felt as if he were 'a lap behind'. This textual silence may be appropriate for the protagonist for whom sex is literally unspeakable – but it clearly demonstrates Garner's approach, which sees narrative as a riddling or code-making process. The novel's title is symptomatic: a reader must grasp the difficult astronomical significance of 'red shift' and consider how that knowledge might assist a reading of a complex book about passion and history.

In the final end-paper of *Red Shift* there is a letter from Tom to Jan composed in a complex code with a shifting key. 'If you can read this, you must care', it says. It is typical of Tom that his farewell letter to his girlfriend should be in code – but it might also stand as Garner's message to his readers. VW

Owl Who Was a Baker's Daughter, The see FOLKTALES AND LEGENDS

Oxenbury, Helen 1938– British PICTUREBOOK author and illustrator who has become closely identified with creating books for pre-reading age-groups onwards. Her three series of board books are regarded internationally as classics which revolutionised the genre. *Tickle, Tickle* (1987; reissued by Walker as a Big Board Book in 1998) was the first winner of the Sainsbury's Baby Book Award, an award whose aim is to encourage authors to write for very young infant children. She has also produced three picturebook series for young children. Sensitive drawing with a highly expressive contour and clarity of communication characterise her style. Oxenbury won the KATE GREENAWAY MEDAL for her illustrations of EDWARD LEAR's *The Quangle Wangle's Hat* (1968). Other award-winning collaborations include *We're Going on a Bear Hunt* (1989) with MICHAEL ROSEN, *Farmer Duck* (1991) with MARTIN WADDELL, and *So Much* (1994), with Trish Cooke. Her interpretation for a lavishly illustrated version of *ALICE'S ADVENTURES IN WONDERLAND* (1999) – winner of both the KURT MASCHLER AWARD and the Kate Greenaway Medal –

enables CARROLL's text to become accessible to a young contemporary audience. Alice, a coltish seven-year-old, is both vital and vulnerable, and the fantastical creatures are treated with good-natured humour.
JD

Oxenham, Elsie J(eanette) see SCHOOL STORIES; see also *LITTLE FOLKS*

Oxford Book of Children's Verse, The (1973) Anthology edited by IONA and PETER OPIE, a canonical collection of poems purportedly addressed to children or adopted by them, from CHAUCER's *Maunciple's Tale* to OGDEN NASH's 'Morning Prayer'. Like the contents, the preface and notes are for accomplished readers. The book appeared just as a new wave of popular poetry for children was beginning. MM

***Oz* series** Popular series of American fantasies written by several authors, beginning with L. FRANK BAUM's *The Wonderful Wizard of Oz* (1900). The land of Oz, America's first notable fairyland, was created by Baum around the turn of the century as a serial bedtime story for his four sons. When he at last published the stories as a book, the imaginary world proved as popular with other children as with his own. Demand for more about Oz, fuelled by the success of the book as well as a musical play version, forced Baum to write a sequel in 1904, *The Marvellous Land of Oz*, despite his desire to focus on other projects. The sequel, which also had its musical play version, lived up to its predecessor in sales; but many children wrote to Baum to express their disappointment at the absence of Dorothy, the Kansas-bred protagonist of the original book. This pattern – of children writing to Baum demanding a book about a certain *Oz* character – was to be the major impetus for the creation and continuation of the *Oz* series. Baum's publishers designed a marketing strategy around the publication of an *Oz* book for every Christmas season, which they continued long after Baum's death in 1919 by employing other authors as new 'Royal Historians' of Oz.

For the most part, each book in the series is arranged, like the original, around a quest of some sort. The importance and resonance of these quests vary, from Dorothy's poignant longing for her Kansas home in the first book, to the considerably less memorable journey to Ozma's birthday party in *The Road to Oz* (1909). Although Oz never became civilised – since that would mean a loss of its fairy qualities – it certainly became domesticated over the years: Ozma, the fairy ruler of Oz, restricted the use of magic, abolished the monetary system present in the original book, and kept a close eye on her subjects through her use of a Magic Picture. Thus, the excitement of Oz increasingly had to come from outside characters (such as Dorothy or the Shaggy Man) entering Oz, most of whom settled there and became domesticated themselves, or from wild and unknown parts of the country which needed Ozma's taming rule. However, enough of these existed for 14 *Oz* books by Baum, 21 by his successor Ruth Plumly Thompson, and several more by various other authors including John R. Neill, who illustrated all the *Oz* books except the first until his death in 1949.

The Oz books continued to sell well throughout the first half of the century, despite some librarians' objections to their uneven style and quality. However, no individual work in the series has lived up to the original, which has spawned countless play and film versions, including the enduring 1939 MGM film with Judy Garland as Dorothy. This film, more than the books, has influenced later productions, including the 1985 film *Return to Oz* and an HBO animated TELEVISION series. KS

P

Paddington Bear (from 1958) Popular British series by MICHAEL BOND, illustrated by Peggy Fortnum, recounting the adventures of a small bear found at Paddington Station in London by Mr and Mrs Brown. He has travelled from 'Darkest Peru', stowed away in a ship's lifeboat, because his guardian, Aunt Lucy, has entered a home for retired bears. It is her note on a label around Paddington's neck that moves the Browns, loosely based on Bond's own parents, to invite Paddington to live with them in a London suburb. Paddington is scrupulously polite and always keen to do others a good turn. However, he also has a knack for attracting trouble and mayhem, often involving his unpleasant and bigoted neighbour Mr Curry. Bond had been deeply affected by news footage of refugees travelling in desperate convoys and gave Paddington a friend, Mr Gruber, who is a Hungarian refugee and who understands him in a way the Browns cannot.

Following the success of the first book, *A Bear called Paddington* (1958), other titles appeared including *More About Paddington* (1959) and *Paddington Abroad* (1961). A series of short animated films of some of the stories was commissioned by the BBC and the first series transmitted in 1975. Paddington also made a number of appearances in *THE BLUE PETER BOOK*.

All kinds of Paddington merchandise have been produced including teddy bears complete with duffel coat, wellingtons and 'best' hat. However, unlike other fictional bears, Paddington is a real bear. His adventures, too, all take place in the real world of taxis, escalators and bath time. The great humour of the books lies in the muddles that Paddington gets himself into, usually through misunderstanding a situation. He is small, curious and inexperienced and this combination has proved irresistible to those most like him: children. AMN

see also MUSIC AND STORY

Paddo, The see SCOTTISH FOLKTALES

Padmanabhan, Manjula 1953– Indian illustrator, painter, cartoonist, fiction writer, playwright and scriptwriter for films. One of the most sophisticated illustrators in the Indian scene, Padmanabhan is a thinking artist who endeavours to mould her work to complement the context in which it appears. Backed by an intimate understanding of the function of illustration, she observes the little details of daily life and incorporates them in her work. Her work displays a dramatic sense of topography, and adeptness at overall composition and pattern. It includes beautiful, tremendously detailed black-and-whites, as well as vibrant colour ILLUSTRATIONS, some of which have ensured the ultimate success of books such as Tara Ali Baig's *Indrani and the Enchanted Jungle* (1979). *Droopy the Dragon* (1984) was another successful example of superb execution reaching consummation after three years of hard work (see p. 540). As author-illustrator of *A Visit to the Market* (1985) she could, with impunity, introduce colouring according to the Indian norm and thus break stereotypical representations of fair heroes and beauties, and dark, ugly villains. Her preferred medium is black ink on paper. Though guided by children's demands, she is one of the rare painstaking and intensive illustrators whose art is issue-based and whose hidden critiques can unsettle the viewer. Dissatisfied with the prevalent ethos in the field, she has formally stopped illustrating. Both as a writer and as an illustrator, she has evinced a deep interest in gender problems, especially those involving the girl child. MBh

***Pagan* series** Australian author CATHERINE JINKS recounts the life of an Arab Christian boy, Pagan, in this prize-winning tetralogy set amidst the Crusades of the 12th and 13th centuries in Palestine and France. Pagan, intelligent and articulate, is the central character of the first three, *Pagan's Crusade* (1992), *Pagan In Exile* (1994) and *Pagan's Vows* (1995) (CHILDREN'S BOOK COUNCIL OF AUSTRALIA Book of the Year: Older Readers, 1996), in which readers are led through the brutalities of the fall of Jerusalem to the beginnings of the Crusade against the Cathars in Provence. *Pagan's Scribe* (1996) depicts this Crusade through the eyes of Isodore, another orphaned boy, mentored by Pagan. CH, HMcC

Page, Thomas Nelson 1853–1922 American fiction writer of the Old South. Born in Virginia, Page was eight years old when his father, a slave owner, rode off to fight in the American Civil War. The remainder of Page's youth was spent in poverty, until he became

Illustration by Marjula Padmanabhan from *Droopy the Dragon.*

successful as a writer and lawyer. Among his works are the novella *Two Little Confederates* (1888), short-story collections *In Ole Virginia* (1887) and *Among the Camps* (1891), and several novels. Many of his stories are told from a child's point of view, and are too sentimental and idealised for modern tastes. CAB

Pai, Anant 1929– Popularly known as 'Uncle Pai', Pai has been associated with publishing comics in India since 1963, when *The Times of India* launched the *Indrajal* comics. A trained chemical engineer, he turned to the publication of the *Amar Chitra Katha* comics series, stimulated by his own traditional upbringing which resulted in a close knowledge of India's literary heritage and a deep-rooted reverence for his country's past. This series, based on Indian culture, mythology and history, was started in 1967 with the aim of highlighting values and teaching young Indians respect for their cultural heritage. Since then, 437 colourful works have been produced in 38 languages, including English and Hindi, ranging even to Swahili and Serbo-Croat, and have sold more than 80 million copies. The first of the series was the story of Lord Krishna, the divine hero of the *Bhagavad Gita*, followed by popular titles like *Shakuntala*, *The Pandava Princes*, *The Sons of Rama* and *Hanuman*, all based on mythological themes. Though success was not instant, sales gradually picked up, with *Krishna* alone going into 80 reprints and reaching sales of more than a million copies. Eventually, the thoroughly researched series diversified from mythological topics to include secular themes from history, FOLK TALES and stories of regional heroes and heroines, motivated by the desire to promote national integration. Engrossing to both children and adults, they have rightly earned Pai the title of 'the father of Indian comics'. MBh

see also COMICS, PERIODICALS AND MAGAZINES; INDIAN MYTHS, LEGENDS AND FOLKTALES

Paikea see MAORI WRITING IN CHILDREN'S BOOKS; ROBYN KAHUKIWA

Paine, Albert Bigelow 1861–1937 American author best known for his BIOGRAPHIES, *Boys' Life of Mark Twain* (1916) and *The Girl in White Armor: the True Story of Joan of Arc* (1927). The first grew out of a collaboration with MARK TWAIN himself, and Paine was able to capture the humorist in a much-admired personal fashion. His portrayal of Joan of Arc, however, challenged him to use records of the woman, her time and nation to produce a living figure. Paine's other children's books include *Arkansas Bear* (1898) about a singing boy and a fiddling bear, and the *Hollow Tree* series in the *Uncle Remus* tradition. KSB

Pair of Jesus-Boots, A (1969) Novel by British author Sylvia Sherry, first published in 1969, reprinted in 1971, 1974 and 1976, and serialised for BBC TELEVI-

SION. Set against the grim backdrop of the Liverpool docks, it tells the story of the spirited Rocky O'Rourke, who hails from a poverty-stricken tenement and aspires to be either a big-time crook or famous footballer. Despite being labelled an 'undesirable' he possesses a heart of gold, helping those shunned by society. His triumph over such inauspicious circumstances is precipitated by his defeat of the criminal Simpson, with the aid of his 'Jesus-boots' – the shabby sandals he always wears that 'help yer to grip'. GD

Palgrave, Francis [Turner] 1824–97 Victorian poet and critic, in 1885 elected Professor of Poetry at Oxford. On holiday with TENNYSON he conceived the idea for his best-known work, *The Golden Treasury of Songs and Lyrics* (1861), never since out of print. This was followed by *The Children's Treasury of English Song* (1875). AHa

Pamela see SAMUEL RICHARDSON; see also ABRIDGEMENT; FAIRY TALES

***Pancha-Tantra* tales** see AFRICAN MYTHOLOGY AND FOLKTALES; FOLKTALES AND LEGENDS; see also INDIAN MYTHS, LEGENDS AND FOLKTALES; PULAK BISWAS

panoramas see MOVABLE BOOKS

Pansy [Isabella MacDonald Alden] 1841–1930 American author of evangelical fiction. In a career lasting over 60 years, Pansy wrote more than 125 novels, including her popular *Ester Ried*, *Chatauqua* and *Life of Christ* series. She also edited the Presbyterian *Primary Quarterly*, published the children's magazine *Pansy*, assisted her minister husband with parish work and taught Sunday school. Pansy wrote 'to win souls for Jesus Christ' and to remedy social problems by promoting temperance, cleanliness and culture. Pansy's sentimental religious fiction lost popularity before her death, but several novels were reprinted in the 1990s in the Grace Livingston Hill Library, named after Pansy's niece. JLB

pantomime A Christmas-time theatrical entertainment designed mainly for children attending with their families. For many British children the annual Christmas pantomime is their only regular experience of live theatre. Pantomime in its modern form is a uniquely British invention, although some Commonwealth countries have adopted the formula successfully. In its British form it has a long history, beginning early in the 18th century, although it has evolved and changed considerably over the three centuries of its existence. Its association with Christmas, and with children, developed gradually, but became firmly established early in the 19th century. During the 19th century attempts were made to transplant it to the United States, and for a short time there was pantomime on Broadway, but the initiative was not successful.

In its modern form pantomime is structured around the telling of a traditional FAIRY STORY, among which *CINDERELLA* is the favourite, or a story from the *ARABIAN NIGHTS*, such as *Aladdin* or *Sinbad the Sailor*, or a well-known fiction such as *ROBINSON CRUSOE*. The story is the pretext for a loosely connected series of incidental entertainments, usually including slapstick comedy, acrobatics, songs, dance and ballet. There is considerable audience participation. Pantomime is thus a hybrid form. In recent years some pantomimes, especially major productions in London, have had a full score and lyrics and have thus copied the integrated form of a stage musical, but provincial pantomimes have remained opportunistically diverse, maintaining traditional features such as the comic Dame played by a male actor, but also serving as a vehicle for one or two star performers. The leading player is often a comedian, but well-known actors in television soap operas, and even sports personalities, often appear. Pantomime remains extremely popular in Britain, and for many provincial theatres it is the chief revenue-earning event of the year.

The origins of British pantomime lie in the Harlequinade, a storytelling dance which was an offshoot of the Italian Commedia Dell'Arte. During the 18th century, this form expanded and gained popularity, notably under the influence of John Rich (1692–1761). The balletic mime of Harlequin and Columbine, fugitive lovers pursued by the aged and comic Pantaloon, was lengthened and also preceded by another story, the Opening, usually derived from classical legend. As pantomime developed, a spectacular 'transformation scene' marked the transitional point between the two elements of the entertainment. Early in the 19th century the great comedian and singer Joseph Grimaldi (1778–1837) amplified the part of Clown, which was henceforth dominant in the Harlequinade, and by this period the now-familiar fairy stories had displaced classical myth and legend as the subject of the Opening. In time the Harlequinade dwindled in importance, though it survived into the 20th century. In the mid-19th century, the pantomime was infiltrated by the ebullient new music halls, and was affected also by the adult satirical form of the burlesque. Out of these disparate origins and influences emerged the curious hotch-potch which we know today. The influence of burlesque survives in comic and bawdy topicalities for adults, but pantomime's great strength lies in the blend of comedy, surprise and visual spectacle for children. PH

see also MUSIC AND STORY

paper engineering see MOVABLE BOOKS

Papers: Explorations into Children's Literature Australian children's literature journal first published in 1990, and originally conceived by Alf Mappin, the editor of *MAGPIES* Magazine. In 1994 the journal came under the auspices of the Centre for Research in Cultural Communication at Deakin University with Clare Bradford as editor. Not restricted to Australian children's literature, the journal, published three times a year, has played a major role in lifting the profile of children's literature as part of the whole literary tradition, by providing 'researchers into the historical background of children's literature, academic theoreticians and literary critics with an outlet for their material'. JAP

Parish, Peggy 1927–88 American writer of books for early readers, best remembered for *Amelia Bedelia* (1963) and its sequels. Amelia Bedelia is a maid who takes everything literally, resulting in a hilarious verbal irony – dressing the turkey, drawing the curtains. Parish created other equally eccentric, but lovable characters, including Granny Gruntry, a feisty grandmother from colonial times, in *Granny and the Indians* (1969). A prolific writer, she produced a mystery series for older readers featuring three clever siblings, numerous non-fiction books on diverse subjects, and craft books. Parish is generally highly regarded as a writer, although her stories about Native Americans have been derided as uninformed and irrelevant to the Native American experience. DLR

Park, (Rosina) Ruth (Lucia) 1923– Australian writer born in New Zealand and latterly living on Norfolk Island. Park is the author of an extensive range of adult novels, many historical, such as the *Harp in the South* trilogy (1948–53). A successful playwright, children's novelist, series writer, screenwriter and author of information texts, Park's most widely known contribution to children's literature is the long-running, popular, eleven-title radio series *THE MUDDLE-HEADED WOMBAT* (1962–81). In the attractive FAMILY STORIES *Callie's Castle* (1974) and its sequel, *Callie's Family* (1988), she presents characters growing in autonomy and their capacity for responsibility.

Come Danger, Come Darkness (1978), set on Norfolk Island in the brutal convict colony, presents an exciting sequence of events involving two young teenagers responding to changes in themselves and the world around them, a theme frequently explored in Park's work. Her award-winning books include the critically and internationally acclaimed *PLAYING BEATIE BOW* (1980, CHILDREN'S BOOK COUNCIL OF AUSTRALIA Book of the Year, 1981; THE BOSTON GLOBE-HORN AWARD, 1982), a TIME-SLIP novel set in Sydney. Park's interest in extending the range of STORYTELLING possibilities is evident again in *My Sister Sif* (1986), featuring merpeople and underwater cities, with an ecological theme and subplot about love and its sacrifices. *Things in Corners* (1989), a collection of short stories, examines ways of facing hidden, eerie and paranormal things in one's family and life.

Her daughters, DEBORAH and KILMENY NILAND, have illustrated many of her PICTUREBOOKS, including *When the Wind Changed* (1980), and *James* (1991). Park believes that the style most appropriate in writing for children is one which opens the imagination outwards. The corpus of her work shows her changing understanding of this. Her own measure of a successful book is not that it wins awards but that it is worn out in library use. CH, HMcC

Parker, Carolyn see *WITCH WOMAN ON THE HOGSBACK*

Parkins, David 1955– Known principally for his line illustrations in DICK KING-SMITH's work, Parkins produced handsome, huge, dark, moody oil illustrations for GINA WILSON's tour-de-force verse story *Prowlpuss* (1994). In the gloom and shadows of what is possibly the darkest PICTUREBOOK ever, one detects rats, bats and watching cats, and through it all stalks the king-size Prowlpuss on his way to court the apparently disdainful white cat. JAG

Parkinson, Siobhán 1954– Irish author who began writing for children with two semi-fictionalised guides to Dublin and to the Irish countryside. *Amelia* (1993), and its sequel, *No Peace for Amelia* (1994), marked her transition to a writer of significance. While there are some memorable set-pieces of Dublin life in these novels about a young Quaker girl in the years 1914 and 1916, neither narrative nor characterisation is sacrificed to historical detail. *All Shining in the Spring: the Story of a Baby Who Died* (1995), illustrated by Donald Teskey, tells through the eyes of young Matthew, the story of his stillborn baby brother, in language which is poignant but never sentimental. *Sisters – No Way* (1996) is a very modern play on the CINDERELLA story presenting the same events from the different perspectives of two teenage girls. *Four Kids, Three Cats, Two Cows, One Witch (Maybe)* (1997), *The Moon King* (1998), and *Breaking the Wishbone* (1999), set among Dublin's homeless population, further display Parkinson's versatility and interesting literary development. VC

Parley, Peter see CENSORSHIP; SAMUEL GRISWOLD GOODRICH; see also PUBLISHING AND PUBLISHERS

Parrish, Anne see DOLL STORIES; see also ROBINSONNADES

Parrish, (Frederick) Maxfield 1870–1966 American muralist, commercial artist and illustrator of children's books. Born in Philadelphia, Pennsylvania, and educated at Haverford College, Pennsylvania Academy of Fine Arts, Drexel Institute of Arts and Sciences and the University of New Hampshire, Parrish studied with illustrator HOWARD PYLE and began his career as a commercial artist by illustrating covers for *Harper's Weekly*, *Century Magazine* and ST NICHOLAS. He also did ILLUSTRATIONS for advertising and commercially successful posters which featured vivid colours. He later illustrated such early 20th-century childhood classics as KENNETH GRAHAME'S *THE GOLDEN AGE* (1900) as well as his *Dream Days* (1902); EUGENE FIELD'S *Poems of Childhood* (1904) and L. FRANK BAUM'S *Mother Goose in Prose* (1905); and a play by Louise Saunders titled *The Knave of Hearts* (1925). However, it is his rich, exotic illustrations for KATE DOUGLAS WIGGIN'S and Nora A. Smith's *ARABIAN NIGHTS ENTERTAINMENT* (1909) that best display his technique in full-colour illustration. Parrish used colour straight from the tube. He began by painting a monochrome background, often using ultramarine or monastral blue; then he would apply different colour and build it up until he was finished. Finally, he would apply a thin coat of varnish to bring out all the colour. DJH

Part of the Pattern see CRITICAL APPROACHES TO CHILDREN'S BOOKS

Partridge, Francesca 1968– and **Dubuc, Franck** 1966– This Australian and French collaboration has created a series entitled *Places for Thinking*, a set of four whimsical philosophical vignettes, with a wandering duck as their linking thread. Published in 1999 the titles are *In a Field*, *On a Path*, *In a Tree* and *On a Plain*. Illustrated in coloured pencil, using natural colours and textures like corrugated cardboard, Partridge and Dubuc pose some deep questions for children to contemplate – based fundamentally on the question: why? They use gentle humour, symbolism and refreshingly challenging vocabulary, with evident respect for children's ability to cope with such abstract concepts and language. They have also illustrated Gretel Killeen's *Cherry Pie* (1998) and *What'll We Get For Grandma?* (1999). RTh

Pascal, Francine see *SWEET VALLEY HIGH*; YOUNG ADULT FICTION

Passage to Freedom: The Sugihara Story see ASIAN AMERICAN CHILDREN'S LITERATURE; see also BIOGRAPHY AND AUTOBIOGRAPHY

Patel, Mickey 1941–94 Indian illustrator, cartoonist, writer and painter, Patel was an accomplished painter and one of India's most gifted and loved illustrators of children's books. Acclaimed both nationally and internationally, he won many awards, including the prestigious UNESCO Noma Concours Award for Children's Picturebook Illustrations. Endowed with a sensitive artistic temperament, he was a pioneer illustrator who evolved a distinctive style that subsequently has been extensively copied. He illustrated books for several leading publishers, and his cartoons and drawings featured in major magazines and newspapers. *The Story of a Panther* (1998) was Patel's last book written and illustrated for children and shows him at the height of his creative powers. The exquisite ILLUSTRATIONS, at times going beyond the needs of a child, are engaged in a dynamic colloquy with the text, making the book a treat for children and adults alike. His illustrations to Umashankar Joshi's *Stories from Bapu's Life* (1973) are some of the best on the subject of Gandhi and are unique. His popular *Procession* (1985) is a beautiful, exquisitely executed number-book without any written text. The animated support of his vibrant illustrations to RUSKIN BOND'S *Snake Trouble* (1991) has been much lauded. MBh

Illustration by Mickey Patel from *Snake Trouble* by RUSKIN BOND.

Paterson, A(ndrew) B(arton) (Banjo) 1864–1941 One of Australia's most popular poets, renowned for his BUSH ballads, many influenced by his childhood years spent in Illalong, New South Wales. Adopting the pen-name 'Banjo', after a family racehorse, Paterson first published his uniquely Australian verses in *The Bulletin*, alongside those of Henry Lawson. Despite some contention, Paterson is generally acknowledged as the writer of WALTZING MATILDA (1895), arguably Australia's most recognised international poem/song. A collection of lively verses for children, *The Animals Noah Forgot* (1933), illustrated by Norman Lindsay, is a celebration of bush animals, from lowly frogs to high-flying cockatoos. His verses and ballads commemorate the people of the bush – the squatters, shearers, drovers and swagmen. Some of his verses have been made accessible to children as PICTUREBOOKS. Notable examples are *Mulga Bill's Bicycle* (1973) by DEBORAH and KILMENY NILAND; *The Man from Ironbark* (1974) and *A Bush Christening* (1974) by QUENTIN HOLE; *The Man from Snowy River* (1977) by ANNETTE MACARTHUR-ONSLOW and *Clancy of the Overflow* (1982) by ROBERT INGPEN. JAP

Paterson, Katherine (Womeldorf) 1932– American novelist, author of HISTORICAL FICTION, contemporary realism, traditional tales and essays about literature and culture. Born in Tsing-Tsiang Pu in China's Jiangsu Province to Southern Presbyterian missionaries George Raymond Womeldorf and Mary (Groethius) Womeldorf, Paterson's first language was Chinese. However, she learned English in early childhood, becoming a refugee to the United States with her family in 1937 and again in 1940. The Womeldorfs moved frequently within the South during Paterson's childhood, living in North Carolina, Tennessee, West Virginia, and Virginia.

Often feeling like an outsider – Paterson says that all of her stories are really about the time she got no valentines in first grade – she read avidly authors ranging from Martha Finley of the *ELSIE DINSMORE* series to DICKENS and GRAHAME. At Kings College in Bristol, Tennessee, she majored in English and experimented with the styles of classical writers. In the best-known of her works, including the NEWBERY winner *Bridge to Terabithia* (1977) and *The Great Gilly Hopkins* (1978), literary allusion shapes the narrative, diction and action. Yet Paterson's birth in China, her own missionary work in Japan from 1957 to 1962, and her daily experience as a woman provide equally important source materials for her writing. Marriage to John Bristow Paterson in 1962, a master's degree in religious education from Union Theological Seminary in the same year, and the rearing of four children (two of them adopted) provided direction as Paterson explored settings and genres, especially mythic realism. This hybrid genre of her own invention allowed Paterson to depict both alienation from a flawed social order and a mysterious universe, and integration into complex history and values, despite the problem of evil, the limited nature of free will, and the necessary search for meanings, material and transcendent. In a way reminiscent of much American canonical and sentimental literature, her books insist on the possibility of hope.

Since 1966, when Paterson published *Who Am I?*, a work for young readers commissioned by the Presbyterian Church to discuss religious concerns (and rewritten for a 1992 edition), she has pursued writing as a profession. Three historical novels set in Japan depict an individual's development into adulthood as a process framed by external social forces but ultimately within the protagonist's control. The third of these novels, *The Master Puppeteer* (1975), refines the narrative ending into a revelation of the problematic nature of social and personal relationships, where one moral choice undercuts other potential choices. A significant set of awards to Paterson began in 1977, with a Newbery Honour designation and a National Book Award for *The Master Puppeteer*. That same year Paterson published *Bridge to Terabithia* followed by *The Great Gilly Hopkins* in 1978 and *Jacob Have I Loved* in 1980, garnering two Newbery Awards and another Honour designation.

Paterson's distinctive use of contemporary social settings and pervasive moral dilemmas in these novels evoked widespread discussion among both young readers and the literary reviewers and scholars who recognised the pain and joy of truthful, if loving, writing. Subjects like the death of a child, the nurture of a foster child, and a tortuous female adolescence were drawn from Paterson's personal life, yet woven into contemporary social settings of a remarkable complexity and clarity. Her reputation for pioneering difficult subjects in children's and youth novels made her seem part of a wider trend towards contemporary problem novels, but Paterson displayed, especially in *Jacob Have I Loved*, a unique interest in historical research and reflective social commentary. Protagonists like Jesse, Gilly and Louise operated from within a social order, markedly different from the earlier search for place and home in the Japanese novels. With the help of her talented editor at Dutton, Virginia Buckley, Paterson produced child protagonists who were artists or meaning-makers. In 1983, *Rebels of the Heavenly Kingdom* allowed Paterson to record an idealistic Chinese struggle of the 19th century as a way of endorsing changes in male and female roles without abandoning focus on intimacy and family life.

Subsequent novels like *Come Sing Jimmy Jo* (1985), *Park's Quest* (1988) and *Flip-Flop Girl* (1994) have contemporary but socially and historically specific settings. In 1995, Paterson wrote an introduction to Virginia Lynn Fry's *Part of Me Died Too*, accounts of how bereaved children and teenagers find ways to deal with their losses. Fry's book seems directly related to *Flip-flop Girl*, which uses tight narrative control to tell the story of a depressed girl enduring the death of her father. *Lyddie*

Illustration from *Winnie the Witch* by Valerie Thomas and Korky Paul.

(1991) and *Jip: His Story* (1996) show Paterson's continuing ability to produce historical novels, now set in 19th-century America and based on research about working-class women and African Americans. The later novels demonstrate Paterson's gift for pioneering the treatment of previously taboo topics like illegitimacy, insanity, depression, war and miscegenation in clear and moving youth literature, grounded in research, personal philosophy and an exacting literary crafting.

International meetings with other artists and editors of children's books have resulted in Paterson's experimenting with the translation, retelling and creation of FOLKTALES, often in partnership with distinguished illustrators. One example is *The King's Equal* in 1992, a feminist story about peace illustrated by Vladimir Vagin. Identifying herself in essays and speeches as a committed writer for children, Paterson has achieved strong recognition from librarians and teachers as an artist who regards social leadership as part of her responsibility. One manifestation of this leadership is her collaboration in 1993 with Ann Durrell and JEAN CRAIGHEAD GEORGE on *The Big Book for Our Planet*, an anthology devoted to the environmental crisis. Though her novels are sometimes censored by conservative Christians for the occasional occurence of profanity – always contextually meaningful – other critics have viewed her work as too religious. Yet it is clear that Paterson demands from her readers a knowledge of how point of view shapes the meaning of a narrative. In return for such understanding, she offers stories that seem almost prophetic in their global, historical and moral vision. NH

Pathfinder, The see *LEATHER-STOCKING TALES*

Patient Griselda see *CONTES DE MA MÈRE L'OYE*

Patmore, Coventry see *CHILDREN'S GARLAND, THE*

Patten, Brian 1946– Liverpool poet who came to the fore during the 1960s through performance poetry, often accompanied by fellow poets ROGER MCGOUGH and ADRIAN HENRI. He has shared his time between adult and child audiences for 15 years, and has been successful and popular with both. *Gargling With Jelly* (1985) and *Thawing Frozen Frogs* (1987) combined outrageous humour with concern for the eco-system and how we deal with death, while *The Utter Nutters* (1994) brings poetry and comic strip together. Patten is also editor of lively anthologies including *The Puffin Book of 20th Century Verse* (1991). JL

Paul, Korky 1951– After what he has described as a wild and privileged childhood in the African bushveldt,

Paul went on to study Fine Arts in Natal before moving on to advertising, film animation and then eventually children's book ILLUSTRATION. The inky, energetic lines of his drawings reveal a humorous and imaginative world which can be revisited again and again to find new details and surprises. Highlighted by a wash of bright colour, his scratchy graphic lines encapsulate the individuality of each character. Paul is particularly proud that the majority of his AWARDS have been voted for by children: he has won THE CHILDREN'S BOOK AWARD twice for *Winnie The Witch* (1987) and *The Rascally Cake* (1994), both written by Jeanne Willis. He has been shortlisted for the KATE GREENAWAY MEDAL, twice in collaboration with Jonathan Long for *The Duck That Had No Luck* (1997) and *The Dog That Dug* (1992) and again for *Captain Teachum's Buried Treasure* (1989), written by PETER CARTER. He has also won several international awards, which again says much about the universal appeal of his distinctive work. Three of Paul's PICTUREBOOKS have been adapted for CD-ROM, *The Fish Who Could Wish* winning him the European Multi-Media Award in 1995, and since 1998 readers have been able to visit the artist on his own website. KJFR

Paul, Lissa see CRITICAL APPROACHES TO CHILDREN'S BOOKS

Paul Bunyan see TALL TALES; GLEN ROUNDS

Paulsen, Gary 1939– Prolific American author who writes for both adults and children. Before becoming an author Paulsen had a variety of occupations, often living in the wild for long periods of time. His own experience provides the basis for many of his novels and he claims to have had first-hand experience of the unlikely situations in which his characters find themselves, telling compelling tales of his encounters with wild animals and the challenge of the long Iditerod sled race. His love of dogs is central to *Dogsong*, a 1985 Newbery Honour Book. Another Newbery Honour Book, *Hatchet* (1987), chronicles the life of a young boy who crash-lands a plane in the wild and has to survive there for months with a hatchet as his only tool. Many of Paulsen's books contain the ingredients of a classic ADVENTURE STORY, depicting a struggle to survive in arduous circumstances. When his characters are placed within a family context the family is often seen as unsupportive and sometimes actively brutal – a trend Paulsen blames on his own unhappy childhood. *Harris and Me* (1993) – in which a child spends a riotous but traumatic summer at his cousin's farm – is based on one of Paulsen's own childhood summers. Few adults are seen to be sources of comfort or wisdom, and those whose views are to be respected tend to come from outside the family circle and often from a very different way of life from the child's own. KA

Pausacker, Jenny 1948– Australian novelist, perhaps best known for *What Are Ya?* (1987), the first Australian young adult novel to explore issues of lesbian sexuality. This book, and its two loosely linked sequels *Mr Enigmatic* (1994) and *Getting Somewhere* (1995), make up the *Central Secondary College* series, and typify Pausacker's insightful, humorous and ultimately positive approach to teenage and social problems and urban realism. Her other young adult novel, the historical adventure *Can You Keep A Secret?* (1989), is the story of a teenage boy torn between right- and left-wing politics in the Depression of the 1930s. Born in Adelaide, Pausacker has a PhD in children's literature, and has written five junior novels, several with the Melbourne-based Women's Movement Children's Literature Co-operative which, in the 1970s, published books combating sexism, racism and class stereotypes. Pausacker has disputed the widely accepted divide between high and low culture as politically motivated (*Viewpoint* 2.1, 1994 and elsewhere) and writes on both sides of this 'divide'. Under the pseudonyms Jaye Francis and Mary Forrest she has written more than 20 teen-romance and children's adventure-series novels, and as Jaye Francis collaborated with author Merrilee Moss on the innovative *Hot Pursuit* romance-thriller series. NLR

Pavey, Peter 1948– Australian writer and illustrator of high-quality PICTUREBOOKS, especially for younger readers. His distinctive illustrative style uses CROSSHATCHING to great effect, and gives his detailed pictures energy and depth. His most successful work, *One Dragon's Dream* (1978), satisfies a number of important demands: it invites the child to look closely, to treat pictures as perceptual puzzles and to practise counting. *I'm Taggerty Toad* (1980) is an adventure which deals with boasting, using frog and toad characters. *Battles in the Bath* (1982) focuses on the imaginative possibilities of bath time. CH, HMcC

Peacock at Home, The (1807) Poem by CATHERINE ANN DORSET, sister of Romantic precursor, CHARLOTTE SMITH, with whom she collaborated on *Conversations Introducing Poetry to Children Chiefly on the Topic of Natural History* (1804). Inspired by Roscoe's *THE BUTTERFLY'S BALL AND THE GRASSHOPPER'S FEAST*, Dorset's verse is funnier and better written, anticipating the work of EDWARD LEAR:

> Each delicate viand that taste could denote,
> Wasps à la sauce piquante, and flies en compote;
> Worms and frogs en friture for the web-footed fowl,
> And a barbecued mouse was prepared for the owl.

MCCS

Peacock Pie (1913) Collection of poetry which established WALTER DE LA MARE as a children's poet. Frequently reissued in differently illustrated editions, the contents seem as fresh and sparkling today. There is the old donkey, Nicolas Nye; the Mad Prince; poor tired Tim 'too tired to yawn, too tired to sleep'; Jim Jay who 'got stuck fast in yesterday'; and the Three Jolly Farmers who 'Once bet a pound / Each dance the other would / Off the ground.' The collection holds mystery, magic and enjoyable tingles of fear: 'Someone came knocking / At my wee, small door', 'Up on their brooms the Witches stream, / Crooked and black in the crescent's gleam.' And there is sometimes a less enjoyable shudder, as in 'The Mocking Fairy': 'And out of her cold cottage never answered Mrs Gill, / The Fairy, mimbling, mambling, in the garden.' In the canon of children's poetry, *Peacock Pie* is as timeless a classic as Blake's *SONGS OF INNOCENCE*, ROSSETTI's *SING-SONG* and STEVENSON's *A CHILD'S GARDEN OF VERSES*. AHa

Peacock Spring, The (1975) Novel by RUMER GODDEN set in India at an unspecified date during the second half of the 20th century. Although now published as an adult novel the book was originally published under a teenage imprint. Una's and Hal's father removes them from their English school and takes them to live with him in India. It becomes clear that he wants them there only as a cover for his relationship with the woman who becomes their governess. Una resents the governess's false pretences and escapes to a relationship with a former student who is now her father's under-gardener; she subsequently becomes pregnant. The book was one of the first young adult novels to deal with the subjects of teenage SEX and pregnancy. Although their sexual relationship is not described in detail the pregnancy and eventual miscarriage are dealt with compassionately and sympathetically. Blame for Una's predicament is seen to rest as much with her father's negligence as with her own actions. Una begins the story as a conventional academic English schoolgirl, uninterested in men and wanting to continue her own education, until she is driven to the relationship by her father's remoteness. KA

see also YOUNG ADULT FICTION

Peake, Mervyn (Lawrence) 1911–68 British writer, painter and illustrator. He is noted for the *Gormenghast* novels which he wrote during his war service, where his black-and-white illustrations match the dark mood of the text. By contrast his *Figures of Speech* (1954) contained only line drawings, appealing to young and old alike. His *RHYMES WITHOUT REASON* (1944) and *Ride-a-Cock-Horse* (1940) are unusual, owing to their bright, flat, decorative shapes of colour which were printed by stencil. Among his best work are the illustrations for LEWIS CARROLL's *THE HUNTING OF THE SNARK* (1941), *ALICE'S ADVENTURES IN WONDERLAND* and *Through the Looking Glass* (1954). In 1996 his *Boy in Darkness* – a brilliantly frightening and baroque work about the Titus of Gormenghast, originally included in *Sometime Never: The Tales of the Imagination* (1956) – was reissued as a book for children, illustrated by P. J. LYNCH. AEW

Peanuts 1950–2000 American comic strip created by Charles Schulz (1922–2000). The strip focuses on a group of small children, who in the half-century of the strip's existence did not age, but who responded to developments in popular culture, thus keeping the tone contemporary. The protagonist of *Peanuts* is CHARLIE BROWN, the lovable but hapless 'failure face' (as his antagonist Lucy calls him); the most popular character is Charlie Brown's free-spirited and imaginative beagle, Snoopy. No adults appear, except from the waist down: this establishes and maintains the children's point of view, though the intellectual content of their dialogue is often itself rather sophisticated. The comic strip has given rise to TELEVISION specials, feature-length ANIMATED FILMS, and two musical plays. The last daily strip appeared in January, 2000 – when Charles Schulz retired for health reasons – and the final Sunday release in February, only a few hours after he died. BH

Pearce, Philippa 1920– British writer, brought up in Great Shelford, a village just outside Cambridge in England. Philippa Pearce's father was the flour-miller and they lived in the house beside the mill on the River Cam, where she swam, fished, canoed and skated. She returned to the area as a parent herself and now lives in a cottage close to her old home. Her living in an area where her family has lived for generations is in keeping with one of the great themes in her writing: it is not nostalgia but an acknowledgement of the continuum between past and present, parents and children, the children and the adults they become. After leaving Cambridge University in 1942, she worked as a civil servant, then an educational and children's book editor at two publishing houses, and finally as a scriptwriter and producer for BBC Radio. One summer, she was hospitalised in Cambridge for TB. The summer was a particularly fine one and she was frustrated at being cooped up in hospital when she could have been enjoying the pleasures of the river. Her first book, *Minnow on the Say* (1955, illustrated by EDWARD ARDIZZONE, published in US as *The Minnow Leads to Treasure*) was the result of her intense day-dreaming about the river.

Commended for the CARNEGIE AWARD, *The Minnow on the Say* describes Adam's and David's search for hidden treasure. Adam's parents are both dead and he lives with his aunt, Dinah Codling, and his grandfather. Miss Codling can no longer afford to keep Adam in the house that the Codling family have lived in for centuries and at the end of the summer is sending him to live with cousins in Birmingham. Adam hopes to prevent this by finding the treasure hidden by an ancestor. The novel is full of the heat and dappled shade of a summer holiday spent on water as the two boys use their canoe called 'The Minnow' to search along the banks of the River Say, following the only clue they have to the whereabouts of the treasure.

Her next novel, *Tom's Midnight Garden* (1958), is certainly her greatest and it won the Carnegie Award. It too is set in the area where Philippa Pearce grew up. Her father had retired and her parents were selling their house and the book is really a celebration of the garden that she, and her father before her, had enjoyed as children. The garden of the title is a description of the one she knew as a child; SUSAN EINZIG's illustrations are based on family photographs and drawings. Part of the richness of Philippa Pearce's writing stems from the vivid sense of place that she creates. She does not simply describe what a place looks like, but what it feels like to be there; she is writing from the inside for she has been there herself.

At the start of the book, all Tom wants to do is spend his summer at home building a tree-house in the garden with his brother Peter; but Peter has measles and Tom is sent to stay with his uncle and aunt in their gardenless flat. When he discovers the beautiful garden, which appears every night at the back of the house, and makes friends with Hatty, the only child who can see him there, he seems to have everything he wants – he even gets to build the tree-house he had longed for. Soon, however, this is not enough: he wants to stay in the garden for ever. Philippa Pearce has said that the walled garden represents the sheltered security of early childhood and it is here that Tom seeks to remain, able to be a boy at play forever. Hatty on the other hand longs to see beyond the garden walls and through the novel, unnoticed by Tom, she grows up and moves out of the garden.

Time and connections between the past and present are the issues at the heart of *Tom's Midnight Garden*. Tom plays in a garden which no longer exists with a girl who, he thinks, is probably now dead. Yet there is never a sense that Tom is going back in time as there is in other novels on a similar theme, e.g. *Charlotte Sometimes* (see PENELOPE FARMER). It is the garden itself that matters to Tom; he does not care when it existed, only that it exists now when he opens the back door. Although he is saddened by the fact that Hatty is probably dead in his own time, his interest in time is essentially practical: he wants to be able to conquer it so that he can stay in the garden.

Tom's Midnight Garden is a powerful book, full of longing and contradictory yearnings: to stay a child forever and yet to be able to grow up and explore the world that lies beyond one's childhood home. The closing lines of the book hint at how these opposing feelings are reconciled as Tom puts his arms around an old woman and embraces the little girl she still is.

A Dog so Small (1962, illustrated by ANTHONY MAITLAND) is also partly set in the area that Pearce grew up in. Again, the River Say is the Cam, the Barleys are the Shelfords and the town of Castleford is Cambridge without the university. The novel opens and closes in London and the dénouement takes place on Hampstead Heath, Pearce's favourite part of London. This splitting of the setting of the novel is fundamental to the plot: Ben wants a dog but, because his family live in central London without easy access to a park, he has to make do with the part-time care of his grandfather's dog during occasional visits to the country. Ben's yearning becomes so great that a dog comes to him, 'a dog so small that you could only see it with your eyes shut'. So Ben closes his eyes and in doing so does not see the changes that are taking place that will eventually allow him to have what he desires. *A Dog So Small* emphasises the dependence of children on the actions of adults and, as in *Minnow on the Say* and *Tom's Midnight Garden*, these actions are the result of the willingness of adults to enable children to gain what they desire.

This is brought out even more strongly in *The Battle of Bubble and Squeak* (1978, illustrated by Alan Baker). Indeed, this short novel – winner of the WHITBREAD AWARD – is as much about Mrs Sparrow as it is about her children. The narrator even refers to the adults by their first names, highlighting that their lives are as tied in with the fate of the gerbils of the title as those of the rest of the family. This novel and the collections of short stories that she wrote in the 1960s and 1970s also demonstrate a shift by Pearce to a simpler writing style. This restraint in style and seeming determination to steer away from FANTASY and stick to the realities of everyday life have been criticised by some. However, she has managed to show that it is possible to write about children's deepest longings and preoccupations using language that they themselves use and understand in contexts that they are familiar with. She highlights the significance that lies behind everyday occurrences: the tensions at the heart of a step-family revealed by the fight over keeping a pair of gerbils; the fear of not living up to a parent's expectations in the running away from a blackberry-picking expedition. The actions of different members of a family reveal not only their individual characters but that of the family as a whole. Children understand this and Pearce never patronises them.

The family at the centre of *The Way to Sattin Shore*

(1983, illustrated by CHARLOTTE VOAKE) is a family in crisis, although at the start not everyone is aware of this. Kate has been told that her father died when she was born. Now she feels hemmed in and restricted by her grandmother's watchful presence. She also longs for her eldest brother Randall to spend time with her as he used to. She has questions she wants to ask and envies Brian, her other brother Lenny's friend, who simply asks when he wants the answer to something. Kate's chief longing, though, is only made explicit in the middle of the book because it is only then that she herself becomes aware of its exact nature. When she sees the sledge that Lenny and Brian have made, she realises that she too could have made one if she had had a father to help her. The gap in her life that is her father's absence is now revealed for her and the reader.

The Way to Sattin Shore differs from the earlier major novels in that it is not based on a fictionalised Cambridgeshire but on Sutton Shore in Suffolk, although again it is a place that Pearce knew as a child. When she revisited it as an adult she had an impression of an emotionally charged meeting between two people of different ages – the meeting which is the climax of the novel.

Descriptions of the countryside do not intrude on the plots of the novels. Yet the settings of her books are never merely background – they are vital characters in themselves, telling tales that interweave with and echo the main plot. Her playful use of a place-name as the name of a minor character in *Minnow on the Say* emphasises this still further. She also included connections between the characters in the first three novels, a result of the reality of the setting for her: if the place is still there, so will the characters be.

Although Pearce has written several collections of short stories – including *The Elm Street Lot* (1969), *The Shadow-Cage and Other tales of the Supernatural* (1977), *The Lion at School* (1985) and *The Rope and Other Stories* (2000), and a retelling of Brian Fairfax-Lucy's *The Children of the House* (1968, later reissued as *The Children of Charlecote*) – she will be remembered for her novels, which with humour, grace and forbearance show children and adults not only learning that when you get your heart's desire you have to learn how to live with it, but also that if you do not have the possible things, then you have nothing. It is this need to reconcile reality with fantasy, the possible with the impossible, that keeps these novels outside the realms of simple wish fulfilment. In each novel it is a case of a 'happier ever after ending'. AMN

Pearse, Susan B. see *AMELIARANNE*; see also *LITTLE FOLKS*

Pearson, Kit 1947– Canadian writer born in Edmonton, Alberta. Pearson has worked as a children's and as a reference librarian and taught writing for children at Simon Fraser University. Her first novel, *The Daring Game* (1986), based upon her own experiences while attending a girls' boarding school in Vancouver, was followed by *A Handful of Time* (1987), a FANTASY woven inside social history. Her World War II trilogy comprises *Looking at the Moon* (1991), *The Sky is Falling* (1989) and *The Lights Go On Again* (1993). Pearson's HISTORICAL FICTION describes young people who are obliged to live in their own society but who suffer displacement and alienation. The trilogy concerns two British young people, Norah and her younger brother, Gavin, who are invited to share the home of a wealthy Canadian woman and her adult daughter until they return home safely to England. Pearson secured a film option for *A Handful of Time* in 1995. Her awards include the Geoffrey Bilson Award in 1995 for Historical Fiction, for *The Lights Go On Again,* and the Ruth Schwartz Award for *Awake and Dreaming* (1996), about a girl who enjoys reading and hides inside her fiction-based day-dreams. MRS

Peck, George Wilbur 1840–1916 American writer and humorist. His *Peck's Bad Boy* (1883) is a humorous chronicle of a boy who plays practical jokes on his father. Despite his penchant for mischief, the boy remains engaging. These stories first appeared in *Peck's Sun*, a Wisconsin newspaper founded and edited by Peck. Later collected in book form as *Peck's Bad Boy and His Pa* (1883), they enjoyed tremendous popularity and provided material for a play, *The Grocery Man and Peck's Bad Boy*, in the same year. His later *Bad Boy Books* did not gain the same following. The author was continuing a genre begun with burlesques of Sunday-school tracts such as *The Story of the Bad Little Boy* and *The Story of a Good Little Boy* (1865) by MARK TWAIN; *THE STORY OF A BAD BOY* (1868) by Thomas Bailey Aldrich, in which the author's memories of his own childhood project a lovable rascal; and of course Twain's *THE ADVENTURES OF TOM SAWYER* (1876). Some believe Peck's reputation as a writer helped him win political recognition and subsequently the election for governor of Wisconsin in 1891. KSB

Peck, Richard 1934– Popular contemporary American poet and writer of YOUNG ADULT FICTION. While teaching at high school in the late 1950s and early 60s, Richard Peck decided to become a writer in order to provide his students with relevant reading material. Since leaving teaching, Peck has successfully published in virtually every genre for young adults. In his realistic novels, he has effectively dealt with a variety of difficult issues, including dysfunctional families in *Father Figure* (1978), suicide and divorce in *Remembering the Good Times* (1985), the death of a friend in *Close Enough to Touch* (1981), and rape in *Are You in the House Alone?* (1976). Peck has also edited anthologies of poetry and essays intended for young adults, including *Sounds and Silences: Poetry for Now* (1970), and written mystery and suspense fiction, such as *Dreamland Lake* (1973). Peck's best-known books are four popular supernatural FANTASIES featuring the independent and eccentric Blossom Culp and her friend, Alexander Armsworth. Set in the early 20th century, *The Ghost Belonged to Me* (1975), *Ghosts I Have Been* (1977), *The Dreadful Future of Blossom Culp* (1983) and *Blossom Culp and the Sleep of Death* (1986) relate Blossom's and Alexander's humorous adventures with ghosts and time travel. JDC

see also YOUNG ADULT FICTION

Peck, Robert Newton 1928– American writer of YOUNG ADULT FICTION, best known for his acclaimed *A Day No Pigs Would Die* (1972), a sensitive and partly autobiographical *Bildungsroman* set on a Shaker farm in Vermont in the 1930s. This book focuses on the clash of cultures between the simple Shaker life led by the protagonist's family and the modern world to which he is constantly exposed at the very borders of the farm. Rob, the central character, idolises his father, but realises he cannot follow in his footsteps; in the end the boy must come to terms with his father's death and accept adult responsibility. The moving story is imbued with a quiet beauty appropriate to its subject and theme. Also particularly popular are Peck's *Soup* stories: the first was *Soup* (1974) and this was followed by many sequels, including *Soup and Me* (1975) and *Soup for President* (1978), and some which have been adapted for TELEVISION. These are humorous bad-boy stories in the tradition of *THE ADVENTURES OF TOM SAWYER* and are aimed at somewhat younger readers than *A Day No Pigs Would Die*. DLR

Peculiar Gift, A see CRITICAL APPROACHES TO CHILDREN'S BOOKS

Peet, Bill (William Bartlett) 1915– Author and illustrator of many PICTUREBOOKS for young readers which have been translated into several languages. He has won numerous regional and children's choice awards. Peet worked for DISNEY Studios from 1937 to 1964 on such animation classics as *PINOCCHIO*, *CINDERELLA*, *Dumbo*, *PETER PAN* and *101 DALMATIONS*. Frustrated by his lack of artistic control on movie projects and the lack of recognition he received as an animator or screenwriter, he began writing and illustrating his own stories. In 1959 his first picturebook was published, *Hubert's Hair-Raising Adventures*. Over 30 other titles have since appeared, including *Chester the Worldly Pig* (1965), *The Whingdingdilly* (1970) and *Big Bad Bruce* (1977).

Peet is primarily admired for his energetic and colourful cartoon-like portraits of animals and inanimate objects. His ILLUSTRATIONS are vigorous and well designed, full of activity and telling detail. As a writer he is frequently compared to DR SEUSS because of his lively verse narrative and the fantastical situations which he creates in his stories. Also like Seuss, he manages to address social problems without overbearing didacticism. *Bill Peet: An Autobiography*, a profusely illustrated story of his life, was honoured by the Caldecott Committee in 1989. EBD

Pellowski, Anne 1933– American children's librarian, author of HISTORICAL FICTION and of STORYTELLING texts, professional storyteller and international consultant. Pellowski was born in Pine Creek, Wisconsin, which is the setting for *The Four Farms* series, historical novels based on her immigrant ancestors, a Polish couple who lived near Pine Creek. Pellowski served as a children's librarian at the New York Public Library and then founded the Information Center on Children's Cultures of the US Committee for UNICEF. Widely recognised and honoured as a goodwill ambassador, educator and advocate for storytelling and story-writing, Pellowski is also a scholar: she has produced the massive international bibliography *The World of Children's Literature* (1968), as well as the definitive scholarly work *The World of Storytelling* (1978, 1990), and *The Story Vine* (1971), which presents objects to accompany narratives from around the world. Pellowski has written several books for children in addition to her historical fiction: *Nine Crying Dolls: A Story from Poland* (1979); *Have You Seen a Comet? Children's Art and Writing from Around the World* (1971); and *The Storytelling Handbook* (1995). Her works reflects the library storyteller's understanding of the nature of storytelling, which includes the use of printed sources and accompanying objects. AL

Pender, Lydia 1907– Gentleness and a delight in the music of language characterise this wordsmith who was one of the first Australian poets to write specifically for children. *Marbles in My Pocket* (1957) captures the joy and drama of everyday happenings in the lives of small children – like 'Splashing Through the Puddles'. In her texts for PICTUREBOOKS such as *Barnaby and the Horses* (1961), *Barnaby and the Rocket* (1972) and *The Useless Donkeys* (1979) – for which she has been well served by her illustrators – Pender successfully intersperses poetic refrains with highly alliterative and 'singing' prose that weave evocative images of childhood and nature. MSax

***Pennington* Series** (1970–80) YOUNG ADULT NOVELS by K. M. PEYTON about an aggressive teenager whose only asset is his incredible talent for playing the piano. The first in the series, *Pennington's 17th Summer* (1970), was one of a crop of novels published in the late 1960s and early 1970s which featured working-class heroes. Pennington is shown to be violent, moody and not averse to breaking the law if the occasion requires it. Despite this the reader rarely feels inclined to judge him harshly since Peyton makes it clear that his behaviour is the result of a miserable home life: '[his mother] was voluble, argumentative, and unpredictable, treating Penn according to her mood with indulgence, indifference or gross injustice, so that in sixteen years he had never known where he stood with her. His father was ... no easier to live with, settling all arguments by means of a good thumping. Pennington's own predisposition to settle arguments by the same means was merely imitative, not a psychological Freudian aggression.' When we learn that Pennington is also disliked by almost all the teachers at school and by the local policeman, the reader's desire for him to succeed is strengthened. The book is unusual in that the story is not presented entirely from the teenage hero's viewpoint; the reader is also privy to discussions that take place in the school staff-room and the police office. The resolution, in which a famous music teacher hears Pennington play and offers to take him on as a pupil, does seem to fall into place too easily, but is nevertheless satisfying.

The two later books do not present the same dramatic tensions and emotional complexity, despite the fact that by the end of the second book Pennington is about to go to prison. Written mainly from the point of view of Ruth Hollis, Pennington's girlfriend and heroine of *Fly-by-Night* (1968), much of *The Beethoven Medal* (1971) is a fairly conventional teenage romance, with Ruth herself desperate to find out how Pennington feels about her, and her parents concerned at her relationship with the surly young man. The fight which results in Pennington's arrest comes almost out of the blue, and since Pennington's time in prison falls between the second and third books, the reader is not unduly troubled by it. In the third book, *Pennington's Heir* (1980), teenage romance fades and gritty realism takes its place as Ruth discovers that she is pregnant, but, despite their poverty and miserable living conditions, the reality of the baby does not really seem to intrude upon their lives.

To a modern audience the series is now dated; the resolution of *Pennington's 17th Summer* is dependent on one of the teachers caning Pennington, and Ruth is irritatingly submissive. Her dependence on Pennington is deliberately exaggerated by the authorial distance from his own thoughts and feelings so that we have little idea whether Ruth's feelings are reciprocated. Despite this, the first novel is still in print and enjoyed by contemporary readers. KA

***Penny Pollard* series** (1983–9) Five titles by Australian ROBIN KLEIN, illustrated by ANNE JAMES, which developed an intimate, humorous continuing conversation about attitudes, language and problems, between Klein and her devoted pre-teen readers in Australia in the 1980s. *Penny Pollard's Diary* (1983), the first of the series, introduces readers to horse-mad Penny, who details her life, her desires and her hassles in attitude-laden, colloquial language. Penny, a tomboy, does not hide her contempt and dislike for the trappings of feminine stereotypes and, while on a school visit to a local nursing home, meets a kindred spirit, in rebellious 80-year-old Mrs Bethany. In *Penny Pollard's Letters* (1984) Penny, sent to stay with Aunt Winifred in the country, writes letters to family, friends and enemies, whining, boastful or aggressive in tone, as she sorts out her sibling rivalry and the other experiences life is dealing her. The letters are full of sketches, jottings, swap cards, photos and souvenirs accumulated for Penny by the series illustrator, Ann James. *Penny Pollard in Print* (1986), *Penny Pollard's Passport* (1988) and *Penny Pollard's Guide to Modern Manners* (1989) relate further tales of Penny, as she variously embraces journalism, travels to the United Kingdom, and completes an enforced school project on 'good manners and etiquette', in which, with assistance from Mrs Bethany, she tackles the problems of life, from bedwetting and beetroot to answering machines, in her own idiosyncratic style.

SNJ

penny dreadfuls Pejorative term for sensationalist story papers of immense popularity from the 1820s to the early 20th century, believed by moralists to incite the working classes to violent crime and dissolute behaviour. Young readers trapped in wretched living and working conditions (and closet devotees from other classes) delighted in such heroes and villains as Varney the Vampyre, Dick Turpin, Sweeney Todd and Jack Harkaway. Hack writers were paid by the line: their stories are often rambling, and wallow in graphic and bloodstained accounts of slaughter, execution and abduction in settings from London's underworld to the pirate-infested Southern Seas. GPF

***Penrod* series** (1914–29) Trilogy comprising *Penrod*, *Penrod and Sam* and *Penrod Jashber*, by the American author BOOTH TARKINGTON. The books relate the adventures of Penrod and his friends as they organise the Society of the In-Or-In, stage a domestic circus, shadow possible criminals, and engage in the great tar fight. Penrod is pleased to be called the 'Worst Boy in Town,' because he feels the epithet is both descriptive and complimentary; it is when he is termed 'little gentleman' that he goes berserk. Tarkington felt the success of the *Penrod* series was due to the fact that

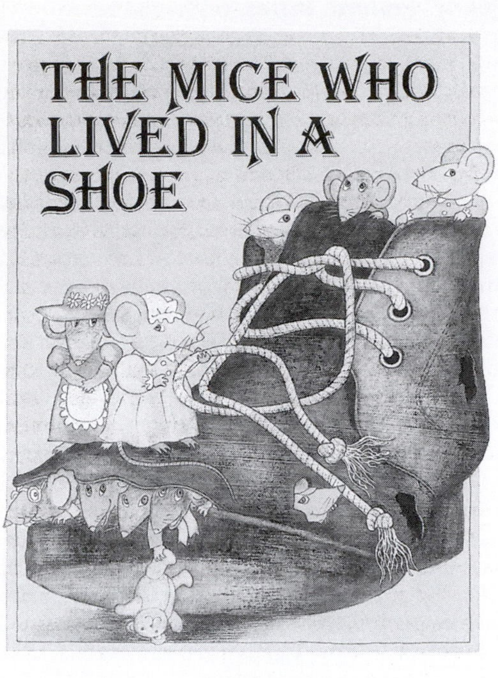

Cover design by Rodney Peppé.

Penrod was a '*true* boy' instead of a 'book-and-stage boy'. Penrod is often linked with *TOM SAWYER*, both because of the ironic narration, and because the books fall into the tradition of bad-boy fiction, popular in America from the 1870s until the 1930s. WH

Pentamerone see 'BLUEBEARD'; FAIRY TALES; 'WARWICK GOBLE'; 'PUSS IN BOOTS'; 'SLEEPING BEAUTY'

Peppé, Rodney 1934– Art-school trained and with an early career in advertising, the British illustrator Peppé comes to the task of creating children's books very much as a graphic designer. His considerable output shows great variety and inventiveness. Solid colours and COLLAGE in the early books (such as his first, *The Alphabet Book*, 1968) give way to detailed pen-and-wash illustrations and the use of toys and models (made by himself) in the later books, as in the several *Mice* books (from 1981). As an author-illustrator he can control the balance of verbal and visual jokes which he supplies to engage even the youngest reader, as in his *Little Toy Board Books* (1983). JAG

Peppermint Pig, The (1975) Novel by NINA BAWDEN and winner of the *GUARDIAN* AWARD. Set during the early years of the 20th century, it describes a family's struggle to adapt to poverty after their father loses his job for a crime he did not commit. Emphasis is placed throughout on the need for absolute morality and independence from strangers, despite the financial difficulties and potential loneliness this may bring, and on the need for honesty, made frighteningly clear by the final episode of the book in which the heroine's beloved pet pig is slaughtered without her prior knowledge. KA

Perceforest see 'SLEEPING BEAUTY'

Percy FitzPatrick Award see AWARDS AND MEDALS

***Percy* Series** PICTUREBOOKS by Nick Butterworth which have gained increasing popularity since the first title, *One Snowy Night*, was published in 1989. Set in the park where Percy the park-keeper tends all the animals, the stories present a comfortable world in which Percy can resolve any difficulty. There is no rivalry between the different animals, who are seen as friendly but not very clever, and everyone is forgiven any minor mistakes. Percy is continually even-tempered, becoming at worst a little disgruntled, even when thrown with his wheelbarrow into the river. The stories are set almost entirely within the safe confines of the park, and the sense of security and familiarity is increased through the warm colours of the ILLUSTRATIONS, many of which are contained within a box a little smaller than the pages of the book, adding to the child reader's sense of security. The first four books in the series are set in the different seasons and the dominant colours in each reflect the time of year. Many of the books make use of some kind of novelty – particularly the fold-out page – while *Four Feathers in Percy's Park* (1998) is a complex pop-up. KA

Perkins, Lucy Fitch 1865–1937 American author and illustrator of the *Twins* series. Beginning with *The Dutch Twins* (1911), Perkins wrote over 25 books about twin children in other countries and other times, in an attempt to encourage 'mutual respect for the best which other nations bring to this shore'. The series was continued by other writers after her death. FEA

Perrault, Charles 1628–1703 French civil servant, member of the Académie Française (1671), essayist and poet. He is best remembered, however, for his *Histoires ou contes du temps passé; avec des Moralitez* (1697), a collection of stories often known in English as 'FAIRY TALES', including such favourites as *CINDERELLA* and *LITTLE RED RIDING HOOD*.

Until the favour of patronage deserted him with the death of Louis XIV's powerful minister Colbert in 1683, Perrault had been employed as Controller General of the King's Buildings, Gardens, Arts and Manufactories – an important office in the reign of 'Le

Roi Soleil', who was determined that his greatness should be reflected in the splendour of his public works. Much of Perrault's early literary output, in the fashion of the times, consisted of poems in praise of the royal family and other potential benefactors.

After the decline of his fortunes in the civil service, Perrault engaged in a series of contentious arguments within the Academy, notably championing the cause of the Moderns in the famous and sometimes bitter 'Quarrel of the Ancients and Moderns'. The *Contes* are to be seen in the context of this debate, for one of Perrault's intentions in publishing them was to demonstrate the qualities of modern tales compared with the fables of classical authors; he argued that his stories were superior both as narratives and as a means of moral instruction. Perrault's energetic contribution to the argument included his 1688 *Parallel of the Ancients and Moderns* which ran to 1,200 pages, followed by a further three volumes under the same title along with two collections of character portraits entitled *Illustrious Men who have lived in Our Century* (1696/1700).

Although it was not judged appropriate to mention the *Contes* in the lengthy funeral eulogy delivered in his praise to the Academy, Perrault's stories have become perhaps the most ubiquitous in the western world. They have been reworked again and again for young readers and listeners by authors, illustrators and storytellers. Literary critics (such as Jack Zipes) and psychoanalytic critics (such as Bruno Bettelheim) have exposed layers of power within the stories Perrault told which account for their longevity and popularity. Andrew Lang expansively declared in 1888: 'No nation owes him so much as we of England, who, south of the Scottish, and east of the Welsh marches, have scarce any popular tales of our own save Jack the Giant Killer.' GPF

Peter (1991) Novel by the Australian author KATE WALKER, which attracted some controversy because of its non-judgemental exploration of themes of masculinity and sexuality. Fifteen-year-old Peter is aware of a growing attraction to David, a university colleague of his elder brother. David's openness regarding his gay identity raises questions for Peter about his own masculinity, as he tries to assert himself in his trailbike group, fails to respond to female sexual advances, fends off his estranged father's and others' homophobic reactions, and attempts to seduce David. Through the character of David, Walker allows Peter to accept that his uncertainty is quite normal, and gives him time to develop and understand his identity, whatever that may be. SNJ

see also GAY AND LESBIAN LITERATURE FOR CHILDREN AND YOUNG ADULTS; SEX IN CHILDREN'S BOOKS

Peter and the Wolf see ABRIDGEMENT; REG CARTWRIGHT; SELINA HASTINGS; MUSIC AND STORY

Peter and Wendy see PETER PAN

Peter Pan and Wendy see PETER PAN

Peter Pan Generic name for a group of texts by J. M. BARRIE, and the name of their chief character. In order of publication in book form, these are *Peter Pan in Kensington Gardens* (1906), consisting of a self-sufficient narrative extrapolated with minimal textual alterations from Barrie's earlier novel for adults, *The Little White Bird* (1902), then *Peter and Wendy*, Barrie's novelisation of his stage play *Peter Pan* (1911), and lastly the stage play itself, which remained unpublished until 1928. An extra scene in the stage play, performed only once in Barrie's lifetime, was finally published in 1957 as *When Wendy Grew Up*. However, the major event in establishing *Peter Pan* in the canon of children's literature was not book publication but the first performance of the play, in December 1904. Over and above the texts in which he appears, the character of Peter Pan has attained an independent life of his own as a universally understood symbol of eternal childhood. Adults and children who have never read the book or seen the play, or even the DISNEY cartoon film, associate the name 'Peter Pan' with folktale shorthand for spirited, mischievous and insistent youthfulness and the wilful renunciation of adulthood. Many critics have associated him with ALICE as a figure from recent literature who has escaped the defining boundaries of text. F.J. Harvey Darton, in his classic study *Children's Books in England*, says that even before the publication of the playscript, 'Peter himself, with Wendy and some of their companions, had become almost as familiar proverbially as Alice'. ROGER LANCELYN GREEN compares his status with that of other celebrated individuals in modern literature. 'Peter alone has crossed the border-land of folklore. Even Alice is only three-dimensional: Peter Pan has broken into the fourth dimension of the imagination.' Barbara Wall, in her study *The Narrator's Voice*, says that the play's success 'released the character into the mythology of childhood', and Marcus Crouch, in *Treasure Seekers and Borrowers*, declares that '*Peter Pan* itself has become embedded deep in the national consciousness'.

The continuing associative power of the symbolic individual figure must somehow be detached as a phenomenon from the texts in which he originates. These give ample scope for confusion in themselves. The figure of Peter Pan in Barrie's work exists in two forms, at two ages and in two places. The Peter Pan of *Peter Pan in Kensington Gardens* is a baby, one week old. The story is a whimsical FANTASY based on the supposition that all children prior to birth were birds, although they naturally lose their wings and hence their ability to fly when born as human children. By the force of imaginative belief Peter Pan retained the powers of his fantasy gestation, escaped from the unbarred windows of his nursery, and flew to Kensington Gardens, where he occupied a position of unique and immortal intermediacy somewhere between bird and baby, becoming in the process an almost god-like nature spirit. From time to time Peter toys with the idea of resuming human form, but delays until it is too late. The second chance of human babyhood has gone, another baby has usurped his place, and the nursery window is barred to him for life.

Peter Pan in Kensington Gardens is often dismissed, even by enthusiasts for the play, as a mere whimsical offshoot of *The Little White Bird*, a curious and disturbing novel in which the narrator engages in the 'innocent' and temporary kidnapping of a small boy, whom as a bachelor he treats with a kind of avuncular motherhood. The 'Kensington Gardens' stories are told as an inset narrative to this small boy. *The Little White Bird* is a strange half-confessional fantasy, rooted in biographical realities, and protected from damaging interpretations of paedophiliac sublimation only by Barrie's customary humour and self-disparagement, his charmingly ingratiating self-contempt, and his persistent habit of disingenuously utilising his personal oddities as the raw material of fictions. Its very openness contains its psychological self-defence. The story's weaknesses are clear, though they are such as to make it (like *Peter and Wendy*) profoundly interesting to modern students of narratology. However, it cannot be ignored as a source of events, ideas and themes which later received classic expression in *Peter Pan*.

The Peter Pan of the play and *Peter and Wendy*, and of folklore symbolism, is not a baby but a boy in middle childhood, and his world is not Kensington Gardens but the Never Never Land. Yet obvious parallels of incident and situation connect the two. The older Peter too has been displaced by a sibling and has found the nursery window barred. An incident in *Peter Pan in Kensington Gardens*, where the fairies build a house round four-year-old Maimie Mannering after she has defied the Lock-Out Time to hide overnight in the Gardens, is the progenitor of the famous Wendy House scene in the play. The ability to fly is still the fugitive children's defining accomplishment. A more significant connection is the power of children's imagination, when coupled with will and confident belief, to create in 'reality' the play-world which it seeks. The two works also share a barbed idealisation of motherhood, as the ultimate protective relationship which yet retains the feared capacity to forget and be forgotten, to betray and be betrayed.

The baby Peter is caught between the conflicting desires for immortal babyhood and human childhood. He wishes to defer re-entry to the nursery, and with it human growth, but while he enjoys immortal babyhood, human time moves on. He can stop his own time in its tracks, but not the world's. 'He knew he could never be a real human being again, and scarcely wanted to be one, but oh! how he longed to play as other children play.' The predicament faced by the older Peter, in *Peter Pan*, is essentially the same. Instead of being caught between immortal pre-nativity and the temporal imperatives of birth, he is caught between immortal boyhood and the temporal necessities of growth. Freed from the mutabilities of natural human process, both the Peters are deprived of its delights. Self-sentenced to immunity from life, they can only play. Seeing that which they desire, but did not desire enough, they can only watch behind the bars of their solitude. At the end of *Peter Pan*, the Darling family are reunited, 'but there was none to see it except a strange boy who was staring in at the window. He had ecstasies innumerable that other children can never know; but he was looking through the window at the one joy from which he must be for ever barred.' You cannot have it both ways, and there is no second chance. The cost of inhabiting the timeless limbo between the unborn and the born, or between boyhood and manhood, is not to be human at all. Barrie called Peter, with accurate irony, 'the tragic boy'.

How, then, did such a complex and in some ways sombre text become a children's classic? The answer, surely, is that the children's classic is the play, and not the printed text at all. *Peter Pan in Kensington Gardens* is for adults. In its whimsical glorying in childhood, its clever pastiche of literary styles, its mock-humble sententiousness, its quick-footed changes of stance, its traces of pagan mysticism, it is shot through with instabilities beyond the reach of children. It stands in a similar relation to *Peter Pan* as KENNETH GRAHAME'S *THE GOLDEN AGE* does to *THE WIND IN THE WILLOWS*. The novelised *Peter and Wendy*, written seven years after the play, is similarly mercurial, with an even more shifting, and shifty, narratorial presence. It is a brilliantly witty, pyrotechnic work, but most children do not know where they stand with it. When Barrie finally published *Peter Pan* in 1928, his stage directions form a complementary satire, lighting yet more torches in his personal no-man's land. The play, however, though not wholly free from subtle infiltration by the dramatist's own persona, exists chiefly as a powerful dramatic action to which child audiences have direct access.

All the *Peter Pan* texts have been subjected to biographical and psychoanalytical interpretations in recent years, and their origins can be confidently traced to elements of Barrie's physical nature, to his early life experiences, and above all to the friendship he formed with the sons of Arthur and Sylvia Llewelyn Davies shortly before they were written. Barrie seems never to have matured physically or sexually. Although he was romantically attracted to women, his marriage to the actress Mary Ansell was unsuccessful and probably unconsummated. He retained a strangely youthful appearance into old age. Childhood experiences too, both negative and positive, may have tied him to boyhood. When he was six his brother David, not quite 14, was killed while skating. Barrie thus acquired an intense emotional image of a boy frozen in time, a tragic prototype of Peter Pan, and may have experienced difficulty in emotionally crossing the barrier of the age at which his brother died. In such ways Barrie was physically and emotionally predisposed to respond imaginatively to the opportunity provided by his meeting with the Llewelyn Davies family.

The story of this relationship has been admirably told by Andrew Birkin in his book *J.M. Barrie and the Lost Boys*. In 1897 Barrie met George and Jack Llewelyn Davies, respectively aged four and three, while walking his dog in Kensington Gardens. Subsequently he met their mother at a dinner party and then, in the years that followed, effectively took possession of the family, which eventually consisted of five boys. Storytelling and games, such as Barrie had enjoyed in his own elongated childhood, were central to the relationship. The Kensington Gardens stories of the infant Peter Pan were evolved during the boys' early childhood, developing naturally as the boys grew older into the bloodthirsty games of redskins and pirates which inspired the older Peter Pan, the eternal boy whose life is wholly consumed by imagination and play.

The biographical connections are only too conspicuous. The 'innocent' kidnapping of David in *The Little White Bird* is a fanciful fulfilment of Barrie's desire to pluck George Llewelyn Davies from his family, and the older Peter's enticement of the Darling children from their nursery to the Never Never Land is another 'innocent' abduction. Oedipal interpretations of the work rest easily on Peter's slaying of Captain Hook and subsequent usurpation of his role as captain, the more so as Captain Hook and Mr Darling are conventionally played by the same actor. The immortal, joyous but ultimately tragic stagnation in endless childhood stands in conflict with growth and natural process through the contrasted figures of Peter and Wendy. Wendy embodies Barrie's preoccupation with motherhood, and especially the child mother.

Such elements are indubitably there in the prose texts, intensified in their complexity by the unstable narratorial persona. The play, however, escapes the complexities which form and underlie it. It too evolved, especially in the course of production and early revivals, generally in ways which simplified the ambiguities of its appeal and made it more obviously a children's play. Although the framing scenes in the Darling household have their embarrassments, the play is predominantly a dramatic collage of traditional children's story – pirates, redskins, mermaids, wolves, secret dens and flying – coupled with original (and to adults ominous) additions such as the ticking crocodile, to make an unforgettable theatrical spectacle and the foundation classic of modern children's theatre.

Except for a short break in wartime, *Peter Pan* was revived annually for over half a century. It is still regularly produced as the Christmas play in provincial theatres, and enjoyed a major production at the National Theatre in 1982. The Disney film, although a travesty of the original, remains popular, and faults of execution rather than of basic appeal undermined STEVEN SPIELBERG's feature film *Hook*. As revivals and adaptations in both theatre and prose narrative abound, it is clear that *Peter Pan* is still a living classic text. PH

see also DRAMA FOR CHILDREN

Peter Pan in Kensington Gardens see PETER PAN; see also ARTHUR RACKHAM

Peter Pan Picture Book, The see ALICE B. WOODWARD

Peter Parley's Annual Peter Parley was the penname of an American writer for children, SAMUEL GOODRICH (1793–1860). His books were reprinted in Britain, but shortly his name was pirated by the publisher Simkin Marshall who introduced the monthly *Peter Parley's Magazine* (January 1839). These issues were bound into a volume, *Peter Parley's Annual* (1840), and subtitled 'A Christmas and New Year's Present for Young People', forming the first Christmas ANNUAL. The monthly paper ran until 1863 but the annual continued until 1892. DG

Petry, Ann (Lane) 1909–97 African American writer and storyteller. Petry is best known for adult novels, YOUNG ADULT FICTION and BIOGRAPHIES for children. Born in the resort town of Old Saybrook, Connecticut, she was married and living in New York City when she wrote her first novel, *The Street* (1946). The novel, about life in Harlem, became a commercial and literary success, and Petry became the first African American woman to write a bestseller. *Tituba of Salem Village* (1964) is perhaps Petry's most enduring legacy to children's literature. It is still used in classrooms as a valuable example of well-written HISTORICAL FICTION. Petry examines the life of Tituba, a young slave, sold to a strict Puritan minister and moved from her home in Barbados to a new and harsh life in New England in 1692. Tituba is an outsider, a woman of courage and intelligence. She brings with her West Indian herbs and practises home arts. Great suspicion arises and leads to eventual accusations of witchcraft. Petry brings into sharp focus many of the factors that contributed to the infamous Salem witchcraft trials. *Harriet Tubman: Conductor on the Underground Railroad* (1955) and *Legends of the Saints* (1970) are biographies for children that reflect Petry's great interest in the motivation for courageous acts in history. Her ability to write with mature intelligence and emotion for children shows great respect for her readers. ESC

see also AFRICAN AMERICAN LITERATURE

Peyton, K.M. see *FLAMBARDS* SERIES; *PENNINGTON* SERIES; see also CHILD AUTHORS

Pfister, Marcus 1960– Swiss author-illustrator born in Berne, where he also studied art, and best known for *THE RAINBOW FISH* (1992). Pfister's work consists of over 20 PICTUREBOOKS, many in series based around characters e.g. *The Rainbow Fish*, *Hopper the Hare*, *Penguin Pete*, as well as several Christmas stories. Pfister's illustrations are distinctive owing to their soft-focus watercolour style, bringing a cosy, reassuring atmosphere to his books. Several of his books, including *The Rainbow Fish*, *Dazzle the Dinosaur* (1994) and *The Christmas Star* (1993) are also notable for their use of holographic foil stamping, which is glitteringly eye-catching. KA

Phantom Tollbooth, The (1961) The American writer Norton Juster's allegorical FANTASY about the precociously bored Milo and his quest to rescue the Princesses Rhyme and Reason from exile, thereby restoring the Kingdom of Wisdom to a proper balance between words and numbers. It is a modern descendant of the quest romance and has been compared with *THE PILGRIM'S PROGRESS* and the *ALICE* books. Like BUNYAN's allegory, *The Phantom Tollbooth* is didactic. However, Milo's 'everyman' appeal and the clever situational puns, striking incidents and distinctive characterisation do much to lighten the educational thrust of the book: Milo's belated discovery that he must eat his own words at a grand banquet in Dictionopolis results in a very unappetising meal; he takes the opportunity to 'direct' the colours of the sunrise and inadvertently causes an entire week to go by; his chief companions are a watch-dog named Tock, whose body is an alarm clock, and a large Humbug who embodies the name admirably. These entertaining qualities and Milo's growth as an intellectual hero over the course of his journey do much to answer the few critics who have found the book's wordplay and conceptual humour too sophisticated for its intended audience. NJW

Phelps, Elizabeth Stuart see *GYPSY BREYNTON* SERIES

Philip, Neil see KING ARTHUR; see also CRITICAL APPROACHES TO CHILDREN'S LITERATURE; SCOTTISH FOLKTALES; *THE STONE BOOK*; *TAM LIN*; *THE WEIRDSTONE OF BRISINGAMEN*

Phillips, Mary South African author of two books written in an experimental form, combining fictional narrative with the retelling of San (Bushman) myths: *The Bushman Speaks* (1961) and *The Cave of Uncle Kwa: A Bushman Fantasy* (1965). Though intended to teach young white readers about the way of life, beliefs and art of the early San, the books are marred by inaccuracies, attitudes which by today's standards are racist, clumsy and dated style, and poor illustrations. However, they mark a stage in the literary rehabilitation of the San and efforts to produce more South African children's books ERJ

see also AFRICAN MYTHOLOGY

Phipson, Joan [Joan Margaret Fitzhardinge] 1912– Few contemporary Australian writers have ranged as widely or explored so many diverse areas of experience as Phipson. Her early realistic FAMILY STORIES set on rural properties were drawn from her own life and a keen observation of her children. But book by book she extended her frame of reference and refined her style. Without resorting to 'issues', Phipson has pursued themes relevant to contemporary youth: a poor self-image and delinquency in *Peter and Butch* (1969) and *Hit and Run* (1986); alienation, hysteria, death and suicide in *A Tide Flowing* (1981) and *Bianca* (1988). She is equally successful whether writing realism as in *Helping Horse* (1974), psychological FANTASY as in *The Watcher in the Garden* (1982), TIME-SLIP FANTASY as in *Dinko* (1985), or dramatising a conservation theme as in *Fly Into Danger* (1978). Her book for younger readers *Hide Till Daytime* (1977), in which two children spend a terrified night locked in a large city department store, has been as acclaimed as her YOUNG ADULT philosophical novels such as *Way Home* (1973). The latter novel postulates that an affinity with the land itself is necessary for human wholeness and personal harmony – a theme that runs throughout Phipson's writing. MSax

Phoenix and the Carpet, The see E. NESBIT; *PSAMMEAD* SERIES; see also FANTASY; H.R. MILLAR

Phoenix Award see AWARDS AND MEDALS

Picard, Barbara Leonie see KING ARTHUR

picturebooks Books which rely for their effects upon an interplay of pictures and words. Unlike illustrated books, where the pictures tend to serve a prior verbal text, picturebooks require that the pictures are as significant within the overall text as the words and that both should be physically close enough together for a reader to apprehend readily their mutual influence. The whole text in picturebooks is thus composite in nature although the form itself is in fact extremely flexible and varied.

The picturebook is a relatively modern invention, since the technical means of printing high-quality pictures in abundance and bringing them into close proximity with the printed text have not always been available. From the beginning printed books were illustrated, but the earliest woodcuts were relatively crude. More sophisticated ILLUSTRATIONS could be produced through engraving on copper, but the placing of engraved images alongside letterpress was costly and difficult. The children of the book-owning élite may have had access to works such as the fables of AESOP or *REYNARD THE FOX*, but there was nothing like a picturebook for children until the publication in 1658 of J.A. Comenius' Latin textbook, *ORBIS SENSUALIUM PICTUS*, first translated into English by Charles Hoole in 1659. The art of 'white line' WOOD ENGRAVING developed by THOMAS BEWICK at the end of the 18th century led to significant improvements in the degree of sophistication in book illustration, and by the latter half of the 19th century colour printing from wood blocks had developed to the point where high-quality picturebooks could be produced relatively cheaply and in quantity.

Despite the fact that a certain technological refinement was necessary before the modern picturebook could begin to develop, its origins lie in the most crude and despised products of the book trade – the CHAPBOOKS. Early picturebooks, such as *The Comic Adventures of Old Mother Hubbard* and *THE BUTTERFLY'S BALL AND THE GRASSHOPPER'S FEAST*, both published by JOHN HARRIS in 1805 and 1807 respectively, were similar to chapbooks both structurally and thematically and were extremely popular with both adults and children. As their popularity waned, colourful picturebooks known as TOY BOOKS began to be produced in great numbers by publishers such as Dean & Son, Routledge and Warne. These continued to recycle traditional chapbook themes right through to the latter years of the century.

A major influence upon the development of the picturebook during the 19th century was the work of narrative artists and printmakers such as William Hogarth, Thomas Rowlandson and GEORGE CRUIKSHANK. Only Cruikshank made a direct contribution to children's literature, most notably through his illustrations to the *German Popular Stories* of JACOB

Illustration from *The Babes in the Wood* by Randolph Caldecott.

and WILLHELM GRIMM (1823–6), but collectively their influence was profound: several generations of artists carried their lively spirit of caricature into book illustration in general and picturebook illustration in particular. A.H. Forrester ('Alfred Crowquill'), RICHARD DOYLE, John Leech and Charles Bennett in the middle years of the century and, later, RANDOLPH CALDECOTT contributed caricatures and illustrations to magazines such as *Punch* and *The Illustrated London News* as well as working on picturebooks and book illustration. Caricature of a different sort entered the bloodstream of the picturebook through the influence of EDWARD LEAR'S *BOOK OF NONSENSE* (1846) and HEINRICH HOFFMAN'S influential *STRUWWELPETER*, translated into English in 1848.

In the last decades of the century Caldecott, along with KATE GREENAWAY and WALTER CRANE, helped transform the toy book into something like the modern picturebook. All three were recruited by the printer and engraver EDMUND EVANS, who not only had an eye for talented illustrators but also possessed the means to render their designs accurately and sensitively through the technique of WOOD ENGRAVING in colour. Caldecott was to prove by far the most influential, for his work transcended the merely decorative or illustrative – he was the interpretative picturebook-maker *par excellence*, his witty and humorous pictorial variations upon rhymes such as *The Queen of Hearts* (1881) and *Hey Diddle Diddle* (1882) setting standards that few picturebook-makers have been able to match. Caldecott's influence reached forward into the 20th century through the work of BEATRIX POTTER and L. LESLIE BROOKE, both of whom were great admirers of the Caldecott toy books. Unfortunately both suffered from further developments in printing technology – the shift from wood engraving to HALFTONE colour printing. Potter was never entirely happy with the glossy, coated paper that this process requires, and in Brooke's most famous works – *Johnny Crow's Garden* (1903) and *Johnny Crow's Party* (1907) – coloured and black-and-white illustrations had to be printed on different kinds of paper.

However, the direction that picturebook design and production in the 20th century was ultimately to take was hinted at in the two small books produced by WILLIAM NICHOLSON in the 1920s, *Clever Bill* (1926) and *The Pirate Twins* (1929). Nicholson's designs for these books, along with the hand-written texts, were reproduced by colour photo-offset LITHOGRAPHY, the process that in time was to supersede all others. The principles of lithography had been developed in the late 18th century by Alois Senefelder, but one of the earliest forms of the process used commercially – chromolithography – tended to produce illustrations that were rather heavy and crude. The great advantage of offset lithography was that a range of effects and art media could be reproduced with a high degree of accuracy and sensitivity. EDWARD ARDIZZONE exploited these possibilities in the 1930s, beginning with his *LITTLE TIM AND THE BRAVE SEA CAPTAIN* (1936). Under the influence of the popular French *BABAR* series Ardizzone cast his first *Little Tim* books as large-scale, folio-sized works, the text being hand-lettered as in Nicholson's earlier books. KATHLEEN HALE adopted a similar format in her *ORLANDO* series published by Country Life.

Perhaps the pioneer of the American picturebook was E. Boyd Smith, a versatile and creative author-illustrator who flourished in the first two decades of the 20th century. One of his most popular and artistic successes was *The Story of Noah's Ark* (1905). However, he had no important followers, and the state of American picturebooks languished in mediocrity, with only occasional luminaries, such as the perennial favourite, Blanche Fisher Wright's *The Real Mother Goose* (1916) and C.B. Fall's much-loved *ABC Book* (1923). It was not until the late 1920s that the American picturebook began to thrive, a phenomenon wrought by several factors. The improvements in offset lithography allowed for more faithful colour reproduction, expanded creative possibilities and attracted many artists, and an influx of talented Europeans, including Miska Petersham (Hungarian), KURT WIESE (German), Ingri and EDGAR PARIN D'AULAIRE (she was Norwegian, he German), FEODOR ROJANKOVSKY (Russian) and Ludwig Bemelmans (Austrian), added vitality to the field.

WANDA GÁG's *Millions of Cats* (1928) is considered a landmark of American picturebook design, justly celebrated for its rhythmical pages with flowing black-and-white illustrations and skilful hand-lettering, all accompanying a story with FOLKTALE qualities and an infectious refrain. It is a story of the castaway, popular during the Great Depression. *The Story about Ping* (1933), written by MARJORIE FLACK and illustrated by KURT WIESE, is one of the first great collaborative picturebooks, filled with humour and poetic imagery and illustrated by an artist familiar with the Chinese setting. ROBERT LAWSON's *The Story of Ferdinand* (1936), illustrated in fine black-and-white drawings by MUNRO LEAF, is about a pacifistic bull, content with the simple things in life. In a similar vein are the works of VIRGINIA BURTON, including *Mike Mulligan and His Steam Shovel* (1938) and *The Little House* (1942), anthropomorphic stories exploring the consequences of urban sprawl and dehumanising technology. The incomparable DR SEUSS (pseudonym for Theodore Geisel) broke the traditional picturebook mould with *And to Think That I Saw It on Mulberry Street* (1937). His fanciful cartoon pictures and his rich language play were bold departures from anything that preceded him. An enduring favourite, he remains loved for both his art and his gentle lessons on life. This period saw two other important developments. One was the rise of the American COMIC book (*SUPERMAN* appeared in 1938), a popular art form long blamed for the nation's declining literary standards (a stigma since passed on to TELEVISION). The other, at the opposite end of the spectrum, was the establishment in 1938 of the CALDECOTT MEDAL, awarded annually for distinguished illustration in an American children's book, an event that seemed to legitimise the field.

In 1942 an American publishing phenomenon emerged – the *GOLDEN BOOKS*, inexpensive hardcover picturebooks selling initially for 25 cents. Among the early contributors to the series were such artists as the author MARGARET WISE BROWN and illustrators Edith Thatcher Hurd, RUTH KRAUSS, FEODOR ROJANKOVSKY, RICHARD SCARRY, LEONARD WEISGARD and GARTH WILLIAMS – all of whom would become noted artists in their own right, dominating the picturebook field in the 1950s. Naturally, many *Golden Book* authors and illustrators were undistinguished, but their influence cannot be discounted. JANETTE SEBRING LOWREY's *The Poky Little Puppy* (1942), one of the earliest selections, remains the bestselling children's book of all time, and five of the top ten bestselling hardcover children's books are *Golden Books*.

From the middle years of the 20th century onwards British picturebooks too were increasingly influenced by COMICS and strip cartoons. Comics had developed out of 19th-century picture sheets and their designers were quick to adapt the graphic techniques of carica-

Illustration from *The Baby's Own Aesop* by WALTER CRANE.

ture – essentially the simplification and exaggeration of form – for their simple narrative ends. They learned much from poster design and the cinema in the early decades of the 20th century about adaptations to perspective and framing, and in time such discoveries were to become a part of the picturebook-maker's design repertoire. Hergé's *TINTIN* and Goscinny and Uderzo's *ASTERIX* did much to bring about this change, as did the popularity of such strips as *RUPERT BEAR*. Contemporary picturebook-makers such as SHIRLEY HUGHES and RAYMOND BRIGGS have thoroughly explored the possibilities offered to the picturebook by the comic strip. The former's *UP AND UP* (1979) and *Chips and Jessie* (1985), and the latter's *FATHER CHRISTMAS* (1973), *Gentleman Jim* (1980) and *When the Wind Blows* (1982) demonstrate the extent to which the techniques can be made to serve much more sophisticated narrative and expressive ends than was originally the intention. The influence of the cinema was also indirect but it can be seen clearly in the close-ups and deep perspectives of *The Story of Ferdinand* (1937) by Americans MUNRO LEAF and ROBERT LAWSON.

Throughout its history the appearance of the picturebook has always been closely tied to the prevailing methods and techniques of printing. Just as the development of WOOD ENGRAVING in the 19th century transformed the picturebook, the progressive refinement of offset lithography, particularly after World War II, enabled illustrators to experiment with an ever-widening range of visual effects. By the 1960s almost any kind of art medium could be reproduced relatively cheaply, in quantity, and more accurately than ever before. In Britain, BRIAN WILDSMITH, VICTOR AMBRUS and CHARLES KEEPING were amongst the first illustrators to explore the possibilities of the more sophisticated technology. Wildsmith is considered to have broken the mould with his first picturebook, *ABC* (1962). Gone was the restraint characteristic of Nicholson and Ardizzone. In contrast Wildsmith's pages blazed with colour and shimmered with the texture of the paint. Keeping and Ambrus were vibrant colourists too but they also had particular strengths as graphic artists and this lent their work – both colour and black and white – a sharp edge and a clear narrative purpose.

Other changes were taking place that had little to do with printing techniques. By 1970 a uniquely late-20th-century form had evolved out of the ever-increasing pictorialisation of culture – the wordless picturebook. Some examples – such as *Vicki* (1968) and *Hide and Seek* (1969) by RENATE MEYER and *Intercity* (1977) and *River* (1978) by her husband, Charles Keeping – offer readers painterly images that have

From *Up and Up* by SHIRLEY HUGHES.

only a slender story to tell. Others – such as *Anno's Journey* (1978) and *Anno's Britain* (1982) by MITSUMASA ANNO, and *The Great Flood* (1978) and *Rain* (1982) by PETER SPIER – invite the reader to examine carefully detailed scenes and panoramas. Still others, such as Raymond Briggs's *THE SNOWMAN* (1978), Shirley Hughes' *Up and Up* (1979) and JAN ORMEROD'S *Sunshine* (1981) are fully-formed narratives that develop characters and tell stories with great skill.

The early 1970s proved to be a time of change in other ways. Raymond Briggs began to draw on the vernacular of the comic and to find his own distinctive style with *Jim and the Beanstalk* (1970) and *FATHER CHRISTMAS* (1974); MICHAEL FOREMAN published his social and political fables *Moose* (1971), *Dinosaurs and All That Rubbish* (1972) and *War and Peas* (1974); non-stereotypical images of black children and their families began to appear in picturebooks as illustrators such as the Jamaican Errol Lloyd began to publish work based upon their own experience. As an exemplar of the changing times, JOHN BURNINGHAM in the 1970s turned his back on his early manner and sought a new direction. In *MR GUMPY'S OUTING* (1970) he adopted a style and an approach that was altogether more spare and light and that allowed him greater freedom to experiment. In picturebook publishing, there was a pronounced shift towards international co-production during the 1970s and 80s, arising in part from the fact that production costs could be kept down through large print runs of pictures, the text, in different languages, being added later.

Recent British illustrators who work within the traditions of caricature have flourished. QUENTIN BLAKE, Raymond Briggs, TONY ROSS, BABETTE COLE, COLIN MCNAUGHTON, BOB GRAHAM and many more have all developed personal variations on the techniques and strategies of the caricaturist. Blake, Cole and McNaughton all suffuse their work with a carefree wit and a spirit of mild subversion. Others such as Tony Ross and COLIN and JACQUI HAWKINS lean towards parody, inverting such forms as the FAIRY TALE and the non-fiction book. Briggs, in *When the Wind Blows* (1982) and *The Tinpot Foreign General and the Old Iron Woman* (1984), returned caricature to its original satirical purpose.

In the United States the post-World-War-II period saw a flowering of quality picturebooks, including such artists as ROBERT MCCLOSKEY, MARCIA BROWN and BARBARA COONEY. McCloskey's *Make Way for Ducklings* (1941) was the first of his notable works in stone lithography (and he most often worked in monochrome). Brown's versatility is phenomenal, working with woodcuts, linocuts, collage and other forms to illustrate primarily folktales. Cooney's hallmarks are muted colours, done in acrylic paints, and painstaking details. By and large, the picturebooks of this period cling to traditional themes, and few can be characterised as daring.

The 1960s saw an explosion of innovative art in children's books. MAURICE SENDAK'S *WHERE THE WILD THINGS ARE* (1963) combines sophisticated visual symbolism with a story probing the psychological depths of the child's mind. Illustrations have become increasingly sophisticated – as in the exquisitely wrought detail of NANCY EKHOLM BURKERT, the naive stylisation of ALICE and MARTIN PROVENSEN, the elegant romanticism of TRINA SCHART HYMAN, the vitality of MARGOT ZEMACH, the dazzling folk art of GERALD MCDERMOTT, and the bold drama of CHRIS VAN ALLSBURG.

A second trend is the recognition of America's cultural diversity. The all-white world of American picturebooks was challenged by EZRA JACK KEATS's *The Snowy Day* (1962), one of the first books to feature an inner-city African American boy. Although Keats himself was white, numerous African American artists and writers have since emerged, including LUCILLE CLIFTON, LEO and DIANE DILLON, ELOISE GREENFIELD, TOM FEELINGS and JOHN STEPTOE. Asian heritage has been celebrated by Ed Young's stunning illustrations for Asian folktales, such as *Lon Po Po: A Red-Riding Hood Story from China* (1989). Hispanic and Native American artists are beginning to appear as well, and a recent trend is the bilingual book, such as Pat Mora's *Uno, Tuo, Tres: One, Two, Three* (1996).

Finally there is the trend towards creative nonfiction – books that are at once informative and artistic. DAVID MACAULEY's books on architecture – for example, *Cathedral* (1973) – and his great work on mechanical principles, *The Way Things Work* (1988), contain meticulous black-and-white drawings. TANA HOBAN is noted for her photographs of multi-layered complexity, as in *So Many Circles, So Many Squares* (1998). The 1980s and 1990s have seen an extraordinary freedom in subject matter, with writers and illustrators venturing into such areas as divorce, homosexuality (see also GAY AND LESBIAN LITERATURE), physical DISABILITY, sexual abuse, and death, even in books for the very young. EVE BUNTING's books for young readers treat such difficult topics as gang violence or the Japanese-American World War II relocation camps, the subject of *So Far from the Sea* (1998), illustrated by Chris Soentpiet. The best picturebook creators today display a deep respect for the sensibilities and the innate wisdom of their young audience, and modern illustrators work with a wide variety of artistic techniques – pulp painting, stencils, computer art, in addition to traditional media. Naturally, alongside these superb artistic achievements are countless cheap storybooks, often with a heavy-handed didacticism and unexceptional art. The American picturebook is nothing if not eclectic.

In Australia, whilst crudely illustrated books for children were published from the early 19th century, it was the publication of Desmond Digby's illustrated interpretation of A.B. PATERSON'S *WALTZING MATILDA* in 1970 that became a landmark in Australian publishing. Its careful attention to overall design and quality illustrations provided an exemplar of the successful picturebook. This book also heralded a spate of picturebook versions of early bush ballads and poems such as *Mulga Bill's Bicycle* (1973) illustrated by KILMENY and DEBORAH NILAND, *The Man from Ironbark* (1974) illustrated by QUENTIN HOLE, and *The Wild Colonial Boy* (1985) illustrated by JOHN ANTHONY KING. During this period, other picturebooks were taking a more irreverent look at Australia's bushranger past. *Bossyboots* (1985) by DAVID COX provides a feminist twist to the more usual masculine bushranger tale through Abigail, 'the bossiest girl in New South Wales', who manages to turn the tables on Flash Fred, while NETTE HILTON's farcical tale *Dirty Dave the Bushranger* (1987) is complemented by ROLAND HARVEY's visual humour, anachronisms and subversive comments.

Pen-and-ink illustration for *Gasp* by TERRY DENTON.

Whilst these picturebooks, with their bush or colonial setting, provide a nostalgic (albeit at times humorous) view of a particular kind of colonial Australian identity, other picturebooks offer alternative versions of what it means to be an Australian. The very popular *POSSUM MAGIC* (1983) by MEM FOX and JULIE VIVAS replaces the bush setting with a tour of the coastal cities as the anthropomorphised possums, Grandma Poss and cheeky Hush, go on a quest to find a cure for Hush's invisibility. The book celebrates a romantic notion of national identity woven around selected traditional Australian/English cuisine (lamingtons, pavlovas) and

Australian symbols and icons (Sydney Opera House, blue apron covered in the stars of the Southern Cross). By contrast, the multicultural and indigenous make-up of Australian society is illustrated in *My Place* (1987) by Donna Rawlins and Nadia Wheatley. This carefully researched and imaginatively constructed picturebook gives an accessible account of 200 years of Australian history by moving backwards in time decade by decade. By focusing on a Sydney suburb, the impact of change on both the physical and social environment is skilfully conveyed.

Prior to the 1970s, stories about indigenous Australians, their culture and stories, were written by white people. This situation was to change with the publication of *The Giant Devil-Dingo* (1973), produced by Aboriginal artist Dick Roughsey and his friend Percy Trezise. This partnership created many fine picturebooks based on Aboriginal Dreaming stories. With their traditional Aboriginal narrative form, vivid colours and stark figures, these books vividly capture the landscape of central and northern Australia and offer all children (and adults) opportunities to view Australia from an Aboriginal perspective. Their second title, *The Rainbow Serpent* (1975), won the Children's Book Council of Australia Book of the Year Award in 1976. Other commendable picturebooks by this partnership include *The Quinkins* (1978) and *The Flying Fox Warriors* (1985). Another successful partnership has been established between two Aboriginal women, Sally Morgan and Bronwyn Bancroft. While Morgan is an acclaimed artist in her own right, she has written a series of picturebooks which have been illustrated by Bancroft. These books, *Dan's Granpa* (1996), *Just a Little Brown Dog* (1997) and *In Your Dreams* (1997), feature indigenous characters. Bancroft's trademark use of bright, vivid colour, dynamic line, and patterned landscapes and motifs provides a modern interpretation of a traditional art form. Bancroft has also illustrated several traditional stories and poems by other Aboriginal writers, including *Minah* (1995) and *Dirrangun* (1994). Another indigenous artist who successfully melds traditional and modern styles is Arone Raymond Meeks. His highly acclaimed picturebooks, *Pheasant and Kingfisher* (1987) and *Enora the Black Crane* (1991), use the traditional colours, yellow ochre, black, red ochre and white, and blend Aboriginal and European styles to offer readers a new interpretation of traditional Aboriginal illustration.

A significant milestone in Australian publishing has been the emergence of postcolonial texts such as *Do Not Go Around the Edges* (1990), by Daisy Utemorrah and Pat Torres, and *Tucker* (1994) by Ian Abdulla. Through prose and poetry, Utemorrah tells of her childhood and early life while Torres's illustrations incorporate images and motifs which are relevant to Utemorrah's land and her people. The interplay and juxtaposition of the three texts – prose, poetry, illustration – break with mainstream literary conventions and challenge the traditional definition of a picturebook. Abdulla's book recalls, in his own distinctive voice, his youth in the South Australian Riverland area during the 1950s. Through naive paintings, Abdulla portrays the stages in catching, preparing and eating the various 'tucker' (food) that could be gathered from the surrounding environment.

Since the 1970s there have been Australian illustrators and writers who were prepared to stretch the boundaries of the picturebook genre. Early picturebooks that were multilayered or dealt with abstract concepts included Ted Greenwood's highly inventive and cerebral *Joseph, Lulu and the Prindiville House Pigeons* (1972) and *The Bunyip of Berkeley's Creek* (1973) by Jenny Wagner and Ron Brooks, which explored the complex notion of personal identity. Increasingly, multilayered and open-ended picturebooks have appeared on the Australian publishing scene. Gary Crew's *The Watertower* (1994), illustrated by Steven Woolman, and *Birdman* (1994), by Jirí Tibor Novák, combine visual symbolism and challenging subject matter to give older readers a challenging and rewarding experience. Others – *The Eleventh Hour* (1988) by Graeme Base; *Whatley's Quest* (1994) by Bruce Whatley and Rosie Smith; *Very Very Odd: A Picture Puzzle Adventure* (1997) by Geoff Kelly; *Bamboozled* (1994) by David Legge; and *Just Another Ordinary Day* (1995) by Rod Clement – deal with complexity of a different kind by using puzzles, codes, and visual tricks and jokes as a way of engaging readers. Challenges to the traditional ways of reading pictures and text as complementary partners in the story construction are also presented in the form of a dual narrative whereby illustrations may tell one story which is in opposition to the story conveyed in words, as in *Drac and the Gremlin* (1988) by Allan Baillie and Jane Tanner. In the case of Ormerod's *The Story of Chicken Licken* (1985), a second layer of pictures in silhouette tells an additional story to the one conveyed by the dominant images and text. Whereas Australian picturebooks once looked to the past and employed idealised notions of predominantly white, Anglo-Celtic family life and childhood, they are increasingly reflecting the complex and culturally diverse world in which children live. Previously taboo topics such as death and ageing are now often treated unsentimentally and openly, as in *The Very Best of Friends* (1989) by Margaret Wild and Julie Vivas, and *Lucy's Bay* (1992) by Gary Crew and Gregory Rogers. The diversity of families and family life is represented in Bob Graham's humorous nuclear-family stories such as *Greetings from Sandy Beach* (1990); divorced but loving parents in *Sam's*

Sunday Dad (1992) by MARGARET WILD and Lorraine Hannay; and ethnic and indigenous families in *Mum Goes to Work* (1992) by LIBBY GLEESON and Penny Azar, and *Pigs and Honey* (1989) by JEANIE ADAMS.

Advanced printing techniques and the diversity of artistic styles, techniques and media offer a range of aesthetic experiences. Some notable examples include the linocuts by NARELLE OLIVER in *The Hunt* (1995) and by PETER GOULDTHORPE in *Hist!* (1991); relief COLLAGE by JEANNIE BAKER in *Window* (1991) and *THE STORY OF ROSIE DOCK* (1995); and torn-paper collage by PATRICIA MULLINS in *V for Vanishing: An Alphabet of Endangered Animals* (1993) and by Sascha Hutchinson in *SNAP!* (Marcia Vaughan, 1994); watercolour and pen by Bruce Whatley in *Detective Donut and the Wild Goose Chase* (1997), co-written with Rosie Smith; crayon and ink by PAMELA ALLEN in *Clippity-Clop* (1994); silk-screen printing and poster paints by Grace Fielding in *Bip, the Snapping Bungaroo* (1990); silk painting by Kim Michelle Toft in *One Less Fish* (1998), co-written with Allan Sheather; charcoal and watercolours by ARMIN GREDER in *Uncle David* (1992), with text by Libby Gleeson, and pencil and watercolours by Di Wu in *Rebel!* (1994), with text by ALLAN BAILLIE. Comic-strip techniques have been used by BRUCE TRELOAR, BOB GRAHAM, DAVID COX, TERRY DENTON, CRAIG SMITH and ALISON LESTER.

Early New Zealand picturebooks included the anthropomorphic *Richard Bird in the Bush* by Mollie Miller Atkinson (1944), illustrated in black-and-white with some colour plates. There were also photo-stories such as Wendy Carnegie's *Finding a Miracle* (1973), which dated quickly owing to the choice of medium. Other books published in the 1970s established a tone of greater respect for the child audience. They were *Pukunui* (1976) by James Waerea and *Mummy, Do Monsters Clean Their Teeth?* (1975) by Jan Farr. The latter title was produced as a small, cheap paperback with illustrations by the new illustrator PAMELA ALLEN. *The Lighthouse Keeper's Lunch* (1977) by RHONDA and DAVID ARMITAGE continues to be popular, and has generated several sequels. The first published titles by New Zealand's best-known author, MARGARET MAHY, were picturebooks. *A Lion in the Meadow* was published in 1969 as part of a five-book international package, which also included *Pillycock's Shop* (1969) and *The Dragon of an Ordinary Family* (1969), which won its illustrator, HELEN OXENBURY, the Kate Greenaway Medal. Two of the best picturebooks by Maori writers are PATRICIA GRACE'S *THE KUIA AND THE SPIDER* (1981), illustrated by ROBYN KAHUKIWA, and *Taniwha* (1986) written and illustrated by Kahukiwa. Although GAVIN BISHOP is well known for his retelling of traditional European folktales in a New Zealand context, an underrated title is the wonderfully surreal *The Horror of Hickory Bay* (1984).

Illustration by JIRÍ TIBOR NOVÁK from *One Big Yo To Go* by Valerie Osborne.

While there have been several highlights since then, including EVE SUTTON'S *My Cat Likes to Hide in Boxes* (1984); Juliet Martin's popular *Boring Mrs Bun* (1986); the *HAIRY MACLARY* books by author/artist Lynley Dodd; and GAELYN GORDON'S *Duckat* (1992), New Zealand picturebooks continue to be criticised for their poor production and design values. The judges of the 1998 *New Zealand Post* Awards commented: '[We] were dismayed by the lack-lustre quality overall. We could see few picturebooks that would excite the imagination of children, books with an integration of text and illustrations, with stories that had tension and resolution, that worked superbly as one unit.' The Australian picturebook, on the other hand, continues to break new ground with innovative and varied approaches to both text and illustration. This fact was acknowledged in the international arena with the Kate Greenaway Medal being awarded to GREGORY ROGERS for his dramatic and creative interpretation of LIBBY HATHORN'S text for *WAY HOME* (1994), a picturebook about a homeless youth.

Canadian picturebooks are a recent phenomenon. In 1967, SHEILA EGOFF lamented that there was 'one important category of writing and illustrating for children that is almost non-existent in Canada: the picturebook' (*The Republic of Childhood*). Little of note was produced prior to 1960, although the first true Canadian picturebook was created in 1859 by Amelia Frances Howard-Gibbon: *An Illustrated Comic Alphabet*. It was drawn for her schoolchildren and not published until 1966. It is after Howard-Gibbon that Canada's annual award for children's book illustration is named. Few Canadian picturebooks used specifically Canadian content until quite recently. Two early examples are Thoreau Macdonald's *A Canadian Child's ABC* (1931), with a text by R.K. Gordon, and Hazel Boswell's *French Canada: Pictures and Stories* (1938). By and large, early Canadian picturebook illustration can be characterised as traditional, representational art with little individual style or experimentalism.

The first Canadian picturebook that can claim to be truly successful is Frank Newfield's *The Princess of Tomboso* (1960), a humorous folktale. Perhaps the first great Canadian picturebook illustrator was ELIZABETH CLEAVER, with such books as William Toye's *The Loon's Necklace* (1977) and *Petrouchka* (1980), both of which demonstrate her superb collage technique. WILLIAM KURELEK and Ann Blades both distinguished themselves with a naive style appropriately suited to their stories of rural Canadian life. The richly diverse Canadian culture is the subject of DAYAL KAUR KHALSA's works, beginning with *Tales of a Gambling Grandmother* (1986), which is based on her family of Russian immigrants. ROBERT MUNSCH's TALL TALES – many, such as *Pigs* (1989), illustrated by MICHAEL MARTCHENKO's cartoons – have universal appeal. Animal fantasies have also proved popular, and TIM WYNNE-JONES's stories about a remarkable cat named Zoom are among the best, including the award-winning *Zoom at Sea* (1983), illustrated with brilliantly detailed pencil drawings by Ken Nutt. Some of the favourite themes in Canadian picturebooks are from native folktales and historical tales of Canadian life. More recently there has been greater diversity, reflecting the country's own diverse culture. Canadian picturebook artists work in many styles, such as MARIE-LOUISE GAY's cartoon art for *Lizzy's Lion* (1984) written by DENNIS LEE, Laszlo Gall's romantic art for numerous retellings of folktales, and Stéphane Poulin's naive art for KATHY STINSON's *Teddy Rabbit* (1988). The artist's medium is equally varied, from acrylics to collage to pen-and-ink – indeed, virtually all forms available to the graphic artist. Given its relatively late start, the Canadian picturebook has made many remarkable contributions to the genre.

A significant number of contemporary picturebooks possess a high degree of self-consciousness about the nature of the form itself. Usually this reflexivity takes the form of a playful testing of limits or subversion of rules and conventions. For example, John Burningham has demonstrated in books such as *COME AWAY FROM THE WATER, SHIRLEY* (1977) and *Where's Julius?* (1986) how the gap between pictures and words can be exploited to create a sense of indeterminacy in the reader. ANTHONY BROWNE regularly draws on a repertoire of surrealist devices to undermine reader expectations, for example in *Bear Hunt* (1979) and *CHANGES* (1990). The AHLBERGS too have shown how reading is a form of play through the use of a conspicuous intertextuality and a free exploration of the book's physical structure. Shirley Hughes, Jill Murphy (see *WORST WITCH* SERIES), DAVID MCKEE and many others have also tested the limits of what is permissible or possible within the pages of a picturebook. That such rule-breaking should take place within a form generally associated with younger children is only apparently paradoxical; children themselves, as they grow and learn, are engaged in the very same exploration of limits. In this respect, playful picturebook-makers are their allies.

The freedoms that picturebook-makers have enjoyed since the 1960s have not been entirely to do with overall appearance and with the technical reproduction of pictorial effects. The picturebook appears to be particularly flexible and varied, with a mutability born of its brevity, its composite nature and its association with childhood, play and the emergence of literacy. Its omnivorousness – its capacity to ingest imagery and text – means that it could respond rapidly to the changes in verbal and visual representation that late 20th-century culture thrust upon us, in much the same way that the chapbook was able to respond to and recycle the cultural produce of its day, both official and unofficial. DL, BN, DLR, KM

see also ALPHABET BOOKS; CHAPBOOKS; COUNTING BOOKS; HALF-TONE PROCESS; ILLUSTRATION; LITHOGRAPHY; MOVABLE BOOKS; PROCESS ENGRAVING; REAL BOOKS

Pied Piper of Hamelin, The (1842) Narrative poem by Robert Browning (1812–89). The celebrated poem, based on a popular German legend, was written for the son of William Macready, the well-known actor. Browning's only serious attempt to write a poem for the young is still regularly anthologised in the late 20th century, a testament to its enduring appeal. A winning combination of wit, spellbinding storytelling and dramatic tension is employed, along with a clever, changing metre and rhyme-scheme. It is a memorable tale which is amusing, moral and sad at the same time, with notable illustrated versions by KATE GREENAWAY (1888), CHARLES ROBINSON (1907) and ARTHUR RACKHAM (1934). MCCS

Pieñkowski, Jan (Michal) 1936– Illustrator and designer, born in Warsaw into a family of architects and artists. He moved to London at the age of ten and was later educated at Cambridge University, where he co-founded a greetings card company. He subsequently worked as an art director in publishing and children's TELEVISION, and his creations have frequently entailed technical innovation and high-

'The nativity' from *Christmas* by Jan Pieñkowski. Pen and ink silhouette and colour background.

quality printing. He began children's book ILLUSTRATION with the refined but vivacious and intricate silhouettes for JOAN AIKEN's *A Necklace of Raindrops* (1968) and *The Kingdom Under the Sea* (1971). The latter won a KATE GREENAWAY MEDAL and has been frequently reprinted, and the style was applied to his illustrations to texts from the King James Bible, beginning with *Christmas* (1984). *MEG AND MOG* arose in 1972 from a TV collaboration with Helen Nicoll. Enormously popular both in and out of school, these pages of saturated colour, heavy lines and pyrotechnic typography have refused to age over a quarter of a century and new titles have continued to appear up to 1990 (*Owl at the Vet*). In design and humour they are a 'seventies' answer to DR SEUSS, but go further in developing credible characters and calamitous plots. Many of his nursery board books have exploited the simplicity of the *Meg and Mog* books, and are worthy of comparison with those of DICK BRUNA. Pieñkowski revitalised the art of the pop-up book (see MOVABLE BOOKS) with equally audacious and inventive ideas in *The Haunted House* (1979), which won a Kate Greenaway Medal, and subsequent *tours de force* in this genre include *ABC Dinosaurs* (1993) and *Botticelli's Bed and Breakfast* (1996). Pieñkowski has subsequently worked in computer graphics, and *The Haunted House* is available on CD-ROM. PC

Pierpont Morgan Library see COLLECTIONS OF CHILDREN'S BOOKS

Pieterse, Pieter 1936– South African writer and broadcaster on both radio and television, who writes and speaks about life in the wild, often drawing on his own experiences. After farming in the bushveld, he moved to South Africa's west coast and lived for some while in a caravan on the sand-dunes. Such environments feature vividly and realistically in his books, which are written in Afrikaans, many translated into English by his wife Jenny, a successful author herself. He writes of the dangers of sea fishing in *Stormy Seas at Clearwater Bay* (1985) and of genuine lion-hunting in *Roar of the Lion* (1992). *Day of the Giants* (1986) tells of two children and a bull elephant struggling to survive in a war-torn Mozambique jungle. *Silver, Jackal of the Namib* (1991) has a similar survival theme with a man and a jackal on the bleak Skeleton Coast of Namibia. In his prize-winning story *The Way to the Sea* (1990) Pieterse combines his knowledge of the wild with some historical research into the agonising cross-country trek of Louis Trichardt and his party. JHe

Piggybook (1986) PICTUREBOOK in which the British author-illustrator ANTHONY BROWNE uses visual puns and mutating imagery to bring a dead metaphor to pictorial life. The Piggott menfolk are pigs of the male chauvinist breed and when Mrs Piggott leaves home in disgust at their behaviour they cannot cope. Their descent into domestic chaos is marked by the transformation of doorknobs, light-switches and wallpaper patterns into pigs' heads. As a tract for its time *Piggybook* was bold and funny, although opinion has always been divided on the appropriateness of the ending, with Mrs Piggott shown happily mending the car. DL

Pike, Christopher Pseudonym for a prolific master of mystery and suspense novels for teenagers. Before launching the teenage thriller genre with *Slumber Party* (1985), Pike worked as a computer programmer, taking his pen-name from a character in the *STAR TREK* TELEVISION series. With his second novel, *Chain Letter* (1986), word of mouth made his books bestsellers. His novels differ from others in the genre in their complicated plots filled with nail-biting suspense, environments void of adults, and the emotional drama with which all teenagers (and their parents) are so familiar. His stories rely heavily on humiliation and revenge themes as well as faked deaths, disappearing characters, and supernatural or unexplained elements. He acknowledges S.E. HINTON, Agatha Christie and Stephen King as greatly influencing him. Though many other writers have attempted to copy Pike's thrillers, none have successfully balanced the elements that continue to make him popular among readers aged from 10 to 18. One main reason is the quality of the writing. His readers identify with characters who not only feel deeply but react in the interests of self-preservation. LAW

Pilgrim's Progess, The (1678) The most popular spiritual allegory in English literature, written in a Bedford gaol by the Baptist preacher JOHN BUNYAN. Drawing on the Christian metaphor of life as an uncertain journey towards salvation, Bunyan's main source for both the style and content of the memorably vivid episodes was the English Bible. But the images – the highway, the country fair, bogs, giants, beasts and goblins – derive as much from FAIRY TALES and romances he had absorbed as a child. This no doubt contributed to the book's popularity and influence, which has lasted into the 21st century and perhaps beyond. DWh

see also *COUNTRY RHIMES FOR CHILDREN*

Pilgrim, Jane see *BLACKBERRY FARM* SERIES

Pillai, Keshav Shankar 1902–89 Indian cartoonist, fiction writer and publisher. Known as 'Shankar', Pillai was the most celebrated cartoonist before and immediately after India's independence. He published a weekly magazine, *Shankar's Weekly*, between 1948 and 1975, which was closed down so that he could concentrate on developing the different facets of his pioneer publishing house for children's books, the Children's Book Trust (CBT), founded in 1957. The CBT has set itself the laudable objective of producing well-written, well-illustrated and well-designed books for children at prices that are within the range of the average Indian child. His books for children, which he generally illustrated himself and which he wrote under several pseudonyms, are delightful evocations of Kerala, *Life with Grandfather* (1965) being one of the most engaging portrayals of a childhood in the coastal state. Shankar started the 'Shankar's International Children's Competition' in 1951, and, as a part of it, the Shankar's 'On the Spot Painting Competition for Children'. He also instituted a competition for writers of children's books. The CBT also has an annual Competition for Illustrators of Children's Books. Perhaps one of the most decorated men in India, he has been honoured by many international organisations for his service to the cause of children and children's literature. MBh

Pilling, Ann 1944– British writer born in Warrington, Lancashire, who also writes under the name Ann Cheetham. She is best known for her second novel *Henry's Leg* (1985) which won the *GUARDIAN* AWARD for Children's Fiction in 1986 and appeared as a Puffin children's classic in 1997. Two other books, *Stan* (1988) and *On the Lion's Side* (1988) were nominated for the CARNEGIE MEDAL.

Pilling is regarded primarily as a writer of novels for children in the 9–13 age-range although her books for younger children have received critical acclaim and are popular classroom choices. Notable titles for that age group are *No Guns, No Oranges* (1993) and *Dustbin Charlie* (1990). She has compiled several collections of stories, including *Realms of Gold* (1993) in which myths and legends from around the world have been retold. *Creation Stories* (1997) and a *Children's Bible* (1993) have been informed and inspired by her interest in Christianity and religion. *Our Best Stories* (1986), which she co-edited, comprises 15 traditional and contemporary stories which were chosen as read-aloud favourites from the responses of five thousand children.

For readers of ten upwards, a set of chilling GHOST STORIES, published now as Ann Cheetham novels and combining aspects of the supernatural with elements of horror, form a distinct aspect of the author's work.

The first title, *Black Harvest* (1983), has become an eponym for the series and, in serving to enlarge the understanding of young readers, is the book which the author feels best represents her as a writer. Set in County Mayo, the sufferings of the past are revealed as terrible local happenings relating to the Irish potato famine begin to trouble and invade the lives of a present-day family. The first of Pilling's contemporary novels, *The Year of the Worm* (1984), won critical favour after it was entered in a competition; its anti-hero, nicknamed Worm, exemplifies elements of human traits and social circumstances which characterise the protagonists of her subsequent novels. The story charts the fatherless Worm's rite of passage from the 'small, pale, and nervous' boy to a more self-assured teenager.

The gaining of personal and peer esteem, opportunities for small acts of heroism or bravery, and the capacity to overcome challenging situations are themes which the author explores in other novels. The commendation given to *Henry's Leg* acknowledged the author's ability to convey 'serious things cheerfully' and, like this stoical hero, Pilling's protagonists are often victims of fractured family life whose situations are perceptively conveyed with characteristic wry humour and sensitive insight. Henry, a collector of junk, longs obsessively to claim the dummy's leg protruding from a dustbin. He also longs with a poignant intensity for the homecoming of his absent father. These two strands of yearning are flavoured with the delights of a knockabout comic narration in which disorganised domesticity and a cast of vivid characters are viewed through the sanguine perspective of Henry's eyes. *Amber's Secret* (2000) – the story of a girl who unluckily smashes the family grandfather clock and must get it repaired without anyone knowing – shows similar features. In a different vein, *Stan* (1998), a compelling thriller for older readers, recounts movingly the physical and psychological journey of a teenager in search of a home and family. CMN

Pingu Series of short, animated films for young children about a penguin. The films, which were directed and animated by the Swiss film-maker Otmar Gutman, enjoyed enormous success in many European countries. In Britain they were broadcast and marketed in video format by the BBC from 1991. As with many modern animal stories for children, Pingu is depicted as growing up within a community of penguins and other creatures which resembles human society. Pingu's family live in an igloo and the child/penguin is shown helping his parents, playing and learning sports such as ice-hockey, in a thoroughly anthropomorphised fashion. The childlike perspective on events is never allowed to become sentimentalised, however, and the strange icecap setting appears to permit the exploration of a greater range of realistic issues within young children's experience than is usual in children's fiction. Pingu is depicted wiping faeces off his baby sister just after she is born, for instance, and nearly destroys the unborn penguin when left looking after the egg. Characteristically, such incidents are related with sensitivity, charm and humour. Another unusual feature of the series is that it makes no use of recognisable words, either as voice-over narration or as dialogue. DWh

Pinkney, (J.) Brian 1961– American author and illustrator of books for children. Born and raised in New York, Pinkney has an MA degree from New York's School of Visual Arts, but he credits his artistic family and particularly the example of his father (the illustrator JERRY PINKNEY) for much of his inspiration. Pinkney has contributed memorable artwork for a variety of FOLKTALE adaptations, such as Robert D. San Souci's *Sukey and the Mermaid* (1992), which was a CORETTA SCOTT KING Honour Book for illustration, and the same adaptor's *The Faithful Friend* (1995), which was a Caldecott Honour Book. His ILLUSTRATIONS also appear in several non-fiction works ranging in genre from poetry to BIOGRAPHY, the latter often written by his wife, Andrea Davis Pinkney, and depicting the lives of significant African Americans. Pinkney also occasionally illustrates his own text, as he did for *The Adventures of Sparrowboy* (1997), which received the BOSTON GLOBE-HORN BOOK AWARD for an outstanding picturebook. Pinkney's artistic style is unmistakable: his signature scratch-board technique suggests white-line WOOD ENGRAVING in its texture, yet the fluid freedom of the lines and the luminosity of his favoured deep hues (Pinkney hand-colours the images in oil paint) provide a vivid immediacy. DS

Pinkney, Jerry 1939– One of America's oustanding illustrators whose distinctive watercolours and pencil drawings are well known. Born in Philadelphia, he was working at a newspaper stand as a 12-year-old when the cartoonist, John Liney – who was to become one of his mentors – discovered him drawing. Pinkney later won a scholarship to the Philadelphia Museum College of Art. The first children's book he illustrated was Joyce Arkhurst's *The Adventures of Spider* (1964). Since that time he has worked with some of the most celebrated writers for children: MILDRED TAYLOR, VIRGINIA HAMILTON, Valerie Flournoy, Robert San Souci, PATRICIA MCKISSACK and VERNA AARDEMA. His collaboration with JULIUS LESTER has produced some of his best work, including four volumes of *Uncle Remus* stories (from 1987); *John Henry* (1994), for which they shared the BOSTON GLOBE-HORN BOOK AWARD for best picturebook; and *Sam and the Tigers* (1996). Pinkney won his third CORETTA SCOTT KING

AWARD for illustration with Alan Schroeder's *Minty: A Story of Young Harriet Tubman* (1996). His adaptation of *The Ugly Duckling* (1999) was a Caldecott Honor Book, his fourth such award. He delves deeply into research of the subject at hand and uses models and photographs for the visual aspect of the characters he wishes to portray.

Pinkney has illustrated books written by his wife, Gloria Jean Pinkney. Their son, BRIAN PINKNEY, already a prominent name in children's books, illustrates books by his wife, Andrea Pinkey. The Pinkney family continues to enrich children's literature with folktales, legends, stories and biographies of African Americans. PDS

Pinkwater, Daniel (Manus) 1941– American author-illustrator of more than 50 PICTUREBOOKS and novels for children and young adults; he is also a regular commentator on National Public Radio and writer of several works for adults. Born in Memphis, Tennessee, but raised in Chicago, Pinkwater occasionally collaborates with his wife, Jill Pinkwater. He applies a Dadaist sensibility to producing hybridised SCIENCE FICTION and FANTASY plots; his equally offbeat characters pursue enthusiasms that often involve unusual animals (a blue moose, mice from space, a canine gourmet chef, a 280-pound chicken). Pinkwater ratchets up the humour of his absurdist situations with deceptively childlike ILLUSTRATIONS, puns (particularly in characters' names), and slapstick references to food, along with sly allusions to cultural icons both classical and popular. For Pinkwater, consumer culture equals conformist culture, and his sympathies clearly lie with his nonconformist protagonists, whether he is writing for young adults and older children (*Lizard Music*, 1976; *Young Adult Novel*, 1982; *The Snarkout Boys and the Baconburg Horror*, 1984), for middle-graders and beginning readers (*Wingman*, 1975; *Second-Grade Ape*, 1998), or for pre-school children (*The Big Orange Splot*, 1977). JMA

Pinky and Perky see COMICS, PERIODICALS AND MAGAZINES

Pinocchio (1883) Story about an accident-prone, stubborn and impetuous wooden puppet created by the sometime editor of a theatrical journal, Carlo Collodi (born Carlo Lorenzini, 1826–90). The episodic narrative – *Pinocchio* was originally published as a serial – draws heavily on the Italian Commedia dell' Arte tradition; the bite of Collodi's satire is evident in his irreverent treatment of figures of authority. Collodi addresses his child audience directly, posing questions and adopting the manner of an oral storyteller. The child reader empathises with Pinocchio throughout his long and difficult journey towards 'growing up' and accepting the responsibilities of love, a quest in which every child is engaged – although in Pinocchio's case this will involve becoming a real boy. He experiences the full range of human emotion on his journey, from laughter and exhilaration to bouts of inconsolable weeping. Through both frightening and hilarious encounters and temptations, Pinocchio carries the burden of guilt and remorse caused by his neglect and deception of his beloved parent Geppetto, until father and son are finally reunited. According to Ann Lawson Lucas *Pinocchio* is revered in Italy as *the* supreme work of children's literature, written by a great stylist in the Italian language. In addition to international recognition as a literary masterpiece, Pinocchio's story – often abridged in translations or retellings – continues to attract a wide audience. There have been many stage versions and the famous WALT DISNEY film, in which Pinocchio's selfishness is toned down. GL

Pip and Squeak Pip (a dog) and Squeak (a penguin) were the 'pets' of 'Uncle Dick' (Bertram Lamb), editor of the children's features that started in the British *Daily Mirror* on 12 May 1919. They soon dominated the page, drawn in a daily comic strip by Austin B. Payne, a brilliant comic artist from Wales who was commissioned by mistake when the *Mirror* editor rang the Amalgamated Press comic department seeking G.M. Payne, another comic artist. A.B. Payne proved ideal for the job and drew the characters for the rest of his life. The strip soon became the nation's most popular children's feature, especially after the introduction of Wilfred (a rabbit) and a club called the W.L.O.G. (Wilfredian League of Gugnuncs). The *Pip & Squeak Annual* ran from 1923 to 1940, and a separate *Wilfred's Annual* ran from 1924 to 1939. DG

***Pippi Longstocking* series** (from 1945) Stories by the Swedish writer Astrid Lindgren (1907–), about a young girl, Pippi, who is able to do exactly as she likes, without the normal constraints of parental authority or social conventions. She lives in Villekulla Cottage, alone, except for her horse and pet monkey, having temporarily mislaid her father on the high seas whilst travelling with him around the world.

Her appearance is eccentric, with her carrot-coloured, sticking-out plaits, her freckles, her odd stockings and shoes twice as long as her feet. No financial problems inhibit her actions, as she has a large suitcase full of gold pieces. She is a strong-minded, stubborn child, with no respect for authority, who does all the naughty things any child would love to do, speaking and acting with spontaneity and questioning accepted values. She is also outstandingly generous and good-humoured, with a great capacity for fun, and a lover of animals who hates all forms of cruelty. On her adventures she is accompanied by her friends,

'And then the frightened girl called loudly upon the name of her lover.' Illustration by Joyce Mercer from *The Play-Hour Book* (no. 2).

Tommy and Annika. What makes Pippi even more amazing is her immense strength, which enables her to pick up horses and subdue tigers. That, coupled with her capacity to tell the most far-fetched stories, makes her an amusing, endearing and fascinating heroine, who has retained her appeal over the years. Astrid Lindgren has made a major contribution to children's literature by inventing this robust female character. JSW

Pirrie, Jill 1939– Retired English teacher and poetry reviewer, best known for her work at Halesworth Middle School, Suffolk, where her pupils regularly won awards in national poetry competitions. She described her teaching methods in *On Common Ground* (1987, 1994) and anthologised her pupils' remarkable poetry in *Apple Fire* (1993). ML

see also CHILD AUTHORS

Pitz, Henry C(larence) 1895–1976 American art teacher and illustrator. A renowned artist, Pitz was the recipient of over 40 awards. He taught art and was an associate editor of *American Artist*. Pitz's *Illustrating Children's Books* (1963) gives a comprehensive history of children's book ILLUSTRATION and clear advice regarding techniques and materials for the would-be artist. He also wrote 'how to draw' books using different media ranging from watercolour to felt-tip pens. Pitz illustrated over 160 books, including Loring McKay's *The Twenty-Fifth Mission* (1944), Mary MacLeod's *The Book of Arthur and his Noble Knights* (1949) and a 1954 edition of ROBERT LOUIS STEVENSON'S *TREASURE ISLAND*. SCWA

Play-Hour Book (from 1927) Annual for children published by Longmans and edited by Stephen Southwold. Editorial policy was committed to high standards of content and design in a manner resembling its contemporary *JOY STREET*. Its contributors included ROSE FYLEMAN, HENRY WILLIAMSON, ELEANOR FARJEON and WALTER DE LA MARE. It published mostly stories, poetry, riddles, puzzles and tricks, with selections from the literature of the past. Its ILLUSTRATIONS were of a high quality – sometimes TIPPED IN – and ranged from the billowy Art Nouveau manner of ANNE ANDERSON to the spiky and vigorous art-deco drawings of Joyce Mercer. VW

Playbox (from 1898) The first ever British children's ANNUAL as we know them today, an original volume featuring the strip stars of a weekly COMIC. *Playbox* was launched as a weekly children's pull-out supplement to the Amalgamated Press women's weekly, *Home Chat*, on 29 October 1898, and later became a coloured comic section of *The World and his Wife*, a family monthly established in May 1905. It then moved to *The New Children's Encyclopaedia* from May 1910. The heroes were Tiger Tim and the Hippo Boys, drawn by Julius Stafford Baker, and they remained as stars of *Playbox Annual*, which had the longest run of any British Christmas book series, from 1909 to 1956. In a reversal of tradition, *Playbox Annual* gave birth to the *Playbox* comic on 15 February 1925, which ran until 11 June 1955, a run of 1279 issues. DG

playground rhymes Ask 7-year-old children to recite a NURSERY RHYME and they will look at you blankly. They have left nursery rhymes behind in their infancy, and the rhymes they know are all concerned with survival in the school playground. Playground rhymes have a variety of functions. Some are aggressive ('You're daft, you're potty, you're barmy, You ought to join the army, You got knocked out with a brussel sprout, You're daft, you're potty, you're barmy!'). Some are defensive ('Sticks and stones may break my bones, But words can never hurt me'). Many are recited because they are 'clever', or 'rude', and their recital brings children prestige among their peers. Children consider rhyme to be clever in itself ('Mrs White had a fright, In the middle of the night'); and they can see that a risqué or lavatorial rhyme is a social success, even if they do not always understand why ('Tarzan swings, Tarzan falls, Tarzan 'urts 'is 'airy balls'; 'Milk, milk, lemonade, Round the corner chocolate's made'). The repetition of 'tangletalk' is an achievement in itself ('One midsummer day in winter, The snow was raining fast, A bare-footed girl with clogs on Stood sitting on the grass'); and the songs they chant to frighten themselves have, naturally, a particularly doom-laden rhythm ('A woman in a churchyard sat, Oo-oo-ah-ah!'). Rhyming lends weight to juvenile legislation ('Finders keepers, Losers weepers'), and a pungency to disapproval ('Liar, liar, your pants are on fire!'). Simple deceptions, like making someone look up, or down, and then slapping their hands, would have no validity if they were not expressed in rhyme: 'Up above, You're in love, Down below, You're so slow.'

The majority of the rhymes in the playground are connected with traditional games. The important business of selecting someone to be the chaser in a game of tig is conducted by 'dipping'. The players stand in a circle; one child recites some little rhyme and, on each accented syllable, points at the players in turn (including herself). The player on whom the word 'out' falls must stand aside, until only one person is left. The rhymes are many and various. Some are dialogues, like the following which requires answers from two players before 'out' is finally reached:

'There's a party on the hill, Will you come?'
'Yes.'
'Bring your own bread and butter and a bun.'
'Can't afford it.'
'So choose your bestest friend, What's she called?'
'Anne.'
'A-N-N-E' [counted round].
'Anne will be there with a ribbon in her hair, What colour shall it be?'
'R-E-D' [counted round].
'You are not IT.'

Others are short, settling the question quite quickly: 'Ip, dip, Bull's shit, You are not IT'. Others again are in the mysterious gibberish known as 'Chinese counting': 'Eeny meeny mackeracka, Rare ri dominaka, Chicka pocka, lolli poppa, Ping pong out!'

Singing games are not as popular as formerly; but girls have a large repertoire of skipping chants, which they use to time the jumps, to limit the length of each turn, or to discover details of the skipper's future. Words such as the following may seem inappropriate, but children are fascinated by unchildish things:

I had a boy and he was double-jointed,
I kissed him and made him disappointed.
That one died, then I had another one,
Bless his little heart, he's better than the other one
Now, now, *Gilly*, I'll tell your mother
For kissing *Michael* around the corner.
How many kisses did he give you?
Five, ten, fifteen, twenty . . .

The charm of movement accompanied by rhyme is also found in another girls' game, two-balls, when the plain action of bouncing a ball against a wall is enlivened by such words as: 'Mrs Brown went to town, With her knickers hanging down; Mrs Green saw the scene, And put it in a magazine.' Clapping chants are just as entertaining:

The Johnsons had a baby, Its name was Tiny Tim, Tim, Tim,
They put him in a bath tub, To see if he could swim, swim, swim.
He drank a bowl of water, He ate a bar of soap, soap, soap,
He tried to eat the bath tub, But it wouldn't fit down his throat, throat, throat.

In each of these activities the songs or chants provide at least as much pleasure as the game itself.

A number of schoolyard rhymes are known to be centuries old ('Tell tale tit', for instance, appeared in *Tommy Thumb's Pretty Song Book*, 1744); others, especially the girls' game rhymes, are relatively modern. Children adopt and adapt, rather than invent. They pick up, from the vast fund of popular song available, whatever catchy songs seem appropriate to their purpose, alter the words, and pass them down to succeeding generations of schoolchildren. The subject matter is usually comical and mundane, but the verse must be strongly rhythmical and include a mechanism for counting skips or ball-bounces, or indications of actions to be performed. Occasionally, the sources of the songs can be found. The widespread clapping routine 'Under the Bram Bush' has a typical history. A student song popular until at least 1960 was composed of fragments from Harry Harndin's comic song 'A Cannibal King', (1895) and Cole and Johnson's 'Under the Bamboo Tree' (1902), and a snappy ending, of unknown origin, beginning 'If you'll be M-I-N-E'. Schoolgirls have perpetuated the middle part of this (the 'Bamboo Tree' part), and have varied the wording – sometimes adding lines from a skipping rhyme – until little of the original remains. Playground rhymes are thus subject to constant change, not only in the process of fission and fusion, but in the alteration of words and phrases through misunderstanding, failure of memory, or deliberate innovation, as when a child chooses to chant 'Under the brown bushes', instead of 'Under the bram bush', and then claims the game as her own, saying 'I made it up'. IO

see also *PLEASE MRS BUTLER*

Playing Beatie Bow (1980) Australian novel by RUTH PARK. A TIME-SLIP FANTASY set in Sydney's historic Rocks area in 1873, it won the CHILDREN'S BOOK COUNCIL OF AUSTRALIA Book of the Year Award (1981) and has been made into a highly successful film. Abigail, a confused and angry teenager, gains a new perspective on her troubled life by returning to the past, where she discovers the potency of love and the meaning of loyalty. Without cluttering the narrative with detail, Park faithfully recreates family and social life as it was, so that Abigail comes to realise that time is 'a great river, always moving, always changing, but with the same water flowing between its banks from source to sea'. MSax

Playschool see *THE BOOK TOWER*; TELEVISION

Please Mrs Butler (1983) First poetry collection by ALLAN AHLBERG. Its authentic recreation of the experiences and voices of the British primary school has made the book a modern classic. Its widespread popularity with teachers as well as children stems from Ahlberg's presentation of school life from both points of view. The poems are funny and perceptive, but also sometimes poignant, as in 'Slow Reader' and 'Reading Test', where the layout suggests the frustrations of struggling readers. Ahlberg uses a variety of poetic forms, excelling in tightly metrical verse and inventive rhyming. In *Heard it in the Playground* (1989), illustrated by FRITZ WEGNER, Ahlberg writes about the same cast of teachers and pupils, adding the parents' voice in some poems ('Parents' Evening'). The long title piece, and others like 'Bags I', use playground chants to create poems which beg to be performed. *The Mighty Slide* (1988) is a collection of five very different narratives in five different verse forms, showing Ahlberg's virtuosity in telling stories in poetry. Ahlberg's most recent collection, *The Mysteries of Zigomar* (1997), combines prose stories and poems, some about school life but others breaking new ground, as in the excellent creation poem 'Worlds'. ML

Plum (1998) First significant poetry collection by the British poet Tony Mitton, a fine new voice in children's poetry. Its distinguishing features include its range from comedy to serious social comment, a capacity to create mood, and a delicate sensitivity to people and places. Mitton has also written raps, picturebook texts and a short book-length poem based on the selkie legend. His latest collection is *The Red and White Spotted Handkerchief* (2000). Like many other distinguished poets for children – CHARLES CAUSLEY, WENDY COPE, ALLAN AHLBERG and others – Mitton was a primary teacher for many years before he became a full-time writer. MCCS

Poems Written for a Child (1868) Collaboration between the sisters Elizabeth Anna Hart and Menella Bute Smedley. Although the verse is close to doggerel, it was popular in its day; LEWIS CARROLL is said to have sent copies to his little girl friends. MCCS

Poet's Tongue, The (1935) Anthology chosen by W.H. AUDEN and John Garrett. Inclusive in style and content, containing NURSERY RHYMES, light verse and folk material, as well as a range of poetry from CHAUCER to T.S. Eliot, this book is the precursor of other anthologies (for example *THE RATTLE BAG* and *A FLOCK OF WORDS*) that serve to widen our view of what poetry can be and do. FRBS

Poetry for Children (1809) Collection of verse by CHARLES and MARY LAMB, one of the many which appeared in the wake of ANN and JANE TAYLOR'S *ORIGINAL POEMS FOR INFANT MINDS*. The Lambs lacked the Taylors's talent for poetry and most of their verse is derivative, pedestrian and didactic, displaying many of the features Lamb deplored in 'that cursed Barbauld crew' – his famous denunciation of female writers of moral tales. MCCS

Poetry in the Making (1967) An anthology of poems and programmes from the radio series *Listening and Writing*. Based on the BBC Radio 4 broadcasts by the British poet TED HUGHES, this book remains accessible to children and inspirational to teachers. It demonstrates Hughes's faith in the genius of the ordinary child, which informs and illuminates his careful analysis of the writer's discipline. JP

Poetry Jump Up (1988) A classic collection of black poetry compiled by GRACE NICHOLS, featuring poets from Britain, Africa, America, Asia and the Caribbean. ZEPHANIAH, Brathwaite, Angelou and TAGORE are represented, but there are also poems from Malawi and Ghana, and one from the 12-year-old daughter of Nelson Mandela, Zinziswa. HT

Pogány, Willy (Vilmos) 1882–1956 Hungarian-born illustrator who worked largely in America from about 1914 and dominatedAmerican ILLUSTRATIONS in the 1930s. Children's books with his illustrations include those by PADRAIC COLUM: *The King of Ireland's Son* (1916), a collection of Irish FOLKTALES woven into one narrative, *The Adventures of Odysseus and the Tale of Troy* (1918), *The Children of Odin: a Book of Northern Myths*

(1920) and *The Golden Fleece and the Heroes who lived before Achilles* (1920). Others include an edition of GULLIVER'S TRAVELS (1917) and *The Golden Cockerel* (1936), a version of a story by Pushkin. KSB

see also CLASSICAL MYTHOLOGY; IRISH MYTHOLOGY AND FOLKLORE

Pogle's Wood see OLIVER POSTGATE AND PETER FIRMIN

Pohl, Victor 1886–1979 South African writer of non-fiction and fiction, mostly for children. Of Boer (originally German) stock, he drew on his family history and his own life to write in English, episodic books about white pioneers, the Boers in the South African War, and hunting adventures. Of the latter type, *Bushveld Adventures* (1940) long remained a popular school reader. His novel, *Farewell the Little People* (1968), is a compassionate though inaccurate tribute to the extinct San. The intrinsic appeal of his material for South African readers outweighed his pedestrian style and anachronistic attitudes about race and hunting. ERJ

***Point* series** Publisher's imprint covering a wide range of different genres aimed at 11- to 14-year-olds. *Point Horror* was introduced by Scholastic in the United States as a new teenage list in the late 1980s. On both sides of the Atlantic the books became extremely popular with teenage readers. Over 30 titles were introduced from the United States into Britain, and within one year two million copies were sold. Scholastic became the top children's publisher in the *Bookseller's* bestselling list for 1993 in Britain. The books can be divided into two distinct kinds – thriller stories such as R. L. STINE'S *The Baby-sitter*, and supernatural stories such as *The Vampire's Promise*, *The Cheerleader* and *Freeze Tag* by Caroline B. Cooney. The narratives deal with conflicts, friendship and trust within a horror framework, and seek the restoration of order and normality after unusual events. A considerable appeal to teenage readers is the marketing package, with more than 60 titles in 1997 for them to choose from, and more being added on a regular basis. The books are designed to grab the readers' attention, with dramatic covers, gold or silver embossed titles and images which demand a response. The *Point Horror* series logo is hand-written with a scratchy fountain pen and underlined for effect. The blurb on the back cover often begins with a statement to intrigue potential readers: 'Two girls . . . one life'; 'This summer's going to be a real killer . . .'.

Riding on the back of the popularity of *Point Horror*, other series have been introduced into the imprint, such as the closely linked *Point Crime*. This series was developed in Britain and then sold back to the United States. These stories involve the reader in solving the crime, thus aiming to hold their attention throughout the story. *Point Romance* is another genre, with titles such as *Winter Weepies* by J. Moffat and *Kiss Me, Stupid* by Alison Creaghan. These are marketed to attract the young female reader, with the use of such lines in the blurb as 'Get out the hankies for a truly romantic read . . .'; 'Will dreams come true in the last story of the series?' The *Point* series imprint now covers a range of popular genres read by adolescents and includes *Point Horror Collections*, *Point Romance*, *Point Crime*, *Point fantasy*, *Point SF* and *Point Nurses*. However, one list, *Point Fiction*, is slightly different in that it publishes books by established authors from a number of different English-speaking countries. Many of these works are more original than other *Point* books, for instance *The Dark behind the Curtain* by GILLIAN CROSS, *Northern Lights* (see HIS DARK MATERIALS) by PHILIP PULLMAN and *Aliens in the Family* by MARGARET MAHY. FMC

See also PUBLISHING AND PUBLISHERS

Poky Little Puppy, The see JANETTE SEBRING LOWREY

Poland [Oosthuisen], Marguerite 1950– Leading South African writer for children and teenagers as well as a novelist for adults. Her first book, *Nqalu, the Mouse With No Whiskers* (1980), marked a significant leap in the quality of South African English children's books. *The Mantis and the Moon* (1979) and *The Wood-Ash Stars* (1983) were the first two books to be awarded the country's most prestigious prize for English children's books, the Percy FitzPatrick Award. Her childhood in the Eastern Cape bush, and her degrees in the Xhosa language and Zulu folklore, give her books an authentic African character which she conveys through a poetic style of writing that uses indigenous words and carries the cadences of indigenous languages. She also has a sharp ear for the English dialogue of modern youngsters, as can be seen in her lively stories for eight-year-olds, *Marcus and the Boxing Gloves* (1984) and *Marcus and the Go-kart* (1988). *The Mantis and the Moon*, *Once at KwaFubesi* (1981), *The Wood-Ash Stars* and *The Small Clay Bull* (1986), all beautifully illustrated, are volumes of stories written in the style of African and San folktales. Of her two novels for young teenagers, *Shadow of the Wild Hare* (1986) deserves to be regarded as a South African classic. It encapsulates many of Poland's concerns: the close ties between humans and nature, her reverence for traditional African beliefs, and a strain of melancholy mitigated by her pervasive faith in the continuity and renewal which is implicit in African and San folklore. Though Poland is highly regarded by critics, it is generally accepted that some of her writing is difficult for her target audiences, though she is a popular choice for reading aloud to young children. ERJ

Politi, Leo 1908–96 American author-illustrator of PICTUREBOOKS and winner of the CALDECOTT MEDAL for *Song of the Swallows* (1948), the story of the swallows of San Juan Capistrano Mission. Politi was among the first to use Hispanic Americans as his subjects, and his works include *Pedro, the Angel of Olvera Street* (1946), a Caldecott Honour Book, and *Juanita* (1948), the story of a Hispanic Easter custom. *Moy Moy* (1960) was one of several books he created celebrating the Asian American culture in California. His ILLUSTRATIONS, typically watercolours done in a naive style, possess a quiet charm and reflect the folk quality of his stories. DLR

Politically Correct Bedtime Stories James Finn Garner's first collection of 'politically correct' FAIRY TALES, which sold almost three million copies in 1994; 1995 saw *Once Upon a More Enlightened Time: More Politically Correct Bedtime Stories*, and *Politically Correct Holiday Stories*. Garner revises the GRIMM BROTHERS, HANS CHRISTIAN ANDERSEN and others to satirise the 'correctness' movement. *SLEEPING BEAUTY* becomes 'Sleeping Person of Better-than-Average Attractiveness'. 'Woman' becomes 'womyn' and 'person' becomes 'persun'. Unlike ROALD DAHL's *Revolting Rhymes*, Garner's revisions are for adults. When LITTLE RED RIDING HOOD bands with the Wolf and the Grandmother at the end of their tale, they axe the Woodsman to death; Little Red exclaims at the Woodsman, 'Sexist! Speciesist! How dare you assume that womyn and wolves can't solve their own problems without a man's help!' This is both funny and disturbing. The satire depends on our belief that the original tales are, ultimately, 'innocent'. Ostensibly, Garner pokes fun at himself in order to say: 'Let's not get too serious about this stuff.' Nevertheless, the original tales are no more innocent than Garner's revisions. Both draw on serious cultural tensions described by historian Todd Gitlin as 'the surface of a deep fault line that reaches an American trauma' about identity, race, gender and childhood. JZo

Polly and the Stupid Wolf see *CLEVER POLLY* SERIES

***Pollyanna* series** Novels by American Eleanor Hodgman Porter (1868–1920), beginning with *Pollyanna* (1913), about an orphaned girl who transforms her aunt's home and town with the 'glad game' that her father had taught her. For Pollyanna, finding something to be glad about is indeed a game, an opportunity to distract oneself by exercising ingenuity rather than a moral duty. Although dictionaries now define a 'Pollyanna' as someone who is foolishly optimistic and blind to realities, the original Pollyanna is shocked to find that many adults in affluent circumstances do nothing but grumble; her naivety allows her to transgress the conventions of good manners and tell adults exactly what she thinks of their behaviour, startling them into a new perspective. In time, though, Pollyanna recognises that her view is a little simplistic. When seriously injured herself, and facing the prospect of never walking again, Pollyanna is unable to play 'the game', until cheered by discovering that the whole town is now playing it. Porter's sequel, *Pollyanna Grows Up*, was published in 1915, and the series was continued after her death by Harriet Lumis Smith and others. FEA

Pomander of Verse, A (1895) Collection of poetry by E. NESBIT. Her verse for children was not as original or well-known as her fiction, but this collection – and others like *Flowers I Bring and Songs I Sing* (1893) and *Songs of Two Seasons* (1891) – tenderly celebrated nature and childhood. MCCS

pony stories Stories about the relationship between a girl and her pony, enormously popular with adolescent pony-lovers, which reached their peak in Britain in the 1940s, 50s and early 60s. Pony stories offer both realism and FANTASY, combining highly detailed, practical and technical information about riding and stable care, with traditional 'transformation' stories, in which shy girl and neglected pony are transformed into top rider and pony in a show. The pony story, part of a far wider range of HORSE STORIES, has frequently been criticised for its limited and often inflexible formula and ridiculed as narrow and middle-class, but the best of these books are coming-of-age stories, in which young riders and their ponies are 'broken in' together.

The genesis of the pony book coincided with the end of the horse's vital role in the working life of Britain in the 1920s and 30s. Riding became part of the new leisure industry, particularly for children, and The Pony Club and the new pony books, which developed during the same period, took on the task of instructing youngsters in all aspects of horsemanship. The values and moral standards of the classic *BLACK BEAUTY* (1877), in which Anna Sewell preached a new compassionate understanding between horse and owner, still influences the genre, although it was almost half a century before the first pony books began to appear. In the 1920s there was a growing interest in native pony breeds and there was no stronger devotee than Allen W. Seaby, Professor of Fine Art at Reading University, who wrote a series of books on the main breeds, starting with *Skewbald the New Forest Pony* (1923), illustrated with his own woodcuts and water colours. These nature books paved the way for scores of minor Black Beautys, the best of which was Golden Gorse's *MOORLAND MOUSIE* (1929), illustrated by the great sporting artist Lionel Edwards.

The anthropomorphic pony story was soon to lose its popularity – although it continued until the 50s in series like ELYNE MITCHELL's *SILVER BRUMBY* books (from 1958) – when the focus of attention shifted from pony to rider, and changed the character of the pony book. Early books like *The Ponies of Bunts and the Adventures of the Children who rode them* (1933), and their sequels, by Marjorie Mary Oliver and Eva Ducat, reflected the new trend, as did the surprising number of CHILD AUTHORS who emerged, like Moyra Charlton, Pamela Hull and Kathleen Whitlock. The two most influential books in the genre were written within a year of each other by writers who were skilled novelists as well as horse lovers. *National Velvet* (1935) was originally intended for adults by its author, Enid Bagnold, but has always been read by children, particularly after the enormous success of the film version in 1944. In 1962 it was chosen by Puffin Books to launch the new Peacock series for older readers. The plot has all the motifs which later became familiar: the poor pony-mad girl who wins a horse in a raffle, and eventually triumphs in the Grand National. The following year, Joanna Cannan wrote *A Pony for Jean* (1936), about a girl learning to ride on a neglected pony, now regarded as the pioneer of the new type of pony novel, and which owed much to E. NESBIT in tone and humour. Cannan dedicated the book to her daughters JOSEPHINE, DIANA AND CHRISTINE PULLEIN-THOMPSON, who became the best-known and most prolific writers in the genre.

The standard of the stories continued to be high with writers like Primrose Cumming, who handled FANTASY in *Silver Snaffles* (1937) as easily as stories of ordinary children in *The Wednesday Pony* (1939); and Mary Treadgold, whose adventure story with ponies, *WE COULDN'T LEAVE DINAH* (1941), won the CARNEGIE MEDAL. However, after the war, when riding became everybody's sport, spurred on by the new phenomenon of TELEVISION, any book with 'pony' in the title would find publishers and readers. Everyone thought they could write the formula – not only teenagers, but equestrian experts like Pamela Macgregor-Morris, Lady Kitty Ritson and Pat Smythe, and writers of adult books, like Catherine Cookson and Monica Dickens (see *FOLLYFOOT*). Series of pony books became popular, like Mary Gervaise's stories about Georgie at the horsey Grange School – one of the few writers to combine school and ponies – and Judith M. Berrisford's *Jacky* series. The granny of them all was the *JILL* series, written between 1949 and 1962 by Ruby Ferguson, whose bouncy heroine and repetitive plots are still going strong.

Just when the genre seemed written out, several good books appeared which broke the mould. K.M. PEYTON proved there was still life in the tired formula with *Fly-by-Night* (1968), whose determined, working-class heroine Ruth Hollis appeared in several books. Peyton continued to write fine pony books, like *Darkling* (1989), and *Poor Badger* (1990), which stress the responsibilities as well as the pleasures of owning horses. Realistic stories were also written by Vian Smith (1920–69), one of the few male authors of pony books, who was as knowledgeable about human behaviour as he was about animals. *Come Down the Mountain* (1967), in which a girl saves a neglected racehorse, and *Martin Rides the Moor* (1965) about a deaf boy, are exceptional books by any standards. A new author, Patricia Leitch, wrote the popular *JINNY* books (from 1976), which remained in print for many years.

In the 1980s, there was new interest in old pony books by established writers, and they were often updated to exclude politically incorrect fox-hunting and signs of upper-class elitism. Caroline Akrill made the most of the growing popularity of three-day eventing with a lively trilogy, starting with *Eventer's Dream* (1981), combining humour, instruction, and an older heroine with a romantic interest. Far inferior is the stereotyped but long-running series of *The American Saddle Club* books. There is still a demand for pony books both here and abroad – particularly in Scandinavia – but like a comparable genre, SCHOOL STORIES, revived after years in the doldrums, they are now being read by younger girls and the several new series reflect this. ARH

see also HORSE STORIES

Pooh Bear see A. A. MILNE

Pooley, Sarah see *A DAY OF RHYMES*

pop-up books see MOVABLE BOOKS

Pope, Elizabeth Marie 1917– American author of TIME-SLIP FANTASY and HISTORICAL FICTION. A Shakespearean scholar and English professor at Mills College in Oakland, California, Pope wrote the first of her two novels for a younger sister who shared her love for the 18th century and the countryside of Orange County in New York State. *The Sherwood Ring* (1958) is an unusual mixture of MYSTERY STORY, GHOST STORY and light-hearted love story, in which a present-day young woman is visited by her 18th-century ancestors; as these friendly ghosts relate their interwoven adventures, played out against the background of guerrilla warfare in the American Revolution, they help her resolve her own thwarted romance. *The Perilous Gard* (1974), a Newbery Honour Book set in Elizabethan England, is darker and more suspenseful, with a more resolute and tough-minded heroine, but equally original in conception–a historical novel bordering on FANTASY. Based on the theories of folklorists, its 'fairies' are frighteningly real, survivors of an older race who still practise human sacrifice. SR

see also TAM LIN

Popeye Sailor hero, originally in comic strips, but best known in short ANIMATED films, at first for cinema, later for TELEVISION. He first appeared in Elzie Seager's comic strip *Thimble Theater* (1929) and in 1933 made his film début in a Betty Boop cartoon, *Popeye the Sailor*, produced by Max Fleisher. He has a girlfriend, Olive Oyl; his enemy is a rival sailor, first called Brutus and later transformed into Bluto. He later adopted a foundling boy, Swee' Pea, whom he and Olive raised. His theme song – 'I'm Popeye the Sailor Man' – became a popular hit; parents used his example to persuade children to eat spinach. Some of the Popeye cartoons used legends, particularly those drawn from the *ARABIAN NIGHTS* (*Sinbad*, *Ali Baba* and *Aladdin*) as the basis for story lines. BH

Porter, Eleanor H. see *POLLYANNA* SERIES

Possum Magic (1983) Australian PICTUREBOOK, which launched the careers of writer MEM FOX and illustrator JULIE VIVAS. Highly commended in the CHILDREN'S BOOK COUNCIL OF AUSTRALIA Picturebook of the Year Awards (1984), the story of Hush the possum and his Grandma as they search for a cure for his invisibility is arguably one of Australia's best-known narratives internationally. While the text is somewhat predictable, the appeal of the theme, a child's cry to be recognised, combined with Vivas's exquisite watercolour paintings of Australian BUSH animals and settings, and with her acerbic touches of humour, have made this into an Australian classic, with global book sales exceeding 500,000 copies, together with an operatic version, and a spin-off industry of associated merchandise. JAP

Postgate, Oliver 1925– and **Firmin, Peter** 1928– British writers and film-makers responsible for some of the most outstanding children's TELEVISION programmes, transmitted under the umbrella of the BBC's *WATCH WITH MOTHER* television series during the late 60s and early 70s. Their productions, especially *NOGGIN THE NOG*, *Bagpuss* and *IVOR THE ENGINE*, formed an important part of daily life in thousands of British homes, with parents and children settling down to programmes that became unmissable. For those that watched, it was also a time for the creation of an invaluable repository of narrative memories to be shared and re-lived for years to come.

With Postgate responsible for the writing and Firmin for the imaginative and varied animations, they made a powerful STORYTELLING combination. They deserve recognition for the innovative ways in which their stories were told. The voice of Oliver Postgate, perfectly suited for storytelling, wove a magical world where cats and engines talked and, deep in the wood, plants drank Bilberry wine. *Bagpuss*, in which an old cloth cat wove stories around various lost items, was particularly strong in this respect. Within each programme, children (and adults) were offered a range of ways to explore stories: FOLK TALES, CLASSICAL MYTHOLOGY, traditional songs and rhymes, none of which were ever considered beyond their audience. A sense of humour pervaded all their programmes; from the wordplay of the mice on the 'mouse organ' (*Bagpuss*) to the dry humour of the carefully written conversations between Noggin the Nog and Thor Nogsen, there was much to make the viewer laugh, the laughter and the 'knowingness' that came with it increasing the viewer's involvement with the stories.

Postgate and Firmin were skilled in the creation of other worlds. Their stories were told somewhere in the no-man's land between the real and the imagined, the balance between the actual and the illusory always carefully constructed. Often this balance was reflected in the ways that the stories were told. In *Pogles' Wood*, for example, each programme began with some real-life film, which led you to the world where the animated Pogles lived. In *Bagpuss*, black-and-white film was transformed into colour as soon as Bagpuss began to wake up and weave his magic with his storytelling. No one was excluded from these programmes as they offered children a myriad of ways into their world of telling and retelling stories. They all had an intellectual quality and were told in ways that offered the youngest children access to some highly complex text forms. Imagination and story were given very high status and were presented as a means of exploring, problem-solving and enjoyment.

Perhaps most importantly, the stories encapsulated the type of magic that appeals whatever the age of the viewer – the magic of pretence. The make-believe worlds of Postgate and Firmin were accessible to everyone because they had their origins in familiar worlds. Oliver Postgate's autobiography, *Seeing Things*, was published in 2000. HB

Postman Pat BBC stop-frame animated puppet series for young children, created for TELEVISION by John Cunliffe and Ivor Wood, and first transmitted in 1981. A vast range of books (illustrated by Joan Hickson, among others), tapes and associated products were developed from the programme. It was explicitly commissioned for its countryside setting and, although supposedly rooted in the reality of the Lake District, the series' cheery signature song about 'happy Pat and his black-and-white cat' sets the tone for a nostalgic portrayal of rural life in 'Greendale' as a pastoral idyll with only occasional echoes of contemporary British culture. John Cunliffe has also written *The Weather Baby* (2000), about how Phil the country baby grew up to become a weatherman. SG

Potok, Chaim 1929– American writer, rabbi and scholar of Jewish texts, Potok is best known for his novels depicting young Orthodox Jews confronting ideological and cultural boundaries within their religious tradition. *The Chosen* (1967) features the son of a Hassidic rabbi rejecting his position as future spiritual leader to become a Freudian psychoanalyst. *The Promise* (1969) continues the story with the protagonist attempting to receive his ordination while practising critical scholarship of the Talmud. *My Name is Asher Lev* (1972) portrays a young Hassid being cast out from his group for using controversial subjects and techniques in his artwork; Lev's redemption is earned by offering his son as an heir to the rabbi in *The Gift of Asher Lev* (1990). Though not marketed as YOUNG ADULT FICTION, Potok's best work shows the difficult juxtaposition of self-definition and community standards faced by children and adolescents. Potok is also known for the ways his American characters confront the horror of the Holocaust, especially as depicted in *In the Beginning* (1975). His first children's book, *The Tree of Here* (1993), presents a young boy overcoming his fear of moving by confessing his fears to a dogwood tree. In *The Sky of Now* (1994), another boy confronts his fear of heights. JJB

Potter, (Helen) Beatrix 1866–1943 British author-illustrator, best known for the *PETER RABBIT* series of books. Beatrix Potter spent most of her childhood in London, her interest in and fondness for the Lake District beginning when her family rented a holiday home there for three months of the year. During these holidays Beatrix and her brother developed a fascination for the study of both plants and animals, through drawing, painting and writing. This fascination was to stay with her all her life, and it undoubtedly made a significant contribution to the success of her books. She brought live animals back to London to keep as pets, including the most famous of all, Peter Rabbit.

Potter's writing talents developed through her use of a journal, which gave her the opportunity not only to keep a record of her discoveries but also to explore her fascination for the creatures that she observed. Her journal writing clearly shows her empathy for the creatures that she drew. This empathy subsequently enabled Potter to represent her PICTUREBOOK characters with perfectly appropriate motivations and behaviours. She began to create stories through writing letters to the son of her former governess, Noel Moore, and it is in this form that *The Tale of Peter Rabbit* first appeared. Her desire for financial autonomy, combined with a strong belief in her books as suitable for young children, resulted in their publication (by Warne). From the royalties, she was able to buy a small piece of land in Sawrey, giving herself some long-needed independence and a permanent base from which to research the illustrations for her books. Many of the landscapes are still identifiable, almost unchanged, today. Hill Top Farm at Sawrey was to provide solace for the author after the death of Norman Warne, to whom she had become engaged, and was to furnish the setting and plots for many of her subsequent books, including *The Tale of Tom Kitten* and *THE TALE OF JEMIMA PUDDLEDUCK*.

Beatrix Potter's combination of talents made her an outstanding author-illustrator of picturebooks for young children. She never underestimated her audience either in the narrative devices or in the vocabulary that she used. Her stories offered a world where, although the animals within it were anthropomorphised, they were never sentimental or simplistic. Her in-depth knowledge of the animals meant that it was never necessary to distort or caricature them in order to enhance their appeal to children. The animals alone had always appealed to Beatrix and she was able to communicate this to her audience through a powerful combination of illustrations and text. Although written over 90 years ago, her stories have a timelessness about them which has made them significant reading for subsequent generations of children and their parents. The tales of Beatrix Potter have spawned many versions, from the original Peter Rabbit toy produced by Harrods, to ballet, animations, bed-linen and crockery. These do not appear to have diluted the power of the original stories, but have merely increased the numbers of ways that children might first encounter Peter Rabbit, and through him, the talents of Beatrix Potter herself. HB

see also ILLUSTRATION; PICTUREBOOKS; *TALE OF MRS TIGGYWINKLE, THE*; *TALE OF PETER RABBIT, THE*; *TALE OF SQUIRREL NUTKIN, THE*

Poulin, Stéphane 1961– Canadian children's illustrator and author. A Montrealer, he began drawing at the age of four and by 19 had received a special mention in a children's ILLUSTRATION contest. At 22 he published *Ah! Belle Cité/A Beautiful City ABC* (1985) to critical acclaim. He has been winning prizes ever since, including a nomination, at the age of 33, for the HANS CHRISTIAN ANDERSEN AWARD. His *Josephine* stories – *Have You Seen Josephine?* (1986), *Can You Catch Josephine?* (1987) and *Could You Stop Josephine?* (1988) – about a mischievous cat whose disappearances worry

Daniel, are full of the sights of the city, school and the country, respectively. Poulin paints even the cityscapes with the colours of nature. Browns often dominate but his pictures are far from dreary. Hopeful and spirited, his stories are about real life. The *Stories and Lies of My Childhood* series – *My Mother's Loves* (1990) and *Travels for Two* (1991) – stretch the truth perhaps, but depict a happy childhood in a large and loving family dominated by the mother. Poulin also shows his fantastical and humorous side in *Benjamin and the Pillow Saga* (1989) in which shy Benjamin makes magical pillows which give sleepers especially sweet dreams. Poulin, who learned to speak English after his success as an author-illustrator, is published simultaneously in French and English. TH

pourquoi stories see AFRICAN MYTHOLOGY AND FOLKTALES

Power, Rhoda (Dolores) 1890–1957 Writer of HISTORICAL FICTION. Early books, such as *Boys and Girls of History* (1927), were written with her sister, the historian Eileen Power. Her work has careful authenticity, often using eyewitness techniques, as in *We Were There* (1955); it also shows a strong sense of story. Power was a pioneer in radio broadcasting for schools; and some of her material – for instance, from the series, *Stories from World History* – later appeared in book form. *Redcap Runs Away* (1953) recounts the adventures of a minstrel boy who hears legends, songs and stories as he roams medieval England. PP

Powling, Christopher 1943– British children's author, teacher, lecturer, and editor for many years of BOOKS FOR KEEPS. His works of fiction for children include *The Phantom Carwash* (1986), *Elf 61* (1990), *Where the Quaggy Bends* (1992) and *Kit's Castle* (1996). Powling's adaptable style means that his stories range from colourful FANTASY, for early readers, to longer novels with strong, vital characters and engaging plots. A serious commitment to his readers marks all his writing and in *Roald Dahl* (1983), a BIOGRAPHY, Powling has a clear sense of writing for an audience of loyal fans who are potential writers themselves. JHD

Practical Princess, The (1968) A collection of liberating fairy tales by Jay Williams. When this writer's fairy godmother gives Princess Bedelia common sense as her christening gift, she sets a precedent for changes which are to gather momentum over the next three decades. Bedelia slays the dragon, rescues the wimpish Prince, sees off Garp the gruesome suitor, and agrees to marriage on her own terms. Although this collection of FAIRY TALES was to become the model for many alternative versions, drawing on and subverting the stereotypes of traditional stories, they have a lightness of touch and understated humour which some of the more recent 'politically correct' versions lack. EAG

Praeger, (Sophia) Rosamond 1867–1954 Irish sculptor, author and illustrator. Praeger wrote and illustrated a number of books for younger children which depict a sharply observed world of Victorian and Edwardian children, some mixed with FANTASY, as in *The Adventures of the Three Bold Babes* (1897) and *The Tale of the Little Twin Dragons* (1900). *The Young Stamp-Collectors* (1985) was published posthumously. VC

Pratchett, Terry 1948– British author best known for his FANTASY *Discworld* novels, aimed at adults but with enormous appeal to readers of all ages. He is also an extremely popular writer for younger readers of both sexes, successfully cutting across stereotypical gendered reading preferences. He assumes his young readers are sharp, witty and thoughtful, ready to take on the intellectual challenges he offers them. TRUCKERS (1989), a fantasy about 'nomes' who inhabit a department store, was developed into a trilogy with the sequels *Diggers* (1990) and *Wings* (1990). In *Only You Can Save Mankind* (1992), Pratchett introduces a teenager, Johnny, whose adventures take place predominantly inside a computer game. *Johnny and the Dead* (1993), in which Johnny mingles with the dead in a local cemetery, was a hugely successful follow-up and won the 1993 Writers' Guild Award.

Whether writing fantasy or SCIENCE FICTION, Pratchett's novels are steeped in contemporary popular culture. His characters inhabit a recognisable world of modern urban life whose science and technology offer some useful literary devices. Young readers are particularly appreciative of Pratchett's humour, which not only mobilises their linguistic and scientific knowledge but also often relies for its effects on an intimacy with the discourses of new technologies and literacies. GCH

Prater, John 1947– British illustrator born in Reading, Berkshire, in 1947. He studied at Brighton College of Art and later at Reading University, graduating in 1972. He worked initially in advertising before taking up the teaching of art in a comprehensive school. His first book was *On Friday Something Funny Happened* (1982), which was runner-up for the MOTHER GOOSE AWARD. His main works have been for very young readers, but they are challenging texts, often playful and interactive, using inventive formats for exploring the recognisable moments of childhood. *The Party* (1983), for example, was one of the first to use the strip-cartoon format, while *The Gift* (1985), an outstanding wordless PICTUREBOOK, used filmic conventions not only to tell its story but for the whole book, including the coda on the back cover. With *Once Upon A Time* (1975) Prater used the double landscape format within which to tell multiple events from well known FAIRY TALES. He has worked with other writers, for example Paul Rogers in *Letters to Granny* (1996) and *Nearly But Not Quite* (1997), and ROGER MCGOUGH in *The Kite and Caitlin* (1996). His other books include *You Can't Catch Me* (1984), *Along Came Tom* (1990), *On Top of the World* (1998), *Walking Around the Garden* (1998) and *Oh Where Oh Where?* (1998). AR

Prefabulous Animiles (1957) Collection of NONSENSE VERSE by British poet JAMES REEVES, illustrated by EDWARD ARDIZZONE. These are poems about the 'almost-and-yet more than animals' about whom 'Darwin knew nothing'. Among these are 'The Hippocrump' ('Along the valley of the Ump / Gallops the fearful Hippocrump'), 'The Amperzand' and, with its echoes of LEAR and CARROLL, 'the luminous Snitterjipe'. *More Prefabulous Animiles* (1975) has a similar blend of whimsy, wordplay and virtuoso rhyming. ML

Prelutsky, Jack 1940– American children's poet, author of numerous collections. Born in New York, Prelutsky has lived in Cambridge, Massachusetts, Seattle and Washington. He has the distinction of being one of the most popular poets in America and successful with young British readers. Prelutsky has edited some substantial anthologies, including *The Random House Book of Poetry for Children* (1983), which appeared in Britain in the same year entitled *The Walker Book of Poetry for Children*; its well-chosen, mainly American and British poetry is engagingly illustrated by ARNOLD LOBEL. Prelutsky's introduction talks of avoiding 'many of the inspirational and the long narrative poems that are so often included in other anthologies, because they no longer seem relevant to today's children . . . the accent is on humour and light verse.' Therein lies the strength and weakness of his own compositions and edited anthologies. A companion volume for younger readers is *The Walker Book of Read-Aloud Rhymes for the Very Young* (1986). *Poems of A. Nonny Mouse* (1992) is a witty title for a book of anonymous verse. Prelutsky's own poetry, which he performs in schools and libraries all over America, is light-hearted and amusing. Well-known titles include *THE NEW KID ON THE BLOCK* (1986), *Nightmares* (1976) and *Something Big Has Been Here* (1991). MCCS

Prentiss, Elizabeth 1818–78 American author. In *Little Susy's Six Birthdays* (1853), Prentiss pleased child readers with cheerful accounts of Susy's birthday celebrations, while offering their parents helpful ideas about the stages of a small child's social, spiritual, physical and psychological development. *Little Susy's Six Teachers* and *Little Susy's Little Servants* (both 1856) show children happily learning about spiritual resources while they also discover the uses of their own eyes, ears, fingers and toes. Many of Prentiss's 25 books were written for children, although she later became well known for her adult fiction, especially *Stepping Heavenward* (1869). FEA

Pretty Lessons in Verse for all Good Children (1834) Collection of poetry by Sara Coleridge. She spent much of her life editing her famous father's work. *Pretty Lessons* does not have the scope or quality of ANN and JANE TAYLORS's *ORIGINAL POEMS FOR INFANT MINDS*, which Coleridge criticises in her preface. It is memorable above all for one wonderful poem, 'The Months of the Year': 'January brings the sleet and snow, / Makes our feet and fingers glow.' MCCS

Price, Evadne see *JUST JANE*

Price, Susan 1955– British writer who was born in Staffordshire and began her long writing career while still in her teens, with *The Devil's Piper* (1973). Although perhaps primarily known as a fantasist and ghost-story writer, winning the CARNEGIE MEDAL for *The Ghost Drum* (1987), her works also show an interest in history: *Twopence a Tub* (1975), which won the Children's Rights Workshop Other Award, focuses on a miners' strike in 1851, *Christopher Uptake* (1981) is set in Elizabethan England, and Price's *The Sterkarm Handshake* (1998), for older readers, is a novel involving time travel between the 16th and 21st centuries. SA

Price, Willard 1887–1983 Born in Peterborough, Canada, Price was a real-life explorer and traveller, drawing upon his own experiences from around the world in his popular *Adventure* series, the first of which was *Amazon Adventure* (1949). The brothers Hal, manly and steady, and Roger, courageous but foolhardy, investigate and capture rare animals for their zoologist father. The stories are full of action and crammed with factual detail in the style of boys' ANNUALS. Although much criticised for their improbabilities of plot and lack of emotional depth, their pacy and undemanding style ensured their continuing popularity with young readers. HCE

primers Prayer books or, later, books of instruction which evolved from the Psalter and Breviary. 'Primer' was the name given to the *Book of Hours of the Blessed Virgin* (*Horae beatae Virginis Mariae*) to which other religious materials were gradually added. By the 12th century it was used principally by the laity for their devotions at church or in the home. Most primers were in Latin, but from the beginning of the 15th century some appeared partly in English, and in those for children an alphabet was inserted. After Henry VIII's primer of 1545, which pleaded that 'yong beginners' should learn their ABC in English, Latin versions became fewer. When the *Book of Common Prayer* appeared in 1549 it superseded all the many varied service books previously allowed, and the primer in its original form was rarely printed after 1585.

In 1666 Benjamin Keach's *The Child's Instructor, or a New and Easy Primer*, and G. and E.H.'s (i.e. George Fox and Ellis Hookes') *A Primmer and Catechism for children; or a Plain and easie way for children to learn to spell and read perfectly in a little time* started a new format for the primer. They were early reading books, with alphabets, syllabariums and token catechisms, prayers and hymns. This development became commercially popular from the late 18th century. The form was given a new lease of life in America as *The New-England Primer*, a fiercely protestant symbol for the Puritan Colonists. It was inspired by *The Protestant Tutor*, published in Cornhill, London in 1679, one of the many anti-Catholic works of the time. PG

Prince and the Pauper, The (1881) A historical romance by Mark Twain [Samuel L. Clemens]. With this book Twain attempted to position himself as a serious writer, rather than a mere humorist, by building on the well-respected Victorian tradition of historical fiction. In the story, Prince Edward, the future Edward VI of England, and pauper Tom Canty accidentally meet, and for a lark they exchange clothes, discovering in the process that they are as alike as twins. Through a mishap, Edward is thrown out of the palace in the pauper's clothes and Tom is left to impersonate the prince. As Prince Edward roams over England trying to establish his true identity, he sees at first hand the dire poverty and wretchedness that mark the lives of so many of his future subjects. He learns as a consequence a greater sense of compassion for the common people and the need for a ruler to govern with sympathy. In a dramatic conclusion, Edward appears just as Tom is about to be crowned king in his stead. The novel is ostensibly a juvenile work, but Twain also intended the story to serve a didactic function and to emphasise the idea that political power must be moderated by compassion. JKB

Prince in Waiting, The (1970–2) Second trilogy by John Christopher, which like his earlier *Tripods* trilogy, recreates the past in a post-cataclysmic future setting. This time, catastrophe has taken the form of a series of natural disasters: volcanic eruptions, earthquakes, increasing solar radiation, and consequent genetic mutation. Technology has been blamed and machines outlawed; in southern England, cut off by a range of volcanoes from the North, the survivors live in warring city states. There are three genetic strains, forming a warrior class, a tradesman's class, and a lower order who are slaves. And there are Seers, who in the first book, *The Prince in Waiting*, choose the hero, Luke, as Prince-to-be of Winchester, with a mission to unite his fragmented country. In the second and third books, *Beyond the Burning Lands* and *The Sword of the Spirits*, Luke succeeds as war leader but his own actions and failings result in his banishment. He joins the people beyond the burning lands and turns rediscovered weapons against his own country.

For younger readers simply pursuing the story, there is strong and varied action; there is also scope for thought on social issues, and there are allusions, especially Arthurian, for those who can pick them up. The 'sword of the spirits', which Luke wields to secure his princedom, is clearly Excalibur. Luke, the flawed hero, a winner in war but a loser in love, victim of his own urge to dominate, is Christopher's best achievement in characterisation. JRT

see also King Arthur

Pringle, Laurence P(atrick) [Sean Edmunds] 1935– American author, editor and photographer who grew up living close to nature in a rural area of western New York. He received degrees in biology from Cornell University and the University of Massachusetts, briefly taught high-school science, and worked as editor for the American Museum of Natural History's *Nature and Science* magazine for children, before becoming a freelance nature-writer and photographer. His books have received critical acclaim and numerous honours for their clear, stimulating writing on sometimes controversial issues. In 1978 Pringle received a Special Conservation Award as 'the nation's leading writer of books on biological and environmental issues for young people'. Topics Pringle has explored include oil spills, acid rain, global warming, nuclear power, forest fires and smoking. His *Taking Care of the Earth* (1996) reports on children who have taken action to protect the environment. In the *Something About the Author Autobiography Series*, vol. VI, Pringle has written: 'My approach to writing a book is like that of a teacher planning to present a subject to students – not "how many facts, dates, and definitions can I jam into their heads" but what are the key ideas and how can I spark some enthusiasm about them.' LH

see also Ecology

printing, history of see Illustration in Children's Books

Prisoner of Zenda, The see Adult Fiction; see also *The Lost Prince*

problem fiction see YOUNG ADULT FICTION

process engraving In 1848 Gillot, a French lithographer, developed a practical method of photographically transferring an artist's drawing to a printing block, although it came to be used to a significant degree only from 1888. A metal plate is coated with a water-soluble photographic emulsion which when exposed becomes insoluble. Strong light is projected through a photographic negative of the artist's drawing onto the plate, which is then coated with greasy, acid-resistant ink, and washed. The unexposed parts of the coating dissolve, taking with them the layer of ink in which they were coated. The plate is immersed in an acid bath and the unprotected parts are etched away, leaving the image in relief. The plate is mounted on a wooden block and is ready for printing.

During the period from 1850 to 1890, when WOOD ENGRAVING was the primary means of reproducing drawings, many established artists were content to provide the engraver with the merest outline, leaving the craftsman to decide the precise line to be cut and to fill in the majority of the detail. However, in the case of the process engraver, the draughtsman could be sure that the line originally made on a sheet of Bristol board would be presented to the reader, perhaps reduced in size, but otherwise unchanged. The effect of this transition was most marked in the impact that it had on the community of illustrators, forcing many of the established men into early retirement, and giving enormous opportunities for younger artists. Amongst those to benefit from the revolution were the ROBINSON brothers, the BROCKS, Hugh Thomson, GORDON BROWNE, J.D. Batten and H.J. FORD, all of whom exploited the new medium to take control of the total design of the books they illustrated, from the BLOCKING on the cover to the layout and decoration of the preliminary pages. Titles such as STEVENSON'S *A CHILD'S GARDEN OF VERSES* became minor works of art, perfectly conceived and crafted. GCB

***Professor Branestawm* series** Based on stories originally written for the BBC's *Children's Hour* and read aloud by Ajax, one of the programme's favourite 'uncles', Norman Hunter's *The Incredible Adventures of Professor Branestawm* appeared in 1933 with the inestimable advantage of accompanying illustrations by W. HEATH ROBINSON, who also illustrated its sequel, *Stories of Professor Branestawm* (1939). Rarely can author and illustrator have been so perfectly matched. Professor Branestawm's various inventions (burglar-catching machine, pancake-making equipment) were lovingly re-created by the artist, with arrows indicating anticipated movement. The professor himself was usually accompanied by Colonel Dedshott of the Catapult Cavaliers: 'A very brave gentleman who never missed a train, an enemy, or any opportunity of getting into danger.' They were both looked after by Mrs Flittersnoop, a cockney house-keeper with a taste for malapropisms but also possessing a strong feeling for common sense. With her help, the professor always made it back to home and a happy ending after his various escapades.

Fourteen more titles followed, illustrated by different artists. Yet the professor is still shown habitually wearing five pairs of glasses all at once on his dome-shaped bald head, with one pair ostensibly there for seeking out the others. This was typical of the author's brand of uncomplicated fun. The professor's own style of speech is sometimes so convoluted it is difficult to be certain what he is getting at. But regular intervals of slapstick and a tight narrative format ensured that young readers usually ended up enjoying yet another of these ever-popular, often near-disastrous adventures, the last of which, *Professor Branestawm's Mouse War*, appeared in 1984. NT

Protestant Tutor, The see *THE NEW-ENGLAND PRIMER*

Provensen, Wilbur 1918– and **Provensen, Alice** 1916–87 American illustrators and writers, who, after their marriage in 1944, collaborated on a number of books, their first being *The Fireside Book of Folk Songs* (1947). *The Glorious Flight: Across the Channel with Louis Blériot*, which celebrates Blériot and early flying machines, won the 1984 CALDECOTT MEDAL. Among their titles are *A Peaceable Kingdom* (1978), *The Provensen Book of Fairy Tales* (1971), *The Golden Serpent* (1971), and a group of four books on their experiences at Maple Hill Farm. They collaborated with NANCY WILLARD on the well-received *A Visit to William Blake's Inn* (1981). Among its honours are the Art Books for Children Citation of the Brooklyn Museum and the Gold Medal for Illustration of the Society of Illustrators. Their work has been exhibited at the American Institute of Graphic Arts and has frequently appeared on the *New York Times* list of Best Illustrated Children's Books of the Year. The Provensens work in full colour gouache, design as well as illustrate their books, and in some cases make special use of lettering as part of their composition. Some have compared them to the British AHLBERGS. Alice Provensen published *The Buck Stops Here* (1990) alone. KSB

see also *SONGS OF INNOCENCE*

proverbs see FABLES; see also AFRICAN MYTHOLOGY AND FOLKTALES

Prøysen, Alf see *MRS PEPPERPOT* SERIES

***Prydain* series** see *CHRONICLES OF PRYDAIN*

***Psammead* series** Three novels by E. NESBIT: *Five Children and It* (1902), *The Phoenix and the Carpet* (1904) and *The Story of the Amulet* (1906). The Psammead is a 'sand-fairy' (from the Greek *psammos* for sand). Nesbit's depiction of the Psammead is of no gauze-winged sprite, but of one closer to the ape than the angel: he is imaged as a chimpanzee with horns, an idiosyncratic being, who is easily offended and irritable. The figures of the Psammead and the Mouldiwarp (the mole-like creature who is the presiding genius of the *Arden* books) represent the continuation of Mrs Molesworth's efforts to de-sentimentalise faery, and their genesis is one indication of the alterations to the aesthetics of children's books which were taking place in the period 1870–1930. The depiction of the children is also in line with these changes; though on the whole much less inventive and unconventional than their BASTABLE predecessors, Cyril, Anthea, Robert and Jane are likeable and high-spirited, real as opposed to idealised children. Rather than wandering around in a saintly haze trailing clouds of glory, they more often trail clouds of dirt from their scrambles in secret passages, and they represent a healthy rejection of the limp and pious ethos found in earlier children's books: as Robert says, when caught in a fire at the theatre in *The Phoenix and the Carpet*, 'No boys on burning decks for me!'

The formula of the first two books is similar: the children come into possession of a wish-granting entity (the Psammead is replaced by the carpet in the second volume) but their wishes bring them no lasting good. The third book of the series is, however, differently conceived: it works on the idea of time-travelling into the past to look for the other, missing half of the amulet – the whole enabling its possessor to achieve his heart's desire; and while the first two are episodic in structure, the third is much more integrated as a narrative, the adventures accreting and building up to a satisfying conclusion.

The Story of the Amulet suggests a different kind of fulfillment from the first two books, where desire is formulated in trivial terms. Wanting to be 'as beautiful as the day' and 'rich beyond the dreams of avarice' are examples of thinking in cliché, and it goes without saying that since even as linguistic constructions the phrases contain little meaning, the fulfillment of the wishes brings scant satisfaction. In the third book, the 'heart's desire', though given in deceptively simple terms, is a various and deeper thing. To the children, it is the reunion of their family, for family wholeness – as the episode of the orphan girl illustrates – is not a thing to be taken for granted. To Rekh-mara and Jimmy, it is knowledge and understanding. The search for utopia is seen to take place on both personal and social levels, the societies of past and future standing in sharp contrast to that inhabited by the children. SA

publishing and publishers Publishing for children in the United Kingdom seems to have had its beginning in CHAPBOOKS – the illustrated tales carried by travelling pedlars in the 17th and 18th centuries that were read for enjoyment by children as well as by their intended adult audience. Their publishers (who were also their printers) sold the books to chapmen on credit, payment to be made (with interest) when the pedlars returned from their summer journeys.

Financial control has always been a crucial element of children's publishing, prices being traditionally lower than for adult books. Immediate return on investment is therefore small, although the life of a book that becomes a classic may be long. As a result, publishers concentrating only on children's books have been few; most have regarded them as a lowly adjunct to their adult list, and the motivation to publish has not been primarily commercial. The dichotomy between instruction and amusement also goes back to the beginning, and the first publishers of books specifically designed for children declared they would combine both: THOMAS BOREMAN and JOHN NEWBERY set up their publishing/bookselling businesses in London in 1730 and 1744 respectively. The 400 books for children produced by John Newbery and his successor JOHN HARRIS between 1740 and 1815 represented just a sixth of the firm's total output.

The inventions and technological advances of the 19th century ensured the rapid expansion of publishing in general. The arrival of the railways and the telegraph in the 1820s speeded up the distribution of books, so that the publisher's function ceased to include printing and selling, leaving him free to specialise in commissioning and promoting his wares, which he often designed and wrote (anonymously). The replacement of the hand-press by steam-driven presses, the invention of photography and electrotyping, the introduction of esparto grass into papermaking – all led to books being produced faster, more cheaply, in larger quantities, and with finer ILLUSTRATIONS and bindings. The century also saw the start of regulation in the trade in Britain – the legal protection of authors' copyright in the mid-1800s and, after much wrangling, the establishment in 1900 of fixed prices by the Net Book Agreement among authors, publishers and booksellers.

Publishers – usually individuals with inherited money – began to produce a wide variety of children's books, many of them market-led by a public desire to teach young people the way to virtue. Such books were called 'rewards' – often given as Sunday-school prizes – and the genre prospered well into the 1930s. Originating in evangelical tracts distributed free to working-class children, they developed into countless fictional series (of ephemeral worth) published principally by the Society for Promoting Christian

Knowledge but also by commercial publishers who found the revenue a means of subsidising more innovative productions.

The change from crude woodcut illustrations to WOOD ENGRAVING and later copperplate engraving meant that publishers could make their children's books as attractive in appearance as they wished. Men such as Joseph Cundall (responsible for the *Home Treasury* series in 1843) and later George Routledge (entrepreneur in the collaboration between artist WALTER CRANE and engraver/printer EDMUND EVANS) were able to 'move up-market' in producing well-designed books for children that gave them status and encouraged artists of repute to work on them.

Between 1850 and 1870 there was an explosion of creative activity in the publishing of illustrated books and magazines for the young, inspired, it seems, by a wish to give pleasure as well as influence readers for their good. George Bell published his friend Mrs Gatty's *AUNT JUDY'S MAGAZINE* (1866) for nearly 20 years but made a profit on only one of them. Alexander Strahan employed GEORGE MACDONALD as editor of *Good Words for the Young*, a sixpenny (2.5 pence) monthly, in 1869 and serialised *At the Back of the North Wind* with ARTHUR HUGHES's illustrations – a method by which many novels for children were first put on the market.

George Routledge and his partner Frederick Warne were the publishers of the famous PICTUREBOOKS (hitherto known as 'TOY BOOKS') by WALTER CRANE, RANDOLPH CALDECOTT and KATE GREENAWAY, and by 1879 Routledge was confident enough to print 20,000 copies of *UNDER THE WINDOW* – remarkable for a first book by a comparative unknown. Also in the 1870s came a spate of novelty MOVABLE BOOKS from the firm of Dean, who had been practising with lift-the-flap books since 1858.

Forster's Education Act of 1870 led to a need for books written solely for schoolroom use – thereafter known as 'educational' publishing – and the Scottish firm of Thomas Nelson was quick to produce a series of *Royal Readers* that sold steadily and in vast numbers. Immediate followers were Edward Arnold and Blackie. Throughout the century, while popular books literally disintegrated (children's books are subject to specially hard wear-and-tear), there was the occasional book every publisher dreams of – the one that proves a favourite with successive generations and becomes a classic.

While educational publishing forged ahead, catering for a school system that required every child in the classroom to have a copy of the same prescribed book, the market for children's books depended on the choice of adults. Children might spend pocket money on COMICS – the publisher Alfred Harmsworth was the first to target children directly in 1904 – and the invention of book tokens in 1932 put spending power in their hands; but it was adults who bought the sumptuous GIFT BOOKS of the early 1900s and the hardback novels of the 1920s and 1930s.

Advances in printing technology were to revolutionise book production, but the opportunities these offered for the picturebook were not fully exploited until the 1960s. The profusely illustrated narratives that publishers such as John Lane and William Heinemann could afford to commission from artists like the ROBINSON brothers and ARTHUR RACKHAM (including colour plates, ENDPAPERS and stamped bindings (see BLOCKING)) survived the 1914–18 war but disappeared in the austerity of World War II. Likewise the publishing of ANNUALS and the 'bumper' book collections of stories, often printed on thick paper to give bulk and the impression of value for money, began to wane. Public LIBRARIES, following the example of the United States, started to make space for children's books in the 1920s, and in the next decade, again following American practice, firms such as Dent, Methuen and Oxford University Press appointed children's book editors, mostly women, to look after this part of their lists.

After World War II children's publishing in Britain suffered the same difficulties as adult publishing; paper rationing continued until 1949. This led to long delays between a new book's conception and its appearance in print, and affected the reprinting of backlist titles, a key part of the children's publishing industry.

During the 1950s most books still reached the hands of the general public by going from publisher to bookseller to customer; bookclubs did not represent a significant market force and few wholesalers were used. British publishing houses began to grow as a result of mergers – partly to fend off possible American takeovers – and the 1950s and 60s saw the gradual emergence of a number of key publishers and editors of children's books. In 1951 Max Reinhardt bought Bodley Head and installed Judy Taylor to develop the children's list there. During the 1960s Tom Maschler worked on the children's list at Cape, publishing many titles still popular today. Meanwhile Paul Hamlyn was determined to broaden the market for children's books, certain that many customers were reluctant to visit traditional bookshops and that the books themselves were not attractive enough. He produced a number of relatively cheap books with colour illustrations, sold not only through bookshops, but also through national British outlets such as Boots the Chemist. Meanwhile LADYBIRD BOOKS grew from strength to strength, keeping their price of two-shillings-and-sixpence a book from the end of the war until 1971, a feat that could be accomplished through growth in sales and consequent larger print-runs.

Of all the figures to emerge in children's publishing during this period, the best-known and most influential is KAYE WEBB, who became editor of the Puffin list in 1961. At Puffin's parent company, Penguin, paperback production was growing under the auspices of Allen Lane. Books were cheaper and more widely available, and people's attitude to them was gradually changing. For children, books were no longer objects of great financial value to be handled with immense care, but became instead purchases that they could buy for themselves and carry around with them. Sales of Puffin paperbacks increased three-fold between 1963 and 1968 and Kaye Webb founded the Puffin Club to promote the list. By 1972 membership of the club was 50,000. Under Webb's direction Puffin published original fiction straight into paperback and encouraged many writers who later came to be viewed as classic children's authors. During the 1970s other publishing houses followed suit and, although the name 'Puffin' continued to be loosely equated with paperback fiction, other companies acquired well-known authors on their growing paperback lists.

Bookclubs became more successful as a result of the growing paperback market; bookclub editions were not subject to the Net Book Agreement and a limited range of titles was sold to customers at a lower price than they would pay in the shops, ensuring the growing popularity of the clubs. Today mail-order clubs hold a dominant position in the marketplace, supplying schools as well as homes. Often reprints of backlist titles are uneconomical unless a club decides to buy the book, thereby increasing its potential sales to a viable total. Many argue that the purchasing power of the clubs has been, at least in part, responsible for the growth of mass-market series fiction and the demise of the literary novel for children, since clubs must look for titles with an established market. Others counter that the clubs are able to get books to a far wider audience than the traditional bookshop.

The Net Book Agreement in Britain effectively ceased to exist in 1995 and became illegal in 1997, encouraging shops as well as clubs to discount high profile titles at the possible expense of work by less well-known authors. Opinion is divided across the trade as to whether the end of the NBA will bring about discounting and therefore make cheaper books more widely available, or whether prices on all books will rise in order to provide the margins necessary to finance discounting on bestsellers.

The 1980s saw many takeovers across the British publishing industry. As hardback and paperback companies merged, a number of authors found that their hardbacks were with one conglomerate while their paperbacks remained with another. As publishers battled to gain market share there were a number of rights reversions, as a result of which many well-known titles changed hands. The growth of the large publishing houses has led to many changes in both the marketing and editing of children's books. In the larger houses the decision to publish titles is often taken by a number of departments, not just editorial, and the immediate profitability of each book is watched very closely. Costs are inevitably higher with the number of personnel needed to provide marketing, design, etc. This can disadvantage a children's list, where sales have traditionally come from the backlist and popularity has grown over the years. Books are now taken out of print and remaindered far more quickly than they were previously, often before they have had a chance to establish themselves in the market-place. At the same time many new titles are published each year, leading to frequent claims of over-productiotion.

A growing emphasis has been placed on the appearance and design of new titles in an attempt to win market share and customer loyalty. The appearance of INFORMATION BOOKS in particular has changed dramatically: text tends to be broken down into small chunks, with little continuous narrative, while illustrations are mainly photographic with a lot of white space on the page. The high cost of producing such material can be offset by large international sales, which means in turn that the books' content has to be suitable for sale overseas. Another key influence on British non-fiction publishing in the late 1980s and 90s has been the development of the National Curriculum. Publishers can now be certain that large numbers of children will be studying the same topic at roughly the same age, and have therefore produced a range of titles covering many areas of the curriculum for sale to the British market. However, publishing takes time and there is often a delay between any change to the Curriculum and the production of material to support it.

Underfunding in British schools and library services – the main purchasers of hardback material – has led to a decline in hardback sales and a greater emphasis on paperback publishing. However, the implementation of the 'Literacy Hour' in British schools from autumn 1998 was accompanied by an influx of government money for books in schools. It has also led to a huge increase in the number of books published in 'big book' format for use with the whole class. Few fiction authors are now published in hardback, and an increasing quantity of non-fiction is being produced in paperback format.

In the United States, Canada, New Zealand and Australia, children's book publishing eventually broke free of British practices and texts in ways unique to each area. In the United States, children's book publishing dates back over 350 years, to the printing in 1646 of the first children's book in America, John Cotton's *Milk for Babes*. Books published during the colonial period were similar to their English prototypes. One of the earliest reprinters of John Newbery's books was Hugh Gaine of New York. The books published in the late 18th century by Isaiah Thomas of Worcester, Massachusetts, were reprints of English publications with American adaptations. In his most productive years of the 1780s, he printed a number of Newbery titles, such as *A Little Pretty Pocket-Book*, the first American collections of nursery rhymes and fairy tales, and assorted school textbooks. Nathaniel Coverly, active in Boston from 1771, published editions of Isaac Watts, John Newbery and *Robinson Crusoe*, as well as collections of moral fables and nursery rhymes.

The development of American children's literature began in the post-Revolution period. Boston, New York and Philadelphia were the leading centres for publishing, with smaller sites in Baltimore, Hartford and New Haven. Philadelphia was prolific in the first two decades of the 19th century, with its production of picturebooks of pirated editions and American adaptations of texts, particularly those by the engraver, William Charles. Jacob Johnson, also of Philadelphia, published information books and moral tales, drawing upon some of Charles's plates. The first known American Christmas book, *A New Year's Present* (1821), was published by William Giley of New York. A renowned New York publisher, Samuel Wood, printed toy books with a distinctive American flavour, such as *The Young Child's ABC, or, First Book* (1806). Contemporary with Wood were New York publishers Mahlon Day (1790–1854) and Solomon King (1791–1832). Edmund Munroe and David Francis of Boston published *Mother Goose's Quarto, or Melodies Complete* (c.1835), which was the largest collection of its kind, followed by Munroe and Francis's *Mother Goose's Melodies* in 1833, which prompted many reprintings. By the 1850s, a series published by the American Sunday School Union, based in Philadelphia, included large picturebooks with lithographs by Augustus Kollner.

Popular literature and textbooks shaped the taste of generations of children in the 19th century. The *Peter Parley* books of Samuel Goodrich provided some of the first recreational reading for American children. His first book with Parley as narrator, *Peter Parley's Tales of America*, was published in 1827 and followed by books on history, geography, astronomy and mythology, among others of the 7 million copies sold by 1860. Jacob Abbott (1805–79) wrote the first two of the *Rollo* series in 1835, published by J. Allen & Co. of Boston; the *Franconia* series, published between 1850 and 1854 by the New York firm of Harper, provided a view of rural New England life. In 1836 the Cincinnati firm, Truman and Smith, began publication of *McGuffey Eclectic Readers*, the most popular American schoolbook for 75 years.

Juvenile periodicals began to appear in America during the late 18th century and flourished throughout the 19th, particularly after the Civil War (see comics, periodicals and magazines). The first distinctive magazine for children was the bimonthly *Juvenile Miscellany*, which began publishing in Boston in 1826 and lasted for a decade. The magazine prominently featured American history, biography, and landscapes; fiction and verse for the young, notably by women writers; and a progressive attitude toward Native Americans, Africans, the poor and the physically handicapped. The most enduring periodical for children – from 1827 to 1929 – was also published in Boston: *The Youth's Companion*, begun by Nathaniel Willis. Other distinguished children's periodicals include *The Riverside Magazine*, edited by Horace E. Scudder, published in Boston from 1867 to 1870, and renowned for its high literary quality; and *St Nicholas*, originally edited by Mary Mapes Dodge, and published by Scribner & Co. of New York.

Until almost the end of the 19th century, American publishers continued to favour European titles over domestic literature for children. However, the passage of the International Copyright Law in 1891 encouraged the growth of American authorship and publishing. By the turn of the century, L. Frank Baum's *The Wonderful Wizard of Oz*, published in 1900 by Geo. M. Hill Co. of Chicago and New York, and illustrated by W.W. Denslow, heralded a new age of fantasy writing with American landscapes and themes.

The juvenile book market grew enough in the early decades of the 20th century to inspire special publishing attention. Firms began appointing editors with the responsibility of developing children's book lists: Louise Seaman Bechtel at Macmillan in 1919 and May Massee at Doubleday in 1922; others, such as Virginia Kirkus at Harper, soon followed. These children's book departments grew in response to the institutional market of libraries and schools, which through their professional organisations encouraged the growth of American children's book publishing by instituting Children's Book Week in 1919, the Newbery Medal in 1922, and the Caldecott Medal in 1938. A professional periodical, *The Horn Book*, begun by Bertha Mahoney Miller in 1924, grew out of the alignment of bookshops and libraries for children, with leaders like Anne Carroll Moore of New York Public Library.

The period from 1920 to 1940 has been called a golden age of American children's book publishing. This was a period of experimentation with new colour-printing techniques and graphics and the incorporation of European styles by immigrant illustrators. Series books proliferated, inspired by the STRATEMEYER SYNDICATE's popular *HARDY BOYS* and *NANCY DREW* mysteries. Despite the Depression, which trimmed lists, children's book publishing flourished until the end of the 1930s, doubling output within two decades. Notwithstanding the slowdown of publishing during World War II, the 1940s witnessed the *GOLDEN BOOKS* series of Simon & Schuster in 1942 and the work of influential children's book editor URSULA NORDSTROM at Harper, who began to publish books by MARGARET WISE BROWN, MEINDERT DEJONG, ELSE HOLMELUND MINARIK, RUTH KRAUSS, CROCKETT JOHNSON, RUSSELL HOBAN, MAURICE SENDAK and E.B. WHITE. A new era was emerging with the development of easy reader books, YOUNG ADULT FICTION, MULTICULTURAL BOOKS, and sophisticated picturebooks.

After World War II, children's book publishing burgeoned like the baby boom. Children's book divisions enjoyed a new prestige within the publishing industry and their growing numbers – over 30 – made it imperative to form a professional organisation; in 1945 the Children's Book Council was established by publishers as a centre for promoting reading and book projects. As the 1950s began, the boom in children's book publishing – largely the results of publisher activity and library sales – resulted in 1,400 new books published annually. As the perception grew that children's books were big business, editors competed for new talent and new formats to publish. E.B. WHITE's *CHARLOTTE'S WEB* and Ruth Krauss's *A Hole is to Dig* were two successful ventures by Ursula Nordstrom at Harper. In 1950 Random House launched Landmark Books, a BIOGRAPHY and history series, which became a popular format for a growing school market. Random House also published DR SEUSS's *THE CAT IN THE HAT* in 1957, inaugurating a new genre in children's books, a limited-vocabulary book for early, independent reading.

In the late 1950s and the 1960s, federal funds accelerated a heady rate of growth. The threat of Sputnik in 1957 prompted a surge of non-fiction, and federal monies were available to schools for the purchase of science and mathematics books through the National Defense Education Act. The passage of the Elementary and Secondary Act in 1965 – 'Title II' – created a surge in children's book publishing of non-textbooks, with demand outstripping supply. The Bologna Children's Book Fair, begun in 1963, created opportunities for international co-productions of children's books. NANCY LARRICK's 1965 *Saturday Review* article, 'The All-White World of Children's Books', stirred the consciousness of creators and publishers of children's books towards an understanding of the need for greater diversity. The new genre of YOUNG ADULT FICTION, inspired, in part, by J.D. Salinger's *CATCHER IN THE RYE* (1951) and BEVERLY CLEARY's *Fifteen* (1957), led to 'problem novels' such as S.E. HINTON's *The Outsiders* (1967), PAUL ZINDEL's *The Pigman* (1968) and JOHN DONOVAN's *I'll Get There, It Better be Worth the Trip* (1969). Two editors associated with the new social realism were Ursula Nordstrom of Harper and Elizabeth Riley at Crowell. After the success of the *THE LORD OF THE RINGS* and the *CHRONICLES OF NARNIA*, FANTASY began to flourish, with American creations such as LLOYD ALEXANDER's *PRYDAIN* books and MADELEINE L'ENGLE's *A WRINKLE IN TIME*. Picturebooks bloomed with the imagery and designs of Maurice Sendak, EZRA JACK KEATS, LEO LIONNI, TOMI UNGERER and WILLIAM STEIG.

The bounty of the 1960s was stunted by recession and declines in federal funding in the 1970s, and several publishing houses pared down their children's book divisions. Inflation created higher printing costs, particularly of hardcover books, while reprint paperbacks of quality children's books flourished. The children's magazine *CRICKET* was launched in 1973, with the intention of becoming a modern periodical similar in quality to *St Nicholas*. The isolationist spirit prompted by the Vietnam War led to fewer translated books entering the market. As library budgets tightened, publishers looked to new sources for sales. As children's bookstores became common, the bookseller (often with a background as a librarian or teacher) became a critical partner to the juvenile editor and the librarian. A growing awareness of feminism and ethnic minorities led to a search for authors and illustrators of 'parallel cultures'. AFRICAN AMERICAN LITERATURE began to be recognised in the top prizes: in 1975 VIRGINIA HAMILTON won the Newbery Medal for *M.C. Higgins the Great*; LEO DILLON in 1976 was honoured with the Caldecott for *Ashanti to Zulu*; and in 1977 the Newbery was given to MILDRED TAYLOR's *Roll of Thunder, Hear My Cry*. ROBERT CORMIER's *The Chocolate War* (1974) – with protagonists defeated rather than triumphant – broke new ground in young adult literature. But, despite these innovations, by 1978 there were 150 fewer titles published annually than in the previous decade.

The 1980s witnessed a recovery in genre paperback series and picturebooks, as institutional markets revived and bookstore sales soared. Larger school populations led to concern about education and reading, and the 'baby boomers', accustomed to buying books of their own, began to fortify their young with literature. In 1987, more than 4,600 new books were published, double the 1978 rate. Children's bookstores increased dramatically over the decade, from a sprinkling to somewhere between 300 and 400. Children's book publishers began to operate in a similar way to their adult book counterparts, with an emphasis on frontlist publishing, big cash advances for star authors and illustrators, and the appearance of a children's bestseller list in *Publishers Weekly*. The whole-language programmes in schools contributed to the rise in paperbacks as the fastest-growing category of children's book sales, with most hardcover publishers selling their own paperback imprints. Series books and books to share with infants and toddlers became competitive, growing fields. Young adult books – such as the *Sweet Valley High* series – returned to romance after a decade of social realism, while new voices were heard in the multicultural milieu of Bruce Brooks, Brock Cole, Chris Crutcher, Cynthia Voigt and Francesca Block. Publishing houses began to be merged into large international conglomerates, a practice soon to overpower the industry.

The 1990s accelerated the trends of the 1980s with heightened attention to marketing. Many of the country's major publishing houses – HarperCollins, Viking Penguin, Bantam Doubleday Dell, Grolier – were now owned by British, German and French corporations. Various publishing houses merged (Penguin Putnam), and other imprints folded (Lodestar and Cobblehill Books). Holiday House remained the sole major independent publisher of long standing. With profitability down in publishing, one bright light was small-press publishing, which grew in sales, with a stronger national commitment to multicultural books and racial equality. While library and institutional sales stagnated or declined along with independent bookstores, the industry looked to non-traditional retail outlets to sell their products. By the end of the 1990s, approximately 5,000 new trade books were published for children and young adults. The recognition of the huge immigrant population base led publishers to seek to produce books for their needs domestically. The children's publishing industry ranged across the country, from coast to coast, to meet an increasingly diverse market. It continued to respond to demographics in its delicate balance between tradition and experimentation, art and commerce.

In Australia, two things characterised early children's book publishing – the view that the local readership was not very interested in things Australian, and that, since most titles were published in London, they must appeal to British tastes for the 'exotic' aspects of Australian life. Hence there was a tendency to write on the outback and on pioneering themes. The first children's book published in Australia was *A Mother's Offering to her Children* (1841), written in the didactic vein characteristic of Victorian books for children. A uniquely Australian imagination was evinced, though, by such writers and illustrators as Ethel Turner, Mary Grant Bruce, Ida Rentoul Outhwaite and May Gibbs. Non-indigenous writers, sensitive to Aboriginal culture, attempted interpretations such as Katherine Langloh Parker's *Australian Legendary Tales* (1896), Mrs Aeneas Gunn's *Little Black Princess* (1905) and the Duracks' *The Way of the Whirlwind* (1941), but Aboriginal people's reflections of themselves did not arrive until much later.

Hodder and Oxford University Press began a 'joint venture' children's list in 1906, and established a Melbourne office in 1908. *Cole's Funny Picturebook* (1876), published by the renowned Melbourne bookseller E.W. Cole, was the most popular seller of this early period. Comics, readers and weekly papers were also enormously popular, and the *Ginger Meggs* annuals were published from 1924 to 1959.

The Great Depression curbed exuberance, and only a few works emerged – notably Dorothy Wall's *Blinky Bill* (1933), Pixie O'Harris' s *Pearl Pinkie and Sea Greenie* (1935) and Frank Dalby Davison's *Man-shy* (1931) and *Children of the Dark People* (1936), though Ion Idriess's books were immensely popular then, too. Angus & Robertson opened a London office in 1938, but Australian children's publishing entered the wartime period in a dejected spirit. However, a shortage of paper and difficulties in importing from the United Kingdom led to the development of a more fertile Australian children's publishing atmosphere during the war. In the post-war period British domination of production declined and the period saw significant growth for Australian educational publishing, with companies like Cheshire, Jacaranda and Rigby beginning to meet the demand for a larger literate audience. Frank Eyre, sent out by Oxford University Press in 1950 to establish an Australian branch, is credited with professionalising the industry, discovering writers such as Nan Chauncy and Eleanor Spence, and developing the Press's educational publishing. An important post-war influence was the influence of the Children's Book Council of Australia awards in educating buyers and promoting books.

The first children's editor was Joyce Boniwell Saxby, appointed in 1963 at Angus & Robertson. Barbara Ker Wilson succeeded her from 1965 to 1974. Ann Ingram, with Collins from 1971, contributed to a growth in picturebook publishing with contributions such as Dick Roughsey and Percy Trezise's award-winning Aboriginal picturebooks, and with artists such as Quentin Hole and Ron Brooks. Improved printing techniques and the advocacy of these new children's editors led to the production of picturebooks of much better quality than in the past. Penguin, though it had begun publishing children's books in 1941, really began its Australian children's list under Kaye Ronai – and later Julie Watts – in 1978.

Mergers in the 70s and 80s not only created stronger foreign ownership but also increased spending on developing the children's market. Such consolidation was accompanied by a surge in the establishment of independent children's lists, notably Omnibus Books, which was enormously successful with early titles such as *Possum Magic* (1983) and *One Woolly Wombat* (1982). Other new publishers were Walter McVitty Books, Margaret Hamilton Books, Mark Macleod Books (Random House), Ros Price's Little Ark imprint (Allen & Unwin), and the University of Queensland Press's Young Adult fiction list created by Barbara Ker Wilson. Lothian Books has developed its list substantially with Helen Chamberlin as editor.

In addition to the economic downturn, other global influences have been the world-wide technology revolution, monopolisation, and a focus on marketing and 'name' publishing; a shift away from British to American and global publishing; the increasing influence of the Children's Book Council Awards; the growing influence of the electronic media on visually literate readers; and social changes such as feminism, multiculturalism and 'issues-based' publishing.

But perhaps the biggest influence in Australia has been Scholastic Australia, with its ownership of bookclubs, trade lists and book fairs. The trends which are currently prevalent are all evinced in Scholastic's 'mass-marketing' (rather than library-oriented) approaches, despite the anomaly that Scholastic has been successful because it has become part of the school culture in every country it has invested in. It engages in niche marketing (e.g. book clubs and targeting of specific age-groups), sales through non-traditional outlets, cross-merchandising and joint food promotions, value-added incentives, and internet sales. The growth of ABC Books as an imprint with integrated media properties is another example of this phenomenon.

Canada began developing an indigenous literature over a century ago. The book trade was slow to start because of a small market, colonial status and the split between English and French cultures. The earliest books were catechisms and ALPHABETS published in Montreal, Quebec City or Halifax, locations of the first printing presses in Canada. William Brown, who established Quebec City's first printing press in 1764, published a catechism and PRIMER. The first Canadian children's magazines were published in Montreal: *The Snow Drop* (1847–52), published by Lovell and Gibson, and its successor, *The Illustrated Maple Leaf*, (1852–3), by Robert W. Lay. Educational publishing began with the importation of textbooks from the United States and Ireland in the 19th century. Canadian school series at this time were published by John Lovell and Son. The 1920s saw a school readers series focusing on Canadian themes published by the Ryerson Press, the oldest publishing house in Canada.

From its beginnings in the 19th century, Canadian publishing for children has struggled with major problems unknown to the British or American publishing industries. The market is composed of a small population divided by language and scattered across a vast distance. Book-buying by the general public and institutions has been weak and reviewing media have been limited. Canada's immense territory makes distribution, promotion and publicity erratic and expensive.

The first Canadian writers for children in the mid-19th century – such as CATHARINE PARR TRAILL, James MacDonald Oxley, James de Mille, MARSHALL SAUNDERS and L.M. MONTGOMERY – were typically published in New York, Boston or London. An impetus to the development of children's publishing was the establishment of a world-renowned library service for children in the Toronto Public Library in 1912 under LILLIAN SMITH. However, between 1921 and 1950, only about ten children's titles, on average, were published annually. The rising Canadian nationalism of the late 1960s and early 70s was the impetus for the establishment of small, Canadian-owned and socially aware presses devoted to indigenous Canadian writing for children, such as The Women's Press; Kids Can Press, under Ricky Englander and Valerie Hussey; Rick Wilkes and Anne Millyard's Annick Press; and Groundwood Books under Patsy Aldana. In the same period, Tundra Books, under May Cutler, pioneered Canadian children's picturebooks as works of art. These houses recognised the critical importance of specialist knowledge in the editing and design of children's books.

Accompanying this birth of cultural nationalism was federal and provincial governmental recognition that the fledgling indigenous publishing industry could not survive in the uneven competitive market without government subsidy. The publishing industry responded with great speed and success, and new and old publishers began to flourish in the 1970s and 80s. This atmosphere of growth continued through the 1970s with a roster of 'firsts' which drew attention to the Canadian children's book world: the Children's Book Store – the first Canadian bookstore to specialise in children's books – opened in Toronto; the first children's literature conferences were held in Canada; *Canadian Children's Literature/Littérature canadienne pour la jeunesse*, the first journal devoted to serious criticism of Canadian juvenile literature, was founded; the Canada Council Children's Literature Prizes (later the Governor General's Awards for Children's Literature) were established; the Canadian Children's Book Centre in Toronto was founded and the first annual Canadian Children's Book Week inaugurated; a children's literature specialist was appointed at the

National Library of Canada; and most critically, new federal and provincial programmes provided grants for authors, illustrators and publishers.

Through the 1980s, a number of small-press children's publishers and alternative publishers came to realise that survival depended on publishing for the international as well as the domestic market. They established high profiles at international book fairs and aggressively sought international co-publication and foreign-rights sales, which lowered expenses and increased publicity. The change in volume of publishing was impressive, from the 30 or 40 books annually of the 1960s to approximately 400 in the late 1990s. Increased numbers of outstanding writers and illustrators were building a substantial body of work.

The 1990s saw major changes in Canadian children's book publishing. The annual Canadian Children's Book Week, sponsored by the invaluable Canadian Children's Book Centre which has done so much for the promotion of Canadian children's literature, brings tens of thousands of children and thousands of adults across Canada in contact with Canadian authors and illustrators. General literary festivals such as the national 'Word on the Street' book fair have large children's components. The nation-wide group of 30 Children's Literature Roundtables (the first was established in Edmonton in 1973) has a wide membership and hosts a variety of programmes.

The gloom in children's publishing in the United States and Britain in the early 1990s (due to a publishing glut in the United States and economic recessions in both regions) did not seem to hit Canadian children's publishers in the same way. But publishing is a risky business, and from 1992, in the United States as well as in Canada, the children's book market went soft. With fewer Canadian children's books in American editions, the ongoing difficulty of penetrating the British market, and decreasing domestic sales at home, many Canadian publishers focused on direct marketing and exporting outside Canada, and the use of sales agents or distributors in the United States, hoping that this direct approach to foreign sales could make up for flat sales to libraries and bookstores in the domestic market and the loss of licensing agreements. Unlike many American and British publishing houses, Canadian children's publishers are still small enough to be independently owned and editorially driven. With this independence, and in the face of the overwhelming wave of globalisation, consolidation and commercialisation swamping children's publishing in other countries, Canadian publishers and editors have continued to focus on thoughtful, individualistic titles that preserve the authorial voice.

Children's publishing is 'different' in that the internal structures which have developed have isolated it, problematically, from the rest of the industry. If concentration of ownership is perceived to represent a threat to cultural diversity, it is also responsible for awakening the children's publishing world to the fact that it is part of a global transition from a library-oriented to a mass market.

However by the year 2000 it was clear that publishing practices were likely to change radically and in unforeseeable ways as on-line publishing became a reality. A number of publishers, including Random House, Penguin and Simon & Schuster, were showing an interest in the e-publishing of adult fiction, with all its commercial advantages – immediate delivery to the buyer, no warehousing costs, no middle men and, consequently, very competitive pricing. But traditional publishers themselves may be bypassed altogether: by 1999 it was already possible for authors to choose between e-publishing sites which edited their work, those which simply hosted it – little more than vanity publishing – and those which allowed serial publication (which is how Stephen King's *Riding the Bullet* (2000) was first issued). One of the first children's authors to publish her work this way was the American Leta Nolan Childers. Alternatively authors discovered that they could form on-line co-operatives, buy copyright protection and publish their own work via a jointly-owned website. (There are already sites where children can publish their own writing (see CHILD AUTHORS)). If this practice is taken up by children's authors, children will become increasingly familiar with two different kinds of reading – the page-turning experience of reading a physical book, and the electronic reading of downloaded text.

KA, MSC, RS, JMS, AL, VW

see also AWARDS AND MEDALS; INFORMATION BOOKS; REVIEWING

Puck see COMICS, PERIODICALS AND MAGAZINES

Puck of Pook's Hill (1906) and its sequel ***Rewards and Fairies*** (1910) Works by RUDYARD KIPLING, whose basic theme is the making of British identity. Dan and Una, thrice acting out 'as much as they could remember of *Midsummer's Night's Dream*' on Midsummer's Eve, discover that they have unwittingly enacted a ritual summoning up Puck, the oldest and last of the Old Things in England. By the power of Oak and Ash and Thorn, and the ritual of *seisin*, the children are given lawful possession of their historical and cultural heritage and the freedom to come and go within time.

Thus begin their excursions with Puck. They meet people from the past who tell them their stories, and these narratives, for the most part, tell the tale of the invasions of the Romans, Normans, etc. and how the invaders become integrated into English society. The invader moves from the position of the antagonist who must be repelled to the defender against other enemies, forging a bond between himself and his erstwhile enemy through mutual defence and marriage. (This was a formula to be followed closely in ROSEMARY SUTCLIFF's historical novels for children.) As de Aquila, one of the Norman leaders says in 'Young Men at the Manor', 'In God's good time . . . there will be neither Saxon nor Norman in England.'

The greater number of the narratives are martial, placing positive value on the soldier figure, and the ethos and stature of the Roman Empire – an 'ancestor' of the British empire – are borrowed to enhance the latter. In 'A British-Roman song', which ends the chapter 'A Centurion of the Thirtieth', the two empires are subtly conflated, and the stirring call to 'guard' gainst home-born ills/ The Imperial Fire' is a call not just to the Roman legions, but to the British serving in overseas postings. The force of the sword, however, gives way to law. In 'The Runes on Weland's Sword', we are told that the sword gathers gold whose economic power is given 'for the Thing', the 'Thing' being the Law that King John is forced to ratify at Runnymede.

However, though the two books are nationalistic in tone and subject matter, the nationalism is not of the crude, jingoistic type. Amidst the martial overtones is something softer, a nostalgia for a gracious past and a determination to preserve that which is precious. The Old Things, of which Puck is the last, represent the romantic vision which is in danger of becoming lost; Puck says that he too will leave when Oak and Ash and Thorn are gone. However, Dan's 'It's all right . . . I'm planting a lot of acorns this autumn too' is not just a covenant to preserve the past but also a gesture towards a future built upon a vision of historical continuity. SA

Puffin Book of Magic Verse, The (1974) Anthology edited by CHARLES CAUSLEY, popular with younger readers and theme-hungry teachers. Here choice encompasses styles, periods and cultures, famous dead poets and modern ones, and runes, chants and spells under headings like 'Enchantments', 'Curses' and 'Creatures of Earth and Air'. The book is full of the sparkle and surprise of Causley's own poetry. Causley's work as an anthology editor will be long-lasting; impeccable taste and breadth of vision are the keys to his success. AHa

Puffin Books see COVER ART; ELEANOR GRAHAM; PUBLISHERS AND PUBLISHING; see also KAYE WEBB

Puffin Picture Books An acclaimed and much-collected British series of small, coloured picturebooks (mostly paperback), suggested during World War II by Noel Carrington. The series was numbered – somewhat haphazardly – from 1 to 120, though no. 116 was never issued. The first three were devoted to the war and most early titles were concerned with rural practices and wildlife, probably to make provision for urban children evacuated to remote and unfamiliar parts of the countryside. Some works of fiction were included (for example, some *ORLANDO* titles by KATHLEEN HALE; *Hamish*, 1944, by Joanna Cannan; *The Story of Ming*, undated, by Chiang Yee) but most of the books were INFORMATION TEXTS on historical, geographical and general topics such as fireworks, printing and steam trains. Some distinguished writers and artists – including Paxton Chadwick and C.F. Tunnicliffe (on wildlife), W.J. Bassett-Lowke (on locomotives and steamships), Lionel Edwards, EDWARD BAWDEN and A.W. Seaby – were commissioned for the series, and the result was an exceptionally high quality of content, design and illustration. Like the roughly contemporaneous *GOLDEN BOOKS* in the United States, the *Puffin Picture Books* were influenced by the innovative and brightly colourful lithographic reproduction used in children's books in Russia during the 1930s. VW

see also LITHOGRAPHY

Pukunui stories see MAORI WRITING IN CHILDREN'S BOOKS; see also PICTUREBOOKS

Pullein-Thompson, Josephine 1924– , **Diana** and **Christine** 1925– Prolific British writers of PONY STORIES, daughters of novelist Joanna Cannan (1898–1961), who wrote the influential pony book, *A Pony for Jean*. Brought up in Oxfordshire with little formal education, the sisters started a riding school and wrote pony stories while still in their teens. Their first book, *It Began with Picotee*, written jointly when Josephine was 17 and the twins 16, was published in 1946. Since then they have written almost 150 pony books between them, selling some 10 million copies worldwide. Although their prodigious output has been of variable quality, their early books set the prototype for the formulaic pony story with few imitators matching their combination of readability and expertise. Josephine's books are unashamedly instructive, full of lively young riders, and her most typical are the *Pony Club* series. Diana, the least prolific, showed from her first book, *I Wanted a Pony* (1946), that she was as interested in her human characters' problems as in the ponies. Christine has written the most books, many without ponies, for children aged 5 to 16. Josephine, who became general secretary, then president, of the English centre of PEN, a world association of writers, was awarded the MBE in 1984. Her sisters are both married, but they are all still writing and several of their older books have been republished. Together they have written six sequels (and prequels) to *BLACK BEAUTY*, *Black Beauty's Clan* (1975) and *Black Beauty's Family* (1978), and an entertaining autobiography, *Fair Girls and Grey Horses* (1996). ARH

Pullman, Philip 1946– British writer who was born in Norwich and read English at Oxford, where he subsequently settled. Though he is best known for the series *HIS DARK MATERIALS*, of which *Northern Lights* (published in America as *The Golden Compass*) has been the recipient of both CARNEGIE and *GUARDIAN* awards, all Pullman's work shares the same wit and intelligence. His writing shows a great diversity both in style and genre, running from historical thrillers (the *SALLY LOCKHART* books), to GRAPHIC NOVELS: *Count Karlstein* (1991), *Spring-Heeled Jack* (1989) and *Clockwork* (1996). *The Firework Maker's Daughter* (1996 winner of the SMARTIES PRIZE Gold Medal) and *Thunderbolt's Waxwork* (1994) are for younger readers. In 1998 Pullman wrote a characteristically vigorous version of *Mossycoat* for Scholastic's series of paperback FAIRY TALES. His more recent work, *I Was A Rat!* (1999), also for younger readers, follows the adventures of one of the rats in the *CINDERELLA* story, who has somehow remained a boy. Despite its essential light-heartedness, the work is also threaded through with irony about happy-ever-after endings. SA

Punch and Judy Glove puppet shows in portable booths, a form of British street theatre dating back to the 17th century and most popular in mid-Victorian times. Punch hurls his shrieking baby into the audience, murders his protesting wife Judy, and vanquishes numerous visitors including the public hangman. He usually succumbs to his final opponent – traditionally the Devil, though sometimes a crocodile in modern versions. Punch derived from the *commedia dell'arte*, but evolved into a typically British knockabout comedian, chiefly delighting adult audiences. Since he became a character in young children's stories and entertainments in the 1870s, his vigour and tongue have become somewhat muted. GPF

***Punchbowl Farm* series** (1947–67) Eleven books written over 20 years by Monica Edwards (1912–98), about the Thornton family and their life on a once derelict farm in Surrey. Perhaps because Edwards was so prolific, producing another 15 books in the *ROMNEY MARSH* SERIES almost back to back, or because, early on, she acquired the pejorative and inaccurate label of writer of PONY STORIES, her reputation is not as high as it should be, although she was extremely popular with young readers. ARTHUR RANSOME's influence is obvious in the self-reliance of the children, their love for the outdoor life, their vigorous ability in dealing with disasters, and the strong sense of place. The stories, based on Edwards's own farm, are firmly rooted in reality and the author's love and knowledge of animals and the countryside, but they are also carefully crafted and atmospheric works of fiction. The first book, *No Mistaking Corker* (1947), is a run-of-the-mill holiday ADVENTURE STORY told in the first person by Lindsey, but from the second, *Punchbowl Midnight* (1950), the action springs naturally from the farm setting, with occasional supernatural touches. The family is central, with characters developed in some depth, particularly Lindsey, who is almost a twin of Tamzin of the *Romney Marsh* series, dreamy, brave, and with a deep feeling for the past; but bossy, clever Andrea, Dion the dedicated farmer, and young Peter, also play their part, as do the animals with their own clearly defined personalities. An unusual feature is that in six books the *Punchbowl* and *Romney Marsh* series converged. ARH

puppet theatre see DRAMA FOR CHILDREN; TONY SARG; TELEVISION

Puranic myth of creation see INDIAN MYTHS, LEGENDS AND FOLKTALES

Pure Tynt Rashiecoat see SCOTTISH FOLKTALES

'Puss in Boots' FAIRY TALE included in CHARLES PERRAULT's *Histoires ou contes du temps passé* (1697) (see *CONTES DE MA MÈRE L'OYE*) entitled 'Le Chat Botté'. On the death of his father the youngest son inherits only a cat. Armed with a pair of boots the cat wins favour for his master with the King, who believes him to be a rich Marquis. A succession of tricks played by the cat – including a fake attempted drowning, servants lying about the name of their master and an ogre being fooled into turning himself into a quickly caught mouse – lead to the cat's master marrying the King's daughter. The story, also known as 'The Master Cat', was translated into English by Robert Samber in 1729. Perrault's tale is similar to an earlier version by Basile in *Pentamerone* (1634/6), in which the grateful master promises that when the cat dies he will have its body preserved in a gold coffin. The cat plays at being dead and the master unceremoniously has the cat thrown out of the window. The cat leaves, furious, and never to be seen again. The story has even earlier versions; Straparola's *The Delightful Nights* (1553) includes a similar story but here the cat is a fairy in disguise and there is no mention of an ogre. More recent storytellers have had difficulty with the morality of this tale; GEORGE CRUIKSHANK referred to it as 'a clever lesson in lying' and in his version changed the character of the cat. JHD

see also SOPHIE MASSON

Pye, Trevor 1952– New Zealand illustrator, sculptor and lecturer in illustrating for children's literature. Pye works mainly in pen and watercolour, and at times in multi-media. His humorous and unconventional characters enliven the script through his use of bold

'The umbrella – a curious present.' Illustration by Howard Pyle from *Harper's New Monthly Magazine* (1881).

colours and a sense of movement. He often uses a cartoon style, with expressive conventions which create a sense of drama and excitement, as in the *Grandma McGarvey* books, written by Jenny Hessell. In addition, Pye has written and illustrated his own books, for example *Mabel and the Marvellous Meow* (1996), and has worked with writers such as JOY COWLEY, RUTH CORRIN and Roger Hall. LL

Pyle, Howard 1853–1911 American illustrator, author and teacher, best known for his revisions of English legends, his original FOLKTALES, and his HISTORICAL FICTION, all lavishly illustrated and ornamented. A descendant of well-established Quaker families in Delaware's Brandywine Valley near Wilmington, Pyle lived there for most of his life. Pyle showed an early aptitude for both writing and drawing; his lack of application in school prompted his parents to enroll him in art classes and employ him in the family leather business.

His professional breakthrough came in 1876, when he recorded in words and pictures the annual wild pony roundup in Chincoteague Island, Virginia. His story was accepted by *Scribner's Magazine*. Encouraged by the editor of *Scribner's*, Pyle moved to New York City in 1876, where he made contact with the editors who would later provide him with his livelihood and vocation. After this apprenticeship, Pyle moved back to Delaware in 1879, an established magazine illustrator whose regular income permitted marriage to Anne Poole in 1881. Over the next 30 years Pyle raised a family, generated thousands of magazine and book ILLUSTRATIONS, published his own books, and began teaching, first at Drexel Institute in Philadelphia, and finally in his own studio in Wilmington. In 1910 Pyle travelled to Europe for the first time. His enjoyment of the Italian masters, however, was marred by increasing illness and terminated by his death in Florence in 1911.

Pyle's work is paradoxical: strongly influenced by his Quaker antecedents, he nevertheless exhibited a lifelong interest in the violent side of human nature. Likewise, although Pyle was vehemently patriotic, actively promoting a distinctively American form of art, his works reveal the influence of European artists, notably the Pre-Raphaelites and Albrecht Dürer. Finally, although Pyle was a deep admirer of the realist school represented by his friend WILLIAM DEAN HOWELLS, the work which made him famous was essentially romantic.

Pyle's first great success was *The Merry Adventures of Robin Hood* (1883), a beautifully designed, illustrated and retold edition of the classic stories. Simultaneously published in England and America, the book won the praise even of William Morris, a disbeliever in American art. Pyle's *Arthuriad* (1903–10) demonstrates his continuing fascination with English tales of chivalry. Pyle altered the stories in order to reinforce his heroes' nobility, chastity and leadership. His editions of retold European folktales, *Pepper & Salt* (1886) and *The Wonder Clock* (1888), were similarly well received and popular. The tales were retold in the colloquial style of the GRIMM BROTHERS and emphasise democratising aspects of the folk tradition. Richly decorated with black-and-white drawings, the collections are as visually engaging as their narratives are entertaining. Pyle's historical narratives, notably *Otto of the Silver Hand* (1888) and *Men of Iron* (1892), recapture the medieval period unsentimentally.

A premier illustrator of the period, Pyle was also a gifted teacher, founding the 'Brandywine School' of American illustration. Among his students were MAXFIELD PARRISH, JESSIE WILCOX SMITH and N.C. WYETH. NJW

Q

Quaye, Kofi Ghanaian writer, one of the new generation of writers who, rather than using materials from oral traditions, prefer to describe contemporary culture, and in the manner of social realism. Quaye writes in a fast-paced style about trendy rich business people, fun-loving youth and crooked criminals, usually set in the city. A very good example of his writing is his junior book, *Foli Fights the Forgers* (1990), in which a student stumbles upon a huge counterfeit operation in the city and fights the criminals with the help of friends. MAs

Quinn, John 1941– Irish author born in County Meath, former teacher, now a broadcaster and novelist. *The Summer of Lily and Esme* (1991) received much acclaim and some commentators felt that it should also be published under an adult imprint. This is largely due to Quinn's delicate evocation of old age in the characters of the sisters, Lily and Esme. Quinn's next book, *The Gold Cross of Killadoo* (1992), is an ADVENTURE STORY set in Viking Dublin. Again he evokes a sense of the period in which the story is set, but its fast pace and focus on action do not provide the thoughtfulness of his previous work. In *Duck and Swan* (1993) he endeavoured to recapture a more reflective note in his writing, raising a number of timely questions related to social issues in Ireland. In *One Fine Day* (1996) the 'troubles' in Northern Ireland resonate throughout the story of a family's escape from Belfast to County Clare in 1974, but the growing maturity of 15-year-old Rossa provides the central motif in this complex novel. Again, social issues are prominent and the rural landscape of Quinn's childhood is a presence as it is in his earlier work. VC

R

'Pussy-cat, pussy-cat, where have you been?' Illustration by Arthur Rackham from *Mother Goose: The Old Nursery Rhymes.*

racism see BIAS IN CHILDREN'S BOOKS; CENSORSHIP

Racketty Street Gang, The (1961) Novel by the Australian writer, L.H. (Len) Evers, winner of the Australian Book of the Year Award. The book is distinctive for its portrayal of strong friendship in an inner-city setting (a departure from the usual outback) and the fact that the protagonist is a post-war German migrant whose family life helps broaden the outlook of the Australian characters. MSax

Rackham, Arthur 1867–1939 British artist. Like his contemporary, Aubrey Beardsley, Rackham started his working life in an insurance office and, also like Beardsley, he was influenced by Japanese prints and the Pre-Raphaelites. His drawings have a certain quality of tension and anxiety owing to his use of a profusion of agitated lines to which he added a dull palette of watercolour. He was strongly influenced by Beardsley but this did not smother the development of his own very particular style which can always be easily recognised. His method was particularly suited to the new means of reproduction through four-colour printing (in cyan, magenta, yellow and black). His low-key palette contrasted with the sweeter colours used by EDMUND DULAC, his main rival in the world of book ILLUSTRATION.

Rackham was born in Lewisham, England, on September 19 1867, the son of an Admiralty Marshal. After a spell as an evening-class student at the Lambeth School of Art in 1884, he began to provide drawings for various illustrated papers. His first work was published in *Scraps.* Among his fellow students were Charles Rickets and Thomas Sturge Moore. By 1892 he had joined the staff of *The Westminster Budget* and by the following year he had started illustrating books. The first of these, *To the Other Side,* was published as a travel brochure. His popularity, lasting from the late 19th century into the first two decades of the 20th, is self-evident from the large number of books he was asked to illustrate. Unfortunately, the depression years of the 1920s and 1930s saw a decline in the number of opportunities.

There is an underlying sinister quality in his illustrations owing to his low-key colours and tortuous wiry line. His dark, atmospheric work remains popular and influential today. He first came to the attention of the public with his illustrations to *Zankiwank and the Bletherwitch* (1896) by S.J. Adair Fitzgerald. This was followed by WASHINGTON IRVING's *Rip Van Winkle* (1905). In 1906 he was awarded a gold medal in Milan, and in 1911 received others in Barcelona and Paris. In 1912 he was elected an associate of the Société Nationale des Beaux-Arts and in 1919 he became a master of the Art Workers' Guild. He gained further success with his illustrations to *Fairy Tales* by the GRIMM BROTHERS in 1909.

Among the long list of his work, one may gain an idea of the very particular qualities of his style from CHRISTINA ROSSETTI's *GOBLIN MARKET* (1933). Other work includes illustrations for *Peter Pan in Kensington Gardens,* by SIR J. M. BARRIE, in 1906; *ALICE'S ADVENTURES IN WONDERLAND,* by LEWIS CARROLL, in 1907; *A Christmas Carol,* published in 1907; and *Aesop's Fables* (see AESOP) in 1912. Rackham produced a series of lavishly illustrated books, most of which were published in signed, limited editions as well as in traditional cloth-bound trade editions. The illustrations were generally printed separately from the main body of the book, each of them printed on fine quality, smoothly finished art paper which was TIPPED-IN by applying glue to one or two edges only. AEW

see also GIFT BOOKS; ILLUSTRATION; PICTUREBOOKS

Radio Fun Weekly British COMIC launched by the Amalgamated Press as a direct competitor against Thomson's *DANDY* and *BEANO*. Clearly inspired by the earlier success of *FILM FUN*, the first issue on 15 October 1938 starred such wireless favourites as Big-Hearted Arthur Askey, Bud Flanagan and Chesney Allen of 'The Crazy Gang', Ethel Revnell and Gracie West – 'The Long and Short of It' (a double-act here playing the parts of Girl Guides) – and Sandy Powell, whose catch-phrase was 'Can you hear me, mother?' The comic was an immediate hit with young radio listeners but, curiously, never carried a feature based on the BBC's own juvenile programme, *Children's Hour*. The related ANNUAL started at Christmas 1939 and ran until 1960, and today is particularly popular with collectors as it illustrates many of the popular radio stars of the past. DG

see also *CHILDREN'S HOUR ANNUAL*

radio for children see ANNUALS; LOUISE SEAMAN BECHTEL; *BOBBY BREWSTER*; MICHAEL BOND; *CHILDREN'S HOUR ANNUAL*; RUTH CORRIN; *EAGLE*; *ELIDOR*; ALAN GARNER; WILLIS HALL; DAVID HILL; SUSAN HILL; ANTHONY HOROWITZ; LIBBY HOUSTON; *JENNINGS* SERIES; JULIUS LESTER; *LISTEN WITH MOTHER*; SPIKE MILLIGAN; LAUREN MILLS; JILL MORRIS; ELAINE MOSS; *THE MUDDLE-HEADED WOMBAT*; MUSIC AND STORY; *POETRY IN THE MAKING*; *RHODA POWER;* RADIO FUN; REVIEWING AND REVIEWERS; MICHAEL ROSEN; DOROTHY L. SAYERS; SOAP OPERAS; SPIDER-MAN; STORY-TAPES; TELEVISION FOR CHILDREN; COLIN THIELE; GEOFFREY TREASE; *WATCH WITH MOTHER*

Rae, Gwynedd see *MARY PLAIN* SERIES

Rag, Tag and Bobtail see *WATCH WITH MOTHER*

***Raggedy Ann* series** Books about a rag doll, written and illustrated by the American Johnny (Barton) Gruelle (1880–1938), and loosely based on stories told to Gruelle's daughter Marcella, who died aged 13 in 1915. Although Marcella did have a rag doll, possibly made by her grandmother, recent research by Patricia Hall shows that the Raggedy Ann doll was designed and patented by Gruelle in 1915, with the intention that it would be marketed by the Vollard Company together with a series of books. The series began with *Raggedy Ann Stories* (1918); Raggedy Andy was added in 1920 to broaden the market appeal, and in 1926 the black doll Beloved Belindy made her appearance. In early stories Raggedy Ann is clearly a doll, living with humans and likely to be put through the washing machine or dropped into a can of paint; later, she and Raggedy Andy spend their time in the 'deep, deep woods' encountering witches, fairies and fantastic creatures like the Snitznoodle. The stories, which have more visual than verbal appeal, were intended to contain 'nothing to cause fright, suggest fear, glorify mischief, excuse malice, or condone cruelty'. New books compiled from newspaper serials continued to appear after Gruelle's death. FEA

Railway Children, The A FAMILY STORY by the British author E. NESBIT, first serialised in *The London* magazine, and published in book form in 1906. Although realistic like its predecessor *The New Treasure Seekers* (1904), *The Railway Children* is more serious, beginning with the crisis of the father's imprisonment, and showing Bobbie, Peter, Phyllis and their mother facing various problems when they move from London to the country. They experience money difficulties; mother falls ill; they meet a sick Russian refugee; they witness a landslide and find a boy injured in a cross-country run. In the process the children develop, learning not only to look after themselves, but how to help other people. The storytelling is not without faults; Nesbit does not probe very deeply into the disagreeable aspects of economic life or the class system, and makes considerable use of coincidences. But though the mother-figure is idealised, the portrayal of the children as neither completely virtuous nor irredeemably wicked is pioneering, with the characterisation of the adolescent Bobbie being particularly poignant. The depiction of the railways and of the railway workers, especially Perks, the independent-minded porter, is also skilful. Above all Nesbit remained optimistic. Without ignoring tragedy, she passionately believed in the possibility of human growth and kindness in a caring society where there was much to laugh at. Perhaps for these reasons the book has remained in print virtually since publication, has been televised by the BBC, and was the subject of a much-loved film directed by Lionel Jeffries in 1970. DB

see also *BASTABLE* SERIES; *PSAMMEAD* SERIES

Rainbow see COMICS, PERIODICALS AND MAGAZINES; see also HELEN JACOBS

Rainbow Fish, The (1992) PICTUREBOOK by MARCUS PFISTER which, along with its sequel, *Rainbow Fish to the Rescue* (1995), has become a modern classic, particularly popular in schools. While Pfister's soft ILLUSTRATIONS, enhanced by the holographic scales of Rainbow Fish, are responsible for making the book eye-catching, it is the stories themselves that underlie the books' success. They are essentially moral tales, the first dealing with vanity and selfishness and the second with hostility to strangers. It is the simplicity of the telling, particularly in the original book, that allows the books to be instructive without becoming didactic. Other titles have followed: *The Rainbow Fish and the Big Blue Whale* (1998), *The Rainbow Fish's Birthday Book* (1999), *The Rainbow Fish's Bath Book* (2000) and *Rainbow Fish and the Sea Monsters' Cave* (2001). KA

Ramayana, The see RELIGIOUS STORIES; see also INDIAN MYTHS, LEGENDS AND FOLKTALES; PULAK BISWAS

***Ramona* series** (1968–84) Books for young readers by American author BEVERLY CLEARY. Ramona first appeared as a minor character in a series of books about her older sister's friend, Henry Huggins. Readers' letters inspired Cleary to write a series in which the characterful younger sister featured more prominently, beginning with *Beezus and Ramona* (1955) and leading eventually to a series about Ramona in her own right. It is unusual that a character who begins in what could be an unpopular role – that of annoying little sister – should have become so popular with children and adults alike. Two of the later *Ramona* books were Newbery Honour Books. Ramona's own series begins as she is about to enter kindergarten. Throughout the series she is desperate to grow older and catch up with her sister. In the first book in which she is the central character, *Ramona the Pest* (1968), she believes that starting school will suddenly make her older, only to learn bafflingly that being in the baby class is not very grown-up. By the end of the series she begins to feel a little grown-up at last. Her family is shown to be a warm and loving one, though always beset by financial worries. Ramona is always conscious of the difficulties of adult life. The family conviction, which Ramona has to learn to share, is spelt out by her father in *Ramona Forever* (1984): 'we can't always do want we want in life . . . so we do the best we can'. KA

Rands, William Brighty 1823–82 English poet and parliamentary reporter, described in the *Dictionary of National Biography* as 'the laureate of the nursery'. He had a good nose for the ridiculous and his NONSENSE VERSE was popular with young readers in his day. Best known were *Lilliput Levee* (1864) and *Lilliput Lectures* (1871). He was a regular contributor to magazines such as *Good Words for the Young*. MCCS

Rankin, Joan see *MANDU AND THE FOREST GUARDIAN*

Ransome, Arthur 1884–67 British novelist, best known for the *SWALLOWS AND AMAZONS* series. Ransome's father was a professor of history whose keen interest in fishing led him to take the family to a farm near Coniston Water every summer. Ransome's love of boating, and of the Lake District in particular, was born in those long holidays. Unhappy both at prep school and at Rugby, Ransome always believed that he was a disappointment to his father. He worked as an office-boy in a publishing firm, but at 19 he tried to establish himself as a freelance writer. In 1909 he married Ivy Walker, and it was partly to escape the unhappiness of that marriage that he left for Russia, where he remained throughout the turbulent years before and during the Revolution. He was near the political centre there and closely acquainted with Lenin and Trotsky. Working as a journalist on the Russian front in World War I, he was also in contact with the British Government and engaged in the difficult task of interpreting the Revolution for British readers. He eventually returned with Evgenia Shelepin, one of Trotsky's secretaries, whom he eventually married. For some years Ransome enjoyed a period of stability with the *Manchester Guardian*, but in 1929 he gave up this secure post to devote himself to writing.

Ransome had been a determined but uncertain writer in his early years: he had tried his hand at literary criticism and edited FOLKTALES for children. In 1915 he had written *Old Peter's Russian Tales*, a collection of 19 stories told by Peter to his two grandchildren. However, in 1923 he published *Racundra's First Cruise*, an autobiographical account of sailing in the Baltic Sea, with pictures, maps, and a great deal of nautical detail. This is the real forebear of his great children's writing, combining a quiet nautical passion with meticulous prose description. Later, when he wrote *Swallows and Amazons* (1930) for the Altounyan children, he discovered the perfect subject and the perfect genre. The book was reprinted ten times in its first six years and has never subsequently been out of print. Ransome went on to write 11 more novels in the series, the last – *Great Northern?* – appearing in 1947. The *Swallows and Amazons* series was also successful in the United States, eventually establishing Ransome as the best children's writer of his time. *Pigeon Post* received the first CARNEGIE AWARD in 1936.

Despite the surface realism of Ransome's writing, the series sustained an altogether magical representation of childhood and landscape, and determined for more than a generation how children's literature was understood. His creative enterprise was not to represent landscape and childhood as they are but as they might be imaginatively transformed within what is ultimately a Wordsworthian vision. But, while *The Prelude* celebrated the perceptions of a solitary male boy, Ransome was altogether more generous in allowing into his stories a variety of approved ways of responding to the experiences of childhood. And he did this so unobtrusively that no young reader was ever likely to be troubled by a sense of bewildering complexities. VW

Ransome, James E. 1961– American illustrator born in North Carolina and educated at Pratt Institute. Ransome is able to bring a wide variety of artwork to his children's books. 'Because each book has a special voice, my approach is different as well', he says. 'Whether it be through my choice of palette, design or perspective, there is always a desire to experiment and explore what makes each book unique.' For example, James Johnson's *The Creation* (1994) features sections bordered by animal and bird patterns and panoramic double-spreads. A reprint of CHARLOTTE ZOLOTOW's *The Old Dog* (1995) presents autumnal colours and borders of fallen leaves to indicate the boy's sadness over his dog's death; William Hook's *Freedom's Fruit* (1995) is lush in vivid colour; *Sweet Clara and the Freedom Quilt* (1993) uses bright greens and yellow to signify hope and freedom. Some of his most recent titles include Michael Rase's *Bovery and Isabel* (1994), Marilee Burton's *My Best Shoes* (1994) and Charlotte Watson Sherman's *Eli and the Swamp Man* (1996). Awards include *Parenting* magazine Reading Magic Award for *Do Like Kyla* (1990) and Parents' Choice Foundation Annual Award for *Aunt Flossie's Hats (and Crab Cakes Later)* (1991). Ransome has also designed jackets for YOUNG ADULT FICTION. KSB

Rao, Shanta Rameshwar 1924– Indian storyteller, fiction writer and experimental educationist. Passionately fond of children, Rao first made her mark when she decided to retell stories from the epics. *The Children's Mahabharata* (1968) is one of the most popular children's versions of the epic and, along with *Tales of Ancient India* (1960), has had many reprints. Her style has the easy rhythm of the oral storyteller. *Seethu* (1980), the story about the intriguing adventures of two children and a doll which can feel and think, explores the enigmatic divisions of class, which make little sense to the children. Her *Matsya, the Beautiful Fish* (1985) and *Mohini and the Demon* (1990) have been extremely popular with smaller children. Her writing, including *Bulbul's Ruby-Nosed Ring and Other Stories* (1970), a collection of well-executed stories on the FOLKTALE pattern, proves that she knows exactly what children want to hear and possesses an intuitive understanding of how they want to hear it. MBh

rap poetry see GILLIAN RUBINSTEIN; GRACE NICHOLS; BENJAMIN ZEPHANIAH

Rapunzel see GRIMM BROTHERS; see also *EGERTON HALL* SERIES; JACQUELINE WILSON; PAUL ZELINSKY

Raschka, Chris 1959– American writer, artist and musician, known for innovative synergy between word, pictures and theme. Raschka's award-winning PICTUREBOOKS show insight into the psychological needs of young children, partly gained through volunteer experience in New York City. A biology major at St Olaf College, Raschka turned down medical school to pursue his interest in art and music. Jazz-related picturebooks, *Charlie Parker Played Be Bop* (1992) and *Mysterious Thelonius* (1997), draw young readers into the beat of the music with a vibrant merger of words, pictures and simulated sound. The symbolic use of colour on warm brown paper in the picture-poem *The Genie in the Jar* (with NIKKI GIOVANNI, 1996), inspired by jazz singer Nina Simone, depicts a young girl's confidence nurtured by a community of black women. Elizabeth in *Elizabeth Imagines an Iceberg* (1993) grows larger as her 'iceberg' gives her strength to flee a threatening adult. Raschka also employs a unique combination of size, position and colour in *The Blushful Hippopotamus* (1996) – about which children eagerly exclaim 'Look he's getting bigger!' – and in *Yo! Yes?* (1993), a Caldecott Honour Book depicting interracial friendship. ETD

see also MUSIC AND STORY

Rasco and the Rats of NIMH see JANE LESLIE CONLY; *MRS FRISBY AND THE RATS OF NIMH*

Rashie Coatie / Rashin Coatie see 'Cinderella'

Raskin, Ellen 1928–84 Innovative American author and illustrator of fiction and PICTUREBOOKS. Born in Milwaukee, Wisconsin, Raskin worked as a commercial illustrator and designer in New York City, taught courses in ILLUSTRATION, and designed her own books. *The Westing Game* (1978), with its clever and complicated puzzle-mystery plot, won the NEWBERY AWARD, and *Figgs & Phantoms* (1974), which some consider a stronger book, was an Honour Book. Although Raskin's work has been called original, difficult, outrageous, exuberant, zany, hilarious and unrestrained, her books have found a continuing audience among young readers. Of *Figgs & Phantoms* she wrote, 'I've never put more into a book – my whole life and dreams.' LH

Raspe, Rudolf Erich see BARON MÜNCHAUSEN

Rathmann, Peggy (Margaret Crosby) 1953– American author and illustrator who won the CALDECOTT MEDAL for *Officer Buckle and Gloria* (1995). Since her first book, *Ruby the Copycat* (1991), her work has become increasingly popular. Extending minimal texts with lively, colourful drawings, she provides humorous actions to carry the stories; none more so than *Good Night, Gorilla* (1994). The detail in *10 Minutes Till Bedtime* (1998) is cleverly conceived as a young boy (together with a family of hamsters) is given the countdown to bedtime. PDS

Rats of NIMH, The see MRS FRISBY AND THE RATS OF NIMH

Rattle Bag, The (1982) An anthology of poetry edited by SEAMUS HEANEY and TED HUGHES. The poems' 'arbitrary alphabetical order' leads to an unexpectedness which transcends time and culture: SHAKESPEARE beside Sylvia Plath, WILFRED OWEN next to Janos Pilinsky. There are also poems from oral cultures whose atavistic force evokes our own beginnings. JP

Raverat, Gwendolen Mary 1885–1957 British illustrator, born in Cambridge, the granddaughter of Charles Darwin. She studied painting at the Slade but she was best known as a wood engraver. Following a period of married life in France she returned to Cambridge after her husband's early death. She admired THOMAS BEWICK's white line engraving. Her work is notable for its use of colour, which had rarely been employed by engravers since EDMUND EVANS and Lucien Pissarro. She illustrated a wide range of books which included *The Cambridge Book of Poetry for Children* by KENNETH GRAHAME and *Four Tales of Hans Andersen* (1935), translated by R.P. Keigwin. AEW

see also WOOD ENGRAVING

Rawlings, Marjorie Kinnan 1896–1953 American novelist and short-story writer, best known for *The Yearling* (1938). *Cross Creek* (1942), a group of autobiographical essays, was a bestseller and subject of a film; *The Secret River*, illustrated by LEONARD WEISGARD, was published posthumously and was a Newbery Honour Book in 1956 (with a stage adaptation by John Cech in 1996). Most of Rawlings's stories and novels are set in rural Florida and describe the lives of the tough but noble Crackers in an attempt to preserve their cultural heritage. Her approach is that of a Romantic with definite Wordsworthian leanings, but she is also a realist, and her stories reflect her attention to detail in her insistence on accuracy. Although all her novels were bestsellers and her short stories published in well-known magazines, her reputation now rests on *The Yearling*, which won the Pulitzer Prize in 1939 and quickly became a children's classic. Once a protégé of Scribner's editor Maxwell Perkins, she was drawn into a legal battle over libel in the mid-1940s (ultimately reduced to invasion of privacy for using a neighbour's real name in *Cross Creek*) that drained her energy and creativity; in her last few years she produced only one novel before her death at the age of 57.

The Yearling was highly praised at its publication, but because of its Thoreau-like descriptions of nature, it is unfortunately not as accessible to children as it once was. Nevertheless, it led to two films: the most recent made-for-TELEVISION version (1994) is too much abridged; the earlier Jane Wyman / Gregory Peck version (1946) is still highly recommended. *The Yearling*, set in 1870s Florida, is the story of a 12-year-old boy, Jody Baxter, whose mother Ora has distanced herself from him (Jody is the first of her children to survive) and whose father has allowed him to stay a child too long (because he had virtually no childhood himself). When Jody adopts a pet deer, hardships and responsibilities come crowding in as he tries to keep the deer away from their crops. When the family is faced with starvation, Jody's eventual forced killing of his pet is the culmination of his new adult role. Jody's transition into adulthood is archetypal, and that he has killed his childhood is painfully obvious. Although the story and characters are poignant and memorable, Rawlings's depiction of carefree childhood being pushed aside by adulthood's work and duties is certainly controversial. CAT

Rawlins, Donna (Belinda) 1956– Australian illustrator, designer and editor, whose vivid images have an understated drama and are often deeply emotive. Her characters are both multicultural and non-stereotypical, her backgrounds frequently rich in detail – especially in MY PLACE (1988). She creates warm depictions of family life in *The Kinder Hat* (1985) and *Tucking Mummy In* (1987) by Morag Loh and, more poignantly, in *My Dearest Dinosaur* (1993), MARGARET WILD'S story of a dinosaur family split apart. Her one self-authored title is the whimsical *Digging to China* (1988), in which Alexis tunnels to China to buy her ageing neighbour a postcard. NLR

Ray, Jane British illustrator and highly successful artist with a recognisable style of her own. Her first book was *A Balloon for Granddad* (NIGEL GRAY, 1989) and her bestsellers include *Noah's Ark* (1991), *The Story of Christmas* (1992) and The *Happy Prince* (1994). Ray's ILLUSTRATIONS glow with jewel-like colours and her style is especially suited to depicting other times and places. She frequently uses a framing device which helps to emphasise the presence of a storyteller and to create pictures in the mind of her audience. She won the SMARTIES PRIZE for *The Story of the Creation* (1992), a dazzling and moving book teeming with the colour and gold of life. AMN

Ray, Satyajit 1921–92 Indian film director, writer, translator, illustrator, designer and composer. With a prolific production of short stories, novellas, poems, LIMERICKS, essays, puzzles, brainteasers and crosswords in Bengali, Ray created a revolution in juvenile fiction in Bengal. His immortal creations, *Professor Shonku*, the scientist (1963; trans. 1994) and *FELUDA* the sleuth (from 1961), are backed by a tremendous variation in plot. It might be Shonku rocking the international circle of science with his astounding inventions and hair-raising escapades, or Feluda chasing criminals across the sands of Rajasthan; or simply a lonely man whose life is changed dramatically by the discovery of a dog who can laugh. He also excelled in the narration of tales of horror. His protagonists are always male, generally lone bachelors with little or no family ties. The magic of Ray's simple, lucid, terse yet warm writing weaves a web that captures children and adults alike without ever becoming patronising or didactic. In addition, the film-maker in him comes through in the way he packs a wealth of detail in a few succinct words. He himself illustrated all his works and designed all the book jackets, a feat few other writers have been able to match. Ray has been translated into English and nine foreign languages. IM

Ray, Sukumar 1887–1923 Indian poet, writer, illustrator, editor, translator and printer. The elder Ray is known to Bengalis as the King of Nonsense and a provider of endless laughter for children. After finishing college, he formed 'The Nonsense Club' and started publishing NONSENSE VERSE in 1914 in the family-run magazine, *Sandesh*. This was later collected in a volume called *Rhymes without Reasons* (1923), the collection for which he is best known. While he made fun of the hypocrisy and self-righteousness of contemporary society, he never deliberately ridiculed or hurt. It is this gentleness and subtlety that won him the admiration of millions. He created a nonsense world startling in its originality and exciting comparisons with LEWIS CAROLL and EDWARD LEAR. His son SATYAJIT RAY and others have carefully preserved this spirit of nonsense in competent translations of his works. IM

Read, Herbert see *THIS WAY DELIGHT*; see also CHILD AUTHORS

Reading Association of Ireland Children's Book Award see appendix; see also AWARDS AND MEDALS

Reading Rainbow (from 1985) A series of daily half-hour programmes on American public TELEVISION stations with the purpose of promoting reading. Actor LeVar Burton has been the host since the series began. Each programme presents a complete PICTUREBOOK, often narrated by a celebrity. Segments introducing related themes use interviews, animation, dramatisations, music and visits to locations around the world to explore cultural, artistic and scientific topics. For example, Burton visits a Renaissance festival after presenting *Rumpelstiltskin* by PAUL ZELINSKY. Each episode includes three short, enthusiastic book reviews written and delivered by children. Four objectives are incorporated into each programme: appreciating good literature through rich verbal and visual experiences with highly acclaimed books, introducing new experiences related to the concepts within featured books, recommending the local library as a resource, and promoting a positive self-concept by showing respectful interaction among adults and children from diverse cultural backgrounds. *Reading Rainbow* stickers on book covers boost sales of featured books. Videos and teaching guides are used in many elementary-school classrooms and homes. The series, which has won many awards for educational television, reflects the trend in education since the 1980s of integrating language arts and the reading of good literature with other subjects. TLH

reading schemes (in North America, also **basal readers**) Texts, usually in a series, written to help children learn to read by grading books according to difficulty, using readability measures. These measures vary because schemes are based on methodological criteria which change according to current beliefs. The earliest schemes usually presented the elements of words removed from meaningful contexts, for example in Lesson 5 of *Reading Disentangled* (1836), where the syllable 'ap' was listed with different initial consonants – 'lap' 'map' 'nap' 'tap' etc., a strictly 'phonic' approach. Nellie Dale, however, in *Reading Without Tears* in 1861, introduced complete stories (of moral import), splitting the long words into syllables: 'What is the mat-ter with that lit-tle boy?' (a whole-word approach). Most subsequent schemes exemplified one or other of these approaches, until the 1970s when a 'whole language' methodology in Britain linked reading with writing (*Breakthrough to Literacy*, 1970). Perhaps the most popular scheme ever in Britain was LADYBIRD BOOKS' *Key Words to Literacy* (from 1964), largely because it was the first series to be made available for parents to buy in local shops.

The most recent schemes in Britain have moved away from tight structural control to include a wide variety of genres and styles, incorporating stories by established children's authors, and including non-fiction as well as fiction.

In North America the pendulum has swung back and forth between the two approaches – an emphasis on learning words as wholes or through sound–symbol relationships. In 1840 Josiah Bumstead published *My*

Little Primer, which adopted a whole-word approach. Also in that year William H. McGuffey previewed McGUFFEY'S ECLECTIC READER, the first of the basal readers so influential in American schools. However, in 1912 Ginn & Company published *Beacon Readers*, among the first to use an extensive phonics approach – an emphasis on the relationships between spelling patterns and speech sounds. Scott-Foresman soon published William S. Gray's *The Elon Readers*, which immortalised 'Dick and Jane' and established Scott-Foresman as the leading producer of reading series from the 1940s to the 1960s.

In 1955 Rudolph Flesch published *Why Johnny Can't Read*, in which he advocated a return to a more intensive phonics approach. This method remained popular until the late 1980s, when the 'whole language' philosophy was adopted by many schools – a teacher-initiated movement which stressed using natural language in whole texts and placed a strong emphasis on an integrated reading-language arts curriculum. The 1990s brought a cry for a 'return to phonics'. Although reading whole texts, and reading and writing across the curriculum, remain popular, phonemic awareness – the awareness that words are composed of separate sounds and the ability to identify and manipulate those sounds – continued to be emphasised for beginner readers in American schools of the 1990s.

In New Zealand the first locally published readers were the *Southern Cross Readers* (c. 1886) by Whitcombe and Tombs Ltd. A New Zealand edition of the *Janet and John* books was published in 1949, and stocks were still held by Whitcombe and Tombs until the early 1980s. The most significant series to be published was the *Ready to Read* scheme (1963), published by the Department of Education. It was one of the first to recognise the use of natural language in beginning reading books. In Australia, in addition to using many of the materials published in the United Kingdom, New Zealand and the United States, several of the states' Departments of Education published carefully structured reading books for use in schools, which were supplemented in the 1960s and 1970s by the use of Australian series such as *Young Australia* and *Endeavour*. In the late 1980s several companies moved to the production of more comprehensive 'language programmes' following the 'whole language' theories of learning then prevailing. Most series produced in the 1990s have responded to the increasing use of multi-media in classrooms. HA, JAP, LSL

see also REAL BOOKS

Reading Time Journal of the CHILDREN'S BOOK COUNCIL OF AUSTRALIA, published quarterly. Originally called *New Books for Boys and Girls*, the name was changed to *Reading Time* in 1967, and from 1970 it became the official journal of the CBCA. It comprises articles on authors and illustrators, and extensive reviews of new books, in a number of categories, both Australian and from overseas. The State Judges' Reports for the CBCA Book of the Year Award are also published, together with the winners' acceptance speeches. The Journal has done much to raise public awareness of children's literature, and has played a significant role in lifting publishing standards. JAP

real books A term at the heart of an educational controversy in Britain in the 1980s. Many teachers had become critical of READING SCHEMES for young readers, with stories artificially constructed on the basis of word-repetition and phonic patterning. They championed the use of 'real books' – books which give free reign to the author's or illustrator's mind, and which offer young readers a similar imaginative freedom. The term was coined by Liz Waterland, an influential teacher who argued that real books provided a child with a chance to be a real reader, not just to say the words aloud. VW

Rebecca of Sunnybrook Farm (1903) KATE DOUGLAS WIGGIN's best novel, a girl's coming-of-age story about the education and tribulations of Rebecca Rowena Randall, sent because of her family's poverty to live at the Brick House with irascible Aunt Miranda and the kinder Aunt Jane Sawyer. Though it resembles other girls' stories of the early 20th century such as ELEANOR PORTER'S *POLLYANNA* and L.M. MONTGOMERY'S *ANNE OF GREEN GABLES*, it is consciously infused with Romantic and transcendentalist ideals. Indeed, many of the chapter titles are drawn from Wordsworth's poetry and the works of Emerson. A Romantic 'divine child', Rebecca is described as a 'black-haired gypsy' with bewitching eyes that contain 'hints of sleeping power and insight' – 'their steadfast gaze . . . had the effect of looking directly through the obvious to something beyond, in the object, in the landscape, in you.' Only Aunt Miranda (an aunt in the tradition of Aunt Fortune, Aunt March and Aunt Em) is oblivious to Rebecca's charms – for her, Rebecca is 'most too lively'. With her 'dull, but dogged' sidekick, Emma Jane, she receives a spotty education until she attends Wareham, where she is taken under the wing of Miss Emily Maxwell (modelled on Wiggin's mentor Emma Marwedel). Miss Maxwell recognises Rebecca as 'a rare pearl', albeit a 'black one'.

But there is a disturbing side to Rebecca's divine innocence. Her hypnotising gaze is particularly powerful in its effect on older men, most notably Adam Ladd (nicknamed 'Mr Aladdin') who is about 30 when he meets 12-year-old Rebecca. Ladd is wealthy, unmarried, and 'so fond of children that he always has a pack of them at his heels'. During Rebecca's years at

Wareham, Ladd virtually courts her, showering her with gifts and endowing a writing prize for her to win. Ladd's affection for Rebecca borders on the obsessive, and he constantly admonishes her not to grow up. Their peculiar relationship has led critic Jerry Griswold to describe the novel as a *Lolita* for children. *Rebecca* was much admired by male contemporaries, especially JACK LONDON, who wrote: 'She is real; she lives; she has given me many regrets, but I love her . . . O, how I envy "Mr Aladdin".'

A tug of war ensues between Ladd and Maxwell over whether or not Rebecca should have a teaching career. But fate intervenes when her mother becomes ill and Rebecca becomes a ministering angel. Her career forestalled, Mr Aladdin sees her as 'all-womanly', yet still a child – his ideal mate. Wiggin, however, leaves us with Rebecca's future 'close-folded still, folded and hidden in beautiful mists'. Like Mr Aladdin, she doesn't want Rebecca to grow up. *New Chronicles of Rebecca* (1907), writes Wiggin, is not a sequel, but a 'further filling in of incidents'. As such it is interesting primarily as a footnote to the haunting – and troubling – original. RF

recontextualisation Term currently used to refer to the re-presentation of a text in another medium, most commonly applied to film versions for television and cinema, though also applicable to other kinds of adaptations such as for stage or opera. The usefulness of the term is that it does not carry the derogatory overtones of the word 'version' and therefore sidesteps the assumption that any such version is secondary to the original work; a 'recontextualisation' should be judged on its own merits, not according to its faithfulness to the original. There is, however, no commonly accepted term for a version which appropriates the title of a well-known children's book but totally disregards its essential characteristics. VW

Red Etin, The see SCOTTISH FOLKTALES

Red Pony, The see JOHN STEINBECK

Red Shift see *OWL SERVICE, THE*; SEX IN CHILDREN'S BOOKS; see also FANTASY

Redmond, Phil see *GRANGE HILL*; see also SCHOOL STORIES; TELEVISION

***Redwall* series** (1986–2000) Set of 13 (to-date) novels by Brian Jacques comprising the hugely popular and highly readable anthropomorphic stories set in and around Redwall Abbey, home to a community of mice and various other animals. These swashbuckling tales of adventure, which began with *Redwall* (1986) and continued with new titles until *Lord Brocktree* (2000), are set during sunny summers and snowy winters, with feasts worthy of ENID BLYTON. Good always wins through in the end but the splendid assortment of villains, ranging from megalomaniac rats to sinister lizards, invariably give the heroes a run for their money before they meet a suitably bloodthirsty end. JEG

Reed, Talbot Baines 1852–93 British creator of the public-school story, who himself famously never attended public school, and son of Sir Charles Reed, type-founder and educationist. Reed ran the family business, was secretary of the Bibliographic Society and wrote *The History of Old English Letter Foundries* (1887), but he is chiefly remembered for his stories of school life first serialised in *THE BOY'S OWN PAPER* and later published as novels, notably *The Master of the Shell*, *The Cock-House at Fellsgarth* and *THE FIFTH FORM AT ST DOMINIC'S* (1881/2, 1887). His own genial and energetic personality informs his fiction. JMM

see also SCHOOL STORIES

Rees, David 1936– British author of novels for teenagers, stories for younger children and critical work on children's literature. Rees draws on his own life history in his work: his Irish heritage is the starting point for *The Green Bough of Liberty* (1980), while childhood experience of wartime London informs *The Exeter Blitz* (1978), winner of the CARNEGIE MEDAL. The history of Exeter – the English city which Rees has made his home – plays a key role in many of his novels. Critical attention has focused on the variable quality of Rees's writing and his pioneering treatment of the theme of homosexual love between adolescent boys in *Quintin's Man* (1976) and *In the Tent* (1979). GL

see also GAY AND LESBIAN LITERATURE

Rees, (George) Leslie 1905–2000 Australian writer of over 40 books for adults and children. Rees was awarded the first CHILDREN'S BOOK COUNCIL OF AUSTRALIA BOOK OF THE YEAR AWARD in 1946 for *The Story of Karrawingi the Emu* (1946), the first of an extensive series of animal life-cycle picture storybooks, all illustrated by WALTER CUNNINGHAM, who also illustrated Rees's popular *Digit Dick* series (1942–57), an Australian *TOM THUMB*. Although laboured and didactic compared with PICTUREBOOKS today, these books were very popular with young readers at the time. Rees also wrote a number of gripping ADVENTURE STORIES. His books have been widely translated and have achieved extensive international sales. Rees's latest picturebook, *The Seagull who Liked Cricket* (1997), was produced at the age of 92 in collaboration with Margaret Wilson, with a story and ILLUSTRATIONS both reminiscent in style of his earlier works. JAP

Reeves, James 1909–78 English poet, anthologist and critic. Humour and vivid characters abound in James Reeves's stories for young children, such as *Pigeons and Princesses* (1956), *Titus in Trouble* (1959) and *Sailor Rumbelow and Britannia* (1962). Reeves also wrote for older children. *The Strange Light* (1964) is about the adventures of eight-year-old Christina who gets through a hedge and meets Wistaria and all the other as yet unborn children who want to be put into books by authors. The FANTASY is perhaps too whimsical here, however, and the book is not as successful as *Mulbridge Manor* (1958), a realistic tale in the vein of *Emil and the Detectives* (see EMIL SERIES) about a gang of children dealing with real if petty criminals. The characters are well drawn, particularly the rather scholarly 12-year-old Richard, but it is the background of the sleepy south-coast town of Mulcaster that gives the book its special quality.

Reeves is best known for his collections of children's poetry, illustrated by EDWARD ARDIZZONE, beginning with *The Wandering Moon* (1950) and *The Blackbird in the Lilac* (1952). Reeves's poetry in these books is meticulously crafted and characterised by lyrical evocations of a childhood lived in 'the garden' rather than 'the street'. *PREFABULOUS ANIMILES* (1957) and *More Prefabulous Animiles* (1975) add a substantial body of *nonsense verse* to his work. Reeves is now best remembered for poems which are examples of unusual technical features, such as the extended metaphors of 'The Sea' ('The sea is a hungry dog'), the kenning-like names in 'The Intruder' ('Two-boots in the forest walks'), and the well-known poem which seeks to find a rhyme for 'W' ('I'm sorry', said he, 'to trouble you'). He also wrote several wise books on teaching poetry which showed his understanding of children, the imagination and poetic language.

Reeves was also a distinguished anthologist, particularly of traditional verse and folksongs, and his reworkings of old tales, such as *English Fables and Fairy Stories* (1954), *Fables of Aesop Retold* (1961) and especially *The Cold Flame* (1967) – a powerful adaptation of a story by the GRIMM BROTHERS – deserve to acquire a classic status for their clarity and wisdom. DB, ML

Reid Banks, Lynne see BANKS, LYNNE REID; see also *INDIAN IN THE CUPBOARD, THE*

Reid, Barbara 1957– Multiple-ward-winning Canadian children's illustrator and author. Barbara Reid is an original and inventive artist; her medium is plasticine. Her technique and meticulous attention to detail – dyeing white plasticine to get the colours she needs, and building layer upon layer, starting with the big pieces and finishing with the tiniest touches – combine to produce three-dimensional ILLUSTRATIONS which are bright, busy and endlessly fascinating. Her work is simultaneously childlike and sophisticated. Her subject matter is diverse: the story of Noah's ark in *Two by Two* (1992); birds in *Have You Seen Birds?* (1986), by Joanne Oppenheim; an ant with a loud voice in *Effie* (1990) by Beverley Allinson; toddler's play in her *Zoe* board books; decorative art for *Sing a Song of Mother Goose* (1987); and, for *The Gift* (1994) by Jo Ellen Bogart, an ageless travelling granny. Her sense of humour and delight in everyday life are apparent in the illustrations, in which jokes abound. *The Party* (1997) is full of rolled sandwiches, jiggling jello, playing children and relatives galore. Her plasticine illustrations are photographed by her husband and – encased in acrylic boxes – are highly sought after by private collectors. TH

Reid, Captain Thomas Mayne 1818–83 Author, soldier and explorer. Reid was born in Ireland, but went to North America in 1838, leading an adventurous life that included hunting and exploring, and fighting with distinction in the war between Mexico and the United States. Recovering in England from injury, Reid wrote *The Rifle Rangers* (1848), the first of many 'thoroughly manly' novels based on his experiences. *The Boy Hunters* (1852) and later novels were written to inspire in boys an interest in nature and a love of books; they combine detailed biological description with exciting conflict on human and animal levels. FEA

Reid, Meta Mayne 1905–91 Born in Yorkshire of Irish parents, Reid settled in Northern Ireland in 1930. She wrote over 20 books for children, some with a contemporary setting but with links to the past, and others which are straightforward historical novels set mainly in the early days of 19th-century Ulster. It is the latter which are now regarded as her strongest works, depicting in some detail a particular phase and place in Irish history, in titles such as *The Two Rebels* (1969), *Beyond the Wide World's End* (1972) and *The Plotters of Pollnashee* (1973). VC

religious stories Stories from religious traditions retold for children, for example, from significant (canonical) texts such as the Bible (Jewish and Christian), or the Ramayana (Hindu). Many such stories are biographical, illustrating religious principles through the lives of significant people, such as the Gurus (Sikh), Muhummad (Muslim), the Buddha or lives of the saints. The intention is often didactic.

However, it is questionable whether such an enterprise is possible without seriously distorting the intention of the original material. Religious story is not primarily for children exclusively, but for a whole community. Narrative theology since the 1970s has illuminated the role of story within faith communities. Religious story has authority within the community to which it belongs and helps to create and maintain a taken-for-granted view of the world and promote the values by which the community lives. Such stories help to create the identity of the community which tells them. Individual religious stories form part of a metanarrative, an overall story which has a theological purpose and tells of the meaning and significance of life and the human response to the mystery of existence.

Although it often has a textual form and some texts are given remarkable status, the story is usually developed orally as a living tradition. Thus the telling of religious story is in a context, often of ritual, which both permits and controls the reinterpretation and adds to the meaning through action; examples can be seen in the retelling of the Exodus story at the Jewish Passover festival, or the story of the Last Supper in the celebration of the Christian Eucharist. Where a story is separated from its metanarrative, its community, its ritual context, and its purpose of nurturing religious identity, it is questionable whether it remains a religious story.

In Britain stories from the Christian tradition, especially BIBLE STORIES, were amongst the first to be published in the 17th century. In the 18th and 19th centuries these were supplemented by moral tales. These stories were primarily intended for Christian children as part of nurturing them within the faith. This strand has continued with publications intended for use within churches and homes. There have been attempts recently to combine the whole Biblical story with scholarly interpretation. The *Jerusalem Children's Bible* (1996) is a successful example of this approach, though its reading level suggests that it is for adolescents or perhaps intended as a resource for parents to introduce their children to the tradition. Other faiths also publish for their own children, though few have the panache of the *Amar Chitra Katha* series of comics published in India, in English as well as other local languages, which provides authentic Hindu stories in an accessible form.

In Britain, the demands of the education system within an increasingly secular society have led to another strand of publication of religious stories for the purposes of information or entertainment. From 1870, the provision of non-denominational Religious Education within the state school system led to books of Bible stories intended for teachers to read to children; however the 'non-denominational' requirement, which was intended to preserve the religious freedom of children – particularly those from Free Church families – led to the omission of theological interpretation from the stories, though sometimes an attenuated moral interpretation would be added.

At the same time, the rise of scientific thinking and of critical analysis of Biblical texts led to a change in adult perceptions of the stories. An increasing literalness linked with rising scepticism led to a loss of understanding of how religious story conveys truth. Such stories became thought of within an increasingly secular society as more fit for children than for adults, to be told for educational purposes so that children would recognise Biblical allusion when they met it within other literature, and they were told in a way which encouraged them to be viewed as fictional.

The development of sophisticated techniques for printing colour ILLUSTRATIONS has led to a genre, often a single story in PICTUREBOOK form, where the artwork has been more significant than the text. This has often led to the production of stories which lend themselves well to illustration rather than which have religious importance. The plethora of books retelling the story of Noah's Ark can perhaps be explained this way, and contains examples which indicate how authors and illustrators often avoid difficult theological or historical questions, rather than considering how to present them. Where major stories are told, the art can suggest that this is a piece for a gallery or a museum rather than of living significance for faith. Despite the merits of BRIAN WILDSMITH's work, for example, his *The Easter Story* (1986) has pictures which with the use of gold and skies filled with angels recall medieval religiosity, and a text which tells the story through the eyes of a donkey; both of these are distancing devices. The problem of how to represent God in illustration is particularly acute, especially when referring to stories from the Jewish Bible or the Islamic tradition which forbid such representation. Issues of gender are also problematic, with many stories and pictures making women even more invisible than in the original.

Since the 1970s there has been a demand led by education for stories from and about other faith traditions. The Ginn *Celebrations* series combines stories told at festivals such as Diwali and Hannukah with contextual material about how the festivals are celebrated. Macdonald published a series in 1987 which includes *Stories from the Jewish World*, *Stories from the Christian World*, and *Stories from the Muslim World*, in which canonical, historical and biographical material are combined. One of the most successful is *Stories from the Sikh World*. Hindu stories are generally more successfully told in material from Hindu sources. For reading aloud, MADHUR JAFFREY's *Seasons of Splendour* (1985) gives a retelling with rich use of language.

Such stories can give children a way in which to imagine themselves into world-views and cultures other than their own and experience the potentially liberating effect of an introduction to alternative values. Most recently, there has been a trend towards religious stories which are not attached to any religion but which encourage a general spirituality, often within an ecological context (see ECOLOGY). *Brother Eagle, Sister Sky* (1991) draws on Native American tradition to deal with responsibility towards the web of life. *Old Turtle* (1992) takes a pluralist view of the nature of God based in a creation-theology. JS

see also BIBLE STORIES

Religious Tract Society One of the most successful and prolific of the evangelical publishing houses, founded in 1799 to promote religious tracts. It had the insight to recognise the limitations of the view that the literacy of the poor should be confined to Bible readings, and, guided by founding member, the Rev. George Burden, it soon identified the market potential of a child readership to which it turned its attentions in 1812.

Burden's *Early Piety* (1814) was a model for the abundance of pious, joyful child-death stories subsequently published by RTS, many of them designed for the Sunday school reward-book market. Urged by George Stokes, RTS began in the 1820s to publish children's books with more palatable secular elements added to the characteristic religious message and, under his editorship, launched *The Child's Companion; or Sunday Scholar's Reward* (1824), the first of its children's periodicals (and read in Florence Nightingale's childhood home). Prolific in publishing children's books, particularly after the 1870 Elementary Education Act, the Society in its guidelines insisted on earnest, moral and natural tales with minimal excitement in order to leave the reader calm in spirit. RTS successfully modified its vigorously Christian style to accommodate juvenile tastes in its magazines, *BOY'S OWN PAPER* (from 1879) and *GIRL'S OWN PAPER* (from 1880). RTS became the Lutterworth Press in the 1930s. BW

see also PUBLISHERS AND PUBLISHING

Remi, Georges see *TINTIN* SERIES

Rendall, Jenny see *FOUR AND TWENTY LAMINGTONS*

Renier Collection see COLLECTIONS OF CHILDREN'S BOOKS

Rescuers, The see *MISS BIANCA* SERIES

Revenge of the Dolls see DOLL STORIES

Revere, Paul see DOROTHY CANFIELD FISHER; ESTHER FORBES; JEAN FRITZ; ROBERT LAWSON; HENRY WADSWORTH LONGFELLOW

reviewing and reviewers In the US and Canada, reviews of children's books have appeared in various publications. Many local newspapers offer periodic reviews of selected children's material, especially around the holidays; some national papers, such as the *New York Times* (in its book review section), regularly devote space to children's titles. Perhaps more significant, however, have been systematic reviews in publications read and written by professionals in various children's literature fields. The best-known early version of such reviews appeared in *Publishers' Weekly* in 1882, and the 20th century has seen a proliferation of reviewing sources, including several standard periodicals.

The American Library Association's own review periodical, *Booklist*, includes a substantial section devoted to new children's books (their *Media* section also reviews non-book materials for children as well as for adults). One of the most venerable of review periodicals, *Booklist* first appeared in 1905. Enhancing its practical merit are frequent annotated thematic bibliographies and cross-references to reviews of adult books with young-adult appeal.

The Bulletin of the Center for Children's Books began in 1945 as an in-house newsletter for an instructional materials collection at the University of Chicago; 1947 marked its official appearance as a subscription journal. It has always retained its academic connection, moving in 1993 from the University of Chicago (where its editors included ZENA SUTHERLAND and BETSY HEARNE) to the Graduate School of Library and Information Science at the University of Illinois. Carrying neither articles nor reviews of adult titles (except for professionally relevant materials), it focuses entirely on reviews of books for children and young adults.

The Horn Book Magazine, founded by BERTHA MAHONY MILLER in 1924, carries articles and several regular columns in addition to lengthy reviews. Many distinguished figures in the field have held the position of editor, including Paul and Ethel Heins, Anita Silvey and Roger Sutton. Maintaining a small staff of regular reviewers for the Magazine, *HORN BOOK* also issues the twice-yearly *Horn Book Guide*, which contains brief coded evaluative annotations of a multitude of titles, most of them not reviewed in the magazine itself. Its news-stand availability and its blend of literary, scholarly and professional appeal has made it one of the most widely known review periodicals.

Originally a section within the *Library Journal*, *School Library Journal* began its life as a full-fledged periodical as *Junior Librarian* in 1955, under the direction of Margaret Saul Melcher. For more than half its life, it has been edited by the legendary Lillian Gerhardt, whose commitment to intellectual freedom and diversity and whose penchant for strong statement have often made *School Library Journal* the site of the most memorable or controversial writings on children's literature. A large stable of volunteer librarians write the bulk of it's reviews, resulting in a greater variation of voices than in most other review periodicals.

There are other significant reviewing venues: *Kirkus Reviews*, founded by editor Virginia Kirkus in 1932, eschews advertisements and articles while retaining a newsletter format and concentrating entirely on reviews of adult and children's books; *Voices of Youth Advocates*, popularly known as *VOYA*, appears six times a year and includes articles on and reviews of literature for young adults, sometimes written by young adult reviewers; *The ALAN Review* includes perforated review cards in addition to critical articles on young adult literature; and *Appraisal*, which assesses science books for young readers, uniquely pairs a review by a librarian with a review on the same title by a scientific expert in the subject field.

The Canadian popular press offers fairly limited reviewing of children's literature. More reliable review sources include *Resource Materials*, which began publication in 1995, and *CM: A Reviewing Journal of Canadian Materials for Young People* (established 1971). The latter, issued by the Canadian Library Association, includes periodic assessments of French-language books as well as its reviews of English-language children's literature. The scholarly journal *Canadian Children's Literature/ Littérature canadienne pour la jeunesse* also includes a large selection of reviews (some in English, some in French) in every issue.

Several of these periodicals have electronic presences on the INTERNET, ranging from selected reviews to special features; complete electronic subscriptions will undoubtedly be available in the near future, and various review compendia are already available on CD-ROM. Some professionals and aficionados have begun to provide electronic-only reviews in forums including electronic newsletters, websites and periodic Usenet postings. The result of this expansion currently seems to be not an undermining of traditional review sources but rather a broadening of review readership.

Though critical articles about children's literature have a long history, in Britain the reviewing of children's books in national newspapers and in specalist magazines or periodicals is largely a post-war development. Before 1939 ELEANOR GRAHAM, then children's bookseller at Bumpus in London's Oxford Street, had recognised the value of promoting children's books to the general public in the national press (*The Sunday Times*). Another bookseller, J.B. Woodfield, started *The Junior Bookshelf* in 1936; but this and *The School Librarian*, first issued in 1937, were directed at the working professional.

World War II was a watershed in the field of children's literature, though what was to become a flood of books towards the end of the century was a mere trickle until the late 1950s. The reviewing of children's books in newspapers and magazines mushroomed, reflecting not only the quality and increasing quantity of books published but also contemporary social ideas and ideals, such as multi-culturalism and feminism. In the 1960s – when MARGERY FISHER was editor of *The Sunday Times* children's book pages, NAOMI LEWIS was at *The Observer*, JOHN ROWE TOWNSEND at *The Guardian*, David Holloway at *The Daily Telegraph* and Brian Alderson at *The Times* – anything other than informed reviewing by experienced panels of reviewers was unthinkable. Often, as in *The Guardian*, this was from authors such as JILL PATON WALSH, LEON GARFIELD and PHILIPPA PEARCE, who believed strongly that children's novels should be regarded as mainstream literature and reviewed without regard to a book's intended readership. This purist view was challenged by pragmatists and, in the 1970s, by ideological activists who began to look at books through the other end of the telescope, believing that the book must be fashioned to come to the child, especially girls and deprived inner-city and ethnic minority children. ROBERT LEESON in *The Morning Star* and Rosemary Stones in *The Children's Book Bulletin* (1979) sowed the seeds of this reviewing *volte face*, which was to influence the like-minded among children's publishers and encourage whole new classes of 'accessible' and 'relevant' children's books. These new developments began to overshadow the children's 'literary' novel, but it was the advance of corporate PUBLISHING in the 1980s and 1990s that threatened to sink literary fiction in Britain beneath giant waves of mediocrity. Publishers' emphasis on quicker returns brought a torrent of indifferent titles onto a shrinking institutional market, and this in the 1990s was reflected in the way the output of publishers was received by literary editors who came to regard children's books as a broadly consumerist rather than a mainly literary commodity. With one or two notable exceptions, batches of children's books tended to be handed over for review not to a specialist, but to any willing parents on the staff.

Specialist magazine editors, however, have ploughed their own furrows with diligence. For parents, there was Margery Fisher's erudite, perceptive and mainly positive GROWING POINT (1962–92). In 1995, a teacher, Anne Wood, founded *Books for Your Children* (now CAROUSEL); it aimed to bring a wide range of families into the know about children's books and authors. Short informed reviews for non-specialist readers were provided in the 1960s and early 70s by Eric Baker's *Children's Book News* and Valerie Alderson's *Children's Book Review*. Radio also played its part: in the 1960s and 70s BBC's *Woman's Hour* had a regular spot called *Children's Books and Writers* which was later developed into a separate, eclectic programme, *Treasure Islands*, presentedby MICHAEL ROSEN.

Schools and LIBRARIES are the places where many children will have their most fruitful contact with a wide range of children's books; selection is therefore vital and the reviewing of children's books in educational media is of great importance. Most educational magazines, like *Child Education* and *Junior Education*, carry book pages; serious review sections are a main feature in the weekly *Times Educational Supplement*. Lighter in tone is a magazine now known as *BOOKS FOR KEEPS*, whose original purpose was to help teachers select books for sale on school bookstalls; but under various editors, and over 20 years, it has become a general source of information for all teachers. Librarians in the public library service tend to have books sent to them by library suppliers for their own assessment; school librarians, however, are more likely to rely on reviews in any of the above media, in addition to *The School Librarian*, published by the School Library Association, a journal comprising articles and reviews by practising teachers or specialists in the various disciplines covered. Much lively reviewing for teachers and librarians used to be found in local authorities' internal publications, such as Hertfordshire's *Material Matters* and the now defunct Inner London Education Authority's *Contact*, which fell victim, respectively, to financial stringency and educational re-organisation.

Booklists can be either a source of considered selection and reviewing or a collection of ill-thought-through suggestions, mundanely annotated. The Thimble Press has led the way in publishing the exemplary series of *SIGNAL Book Guides*; and in *The Signal Reviews* for 1982 and 1983, followed by *The Signal Selections* for 1984 to 1989, it has established a unique exercise in collaborative reviewing. From 1970 to 1994 *Children's Books of the Year* was the annotated catalogue for the National Book League's (later Book Trust's) annual exhibitions of that name, exhibitions that travelled round the United Kingdom and, with the help of the British Council, abroad.

For the children themselves, various attempts at book reviewing have been made, the only successful venture being in *Puffin Post*, the lively child-inviting magazine run by Puffin designed to appeal to children for its own promotional purposes. Children contributed their own views on books, rather like word-of-mouth recommendations in a classroom. Children do not, as a rule, make good book reviewers; however teenagers are different, and Elizabeth Hammill's experiment with adolescent reviewers in Newcastle has been very successful: *In Brief* became a much respected medium in teenage circles and secondary teaching (see CHILD AUTHORS).

In Australia, current Australian titles receive best coverage, but publications from North America and Britain are also included, with New Zealand a growing area of interest. Sources include occasional reviews of children's books in capital-city and national newspapers; a designated section in the prestigious national monthly *Australian Book Review*; and three well-established specialist journals with national and international circulation: *Reading Time*, published quarterly by the CHILDREN'S BOOK COUNCIL OF AUSTRALIA (from 1957); *MAGPIES* (established by David and Rayma Turton, five issues per year, from 1986); and *VIEWPOINT: ON BOOKS FOR YOUNG ADULTS* (from 1993) published quarterly by the Division of Library and Information Studies, University of Melbourne. The quarterly *The Literature Base* (from 1990) and some of the articles in *Viewpoint* discuss books in the context of school library and classroom applications. Departments of Education (States and Territories) produce selection aids for schools, including evaluative annotations and reviews of fiction and INFORMATION BOOKS for children, for example *Scan* (New South Wales), and *Fiction Focus* (Western Australia). Increasingly, these selection aids can be accessed via the INTERNET. Reviews by children and young adults are sometimes included in *Viewpoint* and *The Literature Base*, while school students researched, wrote and edited almost all of the material in the journal *Rippa Reading* (52 issues, 1986?–95), giving young reviewers a voice and a forum. Jonathan Appleton's contribution as writer and editor was widely acclaimed. *React: News, Views and Previews on Teenage Fiction*, published by the Australian Capital Territory Department of Education and Training, consists mainly of reviews by secondary-school students.

National radio and TELEVISION arts programmes review children's books occasionally, usually when awards and/or controversies are involved. Some Community Radio stations have regular coverage, notably Radio 3RPH in Melbourne (reviews and interviews by Krista Bell) and 4MBS Classic FM in Brisbane (reviews by Kerry Neary).

Finding Australian reviews of specific titles is not always easy. The international bibliographic tool *Children's Literature Abstracts* (published by the International Federation of Library Associations, Children's Libraries Section) indexes articles in *Magpies*, *Reading Time* and *Viewpoint*, but not shorter reviews. Only *Magpies* is covered in the international *Children's Book Review Index* (Gale, from 1969). Searching *Reading Time's* comprehensive annual indexes is the surest way of finding reviews of specific Australian children's books.

The importance of reviews is acknowledged by all those with an interest in children's books, and the appropriateness of some reviews is often hotly debated. Questions frequently addressed include the reviewer's responsibilities; the role of the young reader in reviewing children's books; criteria for assessing informational books; variations of reviewing style for different media and different audiences; ways of dealing with contentious issues; the effects of reviews on all concerned with books and reading; and the need for reviewers of PICTUREBOOKS to have a knowledge of art and design. DS, EM, LJL

Revolting Rhymes (1982) Six FAIRY TALES retold in rhyme by ROALD DAHL and illustrated by QUENTIN BLAKE. Dahl's secret is the contemporary flavour of the language: 'Fearing the worst, poor Snow White spake. / She cried, "Oh please give me a break!"' Also, its pacey delivery accentuated by rhyme helps to time the jokes, and the surprising and dramatic endings appeal to children who appreciate scandalous changes to traditional narratives. JL

Reynard the Fox The main protagonist in a series of medieval stories which, with many additions and branches, were gathered under the collective title of the *Roman de Renart*, begun around 1175. The stories became nearly as popular and well-known as AESOP's fables, from which they partly derive, and began to appear in other European languages from the late 12th century. The rapid rise to popularity of the stories is attested by the fact that 'renart' had virtually replaced the common word for fox, 'goupil', in France by the middle of the 13th century. The Reynard stories are generally categorised as *beast epic* rather than *fables*; they tend to be longer than fables and are more consistently satiric in intent, often using mock epic language. Though they may be allegorical or develop moral points, the dominant tone is anarchic: the stories attack institutions and moral norms with zest. Though they contain many memorable animal figures, they are dominated by Renart himself, seen particularly in conflict with Isengrim the wolf. Renart is portrayed as devious, cruel, deceitful, greedy and totally cynical. He has been described as the supreme 'anti-hero' of medieval fiction. DWh

Rhymes for the Nursery see LULLABIES; ANN AND JANE TAYLOR

Rhymes Without Reason (1944) An exuberant but odd collection of NONSENSE VERSE by MERVYN PEAKE, author of the *Gormenghast Trilogy*, with all the hallmarks of this author's extraordinary imagination. Peake suffered from mental illness after disturbing war-time experiences and there is nothing stable to hang onto in the surreal world he created in this volume, where hints of sadness keep seeping through. MCCS

Rice, Alice Hegan see *MRS WIGGS OF THE CABBAGE PATCH*; see also FAMILY STORIES

Richards, Frank see *GREYFRIARS*; CHARLES HAMILTON

Richards, Hilda see CHARLES HAMILTON

Richards, Laura E(lisabeth Howe) 1850–1943 American author and poet whose mother, Julia Ward Howe, wrote 'The Battle Hymn of the Republic'. Richards produced over 90 books of fiction, BIOGRAPHY, and poetry. She contributed verses to the *ST NICHOLAS MAGAZINE* which were added to her first book of poetry, *Sketches and Scraps* (1881). Her best-known collection was *Tirra Lirra: Rhymes Old and New* (1932). PDS

Richardson, Samuel 1689–1761 British author and printer who wrote three of the most successful English novels of the 18th century: *Pamela* (1740), *Clarissa* (1747–8) and *Sir Charles Grandison* (1753–4). He also produced, more specifically for children, a carefully revised and illustrated version of L'Estrange's *AESOP* (1740), in which he gave much thought to the needs of young readers. His novels, though long, were available to a more juvenile audience in abridged versions. Richardson saw the primary task of his writing as being moral instruction, but he tried to achieve this in fiction by instilling dramatic tension and psychological realism into situations which would provoke debate. Richardson aligned himself strongly with women's interests and perspectives, an identification fostered partly through his relatively humble background and lack of classical education. He corresponded regularly with a coterie of women readers and adapted his own writing in the light of their responses or suggestions. The letter, indeed, with its hallmark of reciprocity and concern for the relationship between writer and addressee, became central to Richardson's work: the form of his novels is often epistolary and his first project as a writer was a volume of exemplary letters offered as stylistic models for less experienced writers (*Familiar Letters* 1741). DWh

Richler, Mordecai 1931– Canadian writer, born and educated in Montreal, Canada, though he eventually settled in England. Richler writes primarily for adults, though his well-known autobiographical novel *The Apprenticeship of Duddy Kravitz* (1959) is read by adolescents and was made into a successful film. Richler's *Jacob Two-Two* books – *Jacob Two-Two Meets the Hooded Fang* (1975), *Jacob Two-Two and the Dinosaur* (1987) and *Jacob Two-Two's First Spy Case* (1997) – are appreciated by younger children receptive to Richler's somewhat unsubtle humour. The first of the series won both the CANADIAN LIBRARY ASSOCIATION CHILDREN'S BOOK OF THE YEAR AWARD and the Ruth Schwartz Children's Book Award. *Jacob Two-Two*

Meets the Hooded Fang has been produced on stage and made into a film. MJKP

Riddell, Chris 1962– British illustrator. After graduating from Brighton Polytechnic, Riddell went straight into full-time illustrating and cartooning. A fine draughtsman, who uses an expressive closed line and watercolour, he has illustrated a wide range of texts including ADVENTURE GAME BOOKS, non-fiction, poetry, and titles by TED HUGHES, E.T.A. HOFFMAN, Philip Ridley and HELEN CRESSWELL, in addition to his own PICTUREBOOKS. *Something Else* (Kathryn Cave, 1997) was awarded the new UNESCO Prize for Children's and Young People's Literature in the Service of Tolerance. *The Swan's Stories* (HANS CHRISTIAN ANDERSEN, retold by Brian Alderson, 1997) was shortlisted for the 1997 KURT MASCHLER AWARD, and Riddell's 'illuminations' of Richard Platt's *Castle Diary* were shortlisted for the 1999 KATE GREENAWAY AWARD. JAG

riddles and jokes The age-old pastime of riddling has left a sizeable literature spanning many centuries, from the Anglo-Saxon poetic riddles in the *Exeter Book* (c. 940), and the short prose riddles in *Demaundes Joyous*, printed by Wynken de Worde in 1511, to the rhymed riddles in *The Book of Meery Riddles* (1629) and *Delights for Young Men and Maids* (c. 1745). Rhymed riddles have now taken refuge in NURSERY RHYME books, where verses like 'Hitty Pitty within the wall' (a nettle), 'Little Nancy Etticoat' (a candle), and 'Humpty Dumpty' (an egg) continue to be popular, and the fact that they are riddles is often forgotten. Riddles have also been a memorable feature in some children's books, as when Nutkin teases Old Brown in *The Tale of Squirrel Nutkin* (1903), and Bilbo Baggins engages in a riddling competition with Gollum, the 'small slimy creature' who lives under a mountain, in J.R.R. TOLKIEN's *THE HOBBIT* (1937).

The nomenclature of children's oral humour is confusing. True riddles are now rare in the playground. The verbal jollities which are the staple of juvenile social life, and which are almost entirely based on puns, are known to them simply as 'jokes'. Broadly speaking, there are two categories: questions-and-answers (when success depends more on already knowing the answer than on any brain work), and stories, usually 'rude', which can be admired and told to someone else as soon as possible. The questions-and-answers can be punning riddles, which have punning questions and plain answers ('What runs but never walks? A river'); or conundrums, in which the answers may contain a single pun ('Why are soldiers tired on the First of April? Because they have just had a March of 31 days') or a double pun ('What is the difference between a big black cloud and a lion with toothache? One pours with rain and the other roars with pain'); or catches which sound like riddles and have trick answers, like the immortal 'Why did the chicken cross the road? To get to the other side', with all its train of variations. Joke crazes sweep the country from time to time. 'Knock, knock' jokes, which came to Britain from America in the 1930s, are still as popular as ever. 'Anti-jokes', also American, depend more on surrealism than on puns. They began with the Elephant jokes in the 1960s ('Why do elephants lie on their backs? To trip flying mice') and were followed by 'Colour' jokes and 'Lift' jokes. 'Doctor, doctor' jokes and 'Psychiatrist' jokes came later.

Orthodox jokes – that is, narratives with a witty surprise-ending – often follow well-tried formulas. The device of the misleading name ('There were these three boys called Manners, Mind-your-own-business, and Trouble . . .') was used long ago by Odysseus. Versions of the 'Englishman, Irishman, and Scotsman' stories of the 1920s and 30s are still told. Most of the stories centre around the subjects perennially fascinating to children: the bodily functions, strong drink, sex and death. IO

Ridley, Philip see *KRINKLEKRAX*

Rieu, E. V. 1887–1972 Revered British classical scholar, translator and editor who brought equal skill to his hobby of writing light verse of a particular charm and humour. A range of subjects – fantastical, nonsensical, domestic – was delicately handled, with no straining for effect. Sir Smashum Uppe (an apt name) is sarcastically invited to 'come again. / So glad you're fond of porcelain!' *Cuckoo Calling* (1933) and *The Flattered Flying Fish* (1962) contain all Rieu's poems for children. AHa

Riley, James Whitcomb 1849–1916 American journalist and poet. An Indiana writer with a flair for show business, James Whitcomb Riley published numerous works in Hoosier dialect. His popular poems include 'Little Orphan Annie', 'The Old Man and Jim' and 'The Raggedy Man'. His most famous opening is 'When the frost is on the punkin and the fodder's in the shock / And you hear the kyouck and gobble of the struttin' turkey-cock.' Sometimes derisively called 'a newspaper poet', he nevertheless wrote several verses which became children's favourites. Written in Hoosier dialect, 'Little Orphan Annie' warns:

> the Gobble-uns'll get you
> Ef you
> Don't
> Watch
> Out!

Largely ignored by 20th-century critics, his writings capture a rural America. Collections of his poems include *Rhymes of Childhood* (1890) and *Knee Deep in June* (1912). NV, KSB

Rime of the Ancient Mariner, The (1798) Narrative poem by Samuel Taylor Coleridge. First conceived on a walk with William Wordsworth, this extended BALLAD uses the themes of exile and homecoming, the relationship between human beings and nature, and dream-inspired spiritual journeys which constantly haunted Coleridge. He expertly weaves the plot using dream-like imagery which blends the natural and the supernatural into a beautifully observed landscape of changing weather and shifting seas – part real, part hallucination. Children who manage to penetrate the language love it for its dramatic narrative. Lines like 'Water, water everywhere' are part of popular culture. The poem has been memorably illustrated by MERVYN PEAKE and Gustave Doré. HT

see also LYRICAL BALLADS

Rin Tin Tin (1918–32) German shepherd dog. As a newborn puppy, this star of motion pictures was rescued from a war zone in France by a United States sergeant, Lee Duncan, during World War I, with Tin's mother, herself a German war dog, and four litter mates. Despite snarls of red tape, Rin Tin Tin and Nanette, the two pups allotted to Duncan, came to the United States with the soldier at the end of his tour of duty. In California, Duncan trained Rin Tin Tin with gentle care, and the dog's stardom originated with *Where the North Begins*, filmed in the High Sierra mountains. *Find Your Man* and *The Night Cry* followed. To their fans' pleasure, this champion dog and his devoted owner made numerous personal appearances, including visits to orphanages and hospitals. The sons of Rin Tin Tin carried on his adventuresome tradition, as James W. English describes in *The Rin Tin Tin Story* (1949). A fictional satirical BIOGRAPHY *Won-Ton-Ton – The Dog Who Saved Hollywood* was released in 1976. NV

Ringgold, Faith 1930– African American artist and Caldecott Honour and CORETTA SCOTT KING AWARD winner, who produces PICTUREBOOKS based on her painted, soft-sculpture story-quilts. (*Dancing at the Louvre: Faith Ringgold's French Collection and Other Story Quilts*, 1998, is an illustrated book that tells the story of Ringgold's unique work.)

Ringgold utilises TIME-SLIP FANTASY, magical realism (the flying slave legend), and colour for inscribing readers into a 'mythic' space where African American children learn about their past. In *Tar Beach* (1991), eight-year-old Cassie flies over the scenes of her family's history in a dream-wish memory vision. The art style is naive (flattened perspectives, large expressive eyes) and linear (heavy, bold lines). The colours emphasise the stability of Cassie's family and the sky as human 'hopescape'. In *Aunt Harriet's Underground Railroad in the Sky* (1992), Cassie encounters Harriet Tubman in one of her dream flights and is taken back into slavery days to learn more about her cultural history. Brilliant blue fills the sky world as Cassie journeys back in time; dark green, brown and black fill the narrative spaces of the Underground Railroad cars.

Dinner at Aunt Connie's House (1993) and *Bonjour, Lonnie* (1996) are companion picturebooks. In the first Lonnie, in the attic of his newly-adopted home in America, learns about his heritage from paintings of prominent African Americans telling him their stories. In the second (a prequel), a love-bird takes Lonnie on a journey to Paris to uncover his bi-cultural, international family tree. In *The Dream of Martin Luther King* (1995), 'colour' gives way to black-and-white paintings to emphasise the gravity of the racial struggles of King's life, imagined here by the female child who dreams his BIOGRAPHY. More recently, Ringgold has produced *The Invisible Princess* (1998), a newly minted African American FAIRY TALE set in plantation days, and *If a Bus Could Talk: The Story of Rosa Parks* (1999), a picturebook biography. NM

see also AFRICAN AMERICAN LITERATURE

Rip Van Winkle see IRVING, WASHINGTON; see also F.O.C. DARLEY; GIFT BOOKS

Ritson, Joseph see ROBIN HOOD

Riverside Literature Series for Young People see SCUDDER, HORACE E.

Riverside Magazine for Young People, The: An Illustrated Monthly (1867–70) Magazine published by Hurd & Houghton of New York and Boston, and edited by HORACE SCUDDER, one of America's most influential men of letters, then in his 20s. Scudder attracted writers like MARY MAPES DODGE, FRANK STOCKTON, LUCRETIA P. HALE and Sarah Orne Jewett to his journal. His taste, care and high aesthetic standards made the *Riverside* the most handsome children's periodical America had produced to date, featuring artwork by WINSLOW HOMER, John LaFarge, and Thomas Nast. HANS CHRISTIAN ANDERSEN published 17 stories in the magazine, ten of which had not been published elsewhere. Among Scudder's memorable innovations was an editorial column of reviews and comments on children's reading directed toward adults. Unhappy with the financial performance of their children's periodical, Hurd & Houghton sold it in 1870 to Scribner & Company, publishers of *Scribner's Monthly*. Though it had a short run of only four years, the *Riverside* set a new standard of literary and artistic excellence in the children's periodical and was a worthy predecessor of Scribner and Company's distinguished ST NICHOLAS MAGAZINE which commenced publication in 1873.

SRG

Roberts, Elizabeth Madox 1881–1941 American poet and novelist whose reputation as a children's writer rests on one book of poetry, *Under the Tree* (1922). Born in Perryville, Kentucky, Roberts spent most of her life in the town of Springfield, where her family moved when she was four. The second of eight children, her childhood was filled with hard work, although she found time to write, and she and her brothers and sisters entertained themselves by creating a FANTASY family. She finished high school, briefly attended the State College of Kentucky (now University of Kentucky) and became a teacher to support herself and her family. The quality of some privately printed poems brought her to the attention of an English professor at the University of Chicago, where she enrolled in 1917 at the age of 36, and she at last found encouragement and support for her writing. Her novels, especially *The Time of Man* (1926) and *The Great Meadow* (1930), were extremely successful. The poet DAVID MCCORD, writing on Roberts in *20th-Century Children's Writers* (1983), calls her 'absolutely unique in the field of verse for children' and 'the only poet . . . writing in the English language who possessed and consistently used the undisguised, uninterrupted voice of childhood'.

LH

Roberts, Sir Charles G(eorge) D(ouglas) 1860–1943 Canadian poet and novelist, born in New Brunswick. He wrote nearly 70 books, the most memorable being his realistic animal stories. As a boy, he often roamed in the Tantramar marshes near his home. There he gained expertise in exploring the wilds and a knowledgeable love of animals. He was educated at the University of New Brunswick and served as headmaster in Fredericton, before being appointed a professor at King's College in Windsor, Nova Scotia (1885). After ten years, he turned his attention to fulltime writing. The appearance of ERNEST THOMPSON SETON's *Animals I Have Known* (1898) gave Roberts the impetus to write his own animal stories, the most enduring of which are *The Kindred of the Wild* (1902), a collection of short stories, and *Red Fox* (1905). What separates Roberts and Seton from previous writers is that they do justice to their subjects' animal natures. Red Fox, though the hero, is still very much the fox, whose 'final triumph over the enemies of his kind' – notably man – ensures his freedom in the wilderness. Roberts lived in New York and England for a time and was knighted by George V in 1935.

KSB

see also ANIMALS IN CHILDREN'S FICTION

Robin Having launched EAGLE for boys in 1950 and GIRL in 1951, the Reverend Marcus Morris turned his attention to an untapped area, the younger children not yet ready for space heroes and schoolgirl pony riders. *Robin*, launched on 28 March 1953, ran for a total of 836 weekly issues, and is interesting in that it featured in comic strips several early characters from BBC children's TELEVISION. The front page hero was the puppet Andy Pandy, and inside were the infamous Flowerpot Men, Bill and Ben with Little Weed, much criticised for their unintelligible nonsense talk. Naturally, children loved them. *Robin Annual* was published every Christmas from 1954 to 1976, a run of 23 editions.

DG

see also ANNUALS

Robin Hood Eponymous outlaw hero of innumerable tales and legends set in medieval England. The origins of the Robin Hood legends are uncertain. Despite repeated attempts, no convincing links to an identifiable historical person have been made and, though the earliest surviving stories often localise the hero's exploits with points of specific detail, these are conflicting or contradictory. Although the earliest clear reference occurs around 1370, there are no extant manuscripts from before the end of the 15th century. In these early verse-narratives, the hero is clearly a yeoman; although he carries an embattled sense of social enmity (particularly for the clergy and local judiciary), he is not yet imbued with a mission to rob in order to give to the poor. Robin, at this stage, is more interested in retributive than distributive justice. The shift in his origins to the more romantic image of dispossessed nobleman, the association with nationalist sentiment and the social idealism inspired by his redistributing wealth are all later attributes accreted to this protean and potent legendary figure.

In the 15th century Robin Hood was absorbed into the May game festivities, and an important dimension of his appeal within the modes of play and performance was established. New characters – such as Maid Marion, originally linked to the queen of May – were added to the stories and Robin himself acquired a range of social identities, from outlawed earl to knockabout Jack-the-lad. The performance mode may have assisted the stories being developed in theatrical contexts from the 16th century onwards.

The stories continued to be popular throughout the 17th and 18th centuries, in performance modes, BALLADS and CHAPBOOKS. The first scholarly edition dedicated to the Robin Hood stories was Joseph Ritson's, published in 1795. Ritson, though validating the romantic image of Robin as rebel aristocrat, also gave the stories a politically radical inflection. This edition was the source for most versions of the legend in 19th-century novels. The most popular of these was

Pierce Egan the Younger's *Robin Hood and Little John: or the Merry Men of Sherwood Forest*, which was serialised from 1838 and published in book form in 1840. Egan's book influenced two novels by Alexandre Dumas, published in France in 1872/3, which appeared in English as *Robin Hood, Prince of Thieves* and *Robin Hood the Outlaw* in 1903 and became the source for a number of subsequent film versions.

Although novels based on the Robin Hood material have proliferated in the 20th century, these have rarely matched the quality or impact of the best film and TELEVISION versions. The stories had been popular in the United States from the 19th century and were taken up by Hollywood at an early stage in film production. The 1922 film *The Foresters*, starring Douglas Fairbanks, was a major artistic success. This was followed in 1938 by *The Adventures of Robin Hood*, starring Errol Flynn, regarded for many years as the definitive film version. The stories have provided material for many serious as well as parodic films and television series since. DWh

Robinson Crusoe (1719) Daniel Defoe's first book of fiction, one of the most popular ADVENTURE STORIES in world literature, which influenced the development of the realistic novel and has engendered innumerable abridgements, imitations and adaptations for children and adults. Defoe (1660?–1731), a prolific political journalist critical of society, travelled widely and wrote semi-fictional BIOGRAPHIES as first-person narratives. He heard accounts of Alexander Selkirk's experiences as a sailor left alone on the Island of Juan Fernandez from 1704 to 1709, and when Defoe was nearly 60 and in debt, he completed *The Life and Strange Surprising Adventures of Robinson Crusoe, of York, Mariner . . . Written by Himself*. Following the success of this story about Crusoe's 28 years stranded on a tropical island, W. Taylor of London immediately reprinted it and published Defoe's two less enduring sequels by 1720.

Unauthorised abridgements of the popular first book appeared immediately and continued to the 20th century. CHAPBOOK versions, beginning in the mid-18th century, concealed Defoe's authorship to perpetuate the illusion that Crusoe's story was true. Some were as short as eight pages, with woodcuts. Illustrated abridgements were marketed for children by NEWBERY and CARNAN from 1768, and their text and other versions were sold thereafter by other printers in hundreds of editions, making *Robinson Crusoe* one of the few fictional stories both available to poorer families and recommended for educated children before the mid-19th century. Later high-quality editions were illustrated by prominent artists such as GEORGE CRUIKSHANK, 'Phis' (H.K. Browne) and N.C. WYETH.

Among many writers who recorded the influence of *Robinson Crusoe* on young readers and praised its detailed portrayal of the isolated individual teaching himself how to survive in the wilderness, JEAN JACQUES ROUSSEAU was most influential. Ignoring the 'irrelevant' parts before Crusoe's shipwreck and after his rescue, Rousseau declared in *Émile* (1762) that Defoe's 'complete treatise on natural education' was the only book young boys needed, as imagining themselves in the heroic role of 'solitary adventurer' would instill an eagerness to learn everything useful. Moralists who opposed the castaway's freedom and individuality were overshadowed by generations of readers fascinated with the romance and realism in Crusoe's struggles against natural dangers, loneliness and cannibals. His painstaking efforts to make tools and clothes, build homes, grow food, domesticate animals and rule his self-made kingdom attract readers of all ages and social classes. Many accounts in fiction and non-fiction place *Robinson Crusoe* next to the Bible as a treasured book in households throughout the British Commonwealth. Since the late 18th century, the story has been adapted in drama, opera and poetry. Although Defoe's treatment of 'savages', especially Crusoe's servant Friday, has been questioned by postcolonial critics and 20th-century revisionists such as novelist Michel Tournier, Crusoe's discovery of a native's footprint in the sand after years of solitude is one of the most suspenseful, unforgettable moments in the history of fiction. The worldwide popularity and mythic proportions of this exotic island adventure led to a vast body of related literature called ROBINSONNADES.

TLH

Robinson, Charles 1870–1937 British illustrator. As the son and grandson of wood engravers and one of three gifted artist brothers, Charles Robinson was largely trained within his home and family workshop. In 1895 he illustrated AESOP's fables in a bold, Art Nouveau style, and in 1896 the first illustrated edition of STEVENSON'S *A CHILD'S GARDEN OF VERSES* was published and instantly made Robinson's name. Influenced by WALTER CRANE and William Morris, Robinson surrounds his beautiful children and babies with intricacy, swirling line, detailed borders and hand-written headings. Intertwining illustration and text, and attention to the design of the whole book, characterises all of Robinson's copious output, which consists mostly of FAIRY TALES and NURSERY RHYMES but also includes *ALICE'S ADVENTURES IN WONDERLAND* (LEWIS CARROLL, 1907), the first publication of *THE SECRET GARDEN* (F. HODGSON BURNETT, 1911) and *THE HAPPY PRINCE* (Oscar Wilde, 1913). JAG

see also WOOD ENGRAVING

Robinson, Ian see RUPERT BEAR

Robinson, Tony 1946– Major popular British contributor to children's entertainment through his writing, acting and presenting. Tony Robinson has championed quality children's TELEVISION for many years, believing that young viewers should be stimulated and challenged by the best available. He wrote *Maid Marian and her Merry Men* (1989) and starred in it as the Sheriff of Nottingham, a children's role-reversal comedy with Maid Marian as the leader of the Merry Men and ROBIN HOOD as a weak, fashion-conscious hippie. He has also co-written *Tales From Fat Tulip's Garden, Meet a Dog called Dorian*, and *Never Eat a Tortoise* (all 1985) with Debbie Gates and presented them on ITV for younger children.

Brought to fame largely through his role as *Baldrick* in the *Blackadder* comedy series (now on the INTERNET), Robinson has maintained his collaboration with its co-writer, Richard Curtis, in television adaptations of Greek myths (see CLASSICAL MYTHOLOGY) and Romano-British history, updated for 1990s children, including *The Odyssey* (1986–7), *Theseus: the King who killed the Minotaur* (1988) and *Boodicaa and the Romans* (1989). By creating a direct-to-camera STORYTELLING style, and using actual locations of the story, including the Holy Land in *Blood and Honey: The Story of Saul and David* (1993), Robinson has made traditional and historical characters seem modern and exciting. He is president of the Young Archaeologists' Society, presenting the popular *Time Team* archaeological series for Channel Four. He has made over 1,000 television appearances, and has received a number of accolades for his work, including the International Prix Jeunesse, a BAFTA and two Royal Television Society awards. SET

Robinson, W(illiam) Heath 1872–1944 British cartoonist, illustrator and author, famous for his improbably elaborate machines operated by earnest attendants, which manufacture bizarre products. Robinson thought the surreal humour of his 'contraptions' inappropriate for children who, he wrote, 'have very little humour of their own, but are very, very matter-of-fact little people'. His successful children's story, *Uncle Lubin* (1902), was attractively eccentric in its images and textual design. His illustrations for KINGSLEY'S *THE WATER BABIES* (1915), DE LA MARE'S *PEACOCK PIE* (1916) and several collections of traditional tales are fantastical and exciting. They have something in common with the work of Aubrey Beardsley and his own brother, CHARLES ROBINSON. The meticulous gadgetry he invented for Norman Hunter's *THE INCREDIBLE ADVENTURES OF PROFESSOR BRANESTAWM* (1933) seems driven by the same energy which typified his prolific work for adults. The anarchic humour of his art stood in marked contrast to his gentle reserve as a man. GPF

robinsonnade A story of struggle for survival in an isolated, unfamiliar environment, following the literary tradition established by *ROBINSON CRUSOE*. Soon after the 1719 publication of Defoe's popular novel, Crusoe's story began giving rise to innumerable ADVENTURE STORIES and has remained one of the richest sources of intertextuality in children's literature through the 20th century. For example, generations of children in Britain and America read *The Adventures of Philip Quarll* by Peter Longueville, issued in cheap editions by the late 18th century. Other robinsonnades, such as Joachim Campe's *Robinson der Jüngere* (1779), appeared throughout Europe and colonial regions, with translations and adaptations for children spreading their influence across cultures.

From Defoe's blend of travel literature, heroic quest, pastoral romance, spiritual autobiography and domestic realism, subsequent writers adapted the archetypal story to reflect changing ideologies. JOHANN WYSS'S *The Swiss Family Robinson*, Crusoe's most famous 19th-century descendants, establish a European colony on their island paradise with moral guidance from an authoritarian father. Adventure stories by R.L. STEVENSON, CAPTAIN MARRYAT, WILLIAM HENRY KINGSTON, James Fenimore Cooper and MAYNE REID integrated patriotic masculine virtues, exciting youthful escapades and detailed descriptions of exotic settings. R.M. BALLANTYNE wrote *The Dog Crusoe* (1861) after his very popular robinsonnade, *The Coral Island* (1858). William Golding transformed Ballantyne's protagonists into modern British schoolboys in *LORD OF THE FLIES* (1954), where island isolation produces depravity and violence. JULES VERNE combined robinsonnade and SCIENCE FICTION in *The Mysterious Island* (1874–5).

Survival in the wilderness has been a common theme of colonial children's books, such as CATHERINE PARR TRAILL'S *Canadian Crusoes* (1852), the first noteworthy Canadian children's novel, and IVAN SOUTHALL'S Australian robinsonnade, *To the Wild Sky* (1967). Some writers emphasise the influence of Defoe's novel on young characters adapting to new environments, ranging from an American pioneer farm in ELIZABETH SPEARE'S *The Sign of the Beaver* (1983) to an urban Holocaust hideaway in URI ORLEV'S *Island on Bird Street* (1984) and a new planet in *The Green Book* by JILL PATON WALSH (1982).

Modern castaways also include a doll family in *Floating Island* by Anne Parrish (1930), infants in *Baby Island* by CAROL RYRIE BRINK (1937), and an aristocratic mouse in *Abel's Island* by WILLIAM STEIG (1976). Unlike Robinson Crusoe, who reverts to the middle-class materialism and Christian orthodoxy of his parents, modern young Crusoes often shed traditional values when separated from their societies. A Native American girl in SCOTT O'DELL's *Island of the Blue Dolphins* (1961), and a white boy stranded with a black man in Theodore Taylor's *THE CAY* (1969), form new attitudes toward nature and human relations. Sometimes island isolation is voluntary, as in ARTHUR RANSOME's popular *SWALLOWS AND AMAZONS* (1930), about children vacationing on an English Lake District island. American adolescents in HARRY MAZER's *The Island Keeper* (1981) and GARY PAULSEN's *The Island* (1988) seek solitude to escape family problems. In other survival stories by Paulsen and JEAN CRAIGHEAD GEORGE, characters learn how to live from other animals, rather than attempting to bring civilisation to the wilderness. TLH

Rodda, Emily [Rowe, Jennifer June] 1948– Australian novelist, who writes adult murder mystery books under her real name. Previously editor of *The Australian Women's Weekly*, and a children's editor at Angus and Robertson, Rodda has written a large number of books for children of primary-school age. They include *Something Special* (1984), *Pigs Might Fly* (1986), *The Best Kept Secret* (1988) and *Finders Keepers* (1990), each of which won a CHILDREN'S BOOK COUNCIL OF AUSTRALIA Junior Book of the Year award. In these fantasies, Rodda explores the possibilities of other worlds with laws and dimensions of their own. Rodda is also the author of the popular mystery series *Teen Power Inc.* (1994), and *Deltora Quest* (2000), a serial novel published in eight parts, but it is arguably the *ROWAN OF RIN* series for which she is best known. Her innovative picturebook, *Power & Glory* (1994), is based on the format of an interactive computer game. *Bob the Builder and the Elves* (1998) illustrated by CRAIG SMITH, is a humorous tale of how a very ordinary, good-natured chap deals with an invasion of elves wanting to 'tidy up' his home and then him. Although each of Rodda's books is different, they all capture the imaginations of their readers by quickly bringing them into the world of the book, and making them a part of the challenges experienced by the characters. SAM

Rodgers, Mary see *FREAKY FRIDAY*; see also URSULA NORDSTROM

Rogers, Gregory 1957– Australian illustrator and designer, well-known for draughtsmanship, subtle use of colour and filmic techniques in his coloured pencil and painted illustrations. Already a prolific and lauded book-cover artist before he turned to PICTUREBOOK illustration, he has illustrated *Aunt Mary's Dead Goat* (1990), *The Postman's Race* (1991), *Lucy's Bay* (1992), *Tracks* (1992), *Running Away from Home* (1996) and *The Bent Back Bridge* (1996). Rogers, who describes himself as a 'visual author', is the first Australian to be awarded the KATE GREENAWAY MEDAL, for the elegant and compelling ILLUSTRATIONS of *WAY HOME* (1994). His illustrative style has developed from a workmanlike accompaniment to the print text, to a juxtaposition between visual and print texts of equal artistic status so that they seamlessly inform and extend each other. SNJ

see also COVER ART

Rogers, John see *NEW-ENGLAND PRIMER*

Rogers, Mr (Fred) 1928– American TELEVISION host for children. Creator, writer and producer of the popular *Mister Rogers' Neighborhood*, Fred Rogers came to children's television through his youth work as a minister for a Pennsylvania church. First produced in 1963, the show continues to appear in re-runs on many Canadian and American public television stations. Committed to the teaching of morals and manners along with other simple skills for the pre-school viewer – such as opposites, basic musical concepts and familiar job descriptions – Mr Rogers provides a gentler companion to the fast-paced, often adult wit of other children's television programmes such as *SESAME STREET* or *The Electric Company*. Rogers's multimedia approach is primitive, consisting of dressing up in costumes, playing simple instruments and presenting puppets – which, unlike *Sesame Street*'s MUPPETS, can never be imagined as real. However, his use of repetition and routine provide a safe and soothing environment for child viewers. This reputation for creating a calm setting, combined with his ministerial training in psychology, has allowed Rogers to branch out into other instructional media, a comforting presence for children who are experiencing new situations, such as a first visit to the hospital or the death of a family member. KS

Rojankovsky, Feodor (Stepanovich) [Rojan] 1891–1970 Russian artist and illustrator of over 100 children's books. Rojankovsky was born in Mitava, Russia, one of five children of a teacher who placed great value on education. Rojankovsky studied at the Moscow Fine Arts Academy, served in the Russian Imperial Army, and worked as an illustrator, art director and stage decorator. Moving to Paris in the 1920s, he began working for Esther Averill and Lila Stanley at the Domino Press. His *DANIEL BOONE* (1931), published in both French and English, was, as Barbara Bader writes in *American Picturebooks from Noah's Ark to the Beast Within*, 'a uniquely daring book' with its vivid colours and sure sense of design. In 1941, after the German occupation of Paris, Rojankovsky emigrated to the United States where he illustrated the classic *Tall Book*

'Jonas, I have found a hollow stump here.' Illustration by an unknown artist from *Rollo's Philosophy* by Jacob Abbott.

of Mother Goose (1942) and many other books in association with Georges Duplaix and the Artists and Writers Guild and LITTLE GOLDEN BOOKS. Bader calls *The Three Bears* (1948), with its impish Goldilocks and 'dark, hulking . . . distinctly Russian' bears, Rojankovsky's 'dramatic opus'. However, it was the ILLUSTRATIONS for John Langstaff's *Froggy Went A-Courtin'* (1955), with their rhythmic procession of animals and insects attending the wedding reception of Frog and Miss Mouse, that won him the CALDECOTT MEDAL. LH

Rollins, Charlemae 1897–1979 American children's librarian, author, lecturer and storyteller. Born in Misssissipi, Rollins lived most of her childhood in Oklahoma with her grandmother, a former slave, who inspired her love of reading. Educated at the University of Chicago and Columbia University, she served for 36 years as a librarian in the Chicago Public Library, the George Cleveland Hall branch. Her bibliography, *We Build Together: A Reader's Guide to Negro Life and Literature for Elementary and High School Use* (1938, revised 1948, 1967) raised awareness of the need for quality literature for children and youth that presented positive images of the black experience. Rollins wrote several books for children: *Christmas Gift* (1963), an anthology of poems, songs and stories; *They Showed the Way: Forty American Negro Leaders* (1964); *Famous Negro Entertainers of Stage, Screen and TV* (1967) and *Black Troubador, Langston Hughes* (1971). She was active on the national level in both the National Council of Teachers of English and the ALA. Rollins lectured and started a children's book collection at Roosevelt University in Chicago. Her many honours recognise her leadership in promoting black heritage in children's books and as a role model for librarians like AUGUSTA BAKER. AL

see also LIBRARIES

***Rollo* books** (1835–64) Series of 28 stories by Jacob Abbott. Related books include collections of tales and poetry published under the *Rollo* name and spin-off series about Rollo's cousin Lucy and the hired boy Jonas. Unabashedly didactic, the books reflect the concerns of their author, a New England educator and Congregationalist minister. They also contain amusing and realistic scenes of child life. Forming the first significant children's series in America, the books develop in difficulty and sophistication as Rollo matures. *Rollo Learning to Talk* is a PICTUREBOOK for the three-year-old Rollo. *Rollo Learning to Read* includes stories for and about the five-year-old Rollo as well as instruction in reading. Subsequent books provide episodic narratives about Rollo's daily activities at work, at school and at play, all stressing moral development. Four *Rollo's Philosophy* books emphasise intellectual growth in natural philosophy and science. The ten books comprising the *Rollo's Tour of Europe* series show the 12-year-old Rollo making his own travel arrangements through Europe, caring for his sister, and resisting adult temptations like gambling. The sympathetic narrator, gentle humour and earnest, inquisitive Rollo made the series enormously popular in the 19th century, though it has been largely forgotten since. JLB

Roman mythology see CLASSICAL MYTHOLOGY

***Romney Marsh* series** The 15 books in the series by Monica Edwards (1912–98) cover five years in the eventful lives of Tamzin Grey and her friends on the Romney Marsh. Like the *PUNCHBOWL FARM* series, these books are anchored in real-life experiences which do not appear dated, yet surprisingly, they are now out of print. There is a wider landscape of sea, sky and marsh than in the *Punchbowl* books, and a wider community of farming and fishing characters, like the old ferryman Jim Decks, who is not quite as loveable a rogue as he was intended to be. The first in the series, *Wish for a Pony* (1947), written when Edwards's children requested a pony book without gymkhanas, is a superior version of the formula PONY STORY and remained the most popular of her books. The next, *The Summer of the Great Secret* (1948), a smuggling tale, set the tone for a series of exciting if not wholly credible adventures involving horses bound for slaughter, foot and mouth disease, oiled birds, and a holiday camp development. Ringleader is Tamzin, romantic, loyal and quixotic, whose relationships with her friends Rissa, Meryon and Roger is strongly developed throughout the series. Tamzin's growing closeness to Meryon is treated gingerly – hardly surprising as Tamzin is 14 to Meryon's 17 – but the effect on the four-way friendship is sensitively handled. In the final book, *A Wind is Blowing* (1969), a melodramatic tale in which Meryon is blinded, the relationship is central. ARH

***Rootabaga Stories* series** (1922–93) Literary FAIRY TALES by the American author CARL SANDBURG, which earned him a reputation as a midwestern HANS CHRISTIAN ANDERSEN. The four volumes of this series, *Rootabaga Stories* (1922), *Rootabaga Pigeons* (1923), *Potato Face* (1930) and *More Rootabagas* (1993), were written as bedtime stories for Sandburg's daughters, Margaret and Janet, who are called Spink and Skabooth in the stories. These distinctively American literary FOLKTALES are deeply rooted in the geography, folkways and language of the American Midwest. Sandburg explained, 'I sought the American equivalent of princes and princesses and I sought the American equivalent of elves and gnomes.' The stories are influenced as much by Sandburg's knowledge of the American TALL TALE folk song tradition as his imitation of European fairy tales. His attempt to Americanise fairy tales resembles that of L. FRANK BAUM's *Wizard of Oz* (1900) (see OZ SERIES), although Sandburg's stories are much more poetic, suggest his ear for language, and are much less plot-driven than Baum's FANTASIES. The most successful of Sandburg's fairy tales is 'How to Tell Corn Fairies If you See 'Em', in which hard-working, overall-wearing corn fairies are shown to be responsible for the well-being of the great corn-fields that dot the Midwestern landscape. JCS

Roscoe, William see *BUTTERFLY'S BALL, THE*; JOHN HARRIS

Rose and the Ring, The (1853) Book-length FAIRY STORY by 'Mr. M.A. (Michelangelo) Titmarsh' (W.M. Thackeray's pseudonym), written for his children. The mode of the story is comic and slapstick, tracing the adventures of Prince Giglio, who has been deposed by his uncle, Prince Bulbo, and the Princesses Rosalba and Angelica. The rose and the ring, magical tokens given by the fairy Blackstick which cause people to fall in love with their possessors, act as the catalysts which bring these characters together in a series of (mis)adventures. SA

Rose Blanche see ROBERTO INNOCENTO; MCEWAN, IAN; see also HISTORICAL FICTION

Rose, Gerald 1935– British picturebook author. Both a graduate of and a teacher at a number of art schools, Rose created his first PICTUREBOOK, *How St. Francis Tamed the Wolf*, with his wife Elizabeth in 1958. *Old Winkle and the Seagulls* followed, winning the KATE GREENAWAY AWARD in 1960. *Trouble in the Ark* (1975), *Ahhh said Stork* (1978) and several other titles are still popular with children for their verbal and visual jokes, bright, solid colours and child-like drawing. JAG

Rose, Jacqueline see CRITICAL APPROACHES TO CHILDREN'S BOOKS

Rosen, Michael (Wayne) 1946– British writer, performer and broadcaster, best known for his contibution to children's poetry. Rosen enjoyed a stimulating, secure childhood in Harrow, London, with his elder brother, Brian, and his parents, Connie and Harold Rosen, repected figures in the field of education, all of whom feature in his poems. After a brief spell as a medical student, Rosen graduated with an English degree from Oxford University in 1969.

Rosen began writing for children in the early 1970s. Connie Rosen compiled poetry programmes for schools radio and her son was encouraged to contribute. His first collection of poems, *MIND YOUR OWN BUSINESS* (1974), illustrated by QUENTIN BLAKE, established Rosen as a new and influential voice. This was the first in a series of collaborations with Blake, which produced over the next decade collections with similarly irreverent titles, such as *Wouldn't You Like to Know* (1977), *You Can't Catch Me!* (1981), which won the *SIGNAL* Poetry Award, *Smelly Jelly Smelly Fish* (1986), *Hard-Boiled Legs* (1987) and *Spollyollydiddlytiddlyitis* (1987). In these poems Rosen, for the first time in children's poetry, tried to write not just from the point of view of the child, but in the voice of the child, using the speech rhythms and thought-patterns of the contemporary urban child, usually a boy. At his best, Rosen is able to combine the patterning of poetry with the seemingly artless patter of talk, to produce what he calls, after W.H. Auden, 'memorable speech'. His poems are usually anecdotal, drawing with humour and irony on his childhood experiences and, later, on those of his own children. Rosen's range of moods and styles is larger than he is given credit for by detractors. His poems also deal with sensitive issues, such as the anti-semitism he experienced, and his wider concern for social justice. He uses free verse, one of the first children's poets to do so, but also rhyming formats, including NONSENSE POETRY. Rosen has continued to publish poetry prolifically, working with other illustrators to present his poems in typographically inventive ways, and striving to reproduce his hilarious performances, as with *When Did You Last Wash Your Feet?* (1986) and *Mind the Gap* (1992). He has also edited numerous wide-ranging anthologies.

Rosen has published fiction for children since 1976, in the form of short stories, novels and PICTUREBOOKS for ages ranging from pre-school to teenage. He has a particular interest in FOLKTALES from different traditions, sometimes retelling them, as in *Till Owlyglass* (1989), and sometimes parodying them, as with *Hairy Tales and Nursery Crimes* (1985). His fiction shows the same exuberance, delight in playing with language and love of STORYTELLING as his poems. Rosen has been a regular broadcaster on radio and TELEVISION, being involved in writing and presenting educational programmes, and also presenting for BBC radio *Word of Mouth* and the children's book programme, *Treasure Islands*. His influential book on children's writing, *Did I Hear You Write?* (1989), illustrates how children can find their own voice as writers by following his method of 'oral writing' based on everyday experiences. ML

Rosenbach Museum and Library see COLLECTIONS OF CHILDREN'S BOOKS; see also A.S.W. ROSENBACH

Rosenbach, A(braham) S(imon) W(olf) 1876–1952 American rare-book dealer and children's-book collector. Rosenbach, who gained a PhD in literature from the University of Pennsylvania, was one of the most important book dealers of this century, helping to build the collections of the Huntington, Folger, Houghton, Widener and Morgan libraries. Flamboyant and adept at securing the most dramatic of sales, he brought great attention to the book trade. Adding to the volumes he inherited from his uncle, he collected early American children's books. He twice bought the manuscript for LEWIS CARROLL'S *ALICE'S ADVENTURES UNDER GROUND*, once for a collector and the second time when a fund drive returned it to the British Museum. His reminiscences can be read in *Books and Bidders* (1927) and *Early American Children's Books* (1933). His collection of 800 American children's books from 1682 to 1836 was donated to the Free Library of Philadelphia where it formed the core of their collection of rare children's books. Other significant books and manuscripts including the works of Marianne Moore, MAURICE SENDAK, and the manuscript for James Joyce's *Ulysses* are housed at the last residence of Dr Rosenbach and his brother, now the Philip and A.S.W. Rosenbach Museum and Library, in Philadelphia. GRB

Rosie's Walk (1968) PICTUREBOOK by the British author-illustrator PAT HUTCHINS, a modern classic with a 32-word text, constructed to emphasise dimensional prepositions, about Rosie the hen going for a walk across a farmyard. The illustrations show that Rosie is followed by a fox which makes bungled attempts to catch her. Neither Rosie nor the narrator registers him, or her narrow escapes. However, the beholder sees and knows all. But does the narrator in fact know about the fox? Is the narrator colluding with, or teasing, the beholder? Comedy, irony, visual literacy and language development are shaped for a very young child. The insouciant, folk-art style illustrations, are flat, decorative and bold in effect. JD

Ross, Charles see COMICS, PERIODICALS AND MAGAZINES

Ross, Diana 1910–2000 British writer and illustrator, born in Malta. Many of Ross's stories were broadcast on the BBC's *Children's Hour* and *LISTEN WITH MOTHER*, and she also wrote scripts for the *Camberwick Green* television series. However, she is best known for *Whoo, Whoo, the Wind Blew* (1946), and for her *Little Red Engine* series, the first of which – *The Little Red Engine Gets a Name*, illustrated in brilliant colour by the Polish expatriates George Him and Jan Lewitt – was published in 1942. There were many equally successful sequels, mostly illustrated by LESLIE WOOD. VW

Ross, Tony 1938– British author who has created PICTUREBOOKS with universal appeal, and illustrated juvenile fiction in Britain, France and the United States. His most popular works include the *DR XARGLE* series, the *Towser* series, which has also appeared as a short film, and Ross's humorous updating of classic FAIRY STORIES. JD

see also *I WANT MY POTTY*

Rossetti, Christina 1830–94 English writer, now regarded as one of the finest poets of the Victorian period. The particular blend of apparently artless passion, simplicity and religious fervour which gave her work its originality also marginalised it from serious literary regard for a long time. Her one glorious collection specifically for children, *SING-SONG: A NURSERY RHYME BOOK* (1872), has been reprinted only a handful of times, though individual poems from it are regularly anthologised ('Who has seen the wind?',

'What is pink?', 'A rose has thorns as well as honey', 'Mix a pancake'). *Goblin Market* (1862), full of probably unconscious sexual imagery, was never meant for children, but has regularly been in print since its publication, with many editions tailored to a young audience. MCCS

Roughsey, Dick see Percy Trezise; Aboriginal culture; picturebooks

Round the Twist (1989, 1992) Two 13-part television series based on Paul Jennings' short stories, adapted for the screen by Jennings and Ebsen Storm, and produced by the Australian Children's Television Foundation. The internationally award-winning programme resituates Jennings' bizarre tales in the lighthouse home of the Twist family, and has been shown in over 40 countries. The book of the same title, which includes stories, scripts, actor interviews and author anecdotes, was published in conjunction with the first series. This book was highly successful, but a graphic novel of the second series, with comic-strip images by Glenn Lumsden and David de Vries, was poorly received. NLR

Rounds, Glen 1906– An author and illustrator best known for books depicting the scruffy landscapes, animals and people of the American West. A genuine westerner and teller of tall tales, his first book, *Ol' Paul, the Mighty Logger* (1936), remains one of the most hilarious and popular of all Paul Bunyan collections. Several of his best-known illustrated books feature a nine-year-old cowboy named Whitey. In such books as *Whitey's First Round-Up* (1942) and *Whitey Takes a Trip* (1954), Rounds tells stories that are easy to read but do not seem to be aimed at children in particular. *The Blind Colt* (1941), an enduring classic, presents in realistic detail a wild and difficult terrain as filtered through the perceptions of a sightless young horse. Throughout his long career, his lines, whether drawn or written, are distinguished by their vernacular vivacity. JS

Rountree, Harry see *Little Folks*

Rousseau, Jean Jacques 1712–78 French philosopher and novelist whose work influenced Romanticism. Rousseau's writing stresses the importance of natural feelings: the recovery of authenticity – in a sophisticated society where individuals learn to repress their instinctual selves and become habituated to inequality – is the foundation of freedom, virtue and happiness. Rousseau explored these ideas in relation to children's development in *Émile or On Education* (1762), which describes an imaginary attempt to bring up a young boy – and girl – uncorrupted by society. Rousseau's ideas dismayed many educators towards the end of the 18th century, but inspired a number of others, perhaps most directly Maria Edgeworth and Thomas Day. DWh

Rover Boys at School, The see school stories

Rover Boys see Edward Stratemeyer; Stratemeyer Syndicate

Rover see *'The Big Five'*

***Rowan of Rin* series** (1993–9) Four science fiction novels by the Australian writer, Emily Rodda. *Rowan of Rin* (1993), the first book, begins with a prophecy from the witch Sheba, which foretells disaster for the mountain village of Rin and its inhabitants. Throughout the course of the novel, readers are challenged to try to solve the riddle, along with a young boy, Rowan, on whom falls the task to unravel the mystery, to save his home and his people from destruction. *Rowan and the Travellers* (1996), *Rowan and the Keeper of the Crystal* (1996) and *Rowan and the Zebak* (1999) present further problems to solve, as Rowan faces more dangers in his bid to save his village. SAM

Rowland, Pleasant see *American Girls Collection* series

Rowling, J.K. see Harry Potter

Roy of the Rovers see annuals

Roy, Atanu 1950– Indian illustrator, artist, cartoonist and designer. Spurred by a love of designing and illustrating books for children, Roy has illustrated more than 100 books for children and was the Children's Choice Illustrator of the Year in 1992. He has also won awards at the 1983, 1984 and 1986 Yomiuri Shimbun International Cartoon Contests and is one of the few Indian artists who have contributed to Bob Geldof's book of cartoons, *Cartoonaid*, released at the Seoul Olympics. He worked as an independent art director in Tokyo and subsequently as a freelance designer and artist. His illustrations for children are characterised by the elements of humour, high drama, vivid colours and a heavy emphasis on animation. *Kaju and the Shoe* (1990), which won him the CBT award in 1990, exhibits remarkable delineation of form and a brilliant use of tones that amplify his belief that 'an illustration doesn't just have to interpret, it should stand out on its own and complement the text, so what emerges is a holistic job'. When illustrating for children his effort is to create individual styles for the books

Illustration by Atanu Roy from *Tails* by Hydrose Aaluwa.

according to the age groups and visual literacy of the children. MBh

Roy, Jacqueline see MULTICULTURAL BOOKS

royal gift books Handsomely bound, lavishly illustrated and sold for charity, royal gift books first appeared in the Edwardian era, an early example being *The Queen's Carol*, published in 1905 by the *Daily Mail* to aid the Royal Fund for the Unemployed. It featured work contributed by famous writers, among them Bram Stoker and Algernon Swinburne, and such artists and composers as Sir Lawrence Alma-Tadema and Edward Elgar. It also included a polemical story by Lucy Lane Clifford, author of the memorable children's horror-fantasy, *The New Mother*. 1908 saw *Queen Alexandra's Christmas Gift Book*, an album of Her Majesty's own sublimely dull photographs, published by the *Daily Telegraph*, which also brought out *King Albert's Book* in 1914 to raise money for its Belgian Fund. This 'tribute' to the Belgian people incorporated much opportunistic anti-German propaganda. In the same year Hodder and Stoughton published *Princess Mary's Gift Book*, on behalf of the Queen's 'Work for Women' Fund, possibly the most popular gift book of all, since copies are still relatively easy to find. Original and reprinted texts were contributed by great names of the day, artwork was commissioned especially and there was a noticeable intent to appeal to children as well as adults. *The Princess Elizabeth Gift Book* (1935), entirely child-oriented, included WALT DISNEY illustrations and a *RUPERT BEAR* story. The princess was the present Queen, then aged nine. In 1939, upon the outbreak of World War II, *The Queen's Book of the Red Cross* appeared, the last of its kind. JMM

Rubinstein, Gillian 1942– Australian writer of children's and young adult novels, as well as PICTURE-BOOK scripts. Born in Britain, Rubinstein worked as an editor, freelance journalist and film critic before marrying and emigrating to Australia in 1973. Since the publication of her first, award-winning children's book, *SPACE DEMONS* (1986), Rubinstein has been a high-profile and respected writer – partly because of the undisputed quality of her work, and partly because of the themes she explores. Rubinstein has said that 'children are not seeking escapism or consolation as much as they used to . . . perhaps they no longer believe that consolation is possible. Instead they want to be told the truth and how it really is and that makes them feel strong.'

Her SCIENCE FICTION and FANTASY novels reflect this viewpoint, blending fantasy with a 'real life' in which the protagonists come of age in a dangerous world, burdened by personal anxieties and the threat of nuclear or environmental devastation, and largely unassisted by adults, who are depicted as incompetent, indifferent or cruel. At the same time, the books are often didactic: her characters learn to face facts and fears, and to stand up for themselves. *Beyond the Labyrinth* (1988) received many awards but was controversial in Australia, in part because of its world view, but especially due to the use of swearwords. Brenton (14) is obsessed with the possibility of nuclear annihilation and escapes his fears and uncaring family through role-playing games. In the finale, the reader must roll dice to choose between two endings – one in which Brenton escapes Earth with an alien, and one in which he chooses to stay.

Such toying with genre – in this case, choose-your-own-adventure books – is characteristic of Rubinstein. In *Galax-Arena* (1992) she interrogates the truth (or otherwise) of 'science' in science fiction. In its grim, dog-eat-dog scenario, children are kidnapped – apparently to another planet – to perform in a dangerous circus, where their deaths stimulate the audience. Rubinstein frequently experiments with language, especially dialogue – inventing a pidgin dialect for *Galax-Arena*, 'powerful' chants in *AT ARDILLA*, a partially onomatopoeic fox language in *FOXSPELL*, and a comical cat-speak in the junior novel *Jake and Pete* (1995).

Her early short novels were *Answers to Brut* (1988) and *Melanie and the Night Animal* (1988), both serious works compared to her later junior fiction, which includes the humorous adventures *Flashback, the Amazing Adventures of a Film Horse* (1990), *Squawk and Screech* (1991), *The Giant's Tooth* (1993) and *The Mermaid of Bondi Beach* (1999), a light tale underpinned by a poignant theme of loneliness. Rubinstein has also written several PICTUREBOOK scripts, the most successful of which is perhaps the wordplay *Dog In, Cat Out* (1991), illustrated by ANN JAMES. This book uses only four words – dog, cat, in, out – in varying order, while the images trace the day of a suburban family and their pets. Her other picturebooks include *Keep Me Company* (1992), illustrated by Lorraine Hannay; *Mr Plunkett's Pool* (1992) and *Ducky's Nest* (1999), both illustrated by TERRY DENTON; and the rap poem *Sharon, Keep Your Hair On* (1996) and *Hooray for the Kafe Karaoke!* (1998), both illustrated by David Mackintosh. NLR

Rudhraigheacht see IRISH MYTHOLOGY AND FOLKLORE

'Rumplestiltskin' see GRIMM BROTHERS; see also DRAMA FOR CHILDREN; ENGLISH FOLKTALES; MARIE-LOUISE GAY; *READING RAINBOW*; PAUL ZELINSKY

Runaway Settlers, The (1965) Novel by New Zealand writer ELSIE LOCKE, which established a New Zealand benchmark for high-quality children's HISTORICAL FICTION. Meticulously researched, engagingly written, and successfully bridging the gap between the past and the present, the novel follows the fortunes of the courageous and historically real Small family, as they escape an abusive father and husband in Australia, change their names and make a place for themselves in Governors Bay near Christchurch. BN

running story Minor characters in PICTUREBOOK illustrations, who appear throughout the sequence of pictures and who have a life of their own which flourishes independently alongside that of the main characters. The running story is never referred to in the text. Many examples are to be found in the work of DAVID MCKEE. JD

Rupert and the Frog Song Musical cartoon composed and produced by Paul McCartney, issued as a video in 1985 and in 1986 as a *Ladybird* book, winner of the BAFTA Award for Best Animated Film. The title of the story derives from one of Alfred Bestall's best-known ILLUSTRATIONS, the ENDPAPER design for the 1958 Daily Express *RUPERT* Annual. VW

Rupert Bear Popular British character who first appeared in the *Daily Express* on 8 November 1920, in a story written and drawn by Mary Tourtel. Rupert ANNUALS under various titles have been issued every year since 1936, other Rupert stories have been published by a variety of authors and illustrators in different series-formats, and video-stories are now also available.

Rupert Bear is unique in children's literature. No other series of stories has so successfully appealed both to adults and to children, or remains vigorously imaginative after 80 years. Rupert belongs to popular culture; until the mid-80s his creators were largely unknown, and yet his main illustrator, Alfred Bestall, was a great artist in the tradition of SHEPARD, ARDIZZONE and CALDECOTT. Although Rupert rarely figures in courses on children's literature, the *Annuals* reach thousands of homes every Christmas. Furthermore, Bestall's early *Annuals* are bought and sold by collectors for large sums of money, and the early *Annuals* have been re-issued in facsimile (purged of racial stereotypes). Because new Rupert stories are continually being told, the imaginative landscape and characters associated with his world have grown slowly into what amounts to a powerful and benevolent mythology of innocence and play.

Rupert Bear is not exactly a syndicated property, but he has been associated with several writers and illustrators. The first was Mary Tourtel, whose stories ran daily in the *Daily Express* from 1920 until 1935. Tourtel's rhymed stories in the *Express* were part of a circulation war with TEDDY TAIL in the *Daily Mail* and PIP AND SQUEAK in the *Daily Mirror*. They were really FAIRY STORIES in which Rupert was caught up in magic, witchcraft and wickedness in a medieval setting. Nobody seems to have minded that her verses were dreadful, perhaps because the ILLUSTRATIONS were evocative, clear line-drawings suggesting a tiny faraway world of woods, castles and secret doorways. Tourtel invented many of the other characters, and she established forever Rupert's dress – check trousers with matching scarf, and woolly jumper. When her stories were issued as storybooks, Rupert's jumper was sometimes tinted salmon pink or blue. Later it became established as red. Rupert himself in those early stories was a rather stumpy bear, long-snouted and hairy – in some illustrations a slightly alarming character.

In 1935 failing eyesight compelled Tourtel to give up drawing, and Alfred Bestall took over. His appointment arose amid some confusion: he agreed to provide a present-tense summary in prose of the story-line for editorial approval and was surprised when his summary appeared in the *Express* as the story itself – so establishing the tradition that Rupert stories are told in the present tense. For the next 30 years Bestall provided both the stories and the illustrations. In 1936 the newspaper editor decided to produce an annual totally devoted to Rupert; it was called *The New Adventures of Rupert* and was a large, handsome volume with a dust jacket, printed in black and tinted in salmon pink. The title probably referred to Bestall, the *new* writer/illustrator, but may also have served to distinguish the new publication from the Rupert stories which continued to appear from 1936 to 1939 in the annual *Boys' and Girls' Book*, another *Daily Express* publication.

It was mainly through the long tradition of annuals that Rupert has entered the culture and consciousness of the country, partly because they reached a wider readership and partly because there are greater imaginative possibilities within a large-format book than in a small daily strip. Mary Tourtel had written stories about Rupert; Bestall developed a mythology. From Bestall's first annual in 1936, Rupert began to change slowly: he became a little taller and less hairy, but the illustrator's greatest achievement was in the little bear's face, suggestive of cheerfulness, curiosity, and a well-intentioned, incorruptible innocence. Bestall's Rupert is simultaneously a little bear and a little boy, and combines two almost impossible ideals: a child's ideal of perfect freedom in an expanding but ultimately safe imaginative world, and an adult's ideal of perfect child-behaviour. Rupert is to children what they would like to be, and to parents what they would like their children to become. And the setting appeals strongly to a national pastoral nostalgia: Nutwood is where we would like our children to spend their childhood, endlessly adventuring yet ultimately safe.

The 1940 annual was the first to be printed in full colour. Although the printing was coarse and grainy, the rich colouring transformed Bestall's line drawings. In 1942 the annuals went into paperback because of wartime restrictions, but the quality of the colouring and printing began to improve. It is these paperbacks, from 1942 to 1949, that are most prized by collectors. Bestall's early stories had been rather rambling and shapeless – probably because they were composed with a daily newspaper deadline – but now they became both more imaginative and more controlled, while his sparser drawing, especially when coloured for the annuals, allowed some delicate landscaping. Each illustration was contained within an almost square frame, and, although he occasionally varied the size and proportions, Bestall mainly achieved variety through a range of close-ups, long-shots and panoramas, often composing a picture from an exciting and unusual perspective. The work of the colourists – mostly Doris Campbell – was invaluable in giving texture and depth to a winter snowscape with a fading sunset behind silhouetted trees, or a violent storm at sea, or the menacing shadows of an underground tunnel.

The Bestall annuals all have certain features: they are literally 'MULTILAYERED', with a summary at the top of the page ('Rupert follows the Imp'), the story in four frames, another version in rhyme, and the longer prose telling at the bottom. Two figures from the story are reproduced in miniature at the top of each page; there are puzzles, games and painting pages; and the stories are sequenced in a roughly seasonal pattern, probably a hangover from the *Daily Express Boys' and Girls' Books*, some of which were divided into 12 monthly sections, each with a short single-page *Rupert* story. When the annuals returned to hardback in 1950, Bestall designed an ENDPAPER for each issue, and these too became an obligatory feature. One of them was the inspiration for Paul McCartney's animated cartoon, *RUPERT AND THE FROG SONG*.

Until 1973, the annuals were composed exclusively of Bestall's work. For almost 40 years (anonymously at first), this unknown and unpretentious man enriched the culture of infancy by evolving an extended and extending imaginative world for very young children. And this tradition has been sustained. There were unacceptable race stereotypes in some illustrations, but these have now disappeared. Many of the annuals' characteristics are unashamedly bizarre: the setting suggests rural England between the wars, but with figures from the past or from fairy tales; anthropomorphic animals share adventures with girl guides, postmen and sailors; and many of the tales have deliberately antiquated SCIENCE FICTION features. Journeying provides the structure and the imagery for most of the stories, with Rupert setting out from home at the start and returning safely at the end. His travels may take him all over the world (or even straight through the middle of it), to barren deserts, impenetrable jungles and icy polar wastes. They may take him underground, or to London to see the coronation of the Queen, or back into history. Most frequently of all, they take him into the air – in the claws of a gigantic bird, or by means of a kite, Santa's sledge, a magic flying bicycle, a hot-air balloon, and every conceivable kind of aeroplane. Often, it is enough for Rupert to explore the region around Nutwood, with its forests, wilderness, old castle, village shops and school. Each storyline provides an imaginative space for the versatility of the illustrator, the flying pictures in particular making possible some extraordinary panoramas of mountaintops, cloudscapes and distant horizons. Rupert rarely encounters villainy; mostly, something has just gone wrong – one of the Imps of Spring active in the wrong season, robins who have lost their red breasts, crows scared white by an unfamiliar sight. For very young children, Rupert's face is probably at the centre of their reading, teaching them the appropriate responses and registering the recognisable feelings of ideal childhood. He is often worried, rarely afraid, and only once or twice is he shown crying. He is never deliberately naughty, though he does occasionally get into scrapes. His narratives – journeying outwards towards the horizon and always returning home in time for supper – enact the possibilities of play-and-pretend.

It was difficult to find illustrators to follow in the tradition of Bestall. After 1974, different illustrators were tried, among them Alex Cubie, whose work had much of the vitality of comic strip but was startlingly unlike Bestall's delicate pastoral draughtsmanship. There was a period of uncertainty. In 1985 there was a celebration of the 50th anniversary of the annuals and Rupert Bear became self-conscious. There were articles in magazines about his long-standing cultural significance, and George Perry published *A Bear's Life: Rupert* (1985). In the annuals themselves, there were indications that the editorial staff were becoming more 'bookish'. Bestall, in the spirit of popular journalism, had been anonymous for most of his life, but now Rupert's authors, illustrators, colourists and editors were properly acknowledged. For a time it seemed that the annuals were doomed always to conform to the rigid and unchanging traditionalism of adult collectors and the 'Followers of Rupert', and this would surely have led to a slow death. A failure to acknowledge the needs of Rupert's *young* readers would have destroyed in time the basis of his popularity.

Outwardly, there have been no changes: the arrangement of the annuals, and the layout of each page, remain as they were 40 years ago. The traditionalists seem to have won. But this outward conformity is a counterfeit covering all manner of postmodernist transgressions for today's young readers. For a time the stories were provided by John Henderson; then Ian Robinson became editor and story-writer. These two writers' work brought into the Rupert canon subversive stories-about-stories involving intertextuality, humour and irony. Rupert has passed through an ancient tapestry to visit Tudor England; found some modern-day travellers from Lilliput trying to hijack a long-lost model railway set; and in one extraordinary story he goes back in time, helps Dr Watson capture a thief, is congratulated by Sherlock Holmes, and consults H. G. Wells for help getting home in his time-machine. One new character is the Sage of Um, a brilliantly conceived comic magician in a nightgown, nightcap and pointed slippers, who lives on the Island of Um and travels the world in his inverted Brella. In some of the stories there is hostage-taking, kidnapping, or threatened violence, but the magical air of innocence and security is sustained. Robinson's narratives are outstanding, and the work of the current illustrator, John Harrold (with the help of Gina Hart as colourist), is indistinguishable from Bestall's, and yet it is more than pastiche. Like his predecessor, he understands that the secret of Rupert's lasting appeal is in the varieties of expression in the Little Bear's face, with its trusting expectation of some new revelation in a good world.

Rupert Bear is particularly important because of his unprecented durability and because his narratives combine innovativeness with a surface conservatism. He is perhaps the best-known fictional figure in a genuine popular culture of the young, and yet his survival is sustained by an adult cult following. His future remains uncertain but, at least for the time being, the tension between the pressures for an unchanging fidelity to the tradition, and the need to cater for new young readers in a changing culture, has resulted in a fresh creativity in the Rupert stories. VW

Rushdie, Salman see *HAROUN AND THE SEA OF STORIES*

Rusher, J(ohn) (Golby) 1784–1877 British CHAPBOOK printer. Mayor of Banbury, Oxfordshire, in 1834, and the most successful member of a family of provincial printers and booksellers. His renowned *English Spelling Book* and his series of one penny and halfpenny chapbooks for children, which were informative and charmingly illustrated, proved very popular. Some titles, *Poetic Trifles for Young Gentlemen and Ladies* and *Nursery Rhymes from the Royal Collections*, were cheap and innovative miniature collections of NURSERY RHYMES. Several chapbook stories had local associations: *The History of a Banbury Cake* described a cake's experiences with a family in Oxford until it was eaten. SD

Ruskin, John see *THE KING OF THE GOLDEN RIVER*; see also GEORGE CRUIKSHANK; RICHARD DOYLE; FAIRY FANTASY; KATE GREENAWAY

Russell Clark Award see APPENDIX

She went to the fishmonger's
To buy him some fish;
When she came back,
He was licking the dish.

She went to the ale-house
To buy him some beer;
And when she came back,
He sat in a chair.

From J.G. Rusher's chapbook, *Old Mother Hubbard and Her Dog.*

Rwakasisi, Rose Ugandan author of children's books mainly written to improve children's English, reading and comprehension skills, and to teach young readers about their cultural heritage. Her first book, *How Friends Became Enemies* (1994), is about the Leopard and the Hare, whose friendship breaks up because the Hare cheats. Her second, *The Old Woman and the Shell* (1996), is about an old poor woman who uncovers a shell in her garden with which she becomes wealthy – and will remain so as long as she does not divulge the source of the wealth. Inevitably, she fails this test of confidentiality and the wealth disappears. Both books are for younger children. ABO

Ryan, John see CAPTAIN PUGWASH SERIES; *EAGLE*; *SWIFT*

Rylant, Cynthia 1954– American writer, public-school teacher and children's librarian. Cynthia Rylant has worked in many literary genres, including lyric poetry, short stories, novels and PICTUREBOOKS; within those genres, she writes consistently of the same geography and themes: the Appalachia of her West Virginia childhood. Her books tend to be brief, even anecdotal at times, yet they are remarkably tough and unsentimental in confronting the issues of poverty, alcohol and family violence, and the tension between religion and spirituality in folk communities. Two of her picturebooks, *When I Was Young in the Mountains* (1982) and *The Relatives Came* (1985) were Caldecott Honour Books; she is also the author of the *Henry and Mudge* series of picturebooks. Her two best-known and most highly regarded novels are *A Fine White Dust* (1986, a Newbery Honour Book), which tells the story of a teenage boy 'saved' and then deserted by an itinerant evangelist, and *Missing May* (1992, NEWBERY MEDAL), which confronts the grieving process and the quest for contact with an after-life. Her writing combines the vernacular of her characters with a poetic, even spiritual sensibility. BH

S

Sabre, the Horse from the Sea see CHILD AUTHORS

Sachar, Louis see *HOLES*; see also SCHOOL STORIES

Sachs, Marilyn 1927– American writer known for her sense of humour and concern for social issues. Her first book, *Amy Moves In* (1964), was unusual in its time in that it told a realistic family story without a happy ending. In more than 30 books she has written about children facing real-life issues. *The Bears' House* (1971), a National Book Award finalist, presented the poignant story of a child whose sick mother could not care for her family. *The Big Book for Peace* (1991), co-edited with Ann Durell, is a collection of work emphasising world peace as an antidote to the violence in many children's books. BG

***Sadler's Wells* Series** Stories written by Lorna Hill in the 1950s, belonging to the sub-genre of the BALLET STORY, a type of 'career novel' for girls begun by NOEL STREATFEILD in 1937 with *BALLET SHOES* and added to by Estoril's *DRINA* series. The series opens with *A Dream of Sadler's Wells* (1950). This and the first of the sequels, *Veronica at the Wells* (1951) focus on Veronica Weston's training as a dancer; the subsequent books, *Masquerade at the Wells* (1952), *No Castanets at the Wells* (1953), *Jane Leaves the Wells* (1953), *Ella at the Wells* (1954), *Return to the Wells* (1955) and *Rosanna Joins the Wells* (1956) follow other protagonists, who are however all socially related.

The social world invoked in the books is an upper-class one, but the works quite interestingly juxtapose the values of this class with the single-minded devotion to hard work required of the dancer. While the series tends towards formula, running the full repertoire of the genre's clichés (e.g. the talented and attractive protagonists have to contend with rivals who either get up to underhand tricks in order to halt their rise to fame or who have some character flaw that affects their dancing), it is nonetheless able to communicate – and stimulate in the reader – an interest in the worlds of music and dance. SA

St George, Judith 1931– American author best known for her award-winning non-fiction, which she began to write only after publishing several novels. Her earlier books included HISTORICAL FICTION and mysteries, the kinds of books she says she liked to read as a child. But with the publication of *The Brooklyn Bridge: They Said It Couldn't Be Built* (1982), she found her niche as a writer of non-fiction. Highly acclaimed books about the Panama Canal, the White House and Mount Rushmore followed. Her most recent books have been biographies, including *Dear Doctor Bell* (1992) – the story of the friendship between Alexander Graham Bell and Helen Keller – and books about Crazy Horse (1994), Sitting Bull (1996), and Sacagawea (1997). LH

see also BIOGRAPHY AND AUTOBIOGRAPHY

St George and the Dragon see ROBERT BOLT; see also DRAMA FOR CHILDREN; MARGARET HODGES; TRINA SHART HYMAN

St Nicholas Magazine America's premier children's magazine for over 50 years. In 1873 Roswell Smith of Scribner and Company persuaded MARY MAPES DODGE, editor of the children's page of *Hearth and Home*, to become editor of his company's ambitious new literary magazine for young people, *St Nicholas*. Dodge was a talented writer whose *Hans Brinker; or, the Silver Skates* had been a bestseller. She believed a children's magazine should be, if anything, stronger, bolder and more entertaining than a magazine for adults, and that it should instruct its readers only indirectly. For *St Nicholas* she sought work of the highest literary and artistic quality. She aimed to make the journal a 'pleasure-ground' for its readers, full of wholesome, fresh and hearty fare. As the 'Conductor' of the journal, Dodge maintained close control over every aspect of it. Her personal column, 'Jack-in-the-Pulpit', featured a variety of engaging personae who could speak to her young readers without sounding priggish or preachy. Reformist in its own way, *St Nicholas* extolled the values of self-reliance, hard work, courage, duty and patriotism.

Dodge was a demanding yet sympathetic editor, and many of the magazine's celebrated contributors became close personal friends. RUDYARD KIPLING, who had loved the magazine as a boy, was eager to write for it as an adult and gave Dodge a few of his best

Illustration by Reginald Birch for *St Nicholas Magazine* (1887).

Just So Stories and tales from the *Jungle Books*. Frances Hodgson Burnett's *Little Lord Fauntleroy* and *Sarah Crewe*, Mark Twain's *Tom Sawyer Abroad*, Louisa May Alcott's *Eight Cousins* and *Jack and Jill*, and Dodge's own *Donald and Dorothy* were favourite serials. Among the most popular departments were the 'Letter-Box', the 'Riddle-Box', 'the Agassis Association' and the 'St Nicholas League' for young contributors, whose members over the years included F. Scott Fitzgerald, William Faulkner, and E. B. White.

Dodge's Associate Editor at the outset was Frank R. Stockton, many of whose fanciful tales appeared in the magazine. Stockton's successor, William Fayal Clarke, assisted Dodge faithfully until her death in 1905 and continued to edit the journal until 1927. Clarke did his best to carry on in the Dodge tradition and was especially successful in nurturing the 'St Nicholas League', but the magazine was never quite the same. Later editors included George F. Thompson (1927–9), Albert Gallatin Lanier (1929–30), May Lamberton Becker (1930–2), Eric J. Bender (1932–4), Chesla Sherlock (1934–5), Vertie A. Coyne (1936–40) and Juliet Lit Sterne (1943). Often called the best of all children's magazines, *St Nicholas* for many decades fulfilled its publisher's goal of giving American children 'the best reading that money could buy', 'the finest illustrations procurable at home and abroad', a 'magazine . . . as good as we can make it' with 'something in every number that will interest and instruct every member of every family into which it shall have the good fortune to find its way' (Josiah G. Holland, writing in *Scribner's Monthly*, 1870). SRG

St Trinians see RONALD SEARLE

Salford Road (1979) Acclaimed first collection of poems by GARETH OWEN, published 17 years after he originally wrote them for his pupils. Poems such as 'Ping-Pong' and 'Boredom' appear inventive and original in their use of rhyming and free verse structures despite this delay. Owen's dramatic monologues often use the voice of the child, characteristically that of a boy growing up in post-war urban and suburban Britain, to capture both the concrete details and the fantasies of childhood ('Our School'). There is also wry, ironic humour in the collection and a nostalgia which stops short of sentimentality ('Photograph'). ML

Salinger, J.D. see *CATCHER IN THE RYE, THE*; PUBLISHERS AND PUBLISHING

Salkey, (Felix) Andrew (Alexander) see *HURRICANE*

***Sally Lockhart* series** Four books by Philip Pullman: *The Ruby in the Smoke* (1985), *The Shadow in the North* (1986), *The Tiger in the Well* (1991) and *The Tin Princess* (1994). The series defies definition by genre, combining elements of the historical novel, 'Ruritanian' romance and mystery-thriller. The heroine is a modern woman in a Victorian setting who carries and uses a gun, starts up her own business and has a child out of wedlock. The series is fast-paced and original, the historical elements well researched and convincing, and its concerns, despite its 'historicality', are intensely contemporary. SA

***Sally* series** Trilogy by Irish writer Elizabeth O'Hara (Eilís Ní Dhuibhne, 1954–). In 19th-century Ireland it was not uncommon for agricultural and domestic labourers to be 'bought' at a hiring fair. This is the fate of 13-year-old Sally Gallagher and her sister Katie from Donegal in *The Hiring Fair* (1993), the first in O'Hara's trilogy. It tells the story of the girls, who go to work for families in County Tyrone. *Blaeberry Sunday* (1994) sees 15-year-old Sally back in Donegal in the summer of 1893, and in *Penny-Farthing Sally* (1996), Sally, now older, is working as a governess for a wealthy Dublin family. O'Hara's background as a social historian is obvious in her detailed and fascinating restructuring of both rural and urban Ireland a hundred years ago. The strength of the books lies also in her development of character allied to a narrative which, while never hurried, contains plenty to engage the reader at many levels. These were preceded by two novels for younger children which she wrote as Eilís Ní Dhuibhne, *The Uncommon Cormorant* (1990) and *Hugo and the Sunshine Girl* (1991). VC

'Captain Blacktooth, the dreaded pirate.' Illustration by Michael Salmon from *The Pirate Who Wouldn't Wash*.

Salmon, Michael 1949– Australian writer, illustrator and designer, born in New Zealand, with over 130 titles published and world sales exceeding 13 million copies. His first book, *The Monster Who Ate Canberra* (1972), is probably his best-known, featuring Alexander Bunyip, a character around whom he built an ABC national TELEVISION series for over ten years. This title went on to win the YABBA Picture Story Book of the Year in 1990. With their bright colours, and lively cartoon illustrations, Salmon's book series are extremely popular with children, who enjoy his tongue-in-cheek tales of monsters, dinosaurs, pirates and other FANTASY figures. He is extremely energetic, producing up to 10 titles each year, and involved in many merchandising ventures associated with his books, while maintaining a close contact with his readers through his ongoing school visits. JAP

Salt Water Ballads (1902) A collection of poems about life at sea by the British poet, JOHN MASEFIELD. Most of the ballads take the form of stories told by seamen in forms and rhythms derived from both sea shanties and common speech. Masefield drew on his first-hand experiences as a sailor and wrote about 'The sailor, the stoker of steamers, the man with the clout' and the beauty of ships which 'mark our passage as a race of men'. This new realism broke with the Tennysonian tradition and produced such classics as 'Sea Fever' and 'Cargoes'. HT

Salten, Felix [Siegmund Salzmann] 1869–1945 Austrian novelist born in Budapest, Hungary. Salten moved in infancy with his family to Vienna, where he lived for most of his life, fleeing to Switzerland to escape Nazi persecution. His novels include two that became the bases of popular films produced by WALT DISNEY (*The Hound of Florence*, 1923, which became *The Shaggy Dog* in 1959, and *Perri: The Youth of a Squirrel*, filmed as *Perri* in 1957), but he will always be best remembered as the creator of *BAMBI*, the young deer who was hero of two novels (also making a brief appearance in Salten's *Fifteen Rabbits*, 1929) and of Disney's animated feature film. Salten's literary hero was the French realist novelist Emile Zola, and, like his model, he aspired to reproduce 'life in the woods' with faithfulness and with little sentimentalisation. Such anthropomorphism as there is in his novels seems primarily designed to find novelistic analogues for observable behaviour; while his narrative pushes towards interpretation of these behaviours, the goal always seems to be to allow these animals to have their own authentic existence, separate from the psychology of human interaction. BH

Salway, Lance see CRITICAL APPROACHES TO CHILDREN'S BOOKS

Salwi, Dilip M. 1952– Indian pioneer SCIENCE FICTION writer, dubbed the 'Indian Asimov'. Salwi writes on issues of science and technology for teenagers and children. He has diligently authored 33 books, some recommended as supplementary reading in schools. He gives talks on popular science and teaches science journalism to university students. He has also written science-based plays included in *Dinosaurs! We've Only One Earth* (1996). Though his style is sometimes laboured, his devotion to the popularisation of science through fiction is unmistakable and has won him many awards. His *A Passage to Antarctica* (1986), a travelogue of a teenager in the icy continent at the South Pole, received the Children's Book Trust Award. He has been given an entry in the *Limca Book of Records 1998* for the record sales of his science fiction *Fire on the Moon* (1984), a collection of stories replete with space voyages, modern jungles, mutants and robots. MBh

Samber, Robert see 'Bluebeard'; *CONTES DE MA MÈRE L'OYE*; CHARLES PERRAULT; 'PUSS IN BOOTS'

San folktales see AFRICAN MYTHOLOGY AND FOLKTALES; see also NIKI DALY; MARY PHILLIPS; VICTOR POHL; MARGUERITE POLAND; *THE SOUND OF THE GORA*

Sanctuary (1996) A contemporary New Zealand novel for teenagers by Kate de Goldi, who structures this story around a confessional hero, Catriona, and her psychologist. De Goldi never condescends to her audience, exploiting the interview device fully to achieve a dense, layered novel. She keeps the narrative taut as issues such as large cats in captivity, sexuality and destructive family relationships are teased out. Catriona painfully analyses her life, until she is able to talk about the horror of her young sister's death by fire. One of de Goldi's consistent strengths, evident here, is her open investigation of teenagers' sexually active relationships. MJH

see also SEX IN CHILDREN'S BOOKS

Sandburg, Carl 1878–1967 American poet popular with readers but often marginalised by the literary élite, with whom he fought many battles. The son of a semi-literate Swedish immigrant, he grew up in poverty, but became the friend of presidents (Roosevelt, Kennedy) and the biographer of Abraham Lincoln. He was awarded many honours in his lifetime, though he always felt himself to be a literary outsider and was regarded as a maverick by many for his apparently formless, undisciplined poetry. Sandburg had radical views and was the champion of the underdog. His poems have a simplicity and directness with great appeal to younger readers, for whom they are regularly anthologised:

> The fog comes
> on little cat feet.
> It sits looking
> over harbour and city
> on silent haunches
> and then moves on.

MCCS

see also *ROOTABAGA STORIES*

Sanderson, Ruth 1951– American illustrator whose richly detailed paintings have contributed to the popularity in the late 20th century of FAIRY TALES illustrated with high-quality art that appeals to readers of all ages. After art school and a decade of illustrating textbooks and children's trade books of all kinds in different media, Sanderson concentrated on full-colour oil paintings for PICTUREBOOKS and classic novels such as *HEIDI* (1984) and *THE SECRET GARDEN* (1988). Describing the fairy tale as her 'artistic home', Sanderson believes she is 'best able to capture the romance, the drama, and the beauty inherent in the tale by using oils' in a style that combines naturalistic landscapes and realistic human portraits (based on her photographs of live models in period costumes) with symbolic details and glittering magical elements such as fairies and trees with gold and silver leaves. Many of her paintings are inspired by Pre-Raphaelite art and the Hudson River school of painters. Sanderson began writing her own texts with *The Twelve Dancing Princesses* (1990), and *The Enchanted Wood* (1991) was her first original fairy tale. In brilliant illustrations for *The Nativity* (1993), she adapted the styles of pre-Renaissance religious paintings and illuminated manuscripts. TLH

Sandford and Merton see *THE HISTORY OF SANDFORD AND MERTON*

Sara Crewe or What Happened at Miss Minchin's An early version of FRANCES HODGSON BURNETT's *A LITTLE PRINCESS*, serialised in 1887–8 and later published with the same author's *Editha's Burglar* in 1888. VW

Sarah, Plain and Tall see PATRICIA MACLACHLAN; see also HISTORICAL FICTION

Sarg, Tony 1880–1947 American puppeteer. Sarg was born in Coban, Guatemala, to a German father and an English mother, and educated in Germany at the Lichterfelde Military Academy. At 17, he was commissioned as a lieutenant but he eventually resigned his commission to go to England, where he married Bertha Eleanor McGowan, an American tourist. While working in England as a commercial artist, Sarg became fascinated by puppetry and tried to learn everything he could from the Holden Marionette Troupe. With the advent of World War I, he and his young family migrated to America where he became a naturalised citizen in 1920. There he formed the highly successful Tony Sarg Marionettes, which toured the Unites States until 1940. The troupe performed many tales by the GRIMM BROTHERS, as well as *Ali Baba*, ROBIN HOOD, *Uncle Wiggly's Adventures*, and his signature piece, *ALICE'S ADVENTURES IN WONDERLAND*. Sarg was known for his mechanical inventiveness, his ability to combine cloth and wood construction, and his humour and playfulness. In his production of *Alice's Adventures in Wonderland*, an actress – later replaced by a lookalike puppet – initially plays the role of Alice. This technique was so successful that he later used it in other productions. Many famous American puppeteers started at Sarg's Studio in Greenwich Village, New York, where they learned how to design, build and develop marionette shows. Bil Baird and Margo and Rufus Rose (who created *Howdy Doody*) were members of his troupe until the 1933 World's Fair puppet show. In addition to his marionettes, Sarg had a number of successful ventures with Macy's Department Store in New York City, for which he developed the concept of mechanical window displays. After World War II the demand for his type of entertainment declined and he was forced to declare bankruptcy. His work as a puppeteer was recounted by Tamara Robin Hunt in *Tony Sarg: Puppeteer in America 1915–1942*. DJH

see also DRAMA FOR CHILDREN

Sarland, Charles see CHILDIST CRITICISM

Saro-Wiwa, Ken [Tsaro-Wiwa, Ken] 1941–95 Nigerian author, environmentalist and human-rights activist, born in the Ogoni area of Rivers State. Saro-Wiwa wrote for children as well as adults. Two juvenile novels, *Tambari* (1973) and *Tambari in Dukana* (1973) relate the adventures of a village boy at home and on holiday. Between 1989 and 1991 Saro-Wiwa brought out *The Adventures of Mr B*, a series based on his popular TELEVISION comedy *Basi and Company*. They chronicle the inspired but futile efforts of an unemployed urban dweller to get rich quick. Saro-Wiwa also collected Ogoni folktales for children in *The Singing Anthill* (1991). VD

Saunders, [Margaret] Marshall 1861–1947 Canadian American author. Saunders was encouraged to write by her father, who remarked that she 'had some talent'. It was not until she met the real Beautiful Joe, however, that she became inspired to write her first and most successful book. *Beautiful Joe: An Autobiography* (1894) attempted to arouse pity for mistreated animals (as *BLACK BEAUTY* had previously done) by having an animal narrator relate numerous instances of cruelty. Although Beautiful Joe's first owner cuts off the puppy's ears and tail, Joe is soon rescued and spends the rest of his life with owners who are both kind and sensitive. Other animals Joe meets or hears about, however, are not so fortunate, and he tells their stories as well as his own. *Beautiful Joe* was popular for many years; the poorly conceived sequel, *Beautiful Joe's Paradise; or, The Island of Brotherly Love* (1902), which discusses animal immortality, was not widely successful. Besides her animal books, Saunders wrote *The King of the Park* (1897) in which an arrogant orphan learns that love is more important than riches and station. WH

see also ANIMALS IN FICTION

Saville, (Leonard) Malcolm 1901–82 British writer of nature and ADVENTURE STORIES for children of all ages. Born in Hastings, England, Saville married Dorothy May McCoy in 1926. After school he began a career in publishing, retiring in 1966 to write and lecture. In 1943 he wrote *Mystery at Witchend* (see LONE PINE SERIES) which launched his successful career as a children's author. Through his writings he encouraged children to appreciate the countryside, offering advice on how to explore, as in *Jane's Country Year* (1946) and other, non-fiction, books which were full of information such as his *Countryside* and *Seaside Scrapbooks* and his *Wonder Why* series. He wrote fiction for all ages, from series such as *Susan and Bill* and the *Lone Piners* to the action-packed stories of secret agent *Marston Baines*. His skill at communicating his Christian faith whilst recounting an exciting story is displayed in *King of Kings* (1958), bringing to life the story of Jesus and the crucifixion. In contrast his *Words for all Seasons* (1979) is a collection of his favourite writings of other authors. He encouraged correspondence from his readers, respecting their opinions and giving every child a reply. Sadly, as his values went out of fashion, so too did he as an author. There has been a recent revival of interest in his work, with two of his titles back in print. Malcolm Saville died on 30 June 1982 in Sussex. A Malcolm Saville Society was established in 1994. LW

see also NEGLECTED WORKS

Sawyer, Ruth 1880–1970 American storyteller and writer for children. Born in Boston, Sawyer graduated with a degree in folklore and STORYTELLING from Columbia University. She collected FOLKTALES in Ireland in her twenties and began a storytelling career in the New York Public Library. Her vivid, largely autobiographical novel *Roller Skates* (US, 1936; UK, 1964), set in New York City, tells the story of Lucinda Wyman, an independent and adventurous girl, who explores the city on roller skates one summer when her parents are in Europe. Sawyer continued the story of Lucinda in *The Year of Jubilo* (1940, 1965) and wrote several other novels for children in the 1940s and 50s that display her sympathetic understanding of children struggling against poverty and other difficulties. She also collected folk tales in Spain, which resulted in *Picture Tales from Spain* (1936), and retold stories from Austria, Germany, Serbia and other countries. Her version of the widespread folktale of the pancake under pursuit, *Journeycake, Ho!*, illustrated by her son-in-law, ROBERT MCCLOSKEY, won the CALDECOTT MEDAL (1953). She collected many Christmas stories, such as *The Christmas Anna Angel* (1944), based on a Hungarian refugee's tale and illustrated by KATE SEREDY. Her book *The Way of the Storyteller* (1942, 1962) has been an influential guide for those interested in the art of storytelling. JDS

Say, Allen 1937– Japanese American author and illustrator, who, following the success of *The Bicycle Man* (1982), wrote and illustrated autobiographical works reflecting the relationship between parent and child and between Asian and American cultures. He won the CALDECOTT MEDAL for *Grandfather's Journey* (1993), a PICTUREBOOK BIOGRAPHY in soft-tone watercolours recounting his own grandfather's journeys between Japan and America. Other well-known works include *Tree of Cranes* (1991) and *Tea With Milk* (1999), biographical episodes in his mother's life, as well as *El Chino* (1990), *The Lost Lake* (1989) and *The Ink-Keeper's Apprentice* (1979), and Dianne Snyder's retelling of the Japanese FOLKTALE *The Boy of the Three-Year Nap* (1988). PDS

Say It Again, Granny! (1986) Collection by the British Guyanese poet JOHN AGARD which turns 20 Caribbean proverbs into dialect poems. Speaking directly to the child, these poems combine everyday experience with traditional advice providing wise and witty solutions, often in the form of a punchline – 'Don't Call Alligator Long-Mouth Till You Cross River.' HT

Sayers, Dorothy L(yndon) 1893–1957 British writer of detective fiction, and plays, essays and translations on religious themes. Determined not to write down to children, Sayers's radio plays for *Children's Hour* – a nativity play *He that Should Come* (1938) and a controversially colloquial cycle of plays on the life of Jesus, *The Man Born to be King* (1941–2) – like her illustrated BIBLE STORIES, were based on her own translations, and conceived as historical realism. *Enter the Parrot: Exemplary Conversations for Enlightened Children* (1944) amusingly pastiches 19th-century improving tracts in a wartime setting to debate politics, biology and social planning. SG

Scandinavian mythology see CLASSICAL MYTHOLOGY

Scannell, Vernon 1922– British writer, one-time teacher and boxer. *Collected Poems 1950–93* includes several poems now firmly adopted for children's anthologies. These include 'Gunpowder Plot', 'Dead Dog', 'Uncle Edward's Affliction' (colour-blindness causing the ex-soldier to recall French fields as being blood-green), 'A Case of Murder' (a nine-year-old kills a cat and suffers lifelong guilt), and the unforgettable 'Hide and Seek'. Here the child hiding in the shed is pleased to be undiscovered, until –

> The darkening garden watches. Nothing stirs.
> The bushes hold their breath; the sun is gone.
> Yes, here you are. But where are they who sought you?

The Apple Raid (1974) first introduced Scannell to younger readers. He knows that children respond to painful, disturbing themes within their own range of experience. The section devoted to Scannell in *Poets in Hand* (1985) demonstrates his direct approach and colloquial handling of language. Lines flow; rhyme, nearly always present, is never intrusive. Later writing for children includes three themed collections, *The Clever Potato* (1988), *Love Shouts and Whispers* (1990) and *Travelling Light* (1991). Scannell offers diversity, proving equally comfortable using a grown-up or child voice. His range includes moral tales in the style of HILAIRE BELLOC, poems which wittily instruct, and those which offer insight into adult preoccupations. AHa

Scarlet Pimpernel, The (from 1902) Series of nine novels by Baroness Orczy (Emma Magdalena Rosalia Marie Josefa Barbara, 1865–1947) following the adventures of Sir Percy Blakeney – who acts under the name of the 'Scarlet Pimpernel' – and his friends as they rescue victims of the French Revolution from the guillotine, while their enemy Chauvelin struggles to stop them and to capture Sir Percy. SA

see also ADULT LITERATURE

Scarry, Richard (McClure) 1919–94 Bestselling American author and illustrator of more than 250 PICTUREBOOKS. Born in Boston, Richard Scarry studied at the Boston Museum School, began illustrating books in 1947 and writing them soon after. In 1968, he and his wife moved to Switzerland with their son. At the time of Scarry's death he was, according to *Publishers Weekly*, the author of eight of the top 50 bestselling hardcover children's books of all time. *The Best Word Book Ever* (1963), perhaps his best-known work, contains labelled pictures of over 1,400 objects, and a cast of dozens of lively, colourful, bouncy, cheerful anthropomorphic bears, rabbits, kittens and pigs who demonstrate proper behaviour and good manners. Like many of Scarry's books, this one has been translated into numerous languages, including a Magyar-English-German version with every label printed in three languages. *Busy, Busy World* (1965) contains 33 stories set in as many different countries, and *Cars and Trucks and Things That Go* (1974) is a *tour de force* of real and imaginary vehicles, a page-filling, mind-boggling accident, and a gold bug to look for on every page. Critics have objected to Scarry's cluttered layout, slapstick humour, repetitiveness, excessive violence, and paucity of female characters not wearing aprons, but the books have become classics with pre-school children and their parents. LH

Scheepers Prize see AWARDS AND MEDALS

Schindel, Morton 1918– Pioneer film-maker and entrepreneur born in Newark, New Jersey. After earning his master's degree in curriculum from Teachers College, Columbia University in 1949, Schindel made several curricular films in New York, then moved to Weston, Connecticut, where he founded Weston Woods Studios in 1953. He began making high-quality film adaptations of children's books and quickly earned the respect of writers and illustrators. His productions include *Make Way for Ducklings*, *The Snowy Day* and *WHERE THE WILD THINGS ARE*. *Doctor De Soto* was nominated for an Academy Award in 1984. *Morton Schindel: From Page to Screen* (1981) is a film about Weston Woods Studios.

Schindel is the originator of the iconographic film technique, which uses a moving easel to impose the illusion of movement on still pictures, and the Monaco 'HangUp' system for storing multimedia products in libraries and classrooms. He is the founder of Mediamobiles, a company that transforms recreational vehicles into multimedia learning centres for primary schools; Children's Circle Studios, a distributor of Weston Woods films on video; and the Weston Woods Institute, a non-profit-making organisation for promoting innovation in communications with children. He has received numerous awards and honours for his contributions to education and children's literature. EAM

Schoenherr, John 1935– American author and illustrator of children's books. Although born and raised in New York City, Schoenherr is well known for his wildlife ILLUSTRATIONS. In his early career as an illustrator he worked largely for SCIENCE FICTION magazines, and he has created more than 300 science-fiction book covers. The World Science Fiction Society awarded him the 1965 Hugo for Best Artist. His interest in the natural world began to take precedence over his other work after he and his family moved from New York City to a farmhouse in New Jersey. His black-and-white illustrations for the NEWBERY MEDAL winner, *Julie of the Wolves* (1971) by JEAN CRAIGHEAD GEORGE – and for several other Newbery Honour Books – established him in the field of children's book illustration. His book *The Barn* (1968) was selected as an ALA Notable Book. In 1988, after a hiatus in which he concentrated on wildlife painting instead of children's book illustration, Schoenherr made a dramatic return with his watercolour paintings for the CALDECOTT MEDAL winner, *Owl Moon* by JANE YOLEN. He has since written and illustrated two full-colour children's PICTUREBOOKS with nature themes: *Bear* (1991) and *Rebel* (1995). EHI

Schofield Collection see COLLECTIONS OF CHILDREN'S BOOKS

School Friend, The (from 1919) Amalgamated Press's first schoolgirl weekly story paper, launched in May 1919, edited by Reginald T. Eves and featuring CHARLES HAMILTON's Bessie Bunter (although he was rapidly replaced as a writer). Mainly text, and aiming to entertain rather than inform, the paper focused initially on boarding-school stories but, absorbed into *The Schoolgirl* between 1929 and 1940, it introduced a captivating range of adventurous heroines from air aces to racing drivers. A victim of wartime paper shortages, it reappeared in 1950 as the highly popular schoolgirl picture story weekly, *School Friend*, only to be merged with *June* in 1965. BW

school libraries see LIBRARIES; see also CENSORSHIP; REVIEWING AND REVIEWERS

school magazines and journals In Australia school magazines were the main source of reading material for children before the advent of school libraries. Victoria's *School Paper* was first issued in 1896 and was adapted by the other states. It contained extracts of Australian and overseas writing – poetry, history and geography – as well as things to make and do, and was eagerly received by children. It ceased publication in the 1970s. However, the *New South Wales School Magazine* – first issued in 1916 by the Department of School Education as a 'Magazine of Literature for our Boys and Girls' – is still being published. There are ten issues each year for each of four primary age groups, with the titles 'Countdown', 'Blast-off', 'Orbit' and 'Touchdown'. Each issue contains stories, poems, articles, plays and puzzles, both from Australia and overseas. The *Magazine* is dedicated to providing children with excellence in literature, and has been the launchpad for many well-regarded writers, of both prose and poetry. Contributors in 1998 included ROBERT LEESON, ANNE FINE, WILLIAM JOYCE, ALLAN BAILLIE, NADIA WHEATLEY and JACKIE FRENCH. Illustrators include NOELLA YOUNG and KIM GAMBLE. Previous editors include PATRICIA WRIGHTSON, LILITH NORMAN and ANNA FIENBERG. The *Magazine*, which continues to be popular with children and teachers, has responded to curriculum changes, and now issues accompanying Literacy Teaching Units.

The New Zealand Education Department published the first issues of its *School Journal* in 1907, to provide standardisation of school textbook material. For some years the *Journal* was primarily a history and geography reader, but in the late 1930s the Department realised the importance of reading material that related to children's local environment and engaged their curiosity, interests and imaginations. Since then the *Journal* has evolved into a unique resource that greatly enriches the education of New Zealand children. The editors are committed to providing top-quality New Zealand writing and illustration; over the years the *Journal* has published work by such authors as MARGARET MAHY, JOY COWLEY, ELSIE LOCKE and DAVID HILL, and illustration by artists such as RUSSELL CLARK and Mervyn Taylor. The *Journal* is issued free to all New Zealand schools, published several times a year in four Parts, each Part providing material for a particular reading level from primary to early secondary. Each issue offers a miscellany of stories, articles, plays and poems, and a wide variety of genres and styles. The *School Journal* is a New Zealand institution that has been valued by teachers and children for the last 90 years. LO, JAP

school stories In spite of criticisms of its narrow preoccupation with élitist middle-class education, artificiality and lack of realism, and its frequently but inaccurately forecast demise, the genre has persisted, adapting to changes in educational provision, social attitudes and readership taste. Background, rather than context, characterised the first school stories, such as SARAH FIELDING's *The Governess, Or, the Little Female Academy* (1749) – a collection of tales within the framework of a young ladies' seminary and condemned as frivolous by MRS TRIMMER – and CHARLES and MARY LAMB's *MRS LEICESTER'S SCHOOL* (1809). Few tales about elementary education survive from this period; among the earliest are *Goody Two Shoes* (1765) and DOROTHY KILNER's *The Village School* (1795), a moralising and didactic tale cautioning against the dreadful consequences of carelessness.

Boys' school tales in Britain began with MARIA EDGEWORTH's *The Barring Out* (1796) and Harriet Martineau's *The Crofton Boys* (1841), the first really important boarding-school story, heralding the genre's potential, and its later familiar ingredients: cricket, prefects, fagging, beatings, and a strict code of honour. Nevertheless, the tale is a didactic, harrowing account of the life of a schoolboy hero bearing his afflictions with fortitude. Remarkable because neither writer was able to draw on personal experience, both stories engaged a school setting, but aimed to instruct rather than to entertain. William Adams's *The Cherry Stones* (completed in 1851 by his brother, Henry) successfully launched the genre, but the vitalising key texts were Thomas Hughes's *TOM BROWN'S SCHOOLDAYS* (1857) and Frederick Farrar's *Eric or, Little by Little* (1858). Drawing on their own experience, these writers developed the idea of the public-school ethos, spiritual values and principled behaviour in a self-contained world, separated from the female domain of home and fostering instead muscular Christianity and the values of loyalty and self-sacrifice. The features of the emerging public-school tradition become enshrined in a sentimental and pious fiction. Nevertheless, the two stories differ: Hughes's novel preaches the importance of learning to fit into community and society; *Eric*, a mawkish story popular with parents, focuses on individual conscience and temptation, ending with the beautiful death of the young repentant. Both writers had their imitators, notably Ascott R. Hope (A. R. Hope-Moncrieff) who wrote in the same tradition as Farrar, publishing *Oudendale* in 1865.

By the 1880s the boys' public school in both fact and fiction was securely established. However, with TALBOT BAINES REED's *Fifth Form at St. Dominic's* (serialised in the *BOY'S OWN PAPER* in 1882) and its treatment of schoolboy villainy, the genre's mould of being rather than doing was recast in a revised model, critical of the pious cant of the mainstream tradition, and emphasising plot rather than character. In the same year, the imperfections of the tradition were again exposed in F. Anstey's (Thomas Anstey Guthrie) *Vice Versa* (1882) (described by C. S. LEWIS as the only truthful school story) through the comic exchange of roles between father and son.

Following later developments in girls' education, Sarah Doudney's *Monkesbury College* (1876) marks the tentative start of the girls' boarding-school story, which, adhering to the Victorian ideal of separate spheres and gender-specific literature for juveniles, began appearing in *GIRL'S OWN PAPER* from the 1880s. Mrs George de Horne Vaisey's *Rhoda* (1901, later published by the RELIGIOUS TRACT SOCIETY as *Tom and Some Other Girls*) was the first to explore the difficulties of such schooling and was imitative of some boys' school traditions in its treatment of examination pressure. L.T. MEADE's *A World of Girls* (1886) and *The Beresford Prize* (1890) enjoyed greater success, but both writers, with their leaden and sickly moral tone and emphasis on self-improvement, failed to capture the lighter touch of ANGELA BRAZIL's *The Fortunes of Philippa* (1906), which established the definable, infectiously jolly tone of the genre in Britain. While girls' school stories quickly settled into a recognisable popular formula, those for boys were transformed by a series of anti-tradition novels critical of the idealised, false world of unreal public schoolboy heroes. In H.A. Vachell's *The Hill; a Romance of Friendship* (1905), frequently reprinted in the years following publication, the account of an intense and enduring friendship between two Harrow schoolboys has not stood the test of time. KIPLING's *STALKY AND CO.* (1899), with its tough account of realistic, unregenerate characters who despise and challenge the hypocrisy of school conventions, destroys the naive and reverential tradition of the boys' school story. Less savage, but certainly more witty, P.G. WODEHOUSE's *Mike: a Public School Story* (1909) also attacks the genre's hypocrisy and respect for tradition and its almost risible representation of the schoolboy character.

The readership of full-length boys' school stories declined with fiction which either presented an unattractive realism or launched into improbable adventure. However, weekly story papers like *Magnet* and *Gem* breathed new life into them, particularly in the inter-war years. Attacked by George Orwell as escapist, formulaic and élitist, they were defended and recalled with affection by Robert Roberts. CHARLES HAMILTON's *GREYFRIARS* stories – which made their first appearance in *Magnet* in 1908 – are *primus inter pares* with the enduring comic figure of Billy Bunter, whose sister Bessie (of similar proportions and character) made regular appearances in *SCHOOL FRIEND's* 'Cliff House'.

The genre for girls continued to flourish, peaking in the 1930s, fuelled by tales of Girl Guides (see GUIDING AND SCOUTING), madcaps and schoolgirl sleuths. The indisputable influence of Angela Brazil shaping their work, the remaining 'Big Five' authors created an absorbing and intimate 'world of girls' in their dynastic school-story series. The first were Dorita Fairlie-Bruce (*DIMSIE*) and Elsie Oxenham (who wrote 37 *Abbey Girls* books between 1920 and 1959), followed by Elinor Brent-Dyer (*CHALET SCHOOL*), and ENID BLYTON (*St Clare's*, 1941–5, and *MALORY TOWERS* stories, 1946–51).

Although America had its early school stories, such as Jacob Abbott's *Rollo at School* (1839), the school story never developed there as a genre largely because the United States and Canada had fewer boarding schools. Furthermore, the democratising tendency of the co-educational public school tended to dispel the mystique that made the British school story so attractive. Books of two related genres – the 'bad boy' book and the FAMILY STORY – often featured school scenes; who can forget the punishments meted out to Tom Sawyer and Amy March by their tyrannical schoolmasters? But the responses of the two characters – playing hookey and withdrawing from school entirely – imply a critique or outright rejection of school in favour of individual freedom or the family. Sometimes one book in a popular series would feature the protagonist's life at school, such as SUSAN COOLIDGE's *What Katy Did at School* (1873), Arthur M. Winfield's *The Rover Boys at School* (1899), and, later, L.M. MONTGOMERY's volumes devoted to Anne's experiences as both student and teacher. And the early 20th century saw a rash of college novels, the best-known of which is JEAN WEBSTER's *Daddy Long-Legs* (1912). But only two 19th-century American books entirely set in school qualify as classics: LOUISA MAY ALCOTT's sequel to *LITTLE WOMEN*, *Little Men* (1871), and the Anglo-American FRANCES HODGSON BURNETT's *A LITTLE PRINCESS* (1905).

Much more common in the United States than boarding-school stories have been stories of the public day-school, which has dominated the culture of young people from the 1920s on. In the 1940s and 50s high-school stories portrayed a gentle world of co-operative young people and wise, caring adults. The *BETSY-TACY* books of Maud Hart Lovelace, published in mid-century, were set at the turn of the century. Betsy and her friends live in an ideal small town and enjoy a round of social and school activities, free from any worries except who is going to the dance with whom. By the 1960s children's lives had become more complicated and depictions of school more realistic. *HARRIET THE SPY* (1964) by LOUISE FITZHUGH and *Blubber* (1974) by JUDY BLUME portrayed the real cruelty that can exist in an elementary-school classroom. African American writers such as VIRGINIA HAMILTON (*The Planet of Junior Brown*, 1971) and MILDRED TAYLOR

(*Roll of Thunder, Hear My Cry,* 1976) portrayed the depressing reality of school for black adolescents in the inner-city high school and for black children in the rural South, respectively. In the realistic fiction of the 1970s and 80s, school is often a backdrop to relationship issues. A series by Barthe DeClements (1981–7) follows a class through the middle and upper elementary-grade years, during which the children struggle with problems such as single parents and obesity. However, North America in the last few decades has not been without its share of boarding-school stories. In Canada the most notable are Gordon Kormon's *Bruno and Boots* series, published between 1978 and 1991, and KIT PEARSON's *The Daring Game* (1986). Both Kormon and Pearson feature children who rebel against the system, but the Korman series is played for laughs, while *The Daring Game* explores issues more seriously. And the United States has produced at least two classics of the genre: John Knowles's *A Separate Peace* (1960), a boys' prep-school drama set against the backdrop of World War II, is frequently taught in secondary schools; and ROBERT CORMIER's *The Chocolate War* (1974), a disturbing book in which students and teachers seem equally power-hungry and corrupt, has been the subject of much critical debate.

While in Britain the popularity of the girls' boarding-school series persisted with many reprints – as well as the more recent *TREBIZON* series (from 1979) by Anne Digby – the gender-specific school story itself is less in evidence as the genre has undergone changes in the post-war era, becoming more representative of the day-school experience of most of its British readers. In *No Boats on Bannermere* (1949), GEOFFREY TREASE sets his tale in a Cumbrian grammar school, and the school background to E.W. HILDICK's *Jim Starling* (1958) is Cement Street Boys' Secondary Modern. Nevertheless, some vestige of the traditional school story survives with overtones of Wodehouse's verbal wit in Anthony Buckeridge's *JENNINGS* stories of a prep-school boy – threatened with extinction in 2000 but reprieved after a public outcry – and, with a new authenticity and conviction, in WILLIAM MAYNE's boys' cathedral *CHOIR SCHOOL* stories, beginning with *A Swarm in May* (1955), and the four school stories in Antonia Forest's *MARLOW* SERIES, beginning with *Autumn Term* (1948). Similarly, GEOFFREY WILLAN and RONALD SEARLE's *Down with Skool!* (1953), *How to be Topp* (1954) and *Whizz for Atomms* (1956), featuring Molesworth, exploit a trenchant schoolboy humour. Girls' stories such as PENELOPE FARMER's *Charlotte Sometimes* (1969) and JANE GARDAM's *THE SUMMER AFTER THE FUNERAL* (1973) use the historical dimension imaginatively to interrogate relationships and personal dilemmas within the context of school.

More recent writers have exploited developments in education to write confident and realistic modern school fiction. New ground is broken with the primary-school background of GENE KEMP's *Turbulent Term of Tyke Tiler* (1977) and its sequels, and with GILLIAN CROSS's *Save Our School* (1981). Based on Phil Redmond's TELEVISION series, *GRANGE HILL* stories by a number of writers – notably JAN NEEDLE and David Angus – have transformed the genre with their bold confrontation of issues of contemporary concern such as racism, sexism and bullying. Because of their response to contemporary issues and their consequent immediacy, modern school stories may have an ephemeral quality. Nevertheless, they are more likely to resonate with the educational experience of most readers and, in spite of predictions, the genre survives with a new zest. The world-wide popularity of the *HARRY POTTER* stories has given that zest an entirely unexpected new lease of life.

In the United States contemporary school stories seem to go in two different directions, the realistic and the fantastic, but children are almost always portrayed as capable of handling their own problems. The realistic view of school is taken in a series by the American writer Miriam Cohen (there is no series title), published between 1969 and 1987, which follows a class through the first and second grades. Each book focuses on a different child whose problem is solved by the end of the book. *The Polk Street School* series by Patricia Reilly Giff, published between 1984 and 1992 for slightly older readers, also emphasises problem-solving and co-operation. The adults in both of these series are good role models and help the children develop healthy attitudes about themselves and others. The children are allowed to reach their own decisions about their behaviour, with the adults acting as facilitators.

On the FANTASY side James Allard's *Miss Nelson* series (1977–85) features a group of cartoon characters that get into zany situations. For example, the kind and caring Miss Nelson disappears and returns as Viola Swamp, the evil substitute teacher. A similar classroom situation is created by JAMES MARSHALL in the *Cut-ups* series (1984–92). Two mischievous boys foil or are foiled by a school principal and his favourites in a variety of hilarious ways. In the new series, *Captain Underpants* by Dav Pilkey, kids hypnotise a hapless principal into believing that he is a SUPERHERO who solves crimes in his underwear. In the *Baily School* series by Debbie Dadey and Marcia Thornton Jones (1992–9), a teacher or other adult is routinely suspected of being a vampire, elf, or even an angel. As the title of Bruce Coville's *My Teacher is An Alien* (1989) suggests, the teacher in this book plans to carry several children away on the alien spaceship. Two brave but ordinary kids save the day. The school as a totally weird place is a popular theme with American children. A very popular series of story anthologies demonstrates how far an author can go in this direction: in *Sideways Stories From Wayside School* by Louis Sachar (see *Holes*), a school is built 32 storeys up instead of all on one floor. In the first story a teacher turns her class into apples.

In Australia, the genre of school stories – like that which sprang up in Britain with the publication of *Tom Brown's Schooldays* and flowed through to books by William Mayne and beyond – has not come into existence. No significant title features the closed world of the boarding school. *So Much to Tell You*, by John Marsden, is set in a girls' boarding school where the healing of Marina's pathological shyness begins – but there is nothing unique to boarding-school life essential to the solution of the mystery or to Marina's rehabilitation. The setting serves mainly to isolate her. Marina's story continues a view of boarding schools as an expensive pound for the orphaned, children left homeless by family failure, or for those deserving punishment. In *Seven Little Australians* (1894), Judy's father exiles her to boarding school in the hope that its discipline will reform her. Only children from the outback see boarding school as an advantage, but even then, Norah, of Mary Grant Bruce's *Billabong* series, knows her true education occurs at her home, Billabong. The idea of school as a place that draws together children from diverse backgrounds, and where experiences shape the future adult, is a staple of Australian children's literature from Louise Mack's *Teens: A Story of Australian Schoolgirls* (1897) to Jenny Pausacker's contemporary stories set in a Melbourne school. However, school is treated as an aspect of characters' lives, and not as the centre of narrative focus. BW,MN,CP

Schoolgirl, The see *School Friend*; see also *Girls' Crystal*

Schoolgirls' Own, The see annuals

Schoolgirls' Weekly, The see *Girls' Crystal*

Schulz, Charles see *Peanuts*; see also television

science fiction A genre that speculates about discoveries and developments in science and technology and their effects on the individual and society. Plots revolve around space travel, undersea exploration, time travel, aliens, psionic powers, genetic engineering, nuclear holocaust, utopias, dystopias, or robots running amok, or even all of the above. Plots that emphasise traditional science and technology over powers such as ESP, mind control or telekinesis, are referred to as 'hard', as opposed to 'soft', science fiction.

Contemporary science fiction for children and young adults springs from the same sources as adult science fiction – the works of Mary Shelley, Jules Verne, Edgar Allan Poe and H.G. Wells. Wells's works in particular – known in their time as 'scientific romances' – were widely read by young readers, especially *The Time Machine* (1895), *The War of the Worlds* (1898) and *The First Men in the Moon* (1901). Sir Arthur Conan Doyle – already familiar to young readers because of the *Sherlock Holmes* stories – published *The Lost World* in 1912, and at about the same time in the United States Edgar Rice Burroughs began a series of science-fiction stories later collected under the title *A Princess of Mars*. The *Frank Reade* series, which had first appeared in the late 1870s, also set a pattern for other series, such as the *Great Marvel*, *Tom Swift* and *Rick Brant* volumes that followed. In these, the plots revolve around inventions developed by the protagonist, and his efforts – which might take him all over the world – to keep villains from obtaining or sabotaging the inventions. Young readers also had access to comic strips like *Buck Rogers* and adult pulp science-fiction magazines like *Amazing Stories*.

With the decline of the *Tom Swift* series in the late 1930s and paper shortages during World War II, young American readers did not have much new science fiction from which to choose. After World War II, three events led to a revival of juvenile science fiction. The first was the invention of atomic weapons and their use at the end of the war. This led to a science fiction markedly different from that published earlier; rather than glorifying science and technology as a boon to humanity, authors now approached them warily. Yet it was a wariness mixed with optimism. Hiroshima may have exposed the darker side of science and technology, but it did not eliminate the promise they might hold for humankind. Rocket and atomic science were seen as offering the ability to colonise other planets, thus granting humankind a second chance at survival in the midst of an over-populated, polluted and war-ravaged Earth. Science fiction may have lost some of its innocence as a result of World War II and atomic weapons, but it also matured and paved the way for more interesting themes and complex plots.

The second event to revive interest in juvenile science fiction was the publication and success of *Rocket Ship Galileo* by Robert Heinlein (1947), the first of his successful juvenile works. Unlike the earlier dime novels, pulp serials and Stratemeyer Syndicate offerings, Heinlein's juvenile fiction was warmly welcomed by educators, librarians and parents, as it often explicitly advocated learning and growth. Most importantly, it was also welcomed by its intended readers. Rather than providing plots that move from one adventure to another, Heinlein's juvenile novels offer thoughtful plots and themes that develop naturally, and interesting characters who grow and change. Other publishers launched science-fiction series of their own, such as the Winston Publishing Company's popular *Winston* series.

Finally, the Russian launching of Sputnik in 1957 and the resulting space race pointed up a need to educate and interest children in the space sciences. One way to do this was through science fiction. The *Mike Mars* series (1961–4) tried to motivate young adult readers to support the United States space programme; author Donald Wollheim acknowledges the US Air Force and the National Aeronautics and Space Administration for their help and co-operation. The series follows the protagonist as he trains to become the first American in space and the first man to orbit the moon. A similar aim lay behind the *Young Astronauts* series (1990–1), which recounted the exploits of a group of adolescents training and preparing for a trip to Mars, even as a manned flight was discussed in the public arena. This series is a joint effort of the Young Astronaut Council and Zebra Books.

Most juvenile science fiction was written for boys by men. Female characters peopled the stories only to ask questions so that the scientist could answer, thereby relaying the information to the reader, or to find themselves in distress so that they could be heroically rescued. This began to change slowly after World War II. Heinlein was one of the first male children's science-fiction authors to include capable females among the characters in his books. However, women writers have made notable contributions. ANDRE NORTON was one of the first female authors of children's science fiction and published both hard (*Star* series) and soft (*Witch World* series) science fiction. Ellen MacGregor began the *Miss Pickerell* series in 1951, one of the first series written expressly for children. MacGregor chose a seemingly unlikely candidate for her protagonist – an older, unmarried woman who loves the peace and quiet of her farm, has no ties except her beloved pet cow, but has some scientific interests. MacGregor's elderly female character is old enough to set out on adventures, too old to attract male romantic interest, and eccentric enough to be childlike. MADELEINE L'ENGLE won the 1963 NEWBERY AWARD for *A WRINKLE IN TIME*, one of the first science-fiction children's books to win a prestigious award and one of the first with a young female protagonist. Other notable female authors are ANNE MCCAFFREY, VIRGINIA HAMILTON, MONICA HUGHES and SYLVIA ENGDAHL.

Science fiction intended for children is open to the criticism that its plots seem to rely more on fantasy than on real science; only marginal amounts of hard science can be included because of the limited knowledge of its intended readers. Some authors have found interesting ways to deal with this problem. ELEANOR CAMERON wrote *The Wonderful Flight to the Mushroom Planet*, the first of her *Mushroom Planet* books, in 1954. While much of the science seems more fantastic than speculative, characters Chuck and David do use scientific methods to discover why the Basidiumites' much-needed mushroom-like plant – which contains the necessary element without which they will sicken and die – is no longer thriving. However, the books that follow in the series move farther and farther from hard science and more towards the social sciences and fantasy. JOANNA COLE's *The Magic School Bus*, however, is an exception because it builds the story around a scientific concept and the focus of each instalment is the concept or technology, rather than the characters.

Series make up a large portion of the body of science fiction for young readers. Publishers discovered early that this format was a favourite among young readers, who are attracted by the adventures, predictability of plot, and confident, able and independent protagonists. Most readers eventually tire of this ideal and prefer to read about characters who experience some of the same self-doubts, and who express some of the same questions about the future and their place in it, as the readers themselves. Such readers are more likely to be drawn to Robert Heinlein's fiction, Andre Norton's *Star Ka'at* series, Monica Hughes's *ISIS* trilogy, Virginia Hamilton's *JUSTICE* trilogy, K.A. Applegate's *Animorphs* series or Charles Sheffield's *Jupiter* series. The *DOCTOR WHO* and *STAR TREK* TELEVISION series, and the *Star Trek* and *STAR WARS* movies, continue to create an appetite for science fiction and each has spawned its own juvenile series of books.

Recent American juvenile science fiction emphasises character development, offers more female and minority characters, is less innocent, more violent and more complex, and uses 'ensemble casts'. Bruce Coville's *A. I. Gang* series introduces the 'ensemble' of characters – Wendy, Ray, Tripton, Rachel, Roger and Hap – as the A[rtificial] I[ntelligence] Gang. Each child has a different talent and each is of equal importance to the plot. This provides an interesting reading experience for the child reader: the action does not have to follow a linear pattern and readers learn what all the characters are doing and thinking as the story unfolds. With male and female characters representing various ethnic groups, such books can appeal to a wider audience. This pattern also permits more complex plots capable of exploring ethical questions. Villains become more interesting and harder to identify. In the Cold War days, the villain in juvenile science fiction was stereotyped and flat, often representing the 'evils of Communism' and coming from an Eastern European or Latin American country. Now it is harder to identify who the villains are and which ideology, if any, they are intended to represent. The villains in the *Animorphs* series, for example, are alien slugs who insert themselves into their human host brains in order to control them.

In Australia, Winifred Law's *Through Space to the Planets* (1944) and *Rangers of the Universe* (1946), although crude, were genuine science-fiction novels that predated the first commonly acknowledged children's science-fiction novel, Robert Heinlein's *Rocketship Galileo*. The early years were dominated, however, by IVAN SOUTHALL's rather gung-ho *Simon Black* series of the 1950s – the author later apologised for its 'superficialities and indoctrinations'. From 1979, however, children's science-fiction novels have really taken a hold over both book award judges and readers in Australia. Lee Harding's quasi-science-fiction *Displaced Person* (1979), GILLIAN RUBINSTEIN's *Beyond the Labyrinth* (1988) and CATHERINE JINKS's *Eye to Eye* (1997) all received the CHILDREN'S BOOK COUNCIL OF AUSTRALIA BOOK OF THE YEAR AWARD, while numerous other science-fiction novels have been shortlisted.

These writers, with ISOBELLE CARMODY, JOHN MARSDEN, BRIAN CASWELL and VICTOR KELLEHER, have led the field over the last 20 years. The post-holocaust sub-genre has dominated, with Carmody's mammoth *OBERNEWTYN* series the most successful – and longest – example. More controversially, the subject of Marsden's series of seven novels, which began with *TOMORROW, WHEN THE WAR BEGAN* (1993), is the invasion of Australia by an unnamed Asian power in the immediate future, thus reawakening the old fear of the so-called 'Yellow Peril'. Caswell's *Deucalion* (1995), an allegory of the European treatment of Australia's Aborigines, and Kelleher's *TARONGA* (1986), a novel of human/animal relationships as much as of the post-holocaust Sydney in which it is set, exemplify the interests of these authors in an exploration of morality and the environment.

In Britain during the inter-war years, the usually pessimistic and dystopian scenarios of science fiction had little in common with the predominant optimism in children's literature. However, there was a revival of interest in science fiction in the 1950s. Three British works, deservedly popular in their time but now mostly forgotten, were *Moon Ahead* (1951) by Leslie Greener and John Hutchinson, *The Perilous Descent* (1952) by Bruce Carter, and *The Future Took Us* (1957) by David Severn. More enduring were John Wyndham's *THE DAY OF THE TRIFFIDS* (1951) and RAY BRADBURY's *The Martian Chronicles* (1950) and *Fahrenheit 451* (1953).

Subsequently, although science fiction has for the most part been less popular in Britain than fantasy, several major writers have contributed to the genre. JOHN CHRISTOPHER challenged the prevailing view that science fiction did not deserve serious attention when he published the first of his *TRIPODS* trilogy in 1967, and JOHN ROWE TOWNSEND and JAN MARK – both major children's writers – have developed science fiction for young readers. Some writers prefer to label the genre 'speculative fiction', a term appropriately applied by Jan Mark to her *The Ennead* (1978), *Divide and Rule* (1978), *Aquarius* (1982) and – very appropriately – *The Eclipse of the Century* (1999). NICHOLAS FISK's science fiction has been consistently innovative and popular, and in his stunning *Daz 4 Zoe* (1990) ROBERT SWINDELLS introduced many new readers to the idea of the futuristic dystopia – and its political and social implications. Two respected and popular Indian writers, MARGARET BHATTY and DILIP M. SALWI, have also written science fiction in which subtlety of theme is combined with the representation of characters maturing through danger, crisis and self-doubt.

Thousands of young British readers in the 1950s were introduced to science fiction through COMICS, PERIODICALS AND MAGAZINES and ANNUALS, with many unlikely and outrageous plots. The most successful of these was the *EAGLE* with its famous SUPERHERO comic strip, *DAN DARE, PILOT OF THE FUTURE*. Even more famous – because he is more enduring – is Hergé's TINTIN, whose adventures include *Destination Moon*, *Explorers on the Moon* (both translated in 1959) and *Flight 714* (translated in 1968). According to Harry Thompson, 'When Armstrong and Aldrin stepped out on to the surface of the moon from their Apollo spacecraft, all the world gasped. All, that is, except Tintin readers, who had already known for two decades that the moon looked like that.' Perhaps one of the roles of science fiction is to prepare young readers for science fact. MF, VW, JF

see also ADULT FICTION; FANTASY; SUPERHEROES; TIME-SLIP FANTASY

Scieszka, Jon 1954– The American author whose metafictional texts illustrated by LANE SMITH helped introduce postmodernism into children's literature. Scieszka received an MFA in creative writing at Columbia University, but became an elementary school teacher. He has said that his books are intended for 'hardcore silly kids' and that his two guiding principles in writing for children are 'Never Underestimate the Intelligence of Your Audience' and 'Have Fun and Tell Lots of Bad Jokes as Often as Possible'. *The True Story of the Little Pigs, by A. Wolf* (1989) is the first of Scieszka's revised FAIRY TALES, which developed from a class assignment. His collaborations with Smith – *The Stinky Cheese Man and Other Fairly Stupid Tales* (1992), *Math Curse* (1995) and *Squids Will Be Squids* (1998) – with their ironic sensibilities and goofy sense of humour, are enjoyed by both older children and adults and have been widely celebrated as postmodern PICTUREBOOKS. Scieszka has also written revisionist picturebooks with other illustrators, including *The Frog Prince, Continued* (1991) with Steve Johnson, and *The Book That Jack Wrote* (1994) with Daniel Adel. In addition to their picturebooks, Scieszka and Smith have collaborated on the *Time Warp Trio* series, beginning with *Knights of the Kitchen Table* (1991), which is a time-travel series for middle-school readers that gently parodies genres of boys' ADVENTURES STORIES. JCS

Scorpion, The see COMICS, PERIODICALS AND MAGAZINES

Scott, Bill (William Neville) 1923– Australian folklorist born in Queensland. Scott is passionately devoted to the Australian way of life, which he celebrates in verse, song, folktales and three novels, *Boori* (1978), *Darkness Under the Hills* (1980) – both Aboriginal hero tales – and *Shadow Among the Leaves* (1984), which all pay homage to Aboriginal spirit life. MSax

see also ABORIGINAL CULTURE IN CHILDREN'S BOOKS

Scott, Hugh British writer of the the award-winning *Why Weeps the Brogan?* (1989) and several popular and distinctive horror novels, notably *The Haunted Sand* (1990), *The Camera Obscura* (1990), *A Box of Tricks* (1991), *The Gargoyle* (1991), *A Ghost Waiting* (1993), *The Ghosts of Ravens Crag* (1996), *The Secret of the Pit* (1998), *Giants* (1999), and a number of novels for younger readers, the best-known of which is *Freddie and the Enormouse* (1989).

Many of Scott's novels are set in old houses, with a warm and loving but often eccentric family, and supernatural events provoked by some unresolved historical injustice or tragedy. Three features set Scott's fiction above the common level of horror writing: he constructs most of his novels so that the comforting power and playful seriousness of a same-sex or boy-girl friendship is a cheering counter to the supernatural elements; secondly, evil and cruelty are invariably overcome by the courage, honesty and loyalty of his protagonists; and finally, he is a conscious stylist, constantly rescuing his narratives from formula and cliché with sharp vivid phrasing set in quickly-paced syntax.

Scott's young protagonists experience all the ecstatic and scary intensities of adolescence. However, though there are in some novels hints that the supernatural events are related to their developing sexuality, these are not overtly developed, and they are in any case set against the deep reassurance provided by the atmospheric and convincing evocations of home, family and friendship, and by the almost transcendental joyousness of his endings. VW

Scott, Michael 1959– Prolific and versatile Irish novelist. His work ranges between teenage romantic drama, IRISH MYTHOLOGY, FANTASY and horror. He has combined knowledge of Irish mythology with his STORYTELLING skill in retellings of old Irish sagas. His strongest works, the *De Danann* trilogy – *Windlord* (1991), *Earthlord* (1992) and *Firelord* (1994) – see his modern-day protagonists, Ally and Ken, hurtled into ancient Ireland in a fast-paced fantasy. The same pace is maintained in his horror writing, which includes *October Moon* (1992) and *Vampyre* (1997). Under the name 'Mike Scott' he has written three novels featuring Judith, a girl from a well-off family, and Spider, a young man from the travelling community. VC

Scott, Sir Walter 1771–1832 Novelist and poet. Scott wrote only one book specifically for children: *Tales of a Grandfather* (1827–30), a simplified history of Scotland designed with his six-year-old grandson John Lockhart in mind. But his series of historical novels from *Waverley* (1814) to *The Talisman* (1825) were seized upon by older children starved of ADVENTURE STORIES in their normal reading diet. In these pages they could find romantic locations and deeds of high renown. Irrespective of their various historical inaccuracies, these novels were also popular with adults. Parents were therefore often sympathetic when their children turned to this great writer, either in the original or else in one of the innumerable cut-down versions popular at home or school. In 1888 Scott was nominated third in a poll of boys' favourite authors, after DICKENS and W.H.G. KINGSTON.

As a child in Edinburgh, Scott immersed himself in folklore rather than the classics. His fiction also drew on BALLADS and FAIRY TALES, with ROBIN HOOD and Friar Tuck given important parts in *Ivanhoe* (1819), Scott's most popular book and still read and occasionally televised today. The many descriptions of landscapes and ruins in his novels were an important influence upon the 19th-century Romantic movement. His action-packed historical stories, with their shining heroes and dastardly villains, also helped lay the foundation for the adventure story set in the past, later to be such a feature of older children's reading at the end of the last century. NT

Scottish folktales A group of 19th-century folklorists brought Scottish folktales into prominence. Centuries before, stories were being transmitted orally between Ireland and Scotland, the Fenian Cycle of IRISH MYTHOLOGY being one of the most enduring and popular of this shared lore. The early tales, some said to have come to Scotland's Western Islands and Highlands around 500 AD, reflect this interchange. The continuity of language and culture between the two Gaelic-speaking lands brought about folktales almost parallel in content. Stories came to the Lowland Scots from the North Sea countries, Ireland, and the North of England. Others filtered down from the Highlands. The Scandinavian influence is especially perceptible in the stories from the islands of Orkney and Shetland.

The Red Etin, a tale known to have existed as early as the 16th century, tells of an Irish giant (etin), who has stolen away the king of Scotland's daughter. It has been said that Sir David Lyndsay told this story to the young James V (1512–42), whose father, James IV (1473–1513) encouraged tale-tellers, minstrels, singers and others to contribute to the amusement of his court. *The Complaynt of Scotland* (1548) – described as 'a sort of quaint political pamphlet' – lists (without telling) several tales including *The Red Etin, The Wal at the World's End, The Black Bull of Norroway,* and *Pure Tynt Rashiecoat,* possibly the earliest mention of the CINDERELLA story in the British Isles. These stories are all retold in modern collections today.

Storytellers played an important role in the transmission of FAIRY TALES, in the 19th century especially. Legends, märchen, animal stories, jocular tales, supernatural tales, BALLADS and rhymes all seem to have been part of the storyteller's repertoire. Even TALL TALES were said to have existed. Whether told by nursemaids, local folk, or a traveller passing through the area, these experiences were recalled by those who either heard stories in the nursery, or in the evenings round a blazing peat fire. Alexander Carmichael and Walter Gregor both wrote memorable accounts of STORYTELLING during this period. It was from these sources that collectors gathered much of their material.

SIR WALTER SCOTT (1771–1832) was fascinated by the myths and legends he heard as a boy in the Border Country. His *Minstrelsy of the Scottish Border* (1802–3) reflects his love of this lore, as do his poems and novels. He took great interest in the stories of the GRIMM BROTHERS, carrying on an enthusiastic correspondence with them. He also encouraged and aided Robert Chambers (1802–71), one of the important folklorists of the early 19th century. Chambers first published his *Popular Rhymes of Scotland* in 1826, supplementing it in later editions with a chapter of *Fireside Nursery Stories* which included some of the tales mentioned in *The Complaynt of Scotland.*

The Scottish folktale received the most momentum from John Francis Campbell of Islay (1822–85), who published the four-volume *Popular Tales of the West Highlands* between 1860 and 1862. It has been said that no folklorist could compare in investigative powers, thoroughness of treatment, and acquaintance with the people, combined with a powerful national sentiment and a knowledge of Gaelic. Campbell initiated the technique of folktale collecting in Scotland and was described as a counterpart to the Brothers Grimm.

ANDREW LANG (1844–1912) was a folklore scholar who searched out many tales. He is best known for his 12 volumes of 'COLOURED' FAIRY BOOKS, although it was his wife who was responsible for the retellings; he admitted that he did no more than 'superintend'. Other folklorists of this period involved with collecting Scottish tales included Peter Buchan, John Gregorson Campbell, Walter Traill Dennison, Sir George Douglas, Walter Gregor, Joseph Jacobs, James MacDougall and Donald MacInnes.

Fairy folk have always played important roles in Scottish folktales: bodachs, brollachans, brownies, ferlies, kelpies, selkies, wizards, and worms (sea-serpents) are but a few. From *The Secret Commonwealth of Elves, Fauns, and Fairies,* written in 1691 by Robert Kirk, to the books on fairies by K. M. BRIGGS, these supernatural creatures have been well researched and documented. They continue to provide great interest today.

The Scottish children's writer MOLLIE HUNTER, a very accomplished contemporary storyteller, includes inhabitants of the fairy world in many of her books. Other present-day writers of children's books to draw upon Scottish folklore include K.M. Briggs, SUSAN COOPER, BERLIE DOHERTY, Monica Furlong, FRANCES HENDRY, DIANA WYNNE JONES, ROSEMARY SUTCLIFF and JANE YOLEN.

Collections of Scottish folktales include those of SORCHE NIC LEODHAS, ROSEMARY MANNING-SANDERS, Norah and William Montgomerie, Duncan Williamson and Barbara Ker Wilson, as well as more extensive anthologies edited by Hannah Aitken, Alan Bruford and D.A. MacDonald, David Buchan, Ernest Marwick and Neil Philip. Scottish folklore traditions are actively being kept alive by the School of Scottish Studies in Edinburgh. PDS

Scudder, Horace Elisha 1838–1902 American editor, publisher, critic and writer. Scudder edited the influential *RIVERSIDE MAGAZINE FOR YOUNG PEOPLE: AN ILLUSTRATED MONTHLY* (1867–70). His correspondence with contributors such as MARY MAPES DODGE, FRANK STOCKTON, LUCRETIA P. HALE and Sarah Orne Jewett shows his editorial tact, intelligence and enthusiasm. His concern for the aesthetic effect of ILLUSTRATION and page design made the *Riverside* a trend-setting publication, featuring artwork by WINSLOW HOMER, John LaFarge and Thomas Nast. Scudder's greatest editorial triumph was to persuade HANS CHRISTIAN ANDERSEN to publish 17 stories in the magazine, ten of which had not been published elsewhere. Among Scudder's memorable innovations was an editorial column of reviews and comments on children's reading directed toward adults. Scudder's most popular books of fiction for children were his eight books about the adventures of the Bodley family. But he also edited collections of FABLES, legends and FAIRY TALES for children, and produced *The Riverside Literature Series for Young People,* a series of 200 inexpensive classic texts for the classroom. A pioneer critic of

'Come along, prefects, playtime over.' Illustration of St Trinian's by Ronald Searle.

children's literature, he wrote many articles and reviews, and a collection of lectures, *Childhood in Literature and Art* (1894). SRG

Searle, Ronald 1920– One of the best-known British illustrators of the second half of the 20th century. Searle's first published artwork aimed at a young audience was for such novels as Roy Fuller's *With My Little Eye* (1948). In the same year, Searle produced *Hurrah for St. Trinian's!* (1948), a collection of cartoons depicting the exploits of the young ladies at an infamous academy. Searle's anarchic 'gals' caught the public's imagination and a further five *St Trinian's* volumes, as well as a popular series of films, followed. Searle also provided witty ILLUSTRATIONS for GEOFFREY WILLANS's four *Molesworth* books, which give a boy's-eye-view of England's eccentric public-school system. JC

Sebestyen, Ouida [Igen Sebestyen] 1924– American author of several outstanding novels for children and young adults. Sebestyen was born in Texas and settled in Colorado. After a long apprenticeship, she published her first book, *Words By Heart*, in 1979. The story of 12-year-old Lena and the prejudice her African American family faces in a small town in Texas in the early part of this century was well reviewed and received several awards, but it was also accused of perpetuating racist stereotypes. Despite this negative criticism, the book has become a modern classic, featuring prominently and positively in the novel *Possibles* (1995) by Vaunda Nelson, a young black writer inspired by the book as a child. *On Fire* (1985) continues the story of Tater Haney, a character in *Words by Heart. The Girl in the Box* (1988), unlike Sebestyen's warm FAMILY STORIES, is a stark and intriguing postmodern novel, consisting of notes, letters and reminiscences written on a typewriter by a girl abducted and trapped in a dark room. 'Good words have to be able to make themselves heard over an awful lot of strident and sometimes empty competition', writes Sebestyen in HORN BOOK (December 1995). LH

see also AFRICAN AMERICAN LITERATURE

Secret Diary of Adrian Mole (1982) Extremely popular quartet by SUE TOWNSEND, often found in the adult humour section, partly because the young Adrian is obsessed with SEX – especially the length of his penis – but also because there is a good deal of political comment, some of which is concerned with Margaret Thatcher. He is a spotty youth, a failed poet (he sends poems to the BBC only for them to be rejected), and, caught in the midst of family rows, he retreats into the world of his diary, noting all kinds of disasters and irrelevancies which make up a day in the Mole family household. All the stories are written in the form of a diary, giving them a convincing quality of immediacy, and the mention of contemporary events such as the Falklands War adds to their authenticity. *The Growing Pains of Adrian Mole* (1984) finds him pining for Pandora, the love of his life, and in *True Confessions of Adrian Mole 16 3/4 to 21 & 4 months* (1989), Adrian turns his attentions to – amongst other matters – Sarah Ferguson's lack of taste in choosing Prince Andrew and not himself. *Adrian Mole: The Wilderness Years* was published in 1993 (in US, *Adrian Mole: The Lost Years,* 1994), and *Adrian Mole: The Cappucino Years* followed in 1999. The stories comprise a satirical look at the 1980s and 90s as well as embodying many humiliating and embarrassing adolescent experiences recognised by many readers. The Adrian Mole character has been televised very successfully and adapted for the stage. SET

Secret Garden, The (1911) Novel by FRANCES HODGSON BURNETT, set in Yorkshire at the beginning of the 20th century, about two selfish children, Mary and Colin, and how they are transformed through the agency of the 'secret garden'. The book was one of the earliest works for children to consider not just a single aspect of the child's development – spiritual, physical, social, etc. – but to treat these issues as necessarily integrated. That there is, for example, a link between the physical and emotional states of well-being is suggested quite early on when Colin's unsympathetic nurse says of her 'invalid', 'Half of what ails him is temper and the other half is hysterics.' The movement from isolation and selfishness to social integration finds a correspondence in the movement from weakness to health. The garden itself consitutes a dense and living metaphor for the alterations in Mary and Colin, providing yet another level of correspondence for the changes that occur in the children. Both children and garden have been neglected for ten years and only sporadically attended to. The pruning, weeding, planting and stirring of soil in order that the earth might breathe are not only activities that promote physical health in the plants and children through the exercise involved, but are an external manifestation or enactment of what is happening internally or psychologically within the children. The sense that the garden dramatises for us what is happening intangibly is heightened with the robin's nest-building: Misselthwaite is in the process of becoming a home.

A part of the book's ethos is derived from the Romantic philosophy of Wordsworth and Coleridge. Nature within the text possesses quasi-mystical properties and the Romantic valorisation of Nature as healer, teacher and moral guide informs the text. But the secret garden is more than a magical healing and educational space; it represents both the acknowledgement and fulfillment of the complex needs of children. When Mary asks Mr Craven if she may have a bit of earth, she is asking both for a place to plant things and also, symbolically, for private space (both Colin and Mary hate to be watched) and for something to call her own. As a walled area, the garden is space that is protected and private as well as circumscribed, symbolic of the child's need for freedom as well as discipline; both need to be in balance. As Martha the maid says, never having one's own way or always having one's own way are equally bad for the child. The garden again stands for both work and play, exertion of the body and of the imagination, as in, for example, Colin's 'scientific experiment' designed to test the workings of the 'Magic' (positive thinking) on the body. Finally, the garden is also mythic. But it is not only Eden from which the adult Adam and Eve have been expelled to die or wander sorrowfully over the face of the earth; it is also paradise and lost innocence which the child has reclaimed. The BBC produced a serialised version of the novel in 1952, and it has also been filmed for cinema in 1949, 1987 and 1993. A sequel, *Misselthwaite*, which follows the lives of Colin, Mary and Dickon through World War I and adulthood, was written by Susan Moody in 1995. SA

Secret Seven, The (1949–63) Series of 15 books by ENID BLYTON, inspired by a club organised by one of her publishers' children. Of the Seven, only two seem at all memorable: Peter, the rather autocratic leader, and Janet, his sister. One other character stands out: Susie, a member's sister who is barred from the Seven. She is not only entertaining and subversive, but provides the nearest thing to an ironic stance on the Seven's activities. For post-war adults, the 'SS' might have unfortunate connotations, but for children the series provided well-plotted, simple detective stories which reward any young, perceptive reader. DR

Sedgwick, Catharine Maria 1789–1867 First successful woman novelist in the United States. She grew up in a happy home, with a 'fragmentary' education, spending much of her time in the hills and mountains of Massachusetts. She chose not to marry, enjoying instead close contacts with her siblings and their families. Sedgwick wrote several stories specifically for young adults, such as *The Boy of Mount Rhigi* (1848), but was aware that all her novels had a large readership of 'misses in their teens'. The heroines of Sedgwick's novels conform to 19th-century norms in that their main role is to be a good influence on men, on whom they are usually financially dependent. They may be unsure of themselves when faced with emotional problems: Jane in *A New-England Tale* (1822) falls in love at first with a clearly unworthy man, although she shows great maturity in other ways when orphaned at the age of 12. However, they are usually physically courageous, ingenious in solving problems and firmly independent when they need to make moral decisions. *Hope Leslie* (1827) is particularly interesting in its exploration of the moral, racial and religious problems of early American colonists and the native people they encountered. FEA

Seed, Jenny 1930– South African author of FOLKTALES, local ADVENTURE STORIES and many historical youth novels. Her early work was sent to England for publication, but since the strengthening of the indigenous publishing industry her books are published (and read widely) in South Africa. She does her research carefully and her books teach subtle lessons as well. For example, *The Spy Hill* (1984) tells of a boy involved in the battle of Spionkop between Boers and British in 1900, but its message is that a battle, far from being a boyish adventure, is confusing, frightening and horrible. Her most mature book is *The Great Thirst* (1971), the story of the warring leader Jonker Afrikaner in what is now Namibia. Seed's faith in 'a great hand holding all together' shows clearly in this powerful novel, which does not shrink from showing how white traders brought with them the dangers of alcohol and debt.

Though her writing has been criticised as being informed by a European perspective, she has written many perceptive stories (historical and modern) about black African children. She has written two books on the famous Siege of Mafeking, the award-winning *Place Among the Stones* (1987), and *The Hungry People*

(1992) which exposes the plight of Africans caught in a white man's war. Without doubt, Seed has played an important part in making national history lively and interesting for South African children. JHe

Seeing Stone, The (2000) First part of a proposed trilogy by the British writer KEVIN CROSSLEY-HOLLAND about KING ARTHUR. This narrative, however, is no ordinary retelling of the Arthurian story. It is set in a medieval manor in 1199 and tells in 100 compelling chapters the story of a young boy to whom Merlin has given a magic seeing-stone in which he – the historical Arthur – gradually discovers the story of the great mythical Arthur, slowly beginning to realise that their lives have a number of strange parallels. *The Seeing Stone* is thus a historical novel – graphic, authentic, lucidly detailed, and rich with both the colours and the bleakness of 12th-century England; at the same time, however, it introduces young readers with narrative tact and clarity to the complicated beginnings of the Arthurian story: Uther's desire for Ygerna, the conception and birth of Arthur, the drawing of the sword from the stone, Arthur acknowledged as king, and the background of political instability and the Saxon invasions. It is difficult to think of any other comparable fiction which provides young readers with a stunning wealth of historical and mythical substance with such beguiling narrative appeal. VW

Sefton, Catherine [Martin Waddell] 1941– Irish writer of over 160 books for children, born in Belfast. Taking the surname of his grandmother, Waddell has written his thrillers, GHOST STORIES and novels for older readers under this female pseudonym. The first Catherine Sefton publication, described as 'a pastiche of a Victorian children's book', was *In a Blue Velvet Dress* (1972). Intriguing plots which involve an element of the supernatural are a hallmark of many Sefton novels, but the writer, preoccupied with Irish history, also creates an additional dimension as he explores the ways in which the past, with its legacy of troubles or triumphs, permeates present-day situations and experiences. *The Ghost Girl* (1985) and *Emer's Ghost* (1981) exemplify this fusion of themes, as does *Island of the Strangers* (1983), a book regarded by the writer as clearly most representing his views. *Along a Lonely Road* (1991), a novel of intense suspense and mystery, received critical acclaim and *The Cast Off* (1993) makes a strong statement about the tough issues which confront many alienated young people. Three novels set during the troubles in Northern Ireland form a trilogy: *Starry Night* (1986) won the Other Award and was runner-up for the GUARDIAN AWARD FOR CHILDREN'S FICTION. *Frankie's Story* (1988) and *The Beat of the Drum* (1989) followed. All three stories – re-issued in 2000 as a trilogy by Martin Waddell – focus on the problems faced by young people growing up in Belfast at a time of political and religious hostility and within a volatile atmosphere of mistrust, violence and fear. CMN

see also MARTIN WADDELL

Segal, Lore see MAURICE SENDAK

Segun, Mabel 1930– Nigerian author, born in Ondo in the Yoruba-speaking West. Her first children's book, *My Father's Daughter* (1965), recounts her childhood, as does *My Mother's Daughter* (1987). Segun's books stress responsibility, patriotism and self-reliance, always with a touch of humour. *Olu and the Broken Statue* (1985) concerns the moral dilemma three friends face when they find an antique artwork which could be sold to tourists to clinch a prize. *The Twins and the Tree Spirit* (1991) urges care for the environment, while *Youth Day Parade* (1983) extols co-operative planning. Her other children's books include a FOLKTALE (*The First Corn*, 1989) and two co-edited books of poetry. Long an advocate for children's books, Segun founded the Children's Literature Association of Nigeria in 1978 and has written extensively on children's literature. VD

Selden, George [George Selden Thompson] 1929–89 American novelist, born in Hartford, Connecticut, best known for his series of books featuring Chester Cricket, Harry Cat and Tucker Mouse, beginning with *The Cricket in Times Square* (1960) and ending with *The Old Meadow* (1987). He also wrote a number of other books, including PICTUREBOOKS and adult novels (the latter under a pseudonym, Terry Andrews); none proved as popular as his gentle and wry adventures of animal friends in and out of the city. BH

Selfish Giant, The see *HAPPY PRINCE AND OTHER TALES, THE*

Sendak, Maurice (Bernard) 1928– American PICTUREBOOK maker, illustrator and writer, one of the most important international contributors to the literature of childhood and the first American to win the HANS CHRISTIAN ANDERSEN MEDAL. Born in Brooklyn and brought up in a sheltered Jewish community, he was the youngest child of Polish immigrants who had come to New York before World War I. After leaving school, he worked with a Manhattan window display company whilst attending evening classes in art. A fortuitous meeting with Ursula Nordstrom, the children's book editor, led him to illustrating commissions. His pictures for RUTH KRAUSS's *A Hole is to Dig* (1952) established his name. Sendak illustrated more than 50 books between 1951 and 1961, and consciously expanded his graphic repertoire by emulating the work of master illustrators, both past and present.

Sendak has spoken and written extensively about his art. He sees it as the role of the illustrator to interpret the text, and describes the practice in musical analogies. Sendak has a cherished belief that the child he was still exists within him in the most physical way, thus giving him a dual perception on his experiences. He has a self-confessed absorption with his own childhood, and a curiosity about childhood as a state of being. His own picturebooks record how children live in states of both FANTASY and reality, moving between the two with ease. Sendak, who defines fantasy as that imagined world where disturbing emotional situations are resolved to a child's satisfaction, first maps out this territory in *Kenny's Window* (1956). His best early work, *The Sign on Rosie's Door* (1960), presents the prototype of all Sendak's plucky child-characters, Rosie. This collection of stories about a lively girl, inspired by a real ten-year-old, who entertains her friends and enriches their lives through acting out her fantasies, also acknowledges the price to be paid for taking artistic leaps and imaginative risks. An animated film, *Really Rosie, Starring the Nutshell Kids* (1975) and a Broadway musical, *Broadway Rosie*, in the early 1980s, are evidence of the enduring power of Rosie as character and metaphor.

One of the most popular and evocative of his early collaborations is CHARLOTTE ZOLOTOW's *Mr. Rabbit and the Lovely Present* (1962), in which Sendak adopts a nostalgic style, the dominant influence for which was the American painter, WINSLOW HOMER, and the setting leafy Vermont. This same year also saw the publication of *The Nutshell Library*, Sendak's humorous tribute to CHAPBOOKS: four miniature volumes comprising a reptilian alphabet, a seasons book, a counting book, and a moral tale. One year later Sendak published *WHERE THE WILD THINGS ARE*, which radically changed perceptions of what a children's picturebook might be, in both theme and appearance. *IN THE NIGHT KITCHEN* (1970) and *OUTSIDE OVER THERE* (1981) complete his self-styled trilogy, the central theme of which is the exploration of the shadowy forces of the unconscious. Common elements of all three stories are a journey, extreme dangers to be surmounted by initiative and creativity, and a resolution which is concerned with wholeness or healing rather than a moral imperative.

Sendak credits the birth of the picturebook genre to the 19th-century English illustrator RANDOLPH CALDECOTT, and paid a direct homage to him with *Hector Protector and As I Went Over the Water* (1965), which takes two MOTHER GOOSE rhymes and in each case develops a series of pictures from them, line by line. The marriage of modern interpretation and traditional material is echoed in the graphic style. The illustrations have a quality which relates to WOOD ENGRAVING, whilst the improvised dialogue in speech-balloons brings the costume-drama characters into the style of 1930s COMICS. Sendak's ironic nod to mortality, *Higglety Pigglety Pop! Or, There Must Be More to Life* (1967), also has roots in a NURSERY RHYME and echoes the illustrative style of 19th-century artists. The central character, a Sealyham terrier, Jennie, is dissatisfied with all the material comforts she enjoys, and leaves home. After enigmatic adventures she finds herself, literally and metaphorically, in a childlike heaven, fulfilled through performance-art. *Higglety Pigglety Pop!* was itself transformed into an opera in the 1980s.

At the beginning of the 1970s Sendak worked on illustrated plates for a two-volume collection of the tales of the GRIMM BROTHERS, translated by Lore Segal, to be called *The Juniper Tree* (1973). In preparation he travelled to Europe to steep himself in the landscape and art, responding particularly to Albrecht Dürer. His beautiful brooding black-and-white drawings for the tales are densely worked like etchings, the figures barely contained within their confining frames. *Dear Mili* (1988), Sendak's illustrations of a story by Wilhelm Grimm, is another visual excursion into European territory, this time into the symbols of the Northern Romantic tradition, interwoven with Jewish and Christian imagery and visual references to events in World War II. Mili is a vital descendant of the Romantic child, as portrayed by Philipp Otto Runge: an empirical reality and a lofty symbol, in this case, for the suffering of the innocent in wars. Concern for the plight of vulnerable children beyond tales or dreams, but found in contemporary urban and social decay, fuels *WE ARE ALL IN THE DUMPS WITH JACK AND GUY* (1993). JD

Sengupta, Subhadra 1952– Indian author regarded as one of the most talented, promising and original fiction writers for children in India today. Graduating from initial Indianised versions of formulaic humour, mystery and ADVENTURE STORIES, Sengupta has fallen back on the long sophisticated tradition of children's literature of Bengal, the strongest influences being the writings of the RAY family, and the HISTORICAL FICTION of Sharadindu Bandopadhya. Stimulated by the impulse to popularise the study of history, her historical fiction has strong plots backed by authentic Indian characters and ambience, making them immensely popular with children. Meticulously researched historical location imparts texture and richness to her stories, the major focus falling on the Mughal period, the reigns of the Mauryan Emperor Ashoka and Krishnadeva Raya of Vijaynagar. A fast-paced adventure or mystery story is woven around the exploits of the child protagonists, who are thrown back, in a TIME-SLIP FANTASY, to past times where historical personages like Birbal, Tansen and other court dignitaries become credible flesh-and-blood characters. Scintillating detail of battles, bazaars, palaces, music, painting and food, buoys up the narrative. Her books are about ordinary people. Bishnu, in the popular *Bishnu, the Dhobi Singer* (1994) and *Bishnu Sings Again* (1998), is a washerman's son; the three children in *Mystery of the House of Pigeons* (1993) are the children of a tongawalla and a vegetable-seller. Her books are optimistic with smart children ultimately triumphing after adversity. MBh

Seredy, Kate 1899–1975 American writer and illustrator who moved from Hungary to the United States in 1922. In her fiction, Seredy frequently addresses social problems such as war, poverty, or religious persecution; for example, *A Tree for Peter* (1941) is a gentle story about what happens when a lame boy encourages a poverty-stricken community to plant a garden. Seredy is remembered primarily for her use of the Hungarian past as subject matter, as in her NEWBERY MEDAL winner, *The White Stag* (1938), which is based on ancient legends about the rise of Attila the Hun. Her best-known novels are two that focus on her childhood in Hungary. *The Good Master* (1937) describes the lives of two young cousins growing up in the Hungarian countryside. When high-spirited Kate comes to stay at his horse ranch, Jancsi's life will never be the same. In the sequel, *The Singing Tree* (1939), the cousins have to face what happens to their life when war breaks out; the idyllic world of their ranch changes for ever after World War I begins. Both of these books display Seredy's talent for evoking a vivid vision of the past, creating engaging characters and tackling difficult social issues. SAI

Sergeant Bilko see ANIMATED CARTOONS

Serraillier, Ian (Lucien) 1912–94 Poet and novelist, much of whose work comprised the retelling of ancient myths and FOLKTALES. A schoolteacher for many years, he collaborated on an innovatory READING SCHEME and was founder editor (with Anne Serraillier) of the *New Windmill* series of classic literature for schools. He published ADVENTURE STORIES from 1946, achieving an international reputation with his award-winning *THE SILVER SWORD* (1956), issued in the United States as *Escape from Warsaw* and translated into 12 languages. The narrative skill so evident in his fiction is also a hallmark of Serraillier's verse, which is amusing, kind and loving. All his poetry collections are out of print today, but individual poems such as 'The Rescue' and 'Anne and the Field-Mouse' are still popular in anthologies. His books are characterised by high-quality ILLUSTRATIONS, the work of artists such as C. WALTER HODGES PC

Sesame Street (from 1969) Landmark American public TELEVISION series, created by Joan Gany Cooney, executive director of the Children's Television Workshop. Although the series is set in an urban neighbourhood, expressly to appeal to city children, it has been popular with children from all areas of the country. Its goal is to teach young children letters, numbers and other reading skills, as well as to show them people from all walks of life interacting in harmony with each other. The series uses skits, music and animation to convey its lessons,with deft humour and satire. While adult human actors controlled the programme, one of the major reasons for the series' success was the presence of THE MUPPETS, an ensemble of hand puppets created by JIM HENSON. BH

Seth, Vikram see *BEASTLY TALES FROM HERE AND THERE*

Seton, Ernest Thompson 1860–1946 Canadian author of realistic animal stories for children; he also published as Ernest Seton-Thompson. Born in England, Seton was one of 14 children; the family moved to Canada when Seton was six years old. His father, Joseph Thompson, bitterly opposed Ernest's desire to become a naturalist. At 13, Seton purchased with his own money Ross's *Birds of Canada* only to discover numerous errors in the text; he promptly began correcting and annotating the book. Seton won a scholarship in 1879 to attend the Royal Academy School of Painting and Sculpture in London, where he studied the works of such naturalists as John James Audubon, Henry David Thoreau and John Burroughs. He returned to Canada in the 1880s. Throughout the 1890s, he worked as an illustrator of works such as *The Century Dictionary*. At that time, he became friends with RUDYARD KIPLING. His first marriage, to Grace Gallatin, an American, lasted from 1896 to 1937, although the couple separated in the 1920s. Their marriage produced one daughter, the writer Anya Seton. His second marriage, to his secretary, Julia Moss, also produced a daughter, Beulah. They established a home and a camp near Santa Fe, New Mexico.

Seton is best known for his realistic stories about animals and for founding the Woodcraft League and the Boy Scouts of America. His most famous publication, *Wild Animals I Have Known* (1898), details the lives of animals such as Lobo the Wolf, Silverspot the Crow and Raggylug the Rabbit. Seton insisted that his characterisations were composites of real animals he had observed; nonetheless, he also claimed that his fiction was intended to teach readers that animals were rational creatures entitled to rights similar to those of humans. Initially attacked by John Burroughs as a fraud, Seton invited him to study his notes, photographs and specimens. Eventually, Burroughs revised his published opinion. Seton's natural studies emphasised both the realistic details of animals' lives and man's moral responsibilities for animals. They also encouraged readers to develop a more thorough understanding of human nature through their study of these animals. Well-known nature studies by Seton include *The Biography of a Grizzly* (1900), *Life-Histories of Northern Animals: an Account of the Mammals of Manitoba* in two volumes (1909), and *Wild Animals at Home* (1913). Seton combined his love for the outdoors with his passion for educating young people when he published *Two Little Savages*, subtitled 'A Book of American Woodcraft for Boys', in 1903. This led to *The Book of Woodcraft and Indian Lore* (1912) and *Boy Scouts of America: A Handbook* (1910). In these books, Seton provided for young people a model of the benefits of outdoor life based on Indian customs and beliefs. AKP

see also ANIMALS IN CHILDREN'S FICTION; GUIDING AND SCOUTING

Seuss, Dr (Theodor Seuss Geisel) 1904–91 Probably the most famous and successful American PICTUREBOOK author and illustrator, noted for his bright cartoon graphics and humorous rhymes. Seuss attended Dartmouth College where he edited and drew cartoons for the campus humour magazine, *Jack-o-Lantern*. During his senior year, he was caught drinking on campus and forced to resign as editor, but continued to submit cartoons under his middle name, Seuss. He attended Oxford University for a year but returned to the United States, working as a cartoonist and drawing humorous advertising for Shell Oil. His first picturebook, *And To Think I Saw It on Mulberry Street* (1937), was rejected by 27 publishers until he met a college friend, Mike McClintock, who had recently become a children's book editor. McClintock accepted the manuscript. The grateful Seuss named the protagonist Marco – a boy whose imagination transforms an ordinary horse and cart into an elaborate parade – after McClintock's son. Seuss wrote and illustrated a series of prose FAIRY TALES including *The 500 Hats of Bartholomew Cubbins* (1938), *The King's Stilts* (1939) and, for adults, *The Seven Lady Godivas* (1939). His inspiration for *Horton Hatches the Egg* (1940) was a sketch of an elephant sliding over a drawing of a tree; Seuss wondered what it would be doing in the tree and decided it must be hatching an egg.

During World War II, Seuss was a political cartoonist and made patriotic films for the military under the direction of Frank Capra. This work influenced later books, including *Yertle the Turtle* (1958), in which a dictatorial leader resembles Adolf Hitler, and *Horton Hears a Who* (1954), a FABLE which acknowledges that 'a person is a person no matter how small' and refers to the Japanese need for dignity after the war.

Seuss's best-known book, *THE CAT IN THE HAT* (1957), was written as a controlled vocabulary book after John Hersey complained about dull basal readers (see READING SCHEMES) used by children in school and challenged Seuss and other writers to compose more entertaining texts. The success of *The Cat in the Hat* led to 17 other controlled vocabulary books as part of the *Beginner Books* programme which Seuss supervised. While some of these books, such as *Green Eggs and Ham* (1960) and *Hop on Pop* (1963), were as amusing as the initial book, others were less imaginative. Seuss chose not to illustrate some of his own texts, such as *I Wish I Had Duck Feet* (1965), and in these cases the author appeared as Theo. LeSieg, Geisel spelled backwards.

Other books deal with social issues, such as his environmental *The Lorax* (1971), which warns against the dangers of mass consumption and pollution, and *The Butter Battle Book* (1984), his Pulitzer-Prize-winning fable against nuclear war. *How the Grinch Stole Christmas!* (1958) – and the subsequent TELEVISION special which was first transmitted in 1971 narrated by Boris Karloff – has become a seasonal favourite. *Oh the Places You'll Go!* (1990), with its theme of hope, is a popular graduate gift, and his *You're Only Old Once!* (1986) – with the subtitle 'A Book for Obsolete Children' – shows that Seuss no longer limited his picturebooks to children. He was given the Laura Ingalls Wilder Award in 1980 for his lifetime contribution to children's literature.

Since his death in 1991, his estate has authorised the merchandising of many products featuring Seuss characters. It also released several books, including *Daisy-Head Mayzie* (1994), *My Many Colored Days* (1996) and *Hooray for Diffendoofer Day!* (1998), which Seuss left in manuscript; these texts have ILLUSTRATIONS inspired by Seuss or done by other illustrators, but they do not match Seuss's high standards. Seuss's 47 picturebooks, with their celebration of the subversive and the power of childhood imagination, constitute one of the great contributions to nonsense literature produced in the 20th century. JCS

Seven Champions of Christendom, The see ABRIDGEMENT

Seven Citadels Series (1982–3) Four FANTASY novels by Geraldine Harris (1951–). *Prince of the Godborn* (1982), *The Children of the Wind* (1982), *The Dead Kingdom* (1983) and *The Seventh Gate* (1983) are, on the surface, about the quest of Kerish-lo-Taan to find the keys that will free the Saviour of Galkis, but are in actuality a quest for self. The series, which draws on Eygptian mythology, is deeply thoughtful and sensitively written. Part of what distinguishes the works is the penetrating and luminous quality of its observations on life and human behaviour. SA

Seven Little Australians (1894) First novel by Australian writer ETHEL TURNER. Instead of the BUSH adventures popular at the time, Turner's narrative is set in suburban Sydney and concentrates on character rather than action. The story concerns a family of seven children, whose father, Captain Woolcot, marries a young girl to look after them; their marriage produces another child, 'the little general'. Turner warns the reader that her subjects are not model children, least of all Judy, whose capacity for mischief plunges them all into scrapes. Judy's fearless honesty is contrasted with Bunty's fibs and his failure to take responsibility for his actions, although it is he who finds Judy in the stable loft and steals food from the pantry to feed her.

William Steele wrote to Turner by return mail offering to publish the book, confessing that 'your death of Little Judy very much impressed and affected me'. It was apt that Steele should have fastened so readily and positively on the element in the story that has proved most appealing to readers of every age during the century since the book was written. Turner saw Judy's death from a falling tree as a means of crowning her contribution to the story, preferring this to the conventional solution of having the rebel reform. An early reviewer wrote: 'Her pathos is unforced; there is scarcely a touch of the mawkish sentimentalism with which novelists deal with death.' The death of Judy challenged the axiom that it was the good who died young, while as a plot device it saved Judy from having to mend her ways.

Seven Little Australians is a landmark in the history of Australian children's literature because the perspective from which the story was told and the nature of the story itself contrasted dramatically with previous children's books about Australia, whether written overseas or within Australia itself. The implied reader of earlier books was someone resident in the British Isles; the stories were pioneering adventures demonstrating that the hardy determination of the industrious British settler could tame even the capricious and dangerous Australian environment. In contrast, Turner wrote humorously of domesticity in an urban setting, explicitly championing the right of Australian children to be themselves – mischievous, enterprising, untidy and wary of authority. However, Turner's appeal, both in Australia and overseas, arose as much from her reversal of previous literary models of Victorian childhood as from her nationalism. Her characters' behaviour counterpointed that of the 'ministering angels' of earlier decades. In her portrayal of lively, natural children, Turner preceded E. NESBIT in the world of English-language children's books. While her specifically Australian qualities were greeted enthusiastically at home, it was her ironic treatment of the conventions of Victorian children's literature that won her international fame. ATY, MN

Severn, David see CAMPING AND TRAMPING FICTION; NEGLECTED WORKS; SCIENCE FICTION

Sewell, Anna see *BLACK BEAUTY*; see also ANIMALS IN FICTION; PONY STORIES

Sewell, Helen 1896–1957 American author of nine children's books, editor, and illustrator of several adult and nearly 60 children's books. Born in Mare Island, California, Sewell travelled as a young child to Guam, where her father served as governor. After his death, she and her sister lived with her aunt's family in Brooklyn, New York, where she began art classes at Pratt Institute. She later studied painting with the artist Archipenko. Her first illustrated book, Suzanne Langer's *The Cruise of the Little Dipper and Other Fairy Tales* (1924), brought her work to the attention of LOUISE SEAMAN BECHTEL of Macmillan, who launched Sewell's career and wrote several articles on the artist in *THE HORN BOOK*. Sewell's first book of her own, *ABC for Everyone* (1930), was followed by other PICTUREBOOKS for beginning readers. Among her better-known illustration work are the first editions of WILDER's *THE LITTLE HOUSE* series (1937–43), her collection *A Round of Carols* (1935) and ALICE DALGLIESH's *The Thanksgiving Story*. (1954). A contributor to *The New Yorker*, Sewell also illustrated several fine editions of classics for adults. An esteemed experimental artist, Sewell's illustrations encompass a variety of media and styles, which Louise Seaman Bechtel characterises as 'sculptural'. AL

sex in children's books In children's literature sexual intercourse began not – as the poet Philip Larkin had ironically suggested – in 1963, but in 1975, with the publication of JUDY BLUME's *Forever*. Until the growth of YOUNG ADULT FICTION in the 1970s, sex had rarely been an issue in children's books. Where series took the hero or heroine into early adulthood, sex was not written about either explicitly or metaphorically. In L.M. MONTGOMERY's *Anne's House of Dreams* (1926) Anne, newly married to Gilbert, is expecting their first child but the pregnancy is described in such discreet terms that a young reader could easily miss the clues; we read of Anne's 'exquisite hopes' but nothing more definite is said until baby clothes start to arrive. Other series tend to stop when the hero and heroine marry. Any suspicion of 'unsuitable behaviour' is frowned upon, often by the characters themselves as well as the narrator – in *WHAT KATY DID AT SCHOOL* (1873) Katy and her friends, appalled by the flirtatious behaviour of some of their contemporaries, form a society for the suppression of unladylike conduct.

British children's literature continued to avoid the representation of sex until well after the *Lady Chatterley* Trial in 1961. The increase in young adult novels, combined with society's changing attitude to sex outside marriage, then began to pave the way for a more explicit approach in children's books. As non-fiction about sex and sexuality became more widely available, and as explicit accounts of sexual activity became increasingly frequent in popular adult fiction, authors also began to acknowledge sex as an important factor in teenage relationships, and a number of young adult novels were published in both Britain and America during the early 1970s which tackled the issue. In ALAN GARNER's *Red Shift* (1973) sex is a central issue in Tom's and Jan's relationship (see *THE OWL SERVICE*), but, although attractive in theory, in reality Tom finds sex frightening, and potentially destructive; the dominant image he has of sex is of his parents' love-making in their claustrophobic caravan, an image he tries, but fails, to block out. For the reader, sex is also inextricably linked with rape; soldiers disappear one after another to rape a young girl for 'rest and recreation', and a second rape scene takes place as men are being brutally murdered. Sex is never described explicitly and unless the reader is exceptionally perceptive it is not clear on first reading that Tom and Jan have had sex at all.

Red Shift was seen as a difficult piece of literary fiction and never achieved the widespread popularity of JUDY BLUME's *Forever* (1975), a book that exerted a long-lasting influence on writing about sex for young adults. The novelist set out to write explicitly about sex for teenage readers and wrote what is almost a sex manual with its very factual descriptions of both the physical act and its emotional impact. The book charts Katharine's first sexual relationship and her conviction that it will last forever despite her parents' disbelief. To a modern reader the book is clearly dated; written before the advent of AIDS, it gives little advice on safe sex. The tone remains matter-of-fact throughout as it examines all the possible difficulties of first sex. Although the story is supposedly a romantic one about first love, there is little hint of any love in the prosaic descriptions of Michael's and Katharine's initial fumblings. The tone remains equally pragmatic as the narration describes the act of sex: 'I spread my legs as far apart as I could – and I raised my hips off the bed – and I moved with him.' The implication throughout the book is that sex is a normal teenage activity, and that young readers need to be taught about both the physical and the emotional experience of sex.

AIDAN CHAMBERS's *BREAKTIME* (1978) also deals explicitly with a teenage sexual relationship. Here both language and style are far from mundane, and are perhaps at their most inventive when describing the hero's first sexual encounter. The narrative is divided into three sections: down the right-hand side of the page there runs an extract from Dr Benjamin Spock's *A Young Person's Guide To Life And Love* which opens paradoxically with the statement, 'There is not much / point in trying to / describe lovemaking / . . . it is experienced as / a mixture of emotion / and relationship / more than action.' Dr Spock's text then provides a physical description of love-making set against Ditto's personal response to the experience, described on the left-hand side of the page. In Ditto's account, alternate lines give two different versions: one is written after the event and opens with a factual account which allows Ditto to distance himself from the experience: 'She shifted her position, sitting so that / she could undo the buttons of my / shirt.' The second version, distinguished from the first with a different typeface, reflects the thoughts going through Ditto's mind at the time and is more immediate and less controlled, showing his initial attempts to calm himself – he recites the nine-times-table – and then a series of random word associations, 'thoughts are like broadsides fired / against my bodypleasure . . . why? / o why . . . o sylvan wyesvale'. In a novel which examines the function and value of fiction, Ditto's uncontrolled thoughts turn to other texts and literary language, 'the deflowering of ditto / the cider rosie had'. The split narrative forces readers to re-read the passage several times and to find the links between the different narrative voices for themselves, a marked contrast with the lack of interaction necessary to understand the sex scenes in *Forever*. Both books do, however, give a clear message that the first experience of sex will probably not be with a lifelong partner; in *Breaktime* Ditto's description of love-making is preceded by the thought that 'everybody uses everybody else' and followed almost immediately by a letter from Helen in which she tells him that she is leaving him because they would 'get all serious'. The clear implication is that sex does not have to be associated with love.

Once the way had been paved by novels like *Forever* and *Breaktime*, the early 1980s yielded a crop of novels that determinedly used sex as a way of promoting themselves for a teenage readership. In many cases the titles were more suggestive than the novels themselves, but content too became more explicit. Books like HARRY MAZER's *I Love You Stupid* (1981) were blatant in their approach; the blurb for the British paperback edition states, 'Marcus has two burning ambitions, one is to be a great writer. The other is to get laid . . . Unable to make it with anyone else, Marcus and Wendy decide to make it together. They do and it's wonderful.' As with many such novels, the content is far less explicit than the blurb suggests and sex is not described in any detail.

Although most of the emphasis during the 1980s was on heterosexual sex, a number of titles made use of the new-found freedom – particularly before the spread of AIDS – to write about homosexual relationships, although lesbian relationships still proved an unpopular topic. One of the best-known novels about homosexuality is Aidan Chambers's *Dance On My Grave* (1982), the story of an intense and passionate love affair between two boys, one of whom is killed in a motorbike accident. Although the book, told from the viewpoint of the surviving boy, does not describe their sex life in detail, it is nevertheless made clear to the reader that the two boys are having a physical affair. The narrator uses slang which younger readers probably would not understand, and his boyfriend quotes W.H. Auden's 'Lullaby' when they wake together. JEAN URE's *The Other Side Of The Fence* (1986) is also about a homosexual relationship; readers are obliged to abandon any preconceptions they might have about such a relationship as the narrator leads them to suppose that 'Jan' is a girl, revealing that he is a boy only at the end of the novel. MORRIS GLEITZMAN's *TWO WEEKS WITH THE QUEEN* (1989) is unusual on various counts: it is written for a pre-teenage readership, it deals with the question of AIDS – something few children's novels address – and the homosexual relationship in the book is not the central theme. The book is sympathetic and moving in its portrayal of the gay relationship, although published at a time when the spread of AIDS and resulting homophobia meant that few children's novels were tackling the question of homosexuality. One notable exception was *Jenny Lives With Eric and Martin* by Suzanne Bosche (British edition 1983), an information book, published in PICTUREBOOK format with photographic illustrations, about a little girl who lives with her father and his boyfriend. The book included a photograph of the two men in bed together, and explicitly addressed homophobia. Many adults were outraged that it was aimed at a young readership and called for the book to be banned from schools and libraries.

Reaction to BABETTE COLE's *Mummy Laid an Egg* (1993), published in picturebook format, has been entirely different. The book describes the embarrassed parents' attempts to explain to their young children how babies are made, and uses comic illustrations in an attempt to dispel some of the myths surrounding the subject. Despite the parents' awkwardness, it turns out that the children have known the facts of life all along, and the humorous approach has made the book popular with parents and teachers as well as children.

With the spread of AIDS in the late 1980s and the changing public attitude towards promiscuity, the sexual content of a teenage novel was no longer a strong selling-point. Although authors do not now avoid sex, a sexual relationship tends to be written about explicitly only if it is relevant to the plot or the character development. Towards the end of IAN STRACHAN's *The Boy In The Bubble* (1993) Adam, who has spent all his life in an isolation bubble, emerges knowing that he will die within days and wanting one chance to make love to his girlfriend. Although the sex is the culmination of their relationship, the narrator remains silent about the details, leaving all to the reader's imagination. Again in *The Dividing Sea* (RUTH ELWYN HARRIS, 1989) Julia and Geoffrey finally admit that they have loved one another for years, and then make love while the narrator maintains a discreet distance. ROBERT WESTALL, in *Falling Into Glory* (1993), uses metaphor to avoid the problem of writing explicitly about sex: 'the land [where] you can raise storms, tempests at your will . . . And afterwards a great peace'. In MICHELLE MAGORIAN's *A Little Love Song* (1991) sex without love is 'a nightmare' in which the boy apparently follows a set of instructions while ignoring the heroine's feelings; when Rose falls in love, however, sex is both emotionally and physically fulfilling and she finds herself 'dissolving into a delicious whirlpool . . . rising on such peaks of delight that she almost tipped into unconsciousness'. Magorian is sympathetic in her portrayal of an unmarried girl who becomes pregnant in wartime and encounters considerable prejudice; although Dot and her baby are happy together, other recent novels have been determinedly realistic in their portrayal of teenage pregnancy and single parenthood. In *Tango's Baby* (1995) MARTIN WADDELL gives a very bleak account of teenage parenthood – 'life stopped being a big game for Crystal after the baby'. BERLIE DOHERTY's prize-winning *Dear Nobody* (1991) shows the complex range of emotions experienced by a teenage pregnant girl. In *Junk* (1996) – an award-winning and controversial novel about a group of heroin addicts – MELVYN BURGESS writes explicitly about prostitution; although Gemma initially views sex as 'just something you do with your body' her views are altered dramatically when her friend is violently attacked. In contemporary novels it seems that the lessons are mostly implicit: sex is an accepted part of young adult life, but its consequences cannot be ignored and without love it becomes worthless. KA

see also CENSORSHIP; NUDITY IN CHILDREN'S BOOKS

***Sexton Blake* stories** The fictional detective first appeared in *The Halfpenny Marvel* in 1893 by Hal Meredith (probably Harry Blyth). With his trusty assistant Tinker, Blake outwitted desperate criminals the world over until the 1970s, in prose, comic-strip and film adventures created by over 150 writers. Blake extricated himself from the tightest of corners, whilst his physical prowess – and even his sex appeal – were matched by his unassailable decency. GPF

Shah, Idries see FOLKTALES AND LEGENDS

Shakespeare, William 1564–1616 Although Shakespeare did not write for children, his poetry and songs have been collected for the young since around 1760, when the anonymous editor of *MOTHER GOOSE'S MELODY* included a section of 'the wit and wisdom of Master William Shakespeare'. The most appealing recent version is *Something Rich and Strange* (1995), edited by Gina Pollinger and engagingly illustrated by EMMA CHICHESTER CLARK.

CHARLES and (especially) MARY LAMB established a precedent for fictionalising the plays for children with *Tales from Shakespear: Designed for the use of young persons* in 1807, which was successful in its own time and has stubbornly retained its place in the market despite the proliferation of contemporary versions, many of which are inferior. Exceptions include MARCIA WILLIAMS's lively and accessible cartoon-strip, *Tales from Shakespeare* (1998); Bernard Miles's *Favourite Tales from Shakespeare* (1976), which takes great liberties with the texts but brings an enthusiastic and irreverent actor/director's point of view, brilliantly illustrated by VICTOR AMBRUS; and LEON GARFIELD's elegant volumes, *Shakespeare Stories* (1986), ably illustrated by MICHAEL FOREMAN, which accompany *SHAKESPEARE: THE ANIMATED TALES*, making the plays accessible to children as young as seven.

Shakespearean theatricals take place in a good deal of children's fiction, notably *THE SWISH OF THE CURTAIN* (1941) by Pamela Brown and *Cricket Term* (1974) by Antonia Forest (see *MARLOW* SERIES), and in career novels such as Noel Streatfeild's *Goodbye Gemma* (1969) (see *GEMMA* SERIES), *BALLET SHOES* (1936) and *Curtain Up* (1944). Furthermore, some authors have used the Shakespearean theatre – or specific plays – as a basis for HISTORICAL FICTION: for example, in GEOFFREY TREASE's novel, *Cue for Treason* (1940), a key moment in the narrative occurs during a performance of *Henry V*; both of Antonia Forest's historical novels – *The Player's Boy* and *The Players and the Rebels* – are concerned with the Elizabethan stage; in SUSAN COOPER's *King of Shadows* (1999), a troubled contemporary boy actor travels back in time to take the part of Puck in *A Midsummer Night's Dream* alongside Will Shakespeare himself; and in *Shylock's Daughter* (1999, translated by Brian Murdoch 2000), Mirjam Pressler transforms the story of Jessica's betrayal of her father into a rich and compelling account of Jewish life in Venice.

It could be argued that the works of William Shakespeare have never had a wider readership than at present, with several film versions of the plays currently popular with teenagers: *Shakespeare in Love* (1999) and Baz Luhrmann's *Romeo and Juliet* (1997). MCCS

see also ISAAC ASIMOV; JOHN BENNETT; MICHAEL BOGDANOV; LOUISE BRIERLEY; FARRUKH DHONDY; DRAMA FOR CHILDREN; ROGER LANCELYN GREEN; C. WALTER HODGES; MCGUFFEY ECLECTIC READERS; SIR ARTHUR MEE; NATIONAL YOUTH THEATRE; *THIS WAY DELIGHT*

Shakespeare: The Animated Tales (1992, 1994) Thirty-minute animated versions of 12 of Shakespeare's plays. A multinational venture, the films were commissioned for TELEVISION by Welsh Channel 4, recorded with the voices of leading British actors, and realised visually by the highly sophisticated animators working at the Soyuzmultfilm Studios in Moscow. The plays were abridged by LEON GARFIELD, and the texts subsequently published by Heinemann. Several distinctive techniques were employed in the animation. Highly malleable puppets were used, for example, in *Twelfth Night,* while *Hamlet* was created by painting the scenes on glass, an unusual and very difficult process which produces a more shadowy, mysterious effect than the better-known method of painting on celluloid. The films have been greeted as 'a major contribution to the popularising of Shakespeare', but their usefulness as an introduction for young children, or for those who do not already have some knowledge of the plays, is questionable. Even with extensive narrative links, the stories are not always easy to follow, and the necessarily heavy cutting sacrifices much of the power and beauty of the language. The films are perhaps best appreciated in their own right, for their highly imaginative and witty visual qualities. JFB

Shannon, David 1959– American writer and illustrator. Born in Washington DC, Shannon has created artwork to complement stories written by JULIUS LESTER, JANE YOLEN, Rafe Martin, Audrey Wood, and Robert San Souci. Critics praise Shannon's colourful, bold images for their realism and dramatic details, and his art is often considered stronger than the text it illustrates. Shannon's first PICTUREBOOK that he both wrote and illustrated, *How Georgie Radbourn Saved Baseball* (1994), was named *The New York Times Book Review*'s Best Illustrated Book of the Year and reveals his tendency to incorporate dark humour, irony and didacticism in his text and art.

Shannon emphasises the importance of family and the dangers of excess in *The Amazing Christmas Extravaganza* (1995). In *A Bad Case of Stripes* (1998), Camilla Cream conforms to peer pressure, resulting in her blending into her environment like a chameleon. She regains her identity only when she is true to herself. The autobiographical *No, David!* (1998), a 1999 Caldecott Honour Book, depicts a naughty toddler's relationship with his mother. Based on sketches Shannon drew as a child, his stick-figure ILLUSTRATIONS and repetition of the simple title phrase convey Shannon's theme of unconditional love. The precocious protagonist's adventures continue in *David Goes to School* (1999). EDS

Sharkey, Nimh see IRISH MYTHOLOGY

Sharp, Edith Lambert 1917– Canadian writer. Born in Manitoba, Sharp was raised and educated in British Columbia. She studied at the Vancouver School of Fine Arts and at the Smithsonian Institution in Washington DC. Her only book for children, *Nkwala* (1958), received several prestigious awards. Set in a time before recorded history, the novel recounts the rite-of-passage of a West Coast Indian boy who saves his Salish tribe from destruction during a period of famine through an act of self-sacrifice. Considered one of Canada's best children's novels about early aboriginal society, it has been praised for its historical accuracy, anthropological research and epic qualities. DAC

see also NATIVE AMERICANS IN CHILDREN'S LITERATURE

Sharp, Margery see *MISS BIANCA* SERIES

Sharpe, Richard Scrafton see *ANECDOTES AND ADVENTURES OF FIFTEEN GENTLEMEN*; *A BOOK OF NONSENSE*; EDWARD LEAR; LIMERICKS

Sharratt, Nick British illustrator who has proved to be an ideal line illustrator for the hugely popular sweet-sour novels of JACQUELINE WILSON. His numerous, simple drawings give Wilson's stories immediate accessibility and both reinforce her lightness and underline her seriousness. His characters stare out at the reader, inviting appraisal of their plight, and yet their cartoon nature is also amusing. He frequently explores the literal meaning of Wilson's metaphors and so we see, for instance, a stepfather who is deemed 'as thick as a brick' illustrated as a man-shaped brick wall. Sharratt has also produced many humorous PICTUREBOOKS for younger children, typically using the boldest of colours, no shading, and strong black outlines. In *Ketchup on Your Cornflakes?* (1996) he experiments with split pages, enabling the reader to have all sorts of unpalatable combinations. Sharratt has been shortlisted for a number of awards and has received the Special Artist's Award from the Federation of Children's Book Group. JAG

Shavit, Zohar see FAIRY TALES

Shedlock, Marie 1854–1935 International storyteller and author. Born of English parents at Boulogne, France, Shedlock's childhood was spent in both England and France. After teaching at an English school for 25 years, she left to pursue a career as a professional storyteller. In 1900 she moved to New York and met Mary Wright Plummer of the Pratt Institute, who arranged a series of public recitals which often drew on HANS CHRISTIAN ANDERSEN's stories. ANNE CARROLL MOORE attended and championed Shedlock's storytelling. Shedlock toured America and influenced a succession of leading children's book promoters on the power of STORYTELLING, including BERTHA MAHONY MILLER, who founded *THE HORN BOOK MAGAZINE*, and Anna Cogswell Tyler, who became the first supervisor of storytelling at the New York Public Library, which was the catalyst of library storytelling. Shedlock published a classic work on storytelling, *The Art of the Story-Teller* (1915), as well as a collection of Buddha stories, *Eastern Stories and Legends* (1920). She frequently returned to England and France for tours, and to train teachers and librarians in voice, diction and dramatic power. Shedlock is recognised as the mentor – 'the fairy godmother' – of the storytelling movement in cultural institutions in America and abroad. AL

Sheep in Wolves' Clothing (1995) In this PICTUREBOOK by SATOSHI KITAMURA, the verbal storyline is dominant and can stand on its own, relating the adventures of three sheep who lose their coats to a pack of wolves, a gang of professional knitwear manufacturers. The pictures function more as ILLUSTRATIONS to the text than is usual in Kitamura books, but they still repay close reading in their detail and humour. He draws cartoon-like characters but imbues them with real personality and, with their stick-like limbs, an appealing frailty. He plays with page layout to provide a constantly changing rhythm to the visuals, using the full page with inserts, as well as enclosed and unframed strips. As usual the pictures, drawn on thick absorbent paper, are washed with colour, which provides subtle gradations of hue as colours bleed into each other, while others reveal saturated colour, especially a violet-blue much favoured by Kitamura. AR

Sheep-Pig, The (US, *Babe: The Gallant Pig*) (1983) Novel by British author DICK KING-SMITH, illustrated by Mary Rayner and winner of the *GUARDIAN* CHILDREN'S FICTION AWARD (1984) and the BOSTON GLOBE-HORN BOOK AWARD for Fiction (1985). Mr Hogget, an English farmer, wins a piglet at a fair and takes him home intending to eat him at

Christmas. Once at the farm, the piglet is given to the sheep-dog, Fly, to look after and she proceeds to initiate Babe into the techniques of rounding up sheep. When Babe saves the sheep from rustlers, he is saved from the fate of ending up on the dinner table: as Mrs Hogget says, 'All I know is he saved our bacon and now I'm going to save his.' Consequently Babe is entered for the Grand Challenge Sheep-Dog Trials and wins – with a little help from an older sheep, Ma, and his polite way of speaking to the sheep. Throughout the story there is a strong and comic emphasis on the importance of politeness. The story has been compared with E.B. WHITE's *CHARLOTTE'S WEB*. In 1985 a sequel was published, *Ace: The Very Important Pig* and in 1996 *The Sheep-Pig* was made into an internationally successful film, *Babe*, with special effects cleverly employed to show the animals talking. FMC

see also ANIMALS IN FICTION

Sheldon, Dyan see *THE WHALE'S SONG*; see also GARY BLYTHE

Shepard, E(rnest) H(oward) 1879–1976 British illustrator. Shepard's talent bloomed early and he sustained it over a long working life. Encouraged by his architect father and artistic mother, he trained at Heatherley's and the Royal Academy Schools, to which he won a scholarship. He was a born illustrator; though never a great colourist, he was a master draughtsman who could draw literally anything with beguiling charm. It is easy to take for granted a style which flows with such apparent ease, but Shepard's work is underpinned by formidable powers of observation. With what often appears to be minimal background, he could set his characters firmly in just the right atmospheric landscape, whether a wild wood or a London street. The wind fairly whistles through the pine trees of the Ashdown Forest, the setting for A.A. MILNE's *WINNIE THE POOH* stories, a phenomenal success to which Shepard made such an indelible contribution. It is worth remembering that Shepard, like all his contemporary illustrators in *Punch* magazine, for which he did drawing after drawing in the 1920s and 1930s, worked for hot metal reproduction, which means that all tonality has to be created by means of pen hatching. An airy lightness of touch is essential if the effect is not to become laboured. It may also be that from his experience of the larger magazine format Shepard acquired the idea of dropping small drawings into and around the text setting, thus producing a delightfully ventilated page, as in Milne's collections of children's verse.

Both Shepard and Milne are now thought to epitomise the appeal of the cosy, upper-class nursery with attendant Nanny, elegant, leisured Mummy, and the gently facetious approach to childhood so fashionable in the era following World War I. But Shepard, like Milne, fought with bravery in that war. As a captain in the Royal Artillery he was at the Battle of the Somme and at Ypres, where he won the Military Cross. Perhaps the return to a sweetly idealised, protected childhood can be better understood in this context. Shepard always managed to avoid the sugary, pixilated excesses so popular at the time.

He was above all a master of characterisation. Like ARDIZZONE, he achieved an instantly recognisable style which nevertheless could be adapted over a wide range of interpretations, from Richard Jefferies's *Bevis, the Story of a Boy* (see *WOOD MAGIC*), to his own two-volume autobiography, *Drawn from Memory* (1957) and *Drawn from Life* (1961). As well as his uncanny skill at breathing life into soft toys, he could also handle anthromorphic animals with great sensitivity, a notoriously tricky area where few illustrators truly succeed. Shepard was at the height of his powers with the deceptively simple line illustrations for KENNETH GRAHAME's *THE WIND IN THE WILLOWS*. He got right to the heart of this pre-war arcadia, expressing the yearning to escape, to run off, which all children need to do in their imagination, and the equally strong pull towards the warmth and security of home, of having a little place of their own. He cunningly rigs the scale to make the small animals convincing in the human world. It is a pity that he was later asked to add colour plates; Shepard's line has all the colour and atmosphere that any story could need. SH

Sherry, Sylvia see *A PAIR OF JESUS BOOTS*

Sherwood, Mrs M(ary) M(artha) [Butt] 1775–1851 British writer. The daughter of a clergyman, Mrs Sherwood became an ardent evangelical during the ten years she spent in India after her marriage in 1803. Her most influential works were *The History of Little Henry and His Bearer* (1814), a vivid picture of daily life in colonial India, in which the young English hero converts his Indian servant, and *The History of the Fairchild Family* (three volumes, 1818–47), which remained popular throughout the 19th century. Although her evangelicalism had been substantially moderated by the publication of the second volume in 1842, the first contains the famous scene where the children's father takes them to see the skeleton of a man hanged for fratricide – a lesson in the evils of sibling quarrels. Sherwood's work is marked by a combination of narrative ability – presenting realistic children in a sternly Christian, but still loving, environment – and sheer volume. She wrote over 400 books, tracts and periodical articles and her popularity was long-lasting. JSh

Ship That Flew, The see NEGLECTED WORKS; see also TIME-SLIP FANTASY

Shrinking of Treehorn, The see FLORENCE PARRY HEIDE; see also EDWARD GOREY

Shulevitz, Uri 1935– American PICTUREBOOK artist and author of *Writing with Pictures: How to Write and Illustrate Children's Books* (1985). When he was four, Shulevitz's family left Poland to escape the Nazi uprising. His later childhood was spent in Paris and his teen years in Israel; images of these settings – the city streets of Paris and the lush countryside of Israel – later filtered into his work. At the age of 24 he arrived in New York. His first children's book, *The Moon in My Room* came four years later in 1963, followed by *The Fool of the World and the Flying Ship* in 1968, a Russian FOLKTALE (text by ARTHUR RANSOME), with vivid and finely detailed watercolours that won him the CALDECOTT MEDAL. His picturebooks, including *Hosni the Dreamer* (1997) and *Snow* (1998), a Caldecott Honour Book, are mood pieces, the realistic stories such as *Rain Rain Rivers* (1969) and *Dawn* (1974) presenting fantastic aspects of nature, and the fantasies such as *The Treasure* (1979) and *Fool of the World* dotted with realistic images that embellish the landscape. In the latter, he places readers high in the air with the flying ship; the perspective enhances the feeling of flight and the sweep of air, evoking the breadth of life, and the scope of dreams. NM

Sidney, Margaret see *FIVE LITTLE PEPPERS* SERIES; see also FAMILY STORIES

Signal, Approaches to Children's Books Independent journal founded in 1970 and published thrice-yearly by Aidan and Nancy Chambers through their Thimble Press in South Woodchester, England. Since 1970, under the editorship of Nancy Chambers, formerly of *THE HORN BOOK MAGAZINE* and *Children's Book News*, there have been over 90 issues with more than 400 articles, while the Thimble Press has also produced book guides and other slim critical and educational volumes. In that time, *Signal* has become a major – if not *the* major – children's book journal with immense influence worldwide. Nancy Chambers has established herself as the editor's editor, encouraging young, and perhaps especially non-academic writers, but remaining quite ruthlessly rigorous, regardless of whether she is dealing with new or established writers. In 1984 she described *Signal* as 'a kind of conference in print'.

Signal's critical stance is distinctive. In so far as editorial policy can be summed up in a few words, its contributors are required to have something that *needs* to be said: there is no room for academic solipsism or pretension – and while *Signal* has pioneered the application of modern critical theory to children's books, such theory has had to be genuinely applicable and accessible. Thus *Signal* bridges the huge gaps between the worlds of publishing, teaching, librarianship, history, academic criticism and theory, and children's authors.

The roster of *Signal* writers – many of whom (such as Peter Hunt) began their critical careers here – includes poets and authors, academics and teachers, librarians and booksellers, historians and theorists. *The Signal Companion, a Classified Guide* (to the journal) (1996), prepared by Nancy Chambers and a major contributor, ELAINE MOSS, reads like a directory of experts; among them are GILLIAN AVERY, Hugh Crago, Jane Doonan, MARGERY FISHER, John Goldthwaite, Peter Hollindale, TED HUGHES, JAN MARK, Peter Neumeyer, Lissa Paul, Neil Philip and Victor Watson.

In the closest that Nancy Chambers has allowed *Signal* to come to introspection, Hugh Crago wrote a kind of credo in *Signal* 50 (apropos an article by Charles Sarland): 'It is inclusive rather than exclusive, prepared to tackle the popular as well as the critically approved; it is dissatisfied with established judgements and willing to risk new ones, on different bases; it calls on insights from outside traditional literary scholarship and criticism, while still paying close attention to the facts of an individual text; and it allows the child reader a voice alongside the vastly more knowledgeable and more sophisticated, but not necessarily more "correct" adult reader.'

Among the most influential products of The Thimble Press have been Jill Bennett's *Learning to Read With Picturebooks* (1979), Liz Waterland's *Read With Me: An Apprenticeship Approach to Reading* (1985), MARGARET MEEK's *How Texts Teach What Readers Learn* (1988), Jane Doonan's *Looking at Pictures in Picturebooks* (1993) and AIDAN CHAMBERS's *Tell Me: Children, Reading and Talk* (1993). A valuable selection from the magazine, *The Signal Approach to Children's Books* was published by Kestrel in 1980.

The *Signal* Poetry Award (from 1979) has been 'designed to sharpen response to poetry published for children'. The selectors, who have included John Wain, Margaret Meek and Brian Morse, write annually in *Signal*. See the appendix for a list of award winners. PLH

see also AWARDS AND MEDALS; APPENDIX

Sikuade, Yemi 1948– Nigerian novelist for children and young adults, born in Lagos. *Ehanna and Friends* (1978), the winner of the first Macmillan children's literature competition, relates the adventures of playful children who become victims of a cross-border kidnapping. *Sisi* (1981), a novel for young adults, sensitively portrays young love transcending ethnic and religious barriers. VD

Silver Brumby, The (1958) First title of a series of ten novels by Australian writer ELYNE MITCHELL, with the last, *Brumbies of the Night*, published in 1996. Set in the Snowy Mountains region, Mitchell's home, the stories grew out of her close observation of the wild horses (brumbies) which roam the mountains. *The Silver Brumby*, highly commended in the CHILDREN'S BOOK COUNCIL OF AUSTRALIA Book of the Year Awards (1959), introduced readers to Thowra, 'named for the wind', the future king of all the generations of wild horses in the series. The stories are characterised by adventure, passion and the effort to survive, as the brumbies, often with the help of other wild animals, seek to elude capture by their enemy, the stockmen. *Silver Brumby Whirlwind* (1973), the final episode of the Thowra legend, is the last book to feature dialogue between the horses, whereas in *Moon Filly* (1968) the horses communicate more naturally. A feature film, *The Silver Brumby*, (1992), and a series of animated episodes, have ensured Mitchell's continuing popularity, with many titles being reprinted. *The Silver Brumby* was also selected for a 1995 BILBY (children's choice) award. JAP

Silver Sword, The (1956) Novel by IAN SERRAILLIER which is hailed as a modern classic and regarded as his finest literary achievement, retaining both its popularity as a text for classroom study and its appeal for individual readers. The unobtrusive narration, uncompromising in its glimpses of human suffering, and the vivid characterisation, generated widespread critical acclaim. Based on eyewitness accounts and contemporary records, the novel relates the experiences of a family who become dispersed when Poland is under Nazi occupation. Fictionalised events accord with authentic reports, and fictitious place-names integrate with references to geographical locations. The three Balicki children and companion Jan are forced to leave war-ravaged Warsaw and make their way across Europe to Switzerland where they hope to find their parents. In direct, expressive language and clearly inspired by his pacifist convictions, Serraillier probes the nature of human frailty, loyalty and indomitability as he chronicles the adventures and encounters of these young refugees, whose physical journey charts a transition from oppression to deliverance. The sense of communal pilgrimage and allegorical significance is particularly strong when the children exchange food, homeland stories and tales of escape with fellow travellers on the crowded train which carries them all to exiled freedom. CMN

see also WAR STORIES

Silverstein, Shel 1932–99 American poet, cartoonist, composer and folk singer born in Chicago. Silverstein was the author of popular verse for children, which he both illustrated and wrote, using black-and-white line drawings which are funny, eccentric, outrageous and surreal. Silverstein took the symbiotic nature of word and image seriously and would not allow his verse to be illustrated by anyone else. Superficially, his poems are amusing, featuring a cornucopia of zany characters with a touch of the cautionary (such as 'Sarah, Cynthia, Sylvia Stout / who would not take the garbage out'), but there is often a hint of serious concerns – the environment, the treatment of the very old and young, and outrage at injustice. Essentially humane, though too robust and abrasive for some adults' taste, Silverstein enjoyed a huge following of American and British readers. Key texts include *The Giving Tree* (1972), WHERE THE SIDEWALK ENDS (1974), *A Light in the Attic* (1981) and *Falling Up* (1998). MCCS

Simmonds, Posy 1945– British illustrator, cartoonist and satirist. Simmonds developed a sophisticated comic-strip style for *The Guardian* newspaper, beginning with 'The Silent Three' in 1977. Several collections of these strips were published, such as *Mrs Weber's Diary* (1979). This style has proved to be ideal for her children's books, which although generally benign have retained (often incidentally, or in the background ethos) her intensely perceptive view of the foibles and pretensions of the British middle classes – as in *The Chocolate Wedding* (1990). One of her most original trademarks is the way in which FANTASY does not retreat at the end of the books in the face of reality. In *Lulu and the Flying Babies* (1988) the cherubs who have escaped from paintings in an art gallery are escorted back to their places by an attendant; in *Bouncing Buffalo* (1994), set in an antique shop which disgraces an up-and-coming neighbourhood, the wall demolished by the children's wished-for animals remains demolished. Perhaps her best book has been *Fred* (1987), about the funeral of a cat who was lazy by day, but a feline pop-star by night. A musical version of this book was first performed at the Cheltenham Festival of Literature in 1995. PLH

Simms, George Otto 1910–91 Irish churchman and author, and an acknowledged authority on the *Book of Kells* and early Irish Christianity. He wrote three children's books: *The Book of Kells* (1988), *Brendan the Navigator* (1989) and *St Patrick* (1991). Lively and readable accounts of early Christian Ireland, the books are also distinguished by David Rooney's ILLUSTRATIONS. VC

Simon, Seymour 1931– Award-winning American author of over 150 science books for children, Simon was born and raised in New York City. A science teacher for 23 years for the New York City public schools, he was inspired to write by the lack of good science books to use in his classroom. *Animals in Field and Laboratory: Projects in Animal Behavior* (1968) marked the beginning of his writing career. A sampling of titles reveals the range of his work: *The Paper Airplane Book* (1971), *Pets in a Jar* (1975), *Ghosts* (1976), *The Secret Clocks* (1979), *Strange Mysteries* (1980), *Mad Scientists, Weird Doctors, and Time Travelers* (1981), *How to Talk to Your Computer* (1985) and *Space Worlds* (1991). In the 1990s a *Space Photos* series on planets and stars, and another series on the human body, were characterised by their spectacular photographs accompanied by brief, compellingly written texts. *The Brain* (1997), for example, features stunning images taken by scanners and enhanced by computer codes. The brain, Simon writes, 'is not very big, yet it can do more jobs than the most powerful computer ever made'. He concludes: 'Your brain is really what makes you, *you*.' Simon has also written the *Einstein Anderson* fiction series, about a boy detective who solves mysteries through his knowledge of science. LH

Simont, Marc 1915– French-born American illustrator of nearly 100 PICTUREBOOKS from the 1930s through to the 1990s. Born in Paris to Catalonian parents, Simont spent his childhood moving between Paris, Barcelona and New York City. As a result, school was difficult. 'I was always more concerned with what a teacher looked like than what he said', Simont wrote in *More Junior Authors*. His father, a lifelong illustrator for *L'Illustration*, was an important influence on his career. Since beginning to illustrate children's books in the 1930s, Simont has illustrated the work of such outstanding writers as MARGARET WISE BROWN, MEINDERT DE JONG, Karla Kuskin, DAVID MCCORD and JAMES THURBER. He won a Caldecott Honour award for his dramatic, soft black-and-white ILLUSTRATIONS for RUTH KRAUSS's *The Happy Day* (1949), and the CALDECOTT MEDAL for his glowing coloured pictures for Janice Udry's *A Tree Is Nice* (1956). Many other books have received honours and acclaim, including the illustrations for Karla Kuskin's *The Philharmonic Gets Dressed* (1982). Among books he has both written and illustrated, *The Goose That Almost Got Cooked* (1997) is a satisfying story illustrated with an intriguing combination of atmospheric watercolours and cartoon-like sketches which perfectly suit the text. LH

Simple Simon Old rhyme in which the four verses generally heard in the nursery relate Simple Simon's encounter with the pieman, his attempt to catch a whale by fishing in a pail-full of water, and his search for plums upon a thistle. These form part of the tale of Simple Simon in the CHAPBOOK history, of which editions were printed by Cluer Dicey, Richard Marshall and T. Bachelor (all c. 1810), J. KENDREW (c. 1820), and A. Park (c. 1840). For 'Simple Simon', the *Oxford English Dictionary* quotes Grose's *Dictionary* (1785) 'a natural, a silly fellow', and suggests that the term derives from the NURSERY RHYME. Simon, however, may have been a name for a simpleton for several centuries, perhaps arising from the stories of Simon Peter. The ballad *Simple Simon's Misfortunes and his Wife Margery's Cruelty*, earlier known as *Dead and Alive*, dates at least from c. 1685, and a tune called 'Simple Simon' is included in the third edition of Playford's *The Dancing Master* (1665). The tune Frank Kidson gives for the song in *75 British Nursery Rhymes* (1904) is the old Welsh air 'Ar hyd y nos'. IO

Simpsons, The Animated situation comedy depicting the adventures of the Simpsons and other residents of Springfield. First appearing as a series of interstitials in 1987 on *The Tracy Ullman Show*, it later made its début as a half-hour TELEVISION series in 1989. *The Simpsons* parodies traditional family situation comedies by presenting a father who seldom knows best. Children's animated programming is also parodied in the 'The Itchy and Scratchy show', extremely violent cat-and-mouse cartoon enjoyed by the Simpson children. Many conservative groups have criticised the series for its satire of such institutions as family, school and church. Parental wisdom is twisted: Homer teaches his children the importance of lying, stealing and hating the neighbours. Public education is similarly skewed: teachers are incapable of working without their teacher's editions, and each episode begins with the clichéd punishment of Bart writing prohibitions on the blackboard. Church is also depicted negatively: neighbours desperately attempt to baptise the Simpson children without parental approval, and Sunday-school classes consist of vacuous descriptions of hell and pleas for moral behavior. *The Simpsons* remains extremely popular. It has won several Emmy awards for Outstanding Animated Programme and inspired a wide array of merchandise – another phenomenon parodied in the series. JJB

Sinclair, Catherine see *HOLIDAY HOUSE*; see also *ALICE* IMITATIONS

Sing-Song: a Nursery Rhyme Book (1872) Collection of poems by CHRISTINA ROSSETTI, her only poetry collection aimed at children. Its outstanding merits have never been properly recognised in literary circles. Many poems chime like NURSERY RHYMES from the oral tradition with an cxquisite blend of nonsense and music. Others teach the most harmonious of lessons – months of the year, days of the week, telling the time; and there are RIDDLES aplenty: ('A pin has a head, but has no hair; / A clock has a face, but no mouth there').

Rossetti lived in London all her life, but shows herself a keen observer of nature and is, arguably, one of the earliest 'green' poets ('Hurt no living thing: /

Ladybird, nor butterfly, / Nor moth with dusty wing'). The number of poems about death is a chilling reminder of the high mortality rate for both infants and mothers in childbirth in the Victorian period.

Most wonderful of all, and little remarked on, are simple, tender poems which explore the symbiotic union between mothers and babies in sensuous lyrics:

> Love me, – I love you,
> Love me, my baby;
> Sing it high, sing it low,
> Sing it as it may be.

As writers of PICTUREBOOKS know only too well, writing deceptively 'simple' texts for very young children is very difficult to do well. ARTHUR HUGHES, a member of the Pre-Raphaelite circle and friend to her brothers, William and Dante Gabriel Rossetti, was the perfect choice of illustrator. Hughes's delicate line drawings add to the charm and tenderness of the collection. A facsimile edition of the original remains in print. MCCS

If a pig wore a wig,
What could we say ?
Treat him as a gentleman,
And say 'Good day.'

If his tail chanced to fail,
What could we do ?—
Send him to the tailoress
To get one new.

'If a pig wore a wig . . .' Illustration by ARTHUR HUGHES for *Sing-Song* by Christina Rossetti.

Singer, Isaac Bashevis 1904–91 Recipient of the Nobel Prize in literature (1978). Singer wrote more specifically for children and about his childhood than any other Nobel Prize winner. His vivid, soul-searching fiction and memoirs chronicle the deeply religious but rapidly changing inter-war Eastern Europe of his early years. Yiddish culture and the turmoil of Jewish history provided him with material for a lifetime of writing, often based on his own conflicts confronting modernity as a Hassidic rabbi's son. Whether expanding age-old Yiddish jokes into hilarious stories, writing about his own family of storytellers and the neighbourhood dramas which unfolded in the rabbi's home, or depicting his own rebellions against tradition, Singer never strayed in his writings from the colourful cities and villages of his youth. His often-expressed commitment to ethnicity is significant as a forerunner of contemporary multicultural literature.

His older brother, Israel Joshua Singer, rejected religion and became a famous author in America, greatly influencing Isaac's development and bringing him to New York in 1935. When Singer began writing for children at the age of 62, he was already a world-famous author. Having grown up both in Warsaw and in Jewish *shtetls*, or villages, Singer had first-hand knowledge of old worlds and new. His commitment to his Yiddish setting is also poignant: Singer's portrait of Eastern European Jewry depicts the humane, lively world destroyed by Hitler; many stories are located in the now-vanished Warsaw Ghetto where Singer lived.

Acclaimed in 1962 for *In My Father's Court*, his childhood memoirs for adults, he acceded to Elizabeth Shub, one of his translators (Singer wrote in Yiddish), who suggested he write for children. His first book for young readers, *Zlateh the Goat* (1966), a Newbery Honour Book illustrated by MAURICE SENDAK, is among the very finest of children's story collections. In what became a typical mixture of topic and tone, its seven stories range from the buffoonery of the legendary Fools of Chelm – and their idiotic solutions to Chelm's backwardness and poverty – to the superb realism of 'Zlateh the Goat', about a boy and a goat who help each other survive a Russian snowstorm. Singer also introduced the addle-pated Mr. and Mrs. Shlemiel, who personify the Jewish version of the amiable adult incompetent stereotype which children so enjoy. Singer continued their saga in several subsequent stories, for example in *When Shlemiel Went to Warsaw* (1968), also a Newbery Honour Book. In 1970, Singer selected stories from *In My Father's Court* and wrote several new ones to publish a memoir for children, *A Day of Pleasure*, winner of the National Book Award for Children's Literature. Other collections followed: *Naftali the Storyteller and His Horse, Sus* (1976) and *The Power of Light* (1980), eight diverse stories about Hanukkah. His largest collection, *Stories for Children* (1984), reprinted stories from several sources and belongs with his adult *Collected Stories* (1982) as one of his finest achievements.

His PICTUREBOOKS, such as *The Fearsome Inn* (Newbery Honour Book 1967), *Why Noah Chose the Dove* (1974) and *The Golem* (1982), also demonstrate Singer's singular ability to develop the folkloric, metaphysical and comedic traditions of Jewish literature into universally appreciated children's stories. AA

Singing Grass, The (1975) Translation of the Afrikaans youth novel, *Die Singende Gras*, by its author, Freda Linde (1915–), winner of the Scheepers Prize for Afrikaans children's books. Freda (Christovira Frederika) Linde is one of the mostly highly honoured Afrikaans children's writers, having also won the Tienie Holloway Medal and the C.P. Hoogenhout Award. This book represents the highest quality among the many excellent Afrikaans youth novels of South Africa, to which she does justice with her English prose. One of very few children's books set in Namibia (see also LESLEY BEAKE and *Song of the Surf* by DALE KENMUIR), it gently tells of the love of Lance, a shy Rehoboth Baster boy, for a sickly camel that he is employed to look after at a country hotel. The novel creates a strong sense of the setting in the semi-desert and how this affects the people at the hotel. The grass and the camel symbolise different things to them, and bring out their personalities. With intensity but no melodrama the story takes Lance and the camel on a journey which brings on the death of the camel and with it an opportunity that leads to a new life for him as an apprentice nature conservationist. ERJ

Sinha, Nilima 1936– Indian fiction writer for all age groups, Sinha tries to capture the romance and the magic of childhood in her books and is committed to the creation of an indigenous answer to the imported *NANCY DREW* and ENID BLYTON series. *The Chandipur Jewels* (1981) – winner of the first prize in the Children's Book Trust National Competition for the best fictional work in the year for children – met with immediate success. The popular Chandipur children reappeared in *Vanishing Trick at Chandipur* (1984) and *SOS from Munia* (1990). Colourful descriptions of life on the beautiful Dal Lake in scenic Kashmir, woven into the narrative of *Adventure on the Golden Lake* (1986), make it a mine of information. The struggle for Independence becomes Sinha's focus in several books, such as *Adventure Before Midnight* (1987) and *Kamla's Story – A Saga of our Freedom Struggle* (1997). Steering clear of open didacticism, she yet makes her serious concern for the environment clear in her information-packed novels. With some success, she tries to maintain a balance between a magic sense of wonder and her underlying faith in tradition. She has contributed stories to several collections, has retold FOLKTALES, and written fantasies and BIOGRAPHIES. MBh

Sin[d]bad the Sailor see *ARABIAN NIGHTS' ENTERTAINMENTS*

Sís, Peter 1949– Peter Sís attended the Academy of Applied Arts in Prague and the Royal College of Art in London and has been a United States citizen since 1989. He started his career illustrating the works of others but has now achieved success with highly original PICTUREBOOKS of his own, notably *Follow the Dream: The Story of Christopher Columbus* (1991), whose subject matter – the discovery of a new world – undoubtedly mirrors Sís's own experience. For this book and others, such as his Prague story, *The Three Golden Keys* (1994), Sís researched contemporary maps and sources and wove them into his strange and formal drawings. JAG

Six Little New Zealanders First novel by ESTHER GLEN, published in 1917, with a sequel, *Uncles Three at Kamahi* (1926). The series relates the adventures of the six Malcolm children on their uncle's sheep station in the South Island. Ranging in age from nine to 19, the children are likeable and very realistic characters, whose mishaps are due more to high spirits and natural curiosity than to any mischievous intent. The books are notable for their lighthearted tone, and the absence of the didactic and moralistic themes prevalent in children's literature of the time. LO

see also ESTHER GLEN AWARD; FAMILY STORIES

Sky in the Pie (1983) Poems by ROGER MCGOUGH which won the *SIGNAL* AWARD. McGough creates his own unique blend of wordplay and profundity, a zany humour on which disturbing shadows often fall. McGough is versatile in handling different poetic forms, but shows himself a master of comic, and tragicomic, rhyme. ML

'Sleeping Beauty' A FAIRY TALE included in CHARLES PERRAULT'S *Histoires ou contes du temps passé* (1697) (see *CONTES DE MA MÈRE L'OYE*) entitled 'La Belle au bois dormant'. A princess, having been put under a spell by an offended fairy, pricks her finger and sleeps for a hundred years, surrounded by an enchanted forest, to be awakened by a prince. In modern versions, including the Tchaikovsky/Petipa ballet, PANTOMIMES and numerous retellings, the story ends with a princely kiss which wakes up the princess. There is no kiss in Perrault's version, and the story continues with the birth of the princess's two children, Dawn and Day, who are almost killed along with Beauty by the prince's mother, who is an ogress. The prince arrives in time to save his family, and his mother throws herself into a vat of frightful creatures which was intended for her victims.

The earliest recorded version of the story is 'Troylus and Zellandine' in the 14th-century French romance *Perceforest*, in which a baby, cursed by a goddess, later goes into a deep sleep, is raped by the prince Troylus and wakes to find herself pregnant. In Basile's *Pentamerone* (1634/6) the Princess Talia, whilst in her enchanted sleep, is also raped, this time by a king; she gives birth to twins, Sun and Moon, and awakens only when the splinter is sucked out of her finger by one of the children. JHD

Sleigh, Barbara see CARBONEL SERIES

Slingsby, Peter 1946– Ex-teacher, map-maker and conservation ranger from Cape Town, South Africa, who has designed computerised African pictures, including reproductions of genuine rock art. It is thus hardly surprising that his two latest books have been about the Bushmen, or /Xam as he prefers to call them. *Rock Art of South Africa* (1996) explains rock painting in simple terms for young readers; *The Joining* (1996) is a prize-winning novel about modern children involved in a time-warp who discover the life-values of the /Xam. He wrote several earlier ADVENTURE STORIES of which the best is probably *Leopard Boy* (1989), about a runaway boy in the Cape mountains. JHe

Slobodkin, Louis 1903–75 American author and illustrator. Originally a sculptor who created statues and reliefs for several large cities in the eastern United States, Slobodkin turned his attention in the 1940s to illustrating and writing books for children. He is primarily known for his ILLUSTRATION work, especially in *Many Moons* (1944), which won the CALDECOTT MEDAL, and in the books by award-winning author ELEANOR ESTES, including the popular *Moffats* series. However, Slobodkin also wrote over 40 of his own books for children, beginning with *The Friendly Animals* in 1944, as well as frequent collaborations with his wife Florence. Perhaps his most notable work as a writer-illustrator is his five-volume SCIENCE-FICTION series, beginning with *The Spaceship Under the Apple Tree* (1952), in which a young boy entertains an alien from the imaginary planet Martinea. Slobodkin illustrated the books of many famous authors, including MARK TWAIN and CHARLES DICKENS. His work as a sculptor influenced his illustration technique; his often sketchy drawings and pastel washes give a feeling of animation and movement. He also lends emotion to his artwork by softening his illustrations for serious work, such as Estes's *The Hundred Dresses*, and exaggerating various features in his more humorous tales. KS

Slobodkina, Esphyr 1908– Author, artist and illustrator, born in Chelyabinsk, Siberia, and educated in Manchuria and at the National Academy of Design in New York. Slobodkina ('pronounced Slow-boat-*keen*-a', she always explained) emigrated to the United States with her family following the Russian Revolution. After meeting MARGARET WISE BROWN, who was editing books for William R. Scott, she began to illustrate and write children's books, while continuing to work at wood sculpture, textiles, dolls, interior decoration, still life and abstract painting. Slobodkina illustrated several books by Brown, including *The Little Fireman* (1938). Her own *Caps for Sale* (1940) has become a modern classic, described by Barbara Bader as a model of picturebook design and an example of the difference between 'simplicity and inspired simplification'. *The Wonderful Feast* (1955) uses vibrantly coloured cut-paper COLLAGE to create stunning geometric designs to tell a familiar barnyard story. A founding member of the American Abstract Artist group, Slobodkina brought to children's book ILLUSTRATION her daring cut-paper and COLLAGE designs, and a sensibility arising from her attachment to surrealism and constructivism. Her works are displayed in major art museums and private collections. LH

Smart, Christopher 1722–71 Impecunious English poet who worked for JOHN NEWBERY and married his stepdaughter. His most famous poem is the brilliant and original 'My Cat Jeoffry', wonderfully parodied by WENDY COPE in *Making Cocoa for Kingsley Amis* (1986). Smart's important contribution to children's literature lay in his *Hymns for the Amusement of Youth* (1771), written while in prison for debt, which in their tenderness towards children and apparently artless religious devotion anticipated William Blake's *SONGS OF INNOCENCE*. MCCS

Smarties Book Prize see APPENDIX

Smith, Charlotte 1749–1806 English author and poet who wrote novels to support her family, but poetry for the love of it. Her verse influenced famous Romantic poets, including William Wordsworth. Smith's contribution to children's literature, *Conversations Introducing Poetry, for the use of Children* (1804), includes some exquisite nature poetry amid discussions between a mama and her two children on morals and manners; her sister, Catherine Ann Dorset, supplied several poems. MCCS

Smith, Craig 1955– Australian illustrator whose finely detailed work in his first PICTUREBOOK, CHRISTOBEL MATTINGLEY'S *Black Dog* (1980), has since developed into the relaxed, free-flowing style of his ILLUSTRATIONS for Phil Cummings's *Marty and Mei-Ling* (1995). Smith's versatility is able to represent themes as diverse as the mischievous David in SALLY FARRELL ODGERS'S *Dreadful David* (1985), the slapstick of DOUG MACLEOD'S *Sister Madge's Book of Nuns* (1986), and the poignancy of death in MEM FOX'S

Sophie (1989). With more than 100 published titles and many awards, Craig Smith portrays Australia's cultural diversity entirely without pretension or condescension, and is one of Australia's most popular illustrators. FK

Smith, Dodie [Dorothy Gladys] 1896–1990 British actor, playwright and novelist. Born in Manchester, Smith worked in Heal's furniture shop after realising she would not succeed as a professional actor. She was a highly successful playwright in the 1930s (her play *Dear Octopus* is still performed) but took up novel-writing during World War II, which she spent in America because her husband was a conscientious objector. Her most famous novels, *I CAPTURE THE CASTLE* and *ONE HUNDRED AND ONE DALMATIANS*, are published as children's books but their wit and humour and the sharpness of Smith's observation makes them popular with readers of all ages. JEG

Smith, Emma see NEGLECTED WORKS

Smith, Jessie Wilcox 1863–1935 American illustrator famous for her scenes of charming yet realistic children. It was only by chance that Jessie Willcox Smith became an illustrator instead of a kindergarten teacher. She never drew as a child and was only enticed to try her hand when she chaperoned an art lesson. Immediately a teacher was lost to the profession, but one of the great illustrators was on her way. Smith devoted herself to her chosen field; she never married or had children. She held strong views on the subject, believing that women had to make a choice between motherhood or a career in order for either to be successful.

She began her studies at the School of Design for Women in her hometown of Philadelphia, but soon transferred to the Pennsylvania Academy where she studied with Thomas Eakins, an important American painter. In 1888 her first ILLUSTRATION appeared in *ST NICHOLAS MAGAZINE*. In 1894, after producing advertisements and editorial borders for the *Ladies Home Journal*, she enrolled at Drexel Institute to study with HOWARD PYLE, the legendary illustrator and teacher. Smith found that Pyle's approach encouraged an emotional connection with the subject matter ('live your work') as opposed to Eakin's emphasis on formal composition. Pyle was impressed with Smith and encouraged her, often recommending her for professional commissions. In Pyle's class she also found the friendship of fellow illustrators Violet Oakley and Elizabeth Shippen Green, with whom she lived and worked for most of her life. On Pyles's recommendation, she and Oakley together illustrated the 1897 Houghton Mifflin edition of *Longfellow*, each creating five colour chromolithographs. An extremely successful career followed; her work was so constantly in demand that she was never able to accept any of the teaching positions that were offered her.

Her first book specifically for children was *Rhymes for Real Children* (1903), followed in 1905 by ROBERT LOUIS STEVENSON'S *A CHILD'S GARDEN OF VERSES*, a work particularly well-suited to her vision of childhood as a place of unaffected charm and imagination. Her confident, unsentimental drawings and paintings usually have as their subject children at play, in school, or with their families. She continued to illustrate books for the very young but is also known for classics such as *LITTLE WOMEN*, *The Princess and the Goblin*, and *HEIDI*. One of her best-known works is the 1916 edition of CHARLES KINGSLEY'S *THE WATER BABIES*.

In addition to work for children, Smith created memorable commercial images for such clients as Ivory Soap, Campbell's Soup and Kodak. Her professional association with *Good Housekeeping* made her, until Norman Rockwell and the *Saturday Evening Post*, the only artist consistently featured on the cover of a national magazine. Her original oils and watercolours were widely known and admired, winning numerous awards, including a Silver Medal in St. Louis (1904). MAXFIELD PARRISH, a fellow former student of Howard Pyle, was an enthusiast. The watercolour he purchased from her was the first he owned of another artist's work. MMG

Smith, Lane 1959– Innovative American illustrator best known for his art work in collaboration with JON SCIESZKA in their clever revisions of FAIRY TALES. Smith's bold graphic style is distinguished by his use of COLLAGE, visual puns and parody, and usually dark colours. His first illustrations were for EVE MERRIAM'S *Halloween ABC* (1987), which was widely censored in the United States for its 'satanic' content. His collaborations with Scieszka – in *The True Story of the Three Little Pigs* (1989), told from the wolf's point of view, *The Stinky Cheese Man and Other Fairly Stupid Tales* (1992), with their ironic sensibilities and goofy sense of humour, and *Squids Will Be Squids* (1998) with its Aesopic provision of 'Fresh Morals, Beastly Fables' – are enjoyed by both older children and adults and have been widely celebrated as postmodern PICTUREBOOKS. Smith has also written and illustrated his own picturebooks including *The Happy Hocky Family* (1993), a wicked parody of the basal readers featuring Dick, Jane and Sally (see READING SCHEMES). Smith and Scieszka have also collaborated on the *TIME WARP TRIO* series which began with *Knights of the Kitchen Table* (1991). This time-travel series for middle-school readers gently parodies genres of boys' ADVENTURES STORIES. JCS

Smith, Lillian H(elena) 1887–1983 Canadian children's librarian. Smith worked for the Toronto Public

Library from 1912 to 1952, establishing Boys and Girls House in 1922. In 1949 Edgar Osborne chose to house his collection of 2000 early children's books under her care, and in 1962 the Lillian H. Smith Collection, containing the best children's books published after 1911, was inaugurated. Both collections were moved in 1995 to a new building named in Smith's honour. In several editions of *Books for Boys and Girls*, and in *The Unreluctant Years* (1953), Smith expounded her belief that children's literature deserved serious critical attention. FEA

see also COLLECTIONS OF CHILDREN'S BOOKS

Smith, Lumis Harriet see *POLLYANNA* SERIES

Smith, Maire see *SOMEONE IS FLYING BALLOONS*

Smoky, the Cowhorse (1926) Western ADVENTURE STORY written and illustrated by Will James. This NEWBERY AWARD winner (1927) recounts the career of a black range colt with mustang blood. In Montana, Clint trains Smoky for ranch work, but a horse thief captures him. Known as 'The Cougar' on the rodeo circuit, Smoky ages as the rough life takes its toll. In the nick of time, Clint rescues Smoky (renamed Cloudy) in the Southwest. The horse recovers his broken spirit on the range of his birth where Clint starts his own ranch. James, using authentic cowboy diction, celebrates nature and freedom. NV

see also HORSE STORIES; WESTERNS

Smucker, Barbara 1915– Canadian children's author, primarily an historical novelist sensitive to the suffering of minority groups. Smucker was born in Newton, Kansas, and graduated in journalism from Kansas State University. A New Order Mennonite, she first wrote novels specifically designed to teach Mennonite children their history. After coming to Canada in 1969, however, she began addressing a wider audience. *Underground to Canada* (1977), winner of the Canada Council Children's Literature Prize, is a tense account of the tribulations of black slaves escaping to Canada. It illustrates the need for tolerance and humane values, a theme fundamental to all Smucker's work.

Smucker also made the lives of minority religious groups comprehensible to secular audiences. In *Days of Terror* (1979) and the PICTUREBOOK *Selina and the Bear Claw Quilt* (1995), for example, she explains the beliefs of the pacifist Mennonites who fled revolutionary Russia and Civil War America, respectively. In *Amish Adventure* (1983), she details the internal and external conflicts facing contemporary Amish. Smucker vividly recreates history, but melodrama weakens *Incredible Jumbo* (1991), about a famous elephant, and inadequate characterisation and awkward plotting mar her two TIME-SLIP FANTASIES, *White Mist* (1985) and *Garth and the Mermaid* (1992). REJ

Snoopy see *PEANUTS*

Snow Queen, The see HANS CHRISTIAN ANDERSEN; see also BERLIE DOHERTY; EVA LEGALLIENNE; MUSIC AND STORY

Snow Spider, The (1986–9) Novel by Jenny Nimmo, set in the Welsh mountains. It centres upon the character of Gwyn Griffiths, who has magical powers inherited from his forebears, the magicians Math and Gwydion who feature in the Welsh tales of *The Mabinogion*. *The Snow Spider* (1986) was winner of the Smarties Grand Prix and the Tir na n'Og Award and was adapted for Harlech TELEVISION. Gwyn is given a variety of obscure gifts by his grandmother, who tells him he is a magician. Gwyn's father blames him for the disappearance of his sister Bethan four years before. Through a series of mysterious events a young girl who resembles Bethan comes to stay with the family, and this brings the family together again. The sequel, *Emlyn's Moon* (1987), draws more closely on Welsh life, the community and the landscape. Although Gwyn does use his magic, the story deals more with family relationships. The final book, *The Chestnut Soldier* (1989), returns to FANTASY, with Gwyn being faced by the forces of evil represented by a friend's long-lost uncle coming to stay. Once again Welsh culture and tradition come strongly through with references to *The Mabinogion*, the speaking of Welsh and descriptions of the countryside. All three books have remained in print, reflecting young readers' commitment to the trilogy.

Among Jenny Nimmo's other publications are *The Dragon's Child* (1996) – a mythical story about a young dragon and an orphaned slave girl, illustrated by ALAN MARKS – *The Owl-Tree* (with Anthony Lewis) – which won the 1997 SMARTIES PRIZE – and *Dog Star* (1999) – a magical and engaging girl-and-dog story illustrated by Terry Milne. *The Rinaldi Ring* (1999) was shortlisted for the CARNEGIE AWARD. FMC

see also WELSH FOLKTALES AND LEGENDS

Snow White and Rose Red see GRIMM BROTHERS

Snow White and the Seven Dwarfs see GRIMM BROTHERS; see also NANCY EKHOLM BURKERT; CARTOONS; WALT DISNEY; WANDA GÁG; *EGERTON HALL* SERIES; TRINA SCHART HYMAN; MUSIC AND STORY

Snowman, The (1978) Wordless PICTUREBOOK by RAYMOND BRIGGS, a story of friendship and loss told with great economy of means, and all the more moving for its recognition that love needs no words for its expression. The story is built up through sequences of small square and rectangular pictures rendered in soft coloured pencil and rounded at the edges in keeping with the rotundity and softness of the main character. As the story develops Briggs allows himself more freedom in the size and organisation of the frames and this increasing openness culminates in two double-page spreads depicting a thrilling flight over snowy landscapes. Throughout the snowman is a solid, if slightly blurred, presence whose character is shaped for the reader as much by the reactions of the little boy to his antics as by the shifts in his posture, gesture and facial expression.

The book has been immensely popular, although many younger readers may have come to the story first through the animated film first screened on British TELEVISION at Christmas in 1982. The film differs from the book in a number of ways, notably by extending the characters' flight to the North Pole where they meet Father Christmas, and by disregarding the restraint of the book's ending by having the boy display his grief at the snowman's demise. The soundtrack of the film, and in particular the song 'Walking in the Air' – composed by Howard Blake and sung by Aled Jones – prolonged *The Snowman's* fame, as did the marketing of 'Snowman' products such as mugs, wrapping paper and pyjamas. DL

see also MUSIC AND STORY

Snugglepot and Cuddlepie (1918) Created by MAY GIBBS, these two cherubic gumnut babies, naked except for their gumnut caps, a frilly skirt or a gumleaf waistband, have endeared themselves to generations of Australian children and readers worldwide. Literally born in THE BUSH from the bud of a gumtree, their mentor is wise old Kookaburra who warns them about the ways of humans, bushfire and other hazards. Their friends are bush creatures like Mr Lizard and Mr and Mrs Bear, but their deadly enemy is Mrs Snake, who is aided and abetted by the villainous Banksia men. Their bushland adventures, both happy (visits to the 'Lilly Pilly Picture Palace', exhibitions of 'The Society of Gumnut Artists', a regatta on the river using gumleaf canoes and paddles) and dangerous (the constant battle with the Banksia men), further chronicled in *Little Ragged Blossom* (1920) and *Little Obelia* (1920), were collected in *The Complete Adventures of Snugglepot and Cuddlepie* (1920). In the guise of a bushland FANTASY May Gibbs recreated childhood, investing it with magic through a strong storyline supported by ILLUSTRATIONS that are both dramatic and endearing. Snugglepot and Cuddlepie are archetypal children using creative play to explore the world around them and experimenting with adult roles – preparing the way for the mature years ahead. MSax

Snyder, Zilpha Keatley 1927– American novelist whose career so far spans three decades, from *Season of Ponies* (1964) to *The Gypsy Game* (1997). Snyder has been critically praised for her popular imaginative novels, which often combine psychological realism with magic and FANTASY. The novel for which she is best known is probably *The Egypt Game* (1967), the first of three novels for which she received Newbery Honours. It sets a secret role-playing game, based on ancient Egyptian myth and ritual, among a group of multicultural children, against the backdrop of an urban neighbourhood menaced by a murderer of children. This novel was followed up 30 years later by *The Gypsy Game* (1997), recounting the further adventures of the same children. BH

So Much To Tell You (1987) Novel by JOHN MARSDEN, phenomenally successful in Australia. It is the boarding-school journal of 14-year-old Marina, a terribly disfigured elective mute, depicting her gradual coming-to-terms with family tragedy and the social world of the school. Marsden's portrayal of a damaged but intelligent and witty teenager is linguistically convincing and deeply moving. The sequel *Take My Word For It* (1992), the journal of one of Marina's room-mates, overlaps the time period of *So Much To Tell You* and provides fresh insight into both characters. NLR

So You Want To Be A Wizard First of a highly original series by American author DIANE DUANE. With the exception of the fourth book, *A Wizard Abroad* (1993), which is set in Ireland and is more reliant on the tropes of heroic quest FANTASY and IRISH MYTHOLOGY, the series uses modern idiom with which to refurbish the genre. Wizardry, for example, is conceptualised as a fight against the eventual running-out of the world's energy, and Dairine's wizardry is accomplished by computer technology.

While not using them in any obvious fashion, *So You Want To Be A Wizard* (1983), and its first two sequels contain mythic or religious elements, though these are understated and disguised; for example, in *High Wizardry* (1991) when a creature asks Dairine to name him, saying 'a programme must be given a name to be saved', the word 'saved' is freighted with other meaning as well. The enemy Lone Power is a conflation of Lucifer, Prometheus and Loki, the overreacher and the fallen one. In *Deep Wizardry* (1985), the enacting of a marine Passion Play is necessary to keep the Lone Power bound, and Nita, taking the part of the Silent Lord, is on the verge of sacrificing herself, when the Pale Slayer who was to kill her instead sacrifices himself in her place. In *High Wizardry*, Dairine spells herself onto a planet which has the capacity for sentience. When endowed by Dairine with language and magic, it brings forth creatures who are tempted by the Lone Power but reject him, thus rewriting the myths of Creation and Fall which stand behind the work. SA

soap operas Radio and TELEVISION serials, broadcast regularly, some daily. 'Soaps' are never-ending narratives, with multiple interweaving storylines around a cluster of characters in a set community. They focus on everyday personal lives and talk is central. Each episode leaves a number of tangles to sustain viewers' interest. Popular but long disparaged, soaps offer experienced viewers complex challenges in a pleasurable 'oscillation between engagement and distance' (Christine Geraghty).

Mainstream soaps have taken up a key position in children's lives since the 1980s. In 1985 BBC's controversial *EastEnders* introduced young characters (with former child actors from GRANGE HILL), gripping storylines, outstanding acting and sharp dialogue. In Britain, children eventually wearied of the relentlessly bleak, almost tragic social realism, and fixed on the Australian feel-good alternative, *Neighbours* (1987), comic, bright and unpretentious. Everyday, fast-moving storylines made it accessible to the very young, realism was relieved by humour, while the amicable resolutions, fine weather and teen sex-appeal offered children daily after-school comfort and relaxation nationwide. *Neighbours*' Kylie Minogue set a trend for teenage soap actors becoming pop stars, establishing new cross-overs within youth culture. Child viewers returned to *EastEnders* as its pace and drama heightened, but now held on to their Australian soaps too. Rival soaps like ITV's *Coronation Street* introduced their own younger characters, and new youth soaps appeared in different niches. Television series popular with young people also became more soap-like in their format (UK police series such as *The Bill*, US sitcoms such as *Friends*). At the turn of the century, young viewers watch whole clusters of soaps, like Alice nibbling at various ends of her mushroom.

Soaps bring up complex issues which today's sophisticated children wish to understand and discuss. Few other texts offer children such opportunities for sustained companionship: with a format that allow 'readers' to come and go, and reposition themselves at will as viewers, soaps faithfully provide regular intimate access to known and cared-about people (both fictional characters and real actors) leading ongoing parallel lives on screen, offering identification, vicarious pleasure and pain. At the same time children choose soaps that challenge their active grasp of storying. Soap viewing continues to rise overall: one soap will not necessarily displace another. However children readily pull away once a serial fails to work for them, or they grow out of it; broadcasters are required to stay on their toes as young audiences continue to evolve.

Stories have been served to audiences in deliberately segmented episodes in print media since the 18th century, the serialisation of DICKENS's *Pickwick Papers* being one landmark. The collective audience this device summons, with the active space offered to the reader to speculate about different narrative possibilities and double-guess the intentions of the author, creates a powerful dynamic. Dickens would have recognised the frenzy about 'Who shot JR?', that swept *Dallas* viewers (and non-viewers) across the world in 1980.

The origin of the term 'soap opera' goes back to American daytime radio serials of the 1930s, sponsored by detergent companies advertising to housewife audiences. Combining the low-brow, frothy-cum-gritty connotations of 'soap' with the high-brow melodramatic 'opera', the self-mocking term hints at the contempt with which even fans affectionately disown the genre. The American radio soaps transferred to television in the 1950s, with the longest running, *The Guiding Light*, in continuous production since 1937. Soaps have long been seen as 'women's' programmes, reflecting perhaps the 'untidy' open-ended perspectives of women's lives, rather than the closed 'patriarchal' narratives that would portray individuals as powerful and in control. Soaps trade in the notion of 'happy ever after' for the inevitablity of suffering, as temporary resolutions necessarily unravel and moments of harmony frequently 'serve as the seedbed for future conflicts' (Richard Kilborn). Increasingly popular, many soaps have moved to prime-time hours, and involve the whole family. With communities dwindled in real life, viewers enjoy that 'invigoratingly intimate look into another world' (Jane Root) at the appointed hour. Both cost-efficient and top-rating, soaps and 'telenovellas' (soap-like programmes which conclude after a long run of episodes) are indispensable to broadcasters worldwide. Between the 1980s and 90s 'soap' hours on British terrestrial television doubled while audiences for each soap held up. From the 1980s soaps have played a dominant part in young people's viewing in Britain, who seek their own mix of gritty and escapist programmes.

Successful soaps are intricately managed. Viewers are offered many positions to move between. With continuity of setting and characters, soaps accommodate intermittent or 'distracted' viewing alongside intense involvement. Storylines build up in stages, with repetition adding layers. Restating a previously known fact orients newcomers, but to the faithful viewer it gives useful knowledge about who knows what, with telling ironies and evocations. Diverse characters offer many points of view and opportunities for identification. Interweaving narrative strands ensure that if you dislike this storyline another one will be along in a minute. Light and heavy strands alternate, both to provide relief and to build up the tension, giving a blend of comedy, social realism and melodrama. Rapid cross-cutting between storylines at critical points requires the skilled 'reader' to supply what is happening in the intervals. Far from being overblown as sometimes caricatured, programmes (especially the more recent ones) can be extremely terse, leaving dramatic exchanges to take place in the viewer's imagination. Soaps evolve with changing and sophisticated audiences.

Fans talk self-deprecatingly about their habit ('I know it's rubbish but I enjoy it'). This 'ironic' viewing reveals fans luxuriating in intense involvement whilst remaining lucid and playful about conventions. Whether they package real-life issues in a feel-good or harrowing blend, all provide a safe mix of escapism and reality. The suggestive title of the Latin American soap, *The Rich Also Cry*, echoes an age-old fascination with the ordinary writ large. We have always relished watching our struggling lives magnified in the glamorising 'soaps' of the time, from family squabbles of Ancient Greek deities to the larger-than-life sagas of the *Mahabharata* and the *Medieval Mysteries*. In this parallel world viewers find both friends and characters they love to hate, and there are many strong women characters. Soap events often release powerful emotions, however ironical the viewer. They provide a shared world to discuss in the family and playground, often vital social currency. Soaps tackle informative issues: in 1985 previously inhibited mothers and daughters across Britain were able to communicate feelingly over Michelle's teenage pregnancy in *EastEnders*. Besides being seen as 'rushing our children out of nappies and into condoms' (to quote television producer Nick Wilson), shocking storylines have raised questions about the 'corrupting' effects of soaps. Yet, however dastardly the deeds, soap worlds remain moral places: the darkest secrets do come to light, characters have to live with the consequences of their actions. The basic values that hold communities also hold the programmes together.

Active participation is the key to soap pleasure. Soaps are 'predictable', and they are parodied for it precisely because producers and viewers play by specific rules. It is a vigorous two-way game of resolving enigmas, chasing clues and constraints, being led by teases and false trails. At every point of the ducking and weaving narrative, fans test arrays of possible developments, confirming or readjusting expectations. They juggle fragments of information from multiple sources: plausibility, plot requirements, available narrative devices, personal beliefs about the world, TV listings, media coverage (for example, an actor rumoured to be leaving). For their part producers try not to disappoint their critical and demanding viewers.

Soap fans feel powerful, saying 'I knew that would happen'; enjoying seeing exactly how it does happen goes along with a formal interest in how a soap will pursue certain issues. Young viewers enjoy the concentration of 'drastic' situations: they know it is unrealistic, there 'to make you watch next time'. It is not simply about riding the conventions, developing the expertise. Viewers also play with destinies: with no character central, the viewer is placed in a position of comparative power, knowing more than the protagonists: 'I feel I could go and tell her this secret!' explains one ardent ten-year-old. Average children of today are unlikely to be able to speak about other kinds of narratives with as much nuance, verve and knowledge of storying as they might about soaps. To young viewers soaps are alive – long discussed with others, a cafeteria of experiences, taken for granted, always there. CMP

Sobol, Donald J. 1924– American author who 'tried to write the kinds of books [he] wanted to read when [he] was a boy but could not find'. He has been extremely successful with his *Encyclopedia Brown, Boy Detective* series (from 1963) of over 20 volumes. Leroy Brown, a 'walking encyclopedia in sneakers', is featured in each book of ten mysteries which readers are expected to help solve. At the end of each book there is an explanation of how Encyclopedia has figured out the mysteries. PDS

Solaru, Lanna Nigerian writer of children's books, born in Britain and Nigerian by marriage. Her stories combine exciting adventures with social observation. *Time for Adventure* (1983) is a rare Nigerian work of SCIENCE FICTION in which three students stumble into the year 3500 and are asked to save Planet Earth. Trouble-prone twins have more realistic adventures in *The Twins Are in Trouble* (1983) and *The Twins to the Rescue* (1987), as does Akin in *A Surprise for Auntie* (1986). Solaru's books for younger readers, *Poor Akin* (1985) and *Konko the Naughty Little Monkey* (1991), show seemingly hopeless characters finally saving the day. Solaru has also written *Coconut Palms and Other Poems* (1979) for young children and an autobiographical account of her intercultural marriage. VD

'some easy pleasant book' Phrase from *Some Thoughts Concerning Education* (1693) by JOHN LOCKE. Having written at some length about teaching a child to read, he recommends the provision of 'some easy pleasant Book suited to his Capacity'. He regarded AESOP as ideal for this purpose. Since the philosophical writings of Locke were so influential in the 18th century, this advice has sometimes been seen as the origin of children's books, for in 1744 JOHN NEWBERY published his first book for children along avowedly Lockeian lines.

However, though Newbery was the first printer/publisher to establish a flourishing children's book trade, a considerable number of children's books were published before 1744. Scholarship has only recently begun to understand that the provision of books for children goes back as far as Anglo-Saxon times. Furthermore the discovery of the nursery materials of JANE JOHNSON – which included hand-written books for the author's own children – suggests that Locke may not have been referring only to published material, but also to what might have been a common practice in domestic nurseries where the developing literacy of children was taken seriously. Locke's influence was clearly a major factor in the early development of children's books, but he was not the sole initiator. VW

Some of Us are Leopards, Some of Us Are Lions (1987) The first book to portray black South African children in a school setting with honour and integrity. Enhanced by Nelda Vermaak's delicate pencil drawings which have both compassion and humour, Mike Kantey's story concerns a boy from the country who feels inadequate in a town school – until his ability to cope with a large spider in the classroom earns him the respect he needs. A subsequent prize-winner, the book has been reprinted many times. JHe

Some Other War (1990–2) Trilogy of popular novels by Linda Newbery set during World War I. The war is represented romantically, but its horrors are clearly depicted and the heroine, a nurse in France, eventually becomes a pacifist. Attention is also drawn to the part played by the war in the gradual demise of the British class system. The third novel is set in Ireland and depicts the Easter Rising in 1916. A second trilogy, *The Shouting Wind* (1995–6), describes the lives of later generations of the family from World War II to the present. KA

Someone is Flying Balloons (1983) Anthology of Australian poems selected by Jill Heylen and Celia Jellett, and dynamically illustrated by KERRY ARGENT. Moving from the child's inner world to the child in relation to others, in an Australia past and present, the poems, grouped by sections, represent some of Australia's finest traditional and contemporary poets. A balance of verse styles is complemented by a range of experiences, from the poignancy of Kath Walker's (see OODGEROO NOONUCCAL) *Last of his Tribe*, to the stridency of PETER MCFARLANE's performance poem, 'Automatic Wash Cycle (And Other Noises)', and the sadness of Yen Ha-Chau's 'Do You Believe that a Child Can Die in the Middle of the Pacific Ocean?', an ode to the Boat People. *Rattling in the Wind* (1987), with illustrations by Maire Smith, is a companion volume. JAP

Song of Hiawatha, The (1854) Famous narrative poem by the American poet and Harvard professor of modern languages, HENRY WADSWORTH LONGFELLOW (1807–82). Longfellow had a great interest in the history and folklore of Native Americans and based his poem on the traditions of the Great Lakes tribes. The original Hiawatha was a historical Native American leader, but Longfellow's poem about his life and adventures draws on the subsequent legends which grew up about him. The well-known metre of the poem – trochaic tetrameter ('Sing, O Song of Hiawatha,/Of the happy days that followed') – was borrowed from a collection of Finnish poetry. He uses this rhythm in such a regular, sometimes monotonous way throughout the poem, that it has lent itself to parody, from LEWIS CARROLL's 'Hiawatha's Photographing' to Bill Greenwell's more recent 'Coochi-coochi'. Illustrated versions of the work include those by J. Kiddell-Monroe (1960), ERROL LE CAIN (1985) and SUSAN JEFFERS (1994). ML

Illustration by Joyce Mercer from *The Death of Minnehaha.*

Song of Wirrun, The see WIRRUN TRILOGY; see also THE BUSH

Song Quest (1999) Much-praised novel by the new British writer Katherine Roberts (1962–), the first of a proposed trilogy. *Song Quest* is a compelling and at times deeply moving FANTASY – slightly strained in places – in which issues of power and cruelty drive a highly imaginative narrative. Roberts's second work, *Spellfall* (2000) – about children caught up in a conflict between technology and magic – is a much more assured work, darker and more violent, but with moments of considerable descriptive beauty and a more convincing interest in character. Katherine Roberts is a computer expert and trainer of racehorses; *Song Quest* was the first winner of the Branford Boase Award for a new writer's first children's book, an award established in memory of the author HENRIETTA BRANFORD and the editor Wendy Boase.

VW

Songs of Innocence and Experience: Shewing the Two Contrary States of the Human Soul (1794) A collection of poems by William Blake (1757–1827). The *Songs of Innocence* were published for children as a separate series in 1789 and were reissued as part of the larger collection in 1794. Very few children knew them in Blake's lifetime, and few copies of the *Songs* were made, mainly because he printed and bound his books himself and they were then coloured by hand. Blake was the first major British poet to turn his attention to children, perhaps as a result of his friendship with Mary Wollstonecraft, for whose *ORIGINAL STORIES FROM REAL LIFE* he was at about this time engraving some ILLUSTRATIONS.

Blake was addressing children in ways which were radically new, challenging parents' assumptions about instructional verse. His conception of a book of poetry for children was entirely original; such publications were illustrated – if at all – with occasional woodcuts, but the *Songs* were coloured, and every poem was set within a single-page design or illustration to create a tiny visionary whole. The title-page shows a young woman sharing a book with two children beneath a Tree of Knowledge in which there are spirits and soaring birds. This sets the tone for the rest of the *Songs*, each design placing children in an imaginary pastoral landscape peopled with spirits. The 'Introduction' tells how a 'laughing' child inspired the poet to write, and the emphatic language of joy emphasises how unlike the poetry of JOHN BUNYAN and ISAAC WATTS these *Songs* are intended to be. Some are expressions of a young child's developing sense of goodness; some are poems for bedtime; one is a NONSENSE poem; in others, children take on the language of adults to address creatures smaller than themselves. In 'The Ecchoing Green' every element of the landscape 'echoes' responsively to every other element – the sun, trees, birds, sky, church-bells and villagers; and although one illustration shows a couple of older boys passing some richly suggestive bunches of grapes to a girl below, this hint of growing sexuality is perfectly harmonious within the idyllic security of the pastoral community.

Some of the most evocative of the *Songs* are lyrics expressing the conversation between mothers and small children. To express this quiet maternal intimacy, Blake refined a simplicity and directness of language which seems to resist literary criticism. Early critics believed that this extreme simplicity of style was an oddity arising from his being socially isolated, possibly even unbalanced; but it is more likely that he was the first great poet to draw on the oral traditions of the 18th-century nursery, capturing the gentle child-centred rhetoric of mothers singing and talking with their children. An example of this is 'Infant Joy', which suggests the mysterious love and trust between a mother and her new baby, and becomes at the same time both a blessing and a naming.

I have no name
I am but two days old. –
What shall I call thee?
I happy am
Joy is my name. –
Sweet joy befall thee!
Pretty joy!
Sweet joy but two days old.
Sweet joy I call thee;
Thou dost smile,
I sing the while
Sweet joy befall thee.

Published NURSERY RHYMES were becoming fashionable and several of the *Songs* show Blake's familiarity with their form and imagery. The final verse of 'Spring', for example, has echoes of 'Baa, Baa, Black Sheep' (in print since 1744); and 'The Blossom', with its delicate suggestion of a mother softly speaking to her new-born – or newly-conceived – baby, would sit comfortably alongside the many popular rhymes about robins and linnets. Blake retained the voice and imagery of these traditional rhymes but transformed their rather indeterminate and cheerful brevity into expressions of a single coherent vision of a world seen through innocent eyes.

There are, however, hints of a darker reality in the *Songs of Innocence*. Blake was the first writer to employ a kind of irony unique to children's literature: 'The Chimney Sweeper', while offering a simple reassuring message to a very young child, simultaneously challenges the adult into a different reading about the exploitation of children. Other contemporary moral issues are treated in a similar way, comforting for the child, troubling for the adult: 'The Little Black Boy' deals with race and slavery, and 'Holy Thursday' with the treatment of poor children. In 'The Divine Image', Blake employed a Swiftian satirical 'ambush': the first three verses lull readers with unexceptionable statements about Christian benevolence before luring them into a radical and unequivocal expression of religious tolerance.

Then all must love the human form,
In heathen, turk or jew.

Where Mercy, Love & Pity dwell
There God is dwelling too.

This Song has been popular as a school hymn – sometimes with this last verse omitted.

The *Songs of Experience* were not written for children; only 'The Tyger' has become familiar to them through frequent anthologising. Several of the poems 'partner' a poem from the *Songs of Innocence*, the second addressing the same issue with an explicit despair, or with an angry sense of bafflement. Throughout both series of the *Songs* Blake's thematic use of the word 'play' suggests that he sees a natural connection between a happy and unrestrained childhood and the capacity in adult life for unselfconscious sexual delight; conversely, he saw a cultural link between the repression of sexual desire and the ill-treatment of children.

HONOR APPLETON (1911), Mary and CHARLES ROBINSON (1913), Jacynth Parsons (1927) and HAROLD JONES (1958) have produced editions of the *Songs* with their own illustrations, and ROSEMARY MANNING edited a collection called *A Grain of Sand* (1967), illustrated with pastoral WOOD ENGRAVINGS taken from Blake's other works. In 1981 MARTIN and ALICE PROVENSEN published a tribute to Blake in the form of an illustrated collection of poetry, *A Visit to William Blake's Inn: Poems for Innocent and Experienced Travelers*. But no facsimile of Blake's own text has been published specifically for children. VW

Soper, Eileen (Alice) 1905–90 British writer, illustrator and artist. From an early age, Eileen Soper was encouraged by her father, GEORGE SOPER. She soon rivalled him in talent and surpassed him in popularity by producing etchings of children at play. Increasingly, she moved from treating children as her subject to making them her public, so that from the time of her father's death she worked primarily as an illustrator. She aimed five of her published books at children: four stories, beginning with *The Adventures of Leo the Lion* (1941), and a volume of poetry, *Songs of the Wind* (1948). She also produced wall-posters, guides and primers for use in schools and she collaborated with other authors. She was best known as the favourite illustrator of ENID BLYTON, and worked on the entire series of FAMOUS FIVE adventures (1942–63) and a vast range of her other books, from *The Children's Life of Christ* (1943) to *My First Nature Book* (1952). Latterly, she developed a career as a wildlife writer and artist, a change of emphasis marked by the publication of *When Badgers Wake* (1955). She even encouraged animals into the house which had always been her home, built by her father near Welwyn, in the Hertfordshire countryside. DW

Soper, George 1870–1942 British artist and illustrator. Soper illustrated a series of attractive GIFT BOOKS for Headley Brothers, beginning with THE WATER BABIES (1908), and a number of tales of adventure. DW

***Sophie* series** (1988–95) Six CHAPTER BOOKS for young readers written by the British author DICK KING-SMITH and illustrated in black-and-white by DAVID PARKINS. Sophie, who wants to be a farmer when she grows up, is small and very determined, never failing in anything she sets her mind to. She has very decisive views on things, disliking frilly clothes and spending much of the series dressed in jeans and the same jumper with her name on it, long after it has become too small for her. She labours under misapprehensions common to many young children, believing, for example, that the Scottish Highlands really are a long way up, and often muddling the long words she tries to use, so that she calls her brothers 'ingerent' and 'iterating' when she means 'ignorant' and 'irritating'. The ILLUSTRATIONS often show her looking cross and determined.

The series begins with Sophie aged four and ends just after her eighth birthday, her ageing mirrored in texts which become more difficult as the stories progress. The earlier stories are cheerful, depicting a happy family life where even Sophie's rather annoying brothers are actually very fond of her and where she eventually obtains every animal she wishes for, despite her parents' reluctance. The final story in the book introduces a note of sadness with the death of Sophie's beloved great-great-aunt – an event that experienced readers can predict from the subtle clues in the text. The book has a happy ending, though, as Sophie inherits her aunt's farm and begins to realise her ambition. KA

Sorcerer's Apprentice, The see WALT DISNEY; MUSIC AND STORY

Sorensen, Virginia 1912–91 American author of realistic and historical novels. The author of a variety of adult books, including several which draw on her Mormon background, Sorensen eventually turned to writing children's fiction, often focusing on family life and children who feel like outsiders. Her most enduring children's book, the NEWBERY AWARD winner *Miracles on Maple Hill* (1956), treats a family's renewal of faith in response to a death and their father's return from war. *Plain Girl* (1956), detailing an Amish girl's struggle with her culture, received a Child Study Association of America Children's Book Award. Sorensen's other books for children include *Curious Missie* (1953), *The House Next Door* (1954), *Lotte's Locket* (1964) and *Around the Corner* (1971). JDC

Soto, Gary 1952– Writer of poetry and prose for children and adults. Gary Soto, a third-generation

Mexican American, was born in Fresno, California, and later settled in Berkeley. Soto has been highly praised for his vibrant portrayals of Mexican American life. *Baseball in April and Other Stories* (1990) was Soto's first book written specifically for young readers. Each of the 11 humorous short stories in this collection concerns the coming-of-age of Chicano youths. Today Soto has over 20 books for children in print. Most of his writing springs from memories of growing up in the barrios. His books for younger children are humorous, but there is a wide range of sentiment and mood in his writings which often addresses poverty, violence and racism.

Soto has also written accessible and informal poetry for children, including *Neighborhood Odes* (1992), which explores in verse the emotions of everyday life, and *Canto Familiar* (1955), which reflects the lives of Mexican American children in short-lined free verse. He has delved into the realm of PICTUREBOOKS as well with *Too Many Tamales* (1993), illustrated by ED YOUNG, and *Chato's Kitchen* (1995), illustrated by Susan Guevara. Soto has adapted several of his books for film, including *The Pool Party* (1993), which was awarded the Andrew Carnegie Medal for Excellence in Children's Video. EB

Sound of the Gora, The (1980) A youth novel by Ann Harries (1942–) that has the distinction of having been banned by the South African government of the time as seditious literature. It deals with the historical and religious origins of apartheid, friendship across racial barriers, the existence of 'coloured' members in so-called white families, and black consciousness. It operates within two time frames: clashes between Dutch settlers and indigenous inhabitants in 1800, and the student uprising of 1976. San belief in rebirth and regeneration is shown to effect healing and reconciliation (as it does in the works of MARGUERITE POLAND). ERJ

see also AFRICAN MYTHOLOGY; *GO WELL, STAY WELL*

Sounder (1969) Novel by the American author WILLIAM H. ARMSTRONG which won a NEWBERY MEDAL. This coming-of-age novel set in the Depression era depicts a black share-cropping family. When his father is jailed for stealing food to feed his family, the main character is enabled by a teacher's friendship to make the transition from boyhood to manhood as well as to break the cycle of poverty. To allow readers to identify with the characters, Armstrong left all except the dog, Sounder, unnamed. Although this novel was praised for its literary merit, and his intention was to universalise the experience of poor blacks in the South, Armstrong's first children's book was attacked by some as a white writer's misleading and racist portrayal of black Americans as faceless, nameless and passive victims of oppression. Armstrong, an English teacher and writer of educational materials and BIOGRAPHIES, based *Sounder* and its sequels, *Sour Land* (1971) and *The MacLeod Place* (1972), on stories told to him by an African American teacher. *Sounder* has been translated into 28 languages and adapted as an acclaimed motion picture (1972), described as a 'paean to the resilience and fortitude of the black family'. Despite the controversy it has provoked, *Sounder* remains a staple of school reading lists in the United States and is considered a classic of American children's literature. JB, RSH

Souter, D.H. see *FOUR AND TWENTY LAMINGTONS*

South African mythology see AFRICAN MYTHOLOGY

Southall, Ivan (Francis) 1921– Australian writer of fiction and non-fiction for both adults and adolescents. Southall is highly regarded for his storytelling ability and his empathy with his young characters facing physical and psychological dangers. *Hill's End* (1962), which deals with adolescents caught up in the struggle for survival amidst overpowering storms, and *To The Wild Sky* (1967), which tells of aircraft, accidents and determination, are early examples. The quality of his work, which has been produced for well over 40 years, is reflected by his many national and international awards including CHILDREN'S BOOK COUNCIL OF AUSTRALIA BOOK OF THE YEAR AWARDS in 1966, 1968, 1971 and 1976; Picturebook of the Year, 1969; CARNEGIE MEDAL, 1972; and numerous honour and notable book awards.

Ash Road (1965) tells the story of the survival of young people facing an Australian bush fire. A disabled boy's great courage while facing his inner fears is movingly depicted in *LET THE BALLOON GO* (1968). *Josh* (1971) concerns the life of an alienated and clever adolescent boy living in a rural community. *Bread and Honey* (1970) is about a boy's growing self-perception and alienation, and *Fly West* (1974) is a biography set during World War II. *Sly Old Wardrobe* (1968), illustrated by TED GREENWOOD and concerned with grandmothers, furniture and rejection, gained the CBCA Picturebook of the Year Award (1969). *The Long Night Watch* (1983), an historical mystery, was awarded the Australian National Book Award. While critics have questioned his use of stream of consciousness, flashbacks and multiple points of view for a juvenile readership, his works find many enthusiastic supporters. CH, HMcC

Space Demons (1986) SCIENCE FICTION novel which launched GILLIAN RUBINSTEIN'S career. It tells of four children drawn into a sinister computer game which is fuelled by the hatred and frustration experienced by the children in their real lives – especially in relation to bossiness and parental abandonment. The children must overcome these feelings to escape its clutches. *Space Demons* has been performed and republished as a play. It has two sequels, *Skymaze* (1989) and *Shinkei* (1996), depicting the children in further battles against both emotional weaknesses and artificial intelligence. The last is a more complex, abstract and mature novel than its predecessors. NLR

Spanish Cave, The ADVENTURE STORY for children written by Geoffrey Household (1900–88), best known for his adult thriller *Rogue Male*. First published in 1936 and subsequently reissued by Puffin in 1963, the story is a well-written account of the development of an English schoolboy's maturity as he becomes the hunter of a surviving prehistoric underwater 'beast' in northern Spain. Today a writer would want such a creature rescued for conservation, but in the 1930s heroism required its elimination. The Puffin edition described it as being suitable 'for boys, and some girls'. VW

Speaking to Miranda (1991) Australian novel by CAROLINE MACDONALD, which traces Ruby's efforts to unravel the enigma of her mother's identity. Since her mother's death when she was two, Ruby has lived contentedly with her stepfather, but in the hiatus between the end of school and the start of adult life, she cuts herself off from her known childhood to probe the mystery that precedes it. Ruby's journey, both physical and psychological, intriguingly maps a young woman's exploration of self and identity with a deftness that exemplifies Macdonald's ability to write perceptive and fast-moving stories. MN

Speare, Elizabeth George 1908–94 American historical novelist twice honoured with the NEWBERY MEDAL for her illuminating stories of times past, filled with well-defined characters and enticing plots. *The Witch of Blackbird Pond* (1961) is set in Puritan New England, while her second medal-winner, *The Bronze Bow* (1961), is set in Palestine at the time of Christ. A third novel, *The Sign of the Beaver* (1983), earned her the Newbery Honour award.

Speare was born in Melrose, Massachusetts. She taught English in high school before marrying Alden Speare and settling in Westfield, Connecticut, the setting for her first novel *Calico Captive* (1957). Based on the journal of a woman captured by Indians, its portrayal of Indians is stereotypical. In *The Sign of the Beaver* her rendering of Penobscot Indians is far more accurate. This novel also earned her in 1984 the Scott O'Dell Award for Historical Fiction and the Christopher Award. Her main characters struggle against social injustice while striving for self-identity and learning determination. Her female characters are strong, often forced to act against accepted convention while the adversity they face helps them to mature. She was awarded the 1989 Laura Ingalls Wilder Award for her contribution to children's literature. LAW

see also HISTORICAL FICTION

Spell of Words, A (1997) An outstanding collection of poetry for children by the distinguished English poet, ELIZABETH JENNINGS. The almost luminous quality of some of the verse, the lyric voice, the rich imagery, the haunting resonances are all distinctive and appealing – though perhaps more to literary adults than to children. When it was considered for the *SIGNAL* AWARD FOR POETRY, 1998, critics Lissa Paul and Bob Barton saw its merits but noted that 'the nostalgia was too pervasive' and thought it 'more suited to the adult looking back' than to children. However, some discriminating young readers will find poetry to treasure in this volume. MCCS

Spence, Eleanor (Rachel Therese) 1928– Australian writer, a former librarian and teacher, who has written 14 novels for older children since her first novel, *Patterson's Track* (1958). Highly esteemed for her work, Spence was one of the first writers to recognise and examine DISABILITY in Australian children's fiction. *The Nothing Place* (1972) is centred around a deaf child. *The October Child* (1976), CHILDREN'S BOOK COUNCIL OF AUSTRALIA Book of the Year, explored the very real and heart-wrenching effect of a young autistic child, Carl, upon his family. Her interest in history and a personal spiritual journey led her to Israel to gather material for her two historical novels, *Me and Jeshua* (1984) and *Miranda Going Home* (1985), based upon the young Jesus in Palestine under the Roman occupation. Spence shows enormous integrity as a writer, using exemplary literary prose which has the power to reach across boundaries and speak to a diverse multicultural audience. *A Candle for Saint Antony* (1977) explores both the issue of migrant children adapting to Australian schools, and the complexities of adolescence and friendship. She writes from the heart, and it is this which seems to touch her wide audience. AT

Sperry, Armstrong 1879–1976 American writer and illustrator who continued the tradition of boys' ADVENTURE STORIES begun by such writers as BALLANTYNE and STEVENSON in the 19th century. Born in New Haven, Connecticut, and educated at Yale University School of Fine Arts and the Arts Student League, he drew much of his inspiration as a writer and as an illustrator from his great-grandfather, who told him stories of his days in the South Seas. In 1925

Sperry travelled to Bora Bora, where he spent two years collecting legends and folklore. Though he began as an illustrator, Sperry turned to writing HISTORICAL FICTION and what would today be called 'ethnographic' fiction for younger readers. His two best-known novels were *All Sail Set: A Romance of the 'Flying Cloud'* (1936, Newbery Honour) and *Call It Courage* (1940, NEWBERY MEDAL).

Call It Courage, the only one of Sperry's novels still read with any frequency, is written in the form of a FOLKTALE from the South Seas: Mafatu, a 15-year-old boy, is afraid of the sea and determines to conquer his fear. He survives a storm at sea, kills a shark and escapes from an island of cannibals. Sperry's writing style is simple and direct and possesses some of the cadences of oral formulaic STORYTELLING; similarly, his ILLUSTRATIONS suggest Polynesian drawings. Contemporary critics and readers may question its ethnographic authenticity (some of the descriptions strike today's readers as racist), but Sperry's narrative drive is undeniable. BH

Spider see CRICKET MAGAZINE

Spider-Man *MARVEL COMIC*'s most popular SUPERHERO. Since his 1962 début in *Amazing Fantasy*, Spider-Man, the creation of Stan Lee, has become the best-known costumed superhero of the *Marvel Comics* universe and the star of several comic books and TELEVISION series. Originally a wimpy teenage scientist named Peter Parker, Spider-Man gained strength and agility after being bitten by a radioactive spider. Spider-Man differs from many earlier comic-book crime-fighters because, despite his great powers, he has a number of personal problems, including an often unsuccessful love life, and he has occasionally been misjudged by society. JDC

Spielberg, Steven 1946– American film director and producer, the most commercially successful film maker in the history of cinema. The vast majority of Spielberg's films have been made to include a juvenile audience. Many of his most successful films have been adventure narratives, often reworking familiar genres with ideas derived from older Hollywood films he had loved as a child. Examples are the *Indiana Jones* series (1981, 1984, 1989) and the *Gremlins* and *Back to the Future* films which he produced over a similar period. These series offer a popular mix of thrills, special effects, pastiche and 'in-jokes'. Although this mixture is not unique to Spielberg, he seems to be able to bring a special quality to the most formulaic of genres. In his first world-wide success, *Jaws* (1975), for instance, the care which was exercised in relation to screenplay, soundtrack and special effects particularly, enabled a potentially trite disaster-movie/thriller plot to tap primal emotional chords of fear and wonder in its audiences. Similar qualities are displayed in the more recent *Jurassic Park* (1993). Perhaps Spielberg's quintessential child-oriented film is the story of the little alien *E.T.* (1982), shot almost entirely from a child's viewpoint and undoubtedly one of the most shamelessly and affectingly sentimental films ever made. It drew tears even from the coolly detached novelist Martin Amis, who commented shrewdly that we cry at the end not for the little boy or abandoned alien but 'for our lost selves. This is the primal genius of Spielberg.' DWh

Spier, Peter 1927– Dutch American author and illustrator of PICTUREBOOKS. Born in Amsterdam, he attended the Royal Academy of Arts, but his passion for boats and water led him to the Royal Dutch Navy. In 1952 Spier came to the United States as a reporter for a Dutch magazine. Spier has written and illustrated approximately 100 books, including 50 picturebooks on a wide range of topics. He spends roughly six months researching and visiting locations for each project. As a result each ILLUSTRATION can be a lesson in geography, history and sociology as children enjoy a succinctly worded and entertaining story. *The Erie Canal* (1970) contains a variety of water vessels, people and scenes of rural New York, historically correct and minute in detail. Spier's versatility shows in *Oh Were They Happy* (1978): vivid puddles of colour support the story of siblings who paint the house while their parents are away. Books on folksongs include *The Fox Went Out on a Chilly Night* (1961), a Caldecott Honour Book. The CALDECOTT MEDAL was awarded to *Noah's Ark* (1977) and *London Bridge is Falling Down* (1967) received the BOSTON GLOBE-HORN BOOK AWARD. JRG

Spinelli, Jerry 1941– American novelist, born in Norristown, Pennsylvania. As a child and adolescent, he was interested in sports, and many of his novels centre upon young athletes. His novels are popular and readable and, while most have male protagonists, they appeal to both sexes. Many of his novels – such as *Space Station Seventh Grade* (1982) and its sequel *Jason and Marceline* (1986) – are aimed at middle-school readers. Recent novels retain the sense of humour that made earlier novels popular but also address more complex social and cultural issues, such as the link between sports and violence (*Crash*, 1996) and homelessness and illiteracy (*The Library Card*, 1997, a collection of four linked short stories). His best-known and most critically-praised novel, *Maniac Magee* (1991, NEWBERY MEDAL and BOSTON GLOBE-HORN BOOK AWARD), combines sports, social activism and homelessness in the story of Jeffrey Magee, a homeless boy whose speed as a racer becomes legendary in the mill-town in which he lives and whose own liminality allows him to become a cultural hero to both blacks and whites and to bring them together in harmony. The very short chapters prevent Spinelli from developing any of the characters with much psychological depth and instead emphasise the legendary elements of the plot. Spinelli's later novel, *Wringer* (1997), was awarded Newbery honours. BH

Spiritual Milk for Babes see *THE NEW-ENGLAND PRIMER*

sports stories see RALPH HENRY BARBOUR; MICHAEL HARDCASTLE; ROBERT LIPSYTE; CLAIRE MACKAY; SUZANNE MARTEL; JOHN TUNIS; JERRY SPINELLI

Spot Series by Eric Hill consisting of board, cloth and bath books for very young children, and lift-the-flap books for older pre-school children. Hill made a major contribution to the recent popularity of flapbooks with his first flapbook, *Where's Spot?* (1980). The series features a small dog called Spot in various situations familiar to young children. The illustrations are confident and bright, with uniform blocks of colour within simple lines on a white background. The stories are told in large, bold print with no more than a couple of sentences on each page. There are no overt lessons to be learnt, just a simple story to visually engage a small child. AW

see also MOVABLE BOOKS

Springheel Jack see SUPERHEROES

Spyri, Johanna see *HEIDI*

Srivastav, Sigrun 1943– Indian fiction writer, scriptwriter, sculptor, painter and illustrator. Endowed with a multifaceted personality, Srivastav is rated as one of the most committed writers for children in India. She addresses the problems that confront children in the process of growing up in such contemporary contexts as terrorism, corruption and competitiveness. She brings to these difficult issues a rare compassion and understanding rooted in a heartfelt respect for teenagers. For instance, 'The Lost Case' – a short story included in *Trapped and Other Stories* (1995) and a personal favourite of the author – is about a teenager's relationship with his mother who is dying of cancer. Her faith in the realistic novel makes her pay careful attention to the specificities of the setting, which she draws with the unerring judgement of a painter. This is buttressed with real, bubbly dialogue.

Srivastav has written more than 30 books for children, quite a few of which she has innovatively illustrated herself. These include the popular *What's Right and What's Wrong* (1986) and *I am Better than You* (1992). Lauded for a mellifluous style, her restrained technique is dramatically offset by her unexpected climactic twists. Her ability to get under the skin of her child characters makes them credible individuals with real-life feelings, fears and problems. Her popularity can be gauged by the fact that she received the Children's Choice Award in 1989 for *The Ghost Rider of Darbhanga* (1989). *Grin and Bear It, Abhy* (1993) is a rib-tickling entertainer with a healthy element of suspense. MBh

Stables, Gordon see *BOY'S OWN PAPER*

Stackpool, Walter see COVER ART

Stacpoole, H[enry] de Vere 1863–1951 Prolific American writer of sea tales, murder mysteries and romances. He is best remembered for *The Blue Lagoon* (1908), the story of two shipwrecked children growing up on a Pacific island. *The Garden of God* (1923) and *The Gates of Morning* (1925) are sequels. Stacpoole is also the author of *Pierrette* (1899), a collection of children's stories, enlarged and republished as *Poppyland* (1914). *The Cruise of the Kingfisher* (1911) is a novel for young readers. Stacpoole's novels of high-sea adventure and island life were popular reading for children during the first half of the 20th century. However, young people in the 1990s know Stacpoole's work primarily through film: *The Blue Lagoon* was filmed in 1923, 1949 and 1980, and *The Garden of God* was filmed as *Return to Blue Lagoon* in 1991. EAM

Stafford, Ann see CAMPING AND TRAMPING FICTION

Stagg, Paul see NAOMI LEWIS

Stalky and Co. (1899) Novel by RUDYARD KIPLING, belonging superficially to the genre of the SCHOOL STORY, humorously detailing the exploits of Stalky, Beetle, and M'Turk at the College, as they attempt to outwit the unfortunate master, Prout. While contemptuous of such things as games, upholding the honour of the school house and cant, *Stalky and Co.* espouses the values of 'officer and gentleman', the creed of country. The education with which the book is concerned has to do with the making of men for the Empire – as the coda to the work, which narrates Stalky's heroic doings in India, makes clear. SA

Standards of Criticism for Children's Literature see CRITICAL APPROACHES TO CHILDREN'S BOOKS

Stanley, Diane 1909– British illustrator. Stanley is best known for her line illustrations in MARY NORTON'S *BORROWER* novels (*The Borrowers*, 1952, *The*

Borrowers Afield, 1955, *The Borrowers Aloft*, 1961) but she also contributed eight watercolours to an edition of *ALICE'S ADVENTURES IN WONDERLAND* in 1954. JAG

Stannard, Russell see *UNCLE ALBERT* SERIES

Staples, Suzanne Fisher see *DAUGHTER OF THE WIND*

Star Trek 1966– SCIENCE FICTION series optimistically set in the space-faring future, created for TELEVISION by American Gene Roddenberry. *Star Trek* dramatises the adventures of Captains Kirk and Spock and the ethnically diverse crew of the *USS Enterprise* as they explore 'Space, the final frontier'. Despite the original series' cancellation (1969), *Star Trek* attracted idealistic fans (or 'Trekkers') whose demand resuscitated the programme through international syndication; it became a global phenomenon. In 1979, *Star Trek: the Motion Picture* was released, the first of eight profitable films. Conventions, books and merchandise followed, as well as three spin-off series: *Star Trek: the Next Generation* (1987), *Deep Space Nine* (1993) and *Voyager* (1995). AA

***Star Wars* Trilogy** Films written and directed by George Lucas. *Star Wars* (1977), *The Empire Strikes Back* (1980) and *Return of the Jedi* (1983) comprise the futuristic paradigm of the battle between good and evil. Set 'a long time ago in a galaxy far, far away', the trilogy depicts the quest of the archetypal hero Luke Skywalker, who uses 'the Force' to fight to save the galaxy from the evil Imperial forces, led by Darth Vadar. Joined by his sister Princess Leia and Captain Han Solo, Skywalker ultimately vanquishes the empire and Vadar is revealed as the repentant Faustian father who had succumbed to the darker side. CLR

Starting School (1988) This warm, witty and reassuring book by British author-illustrators JANET AND ALLAN AHLBERG had its origins in an idea from the Ahlbergs' daughter's first schoolteacher, who wanted to welcome and inform new entrants to primary school. The Ahlbergs do more than induct readers into the rhythms and rituals of school. Seven children start school together and, through the tiny, detailed illustrations, we can detect their personalities and follow their individual stories. Red-haired Sophie, for instance, develops into a confident and independent child, not above sniggering in prayers and capable of hurling the odd wooden block and attempting to throttle a classmate. Thumb-sucking, solemn, bookish Gavin comes to school with his pregnant Mum; by the time of the Christmas play, he has relaxed, and in the audience is his new baby sibling. The pre-school child is unlikely to miss these extra details. JAG

Steadfast Tin Soldier, The see HANS CHRISTIAN ANDERSEN; see also MARCIA BROWN; P.J. LYNCH; MUSIC AND STORY

Steadman, Ralph 1936– Though principally known for his political cartoons and caricatures, the British illustrator Ralph Steadman has frequently returned to illustrate children's books, winning numerous prizes in the process. *Emergency Mouse*, *Inspector Mouse* and *Quasimodo Mouse* (Bernard Stone, 1978, 1980 and 1984) are illustrated in wash, stipple and ink in vigorous and sophisticated style. *That's My Dad* (1986) and *Teddy, Where Are You?* (1994) are titles both written and illustrated (more gently) by Steadman. He provided magnificent and uncompromising illustrations to *ALICE'S ADVENTURES IN WONDERLAND* (1967), *Through the Looking Glass* (1972), TREASURE ISLAND (1985) and *Animal Farm* (1995). JAG

Steamboat Willie see WALT DISNEY; *MICKEY MOUSE*; see also ANIMATED CARTOONS

Steele, Mary (de Chair) 1930– Australian author whose first book, *Arkwright* (1985), was awarded the CHILDREN'S BOOK COUNCIL OF AUSTRALIA Book of the Year: Younger Readers Award (1986). The book's absurd humour and distorted picture of reality prompted the judges to describe it as 'A jolly good read!' The well-received sequel, *Citizen Arkwright* (1990), continues the heroes' ridiculous but endearing battles over the wrongs in their world. *Mallyroots' Pub at Misery Ponds* (1988) is filled with humour and littered with Australiana, colloquialisms, and blatantly amusing stereotypes. The sensitive *Featherbys* (1993), her most successful book to date, and one which won international acclaim, is a change of pace and style, with a more realistic and thought-provoking narrative about some children who work with two ageing sisters to save their family home. *A Bit of a Hitch* (1991) is a collection of eight stories about ordinary people who find themselves in extraordinary, often comic, situations. Steele has also contributed to a number of short-story anthologies, which include *Dream Time* (1989), *Into the Future* (1991) and *Bittersweet* (1992). AT

Steele, Susannah see *INKY PINKY PONKY*; *MOTHER GAVE A SHOUT*

Steele, William O(wen) 1917–79 American writer of HISTORICAL FICTION. Born in Tennessee, Steele was keenly interested in the pioneering history of his native state. His books try to convey not events, but the people who make events, including notable figures like DAVY CROCKETT and DANIEL BOONE. Steele was fascinated by the clash of Indian and white cultures in the old Southwest and many of his award-winning earlier books, including *Winter Danger* (1954), *Flaming Arrows* (1957) and *The Lone Hunt* (1958), all illustrated by P. GALDONE, told of matters from the frontiersman's point of view. However, in later life Steele chose to write from the perspective of his Indian characters, as in *The War Party* (1978). SCWA

Steig, Michael see CRITICAL APPROACHES TO CHILDREN'S LITERATURE

Steig, William 1907– American children's author and illustrator, as well as sculptor and popular adult cartoonist. Steig's cartoons appeared regularly in *New Yorker* magazine from 1930, but it was not until 1968 that he wrote and illustrated his first children's book, *Roland the Minstrel Pig*. Several years later, his *Sylvester and the Magic Pebble* (1969) won both the CALDECOTT MEDAL and the American Book Award. Although some criticised his use of pigs as police in *Sylvester*, Steig maintains he tries to remain politically neutral in his children's books. Many critics have praised the author for his use of rich language, imaginative story lines and fanciful illustrations. His characters are typically intelligent, anthropomorphic animals – *Abel's Island* (1976) is a notable example – and his whimsical tales always end happily. For example, *Doctor De Soto*'s mouse dentist outsmarts a selfish – and hungry – fox who complains of a toothache (1982). *Doctor De Soto Goes to Africa* was published in 1992. Children especially enjoy his stories in which smaller creatures overcome large obstacles, while adults can appreciate Steig's sophisticated humour and dialogue. Steig has written CHAPTER BOOKS for older children in addition to picture stories, many of which have been adapted into videos, filmstrips and various other media forms. CHW

see also ROBINSONNADES

Stein, Gertrude see *THE WORLD IS ROUND*; see also MARGARET WISE BROWN

Steinbeck, John 1902–68 Native Californian and winner of the Nobel Prize for Literature in 1962. His most famous book, *The Grapes of Wrath* (1939), is an epic of the 'Okies', the poor and hungry who left the dust bowl of the Midwest and sought the Promised Land of California in the 1930s. Jim Casy can be seen as a Christ figure, whereas Ma Joad, the 'citadel' of her family, epitomises the life spirit; she labours to pass on the mystery of the cycle of life to her daughter, Rose of Sharon. Another significant title is *The Red Pony* (1949), in which Jody observes the cycle of birth and death as part of a three-generational farm family. He loses his beloved pony, Gabilan, in the novella, and he watches as Nellie is sacrificed for her foal. Also important are *The Pearl* (1948), *Tortilla Flat* (1935), *Of Mice and Men* (1937) and *Cannery Row* (1945). The theme of the land assaulted by mechanisation, technology and profit barons runs through his works. Politically, he aroused controversy, but his fiction has been much read by adolescents both in and outside the classroom. NV

Stephens C[harles] A[sbury] 1844–1931 American author who, from 1870, wrote extensively for *THE YOUTH'S COMPANION*, where for nearly 60 years he was immensely popular with a wide readership. He contributed over 2,500 short stories, many under a variety of pen-names; some of his serials and collections of stories were later published as novels. Stephens wrote ADVENTURE STORIES for boys (the *Knockabout Club* series and the *Camping Out* series), but his best work occurs in the *Old Squire* series. In these, six orphan cousins are raised by their grandparents on a farm in Maine. Recurring themes are the value of education and hard work, the benefits of a simple wholesome life, the importance of the democratic process, the inevitability of the entrepreneurial spirit and the acceptance of personal responsibility. In spite of having to deal with these weighty issues, the cousins enjoy many adventures on the Old Farm and in the surrounding countryside, playing pranks on their rivals, extricating themselves from delicate situations, and foiling the evil schemes of the less than virtuous. Although the boys tend to have more adventures than the girls, girls are represented as brave, intelligent and competitive. WH

Stephens, James 1882–1950 Irish writer best known for his novel *The Crock of Gold* (1912). His *Irish Fairy Tales* (1920) was illustrated by ARTHUR RACKHAM. *Collected Poems* (1926) includes imaginative, vivid writing on themes of nature and the folklore of an Ireland of giants and leprechauns. Still occasionally appearing in anthologies, Stephens's work deserves greater recognition. AHa

see also IRISH MYTHOLOGY AND FOLKLORE

Stephens, John see CRITICAL APPROACHES TO CHILDREN'S LITERATURE

Stephens, Michael see also KIM GAMBLE

Steptoe, John (Lewis) 1950–89 African American author and illustrator of PICTUREBOOKS and fiction. Born in Brooklyn, Steptoe gained national recognition at the age of 19 when his first book, *Stevie*, was published in *Life* magazine in 1969 prior to its release by Harper and Row. Steptoe stated that the book was 'not directed at white children' but was 'something black children could read without translating the language, something real, which would relate to what a black child would know'. The book was greeted with great acclaim, and Steptoe followed it with other picturebooks depicting the everyday lives of inner-city black children, including *Uptown* (1970), *Train Ride* (1971), *My Special Best Words* (1974) and *Daddy Is a Monster . . . Sometimes* (1980). He also wrote a fascinating but under-appreciated young adult novel, *Marcia* (1976). In the 1980s Steptoe experimented with different styles of art and writing. *The Story of Jumping Mouse: A Native American Legend* (1984) was written in a traditional style and illustrated in black, white and shades of gray with finely-detailed pictures of plants and animals. *Mufaro's Beautiful Daughters* (1987), a lyrically, colourfully illustrated retelling of an African CINDERELLA story, won the BOSTON GLOBE-HORN BOOK AWARD for ILLUSTRATION, the CORETTA SCOTT KING AWARD for illustration, and a Caldecott Honour medal. LH

Sterling, Dorothy 1913– American writer of fiction, INFORMATION BOOKS and young adult BIOGRAPHY. Born in New York to a German Jewish family, Sterling attended college early. Starting work as an editor, she later researched for *Life*, before turning to freelance writing. Her first book, primarily a photo-essay, was *Sophie and Her Puppies* (1951), with photographs by Myron Ehrenberg. Although Sterling has written children's fiction, such as *The Brownie Scout Mystery* (1955), she sees herself more as a gatherer of information than a writer. Among her well-researched natural history books are *Trees and their Story* (1953) and *Creatures of the Night* (1960).

Fascinated by how African American accomplishments have been ignored by the larger society, Sterling determined to rectify this. Her biographies, including *Freedom Train* (1954) and *Black Foremothers* (1979), mostly feature female African Americans, although the award-winning *Captain of the Planter* (1958) was about the ex-slave turned congressman, Robert Smalls. After visiting the South, she wrote her award-winning novel, *Mary Jane* (1959), a fictional tale of an African American girl entering an all-white school. By the 1970s Sterling decided to let African Americans speak for themselves, and began editing collections of letters, stories and memoirs, including *Speak Out in Thunder Tones* (1973) and *The Trouble They Seen* (1976). SCWA

see also YOUNG ADULT FICTION

Stevenson, James 1929– American author, illustrator and cartoonist. Stevenson grew up in Croton-on-Hudson, New York, and graduated from Yale University. His first job was developing cartoon ideas for the *New Yorker* where he continued to write features. He illustrated the friendly monsters in JACK PRELUTSKY's *Baby Uggs Are Hatching* (1982) and also Prelutsky's poetry books, including the now classic *NEW KID ON THE BLOCK* (1984), with its zany creatures like Baloney Belly Billy. Many of Stevenson's own books feature older people in reassuring roles for children. One series features Grandpa, his brother, Wainright, and young Mary Ann and Louie. Grandpa always appears in a suit, even in his childhood recollections when he sports short pants. An example of the series, *Worse Than Willie* (1984), sensitively tells of adjusting to a new baby at home. Another popular series, including *Emma* (1987) and *Emma at the Beach* (1990), features a young witch trying to outwit two older witches who are tormenting her. Animals with human characteristics and human names are the sponsors in *Mud Flat Olympics* (1994). Stevenson's fictional characters, winners and losers alike, learn the values of friendship, good sportsmanship and perseverance; he introduces young readers to life's issues in humorous and reassuring ways. JRG

Stevenson, Robert Louis 1850–94 Scottish writer whose published work included and transformed most genres current in his lifetime. Coloured in part by his self-deprecation as an author 'read by journalists, by my fellow novelists and by boys', Stevenson's reputation has varied in the shifting focus of critical appraisal of his romantic life-story, the strength and imaginative versatility of his narratives, and his Scots language and heritage.

His father, Thomas, was a civil engineer who designed and illuminated lighthouses. Towards his only child he was both devotedly indulgent and god-fearingly Victorian. Of the same Calvinist strain, but more easy-going, was his mother, Margaret Balfour. Her ill-health during Louis's early years meant that he saw more of his nurse, Alison Cunningham (Cummy), whose stories furnished his nightmares with visions of hellfire and the bleaker morbidities of Scottish Covenanting history. (She is acknowledged as the main character in the story *Thrawn Janet*). The dualities and ambivalences characteristic of many of Stevenson's writings are usually traced to the double binds of his Edinburgh childhood. Too delicate to play games, he spent time with Skelt toy theatres. Yet he won his place in a gang of sorts by devising stories for his companions and after-dark outings with bull's-eye lanterns. His formal education was intermittent; chest illnesses and bohemian distractions in Edinburgh's Old Town are differentially reported as the cause. His decision to became a writer rather than an engineer in the family tradition provoked serious conflict between father and son, exacerbated by Louis's professed atheism and his financial dependence.

Accounts of Stevenson's life after 1873 combine nomadic restlessness, illness and money problems with details of a rigorous and varied output of writing. In France he met Fanny Osbourne, an American with two children, estranged from her husband. When she returned to America in 1878, Stevenson went on a solitary journey which became his first important book, *Travels with a Donkey in the Cevennes* (1979), which still provides a model of romantic adventure for the young: wild landscape, subsistence living, unexpected encounters, solitude and the traveller's interior dialogues. (The first edition had a frontispiece by WALTER CRANE.) Thereafter, Stevenson, seriously ill, followed Fanny to California by emigrant ship and train to bring her back to Scotland as his wife.

In Braemar during the summer of 1881, he wrote 15 chapters of *TREASURE ISLAND* and read them to his delighted father and stepson, a generational partnership in reading now less common. Although there are echoes of Stevenson's own boyhood reading of James Fenimore Cooper and J.M. BALLANTYNE, this tale, his first full-length novel, is, in his own words, as 'original as sin'. Its novelty lies in the pace of the action, the attractiveness of the villain, a complete lack of didacticism and more than a little moral ambiguity. Its immediate appeal made it the paradigm for a succession of piratical adventures, including *MOONFLEET* (J. Meade Falkner, 1898) and a sequel to the original, *Silver's Revenge* (ROBERT LEESON, 1979).

Having found a voice with which to address a double audience, Stevenson varied its use. *The Black Arrow* (serialised in 1883; a book in 1888), a potboiling historical novel about the Wars of the Roses was, he said, 'tushery'. A more significant venture, *A CHILD'S GARDEN OF VERSES* (1885), has overtones of MOTHER GOOSE and ANN and JANE TAYLOR's *Original Poems for Infant Minds* (1804), but, as an enchanting and metrically skilful celebration of childhood for Victorian adults, it is wholly distinctive. Successive editions were illustrated by CHARLES ROBINSON (1896), Kate Elizabeth Olver (1927), BRIAN WILDSMITH (1966) and MICHAEL FOREMAN (1985). During convalescence in Bournemouth, where his nostalgia for Scotland was the theme of many letters to an increasing number of literary friends, including Henry James, Stevenson also wrote, in six days, *The Strange Case of Dr Jekyll and Mr Hyde* (1886). With concentrated power and originality he represents one character as two personalities. The story made him famous; its title became an extended metaphor for contemporary and subsequent interest in dualities of different kinds. Karl Miller detected in its author 'the two natures of the uncertain son'. In the same year, *KIDNAPPED*, probably the most exciting ADVENTURE STORY of its kind, richly developed the same theme in the contrasted main characters, with their conflicting political and religious allegiances derived from their origins in the highlands and lowlands of the Scottish countryside.

After his father's death in 1889, Stevenson and his family sailed to America for good, but Scotland remained his inner landscape. During a severe winter in the Adirondacks he began *The Master of Ballantrae* (1889), another Scots tale of family conflict which has had a restricted readership amongst young people. It was finished in Honolulu before the last stage of the voyage to Samoa. By this time Stevenson was writing at a great pace, extending his literary contacts and experimenting with different styles. Less successfully, he collaborated with his stepson, Lloyd Osbourne, in *The Wrong Box* (1889) and *The Wreckers* (1892). *Catriona* (1893), planned as a sequel to the unsettled ending of *Kidnapped*, is a convincing love story, but, more obviously, a confident political novel showing Stevenson's mature interests. The distinctive stylistic changes of the period before his death in Samoa in 1890 are shown best in *The Beach of Falesá* (1893), a more challenging piece than anything by JOHN BUCHAN, usually seen as Stevenson's successor. When he died suddenly of a brain haemorrhage, Stevenson was writing *Weir of Hermiston* which, even in its unfinished state, is now regarded as his most subtle, complex and powerful work.

Revisions and reconsiderations in critical judgements of Stevenson have been most marked since 1990, the centenary of his death. Although, like other writers since, he did not want to be regarded as a writer of adventure stories for the young, his narratives are amongst the best of the genre. MM

Stig of the Dump (1963) A modern classic by CLIVE KING, illustrated by EDWARD ARDIZZONE. A series of adventures features Barney's friendship with Stig, a caveman, whom other children (Barney's sister Lou and the proletarian Snargets) can see, but adults cannot. Through the eyes of a caveman, the author can express a sense of wonderment at the complexities of modern life and its inventions. The book concludes with a dream sequence as reality blurs into FANTASY at the midsummer solstice. Although written in a concise sentence structure and language, some of the dialogue now seems anachronistic, particularly the phonetically reproduced speech of the Snargets family. MSS

Stine, R(obert) L(awrence) 1943– Popular and prolific author of horror fiction for adolescent and middle-school readers. Called 'the Jekyll and Hyde' of children's books, Stine is a humour writer turned horror writer, having compiled nearly 40 joke books, often under the name Jovial Bob Stine. He was asked by an editor to write a scary book for adolescents (*Blind Date*, 1986) and has been writing horror fiction ever since. Along with CHRISTOPHER PIKE, Stine helped to make teen-horror novels the most popular genre of the 1990s. With emphasis on violence and mayhem, his *Fear Street* series, beginning with *The New Girl* (1989), has become one of the most popular horror series for adolescent readers. In 1992, Stine began

'The two giants bring in the sedan-chair.' Illustration by Frank Stockton from 'The Floating Prince', *St Nicholas Magazine* (1880).

writing the controversial *Goosebumps* series for midde-school readers. Unlike his horror novels for adolescents, *Goosebumps* tends to combine large doses of humour with scariness and celebrates gross humour rather than gore. JCS

Stinson, Kathy 1952– Canadian children's writer from Toronto. Kathy Stinson held a variety of jobs until she found her calling. Her inaugural PICTUREBOOK, *Red is Best* (1982), won the IODE Award and remains her most enduring work. Stinson captures the feelings of small children with honesty, integrity and understanding. Stories such as *Big or Little?* (1983), *Mom and Dad Don't Live Together Any More* (1984) and *Who is Sleeping in Auntie's Bed?* (1991) gently offer young readers real-life experiences. Innocent and celebratory, *The Bare Naked Book* (1986) created a controversy because of its open exploration of the human body. Stinson writes both fiction and non-fiction for all ages. Her early works, such as *Seven Clues in Pebble Creek* (1987), make for light and pleasurable reading. Her YOUNG ADULT FICTION confronts relevant issues; for example, *One Year Commencing* (1997) deals with court-ordered child-custody. Her short stories have appeared in young adult anthologies, most recently 'Babysitting Helen' in *Takes* (1996), which won the CANADIAN LIBRARY ASSOCIATION Young Adult Book Award. Stinson is a popular speaker, has been a writer-in-residence and teaches children's writing to adults. TH

Stobbs, William 1914–2000 British illustrator, engineering draughtsman and teacher, from 1950 to 1958 head of the Design Department at the London School of Printing, and finally Principal at the Maidstone School of Art. Stobbs was born in South Shields and studied at the Durham School of Art. He won the KATE GREENAWAY AWARD for his illustrations for RUTH MANNING-SANDERS's *A Bundle of Ballads* (1959) and for a translation of Anton Chekhov's *Kashtanka* (US 1961). He contributed powerfully dramatic full-page black-and-white illustrations for David Severn's *The Future Took Us* (1957) and for RONALD WELCH's CARNEGIE AWARD winner, *Knight Crusader* (1954). In response to improved colour printing in the 1960s, he developed his talent for vibrant use of colour in a number of traditional stories, such as *Rumpelstiltskin* (1970) and *Old Mother Goose and the Golden Eggs* (1977). VW

see also NATIVE AMERICANS IN CHILDREN'S BOOKS

Stockton, Frank 1834–1902 American author best known for his humorous stories for adults and his FAIRY TALES for children. From 1873 to 1878 Stockton was MARY MAPES DODGE's assistant editor for the new children's magazine *St Nicholas*, for which he wrote non-fiction and TALL TALES as well as fairy tales. Meanwhile he delighted adult readers with the wit and ingenuity of *Rudder Grange* (1879) and *The Casting Away of Mrs Lecks and Mrs Aleshine* (1886), and baffled them with 'The Lady or the Tiger?' Stockton was pivotal in the development of American children's FANTASY, as the first to create original fairy tales with an American flavour. His ironic, common-sense treatment of familiar plots and characters seems to reflect both the scepticism of the New World towards tradition and the supernatural, and his own sardonic view of life. Quests are twisted awry or end in failure; happy endings are often ambiguous – as in his most famous tale, 'The Griffin and the Minor Canon', in which one's relief at the death of the monster is overshadowed by a sense of loss. His major fairy-tale collections were *The Floating Prince* (1881), *The Bee-Man of Orn* (1887), *The Queen's Museum* (1887) and *The Clocks of Rondaine* (1892). SR

Stolz [Slattery], Mary 1920– American author of numerous contemporary novels, as well as several PICTUREBOOKS and HISTORICAL FICTION. Critics in the 1950s considered Stolz in a class by herself among writers for teenage girls. While she, like the rest, explored family relationships and the problems of first love, the subtlety and perceptivity of her writing, her probing characterisations, and her avoidance of simplistic solutions made such novels as *To Tell Your Love* (1950), *Ready or Not* (1953) and *Who Wants Music on Monday?* (1963) comparable to good novels for adults. They have since acquired additional interest, preserving as though in crystal the youthful sensibility of their period. Finding herself less in tune with adolescents of the 1960s, Stolz began focusing on younger readers, establishing a new reputation for excellence with a double *tour de force*, *A Dog on Barkham Street* (1960) and *The Bully of Barkham Street* (1963) – which tell the same story from opposing perspectives – and stories of friendship under stress, *The Noonday Friends* (1965) and *A Wonderful, Terrible Time* (1967). Though never descending to the problem novel, she has also dealt with such formerly taboo topics as the effects on families of death or divorce. SR

Stone Book Quartet, The (1976–7) Stories by the acclaimed British writer Alan Garner. Each story describes the events of a single day through four generations of a family living in Cheshire, the main character in each case being a child seeking a place and a value in a changing adult world. In *The Owl Service* and *Red Shift*, Garner had been concerned with the ways in which education can alienate the young from their own culture; in the *Quartet*, this division is understood and healed.

The Stone Book (1976), set in the summer of 1864, is the only one of the four stories in which the main character is a girl. Mary, the daughter of a stonemason, has to take her father's dinner to where he is working at the pinnacle of a church spire. Garner's account of her solitary climb to the platform under the weathercock is one of the finest pieces of description in English and exemplifies his narrative approach in the *Quartet*. He has eschewed those narrative features which emphasise the pastness of the past, and has developed a prose style which intensifies the dramatic quality of new experience touched with uncertainty. Mary wants to gain some of the education the parson has, but her father casts doubt on such book knowledge. 'When you cut stone, you see more than the parson does,' he says. He sends Mary deep underground in a kind of rite of passage to discover for herself some ancient cave art, and cuts her a 'stone book', perfect in form and appearance, and a precise symbol for his belief in an alternative to book knowledge. Given that Darwin's *Origin of Species* was published in 1859, this illiterate craftsman's 'stone-knowledge' is more progressive than the parson's.

Mary disappears from the sequence, and in the next story it is clear that the little girl who fearlessly rode astride the weathercock on the steeple grew up to have an illegitimate son, brought up by his grandmother. *Granny Reardun* (1977) is the story of young Joseph's realisation that he wants to become a blacksmith and 'get aback of' his grandfather. This is not easy; the entire landscape has been shaped by the old man's stonework, just as stone encircles the boy as he stands in the porch of the school. But the stone would be useless without the ironwork of latches, hinges and locks – and Joseph joyously realises exactly what he wants to do and goes to the smithy to arrange an apprenticeship.

Stone book: illustration by Michael Foreman from *Granny Reardun* by Alan Garner.

Granny Reardun is a celebratory story of a boy whose needs are precisely met by the community and landscape he belongs to. In *The Aimer Gate* (1978), however, there is only frustration and baffled enquiry. It is set in 1916 against the waste and brutalities of World War I, and Joseph – a father and blacksmith now – has to set aside his craft to make thousands of horseshoes for the war effort. His son, Robert, is doomed to frustration, finding nothing in his family life to provide the understanding and knowledge he seeks. He is preoccupied with a home-made go-cart – its load-carrying, its capacity to free-wheel downhill, its need for lubrication. But when he asks what makes wheels go round, his father can give him only an incomprehensible account of a clock's escapement. In a reversal of Mary's triumphant climb to her father at the top of the church spire, Robert climbs the *inside* of a spire *alone*. With his head pressed under the capstone, 'he was wearing the steeple. It fitted like a hat . . . a stone dunce's cap.' But Robert is no dunce; he simply wants to know things that his world cannot explain. We are not told what happens to Robert: his preoccupation with wheels perhaps suggests that he simply left home.

Tom Fobble's Day (1979) recounts the death of Joseph on the day he stops working at his forge. His last job, on a snowy day in 1941, is to make a sledge for his grandson, William. It is an act rich with symbolism, for the sledge is meticulously constructed from leftover scraps from the early stories, and from the ash handle of Joseph's forge. The making is described in simple and sacramental language, for the sledge is more than a plaything. It affirms William's stature among his peers and articulates his sense of belonging to a continuing family and an abiding place: 'The line did hold. Through hand and eye, block, forge and loom to the hill and all that he owned.' Neil Philip believes that the actual writing of the *Quartet* amounts to an 'implied' fifth story in which Garner rejoins his ancestors 'by putting his learned skills at the service of theirs'.

The unity of the four stories lies partly in the character of Joseph, partly in the language, and partly in Garner's provision of simple continuities: a clay pipe dropped in the first story is dug up in the last; a hump under the snow in the final story was a half-buried supply of stone in the third, and a demolished cottage in the second. Garner's love of planting clues suggests the ways in which the young learn remembered anecdotal fragments of their family history. And his riddling narratives now serve not to baffle the reader but to suggest the deep complexity of character, the importance of things unsaid, and the frequent bafflement of the young in the face of their elders. MICHAEL FOREMAN's illustrations for later editions of the stories are suggestive and mysterious, emphasing by means of simple line and dense cross-hatching energetic human figures against the bulk of hillside, building or sky. The *Quartet* is one of the great originals of children's literature alongside *ALICE'S ADVENTURES IN WONDERLAND* and *PETER PAN*. Garner has developed a new form and style perfect for expressing a child's view of time and place, and for admitting into narrative the voices of ordinary people with a habit of saying little and enduring much. VW

Stone Cold (1993) Novel by the British author ROBERT SWINDELLS. Link, aged 16, leaves Bradford after being thrown out by his family. He ends up on the streets of Camden in London, suffering the intense privation and humiliation of the homeless, losing his only friend Ginger and finding that his new girfriend Gail is an undercover reporter. Ginger is a victim of Shelter, a serial killer: only Gail's intervention saves Link from a similar fate and ensures Shelter's arrest. The plot, however, is incidental to the vivid directness and moral indignation which lies behind this account of the reality of homelessness and rejection of conventional attitudes towards it. Swindells spent time on the streets himself before writing: the balance between fierce direct involvement and dispassionate portrayal of actuality is finely kept, though there were initially some accusations of sensationalism. The first-person narrative has the immediacy of individual utterance as well as articulate, moving eloquence. A problem for many 'issue' books is that concentration on the issue distorts the narrative. This is not true of *Stone Cold*; the issue *is* the narrative and the force of felt experience speaks directly to young readers. *Stone Cold* won the CARNEGIE MEDAL in 1994 and was highly praised for its authenticity in *The Big Issue*, the magazine concerned with homelessness. DCH

Stone Soup (from 1976) International magazine of the arts based in the United States, written and illustrated by English-speaking children up to the age of 13. The magazine, published and edited by William Rubel and Gerry Mandel, is operated under the auspices of *The Children's Art Foundation* which consists of the magazine, a museum and an art school. To maintain its freedom and independence from outside influence, the organisation has never accepted grants or donations. Instead, the *Foundation* is supported by magazine subscriptions and its art-school tuition fees. *Stone Soup*, first published in 1976, continues to encourage children around the world to become familiar with the tools and the habit of writing, thinking and drawing, using the material of their own lives and environments. The content of *Stone Soup* allows its readers to see stories and ILLUSTRATIONS created by other young writers and artists and encourages them to think, read and observe what is happening, not only to themselves, but to other children in the world around them. MRS

see also CHILD AUTHORS

Stone Soup This centuries-old FOLKTALE, probably originally French, has evolved into a wide variety of retellings, using various geographical settings, cultures and characters as well as different 'magical' tokens or symbols. In the original story, three hungry soldiers – or a travelling pedlar – trick villagers into believing they have enough food for the entire village or community by introducing a stone as the basis for soup. Sceptical villagers gradually relinquish hidden supplies, which provides a rich, nourishing soup for everyone. In *The Sandwich* (1975) by IAN WALLACE and Angela Wood, *Stone Soup* (1973) by Carol Pasternak and Allen Sutterfield, illustrated by Katya Jacobs, and Aubrey Davis's *Bone Button Borsht* (1995), illustrated by Dusan Petricic, acceptance and tolerance of others is also evidenced by the public sharing of a wide variety of ethnic food. In *The Soup Stone* (1988) by Iris Van Rynbach, as the soldier leaves he picks up another 'magic' stone, an act which confirms not merely the gullibility of human nature but also an underlying belief in people's need for community and compassion. One of the most enduring versions of the story is *Stone Soup* (1947) by MARCIA BROWN.

MS

Stones, Rosemary see REVIEWING AND REVIEWERS; see also *BOOKS FOR KEEPS*

Stories by the Fireside (1985) Collection of stories by Kenyan author Jedida Kivali Mandara. The book is lavishly and beautifully illustrated with interesting and humorous adventures to stimulate and entertain young readers.

ABO

Storm Boy (1963) Novel by Australian author COLIN THIELE, which earned him the label of 'environmental writer'. Storm Boy lives in a fishing shack with his father, Hide-Away Tom, on the Coorong in South Australia. Local Aborigine, Fingerbone Bill, teaches Storm Boy much about his traditional land. 'Mr Percival', one of three hand-reared pelicans saved by Storm Boy when their rookery was vandalised, refuses to return to the wild and becomes famous by helping with the fishing. The innocence which seems possible when living in a state of harmony with nature is destroyed when Mr Percival is shot by hunters. *Storm Boy* was made into a film in 1976, has been translated into nine languages, and has received awards in Australia and the Netherlands.

FK

Storm, Ebsen see *ROUND THE TWIST*

Storr, Catherine 1913–2001 British author, doctor and psychiatrist, best known for *MARIANNE DREAMS* (1958) and the *CLEVER POLLY* series (from 1955). She wrote more than 30 books for children, covering a wide range of genres for different age groups. Storr's psychiatric background gave her insight into problems of isolation, rejection and low self-esteem. Her interest lay in what she called 'the different faces of reality' and 'the possibilities of explaining events in more than one way.' Accordingly her characters' perceptions shift as imagination, appearance and reality work side by side.

Thursday (1971) and *February Yowler* (1982) deal with the issue of isolation and the consequences of being unable to communicate emotional stress. This leads the children into dream worlds, secret languages or, more seriously, psychotic behaviour. Conflicts of loyalties, lack of communication between generations, loss of parents, and charged perceptions of reality pervade other stories; in *Winter's End* (1978), an adolescent dealing with parental loss is living in a sterile environment in which expression of deep emotion is impossible. The introspective and slow-moving *Two's Company* (1984) shows the disturbing influence of parental conflict not shared with or explained to the children. Storr's DETECTIVE FICTION includes *The Catchpole Story* (1965) and, more menacing, *The Underground Conspiracy* (1987), in which a child is unwittingly drawn into drug-running. Amongst her ADVENTURE STORIES for younger readers are *Lucy* (1961) and *Lucy Runs Away* (1962). Storr, though able to write with pace and excitement, was never afraid to deal with difficult issues, or to move her stories at a pace in which contemplative exploration of emotion is possible. Her latest publications include *The Mirror Image Ghost* (1994), *Stephen and the Family Nose* (1995) and *The Watcher at the Window* (1995).

JSW

Story About Ping, THE see MARJORIE FLACK; KURT WIESE; see also ILLUSTRATION IN CHILDREN'S BOOKS; PICTUREBOOKS

Story of a Bad Boy, The (1869) Fictionalised AUTOBIOGRAPHY of Thomas Bailey Aldrich, American writer and editor. An adult narrator recalls three years spent as a boy in Rivermouth, a New England town modelled on Portsmouth, New Hampshire, where he is taken to be educated. After his parents return to New Orleans, he lives with his grandfather, Captain Nutter, and great-aunt. Tom Bailey joins in the life of his new community, enduring the funeral-like Sabbaths, celebrating holidays, organising a secret society, fighting the school bully, reuniting his grandfather's maid with her long-lost husband, falling in love with an older woman and plotting numerous pranks. The episodic novel is light and humorous, dealing only briefly with serious events such as Tom's separation from his parents and a friend's drowning. It ends when Tom must earn his living in New York after the death of his father and reversal of the family finances. Contemporary readers praised the book for its realistic portrayal of American boyhood and its natural protagonist, created as a reaction against the usual 'improbable little prig' set up as a model boy in juvenile literature of Aldrich's time. The novel, which

'The Centipedes.' Illustration by Thomas Bailey Aldrich from *The Story of a Bad Boy.*

preceded Twain's THE ADVENTURES OF TOM SAWYER (1876), helped establish the 'bad boy' genre in America. JLB

Story of Chicken Licken, The (1985) JAN ORMEROD's written text is a straight forward retelling of the traditional tale, which here comes from the mouths of children in a school performance. The action on the stage hardly engages us, however (though we admire Ormerod's inventive costumes); of far more interest is the activity revealed, through ILLUSTRATION, in the silhouetted audience where we track the father as he intermittently dozes off, the noisy toddler told to shush, and particularly the baby in the yellow baby-gro who, grown tired of rummaging in an unattended handbag, spies the 'acorn' (a tennis ball) on stage and sets off to claim it. On stage and in the house lights, he also finds his brother, Chicken Licken himself, clad in identical yellow baby-gro. Applause all round. For many literate and non-literate children, the tracking of these pictured stories generates a special pleasure which ensures that they return again and again to the book. JAG

Story of Dr Dolittle, The see *DOCTOR DOLITTLE* SERIES

Story of Little Black Sambo, The see *LITTLE BLACK SAMBO*; see also ILLUSTRATION IN CHILDREN'S BOOKS

Story of Rosy Dock, The (1995) A PICTUREBOOK by JEANNIE BAKER which raises ecological issues by showing how an elderly European settler who introduces Rosy Dock in her garden unwittingly changes the environment of central South Australia. Double-spread COLLAGE constructions using natural materials, coloured in burning orange-red, ochre and cobalt, capture the desert and sky. The poetic text uses a mixture of continuous present tense to imply the timelessness of the setting, and a past tense to recount events. *The Story of Rosy Dock* won the CHILDREN'S BOOK COUNCIL OF AUSTRALIA Picturebook of the Year Award, and also exists in short film form. JD

see also ECOLOGY

Story of the Amulet, The see E. NESBIT; *PSAMMEAD* SERIES; see also *CHRONICLES OF NARNIA*; FANTASY; see also TIME-SLIP FANTASY

Story of the Treasure Seekers, The see *BASTABLE* SERIES

story papers see *'THE BIG FIVE'*; COMICS, PERIODICALS AND MAGAZINES; GIRL; *GIRLS' CRYSTAL*; *GIRL'S OWN PAPER; THE SCHOOL FRIEND*

storytapes Full-length or abridged readings and dramatisations of books and stories recorded as audiotapes and marketed either as stand-alone products or packaged with a book, magazine or character toy, generally available in a range of retail outlets as well as bookshops. The post-war development of portable cassette players allowed oral traditions of STORYTELLING to combine with contemporary technologies which children could control themselves, producing an increasingly popular medium by which to encounter children's literature, either alongside, or instead of, the original book.

Audio-publishing initially flourished in the early 1980s, when the cassette replaced the LP because of advances in sound quality. Numerous storytapes are now available, from imaginative interpretations of such wordless PICTUREBOOKS as *THE SNOWMAN* (1995) to spooky renderings of the popular *POINT HORROR* books or the multi-voiced adaptations of the *Roald Dahl Theatre Collection*. Many publishers record works in full, though scrupulous ABRIDGEMENTS are often more appropriate for restless young listeners.

Long before the literary transcription of narrative into authored books, tales were part of a vibrant oral culture and while currently the written book is the transcendent literary form, oral narrative retains its place in the nursery. Audio-cassettes allow children to listen at will. The possibility that tapes will substitute for books sometimes makes them controversial, but in general they are regarded as providing an experience closer to book-reading, with its encouragement of concentration and imagination, than that offered by video.

Such confidence in the authenticity of storytapes overlooks the fact that the codes and conventions of sound reinterpret those of the book as fundamentally as any other media transposition. After any editing of the story, the choice of narrator or actors, together with the quality and accent of voice, is the most important element, followed by the deployment of music or sound effects to create pace, atmosphere or realism of setting. The narrator may seek to present a persona appropriate to the action, period or location of the story, or adopt a more neutral 'storyteller' role, and in some cases authors read their own stories.

The recording of a book in several versions often indicates actual or potential classic status. Indeed, most storytapes are derived from familiar traditional tales or already successful children's books. In 1998 there were 13 versions of *The Secret Garden* available, and Beatrix Potter, Enid Blyton and Roald Dahl are always popular. Since its experimental release of a multi-voice recording of Tolkien's *The Lord of the Rings* in 1987, the market-leading BBC has mined its extensive archives for radio dramatisations and readings featuring well-known authors from Rudyard Kipling and E. Nesbit to Philippa Pearce and Dick King-Smith. There is also a growing trend for 'tie-in' titles derived from media culture. The award-winning *Dark Forces* is based on *Star Wars* and Disney now produces audio versions of its animated films. These are 'audio movies' rather than 'performance literature', in which sound offers exciting imagined spectacle as well as intimate listening.

Storytapes are produced for all age-groups, though a survey by the Roehampton Institute in England in 1996 suggested that, while young children enjoy listening, a steep decline in use is apparent among readers above the age of seven. The early demand for orally rendered narrative is perhaps a projection of the infant's lack of linguistic confidence. Conversely, the later rejection of cassettes possibly concurs with the maturing reader's increasingly private relationship with books in which the storyteller's interpretation is likely to conflict with individual textual experience. Regardless of age, however, storytapes provide an invaluable narrative resource for anyone experiencing reading difficulties; the interpretative skills of the storyteller can liberate the struggling reader from the complexities of written texts. SG, LS

storytelling Probably as highly valued in schools and libraries at the beginning of the 21st century as at any time in the previous hundred years. There is a theorised basis for the view that children and young people need stories; an increasing number of skilled professional and amateur storytellers; and an emerging awareness that those who used simply to listen have stories to tell.

Belief in the importance of storytelling is underpinned by the knowledge that early cultures defined their identity through the stories they told themselves. The storyteller was afforded particular respect, since a settlement or nomadic tribe which was not sustained by well-told, powerful stories felt ill-at-ease with itself. The privileged position of the storyteller is evident in later societies, whether the tales were heard in a Viking mead hall, a medieval castle or cottage, or in the meeting place of a Native American band. Adults needed and enjoyed stories as much as children; the oldest known oral versions of what are now thought of as Fairy Tales are sometimes charged with a sexual energy apparent to any listener except a young child.

The spread of literacy and the provision of sophisticated and popular reading matter, coupled with the withdrawal into family rather than communal life, no doubt weakened the oral tradition. However, the recognition that oral stories should be preserved led, especially in the 19th century, to the energetic collecting of tales which continues to the present day; in some senses, there is even greater urgency as the influence of bland western popular culture through electronic media reaches out into less developed regions.

By the early years of the 20th century, there were calls for a revival in the art of storytelling by educators and librarians such as Marie Shedlock in her classic *The Art of the Storyteller* (1915), still in print in paperback format and used in university courses in North America today. Katherine Dunlap Cather was able to recommend no fewer than 15 titles on how best to tell stories in *Educating by Story Telling* (1910). The revival they hoped for seems not to have taken deep root in schools, although in libraries and Sunday schools storytelling remained staple fare.

In the latter part of the century, the faith of teachers and librarians who found even normally restless listeners gripped by stories has been confirmed and illuminated by two main sources. Firstly, myths, legends and fairy tales have increasingly attracted the interest of literary and psychoanalytic scholars. Secondly, sociolinguists in the 1960s and 70s argued that the stories we tell ourselves, and each other, about our everyday concerns are of crucial value. In a fragmented society, they suggested, it is necessary for individuals to make sense of their pasts, presents and possible futures through framing their experience in narrative. Without this capacity, there can be no empathy for those with whom we live and work, no understanding of ourselves. For a generation of English teachers in Britain, it was important to attend closely to what children said, inside and outside the classroom, from their anecdotes to their fantasies, whether spoken or written. In the 1980s, the National Oracy Project further emphasised the importance of story.

This is the context in which a revival of storytelling in schools and libraries continues to develop. Even in stringent financial times, schools and libraries have financed visits by professional storytellers, who work in clubs, pubs and arts centres as well as with young people. There are many enthusiastic amateur tellers, for the mystique surrounding the telling of tales has been usefully challenged. Courses for teachers, librarians and students in training institutions give confidence to many who thought the work beyond them. Stories are used in many ways: children might hear first-hand accounts of life during World War II; or be told the wanderings of Odysseus by a role-playing teacher who pulled on an oar through all the desperate voyages. Listening children commonly say – since they *want* to share in the game – 'You really were there, weren't you?'; and empirical evidence indicates that information carried within a powerfully recounted narrative will be long retained by the listener.

In the United States and Canada, storytelling groups and associations have existed for many years, while Britain has a Society of Storytelling. There are large storytelling festivals and, perhaps more important, cells of enthusiasts sharing stories around the country. Sometimes tales are simply heard and passed on. The most useful sources are sparely told collections from all over the world, leaving space for storytellers to imprint their own style on the tale. Storytelling has become one of the most dynamic ways of sharing knowledge and promoting understanding between ethnic groups.

The told story sits comfortably enough alongside the story read aloud. Told stories are immediate, flexible, uniquely of the moment, a once-only gift from teller to listener. They conjure up pictures and voices through timing, gesture, eye contact and vocal agility. They have a particular social value. Sara Cone Bryant wrote in 1910 of stories relaxing 'the tense schoolroom atmosphere' and establishing 'a happy relation between teacher and children'. Many present-day teachers would concur.

Children and young people themselves are taking an increasing part in such storytelling communities. Although the importance of anecdotes of children and adolescents has been recognised for some 30 years, their ability to tell shaped stories about matters which do not arise from their personal experience is a more recent discovery. Vivian Gussin Paley's account of her work in the Laboratory Schools of the University of Chicago demonstrates the value of stories told by pre-school children. Betty Rosen described her powerful work with a storytelling class in a North London comprehensive school. Michael Wilson has explored how young people tell each other a range of stories very similar to urban myths and traditional tales. It may well be that this is an area which will yield much interest and excitement in the future. GPF

Stowe, Harriet Beecher see *Uncle Tom's Cabin*; see also *McGuffey Eclectic Readers*; *Our Young Folks*; *The Youth's Companion*

Strachan, Ian 1938– British novelist who won the *Observer* Award for *Moses Beech* (1981) and has been shortlisted for the Whitbread Children's Award. His novels tackle difficult situations and controversial issues. *Throwaways* (1992) examines the lives of children living on a rubbish dump after being abandoned by their parents, and *Journey of 1000 Miles* (1984) was written about the Vietnamese boat people. Several novels deal with family problems and the family always plays an important role. Sometimes it provides characters with a strong base from which to forge their own independence, but often it is the absence of a happy family which encourages the characters to develop. In *Moses Beech* Peter leaves home because he cannot bear the prospect of becoming like his parasitic father, while *Kidnap* (1994) describes children's misery after their parents' acrimonious divorce. In *Which Way Is Home?* (1996) Toby sets out to choose his own foster family. *The Flawed Glass* (1989) and *The Boy in the Bubble* (1993) depict the lives of severely handicapped teenagers. *The Flawed Glass* has a happy outcome with a magical but satisfyingly plausible resolution. However, such endings are rare in Strachan's works, which offer the reader few easy solutions. KA

see also Family Stories

Stratemeyer Syndicate A literary syndicate founded around 1905 by Edward Stratemeyer producing boys' and girls' series for an audience of millions. *Bomba the Jungle Boy*, *Boys of Pluck*, *Boys of Columbia High*, *Dave Dashaway*, *Doris Force*, *Happy Hollisters*, Hardy Boys, *Honey Bunch*, *Motion Picture Chums*, *Moving Picture Girls*, *Blythe Girls*, Nancy Drew, *Outdoor Girls*, *Rover Boys*, *Tom Swift* and *Ruth Fielding* – these are a few of the numerous series produced by the Syndicate.

Stratemeyer helped to make series book publishing into a rationalised business in which books were produced like any other commodity. Although Stratemeyer's novels were often awkwardly written, sometimes implausible and formulaic, that did not prevent their tremendous success with young readers, who could not seem to get enough of the adventure-filled works and bought them by the score – which they had to do since many children's librarians would not allow the cheap, sensation-filled

Stratemeyer books into their libraries. After Stratemeyer's death in 1930, his daughters, Harriet and Edna, ran the business, with Edna becoming an inactive partner in 1942. Harriet ran the company for over 50 years, sharply curtailing the range of series, but still managing to do well with the *Nancy Drew* and *Hardy Boys* books. Upon her death in 1982, the Syndicate was run for two years by Harriet's three junior partners, until they sold the business to Simon & Schuster, which continued to publish a wide range of *Nancy Drew* and *Hardy Boys* books. SAI

Stratemeyer, Edward 1862–1930 American series publisher. A prolific writer, Stratemeyer began his career in the 1890s writing DIME NOVELS. He moved over into publishing and established himself as a major force in the development of series books. He is credited with writing numerous series books under 83 different pseudonyms (including Victor Appleton, Captain Ralph Bonehill, Franklin W. Dixon, Laura Lee Hope and Carolyn Keene) in such series as the *BOBBSEY TWINS*, *Dorothy Dale*, *Rover Boys*, *Tom Swift*, *The Flag of Freedom* and *Old Glory*, but his main claim to fame is as the originator of the *NANCY DREW* and *HARDY BOYS* series.

Stratemeyer produced these books and many others while serving as the head of the STRATEMEYER SYNDICATE, a company he founded that was responsible for publishing dozens of girls' and boys' series. Stratemeyer had a stable of ghost-writers working for him to turn out the countless volumes that young readers demanded. Featuring fast-paced action and adventure, Stratemeyer's books were a hit with young readers, if not with librarians, who worried about the influence of the books and doubted their deserving a place on library shelves. However, the condemnation of his books by educators and librarians did not prevent them from selling in millions. Upon Stratemeyer's death in 1930, his daughters, Harriet Stratemeyer Adams and Edna Stratemeyer, took over the Syndicate. Edna left in 1942, leaving her sister to steer the company until her death in 1982. SAI

Stratton, Helen see *BLACKIE'S CHILDREN'S ANNUAL*; see also NUDITY IN CHILDREN'S BOOKS

Stratton-Porter, Gene 1863–1924 American naturalist and novelist. The youngest of 12 children, she spent much of her childhood outdoors and developed a great affinity for forest wildlife. She never graduated from high school, but she discovered there that she loved to write and to read her work to an audience. In 1881, she attended her first Chautauqua – an outdoor camp meeting that emphasised spiritual devotion, educational improvement and the arts – and found it a profound experience. She met her husband, Charles Dorwin Porter, through a Chautauqua; they married in 1886. Relocating to Geneva, Indiana, to be near Charles's business, they built 'Limberlost Cabin' so that Gene could pursue her interests in writing, photography and nature studies in close proximity to the Limberlost, a prodigious swamp in east-central Indiana. By 1912, much of the swamp had been destroyed by farmers and oil companies. Stratton-Porter then designed and built Wildflower Woods, a wildlife habitat and preserve, near Rome City in northern Indiana. Eventually, she moved to California, where she dabbled in poetry and wrote extensively for contemporary women's magazines such as *McCalls* and *Good Housekeeping*. She also became active in the film industry, establishing her own company to produce film versions of her novels. She died when her car was struck by a trolley in December 1924.

Stratton-Porter is best-known for her novels about the Limberlost, particularly *Freckles* (1904) and its sequel, *A Girl of the Limberlost* (1909). She regarded these works as 'nature studies coated with fiction' designed to teach her readers to love and to protect the natural world and to establish a spiritual connection with God through nature. Freckles, an orphan from Chicago who is hired to guard valuable timber within the swamp, develops an intimate relationship with the birds of the Limberlost; studying them, he comes to know himself. Elnora, the protagonist of the sequel, collects the moths of the Limberlost; her collections enable her to attend high school and to demonstrate her knowledge of natural history so thoroughly that the school board establishes a teaching position for her. Stratton-Porter's highly accurate and engaging descriptions of nature are not the only reason these books were bestsellers: in her novels, she also provides powerful psychological drama, particularly in Freckles's love for the Swamp Angel and Elnora's relationship with her embittered, widowed mother.

Stratton-Porter's magazine columns are collected in *Let Us Highly Resolve* (1927). Selections from her nature studies were republished as *Coming Through the Swamp: The Nature Writings of Gene Stratton Porter* (1996). Both Limberlost Cabin and Wildflower Woods are maintained as Indiana state historical sites. AKP

Streatfeild, Noel 1895–1986 Hugely prolific British author of almost 90 works for both adults and children, some written under the pseudonym 'Susan Scarlett'. She is remembered mainly for her work for children, in particular her first, *BALLET SHOES* (1937), though *Tennis Shoes* (1938), *White Boots* (1951), the GEMMA books and *The Painted Garden* (1949) are also worth special mention.

Streatfeild's early life in the household of an Anglican clergyman is reflected in *A Vicarage Family* (1963). She was the middle one of three sisters, and, as

Illustration by MARGERY GILL from *Apple Bough* by Noel Streatfeild.

Angela Bull's biography of her (1984) tells us, felt herself to be unattractive and the odd one out, this suggesting that Petrova of *Ballet Shoes* might be a self-portrait. After working in a munitions factory during World War I she turned to a career in the theatre, where she worked for ten years; her love for drama informs her best work.

Streatfeild is generally considered one of the pioneers of the 'career novel'; a good many of her books are about children at work or in training for an occupation, on the stage, making films, on the ice-rink and tennis courts, in the recording studio. And though Petrova is depicted as an aspiring mechanic/inventor/explorer, the 'careers' considered in Streatfeild's work tend for the most part to be attractive, glamorous and lucrative ones. Streatfeild's work, however, seldom dwells on the strenuousness of work: talent appears to carry the day for most of Streatfeild's children; Petrova and Jane Winter of *The Painted Garden* are two of the few who have to struggle to accomplish what they do. The ordinary child without a special gift is not well represented in Streatfeild's work.

Though very readable and enjoyable, Noel Streatfeild's fiction deals little with serious issues, and most of her characters are superficially outlined and develop only marginally. As Mary Cadogan and Patricia Craig note in *You're a Brick Angela!* (1976), the grown-up Fossils who make a guest appearance in *The Painted Garden* have not changed or deepened.

This work is, however, perhaps the most deeply satisfying of all Streatfeild's books. While her writing is markedly intertextual, opening up a dialogue between her work and other works, *The Painted Garden* does more than merely (re)present other texts within itself. Jane Winter, an unhappy child, is given the part of Mary in a film version of FRANCES HODGSON BURNETT's *THE SECRET GARDEN*, not because of dramatic talent, but because of her disagreeableness which lends her resemblance to Mary. As the film-making progresses, the changes that come about in Mary in Burnett's book are duplicated in Jane. There is no magic element at work here as in the original text, except the spell of human liking, but the friendship that grows up between Jane and the boy playing Dickon softens the edge of her disagreeableness. Being liked and appreciated makes her 'better not worse', and the conclusion of *The Painted Garden* reaffirms the meaning of its guest text. SA

see also LITERATURE IN CHILDREN'S LITERATURE

Street Musician, The see *HUNDRED MILLION FRANCS, A*

Stretton, Hesba [Smith, Sarah] 1832–1911 Evangelical writer of over 60 stories, mostly about street life in the London slums. A founder of the London Society for the Prevention of Cruelty to Children, Stretton was concerned with child poverty, a theme enlarged in her most popular works, *Jessica's First Prayer* (1867) and *Little Meg's Children* (1868), published by the RELIGIOUS TRACT SOCIETY in spite of her prejudice against the over-zealous piety of some of its members. Both novels, favourites as Sunday-School prizes, dwell on the redeeming power of the intrinsic and artless goodness of the child-heroine. BW

Strong, Jeremy 1949– Popular and prolific British writer for young children, his work often illustrated by NICK SHARRATT. Strong's mastery of the farcical slapstick chase and resulting catastrophic chaos makes his work outstanding. In the *Karate Princess* series (from 1986) he subverts the conventions of traditional tales with his powerful heroine, Princess Belinda, who is fearless and decisive with a temper to match. She deals with her enemies by using her brains and her amazing karate skills. The stories are imaginative, with a good narrative pace and a richer range of language than is usual in books for younger readers. The *Viking* series, beginning with *There's a Viking in my Bed* (1992), features a large, shaggy and undisciplined Viking who comes through the mists of time to the 20th century. His hilarious misadventures result from linguistic misunderstandings and cultural differences. As ever in Strong's work, authority – particularly in the form of the police – is treated with scant respect.

Other stories strike a more serious note, touching on issues of bullying, low self-esteem, friendship, insecurity and family loyalty, as in his first book, *The Air-Raid Shelter* (1986), and in *Dinosaur Pox* (1999) where the usual comic elements are somewhat muted. *I'm Telling You, They're Aliens!* (2000), again showing Strong's empathy with children, is about a 'loner' hero who, in his over-anxious state, sees problems of epic proportions around every corner. *The Hundred-Mile-An-Hour Dog* (1996) was shortlisted for the CHILDREN'S BOOK AWARD and *My Granny's Great Escape* won the same award in 1997. JSW

Struwwelpeter (1845) *The English Struwwelpeter* was first published in translation in 1848. Its author and illustrator, DR HEINRICH HOFFMANN (1809–94), manager of a 'progressive' mental hospital, made a book for his own child when he could not find a suitable PICTUREBOOK to buy. His CAUTIONARY TALES are strongly moralistic, and the pictures are terrifying for most adults, although Hoffman subtitled his book *Pretty Stories and Funny Pictures for little Children*, seeing them as therapy rather than threat. The tale of Augustus, an early victim of anorexia, and the anti-racist admonitions in the 'Story of the Inky Boys', are more topical than one would have imagined. HA

Studdy, George Ernest 1878–1948 British illustrator. Studdy followed a course at Calderon's School of Animal Painting which set him up for an illustrating career in which drawings of animals dominate. With a career pattern similar to that of LOUIS WAIN and LAWSON WOOD, he became known for a character, in his case Bonzo the dog, created initially for the *Sketch* (1922 onwards) but later to appear in ANNUALS and books. 'Bonzo' memorabilia was abundant in the 1920s. JAG

Styles, Morag see *BOOKS FOR KEEPS GUIDE TO POETRY*; CRITICAL APPROACHES TO CHILDREN'S BOOKS; *I LIKE THAT STUFF*

Subtle Knife, The see *HIS DARK MATERIALS*

***Sula* series** (from 1969) Four stories by Lavinia Derwent set on the imaginary Scottish island of Sula. Each follows the gradual taming of Magnus MacDuff, through his affinity with animals and his talent for drawing. As he fends off attempts to educate him, the island fends off threats to its tranquil way of life. With its community spirit and ever-ready hospitality extended even to those visitors who seek to exploit its fragile beauty, the view of Sula is romanticised yet compelling. While the action visits the mainland, Glasgow and London, the best passages are reserved for Sula – lovingly and poetically described in all its moods. A gallery of characters, developed with insight and humour, moves through all four lively stories – for example the eccentric Duke whom the island inspires to compose a symphony; the hermit, Mr. Skinnymalink; and taciturn Gran in her tackety boots. Young readers would readily identify with the children, including Tair with his imaginary friend, Avisandum; the precociously bright Jinty Cowan; the mischievous 'Ferret' and the rebellious Magnus, with his friend, Old Whiskers, the seal. In the cadences of their dialogue, with its use of Scots words and speech patterns, is reflected the rhythm of life on Sula. MSS

Sullivan, Jenny see *GWYDION* TRILOGY

Summer After the Funeral, The (1973) Much-admired novel by the British author JANE GARDAM; it confirmed her reputation as a witty, stylishly entertaining writer about the tribulations of adolescent girls whose inevitable rites of passage are complicated by a dangerous lack of awareness in their elders. Beautiful, clever Athene, bereaved and homeless after the death of her adored, very old, clerical father, is ensconced in her fantasy life as EMILY BRONTË. Sketchy arrangements for her summer holiday made by her scatty mother lead Athene into three potentially non-platonic encounters with men: a silent youth in an overheated hydropathic hotel, a painter in a seaside cottage and a youngish schoolmaster in an empty school. Growing awareness of sexuality and other social hazards of precipitated independence emerge in a subtly controlled plot. A string of late-1940s characters, offering painfully clear glimpses of the heroine from their differently situated perspectives, let the reader admire the author's skill and tremble for Athene's fate.

In Gardam's writing, what is implied or thrown away in passing is more resonant than what is actually said. This challenges developing readers. Although SEX was already an accepted topic when the book first appeared, these writerly features were generally less common. Accomplished readers detect a dark side, a whiff of threat, especially when adult repressions are bitingly, if humorously, contrasted with explosive youthful passion. The reissue of the novel in 1986 on the publisher's adult list seems to justify an earlier critic's comparison of it with the satire of Iris Murdoch. MM

Summerfield, Geoffrey see MIROSLAV HOLUB; *JUNIOR VOICES*

Summerly, Felix [Cole, Sir Henry] 1808–82 British editor of FOLKTALES and FAIRY TALES. Reacting against the utilitarian tendency in children's books, especially those by 'PETER PARLEY', in 1843 Cole began to produce *The Home Treasury*, a series of booklets, pictures and toys intended to cultivate the affections, imagination and taste of children. Illustrated by some of the best contemporary artists, the series retold such traditional tales as JACK THE GIANT-KILLER and LITTLE RED RIDING HOOD. Cole, who also invented the Christmas card in 1846, is widely credited with helping lead the revolution in children's books in the Victorian era. DB

Sun on the Stubble (1961) Collection of 12 interconnected short stories by Australian writer COLIN THIELE. The stories, which express a variety of moods, are set in a German farming community in the Barossa Valley of South Australia in the 1920s. The main character, 12-year-old Bruno, is completing his last years of primary schooling before bidding farewell to his childhood and leaving for the city to attend high school. Some of the stories have been adapted for TELEVISION and were released internationally in 1996. The collection has also been translated into German and Swedish. FK

Sunday-School prizes see DIDACTICISM; PUBLISHING AND PUBLISHERS; RELIGIOUS TRACT SOCIETY

Sunita Experiment, The see ASIAN AMERICAN CHILDREN'S LITERATURE; BIAS IN CHILDREN'S BOOKS

Sunny Stories A children's magazine founded and written by ENID BLYTON for the publisher Newnes. Over the years it changed in both frequency (between fortnightly and weekly) and title: from *Sunny Stories for Little Folks* (1926–36) to *Enid Blyton's Sunny Stories* (1937–42), thence to *Sunny Stories*. In 1953, Blyton withdrew to write her own *Enid Blyton's Magazine* (Evans), reputedly because Newnes would not allow her to advertise any non-Newnes works. Newnes chose not to announce her departure, hence Blyton's disclaimer in her new magazine – 'the only magazine I write'. *Sunny Stories* did survive, though, attracting MALCOLM SAVILLE's editorship in the late 1950s. DR

Sunshine (1981) Wordless PICTUREBOOK by JAN ORMEROD, which betrays media influences in the freeze-frame techniques used to depict a sequence of events – a child and her family's early morning routines – in a visually active way. It was winner of the CHILDREN'S BOOK COUNCIL OF AUSTRALIA Picturebook of the Year Award in 1982. It was followed by a sequel, *Moonlight*, in 1983. RS

superheroes Characters that grew out of the pulp fiction COMICS, PERIODICALS AND MAGAZINES proliferating in America in the 1920s and 30s. A landmark was the launch of SUPERMAN in *ACTION COMICS* 1 in 1938. The cutting edges of this tradition is now to be found in increasingly sophisticated comic-book narratives for a (young) adult audience, but the genre still permeates popular culture more generally, from mass-made cartoon series to blockbuster movies and parodies.

Superheroes are 20th-century replacements for the gods and superior beings that once walked the earth and intervened in human affairs, from Rama and the Archangels of the Bible, to Gilgamesh and Siegfried. 'SHAZAM', the word Billy Batson has to utter to turn into the eponymous *Captain Marvel* (1940), stands for **S**olomon's wisdom, **H**ercules strength, **A**tlas' stamina, **Z**eus' power, **A**chilles' courage, **M**ercury's speed.

Superman took to the news-stands at the beginning of a century anticipating enormous human and scientific expansions. Speed, purity, audacity, struggle, and the power of human will were the ardent thoughts of the new self-reliant working-class hero, celebrated from monuments in Leningrad to Hollywood's 1925 *Ben-Hur*. Hopes for the betterment of society and the perfectibility of human nature found expression in Marxism and fascism, together with a belief in strong leadership. Interest in athletics (the Olympics were restarted in 1896) reflected a new cult of the body, a striving for physical perfection as 'Übermensch', made more possible by improving nutritional standards. Enterprises on a grandiose scale created the soaring modern architecture found on the vertical panels of superhero comics, while faith in the magic of science and technology pervaded every gadget and invention-riddled superhero plot.

Individualism both springs from and subverts this triumphant collective idealism, as utopian optimism jostles with disenchantment. Superheroes are indeed the unfettered 'Übermensch', but solitary, alienated, rising above the wretched human condition, battling against ever-surging evil and corruption. With roots in the outsider figure, superheroes draw on narrative traditions that range from Jesus, knights-errant, ROBIN HOOD and highwaymen like Dick Turpin, to the tormented adolescent hero of 19th-century Romanticism and the outlawed lone ranger of westerns. Set in the modern wilderness of urban landscapes, superhero narratives crawl out of teeming, decadent Dickensian worlds. PENNY DREADFULS were direct precursors of the garish early superhero comic-books, the Victorian pulp-hero *Springheel Jack* an early *Superman*.

To qualify as a superhero in the narrow 20th-century definition, certain criteria have to be met. Superheroes have dual identities, combining human and divine (or animal) aspects. Unassuming alter egos protect superhero operations: either a disguise

(*Superman* stoops and fumbles deliberately, and wears glasses), or simply the transformed self (schoolboy Billy Batson changes into fully-grown *Captain Marvel*, mild-mannered scientist Bruce Banner changes into the *Incredible Hulk*, 1962, when stressed). Alter egos, possibly unattractive and despised, can contrast radically with superhero personas. The split draws on cultural and psychological notions of the Jungian 'shadow', as in the 'Jekyll and Hyde' archetype. Dualism occurs in many forms: blending human and animal nature (a man with the power of a bat or spider), or mirroring and merging with the evil nature of the foe to understand it. The latter is salient in the sombre, troubled BATMAN (1939), whose protagonist is drawn to and almost obsessed with darkness and evil, as are the heroes of *The Shadow* (1931) or *Spectre* (1940). Being frequently perceived by the public as causing the evil they are fighting is another aspect of the superheroes' ambiguous nature. Crucially, dual nature highlights the 'divided self' of modern souls, with the colourful superhero form, in 'natural' body-moulding outfit, bursting out of the repressed grey pedestrian guise of the alter ego. Superheroes are striking forms, simple to draw within the constraints of early comic-book printing technology (in lurid coal tar dyes). Many wear masks or goggles, and (animal) talismans, just as shamans or warriors assume masks and symbolic attire to invoke the power of gods.

Superheroes are often wounded or traumatised, like shamans transformed and set apart through an alchemy of suffering. Loss is one catalyst, and many are orphans: *Batman* saw his parents murdered, which fuels his solitary and haunted vocation, while others include *Superman*, SPIDER-MAN *(1962)*, *Captain America* (1941). Childhood can be a crucible: the hero of *The Atom* (1940) is teased for being small and shrinks at will to molecular size; *Superted* (UK, 1983) is discarded from the teddy bear production line. Heroes also experience searing events in adulthood, even death itself: *Dr Mid-Nite* (1941) is blinded by criminals and now sees in the dark; *Nighthawk* (1969) is redeemed like Hercules after crippling a girlfriend while drunk-driving. Many 1950s superheroes were exposed to radiation or scientific accidents, opening cracks in the fabric of normality: *The X-Men* (1963) became gifted mutants at adolescence. Alien origins also confirm status (*Superman*).

Wounding, mutant or extra-terrestrial natures confer on superheroes specific powers of every conceivable kind – speed, invulnerability, heightened senses, total recall, weather-conjuring. Deliciously effortless, they are effectively 'magical', yet many characters acquire exceptional faculties through relentless discipline, solitude or spiritual apprenticeship: the popular mutant loner Wolverine of *The X-Men* has constantly to work at subduing his violent temper. Science usually replaces magic and religion as vehicle of the fantastic: unlike *Aladdin*, *Green Lantern*'s lamp and ring derive awesome powers from 'natural' properties of the meteorite they came from. Powers lie within or depend on special devices: *Wonder Woman*'s lasso (1942) forces captives to tell the truth. *Green Arrow* (1941) uses boxing-glove arrows, tipped with tiny leather fists, that knock out rather than kill. *Batman* and *Spiderman* (amateur scientists, like many others) painstakingly perfect their own inventions. Utility belts are inexhaustibly stocked with astonishingly compact revolutionary gadgets.

A superhero's 'Achilles' heel' maintains suspense (*Green Lantern* is helpless against yellow, *The Avenger*, 1939, has a fatal mania for cleanliness), while entertaining sidekicks (love interests, trusty 'kid' partners, comic dimwits) provide a human touch. However, villains are the key players, whether comical, glamorous, resourceful or chilling. Splendid arrays of perennial foes and unlimited supplies of expendable deranged monsters – with names like Ultrahumanite, Mr Mxyztplk, The Puppet Master, Dr Octopus and Red Skull – supply the colour and variety needed for long-running titles.

Superhero stories conjure the fantastical inside everyday believable settings. Crime-rife American cities provide visually dramatic levels ranging from skyscraper to subway. Superheroes fight crime and villains, restoring the status quo in society but doing no more – they do not question or take on the social system itself. Fighting for right, they are themselves beyond the law and share with the criminal self-reliance and freedom. Classic superheroes do not kill or inflict more pain than necessary. Ascetic codes of honour often mean sacrificing ordinary human comforts like family and sexual fulfilment. When framed or misunderstood, they suffer in silence.

Superheroes are reinvented to express current aspirations and fears. On the heels of the Depression, early *Superman* championed the oppressed, fighting lynchings and illegal arms dealers. As readership widened, stories shifted towards blander, physical exploits and avoided politics. World War II boosted output: 'The idea of the Superhero, who gave up his ordinary life and put on a uniform to battle the bad guys, had special resonance' (Les Daniels). During the 1930s and 40s, the 'Golden Age of Comics', hundreds of different superheroes were on news-stands.

In 1954 the axe fell on the comic-book industry as *Seduction of the Innocent* by psychologist Dr Fredric Wertham created hysteria and brought comics into disrepute. From an all-time high, sales dropped by 7 per cent in a single year. A regulatory body was set up; some 'clean' superheroes survived. However, after the war drive, fatigue with one-dimensional superheroes had set in. TELEVISION was becoming chief purveyor of popular entertainment; comics specialised, making way for a new age. MARVEL COMICS did most to reinvent the genre, with humorous, well-written dialogue and complex characters such as *The Fantastic Four* (1961), who had irritating sides to them, and relationship problems. Rejecting the imaginary 'Metropolis' or 'Gotham City' of *Detective Comics*, *Marvel* relocated to real New York and created superheroes with problems, such as *Spider-Man*, the flawed everyman who catches colds, is always short of money and mends his own costumes ('I'll just shoot my web . . . Oh no! The ejector is empty!'). Questioning himself and what he is fighting for, he embodies teenage angst, heralding a 1960s return to social consciousness, and a progressive loss of moral certainty. *Watchmen* (1986) explored a dark scenario where New York is 'infested' with obsessed and exhausted superheroes operating beyond control, unleashing disasters.

From the 1950s, superhero stories tapped the massive interest and fear of 'superscience' – nuclear power, radiation, space travel. The 'Silver Age' of comics (from 1956) also saw many superheroes teaming up (*Justice League of America*, 1960). Original 'Golden Age' heroes were brought up to date, but also resurrected in their original form in a parallel universe, 'Earth Two'. Different superheroes popped in and out of each other's comic-book titles (good for business), creating intricacies that only the initiated could appreciate. Ever more parallel universes were needed to interrelate events and accommodate discrepancies. Finally 'the interdimensional turnpikes got so crowded' (Jeff Rovin) that in 1985 *Detective Comics* organised a 'Crisis on Infinite Earths', a cosmic meltdown reuniting in a single world all the heroes DETECTIVE COMICS chose to save, giving them a clean slate.

The familiar conventions of the genre have been widely borrowed, from road safety and public health campaigns to advertisements and parody (*Thunder Bunny*, 1982, and actor Richard Pryor's 1976 'Supernigger', just two of many characters ranging from the absurd to the challenging).

In comics and television cartoons established characters like Marvel's *X-Men* are still going strong, while new permutations tackle fresh concerns: mutation (the hedonistic *Teenage Mutant Ninja Turtles*), toxic and environmental threats (*Captain Planet*, *Toxic Avengers*). Hero teams are ubiquitous, like the *Mighty Morphin Power Rangers* and *Biker Mice from Mars*. Superheroes provided hits for cinema and television, while influences can be traced in many heroes of mainstream cinema, from wounded avengers like *Mad Max* (1979) and *Robocop* (1987), prefigured in *Robotman* (1942), to *Lethal Weapon*'s crazy cop team operating outside, but on behalf of, the law (1987). Mad scientists and power-crazed despots continue to torment *James Bond* and others, *The Fantastic Four*'s 'Dr Doom' lives again in STAR WARS' 'Darth Vader' (1977). The best superhero fictions are still where they started – in comics. The trend towards older audiences continues with GRAPHIC NOVELS exploring powerful visuals, two classics being *Batman – the Dark Knight Returns* (1986), about a tortured, aged *Batman*, and *Watchmen*.

One of the few females to become a major superhero in her own right, *Wonder Woman*, was to 'possess all the strength of Superman, all the allure of a good and beautiful woman' (creator Marston). Erotically attired like other superwomen (for a predominantly male readership), her sexiness is in practice completely overlooked by other characters as she gets on with battling evil. As a male fantasy blend of good woman and dominatrix, *Wonder Woman* has spent an inordinate amount of time in chains, but she has also inspired a devoted following in many young girls, who have found in her a role model both powerful and compassionate. Different cultures have evolved their own superheroes, Britain for example preferring more gritty and characterful scenarios such as *Judge Dredd* to the more action-packed American models. Japanese influence, with powerful samurai and supernatural traditions blossoming in manga comics and cartoons, is spreading widely.

Stan Lee mentions the imaginative appeal of comics to 'intelligent kids, introverted readers and dreamers who have fantasies of acquiring brawn to match brain'. From impotent childhood to troubled adolescence, superheroes express young people's longings to be powerful, smart, a law unto oneself. Rituals such as the mystique conferred by gadgets help fans weave their own sheltering *Doppelgänger* worlds: the Batcave, *Batman*'s intricate hideout equipped with every possible magical device, is the perfect dreamer's den. The child knows that under the unappreciated exterior a talented and powerful person is waiting to be let loose. In the words of that 'superhero' precursor, *Zorro* (1919): 'I've convinced my father I'm a spineless weakling. Now I'm free to act alone!' CMP

Superman 1938– The most influential of American comic book SUPERHEROES. When the character, Superman, made his first appearance in *Action Comics* no. 1 in 1938, he both popularised and defined the conventions of the comic-book 'superhero', a term derived from his name. The creation of two teenagers, Jerry Siegel and Joe Shuster, Superman has appeared in a variety of comics, novels, motion pictures, cartoons, and TELEVISION series and has been widely imitated. Part of Superman's appeal derives from his double life as both mild-mannered reporter, Clark Kent, and a costumed crime-fighter with extraordinary powers such as x-ray vision, superhuman strength and the ability to fly. JDC

see also COMICS, PERIODICALS AND MAGAZINES

Illustration by CHARLES KEEPING from *Dragon Slayer: The Story of Beowulf* by Rosemary Sutcliff.

Sutcliff, Rosemary 1920–92 Writer of HISTORICAL FICTION for children and adults, born in West Clandon, Surrey, and brought up in Malta until she was ten, when her family returned to England. She was first educated at home owing to her having contracted Still's Disease (a condition which left her wheelchair-bound for many years) at the age of two, and she joined the Bideford Art School at 14. Her first novel, *The Chronicles of Robin Hood*, was published in 1950 and more than 30 other works have since appeared. A proportion of Sutcliff's work is concerned with the retelling of legends; these range from the IRISH MYTHOLOGY AND FOLKLORE concerning Finn Mac Cool to the Arthurian legends (see KING ARTHUR) and the tale of BEOWULF. Her best-known novels are those set in Roman Britain (*The Lantern Bearers*, 1959, which won the CARNEGIE MEDAL), though *WARRIOR SCARLET* (1950) and *The Mark of the Horse Lord* (1965), which do not come under this heading, also deserve special mention. She was awarded the OBE in 1975 for her services to children's literature.

The tone of much of Sutcliff's work is sombre; her themes are those of alienation and self-making in a world of hard choices. Many of her characters are outsiders and exiles for reasons of race, physical disability or emotional damage. Drem of *Warrior Scarlet* and Marcus of *THE EAGLE OF THE NINTH* (1954) are crippled, Lovel of *The Witch's Brat* (1970) is ostracised as a hunchback and witch, Justin and Flavius of *The Silver Branch* (1957) are outlawed, Beric of *Outcast* (1955) is a Roman outsider in a British community – the list continues. These works proclaim that the achievement of self is a thing needing to be wrought rather than a thing inherited or shaped by society. They also acknowledge that even if 'the struggle availeth' it can never quite cease: DISABILITY does not magically disappear but has to be accommodated.

Sutcliff's work is an examination of liminality: what it means to be marginalised by a society, and also what it means to traverse the region away from the centre: this not only physically but in other ways as well. Marcus's quest to find the lost eagle of the Ninth Hispana in *The Eagle of the Ninth* takes him well away from Hadrian's Wall, the circumscribing marker of Roman civilisation, into terra incognita. *The Lantern Bearers*, perhaps the most complex of her works, explores through the experiences of its protagonist, Aquila, the utter loneliness that comes not just from losing one's family to death and perceived betrayal, but also from slavery and exile, from being emotionally shut off, and from moral choice. For Aquila at the outset of the book deserts the Eagles in order to keep faith with family and, in a strange way, with himself. His lighting of the Rutupiae beacon one last time, a symbolic thrusting back of the dark, also highlights the lonely courage of the individual whose actions can know no other validation but that of his own conscience. SA

Sutherland, Zena B(ailey) 1915– American critic and teacher of children's literature. From 1958 to 1985 the editor of *The Bulletin of the Center for Children's Books*, Sutherland has been one of the most influential professional voices in American children's literature. Sutherland became co-author of the important textbook *Children and Books*, with its fourth edition in 1972, and was its main author for five more editions. Instrumental in the creation of the Scott O'Dell Award for Historical Fiction, she remains chair of that award's committee, as well as having founded the annual lecture bearing her name. In 1996, she received the Arbuthnot Honour Lecture Award. DS

Sutton, Eve 1906–92 Having emigrated from England to New Zealand in 1949, Sutton published her first book at the age of 67. Her PICTUREBOOK, *My Cat Likes to Hide in Boxes* (1973), illustrated by Lynley Dodd, won the ESTHER GLEN AWARD for its classic combination of humour and imagination. It was followed by eight novels, most of them set in colonial New Zealand. The historical novels are carefully crafted, with *Moa Hunter* (1978) being the result of five years of research and writing. Sutton's last book, *Valley of Heavenly Gold*, was published in 1987. LO

Swallows and Amazons Series of 12 related novels by the British author ARTHUR RANSOME, mostly concerned with children sharing the activities of boating, camping and exploring. How Ransome came to write *Swallows and Amazons* (1930) is described by Hugh Brogan in his account of the author's friendship with the Altounyan family. It introduced the four Swallows, John, Susan, Titty and Roger Walker, whose rather orderly make-believe activities are disrupted by the more boisterous Amazons, Nancy and Peggy Blackett. (Nancy's real name is Ruth, but pirates must be ruth-less.)

Central to the story is the children's devotion to make-believe. The most imaginative of them is Titty, a reader of poetry and sea stories, who enriches their pretending with literary possibilities. Details of landscape and the practicalities of sailing are described with a convincing authenticity. The behaviour of the children, on the other hand, is idealised; nobody sulks, nobody is ever malicious, for such realism would work against the book's gentle imagery of innocence. These children are their own safe family. There are no enemies in this story, and no wickedness – only a burglary which is kept at a safe distance from the children. Early editions of *Swallows and Amazons* had rather stylised line drawings by Clifford Webb, but from *Peter Duck* onwards all the novels had maps and crude but vigorous illustrations by Ransome himself ('I have to thank Miss Nancy Blackett for much earnest work on the illustrations'). *Swallows and Amazons* sold slowly at first, probably because it was so unlike other children's books at that time.

Encouraged by slightly better publishing figures in the United States, Ransome wrote a sequel. In *Swallowdale* (1931), there is again no wickedness and all the adults are true, honest, skilled and kind. The children's boat inspires them almost to poetry: the account of *Swallow's* sinking and subsequent salvage employs a mixture of the practical and the lyrical which is a distinguishing feature of Ransome's writing. Next came *Peter Duck* (1932), supposed to be a story made up by the children. In this deep-sea ADVENTURE STORY, with its pirates and hidden treasure, Ransome brings the six children face to face with real danger, for although Black Jake is a stereotypical villain deriving from Titty's reading, the account of his brutality is lucid and grim. The 'Wild Cat' combines the security of home with the uncertainties of voyaging and its crew is an idealised community in danger. Despite its fantastic nature (its earthquakes, storms, tornadoes and water-spouts), *Peter Duck* thematically completes *Swallows and Amazons* and *Swallowdale*; the three books are like a trilogy, defining a social ideal of companionship based on respect, loyalty and love of seascape and landscape.

According to Hugh Brogan, Ransome insisted that the fourth in the series, *Winter Holiday* (1933), was to be the last about the Walkers and the Blacketts. In it, Ransome shifts his imaginative sympathy to two new children, Dick and Dorothea Callum – 'the Ds' – and removes Nancy from most of the action by giving her mumps. The themes of innocence and discovery are handed over to the two town-children, outsiders at first, but generously initiated by the others into a bewildering world of coded messages. Dorothea and Dick construct meanings according to their different natures, he scientific, she imaginative. They are profoundly serious and heroically loyal to each other, and their silent and almost telepathic mutual concern is in stark contrast to their rather noisy companions.

Coot Club (1934) was a fresh start. It is set in the Norfolk Broads and Dick and Dorothea are now the main characters. The Swallows and Amazons are not present, and there are a number of new characters, notably Tom Dudgeon and the 'Death and Glories'. However, Ransome's artistic commitment is to the Broads themselves – its waters, its people, and especially its birds – and accordingly there is a great deal of his characteristic and carefully stated observation. The villages and waterways are given their real names, not fictional ones. All the plots and sub-plots are about voyaging: while Mrs Barrable is boating down to Beccles, the twins are making their own unorthodox journey by hitching lifts on boats, and the Death and Glories are either cycling all over the area or rowing frantically about in their makeshift craft. *Coot Club* is an extraordinarily visual story, with a serious ecological message about wildlife; yet it stands apart from the main thrust of the series because the children in it are of less interest than the author's pleasure in the unique visual appeal of Norfolk.

However, in *Pigeon Post* (1936), the first winner of the CARNEGIE MEDAL, Ransome returned to the more robust mode of the Lake District novels, with the Swallows and Amazons and the Ds together. It is a far less 'safe' novel than its predecessors: four of the children are almost buried alive in a derelict mine-working, all of them are almost burned to death in a fell-fire of terrifying ferocity, and in a drought-baked landscape Ransome has his children trying to heat a furnace to 2060 degrees. In this story Ransome is risk-taking, pressing close to the edge of the acceptable boundaries of comfortable children's fiction. These children are dangerous – especially Roger. In the earlier books he tagged on, an enthusiastic little boy with an egocentric and uncertain grasp of what was happening; but in *Pigeon Post* he is subversive, disobedient and dangerous.

There is an even greater authorial interest in danger in the next novel, *We Didn't Mean to Go to Sea* (1937), which many readers regard as the best of the series. Its structural simplicity focuses exclusively on the four Swallows, alone at sea in a cutter, forced to employ their sailing skills to survive thick fog, impenetrable darkness and hurricane-force winds, and grimly aware of the price of failure. Ransome made the trip himself to ensure authenticity in his fictional account. There is in the description of the children's terrible night at sea some of his best writing, an authentic and compelling account of John's mistakes, his generosity and his boyish heroism. There is a new note of urgency in the prose and a commitment to details of seamanship, with no over-statement or sentimentalism. The dangers press upon the children with unrelenting ferocity, and each is faced, endured and survived. It is also Susan's story, for in her domesticated and law-abiding heart there resides a spirit of stormy rebellion which pits her passionately against her brother. In *We Didn't Mean to go to Sea*, Susan herself is the most stormy element that John has to contend with.

The next two novels returned to East Anglia and are less urgent and less tense. *Secret Water* (1939) is a sedate and untroubled account of the children as an idealised group of children behaving with exemplary good-nature. There are many muted pleasures in this gentle novel – such as the Mastodon's den, or little Bridget's indignation when she is *not* to be a human sacrifice. *The Big Six* (1940) has a similarly reduced imaginative horizon. Its plot revolves around detection, to which Dick brings a scientific and practical approach to the discovery and recording of evidence, while Dorothea provides an imaginative insight which to the three local boys is comically incomprehensible.

The next novel of the series marked a return to Ransome's earlier controlled and impassioned excitement. Despite its stereotypes of race, *Missee Lee* (1941) is a powerful thriller-romance set in a distant exotic place, vividly and economically described, among strange and ferocious people. There are no Ds, no Coots, no extras – just the old fellowship of the Swallows and Amazons and Captain Flint. There is a good deal of humour in *Missee Lee*, but with a sharp edge of danger. At one point Captain Flint is in a bamboo cage and the children are awaiting execution; yet Ransome conducts his readers through this grimness, finding comedy at every turn. Missee Lee herself is the strangest adult character in the series (based partly on Madame Sun Yat Sen, the wife of the Chinese revolutionary) – a piratical tyrant conducting with ruthless skill the politics of gangsterism while pining for her lost undergraduate days at Cambridge.

In the next novel, *The Picts and Martyrs* (1943), Ransome returned to the Lake District. For rather contrived reasons, Dorothea and Dick must live a secret life in the woods (like Picts) while Nancy and Peggy must behave for ten days like model schoolgirls (hence, Martyrs). This novel is a sustained demonstration of Nancy's goodness. She assumes a protective responsibility for Dorothea and Dick, combining adult caring with her usual cheerful inventiveness. With the Ds, Ransome has rediscovered his original commitment to newness. 'We've got to learn everything,' Dorothea says, and this takes us back to the early stories in which Roger learned to swim and Titty sailed alone at night.

Great Northern? (1947) is the last of the series. The question-mark indicates the ornithological puzzle Dick must solve: are there really Great Northern Divers nesting on a Scottish lake? At the imaginative heart of this story is Dick's self-effacing and patient bird-watching and his entirely innocent eagerness to understand the world. But *Great Northern?* is also concerned with the moral and psychological uncertainties of watching; its plot is a web of strategies of surveillance. In its closing account, when Titty and Dick replace the stolen eggs in the divers' nest and the great birds return to it, some of Ransome's best writing is to be found, suggesting a powerful symbolism and great depth of feeling while apparently using unremarkable language to describe simple activities.

The series ended there, though there might have been a 13th story: in 1988 Hugh Brogan edited a collection of little-known and unpublished works by Ransome, one of which consisted of some unfinished fragments and an outline of another story which Brogan called *Coots in the North*. It was to have taken the three East Anglian 'Death and Glories' to the Lake District for a shared adventure with Nancy and the others.

The qualities which distinguish Ransome's work are his unpretentious and exact prose, his love of landscape and seascape, and his belief in the goodness of people. He is an unusually 'literary' writer for children; his writing drew sustenance from a wide cultural tradition embracing CLASSICAL MYTHOLOGY, FOLKTALES and FAIRY TALES, the *ARABIAN NIGHTS*, sea-shanties, Romantic poetry, ROBINSON CRUSOE, KIPLING, Conrad and STEVENSON. He mediates for young readers a cultural continuity and a long literary tradition. His influence on the development of children's books is incalculable. MALCOLM SAVILLE'S *LONE PINE* series was almost certainly inspired by him, and so were ENID BLYTON'S *FAMOUS FIVE* and *SECRET SEVEN* stories. And the 1930s and 40s saw the publication of dozens of now-forgotten children's stories about CAMPING AND TRAMPING and other countryside activities. The first of Ransome's series was made into a film, and *Coot Club* and *The Big Six* have been filmed for television.

The *Swallows and Amazons* series has been criticised for a lack of realism. JOHN ROWE TOWNSEND pointed out that Ransome's young characters 'maintain a sexless companionship which does not quite accord with the facts of adolescence'. It is also true that none of the novels – written between 1930 and 1947 – makes any reference to the realities of World War II. But such criticisms miss the point, for the 12 linked novels are closer to the quality of magical fairy tales than their surface realism seems to indicate. They constitute a kind of mythology of perpetual voyaging in an extended holiday of expanding childhood. His main child-characters are a fellowship of innocence, a company of magical children sailing in search of experience, yet never losing their innocence. They learn new knowledge, yet are never disillusioned. His narratives are composed of possibilities for pretending and ideas for imagining; many adult readers recall that they used them as resource-books for play. VW

Swami and Friends (1935) Written by the most famous Indian writer in English, R.K. Narayan, *Swami and Friends* was hailed by GRAHAM GREENE as 'a book in ten thousand'. This is an unpretentious first novel about an impetuous ten-year old boy, Swami. The charming, entertaining stories of his escapades graduate from a simple narrative to a deep, sympathetic analysis of the relationship between the child's world and that of the adult. Scrupulous detail establishes both the child's world as he himself sees it, and the adult community of the fictional town of Malgudi, which provides the setting for almost all of Narayan's later novels. Much anthologised, the stories work successfully as entertaining children's fiction while continuing to have a more general appeal. MBh

Swan Lake see BALLET STORIES; RACHEL ISADORA; CHRIS VAN ALLSBURG

Swarm in May, A see *CHOIR SCHOOL* SERIES

Sweeney, Matthew 1952– Irish poet born in Donegal. He has written fiction for children but is better known for poetry collections, including *The Flying Spring Onion* (1992) and *Fatso in the Red Suit* (1995). His poetry is unconventional, offbeat, funny, sometimes edging towards the surreal, often considering subject matter from unusual perspectives. *Emergency Kit* (edited with Jo Shapcott, 1996) is considered a defining anthology for the latter part of the 20th century and has been adopted by some enterprising English teachers of young adults. MCCS

***Sweet Valley High* series** (from 1984) American paperback fiction. Created by Francine Pascal, the *Sweet Valley High* series chronicles the lives of identical twins, 16-year-olds Jessica and Elizabeth Wakefield. Both are blonde, beautiful Californian girls, but Elizabeth is serious and responsible, maintaining a steady relationship with one boy at a time, while daring Jessica is a flirt and a troublemaker, though essentially good-hearted and loyal to her sister. The books are penned by a stable of writers according to outlines written by Pascal herself (new titles are issued monthly), but the pseudonymous Kate William remains the official author of all the titles. Though often criticised for its shallowness and unrealistic glamour (which may be the keys to its popularity), the series occasionally focuses on issues such as racism and DRUG use and has permitted growth and change; the girls eventually go off to college and Jessica becomes sexually active. Special issues and contests fuelled the tremendous popularity of the series, which spun off into *Sweet Valley Twins* (Jessica and Elizabeth in sixth grade), *Sweet Valley Kids* (Jessica and Elizabeth at seven years of age), *Sweet Valley University*, and finally – perhaps inevitably – became a syndicated TELEVISION series. DS

Swift (from 1954) Comic created by the Reverend Marcus Morris to bridge the gap between very young readers of *ROBIN* and older readers of *EAGLE*. The first issue was published on 20 March 1954, and the comic ran for 477 weekly editions. Printed with pages in full-colour photogravure, its pages were enlarged from 9 April 1960, when publication was taken over by Longacre/Odhams. Early heroes included cover star Tarna the Jungle Boy (a junior TARZAN), Koko the Bush Baby and Sir Boldasbrass by John Ryan. Later came Michael Bentine and *The Bumblies* from BBC TELEVISION, and adventure strips by the great Frank Bellamy, including *ROBIN HOOD*. *Swift Annual* was published every Christmas from 1955 to 1963. DG

Swift, Jonathan see *GULLIVER'S TRAVELS*; see also PAT LYNCH; *TWEEDLEDUM AND TWEEDLEDEE*

Swindells, Robert 1939– Yorkshire-born British novelist many of whose stories are characterised by an acute historical sense and an unease about contemporary society. After local newspaper work and RAF service Swindells trained as a teacher. His first book, *When Darkness Comes* (1973), started as a thesis. He writes engagingly exciting FANTASIES such as *World Eater* (1981) and the award-winning *Room 13* (1989). However, early novels such as *A Candle in the Dark* (1974) are more typical of his output. The evocation of child labour in Victorian coalmines exhibits pessimism about society's outcomes, presaging the finely dramatised anger of *Daz 4 Zoe* (1990), a brilliantly written novel set in a dystopian society which logically extended the contemporary dread of a growing underclass. *Staying Up* (1986) sees the local football team as a metaphor of social disintegration. *A Serpent's Tooth* (1988) and *Follow a Shadow* (1989) use the supernatural and aspects of the past (the Black Death and Branwell Brontë respectively) as reference points for continuity, while *Invisible!* (1999) is a taut cliff-hanging narrative dealing with crime and violence. Swindells's most influential novel, apart from STONE COLD (1993), was the award-winning *Brother in the Land* (1984), a post-holocaust vision countering unrealistic optimism in other such stories. Other concerns depicted are cults (*Unbeliever*, 1995), racism (*Smash*, 1997), deprivation (*Abomination*, 1999) and teenage alcoholism (*Wrecked*, 2000). Swindells's uncompromising honesty – together with his unerring construction and flexible prose – ensures his compulsive readability. DCH

Swish of the Curtain, The (1941) Novel by PAMELA BROWN, begun when she was only 14. It tells the story of a group of children who start their own theatre in a disused chapel. In spite of its unconscious snobbishness and clumsy drawing of the adult comic characters, it rocks along with real energy, and the descriptions of the preparations for the shows are convincing and absorbing. Parents are satisfyingly absent from most of the action, and readers can lose themselves in an innocent world of exercise-book scripts, raspberry-juice wine and homemade costumes. The story builds to a gripping climax as the children enter a drama contest which they have to win in order to realise their dream of a career in the professional theatre. The novel was reissued many times in popular editions and there were several sequels. VWo

see also CHILD AUTHORS; BALLET STORIES

Swiss Family Robinson, The (1812) Novel by the Swiss author, J.D. Wyss (1743–1818). The story of a family shipwrecked on a desert island was first published in Zurich in 1812, and translated as *The Family Robinson Crusoe* in 1814. One of the first ROBINSONNADES for young people, the book became popular as *The Swiss Family Robinson* and about 300 different editions have been published in England and America. Despite the father's moralising and the implausibility of so many different plants and animals being found on one island, the lively behaviour of the boys and the father's unflagging resourcefulness still give the book an interest. A version was filmed by WALT DISNEY in 1960. DB

Sword in the Stone, The see THE ONCE AND FUTURE KING; see also ANIMALS IN FICTION; KING ARTHUR; ROSEMARY SUTCLIFF

syllabaries see ALPHABET BOOKS

syllabarium see HORNBOOKS AND BATTLEDORES

T

Tagore, Rabindranath 1861–1941 Bengali poet, playwright, fiction writer, thinker and educationist who wrote more about children than for them. Tagore's few children's books focus on the sensitive depths of the child's mind. His unhappy childhood casts its sombre shadow in these works and precludes the presence of the lightness that is normally associated with children's writing. Consequently, adult life as seen through the eyes of an imaginative child remains the substance of his most poignant poems. Most of his child poems are collected in *Sisu* (1902), subsequently translated as *The Crescent Moon*. He has also penned stirring stories that have been popular with both children and adults, like *Cabulliwallah* (translated in 1912 by Sister Nivedita), as well as some short humorous prose sketches, and some plays about boyhood. MBh

Tailor of Gloucester, The (1903) The second of BEATRIX POTTER's tales and her personal favourite. It began life as a story that she had heard on a visit to friends in Gloucestershire. In Potter's version a tailor is unwell and cannot complete an important order. He is helped by some mice that he has freed after they had been imprisoned by his cat, Simpkin. It is different from other Beatrix Potter tales in two particular respects. Firstly, it contains an unusual mixture of human and FANTASY elements, and secondly it is given a definite period setting 'in the time of swords and periwigs'. This places the reader firmly in the past, whereas most of her books had a timeless quality about them, allowing readers to place the story wherever they wished. It is notable for the number of NURSERY RHYMES included in the text, reflecting Beatrix Potter's fascination with such rhymes. It also gives young readers the opportunity to join in with what is quite a lengthy story, and to delight in sharing such knowledge with the author. HB

tailpiece A small decorative design or illustration used to fill the blank space at the end of a chapter or poem. GCB

Talbot, Ethel 1880–1944 A prolific British writer of girls' school and GUIDING stories of the 1920s and 30s. Despite an unquestioning conformity to the morality of the genre ('Don't you know how to be sporting, and clean, and straight?'), she often touches on the deeper emotional relationships between younger and older girls. EAG

Tale of Benjamin Bunny, The see *TALE OF PETER RABBIT, THE*

Tale of Jemima Puddle-Duck, The (1908) Story by BEATRIX POTTER. Described by the author as 'a farmyard tale for Ralph and Betsy', *Jemima Puddle-Duck* is far more than that. There are shades of RED RIDING HOOD and of FABLES warning of the consequences of wandering into the unknown. Jemima is undomesticated, naive and incautious. There is much in this tale to teach children about irony: the bed of feathers offered by the villainous fox, his remarks about 'loving eggs and ducklings', and the way in which Jemima dutifully gathers sage and onion for her own stuffing. There is also the challenge of a story told from differing perspectives, that of the fox and the duck. This, combined with the use of parallel time frames (the collie marshalling support for a rescue, whilst at the same time Jemima is witnessing a dramatic change in the fox's personality), makes for a challenging read. The change in the fox's behaviour, from almost obsequious politeness to an offensive abruptness, is an excellent example of Beatrix Potter's careful attention. The illustrations in *Jemima Puddle-Duck* show the author's ambivalent attitude towards dressing her animal characters: when they revert to their natural behaviour all clothes are shed, and Kep (the rescuer) has no clothes at all. Uncharacteristically, the heroine, although rescued in fine tradition, meets a rather unjust and quite distressing fate – the loss of her eggs. This loss seems all the worse as it happens at the hands of her rescuers. HB

Tale of Mr Tod, The see *TALE OF PETER RABBIT, THE*

Tale of Mrs Tiggywinkle, The (1905) Story by BEATRIX POTTER about little Lucie from Newlands, who loses her handkerchiefs and her pinafore and goes off in search of them. Through a door in the hillside she finds Mrs. Tiggywinkle's kitchen, in which the hedgehog washerwoman is finishing off the local laundry, the majority of her customers being the local animals. There is delightful use of intertextuality here: 'a red tailcoat with no tail, belonging to Squirrel Nutkin; and a very much shrunk jacket belonging to Peter Rabbit'. These references leave gaps to be filled and connections to be made, allowing knowledge gained from reading her other volumes to be used for the satisfaction of the young reader. With all her lost items safely returned, Lucie sets off with Mrs Tiggywinkle to return the laundry to the other customers, including Peter Rabbit and Benjamin Bunny.

The ending of the story is particularly well constructed. As Lucie watches Mrs Tiggywinkle run up the hill she realises that 'Mrs Tiggywinkle was nothing but a HEDGEHOG'. The character of Mrs Tiggywinkle has been so strongly and sympathetically created that it is unthinkable that she should not exist at all. To overcome this difficulty, Potter adds a postscript contained in parentheses and written in tiny print, just like a secret, confirming the existence of Mrs Tiggywinkle through an eye-witness account. Perhaps the realism of Mrs Tiggywinkle owes much to her origins, the drawings being based on one of Beatrix Potter's favourite pets, and her character owing much to Kitty Macdonald, a Scottish Washerwoman employed by the Potters from 1871. HB

Tale of Peter Rabbit, The (1902) The first of BEATRIX POTTER's books for children, published by Frederick Warne after considerable effort by both the author and her friend Canon H.D. Rawsley. Warne agreed to publish the book, insisting that it should be in colour, and not in black-and-white as had originally been intended. Beatrix Potter was equally insistent that it should be sold at a price that 'little rabbits could afford' even though this meant 'losing' some of her original illustrations and accompanying text. However, these were not lost altogether, as two years later she was able to use them in *The Tale of Benjamin Bunny*.

The story contains an amazing range of emotion and excitement. Peter flies in the face of authority, in the form of his mother, who has been cleverly removed from the scene on a trip to the baker. It is a masterpiece of tension-building, with its central chase scene, involving Peter Rabbit and Mr McGregor, extremely well constructed, keeping readers on the edge of their seats. Despite being advised to the contrary, Peter enters Mr McGregor's garden, feasts himself on vegetables, is pursued, almost caught, manages to escape, but without his shoes and 'blue jacket with brass buttons, quite new'. On reaching the safety of home, he is treated with relative kindness by his mother, who wonders (as all mothers would) how he could have lost two sets of clothes in a fortnight, but nevertheless tucks him up in bed and makes him camomile tea for his indigestion – a satisfying and just conclusion.

Peter Rabbit also makes appearances in other Potter tales. He features in *The Tale of Benjamin Bunny* and *The Tale of Mr Tod*. Close observation of the other books reveals that his laundry is done by Mrs Tiggywinkle, that he shops at Ginger and Pickles, and that he has a nursery garden from which he 'lent' cabbages to the father of the Flopsy Bunnies.

The Tale of Benjamin Bunny acts as a sequel to *Peter Rabbit*, the story telling of the attempt to rescue Peter's clothes, which are adorning Mr McGregor's scarecrow. As with all her books, the illustrations show the care that Beatrix Potter gave to detail and exemplify the way in which she carefully mixed FANTASY and reality. The success of the animal characters owes much to the fact that she always drew from real animals; her characters were not people with animal heads.

The theme of escaping from Mr McGregor is continued in *The Tale of the Flopsy Bunnies*, which in many ways is another version of *Peter Rabbit* or *Benjamin Bunny*. What distinguishes this book, however, is the way in which Beatrix Potter uses the sounds of words to such great effect. It is this tale which famously includes 'soporific' in the opening lines. Seen as a trilogy, these books give readers the opportunity to develop character-loyalty and to re-visit familiar characters in new adventures. HB

Tale of Squirrel Nutkin, The (1903) Like many of BEATRIX POTTER's books, this story began life as a letter to Noel Moore. It tells the story of those ultimate childhood crimes – rudeness and disobedience. Nutkin and his friends travel to Owl Island in order to gather nuts. He is uncompromisingly naughty, taunting Old Brown with RIDDLES, until the owl is able to bear this no longer. The squirrel is captured but manages to escape – without his tail. The inclusion of the riddles is cleverly done. The reader is given clues through the careful use of italics, either in the prelude to, or in the piece of text immediately following, the riddle. This use of riddles, as with the NURSERY RHYMES in *THE TAILOR OF GLOUCESTER*, reflects Potter's interest in the language and rhyme of childhood. It also shows her awareness of a variety of devices for involving the reader in the story. Another such device employed effectively in this book is the positioning of words on the page. When Nutkin is caught, the seriousness of the situation is emphasised by the use of italics: '*Nutkin was in his waistcoat pocket!*' This is then followed, equally dramatically, with very few words on an expanse of white page: 'This looks like the end of the story; but it isn't.' Hoping for a happy ending, the reader discovers, on turning the page, that Squirrel Nutkin escapes, but without his tail. The final page, which offers the story as an explanation for squirrels' natural behaviour, makes for a satisfying ending. HB

Tale of the Flopsy Bunnies, The see TALE OF PETER RABBIT, THE

Tales from Shakespear (1807) Short prose adaptations, by CHARLES and MARY LAMB respectively, of six tragedies and 14 comedies. Intended as an introduction to SHAKESPEARE for 'very young children' and 'young ladies', the *Tales* were soon widely translated, and adopted for use in their own right in schools and colleges. They have been frequently, in many cases annually, reprinted, inspiring many successors among both scholars and children's writers such as E. NESBIT and LEON GARFIELD. Recognising the paradoxical nature of their undertaking in 'the necessity of changing many of [Shakespeare's] excellent words into words far less expressive of his true sense', the Lambs tried to retain much of Shakespeare's language. In Charles's hands this resulted in overloaded paragraphs often more difficult than the original text, while Mary, bringing a lighter touch to the comedies, cut plots and characters – especially the 'clowns' – ruthlessly. Since the Lambs' interpretations inevitably reflect the attitudes of their own time, their handling of issues of gender and of race also raises some awkward questions about the way they are offered to children today. In spite of their faults, however, the *Tales* have undoubtedly fulfilled the Lambs' hopes in leading many people to discover Shakespeare's plays for themselves. JFB

Taliesin Court poet of King Urien of Rheged in the 6th century, whose adventures are recounted in *The Mabinogion*. Urien was one of the four North British kings who fought against the Anglo-Saxon rulers of Northumbria. Opinions differ on whether most of Rheged was in what is now southern Scotland or what is now northwest England. The 'North Britons' spoke the language that is now called Welsh and, when the North British kingdoms fell, many of the people resettled in Wales, bringing their poetry and traditions with them. In their legends, Taliesin became a prophet born of water stolen from the Cauldron of Inspiration and Knowledge. His famous harp was credited with magical powers of its own. The story of Taliesin has been retold in *Gwion and the Witch* (1996), a PICTUREBOOK by Jenny Nimmo (see *THE SNOW SPIDER*) and Jac Jones. GHP

scc also WELSH LEGENDS AND FOLKLORE

tall tales Comic stories, mostly American, featuring deliberately exaggerated details and a deadpan delivery. In the United States, tall tales flourished as a literary genre between 1830 and 1860, appearing in newspapers, almanacs, popular plays and songs.

Tall tales usually reflect the concerns and professions of specific geographical regions. Stories about the logger Paul Bunyan and Babe, his great blue ox, are set in Maine, the Old Northwest and the Pacific Northwest, where logging was and is an important industry. Pecos Bill, a cowboy, has his adventures in the American Southwest. Tall tales about DAVY CROCKETT and his hunting ability are set in the old Southwest of Tennessee, Arkansas and Missouri. Febold Feboldson struggles with natural phenomena such as heat, fog, grasshoppers and prairie dogs on the Great Plains. Mike Fink's exploits as a keelboatman take place on the Ohio and Mississippi Rivers. Stories of John Henry, the famous railroad worker, are set in the Allegheny Mountains of western Virginia. Captain Stormalong, the clippership sailing expert, makes his home in New England. Tales about Johnny Appleseed sprang up in the fertile farmland of the Ohio River Valley.

The characters are often portrayed as larger-than-life to suggest their super-human abilities; Paul Bunyan, for example, is gigantic. The tall-tale heroes, besides being able to sail, hammer, fight, hunt or chop better than any other person, also help shape the landscape of the United States. Many tales explain geographic features such as the Great Lakes or the Grand Canyon as the result of a hero's exploits or embarrassments.

The tall tale has been an important aspect of American oral folk culture, establishing community and distinguishing members of the community from outsiders through humour and exaggeration. EBD

Tam Lin The story of Tam Lin, which dates back to the 14th century, may be found in F.J. Childe's *English and Scottish Ballads* (1857–8). Tam Lin is carried off to Elfland by the Fairy Queen, to be used at the end of seven years to pay the teind (tax) to hell. However, he is saved by Janet, who has to keep hold of him while he is turned into a snake, a deer, and hot iron, until at last he is restored to his old self.

Andrew Lang's *The Gold of Fairnilee* (1888) incorporates certain of its elements, although Randal, the Tam Lin figure, is (by comparison, tamely) changed by the Fairy Queen only into a dwarf and is restored by Jean's thrice making the sign of the cross. ELIZABETH MARIE POPE's *The Perilous Gard*, which unlike Lang's adaptation does not gloss over the darker aspects of the tale – such as the threat of human sacrifice – is a noteworthy reshaping of the story. Set in the last days of Mary Tudor, the novel's characters are immensely likeable, and the bare narrative outline is also fleshed out in a very satisfactory way. Both DIANA WYNNE JONES and Pamela Dean, in *FIRE AND HEMLOCK* (1985) and *Tam Lin* (1991) respectively, give modern settings to the story, Wynne Jones's work managing to be both a recognisable reworking and a blending of 'Tam Lin' and 'Thomas the Rhymer' (a ballad sharing some elements with 'Tam Lin') and an original FANTASY in its own right. It has also been noted by Neil Philip in *A Fine Anger* (1981) that the Tom–Jan relationship in ALAN GARNER's *Red Shift* may be illuminated by referencing it against the Tam Lin story, except that in Garner's novel, Jan is unable to keep hold of Tom during his (metaphorical) transformations. SA

Tan, Shaun 1974– Australian illustrator, writer and editor, whose illustrations for *The Viewer* (1997), written by GARY CREW, won the 1998 Children's Book Council Crichton Award for new PICTUREBOOK illustrators. Art director of *Eidolon*, a SCIENCE FICTION magazine, Tan's keen interest in this genre is evident in his experimental and unconventional approach to picturebook design. Tan admits to an interest in 'seeking out the strangeness in familiar things', and pushing up the 'voltage' between words and pictures as separate reactive elements. This is exemplified magnificently in his illustrations for JOHN MARSDEN's *The Rabbits* (1998), an allegory about the European invasion of Australia, where his surreal and often visually sombre images, which draw on the style of 19th-century art, achieve multiple layers of meaning. In quite a different approach and style, Tan uses COLLAGE and mixed media – including wood, metal, glass and leaves – in his illustrations for GARY CREW's *Memorial* (1999), a reflection on war and communal memory through the metaphor of a huge old tree about to be cut down. Tan has also illustrated a number of short stories in the *After Dark* series, including his own novel, *The Playground* (1998). JAP

Tanglewood Tales see HAMMAT BILLINGS; CLASSICAL MYTHOLOGY; NATHANIEL HAWTHORNE

Tanner, (Barbara) Jane 1946– Australian illustrator whose aim – 'to achieve a feeling of denseness, depth and monumentality' – has underpinned her acclaimed interpretations of many PICTUREBOOK texts. *There's a Sea in my Bedroom* (1984), written by MARGARET WILD, which traces a young boy's coming to terms with his fear of the water within the safety of a FANTASY in his own room, is graphically realistic, an approach which involves Tanner in considerable research, including taking photographs. Tanner shows a deep awareness of a story's rhythms and sub-text, powerfully exemplified in *Drac and the Gremlin* (1988), written by ALLAN BAILLIE, which won the CHILDREN'S BOOK COUNCIL OF AUSTRALIA Picturebook of the Year Award in 1989. This book gained immediate acceptance by children, who can relate to the topic of two young children engaged in adventurous role play in their suburban garden. While the words soar into the imagination, the illustrations, with their discerning use of angles, are firmly grounded in reality. For

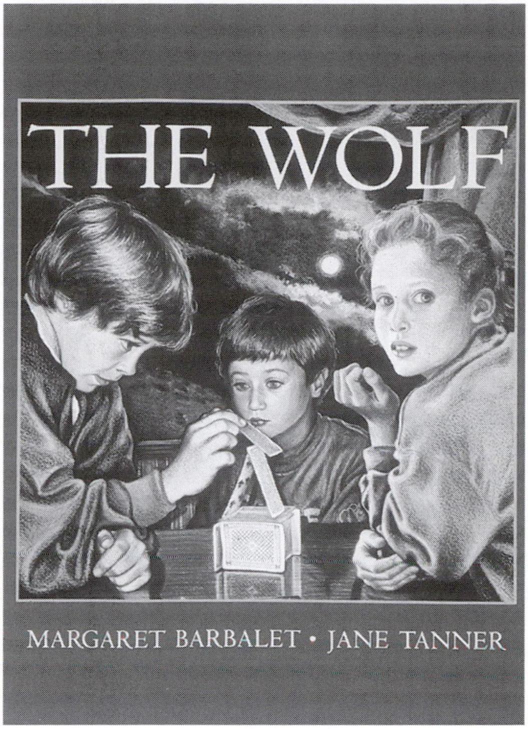

Cover by Jane Tanner of *The Wolf* by Margaret Barbalet.

Margaret Barbalet's psychological thriller, *THE WOLF* (1991), Tanner plays with darkness and light to reveal subtle changes of the characters' inner feelings. Contrasts of dark and light are also used in *THE FISHERMAN AND THE THEEFYSPRAY* (1994), written by PAUL JENNINGS. Tanner's use of rich colour and command of textures adds to the emotional power of this thoughtful story. JAP

Tarka the Otter (1927) Novel by Henry Williamson (1895–1977) about the birth, life and death of an otter, set, with extraordinarily accurate detail, around the rivers and landscape of North Devon. Extending the tradition of detailed observation of the countryside established by Gilbert White and, particularly, Richard Jefferies, Williamson builds up a graphic, compelling sense of his animal protagonists that relies on a minimum of anthropomorphic sentiment. Drama – indeed an almost epic quality – is imbued into the life-history through a succession of otter hunts that impart an heroic sense of the animal and its eventual, moving death. DWh

Tarkington, [Newton] Booth 1869–1946 American author whose interest in the way children think and the reasons behind their behaviour is especially apparent in *Little Orvie* (1934), *Seventeen* (1902) and the

PENROD SERIES (1914–29). In these books he examines different stages of childhood, and the contradictions that attend growth and maturation, in a comic style that is still fresh and amusing. Tarkington is particularly interested in relationships between children and their parents, their pets and their peers. A theme which is always present is the absolute impossibility of understanding between generations, even though both sides may be well-intentioned. Children and adults are simply too different for either group to appreciate what motivates the other. At seven, the title character of *Little Orvie* does not realise that adults can know calamity, 'because they were grown people, all powerful and therefore impervious'. On the other hand, Willie Baxter's parents, in *Seventeen*, are nonplussed over their son's constant devotion to a vain and shallow young woman whose vocabulary does not extend beyond baby talk. Although Tarkington more frequently focuses on boys than girls, characters like the imperturbable Jane Baxter in *Seventeen*, and the offensively perfect Little Marie in *Little Orvie*, are memorable, while Cornelia, in *Women* (1925), demonstrates the same sort of intense but misplaced affection in her experience of first love that characterises Willie Baxter. Tarkington's depiction of ethnicity reflects the common attitudes and vocabulary of his time. WH

Taronga (1986) Novel by Australian author VICTOR KELLEHER, which follows a theme noticeable in a number of his other works, namely life after an apocalyptic event. In *Taronga* this is called Last Days, and has left survivors to eke out an existence without many of the essentials formerly taken for granted. This new world is apparently divided into two distinct groups – those whose daily existence is a hazardous affair, and those who are fortunate to live within the safe and secure confines of Taronga Zoo. Kelleher raises many questions about the fragility of human existence as we know it, good versus evil, and the ease with which the niceties of human behaviour disappear under pressure. SAM

Tarrant, Margaret Winifred 1888–1959 One of a number of British women illustrators of the 20th century who appealed to the romantic culture of the inter-war years. Tarrant's first illustrated book was an edition of KINGSLEY's *THE WATER-BABIES* in 1908. Following this she worked with Marion St John Webb illustrating her stories about fairies such as *The Heath Fairies* (1927). In 1936 Tarrant travelled to Palestine where she collected material which was used to show children in religious settings, particularly in postcards published by the Medici Society. She also illustrated NURSERY RHYMES in vibrant watercolours capturing the essence of the verses. SM

Tartar, Maria see CRITICAL APPROACHES TO CHILDREN'S LITERATURE

Tarzan (John Clayton III, Lord Greystoke) Fictional character and cultural icon created by American author Edgar Rice Burroughs (1875–1950). Burroughs began publishing *Tarzan of the Apes* in *All-Story Magazine* in October 1912. It was an overwhelming success, spawning a hardcover book in 1914 and a highly profitable film in 1918. Burroughs wrote 25 *Tarzan* novels. Other authors, including Fritz Leiber and Philip José Farmer, have also written *Tarzan* novels.

Tarzan's story begins when his parents, John and Alice Clayton, become stranded in the African jungle. Alice dies after giving birth and John is soon killed by a great ape. A female ape adopts the baby, giving him the name Tarzan. Tarzan grows up a jungle hero, learning about humans through his late father's belongings left in the jungle. After a series of adventures illustrating the theme of civilisation versus nature and popular scientific theory of the time, Tarzan is reunited with his human family, becomes Lord Greystoke, and marries Jane Porter. Later books chronicle Tarzan's further adventures. The novels display a depth and complexity of character and theme unusual for this mode of writing. There have been radio series, four live-action and animated TELEVISION series, approximately 86 live-action and animated films, and several comic-strip series detailing Tarzan's exploits. ELPB

***Tashi* series** see ANNA FIENBERG; see also KIM GAMBLE

Tashjian, Virginia 1921– American writer of juvenile FOLK TALES. Born in Massachusetts, Tashjian is of Armenian descent, and it is the folk heritage of that country which she tries to preserve and pass on through her writing. Working as a librarian and involved in numerous library associations, Tashjian's life has revolved around books. Her first publication was *Sing and Pray: A Book of Armenian Hymns and Prayers* (1961). Seeing herself as more of a storyteller than an author, she wrote the award-winning *Once There Was and Was Not* (1966), based on stories by Hovhannes Toumanian, which her mother had told her as a child, and *Three Little Apples* (1971), both illustrated by NONNY HOGROGIAN. She also put together selections of rhymes, songs, poems and RIDDLES designed for group work with young children, including *Juba This and Juba That* (1969), illustrated by Victoria de Larrea, and *With a Deep Sea Smile* (1974), illustrated by ROSEMARY WELLS. Tashjian has also written DRAMA, such as *Miller-King* (1971), and articles for *Armenian Weekly*, *Boston Globe* and *Washington Post*. Her writing is most notable for its air of wisdom and quiet humour, and for its making accessible to the English-speaking world some of the rich body of Armenian folklore.

SCWA

Taylor, Ann 1782–1866 and **Taylor, Jane** 1783–1824 English writers. The sisters were born into an industrious, nonconformist, literary family living at various times in London, Lavenham and Ongar. Together they wrote three collections of poetry which sold in large numbers and influenced children's poetry in a more child-centred direction. Harvey Darton described *Original Poems for Infant Minds* (1804) as 'the book that awoke the nurseries of England'; it was followed by *Rhymes for the Nursery* (1806) and *Hymns for Infant Minds* (1810), the latter producing £150 profit for the sisters in its first year. They also wrote *The World Turned Upside Down* (1810) and other minor works. Their collaboration ended with Ann's marriage in 1813.

Ann's most popular poem, 'My Mother' (wickedly parodied by Thomas Hood) was sold in many versions throughout the 19th century, while Jane's 'Twinkle, twinkle, little star, / How I wonder what you are' is now part of western culture. Their contribution to children's literature was important and lasting. Poems like 'The Kind Mamma' and 'The Baby's Dance' ('Dance little baby, dance up high, / Never mind baby, mother is by') explored the affectionate relationship between mothers and babies as no one had done before, a theme which Christina Rossetti would bring to high art in *Sing-Song* (1872).

MCCS

Taylor, Clark see drugs in children's books

Taylor, Cora 1936– Award-winning Canadian writer, born in Fort Qu'Appele, Saskatchewan. After attending the University of Alberta, she became a teacher and raised a family. In her first novel, *Julie* (1985), Julie Morgan's psychic ability allows her to move back and forth in time to see sights such as sailing ships, and buffalo stampedes on the Canadian prairies. In the sequel, *Julie's Secret* (1991), Julie moves outside the realm of innocence to confront the presence of evil. *The Doll* (1992) is a blend of fantasy and prairie social history; while *Ghost Voyages* (1992) is a time-slip fantasy. *Summer of the Mad Monk* (1994) is based upon the historical Rasputin. *Vanishing Act* (1997) is a mystery. Taylor's subjects include family and marriage breakdown, physical illness and fear of identity loss. She won the 1985 Canada Council Children's Literature Prize for *Julie*. Awards for *Summer of the Mad Monk* include the Mr Christie's Book Award, the Canadian Library Association Award, and the Children's Book of the Year Award.

MRS

Taylor, Helen see *There's a Poet Behind You*

Taylor, Marilyn 1940– Novelist, born in London and subsequently living in Dublin. Working as a school librarian and observing the popularity of teen fiction series, she wrote a series set around the lives of a group of young Dubliners. Her three titles – *Could This Be Love? I Wondered* (1994), *Could I Love a Stranger?* (1995) and *Call Yourself a Friend?* (1996) – explore social issues and show more depth and development in their central characters than is usual in such series. *Faraway Home* (1999) – winner of the 1999/2000 CBI/Bisto Award – is based upon the true story of the evacuation of young Jewish refugees to Northern Ireland during World War II.

VC

Taylor, Mildred 1943– African American writer who produces both suspenseful bestsellers and unforgettable award-winning books, the result of an accessible writing style, rich storytelling power, and the ability to address important themes about the historical American black experience.

A strong father–daughter relationship prompted Mildred Taylor to produce, as her major body of work, a fictional saga of the Logan family. The series currently includes seven books (three novels and several illustrated storybooks), nearly all of which are centred on a young African American girl living in Mississippi in the 1930s, Cassie Logan. The most famous is *Roll of Thunder, Hear My Cry* (1976), a Newbery Award winner and companion volume to the much shorter works, *Song of the Trees* (1975), *The Friendship* (1987) and *Mississippi Bridge* (1990). Taylor has also produced two sequels to *Roll of Thunder*, both of which won the Coretta Scott King Award: *Let the Circle Be Unbroken* (1981) and *The Road to Memphis* (1990), as well as a prequel to the entire group, *The Well* (1995), a short work about David Logan, Cassie's father, when he was a child. David, as well as Stacey Logan, Cassie's older brother, are both based on Taylor's own father, Wilbert Lee Taylor, whom Mildred remembers as a master storyteller, and the one who supplied her with so many of the tales for this saga. (Only *The Gold Cadillac*, 1987, set in Toledo, where she moved from Mississippi as an infant, is based on the author's own childhood experiences.)

Taylor's father also taught her to question discrimination and to value strong family ties. In her Newbery acceptance speech of 1977, she told of the trips back from Ohio to the 'rich farm country of Mississippi' where she was born, where relatives would gather and tell the stories she would later retell in her own children's books. Those stories encompassed 'a history of Black people' and if readers believe her books to be biographical, the reason is that she has tried 'to distill the essence of Black life, so familiar to most Black families [and] to make the Logans an embodiment of that spiritual heritage'.

In the stories that Taylor had read as a child in her history books, there was nothing about the 'small and often dangerous triumphs of Black people', nothing about 'human pride and survival in a cruelly racist society'. There were no black heroes in her books, only the tales of a 'docile, subservient people happy with their fate who did little or nothing to shatter the chains that bound them, both before and after slavery'. Books about black families were often written by white writers who did not understand the black experience nor the 'principles upon which Black parents brought up their children and taught them survival'.

Knowing this ethnic experience so well, she felt driven to 'paint a truer picture of Black people . . . to show the endurance of the Black world, with strong fathers and concerned mothers . . . [and] happy, loved children'. Years later, after Taylor completed a stint in the Peace Corps and attended graduate school, she found a way to fulfill her literary quest. One year, an alter ego in the form of a 'spunky eight-year-old, innocent, untouched by discrimination, full of pride, and greatly loved' appeared in Taylor's mind. The child's name was Cassie Logan, 'and through her I discovered I now could tell one of the stories I had heard so often as a child,' Taylor says.

Song of the Trees was the result, and in writing it she discovered how she could incorporate the teachings and family stories of her childhood. She also found that she could interweave factual events that she had heard and read about with her own feelings from earlier days. Taylor went on to produce the Logan family saga to fulfill her hope of 'teaching children of all colors the tremendous influence that Cassie's generation – [Mildred's] father's generation – had in bringing about the great Civil Rights movement of the fifties and sixties'. Without understanding that generation, she says, today's children will never understand the rights they now have. If children can relate to the Logans, 'perhaps they can better understand and respect themselves and others'.

Self-respect – developing it and maintaining it in the face of the intimidation and harassment that prevails in this time and place for black people – is a major theme running through all these books. The three larger novels of the saga present Cassie at ages nine, 11 and 17 learning more and more about how institutionalised racism leads to inequities and injustices for black people. For Taylor, their only weapon in this struggle, she sees, is their strong belief in the importance of family and in the black community as extended family (taking care of one's own).

In *Roll of Thunder, Hear My Cry* when Stacey's friend T.J. is facing an angry crowd of white supremacist males, David Logan sacrifices the one thing that gives him self-respect in this era, his land. Thus he saves T.J. from being lynched. (The men rush away to save the Logan land; in doing so, they save their own adjacent farms.) In *Let The Circle Be Unbroken*, when Stacey is recruited for excruciatingly hard labour in the sugar cane fields of Louisiana, the Logan family, after ceaseless searching, makes the long journey to retrieve him and save his life.

In *The Road to Memphis*, when their friend Moe must escape to Chicago after an interracial fight, Cassie and Stacey have to take to the road, with all the racial harassment that highway travel in the early 1940s entailed, in order to save him. This time they are aided by their ever-present white friend, Jeremy Simms. Pale, shy, tow-headed Jeremy, who becomes an expert liar early in life in order to do what is right, realises his talents are crucial for helping his friends. But to do so, he, like Moe, must sacrifice home and community, thus exemplifying the no-win situation of racism, for both blacks and whites. NM

Taylor, Theodore see BIAS IN CHILDREN'S BOOKS; *THE CAY*; see also ROBINSONNADES

Taylor, William 1938– Prolific New Zealand novelist, former primary-school principal and Mayor of Ohakune. Born in Lower Hutt, Taylor had already written six adult novels before he became a full-time writer for children in 1986. His first books, *Pack Up, Pick Up and Off* (1986) and *Shooting Through* (1987), drew on his passion for outdoor life. With *Possum Perkins* (1987), which deals with incest, he found his voice as a serious writer especially sympathetic to society's young victims and underdogs in small-town life. With *The Worst Soccer Team Ever* series (1987–9), *Agnes the Sheep* (1991), *Annie & Co and Marilyn Monroe* (1995), and the trilogy of *Knitwits* (1992), *Numbskulls* (1995) and *Hark the Herald Angel* (1997), his abilities as a gifted comic writer were fully realised. His work is characterised by its precise, sparse language, a wide range of characters observed with a sometimes acerbic wit, and an unfailing sense of structure. Among his serious young adult books, *The Blue Lawn* (1994) broke new ground in New Zealand as a compassionate study of a (possibly) gay friendship between two teenage boys, while *Circles* (1996) further extended his range into (partly) HISTORICAL FICTION. He has also written short stories and has pleaded effectively for the status of comic writing in children's literature. TD

Te Kura Pounamu Maori Book Award see APPENDIX

Teddy Tail Cartoon character. Created by the famous artist CHARLES FOLKARD, Teddy Tail – a besuited mouse – began his adventures in the British *Daily Mail* children's section on 5 April 1915, went missing during World War II, and then returned, drawn by Arthur

'Spot' Potts. The best-remembered artist, however, is Herbert Foxwell, who had been drawing *Tiger Tim* for the *Rainbow* comic, and was lured by the *Mail* to draw their comic supplement from 1933 until 1939. There were many *Teddy Tail* books of reprints running from 1915 to 1926, followed later by the delightful *Teddy Tail Annual* (1934–42), revived after the war from 1945 until 1962. Young readers could also join the Teddy Tail League; the pre-war coloured badge is currently a highly desirable collectors' item. DG

see also COMICS; ANNUALS

Teenage Mutant Ninja Turtles see TELEVISION

teenage fiction see YOUNG ADULT FICTION

Teletubbies Popular but controversial educational TELEVISION programme for pre-nursery children created by Anne Wood and Andrew Davenport. Developed as educational programming for infants, *Teletubbies* was first transmitted in England on the BBC in 1997 and subsequently on PBS in the United States in 1998.

Living in the pastoral Teletubbyland, surrounded by rabbits and talking flowers, the four Teletubbies – each with a distinctive personality – communicate in simple language which imitates the speech patterns of a one-year-old. The baby talk of the Teletubbies has raised concerns by some adults, although only 15 per cent of the programme is delivered in this language. Each Teletubby has a television screen on his/her stomach which allows them to view short, live-action programmes of real children, at the end of which the group demands, 'Again, again', and the segment is repeated. Living in an adult-free world that combines FANTASY with contemporary technology, the Teletubbies directly address and interact with the audience, share frequent group 'big hugs', and are reluctant to say goodbye at the end of the programme.

The largest and most gentle Teletubby is Tinky Winky, who is purple and has a handbag which he takes with him on walks. Dipsy is green and the second largest character; he frequently wears a top hat and is the most accomplished dancer of the group. Laa-Laa is the most cheerful and group-oriented Teletubby and likes playing with her ball. Po is red, the smallest and most independent Teletubby, who enjoys riding her scooter.

Teletubbies acknowledges that many very young children watch television and attempts to provide entertaining and educational programming for them through frequent and carefully researched use of repetition, large movements, bright colours and deliberate pacing. The programme boldly defies its detractors in its serious concern to provide for its very young viewers. JCS

television for children In the United States television programmes for children were first aired in the 1940s and 50s. Most of the early programmes were live and many were regional productions. These were entertaining half-hour slots led by a star performer with a supporting cast and often performed before a studio audience. *Howdy Doody Show* (1947–60) was the first nationally recognised success, featuring Buffalo Bob Smith as the master of ceremonies, the marionette Howdy Doody, and other comic characters, as well as a children's audience called 'The Peanut Gallery'. Other shows from this era were *Kukla, Fran, and Ollie* (1948–57) with Burr Tillstrom's puppetry; *The Ding Dong School* (1952–6), created by educator Frances Horwich; *Sky King* (1951–66), a western featuring aerial photography of the Flying Crown Ranch; and science experiments with Don Herbert as *Mr Wizard* (1951–65, 1971–2). WALT DISNEY's important television contribution was the *Mickey Mouse Club* (1955–9), featuring the talented Mouseketeers and popular Disney animation and live-action films.

The three most prominent personalities in 1960s children's television were Walt Disney, Bob Keeshan and Fred Rogers. Disney hosted the Sunday evening, hour-long show *Walt Disney's Wonderful World of Color* (1959–81), which featured serialised stories, scientific and live-action films, and animation. Keeshan, who began as Clarabell the clown on *Howdy Doody*, hosted *Captain Kangaroo* (1955–81); the hour-long morning show combined amusing skits, cartoons, puppetry, art, and children's books. One of the first important children's shows on non-commercial television was *Mister Rogers' Neighborhood*, a reworking of Rogers's 1954 *Children's Corner*. The *Neighborhood* first appeared in 1965 with dual sets of Mister Rogers's home and a make-believe puppet kingdom.

In 1962, Congress passed the Educational TV Facilities Act which prompted the development of public broadcasting in which many important children's shows originated. In 1970, the Public Broadcasting System (PBS) was formed. The Children's Television Workshop became a major force on PBS with the début in 1969 of *SESAME STREET*, a fast-paced, hour-long show for children ranging from pre-school to first-graders. Its working-class, urban neighbourhood set and multicultural cast tried to encourage learning and appeal to a diverse audience. Jim Henson's puppets include favourites such as Ernie and Burt, the Cookie Monster, Oscar the Grouch and Big Bird.

On commercial television, much of children's programming in the 1960s and 70s appeared in the form of cartoons with advertisements aimed at children. Hanna-Barbera's *The Flintstones* (1960–6), set in a Neanderthal suburb, was a successful early prime-time cartoon. Charles Schulz brought his newspaper comic strip to television with a series of *CHARLIE BROWN* specials. Saturday mornings were usually devoted to cartoons, such as Jay Ward's *The Bullwinkle Show* (1961–73), *Scooby-Doo* (1969–72) and programmes featuring various SUPERHEROES.

In the 1960s and 70s, parents and researchers became concerned about the violence and inanity which children could view. Television was blamed for anti-social behaviour, shorter attention spans and reduced test scores. The controversy continued with investigations into television and child behaviour. To remedy these problems, Congress and the Federal Communications Commission – which oversees broadcasters – has tried to legislate on the air-time and content of children's programming. Peggy Charren, founder of Action for Children's Television, had advocated improving children's programming for decades when she finally succeeded with the Children's Television Act of 1990.

Some parents and teachers advocate little television-viewing, or none at all; for others, television and pre-recorded videos have become surrogate baby-sitters. Children often watch adult fare including SOAP OPERAS, wrestling, music videos, sit-coms or talk shows. In the 1990s, networks decided to self-regulate with a rating system similar to that employed by the film industry, and politicians discussed the V-chip as a way of enabling parents to prevent violent shows being shown on family sets.

In the 1980s, PBS continued its innovative children's television programming. LaVar Burton began hosting *READING RAINBOW* (from 1981), which features children's books. SHARI LEWIS, the ventriloquist, introduced her puppet Lamb Chop in 1957 on *Captain Kangaroo* and soon had her own network television programme. She attained success in the 1960s, and found popularity again on PBS in the 1980s. PBS stations scheduled large time-blocks for young children's programmes in the morning and programmes for elementary children in the afternoon. Programming for older children is often difficult as they reject overtly educational content.

Both PBS and commercial networks found that marketing products connected to shows increased revenues and reinforced their impact and ratings. Products have included books, games, toys, clothes and movies. Popular network and syndicated cross-marketed programmes in the 1980s and 90s included *Teenage Mutant Ninja Turtles* (1987–96), *The Smurfs* (from 1981) based on Belgian comics, and *Mighty Morphin Power Rangers* (from 1993), which originated in Japan.

As cable television segmented into audience-specific networks, Nickelodeon started the first network for children. Nickelodeon developed its own programming for many age levels featuring a mix of non-violent cartoons, sit-coms, game shows and educational shows. Some cable channels devoted mornings to children's shows, while the Disney channel became a home for re-runs of its movies and television shows as well as new programming.

In the 1990s, PBS continued airing important shows for children. *Where in the World is Carmen Sandiego?* (from 1994) challenges middle-schoolers with a geography quiz based on Broderbund's computer game. The experiments of *Bill Nye the Science Guy* (from 1993) are aired on PBS and Disney. *BARNEY AND FRIENDS* (from 1989) features a large purple dinosaur singing heart-warming tunes with children on a nursery school set. The BBC has begun broadcasting several of its popular shows on PBS, including *Shining Time Station* with *THOMAS THE TANK ENGINE* (from 1984), based on W. Awdry's series, and the technologically friendly *TELETUBBIES* (from 1998) for children under two.

In Britain, one or two experimental programmes for children were transmitted in the pre-war period, labelled 'for the youngsters', while some other shows had obvious appeal for young viewers. These included regular visits to the Regents Park Zoo with David Seth-Smith, who had many years' experience on BBC radio's *Children's Hour*, and West End comedian Richard Hearne, who appeared in walrus whiskers as 'Mr Pastry' and eventually became a post-war television star in many series for children.

Children's television as a separate service for British children began with the BBC's opening of their new children's production unit (a conversion of the former Lime Grove film studios) in 1950. There were three cameras and equipment was largely rudimentary and in short supply. Very few of the production team, including actors, had any television experience and there was inevitably a substantial crossover from radio in many of the early programmes. The weekday afternoon series *WATCH WITH MOTHER* was modelled on radio's *LISTEN WITH MOTHER*; characters such as Larry the Lamb came from the radio programme *Toytown*, while *MUFFIN THE MULE* graduated from theatre. Nevertheless there was considerable ambition and innovation in early programme development for children's television: full-scale original productions of *THE RAILWAY CHILDREN* and *THE SECRET GARDEN* were broadcast live under these conditions.

With the appointment of Freda Lingstrom as Head of Children's Television in 1951, there was a move towards an increasing professionalisation of the television output. Lingstrom had moved across from schools programmes and was determined to develop within the new medium a distinctive child-centred style which was not overly educational in intention and did not treat children like small adults. She is best known as the creator, with her colleague and companion Maria Bird, of *Andy Pandy* and *The Flowerpot Men* for the *Watch With Mother* series. Although innovative and widely respected, she was also passionate about 'correct' standards and helped set both a house style and an agenda for BBC children's programmes – which left it vulnerable to the charge of élitism and to competition from commercial television when this was licensed from 1955. She had a deep disdain for anything she regarded as tasteless or which had a hint of commercialism about it. Prior to Lingstrom's appointment, plans had been discussed for screening some of ENID BLYTON's stories and W.E. John's *BIGGLES* books; but such forays into the realm of popular literary culture were unthinkable to her. It was not until 1992 that Enid Blyton's *NODDY* was finally admitted within the ranks of the BBC's children's programmes.

By the late 1950s most of the genres which were to define children's television in Britain were well established. The dramatised school story was represented by *Billy Bunter* and *JENNINGS*. It was not until the late 1970s that this genre was prised out of its traditional private school setting, however, with the advent of the more realistic and demotic *GRANGE HILL* (from 1977), devised by Phil Redmond. *Grange Hill* itself influenced a number of drama series aimed at slightly older children which attempted to take up contentious issues realistically from a child perspective. These have included *Press Gang* (Central), *Children's Ward* (Granada) and *Byker Grove* (Zenith North for the BBC). A version of soap opera for children was launched in the 1950s with *The Appleyards*, though more recently children's interest in this genre has tended to be taken up with early evening 'family' soaps, such as the Australian produced *Neighbours* and *Home and Away*. Children's magazine programmes and game shows (*Whirligig*, 1950; *Crackerjack*, 1955; *Blue Peter*, 1958 (see *THE BLUE PETER BOOK*)) made their first appearance in the 1950s, as did information programmes on current issues, although the first regular news programme for children did not appear until the ground-breaking *John Craven's Newsround* (BBC) was launched in 1972. Animal programmes (*Zoo Time*, 1956; *Animal Magic*, 1962), animation and puppet series, together with drama based on children's literature, have also figured strongly since the earliest period of children's television. An interesting feature of some children's programmes, at least since the 1960s, has been their potential to engage a cult following of viewers considerably beyond the age group for which the programmes were originally intended. *Thunderbirds* (1965), *THE MAGIC ROUNDABOUT* (1965) and, more recently, *Teletubbies*, all fall into this category, while perhaps the most spectacularly successful of all series, DOCTOR WHO, succeeded in creating an audience within which age was practically irrelevant.

Cultural change, commercial competition and the availability of different kinds of children's programmes from other countries – particularly the United States – have led to some quite profound changes in the presentational style and attitudes conveyed within most of the genres of children's television. When independent television was first licensed in 1955, its policy was to attract a child audience particularly through broadcasting popular westerns and adventure series. Many of these – such as *Roy Rogers*, *Hop Along Cassidy*, RIN TIN TIN and *LASSIE* – were bought in from the United States, though the most popular of ITV's early series had a more home-grown subject in *The Adventures of Robin Hood* (1957) (see ROBIN HOOD), starring Richard Greene. When Owen Reed took over as Head of the Children's Department at the BBC in 1956, he responded to the steady leaching of child audience numbers to ITV by gradually building up the proportion of drama programmes. He also started to buy in, from what was perceived to be the quality end of American children's broadcasting, series such as *Champion the Wonder Horse*. A similar process of evolution and debate over style and values took place in the 1970s when the BBC refused an option to broadcast the innovative American children's programme *Sesame Street*, partly on the grounds that its fast-cutting, visually arresting style was derived from advertising and was felt to be incompatible with the production values and more reflective quality of the BBC's children's output. *Sesame Street* was eventually transmitted to British audiences by London Weekend Television and later by Channel 4.

Perhaps the oldest, and at first sight least likely, genre to have been transferred to the television medium was the traditional, orally delivered story. In the early period of children's television a considerable amount of time was given over to STORYTELLING in this mode, often making relatively little use of the visual medium. No doubt the fact that this form was simple and cheap to produce was part of its attraction, but storytelling on television has maintained its appeal for generations of young viewers despite the competition of more visceral stimulation from other programmes. *JACKANORY* (from 1965) in particular, though it began only as a short-term experiment, managed to attract hundreds of well-known actors and actresses to perform in its storytelling slot over a period of 30 years. As the technology for reading from autocue became more sophisticated, so the dramatic context of the storytelling began to be exploited in more complex ways using film inserts, more elaborate sets and so on. The stories were generally accompanied by pictures and the programmes gradually became showcases for a range of distinguished illustrators such as QUENTIN BLAKE, Gareth Floyd and Barry Wilkinson. Other programmes with substantial elements of storytelling have included *Picturebook*, *Playschool*, and *The Hot Chestnut Man* (1955) presented by Johnny Morris.

Children's television in Britain has maintained a particularly strong relationship with children's literature. In addition to traditional storytelling, the BBC in particular has been committed to producing dramatisations of classic and historically based fiction, as well as a range of significant works by contemporary children's authors. Many classic adaptations such as *Great Expectations*, *The Secret Garden*, *Little Women* and *Treasure Island* were produced from the inception of children's television in the 1950s, alongside specially commissioned series such as *Paradise Walk* and *A Long Way Home*.

The high cost of setting up a production has always meant that series and serialisations have been heavily favoured over single-episode dramatisations. For many years the prime slot for such serialisations was the BBC's Sunday afternoon programming, where classic serials particularly came to figure as a central, and shared, cultural experience for many British families. The Sunday serial tradition was continued when, during the mid-1960s, all drama production was shifted to the Drama Department at the BBC and much less new drama was aimed specifically at children (though a separate production unit for children's drama was revived and grew steadily from around 1968). From the late 1980s onwards, however, the costs of producing period drama for a mixed adult/child audience began to be perceived as prohibitive: *Vanity Fair* (1987) was one of the last classic serials produced for the family entertainment Sunday afternoon slot. Notable productions have included Nina Bawden's *Carrie's War* (1974) and C.S. Lewis's *The Chronicles of Narnia* series, produced using the latest special-effects technology during the 1980s. While increasingly sophisticated special-effects have extended film producers' capacity to reproduce magical elements within children's fantasy narratives (see also *The Borrowers*), expectations of realism have also expanded as studio production has tended to be replaced by location shooting in children's television drama. Ultimately the quality of productions is not dependent on technology but, combined with cultural change, this has undoubtedly produced some profound shifts in the style and texture of experience available to contemporary children through the medium of television.

A national television service for Canada was launched in 1952 when the Canadian Broadcasting Corporation (CBC) began regular programming from Montreal and Toronto. The first children's programme – the French production of *Pepinot & Capucine* – was dubbed in French and English. A schedule emerged with the addition of a children's newsreel, an audience-participation programme called *Children's Corner*, and an evening magazine entitled *Let's See*, featuring the hugely popular Uncle Chichimus. From the beginning, drama presentations were a central concern. Following the precedent of the BBC, the CBC undertook the dramatisation of classic novels and stories, including Jules Verne's *Twenty Thousand Leagues Under the Sea*, Wilkie Collins's *The Moonstone*, and the Canadian author Thomas Raddell's *Roger Sudden*. The first original dramatic series was *Space Command*, of which more than 150 episodes were transmitted in the CBC's first year of broadcasting.

In 1954, Fred Rainsberry, supervising producer of children's television at CBC Toronto, developed a policy that emphasised the enlightenment and enrichment of Canadian children. Rainsberry insisted that the American-inspired *Howdy Doody Show* be rewritten and recast to fit child-development goals set by CBC. The Canadian version was less chaotic and encouraged problem-solving and learning. In fact, the informal education of young viewers has been a goal of CBC English-language television through to the present day. *The Friendly Giant* (1958–86), created and hosted by Bob Homme, encouraged a respect for words and music, a love of listening and a concern for others. Another long-running programme, *Chez Hélène* (1959–73), hosted by the folk-singer Hélène Baillargeon, introduced pre-school children to the French language through stories, songs and games.

When, in the early 1960s, CTV began to compete with CBC for the children's television market, CBC discovered that the best way to hold a child audience was with a daily magazine show. *Junior Magazine* and *Razzle Dazzle* presented a community of young people who were friends of the viewer. *Razzle Dazzle* had over half a million viewers every day and there were over 100,000 members of the *Razzle Dazzle Club*. The period was also noteworthy for the CBC's diminished reliance on outside programming; in-house productions such as *Homemade TV*, *Butternut Square* and the Canadian legend *Mr Dressup* accounted for 85 per cent of the children's schedule.

In 1966, when Dan McCarthy took over children's programmes, budget pressures required CBC to relax policy and purchase syndicated American films such as *Sesame Street*; and in the 1970s the new head, Dodie Robb, devoted her even more limited funds to an hour-long weekly drama. The series *W.O.W.* (*Wonderful One-of-a-kind Weekend Show*), included original drama and opera. At this time, The Ontario Education Communications Authority (later known as TVOntario or TVO), Canada's first full-time educational television station, originated its longest-running series, *Polka Dot Door*, as well as *Today's Special*, *Cucumber* and *Monkey Bars*, which combined information and entertainment for out-of-school viewing.

By 1982, educational broadcasters such as TVO, the Knowledge Network, Radio Quebec and ACCESS Alberta moved in to fill what they perceived as a cultural and informational gap in the Canadian broadcasting system. Meanwhile, at CBC, Nada Harcourt, Head of Children's Programming, looked to private film companies to co-produce programming for children. One result was *The Kids of Degrassi Street*, a series dealing with issues such as divorcing parents, weight concerns and social dilemmas. In 1988 it became Canada's top-rated series with up to 1.9 million viewers. At about the same time pre-school programming re-emerged as a priority; in 1985, CBC introduced *Fred Penner's Place*, a 15-minute music-based educational programme for young viewers. Co-productions *Under the Umbrella Tree* – featuring the freelance artist Holly and her puppet friends – and *Theodore Tugboat* – a live-action animation series – followed. By the 1990s programmes that emphasised early childhood development dominated children's television at CBC and TVO. Both broadcasters provided a television oasis for both children and parents, with lengthy blocks of commercial-free, non-violent programmes for pre-schoolers and support to the adults caring for them.

In Australia, early children's television programmes were mostly imported from the United States and Britain. In the 1960s and 70s, however, there was a growth in local productions. Notable examples include *Skippy the Bush Kangaroo*, which achieved international recognition, and the 1973 drama series *SEVEN LITTLE AUSTRALIANS*. In the 1980s, the advent of colour television and the increased use of the video cassette recorder in the home led to a greater diversity in local productions, and to an emphasis on multicultural and multilingual programming with the establishment of the Special Broadcasting Service (SBS). Popular young children's programmes include the long running *Playschool*, based on the English model; *Bananas in Pyjamas*, and Channel Nine's *Here's Humphrey*.

The quality of children's television and film production was, and continues to be, influenced by the creation of the independent body, the Australian Children's Television Foundation (ACTF) in 1982. Funded by the Commonwealth Government and the Governments of all States and Territories, the Foundation has a number of roles, both in the development and production of television programmes and other media, and in undertaking research in promoting and improving children's programmes. Dr Patricia Edgar, Director of the Foundation since its inception, has guided it to international recognition for its work, through overseas sales and awards. There has been a major emphasis on the development of children's drama, using well-known children's writers and independent producers. Notable productions include the *ROUND THE TWIST* series, based on the comic short stories of PAUL JENNINGS; *Touch the Sun*, a series of six telemovies made to mark the Australian Bicentennial in 1988; and the *Lift-Off* series for younger children, which combines live and animated performers. Known for its innovative use of technology, the ACTF released *Li'l Elvis and the Truckstoppers* in 1998, an animated series which involved over 150 animators in its production. In 1998 the Foundation launched *Planet KAHooTZ*, which combines CD-ROM and internet technology and allows children to create an environment where members can explore and communicate using state-of-the-art software tools.

EBe, DG, DWh, JAP, JAS

Tempest, Margaret Mary 1892–1982 Prolific British illustrator of children's books from the 1920s to the 70s. Tempest created and illustrated 20 books herself, and produced several series of NURSERY RHYMES and wall friezes for the Medici Society in the 1920s and 30s. She is perhaps best known for her enduring work with ALISON UTTLEY, in their creation of the *LITTLE GREY RABBIT* SERIES. Here Tempest gave form to a family of woodland animals in soft watercolours. The surroundings of the characters sometimes lack definition, but the personality given to Grey Rabbit by Uttley is loyally expressed in Tempest's illustrations.

SM

Temple, Frances 1945–95 American author of books for children, teacher and educational writer. Temple was born in Washington DC and spent much of her youth in France and Vietnam and later served in the Peace Corps in Sierra Leone. Her own international experiences are reflected in the global vision of her fiction. She authored one PICTUREBOOK, *Tiger Soup* (1994), a retelling of a Jamaican TRICKSTER TALE which she illustrated with colourful COLLAGE. However, she is better known for her novels, which convey the day-to-day lives of protagonists and their confrontations with adversity. Two of these novels, *The Ramsay Scallop* (1994) and its sequel, *The Beduin's Gazelle* (1995), are set in medieval times. Her other novels focus on recent historical events in the Caribbean and Central America. *Grab Hands and Run* (1993) concerns a boy and his family who have to flee from El Salvador after the father has been taken away by army thugs. Temple became interested in Haiti during the election of Jean-Bertrand Aristide, and her desire to present current events from that region to young people in the United States resulted in two novels, *Taste of Salt* (1992) and *Tonight by Sea* (1995). Temple died in 1995 with several novels still in process.

EB

Tennant, Kylie 1912–88 Australian writer of three books for children, as well as successful novels, short stories, plays and works of non-fiction for adults. Her life was greatly affected by the 1930s Depression and, after producing children's radio programmes, raising chickens and living as an itinerant, she wrote about her experiences in her works for adults. The most successful of her books for children, *All the Proud Tribesmen* (1959), was based on her visit to the islands of the Torres Strait, north of Australia. This novel of positive intercultural relations – though emphasising aspects of European 'superiority' – won the CHILDREN'S BOOK COUNCIL OF AUSTRALIA BOOK OF THE YEAR AWARD in 1960. JF

Tenniel, Sir John 1820–1914 Cartoonist and illustrator, who drew for the distinguished satirical journal *Punch*. He excelled in drawings of allegorical beasts and grotesque subjects, and his whimsical inventiveness appealed to LEWIS CARROLL, who commissioned him to illustrate *ALICE'S ADVENTURES IN WONDERLAND* (1865) and *Through the Looking Glass* (1872). On first publication, the illustrations received more notice than the text, and despite later versions such as those by ARTHUR RACKHAM, Tenniel's wiry and surreal images remain integral to the popular notion of 'Alice'. PC

Tennyson, Alfred Lord 1809–92 Successor to William Wordsworth as poet laureate who exemplified the Victorian age through his epic and lyrical poetry. 'In Memoriam', 'The Charge of the Light Brigade' and *Idylls of the King* made him famous from court to cottage. His ability to tell a dramatic tale in musical verse makes some of his lyrics accessible to children and his poetry has accordingly been regularly included in children's anthologies. HT

see also KING ARTHUR

Terhune, Albert Payson 1872–1942 American author. Terhune did not intentionally write books for children, but his books about dogs, especially collies, were widely read by American children for nearly 50 years. Like JACK LONDON's Buck, Terhune's dogs are often successful because of atavistic impulses; at the same time, they are often more civilised than the human beings who own them. They are loyal, wise, affectionate and especially understanding of the young and/or helpless. *Lad, a Dog* (1919) is often cited as Terhune's best book; in fact, although it is the book that assured his success as an author, it is less developed and consciously shaped than some of his later works, such as *Gray Dawn* (1927). The books tend to be episodic as chapters were often initially published individually as short stories. Loyal readers coveted every scrap of information about The Place, The Master, The Mistress and the collies of Sunnybank; a story of Wolf's heroic death was printed in *The New York Times*. Today, Terhune's appeal has definitely lessened because of the clichés, repetitious plots and anthropomorphising of canine characters. Nevertheless, his dog stories still have fans, while his mysteries, religious essays and travel stories are largely forgotten. WH

text-books see INFORMATION BOOKS

Thackeray, W.M. see FAIRY TALES; FANTASY; *THE ROSE AND THE RING*; see also *MARLOW* SERIES

Thesen, Hjalmar 1925– A South African novelist usually included in lists for young readers, admired for his knowledgeable and compelling writing about nature. After two historical novels about the Khoikhoi and the arrival of white people in the country, *The Echoing Cliffs* (1963) and *Strangers from the Sea* (1969), he wrote his best and most successful novel, *A Deadly Presence* (1982), about the effect that a marauding black leopard has on people. This was made a Reader's Digest Condensed Book. *Bond of the Sea* (1991) and *The Way Back* (1993) are animal stories in which scientific information replaces the lyrical descriptions and social analysis of his earlier work. ERJ

Thiele, Colin (Milton) 1920– Australian writer and educator who has written over 60 books for children. The fourth of five children, Thiele grew up in a German farming community near Eudunda in South Australia's Barossa Valley. The world-wide economic depression prior to World War II destined him for teaching, rather than a farming career. While a student at Adelaide University, Thiele began writing poetry and radio scripts and, following active war service in New Guinea, he published several collections. From 1945 to 1955 he taught at Port Lincoln High School on South Australia's remote Eyre Peninsula and wrote extensively for the ABC's national radio.

His themes are consistent: growing up, accepting change, and respect for the natural environment. *SUN ON THE STUBBLE* (1961), a series of interconnected stories based on Thiele's Germanic farm upbringing, has been in print since publication. Later titles, *Uncle Gustav's Ghosts* (1974), *The Shadow on the Hills* (1977) and *The Valley Between* (1981), are based on his childhood. *STORM BOY* (1963) earned Thiele the label of environmental writer. Humankind's ability to commit senseless acts of destruction is a theme which runs through much of his work. *Blue Fin* (1969), one of his best works, immortalised the tough heroism of the tuna-fishing families on the ruggedly beautiful coast near Port Lincoln. Thiele greatly admired the skill of the young crews. These boys were often regarded as failures in the school system, but could handle boats on the high seas with skill and dexterity. *The Hammerhead Light* (1976), *Magpie Island* (1974) and *Seashores and Shadows* (1985) are other sea stories which followed.

After 1955, Thiele battled with rheumatoid arthritis. At the request of a young sufferer he wrote *Jodie's Journey* (1988), the fictional story of an authentic case of juvenile rheumatoid arthritis. In this work, as well as in the earlier *February Dragon* (1965), he explored the devastation caused by bush fires. *Storm Boy, Blue Fin* and *Fire in the Stone* (1973) – the latter set in the opal mining fields of far northern South Australia – were all made into successful feature films and are still viewed world-wide. A TELEVISION series based on *Sun on the Stubble, The Shadow on the Hill* and *The Valley Between* was broadcast in 1996.

Most of Thiele's children's books are set in the varied terrains of rural Australia, the majority in South Australia where Thiele lived until 1993. His sensitive perceptions of people and his deep love and respect for the natural environment permeate his work. He has won numerous national and international awards, and in 1977 was made a Companion of the Order of Australia for services to literature and education. FK

Thimble Press see REVIEWING AND REVIEWERS; see also *SIGNAL*

This Way Delight: a book of poetry for the young (1957) Anthology edited by Herbert Read. 'Literature', said Read in *What is poetry?*, 'is an ugly word invented by schoolmasters . . . poetry should be a deep delight.' The influential art historian and critic advised young readers to develop the poet's ear and eye and write their own verse. Although his selection features some wonderful lyrics from the adult canon – from SHAKESPEARE and Jonson to Yeats and KIPLING – only five women poets are included in this book of more than 100 poems. MCCS

Thomas, Dylan see *CHILD'S CHRISTMAS IN WALES, A*

Thomas, Edward 1878–1917 English poet who started writing verse only three years before he was killed at the Battle of Arras in World War I, but who produced poetry of lasting value which is regularly anthologised for children. He was a great observer of nature and could evoke the 'sweetness of a shower' on dusty nettes ('Tall Nettles'), or 'the child crying for the bird of the snow' ('Snow'), or note the passing of winter by listening to 'the speculating rooks' ('Thaw') or, most famously and 'unwontedly', remember a train stopping at Adlestrop. MCCS

see also ELEANOR FARJEON

Thomas, Isaiah 1750–1831 American printer and publisher of a large number of children's books. Born in Boston, Massachusetts, Thomas survived the death of his father with a penniless mother and became a printer's apprentice at the age of six, setting up a broadside, *The Lawyer's Pedigree*, before he could read. By the time he was in his teens, he was managing a shop for his master. A newspaper career interested him briefly, and he established the *Massachusetts Spy*, but when the British occupied Boston in 1776 Thomas moved his printing operation to Worcester, where he became a leading publisher with his own paper mill and bindery. He appropriated many of JOHN NEWBERY's English publications, taken surreptitiously, and printed his own editions of them among his more than 100 titles for children (1785–8): *Goody Two-Shoes*, MOTHER GOOSE (attributed to Goldsmith), *ROBINSON CRUSOE*, *Be Merry and Wise, A Little Pretty Pocket Book, Nurse Truelove's New Year's Gift, The Lilliputian Masquerade* and many others. The volumes were small books with marbled or embossed paper for bindings. Acquiring enough wealth to retire in 1802, Thomas wrote *The History of Printing in America* (two volumes, 1810) and established the American Antiquarian Society. KSB

Thomas, Joyce Carol African American poet, novelist, playwright, critic and ethnic feminist. Thomas has lived in Oklahoma and California, and these regions are often featured in her work. Her earliest YOUNG ADULT novel, a National Book Award winner, *Marked By Fire* (1982), was followed by two sequels, *Bright Shadow* (1983) and *Water Girl* (1986). This coming-of-age series has strong, inquisitive, western and southwestern African American teenage females as protagonists. But though her fiction is authentic, well-realised and thought-provoking, it is her poetry that shines because of its imagery and the strong feeling it evokes of growing up as an African American. *Brown Honey in Broomwheat Tea* (1993) focuses on a year – a poem for each month – in a young boy's life. *I Have Heard of a Land* (1998) celebrates the pioneer spirit as a freed slave tells of her life as a settler of the Oklahoma Territory in the late 1800s.

Thomas has also produced an important edited collection of multi-ethnic short stories for young adults, *A Gathering of Flowers* (1990), and a lyrical novel, *The Golden Pasture* (1986), about a 12-year-old boy's experience on his grandfather's ranch. Of equal importance are *When the Nightingale Sings* (1992), an African American CINDERELLA novel, haunting and multilayered, and *The Gospel Cinderella* (2000), illustrated by David Diaz. NM

Thomas, R(onald) S(tuart) 1913–2000 Welsh vicar and poet whose only children's collection, *Young and Old* (1977), contains bleak, unrhymed pieces less attractive than much of his adult work. More popular and frequently anthologised are poems such as 'The Evacuee', and a particular favourite, 'Cynddylan on a

Tractor' – whose hero is 'a new man now, part of the machine'. AHa

Thomas, Ruth 1927– British writer born in Wellington, Somerset, author of several books for children and winner of the GUARDIAN AWARD FOR CHILDREN'S FICTION for her first novel *The Runaways* (1988), which has been translated into several languages. The story concerns two unpopular and isolated children who are drawn together in mutual dependence after their discovery of hidden money. In running away from the suspicion which arises from their naive attempts to buy peer acceptance with the wealth, their enforced mutual dependence enables each child to learn about the nature of true friendship.

Inspired by real situations and set in inner-city London and West Country landscapes familiar to the author, the novels feature children who are, and feel, disadvantaged. The mixture of action, excitement and adventure which drives the narratives does not overwhelm the deft handling of character. Complex inner worlds of children are captured and conveyed as individuals experience the daily confrontations of life and face unexpected points of crisis. *The Secret* (1991) has been dramatised by Thames Television and a Channel Four documentary featured the writer and her work. Her popularity among young readers was acknowledged when a London school chose her name for one of its classes. CMN

Thomas the Rhymer see *FIRE AND HEMLOCK*; see also *TAM LIN*

***Thomas the Tank Engine* Series** (1946–72) Stories by the British writer the Reverend W. Awdry (1911–97). Awdry started his Railway Series in 1945, and his most famous story, *Thomas the Tank Engine*, appeared one year later. In this tiny PICTUREBOOK, illustrated in bold colours by C. Reginald Dalby, Thomas begins as a mere shunting engine, easily intimidated by the Fat Controller and beneath the notice of grand locomotives like Gordon, the big engine. But when Thomas is awarded his own branch line, he visibly grows in confidence, the human face superimposed on the smoke box of an otherwise strictly accurate drawing of an 0–6–0 tank engine now set in a permanent smile. Other adventures followed, many inspired by stories that Awdry had read in *The Railway Gazette*. Rural scenery throughout was always idyllic, and should things ever look like going badly wrong, the Fat Controller always sorted everything out by the end. Some critics in the 1970s drew attention to the sexist structure of these stories, where male engines do all the work while dragging along silly, gossiping female carriages in their wake. There was also controversy over the use of the word 'nigger' in one tale, and it was eventually withdrawn.

Awdry finished writing his stories in 1972 with his 26th title, *Tramway Engines*. More railway stories have subsequently been written by the author's son Christopher, starting with *Really Useful Engines* in 1983. Thomas meanwhile began appearing frequently in toyshops, either as himself or as part of different types of merchandising. He also became the hero of a TELEVISION series. Asked about the connection between the church and the railway, Awdry is said to have replied that both owned a good deal of gothic architecture which was expensive to maintain, were regularly assailed by critics, and were firmly convinced they were the best means of getting men and women to their ultimate destination. NT

Thompson, Colin (Edward) Australian writer and illustrator, born in the United Kingdom, whose vivid imagination and delight in the bizarre are reflected in his sought-after FANTASY PICTUREBOOKS, many published internationally. His finely drawn and coloured illustrations, often consuming every millimetre of space on the page, owe much to the surrealists – with unexpected juxtapositions, distortions, impossible realities – and provoke child and adult readers into many hours of close inspection. His books usually involve an adventurous search or challenge for the main character, and although an underlying message can be read into many of the stories, Thompson claims his starting points are often just an idea of a place, or a drawing – the impressive British Museum Reading Room was the springboard for *How to Live Forever* (1995), while childhood visits to Kew Gardens inspired *The Paradise Garden* (1998). An idea for drawing a tower incorporating every other kind of building was the launching pad for *The Tower to the Sun* (1996). Other titles include *Looking for Atlantis* (1993) and *Ruby* (1994). Picturebooks written by Thompson and illustrated by other artists include *Sailing Home* (1997) with Matt Ottley, *The Last Circus* (1997) with KIM GAMBLE, *The Staircase Cat* (1998) illustrated by Anna Pignaturo, and *The Puzzle Duck* (1999) illustrated by Emma Quay. JAP

Thompson, Kay 1913–98 America author of the renowned *ELOISE* books. Born in St Louis, Missouri, Thompson worked as a singer, pianist, actress, songwriter and author. She once said to an interviewer, 'If artistically you are able to do one thing, you are more than likely able to do them all.' This proved exceptionally true for Thompson. Her celebrated fictional character, Eloise, was born during her nightclub act with the Williams Brothers. After arriving late to rehearsal, Thompson apologised in a high, childlike voice that her name was Eloise and she was only six years old. Her first book about Eloise, *Eloise: A Book for Precocious Grown Ups*, illustrated by HILARY KNIGHT, was published in 1955. In the two years after it was released, this book about a poor little rich girl who lives in the Plaza Hotel with her nanny, her dog and her turtle, had already sold 150,000 copies. Thompson went on to write *Eloise in Paris* (1957), *Eloise at Christmastime* (1958) and *Eloise in Moscow* (1959). She also wrote *Kay Thompson's Miss Pooky Peckinpaugh and Her Secret Private Boyfriends Complete With Phone Numbers* (1970), illustrated by Joe Eula. NC

Thomson, David see DANNY FOX

Thousand and One Nights, The see ARABIAN NIGHTS' ENTERTAINMENT

Three Bears, The see GOLDILOCKS AND THE THREE BEARS; see also FEODOR ROJANKOVSKY

Three Billy Goats Gruff FOLKTALE with Norwegian origins first put into print by Asbjørnsen and Moe in the 1840s. It is the story of three goats who have to cross a bridge in order to get to their field. In some editions it is a family of goats including a father, a mother and a baby goat, and in others they are simply three goats of various sizes. Under the bridge there lives an aggressive troll. One by one, beginning with the smallest, the goats 'trip, trap! trip, trap!' over the bridge. On each occasion the troll asks who is crossing his bridge. The small and the middle-sized goats ask not to be eaten, adding that a fatter, tastier goat is following. When it comes to the turn of the biggest goat it kills the troll. In England the best-known version of this tale is the translation by Sir George Dasent (1859). The troll is a common feature of Norwegian tales (see CLASSICAL MYTHOLOGY) and this unfriendly and often dangerous creature is a development of the giants of Norse mythology found in the *Eddas*. JHD

Three Little Kittens see ELISA LEE FOLLEN; GOLDEN BOOKS

Three Little Pigs, The Nursery tale in which three young pigs, making their way in the world, each build a house, one of straw, one of furze and one of bricks. The first two pigs, in their insubstantial houses, are easy prey for the wolf who blows down their dwellings when they refuse him entry. The request is repeated: 'Little pig, little pig, let me come in.' 'No, no, by the hairs of my chiny chin chin.' 'Then I'll puff and I'll huff, and I'll blow your house in.' But the sturdy house of the third pig remains standing. Three attempts at trickery follow but the wily pig circumvents each one; the wolf is lured down the chimney and into the cooking pot over the fire.

The story has links with *The Fox and the Geese* and *The Fox and the Pixies*; the word 'pixies' in the latter, a Devonian tale, may as KATHARINE BRIGGS (*A Dictionary of British Folk-Tales*, 1976) suggests, have been confused with 'pigsies'. Joseph Jacobs (*English Fairy Tales*, 1890) hypothesised that, since pigs do not have hairy chins, the tale might have originally been one about kids; indeed parallels can be drawn with the GRIMMS' *The Wolf and the Seven Little Little Kids*. The tale remains popular, and humorous recent PICTUREBOOKS – such as *THE TRUE STORY OF THE THREE LITTLE PIGS, BY A. WOLF* (JON SCIESZKA and LANE SMITH, 1990) and *The Three Little Wolves and the Big Bad Pig* (Eugene Trivisas and HELEN OXENBURY, 1993) – capitalise on its familiarity. MSut

Three Mulla-Mulgars, The see DOROTHY LATHROP; NEGLECTED WORKS

Three Wishes, The Traditional FAIRY TALE translated from MADAME JEANNE-MARIE LEPRINCE DE BEAUMONT and first printed in English in *The Young Misses Magazine* (1761). It is the story of a couple who are visited by a beautiful fairy lady who grants them three wishes. The first is wasted by the wife unthinkingly wishing for a yard of black pudding. The husband is so vexed that he wishes that the black pudding was stuck to her nose. Knowing they have only one chance left the husband suggests that they wish for vast riches and make a gold case to hide the pudding. The wife declares that if she has to live with the pudding on her nose she will kill herself and so the final wish is used to remove it. The tale had been published in verse by CHARLES PERRAULT as *Les Souhaits Ridicules* in 1693/4, differing from Beaumont's in that the granter of wishes is Jupiter. Other similar tales include one collected by the GRIMM BROTHERS in which a poor man makes good use of three wishes granted to him by the Lord and a rich man wastes them.

The oldest version is in the *Book of Sindibâd* (c. 9th century) in which a man has three wishes: his wife requires that his first wish should be to have more penises. The result is so embarrassing that the man wishes them all gone. He is now left with none and so the last wish is used to return him to his original state. JHD

Through the Looking Glass see *ALICE'S ADVENTURES IN WONDERLAND*

Thunder and Lightnings (1976) First novel by the British author JAN MARK, winning both the Penguin/*Guardian* competition and the CARNEGIE MEDAL. Andrew and his family move to Norfolk. At his new school Andrew meets Victor, cheerfully dislocated from the classroom but profoundly knowledgable about aircraft and with a motivation to learn reminiscent of Billy Caspar in KES. Victor's passion is for the English Electric Lightning: their phasing out provides an overarching structure, a potent image of change and an index of Victor's capacity to adapt. The wit, immaculately pointed prose, ear for dialogue, acute sense of place, subtly accurate picture of family relationships, appreciation of the significance and poetry in inanimate objects, and unsentimental empathy with children's minds are features of Mark's subsequent work.

The character of Victor was perhaps the first significant fictional portrayal of a child with learning difficulties: he becomes not only a great comic character but a profoundly sympathetic study. Certain passages – the Lightnings at RAF Coltishall and Andrew's first meeting with Victor – are very effective. The novel has become a *locus classicus* for teachers, warning about the dangers of project work. The novel has little active plot but a clear, satisfying structure. The ending is memorable: the Lightnings go, 'tamed and shabby tigers slinking into the hangar'. But one makes a last flourish: 'It went up and up, hung for a second, then the nose came down and it fell in a long solitary dive ... Victor grinned, his old and famous grin ... "What a way to go out, eh? Whaaaaaaam!"' DCH

Thunderbirds see COMICS, PERIODICALS AND MAGAZINES; see also TELEVISION

Thurber, James 1894–1961 American humorist and cartoonist associated with *The New Yorker*, who wrote five literary FAIRY TALES and two collections of modern FABLES for older children and adults. Thurber's fables first appeared in *The New Yorker* and were subsequently published in *Fables for Our Times and Famous Poems Illustrated* (1940) and *Further Fables for Our Times* (1956). His simple but expressive line-drawings accompany these revisions of AESOP and traditional fairy tales: 'The Little Girl and the Wolf' argues that it is not so easy to fool little girls any more, while 'The Unicorn in the Garden' suggests that imagination can outwit dull facts.

In his best-known children's book, *Many Moons* (1943, illustrated by LOUIS SLOBODKIN; reillustrated by MARC SIMONT, 1990), which won the CALDECOTT MEDAL in 1944, the court jester cleverly honours the young princess's request for the moon. *The Great Quillow* (1944) is another fairy tale, in which a humble toy-maker defeats a giant by a ruse of creative STORYTELLING. *The White Deer* (1945) is the longest and most bitter of Thurber's fairy tales and reveals the author's increasingly misanthropic attitude towards American culture. In *The 13 Clocks* (1950) romantic love and the imagination triumph over the cold world of reality. All Thurber's fairy tales celebrate wordplay and wit, but it is most apparent in *The Wonderful O* (1957), a didactic tale in which the villain obsessively wishes to rid the world of the letter o but is defeated by the spirits of imagination – a veiled meditation on McCarthyism. His first book, *Is Sex Necessary?* (1929), was written in collaboration with his long-time friend and *New Yorker* colleague, E.B. WHITE, whose children's books also celebrate language and the imagination. JCS

Tibo, Gilles 1951– Canadian illustrator and author who was born in Nicolet, Quebec. Tibo is a self-taught artist who published a 40-page comic book *L'Oeil Voyeur* (1970) at the age of 18. His first PICTUREBOOK was *Le Prince Sourire et le Lys Bleu* (1975). His developed style features atmospheric landscapes created with airbrush and coloured pencils. He first gained national and international attention with a series of seasonal picturebooks about a little boy in a baseball cap named Simon; in 1988, *Simon and the Snowflakes* was nominated for a Governor General's Literary Award for English ILLUSTRATION, and also received Japan's Owl Award. The French edition of a later title, *Simon et la Ville de Carton* (1992), won the Governor General's Literary Award for French illustration. Notable picturebooks he illustrated for other writers include Felix Leclerc's *Le Tour de l'Ile* (1980) and ROBERT MUNSCH's *Giant* (1989). Adult illustration credits include a French edition of Edgar Allan Poe's *Annabel Lee* (1987), set in Quebec's Gaspé, and an English translation of Louis Hemon's *Maria Chapdelaine* (1989). As an author, Gilles Tibo also won the Governor General's Literary Award for French text for *Noèmie: Le Secret de Madame Lumbago* (1996), illustrated by Louise-Andrée Laliberté. MB

Tienie Holloway Medal see AWARDS AND MEDALS

Tiger Tim see ANNUALS, COMICS, PERIODICALS AND MAGAZINES; *PLAYBOX ANNUAL*; ANNUALS

Till Eulenspiegel see FOLKTALES AND LEGENDS

Till Owlyglass see MICHAEL ROSEN; FRITZ WEGNER

Time to Get Out of the Bath, Shirley see *COME AWAY FROM THE WATER, SHIRLEY*; see also JOHN BURNINGHAM

***Time Warp Trio* series** Four short books written by the American writer, JON SCIESZKA, which employ the TIME-SLIP device. The charcoal drawings by LANE SMITH are integral to the works and add immeasurably to their humour. Three modern American youngsters, Fred, Sam and Joe, travel to times of their choice by means of a magic book given to Joe on his birthday;

the only way of returning to the present is by finding the book in the time they currently happen to be in. As they note in *Your Mother was a Neanderthal* (1993), this can provide cause for worry, when books have not yet been invented in prehistoric times. In *The Not-So-Jolly Roger* (1991), they travel to the 18th century, and in the other two books, the settings are the Wild West and Camelot. The humour of the series is generated by discrepancy, modern idiom and assumptions clashing with those of the periods travelled to. It is further fuelled by wisecracks and situation comedy of a deliberately silly kind, as when, in *Knights of the Kitchen Table* (1991), the Black Knight attempts to ride them down, and they jump out of the way, repeating this manouevre till he falls, exhausted. SA

time-slip fantasy The strict notion of 'genre' in connection to works falling into this 'category' is not an easy one to sustain. The term may be held to refer to works whose only common feature is the trope of 'time-slipping' itself; there is little that is otherwise formally or structurally necessary in works gathered under this umbrella.

Time-slipping can happen 'spontaneously', as in *ALISON UTTLEY'S A TRAVELLER IN TIME* (1939), or require a ritual or agent, as in the laying out of Dickie's rattler and the moonflower seeds in E. NESBIT'S *Harding's Luck* (1909), the thyme in EDWARD EAGER'S *The Time Garden* (1958) or the book in JON SCIESZKA'S *TIME WARP TRIO* SERIES. The narrative structure of such fantasies can be episodic, as in many of Nesbit's works and RUDYARD KIPLING'S *PUCK OF POOK'S HILL* (1906) and *Rewards and Fairies* (1910). (These two authors – friends whose work proved mutually inspiring – are probably the earliest essayists into the field of time-slip fantasy for children.) Alternatively, the adventure in time can be continuous and complete, as in RONALD WELCH'S *The Gauntlet* (1951), where Peter slips back to the Middle Ages, returning to the present when his historical persona is killed in battle. History is presented as immutable in works like Uttley's *A Traveller in Time*, where Penelope, slipping to the time of Elizabeth I and the Babington plot, can only witness but not change the past, while in other works, such as MADELEINE L'ENGLE'S *A Swiftly Tilting Planet* (1978) the raison d'être of time-travel is to avert a crisis in the present by altering events in the past; entirely different philosophies are obviously implicit here. All this should be sufficient to demonstrate the lack of homogeneity in works placed under this heading.

The problems involved in defining 'time-slip fantasy' may also be seen when, for example, one considers the question of the direction in which time slips. Not all time-slip novels involve travelling to the past. LUCY BOSTON'S *The Stones of Green Knowe* (1976), Hilda Lewis's *The Ship that Flew* (1939) and Nesbit's *The Story of the Amulet* (1906), for example, involve journeys taken in both directions, and DIANA WYNNE JONES'S *A Tale of Time City* (1987) operates on the principle of time itself being circular. It is nonetheless true that most works one would instinctively place under the heading of 'time-slip fantasy' gravitate towards the past, works which predominantly concern themselves with futuristic travel tending instead to be thought of as SCIENCE FICTION. Further difficulties emerge if one includes GHOST STORIES, for in these it is also possible to observe people of one era inhabiting a time not theirs. Thus the boundaries which time-slip fantasy shares with other literary categories are rather porous.

In works belonging to this fluid category, the notion of 'dialogue' is surely an important one, as suggested by the juxtaposition of various times and their denizens, although the purpose of such dialogue and the manner of its manifestation vary widely. The frequent end of the experience is a modification or transformation of the consciousness of the time-travellers by their experience of the period to which they have travelled and the people in it, though ideally, in a dialogue, such modification should be mutual. PHILIPPA PEARCE'S *Tom's Midnight Garden* (1958), in which two lonely children from different times, Tom and Hatty, meet and befriend each other is perhaps a paradigm of such reciprocality. That Tom later finds out that the old lady in the house is actually Hatty, and that the friendship rooted in 'other' time flowers lovingly in this, strengthens the sense of dialogue, both between people and between times. The *GREEN KNOWE* books also emphasise this kind of mutuality, shown in the way the children of the different centuries seem not so much to slip through time (though this happens too), as companionably inhabit and share the same time and space. Though this is left understated, the time-slipping here is also seen to ameliorate Tolly's initial sense of displacement and loneliness in the first book of the series. It is, however, easy to mismanage this aspect of time-slip fantasy and to turn it into something merely escapist, over-simplifying or brutalising complex emotions or situations by glibly allowing the time-adventure to work some kind of inner cure. This happens in Julia Jarman's *The Time-Travelling Cat* (1992), where Topher, who has lost his mother in an accident, gains, through an adventure in ancient Egypt, some kind of inner strength with which to cope.

The time-slip format has also been used for what might be called ideological purposes. Time-slip novels, by virtue of the fact that they straddle different times, may be useful in rendering oblique commentary on particular times through their juxtaposition with other historical periods, and also in working through ideas about historical process. Underpinning *The Story of the Amulet*, for instance – as Julia Briggs has pointed out in her biography of Nesbit, *A Woman of Passion* (1989) – is a critique of society which emerges through comparisons of Edwardian England with Roman Britain (an unwanted child in one time finding a loving home in the other), ancient Babylon, a future Utopian society and so forth.

Perhaps the most interesting change to be rung in recent years on time-slipping, however, is Diana Wynne Jones's *Hexwood* (1993), where for the best part of the novel, the characters (and hence the readers) think they are experiencing (and reading about) time-slipping, only to discover at the end that their apparent wanderings in time and the personalities in which they wander have been experiences created by the Bannus, a device which works by creating virtual-reality fields. SA

Times Educational Supplement see REVIEWING AND REVIEWS; INFORMATION BOOKS

Tinderbox, The see HANS CHRISTIAN ANDERSEN; NICHOLAS STUART GRAY

Tintin Eponymous hero of a series of stories in comic-strip form by the Belgian artist Hergé (1907–83), whose name is formed from the pronunciation of the reversed initials of his real name, Georges Remi. Hergé's first work, featuring a resourceful and adventuring character called Totor, appeared in the magazine *Le Boy Scout*. This led to a longer engagement with a Catholic newspaper called *Le Vingtième Siècle*, which in 1928 began issuing a weekly comic supplement with Hergé as editor. This was to feature comic strips drawn in the American style – with speech balloons in the pictures instead of a text running underneath. The first adventure of Tintin himself, *Tintin in the Land of the Soviets*, began in January 1929 and soon became immensely popular.

This first story was crude by Hergé's later standards, and so was the second, *Tintin in the Congo* (in newspaper form, 1930; as a book, 1931). But Hergé was developing as an artist, and *Tintin in America* (1931/2), the third adventure, marks a technical advance which is almost fully consolidated by *The Cigars of the Pharaoh* (1932/4). By this time the books were being issued by the Franco-Belgian publisher Casterman, and in 1942 came *The Shooting Star*, the first to be conceived from the start as a 62-page book in full colour, with four lines of frames on each page. It had taken Hergé some time to arrive at this format, but it suited him well, and from then on he did not diverge from it.

Hergé's particular strength is clarity, both in his drawing and in his storytelling. There are no lazy or ambiguous passages in his frames: every line has a purpose. Similarly, each page ends either in a joke or in a miniature cliff-hanger: everything is subordinated to the narrative. When he discovered that having a character move from left to right advances the story more successfully, for example, he went back and re-drew earlier stories to take account of the fact; and when later he could afford the help of studio assistants, he would prepare large-scale models of the ships and rockets in his stories so that they could be drawn accurately from any angle. Only the faces of his characters are caricatures: their bodies and the physical spaces they move in are meticulously realistic.

The appeal of the stories is international – there are translations into over 40 languages. Tintin's very blandness is perhaps one reason for this success: he is a blank and amiable space rather than a fully-rounded character. His quiff and his plus-fours are the only eccentricities he has, though the other characters more than make up for it: the whisky-bibbing Captain Haddock, the bowler-hatted detectives Thomson and Thompson, the absurd inventor Professor Calculus. Some of the 23 stories – *The Castafiore Emerald* (1961/3) in particular – are masterpieces of comic invention, and Hergé has been a profound influence on generations of comic artists. The stories are very well translated into English by Leslie Lonsdale-Cooper and Michael Turner. PNP

Tiny Tots see ANNUALS

tipping in Illustrations printed on brittle ART PAPER could not be folded and sewn into a book. They were therefore printed on single sheets stuck, or 'tipped', with a thin line of paste on one edge, to the following page or, for GIFT BOOKS, onto a CARD MOUNT which was sewn into the book. GCB

tissue guards Sheets of tissue paper inserted between illustrations and the facing pages to prevent offsetting. In GIFT BOOKS they often bore the captions to the illustrations. GCB

title appropriation A term proposed here to refer to the practice by the film industry of using the title of a well-known novel or series for a film that disregards the essential features of the original work. Although the view that a film or television version of a novel is necessarily secondary to or dependent upon the original is now generally and rightly rejected, a critical term is needed for films which are neither adaptations nor RECONTEXTUALISATIONS. The 1998 film of *DOCTOR DOLITTLE* had – literally – little more than a nominal connection with its purported source. In a film of *THE BORROWERS*, the central idea of smallness, and some names of characters, were the only features that the film shared with MARY NORTON's series; the narrative incidents were newly contrived, and there was no attempt to engage with either the melancholy or the psychological and poetic aspects of the original. VW

To Kill a Mocking Bird (1960) Novel by the American author Harper Lee (1926–) concerning racism and moral courage in a small Alabama town as seen through the eyes of children. *To Kill a Mocking Bird* won the Pulitzer Prize in 1961 and remains a popular novel with adolescent readers throughout the English-speaking world.

Lee attended the University of Alabama Law School and her novel is loosely based on the infamous Scotsboro Trial of 1931 in which nine African American men were accused of raping two white women and eight of the men were found guilty and sentenced to death. Lee's novel focuses on the trial of Tom Robinson, an African American accused of raping a poor white woman, Mayelle Ewell. Atticus Finch is asked to confront community standards and defend a 'negro' accused of raping a white woman. While Atticus fails in this task, his defence makes it clear that rape by Robinson was physically impossible and instead Mayelle had attempted to kiss him. Humiliated, Mayelle's father swears revenge and attempts to kill Atticus' children, Scott and Jem, who are saved by the town hermit, Boo Radley. The novel was made into a 1962 film starring Gregory Peck, who won the Academy Award for Best Actor, while Horton Foote won the Academy Award for Best Screenplay. JCS

Toad of Toad Hall (1929) A. A. MILNE's stage adaptation of KENNETH GRAHAME's *THE WIND IN THE WILLOWS*. Milne's introduction to the play explains his decision to restrict his adaptation to the story of Toad, omitting the Riverbank scenes and the mystical chapter 'The Piper at the Gates of Dawn', on the grounds that only the Toad plot could be successfully staged. Therefore the play largely follows the original story as it was first told to Alastair Grahame, and much of the dialogue is transposed directly from the book. Milne added framing scenes at the beginning and end which present the story as a little girl's summertime dream, a device modelled closely on *ALICE'S ADVENTURES IN WONDERLAND*. He made sparing additions of new characters, the most notable of whom is Alfred, the horse who draws the caravan, who closely resembles Eeyore in *Winnie the Pooh*. However, his major change to the original is probably the ending. Rather than curtailing Toad's incorrigible conceit, as his friends do in the original story, Milne causes all the characters, both animal and human, to join in a celebratory song and dance in salutation of the eponymous hero. Omitting Grahame's nature mysticism and pastoral idyll, Milne produced a witty and vigorous comedy of enduring appeal. PH

Todd, Barbara Euphan see *BLACKIE'S CHILDREN'S ANNUAL*; CAMPING AND TRAMPING FICTION; *WORZEL GUMMIDGE* SERIES

Todd, H(erbert) E(atton) see *BOBBY BREWSTER* SERIES

Todd, Justin 1932– British illustrator who attended the Royal College of Art, where one of his tutors was EDWARD BAWDEN with whom he later worked on a set of murals at Morley College. In 1982, Todd was runner-up for the Francis Williams Memorial Prize for children's book ILLUSTRATION and in 1987 he won second prize in the W.H. Smith Illustration Award for his two *ALICE* books, which have highly finished, detailed colour plates. He also gave a set of bright colour plates to *THE WIND IN THE WILLOWS* (1988) and produced soft, decorative, mysterious pictures for Jenny Nimmo's *The Starlight Cloak* (1993). JAG

Token for Children, A (1671/2) Popular devotional text for children, written by JAMES JANEWAY and published by Dorman Newman in two volumes. Janeway had been a nonconformist preacher, and the full title of his book – *being an Exact Account of the Conversion, Holy and Exemplary Lives, and Joyful Deaths of several young Children* – gives some idea of its contents and of its Puritan, exhortatory purpose in saving children from Hell. The book, which remained in print until the late 19th century, was extremely popular between about 1670 and 1720, when it was extended, with additional prayers for young children, and illustrated. DWh

Tolkien, J(ohn) R(onald) R(euel) 1892–1973 English writer born in Bloemfontein, South Africa. He was brought up in Birmingham where he received his basic education, going on to read English Language and Literature at Oxford. It was here that he returned at the age of 33 as Professor of Anglo-Saxon, after an interlude spent serving with the Lancashire Fusiliers during World War I. Here he made friends with C.S. LEWIS and Charles Williams, who with him were members of the writing group known as the Inklings. His marriage to Edith Mary Bratt in 1916 produced four children, who were the audience for whom *THE HOBBIT* (1937) was written.

Tolkien was much honoured for his writing, becoming a Fellow of the Royal Society of Literature in 1957, and was awarded the CBE the year before he died. He was a scholar and translator of some note; however, his academic achievements have been somewhat overshadowed by his literary productions, in particular his fantasies, *The Hobbit* and *The Lord of the Rings* (1954–6). The latter gathered Tolkien a cult following in the 1960s and gave immense impetus to the genre of

FANTASY, which expanded enormously in the decades thereafter. It has become an archetype of heroic fantasy (fantasy writers now appear, for instance, to consider the trilogy format to be *de rigeur*), whose tropes are frequently repeated. An example is the apparent death of the wizard figure who later returns, which is a motif used in Terry Brooks's *The Sword of Shannara*, Barbara Hambly's *Darwath* trilogy and also in LLOYD ALEXANDER's *The Book of Three*.

The amplitude and thoroughness of Tolkien's world-building cannot be overstated. His creation of entire languages for the different races of Middle-Earth is well-documented, and he produced an enormous amount of 'background' material (history and mythology) to *The Lord of the Rings*. The most important of these writings is the *Silmarillion* (1977), a work already conceived during World War I; sadly, with the eight volumes of the *History of Middle-Earth* (1984–92), it remained unpublished at Tolkien's death. The *Silmarillion* and the *History of Middle-Earth* were subsequently edited for publication by his son Christopher Tolkien.

Tolkien also wrote two books of verse: *The Adventures of Tom Bombadil and Other Verses from the Red Book* (1962) and *Bilbo's Last Song* (1974). Both were illustrated by PAULINE BAYNES, known for her work with the NARNIA books. The verse is whimsical and its interest derives from its connection to Middle-Earth rather than from any great poetic merit. His other works for children are *Farmer Giles of Ham* (1949) (another dragon tale), *Smith of Wooton Major* (1967), *The Father Christmas Letters* (1976) and *Mr Bliss* (1982). These belong to an earlier period of writing than *The Hobbit*, and, though charming, are slight works. SA

Tom and Jerry (from 1940) A series of animated shorts in which a cartoon cat struggles with a small mouse and inevitably loses. Featuring virtually no dialogue, these popular cartoons were a mainstay of MGM from 1940 to 1957, won seven Academy Awards and were even integrated into live-action motion pictures like *Anchors Away* (1945). They inspired numerous imitations and sequels and launched the careers of their creators, Bill Hanna and Joseph Barbera, who went on to dominate American children's TELEVISION programming thorough the 1970s with such creations as *Huckleberry Hound* (1958), *The Flintstones* (1960) and *Scooby-Doo, Where Are You?* (1969). JDC

Tom Brown's Schooldays SCHOOL STORY 'by an Old Boy', published in 1857 by Thomas Hughes (1822–96). Though not the first school story – preceded for example, by Harriet Martineau's *The Crofton Boys* (1841) – it was an instant success, reaching five editions within a year, and established many of the conventions of the school-story genre which soon developed. From rural Berkshire Tom goes up to Rugby where 'Scud' East introduces him to the school's rules; he quickly learns its régime of lessons, sports and bullying, and is deeply impressed by the character of the Headmaster, the great Doctor Arnold. Involved in various scrapes, the boys narrowly avoid being expelled, but Tom is asked to share his study with Arthur, a timid but devout newcomer, whose Christianity gradually influences him and helps him to mature. Written for Hughes's eight-year-old son, and partly to praise Arnold's character-building reforms, the book has rarely been out of print, and has become the subject of film and TELEVISION adaptations. Though sometimes criticised for its 'muscular Christianity' and nationalism, the book's graphic picture of schoolboy life in 19th-century England, its characterisation, crowded incidents and robust vitality have helped it survive. DB

Tom Hickathrift Popular folk hero of CHAPBOOKS in the 17th and 18th centuries, with a long oral tradition. The first known copy is a late 17th-century chapbook in the Samuel Pepys Library in Cambridge. Tom, a lazy boy from Ely in the Cambridgeshire Fens, grew to great size. Discovering his strength carting beer for a brewer, he performed mighty deeds which included killing a rich giant who had terrorised the neighbourhood. The giant's fortune enabled him to build a house and call himself 'Mr' Hickathrift. He excelled at country sports and in later stories put down a rebellion and was knighted by the king. SD

Tom Merry and Co see GREYFRIARS

Tom Sawyer see THE ADVENTURES OF TOM SAWYER

Tom Thumb Story of a thumb-sized man, whose amazing adventures included being swallowed by a giant, falling into a pudding mix, and visiting KING ARTHUR's court inside a fish. His size made his mischievous exploits more exciting since he could seem invisible. The story is very old and similar versions are recorded in many other countries. Originally a FOLK TALE, it was written down in England in 1621 by Richard Johnson, and was reprinted continually as a nursery tale, a CHAPBOOK, in verse, and for the stage. 'Tom Thumb' became a popular name in the 18th century to describe anything small. SD

Tomlinson, Jill 1931–76 British writer of fiction for young children in the 5-to-7 age range, who trained as an opera singer and took up writing after illness cut short her career. Her first story, *The Bus that Went to Church* (1965), provided her with a distinctive formula for a succession of similarly titled books of which *The Owl who was Afraid of the Dark* (1968) remains a favourite choice for beginning readers. Animals who face gently amusing challenges commonly feature in the stories, and other publications include *Hilda the Hen* (1967), *Lady Bee's Bonnets* (1971) and *The Aardvark Who Wasn't Sure* (1973). CMN

Tomlinson, Theresa 1946– British novelist distinguished for the way she encourages young readers to connect present and past. In her historical novel, *The Flither Pickers* (1987), set in a northeastern fishing community, the story of fictional narrator Lisa Wexford is threaded through with actual events. Characterisation is further enhanced by Frank Meadow Sutcliff's turn-of-the-century photographs. In her contemporary novels, Tomlinson uses devices such as a history project in *Riding the Waves* (1990) or patterning on an ancient vase in *Dancing Through the Shadows* (1997) as means by which characters discover something of their personal or cultural histories, gaining an enlarged understanding of their present. In *Child of the May* (1998), male and female roles are explored in the context of the ROBIN HOOD stories. GCH

Tommy Thumb's Pretty Song Book (1744) The first collection of NURSERY RHYMES for English children known to exist: only one copy survives. It was published by Mary Cooper in a tiny book whose title page indicates that this is the second of two volumes, the first now lost (see also *TOMMY THUMB'S SONG BOOK*). The book is edited in a light-hearted fashion with mock musical directions. Its contents are largely what have become nursery rhyme classics: 'London Bridge is broken down', 'Hickere, Dickere, Dock', 'Oranges and Lemons' and other favourites. DWh

Tommy Thumb's Song Book No copy of this volume has been found, though it was advertised by Mary Cooper in *The London Evening Post* in March 1744. Its importance lies in the hypothesis that this may have been the now lost first volume to *TOMMY THUMB'S PRETTY SONG BOOK* (vol. II), also produced by Mary Cooper in 1744, which is the first extant collection of NURSERY RHYMES known to exist. An American book entitled *Tommy Thumb's Song Book* was published by ISAIAH THOMAS of Massachusetts in 1788, however, and it remains possible that the 1744 English book was the original for this, rather than the fabled lost volume of nursery rhymes. DWh

Tomorrow, When The War Began (1993) The first in a series of seven novels by Australian writer JOHN MARSDEN, in which seven teenagers must fight for themselves when Australia is invaded. A gripping, youth-centred adventure, ostensibly written by teenage Ellie, the complete series comprises *The Dead Of The Night* (1994); *The Third Day* (1995); *The Frost* (1995); *Darkness, Be My Friend* (1996); *Burning for Revenge* (1997); *The Night is for Hunting* (1998) and *The Other Side of Dawn* (1999). Marsden does not shrink from involving his heroes in the realities of war – pain, violence and death – but at the same time he offers hope, and the ending shows Ellie's awareness that life is about more than living 'happily ever after'. NLR

Tonkin [Legge], (Elizabeth) Rachel 1945– Australian illustrator of PICTUREBOOKS and information texts for both children and adults. Tonkin's concern for accurate detail is most apparent in her gentle watercolour evocations of an early 20th-century country general store in *Papa and the Olden Days* (1989), based on her father's reminiscences, and written by Ian Edwards. Her non-fiction picturebook *What Was the War Like, Grandma?* (1996) recreates everyday life for children and adults during World War II, from ration books to gas masks, with lifelike watercolour images and an informative caption text. Tonkin strives to show that children of the past, despite outward differences, had the same fears, hopes and loves as current readers. *Willy and the Ogre* (1991) offers readers multiple narratives, as Willy takes a walk with his Grandpa through a forest with hidden characters, each with a story to be discovered. JAP

***Topsy and Tim* series** In an age where male characters dominated children's books, this hugely popular series was started in 1959 by British authors Jean and Gareth Adamson with the aim of ensuring that both male and female characters would have equal status. The stories were simply told domestic adventures written by Gareth and illustrated by Jean. Each story tackles a subject of interest to young children or an issue which will help them understand their own lives, for example *Topsy and Tim's New School* (1976). Gareth died in 1982 and Jean continued the series on her own. So far there are over 40 titles. They are particularly popular with libraries. AEW

Torrence, Jackie 1945– African American storyteller. Torrence grew up in Salisbury, North Carolina, the great-granddaughter of a slave freed in 1869. Employed by the High Point Public Library, she developed a special programme of North Carolina GHOST STORIES, TALL TALES and mountain legends which she added to her own repertoire of African American FOLKTALES. Soon she found herself in demand regionally, and then nationally and internationally, as a concert performer and artist for Weston Woods films. In a unique genre-blending of autobiography, BIOGRAPHY, folktales, family history, slave history and personal reminiscence, entitled *The Importance of Pot Liquor* (1994), she tells stories that nurtured and nourished her as a child, particularly the talking animal stories told in her family as well as those by JOEL CHANDLER HARRIS. ('Forget the Remus "frame" and tell the stories', Torrence has always advised; they 'convey philosophies, values, attitudes ... You don't have any pride unless you know where you come from.') Framing the animal stories are gripping accounts of her own childhood life, the family members who told her the tales, and the occasion of the telling. NM

Tourtel, Mary see *RUPERT BEAR*

Townsend, John Rowe 1922– British novelist and critic, born in Leeds, England. He read English at Emmanuel College, Cambridge, and after working as a reporter, became Children's Editor of *The Guardian* until 1978. His critical history of children's literature in English, *Written for Children* (1965; 6th edition, 1996), is a standard introductory text. He has also written two collections of essays on contemporary writers for children: *A Sense of Story* (1971) and *A Sounding of Storytellers* (1979). He has lectured on children's books in Britain, Canada, Australia, Japan and the United States. A recent work is a collection of writings on JOHN NEWBERY: *Trade and Plumb-cake for Ever; Huzza!* (1994).

Townsend has published more than 20 books for children and young people and has won several AWARDS, including the BOSTON GLOBE-HORN BOOK AWARD (1970), the Silver PEN Award (1979) and the Christopher Award (1982). He was also runner up for the CARNEGIE MEDAL in 1963 with *Hell's Edge* and in 1969 with *THE INTRUDER*.

The author's sense that there was a lack of books for children in Britain which dealt with poverty and other contemporary social problems led to his first books, beginning with the innovative and influential *GUMBLE'S YARD* (1961), *Hell's Edge* (1963) and *Goodbye to Gumble's Yard* (originally published as *Widdershins Crescent*, 1965). Like these, several of his subsequent books are set around the area of an imaginary small town called Cobchester where an abandoned warehouse by a canal shelters both shadowy characters and the young protagonists. He has since continued writing about the difficulties and joys of growing up but has employed FANTASY and SCIENCE FICTION in some of his narratives, such as in *Gone to the Dogs* (1984), where in an eye-opening reversal dogs have people as pets. In all these genres, fast-paced action and the realistic rendering of dialogue are characteristic of his work.

Whatever the setting, in the past, present or future, the children and young people in Townsend's books are usually faced with making difficult choices which may alienate them from grown-ups or the world as they know it. This occurs when, in their apparently stable lives, something happens which forces them to realise that their situation is precarious and the future is menacing. Loyalty, love and compassion begin to be questioned and they must choose between ensuring their own survival or acting upon their compassion to others. This is the case of Barry, in *Noah's Castle* (1975), who must make a choice between his loyalty to his father and helping others to survive during an extreme economic depression in Britain.

First love is also a theme in many of his books for young people, always presented with humour. Usually it is the boys who have to do most of the growing up, as the girls seem to be more mature, determined and aware of the future of their relationship, as in *King Creature Come* (1980) or *Cloudy/Bright* (1984). Although he often makes use of a gentle irony in narrating events, Townsend leaves the reader with an optimistic view of the future of his young characters. EA

see also *GOODNIGHT, PROF, LOVE*; REVIEWERS AND REVIEWING

Townsend, Sue see *SECRET DIARY OF ADRIAN MOLE 13¾, THE*

toy books A term used mostly to refer to PICTUREBOOKS published in the second half of the 19th century, in particular by Dean and Son, and by EDMUND EVANS for Frederick Warne and Co., and associated especially with WALTER CRANE and RANDOLPH CALDECOTT. VW

see also ILLUSTRATION; LITHOGRAPHY; PICTUREBOOKS; PROCESS ENGRAVING; WOOD ENGRAVING

toy theatres see DRAMA FOR CHILDREN; MOVABLE BOOKS; see also ROBERT LOUIS STEVENSON

Toye, William see PICTUREBOOKS

***Toytown* series** Created by Sydney Hulme Beaman (1886–1932) as a comic strip based on wooden figures he had constructed as a toymaker, the first *Toytown* story was published in 1925. In 1929 a dramatised version appeared on the BBC's *Children's Hour*, where it remained ever after a firm favourite. Set in a small town run by a mayor never above a certain level of municipal corruption, the series' unforgettable figures – such as Larry the Lamb, Dennis the Dachshund and Mr Growser – gladdened the lives of innumerable children. Comic misunderstandings allied to persistent mischief from the deceptively well-meaning Larry and his friend always made excellent entertainment. NT

see also *BLACKIE'S CHILDREN'S ANNUAL*

Traill, Catharine Parr (Strickland) 1802–99 Author of Canada's first important children's book, *Canadian Crusoes* (1852). Born in Kent, England, Traill became a botanist and an established author of children's material. She was born into a family in which writing and education were taken seriously; her brother Samuel and her sisters Susanna, Jane Margaret and Agnes [Strickland] all became published authors. In childhood she and Susanna, like the young CHARLOTTE, EMILY AND ANNE BRONTË, wrote numerous stories, a few of which were sent to John Harris and published by him in 1818.

Before arriving in Canada in 1832, Traill had written *The Young Emigrants; or, Pictures of Canada. Calculated to Instruct the Minds of Youth* (1826), using first-hand pioneer accounts. Traill's themes, instructional and descriptive, are based upon survival information and the need for harmony between native people and settlers arriving from other cultures and countries. Her other non-fiction work, *The Backwoods of Canada* (1836), suitable for all ages, describes Traill's life in Upper Canada. Her memorable first children's book, *Canadian Crusoes: A Tale of the Rice Lake Plains*, is, as its title suggests, an ADVENTURE STORY. This book was republished as *Lost in the Backwoods* and did not appear again under its original title until 1923. *Lady Mary and Her Nurse or, A Peep into Canadian Forests* (1856), republished as *Afar in the Forest* and *In the Forest*, was not as popular with her readers. Traill's *Cot and Cradle* (1895), a selection of nature stories, is now viewed as sentimental and anthropomorphic. MRS

see also ROBINSONNADES

Train, The: the Amazing Train Chase that Unfolds into one of the Longest Books in the World (1982) Australian Withold Generowicz's wordless PICTUREBOOK in the innovative form of a frieze story about a chase along the length of a goods train. The work literally unfolds in a long chain of pictures each connected to the previous and following illustrations. Each of the frames, full of details of a train and its contents, invites close attention and discussion of how each event is connected in a narrative. Though there is only one actual train, there are in fact many trains of narrative for those willing to search for them in objects, events and characters. CH, HMcC

Traveller in Time, A (1939) Novel by ALISON UTTLEY which is FANTASY, historical novel and romance in one. Penelope, a visitor to Thackers, moves between her own time and the reign of Elizabeth I, finding herself in the household of Sir Anthony Babington, whose (historical) plot to rescue Mary, Queen of Scots, failed. Part of the book's interest lies in its depiction of the period, but its atmosphere, combining a certain dream-like quality, lyricism, and doom connected to the sense of a past that cannot be rewritten and cannot be quite recalled, is what makes this a haunting and memorable work. SA

Travers, P(amela) L(yndon) see MARY POPPINS SERIES

Treadgold, Mary 1910– British writer, author of *We Couldn't Leave Dinah* (1941), winner of the CARNEGIE MEDAL and one of the first – and best – children's books written about World War II. It is set on the fictional Channel Island of Clerinel and is both a PONY STORY and a WAR STORY of the German occupation. National stereotypes are largely avoided and difficult wartime issues are resolutely faced – danger, fear, intimidation and divided loyalties. The sentence construction is at times archly complex: 'Even in this semi-comatose state the hazily perceived rapture upon her brother's usually phegmatic countenance silenced upon her lips the righteous fury of the thus rudely awakened.' However, the writing evokes with great skill the atmosphere of the island in the late summer of 1940 and the chapter 'Caroline Rides to Town' is a masterpiece of suspense. Despite the title, Dinah does get left behind.

Treadgold wrote several more novels, often exciting, always reflective and with a strong sense of place. She has, however, unjustly gained a limiting reputation as a writer of pony stories; in fact, *No Ponies* (1946), set in France in 1944 after the retreat of the occupying German forces, is an ADVENTURE STORY more concerned with the repercussions of collaboration than with horses, and *The 'Polly Harris'* (1949) – in which the author returns to the Clerinel children – is an adventure story about urban terrorism in post-War London. Treadgold subsequently wrote a group of three related novels: *The Heron Ride* (1962) and *Return to the Heron* (1963) – set in the English Downs – are about an orphaned brother and sister passionately longing for a home; *Journey from the Heron* (1982) lovingly evokes the atmosphere of London during World War I. VW

Trease, (Robert) Geoffrey 1909–98 British writer. The diversity of Geoffrey Trease's achievements is without parallel. Over seven decades, he wrote some 120 books, published in 26 countries and in 20 languages. He is best known as an historical novelist, but he was also a playwright (for stage, TELEVISION and the much-loved BBC radio *Children's Hour*), a biographer, editor, travel writer, author of information books, adult novelist, critic and reviewer. For many years, he was a tireless lecturer to young people, teachers and librarians, visiting schools and contributing to festivals, book weeks and conferences. He chaired the British Children's Writers' Group and the Society of Authors, and was a Fellow of the Royal Society of Literature.

Such a chronicle conceals the innovative, often pioneering nature of his work: he brought a new realism to HISTORICAL FICTION; wrote stories set in state day-schools rather than private boarding schools; and produced the first critical survey of British contemporary literature for children.

The son of a wine merchant, he was educated at Nottingham High School, winning an open scholarship in Classics to Oxford, which he abandoned after only one year, disenchanted by the quality of the teaching. He worked for brief periods with children in London's East End, as a journalist and then as a teacher in a south-coast private school. Given that he had recently married, and in the economic circumstances of the day, his decision to become a full-time writer in 1933 was a bold one. With interludes during World War II when he returned to teaching on the edge of the Lake District (later to become a favourite setting for his novels) and for service in the army (which took him as an education sergeant to India), Trease earned his living through writing.

The historical novels and ADVENTURE STORIES available to children in the early 1930s had changed little in spirit from the jingoistic tales of empire enjoyed by their fathers and grandfathers. Trease wrote in deliberate reaction against what he saw as sentimental romanticism. Politically, he stood well to the left, and the ROBIN HOOD and his comrades of Trease's first novel, *Bows Against The Barons* (1934), would have been more at home in Moscow than in Hollywood.

Cue for Treason (1940) exemplifies many of the qualities which remained hallmarks of his fiction. The narrative is swift and exciting. His cast is small; the hero and heroine are of an age similar to that of the reader – or perhaps a year or two older. They are drawn close to events and characters of national importance. Here, Peter Brownrigg and Kit Kirkstone (disguised as a boy) are on the run. They fall in with a troupe of travelling actors and eventually perform at the Globe, where Kit is a brilliant Juliet. SHAKESPEARE, Burbage and the court naturally become prominent players in Trease's plot. Thanks to Kit and Peter, Queen Elizabeth is saved from the assassin's pistol – due to be fired under cover of stage artillery in Act III of *Henry V*. (Trease's love of the stage was to take his young readers on numerous theatre trips from a comedy by Aristophanes at an Athenian Festival to an opera in London disrupted by suffragettes.) Kit is the kind of girl Trease enjoyed writing about – active, independent and witty, a courageous participant in an adventure, but ready to deploy more feminine manners when the situation demanded. The final paragraph finds Peter looking back from the security of a happy marriage to Kit; and throughout his writing, Trease often liked to suggest early feelings between the sexes – a stirring of jealousy, a sudden appreciation of a girl's beauty.

Also evident in *Cue for Treason* is his characteristic style. At once, we are in the middle of things. The language is economical, unmannered, hurrying the reader along to the next adventure; the dialogue is free from affected archaisms. There is little doubt that all will turn out well – though there may be prices to be paid – whether we are in revolutionary Russia (*The White Nights of St Petersburg*, 1967), occupied Guernsey (*Tomorrow is a Stranger*, 1987), a grim monastery in 16th-century Albania (*The Hills of Varna*, 1948), or industrial Victorian England (*No Horn at Midnight*, 1995).

Along the way, the young reader may well pick up, almost unawares, intriguing information. Trease's careful research took him into fields which history text books used to avoid – the detail of daily life in cottage or court, theatre or street. He concentrated upon European history and his settings are often underpinned by notebook jottings made on regular expeditions with his wife and daughter, undertaken by public transport long before the tourist industry distanced the traveller from the events and customs of the local population. His curiosity never waned: a trip to communist Romania in the 1980s enabled him to set the scene for young Greg and his attractive Romanian cousin Nadia to be in Bucharest and Timisoara to witness the fall of Ceausescu (*Song for a Tattered Flag*, 1992).

Trease's five *Bannermere* stories (1949–56) also broke new ground. He wrote about four children who attended the boys' and girls' grammar schools in a small Lakeland town. Unlike ARTHUR RANSOME'S SWALLOWS AND AMAZONS, these are term-time children with parents and teachers (of engaging eccentricity) who are integral to the plot. Days are crowded with lessons, sports days, cadet corps exercises and, inevitably, a school play which tours France at a time when, for most of Trease's readers, crossing the channel was the height of adventure. Unlike the denizens of *MALORY TOWERS* or *GREYFRIARS*, the children move up the school through the series, which finishes as they are starting at university.

Tales Out of School (1949) was the first critical survey of living British writers for children. Characteristically, Trease found it 'an exhilarating exercise, very different from anything I had done before'. He read assiduously and corresponded with some of the bestselling authors of the day, including W.E. Johns and MALCOLM SAVILLE, but that did not preclude firm judgements. ENID BLYTON'S 'exclamation marks, which often splash across the page like raindrops, suggest the kindergarten teacher telling the story "with expression"'. Arthur Ransome's children, he thought, 'take plenty of soundings at sea, but they plumb no emotional depths'. The book was so well received that he opened a way for the serious discussion of children's books which was to develop in the next two decades. When he came to revise the book in 1964, he found extensive changes were necessary to reflect the transformation which had taken place in the numbers and quality of children's books. Not without justification, he liked to think 'that this need for wholesale revision was, at least in part, my own fault'.

Throughout his extraordinarily various and numerous work, there is a quiet, uncondescending respect for his reader; he remained responsive to changing mores among the young, without compromising his own concern for 'continuing, common humanity'. His malevolent and sinister villains meet deserved and often dramatic ends, and there is plenty of satisfying play with sword and pistol; but, as Trease noted: 'It's not the splitting of skulls with battle axes that inspires me, it's the opening of minds in a gentler sense.' GPF

Treasure Island (1883) Novel by ROBERT LOUIS STEVENSON, a landmark book in the history of children's literature. It is both the apotheosis of the sea story and the ADVENTURE STORY of the 19th century, and a precursor of the more psychologically subtle books of the 20th century. Its inception is described by the author in his essay 'My First Book':

> On a chill September morning, by the cheek of a brisk fire, and the rain drumming on the window, I began *The Sea Cook* . . . It seemed to me original as sin; it seemed to belong to me like my right eye . . . It seems as though a full-grown experienced man of letters might engage to turn out *Treasure Island* at so many pages a day and keep his pipe alight. But alas! . . . fifteen days I stuck to it, and turned out fifteen chapters; and then, in the early paragraphs of the 16th, ignominiously lost hold . . . and here were the proofs of the beginning already waiting me . . . [*Young Folks* had begun to publish the book as a serial in October 1881] . . . I was thirty-one; I was head of a family; I had lost my health; I had never yet made £200 a year . . . was this to be another . . . fiasco? . . . I arrived at [Davos, where he was to pass the winter] . . . and behold! it flowed from me like small talk: and in a second tide of delightful industry, and again at the rate of a chapter a day, I finished *Treasure Island*.

Stevenson had, up to this point been a dilettante writer, partly supported by his father. Although his health was not good, he had romantically pursued Fanny Osborne across America, and it was for her son, now his step-son, Lloyd, that he began his 'first book'.

Treasure Island is on the surface a thriller, which skilfully increases the tension in each episode of the breathless adventure to find the murderous Captain Flint's gold. It has been pointed out that many of its effects depend on grotesquerie – Blind Pugh, Ben Gunn, Long John Silver – while Stevenson admitted that he had unconsciously plagiarised several writers, notably WASHINGTON IRVING. But the book's longevity may well be owing to its paradoxes. The villain, Long John Silver, a devious and brutal murderer, emerges as the closest thing in the book to a hero. The narrator, Jim Hawkins, and the supposedly 'good' characters – Doctor Livesey and Squire Trelawney – are all flawed, and a good deal less attractive.

Treasure Island was followed by the highly influential *A CHILD'S GARDEN OF VERSES* (1885) and *KIDNAPPED* (1886) before *The Strange Case of Dr Jekyll and Mr Hyde* (1886) – again exploring contrasting sides of human nature – sealed Stevenson's success. His two other children's books, *The Black Arrow* (1888) – described by ARTHUR RANSOME as 'a poor machine-made thing' – and *Catriona* (1893), sequel to *Kidnapped*, are generally considered to be inferior performances. Stevenson spent his final years, much revered by the natives, on Samoa. PLH

Treasure Islands see REVIEWING AND REVIEWERS; see also MICHAEL ROSEN

Treasure Seekers see *BASTABLES* SERIES

treasuries see MISCELLANIES

***Trebizon* series** Sequence of SCHOOL STORIES by British writer Anne Digby, following Rebecca Mason's progress at a fictional girls' boarding school, Trebizon, on the west coast of England. The first book in the series *First Term at Trebizon* is less conventional than its sequels. Rebecca is introduced to us as a 13-year-old who wants to be a writer and who already finds release and solace in writing. As the series develops, however, Rebecca becomes a more usual boarding-school heroine by being discovered to be a talented athlete. A career as a professional tennis player seems assured, but Rebecca chooses instead to stay at school and gain qualifications. Although this choice returns us to Rebecca the thinker, the action remains strictly outside her head rather than within it.

These are first and foremost ADVENTURE STORIES for girls. Through the series, Rebecca and her friends Tish and Sue brave the usual trials of life at a fictional boarding school: kidnappings, theft, near-expulsions, matters of honour. Their motives are always good even if their actions appear strange and hurtful. Only outsiders are selfish or unkind. Despite this lack of psychological depth, the stories are often gripping and it is not surprising that this has been a very popular series with young girls. AMN

Treece, Henry 1912–66 British poet and historical novelist, whose detailed knowledge of history, archaeology and anthropology began with the colourfully illustrated historical works which he was given as a boy. English, however, was the subject he taught at school for 24 years. As a poet he was co-founder of the 'New Apocalypse' Romantic literary movement,

Snorre Pig had big brown eyes,
Big brown eyes, big brown eyes,
And he was the Jarl of all the sties.
Hey up, for Snorre Pig!
When Snorre Pig met a lady sow,
A lady sow, a lady sow,
He'd smile and bend his knee full low;
Hey up, for Snorre Pig!
But when he met another boar,
Another boar, another boar,
He'd tread him into the farmyard floor;
Hey up, for Snorre Pig!

Illustration by CHARLES KEEPING from *Horned Helmet* by Henry Treece.

opposed to totalitarianism and committed to freedom of expression, and he began to publish poetry in 1939. After war service as an intelligence officer, his first historical novel for adults appeared in 1952, and two years later he launched his prodigious output of children's historical fiction, 31 titles in all.

In his introduction to *Legions of the Eagle* (1954), a Celtic boy's experiences of the Roman invasion in AD 43, he expressed his aspiration to write 'for the pleasure of boys and girls between the ages of nine and twelve', but there was also a didactic intent: 'This is a story of battle and treachery, as might be expected when so many peoples were living together, each with its own kings and heroes and beliefs. But at the end . . . it doesn't matter what colour your hair is, or what language you speak. The important thing is – what sort of person are you?' That philosophy infused all his children's fiction, epitomised in his masterpiece, the trilogy: *Viking's Dawn* (UK, 1955; USA, 1957), *The Road to Miklagard* (1957) and *Viking's Sunset* (UK, 1960; USA, 1961), republished posthumously in one volume entitled *THE VIKING SAGA* in 1985. Most of his stories are set in Roman or Viking Times (*The Centurion*, 1967; *The Horned Helmet*, 1963) but he also turned his attention to other periods, including ancient Greece (*The Windswept City: A Novel of the Trojan War*, 1967), the Norman conquest (*Man With a Sword*, 1962) and the medieval crusades (*The Children's Crusade*, 1958) and to the tale of ROBINSON CRUSOE: *The Return of Robinson Crusoe* (1958), issued in the United States as *The Further Adventures of Robinson Crusoe* (1959).

The historical detail in these stories is founded on extensive knowledge which Treece also displayed in a number of non-fiction books for children on castles and warfare, though some details have inevitably been overtaken by more recent archaeology. A realistic and harsh tone in relation to the brutal conditions of life in the periods of which he wrote is more tempered in his writing for children than in his adult novels, and is mitigated by serious reflection on morality, anthropology and comparative religion. His plots are fast-moving and dramatic, but less elaborate than those of ROSEMARY SUTCLIFF, and more conservative in interpretation than GEOFFREY TREASE, but Henry Treece belongs with these writers as a major exponent of the children's HISTORICAL FICTION which flourished in Britain especially in the period after World War II. PC

***Treehorn* trilogy** see FLORENCE PARRY HEIDE

Trelease, Jim 1941– American journalist and champion of children's reading. After 20 years as a journalist, he began visiting community classrooms and talking with children. He and his wife were also raising two children, reading aloud to them nightly. Students he met did not read much; those who did seemed to have teachers who read aloud daily. Seeing a connection, Trelease investigated available research, finding studies he thought inaccessible to lay readers. This inspired him to write and self-publish *The Read-Aloud Handbook* in 1979, a combination of practical tips and annotated booklist. Picked up by the publishers Penguin and touted by the advice column 'Dear Abby', it spent 17 weeks on the *New York Times* bestseller list. Three more American editions – plus British, Australian and Japanese versions – followed, and it became the all-time bestselling guide to children's literature for parents and teachers. A total of 1.6 million copies were sold. Two companion volumes followed, *Hey! Listen to This* (an anthology for children) and *Read All About It!* (for preteens and teens). In 1989, Trelease was honoured by the International Reading Association for his major contribution to reading in the 1980s. In 1984, he left journalism to become a much sought-after educational speaker. SMV

see also STORYTELLING

Treloar, Bruce 1946– Australian painter, and illustrator and writer of PICTUREBOOKS, born in New Zealand. *Kim* (1978), set on Norfolk Island, was awarded the RUSSELL CLARK AWARD in 1987. *Bumble's Dream* (1981), a commended CHILDREN'S BOOK COUNCIL OF AUSTRALIA Picturebook of the Year, was ahead of its time, creating a positive image for recycling, as the eccentric Mr Bumble builds a flying machine from junk. Further adventures are recounted in *Bumble's Island* (1984) and *Bumble's Journey* (1986). Treloar's large, crowded CROSS HATCHED ink drawings, in earthy colours, sprawl across the pages. *Cake I Hate* (1984) is an energetic book, with a brother and sister voicing their likes and dislikes in gigantic speech bubbles, while engaged in active pursuits, both clothed and boldly naked. Other titles include *Toby Jug and It* (1986), *Beware, Take Care* (1988) and *Only Me From Over the Sea* (1988). Treloar has also illustrated books for KATE WALKER, EDEL WIGNELL and JEAN CHAPMAN. JAP

Tresselt, Alvin 1916–2000 American writer born in New Jersey. After finishing Passaic High School, Tresselt held a number of jobs from 1934 to 1942. Rejected by the army for poor health, he worked at various defence jobs until 1946, when he joined the interior display team at Altman's in New York City, where he later became a copy-writer for the home furnishings department. He served as editor of *Humpty Dumpty Magazine* from 1952 to 1965 and editor of the *Parents' Magazine Press* from 1965 to 1967, eventually becoming executive editor and vice-president. His *White Snow Bright Snow*, illustrated by ROGER DUVOISIN, won the CALDECOTT MEDAL, 1948; *Bonnie Bess, the Weathervane Horse*, illustrated by Marilyn Hafner, won first prize in the PICTUREBOOK division of the *New York Herald Tribune*'s Children's Spring Book Festival, 1949; *The Dead Tree* won the Irma Simonton Block Award, 1973; *Rain Drop Splash*, illustrated by LEONARD WEISGARD, and *Hide and Seek Frog*, illustrated by Roger Duvoisin, were both Caldecott Honour Books. In addition to some 35 books of his own, he edited a group of English retellings of Japanese and German favourites, such as *Tears of the Dragon* (1967), *Crane Maiden* (1968), *Land of Lost Buttons* (1970), *Ogre and His Bride* (1971), *Lim Fu and the Golden Mountain* (1971) and *Little Mouse Who Tarried* (1971). KSB

Tretis, Le (c. 1275) Extant in 16 manuscripts, this 1,140-line poem by Walter de Bibbesworth [or Biblesworth], in Anglo-Norman with Middle-English interlinear glosses, was intended to teach French to the children of the English nobility and gentry. Written at the request of Lady Dionysia de Monehensey so that the rising generation might know the language from early childhood, it begins with an account of the child from birth, follows with the body, clothing, children's manners, diet, the barn, weaving, brewing, the weather, familiar flora and fauna, rural occupations, building and houses, and cooking; it closes with a feast. It was a popular elementary text in its time. GA

Treviño, Elizabeth Borton de 1904– American author of HISTORICAL FICTION and INFORMATION BOOKS. In the 1920s, Borton studied violin at the Boston Conservatory and became the only woman reporter on the Boston *Herald*. Left jobless by the Depression, she was invited to write an addition to the popular *POLLYANNA* SERIES. As four sequels followed *Pollyanna in Hollywood* (1931), her writing steadily improved, well beyond the usual level of formula fiction. In 1935 she married Luis Treviño Gomez; her account of married life in Mexico, *My Heart Lies South*, became a 1953 bestseller. A lifelong interest in Spain and Latin America, deepened by her marriage and the rearing of two Mexican sons, and a desire to further inter-cultural understanding, inspired several children's books. *Nacar, the White Deer* (1963) came from historical records of a white deer shipped from Mexico to the King of Spain, *Casilda of the Rising Moon* (1967) from a little-known girl saint of medieval Spain; both stories celebrate the power of faith and gentleness. *I, Juan de Pareja* (1965), winner of the NEWBERY AWARD, based on the true story of the slave of Velasquez who became a painter, evokes both 17th-century Spain and the possibility of interracial friendship. SR

Trevor, William see *JULIET'S STORY*

Trezise, Percy (James) 1923– Australian writer and artist, whose earlier career as a pilot in the outback introduced him to the country and to the Aboriginal rock art which has become the subject of his art, his leisure and his livelihood. In the 1960s he documented many Aboriginal stories and with his friend Dick Roughsey, an Aboriginal artist from Mornington Island, he began to write and illustrate a series of PICTUREBOOKS which were unique in Australian publishing. Two of their books won the CHILDREN'S BOOK COUNCIL OF AUSTRALIA Picturebook of the Year Award: *The Rainbow Serpent* (1975) and *The Quinkins* (1977). The stories relate directly to the images painted in the rock art preserved in the Far North Queensland caves. After Roughsey's death, Trezise continued the books, some jointly produced with Mary Haginikitas, another North Queensland artist and BUSH guide. Other memorable titles have been *The Giant Devil Dingo* (with Dick Roughsey, 1973), *Peopling of Australia* (1987), *The Last of his Tribe* (with Haginikitas, 1989), and *Children of the Great Lake* (1992). Titles in his *Journey of the Great Lake* series include *Land of the Dingo People*

'Brown Bruin was a solemn, dignified bear.' Illustration by Palmer Cox from *The Monkey's Trick* by E. Veale.

(1997) and *Land of the Emu People* (1998). He has also published an autobiography, *Dream Road: Journey Among Men* (1991), and received an Order of Australia. RS

see also Aboriginal culture in children's books

Triads of the Island of Britain, The see Welsh mythology and folklore

trickster A comic figure in many folk literatures, associated with disruption and disorder, and dominated by appetites. Frequently, but not exclusively male, the trickster inhabits the margins of society or the border between the divine and the mortal. His ability to transform his shape underscores his ambiguous character. He is characterised by deceitfulness, vanity, immense appetites and foolishness as well as beneficent power and purpose. He brings chaos and disorder into stable societies through cheating, thievery and even murder. In Greek myth, he is Hermes and Prometheus. In African and African diaspora literatures he is the Monkey, Anancy the spider, or the Hare. In Native American tales he is, among others, the Coyote, the Raven, the Hare or the Wolverine. Probably the best-known example of a trickster is Brer Rabbit in Joel Chandler Harris's *Uncle Remus Stories*. But trickster figures appear in various guises, from Puss in Perrault's 'The Master Cat, or Puss in Boots' to Iktomi in Paul Goble's recent series of Native American legends. EBD

see also Native Americans in children's literature

Tricksters, The (1996) New Zealand novel by Margaret Mahy which interweaves three gripping mysteries: 17-year-old Ariadne's secret imaginative power as a romance writer; her family's secret concerning fatherhood; and Teddy's murder 80 years ago. One summer Christmas holiday, Harry (Ariadne) invokes Teddy's ghost out of the sea, representing her deepest desires. Three Tricksters appear, embodying Teddy's mind, body and spirit. They become the catalyst for explosive denouements leading to forgiveness and healing. Mahy gains imagistic power from linking Greek myth to her internalised New Zealand setting, Lyttelton harbour – an extinct volcanic crater. The beach symbolises lines repeatedly crossed in relationships, creativity, reality and illusion. DAH

Trimmer, Sarah 1741–1810 Writer, educator and mother of 12. Trimmer's earliest publication (following the example of Anna Barbauld) was of the lessons she gave her own children: *Easy Introduction to the Knowledge of Nature* (1782) reached its eleventh edition by 1802. This was followed by *Sacred History, Selected from the Scriptures, with Annotations and Reflections Adapted to the Comprehension of Young Persons* (6 volumes, 1782–84). Engaged in the promotion of Sunday schools and a 'school of industry' for girls, she developed the idea of 'series of prints . . . designed as ornaments for those apartments in which children receive the first rudiments of the education'. Accompanied by simple but effective explanatory texts, these dramatic little wood engravings illustrate scenes from ancient history, Roman history, scripture history and English history and were frequently republished in the early decades of the 19th century. Her periodical *Guardian of Education* (1802–6) was perhaps the earliest critical journal of children's literature in English. Mrs Trimmer is best remembered, however, for her *Fabulous Histories* (1786), later retitled *The History of the Robins*, in which Christian piety accompanies a sympathy for nature undoubtedly influenced by Jean Jacques Rousseau and Enlightenment values. PC

***Tripods* Trilogy** (1967–8) Novels written by British author John Christopher in response to a request from a publisher to write a science fiction book for children. Tired of producing science fiction, and more interested in the past than the future, Christopher blended requirement with inclination by writing about a future that had gone back to the past. This trilogy was the result. The earth's technology has been destroyed and people live in a dull medieval peace imposed by the Masters, superior beings from a distant world, whose visible representatives are the Tripods, great gleaming metal hemispheres on articulated legs. The Masters keep people in order by 'capping', a kind of mental castration carried out at adolescence. The theme of the trilogy is the rebellion and eventual triumph of a small group of free humans. In *The White Mountains* (1967), the protagonist, Will, escapes being capped and runs away with two other boys to join the rebels in their mountain fastness. In *The City of Gold and Lead* (1967), Will and a friend gain access to the Masters' city which is built under a great crystal dome because the Masters cannot breathe Earth air. In the third book, *The Pool of Fire* (1968), the Masters are destroyed. Yet a world conference held afterwards cannot decide on a system for the future. In these books, Christopher combined the page-turning grip of an expertly told ADVENTURE STORY with an unusual distinction of style and interest in ideas. JRT

Trites, Roberta Seelinger see CRITICAL APPROACHES TO CHILDREN'S LITERATURE

Tritten, Charles see *HEIDI*

Trouble Half-Way (1985) Novel by the British author JAN MARK. Amy lives on a Gravesend Council Estate. Her relationship with Richard, her new stepfather and long-distance lorry driver, is shy and slightly hostile; her mother is possessive of her. Amy's life, defined by family, school and ambitions in gymnastics, is sheltered and confined. When Mum has to go to Amy's sick grandfather, Amy is left with Richard who, forced by economics, against her will and her mother's wishes, takes her on a roundabout journey to Manchester. A sight of an Oldham cotton mill called 'Amy' becomes her justification, a quest nearly prevented when the lorry breaks down. However, she travels on alone by train, a shaping experience. She gains new insights, breaks many childhood bonds and understands both herself and Richard better: she will be radically changed. The novel works at many levels: humorous, with concrete, perfectly shaped prose and sharp dialogue, insightful about family relationships, loyalties and children's minds, structurally providing both a reverberating image of growing up and a quirkily sympathetic celebration of many facets of England, exhibiting fascination with and understanding of concrete processes and objects – all representative virtues of Mark's work. DCH

Trouble with Donovan Croft, The (1974) Novel by British author BERNARD ASHLEY. A deeply confused West Indian boy, temporarily separated from his parents and fostered by a white family, responds by retreating into mutism and then trying to run away from school. He is found and returned, but then encounters wounding racist attitudes before finally finding his voice in order to shout a warning to his foster-brother Dick. One of the first British novels to tackle racism and also to feature a black child as hero, this stirring and exciting story has the typical toughness and authenticity found in all of Ashley's novels. NT

see also BIAS IN CHILDREN'S BOOKS

Troughton, Joanna 1947– British illustrator and writer. Troughton is known for her retellings and ILLUSTRATIONS of myths and legends, such as *The Little Mohee* (1971) and *Sir Gawain and the Loathly Damsel* (1972). In the *Folk Tales of the World* series, which includes titles such as *How the Birds Changed their Feathers* (1976), *What Made Tiddalik Laugh* (1977) and *Tortoise's Dream* (1980), she successfully conveys the atmosphere of each tale's country of origin, using boldly executed artwork, with dramatic colour, design and decoration. JAG

Trowbridge, John Townsend 1827–1916 American novelist, poet and co-editor of *OUR YOUNG FOLKS* from 1865 until its absorption by *ST NICHOLAS* in 1873. Known by adult readers for his abolitionist novel *Cudjo's Cave* (1864), Trowbridge became one of America's most popular authors of boys' stories with his *Jack Hazard* series (1871–5). *His One Fault* (1886) and *Two Biddicut Boys* (1898) show him at his best. In both, long chases – pursuing a stolen horse and an elusive con-man – test the intelligence and determination of his Yankee heroes through a succession of amusing and unexpected twists of plot. SR

Truckers (1989) First volume in a FANTASY trilogy by the British author TERRY PRATCHETT, centred on tiny 'nomes' who inhabit a department store. The store's slogan, 'All things under one roof', suggests a store-as-universe, the nomes' beliefs reinforced by the predictable round of seasonal special offers. The store as a microcosmic world offers readers a different perspective from which to reflect on reality. In the sequels, *Diggers* (1990) and *Wings* (1990), the nomes, guided by their 'black box', endeavour to be reunited with their spaceship. Pratchett presents society from a four-inch-high vantage point, resulting in the reader seeing both the global and the commonplace in new ways. Pratchett does not shy away from dealing with large issues such as religion or cultural difference. He assumes an intellectual curiosity in his readers but seriousness of purpose is tempered by humour and verbal wit. In *Truckers*, the black box challenges the nomes to decide whether they consider themselves to be 'intelligent nomes or just clever animals'. Readers are offered the chance to reflect on the difference. The posing of such a question shows Pratchett's respect for his readers' intelligence, providing one possible clue to his bestselling success. GCH

Tucker, Nicholas see CHILDIST CRITICISM; CRITICAL APPROACHES TO CHILDREN'S LITERATURE; see also FAIRY TALES; YOUNG ADULT FICTION

Tudor, Tasha (Natasha Burgess McCready) 1915– American illustrator, anthologist, and author-illustrator of PICTUREBOOKS. As a young girl, Tudor planned to have a farm and felt more comfortable in long dresses than in modern clothes. As a divorced mother of four, she brought to life her idealised version of a 19th-century New England farm and used it as material. *Beeky's Christmas* (1961), for example, seems to depict a 19th-century family's Christmas celebration; the family, its customs and its corgis, however, are Tudor's own. In her old age, Tudor herself became an icon, her deliberately anachronistic way of life recorded by Richard Brown's lavish colour photographs in *The Private World of Tasha Tudor* (1992). After *Pumpkin Moonshine* (1938), Tudor illustrated over 70 books, including *MOTHER GOOSE* (1944), RUMER GODDEN's *The Dolls' House* (1947) and *THE SECRET GARDEN* (1962), as well as her own anthologies and picturebooks. Her work is instantly recognisable: soft colours; decorative borders; bright-eyed, innocent children in quaint, old-fashioned clothes; exquisitely detailed plants, birds and animals in unspoiled natural settings; cosy, firelit interiors; corgis and dolls. Her appeal is somewhat like that of KATE GREENAWAY. SR

Tulloch, Richard (George) 1949– Australian TELEVISION scriptwriter of more than 100 *Bananas in Pyjamas* episodes (1992–6) and ten books in the series, including *Banana News* and *Doctor Bananas*. A skilful writer of stage adaptations, including ROBIN KLEIN's novel *Hating Alison Ashley* and GILLIAN RUBINSTEIN's *SPACE DEMONS*, he has also created original youth-orientated plays such as *Year 9 are Animals* (1981) and *Could do Better* (1989). HE

Tunis, John 1889–1975 American novelist, born in Boston and educated at Harvard. A prolific writer, primarily of sports novels for boys, Tunis began as a sports commentator and writer. He originally aspired to write novels for adult readers, but when in 1938 he submitted *The Iron Duke* for publication, he was advised to consider revising it for younger readers. While he initially balked at such an idea, he quickly became one of the most popular and productive novelists in the boys' sports genres. His novels argue for an ideal, classical and anti-commercialist view of sports, in which athletic competition teaches enobling values and builds character. BH

Tunnel, The (1989) PICTUREBOOK by the British illustrator ANTHONY BROWNE that transposes FAIRY TALE themes into a modern, urban setting. There is little here of Browne's trademark surrealist imagery but a good deal of pointed symbolism. For example, the first time we meet the symbolically named Jack and Rose – the brother and sister protagonists of the tale – we see them posed against contrasting backgrounds: a brick wall for the tough, football-playing Jack and a William-Morris-like wallpaper for the dreamy, fairy-tale-obsessed Rose. The story itself has a schematic air, the latter half being acted out against some of the props and scenery of Rose's beloved tales. Sent out to play together by their mother, the siblings become separated when Jack crawls down a tunnel and disappears. The red-coated Rose courageously follows and finds her brother turned to stone in a forest clearing. She embraces him, her bravery, loyalty and love restoring the effigy to flesh and blood. *The Tunnel* is thus not a retelling of any one fairy tale, and is relatively cool and humourless in tone, but the lack of specificity, combined with numerous allusions to traditional tales, allows for many intertextual resonances. DL

Tunnicliffe, C.J. see LADYBIRD BOOKS; *PUFFIN PICTURE BOOKS*

Turbulent Term of Tyke Tiler, The see *CRICKLEPIT COMBINED SCHOOL* SERIES; see also CAROLYN DINAN

Turkle, Brinton 1915– American illustrator and writer praised for his ability to breathe life into history for young readers. In a career spanning over three decades, Turkle has written and illustrated books that address a broad variety of topics. *The Fiddler of High Lonesome* (1968) recreates Appalachian life, while *Do Not Open* (1981) is a FAIRY TALE about an old woman who finds a magical bottle with a genie in it washed up on the beach. Turkle's best-known books are the four that feature young Obadiah, a Quaker boy living in 19th-century Nantucket. Children find the Obadiah stories intriguing because he faces many of the problems that children of any period must confront. In *Obadiah the Bold* (1965), he dreams of being a fierce pirate when he grows up; in *Thy Friend, Obadiah* (1969), he deals with the attention of an unwanted friend – a seagull; in *The Adventures of Obadiah* (1972), he must learn the difference between truth and lies; and in *Rachel and Obadiah* (1978), he learns a lesson when his little sister wins a race with him. All of the Obadiah stories show

Turkle's ability to tell lively, engaging stories that bring a host of different settings and characters to life. SAI

Turner [Burwell], Ethel (Mary) 1870–1958 Australian novelist and journalist, creator of *SEVEN LITTLE AUSTRALIANS* (1894). Turner migrated to Sydney with her mother, Sarah, and siblings in 1880, after her father died. Ethel and her elder sister Lilian became part of the first class formed at Sydney Girls High in 1883. At school she founded the *Iris*, a lively magazine that sold advertisements, and when she left school in 1888, the two sisters established the *Parthenon*, a literary magazine. Turner's first story for the *Sydney Bulletin*, *The Little Duchess* (1892), made it clear that a new talent had arrived. Her story of the back streets, *Wilkes of Waterloo* for the *Daily Telegraph* (1893), was quite daring in exposing wife beaters.

With her crowning literary achievement, *Seven Little Australians* and its sequel, *The Family at Misrule* (1895), Australian children had stories that they could enjoy and relate to. *The Little Larrikin* (1896) was based on Turner's half-brother Rex, whose adventures were legion. She wrote, 'There is hardly anything I find that you can put it past a child to say – or do.' Herbert Curlewis, a law student and contributor to the Turner girls' magazine, courted Ethel for years, but it was only in 1896 when her career as a writer was clearly established that she agreed to marriage.

Most of Ethel's 44 books were published by Ward Lock of London, including the semi-autobiographical *Three Little Maids* (1900). *In the Mist of the Mountains* (1906) was the first of the stories celebrating the family's love of the Blue Mountains, where her special friends, Sir William and Lily Cullen, remarkable for their concern to protect the environment, had established a lovely home. During World War I, Ethel devised the *Cub* series (from 1915) with a patriotic theme; at the same time she was writing articles, including *Belgium, Our Tears*, and poems for metropolitan papers. In 1921 she began editing *Sunbeams*, devising, with the help of Jimmy Bancks, the character who went into history as *GINGER MEGGS*. ATY

Turner, Ann [Warren] 1945– American writer of children's books for all ages. Born in Northampton, Massachusetts, Turner has published a wide range of books, including non-fiction, poetry, FANTASY, and realistic and HISTORICAL FICTION. Turner's own family has served as the source of some of her stories. *Katie's Trunk* (1992) is a PICTUREBOOK about the Revolutionary War drawn from events in her family's history, and the description of slavery in *Nettie's Trip South* (1987) was inspired by a diary account of Turner's great-grandmother. The past, and tensions between the past and present, are often themes in her work. In *Rosemary's Witch* (1991) Turner uses a fantasy story about an abandoned witch to explore the issue of social outcasts. Throughout her varied writings, Turner captures the cadences of sound and underpins her descriptions with a keen sense of poetic imagery. In *Katie's Trunk*, the narrator describes her anticipation of coming troubles: 'I could feel the itchiness in the air . . . / the clouds tumbling over the trees/ bringing rain– a sour rain.' Whether in her poems about children or novels for adolescents, Turner creates tangible scenes and strong characterisation using simple and poetic language. PTC

Turner, Elizabeth 1775–1846 British author of moral tales in verse, such as *The Daisy* (1807) and *The Cowslip* (1811). She tempered her didactic intentions with a sense of fun, resulting in poems which anticipate the full-blown CAUTIONARY VERSE of writers like HILAIRE BELLOC. MCCS

Turska, Krystyna 1933– Turska arrived in England at the age of 15 after a childhood in Poland and some time in a concentration camp in Russia. She has contributed expressive line drawings to the work of many authors, including WILLIAM MAYNE, JAMES REEVES, ALAN GARNER, GEOFFREY TREASE, BARBARA WILLARD and GILLIAN AVERY. Her dramatic, richly coloured PICTUREBOOK *Pegasus* was runner-up for the KATE GREENAWAY MEDAL in 1970, which she won in 1972 for *The Woodcutter's Duck*. JAG

Twain, Mark [Samuel Langhorne Clemens] 1835–1910 American lecturer, satirist and author. Born in Florida, Missouri, on 30 November 1835, Clemens moved to Hannibal in 1839 and spent his youth on the river and exploring the surrounding area. When his father died in 1847, he quit school and apprenticed himself in a printshop. At 18, Clemens left Hannibal to work as a journeyman printer; then in 1857, he signed on with Captain Horace Bixby as a riverboat pilot apprentice and subsequently as a licensed riverboat pilot. When the Civil War closed the Mississippi to travel, Clemens served two weeks in a small band of Confederate volunteers, but left the war for the Nevada Territory. Working for the Territorial Enterprise, he assumed the pen-name Mark Twain, a riverboat term meaning 'two fathoms deep'.

During this time, he associated with other rising literary figures, including Bret Harte, and wrote the immediately acclaimed 'The Celebrated Jumping Frog of Calaveras County' in 1865. He further developed his literary career with letters and lectures about his travels to the Sandwich Islands, Europe and the Holy Land. He met the brother of his future wife, Olivia

Langdon of Elmira, New York, on the latter trip. After a two-year courtship, he married Olivia in 1870; they settled in Hartford, Connecticut, and spent their summers in Elmira where Twain wrote in his Quarry Farm study.

Twain published the nostalgic remembrance of his boyhood, *The Adventures of Tom Sawyer*, in 1876 and thereby emerged as a writer of children's books. Departures from the previously idealised literary view of childhood, *Tom Sawyer* and its sequel, *The Adventures of Huckleberry Finn* (1884), present a realistic view of the antebellum South. His other successful children's books were published during this decade: *The Prince and the Pauper* in 1882 and *A Connecticut Yankee in King Arthur's Court* in 1889. Despite these successes, Twain suffered bankruptcy after investing in an unsuccessful typesetting machine and in his own failed publishing house. After the publication of *The Tragedy of Pudd'nhead Wilson* (1894), he embarked on a successful lecture tour of Europe.

Although Oxford University presented Twain with an honorary doctorate, he was embittered by the decade's misfortunes, including his wife's prolonged illness, the death of his daughter Susy, and the continued attempts to ban his works because of their harshness and realism. His long-time friendship with William Dean Howells notwithstanding, Twain was never fully accepted by the élitist literary culture of New England. The writings of his last decade are marked by bitterness and lack the quality of his earlier successes. His beloved 'Livy' died in 1904, and his daughter Jean died in 1909. Samuel Langhome Clemens died on 21 April 1910.

Ernest Hemingway said of Clemens: 'All modern American literature comes from one book by Mark Twain called *Huckleberry Finn*.' More specifically, through his realistic and humorous depiction of real children in real settings who speak in authentic dialect, Twain set the stage for the next generation of children's books. CLR

'Twas The Night Before Christmas see *A Visit from St Nicholas*

Tweedledum and Tweedledee An old song, the words of which Alice, in *Through the Looking Glass* (see Alice's Adventures in Wonderland), could not help recalling when she met the two characters marked 'DUM' and 'DEE'. The version Alice remembered concerned a quarrel over a 'nice new rattle', but in 1725 a bitter feud had arisen between Bononcini and Handel in which, according to the onlookers, it was difficult to distinguish what difference there was between the opposing parties. John Byrom wrote:

> Some say, compar'd to Bononcini,
> That Mynheer Handel's but a Ninny;
> Others aver, that he to Handel
> Is scarcely fit to hold a Candle:
> Strange all this Difference should be
> 'Twixt Tweedle-dum and Tweedle-dee!

Byrom is said to have coined the words 'Tweedledum' and 'Tweedledee'. However, the final couplet has also been attributed to both of the contemporary satirists, Jonathan Swift and Alexander Pope. The nursery rhyme was not found in print till 80 years later, in *Original Ditties for the Nursery*, published by John Harris (c. 1805). It is not clear whether the rhyme was first composed to describe the feud, or whether a version existed already and gave Byrom the idea for his lines. IO

Twelve and the Genii, The see Pauline Clarke; see also literature within children's literature; Charlotte, Emily and Anne Brontë

Twelve Dancing Princesses, The see Grimm brothers; Errol le Cain; see also Janet Lunn; Ruth Sanderson

Twinkle, Twinkle, Little Star see nursery rhymes; see also Ann and Jane Taylor

Twizzle see comics, periodicals and magazines

Two Weeks with the Queen (1989) Innovative Australian novel by Morris Gleitzman which deals unflinchingly with the tragedy of childhood death. It begins as comedy: Colin is irritated by the favouritism his parents show his younger brother, until he learns that Luke is dying of leukemia. In searching for a way to save Luke, Colin is brought face to face with the realities of Aids (hence the 'queen' of the title) – and the hard lesson that love and friendship are essential when the limits of the human power to deal with illness are reached. Gleitzman's extraordinary ability to treat humorously such a topic in a manner which is at once honest, unsentimental and suited to his intended audience is the trademark of his distinctive and uncompromising style. *Two Weeks with the Queen* has been particularly popular with young readers in the United Kingdom. MN

Two's Company (1992) First children's collection by Jackie Kay, which won the *Signal* Award. Kay writes about her childhood and that of her young son. The opening poem introduces the theme of double identity which runs through the collection: 'People don't understand: there are two Carla Johnsons./The one with wings and the one with hands.' Written in the first person and in a free verse close to speech, Kay's poems use real and imaginary voices to give immediacy to experiences of duality, whether having an imaginary friend, sharing the two houses of divorced parents or having two mothers. ML

Tyger, The see *SONGS OF INNOCENCE AND EXPERIENCE*; see also KENNETH KOCH; ADRIAN MITCHELL

Tyler, Anna Cogswell see MARIE SHEDLOCK

typography In PICTUREBOOKS, the design of the whole book, including the choice of format, size, typeface, position of display lettering, length of lines (justified or unjustified), spacing between lines, and break of lines to facilitate reading. JD

U

Uchida, Yoshiko 1921–92 Revered American children's writer who was one of the first to explore the depths of her Japanese cultural heritage in her books. Her retellings of Japanese FOLKTALES were collected in *The Dancing Kettle and Other Japanese Folk Tales* (1949) and *The Magic Listening Cap: More Folk Tales from Japan* (1955), as well as in individual titles such as *Rokubei and the Thousand Rice Bowls* (1962) and *The Two Foolish Cats* (1987). She wrote realistic and fictional works about life in relocation camps during World War II, based on her own experiences: *Journey to Topaz* (1971), *Desert Exile* (1982), and *Journey Home* (1978). In a PICTUREBOOK, *The Bracelet* (1993), she told of the camp experience through the friendship of two young girls, one who stayed behind and one who was sent away. In *The Invisible Thread: A Memoir* (1991) Uchida describes what her family endured during the war years when they were taken from their home in Berkeley, California, and forced to live in horse stables before being sent to a relocation centre in Utah. Uchida brought her readers a broader picture of the world through her moving and sensitive stories of a painful time in American history. BG

see also WAR STORIES

Uderzo, Albert see *ASTERIX*

Ugly Duckling, The see HANS CHRISTIAN ANDERSEN; JONATHAN HEALE

Ukoli, Neville 1940– Nigerian journalist and author of children's books, born in Warri, Delta State. His children's books reflect a concern for traditional culture but not an uncritical acceptance. In *The Twins of the Rain Forest* (1969) a young man rescues his twin sisters at a time when twins were often left to die. Ukoli's PICTUREBOOK, *The Antelope That Hurried* (1974), teaches the virtue of making haste slowly. His other works include *Softly, Softly* (1982), a story and two FOLKTALES from the Itsekiri people, and *Home to the River* (1975), a play set in the riverine area of Nigeria. VD

Ulster Cycle, The see IRISH MYTHOLOGY AND FOLKLORE

Umelo, Rosina Nigerian author of British birth, Nigerian by marriage, best known for her perceptive YOUNG ADULT FICTION which often focuses on adolescent girls. The heroine of *Felicia* (1978) comes home from the Nigerian Civil War, sad and pregnant, refusing to name the father. Withstanding all pressures, she gains some grudging respect for her perseverance and courage. *Something to Hide* (1986), a novel set in Kenya, traces the maturing of two young women, a poor relation and her more favoured cousin, who both learn to accept responsibility for their actions. *The Finger of Suspicion* (1984) addresses the dangers of superstition: when everything begins to go right for a young couple, neighbours suspect they have sacrificed their housemaid. More recent novels for young adults include *Please Forgive Me* and *Forever*. During her long career as an educator, writer and editor, Umelo has also produced a volume of short stories (*The Man Who Ate the Money*, 1978), literature anthologies and, in the 1990s, books for less mature readers. VD

Uncle Albert Series of novels by British author and professor of physics, Russell Stannard. The first novel, *The Time and Space of Uncle Albert* (1989) received great critical acclaim. It explains Einstein's second theory of relativity to children in a fictional form; Gedanken – her name means 'experiments' – comes home from school with a science project to complete. Uncle Albert dreams her a spaceship which takes her into space and demonstrates the effects of relativity so that she can see and understand them. Later books follow the same format, explaining the General Theory of Relativity and Einstein's theories about the nature of electrons. Each book ends with a series of questions about the ideas explained in the text. These are still contained within the fictional format, but are used to revise and clarify the issues raised in the text and are followed by a set of brief explanations. The books end with a section entitled 'a bit of real science'. Further explanations are published in Stannard's books of letters children have written to Uncle Albert. Although the fiction exists only as a vehicle for the scientific explanations, it is nevertheless convincing enough to engage the reader's attention. KA

Uncle Remus see JOEL CHANDLER HARRIS; see also AFRICAN MYTHOLOGY AND FOLKTALES; ANIMALS IN FICTION; A. B. FROST; JULIUS LESTER

***Uncle* series** see MARTIN, J. P.

Uncle Tom's Cabin (1852) The best-known abolitionist novel ever written, famous for its depiction of the saintly child Little Eva and the slave child Topsy, as well as the eponymous hero. Harriet Beecher Stowe (1811–96) claimed that she wrote it under 'God's influence'. Uncle Tom remains loyal to his master, even after Mr Shelby sells him 'down the river' and separates him from his family. Tom is finally purchased by Simon Legree, a slave-owner in the deep south who works his slaves to death, including Uncle Tom. Stowe's portrayal of the slave-owning south as a place of violence and inhumanity struck an emotional cord with abolitionists all over the world. Though Stowe depicts the physical violence slaves endure, it is the emotional violence they suffer that is central to her abolitionist vision. The narrative works upon the sentiments of the reader to such a degree that the book has been labelled – and often scorned – as 'sentimental'. Because of Uncle Tom's pacifism, JAMES BALDWIN, Richard Wright and others have criticised the novel as racist. Still, Stowe's work remains popular and controversial today in part because, as one critic wrote, the novel demonstrates that, regarding human dignity, 'it is the women and the slaves and the children, if anyone, who care'. JZo

***Uncle Wiggily* series** A humorous series of American books centred on the character Uncle Wiggily, an anthropomorphic rabbit who lives with his family in a 'hollow stump bungalow' in Woodland, near the Orange Ice Mountains. The character was created in 1910 for the *Newark News* (New Jersey) by newspaperman Howard R. Garis (1873–1962), who later became a full-time novelist for the STRATEMEYER SYNDICATE. For more than 50 years, stories appeared six days a week, and in 1912 the first volume of collected tales was published. Approximately 40 volumes were produced through the late 1940s, with new editions appearing as late as 1976. The series changed with the times, as *Uncle Wiggily's Rheumatism* (1920) gave way to *Uncle Wiggily's Automobile* (1939), reflecting the events and interests of Garis's readers. The popularity of this irascible rabbit is due in no small part to Garis's own personality, showmanship and talents for marketing. MS

see also ADVENTURE STORIES

Under The Window (1878) Illustrated collection of verse which launched the phenomenal success of KATE GREENAWAY. Subtitled 'Pictures and Rhymes for Children', the quality of the book lies in its charming variety of page design. Simple rhymes with a tripping metre and the singing quality of traditional NURSERY RHYMES are integrated in a lively way with pictures of prosperous children in joyful and innocent play: 'The little boys dance and the little girls run: If it's bad to have money it's worse to have none.' The darkest moment is the burial of a bird: 'Poor Dicky's dead . . .' These verses celebrate the exuberance and imagination of young children with little condescension or moralising. PC

Underhill, Liz see *MISS TAFFERTY'S CATS*

Ungerer, Tomi 1931– For much of his illustrating life, Ungerer lived in the United States but his youth was spent in some poverty, hardship and trauma in and around Strasbourg. The gruesome slant that is clearly visible in his work possibly springs from his early life but it is always, at any rate in his books for children, relieved by comedy, inventiveness and affection. The hat, in the highly fantastical and circular comedy *The Hat* (1970), is put to various inventive and lucrative uses in a story packed with understated visual and verbal jokes. Despite the success of this PICTUREBOOK and others such as *Zeralda's Ogre* (1987) and *The Beast of Monsieur Racine* (1971), in which bold pictures (solid colours and black outlines) keep pace with precisely written texts, Ungerer has mostly worked for adults. He contributed lively line drawings to the children's novel *FLAT STANLEY* (Jeff Brown) and to collections by WILLIAM COLE of comic verse. JAG

Up and Up (1979) Wordless strip-cartoon PICTUREBOOK by the British illustrator SHIRLEY HUGHES, about a little girl who is determined to fly like a bird. Ingenuity – in the form of paper wings, a leap from a ladder, and holding up a cluster of balloons – fails; FANTASY – every child's magic resource – succeeds. After defying gravity, astonished parents, astounded bystanders and abortive attempts to catch her, she finally comes down to earth to receive congratulations and a boiled egg for breakfast. The ENDPAPER sets the scene with a bird's-eye view of the little aerobat's natural habitat, and the first page-opening – a bird in flight and a sequence of eight small strips – propels us into the action with a wing-beat and a running jump. When it suits her visual narrative needs, Hughes ignores the traditional arrangement, shape and scale of comic-strip frames and stretches the latter vertically and horizontally. This extends the drawing area for showing sustained actions. In effect it also adds an implied temporal dimension and varies the visual rhythms of the page-openings. The viewpoint alternatively keeps us grounded or has us swooping about. The simple medium, intensely vigorous black line drawings on a sepia background, catches the power of the child's imagination. JD

Up in the Tree (1978) PICTUREBOOK written, illustrated and hand-lettered by the Canadian poet and novelist Margaret Atwood and dedicated to her daughter, Jess. Her first book for children, it is simple in word choice, story line, and ILLUSTRATION. The gender of the characters is not specific, perhaps in keeping with Atwood's feminist views. Themes of environmental sensitivity, a concern for equality, and the importance of adjusting to change emerge in the rhythmic verse geared to beginning readers. Even in the halting rhythm with which new readers sound out the monosyllabic words, the drama and enthusiasm of two little people living in an apple tree unfolds. 'We swing in the spring/and we crawl in the fall/and we dance in the branches.' The cadence of the words matches the tone of the story as it progresses. When two beavers chew on the ladder the children have used to climb their tree, they are stranded. They must solve their dilemma alone, as no adults are present in this world of living happily among the tree heights. With the help of a bird they are able to get down and devise new stairs – tacked to the tree – so they can continue their adventure in the tree above. LAW

Upton, Florence K. see *GOLLIWOGG*; see also ILLUSTRATION IN CHILDREN'S BOOKS

urchin verse Term employed by JOHN ROWE TOWNSEND in *Written for Children* (1987) to describe the 'demotic' movement in British children's poetry initiated by MICHAEL ROSEN'S *MIND YOUR OWN BUSINESS* (1974) and developed by ROGER MCGOUGH, KIT WRIGHT and GARETH OWEN. It deals unromantically with family and street life, rather than with nature. ML

Ure, Jean 1943– Prolific British writer for both adults and children, best known for her YOUNG ADULT novels. Ure trained at the Weber-Douglas Academy of Dramatic Art and a number of her books are set in the world of the theatre. Many of the characters are working-class, and few are shown eating since, according to *BOOKS FOR KEEPS*, Ure is a strict vegetarian and will not show her characters eating meat. Her novel *A Proper Little Nooryeff* (1982) takes a humorous look at the world of the ballet school when a reluctant boy is cajoled into dancing. Other novels tackle more serious issues: *See You Thursday* (1981) and its sequels examine the relationship between a teenage girl and her family's blind lodger; in *One Green Leaf* (1987) Ure makes it clear that there are no easy solutions when one of a group of friends becomes seriously ill; and in *The Other Side of the Fence* (1986) the protagonist turns out to be homosexual, although this is not revealed until the end of the book. *Plague 99* (1989) and its sequels show a world in which society has completely disintegrated and has to be rebuilt differently if it is to survive. KA

US Latino children's literature A body of writing in the United States built on the work of American authors and illustrators from a variety of Latin American cultures including, but not limited to, Mexican, Puerto Rican, Peruvian, Guatemalan, Cuban and Dominican. US Latino children's writers and illustrators tell stories through a diversity of genres, including poetry, such as GARY SOTO's *Canto Familiar* (1995) or Carlos Cumpian's *Latino Rainbow: Poems About Latino Americans* (1994); folklore, such as Lucia Gonzalez' bilingual *The Bossy Gallito* (1994), illustrated by Lulu Delacre; PICTUREBOOKS, such as Rudolfo Anaya's historical tale *The Farolitos of Christmas* (1995), illustrated by Edward Gonzales; ALPHABET BOOKS like Alma Flor Ada's bilingual *Alphabet in Spanish and English* (1997), illustrated by Simon Silva; anthologies of fiction, essays and poetry, such as *Growing up Latino* (1993) or *Hispanic, Female and Young* (1994); short-story collections by such writers as NICOLASA MOHR (*El Bronx Remembered*, 1975); and novels such as Ada's *My Name is Maria Isabel* (1993), Mohr's *The Magic Shell* (1995), illustrated by Rudy Gutierrez, and Esmeralda Santiago's *When I was Puerto Rican* (1993).

Many of the books in this field are bilingual or published simultaneously in Spanish and English. For example, Arthur Dorros's picturebook *Abuela* (1991) was published in English and translated into Spanish by his wife, Sandra Marulanda. In *Family Pictures* (1990), Carmen Lomas Garza tells the story of her family's life on either side of the Rio Grande (as told to Harriet Rohmer), and her voice is echoed in a Spanish translation by Rosalma Zubizaretta. Gloria Azaldua's *Friends from the Other Side* (1995) – a bilingual picturebook about intra-cultural discrimination, illustrated by Consuelo Mendez – tells the story of a young Chicana's friendship with a Mexican boy who is living illegally in Texas.

US Latino illustrators like the CALDECOTT AWARD winner David Diaz (*Smoky Nights*, 1994), Gonzalez, Mendez, Ray Cruz (Mohr's *Felita*, 1979), Lomas Garza, Delacre, Silva and Guevara (Soto's *Chato's Kitchen*) have worked to improve the cultural accuracy of visual portrayals of US Latinos and to demonstrate the diversity of their own artistic visions. To honour the work of US Latino writers and illustrators who accurately portray and celebrate the Latino cultural experience in children's books, REFORMA, a division of ALA, established the Pura Belpré Award in 1996; Pura Belpré (1899–1982) was a pioneer in the preservation and dissemination of Puerto Rican folklore as New York City's first Latina children's librarian, a storyteller and an author. In 1998, Stephanie Garcia won a Belpré Award for illustrating Soto's *Snapshots from the Wedding* and Victor Martinez also earned one for *Parrot in the Oven* (1996).

The importance of celebrating Latino cultural traditions, biculturalism, cultural discrimination, the value of family, the trials and triumphs of urban life, and the joys and difficulties of living and moving across geographical and cultural borders are common issues in the work of US Latino writers and illustrators. But like all artists, they have stories to tell that both express their own cultural individuality and cross cultural boundaries to become accessible to a diverse audience. ARTL

Utemorrah, Daisy 1922–94 Australian poet, an elder of the Wunumbal people of Western Australia. *Do Not Go Round the Edges* (1990) combines her autobiography, told along the bottom of each page, with her powerful verses in borders above, surrounded by richly coloured, dramatic illustrations by Pat Torres. Winner of the Australian Multicultural Children's Literature Award in 1992, the collection embraces aspects of her life such as growing up on a mission, going to church and to school, and the influences of white people's religion and laws on traditional family life. *Moonglue* (1993) is a retelling of a story remembered from her own childhood at Kunmunya mission. Two children, told to go to sleep, only pretend, and the 'moon was on their faces and they were stuck together', just as their mother had warned. Susan Wyatt's densely coloured images reflect the earthy colours of the Kimberley region and the traditional lifestyle. JAP

Uttley, Alison [Alice Jane Taylor] 1884–1976 British writer. Born at Castle Top Farm in the Derbyshire Peak District, she used 'Alison' for her first book in 1929. Studying mathematics and physics at Manchester University, and English at the Ladies' Training College, Cambridge, she then taught science in Fulham. She married James Uttley in 1911 and had a son, John, in 1914. Tragically, her husband drowned himself in 1930, and she turned to her writing to cope. She wrote over 90 children's books, including the famous *LITTLE GREY RABBIT* series, the *Sam Pig* stories, a number of plays, two novels for adults, and other countryside tales. SET

see also *COUNTRY CHILD, THE*; CAMPING AND TRAMPING FICTION; *LITTLE BROWN MOUSE* SERIES; *A TRAVELLER IN TIME*

Uwemedimo, Rosemary 1933– Nigerian teacher and writer of children's books, born in London and Nigerian by marriage. She recounts the experience of her marriage in *Mammy Wagon Marriage* (1961). Her best-known book is *Akpan and the Smugglers* (1965), illustrated by BRUCE ONOBRAKPEYA, the story of a boy who sets out to clear his father's name by discovering the real criminals. Uwemedimo has also written *Boma and His Friends* (1977) for younger readers. VD

V

Vallone, Lynne see CRITICAL APPROACHES TO CHILDREN'S LITERATURE

Van Allsburg, Chris 1949– American sculptor who found fame as a PICTUREBOOK writer and artist. Van Allsburg was born in Grand Rapids, Michigan. He discovered his career in children's picturebooks when he was encouraged to submit some of the drawings done in his spare time to a publisher. His first book, *The Garden of Abdul Gasazi* (1979), earned lavish critical praise and was named a Caldecott Honour Book. This picture tale of an encounter between a young boy and a magician who seems to have turned a dog into a duck established Van Allsburg's special genre: the dream-like picture tale in which surrealism of image inspired by the fine arts is combined with the strangeness of urban legend and twighlight-zone stories. Among his most celebrated books are his two CALDECOTT MEDAL winners, *Jumanji* (1991) and *The Polar Express* (1985). The gorgeous stillness of Van Allsburg's depictions of a brother and sister playing an oddly dangerous jungle game called Jumanji became the inspiration for raucous reinterpretations of the story as a 'major motion picture' film and a cartoon TELEVISION series. *The Polar Express* – the story of a boy who is granted a miraculous train ride to the realm of Santa – has been Van Allsburg's best-selling book by far, in part because it sells well every Christmas.

Though Van Allsburg established his initial reputation through works that display a marvellously sculpturesque use of black-and-white, he has developed a variety of styles and techniques in subsequent works. Perhaps the most distinctive and characteristic of his black-and-white books is his *The Mysteries of Harris Burdick* (1984), which presents an array of story fragments, each illustrated by a compelling, bizarre single image. A similar array of graphically powerful oddities is provided in his ALPHABET BOOK, *The Z Was Zapped* (1986). Colour has also played an important role in several of his most striking works, including *The Wreck of the Zephyr* (1983), in which a boy masters the art of flying boats, and *The Stranger* (1986) in which a Jack-Frost-like character suffers amnesia, causing autumn to linger in suspended animation at the farm where 'the stranger' is nursed back to health. Rich panoramas of harvest scenery and autumnal trees make *The Stranger* a feast for the eyes. An ongoing feature of his work has been the continuing presence of a bull terrier who was the trouble-causing central character in his first book. Van Allsburg's fans look forward to searching for the increasingly well-hidden terrier in book after book.

Among his best illustrations for the books of others are his pictures for Mark Helperin's novella-length fantasies *Swan Lake* (1989) and *A City in Winter* (1996). He has also contributed cover illustrations to reissues of children's classics, including an edition of ROALD DAHL'S *James and the Giant Peach* (1988) and a seven-volume boxed set of C.S. LEWIS'S *THE CHRONICLES OF NARNIA* (1994). Van Allsburg's 1995 transmutation of a Wild West colouring book into a hilarious alternative reality in *Bad Day at Riverbend* shows that his unique instinct for the bizarre continues to lead him in surprising directions. JS

see also COVER ART

Van Loon, Hendrik (Willem) 1882–1944 Author, journalist and history professor. He was born in the Netherlands, but came to America in 1903 to study at Cornell and Harvard. He wrote a number of books of instruction for children, the best-known of which is *The History of Mankind* (1921), a panoramic history of the world from prehistoric times to the present. The book was much admired for its fresh approach to history for children and awarded the first NEWBERY MEDAL. Well blended with the ILLUSTRATIONS, the text approaches the history of mankind as an ever-onward march toward higher goals and improved circumstances. Van Loon presents the human adventure as one in which man corrects tyrannical wrongs with appropriate resistance and heroic action. Today, Van Loon is regarded as having taken an unduly optimistic view of human history, one which, in retrospect, seems ironic. For example, he describes World War I as having 'brought about the coming of a new day'. Despite the challenge of contemporary judgement, *The History of Mankind* remains a milestone in the presentation of history for children in that it sought to be entertaining as well as informative. KSB

Van Stockum, Hilda 1908– Author, illustrator and translator of children's books. Born in Rotterdam in the Netherlands, Van Stockum attended art schools in Dublin and Amsterdam. She wrote and illustrated her first book, *A Day on Skates: The Story of a Dutch Picnic,* in 1934 (Newbery Honour Book 1935). Her most important works are *The Winged Watchman* (1962) and *The Borrowed House* (1975), both set in World War II Netherlands. The settings of her other stories were influenced by her study abroad and migration after marriage – in Ireland, the United States and Canada. Family life and relationships are her primary themes. EAM

Van Straten (Luck), Cicely 1947– South African author with an East African background. Strongly influenced by AFRICAN MYTHOLOGY AND FOLKTALES, she has written stories which imitate them, and introduced elements of MYTH in two quest novels for young readers, *Tajewo and the Sacred Mountain* (1983) and *Torit of the Strong Right Arm* (1992), about East African boys who go on dangerous missions. *Kaninu's Secret* (1981) and *The Great Snake of Kalungu* (1981) contain lively stories about little East African children. Her youth novel, *Flowers of the Thorn* (1986), is a semi-autobiographical story narrated by the daughter of settlers at the time of the Mau Mau uprising in Kenya.

Van Straten is particularly admired for her style and her ability to evoke the colours, smells and sounds of the African veld. Here, in *Huberta's Journey* (1988) – a partly fictionalised account of a famous wandering South African hippopotamus – a hippo introduces her calf to the herd: 'The calf pressed close to Novikela. All round her the sand was churned by great horn-toed feet. Vast grey bellies loomed, criss-crossed with scars and fat skinfolds, with now and then rosy-brown flashes of underlegs. Belching, rumbling, sighing, the cows milled round to welcome Novikela and her newborn. Huge bristled maws nudged the calf, acknowledging her with pleasure, binding her into the group.' ERJ

Van Wyk, Chris 1957– South African author and poet, born in Soweto, near Johannesburg. Chris van Wyk always wanted to be a writer. When he was nine, he recalls, 'Whenever my teacher left the classroom she would ask me to tell the class a story to keep them quiet.' Now an experienced writer, he is editor of the *They Fought for Freedom* series, which provides young South Africans with brief biographies of such heroes as Steve Biko and Chris Hani. His youth novel *A Message in the Wind* (1982) won the Adventure Africa Award with its message of 'living together in love and peace'. JHe

Varley, Susan 1961– British illustrator. Tutored by TONY ROSS at Manchester Polytechnic, Susan Varley had an early outstanding success with her first PICTUREBOOK, *BADGER'S PARTING GIFTS* (1985). This gentle exploration of coming to terms with death won no fewer than four international prizes, including the MOTHER GOOSE AWARD for new illustrators. Many of the subsequent picturebooks she has illustrated – such as *After Dark* (Louis Baum, 1984), *The Monster Bed* (Jeanne Willis, 1986), *The Long, Blue Blazer* (Jeanne Willis, 1987), *Jack and the Monster* (Richard Graham, 1988) and *Princess Camomile Gets Her Way* (HIAWYN ORAM, 1998) – demonstrate a sure response to sensitive issues, for which her wavering line and gentle colour washes seem highly suitable. JAG

Vasil, Lisa 1972– New Zealand writer who achieved the remarkable feat of publishing her first book at the age of 13. *Just an Ordinary Kid* (1988) is a poignant account of Carol, who has cerebral palsy, striving to be treated like everyone else. Three more novels for teenagers were published by the time Vasil was 20. *Dark Secret* (1989) tells the story of twin girls, one of whom is blind while the other nurses a terrible guilt. *Escape From the Future* (1991) and *The Apprentice Devil* (1993) are FANTASIES. The last three books address universal adolescent themes, but Carol's story is the one that has retained a special and long-lasting appeal. LO

See also CHILD AUTHORS

Vatsa, Mamman 1944–86 Nigerian army general and writer of poetry and PICTUREBOOKS for children. *Stinger the Scorpion* (1980), amusingly illustrated in full colour by Anne Nwokoye, takes a humorous look at a feared animal. Vatsa also edited *Soldiers' Children as Poets* (1980), a collection of poems by Nigerian children with impressionistic watercolours by Oseha Ajokpaezi. VD

Velthuijs, Max 1923– Dutch author and illustrator who studied art in Arnhem and worked as an artist and designer until his first picturebook appeared in 1969. His Frog, an instantly recognisable and loveable character, first appeared in all his plain, green, graphic simplicity in a typically plaintive but warm and reassuring story, *Frog in Love*, in 1989. The many *Frog* titles that have followed have been translated into many different languages. He has won the Dutch Golden Paintbrush award twice and, amongst many other awards, has received the American Graphic Award of the Society of Illustrators. JAG

Velveteen Rabbit, The, or How Toys Became Real (1922) PICTUREBOOK by Margery Williams Bianco which tells of the enchanted world of play where toys come to life in the minds of children to become, for a while, their closest and dearest friends. This special companionship is explored through a mixture of humour and pathos which highlights the complex overlap between the real and the imagined worlds explored by childhood fantasies. Basing the story on her own memories of her beloved rabbit, Fluffy, and inspired by the experiences of her own young children, Bianco celebrates the way in which important truths about love and loss can be learned through play. 'The Boy' remains nameless throughout, acting as an allegory for all children and adults who once loved toys. The story has been retold and reillustrated many times since its conception. The original edition was illustrated by WILLIAM NICHOLSON with his distinctive colour lithographs. Each plate is personalised by the artist's own short annotation and the sketchy texture of his drawings captures the crude simplicity of the little ragged toy rabbit. KJFR

see also LITHOGRAPHY

Vermaak, Nelda see *SOME OF US ARE LEOPARDS, SOME OF US ARE LIONS*

Verne, Jules 1828–1905 French writer who, with his publisher Jules Hetzel, developed SCIENCE FICTION. Seeing the potential of this new genre, Hetzel advised Verne to include scientific detail in his first novel, *Cinq semaines en ballon* (1862). Others followed, including *Voyage au centre de la terre* (1864), *Vingt mille lieues sous les mers* (1870) and *Le tour du mond en quatre vingts jours* (1873), the inspiration usually being the exploits of real-life adventurers. Although written as ADULT FICTION, these novels have always appealed to young readers and are still read today because, at heart, Verne was more interested in adventure and mysterious adventurers than the science that is used to help them. AMN

Verney, Sir John 1913– British author and illustrator born in London and educated at Eton and Christ Church, Oxford, where he read history. Verney served in the Special Air Service during World War II; he was twice decorated, receiving the Military Cross in 1944 and the Legion of Honour (France) in 1945. He enjoyed a career not only as a novelist for both adults and children, but also as an artist and illustrator: the style of the illustrations in his books is reminiscent of the work of EDWARD ARDIZZONE.

Verney's stories about the Callendar family began in 1959 with *Friday's Tunnel*. The series, which, sadly, has been neglected and fallen out of print, continued through *February's Road* (1966), *ismo* (1967), *Seven Sunflower Seeds* (1969) and *Samson's Hoard* (1973). It is lively, humorous and original, and its characterisation is particularly vivid. There is a peculiarly adult flavour to the works, perhaps as a result of the subjects of the plots which all address political and social issues, for example the entrance of Britain into the European Common Market. The issues are treated seriously though never heavily, and the Callendar children, in their engagment with these matters, emerge as intelligent and socially aware young people. SA

Very Best of Friends, The (1989) Australian PICTUREBOOK by MARGARET WILD and JULIE VIVAS, about an elderly couple, Jessie and James, and their cat William, who live on a farm with many other animals. After the death of James, Jessie ceases to pay attention to William, who is driven to feral life. The story examines the caring relations between animals and humans. It explores the impact of death and the need for friendship, evoking a sense of loneliness, grief and rejection and suggesting the ultimate triumph of the mutuality of friendship. CH, HMcC

viewpoint In PICTUREBOOK illustration, the position chosen by the artist for the viewer in relation to the picture. The viewpoint establishes the point of view both literally and psychologically, affecting the relations between the depicted participants and the viewer, and between the artist and the viewer via the depicted participants. A low viewpoint (worm's eye) gives the image elevated importance, whilst a high viewpoint (bird's eye) gives power to the viewer. Multiple viewpoints at a fixed level allow the viewer to travel in stages along the picture, while no fixed viewpoint favours every area of the picture plane and allows the viewer to wander freely. JD

Viewpoint: On Books for Young Adults Australian journal, first issued in 1993, in response to the growing field of YOUNG ADULT FICTION. It includes reviews, comments and discussion forums on books from Australia and overseas. Edited by Pam MacIntyre, there are four issues per year. JAP

see also REVIEWING AND REVIEWERS

vignette A small isolated design or depiction, looking like a cut-out shape, traditionally in line, and more recently in PICTUREBOOKS in line and colour as well. This decorative feature, coming from the French word for 'vine', can be seen clinging to the pages of the GRIMMS' fairy tales illustrated by ARTHUR RACKHAM, and in *I SAW ESAU*, the pocket book of rhymes edited by IONA AND PETER OPIE and illustrated by MAURICE SENDAK. JD

Viking Saga, The (1985) Title given to the posthumous republication in one volume of the Viking trilogy by HENRY TREECE, comprising: *Viking's Dawn* (UK, 1955; USA, 1957), *The Road to Miklagard* (1957) and *Viking's Sunset.* (UK, 1960; USA, 1961). Through the three novels, Harald Sigurdson progresses from a young seafarer to old age and death. In *Viking's Dawn*, his first voyage takes him to Scotland,

Ireland and the west coast of England. Vigorous narrative is enriched with poetic descriptions of fighting, of the sea and of the harsh conditions of seafaring. Relations between Christians and Vikings and their contrasting views of the afterlife are discussed: 'We are a people not yet born', says Harald. But Viking leaders are sympathetically observed: 'They are not saints . . . yet there is a strange good in them . . . if a man will only try to look for it.' A rare footnote to the text reflects on cultural tolerance and the lessons of history in this regard. In the closing chapters of *Viking's Dawn*, Harald Sigurdson begins to glimpse the truth of Christianity through his admiration for John the Priest, but in the next books of the series he ponders on John's death and muses: 'Dear John, Alas that I shall never see you again. Your heaven is not my own.'

The Road to Miklagard takes Harald south, through the Mediterranean to Constantinople, returning to the Baltic by way of the Black Sea. His journey is enlivened by more exciting incidents and more exotic locations than in the previous volume, and the turns of fate are more dramatic than in *Viking's Dawn*. Treece's instructional intent again shows through, as in the Vikings' knowing but stilted references to world geography, thus demonstrating the impressive knowledge acquired by word of mouth in a society occupied with seafaring and trade. Literary traditions of the schoolboy hero survive in Harald Sigurdson: 'This quiet Viking who assumed power so easily without assuming the arrogance which too often goes with it', as do traditions of 'innocent' sexism in statements like: 'most girls are foolish, I have been led to understand'.

In *Viking's Sunset* the global scope of Viking travels is completed when Harald voyages to Iceland, Greenland and North America. Encounters with Innuit and Native American Indians reveal the Vikings' confrontation with peoples as hardy and resourceful as themselves. Where the first two books narrated encounters with Christianised peoples of Western Europe and the Mediterranean, the Native Americans share their familiar paganism, offering rich scope for comparison as well as contrast. Underlying the pagan cultures, however, in Treece's telling, lies a basic 'decency' in the heroic figures, that echoes the 'muscular christianity' of *TOM BROWN'S SCHOOLDAYS*. A distinctive feature of this third volume is Treece's attempt to recapture the flavour of the Vikings' own STORYTELLING style – tales told with gusto and exaggeration, sometimes laconic, sometimes repetitious in the manner of FAIRY TALES, and with a grim sense of humour. Beneath all the ruggedness and brutality of seafaring adventure and piracy lies a morality, a gentleness and nobility of human spirit and a reaffirmation of human nature. PC

Vincent, Gabrielle British illustrator. Vincent's *Ernest and Celestine* PICTUREBOOKS, which were published regularly throughout the 1980s, are tender tales of the bear Ernest and his small charge, the mouse Celestine. Everything is understated, both the spare text which is mostly dialogue, and the drawings, which, in the E. H. SHEPARD tradition, rely on superb line drawing. Vincent also makes subtle use of colour. JAG

Viorst, Judith (Stahl) 1931– American author and poet, well known for her PICTUREBOOKS portraying relationships between siblings. *Alexander and the Terrible, Horrible, No Good, Very Bad Day* (1972) is probably the best-known of the three 'Alexander' stories, now combined into one volume as *Absolutely Positively Alexander* (1997). *The Tenth Good Thing About Barney* (1971) handles the concept of death through the grieving of a young boy over the loss of his cat. Viorst has also published books of poetry for children and their parents. PDS

Vipont, Elfrida 1902–92 British biographer and author of several children's novels, four of which deserve to be better known as a quartet: *The Lark in the Morn* (1948) and its sequels *The Lark on the Wing* (1950), *The Spring of the Year* (1957) and *Flowering Spring* (1960). The second won the CARNEGIE MEDAL, though the first of the titles is a better children's book. The fourth was illustrated by SHIRLEY HUGHES. They tell the story of a Quaker family – and in particular of one girl whose musical gifts are unappreciated. The appeal of the novels lies largely in the way they communicate the pleasures of a serious devotion to music, an unusual theme in children's books. VW

see also *ELEPHANT AND THE BAD BABY, THE*; KITTY BARNE; MUSIC AND STORY

Visit from St Nicholas, A (1822) Classic Christmas poem best known by its first line: ''Twas the night before Christmas . . .' Probably written by Clement Clarke Moore for his sick daughter, he first recited it in 1822 at a Christmas Eve party. Many modern Christmas symbols have their origin in this poem. (Illustration over page.) LAW

Visitors Who Came to Stay, The (1984) PICTUREBOOK written by Annalena McAfee and illustrated by ANTHONY BROWNE, with Browne's imagery serving to counterpoint and enlarge the tale. Katy and her father live quiet lives in a seaside town, but their routines are disrupted when Mary and her practical joker son, Sean, come to stay. In the full-page recto ILLUSTRATIONS Browne uses colour, framing, the position of his subjects and VIEWPOINT to suggest the quietness and simplicity of Katy's and her father's lives. The

'The Coming of Santa Claus.' Illustration by Thomas Nast for *A Visit from St. Nicholas* (1872).

arrival of Sean and his giddy mother is signalled by an eruption of surreal imagery, and the cluttered seaside scenes that follow provide Browne with suitably carnivalesque subject matter. McAfee's text deals with Katy's mental states as well as with the mundane details of her life, and Browne reflects this in his imagery. The growing affection of the grown-ups for each other – the cause of the chaos in Katy's life – is only hinted at, both in the text and the pictures, and this adds to the layered nature of the text. Browne and McAfee have also collaborated on *Kirsty Knows Best* (1987). DL

Vivas, Julie 1947– Australian illustrator who achieved instant success with her pictures for POSSUM MAGIC (1983). Vivas is one of Australia's most recognised illustrators. Her work has continued to excite readers with its ability to tantalise and with its extraordinary humanity. No sentimentalism is allowed in her depictions of figures, elongated in face and limb and exuding vibrant emotional responses to circumstances. Her many awards include the Dromkeen Medal (1992) for her contribution to Australian Children's Literature, and her CHILDREN'S BOOK COUNCIL OF AUSTRALIA Picturebook of the Year Award (1990) for THE VERY BEST OF FRIENDS (1989). In 1986 she won an Ibby Australia Honour Diploma, and she has received several other overseas citations and awards. Memorable works include *Wilfrid Gordon McDonald Partridge* (1987) and THE NATIVITY (1986). The latter demonstrates her ability to translate a well-known text into a new work – she tells the story of Christ's birth with startling originality and a subversive wit and humour. She is also prepared to takes risks with her subjects, as in LET THE CELEBRATIONS BEGIN! (1991). In *Hello Baby* (1999), written by Jenni Overend, Vivas uses coloured pencil and watercolour to capture a powerful family experience, the birth of a baby brother, told through the eyes of Jack, until then the youngest member of the family. Vivas deals with the subjects of loss, death and the power of memory and hope in the human spirit. RS

Voake, Charlotte 1957– British illustrator. Despite having received no formal art training, Voake's titles are enthusiastically received, and several PICTUREBOOKS have been shortlisted for prizes. *Ginger* (1997), won the Gold Medal for the Under-five Category of the SMARTIES PRIZE and reveals her special qualities: light, airy line-and-wash drawings, minimal back-

Illustration by Julie Vivas from *Let's Eat* by Ana Zamorano.

ground and yet a whole and convincing world established. An unusual typeface, coupled with sensitive page design and high-quality paper, produce a rare end-product. Voake has contributed discreet drawings to ALLAN AHLBERG's *The Mighty Slide* (1988) and to PHILIPPA PEARCE's *The Way to Sattin Shore* (1983), and her picturebook version of ELEANOR FARJEON's *Elsie Piddock Skips in her Sleep* was published in 2000. JAG

Voigt, Cynthia 1942– Award-winning American author of young adult literature. One of the most prolific and widely respected contemporary American writers for young adults, Cynthia Voigt decided to become a writer at an early age, but began her work in earnest while teaching in a private school. Many of Voigt's books can be defined as 'problem novels' and treat realistically the difficulties of young adults, often outsiders, who are trying to find their place in the world. For example, *Tell Me if the Lovers Are Losers* (1982), which grew out of Voigt's experiences as a college student, deals with the maturation of three young women, while *David and Jonathan* (1992) is about the aftermath of war, as well as death and suicide. While the majority of Voigt's novels are realistic, she often draws on classical and religious sources such as *The Odyssey* and the Bible to provide structure and depth to her work. Virtually all of Voigt's work has won universal praise from critics, who have noted in particular her appealing characters, poetic style, detailed descriptions and vivid settings, along with her sympathetic treatment of orphans and outsiders searching for the stability of family life.

Voigt's most ambitious and well-known works are the seven books about the Tillermans and their friends set in Crisfield, Maryland (see DICEY'S SONG SERIES). In these works, Voigt interweaves characters and overlaps plots, occasionally presenting the same scene in another book, but from a different point of view. Voigt has also experimented in a variety of genres, including mysteries (*The Callendar Papers*, 1983, and *The Vandemark Mummy*, 1991) and FANTASY (*Building Blocks*, 1988). Voigt's long interest in myth and hero tales has given rise to a series of three popular medieval fantasies beginning with *Jackaroo* (1985) and continuing with *On Fortune's Wheel* (1990) and *The Wings of a Falcon* (1993). JDC

W

Wace, Muriel see *MOORLAND MOUSIE*

Waddell, Martin 1941– Irish author best known for his numerous prize-winning PICTUREBOOKS which are illustrated by a variety of well-known illustrators. He won the SMARTIES PRIZE for *Farmer Duck* (1991), a children's version of the *Animal Farm* story illustrated by HELEN OXENBURY, and for *Can't You Sleep Little Bear?* (1988), illustrated by BARBARA FIRTH. This endearing picturebook, in which Big Bear deals kindly but firmly with Little Bear's fear of the dark, has now become a classic bedtime story; there have been three further stories – *Let's Go Home, Little Bear* (1991), *You and Me, Little Bear* (1996) and *Well Done, Little Bear* (1999). Other books deal with familiar childhood worries, including new babies, loneliness and the death of a grandparent. *Night Night, Cuddly Bear* (2000), illustrated by PENNY DALE, is a picturebook about bedtime; *The Hollyhock Wall* (1999), illustrated in COLLAGE by Salley Mavor, tells the story of a little girl whose 'pretend' garden comes magically to life.

Although Waddell's picturebooks often reassure children about their fears, his YOUNG ADULT novel, *Tango's Baby* (1995), is far from reassuring, providing a depressing account of teenage motherhood. He has also written fiction for older children under the pen name of CATHERINE SEFTON. Many of these novels, like the prize-winning *Starry Night* (1986), are set in Northern Ireland against the background of the troubles. While the fiction Waddell writes under his own name is usually about boys and traditionally 'male' preoccupations, like the football of the *Napper* series, when he writes as Sefton, Waddell often features girls in the central roles. KA

Wade, Barrie see *BOOKSTART*

Waera, James see MAORI WRITING IN CHILDREN'S BOOKS; PICTUREBOOKS

Wagner, Jenny 1939– Acclaimed for the texts of her award-winning Australian PICTUREBOOKS, Wagner has also written magic realism for older readers. Each book addresses an ongoing human concern expressed unconventionally: the search for identity; the need for acceptance, for self-expression, for love and trust; the power of love to transform; and the true nature of integrity. Wagner embodies her profoundly philosophical ideas in engaging stories and has been well served by her illustrators, especially RON BROOKS who in *Motor Bill and the Lovely Caroline* (1994) shows Caroline and Bill as dressed-up animal characters, thus underscoring the FABLE-like quality of Wagner's text. *The Machine at the Heart of the World* (1983) has appealed less to children than to symbol-seeking adults who variously interpret Theobald, the machine-keeper, as God or an abstract scientific principle. In *The Werewolf Knight* (1995) Wagner, as the title indicates, plays with the idea of someone who can develop both sides of his character. *The Nimbin* (1978) and *Return of the Nimbin* (1992) elaborate the Aboriginal concept of a spirit which impinges on human destiny, and in *Message from Avalon* (1990) Avalon is no Arthurian paradise but rather a house haunted by a ghost that brings insight and courage to a girl who lives in the present. MSax

see also ABORIGINAL CULTURE IN CHILDREN'S BOOKS

Wain, Louis 1860–1939 British illustrator. Known as 'the man who drew cats', Wain illustrated (nearly always with cats as characters) and wrote over 100 children's books, starting with *Madame Tabby's Establishment* in 1886. Very popular in his time and still readily recognised, Wain's cats remain feline despite their enjoyment of human pastimes such as boating and tennis and despite their bowler hats, bow ties and beaded handbags. Wain also used his cats to comment on contemporary society, choosing often to satirise the forces of law and order. Louis Wain ANNUALS and memorabilia have flourished, both in Britain and in the United States. H.G. Wells said in a broadcast: 'He has made the cat his own. He invented a cat style, a cat society, a whole cat world. English cats that do not live like Louis Wain cats are ashamed of themselves.' JAG

Wakefield, S.A. see *BOTTERSNIKES AND GUMBLES*

Wal at the World's End, The see SCOTTISH FOLKTALES

Walk in the Park, A (1977) The British illustrator ANTHONY BROWNE's second PICTUREBOOK develops thematic and stylistic elements which were introduced in *Through the Magic Mirror* (1976) and which continued to dominate almost all which followed: resourceful child protagonists, the exploration of social relationships, together with the use of surreal imagery to symbolise emotional mood. Smudge, her yobbish dad and Albert their dog, and Charles, his snobbish mother and Victoria their bitch, converge daily in the park. Over time, despite the obdurate unsociability of the adults, the children and animals come together and win for themselves a rainbow-blessed period of happiness before being dragged apart again. In 1998 the same characters and events were revisited in *Voices in the Park* – winner of the KURT MASCHLER AWARD – a sad and complex exploration of the inner lives of characters caught up in class mistrust. JD

Walker, Kate (Dianne Maria Catherine) 1950– Australian author of novels, PICTUREBOOKS and short stories, whose earlier works were published under educational imprints. Walker draws upon European FOLK-TALE traditions in several stories: *The Frog Who would be King* (1988), *King Joe of Bogpeat Castle* (1988), *Tales from the Good Land* (1989), and *The Dragon of Mith* (1989), in which a town and a dragon learn to cohabit peacefully. PETER (1991), her first book for teenagers, was – in spite of some controversy – widely commended for its sensitivity and accuracy in capturing an adolescent slice of life. In *Changes* (1995), also intended for an adolescent audience, the stories have emotional punch and veracity, and explore events and characters which confront readers with issues of life and death, growth and change, identity and responsibility. *I Hate Books* (1995) focuses upon family, self-esteem and childhood confidence; Hamish is a great teller of, and listener to, stories until he goes to school and is convinced that he cannot read. A recipient of several CHILDREN'S BOOK COUNCIL OF AUSTRALIA Honour Book awards, Walker is a versatile craftsperson of stories and novels about people coming to self-awareness. She writes perceptively and sensitively, using unsentimental language. SNJ

Wall, Barbara see CRITICAL APPROACHES TO CHILDREN'S BOOKS; see also *PETER PAN*

Wall, Dorothy 1894–1942 Australian author and illustrator who migrated from New Zealand in 1914, and in 1920 produced the first of her 13 books. Her greatest successes were *BLINKY BILL* (1933) and its three sequels, which centred upon the escapades of a mischievous koala, and the rabbit tale *Brownie* (1935). Wall's strength was her ILLUSTRATION, which was influenced by Art Nouveau, though it had realistic settings and featured accurately drawn (if clothed) animals. Her writing was often clumsy and the books didactic in their treatment of animal conservation, but their appeal to children was still great. JF

'Six black pussy cats all in a row.' Illustration by Louis Wain for *BLACKIE'S CHILDREN'S ANNUAL*.

Wallace and Gromit see BOB KERR

Wallace, Ian 1950– One of Canada's premier illustrators of books for children. Growing up in a family of storytellers and readers in Niagara Falls, Ontario, Wallace began drawing almost as soon as he could hold a crayon. He later moved to Toronto to attend the Ontario College of Art where he won a scholarship. Whether Wallace illustrates his own stories or the work of others, his art coalesces with the words and expands the text in provocative ways. In Jan Andrews's *The Very Last First Time* (1985), he subtly incorporates the Inuit spirit world in his work. He returns to spirit imagery in W.D. Valgardson's *Sarah and the People of Sand River* (1996).

Wallace is a painstaking researcher and the breadth of his subject matter is awe-inspiring. He spent months in Toronto and Vancouver's Chinatowns to create authentic ILLUSTRATIONS for *Chin Chiang and the Dragon's Dance* (1984), a multiple-award-winning book. The illustrations for Celia Barker Lottridge's *The Name of the Tree* (1989), for which he again won awards, also required extensive research. From traditional FOLKTALES (*HANSEL AND GRETEL*) to contemporary issues such as homelessness (*Mr Kneebone's New Digs*,

1991), the variety of themes he tackles is impressive. In 1994 IBBY-Canada nominated him for the prestigious HANS CHRISTIAN ANDERSEN AWARD. TH

Walsh, Jill (Gillian) Paton 1937– British novelist who was born in London and received an honours degree in English and a Diploma in Education from St Anne's College, Oxford. She taught English for several years before beginning her writing career. She is the author of three adult novels, one of which, *Knowledge of Angels* (1994), was shortlisted for the Booker Prize. She has written more than 20 books for children and has won numerous awards, including the Book World Festival Award (1970) for *FIREWEED* (1969); the WHITBREAD AWARD (1974) for *The Emperor's Winding Sheet*, the BOSTON GLOBE-HORN BOOK AWARD (1976) for *Unleaving*; the Universe Literary Prize (1984) for *A Parcel of Patterns*; and the SMARTIES PRIZE Grand Prix (1986) for *GAFFER SAMSON'S LUCK*. She has also served on committees and jury panels concerned with children's literature.

The events in Walsh's novels are set in a wide range of contexts, some taking place in identifiable historical periods, such as the London Blitz or the siege of Constantinople, others in imaginary settings. A distinctive characteristic is her fascination for landscape; her detailed descriptions create an atmosphere particular to each of her narratives, including those for her youngest readers, such as in the PICTUREBOOK *Babylon* (1981), where three children discover a garden on top of an abandoned London viaduct. The appreciation of the beauty of nature is at times sharply contrasted with an awareness of its potential threat, as characters attempt to survive stormy seas and cross inhospitable mountains.

As well as evoking landscape, Walsh evokes a sense of history for her readers. The events of the past and the present are linked through the actions of children in the same places throughout different periods. This is evident in *Lost and Found* (1984), where children, from the Stone Age to modern times, lose things that are eventually found by children in another age; and in *The Butty Boy* (1975), where a young girl experiences life in the canals in the 1880s. Christopher also discovers history through the canals while trying to find his brother in *A CHANCE CHILD* (1978). Walsh recovers traditional children's games through a series of stories for younger readers called *Can I Play . . .?* (1990).

The narratives tend to be deceptively simple, as they relate the adventures of children and adolescents who must overcome some form of obstacle to their survival or their happiness. Underneath the surface, however, lies the real task for the characters: dealing with complex moral issues and values such as loyalty, unselfishness, courage and – particularly for the female characters – strength and independence. As the narratives progress, the young protagonists experience joy, sadness, wonder, horror and other feelings from which they would normally be protected. They must endure parting from those they love, as few relationships and friendships seem to survive in her novels. This includes having to deal with the meaning of death through war (in *THE DOLPHIN CROSSING*, 1967) or through the Plague (in *A Parcel of Patterns*, 1983). Yet they manage to emerge from these situations, developing a more mature understanding of themselves and others. EA

see also *GRACE*

Walsh, John 1911–72 British teacher and poet whose collections *The Roundabout by the Sea* (1960) and *The Truants* (1965) bridge the years between the era of DE LA MARE, FARJEON and REEVES, and the 1970s. Walsh was able to turn incidents of home and school life into entirely believable, well-crafted poetry. He skilfully recaptured moments of guilt and joy, sounds, smells, journeys, arrivals and recognisable characters – like the bully, Bill Craddock, 'his dark eyes cruel / And somehow sad'. Walsh continues to be represented in the occasional anthology but, although *Poets in Hand* (1985) featured 28 of his poems, his achievement has not been sufficiently recognised. AHa

Walter, Mildred Pitts 1922– African American writer who has produced 14 children's books – five YOUNG ADULT novels, eight illustrated books for younger readers, and an INFORMATION BOOK on the history of voting (*Mississippi Challenge*, 1992) – many of which reflect her experiences as a teacher and civil rights activist in California and her upbringing in Louisiana. Depth of character is Walter's literary strength. For young readers, she focuses on the way children work through their personal conflicts as they grapple with family responsibilities. A child may be adjusting to a new baby in the house, as in *My Mama Needs Me* (1983), or dealing with the consequences of a bad decision, as in *Lillie of Watts* (1969). But always the adults are warm, comforting and understanding cultural teachers, as is Granpa in *Justin and the Best Biscuits in the World* (1985), who tells Justin about black cowboys and his own family history during the Reconstruction period.

For young adult readers, Walters focuses on the difficult choices her characters must make in order to grow and change. In *Trouble's Child* (1985), Martha leaves her isolated island home and her beloved grandmother to attend high school on the Louisiana mainland. In *The Girl on the Outside* (1982), Sophia takes a stand against the racist beliefs of her friends, when she befriends a black student entering her all-white Arkansas high school. In *Because We Are* (1983), Emma Walsh discovers class differences in the wider black community when she enters a new school, leaving behind her snobbish friends. In *Second Daughter; The Story of a Slave Girl* (1996), Aissa and Bett endure painful consequences when they resist authority to create change in the world. NM

Waltzing Matilda (1970) Australia's most famous song, written in 1895 by A. B. (BANJO) PATERSON and given pictorial life in 1970 by the artist Desmond Digby. Not only did Digby's book win the CHILDREN'S BOOK COUNCIL OF AUSTRALIA Picturebook of the Year Award, but it became, because of its format, production and the quality of the art work, the progenitor of the modern Australian PICTUREBOOK. A successful landscape painter, Digby captures in oils the essence of the Australian countryside, and as an experienced stage and set designer, he gave his depiction of the swagman the earthy quality of Paterson's original that epitomises the defiant larrikin element in Australian culture. MSax

war stories Tales featuring armed conflict, usually from an anti-war perspective – as in 'Things by their Right Names' and 'The Price of a Victory' in ANNA BARBAULD and John Aikin's *Evenings at Home* (1792–6). Such stories have contributed to juvenile literature since the late 18th century. War stories are inherently didactic: they inculcate patriotic moral values or, more often, question the morality of war. Most are variants of the oldest adult genre, the *ROBINSONNADE*, and *ROBINSON CRUSOE* is often directly alluded to within the text, as in URI ORLEV'S *The Island on Bird Street* (1981, trans. Hillel Halkin).

Some commonplace views that may have been relevant to older stories are now no longer necessarily applicable: for example, that war books fascinate young readers because they provide real events that are more exciting than any make-believe yet appealingly predictable because the audience knows who won; that they evade serious moral issues or reduce them to the 'good guys' versus the bad, thus serving as conduits for national ideologies; or that they are usually escapist (combat books for boys) or gendered (stories for girls on domestic contribution on the home front). The current proliferation of war fiction for the young coincides with accelerating contemporary violence and reflects adult preoccupations with human evil – all forms of moral, psychological and material destruction; past and present genocides, from the Holocaust to more recent 'ethnic cleansings'; and the ever-present possibility of nuclear disaster. Adult social history, cultural studies and postmodern/postcolonial literary theory – all much concerned with redefining what counts as 'war' and with exploring how conflicts escalate and how war is represented in history, memory and words – filter into the expanding and impressive body of war stories for the young. Not always comfortable or reassuring, many recent publications contrast sharply with previous simpler works that were in essence forms as familiar as SCHOOL STORIES or PONY STORIES.

War stories written for British children originally belonged to a tradition of patriotic literature designed to sustain the war effort, and promote a positive national image in peacetime. Children's books and magazine stories on the subject followed a clear gender division in their implied audience: war in boys' books was regarded as an opportunity for adventure and heroic exploits, with an emphasis on the role of adult combatants. The *BIGGLES* books, written by Captain W. E. Johns and set in both World Wars, exemplify this approach and were read avidly by generations of boys. Girls' stories set in the two World Wars highlighted fortitude, adventure and gentleness, as typified in two well-known examples published during World War II: Elinor Brent-Dyer's *The Chalet School in Exile* (1940) (see CHALET SCHOOL SERIES) and Dorita Fairlie Bruce's *Dimsie Carries On* (1946) (see *DIMSIE* SERIES). Both boys' and girls' fiction written at the time of World War II and during the early post-war period generally maintained a tone consistent with that of contemporary propaganda, with spy-catching and evacuation as the two main themes. Although children's fiction set in World War I continues to be published – MICHAEL MORPURGO'S *War Horse* (1990) is one notable example – it is World War II which has generated a volume of children's fiction far in excess of that inspired by any previous conflict, and which is of particular interest to young readers in the United States, where evacuation and blitz have not been part of the national experience.

In the decades since the war, combat and spy stories have found a niche in boys' COMICS, MAGAZINES AND PERIODICALS, while evacuation and the experience of bombing have remained key themes in children's fiction. New dimensions of psychological insight have characterised the evacuation novel, which has maintained to the present day its high profile in children's World War II novels. MICHELLE MAGORIAN, for example, offers a sensitive portrayal of the developing relationship between an emotionally deprived evacuee and his host in *GOODNIGHT MISTER TOM* (1981). Other recurring topics include the discovery by children of a stray German pilot or sailor (*The Missing German*, 1975, by DAVID REES), and the occupation of the Channel Islands, which featured in contemporary novels (*We Couldn't Leave Dinah*, 1941, by MARY TREADGOLD) as well as more recent publications (*Tomorrow is a Stranger*, 1987, by GEOFFREY TREASE). In recent fiction time-travel has become a popular means of access to the war years; children of the 1970s and 80s are magically transported to the Britain of the 1940s in

Conrad's War (1978) by ANDREW DAVIES and *An Angel for May* (1992) by MELVYN BURGESS.

There is no longer a strict divide between girls' and boys' war fiction; children of either sex are central figures in realistic novels written from the child's perspective. A retrospective narrative framework is often employed to accentuate the child's point of view and the lingering effects of evacuation or bombing within the narrator's life; examples can be found in novels by JILL PATON WALSH (*FIREWEED*, 1969), PENELOPE LIVELY (*Going Back*, 1975), and NINA BAWDEN (*CARRIE'S WAR*, 1973 and *Keeping Henry*, 1987). Indeed, several writers have recast their own childhood wartime experience in the form of autobiographical fiction. Nina Bawden uses insights into her own dawning adolescence in her two evacuation novels; JOAN LINGARD expiates the childhood persecution of a German-Jewish teacher she had assumed to be a spy in *The File on Fräulein Berg* (1980), and ROBERT WESTALL revisited many times in fictional form (from *THE MACHINE-GUNNERS*, 1975, to *A Time of Fire*, 1994) a period which he declared to be the most exciting of his life: his childhood experience of the bombing of Tynemouth. Westall's adaptation of the adventure story genre in *The Machine-Gunners* and of the spy story in its sequel, *Fathom Five* (1979), illustrates the tension in his work between traditional approaches to war stories and an attempt to develop children's understanding of the complexities of war, for example, by introducing a 'good German', the pilot Rudi in *The Machine-Gunners*. This theme of the stray German pilot, found in the novels of Westall and in Michael Morpurgo's *Friend or Foe* (1977), represents an invitation to readers to reassess their responses to 'the enemy'. Westall turned his attention to a more recent conflict in *Gulf* (1993), abandoning traditional genres in a subtle and powerful indictment of the effects of war on the individual psyche.

Westall's recurrent motifs of the lone German and the problematic father also characterise perhaps the most often cited American World War II fiction, BETTE GREENE'S *The Summer of My German Soldier* (1973) and its sequel, *Morning is a Long Time Coming* (1978). Greene's Jewish heroine is persecuted by a punitive father and by the Arkansas community; when she falls in love with a German prisoner of war and hides him after his escape, she is sentenced to a reformatory. Like the novels of Westall, Greene and Magorian, Mary Downing Hahn's *Stepping on the Cracks* (1991) and *Following My Own Footsteps* (1996), and most recently Carolyn Reeder's *Foster's War* (1998), link abusive parents with international abuses of power. The parallels between youthful war games at home and bloody combat abroad, and the exploration of how war develops and of the human capacity to hate, are worked through in John Malcolm Rae's *The Custard Boys* (1960), SUSAN COOPER'S *Dawn of Fear* (1970) and Marion Dane Bauer's *Rain of Fire* (1983).

Children's appreciation of the extent and nature of human suffering during World War II has also been extended by literature set in the Far East and continental Europe. Judith Elkin's retelling in English of TOSHI MARUKI'S uncompromising *The Hiroshima Story* (1983) and MEINDERT DE JONG'S tale of a Chinese war orphan in *The House of Sixty Fathers* (1956) are notable examples of an aspect of the war largely neglected in children's books. There is, on the other hand, a considerable body of British fiction on the fate of refugees and Jewish children across Europe. IAN SERRAILLIER'S groundbreaking novel *THE SILVER SWORD* (1956) follows a group of Polish children across a devastated Europe as they search for their parents; Elizabeth Mace explores the identity crises of a refugee Jewish boy in *Brother Enemy* (1979); and Joan Lingard has fictionalised her Latvian husband's refugee childhood in *Tug of War* (1989) and *Between Two Worlds* (1991). The dangers, hostility and alienation of a childhood spent in hiding, in exile or with a concealed identity, are revealed in several autobiographical novels by Jewish authors written in English, their adopted language. These include *The Upstairs Room* (1972) by Johanna Reiss and its sequel on the aftermath of war, *The Journey Back* (1976), *Mischling, Second Degree* (1977) by Ilse Koehn (the last two both first published in the United States), and Judith Kerr's *When Hitler Stole Pink Rabbit* (1971) (see *OUT OF THE HITLER TIME* series).

Translations into English of children's books from continental Europe also broaden children's understanding of the affective consequences of World War II, in particular the systematic persecution of the Jews during the Third Reich. In her bestselling and emotionally intense novel *I AM DAVID* (1963, trans. L.W. Kingsland), the Danish writer Anne Holm distils the psychological suffering of millions of refugees and concentration camp inmates in the decontextualised story of David, the archetypal victim and refugee. Claude Gutman details in the specific historical setting of occupied France the secret and constantly threatened life of a young Jew in two novels based on family experience, *The Empty House* and *Fighting Back* (1990, 1991, trans. Anthea Bell). The fate of Jews within Germany itself is the subject of both Hans Peter Richter's novel *Friedrich* (1970, trans. Edite Kroll), loosely based on his own childhood, and the even more directly autobiographical *I Was There* (1972, trans. Edite Kroll). Richter's honest attempt to portray his own youthful enthusiasm for the Hitler Youth and participation in the persecution of the Jews is an important contribution to an understanding of the powerful effect of National Socialist rhetoric on the young. In contrast to Richter's spare, distanced and guilt-driven account of childhood in the Third Reich, Austrian writer Christine Nöstlinger adopts a characteristically robust and humorous perspective on life in Vienna during the last chaotic days of the war in her autobiographical novel *Fly Away Home!* (1973, trans. Anthea Bell). Two other translated works which have set a high standard for stark realism, formal experiment and moral engagement are Rudolf Frank's *No Hero for the Kaiser* (1931; trans. Patricia Crampton, 1986) and Max Von Der Grün's *Howl Like the Wolves: Growing Up in Nazi Germany* (trans. Jan Van Heurck, 1980). Gudrun Pausewang – in *The Final Journey* (1992; trans. Patricia Crampton, 1996), winner of the Marsh Award for best translated work of the year – sends her uncomprehending Alice to the gas chamber expecting a cleansing shower, a wake-up call to readers who know what she does not.

Within the exciting and comfortably familiar conventions of quest narratives, war stories move from harrowing escape and survival to a redemptive re-establishment of home, family and friendship, whether in Siberia – as in Esther Hautzig's *The Endless Steppe: Growing Up in Siberia* (1968) and Tamar Bergman's *Along the Tracks* (1988; trans. Michael Swirsky, 1991) – or in the refugee trilogies of Sonia Levitnin and Judith Kerr, whose German Jewish families came, respectively, to America and England. Clever children and cross-cultural friendships elude Nazi terror in Claire Huchet Bishop's *Twenty and Ten* (1952), Doris Orgel's *The Devil in Vienna* (1978) and Lois Lowry's *Number the Stars* (1989). The difficulties of growing up German are explored by Barbara Gehrts in *Don't say a Word* (1975; trans. Elizabeth B. Crawford, 1986); and Laura E. Williams's *Behind the Bedroom Wall* (1996). Through brilliant time-slip narratives of switched identities, Jane Yolen in *The Devil's Arithmetic* (1988) and Han Nolan in *If I should Die Before I Wake* (1994), transport into the concentration camps, respectively, a modern Jewish girl bored with old woes, 'tired of remembering', and a post-modern neo-Nazi skinhead. Confusions of national identity and religious affiliation, especially when Jewish youngsters grow up abroad or hide out as Christians, are often found in refugee tales, as in Renée Roth-Hano's *Touchwood: A Girlhood in Occupied France* (1988) and Anita Lobel's *No Pretty Picture: A Child of War* (1998). Returning to a devastated homeland after the war, strong young people nevertheless locate alternative 'relatives' to love in T[amar] Degens's *Transport 7–41–R* (1974); and Peter Härtling's *Crutches* (1986; trans. Elizabeth D. Crawford, 1988); or finally 'get home' only to discover that their solitary heroism has matured them beyond the adults, as does the astonishingly resilient protagonist in Tatjana Wassiljewa's *Hostage to War: A True Story* (1992; trans. Anna Trenter from the German translation of the original Russian, 1996).

The lone child traversing combat zones has long been a motif of exciting stories that implicitly question war ideologies, as in Tomiko Higa's *The Girl With the White Flag* (1991, trans. Dorothy Britton), the title referring to the child behind the famous army photograph of a youngster amidst battle on Okinawa. Boys in modern works typically learn that combat sickens; girls reveal great resilience and courage; both frequently show themselves to be wiser than their elders, able to rekindle hope. Disenchanted soldiers star in Harry Mazer's *The Last Mission* (1979); Walter Dean Myers's *Fallen Angels* (1988); Cynthia Rylant's *I Had Seen Castles* (1993); and Robert Cormier's *Heroes* (1998), the latest in his trademark positioning of young people in contexts dominated by institutionalised violence.

In New Zealand, novels like Eve Sutton's *Moa Hunter* (1978) and Joanna Orwin's *The Guardian of the Land* (1985) go back to early Maori inter-tribal warfare, whereas Ronald Syme's *The Spaniards Came at Dawn* (1959) invents a Maori-English repulsion of a 17th-century Spanish invasion. The 1845–70 New Zealand Wars over land and sovereignty have inspired several novels, such as Mona Tracy's *Rifle and Tomahawk* (1927), which champions English success. However, Anne de Roo's *Jacky Nobody* (1983) and *The Bats' Nest* (1985) present the Maori point of view, the plight of racially mixed children and the stupidity of war. The siege of Orakau invigorates Ron Bacon's time-shift novel *Again, the Bugles Blow* (1973), evoking Maori heroism and hopes for racial unity. Beverley Dunlop's time-shift *Spirits of the Lake* (1988) de-activates a curse laid down during the Land Wars. The huge impact of World War I and II on New Zealand society is most notably represented in Maurice Gee's *The Fire-Raiser* (1986) and *The Champion* (1989) through the themes of nationalism, racism, heroism, and a black American's terror of Pacific battles. Terror of Japanese invasion in 1941 tragically drives children into hiding in Jack Lasenby's *The Mangrove Summer* (1988), which also individualises the suffering of thousands of New Zealand wounded. German aggression at sea dominates Winifred Owen's *Captives and Castaways* (1984). *The Bantam and the Soldier* (1996), Jennifer Beck's and Robyn Belton's picturebook set in France, emphasises hope in combat, whereas J.L. Sutherland's *Rundle's Hill* (1984) portrays a farmer's despair when his only son is killed overseas. William Taylor's *The Blue Lawn* (1994) tellingly recalls a grandmother's war experiences. Michael Joseph's *Kaspar's Journey* (1988) spotlights the European Children's Crusade, Ken Catran's time-shift *Neo's War* (1995) reinterprets the Trojan War, and Kate de Goldi's complex *Love, Charlie Mike* (1997) sends her Maori soldier to confusion and humiliation in Bosnia.

The first international war in which Australians were involved, the Boer War (1899–1902), did not generate any significant contemporary children's literature, but Bruce Tanton's *Time's Lost Hero* (1990) provides both an historic and realistic account of the true horrors of that war. Based on the characters from her BILLABONG series, MARY GRANT BRUCE captures the lives of ordinary Australians in World War I in her trilogy, *From Billabong to London* (1915), *Jim and Wally* (1916) and *Captain Jim* (1919). In ETHEL TURNER's patriotic trilogy, *The Cub* (1915), *Captain Cub* (1917) and *Brigid and the Cub* (1919), an observer's view of the war is given through the eyes of the central character, John Calthorp, the embodiment of the Australian soldier – informal, undisciplined and lacking class consciousness. A different perspective on war is evident in *Boy Soldiers* (1990) by Cliff Green; set just before World War I, the novel, based on Green's screenplay for the television series, *More Winners*, describes a 14-year-old who 'conscientiously objects' to undertaking the Government's compulsory military training, with dire consequences.

Life during World War II in country-town Australia is reflected in MAX FATCHEN's novel *Closer to the Stars* (1981), which recounts the story of a young girl who meets a serviceman in 1941. Michael Noonan addresses the fighting in New Guinea in the early 1940s in *MacKenzie's Boots* (1987), while Maureen Pople's *The Other Side of the Family* (1986) gives a realistic view of Sydney life in 1942 through the eyes of a young English evacuee, Katherine. Another English evacuee, Tommy, is the protagonist of Deirdre Hill's *Flight from Fear* (1988). RACHEL TONKIN's well-researched picturebook, *What was the War Like, Grandma?* (1996), represents life in Australia during the war years, as seen from the point of view of a young child. It gives a realistic and nostalgic insight into school and home life at that time. Based on her own wartime experiences, JUNKO MORIMOTO's picturebook, *My Hiroshima* (1987), is a poignant and moving account of her childhood, recreating that terrible event. MARGARET WILD provoked some controversy with her picturebook *LET THE CELEBRATIONS BEGIN* (1991), illustrated by JULIE VIVAS; based on a true event – the making of stuffed toys by Polish women in Belsen concentration camp for the first children's party held after the liberation – the book treads a fine line between realism and horror.

CHRISTOBEL MATTINGLEY conveys a strong anti-war message in her books, which show the impact of wars on the lives of ordinary families and their children: *The Angel with a Mouth-Organ* (1984), the first picturebook published in Australia about World War II, recounts the sorrows of a European family, while another picturebook, *The Miracle Tree* (1985), relates the suffering which followed the dropping of the atomic bomb on Nagasaki. The novels which form Mattingley's *ASMIR* SERIES are true stories based on Mattingley's personal contact with a family, and tell with great compassion the story of Asmir and his family living in Sarajevo, and the changes to their lives wrought by the war in Bosnia-Herzegovina.

The Vietnam War led to Australia's biggest anti-war demonstrations, particularly in relation to conscription, a topic explored in J.M. Couper's *The Thundering Good Day* (1985). ALLAN BAILLIE's *Little Brother* (1985) is a moving account of Vithy and his brother Mang as they flee the Khmer Rouge, from Cambodia into Thailand. Baillie's powerful adolescent novel, *THE CHINA COIN* (1991), encompasses the terrible massacres in Tiananmen Square in 1989, an event which Baillie witnessed. MMy, DAH, GL, JAP

See also HISTORICAL FICTION; ANNE FRANK

Warburton, Nick 1947– British author of drama and fiction for children, born and brought up in Essex, England. After ten years as a teacher, Warburton became a full-time writer. He has written TELEVISION plays and published a number of playscripts for children, winning the 1985 BBC *Radio Times* Drama Award for *Conversation from the Engine Room*.

His school and family stories – including *Normal Nesbitt: The Abnormally Average Boy* (1992), *The Battle of Baked Bean Alley* (1992) and *You've Been Noodled!* (1998) – are fast-paced narratives with lively dialogue, stereotypical or larger-than-life characters, and a good deal of humour, farce and slapstick, though the central character (often the narrator) is often more complex and serious issues underlie the humour. Warburton's understanding of issues important to children is also apparent in his stories for younger readers, such as *Hopping Mad* (1992) and his 'Roman' story *Gladiators Never Blink* (1999).

Warburton is an unusually versatile writer and has written a number of distinguished works for older readers. *The Thirteenth Owl* (1993) mixes FANTASY and reality in a powerfully told account of a young girl's discovery of adult passions and her own special power; both the theme and the narrative mode are reminiscent of the work of ALAN GARNER. *To Trust a Soldier* (1995), set during a future war in the British Isles, concentrates on the experiences of a young woman slowly coming to understand the humanity and vulnerability behind the soldierly codes of her companions. *Ackford's Monster* (1996), set in 1914, is a compelling but strange fantasy. Warburton's most assured work to date is an ADVENTURE STORY, *Lost in Africa* (2000), which describes in the words of the young narrator what happens when she and her father take off into remote West Africa in the 1960s. This narrative about racial anger and confusion is simultaneously a story of Natasha's struggle with her wilful and foolish father; political intimidation is described in carefully understated language, achieving authenticity while avoiding melodrama and cliché. VW

see also DRAMA FOR CHILDREN

Ward, Lynd (Kendall) 1905–85 American PICTUREBOOK artist, wood engraver and artist of wordless novels. Following a tradition of often politically radical artists such as the Flemish Frans Masereel (1889–1920) – who created novels with monotone woodcuts, most notably *Passionate Journey* (1919) – Ward's own contributions include *God's Plan: A Novel in Woodcuts* (1929), *Madman's Drum* (1930), *Wild Pilgrimage* (1932) and *Song Without Words* (1936), based on Masereel's *Story Without Words* (1924). These small morality plays, in stark black-and-white, usually show man or woman dwarfed and thwarted by the forces of the capitalist city. His pictures are hard-edged, stylised, sinuous, with little shading. He also illustrated other writers' books for children, such as ELIZABETH COATSWORTH's NEWBERY AWARD winner, *The Cat Who Went to Heaven* (1930). By contrast, his works for children are often more rural and feature animals, of which he was an adept draughtsman. For example, he won the CALDECOTT AWARD for *The Biggest Bear* (1952). Like *The Silver Pony: A Story in Pictures* (1973), it tells a parable using naturalistic depictions of a boy living on a farm. His works are collected in *Storyteller Without Words: The Wood Engravings of Lynd Ward* (1974). GRB

see also WOOD ENGRAVING

Wardell, Phyl(lis Ruth Margaret) 1909–94 New Zealand writer of traditional holiday ADVENTURE STORIES set in recognisable local landscapes. In the tradition of this genre there are plenty of mysterious strangers and coincidences, but the books are strengthened by Wardell's pioneering awareness of conservation issues, her concern to identify local flora and fauna, including the use of appropriate Maori names, and her treatment of local history and geography. *Gold at Kapai* (1960) is set on New Zealand's West Coast; *The Secret of the Lost Tribe* (1961) in Te Anau; and *Passage to Dusky* (1967) in Fiordland. All these stories generate a strong sense of place. Three later books – *Hazard Island* (1976), *The Nelson Treasure* (1983) and *Beyond the Narrows* (1985) – are similarly motivated, but the freshness found in the earlier books is compromised by a failure to move away from the constraints of the genre, despite the introduction of topical concerns, such as genetic engineering in *Beyond the Narrows*. Originality is sacrificed for repetition, especially in the basic patterning of the characters – father, sister, brother, English cousins, and an unexplained absence of mothers. BN

Warden's Niece, The (1957) Historical novel by GILLIAN AVERY, set in Oxford in 1875 and deservedly popular for many years. It has many of the best features of E. NESBIT's stories, the central character being an orphaned girl who is intelligent, shy and determined. The story begins with her escape from a boarding-school, and then turns into a kind of career story, showing Maria's growing interest in historical research and her bizarre but convincing adventures in – among other places – the Bodleian Library. It concludes, very satisfyingly, with the young heroine giving an academic paper to the Kentish Historical Association. VW

Warlow, Aidan see *THE COOL WEB*

Warner, Marina see 'Bluebeard'; see also FAIRY TALES; LULLABIES

Warner, Susan (Bogert) 1819–85 American author of domestic novels published under the pseudonym Elizabeth Wetherall. Born into a wealthy New York City family, Warner moved in her late teens with her family to an isolated farm after her father lost his fortune. The family's comparative poverty was the impetus for Warner's writing. Her first novel, *The Wide, Wide World* (1850), was second only to *UNCLE TOM'S CABIN* in popularity among 19th-century American novels. In it young Ellen Montgomery is sent to live on her unsympathetic Aunt Fortune's farm while her parents go abroad. After many trials, including the deaths of her parents and a close friend, Ellen develops an attitude of religious submission, shedding many tears of sorrow and self-reproach in the process. She is adopted by wealthy relatives in Scotland, but returns to America to marry her spiritual mentor. *Queechy* (1852) follows a similar formula of a young heroine suffering trials which demand domestic skills and spiritual strength, and being rewarded for her spiritual fortitude with an advantageous marriage. Warner wrote more than 30 novels, all overtly didactic and fervently evangelical. Though notoriously sentimental, Warner's works display her skill as a talented local colour writer, showing realistic details of life – particularly women's life – in 19th-century New England. JLB

Warrior Scarlet (1958) Acclaimed novel by ROSEMARY SUTCLIFF, illustrated by CHARLES KEEPING and set in Britain in the Bronze Age. The book tells the story of Drem, a young boy determined to win his warrior scarlet and be taken into the Men's side, despite the fact that he cannot use his spear-arm. As a child Drem has not been unduly troubled by his DISABILITY and has accepted it until he realises that, unless he can find 'ways round, and ways through, and ways over' he will have to leave his ruling tribe and be a shepherd with the Little Dark People.

The worlds of the warriors and the Dark People at first appear to be in sharp contrast. The world of the ruling warriors is made up of bright, fiery colours, reds, copper and gold, symbolised most clearly by the warrior scarlet, while the Dark People are associated with earthy greys and browns. Although Drem is determined not to be one of them, there is considerable sympathy for the little Dark People, who appear in many of Sutcliff's novels about Ancient Britain. Drem is an outsider himself and has divided his early life between his own tribe and the Dark People, learning a little of what it is like to be one of them and to be ruled by outsiders.

Like Marcus in *The Eagle Of The Ninth* (1954), Drem fights his disability with a determination that is common to all Sutcliff's heroes. Although the author claims in her 'historical note' that 'this story is not about Kings or heroes or battles', Drem has all the qualities of a hero but is unusual in that the challenge he faces is not created by external events but by his need to prove his capabilities to himself, meeting fear with anger. He has to slay his symbolic wolf on his own and is bitterly angry when his friend's intervention saves his life, but loses him the sought-after scarlet. To become a warrior Drem needs not only to prove his strength on his own, but also to win the co-operation of the rest of the tribe who must bend the rules to permit a second attempt.

The themes of reconciliation and compromise run throughout the book. Drem has to find alternatives to the skills needed by other warriors and when he fails in his wolf-slaying he has to come to terms with his situation before he can be reunited with his tribe. When it comes to his second wolf-slaying challenge Drem saves the life of Doli, one of the Little Dark People, slaying the same wolf that had defeated him in his earlier attempt and using Doli's dog rather than his own. The two peoples have to work together to survive in a dangerous environment, and it is satisfying that by the end of the book Drem has gained enough understanding to be united with Blai, a woman who is also an outsider KA

Watch With Mother Much-loved BBC TELEVISION programming slot for very young children, originally titled *For the Children*, scheduled on weekdays from 1950 until 1973 (though individual programmes were transmitted well after this). Devised and often written by Maria Bird as a visual equivalent to the STORYTELLING tradition established by radio, it developed into different 15-minute animation and puppet series for each day of the week, all introduced by tinkling music and an opening flower logo. *Picturebook* was the most overtly educational, employing the magazine format of stories, activities and short films which was to be the mainstay of many future pre-school programmes. The use of (very visible) string puppets in *Andy Pandy*, *The Flowerpot Men* and *The Woodentops*, and glove puppets of wild animals in *Rag, Tag and Bobtail* reflected producer Freda Lingstrom's passion for puppetry, establishing a lasting trend in children's television.

In spite of controversies over the supposedly incomprehensible 'flobbadob' language of the Flowerpot Men, *Watch with Mother*'s original scheduling as part of women's programmes, its representation of traditional family values, and use of mainly female narrators arguably helped to legitimate the new concept of television for very young children. The Flowerpot Men were re-introduced to the British screen, without the puppet-strings, in 2001. SG

Water-Babies, The: A Fairy Tale for a Land-Baby (1863) Story by the British author CHARLES KINGSLEY, one of the earliest children's books to work even more powerfully for adults. It follows the adventures of Tom Grimes, the chimney-sweep's boy, who flees to the Other-end-of-Nowhere and back. Tom, sweeping the chimneys at Harthover Place, finds himself by accident in the white room of the beautiful, clean Miss Ellie, and catches sight of his image, a little black ape, in the mirror. Pursued from the house, he is hunted into Vendale, where he tumbles into a river, and falls asleep. Underwater, he is transformed into an 'eft'. As an amphibious water-baby, he travels downstream towards the salt water, the 'mother of all living things', and tracks back through evolutionary stages on what becomes a moral search. The presiding spirit who watches over Tom's sometimes painful adventures is a kind of goddess of human nature who features within the story in different guises, as the Irishwoman, as Mrs Doasyouwouldbedoneby and her sister Mrs Bedonebyasyoudid, and as Mother Carey. Tom is finally redeemed 'because he has done the thing he did not like' – helping Grimes see the light – and allowed to go home with Miss Ellie on Sundays. Eventually, like a good Victorian, he becomes a great man of science.

Kingsley, inspired by Rabelais, injects amazing diversions into his episodic narrative. The book can be read at one level as an attempt to reconcile the implications of Darwin's *The Origin of Species* with Kingsley's own blend of Anglicanism and Christian Socialism. This is more a leap of faith than of logic, but Kingsley's optimism that the ultimate purpose of everything in life is good provides a thrust which propels the story through its many inconsistencies. The imaginative energy, the digressions, the swoops of tone, the vivid descriptions of landscape and seascape, and the vigorous language triumph over the didactic purpose – and even that is presented with touches of humour.

It is difficult to calculate how far *The Water-Babies* is, or was intended to be, a book for children. Mrs Kingsley claimed that the first chapter about little Tom came in response to her comment over breakfast at Eversley Rectory that 'Rose, Maurice, and Mary have got their book, and baby must have his'. Kingsley rapidly fleshed out his April scenario so that publication could begin in the August 1862 number of *Macmillan's Magazine* and continue in the seven succeeding issues. The following summer it was published in book form with two plates by J. Noel Paton, after considerable revision and some significant additions, notably the figure of the Irishwoman.

Once out of copyright, publishers seized on the story featuring winged water-babies as an ideal opportunity for illustration, and WARWICK GOBLE, JESSIE WILLCOX SMITH, MABEL LUCIE ATTWELL and MARGARET TARRANT took full sentimental advantage. Macmillan's chose a far more appropriate artist for their 1886 edition, in which the wood engravings based on Linley Sambourne's drawings provide a tough, satiric and often disturbing visual accompaniment to Kingsley's bizarre tale. PR

Waterhouse, Keith (Spencer) 1929– English novelist, playwright and journalist. He has, he says, never written children's books. His place here is owing to his first two novels: *There is a Happy Land* (1957) and *Billy Liar* (1959). Both are set in a city in Yorkshire, in the North of England. (Waterhouse was born in Hunslet, an area of Leeds.)

Both novels have first-person narrators who describe the disparity between their lives and their aspirations. The first is unnamed, a boy of about 11; the second is Billy Fisher, old enough to be thinking of leaving home. *There is a Happy Land* – taking its ironic title from a song in the novel, 'Where they have jam and bread three times a day' – opens with children's games in the street and ends in a cemetery. In between are the narrator's loneliness, the cruelties and precarious friendships of childhood, capricious adults, Uncle Mad who may be a child-molester, and the murder of a young girl. The narration and dialogue are funny, acute, unsentimental and realistic. The narrator of *Billy Liar* might be the same boy grown older. Like Walter Mitty, he escapes from the mundane awfulness and complications of his life (his family, his two fiancées, Shadrack the undertaker) into what he calls Number One thinking, the happy land. He is witty and clever. His novel is funny and farcical. But it, too, ends with a death and sadness. *Billy Liar* (with WILLIS HALL) was dramatised in 1960 and filmed by John Schlesinger in 1963. RC

Waterland, Liz see REAL BOOKS

Watership Down (1972) Novel by Richard Adams. Its publishing history is an interesting one: turned down by all the major publishing houses and finally published by Rex Collings, its sales have been enormous; it has won both the CARNEGIE MEDAL and *GUARDIAN* AWARD and has also been filmed. To its influence may be attributed the popularity that has since attended recent ANIMAL STORIES, inspiring works such as Horwood's *DUNCTON CHRONICLES* and the *REDWALL* SERIES.

Watership Down may be described as a utopian quest. It details the search of Hazel, Fiver and other rabbits for a new warren when theirs is destroyed to make way for a building site. While this might appear to suggest a politics of anti-industrialisation, the novel is not conceived in terms of the Romantic city–country dichotomy: enemies are rife (or *hrair* as the rabbits themselves would say), from man and his traps, dogs and natural predators, to other rabbits with different ideological outlooks. The novel has been accused of both sexism and fascism; its accusers might be forgiven for projecting a human value system onto the rabbits, for Adams endows them with both language and the power of political thought. On the other hand, he simultaneously takes care to emphasise their 'rabbitness' (for example, showing doe rabbits reabsorbing their young). SA

Watertower, The (1994) Australian PICTUREBOOK written by GARY CREW and illustrated by STEVEN WOOLMAN, aimed at older readers. It is a sparsely told horror story, wherein a boy meets with an unexplained, uncanny event at a small-town watertower, and returns home strangely changed. Woolman's eerie ILLUSTRATIONS imply that the entire town colludes in the watertower's evil, with many visual clues for the reader to discover. The book's design is exceptional and appropriate: the watertower bears a spiral-like symbol, and the reader must turn the book 180 degrees to follow the story. NLR

Watkins Pitchford, D.J. see B. B.

Watson, Clyde 1947– A New Englander whose stories and rhymed books are filled with distinctly American folk details drawn from her Vermont childhood. Her interest in music, which she teaches and performs professionally, is reflected in her books of original NURSERY RHYMES and songs, including *Fisherman Lullabies* (1968), *Hickory Stick Rag* (1976) and the award-winning *Father Fox's Pennyrhymes* (1971), illustrated, as are most of her books, by her sister, Wendy Watson. Other books include *Applebet* (1982) – an ALPHABET BOOK with a unified storyline – and fiction, such as *Tom Fox and the Apple Pie* (1972). SCWA

Watson, John see COMICS AND MAGAZINES

Watson, Victor see CRITICAL APPROACHES TO CHILDREN'S BOOKS

Watts, Isaac 1674–1748 Nonconformist minister and hymn writer, and author of *DIVINE SONGS* (1715), a popular book of religious poems written for children. He was also the writer of many well-known adult hymns, such as 'When I survey the wondrous cross' and 'Jesus shall reign where'er the sun'. ML

Waugh, Sylvia see *MENNYM* SERIES

***Waverley* novels** see SIR WALTER SCOTT; see also ADULT FICTION; HISTORICAL FICTION

Way, Brian see DRAMA FOR CHILDREN

Way Home (1994) Australian PICTUREBOOK, with words by LIBBY HATHORN, and ILLUSTRATION and design by GREGORY ROGERS, for whom it won the KATE GREENAWAY AWARD. Shane, homeless and needy, rescues a stray kitten, and journeys across the shadows and decay of an inner city, against a profligate, electrified landscape of advertising and business premises, to shelter in a discarded packing crate. Crumpled ENDPAPERS allude to the fate of the homeless in throwaway consumer- and market-driven societies, and Rogers uses charcoal and crayons to contrast light and dark, hope and despair, in sweeping, grainy illustrations. Intertextual allusions and quotations (for example, the repeated hands image from Michelangelo's 'Creation of Adam') signal the richness of meanings constructed within the text and the creators' intention to critique a society which produces homeless children. Libby Hathorn's lyrical print text, which plays with speech patterns, pace and suspense, integrates seamlessly with the illustrations, to present dangers, hopes and fears in evocative detail. *Way Home* is a landmark picturebook addressed to an older audience, multilayered in meanings and rich in symbolic allusion, exploring a controversial and contemporary theme, but never glamorising or sensationalising the position of homeless children. SNJ

see also *WE ARE ALL IN THE DUMPS*; *STONE COLD*

Way of the Whirlwind, The (1941) Australian PICTUREBOOK written and illustrated by Mary (1913–94) and Elizabeth (1916–) Durack. Combining the traditions of a European FOLKTALE with ABORIGINAL myth, the FANTASY story centres on two children, Nungaree and Jungaree, looking after their baby brother, Woogoo, who vanishes while they sleep. The richly poetic language, reminiscent of oral traditions, is complemented by Elizabeth Durack's black-and-white drawings and her TIPPED IN colour plates which use vibrant swirling colours. The sumptuous production – it was the last children's book to feature such plates – was well received, particularly as it was seen to reflect contemporary feelings about Australian identity. JAP

We Are All in the Dumps with Jack and Guy (1993) PICTUREBOOK by MAURICE SENDAK confronting social, political and economic realities of the world today as experienced by the least fortunate children on the streets of America, and, by implication, by children, on the wrong side of the tracks anywhere. The picturebook had its genesis when Sendak came upon a bare-footed boy sleeping in a box on the streets of Los Angeles. The fantasy which this experience prompted is set in a cardboard city occupied by a group of homeless children, dressed in rags and wrapped in newspapers. Their leaders, Jack and Guy, become unwillingly involved in the rescue of a black baby, an image of famine and plague, who is kidnapped by rats. Sendak unites two cryptic NURSERY RHYMES, adds dialogue in speech bubbles, and places words on newspapers and signs for the text. The picturebook has the immediacy of a theatrical performance with characters appearing as if on a shallow stage against backdrops, set down in fluid outline, with colour affecting the mood and controlling the pace. The FANTASY, which is a testimony to the tenacious need that children have to survive, reads on a symbolic level like a FOLKTALE shaped to encourage resourcefulness; it exemplifies the redemptive power of love through the changing and developing relationships between Jack, Guy and the baby. Sendak offers this main theme emblematically in the COVER ART for the jacket with his reinterpretation of the 15th-century painting 'Descent into Limbo' by Andrea Mantegna. JD

Weary Willie and Tired Tim see COMICS, MAGAZINES AND PERIODICALS

Webb, Clifford (Cyril) 1895–1972 Artist, illustrator and writer. Webb made his name as an illustrator with woodcuts to ARTHUR RANSOME'S *SWALLOWS AND AMAZONS* (1931). He then provided striking images in gouache and scraperboard, including many of animals, for the exemplary children's books that he produced with his wife Ella Monckton. DW

Webb, Kaye 1914–96 British writer and editor whose career in journalism included editing the innovative magazine *THE YOUNG ELIZABETHAN* in the 1950s. In 1961 she became editor of Puffin Books. Her tireless enthusiasm, concern for children's reading and flair for publicity established her as a leading force in children's literature. In 1967 she founded the Puffin Club, and by 1974 120,000 members, world-wide, joined in literary events, read *Puffin Post* and entered competitions. She edited *I LIKE THIS POEM* (1979), a collection 'chosen by children for children'. AHa

see also PUBLISHING AND PUBLISHERS

Webb, Marion St John see MARGARET TARRANT

Webster, Jean 1876–1916 American novelist and playwright best known for her epistolary novels *Daddy-Long-Legs* (1911) and its sequel, *Dear Enemy* (1915). A grand-niece of MARK TWAIN, Webster was a gifted humorist. Her first novel, *When Patty Went to College* (1903), depicts life at a private women's college (based on her own experiences at Vassar, where she matriculated in 1901). Although her works have been regarded as light romances, Webster incorporates into her novels much of the contemporary social theory of her day. *The Wheat Princess* (1906) studies the economic impact of American business on Italian peasants, while *Dear Enemy* concerns the care of dependent children. Webster wrote the theatrical version of *Daddy-Long-Legs* in 1913/14 and travelled with the road company throughout the East and Midwest. The play was a tremendous hit, spawning numerous regional touring companies and four films. A film of *Dear Enemy* was produced by the BBC in the early 1990s. In 1966 *Daddy-Long-Legs* was reissued in the United Kingdom with ILLUSTRATIONS by EDWARD ARDIZZONE. Webster gave birth to a daughter in June, 1916; she died the following day. An authorised biography, *Jean Webster, Storyteller*, was published by Alan Simpson in 1984. AKP

Webster, Noah see *THE AMERICAN SPELLING BOOK*; *MCGUFFEY ECLECTIC READERS*

Weetzie Bat see *DANGEROUS ANGELS* SERIES; see also GAY AND LESBIAN LITERATURE

Illustration by Fritz Wegner from *Giant Kippernose* by John Cunliffe.

Wegner, Fritz 1924– Born in Vienna, Wegner came to England in 1938. After studies at St Martin's school of Art, once the war was over he became a freelance illustrator, producing his first work in 1949. His witty pen-and-ink drawings enhanced such books as *Fattypuffs and Thinifers* (André Maurois, 1968), *Dribblesome Teapots* (Norman Hunter, 1969), *The Strange Case of Adelaide Harris* (LEON GARFIELD, 1971) and *Jacob Two-Two Meets the Hooded Fang* (MORDECAI RICHLER, 1975). More recently, he has worked closely and inventively with ALLAN AHLBERG on around ten titles, including *PLEASE MRS BUTLER* (1983), *Heard it in the Playground* (1989), *The Giant Baby* (1994) and *The Better Brown Stories* (1995). *The Wicked Tricks of Till Owlyglass* (retold by MICHAEL ROSEN, 1990), illustrated with fastidious detail, great crowd scenes and subtle colouring, was shortlisted for the KURT MASCHLER AWARD. *The Tale of the Turnip*, retold by Brian Alderson, was published in 1999. JAG

Weirdstone of Brisingamen, The (1960) First novel by the British writer ALAN GARNER, which excited a generation with its fast-moving and unflinching descriptions of danger. It begins with a brother and sister, Colin and Susan, arriving by train to stay at a farm near Alderley Edge. There is a tradition of English children's stories beginning in this predictable way, but this novel quickly changes into an extraordinary FANTASY in which a precious stone belonging to Susan turns out to be a stone of power which evil forces seek to possess. Garner, like JOHN MASEFIELD in *THE MIDNIGHT FOLK* and *The Box of Delights* – but without Masefield's comic relish – used myth and legend to provide a structure for conflict. His innovativeness lay mostly in the narrative pace, an uncompromising magic realism in which the fantastic breaks in upon convincing naturalistic settings, and what Neil Philip calls his 'assured, poetic command of English'.

Colin and Susan are unremarkable characters borrowed from the conventions of hundreds of children's ADVENTURE STORIES. Garner himself described his first work as 'a fairly bad book', claiming that when he deliberately wrote for children the result was 'the usual condescending pap'. Such dismissive severity was characteristic of children's literature in the 1960s. 'It is my job to show, not tell', he said, and his unequivocal commitment to authentic description was especially apparent in the account of the children's terrifyingly claustrophobic journey underground through collapsing tunnels.

The Moon of Gomrath (1963), the sequel, is a better novel. The writing is evocative, visual and precise; racing clouds, for example, are described as 'breaking into separate glories that whisped and sharpened to skeins of starlight . . .'; and, although the characterisation of Colin remains sketchy, there is a more imaginative interest in Susan. Her magic is represented as a specifically female power associated with the moon. The fantasy arises from a magic of place and prehistory, and Garner creates an archaeology of ancient modes of knowledge – the Old Magic, Cadellin's High Magic, and modern Reason. Susan belongs to the Old Magic, intuitive, dangerous and unpredictable. Each catastrophe is precipitated by her disruptive recklessness. At the end, when everything has failed and elves and dwarfs are running away, Susan has the battle-madness in her and returns to the conflict alone. In a triumphant climax, she briefly joins nine magical huntresses, 'the Shining Ones, the Daughters of the Moon' – but they leave her behind, 'waking from the dream of a long yearning fulfilled', aware of promised mysteries but for the time being 'left as dross upon the hill'.

Similar modes of fantasy were later to be developed with more psychological authenticity by JOHN GORDON, HUGH SCOTT, ANNIE DALTON and DIANE DUANE, but in the 1960s Garner's first two novels signalled a fresh urgency and seriousness in a new generation of children's writers who wanted to put behind them what they saw as the slack and comfortable fiction of the past. VW

Weisgard, Leonard (Joseph) 1916–2000 American illustrator of nearly 200 books. Weisgard was born in New Haven, Connecticut, and spent part of his childhood in England among his father's many relatives, and from 1970 lived in Denmark. He attended Pratt Institute and the New School for Social Research and then worked as an illustrator for various magazines before breaking into children's books with *Suki, the Siamese Pussy* (1937), which he both wrote and illustrated. Shortly afterwards he began working with MARGARET WISE BROWN, collaborating on *The Noisy Book* (1939). Brown greatly influenced Weisgard's career in children's books. He eventually collaborated with her on 25 more books. He received a Caldecott Honour Award for Brown's *Little Lost Lamb* (1945) and the CALDECOTT MEDAL for his expressionistic ILLUSTRATIONS for her *The Little Island* (1946), painted with a mixture of zinc and egg-white on wood. The most widely known Brown/Weisgard book, however, may be the lavishly illustrated *The Golden Egg Book* (1947) about a lonely little rabbit and an egg.

In the 1950s Weisgard wrote and illustrated several books under the name Adam Green. He has also illustrated non-fiction and novels, including MARJORIE KINNAN RAWLINGS's *The Secret River*, which was given an award by the American Society of Graphic Arts. LH

Welch, Ronald [Ronald Felton] 1909–82 British author of largely forgotten HISTORICAL FICTION for children, who chose his pseudonym from the regiment in which he served during World War II. Each novel of the *Carey* series follows the adventures of a particular member of the family at different points in history; the first of these, *Knight Crusader* (1954), won the CARNEGIE MEDAL. *The Gauntlet* (1951) is also a historical novel, but with a difference: its modern protagonist, Peter, finds himself back in the Middle Ages where he appears to belong, and has to be 're-educated' into its ways. SA

Well at [of] the World's End see THE FROG PRINCE

Wells, H.G. see SCIENCE FICTION

Wells, Rosemary 1943– American author-illustrator well known for her child-pleasing books dealing with family conflict and sibling rivalry for young children. She has also written several successful novels for older readers. Her books have won many awards and citations, including the 1989 BOSTON GLOBE-HORN BOOK AWARD for *Shy Charles* (1988), the Irma Simonton Black Award for *Benjamin and Tulip* (1973), and Edgar Allen Poe runner-up awards from Mystery Writers of America for *When No One Was Looking* (1980) and *Through the Hidden Door* (1987).

Wells was born in New York City. A fan of theatre, especially musicals, her first publishing success was an illustrated book of a Gilbert and Sullivan song from *Yeoman of the Guard – A Song to Sing, O!* (1968). Max and Ruby are two of her best-known characters, from the *Max* series established in 1979. Her novels for older readers demonstrate her versatility; using gripping and intricate plots, she reveals a true understanding of teenage friendship and burgeoning maturity. LAW

Welsh mythology and folklore For centuries after the Saxon invasion, the myths and legends of the British people were kept alive in the oral tradition of Wales. Poems were composed and sung to harp accompaniment by various grades of bard, while STORYTELLING was mainly left to popular entertainers known as *cyfarwyddiaid*. Poems in Old and Middle Welsh contain some of the earliest references to KING ARTHUR and many allusions to other characters and incidents from MYTH AND LEGEND. Another rich source for Welsh mythology is *The Triads of the Island of Britain*. Headings such as 'Three Red Ravagers of the

Island of Britain' or 'Three Golden Shoemakers of the Island of Britain' are followed by names and brief explanations. These and other descriptive lists, such as *The Thirteen Treasures of the Island of Britain* (which actually number 16) and *The Twenty-Four Knights of Arthur's Court*, acted as an index to the tales that a bard or storyteller was expected to know. Very few of these tales survive in written versions.

One collection of 11 stories written in Middle Welsh is preserved in two medieval manuscripts. This collection was named *The Mabinogion* by Lady Charlotte Guest, who edited the first English translation (1838–49). The stories range in date from the 11th to the 13th century, but they draw on much older oral versions. The tales of Pwyll, Branwen, Manawydan and Math are called 'the Four Branches of the Mabinogi'. The gifted compiler of the 'Four Branches' drew on myth, legend, genealogy and local tradition to create four interlaced stories set in a realm of brave warriors, cunning wizards, enchanted animals and magic cauldrons. The 'Four Branches' have lively dialogue, subtle characterisation, and several outstanding heroines who endure cruel fates with dignity, courage and dry humour. Some of the main characters, such as Math, Gwydion and Bendigeidfran seem to be Celtic deities in origin, and the Children of Don who appear in the 'Fourth Branch' are cognate with the Tuatha Dé Danann of IRISH MYTHOLOGY. These characters are mostly treated as if they were human, but they retain some supernatural powers: Math can turn people into animals, Gwydion can create a woman out of flowers, and Bendigeidfran's severed head continues to protect Britain after his death.

The remaining stories in *The Mabinogion* are of diverse date and authorship. 'Culhwch & Olwen' is set in the time of Arthur but includes pre-Christian elements. A complicated quest to win a princess is described in exuberant prose, culminating in a confrontation with an irascible giant whose eyelids have to be propped up with pitchforks. 'Lludd and Llefelys' tells how King Lludd cleverly overcame the Three Plagues of Britain, while 'The Dream of Macsen' involves the historical characters of St Helena and the Roman general Magnus Maximus in a colourful romance. 'The Dream of Rhonabwy' seems to be a satire on traditional storytelling and jokes about the nostalgia for a lost heroic age which had become typical of Welsh literature. The collection is completed by three Arthurian romances which are very similar to poetic versions of the same stories in Norman French. Lady Guest added to *The Mabinogion* a story from a 16th-century manuscript about the youthful adventures of the poet TALIESIN. He was a real person who lived in what is now southern Scotland in the sixth century. In legend, Taliesin became a prophet born of water stolen from the Cauldron of Inspiration and Knowledge. His famous harp was credited with magical powers of its own.

Retellings for children of stories from *The Mabinogion* include SIDNEY LANIER's *The Boy's Own Mabinogion* (1881), PADRAIC COLUM's *The Island of the Mighty* (1924), Robert Nye's *Taliesin* (1967), and Gwyn Thomas and KEVIN CROSSLEY-HOLLAND's *Tales from the Mabinogion* (1984). *The Mabinogion* has inspired FANTASY series by Kenneth Morris and Evangeline Walton, PICTUREBOOKS by Jenny Nimmo (see *THE SNOW SPIDER*) and Jac Jones, and some notable books for children and young adults. LOUISE LAWRENCE drew on the *The Mabinogion* for *The Earth Witch* (1981), a novel about a teenage girl who is taken over by an ancient Celtic goddess. Taliesin and his harp feature in *The High King* (1968) and *The Truthful Harp* (1971) by LLOYD ALEXANDER, *Silver on the Tree* (1971) by SUSAN COOPER (see *THE DARK IS RISING*) and *A String in the Harp* (1977) by NANCY BOND. ALAN GARNER's *THE OWL SERVICE* (1967), centred on an incident from 'The Fourth Branch of the Mabinogi', reflects the strong association of place and story that is typical of Welsh myth. Some characters from the lost body of Welsh stories listed in *The Triads of the Island of Britain* appear in Garner's *The Moon of Gomrath* (1963) (see *THE WEIRDSTONE OF BRISINGAMEN*). In *THE CHRONICLES OF PRYDAIN* (1964–73) Lloyd Alexander uses characters, objects and incidents from *The Mabinogion*, *The Triads* and *The Thirteen Treasures of the Island of Britain* to create his own fantasy version of early Wales. GHP

see also *GWYDION* TRILOGY

Welsh National Centre for Children's Literature see COLLECTIONS OF CHILDREN'S BOOKS

Wersba, Barbara 1932– American writer of PICTUREBOOKS, verse and novels. Introduced to acting when she moved from Chicago to New York City as a child, Wersba pursued a stage career for 15 years. After writing her first book, *The Boy Who Loved the Sea* (1961), she decided to become a full-time writer. *The Dream Watcher* (1968), the story of loner Albert Scully who gains self-worth through a relationship with an eccentric old woman, established her reputation. Drawing from her own experiences, Wersba writes honestly about outsiders with artistic interests, unusual older mentors and teenage sexuality (including homosexuality). Her newest book, *Whistle Me Home* (1997), addresses teenage alcoholism. ARTL

see also SEX IN CHILDREN'S BOOKS; GAY AND LESBIAN LITERATURE

Wesley, Charles 1707–88 English writer of hymns, closely associated with his evangelist brother, John Wesley. He has been aptly described by IONA AND PETER OPIE as 'one of the most inspired and prolific hymn writers of all time', who encouraged others to turn their attention to the young with verses 'flowing with cheerfulness, and without the solemnities of religion . . . so that children might find delight and profit together'. Wesley's exquisitely beautiful, musical hymns influenced other writers, including William Blake, whose poem, 'The Lamb', for example, is very close to Wesley's 'Gentle Jesus, meek and mild'. Wesley's *Hymns for Children* (1763) contain many of his best-loved hymns, a good number of which are still regularly sung today. MCCS

see also LULLABIES; *SONGS OF INNOCENCE AND EXPERIENCE*

West, Colin 1951– British nonsense poet and illustrator. In *Not To Be Taken Seriously* (1984), *It's Funny When You Look at It* (1982) and *What Would You Do with a Wobble-dee-Woo?* (1988) West's wry and quirky verse is reminiscent of SPIKE MILLIGAN and OGDEN NASH. He excels at skilful tongue-twisters, shape poems and general delightful silliness. JL

see also NONSENSE VERSE

West, Joyce 1908–85 New Zealand author whose books vividly describe the life in the small isolated communities on the east coast of New Zealand that she knew intimately. *Drovers Road* (1953) and its sequels *Cape Lost* (1963), *The Golden Country* (1965), *The Year of the Shining Cuckoo* (1961) and *The River Road* (1980) tell of children whose love of horses dominates their isolated lives, while in *The Sea Islanders* (1970) young children survive on their own in a beach cottage. West's books are notable for their warm extended families whose daily work routines are often complicated by harsh weather, but lightened by time spent with their beloved horses. FP

Westall, Robert 1929–93 Award-wining and popular British fiction author who described himself as 'a working class lad with middle class vices'. His ambitious parents sent him to grammar school but were nervous of what he had learnt there. Many of his novels reflect a sense of exclusion from family life; World War II, a favourite theme in Westall's writing, provides plausible reasons for the loss of home and family in his narratives. In *The Kingdom by the Sea* (1990), winner of the GUARDIAN AWARD, Harry is made homeless after an air raid and struggles to fend for himself, while in *Blitzcat* (winner of the 1989 SMARTIES PRIZE for the 9–11 age range) a cat who has lost its home travels for miles across the country to find its owner. *A Place for Me* (1993) also looks at the theme of the lost home, though this time the heroine is sent away to avoid trouble. She is older than many of Westall's heroines, and capable of setting up her own home, but nevertheless the sense of loss is still pervasive.

Those heroes and heroines who remain with their families often demonstrate a fierce need to be independent and to establish their own moral code and way of life. Chas McGill in *THE MACHINE GUNNERS* (1975) creates a second home where he is in charge. Independence does not necessarily come easily though; there is often a high price to be paid for it and its loss by the end of each novel is almost inevitable.

Westall's native Tyneside provides the setting for many of his novels. A handful of stories – including *The Christmas Cat* (1991) and *The Christmas Ghost* (1993) – are set there during the 1920s and 1930s and much of his work features the area during World War II. Another novel, *Falling into Glory* (1993), retains the same local setting, although the time is now the 1950s: Robbie Atkinson, a grammar-school boy, falls in love with his teacher and the two begin a passionate but potentially dangerous affair. The novel is partly autobiographical, featuring Westall's home town and his own name. Although Emma is initially in the position of power, being a teacher and ten years older than Robbie, as the relationship develops the balance of power shifts and Robbie swings between being a pathetic little boy and a manipulative adult. Many of Westall's heroes exhibit a similar need to be in control; when Westall was asked why he made his male characters so macho his answer was that he 'wrote about the real world'.

Another strong influence on Westall's writing was his son, who died tragically in a biking accident at the age of 18. He had been a stern critic of his father's work and encouraged him to develop his fast-paced style with its snappy dialogue. *Devil on the Road* (1978) is about a biker who goes back in time and explores the theme of the supernatural, another frequent motif in Westall's work. KA

see also WAR STORIES

Westerman, Percy F. 1876–1959 Prolific British writer of ADVENTURE STORIES. Beginning with historical tales in the manner of G.A. HENTY, such as *A Lad of Grit* (1908), Westerman began to introduce aspects of new technology, such as aeroplanes, tanks and wireless, into books like *Winning his Wings: a story of the R.A.F.* (1919), which became extremely popular in the 1930s. DB

westerns Stories set in the American West during the second half of the 19th century that feature stock characters, incidents and settings. Westerns have dominated American popular culture in print as well as in radio plays, movies and TELEVISION shows. The typical western features a cowboy or drifter who battles Indians or outlaws in order to defend a helpless or oppressed character, frequently female. The antecedents of the genre can be traced to the Puritan writers who demonised the wilderness landscape, but the genre owes more to James Fenimore Cooper's *Leather-Stocking Tales*, as well as the TALL TALES associated with southwestern humorists and the sentimental stories and sketches of Bret Harte. Westerns – especially those by Edward Ellis, Ned Buntline and Edward L. Wheeler – were very popular in the pulp story papers and DIME NOVELS at the turn of the 20th century. Owen Wister's *The Virginian* (1902), often considered the quintessential western, solidified into types such genre elements as the 'walkdown' and 'shoot-out', the relationship between a cowboy and his horse, the clothing of the cowboy, his natural and graceful movement, his stoicism in the face of hardship, and his adherence to a chivalric code. EBD

Weston Woods Studios see MORTON SCHINDEL

Westward Ho! see CHARLES KINGSLEY

Whaanga, Mere 1952– New Zealand writer and illustrator. Having realised that the old Maori legends were in danger of being lost, Whaanga wrote, illustrated and published a bilingual PICTUREBOOK, *The Legend of the Seven Whales of Ngai Tahu Matawhaiti = He Pakiwaitara o Ngaa Taahora Tokowhitu a Ngai Tahu Matawhaiti* (1988). This was followed by *Tangaroa's Gift = Te Koha a Tangaroa* (1990) and *Te Kooti's Diamond = Ta Tiamana a Te Kooti* (1991). Whaanga is committed to bilingual publication in order to share the legends as widely as possible. Their poetic language and evocative illustrations make Whaanga's books a pleasure to read, as well as valuable language resources. LO

see also MAORI WRITING FOR CHILDREN

Whale's Song, The (1990) Popular and influential story by Dyan Sheldon with illustrations by GARY BLYTHE. Lilly wishes to repeat her grandmother's childhood experiences of hearing the whales sing, though Uncle Frederick believes she should be given a realistic view of the uses of these creatures. The story is told with the poetic cadence of a traditional storyteller, perfectly complemented by Gary Blythe's oil paintings, a series of powerful and often detailed illustrations, full of subtle colour and light. Using dry paint effects and the canvas weave itself, he captures the textures of fabric, skin and moss-encrusted planking. Blythe won a KATE GREENAWAY MEDAL for his paintings. AR

What is the Truth? (1984) A farmyard FABLE for the young by TED HUGHES, which won the *SIGNAL* AWARD FOR POETRY. God and his son visit earth and summon the sleeping villagers to speak the truth of their best-known creature. So begins a dream sequence of poems in which lies the tantalising possibility of ultimate truth. The foal, for instance, is 'a warm heap / Of ashes and embers, fondled by small draughts'. Each of R.J. Lloyd's ILLUSTRATIONS has a moon or a sun, giving a numinous backdrop to a creature of earth, which is entirely appropriate to a fable with linguistic as well as environmental implications. It was reissued in 1995 in a smaller format, with illustrations by Lisa Flather. JP

What Katy Did (1872) First of a series of popular books by American author SUSAN COOLIDGE (Sarah Chauncy Woolsey). *What Katy Did* was published in 1872 and may have been influenced by the success of *LITTLE WOMEN* (1868). Its heroine, Katy Carr, resembles Jo March in her independence and spirit of fun, but further similarities may in part be due to the fact that Susan Coolidge shared an editor with LOUISA MAY ALCOTT.

Katy Carr is 12 when the series begins, a bossy big sister full of splendid ideas and great intentions to be good and beautiful one day. She is headstrong and enthusiastic but often forgets to think of the consequences of her actions. The absence of a mother allows the children an unusual degree of freedom and Katy initially has little respect for her Aunt Izzy, who looks after them. When Katy ignores her aunt's instructions she pays heavily for her disobedience and has to spend four years confined to her bed unable to walk. Her virtuous Cousin Helen, herself paralysed, counsels her not to resent her paralysis but to learn in the 'School of Pain'. When Aunt Izzy dies unexpectedly Katy, who has learnt patience and understanding, is able to take on the maternal role.

In many ways *What Katy Did* appears to conform to the pattern of a Sunday-school story in which the disobedient child is severely punished for her naughtiness and learns patience and humility in the process. However, the pattern is actually less clear-cut than it first appears; although Katy's father has tried to check her headstrong temperament, he also allows her an unusual degree of freedom so that we do not expect her to behave in a model way. The accident is shown to be, at least in part, Aunt Izzy's fault, since she expected blind obedience from the children without explaining her reasons to them – 'This was unwise of Aunt Izzy. It would have been better had she explained further . . . If she had told this to the children all could have been right: but Aunt Izzy's theory was that young people must obey their elders without explanation.'

Both *What Katy Did* and its sequel *What Katy Did at School* (1873) have been in print in Britain since their first publication there, although they have had less success in the United States. Perhaps the second novel's enduring popularity with British readers is due in part to the fact that it is an early example of the

'It was after my third donut that I had my first break. Unfortunately, it was my big toe.' Illustration from *Detective Donut and the Wild Goose Chase* by Bruce Whatley and Rosie Smith.

girls' SCHOOL STORY and combines a healthy sense of fun with strong moral values. *What Katy Did Next* (1886) describes a trip round Europe and culminates in a conventional happy ending as Katy plans to marry, thereby fulfilling the traditional womanly role. In many respects this novel is less successful than the earlier two, at times seeming little more than a guide to Europe. However, it remains in print in Britain. Two later novels about the Carr family, *Clover* (1888) and *In The High Valley* (1891), never attained the same popularity as the earlier three. KA

Whatley, Bruce Australian writer and illustrator, who enjoys sharing his tongue-in-cheek sense of humour with his young readers in his popular PICTUREBOOKS. *The Ugliest Dog in the World* (1992) – his first title – and *That Magnetic Dog* (1994) feature his own boxer dog. *Looking for Crabs* (1992) depicts a family at the beach looking (fruitlessly) for crabs, which the reader can see, hiding under the rocks. As with *ROSIE'S WALK*, young children relish the chance to be more knowledgeable than the characters in the book. *Whatley's Quest* (1994) is a puzzle and ALPHABET BOOK, with well-defined, imaginative watercolour and gouache illustrations, a style Whatley has honed to perfection in *Detective Donut and the Wild Goose Chase* (1997), shortlisted for the CHILDREN'S BOOK COUNCIL OF AUSTRALIA Awards for 1998. With a bear as detective, and a mouse assistant, this is a splendid witty parody of the classic private investigator genre of Raymond Chandler's 1940s America, instantly recognisable from the dry, terse first-person narration and the flawless visual evocation of the period, with the shabby, cluttered office, sombre streets and Humphrey Bogart film posters. Australian humour underpins both *The Flying Emu* (1999) and *The Boing Boing Races* (1999), with their caricatured yet believable animals. JAP

Wheatley, Nadia 1949– Australian historian and writer of overtly political quality fiction. Her first novel, *Five Times Dizzy* (1982), about a Greek girl and her family settling into urban Sydney, reputedly heralded the arrival of the non-Anglo-Saxon protagonist in Australian children's fiction. The sequel *Dancing in the Anzac Deli* was published in 1984, and both books were televised. An advocate of social history, Wheatley wrote of 1930s Sydney eviction battles in the historical FANTASY *The House That Was Eureka* (1985), and of ordinary Australian life in the PICTUREBOOKS *MY PLACE* (1987), illustrated by DONNA RAWLINS, and *Highway* (1997), illustrated by ANDREW MCCLEAN. These books reflect her interest in narrative and structural innovation, as does *The Blooding* (1987), which blends diary entries, letters, songs and newspaper reports to tell of a teenager torn between environmental concerns and his local logging community. *Lucy in the Leap Year* (1993) is structured around a child's calendar, depicting a difficult year in which Lucy's focus shifts from the local to the universal. Place is carefully depicted in Wheatley's novels, and deeply entwined with the narrative; she has said that for her, place gives rise first to characters, then to plot. Her picturebook *Luke's Way of Looking* (1999), illustrated by Matt Ottley, is about art and schooling as Luke breaks free from his repressive teacher's views. *Vigil* (2000), a novel for older readers, revolves around Nathan's grief after the death of two friends. Wheatley is also a noted short-story writer, publishing the collection *The Night Tolkien Died* in 1994. NLR

Whelan, Gerard 1957– Irish author. His first two books, *The Guns of Easter* (1996) and *A Winter of Spies* (1998), vividly capture the Dublin of the 1916 Rising and the subsequent War of Independence. *Dream Invader* (1997), a FANTASY thriller, won the CBI/BISTO

BOOK OF THE YEAR AWARD. *Out of Nowhere* (1999) is another fantasy, which despite a gripping beginning falls away in the second half. VC

When Hitler Stole Pink Rabbit see OUT OF THE HITLER TIME SERIES

When I Dance (1988) First collection of poems for children by JAMES BERRY, drawing on experience of inner-city life in Britain and from the rural Caribbean. The title poem exemplifies Berry's intentions: 'I'm costumed in a rainbow mood . . . And I celebrate all rhythms.' These poems promote diversity and integration, introducing black writing into mainstream children's literature. The collection won the *SIGNAL* POETRY AWARD in 1989. HT

When Sheep Cannot Sleep (1987) Picturebook by SATOSHI KITAMURA, which is both a counting book dealing with consecutive numbers up to 22 (but only if the young reader wants it to be) and the story of Woolly's insomniac night-time wanderings. Woolly is represented as an endearing character, sheep-like without being sheepish, who finally gets to sleep counting sheep. The artwork is a fusion of western and Japanese traditions. Kitamura chooses a rich colour palette, adding strong reds and oranges to a range of earth colours, and he gives full play to a particular bluish purple in his increasingly darkening night skies. He draws clear, closed outlines with pen and ink on thick textured paper and then fills them in with watercolour. He achieves a range of effects, such as colour fading and fringing, allowing the paint to bleed into the paper. He adds to these effects by using clear water washes. He often combines western three-dimensional perspective effects with the Japanese drawing tradition which appears to tip up an object such as a table or a floor in an attempt to provide maximum information about it. *When Sheep Cannot Sleep* received the Parents' Choice Illustrations Award and an award from the New York Academy of Sciences. AR

When We Were Very Young Published in 1924, this collection of verse, the first of A.A. MILNE's four famous books for children, was reprinted six times in the two months from publication and has since become a classic. It is dedicated to the author's four-year-old son Christopher Robin, each poem describing typical childhood happenings in a way that both adults and children could relish. Already a skilled and practised versifier, Milne brought consummate professionalism to his writing. Insistent rhythms, in which the naturally metrical name Christopher Robin often played a part, were allied to the briefest stories where every word is made to count. Situations described include ever-popular events such as changing the guard at Buckingham Palace, feeding elephants in the zoo and episodes of mild childish disobedience.

Affectionately illustrated by E.H. SHEPARD, these short poems celebrate a childhood portrayed as totally secure, privileged and imaginative. Set to music by H. Fraser-Simpson, they sang of a world which seemed largely trouble-free – a welcome respite for those who, like Milne himself, had suffered in World War I. Unjustly accused of sentimentality, the poems themselves are in fact quite caustic about a child's egocentricity. But ILLUSTRATIONS and music combined to give this book an undeserved reputation for sickly fantasy. In his autobiography *The Enchanted Places* (1974) Christopher Robin accused the poems of getting him wrong. But his father was often, in fact, recalling his own childhood in this book, which never pretended to be anything other than a light-hearted work written to give pleasure. NT

Where the Forest Meets the Sea (1988) A PICTUREBOOK by JEANNIE BAKER, which won the Friends of the Earth Earthworm Award and chronicles the reflections of a young boy exploring a rainforest in North Queensland. He imagines the people and animals which have been there before him, and those of the future. Their presence is manifested in ghostly images on the textured, densely worked COLLAGE compositions. The final illustration displays the true cost of development: superimposed on the creek and forest are spectral forms of a motor boat, cars, and children watching television beside an outdoor pool. JD

see also ECOLOGY

Where the Sidewalk Ends (1974) Collection of poems and drawings by SHEL SILVERSTEIN, a modern classic full of nonsense and humour with a hint of the cautionary now and again, promoting peace, love, friendship and general silliness. The jokes and crazy characters and occurrences are delivered in truly great rhymes. The ILLUSTRATIONS have a symbiotic relationship with, and are as inventive as, the words themselves. JL

Where the Wild Things Are (1963) PICTUREBOOK by MAURICE SENDAK, the first of his picturebook trilogy. Sendak's emphasis is not on the morality of the hero's behaviour, but rather on the internal dynamics of his experience. In content and theme the picturebook was controversial, setting a new precedent, and provoking a major debate about the content of children's books in the 1960s. Max, about six years old and wearing a wolf suit, is sent to bed supperless for misbehaving. He has been a perfect little monster. Impotent, he resorts to FANTASY. His bedroom is transformed, he sails away to the land of the Wild Things. Max tames them with a charm and leads them in a rumpus of dancing and shouting; then, on his own terms, he returns to the real world, sleepy, hungry and at peace with himself.

The spare text, set down in a small segment on each page, has a discernible pattern and rhythm which dramatise events. Three particularly long sentences run on and on to mimic continuous action both external and internal, the seamless passage between reality and fantasy. The illustrations gradually grow in size until their restraining borders disappear altogether, in partnership with the action building towards its climax – the three commanding textless double-spread openings of the orgy scene. Throughout, the shapes and scale of figures, and the saturation and tones of colour, show Max's moods pictorially, and CROSSHATCHING in ink of black or dark shades give Max's monsters density, weight and seeming movement. The monsters' appearance is not as terrible as the text implies, and they are often depicted smiling and looming as elderly relatives might be perceived through a child's eyes – as indeed Sendak remembered his Brooklyn aunts.

At the time of its publication, Sendak's picturebook about a young 'Wild Thing' and his monsters was thoroughly subversive in depicting behaviour and expressing feelings not generally approved of by adults. It drew some negative responses, including the charge that the monsters were frightening. However the majority of critical voices applauded the picturebook. A few months after it was published *Where the Wild Things Are* won the CALDECOTT AWARD, and since then it has sold millions of copies and has also been turned into an opera. The narrative and graphic devices which were so bold, fitting and innovative at the time have become what is now fundamental practice for picturebook form at its most expressive. JD

Where's Wally? (1987) First of a commercially successful series by Martin Handford, which by 1995 had sold 30 million copies world-wide, its popularity confirmed by Wally's role in a televised cartoon, and *Wally's World*, a children's magazine launched in 1997. Later books include: *Where's Wally Now?* (1988), *Where's Wally? 3: The Fantastic Journey* (1989), *Where's Wally in Hollywood?* (1993) and various companion titles, such as *Where's Wally? The Wonder Book* (1997).

The books involve seeking out the ubiquitous Wally, distinctive in spectacles and candy-striped attire, hidden amid the chaos of Handford's detailed artwork. The series reflects a contemporary culture which demands high standards of visual literacy, for Handford's pictures function variously as puzzle, information source and narrative. Handford foregrounds the impulse to discovery, encouraging children to detect Wally themselves, in a process of self-empowerment. His illustrations also provide lessons in geography, history, mythology and, of particular significance, the art of STORYTELLING. While the books lack central stories, each illustration contains numerous narrative tableaux requiring development by observant readers. Handford's work has a literary precedent in MITSUMASO ANNO's series of pictorial journeys, which begins with *Anno's Journey* (Japan, 1997; UK, 1978); both artists conceal a nomadic protagonist in a frenetic context of human interaction and slapstick humour, to be interpreted as narrative by the child reader. LS

Where's Spot? see SPOT SERIES

Whitbread Children's Book of the Year see APPENDIX

***Whitby* trilogy** (1991–4) Three works by British author Robin Jarvis telling how two orphans, Jennet and her 'second-sighted' brother Ben, aided by eccentric 92-year-old Alice Boston, are caught in a web of mystery, magic and evil, from which the victory of good often seems impossible. A tapestry combining historical fact and legend has been woven around a modern-day story of vivid and exciting proportions. The story is carried through to dramatic cliff-hangers at the end of the first and second books – *Whitby Witches* (1991) and *Warlock in Whitby* (1992) – and a satisfactory conclusion is reached only in the final chapters of the third, *Whitby Child* (1994). Unlike some similar FANTASIES, this trilogy has not become an adult cult book, but it has remained consistently popular with children. KH

see also *THE DEPTFORD MICE*

White Fang see JACK LONDON; see also ANIMALS IN FICTION

White, E(lwyn) B(rooks) 1899–1995 American writer of essays, poems and articles for *The New Yorker* magazine and three celebrated books for children. His first, *Stuart Little* (1945), came to him in a dream which he shared with his nieces and nephews before expanding it into a book. Stuart, two inches tall and looking very much like a mouse, is born into a normal human family of average height. His adventures end in a search for his friend, Margalo, the bird with a 'streak of yellow on her bosom', and we never discover whether Stuart finds her. When children wanted to know what happened to him, White explained that it was the search that mattered. His next book for children, *CHARLOTTE'S WEB* (1952), continues to be read and loved by children and adults as a story about nature, love, life and death. Many critics believe he will be remembered as the writer of this book rather than as one of the most important essayists of the 20th century.

Charlotte's Web was a Newbery Honour Book in 1953, and in 1970 White received a Laura Ingalls Wilder Award for a 'lasting contribution to children's literature'. In 1971 he was awarded the National Medal for Literature and in 1978 he was given a Pulitzer Prize Special Citation for the body of his work. He rarely attended the awards; his fear of an audience began when he was a boy and he vowed never to appear before groups again.

His third book for children, *Trumpet of the Swan* (1970), tells the story of a trumpeter swan born without a voice. White successfully created magical worlds in all his books and drew his young readers into them without question; they accepted Louis's trumpet-playing, just as they accepted Charlotte's spinning words in her web and Stuart's driving a miniature roadster.

White continued to write his essays and columns for *The New Yorker* and to respond to the letters sent him by both children and adult fans. He admitted that it was hard work for him to write. 'When I want some fun, I don't write, I go sailing.' He insisted he was a lucky man, born in the seventh month, on the eleventh day – and he felt especially lucky that children liked his books. BG

White, Robb 1909– American author who drew on his extensive knowledge of seamanship to write his many novels set at sea; in addition, his naval experience provided him with authentic and effective settings for his World War II novels. *Up Periscope* (1956), for example, is a fine evocation of the claustrophobic world of the submariner, while *The Frogmen* (1973), with its graphic descriptions of underwater demolition work, provides insight into the emotions and motivations of the men who volunteer for hazardous underwater missions. By far the most popular of White's works is *Deathwatch* (1972), a classic struggle between good and evil, as Ben, a young hunting guide, is hunted by Madec, his dangerous and unscrupulous client. Although this novel takes place in the Mojave Desert, not familiar to the author as the ocean is, White's descriptions of the desert are entirely convincing and authentic. The two main characters are well developed, the narrative is tightly written, and there is an intense level of suspense throughout the entire book. Ben shares his convictions, idealism and courage with other White protagonists who choose to do the right thing in a variety of perilous situations. White sees these traits as characteristic of the young and believes they should be celebrated. WH

White, T(erence) H(anbury) 1906–64 British author and naturalist, best known for his historical fantasy *The Sword in the Stone* (1938) which grew into THE ONCE AND FUTURE KING (1958). Psychologically troubled but a brilliant student of English at Cambridge, White later led a reclusive life in the country. Wit and irony suffuse his work in which a pessimistic view of human nature coincides with his admiration for animal life. His prolific output included only one other work celebrated as a children's book, *MISTRESS MASHAM'S REPOSE* (USA, 1946; UK, 1947). PC

Whitlock, Pamela see CHILD AUTHORS; *THE FAR DISTANT OXUS*; see also NEGLECTED WORKS

Whitney, Mrs Adeline Dutton (Train) 1824–1906 American writer of advice books and stories for girls. Whitney's digressive style and humour in depicting day-to-day female concerns gave her writing an attractive immediacy. The additional strong basis in Christian morality and common sense made books like *Faith Gartney's Girlhood* (1866) and *Patience Strong's Outings* (1881) – or collections like *Homespun Yarns* (1887) and *Odd, or Even* (1908) – very popular; her publisher even printed and sold a Whitney calendar. Her *Mother Goose for Grownups* (1882) offered NURSERY RHYME extracts coupled with commentaries for contemporary adults. SCWA

Whittier, John Greenleaf 1807–92 Massachusetts poet particularly remembered for his impassioned abolitionist beliefs during the Civil War, his strong Quaker religion, and his BALLADS and long narrative poems. Several generations of American children have been brought up reading, memorising and declaiming such popular works as 'Skipper Ireson's Ride' (1828), 'The Barefoot Boy' (1855), 'Telling the Bees' (1860) and 'Barbara Frietchie' (1863). But Whittier's interest in rural life, nature and justice, and his deep religious faith, are probably most stunningly displayed in his masterpiece 'Snowbound' (1866), a narrative poem depicting the simple duties, pleasures and hardships of a New England farm family during a blizzard.

In 1871, Whittier edited a well-received anthology of children's poetry, *Child Life*, followed in 1872 by its companion, *Child Life in Prose*. A number of his religious poems have been set to music as hymns and are still sung in churches. When he turned 70, the *Atlantic Monthly*, which he had helped to found in 1870, hosted a birthday party attended by almost every important American author, and on his 80th birthday a national proclamation extolling his writings and efforts on behalf of his country marked the celebration. Whittier, the simple rural boy who had never travelled beyond Pennsylvania, had touched the hearts and spirits of multitudes of Americans with his lyricism and passionate beliefs. MS

Whizzer and Chips see ANNUALS

Who Killed Cock Robin? see COCK ROBIN

Why the Sun Lives in the Sky (1998) Story by Ugandan author Tumusiime Mwije. When man lived on earth with the sun, life was easy. The sun provided everything man needed for his comfort. Man was warned against laziness but he did not listen. The sun is finally upset and moves up into the sky, taking food and all. The moral of this FABLE is that people must work and must not waste food. ABO

Why Weeps the Brogan? (1989) Exceptional post-holocaust novel written and illustrated by the British writer HUGH SCOTT, about Saxon and Gilbert, sister and brother, living a bizarre and ritualised existence inside a museum. The postmodern narrative requires readers to construct explanations for the children's presence and their relationship with the creature they call the 'Brogan', who also inhabits the museum. The gaps in the narrative mirror gaps in the children's knowledge and memories. Gradually it becomes clear that the Brogan is their mother, grotesquely injured while trying to get her children into the safety of the museum (which has been prepared for just such a situation). The traumatic events have resulted in the children's repressing the relationship and turning their mother into a monster who must be propitiated. The museum setting compares interestingly to that in H.G. Wells's *The Time Machine* – objects recapitulate human knowledge and life on earth until what appears to be its annihilation. The novel ends with the return of the children's memories; they recognise their mother as the Brogan falls to her death and a rescue team enters the museum, throwing into doubt the need for the children's incarceration. The challenging narrative stance, sustained use of ambiguity, and attempts to explore the natures of knowledge and childhood make this an important end-of-century text and a worthy winner of the WHITBREAD AWARD in 1989. KR

Wibberley, Leonard (Patrick O'Connor) 1915–83 Irish-born American writer best remembered for *The Mouse That Roared* (1955), a rolicking Cold War satire for adults, but also enjoyed by young readers. Wibberley, a prolific writer, lived most of his life in the United States. His books for children include numerous BIOGRAPHIES and INFORMATION BOOKS, as well as HISTORICAL FICTION, notably the *Treegate* series – *Johnny Treegate's Musket* (1959) and others – set in post-Revolutionary America. *The Mouse That Roared* and its sequel *The Mouse on the Moon* (1962) were made into popular films. Wibberley wrote under several pseudonyms, including Leonard Holton, Christopher Webb and Patrick O'Connor. DLR

Wiese, Kurt 1887–1974 A major figure in the development of American PICTUREBOOKS. With more than 300 books to his credit, Wiese is particularly known for his Chinese ILLUSTRATIONS. MARJORIE FLACK's *Story about Ping* (1933) and CLAIRE HUCHET BISHOP's *Five Chinese Brothers* (1938) are among the most widely read and reveal his mastery of lithographic technique, the horizontal two-page spread format, and the interplay of image with text. Two books that he both illustrated and authored – *You Can Write Chinese* (1945) and *Fish in the Air* (1948) – were Caldecott Honour Books. Wiese also developed a great knack for portraying woodland animals. His illustrations for Phil Stong's *Honk the Moose* (1966) depict a hilariously expressive personality without sacrificing essential realistic detail, and also demonstrate the possibilities of colour LITHOGRAPHY. JS

Wiesner, David 1956– American illustrator, an important innovator in the area of the wordless, and almost-wordless, PICTUREBOOK. Wiesner grew up in Bridgewater, New Jersey, a suburban area much like the one depicted in his partly autobiographical *Hurricane* (1990). Although surrealism and FANTASY comic books are often said to have been influences in Wiesner's work, his wild rides often have a child-satisfying neatness to their punchlines. In *Free Fall* (1988), Wiesner's dreaming transformations are suggestive of the mathematical metamorphoses of M.C. Escher. *Free Fall* is a richly allusive celebration of the imagination, with unobtrusive references to LEWIS CARROLL's Wonderland, Winsor McCay's Dreamland and JONATHAN SWIFT's Lilliput. In his 1991 CALDECOTT MEDAL winner, *Tuesday*, Wiesner's frogs absurdly acquire the power to fly but lose their magic after one great night and must make it home to their humdrum pond as best they can. *June 29, 1999* (1992) has a grandiose B-movie premise: a young girl's science project seems to have caused gigantic vegetables to fall from the sky. Wiesner's evocative and often spooky ILLUSTRATIONS for the books of others include his pictures for LAWRENCE YEP's collections of FOLKTALES, *Tongues of Jade* (1991) and *The Rainbow People* (1989), and his gorgeously weird depictions of gargoyles at play for the haunted pages of EVE BUNTING's *Night of the Gargoyles* (1994). JS

Wiggin, Kate Douglas 1856–1923 American writer for children and educational theorist. Best remembered for the children's novel *REBECCA OF SUNNYBROOK FARM* (1903) and its sequel, *New Chronicles of Rebecca* (1907), Wiggin became a writer because of her involvement with the kindergarten movement in the late 19th century. Moving from her home in Maine to California at the age of 17, Wiggin (then Kate Smith) helped establish the Silver Street

Kindergarten in the Tar Flats slum in San Francisco. Though she had published a story in ST NICHOLAS magazine in 1876, her career as a writer began in earnest when she wrote the tear-jerker *The Story of Patsy* (1881) to raise money for the school. In the same year, she married lawyer Samuel Bradley Wiggin. Wiggin, in collaboration with her sister, Nora Archibald Smith, became a leading proponent of the theories of Friedrich Froebel, the German inventor of the kindergarten. In *Children's Rights* (1892), she promoted the cause of early childhood education, emphasising 'The Relationship of the Kindergarten to Social Reform', as well as the responsibility of middle- and upper-class adults to provide for 'Other People's Children'. Extremely prolific, Wiggin wrote or edited over 60 books in her lifetime; most of her fiction, such as *Timothy's Quest* (1890) and *A Cathedral Courtship* (1893), is little read today because of its sentimentality. In her AUTOBIOGRAPHY, *My Garden of Memory* (published in the year of her death), Wiggin admits that 'Rebecca's origin was peculiar to itself' – inspired by a dream that haunted her. Though her major legacy is one extraordinary novel, she could not have written it without the preparation of her active and extraordinary life. RF

Wigglesworth, Katherine see *LITTLE BROWN MOUSE* SERIES; *LITTLE GREY RABBIT*

Wignell, Edel 1936– Australian author whose novel *Escape by Deluge* (1989) about a young swimmer combines the power of ABORIGINAL mythology with realistic city life. The TIME-SLIP novels *The Ghost Wagon Mystery* (1996), *Ghost Dog* (1991) and *Midnight Monster* (1997) employ folklore, history and FANTASY in a setting of everyday family life. Australiana collections *A Boggle of Bunyips* (1981) and *A Bluey of Swaggies* (1985), and folklore-based scripts *The Hobyahs* (1995) and *The Raven's Magic Gem* (1997), indicate Wignell's historical strengths, while her humorous handling of fantasy is apparent in PICTUREBOOKS such as *Spider in the Toilet* (1987). HE

Wijngaard, Juan 1951– Illustrator of Dutch parentage and born in Argentina, who came to England in 1970 and subsequently lived in California. Wijngaard studied illustration at the Royal College of Art and won the MOTHER GOOSE AWARD for *Greenfinger House* (Rosemary Harris, 1981). *Sir Gawain and the Loathly Damsel* (SELINA HASTINGS, 1985), Wijngaard's second *Sir Gawain* title, won the KATE GREENAWAY AWARD and displays his handsome, highly wrought, intensely coloured style. Striking use of FRAMES, decorative borders, cameos and motifs characterise *The Blemyah Stories* (WILLIAM MAYNE, 1987), *Hannukah* (Jenny Koralek, 1989), *The Nativity* (1989), *Tales of Wonder and Magic* (BERLIE DOHERTY, 1997) and Ruskin's *THE KING OF THE GOLDEN RIVER* (2000). JAG

Wild Bill Hickok 1837–79 A gunman who became famous for his skill with a pistol. James Butler Hickok worked variously as a gambler, wagonmaster, spy during the Civil War, scout for military expeditions, detective, and deputy United States marshal. His sharpshooting skill and the adventures associated with his various jobs led to DIME NOVELS and articles in popular magazines emphasising the number of men he killed; records, however, show that he killed seven rather than the 100 sometimes assigned to him. He was murdered in Deadwood while playing poker. The cards he held, aces and eights, became known as 'The Dead Man's Hand'. EBD

Wild, Margaret 1948– Australian writer born in South Africa, who has made an important contribution to the Australian PICTUREBOOK for younger readers. Her most successful picturebooks include: *There's a Sea in My Bedroom* (1984) illustrated by JANE TANNER, which examines a child's deep-seated fear of the sea; *Creatures in the Beard* (1986, with Margaret Power), a humorous FANTASY of a father who shaves off his beard and renders homeless its animal inhabitants; *Mr. Nick's Knitting* (1988, with Dee Huxley), a very simple but compassionate tale of two elderly people; the poignant *THE VERY BEST OF FRIENDS* (1989), which won the CHILDREN'S BOOK COUNCIL OF AUSTRALIA Picturebook of the Year Award in 1990, and *Old Pig* (1996), both of which confront dying and grief; and *Jenny Angel* (1999) with ink-and-wash ILLUSTRATIONS by Anne Spudvilas, in which a young child's death is movingly depicted. In *LET THE CELEBRATIONS BEGIN!* (1991), set in a concentration camp, Wild shows the power of the human spirit in the face of adversity. *Fox* (2000), illustrated by RON BROOKS, breaks new ground in its multilayering of both words and illustration. These works are indicative of the range of complex matters which she makes accessible for young readers, without undue sentimentality, but always challenging their emotions. *Miss Lily's Fabulous Pink Feather Boa* (1998), illustrated by KERRY ARGENT, is a warm tale of friendship, when the Last Potoroo goes to stay at Miss Lily's Tropical Holiday House. CH, HMcC

Wilde, Oscar see *THE HAPPY PRINCE AND OTHER TALES*; see also BALLADS; P.J. LYNCH; LISBETH ZWERGER

Wilder, Laura (Elizabeth) Ingalls 1867–1957 American author of the *LITTLE HOUSE* books, born in Pepin in the Big Woods of Wisconsin on 7 February 1867, the second child (after Mary) of Charles Philip

Ingalls and Caroline Quiner ('Pa' and 'Ma'). In 1868 the family sold their farm, and travelled from Wisconsin to Kansas in a covered wagon, as described in *Little House on the Prairie* (USA, 1937; UK, 1957). Laura's sister, Carrie, was born in 1870, although her birth and those of the other three children are not documented in the novels. Pa's encounters with Indians and the subsequent troubles are vividly described in the novel. The Ingalls family returned to Pepin to repossess the farm in the spring of 1871, when Laura was four, and it is this period that is described in *Little House in the Big Woods* (1932; 1956). In 1873, Pa sold the farm again and made a second journey, to Walnut Grove, Minnesota.

This stage in Laura's childhood is described in *On the Banks of Plum Creek* (1937; 1958); however, the following episodes are not included in the novels. In 1875 a fourth child, Charles Frederick, was born, and after failing to make the farm pay, the family moved to Burr Oak, Iowa to join friends in running a hotel. Before moving to Iowa, the Ingalls family spent the summer with Charles's brother Peter and his wife Eliza, and while they were there baby Freddie, who had been frequently ill, died on 27 August 1876. Grace was born in Iowa, and the family moved back to Walnut Grove and stayed with friends while Charles established himself by taking on a variety of jobs until he had bought land and built their own house. Laura and Mary went to school and made childhood friends and rivals, including the storekeeper's daughter Nellie Owens, who became the character Nellie Oleson. *By the Shores of Silver Lake* (1939; 1961) begins with the events of 1879. Mary became blind after an illness described as scarlet fever but which was probably spinal meningitis. Pa took a job as timekeeper and paymaster for the railroad camps as they progressed west. In Spring 1880 the new town of De Smet, South Dakota, was laid out and the family built a house there in addition to their claim shanty.

At the beginning of the severe winter of 1880, the Ingalls family moved back to town, and when the railroad could not be kept free of snow, they began to be short of food; they were helped by Laura's future husband, Almanzo Wilder. Although fictionalised in *The Long Winter* (1940; 1962), the struggle for survival is very close to the facts. The storms continued until April and the first train arrived in De Smet on 10 May. Mary left home in the autumn of 1881 when she was 16, to study at the College for the Blind in Vinton, Iowa. The family lived in De Smet each winter and Laura made friends with local people, including Mary Power, Minnie Johnson and Ida Brown, all of whom appear briefly in the book *Little Town on the Prairie* (1941; 1963). The episode dealing with Laura's conflict with the schoolteacher Eliza Jane Wilder is a close parallel to actual events. Laura's subsequent education culminated in her appointment as teacher in late December of 1882. The beginning of *These Happy Golden Years* (1943; 1964) describes Laura's first school (the Bouchie school, fictionalised as the Brewster school) and the book gives realistic details of her working and social life. In the summer of 1884 Almanzo and Laura became engaged. She was 17, he was 27, and they were married on 25 August 1885.

The first four years of Laura's married life included the birth of their daughter Rose in December 1886, repeated crop failure, illness in the family, and the birth and death of their infant son in August 1889. Both Laura and Almanzo caught diphtheria which left Almanzo permanently disabled. These circumstances, combined with a fire which burnt their house and most of their belongings, forced the Wilders to leave Dakota. They went first to Almanzo's family farm in Minnesota, and then to Florida. However, Laura and Almanzo were unable to settle, and returned to De Smet to prepare for their final journey to Missouri, a place which promised good farming and a better climate. Laura's diary entries which describe that journey were published as *On the Way Home* (1962).

As Rose grew up, Laura became known as a local author, writing about poultry-keeping and general farm matters and also feature-stories about the Ozarks. In 1909 Rose married Gillette Lane, and the couple moved to California where Rose became established as a writer for the *San Francisco Bulletin*. In 1915 Laura visited San Francisco for two months and Almanzo saved all her letters (these were published in 1974 as *West From Home*). Rose encouraged her to write her autobiography, and Laura believed that her experiences were 'altogether too good to be lost'. The original manuscript, *Pioneer Girl*, was written in pencil in blue-lined school exercise books and covered her life up to her wedding. Rose added suggestions, the publishers Harper and Brothers encouraged Laura to rewrite the material, and *Little House in the Big Woods* was the result. This was followed by the story of Almanzo's boyhood, *Farmer Boy* (1933; 1965). Laura relied on Rose's advice and encouragement and researched the background of her books carefully. *Little House on the Prairie* was written at the request of her readers, the rest of the series followed rapidly, and the last book, *These Happy Golden Years* was written when she was 76.

The last years of Laura and Almanzo's life together were spent on their farm and in the local community. On 23 October 1949 Almanzo died after two heart attacks. After his death Laura lived alone enjoying her recognition as a writer until her death on 10 February 1957. ASTH

Wildsmith, Brian (Lawrence) 1930– British illustrator, among the first in the field to establish new conventions for the modern PICTUREBOOK. For over three

'Joseph rejects Potiphar's wife.' Drawing for *Joseph* (1997) by Brian Wildsmith.

decades his work has exhibited a sustained creative energy and gained a world-wide reputation. Born in the North of England, and educated there, he was gifted in both music and art. He trained as a painter in London. After working as a teacher and a line draughtsman, his breakthrough came with the colour plates for *Tales From The Arabian Nights* (1961). He was attracted to picturebooks, believing they offered the opportunity for a union between painting and illustration. Painterly values permeate his work. His concern for the mental, aesthetic and moral development of a child is displayed through the range of his work: concept books, FABLES, poetry anthologies and stories – including BIBLE STORIES – which deal with fundamental aspects of human behaviour. Wildsmith's *ABC* (1962), demonstrating his daring colour sense and fresh approach, won the KATE GREENAWAY MEDAL. The concept books *Fishes* (1968) and *What the Moon Saw* (1978) celebrate the act of painting whilst teaching language development. Pattern and texture are varied for expressive and structural purposes. In *Mother Goose: A Collection of Nursery Rhymes* (1964) the patterning recalls folk art, whilst in *Professor Noah's Spaceship* (1980) texture suggests the natural world, and geometric patterns represent intellectual and technological wonders. Wildsmith is master of the split-page format which advances action, varies pace and introduces suspense, as in *Give a Dog a Bone* (1985), a story exemplifying perseverance and resourcefulness. More recent publications include *The Bremen Town Band* (1999) and the FAIRY TALE *The Seven Ravens* (2000). JD

Willans, Geoffrey 1911–58 English author of the *Molesworth* series. *Down With Skool* (1953), *How To Be Topp* (1954), *Whizz For Atoms* (1956) – compiled as *The Compleet Molesworth* (1958) – and *Back In The Jug Agane* (1959) are based on his experience as a teacher in a private prep school for boys. They are wonderfully illustrated by RONALD SEARLE. Set in St Custard's, they are narrated and, unforgettably, spelt by Nigel Molesworth himself, who first appeared in *Punch* in the 1940s. The spelling shows glimmerings of the realisation that English spelling is irrational: typical of the unreasonable impositions placed on schoolchildren. *Tough*, therefore, is *tuough*, not *tuff*; *toffee* is *tooffe*, not *toffy*. Molesworth's prose and punctuation ('a chis is a swis or a swindle as any fule kno') and his depictions of adults and the conventions of teaching are just as funny, even to those unfamiliar with English prep schools. RC

see also SCHOOL STORIES

Willard, Barbara see *MANTLEMASS SERIES*; see also HISTORICAL FICTION; ANTONY MAITLAND

Willard, Nancy 1936– American poet, teacher, novelist, illustrator and writer of PICTUREBOOKS. Born in Michigan, Willard gained a PhD in literature from

'This is me e.g. nigel molesworth the curse of st custard's which is the skool i am at.' Illustration from *Down With Skool!* by Ronald Searle and Geoffrey Willans.

Stanford University. Her picturebook *A Visit to William Blake's Inn: Poems for the Innocent and Experienced Travelers* (1981), illustrated by ALICE AND MARTIN PROVENSEN, was awarded the NEWBERY MEDAL. Rather than describing Blake factually, the book evokes the spirit of his writing in FANTASY and poetry which celebrates language and challenges its readers. While much poetry for children is narrative, Willard's tends to be lyrical and full of colourful, almost surrealistic, connections. Her award-winning trilogy – *Sailing to Cythera* (1974), *The Island of the Grass King* (1979) and *Uncle Terrible* (1982), illustrated by David McPhail – recounts the adventures of a small boy named Anatole, who is tested against evil in fantasy worlds reminiscent of the stories of C.S. LEWIS. Her own photographs illustrate *An Alphabet of Angels* (1994). Her work is collected in *A Nancy Willard Reader: Selected Poetry and Prose* (1991). GRB

see also *SONGS OF INNOCENCE AND EXPERIENCE*

***William Brown* series** see *JUST WILLIAM*

William Tell Legendary figure in the 14th-century Swiss struggle for independence from Austrian Hapsburg authority who, like Britain's ROBIN HOOD, has become a hero of children's stories. The famous set-piece where Tell is forced to shoot an apple from his son's head has entered folk memory and features as the climax of many popularised versions of the tale which bear little relation to Swiss history. GL

Williams, Garth 1912–96 American illustrator and writer known for his expressive line ILLUSTRATIONS of modern children's classics. The illustrator of such great American works as *CHARLOTTE'S WEB* and many of the *LITTLE HOUSE ON THE PRAIRIE* series, he lived a cosmopolitan life. Born in New York City, he spent a few years on a farm in New Jersey, then moved to Canada and on to England with his family. His English education included study at the Westminster School of Art and the Royal College of Art. Awarded the British Prix de Rome, he travelled and studied in Italy, France and Germany, where he met the first of his four wives. His long association with children's books began in 1945 when Harper and Row's legendary editor, URSULA NORDSTROM, assigned him E.B. WHITE's *Stuart Little*. Other commissions followed, including *Little Fur Family*, the first of 11 books with MARGARET WISE BROWN. *The Little House* books took him six years, and included travel to all but one of the locations, as well as a meeting with the 80-year-old LAURA INGALLS WILDER. He wrote several books of his own, including the unintentionally controversial *Rabbit's Wedding* (1958), in which the marriage between black and white rabbits was seen as inflammatory and banned by some Southern librarians. MMG

Williams, Jay see *THE PRACTICAL PRINCESS*; see also FAIRY TALES; MERCER MAYER

Williams, Marcia 1945– British children's author and illustrator of PICTUREBOOKS. Before writing her first book she worked as librarian, interior designer and nursery-school teacher. Her books include *Greek Myths for Young Children* (1991), *The Adventures of Robin Hood* (1995), *King Arthur and the Knights of the Round Table* (1996) and *Mr William Shakespeare's Plays* (1998). Williams's work, with its strip-cartoon style in pen, ink and water-colour, brings humour to traditional stories from the Bible, folklore and CLASSICAL MYTHOLOGY. Energetic illustrations, including sumptuous borders and ENDPAPERS, are combined with witty speech bubbles and clear text to create retellings which are both spirited and informative. Marcia Williams retold seven more of Shakespeare's plays in *Bravo, Mr William Shakespeare!* (2000). JHD

Williams, Ursula Moray 1911– Prolific British author, occasional playwright and illustrator. She is best remembered for the 1939 classic *Adventures of the Little Wooden Horse*, a heartbreaking but happily resolved episodic tale whose theme is loyalty, love and gratitude winning through against almost over-

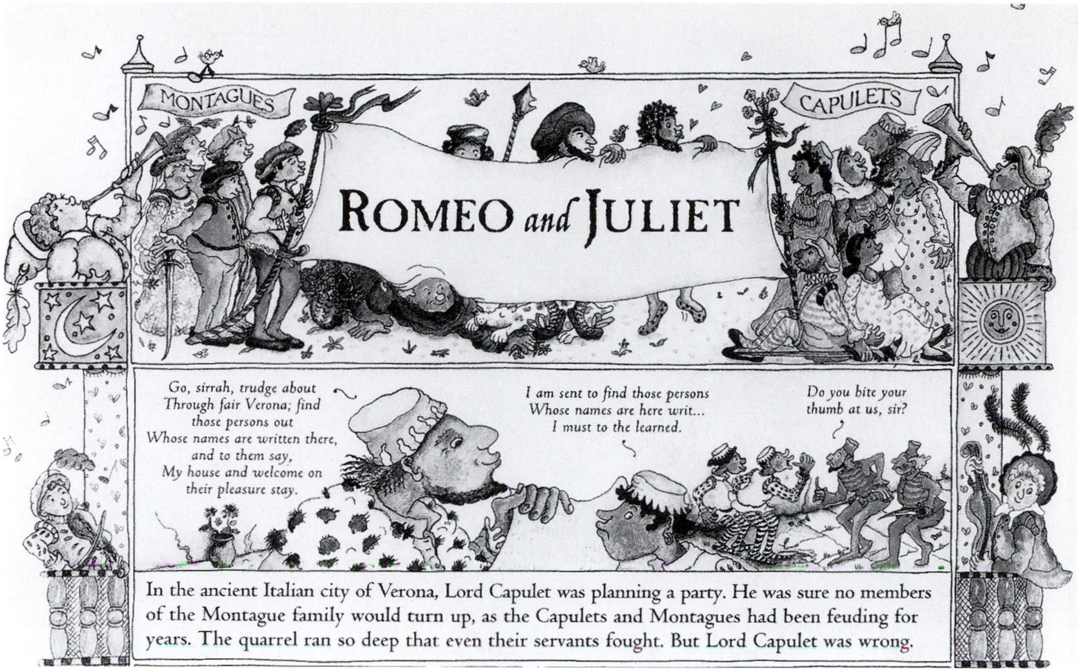

MONTAGUES
CAPULETS
ROMEO and JULIET
Go, sirrah, trudge about Through fair Verona; find those persons out Whose names are written there, and to them say, My house and welcome on their pleasure stay.
I am sent to find those persons Whose names are here writ... I must to the learned.
Do you bite your thumb at us, sir?
In the ancient Italian city of Verona, Lord Capulet was planning a party. He was sure no members of the Montague family would turn up, as the Capulets and Montagues had been feuding for years. The quarrel ran so deep that even their servants fought. But Lord Capulet was wrong.

From *Mr William Shakespeare's Plays* by Marcia Williams.

whelming odds. Highly moral and deeply emotional, it was published on Harrap's general list (as ARTHUR RANSOME was on Cape's and J.R.R. TOLKIEN on Allen & Unwin's) in the days before there were children's departments in publishing. With *Gobbolino the Witch's Cat* (1942), a well-controlled, humorous FANTASY, and *Bogwoppit* (1978), a deliciously absurd *PSAMMEAD*-like creation for older children, she maintained a popularity that stretched over five decades.

EM

Williams, Vera B. 1927– American author of innovative children's books. Williams was born in Los Angeles but grew up in New York City, where she attended the High School of Music and Art. Greatly influenced by her education at Black Mountain College, Williams joined a group that founded a co-operative community at Stony Point, New York, and taught nature study, art, writing, cooking and crafts at a small independent school. After the school closed she moved to Canada and there had the experiences that inspired *Three Days on the River in a Red Canoe* (1981). Praised for its innovative journal-like format, the book combined story and information, such as recipes and a diagram showing how to set up a tent. Another successful book, *Stringbean's Trip to the Shining Sea* (1988), is told through postcards, and was illustrated in collaboration with her daughter Jennifer Williams. *A Chair for My Mother* (1982) and two sequels were praised for their vibrant colours and warm yet realistic portrayals of life in a struggling, single-parent family. *Scooter* (1993), the story of the irrepressible Elana Rose Rosen, was lovingly told and lavishly decorated with doodles, drawings and acrostics. It marked Williams's venture into longer fiction, and received the BOSTON GLOBE-HORN BOOK AWARD.

LH

Williamson, Henry see *TARKA THE OTTER*

Willis, Jeanne see *DR XARGLE* SERIES; KORKY PAUL; SUSAN VARLEY; see also NUDITY IN CHILDREN'S BOOKS

Willis, Nathaniel see *THE YOUTH'S COMPANION*; see also PUBLISHING AND PUBLISHERS

Willy the Wimp (1984) This PICTUREBOOK by ANTHONY BROWNE, winner of the KATE GREENAWAY MEDAL, allows Browne to indulge his interest in primates. It tells of a timid gorilla, terrorised by a gang of urban gorillas, who is finally provoked into action by their nicknaming him Willy the Wimp. In Willy, Browne has created a well-rounded character, immediately recognisable in his fairisle pullover, cord trousers and his general air of anxiety. The words carry the main narrative but most of the

Illustration from *Willy the Wimp* by Anthony Browne.

comedy and the emotional content rests with the pictures. Colour and textures are very important in Browne's work, with painstaking depiction of hair and fur, of brick or wooden surfaces, and of patterning in clothes and wallpapers. With the changes to Willy's leotard, Browne uses colour symbolically to suggest Willy's increasing strength. The story combines elements of FAIRY TALE, its moral tinged with modern cynicism. Willy saves his sweetheart from the gang and earns himself a kiss – but learns that 'pride comes before a fall' when he marches straight into a lamppost and reverts to his meek behaviour. Browne links the last image with the front cover to suggest that this is a circular story, and perhaps that transformations are not instant. Browne has produced a number of sequels: *Willy the Champ* (1985), *Willy and Hugh* (1991), *Willy the Wizard* (1995) and *Willy the Dreamer* (1997). AR

Wilson, Barbara Ker (Tahourdin) 1929– Australian writer, editor and children's publisher whose work has been influential in the United Kingdom and Australia. While children's editor for Angus and Robertson from 1965 to 1974 she became the first Australian to take children's books to the Bologna Book Fair. She edited acclaimed writers such as IVAN SOUTHALL and HESBA BRINSMEAD. Later she worked for *Readers' Digest Condensed Books* and Hodder and Stoughton before being asked to establish the Young Adult Fiction list for University of Queensland Press. She also created their Storybridge list for younger readers. With these two lists she brought to light the now highly regarded writers JAMES MOLONEY, BRIAN CASWELL and JUDITH CLARKE.

Wilson has also written many books, which include the PICTUREBOOKS *Willow Pattern Story* (1978) and *Acacia Terrace* (1988); adult novels such as *Jane Austen in Australia* (1984) and YOUNG ADULT FICTION such as *Last Year's Broken Toys* (1962). Her collections of FOLKTALES are innumerable and many are still in print. Other edited collections include *Wishbones* (1994) and *Hands Up* (1994). Her skills as a writer are informed by a highly developed interest in historical research, and through her eclectic reading she draws upon a wealth of knowledge relating to literature and history, combined with a great passion for foreign travel. RS

Wilson, Bob see *GING GANG GOOLIE, IT'S AN ALIEN*

Wilson, Budge 1927– Canadian writer born in Halifax, Nova Scotia. Wilson attended Dalhousie University, had two daughters, and then worked as a teacher, commercial artist, photographer and fitness instructor prior to becoming a writer. Wilson writes short stories, PICTUREBOOKS and novels. Her first book, *The Best Worst Christmas Present Ever*, was published in 1984. Wilson stresses 'trust and communication especially between between those to whom one is closest'. *A House Far From Home* (1986) describes, as Wilson says, 'how difficult and rewarding relationships can be'. *Breakdown* (1987) conveys her belief 'that people sometimes emerge wiser and more thoughtful after recovery'. In *Thirteen Never Changes* (1989) Lorinda reads her grandmother's journal and discovers adolescent concerns never change, while in *Oliver's Wars* (1992), Oliver adjusts to the faults of himself and other people and also learns trust and acceptance. Wilson's awards include the 1991 City of Dartmouth and the Canadian Library Association Young Adult Book Award for *The Leaving* (1991) and the 1993 Ann Connor Brimer Award for *Oliver's Wars*. MRS

Wilson, Gina 1943– British novelist and poet, best known for her perceptive young adult stories. *Cora Ravenwing* (1980) concerns peer group rejection of an outsider and the narrator's consequent conflict of loyalties. Themes of friendship and jealousy are developed in *A Friendship of Equals* (1981) and *The Whisper* (1982). *All Ends Up* (1984), *Family Feeling* (1986) and *Just Us* (1988) depict tensions within families and between generations. *Riding the Great White* (1991), in form and setting recalling *Cora Ravenwing*, powerfully chronicles the end of adolescence. Work for younger children includes *Wompus Golompus* (1990), the narrative poem *Prowlpuss* (1994), and *Ignis* (2001), about a dragon. DCH

Wilson, Jacqueline 1945– Influential and enormously popular British children's author who won the 1995 SMARTIES PRIZE for her novel *Double Act*, a story of identical twins with very different personalities. Although Wilson has been writing for some years it is her recent novels, illustrated by Nick Sharratt, which have brought her widespread critical acclaim and popularity. Like her earlier YOUNG ADULT FICTION, her recent younger children's fiction deals with difficult situations in which children may find themselves. The settings are almost always urban and the books owe their outstanding popularity to Wilson's eye for the detail of children's ordinary lives and her ability to present these lives humorously and from a child's perspective.

In 1991 Transworld published *The Story of Tracy Beaker*, a first-person narrative about a girl living in a children's home who longs to be adopted but finds it hard to behave as well as she should if she wants prospective parents to like her. The book is written as if the heroine were filling in 'my book about me' and Nick Sharratt's ILLUSTRATIONS subtly show her untruths, so that while Tracy claims she 'sort of clung a bit' when a visitor returns her to the home, the illustrations show her having to be prised away. No simple solution is offered, and although Tracy ends the novel hoping that the visitor will adopt her there is no certainty that this will happen. A sequel, *The Dare Game* (2000), shows Tracey living with her foster mother but still dreaming of a fairy-tale lifestyle. Only at the end of the book does she finally come to accept that there is a very real possibility of happiness to be found in her ordinary life.

Since 1991 Wilson has written a number of novels which follow the same format as *The Story of Tracy Beaker* and which cover a range of issues; many of the children she depicts lead difficult lives, while the adults are often either absent or bullies. At best the parents tend to be well-intentioned but with little idea of how their children really feel, and it is often an outside adult who has to step in to remedy the situation. The children themselves are generally tough and resourceful, though rarely prepared to conform to what the adult world expects of them. *The Suitcase Kid* (1992) offers an unusually happy ending as Andy comes to enjoy staying with both her sets of parents and finds herself a third home to visit when she gets fed up with the first two. All the novels retain a strong sense of humour, despite the adverse circumstances in which the heroes and heroines find themselves. In *The Bed and Breakfast Star* (1994) the heroine, who lives in a bed-and-breakfast hostel with her depressed mother and aggressive stepfather, is continually seeing the funny side of life and cracking jokes. Adult readers may become irked by the incessant and repetitive jokes, but children enjoy them.

The stories are rarely written in straightforward chapters and each has some novelty aspect: they may follow the colours of the rainbow, or be written by different characters with different illustrators. In 1999 Wilson's *The Illustrated Mum* received widespread acclaim and was shortlisted for the CARNEGIE AWARD, but it also excited some controversy with its disturbing picture of life for two girls whose single mother suffers from depression. Wilson's *Girls* trilogy (1997–99) is written for a teenage readership. It charts the lives of three girls in their first three years at secondary school. With the honesty and absence of patronising typical of Wilson's writing it tackles the difficult issues familiar to many teenage girls: anorexia, drugs, and pressure from boyfriends and anxious parents. The trilogy has ensured her popularity among teenagers as well as younger readers. *Lizzie Zipmouth* won the SMARTIES BOOK PRIZE in 2000.

Wilson's version of *Rapunzel* (1998) for Scholastic's series of FAIRY TALES is characteristically vigorous, with a particular and amusing interest in the difficult practicalities of the long hair, and a sympathetic understanding of the growing girl's frustration at being imprisoned for so long. KA

Wilson, Raymond 1925–95 English poet, anthologist and Professor of Education. He published *Daft Davy: A Story in Verse* (1987), an original collection which follows Davy from birth through a luckless life to his epitaph. Wilson edited many anthologies, including classic verse, story poems, and *Nine O'Clock Bell* (1985), about school. His endowment established a Memorial Prize for children's poetry at Reading University. ML

Wind in the Willows, The (1908) This classic of children's literature began as bedtime stories told by KENNETH GRAHAME to his four-year-old son Alastair. Over three years these included mentions of moles, water-rats and toads, recalling Grahame's own interest as a child in observing wildlife near the Thames in Berkshire, a habit he continued as an adult. In May 1907 Alastair went on a holiday to the South Coast with his governess but without his parents, who chose to go elsewhere. Perhaps as a peace offering, Grahame sent his son a series of letters detailing the adventures of Toad. In 1908, after chivvying by Constance Smedley, a journalist and neighbour, Grahame finally integrated these into a full-length version. Appearing to no great critical acclaim, the book's reputation soon picked up, resulting in a new, illustrated edition in 1913. By 1926 the book was in its 21st printing, with E.H. SHEPARD's illustrations in 1931 leading to a new wave of popularity which has lasted to this day. Its appeal extended to readers of all ages.

Toad is a very funny character, infantile in his boasting, impulsiveness, ready tears and instant enthusiasms. Grahame partly based him on the volatile personality of his son Alastair when young. Mole, Rat and Badger in their turn represent instead a dream of perfect fellowship, where middle-aged bachelors settle down with each other in a life of picnics and agreeable conversation. All share an abiding love of home, one of the main threads of this story and a theme easily picked up by children, also often deeply attached to the place they first remember. Much else appeals as well. Toad's escapades with stealing motor cars, escaping from prison and journeying back are the stuff of picaresque adventure. These events are largely separate from the doings of Mole, Rat and Badger, which share a less hectic, more mystical atmosphere. Rat has yearnings to become a traveller; Mole only just stops him from decamping for good while in a trance. Both animals get to meet the Great God Pan in a highly wrought episode, not unlike some of the pagan fantasies found in *The Yellow Book* during the 1890s, to which Grahame occasionally contributed. The final desperately exciting show-down where the riverbankers force out the invading stoats and weasels from their illegal occupation of Toad Hall contains mock-Homeric overtones. Toad's subsequent renunciation of his bad old ways has genuine pathos, reminiscent of Henry V's dismissal of Falstaff, a character with whom the unreformed Toad has much in common.

All this happens against a background of nature at its most idyllic. There are no deaths in the story; the riverbankers live in harmony with each other. Nor is there much evidence of the female sex. Unhappily married himself, Grahame preferred male company in fiction as in life. The only threat lies in the darkness of the Wild Wood – a place where feral animals lurk behind trees promising no good at all, as Mole discovers on an unwise late-night trip. The villainous stoats and weasels who smell as well as dropping their h's are seen by Grahame's biographer Peter Green as a projection of the author's fear of the lower classes, and the perpetual threat they offer to a social stability based on the wealthy retaining all their privileges. Others view the Wild Wood as symbolising the depression that haunted Grahame all his life, finally cutting down his creativity to total inactivity.

Choosing animal rather than human characters enabled Grahame to avoid all the mundane details that can so easily bog down an otherwise lively adventure story. As it is, his characters change size according to the demands of the moment: Toad can both drive a car and be picked up and carelessly flung away by the irate barge-woman. There is also no sense of economic or social realities. Meals simply turn up, money is invisibly earned and no one ever does anything like work. But beneath this surface unreality resides a personal FANTASY of happiness and fulfilment so strong and poignantly expressed as to banish disbelief in all but the most sceptical reader. Humour is also always on hand to avoid any hint of mawkishness, and Grahame can be very witty indeed. Some of this humour was subsequently transcribed by A.A. MILNE into a stage edition, *TOAD OF TOAD HALL*. Also very popular, it is as captivating on the stage as it is in print, in spite of the few liberties that Milne takes with the text, such as introducing a talking horse. Subsequent film versions miss the spirit of the original altogether. Ultimately it is perhaps the charm of Grahame's prose that is still the most important factor in making this book the classic it continues to be.

In 1981 JAN NEEDLE wrote *Wild Wood*, a clever sequel written from the point of view of the stoats and weasels, pictured here as in a state of righteous rebellion against the selfishness of the traditional riverbankers. William Horwood's *The Willows in Winter* (1993) also provided a sequel to this great story, mainly concentrating on further adventures of the ever-popular Toad. Numerous illustrated editions have been issued, one of the most appealing being the version tactfully abridged and beautifully illustrated by Inga Moore (2000), first published in two separate parts in 1996 and 1998. NT

Wind on Fire, The Proposed trilogy by the British dramatist and TELEVISION scriptwriter, William Nicholson (1948–), the first volume of which – *The Wind Singer* – was published in 2000, to be followed by *Slaves of the Mastery* in 2001 and, ultimately, *Song of Fire*. Nicholson is well known as a dramatist and documentary film-maker, and in particular for his *Shadowlands* (1985) – winner of the BAFTA Award for best television play – which explored the relationship between C.S. LEWIS and the American Joy Davidman. *The Wind Singer*, which won the SMARTIES BOOK PRIZE, is a vivid and fast-paced FANTASY thriller. Apart from one or two slightly implausible special effects, the novel is a compelling account of a utilitarian tyranny which is exposed and overthrown by two children strengthened by their loyalty to each other and – unusual in recent children's books – the love of their family. VW

Winnie ille Pu see WINNIE-THE-POOH; see also LATIN VERSIONS

Winnie-The-Pooh (1926) and ***The House at Pooh Corner*** (1928) Stories by A.A. MILNE with an enduring and universal appeal. They have been translated into many languages (even into a purportedly 'dead' language, Latin, as *Winnie Ille Pu* and *Domus Anguli Puensis*), inspired mock-philosophy, and been adapted for an animated film cartoon by WALT DISNEY, who for some reason clothed Pooh in a red vest. The original soft-pencil illustrations by E.H. SHEPARD, which show Pooh and his friends not as animals naturalistically rendered but as deriving from 'toys', contribute significantly to their appeal.

The 'Pooh' books are generally thought of as works for younger children, containing an idyllic world undisturbed by adults or unpleasantness. Here, the child is king; Christopher Robin is the presiding deity of the Hundred Acre Wood to whom Pooh, Piglet and the rest look to solve problems and give advice. He is the reader of Sustaining Books to Wedged Bears in Great Tightness, the leader of Expotitions to the North Pole and the one to whom the rest appeal for judgement when Tigger bounces Eeyore. This role is suggested in the episode where Pooh and Piglet hunt the Woozle: sitting up in the tree, he has been in a position to see Pooh and Piglet making the 'Woozle' tracks, and is therefore able to elucidate the mystery, a quasi-omniscient 'god'.

The humour of the 'Pooh' books is, however, complex and possibly more accessible to the adult than the child. The books are highly aware of language, and without being patronising they play on the imperfections of the child's vocabulary; this kind of humour requires awareness of what is being played upon. The first chapter of *The House at Pooh Corner* is entitled 'Contradiction', which is explained as follows:

> Owl kept his head and told us that the opposite of an Introduction, my dear Pooh, was a Contradiction . . .

A proportion of this humour also turns on differences in perception: the transparency of the child's strategems and ways of thinking to the adult who finds them funny yet endearing. An example may be found in the opening sections, where Christopher Robin asks for a story:

> 'Could you very sweetly tell Winnie-the-Pooh one?'
> 'I suppose I could,' I said. 'What sort of stories does he like?'
> 'About himself. Because he's *that* sort of Bear.'
> 'Oh I see.'
> 'So could you very sweetly?'

The 'Pooh' books represent a compact between child and adult and this accounts for the sense of affection and trust that strongly emerges from the text; the faith that Pooh, Piglet and the rest have in Christopher Robin's ability to put everything right is a reflection of children's own relationship with their parents. SA

Winton, Tim(othy) (John) 1960– Australian novelist, best known for his adult novels, which include *Cloudstreet* (1992) and *The Riders* (1994). For young readers he has written the PICTUREBOOK *Jesse* (1988), illustrated by Maureen Prichard, the gentle tale of a child's morning walk, and *The Bugalugs Bum Thief* (1991), illustrated by Carol Pelham-Thorman, the comic story of a town whose inhabitants' bottoms are stolen. His YOUNG ADULT novels *Lockie Leonard, Human Torpedo* (1990) and *Lockie Leonard, Scumbuster* (1993) depict the fast-moving, vernacular adventures of a surfer coming to terms with SEX, love and friendship, and are very popular among teenagers. NLR

Wirrun Trilogy, The Multi-award-winning trilogy by Australian author PATRICIA WRIGHTSON, comprising *The Ice is Coming* (1977), *The Dark Bright Water* (1979) and *Behind the Wind* (1981). It is an epic hero tale with an Australian locale. Using the Aboriginal spirit creatures that first appeared in *An Older Kind of Magic* (1972) and were central to *The Nargun and the Stars* (1973), but working now on a vast canvas that stretches across the continent, Wrightson incorporates universal archetypes and narrative patterns into the Australian landscape. The land, as in all her writing, claims all its inhabitants, black or white, and forges their destiny. So Wirrun, accompanied by the Mimi, a stick-like rock spirit, rides the wind and travels the continent to find and contain the Eldest Nargun that is threatening to freeze the land with its frosty hands. His second task in *The Dark Bright Water* forces Wirrun to come to terms with the dark side of his nature, a journey of self-discovery that is to culminate in the third book when he defeats Wulgaru, 'who took its power from men' and embodies the final enemy – death. In overcoming this mysterious thing Wirrun attains the stature of immortal Hero, belonging to the world, but remaining essentially Australian. MSax

see also ABORIGINAL CULTURE IN CHILDREN'S BOOKS

Witch Woman on the Hogsback (1987) Novel by Carolyn Parker (1956–), one of a small number of South African youth novels that introduce African myth in the lives of modern children – sometimes, as in this case, in obvious FANTASY, at other times as part of a realist plot. A black boy and a white girl become embroiled in a battle against a European witch who seeks with the help of African evil spirits to control the natural world. The children's friendship and the victory of their combined powers have an obvious message for racial harmony in South Africa. ERJ

Witches, The (1983) Novel by ROALD DAHL, almost the sexual mirror-image of *THE BFG*, with a courageous boy and his remarkable grandmother fighting female evil. In view of the strong role of the grandmother, attacks on the book as misogynistic seem difficult to sustain. Love and friendship are emphasised by the ending (suggested by Dahl's editor) where the boy, who has been turned into a mouse, remains one – happy that his short life will coincide with that of his grandmother. Nicholas Roeg's film version (1990), which Dahl called a 'stupid horror film', changes mouse back into boy at the end. PLH

Without a Silver Spoon (1981) Story by Nigerian novelist Eddie Iroh about an honest boy who succeeds in school despite his poverty and the machinations of others. It was named a notable book by IBBY. A cartoon version illustrated by Femi Arowolo was published in 1996. VD

Wizard of Earthsea see *EARTHSEA QUARTET*

Wizard see *'THE BIG FIVE'*

Wodehouse, P(elham) G(renville) 1881–1975 English comic novelist, lyricist and playwright. He published early stories (in *Captain*) and novels of English public-school life: for example, *The White Feather* (1907). But he is best known for the *Jeeves* series of short stories and novels, set in an idyllic and innocent world made comic by its parody of the conventions of popular fiction and what have become the clichés of serious literature. The plots are farcical and meticulously contrived, the prose immaculate and rich in inventive similes. RC

Wojciechowska, Maia (Teresa) [Maia Rodman] 1927– Winner of the NEWBERY MEDAL in 1965 for *Shadow of a Bull*. Born in Warsaw, Poland, Wojciechowska emigrated to the United States in 1942. She worked as a detective, a professional tennis player, a translator, a ghost writer, and an author and editor. Her varied writing includes translations, FOLKTALES, books for younger children, YOUNG ADULT FICTION, BIOGRAPHY AND AUTOBIOGRAPHY, poetry, and film and TELEVISION adaptations. *Shadow of a Bull*, the moving story of a young Spanish boy who struggles to find his own role in life while pressured to follow the footsteps of his famous bullfighter father, remains her best-known book. LH

Wolf (1990) Multilayered and intertextual novel by British writer GILLIAN CROSS, for which she deservedly won the CARNEGIE MEDAL. Reaching adolescence, Cassy, hitherto sensible and untroubled, finds herself in a FAIRY TALE allegory in which her role as RED RIDING HOOD forces her to confront her own identity. Who and what is the wolf – her terrorist father or the ambiguous Lyell, her fey mother's lover? And are wolves to be feared or respected? Lyell's theatre group explores this theme, presenting the wolf, real and imaginary, facts and prejudices, to school children. Cross's research is impeccable, feeding into a dramatisation of the distortions and dangers of half-knowledge and prejudice. In a reversal of the fairy tale, Cassy is sent by her Nan to find her mother; the basket she carries contains a lethal package. Stalked by her father, she moves from the reality to the dream world of her mother's scruffy squat, where imagination and fantasy count for more than the common-sense values of her previous life. The reader is faced with contradictions and required to question the nature of violence, of fear itself, of loyalty and responsibility, of risk-taking and imagination. Cross presents readers with uncomfortable options in an uncompromising style. EAG

Wolf, Shelby see CRITICAL APPROACHES TO CHILDREN'S LITERATURE

Wolf, The (1991) Australian PICTUREBOOK by Margaret Barbalet, illustrated by JANE TANNER, which won the CHILDREN'S BOOK COUNCIL OF AUSTRALIA Book of the Year Award: Younger Readers (1992). Set in a one-parent family with a mother and three children, in a house closed against the outside world, the story deals with a boy threatened by some external force represented by a wolf which never appears. At the end, golden light shining through the family's door removes the pervasive air of menace. The wolf may be interpreted as symbolic of the threats which this family faces, overcome by the warmth of family affection and mutual support. The ending is left open. CH, HMcC

Wolff, Virginia Euwer 1937– American writer whose *Bat 6* (1988) explores, through preparations for a girls' annual softball game, the repercussions which World War II had on a small Oregon town. In books such as *Probably Still Nick Swansen* (1988), *The Mozart Season* (1991) and *Make Lemonade* (1993), Wolff writes of young people with lives different from ordinary adolescents' – one with learning disabilities, another a gifted violist, and finally a teenage mother living in poverty with her two children – who must prove themselves to win acceptance in today's world. PDS

Wollstonecraft, Mary see *ORIGINAL STORIES FROM REAL LIFE*; *SONGS OF INNOCENCE AND EXPERIENCE*

Wolves of Willoughby Chase, The see *JAMES III* SERIES; see also JOAN AIKEN

***Wombles* series** see ELIZABETH BERESFORD

Wonder Book for Boys and Girls, A see NATHANIEL HAWTHORNE; CLASSICAL MYTHOLOGY; HAMMATT BILLINGS

Wonder Woman see SUPERHEROES

Wonderful Adventures of Nils, The (1901) A lengthy two-volume story written by Selma Lagerlöf (1858–1940) when she was requested by a committee to produce a reader for Swedish schoolchildren designed to inspire in them a greater understanding of and love for their native country. Her hero, Nils, joins the migrating wild geese on their journey to the mountains of Lapland. Riding on the back of a tame gander, Nils literally has a bird's eye view of Sweden's climate, terrain, agriculture and early industrial development. Nils's varied adventures maintain narrative interest, but it is the revelation to the young of the beauty of Sweden's landscape and the richness of its culture which have made this story a national icon. The English translation by Velma Swanston Howard (1921) was illustrated in a distinctively stylised manner by Mary Hamilton Frye. GL

Wonderful Wizard of Oz, The see OZ SERIES

Wood, Anne see REVIEWING AND REVIEWERS; *TELETUBBIES*

'A Happy Family.' Wood engraving by John Greenaway, father of KATE GREENAWAY, for *Little Folks* (1880).

Wood, David 1944– British dramatist and novelist. Wood has also composed the music for a number of his own plays, and has frequently directed them in the theatre. He has been active in promoting the cause of companies and productions dedicated to children. Many of his works are adaptations of well-known FAIRY TALES and traditional tales, usually with some original perspective and with a sympathy for the underdog which appeals to young audiences. Works such as *Aladdin* (1981) and *Dick Whittington and Wondercat* (1982) occupy the territory of PANTOMIME and reconvert it to true musical theatre (see MUSIC AND STORY) addressed directly to the child's world, rather than playing indirectly to the adults in the audience as commercial pantomime often does. Wood has also dramatised ROALD DAHL'S *THE BFG* (1991) and *THE WITCHES* (1994), and Prince Charles's *The Old Man of Lochnagar* (1986). His original work includes *The Gingerbread Man* (1977), a popular and original variation on the well-known theme of the life that toys and inanimate objects take on at night when human beings are asleep; a novelised version was published in 1985. *The Selfish Shellfish* (1983) is a light-hearted yet serious treatment of ecological issues. Music and songs are important in most of Wood's plays, and they make imaginative use of lighting, movement and spectacle. With Janet

Grant, Wood has published an important handbook on children's theatre, *Theatre for Children: A Guide to Writing, Adapting, Directing and Acting* (1997). PH

Wood, Ivor see POSTMAN PAT SERIES

Wood, (Clarence) Lawson 1878–1957 British illustrator. Wood is remembered for his humorous pen-and-ink drawings in several magazines and especially for his cartoon chimpanzee character, 'Gran'pop', which appeared over many years in the *Sketch*, in a Christmas annual in the 1930s, and in books in the 1940s. Just as LOUIS WAIN is associated with cats and Cecil Aldin with dogs, so Wood is known for his comical monkeys in books such as *Meddlesome Monkeys* (1946), though he also illustrated *The Old Nursery Rhymes* in 1933 with more classical images. JAG

Wood, Leslie 1920– British illustrator. Wood is mostly known for his lithographed colour ILLUSTRATIONS for *The Story of a Little Red Engine* (DIANA ROSS, 1945) which was followed by eleven more *Red Engine* titles up to 1971. Wood has also illustrated WILLIAM MAYNE's five volumes of *Dormouse* tales (1966) and titles by HELEN CRESSWELL, LEILA BERG and others. JAG

wood engraving Wood engraving became popular as a means of producing book ILLUSTRATIONS towards the end of the 18th century through the work of THOMAS BEWICK. In the 19th century it quickly and effectively replaced metal engraving and etching (intaglio), for economic as well as practical reasons. Its nearest rival, LITHOGRAPHY, was used mainly for printing posters, labels, packages and some book illustration. For nearly a century wood engraving was the method by which illustrations and drawings were reproduced in most books, newspapers and magazines.

Wood blocks could be made so that they were exactly the same height as the type and both could be printed in the form of a single page by the same relief printing press. Books containing illustrations produced by intaglio methods required two different presses and it was therefore difficult to print the text and the image on the same page. As the demand for books increased it became important to restrict the cost and increase the speed of production. Hundreds, possibly thousands of prints could be taken from wood blocks, while the intaglio image wore out much more rapidly.

The technique used for wood engraving differs from that of the woodcut in that the former is engraved on the end grain while the latter is cut along the plank of the wood. While the tools employed for the woodcut were gouges and knives, the tools used in wood engraving were similar to those used in metal engraving. By tradition the wood-block engraver was a highly skilled craftsman or craftswoman who reproduced the work of another artist by using the burin, spitstiker and tint tool to work the polished surface of the wood block until it accurately reproduced the intricate tracery of cross-hatched lines and patterns of the original drawing. Once the block had been engraved the print was transferred onto paper from the inked surface of the engraved block by using an Albion or a similar relief printing press. There was a restriction on the size of the block, but in many cases several blocks were ingeniously joined together in order to produce a larger print.

Bewick developed a technique which was called 'white line' which allowed dark, flat tonal areas to be contrasted against areas of lighter tone. Apart from the followers of Bewick, this approach was not used again until the 20th century. The technique that dominated wood engraving throughout the 19th century was one that emphasised the use of line. In the majority of cases two talents were involved – that of the artist and that of the engraver. The latter interpreted as well as followed the pen or pencil line and cross-hatching of the artist. An example can be seen in the relationship between the DALZIEL BROTHERS and SIR JOHN TENNIEL, who worked together to produce the masterpieces that illustrated LEWIS CARROLL's *ALICE'S ADVENTURES IN WONDERLAND* and *Through the Looking Glass*. No less inspirational are the illustrations to Carroll's *THE HUNTING OF THE SNARK*, where Henry Holland translated Tenniel's drawing.

The Dalziel brothers' substantial output included work for magazines as well as a number of children's books. This was a period when many of the most notable artists of the day produced drawings for publication as well as paintings for exhibition. In the first of their publications for Ward and Lock, *THE ARABIAN NIGHTS' ENTERTAINMENTS* (1865), the Dalziels employed many famous artists, such as John Everett Millais. This very substantial volume contained 200 illustrations. Tenniel produced eight of them and George Pinwell contributed ten.

ARTHUR HUGHES, like other members of the Pre-Raphaelite Brotherhood, produced a number of evocative book illustrations that were engraved by the Dalziel Brothers. The most memorable examples are those for GEORGE MACDONALD's *At the Back of the North Wind*, for which he produced 76 magical drawings. This was first published in *Good Things for the Young of All Ages* (1872) and republished in 1884 in book form.

Towards the end of the century the entrepreneur publisher and engraver EDMUND EVANS produced a whole series of children's books illustrated by such renowned artists as RANDOLPH CALDECOTT, KATE

GREENAWAY, WALTER CRANE and RICHARD DOYLE. Evans made effective use of engraving for colour printing. Each colour had to be printed from a separately engraved block, and there were often between five or ten blocks. Nevertheless, by producing large editions, Evans was able to publish the work of these artists at reasonable prices. Until recently the same blocks were used for reprints of many of these books, having remained in continuous use for over a century.

Engraving suffered a rapid decline in the commercial printing world with the introduction of photography as a method of reproducing images, first on wood and then onto zinc or copper. Black-and-white line images, monochrome HALF-TONE and full-colour images all meant that the artist's work could be reproduced accurately without the intervention of the craftsman. By the latter part of the 20th century full colour lithography meant that children's books could be printed entirely in colour.

However, wood engraving remained alive in the 20th century through the private presses and artists who usually cut their own blocks. Examples include Eric Gill, GWEN RAVERAT, Clare Leighton and Paul Nash, but most of these worked as printmakers or illustrators of adult publications. While a new generation of children's illustrators was content to see its work reproduced through four-colour process printing, there are a few good examples of the tradition of engraving being sustained in recent times, such as in JOHN LAWRENCE's *Rabbit and Pork* (1974). His work, like many others who still use the medium, was published in Britain by the Folio Society. Today, wood engraving has become too closely associated with its past traditions and as such it is a craft with a limited range; contemporary printmakers and illustrators require a more flexible medium. Nevertheless, wood engraving is a process with an extraordinary history.

AEW

Wood Magic, a Fable (1881) The only book written specifically for children by the English nature-writer and mystic, Richard Jefferies (1848–87). It is a mawkish, fatalistic and uneasy blend of the animal fable and Victorian melodrama. Jefferies's attempt to make the central child-character, Bevis, into a mystic innocent only succeeds in presenting him as precocious. Bevis reappears in the naturalistic *Bevis, the Story of a Boy* (1882), which, although intended for adults, was for many years regarded as a children's classic, and influenced ARTHUR RANSOME. An edition illustrated by E. H. SHEPARD appeared in 1932. PLH

Woodson, Jacqueline 1963– American author, listed as one of *Granta*'s 50 Best American Authors Under 40 in 1996. Her books *I Hadn't Meant to Tell You This* (1994) and *From the Notebooks of Melanin Sun* (1995) were named CORETTA SCOTT KING Honour Books in 1995 and 1996. All her books treat the child and adolescent reader with tremendous respect, recognising that writing for that audience requires a non-reductive ear for the voice of the child. Woodson seeks to empower her readers, to remind them to like themselves. She portrays strong girls, aware that such role-models are essential in today's world, and represents their friendships with one another as deep and believable. Her characters speak to her readers of love and loss and the joy of being together. Woodson often addresses the issues of race, class, abuse and sexuality; she explores these issues gently, but fully, and never offers easy answers. Her spare use of language lends a poetic feel to her narratives and, though critics might be tempted to classify her as an issues writer, such limited classification does a disservice to her artistry with words and ideas. Other titles include *The House You Pass on the Way* (1997), *If You Come Softly* (1998), *Lena* (1999) – a sequel to *I Hadn't Meant to Tell You This* – and *Miracle's Boys* (2000).

CEJ

Woodward, Alice B(olingbroke) 1862–1951 British illustrator best known for her illustrations to *The Peter Pan Picturebook*, first published by George Bell and Sons in 1907, which remained in print in various forms until 1982. She spent her early years in Chelsea, training at the Westminster and South Kensington schools. She was one of the young artists to benefit from the introduction of PROCESS ENGRAVING, designing a series of striking and original children's books with black-and-white ILLUSTRATIONS for Blackie and other leading publishers. These included such classics as *To Tell the King the Sky is Falling* (c. 1896), *Princess of Hearts* (c. 1910) and *Adventures in Toyland* (c. 1897). From 1907 she worked primarily in colour for Bell, following *Peter Pan* with two Gilbert and Sullivan books, *The Pinafore Picturebook* (1908) and *The Story of the Mikado* (1921?). She illustrated a number of titles in Bell's *Queen's Treasure Series* including *ALICE IN WONDERLAND*, *THE WATER BABIES* (1909) and *BLACK BEAUTY*. During World War I she was CICELY MARY BARKER's tutor. After a short period working for Naval Intelligence she went to live in Bushey. She was noted for her graceful and economical line and for her drawings of lively and attractive children. Her work was signed with a stylised monogram which she frequently integrated into the drawing, for example as a carving on a tree or piece of furniture. GCB

Wool Pack, The see CYNTHIA HARNETT; see also HISTORICAL FICTION

Woolman, Steven 1969– Australian illustrator and designer, best known for illustrating GARY CREW's

The Watertower (1994) and *Caleb* (1996), books which demonstrate Woolman's talent for evoking the macabre. The first uses full-colour American Gothic realism, the second employs eerie, distorted black-on-white pen drawings reminiscent of Victorian engravings. Woolman has a broad stylistic repertoire: humorous line drawings and cartoons for poetry collections; endearingly comical images in *Peter and the Polar Bear* by Elizabeth Best (1994); muted colours and soft lines in Dyan Blacklock's *The Lighthouse*; and rich, delicate illustrations in the Chinese folktale *Kuanyin* (1995), retold by Kath Lock and Frances Kelly. NLR

Woolsey, Sarah Chauncy see SUSAN COOLIDGE; see also *WHAT KATY DID* SERIES

Word Party, The (1986) First collection by RICHARD EDWARDS. The title poem – describing words as party-goers ('Loving words clutch crimson roses, / Rude words sniff and pick their noses') – shows Edwards's imagination, verbal wit and skill in traditional forms characteristic of the collection, evoking echoes of DE LA MARE and CARROLL. ML

wordless picturebooks see PICTUREBOOKS; see also PETER COLLINGTON; SHIRLEY HUGHES; RENATE MEYER

Wordsworth, Dorothy 1771–1855 English diarist, best known as the companion of Romantic poets Samuel Taylor Coleridge ('In every motion her most innocent soul / Outbeams so brightly'), Thomas de Quincy ('the wildest person I have ever met') and William Wordsworth ('and in thy voice I catch / The language of my former heart'), to whom she was also sister and muse. She deserves recognition entirely on her own merits as an outstanding writer of everyday country life, as her journals testify. *Home at Grasmere* (1960) is the best known, documenting several years spent with William in the Lake District (1800–3) before his marriage to Mary Hutchinson. Some of the best features of her writing include tenderness towards children, sympathy for the poor, a fine eye for detail, enjoyment of domesticity and gardening, as well as an appreciation of nature. She wrote some exquisite poems for William's children, including 'Address to a Child during a Boisterous Winter Evening', 'Loving and Liking' and 'The Cottager to her Infant'. She died after many years of an illness similar to senile dementia. MCCS

Wordsworth, William see *LYRICAL BALLADS*; see also DOROTHY WORDSWORTH

World is Round, The (1939) The American author Gertrude Stein's best-known book for children. Stein was invited by MARGARET WISE BROWN, children's book editor for the publisher William R. Scott, to submit a children's book. Stein's story is a mixture of poetry and prose which traces the journey of nine-year-old Rose to the top of a mountain where she triumphantly celebrates her achievement. The book's circular dedication reproduced Stein's famous phrase 'Rose is a Rose is a Rose', which Rose carves on the base of a tree. *The World is Round* is a stunning innovative text printed on pink paper – Rose's favourite colour – with the text and ILLUSTRATIONS by CLEMENT HURD printed in blue ink. The illustrations emphasise the roundness and repetition that is apparent in Stein's language. Despite the influential librarian ANN CARROLL MOORE calling the book 'genuine child stuff' and a good deal of initial acclaim, it never became popular. Brown continued to support Stein's writing, which strongly influenced her own, but William R. Scott declined to publish Stein's second children's manuscript, *To Do: A Book of Alphabets and Birthdays*. JCS

world wide web see INTERNET; CD-ROMs

Wormell, Christopher 1955– Self-taught engraver, son of a landscape painter. Inspired by THOMAS BEWICK, he bought a couple of engraving tools and a boxwood block, and, in 1983, began to send prints off to publishers. His first book for children was the hand-printed, linocut *An Alphabet of Animals* (1990) which won the Graphics Prize in that year at Bologna. The delicate woodcut *Mowgli's Brothers* (RUDYARD KIPLING, 1992) and the bold, block-printed *A Number of Animals* (1994) followed, to wide critical acclaim. JAG

see also WOOD ENGRAVING

Worrals of the WAAF see *BIGGLES AND WORRALS* SERIES

***Worst Witch* series** (1974–93) Four CHAPTER BOOKS written and illustrated by JILL MURPHY; *Worst Witch Novelization* followed in 2000. The stories of Mildred Hubble, the worst witch at Miss Cackle's Academy, are deservedly popular with young readers and adults alike with their mixture of conventional images of witches – dressed in black and living in a cold dark castle – and the humour of Mildred's attempts to do things properly. Mildred's rivalry with her arch enemy Ethel provides a recurring theme, as does Mildred's own ability to get out of scrapes and save the day at the very last minute. KA

Wortis, (Avi) see AVI

***Worzel Gummidge* series** Popular stories, beginning with *Worzel Gummidge or The Scarecrow of*

Scatterbrook (1936), by the prolific British children's author Barbara Euphan Todd (1890–1976). The series was illustrated initially by Elizabeth Alldridge and later by Will Nickless and Jill Crockford, and was continued, and popularised on TELEVISION, by KEITH WATERHOUSE and WILLIS HALL. The stories, told with humour and interwoven with realistic details of country life, describe the wide-ranging adventures of a scarecrow, Worzel Gummidge, and his motley collection of friends, who are able to come alive. Worzel himself, though larger than life, is a fully rounded character, often quick to anger and prone to sulking, yet generally good-humoured, with a zest for life. The mixture of slap-stick humour and down-to-earth, if wayward, philosophy makes him an appealing character. The children in the stories take an almost adult moral high ground in their efforts to protect Worzel and to modify his behaviour, even though this leads to much trouble and misunderstanding for themselves. Other figures, like Saucy Nancy and Earthy Mangold, add to the humorous diversity of the stories, which uncover pretensions and debunk pomposity. The follow-up stories, written in simpler language, are more accessible to a young, modern audience. JSW

Wouldbegoods, The see BASTABLES SERIES

Wright, Kit 1944– British writer of children's poetry, including the collections *Rabbiting On* (1978), *Cat Among the Pigeons* (1987) and *Great Snakes* (1994), who calls himself 'the tallest poet in Christendom'. Wright's verse exploits wordplay to the full, especially in the use of alliteration, repetition and rhyme, conveying a humour which is often sardonic. *Rabbiting On* centres on domestic situations and familiar community figures, who have their own strange foibles. In *Great Snakes* the themes widen to include human origins, old age and death. All the books are illustrated by POSY SIMMONDS, who underlines mainly the humour but occasionally the pathos of the poetry. Wright has won many major poetry prizes, has taught in America and Britain, and is a tutor on Arvon Foundation Writing Workshops. In 1998 he wrote a version of *Rumpelstiltskin* for the Scholastic paperback series of FAIRY TALES. HA

Wrightson, Patricia (Alice) 1921– Acclaimed Australian writer for children, awarded the HANS CHRISTIAN ANDERSEN MEDAL for writing in 1986. Wrightson's immense success is due to the range of her subject matter, her evocation of the Australian countryside, her insight into both rural and urban life, her wise understanding of the human predicament that transcends national and cultural barriers, along with the richness and versatility of her style.

Running throughout Wrightson's work is her respect for the land and its creatures, its invisible forces and the way it shapes life and destiny. In the early novels human beings are seen as responsible guardians of their heritage. An affinity with 'the patient, knowing land' is the mark of wisdom, as the Aboriginal boy Eustace, in *The Rocks of Honey* (1960), acknowledges: 'He knew that this old country would fashion its people, all of them, to its own shape in its own good time.' Even when she moves to inner-city settings, as in *An Older Kind of Magic* (1972), life is driven by an energetic force, which in that book is seen as coming partly from the normally invisible ancient Aboriginal spirits: Pot-Kooroks, Nyols and Net-Nets – which for hundreds of years had crept around Aboriginal campfires at night. And from this point on Wrightson was to explore the place of such spirits in the secret life of those who inhabit her 'old south land'. It is his engagement with the Nargun, a huge lumbering stone figure, that, in *The Nargun and the Stars* (1973), brings healing and wholeness to the emotionally wounded Simon. The destiny of Wirrun, the Aboriginal hero of the *SONG OF WIRRUN* TRILOGY, is bound up with the life-force of the land as embodied in its ancient spirits. The doughty old Mrs Tucker in *A Little Fear* (1983) and the fair-skinned Jo Murray in *Balyet* (1989) grow in self-knowledge and resolution as they interact, respectively, with the belligerent Njimbin and with Echo, or Balyet, the ghost of an Aboriginal girl. *Shadows of Time* (1994) moves across the period of white settlement, the land and its spirits providing the constant that binds its inhabitants together and gives their life a focus. MSax

see also ABORIGINAL CULTURE IN CHILDREN'S BOOKS

Wrinkle in Time, A (1962) Novel by MADELEINE L'ENGLE, a NEWBERY MEDAL winner and the first of the books about the Murry and O'Keefe families. The series continues through *A Wind in the Door* (1973), *A Swiftly Tilting Planet* (1978), *Many Waters* (1986), *The Arm of the Starfish* (1965), *Dragons in the Waters* (1976), *A House Like A Lotus* (1984), and *An Acceptable Time* (1989). The first four in the series, which are sometimes known as the *Time* quartet, have a mystical, fantastic quality to them, as does *An Acceptable Time*, but the other three are written in a different mode. *Dragons in the Waters* and *The Arm of the Starfish* are mystery thrillers, and *A House Like a Lotus* has closer affiliations with the teenage 'problem' novel.

When *A Wrinkle in Time* begins, Dr Murry, Meg's father, is 'missing', supposedly on a top-secret mission for the government; however, as Meg learns from her mother, also a scientist, the Murrys have been working on a mode of super-speed travel across space and it is suspected that Dr Murry's disappearance is somehow connected to the 'tesseracts'. Meg, her brother Charles and a friend, Calvin, meet three strange ladies, Mrs

Who, Mrs How and Mrs Whatsit, who tell them that Dr Murry is a prisoner on the planet of Camazotz and enable them to travel there to rescue him. On arrival, Charles, confident in the power of his superior intellect, is taken over by IT, the evil entity who rules the planet, but is reclaimed by the power of Meg's love for him. They then rescue their father and return home.

What is interesting about *A Wrinkle in Time* is that it appears to support, or be constructed upon, two different logics or aesthetics: the scientific and the quasi-religious. The novel is usually described as SCIENCE FICTION, and one would expect in a work predicated upon scientific principles to find the resolution or the answer to the situation given in scientific terms. Yet, while a good part of its terminology (e.g. 'tesseracts' – the 'wrinkle' of the title) is 'scientific', the work is essentially dramatised in terms of the conflict between good and evil, and may be argued, at its most basic, to be about the redemptive power of love. Science, then, seems to provide a framework for the narrative without significantly contributing to the meaning of the text. The same is also true of the first of the sequels, *A Wind in the Door*, which uses biology rather than physics as its basic 'metaphor'. By *A Swiftly Tilting Planet*, the scientific framework had been nearly altogether abandoned for something closer to FANTASY, although the quasi-religious element continued to be important in the series.

Apart from its main theme, the series also conducts an examination of the pains of growing up, allowing it to be considered in a limited way as adolescent 'problem' literature. Two of the three protagonists, Meg and Charles are depicted as 'sports', outsiders whose difference from the ordinary child/teenager causes them to be ostracised. Meg despairs over her looks; Calvin has to cope with the problems of what is nowadays called a 'dysfunctional' family. Never treated too heavily, this aspect of the series amplifies and enriches it greatly. In the last of the novels, *A House Like A Lotus*, the problem novel elements predominate as Polly – Meg's and Calvin's daughter, and the work's protagonist – has to learn to cope not just with her own sexual awakening and relationships, but with her mentor's lesbianism. SA

Written for Children see JOHN ROWE TOWNSEND; see also BIOGRAPHY AND AUTOBIOGRAPHY; URCHIN VERSE

Wyatt Earp 1849–1929 Frontier lawman famous for his participation in the 'Gunfight at the OK Corral' in Tombstone, Arizona. In 1881, Wyatt assisted his brother Virgil, the marshal of Tombstone, in a confrontation with the Clancy and McLaury brothers, which resulted in several deaths. Wyatt subsequently left Tombstone and lived the rest of his life quietly as a business man. Over two dozen movies have variously portrayed him as hero and anti-hero, including *My Darling Clementine* (1948), *Gunfight at the OK Corral* (1957) and *Cheyenne Autumn* (1964). EBD

Wyeth, Newell Convers 1882–1945 American illustrator and painter, especially known for his dramatic and heroic scenes. Wyeth was born in Massachusetts to a family whose Welsh ancestor had settled there in 1647. His outdoor boyhood on a Charles River farm made him a child 'who saw things as they were'. A teacher recognised his talent for drawing and suggested he try ILLUSTRATION, but he bridled at his first regimented training. He applied to study with HOWARD PYLE, who accepted him on probation, and he began the hard work of learning Pyle's lessons in character and art. In 1903 his first professional submission, a *Saturday Evening Post* cover, was accepted just as he won full admission to Pyle's school on the condition that he drop everything else for one year. Afterwards he travelled through the American West, gathering a rich store of material. In 1907 he married, beginning the family of artists that includes his son Andrew and grandson Jamie. In 1911, Scribner commissioned Wyeth for *TREASURE ISLAND*, the first in a 30-year contract for the *Illustrated Classics* series. This was one of many highly successful books in an illustrious career, which included *TREASURE ISLAND* (1911), *KIDNAPPED* (1913), *The Boy's King Arthur* (1917), *ROBIN HOOD* (1917), *THE LAST OF THE MOHICANS* (1919), *ROBINSON CRUSOE* (1920) and works by MARK TWAIN. Wyeth was killed with a grandson in a train accident in 1945. MMG

Wyndham, John see *THE DAY OF THE TRIFFIDS*; SCIENCE FICTION

Wynken de Worde see BARTHOLOMAEUS ANGLICUS; ELUCIDARIA; *GESTA ROMANORUM*; RIDDLES AND JOKES

Wynken, Blinken, and Nod, and Other Child Verses see EUGENE FIELD

Wynne Jones, Diana see JONES, DIANA WYNNE

Wynne-Jones, Tim 1948– British-born Canadian writer. Wynne-Jones grew up in Kitimat, British Columbia, and, after attending the University of Waterloo and York University, he worked as a book designer and an editor. His first book, *Odd's End* (1980), was an adult mystery novel, which won the Seal First Novel Award in 1980. It was followed by other adult novels, radio drama and newspaper columns. He has also written poetry (*Mischief City*, 1986), short stories, PICTUREBOOKS, FANTASY and mysteries for children. Wynne-Jones depicts warm, believable characters, animals and individuals who set out on journeys as they search for self-identity and adventure. His picturebooks series, which includes *Zoom at Sea*, featuring a cat named Zoom, are also 'traditional fantasy quest' stories. His writing stresses the importance of communication, love, friendship, redemption and the power of the creative imagination. *Some of the Kinder Planets* (1993) won the 1993 Governor General's Award and also the BOSTON GLOBE-HORN BOOK AWARD. Wynne-Jones won the Governor General's Award (text) and the CLA YA Book Award for *The Maestro* (1996) and also the Vicky Metcalf Award for a Body of Work Inspirational to Young People. MRS

Wyss, J.D. see *SWISS FAMILY ROBINSON*; see also ROBINSONNADES

Y

Yankee Doodle American NURSERY RHYME, originating in a popular dance tune of the pre-Revolutionary War years. Although hundreds of verses for the song may exist, the most common is still the one in which the foolish Doodle 'stuck a feather in his hat and called it macaroni'. During the American Revolution, the British at first used the song to ridicule American soldiers, but as the tide of the war turned, the Americans took it up as a battle cry. The song has continued to be popular ever since, and the phrase 'Yankee Doodle Dandy' is colloquial for a patriotic American. KS

Yarmak see COMICS, PERIODICALS AND MAGAZINES

Yashima, Taro (Jun Atsushi Iwamatsu) 1908–94 Artist, illustrator, translator and author of PICTUREBOOKS and novels for children. Born in Kagoshima, Japan, Yashima immigrated to the United States in 1939. He studied art at the Imperial Art Academy in Tokyo and at the Art Students League in New York City. As an artist, Yashima illustrated most of his books, including his first novel, an autobiographical book entitled *The New Sun* (1943). His first children's book, *The Village Tree* (1953), about his childhood in Japan, was written for his daughter. Three of his books, *Crow Boy* (1925), *Umbrella* (1958) and *Seashore Story* (1967), were runners-up for the CALDECOTT MEDAL, and he was honoured in 1968 by the Southern California Council on Literature of Children and Young People for his significant contribution in the field of ILLUSTRATION. Known primarily for his impressionistic drawings, his work reflects both his cultural heritage and his love for children. *Crow Boy, The Village Tree* and *Umbrella* have been made into educational movies and filmstrips for children. In 1954, with his wife Mitsu Yashima, he published *Plenty to Watch*. He has also illustrated and translated Hatoju Muku's *The Golden Footprints* (1960), and in 1965 he illustrated June Beherns's *Soo Ling Finds a Way*. JGJ

Yasin in Trouble (1990) School story by Tanzanian author Martha Mvurungi, one of the few Tanzanian writers who have written in English for children. It is the story of a high-school boy who frequently sneaks out to go and dance. One night he finds gangsters stealing money from the headmaster's office, and through his bravery he recovers the money. The question is: should he keep the money for himself or give it to the headmaster? And how is he going to explain to the teachers why he was out when he met the gangsters? ABO

Yates, Elizabeth 1905– American writer born in Buffalo, New York. Yates received the Sarah Josepha Hale Medal for writing that reflects the literary tradition of New England. She wrote *Pebble in a Pool* (1958) about DOROTHY CANFIELD FISHER, a native of Lawrence, Kansas, and a neighbour of ROBERT FROST in Vermont. Yates's most famous book, *Amos Fortune, Free Man* (1951) won the NEWBERY MEDAL. This book is a pre-Civil-War story celebrating freedom: a young king is captured by slavers in Africa; then in America, At-mun (Amos) spends his life helping others gain freedom, refusing to hate. *Prudence Crandall, Woman of Courage* (1955) is a companion story. A researcher, biographer and owner of Shetland sheepdogs, Yates wrote *Skeezer: Dog with a Mission* (1973) about a 'canine co-therapist' at the University of Michigan psychiatric hospital for children, a story also filmed. Skeezer lives on the sixth floor with troubled residents; she has puppies there and promotes acceptance and healing. Many of Yates's books are illustrated by Nora S. Unwine. A prolific writer and woman of faith, Yates wrote religious titles such as *Children of the Bible* (1950). She also received the Jane Addams Children's Book Award for *Rainbow 'Round the World: A Story of UNICEF* (1954). NV

Yearling, The see MARJORIE KINNAN RAWLINGS; see also ANIMALS IN FICTION

Yeats, Jack Butler 1871–1957 Irish artist and author. He was the youngest child of John Butler Yeats and brother of the poet William Butler Yeats. He spent his childhood in Sligo, but studied and lived in England before finally returning to settle in Ireland. He wrote plays and novels for children and adults but is mainly known as an outstanding painter. He illustrated a number of children's books by PADRAIC COLUM and PATRICIA LYNCH. VC

Yeats, William Butler see IRISH MYTHOLOGY AND FOLKLORE; see also EDMUND DULAC; VACHEL LINDSAY; P.J. LYNCH

Yellow Dwarf, The see AULNOY, MARIE-CATHERINE LE JUMEL DE BARNEVILLE DE LA MOTTE; see also FAIRY TALES

Yep, Laurence 1948– Asian American author of many thought-provoking, artistic, authentic and innovative books. No other Asian American writer for children and young adults has given American children of all ethnicities such breadth and depth of exposure to Chinese history; the quality and variety of his canon is superseded by few writers in the field.

His realistic fiction – *Child of the Owl* (1978) and its sequel *Thief of Hearts* (1995); *Sea Glass* (1979); *Ribbons* (1966) and its sequel *The Cook's Family* (1998); and *The Amah* (1999) – reveals characters whose voices and experiences are decidedly Asian American but whose personalities and preoccupations (peer pressures, friendships, conflicts with parents, assuming adult responsibilities) are those of young adults everywhere. His books have a MULTICULTURAL emphasis, with protagonists coming of age as members of two cultural traditions, either due to the immigrant experience or as the product of a bi-cultural marriage, such as Yep's own. (His wife, Joanne Ryder, is also a children's book writer.)

Yep has created a FANTASY series of four books, beginning with *Dragon of the Lost Sea* (1982), and continuing with *Dragon Steel* (1985), *Dragon Cauldron* (1991) and *Dragon War* (1992), which focuses on the quest of a dragon princess to recover her dragon homeland. In addition, he has produced an excellent autobiography of his own childhood which shows him growing up between two cultures, Chinese and American: *The Lost Garden* (1991); and a well-received anthology of stories focused on young Asian Americans: *American Dragons* (1993). He has also produced several collections of FOLKTALE retellings: *The Rainbow People* (1989), *Tongues of Jade* (1991) and *Tree of Dreams* (1995), and a SCIENCE FICTION novel, *Sweetwater* (1973).

However, Yep's special strength is HISTORICAL FICTION. *The Star Fisher* (1992), a story of second-generation Asian Americans living in Clarksburg, West Virginia, is a touchstone of excellence in this genre, as well as a strong and authentic portrait based on his grandmother's life. Two other historical novels of immigrant experience set in America have been Newbery Honour Books: *Dragonwings* (1975) – which also won the Phoenix Award – and *Dragon's Gate* (1994). Yep's historical fiction set in China is particularly sensitive and informative: *The Serpent's Children* (1984) and its sequel *Mountain Light* (1985) are an excellent introduction to *Dragon's Gate*. *The Ghost Fox* (1994) is an interesting blend of folk realism for younger readers.

Whether in historical fiction like *The Star Fisher* or contemporary novels like *Thief of Hearts* or *Ribbons*, Yep's special subject is what it means to be Chinese, especially in America. Many of his stories focus on the immigrant experience and the way Chinese immigrants can adopt American customs while continuing to honour their Chinese heritage. These three books are the most accessible of Yep's works for today's young adult readers. Focusing on the pivotal moments in the lives of young adults of Chinese American heritage, they emphasise such themes as mother–daughter relationships, mutual respect in friendships, the sacrifices parents make to keep families going, inter-generational relationships, accepting one's personal or cultural identity, discovering what it means to help others, and accepting and recognising the weaknesses and strengths of other people, adults or peers.

Yep's special stylistic trait, one he shares with SOOK CHOI, is the small embedded image (a story, object or artifact) that he places at the heart of a book and allows to unfold gently, in order to reveal that although children may be caught between two worlds, they are stronger for the cherished place they can discover in each. NM

Yolen, Jane 1939– Prolific American writer and editor of children's books, including fantasies and poems for all ages. Yolen has worked as a reporter, storyteller, lecturer, college professor and editor. Born in New York City, she settled in rural Massachusetts to devote herself to writing and family. Her first award-winning book, *The Emperor and the Kite* (1967), illustrated by ED YOUNG, was followed by many other PICTUREBOOKS based on myth, folklore and history. Her favourite themes include Arthurian legends, dragon lore, magical transformations, the natural world and adventures of strong women. In *Dove Isabeau* (1989), a woman who is transformed into a dragon becomes more powerful than her predecessor in traditional ballads. Yolen says the literary or art FAIRY TALES for which she is best known 'use the elements of old stories – the cadences, the magical settings or objects – but concern themselves with modern themes'. *The Girl Who Cried Flowers and Other Tales* (1974) helped begin a revival of literary fairy tales in the late 20th century. Later collections of tales and poems include volumes focusing on dragons, unicorns, witches, angels, the moon and the life of Merlin.

Although Yolen speaks out against CENSORSHIP and her writing reflects her progressive social and political views, her fiction is not intentionally didactic; it derives from personal experience and the emotional exploration she describes as 'going down into the heart's cavern'. In *The Moon Ribbon* (1976), one of her most successful tales, a heroine akin to CINDERELLA is not beautiful, but she uses her dead mother's magic legacy to escape enemies and learn to love wisely. Striving to appeal to both the ear and the eye, Yolen skilfully uses evocative language and archetypal symbols to explore the mysterious shadows of the human heart as well as the utopian dreams of traditional fairy tales. In *Touch Magic* (1981) and shorter essays, she affirms the enduring value of FANTASY and fairy tales in children's literature.

Yolen's humorous picturebooks for beginning readers, such as *Sleeping Ugly* (1981), the *Commander Toad* series, and the *Piggins* books, contain gentle satire of fairy tales, outer-space adventures and mysteries set in Edwardian mansions. Her novels include *The Gift of Sarah Barker* (1981), about star-crossed young lovers among the Shakers; *Children of the Wolf* (1984), based on a true story of feral children in India; and a series about inter-planetary dragon tamers. Through time travel in *The Devil's Arithmetic* (1988), and fairy-tale motifs in *Briar Rose* (1992), a novel for older readers, fantasy elements are woven into modern stories of the Holocaust. Among Yolen's more realistic picturebooks emphasising family and nature are *Owl Moon*, winner of the 1988 CALDECOTT MEDAL (illustrated by JOHN SCHOENHERR); *Letting Swift River Go* (1992), about a New England town drowned by a reservoir; and *Welcome to the Green House* (1993), on the tropical rainforest. Yolen also writes LULLABIES, folk songs, ALPHABET BOOKS, SCIENCE FICTION and horror stories, as well as editing volumes of FOLKTALES, fantasy, science fiction and poetry. TLH

see also KING ARTHUR

Yonge, Charlotte Mary 1823–1901 Prolific British writer producing novels, essays and biographies and working as both an editor and a historian. Felt by many to be a pioneer writer of girls' books, she is perhaps best known today for her historical tales chronicling the days of chivalric endeavour. An archetypal Victorian, she attached to her works a highly moral tone, preached self-denial and proclaimed the inferiority of women. Her work as a Sunday-school teacher prompted the production of articles in 1842 for the *Magazine for the Young*. The success of this earned her the editorship in 1851 of a new juvenile periodical, *The Monthly Packet*, which remained under her supervision until 1890. This work was supplemented by the publication of over 160 books, the majority of which were novels. *Abbeychurch* (1844) was Yonge's first published title. *The Heir of Redclyffe* (1853), billed as a 'modern romance', became one of the most widely read novels of the 19th century, with its hero, Sir Guy Morville, providing a sound model for the nation's young men. Perhaps her most famous and bestselling work, though, was *The Daisy Chain* (1856). Representative of her preoccupation with self-sacrificing heroines, it was also the first of her long series of stories recounting family life in Victorian times. The heroine, Ethel May, a virtuous girl, became the idol of every female reader as the experiences of the widowed Dr May and his family were unfolded by Yonge. Her social novel *Heartsease* (1844) was illustrated by KATE GREENAWAY. GD

see also FAMILY STORIES

Yoruba folktales see CHRISTIE ADE AJAYI

Young, (Rev.) Egerton R(yerson) 1840–1909 Collector and translator of Native American folklore. Young wrote books, including *By Canoe and Dog Train* (1890) and *On the Indian Trail* (1897), telling of his work for more than 30 years as a missionary among such Northern Native American tribes as the Cree and the Saulteaux. He also assembled anthologies of their myths and legends, which he collected on his travels, including *Stories from Indian Wigwams and Northern Campfires* (1892) and *Algonquin Indian Tales* (1903), illustrated by J. E. Laughlin and including some of Young's own photographs. Fascinated by the social and political importance of myths and legends, Young was one of the first writers to convey Native American folklore to the youth of America in the hope that they would find it as 'attractive and interesting' as he had done. SCWA

Young, Ella 1865–1956 Irish novelist who was born in County Antrim. Young attended university in Dublin where she became involved in the Irish Literary Revival. This resulted in several collections of stories based on Celtic myths. Initially, these were very much retellings, as in *Celtic Wonder-Tales* (1910), and *The Tangle-Coated Horse* (1929), a collection of tales of Fionn McCool. In other work, she displays a more imaginative approach, loosely based on ancient IRISH LEGENDS, such as *The Wonder-Smith and his Son* (1927) and *The Unicorn with Silver-Shoes* (1932). She emigrated to the United States where her work won considerable popularity. VC

Young, Noela 1930– Australian award-winning illustrator of well over 50 books, including the popular *THE MUDDLE-HEADED WOMBAT* SERIES by RUTH PARK. Since her first ILLUSTRATIONS for *David and his Australian Friends* (1953), by Enid Bell, Young has illustrated the works of writers such as PATRICIA WRIGHTSON, HESBA BRINSMEAD, EMILY RODDA, CHRISTOBEL MATTINGLEY and SALLY ODGERS, as well as contributing to the New South Wales *SCHOOL MAGAZINE*. A versatile artist, with considerable drawing talent and a strong sense of form, she depicts people (especially children), real and imaginary animals, and natural or suburban settings with confidence and empathy. The child figures for her own text, *Keep Out* (1975), set in the inner city, were described by Saxby as 'among the best ever drawn for an Australian picturebook: leggy, cheeky, nonchalant, eager, vociferous – never resting'. She has also written and illustrated *Flip the Flying Possum* (1963), *Mrs Pademelon's Joey* (1967) and *Torty Longneck* (1977). JAP

young adult fiction As a genre young adult fiction did not exist until well after World War II. Before then a number of classic children's series such as *ANNE OF GREEN GABLES* (1925) or *LITTLE HOUSE IN THE BIG WOODS* (1932) had taken their heroines into early adulthood and marriage, but the later novels were not regarded as a separate genre, partly because society was less concerned with teenagers as a separate group, and perhaps partly because many of the series began when their protagonists were still young children.

One of the first pieces of writing for the young adult genre was American writer BEVERLY CLEARY's *Fifteen* (1956), a title still in print in Britain, about a teenage girl, her desire for a boyfriend and her eventual relationship with a particular boy. By modern standards the book is very tame; the boy and girl meet at the beginning of the book, the central part of the book features all the familiar dilemmas about clothing, parents and phone calls, and the book ends when the two, who have by now been seeing each other for some time, decide to go steady and have their first kiss. Sex, needless to say, does not feature and the emphasis is on romance throughout. *Fifteen* was not published in Britain until 1962 when it became one of the first titles on the Penguin teenage imprint, Peacock. Despite its lack of drama, the book set some of the patterns for subsequent teenage novels; Jane's desperate desire for a boyfriend, her continual and acute embarrassment, and her sense that her parents cannot possibly understand what she is going through, are all themes that have been reworked in many later young adult novels.

The popular conception of teenage literature is that it is about romance, relationships, and the difficulties of family life. It is predominantly concerned with real life rather than FANTASY and frequently examines 'issues' considered to be of interest to teenage readers. It deals with a teenage identity which is separate from that of either adulthood or childhood, and often takes its cue from J.D. Salinger's influential *CATCHER IN THE RYE* (1951). Often characters experience a sense of isolation and exclusion from the rest of the world which has to be worked through before they can establish their own identity. Young adult literature is often concerned with teenagers' search for this identity as they struggle against the apparent restrictions of adult authority, seeking to develop their own set of values, establish their autonomy, and build new relationships with family and friends.

Young adult literature developed initially in America, where the idea of being a teenager was more quickly established than in Britain. Early American contributors to the genre included PAUL ZINDEL, whose *The Pigman* (1968) was an example of the teenage novel's preoccupation with the relationship between adolescents and their parents. In *My Darling, My Hamburger* (1969) the relationship between the girl and her father is so poor that it leads indirectly to her becoming pregnant; his over-strict attitude is clearly viewed as being as much to blame for her predicament as the choices she makes herself. It is the apparent absolution of the teenagers from responsibility for their own lives, coupled with an emphasis on trauma and disaster, that can make teenage novels unpalatable to adult readers, a number of whom have echoed the criticism voiced by Nicholas Tucker in relation to PAULA FOX's *A Place Apart* (1978) – 'A 14-year-old . . . first loses her father and then a best friend and never stops whining as a result. Teenagers may think (and write) like this in the privacy of their own homes or diaries, but there is no reason why other children should want to tune in to quite such relentless self-absorption' (*Books For Your Children*, Spring 1982).

Certainly many novels written for teenagers in the 1960s and 70s were sympathetic towards the teenager in his/her rebellion against adult authority. In many of the best novels this criticism of adult authority is clearly justified, as in the narrator's implicit criticism of Una's father in *THE PEACOCK SPRING* (1975) or K.M. Peyton's criticism of Pennington's violent father in *Pennington's Seventeenth Summer* (1970) (see PENNINGTON SERIES). However, at times the teenager's apparently pointless rejection of all adult values has led to further criticism of the genre by adult readers.

In Britain the Peacock list was set up in the early 1960s to publish paperback fiction for young adults. Writing in *The Best Children's Books of 1963* NAOMI LEWIS described the list as being 'generally speaking, for twelves and upwards', although to a modern reader some of the titles might now look better suited to the Puffin list for the under-twelves. Early Peacock titles included *Walkabout* (1959), *STIG OF THE DUMP* (1963) and *THE COUNTRY CHILD* (1931), although *THE WEIRDSTONE OF BRISINGAMEN* (1960) – in many respects a more complex and difficult book – was published as a Puffin. MARGERY FISHER in her book *Intent Upon Reading* (1961) included a chapter on 'Growing Up' and commented that 'writers need not always pretend that parents are always kind and tolerant, always interested in what their children are doing: their readers know otherwise'. In 1965 Naomi Lewis described *Young Mother* by Josephine Hamm as 'a detailed and helpful document' believing that it 'had to come sooner or later; this author has managed it not only sooner, but well' (*The Best Children's Books of 1965*). Such commentary from critics was indicative of the changing attitude of adult readers to the new genre.

During the 1970s and 80s publishers became increasingly conscious of the role of teenagers in the market-place. Many publishers set up separate teenage imprints with covers and blurbs designed to attract the young adult market, often drawing attention to the books 'adult' content. The clear signals that these books were not suitable for younger children were designed both to appeal to the teenage audience and to warn parents against buying such books for their younger children. The age of the readership has always been a problem for publishers of young adult fiction, since many of the novels are read not by teenagers, but by children in the 10–13 age group, whose parents are often reluctant to have their offspring reading about young adult relationships. Critics, however, were becoming increasingly tolerant of the new genre, at least of its best manifestations. Nicholas Tucker wrote of teenage fiction in the spring 1985 edition of *Books For Your Children*: 'Gone are the days when writing for children regularly harked back to memories of years when the authors themselves were young; today's paperback novels are often as immediate as this week's newspapers or magazines. If the best of these can't persuade teenagers that fiction has the ability to put their present bewildering reality into more meaningful patterns I doubt if any other writing will.'

Tucker went on to comment that sadly not all teenagers have access to such fiction. Many authors were conscious that much of the earlier literature for children had been aimed at a primarily middle-class audience and therefore risked alienating many of their potential readers. A determined effort was made to broaden the scope of teenage fiction. K. M. Peyton's *Pennington* series featured a working-class hero who meets – and eventually marries as a result of her pregnancy – a middle-class girl whose parents are far from delighted at their relationship. In Britain class is often seen as an issue that divides parents and offspring; in LYNNE REID BANKS's *My Darling Villain* (1977) the heroine's parents obviously disapprove of her relationship with Mark, partly because the relationship is potentially sexual, but mainly because of his class.

As more novels came to feature teenage sex and pregnancy some of the taboos surrounding children's fiction were lifted. A number of authors began to write fiction about the sexual abuse of children. Gloria D. Miklowitz's *Secrets Not Meant To Be Kept* (UK, 1989) is a harrowing account of a Satanic ring of abuse perpetrated through a nursery school. CYNTHIA VOIGT's *When She Hollers* (1994) is perhaps one of the best-written examples of its kind, managing to describe the horrors of a daughter's abuse by her father without becoming voyeuristic or sensational. Most of these novels are clearly designed to provide reassurance and advice for teenage readers, but some seem intended to provide little more than an unpleasant source of entertainment. *Are You In the House Alone?* (1974) by RICHARD PECK is an account of a girl who, after a series of obscene phone calls, is raped by a boy she knows, and seems written to thrill rather than to reassure.

Almost all major publishers have experienced some degree of difficulty in marketing their books to the notoriously difficult teenage audience and have spent time and money adjusting imprint names, covers and blurbs in an attempt to woo the market. Few 'looks' have achieved long-term success, if only because of the fashion-conscious and transient nature of the readership. Even well-known and popular authors like JUDY BLUME have to be regularly 'rejacketed'. However a few series published in the second half of the 1980s were phenomenally successful on both sides of the Atlantic, most notably the *SWEET VALLEY HIGH* books developed by Francine Pascal. The series was designed as mass-market fiction which would be purchased by teenagers themselves, although their commercial success led to the development of titles for younger readers. The books were not intended to place great demands upon their readers, being mainly concerned with romance and friendships. The problems set up within each novel are easily resolved; for example, when one of the heroines invents a boyfriend to gain popularity she manages to end the novel with a group of friends who forgive her for lying to them as well as a desirable boyfriend who materialises out of nowhere at the school dance (*Love Letters*, 1985). Although the overt message is that she does not need a boyfriend to win friends, the implication is that the appearance of the young man will complete her happiness. The *Sweet Dreams* series, also successful in both Britain and America, concentrated even more heavily on romance. Although ostensibly intended for a slightly older readership than *Sweet Valley High*, the actual age of its readers is clearly reflected in titles like *Blue Ribbon Romance* (1990), where the heroine's greatest dilemma occurs when the boy she fancies is competing for the same riding trophy that she herself wants to win.

A number of American series have attempted to woo older readers by taking their heroines on to college, most notably in the *Sweet Valley University* series. However, such series have proved less popular than their younger counterparts, particularly in Britain where the *Freshman Dorm* series, for example, has had only limited sales. Very few British teenage novels have been set at university, though PETER HUNT has described the experience of starting college in his book *Going Up* (1989).

A common catalyst for the search for a new identity in teenage novels is the death of a friend or family member and the hero/heroine's need to come to terms with grief. HONOR ARUNDEL's *The High House* (1967) – an early British example of the young adult novel – begins with the death of both Emma's parents in a car crash. The book is written in the first person and, although it is about her need to adapt to a new way of life, Emma refuses to discuss with the reader her feelings about her parents – 'Mother and Father had been killed in a car smash on their way back from visiting friends. I can't write about it.' Later novels tend to be more explicit about the teenager's feelings and many seem deliberately written as an aid for either the grieving teenager or his/her friends.

Several young adult novels have examined teenagers' reactions to the adult society in which they live, and which they often deplore. The threat of nuclear disaster during the 1970s and 80s led to a spate of novels about nuclear power, life after a nuclear holocaust, and ecological issues. One of the best-known of these was *Z For Zachariah* (1975) by ROBERT C. O'BRIEN, a novel about the survivor of a nuclear holocaust. Many such novels were depressing in outlook, suggesting that there was little teenagers could do to change the ways of the adult world, although some, such as JEAN URE's *Plague 99* (1989), offer hope as a new society rises from the ashes of the old.

In recent years there have been fewer overtly political novels written for young adults, but a number of writers have examined the theme of homelessness among young people, most notably ROBERT SWINDELLS in his award-winning *Stone Cold* (1993). The books sometimes have a contemporary, realistic setting, but are more often set in a futuristic society. A number of books have featured children living on or around large municipal rubbish dumps where they can gather food and a few belongings. Adult society tends to be threatening, as in IAN STRACHAN's *The Throwaways* (1992) where the alternative to living on the dump is to be disposed of by the 'Catchers', whose ugly and sinister presence haunts the children. The strength of many of these novels comes from the fellowship which develops amongst the children who live outside society; in GARY KILWORTH's *The Electric Kid* (1991) a boy with an astonishing gift for electrical gadgets teams up with a blind child who has phenomenal hearing so that together they can take on the adult world. The atmosphere in MELVYN BURGESS's award-winning *Junk* (1996) is much bleaker: two young teenagers run away from home and become involved with drugs and, eventually, prostitution. Again they receive support from their contemporaries when they first leave home, and their deliberate rejection of this support adds to the overwhelming sense of misery within the novel. Adult critics had very mixed views about the book's subject matter; when it was given the prestigious CARNEGIE AWARD by a panel of adult judges the award made front page news in the United Kingdom, with headlines like, 'Sex and Drugs and A Damn Good Read' (*The Times*, 18 July 1997) and photo captions such as 'Would you let your child read this?' (*The Guardian*, 18 July 1997).

Many authors have used the popular diary format to portray the rapidly changing emotions of adolescence. Best known is Sue Townsend's *SECRET DIARY OF ADRIAN MOLE AGED 13¾* (1982), which is unusual in that it has been widely read and enjoyed by adults as well as teenagers, perhaps partly because of its humorous look at adult behaviour. A number of other diaries followed the success of *Adrian Mole*, some of which were deliberately intended to provide adolescents with information about their emotions and developing sexuality; most notable amongst these was the *Diary of a Teenage Health Freak* (1987) written by two doctors and providing information on such topics as menstruation, acne and smoking. A more recent success has been Yvonne Coppard's *Not Dressed Like that You Don't* (1991) in which the diaries of a teenage girl are interspersed with those of her mother, showing both the huge gaps in their understanding of one another and the similarity in their experiences.

Recently young adult publishing appears to have been dominated by horror novels, with the phenomenal success of Scholastic's *Point Horror* series (see POINT SERIES). Many adults have viewed the growth of the horror novel as an unfortunate development in teenage fiction, believing that such novels encourage both violence and a belief in the occult, while their easy readability and widespread availability is believed to discourage children from reading more literary fiction. Horror novels are always very clearly signalled through their jackets and titles; jackets are almost always predominantly black, with embossed lettering often in coloured foil, while the horror of the content tends to be exaggerated, so that the blurb is frequently more lurid than the contents. Teenage horror novels are often more moral than they at first appear; the good characters often have a happy outcome and the bad an unhappy one.

Although horror novels have predominated in recent years, there has nevertheless been a steady flow of literary teenage fiction, much of which has won widespread adult acclaim as well as being enjoyed by teenage readers. *Junk* is now published under an adult imprint, while BERLIE DOHERTY's *Dear Nobody* (1991) has been praised by critics, parents and teachers alike for its thought-provoking account of teenage pregnancy. ANNE FINE's *Flour Babies* (1992) is an entertaining book which, without being overtly didactic, encourages young adults to consider the far-reaching implications of having a baby. Fine's most successful novels for this age group all tackle issues of relationships with family and friends. MADAME DOUBTFIRE (1987) gained huge popularity when it was made into a film, while *The Tulip Touch* (1996) won the WHITBREAD CHILDREN'S NOVEL AWARD for its powerful portrayal of a disturbing friendship. Many of the most successful authors choose not to write specifically for teenagers, but produce books which deal with a range of issues and can be enjoyed by children and adults alike. In America SHARON CREECH and KAREN CUSHMAN have both received critical acclaim for novels which tackle many of the themes common to young adult literature, while Cynthia Voigt's DICEY series has become a modern classic. None of these novels have been written specifically for the teenage audience but all examine the young heroine's progression from childhood to adulthood and her growing autonomy. Although both Creech and Voigt deal with subject matter apparently similar to that of the issue-based teenage novels of the 1970s, here it is the stories rather than the issues which predominate. Both create strong and plausible heroines whose reactions to situations are not based on stereotypes of teenage behaviour but on intelligent responses to difficult situations.

In the late 1960s and the 1970s, Australian authors enthusiastically embraced the new trends in writing for teenagers that marked the advent of the modern adolescent novel. Books for young adults were distinguished from their predecessors by the construction of adolescence on which they were based and the features which sprang from that construction. Whereas adolescence had previously been seen as a time of induction into the adult world, now it was conceptualised as a time of conflict with the older generation that led protagonists not merely to question established values, but to reject past experience as relevant to the dilemmas of contemporary youth. Plots became focused on social issues perceived as relevant to the intended audiences and authors explored previously taboo areas. ELEANOR SPENCE, for example, delicately touched on homosexual attraction in *A Candle for St Antony* (1977).

On the other hand, in many works throughout the 1970s and much of the 1980s, a specifically Australian context was given to the individual's struggle to develop an assured sense of self by the use of national and historical landscapes. IVAN SOUTHALL threw young people upon their own resources to face fire, flood and accident, while PATRICIA WRIGHTSON made them conscious of the different ways of valuing the world around them, embedded in settler and indigenous traditions. The success of Southall's *Josh* (1971) in winning the CARNEGIE MEDAL in 1972 demonstrates its relevance and appeal across English-speaking countries.

The 1990s have been marked by diversity, innovation and controversy. GARY CREW's fascinating but demanding *Strange Objects* (1990) implies sophisticated readers who are willing to question received wisdom and able to appreciate various narrative devices. It stretched the projected audience beyond the age limit usual for adolescent literature. SONYA HARNETT also wrote 'cross-over' literature, books for those aged from 16 to 21. Her novel, *Sleeping Dogs* (1995), is a parable of relationships, and challenges conventional morality. JAMES MOLONEY refused to simplify relationships between black and white Australians in his books of the lives of Dougy and Gracey, while Glynn Parry's creation of *Monster Man* explored the psychotic. CATHERINE JINKS produced a popular hero set in Crusader times with her PAGAN SERIES of novels. BRIAN CASWELL's novels illustrate the ways authors have transformed writing styles to interest readers accustomed to interactive texts. In the series which began with TOMORROW, WHEN THE WAR BEGAN (1993) JOHN MARSDEN has revived the romantic male adventure, though his cast of characters is both gender-balanced and multiculturally inclusive. The success of Melina Marchetta's LOOKING FOR ALIBRANDI (1992) attests to the continued popularity of romantic fiction about male–female relationships.

Young adult fiction at the end of the century is now reaching a wider audience, both in terms of a broader age range and a wider section of the teenage population itself. While horror titles are often read by young adults who might not otherwise consider a book as an enjoyable from of entertainment, the literary novel is also flourishing and being enjoyed by adults and children as well as the teenage audience for which it is intended. KA, MN

Young Elizabethan, The (1948–73) British monthly magazine that went through several title changes. Beginning life as *Collins Magazine for Boys and Girls*, it changed shortly before the Coronation in 1953 to *The Young Elizabethan* and, later, to *The Elizabethan*. What distinguished it from other children's periodicals was monthly publication, its relatively high price (two shillings, rising eventually to four), the targeting of both boys and girls, its middle-class ethos, and, especially, the magazine's literary emphasis – factors that made its comparative longevity all the more surprising. Its literary character is evident not only in stories by such distinguished writers as RUMER GODDEN, NOEL STREATFEILD, CYNTHIA HARNETT and EDMUND BLISHEN, but also in its book REVIEWS and literary criticism, as well as regular sections devoted to readers' essays, poetry and fiction. The magazine remained true to its aim of promoting a well-informed and literate readership, and though falling circulation in the 1960s led to more extensive coverage of media events and personalities in an attempt to broaden its appeal, the guiding principles were never abandoned. When the magazine finally ceased publication in 1973, a valedictory editorial acknowledged: 'We had a chance to live – by reviewing pornographic books and films. We chose to die.' DJ

Young Marvelman see COMICS, PERIODICALS AND MAGAZINES

Young Visiters, The see ASHFORD, DAISY; see also CHILD AUTHORS

Youth's Companion, The (1827–1929) One of America's most popular and long-lived children's periodicals, founded by Nathaniel Willis (1780–1870), as an outgrowth of his religious paper, *The Recorder*. According to its Prospectus, the *Companion* prepared children for life in a 'far advanced period of the church and the world' by forming their minds, hearts and characters 'for the scenes and the duties of a brighter day'. At first overwhelmingly religious and didactic, it became a weekly under Daniel Ford (1857–99), offering a lively mix of features, fiction and ILLUSTRATION to a family audience. Authors published in the magazine included LOUISA MAY ALCOTT, JOHN TOWNSEND TROWBRIDGE, FRANCES HODGSON BURNETT, L. FRANK BAUM, Harriet Beecher Stowe, JACK LONDON and the indefatigable CHARLES ASBURY STEPHENS, a contributor for 60 years. *The Youth's Companion*'s circulation in the 1880s was among the highest in the country, considerably greater than that of *ST NICHOLAS* or most adult magazines. Editors after Ford included Edward Stanwood (1899–1911), Charles M. Thompson (1911–25) and Harford Powel, Jr. (1925–9). In 1928 the *Youth's Companion* became a monthly, and in 1929 it was merged with *The American Boy*. SRG

see also COMICS, PERIODICALS AND MAGAZINES

Youth's Friend, The see AMERICAN SUNDAY SCHOOL UNION

Z

Zelinsky, Paul 1953– Born in Illinois, educated at Yale University and the Tyler School of Art, where he was taught by MAURICE SENDAK, Zelinsky is an illustrator of many award-winning books. His *Hansel & Gretel* (1984) and *Rumpelstiltskin* (1986), both Caldecott Honour Books, are illustrated with rich, romantic and traditional paintings, but he also experiments with very original, cleverly designed PICTUREBOOKS, varying his medium to suit the text. He has line-illustrated BEVERLY CLEARY'S *Ralph S. Mouse* (1982) and *Dear Mr. Henshaw* (1983). In 1998 he won the CALDECOTT MEDAL for *Rapunzel*. JAG

Zemach, Margot 1931–89 American writer and illustrator called 'a national treasure' by one critic. In 1980 she was a nominee for the HANS CHRISTIAN ANDERSEN AWARD. She received the CALDECOTT MEDAL for *Duffy and the Devil: A Cornish Tale* (1974). Her Yiddish FOLKTALE *It Could Always Be Worse* was a Caldecott Honour Book in 1978. Zemach's ILLUSTRATIONS are full of movement and action. She described her creative process as follows: 'When there is a story I want to tell in pictures, I find my actors, build the sets, design the costumes and light the stage . . . If I can get it all together and moving, it will come to life.' BG

Zephaniah, Benjamin 1958– Poet and dramatist born in Birmingham, England, and raised in Jamaica. He has produced two collections of poetry for younger readers, *Talking Turkeys* (1994) and *Funky Chickens* (1996), after previously publishing poems and plays for adults. These rap poems are written for performance, and Zephaniah has established a reputation as a mesmerising performance poet on stage. On the page the poems are presented in a wildly inventive typographical and pictorial style which tries to capture visually some of the energy of his performances ('According to my Mood'). Serious causes (the environment, veganism) are championed through the zany humour. ML

Zindel, Paul 1936– A prolific, award-winning American novelist of YOUNG ADULT FICTION. After winning the Pulitzer Prize for his play *The Effect of Gamma Rays on Man-in-the-Moon Marigolds* (1965), Zindel turned to writing realist juvenile novels – often about life in New York City and its environs – beginning with his first novel, *The Pigman* (1968), a sensitive portrayal of the growing relationship between two teenagers, John Conlan and Lorraine Jensen, and a lonely old man whom they befriend. After the tremendous success of *The Pigman*, which is now considered a classic, Zindel went on to write numerous novels that address the themes he explored in his first novel, including the difficulties of romantic love and the problems associated with being a misfit as a teenager.

His novels are notable for discussing many issues of particular importance to teenagers, such as romance, sexuality, death and alcohol abuse. For instance, in *Pardon Me, You're Stepping on My Eyeball!* (1976), Marsh Mellow and Edna Shinglebok are alienated, isolated teenagers who fall in love after meeting at their school's group-therapy session. Like many of Zindel's characters, Edna and Marsh are tormented by their peers and parents alike, and the two have dysfunctional, non-traditional families. In *The Pigman's Legacy* (1980), Zindel continues to chart the adventures of John and Lorraine as they befriend another old man and recognise their love for each other. In *The Girl Who Wanted a Boy* (1981), Sibella Cametta envies her sister Maureen, who is 'gorgeous, terrific' and has flocks of boys pursuing her. Sibella wants a boyfriend and is willing to do almost anything to get one, even if it means falling in love with a boy whom she does not even know; like many of Zindel's characters, she discovers that the course of true love is a rockier path than she had assumed. In *The Amazing and Death-Defying Diary of Eugene Dingman* (1987), 15-year-old Eugene works as a waiter at a resort in the Adirondack Mountains and learns the difficulties of loving someone who does not return your affection. Eugene must also learn how to deal with a father who has abandoned his family. In *A Begonia for Miss Applebaum* (1989), two teenagers must learn how to handle the terminal illness and death of Miss Applebaum, their former biology teacher. She shows them that death should be accepted as part of life's natural process. In *David and Della* (1993), David, a young teenager with writer's block after his girlfriend tries to commit suicide, falls in love with Della, a young alcoholic who ultimately helps David to get over the pain associated with his girlfriend's suicide attempt.

In these books and others, Zindel shows young people confronting difficult problems and overcoming them; his fiction charts a path through the troubled waters of adolescence. He also has a talent for capturing teenage life in a plausible, realistic fashion, with a good deal of humour, often bitter and satirical. SAI

Zion, (Eu)Gene 1913–75 American author of 13 PICTUREBOOKS illustrated by his wife, Margaret Bloy Graham. Born in New York City, Zion created his most memorable character in *Harry the Dirty Dog* (1956) and three sequels. Whether getting increasingly dirty in his début story, trying to lose an embarrassing sweater in *No Roses for Harry* (1958), or accidentally frightening beachgoers in *Harry by the Sea* (1965), Harry is always rescued by his loving family. Graham's ILLUSTRATIONS play an essential role in making the mischievous black-and-white dog an appealing and enduring picturebook character so that children can relate easily to Harry's predicaments. KKP

Zipes, Jack see CRITICAL APPROACHES TO CHILDREN'S LITERATURE; 'LITTLE RED RIDING HOOD'; CHARLES PERRAULT

Zolotow, Charlotte 1915– Distinguished American author and editor. Born in Norfolk, Virginia, Zolotow studied at the University of Wisconsin before coming to New York. Her first book, *The Park Book* (1944), was published while she was working at Harper as an assistant to children's book editor, URSULA NORDSTROM, her mentor and strongest influence. As Zolotow continued to write books for young children, she assumed more responsibilties as an editor and vice-president, culminating in 1987 with her own Harper imprint, Charlotte Zolotow Books. Most of the subject matter of her books for young children is realistic, with *Mr Rabbit and the Lovely Present* (1963), illustrated by MAURICE SENDAK, a rare piece of FANTASY. Among other well-known titles are *The Storm Book* (1953), *The Hating Book* (1969), *William's Doll* (1972), *My Grandson Lew* (1974), and her two anthologies of stories for young adults: *An Overpraised Season* (1973) and *Early Sorrows* (1986). Her books have been illustrated by a pantheon of artists, such as LEONARD WEISGARD, ROGER DUVOISIN, Sendak, ARNOLD LOBEL and WILLIAM PÈNE DU BOIS. Her more than 70 children's books are distinctive in their perception of childhood emotions and personal relationships, told in humorous and spare prose. AL

Zoo (1992) PICTUREBOOK by the British illustrator ANTHONY BROWNE, returning to the issues raised in the middle section of *GORILLA* concerning the nature and purpose of zoos. The caged hamster in its barren environment depicted on the title page indicates an interest in the wider issue of the treatment and caging of animals. *Zoo* describes a family outing to London Zoo told from the viewpoint of the elder son, but it is in the difference between what the readers are told by the boy and what they are shown by the pictures that the real story is realised. Browne sets up a series of parallels with which to make his point: the children's behaviour reflects events inside the cages and the constant escape from boredom by the human beings is set against the unrelenting boredom of the animals caged in a world of concrete. There is a strong and pointed contrast between the conventional depiction of the family and the almost photographic realism of the animals. The father is odious and his behaviour at the zoo embarrassing. The framing of the pictures acts as a metaphor for freedom: the human activities are enclosed by fine hand-drawn frames while the animals are contained in thick machine-made borders except on the final double spread where night and darkness bring a kind of liberty. AR

Zulu tales see AFRICAN MYTHOLOGY AND FOLKTALES; see also MARGUERITE POLAND

Zwerger, Lisbeth 1954– Austrian artist born in Vienna, where she studied at the College of Applied Art. Since the publication of her first book in 1977, *The Strange Child* by E.T.A. Hoffman, she has illustrated many classic texts, mostly FAIRY TALES and other fantastic stories. Zwerger is an illustrator in the true sense: her work interprets the text closely. Thus, while the influence of illustrators such as ARTHUR RACKHAM, HEATH ROBINSON and EDMUND DULAC is clear, so is the influence of writers like ANDERSEN, DICKENS, Wilde and the BROTHERS GRIMM. Her pictures always capture the atmosphere of a text successfully; for example, the loose, ethereal illustrations for fairy tales such as Clemens Brentano's *The Legend of Rosepetal* (1978) convey their essential strangeness well. There is a distinct evolution from early works such as *Hansel and Gretel* (1979), *The Seven Ravens* (1981) and *The Swineherd* (1982), which clearly reveal her classical influences, to the increasingly surreal pictures she has produced in more recent books, such as *The Wizard of Oz* (1996) (see also OZ SERIES), *Noah's Ark* (1997) and *Alice in Wonderland* (1999). Zwerger has won many AWARDS for her work, the most notable being the HANS CHRISTIAN ANDERSEN MEDAL, awarded for lifetime achievement and contribution to children's literature. MSed

see also CHRISTIAN MORGENSTERN

Appendix: selected literary prizes

Boston Globe-Horn Book Award

Sponsored jointly by *The Boston Globe* and *The Horn Book, Inc.*, this annual award was established in 1967 for excellence in children's or young adult literature. In early years, the categories were text and illustration; they later became fiction and picturebooks, and a non-fiction category was added in 1976.

Winners:

1967	Text: Erik Christian Haugaard, *The Little Fishes* Illustration: PETER SPIER, *London Bridge is Falling Down!*
1968	Text: John Lawson, *The Spring Rider* Illustration: Arlene Mosel, *Tikki Tikki Tembo*, illustrated by BLAIR LENT
1969	Text: URSULA LE GUIN, *A Wizard of Earthsea* Illustration: JOHN S. GOODALL, *The Adventures of Paddy Pork*
1970	Text: JOHN ROWE TOWNSEND, *The Intruder* Illustration: EZRA JACK KEATS, *Hi, Cat!*
1971	Text: ELEANOR CAMERON, *A Room Made of Windows* Illustration: Kazue Mizumura, *If I Built a Village*
1972	Text: ROSEMARY SUTCLIFF, *Tristan and Iseult* Illustration: JOHN BURNINGHAM, *MR. GUMPY'S OUTING*
1973	Text: SUSAN COOPER, *The Dark is Rising* Illustration: TRINA SCHART HYMAN, *King Stork*
1974	Text: VIRGINIA HAMILTON, *M.C. Higgins, the Great* Illustration: MURIEL FEELINGS, *Jambo Means Hello*, illustrated by TOM FEELINGS
1975	Text: T. Degens, *Transport 7-41-R* Illustration: MITSUMASO ANNO, *Anno's Alphabet*
1976	Fiction: JILL PATON WALSH, *Unleaving* Non-fiction: Alfred Tamarin and Shirley Glubok, *Voyaging to Cathay: Americans in the China Trade* Illustration: Remy Charlip and Jerry Joyner, *Thirteen*
1977	Fiction: LAURENCE YEP, *Child of the Owl* Non-fiction: PETER DICKINSON, *Chance, Luck and Destiny* Illustration: Wallace Tripp, *Granfa Grig Had a Pig and Other Rhymes Without Reason from Mother Goose*
1978	Fiction: ELLEN RASKIN, *The Westing Game* Non-fiction: Ilse Koehn, *Mischling, Second Degree: My Childhood in Nazi Germany* Illustration: MITSUMASO ANNO, *Anno's Journey*
1979	Fiction: SID FLEISCHMAN, *Humbug Mountain* Non-fiction: David Kherdian, *The Road From Home: The Story of an Armenian Girl* Illustration: RAYMOND BRIGGS, *THE SNOWMAN*

1980 Fiction: ANDREW DAVIES, *Conrad's War*
Non-fiction: Mario Salvadori, *Building: The Fight Against Gravity*
Illustration: CHRIS VAN ALLSBERG, *The Garden of Abdul Gasazi*

1981 Fiction: Lynn Hall, *The Leaving*
Non-fiction: KATHRYN LASKY, *The Weaver's Gift*
Illustration: MAURICE SENDAK, *OUTSIDE OVER THERE*

1982 Fiction: RUTH PARK, *PLAYING BEATIE BOW*
Non-fiction: Aranka Siegal, *Upon the Head of the Goat: A Childhood in Hungary 1939–1944*
Illustration: NANCY WILLARD, *A Visit to William Blake's Inn: Poems for Innocent and Experienced Travelers*, illustrated by ALICE AND MARTIN PROVENSEN

1983 Fiction: VIRGINIA HAMILTON, *Sweet Whispers, Brother Rush*
Non-fiction: Daniel S. Davis, *Behind Barbed Wire: The Imprisonment of Japanese Americans During World War II*
Illustration: VERA B. WILLIAMS, *A Chair for My Mother*

1984 Fiction: PATRICIA WRIGHTSON, *A Little Fear*
Nonfiction: JEAN FRITZ, *The Double Life of Pocahontas*
Illustration: WARWICK HUTTON, *Jonah and the Great Fish*

1985 Fiction: Bruce Brooks, *The Moves Make the Man*
Non-fiction: Rhoda Blumberg, *Commodore Perry in the Land of the Shogun*
Illustration: Thatcher Hurd, *Mama Don't Allow*

1986 Fiction: ZIBBY ONEAL, *In Summer Light*
Non-fiction: Peggy Thomson, *Auks, Rocks and the Odd Dinosaur: Inside Stories from the Smithsonian's Museum of Natural History*
Illustration: MOLLY BANG, *The Paper Crane*

1987 Fiction: LOIS LOWRY, *Rabble Starkey*
Non-fiction: Marcia Sewall, *Pilgrims of Plimoth*
Picturebook: JOHN STEPTOE, *Mufaro's Beautiful Daughters: An African Tale*

1988 Fiction: MILDRED TAYLOR, *The Friendship*, illustrated by Max Ginsburg
Nonfiction: VIRGINIA HAMILTON, *Anthony Burns: The Defeat and Triumph of a Fugitive Slave*
Picturebook: Dianne Snyder, *The Boy of the Three-Year Nap*, illustrated by Allen Say

1989 Fiction: PAULA FOX, *The Village by the Sea*
Non-fiction: DAVID MACAULAY, *The Way Things Work*
Picturebook: ROSEMARY WELLS, *Shy Charles*

1990 Fiction: JERRY SPINELLI, *Maniac Magee*
Non-fiction: JEAN FRITZ, *The Great Little Madison*
Picturebook: Ed Young, *Lon Po Po: A Red Riding Hood Story from China*

1991 Fiction: AVI, *The True Confessions of Charlotte Doyle*
Non-fiction: Cynthia Rylant, *Appalachia: The Voices of Sleeping Birds*, illustrated by Barry Moser
Picturebook: KATHERINE PATERSON, *The Tale of the Mandarin Ducks*, illustrated by LEO AND DIANE DILLON

1992 Fiction: Cynthia Rylant, *Missing May*
Non-fiction: Pat Cummings, *Talking with Artists*
Picturebook: Ed Young, *Seven Blind Mice*

1993 Fiction: JAMES BERRY, *Ajeemah and His Son*

	Non-fiction: Patricia C. and Frederick McKissack, *Sojourner truth: Ain't I a Woman?*
	Picturebook: LLOYD ALEXANDER, *The Fortune Tellers*, illustrated by TRINA SCHART HYMAN
1994	Fiction: Vera B. Williams, *Scooter*
	Non-fiction: RUSSELL FREEDMAN, *Eleanor Roosevelt: A Life of Discovery*
	Picturebook: ALLEN SAY, *Grandfather's Journey*
1995	Fiction: TIM WYNNE-JONES, *Some of the Kinder Planets*
	Non-fiction: Natalie S. Bober, *Abigail Adams: Witness to a Revolution*
	Picturebook: JULIUS LESTER, *John Henry*, illustrated by JERRY PINKNEY
1996	Fiction: AVI, *Poppy*
	Non-fiction: Andrea Warren, *Orphan Train Rider: One Boy's True Story*
	Picturebook: Amy Hest, *In the Rain with Baby Duck*, illustrated by Jill Barton
1997	Fiction: Kazumi Yumoto, *The Friends*
	Non-fiction: Walter Wick, *A Drop of Water: A Book of Science and Wonder*
	Picturebook: BRIAN PINKNEY, *The Adventures of Sparrowboy*
1998	Fiction: Francisco Jiménez, *The Circuit: Stories from the Life of a Migrant Child*
	Non-fiction: Leon Walter Tillage, *Leon's Story*
	Picturebook: Kate Banks, *And if the Moon Could Talk*, illustrated by Georg Hallensleben
1999	Fiction: Louis Sachar, *HOLES*
	Non-fiction: Steve Jenkins, *The Top of the World: Climbing Mount Everest*
	Picturebook: JOY COWLEY: *Red-Eyed Tree Frog*, illustrated by Nic Bishop
2000	Fiction: Franny Billingsley, *The Folk Keeper*
	Non-fiction: Marc Aronson, *Sir Walter Ralegh and the Quest for Eldorado*
	Picturebook: D. B. Johnson, *Henry Hikes to Fitchburg*

Caldecott Medal

An award presented annually by the American Library Association to the illustrator of the most distinguished American picturebook for children published in the United States in the preceding year. The recipient must be a citizen or resident of the United States. The award was established in 1938.

1938	DOROTHY P. LATHROP, *Animals of the Bible*
1939	Thomas Handforth, *Mei Li*
1940	INGRI AND EDGAR PARIN D'AULAIRE, *Abraham Lincoln*
1941	ROBERT LAWSON, *They Were Strong and Good*
1942	ROBERT MCCLOSKEY, *Make Way for Ducklings*
1943	VIRGINIA LEE BURTON, *The Little House*
1944	LOUIS SLOBODKIN, *Many Moons* (Text: JAMES THURBER)
1945	Elizabeth Orton Jones, *Prayer for a Child* (Text: RACHEL FIELD)
1946	Maud and Miska Petersham, *The Rooster Crows*

1947 LEONARD WEISGARD, *The Little Island*
1948 ROGER DUVOISIN, *White Snow, Bright Snow* (Text: ALVIN TRESSELT)
1949 BERTA AND ELMER HADER, *The Big Snow*
1950 LEO POLITI, *Song of the Swallows*
1951 Katherine Milhouse, *The Egg Tree*
1952 Nicolas Mordvinoff, *Finders Keepers* (Text: William Lipkind)
1953 LYND K. WARD, *The Biggest Bear*
1954 Ludwig Bemelmans, *Madeline's Rescue* (see MADELINE SERIES)
1955 MARCIA BROWN, *Cinderella, or The Little Glass Slipper* (Text: CHARLES PERRAULT trans. by Marcia Brown)
1956 FEODOR ROJANKOVSKY, *Frog Went A-Courtin'* (Text: John Langstaff)
1957 MARC SIMONT, *A Tree is Nice* (Text: Janice May Udry)
1958 ROBERT MCCLOSKEY, *Time of Wonder*
1959 BARBARA COONEY, *Chanticleer and the Fox* (Text: adapted from GEOFFREY CHAUCER)
1960 MARIE HALL ETS, *Nine Days to Christmas* (Text: Marie Hall Ets and Aurora Labastida)
1961 Nicolas Sidjakov, *Baboushka and the Three Kings* (Text: Ruth Robbins)
1962 MARCIA BROWN, *Once a Mouse*
1963 EZRA JACK KEATS, *The Snowy Day*
1964 MAURICE SENDAK, *WHERE THE WILD THINGS ARE*
1965 BENI MONTRESOR, *May I Bring a Friend?* (Text: BEATRICE SCHENK DE REGNIERS)
1966 NONNY HOGROGIAN, *Always Room for One More* (Text: SORCHE NIC LEODHAS)
1967 EVALINE NESS, *Sam, Bangs & Moonshine*
1968 ED EMBERLEY, *Drummer Hoff* (Text: Barbara Emberley)
1969 URI SHULEVITZ, *The Fool of the World and the Flying Ship* (Text: ARTHUR RANSOME)
1970 WILLIAM STEIG, *Sylvester and the Magic Pebble*
1971 GAIL E. HALEY, *A Story A Story*
1972 NONNY HOGROGIAN, *One Fine Day*
1973 BLAIR LENT, *The Funny Little Woman* (Text: Arlene Mosel)
1974 MARGOT ZEMACH, *Duffy and the Devil* (Text: Harve Zemach)
1975 GERALD MCDERMOTT, *Arrow to the Sun: A Pueblo Indian Tale*
1976 LEO AND DIANE DILLON, *Why Mosquitoes Buzz in People's Ears: A West African Tale* (Text: VERNA AARDEMA)
1977 LEO AND DIANE DILLON, *Ashanti to Zulu: African Traditions* (Text: Margaret Musgrove)
1978 PETER SPIER, *Noah's Ark*
1979 PAUL GOBLE, *The Girl Who Loved Wild Horses*
1980 BARBARA COONEY, *Ox-Cart Man* (Text: DONALD HALL)
1981 ARNOLD LOBEL, *Fables*
1982 CHRIS VAN ALLSBURG, *Jumanji*
1983 MARCIA BROWN, *Shadow* (Text: Blaise Cendrars)
1984 ALICE AND MARTIN PROVENSEN, *The Glorious Flight: Across the Channel with Louis Blériot*
1985 TRINA SCHART HYMAN, *Saint George and the Dragon* (Text: MARGARET HODGES)
1986 CHRIS VAN ALLSBURG, *The Polar Express*

1987	RICHARD EGIELSKI, *Hey, Al* (Text: Arthur Yorinks)
1988	JOHN SCHOENHERR, *Owl Moon* (Text: JANE YOLEN)
1989	STEPHEN GAMMELL, *Song and Dance Man* (Text: Karen Ackerman)
1990	ED YOUNG, *Lon Po Po: A Red-Riding Hood Story from China*
1991	DAVID MACAULAY, *Black and White*
1992	DAVID WIESNER, *Tuesday*
1993	EMILY ARNOLD MCCULLY, *Mirette on the High Wire*
1994	ALLEN SAY, *Grandfather's Journey* (Text: edited by Walter Lorraine)
1995	David Diaz, *Smoky Night* (Text: EVE BUNTING)
1996	PEGGY RATHMANN, *Officer Buckle and Gloria*
1997	David Wisniewski, *Golem*
1998	PAUL ZELINSKY, *Rapunzel*
1999	Mary Azarian, *Snowflake Bentley* (Text: Jacqueline Briggs Martin)
2000	Simms Taback, *Joseph Had a Little Overcoat*
2001	David Small, *So You Want to Be President* (Text: JUDITH ST GEORGE)

Canadian Library Association Book of the Year for Children

A medal presented annually to the author of the best children's book published in Canada. The award was established in 1947. The author must be a citizen or resident of Canada. (In some years, no award was made.)

1947	RODERICK HAIG-BROWN, *Starbuck Valley Winter*
1948	Mabel Dunham, *Kristli's Trees*
1950	Richard S. Lambert, *Franklin of the Arctic*
1952	Catherine Anthony Clark, *The Sun Horse*
1956	Louise Riley, *Train for Tiger Lily*
1957	Cyrus Macmillan, *Glooskap's Country and Other Indian Tales*
1958	FARLEY MOWAT, *Lost in the Barrens*
1959	JOHN F. HAYES, *The Dangerous Cove*
1960	Maruis Barbeau and Michael Hornyansky, *The Golden Phoenix and Other Fairy Tales from Quebec*
1961	William Toye, *The St. Lawrence*
1963	Sheila Burnford, THE INCREDIBLE JOURNEY
1964	RODERICK HAIG-BROWN, *The Whale People*
1965	Dorothy M. Reid, *Tales of Nanabozho*
1966	James McNeill, *The Double Knights: More Tales from Round the World* and JAMES HOUSTON, *Tikta' liktak: an Eskimo Legend*
1967	CHRISTIE HARRIS, *Raven's Cry*
1968	JAMES HOUSTON, *The White Archer: an Eskimo Legend*
1969	Kay Hill, *And Tomorrow the Stars*
1970	Edith Fowke, *Sally Go Round the Sun*
1971	William Toye, *Cartier Discovers the St. Lawrence*
1972	Ann Blades, *Mary of Mile 18*
1973	RUTH NICHOLS, *The Marrow of the World*
1974	ELIZABETH CLEAVER, *The Miraculous Hind*
1975	Dennis Lee, *Alligator Pie*
1976	MORDECAI RICHLER, *Jacob Two-Two Meets the Hooded Fang*
1977	CHRISTIE HARRIS, *Mouse Woman and the Vanished Princesses*
1978	DENNIS LEE, *Garbage Delight*
1979	KEVIN MAJOR, *Hold Fast*

1980 JAMES HOUSTON, *River Runners*
1981 DONN KUSHNER, *The Violin-Maker's Gift*
1982 JANET LUNN, *The Root Cellar*
1983 BRIAN DOYLE, *Up to Low*
1984 Jan Hudson, *Sweetgrass*
1985 JEAN LITTLE, *Mama's Going to Buy You a Mockingbird*
1986 CORA TAYLOR, *Julie*
1987 JANET LUNN, *Shadow in Hawthorn Bay*
1988 KIT PEARSON, *A Handful of Time*
1989 BRIAN DOYLE, *Easy Avenue*
1990 KIT PEARSON, *The Sky is Falling*
1991 MICHAEL BEDARD, *Redwork*
1992 KEVIN MAJOR, *Eating Between the Lines*
1993 Celia Barker Lottridge, *Ticket to Curlew*
1994 TIM WYNNE-JONES, *Some of the Kinder Planets*
1995 CORA TAYLOR, *Summer of the Mad Monk*
1996 Maxine Trottier, *The Tiny Kite of Eddie Wing*
1997 BRIAN DOYLE, *Uncle Ronald*
1998 Kenneth Oppel, *Silverwing*
1999 TIM WYNNE-JONES, *Stephen Fair*
2000 Kenneth Oppel, *Sunwing*

Carnegie Medal

An award presented annually by the Library Association of Great Britain for an outstanding book published in the previous year in the United Kingdom. The award was first made in 1937. Restricted to British writers until 1969, it has subsequently been awarded for any book written in English and published first, or concurrently, in the United Kingdom.

1936 ARTHUR RANSOME, *Pigeon Post*
1937 EVE GARNETT, *The Family from One End Street*
1938 NOEL STREATFEILD, *The Circus is Coming*
1939 Eleanor Doorly, *The Radium Woman*
1940 KITTY BARNE, *Visitors from London*
1941 Mary Treadgold, *WE COULDN'T LEAVE DINAH*
1942 BB [Denys Watkins-Pitchford], *THE LITTLE GREY MEN*
1943 no award
1944 ERIC LINKLATER, *The Wind on the Moon*
1945 no award
1946 ELIZABETH GOUDGE, *The Little White Horse*
1947 WALTER DE LA MARE, *Collected Stories for Children*
1948 Richard Armstrong, *Sea Change*
1949 Agnes Allen, *The Story of Your Home*
1950 ELFRIDA VIPONT, *The Lark on the Wing*
1951 CYNTHIA HARNETT, *The Wool-Pack*
1952 MARY NORTON, *THE BORROWERS*
1953 Edward Osmond, *A Valley Grows Up*
1954 RONALD WELCH, *Knight Crusader*
1955 ELEANOR FARJEON, *The Little Bookroom*
1956 C.S. LEWIS, *The Last Battle*
1957 WILLIAM MAYNE, *A Grass Rope*
1958 PHILIPPA PEARCE, *Tom's Midnight Garden*
1959 ROSEMARY SUTCLIFF, *The Lantern Bearers*

1960 I.W. Cornwall, *The Making of Man*
1961 LUCY BOSTON, *A Stranger at Green Knowe*
1962 PAULINE CLARKE, *The Twelve and the Genii*
1963 HESTER BURTON, *Time of Trial*
1964 Sheena Porter, *Nordy Bank*
1965 Philip Turner, *The Grange at High Force*
1966 no award
1967 ALAN GARNER, *THE OWL SERVICE*
1968 Rosemary Harris, *The Moon in the Cloud*
1969 K. M. PEYTON, *The Edge of the Cloud*
1970 LEON GARFIELD and EDWARD BLISHEN, *THE GOD BENEATH THE SEA*
1971 IVAN SOUTHALL, *Josh*
1972 Richard Adams, *WATERSHIP DOWN*
1973 PENELOPE LIVELY, *The Ghost of Thomas Kempe*
1974 MOLLIE HUNTER, *The Stronghold*
1975 ROBERT WESTALL, *THE MACHINE-GUNNERS*
1976 JAN MARK, *Thunder and Lightnings*
1977 GENE KEMP, *The Turbulent Term of Tyke Tiler*
1978 DAVID REES, *The Exeter Blitz*
1979 PETER DICKINSON, *Tulku*
1980 PETER DICKINSON, *City of Gold*
1981 ROBERT WESTALL, *The Scarecrows*
1982 MARGARET MAHY, *THE HAUNTING*
1983 JAN MARK, *Handles*
1984 MARGARET MAHY, *The Changeover*
1985 KEVIN CROSSLEY-HOLLAND, *Storm*
1986 BERLIE DOHERTY, *Granny Was a Buffer Girl*
1987 SUSAN PRICE, *The Ghost Drum*
1988 GERALDINE MCCAUGHREAN, *A Pack of Lies*
1989 ANNE FINE, *GOGGLE-EYES*
1990 GILLIAN CROSS, *Wolf*
1991 BERLIE DOHERTY, *Dear Nobody*
1992 ANNE FINE, *Flour Babies*
1993 ROBERT SWINDELLS, *STONE COLD*
1994 THERESA BRESLIN, *Whispers in the Graveyard*
1995 PHILIP PULLMAN, *NORTHERN LIGHTS* (see *HIS DARK MATERIALS*)
1996 MELVIN BURGESS, *Junk*
1997 Tim Bowler, *River Boy*
1998 David Almond, *SKELLIG*
1999 AIDAN CHAMBERS, *Postcards from No Man's Land*

CBI/Bisto Book Award

The Bisto Book of the Decade Award, given to TOM MCCAUGHREN in 1990, led to the establishment of an annual award made by CHILDREN'S BOOKS IRELAND for books by an author or illustrator born or resident in Ireland.

1990–1 EILÍS DILLON *The Island of Ghosts*
1991–2 JOHN QUINN *The Summer of Lily and Esme*
1992–3 MARITA CONLON-MCKENNA *The Blue Horse*
1993–4 JANE MITCHELL *When Stars Stop Spinning*

1994–5 Elizabeth O'Hara *Blaeberry Sunday*
1995–6 P. J. LYNCH (illus) *The Christmas Miracle of Jonathan Toomey*
1996–7 SIOBHÁN PARKINSON *Sisters . . . No Way!*
1997–8 Gerard Whelan *Dream Invader*
1998–9 Niamh Sharkey (illus) *Tales of Wisdom and Wonder*
1999–2000 MARILYN TAYLOR *Faraway Home*

Other awards:

1990–1 Best emerging author: MORGAN LLYWELYN for *Brian Boru*
Book for young readers: *Grandma's Bill* by MARTIN WADDELL
Illustration: P. J. LYNCH for *Fairy Tales of Ireland* by W. B. Yeats
1991–2 Historical Fiction: *Wildflower Girl* by MARITA CONLON-MCKENNA
Picturebook: *THE SLEEPING GIANT* by Marie-Louise Fitzpatrick
First children's novel: *The Secret of the Ruby Ring* by Yvonne MacGrory
1992–3 Information Book: *Tamall Sa Chistin* by Mairin Uí Chomain, illustrated by Deiri and Bébhinn Ó Meadhra
Teenage Fiction: *Put a Saddle on the Pig* by SAM MCBRATNEY
Historical Fiction: *Strongbow* by MORGAN LLYWELYN

From 1993 awards were no longer made in categories and were replaced by the Bisto Merit Awards:
1993–4 *The Chieftain's Daughter* by SAM MCBRATNEY
The Hiring Fair by Elizabeth O'Hara
The Pony Express by Máirín Johnston
1994–5 *Goodbye Summer, Goodbye* by Rose Doyle
Catkin illustrated by P. J. LYNCH
Ecstasy agus Scéalta Eile by Ré Ó Laighléis
1995–6 *Hannah or Pink Balloons* by Mary Beckett
Sceoin Sa Bhoireann by Ré Ó Laighléis
Lockie and Dadge by Frank Murphy
1996–7 *An Eala Dubh* by Cliodna Cussen and Cormac Ó Snodaigh
The Guns of Easter by Gerard Whelan
The Lantern Moon by MAEVE FRIEL
1997–8 *Four Kids, Three Cats, Two Cows, One Witch (maybe)* by SIOBHÁN PARKINSON
The Hungry Wind by Soinbhe Lally
When Jessie Comes Across the Sea illustrated by P. J. LYNCH
1998–9 *An Rógaire agus a Scáil* by Gabriel Rosenstock, illustrated by Piet Sluis
The Long March by Marie-Louise Fitzpatrick
The Moon King by SIOBHÁN PARKINSON
1999–2000 *Siúlóid Bhreá* by Mary Arrigan
Fierce Milly by Marilyn McLaughlin
Silent Stone by MARK O'SULLIVAN

From 1994 an additional award, the Eilís Dillon Award, was presented to the author of an outstanding first book for children:
1994–5 Mark O'Sullivan for *Melody for Nora*
1995–6 Frank Murphy for *Lockie and Dadge*
1996–7 Gerard Whelan for *The Guns of Easter*
1997–8 Ed Miliano for *It's a Jungle Out There*

1998–9 Caitríona Hastings for *Dea-Scéala*
1999–2000 Marilyn McLaughlin for *Fierce Milly*

Children's Book Award

The first award in the UK to take seriously the views of young readers. This annual prize for the best book of the year judged by children was originated in 1980 by the former Chair of the Federation of Children's Book Groups, Pat Thomson, and is currently administered by the Federation. Titles are submitted by publishers to be judged by thousands of children in 12 testing areas in the UK.

1981 *Mister Magnolia* by QUENTIN BLAKE
1982 *Fair's Fair* by LEON GARFIELD and Margaret Chamberlain
1983 *THE BFG* by ROALD DAHL
1984 *The Saga of Eric the Viking* by TERRY JONES and MICHAEL FOREMAN
1985 *Brother in the Land* by ROBERT SWINDELLS
1986 *Arthur* by Amanda Graham and Donna Gynell
1987 THE JOLLY POSTMAN by JANET and ALLAN AHLBERG
1988 *Winnie the Witch* by Valerie Thomas and KORKY PAUL
1989 *MATILDA* by ROALD DAHL
1990 *Room 13* by ROBERT SWINDELLS
1991 *Threadbear* by MICK INKPEN

After 1991, the Award was split into three categories – picturebooks, shorter novels and longer novels, with an overall winner (identified by an asterisk):

1992 *Shhh!* by Sally Grindley and Peter Utton
Find the White Horse by DICK KING-SMITH
**Kiss the Dust* by ELIZABETH LAIRD

1993 *Snowy* by BERLIE DOHERTY
**The Suitcase Kid* by JACQUELINE WILSON
Gulf by ROBERT WESTALL

1994 *Amazing Anthony Ant* by Lorna and Graham Philpot
The Finders by NIGEL HINTON
**The Boy in the Bubble* by IAN STRACHAN

1995 *The Rascally Cake* by Jeanne Willis and KORKY PAUL
**Harriet's Hare* by DICK KING-SMITH
Walk Two Moons by SHARON CREECH

1996 *Solo* by Paul Geraghty
**Double Act* by JACQUELINE WILSON
Wreck of the Zanzibar by MICHAEL MORPURGO

1997 *Mr. Bear to the Rescue* by Debi Gliori
**The Hundred-Mile-an-Hour Dog* by JEREMY STRONG
Which Way is Home? by IAN STRACHAN

1998 *The Lion Who Wanted to Love* by Giles Andreae and David Wojtowycz
Nightmare Stairs by ROBERT SWINDELLS
**Harry Potter and the Philosopher's Stone* by J. K. Rowling [see HARRY POTTER SERIES]

1999 *What!* by Kate Lum and Adrian Johnson
Little Dad by Pat Moon and NICK SHARRATT
**Harry Potter and the Chamber of Secrets* by J. K. Rowling [see HARRY POTTER SERIES]

2000 *Demon Teddy* by NICHOLAS ALLAN
Kensuke's Kingdom by MICHAEL MORPURGO
Harry Potter and the Prisoner of Azkaban by J. K. Rowling [see HARRY POTTER SERIES]

Children's Book Council of Australia Book of the Year Award

Presented annually by the Children's Book Council of Australia for a book written by an Australian, or a resident of Australia. The award is made for different categories.

Older readers category:

1946 LESLIE REES, *The Story of Karrawingi, the Emu*
1948 Frank Hurley, *Shackleton's Argonauts*
1950 Alan Villiers, *Whalers of the Midnight Sun*
1951 Ruth Williams, *Verity of Sydney Town*
1952 Eve Pownall, *The Australia Book*
1953 J.H. and W.D. Martin, *Aircraft of Today and Tomorrow* and Joan Phipson, *Good Luck to the Rider*
1954 K.L. Parker, *Australian Legendary Tales*
1955 H.A. Lindsay and N.B. Tindale, *The First Walkabout*
1956 PATRICIA WRIGHTSON, *The Crooked Snake*
1957 Enid Moore-Heddle, *The Boomerang Book of Legendary Tales*
1958 NAN CHAUNCY, *Tiger in the Bush*
1959 NAN CHAUNCY, *Devil's Hill* and John Gunn, *Sea Menace*
1960 KYLIE TENNANT, *All the Proud Tribesmen*
1961 NAN CHAUNCY, *Tangara*
1962 H.L. Evers, *THE RACKETTY STREET GANG* and Joan Woodberry, *Rafferty Rides a Winner*
1963 JOAN PHIPSON, *The Family Conspiracy*
1964 ELEANOR SPENCE, *The Green Laurel*
1965 HESBA F. BRINSMEAD, *Pastures of the Blue Crane*
1966 IVAN SOUTHALL, *Ash Road*
1967 MAVIS THORPE CLARK, *The Min Min*
1968 IVAN SOUTHALL, *To the Wild Sky*
1969 Balderson, Margaret, *When Jays Fly to Barbmo*
1970 ANNETTE MACARTHUR-ONSLOW, *Uhu*
1971 IVAN SOUTHALL, *Bread and Honey*
1972 HESBA F. BRINSMEAD, *Longtime Passing*
1973 Noreen Shelly, *Family at the Lookout*
1974 PATRICIA WRIGHTSON, *The Nargun and the Stars*
1975 no award
1976 IVAN SOUTHALL, *Fly West*
1977 ELEANOR SPENCE, *The October Child*
1978 PATRICIA WRIGHTSON, *The Ice is Coming*
1979 Ruth Manley, *The Plum-Rain Scroll*
1980 Lee Harding, *Displaced Person*
1981 RUTH PARK, *PLAYING BEATIE BOW*
1982 COLIN THIELE, *The Valley Between*
1983 VICTOR KELLEHER, *Master of the Grove*
1984 PATRICIA WRIGHTSON, *A Little Fear*
1985 JAMES ALDRIDGE, *The True Story of Lilli Stubeck*
1986 THURLEY FOWLER, *The Green Wind*
1987 SIMON FRENCH, *All We Know*

1988 John Marsden, So Much to Tell You
1989 Gillian Rubinstein, *Beyond the Labyrinth*
1990 Robin Klein, Came Back to Show You I Could Fly
1991 Gary Crew, *Strange Objects*
1992 Eleanor Nilsson, *The House Guest*
1993 Melina Marchetta, Looking for Alibrandi
1994 Isobelle Carmody, *The Gathering* and Gary Crew, *Angel's Gate*
1995 Gillian Rubinstein, Foxspell
1996 Catherine Jinks, *Pagan's Vows* (see Pagan series)
1997 James Moloney, *A Bridge to Wiseman's Cove*
1998 Catherine Jinks, *Eye to Eye*
1999 Phillip Gwynne, *Deadly, Unna?*
2000 Nick Earls, *48 Shades of Brown*

Eve Pownall Award for Information Books:

1993 Gracie Greene and Joe Tramacci, *Tjarany Roughtail: The Dreaming of the Roughtail Lizard and Other Stories Told by the Kukatja*, illustrated by Lucille Gill
1994 Patricia Mullins, *V is for Vanishing: An Alphabet of Endangered Animals*
1995 Robin E. Stewart, *New Faces: The Complete Book of Alternative Pets*
1996 John Nicholson, *The First Fleet: a New Beginning in an Old Land*
1997 Gordon Cheers and Julie Silk, *Killer Plants*, illustrated by Margaret Crosby-Fairall
1998 John Nicholson, *A Home Among the Gum Trees*
1999 Yvonne Edwards and Brenda Day, *Going for Kalta*
2000 John Nicholson, *Fishing For Islands: Traditional Boats and Seafarers of the Pacific*

Younger readers category:

1982 Christobel Mattingley, *Rummage*, illustrated by Patricia Mullins
1983 Robin Klein, *Thing*, illustrated by Alison Lester
1984 Max Dann, *Bernice Knows Best*, illustrated by Ann James
1985 Emily Rodda, *Something Special*, illustrated by Noela Young
1986 Mary Steele, *Arkwright*
1987 Emily Rodda, *Pigs Might Fly*, illustrated by Noela Young
1988 Nadia Wheatley, *My Place*, illustrated by Donna Rawlins
1989 Emily Rodda, *The Best-Kept Secret*
1990 Jeanie Adams, *Pigs and Honey*
1991 Emily Rodda, *Finders Keepers*
1992 Anna Fienberg, *The Magnificent Nose, and Other Marvels*, illustrated by Kim Gamble
1993 Garry Disher, *The Bamboo Flute*
1994 Emily Rodda, *Rowan of Rin*
1995 Wendy Orr, *Ark in the Park*, illustrated by Kerry Millard
1996 James Moloney, *Swashbuckler*
1997 Libby Gleeson, *Hannah Plus One*, illustrated by Ann James
1998 Elaine Forrestal, *Someone Like Me*
1999 Meme McDonald and Boori Pryor, *My Girragundji*
2000 Jackie French, *Hitler's Daughter*

Picture Book of the Year award (in some years, no award was made):

1956 Sheila Hawkins, *Wish and the Magic Nut* (Text: Peggy Barnard)
1958 Axel Poignant, *Piccaninny Walkabout*
1965 Elisabeth MacIntyre, *Hugh's Zoo*
1969 TED GREENWOOD, *Sly Old Wardrobe* (Text: IVAN SOUTHALL)
1971 Desmond Digby, WALTZING MATILDA (Text: A.B. PATERSON)
1974 RON BROOKS, *The Bunyip of Berkeley's Creek* (Text: JENNY WAGNER)
1975 QUENTIN HOLE, *The Man from Ironbark* (Text: A.B. PATERSON)
1976 Dick Roughsey, *The Rainbow Serpent*
1978 RON BROOKS, JOHN BROWN, ROSE AND THE MIDNIGHT CAT (Text: JENNY WAGNER)
1979 PERCY TREZISE and Dick Roughsey, *The Quinkins*
1980 PETER PAVEY, *One Dragon's Dream*
1982 JAN ORMEROD, SUNSHINE
1983 PAMELA ALLEN, *Who Sank the Boat?*
1984 PAMELA ALLEN *Bertie and the Bear*
1986 TERRY DENTON, *Felix & Alexander*
1987 JUNKO MORIMOTO, *Kojuro and the Bears* (adapted by Helen Smith)
1988 BOB GRAHAM, *Crusher is Coming*
1989 JANE TANNER, *Drac and the Gremlin* (Text: ALLAN BAILLIE)
1990 JULIE VIVAS, THE VERY BEST OF FRIENDS (Text: MARGARET WILD)
1991 BOB GRAHAM, *Greetings from Sandy Beach*
1992 JEANNIE BAKER, *Window*
1993 BOB GRAHAM, *Rose Meets Mr. Wintergarten*
1994 PETER GOULDTHORPE, *First Light* (Text: GARY CREW)
1995 STEVEN WOOLMAN, THE WATERTOWER (Text: GARY CREW)
1996 NARELLE OLIVER, *The Hunt*
1997 ELIZABETH HONEY, *Not a Nibble*
1998 JUNKO MORIMOTO, *The Two Bullies*
1999 SHAUN TAN, *The Rabbits* (Text: JOHN MARSDEN)
2000 LIBBY GLEESON and ANN JAMES, *Hannah and the Tomorrow Room*

Coretta Scott King Award

An award presented by the ALA to commemorate the life and work of the late Dr Martin Luther King and to honour Mrs Coretta Scott King for her courage and determination in continuing to work for peace and world brotherhood. The award is presented annually to an African American author and – from 1979 – an African American illustrator for an outstandingly inspirational and educational contribution.

1970 Lillie Patterson, *Martin Luther King, Jr.: Man of Peace*
1971 CHARLEMAE H. ROLLINS, *Black Troubador: Langston Hughes*
1972 Elton C. Fax, *Seventeen Black Artists*
1973 Alfred Duckett, *I Never Had It Made: The Autobiography of Jackie Robinson*
1974 SHARON BELL MATHIS, *Ray Charles* (Illustration: George Ford)
1975 Dorothy Robinson, *The Legend Of Africania* (Illustration: Herbert Temple)

1976 Pearl Baily, *Duey's Tale*
1977 JAMES HASKINS, *The Story Of Stevie Wonder*
1978 ELOISE GREENFIELD, *Africa Dream* (Illustration: Carol Byard)
1979 Author: Ossie Davis, *Escape To Freedom: A Play about Young Frederick Douglass*
Illustration: TOM FEELINGS, *Something On My Mind* (Text: Nikki Grimes)
1980 Author: WALTER DEAN MYERS, *The Young Landlords*
Illustration: Carole Byard, *Cornrows* (Text: Camille Yarbrough)
1981 Author: Sidney Poitier, *This Life*
Illustration: ASHLEY BRYAN, *Beat The Story-Drum, Pum-Pum*
1982 Author: MILDRED D. TAYLOR, *Let the Circle Be Unbroken*
Illustration: JOHN STEPTOE, *Mother Crocodile: An Uncle Amadou Tale From Senegal* (text adapted by ROSA GUY)
1983 Author: VIRGINIA HAMILTON, *Sweet Whispers, Brother Rush*
Illustration: Peter Magubane, *Black Child*
1984 Author: LUCILLE CLIFTON, *Everett Anderson's Goodbye*
Illustration: Pat Cummings, *My Mama Needs Me* (Text: Mildred Pitts Walter)
1985 Author: WALTER DEAN MYERS, *Motown and Didi*
Illustration: no award given.
1986 Author: VIRGINA HAMILTON, *The People Could Fly: American Black Folktales*
Illustration: JERRY PINKNEY, *The Patchwork Quilt* (Text: Valerie Flournoy)
1987 Author: MILDRED PITTS WALTER, *Justin and The Best Biscuits In The World*
Illustration: JERRY PINKEY, *Half A Moon And One Whole Star* (Text: CRECENT DRAGONWAGON)
1988 Author: MILDRED D. TAYLOR, *The Friendship*
Illustration: JOHN STEPTOE, *Mufaro's Beautiful Daughters: An African Tale*
1989 Author: WALTER DEAN MYERS, *Fallen Angels*
Illustration: JERRY PINKNEY, *Mirandy And Brother Wind* (Text: PATRICIA MCKISSACK)
1990 Author: PATRICIA and FREDERICK MCKISSACK, *A Long Hard Journey: The Story of the Pullman Porter*
Illustration: JAN SPIVEY GILCHRIST, *Nathaniel Talking* (Text: Eloise Greenfield)
1991 Author: MILDRED D. TAYLOR, *The Road To Memphis*
Illustration: LEO and DIANE DILLON, *Aida* (Text: Leontyne Price)
1992 Author: WALTER DEAN MYERS, *Now Is Your Time! The African-American Struggle for Freedom*
Illustration: FAITH RINGGOLD, *Tar Beach*
1993 Author: PATRICA MCKISSACK, *The Dark Thirty: Southern Tales of the Supernatural*
Illustration: Kathleen Atkins Wilson, *The Origin Of Life on Earth: An African Creation Myth* (Text: David A. Anderson)
1994 Author: Angela Johnson, *Toning the Sweep*
Illustration: TOM FEELINGS, *Soul Looks Back in Wonder*
1995 Author: PATRICIA and FREDERICK MCKISSACK, *Christmas in the Big House, Christmas in the Quarters*

	Illustration: JAMES RANSOME, *The Creation* (Text: James Weldon Johnson)
1996	Author: VIRGINIA HAMILTON, *Her Stories* (Illustrated by LEO AND DIANE DILLON)
	Illustration: TOM FEELINGS, *The Middle Passage: White Ships Black Cargo*
1997	Author: WALTER DEAN MYERS, *Slam!*
	Illustration: JERRY PINKNEY, *Minty: A Story of Young Harriet Tubman* (Text: Alan Schroeder)
1998	Author: Sharon M. Draper, *Forged by Fire*
	Illustration: Javaka Steptoe, *In Daddy's Arms I Am Tall: African Americans Celebrating Fathers* (Text: Alan Schroeder)
1999	Author: Angela Johnson, *Heaven*
	Illustration: Michele Wood, *i see the rhythm* (Text: Toyomi Igus)
2000	Christopher Paul Curtis, *Bud, Not Buddy*
	Illustration: BRIAN PINKNEY, *In the Time of the Drums* (Text: Kim L. Siegelson)
2001	Author: JACQUELINE WOODSON, *Miracle's Boys*
	Illustration: Brian Collier, *Uptown*

Esther Glen Award

An award made by the Library and Information Association of New Zealand Aotearoa, established in 1945, and given for a distinguished contribution to New Zealand literature for children and young adults. (In some years, no award was made.)

1945	Stella Morice, *The Book of Wiremu*
1947	A.W. Reed, *Myths and Legends of Maoriland*
1950	Joan Smith, *The Adventures of Nimble, Rumble and Tumble*
1959	Maurice Duggan, *Falter Tom and the Water Boy*
1964	Lesley C. Powell, *Turi, The Story of a Little Boy*
1970	MARGARET MAHY, *A Lion in the Meadow*
1973	MARGARET MAHY, *The First Margaret Mahy Story Book*
1975	EVE SUTTON and Lynley Dodd, *My Cat Likes to Hide in Boxes*
1978	RONDA ARMITAGE, *The Lighthouse Keeper's Lunch*
1979	JOAN DE HAMEL, *Take the Long Path*
1981	Katherine O'Brien, *The Year of the Yelvertons*
1982	MARGARET MAHY, THE HAUNTING
1983	ANNE DE ROO, *Jacky Nobody*
1984	CAROLINE MACDONALD, *Elephant Rock*
1985	MARGARET MAHY, THE CHANGEOVER
1986	MAURICE GEE, *Motherstone*
1988	TESSA DUDER, *Alex*
1989	JACK LASENBY, *The Mangrove Summer*
1990	TESSA DUDER, *Alex in Winter*
1991	WILLIAM TAYLOR, *Agnes the Sheep*
1992	TESSA DUDER, *Alessandra: Alex in Rome*
1993	MARGARET MAHY, *Underrunners*
1994	PAULA BOOCK, *Sasscat to Win*
1995	MAURICE GEE, *The Fat Man*
1996	JANICE MARRIOTT, *Crossroads*
1997	Kate De Goldi, SANCTUARY
1998	DAVID HILL, *Fat, four-eyed and useless*
2000	no award

Guardian Award for Children's Fiction

A British award given annually by *The Guardian* for an outstanding work of fiction by a British or Commonwealth author.

1967 LEON GARFIELD, *Devil-in-the-Fog*
1968 ALAN GARNER, *THE OWL SERVICE*
1969 JOAN AIKEN, *The Whispering Mountain*
1970 K. M. PEYTON, The *FLAMBARDS* Trilogy
1971 JOHN CHRISTOPHER, *The Guardians*
1972 GILLIAN AVERY, *A Likely Lad*
1973 Richard Adams, *WATERSHIP DOWN*
1974 Barbara Willard, *The Iron Lily* (see *MANTLEMASS* SERIES)
1975 Winifred Cawley, *Gran at Coalgate*
1976 NINA BAWDEN, *THE PEPPERMINT PIG*
1977 PETER DICKINSON, *The Blue Hawk*
1978 DIANA WYNNE JONES, *Charmed Life*
1979 ANDREW DAVIES, *Conrad's War*
1980 Ann Schlee, *The Vandal*
1981 PETER CARTER, *The Sentinels*
1982 MICHELLE MAGORIAN, *GOODNIGHT MISTER TOM*
1983 ANITA DESAI, *The Village by the Sea*
1984 DICK KING-SMITH, *THE SHEEP-PIG*
1985 TED HUGHES, *WHAT IS THE TRUTH?*
1986 ANN PILLING, *Henry's Leg*
1987 JAMES ALDRIDGE, *The True Story of Spit MacPhee*
1988 RUTH THOMAS, *The Runaways*
1989 GERALDINE MCCAUGHREAN, *A Pack of Lies*
1990 ANNE FINE, *GOGGLE-EYES*
1991 ROBERT WESTALL, *The Kingdom by the Sea*
1992 Rachel Anderson, *Paper Faces* and Hilary McKay, *The Exiles*
1993 WILLIAM MAYNE, *Low Tide*
1994 Sylvia Waugh, *THE MENNYMS*
1995 LESLEY HOWARTH, *Maphead*
1996 PHILIP PULLMAN, *Northern Lights* (see *HIS DARK MATERIALS*)
1997 MELVIN BURGESS, *Junk*
1998 HENRIETTA BRANFORD, *Fire, Bed and Bone*
1999 SUSAN PRICE, *The Sterkarm Handshake*
2000 JACQUELINE WILSON, *The Illustrated Mum*

Hans Christian Andersen Medal

Awarded by the IBBY, established in 1956 and awarded every two years to an author and – from 1966 – an illustrator in recognition of an entire body of work.

1956 Author: ELEANOR FARJEON (UK)
1958 Author: Astrid Lindgren (Sweden) (see *PIPPI LONGSTOCKING* SERIES)
1960 Author: Erich Kästner (West Germany) (see *EMIL AND THE DETECTIVES*)
1962 Author: MEINDERT DEJONG (USA)
1964 Author: René Guillot (France)
1966 Author: Tove Jansson (Finland) (see *MOOMIN* SERIES)
Illustrator: Alois Carigiet (Switzerland)
1968 Authors: James Krüss (West Germany) and José Maria Sanchez-Silva (Spain)

	Illustrator: Jirí Trnka (Czechoslovakia)
1970	Author: Gianni Rodari (Italy)
	Illustrator: MAURICE SENDAK (USA)
1972	Author: SCOTT O'DELL (USA)
	Illustrator: Ib Spang Olsen (Denmark)
1974	Author: Maria Gripe (Sweden)
	Illustrator: Farshid Mesghali (Iran)
1976	Author: Cecil Bødker (Denmark)
	Illustrator: Tatjana Mawrina (USSR)
1978	Author: PAULA FOX (USA)
	Illustrator: Svend Otto Sorensen (Denmark)
1980	Author: Bohumil Ríha (Czechoslovakia)
	Illustrator: Suekichi Akaba (Japan)
1982	Author: Lygia Bojunga Nunes (Brazil)
	Illustrator: Zbigniew Rychlicki (Poland)
1984	Author: Christine Nöstlinger (Austria)
	Illustrator: MITSUMASO ANNO (Japan)
1986	Author: PATRICIA WRIGHTSON (Australia)
	Illustrator: ROBERT INGPEN (Australia)
1988	Author: Annie M.G. Schmidt (Netherlands)
	Illustrator: Dusan Kállay (Czechoslovakia)
1990	Author: Tormod Haugen (Norway)
	Illustrator: LISBETH ZWERGER (Austria)
1992	Author: VIRGINIA HAMILTON (United States)
	Illustrator: Kveta Pacovská (Czechoslovakia)
1994	Author: Michio Mado (Japan)
	Illustrator: Jörg Müller (Switzerland)
1996	Author: URI ORLEV (Israel)
	Illustrator: Klaus Ensikat (Germany)
1998	Author: KATHERINE PATERSON (USA)
	Illustrator: TOMI UNGERER (USA)
2000	Author: Ana Maria Machado (Brazil)
	Illustrator: ANTHONY BROWNE (Great Britain)

Kate Greenaway Medal

An award presented annually in Britain by the Library Association for the most distinguished work in the illustration of children's books published the previous year in the United Kingdom.

1955	no award
1956	EDWARD ARDIZZONE, *Tim All Alone* (see LITTLE TIM SERIES)
1957	V.H. Drummond, *Mrs. Easter and the Storks*
1958	no award
1959	WILLIAM STOBBS, *Kashtanka* (Text: Anton Chekov), and *A Bundle of Ballads* (compiled by: RUTH MANNING-SANDERS)
1960	GERALD ROSE, *Old Winkle and the Seagulls* (Text: Elizabeth Rose)
1961	ANTONY MAITLAND, *Mrs. Cockle's Cat* (Text: PHILIPPA PEARCE)
1962	BRIAN WILDSMITH, *Brian Wildsmith's ABC*
1963	JOHN BURNINGHAM, *Borka: The Adventures of a Goose With No Feathers*
1964	C. WALTER HODGES, *Shakespeare's Theatre*
1965	VICTOR AMBRUS, *Three Poor Tailors*
1966	RAYMOND BRIGGS, *Mother Goose Treasury*

1967	Charles Keeping, *Charley, Charlotte and the Golden Canary*
1968	Pauline Baynes, *A Dictionary of Chivalry* (Text: Grant Uden)
1969	Helen Oxenbury, *The Quangle-Wangle's Hat* (Text: Edward Lear) and *The Dragon of an Ordinary Family* (Text: Margaret Mahy)
1970	John Burningham, *Mr. Gumpy's Outing*
1971	Jan Pieñkowski, *The Kingdom Under the Sea*
1972	Krystyna Turska, *The Woodcutter's Duck*
1973	Raymond Briggs, *Father Christmas*
1974	Pat Hutchins, *The Wind Blew*
1975	Victor Ambrus, *Horses in Battle* and *Mishka*
1976	Gail E. Haley, *The Post Office Cat*
1977	Shirley Hughes, *Dogger*
1978	Janet Ahlberg, *Each Peach Pear Plum* (Text: Allan Ahlberg)
1979	Jan Pieñkowski, *The Haunted House*
1980	Quentin Blake, *Mister Magnolia*
1981	Charles Keeping, *The Highwayman* (Text: Alfred Noyes)
1982	Michael Foreman, *Long Neck and Thunder Foot* (Text: Helen Piers), and *Sleeping Beauty and other Favourite Fairy Tales* (Text: Angela Carter)
1983	Anthony Browne, *Gorilla*
1984	Errol Le Cain, *Hiawatha's Childhood*
1985	Juan Wijngaard, *Sir Gawain and the Loathly Lady* (Text: Selina Hastings)
1986	Fiona French, *Snow White in New York*
1987	Adrienne Kennaway, *Crafty Chameleon* (Text: Mwenye Hadithi)
1988	Barbara Firth, *Can't you Sleep, Little Bear?* (Text: Martin Waddell)
1989	Michael Foreman, *War Boy: A Country Childhood*
1990	Gary Blythe, *The Whales' Song* (Text: Dyan Sheldon)
1991	Janet Ahlberg, *The Jolly Christmas Postman* (Text: Allan Ahlberg)
1992	Anthony Browne, *Zoo*
1993	Alan Lee, *Black Ships before Troy* (Text: Rosemary Sutcliff)
1994	Gregory Rogers, *Way Home* (Text: Libby Hathorn)
1995	P. J. Lynch, *The Christmas Miracle of Jonathan Toomey* (Text: Susan Wojciechowski)
1996	Helen Cooper, *The Baby Who Wouldn't Go To Bed.*
1997	P. J. Lynch, *When Jessie Came Across the Sea* (Text: Amy Hest)
1998	Helen Cooper, *Pumpkin Soup*
1999	Helen Oxenbury, *Alice's Adventures in Wonderland* (Text: Lewis Carroll)

Kurt Maschler Award

Annual award – sometimes known as the Emil award because of the bronze figure of Erich Kästner's character presented to winners – given to the author and illustrator of a children's book combining excellence in both text and illustration.

1982	Angela Carter, *Sleeping Beauty and Other Favourite Fairy Tales*, illustrated by Michael Foreman
1983	Anthony Browne, *Gorilla*

1984 JOHN BURNINGHAM, *GRANPA*
1985 TED HUGHES, *THE IRON MAN*, illustrated by ANDREW DAVIDSON
1986 ALLAN AHLBERG, *THE JOLLY POSTMAN*, illustrated by JANET AHLBERG
1987 CHARLES CAUSLEY, *Jack the Treacle Eater*, illustrated by CHARLES KEEPING
1988 LEWIS CARROLL, *ALICE'S ADVENTURES IN WONDERLAND*, illustrated by ANTHONY BROWNE
1989 MARTIN WADDELL, *The Park in the Dark*, illustrated by BARBARA FIRTH
1990 QUENTIN BLAKE, *All Join In*
1991 COLIN MCNAUGHTON, *Have You Seen Who's Just Moved In Next Door to Us?*
1992 RAYMOND BRIGGS, *The Man*
1993 Karen Wallace, *Think of an Eel*, illustrated by Mike Bostock
1994 Trish Cooke, *So Much*, illustrated by HELEN OXENBURY
1995 Kathy Henderson, *The Little Boat*, illustrated by PATRICK BENSON
1996 BABETTE COLE, *Drop Dead*
1997 WILLIAM MAYNE, *Lady Muck*, illustrated by JONATHAN HEALE
1998 ANTHONY BROWNE, *Voices in the Park*
1999 LEWIS CARROLL, *ALICE'S ADVENTURES IN WONDERLAND*, illustrated by HELEN OXENBURY

Library and Information Association of New Zealand Aotearoa (LIANZA) Young People's Non-Fiction Award

Established in 1987 and given for the most distinguished contribution to non-fiction for young people. (In some years no award was given.)

1987 Olive and Ngaio Hill, *Gaijin, Foreign Children in Japan*
1989 Claire Patterson, *It's OK to be You! Feeling Good About Growing Up*
1990 Deborah Furley, *The Web: The Triumph of a New Zealand Girl over Anorexia*
1991 John Reid Model, *Boats That Really Go*
1992 Peter Garland, *The Damselfly*
1993 Kim Westerskov, *Albatross Adventure*
1994 ROBYN KAHUKIWA, *Paikea*
1995 Barbara Cairns and Helen Martin, *Shadows on the Wall*
1996 Laura Ranger, *Laura's Poems*
1997 DIANA NOONAN, *I Spy Wildlife: The Garden*, photographs by Nic Bishop
1998 Andrew Crowe, *The Life-size Guide to Native Trees and Other Common Plants of New Zealand's Native Forest*
1999 no award

Mother Goose Award

An award presented annually to the most exciting newcomer to British children's book illustration, discontinued in February, 2000.

1979 Michelle Cartlidge, *Pippin and Pod*
1980 REG CARTWRIGHT, *Mr. Potter's Pigeon* (Text: Patrick Kinmonth)
1981 JUAN WIJNGAARD, *Green Finger House* (Text: Rosemary Harris)

1982 Jan Ormerod, *Sunshine*
1983 Satoshi Kitamura, *Angry Arthur* (Text: Hiawyn Oram)
1984 Patrick Benson, *The Book of Hob Stories* (Text: William Mayne)
1985 Susan Varley, *Badger's Parting Gifts*
1986 no award
1987 Patrick James Lynch, *A Bag of Moonshine* (Text: Alan Garner)
1988 Emma Chichester Clark, *Listen to This* (Text: Laura Cecil)
1989 Charles Fuge, *Bush Vark's First Day Out*
1990 David Hughes, *Strat and Chatto* (Text: Jan Mark)
1991 Amanda Harvey, *A Close Call*
1992 Ted Dewan, *Inside the Whale and Other Animals* (Text: Steve Parker)
1993 Claire Fletcher, *The Seashell Song* (Text: Susie Jenkin-Pearce)
1994 Lisa Flather, *Where the Great Bear Watches* (Text: James Sage)
1995 Flora McDonnell, *I Love Animals*
1996 Bruce Ingman, *When Martha's Away*
1997 Clare Jarrett, *Catherine and the Lion*
1998 Mary Fedden, *Motley the Cat*
1999 Niamh Sharkey, *The Gigantic Turnip and Tales of Wisdom and Wonder*
2000 no award

Newbery Medal

Annual award made by the Association for Library Services to Children, a divison of the ALA. It was established in 1922 and presented to the author of the most distinguished contribution to American literature for children published in the United States in the preceding year.

1922 Hendrik Van Loon, *The Story of Mankind*
1923 Hugh Lofting, *The Voyages of Doctor Dolittle*
1924 Charles Hawes, *The Dark Frigate*
1925 Charles Finger, *Tales from Silver Lands*
1926 Arthur Chrisman, *Shen of the Sea*
1927 Will James, *Smoky, the Cowhorse*
1928 Dhan Gopal Mukerji, *Gay-Neck, the Story of a Pigeon*
1929 Eric P Kelly, *The Trumpeter of Krakow: A Tale of the Fifteenth Century*
1930 Rachel Field, *Hitty, Her First Hundred Years*
1931 Elizabeth Coatsworth, *The Cat Who Went to Heaven*
1932 Laura Adams Armer, *Waterless Mountain*
1933 Elizabeth Lewis, *Young Fu of the Upper Yangtze*
1934 Cornelia Meigs, *Invincible Louisa: The Story of the Author of Little Women*
1935 Monica Shannon, *Dobry*
1936 Carol Ryrie Brink, *Caddie Woodlawn*
1937 Ruth Sawyer, *Roller Skates*
1938 Kate Seredy, *The White Stag*
1939 Elizabeth Enright, *Thimble Summer*
1940 James Daugherty, *Daniel Boone*
1941 Armstrong Sperry, *Call It Courage*
1942 Walter D. Edmonds, *The Matchlock Gun*

1943 Elizabeth Janet Gray, *Adam of the Road*
1944 Esther Forbes, *Johnny Tremain*
1945 Robert Lawson, *Rabbit Hill*
1946 Lois Lenski, *Strawberry Girl*
1947 Carolyn S. Bailey, *Miss Hickory*
1948 William Pène du Bois, *The Twenty-One Balloons*
1949 Marguerite Henry, *King of the Wind*
1950 Marguerite de Angeli, *The Door in the Wall*
1951 Elizabeth Yates, *Amos Fortune, Free Man*
1952 Eleanor Estes, *Ginger Pye*
1953 Ann Nolan Clark, *Secret of the Andes*
1954 Joseph Krumgold, *. . . And Now Miguel*
1955 Meindert DeJong, *The Wheel on the School*
1956 Jean Lee Latham, *Carry On, Mr, Bowditch*
1957 Virginia Sorensen, *Miracles on Maple Hill*
1958 Harold V. Keith, *Rifles for Watie*
1959 Elizabeth George Speare, *The Witch of Blackbird Pond*
1960 Joseph Krumgold, *Onion John*
1961 Scott O'Dell, *Island of the Blue Dolphins*
1962 Elizabeth George Speare, *The Bronze Bow*
1963 Madeleine L'Engle, *A Wrinkle in Time*
1964 Emily C. Neville, *It's Like This, Cat*
1965 Maia Wojciechowska, *Shadow of a Bull*
1966 Elizabeth Borton de Treviño, *I, Juan de Pareja*
1967 Irene Hunt, *Up a Road Slowly*
1968 E.L. Konigsburg, *From the Mixed-Up Files of Mrs. Basil E. Frankweiler*
1969 Lloyd Alexander, *The High King*
1970 William H. Armstrong, *Sounder*
1971 Betsy Byars, *The Summer of the Swans*
1972 Robert C. O'Brien, *Mrs. Frisby and the Rats of NIMH*
1973 Jean Craighead George, *Julie of the Wolves*
1974 Paula Fox, *The Slave Dancer*
1975 Virginia Hamilton, *M.C. Higgins, the Great*
1976 Susan Cooper, *The Grey King*
1977 Mildred D. Taylor, *Roll of Thunder, Hear My Cry*
1978 Katherine Paterson, *Bridge to Terabithia*
1979 Ellen Raskin, *The Westing Game*
1980 Joan Blos, *A Gathering of Days: A New England Girl's Journal, 1830–32*
1981 Katherine Paterson, *Jacob Have I Loved*
1982 Nancy Willard, *A Visit to William Blake's Inn: Poems for Innocent and Experienced Travelers*
1983 Cynthia Voigt, *Dicey's Song*
1984 Beverly Cleary, *Dear Mr. Henshaw*
1985 Robin McKinley, *The Hero and the Crown*
1986 Patricia MacLachlan, *Sarah, Plain and Tall*
1987 Sid Fleischman, *The Whipping Boy*
1988 Russell Freedman, *Lincoln: A Photobiography*
1989 Paul Fleischman, *Joyful Noise: Poems for Two Voices*
1990 Lois Lowry, *Number the Stars*
1991 Jerry Spinelli, *Maniac Magee*
1992 Phyllis Reynolds Naylor, *Shiloh*

1993	CYNTHIA RYLANT, *Missing May*
1994	LOIS LOWRY, *The Giver*
1995	SHARON CREECH, *Walk Two Moons*
1996	KAREN CUSHMAN, *The Midwife's Apprentice*
1997	E. L. KONIGSBURG, *The View From Saturday*
1998	KAREN HESSE, *Out of the Dust*
1999	Louis Sachar, HOLES
2000	Christopher Paul Curtiss, *Bud, Not Buddy*
2001	RICHARD PECK, *A Year Down Yonder*

New Zealand Post Children's Book Award

Formerly known as the AIM Children's Book, these awards were established in 1990 and presented to New Zealand books in six categories, plus a 'Book of the Year'.

Winners of the Picture Book Category:

1990	Miriam Smith, *Annie and Moon*, illustrated by Lesley Moyes
1991	PAMELA ALLEN, *My Cat Maisie*
1992	Lynley Dodd, *Hairy Maclary's Showbusiness* (see HAIRY MACLARY SERIES)
1993	Christine Ross, *Lily and the Present*
1994	GAVIN BISHOP, *Hinepau*
1995	DIANA NOONAN, *The Best-Loved Bear*, illustrated by Elizabeth Fuller
1996	JOY COWLEY, *The Cheese Trap*, illustrated by Linda McClelland
1997	JENNIFER BECK, *The Bantam and the Soldier*, illustrated by ROBYN BELTON
1998	Lesley Moyes, *Alphabet Apartments*
1999	MARGARET MAHY, *A Summery Saturday Morning*, illustrated by Selina Young
2000	GAVIN BISHOP, *The House that Jack Built*

Winners of the Fiction Categories:

1990	TESSA DUDER, *Alex in Winter* (see ALEX QUARTET)
1991	SHERRYL JORDAN, *Rocco*
1992	JOY COWLEY, *Bow Down Shadrach*

Winners of the Junior Fiction category:

1993	MARGARET MAHY, *Underrunners*
1994	DIANA NOONAN, *A Dolphin in the Bay*
1995	MAURICE GEE, THE FAT MAN
1996	JACK LASENBY, *The Waterfall*
1997	JACK LASENBY, *The Battle of Pook Island*
1998	JOY COWLEY, *Ticket to the Sky Dance*
1999	JOY COWLEY, *Starbright and the Dream Eater*
2000	Vince Ford, *2MUCH4U*

Winners of the Senior Fiction category:

1993	TESSA DUDER, *Songs for Alex*
1994	Pat Quinn, *The Value of X*
1995	WILLIAM TAYLOR, *The Blue Lawn*
1996	JANICE MARRIOTT, *Crossroads*
1997	Kate De Goldi, SANCTUARY

1998 PAULA BOOCK, *Dare Truth or Promise*
1999 JACK LASENBY, *Taur*
2000 TESSA DUDER, *The Tiggie Thompson Show*

Winners of the Non-Fiction Category:

1993 CHRIS GASKIN, *Picture Magic*
1994 Mary Taylor, *Old Blue: The Rarest Bird in the World*
1995 Andrew Crowe, *Which Native Forest Plant?*
1996 Jenny Scown, *Aya's Story*, photographs by Trish Gribben
1997 CHRIS GASKIN, *Picture Book Magic*, photographs by Denis Page
1998 DIANA NOONAN, *The Know, Sow & Grow Kids' Book of Plants*, illustrated by Keith Olsen
1999 Gerard Hutching, *The Natural World of New Zealand*
2000 Hirini Melbourne, *Te Wao Nui a Tane*, illustrated by Te Maari Gardiner

Winners of the Children's Choice Award:

1997 BOB KERR, *Mechanical Harry*
1998 Lesley Moyes, *Alphabet Apartments*
1999 GAELYN GORDON, *The Life-Sized Inflatable Whale*, illustrated by John Tarlton
2000 LYNLEY DODD, *Hairy Maclary and Zachary Quack*

Winners of the Supreme Award, chosen from among the other category winners:

1995 MAURICE GEE, *The Fat Man*
1996 JANICE MARRIOTT, *Crossroads*
1997 JENNIFER BECK, *The Bantam and the Soldier*, illustrated by ROBYN BELTON
1998 PAULA BOOCK, *Dare Truth or Promise*
1999 MARGARET MAHY, *A Summery Saturday Morning*, illustrated by Selina Young
2000 GAVIN BISHOP, *The House that Jack Built*

Reading Association of Ireland Children's Book Award

A biennial award for children's books published in Ireland. A second award, the RAI Special Merit Award, is made for any book which has made a significant contribution to publishing for children in Ireland.

1985 TOM MCCAUGHREN, *Run With the Wind*
1987 Eugene McCabe, *Cyril: the Quest of an Orphaned Squirrel*
1989 Marie-Louise Fitzpatrick, *An Chanáil*
1991 MARITA CONLON-MCKENNA, *Under the Hawthorn Tree*
1993 MORGAN LLYWELYN, *Strongbow*
1995 Elizabeth O'Hara, *The Hiring Fair*
1997 Susan Wojciechowski and P.J. LYNCH, *The Christmas Miracle of Jonathan Toomey*
1999 MARK O'SULLIVAN, *Angels Without Wings*

Winners of the Special Merit Award:

1989 GEORGE OTTO SIMMS, *Exploring the Book of Kells*
1991 Joan O'Neill, *The Daisy Chain War*
1993 MARGRIT CRUICKSHANK, *Circling the Triangle*

1995 P. J. LYNCH, *Catkin*
1997 The O'Brien Press (for its contribution to raising the standard of publishing children's books in Ireland)
1999 Marie Louise Fitzpatrick, *The Long March*

Russell Clark Award

First presented in 1978 in honour of the prominent New Zealand illustrator RUSSELL CLARK and given for the most distinguished illustrations for a book for children or young adults. (In some years, no award was made.)

1978 Robert F. Jahnke, *The House of the People* (Text: RON L. BACON)
1979 BRUCE TRELOAR, *Kim*
1982 GAVIN BISHOP, *Mrs McGinty and the Bizarre Plant*
1984 Gwenda Turner, *The Tree Witches*
1985 ROBYN BELTON, *The Duck in the Gun* (Text: JOY COWLEY)
1986 PAMELA ALLEN, *A Lion in the Night*
1987 ROBYN KAHUKIWA, *Taniwha*
1988 Dick Frizzell, *The Magpies* (Text: Denis Glover)
1989 CHRIS GASKIN, *Joseph's Boat* (Text: CAROLINE MACDONALD)
1990 CHRIS GASKIN, *A Walk to the Beach*
1991 David Elliot, *Arthur and the Dragon* (Text: PAULINE CARTWRIGHT)
1992 Sandra Morris, *One Lonely Kakapo*
1993 Christine Ross, *Lily and the Present*
1994 Kerry Gemmill, *The Trolley* (Text: PATRICIA GRACE)
1995 CHRIS GASKIN, *Kotuku: The Flight of the White Heron* (Text: Philip Temple)
1996 Linda McClelland, *The Cheese Trap* (Text: JOY COWLEY)
1997 Murray Grimsdale, *George's Monster* (Text: Amanda Jackson)
1998 Sue Hitchcock Pratt, *Emily's Wonderful Pie* (Text: Jane Cornish)

Smarties Book Prize

A British annual sponsored award for which the shortlist is compiled by adults and the winner chosen by children. An asterisk indicates an overall winner.

Winners:

1985 JILL PATON WALSH, *GAFFER SAMSON'S LUCK*
SUSANNA GRETZ, *It's Your Turn, Roger!*
Ray Marshall and John Bradley, *Watch it Work! The Plane*
1986 Jenny Nimmo, *THE SNOW SPIDER*
Geoffrey Patterson, *The Goose that Laid the Golden Egg*
Michael Palin, ALAN LEE and Richard Seymour, *The Mirrorstone*, and Miss Pinnell and the Children of Sapperton School, *Village Heritage*
1987 JAMES BERRY, *A Thief in the Village**
PETER COLLINGTON, *The Angel and the Soldier Boy*
Benedict Blathwayt, *Tangle and the Firesticks*
1988 MARTIN WADDELL, *Can't You Sleep, Little Bear?*, illustrated by BARBARA FIRTH*
SUSAN HILL, *Can It Be True?*, illustrated by ANGELA BARRETT
Theresa Whistler, *Rushavenn Time*
1989 MICHAEL ROSEN, *We're Going on a Bear Hunt*, illustrated by HELEN OXENBURY*

	ANNE FINE, *Bill's New Frock*
	ROBERT WESTALL, *Blitzcat*
1990	Pauline Fisk, *Midnight Blue**
	Inga Moore, *Six Dinner Sid*
	ROALD DAHL, *Esio Trot*, illustrated by QUENTIN BLAKE
1991	MARTIN WADDELL, *Farmer Duck*, illustrated by HELEN OXENBURY*
	Magdalen Nabb, *Josie Smith and Eileen*, illustrated by Pirkko Vainio
	Philip Ridley, *KRINDLEKRAX*
1992	GILLIAN CROSS, *The Great Elephant Chase**
	Hilda Offen, *Nice Work, Little Wolf*
	JANE RAY, *The Story of the Creation*
1993	MICHAEL FOREMAN, *War Game**
	Rita Phillips Mitchell, *Hue Boy*, illustrated by CAROLINE BINCH
	Maeve Henry, *Listen to the Dark*
1994	Hilary McKay, *The Exiles at Home**
	Trish Cooke, *So Much*, illustrated by HELEN OXENBURY
	HENRIETTA BRANFORD, *Dimanche Diller*, illustrated by Lesley Harker
1995	JACQUELINE WILSON, *Double Act*, illustrated by Nick SHARRATT*
	JILL MURPHY, *The Last Noo Noo*
	JILL PATON WALSH, *Thomas and the Tinners*, illustrated by ALAN MARKS
	LESLEY HOWARTH, *Weather Eye*
1996	PHILIP PULLMAN, *The Firework-Maker's Daughter*
	MICHAEL MORPURGO, *The Butterfly Lion*
	COLIN MCNAUGHTON, *Oops!*
1997	J.K. Rowling, *Harry Potter and the Philosopher's Stone* (see HARRY POTTER)
	CHARLOTTE VOAKE, *Ginger*
	Jenny Nimmo, *The Owl Tree*, illustrated by Anthony Lewis
1998	Sue Heap, *Cowboy Baby*
	Harry Horse, *The Last of the Gold Diggers*
	J.K. Rowling, *Harry Potter and the Chamber of Secrets* (see HARRY POTTER)
1999	Julia Donaldson, *The Gruffalo*, illustrated by Axel Scheffler
	LAURENCE ANHOLT, *Snow White and the Seven Aliens*, illustrated by Arthur Robins
	J.K. Rowling, *Harry Potter and the Prisoner of Azkaban* (see HARRY POTTER)
2000	BOB GRAHAM, *Max*
	JACQUELINE WILSON, *Lizzie Zipmouth*
	William Nicolson, *The Wind Singer* (see THE WIND ON FIRE)

Te Kura Pounamu Maori Book Award

An award established in 1996 by the Library and Information Association of New Zealand Aotearoa, presented to the author of a book for young people written in the Maori language.

1996	Katerina Mataira and Terewai Kemp, *Marama Tangiweto*
1997	Katerina Mataira, *He tino Kuia taku Kuia*

1998 Mere Clarke, *Whirikoki me tana Kekeno*, illustrated by Manu Smith
1999 no award

Whitbread Children's Book of the Year

An award sponsored by Whitbread Breweries, administered by the Booksellers Association of Great Britain and Ireland. Books for children of seven and up are eligible, written by a British or Irish author.

Winners:

1972 RUMER GODDEN, *The Diddakoi*
1973 Alan Aldridge and William Plomer, THE BUTTERFLY BALL AND THE GRASSHOPPER'S FEAST
1974 RUSSELL HOBAN, *How Tom Beat Captain Najork and His Hired Sportsmen*, illustrated by QUENTIN BLAKE; and JILL PATON WALSH, *The Emperor's Winding Sheet*
1975 no award
1976 PENELOPE LIVELY, *A Stitch in Time*
1977 Shelagh Macdonald, *No End to Yesterday*
1978 PHILIPPA PEARCE, *The Battle of Bubble and Squeak*
1979 PETER DICKINSON, *Tulku*
1980 LEON GARFIELD, *John Diamond*
1981 JANE GARDAM, *The Hollow Land*
1982 W.J. Corbett, *The Song of Pentecost*
1983 ROALD DAHL, *The Witches*
1984 BARBARA WILLARD, *The Queen of the Pharisees' Children*
1985 JANNI HOWKER, THE NATURE OF THE BEAST
1986 Andrew Taylor, *The Coal House*
1987 GERALDINE MCCAUGHREAN, *A Little Lower Than the Angels*
1988 JUDY ALLEN, *Awaiting Developments*
1989 HUGH SCOTT, WHY WEEPS THE BROGAN?
1990 PETER DICKINSON, *AK*
1991 Diana Hendry, *Harvey Angell*
1992 GILLIAN CROSS, *The Great Elephant Chase*
1993 ANNE FINE, *Flour Babies*
1994 GERALDINE MCCAUGHREAN, *Gold Dust*
1995 MICHAEL MORPURGO, *The Wreck of the Zanzibar*
1996 ANNE FINE, *The Tulip Touch*
1997 ANDREW NORRISS, *Aquila*
1998 DAVID ALMOND, *Skellig*
1999 J. K. Rowling, *Harry Potter and the Prisoner of Azkaban* (see HARRY POTTER)
2000 JAMILA GAVIN, *Coram Boy*

Contributors

SCWA	Sue Abbotson	Rhode Island College, USA
GA	Gillian Adams	Editor and independent scholar, USA
JCA	Jim Addison	Western Carolina University, USA
KA	Kate Agnew	Writer and bookseller, UK
JMA	Janice M. Alberghene	Fitchburg State College, USA
AA	Alida Allison	San Diego State University, USA
AHA	Anne Hiebert Alton	Central Michigan University, USA
SA	Susan Ang	National University of Singapore
EA	Evelyn Arizpe	Independent researcher, UK and Mexico
FEA	Frances Armstrong	Independent scholar, Canada
MRA	Mark Armstrong	Scholar, USA
HA	Helen Arnold†	Writer, UK
MAs	Meshak Asare	Author and artist, Ghana and UK
VAG	Viki Ash-Geisler	Texas Woman's University, USA
JMB	John Ball	Homerton College, Cambridge, UK
KB	Keith Barker†	Westhill College of Higher Education, Birmingham, UK
JJB	Jason Barker	United States of America
JLB	Jani L. Barker	United States of America
EBe	Ellen Bear	Writer and producer, Canada
GCB	Geoffrey Beare	Chairman of the Imaginative Book Illustration Society, UK
ECB	Eve Bearne	Homerton College, Cambridge, UK
MB	Mary Beaty	Freelance librarian, New York City, USA
CB	Chris Beetles	Chris Beetles Ltd., London, UK
MBh	Meenakshi Bharat	University of Delhi, India
VB	Valerie Bierman	United Kingdom
CAB	Cynthia Bily	Adrian College, Michigan, USA
GRB	George Bodmer	Indiana University Northwest, USA
KSB	Katharine Boling	Francis Marion University; author, USA
JB	Jennifer Bolton	Hollins University, USA
EB	Ernie Bond	Salisbury State University, USA
FB	Frieda Bostian	Virginia Polytechnic Institute & State University, USA
RBB	Ruth Bottigheimer	State University of New York at Stony Brook, USA
JFB	Janet Bottoms	Homerton College, Cambridge, UK
CWB	Celia Boyd	United Kingdom
JKB	Johanna Bradley	University of Illinois, USA
LEB	L. Elisabeth Brewer	Author, UK
ELPB	Elizabeth L. Pandolfo Briggs	University of Wales, Cardiff, UK
HB	Helen Bromley	Homerton College, Cambridge, UK
MBu	Melvyn Burgess	Author, UK
DB	Dennis Butts	University of Reading, UK

MJC	Mike Cadden	Missouri Western State College, USA
JEDC	Joan Carris	Duke University instructor; independent author and reviewer, USA
NC	Nancy Castaldo	Author, USA
JDC	Joel D. Chaston	Southwest Missouri State University, USA
DAC	Diana Chlebek	The University of Akron, Ohio, USA
MSC	Margaret S. Clark	Formerly of The Bodley Head, UK
GCH	Gabrielle Cliff Hodges	Homerton College, Cambridge, UK
VC	Valerie Coghlan	Librarian, Church of Ireland College of Education
FMC	Fiona Collins	University of Surrey, Roehampton, UK
WC	William Connelly	Retired teacher, UK
PTC	Paula Connolly	University of North Carolina at Charlotte, USA
RC	Richard Cook	United Kingdom
JC	Jonathan Cooper	University of Cambridge, UK
MC	Margaret Courtney	The Guide Association Archivist, UK
JRC	J. Randolph Cox	Editor, Dime Novel Round-Up, USA
ESC	Elizabeth S. Crane	Reviewer and independent researcher, USA
PC	Peter Cunningham	Homerton College, Cambridge, UK
JDan	Jenny Daniels	United Kingdom
JHD	Jane Dartnall	Picture book editor, UK
LD	Lawrence Darton	Independent researcher, UK
GD	Gayle Digby	United Kingdom
VD	Virginia Dike	University of Nigeria
SD	Sue Dipple	Independent researcher, UK
EBD	Ellen Donovan	Middle Tennessee State University, USA
JD	Jane Doonan	Author; University of Bath, UK
CD	Christine Doyle	Central Connecticut State University, USA
ETD	Eliza T. Dresang	Florida State University, USA
TD	Tessa Duder	Writer/ reviewer, New Zealand
HE	Hazel Edwards	Author and journalist, Australia
HCE	Helen Entwistle	Independent researcher, UK
ME	Margaret Evans	Loughborough University, UK
RF	Richard Flynn	Georgia Southern University, USA
JF	John Foster	University of South Australia
GPF	Geoff Fox	Honorary Fellow, University of Exeter, UK
MF	Marietta Frank	Reference Librarian, University of Pittsburgh at Bradford, USA
SRG	Susan R. Gannon	Pace University, USA
JEG	Jane Gardiner	Bottisham Village College, UK
PG	Pat Garrett	Secretary, Children's Books History Society, UK
BG	Beverly Gherman	Author and reviewer, USA
DG	Denis Gifford†	Writer, UK
AG	Annette Goldsmith	Miami-Dade Public Library System, USA
JRG	Jane R. Goldstein	Independent researcher, USA
EG	Elizabeth Goodenough	University of Michigan, USA
JG	Joan Goody	Teacher, retired, UK

JAG	Judith Graham	University of Surrey, Roehampton, UK
LG	Linda Granfield	Writer, Canada
SG	Susan Greenhalgh	University of Surrey, Roehampton, UK
EAG	Elizabeth Grugeon	De Montfort University, Bedford, UK
DCH	Dennis Hamley	Author/reviewer, UK
EMH	Elizabeth Hammill	Centre for the Children's Book, UK
VCH	Veronica Hanke	Swaffham Prior Primary School, UK
TLH	Bettina L. Hanlon	Ferrum College, Virginia, USA
AH	Anne Hanzl	RMIT University, Melbourne, Australia
AHa	Anne Harvey	Anthologist, broadcaster and actress, UK
ARH	Alison Haymonds	Writer and journalist, UK
JHe	Jay Heale	Editor, Bookchat, South Africa
DAH	Diane Hebley	Writer/ freelance tutor, New Zealand
KH	Kate Hellen	R. A. Butler School, UK
DJH	Dona Helmer	College Gate School, Alaska, USA
BH	Bruce Henderson	Ithaca College, New York, USA
LH	Linnea Hendrickson	Independent scholar, USA
TH	Theo Heras	Toronto Public Library; MaryContrary Associates, Canada
MLH	Margot Hillel	Australian Catholic University, Melbourne
CH	Claire Hiller	University of Tasmania
MPH	Martha Hixon	Middle Tennessee State University, USA
PH	Peter Hollindale	Freelance writer and lecturer; formerly University of York, UK
MJH	Jill Holt	Auckland College of Education, New Zealand
JCH	Jackie C. Horne	Center for the Study of Children's Literature, Simmons College, Boston, USA
WH	Winona Howe	La Sierra University, California, USA
SH	Shirley Hughes, OBE	Artist and author; Fellow of the Royal Society of Literature, UK
JHu	Julia Hunt	Ernest Nister Bibliographer, UK
PLH	Peter Hunt	University of Wales, Cardiff, UK
ASTH	Sarah Hunt	University of Reading, UK
NH	Nancy Huse	Augustana College, Illinois, USA
SAI	Sherrie Inness	Miami University, Ohio, USA
EHI	Beth Irvine	United States of America
SPI	Sylvia Iskander	University of Louisiana at Lafayette, USA
ERJ	Elwyn Jenkins	Vista University, South Africa
SJ	Sharon Jennings	Author, Canada
JGJ	Judith John	Southwest Missouri State University, USA
SNJ	Scott Johnston	Riverside High School, Tasmania; reviewer
DJ	Dudley Jones	University of Reading, UK
CEJ	Caroline E. Jones	Illinois State University, USA
REJ	Raymond E. Jones	University of Alberta, Canada
KK	Kara Keeling	Christopher Newport University, Virginia, USA
FK	Frances Kelly	Independent researcher

SKS	Samantha Kerr-Smiley	Independent researcher, Australia
KBK	Kenneth B. Kidd	University of Florida, USA
MJKP	Marty Korwin-Pawlowski	Writer, USA
VK	Valerie Krips	University of Pittsburgh, USA
GIK	Gabriele Kupitz	Librarian, Brigham Young University, USA
MDK	M. Daphne Kutzer	State University College at Plattsburgh, USA
ARTL	Alexandria LaFaye	California State University, San Bernardino, USA
LSL	Lorraine S. Lange	Hollins University, Virginia, USA
GL	Gillian Lathey	University of Surrey, Roehampton, UK
DL	David Lewis	Independent researcher, UK
LL	Libby Limbrick	Auckland College of Education
FL	Frieda Ling	United States of America
LJL	Lyn Linning	Queensland University of Technology
ML	Michael Lockwood	University of Reading, UK
AL	Anne Lundin	United States of America
JL	John Lynch	Tattingstone Primary School, Suffolk, UK
HMcC	Hugo McCann	University of Tasmania
MMcC	Mike McCausland	University of Tasmania
MMG	Marilyn MacGregor	Artist, writer and teacher, USA
TM	Tim Maddren	Independent researcher, UK
IM	Indrani Mahumdar	Independent researcher, India
SM	Sarah Mahurter	London College of Printing and Distributive Trades, UK
KM	Kerry Mallan	Queensland University of Technology
EAM	Edward Malone	Missouri Western State College, USA
LSM	Leonard S. Marcus	Children's books historian, author, critic, USA
JMM	Jan Mark	Writer and critic, UK
CM	Claudia Marquis	University of Auckland
MM	Margaret Meek	Reader in Education, London Institute of Education, UK
EJM	Liz Mellor	Homerton College, Cambridge, UK
MUiM	Maire Mhaicin	Writer, Ireland
NM	Nina Mikkelsen	Independent researcher and writer, USA
SAM	Sally Milbourne	Independent researcher, Australia
RAM	Robin Morris	University of Massachusetts, Amherst, USA
EM	Elaine Moss	Writer, UK
PM	Paul Moynihan	Archivist, The Scout Association, UK
MMy	Mitzi Myers	University of California, Los Angeles, USA
BN	Bill Nagelkerke	Christchurch City Libraries, New Zealand
AMN	Mary Nathan	Teacher, editor and consultant, UK
CMN	Catriona Nicholson	University of Reading, UK
AN	Agnes Nieuwenhuizen	Director, Australian Centre for Youth Literature, State Library of Victoria; writer and reviewer

MN	Maureeen Nimon	University of South Australia
ABO	Asenath Odaga	Author and teacher, Kenya
MSO	Marilynn Olson	Southwest Texas State University, USA
IO	Iona Opie	Independent scholar, UK
LO	Lorraine Orman	Freelance writer, New Zealand
CP	Connie Parker	Cuyahoga County Public Library, USA
JAP	Juliet Partridge	University of Tasmania
PP	Philippa Pearce	Author, UK
AKP	Anne K. Phillips	Kansas State University, USA
KKP	Kathy Piehl	Minnesota State University, Mankato, USA
GHP	Geraldine Harris Pinch	University of Cambridge, UK
PAP	Pat Pinsent	University of Surrey, Roehampton, UK
JP	Jill Pirrie	Reviewer, writer and speaker, UK
FP	Frances Plumpton	Waitakere Libraries, New Zealand
CMP	Cathy Pompe	The Red Balloon Learner Centre, Cambridge, UK
KP	Kate Pretty	Homerton College, Cambridge, UK
SDP	Susan D. Price	Curator of the Susan Price Collection of 20th Century Children's Books, National Library of New Zealand
PNP	Philip Pullman	Author, UK
KJFR	Kate Rabey	United Kingdom
PR	Peter Raby	Homerton College, Cambridge, UK
SR	Suzanne Rahn	United States of America
DWR	Dan Reagan	St Anselm College, New Hampshire, USA
KR	Kimberley Reynolds	University of Surrey, Roehampton, UK
HR	Hannah Reynolds	Homerton College, Cambridge, UK
CLR	Carolyn Leutzinger Richey	San Diego State University, California, USA
NLR	Nicola Lynne Robinson	Freelance children's book reviewer and editor, Australia
TR	Teya Rosenberg	Southwest Texas State University, USA
AR	Anne Rowe	Independent writer and reviewer, UK
PJR	Peter Rowe	Furze Platt School, UK
DR	David Rudd	United Kingdom
DLR	David Russell	Ferris State University, Michigan, USA
MS	Marion Sader	Hollins University, USA
LS	Lisa A. Sainsbury	University of Surrey, Roehampton, UK
JMS	Judith Saltman	University of British Columbia, Canada
MSS	Monique S. Sanders	Lecturer and writer, UK
KS	Karen Sands O'Connor	Buffalo State College, USA
MSax	Maurice Saxby	Historian, Australian children's literature
PDS	Pat Schaefer	Children's librarian, UK and USA
EDS	Elizabeth Schafer	Independent scholar, USA
FRBS	Fred Sedgwick	Freelance lecturer and writer, UK
MSed	Marcus Sedgwick	Author, UK
RS	Robyn Sheahan-Bright	Freelance writer, critic, editor, Australia
JSh	Jill Shefrin	Independent scholar, Toronto, Canada
CS	Carolyn Sigler	Kansas State University, USA
JAS	Jodie Slothower	Heartland Community College, USA

JDS	J. D. Stahl	Virginia Polytechnic Institute & State University, USA
JS	Joseph Stanton	University of Hawai'i at Manoa, USA
DS	Deborah Stevenson	University of Illinois at Urbana-Champaign, USA
MRS	Margery R. Stewart	Writer and reviewer, Canada
RSH	Ru Story-Huffman	Cumberland College, Williamsburg, Kentucky, USA
JCSt	Jon C. Stott	Western Washington University, USA
MCCS	Morag Styles	Homerton College, Cambridge, UK
JCS	Jan Susina	Illinois State University, USA
MSut	Mary Sutcliffe	Westminster College, Oxford, UK
MT	Mihoko Tanaka	Translator and teacher, Japan
CAT	Anita Tarr	Illinois State University, USA
HT	Helen Taylor	Homerton College, Cambridge, UK
JAT	Judy Teaford	The College of West Virginia, USA
AT	Angela Thomas	University of Tasmania
RTh	Roie Thomas	University of Tasmania
SET	Sue Tibbles	Bodleian Library, Oxford, UK
JRT	John Rowe Townsend	Author and historian of children's literature, Cambridge, UK
RT	Ryoji Tsurumi	Seijo University, Japan
NT	Nicholas Tucker	University of Sussex, UK
SMV	Sylvia Vardell	University of Texas at Arlington, USA
CV	Constance Vidor	The Cathedral School, USA
NV	Nancy Vogel	Fort Hays State University, Kansas, USA
KKW	Karla Walters	Independent researcher, USA
JSW	Judith Watson	R. A. Butler School, UK
VW	Victor Watson	Homerton College, Cambridge, UK
DHW	David Watters	University of New Hampshire, USA
AEW	Arvon Wellen	Artist and writer, UK
BW	Bobbie Wells	Homerton College, Cambridge, UK
AW	Alison White	Teacher, UK
DWh	David Whitley	Homerton College, Cambridge, UK
CHW	Carol H. Williams	Writer, Tennessee, USA
ALW	Andrea L. Williams	Moffett Library, Midwestern State University, USA
LW	Louise A. Winterbottom	United Kingdom
IW	Irene Wise	Illustrator; University of Surrey, Roehampton, UK
NJW	Naomi Wood	Kansas State University, USA
VWo	Victoria Wood	Writer and comedienne, UK
DW	David Wootton	Chris Beetles Ltd., London, UK
LAW	Lisa A. Wroble	Redford (Mich.) District Library; author, USA
ATY	Alexander Yarwood	Australia
JZ	Joan Zahnleiter	Education Queensland, Australia
LMZ	Laura Mandell Zaidman	University of South Carolina Sumter, USA
JZo	Joe Zornado	Rhode Island College, USA

Illustration acknowledgements

The publishers gratefully acknowledge the following for supplying illustrations and granting permission for their use. In particular, the publishers appreciate the goodwill of those illustrators who have provided samples of their illustrations. Pat Schaefer and Victor Watson have kindly provided illustrations from their own collections. Every reasonable effort has been made to obtain permissions to use illustrations; if any errors or omissions have occurred the publishers would welcome these being brought to their attention.

Aboriginal culture in children's books: by kind permission of Lisa Kennedy.
Allan and Janet Ahlberg: by kind permission of the artist © Janet and Allan Ahlberg, 1977.
Pamela Allen: by kind permission of the artist.
Animalia: by kind permission of Penguin Books Australia.
Arabian Nights: by kind permission of the artist, Pauline Baynes.
Edward Ardizzone: by permission of Scholastic Ltd.
Kerry Argent: by kind permission of the artist.
Meshak Asare: by kind permission of the artist.
Allan Baillie: by kind permission of the artist, Di Wu.
Jeannie Baker: by kind permission of the artist.
Suddasattwa Basu: by kind permission of the artist.
Nicola Bayley: © 1990 Nicola Bayley.
Ian Beck: by kind permission of Scholastic Children's Books.
Gavin Bishop: by kind permission of the artist.
Pulak Biswas: by kind permission of the artist.
Quentin Blake: by permission of Jonathan Cape.
Louise Brierley: by kind permission of the artist.
Catherine Brighton: by kind permission of the artist.
Ruth Brown: by kind permission of the artist.
John Burningham: by permission of Jonathan Cape.
Nan Chauncy: by kind permission of the illustrator, Annette Macarthur-Onslow.
Judith Crabtree: by kind permission of the artist.
Day of Rhymes: by kind permission of the artist.
Carolyn Dinan: by kind permission of the artist.
Philippe Dupasquier: reproduced by permission of Walker Books, London.
Ecology: by kind permission of the artist.
Father Christmas: © Raymond Briggs 1973, by permission of Hamish Hamilton.
Michael Foreman: by kind permission of the artist.
Frog Prince: by kind permission of the artist.
A. B. Frost: illustration for *Uncle Remus: His Sayings* by Joel Chandler Harris.
Kim Gamble: by kind permission of the artist.
Peter Gouldthorpe: by kind permission of the artist.

Bob Graham: © 1999 Robert Graham, by permission of Walker Books, London.
Armin Greder: by kind permission of the illustrator.
Green Knowe series: by kind permission of the artist's family.
Ted Greenwood: by kind permission of the artist.
Bluebeard; *Cock Robin*; Chapbooks; *Children in the Wood*; Wanda Gág;
Grimm Brothers; Joel Chandler Harris; Illustration (William Cobbett's School); *Jack the Giantkiller*; James Otis; *Story of a Bad Boy*; Frank Stockton; Trickster; *Visit from St Nicholas* by permission of the Syndics of Cambridge University Library.
Tapas Guha: by kind permission of the artist.
Quentin Hole: by kind permission of the artist.
Shirley Hughes: by kind permission of the artist.
Pat Hutchins: by kind permission of the artist.
Illustration: Shirley Hughes: by kind permission of the author/artist.
Robert Ingpen: by kind permission of the illustrator.
Ann James: by kind permission of the artist.
Faith Jaques: by kind permission of the artist.
Charles Keeping: by kind permission of Renate Keeping.
Satoshi Kitamura: by kind permission of the artist.
Lynton Lamb: by kind permission of the Estate of Lynton Lamb.
Alison Lester: by kind permission of the artist.
Annette Macarthur-Onslow: by kind permission of the artist.
Ruth Manning-Sanders: by kind permission of the artist.
Midnight Folk: first published by William Heinemann and used with permission of Egmont Children's Books, London.
Junko Morimoto: by kind permission of the artist.
Patricia Mullins: by kind permission of the artist.
Noggin the Nog: by kind permission of the artist.
Nudity in children's books: illustration by Helen Stratton
Nursery rhymes (1) Illustration by Katherine Robertson
Pixie O'Harris: by kind permission of the artist's family.
Narelle Oliver: by kind permission of the illustrator.
Orlando the Marmalade Cat: with kind permission of David Higham Associates.
Marjula Padmanabhan: by kind permission of the artist.
Mickey Patel: by kind permission of the artist.
Korky Paul: by kind permission of Korky Paul.
Rodney Peppé: by kind permission of the artist.
Picturebooks: *Up and Up* by kind permission of Shirley Hughes; *Gasp*: by kind permission of Terry Denton; *One Big Yo To Go*: by kind permission of Jirí Tibor Novák.
Jan Pieńkowski: by kind permission of the artist.
Arthur Rackham: by permission of the artist's family.
Atanu Roy: by kind permission of the illustrator.
Michael Salmon: by kind permission of the artist.
Ronald Searle: © Ronald Searle 1950, by kind permission.
Stone Book Quartet: by kind permission of Michael Foreman.
Rosemary Sutcliff: by kind permission of Renate Keeping.
Henry Treece: by kind permission of Renate Keeping.
Julie Vivas: by kind permission of the artist.
Fritz Wegner: by kind permission of the artist.
Bruce Whatley: by kind permission of the illustrator.
Brian Wildsmith: by kind permission of the artist.
Geoffrey Willans: © Ronald Searle, 1953, by kind permission of the illustrator.
Marcia Williams: © 1998 Marcia Williams.
Willy the Wimp: by kind permission of Anthony Browne.